lonely planet

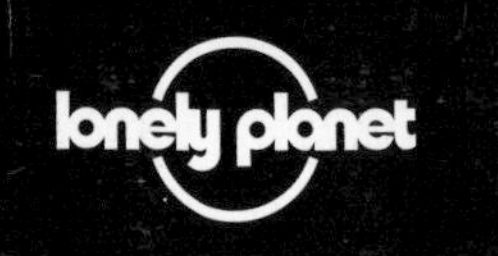

USA

Jeff Campbell, Loretta Chilcoat, Susan Derby, Beth Greenfield, Carolyn B Heller, Sam Martin, Debra Miller, Bob Morris, Becky Ohlsen, Andrea Schulte-Peevers, Kurt Wolff, Karla Zimmerman

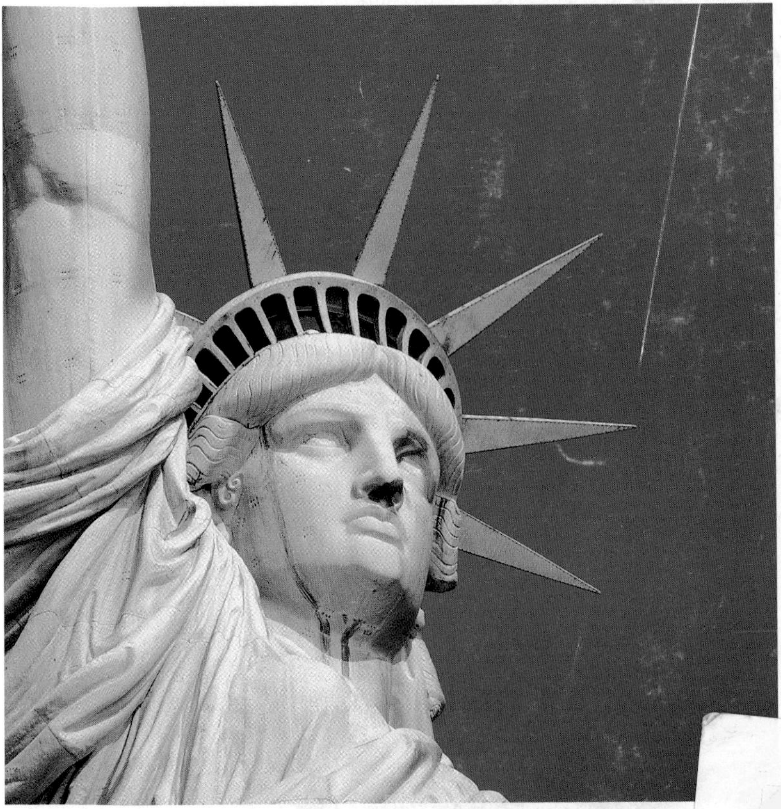

Contents

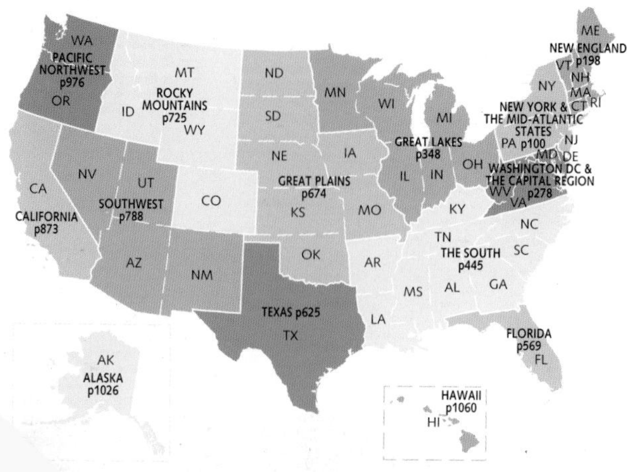

Lonely Planet books provide independent advice. Lonely Planet does not accept advertising in guidebooks, nor do we accept payment in exchange for listing or endorsing any place or business. Lonely Planet writers do not accept discounts or payments in exchange for positive coverage of any sort.

Destination: USA

Families land-cruising in ponderous Winnebagos, college students lead-footing it to spring break beaches, Jack Kerouac hitchhiking west on the back of a flatbed truck, Mark Twain seeking his fortune in the gold rush, Lewis and Clark traversing the wilderness and claiming it for a new republic: whatever the reason, in every age since its founding, the United States isn't a place that you come to and stand still.

America has always called out for exploration and discovery. And whether the goal has been to take the measure of an unmapped and unruly nation or simply to kick back along endless ribbons of highway, any trip invariably entails taking stock of oneself. In ways large and small, America is and has always been about the journey. It is a gloriously defiant work in progress.

Today, some come to revel in America's kitsch and omnipresent pop culture – in the fast-food hamburgers, reality TV, comic book heroes and small-town Americana. Some head for the cities to experience first-hand the grand canyons of Manhattan, Chicago's blues joints and Los Angeles' sun-drenched boulevards. Still others don't stop until the highways and trails peter out, leaving them in solitary contemplation of the continent's awesome natural beauty and vast wilderness.

But if the well-trodden journey across America never fails to be rewarding, it's because of her people, whose energy and restless reinvention never cease, and who keep moving in the dogged belief that they will eventually reach the place where the country makes good on its promise of prosperity, freedom, equality, justice and even happiness for all.

In America, the road always beckons.

RICHARD CUMMINS

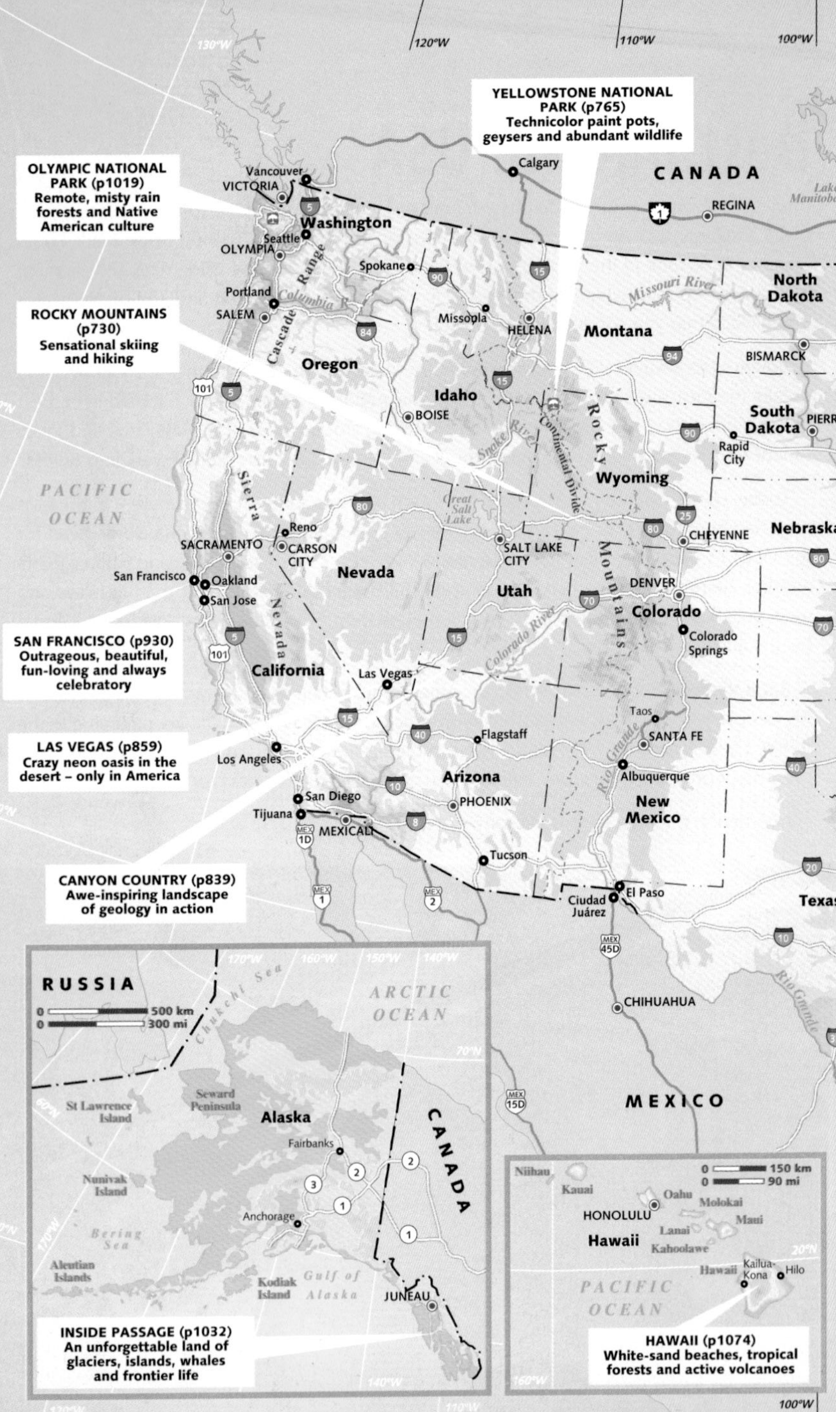

YELLOWSTONE NATIONAL PARK (p765)
Technicolor paint pots, geysers and abundant wildlife
OLYMPIC NATIONAL PARK (p1019)
Remote, misty rain forests and Native American culture
ROCKY MOUNTAINS (p730)
Sensational skiing and hiking
SAN FRANCISCO (p930)
Outrageous, beautiful, fun-loving and always celebratory
LAS VEGAS (p859)
Crazy neon oasis in the desert – only in America
CANYON COUNTRY (p839)
Awe-inspiring landscape of geology in action
INSIDE PASSAGE (p1032)
An unforgettable land of glaciers, islands, whales and frontier life
HAWAII (p1074)
White-sand beaches, tropical forests and active volcanoes
CANADA
MEXICO
PACIFIC OCEAN
Washington
Oregon
California
Nevada
Idaho
Montana
Wyoming
Utah
Colorado
Arizona
New Mexico
Texas
North Dakota
South Dakota
Nebraska
Vancouver
VICTORIA
Seattle
OLYMPIA
Portland
SALEM
Spokane
Missoula
HELENA
Calgary
REGINA
BISMARCK
PIERRE
Rapid City
BOISE
Reno
CARSON CITY
SACRAMENTO
San Francisco
Oakland
San Jose
SALT LAKE CITY
CHEYENNE
DENVER
Colorado Springs
Las Vegas
Los Angeles
San Diego
Tijuana
MEXICALI
Flagstaff
PHOENIX
Tucson
Taos
SANTA FE
Albuquerque
El Paso
Ciudad Juárez
CHIHUAHUA
Cascade Range
Sierra Nevada
Rocky Mountains
Continental Divide
Columbia R
Snake River
Missouri River
Colorado River
Rio Grande
Great Salt Lake
Lake Manitoba
130°W
120°W
110°W
100°W
40°N
30°N
RUSSIA
0 500 km
0 300 mi
ARCTIC OCEAN
Chukchi Sea
Alaska
Seward Peninsula
St Lawrence Island
Nunivak Island
Bering Sea
Aleutian Islands
Kodiak Island
Gulf of Alaska
Fairbanks
Anchorage
JUNEAU
170°W
160°W
150°W
140°W
70°N
60°N
20°N
0 150 km
0 90 mi
Niihau
Kauai
Oahu
HONOLULU
Molokai
Lanai
Maui
Kahoolawe
Hawaii
Kailua-Kona
Hilo
20°N
160°W

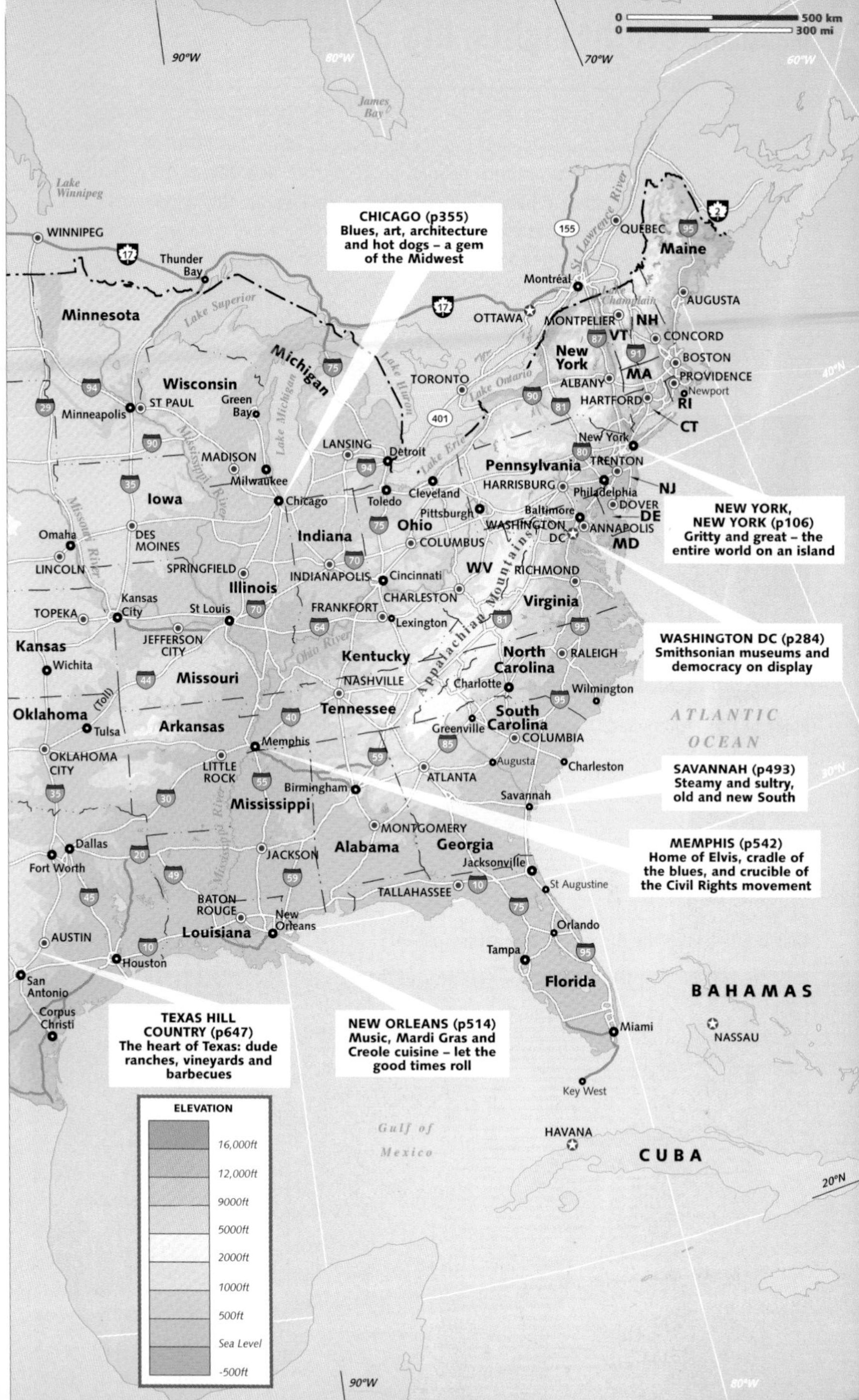

0 500 km
0 300 mi
90°W
80°W
70°W
60°W
40°N
30°N
20°N
James Bay
Lake Winnipeg
CHICAGO (p355)
Blues, art, architecture and hot dogs – a gem of the Midwest
WINNIPEG
Thunder Bay
Minnesota
Lake Superior
Michigan
Lake Michigan
Lake Huron
Wisconsin
Minneapolis
ST PAUL
Green Bay
MADISON
Milwaukee
Chicago
Iowa
Omaha
DES MOINES
LINCOLN
SPRINGFIELD
Illinois
Kansas City
TOPEKA
St Louis
JEFFERSON CITY
Kansas
Wichita
Missouri
Oklahoma
Tulsa
(Toll)
Arkansas
OKLAHOMA CITY
LITTLE ROCK
Memphis
Mississippi River
Missouri River
Mississippi
Dallas
Fort Worth
JACKSON
BATON ROUGE
Louisiana
New Orleans
AUSTIN
Houston
San Antonio
Corpus Christi
TEXAS HILL COUNTRY (p647)
The heart of Texas: dude ranches, vineyards and barbecues
NEW ORLEANS (p514)
Music, Mardi Gras and Creole cuisine – let the good times roll
ELEVATION
16,000ft
12,000ft
9000ft
5000ft
2000ft
1000ft
500ft
Sea Level
-500ft
Gulf of Mexico
HAVANA
CUBA
BAHAMAS
NASSAU
Key West
Miami
Florida
Tampa
Orlando
St Augustine
Jacksonville
TALLAHASSEE
Georgia
Alabama
MONTGOMERY
Birmingham
ATLANTA
Augusta
Savannah
Charleston
COLUMBIA
South Carolina
Greenville
Charlotte
North Carolina
RALEIGH
Wilmington
Tennessee
NASHVILLE
Kentucky
FRANKFORT
Lexington
Ohio River
INDIANAPOLIS
Indiana
Cincinnati
Ohio
COLUMBUS
CHARLESTON
WV
Virginia
RICHMOND
Appalachian Mountains
LANSING
Detroit
Toledo
Cleveland
Lake Erie
Pittsburgh
Pennsylvania
HARRISBURG
Philadelphia
TRENTON
New York
NJ
DOVER
DE
Baltimore
WASHINGTON DC
ANNAPOLIS
MD
TORONTO
Lake Ontario
Montréal
OTTAWA
QUEBEC
St Lawrence River
Lake Champlain
Maine
AUGUSTA
MONTPELIER
NH
VT
CONCORD
New York
ALBANY
MA
BOSTON
PROVIDENCE
Newport
RI
HARTFORD
CT
NEW YORK, NEW YORK (p106)
Gritty and great – the entire world on an island
WASHINGTON DC (p284)
Smithsonian museums and democracy on display
ATLANTIC OCEAN
SAVANNAH (p493)
Steamy and sultry, old and new South
MEMPHIS (p542)
Home of Elvis, cradle of the blues, and crucible of the Civil Rights movement

Bright Lights, Big City

Some US cities justify a trip for themselves alone. **Boston** (p206) is a youthful university town with Revolutionary history. **New Orleans** (p514) is the Big Easy, a picture of insouciant decadence. The Emerald City, hip **Seattle** (p1002), enjoys a gorgeous setting. **San Francisco** (p930) is a living history of wild times, while sophisticated **Los Angeles** (p879) is famously the home of Hollywood and celebrity-strewn beaches.

JON DAVISON

Pulse to the Latin beat of **Miami** (p575)

Hit **Chicago** (p355) for its music, architecture, art and food

RICHARD CUMMINS

Take a bite out of the Big Apple, **Manhattan** (p110)

ANGUS OBORN

Purple Mountains Majesty

America's landscape is still wild and abundant in natural beauty. Picking highlights is a fool's errand. The **red-rock desert of Utah** (p839) has geological magnificence to spare, and lovers of desert landscapes should not miss South Dakota's eroded **Badlands** (p715). In the Sierra Nevada, **Yosemite** (p969) is pure granite majesty. Want extremes? Compare the glaciers and primeval forests of Alaska's **Inside Passage** (p1032) with the gator-infested primeval swamps of Florida's **Everglades** (p591).

JOHN ELK III

View the never-ending vistas at **Glacier National Park** (p780)

Marvel at the geothermal delights of **Yellowstone** (p765)

JIM WARK

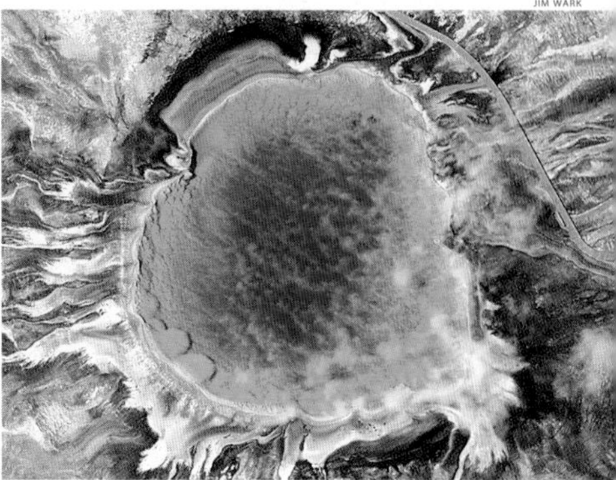

RICHARD CUMMINS

Find out why the **Grand Canyon** (p826) gets so much press

Roadside Attractions

Where to begin? In Mitchell, South Dakota, the **Corn Palace** (p714) is decorated annually with 275,000 ears of corn. Off Hwy 17 in southern Colorado is the **UFO Watchtower** (p755), where folks await abduction. North of Missoula, Montana, the **Miracle of America Museum** (p777) is a random sample of unique Americana, while Dr Evermor's **Sculpture Park** (p426), near Madison, Wisconsin, includes his enormous scrap-metal Forevertron. Houston is a veritable folk art bonanza, with its **Beer Can House** (p658) and **Art Car Museum** (p658), among others. In California's Santa Cruz, the laws of gravity need not apply at the **Mystery Spot** (p929), a world of odd-ball Americana.

RICHARD CUMMINS

Enter another dimension at **Biosphere 2** (p837), outside Tucson, Arizona

Slow down for Amarillo's **Cadillac Ranch** (p673), Texas

CHARLES COOK

Face the four US presidents carved into the Black Hills at **Mt Rushmore** (p718), South Dakota

STEPHEN SAKS

HIGHLIGHTS One Nation, Many Peoples

One definite highlight of any US trip is America's diverse peoples. For the most evocative experience, simply stroll multicultural **New York City** (p106), though arriving for Manhattan's **Harlem Week** (p137) in August is a standout. San Francisco also exemplifies US diversity, particularly in its **Chinatown** (p937) and Hispanic **Mission District** (p938). Miami's **Little Havana** (p579) is a lively Cuban-American enclave. **Pennsylvania Dutch Country** (p186) is famous for its old-world Amish and Mennonite communities. Native American communities include **Acoma** (p799) and **Zuni Pueblos** (p800) in central New Mexico and the **Hopi Indian Reservation** (p832) in Arizona. **San Antonio** (p649) is a great place to experience the USA's hybrid Tex-Mex culture.

LEE FOSTER

Connect with Asian-American culture in **Little Tokyo** (p885), Los Angeles

Get a feel for **Navajo heritage** (p830)

DALLAS STRIBLEY

Celebrate **Cinco de Mayo** (p895) with style on Olvera St, Los Angeles

RAY LASKOWITZ

Strike Up the Band

Whether you're interested in America's musical heritage or its living present, your choices are many. For blues, head to the **Mississippi Delta** (p508) or catch the June **Chicago Blues Festival** (p370). For country, head straight for **Nashville** (p549) and the **Grand Ole Opry** (p555). Contemporary music – rock, hip-hop and the many permutations – can be found in **New York City** (p150), **Austin** (p646), **San Francisco** (p948) and many other cities, while Cleveland houses the **Rock & Roll Hall of Fame & Museum** (p392).

Head to Beale St, **Memphis** (p542), where blues is king

GREG ELMS

Experience Salt Lake City's wonderful **Mormon Tabernacle Choir** (p843)

LEE FOS

Catch the jazz masters in **New Orleans** (p526)

THOMAS DOWNS

Architectural America

America is a young country, and its most interesting architecture is modern. **Chicago** (p355) is a prime destination for its early skyscrapers and its many Frank Lloyd Wright buildings. **Manhattan** (p110) is also notable for its tall buildings and its art deco masterpieces, such as **Rockefeller Center** (p123) and **Radio City Music Hall** (p123). North Carolina's **Biltmore Estate** (p457) is an unbelievable beaux arts mansion, and Thomas Jefferson's home, **Monticello** (p317), epitomizes the colonial neoclassical style.

Wander among the Victorian homes of **San Francisco** (p930)

CURTIS MARTIN

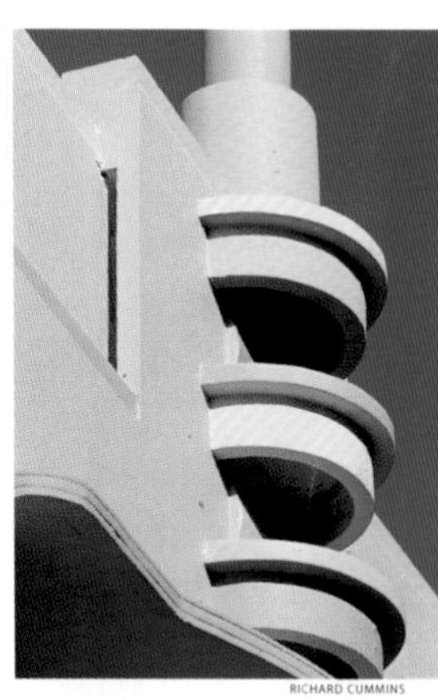

RICHARD CUMMINS

Dream of art deco in **Miami Beach** (p575)

Experience true postmodernism at the Frank Gehry–designed **Weisman Art Museum** (p434), Minneapolis

RICHARD CUMMINS

Adrenaline Highs

Outdoor adventure awaits travelers at every bend in the road. Southern California beaches are world famous for their **surfing** (p893). For world-class skiing, try **Lake Tahoe** (p967), Utah's **Wasatch Mountains** (p846), and the Rocky Mountain slopes of **Aspen** (p753) and **Sun Valley** (p785). Many ski slopes become mountain-biking trails in summer; particularly famous is the Sierra Nevada's **Mammoth Mountain** (p974). Sea kayak in Washington's **San Juan Islands** (p1022). For heart-pumping rafting, try the **Colorado River** (p828) through the Grand Canyon, the **Arkansas River** (p754) in Colorado, and around **Nantahala** (p458) in North Carolina. If you like to run, catch up with April's **Boston Marathon** (p215) or October's **New York Marathon** (p137).

Climb to the top at **Yosemite National Park** (p969)

ANDREW PEACOCK

Race to **Vail** (p750) for incredible skiing

MARK & AUDREY GIBSON

Scuba dive and snorkel in the **Florida Keys** (p594)

WILLIAM HARRIGA

Getting Started

Traveling in the USA is easy. Tourists are well cared for and accommodations and transportation options are plentiful. The only thing to keep in mind – besides costs – is the continent's immense scale. Texas alone is twice the size of Germany. When planning what to see, don't be overambitious, and when deciding how to get around, carefully compare transport costs versus travel time and flexibility. If time is short, staying in one place, renting a car or flying between destinations are a few ways to make the most of it.

WHEN TO GO

The USA is so big it doesn't matter what time of year it is, you can always find some place where the weather is perfect and it's the ideal time to visit. In general, the main holiday season is summer, which is bounded by Memorial Day (the last Monday in May) and Labor Day (the first Monday in September). In summer, hotel rates will be at their highest and crowds will be at their most dense, but sometimes you just have to strike while the iron is hot: mountain parks and gorgeous beaches are just not the same without the presence of a warm, beaming sun.

Still, regional variation is huge, and one place's high season is another's hell: July in the Pacific northwest is wonderful, but in the deserts of the Southwest it's brutal. The main indicators of weather and season will be latitude and altitude: the higher you go, and the further north, the later summer arrives and the earlier winter. But even this is not foolproof. See the Geography & Climate sections at the beginning of each regional chapter for destination-specific advice, and for current information, visit www.weather.com.

One travel truism is that spring and fall are often the best times to visit. The shoulder seasons – roughly March to May (spring) and September to November (fall) – tend to avoid the extremes of weather, prices sometimes drop and scenery is often at its peak. Again, check your destination: spring in the Rocky Mountains or Sierra Nevadas may not arrive until May or June, or it may bring an off-putting amount of rain, as in Seattle.

See Climate Charts (pp1090–1) for more information.

Winter is high season in ski areas, and drives the snow birds from north to south. With careful planning, however, a successful winter trip can yield the riches of America's landscape virtually all to yourself.

Whether you're planning to join them or avoid them, holidays (p1095) and festivals (p1094) are another thing to consider before making plans.

DON'T LEAVE HOME WITHOUT...

- Checking the visa and US entrance requirements (p1103). These may change.
- A copy of your travel insurance policy (p1096)
- Car, hotel or camping reservations. Sometimes, everything's booked!
- Plenty of cash. Every budget needs a backup, just in case.
- An open mind. Refreshingly, real Americans are much more interesting than the ones on TV.

TOP TENS

AMERICA IN PICTURES

Foreigners often ask, Is America really like it is in the movies? And the answer is, Of course, only more so! Here are 10 films that have revealed the US to the world.

- *Citizen Kane* (1941) Director: Orson Welles
- *Casablanca* (1942) Director: Michael Curtiz
- *Some Like It Hot* (1959) Director: Billy Wilder
- *The Graduate* (1967) Director: Mike Nichols
- *The Godfather* trilogy (1971–1990) Director: Francis Ford Coppola
- *Blade Runner* (1982/1991) Director: Ridley Scott
- *Blue Velvet* (1986) Director: David Lynch
- *Do the Right Thing* (1989) Director: Spike Lee
- *Fargo* (1995) Director: the Coen brothers

NOTHING LIKE A GOOD BOOK

Like a multifaceted diamond, America has many sides. Here is a selection of literature, memoirs and essays that polish the jewel and let it shine. See p62 for more on American literature.

- *Leaves of Grass* (1855–92) Walt Whitman
- *Huckleberry Finn* (1884) Mark Twain
- *Travels with Charley* (1962) John Steinbeck
- *A Supposedly Fun Thing I'll Never Do Again* (1997) David Foster Wallace
- *'Tis* (1999) Frank McCourt
- *That Old Ace in the Hole* (2002) Annie Proulx
- *Brown* (2003) Richard Rodriguez
- *Drop City* (2003) T Coraghessan Boyle
- *Ten Little Indians* (2003) Sherman Alexie
- *Cosmopolis* (2003) Don DeLillo

PARTY IN THE STREETS

Whatever troubles may afflict the nation, Americans never forget to have fun. The following festivals and events are celebrations of the highest order, when Americans let loose with their most exuberant and uninhibited selves. See also Highlights (p6) and Festivals & Events (p1094).

- Tournament of Roses Parade, Los Angeles (CA), January 1 (p895)
- Mardi Gras, New Orleans (LA), February or March (p522)
- St Patrick's Day, Boston (MA), March 17 (p215)
- South by Southwest, Austin (TX), March (p645)
- Chicago Blues Festival, Chicago (IL), June (p370)
- Gay Pride Month, San Francisco (CA), June (p944)
- Independence Day, Washington DC, July 4 (p295)
- Woodward Dream Cruise, Detroit (MI), August (p409)
- Los Angeles County Fair, Los Angeles (CA), September (p895)
- Thanksgiving Day Parade, New York City (NY), November (p137)

COSTS

The USA can be an expensive place to visit. The standard of living is higher than in many places in the world, but costs are too, particularly for hotels and transport.

Still, almost any budget can be accommodated. At a minimum – staying in hostels and making your own food or eating fast food – you can scrape by on about $40 a day, not counting transportation. If you want to stay in decent motels or hotels and eat at decent restaurants, you should plan on $100 or so a day (per person traveling as a couple). If you will be staying in a major city, such as New York, Chicago or Los Angeles, costs can jump dramatically, and planning on $150 a day per person would not be lavish. Rental cars, which can be a travel necessity, cost from $35 to $45 a day for compact models (not including gas).

PREDEPARTURE READING

The American travelogue is its own literary genre, and many of the classics remain not only enjoyable but relevant. In *Democracy in America* (1835–40), Alexis de Tocqueville distilled the philosophical underpinnings of the then-new American experiment, and it remains a first-rate, even pithy assessment of American sensibilities.

Mark Twain spent seven years going west – from St Louis to Virginia City and thence to San Francisco and Hawaii – in the hopes of making his fortune, and *Roughing It* (1872) is his hilarious account of every indignity suffered along the way.

Celebrated travel writer Jan Morris was clearly smitten with America in *Coast to Coast* (1956/2002); her account is crisp, clear and elegantly thoughtful, but not naive. Her experiences in the pre–Civil Rights South are truly poignant.

No book has done more to spur cross-country travel than Jack Kerouac's *On the Road* (1957). His headlong jazz style and lust for life inspire people still.

You could wish for no better companion and guide than John Steinbeck, who late in life set out with his poodle in a makeshift camper to reacquaint himself with America. *Travels with Charley* (1962) is sharp, funny, noble and filled with wise, road-tested advice.

At a crossroads in life, William Least Heat-Moon set out on a 13,000-mile circuit of America's back roads. The poetic result, *Blue Highways* (1982), is a moving pastiche of everyday Americans as it follows one man's attempt to find himself by losing himself.

Everybody knows humorist Bill Bryson, or should. Nobody is funnier having a bad time, and in *The Lost Continent* (1989) he has a terrible one. In his quixotic search for the great American small town, he is by turns acidic and melancholy, but ever accurate.

In *Roads* (2000), Larry McMurtry has no grand pretensions, just an abiding wanderlust. Reading his account – a meditation on highways, the West and his own life and inspirations – is to hitchhike a ride with one of America's best writers.

For a compendium of great contemporary travel writing, pick up *America* (1999) by Travelers' Tales.

LONELY PLANET INDEX

Gallon/liter of gas: $1.54/$0.40

Liter of bottled water: $0.95

Bottle of Budweiser: $0.95

Souvenir T-shirt: $7

New York hot dog: $1.50

HOW MUCH?

Hotel double: $70–100

Restaurant meal: $25–40

Print film: $5

Pound of ground beef (mince): $1.85

Loaf of whole wheat bread: $1.45

INTERNET RESOURCES

Connected Traveler (www.connectedtraveler.com) Humorous and opinionated travel stories and advice, from the esoteric to the mundane, and a ton of US and world travel resources.

Firstgov.gov (http://firstgov.gov) The US government's official website is a great all-round resource; links to all federal and state agencies.

Lonely Planet (www.lonelyplanet.com) US travel news and summaries, the Thorn Tree bulletin board, and links to more web resources.

Map Quest (www.mapquest.com) Maps and directions for any place in the USA, plus a trip planner.

Recreation.gov (www.recreation.gov) Comprehensive information on the nation's public lands, plus links, reservations, news, outdoor advice and more.

Roadside America (www.roadsideamerica.com) A one-stop shop for all that wacky, one-of-a-kind Americana.

Itineraries

CLASSIC ROUTES

EASTERN SEABOARD — 2 weeks–1 month / Boston to Miami

The USA's crowded eastern seaboard packs in as much bustle, culture and history as most visitors would want. I-95 is the principal route.

Boston (p206) is a major arrival point in general, and its Revolutionary history and university life make it a fine introduction to the USA. Next up is **New York** (p106), which needs no introduction; if you've never been, plan on four days. Less can feel rushed, more can get overwhelming.

Depending on your interest in historic places and museums, **Philadelphia** (p174), **Baltimore** (p325) and **Washington DC** (p284) will either fascinate you endlessly or sate you quickly.

When you get to **Richmond, Virginia** (p305), you abruptly enter the antebellum South and begin a tour of Civil War history. Further south, North Carolina's **'Research Triangle'** (p452) is the state's most vibrant cultural center, while in Georgia, **Savannah** (p493) weaves a sultry, intoxicating spell.

Daytona Beach (p604) has miles of flat beaches and spring-break atmosphere, as does **Miami** (p575), one of the USA's great multicultural cities.

It's about 1500 fast highway miles from Boston to Miami along I-95. In two weeks, you can hit all the major cities, but three weeks to a month will be more relaxed.

PACIFIC COAST HIGHWAY

3–6 weeks / Seattle to San Diego

Traversing the USA's West Coast is a dream trip, including a wealth of natural and cultural highlights. However, it can be extremely slow. You might want to pick and choose destinations, and then leave the coast in between (inland on I-5) to make better time.

Seattle (p1002) is the main entry point in the Pacific Northwest. Grab a coffee, then head straight for the ancient rain forests of the **Olympic Peninsula** (p1018). From here, take Hwy 101 south along the rugged, scenic **Oregon Coast** (p999). It's also worth a sidetrip to livable, liberal **Portland** (p983).

When you reach **California's North Coast** (p958), you pass through towering old-growth redwood forests. If you have time, stick to the coast along the Pacific Coast Hwy (Hwy 1), or zip more quickly along Hwy 101 to **San Francisco** (p930). Vibrant, beautiful and hedonistic, the 'City that Knows How' is worth three to four days.

Next are **Santa Cruz** (p928) and the beautiful **Monterey Peninsula** (p926), which offer lots of opportunities to play outdoors. Whatever you do, don't miss the stretch of Hwy 1 through the natural splendor of **Big Sur** (p924).

Los Angeles (p879) is the next major destination, and it's worth at least four days to experience its fine art, Hollywood glamour and warm beaches. For an entirely different cultural experience, don a pair of mouse ears at **Disneyland** (p903), then complete the journey in **San Diego** (p904), which has interesting museums and great beaches and allows for an easy jaunt into **Tijuana, Mexico** (p914).

It's about 1500 winding miles hugging the West Coast between Seattle and San Diego, though side routes add mileage and time. If you want to do the whole route, don't rush it; take a month or more and explore. Otherwise, tackle only a portion.

THE GREAT MOTHER ROAD

1 week / Chicago to Los Angeles

Route 66, once the 'Main Street of America,' is a nostalgic driving tour that still passes enough quintessential, wacky, shake-your-head-in-disbelief Americana to make it a highlight. Only portions of the original highway remain; today it has either been paralleled or replaced by newer interstates. Consult good state maps for details.

In Illinois **Route 66** (p382) parallels I-55 from **Chicago** (p355) to **St Louis** (p680). Through Missouri and into Oklahoma it parallels **I-44** (p688). A long original stretch exists between **Tulsa** (p696) and **Oklahoma City** (p693), and west of Oklahoma City the route parallels **I-40** (p799) the rest of the way to California.

In the Texas panhandle **Amarillo** (p672) boasts the famous Cadillac Ranch. Through New Mexico good Route-66 stops, with museums and memorabilia, are **Albuquerque** (p794) and **Gallup** (p800), while in Arizona major destinations are **Flagstaff** (p824), **Williams** (p826) and **Kingman** (p832), which has another sizable original portion.

Nostalgia trails off markedly once you enter California, though a final named stretch will take you the last few miles into **Los Angeles** (p879).

Route 66 is about 2200 miles from Chicago to Los Angeles. It's easy to go as fast or as slow as you wish, stopping for every quirky roadside attraction or simply smiling as you pass. A week is plenty of time to do the road itself.

THE BLUES HIGHWAY

10 days–2 weeks / Minneapolis to New Orleans

The Mississippi River marks a physical and psychological divide, and along this spine runs America's greatest music: blues, jazz, and rock 'n' roll. Hwy 61 is the legendary route, though numerous other roads join up, run parallel and intersect with it.

Progressive, artistic, youthful **Minneapolis** (p430) is the easiest starting point, though some might want to start farther north in **Hibbing** (p444), Bob Dylan's birthplace. Hwy 61 then winds scenically on either side of the Mississippi River to **Hannibal, Missouri** (p687), the birthplace of Mark Twain. Gateway to the West, **St Louis** (p680) also bills itself as the 'Home of the Blues,' and not without cause.

The next major destination is **Memphis** (p542), where you can pay homage to Elvis Presley at Graceland and to rock 'n' roll at Sun Studio. South of here Hwy 61 runs through the **Mississippi Delta** (p508), where the blues was born; **Clarksdale** (p508) has still-jumpin' blues joints and **Natchez** (p511) is full of antebellum homes.

South of Baton Rouge a detour along Hwy 1 leads past the famous 19th-century **Mississippi River Plantations** (p529). Then you get to **New Orleans** (p514), birthplace of jazz. It's easy to lose track of time in the 'Big Easy,' with lazy mornings blending into late nights, and you should leave plenty of time here to go with the flow.

It's about 1200 miles from Minneapolis to New Orleans on Hwy 61; south of St Louis, parallel I-55 makes swifter going if time is short. It's not hard to do this route in a little over a week, but you'll always wish for an extra day or two in New Orleans.

BLUE RIDGE PARKWAY

1 week / Harpers Ferry to Great Smoky Mountains National Park

This popular, easy route is a trip back in time: to the Civil War and to old-time Appalachia. People do this as a scenic driving tour in a couple of days – particularly for spring wildflowers and fall colors – but it's worth a week if you want to poke around historic sites and catch some bluegrass in the small towns. For more complete descriptions of the Blue Ridge Parkway, see p322 and p456.

It's not officially part of the parkway, but **Harpers Ferry** (p344), in West Virginia, is a good starting point, since events here sparked the Civil War. Take Hwy 340 south to **Shenandoah National Park** (p319), in Virginia, and take Skyline Dr; check out some of the **famous caverns** (p321) along the way. Make a detour to beautiful **Charlottesville** (p317) and visit Thomas Jefferson's home, **Monticello** (p317).

After rejoining the parkway, make another detour to **Appomattox** (p318), where General Lee surrendered and ended the Civil War. South of here the Blue Ridge Parkway leads past tiny **Floyd** (p322), with bluegrass jamborees, and into North Carolina, where **Boone** (p457) has the great Appalachian Cultural Museum.

Near the end, **Asheville** (p457) is a relaxing town to spend a night or two. The parkway ends at the stunning **Great Smoky Mountains National Park** (p458), which straddles the border with Tennessee and is the USA's most-visited national park.

The Blue Ridge Parkway is 469 miles, but crowds and low speed limits mean that it takes longer than you'd think. A week allows time for dawdling.

THE CROSS-COUNTRY JOURNEY 2 weeks–1 month / Boston to Seattle

It's over 3000 miles coast to coast, Boston to Seattle. While some people enjoy logging 600 miles in a day, plan an itinerary that's half that, and leave room for detours. Two weeks is just enough time to experience more than the road; take a month if you want to explore along the way.

I-90 is one of several epic routes across the continent. People in a hurry do it in a week or less, and sometimes the rhythm of driving just takes over and you forget to stop. If you find yourself in Seattle long before you meant to be, you can always turn around and go back.

I-90 begins in **Boston** (p206), then traverses the width of Massachusetts and New York to **Niagara Falls** (p154). Then it skirts Lake Erie to **Cleveland** (p390), where the Rock & Roll Hall of Fame beckons. From here, it's a straight shot to **Chicago** (p355), a perfect spot to stretch your legs and rest up.

The college town of **Madison** (p425) rewards lingering, and nearby **Baraboo** (p426) sports some rather pause-worthy Americana. Then I-90 straightens out again as it crosses the fertile flatlands of Minnesota and the bone-dry flatlands of South Dakota, broken up only by signs for **Wall Drug** (p715).

The **Black Hills** (p715) rise like a mirage in the distance, and they and **Badlands National Park** (p715) provide awesome vistas and buffalo herds. Heading west, leave I-90 for Hwy 16 and visit **Yellowstone National Park** (p765). Rejoin I-90 to the north and cut across western Montana. **Missoula** (p775) is a good place to park the car and jump in a raft for a day.

Then the **Idaho Panhandle** (p787) has some western-flavored towns, and gritty **Spokane** (p1024) offers some nightlife, but not much slows you down till **Mt Rainier National Park** (p1016) and, finally, **Seattle** (p1002). Whew!

ROADS LESS TRAVELED

THE LEWIS & CLARK TRAIL

2–3 weeks / St Louis to Astoria

The 200th anniversary of Lewis and Clark's famous 1804–06 journey – which hoped to follow the Missouri River to the Pacific Ocean – is being marked by numerous events until 2006; see www.lewisandclark200.org to find out what's happening while you're here. It makes a great excuse to retrace their route; all the stops below have parks and museums, or will have temporary special exhibits, dedicated to these historic explorations.

The expedition gathered in **St Louis** (p680) and set off from **St Charles** (p686); follow I-70. At **Kansas City** (p689) and Leavenworth, the Missouri River turns north; follow I-29 to **Omaha** (p708) and **Sioux City** (p707). North of Sioux City, a series of smaller roads follows the Missouri as it winds north to **Bismarck, North Dakota** (p722).

From here go north on Hwy 83, west on Hwys 2 and 87, and at Great Falls, Montana, south on I-15. Or save time and, following the expedition's return route, go west from Bismarck on I-94 through **Billings** (p773) to Three Forks, Montana.

Lewis and Clark crossed the Continental Divide south of Dillon and then went north (follow Hwy 93) to **Missoula** (p775). From here, follow Hwy 12 to Lewiston and Clarkston, on the Idaho-Washington border, and then to the I-84 junction. Take I-84 west to **Portland** (p983), where you pick up Hwy 30 to **Astoria** (p999) on the Pacific Coast.

This winding trip is 2500 to 2800 miles, some of it fast, some slow. How long it will take depends in part on your fidelity to Lewis and Clark's original route. Still, allow at least two weeks, and keep your eye on the weather reports.

MOUNTAIN VALLEYS & RIVER CANYONS

1 month / Glacier National Park to Phoenix

This route is all about nature, and it passes through some of the USA's most dramatic, wild and superlative terrain, from Glacier National Park to the Grand Canyon, and on to Phoenix. Hwy 89 is the route described here, though I-15 can be used if time is tight or weather turns bad. Early summer to early fall is the best time to do this trip.

In Montana, **Glacier National Park** (p780) is wondrous to behold; it also has an airport near Whitefish. Hwy 89 then edges the **Bob Marshall Wilderness Complex** (p779), which will call to backpacking adventurers. Farther south, **Bozeman** (p772) is a picturesque agricultural town, while **Chico Hot Springs** (p773) will ease aching muscles.

The next stops are **Yellowstone National Park** (p765) and **Grand Teton National Park** (p768), which are so varied they could fill a week.

Hwy 89 is gorgeous going south, particularly through Utah's **Logan Canyon** (p849). **Salt Lake City** (p840) is a great introduction to the country's most sober pioneers, the Mormons. From here **Hwy 89** (p850) passes a number of attractive, small Mormon towns before getting to the next pair of blockbusters, **Bryce Canyon National Park** (p856) and **Zion National Park** (p858).

Hwy 89 then offers access to **Lake Powell** (p830) before reaching that icon of the Southwest, **Grand Canyon National Park** (p826). Funky **Flagstaff** (p824) and **Sedona** (p823) make nice places to rest tired legs before taking I-17 to **Phoenix** (p815) and catching a flight home.

It's over 1500 miles from Glacier National Park to Phoenix on Hwy 89. Portions of the route can be slow and mountainous. If you only have two weeks, pick a portion of this route and take your time; these are places that reward lingering and long hikes.

ALASKA'S INSIDE PASSAGE

1–3 weeks / Bellingham to Skagway

You can take a car, but if you are looking for an unforgettable journey that doesn't involve an automobile, consider cruising Alaska's Inside Passage. Glaciers and fjords, whales and wildlife, Native American history and Russian frontier heritage: it could add up to the most memorable trip you ever take. In summer the Alaska Marine Hwy ferries stop at towns nearly every day, and with advance notice you can get on and off at every one, so long as you keep going in the same direction. See p1033 for ferry information.

Fly into **Seattle, Washington** (p1002), and linger there or take a shuttle directly to **Bellingham** (p1021), where you catch the Alaska Marine Hwy. The first stop is **Ketchikan** (p1033), which still has a rugged western feel. It might be worth renting a car once you land on **Prince of Wales Island** (p1034), which is the third-largest island in the USA.

Wrangell (p1035) was founded by Russians, while pretty **Petersburg** (p1035) has a Norwegian heritage. Rich with Native American culture and beautifully situated, **Sitka** (p1036) shouldn't be missed. Busy **Juneau** (p1037) is Alaska's capital, and from here it's easy to get close to magnificent **Mendenhall Glacier** (p1038).

Haines (p1040) is another sizable town, and **Skagway** (p1041) is the end of the line. It is a well-preserved, nonthreatening version of its once lawless Gold Rush self.

You can also fly into or out of Juneau, or make it a round-trip and take the ferry back to Bellingham.

Some people take weeks to complete the ferry trip through the Inside Passage, spending a few days in each town. Or you can do a one-way journey in a week. Even if that's all the time you have, you won't be sorry.

TAILORED TRIPS

CHEERS!

Americans like to drink. The US Constitution's 21st Amendment (which ended the 14-year Prohibition experiment) establishes that emphatically, even legally. And they've become quite good at making the stuff, too.

Everyone knows about California's justly famous **Wine Country** (p955), where sun, wine, art and gourmet dining make an intoxicating combination. But great wines can be found all over the USA. Oregon's **Yamhill County** (p966) and Washington's **Walla Walla** (p1017) are both notable. New York's **Finger Lakes region** (p163) has a wealth of attractive wineries, and to a lesser degree Long Island's **North Fork** (p158). Cowboys knocking back merlot? They do in **Texas Hill Country** (p647), one of the USA's largest wine regions.

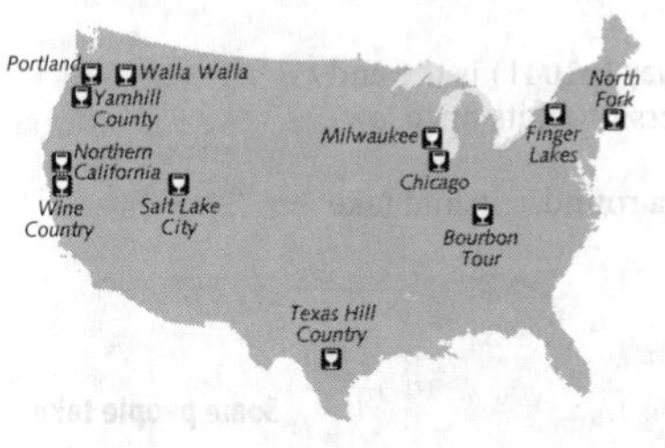

There's plenty of fine beer to be had as well. Despite building its reputation by producing bland major-label brews (such as Pabst and Miller), **Milwaukee** (p424) is still a beer-lover's destination, as is **Chicago** (p375). The microbrewery renaissance began in the West: **Portland** (p990) is a mecca, and **northern California** (p955) is studded with fantastic microbreweries. Surprisingly, the Mormon capital **Salt Lake City** (p845) supports several excellent microbreweries.

Those who like the hard stuff should get to Kentucky, renowned for its **bourbon tour** (p562). It makes for a genteel Southern experience.

ISLAND HOPPING

Everybody wants to go across the USA, but traveling around it may be an even better trip. Start at Maine's **Acadia National Park** (p274) for a sunrise hike. Then go to historic **Martha's Vineyard** (p230), from whence it's a quick tack to the USA's most famous island, **Manhattan** (p110). Off the Virginia coast is **Chincoteague Island** (p317), famous for its wild horses, and off North Carolina are the **Outer Banks** (p459) and **Cape Hatteras National Seashore** (p460), where the Wright brothers learned to fly, and you can too – by hang gliding.

Florida boasts the long white stretches of **Daytona Beach** (p604) and off the continent's tip, the **Florida Keys** (p594) are like a string of skipped stones. South of Mississippi, **Gulf Islands National Seashore** (p513) is a place to get away from it all, while **South Padre Island** (p666), off the Texas coast, is a place to let loose.

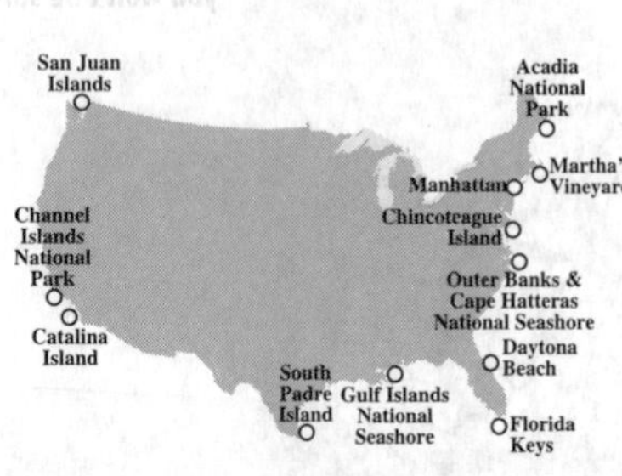

At this point you'll have to sail through the Panama Canal or go overland. Once off the southern California coast, **Catalina Island** (p902) has great snorkeling, and **Channel Islands National Park** (p920) is so diverse it's been nicknamed 'California's Galápagos'. Don't miss Washington's **San Juan Islands** (p1022), perfect for sea kayaking – keep an eye out for orcas!

INDIEWOOD, HOLLYWON'T

Multiplex cinemas are a tease: so many screens, so few choices. For real variety, hit a film festival; the biggies last two to three weeks, while smaller ones might run for a week. No one has done the calculations, but the USA has so many film festivals, it's possible one is happening *every single day*. If these high-profile ones aren't enough, check www.filmfestivals.com to fill up your calendar.

In January bundle up and arrive in Park City for the festival that defined independent film, **Sundance** (p847). In April **San Francisco** (p944) hosts the biggest of its many film festivals. In May, first there is New York's celebrity-packed **Tribeca Film Festival** (p137), and then, near the end of the month, **Seattle** (p1013) does its thing. **Los Angeles** (p895) hosts its major film festival in mid-June (which is not to be confused with March's Oscar ceremony). **Boston** (p215) happens in mid-September, **New York** (p137) in late September, and the major film festival in **Chicago** (p370) is in mid-October.

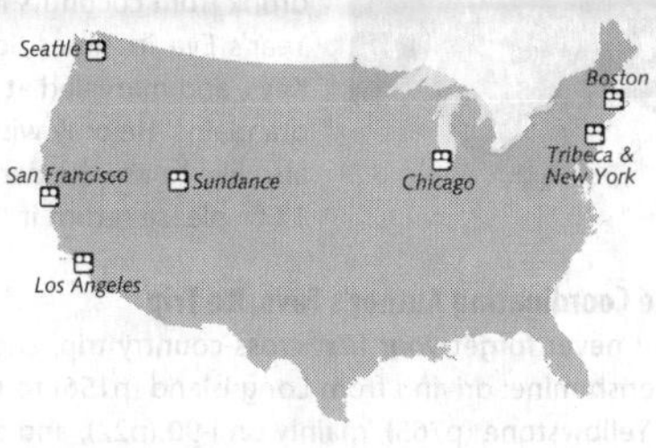

FAMILY FUN

It's easy to travel with kids in the United States – and there's loads of fun designed just for them. Every large city has a good selection of amusements and kid-friendly museums. Here is a quick list of other places, both famous and, perhaps, unexpected.

Just to get started, here's a shout out to **Walt Disney World** (p619) in Orlando, Florida. Near the original **Disneyland** (p903) in southern California is **Legoland** (p915), while further north **Santa Cruz** (p928) has a classic boardwalk, beaches and other teen fun. **Las Vegas** (p859) is actually packed with kid-friendly stuff. Of the national parks, **Yellowstone** (p765) is strange enough to qualify as an amusement. If you've got horse fanatics, take them to **Tennessee walking horse country** (p556). Outside Minneapolis is the **Mall of America** (p435), which is just a mall the way the QE2 is just a boat. If you're in Manhattan, do whatever everybody else does and go to **Jones Beach** (p156) on Long Island; afterward, you can bet the kids will fall asleep on the ride back to the hotel.

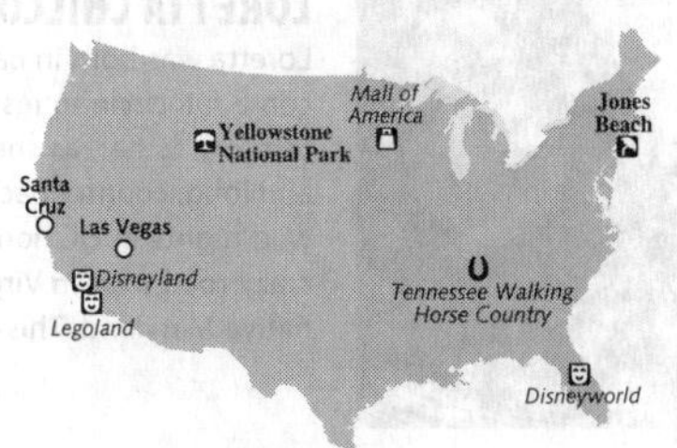

The Authors

JEFF CAMPBELL

Coordinating Author & California

Jeff has worked, lived and traveled nearly his entire life in the United States. He was born in Texas, educated on the East Coast, and now resides in San Francisco. He's gutted salmon in Alaska, camped on a Hawaiian volcano, drunk from coconuts in Puerto Rico, bowled his way to Reno, survived New Year's Eve in Times Square, been intimidated by barracuda in the Florida Keys, and marveled at the Black Hills rising out of the dead level South Dakota plains. He only wishes he got into the mountains more often. He would also like to ask the person who stole his rock album collection when he was 15 to please return it.

The Coordinating Author's Favorite Trip

You never forget your first cross-country trip, and I will always cherish mine: driving from Long Island (p156) to the paint pots of Yellowstone (p765), mainly on I-90 (p22), and along the way getting surrounded by bison in the Badlands (p715). Then north: practically petting bighorn sheep in Glacier National Park (p780) and on to Alaska via the Alcan Hwy. Perhaps my best July 4 was positioned on Mt Marathon near Seward (p1050), watching its incredible annual foot race. Returning through the Inside Passage (p1032) was an all-time high, hiking next to glaciers and watching pods of blue whales. My trip ended in San Francisco (p930), where my first stops were Twin Peaks, an organic grocery and Cafe du Nord – and I've been a resident ever since.

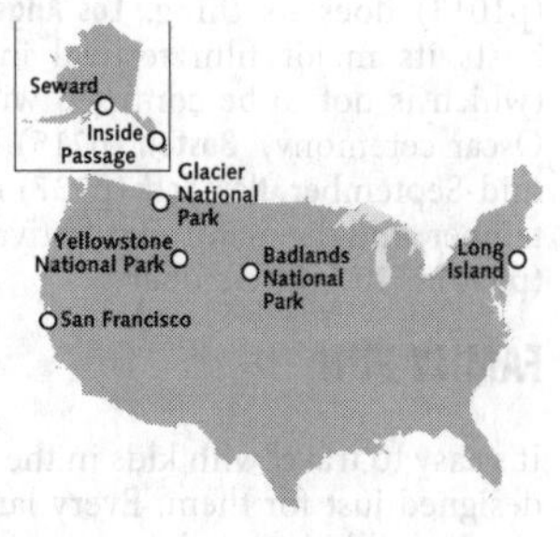

LORETTA CHILCOAT

Washington DC & the Capital Region

Loretta was born in Baltimore, grew up on Maryland's Eastern Shore and has come full circle to reside back in 'Charm City.' The Capital Region is familiar territory to her, as she has spent most of her life exploring the hectic cities and long, country back roads. She has spent summers on Delaware beaches, wild nights in DC, long lazy weekends in the West Virginia mountains, and crazy road trips in Virginia, and of course has the insider knowledge on her native Maryland. This is her first Lonely Planet guidebook.

SUSAN DERBY

Rocky Mountains

Susan spent a summer as a seasonal worker in Glacier National Park at the age of 19 and fell in love with the region during wanders through the backcountry. She has road-tripped extensively through the Rocky Mountain states, and along the way has become acquainted with extreme weather, wild wildlife, intriguing humans and more mountains than Wal-Marts. When not on the road, Susan gets closer to sea level in beautiful San Francisco, where she is a freelance writer.

BETH GREENFIELD

New York & the Mid-Atlantic States

Like many teens growing up in New Jersey, Beth spent weekends hopping trains into New York City to get big doses of culture and observe all kinds of fascinating characters. She moved there right after college to attend journalism school at NYU, and has lived in Chelsea, the East Village and Brooklyn; she now resides on the Upper West Side with her girlfriend Kiki. To quell her passion for travel – going everywhere from India and Cuba to Cape Cod and Oregon – Beth leaves whenever she can pry herself away from city life. She has even made recent peace with her suburban past, discovering a renewed sense of appreciation for the Jersey Shore area that surrounds her hometown, Eatontown.

CAROLYN B HELLER

New England

Carolyn first caught the travel bug years ago when she lived for a summer with a family in France, and, since then, she's journeyed to more than 30 countries on six continents and throughout most of the USA. But she has a soft spot for New England, where she lived, traveled and wrote for more than 20 years. She now lives with her husband and daughters in Vancouver, British Columbia.

SAM MARTIN

Texas

After moving to Texas from London, England, at the age of eight, Sam quickly lost his accent under the withering criticism of his fellow first graders. From then on he lived, attended classes or worked in several Texas towns, including Houston, Waco, Dallas and Austin, while taking extended breaks in Western Europe, Central America, Mexico, Australia, Southeast Asia, Nepal and Canada, where he planted nearly 80,000 trees in the forests of Ontario and British Columbia. Sam has worked as a writer for the *Austin Chronicle* and then as an editor at *Mother Earth News* and *This Old House* magazines. He now works as a freelance writer and lives with his wife, Denise, and two-year-old son, Ford, in Austin.

DEBRA MILLER

The South

As a contributing editor to *Atlanta* magazine, Debra writes about Atlanta and the 'new South' experience. As a road-tripper and Harley rider, she's logged many miles traveling lazy back roads where the 'old South' pops up like cotton. Though ideas and opinions vary wildly in the South, Debra has learned that wherever you journey there's always intense curiosity and generous conversation, both things that helped her write the chapter for this guide. Good food is as essential to Southerners as football and beer, while great music tinges the air revealing history and character. Along with magazine writing, Debra has authored several Lonely Planet guidebooks, including *Savannah, Georgia & the Carolina Coast*.

BOB MORRIS

Florida

Bob is an award-winning journalist who lives in Florida and regularly contributes articles on Florida and the Caribbean to *National Geographic Traveler, Arthur Frommer's Budget Travel* and *Islands*, among other magazines. He's also the author of *True Floridians & Other Passing Attractions* and *Greetings from Florida.*

BECKY OHLSEN

Pacific Northwest

Becky grew up in a microscopic village in the Colorado Rockies, but she's lived in the Pacific Northwest long enough to have moss behind her ears. From her cloud-covered lair in Portland, Oregon, she writes and copyedits for a number of newspapers and websites, exploring the area's urban landscapes and wild nature with equal enthusiasm. This is her first Lonely Planet assignment.

ANDREA SCHULTE-PEEVERS

California

Andrea is a writer, editor and translator who caught the travel bug early in life, hitting all continents but Antarctica before turning 18. A fan of big cities and sunny skies, she has made her home in Los Angeles for the past 17 years and feels strongly that California is the most perfect place on earth. A graduate of UCLA, she shares her enthusiasm by writing extensively about the state and its cultural and natural treasures. Among other titles, she has authored several Lonely Planet guidebooks, including *Los Angeles* and *San Diego & Tijuana,* and has also coordinated *California.*

KURT WOLFF

Southwest

Born and raised in the flatlands of central Ohio, Kurt first saw the Grand Canyon, the Great Salt Lake and other Southwestern landscapes and landmarks from the back of a VW Microbus, and because he's been smitten with the region ever since, he was ready to write about it. He settled in San Francisco, but still dreams of owning a cabin in New Mexico's Sangre de Cristo mountains. When he's not driving desert byways, meandering mountain trails or scouring junk stores, he works as a freelance writer and editor. He wrote about Nevada and northern California for the previous editions of Lonely Planet's *USA* and *California,* and was coordinating author on the *Yosemite National Park* guide.

KARLA ZIMMERMAN

Great Lakes

Karla is a life-long Midwesterner, weaned on a diet of corndogs and cheese. She became a rabid traveler young, seeing most of the 50 states from the back seat of her parents' station wagon. Even her first job – writing about cement for a trade magazine – didn't seem so bad since it involved treks across the country to quarries. Karla has written travel features for books, newspapers, magazines and radio. She lives in Chicago with husband Eric, the ultimate travel companion, who never says no and pays for it by having to endure everything from bus crashes in the highlands of Vietnam to polka-music bars in deep Chicago.

CONTRIBUTING AUTHORS

Ryan Ver Berkmoes is the author of the History chapter. Although his long association with Lonely Planet could be a historical drama in itself, he prefers the greater drama of American history. His interest came early, which proved useful when the history teacher hired at the last moment thought that a constitution was something you needed on a long car trip. The high school principal asked Ryan to take over the teaching duties for his own class and he cheerfully did. Anything for an A.

Tara Duggan, author of the Food & Drink chapter, was a travel writer and editor before attending San Francisco's California Culinary Academy and becoming a food writer. She is now a staff writer for the *San Francisco Chronicle* Food section, where her reporting has won the James Beard Foundation award. Tara also teaches cooking classes for the *Chronicle*.

Dr David Goldberg, MD, is the author of the Health chapter. He completed his training in internal medicine and infectious diseases at Columbia-Presbyterian Medical Center in New York City, where he has also served as voluntary faculty. He is now an infectious diseases specialist in Scarsdale, New York State, and the editor-in-chief of www.mdtravelhealth.com.

Alex Hershey was able to contribute to the research of several chapters in this book, with good reason. As a sulky teenager, she was tossed into a Dodge minivan and driven from Seattle to Alaska (and back). A year later, a 500-mile bike ride across Iowa opened her eyes to the greatness of the Great Plains. Alex now does all sorts of stuff for the LP publishing department in Oakland, California.

Snapshot

FAST FACTS

Population: 288.4 million, or about 5% of the world population

Inflation: 2.4%

Unemployment: 6+%

Gross domestic product: $10.4 trillion

Median per capita income: $21,587

Average hourly wage: $15.33

Of the amount spent globally every year, the USA accounts for 31% of the economic output, 36% of defense spending and 40% of research and development.

As America enters the 21st century, it is beset with troubles, both from within and without. By far, the two biggest issues are the ongoing threat of foreign terrorism and the economic downturn, which as of 2003 had yet to show lasting signs of real improvement.

Even though much about American life has returned to normal, the devastating terrorist attacks of September 11, 2001, have in some ways changed the United States forever. The American people have a resiliency of spirit that remains remarkably undaunted, but lingering grief and memories of the tragedy hover close to the surface. The destruction of one of the United States' major landmarks – the World Trade Center buildings in New York City – and the construction of a new monument on the site ensures that there will always be a visible reminder of this event.

One of the understandable first reactions to the attacks has been to tighten security at the nation's borders and to increase monitoring of foreign visitors. To oversee this, a new federal bureau was created in 2002 – the Department of Homeland Security. At the same time, the much-maligned US Immigration and Naturalization Service (INS) was shut down and its responsibilities absorbed into the new department. For the great majority of foreign visitors to the United States, the new security measures and regulations amount to only minor inconveniences; for a detailed description, see Visas (p1103).

The other major piece of post-9/11 legislation was the 2001 Patriot Act, which for a limited time has greatly expanded the federal government's surveillance and search powers and its ability to detain noncitizens. The Patriot Act is due to expire in 2005, and there is an ongoing debate about whether some less sweeping version of it should then be approved permanently.

Indeed, most of the government's initial domestic security responses have sparked heated debate and it's generally recognized that the government, in its anxious zeal to find more terrorists, initially went too far in its detainment and harsh treatment of Arab nationals in this country. In addition, proposed federal programs like 'Terrorism Information Awareness,' which if approved would create files on all American citizens, have raised concerns that in its fear the United States may be sacrificing the very ideals it holds sacred.

The USA has traditionally been the most open country in the world, and its citizens cherish their personal freedoms and right to privacy. The question of the day is should civil liberties and the country's openness be modified to achieve a higher level of national security? Americans have never had to ask this question in quite this way before, and they may never agree on an answer. For now, visitors to the USA get to witness one of the nation's periodic, highly emotional arguments over the meaning of US democracy itself.

The year 2001 also saw the decline of the country's economy, which was precipitated by the collapse of the stock market beginning in 2000. From 1994 to 1999, the stock market experienced a record-setting meteoric rise, built largely on overvalued high-tech and Internet stocks. When the tech bubble burst, it did so in equally spectacular fashion, with stocks losing more value in three years than at any time since the Great Depression.

The federal government went from predicting a $1.5 trillion budget surplus between 2003 and 2008 to predicting a deficit of over $1 trillion in the same period, and after four years of annual budget surpluses, 2002 began the first of what will surely be a string of federal budget deficits. Of course, state governments are also bleeding red ink, none worse than California, which gained the most during the dot-com mania, because of Silicon Valley's high-tech industry, and has since fallen the furthest.

President George W Bush's strategy for improving the economy has been to lower taxes, increase defense spending and allow for record-setting annual deficits, an approach similar to President Ronald Reagan's in the 1980s. Conservative Republicans applaud this strategy, while liberal Democrats predict that it will lead to long-term fiscal disaster.

Such divisive reactions have accompanied many of the decisions of the Bush presidency. Perhaps the most controversial has been the declaration that the USA will now take preemptive military action against threatening nations, which is a reversal of long-standing US military policy. This strategy was put into practice in early 2003 when the USA declared war on Iraq and overthrew the Hussein regime based on its hostile stance and presumed possession of weapons of mass destruction. As of late 2003, no such weapons had been found, and the USA was struggling to restore a working government in Iraq so that it could remove its military from the country.

Other controversial policies include the revival of the nation's nuclear weapons program, the refusal to sign the international Kyoto Protocol limiting greenhouse gases, and various administration efforts to open up public lands to increased logging and human use (for more, see p81). Add to this several recent corporate accounting and insider-trading stock scandals, such as Enron in 2002, and it's no surprise that Americans are feeling a certain fatigue. Trust in public institutions is at a low ebb, and despite the patriotism that rose to prominence during the Iraq war, there is an uncomfortable acknowledgment that the nation needs to do better, both at home and abroad.

There are indications, though, that America remains committed to its founding principles and ideals. In a surprise move, President Bush has tripled the USA's spending on AIDS prevention worldwide – raising it to $15 billion over five years – and so far has put few stipulations on the type of AIDS programs it funds. And in 2003, the Supreme Court handed down two landmark rulings related to diversity and equality. The first affirmed the legality of affirmative action programs in college admissions, in effect confirming that such programs are still necessary to achieve racial and ethnic equality, and that when conducted within certain limits they do not amount to racial discrimination. The second ruling struck down a Texas anti-gay sodomy law, declaring that gay Americans have a constitutional right to privacy and equality. This ruling paves the way for a potential tide of gay civil rights legislation that could become a mirror of the 1960s black Civil Rights movement.

FAST FACTS

Percentage of US consumption of all the oil produced worldwide annually: 25%

Since 1990, number of new food and beverage products introduced in the US market: 116,000

A 2002 US study of 18- to 24-year-olds found that half couldn't locate New York on a map, two-thirds couldn't locate New Jersey, and one-tenth couldn't find the United States.

Percentage of Americans who say they are 'very happy': in 1957, 53%; in 1982, 50%; in 2000, 47%

History by Ryan Ver Berkmoes

> *A People's History of the United States* by Howard Zin is a delightful read that looks at history not from the perspective of rich white men but from that of the overlooked people who actually lived it: women, children, minorities, the poor and more.

EARLY ARRIVALS

Humans first arrived in North America some 20,000 to 30,000 years ago. Most likely they migrated from Asia over a land bridge that existed between today's Siberia and Alaska. In what has become the USA, evidence of the large and flourishing cultures created by these people can be found at Cahokia Mounds in Illinois (p382) and at Chaco in New Mexico (p809), among other places.

Europeans only washed ashore – literally – in the last 1000 years. The big name here is Christopher Columbus, the Italian navigator who made three voyages west in search of the Orient and instead stumbled upon some small islands in the Bahamas. But unlike previous European seafarers (Vikings, Celts and even an Irish priest are thought to have visited the Americas in the centuries before Columbus's 1492 adventure), Columbus had the backing of Spain, which meant that news of his 'discoveries' was disseminated widely.

Spain followed up with a gaggle of explorers who claimed much of the Americas for the empire. Among them were Cortés, who conquered much of today's Mexico and set the stage for Spain's colonization of California, and Ponce de León, who stumbled around Florida looking for the fountain of youth.

Meanwhile the other European powers didn't sit back while Spaniards ran unchecked about the 'New World.' In 1524 Giovanni de Verrazano led a French group which explored the coast of North America from the Carolinas to Canada. Later expeditions pushed further into Canada and the fur-rich regions of today's Midwest, as well as north from Louisiana. The Dutch got in on the act late but scored a real deal in today's New York; in 1609 Henry Hudson claimed much of the region around the river that today bears his name, and in 1624 a group of Dutch settlers bought Manhattan Island from local Native American tribes for a few beads and trinkets.

It was the English who were ultimately to have the most impact on colonizing the land that became the USA. In 1497 John Cabot charted the eastern coast of Canada. This led to an almost routine claim by the English to North America. However, their interests were elsewhere and for much of the 16th century they mostly ignored their 'claim.' The exceptions were the result of Queen Elizabeth I, who didn't like her rivals the Spanish, but who did have a thing for pirates. She sent several, including the rather flirtatious Sir Francis Drake, to harass the Spanish in the New World. Drake helped himself to heaps of Spanish booty and even got as far as today's San Francisco in his maraudings.

The paltry English efforts to colonize the eastern seaboard of America were marked by starvation and failure for much of the 16th century. However, victory over the Spanish Armada in 1588 helped focus attention on the New World. A group of businessmen started a colony at Jamestown, Virginia (p313), in 1607. A second colony was started in 1620 at Plymouth, Massachusetts (p223), by the Pilgrims, a group of

TIMELINE

Before 10,000 BC	1492
Migration from Asia to North America across Bering Strait	Columbus 'discovers America,' making landfall in the Bahamas

conservative protestants fleeing the Church of England. Unfortunately in both cases, the English repeated their mistakes. Jamestown was actually sited in a malarial swamp. Worse, the businessmen were definitely not farmers. They planted the wrong crops too late in the season to grow and they tried to get their equally unskilled butlers to do much of the work. In short order half of the colonists were dead of disease or starvation. Meanwhile the Pilgrims were faring little better. Sick from their voyage across the Atlantic in the notoriously leaky *Mayflower* (they had rather gullibly bought the boat from a used boat dealer who gave them a 'deal'), they poked at the ground futilely and starved.

In both Jamestown and Plymouth, it was the local tribes of Native Americans who saved the settlers by giving them food and showing them how and when to grow local crops. So successful was this relationship that the thankful Pilgrims threw a harvest festival that has come to be celebrated every year as Thanksgiving. (The original holiday was celebrated closer to the true harvest season of October but in the 1940s it was moved to late November.)

'It was the local tribes of Native Americans who saved the settlers by giving them food'

Ultimately, relations between the colonists and the Indians took a fateful and what would come to be an all-too-familiar turn: after a few successful harvests, the newcomers turned on the tribes, stealing their land and breaking treaties. And the Europeans gave the locals diseases such as smallpox to which they had no natural immunity.

Jamestown was also the setting for two events in 1619 that were to shape the future USA. The settlers established a nascent form of representative democracy called the House of Burgesses (citizens) to decide local matters. And in order to cope with the chronic labor shortage – crops of tobacco had found an eager market back in England and the settlers were still dying at a rapid rate – the first boatload of African slaves arrived.

GROWING PAINS

During the 17th and early 18th centuries, the English set up colonies along the Eastern Seaboard. In 1664 they booted the Dutch out of New Netherland and promptly changed the name to New York. In 1733 Georgia became the last of the 13 original colonies, which stretched south from New Hampshire. Virginia's House of Burgesses was used by the colonies as a model for local government, although participation was limited to men who either owned property, paid taxes or both. Economically, the colonies began exploiting their natural strengths. In New England – as the colonies northeast of New York came to be called – the short growing season and wealth of lumber combined to drive a move away from farming to boat-building, manufacturing and fishing. The rolling hills of New Jersey and Pennsylvania were well suited to crops such as grain, while further south in the Carolinas and Georgia, large tobacco farms flourished.

The population grew rapidly as the colonies became economically sound and such accoutrements of civilization as roads, governments and towns were established. In 1700 there were 250,000 colonists living in today's USA. Word of the opportunities spread around Europe and immigrants primarily from Germany, Scotland, Ireland as well as

1607
First permanent English settlement at Jamestown, Virginia

1620
Mayflower lands in Cape Cod with 102 English Pilgrims

England swelled the population to over 1.6 million by 1760. But not all of these newcomers were there by choice – slaves outnumbered whites in the Carolinas by two to one.

'By the mid-1700s, much of the land east of the Appalachian Mountains had been colonized'

With a growing population, it was natural for the colonies to expand westward, a process that lasted for 150 years until the tide of settlement hit the Pacific. By the mid-1700s, much of the land east of the Appalachian Mountains had been colonized. As settlers pushed into what is today the Midwest, they ran into the French, who were making money from the fur trade with the Indians as well as exploiting the many natural resources along the Mississippi and other rivers south of the Great Lakes. Just as the two nations were in near constant conflict in Europe, so too they were in North America. War broke out in 1756 and lasted for seven years. In the French and Indian War – a name that has flummoxed schoolchildren (and adults) ever since – the British successfully battled the French and their Indian allies, winning control of territory east of the Mississippi and north through Canada.

For the colonies, victory fuelled expansion westward, but it also came at a cost – literally. The British government, which had kept the colonies at arm's length, decided it needed help paying for the war and that some of the colonies' wealth should find its way back to London. The colonists reacted to these new taxes in a manner that has formed the basis of the average American's view of taxes ever since: they were not impressed. Knowing that simply saying they did not want to pay the taxes would not get them far, the colonists seized on the principle that the taxes were being imposed by the British Parliament, which had no representatives from the colonies. The slogan 'No taxation without representation!' was born. Protests and boycotts of imported English goods followed, and led the English to send in the troops.

Not surprisingly, tensions grew. In 1770 a bunch of drunken seamen attacked a group of British soldiers on the wintry Boston waterfront (see Boston Tea Party Museum, p214). A hail of seamen-tossed snowballs brought a response of gunfire and five colonials were killed. Colonists quickly made martyrs of the five in an incident that became known as the 'Boston Massacre.' London responded by half-heartedly rescinding some of the taxes and other repressive laws. But the colonists, led by Samuel Adams (for whom the pretty decent beer is named), believed that the colonies' brightest future lay with independence and they were not pacified. Things worsened in 1773 when England granted the East India Company a legal monopoly on tea sales to the colonies. Here was an issue the tea-drinking colonists could rally around. A band of Bostonians dressed up like Indians – fooling no one – boarded three British tea-laden ships in the harbor and tossed all their cargo overboard.

Boycotts and protests were one thing but spilling tea was another. The British clamped down hard with more troops and new repressive laws and taxes (one outcome of the tea party is that to this day America is a nation of coffee-drinkers). In 1774 colonial representatives met at the First Continental Congress in Philadelphia's Independence Hall (p178) to discuss what to do next. Those from New England and Virginia, from whence came an inordinate number of early American leaders, favored full independence while the rest of the colonies preferred more boycotts of British goods.

1776	1783
American colonies sign Declaration of Independence on July 4	Treaty of Paris; US independence from Britain

By the following year the upstart colonists in Massachusetts were preparing for war. The British response was to raid towns throughout the colony to seize weapons. Seeing that the British were about to march, Paul Revere made his famous ride to warn colonists in Lexington and Concord (p222). A series of gun battles ensued and the American Revolution had begun.

Benjamin Franklin: An American Life by Walter Isaacson is a biography of one of the most brilliant and definitely the most entertaining of the founding fathers. Franklin squeezed several lifetimes of joy and accomplishment into his.

BREAKING THE SHACKLES

In May 1775 the Second Continental Congress met in Philadelphia. There a leader for the American 'army' (really a ragtag collection of poorly armed farmers, hunters and merchants) was chosen. George Washington, a wealthy Virginia farmer who had been a somewhat successful commander in the French and Indian War, volunteered to be general for free. It was a deal too good for the Congress to pass up.

But the colonists still didn't like taxes – even if those taxes were funding their fight for independence. Washington found himself in charge of an army that was poorly paid (his troops regularly quit and returned to their farms for lack of pay) and very poorly equipped. In one low moment, the 'army' almost starved while holed up in Valley Forge, Pennsylvania, during the winter of 1777. At no point during the war were more than 5% of adult males in the colonies active in the army.

Fortunately for Washington, British commanders helped the colonial cause by usually behaving like a bunch of fools. Even the nickname 'redcoats' given to the British soldiers by the colonials was based on a strategic blunder. The British Army's bright red uniforms made the soldiers easy targets for the colonials who did the ungentlemanly thing of hiding behind shrubs and picking the Brits off from behind.

Working through the stifling summer of 1776, the Second Continental Congress proved to be a remarkable gathering of intellects that counted Benjamin Franklin, Thomas Jefferson and John Hancock among the group. The congress produced the Declaration of Independence, which the delegates signed on July 4, 1776. The document – largely written by Jefferson – set out the principles that would be fundamental to the new nation. Passages such as 'We hold these truths to be self-evident, that all men are created equal, that they are endowed by their Creator with certain unalienable Rights, that among these are Life, Liberty and the pursuit of Happiness' have inspired generations since. At the last moment the Congress bowed to pressure from southern colonies and removed anti-slavery passages, a move that made the grand prose hollow and which was to have horrific consequences for the new nation in the decades to come.

Washington's army scored a major victory against the British at Saratoga, New York, in 1777. France, always looking for a chance to rub the British noses in it, began providing vital troops and supplies to the colonists. In 1781 the British surrendered at Yorktown, Virginia. Two years later the Treaty of Paris was signed, which gave the 'United States of America' full independence.

Looking forward to setting up shop after the war, the Second Continental Congress had drawn up the Articles of Confederation, which would form the basis of the new nation's government. The articles called for a loose

1787
Constitutional Convention in Philadelphia draws up the US Constitution

1791
Bill of Rights adopted as constitutional amendments

confederation of states, as the colonies were now known. This arrangement quickly proved unworkable as the states started printing their own money, engaging in trade battles, squabbling about foreign policy and otherwise behaving like a bunch of chickens at feeding time. In 1787 another convention was held in Philadelphia and this produced a new scheme that had a strong federal government at its core. A complex array of checks and balances were built into the system, which called for a government of three branches: a Congress of elected representatives, an executive branch under a president, and a Supreme Court. The Constitution came with an initial 10 amendments that were called the Bill of Rights and included freedoms of the press, religion and speech. Battles to implement and interpret these rights have been a continuing part of American history.

George Washington (p303) was elected the first president in 1789. Meanwhile, Americans were breeding like rabbits and the population kept expanding west. The Constitution allowed for the formation of new states and in 1792 Kentucky became the first state west of the Appalachians. President Thomas Jefferson (p317) offered to buy the vital port of New Orleans and today's Louisiana and Mississippi from the French in 1803. But in a curious bit of bargaining the French responded by throwing in all their lands, including huge tracts of land in the Northwest. With the stroke of a pen the United States doubled in size. In order to see what he'd got for the taxpayers' $15 million, Jefferson ordered an expedition across the new territory to the Pacific. Named after its leaders, the Lewis and Clark expedition (p686) was an epic journey that has become iconic in American lore. Among their discoveries were the Missouri River and the Rocky Mountains.

Undaunted Courage by Stephen Ambrose follows the Lewis and Clark expedition on its extraordinary journey west to the Pacific and back again. You can follow much of their route today.

Although the British had signed the peace treaty, relations between the two nations remained testy. London didn't like the USA's cozy relationship with the French, and the British Navy regularly harassed American ships worldwide. In 1812 the USA declared war on the British in an inconclusive conflict that lasted a little over two years. Two events in 1814 were notable: the British marched on the new American capital of Washington, DC, and just for spite torched the newly built home for the president, the White House; and while watching the Americans successfully defend Fort McHenry (p329) and Baltimore from the British Navy, Francis Scott Key wrote what was to become the national anthem, the 'Star Spangled Banner.'

Although the War of 1812 hadn't resulted in many tangible outcomes, it did fuel American desire for the Europeans to stay home in Europe. In 1823 President James Monroe issued the Monroe Doctrine, which said North and South America were now closed to European colonialism. This became a key part of US foreign policy and led to the first major build-up of the American army and navy.

FEELING THEIR OATS (AND SOWING THEM)

Commercially the USA took off in the first part of the 19th century. In 1825 the Erie Canal linked New York City, which had emerged as the commercial center of the country, with the raw materials of the Great Lakes. And the Americans took a British invention, the railroad, and

1803
Louisiana Purchase from France doubles the area of US territory

1812
War of 1812 starts with battles against British and Indians around Great Lakes

made – well, tracks. Beginning in the 1830s hundreds of miles of lines were built. The remote Midwest was now linked to the markets of the East Coast.

Inventors were busy as well. The cotton gin, first demonstrated by Eli Whitney in 1793, turned growing cotton into a fabulously wealthy pursuit. Plantations spread through the south and drove trade in both goods and slaves. The mechanical reaper made family farms viable and grain-growing settlers busily carved up new states such as Ohio, Indiana and Illinois. Much of the nation's growing industrial strength came from the factory towns springing up throughout the Northeast.

Winchester '73 (1950): James Stewart stars in this beautifully shot, taut drama about a pioneer who loses his gun and what he goes through to get it back. Easily one of the best of the 1950s westerns.

The continental USA took most of its final shape in the 1830s and '40s under a philosophy known as Manifest Destiny, which was based on the assumption that since much of North America was bound to become part of the US, why wait for the inevitable? Among the roadblocks on the road to this destiny was Mexico, which had won independence from Spain and controlled today's Texas and California. In 1836 a group of Texans started a revolution and the Mexicans responded with an assault on the Texan stronghold at the Alamo in San Antonio (p651). The resulting battle lasted two weeks and all but one of the defenders, who included the likes of Davy Crockett, were annihilated. But the Mexicans were so sapped by this victory that they ultimately lost the war. Although much of the mystique of the Alamo pervades Texas culture to this day, less is said about Texas' subsequent tough time as an independent nation; it begged to join the US, which it did in 1845.

Out West a string of Spanish missions (there's a great example in Santa Barbara, p921) built in the 18th century had formed the first part of the European colonization of California. In the 1840s the growing population of immigrants from the eastern US began clamoring for independence from Mexico. One word, gold, made it a done deal. The swarms of gold seekers (mostly Americans) who rushed into California via San Francisco so weighted the population against Mexico that it gave up without a fight. California became a state in 1850. Up north, settlers pounding the Oregon Trail (p771) caused the British to relinquish claims to today's Washington and Oregon in 1846.

BROTHERS FIGHT BROTHERS

Even as the USA expanded west and its economy grew, slavery remained a major source of contention; during the first half of the 19th century debate raged for and against on this issue. States north of Maryland banned slavery in 1804. After that, one compromise after another was tried to placate the competing forces. Some states were admitted as 'free states,' others as slave states, while yet others were allowed to hold referenda to decide. The so-called Underground Railroad, a loose-knit confederation of people opposed to slavery, assisted slaves escaping to the free north. In the meantime the southern states' agrarian economies became increasingly dependent on slave labor to farm the vast cotton and tobacco plantations.

Lincoln by David Herbert Donald is easily the best biography of the man many consider the greatest American president. Humble yet driven, compassionate but fearless, Lincoln rose from nothing to save his nation.

Abraham Lincoln, a country lawyer from Springfield, Illinois (p234), and a member of the anti-slavery Republican party, was elected president in 1860 after a bitter campaign in which slavery was the main issue. The

1823
Monroe Doctrine warns European countries against interference in the Americas

1841
First wagons follow new immigrant trails to California

southern states decided it was time to fight rather than switch and in 1861 formed the Confederate States of America and declared war on the United States by attacking Fort Sumter in Charleston, South Carolina (p469). The Civil War was fiercely fought. Perhaps it was the raw emotion that led brother to literally fight brother, but over the next four years the carnage was incalculable. Developments such as machine guns helped kill upward of one million people. Although the Confederates (or Grey) had the better generals, ultimately the Union (or Blue) won, primarily on its inherent industrial might and a reckless use of troops that saw casualties exceed the South's by a factor of six to one. As would be the case in later wars, the US was able to overpower the Confederates on brute strength alone. Sitting on a plantation porch sipping a mint julep and talking about valor was no match for trainloads of cannons, flotillas of iron-clad warships and waves of troops.

Gone With the Wind (1939): The original Civil War epic is also an American icon. Clark Gable as Rhett Butler and Vivien Leigh as Scarlett O'Hara – frankly, my dear, what more do you need? (Except maybe the damn fine burning of Atlanta…)

Union victories in 1863 at Gettysburg, Pennsylvania (p188), and Vicksburg, Mississippi (p510), sealed the Confederates' fate. A year later General William T Sherman made his notorious 'march to sea' through the heart of the South. The plunder and pillage were epic and included the burning of Atlanta. In April 1865 General Robert E Lee surrendered for the South at the courthouse in Appomattox, Virginia (p319).

Bygones were not bygones after the war. The north extracted reparations from the southern states and readmitted them to the union only begrudgingly and at great cost. Southern anger festered for decades and it was more than 100 years before the Republican Party could win elections in the South even though its conservative policies were more in tune with local beliefs than those of the Democratic Party. To this day the Confederate flag remains an unofficial talisman for white supremacists. Union victory also did little to improve the lot of Southern blacks. Slavery was replaced by a system of 'sharecropping' that kept the former slaves indentured to land they farmed for someone else in return for a measly share of the crops. Enjoying the fruits of American life enshrined in the Constitution was a battle for African-Americans through the Civil Rights era of the 1960s and continues to be so now.

Glory (1989): America's first black army unit fought against more than a few Johnny Rebs in the Civil War. Denzel Washington won an Oscar for his work in one of the best historical dramas ever made.

America's feverish growth accelerated further after the Civil War. The joining of the first transcontinental railroad near Promontory, Utah (p848), in 1869 opened up much of the unsettled West to pioneers. Until then movement west had often been by wagon train where misfortune was common. Industry's omnivorous appetite for new workers and the seemingly boundless frontiers available for settlers gave the US its reputation as a land of opportunity. Word spread worldwide and an open immigration policy meant that during a 50-year period beginning in the 1870s tens of millions of immigrants arrived from Europe and Asia (see the Immigration Museum, p118). Many found livelihoods in the ethnic neighborhoods of the cities. Others set out on their own to claim land for 40-acre farms they could work with their family and a mule. These forces came together spectacularly in the fast-growing city of Chicago (p355) where commodities such as grain and cattle produced in America's heartland were sold, industries produced everything from steel to machinery and the nation's railroads converged. The hub of the nation, Chicago was a magnet for immigrants.

1849	1861
California Gold Rush; 80,000 immigrants arrive	Abraham Lincoln becomes president; Southern states secede; attack on Fort Sumter starts Civil War

But one group, the Native Americans, not only did not enjoy this growing prosperity but were almost eradicated by it. In a process that had begun at Jamestown, a familiar pattern was repeated endlessly: new settlers to an area made compacts with the local tribes until the new population grew and the tribes were pushed out. The Indians would fight back but were ultimately no match for the superior numbers and weapons of the settlers. To bring peace, the government would offer the tribes their own lands further west if they would simply go away. All would be fine until settlement reached these lands and the process would begin again. Scores of promises made by the 'forked-tongues' of the government were broken and whole tribes vanished (see the National Museum of the American Indian, p290).

The Searchers (1956): Probably John Wayne's best film; he spends years hunting for his niece (Natalie Wood) who was kidnapped by the Comanches. The morals are complex and the Indian perspective surprisingly sympathetic for the time.

By the 1870s few Great Plains tribes had not fallen to this genocide. For two decades the Indian wars raged across the plains, spawning little but tragedy (and much later scores of awful movies). Although the Indians had many successes – most notably against the spectacularly incompetent General George Custer and his troops at Little Big Horn in South Dakota in 1876 (p712) – the force of expansion eventually overwhelmed them and the few survivors were carted off to desolate reservations.

WEALTH, WORK & POVERTY

The huge growth of the American economy in the latter part of the 19th century led to the emergence of some industrial behemoths. Notable were US Steel run by Andrew Carnegie from its base in Pittsburgh, Pennsylvania, and the enormous near-monopoly of John D Rockefeller's Standard Oil Company. Inventions such as the automobile led to other empires, including the one created by Henry Ford at the turn of the 20th century. Industrial technology replaced the quaint notion of craftsmen making goods. At factories such as Ford's in Detroit, Michigan (p412), legions of unskilled workers performed simple tasks on assembly lines that resulted in complex products such as a car. Although jamming peg A into hole B over and over could be mind-numbing, it was also steady work. The crafty Ford paid his workers above-average wages, not out of beneficence but because he and other industrialists realized that if they gave workers more money to spend, they would buy the very products they produced. Industrialization created the vast American middle class and spurred the movement of people from back-breaking and unpredictable lives on farms to greater economic security in the cities.

The Chief by David Nasaw chronicles the life of William Randolph Hearst, America's first media mogul. From the Spanish-American War through World War II Hearst hobnobbed with politicians and celebrities and changed US history.

But it wasn't all happy workers at the factories either. Work was often dangerous, hours long and those easiest to exploit such as women, children and recent immigrants were treated little better than slaves. In 1906 Upton Sinclair published *The Jungle* to the acclaim of the growing reform movement and to the horror of almost everyone else. Although it was primarily a political work promoting socialism, it gained notoriety for its section describing the grotesque and decidedly unsavory conditions in Chicago's meat-packing plants (among the horrors revealed was that workers often contributed far more than just their labor to the cans of meat they packed). Spurred by labor unions and other reformers, government reforms on industry included anti-trust laws that broke up monopolies like Standard Oil, labor laws that guaranteed the 40-hour

1876
Custer's Last Stand at Little Big Horn, South Dakota

1898
Victory in Spanish-American War gives USA control of Philippines, Puerto Rico and Guam

work week and banned the exploitation of children and women, and regulations ensuring the safety of foods and other goods. A growing women's rights movement drove the passage of the 19th amendment in 1919 which gave women the right to vote.

Growing prosperity at home meant that the US could also define its role in the rest of the world. A rambunctious war movement in the 1890s caused the declaration of war in 1898 against the teetering Spanish empire. The results were quite one-sided and America took possession of Puerto Rico and Guam while picking up the Philippines for a pittance. Ostensibly about freedom for Cuba, the war caused the dictatorial Spanish government to be replaced by one supported by US corporations.

Further south the French had been literally stuck in the mud for years trying to dig a canal across Panama. The US played politics shrewdly and got 'freedom' for Panama from its Colombian rulers, and in return won the right to complete the Panama Canal and run it as a monopoly link between the Atlantic and Pacific Oceans right from the time it opened in 1914.

Across the Atlantic events were unfolding that would eventually propel the US to its position of prominence. The Great War between the European powers that began in 1914 slowly sucked in the Americans. Known as WWI only after an even worse cataclysm became WWII, the conflict forced the US to choose sides between the Allies (mainly Britain and France) and the Central Powers led by Germany. By historical association, and because they were major trading partners, the US tended to side with the Allies. Most Americans, however, wanted to stay isolated and President Woodrow Wilson won re-election in 1916 on the slogan of 'He kept us out of the war.' Meanwhile America profitably sold armaments to the Allies, which caused the Germans to order their U-boats to sink American freighters thought to be carrying weapons. A string of sinkings, along with the realization by the government that it would be important to have a place at the post war table where the spoils would be divvied up, led the US to declare war on the Central Powers in 1917.

Sergeant York (1941): Gary Cooper shines in this true story of an archetypical American hero. Alvin York didn't want to fight in WWI because he thought killing was wrong, but once in the trenches he single-handedly wins the battle.

America mobilized rapidly: in 18 months the army trained and sent over two million men to Europe and the air force grew from 55 planes to over 17,000. The American army tipped the balance to the Allies, who ended years of futile trench-fighting carnage and overwhelmed the exhausted Germans.

Isolationists regained their political strength after the war and kept the US from joining Wilson's brainchild, the League of Nations. A disappointed Wilson died a broken man and, hobbled by the lack of US participation and other woes, the League never became the force for world peace that had been envisaged.

FALSE MORALITY & FALSE PROSPERITY

Although the decade that followed WWI has earned the sobriquet 'the Roaring '20s' for its flappers, jazz and supposed 'anything goes' culture, the 1920s were in reality a time of great contrasts. In 1920 the federal government began enforcing the 18th amendment to the Constitution, which prohibited the sale of alcohol. Driven by the religious conservatives who had been a part of American life since the Pilgrims, prohibition

1908
The first model T car is built; Ford is soon selling one million a year

1917–18
US involvement in WWI

overnight made a majority of Americans lawbreakers. It also spawned a new industry of organized crime that supplied the thirsty populace. Entrepreneurs such as Joseph Kennedy (father of a future political dynasty) in Massachusetts made fortunes off illegal sales of alcohol. But it was in Chicago that the effects of Prohibition were seen most colorfully. Gangs such as Al Capone's battled openly for domination of the trade, spawning corruption at all levels of public life. Although mythologized in countless movies and lore, Chicago's gangs were trigger-happy thugs whether they were blasting flower shops or gunning down mourners at funerals. After Prohibition was repealed in 1933 (although to this day some conservative enclaves, including Utah, retain local restrictions on alcohol consumption), the gangs found it easy to shift to new ventures in prostitution and drug-running.

The Untouchables (1987): David Mamet wrote the script for this familiar but in this case thrilling saga of good (Kevin Costner as Elliot Ness) versus evil (Robert De Niro as Al Capone). Scores of great scenes include the famous one shot on the steps of Chicago Union Station.

Obtaining a drink wasn't the only game Americans were willing to play in the 1920s; they also played the stock market by the millions to the tune of billions in the hopes of making zillions. This financial free-for-all extended throughout the economy with banks making dubious loans to farmers, businessmen and almost anyone else who wanted cash. Citizens became 'consumers' by getting credit to buy whiz-bang inventions like refrigerators, clothes washers, automobiles, radios and all the other accoutrements of a modern and increasingly comfortable life.

But what goes up must come down; spurred by a gloomy global economy, the stock market collapsed in October 1929 as panicked investors tried to sell off their stocks and share prices plummeted. The ripple effects were devastating. Millions lost their homes, farms and businesses as the teetering banks called in their dodgy loans, and millions more lost all of their savings as the banks collapsed. This was the beginning of the Great Depression that ultimately saw perhaps as much as 50% of the American workforce unemployed. Scores took to the roads in search of work.

The Grapes of Wrath (1940): John Steinbeck's saga of Okies trying to escape the Dust Bowl for the promised land of California during the Depression is beautifully acted by a cast led by Henry Fonda.

Democrat Franklin Roosevelt (p159) was elected president in 1932 on the ill-defined promise of a 'New Deal' to get the US out of its crisis. (Even a vaguely talented dog-catcher could have been elected president against the Republicans, whose president, Herbert Hoover (p705), had happily fiddled away while the economy crashed and burned.) Not widely known or highly regarded when elected, Roosevelt quickly became one of the pivotal figures in American history. After taking office he led the passage of laws to stabilize the economy. But more radical were his creation of social programs, which had previously been anathema to independent-minded Americans. Social security, the government-run retirement program, is one example of how Roosevelt gave the federal government a role in almost every aspect of Americans' lives. In addition federal spending projects resulted in everything from the enormous Hoover Dam (p868) on the Arizona–Nevada border to the Civilian Conservation Corps, which put talented Americans to work creating such things as the magnificent stone structures that grace national parks as well as public murals and other lasting works of art.

WORLD WAR II

With so many troubles at home, it was no wonder that Americans were more isolationist than ever during the 1930s. The rise of Hitler and fascism

1920

18th amendment bans alcohol, Prohibition starts; 19th amendment gives women the vote

1933

Franklin D Roosevelt introduces New Deal economic initiatives to counter the Great Depression; Prohibition ends

The Good War by Studs Terkel tells the story of WWII using the voices of Americans who lived through it. Those who fought and those who were left behind tell stories that are at once common yet deeply moving.

Tora Tora Tora (1970): Rigorously accurate albeit at times dry, the events that brought America into WWII are faithfully chronicled right down to the heroics of Doris Miller (a black mess attendant who shot down a Japanese plane). Miles better than the execrable *Pearl Harbor* (2001).

around the world received coverage in the media, but for most Americans it was another reason to let foreigners deal with their own problems. However, Roosevelt and a few others in government recognized the threats from both Germany and Japan. After WWII broke out in 1939, Roosevelt used every trick he could think of to lend support to Britain and his close friend Winston Churchill while beginning a military build-up at home. Programs such as the Lend-Lease Act, which virtually gave Britain military supplies, barely skirted the law and Roosevelt had to rely on his immense popularity with voters to keep the isolationist Congress on board.

Indeed it was Roosevelt's popularity with Americans – his ability to communicate and reassure the average person throughout the Depression was unmatched – that allowed him to run for an unprecedented third term in 1940. Republicans were quick to point out that George Washington's refusal to run for a third term as president had helped preserve the nascent democracy in 1796, but this argument found no traction with the populace.

The war many expected came in a manner nobody expected on December 7, 1941 when the Japanese launched a surprise attack on Pearl Harbor in Hawaii (p1071). Although more than 2000 Americans were killed, the attack had more symbolic than strategic importance (the ships sunk were mostly old battleships that would have had little value in the war to come). Any thoughts of isolationism were erased as 'Remember Pearl Harbor!' became a rallying cry across the nation. Roosevelt gave an eloquent address to Congress the next day, which included the line 'Yesterday, December 7th – a date which will live in infamy…'

Although American emotion demanded that the Japanese be dealt with immediately, Roosevelt understood that Germany and the Axis powers represented the more immediate threat. Making the defeat of Germany the strategic priority was helped by Germany's (and its somewhat unreliable ally Italy's) declaration of war on the US on December 11, 1941.

The war in the Pacific went poorly until June 1942 when a combination of luck, tenacity and cleverness gave the US Navy an incredible victory over the much larger Japanese Navy at the Midway Islands. From there began a long and bloody counterattack recapturing islands from the Japanese all the way back to Tokyo.

In Europe a series of missteps in the air and in Africa initially hindered US efforts, but most importantly the Americans ensured the safety of the British and with time came the experience and materials that allowed the Americans to successfully attack the Axis by air, land and sea. Led by American General Dwight Eisenhower (see Abilene, p702), the Allies launched their assault on Germany with the D-Day invasion (p519) of France on June 6, 1944; this brought some relief to the Soviet Union, which had been savagely fighting the Germans in Eastern Europe for three years.

Over 25% of Americans joined the military during WWII; men were eligible for the draft up to the age of 46. But every American played a role, from children who collected recyclable goods for the war effort to women who, as popularized by the iconic Rosie the Riveter, took on traditional male jobs throughout industry. This mobilization of women had profound effects on American society following the war as

1941
Pearl Harbor bombed; USA enters WWII

1951
I Love Lucy premiers on CBS and is number one in the ratings; television becomes a national obsession

women no longer expected to spend their lives working in the home. The segregated military meant that African-Americans had to serve in support roles although a few did see combat in all-black units. Their success in battle helped drive the desegregation of the military shortly after the war, an early victory in the Civil Rights struggle.

Germany surrendered in May 1945. Full attention then shifted to the Pacific where American experience with Japanese tactics such as the kamikaze suicide attacks made it certain that an invasion of the Japanese mainland would result in unprecedented death and carnage. But a vast yet secret government program called the Manhattan Project provided an alternative. Scores of scientists, many of whom were Jews who had escaped the Nazis, produced the atomic bombs that were used to vaporize Hiroshima and Nagasaki in August 1945. Japan surrendered a few days later.

Shortly before the war ended and right after winning a fourth term as president, Roosevelt, clearly aged beyond his years, died. The new president, Harry S Truman (see Independence, p692), said he never had any qualms about ordering the use of the atomic bombs as the alternative was the possible deaths of thousands if not millions of American troops in an invasion.

The Making of the Atomic Bomb by Richard Rhodes takes an almost lyrical look at the Manhattan Project and the moral issues that haunted some of the inventors and inspired others.

SUPERPOWER TRIALS & TRIUMPHS

The end of the war did not bring real peace, however, as the US and its wartime ally the Soviet Union soon became caught in a struggle of wills and influence to control the course of the world. The four-decade-long conflict came to be known as the Cold War. It was capitalism versus communism on a global stage with only the threat of mutual nuclear destruction keeping the two superpowers from direct war. Instead the conflict played out in other nations worldwide. In Korea, the Soviet- and Communist Chinese-supported North Korea invaded the south and only the US and its allies prevented South Korea from being overrun. The war ended in a stalemate in 1953. In Europe the US-led West faced off against the East in divided Germany for decades. Meanwhile the divided United Nations (p126), which had been chartered in San Francisco in 1945, was largely ineffectual in preventing conflict.

The Fifties by David Halberstam explores a decade marked by both upheaval and complacency. Television, repression, Civil Rights, suburbanization, the Beat poets and more were intertwined in the decade that spawned modern America.

At home, the US economy had exploded in size during and after the war. Returning servicemen could choose between nearly free college educations and immediate employment in a plethora of well-paying jobs. Affluence brought a near obsession with modern comforts, foremost of which was the single-family home. Millions of Americans left the crowded cities in a suburban migration made possible by cheap cars, cheap gas, vigorous government road-building (the Interstate highway system was begun in the 1950s) and zoning policies – or lack thereof – that encouraged construction of homes and shopping malls on former farmland surrounding cities. Another American obsession reached prominence during the early 1950s: television. Movies and radio were rapidly supplanted by the ubiquitous tube, which soon held sway over popular American culture.

The 1960s saw the Cold War move to two new theaters: space and Vietnam. In the former the US had been embarrassed by a string of failures

1955
The first McDonald's and Disneyland both open

1963
President John F Kennedy assassinated in Dallas, Texas

while the Soviets enjoyed a string of successes. At his inaugural address in 1961 President John F Kennedy promised to regain the lead and land an American on the moon before the end of the decade. Few thought it was possible and even fewer had any idea about how to do it but in a dramatic and still awe-inspiring effort that symbolized the swaggering confidence of the USA, Neil Armstrong and Buzz Aldrin landed on the moon July 20, 1969. (See Kennedy Space Center, p602; Johnson Space Center, p663; and National Air & Space Museum, p290.) Concurrently, however, the US was getting a lesson in humility in Vietnam.

A Man on the Moon by Andrew Chaikin captures the invention, drama and sheer luck that were the hallmarks of the US space program and its goal of landing men on the moon.

President Lyndon B Johnson, who had succeeded Kennedy after he was assassinated on November 22, 1963, presided over remarkable change at home. He used his forceful personality to push through major Civil Rights legislation that came after years of often violent struggles in the South and which saw the emergence of forceful black leaders such as Martin Luther King (p479 and p544). But Johnson met his Waterloo in Vietnam where he committed half a million American troops to stop a takeover of South Vietnam by communist North Vietnam. It was a classic Cold War confrontation, and the Americans ultimately lost due to miscalculation, hubris and eroding support at home.

Freedom's Daughters: A Juneteenth Story by Lynne Olson is a page-turner about black women such as Rosa Parks, Diane Nash and Ida Mae Holland who were real heroes of the Civil Rights movements.

Growing anger over the war divided Americans and led to huge protests on college campuses. It also led to the 1968 election of Richard M Nixon, possibly the most cynical and manipulative president in US history. Certainly he was one of the darkest; aides presented Nixon with a jovial Irish setter in an effort to humanize the president but the dog growled and barked whenever it was near Nixon. During the election campaign, Nixon claimed to have a 'secret plan' to end the Vietnam war, but once in office he expanded the war and began secret bombing raids on Laos and Cambodia. Paranoid beyond reason, Nixon led a White House culture that ordered the 1972 burglary of Democratic Party offices at the Watergate office complex in Washington. Although it took months for dogged journalists to uncover the conspiracy behind the break-in, the resulting scandal eventually consumed the administration and Nixon himself. He became the first president to resign from office, in August 1974.

These dramatic events at home and abroad were but some of the forces shaking American society. Women's liberation, the sexual revolution and the hippies who emerged from San Francisco in the mid-1960s all confronted traditional American values. The 1970s was an unrestrained time for many Americans, marked not just by the birth control pill and an end to cultural censorship but also by a certain narcissism that reached an unfortunate extreme at the end of the decade with the Bee Gees, disco and polyester. But this social exuberance was not found throughout society where there was widespread malaise brought on by the aftereffects of Vietnam and Watergate, a stagnant economy and recurring energy shortages that put a crimp on the suburban lifestyle.

Platoon (1986): There have been scores of movies about Vietnam but this autobiographical account by Oliver Stone of his own time as a soldier is wrenching. It unflinchingly captures the moral ambiguities faced by Americans during the war.

In 1980 Ronald Reagan, a modestly talented and moderately successful actor who had gone on to some fame as the governor of California, ran for president. His campaign was simple: make Americans feel good about America again. The ever-cheerful Reagan won handily and it soon became apparent that taking care of the Commies once and for all was

1969
Two Americans land on the moon, culminating the space race

1973
Last US forces leave Vietnam

also going to be high on the agenda. He launched a defense build-up of such monumental proportions that the Soviets went broke trying to keep up. Meanwhile he enacted policies, such as huge tax cuts, which brought comfort and solace to conservatives and business interests who had been left quite addled by the events of the previous two decades.

The US enjoyed huge economic growth in 1980s as Reagan's optimism proved infectious. The nation also enjoyed record budget deficits brought on by the binge-spending on weapons coupled with the tax cuts. The hangover for these good times fell to Reagan's hapless successor, George Bush. Despite a successful war to liberate Kuwait after an Iraqi invasion, Bush never caught on with the public and was easily trounced by the previously unknown Bill Clinton in 1992. A political moderate, Clinton proved an able communicator who easily connected with the populace. He also had the good fortune to catch the technology boom that had started with personal computers in the 1980s and moved on to the Internet in the 1990s. The US enjoyed unprecedented economic growth, which erased government budget deficits and sent unemployment below 2%.

However, despite record popularity – he was re-elected in a landslide in 1996 – Clinton had no shortage of enemies among conservatives. With a hatred that was almost fanatical, conservatives used radio talk shows and other media to launch an all-out assault on Clinton and his prominent wife Hilary. Unfortunately for Clinton, he proved to be his own worst enemy. The Clinton administration provided fodder for the opposition with a string of minor scandals. But the lowest moment came after Clinton admitted he had lied about an affair with a comely White House intern. While much of the world looked on in disbelief, he narrowly managed to avoid being tossed out of office by the Republican-controlled Congress.

By the start of the 2000 presidential race, conservative politics and religion were dominant forces in American life. With vast wealth that helped shape public opinion as well as voter apathy stemming from the disenfranchisement of scores of Americans, conservatives managed to get their chosen man, George W Bush, elected president in an election marred by a voting fiasco in Florida that left the result in doubt for weeks.

The son of the former President Bush, George W had previously done little of note as a businessman, barely traveled outside of the US and had been governor of Texas at a time when the economy would have made almost anyone look good. Seizing on the disinterest that many Americans have in the affairs of their own country – fewer than 50% of those eligible vote – Bush installed a government that launched a crusade against the environment, personal freedoms, Civil Rights and other liberties that polls showed most Americans actually favored. At the same time he granted billions of dollars in tax cuts and government contracts to his wealthy supporters.

Everything changed on September 11, 2001. Terrorists launched catastrophic attacks on the World Trade Center (p108) in New York and the Pentagon in Washington that killed 3000 people. Americans rallied behind the president and called for revenge but, unlike after Pearl Harbor, there was no foreign government to easily blame. Instead the enemy was a shadowy radical Islamic terrorist group called Al-Qaeda that operated

Barbarians at the Gates (1993): The true story of a huge American business merger oozes with the greed that was officially sanctioned during the Reagan 1980s. Fire thousands of loyal employees to enjoy a minor gain in share price? You bet!

Hard Drive by James Wallace and Jim Erickson looks at the often unsavory manners of Bill Gates as he borrowed ideas from others to dominate an industry that now dominates the economy.

1974

Nixon resigns over Watergate

1977

The Apple II computer goes on sale, starting the personal computer boom out of remote regions of Third World countries. The US launched an invasion of Afghanistan in an effort to root out the terrorists thought to be hiding there. Results were mixed and in the meantime Bush and his advisors were arguing for a war against Saddam Hussein and Iraq. Having been let off the hook by the senior Bush 10 years previous, Hussein spent the 1990s taunting the US and serving as a rallying point for those against US unilateralism around the world. The Bush administration claimed the Iraqis had 'weapons of mass destruction' and used this as a reason to invade Iraq in April 2003. Notably scores of traditional American allies (with the exception of the ever-loyal British) opposed the war. The battles were over quickly, but in the aftermath a shattered Iraq, like Afghanistan before it, waited with increasing anger for the US to put the nation in order again. Concurrently the American rationale for the war came into doubt.

'American isolation is again popular even as America's role in the world makes this impossible'

Although the world gobbles up American pop culture in the form of fast food, logo-covered clothes and mass entertainment, there is a growing hatred for American policies. While at home, American isolation is again popular even as America's role in the world makes this impossible.

1991

The World Wide Web debuts on the Internet; boom and bust over the next 10 years is the largest ever

2001

Terrorists hijack four planes and crash into the World Trade Center and Pentagon, killing thousands

The Culture

THE NATIONAL PSYCHE

As a nation, America was an idea before it became a place, and the same can be said of the creation of its citizens: being an American is as much a state of mind as a statement of birth or heritage.

Despite any claims otherwise, it is impossible to describe a single national character. America is simply too diverse – ethnically, geographically and economically. The list of differences and disagreements is so long, in fact, that the principal question is not 'What is the typical American like?' but 'Is there any common trait that's shared by all?'

Put a native Puebloan, a Bronx plumber, a Mennonite farmer, a Hollywood starlet, an African-American senator, an Afghan-born teacher and a Korean-born grocery clerk in the same room, and what, besides the legal right to live here, connects them? It is not shared history, values or morality. It is not a shared ethnicity or race. It is not an evolved, open-minded brother- or sisterhood, despite two centuries of trying.

Paradoxically, what has become one of America's defining connections is otherness and individualism. Now as much as ever, most citizens are Americans – and something else. One's 'Americanness' is rarely total. As well, the American mandate – the freedom to pursue one's own ideals – is pointedly at odds with the common human urge, exhibited in societies throughout history, to have all members conform to similar standards. For some in America, eccentricity is a fact to be tolerated; for others, it's a point of pride.

Which leads to the nation's most unifying concept. If Americans lack a shared past or a common present, together they hold the future: fully three-quarters of Americans still claim to believe in the American Dream. This revolutionary set of aspirations may be nothing more than the desire for a better, more just life, but it is, remarkably, the same essential set of hopes the Pilgrims had when they fled from Europe in the 16th century.

America's history has indeed left its mark on the nation's psyche. Those first European immigrants developed America's much-vaunted 'pioneer spirit,' that combination of self-reliant individualism, practical creativity, disregard for social convention, mistrust of authority and courage in the face of adversity – what would become, in other words, good-old Yankee pragmatism and Silicon Valley know-how. Little has changed. Each immigrant who arrives from Pakistan or Mexico, each citizen who packs up, moves along and tries again, must carve for themselves a home out of a strange and sometimes inhospitable land – and it helps if they've packed similar traits in their luggage.

What people desire from America has also been notably consistent, embedded as these desires are in the rights and freedoms promised by the Constitution. People want to share in the nation's wealth and prosperity and to say what they like and worship how they wish without persecution. This set of expectations forms the egalitarian contract that binds – and as often divides – the nation.

The other primary influence on the American mind has been the Protestant religion. When the Puritans arrived, their most valuable possession was their faith, and they tilled its hard-working, plain-spoken and conservative sensibilities deep into the American soil. Today, whether they hold religious beliefs or not, many Americans value these same qualities,

Coming of Age (1995) by Studs Terkel: No journalist gets inside the average American and busts the stereotypes any better than Studs. His most recent collection – interviewing a gathering of America's elders – is typically brilliant and inspiring.

Made in America (1994) by Bill Bryson: What is more revealing than a country's language? With consummate skill and his trademark wit, Bryson explains the native tongue, and the American mind, with a blizzard of clever, delightful and revealing anecdotes.

and they espouse the central 'I' of Protestant doctrine: that the divine – whether in the form of God, art or ecstatic nature – is experienced by the individual directly. Each person becomes a locus, an expert. To be right does not require a consensus.

Given all these influences, a portrait of the 'typical American' begins to come into focus – and yet it never completely resolves itself, mainly because the nation is too big, too diverse, too cantankerous and contradictory. Most people – due to the omnipresence of American media – are already well familiar with the common stereotypes: the 'ugly' American and the 'good' American. These clichés are in fact two sides of the same shiny coin, and how satisfying it would be to flip it and have one side turn out to be true.

Instead, America, as a nation, has the curious ability to appear, at one and the same time, both generous and greedy, altruistic and self-serving, open and prejudiced, radically inventive and rabidly conservative, intellectually curious and ignorant of history, exultant in individualism and prizing conformity, devoutly spiritual and cynically materialistic. Natives fancy themselves doers and dreamers, simple and smart, trailblazers and fence menders, and eternally optimistic.

A traveler to America will meet all of these faces and many more that don't fit into neat postcard images. America is finally a stubborn nation, if only because it never holds still long enough to take a picture.

LIFESTYLE

Lifestyles in America are as varied as her citizens, and they are almost as impossible to generalize about. In comparison with other advanced democracies, the USA ranks among the very best or the very worst in a wide range of economic and social criteria, with very little in between. On the one hand, it is without question the largest, most robust and technologically advanced economy in the world; it has the most Nobel laureates, patent applications, business start-ups and charitable giving.

THE RICH GET RICHER...

It's a story as old as human history, but in egalitarian America, it's threatening to pull apart the country's beloved democratic center. The growing gap between America's rich and poor is now so pronounced and ingrained it's astonishing: since 1975, nearly all gains in household income have gone to the top 20%. This same one-fifth of the population earns approximately 55% of the nation's annual income and owns over 80% of its wealth (which includes assets like land, homes, businesses and investments). The top 1% – America's upper class – earns around 17% of income and controls 38% of wealth. Over the last two decades, the number of millionaires has doubled to 4.8 million.

By contrast, the bottom 40% of households earn only 10% of income and own less than 1% of wealth; the bottom 60%, which includes a large portion of the middle class, earn only 23% of income and own less than 5% of wealth. The definition of what constitutes America's 'middle class' is broad and extremely subjective, but the numbers don't lie. Being in the middle is closer to the bottom than it has ever been.

And what of the poor? In 2001, the poverty rate was 11.7%, or 32.9 million people; as a percentage of their populations, 7.8% of non-Hispanic whites were in poverty, 22.7% of blacks, 21.4% of Hispanics and 10.2% of Asians.

Each year the government sets the official poverty threshold; in 2003, it was just under $9000 for a single person, and $15,260 for a family of three. Officially, a family earning $18,000 a year would not be counted in the poverty totals, though there would be little practical difference in their circumstances. As a comparison, in 2000 the Economic Policy Institute estimated that a 'living wage' for a family of three would be $30,000. What would the official US poverty rate look like if this were the standard of measure? It gives one pause.

On the other hand, compared with other industrialized countries, it has one of the largest gaps between rich and poor, the highest rates of poverty and infant mortality, the most uninsured citizens and one of the least successful K–12 public education systems.

First and foremost, though, America has long been distinguished by its large, stable, homogenous middle class, which since the 1950s has been anchored by the 'nuclear family': that is, two parents, two kids, a pet, a car and a house. Toss in a well-paid job and an annual vacation, and for many what you still get is their ideal vision of the American Dream. Statistics bear this out: the average family is 3.17 persons, three-quarters of families are headed by a married couple, and two-thirds of families own their own home.

Fast Food Nation (2001) by Eric Schlosser: This muckraking exposé of the American fast-food industry is not just about hamburgers. It's a kaleidoscopic account of the modern-day transformation of American business, society and agriculture. It's a must-read.

And yet, the sameness of averages doesn't do justice to the diversity of America's families. Behind the sometimes faceless tract houses of the suburbs live a multitude: from large Mormon or Catholic families with oodles of kids to single-parent families to same-sex couples raising adopted children. Multigenerational families living under one roof are becoming more common again, particularly in immigrant communities. These days, there's little social or cultural pressure to pursue any one idealized lifestyle: more and more Americans are marrying later and having fewer or no kids, and some are happy not to marry at all. In cities especially, young adults strike out on their own, share housing, and make 'families' of friends instead.

Nickel and Dimed (2001) by Barbara Ehrenreich: This slim volume says more about the struggles of America's minimum-wage workers than a compendium of statistics. Ehrenreich asked herself a simple question: Could I survive on these wages myself? This is her story.

However, recent decades have not been kind to the USA's middle class. Despite living in a land of plenty, most Americans are struggling harder just to maintain what they've got, much less realize their upwardly mobile aspirations. Job and lifestyle choices are increasingly necessitated by harsh economics, not desire. Just one indicator of this is that in 2001, for the first time in US history, consumer debt surpassed disposable income, meaning that Americans are spending more than they're making, and saving less and less.

Poverty is a real and growing concern, for Americans both personally and as a society. US politicians have congratulated themselves that an estimated 6 million people have left the welfare rolls since the 1996 Welfare Reform Act was passed, but there has been no follow-up assessment to determine what their lives are like. In 1997, one estimate was that one-fifth of the homeless were actually employed full- or part-time. While homelessness itself is the result of very complex social causes, clearly, in the USA a job is not always enough to keep you off the streets.

The United States is practically alone among industrialized democracies in requiring citizens to survive solely on wages (and accumulated wealth), and this is a large reason why poverty, by any definition, remains so pervasive. Despite the occasional effort to nationalize a major public service – such as education, childcare or healthcare – the country resists because of its aversion to more taxes and federal intrusions into the private sphere.

Hunting Mister Heartbreak (1990) by Jonathan Raban: Though politically dated, Englishman Raban's chronicle of his experience living in America is still provocative and insightful, as he copes with his own preconceptions and gets beyond the cultural clichés.

The jobs that are available are changing too. Blue-collar work in manufacturing, agriculture and industry is disappearing and being replaced by white-collar service and information sector jobs. For a short time, it seemed like the 1990s 'New Economy' – based on financial services and technology – would complete the USA's postindustrial transformation, but the 'dot-bomb,' or economic crash, at the turn of the 21st century has cooled such talk. The great majority of service industry jobs are at or just above the minimum wage, and this is simply not enough to get by. Americans respond by working longer hours, taking more than one job and having more family members work. An older generation, whose retirement savings have been decimated by the stock market plunge, now

...posedly Fun Thing I'll Never Do Again (1997) by David Foster Wallace: If you read only one book before you travel, let this be it. Wallace is the most protean, gifted, drop-dead funny writer America's got. These idiosyncratic essays on American life are priceless.

has to compete with teenagers for work flipping burgers and folding jeans in department stores.

Coupled with this is the looming crisis in health care, which short of finding a job itself is the single biggest financial challenge facing Americans. The United States has, by most measures, the best and most sophisticated medical facilities in the world, but an ever-increasing number of Americans simply can't afford access to them: in 2002, one in seven Americans, or 41 million people, had to go without health insurance. This is not just a problem for the poor; one-third of the uninsured live in households with incomes over $50,000. It's now estimated that each year 18,000 people die prematurely as a result of being uninsured.

The problem isn't one of spending. In 2002, Americans spent two to four times the per capita rate in other developed countries on health care. The problem is part method of delivery and part costs. Since WWII, all large employers have been required to provide health insurance for workers, but this has left out an ever-growing number of citizens whose only access to health care or insurance is to pay for it themselves. Many in this position must play a financial shell game between rent, food and insurance.

DID YOU KNOW?

The hottest new dating fad is 'speed dating,' in which 50 romantically challenged singles meet in pairs, round-robin style, for three minutes each in the hopes of finding the perfect match.

Health care costs, meanwhile, are rising by about 10% a year, driven mainly by prescription drugs. In light of this, one can't help but note the health of the pharmaceutical industry, which enjoys after-tax net profits of 19%, or nearly four times the average of Fortune 500 companies, making it the nation's most profitable business.

As for the health of the average American, he or she would love to be in such good shape. Instead, Americans are, plainly put, getting fatter. Today, two out of three adults are overweight or obese, and the US surgeon general has called this an epidemic. The number of overweight kids has jumped 50% in the last decade, and all evidence points to computers,

DOS & DON'TS

Americans are overall a pretty easygoing bunch. By and large, their motto is to live and let live. But as in any society, there are certain norms of behavior and cultural taboos that foreign visitors should be aware of.

- Do return friendly greetings. 'Hi. How are you?' is expected to receive a cheerful 'Thanks, I'm fine,' not actual complaints.
- Don't be overly physical when you first meet someone. Some Americans will hug, but many more, especially men, will just shake hands.
- Do be on time. Americans are a punctual lot, and they consider it rude to be kept waiting.
- Don't take your clothes off in public. Especially on beaches, make sure you don't disrobe entirely, or for women go topless, unless others are doing so.
- Do tip your waiter, bartender and taxi driver.
- Don't smoke inside a building or home without asking first. Most states now have some kind of nonsmoking law.
- Do use a trashcan. City streets may be dirty, but littering is seriously frowned upon.
- Don't expect Americans to know much about your country. Americans are usually excited to meet foreign visitors, but their world knowledge may be quite slim.
- Do be respectful of police officers. Americans address each other casually, but the police expect to be called 'Sir,' 'Ma'am' or simply 'Officer.'
- Don't criticize the country or the president unless the person you're with takes the lead. Americans display a lot of patriotism and national pride, and while they respect the views of others, they may take offense if they feel you're 'bashing America.'

TV and fast food as the main culprits. How serious is this epidemic? It's estimated that a quarter of a million Americans die every year as a result of health problems brought on by being overweight, which makes it one of the nation's leading causes of death.

It's an odd problem for a nation as obsessed with fitness and personal image as the US. In fact, the number of Americans engaged in sports and outdoor activities is on the rise; the number of people participating in yoga almost doubled from 1998 to 2002, when it reached nearly 10 million. In addition, for many, dieting has taken on the seriousness of a religion, with every aspect of nutrition and health publicly debated with scientific precision. But like a cosmic scale with a supermodel on one end and a supersize hamburger, fries and soda on the other, the desired image and the dumpy reality never quite balance.

DID YOU KNOW?

In 1960, 70% of American families had one working and one stay-at-home parent, but in 2000 only 30% did, while both parents worked in 70% of families.

The last in the set of seemingly intractable problems facing the United States is education. While US universities are justifiably famous for their quality, drawing the top tier of international and US students, US public K–12 schools, which serve 47 million children, lag behind other developed countries. Even measured against itself, US public school education has shown no, or only slight, improvement in test scores over the last 20 years. In addition to this, there is a persistently wide disparity in quality between schools. Since the greater part of public school funding is local, where children live currently has a tremendous impact on the education they receive, and, as a consequence, on the opportunities that will be available as they grow up.

While nearly every US politician recognizes that wide disparities in wealth, health care and education are urgent problems – and they are on record as saying that the future of the nation depends on fixing them – solutions have so far been either elusive, unpalatable or inadequate. These problems existed before the latest economic downturn, and they will be waiting when the country is on better financial footing. It remains to be seen if, at that time, the political courage, and the public outrage, will then rise up to meet them.

POPULATION

The real story behind US population statistics is immigration, which for the last three decades has been occurring at historically unprecedented levels and now accounts for over half of the country's annual population growth. So far, the events surrounding 9/11 and the down economy have done nothing to slow the desire of foreigners to reach these teeming shores.

As of July 2002, the total US population was estimated at 288.4 million, making it the world's third most populous country, but still well behind India at 1.03 billion and China at 1.29 billion. Largely because of immigration, for the decade between 1990 and 2000, the USA grew by 13%, a rate five times higher than other industrialized countries (who averaged 2.5%). The US population is projected to increase 23% by 2025, compared with a worldwide increase of 29%.

Since 1980, both the total number of immigrants and their percentage in the population have doubled. This rate of increase is even higher than it was during the great waves of immigration at the turn of the 20th century, and such raw numbers have never been seen before. By 2002, the US foreign-born population stood at 33.1 million and was adding about a million a year; the Census Bureau estimated 8 to 9 million were illegal immigrants. Overall in 2002, immigrants represented 11.5% of the total population.

For US population details and updates, visit the US Census Bureau: www.census.gov.

Immigrants primarily cluster in gateway cities and counties. The states with the largest number of immigrants (in order) are California, New

AMERICA BY THE NUMBERS

In 2000, the year of the last official US census, the country's median age was 35.3, with 14% under 10 and 12.5% over 65. Racially, the US was approximately 75% white, 12.5% black, 3.5% Asian, 1% Native American and 2.5% of mixed race. Hispanics or Latinos, of any race, accounted for 12.5% (of which 7.3% were Mexican). Since 2000, the Hispanic and Asian populations have both grown by around 10% (four times faster than the national average), and by some 2003 measures, Hispanics have now surpassed blacks as the nation's 'largest minority.'

York, Florida, Texas, New Jersey and Illinois, though California, with 9.1 million, has as many as the next three states combined.

This settlement pattern reflects the spread of the general population as well, which is gathered along the coasts, leaving many of the middle states only sparsely inhabited. The Great Plains, which accounts for 20% of the US landmass, has only 4% of the population, and North Dakota has the dubious distinction of being the only state to lose population from 2001 to 2002.

Or, to put it another way: the average population density of the USA is 76 people per sq mile (psm); for Europe it's 134 psm, and Asia 203 psm. But in the northeast US, population density is 654 psm (about the same as Germany), and in 2010, the California coast will have 1050 psm. Go west, indeed.

SPORTS

You'd be hard-pressed to overestimate the importance of sports in the everyday life of Americans. They don't just love sports, they live and breathe them, with a passion and fidelity that defies scandal, strikes, defeat, cynicism and the corruption of big money. For even casual fans, the seasons of nature and of sports are inextricably intertwined, forming a comforting backdrop that colors the ongoing bustle of the world. And for some, the identification with a particular team can become so intense and enduring that it defines a lifetime.

Professional baseball, football and basketball form the holy trinity, though collegiate football and basketball are also widely, and perhaps even more obsessively, followed. In some regions, even high school sports draw this level of attention. Americans love to play sports, too, and the joyous zeal for competition is a hallmark of the national character.

In fact, there is nary a contest of any kind – so long as it ends in winning and losing – that doesn't have an organized professional league, ardent supporters, and in this day and age, television coverage. Hockey, tennis, golf, soccer (what the rest of the world may call 'football'), car racing, horse racing, rugby, bowling, boxing, skiing, skating, softball, track and field, surfing and beach volleyball all have sizable audiences, and the list goes on. Any traveler to the United States should make an effort to attend at least one sporting event, for it will provide the quickest and perhaps most vivid portrait of Americans.

Because sports are a common focus at all levels of society, they often mirror the nation to itself. This is particularly true regarding issues of race and gender, but it also includes issues of poverty, education, ethics and leadership. Sports are not just an arena for competition, but a microcosm where America debates and attempts to address its prejudices and inequities.

For instance, in 1947, Jackie Robinson began the racial integration of baseball when he joined the Brooklyn Dodgers, becoming the first African-American to play for a major league team. This not only opened

THE PAY OF PLAY

In terms of easy money, being a movie star is the best career move. Still, being a ballplayer's not bad. In 2003, the average salary for an NBA basketball player was $4.54 million, tops of any team sport. Professional baseball players averaged $2.5 million annually, and pro football players $1.25 million. These numbers are a bit skewed by the top earning players. In baseball, the top annual salary in 2003 was $22 million (earned by Alex Rodriguez), and in his prime, basketball star Michael Jordan dusted everybody, making approximately $33 million a year, which more than doubled with endorsement contracts.

the door for black athletes, but was a signature moment in the ongoing nationwide debate over integration itself. Today, when players reflect a broad, even international diversity, the issue of race has shifted to ownership, which is still overwhelmingly white.

A landmark for women occurred in 1972, when the Title IX law was passed; it mandated that colleges and high schools receiving federal funds create equal athletic opportunities for both genders. Up to then, women had been virtually ignored as athletes. Now, just thirty years later, women participate in nearly every sport at every level, though public interest in professional leagues remains tepid: the Women's United Soccer Association shut down in 2003, and the Women's National Basketball Association has yet to become profitable.

In recent decades, college football and basketball programs have become essentially training grounds for professional teams; unlike baseball, football and basketball have no minor league system. Numerous scandals involving payment of student athletes and tampering with academic records have led to fines, sanctions and calls for reform.

The world's first 24-hour sports TV network runs the definitive sports website: www.espn.com.

Baseball

The 'National Pastime' is synonymous with America itself, conjuring sepia-toned images of grass fields in summer, gangly youth chasing fly balls and drowsy contests suddenly electrified by the whip-crack of a bat. This befits a game that developed organically out of the backlots and playfields of the northeast USA in the mid-19th century.

Baseball was not so much invented as codified out of several informal variations that had developed, which were partly based on the English 'rounders,' children's games and other local contests. To facilitate competition, the field and many game features were standardized in the 1840s, and the first rulebook was written in 1858. The first professional league was formed in 1871.

Today, Major League Baseball (MLB; www.majorleaguebaseball.com) is composed of 30 teams in two leagues; the winners of each league meet in the World Series, held in October. Teams play 162 games during the April-to-September season. In other words, they play nearly every day, which is one of the game's enduring appeals.

Baseball has been called a 'thinking man's game.' As in English cricket, most of the drama concerns the subtleties of strategy, such as the type of pitch being thrown and the approach of the hitter. To the uninitiated, however, it can simply look like nine men standing around waiting for something to happen, which is not altogether untrue.

Perhaps because of this, baseball, at least in terms of TV audience, has been eclipsed in popularity by football and basketball, though judging by the ample number of little league teams for kids, it's in no danger of ceding its nostalgic pride of place.

FIVE GREAT SPORTS BOOKS

The Boys of Summer (Roger Kahn, 1971) A classic on baseball and America in the 1950s.
Friday Night Lights (HG Bissinger, 1990) Texas + high school + football = obsession.
Only the Ball Was White (Robert Peterson, 1970) On the negro baseball leagues.
Road Swing (Steve Rushin, 1998) A wacky travelogue of America as seen through its sports.
A Season on the Brink (John Feinstein, 1986) Famous coach Bobby Knight and Indiana college hoops.

Baseball remains the cheapest sport to attend (seats average $10 to $40), but ticket prices have been rising, and the cost of ballpark concessions is practically extortionary.

Football

As a spectator sport, football is the USA's most popular pastime, with the collegiate version every bit as popular as the professional one.

American football has the same ancient Greek and Roman roots as rugby and international football (what Americans call soccer), though its particular rules emerged out of Ivy League college games in the 1870s. Today, the National Football League (NFL; www.nfl.com) is composed of 32 teams in two conferences; the winners of each conference meet in the Super Bowl, held in January. Teams play 16 games, mainly on weekends, during the regular August-to-December season.

The appeal of football is visceral and immediate – and makes great TV – as opposing 11-man teams square off on each play with violent results. Strategy is just as important in football as it is in baseball, though its application is more complicated and less refined.

Football is the most expensive sport to attend (tickets begin around $50 and go way, way up). Tickets for successful teams can be almost impossible to acquire.

'Basketball is the sport of choice for black urban kids, and college basketball may be even more popular than the pros'

Basketball

Basketball truly was invented: in 1891, a Massachusetts YMCA instructor created it as a way to condition athletes in winter. Though it was played professionally throughout the early 20th century, it didn't really find success until after WWII. And it wasn't until the 1980s – and the marketing of charismatic stars like Magic Johnson and Michael Jordan – that professional basketball emerged as one of the USA's premier sports.

The National Basketball Association (NBA; www.nba.com) is composed of 29 teams in two conferences; winners in each conference play for the NBA Championship in June. The 82-game regular season runs from October to April.

Basketball is the sport of choice for black urban kids, and college basketball may be even more popular than the pros. The college playoffs have been dubbed 'March Madness,' and are one of the USA's top sports spectacles.

Established in 1997, the Women's National Basketball Association (WNBA) is the most popular professional women's team sport.

Basketball is also expensive to attend (tickets usually begin around $40), though tickets are easier to get than for football.

MULTICULTURALISM

The United States is famously a nation of immigrants and takes great pride in being so. Each year, the calendar bursts with ethnic and cultural celebrations, as if strewn with bright handfuls of confetti – from St Patrick's Day to Carnival, from Cinco de Mayo to Martin Luther King

Day, from Thanksgiving to Mardi Gras to the Chinese New Year. The USA is without a doubt the world's most diverse country – seemingly every nation has representatives here – and Ellis Island is its navel as much as Plymouth rock or the Constitution oak.

However, for Americans there is no more loaded topic than race and ethnicity, which amounts to a national obsession. No other social or political terms stir Americans as deeply – not class, gender or age, not economics or foreign policy. When the country divides, racial fault lines crack the widest.

The reason is that, although multiculturalism is central to the USA's identity, the issues surrounding it mark an enormous rift in the nation's psyche – for it is the place that holds the country's greatest pride as well as its greatest shame. The Statue of Liberty, torch held high, clutching the famous sonnet by Emma Lazarus, is America's symbol of openness; it is a symbol of its founding belief in the essential dignity of every human being. This belief is made real in countless ways, large and small, every day.

And yet, racism and xenophobia run like electric currents through US society and history, which stand as a rebuke to easy sentiment and complacency. In the USA, race has most often been discussed in black-and-white terms, literally, because of the terrible legacy of slavery and Jim Crow. This legacy remains very much alive because of the persistent inequalities that remain in the circumstances of many black Americans. The country has eliminated its once-racist laws; it has made attempts (through legislation like affirmative action) to redress historic wrongs. But the black experience will most likely remain the needle of America's moral compass until its reality matches that of whites, not to mention the realities of Native Americans, Hispanics, Asians and every other American ethnicity.

Indeed, the very idea of 'multiculturalism' – of the peaceful coexistence of equal but distinct cultures – arose out of the black Civil Rights movement in the 1960s. This is the ideal that America strives for. To achieve it, the USA will have to untangle an exceedingly complex knot of political, social and personal issues that go well beyond black and white. It's an effort that holds important lessons for the world's 'global village.'

Other historic examples of racism in the United States – for instance, the shameful slaughter and dispossession of Native Americans, the 1882 Chinese Exclusion Act (the only immigration law ever to exclude a specific race) and the WWII internment of Japanese Americans – are vivid reminders that what is foreign and celebrated and foreign and feared often shifts with the larger political winds. Today, Middle East terrorism directed at the United States is causing a backlash of anger and suspicion against Arab-American citizens at home.

Ethnic groups, furthermore, are not always kind to each other. More established ethnicities can meet newer immigrants with resistance and mistrust; they are often seen as interlopers competing for the same low-wage jobs. Until they themselves become established, new arrivals also frequently suffer all the common prejudices that greet the unfamiliar.

Perhaps the most interesting dynamic, though, involves the immigrant experience itself, which opens up very intimate questions of personal identity. An individual, new to the United States, immediately faces a vexing conundrum: How much or how little should you, or can you, assimilate? Which customs, ways of thought and values do you drop and which keep – and how do you negotiate the prejudices and assumptions that your skin inevitably inspires? In many ways, the USA is the sum of all the myriad answers to this question.

Interracial Intimacies (2003) by Randall Kennedy: A law professor and passionate academic, Kennedy is not just interested in charting the history of 'transgressive' black-white relationships in America, but in ensuring that laws protect all interracial couples.

The Chinese in America (2003) by Iris Chang: This scholarly but wonderful account of the somewhat neglected history of Chinese Americans highlights all of the push-pull complexities of the US immigrant experience.

'Tis (1999) by Frank McCourt: McCourt won the Pulitzer Prize for his memoir of growing up in Ireland, *Angela's Ashes*. With *'Tis*, McCourt finishes his remarkable story: 19, fresh off the boat in America, and ready to test his Hollywood-spun dreams.

THE NEW COLOSSUS

Give me your tired, your poor,
Your huddled masses yearning to breathe free,
The wretched refuse of your teeming shore,
Send these, the homeless, tempest-tost to me:
I lift my lamp beside the golden door.

This sonnet was written by Emma Lazarus in 1883 as the inscription for the Statue of Liberty.

One of the first displacements immigrants experience is recategorization. Their ethnicity is instantly recast into American terms, which are broad and simplistic. Arrivals from Mexico, Brazil and Cuba all become 'Hispanic,' though they may be strangers to each other. The same occurs for Koreans, Japanese, Chinese and Malaysians – who are placed under a tent called 'Asian' that has no meaning where they come from.

In sufficient numbers, immigrant communities can isolate themselves from the larger US culture, and even from their ethnic umbrella, maintaining distinctions of language and custom that mirror their towns or even clans of origin. Very quickly, no matter what their choices, communities and individuals come to occupy a unique netherworld, one that is neither here nor there, neither one thing nor another. This duality is potently symbolized by each immigrant's new compound name – Greek American, Italian American.

The Center for Immigration Studies, a conservative-leaning independent research center, is a good place for up-to-date immigration statistics and topical discussions: www.cis.org.

And each generation makes its own choices. If a first-generation immigrant tries to shed his or her heritage like a tattered, unwanted coat, the second, third or fourth generation will reclaim it vigorously. Time may dilute first-hand experience, but otherwise it seems to exert little influence over people's self-identity: many longtime Americans, those whose roots extend to the American Revolution and beyond, lovingly claim their original ethnic selves – be they English, Scottish or Irish, Scandinavian, Russian or German – even when the pulse of genetic memory has grown so faint as to be barely audible.

As if all this weren't complicated enough, increasing rates of intermarriage among ethnicities, and their resulting children, are slowly forcing the United States to rethink the very terms of the debate.

DID YOU KNOW?

Pro golfer Tiger Woods coined the term 'Cablinasian' to describe his unusual ethnic heritage, a combination of Caucasian, Black, Indian and Asian.

For most of US history, state antimiscegenation laws (mainly regulating sex and marriage between whites and blacks, but at some point targeting every race) have been the rule rather than the exception. These were all finally struck down as unconstitutional in 1967. Since then, the number of black-white marriages has quadrupled (they totaled 330,000 in 1998). Additionally, studies show that, among immigrants, each successive generation is more likely to marry outside of their ethnic group, and Mexican and Asian immigrants, who have been arriving in the greatest numbers recently, already bring a much more accepting attitude toward intermarriage.

Because of this, it's predicted that over the next hundred years in the USA fully 70% of Hispanics, 40% of Asians and 35% of both blacks and whites will in fact be multiethnic or multiracial. Little wonder that for the first time in 2000, the US Census Bureau decided to acknowledge the USA's emerging reality by allowing citizens to identify themselves with as many racial and ethnic categories as they wished.

However one characterizes America – as a melting pot, or a rainbow of not-yet-equal colors, or a mestizo nation – one thing is certain: something new is being created, and it has the countenance of the future.

MEDIA

One area that has come to epitomize the occasional looking-glass quality of American life is its media, which in the last decade has gone through a phenomenal transformation in two opposing directions: the number of media outlets has proliferated at a dizzying pace (mainly due to the Internet) at the same time that media ownership has consolidated at an equally dramatic clip.

Nearly every American home has a TV (with its hundreds of cable channels), and over half have access to the Internet and its riotous freedom of expression. Up until the nationwide economic troubles in 2001, magazines and newspapers were experiencing steady revenue growth, and for magazines, this included circulation growth. In addition, US citizens are buying more books than ever before. With the availability of so many channels, websites, stations, periodicals and books, America's media would seem to be a delightfully diverse, egalitarian symbol of democracy in action.

The Onion is a drop-dead funny parody of mainstream news, but it also carries no-kidding reviews of current entertainment: www.theonion.com.

And it is, sort of. In an irony worthy of Lewis Carroll, the Federal Communications Commission (FCC) has cited this very abundance of media as the primary reason that it has – through a series of rulings in recent years – progressively deregulated media ownership.

In 1996, the FCC deregulated radio station ownership, and since that time one company has come to dominate the industry, Clear Channel, which has grown from 40 to 1200 stations nationwide (or about half of all radio stations). Clear Channel also now owns many major concert venues and ticketing agencies, and as a result, they can and do wield a huge, homogenous influence over the music industry.

In 2001, the FCC allowed major TV networks to merge with newer TV networks – though the top four networks (ABC, CBS, NBC and Fox) are still not allowed to merge.

In 2003, the FCC took the next logical step and proposed weakening the rules that limit the overall concentration of media ownership as well as the rules governing cross-ownership of TV stations and other media in the same market. The upshot of these changes, if approved, is that, in larger cities, a single company could own up to three TV stations as well as the major daily newspaper and up to eight radio stations.

In the next few years, it is expected that the new legal levels of media concentration will be reached in most markets. Further, it's expected that the same handful of multinational corporations will be involved, since smaller companies will not have the resources to compete. These companies, which already dominate American media ownership, are News Corp (Fox), Walt Disney Corp (ABC), General Electric (NBC), AOL Time Warner and Viacom (CBS). In addition, these conglomerates also own most of the nation's top magazines, TV cable companies and movie studios, thus ensuring that they can 'leverage' news, ideas and entertainment properties across the gamut of media outlets.

Considering all this, America's media could just as easily be a symbol of the power and influence of US corporations. And it is because of this that the American public now increasingly regards the media with, at best, a critical distance, and at worst, outright skepticism. Alice would feel right at home.

RELIGION

The USA has no official state religion – indeed, freedom of religion is one of the country's founding rights – but it is predominantly a Christian society. In 2000, it was 54% Protestant, 24% Roman Catholic, 2.2% Jewish and 14% none. Numerous other religions are also represented – such as

Islam, Buddhism, Hinduism and others – but together they account for less than 6% of the population. Native American religions are still practiced, sometimes with traditional ceremonies open to the public.

In general, it has been proposed that the US contains a 'religious equilibrium' whereby one-quarter of its citizens are devout, one-quarter secular and one-half mildly interested.

DID YOU KNOW?

In most parts of the US, businesses are closed on Sunday, the Christian day of rest.

The Constitution mandates separation of church and state, and the First Amendment says that congress 'will make no law respecting an establishment of religion.' Thus, prayers are not permitted in public schools. However, the phrase 'In God We Trust' has been stamped on the currency since 1864 and was officially adopted by congress in 1956 as the national motto. And the words 'under God' were added to the pledge of allegiance in 1954. As a sign of how seriously this issue is regarded by all sides, a federal court ruled in 2003 that the words 'under God' were unconstitutional when the pledge was recited in public schools – and so should be removed – and the Bush administration vowed to appeal the ruling to the Supreme Court, which opens with a prayer before every session.

The main Protestant sects are (in descending order of number of adherents) Baptist, Methodist, Lutheran, Presbyterian and Episcopalian. The so-called Bible Belt stretches roughly through Oklahoma, Arkansas, Mississippi, Tennessee and Kentucky, and is the heartland of the fundamentalist Southern Baptist church, known for its literal interpretation of the Bible, full-body baptisms and fire-and-brimstone sermons. Some Christian denominations have almost exclusively African-American adherents, including the African Methodist Episcopal Church, the National Baptist Convention USA and the National Baptist Convention of America.

Other religions of interest include the Nation of Islam, a black American Muslim sect, and the Religious Society of Friends, or Quakers, who were among the first immigrants to the USA. The country also has a handful of homegrown religions, including the Shakers, of whom only a few in Maine survive; the Amish in Pennsylvania and Ohio; Mormons, headquartered in Utah; and the Christian Scientists, Seventh-Day Adventists and Jehovah's Witnesses.

ARTS

For the better part of the last century, America was a leader in the arts worldwide. The country has been at the forefront of modern movements in dance, literature, architecture, music, performance, painting and film. Americans have introduced new forms and new genres that have since been eagerly gobbled up by other cultures everywhere: West Africans play the blues, Germans write cowboy poetry and Japanese make sci-fi noir films.

'Americans have introduced new forms and new genres that have since been eagerly gobbled up by other cultures everywhere'

A traveler looking to experience America's arts will hardly know where to begin. The USA's great cultural cities – New York, Chicago, LA, San Francisco – remain epicenters of fine and avant-garde art, but many other robust arts scenes exist. Try New Orleans and Nashville, Houston and Austin, Minneapolis, Pittsburgh, Detroit, Seattle, Salt Lake City and even such smaller towns as Chapel Hill, North Carolina, Athens, Georgia, and Cedar Rapids, Iowa. Scratch the surface of the Heartland, and you are as likely to find a screeching punk band, political Latino artists or gay playwrights as you will the tight-lipped, grim farmers in *American Gothic.*

In fact, this is perhaps the highlight of the American arts today – its increasingly vibrant expression throughout the country and its wealth of new, diverse voices.

REFLECTIONS OF 9/11

The 9/11 terrorist attacks are still a fresh memory, but they will also remain a transformative moment in American history. Here are some of the ways Americans have responded to it, both artistically and personally.

American Ground: Unbuilding the World Trade Center (2002) by William Langewiesche: This is the definitive book about the destruction of the World Trade Center and its aftermath. Langewiesche was the only reporter given complete access to ground zero in the immediate wake of the attacks, and he's written an astonishing account: it takes readers through the day of September 11, 2001, and then follows the superhuman effort to find survivors, which is by turns sobering, inspiring and all too human.

Sonic Memorial (sonicmemorial.org): Part of National Public Radio's Lost & Found Sound series, this is a powerful, ongoing collection of voices, ambient sounds, memories, music and interviews that vividly evoke the day itself and the range of emotional responses. People who lost family members testify to their grief while also pleading for peace.

West of Kabul, East of New York (2002) by Tamim Ansary: This Afghanistan-born American writer wrote a passionate email to friends immediately following 9/11 that was copied and made famous around the world. It inspired him to write this elegant memoir, which is a searching, very personal look at the fractious divide between conservative Islam and the West.

On the Transmigration of Souls (2002) by John Adams: Commissioned by the New York Philharmonic, Adams created a 25-minute musical composition that he prefers to call a 'memory space' rather than a memorial. This moving piece, which won the Pulitzer Prize, includes orchestra, adult and children's choirs, and text taken from missing-person posters, quotes and names of victims.

The Rising (2002) by Bruce Springsteen: Springsteen's album was written to heal a nation. It is at once prayerful, solemn and inspiring, and filled with poetic imagery that crystallizes the complex emotions and hurt surrounding 9/11.

Jerusalem (2002) by Steve Earle: Righteous anger rarely yields such brilliant songwriting. This album showcases Earle's biting wit, trenchant political observations and self-deprecating humor, but in the end Earle offers faith, not bitterness.

25th Hour (2003) by Spike Lee: This meditation on loss and lost chances resonates with elegiac images of ground zero and post-9/11 NYC. Lee's in complete mastery, tempering his usual provocative examination of racism and self-delusion with aching sorrow. Lee may now be the best filmmaker about America.

World Trade Center Memorial Site: View architect Daniel Libeskind's design for the WTC site at www.renewnyc.com. The complex of buildings and open spaces (allowing views of the now-exposed slurry walls) will include the world's tallest structure, a spire rising a patriotic 1776ft. Once finished, this will surely become one of America's icons and a permanent reminder of these events.

But in several ways as they enter the 21st century, the arts in United States are going through an awkward transition. The recent economic recession has hurt arts organizations across the board. Public funding is down, and staffing and programming are being cut; smaller companies, with no margin for error, have been the first to close, but even a few larger companies (like San Jose's symphony) have had to file for bankruptcy.

To make matters worse, as finances have gotten tighter, so has access to the general public. In the last 10 years, ownership of the major media has become increasingly concentrated, so that now a handful of multinational corporations have become the main gatekeepers of popular culture – and they tend to favor those with the widest appeal and the safest opinions. (For more, see p59.)

Then there's digital technology, which is currently revolutionizing many of the arts, and no one knows where it will end. For instance, in the next decade it's quite likely that CDs and celluloid film – and maybe even magazines and books – will join the phonograph, the vacuum tube and the typewriter in the junk pile of quaint, 20th-century anachronisms.

And yet, digital technology is also putting the means of professional-quality production (and sometimes of distribution) into the hands of individuals – and this is exerting radical, democratizing changes in the music, film and publishing industries. The current angry music industry debate over the legality and ethics of free Internet file-sharing is just the first battle in a growing war over the control of digitized art that will include everyone: makers, sellers and consumers.

Finally, the content of the arts in America are in flux like never before. New media, the Internet and digital technology continue the deconstructive process set in motion by modernism and postmodernism, both periods of epic creativity in the US. The already-blurred lines between high culture and pop culture are being erased, genres and styles are mixed and matched at will, and no overarching philosophy now galvanizes artists or presents a coherent vision of the future.

Cosmopolis (2003) by Don DeLillo: An ambitious novelist who tackles great American events and themes, DeLillo uncorks a brilliant epic on the late 1990s 'new economy,' which he frames within the context of a young billionaire's doomed limo ride.

The start of the 21st century is, in other words, both a very exciting and a very confusing time for American art and culture. The future is coming, but it hasn't arrived just yet.

Literature

America first articulated a vision of itself through its literature, and whatever else may be said about America's tastes, it has always been a nation of readers. Competition from other media – most particularly from television – has hurt the publishing industry overall in recent decades, and digital books may one day remake it entirely, but it's doubtful Americans will ever lose their love of a well-told tale. Sure, they play a lot of video games, but Americans also spent $10 billion on books in 2002, and they weren't all shopping at Wal-Mart for the latest trashy romance – independent bookstores had rising sales from 2000 to 2002.

Reading is still the best way for the traveler to get inside the American experience. It may safely be said that never before has America seen the breadth and diversity of its people represented so completely and so skillfully. Seemingly every region and subregion of the country, every immigrant community, every hybrid ethnicity and social strata has now elbowed its way onto the shelves of America's library. Travelers wanting literary companionship need only run their fingers across the spines until they find the authors who match their interests and itinerary.

DISCOVERING AMERICA'S VOICE

American culture took some time to come into its own. Indeed, before the American Revolution, the continent's citizens identified as British, and all of their arts were imitative of Europe, whose long artistic traditions were the very definition of culture. Then, once independence was won, an immediate call went out to develop a new national identity, a wholly American voice. Despite much parochial hand-wringing, little progress was made until around the 1820s, when writers and artists began to take up the two aspects of American life that had no counterpart on the continent: wilderness and the frontier experience.

James Fenimore Cooper is credited with creating the first truly American literature when he wrote *The Pioneers* in 1823 (the first in what would become his famous Leatherstocking series of adventures), and it made him a national hero. Cooper esteemed raw nature, and he portrayed the humble pioneer, gathering ethical and spiritual lessons through his close association with wilderness, as a more authentic and admirable figure than the refined European. This idea went over well, and it signaled a historic philosophical shift that would be developed over the course of the century.

In his 1836 essay *Nature,* Ralph Waldo Emerson articulated this explicitly in intellectual terms. Emerson claimed that nature was not only connected to the divine, as late-18th-century Romanticism held, but that it reflected God himself; nature was where humankind could read God's instructions. The essay, with its emphasis on rational thought and self-reliance, in essence made a spiritual philosophy out of the Puritan religion, and the ideas became the core of the Transcendentalist movement, which Henry David Thoreau would later champion in *Walden* (1854).

Emerson's tragic opposite was Herman Melville, whose ambitious masterpiece *Moby Dick* (1851) was, in part, a cautionary tale of what happens when the individual accepts Transcendentalist beliefs, and can thus distinguish good from evil with God-like authority. Similarly, Nathaniel Hawthorne (*The Scarlet Letter*, 1850) examined the dark side of conservative Puritan New England.

Standing oddly off by himself, somewhat outside this dialogue, was Edgar Allen Poe, who was the first American poet to achieve international acclaim. His gruesome stories (such as 'The Tell-Tale Heart,' 1843) helped popularize the short-story form, and he is credited with inventing the detective story, the horror story and science fiction, all genres that bear a distinctly American stamp and remain extremely popular.

The celebration of the common man and nature would reach its apotheosis in Walt Whitman, whose epic poem *Leaves of Grass* (1855) signaled the arrival of a literary master and an American visionary. Americans themselves did not recognize it immediately, but here – in Whitman's informal, intimate, rebellious free verse – were songs of individualism, democracy, earthly spirituality, taboo-breaking sexuality and joyous optimism that encapsulated the heart of the new nation, and would become the touchstone for all subsequent American poets.

Ten Little Indians (2003) by Sherman Alexie: An exuberant writer, Alexie has been the country's literary trickster for the last 10 years, spinning tough, funny, provocative, unexpected stories about Native Americans. His latest stand with his best.

Drop City (2003) by T Coraghessan Boyle: Just what the heck happened to 1960s idealism? Only a true rebel and iconoclast like Boyle could do justice to America's wackiest, most heartfelt decade. He's unsparing, unsentimental and unforgettable.

THE GREAT AMERICAN NOVEL

After the Civil War (1861–65), two main and lasting trends emerged: realism and regionalism. Stephen Crane's *The Red Badge of Courage* (1895) was one of the first great books to depict the horror of war itself, and Upton Sinclair's *The Jungle* (1906) was a shocking exposé of Chicago's meatpacking industry. At the same time, the rapid, late-19th-century settlement of the West led to increasing interest in 'local colorist' writing; two of the more popular regionalists were western humorist Bret Harte and novelist Jack London, who wrote Alaskan adventures (*Call of the Wild*, 1903).

However, it was Samuel Clemens, better known as Mark Twain, who would come to define American letters. Twain wrote in the vernacular, capturing the dialects and common speech of Americans. As a lover of 'tall tales,' he embraced satirical humor and absurdity, and his colloquial storytelling and 'anti-intellectual' stance endeared him to everyday readers. And with *Huckleberry Finn* (1884) he wrote the seminal modern American novel, from which, as Ernest Hemingway once contended, all subsequent American literature has flowed. Huck's journey embodies the quintessential American narrative: necessitated by a primal moment of rebellion, Huck embarks on a search for authenticity through which he discovers himself. The image of Huck and Jim, a poor white teenager and a runaway black slave, standing outside society's norms and floating together toward an uncertain future down the Mississippi River, reverberates through the culture still.

Interpreter of Maladies (1999) by Jhumpa Lahiri: In the increasingly crowded arena of immigrant fiction, Lahiri stands out for the sensitive beauty of her stories, which are aching, nuanced pictures of Indians and Pakistanis as they 'become American.'

The Master Butchers Singing Club (2003) by Louise Erdrich: Known as a preeminent writer of the Native American experience, Erdrich here tackles her German immigrant heritage with the same gorgeous prose and indelible characters.

DISILLUSIONMENT & DIVERSITY

The horrors of WWI affected cultures worldwide, and American literature, reflecting the widespread disillusionment with modern industrialized society, came into full bloom.

Dubbed the Lost Generation, a number of US writers became expatriates in Europe, most famously Ernest Hemingway. His novel *The Sun Also Rises* (1926) exemplified the era, and his spare, stylized realism influenced several generations of writers.

While F Scott Fitzgerald (*The Great Gatsby*, 1925) captured the hollowness of East Coast society life, John Steinbeck (*The Grapes of Wrath*, 1939) became the great voice of the rural and working poor in the West, and his novels dug deep into the growing personal, social and political discontents of America. In the South, William Faulkner (*The Sound and the Fury*, 1929) continued the examination of troubled racial relations and social rifts, and his dense but mordantly funny prose is rich with the flavor of southern speech.

In the 1930s, Poe's detective story got a good once-over by Dashiell Hammett (*The Maltese Falcon*, 1930) and Raymond Chandler (*The Big Sleep*, 1939), who minted a brand of hard-boiled urban realism, called 'noir,' that has yet to go out of style.

Meanwhile, the Harlem Renaissance flourished between the world wars, and a generation of African-American intellectuals emerged who caught the attention of the wider white society. Based mainly in New York, these writers sought to instill pride in American black culture and to undermine racist stereotypes. Among the most well known were poets Langston Hughes and Claude McKay, and novelist Zora Neale Hurston (*Their Eyes Were Watching God*, 1937), who captured the resilient dignity of rural black life.

After WWII, these trends continued and only became more pronounced: American writers displayed a fully rebellious questioning of middle-class society's values, represented increasingly varied regional and multicultural perspectives, and experimented with a wealth of literary styles and genres.

The Beat Generation of the 1950s took up where the Lost Generation left off: no longer just questioning but overturning social and literary conventions. Their mantras were individualism and nonconformity, and they explored free-form and stream-of-consciousness writing. The main authors included Jack Kerouac (*On the Road*, 1957), poet Allen Ginsberg (*Howl*, 1956) and William S Burroughs (*Naked Lunch*, 1959).

JD Salinger (*The Catcher in the Rye*, 1951) and John Updike (*Rabbit, Run*, 1960) were two of the writers who captured the ironic disaffections of modern urban and suburban life with great humor, while those who charted a more brutal, unflinching realism included Norman Mailer, whose *The Naked and the Dead* (1948) is one of the great books about WWII, and Nelson Algren, who scoured the underside of Chicago in *The Man with the Golden Arm* (1949).

The South, never at a loss for contradictions and paradoxes, continued to be ripe pickings for writers, and two of the most masterful were Flannery O'Connor (*Wise Blood*, 1952) and Eudora Welty (*The Optimist's Daughter*, 1972). The mythic rural West found its modern-day poet laureate in Larry McMurtry (*Lonesome Dove*, 1986).

After WWII, African-American writing grew in complexity and urgency. Richard Wright (*Black Boy*, 1945) and Ralph Ellison (*Invisible Man*, 1952) wrote passionately about racism, while James Baldwin became perhaps the most acclaimed African-American writer (*Go Tell It on the Mountain*, 1953). He was also one of America's first openly gay writers (*Giovanni's Room*, 1956). Over the next decades, black women writers came to prominence, most significantly Toni Morrison (*Beloved*, 1987) and Alice Walker (*The Color Purple*, 1983).

Highly talented contemporary writers who reflect some of the many faces of America include Native American novelist Barbara Kingsolver (*Animal Dreams*, 1990); Chinese-American Amy Tan (*The Joy Luck Club*, 1989); Korean-American Kim Ronyoung (*Clay Walls*, 2001); Cuban-American Oscar Hijuelos (*The Mambo Kings Play Songs of Love*, 1990); and Calcutta-born Bharati Mukherjee (*Jasmine*, 1988).

Drama

American drama was not particularly notable until after WWI, when the Little Theater movement arose. Emulating the progressive theater of Europe, it sought to provide an alternative to commercialized Broadway plays, and this eventually developed into New York's 'off-Broadway' theater scene. Still today, New York has the largest and most vibrant theater community in the country, though most cities of any size have their own active theater troupes. In addition, notable regional theaters – like the Shakespeare festivals in Ashland, Oregon, and Cedar City, Utah – and touring Broadway productions mean that you don't necessarily need to bite the Big Apple if you want good drama.

Angels in America (1990s) by Tony Kushner: This epic, cathartic, furiously funny two-part play tackles the AIDS epidemic in America, but it's also about identity, authenticity and faith. On the lighter side, it's got Mormons and drag queens.

The 1920s also saw the arrival of Eugene O'Neill, who is regarded by many as America's best playwright. His magnificent trilogy *Mourning Becomes Electra* (1931) is a retelling of the tragic Greek myth about the murder of Agamemnon but set in post–Civil War New England. *The Iceman Cometh* (1946), about the self-delusions of a group of outcasts, is considered his greatest work, though the posthumously produced, autobiographical play *Long Day's Journey into Night* (1956) is also a masterpiece.

American playwrights joined in the creative flowering in all the arts after WWII. Arthur Miller's *Death of a Salesmen* (1949) was a moving tragedy about a quietly desperate ordinary man. The great Southern playwright Tennessee Williams achieved fame with his first play, *The Glass Menagerie* (1945), and didn't look back. Many of his plays – including *A Streetcar Named Desire* (1947) and *Cat on a Hot Tin Roof* (1955) – have been made into successful movies.

As in Europe, the 1960s in America were marked by absurdist, avant-garde theater. Edward Albee established himself as one of the nation's leading playwrights with such stylized dramas as *Who's Afraid of Virginia Woolf?* (1962) and *A Delicate Balance* (1967). Prominent dramatists to emerge during the 1970s were David Mamet (*American Buffalo*, 1975) and Sam Shepard (*Buried Child*, 1978), both of whom continue to set the highest standards on stage and screen.

More recently, Suzan-Lori Parks' *Topdog/Underdog* (2001) signaled the emergence of a major American playwright, and one-person plays have become increasingly popular: Sarah Jones brings a hip-hop sensibility and slam-poetry credentials, and Margaret Cho is a bitingly hilarious Chinese-American comedian.

The All Music Guide lives up to its name, with comprehensive categories (from Riot grrrl to Twee-pop) and 'music maps' that relate trends and artists: www.allmusic.com.

Music

American popular music is the great soundtrack of the 20th, and now the 21st, century. Blues, jazz, folk, country, rock 'n' roll, hip-hop: all of these forms are indigenous to the USA, and they have since spread and changed music throughout the world. Any journey across America will be accompanied by this toe-tapping score – and some of the finest trips involve pilgrimages to the country's musical birthplaces.

Most of these journeys lead through the South, which is the mother of American music. However, these days you can hear just about any style anywhere, and the hottest new artists are as likely to come out of Omaha, Austin or Chapel Hill as New York, Nashville or New Orleans.

The music industry itself is going through tremendous upheaval. Record sales have been dropping for the last three years, consumer-friendly computer programs (particularly Pro Tools) are making traditional recording studios obsolete and industry consolidation has meant fewer opportunities for new, unproven musicians. The music industry blames much of its woes on the rampant 'piracy' of songs through free Internet file-sharing programs, but even if legal or technical solutions are found to control this, it's doubtful the current industry will survive as is for long. History demonstrates that music is nothing if not a relentless and notoriously democratic force for change.

BLUES

The blues is a simple-seeming music with complex roots. It developed primarily out of the work songs, or 'shouts,' of black slaves and out of black spiritual songs and their 'call-and-response' pattern, both of which were adaptations of African music. These unformalized musical styles were, perhaps obviously, an entirely oral tradition until after the Civil War.

Blues People (1963) by LeRoi Jones: This was the first book on blues and jazz by an African American writer, and it's still one of the best. The uncompromising Jones grounds the history of the music in the history of black life in unforgettable fashion.

Once blacks were liberated from slavery, they had the freedom to develop their own cultural expressions. Black Christian choral music evolved into gospel, whose greatest singer, Mahalia Jackson, arrived in the 1920s.

Transformed by the crucible of African-American life in white US society, slave work songs became the blues. Largely improvisational and intensely personal, the blues could be played by anyone, and they remain at heart an immediate expression of individual pain, suffering, hope, desire and pride.

Across the South, but particularly in the Mississippi River Delta (see p508), individuals around the turn of the 20th century began to gain fame, and employment, as traveling blues musicians and singers; some of these early pioneers were Robert Johnson, WC Handy and Leadbelly. However, it was female blues singers – particularly Bessie Smith, who is considered the best blues singer who ever lived – who initially gained the most widespread attention.

After WWII, the blues dispersed north, particularly to Chicago, in the hands of a new generation of musicians – such as Muddy Waters, Bo Diddley, Buddy Guy and John Lee Hooker.

Much of the rest of American music has since drawn from the blues and by extension the African-American experience, most particularly rhythm and blues, soul (which also came out of gospel), rock 'n' roll and hip-hop.

JAZZ

Hear Me Talkin' to Ya (1955/1966) by Nat Shapiro and Nat Hentoff: It's worth tracking down this book of interviews, which includes every famous and semi-famous jazz musician from then to jazz's birth talking about music, life and each other.

Jazz is more of a sibling to the blues than a child of it. Both developed concurrently, one more instrumental, one more vocal, out of the same roots.

Congo Sq in New Orleans (see p518) – where slaves gathered to sing and dance in the early 19th century – is commonly sighted as the 'birthplace' of jazz, but like the blues, its actual origins are more diffuse. However, New Orleans was central to its development because of its unique mix of cultures. Here, ex-slaves adapted the reed, horn and string instruments used by the city's black Creoles – who were themselves more interested in playing formal European music like quadrilles – to play their own 'primitive,' African-influenced music, and this fertile cross-pollination produced a steady stream of innovative sound.

The first variation was ragtime, which got its name from the 'ragged' style of its syncopated African rhythms. Ragtime was popularized by Scott Joplin and Irving Berlin beginning in the 1890s, and made widely accessible through sheet music and player-piano rolls.

Money Jungle (1962) by Duke Ellington, Charles Mingus and Max Roach: A holy summit of jazz greats from the swing and bop eras, this trio plays original Ellington tunes and reimagines classics, like 'Caravan.' It's a jam session from heaven.

Dixieland jazz, centered in New Orleans' infamous Storyville district, closely followed. Buddy Bolden is credited with being the first true jazz musician, although Jelly Roll Morton also played an extremely significant role (in fact, he frequently boasted that he was the one who created jazz).

In 1917, Storyville was shut down, and New Orleans jazz musicians dispersed. In 1919, bandleader King Oliver moved to Chicago, and his star trumpet player, Louis Armstrong, followed in 1922. Armstrong's distinctive vocals and talented improvisations led to the establishment of the solo as an integral part of modern jazz music, and his own bands would remain extremely popular throughout his life.

The 1920s and 1930s have come to be known as the Jazz Age, which not incidentally coincided with the Harlem Renaissance of African-American culture in New York. Swing – a new, urbane, big-band jazz style – swept the country, and Harlem bandleader Duke Ellington and Kansas City bandleader Count Basie were its most innovative practitioners. Jazz singers Ella Fitzgerald and Billie Holiday, as well as guitarist BB King, combined the blues with jazz.

After WWII, 'bebop' or 'bop' arose as a reaction against the smooth melodies and confining rhythms of big-band swing. Swing saxophonist Lester Young was a major influence on this new crop of musicians, who included Charlie Parker, Dizzy Gillespie and Thelonious Monk. Music critics at first derided bop and most of its other permutations in the 1950s and 1960s – such as cool jazz, hard-bop, free or avant-garde jazz and fusion (which combined jazz and Latin or rock music) – but there was no stopping the tide of postmodernism, which kept deconstructing and then remaking jazz music. Pioneers of this era include Miles Davis, Charles Mingus, John Coltrane and Ornette Coleman.

Today, no particular style of jazz predominates. Ragtime, Dixieland and swing have all experienced popular revivals, while other jazz musicians continue to push the boundaries of this ever-malleable, resilient form.

FOLK & COUNTRY

Early Scottish, Irish and English immigrants brought their own instruments and folk music to America, and what emerged over time in the secluded Appalachian Mountains was foot-stompin', fiddle-and-banjo hillbilly or 'country' music; in the Southwest, 'western' music was distinguished by steel guitars and larger bands. In the 1920s, these styles merged into 'country-and-western' music, and became centered in Nashville, Tennessee, particularly once the Grand Ole Opry began its radio broadcasts in 1925 (see p552).

World Without Tears (2003) by Lucinda Williams: Williams' roots are as a country/bluegrass singer-songwriter, but now she's in a class by herself: worldly, honest, sensual and lyrical, mixing slashing guitars, her soulful voice and even hip-hop rhymes.

Jimmie Rodgers and the Carter Family were some of the first country musicians to become widely popular. In Kentucky, Bill Monroe and his Blue Mountain Boys mixed country with jazz and blues to create 'bluegrass.' Other famous country musicians were Hank Williams, Johnny Cash and Willie Nelson. Like the blues, country songs were most often personal paeans to love, loss and tough times.

The tradition of American folk music was crystallized in the person of Woody Guthrie, who traveled through the USA during the Depression singing politically conscious songs about the poor and downtrodden. In the 1940s, he was joined by Pete Seeger, who was a tireless preserver of America's folk heritage. Folk experienced a revival during the protest movements of the 1960s, led by musicians like Joan Baez and Bob Dylan, who went on to experiment with fusions of folk, country and rock.

Country music influenced the development of rock 'n' roll in the 1950s and 1960s, while rock-flavored country was given the name 'rockabilly.' During the 1970s and 1980s, country-and-western music became a major commercial industry, and musicians like Garth Brooks achieved record sales only rock stars had previously known. In the last decade, the Dixie Chicks, Shania Twain and Faith Hill have been major country artists, though Twain and Hill have received periodic criticism from the country faithful for dipping too deeply into the pop music well.

ROCK 'N' ROLL

Some say rock 'n' roll was born when Bill Haley and the Comets released 'Rock Around the Clock' in 1954; others say it was when Elvis Presley recorded 'That's All Right' in Sam Phillips' Sun Studios the same year. Either way, in 1956, Presley scored his first big breakthrough with 'Heartbreak Hotel,' shocking and thrilling the entire country with his rebellious sexuality – and rock 'n' roll, as the song goes, was here to stay.

Rock 'n' roll was a complex hybrid that both signaled and abetted a cataclysm of social change. As a musical form, it was a combination of guitar-driven blues, black rhythm and blues (R & B), and white country-and-western music. R & B, which evolved in the 1940s out of swing and the blues, was then categorized as 'race music' and listened to almost exclusively by black audiences. With rock 'n' roll, white musicians (and a few black musicians) took up these black musical styles and made them popular and acceptable to white audiences.

DID YOU KNOW?

Elvis Presley has sold over a billion records worldwide, more than any other artist, and Graceland, his home, is the most well-known residence in America after the White House.

However, rock 'n' roll, more than any other music before it, was aimed at youth. An entire generation was questioning American society's values, and rock music became its call to arms. Critics considered it a fad, but beneath its loud, hip-shaking, easily commercialized surface, rock embodied an urgent countercultural force. This tension – between commerce and authenticity, between hedonistic fun and seriousness – has defined rock music ever since.

Each generation has made rock their own. In the 1960s, the 'British invasion,' led by the Beatles and the Rolling Stones, took US rock even closer to its blues roots, while San Francisco's drug-inspired psychedelic sound, epitomized by the Grateful Dead and Jefferson Airplane, shattered social and musical conventions. Other notable 1960s musicians, whose lifestyles and personalities were sometimes as influential as their songs, were Janis Joplin, Jimi Hendrix, Bob Dylan and Patti Smith.

In the late 1970s and 1980s gritty punk turned up the anti-establishment volume, along with its more style-conscious cousin, 'new wave.' Influential musicians were the Ramones, Blondie, the Dead Kennedys, the Talking Heads and REM. Tom Petty and Bruce Springsteen epitomized authentic classic rock, while angry, speed-driven heavy metal, in the hands of groups like Metallica, filled arenas with a sea of raised fists.

Odelay (1996) by Beck: Mixing musical genres like a carny wheel-of-fortune, Beck creates a sonic collage that recalls much but mimics none: folk, rock, techno, disco, hip-hop, electronica and more. Best of all, he's a great songwriter.

Plaid-clad grunge rock came out of Seattle in the 1990s, led by supergroups Nirvana and Pearl Jam, at the same time that worldbeat and international sounds insinuated themselves into rock's lexicon. However, despite this, rock music suffered in the decade, leading some to proclaim that 'rock is dead.' The success of bubble-gum pop – most particularly Britney Spears and the boy bands 'N Sync and Backstreet Boys – and the emergence of hip-hop as a cultural force took away much of rock's currency.

Never fear. Rock remains alive and well in the hands of many new groups – such as Wilco, Interpol and the Yeah Yeah Yeahs – who are carrying this definitive American music into the 21st century.

Elephant (2003) by the White Stripes: This Detroit duo gets back to basics: noisy, electric, blues-inflected punk rock that's sufficiently ironic for today and yet authentically heartfelt to be moving. Rock, they remind us, is elemental.

HIP-HOP

Hip-hop arose out of black and Puerto Rican street culture in New York's South Bronx in the 1970s, where turntable DJs punctuated disco-influenced dance songs with a rhythmic scratching of the disc. It was at first known as rap, and Harlem's Sugar Hill Gang had the first major hit with 'Rapper's Delight' (1979). As in the blues, lyrics came to dominate the repetitive structure of the music, which often included snatches or 'samples' of other well-known songs, with groups like Public Enemy, De La Soul and Run-DMC giving urgent voice to contemporary political, racial and urban problems.

In the 1990s, hip-hop culture spread like wildfire through America's youth – black, white and Hispanic – to whom it spoke with a fresh authenticity and authority. The music, as a result, became a commercial juggernaut and has come to mix with nearly every other musical genre: R & B, pop, punk, metal, techno, rock and even country.

'Gangsta rap' became the most notorious style, as groups like NWA glorified guns and killing, prostitution and drug use; however, the murders of Tupac Shakur and Biggie Smalls in 1997 have since tempered its popularity. The extremely successful white rapper Eminem has been called the Elvis of hip-hop because of his central role in making hip-hop popular with white teenagers. Missy Elliott has exemplified the crossover of pop and hip-hop, and Jay-Z is another major artist. In many ways, hip-hop is a producer's medium (like Jamaican reggae), and Dr Dre and Snoop Dogg have been extremely influential behind the consoles.

Get Rich or Die Tryin' (2003) by 50 Cent: Produced by Eminem, 50 Cent arrives with all the street cred and proud, tough, violent swagger necessary to be the biggest gangster rap star in a decade.

Dance

Perhaps it shouldn't be a surprise that it was rule-breaking Americans who were the innovators of modern dance. Without a doubt, dance lovers should head first to New York City, which is the base for many of the nation's premier choreographers and dance companies, not to mention all the superior hoofin' on Broadway. However, the San Francisco Bay Area is a close second in importance for modern dance, and Minneapolis, Chicago and Philadelphia have active scenes. In addition, most major cities have high-quality professional ballet companies.

BALLET

The School of American Ballet was founded in 1934 by Russian-born choreographer George Balanchine. He then became artistic director of the New York City Ballet when it was founded in 1948 and turned it into one of the best ballet companies in the world. He adapted traditional ballet to modern influences and set new standards in performance. Jerome Robbins took over from Balanchine in 1983, after Robbins had achieved his own fame as a collaborator with Leonard Bernstein on several of Broadway's biggest musicals, including *West Side Story* (1957).

MODERN DANCE

The pioneer of modern dance, Isadora Duncan didn't find success until she began performing in Europe at the turn of the 20th century. Basing her ideas on ancient Greek concepts of beauty, she challenged the strictures of classical ballet and sought to make dance an intense form of self-expression.

In the 1920s and 1930s, New York–based Denishawn was the nation's leading modern-dance company, and its most famous and influential

Voice of Dance is San Francisco–based and focuses on the modern dance scene, with a comprehensive list of links to groups across the country: www.voiceofdance.com.

student was Martha Graham. She founded the Dance Repertory Theater in New York, and most of the major American choreographers of the late 20th century developed under her tutelage. In her long career she choreographed more than 140 dances and developed a new dance technique, now taught worldwide, aimed at expressing inner emotion and dramatic narrative. Her two most famous works were *Appalachian Spring* (1944), dealing with frontier life, and *Clytemnestra* (1957), based on Greek myths.

Merce Cunningham, Paul Taylor and Twyla Tharp succeeded Graham as the leading exponents of modern dance, but all differed from her and remain very active. In the 1960s and '70s, Cunningham explored Abstract Expressionism as it related to movement, and he collaborated famously with musician John Cage. Taylor and Tharp are known for borrowing themes from popular culture; in 2003, Tharp won the Tony Award for best choreography for the musical *Movin' Out*. Another student of Martha Graham, Alvin Ailey set up the Alvin Ailey American Dance Theater in 1958. His most famous work is *Revelations* (1960), a dance suite set to gospel music. San Francisco Bay Area–based Anna Halprin and New York–based Mark Morris are two other celebrated postmodern dancers and choreographers working today.

The website for the American Institute of Architects can lead you to more information on contemporary topics and architects: www.aia.org.

Architecture

The story of any nation can be told through its buildings, and the USA is no exception. American architecture is marked by eclectic diversity and regional variations. With a few exceptions, it mainly followed revivalist trends and adopted European tastes until well into the 20th century, when it championed postmodern aesthetics. It is fitting that America's most prominent architectural contribution to the world – the skyscraper – is a symbol of its technical achievements, commerce and grand aspirations.

THE COLONIAL PERIOD

The only lasting indigenous influence on American architecture originated in the Southwest, where 17th- and 18th-century Spanish colonial and mission buildings incorporated elements of Pueblo Indian design and construction, notably the flat-roofed, thick-walled adobe building (see p806). The hybrid Spanish-Indian influence reappeared in 20th-century architecture as mission-revival style in Southern California and Pueblo style in the Southwest.

On the East Coast, early colonists brought European architectural influences, though the first buildings reflect necessity as much as style. In Virginia and the Carolinas, the would-be gentry aped grander English homes (based on pictures of them), and bricks replaced timber. Present-day Williamsburg, Virginia, is an accurate reconstruction.

After the Revolutionary War, the nation's leaders adopted neoclassicism as a style befitting the new republic, since it embodied the ideals of Greece and Rome. The Virginia State Capitol, designed by the multitalented Thomas Jefferson, was modeled on a Roman temple, and his home, Monticello, had a Romanesque rotunda.

Professional architect Charles Bulfinch helped develop the similar but more monumental Federal style, which paralleled the English Georgian style. The grandest example is the US Capitol in Washington, which became the model for many state legislative buildings, from Georgia to California.

In the early 19th century, mirroring the fashion in England, American tastes preferred the heavier Greek-revival style. Public buildings and mansions all over the country took the form of Greek and Roman temples or had a mini-Parthenon-shaped portico tacked on the front. Around

1850, Gothic-revival style became popular for church and college buildings, again following the English lead.

SUBURBS & SKYSCRAPERS

In the mid-19th century, small-scale building was revolutionized by 'balloon-frame' construction: a light frame of standard-milled, 2-by-4-inch timber was joined by cheap, mass-produced nails. Easy and economical to build, balloon-frame stores and houses were thrown up in towns and cities all over the expanding West and Midwest. Eventually condemned as a fire hazard in the inner cities, this type of house proliferated in the suburbs, putting home ownership within reach of middle-class Americans; the technique is still used today.

A notable variation on the balloon-frame house was the more well-to-do 'Victorian' (Queen Victoria reigned from 1837 to 1901), which appeared in San Francisco and other cities. Larger and fancier, these homes added balconies, towers and ornate, colorful trim reflecting a mix of neoclassical, Queen Anne, Gothic and Italianate styles.

After the Civil War, influential architects studied at the École des Beaux-Arts in Paris, and American buildings showed increasing refinement and confidence. Richard Morris Hunt's Biltmore Estate in North Carolina epitomizes this style. Major beaux-arts-style public buildings include the railway station in Washington, DC, and City Hall in San Francisco.

Iron-frame buildings first began to appear in New York City in the 1850s; the internal iron frame (which meant the walls no longer supported the building) allowed greater freedom of design. Along with the invention of the Otis elevator, tall buildings became possible. The Chicago School crossed these innovations with beaux arts style and produced the skyscraper, the first 'modern' architecture.

A leading exponent of functionalism, Louis Sullivan built the first true skyscraper (actually in Buffalo, New York): the 13-story Guaranty Building. Among Chicago's early skyscrapers is Sullivan's intriguing Carson Pirie Scott & Co department store in Chicago, featuring ornate metalwork at street level. Soon, however, Chicago was eclipsed by New York, where the skyscraper was pushed ever higher by the pressures of profit and high-priced real estate.

A Field Guide to Contemporary American Architecture (2001) by Carole Rifkind: This is a very good, accessible primer, with lots of helpful line illustrations, of American architecture from WWII to the present.

FRANK LLOYD WRIGHT

Initially an apprentice to Sullivan's firm, Frank Lloyd Wright created an architectural style all his own and is considered one of the 20th century's great visionaries. Working mainly on private houses, he abandoned all the historical elements of architecture, making each building a unique sculptural form characterized by strong horizontal lines. Wright called them 'prairie houses,' though invariably they were built in the suburbs.

Interior spaces flowed from one to another, rather than being divided into rooms, and the inside was connected to the outside rather than separated by solid walls. Texture and color came from the materials themselves, not from applied decoration. Wright was innovative in his use of steel, glass and concrete, creating shapes and structures like nothing in the past, and he pioneered panel heating, indirect lighting, double glazing and air-conditioning.

As well as visiting the revolutionary Guggenheim Museum in New York City, Wright fans should check out Buffalo, New York; southern Wisconsin; eastern Pennsylvania; and, of course, Chicago.

From Bauhaus to Our House (1981) by Tom Wolfe: New journalist and cultural critic Wolfe takes modern American architecture and aesthetics to task in his usual wry, witty fashion. Wolfe is an entertaining scourge of intellectual pretensions.

THE MODERN AGE

Influenced by Wright's breaking of traditions and by art deco – which became instantly popular in the US after the 1925 Paris exposition – tall city buildings took on new appearances. The horizontals and especially the verticals of the structural grid and the surfaces of concrete, glass and steel became the main design elements. Notable examples are the 1930 Chrysler Building and the 1931 Empire State Building. Art deco was also a feature of the 1932 Rockefeller Center and its Radio City Music Hall, and it set the tone for movie houses, gas stations and resort hotels, most notably in Miami.

European architects absorbed Wright's ideas, and that influence bounced back when the Bauhaus School left Nazi Germany to set up in the USA. In America, Bauhaus became known as the International style, and its principles were taught at Harvard by Walter Gropius and practiced in Chicago by Ludwig Mies van der Rohe. By using glass 'curtain walls' over a steel frame, the best International-style buildings became abstract, sculptured shapes and the worst became ugly glass boxes. The Seagram Building in New York and the North Lake Shore Dr Apartments in Chicago are two of the best.

One response to the starkness of the International style was postmodernism, which re-introduced decoration, color, historical references and even whimsy. In this, American architects like Michael Graves and Philip Johnson took the lead, and two excellent examples are Graves' Portland Building (in Portland, Oregon) and Johnson's AT&T Building in New York City.

Arguably the best American architect today is Canadian-born Frank Gehry. A truly 21st-century designer, he has been greatly influenced by installation art, and his firm has pioneered computer-design techniques that allow the conception and construction of perfectly composed asymmetrical buildings, such as the Weisman Art Museum in Minneapolis (see p434).

Painting & Sculpture

The coolest feature of the helpful International Sculpture Center's website is the list of major US sculpture parks and gardens, with descriptions and contact information: www.sculpture.org.

Painting and sculpture have always had a rough row to hoe with the American public. This is perhaps a vestige of Puritan prejudices; America's first settlers actively prohibited religious art and had little use or time for art otherwise. Today, the average American remains somewhat skeptical of contemporary art: it's obscure, expensive and feels like an upper-class luxury rather than a cultural necessity.

That said, there has always been a sizable segment of Americans deeply devoted to the fine arts, and the quality of American art is exceptional. The richness of America's art museums – which contain all periods, styles and artists – is stunning, and these museums enjoy a widespread popularity that never quite translates into everyday art appreciation. Outstanding museums devoted to American art exist all over the country, but two of the most comprehensive collections are at the Whitney Museum in New York City and the Corcoran Gallery in Washington, DC.

NATIVE AMERICAN ARTS

Most Native American arts and crafts were personal adornments and decoration of everyday tools and weapons, but several cultures produced work of exceptional interest. In the Pacific Northwest, the coastal societies carved religious masks and totem poles with semi-abstract depictions of gods and deities in the form of whales, fish and 'thunderbirds.' In the Southwest, Pueblo people became skillful at pottery, which they painted in distinctive, abstract designs. Influenced by the Spanish missionaries, the Navajo learned to weave blankets using ancient designs, and to make silver jewelry.

AMERICAN LANDSCAPES & THE WEST

Since the 18th century, talented American artists have participated in most of the European artistic movements. In fact, in the late 18th and 19th centuries, some of the most famous – such as Benjamin West, John Singer Sargent, James Whistler and Mary Cassatt – worked most of their lives in Europe. It wasn't until the 1820s that the first distinctly American artistic trends emerged. As with American writers, American artists responded to the call to develop a new national culture by embracing wilderness and the frontier, and they embodied in sometimes allegorical images all of the Romantic and Transcendentalist beliefs that were then firing the American imagination.

Thomas Cole inspired the influential Hudson River School with his magnificent landscape paintings of the Catskill Mountains near New York in 1825. Asher Durand was another of the school's leading figures, and their 'luminist' emphasis on atmosphere and light was further developed in the famous landscapes of Cole's student Frederick Church.

The first images of the West were the monumental landscapes of Albert Bierstadt, a German-born, European-trained artist who went west with surveyors in 1859. He painted most of the prominent western landmarks – Yosemite, Yellowstone, the Grand Canyon – in an overly dramatic, highly emotional style. Along with Thomas Moran's paintings, these depictions helped spur political efforts to preserve these areas as 'national parks.'

After the Civil War, landscapes and seascapes were increasingly populated, serving more frequently as backdrops for human drama rather than solely as allegories of nature. The postwar work of Winslow Homer emphasized rural renewal, and from the 1880s, he painted powerful, unsurpassed watercolors of the sea.

Nineteenth-century paintings also echoed the mythologies of frontier life that were being developed in American literature. Western art promulgated the rugged heroism of the cowboy and the humble virtues of the pioneers – most often at the expense of Native Americans. George Catlin went west in 1832 to document Indian life, and his numerous paintings (many are in the Smithsonian's National Gallery of Art) are not unsympathetic records of Indian society, though their ultimate accuracy has been questioned.

The two great 19th-century romanticizers of the West were Frederic Remington and Charles Russell. Both spent portions of their lives on the frontier, and their exciting paintings and bronze statues capture all of the glorious, galloping adventure of cowboy life. However, despite the seeming realism of their work, their depictions of Indians and of Indian battles are, by and large, historically false. Good places to see this art are the western museums in Fort Worth, Texas; Oklahoma City and Tulsa, Oklahoma; and Remington's birthplace, Ogdensburg, New York.

American Visions (1999) by Robert Hughes: It's hardly airplane reading, but this is the best, most comprehensive and fully illustrated overview of American art.

AMERICAN REALISM

American art's rampant romanticism was dealt its first serious blow in the late 19th century by Thomas Eakins, who spent most of his controversial career in Philadelphia and is now considered one of the 19th century's greatest painters. He sought to capture not idealized beauty but the beauty inherent in real life. *The Surgical Clinic of Professor Gross* (1875) initially caused a scandal, and he revived American portraiture and was one of the first to use the new medium of photography.

As in literature, realism and stylistic experimentation came to dominate 20th-century American art. Early in the century, a diverse group of New York City artists, later known as the Ashcan School, worked like muckraking journalists, undermining accepted notions of appropriate subject matter. George Bellows' paintings of the poor and of boxers are quintessential examples. It was the Ashcan artists who organized the infamous 1913 Armory Show in Manhattan that introduced the country to the shocking force of European modernism.

Another definitive American realist was Edward Hopper, whose bleak urban landscapes from the 1930s and '40s are rich psychological images.

Often called 'regionalists,' other realist painters sought to capture small-town and rural life; these included Grant Wood (*American Gothic,* 1930) and Thomas Hart Benton, who was a renowned muralist. Reminiscent of Soviet social-realist paintings, regionalism dominated the work of Works Progress Administration (WPA) artists during the 1930s.

Though a realist in style, Norman Rockwell largely idealized American life, often patriotically. His wildly popular illustrations appeared on the covers of family magazines from the 1920s to the 1960s.

MODERNISM & BEYOND

American artists followed the early-20th-century European trends toward abstract art – such as fauvism and cubism. Artists such as Joseph Stella, Charles Demuth, Charles Sheeler and Stuart Davis began to 'abstract' colors and forms from urban landscapes and still-life objects. In the southwest, Georgia O'Keeffe did the same using desert flowers and landscapes, and she remains one of the USA's most popular artists.

You don't have to subscribe to the Art Renewal Center's ideology – rescuing contemporary art from modernism – to be impressed by its website: tons of high-quality art, articles and profiles of current US realists: www.artrenewal.org.

After WWII, New York became a world center for the avant-garde, and American Abstract Expressionism became the dominant trend. Artists pushed abstraction to its ultimate end, notably in Mark Rothko's bold squares of color, Willem de Kooning's improvisations and Jackson Pollock's rhythmic, process-driven 'action paintings.'

As abstraction deconstructed the image, Pop Art emerged to tear down the wall separating high art from popular culture. Roy Lichtenstein parodied comic book art, Jasper Johns co-opted the American flag and Andy Warhol appropriated advertising, everyday items and the images of celebrities. Irony and commercialization reached into the fine arts and shook their foundations.

Today, American and international avant-garde art movements – such as installation and performance art – continue the deconstructive process. Whatever the current fad, contemporary American art is rarely still – it mixes media, adds moving images, invites viewer participation or celebrates process over result. However, some American artists have also begun calling for a revival of 'classical' notions of beauty, ethics and form – charging that art movements that once sought to undermine elitism have themselves become elitist.

It's anyone's guess what will emerge from this worldwide artistic dialogue, but the ideas and sensibilities of American artists are certain to help shape it into the new century.

Film

It's hard to say which of America's arts has had the greatest influence on world culture, but this much we know: movies have had far and away the biggest impact on how the world sees America, and even on how Americans view themselves.

The Graduate (1967) by Mike Nichols: It's become a nostalgia piece of the 1960s, but Anne Bancroft's performance as a mother having an affair with graduate Dustin Hoffman keeps this movie feeling edgy and urgent.

Movies are the repository of the country's dreams. They project America's fears, fantasies and hopes, and occasionally its unadorned reality. They have become, without a doubt, the most popular of the popular arts. In the crowded, noisy rec room of American entertainment, only film, and occasionally TV, still has the power to get everybody's attention at once.

In many ways, the movie industry has never been in better shape. Americans spend more on seeing movies than on any other form of entertainment; in 2001, they spent a combined $29 billion on theater admissions, videos and DVDs, and that spending is predicted to keep rising. Almost all of this growth is due to DVDs, which is becoming the fastest-adopted new technology ever.

In addition, the advent of digital cameras, digital editing and digital projection is reinventing filmmaking itself, making it cheaper, faster, easier and more flexible. The creative possibilities are literally endless, since all the traditional limitations of celluloid are gone. However, digital equipment doesn't just help Hollywood make bigger special effects; most excitingly, it also allows low-budget, independent filmmakers access to this very expensive artform. These independent films rarely reach the local multiplex, but attend any one of the many film festivals across the country and you will find an explosion of new ideas and voices.

Annie Hall (1977) by Woody Allen: Allen is one of America's most prolific, energetic and skillful directors. In the first of his many love letters to New York, he proved he could marry his comedy shtick to genuine romantic pathos.

DOES A HORSE REALLY LIFT ITS FEET?

In California in the 1860s, Eadweard Muybridge set up a row of cameras with trip wires to study animal and human movement. One of the things he hoped to prove was that horses lift all four feet when they run. They do, and his tiny experiment opened up a whole new way of seeing the world.

Blue Velvet (1986) by David Lynch: Sure, others have come along to peel the overripe fruit of middle-class suburban America, but none get under your skin like Lynch. Almost 20 years later, it's still disturbing.

Motion picture cameras and projectors were developed simultaneously in France and the USA in the late 19th century, though Thomas Edison was the first to use sprocketed celluloid film. The first movie house opened in Pittsburgh in 1905, and because shows cost a nickel, it became known as a nickelodeon.

The potential of moving pictures for storytelling was quickly realized; the 1903 film *The Great Train Robbery* is famous because it was the first to use editing for dramatic effect – it cut to the chase. Almost as quickly, movie-makers realized the power of genres and of stars to entertain and draw audiences. Actors were promoted and fan clubs encouraged. In the 1910s, Charlie Chaplin became the first true movie star, and Mack Sennett's slapstick comedies – and his ever-bumbling Keystone cops – became cultural institutions.

DW Griffith was a pioneer of cinematic techniques, and his landmark films *Birth of a Nation* (1915) and *Intolerance* (1916) introduced much of cinema's now-familiar language, such as the fade, the close up, the moving shot and the flashback.

Do the Right Thing (1989) by Spike Lee: It's a hot, hot summer in Brooklyn, and something's gotta give. Lee smoothly and stylishly builds a latticework of racial tension, then delivers an explosion. Lee hasn't stopped since.

At the same time, increased competition led to the studio system, which began in New York City, where Edison tried to create a monopoly with his patents. This drove many independents to move to a suburb of Los Angeles, where they could easily flee to Mexico in case of legal trouble – and thus, Hollywood was born.

In 1927, sound was first introduced in *The Jazz Singer* (starring Al Jolson), and the 'talkies' ushered in the golden age of the movies, from the 1930s to the 1950s. Movie palaces and drive-in theaters sprung up everywhere; in 1938 alone, it was estimated 65% of the population saw a film. Glamorous stars enthralled the nation, and their names still conjure flutters: Humphrey Bogart, Cary Grant, Ingrid Bergman, Katherine Hepburn, James Stewart. The Hollywood studios locked these stars into exclusive contracts, ran production departments that handled every aspect of filmmaking, and controlled distribution and exhibition in theaters. It was the perfect racket.

Then, in the 1950s, competition from TV siphoned audiences, and federal authorities broke up Hollywood's monopoly on distribution and exhibition. In the 1960s, in order to survive, studios cut costs, ended

Easy Riders, Raging Bulls (1998) by Peter Biskind: Admit it. You want Hollywood gossip with your film criticism. Biskind rips the lid off the 1970s in this deliciously dishy examination of Hollywood's last radical era.

Citizen Kane (1941) by Orson Welles: Many critics feel it's the best film of all time. But don't be put off by ponderous expectations. A journalist's search to find the 'truth' about a dead newspaper tycoon still yields honest drama and a biting critique of the American Dream.

actor contracts, sold off production departments, and still sometimes went under.

In the 1970s, desperate studios took a risk on a generation of young, anti-establishment filmmakers who, reflecting the times, were interested in social realism, not musicals, romantic comedies or westerns. They included Martin Scorsese, William Friedkin, Robert Altman and Francis Ford Coppola, and their provocative films were a catalyst for America's current independent-film movement.

The other lasting legacy of the '70s is the blockbuster, and it arrived courtesy of two innovative young filmmakers whose names are now synonymous with pop culture: Steven Spielberg and George Lucas. In particular, Lucas' *Star Wars* (1977) became such an unexpected cultural phenomenon, and its pleasures were so visceral and eye-popping, that studios now had a blueprint for the future: keep the heroes simple, the action fast, ladle on the special effects and open big.

In the 1980s and 1990s, glamour returned to Hollywood, the studios reinforced their dominance and all of America turned out for the show.

IT'S A GENRE WORLD OUT THERE

If you judged American life by its films, you'd think everyone lived by a preset formula. Genres have defined American cinema since its birth, and the following are either original to America or are distinctive expressions of it.

The Western

In pop cinema terms, the mythic West is America: good guys versus bad guys, law versus lawlessness, all duking it out on the rugged frontier. The 1940s and '50s were the western's heyday. For an unironic paragon of manhood, check out Gary Cooper in *High Noon* (1952), while John Ford's influential *The Searchers* (1956) is pure western poetry: John Wayne, Monument Valley and a deadly score to settle. Sam Peckinpah's ode to nihilistic violence, *The Wild Bunch* (1969), dragged the western into the antiheroic modern day, as did Clint Eastwood's *Unforgiven* (1992).

The Musical

The golden age of Hollywood was defined by the musical. *42nd Street* (1933) encapsulates the entire genre. Fred Astaire and Ginger Rogers were a match made in heaven, and *Top Hat* (1935) adds a classic Irving Berlin score. *Meet Me in St Louis* (1944) is a showcase for Judy Garland, while Gene Kelly's impish grin and athleticism make *Singin' in the Rain* (1952) an exuberant confection. The musical has largely fallen out of favor since then, though *Moulin Rouge* (2001) and *Chicago* (2002) show there is still life left in it.

TOP FIVE ALL-AMERICAN FREAK SHOWS

These singularly strange classics have come to define America's fringe. Blame it, mostly, on the '70s:

Eraserhead (David Lynch, 1977) Ruined plots.
Pink Flamingos (John Waters, 1972) Ruined taste.
The Rocky Horror Picture Show (Jim Sharman, 1975) Ruined theaters.
The Texas Chainsaw Massacre (Tobe Hooper, 1974) Ruined appetites.
This Is Spinal Tap (Rob Reiner, 1984) Ruined audiences.

Gangsters & Crime

The outsider status of the urban gangster is an often-explicit metaphor for the immigrant experience, and the crime genre includes many of America's greatest films. The original tough guy was Edward G Robinson in *Little Caesar* (1930). The influential subgenre 'film noir,' in which ambiguous, flawed heroes traipse through a dark underworld, got the star treatment in John Huston's *The Maltese Falcon* (1941); in Orson Welles' unsettling masterpiece *Touch of Evil* (1958); and in Roman Polanski's *Chinatown* (1974), which evokes 1930s LA. Francis Ford Coppola's *Godfather* trilogy (1971–90), which refracts immigrants and American society through the prism of organized crime, stands as an almost unrivaled American cinematic achievement. Through numerous crime films, Martin Scorsese has sifted the New York Italian-American experience, perhaps never more urgently than in *Mean Streets* (1973). In the 1990s, pop culture and wicked irony met the crime genre most famously in *Pulp Fiction* (1994) by Quentin Tarantino, and *Fargo* (1996) by the talented Coen brothers.

Science Fiction

An extremely popular genre of American fiction, sci-fi is a cinematic natural. Beneath the futuristic jargon and cool sets lie a range of postmodern concerns, such as fear of otherness and the unknown, existential dread, and the relationship of humans to technology. The original *Star Wars* trilogy (1977–82) trailblazed an archetypal mytho-spiritual terrain that has been rewired for the virtual-reality 21st century by *The Matrix* films (1999, 2003). Other sci-fi highlights include the first two *Alien* films (1979, 1986) and Ridley Scott's *Blade Runner* (1982).

Blade Runner (1982/1991) by Ridley Scott: It's hard to say who gets the tougher workout in this sci-fi noir detective thriller: LA or American hero Harrison Ford. Both evoke a moody sadness that stays with you. See the 1991 director's cut.

Comic Books

Condescended to by critics as juvenile fare, American comic books have long existed in a cultural limbo, that is until Hollywood began turning superheroes into movie stars. It began with *Superman* (1978), and now includes all the favorites: Batman, Spiderman, the X-Men and more. Close to sci-fi, they engage universal issues of personal identity, but take these movies for what they most often are: pure unadulterated escapism that is as American as apple pie.

Television

Television was developed in the USA and Britain in the 1920s and 1930s, and the first commercial TV set was introduced at the 1939 New York World's Fair. Today, nearly every home in the USA has one, making TV perhaps the defining medium of the modern age. While the recent arrival of another box-like screen – the personal computer – has partially upset this claim, neither may resemble itself for long. All signs point to the eventual merging of these icons in the not-too-distant future.

Sex and the City: Debuted in 1998, this HBO series overturns any lingering 1950s sex-and-the-single-girl stereotypes. It brilliantly encapsulates the modern-day search for love and the state of contemporary sexual politics, and New York City never looked better.

TV programming has long been known as the soft middle of American culture. Like a bag of potato chips, it's easy to consume, dependable and addictively inoffensive, but by itself, a terrible diet. This is largely because, unlike other media, TV has always been, and will most likely remain, almost solely a corporate-run enterprise whose success depends upon attracting the widest possible audience. Even the advent of cable in the 1980s, which exploded the number of available channels to literally hundreds, at first did little to change TV's formulaic sameness.

Then, things did change. Video brought movies into the home, and the stigma Hollywood once attached to TV acting faded. In the late 1990s, pay cable channels began to produce their own content, tackling

The Simpsons: Debuted in 1989, this cartoon series takes every cliché, stereotype and pop culture reference that America offers, stuffs them in a blender of modern irony, and hits purée. It's a postmodern crash course, American-style.

controversial topics in TV-size bites but with film-quality explicitness. Now videos and DVDs package TV shows for repeat viewing. If all of America's arts have become a mix of high culture and pop culture, TV should be included among them.

High quality and occasionally radical TV programs have always existed – those bright moments when the medium's reach has been met by equally lofty aims. Here are just a few.

The original *I Love Lucy* show (1951–57) was groundbreaking in numerous ways: it was the first show to shoot on film, using three cameras, before a live audience, and then to be edited before airing. This allowed for syndication (or rebroadcast). As a 'situation comedy,' it established the sitcom formula, and not only that, it revolved around the hilarious antics of a strong woman in an inter-ethnic marriage. Every major female TV star since, from Mary Tyler Moore to Roseanne, owes a debt to Lucille Ball.

In the 1970s, *All in the Family* was nominally a comedy, but in its unflinching examination of prejudice – in the form of Carol O'Connor's bigoted patriarch Archie Bunker – it tread ground no TV show had until then dared enter. Similarly, the sketch-comedy show *Saturday Night Live*, which debuted in 1975, pushed the envelope of propriety, became required viewing on college campuses, and launched the careers of numerous actors.

In the 1980s, *The Cosby Show,* starring comedian Bill Cosby, became the nation's highest-rated program, and while it was not the first successful black show, it was revolutionary in its portrayal of a middle-class black family with whom the entire country could identify.

From the 1990s to today, there has been a growing list of more diverse, intense and well-written dramas and comedies – including pay cable programs like Showtime's *Queer as Folk* and HBO's *Sex and the City* and *The Sopranos*. However, the last decade's most influential show has turned out to be a cartoon: *The Simpsons*, with its fractured nuclear family. For travelers, it makes singularly ideal predeparture viewing.

Environment

The USA, without its land, might never have been more than a political experiment of small historical consequence. Instead, through luck, wars and purchase, it acquired the entire lower half of the North American continent, which contained riches beyond a pharaoh's wildest dreams. This land fueled the nation's incredibly rapid growth and wove itself into the fabric of the nation's identity. For most of its history, America has spent its natural wealth recklessly, like a drunken gold miner, but as it has grown, it has also sought to hoard its last remaining wild places and to protect and restore damaged landscapes and wildlife. America's land is its soul – as well as its body – and whatever conflicts arise over resources, all Americans consider the continent's unsurpassed beauty and radiant natural wonders a national treasure.

Where the Bluebird Sings to the Lemonade Springs (1993) by Wallace Stegner: These essays make a great introduction to one of America's greatest environmentalists and writers about the West. Here, Stegner dismantles all the Western clichés.

Despite the vast changes that humans have wrought on the landscape in the last three hundred years, there are still many places where travelers can experience vast stretches of nearly pristine wilderness, sometimes not much different than they were thousands or even millions of years ago. America's national park system is the envy of the world, and the USA has done more to preserve its land than any other nation. Not only is visiting America's parks and refuges one of the highlights of any visit, but nature writing has become one of the richest genres of American nonfiction. Poets range the countryside and bring to life America's distinctive spirit and its inextricable relationship to the land.

THE LAND

The USA covers about 3,787,000 sq miles and is the fourth-largest country in the world in area. Continental USA is made up of 48 contiguous states ('the lower 48'), while Alaska, its largest state, is northwest of Canada, and the volcanic islands of Hawaii, the 50th state, are 2100 miles southwest in the Pacific Ocean. In addition, the USA has a number of external territories (not covered in this book) including Puerto Rico, Guam, American Samoa, Navassa Island, Northern Mariana Islands and the US Virgin Islands.

Annals of the Former World (1998) by John McPhee: Geology rarely makes for a page-turner, but the gifted McPhee turns the history of North American plate tectonics into a thrilling, human spectacle of discovery. It's an epic masterpiece.

The country encompasses an extensive range of geographic regions and climates. Most of the continental USA is temperate, particularly in the east, but Hawaii and Florida are tropical, Alaska is arctic, the Great Plains are semiarid, and large portions of the West are bone-dry desert. The continental USA has three main mountain systems: the Appalachian Mountains are a string of ancient, eroded ranges that parallel the east coast; the dramatic Rocky Mountains are younger and taller and run north–south from Montana to New Mexico; and the volcanic Cascade and granite Sierra Nevada mountains parallel the Pacific coast.

Alaska has the wildest, and most protected, terrain of any state: it contains North America's highest point (Mt McKinley, 20,320ft), an interior rainforest and glaciers and wildlife aplenty. Hawaii is noted for its active volcanoes, lush greenery, endemic species and miles of beaches.

Geologically, the current North American topography was shaped about 50 to 60 million years ago, when ice sheets covered the continent and the modern Rocky Mountains began to rise (replacing an ancestral range that had already eroded away). In the last several million years, rivers, rain, ice and wind have carved and polished the results – to the most dramatic effect in the Southwest desert canyons.

The Solace of Open Spaces (1985) by Gretel Ehrlich: These essays capture the vast lonely expanses of Wyoming and their influence on the people who live there: Native Americans, cowboys and at one time, Ehrlich herself.

When America's first pioneers arrived, the east was blanketed in deciduous forests. In a relatively short time most of these were cut down for timber and fuel and to make room for agriculture. West of the Appalachians, the fertile Interior Plains became the nation's breadbasket, divided roughly into the northern 'corn belt' and the southern 'cotton belt.' As the plains continue west, they become more arid, and the northern Great Plains – a vast, treeless plateau of sweeping grasslands east of the Rocky Mountains – were used for cattle ranching and, with irrigation, turned over to more agriculture.

The Western deserts were some of the last areas to be settled in any significant numbers, and then only through great effort. From very early on, the nation dreamed of converting its deserts into green pastures, and it spared little in this quixotic quest. Dam building, water reclamation and irrigation projects were pursued at high monetary and environmental cost. These helped make California into an agricultural powerhouse, and allowed the creation of cities such as Los Angeles, Las Vegas and Phoenix, but on the whole, the Western deserts remain largely unpopulated except in pockets, and are only minimally conducive to farming. Travelers should be thankful for this, for in addition to their astonishing beauty, these inhospitable deserts are also an open book of geology, where billions of years of the continent's history remain on vivid display.

WILDLIFE

The story of America's wildlife is intertwined with the nation's settlement. When the pioneers arrived, unimaginably vast herds of bison (perhaps totaling as many as 100 million) roamed the plains from the Mississippi River to the Rocky Mountains; brown bears (or grizzlies) ruled the west from Alaska to Mexico; and black bears, gray wolves and bald eagles (the only eagle unique to North America) ranged across the entire continent. But as the forests gave way to the hatchet and the farm, and as predators were destroyed to protect livestock, the range and numbers of America's indigenous plants and animals shrank. Some were driven or hunted to extinction, and others, like the gray wolf and bison, very nearly so.

The continent's incredibly rich biodiversity was not completely destroyed, however, even as it suffered under the steady march of civilization, and later, industrial pollution. From the mid-19th century onward, calls for conservation arose and grew only louder. By 1871, the USA became concerned about its fisheries, and established what would become the US Fish & Wildlife Service (www.fws.gov). Then, in 1903, President Teddy Roosevelt set aside Florida's Pelican Island as the nation's first bird sanctuary, and thereby gave birth to the National Wildlife Refuge System (NWRS).

Managed by the US Fish & Wildlife Service, the NWRS currently includes around 540 refuges totaling 95 million acres (most of it in Alaska), making it the world's largest system of land and water preserves dedicated primarily to conserving wildlife and habitat. It protects over 700 bird species, 200 mammal species, 250 reptile and amphibian species and over 200 kinds of fish.

In 1964 the Wilderness Act was passed in an effort to preserve whole biospheres (not just significant natural features), and the 1973 Endangered Species Act remains a landmark of wildlife conservation and a powerful tool for environmental protection. The cumulative effect of all these efforts has been that notable portions of America's indigenous flora and fauna have been saved and in some cases restored.

Success stories include the American alligator, which lost so much of its wetland habitat it nearly became extinct, but has recovered so well it has been removed from the endangered species list and can be found throughout the southeast, particularly in Florida. Peregrine falcons, bald eagles, grizzly bears and bison dwindled to the hundreds and have all recovered to sustainable levels in portions of their original range. In the last decade, the reintroduction of the gray wolf into the Rocky Mountains and Southwest has been controversial but so far successful; gray wolf populations are growing, and livestock compensation has mollified worried ranchers.

Plant and ecosystem recovery is less dramatic and more complex. Of the once-vast Great Plains' tallgrass prairies, only 1% remain today; of the old-growth redwood forests, only 4% remain. At least a third of the nation's wetlands have been lost. Many native plant species survive only in tiny, isolated, federally protected remnants where, especially in the prairies, they continue to wage desperate battles against invasive non-native species. Restoration is expensive, but sometimes remarkable: done properly, grasslands can be restored to a relatively natural state within a decade.

The USA has so many diverse refuges and national parks, it's hard to characterize all that they contain or to single out any one; those interested in specific species or ecosystems should visit the federal and other recommended websites for details. However, for the sheer breadth of their diversity, Yellowstone and Great Smoky Mountains National Parks should not be missed. They are the best microcosms of what the continent used to be.

Wildlife in America (1957) by Peter Matthiessen: This remains the seminal text on North American wildlife, with detailed histories of indigenous species; more recent additions have updates on conservation efforts.

NATIONAL PARKS

Today, the National Park Service (NPS; www.nps.gov) manages over 380 federally protected areas covering approximately 83 million acres. These lands are divided among nearly 20 types of designations that preserve unique geographical features and outstanding natural areas, seashores and rivers, in addition to preserving historic sites, battlefields, cemeteries, buildings, landmarks and trails. See p86 for an overview of how the NPS came to be and of the different types of federal lands.

The USA's 53 national parks are the crown jewels of the system. They range in size from 40 sq miles to 1300 sq miles, and cover the length and breadth of the USA's natural highlights, including caverns and swamps, mountains and deserts, volcanoes, islands and rainforests. Many are clustered in the USA's most dramatic regions: the Southwest desert, the western mountain ranges and Alaska.

National parks are extremely popular, particularly in summer, and in an effort to keep them from being loved to death, the NPS regulates them with varying degrees of strictness. A few, like Zion, don't allow cars during the summer months, and most have tight controls on backcountry camping, among other activities. Facilities range from absolutely minimal – a ranger station and some exhibits – to quite comfortable, including museums, grocery stores, lodges and gourmet restaurants. Pretrip research, and lodging or camping reservations are essential for successful visits.

In general, interpretive services and publications are excellent, and rangers are very dedicated, knowledgeable and eager to help. However, the NPS budget is perpetually being tightened, and the Interior Department is in the process of privatizing a great number of park service jobs (mostly excluding rangers). Nevertheless, national parks tend to be the best protected and served of all the USA's public lands.

American Park Network has comprehensive details on all the national parks (including surrounding areas), and publishes free guides to the most popular: www.americanparknetwork.com.

Note that the National Parks map (pp82–3) and the National Parks Table (pp84–5) only include parks that are covered in this guide.

THE ENVIRONMENTAL MOVEMENT

America's political and social revolutions are well known, but the USA also birthed environmentalism, which was, and is, every bit as revolutionary.

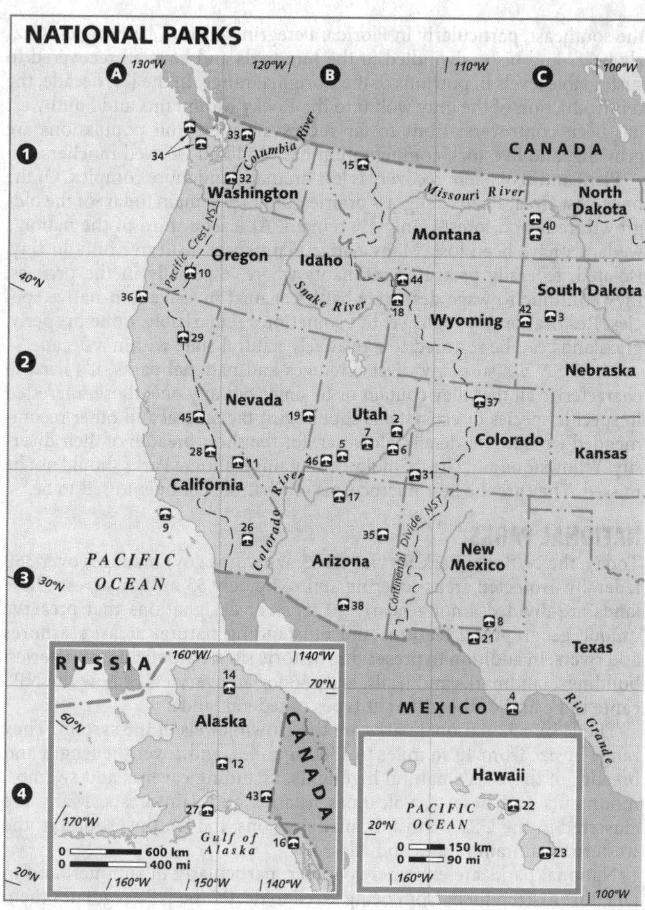

Before the USA did so, no nation had thought to preserve its wilderness, and still today, the US environmental movement often leads preservation efforts worldwide.

Wilderness and the American Mind (1967/2001) by Roderick Nash: This marvelous account traces how the concept of wilderness evolved in America, and demonstrates why environmentalism should be considered one of the world's great intellectual revolutions.

The idea that nature was anything but a commodity did not occur to most Europeans or American pioneers until the 19th century. Indeed, to America's settlers, wilderness was both deadly dangerous and a symbol of wild, godless impulses, and they took great pride in subduing them both. This was, they felt, civilization's holy mandate.

Then, in the 19th century, European Romanticism embraced the natural world for its poetic inspiration, and the USA's Transcendentalist movement took this one step further: it claimed that nature actually embodied God, and its workings provided transcendent, heavenly instruction. In *Walden* (1854), iconoclast Henry David Thoreau described living two years in the woods, blissfully free of civilization's comforts, and he persuasively argued that human society was harmfully distant from nature's essential truths. All this led to a profound philosophical shift: God came to speak through wilderness, not the ax.

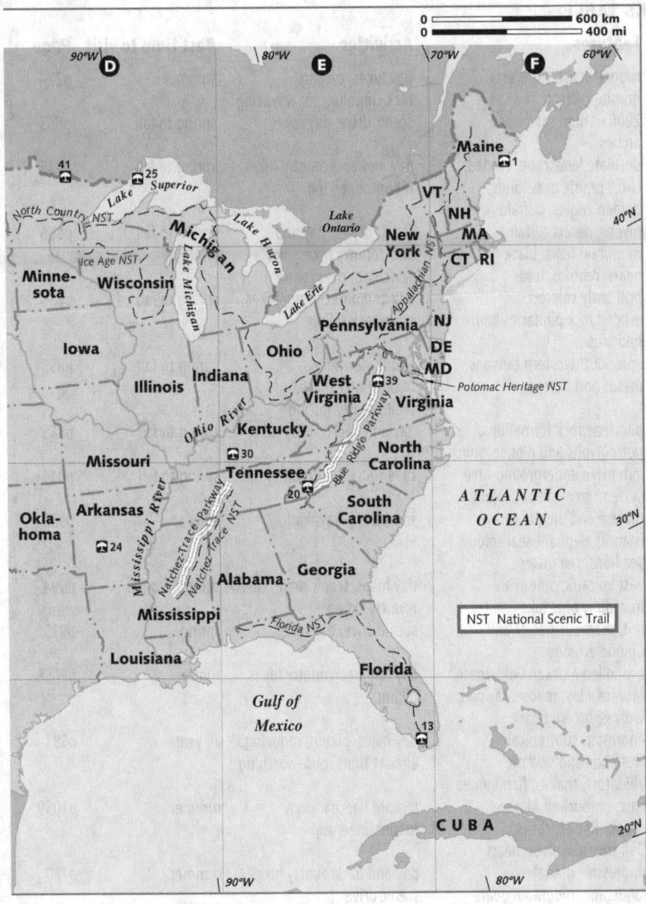

Park	No.	Grid
Acadia	1	F1
Arches	2	B2
Badlands	3	C2
Big Bend	4	C4
Bryce Canyon	5	B2
Canyonlands	6	B2
Capitol Reef	7	B2
Carlsbad Caverns	8	C3
Channel Islands	9	A3
Crater Lake	10	A2
Death Valley	11	B2
Denali	12	B4
Everglades	13	E4
Gates of the Arctic	14	B3
Glacier	15	B1
Glacier Bay	16	B4
Grand Canyon	17	B3
Grand Teton	18	B2
Great Basin	19	B2
Great Smoky Mountains	20	E3
Guadalupe Mountains	21	C3
Haleakala	22	C4
Hawaii Volcanoes	23	C4
Hot Springs	24	D3
Isle Royale	25	D1
Joshua Tree	26	B3
Kenai Fjords	27	A4
Kings Canyon & Sequoia	28	A2
Lassen Volcanic	29	A2
Mammoth Cave	30	E2
Mesa Verde	31	B3
Mt Rainier	32	B1
North Cascades	33	B1
Olympic	34	A1
Petrified Forest	35	B3
Redwood	36	A2
Rocky Mountain	37	C2
Saguaro	38	B3
Shenandoah	39	E2
Theodore Roosevelt	40	C1
Voyageurs	41	D1
Wind Cave	42	C2
Wrangell-St Elias	43	B4
Yellowstone	44	B2
Yosemite	45	A2
Zion	46	B2

The continent's natural wonders – vividly captured by America's 19th-century landscape painters – also had a way of selling themselves, and rampant nationalism led to a desire to promote them. In 1864, a 10-sq-mile

The Practice of the Wild (1990) by Gary Snyder: One of the great Beat poets, Snyder recalls, the spirit of Thoreau in these essays on wilderness and place, with prose that is eloquent, spare and sharp as diamonds.

NATIONAL PARKS TABLE

Park	Features	Activities	Best time to visit	Page
Acadia	rugged coast, fir forests, granite cliffs	day hikes, cycling, rock climbing, sea kayaking	summer	p274
Arches	2000 natural sandstone arches	scenic drive, day hikes	spring to fall	p853
Badlands	desolate landscape, eroded cliffs, prairie grasslands; golden eagles, buffalo	day and backcountry hikes, mountain biking	spring to fall	p715
Big Bend	diverse desert terrain; mountain lions, black bears, reptiles, birds	scenic drives, day and backcountry hikes, bird-watching, river running	spring to fall	p666
Bryce Canyon	brilliantly colored, eroded rock pinnacles and hoodoos	day and backcountry hikes, horseback riding	spring to fall	p856
Canyonlands	epic Southwestern canyons, mesas and buttes	scenic viewpoints, backcountry hikes, white-water rafting	spring to fall	p853
Capitol Reef	painterly rock formations, petroglyphs and pioneer ruins	day and backcountry hikes	spring to fall	p855
Carlsbad Caverns	extensive underground cave system; free-tail bat colony	cave tours, backcountry hike	spring to fall	p814
Channel Islands	diverse and unique rocky islands; elephant seal colony, sea lions, sea otters	snorkeling, kayaking,	all year	p920
Crater Lake	vast volcanic cone with incredibly blue lake	day hikes, scenic drive, cross-country skiing	summer to fall	p994
Death Valley	hot, dramatic desert and unique ecology	scenic drive, day hikes	spring	p919
Denali	unspoiled Alaskan wilderness, Mt McKinley; moose, caribou, wolves, brown bears	day and backcountry hikes, biking	summer	p1056
Everglades	enormous subtropical wetlands and swamp; alligators, snakes, flamingoes	day hikes, biking, canoeing, airboat tours, bird-watching	all year	p591
Gates of the Arctic	vast, untouched Alaskan Brooks Range; caribou, Dall sheep, wolves, bears	remote backpacking, mountaineering	summer	p1059
Glacier	impressive glaciated landscape; mountain goats	day and backcountry hikes, scenic drive	summer	p780
Glacier Bay	remote Alaskan bay filled with icebergs, 16 glaciers	boat tours, sea kayaking	summer	p1039
Grand Canyon	spectacular 277-mile-long, 1-mile-deep river canyon	day and backcountry hikes, mule trips, river running	spring to fall	p826
Grand Teton	towering granite peaks mirrored in lakes; moose, bison, wolves	day and backcountry hikes, rock climbing, fishing	spring to fall	p768
Great Basin	remote 13,000ft Wheeler Peak, ancient bristlecone pines, limestone caves	day hikes, scenic drives	spring to fall	p872
Great Smoky Mtns	wildly diverse Appalachian forest, wildflowers and mammals; bears	day and backcountry hikes, biking	all year	p858
Guadalupe Mtns	high desert country, fall foliage	day and backcountry hikes	spring to fall	p668
Haleakala	world's largest dormant volcano, lunar landscape	day hikes, scenic views	all year	p1079
Hawaii Volcanoes	two active volcanoes, tropical beaches, icy summit, lava flows	day hikes, scenic drives	all year	p1076

Park	Features	Activities	Best time to visit	Page
Hot Springs	47 natural springs, historic bathhouses, Hot Springs Mountain	bathing, sightseeing, day hikes	all year	p538
Isle Royale	remote, undeveloped island in Lake Superior, diverse wildlife	backcountry hikes, canoeing	summer	p420
Joshua Tree	sprawling rocky desert, the spiky Joshua tree	day and backcountry hikes, rock climbing	spring to fall	p917
Kenai Fjords	huge Harding Icefield, tidewater glaciers, diverse marine life	day hikes, boat trips	summer	p1051
Kings Canyon & Sequoia	Sequoia redwood groves, granite canyon	day and backcountry hikes, cross-country skiing	summer to fall	p972
Lassen Volcanic	volcanic peak and terrain, geothermal activity, hot springs	day and backcountry hikes	summer to fall	p967
Mammoth Cave	world's most extensive cave system, delightful river and forest	NPS-led cave tour, day hikes	all year	p563
Mesa Verde	preserves Ancestral Puebloan cliff dwellings, mesa and canyons	visit historic sites, short hikes	spring to fall	p759
Mt Rainier	volcanic mountain with glaciers, alpine meadows	day and backcountry hikes, mountaineering, skiing	spring to fall	p1016
North Cascades	undeveloped, glaciated landscape, Skagit River	day and backcountry hikes, rafting	summer	p1024
Olympic	temperate rainforests, alpine meadows, Mt Olympus	day and backcountry hikes	spring to fall	p1019
Petrified Forest	fossilized trees, petroglyphs, Painted Desert scenery	day hikes	spring to fall	p832
Redwood	177 sq miles of virgin redwood forest, world's tallest trees; Roosevelt elk	day and backcountry hikes	spring to fall	p961
Rocky Mountain	stunning peaks, alpine tundra, the Continental Divide; elk, bighorn sheep, moose, beaver	day and backcountry hikes, cross-country skiing	summer to fall	p742
Saguaro	large stands of giant saguaro cactus, desert scenery	day and backcountry hikes	spring to fall	p837
Shenandoah	Blue Ridge Mountains, Skyline Dr, Appalachian Trail	day and backcountry hikes, scenic drive, horseback riding	spring to fall	p319
Theodore Roosevelt	two units, prairie grasslands, desert badlands; birds, wild horses, bighorn sheep, bison	scenic drives, day and backcountry hikes, horseback riding	spring to fall	p722
Voyageurs	lake and forest area with moose, black bear and timber wolf; limited access, usually explored by motorboat	day hikes, canoeing	summer to fall	p444
Wind Cave	98-mile-long cave, prairie grassland and forest; elk, bison, prairie dogs	cave tours, day hikes	spring to fall	p720
Wrangell-St Elias	three mountain ranges meet amid ice fields and glaciers	scenic drives, day and backcountry hikes	summer	p1054
Yellowstone	numerous geysers and geothermal phenomena, impressive canyon, prolific wildlife	day and backcountry hikes, cycling, cross-country skiing	all year	p765
Yosemite	sheer granite-walled valley, waterfalls, alpine meadows	day and backcountry hikes, rock climbing, skiing	all year	p969
Zion	immense red-rock canyon, Virgin River	day and backcountry hikes, canyoneering	spring to fall	p858

portion of Yosemite Valley was set aside as a state park; then in 1872 President Ulysses S Grant designated two million acres as Yellowstone National Park, the first such large-scale preserve in the world.

The main reason given for establishing Yellowstone was to preserve its unique features for human enjoyment. But nature's greatest cheerleader, John Muir, soon emerged to champion the preservation of wilderness for its own sake, regardless of its benefit to humankind. For Muir, wilderness was superior to civilization, and he spent much of his life wandering the Sierra Nevada (he founded the Sierra Club in 1892) and passionately advocating on behalf of the mountains and forests. Muir was central in developing the nation's first true conservation movement, which secured its first big victory in 1890, when Yosemite National Park was established expressly to preserve its wilderness.

By the end of the 19th century, the nation was also realizing the limits of its once seemingly endless resources. Civilization had won; the continent was subdued. In 1891 the Forest Reserve Act was passed in order to manage forests so they would continue to house and fuel the growing nation. This, then, epitomized the central conflict of the early conservation movement – whether to preserve nature for human use and utility or for its spiritual sanctity. These mutually exclusive aims continue to underlie many conflicts today.

In the early 20th century, the increasingly dark scars of industrial progress raised urgent new concerns. The 1916 National Park Service Act established a permanent federal mechanism for wilderness preservation, and more importantly, the science of ecology emerged. Ecology would prove to be the final humbling of humankind – already knocked from the

US WORLD HERITAGE SITES

For more information on World Heritage Sites, visit Unesco's website: whc.unesco.org/heritage.htm.

- Cahokia Mounds State Historic Park (p382)
- Carlsbad Caverns National Park (p814)
- Chaco Culture National Historic Park (p809)
- Everglades National Park (p591)
- Grand Canyon National Park (p826)
- Great Smoky Mountains National Park (p858)
- Hawaii Volcanoes National Park (p1076)
- Independence Hall (p178)
- La Fortaleza and San Juan Historic Site in Puerto Rico
- Mammoth Cave National Park (p563)
- Mesa Verde National Park (p759)
- Monticello and University of Virginia in Charlottesville (p318)
- Olympic National Park (p1019)
- Redwood National Park (p961)
- Statue of Liberty (p117)
- Taos Pueblo (p824)
- Yellowstone National Park (p765)
- Yosemite National Park (p969)

center of the universe and arm in arm with monkeys – with its assertion that people were in fact interdependent with nature, not in control of it. With ecology, America's 19th-century conservation movement became the modern environmental movement.

The Sierra Club was the USA's first conservation group and remains the most active, with educational programs, organized trips and information: www.sierraclub.org.

Aldo Leopold was the first writer to popularize an ecological worldview with his idea of a 'land ethic,' which proposed that humans must act with respectful stewardship toward all of nature, rather than saving the parts they like and abusing the rest. The 1962 publication of *Silent Spring* by Rachel Carson provided the shocking proof: this exposé of how chemicals such as DDT were killing animals and poisoning the land and us horrified the nation and inspired an army of activists.

Since then, the US environmental movement has focused on combating pollution as well as preserving wilderness. Landmarks include the 1964 Wilderness Act; the 1968 National Wild and Scenic River Systems Act, designed to preserve free-flowing rivers; the 1969 National Environmental Policy Act; in 1970, the Clean Air Act and the first Earth Day; several 1972 water pollution and marine protection acts; and the 1973 Endangered Species Act. In 1980, President Jimmy Carter authored the greatest single act of wilderness preservation in history when he set aside 104 million acres in Alaska as federal lands. Taken together, America's environmental and wilderness legislation has resulted in significant improvements in the nation's water and air quality, and in the restoration of many once-threatened landscapes and wildlife.

The Wild Muir (1994) edited by Lee Stetson: Muir's prose can seem a little purple today. By highlighting his wildest adventures, this collection provides an evocative taste of what made Muir so influential while keeping things fun.

Today, nearly 700 million acres, or over a quarter of the USA, is owned and managed by the federal government. The Bureau of Land Management (BLM; www.blm.gov) controls the most, 262 million acres, managing resources like minerals and timber and conserving the land for recreation and sustainability. The US Forest Service (USFS; www.fs.fed.us) does nearly the same thing with 191 million acres of national forests. The most strictly preserved lands are held under the National Park Service and within the National Wildlife Refuge System. These allow very little use of resources, if any, as their main mandates are to preserve the land's wilderness quality and its wildlife habitats, and as much as possible to allow for its enjoyment by people.

ENVIRONMENTAL ISSUES

Environmental problems in the USA fall into two main categories: use of resources and pollution. Because the USA is so big, many issues are regional even when the effect is felt nationally. Some of the biggest issues are water use in the West, automobile dependence and air pollution, effective monitoring and clean up of industrial pollution, the fact that numerous landfills may soon reach their capacity, and continued dependence on fossil fuels and nuclear power.

When Smoke Ran Like Water (2002) by Devra Davis: By all rights, this book should become the *Silent Spring* for the new century. Readable and provocative, it's a modern history of how scientists study environmental pollution and how politics and industry undermine them.

The Environmental Protection Agency (EPA; www.epa.gov), established in 1970, is the main federal agency in charge of enforcing the USA's many environmental pollution laws and standards. Unfortunately, it is chronically underfunded and hampered by powerful industrial lobbies, and so many polluters are not called to task or fined to the extent that current laws allow.

In addition, each presidential administration exerts its influence every four years. The Bush administration has been notorious for its many efforts to loosen federal protections for wilderness (to allow for increased logging and oil drilling, among others) and to weaken federal pollution standards and enforcement for the benefit of industry. In some cases, Bush has pointedly reversed protective, Clinton-era wilderness legislation,

ARRIVE PREPARED, LEAVE NO TRACE

If you are planning an exciting adventure in America's wilderness, remember to do so responsibly. One thoughtless gesture – hiking off-trail through fragile soil or building an illegal fire – can take years for nature to repair. The cumulative effect of tens of millions of feet in America's parks every year is taking its toll. Each person does indeed make a difference.

Most hiking and camping advice is common sense. First, know what you are getting into. Know what weather to expect and pack accordingly, even if it's just for a few hours. Get trail maps, and take five minutes to talk to a ranger before plunging ahead. Rangers can alert you to crowds, landmarks, trail conditions and dangers, and they can confirm that your abilities, equipment and plans match the needs of your trip.

Once in the wild, do everything possible to minimize your impact. As the old saying goes, leave only footprints, take only pictures. Stick to established trails and campsites. Be particularly sensitive to riparian areas: don't wash yourself or your dishes in streams or rivers, and camp at least 200ft away from them. Use a stove for cooking, and make fires only in established fire rings. When you leave, take out everything you packed in and clean up every trace of your visit.

Conduct yourself as if you were a guest in someone's home – which in fact you are. Observe wildlife, but do not approach or feed it. If you find cultural or historic artifacts, leave them untouched. And finally, be aware and respectful of other visitors. Human noise travels far and is the fastest way to spoil a whole valley's worth of experiences.

For more information and advice, visit the Leave No Trace Center website at www.lnt.org.

and the two administrations exemplify, among other things, the perennial tension between America's desire to preserve and its eagerness to use its highly valuable land.

Water

Water usage in the West has always been, and will continue to be, a huge issue. About a quarter of a million dams were built across the country in the last century, many to divert precious water to western cities and farms. This dam building ended about 20 years ago because of its unprofitable expense and damaging environmental impact. Now, the West is using up its large underground aquifer at a phenomenal rate, and increasing water salinity is creating havoc with farms. If solutions are not found, in the next 20 to 30 years, the West may find itself at a very thirsty crossroads.

Water pollution also remains a large problem. Despite significant and notable progress in the 30 or so years since the Clean Water Act was passed, the EPA estimates that more than 40% of US waters remain polluted. Most recently, in 2003 it was discovered that perchlorate, a chemical used in missile and rocket fuel, now contaminates much of the lower Colorado River. Though the extent of the danger is still being determined, it's a potentially disastrous health hazard for the entire Southwest.

In addition, an internal EPA study in 2003 found that its own clean water enforcement has been horrendously bad. The EPA estimates that only 15% of serious industrial offenders ever face formal enforcement actions, and of these, only half result in fines, which themselves average no more than $6500.

Air Pollution

The USA is the world's single largest emitter of carbon dioxide from the burning of fossil fuels; and in the last decade, US greenhouse gas emissions have risen 14%, with most of the increase due to SUVs (sport utility vehicles) and residential energy use. However, acid rain in the northeast has actually become less of a problem since the 1990 amendment to the Clean Air Act, which raised emission standards for US factories.

In terms of air pollution, the internal combustion engine is the main culprit, and yet the two 'easiest' remedies – raising auto emissions standards and fuel efficiency – have been continually rebuffed by the auto industry. Americans, who in recent years have embraced the gas-guzzling sports utility vehicle (SUV), have not been noted for their environmentally friendly car choices either. However, low-emission hybrid cars, which use gas and electricity, are slowly increasing in sales, particularly in California, and the Bush administration has proposed funding research into zero-emission, hydrogen-powered cars, although these are at least a decade away from becoming a commercially viable option.

SUVs average 15 to 18 miles per gallon, take up as much space as 1.4 regular cars, are prone to rollovers (which cause one-quarter of all highway fatalities) and accounted for five of the top 10 selling cars in the US in 2002.

More immediately, in 2003 the EPA proposed tough new emissions standards for off-road diesel-powered vehicles, such as farm equipment, which are now virtually unregulated. It's estimated that 70% of the cancer risk from air pollution is due to diesel exhaust, and if passed, this legislation would have a dramatic impact on rural air quality and human health.

Energy

Over two-thirds of the USA's electricity comes from burning fossil fuels, and this dependency on oil is why there are continual calls to open up more federal lands in Alaska and off the coasts for increased drilling. Coal is also still used, and nuclear power plants generate about 18% of the USA's energy supply. While all of these pollute the environment, none is more lasting than nuclear waste.

In 2001, Yucca Mountain in Nevada was chosen as the nation's sole permanent nuclear waste storage site. Until it is built and operational, tentatively in 2010, nuclear waste will remain in 'temporary' storage at nuclear plants and other sites, where it has lived for years. The creation of the permanent storage site, however, means that nuclear plants can continue to operate in the meantime, saving the nation from power shortages.

Renewable energy sources – such as wind and solar power – account for only a tiny fraction of the USA's power generation, and if the Bush administration's energy plans are adopted, they will remain a tiny fraction for decades to come.

Food & Drink

by Tara Duggan

The USA may not have always had a stellar reputation for food, but this is changing quickly. While a burger, fries and Coke effectively make up the national meal, and fast-food chains threaten to consume what is distinctive about food across the country, there also is a rich tradition of quality regional cooking. The increasingly diverse population continues to improve the number of interesting restaurant options, and a burgeoning interest in restaurant chefs has brought excitement to the culinary scene.

In the past few decades, the country basically experienced a food revolution. Up through the 1960s and 1970s, ethnic foods were still mostly an anomaly and haute cuisine was all about nondescript 'continental' menus and stuffy service. But then groundbreaking cookbook authors and teachers like Julia Child and James Beard introduced Americans to the wonders of real French food and other culinary traditions, creating a demand for better quality in restaurants and supermarkets. In the early 1980s Alice Waters of Chez Panisse in Berkeley, California, and other chefs from that state created a new type of cuisine based on quality local produce, teaching people to become aware of the sources of their food.

No cross-country road trip would be complete without Jane and Michael Stern's *Road Food: The Coast-to-Coast Guide to 500 of the Best Barbecue Joints, Lobster Shacks, Ice Cream Parlors, Highway Diners and Much More*. Then again, you can get a lot of it for free at www.roadfood.com.

Now, chefs have a celebrity status akin to rock stars, especially the better-looking ones that appear on the Food Network, a 24-hour cable television station. In supermarkets throughout the country, shoppers can pick up organic baby greens and frozen Thai chicken pizza. All this fuss about food is causing some Americans to return to the kitchen, so there's hope that the country's regional traditions won't be lost amid a sea of french fries.

STAPLES & SPECIALITIES

It's difficult to generalize about what Americans eat. Most people eat three meals a day, with a snack or two in between. The traditional American breakfast grew out of the country's origins as an agricultural society, where hearty plates of eggs, bacon and pancakes helped farming families start the day. Today, most people have office jobs and can only handle a bowl of cold cereal, toast or pastry with coffee.

Lunch used to be more of an important meal, and on weekends, some people still take their main meal in the middle of the day. But workers' lunch breaks only last between 30 minutes and one hour, so most people grab a quick burger, soup or hearty salad. Dinner is when people take the main meal of the day. Traditional home-style dinners include baked casseroles, roast or grilled meat with potatoes, rice or noodles, bread and a vegetable or salad.

DID YOU KNOW?

Americans eat almost 50% of their meals in restaurants. On average, an American eats three hamburgers per week. And around 90% of children aged between three and nine dine at McDonald's once a month.

Most folks take a coffee (or Coke) break mid-morning or late afternoon with a cookie, candy bar or bag of chips. Traditional desserts are very sweet, and like everything else come in big servings, such as an ice-cream sundae or a slice of frosting-coated layer cake.

New England

This is where to find seafood specialities like Maine's prized lobster and New England clam chowder. Clams also come fried, steamed and completely uncooked, the latter at 'raw bars' that also serve oysters cold and briny from the sea. The clambake is an almost ritual meal, originated from

THE BAGEL PHENOMENON

Bagels are big these days, and if you buy one in an Iowa supermarket you may wonder why all the fuss about a bread roll with a hole in the middle. But certain bakeries in New York City still make bagels the old-fashioned way, and if you try one of these you might understand how it came to be that McDonald's now serves a ham, egg and cheese bagel for breakfast.

A true bagel, which really became a Jewish delicacy in this country, is made of just flour, water, salt, and malt for a little sweetness, and often is still rolled by hand. It is boiled, then baked, making it slightly crisp on the outside and deliciously dense and chewy inside. Traditional flavors include plain, poppy seed, sesame seed, onion, pumpernickel and egg, but modern-day bakeries have added things such as blueberries and sun-dried tomatoes.

Bagels are split in half and toasted, unless right out of the oven, then spread with cream cheese and often topped with smoked salmon, or lox (cold salmon). If you're in New York City, find out why Americans love bagels at one of these popular spots:

Absolute Bagels (☎ 212-932-2052; 2788 Broadway)
Columbia Hot Bagels (☎ 212-222-3200; 2836 Broadway)
Ess-a-bagel (☎ 212-980-1010; 831 Third Ave; ☎ 212-260-2252; 359 First Ave)
H & H Bagels (☎ 212-595-8003; 2239 Broadway)
Murray's Bagels (☎ 212-462-2830; 500 Sixth Ave)

Native Americans, where the shellfish are buried in a pit fire with corn, chicken and sausages. Cranberries, one of the essential parts of Thanksgiving dinner, are grown in Massachusetts and Rhode Island. The state of Vermont is known for its specialty aged cheddar cheese and maple syrup.

New York

Go to New York City and find almost any cuisine known to humankind. Because it continues to be a huge melting pot, it's a wonderful place to sample hard-to-find ethnic cuisines, from Jamaican to Ukrainian. Long-established ethnic treats include Chinese dim sum, Puerto Rican rice and beans, wood-fire charred 'New York'–style pizza, and pastrami sandwiches, pickles and bagels from Jewish delis. Many argue that New York is the country's center of haute cuisine, where restaurants run by the trendiest chefs uphold impeccable standards of food and service.

Mid-Atlantic

Like New England, the mid-Atlantic areas (DC, Virginia and Chesapeake Bay) have a lot to offer in terms of seafood, with oysters along the coast and delicious blue crab from Chesapeake Bay. Philadelphia gave the world the Philly cheesesteak, a gooey mouthful of a roll stuffed with beef, onions and melted cheese. At Amish restaurants, the Pennsylvania Dutch serve home-style, Germanic foods such as stews, pickles and shoofly pie at family-style, communal tables.

Southern

Southern cooking is a wonderful amalgamation of European, Native American and African traditions. Breakfast is as heavy as it could be, with eggs surrounded by buttery biscuits and gravy and ham. The ultimate Southern dish is barbecue: usually pork, sometimes chicken or beef, which is rubbed with spices, cooked slowly in a smoker until tender and then slathered with sauce. Every region of the South argues that their cuisine is best, from Texas' beef brisket to North Carolina's pulled pork. Tooth-achingly sweet desserts like cobblers, pies and layered cakes are a treat.

The Southern Belly: The Ultimate Food Lover's Companion to the South, by John T Edge, is the current favorite guide to the region.

Louisiana

If you thought a trip to New Orleans was all about drinking and taking your clothes off during Mardi Gras, you'd be missing something. This region has some of the best food in the country: Cajun food is heavy and spicy, a wild combination of French, Spanish, African and Native American influences. Specialties include gumbo, a stew of chicken and shellfish or sausage, and often okra; jambalaya, a rice-based dish with tomatoes, sausage and shrimp; blackened catfish; and alligator anything. For dessert try gooey, rum-laced bananas foster, or a fried beignet washed down with a chicory-scented café au lait.

Midwest

Swedes, Germans, Poles and Norwegians flocked to the Midwest in the 19th century to farm. The influence of their hearty cuisines, known as heartland cooking, and hard-working lifestyle means you'll find lots of homespun Americana on the menu – potato salads, fruit pies and hefty loaves of bread. Both beef cattle and dairy cows are huge industries here, so it's a good place to sample steak and cheese. For something with a little more spice, try Kansas City barbecue, or head to Chicago, an ethnically diverse culinary center with some of the country's top restaurants.

Southwest

This region was Spanish territory for some time and still has a large Chicano population, so the Mexican (and Mexican-American) food is excellent. Northern New Mexico makes delicious green and red chili sauces, which are pooled over enchiladas, tacos and eggs for breakfast. Native American specialties like fry bread are easy to find here. Utah, with its strong Mormon tradition, favors old-fashioned, standard American fare, but Las Vegas is the USA's most up-and-coming culinary center, where top chefs from New York, San Francisco and Los Angeles have set up satellite restaurants.

California

A concept that was born in the 1980s in the San Francisco Bay Area, California cuisine is all about using quality local ingredients in simple preparations. French and Italian bistro-style food was the first inspiration,

TRAVEL YOUR TASTEBUDS

Travel is an adventure for all the senses. While in the US make sure you try:

- Peanut butter and jelly sandwich – a savoury-sweet school lunchbox favorite made of white bread spread with peanut butter and jam.
- Tuna casserole – popularized in post-war America, when convenience foods became chic, this is a jumble of egg noodles, canned tuna and creamy condensed soup mix, with a crunchy topping.
- Burrito – a Mexican-American creation consisting of a large flour tortilla rolled around beans, meat, salsa and rice, usually enough food for two meals.
- S'mores – a camping treat, this interactive dessert involves roasting a marshmallow on a stick over the fire, then placing it between graham crackers with a piece of chocolate, which melts on impact.

We dare you to try Rocky Mountain oysters, a euphemistically named dish of battered and fried sheep or calf testicles served with a spicy dipping sauce to help it go down easier.

SAN FRANCISCO'S TOP FIVE

Chez Panisse Everyone should make a pilgrimage to Alice Waters' Berkeley shrine to California cuisine (p953).
Delfina One of the best values in San Francisco with excellent, California-inspired Italian food (p947).
Gary Danko The New French cuisine at this impeccable restaurant is as sophisticated and elegantly stylish as the best Armani suit (p947).
Slanted Door Moderately priced Vietnamese restaurant serving some of the most delicious food in the Bay Area (p947).
Zuni Café Specializes in cocktails and American/Mediterranean food, but most people come for the hip – yet classic San Francisco – atmosphere (p946).

but Latin and Asian influences have become part of the mix. The natural resources are overwhelming, with wild salmon, Dungeness crab, oysters and halibut coming from local waters; excellent produce year-round; and artisanal products like cheese, bread, olive oil and, of course, wine. The state is so ethnically diverse that you can eat almost anything here, especially in the Los Angeles area.

Pacific Northwest & Hawaii

These are the regions of Pacific Rim food. The cool, wet climate of the Pacific Northwest produces wonderful wild mushrooms, berries, stone fruits, apples and wine grapes. The entire northern coast, all the way to Alaska, has an abundance of wild king salmon and oysters. Seattle is home to Starbucks and has an espresso stand on every corner; it also brews a lot of boutique beer. With its heavily Asian-American population, Hawaii offers a combination of native foods and Chinese, Filipino and Japanese influences. Kalua pig, which is cooked in an underground fire pit, is usually the showcase dish at a traditional *luau* (multicourse feast).

Chowhound.com (www.chowhound.com) 'For those who live to eat.' Come here to ask locals about important issues from the best all-beef hot dogs in Chicago to the tastiest beef tongue tacos in Oakland, California.

DRINKS

Alcoholic drinks have had an interesting history in this country. In 1791, German and Scots-Irish farmers who grew rye for whiskey staged a rebellion to protest taxes. They fled to Kentucky and made their booze with corn instead, creating bourbon, the country's only original spirit.

In 1919, a growing temperance movement caused Congress to pass an act outlawing the sale and manufacture of alcohol. Prohibition lasted from 1920 to 1933, when it was finally rescinded.

California missionaries began making wine in the 18th century, when they needed fermented grape juice for communion. Today, some wineries in California still have 100-year-old vines as a result of that early culture. The state's wine industry suffered a blow during both a 1916 phylloxera (grapevine louse) epidemic and Prohibition, and wasn't really taken seriously until the 1970s, when a blind tasting of French and California cabernet sauvignon (by French wine tasters) put California wine on top for the first time. California makes 90% of the wine in the country. Other top wine-producing states are Washington, Oregon, Texas, Virginia and New York.

DID YOU KNOW?

Jack Daniels whiskey is distilled in Moore County, Tennessee, which has been a dry county since Prohibition days.

Meanwhile, it was German and Czech settlers who turned the Midwest into a beer-making center. Today, the top four US beer makers, three of which are located in the Midwest, brew 80% of the beer drunk in the USA, most of which is light in body and flavor. Seattle and other parts of the Northwest are part of the microbrewery movement, producing more European-quality beers.

Cocktails are making a popular comeback, and some of the top native creations include the mint julep (bourbon, mint, sugar and crushed ice), martini (gin and vermouth), Irish coffee (coffee, Irish whiskey, sugar and cream), and Bloody Mary (vodka, tomato juice, Tabasco sauce, horseradish and other flavorings).

Most nonalcoholic beverages are quite sweet and served over ice, from Southern-style iced tea to the ultimate American beverage: Coca-Cola from Atlanta, Georgia.

Want to know how to make something you ate during your travels? Epicurious (eat.epicurious.com) has 15,000 recipes from the popular cooking magazines *Gourmet* and *Bon Appetit*.

CELEBRATING WITH FOOD

Birthdays

The birthday boy or girl is presented with a decorated layered cake topped with flaming candles, which they have to blow out as they make a wish. The cake is usually served with ice cream, and also appears at other big occasions like wedding anniversaries.

Weddings

The bride and groom also celebrate with a cake, but one that's much larger and more multilayered. Tradition goes that they feed each other the first bite by hand.

New Year's Day

Especially in the South, people eat Hoppin' John, a plate of black-eyed peas and rice and often collard greens, for good luck.

Superbowl Sunday

Die-hard football fans will be glued to the television, but everyone else cares more about what's to eat and drink, which is as many snacks and as much beer as possible.

Chinese New Year

During this food-centric holiday, restaurants in Chinatowns are packed with celebrating families eating foods with names that sound like words for good fortune in Chinese, such as whole fried fish, noodles and dumplings.

Mardi Gras

In Louisiana, revelers eat King cake, with a good luck charm hidden inside, and head to gumbo parties or crayfish boils.

St Patrick's Day

On this day of celebrating Irish-American culture, some restaurants serve corned beef and cabbage, and maybe green-colored beer.

Easter

Most people of a Christian heritage celebrate with a big Sunday roast and Easter egg hunt, where adults hide egg-shaped chocolate and jelly candies around the house and yard for children to find.

Memorial Day, Independence Day & Labor Day

These summer holidays bring friends and family together in backyards or parks around the barbecue, surrounded by dishes of potato salad, coleslaw, Jello and apple pie. If you're lucky, someone will bring homemade fried chicken.

Halloween

Children dress up in costumes to scare away demons and go trick-or-treating, which means knocking on neighbors' doors and asking for candy.

Thanksgiving & Christmas

Both of these holidays are celebrated with large feasts involving a big roast and a spread of side dishes. Thanksgiving is based on a mythic celebratory harvest meal between early New England settlers and Native Americans. The traditional dishes are European in nature but made with native ingredients, such as turkey, cranberry sauce, roast sweet potatoes, mashed potatoes and pecan and pumpkin pies. Christmas is marked with many of the same foods, but maybe with a ham or beef roast instead of the turkey.

To make online restaurant reservations in advance of a trip, head to Foodline (www.foodline.com) or OpenTable.com (www.opentable.com/home.asp), which each serve 16 major US cities.

WHERE TO EAT & DRINK

Though what you find at a random roadside diner won't usually compare with the equivalent in, say, France, if you do some research you will come across some excellent food on your travels. For a more authentic experience, head to neighborhoods where locals really live and work, whether an ethnic district in a big city or a small rural town. A sign of a tourist trap is when the menu has photos of the food, or a long-winded text telling the history of the establishment. Sometimes these places can be charming, but they are usually avoided by locals.

Lunch can be a good time for bargains at quality restaurants, when prices can be much lower than at dinner; though keep in mind that the first-rate cooks usually work the night shift.

If you're looking for a quick meal, one option is to join the overwhelming number of Americans who eat in fast-food restaurants. Most of the food in these establishments is prepared and frozen at a central commissary then reheated before serving. The reheating involves a lot of frying, which makes the food pretty darn tasty but not too healthy.

A step up from fast food is the cafeteria or buffet, where you load up a tray with dishes from various steam tables, then carry it to your table. The all-you-can-eat buffet is a stunning phenomenon: for a set price you can revisit the buffet as many times as you like, until you're completely stuffed or just plain embarrassed.

'Family-style' restaurants or coffee shops are also very popular. Epitomized by the chain Denny's, they provide table service and homey foods like salads, soups, sandwiches, meatloaf dinners and ice-cream sundaes. Kids are very welcome.

Similar food is on the menu at old-fashioned diners and lunch counters, many of which are authentically retro, complete with vinyl booths, Formica counters and wise-cracking locals. Big breakfasts are an important part of the roster and often are available all day.

CHOICES, CHOICES

Americans like to have independence and freedom of choice, down to the toast they eat in the morning. When dining out, be prepared to make a lot of choices. Here are some of the decisions your server might ask you to make.

Breakfast: what kind of bread would you like with your eggs – toasted whole wheat, sourdough or white, English muffin (similar to a crumpet), bagel, biscuit? Home fries (fried, seasoned potato wedges), hash browns (shredded fried potatoes) or a fruit salad? Bacon or sausage? Orange, grapefruit, tomato or apple juice? Decaf or regular coffee, cream and sugar?

Lunch/dinner: soup of the day or salad? If a salad, which dressing – blue cheese (creamy), ranch (similar but without the cheese), Italian (oil and vinegar) or French (red, gloppy and sweet)? With that steak, a baked potato, mashed potato, rice or french fries?

The word café can mean many things in the US. Sometimes it's just a coffee and teahouse in the European tradition, with pastries and light snacks, other times it sells heartier sandwiches and soups.

A bar and grill is a casual dinner place specializing in – surprise, surprise – cocktails and grilled steak. Brewpubs are a relatively new, but popular venue, where you can sit right next to gleaming beer tanks and drink the house brew with burgers and pizza.

For a slower-paced meal, you may have to spring for a more high-end restaurant, such as a steakhouse. These low-lit taverns are devoted to huge cuts of beef and potatoes, with a little lobster thrown in for good measure. In bigger cities you'll find restaurants with European-style service and prix fixe menus where you can happily linger over your *crème brûlée.*

Fast-food restaurants, diners and coffee shops tend to be open from breakfast through dinner, sometimes 24 hours, while other restaurants take a break between lunch and dinner. Breakfast is usually 6am to 11am (except on weekends when it starts later and is offered longer), lunch 11:30am to 2pm and dinner 5pm to 10pm at the latest, except in bigger cities.

Quick Eats

On the lower end of the dollar-for-dinner quotient, street stands sell everything from hot dogs to meat kebabs. You can even find what are called 'lunch trucks' or taco trucks that serve hot foods and drinks. It's a gamble: these vendors can be the place for an authentic, delicious, bargain-priced meal, or you might just end up with tasteless, cheap grub.

Look to outdoor summer fairs, festivals and farmers markets for some of the better street foods. County fairs have stands devoted to culinary Americana like corn dogs, candy apples and funnel cakes. Farmers markets and food festivals might have anything from crepes to meat barbecued in an outdoor smoker. Some food festivals are wonderful, with local traditions that go back forever, while others are nothing more than gimmicky commercial enterprises. Do some research before handing over your cash at one of these events.

DID YOU KNOW?

The Vegetarian Resource Group has found that only 2.5% of Americans are completely vegetarian but 57% of the population regularly chooses to eat meatless.

VEGETARIANS & VEGANS

Vegetarianism in the USA has come a long way since the 1970s, when those who ate tofu were considered weird, if not suspect. Many from the younger generations are turning to vegetarianism and veganism, and even carnivores regularly skip the meat for health reasons. Most medium-size cities, especially those with universities, have at least one vegetarian restaurant, and cosmopolitan areas like the San Francisco Bay Area and New York City have upscale restaurants devoted to the art of meatless cooking. In addition, nonvegetarian restaurants in urban areas tend to have creative vegetarian offerings. Chinese, Indian and Italian restaurants are usually good bets for vegetarians.

Some things to look out for: traditionally, tortillas and beans are made with lard, though many Mexican restaurants now make them with vegetable oil instead. Be sure to ask if that vegetable soup or risotto you're looking at contains chicken broth. Also, most Vietnamese and Thai dishes contain fish sauce, but the kitchen might make them with soy sauce instead if you ask your server.

WHINING & DINING

At family-style restaurants and coffee shops, paper placemats and crayons are distributed at the door, and kids get their own menu. These menus offer children under 10 or 12 small servings of things like cheese sandwiches, spaghetti, pizza and chicken nuggets, at the cost of a few dollars. Fast-food chains also snare weary parents with kid-size meals and even playgrounds.

Restaurants without a children's menu don't necessarily discourage kids, though higher-end restaurants might. Ask if the kitchen will make a small order of pasta with butter and cheese (also ask how much it will cost) or if they will split a normal-size order among two plates for the kids. Restaurants usually provide high chairs and booster seats.

If you'd like to pick up snacks at the grocery store, beware that many food products aimed at kids contain less-than-healthy ingredients: for example, kids' breakfast cereals are loaded with sugar. Pure juices, fresh and dried fruits, carrot sticks, string cheese, granola bars, and small containers of yogurt, cottage cheese and apple sauce are some good snack options that are readily available. Supermarkets also carry a wide range of jarred baby foods, some of them even organic.

HABITS & CUSTOMS

Americans love to eat out, whether it's taking the kids to a coffee shop or showing off a date at a swanky, trendy restaurant. But eating out may be more of a necessity than a choice. Americans tend to work long hours and that leaves little time to cook a meal at home.

Like most other things they do, Americans eat very quickly, often spending only a half hour to an hour on their meal depending on the type of restaurant and the occasion. Many skip breakfast entirely and just grab a quick cup of coffee, gaining their sustenance from lunch and dinner.

But there are times when people slow down to eat, especially on weekends or for holiday meals. In religious households, a family member often leads grace before the meal begins, while the rest of the group bow their heads or close their eyes. At formal dinners of any denomination, guests may offer a toast to the host or guest of honor before the meal begins or in between courses. After a toast, everyone usually says 'cheers' or – even 'bon appètit' since there isn't a good equivalent in English – and clinks glasses around the table.

The hostess is supposed to be the first to take a bite, and will most likely offer second helpings. It's not exactly rude to leave food on your plate, but the cook may say something about it (in a friendly way), so be prepared to have a good excuse.

Religious occasions and festivals such as Lent, Chinese New Year and Ramadan can affect when sections of the population are eating what, but only major holidays such as Thanksgiving and Christmas close down the majority of restaurants, and some even stay open on those days.

Big Night (1996) is a wonderful film about two Italian brothers who struggle to run an authentic, refined Italian restaurant in 1950s America, which only seems to want spaghetti and meatballs and loud Louis Prima.

TAXES & TIPPING

Unless noted, service is not included in restaurant checks, and servers depend on tips to survive on their minimum-wage salaries. Those who fail to tip at least 15% will receive a frosty, if not hostile, farewell. The exceptions: great service (especially at high-end restaurants) merits a 20% tip, while anyone providing sloppy, careless service can get more like 10%. There's no need to tip at self-service or fast-food restaurants.

Except in areas that have no sales tax, state, local and/or city taxes are added to your bill at the end of the meal.

DOS & DON'TS

Americans are generally fairly casual when it comes to dining, but there are some important customs to honor. Dinner guests should bring a small gift such as flowers or chocolates. For more informal dinners, you can offer to bring something for the meal, such as a bottle of wine or a loaf of good bread.

The method for holding cutlery seems extremely complicated at first: hold your fork in your right hand, and rest your left hand in your lap. When you need to use a knife, switch your fork to your left hand and cut with your right. Or just eat European-style – it won't be considered rude unless you rest your left hand on the table. It's OK to eat with your hands when burgers or pizza are on the menu.

Definitely ask your dining companions as well as the restaurant staff if it's OK to smoke. Many states require that restaurants have smoking and nonsmoking seating areas, while some, like California, don't even allow smoking in bars or in outdoor patios. It's considered rude to chat on cell phones in a restaurant, but plenty of people do it anyway.

Usually, servers simply drop off the check after you've ordered dessert, but it's déclassé to do this in more formal establishments, where you must request the bill. Leave the tip on the table, and don't hand cash directly to the server.

COOKING COURSES

There has been a proliferation of cooking courses in the past decade, as more Americans realize they don't know how to cook and as cooking shows become more popular on television. One type of class is offered at high-end cookware shops such as Sur La Table (www.surlatable.com). Here is a sampling of cooking schools that offer courses to amateur chefs on holiday. For more on professional cooking programs, visit www.cooking-schools.net.

California

Culinary Institute of America (www.ciachef.edu) At Greystone in the Napa Valley (see p956).
Tante Marie's (www.tantemarie.com) A small school in San Francisco.

Southwest

Jane Butel's Southwestern Cooking School (www.janebutel.com) In Albuquerque, New Mexico.
Santa Fe School of Cooking (www.santafeschoolofcooking.com) In Santa Fe, New Mexico, (see p802).

New Orleans

Cookin' Cajun Cooking School (www.cookincajun.com)

New York City

French Culinary Institute (www.frenchculinary.com)
Natural Gourmet Cookery School (www.naturalgourmetschool.com) Focusing on vegetarian and healthy cooking.

GLOSSARY

eggplant – aubergine
bagel – a New York speciality, rolled bread that is boiled, then baked, giving it a chewy texture
barbecue – officially refers to Southern style of slow-cooking spice-rubbed meat with smoke, but sometimes refers to a grill
biscuit – flaky, buttery roll served in the South at dinner or breakfast
blue plate – special of the day

BLT – bacon, lettuce and tomato sandwich
brownie – fudgy, cake-like bar cookie rich with chocolate and sometimes nuts
Caesar salad – Romaine lettuce tossed with croutons and shaved Parmesan cheese in a dressing laced with raw egg and anchovy
chicken-fried steak – thin steak battered and fried like chicken
chili – hearty, meaty stew spiced with ground chilis, sometimes with vegetables and beans
chips – thin, deep-fried potato slices or tortilla wedges
cilantro – coriander
clam chowder – chunky, potato-based soup full of clams and vegetables, sometimes bacon, and thickened with milk
club sandwich – white sandwich bread stacked in three layers with chicken or turkey, bacon, lettuce and tomatoes
cobbler – fruit dessert with a biscuit or pie crust topping, baked until bubbly and served with whipped cream or ice cream
continental breakfast – coffee or tea, pastry, and juice or fruit
corn dog – hot dog on a stick wrapped in a crisp, cornmeal batter
crab cake – crab meat held together with breadcrumbs and eggs, then fried
cranberry – very tart, crimson berry made into a sauce or jelly for Thanksgiving dinner
crisp – similar to cobbler, except with a crunchy, streusel-like topping
French toast – egg-dipped bread that is fried and served with maple syrup for breakfast
fries or french fries – deep-fried potato wedges
granola – breakfast cereal of oats baked with honey and nuts, usually served with yogurt or milk and fresh fruit
grits – white cornmeal made into a porridge for a Southern breakfast or side dish
guacamole – dip of mashed avocados with lime juice and often tomatoes, onions, chilis and cilantro, served with tortilla chips or in Mexican-American dishes
hash browns – shredded fried potatoes, served with eggs
huevos rancheros – Mexican breakfast of corn tortillas topped with fried eggs and chili sauce
Jello – trademarked name for a molded gelatin fruit dessert or salad
jelly – fruit preserves with a thinner consistency than jam
lemonade – cold drink made of sweetened lemon juice diluted with water
maple syrup – unctuous, deeply flavored syrup that is drizzled over waffles, pancakes and French toast, made from the maple tree's spring sap
marshmallow – whipped sugar confection in fluffy, spongy cube shapes
milkshake – ice cream frothed up with milk
pickle – unlike Britain's piquant condiment, this refers to a pickled cucumber
pretzel – twisted salty snack in two forms: a crunchy, thin kind made commercially, and a much larger, bready variety that's sold as a street food
smoothie – cold, thick drink made with purèed fruit, ice and sometimes yogurt
submarine sandwich – also called the hoagie, po'boy, hero or grinder in various regions, this sandwich is served on a thick roll slathered with mustard and mayonnaise and filled with thinly sliced deli meats and cheeses, as well as lettuce, onions, pickles and tomatoes
surf 'n' turf – plate of both seafood (often lobster) and steak
wrap – modern-day offshoot of the burrito, with a vibrantly colored tortilla stuffed with fillings of practically any origin

Foodnetwork.com (www.foodtv.com), from the 24-hour cable television channel, is a great site featuring discussions with celebrity chefs, video cooking demos and 25,000 recipes.

Zagat Survey (www.zagat.com) is based on the popular series of guidebooks that lists restaurants based on reader approval ratings. The site requires registration, but it's free.

New York & the Mid-Atlantic States

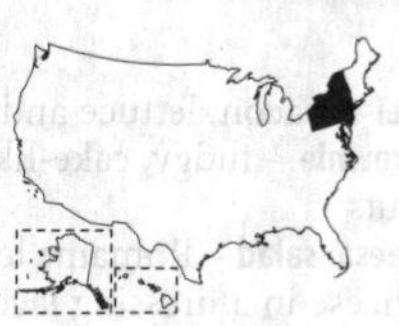

CONTENTS

OK, so New York City is often regarded as the center of the universe. But can that make up for neighboring New Jersey, Pennsylvania and the rest of New York state? Luckily, it doesn't have to. While the three-state region may appear to be stuck in the great city's shadow, those who have discovered the area's riches couldn't disagree more. These are the country's most densely populated states, after all, and while all those people could be wrong, a glance at their surroundings makes it seem pretty doubtful.

The area offers a range of urban settings, from river-rich Pittsburgh and bohemian Buffalo to the historic gem of Philadelphia and the casino-jammed metropolis of Atlantic City. Of course, NYC is home to some of the top cultural offerings in the world. Perhaps most lovable about all of the region's cities, though, are its multi-culti mixes of inhabitants, globe-trotters who have often emigrated from places as varied as Cambodia, Jamaica, Mexico and India.

Outside the cities, you'll be lured by tranquil rural hideaways. This is where you'll find the spellbinding Niagara Falls, the gorgeous Jersey Shore, the sumptuous Brandywine Valley and the mountainous Adirondacks, reaching skyward just a few hours north of New York City. With its strikingly diverse offerings in both people and landscapes, the entire area is a microcosm of the rest of the country in 100,000 sq miles – just 7% of America.

HIGHLIGHTS

- Being in **New York, New York** – duh! (p106)
- Chowing on ethnic foods in New York City's **outer boroughs** (p149)
- Strolling through **Newark's** blossoming cherry trees in April (p168)
- Hiking to the highest peaks of the **Adirondacks** (p162)
- Laying eyes on that massive, cracked **Liberty Bell** in Philadelphia (p178)
- Exploring **Pittsburgh**, where Andy Warhol fled and hipsters have arrived (p188)
- Glimpsing the mighty **Niagara Falls** from high above, in your hotel room-with-a-view (p165)

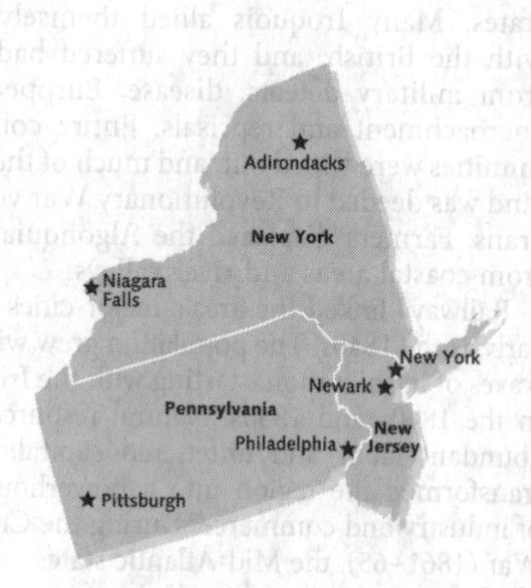

HISTORY

Native American settlement was sparse when Europeans first arrived here. The area was probably home to fewer than 100,000 people, comprising two major cultural groups: the Algonquians and the Iroquois.

French fur trappers and traders on the St Lawrence River reached the region by the mid-16th century, and in 1609, Henry Hudson found, named and sailed up the Hudson River, claiming the land for the Dutch, who started several settlements in 'New Netherlands.' The Iroquois soon controlled the booming fur trade, selling to Dutch, English and French agents.

The tiny Dutch settlement on Manhattan Island surrendered to a Royal Navy warship in 1664, in the midst of a series of Anglo-Dutch wars. The new colonial power created two territories, called 'New York' and 'New Jersey.' In the prolonged French and Indian War (1754–63) the British defeated the French to secure control of northeast America. The shift of Indian allegiances away from the French was a crucial factor in the British victory. The new British territory, extending to the Mississippi, was made a short-lived Indian reserve.

Pennsylvania played a leading role in the Revolutionary War (1775–83). New York and New Jersey loyalties were split, but important battles still occurred in all three states. Many Iroquois allied themselves with the British, and they suffered badly from military defeats, disease, European encroachment and reprisals. Entire communities were wiped out, and much of their land was deeded to Revolutionary War veterans. Farmers displaced the Algonquians from coastal areas and river valleys.

Railways linked the area's major cities as early as the 1840s. The population grew with waves of immigration, starting with the Irish in the 1840s and 1850s. Natural resources, abundant labor and unfettered capitalism transformed the region into a powerhouse of industry and commerce. During the Civil War (1861–65), the Mid-Atlantic states supplied men and material for Union forces.

After the Civil War, the West was opened by steel railroad tracks made in Pittsburgh, the engines of growth used Pennsylvania coal and oil, and the profits went back to the 'robber barons' (the super-rich industrialists and financiers) in New York. All the region's cities were swollen with immigrants – blacks from the South, Chinese from California, and over 12 million Europeans who arrived at Ellis Island, in the middle of New York harbor. The growth, industry, wealth, cultural diversity and constant flow of people continue in the Mid-Atlantic states to this day.

GEOGRAPHY

Most big cities are on the main rivers of the eastern coastal plain, including the Hudson, Delaware, Susquehanna and Ohio Rivers. Low mountain ranges extend across the region's interior, heavily forested with pine, red spruce, maple, oak, ash and birch. Further inland, the waterways of the Great Lakes and the Ohio River link many smaller industrial cities.

INFORMATION

The basic state sales tax is 4%, but varying local taxes increase the bite – up to 13.25% in New York City.

The following are very useful sources of information:

New Jersey Division of Travel & Tourism (☎ 609-292-2470, 800-537-7397; www.state.nj.us/travel)
New York State Tourist Bureau (☎ 518-474-4116, 800-225-5697; www.iloveny.com; PO Box 2603, Albany, NY 12220-0603)

For information about Pennsylvania, refer to the following:

Lancaster Counter Center (☎ 800-723-8824; www.padutchcountry.com)
Northeast Pennsylvania Conventions & Visitors Bureau (☎ 570-963-6363; www.visitnepa.org)
Welcome to Chester County (www.brandywinevalley.com)

NATIONAL & STATE PARKS

New York has protected parklands that offer everything from beach camping to mountain climbing. For entrance to state-run parks, it offers the $59 Empire Passport, which gives you access to almost all of the 164 state parks and 50 Department of Environmental Conservation forest preserve areas for one year. In New Jersey, the Wharton State Forest, with more than 110,000 acres, is notable for being the largest single tract of land within the state's park system. Pennsylvania's Lake Erie region has the only surf beach in the state.

The following places provide useful information about national and state parks:

Fish, Game & Wildlife Commission (☎ 609-292-2965) For fishing licenses.

Gateway National Recreation Area (☎ 718-338-3338; www.nps.gov/gate) For details about beachfront state parks.

National Park Service (www.nps.gov)

New Jersey State Park Service (www.state.nj.us/dep/forestry) For New Jersey state park and forest maps and regulations.

New York State Parks (http://nysparks.state.ny.us/)

Pennsylvania Department of Conservation & Natural Resources (www.dcnr.state.pa.us/) Has information about all state parks, forests and trails.

State Park Service (☎ 800-843-6420) Lists campgrounds.

ACTIVITIES

The 2158-mile Appalachian Trail passes through New York north of Pawling and heads southwest through the Taconic Mountains, Hudson Highlands, Ramapo Mountains and Hudson Valley. From there, it continues through the Pocono Mountains and Delaware Water Gap National Recreational Area into central Pennsylvania. In Adirondack Park, one of the best-known trails is the Johns Brook Trail, which covers 9.5 miles from Keene Valley to the summit of Mt Marcy. In Pennsylvania, walks include the Susquehannock Trail System and the Laurel Highlands Hiking Trail.

Hiking and backpacking information can be obtained from the following sources:

Adirondack Mountain Club (☎ 518-668-4447; www.adk.org)

Appalachian Mountain Club Manhattan Resource Center (☎ 212-986-1430; www.outdoors.org; 5 Tudor City Pl, New York, NY 10017)

Finger Lakes Trail Conference (☎ 585-288-7191; PO Box 18048, Rochester, NY 14618). Finger Lakes maintains an east–west trail from the Alleghenies to the Catskills.

Sierra Club (www.sierraclub.org) New York (☎ 518-426-9144); New Jersey (☎ 609-656-7612); Pennsylvania (☎ 717-232-0101)

A bicycling highlight is the spectacular 35-mile Mohawk–Hudson Bike/Hike Trail along former railroads and canal towpaths. You can also cycle on long stretches of the scenic Seaway Trail, which runs parallel to the St Lawrence River, Lake Ontario, Niagara River and Lake Erie. Whiteface Mountain, near Lake Placid in the Adirondacks, has twice hosted the Alpine events of the Winter Olympics and offers the region's best downhill skiing. In the Catskills, Ski Windham and Hunter Mountain are good ski areas fairly close to New York City.

Rafts and canoes go down the Delaware, a National Wild & Scenic River, which flows through all three states. In Pennsylvania's Laurel Highlands, the Youghiogheny River has Class I to Class IV rapids. The St Regis Canoe Area, in the Adirondacks, is a network of 58 interconnected lakes and ponds, linked primarily by the Raquette, St Regis and Saranac Rivers.

GETTING THERE & AWAY

The big cities all have airports, but New York's John F Kennedy (JFK) is the region's major international gateway. Alternatives include Newark International Airport; La Guardia, in Queens, with mostly domestic flights; and the Long Island MacArthur Airport in Islip, also offering domestic travel.

Greyhound buses serve main US towns, as well as Canada. **Peter Pan Trailways** (☎ 800-343-9999) and **Adirondack Trailways** (☎ 800-225-6815) are both regional bus lines. Amtrak provides commuter rail services throughout the New York metropolitan area. The main northeast coastal rail corridor (Boston–Providence–New London–New York–Newark–Philadelphia–Washington, DC) has frequent services, including several per day with the high-speed Acela trains. For car trips out of town, hit the rental agencies in New Jersey for better deals (see p1121).

GETTING AROUND

A car is the best way to see the countryside, but you don't want one in New York City. Rentals are expensive in New York State (with a 13.25% state tax), and especially New York City (where all 'deals' are usually voided). Hitchhiking is not only illegal on major highways, it's just not done these days for fear of being picked up by a lunatic. So to save money while traveling within the area, look into bus and rail options.

NEW YORK STATE

A cross-state drive through huge New York is like a cross-country trek: you encounter farmlands, quaint artsy towns, backwater

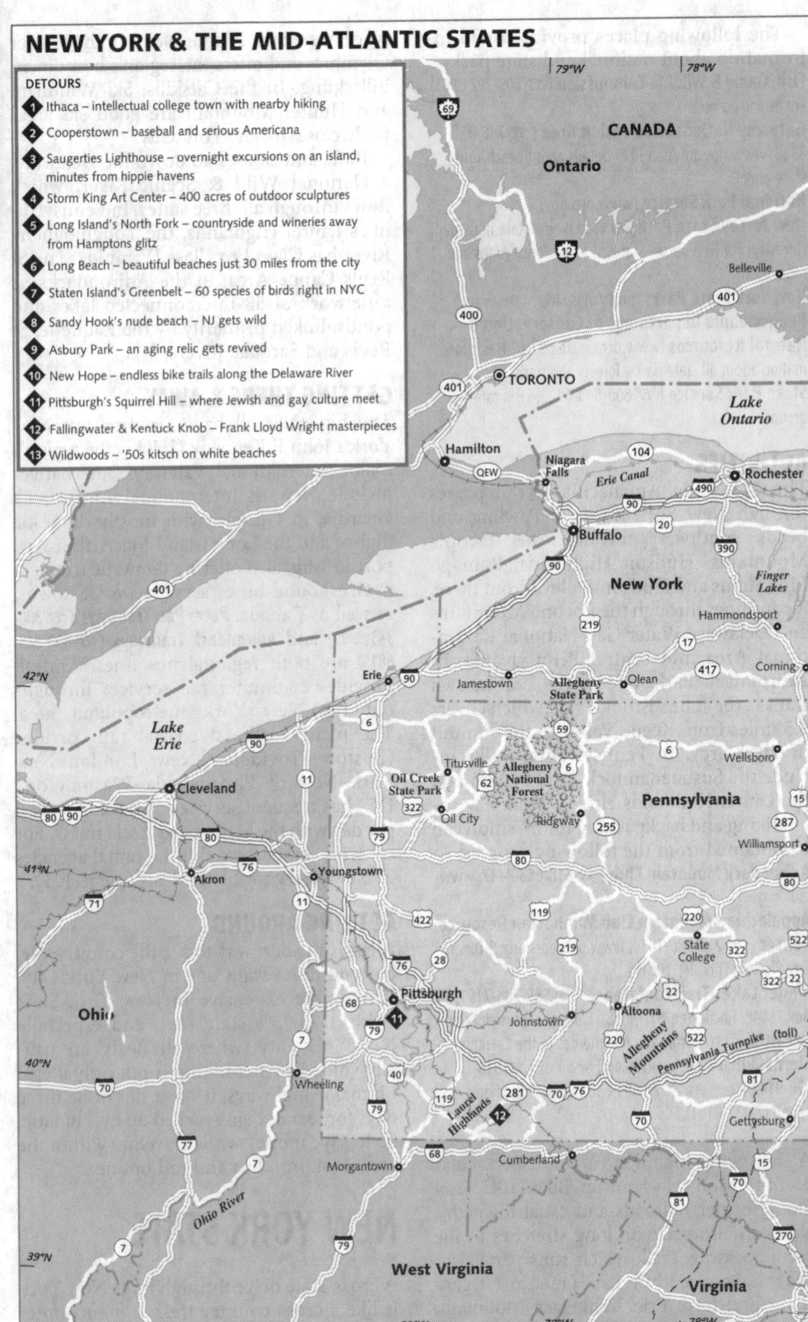
NEW YORK & THE MID-ATLANTIC STATES
DETOURS
1 Ithaca – intellectual college town with nearby hiking
2 Cooperstown – baseball and serious Americana
3 Saugerties Lighthouse – overnight excursions on an island, minutes from hippie havens
4 Storm King Art Center – 400 acres of outdoor sculptures
5 Long Island's North Fork – countryside and wineries away from Hamptons glitz
6 Long Beach – beautiful beaches just 30 miles from the city
7 Staten Island's Greenbelt – 60 species of birds right in NYC
8 Sandy Hook's nude beach – NJ gets wild
9 Asbury Park – an aging relic gets revived
10 New Hope – endless bike trails along the Delaware River
11 Pittsburgh's Squirrel Hill – where Jewish and gay culture meet
12 Fallingwater & Kentuck Knob – Frank Lloyd Wright masterpieces
13 Wildwoods – '50s kitsch on white beaches
CANADA
Ontario
Belleville
TORONTO
Lake Ontario
Hamilton
Niagara Falls
Erie Canal
Rochester
Buffalo
New York
Finger Lakes
Hammondsport
Corning
Jamestown
Allegheny State Park
Olean
Erie
Lake Erie
Cleveland
Titusville
Oil Creek State Park
Allegheny National Forest
Oil City
Ridgway
Wellsboro
Pennsylvania
Williamsport
Akron
Youngstown
State College
Pittsburgh
Ohio
Johnstown
Altoona
Allegheny Mountains
Pennsylvania Turnpike (toll)
Wheeling
Laurel Highlands
Gettysburg
Morgantown
Cumberland
Ohio River
West Virginia
Virginia
42°N
41°N
40°N
39°N
82°W
81°W
80°W
79°W
78°W

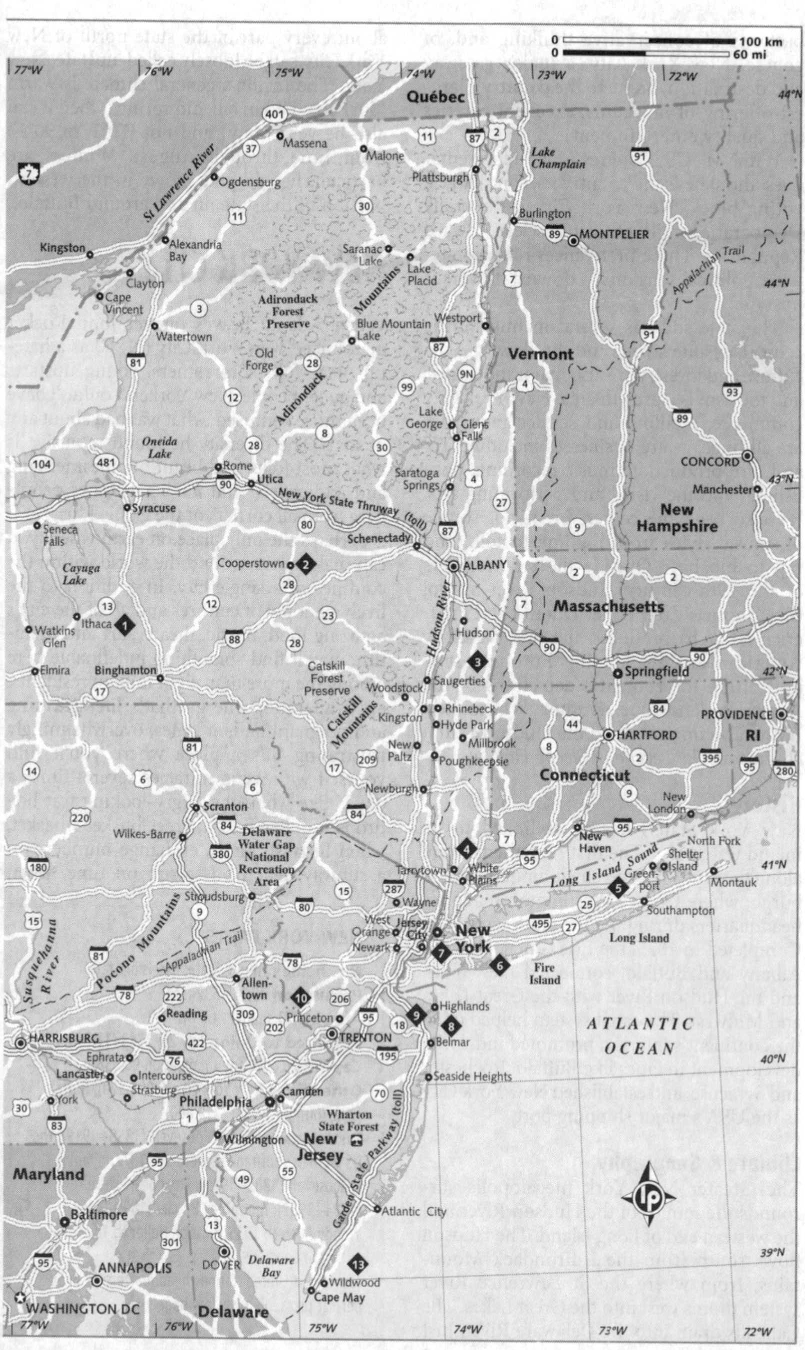
0 100 km
0 60 mi
Québec
Lake Champlain
Vermont
New Hampshire
Massachusetts
Connecticut
RI
New Jersey
Maryland
Delaware
ATLANTIC OCEAN
Long Island Sound
Long Island
Fire Island
Adirondack Forest Preserve
Adirondack Mountains
Catskill Forest Preserve
Catskill Mountains
Pocono Mountains
Delaware Water Gap National Recreation Area
Wharton State Forest
Appalachian Trail
St Lawrence River
Hudson River
Susquehanna River
New York State Thruway (toll)
Garden State Parkway (toll)
Oneida Lake
Cayuga Lake
Delaware Bay
MONTPELIER
CONCORD
ALBANY
HARTFORD
PROVIDENCE
TRENTON
HARRISBURG
ANNAPOLIS
DOVER
WASHINGTON DC
New York
Philadelphia
Baltimore
Kingston
Massena
Malone
Plattsburgh
Burlington
Ogdensburg
Alexandria Bay
Clayton
Cape Vincent
Watertown
Saranac Lake
Lake Placid
Blue Mountain Lake
Westport
Old Forge
Lake George
Glens Falls
Saratoga Springs
Rome
Utica
Syracuse
Seneca Falls
Schenectady
Cooperstown
Ithaca
Watkins Glen
Elmira
Binghamton
Hudson
Saugerties
Woodstock
Rhinebeck
Kingston
Hyde Park
Millbrook
New Paltz
Poughkeepsie
Newburgh
Springfield
Manchester
New London
New Haven
North Fork
Shelter Island
Greenport
Montauk
Southampton
Tarrytown
White Plains
Wayne
West Orange
Jersey City
Newark
Scranton
Wilkes-Barre
Stroudsburg
Allentown
Reading
Princeton
Highlands
Belmar
Ephrata
Lancaster
Intercourse
Strasburg
York
Camden
Seaside Heights
Wilmington
Atlantic City
Wildwood
Cape May
77°W
76°W
75°W
74°W
73°W
72°W
44°N
43°N
42°N
41°N
40°N
39°N

bastions of conservative thinking and, of course, New York City, a major gateway and destination, home to the country's largest offering of museums, excellent eateries and quality entertainment.

With 31 US Congressional representatives, the state is the country's second-largest voting block. New York City is generally Democratic, while other parts lean toward Republican. These preferences reflect state-wide political tensions – downstate versus upstate.

The state still has several manufacturing centers, despite layoffs and shutdowns. Agriculture and forestry are also major industries, and tourism is a growth area. New York City commerce, retailing and service industries are all huge, as are businesses including TV and film production, music recording, publishing, and the visual and performing arts. It's also been the center for, if not source of, music styles from ragtime to folk, and rap to hip hop. Outside the city, painters of the 19th-century Hudson River school (like Thomas Cole, Asher Durand and Frederick Church) produced the first distinctly American art, abandoning European-style portraiture for romantic depictions of the American landscape. Author Washington Irving also immortalized the Hudson's rural charms in *The Legend of Sleepy Hollow*.

History

New York State's history is linked to its inland waterways. The first settlements were along the Hudson River, including tiny Newburgh, where George Washington made his headquarters during the Revolutionary War. Completed in 1825, the Erie Canal, between Albany and Buffalo, connected New York and the Hudson River with the Great Lakes and Midwest. The canal system helped open the continent's interior, promoted industrial development in cities like Buffalo, Rochester and Syracuse, and established New York City as the USA's major shipping port.

Climate & Geography

The Greater New York megalopolis surrounds the mouth of the Hudson River and the western end of Long Island. The Hudson flows south from the Adirondack Mountains, from where the St Lawrence River system drains west into the Great Lakes. The Catskills drain into the Delaware River. Just about every part of the state north of New York City can be loosely called 'upstate' New York. The region's general climate is warm (50°F to 60°F) in fall and spring (when it can also be very rainy) and hot (70°F to 90°F) from June through August. Winters are particularly cold and snowy in the western portion of the state, in and around Buffalo.

NEW YORK CITY

When Atlanta Braves pitcher John Rocker denounced New York City (NYC) as a hateful place full of foreigners, young upstarts and queer people, New Yorkers couldn't have been more confused: what was bad about any of that? The diversity he found repulsive is what most folks find beautiful, mesmerizing and addictive – and it's what draws people here from all corners of the globe. Plus, NYC is perhaps the only place on earth where you can make a trip around the world within the confines of a single city. In addition to the lively panoply of cultures and all of the city's amazing food, music, theater, art and literature, you'll find something indefinable here among the more than eight million residents: an exhilarating energy that's life-affirming and poignant and, at times, overwhelmingly frustrating. It's a place where you'll find yourself witnessing miracles several times a day – like when the angry-looking frat boy drops a dollar into a street busker's basket, when flirty strangers exchange numbers on a subway, when buses run on time, when

NEW YORK FACTS

Nicknames Empire State, Excelsior State
Population 19,157,532 (3rd)
Area 54,471 sq miles (27th)
Admitted to Union July 26, 1788 (11th)
Capital city Albany (population 96,658)
Other cities New York City (8,008,300), Buffalo (292,700), Rochester (219,800)
Birthplace of Teddy Roosevelt (1858–1919); the US women's suffrage movement (1872); Franklin D Roosevelt (1882–1945); Eleanor Roosevelt (1884–1962); Humphrey Bogart (1899–1957); Woody Allen (b 1935); Joseph Heller (b 1923), author of *Catch 22*
Home of United Nations headquarters, Wall St, perfect pizza, blemish-free bagels

new skyscrapers are built, and when you stumble into a hole-in-the-wall pub to find the most brilliant poetry reading you could ever imagine. It's brash, it's sexy, it's brilliant. It's NYC.

History

When Henry Hudson first claimed this land for his sponsors, the Dutch East India Company, in 1609, he reported it to be 'as beautiful a land as one can hope to tread upon.' And, though it's gorgeous today in an urban-jungle sort of way, it may be difficult to picture today's New York City as it was for 11,000 years, when the land was occupied by Native Americans. The name 'Manhattan' was indeed derived from local Munsee Indian words, meaning 'Island of Hills.'

COLONIAL ERA

New Yorkers have fancied themselves as fabulous right from the start: the aristocracy here, according to Howard Zinn's *A People's History of the United States*, was the most ostentatious of all the colonies. Folks had window hangings of camlet, gold-framed mirrors, richly carved furniture and silver. The colonial period was run much like a feudal kingdom, with the Dutch setting up a patroon-ship system along the Hudson River and their first trading post, Nieuw Amsterdam, in 1624. Governor Peter Stuyvesant was sent to impose order on the unruly colony, but his ban on alcohol and curtailment of religious freedoms caused unrest, and after a struggle, the colony was taken over by the British in 1664.

Renamed 'New York,' the town retained much of its Dutch character well into the mid-18th century. Soon, residents started expressing their opposition to British colonial rule in newspapers and by protest marches on New York's Commons. However, New York was a British stronghold, and George III's troops controlled the city for most of the Revolutionary War.

BOOM YEARS

George Washington was sworn in here as the republic's first president in 1789, but the founding fathers disliked New York City; Thomas Jefferson (just like John Rocker!) described the city as 'a cloacina of all the depravities of human nature.' The city was then a bustling and dirty seaport of 33,000 people. The Erie Canal, opened in 1825, linked New York to the Great Lakes and made it the main port for the whole country, as well as the major center for trade and finance. By 1830 New York had grown eightfold, to a metropolis of 250,000.

The following decades were occupied with commerce and the building of infrastructure. The Planning Commission of 1811 imposed Manhattan's distinctive street grid, and the Croton Aqueduct, completed in 1842, brought 72 million gallons of fresh water daily into the city, greatly improving public health.

GROWING PAINS

New York's explosive growth continued in the late 19th century, from 515,000 residents in 1850 to 1.1 million in 1880. Corrupt politicians milked millions from public works projects, while industrial barons amassed tax-free fortunes. The poorest New Yorkers worked in dangerous factories and lived in squalid apartment blocks, where a tenement culture developed. Journalist Jacob Riis chronicled their miseries, and his reports shocked the city and led to the establishment of an independent health board and a series of workplace reforms. Another newspaperman, William Cullen Bryant, championed the establishment of Central Park, which opened on the swampy northern outskirts of the city in 1876. Meanwhile, multimillionaire philanthropists began pouring money into public institutions like the New York Public Library and Carnegie Hall.

The severely limited space in the downtown business district left no room for growth. The only way to go was up, and by the late 19th century Manhattan had a cluster of new multistory office buildings called 'skyscrapers.' A growing network of subways and elevated trains ('els') made the city's outer reaches accessible. Growth beyond the official borders led to the 'consolidation movement,' and in 1898 the independent districts of Manhattan, Queens, Staten Island, the Bronx and Brooklyn became the five 'boroughs' of a consolidated New York City.

With another wave of European immigrants, the population leapt from three million in 1900 to seven million in 1930. The Depression caused residents enormous distress, but Mayor Fiorello La Guardia fought municipal corruption and expanded the social service network. Autocratic civic planner, Robert Moses, remade the city's landscape – whole working-class neighborhoods were destroyed to make room for new parks, roads and bridges.

DECLINE & RENEWAL

After WWII New York was the premier city in the world, but it suffered from a new phenomenon: the middle-class flight to the suburbs. Television production, manufacturing jobs and even the fabled Brooklyn Dodgers baseball team moved to the West Coast. By the 1970s the unreliable, graffiti-ridden subway system had become a symbol of New York's civic and economic decline. Only a massive federal loan program saved the city from bankruptcy.

New York regained much of its swagger in the 1980s, led by colorful three-term mayor Ed Koch – still to this day a verbose character and father figure for many New Yorkers, who insist on calling him 'mayor.' The city elected its first African-American mayor, David Dinkins, in 1989. After his largely ineffectual single term, the city's overwhelmingly Democratic voters ousted Dinkins in favor of liberal Republican Rudolph Giuliani, who was a strong and colorful character during his reign.

In 2001 New York elected the current mayor, Republican Michael Bloomberg, a wealthy philanthropist and president of his own financial empire; Bloomberg LP expanded into publishing, radio, new service and television operations. He campaigned on issues, including improving education and strengthening law enforcement. Bloomberg has built upon Guiliani's attempts to clean up the joint by signing into law several quality-of-life bills – from the new smoking ban in all bars and restaurants, to one that slaps bicyclists with a $100 fine if they ride on sidewalks. His true effect on the Big Apple, however, remains to be seen.

CATASTROPHE

By now, '9/11' is a catchphrase known around the world. But to New Yorkers who were here on September 11, 2001 – especially to those who witnessed the terrorist attacks – the numbers are weighted with psychological baggage. The late summer day was marked by a brilliant blue sky and balmy weather, but by mid-morning, Al-Qaeda terrorist hijackers had flown a pair of passenger jets into the two towers of the World Trade Center in Manhattan's Financial District, killing more than 3000 people. Thousands watched as the 110-story twin towers of the Trade Center became engulfed in balls of fire and then collapsed, seemingly in ultraslow motion. The impact of the crumbled towers wrecked other buildings in the surrounding blocks, which will be a construction zone for years to come. Hundreds of rescue workers died as heroes, fearlessly entering the doomed towers, which then collapsed on top of them. Mayor Giuliani was conspicuous throughout as a compassionate, cool and effective leader.

An **observation deck** (Map pp114–16), for relatives of the deceased and curious onlookers, still stands across from the now-empty lot. Street vendors sell tacky American-flag baseball caps and pictures of the Twin Towers to tourists. In an attempt to move beyond the wreckage, the Lower Manhattan Development Corporation (LMDC) is moving forward on plans for the new construction. Memory Foundations, by Studio Daniel Libeskind, includes a memorial, museum and a tower with a 1776ft-tall spire. The LMDC made its choice after working closely with community leaders and citizens to gain input, and are doing the same for the next phase of the project – choosing a design for the 9/11 memorial (visit www.renewnyc.com for updates).

Orientation

New York City lies near the mouth of the Hudson River, at the west end of Long Island Sound, linked to the Atlantic Ocean through the Verrazano Narrows. The metropolitan area sprawls east into the neighboring state of Connecticut and is linked to urban areas of New Jersey, on the west side of the Hudson. That whole area, known as the 'Tri-State Area,' is home to over 17 million people.

The City of New York proper comprises five boroughs: Manhattan (the densely packed heart of NYC and the epicentre of its attractions), Staten Island (a suburban appendage with an inferiority complex), Brooklyn (the place where most hipsters choose to live, after Manhattan), Queens (the largest borough, with endless foreign cultural perks)

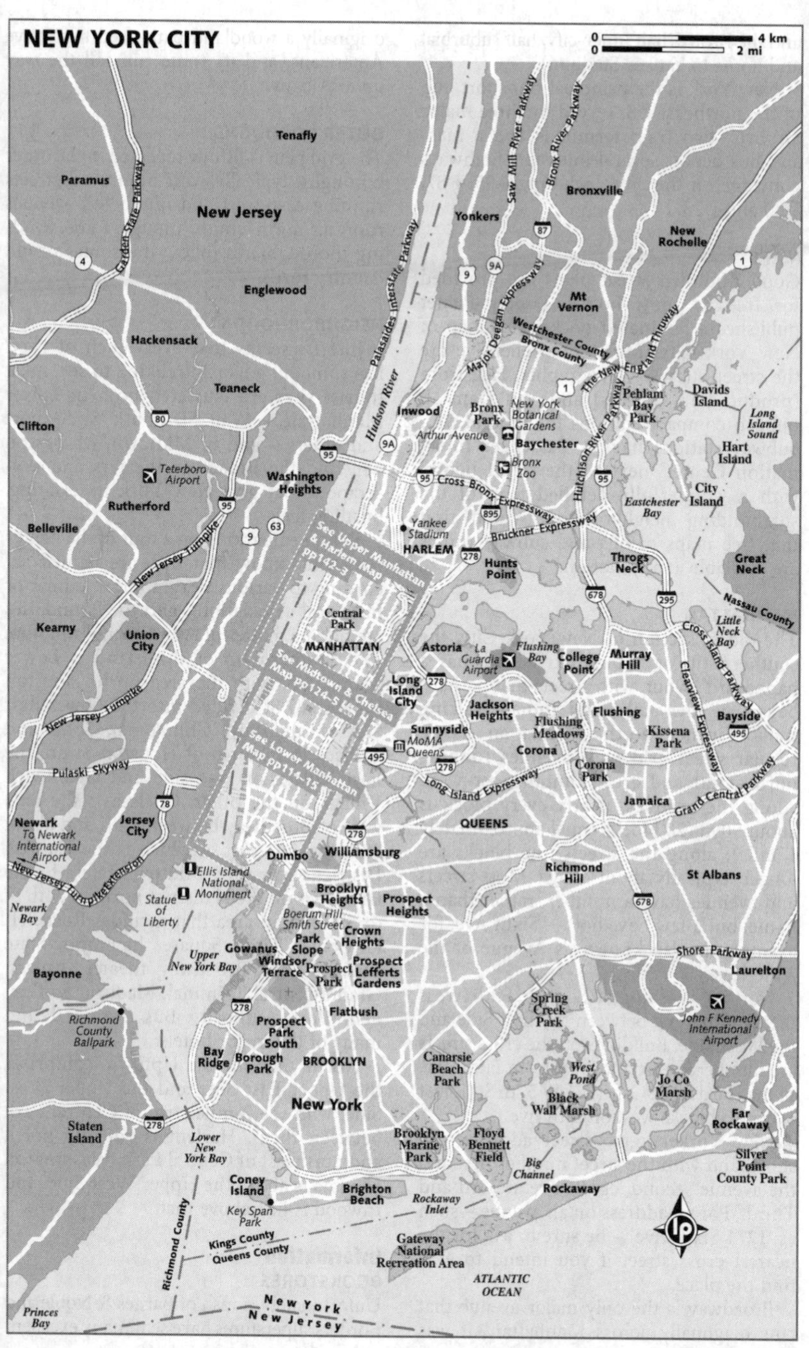
NEW YORK CITY
0 4 km
0 2 mi
Tenafly
Paramus
New Jersey
Garden State Parkway
Englewood
Hackensack
Teaneck
Clifton
Teterboro Airport
Rutherford
Belleville
Kearny
Union City
Washington Heights
New Jersey Turnpike
Palisades Interstate Parkway
Hudson River
Yonkers
Saw Mill River Parkway
Bronx River Parkway
Bronxville
New Rochelle
Mt Vernon
Major Deegan Expressway
Westchester County
Bronx County
The New England Thruway
Inwood
Bronx Park
New York Botanical Gardens
Arthur Avenue
Baychester
Bronx Zoo
Hutchinson River Parkway
Pelham Bay Park
Davids Island
Long Island Sound
Hart Island
City Island
Eastchester Bay
Cross Bronx Expressway
Bruckner Expressway
Yankee Stadium
HARLEM
Hunts Point
Throgs Neck
Great Neck
Nassau County
See Upper Manhattan & Harlem Map pp142-3
Central Park
MANHATTAN
See Midtown & Chelsea Map pp124-5
See Lower Manhattan Map pp114-15
Astoria
La Guardia Airport
Flushing Bay
College Point
Murray Hill
Little Neck Bay
Cross Island Parkway
Clearview Expressway
Long Island City
Jackson Heights
Flushing
Sunnyside
MoMA Queens
Flushing Meadows
Kissena Park
Bayside
Corona
Corona Park
Long Island Expressway
Grand Central Parkway
Jamaica
QUEENS
Pulaski Skyway
Newark
To Newark International Airport
New Jersey Turnpike Extension
Jersey City
Dumbo
Williamsburg
Ellis Island National Monument
Statue of Liberty
Richmond Hill
St Albans
Newark Bay
Brooklyn Heights
Boerum Hill
Smith Street
Prospect Heights
Crown Heights
Park Slope
Gowanus
Upper New York Bay
Windsor Terrace
Prospect Park
Prospect Lefferts Gardens
Shore Parkway
Laurelton
Bayonne
Richmond County Ballpark
Flatbush
Prospect Park South
Spring Creek Park
John F Kennedy International Airport
Bay Ridge
Borough Park
BROOKLYN
Canarsie Beach Park
West Pond
Black Wall Marsh
Jo Co Marsh
New York
Staten Island
Lower New York Bay
Brooklyn Marine Park
Floyd Bennett Field
Far Rockaway
Big Channel
Silver Point County Park
Coney Island
Key Span Park
Brighton Beach
Rockaway Inlet
Rockaway
Richmond County
Kings County
Queens County
Gateway National Recreation Area
ATLANTIC OCEAN
Princes Bay
New York
New Jersey

and the Bronx (half inner-city, half suburbia, and home to Yankee Stadium).

New York is the principal transport hub of the northeast US, served by three major airports, two train terminals and a massive bus depot. Several interstate highways converge on the city, including I-95, I-87, I-80 and I-78.

MAPS

Good Midtown street plans are provided for free by most hotels. Lonely Planet publishes a laminated pocket-size map of New York City. Most comprehensive are the street atlases – Geographia, Hagstrom (produced in Queens) and Van Dam all publish compact editions for around $13. Subway stations have a 'Passenger Information Center' next to the ticket booth, with a wonderfully detailed map of the surrounding neighborhood. You'll find that free maps of bus and subway routes are available at any station.

MANHATTAN

The oldest section of New York City, the southern tip of Manhattan Island, has a haphazard layout, with streets that perhaps began as cow paths and Indian walking trails. Further north, Manhattan has a regular street grid with avenues running north–south and streets running east–west. Along the avenues, nearly every block is about 90yd (20 blocks equal approximately 1 mile); along the streets, the blocks are longer, typically about 350yd. Most streets and avenues have a number, rather than a name, but a few have both – Sixth Ave, for example, is also known as Avenue of the Americas.

North of Washington Sq Park, Fifth Ave is the dividing line between the East Side and the West Side. Buildings on the cross streets are numbered east and west from Fifth Ave, so the Hard Rock Cafe (221 W 57th St) is just over two blocks west of Fifth Ave.

New Yorkers give street addresses in shorthand with the street number first and the avenue second, eg, 'We're at 33rd and Third.' For an address on an avenue – such as '1271 Sixth Ave' – be sure to ask for the nearest cross street if you intend to ever find the place.

Broadway is the only major avenue that cuts diagonally across Manhattan. It was originally a woodland path used by Native Americans, and its route runs all the way up to Albany.

OUTER BOROUGHS

The grid plan is fitfully repeated in the other boroughs, typically with numbered streets running east–west and numbered avenues running north–south, though some winding thoroughfares follow the routes of old country roads.

NEIGHBORHOODS

While its seems that every inch of NYC has something worth trekking to see, most tourist sites are clustered both in Lower Manhattan – Wall St, South St Seaport and others – and in Midtown, where you will find the Broadway theaters and skyscrapers that give New York its exciting, bustling feel.

Before embarking on a tour of the neighborhoods, know that they are named according to various geographical, ethnic or historical associations, and the boundaries are often a matter of (very strong) opinion. The southern tip of the island is Lower Manhattan, with the area up to Houston (*how*-sten) St divided into the Lower East Side, Little Italy, Chinatown, Soho and Tribeca. Just north of Houston St are the East Village on one side and Greenwich Village on the other. Chelsea is the area west of Broadway between 14th and about 28th Sts, just east of which is the Flatiron District. Generally, Midtown refers to the largely commercial district north of 34th St to 59th St, an area that includes Rockefeller Center, Times Square, the Empire State Building, the Broadway theater district, Grand Central Terminal, Madison Sq Garden, Port Authority Bus Terminal and many of the major hotels.

North of 59th St, Uptown comprises the Upper East Side and the Upper West Side, with the 2-mile strip of Central Park between them. Harlem is roughly north and northeast of Central Park, Washington Heights is above the Upper West Side, and Inwood is just above that.

Information

BOOKSTORES

Unfortunately, a rash of Barnes & Noble and Borders superstores have sent many excellent indie shops to early graves. But luckily, many do still exist:

Bluestockings Bookstore (Map pp114-16; ☎ 212-777-6028; 172 Allen St) A homegrown women's book-store-café with frequent readings and other events.

Book Court (☎ 718-875-3677; 163 Court St) Excellent stock of new fiction and nonfiction, right in the heart of hip Boerum Hill.

Complete Traveller (Map pp124-6; ☎ 212-685-9007; 199 Madison Ave)

Gotham Book Mart (Map pp124-6; ☎ 212-719-4448; 41 W 47th St)

Oscar Wilde Bookstore (Map pp114-16; ☎ 212-255-8097; 15 Christopher St) The better of the city's two remaining gay bookstores.

St Marks Bookshop (Map pp114-16; ☎ 212-260-7853; 31 Third Ave)

Shakespeare & Company (Map pp114-16; ☎ 212-529-1330; 716 Broadway)

Strand Bookstore (Map pp114-16; ☎ 212-473-1452; 828 Broadway) Great for used books.

Urban Center Books (Map pp124-6; ☎ 212-935-3595; 457 Madison Ave) Massive selection of NYC, architecture and design titles; part of the Municipal Arts Society.

EMERGENCY

Crime victims services (☎ 212-577-7777)

Emergency number (☎ 911)

Gay & Lesbian Anti-Violence Project (☎ 212-714-1141) Twenty-four-hour hotline for bias crimes.

Legal Aid Society (☎ 212-577-3300)

New York Police Department (☎ 212-374-5000)

INTERNET ACCESS

Like every other major city, NYC has a plethora of Internet cafés. To avoid hourly rates of up to $15, try these options:

EasyEverything (Map pp124-6; ☎ 212-391-9611; 234 W 42nd St at 7th Ave) Eight hundred PCs, with 24-hour service for as little as $1.

LGBT Community Center (Map pp114-16; ☎ 212-620-7310; 208 W 13th St) Brand-new Cyber Center has 15 computers, open to all, with Internet access for only a $3 suggested donation.

Net Zone (Map pp124-6; ☎ 212-239-0770; 28 W 32nd St) Special rate 9am-1pm, $2 per hour.

New York Public Library (Map pp124-6; ☎ 212-930-0800; Fifth Ave at W 42nd St) With various branches, the library offers 30 minutes of free Internet access, but all terminals may be busy.

INTERNET RESOURCES

www.findagrave.com New York City cemetery locations for the famous departed, from Leonard Bernstein to Louis Armstrong.

www.flavorpill.com A trés-hip city culture guide.

www.menupages.com On-screen and printable menus for countless NYC eateries; for the food-obsessed only!

www.newyork.citysearch.com Restaurants, shops, bars and more, all searchable by neighborhood, price or cuisine.

www.strangeny.com Haunted houses, odd public sculptures and weird news reports for an alternative look at the city.

www.timeoutny.com An archive of useful articles and listings at this online version of *Time Out New York* magazine.

LAUNDRY

You'll find standard Laundromats in every residential 'hood. Average washing-machine prices are $1.75 per load; dryers are about $1.50 per 25 minutes. Note that, oddly, most places won't allow you to dry a wet load of washing elsewhere; you must both wash and dry on the premises. Laundromats also offer a drop-off service for an average of $1 per pound (dry weight).

LIBRARIES

New York Public Library (Map pp124-6; ☎ 212-930-0800; Fifth Ave at W 42nd St; 🕑 10am-6pm Thu-Sat, 11am-7:30pm Tue-Wed) The main branch at Fifth Ave is really worth a visit for its famous 3rd-floor reading room and temporary exhibitions.

Brooklyn Library (☎ 718-230-2100; www.brooklynpubliclibrary.org; Grand Army Plaza, Brooklyn) Brooklyn's main branch, located alongside the sprawling Prospect Park, is also grand and worth a look-see.

Neighborhood branches, dotted around the city, have sporadic hours but can be great places to get in some quiet reading time.

MEDIA

Daily News (www.nydailynews.com; 50¢; daily) A tabloid publication with a heavy emphasis on media gossip and the sports market.

New York ($3) Similar to the *New Yorker*, but for a younger, more restaurant-oriented readership.

New Yorker (www.newyorker.com/; $4; weekly) Venerable magazine that publishes news, fiction and critical reviews. Its 'Goings on about Town' section lists major art, cinema and music events.

New York Observer (www.observer.com; $1; weekly) Specializes in local media and politics.

New York Post (www.nypost.com; 25¢; daily) Another tabloid covering media scandal and sports.

New York Times (www.nytimes.com; $1 Mon-Sat, $3 Sun; daily) For thorough world and local news coverage

Time Out New York (www.timeoutny.com; $3; every Tue) Comprehensive listings, including gay and lesbian events.
Wall Street Journal (www.wsj.com; $1; daily) For financial reading.
Village Voice (www.villagevoice.com; $1; every Wed) Well known for its listings of clubs and music venues, it's also the best source for rental apartments and roommate listings.

There's also plenty of gay and lesbian street press in New York: gay clubs and bars are listed in *HX* and *Next*, free at most restaurants and bars. *Go* is a free listings magazine for lesbians, available at most dyke bars.

Where New York, which is available at most hotels, is the best free monthly guide to mainstream city events and museums.

National Public Radio's local affiliate station is WNYC, either 820 AM or 93.9 FM. Bronx's Fordham University has the area's best alternative-music radio station (WFUV-90.7 FM).

An excellent source of local news is NY1, the city's all-day news station on cable's Channel 1.

MEDICAL SERVICES

24-hour Rite-Aid pharmacies (☎ 800-748-3243) A free locator service.
Callen-Lorde Community Health Center (Map pp124-6; ☎ 212-271-7200; 356 W 18th St) Focuses on the lesbian, gay, bisexual and transgender (LGBT) community, but open to all.
Columbia-Presbyterian Eastside (Map pp142-7; ☎ 212-326-8500; 16 E 60th St) Uptown hospital.
New York University Medical Center (Map pp124-6; ☎ 212-263-5550; 462 First Ave)
St Vincent's Medical Center (Map pp124-6; ☎ 212-576-6000; Sixth Ave at Greenwich St) In the Village.
Travel MD (☎ 212-737-1212; 952 Fifth Ave) A 24-hour medical service for travelers.

MONEY

Thousands of ATMs are linked to Cirrus, Plus and other international networks. Withdrawal fees average about $3 at ATMs in convenience stores.

Banks are normally open from 9am to 3:30pm weekdays, though the popular **Commerce bank** (☎ 888-751-9000), with locations throughout Manhattan, is open seven days a week. Many of the Chase Manhattan Bank branches offer commission-free currency-exchange services; the one in Chinatown at Mott and Canal Sts is open daily.

POST

The **general post office** (421 Eighth Ave at 33rd St) is open 24 hours; however, its general delivery service is unreliable and not recommended. Find a local branch, with regular daytime hours, by checking www.ny.com/general/postoffices.html.

TELEPHONES

Thousands of pay telephones line the streets, but roughly half of them are out of order – a problem often ignored by phone companies in this day of cell phones. Those maintained by Verizon are usually the most reliable. Many pay phones accept credit cards, but some will bill you an outrageous amount for a long-distance call.

For many years Manhattan's telephone numbers carried the area code 212, the quickest digits for fast-living New Yorkers to dial on a rotary phone. In 1998 Manhattan got a new area code, 646, to cope with the huge demand for new lines. The four other boroughs carry the 718 and 347 area codes. Now, as of 2003, you must always dial the area code, even if you are calling from a borough that uses the same one you're calling.

TOILETS

Public toilets are almost nonexistent, and those in commercial establishments are for customers only. It's sometimes possible to slip into the bathroom of a busy bar or restaurant if you are discreet and well dressed. If you're in distress, head to a Starbucks (there's one on every other corner) and ask the indifferent counter person for the restroom key.

TOURIST OFFICES

Dairy building (Map pp142-7; ☎ 212-794-6564; www.centralpark.org/find/dairy.html; Central Park at 65th St; 🕑 11am-4pm Tue-Sat) In the middle of Central Park, along the 65th St pathway.
Lesbian, Gay, Bisexual & Transgender (LGBT) Community Center (☎ 212-620-7310; www.gaycenter.org; 208 W 13th St; 🕑 9am-11pm) Gay and lesbian travelers receive queer-themed visitor information and a grand welcome at this visitors center in Greenwich Village.
New York City & Company (Map pp124-6; ☎ 212-484-1222, 24hr toll-free ☎ 800-692-8474; www.nycvisit.com; 810 Seventh Ave at 53rd St; 🕑 8:30am-6pm Mon-Fri; 9am-5pm Sat & Sun) The official information service of the Convention & Visitors Bureau,

NEW YORK CITY IN...

Two Days

Get a small dose of all the major tourist spots, plus the lay of the land, by taking a guided tour, either on the Circle Line or a double-decker bus. Have an early dinner in **Koreatown**, go to a **Broadway show** in the evening and then, for the perfect nightcap, head to the top of the **Empire State Building** to see the city aglow. The next day, focus on walking around the diverse neighborhoods of **downtown**. Splurge for brunch at **Balthazar**, wander around the **West Village**, then meander over to the **East Village**. People-watch in **Tompkins Sq Park**, check out the boutiques and grab dinner at **Prune** (expensive) or **Bereket** (cheap). Go see some live music, or have cocktails at a downtown spot of your choice.

Four Days

Follow the two-day itinerary, then hit the **Metropolitan Museum of Art** on the third day. Grab a picnic when you're through exploring, and head into **Central Park**. Stroll around when you're done, or even rent bikes. That night, after dinner, enjoy a jazz or comedy show. Head to an outer borough on your final day – either Queens, where you can see the new **MoMA** along with the **PS 1 Contemporary Art Center** and **Socrates Sculpture Park**, or Brooklyn, where the **Brooklyn Museum of Art** and **Botanic Gardens** await. Have an outstanding dinner no matter where you are – Greek food in Astoria, Queens, or eclectic American in Boerum Hill, Brooklyn.

it has helpful multilingual staff. The 24-hour toll-free line provides information on special events and reservations.

Times Square Visitors Center (Map pp124-6; ☎ 212-869-1890; 1560 Broadway; 🕑 8am-8pm) Runs a free two-hour walking tour at noon every Friday and is a useful source of information.

TRAVEL AGENCIES

Apart from regular and discount agencies, such as Council Travel and STA Travel (which have several offices), there are consolidators selling last-minute flights. Most are in Midtown office buildings and advertise weekly in the *Village Voice* and the Sunday *New York Times*. The more reliable agencies take credit cards and can book tickets on scheduled carriers.

UNIVERSITIES

The city has several colleges and universities in each borough, each with its own surrounding community and cultural offerings. In Manhattan, Columbia University, its grand ivy-league campus an oasis in the craziness of NYC, is definitely worth a visit, if just to sit and people-watch on the grand steps of the school library. Downtown, New York University (NYU) surrounds Washington Sq Park, and offers concerts, plays and art openings to the public. (See p111 for event listings).

Dangers & Annoyances

Statistically, New York has become a very safe city by US standards, but it doesn't hurt to watch your back. You're probably safest in any of the areas frequented by tourists, especially during daylight hours, but watch for pickpockets. At night, avoid places that are largely deserted or badly lit. Steer clear of Central Park at night, unless you're heading to a well-populated concert, play or other event. In general, don't flaunt money or valuables, especially in poor areas.

Drug dealing has virtually disappeared from Manhattan streets. Plenty of panhandlers and hustlers remain – especially on the subways and in subway stations – and some give a very polished presentation. All New Yorkers handle such situations differently, but if you really want to help those in need and avoid supporting a drug habit, contact **Citydishes-on-Wheels** (☎ 212-687-1234).

SCAMS

Three-card monty may not be as rampant as it used to be, but it still draws crowds in tourist areas like Midtown. There's just one thing you need to remember about the shell game: nobody ever wins! Other scams include folks on the street approaching you with a story about having an appointment to pick up a check at their social worker's office

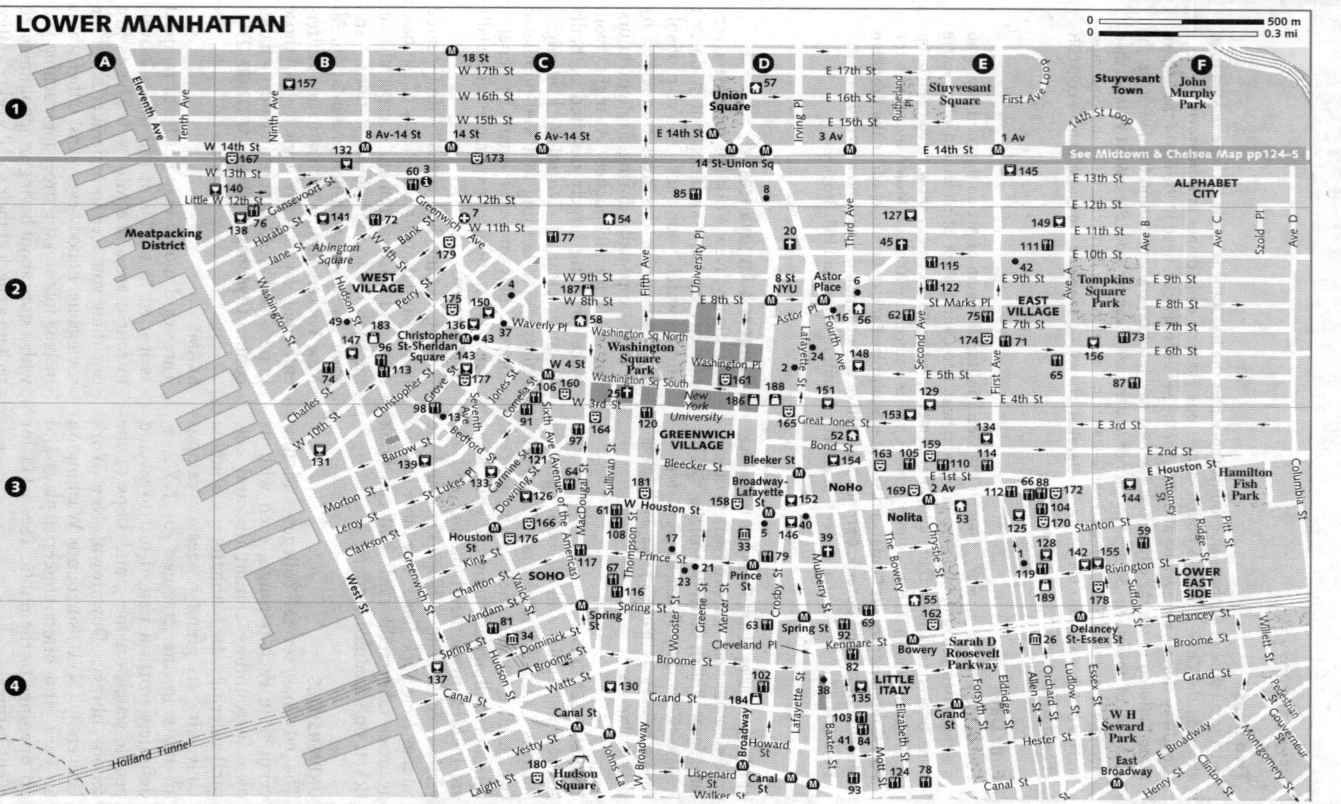

LOWER MANHATTAN
500 m
0.3 mi
See Midtown & Chelsea Map pp124-5
Stuyvesant Town
John Murphy Park
ALPHABET CITY
Tompkins Square Park
EAST VILLAGE
Stuyvesant Square
Union Square
Washington Square Park
New York University
GREENWICH VILLAGE
WEST VILLAGE
Abingdon Square
Meatpacking District
NoHo
Nolita
SOHO
LITTLE ITALY
LOWER EAST SIDE
Hamilton Fish Park
Sarah D Roosevelt Parkway
W H Seward Park
Hudson Square
Holland Tunnel
Eleventh Ave
Tenth Ave
Ninth Ave
West St
Washington St
Hudson St
Greenwich St
Seventh Ave
Sixth Ave (Avenue of the Americas)
Fifth Ave
Broadway
Lafayette St
Fourth Ave
Third Ave
Second Ave
First Ave
Ave A
Ave B
Ave C
Ave D
E 14th St
W 14th St
E Houston St
W Houston St
Bleecker St
Prince St
Spring St
Broome St
Grand St
Canal St
Delancey St
The Bowery
Bowery
Chrystie St
Forsyth St
Eldridge St
Allen St
Orchard St
Ludlow St
Essex St
Columbia St

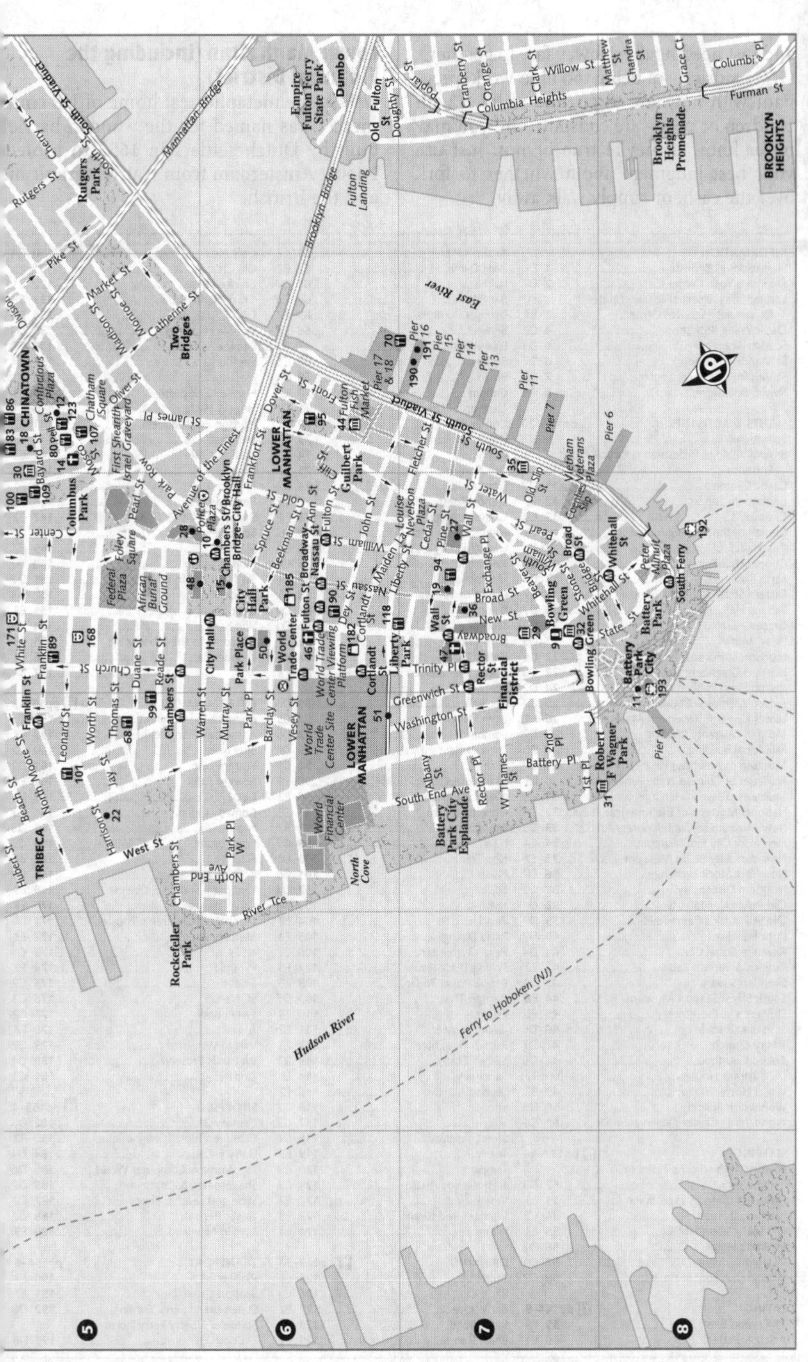

TRIBECA
CHINATOWN
Columbus Park
Two Bridges
Rutgers Park
LOWER MANHATTAN
Financial District
City Hall Park
Federal Plaza
Foley Square
African Burial Ground
World Trade Center Site
World Financial Center
Battery Park City Esplanade
Robert F Wagner Park
Battery Park
Bowling Green
Liberty Park
Guilbert Park
Rockefeller Park
North Cove
Peter Minuit Plaza
Vietnam Veterans Plaza
Louise Nevelson Plaza
Confucious Plaza
Chatham Square
First Shearith Israel Graveyard
Police Plaza
Fulton Fish Market
Empire Fulton Ferry State Park
Dumbo
Fulton Landing
Brooklyn Heights Promenade
BROOKLYN HEIGHTS
East River
Hudson River
Ferry to Hoboken (NJ)
Brooklyn Bridge
Manhattan Bridge
South St Viaduct
Pier 6
Pier 7
Pier 11
Pier 13
Pier 14
Pier 15
Pier 16
Pier 17 & 18
Pier A
West St
Broadway
Wall St
Chambers St
City Hall
Park Place
Fulton St
Cortlandt St
Rector St
Whitehall St
South Ferry
Franklin St
Canal St

and just needing the subway fare to get there. Other stories – of being too ill to work, pregnant with nowhere to go, and saddled with children or pets – are constant, and you may never know if they're true or not. Just use your best judgment about whether to fork over the cash, or simply walk away.

Lower Manhattan (Including the Financial District)

Wall St, the metaphorical home of US commerce, was named for the wooden barrier built by Dutch settlers in 1653 to protect Nieuw Amsterdam from Native Americans and the British.

INFORMATION

- Bluestockings Bookstore 1 E3
- Jivamukti Yoga Center 2 D2
- Lesbian, Gay, Bisexual & Transgender Community Services Center 3 B1
- Oscar Wilde Bookshop 4 C2
- Scratch Academy 5 D3
- St Mark's Bookshop 6 D2
- St Vincent's Medical Center 7 C2
- Strand Bookstore 8 D1

SIGHTS & ACTIVITIES pp116–20

- Bronze Bull 9 D7
- Brooklyn Bridge Pedestrian & Bicycle Path Entrance 10 D6
- Castle Clinton 11 D8
- Chinatown Tunnel 12 E5
- Chumley's 13 C3
- Church of the Transfiguration 14 E5
- City Hall 15 D6
- Cooper Union 16 D2
- Earth Room 17 D3
- Eastern States Buddhist Temple 18 E5
- Federal Hall 19 D7
- Grace Church 20 D2
- Haas' Mural 21 D3
- Harrison St Houses 22 C5
- Howard Greenberg Gallery 23 D3
- Joseph Papp Public Theater 24 D2
- Judson Memorial Church 25 C2
- Lower East Side Tenement Museum 26 E4
- Morgan Guaranty Building 27 D7
- Municipal Building 28 D5
- Museum of American Financial History 29 D7
- Museum of Chinese in the Americas 30 E5
- Museum of Jewish Heritage 31 C8
- National Museum of the American Indian 32 D7
- New Museum of Contemporary Art 33 D3
- New York City Fire Museum 34 C4
- New York City Police Museum 35 E7
- New York Stock Exchange 36 D7
- Northern Dispensary 37 C2
- Old Police Headquarters 38 D4
- Old St Patrick's Cathedral 39 D3
- Puck Building 40 D3
- Ravenite Social Club 41 D4
- Russian & Turkish Baths 42 E2
- Sheridan Square 43 C2
- South Street Seaport Museum 44 E6
- St Mark's in-the-Bowery 45 E2
- St Paul's Chapel 46 D6
- Trinity Church 47 D7
- Tweed Courthouse 48 D6
- US Customs House (see 32)
- White Horse Tavern 49 B2
- Woolworth Building 50 D6
- World Trade Center Observation Deck 51 C6

SLEEPING pp137–44

- Bowery's Whitehouse Hotel of New York 52 D3
- Howard Johnson's Express Inn 53 E3
- Larchmont Hotel 54 C2
- Off SoHo Suites Hotel 55 E3
- St Marks Hotel 56 D2
- W Union Square 57 D1
- Washington Square Hotel 58 C2

EATING pp144–9

- 71 Clinton Fresh Food 59 F3
- A Salt & Battery 60 B1
- Arturo's Pizzeria 61 C3
- B&H Dairy 62 E2
- Balthazar 63 D4
- Bar Pitti 64 C3
- Benny's Burritos 65 E2
- Bereket 66 E3
- Blue Ribbon 67 C3
- Bouley 68 C5
- Bread 69 D4
- Cabana 70 E7
- Caravan of Dreams 71 E2
- Corner Bistro 72 B2
- Dawgs on Park 73 F2
- Delicia 74 B2
- Dok Suni's 75 E2
- Florent 76 B2
- French Roast 77 C2
- Grand Sichuan 78 E4
- Hampton Chutney Co 79 D3
- Hay Wun Loy 80 E5
- Herban Kitchen 81 C4
- Hoomoos Asli 82 D4
- House of Vegetarian 83 E5
- Il Fornaio 84 D4
- Japonica 85 D1
- Kam Chueh 86 E5
- Kate's Joint 87 F2
- Katz's Delicatessan 88 E3
- Kori 89 D5
- Les Halles 90 D6
- Little Havana 91 C3
- Lombardi's Pizza 92 D4
- Luna Restaurant 93 D4
- Mangia 94 D7
- Mark Joseph Steakhouse 95 E6
- Mexicana Mama 96 B2
- Minetta Tavern 97 C3
- Moustache 98 B3
- Nam 99 C5
- Nha Trang 100 D5
- Nobu 101 C5
- Ñ 102 D4
- Nyonya 103 D4
- Paladar 104 E3
- Patio Dining 105 E3
- Pearl Oyster Bar 106 C2
- Peking Duck House 107 E5
- Peppe Rosso To Go 108 C3
- Ponsgri Thai 109 D5
- Prune 110 E3
- Quintessence 111 E2
- Russ & Daughters 112 E3
- Sacred Chow 113 B2
- Sanctuary 114 E3
- Second Ave Deli 115 E2
- Snack 116 C3
- Souen 117 C3
- Street Vendors 118 D6
- Teany 119 E3
- Temple In 120 C3
- Trattoria Spaghetto 121 C3
- Veselka 122 E2
- Vietnam Restaurant 123 E5
- Wong Kee 124 E4

DRINKING pp149–50

- Angel 125 E3
- Bar d'O 126 C3
- Bar Veloce 127 E2
- Barramundi 128 E3
- Boiler Room 129 E2
- Cafe Noir 130 C4
- Chi Chiz 131 B3
- Chicago Blues 132 B1
- Crazy Nanny's 133 C3
- DBA 134 E3
- Double Happiness 135 D4
- Duplex 136 C2
- Ear Inn 137 C4
- Hell 138 B2
- Henrietta Hudson 139 B3
- Hogs & Heifers 140 B1
- Hudson Bar & Books 141 B2
- Magician 142 E3
- Marie's Crisis 143 C2
- Meow Mix 144 F3
- Phoenix Bar 145 E1
- Puck Fair 146 D3
- Rubyfruit's Bar & Grill 147 B2
- Scratcher 148 D2
- Starlight 149 E2
- Stonewall Inn 150 C2
- Swift Hibernian Lounge 151 D2
- Temple Bar 152 D3
- Urge Lounge 153 E3
- Von Bar 154 D3
- Welcome to the Johnson's 155 F3
- Wonder Bar 156 F2
- XL 157 B1

ENTERTAINMENT pp150–3

- Angelika Film Center 158 D3
- Anthology Film Archives 159 E3
- Blue Note 160 C2
- Bottom Line 161 D2
- Bowery Ballroom 162 E4
- CBGB 163 E3
- Comedy Cellar 164 C3
- Fez 165 D3
- Film Forum 166 C3
- Filter 14 167 B1
- Knitting Factory 168 D5
- Landmark Sunshine Cinema 169 E3
- Luna Lounge 170 E3
- Manhattan Children's Theater 171 D5
- Mercury Lounge 172 E3
- Nell's 173 C1
- Pyramid 174 E2
- Smalls 175 C2
- SOB's 176 C3
- Sweet Basil 177 C2
- Tonic 178 F3
- Village Vanguard 179 C2
- Wetlands Preserve 180 C4
- Zinc Bar 181 C3

SHOPPING pp153–4

- Century 21 182 D6
- Creative Visions/Gay Pleasures 183 B2
- Daffy's 184 D4
- J&R Music & Computer World 185 D6
- Shakespeare & Company 186 D2
- Shoe and Leather Shops 187 C2
- Tower Records 188 D2
- Toys in Babeland 189 E3

TRANSPORT pp154–6

- Pioneer 190 E7
- Seaport Cruise Line 191 E7
- Staten Island Ferry Terminal 192 D8
- Statue of Liberty Ferry Ticket Booth 193 D8

Further east is **Federal Hall** (Map pp114-16; ☎ 212-825-6888; 26 Wall St; 9am-5pm), New York City's 18th-century city hall, distinguished by a huge statue of George Washington on the steps. This is where the first US Congress convened and Washington was sworn in as the first president, though it is not the original building.

The **New York Stock Exchange** (Map pp114-16; ☎ 212-656-3000; www.nyse.com; 20 Broad St) has a facade like a Roman temple. The visitors center, unfortunately, is closed indefinitely due to security concerns.

South St Seaport is an 11-block enclave of shops and historic sights. The **South St Seaport Museum** (Map pp114-16; ☎ 212-748-8600; www.southstseaport.org; adult/child $6/3; 10am-5pm) includes three galleries, a children's center and the three historic ships just south of the pier. A booth on Pier 16 sells tickets for an hour-long riverboat cruise with the **Seaport Cruise Line** (Map pp114-16; ☎ 212-630-8888; Pier 16; adult/child $13/7; tours three daily Mar-Nov), highlighting Manhattan's maritime history. Better yet, take a sail on the 1885 wooden schooner **Pioneer** (Map pp114-16; ☎ 212-748-8786; www.southstseaport.org; Pier 16; adult/child $25/15; sail times vary).

At **Bowling Green Park** (Map pp114-16; State & Whitehall Sts), British residents relaxed with quiet games in the late 17th century. The large bronze bull here is a tourist photo stop. Nearby, the old Standard Oil Building was built in 1922 by John D Rockefeller and now houses the **Museum of American Financial History** (Map pp114-16; ☎ 212-908-4110; 26 Broadway; admission $2; 10am-4pm Tue-Sat). **City Hall** (Map pp114-16; City Hall Park, Broadway), in the Civic Center precinct, has been home to New York City's government since 1812. **Tweed Courthouse** (Map pp114-16), just behind (north of) City Hall, is what the 1872 County Courthouse building is commonly called, after the notoriously corrupt 'Boss' Tweed, the Tammany Hall political organizer who embezzled $10 million of the $14 million construction cost. The opulent structure has just undergone extensive renovation. On the corner of Chambers St, the **Woolworth Building** (Map pp114-16; 233 Broadway) was the world's tallest building when it opened in 1913, and the lobby has a relief of proprietor Frank Woolworth counting his change. Historic church fans will love **St Paul's Chapel** (Map pp114-16; Broadway at Fulton St), built in 1766, and **Trinity Church**.

There are two nearby museums that are worth a visit: the **New York City Police Museum** (Map pp114-16; ☎ 212-480-3100; www.nycpolicemuseum.org; 100 Old Slip; admission free; 10am-5pm Tue-Sat), which covers cops, Capone and killers; and the **National Museum of the American Indian** (Map pp114-16; ☎ 212-514-3700; www.nmai.si.edu; 1 Bowling Green; admission free; 10am-5pm), housing quite an extensive collection of Native American arts, crafts, exhibits, a library and a gift shop.

STATUE OF LIBERTY

This great statue, Liberty Enlightening the World, is an American icon and New York's best-known landmark. As early as 1865, French intellectual Edouard Laboulaye conceived a great monument to the republican ideal in France and the USA. French sculptor Frédéric-Auguste Bartholdi traveled to New York in 1871 to select the site. He then spent more than 10 years in Paris, designing and making the 151ft figure, which was then shipped to New York, erected on a small island in the harbor, and unveiled in 1886. Structurally, it consists of an iron skeleton (designed by Gustave Eiffel) with a copper skin attached to it by stiff, but flexible, metal bars. Corrosion of the copper became a serious problem, and more than $100 million was spent restoring Liberty for her centennial in 1986.

The **Statue of Liberty National Monument** (☎ 212-363-3200; www.nps.gov/stli/; New York Harbor, Liberty Island; adult/child $10/8; 9:30am-5pm) is a major attraction and can be overcrowded. It's usually visited in conjunction with nearby Ellis Island, and the trip involves pleasant ferry rides with spectacular views of downtown Manhattan. You can climb 354 steps (22 stories) to the statue's crown, though this may involve hours of waiting for a very brief moment at the top. It's wonderful to see the statue from the inside and close up, and to share the experience in a confined space with a few thousand other pilgrims – and you'll never forget your glimpse of New York Harbor as Liberty sees it. The fine museum in the base is well worth seeing for its fascinating exhibits on the statue's structure, restoration and cultural significance.

Ferries (☎ 212-269-5755) leave from Battery Park every 30 minutes 8:30am to 3:30pm, with extended hours during summer. South

Ferry and Bowling Green are the closest subway stations.

See also Tours, p137.

ELLIS ISLAND

Ferries to the Statue of Liberty make a second stop at Ellis Island, the country's main immigration station from 1892 to 1954, where more than 12 million immigrants first set foot in the New World. The handsome main building is now restored as an **Immigration Museum** (Map pp114-16; ☎ 212-269-5755; www.ellisisland.com; New York Harbor; adult/child $7/3, audio tours $3.50; 🕘 9:30am-5:15pm), with exhibits and a film about immigrant experiences, the processing of immigrants and how the influx changed the USA. You can listen to fascinating narratives with actors reading from immigrants' letters, or take a 50-minute audio-guided tour of the vast, light-filled space. Try to leave the Statue of Liberty before 2pm to allow enough time at Ellis Island, or else make a separate trip here – it's worth it. The last ferry heads back to Battery Park around 5pm.

BROOKLYN BRIDGE

This was the world's first **steel suspension bridge**, with an unprecedented span of 1596ft. It remains a compelling symbol of US achievement and a superbly graceful structure, despite the fact that its construction was plagued by budget overruns and the deaths of 20 workers. Among the casualties was designer, John Roebling, who was knocked off a pier in 1869 while scouting a site for the western bridge tower and later died of tetanus poisoning. Then, at the bridge's opening in 1883, there was a sudden fear of imminent collapse, and 12 pedestrians were trampled to death in the ensuing panic.

The bridge was extensively renovated in the early 1980s, and the pedestrian/bicyclist path, beginning just east of City Hall, affords wonderful views of Lower Manhattan and Brooklyn. Observation points under the two stone support towers have illustrations showing panoramas of the waterfront at various points in New York's history. For a romantic nightcap, try an early evening stroll (it's well lit and patrolled by cops on bikes), when you'll see the sparkling lights of the city begin to come to life.

BATTERY PARK AREA

The southwestern tip of Manhattan Island has been extended with landfill over the years to form Battery Park. **Castle Clinton**, a fortification built in 1811 to protect Manhattan from the British, was originally 900ft offshore but is now at the edge of Battery Park, with only its walls remaining. Come summertime, it's transformed into a gorgeous outdoor stage for concerts.

West of the park, the **Museum of Jewish Heritage** (Map pp114-16; ☎ 212-509-6130; www.mjhnyc.org; 18 1st Pl, Battery Park City; admission $7; 🕘 10am-5:45pm Sun-Wed, until 8pm Thu, until 3pm Fri) depicts many aspects of New York Jewish history and culture, and includes a holocaust memorial.

Chinatown & Little Italy **Map pp114–16**

These two long-standing ethnic enclaves are just north of the Financial District. **Chinatown** is a thriving community of more than 120,000 residents, many living and working in this minisociety without using a word of English. Throughout the 1990s Chinatown saw an influx of Vietnamese immigrants, who set up their own shops and some incredibly cheap restaurants. **Little Italy**, on the other hand, has lost much of its ethnic character in recent years. Mulberry St is a tourist-trap enclave of cheap (and not necessarily good) pasta restaurants and overpriced tobacco shops. (For a more authentic Chinatown *and* Little Italy, see Keepin' It Real: New York City's Most Authentic Ethnic 'Hoods p131.)

While the best reasons to visit Chinatown are simply to stroll in a bustling environment, eat from street stalls and cheapo restaurants, and browse the strange and wonderful herbal shops, there are a few sites, too. The **Museum of Chinese in the Americas** (☎ 212-619-4785; www.moca-nyc.org; 70 Mulberry St at Bayard St; admission $3; 🕘 noon-5pm Tue-Sun) has exhibits and sponsors walking tours and workshops on Chinese crafts. **Columbus Park** (Worth St btwn Mulberry, Baxter & Bayard Sts), especially in the wee hours of the morning, gives you an excellent taste of local life, as you'll no doubt find folks playing games of mah-jongg and practicing tai chi. **Chatham Sq** (Park Row, The Bowery & St James intersection), where the goods of Irish debtors were auctioned in the early 19th century, now houses a monument to Chinese-Americans who were killed in war.

A stroll along Mulberry St will give you a taste of what's left of the Italian 'hood.

NEW YORK'S BEST BARGAINS

After paying for food and lodging, budget travelers will be wilting at the expense of visiting New York City. However, many of the finest attractions are free or cost only a few dollars. It costs nothing to walk across the iconic Brooklyn Bridge, to stroll through picture-perfect Central Park or to browse at the Union Sq Greenmarket (where vendors offer free tastes of cheese, baked goods and produce). For fantastic, free people watching, visit Washington Sq Park (at weekends), Wall St (weekday lunchtimes), Fifth Ave, Harlem, Chinatown and the Chelsea and Soho gallery scenes. Some of the city's finest buildings are free, too, such as Tweed Courthouse, the old Customs House, the New York Public Library and Grand Central Terminal (even the Met, technically, which only charges a 'donation'). In the summer months, Bryant Park shows free outdoor movies on Monday, while Central Park and Prospect Park are hosts to free concerts by the New York Philharmonic Orchestra.

To access much of New York's best, you need chutzpah and a presentable appearance more than you do money. Why not browse in Cartier or Tiffany's, admire the fashions in Saks Fifth Ave, and check out exquisite antiques on E 12th, W 32nd or E 59th Sts? You can sit in the lobbies of the swankiest hotels, and hang out in an opulent bar for the price of a drink.

For a free harbor cruise past the Statue of Liberty, just catch a Staten Island Ferry. Many of the great cultural institutions offer admission by donation, free days or pay-what-you-can entry times (eg, Friday evening at the MoMA and the Guggenheim, Thursday evening at the Whitney, Tuesday evening at Cooper-Hewitt). Some attractions are always free, like the National Museum of the American Indian, New York City Police Museum or a tour of the New York Stock Exchange. The New York CityPass ($28) gets you into five big attractions (the Empire State Building, Guggenheim, MoMA, American Museum of Natural History and *Intrepid* Sea-Air-Space Museum).

One of the best bargains of all is the weekly MetroCard ($21). It lets you use the whole subway and the bus system over all five boroughs, 24 hours a day. Creative advertising, outstanding people-watching and impromptu entertainment are included, and the ticket can get you to the airport at the end of your stay.

The **Old St Patrick's Cathedral** (263 Mulberry St) became the city's first Roman Catholic cathedral in 1809 and remained so until 1878, when its more famous uptown successor was completed.

The former **Ravenite Social Club** (247 Mulberry St), now a gift shop, is a reminder of the not-so-long-ago days when mobsters ran the neighborhood. Originally known as the Alto Knights Social Club, where big hitters like Lucky Luciano spent time, the Ravenite was a favorite hangout of John Gotti (and the FBI) before his arrest and life sentencing in 1992.

Tribeca

The 'TRIangle BElow CAnal St,' bordered roughly by Broadway to the east and Chambers St to the south, has old warehouses, very expensive loft apartments (JFK Jr's was among them before he died) and funky restaurants. It's not as established or as architecturally significant as Soho, but its retro-industrial look and see-and-be-seen lounges and eateries has made it a super-trendy area. The **townhouses** (Map pp114-16; Harrison St) west of Greenwich St were built between 1804 and 1828 and are New York's largest remaining collection of Federal architecture. Only those at Nos 31 and 33 were actually built here, though; the others were relocated from a nearby development site.

Soho

Map pp114–16

This neighborhood 'SOuth of HOuston St,' extending down to Canal St, is a paradigm of inadvertent urban renewal. The many blocks of cast-iron industrial buildings originally housed textile and clothing factories, but retail businesses relocated uptown and manufacturing moved out of the city. In the 1950s the huge lofts and low rental properties attracted artists and other members of the avant-garde, whose influence and political lobbying saved the neighborhood from destruction. The 26-block area was declared a 'protected historic district' in 1973, and today Soho is a retail-heavy center for clothing stores, boutiques and established art galleries (though several big-name galleries have relocated to Chelsea or further uptown). On weekends W Broadway and nearby Prince

St are packed with tourists and street artists. The **New Museum of Contemporary Art** (☎ 212-219-1222; www.newmuseum.org; 583 Broadway; admission $6; ⌚ noon-6pm Tue-Sun, until 8pm Thu) displays works less than 10 years old.

Southwest of central Soho, the **New York City Fire Museum** (☎ 212-691-1303; www.nycfiremuseum.org; 278 Spring St; suggested donation $5; ⌚ 10am-5pm Tue-Sat, until 4pm Sun) is a grand old firehouse dating back to 1904. Gleaming gold horse-drawn fire-fighting carriages, modern-day fire engines, pictures and documents tell the story of New York's fire-fighting history, including the heroic rescues made on 9/11.

Greenwich Village

One of New York's most popular neighborhoods, Greenwich Village is bounded by 14th St, Lafayette St/Fourth Ave, Houston St and the Hudson River. The center of 'the Village' is dominated by New York University (NYU), which owns most of the property surrounding Washington Sq Park. Southwest of the park is a lively, crowded collection of cafés, shops and restaurants; west of Seventh Ave, the West Village is a delightful neighborhood of quaint, crooked streets and restored townhouses.

After the Civil War, Greenwich Village became New York's most prominent black neighborhood, but in the early 1920s many of these residents moved to Harlem. The early 20th century also saw artists and writers move in, and from the 1940s the neighborhood drew anyone and everyone from the fringes of society – gays and lesbians, beats, artists and musicians.

South of the park on Thompson St, **Judson Memorial Church** stands on the corner. Designed by Stanford White, it's a national historic site with notable stained-glass windows and a marble facade. Along Thompson, you'll pass a series of chess shops where Village denizens meet to play the game ($1.50 per hour). **Bleecker St** (spelled 'Bleeker' on some city signs) has several coffeehouses, including Le Figaro, associated with the beatniks of the 1950s. But steer clear of the strip at night, when hawkers try to pull you into dark and generic bars, mobbed with drunk college kids, to hear third-rate bands. The nearby **Minetta Lane** and **Minetta St** takes you past a block of 18th-century slums, now preserved and improved. The old Minetta Brook still runs under some of the row houses.

The western edge of the Village holds **Sheridan Sq** (also called 'Stonewall Place'), a small, triangular park where life-size white statues honor the gay community and gay pride movement that began in the nearby Stonewall Inn. East of the 'square,' the triangular brick building is the **Northern Dispensary**, built in the cholera epidemic of the 1830s. A block further east, a bent street is officially named Gay St (prompting titillated gay folks to periodically swipe the street sign). Although gay social scenes have in many ways moved a bit further uptown to Chelsea, **Christopher St** is still the center of gay life in the Village. On Bedford St, there's a wonderful 1894 horse stable that has been turned into a brewery at No 95, and **Chumley's** (86 Bedford St), a onetime speakeasy enjoyed by socialists and writers in the late 1920s.

If you want to walk further into the West Village, go three blocks north on Hudson St to the **White Horse Tavern** (Map pp114-16; 567 Hudson St), where Dylan Thomas reputedly drank himself to death in 1953 (he actually died in the hospital). Continue north about four blocks, past Abington Sq, and turn left on Jane or Horatio Sts; both have lovely old stone row houses heading down to the Hudson River running path. The latest part of the Village to become gentrified is the **Meatpacking District**, around Gansevoort–Little W 12th St. Though it's still active and odorous on weekday mornings, evenings and weekends draw the trendy set to high-ceilinged wine bars, Belgian and Cuban eateries, nightclubs and high-end 14th-St designer clothing stores (including the popular Jeffrey and Stella McCartney).

WASHINGTON SQUARE PARK & AROUND

This park began as a 'potter's field' – a burial ground for the penniless – and its status as a cemetery protected it from development. It is now an incredibly well-used park, especially on the weekends. Children use the playground, NYU students catch some rays and friends meet 'under the arch' – the landmark on the park's northern edge, designed in 1889 by society architect Stanford White. The row of townhouses along Washington Sq North was the inspiration for Henry James' novel of late 19th-century mores, *Washington Square,* though James never actually lived here. Around the now-dry central 'fountain,' street comedians and musicians do their thing and food carts cater to the snack-needy. All sorts of canines frolic and hump in the dog run on the southwest corner.

East Village

Bordered roughly by 14th St, Lafayette St, E Houston St and the East River, the East Village has gentrified rapidly in the last decade. Old tenements, especially those in the blocks bordering Greenwich Village, have been taken over by artists, restaurateurs and real-estate developers. And, though it's trendier than Greenwich Village, the ambience is different (more fashionable-grunge) and its restaurants cater to a rich ethnic mix.

To explore the recently reinvented East Village, walk along First, Second or Third Ave between 14th and Houston Sts. They're lined with laundries, bars, coffee shops, delis and multiethnic restaurants.

Poorer residents have moved further toward the East River into **Alphabet City** (Aves A, B, C and D), where Latino culture still prevails (but probably not for long). Despite the general upmarket movement, the areas east of Ave C can still feel a bit threatening at night.

Tompkins Sq Park is an unofficial border between the East Village (to the west) and Alphabet City (to the east). Once an Eastern European immigrant area, you'll still see old Ukrainians and Poles in the park, but they'll be alongside punks, students, panhandlers and dog-walking yuppies. And on E 10th St, **Grace Church** (Map pp114-16; E 10th St) was designed by James Renwick and built mostly in the 1840s. The steeple was added in 1888, and the church's white marble exterior glows beautifully when it's floodlit at night; the church is among dance clubs, record stores and pizza parlors.

The historic **Russian & Turkish Baths** (Map pp114-16; ☎ 212-473-8806; www.russianturkishbaths.com; 268 E 10th St; admission $22; 🕑 11am-10pm Mon, Tue, Thu & Fri, 7:30am-10pm Sat, 7.30am-2pm Sun) still offer a traditional massage followed by an ice-cold bath. It's ladies-only from 9am to 2pm Wednesday, men-only from 7:30am to 2pm Sunday and coed the rest of the time.

At the west end of St Mark's Place, **Astor Place** was once an elite neighborhood, and some of its impressive original Greek Revival residences remain. Across the street, in the public library built by John Jacob Astor, is the **Joseph Papp Public Theater** (Map pp114-16), home to the New York Shakespeare Festival. The large brownstone **Cooper Union** (Map pp114-16) is a public college founded by glue millionaire Peter Cooper in 1859. Abraham Lincoln gave his 'Right Makes Might' speech condemning slavery before his election to the White House in the college's Great Hall. The Astor Place subway station is decorated with beaver mosaics, a reminder that John Jacob Astor's first fortune came from the fur trade.

Lower East Side

First came the Jews, then the Latinos, and now…the hipsters, of course. In the early 20th century, about half a million Jews from Eastern Europe lived in tenements and worked in the factories of the Lower East Side. The neighborhood had 400 synagogues then, but only a few of them still stand, serving the few remaining Jewish residents. Those living behind the crumbling doorways are now as likely to be young people in their first city apartment as long-term residents holding onto a place with rent control. The four-block area on and around **Ludlow St** is packed Saturday nights with grunge rockers, dance-club addicts, late-night eaters and underage drinkers. Recently, a slew of excellent restaurants, lounges and boutiques have crowded into the vicinity, along with a burgeoning art-gallery scene.

The **Orchard St Bargain District**, the market area around Orchard, Ludlow and Essex Sts, north of Delancey St, is where Eastern European merchants sold their wares from pushcarts when this was a largely Jewish neighborhood. Today shops sell an odd array of sporting goods, belts, hats and off-brand 'designer fashions.' While the businesses are not exclusively owned by Orthodox Jews, they still close early Friday afternoon and remain shuttered Saturday. The local speciality is kosher food products; it's worth visiting **Russ & Daughters** (☎ 212-475-4880; 179 E Houston St), an institution since 1914, where you'll find smoked fish, caviar, herring, imported cheeses and dried fruits.

For a fascinating glimpse into tenement life, take a tour of an authentically restored tenement building conducted by the **Lower East Side Tenement Museum** (Map pp114-16; ☎ 212-431-0233; www.tenement.org; 90 Orchard St; tours $7.50; tours 10am & 11:30am Mon-Fri, 10am Sat & Sun, by appointment Mon). The museum itself shows an interesting video and sells some good social-history books, but the real highlight is the tenement house tour.

Chelsea

It's all about gay men here – muscled guys who frequent gyms and bars and are well known semi-endearingly as 'Chelsea boys.' Of course, anyone is welcome at any of these places, and many non–Chelsea boys make it a destination for shopping and dining and, especially in recent years, gallery hopping.

The red-brick **Chelsea Hotel** (Map pp114-16; ☎ 212-243-3700; www.chelseahotel.com; 222 W 23rd St) has long been notorious as a hangout for writers and musicians, including Mark Twain, Dylan Thomas, Arthur Miller, Jack Kerouac, Andy Warhol and Sid Vicious (who overdosed in his room here).

Chelsea's burgeoning art-gallery scene is mostly between Tenth and Eleventh Aves, from 22nd through 26th Sts. One of the stars is the **DIA Art Foundation** (Map pp114-16; ☎ 212-989-5566; www.diacenter.org; 548 W 22nd St; admission $10; 🕑 11am-6pm Thu-Mon May-Oct, 11am-6pm Wed-Sun Sep-Jun, 11am-4pm Fri-Mon Nov-Apr), a warehouse dedicated to large-scale installations.

In Chelsea's southeast corner, just where Broadway meets 14th St, **Union Sq** was the site of many 19th-century workers' rallies, hence the name. A pleasant garden square, it has the city's largest open-air produce market, the **Greenmarket** (Map pp114-16; 🕑 Mon, Wed, Fri & Sat), and the surrounding streets are thick with bars and restaurants.

At the intersection of Broadway, Fifth Ave and 23rd St, the famous (and absolutely gorgeous) 1902 **Flatiron Building** has a distinctive triangular shape to match its site. It was New York's first iron-frame high-rise, and the world's tallest building until 1909. The surrounding Flatiron District is a fashionable area of boutiques and loft apartments. The city's newest museum, the **Museum of Sex** (Map pp114-16; ☎ 212-689-6337; www.museumofsex.org; 233 Fifth Ave at W 27th St; after/before 2pm $17/12; 🕑 11am-6:30pm Mon-Fri, 10am-9pm Sat, 10am-6:30pm Sun). Not as racy as you might imagine, this house of culture intellectually traces the history of NYC and sex – from tittie bars and porn to street hustling and burlesque shows.

Midtown

Teeming Midtown is archetypical New York, boasting many of the best-known buildings and most popular attractions, as well as some old industrial and ethnic neighborhoods. The depressingly dingy Port Authority Bus Terminal, on Eighth Ave at 41st St, is, unfortunately, one of the city's main gateways. The stretch of 42nd St east of the terminal was once a sleazy strip, but is now cleaned up, or 'Disneyfied,' and leads directly to New York's best-known junction, Times Square.

TIMES SQUARE & THEATER DISTRICT

Actually a triangle at the junction of 42nd St, Seventh Ave and Broadway, Times Square is a showplace for spectacular billboard advertising, crowded with visitors late at night bathing in the flashy electric glow of giant screens, corporate logos and nonstop banner headlines. Up to a million people gather here every New Year's Eve to see the same thing, with added fireworks, and the never-aging host Dick Clark. The blocks to the north, up to 53rd St, are home to New York theater – Broadway, off-Broadway and off-off-Broadway (see p150).

If you come during the day, look for the variety of architectural styles, from the art deco **McGraw Hill Building** (Map pp124-6; 330 W 42nd St) to the **Greek Revival Town Hall** (Map pp124-6; 113 W 43rd St), a lavish performance space. Of course you won't be able to miss the more recent and garish office blocks on Broadway itself, like the **Morgan Stanley Building** (Map pp114-16; 1589 Broadway).

The Times Square Visitors Center also runs walking tours of the neighborhood (for contact details, see Tourist Offices p112).

EMPIRE STATE BUILDING

A long-standing symbol of New York's skyline, the classic **Empire State Building** (Map pp124-6; ☎ 212-736-3100; www.esbnyc.org; 350 Fifth Ave at E 34th St; admission $11; 🕑 9:30am-midnight), 1454ft high (including antennae), was the world's tallest from 1931 to 1977. Built in 410 days during the depths of the Depression at a cost of $41 million, it features a stepped shape that was primarily a response to the 'air rights' planning regulations, requiring tall buildings to be set back from street frontages in proportion to their height. Observatories on the 86th and 102nd floors are a major attraction. There may be a long wait, so come very early or very late; a night trip to the top is quite romantic. Don't miss the art deco medallions around the lobby.

GRAND CENTRAL TERMINAL

Built in 1913 as a prestigious terminal by New York Central and Hudson River Railroad, **Grand Central Station** is no longer a romantic place to begin a cross-country journey – it's the terminus for Metro North commuter trains to the northern suburbs and Connecticut. The huge Romanesque south facade is marred by an ugly car ramp, but it's worth looking inside at the vast, vaulted main concourse – and at the recently restored ceiling, decorated with a star map that is actually a 'God's eye' image of the night sky. Towering over the terminal, the 60-story **MetLife Building** (Map pp124–6) was a controversial but innovative structure in 1963, when it was built as the Pan Am headquarters.

CHRYSLER BUILDING

Just east of Grand Central Terminal, the **Chrysler Building** (Map pp124-6; 405 Lexington Ave), an art deco masterpiece that's adorned with motorcar motifs, was designed by William Van Alen and completed in 1930. Luckily, it's most magnificent when viewed from a distance, because visitors can't go up in the building, and some details are barely visible from the ground. In the lobby, admire the African marble, onyx lights and other decorative elements.

NEW YORK PUBLIC LIBRARY

The superb beaux arts–style **New York Public Library** (Map pp124-6; Fifth Ave at 42nd St) is a wonderful retreat from the Midtown bustle. The stately lion sculptures at the front entrance, elegant lobby, marble stairs and impressive halls lead to the brilliant 3rd-floor reading room with its natural light and magnificent ceiling. This, the main branch of the library, has galleries of manuscripts on display, as well as fascinating temporary exhibits.

ROCKEFELLER CENTER

Known for its ice rink, Christmas tree, statuary and decorated facades, this **art deco complex** was started in 1931 and took nine years to complete. Some 200 dwellings were removed to make way for the project, but at the time that was less controversial than the lobby mural, painted by Mexican artist Diego Rivera, which depicted Lenin; it was covered up during the opening ceremonies and then later destroyed. Its replacement, painted by José María Sert, features the more acceptable figure of Abraham Lincoln. Look for the tile work above the Sixth Ave entrance to the GE Building, the entrance to the East River Savings Bank building at 41 Rockefeller Plaza, the triptych above the entrance to 30 Rockefeller Plaza and the statues of Prometheus and Atlas.

The 1932 **Radio City Music Hall** (Map pp124-6; ☎ 212-247-4777; www.radiocity.com; 1260 Sixth Ave; tours $17; tours 11am-3pm Mon-Sun), a 6000-seat theater, is a protected landmark perfectly restored in all its art deco grandeur. Guided tours leave the lobby every half-hour.

NBC Studios (Map pp124-6; ☎ 212-664-3700; 70th Fl, GE Building; studio tours $17.50; 🕒 8:30am-5:30pm Mon-Sat, 9:30am-4:30pm Sun) and the NBC television network headquarters are in the GE Building (formerly the RCA Building, and not to be confused with the art deco GE Building at 50th St and Lexington Ave), at the top of which the Rainbow Room offers priceless views and pricey drinks. The *Today* show broadcasts 7am to 9am daily from a glass-enclosed street-level studio near the fountain area and ice rink. Children under six aren't allowed to participate in studio tours.

ST PATRICK'S CATHEDRAL

Just across the street from the Rockefeller Center, **St Patrick's Cathedral** (Map pp124-6; Fifth Ave at 50th St; 🕒 6am-9pm) serves the 2.2 million Roman Catholics in the New York diocese. It was built mostly during the Civil War, but the two front spires were added later, in 1888. Look for the handsome rose window above the 7000-pipe organ.

HERALD SQUARE & AROUND

This crowded convergence of Broadway and Sixth Ave at 34th St is where you'll find Macy's, the city's largest Gap and a couple of nearby shopping malls. West of Herald Sq, the **Garment District** has most of New York's fashion design offices, though not much clothing is actually made here anymore. Stores on 36th and 37th Sts immediately west of Seventh Ave sell 'designer clothing,' perfume, purses and various other accessories at wholesale prices.

Nearby Pennsylvania Station (Penn Station), on 33rd St between Seventh and Eighth Aves, is not the original, grand entrance to the city, but tens of thousands of commuters and travelers do pass through daily. Built over Penn Station, **Madison Sq**

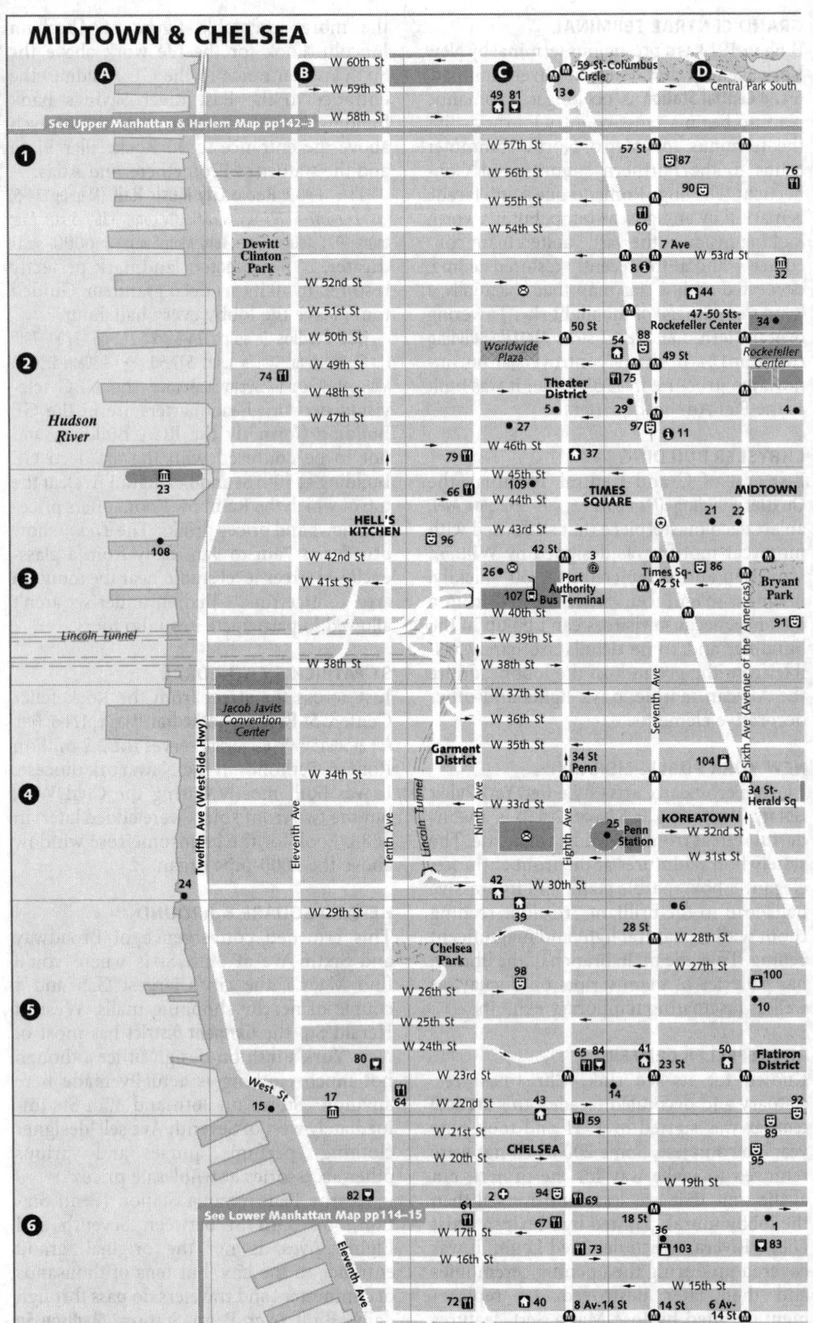
MIDTOWN & CHELSEA
See Upper Manhattan & Harlem Map pp142-3
See Lower Manhattan Map pp114-15
Hudson River
Dewitt Clinton Park
HELL'S KITCHEN
Theater District
TIMES SQUARE
MIDTOWN
Worldwide Plaza
Rockefeller Center
Port Authority Bus Terminal
Bryant Park
Lincoln Tunnel
Jacob Javits Convention Center
Garment District
KOREATOWN
Penn Station
Chelsea Park
CHELSEA
Flatiron District
Twelfth Ave (West Side Hwy)
Eleventh Ave
Tenth Ave
Ninth Ave
Eighth Ave
Seventh Ave
Sixth Ave (Avenue of the Americas)
West St
Central Park South
59 St-Columbus Circle
47-50 Sts-Rockefeller Center
Times Sq-42 St
34 St-Penn
34 St-Herald Sq
8 Av-14 St
6 Av-14 St

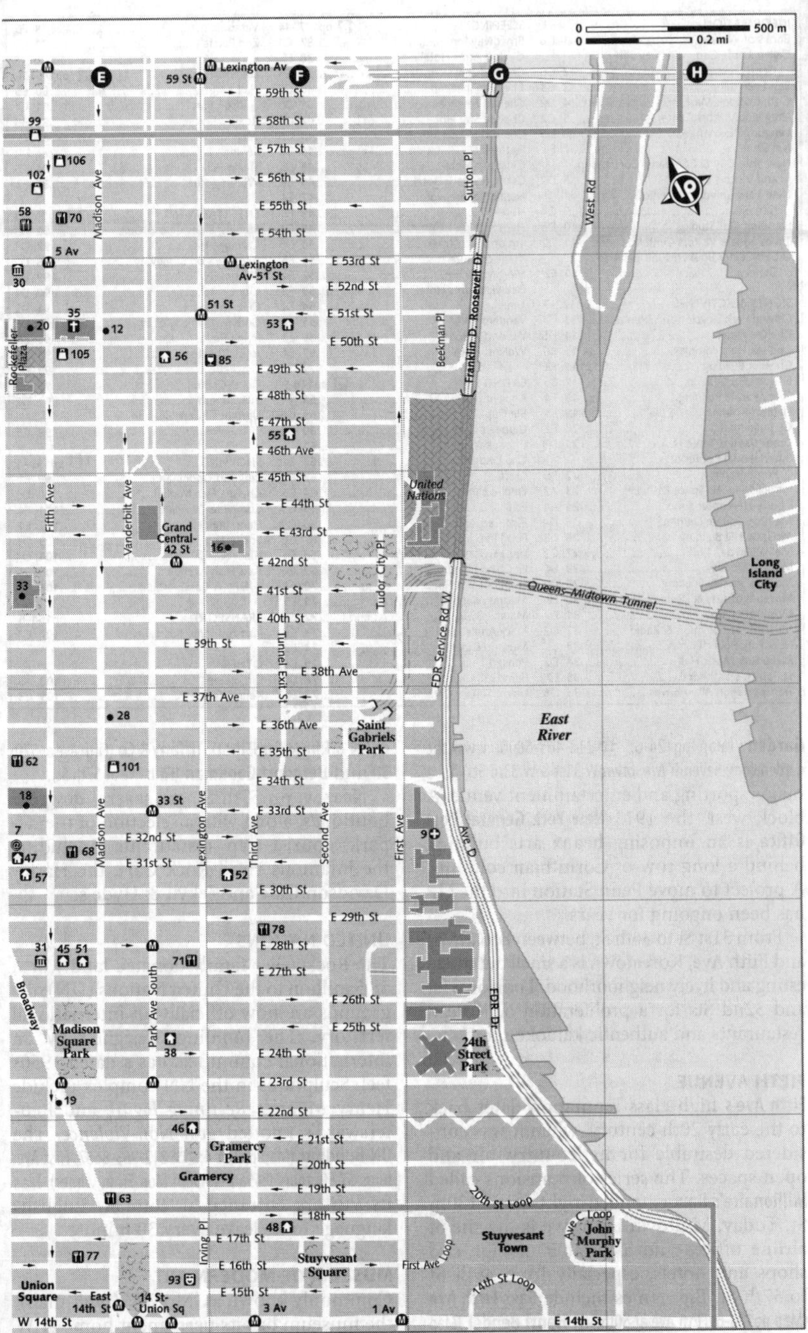

0 500 m
0 0.2 mi
Lexington Av
59 St
E 59th St
E 58th St
E 57th St
E 56th St
E 55th St
E 54th St
5 Av
Lexington Av-51 St
E 53rd St
E 52nd St
51 St
E 51st St
E 50th St
Rockefeller Plaza
E 49th St
E 48th St
E 47th St
E 46th Ave
E 45th St
E 44th St
E 43rd St
E 42nd St
E 41st St
E 40th St
E 39th St
E 38th Ave
E 37th Ave
E 36th Ave
E 35th St
E 34th St
33 St
E 33rd St
E 32nd St
E 31st St
E 30th St
E 29th St
E 28th St
E 27th St
E 26th St
E 25th St
E 24th St
E 23rd St
E 22nd St
E 21st St
E 20th St
E 19th St
E 18th St
E 17th St
E 16th St
E 15th St
W 14th St
E 14th St
Madison Ave
Fifth Ave
Vanderbilt Ave
Grand Central-42 St
Lexington Ave
Third Ave
Second Ave
First Ave
Tunnel Exit St
Tudor City Pl
Beekman Pl
Sutton Pl
Franklin D. Roosevelt Dr
FDR Service Rd W
FDR Dr
Ave D
West Rd
United Nations
Queens-Midtown Tunnel
Long Island City
East River
Saint Gabriels Park
Park Ave South
Broadway
Madison Square Park
24th Street Park
Gramercy Park
Gramercy
Irving Pl
Stuyvesant Square
Stuyvesant Town
John Murphy Park
20th St Loop
Ave C Loop
First Ave Loop
14th St Loop
Union Square
East 14th St
14 St-Union Sq
3 Av
1 Av
E
F
G
H

INFORMATION		
Books of Wonder	1	D6
Callen-Lorde Community Health Center	2	C6
EasyEverything	3	C3
Gotham Book Mart	4	D2
Gray Line Visitors Center	5	C2
Language Exchange	6	D5
Net Zone	7	E4
New York City & Company/Convention and Visitors Bureau	8	D2
New York University Medical Center	9	G4
Stepping Out Studios	10	D5
Times Square Visitors Center	11	D2
Urban Center Books/Municipal Arts Society	12	E2

SIGHTS & ACTIVITIES	pp122–7	
Central Park Bicycle Tours/Rentals	13	C1
Chelsea Hotel	14	D5
Chelsea Piers complex	15	B6
Chrysler Building	16	F3
DIA Art Foundation	17	B5
Empire State Building	18	E4
Flatiron Building	19	E5
GE Building	20	E2
Greek Revival Town Hall	21	D3
International Center of Photography	22	D3
Intrepid Sea-Air-Space Museum	23	A3
Liberty Helicopter Tours	24	A4
Madison Square Garden	25	D4
McGraw Hill Building	26	C3
Metro Bicycle	27	C2
Morgan Library	28	E4
Morgan Stanley Building	29	D2
Museum of Arts & Design	30	E2
Museum of Sex	31	E5
Museum of Television & Radio	32	D2
New York Public Library	33	E3
Radio City Music Hall	34	D2
St Patrick's Cathedral	35	E2
Transportation Alternatives	36	D6

SLEEPING	pp137–44	
Broadway Inn	37	C2
Carlton Arms Hotel	38	E5
Chelsea Center Hostel	39	C5
Chelsea Pines Inn	40	C6
Chelsea Savoy Hotel	41	D5
Chelsea Star Hotel	42	C4
Colonial House Inn	43	C5
Flatotel	44	D2
Gershwin Hotel	45	E5
Gramercy Park Hotel	46	E6
Herald Square Hotel	47	E4
Hotel 17	48	F6
Hudson	49	C1
Inn on 23rd Street	50	D5
Madison Hotel	51	E5
Murray Hill Inn	52	F4
Pickwick Arms Hotel	53	F2
Time	54	D2
Vanderbilt YMCA	55	F2
Waldorf Astoria	56	E2
Wolcott Hotel	57	E4

EATING	pp144–9	
Aquavit	58	E1
Big Cup	59	C6
Carnegie Deli	60	D1
Chelsea Market	61	C6
Cho Dang Goi	62	E4
Craft	63	E6
Empire Diner	64	B5
F&B	65	C5
Film Center Café	66	C3
Food Bar	67	C6
Hangawi	68	E4
La Chinita Linda	69	C6
Lespinasse/St Regis	70	E1
Madras Mahal	71	E5
Markt	72	C6
Mary Ann's	73	C6
Munson Diner	74	B2
Ponsgri Thai	75	D2
Pump	76	D1
Union Square Café	77	E6
Vatan	78	F5
Zen Palate	79	C2

DRINKING	pp149–50	
Half King	80	B5
Hudson Bars	81	C1
Roxy	82	B6
SBNY	83	D6
Serena	(see 14)	
Trailer Park Lounge & Grill	84	C5
Whiskey Blue	85	F2

ENTERTAINMENT	pp150–3	
BB King Blues Club & Grill	86	D3
Carnegie Hall	87	D1
Caroline's on Broadway	88	D2
Centro-Fly	89	D6
City Center	90	D1
Club Shelter	91	D3
Gotham Comedy Club	92	D5
Irving Plaza	93	E6
Joyce Theater	94	C6
Limelight	95	D6
Ticket Central	96	C3
TKTS Booth	97	D2
Upright Citizens Brigade Theatre	98	C5

SHOPPING	pp153–4	
Bergdorf Goodman	99	E1
Chelsea Flea Market	100	D5
Complete Traveller	101	E4
Henri Bendel	102	E1
Loehmann's	103	D6
Macy's	104	D4
Saks Fifth Avenue	105	E2
Tiffany & Co	106	E1

TRANSPORT	pp154–6	
Port Authority Bus Terminal	107	C3

OTHER		
Circle Line	108	A3
Kenny Kramer	109	C3

Garden (Map pp124-6; ☎ 212-465-5800; www.thegarden.com; Seventh Ave, btwn W 31st & W 33rd Sts) is a major sporting and entertainment venue. A block west, the 1913 **New York General Post Office** is an imposing beaux arts building behind a long row of Corinthian columns. A project to move Penn Station into the GP has been ongoing for years.

From 31st St to 36th St, between Broadway and Fifth Ave, Koreatown is a small but interesting and lively neighborhood. Look on 31st and 32nd Sts for a proliferation of Korean restaurants and authentic karaoke spots.

FIFTH AVENUE

Fifth Ave's high-class reputation dates back to the early 20th century, when it was considered desirable for its 'country' air and open spaces. The series of mansions called **Millionaire's Row** extended right up to 130th St. Today, Midtown Fifth Ave is the site of airline offices and a number of high-end shops and hotels, especially from 49th St to 57th St. Big names include **Saks Fifth Ave** (Map pp124-6; Fifth Ave at 50th St), **Henri Bendel** (Map pp124-6; Fifth Ave at 55th St), **Tiffany & Co** (Fifth Ave at 57th St) and **Bergdorf Goodman** (Fifth Ave at 57th St).

Nearby, on 57th St, are several designer boutiques, along with a selection of theme-park, tourist-trap restaurants, including the infamous Hard Rock Cafe, the Harley Davidson Cafe and Jekyll & Hyde's.

UNITED NATIONS

The Rockefeller family donated land worth $8.5 million to the United Nations (UN); the grounds are now officially an international territory. The building, designed by an international committee, has a dated 1950s feel. Sculptures in the UN complex include Henry Moore's *Reclining Figure* and Reutersward's knotted gun *Non-Violence*. The **UN Building** (Map pp124-6; ☎ 212-963-8687; First Ave; tours $7.50; tours 9:15am-4:45pm Mon-Fri in winter) has its visitors entrance at 46th St. English-language tours leave every 30 minutes.

MUSEUM OF MODERN ART

Commonly known as 'MoMA' (*moh*-mah), the museum has its permanent home at W

53rd St, but because of extensive renovations (scheduled for completion in 2005) it's temporarily located at Long Island City, Queens (see p132). Its permanent listing is **Museum of Modern Art** (Map pp124-6; ☎ 212-708-9400; www.moma.org; 11 W 53rd St). Check out the website to see what stage the construction is at.

OTHER MUSEUMS

Across the street from the MoMA, the **Museum of Arts and Design** (Map pp124-6; ☎ 212-956-3535; www.americancraftsmuseum.org; 40 W 53rd St; admission $8; 🕒 10am-6pm Tue-Sun), formerly known as the American Crafts Museum, displays crafts in wood, textiles, metal, ceramics and more, from colonial times to the present.

More than 100,000 US TV and radio programs and advertisements are available at the click of a mouse in the **Museum of Television & Radio** (Map pp124-6; ☎ 212-621-6600; www.mtr.org; 25 W 52nd St; admission $10, theater $6; 🕒 noon-6pm Tue, Wed, Sat & Sun, until 8pm Thu, until 9pm Fri). You search the extensive catalogue on computer, and staff will find and play your selection. A small theater shows some great specials on broadcasting history.

Perhaps New York City's most important photography showplace, the **International Center for Photography** (Map pp124-6; ☎ 212-857-0001; www.icp.org; 1133 Sixth Ave at 43rd St; admission $10; 🕒 10am-5pm Tue-Thu, 10am-8pm Fri, 10am-6pm Sat & Sun) has regularly rotating exhibitions by major photographers – always interesting, sometimes stunning.

Once banker, financier, railroad and steel magnate JP Morgan's mansion, the three-tiered **Morgan Library** (Map pp124-6; ☎ 212-685-0008; www.morganlibrary.org; 29 E 36th St; suggested donation $8; 🕒 10:30am-5pm Tue-Thu, 10:30am-6pm Sat, noon-6pm Sun), off Madison Ave, features JP Morgan's collection of Italian Renaissance artwork, manuscripts, tapestries and books, including three Gutenberg Bibles. The rooms themselves are magnificent.

Most of the exhibits in the **Intrepid Sea-Air-Space Museum** (☎ 212-245-0072; www.intrepidmuseum.org; Pier 86, W 46th St; admission $14; 🕒 10am-5pm Mon-Fri, until 7pm Sat & Sun) are in, or actually on, a behemoth WWII aircraft carrier, and include fighter planes, helicopters, a space capsule and artifacts from the military-industrial complex. The museum also includes a submarine and a destroyer.

Central Park

This enormous rectangular park, right in the middle of Manhattan, is for many what makes New York livable and lovable. On warm weekends it's packed with joggers, skaters, musicians and tourists. Though it's heavily used, and quite safe during the day, New Yorkers avoid walking through the park after dark.

The park's 843 acres were set aside in 1856 on the marshy northern fringe of the city. The landscaping (the first in a US public park), by Frederick Law Olmsted and Calvert Vaux, was innovative in its naturalistic style, with forested groves, meandering paths and informal ponds. The **Ramble**, a lush wooden expanse, is headquarters for a strange confluence of folks: dog owners, bird-watchers and, the most infamous Ramble group, gay men cruising for sex. At the W 72nd St entrance, **Strawberry Fields**, with plants from 100 nations, is dedicated to John Lennon, who lived at (and was murdered in front of) the nearby apartments of the **Dakota building**. Other highlights are the sparkling **Jacqueline Kennedy Onassis Reservoir**, often circled by joggers; the **zoo** (feeding times adult/child $3.50/0.50), particularly the polar bears and feeding times; **Wollman Skating Rink** (☎ 212-439-6900; admission $8.50 Mon-Fri, $11 Sat & Sun, plus skate rental fee $4.75; 🕒 from 10am, closing times vary), for ice skaters in winter and bladers in the warmer months; Shakespeare in the Park performances in the **Delacorte Theater**; and the formal promenade called **the Mall**, which culminates at the elegant **Bethesda Fountain**. The Central Park roadway is regularly closed to traffic and is popular for running, cycling and skating. The most touristy activity is to rent a **horse-drawn carriage** (per half-hr $40, plus a generous tip for the driver) at 59th St (Central Park South). A better option is to rent a bike at **Loeb Boathouse** (☎ 212-517-2233; per hr $10).

The park offers concerts and performances in the summer. For information, visit www.centralpark.org or the **Dairy building visitors centre** (Map pp142-4; ☎ 212-794-6564; Central Park at 65th St; 🕒 11am-4pm Tue-Sat), in the middle of Central Park along the 65th St pathway.

Upper West Side & Morningside Heights

Many celebrities – Jerry Seinfeld, Meg Ryan and Woody Allen among them – live in the massive apartment buildings that line

Central Park West all the way up to 96th St. Along with them, you'll find mommies pushing jogging-designed strollers, ladies who lunch and a diverse mix of stable, upwardly mobile folks.

A complex of performance spaces built in the 1960s, **Lincoln Center** (Map pp142-4; ☎ 212-875-5370; www.lincolncenter.org; Columbus Ave & Broadway) is uninspiring during the day, but its chandeliered interiors, featuring winding staircases and huge Chagalls, look simply beautiful at night. See Entertainment (p150) for information about the various theater, film, opera, music and dance performances. Tours of the complex leave from the concourse level daily and explore at least three of the **theaters** (☎ 212-875-5350; admission $12.50).

The antiquated, hyphenated **New-York Historical Society** (Map pp142-4; ☎ 212-873-3400; www.nyhistory.org; 2 W 77th St; ⏰ 10am-6pm Tue-Sun) is the city's oldest museum, founded in 1804. The original watercolors for John James Audubon's *Birds of America* are displayed in a 2nd-floor gallery. The quirky permanent collection is like New York City's attic – **George Washington's old army cot** (admission $5; ⏰ 11am-5pm Tue-Sun) is in here somewhere.

Meanwhile, you'll find more than 30 million artifacts in the **American Museum of Natural History** (Map pp142-4; ☎ 212-769-5100; www.amnh.org; Central Park West at 79th St; suggested donation adult/child $12/7; ⏰ 10am-5:45pm), but the three dinosaur halls are by far the most popular. Knowledgeable guides are ready to answer questions, and 'please touch' displays will captivate kids.

Part of the Rose Space Center, the recently rebuilt **Hayden Planetarium** (Map pp142-4; ☎ 212-769-5100; www.haydenplanetarium.org; 79th St) is the amazing sphere-in-a-cube structure beside the Museum of Natural History; at night it's illuminated in an eerie blue and looks extraterrestrial. Most of the exhibits at Hayden are included in the normal museum entry, but the shows inside the spherical Space Theater cost $9 extra. Free guided tours run several times daily.

The gated campus of **Columbia University** is on upper Broadway between 114th and 121st Sts, where the Upper West Side morphs into its northern neighbor, Morningside Heights. The spacious central quadrangle is dominated by the 1895 Low Library, one of several neoclassical campus buildings by McKim, Mead & White.

The surrounding neighborhood is filled with inexpensive restaurants, good bookstores, cafés and the dark and massive Episcopal **Cathedral of St John the Divine** (Map pp142-4; ☎ 212-316-7540; 1047 Amsterdam Ave at 112th St; ⏰ 8am-6pm). The church is the largest place of worship in the USA. Though the cornerstone was laid in 1892, the cathedral is nowhere near completed. Still, it's an active place of worship and the site of holiday concerts, lectures and memorial services for famous New Yorkers. The peaceful outdoor cathedral garden features bronze animal sculptures crafted by children. High Mass, held at 11am Sunday, often features sermons by well-known intellectuals.

Nearby, **Riverside Church** (Map pp142-4; ☎ 212-330-1234; www.theriversidechurchny.org; 490 Riverside Dr at 122nd St; ⏰ 7am-10pm), a 1930 Gothic marvel, is famous for its 74 carillon bells, rung every Sunday at noon and 3pm. The church's observation deck affords a superb view of the Hudson River.

Upper East Side — Map pp142–4

Often dismissed by Upper West Siders as the uptight and conservative area across Central Park, the area is actually home to New York's greatest concentration of cultural centers: Fifth Ave above 57th St is called 'Museum Mile.' The area also has many of the city's most exclusive hotels and residential blocks. Look on the side streets from Fifth Ave east to Third Ave between 57th and 86th Sts for elegant brownstones, especially at nightfall, when you can peer into grand libraries and living rooms.

METROPOLITAN MUSEUM OF ART

Commonly called 'The Met,' this vast **museum** (☎ 212-879-5500; www.metmuseum.org; 1000 Fifth Ave at 82nd St; suggested donation $12; ⏰ 9:30am-5:30pm Tue-Thu & Sun, until 9pm Fri & Sat), surrounded by Central Park, is New York's most popular single-site attraction – and deservedly so. It receives about five million annual visitors, and crowds can be impossible, but on a Friday evening in winter the place might be nearly deserted. It always helps to arrive early. The suggested donation includes same-day admission to the Cloisters (see p130). Highlights include Egyptian Art, the American Wing, Arms & Armour, 20th-Century Art, Greek & Roman Art and the Impressionists.

OTHER MUSEUMS

On the east side of Fifth Ave, the **Museum of the City of New York** (☎ 212-534-1672; www.mcny.org; 1220 Fifth Ave at 123rd St; suggested donation adult/child/family $7/4/12; ⏲ 10am-5pm Wed-Sat, from noon Sun) is a northern Museum Mile institution. It traces the city's history from beaver trading to futures trading.

The **Jewish Museum** (☎ 212-423-3200; www.jewishmuseum.org; 1109 Fifth Ave at 92nd St; admission $8, donation 5-8pm Thu; ⏲ 11am-5:45pm Sun-Wed, until 8pm Thu, until 3pm Fri) examines 4000 years of Jewish history, ceremony and art.

Billionaire Andrew Carnegie built a sumptuous 64-room mansion in 1901, off Fifth Ave and far from the downtown bustle, but it was soon surrounded by other homes of the super-rich. Now the **Cooper-Hewitt National Museum of Design** (☎ 212-849-8400; www.ndm.si.edu/; 2 E 91st St; admission $8; ⏲ 10am-5pm Wed-Fri, 10am-6pm Sat, noon-6pm Sun), Carnegie's home is a branch of the Smithsonian Institution and a must for anyone interested in architecture, engineering, jewelry, textiles, and even domestic design.

The opulent 1914 mansion housing the **Frick Collection** (☎ 212-288-0700; www.frick.org; 1 E 70th St; admission $12; ⏲ 10am-6pm Tue-Thu & Sat, 10am-9pm Fri, 1-6pm Sun), off Fifth Ave, was part of the Fifth Ave Millionaires Row in the age of the robber barons, of whom Henry Clay Frick was among the most ruthless. Outstanding European paintings include works by Holbein, Titian, Vermeer, Gainsborough and Constable. A useful little guide explains the significance of the paintings.

One of the few museums that concentrates on American works of art, the **Whitney Museum of American Art** (☎ 212-570-3676; www.whitney.org; 945 Madison Ave at 75th St; admission $12; ⏲ 11am-6pm Tue-Thu, Sat & Sun; 1-9pm Fri) is actually a block east of Fifth Ave. The distinctive concrete and stone building, designed by Marcel Breuer in the late 1950s, has been variously described as 'odd,' 'brutal' and 'extraordinarily ugly.' The collection specializes in 20th-century and contemporary art, with works by Hopper, Pollock, de Kooning, O'Keeffe, Rothko, Johns and others, as well as brilliant temporary shows. The Whitney's important biennial exhibitions serve as a status report on contemporary American art.

The inspired work of Frank Lloyd Wright, the sweeping spiral of the **Solomon R Guggenheim Museum** (☎ 212-423-3500; www.guggenheim.org; 1071 Fifth Ave; admission $15, donation 6-8pm Fri; ⏲ 10am-5:45pm Sat-Wed, until 8pm Fri) is a superb sculpture, in which the excellent collection of 20th-century paintings is almost an afterthought. The museum's permanent collection includes work by Picasso, Pollock, Chagall, Cézanne and (especially) Kandinsky. A controversial 1993 extension allows for more works to be displayed, and for special exhibitions in the spiral.

> **THE AUTHOR'S CHOICE**
>
> **Neue Galerie** (Map pp142-4; ☎ 212-628-6200; www.neuegalerie.org; 1048 Fifth Ave at E 86th St; adult $10; ⏲ 11am-6pm Sat-Mon, until 9pm Fri) New York City is so rife with museums that choosing the ones worth visiting can be an overwhelming experience. For the best small museum, here's our pick: an intimate but well-hung museum housed in a former Rockefeller mansion and dedicated to German and Viennese art c 1900. It has an impressive collection of works by Gustav Klimt and Egon Schiele, plus a grand, romantic street-level café serving Viennese pastries and other treats. Children under 12 years of age are not admitted in the gallery.

Harlem Map pp142–4

Once New York's most famous African-American neighborhood, Harlem is an area in transition. It's still a predominantly black area, but the people you see are as likely to be from the Dominican Republic, Ivory Coast, Senegal – or the East Village. Trendy, bargain-seeking white folks are moving in at growing (and alarming, say many longtime residents) rates, restoring and redeveloping old houses from Central Park to Sugar Hill. One notable arrival is ex-President Bill Clinton, who has an office in the heart of Harlem (but is rarely, if ever, seen hobnobbing around the 'hood). Groups of European and Japanese tourists are a common, and sometimes intrusive, presence. There are still racial tensions and rundown buildings, but the latter are now viewed as development opportunities rather than urban blight, and the areas that most tourists visit are now as safe as any other part of the city.

A slew of new sleek eateries and cocktail lounges reflect this shift. But for a more traditional view of Harlem, visit on Sunday morning, when well-dressed locals flock to small neighborhood churches. On Wednesday the Apollo Theater has its famous amateur night; it's still good, tourists notwithstanding. Weekends are best for visiting Harlem's jazz clubs. Many guided tours and bus trips offer a voyeuristic approach to the area, but it's better (and cheaper) to go by subway or bus and look around for yourself. The A and D trains take you to 125th St, within a block of the Apollo Theater and two blocks of Lenox Ave, while the 2 and 3 trains stop on Lenox Ave at 116th and 125th Sts.

Harlem's major avenues have been renamed in honor of prominent blacks, but some locals still call streets by their original names – Eighth Ave/Central Park West is Frederick Douglas Blvd, Seventh Ave is Adam Clayton Powell Jr Blvd, Lenox Ave is Malcolm X Blvd and 125th St is Martin Luther King Jr Blvd.

APOLLO THEATER

Virtually every major black artist of note in the 1930s and 1940s performed at the landmark **Apollo Theater** (☎ 212-749-5838; www.apollo showtime.com; 253 W 125th St), including Duke Ellington and Charlie Parker. In 1983 the Apollo was revived as a live venue, and it still holds its famous weekly amateur night (tickets $16 to $24, 7:30pm Wednesday), 'where stars are born and legends are made.' On other nights the Apollo hosts performances by established R & B, rock, hip-hop and comedy artists.

STUDIO MUSEUM IN HARLEM

The small **Studio Museum** (☎ 212-864-4500; www .studiomuseumorg; 144 W 125th St; suggested donation $7; 🕑 noon-6pm Wed-Fri & Sun, from 10am Sat) has given exposure to the crafts and culture of African-Americans for 30 years. Look for the photos of James VanDerZee, who chronicled the Harlem Renaissance of the 1920s and 1930s.

SCHOMBURG CENTER FOR RESEARCH IN BLACK CULTURE

The **Schomburg Center for Research in Black Culture** (☎ 212-491-2200; www.nypl.org/research/sc /sc.html; 515 Lenox Ave; admission free; 🕑 noon-6pm Tue-Sat), which is a branch of the New York Public Library, has the nation's largest collection of documents, rare books and photographs on black history and culture. It mounts changing exhibitions on black cultures from around the world and has regular lectures and concerts.

SUNDAY GOSPEL SERVICES

Tour-bus loads of sometimes insensitive visitors pack several Harlem churches on Sunday; the churches do charge the tour company heavily *and* expect donations from the visitors. It's better to go on your own, be respectfully well dressed and leave your camera in the hotel. Unless you're invited by a member of the congregation, stick to the bigger churches like the one mentioned here, which is accustomed to visitors. **Abyssinian Baptist Church** (☎ 212-862-7474; www.abyssinian.org/; 132 W 138th St), with its superb choir and charismatic pastor, Calvin O Butts, welcomes tourists and prays for them. Sunday services start at 9am and 11am – the later one is *very* well attended.

SPANISH HARLEM

Spanish Harlem, which is also called 'El Barrio' (Neighborhood), is a former Italian area that now contains one of the biggest Latino communities, predominantly Puerto Rican, in the city. Just north of 110th St, **La Marqueta** (Park Ave at W 112th St) is a colorful collection of produce stalls. In an unprepossessing old school building, **El Museo del Barrio** (☎ 212-831-7272; www.elmuseo.org; 1230 Fifth Ave at 104th St; admission $6; 🕑 11am-5pm Wed-Sun) began in 1969 as a celebration of Puerto Rican art and culture, and has since expanded to include the folk art of Latin America, the Caribbean and Spain. It also has pre-Columbian artifacts, hand-carved wooden *santos* (saints) and temporary exhibitions of work by local artists.

Washington Heights

The northern end of Manhattan has some surprisingly rural landscapes, especially around Fort Tryon Park and Inwood Hill. Visitors come mainly to see the Cloisters and a few other attractions, which are linked by free shuttle buses on Sunday (call the Cloisters for details).

A branch of the Metropolitan Museum of Art, the **Cloisters** (☎ 212-923-3700; www.met museum.org; Fort Tryon Park at 190th St; admission $12; 🕑 9:30am-4:45pm Tue-Sun Nov-Feb, until 5:15pm Mar-Oct) was constructed in the 1930s using stones and fragments from several French and Spanish medieval monasteries. It looks remarkably authentic, and the courtyards and herb gardens are delightful, especially on warm, sunny days. Inside, the Met's fine collection of medieval frescoes, tapestries and paintings is on display.

The Bronx

This borough includes the rundown South Bronx (the home of hip-hop and rap and the site of a massive low-income housing proect), suburban Riverdale in the west, and Fieldston in the north, with its posh pseudo-Tudor homes.

The **Bronx Tourism Council** (www.ilovethebronx.com) has a visitors guide, and the **Bronx County Historical Society** (☎ 718-881-8900; 3266 Bainbridge Ave) sponsors weekend walking tours.

Don't pass up a pilgrimage to baseball's mecca, **Yankee Stadium** (☎ 718-293-6000; www.yankees.com; 161st St at River Ave), 15 minutes from downtown Manhattan via the 4 and D trains. Fans arrive when the gates open, 90 minutes before game time. **Memorial Park** has plaques dedicated to baseball greats, and shops across the street sell all kinds of memorabilia.

The 250-acre **New York Botanical Gardens** (☎ 718-817-8705; www.nybg.org; Bronx River Parkway at Fordham Rd; admission $3, free 10am-noon Wed-Sat; 🕑 10am-6pm Tue-Sun & Mon holidays Apr-Oct, until 5pm Tue-Sun & Mon holidays Nov-Mar) feature the restored Victorian-era Enid A Haupt Conservatory and glasshouses full of tropical

KEEPIN' IT REAL: NYC'S MOST AUTHENTIC ETHNIC 'HOODS

Sure, Manhattan's Little Italy and Chinatown are fine – if you like mobs of tourists desperately seeking authenticity. But you can truly find it in the outer boroughs, where the latest waves of immigrants have settled and continue to arrive. Below, a guide to going round the world in six neighborhoods:

China

Sunset Park, Brooklyn, instead of Chinatown. Replace mobs of New Jersey tourists buying Hello Kitty wallets with Asian crowds, top-notch eateries (including 24-hour dim-sum spots) and a feeling that you're far, far away. Take the N train to Eighth Ave.

India

Jackson Heights, Queens, instead of E 6th St. Dirt-cheap chicken tikka, sari shops, thali plates and Bollywood theater. Take the 7, E, F, G, R to Roosevelt Ave.

Ireland

Woodlawn in the Bronx, instead of Manhattan's Third Ave Irish bars. Say goodbye to drunken frat boys and hello to correctly poured pints of Guinness, authentic bangers 'n' mash, just-arrived youngsters and, of course, about a dozen great pubs. Take the 4 subway to Woodlawn.

Italy

Belmont in the Bronx, instead of Little Italy. Trade in mediocre restaurants for excellent eateries, samples of fresh mozzarella in the Arthur Avenue Retail Market, to-die-for cannoli and serious Soprano-character dead ringers. Take the B, D or 4 subway to Fordham Rd, then the Bx 12 bus to Hoffman St.

Korea

Flushing, Queens, instead of Koreatown. Goodbye Macy's shoppers, hello kimchi buyers. Take the 7 train to Flushing-Main St.

Russia

Brighton Beach, Brooklyn, instead of Midtown restaurants. No more vodka-tinis, please – just the rudely staffed food markets, bustling nightclubs and the boardwalk that feels like Odessa on the sea. Take the D to Ocean Parkway.

and desert plants. There are 40 acres of original forest and a garden of 2700 roses.

It's officially been renamed the Bronx Wildlife Conservation Park, but almost everyone still calls it the **Bronx Zoo** (☎ 718-367-1010; www.bronxzoo.com; Bronx River Parkway at Fordham Rd; adult/child $11/6; 🕑 10am-5pm Apr-Oct), which is one of the biggest, best and most progressive zoos anywhere. Monorail and aerial tram rides take you through naturalistic settings that are home to some 6000 animals.

Just south of Fordham University, the Belmont section of the Bronx is New York City's most authentic Italian neighborhood and is great for gastronomic exploration, especially along **Arthur Ave** (see p131).

Queens

Queens is the largest (282 sq miles), most ethnically diverse and fastest-growing borough in the city, with over two million people speaking 120 different languages. The **Queens Tourism Council** (☎ 718-286-2667; www.queensbp.org/depts/tourism/tourism.html) has information on attractions, special events and accommodations.

ASTORIA & LONG ISLAND CITY

The largest Greek community in the USA (with amazing restaurants), Astoria also has a smattering of Eastern Europeans. It is still proudly working class, with brick-and-concrete apartment blocks and two-story wooden homes. Long Island City, a waterfront neighborhood with a very industrial feel, is home to many local artists. In very recent years it has become quite the hub of art museums.

MoMA Queens (☎ 212-708-9400; www.moma.org; 33rd St at Queens Blvd; admission $12; 🕑 10am-5pm Mon & Thu-Sun, until 7:45pm Fri) is the home of the venerable Museum of Modern Art, until 2005. It is a New York highlight, with an all-star collection of more than 100,000 paintings, sculptures, design pieces and weird stuff from the early impressionists to the early 2000s. Exhibitions focus on a selected major artist or theme, and the film and photography collection is excellent. Because of its relocation, however, only selected highlights are currently on view.

Movie making started in Astoria in the 1920s, and the **American Museum of the Moving Image** (☎ 718-784-0077; www.ammi.org; 35th & 36th Ave; admission $10; 🕑 noon-5pm Tue-Fri, 11am-6pm Sat & Sun) exposes some of the mysteries of the craft. There are galleries and interactive displays that let you create your own video backdrop or redub dialogue from famous films.

The **PS 1 Contemporary Art Center** (☎ 718-784-2084; www.ps1.org; 22-25 Jackson Ave at 46th Ave; suggested donation $5; 🕑 noon-6pm Thu-Mon), sister museum to MoMA, was founded in 1971 as one of the largest US institutions dedicated solely to contemporary art. Its cutting-edge approach and appearance, wild rotating exhibits, funky outdoor space and hip, clubbish dance events on summer nights has put it at the top of many culture hounds' lists.

Museum for African Art (☎ 718-784-7700; www.africanart.org; 36-01 43rd Ave; admission $5; 🕑 10am-6pm Mon, Thu & Fri, noon-5pm Sat & Sun), an intimate space on the main drag, features African religious works, tribal crafts and traditional musical instruments.

If the weather is pleasant, don't miss the waterside **Socrates Sculpture Park** (☎ 718-956-1819; www.socratesculpturepark.org; Broadway at Vernon Blvd; admission free; 🕑 dusk-dawn), an outdoor museum of massive, always-rotating sculptures by greats including Mark DeSuvero, who founded the space. You can climb on the creations, enjoy straight-on views of Manhattan's east side, and see outdoor film screenings on some summer evenings.

Just a few blocks away is the peaceful **Isamu Noguchi Museum** (☎ 718-204-7088; www.noguchi.org; 36-01 43rd Ave; suggested donation $5; 🕑 10am-5pm Mon, Thu & Fri, 11am-6pm Sat & Sun), a beautiful outdoor garden exhibit of sculptures by this Japanese artist. Because of renovations, however, the museum has been temporarily relocated to an indoor space in nearby **Sunnyside** (46-01 43rd Ave). In between all the sculpture viewing, you can refuel with Greek food by choosing from the various cafés, tavernas and bakeries along Astoria's **Broadway**.

FLUSHING

This now-bustling neighborhood (Main St–Flushing) was a secluded forest that 17th-century Quakers used for secret meetings. It was later used for junkyards and a huge commercial ash heap before being redeveloped for the 1939 World's Fair. With many Asian immigrants, most recently from Korea and China, **Main St** is a bustling, diverse area known mainly for its cheap and delicious gastrointestinal wonders.

Site of Shea Stadium, the National Tennis Center and the new Arthur Ashe Stadium, **Flushing Meadows–Corona Park** was used for the 1939 and 1964 World's Fairs, of which there are quite a few faded leftovers. The park was also the site of the first New York City sessions of the United Nations. The **Queens Museum of Art** (☎ 718-592-9700; www.queensmuse.org; New York City Building; suggested donation $5; 🕑 10am-5pm Tue-Fri, from noon Sat & Sun) contains displays on both fairs and the UN. The *Panorama of New York City* is a detailed and up-to-date model of the metropolis, with 835,000 tiny buildings and a lovely sunset every 15 minutes.

Brooklyn

With 2.3 million people, Brooklyn is the most populous of the outer boroughs, and it would be a significant destination city but for the overwhelming attractions of adjacent Manhattan. The northern portion of the borough, especially the Boerum Hill and Carroll Gardens area, has become the most popular of bedroom communities for the mid-thirties set. A walk across the Brooklyn Bridge is an experience in itself. For information, especially about the special events, contact **Brooklyn Information & Culture** (☎ 718-855-7882; www.brooklynX.org; 647 Fulton St).

BOERUM HILL & CARROLL GARDENS

While just five years ago this area was an unassuming residential spot filled with families, its tree-lined streets are now the latest haven for hipsters. Cheap rents brought the first couple of waves from Manhattan, although now prices have skyrocketed, with a never-ending parade of boutiques, pubs and eateries pushing out every last bodega, deli and dive bar that catered to the Puerto Rican and Italian families, who have populated the area for generations. **Smith St**, the main artery connecting Carroll Gardens (which still maintains some of its old-school Italian charm through fresh-mozzarella shops and red-sauce restaurants) to Boerum Hill, has been dubbed the city's latest 'restaurant row,' and draws fabulous crowds from Manhattan on weekends.

DUMBO

Dumbo's nickname is an anagram for its location: 'Down Under the Manhattan–Brooklyn Bridge Overpass.' This north Brooklyn slice of waterfront used to be strictly for industry, but now the huge loft spaces are occupied by artists and artist wannabes. Its quirky cobblestone streets are traversed by edgy culture seekers heading to the latest gallery show, rave-like party or performance-art piece. A few cafés and shops have even opened very recently, making the after-dark trek from the subway on the still-desolate sidewalks seem a little less scary than before.

BROOKLYN HEIGHTS

When Robert Fulton's steam ferries started regular service across the East River in the early 19th century, well-to-do Manhattanites began building comfortable houses at Brooklyn Heights. Don't miss the 1848 beaux arts **Brooklyn Borough Hall**.

Two blocks south, the **New York Transit Museum** (☎ 718-694-5100; www.mta.info; Boerum Pl & Schermerhorn Row) has an amazing collection of original subway cars and transit memorabilia dating back 100 years. It's currently closed for renovations, but scheduled to reopen by late 2003, with new hours to be determined.

Montague St is the main avenue for cafés and bars; follow it down to the waterfront until you hit the **promenade**, offering stunning sunset views of Lower Manhattan.

PROSPECT PARK & PARK SLOPE

Created in 1866, 526-acre **Prospect Park** (☎ 718-965-8999) is considered the greatest achievement of landscape designers, Olmsted and Vaux, who also designed Central Park. Attractions include ice skating, boating, strolling, a small zoo, the Children's Museum and the immense art deco Brooklyn Public Library. The excellent 52-acre **Brooklyn Botanic Garden** (☎ 718-622-4433; www.bbg.org; 1000 Washington Ave; admission $3, free Tue; 🕑 8am-6pm Tue-Fri, from 10am Sat & Sun) is on the eastern side of Prospect Park.

Beside the Botanic Gardens, the **Brooklyn Museum of Art** (☎ 718-638-5000; www.brooklynart.org; 200 Eastern Parkway; admission $6; 🕑 10am-5pm Wed-Fri, 11am-6pm Sat & Sun) has some comprehensive collections of African, Islamic and Asian art, Egyptian mummy casings and classical antiquities, plus popular temporary shows. The first Saturday of each month brings extended hours (11am to 11pm), free admission and special events including films and performances.

Immediately west of Prospect Park, the **Park Slope** neighborhood has some classic brownstones and a literary atmosphere. Bookstores, cafés and restaurants are interspersed along nearly 20 blocks of Fifth Ave and Seventh Ave, which is always bustling with its Slope-style mixture of Manhattan transplants: bookish, hand-holding lesbians and mommies pushing strollers.

CONEY ISLAND

Now just a ghostly shadow of its former summer-playground self, the home of the old Dreamworld amusement park retains a certain skanky fascination. You emerge from the colorfully decrepit Coney Island subway station (check out the all-night diner inside) onto Surf Ave, with flea-market stalls and Nathan's historic hot-dog stand. Along the **boardwalk**, the bright-red 1930s 'parachute jump' is now defunct, but the famous 1927 Cyclone roller coaster, in **Astroland Amusement Park** (☎ 718-265-2100), still offers a five-dollar thrill from mid-June to Labor Day. Plus, come summertime, public fireworks light up the sky every Friday night, and frequent concerts bring a diverse crowd to the beach on weekend evenings.

Further along the boardwalk, the **New York Aquarium** (☎ 718-265-3474; www.nyaquarium.com; W 8th St at Surf Ave; adult/child $9/5; 🕑 10am-5pm) has a touch pool, dolphin shows and 10,000 specimens of sea life. A five-minute walk north of the beach, Brighton Beach Ave in **Brighton Beach** ('Little Odessa') is lined with Russian shops, bakeries and restaurants.

WILLIAMSBURG

Just cross the Williamsburg Bridge, east of Manhattan, and you'll land in the middle of an Orthodox Jewish community. But the northern part of Williamsburg has long been augmented by artists and writers seeking low rent and a cool scene. The result is hyper-hipster: cafés, restaurants and an arty (read: slouchy, chain-smoking 20-somethings with perfectly messed-up hair) ambience prevail on and around **Bedford Ave**. Get a great sunset view of Manhattan from Kent Ave along the undeveloped waterfront and be sure to visit the excellent **Brooklyn Brewery** (☎ 718-486-7422; www.brooklynbrewery.com; 79 N 11th St; admission free; tours noon-5pm Sat), which hosts tours, special events and the Friday night Tasting Room, a community pub night – from 6pm to 10pm.

Staten Island

The 'forgotten borough' was mostly farmland until the 1960s, when the Verrazano Narrows Bridge provided a land link with the rest of the city. The population grew by 15% in the 1990s, to around 450,000. The Staten Island **Chamber of Commerce** (☎ 718-727-1900; www.sichamber.com; 130 Bay St) has information about events and attractions. Today, while the borough is still the butt of many a joke for being decidedly suburban and relatively unhip, it's home to an impressive array of cultural attractions, ethnic enclaves and close to 4000 acres of waterfront parkland.

The free **Staten Island Ferry** (☎ 718-727-2508; www.dot.com) provides a wonderful 6-mile ride, passing close to the Statue of Liberty and offering breathtaking views of Manhattan and Brooklyn Heights. Just next door to the ferry terminal is the newly completed **Richmond County Bank Ballpark** (718-720-9200; www.siyanks.com; Richmond Tce), home to the minor-league Staten Island Yankees.

Originally a home for retired sailors, the **Snug Harbor Cultural Center** (☎ 718-448-2500; www.snug-harbor.org; 1000 Richmond Tce) has some fine Greek Revival structures, and you can explore the Botanical Garden, Children's Museum and the Newhouse Center for Contemporary Art. And make sure you don't miss the beautifully preserved **Alice Austen House Museum** (☎ 718-816-4506; www.aliceausten.8m.com/museum/; 2 Hylan Blvd; suggested donation $2; 🕑 noon-5pm Thu-Sun Mar-Dec), home of the famed photographer who lived here with her lesbian lover back in the Victorian era.

In the middle of Staten Island, the 2500-acre **Greenbelt** (☎ 718-667-2165) environmental preserve is one of New York City's natural treasures, with miles of walking trails and 60 bird species.

Activities

The **Chelsea Piers Complex** (Map pp124-6; ☎ 212-336-6666; Hudson River at 23rd St) has a four-level driving range, indoor ice-skating rink, running track, swimming pool, workout center, rock-climbing wall and even sand **volleyball courts** (day pass $40; 🕑 6am-11pm Mon-Fri, 8am-8pm Sat & Sun). Gyms around the city, which are plentiful, charge at least $20 for day use. YMCAs are about $25, while many fancy gyms require subscriptions.

Central Park's 6-mile roadway is closed to cars from 10am to 3pm weekdays and all weekend, which is perfect for **running**. Also in Central Park, the Jacqueline Kennedy Onassis Reservoir is encircled by a soft 1.5-mile path. Another runner's pathway goes along the Hudson River from Battery Park City up to Washington Heights, with just a few construction detours along the way. **New York Road Runner's Club** (Map pp142-4; ☎ 212-860-4455; www.nyrrc.org; 9 E 89th St) organizes weekend runs and the October New York Marathon.

Bicycling on the streets can be a high-risk activity in Manhattan, but Central Park has lovely cycling paths. Also try the straightaway path that runs alongside the western edge of Manhattan (shared by runners); the auto-free road that runs round the perimeter of Brooklyn's Prospect Park; and the Franklin D Roosevelt Boardwalk in Staten Island, hugging 4 miles of unspoiled beaches.

For cycling tips and weekend trips, contact **Five Borough Bicycle Club** (Map pp142-4; ☎ 212-932-2300, ext 115; 891 Amsterdam Ave at 104th St). **Transportation Alternatives** (☎ 212-629-8080; www.transalt.org; 115 W 30th St), a nonprofit bicycle lobbying group, is also a good source of information. Gay cycling enthusiasts should check the website of **Fast & Fabulous** (www.fastnfab.org), a gay bicycling club that organizes long weekend rides. For bike rentals, **Metro Bicycle** (Map pp124-6; ☎ 212-581-4500; W 47th St at Ninth Ave) has several locations, or you can try **Central Park Bicycle Tours/Rentals** (Map pp124-6; ☎ 212-541-8759; 2 Columbus Circle), at Broadway and 59th St.

In-line skating is also popular in Central Park and on the path along the west side of Manhattan. For rentals, try **Blades West** (Map pp142-4; ☎ 212-787-3911; 120 W 72nd St), two blocks from Central Park.

Walking Tour

New York City has been used in countless films over the decades. While most classic scenes have been shot at uptown locations, like the famed Dakota building on Central Park West *(Rosemary's Baby)* and the Museum of Natural History *(Annie Hall)*, there have been plenty of films, especially in recent years, shot all over downtown. This walk takes you to some of the cool movie locations that lie in the East Village area. Even if you're not familiar with the flicks or the scenes, the journey from one

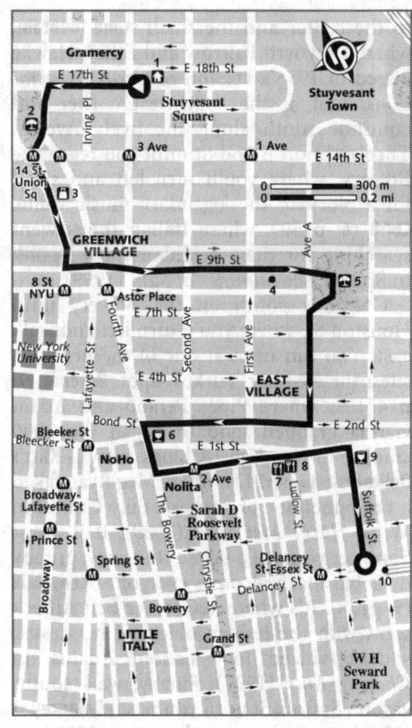

to the next adds up to a lively, fun walk through one of Manhattan's most colorful neighborhoods.

Start at **Hotel 17** (**1**; p139), the way-cool dive hotel that Woody Allen used as his location for *Manhattan Murder Mystery* (1993). Then head southwest to **Union Sq Park** (**2**), site of a dramatic helicopter landing in the 1997 film *Conspiracy Theory*, which starred Mel Gibson and Julia Roberts. Exit at the south of the park and continue onto Broadway. Stroll south till you arrive at the **Strand Bookstore** (**3**; 828 Broadway), a favorite used-book haunt, which made a notable appearance in *Six Degrees of Separation* (1993), starring Stockard Channing.

Continue south on Broadway and turn left on E 9th St. Walk until you reach the block between First Ave and Ave A. Take note of **building No 422** (**4**), the stoop where a very young Leonardo Di Caprio teased a junkie prostitute (Juliette Lewis) in the *Basketball Diaries* (1995). At the corner is the bustling **Tompkins Sq Park** (**5**; p121); head to the center and the small **stone fountain**, where Gwyneth Paltrow and Ethan Hawke kissed in 1998's version of *Great Expectations*. Exit at the southwest corner and continue south along the lively Ave A. Turn right on E 2nd St until you reach the Bowery, where you'll turn left and stroll for a block to the legendary music venue **CBGB** (**6**; p152), where Italian thugs went searching for their neighbor-turned-punk in Spike Lee's *Summer of Sam* (1999).

Continue south on the Bowery until Houston St, where you'll turn left and walk east. You can nosh at one of the next two sites: the 24-hour Turkish spot, **Bereket** (**7**; p147), is where Piper Perabo and Adam Garcia grabbed food to go in the 2000 clunker *Coyote Ugly*. A block away is **Katz's Delicatessen** (**8**; p147), where Meg Ryan faked a rambunctious orgasm for Billy Crystal in *When Harry Met Sally* (1989). If it's past 5pm, get yourself a beer at the cozy, grubby dyke bar that welcomes everyone, **Meow Mix** (**9**; p138). It's where newcomer Ben Affleck went with the lesbian object of his desire, squeaky-voiced Joey Lauren Adams, in *Chasing Amy* (1997). Finally, walk southeast on Suffolk St until you reach **Delancey St** (**10**), the strip that gave the syrupy 1988 love story *Crossing Delancey* its name. The flick, starring Amy Irving, featured several beautiful shots of the **Williamsburg Bridge**, which crosses into Brooklyn. You'll be practically at the foot of the span here, where you'll enjoy your own great glimpse of it.

Courses

It's hard to walk more than five blocks without stumbling over a yoga studio these days, but popular downtown is a good place to start. Cooking classes are listed on p98. For yoga and other courses, check out the following:

Jivamukti Yoga Center (Map pp114-16; ☎ 212-353-0214; www.jivamuktiyoga.com; 404 Lafayette St; per class $17) Free introductory classes held the last Sunday of the month at 11:45am, second Saturday of the month at 1:30pm.

Language Exchange (Map pp124-6; ☎ 212-563-7580; www.language-exchange.com; 135 W 29th St btwn Sixth & Seventh Aves; average class $250) Get a quick, intensive lesson in conversational English – or Russian, Italian, Spanish or anything else.

Scratch Academy (Map pp114-16; ☎ 212-625-3881; www.scratch.com; 600 Broadway at Houston St; six beginner classes $300) Learn the foundations of DJ-ing at the unique Scratch Academy, co-founded by the late Jam Master Jay of Run-DMC and equipped with 15 turntables.

SteppingOut Studios (Map pp124-6; ☎ 646-742-9400; www.steppingoutstudios.com; 37 W 26th St at Sixth Ave) Holds frequent free open-house classes and dance parties in swing, salsa and ballroom, plus special events and classes – Outdancing – for same-sex partners.

New York for Children

The old and marvelous standby for kids, with its huge dinosaur skeleton, planetarium and big, blue whale is the **American Museum of Natural History** (p128). The city's various zoos, from the **Bronx Zoo** (p132) to the **Central Park zoo** (p127), are always big hits. For special events, from concerts to puppet shows, be sure to check the Kids section of the weekly magazine *Time Out New York*.

However, a few places are specifically for children (and their parents, of course!):

Books of Wonder (Map pp124-6; ☎ 212-989-3270; www.booksofwonder.net; 16 W 18th St btwn Fifth & Sixth Aves; 🕒 11am-7pm Mon-Sat) The city's largest and oldest children's bookstore, it often has readings by authors popular with the 12-and-under set.

Brooklyn Children's Museum (☎ 718-735-4400; www.bchildmus.org/; 145 Brooklyn Ave; admission $4; 🕒 2-5pm Wed-Fri, from 10am Sat & Sun) For children five and over, the museum has exhibits on sleep and dreams, tools and nutrition.

Children's Museum of Manhattan (Map pp142-4; ☎ 212-721-1234; www.cmom.org/; 212 W 83rd St; admission $6; 🕒 1:30-5:30pm Mon, Wed &Thu, 10am-5pm Fri-Sun) Features hands-on exhibits, discovery centers for toddlers, a 'Brainatarium' and a postmodern Media Center for older children.

Manhattan Children's Theatre (Map pp114-16; ☎ 212-352-3101; www.manhattanchildrenstheatre.org; 380 Broadway at White St) Presents musicals and dramas just for the little ones.

Quirky New York

Chinatown Tunnel (Map pp114-16; 8-9 The Bowery btwn Mott & Doyer Sts) Head through the unmarked door and down the staircase. While the tunnel houses a cheesy mall today, it's rumored to have been a stop on the Underground Railroad in the early 1800s, and later was a secret escape route for members of warring Chinatown gangs.

Earth Room (Map pp114-16; 141 Wooster St; 🕒 noon-6pm Wed-Sat) This roomful of dirt in Soho is just what it says it is – a gallery space filled with dug-up earth. It's probably the sweetest-smelling spot in the city – oh, and it's art!

Maxilla & Mandible (☎ 212-724-6173; www.maxillaandmandible.com; 451-455 Columbus Ave at 81st St) The glass cases in this small, odd store are filled with gory

delights: bones from every imaginable animal (human included), preserved insects and some taxidermy specials.
TV tapings (www.gonyc.about.com/cs/tvtapings/ for information about various shows) From the *View* and the *Late Show With David Letterman* to the *Ricki Lake Show* and *Saturday Night Live*, being a part of a studio audience is a downright bizarre way to spend your time.

Tours

Though bus tours may offer a quick introduction to the city, many have non-native guides who aren't well informed. This is especially true of some foreign-language tours.

Gray Line (☎ 212-397-2620; www.graylinenewyork.com; tours $26-60) This is a reliable foreign-language option, which runs nearly 30 different tours from its main terminal at the **Port Authority Bus Terminal** (Map pp124-6; www.portauthorityny.com; 625 Eighth Ave) and from its **visitors center** (Map pp124-6; 777 Eighth Ave at 48th St), including a hop-on, hop-off loop of Manhattan. Short loop tours cost from $26, while the comprehensive 'Essential New York' tour for adult/child costs $60/44.

Many companies and organizations conduct urban treks:
Big Apple Greeters Program (☎ 212-669-8198; www.bigapplegreeters.org; tours free) Volunteer-led tours of lesser-known neighborhoods. Some greeters are multilingual and specialize in helping the disabled (book at least two days ahead).
Big Onion Walking Tours (☎ 212-439-1090; www.bigonion.com; adult $12) Popular and quirky guided tours specializing in ethnic New York operating year-round.
Municipal Art Society (☎ 212-935-3960; www.mas.org; 457 Madison Ave; adult $10) Various scheduled tours focusing on architecture and history.

Other quite specialized tours include the following:
Beast (☎ 212-563-3200; www.ridethebeast.com; adult $16) For a 30-minute rush, the Beast will take you round the Statue of Liberty at 45mph. For a free, but slower, ride take the Staten Island Ferry (see p117). Departs from Piers 83 and 16.
Circle Line (Map pp124-6; ☎ 212-563-3200; departs Pier 83 at W 42nd St; adult $24; Mar-Dec) Three-hour, 35-mile boat cruise around Manhattan on the Hudson River. A popular and informative tour, especially attractive when the weather is good, though it's still OK if it's not – boats are covered and heated. Shorter tours are offered, but go the whole way if you can.
Kenny Kramer (☎ 212-268-5525, 800-572-6377; www.kennykramer.com; 358 W 44th St; adult $38; noon Sat & Sun) The real-life inspiration for the *Seinfeld* character, Kenny Kramer offers fun three-hour tours past major sites from the TV series. Reservations required.
Liberty Helicopter Tours (Map pp124-6; ☎ 212-967-6464; www.libertyhelicopters.com; 12th Ave at W 30th St; adult from $56; 9am-7pm) A bird's-eye view of the city, whisking you high above the skyscrapers – for a price. Five- to seven-minute tours cost $56 per person, 30-minute flights go for $275, while private, 15-minute 'Romance Over Manhattan' rides are a whopping $849 per couple.

Festivals & Events

Some 50 officially recognized annual parades honor various causes or ethnic groups. There are also several hundred annual street fairs, mostly in summer. Fifth Ave shuts down for the major parades. Here's just a sample:
Carnaval Memorial Day weekend (last Monday in May); a celebration of Hispanic culture.
Chinese New Year (☎ 212-619-4785) Fireworks and parades in and around Chinatown. Held the end of January or beginning of February.
Comedy Festival (☎ 888-338-6968) In early June comedians perform on stage at Carnegie Hall, and at a host of clubs.
Fleet Week (☎ 212-245-2533) Annual convocation of sailors, naval ships and air rescue teams. Late May.
Harlem Week Celebration of Harlem's history and culture held through most of August.
Jazz Festival (☎ 212-501-1390) All the concert halls in town are jumping with the top names in jazz. Mid- to late June.
Lesbian & Gay Pride Week Last weekend in June.
Macy's Thanksgiving Day Parade Huge balloons and floats paraded down Broadway. Held the fourth Thursday in November.
Mermaid Parade On the last weekend in June mermaid-wearing marchers parade along the Coney Island boardwalk.
New Year's Eve On December 31 there are festivities in Times Square and a 5-mile midnight run through Central Park.
New York Film Festival Major event at the Lincoln Center held late September.
New York Marathon Road-race through all five boroughs. Held the first weekend in November.
Rockefeller Center Christmas Tree Lighting Marks the start of the Christmas season. Held the Tuesday after Thanksgiving.
Tribeca Festival (☎ 866-941-3378; www.tribecafilmfestival.com) One week in May.
US Open Tennis Tournament Grand Slam event in Flushing Meadows. Held September.

Sleeping

It's an urban myth that it's nearly impossible to find a good, affordable place to stay in NYC. As long as you book in advance – and are flexible when it comes to details like location and decor – there's no reason why you can't enjoy a comfortable stay and still have enough money left over to reap the cultural benefits of the city.

If you arrive without a reservation, and have a limited budget, stay the first night in a pricier hotel (or hostel), then phone around for somewhere cheaper (or more comfortable). Note that prices are flexible; it's usually more expensive on Friday and Saturday nights, and during spring and fall. Tax is 13.25% plus $2 per night, in addition to the prices quoted here.

Several companies handle B&B reservations, some offering spots in 'outlaw' B&Bs

GAY & LESBIAN NEW YORK

Sometimes it feels like *everyone* in New York is gay – ask any straight girl looking for a husband. Downtown, same-sex, hand-holding couples are a dime a dozen, and in recent years it's even become a common sight on the Upper West Side and other more family-oriented 'hoods. Basically it's because New Yorkers just don't seem to give a damn. Nevertheless, there are plenty of spots, from bars and clubs to eateries and bookstores, reserved just for dykes and fairies.

For all things gay – from 12-step groups and lecture series to gay bingo parties and transgender movie nights – head to the **LGBT Community Center** (p112), housed in a stylish, light-filled, recently renovated building in the Village. For gay literature, head to **Creative Visions** (Map pp114-16; 548 Hudson St), **Oscar Wilde Bookstore** (p111) or **Bluestockings Bookstore** (p111) for women. Shopping at the queer-leaning **Toys in Babeland** (Map pp114-16; ☎ 212-375-1701; www.babeland.com; 94 Rivington St) is an erotic adventure, with every dildo, vibrator and cock ring displayed in ways that let you test out the merchandise before buying. The place also hosts occasional sex workshops.

The homo-filled Chelsea neighborhood has two excellent gay inns: **Chelsea Pines Inn** (p141) and **Colonial House Inn** (p141). The huge **LGBT Pride Weekend**, held during the last weekend in June, features countless parties and the main Pride March along Fifth Ave. While that parade has gotten a bit mainstream (recent years have seen floats sponsored by corporations including beer companies and banks), an edgier, passion-filled alternative is the fabulous Dyke March on Saturday at 5pm.

As far as drinking and dancing spots go, New York has about 75 gay and lesbian bars and clubs, with countless other queer nights held at otherwise straight venues.

For complete listings, pick up a copy of *HX* and *Next* magazines at any gay establishment. Here's a sample. The East Village, with one of the highest concentrations of gay spots by neighborhood, has **Meow Mix** (Map pp114-16; ☎ 212-254-0688; 269 E Houston St; admission $5-12) for chicks, attracting mostly cute, messy, short-haired girls in their twenties; Thursday night's Gloss, for femmes and the butches who love them, is very popular. **Boiler Room** (Map pp114-16; ☎ 212-254-7536; 86 E 4th St) is a low-key, standard stop on the East Village circuit, as are **Phoenix Bar** (Map pp114-16; ☎ 212-477-9979; 447 E 13th St), **Urge Lounge** (Map pp114-16; ☎ 212-533-5757; 33 Second Ave), **Wonder Bar** (Map pp114-16; 505 E 6th St) and **Starlight** (Map pp114-16; ☎ 212-475-2172; 167 Ave A), which hosts the city's slickest lesbian night, Starlette, on Sunday. Chelsea's Chelsea boys have the pick of the city's litter, with the glossy **XI** (Map pp114-16; ☎ 212-995-1400; 357 W 16th St) and **G** (☎ 212-929-1085; 225 W 19th St) lounges, and the hugely popular **SBNY** (Map pp114-16; ☎ 212-691-0073; 50 W 17th St; admission $5-20) and **Roxy** (Map pp124-6; ☎ 212-645-5156; 515 W 18th St; admission $10-20) dance clubs. In the West Village, the bars are too numerous to mention, but all types of women should visit **Henrietta Hudson** (Map pp114-16; ☎ 212-924-3347; 438 Hudson St) or **Rubyfruit's Bar & Grill** (Map pp114-16; ☎ 212-924-3343; 531 Hudson St), also a restaurant; the old-school boys have the cabaret bars **Duplex** (Map pp114-16; ☎ 212-255-5438; 61 Christopher St) and **Marie's Crisis** (Map pp114-16; ☎ 212-243-5438; 59 Grove St), and an African-American crowd hangs at **Chi Chiz** (Map pp114-16; ☎ 212-462-0027; 135 Christopher St).

Brooklyn's got its own thriving scene, with the monthly **Steam at Bar Below** (☎ 718-694-2277; 209 Smith St) in Boerum Hill. Park Slope's cute-boy venue is **Excelsior** (☎ 718-832-1599; 390 Fifth Ave), which sits right across the street from the softball-dyke girl spot, **Ginger's Bar** (☎ 718-788-0924; 363 Fifth Ave). In Williamsburg, check out the super-hip **Luxx** (☎ 718-599-1000; 256 Grand St; admission $10) on Saturday. Meanwhile, **Spectrum** (☎ 718-238-8213; 802 64th St; admission $10-15), amusingly cheesy and way out in Bay Ridge, is the nightclub used in the classic '70s film *Saturday Night Fever* – original light-up dance floor and all!

not registered with the city. B&Bs are not a cheap alternative in NYC, as rooms cost about the same as mid-range hotels ($100 to $200), with a two-night minimum stay in summer. As B&Bs are small, with flexible prices and opening dates, it's best to book through an agency, which should give a detailed description of the accommodations, the neighborhood and the level of contact with the host.

Bed & Breakfast Network of New York (Map pp114-16; ☎ 212-645-8134, 800-900-8134) An accommodations agency with a good selection of sleeping options in Greenwich Village.

For stays of a week or more, an apartment rental or sublet can be the best option (there's no tax on rentals, so you're already 13.25% ahead). Agencies include the following:

Gamut Realty (☎ 212-879-4229; www.gamutnyc.com)
Hospitality Company (☎ 212-965-1102)

Note that even when parking is provided by hotels, it's never free; usually, the hotel is affiliated with a nearby parking lot and can offer a discount (around $25 per 24 hours).

Recent antismoking laws passed in the city mean that all hotels, inns and hostels are nonsmoking.

Sleeping – Budget

Most hostels require guests to have a passport, hostel card, international air ticket or other proof that they're genuine travelers. Some places limit the length of stay to a couple of weeks. The better hostels have a laundry service, Internet access, kitchen facilities and sociable common room.

Some of the basic budget hotels listed resemble backpacker hostels, but with private rooms (sometimes with shared bath) and a few dorm beds, if any. A double under $100 is a budget room in Manhattan.

LOWER MANHATTAN, MIDTOWN & CHELSEA

Murray Hill Inn (Map pp124-6; ☎ 212-683-6900; 888-996-6376; www.murrayhillinn.com; 143 E 30th St; s/d $75/$125; ❄) Sitting peacefully on a tree-lined street, Murray Hill Inn offers rooms that are small but tidy.

Madison Hotel (Map pp124-6; ☎ 212-532-7373; www.madison-hotel.com; 21 E 27th St; s $60-99, d $88-145; ❄) Within walking distance to the East Village, and just a couple blocks away from peaceful Madison Park, this spot has clean, basic rooms (even if they are a bit drab) and a slightly crazed staff.

Gershwin Hotel (Map pp124-6; ☎ 212-545-8000; www.gershwinhotel.com; 3 E 27th St; dm $40, s/d $100/200) Long-running and popular, the Gershwin features a funky lobby and eclectic, international clientele.

Vanderbilt YMCA (Map pp124-6; ☎ 212-756-9600; www.ymcanyc.org; 224 E 47th St; s/d $64/84; 🏊) This Midtown flop offers tiny but adequate rooms as well as an inexpensive restaurant. Guests can use the gym and pool free of charge.

Carlton Arms Hotel (Map pp124-6; ☎ 212-684-8337; www.carltonarms.com; 160 E 25th St; s $70-85, d $90-100; ❄) Definitely one of the quirkiest spots in town. Each room is a floor-to-ceiling walk-in artwork, based on themes from English cottage to rhinos (you'll have to see for yourself).

Chelsea Star Hotel (Map pp124-6; ☎ 212-244-7827; www.starhotelny.com; 300 W 30th St; dm/s/d $35/59/79, ste $129-175; ❄ 💻) Best known for its history as one of Madonna's first homes, the Star has small, clean rooms dedicated to various TV shows and theater productions.

Bowery's Whitehouse Hotel of New York (Map pp114-16; ☎ 212-477-5623; www.whitehousehotelofny.com; 140 The Bowery; s/d/tr $27/53/70; ⊠ 💻) A popular East Village choice for its clean and spartan rooms, funky café-like lobby hung with authentic subway signs, and the 40-odd old-timer residents who will tell you a tall tale or two about how things used to be. It's safe, too, as the hard-nosed front-desk guy doesn't miss a beat.

THE AUTHOR'S CHOICE

Hotel 17 (Map pp124-6; ☎ 212-475-2845; www.hotel17.citysearch.com; 225 E 17th St; s/d $75/90; P ❄ 💻) While bargain hotels and charming hotels are not hard to find in NYC, an inn that features both can be a bit of a challenge. That's why Hotel 17 is such a fabulous find. Quirky enough to be used as the set for Woody Allen's *Manhattan Murder Mystery*, it has plenty of old-fashioned grace, highlighted by some cool chandeliers in the lobby. The clean rooms come with firm beds, pleasant wood accents and desks, and you're in walking distance to some of the city's trendiest cafés and restaurants. Where are we, Europe?

Chelsea Center Hostel (Map pp124-6; ☎ 212-643-0214; www.chelseacenterhostel.com; 313 W 29th St; dm $25-30; 🖳 ☒) The 22 beds and convivial atmosphere make the Chelsea Center feel like college housing.

International Student Hospice (Map pp124-6; ☎ 212-228-7470; 154 E 33rd St; dm $25) More like a private boarding house than a hostel, the small and funky International fits 15 bunks (30 beds) among its stacks of old books and dusty decor. Only students aged under 30 are allowed to stay.

UPPER MANHATTAN & HARLEM Map pp142–4

Several places on the Upper West Side are close to the subway and Central Park.

West Side YMCA (☎ 212-875-4100; www.ymcany.org; 5 W 63rd St; s/d $85/95; ❄ 🖳) Right near Lincoln Center, this has the usual YMCA facilities, and small, quiet rooms.

Harlem Flophouse (☎ 212-662-0678; www.harlemflophouse.com; 242 W 123rd St; s/d $65/90; ❄) Housed in a beautiful brownstone, it has tin ceilings and antique furnishings.

Jazz on the Park (☎ 212-932-1600; www.jazzhostel.com; 36 W 106th St; dm/d $30/80; ❄ 🖳) This slick place has tiny rooms (use the lockers), a 2nd-floor terrace and occasional live jazz.

HI New York (☎ 212-932-2300; www.hinewyork.org; 891 Amsterdam Ave; dm $29-32; ❄ 🖳) This behemoth – the biggest hostel in the world – fills its 624 beds quickly during summer. It's open for check-in 24 hours a day, has a cafeteria, laundry, Internet access, tours, guest speakers, a sprawling outdoor patio and a busy, sociable atmosphere despite its large size.

Central Park Hostel (☎ 212-678-0491; www.centralparkhostel.com; 19 W 103rd St; dm $25; ❄ 🖳). Renovated, well run and right near Central Park.

Sugar Hill International House (☎ 212-926-7030; www.sugarhillhostel.com; 722 St Nicholas Ave; dm $20; 🖳) Featuring a friendly, in-house dog, Sugar Hill is a basic, well-run place.

Sleeping – Mid-Range

Mid-range hotels in New York will cost you between $100 and $200. Hotel discounters or consolidators can be helpful when seeking places in these ranges. Check out:

Hotel Reservations Network (☎ 800-964-6835; www.180096hotel.com) Covers many inexpensive Manhattan hotels. You must pay in advance, though the room can be canceled upon 24-hour notice.

Accommodations Express (☎ 800-444-7666; www.hotels.com) Offers smaller discounts (around 15%), but deals with a larger number of rooms in every price category.

Quikbook (☎ 800-789-9887; www.quikbook.com) Discounts moderate Midtown hotels, including many that are listed in this guide.

LOWER MANHATTAN Map pp114–16

Hotels below Houston St cater to businesspeople, so most offer good deals at weekends. However, the neighborhood is dead once the office workers go home – even the restaurants are closed.

Off Soho Suites Hotel (☎ 212-979-9808, 800-633-7646; www.offsoho.com; 11 Rivington St; ste $119-209; ❄ 🖳) On the lively Lower East Side, Off Soho offers a variety of clean and bright 'efficiency units,' with wood-beam floors.

Howard Johnson's Express Inn (☎ 212-358-8844; www.hojo.com; 135 E Houston St; s/d $109/169; ❄) An excellent new option, even if you're usually averse to chains, as it has spankin' clean rooms, complimentary morning muffins and the Landmark Sunshine Cinemas and legendary Yonah Schimmel's Knishes right next door.

St Marks Hotel (☎ 212-674-2192; stmarkshotel@aol.com; 2 St Marks Place; s/d $80/100; ❄) Though the block is a bit noisy, St Marks has a great East Village location. Ignore the beat-up stairwell that takes you up to the lobby – rooms are clean and have character, with teeny sinks, black-and-white-checked bathroom floors, mounted TVs and wide, full-length mirrors.

Washington Square Hotel (☎ 212-777-9515; www.washingtonsquarehotel.com; 103 Waverly Pl; s/d $130/150; ❄) Practically on NYU's campus, Washington Square Hotel is well regarded for its elegant lobby, great location and a variety of cozy rooms; book well ahead.

Larchmont Hotel (☎ 212-989-9333; www.larchmonthotel.com; 27 W 11th St; s $70-95, d $90-115; ❄) Another good choice, on a quiet block just off Fifth Ave. The clean rooms, housed in renovated beaux arts buildings, feel like private apartments.

MIDTOWN & CHELSEA Map pp142–4

Wolcott Hotel (☎ 212-268-2900; www.wolcott.com; 4 W 31st St; s/d $100/120; ❄) This good bargain is a 280-room beaux arts building with a classy, gilded lobby and nice but small quarters.

Herald Square Hotel (☎ 212-279-4017, 800-727-1888; www.heraldsquarehotel.com; 19 W 31st St; r $60-120; ❄) The no-frills Herald Square is recommended for its choice of rooms and reasonable rates. Its hallways are lined with framed illustrations from *Life* magazine, as the building used to be home base for the publication.

Pickwick Arms Hotel (☎ 212-355-0300; www.pickwickarms.com; 250 E 51st St; s $79-109, d $129-150; P ✱ 💻) This 400-room inn offers a variety of spotless rooms at reasonable prices. Plus, the place features two restaurants and a rooftop garden.

Broadway Inn (☎ 212-997-9200; www.broadwayinn.com; 264 W 46th St; s/d $100/130; P ✱) Though it looks like a motor inn that you'd find off a highway in Des Moines and the rooms are still a bit stuck in the '70s, it's clean, friendly and well located.

Chelsea Hotel (☎ 212-243-3700; www.chelseahotel.com; 222 W 23rd St; s/d from $135) This place is cashing in on its notoriety (the room where Sid Vicious died has been redone – don't ask). The decor is lively and art-filled, and 'Serena,' the downstairs lounge, is a dark and cushy den with weekly gay parties.

Colonial House Inn (☎ 212-243-9669; www.colonialhouseinn.com; 318 W 22nd St; s $80-99, d $125-140; ✱ 💻). This popular gay inn is housed in a brownstone on a quiet residential block. The inn is filled with modern art by the proprietor (owner of the now-defunct, classic Paradise Garage club). Rates include breakfast served in a sunny nook, and the cozy rooms are spotless, some with working fireplaces.

Chelsea Pines Inn (☎ 212-929-1023; www.chelseapinesinn.com; 317 W 14th St; s/d $99/139; ✱ 💻) Nearby is another gay spot, this one with comfy rooms, each named after film stars and adorned with vintage movie posters. The staff is friendly and helpful, and a backyard garden is a peaceful place to chill before checking out the nightlife scene.

Also recommended:

Gramercy Park Hotel (☎ 212-475-4320; www.gramercyparkhotel.com; 2 Lexington Ave; s/d $160/185; ✱ 💻)
Chelsea Savoy Hotel (☎ 212-929-9353; www.chelseasavoynyc.com; 204 W 23rd St; s/d $99/135; ✱)

UPPER MANHATTAN

Map pp142–4

Close to Central Park, and a short subway ride from Midtown, the Upper West Side has some of Manhattan's best-value accommodations.

Hotel Belleclaire (☎ 212-362-7700; www.hotelbelleclaire.com; 250 W 77th St; s/d $99/159; P ✱ 💻) The renovated inn is in a landmark building and has very basic rooms right near the park.

The following are also recommended:

Quality Hotel (☎ 646-698-0500; 215 W 94th St; s/d $80/180; ✱ 💻)
Empire Hotel (☎ 212-265-7400; www.empirehotel.com; 44 W 63rd St; s & d $100-249; P ✱ 💻)
Hotel Beacon (☎ 212-787-1100; www.beaconhotel.com; 2130 Broadway; s/d $145/185; P ✱)

Close to Central Park and Museum Mile, the Upper East Side has some of New York's most elegant and expensive hotels.

Habitat Hotel (☎ 212-753-8841; www.habitatny.com; 130 E 57th St; s/d $89/129; ✱) A reasonably priced option is the Habitat Hotel, now a stylish spot, following its makeover from a dusty old women's residence.

OUTER BOROUGHS

Angelique Bed & Breakfast (☎ 718-852-8406; 405 Union St; s/d $100/150; P ✱) Nestled in the peaceful neighborhood of Carroll Gardens, this country-ish B&B is housed in an 1889 brownstone and features Victorian-type furnishings. It welcomes pets and kids, and is right nearby Smith St's restaurant row.

Le Refuge Inn (☎ 718-885-2478; 620 City Island Ave; d/ste $105/210; P ✱) For a true country getaway right in NYC, head up to City Island, where you'll dine on fresh lobster, stroll on the beach and stay in this cozy, quirky and welcoming hotel.

Sleeping – Top End

Top-end spots are usually around $200 – sometimes a lot more; they are also in large supply. If you're not on a limited budget, the bedtime world is your oyster.

MIDTOWN & CHELSEA

Map pp124–6

Waldorf Astoria (☎ 212-355-3000; www.waldorf.com; 301 Park Ave; r & ste from $300; P ✱) This legendary spot, where British royals host fundraising dinners, is all art deco and high class. Bonuses include an on-site beauty parlor, fitness center with steam rooms, and a cellphone rental service.

Hudson (☎ 212-554-6000; www.ianschragerhotels.com; 356 W 58th St; s/d $175/260; ✱) This Ian Schrager joint – one of three in NYC – has ultramodern, edgy designer ambience. It features a gorgeous interior courtyard, a rooftop terrace and two sleek bars that are mobbed with models and their cohorts.

Time (☎ 212-320-2900; www.thetimeny.cm; 224 W 49th St; s & d $189-239; ✱) Every room is

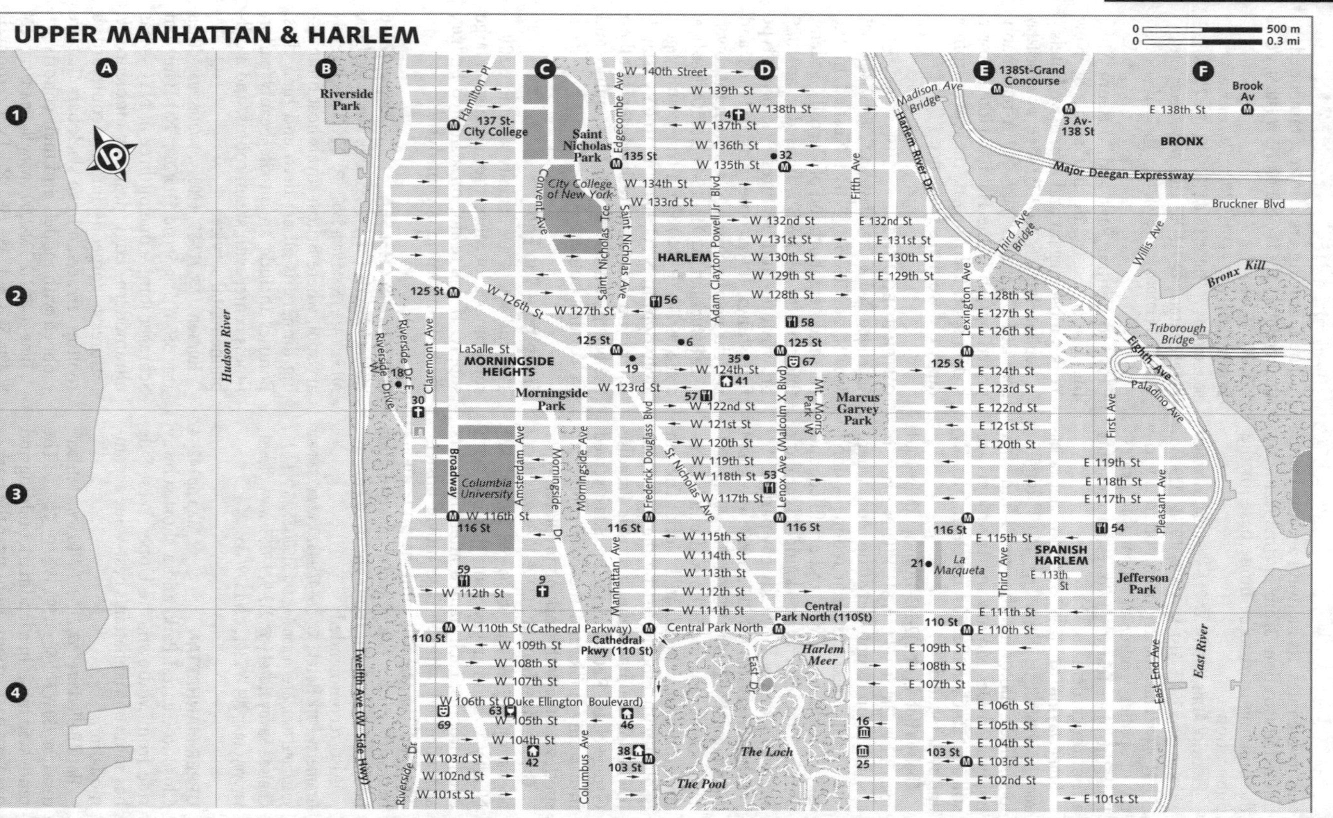
UPPER MANHATTAN & HARLEM
0 500 m
0 0.3 mi
Hudson River
East River
Harlem River Dr
Bronx Kill
BRONX
HARLEM
SPANISH HARLEM
MORNINGSIDE HEIGHTS
Riverside Park
Morningside Park
Saint Nicholas Park
Marcus Garvey Park
Mt Morris Park W
Jefferson Park
Harlem Meer
The Loch
The Pool
City College of New York
Columbia University
La Marqueta
Triborough Bridge
Madison Ave Bridge
Third Ave Bridge
Major Deegan Expressway
Bruckner Blvd
Willis Ave
Twelfth Ave (W Side Hwy)
Riverside Drive
Broadway
Amsterdam Ave
Columbus Ave
Manhattan Ave
Morningside Ave
Frederick Douglass Blvd
Adam Clayton Powell Jr Blvd
Lenox Ave (Malcolm X Blvd)
Fifth Ave
Lexington Ave
Third Ave
First Ave
Pleasant Ave
East End Ave
Paladino Ave
St Nicholas Ave
Convent Ave
Central Park North (110St)
Cathedral Pkwy (110 St)
W 110th St (Cathedral Parkway)
W 106th St (Duke Ellington Boulevard)
W 126th St
125 St
116 St
110 St
103 St
135 St
137 St-City College
138St-Grand Concourse
3 Av-138 St
Brook Av

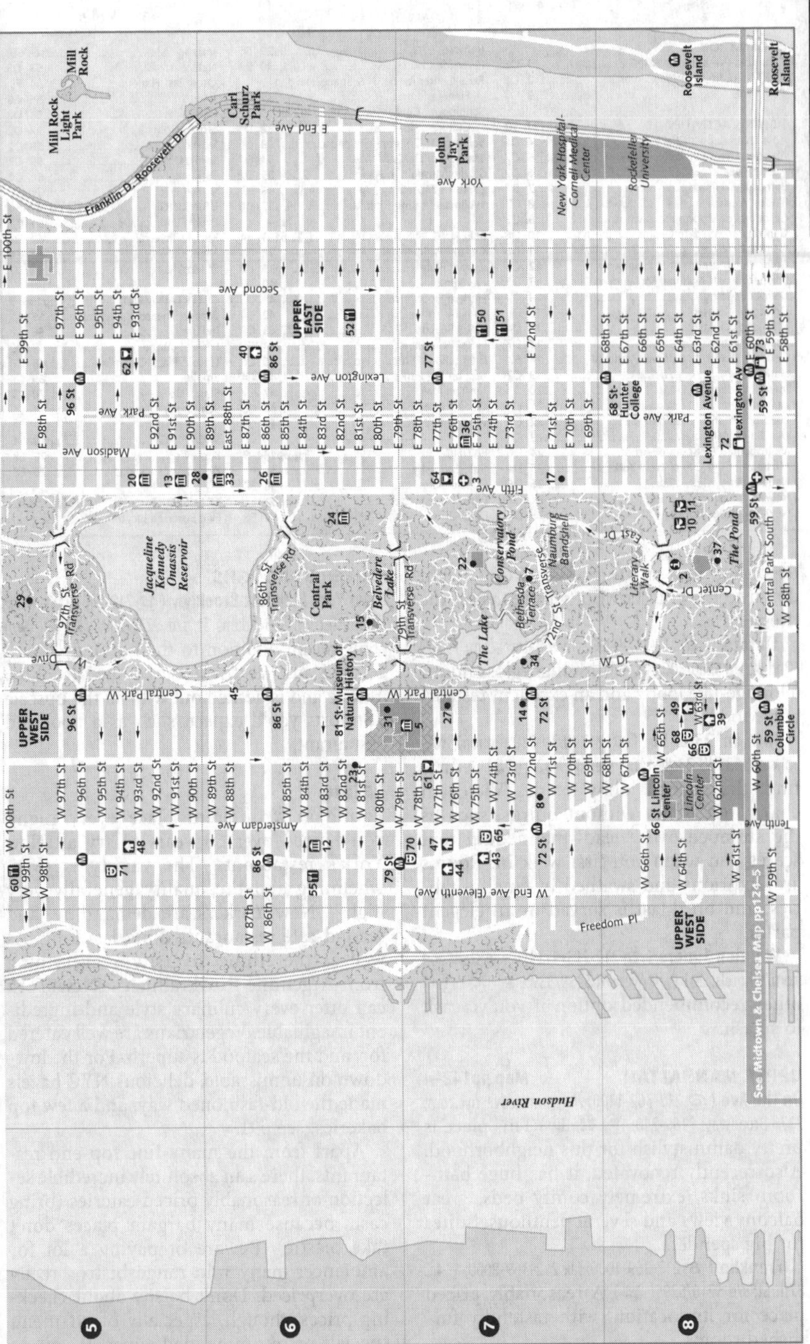
Mill Rock
Mill Rock Light Park
Carl Schurz Park
Franklin D. Roosevelt Dr
E End Ave
John Jay Park
York Ave
New York Hospital-Cornell Medical Center
Rockefeller University
Roosevelt Island
E 100th St
E 99th St
E 98th St
E 97th St
E 96th St
E 95th St
E 94th St
E 93rd St
E 92nd St
E 91st St
E 90th St
E 89th St
East 88th St
E 87th St
E 86th St
E 85th St
E 84th St
E 83rd St
E 82nd St
E 81st St
E 80th St
E 79th St
E 78th St
E 77th St
E 76th St
E 75th St
E 74th St
E 73rd St
E 72nd St
E 71st St
E 70th St
E 69th St
E 68th St
E 67th St
E 66th St
E 65th St
E 64th St
E 63rd St
E 62nd St
E 61st St
E 60th St
E 59th St
E 58th St
Second Ave
Lexington Ave
Park Ave
Madison Ave
Fifth Ave
UPPER EAST SIDE
96 St
86 St
77 St
68 St-Hunter College
Lexington Avenue
Lexington Av
59 St
Jacqueline Kennedy Onassis Reservoir
97th St Transverse Rd
86th St Transverse Rd
79th St Transverse Rd
72nd St Transverse
Central Park
Belvedere Lake
Conservatory Pond
The Lake
Bethesda Terrace
Naumburg Bandshell
Literary Walk
East Dr
Center Dr
W Dr
W Drive
The Pond
Central Park South
Central Park W
81 St-Museum of Natural History
72 St
UPPER WEST SIDE
W 100th St
W 99th St
W 98th St
W 97th St
W 96th St
W 95th St
W 94th St
W 93rd St
W 92nd St
W 91st St
W 90th St
W 89th St
W 88th St
W 87th St
W 86th St
W 85th St
W 84th St
W 83rd St
W 82nd St
W 81st St
W 80th St
W 79th St
W 78th St
W 77th St
W 76th St
W 75th St
W 74th St
W 73rd St
W 72nd St
W 71st St
W 70th St
W 69th St
W 68th St
W 67th St
W 66th St
W 65th St
W 64th St
W 63rd St
W 62nd St
W 61st St
W 60th St
W 59th St
W 58th St
Amsterdam Ave
W End Ave (Eleventh Ave)
Tenth Ave
66 St Lincoln Center
Lincoln Center
59 St Columbus Circle
79 St
Freedom Pl
Hudson River
See Midtown & Chelsea Map pp124-5
5
6
7
8

INFORMATION
Columbia-Presbyterian Eastside 1 D8
Park Visitor Information Center 2 D8
Travel MD 3 D7

SIGHTS & ACTIVITIES pp127–30
Abyssinian Baptist Church 4 D1
American Museum of Natural History 5 C7
Apollo Theater 6 D2
Bethesda Fountain 7 D7
Blades West 8 C7
Cathedral of St John the Divine 9 C3
Central Park Wildlife Center 10 D8
Central Park Zoo 11 D8
Children's Museum of Manhattan 12 C6
Cooper-Hewitt National Museum of Design 13 D5
Dakota Building 14 C7
Delacorte Theater 15 D6
El Museo del Barrio 16 D4
Frick Collection 17 D7
General US Grant National Memorial 18 B2
Harlem USA 19 C2
Jewish Museum 20 D5
La Marqueta 21 E3
Loeb Boathouse 22 D7
Maxilla & Mandible 23 C6
Metropolitan Museum of Art 24 D6
Museum of the City of New York 25 D4
Neue Galerie 26 D6
New York Historical Society 27 C7
New York Road Runner's Club 28 D6
Ramble 29 D5
Riverside Church 30 B2
Rose Center for Earth & Space/Hayden Planetarium 31 C6
Schomburg Center for Research in Black Culture 32 D1
Solomon R Guggenheim Museum 33 D6
Strawberry Fields 34 D7
Studio Museum in Harlem 35 D2
Whitney Museum of American Art 36 E7
Wollman Skating Rink 37 D8

SLEEPING pp137–44
Central Park Hostel 38 C4
Empire Hotel 39 C8
Franklin 40 E6
Harlem Flophouse 41 D2
HI New York 42 C4
Hotel Beacon 43 C7
Hotel Belleclaire 44 C7
International Student Hospice 45 C6
Jazz on the Park 46 C4
On The Ave 47 C7
Quality Hotel 48 C5
West Side YMCA 49 C8

EATING pp144–9
Café Sabarsky (see 26)
Candle Cafe 50 E7
EJ's Luncheonette 51 E7
Etats-Unis 52 E6
Josie's (see 65)
Native 53 D3
Orbit East Harlem 54 F3
Ouest 55 C6
Revival 56 D2
Strictly Roots 57 D2
Sylvia's 58 D2
Tom's Diner 59 C3
Turkuaz 60 C5

DRINKING pp149–50
Evelyn Lounge 61 C7
Kinsale Tavern 62 E5
Night Cafe 63 C4
St Mark's 64 D7

ENTERTAINMENT pp150–3
Beacon Theater 65 C7
Iridium 66 C8
Lenox Lounge 67 D2
Lincoln Plaza Cinemas 68 C8
Smoke 69 C4
Stand-Up New York 70 C7
Symphony Space 71 C5

SHOPPING pp153–4
Barney's 72 E8
Bloomingdale's 73 E8

TRANSPORT pp154–6
Five Borough Bicycle (see 42)

decorated in a single primary color (right down to the cool bowl of jellybeans on the dresser).

Flatotel (212-887-9400; www.flatotel.com; 135 W 52nd St; s/d $200/300;) With high-gloss floors, a lounge-like lobby and an excellent restaurant, Moda.

Inn on 23rd St (212-463-0330; innon23rd@aol.com; 131 W 23rd St; r & ste $179-329;) A true find: the hushed lobby exudes Victorian charm but is not without quirks, such as the slumped-over 'dead' mannequin that scares you when you first walk in. Rooms are luxurious and swathed in fanciful fabrics, and breakfast is served in an elegant parlor.

W Union Square (212-253-9119; www.starwood.com/whotels; 201 Park Ave; s/d $259/339; P) Another recommended option if you've cash to splash.

UPPER MANHATTAN Map pp142–4

On the Ave (212-362-1100; www.ontheave-nyc.com; 2178 Broadway; $165-240; P) This place is pretty damn stylish for this neighborhood. Also recently renovated, it has huge bathroom sinks, extremely comfy beds, great balcony views and several penthouse suites for big spenders.

Franklin (212-369-1000; fax 212-369-8000; 164 E 87th St; s/d $210/$295;) A reasonably priced place for its location, with tastefully furnished rooms.

OUTER BOROUGHS

New York Marriott Brooklyn (718-246-7000; www.marriott.com; 333 Adams St; s/d $239/289; P) This recent addition to the borough is well located just at the foot of the Brooklyn Bridge and is decked out with all the upscale comforts you'd expect, such as a pool and restaurant.

Eating

Eating in a different place every night, you'd need over 60 years to try all New York's restaurants. The variety is overwhelming and the quality generally very high – New Yorkers are demanding, and second-rate restaurants don't last long. As well as the ethnic diversity – everything from Argentine to Ukrainian – New York can offer every culinary style and ingredient imaginable. Vegetarians are well catered for, and the seafood is superb. For the lowdown on unmissable, delicious NYC bagels made the old-fashioned way, and a few top bakeries, see p91.

Apart from the many fine top-end restaurants, there's an absolutely incredible selection of reasonably priced eateries (bring cash, because many bargain places don't take plastic). Beware of paying a lot for ambience: many mid-range bistros really are overpriced. Don't be shy about checking prices, though, especially of off-menu specials or recommended wines. If you do

STREET EATS

Apart from its many restaurants, the city has hundreds of **street vendors** serving food. They sell the quintessential hot dog ($1) or hot dog with onions ($2), as well as hot pretzels ($1). Also on offer are soups, sandwiches, falafel, focaccia, noodles, gyros, knishes, kebabs, souvlakia, chicken, chips and Philly cheesesteaks (all around $2 to $5). You'll find lots of stands in the side streets of Midtown. A filling meal near museums and tourist sites is slightly more expensive (around $3 to $5).

want to enjoy a few drinks, you should do it at a bar, not a restaurant, where speciality drinks can be especially expensive.

Time Out New York's Eating and Drinking Guide, available at most newsstands, is the best source of dining information. *Zagat Survey*, which offers a collection of diners' comments, is also useful.

Note that, under city law, there is no smoking permitted in any dining establishment.

LOWER MANHATTAN **Map pp114–16**

Not exactly a foodie's heaven, many places here are open only for lunch, and proper restaurants tend to be expensive and boringly steak-heavy. If you like this, you're in luck.

Les Halles (☎ 212-285-8585; 15 John St; dishes $15-30) A noted French restaurant, featuring famous Food Network pastry chef, Anthony Bourdain.

Mark Joseph Steakhouse (☎ 212-277-0020; 261 Water St; dishes $20-35) While it is, yes, a steakhouse, it ranks among the city's best.

Mangia (☎ 212-425-4040; 40 Wall St; dishes $7-10) Part of a small city chain, Mangia has excellent sandwiches (try the pecan-crusted chicken cutlet), salads and pastas.

CHINATOWN **Map pp114–16**

Every New Yorker has a favorite Chinatown restaurant.

Peking Duck House (☎ 212-227-1810; 28 Mott St; dishes $10-16) The definitive Peking duck is still done at Peking Duck House, proudly patronized by former mayor, Ed Koch, and now in more opulent premises.

The following are suggested for taste and price, not for decor.

Hay Wun Loy (☎ 212-285-8686; 28-30 Pell St; dishes $10-15) Specializes in dim sum and fish fresh from the tank.

Wong Kee (☎ 212-966-1160; 113 Mott St; dishes $9-15) For Cantonese.

Grand Sichuan (☎ 212-625-9212; 125 Canal St; dishes $9-15) For Szechuan.

Kam Chueh (☎ 212-791-6868; 40 The Bowery; dishes $7-12) For seafood.

House of Vegetarian (☎ 212-226-6572; 68 Mott St; dishes $7-15) Vegans should check out this place.

Nyonya (☎ 212-334-3669; 194 Grand St; dishes $7-12) Good Malaysian can be had at Nyonya.

Ponsgri Thai Restaurant (☎ 212-349-3132; 106 Bayard St; dishes $5-12) For yummy Thai.

Get a cheap and excellent Vietnamese meal for under $15 from the following:

Vietnam Restaurant (☎ 212-693-0725; 11 Doyers St; dishes $5-8)

Nha Trang (☎ 212-233-5348; 87 Baxter St; dishes $5-8).

LITTLE ITALY **Map pp114–16**

In summer the two blocks of Mulberry St north of Canal St close to traffic, allowing more space for outdoor dining.

Il Fornaio (☎ 212-226-8306; 132a Mulberry St; dishes $7-12) Mulberry St isn't a cheap-eats street, but Il Fornaio comes close, with substantial servings of Italian standards.

Luna Restaurant (☎ 212-226-8657; 112 Mulberry St; dishes $7-12) A good standard red-sauce place, serving very affordable mains.

Bread (☎ 212-334-1015; 20 Spring St; dishes $7-10) Bread is a lovely paninoteca wine bar.

Lombardi's Pizza (☎ 212-941-7994; 32 Spring St; pies $14) Between Mott and Mulberry Sts, legendary Lombardi's is the oldest, and some say the best, pizza place in town.

SOHO & TRIBECA **Map pp114–16**

Always a pretty trendy eating scene, Soho, in recent years, has gained some quality to boot.

Balthazar (☎ 212-965-1414; 80 Spring St; dishes $12-20) Enjoy excellent bistro fare at Balthazar – if you can even get in, that is.

Blue Ribbon (☎ 212-274-0404; 97 Sullivan St; dishes $12-25) Many New Yorkers swear Blue Ribbon has the best brunch in town and, because of the no-reservations policy, they'll wait hours to get it.

Hoomoos Asli (☎ 212-966-0022; 100 Kenmare St; dishes $5-11) This place is great for lunch;

Hoomoos serves flawless Israeli food in no-frills surroundings.

Hampton Chutney Co (☎ 212-226-9996; 68 Prince St; dishes $7-10) Offering huge South Indian dosas, stuffed with everything from masala to turkey.

Snack (☎ 212-925-1040; 105 Thompson St; dishes $5-8) Tiny, but with a delicious twist on Greek food, Snack is another great lunch stop.

Ñ (☎ 212-219-8856; 33 Crosby St; tapas $6-8) A tasty tapas bar.

Herban Kitchen (☎ 212-627-2257; 290 Hudson St; dishes $11-22) Herban serves excellent organic and vegetarian fare (and organic wine) in a space with more ambience than you'd expect from a natural foods eatery.

Peppe Rosso To Go (☎ 212-677-4555; 149 Sullivan St; dishes $7-12) A shoebox-sized spot with irresistible pasta dishes.

Trendy Tribeca is where you'll find some of the city's most hyped, celebrity-packed, pricey – but inarguably superior – options:

Nobu (☎ 212-219-0500; 105 Hudson St; dishes $18-35) For the best sushi in town.

Bouley (☎ 212-924-6565; 120 W Broadway; dishes $25-33) David Bouley's is a four-star French destination.

Nam (☎ 212-267-1777; 110 Reade St; dishes $6-13) Cheap and delicious Vietnamese.

Kori (☎ 212-334-0908; 253 Church St; dishes $10-15) Serves up creative Korean fare.

GREENWICH VILLAGE & WEST VILLAGE

Map pp114–16

There are lots of restaurants to choose from around Bleecker St, between Broadway and Seventh; some are much better than others.

Trattoria Spaghetto (☎ 212-255-6752; 232 Bleecker St; dishes $10-15) A reliable, inexpensive Italian restaurant.

Arturo's Pizzeria (☎ 212-677-3820; 106 W Houston St; dishes $8-19) With its live piano music most nights and thin-crusted, delicious pizza on others, Arturo's is a blast.

Bar Pitti (☎ 212-982-3300; 268 Sixth Ave; dishes $10-15) Bar Pitti serves excellent Italian fare.

Japonica (☎ 212-243-7752; 100 University Pl; $17-30) For excellent sushi.

French Roast (☎ 212-533-2233; 78 W 11th St; dishes $6-12) A 24-hour café serving light sandwiches and desserts at reasonable prices.

Vegetarians should head to **Souen** (☎ 212-807-7421; 210 Prince St) for superb organic fare, or **Temple In** (☎ 212-475-5670; 74 W 3rd St) the Village, for its amazingly tasty salad-bar options.

Florent (☎ 212-989-5779; 69 Gansevoort St; dishes $9-13) In the West Village, Florent is a nouvelle diner that attracts all sorts with its excellent French food, hip ambience and all-night hours.

A Salt & Battery (☎ 212-691-2713; 112 Greenwich Ave; dishes $7-16) Great fish-and-chips.

Corner Bistro (☎ 212-242-4502; 331 W 4th St; burgers $4-7) The corner is known for its unforgettably juicy burgers.

Delicia (☎ 212-242-2002; 322 W 11th St; dishes $12-16) Wonderful Brazilian fare, but be prepared to settle in, as service is leisurely.

Little Havana (☎ 212-255-2212; 30 Cornelia St; dishes $12-16) A Cornelia St star, Little Havana serves cheap Cuban fare.

Pearl Oyster Bar (☎ 212-691-8211; 18 Cornelia St; dishes $8-17) For mammoth lobster rolls.

Mexicana Mama (☎ 212-924-4119; 525 Hudson St; dishes $9-14) Head to Mexicana Mama for intense guacamole.

Moustache (☎ 212-229-2220; 90 Bedford St; dishes $5-10) For great Middle Eastern food.

Sacred Chow (☎ 212-337-0863; 522 Hudson St; dishes $6-12) For amazing (if overpriced) takeout vegetarian food.

EAST VILLAGE & LOWER EAST SIDE

Map pp114–16

For value and choice, these are the best areas in the city. East 6th St's India row may seem charming, but the cheap fare, actually Bangladeshi, is nothing to write home about. Instead, hit Little India in the E 30s.

Benny's Burritos (☎ 212-254-2054; 93 Ave A; dishes $5-11) Features minimalist-Mex decor, filling Cal-Mex food and lethal margaritas.

Second Ave Deli (☎ 212-677-0606; 156 Second Ave; dishes $9-18) Quintessentially Jewish, this deli serves up delicious dishes like motza-ball soup and fat turkey sandwiches.

B&H Dairy (☎ 212-505-8065; 127 Second Ave; dishes $3-6) A tiny hole-in-the-wall kosher place with cheap, yummy soups and fresh juices.

Veselka (☎ 212-228-9682; 144 Second Ave; dishes $6-10) A Ukrainian diner that's popular with local artists. It serves hearty breakfasts 24 hours a day.

Dok Suni's (☎ 212-477-9506; 119 First Ave; dishes $9-15) Dok Suni attracts crowds with its delicious Korean dishes.

Prune (☎ 212-677-6221; 54 E 1st St; dishes $8-24) Prune is beloved for its creative American food.

Patio Dining (☎ 212-460-9171; 31 Second Ave; dishes $10-15) For excellent, eclectic organic fare.

Bereket (☎ 212-475-7700; 187 E Houston St; dishes $6-12) A 24-hour kebab cafeteria for cabbies and cops, with a great selection of Turkish and vegetarian dishes.

Katz's Delicatessen (☎ 212-254-2246; 205 E Houston St; dishes $7-11) This East-side institution makes huge pastrami sandwiches – you can eat what Meg Ryan ordered in *When Harry Met Sally*.

Teany (☎ 212-475-9190; 90 Rivington St; dishes $4-10) Owned by Moby, Teany is a fun little organic teahouse serving organic vegan treats.

Paladar (☎ 212-473-3535; 161 Ludlow St; dishes $10-19) Tasty food and a trendy, Latin-American scene.

71 Clinton Fresh Food (☎ 212-614-6960; 71 Clinton St; dishes $17-25) Head here for a taste-treat extravaganza of creative American fare.

Herbivores can't go wrong at any of the following:

Caravan of Dreams (☎ 212-254-1613; 405 E 6th St; dishes $9-14) A hippie-ish, homey spot with live music and a huge menu.

Quintessence (☎ 646-654-1823; 263 E 10th St; dishes $8-15) A haven for raw foodies.

Kate's Joint (☎ 212-777-7059; 58 Ave B; dishes $6-10) Guilty pleasures like greasy veggie burgers and organic beers.

Sanctuary (☎ 212-780-9786; 25 First Ave; dishes $7-11) Ashram-run spot with international dishes.

Dawgs on Park (☎ 212-598-0667; 178 E 7th St; hot dogs $2-4) Feast on great franks (veggie ones too!) before relaxing in Tompkins Sq Park.

CHELSEA & AROUND Map pp124–6

Chelsea has an excellent variety of eateries, but you'll have to book early and spend a lot for the trendy places.

Markt (☎ 212-727-3314; 401 W 14th St; dishes $17-23) A barn-size Belgian brasserie that features fine seafood, a big beer list and lots of beautiful people.

Big Cup (☎ 212-206-0059; 228 Eighth Ave; dishes $3-6) The see-and-be-seen gay café.

Mary Ann's (☎ 212-633-0877; 116 Eighth Ave; dishes $8-12) This is an always-packed haven and the place for sloppy, tasty Mexican food.

La Chinita Linda (☎ 212-633-1791; 166 Eighth Ave; dishes $7-12) Cheap and untrendy Chelsea eats, the Cuban-Chinese food here will fill you up for under $10.

Empire Diner (☎ 212-243-2736; 210 Tenth Ave; dishes $10-14) Late-night clubbers hit the 24-hour Empire Diner.

Food Bar (☎ 212-243-2020; 149 Eighth Ave; dishes $7-15) Food Bar has an imaginative menu, consistent quality and really comfortable surroundings.

Craft (☎ 212-780-0880; 43 E 19th St; dishes $25-35) In the Flatiron District, Craft serves exquisite organic, seasonal fare with a big price tag. But for an unforgettable dining experience, it's worth it.

Union Square Cafe (☎ 212-243-4020; 21 E 16th St; dishes $18-28) Arguably the city's finest food is served here, where the imaginative gourmet fare and fine wines are enhanced by an unpretentious atmosphere.

MIDTOWN Map pp124–6

Carnegie Deli (☎ 212-757-2245; 854 Seventh Ave; dishes $11) An institution with small tables, huge pastrami sandwiches and full Manhattan prices – for tourists only.

Lespinasse (☎ 212-339-4100; 2 E 55th St; dishes from $42) In the St Regis, Lespinasse is perhaps the finest, fanciest and priciest restaurant in New York.

Aquavit (☎ 212-307-7311; 13 W 54th St; 3-course prix fixe $69) Slightly less expensive than Lespinasse, Aquavit is also acclaimed and serves classic Scandinavian seafood in a stunning six-story atrium.

Pump (☎ 212-246-6844; 40 W 55th St; dishes $9) If you like to stay in shape, even while you're traveling, fuel up at the Pump, serving high-protein, low-fat lunches.

THE AUTHOR'S CHOICE

F&B (Map pp124-6; ☎ 212-486-4441; 269 W 23rd St; dishes $4-7) Here's a New York dilemma for you: you're a busy sightseer, vegetarian and hungry. F&B is New York's answer. This wonderful 'European street food' takeout joint and café serves excellent *frites* (french fries), beers, desserts, lemonades and, best of all, tofu dogs (with toppings from sauerkraut to hummus). It's a refreshingly delicious and convenient pit stop in a city where fast veggie food usually means a tasteless, protein-free pretzel from a street vendor. Oh, and your carnivore pals will be satisfied, as F&B has a slew of options and makes pure beef hot dogs too.

Zen Palate (☎ 212-582-1669; 663 Ninth Ave; dishes $5-9) Serves unique Asian vegetarian fare.

Munson Diner (☎ 212-246-0964; 600 W 49th St at Eleventh Ave; dishes $3-6) On the west side of Midtown, in the Hell's Kitchen neighborhood, this classic diner is an authentic New York experience. Cops and cab drivers get greasy burgers in stainless-steel surroundings.

In Koreatown, try the following:

Cho Dang Goi (☎ 212-695-8222; 55 W 35th St; dishes $7-10) Its remarkable homemade *dooboo* (tofu) attracts scores of Koreans.

Hangawi (☎ 212-213-0077; 12 E 32nd St; dishes $7-10) Excellent veggie Korean meals can be had here in tranquil surrounds.

In Little India, Indian restaurants abound along Third and Lexington Aves, between 27th and 29th Sts. The following are recommended:

Madras Mahal (☎ 212-684-4010; 104 Lexington Ave; dishes $8-12) Kosher vegetarian food and a cheap lunch buffet.

Vatan (☎ 212-689-5666; 409 Third Ave; prix fixe $22) A great Indian vegetarian joint serving hearty Gujurati *thalis*.

In the Theater District, 'Restaurant Row' is the block of W 46th St between Eighth and Ninth Aves, featuring many mediocre and overpriced eateries providing pre-theater sustenance. If you're rushing to the theater, or hungry after a show, try the following:

Film Center Café (☎ 212-262-2525; 635 Ninth Ave; dishes $5-12) Quirky café serving typical American grub.

Ponsgri Thai (☎ 212-582-3392; 244 W 48th St; dishes $8-13) Also has a Lower Manhattan outlet.

Chelsea Market (☎ 212-620-7500; 75 Ninth Ave) Self-caterers should head here. This classy indoor market features high-quality baked goods, gourmet cheeses, produce, seafood, flowers and wine.

UPPER WEST SIDE

Map pp142–4

You'd have been hard-pressed to find decent fare up here just a few years ago, but now all that's changed. Many credit Ouest for that, but several other places are worth hitting as well.

Ouest (☎ 212-580-8700; 2315 Broadway; dishes $16-23) The fancy, eclectic French fare certainly draws crowds.

Josie's (☎ 212-769-1212; 300 Amsterdam Ave; dishes $9-17) For healthy fare, go to Josie's where creative and satisfying vegetarian dishes are served to a cheerful, bustling crowd.

Café con Leche (☎ 212-595-7000; 424 Amsterdam Ave; dishes $7-12) Serves satisfying Dominican dishes in a buzzing, colorful setting.

Turkuaz (☎ 212-665-9541; 2637 Broadway; dishes $9-28) Offering authentic Turkish food in a cavernous, sexy dining room, featuring belly dancers on weekends.

Tom's Restaurant (☎ 212-864-6137; 2880 Broadway at W 112th St; dishes $4-10) Attracts students and *Seinfeld* fans (the show uses the exterior shot for the gang's gathering place) with typical American fare and low prices.

UPPER EAST SIDE

MAP pp142–4

Dozens of moderately priced American restaurants on Second and Third Aves, between 60th and 86th Sts, do offer lunch specials for under $10 and are packed for weekend brunches.

EJ's Luncheonette (☎ 212-472-0600; 1271 Third Ave at 73rd St; dishes $7-12) Features classic diner food in a 1950s retro setting.

Café Sabarsky (☎ 212-228-0655; 1048 Fifth Ave; dishes $12-18) Housed in the Neue Galerie, Sabarsky is an elegant and delicious Austrian restaurant.

Candle Cafe (☎ 212-472-0970; 1307 Third Ave; dishes $9-15) Between 74th and 75th Sts, vegetarians fill up here at this very good café.

Etats-Unis (☎ 212-517-8826; 242 E 81st St; dishes $18-26) Etas-Unis presents a market-fresh blend of French and American cuisines.

HARLEM

Map pp142–4

Surprisingly few restaurants serve up soul food in Harlem, and even fewer represent the growing West African influence.

Sylvia's (☎ 212-996-0660; 328 Lenox Ave; dishes $9-17) Harlem's most famous soul-food restaurant known for its Sunday gospel brunch (reservations required). The food's authentic, but the ambience suffers when the tour buses turn up.

Several new arrivals have been thrilling those with sophisticated palates. Check out:

Orbit East Harlem (☎ 212-348-7818; 2257 First Ave; dishes $7-17) You can enjoy a juicy pork chop with a side of celery-root slaw as the bartender MCs for nightly jazz shows.

Revival (☎ 212-222-8338; 2367 Frederick Douglas Blvd; dishes $13-26) Revival serves up modern takes on soul food (with great veggie options).

Native (☎ 212-665-2525; 161 Lenox Ave; dishes $9-14) Native offers inventive French-Moroccan dishes.

Strictly Roots (☎ 212-864-8699; 2058 Adam Clayton Powell Jr Blvd; dishes $7-10) Join the vegetarian Rastas enjoying vegan takes on soul food at the cafeteria-style Strictly Roots.

OUTER BOROUGHS

Smith St in Boerum Hill, Brooklyn, is a happening destination point for foodies, with at least two dozen excellent options.

Café LuluC (☎ 718-625-3815; 214 Smith St; dishes $9-13) Convivial, neighborhood atmosphere and tasty bistro meals at great prices.

Banania Café (☎ 718-237-9100; 241 Smith St; dishes $12-17) The more expensive, upscale sister eatery of Café LuluC – top-notch French fare.

Patois (☎ 718-855-1535; 255 Smith St; dishes $16) For excellent bistro fare.

Panino'teca 275 (☎ 718-237-2728; 275 Smith St; dishes $5-8) Romantic, affordable café serving pressed sandwiches and excellent wines.

Zatyoons (☎ 718-875-1880; 283 Smith St; dishes $6-11) Good, cheap Middle Eastern food.

Robin des Bois (☎ 718-596-1609; 195 Smith St; dishes $7-11) Serves down-home French food in truly eclectic surroundings.

Boerum Hill Food Company (☎ 718-222-0140; 134 Smith St; dishes $8-13) Excellent muffins, frittatas and pancakes for brunch.

Go all-out Greek on Astoria's Broadway in Queens:

Uncle George's (☎ 718-626-0593; 33-19 Broadway; dishes $7-11) Spicy dips and cheap specials 24 hours a day.

Omonia (32-20 Broadway; dishes $2-4) Just across the street from Uncle George's. A sleek, Greek espresso bar.

Elia's Corner (☎ 718-932-1510; 24-02 31st St; dishes $10-15) The best place in the city for fresh fish. Elia's is inelegant, inexpensive and exquisite.

Drinking

BARS

Here's a highly selective list of assorted and well-established Manhattan bars. Most stay open until 2am, sometimes until 4am Friday and Saturday. And thanks to a controversial city law passed in 2003, there is absolutely no smoking allowed.

Cabana (Map pp114-16; 89 South St Seaport) Probably the coolest bar at South St Seaport; chow down on Latino snacks with your ice-cold Corona.

Double Happiness (Map pp114-16; ☎ 212-941-1282; 173 Mott St) North of Chinatown proper, between Broome and Grand Sts, is a cavernous, crowded one-time speakeasy.

Barramundi (Map pp114-16; ☎ 212-529-6900; 147 Ludlow St) Convivial Barramundi serves reasonably priced drinks and is a good place to start a Lower East Side bar crawl.

Angel (☎ Map pp114-16; ☎ 212-780-0313; 174 Orchard St) Curvy couches and ambient music from DJs.

Magician (Map pp114-16; ☎ 212-673-7851; 118 Rivington St) A vintage-furnished spot named after an Ingmar Bergman film of the same name.

Welcome to the Johnson's (Map pp114-16; ☎ 212-420-9911; 123 Rivington St) Has Pabst Blue Ribbon and a 1970s rec-room feel.

Bar Veloce (Map pp114-16; ☎ 212-260-3200; 17 Cleveland Pl) A lovely Italian wine bar.

Puck Fair (Map pp114-16; ☎ 212-431-1200; 298 Lafayette St) A sleek Irish pub serving bangers and mash with pints of Guinness.

Temple Bar (Map pp114-16; ☎ 212-925-4242; 332 Lafayette St) Temple Bar has high-priced, top-shelf booze for a fancy after-hours crowd.

Von Bar (Map pp114-16; ☎ 212-473-3039; 3 Bleecker St) Worn old wooden floors and a wonderful beer and wine (only) selection.

DBA (Map pp114-16; ☎ 212-475-5097; 41 First Ave) In the East Village, DBA has endless imported beer, single-malt scotch and high-end tequila options, plus a back patio.

Ear Inn (Map pp114-16; ☎ 212-226-9060; 326 Spring St) On the edge of Soho, this old and cozy place, with an old-fashioned pub atmosphere and inexpensive food, attracts a mixed clientele.

Cafe Noir (Map pp114-16; ☎ 212-431-7910; 32 Grand St) The somewhat trendy Cafe Noir has North African appetizers and a bar overlooking the passing parade.

Chumley's (Map pp114-16; ☎ 212-675-4449; 86 Bedford St) Hard-to-find Chumley's, in Greenwich Village, is a former speakeasy serving decent pub grub and US microbrews.

Scratcher (Map pp114-16; ☎ 212-477-0030; 209 E Fifth St) The East Village specializes in Irish pubs like this one, pleasantly quiet by day and suitably raucous at night.

Swift Hibernian Lounge (Map pp114-16; ☎ 212-260-3600; 34 E 4th St) Live music and the best pint of Guinness in town.

Hogs & Heifers (Map pp114-16; ☎ 212-722-8635; 8859 Washington St) In the Meatpacking District, this animal act sells cheap booze to a rowdy crowd.

Half King (Map pp124-6; ☎ 212-462-4300; 505 W 23rd St) In north Chelsea, the Half King features poetry readings as well as outdoor seating in warm weather.

Night Cafe (Map pp142-4; ☎ 212-864-8889; 938 Amsterdam Ave at 106th St) On the Upper West Side, Night Cafe is supported by Columbia students.

Kinsale Tavern (Map pp142-4; ☎ 212-3348-4370; 1672 Third Ave) On the Upper East Side, look for scores of Irish pubs, such as Kinsale Tavern, which has 20 beers on tap and live satellite broadcasts of European rugby and soccer.

LOUNGES

Lounges are classier than bars and often provide entertainment.

Hudson Bar & Books (Map pp114-16; ☎ 212-229-2642; 636 Hudson St) In Greenwich Village, Hudson is a narrow faux library with free jazz on weekends.

Bar d'O (Map pp114-16; ☎ 212-627-1580; 29 Bedford St) Slick Bar d'O has drag acts and a chic, mixed crowd.

Happy Ending (Map pp114-16; ☎ 212-334-9676; 302 Broome St) This hip spot is housed in a two-story, former Asian massage parlor.

Hell (Map pp114-16; ☎ 212-727-1666; 59 Gansevoort St) In the Meatpacking District, Hell is dark and sultry, with a mostly gay clientele.

Trailer Park Lounge & Grill (Map pp114-16; ☎ 212-463-8000; 271 W 23rd St) In Chelsea, with a kitschy feel that would make John Waters proud.

Serena (Map pp124-6; ☎ 212-255-4646; 222 W 23rd St) In the basement of the Chelsea Hotel, Serena is all cushy couches, moody lighting and DJs.

Whiskey Blue (☎ 212-407-2947; 541 Lexington Ave) Head off to Whiskey Blue, which is at the W Hotel.

Hudson Bars (Map pp124-6; ☎ 212-554-6343; 356 W 58th St) In Ian Schrager's Hudson hotel, this is where you come for swanky swilling.

Evelyn Lounge (Map pp142-4; ☎ 212-724-5145; 380 Columbus Ave at 78th St) On the Upper West Side, Evelyn is a clubby multiroom cellar, with a classy cigar lounge and a long martini list.

Turkuaz (Map pp142-4; ☎ 212-665-9541; 2637 Broadway) The front lounge of the Turkish restaurant by the same name, this lounge has low couches and belly dancing shows.

Halcyon (☎ 718-260-9299; 227 Smith St) In Boerum Hill, Brooklyn, make sure you don't miss the techno-trendy Halcyon, with a rotation of acclaimed DJs always on tap.

Entertainment

Time Out New York is the best guide to the city's nightlife. High culture is well covered in the Sunday and Friday editions of the *New York Times* and *New Yorker*. Dance clubs, smaller music venues and alternative happenings advertise in the *Village Voice*.

NYC On Stage (☎ 212-768-1818) A 24-hour information line for music and dance. It's connected to TKTS.

TKTS (Map pp124-6; Times Sq) Sells same-day tickets to Broadway and off-Broadway musicals, and drama, from a conspicuous booth in Times Square. Tickets are up to 75% off regular prices, and evening tickets go on sale at 3pm. A line starts forming at 2pm, but the best seats become available at 7pm (no credit cards).

You can also buy tickets from the following places:

Ticketmaster (☎ 212-307-7171; www.ticketmaster.com)

Telecharge (☎ 212-239-6200; www.telecharge.com) Handles tickets for most performances, major concerts and sporting events.

Ticket Central (Map pp124-6; ☎ 212-279-4200; 416 W 42nd St) Sells Broadway and off-Broadway theater tickets.

Broadway Ticket Center (Map pp124-6; 1560 Broadway) At the Times Square Visitors Center. Has Broadway tickets for sale and information.

Broadway Line (☎ 212-302-4111; www.broadway.org/league.html).

CenterCharge (☎ 212-721-6500) Books Lincoln Center events.

Major concerts are usually held at:

Madison Sq Garden (Map pp124-6; ☎ 212-465-5800; www.thegarden.com; Seventh Ave, btwn W 31st & W 33rd Sts)

Radio City Music Hall (Map pp124-6; ☎ 212-247-4777; www.radiocity.com; 1260 Sixth Ave)

Beacon Theater (Map pp142-4; ☎ 212-496-7070; 2124 Broadway at 74th St)

THEATER

The center of the New York theater district, Times Square, is dominated by big-budget spectaculars. The so-called Broadway shows are those in the large theaters around Times Square (tickets $40 to $100). 'Off-Broadway' refers to dramas in smaller spaces (200 seats or less) elsewhere in town – still big business ($20 to $50). 'Off-off-Broadway' events are readings, experimental performances and improvisations in spaces with less than 100 seats ($12 to $30).

Lincoln Center Theater group (☎ 212-239-6200; www.lincolncenter.org; Columbus Ave & Broadway) Runs the 1000-seat Vivian Beaumont Theater and the smaller, more intimate Mitzi Newhouse Theater.

CINEMAS

New Yorkers take film seriously, and new-release films (tickets around $10) sell out early Friday and Saturday nights. To save the wait, you can call ☎ 212-777-3456 and prepay ($1.50 extra) for a ticket.

Angelika Film Center (Map pp114-16; ☎ 212-777-3456; 18 W Houston St at Mercer St) Specializes in foreign films, crowded at weekends.

Lincoln Plaza Cinemas (Map pp142-4; ☎ 212-757-2280; 1886 Broadway) Opposite the Lincoln Center, this cinema specializes in foreign films and is always crowded on weekends.

Landmark Sunshine Cinema (Map pp114-16; ☎ 212-358-7709; 143 E Houston St) Newly renovated and in a former Yiddish theater, Landmark shows first-run indies.

Brooklyn Academy of Music Rose Cinemas (☎ 718-777-FILM; 30 Lafayette Ave) In Brooklyn, BAM is comfortable as well as popular, shows new-release indie films and is well worth the trip.

Film Forum (Map pp114-16; ☎ 212-727-8110; 209 W Houston St) Shows revivals and independent and classic movies.

Walter Reade Theater (Map pp142-4; ☎ 212-875-5600; 70 Lincoln Center Plaza) Independent films as well as career retrospectives are shown at the Lincoln Center's Walter Reade Theater, which also hosts the New York Film Festival every September.

Symphony Space (Map pp142-4; ☎ 212-864-5400; Broadway at 95th St) This recently renovated complex provides similar programming to the Walter Reade, along with theater and literature events.

Anthology Film Archives (Map pp114-16; ☎ 212-505-5181; 32 Second Ave at 2nd St) For far-out fringe works and otherwise unreleased fare.

CLASSICAL MUSIC & OPERA

New York Philharmonic (Map pp142-4; ☎ 212-721-6500; Lincoln Center, Columbus Ave & Broadway; tickets $19-80) Performs at the Lincoln Center's Avery Fisher Hall.

Carnegie Hall (Map pp124-6; ☎ 212-247-7800; 881 Seventh Ave at 57th St; tickets $15-90) Visiting orchestras and the New York Pops play at Carnegie Hall.

Alice Tully Hall (Map pp142-4; ☎ 212-875-5050; Lincoln Center, Columbus Ave & Broadway) The American Symphony Orchestra, Chamber Music Society of the Lincoln Center and the Little Orchestra Society hold their seasons at Lincoln Center's Alice Tully Hall.

Metropolitan Opera (Map pp142-4; ☎ 212-239-6200; Lincoln Center, Columbus Ave & Broadway; tickets $18-250) The season is from September to April at the Lincoln Center theater. It's extremely difficult to get tickets for the big-name performances, but it might be possible later in the season.

The more daring and affordable **New York City Opera** (☎ 212-870-5630) performs at the **New York State Theater** (☎ 212-870-5570; Lincoln Center, Columbus Ave & Broadway) for a few weeks in early autumn and again in late spring.

DANCE & BALLET

The **New York City Ballet** (Map pp142-4; ☎ 212-870-5570) performs in winter at the **New York State Theater** (☎ 212-870-5570; Lincoln Center, Columbus Ave & Broadway; tickets $16-85).

American Ballet Theater (☎ 212-875-5766; Lincoln Center) In spring the American Ballet Theater takes over at the Metropolitan Opera House for a short season.

City Center (Map pp124-6; ☎ 212-581-1212; 131 W 55th St btwn Sixth & Seventh Aves) Home to the Alvin Ailey American Dance Theater every December, and it also hosts visiting foreign companies.

Joyce Theater (Map pp124-6; ☎ 212-242-0800; 175 Eighth Ave at 19th St) A popular, offbeat dance venue that's located in a renovated Chelsea cinema.

Brooklyn Academy of Music (BAM; ☎ 718-636-4100; 30 Lafayette Ave) Also boasting avant-garde dance programming is BAM, in Fort Greene, Brooklyn.

JAZZ

Cover charges at jazz venues vary with the popularity of the performer; late-night sets can be cheaper. 'Music charges' may be added to your bill, but you're not obliged to pay tips as well.

Village Vanguard (Map pp114-16; ☎ 212-255-4037; 178 Seventh Ave at 11th St) The famous Village Vanguard has featured major stars for 50 years.

Blue Note (Map pp114-16; ☎ 212-475-8592; 131 W 3rd St) By far the most expensive club, where big stars play short sets.

Sweet Basil (Map pp114-16; ☎ 212-242-1785; 88 Seventh Ave) Between Grove and Bleecker Sts, there's a jazz brunch here on Sunday.

Small's (Map pp114-16; ☎ 212-929-7565; 183 W 10th St; tickets $10) This unique place without a liquor license hosts a 10-hour jazz marathon ($10) every night from 10pm that attracts top talent.

Zinc Bar (Map pp114-16; ☎ 212-477-8337; 90 W Houston St) Hosts new and established jazz acts and definitely serves liquor.

Knitting Factory (Map pp114-16; ☎ 212-219-3055; 74 Leonard St) You can hear acid jazz and other fringe music at this place in Tribeca.

Fez (Map pp114-16; ☎ 212-533-2680; 380 Lafayette St) Has experimental music.

Iridium (Map pp142-4; ☎ 212-582-2121; 44 W 63rd St) Features new jazz acts.

Smoke (Map pp142-4; ☎ 212-864-6662; 2751 Broadway) Near Columbia University, Smoke often has great free shows.

Harlem's Cotton Club era is long gone, but several places still present modern and traditional jazz, mostly at weekends; call ahead to check times and prices.

Lenox Lounge (Map pp142-4; ☎ 212-427-0253; 288 Lenox Ave at 125th St) Worth visiting anytime for its art deco interior.

St Nick's Pub (☎ 212-769-8275; 773 St Nicholas Ave at 149th St) A cramped, smoky Harlem hangout with great jazz acts and atmosphere.

ROCK, BLUES & WORLD MUSIC

Bottom Line (Map pp114-16; ☎ 212-228-6300; 15 W 4th St) In the Village, this is a rock cabaret-style music hall with mainly name acts.

CBGB (Map pp114-16; ☎ 212-982-4052; 315 The Bowery) This prototypical punk club is still going strong after 25 years.

Wetlands Preserve (Map pp114-16; ☎ 212-966-4225; 161 Hudson St) Where the Deadhead tradition continues, with everything from classic 1960s rock to reggae, ska and hip-hop.

Mercury Lounge (Map pp114-16; ☎ 212-260-4700; 217 E Houston St) Big names play at the small Mercury Lounge.

Irving Plaza (Map pp124-6; ☎ 212-777-6800; 17 Irving Pl) Big names play here.

Luna Lounge (Map pp114-16; ☎ 212-260-2323; 171 Ludlow St) On the Lower East Side, the Luna Lounge has a small room in back for garage bands, local musicians and new indie talent.

Bowery Ballroom (Map pp114-16; ☎ 212-533-2111; 6 Delancey St) Between the Bowery and Chrystie St, the Ballroom hosts popular touring acts and top local talent in a big, atmospheric venue.

Tonic (☎ 212-358-7503; 107 Norfolk St) The place to hear the latest in electronic, underground and inventive rock.

Southpaw (☎ 718-230-0236; 125 Fifth Ave) In Park Slope, Brooklyn, Southpaw has very quickly put itself on the map as a worthy rock-music destination.

Chicago Blues (Map pp114-16; ☎ 212-924-9755; 73 Eighth Ave at 13th St) Blues masters play here and the Monday-night blues jam is good.

BB King Blues Club & Grill (Map pp124-6; ☎ 212-997-4144; 237 W 42nd St) This flash 500-seat venue hosts quality blues, jazz and rock acts – drinks are expensive and the cover is high, but it's sometimes free after 11pm. There's a Sunday gospel brunch from 1pm.

SOB's (Map pp114-16; ☎ 212-243-4940; 204 Varick St) This place specializes in Afro-Cuban and salsa music.

DANCE CLUBS

Time Out New York (www.timeoutny.com) is the best source for the ever-changing club scene – check out its annual Clubs issues, published in spring, online. Also watch for flyers in the East Village, on walls and in cool record shops.

Tough drug laws keep the real rave scene under wraps. One long-standing club, periodically closed down by the authorities, is Limelight.

Limelight (Map pp114-16; ☎ 212-807-7780; 47 W 20th St at Sixth Ave) Reinventing itself again as a multimusic venue, variously offering deep house, tech house, soul, funk, hip-hop etc.

Filter 14 (Map pp114-16; ☎ 212-366-5680; 432 W 14th St) Friendly Filter 14 is for dancing, especially Tuesday and Saturday party nights and Thursday's '80s night.

Nell's (Map pp114-16; ☎ 212-675-1567; 246 W 14th St) The original European velvet lounge.

Centro-Fly (Map pp124-6; ☎ 212-627-7770; 45 W 21st St) Attracts island groovers midweek and assorted dance bunnies on weekends – it's big, cool and popular.

Club Shelter (Map pp124-6; 20 W 39th St) Deep house and garage, with classic DJs.

Pyramid (Map pp114-16; 101 Ave A) In the East Village, Pyramid hosts a popular Friday night kitsch fest, c 1984.

Water Street Bar (66 Water St) In Dumbo, Brooklyn, Water St is home to the monthly dance party, 718 Sessions, featuring DJ

Danny Krivit of the sadly defunct and very popular Body & Soul.

COMEDY

See gig guides for comedy nights and performances at many bars, lounges and clubs. For guaranteed laughs, go to one of the big-name stand-up comedy clubs. With cover charges and two-drink minimums, these clubs can make for an expensive night.

Caroline's on Broadway (Map pp124-6; ☎ 212-757-4100; 1626 Broadway; admission $10-20) The best-known place.

Comedy Cellar (Map pp114-16; ☎ 212-254-3480; 117 MacDougal St) Between 3rd and Bleecker Sts, Comedy Cellar has high-profile comics and surprise guests.

Stand-Up New York (Map pp142-4; ☎ 212-595-0850; 236 W 78th St; tickets $5-12) Make a reservation for Stand-up New York, which features funny theme nights like Southern-Fried Humor and also gets surprise appearances from star comedians.

Gotham Comedy Club (Map pp114-16; ☎ 212-367-9000; 34 W 22nd St) For innovative acts.

Upright Citizens Brigade Theatre (Map pp114-16; 307 W 26th St) For innovative acts.

SPECTATOR SPORTS

Baseball fans should check out the **National League New York Mets** (☎ 718-507-8499) playing baseball at the windswept Shea Stadium in Flushing Meadows, Queens. The **American League New York Yankees** (☎ 718-293-6000; Yankee Stadium, S 161st St; tickets $8-45) throw ball at Yankee Stadium in the Bronx (tickets are generally available), while for minor-league baseball action, take in a game of the **Staten Island Yankees** (☎ 718-720-9200; Richmond County Bank Ballpark, 75 Richmond Tce) or **Brooklyn Cyclones** (☎ 718-49-8497; KeySpan Park, Coney Island boardwalk).

Basketball fans can get courtside with the **NBA New York Knicks** (☎ 212-465-6741; tickets $35-1500) at Madison Sq Garden, though when the team is doing well, seats are more than scarce; try Ticketmaster (p150). The women's league **WNBA New York Liberty** (☎ 212-465-6741) is also based at Madison Sq Garden, while the **NBA New Jersey Nets** (☎ 800-765-6387) call the Meadowlands sports complex in Rutherford, New Jersey, home.

For fans of ice hockey, **NHL New York Rangers** (☎ 212-465-6000) hit the ice running at Madison Sq Garden; the New York Islanders play at **Nassau Coliseum** (☎ 516-794-4100).

New York City's NFL (pro football) teams, the **Giants** (☎ 201-935-8222) and **Jets** (☎ 516-560-8200), share the Giants Stadium in Rutherford's Meadowlands complex.

Shopping

CLOTHING

New York's famous department stores include the following:

Bloomingdale's (Bloomie's; Map pp142-4; ☎ 212-705-2000; 59th St & Lexington Ave)

Macy's (Map pp124-6; ☎ 212-695-4400; Broadway at 34th St)

Barney's (Map pp142-4; ☎ 212-339-7300; 660 Madison Ave) An upscale department store.

Dozens of shops sell wholesale off-brand clothing in the Garment District, mainly on W 37th St between Eighth and Ninth Aves.

Soho has been bombarded by a recent influx of every chain store on the planet, from Express to Kenneth Cole, although it used to be known for its funky, indie boutiques (you'll still find a few). Now that distinction goes to neighborhoods of the East Village and Lower East Side, where you'll also find a good selection of thrift and vintage shops.

Madison Ave on the Upper East Side has the big-name designer stores, such as Armani and DKNY, and you'll find hyped superstores, such as the multilevel Niketown, on W 57th St.

For New York–style bargains on coveted designer-label clothing, shoes and accessories, try the following always-mobbed city 'secrets':

Century 21 (Map pp114-16; ☎ 212-227-9092; 22 Cortlandt St) With prices up to 75% lower than standard retail.

Daffy's (Map pp114-16; ☎ 212-334-7444; Broadway & Grand St) In Soho, with various locations around the city.

Loehmann's (Map pp124-6; ☎ 212-352-0856; Seventh Ave at 16th St)

OTHER

J&R Music & Computer World (Map pp114-16; ☎ 212-238-9000; Park Row) For computers and a huge range of electronics at discount prices, hit the mammoth J&R, across from City Hall Park.

Chelsea Flea Market (Map pp124-6; ☎ 212-647-0707; Sixth Ave at W 26th St; 🕑 7am-5pm Sat & Sun year-round). For antique furniture, vintage appliances, books and more. Get there early to snag the best bargains. (Also see p148.)

Low-cost (but often low-quality) leather goods are available along Broadway just above Houston St, on Bleecker St and on W 4th St immediately off Sixth Ave.

A dozen stores sell sturdy footwear on W 8th St between Fifth and Sixth Aves, but you'll find more stylish, high-quality options in Soho, mainly on Prince St, and on Broadway between Houston and Canal Sts.

For competitively priced diamonds and pearls, visit the Diamond District on W 47th St off Fifth Ave (closed Saturday and Sunday).

Getting There & Away

AIR

Most airlines have an office downtown or at one of the three airports that serve New York City. For lowest airfares, search discount travel websites (see p1110).

In southeastern Queens, 15 miles from Midtown Manhattan, **John F Kennedy International Airport** (JFK; Map p109; information line ☎ 718-244-4444; Queens) is where most international flights land. A few airlines have their own terminals, but most use the International Arrivals Building. The airport information line is not especially helpful.

In northern Queens, **La Guardia Airport** (Map p109; ☎ 718-533-3400; Guardia) has mostly domestic flights, including shuttles to Boston and Washington, DC. It's more convenient than JFK.

Though it's in New Jersey, about 10 miles west of Manhattan, **Newark International Airport** (Map p109; ☎ 973-961-6000; Newark, New Jersey) is just as accessible as JFK or La Guardia. It has a large, new international terminal, is making further improvements and is the hub for Continental Airlines, used by many major carriers.

BUS

All suburban and long-haul buses arrive and depart from the **Port Authority Bus Terminal** (Map pp124-6; ☎ 212-564-8484; 41st St & Eighth Ave); you may still be confronted by beggars here.

Greyhound (☎ 212-971-6300; Port Authority) links New York with major cities across the country. Regular buses go to Albany ($32, 2½ hours); Buffalo ($69, nine hours); Boston, Massachusetts ($30, 4½ hours); Philadelphia, Pennsylvania ($21, two hours); and Washington, DC ($42, 4½ hours).

Peter Pan Trailways (☎ 800-343-9999) runs buses to the nearest major cities, including a daily express to Boston ($42).

Short Line (☎ 212-736-4700) offers numerous departures to towns in northern New Jersey and upstate New York. **New Jersey Transit** (☎ 973-762-5100) serves all of that state.

CAR & MOTORCYCLE

See p1121 for information about vehicle rentals.

TRAIN

Pennsylvania Station (Penn Station; Map pp124-6; 33rd St btwn Seventh & Eighth Aves) is the departure point for all **Amtrak trains** (☎ 800-872-7245). There are regular services to Albany ($43, 2½ hours); Buffalo ($63, 7½ hours); Boston, Massachusetts ($64, 4¼ hours); Philadelphia, Pennsylvania ($48, 1¼ hours); and Washington, DC ($72, 3½ hours). Acela high-speed trains, with all business- or 1st-class seating, are available on some routes. Destinations include Boston ($99, 3½ hours), Philadelphia ($102, one hour) and Washington, DC ($157, 2¾ hours).

The **Long Island Rail Road** (LIRR; ☎ 718-217-5477) has its own platform at Penn Station for commuters to Brooklyn, Queens and the suburbs of Long Island. **New Jersey Transit trains** (☎ 973-762-5100) go from Penn Station to the Jersey suburbs and Jersey Shore.

Metro North Rail Road (☎ 212-532-4900; Grand Central Station), which serves northern suburbs and Connecticut, is the only commuter train company using Grand Central Station.

PATH (☎ 800-234-7284) has a separate subway system that runs up Sixth Ave to 33rd St and then on to Hoboken, Jersey City and Newark. These reliable trains ($1.50; every 15 minutes) run 24 hours.

Getting Around

Manhattan's street-grid system carries a lot of traffic, but outside rush hours it is rarely gridlocked. The worst traffic jams are on the roads leading in and out of the city. Cyclists will find wide wheels are best for the city's pockmarked streets. Wear a helmet and watch for taxi doors.

TO/FROM THE AIRPORT

The **Air Ride line** (☎ 800-247-7433) has information on transportation to and from all three airports. Do not accept transport from, or entrust your baggage to, anyone except uniformed airport staff.

At JFK, staff at Ground Transportation desks, near the baggage claim areas, sell taxi vouchers and shuttle bus tickets, and can explain how to get into town on the subway. An official yellow taxi from JFK into Midtown charges a fixed rate of $30; bridge and tunnel tolls, and a tip are extra. From Midtown to JFK a taxi costs about $45 to $55, plus tolls and a tip (allow at least 1½ hours). Airport shuttle bus services with **Gray Line** (☎ 212-315-3006, 800-451-0455) or **Super Shuttle** (☎ 212-209-7000, 800-258-3826) cost about $18 per person and take a circuitous route around Manhattan to drop off passengers at their various destinations. Going to the airport, you might have to leave more than two hours before check-in time.

The cheapest way to JFK is to take the A train to Howard Beach–JFK (at least an hour), then a free yellow and blue bus to the terminals (another 15 minutes). It's a hassle with luggage.

Taxis to and from La Guardia are metered, so the cost depends on time and distance – about $45 from Midtown in light traffic, plus tolls and a tip. Gray Line or Super Shuttle airport shuttle-bus services cost about $15. New York Airport Service buses run every 15 to 30 minutes to and from Midtown ($10).

To get to La Guardia via public transportation, take an A, B, C, D, 2 or 3 subway to 125th St in Harlem, then an M60 bus right to the terminals. Alternatively, take an E, F, G, R or 7 subway to Roosevelt Ave–Jackson Heights or 74th St–Broadway stops in Queens, then a Q33 bus to the main terminals. It takes well over an hour, and it's difficult with luggage.

A taxi from Midtown to Newark International Airport costs about $55, plus tolls and tip. Allow 40 minutes to an hour. Gray Line or Super Shuttle airport shuttle bus services cost about $18. Or take a bus from the Port Authority Airport Bus Center ($11).

BUS

Blue-and-white city buses operate 24 hours a day, generally along avenues in a south or north direction, and across town along the major thoroughfares. You need exact change of $2 (no pennies or bills) or a MetroCard to board the bus. If you intend to take a connecting bus, ask for a 'transfer' when boarding – a transfer ticket is good for two hours. Drivers can tell you if their bus stops near a specific site. Bus maps are available at subway and train stations.

Some 'limited stop' buses pull over only every 10 blocks or so, but at night you can ask to be let off at any point along a bus route. 'Express' buses are for outer-borough commuters.

CAR & MOTORCYCLE

Parking in Manhattan is difficult or very expensive. Street-cleaning rules require you to move your car several times a week. Parking garages in Midtown charge at least $35 during daylight hours. Cheaper lots can be found along West St in Chelsea (around $18). Hotel parking lots charge $35 to $45 a day for guests' cars.

PEDICAB

A fairly new addition to the already crazed streets are bicycle taxis, similar to rickshaws, which are used mostly as novelty rides by tourists. The general rates are 50¢ per minute, but can go up based on distance and the number of passengers. Two companies that operate pedicabs are **Manhattan Rickshaw** (☎ 212-604-4729) and **PONY** (☎ 212-965-9334).

SUBWAY

Generally, the subway is the cheapest, most reliable way to get around Manhattan and the adjacent boroughs, 24 hours a day – four million people a day can't be wrong. Run by the MTA (Metropolitan Transit Authority), **New York City Transit Authority** (☎ 718-330-1234), New York's subway system, began as privately operated lines designed to compete with, rather than complement, each other. The city wound up owning all the lines (depicted in different colors on the subway map), which form 26 different subway routes, designated by letters and numbers. A funding boost in the 1980s resulted in quieter, more reliable, graffiti-free trains. Much-needed renovation of subway stations is under way.

Almost every subway booth offers a good bus and subway map, and the subway clerks are generally helpful. A common mistake is boarding an express train that doesn't stop at the station you want – on subway maps, local stops are solid black dots, while express stops are white dots.

A subway ride costs, basically, $2 for any distance. Tokens have been phased out in favor of plastic MetroCards – a $15 MetroCard gets you 11 rides (one free ride!). A MetroCard ride includes free transfers from subway to a city bus within two hours. Even better value is the $7 MetroCard, good for a day of unlimited travel on subways and city buses. For safety, wait in the middle of the platform so you can board near the conductor's car. Do not leave your wallet in your back pocket on a crowded subway, and secure your daypack with a safety pin.

TAXI

Taxi flagfall is $2, plus 30¢ for every fifth of a mile and 20¢ a minute while stuck in traffic; 8pm-6am, a 50¢ nighttime surcharge is tacked on to your fare. The passenger must pay any bridge or tunnels tolls and tip 10% to 15% (minimum 50¢), and don't expect many thanks for it.

For trips of 50 blocks or more, ask the driver to take a road well away from Midtown traffic – it will be quicker and cheaper. Any taxi with its rooftop license number lit is available for hire, though it's hard to see it from a distance. Taxi drivers are required to take you anywhere in the city and to all airports. The city's **Taxi & Limousine Commission** (☎ 212-NYC-TAXI) is a strong regulator, and the threat of a complaint should deter any abuses.

LONG ISLAND

The crowded boroughs of Brooklyn and Queens occupy the western tip of Long Island, but the rest of the land mass, which extends about 120 miles east from the mouth of the Hudson River, is filled with diverse bedroom communities of the city. The first county east, Nassau, is mostly suburban housing and strip malls, built up as commuter trains linked the area to Manhattan. Partly rural Suffolk County covers the eastern two-thirds of the island; its tip splits into the North Fork, home of vineyards and farmland, and the South Fork, otherwise known as the Hamptons.

The first European settlements on the island were whaling and fishing ports, established as early as 1640. In the late 19th and early 20th centuries, the ultrarich built big estates along the secluded coves and cliff tops of the north shore.

Now a trip to Long Island means a trip to the beach – crowded Jones Beach, frenetic Fire Island, quiet Shelter Island or the posh East Hampton, all accessible by train or bus. To explore the rural areas, it's best to have a car, though traffic to and from the city can be hellish in summer.

The **Long Island Convention & Visitors Bureau** (☎ 631-951-3440, 877-386-6654; www.licvb.com) publishes an annual free travel guide. Local chambers of commerce provide maps, restaurant listings and lodging guides.

Activities

For bicycling, try Rte 25 on the North Fork, side roads in the Hamptons, the 7-mile Rte 114 from East Hampton to Sag Harbor, or the boardwalk at Long Beach in Nassau County. There's pleasant hiking in October and April on Fire Island, Shelter Island and along the shoreline from East Hampton to Montauk. Montauk and Long Beach are the main surfing spots.

Getting There & Away

From Manhattan, **Hampton Jitney buses** (☎ 800-936-0440; www.hamptonjitney.com) head off to the South Fork ($48 round-trip) several times daily. **Sunrise Coach Lines** (☎ 800-527-7709) services the North Fork (around $22 one way).

Long Island Rail Road (LIRR; ☎ 718-217-5477) trains run from New York City's Penn Station to 134 stations throughout Long Island, as far as Greenport on the North Fork and Montauk on the South Fork. Fares are similar to the buses.

In summer LIRR offers round-trip deals to the south-shore beaches (buy tickets the day before to avoid long lines just before departure).

ATLANTIC SHORE

Long, narrow rows of sand dunes form a stretch of islands with remarkably clean and pleasant beaches, though the ones closest to New York get very crowded.

On summer weekends it's quite a mob scene – but a fascinating one – on the 6-mile stretch of massive, pretty **Jones Beach**, which attracts young surfers, wild city folk, local teens, nudists, staid families, gay men, lesbians and plenty of old-timers. There's a long boardwalk that's great for strolling or running along, concessions, miniature and standard golf courses, a massive swimming pool and a small Jones Beach museum called **Castles in the Sand** (☎ 516-785-1600; admission $1; 10am-4pm). Oh, and there are parking lots for 25,000 cars. LIRR makes a bus connection to Jones Beach.

Beautiful **Long Beach**, even closer to the city and also accessible by train, has clean beaches, a hoppin' main town strip, a surfers' scene and many city hipsters; even rock 'n' roll bad girl Joan Jett calls the town home.

The stretch of dunes forming gorgeous **Fire Island** includes **Fire Island National Seashore** (☎ 631-289-4810) and several summer-only villages accessible by ferry from Long Island. The villages of the exclusive Pines and the more down-to-earth Cherry Grove make up the major local gay summer scene, while other areas cater to straight singles and families. Ferry terminals to Fire Island beaches and the national seashore are close to LIRR stations at Bayshore, Sayville and Patchogue ($12 round-trip, May to November). There are limited places to stay, and booking in advance is strongly advised (check www.fireisland.com for information). Beach camping is allowed in **Watch Hill** (☎ 631-289-9336; www.watchhillfi.com; campsites $15; camping from May 16–Oct 14), though mosquitoes can be fierce and reservations are a must. At the western end of Fire Island, **Robert Moses State Park** is the only spot accessible by car and can get very crowded.

The Hamptons

What began as a tranquil hideaway for city artists, musicians and writers has developed into a frenetic summer getaway mobbed with jet-setters, celebrities and throngs of curious wannabes. That said, there is still plenty of the original peace and beauty to discover. The beaches and farmlands (what's left of them) are indeed beautiful, the restaurants are top notch and there's plenty of opportunity for outdoor activities, from kayaking to mountain biking. However, bargain travelers should be warned: absolutely everything costs a pretty penny out here, with most inns charging well over $200 per night in high season. Prices drop a bit and traffic jams disappear about a month after Labor Day. Pick up a copy of the *East Hampton Star* or the *Southampton Press* for local arts listings.

The Hamptons is actually a series of villages, most with 'Hampton' in the name.

SOUTHAMPTON

The village of Southampton has 'old money' and is rather conservative compared to some of its neighbors. Within the town is a small Native American reservation, home to the Shinnecocks, who run a tiny **museum** (☎ 631-287-4923) with unpredictable opening hours. The **Parrish Art Museum** (☎ 631-283-2111; 25 Jobs Lane; admission $4; 11am-5pm Mon-Sat, 1-5pm Sun) has quality exhibitions.

La Parmigiana (☎ 631-283-8030; 48 Hampton Rd; dishes $12-18) For an excellent meal that won't empty your wallet, join the locals at La Parmigiana for huge plates of pasta and meatballs.

BRIDGEHAMPTON

To the east, Bridgehampton has the shortest of all main drags, but it's packed with trendy boutiques and restaurants.

Enclave Inn (☎ 631-537-0197; Montauk Hwy; r low season $75-249, r high season $99-349;) A relative bargain that's stylish and comfortable, and just a short walk from the beach.

SAG HARBOR

Seven miles north of Bridgehampton on Peconic Bay is the old whaling town of Sag Harbor. Check out its **Whaling Museum** (☎ 631-725-0770; admission $3; 10am-5pm Mon-Sat, from 1pm Sun May 17–Oct 1, noon-4pm Sat & Sun only Oct-Dec), while its tiny Cape Cod–like streets are a joy to stroll through. It's also got several excellent restaurants worth checking out.

Espresso (☎ 631-725-4433; 184 Division St; dishes $9-15) A tiny Italian deli tucked into a quiet residential street where you can pick up outrageously good sandwiches and desserts for a beach picnic.

Sen (☎ 631-725-1774; 23 Main St; dishes $15-20) A popular sushi den.

EAST HAMPTON

Long Island's trendiest town is East Hampton, where you can catch readings and art exhibitions at **Guild Hall** (☎ 631-324-0806; 158 Main St).

Babette's (☎ 631-537-5377; 66 Newtown Lane; dishes $9-18) An outstanding organic and mostly vegetarian eatery where former-president Bill Clinton stopped in to visit the active Democratic owner when he was in town.

The eateries where you'll most likely spot celebrities are as follows:

Della Femmina (631-329-6666; North Main St; dishes $18-27)

Nick & Toni's (☎ 631-324-3550; 136 North Main St; dishes $18-27) Italian-influenced dishes are flawless.

MONTAUK & AROUND

More honky-tonk than the rest of the Hamptons, Montauk has relatively reasonable restaurants and a louder bar scene, largely because all the service personnel – mainly students – live here in communal housing.

Memory Motel (☎ 631-668-2702; 692 Montauk Hwy; r $95-120;) For a 'bargain,' try staying at this scruffy but comfortable spot where Mick Jagger often stayed in the 1970s and was inspired to write the Rolling Stones song of the same name.

Covering the eastern tip of the South Fork is **Montauk Point State Park**, with its impressive Montauk Lighthouse.

Hither Hills State Park (☎ 631-668-2554; New York residents/nonresidents $24/48; Apr-Nov) You can camp in the sand here.

Cedar Point Park (☎ 631-852-7620; campsites $24) You can also try Cedar Point Park in the Springs section of East Hampton on the calm Northwest Harbor. Just be sure to call ahead, as sites tend to fill up fast.

NORTH FORK

The main North Fork town and the place for ferries to Shelter Island, **Greenport** is friendly and more affordable than South Fork villages, though the restaurants that are around the marina are still pretty pricey. North Fork is known mostly for its wineries, and the **Long Island Wine Council** (☎ 631-369-5887) provides details of the local wine trail, along Rte 25. A drive along the back roads of the North Fork affords some beautiful, unspoiled vistas of farms and rural residential areas.

The **Always In Bed & Breakfast** (☎ 631-765-5344; r $135-150;) is an elegant, cozy and reasonable B&B in the woods of nearby **Southold**.

SHELTER ISLAND

Between the North and South Forks, Shelter Island, accessible by ferry, is home to a cluster of Victorian buildings and the **Mashomack Nature Preserve**. It's a great spot for hiking or kayaking.

B&Bs include the following:

Azalea House (☎ 631-749-4252; 1 Thomas Ave; r $60-250;)

Ram's Head Inn (☎ 631-749-0811; r low season from $70, r high season from $200;) A large, columned spot overlooking the water.

Sunset Beach (☎ 631-749-2001; 37 Shore Rd; Jun-Aug) A summer hotspot, this club and eatery serves French-Asian cuisine to trendies who stay to dance until the sun comes up.

UPSTATE NEW YORK

New York State has some magnificent wilderness and surprisingly rural areas, plus a rich history preserved in many pretty towns and grand estates. You can reach the main towns by bus or train, but to explore the countryside, you need a car. Take a train to a town like Albany and rent one there – you'll avoid driving in the metropolis. Many museums and historic sites are open only from May to October, or keep shorter hours off-season – call for details. Most campgrounds are closed in the winter.

HUDSON VALLEY

Winding roads along the Hudson River take you by picturesque farms, Victorian cottages, apple orchards and old-money mansions built by New York's elite. **Hudson Valley Tourism** (☎ 800-232-4782; www.hvnet.com) has regional information about sites and events. Painters of the Hudson River school romanticized these landscapes – you can see their work at museums in Albany, Poughkeepsie and New York City.

Lower Hudson Valley

On the west side, 40 miles north of New York City, **Harriman State Park** covers 72 sq miles and offers swimming, hiking, camping and a **visitors center** (☎ 845-786-5003). Adjacent **Bear Mountain State Park** (☎ 845-786-2701) offers great views from its 1306ft peak. The Manhattan skyline looms beyond the river and surrounding greenery. You can enjoy hiking in summer, wildflowers in spring, gold foliage in fall and cross-country skiing in winter.

West of Rte 9W, the **Storm King Art Center** (☎ 845-534-3115; www.stormkingartcenter.org; admission $9; 11am-5pm Wed-Sun Apr-Nov), on Old Pleasant Hill Rd in Mountainville, is well worth a visit. It showcases stunning avant-garde sculpture by Calder, Moore and Noguchi, among others. Tucked among rolling hills, this outdoor park occupies 400 acres, successfully combining art and nature. Nearby **Newburgh**, once an important New York whaling village, was George Washington's longest-lasting wartime headquarters during the Revolutionary War. **Washington's Headquarters State Historic Site** (☎ 845-562-1195; cnr Liberty & Washington Sts, Newburgh; admission $3; 🕑 1-5pm Wed-Sat Apr-Oct) has a museum, galleries and maps.

Another excellent stop for war historians is **West Point**, where the Revolutionary War's colonial troops stretched a massive iron chain across the Hudson River to blockade British ships. The strategic fort became the US Military Academy in 1802. West Point's graduates include Generals Ulysses S Grant, Douglas MacArthur and H Norman Schwarzkopf. The **visitors center** (☎ 845-938-2638; 🕑 9am-4:45pm) in Highland Falls has exhibits and maps and can tell you when cadets will parade in their finery.

Middle Hudson Valley

The largest town on the Hudson's east bank, **Poughkeepsie** (puh-*kip*-see) is famous for **Vassar**, a private liberal-arts college that admitted only women until 1969. Its modern **Francis Lehman Loeb Art Center** (☎ 845-437-5632; 124 Raymond Ave; 🕑 10am-5pm Tue-Sat, 1-5pm Sun) features Hudson River–school paintings and contemporary work. **Dutchess County Tourism Office** (☎ 800-445-3131; www.dutchesstourism.com; 3 Neptune Rd; 🕑 9am-5pm Mon-Fri) has regional information. Cheap motel chains in Poughkeepsie are clustered along Rte 9, south of the Mid-Hudson Bridge. For a stay with much more character, try the **Copper Penny Inn** (☎ 845-452-3045; www.copperpennyinn.com; 2406 Hackensack Rd; r $90-150), a well-run B&B in a converted 1860s farmhouse.

Hyde Park (reservations ☎ 800-967-2283) has long been associated with the Roosevelts, a prominent family since the 19th century. Recommended is a combination ticket ($18), which you can use for all three following sites. The **Franklin D Roosevelt Library & Museum** (☎ 845-229-8114; www.fdrlibrary.marist.edu/; 511 Albany Post Rd/Rte 9; admission $10; 🕑 9am-5pm) features exhibits on the man who created the New Deal and led the USA into WWII. Eleanor Roosevelt's cottage, **Val-Kill** (845-229-5302; www.ervk.org; admission $5; 🕑 9am-5pm), was her retreat from Hyde Park, FDR's mother and FDR himself. The **Vanderbilt Mansion** (☎ 800-967-2283; Rte 9; admission $8; 🕑 9am-5pm), a national historic site 2 miles north on Rte 9, is a spectacle of lavish beaux arts and eclectic architecture. A nearby country inn, the **Village Square** (☎ 845-229-7141; 4159 Albany Post Rd; r $40-100), has exceptional country-style rooms.

The well-regarded **Culinary Institute of America** (☎ 800-285-4627; www.ciachef.edu/; 1964 Campus Dr) trains future chefs and can satisfy absolutely anyone's gastronomic cravings. Its four student-staffed restaurants are formal, but **St Andrew's Cafe** (☎ 845-471-6608; mains around $30) is more casual and the least expensive. Reservations are required.

CATSKILLS

This scenic region of small towns, farms, resorts and forests has become the latest playground for NYC publishing types and various celebrities who have tired of the Hamptons glitz. They've been snapping up historic houses here to serve as second-home getaways, but so far the rural feel of the area has not been compromised. You'll still find quaint small towns galore, and gorgeous countryside.

The focus of the Catskills has moved north in recent years. While the Southern Catskills, and its 'Borscht Belt' resorts, were once enormous holiday spots for New York's Jewish families, most destinations have closed. Today Manhattanites needing escape stick to Rte 28, which crosses the Catskills west of Woodstock, then winds past the Ashokan Reservoir and through the 'French Catskills' (an area settled by the French). Along this route are great restaurants, campgrounds, inexpensive lodgings and character galore.

The **Kaatskill Kaleidoscope** (☎ 888-303-3936; Mt Tremper; admission $5) is the world's largest. The 60ft tube, an old farm silo, is touristy, but the 10-minute presentation is worthwhile, featuring US history, psychedelic colors and, of course, images of marijuana leaves.

In Arkville, take a scenic ride on the historic **Delaware & Ulster Rail Line** (☎ 845-652-2821; www.durr.org; Hwy 28; adult $10; 🕑 Sat & Sun May-Aug). Nearby, Fleischmans hosts an old-fashioned **auction** every Saturday night, where locals pack the rafters to snap up bargains from old records to furniture. Take a load off at the **River Run Bed & Breakfast** (☎ 845-254-4884; www.catskill.net/riverrun/; 882 Main St; r $75-165), which has beautiful oak floors, stained-glass windows, a big porch and comfortable rooms. **Belleayre Hostel** (☎ 845-245-4200; Pine Hill; dm $10), off Main St, is very rustic with cheap bunks.

Keen skiers should head further north, where Rtes 23 and 23A lead you to **Hunter Mountain Ski Bowl** (☎ 518-263-4223), a year-round resort with challenging runs and a 1600ft vertical drop; and **Ski Windham** (☎ 518-734-4300), with more intermediate runs.

Woodstock & Saugerties

Ten miles northwest of Kingston, **Woodstock** symbolizes the tumultuous 1960s, when US youth questioned authority, experimented with freedom and redefined popular culture. Today it's a combination of quaint and hip. The town has been an artists' colony since the early 1900s, and you'll see an eclectic mix of young Phish fans sporting dreadlocks, and old-time, graying hippie throwbacks. The famous 1969 Woodstock music festival actually occurred in Bethel, a town over 40 miles southwest, where a simple plaque marks the famous spot. Two not-so-peaceful spin-offs, also named 'Woodstock,' took place in nearby Saugerties (1994) and Rome (1999). **Saugerties**, just a few miles from the town of Woodstock, offers a similar downtown area, with fewer galleries, cafés and eateries.

You'll find plenty of fine inns in the area, but only a couple stand out from the frilly Victorian masses. The **Villa at Saugerties** (☎ 845-246-0682; www.thevillaatsaugerties.com; 159 Fawn Rd; r Jun-Oct $110-160, r Nov-May $95-140; ⊠ ⁙ ⚇), opened recently by a young city couple who escaped the rat race, is the sleekest place around. The four amazing rooms are more urban boutique hotel than country B&B. In Woodstock, **Twin Gables** (☎ 845-679-9479; 73 Tinker St; s/d $59/99; ⊠ ⁙) is central, with nicely furnished rooms that have a shared bathroom. Backpackers should head to the nearby **Rip Van Winkle Campground** (☎ 845-246-8334; 149 Blue Mountain Rd; campsites $24-28) for cheap, well-maintained sites. For a true adventure, stay at remote **Saugerties Lighthouse** (☎ 847-247-0656; www.saugertieslighthouse.com; r Nov-Mar $135, r Apr-Oct $160), an 1869 lighthouse that sits on a small island in the Esopus Creek. The Saugerties Lighthouse Conservancy operates it as a year-round B&B, taking guests out to one of the three spare and tidy rooms, all with sweeping water views, by boat.

The **Blue Mountain Bistro** (☎ 845-679-8519; Glasco Turnpike; Saugerties; dishes $12-17) serves up four-star French-Mediterranean cuisine as well as Spanish tapas to a sophisticated crowd. **New World Home Cooking Co** (☎ 845-246-0900; Rte 212; Woodstock; dishes $10-16) focuses on fresh and tasty organic food in a quirky setting. **Heaven** (☎ 914-679-0111; 17 Tinker St; dishes $4) is a hip coffee hang, offering organic blends, affordable soups and sandwiches and scrumptious baked goods.

Getting There & away

Adirondack Trailways (☎ 800-858-8555) operates daily buses to Kingston, the Catskills' gateway town, as well as to Saugerties, Catskills, Hunter and Woodstock. Buses leave from the Port Authority.

ALBANY

While the New York State capital is far from a high-culture destination, the town (nicknamed 'Smallbany' by jaded locals) has revived its northeastern charm in several neighborhoods. **Lark St** (www.larkstreet.org) is the most hoppin' strip, with plenty of good shops, restaurants and trendy lounges, including several gay bars and clubs. The main **visitors center** (☎ 518-434-0405; 25 Quackenbush Sq; ⌚ 9am-5pm Mon-Fri, until 4pm Sat & Sun) has information about the city's mansions and churches. It's easy to get around on foot or by car. However, the downtown empties after business hours, and walking between neighborhoods can feel creepy after dark. For entertainment information, pick up a copy of *Metroland*, the free alternative weekly.

SIGHTS

The **Empire State Plaza** houses legislative offices, state agencies, modern art and a performing-arts center, and is dubbed 'the Egg' for its oval architecture. It also has an **observation deck** (☎ 518-473-7521; Corning Tower; admission free; ⌚ 10am-3:45pm) that overlooks the city and the Hudson River, and the **New York State Museum** (☎ 518-474-5877; www.nysm.nysed.gov; admission by donation; ⌚ 9:30am-5pm), which documents the state's political, cultural and natural history. East of the plaza, **Albany Institute of History & Art** (☎ 518-463-4478; www.albanyinstitute.org; 125 Washington Ave; admission $5; ⌚ 10am-5pm Tue & Thu-Sat, 10am-8pm Wed, noon-5pm Sun) houses decorative arts and works by Hudson River–school painters, including the likes of Thomas Cole and Asher Durand.

SLEEPING

Chain motels along Central Ave, west of I-87 exit 2, are only about a 10-minute drive from downtown, and prices are low. A good downtown option is **Pine Haven B&B** (518-482-1574; 531 Western Ave; r $59-89;), a Victorian home with feather beds and surprisingly reasonable rates. **Kittleman House** (518-432-3979; 70 Willett St; r $95;) has antique-furnished rooms and views of Washington Park, and the **State House** (800-427-6063; 393 State St; r $135-260;) is a more upscale option.

EATING & DRINKING

For the best fare in town, stick to the Lark St area:

Shades of Green (518-434-1830; 187 Lark St; dishes $8-13) Albany's haven for vegetarians.

A Taste of Greece (518-426-9000; 193 Lark St; dishes $9-13) A bustling storefront offering authentic Greek food.

Justin's (518-436-7008; 301 Lark St; dishes $13-19) An upscale dining scene.

For drinking, check the following:

Daily Grind (518-427-0464; 204 Lark St) Doles out freshly brewed coffee.

Waterworks Pub (518-465-9079; 76 Central Ave) A gay crowd flocks here for late-night snacks, but mostly dancing and drinking.

GETTING THERE & AWAY

From the **bus terminal** (34 Hamilton St), **Trailways** (518-436-9651) and **Greyhound** (518-434-8095) head to/from New York City ($33, three hours), Long Island, the Catskills, the Adirondacks, Buffalo ($53, six hours) and Montreal, Canada ($53, five hours). The **Amtrak train station** (518-462-5763; 555 East St) is 2 miles from downtown and has regular trains to New York ($41, two hours), Buffalo ($56, five hours) and north to the Adirondacks and Montreal.

AROUND ALBANY

Cooperstown

Fifty miles west of Albany, Cooperstown is pure Americana, thanks to its brick buildings and national baseball institution. The **chamber of commerce** (607-547-9983; 31 Chestnut St; 9am-7pm) provides visitors information.

The **National Baseball Hall of Fame & Museum** (607-547-7200; 25 Main St; www.baseballhalloffame.org; admission $9.50; 9am-5pm Sep-May, until 9pm Memorial Day–Labor Day), a shrine to the national sport, is what this town is all about. It has exhibits on players, uniforms and equipment; a theater; library; and an interactive statistical database. The **Farmer's Museum & Village Crossroads** (607-547-1450; www.farmersmuseum.org; Lake Rd; admission $9; 10am-4pm Tue-Sun Apr, May, Oct & Nov, until 5pm Jun-Sep) consists of a dozen relocated 19th-century buildings, including a store, printing office and barn. The old stone **Fenimore Art Museum** (607-547-1400; www.fenimoreartmuseum.org; Lake Rd; admission $9; 10am-4pm Tue-Sun Apr, May, Oct & Nov, until 5pm Jun-Sep) has an outstanding collection of Americana.

Accommodations range from homey B&Bs to more basic campgrounds. The **Middlefield Guest House** (607-286-7056; mghcjt@webtv.net; Hwy 166; s/d $40/60;) is in a restored farmhouse. **Cooperstown Beaver Valley Campground** (800-726-7314; Rte 28; campsites $17-31) has full facilities, rustic sites and cabins. Don't bother with its dreadful 'camp cabins' or 'log cabin' trailers, overpriced at $58 and $100, respectively.

Several restaurants along Main St serve inexpensive 'family-style' American food.

Pine Hills Trailways (914-633-7174) and **Adirondack Trailways** (800-858-8555) stop in front of the Chestnut St Deli.

Saratoga Springs

This gracious Victorian town is known for mineral springs, performing arts, horse racing and its liberal-arts college, Skidmore. It's blessed with the artsy, intellectual feel of a college town and the removed feel of a rural, pioneering community. The town's **visitors center** (518-587-3241; 9am-4pm Mon-Sun) is in a former trolley station across from Congress Park.

Most of the famous springs are in **Saratoga Spa State Park** (518-584-2535; 19 Roosevelt Dr; per car $4; dawn-dusk), which offers the soothing Lincoln and Roosevelt mineral baths, along with golf courses, an Olympic-sized pool complex, multi-use trails and ice rinks. It's also where you'll find the **Saratoga Performing Arts Center** (518-587-3330; www.spac.org; Hall of Springs), the summer home of the New York City Ballet and Philadelphia Orchestra, offering world-class cultural performances (tickets around $15 to $53). The **National Museum of Dance** (518-584-2225; www.dancemuseum.org; 99 South Broadway; admission

$6.50; 10am-5pm Tue-Sun), the only national museum dedicated to professional American dance, is next to the Lincoln Baths.

From late July through September, fans of horse racing flock to the **Saratoga Race Course** (518-584-6200), the country's oldest active thoroughbred racetrack. The **National Museum of Racing & Hall of Fame** (518-584-0400; www.racingmuseum.org; admission $7; 10am-4:30pm Mon-Sat, from noon Sun) is across from the track.

The nearest campground is **Cold Brook Campsites** (518-584-8038; 385 Gurn Springs Rd; campsites $20), about 10 miles north in Gansevoort. Independent motels along Rte 9/S Broadway (exit 13N) are the cheapest, but there is a good selection of affordable B&Bs, especially **Brunswick Bed & Breakfast** (518-584-6751; www.brunswickbb.com; 143 Union Ave; r from $79). The **Saratoga Downtowner** (518-584-6160; www.saratogerdowntowner.com; 413 Broadway; s/d $69/89;) is a standard motor lodge in the heart of town; during racing season, from July 23 to September 1 singles/doubles cost $169/199. The **Adelphi** (518-587-4688; www.adelphihotel.com; 365 Broadway; r $115-300;) is a wonderfully opulent Victorian inn; room rates vary depending on local events and the season.

Plenty of cafés and restaurants line Broadway and the intimate side streets. **Four Seasons Natural Foods Store & Café** (518-584-4670; 33 Phila St; dishes $6) has a tiny seating area where local college kids and other veggies fuel up on outrageously delicious brunch and lunch buffets. Meanwhile, the cool **Wine Bar** (518-584-8777; 417 Broadway; snacks $10) serves 50 wines by the glass, along with nibbles like cheese plates.

Greyhound (518-434-9651) and **Adirondack Trailways** (800-858-8555) stop at 133 S Broadway. Amtrak has daily trains from Montreal and New York City.

THE ADIRONDACKS

Adirondack Park's 6 million acres include towns, mountains, lakes, rivers and more than 2000 miles of hiking trails. The Adirondack Forest Preserve covers 40% of the park; the state constitution designates it as 'forever wild' – a good thing, because the peaks and valleys and lakes rival the best in the state. There's good trout, salmon and pike fishing, along with excellent camping spots (despite the biting black flies, a summer nuisance). In colonial times, settlers exploited the forests for beaver fur, timber and hemlock bark, but by the 19th century, wilderness retreats became fashionable, and large hotels and millionaires' estates adopted the rustic Adirondack style: log cabins on a grand scale.

Lake George

At the park's southeastern entrance, 32-mile-long Lake George has clear blue water and wild shorelines. The village of Lake George is tacky and touristy; still, it's a gateway to the Adirondacks. The **Great Escape Fun Park** (518-798-1084; adult/child $29/15) features raft rides, roller coasters, shows and a beautiful Adirondack backdrop. In nearby Glens Falls, the remarkable Hyde Collection, housed in the **Hyde Collection Art Museum** (518-792-1761; www.hydeartmuseum.org; 161 Warren St; admission free; 10am-5pm Tue-Sat, 10am-7pm Thu, noon-5pm Sun), an impressive 1912 Florentine Renaissance-style villa, includes works by Rembrandt, Degas and Matisse.

The state maintains wonderfully remote **campgrounds** (reservations 800-456-2267) on Lake George's islands. One of several local tourist offices is the **Adirondack Mountain Club** (518-668-4447; 814 Goggins Rd), which publishes excellent guides. **Lake George Battleground Public Campground** (518-668-3348; campsites $10-16), at the southern end of town, has 50 shaded sites. Canada St/Rte 9 is lined with motels. Friendly **Georgian Motel** (518-668-5408; fax 518-668-5870; 384 Canada St; r $49-200) has basic, clean rooms. Accommodations rates are highest in summer.

Lake Placid

This mountain resort hosted the Winter Olympics in 1932 as well as 1980, and elite athletes still train here. The **visitors center** (518-523-2445; www.lakeplacid.com; 216 Main St; 8am-4pm Mon-Fri, from 9am Sat & Sun) has maps and information about skiing, fishing, cycling and hiking. For information about all the Olympic sports centers open to visitors, check out www.orda.org.

On Main St, the **Olympic Center Ice Arenas** (518-523-3325; Main St; admission $5) has four ice rinks that are now used for training, hockey and ice shows (tours available). Ski jumpers train year-round at the **Olympic Ski Jump Complex** (518-523-2202; Rte 73), which is southeast of town. The **Mt Van Hoevenberg Olympic Sports Complex** (518-523-4436; adult in winter $125;

by appointment only), for the most adventurous travelers, lets you shoot through the bobsled or luge runs with a professional driver, weather permitting.

Lake Placid has expensive accommodations, especially in summer and in the ski season. Wilmington, 15 miles east, is cheaper. South of town, the Adirondack Mountain Club's (ADK) **Adirondack Loj** (518-523-3441; www.adk.org; dm/r $34/55) is a large house beside a small lake – it is a lovely, rustic retreat with great atmosphere and good breakfasts. For a place with character, check **Hotel St Moritz** (518-523-9240; 31 Saranac Ave; r $45-55). **Paradox Lodge** (877-743-9078; 76 Saranac Ave; r $80-125), an all-seasons inn housed in a renovated 1950s lodge, has rustic furniture, tidy rooms and a peaceful, covered porch.

ST LAWRENCE RIVER

East of Lake Ontario, over 1890 tiny islands dot the wide St Lawrence River in what's called the **Thousand Islands** region. Once a summer playground for the very rich, it's now a popular area for boating, camping and even scuba diving, promoted by the **1000 Islands International Tourism Council** (800-847-5263; www.visit1000islands.com; 9am-5pm).

The relaxing village of **Cape Vincent** is at the western end of the St Lawrence River, where it meets Lake Ontario. Its **Burnham Point State Park** (315-654-2324; Rte 12E; campsites $20) has small, wooded, lakeside campsites. Further east, Alexandria Bay (Alex Bay), an early-20th-century resort town, has lost its charm but remains the departure point for ferries to Heart Island, where **Boldt Castle** (800-847-5263; admission $4.75; 10am-6:30pm mid-May–Sep) marks the sad love story of a rags-to-riches New York hotelier who built the castle for his beloved wife, who then died before its completion. The same hotelier once asked his chef to create a new salad dressing, which was popularized as 'Thousand Island' – an unfortunate blend of ketchup, mayonnaise and relish.

Ogdensburg is the unlikely birthplace of artist Frederic Remington (1861–1909), chronic romanticizer of the American West. The **Frederic Remington Art Museum** (315-393-2425; www.remington-museum.org; admission $5; 11am-5pm Wed-Sat, 1-5pm Sun) is the place to view his sculptures, paintings and personal effects.

FINGER LAKES REGION

Eleven long, narrow lakes stretch north to south and form the fingers of this western New York region. It's an ideal place for boating, fishing, cycling, hiking and cross-country skiing, and the rolling hills are the state's best wine-growing region. With more than 65 vineyards, you can sample an array of palate-pleasing whites and reds. The **New York Wine & Grape Foundation** (315-536-7442; www.newyorkwines.org), in Penn Yan, distributes free brochures about wine trails.

Seneca Falls

This sleepy, tiny town is where the USA's organized women's rights movement was born. After being excluded from an antislavery meeting, Elizabeth Cady Stanton and her friends drafted an 1848 declaration asserting that 'all men and women are created equal.' The inspirational **Women's Rights National Historical Park** (315-568-2991; www.nps.gov/wori; 136 Fall St; admission $5; 9am-5pm) has a small but fairly impressive museum with an informative film available for viewing, plus a visitors center offering tours of Cady Stanton's house. The surprisingly tiny **National Women's Hall of Fame** (315-568-8060; www.greatwomen.org; 76 Fall St; admission $5; 9:30am-5pm Mon-Sat May-Oct, 10am-4pm Wed-Sat Nov-Apr, noon-4pm Sun Nov-Apr) honors American women such as first lady Abigail Adams.

Ithaca & Around

This fun, diverse and handsome college town has pedestrian-friendly streets lined with bookstores, eateries, art-house cinemas and a summertime farmers' market. For tourist information, head to the **visitors center** (800-284-8422; 904 E Shore Dr; 9am-5pm Mon-Fri, from 10am Sat).

Ithaca's suburbs and surrounding countryside are interspersed with waterfalls, gorges and gorgeous parks, popular with hikers and rock climbers. Eight miles north on Rte 89, the spectacular **Taughannock Falls** spill 215ft into the steep gorge below; **Taughannock Falls State Park** (607-387-6739; Rte 89) has two major hiking trails, craggy gorges, tent-trailer sites and cabins.

Founded in 1865, **Cornell University** boasts a lovely campus, mixing traditional and contemporary architecture, that sits high on a hill, overlooking the picturesque town below. The striking, modern **Johnson Museum**

of Fine Art (☎ 607-255-6464; www.museum.cornell.edu; University Ave; admission free; ⏲ 10am-5pm Tue-Sun), which was designed by IM Pei, has a major Asian collection, pre-Columbian, American and European exhibits, and a nice view from its top floor.

For sleeping, a gem of a find is the **Elmshade Guest House** (☎ 607-273-1707; 402 South Albany St; r $35-125; ⊠ ⁂), a private home on a quiet street offering eight spotless, tasteful rooms, all with televisions, for remarkably low rates that include a hearty breakfast. For a more luxurious stay, head to the grand **William Henry Miller Inn** (☎ 607-256-4553; www.millerinn.com; 303 North Aurora St; r $95-155; ⊠ ⁂), a historic B&B (with wheelchair access), built by Cornell University's first student of architecture, William Henry Miller.

Ithaca has a great variety of international, gourmet and vegetarian restaurants. Popular **Moosewood Restaurant** (☎ 607-273-9610; www.moosewoodrestaurant.com; 215 N Cayuga St; mains $12) offers fixed-price menus that change daily, including salad, soup and dessert; it's famous for its vegetarian dishes and recipe books by founder Mollie Katzen. The bustling **Just a Taste Wine & Tapas Bar** (☎ 607-277-9463; 116 N Aurora St; tapas $4-7) incorporates food and wines from local merchants into its daily changing menu. **Common Ground** (☎ 607-273-1505; www.ithacacommonground.com; 1230 Danby Rd) has a mixed gay clientele that comes for the live music, dancing and a variety of shows.

WESTERN NEW YORK

The Erie Canal spawned a number of early industrial centers along its route between Albany and Buffalo. Tracing the canal is an alternative to the I-90 toll route, and a more interesting way to get to Niagara Falls, 430 miles northwest of New York City. Plus, the canal's towpaths are ideal for easy-going cycling trips. Unfortunately, two of the region's biggest cities, Syracuse and Rochester, don't really warrant visits. The cities, filled with chain motels, are a cultural void, and the food isn't great (Rochester's local speciality is the 'garbage plate,' a pile of macaroni, beans, french fries and a hot dog).

Niagara Falls

Misty sprays and the majestic scale of this roaring cascade make it a marvelous spectacle – assuming you don't get so distracted by the tacky theme-park restaurants, flashy arcades and high-rise hotels that you forget to look at the natural wonder. To keep tourists and their dollars for longer than it takes to see the falls, the Canadian side – the much worthier side for visiting, as it's where you'll find the stunning views – offers a whole strip of Vegas-like attractions, including a towering casino (see Canadian Niagara Falls p165). The New York side, which has a handful of low-key, natural-park offerings (and now a casino of its own) is a depressing town with not much going for it – mainly because its view of the cascade is limited (but there's a perfect one of Ontario's tacky skyline).

If you can strap on some mental blinders and focus on the falls, you'll be glad you came. Long before tourism invaded, Seneca Indians populated the area, leading French priest Louis Hennepin here in 1678. His description, widely read in Europe, was quite apt: 'The universe does not afford its parallel.'

ORIENTATION & INFORMATION

Here there are two separate towns: Niagara Falls, New York (USA), with 61,800 people; and Niagara Falls, Ontario (Canada), with 75,400 people. The towns face each other across the Niagara River, which is spanned by the Rainbow Bridge.

On the US side, the convention and **visitors bureau** (☎ 800-338-7890; 4th & Niagara Sts; ⏲ 8:30am-5pm) is next to the NFTA bus terminal. The **Orin Lehman State Park Visitors Center** (☎ 716-278-1796; Prospect Park; ⏲ 9am-5pm), adjacent to the falls, stays open later and shows a good film on the falls ($3).

SIGHTS & ACTIVITIES

If you must stay on the US side, you can see side views of the **American Falls** and their western portion, the Bridal Veil Falls, dropping 180ft. Take the Prospect Point Observation Tower elevator up for a vista (50¢). Cross the bridge to **Goat Island** for other viewpoints, including Terrapin Point, which has a fine view of Horseshoe Falls and pedestrian bridges to the Three Sisters Islands in the upper rapids. From the north corner of Goat Island, an elevator descends to the **Cave of the Winds** (☎ 716-278-1730; admission $6), where walkways go within 25ft of the cataracts (raincoats provided). The **Maid of the Mist** (☎ 716-284-8897; tours $8.50; Apr-Oct) boat trip around the bottom of the falls has been a major attraction since 1846 and is highly recommended. Boats leave every 15 minutes from the base of the Prospect Park Observation Tower on the US side.

TOURS

Many tours stop at major sights on both sides and include a Maid of the Mist ride. Check out the following:

Bedore Tours (☎ 716-285-7550; tours $45-130)

Niagara Helicopters (☎ 905-357-5672) Does similar chopper trips from Canada.

Rainbow Air (☎ 716-284-2800; tours $50) Runs 10-minute sightseeing flights over the falls.

SLEEPING & EATING

Besides some of the usual chains, the US side doesn't have many options. You're better off making a day trip from a home base in Buffalo – or heading over to Canada if you get tired or hungry.

Hanover House B&B (☎ 716-278-1170; 610 Buffalo Rd; r $80-125; ⊠ ⊠) One quirky choice, though, is this Italian-villa style home with four cozy, Victorian-style rooms.

GETTING THERE & AROUND

From the **NFTA terminal** (4th & Niagara Sts), frequent No 40 buses go to Buffalo ($1.85, one hour) for air and bus connections. The **Amtrak train station** (☎ 716-285-4224) is about 2 miles northeast of downtown. And from Niagara Falls, daily trains go to Buffalo, Toronto and New York City ($60, eight hours). The Canadian-side **Greyhound & Trailways terminal** (☎ 905-357-2133; 4555 Erie Ave) has buses to Toronto (US$15.50, 1½ hours).

Avoid driving around on either side. You can park free at the downtown Rainbow Mall and walk around. Parking near the falls costs $5 on the US side, and US$6.50 on the Canadian side. The **Viewmobile trolley** (☎ 716-282-0028; per day $5) does a loop around the US side, and the **People Mover** (per day $3.50) shuttles up and down the riverfront on the Canadian side of the falls.

Crossing the Rainbow Bridge to Canada costs US$2.50/50¢ for cars/pedestrians. There are customs and immigration stations at each end – carry proper papers (see Visas p1103).

Buffalo

Known for its spicy chicken wings and painfully cold and snowy winters, Buffalo has quite a bit more going for it, from impressive art museums and architecture to bustling shopping areas and sprawling university campuses. There's an inspiring presence of young, hip and stylish college students, no doubt influenced by native local hero Ani DiFranco, who has chosen

CANADIAN NIAGARA FALLS

You get a great panorama of the falls by strolling over Rainbow Bridge to Canada. Canada's **Horseshoe Falls** are wider, and the curved shape makes them especially photogenic from Queen Victoria Park; at night they're illuminated with a colored light show. The **Journey Behind the Falls** gives access to a spray-soaked viewing area beneath the falls (US$7).

Clifton Hill St has kitschy attractions and a carnival atmosphere, and can provide some tongue-in-cheek fun (and great people-watching opportunities) in the evening. At **Casino Niagara** (☎ 905-374-3598; 5705 Falls Ave), you can gamble in two currencies.

For sleeping, your best bet is to bite the bullet and stay in one of the high-rise chain hotels. The swank rooms, positioned 20 and 30 stories above the falls, offer such mesmerizing views that observatories, trips and helicopter rides become redundant. Big names like **Sheraton** and **Marriott** all have great rooms with comparable views, averaging at about US$125. For comfortable quarters without views, try one of the many standard, well-located motels like the **Inn By the Falls** (☎ 800-263-2571; 5525 Victoria Ave; r US$49-119). Backpackers should head to the **HI Niagara Falls Hostel** (☎ 905-357-0770; 4549 Cataract Ave; dm US$25).

When you get hungry, skip the obvious tourist traps. **Four Brothers Italian Restaurant** (☎ 905-358-6951; 5283 Ferry St; dishes around US$12) is pretty good for a decent pasta dinner. **Taki Japanese Restaurant & Sushi Bar** (☎ 905-357-7274; 5500 Victoria Ave; dishes around US$15) has sushi and saki, and vegetarians will be thrilled with the vegan-Chinese **Xin Vego Café** (☎ 905-353-8346; 4939 Victoria Ave; dishes around US$8). Locals pack into **Falls Manor** (☎ 905-358-3211; 7104 Lundy Lane; dishes around US$6) for breakfast, served all day long.

her hometown as the place to base her indie music label, Righteous Babe Records.

Settled by the French in 1758 – its name is believed to derive from beau fleuve (beautiful river) – Buffalo became a shipping nexus between the Great Lakes and eastern USA when the Erie Canal was opened in 1825. Railroads boosted the area further, and the city thrived as an industrial center, acquiring fine buildings, parks and well-endowed museums.

A post-WWII decline in its traditional industries hit the city hard, the population fell, and much of the inner city became badly run-down, the evidence of which is still obvious in several areas of town. Recent urban renewal has improved the downtown area, and the huge student population adds another dimension to a city still known for its working-class roots and football fanatics.

The helpful **visitors center** (☎ 716-852-0511; 617 Main St) has some good walking-tour pamphlets. Despite harsh winters, the city is dubbed 'the Miami of the North' because of its pleasant, sunny weather during May to September.

SIGHTS

Architecture fans will have a field day. The **Prudential Building** (28 Church St), designed by Louis Sullivan in 1895 as the Guaranty Building, used an innovative steel-frame construction to create the first modern skyscraper; it's elaborately decorated with terra-cotta tiles. The stunning art deco **city hall** (65 Niagara Sq) was built in 1931 and boasts a roof observatory with excellent views of the city. The neo-Gothic **Old Post Office** (121 Ellicot St) was built in 1894; and the **M&T Bank** (545 Main St) is topped with a gilded dome of 140,000 paper-thin sheets of 23.75-carat gold leaf. Six **Frank Lloyd Wright houses** are a highlight; most are privately occupied, but the 1904 **Darwin Martin House** (125 Jewett Parkway) and neighboring **Barton House** (☎ 716-856-3858; 118 Summit Ave) are being restored and may be accessible by appointment.

North of downtown, the beautiful Delaware Park was designed by Frederick Law Olmsted. Its jewel is the not-to-be-missed **Albright-Knox Art Gallery** (☎ 716-882-8700; www.albrightknox.org; 1285 Elmwood Ave; admission $6, free Wed; h 11am-5pm Tue-Sat, from noon Sun), which is actually a sizeable museum including some of the best French impressionists, as well as American works by Pollock, O'Keefe, Lichtenstein, Ernst and Warhol. Buffalo also has good science, history and children's museums and a fine zoo. The Elmwood neighborhood, stretching along Elmwood Ave, between Allen St and Delaware Park, is dotted with hip cafés, restaurants, boutiques and bookstores. Another cool stretch is the Main St, between Hertel and Kenmore, which is quickly becoming gentrified. Not far from here is the charming **Guercio & Sons** (☎ 716-882-7935; 250 Grant St), an old-school Italian gourmet shop.

History buffs are sure to enjoy the fascinating **Theodore Roosevelt Inaugural National Historic Site** (☎ 716-884-0095; 641 Delaware Ave; admission $5; 9am-5pm Mon-Fri, from noon Sat & Sun) in the Ansley-Wilcox house, which tells the tale of Teddy's emergency swearing-in here following the assassination of William McKinley.

SLEEPING

Hotel Lenox (☎ 716-884-1700; 140 North St; s/d from $60/75;) Old-style Hotel Lenox, in the historic Allentown district, has some character.

Mansion on Delaware Avenue (☎ 716-886-3300, www.mansionondelaware.com; 414 Delaware Ave; r from $175;) Highly recommended for its grand style, luxurious quarters and complimentary cocktails each evening from 5pm to 7pm.

HI Buffalo Hostel (☎ 716-852-5222; 667 Main St, d members/nonmembers $17/19) Conveniently located right in the middle of downtown.

EATING

The local speciality is Buffalo wings – deep-fried chicken wings covered in a spicy sauce and served with blue-cheese dressing and celery.

Anchor Bar (☎ 716-886-8920; 1047 Main St; 10 wings $7) Claims credit for the innovation of Buffalo wings, and still serves them up.

Amy's Place (☎ 716-832-6666; 3234 Main St; dishes $3-6) Popular with students for its Middle Eastern–style food.

¡Toros! Tapas Bar (☎ 716-886-9457; 492 Elmwood Ave; dishes $9-14) Excellent tapas, wine and cocktails and ambience; it serves till 2am on weekends.

Saigon Café (☎ 716-883-1252; 10998 Elmwood Ave; dishes $7-12) Fresh, affordable Thai and Vietnamese cuisine.

Spot Coffee (☎ 716-854-7768; 227 Delaware Ave; lishes $4-7) This hip, funky café offers deli-:ious coffee drinks, salads, sandwiches and pastries.

DRINKING

Everyone should steer clear of the mobbed Chippewa St pub strip, packed with trashed rat boys and sorority girls (as proven on MTV's series *Sorority Life*, filmed here).

Bacchus (☎ 716-854-9463; 56 W Chippewa St) One oasis in the Chippewa St hell includes this leek wine bar and eatery, serving several classy wines by the glass.

Cecilia's Restaurant & Martini Bar (☎ 716-883-066; 716 Elmwood Ave) More than 50 varieties of ce-cold martinis.

Several gay bars are clustered around he south end of Elmwood, including **Fuazi** (☎ 716-881-3588; 503 Franklin St) and **Friends** ☎ 716-883-7855; 16 Allen St).

PECTATOR SPORTS

Locals worship the **NFL Buffalo Bills** (☎ 716-648-800) football team, who play at **Ralph Wilson tadium** (☎ 716-648-1800; www.buffalobills.com; 1 Bills r, Orchard Park).

Other franchises include the **Buffalo Sabres** ☎ 716-855-4100) ice-hockey team, **Buffalo Bisons** ☎ 716-846-2000) minor-league baseball team, **uffalo Bandits** (☎ 716-855-4100) lacrosse team nd the **Buffalo Blizzard** (☎ 716-855-4151) indoor occer team.

ETTING THERE & AROUND

Buffalo's **Niagara International Airport** (☎ 716-30-6000), about 16 miles east of downtown, is regional hub. Jet Blue Airways has round-rip fares from New York City for less than 200, and the flight takes just under an our. Buses arrive and depart from the **reyhound terminal** (☎ 716-855-7531; 181 Ellicott St). **FTA** (☎ 716-285-9319) local bus No 40 goes to Niagara Falls ($1.85). From the downtown **mtrak train station** (☎ 716-856-2075; 75 Exchange St), ou can catch trains to New York City ($60, ½ hours). Car rentals are reasonable (see 1121 for more information on renting).

NEW JERSEY

New Jersey (NJ) is often the butt of jokes – or its preponderance of suburbanite-filled malls, its nasal dialect and, most of all, for its polluted (and very smelly) manufacturing district off the Jersey Turnpike. But when you take the time to exit the highways and flee the malls, you are privy to a beautiful side of New Jersey: a surprising 40% of the state is forest, and a quarter is farmland. It has 127 miles of beaches, extensive parkland and beautiful Victorian buildings. Its urban areas and many of its small towns are filled with progressive people, top-rated restaurants and a thriving cultural scene.

New Jersey is the most urbanized, most densely populated state in the USA. About two-thirds of the population live within 30 miles of New York City, and much of the state can be regarded as part of the great metropolis: most of New York's port facilities are here, along with its second international airport, the bulk of its industry and many of its workers. Two of New York's greatest icons, the Statue of Liberty and Ellis Island, are actually in New Jersey, as is the home stadium for New York's two pro football teams, the Giants and the Jets.

In presidential politics, New Jersey is a bellwether state, tending to support the winner. In 1993 Republican Christine Todd Whitman became the state's first female governor; Democrat James E McGreevy is the current governor.

The busy Port of New York and New Jersey, and the Delaware River Port are both major container ports. Heavy industry has declined in importance, but manufacturing still employs 17% of the workforce.

NEW JERSEY FACTS

Nicknames Garden State, Clam State
Population 8,590,300 (9th)
Area 8722 sq miles (47th)
Admitted to Union December 18, 1787 (3rd)
Capital city Trenton (population 85,403)
Other cities Newark (273,546), Jersey City (240,055)
Birthplace of 22nd and 24th US president Grover Cleveland; athlete, entertainer and social activist Paul Robeson (1898–1976); jazz musician Count Basie (1904–84); Frank Sinatra (1915–98); astronaut Buzz Aldrin (b 1930); Meryl Streep (b 1949); Bruce Springsteen (b 1949); Lauryn Hill (b 1975); Queen Latifah (b 1970)
Home of the first movie (1889), professional basketball game (1896), drive-in theater (1933)

Pharmaceuticals, petrochemicals, high-tech industry, tourism, trade and services constitute big employers. The state's per capita income is among the country's highest.

Resident-wise, the state runs the gamut from waterfront workers to Ivy League intellectuals. The state has been home to two US presidents (Woodrow Wilson and Grover Cleveland), physicist Albert Einstein, inventor Thomas Edison and hard-rocker Bruce Springsteen. All in all, New Jersey has America's diversity in a concentrated form.

History

The state's original residents were called *lenni lenape* (original people), a group of Delaware speakers, probably numbering less than 20,000 when European settlers arrived in the early 17th century. Dutch settlers built a trading post at Bergen (now Jersey City) in 1618 and another at Camden in 1623. When the British took over New Netherlands in 1664, the new colony of New Jersey offered generous terms and religious freedom to attract new settlers. Like the harsh 'removals' that took place in all colonies at the time, the surviving Native Americans were placed in the Brotherton reservation and later moved to the states of New York and Wisconsin.

New Jersey saw many Revolutionary War battles, and George Washington placed his Continental Army headquarters at Morristown during the winters of 1776–77 and 1779–80. New Jersey's population grew from 15,000 in 1700 to more than 185,000 by 1795, and industry boomed. Post–Civil War industrial expansion also spawned a movement to improve working conditions. One of its leaders, Democratic Governor Woodrow Wilson, a former Princeton University president, later served as US president (1913–21). After WWII Newark and Jersey City saw influxes of immigrants. By the mid-1980s, New Jersey had some of the country's fastest-growing urban areas. Decline in traditional industries has been offset by new activities like chemicals and services, and by the benefits of being part of the thriving New York conurbation.

Getting There & Around

The proximity of **Newark International Airport** (☎ 973-961-6000; www.newarkairport.com) to Manhattan (see p154 for transport details) makes it a worthwhile option.

New Jersey Transit (☎ 973-762-5100, 800-772 2222; www.njtransit.com) trains from New York City's Penn Station service the Jersey Shore as far as Bay Head, and also make connections to the Trenton and Princeton areas buses serve an even larger area. Amtrak trains from New York City to Washington DC stop at Princeton Junction and Philadelphia. The 24-hour underground PATH train, with several train stations along the west side of New York City, connects with Hoboken, Newark and Jersey City ($1.50).

When it comes to getting around, it's al about having a car in New Jersey. Towns are connected by unreliable bus lines, i they're linked at all. The main roadways are the New Jersey Turnpike, which crosses the state diagonally from New York, leading to Philadelphia, and the much more pleasant Garden State Parkway, which runs along the Jersey Shore all the way south to Cape May. Both are toll roads. Car rentals are cheaper here than in New York; the average rate is $30 per day (see p1121 for more information on renting).

Seastreak ferries (☎ 800-262-8743) depart from Pier 11 and E 34th St in Manhattan crossing to Highlands (near Sandy Hook) on the Jersey Shore several times a day (one wa $17). This is a good option for cyclists.

NORTHERN NEW JERSEY

Newark

Because of its airport, Newark is the startin or finishing point for many visitors, which i why it's often quickly passed over by folks i a hurry to get elsewhere. And that's a shame The city itself, long considered off-limits b many people – following a serious declin that stemmed from its infamous 1969 rac riots – is back in business. Efforts have lea to a new safety level and brand-new ente tainment facilities. A 10-minute trip fro NYC's Penn Station on New Jersey Trans gets you into Newark's stunning, neoclassi Penn Station, the logical starting point f exploration.

Among the best reasons to visit Newar is the Ironbound District surroundin Penn Station. With a vibrant Portugues community, its Ferry St is lined with exce lent restaurants, pastry shops and mus stores. The **Newark Museum** (☎ 973-596-655 www.newarkmuseum.org; 49 Washington St; suggest donation $5; 🕐 noon-5pm Wed-Sun) has a renowne

Tibetan Collection. The recently built **New Jersey Performing Arts Center** (973-642-0404; www.njpac.org; One Center St) is the city's proud gem; it hosts national orchestras, operas, dance, cabaret, theater, jazz and world-music concerts. Other attractions in the area include the grand, Europe-worthy **Cathedral Basilica of the Sacred Hearts** (973-484-4600; www.cathedralbasilica.org; 89 Ridge St), the 400-acre, Frederick Law Olmstead–designed Branch Brook Park, with some 2700 cherry trees that blossom in April; and the single-car Newark City Subway, Newark's best-kept secret.

The best place to stay in town is the **Robert Treat Hotel** (973-622-1000; 50 Park Pl; www.rthotel.com; $95-110; P), although a day trip to Newark while staying in NYC should be sufficient.

For a cheap, classic Newark meal, grab a giant pastrami-on-rye at **Hobby's Delicatessen** (973-623-0410; 32 Branford Pl; dishes around $8), an 85-year-old Jewish deli.

Delaware Water Gap National Recreation Area

The Delaware River meanders through 40 miles of this national recreation area, carving the 1400ft-deep Kittatinny Ridge chasm at the southern end. Activities include canoeing, swimming, rock climbing, horseback riding and hiking – the Appalachian Trail passes through the area. The park straddles the New Jersey–Pennsylvania border – from New Jersey, exit I-80 at the **Kittatinny Point Visitors Center** (908-496-4458; 9am-5pm).

CENTRAL NEW JERSEY

The tony town of **Princeton** and its Ivy League university, Princeton, have lovely architecture and noteworthy historic sites. Nassau and Witherspoon Sts are the main streets. Princeton was the site of the 1777 Battle of Princeton, which proved a decisive victory for General Washington's troops during the Revolutionary War, now commemorated at Princeton Battlefield State Park. The **Historical Society of Princeton** (609-921-6748; 158 Nassau St) has maps and brochures. **Orange Key Guide Service & Campus Information Office** (609-258-3603) arranges free university tours.

Accommodations are expensive and hard to find during graduation time in May and June. The most affordable motels are along Rte 1 and include the usual chains, which charge an average of $80. The landmark and atmospheric **Peacock Inn** (609-924-1707; 20 Baynard Lane; r from $160) has counted Albert Einstein and F Scott Fitzgerald among its illustrious guests.

Grab some breakfast or affordable lunchtime sandwiches at **PJ's Pancake House** (609-924-1353; 154 Nassau St; mains $6-10), an institution. **Lahiere's** (609-921-2798; 11 Witherspoon St; dishes $20) is the posh, grand dame of town.

JERSEY SHORE

When north-Jersey locals say they're 'goin' down the shore,' they're headed to one of the beaches along the 127-mile stretch from Sandy Hook to Cape May. The surrounding vacation towns range from seedy to beautiful, with architecture from tacky to spectacular. During summer weekends, some towns see up to about 100,000 visitors; weekdays are almost as busy, and reservations are highly recommended – many New Yorkers rent a house for the whole summer. In September crowds diminish, and lots of places close after Labor Day.

In the north, beaches are narrow, while further south they are wider and whiter – although all Jersey beaches are fatter than they were even 10 years ago, following extensive dredging and widening projects conducted by the Army Corps of Engineers to counteract erosion. Most towns make you buy a 'beach badge' ($3 to $5) to use the beach during the day in summer, and there are extensive regulations about where you can surf, when you can have a picnic and when your dog is welcome. Parking regulations are strictly enforced.

SANDY HOOK

At the north tip of the Jersey Shore, **Sandy Hook National Recreation Area** (732-872-5970; per car $10; dawn-dusk) is a sandy, 6-mile-long peninsula at the entrance to New York Harbor. Most of the area is undeveloped, and the ocean side of the peninsula has massive **beaches** (including a nude beach at parking lot G), lined on the inland side by an extensive system of bike trails. At the northern end is the coastguard station and **Fort Hancock** – an absolutely amazing, abandoned defense complex, with empty army buildings and enormous gun emplacements. The closest place to stay is the gay-owned **Sandy Hook Cottage** (732-708-1923; www.sandyhookcottage.com; 36 Navesink Ave;

r $100-200; ⊠ ❋), which has been done up with a tasteful, beach-house decor.

RED BANK

About 10 miles inland is the artsy town of Red Bank, on the gleaming Navesink River, easily accessible from New York by the New Jersey Transit train and bus service. The small town has an intact main street in a county that has seen much of its downtowns lost to big malls. The **Count Basie Theater** (☎ 732-842-9000; 99 Monmouth St), named in honor of local jazz great William 'Count' Basie, is an 80-year-old venue for quality dance, music and productions. And the waterfront parks are great for strolls or picnics, while the town is full of quality boutiques and eateries. Try the **Bistro** (☎ 732-530-5553; 14 Broad St; dishes $10-15) for high-quality, eclectic bistro fare, and **Down to Earth** (☎ 732-747-4542; 7 Broad St; dishes $7-12) for creative vegetarian meals.

ASBURY PARK

Asbury Park experienced passing prominence in the 1970s, when Bruce Springsteen 'arrived' at the **Stone Pony** (☎ 732-502-0600; 913 Ocean Ave) nightclub (still offering live music at weekends). After that, the town went through a fairly major decline, becoming a depressingly skanky spot rife with drugs, political corruption and derelict buildings. However, the past few years have seen Asbury Park make a major comeback, lead by rich gay men from NYC who have snapped up blocks of forgotten Victorian homes and storefronts. While it's still a work in progress, and has areas that should be avoided after dark, a visit to Asbury Park is rewarding. The sprawling **Antique Emporium of Asbury Park** (☎ 732-774-8230; Cookman Ave) has two floors of amazing finds. **Moonstruck** (☎ 732-988-0123; 517 Lake Ave; mains $17-25) is a top-notch Italian restaurant, while **Sonny's** (☎ 732-774-6262; 574 Cookman Ave; mains $9-13) serves authentic Southern cuisine. **Paradise** (☎ 732-988-6663; 101 Asbury Ave), a big gay nightclub, is owned by Madonna's former producer Shep Pettibone.

OCEAN GROVE

This is a fascinating place to wander. Founded by Methodists in the 19th century, and keeping itself nice ever since, the town retains its Victorian architecture and a 6500-seat wooden auditorium, which featured in Woody Allen's *Stardust Memories* and now hosts concerts and religious events.

BELMAR & SPRING LAKE

Not-so-straitlaced **Belmar** attracts a younger crowd, and can get pretty rowdy when the bars close at 2am. **Carol's Guest House** (☎ 732-681-4422; 201 11th Ave; r from $30) is friendly and inexpensive.

Spring Lake, a very classy community once called the 'Irish Riviera,' has lush gardens, Victorian houses and elegant accommodations. The **Hollycroft Bed & Breakfast** (☎ 800-679-2254; fax 732-280-8145; 506 North Blvd; r from $125; ⊠ ❋) is romantic.

BARNEGAT PENINSULA

This narrow barrier island/sand spit extends some 22 miles south from Point Pleasant. In its center, **Seaside Heights** sucks in the wild twenty-something summer crowds with beaches, boardwalks, bars and two amusement piers. Occupying the southern third of Barnegat Peninsula is **Island Beach State Park** (☎ 732-793-0506; per car $7), a flat 3000-acre stretch of dunes and wetlands.

Atlantic City

When the railway arrived on Absecon Island in the 1850s, city dwellers came here for the wide white beach and the seaside atmosphere. By 1900 the resort was a hot spot that catered to the affluent; in the 1920s it was a hotbed of vice, with smuggled liquor, speakeasies and illegal gambling. After WWII faster transportation made other destinations more accessible, and Atlantic City went into steep decline. In 1977 the state approved casinos to revitalize the place, and the city has since reemerged as a high-profile gamblers' destination. If you can get past the mobs of blue-haired ladies, high-rolling businessmen, Disney-type tourists and the generally greedy atmosphere, you'll find some hidden gems and get a fascinating glimpse into American culture.

The **visitors center** (☎ 609-449-7130; Atlantic City Expressway; ⏲ 9am-5pm), under the giant teepee in the middle of the Atlantic City Expressway, can provide you with maps and accommodation deals.

As in Las Vegas, the casinos have themes, from the Far East to Ancient Rome, but they're very superficially done. Inside they're all basically the same, with clanging slot machines and flashing lights and all-you-can-eat food buffets. Staying in the towering hotels can be cheap or extravagant, depending on the season, with rooms ranging from $50 in winter to $300 in summer.

Built in 1870, the **Boardwalk** was the first in the world. Enjoy a walk or a hand-pushed rolling chair ride ($20) and drop in on the informative **Atlantic City Historical Museum** (☎ 609-347-5839; cnr Boardwalk & New Jersey Aves; admission free), run by a quirky old-timer. The **Miss America Pageant**, held every September in the city's Convention Hall – which is worth a visit if only for its claim to the 'world's largest' pipe organ – remains a very popular draw.

Good food can be found away from the casino strip. A few blocks inland, **Mexico Lindo** (☎ 609-345-1880; 2435 Atlantic Ave; dishes $7-11) is a favorite offering among the Mexican locals. **Hannah G's** (☎ 609-823-1466; 7310 Ventnor Ave; dishes $5-9) is a family-owned, excellent breakfast and lunch spot in Ventnor. **Maloney's** (☎ 609-823-7858; 23 S Washington Ave) is a popular seafood-and-steak place, and **Ventura's Greenhouse Restaurant** (☎ 609-822-0140; 106 Benson Ave), in next-door Margate City, is an Italian restaurant loved by locals.

Atlantic City 'International' Airport (☎ 800-645-7895) is a 20-minute drive from the city center. Greyhound and New Jersey Transit buses run from New York ($20 round-trip, six hours return); Greyhound, Capitol Trailways and New Jersey Transit run from Philadelphia (about $14 round-trip, 1½ hours one way). A casino will often refund the fare (in chips, coins or coupons) if you get a bus directly to its door. New Jersey Transit trains from Philadelphia for a one-way/round-trip cost $10/11.50. Casino parking garages cost about $2, but will waive the fee if you have a receipt showing you spent money inside the casino.

The Wildwoods

Just north of Cape May, the three towns of **North Wildwood**, **Wildwood** and **Wildwood Crest** are an archaeological find – whitewashed motels with flashing neon signs, turquoise curtains and pink doors. Wildwood Crest really is an especially kitschy slice of 1950s Americana. Wildwood is the main focus, a party town popular with teens and young overseas visitors. The Wildwood **tourist office** (☎ 609-729-4000; www.gwcoc.com) hands out information on self-guided tours around the 'doo-wop' motels. The beach is free, and there are rides on the pier. About 250 motels offer rooms for $50 to $200, making it a good option if Cape May is booked.

Cape May

Founded in 1620, Cape May is on the state's southern tip and is the country's oldest seashore resort. Its sweeping beaches get crowded in summer, but the stunning Victorian architecture is attractive year-round. In addition to 600 gingerbread-style houses, the city boasts a 157ft lighthouse, the Cape May County Park & Zoo, antique shops, whale watching and bird-watching. It's also the only place in the state where the sun rises and sets over the water. The quaint area attracts everyone from suburban families to a substantial gay crowd, who flock to the many gay-owned and gay-friendly inns. It can be expensive, but the quality accommodations and eateries are well worth a splurge.

New Jersey Transit buses come from New York City and Philadelphia, and the daily **Cape May–Lewes Ferry** (☎ 800-643-3779; www.capemaylewesferry.com; per car & driver $25, per passenger $8) connects Cape May with Lewes, Delaware, across the Delaware River.

The white, sandy **beach** ($4/8/11 day/three-day/week pass) is the main attraction in summer months. **Cape May Whale Watcher** (☎ 609-884-5445) 'guarantees' sighting a marine mammal on its ocean tour ($17 to $26).

The majority of Cape May's B&Bs are upscale, and many places have a two- to three-night minimum stay at summer weekends. The best budget option remains **Hotel Clinton** (☎ 609-884-3993, off-season 516-799-8889; 202 Perry St; r $40-50). Classy **Virginia Hotel** (☎ 609-884-8690; 635 Columbia St; r $80-365; ⊠ ❄) has gorgeous old-fashioned rooms with costs that vary wildly depending on the season. The sprawling, just-renovated **Congress Hall** (☎ 609-884-8422; 251 Beach Ave; r $80-400; ⊠ ❄ ♿), run by the same owners as Virginia Hotel, has a range of quarters to suit various budgets, plus a long, oceanfront porch lined with rocking chairs. The town is overflowing with smaller B&Bs; try the darling **Gingerbread House** (☎ 609-884-0211; 28 Gurney St; r $98-260).

Brad's Beachfront Cafe (☎ 609-898-6050; 314 Beach Dr; dishes $8) is good for sandwich wraps and salads at lunchtime. **Louisa's Café** (☎ 609-884-5884; 104 Jackson St; dishes $10-18), with a tiny, low-ceilinged dining room, is the town's prize eatery, serving up seasonal eclectic specialities; the casual **Blue Pig Tavern** (☎ 609-884-8422; Congress Hall, 251 Beach Ave; dishes $12-18) is comparable. Upscale diners should reserve a table at the award-winning **Ebbitt Room** (☎ 609-884-5700; 25 Jackson St; dishes $19-24) in the Virginia Hotel.

PENNSYLVANIA

Though often bypassed between New York and Washington, the massive state of Pennsylvania is worth a visit whether you're an urban hipster, outdoorsy type or history buff. The culturally and historically rich cities of Pittsburgh and Philadelphia satiate those in search of art, culture or cuisine, while the quaint Pennsylvania Dutch communities and the Civil War battlefield of Gettysburg provide fascinating and beautiful educational journeys.

In politics, Pennsylvania is a Democratic stronghold, while the state legislature is generally split evenly between the two parties. The current governor, Edward Rendell, is a moderate Democrat.

Industry includes coal, which is still mined, along with oil, natural gas, building stone, clay and sand. Manufacturing is important, as are forest products. Some 30% of the state is productive farmland, used mostly for poultry and dairy farming. Other crops include hay, corn, mushrooms, fruits and Christmas trees.

The art history here is rich, and Philadelphia is important in the early history of American painting. Benjamin West (1738–1820) and Charles Willson Peale (1741–1827) both produced portraits and scenes of early American life. Thomas Eakins (1844–1916) specialized in water scenes around Philadelphia and contemporary portraits. Some Pennsylvanian artists achieved fame outside their home state, including native impressionist Mary Cassatt (1845–1926), who lived in Europe, and Andy Warhol (1928–87), who lived in New York (the Warhol museum is in Pittsburgh).

History

In 1681 King Charles II gave William Penn a charter for land west of the Delaware River. Penn, a Quaker, founded his colony as a 'holy experiment' that respected religious freedom and liberal government. William Penn also did the unthinkable and showed some respect for indigenous people, purchasing land, rather than seizing it. However, it didn't take long for the European settlers to displace those communities.

The 1701 Charter of Privilege was the colony's constitution, giving its elected assembly more power than any equivalent British body. Pennsylvania became the richest and most populous British colony in North America and had a major role in the independence movement. The First and Second Continental Congresses met in Philadelphia, and colonists adopted the Declaration of Independence in its State House in July 1776, when Philadelphia became the new nation's capital. But in one of the Revolutionary War's first battles, British troops defeated Washington's forces at Brandywine Creek. In September 1777 they occupied Philadelphia, forcing Washington to withdraw to Valley Forge. Postwar, state representatives met again in Philadelphia for the 1787 federal constitutional convention. Pennsylvania accepted the new national constitution and adopted a new state constitution in 1790.

Development of canals, turnpikes and, later, railroads enabled the residents to relocate to the west and north. Pennsylvania became the country's main supplier of coal, iron and timber, while Philadelphia and Pittsburgh became important industrial centers. Slavery was not deeply entrenched in Pennsylvania because of Quaker opposition, and border towns close to Maryland became havens on the Underground Railroad, which helped slaves escape from the South. About 350,000 Pennsylvanians, which included 8600 black men, served in the Union army

PENNSYLVANIA FACTS

Nicknames Keystone State, Quaker State
Population 12,335,091 (6th)
Area 46,058 sq miles (33rd)
Admitted to Union December 12, 1787 (2nd)
Capital city Harrisburg (population 53,500)
Other cities Philadelphia (1,517,550), Pittsburgh (334,563), Erie (103,717)
Birthplace of the US Constitution (1787), writer Louisa May Alcott (1832–88), comedian WC Fields (1880–1946), Andy Warhol (1928–87), actress Grace Kelly (1929–82), Bill Cosby (b 1937)

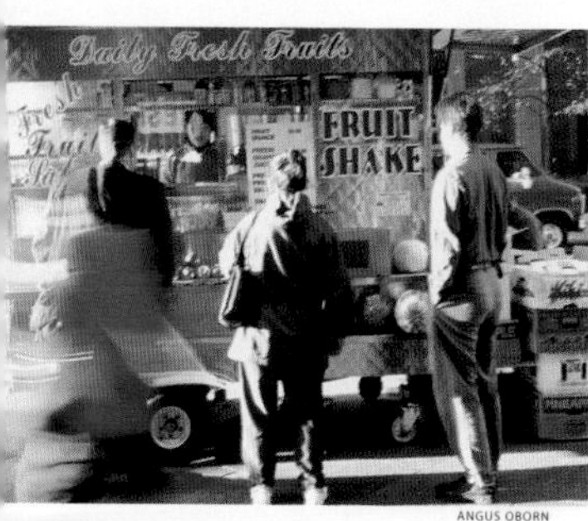

ANGUS OBORN

Street vendors (p145), New York City

ANGUS OBORN

Baseball at **Yankee Stadium** (p131), New York City

ESBIN ANDERSON PHOTOGRAPHY

Chrysler Building (p123), New York City

Brooklyn Bridge (p118), New York City

ESBIN ANDERSON PHOTOGRAPHY

JON DAVI

Niagara Falls (p165), New York State and Ontario

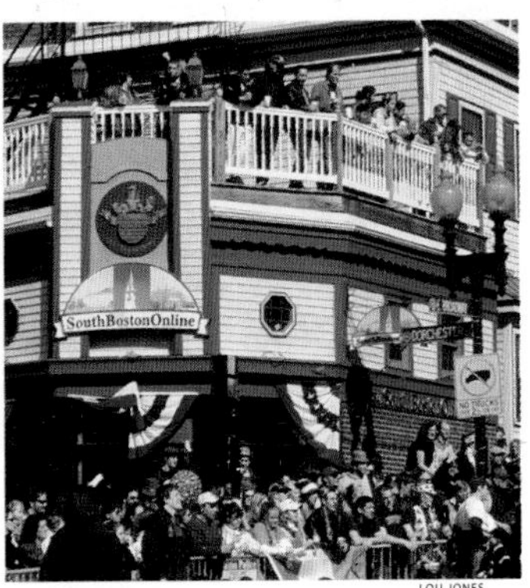

LOU JONES

St Patrick's Day parade (p215), Boston

JON DAVISON

Portland Head Light (p270), Portland, Maine

Fall foliage, **Waitsfield** (p254), Vermont

MARK NEW

during the Civil War, and the state's industries were vital to the North's war effort. Southern forces attacked along Pennsylvania's Cumberland Valley, and then, in July 1863, the North halted the biggest invasion at the three-day battle of Gettysburg.

After the Civil War, Pennsylvania's political influence waned, but its industrial importance expanded. European immigration provided factory fodder for the booming industries, and the state saw the emergence of national labor unions. During WWI and WWII, Pennsylvania supplied massive raw material and labor. In the postwar period its industrial importance gradually declined. Urban renewal programs and the growth of service and high-tech industries have boosted the economy, most notably in Philadelphia and Pittsburgh.

Quakers founded Pennsylvania on the principle of religious tolerance, and that tolerance attracted other minority religious sects. Many Quakers still live here, along with the well-known communities of Mennonites and Amish in the Pennsylvania Dutch Country.

Climate & Geography

The Appalachian Plateau (also known as the Allegheny Plateau) occupies most of western and northern Pennsylvania. A series of ridges and valleys curves northeast through the state's central part. Some fertile lowlands cover the southeastern segment, with the Atlantic Coastal Plain extending into New Jersey and Delaware, bringing nice cool breezes in summer and chilly ones in winter. Most people live around Philadelphia in the southeast and around Pittsburgh in the southwest. Once severely polluted, Pennsylvania's environment has improved with state and federal legislation and the decline of old industries.

Pennsylvania for Children

Pennsylvania has draws for everyone from aged naturalists to teenage historians – and it hasn't left out children. While most attractions are in Philadelphia or Pittsburgh, you'll find plenty of great ones scattered around in between.

Thirty minutes from Philadelphia in Langhorne is **Sesame Place** (☎ 215-752-7070; www.sesameplace.com; admission $37; ⌚ May-Oct), a popular theme park that has water rides, massive play areas, and shows starring Big Bird, Elmo and the rest of the gang.

At the **Crayola Factory** (☎ 610-585-8000; www.crayola.com/factory; admission $9; ⌚ 9:30am-5pm Tue-Sat, from noon Sun Sep-Jun, until 6pm July-Aug) in Easton, 70 miles from Philly, the little ones can see how the hot wax gets turned into their favorite crayons. There's also a big, curvy see-through wall to draw on with markers.

PHILADELPHIA

At the **Please Touch Museum** (☎ 215-963-0667; www.pleasetouchmuseum.org; 210 N 21st St; admission $9; ⌚ 9am-4:30pm Sep-Jun, until 5pm Jun-Aug), Philadelphia is blessed with hands-on exhibits about Maurice Sendak, *Alice in Wonderland*, baby animals and science. Admission to the Science Park is included in the admission fee.

Just behind the Please Touch Museum you will find **Core States Science Park** (☎ 215-448-1200; ⌚ 10am-3:30pm May-Sep), a 25,000 sq-ft playground with play structures, a maze and three-dimensional optical illusions.

For a bit of culture once the playing is out of their system, head to the productions at **Arden Children's Theatre** (☎ 215-922-1122; www.ardentheatre.org; 40 N 2nd St; admission $20-35). The theatre puts on performances followed by Q&A sessions, during which kids can ask the actors questions about their profession.

PITTSBURGH

Pittsburgh has a preponderance of accessible museums, parkland and festivals.

Pittsburgh Children's Museum (☎ 412-322-5058; www.pittsburghkids.org; Allegheny Sq; adult/child $5/4.50; ⌚ 10am-5pm Mon-Sat, from noon Sun) features a climbable space sculpture, exhibits about Jim Henson and Mister Rogers and some child-friendly artwork of Andy Warhol.

Carnegie Science Center (p192) has hands-on exhibits about anatomy, outer space and underwater life.

The **National Aviary** (p192) is well stocked, with guides who are trained to answer to wonderfully curious questions of the under-12 set.

A large array of creatures can be visited at the **Pittsburgh Zoo & Aquarium** (☎ 412-665-3640; www.pittsburghzoo.com; 1 Wild Pl; adult/child $8/6; ⌚ 9am-4pm Oct-Mar, until 5pm Apr-Sep).

In the summer head to **Sandcastle Waterpark** (☎ 412-462-6666; www.sandcastlewaterpark.com; 1000 Sandcastle Dr; admission $22; ⌚ 11am-6pm Jun-Sep),

Pittsburgh's water theme park, right in the city. It features the Mon Tsunami tidal wave pool, Thunder Run inner-tube river and Boardwalk Blasters shotgun slides.

If it's raining, bring your tots to Station Sq, at the base of Mt Washington's Duquesne Incline funicular railroad, where you can get in some shopping and they can take advantage of the indoor **Station Square Express Kiddie Train Rides** (☎ 412-261-2811; child $1; ⌚ noon-9pm Mon-Fri, until 5pm Sun Memorial Day–Labor Day). Rides start on the hour, at 20 minutes after and at 20 minutes till.

PHILADELPHIA

While it's famous for historic sites such as the Liberty Bell and Independence Hall (and those tasty, greasy cheesesteaks), Philly often gets brushed aside as a worthy city destination because NYC, just over an hour away, steals the limelight. It would be a shame to miss this lovely and manageable urban center, chock full of world-class museums, performing-arts centers, terrific restaurants and a thriving nightlife scene.

History

William Penn made Philadelphia his capital in 1682, basing its plan on a grid with wide streets and public squares – a layout copied by many US cities. For a time the second-largest city in the British Empire (after London), Philadelphia became a center for opposition to British colonial policy. It was the new nation's capital at the start of the Revolutionary War and again after the war until 1790, when Washington, DC, took over. By the nineteenth century New York had superseded Philadelphia as the nation's cultural, commercial and industrial center, and Philly never regained its early preeminent status. In the 1970s the nation's bicentennial prompted an urban renewal program that continues to this day.

Orientation

Philadelphia is easy to get around. Most sights and accommodations are within walking distance of each other, or a short bus ride away. East–west streets are named;

BENJAMIN FRANKLIN

In order for three people to keep a secret, two must be dead.

Benjamin Franklin

This colonial Renaissance man had a bald spot, locks of long, flowing hair and a quirky wit. He started off different right away, when he was born on a Sunday – something considered a sin in Puritan times. His father had him baptized on the same day to try to make things right. When he was 16, he became a vegetarian for a while so he could save up money to buy more books. Best known for flying his kite during a storm, this oddity began to attract curious onlookers; Franklin, not wanting an audience, sent a powerful but harmless surge of electricity through a nearby iron fence to move them along. An obsessed inventor, his creations included, but were not limited to, bifocals, the catheter, odometer, Franklin stove and political cartoons.

His love for literature continued as he served as an apprentice in his brother's print shop; eventually he started the *Pennsylvania Gazette,* which went on to become the colonies' top newspaper. He pushed for cleaner city streets in Philadelphia, started the country's first circulating library, and founded the American Philosophical Society and the University of Pennsylvania. After representing the colonies in Britain, Franklin came to resent the corruption in colonial administrations. While in the motherland, he became a curiosity for consuming great amounts of water, rather than beer, which earned him the nickname 'Water American' among bemused pals.

Upon his return to America in 1775, he broke with London, opposed British taxes and openly supported independence. Franklin eventually helped write the Declaration of Independence with Thomas Jefferson, and, at age 70, was the document's oldest signer. A few years later Franklin had the gumption to propose to a Parisian widow, although she turned him down. After his return from France in 1784, he worked on the final version of the US Constitution and went about his final public – and brazen – act: petitioning congress calling for an end to slavery. Talk about being ahead of your time.

north–south streets are numbered, except for Broad and Front Sts.

Historic Philadelphia includes Independence National Historic Park and Old City, which extends east to the waterfront. West of the historic district is Center City, home to Penn Sq and City Hall. The Delaware and Schuylkill (*skoo*-kill) Rivers border South Philadelphia, which features the colorful Italian Market, restaurants and bars. West of the Schuylkill, University City has two important campuses as well as a major museum. Northwest Philadelphia includes the genteel suburbs of Chestnut Hill and Germantown, plus the hip and growing Manayunk, with plenty of bustling pubs and eateries. The South St area, between S 2nd, 10th, Pine and Fitzwater Sts, has bohemian boutiques, bars, eateries and music venues.

Information

BOOKSTORES

Giovanni's Room (☎ 215-923-2960; 345 S 12th St) Gay and lesbian books and periodicals.

House of Our Own (☎ 215-222-1576; 3920 Spruce St) Used books, small-press publications and frequent readings.

Robin's Bookstore (☎ 215-735-9600; 108 S 13th St) Philly's oldest independent bookstore.

EMERGENCY

Emergency number (☎ 911)

Philadelphia Operation Town Watch (☎ 215-686-1459) Call to report a not-so-urgent safety problem.

Women Organized Against Rape (☎ 985-3333) The local rape-crisis center hotline.

INTERNET ACCESS

Internet access isn't everywhere yet, but it's free to $8 an hour in most places.

Digital Age Café (☎ 215-389-4030; 1814 S 13th St) Coffee bar with access for $8 per hour, $4 minimum.

Free Library of Philadelphia (☎ 215-686-5322; 1901 Vine St) Free Internet access.

Intermezzo Café & Lounge (☎ 215-222-4300; 3131 Walnut St) University City café with 15 free, high-speed hook-up ports.

MEDIA

City Paper (www.citypaper.net) Free weekly available at street boxes around town.

Philadelphia Inquirer (www.philly.com/mld/inquirer; 55¢) The region's top daily newspaper.

Philadelphia Weekly (www.philadelphiaweekly.com) Free weekly available at street boxes around town.

MEDICAL SERVICES

CVS (☎ 215-465-2130; cnr 10th & Reed Sts) Twenty-four-hour pharmacy in South Philadelphia.

Dentist referral line (☎ 215-925-6050)

Doctor referral line (☎ 215-563-5343)

Graduate Hospital (☎ 215-893-2350; 1800 Lombard St) Close to the business district.

Thomas Jefferson University Hospital (☎ 215-955-6840; 11th & Walnut Sts) Closest to downtown, with round-the-clock emergency services.

MONEY

Thomas Cook (☎ 800-287-7362; 18th St & JFK Blvd) can organize currency exchange.

ATMs are plentiful, but if you're having trouble finding one, call the **ATM locator service** (☎ 800-248-4286).

POST

Main US Post Office (☎ 215-895-8000; 30th & Market Sts) Open 24 hours.

TOURIST OFFICES

Independence Visitors Center (☎ 215-636-1666; www.gophila.com; 6th & Market Sts; 🕒 8:30am-5:30pm) Run by the National Park Service, distributes the useful *Philadelphia Official Visitors Guide,* maps and brochures; sells tickets for the various official tours that depart from nearby locations. Staff is helpful and knowledgeable.

Philadelphia Convention & Visitors Bureau (☎ 215-636-3327; www.pcvb.org; 1515 Market St) Has information about businesses, tours, hotels and package deals.

Visitors Center (☎ 215-636-1666; 15th St & JFK Blvd; ☎ 9am-5pm) Distributes the helpful *Philadelphia Running Map*.

UNIVERSITIES

University of Pennsylvania (U Penn), in University City, is an Ivy League school with 30,000 students and a gorgeous campus.

Dangers & Annoyances

Downtown, the Walnut and S 13th Sts area can be sleazy at night, particularly at weekends. Avoid West Philadelphia, west of University City, and North Philadelphia. Also avoid the subway at night, unless you're with a few thousand fans attending a sports event in South Philly.

Sights

While most of Philly's better-known historic sites – the Liberty Bell, Carpenters' Hall etc – are concentrated in the Independence National Historic Park, there's something to

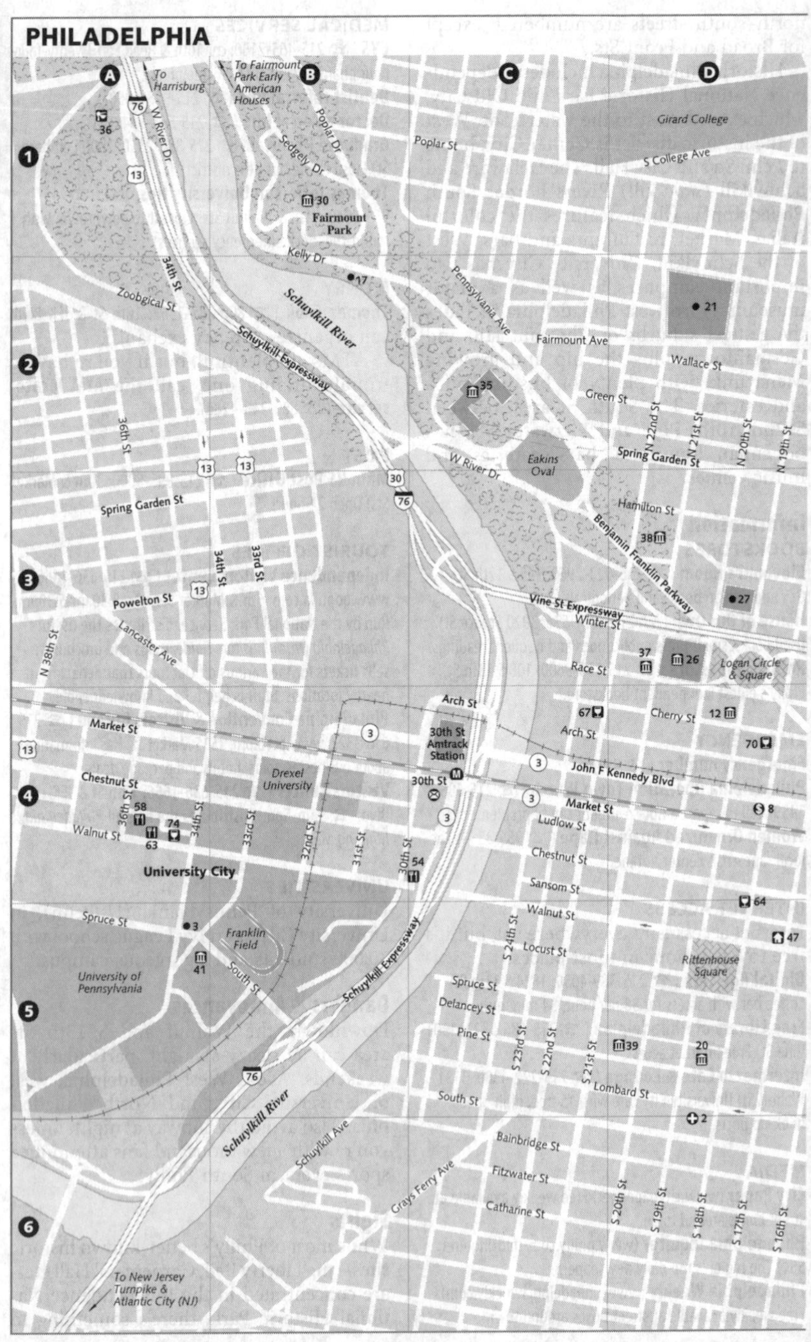

PHILADELPHIA
To Harrisburg
To Fairmount Park Early American Houses
Girard College
Poplar St
S College Ave
Sedgely Dr
Poplar Dr
W River Dr
Fairmount Park
Kelly Dr
34th St
Zoological St
Schuylkill River
Schuylkill Expressway
Pennsylvania Ave
Fairmount Ave
Wallace St
Green St
N 22nd St
N 21st St
N 20th St
N 19th St
Spring Garden St
Eakins Oval
W River Dr
36th St
Spring Garden St
Hamilton St
Benjamin Franklin Parkway
33rd St
Powelton St
Lancaster Ave
Vine St Expressway
Winter St
N 38th St
Race St
Logan Circle & Square
Arch St
Cherry St
Market St
30th St Amtrack Station
Arch St
John F Kennedy Blvd
Chestnut St
Drexel University
30th St
Market St
Ludlow St
Walnut St
32nd St
31st St
Chestnut St
University City
Sansom St
Walnut St
Spruce St
Franklin Field
Locust St
S 24th St
University of Pennsylvania
South St
Schuylkill Expressway
Rittenhouse Square
Spruce St
Delancey St
Pine St
S 23rd St
S 22nd St
S 21st St
Lombard St
South St
Bainbridge St
Schuylkill River
Schuylkill Ave
Grays Ferry Ave
Fitzwater St
Catharine St
S 20th St
S 19th St
S 18th St
S 17th St
S 16th St
To New Jersey Turnpike & Atlantic City (NJ)

0 0.5 km
0 0.3 mi
E
F
G
H
1
2
3
4
5
6
611
Thompson St
Girard
Girard Ave
Poplar St
Ridge Ave
Brown St
Fairmount
N 13th St
N 12th St
N 11th St
N 10th St
Fairmount Ave
Wallace St
N 18th St
N 17th St
N 16th St
N 15th St
N Broad St
N 7th St
N 6th St
N 5th St
To Trenton (NJ) & New York City (NY)
83
N American St
N 2nd St
22
Spring Garden
Spring Garden St
59
95
Spring-Garden
N 8th St
N 9th St
N 4th St
N 3rd St
Callowhill St
75
Delaware Expwy
Vine St
Vine St
30
676
Race-Vine
62
Chinatown
Chinatown
Franklin Square Hospital
Franklin Square
N Front St
N Water St
Columbus Blvd
Suburban Septa Station
34
10
JFK Plaza
Pennsylvania Convention Center
Florist St
To Camden (NJ)
84
87
92
13
Old City
42
24
Benjamin Franklin Bridge (toll)
15th St
Penn Square
City Hall
89
City Hall
13th St
11th St
Independence National Historic Park
66
15
23
14
33
80
8th St
5th St
19
2nd St
48
Christopher Columbus Blvd (Delaware Ave)
Gazela of Philadelphia
51
7
90
56
4
31
86
25
65
71
Center City
9
Chestnut St
45
81
68
88
85
78
79
50
Walnut-Locust
76
57
55
Jewelers' Row
28
Thomas Jefferson University
Walnut St
40
Independence Square
32
18
5
16
77
82
91
Ferry
Washington Square
52
11
61
Penn's Landing
46
44
29
1
43
53
Society Hill
6
International Sculpture Garden
69
Antique Row
Lombard-South
Delaware River
S 15th St
Broad St (Ave of the Arts)
South St
S 13th St
S 12th St
S 11th St
S 10th St
S 9th St
S 8th St
S 7th St
S 6th St
60
S 5th St
S 4th St
S 3rd St
S 2nd St
Front St
South Philadelphia
73
72
49
611
To Italian Market (3mi)
To Mummers' Museum (3mi)
To Philadelphia International Airport & Wilmington (DE)

INFORMATION

Giovanni's Room 1 E5
Graduate Hospital 2 D6
House of Our Own 3 A5
Independence Visitors Center 4 G5
National Park Service Visitors Center 5 G5
Pennsylvania Hospital 6 F5
Robin's Bookstore 7 E5
Thomas Cook 8 D4
Thomas Jefferson University Hospital 9 F5
Visitors Center 10 E4
William Way Lesbian, Gay, Bisexual and Transgender Community Center 11 E5

SIGHTS & ACTIVITIES pp175–81

Academy of Natural Sciences Museum 12 D4
African American Museum in Philadelphia 13 G4
Arch St Meeting House 14 G4
Betsy Ross House 15 H4
Blue Cross River Rink 16 H5
Boathouse Row 17 B2
Carpenters' Hall 18 G5
Christ Church 19 H5
Civil War Library & Museum 20 D5
Congress Hall (see 28)
Eastern State Penitentiary 21 D2
Edgar Allan Poe National Historic Site 22 G3
Elfreth's Alley 23 H4
Fireman's Hall 24 H4
Franklin Court 25 G5
Franklin Institute Science Museum 26 D3
Free Library of Philadelphia 27 D3
Independence Hall 28 G5
Independence Seaport Museum 29 H5
Lemon Hill Mansion 30 B1
Liberty Bell Pavilion 31 G5
Library Hall 32 G5
Mantua Maker's Museum House (see 23)
National Museum of American Jewish History 33 G5
National Portrait Gallery (see 40)
Old City Hall Philosophical Hall (see 28)
Pennsylvania Academy of the Fine Arts 34 E4
Philadelphia Museum of Art 35 C2
Philadelphia Zoo 36 A1
Please Touch Museum 37 D3
Rodin Museum 38 D3
Rosenbach Museum & Library 39 D5
Second Bank of the US 40 G5
University Museum of Archaeology & Anthropology 41 A5
US Mint 42 G4
US Postal Service Museum (see 25)

SLEEPING p182

Alexander Inn 43 E5
Antique Row B&B 44 E5
HI Bank St Hostel 45 G5
Inn on Locust 46 E5
Latham Hotel 47 D5
Penn's View Hotel 48 H5
Shippen Way Inn 49 G6
Society Hill Hotel 50 G5

EATING p183

Capogiro Gelato Artisans 51 E5
City Tavern 52 H5
Effie's 53 F6
Intermezzo Café 54 C4
Joe 55 F5
Le Bec-Fin 56 E5
Millennium Coffee 57 E5
Pod 58 A4
Silk City Diner 59 G3
St Gianna's Grille 60 F6
Valanni's 61 E5
Vietnam Restaurant 62 F4
White Dog Café 63 A4

DRINKING pp183–4

Bar Noir 64 D5
Bijou 65 G5
Café Olé 66 H4
Cherry Street Tavern 67 C4
Continental 68 H5
Dirty Frank's 69 E6
Dock St Brewing Company 70 D4
Five Spot 71 H5
Fluid 72 G6
Last Drop Coffee House (see 69)
Manny Brown's 73 G6
New Deck Tavern 74 A4
Shampoo 75 G3
Sisters 76 E5
Uncles 77 E5
Woody's Bar & Restaurant 78 E5

ENTERTAINMENT p184

2-4 Club 79 E5
Arden Children's Theater 80 H4
Khyber Pass 81 H5
LaTazza 108 82 H5
Ortlieb's 83 H2
Trocadero Theater 84 F4
Zanzibar Blue 85 E5

SHOPPING p184–5

Bourse 86 G5
Reading Terminal Market 87 F4
Shops at Bellevue 88 E5
Shops at Liberty Place 89 E4
Sparacino Men's 90 E5

TRANSPORT p185

Ferry to New Jersey State Aquarium 91 H5
Greyhound Bus Terminal 92 F4

see in plenty of other neighborhoods, too. The Old City is rich with history, Center City is bursting with arts and culture, South Philadelphia is home to the Italian Market, and University City feels like an entirely other town in itself. Plan well, and you'll get to see it all.

INDEPENDENCE NATIONAL HISTORIC PARK

This L-shaped 45-acre park, along with Old City, has been dubbed 'America's most historic square mile,' and can feel like a stroll back through time. Most sites are open every day from 9am to 5pm. The **National Park Service visitors center** (☎ 215-597-8974; 3rd & Chestnut Sts; 9am-5pm) has maps and information. **Carpenters' Hall** (closed Mon), owned by the Carpenter Company, the USA's oldest trade guild (1724), is the site of the First Continental Congress in 1774. **Library Hall** is where you'll find a copy of the Declaration of Independence, handwritten in a letter by Thomas Jefferson, plus first editions of Darwin's *On the Origin of Species* and Lewis and Clark's field notes.

Independence Hall (9am-5pm) is the 'birthplace of American government,' where delegates from the 13 colonies met to approve the Declaration of Independence on July 4, 1776. An excellent example of Georgian architecture, it sports understated lines that reveal Philadelphia's Quaker heritage. To get inside, you must join one of the frequent free tours. Behind Independence Hall is Independence Sq, where the Declaration of Independence was first read in public. **Congress Hall** (S 6th & Chestnut Sts; 9am-5pm), meanwhile, was the meeting place for US Congress when Philly was the nation's capital. **Old City Hall** (11am-5pm), finished in 1791, was home to the US Supreme Court until 1800. **Philosophical Hall** (☎ 215-440-3400; 10am-5pm Wed-Sun Mar–Labor Day, until 4pm Thu-Sun Labor Day–Mar), south of Old City Hall, is the headquarters of the American Philosophical Society, founded in 1743 by Benjamin Franklin.

The glassed-in **Liberty Bell Pavilion** is home to Philadelphia's top tourist attraction. Made in London and tolled at the first public reading of the Declaration of Independence, the bell became famous when abolitionists adopted it as a symbol of freedom. It's inscribed, ' "Proclaim liberty through all the land, to all the inhabitants thereof." (Leviticus 25:10).' Cracking eventually made the bell unusable in 1846, and it was moved to its present site in 1976.

The **Franklin Court** (🕑 9am-5pm) complex, a row of restored tenements, pays tribute to Benjamin Franklin with an underground museum displaying his inventions. At the **B Free Franklin Post Office** (☎ 215-592-1289; 316 Market St; 🕑 9am-5pm), which has a small US Postal Service Museum, mail receives a special handwritten Franklin postmark. (In addition to being a statesman, author and inventor, the multitalented Franklin was a postmaster.) **Christ Church** (☎ 215-922-1695; S 2nd St), completed in 1744, is where George Washington and Franklin worshipped.

The **Greek Revival Philadelphia Exchange**, a really beautiful Episcopal church designed by William Strickland, is the home of the country's first stock exchange (1834). It's closed to the public.

OLD CITY

Along with Society Hill, Old City – the area bounded by Walnut, Vine, Front and 6th Sts – was early Philadelphia. The 1970s saw revitalization, with many warehouses converted into apartments, galleries and small businesses.

Elfreth's Alley is believed to be the oldest continuously occupied street in the USA; on it, **Mantua Maker's Museum House** (☎ 215-574-0560; 126 Elfreth's Alley; admission $2; 🕑 10am-4pm Sat, from noon Sun) offers displays of period furniture, and **Windsor Chair Maker House** (☎ 215-574-0560; 126 Elfreth's Alley; admission $2; 🕑 10am-4pm Sat, from noon Sun) produced the chairs in Independence Hall. **Fireman's Hall** (☎ 215-923-1438; 147 N 2nd St; admission by donation) is where you'll find the nation's oldest fire engine and an exhibit on the rise of organized volunteers led by Ben Franklin. **Betsy Ross House** (☎ 215-686-1252; 239 Arch St; admission by donation) is where Betsy Griscom Ross (1752–1836), upholsterer and seamstress, may have sewn the first US flag.

National Museum of American Jewish History (☎ 215-923-3811; www.nmajh.org; 55 N 5th St; admission free; 🕑 10am-5pm Mon-Thu, 10am-3pm Fri, noon-5pm Sun) features exhibits that examine the historical role of Jews in the USA. At the nearby **US Mint** (☎ 215-408-0114; Arch St, btwn 6th & 7th Sts; admission free; closed Sat & Sun Sep-May), tours are now only available on a limited basis, mainly to school groups, because of security concerns. **Arch St Meeting House** (320 Arch St; admission by donation; closed Sun) is the USA's largest Quaker meeting house, and the **African American Museum in Philadelphia** (☎ 215-574-0380; www.aampmuseum.org; 701 Arch St; admission $6; 🕑 10am-5pm Thu-Sun, 10:30am-5pm Tue, 10:30am-7pm Wed) has excellent collections about black history and culture.

Waterfront

The 1.8-mile Benjamin Franklin Bridge, the world's largest suspension bridge when completed in 1926, spans the Delaware River. Its lights dominate the skyline. Along the Penn's Landing riverfront area, between Vine and South Sts, is the **Independence Seaport Museum** (☎ 215-925-5439; www.seaport.philly.com; 211 S Columbia Blvd; admission $8; 🕑 10am-5pm) highlighting

PHILADELPHIA IN...

Two Days

Start in Independence National Historic Park, taking in everything from the **Liberty Bell** to the **National Portrait Gallery**. Then wander over the **Rittenhouse Sq** for some people watching before strolling through South St and to the **Italian Market** to sample some cheese and salami. Head to **Chinatown** for dinner. On day two, enjoy brunch at **Society Hill** followed by a stroll that includes **Antiques Row** and the sites of the **Old City**. Spend the rest of the afternoon in the **Philadelphia Museum of Art** (or other museums of your choice along the Benjamin Franklin Parkway). Have dinner in Society Hill.

Four Days

Follow the two-day itinerary, and on the third day, stroll over to **University City**. Have brunch at the White Dog Café, followed by a stroll around the lovely U Penn campus and the nearby 30th St Station. Walk back into the **Old City** and then to the **Reading Terminal Market**, where you'll eat yourself silly. Treat yourself to a musical or theater performance at night, or just have drinks in **Center City**. On your final day, head out to **Manayunk** for some leisurely shopping, strolling, eating and drinking.

Philadelphia's role as an immigration hub; its shipyard closed in 1995 after 200 years.

In nearby Camden, New Jersey is the excellent **New Jersey State Aquarium** (☎ 800-616-5297; www.njaquarium.org; admission $13; ⌚ 9:30am-4:30pm Mon-Fri, 10am-5pm Sat & Sun).

RiverLink Ferry (☎ 215-925-5465) runs hourly from Penn's Landing ($5 round-trip).

Society Hill & South Philadelphia

Architecture from the 18th and 19th centuries dominates the lovely residential neighborhood of Society Hill. An interesting mix of colonial and contemporary homes can be seen along Delancey, American, Cypress and Philip Sts. **Washington Sq** was conceived as part of William Penn's original city plan, and offers a peaceful respite from sightseeing.

The **Italian Market** (⌚ Tue-Sat) is a highlight of South Philadelphia, where museums and restaurants reflect the area's diversity. It's the country's largest outdoor market, hawking fresh produce and cheese, homemade pastas, fish and butchered treats from lamb to pheasant.

In the midst of it all is the **Mummers' Museum** (☎ 215-336-3050; 1100 S 2nd St; admission $2.50; ⌚ Tue-Sun Sep-Jun, Tue-Sat Jul & Aug), celebrating the tradition of disguise and masquerade. It has an integral role in the famed Mummers Parade, taking place here every New Year's Day.

Center City & Around

Rittenhouse Sq is the most well known of William Penn's city squares, with its wading pool, trees and fine statues. **City Hall** (☎ 215-686-1776; Broad & Market Sts; admission by donation; ⌚ 12:30-2pm) stands tall in Penn Sq, and was completed in 1901. It's probably Philadelphia's architectural highlight, at 548ft high, and topped by a bronze statue of William Penn. **Pennsylvania Academy of the Fine Arts** (☎ 215-972-7600; www.pafa.org; 118 N Broad St; admission $5) is a prestigious academy that has a museum with works by American painters, including Charles Willson Peale and Thomas Eakins. Highly recommended for Civil War buffs is the comprehensive **Civil War Library & Museum** (☎ 215-735-8196; 1805 Pine St; admission $5; ⌚ 11am-4:30pm Wed-Sun) boasting artifacts and exhibitions. **Rosenbach Museum & Library** (☎ 215-732-1600; www.rosenbach.org; 2010 Delancey St; admission $5; ⌚ 10am-5pm Tue & Thu-Sun, until 8pm Wed), meanwhile, is for bibliophiles, as it features rare books and manuscripts, including James Joyce's *Ulysses* manuscript and pages from Bram Stoker's *Dracula*. **Edgar Allan Poe National Historic Site** (☎ 215-597-8780; 532 N 7th St; admission free), a slightly spooky spot, is where Poe wrote the *Black Cat*.

Benjamin Franklin Parkway

Modeled after the Champs Elysées in Paris, the parkway is a center of museums and other landmarks. **Philadelphia Museum of Art** (☎ 215-763-8100; www.philamuseum.org; 26th St; admission $10, pay-what-you-can Sun; ⌚ 10am-5pm Tue-Sun, until 8:45pm Wed & Fri) is the highlight. It's one of the nation's largest and most important museums, featuring some excellent collections of Asian art, Renaissance masterpieces, post-impressionist works and modern pieces by Picasso, Duchamp and Matisse. The grand stairway at its entrance was immortalized when star Sylvester Stallone ran up the steps in the 1976 flick *Rocky*. **Academy of Natural Sciences Museum** (☎ 215-299-1000; 1900 Benjamin Franklin Parkway; $9) features a terrific dinosaur exhibition, where you can dig for fossils on weekends. **Franklin Institute Science Museum** (☎ 215-448-1200; 20th St; adult/child $13/10; ⌚ 9:30am-5pm) is where hands-on science displays were pioneered; a highlight is the Ben Franklin exhibit. Downstairs in Fels Planetarium, laser rock shows feature the standard Pink Floyd–type sounds. The Mandell Futures Center (tickets $10 to $15) highlights computers, health issues and environmental problems. At the **Rodin Museum** (☎ 215-763-8100; 22nd St; suggested donation $3; ⌚ 10am-5pm Tue-Sun), you'll find Rodin's great works the *Thinker* and *Burghers of Calais*.

A few blocks from the parkway, the old **Eastern State Penitentiary** (☎ 215-236-3300; 22nd St & Fairmount Ave; admission $7) features Al Capone's cell and death row. The penitentiary opened in 1829 and was so effective that 300 other prisons were modeled after it.

University City

University of Pennsylvania, commonly called 'U Penn,' was founded in 1740. The Ivy League school, along with nearby Drexel University, gives the area 30,000 students. The campus makes a pleasant afternoon stroll. While you're here, don't miss the romantic, neoclassical **30th St Station**, beautifully lit at night. **University Museum of Archaeology & Anthropology** (☎ 215-898-4000; 33rd & Spruce Sts; admission $5; ⌚ 10am-4:30pm Tue-Sat, 1-5pm Sun) is Penn's magical museum, containing archaeological treasures from ancient Egypt, Mesopotamia, the Mayan peninsula, Greece, Rome and North America. Its fragments of Sumerian script are among the oldest examples of writing ever found.

Fairmount Park

The snaking **Schuylkill River** divides this expansive park into east and west. On the east bank, **Boathouse Row** has Victorian-era rowing-club buildings that are illuminated at night. And **Philadelphia Zoo** (☎ 215-243-1100; www.phillyzoo.com; 3400 W Girard Ave; adult/child $11/8; 9:30am-5pm), the country's oldest zoo, has been modernized with naturalistic habitats.

The historic **Fairmount Park** (admission $2.50; Tue-Sun) early American houses open to the public include the following:

Laurel Hill (☎ 215-235-1776)
Lemon Hill Mansion (☎ 215-232-4337) 'The most elegant seat in Pennsylvania.'
Mount Pleasant (☎ 215-763-8100)
Strawberry Mansion (☎ 215-228-8364) The largest mansion; offers an antique-toy exhibit.
Woodford (☎ 215-229-6115) A Georgian mansion.

Barnes Foundation Gallery (☎ 610-667-0290; 300 N Lodges Lane; admission $5; by appointment only) is beyond Fairmount Park, 6 miles northwest of downtown. The gallery has an exceptionally fine collection of impressionist, post-impressionist and early French modern paintings, including works by Cézanne, Matisse, Monet, Picasso, Renoir and van Gogh.

Activities

Great spots for cycling and rollerblading include the vast expanse of Fairmount Park and the towpaths that run alongside the neighborhood of Manayunk. For advice and group rides, contact the **Bicycle Club of Philadelphia** (☎ 215-843-1093; www.phillybikeclub.org), which leads rides for all skill levels.

Runners should also head to the park, which has tree-lined trails that range from 2 to 10 miles in length. For some excellent urban runs, stick to the quaint residential blocks around Antique Row or Center City; Kelly Drive, off Benjamin Franklin Parkway, is also a great spot to sprint, as is the all-weather track at University of Pennsylvania (Franklin Field, corner of 33rd and Spruce Sts). Also see the visitors center (p175).

Front Runners (www.frontrunnersphila.org) is a gay and lesbian runners club that sponsors treks all around the city. The umbrella group **Middle Atlantic Road Runners Club** (☎ 609-964-6232), based in Lafayette Hill, provides course and race information for locals as well as visitors. Urban hikers should check out Fairmount Park's dirt path extensions toward Wissahickon Creek, far from any noisy city traffic. Take to the ice at **Blue Cross River Rink** (☎ 215-925-RINK; cnr Chestnut St & Christopher Columbus Blvd; Nov-Mar), Penn's Landing.

Tours

Philadelphia Trolley Works (☎ 215-925-8687; adult/child $20/5) The most complete tour of the city is the 90-minute narrated trolley trip during which you can hop on and off at designated stops to stroll and then reboard when you're ready.

76 Carriage Company (☎ 215-923-8516; tours $25-70) For a unique way of getting around, take a tour of various areas by horse-drawn carriage. Prices vary according to length and the size of the group.

Phlash visitor shuttle (☎ 215-4-PHLASH; all-day pass $4) An affordable option is the one-hour, do-it-yourself tour that takes you to about 25 sites in a bright purple van; you can hop on and hop off when you want. There is no tour guide, but you are equipped with a color-coded, easy-to-follow map of the journey.

Mural Tours (☎ 215-685-0754; tours $13; 11am Sat Jun-Oct) Guided walking tour of the city's colorful outdoor murals, the largest collection in the country.

Centipede Tours (☎ 215-735-3123; tours $5) Summer walking tours around Society Hill on Friday and Saturday evenings, with guides in period costume.

Preservation Alliance for Greater Philadelphia (☎ 215-546-1146; tours $15) Contact for architectural tours. Tours don't operate during the summer months.

Festivals & Events

Mummers Parade A very Philly parade, an elaborate celebration of costumes. January 1.
South St Mardi Gras for Fat Tuesday Music and booze in the streets. Mid-February.
Dad Vail Regatta Serious sailing boats. Held May.
Annual Jam on the River Excellent music lineup, from folkies to jam bands. Memorial Day weekend.
Gay Pride Weekend A huge parade, festival and series of parties. First weekend in June.

GAY & LESBIAN PHILADELPHIA

Philly's a pretty gay city, which isn't surprising considering its proximity to New York and its history of tolerance. Most gay venues are within a few blocks of each other west of Society Hill in the heart of **Center City**, although there's a gay-owned hotel, the **Alexander Inn** (p182), on Antique Row. The first Sunday in June is the annual **Gay Pride Weekend** (www.phillypride.org) celebration, featuring a parade, street festival and various parties all over town. The **William Way Lesbian, Gay, Bisexual & Transgender Community Center** (☎ 215-732-2220; www.waygay.org; 1315 Spruce St) offers lectures, support groups and a slew of other events. **Giovanni's Room** (p175) is a large, well-stocked gay bookstore on Antique Row.

Bars and clubs, catering mostly to men, are all close together, which creates a festive scene on weekend evenings. **Bump** (☎ 215-732-1800; 13th & Locust Sts) is the newest luxe lounge, serving continental cuisine till about 10pm, when beefy boys muscle their way in for cocktails and cruising to the sounds of a live DJ. **Woody's Bar & Restaurant** (☎ 215-545-1893; 202 S 13th St) is an always-crowded neighborhood watering hole; nearby **Uncles** (☎ 215-546-6660; 1220 Locust St) caters to a 40-and-over crowd. **Shampoo** (☎ 215-922-7500; 417 N 8th St) is a happenin' club drawing drag queens, hotties and international DJs. While the two-level **2-4 Club** (☎ 215-735-5722; 1221 St James Pl) is everybody's dance club, with a mellow lounge in the basement, its lesbian headquarters one night a month. Besides that, **Sisters** (☎ 215-735-0735; 1320 Chancellor St) is the city's sole dyke bar. **Millennium Coffee** (☎ 731-9798; 212 S 12th St) is a hip, queer java hang.

Equality Forum Formerly PrideFest America; conference on equality issues with national participants. Late April to early May.
Philadelphia Fringe Festival Catch the latest in edgy theater. Held September.
Philadelphia Annual Marathon Runners flock to Philly in fall (November).

Sleeping

Downtown, upscale hotel chains are quite expensive, but some do offer discounted weekend packages. And although there are several quaint B&Bs to choose from, the city is sorely lacking classy boutique-style hotels.

Penn's View Hotel (☎ 215-922-7600; www.pennsviewhotel.com; cnr Front & Market Sts; r from $165; P ⁂ 💻) This old-fashioned inn overlooks the water. It offers a range of rooms featuring Chippendale-style furniture and pleasant, if quite masculine, decor. Many of the rooms have exposed-brick walls and working fireplaces, and all come with plush robes for you to wear during your stay. A continental breakfast is included.

Latham Hotel (☎ 215-563-7474; www.lathamhotel.com; 135 S 17th St; r from $109; P ⁂) A classy, European-style hotel with Victorian rooms.

Shippen Way Inn (☎ 215-627-7266; 416-418 Bainbridge St; r $80) This 1750s colonial house has nine rooms with quilted beds, free wine and cheese in the kitchen and a cozy B&B atmosphere.

Antique Row B&B (☎ 215-592-7802; www.antiquerownbb.com; 341 S 12th St; r $65-110) You'll find quirky, period-furnished rooms and good breakfasts on hoppin' Antique Row.

Alexander Inn (☎ 215-923-1004; www.alexanderinn.com; 301 S 12th St; r $99; P ⊠ ⁂ 💻) Gay-owned, with a classy lobby and basic, good-sized rooms. Breakfast is included.

Inn on Locust (☎ 215-985-1905; www.innonlocust.com; 1234 Locust St; s/d $125/200; P ⊠ ⁂) This intimate inn, which is near all the gay clubs, gears itself to a business clientele with quarters that convert into boardrooms or offices. Features high-speed Internet service and modern room decor, although the lobby is a bit off-putting. Rooms at the back of the building feel stuffy, but rooms in the front have great views of one of Philly's huge and colorful outdoor murals.

Society Hill Hotel (☎ 215-925-1919; www.societyhillhotel.com; 301 Chestnut St; r $88-155; P ⁂) Philly's smallest hotel has a European atmosphere, a friendly staff and is right near Independence Park. Its very small but quaint rooms feature brass beds and private baths, and the 1st floor of the place is a popular bar and restaurant.

HI Bank St Hostel (☎ 215-922-0222; 32 S Bank St; dm $18-21) An excellent hostel in a safe neighborhood, a short walk from 2nd St Station and major sights, with Internet access for $8 an hour. It's got 70 dorm beds and a rec-room-type lounge area.

Eating

CHINATOWN & SOUTH STREET AREA

Chinatown has many cheap options.

Vietnam Restaurant (☎ 215-592-1163; 221 N 11th St; dishes $8-10) An always-crowded favorite serving authentic Vietnamese food such as summer rolls and vermicelli.

St Gianna's Grille (☎ 215-829-4448; 507 S 6th St; dishes $5-8) Off of South, this place has good, cheap pizzas, salads, calzones and vegetarian specials – like the vegan cheesesteak sandwich topped with soy cheese!

Here are two of Philly's most popular cheesesteak places, both open 24 hours:

Geno's (☎ 215-389-0659; S 9th St & Passyunk Ave)

Pat's King of Steaks (☎ 215-468-1546; S 9th St & Passyunk Ave)

In south Philadelphia, the **Italian Market** (see p185) is the best option.

CENTER CITY & AROUND

Reading Terminal Market (☎ 215-922-2317; www.readingterminalmarket.org; 12th & Arch Sts; dishes $2-8) At the budget end, the huge indoor market is the best you'll find. Pick up a map of the place inside one of the entrances and choose your favorite, from fresh Amish cheeses and Thai desserts, to falafel, cheesesteaks, salad bars, sushi, Peking duck and great Mexican.

Le Bec-Fin (☎ 215-567-1000; 1523 Walnut St; prix fixe lunch/dinner $38/120) On the high end, many gourmets rate Le Bec-Fin as the country's best restaurant for its setting, service and superb French food. It's quite expensive, of course, but the fixed-price lunch or dinner are comparative bargains.

Valanni (☎ 215-790-9494; 1229 Spruce St; dishes $13-18) Popular with 50-something theatergoers in the early part of the evening, and sassy gay men in the latter, who come for solid Medi-Latin cuisine.

Effie's (☎ 215-592-8333; 1127 Pine St; dishes $12-15) On Antique Row, Effie's has Greek specialities in an intimate setting.

Joe (☎ 215-592-7384; Walnut & 11th St; coffee $2) Serves only 'organic, fair-trade, shade-grown' coffee and light fare.

Silk City Diner (☎ 215-592-8838; 425 Spring Garden St at N 5th St; dishes $6-11) A 1940s classic open 24 hours, with entertainment some nights.

Capogiro Gelato Artisans (☎ 215-351-0900; 119 S 13th St; ice cream $4) Whatever you do, if you are up for dessert, don't skip Capogiro, which is not your average ice-cream shop.

> **PHILLY CHEESESTEAK**
>
> A stack of tender, juicy, thinly sliced beef, topped with lashings of freshly fried onion rings, covered with gorgeous, gooey melted cheese, served in a soft, warm, white bread roll – that's the city's namesake taste sensation. Among Philadelphia's contributions to American civilization, it ranks right up there with the Declaration of Independence.

The design here is slicker than a Barcelona nightclub, and the gelato, in dozens of outrageous flavors, is perfection; it's made only from grass-fed, hormone-free cows. Moo!

UNIVERSITY CITY

White Dog Café (☎ 215-386-9224; 3420 Sansom St; dishes $8-13) For an amazing brunch, join the swarms of U Penn students and professors. Made famous by its cookbook and reputation for social activism, it offers omelettes, pastries and even tofu scramble for vegans.

Intermezzo Café & Lounge (☎ 215-222-4300; 3131 Walnut St; dishes around $5) Has good coffee, sandwiches, sushi and desserts.

MANAYUNK

Main St is a bustling restaurant row.

Sonoma (☎ 215-483-9400; 4411 Main St; dishes $15-22) Cooks up organic, seasonal dishes including organic Philly cheesesteak and shrimp ravioli in lobster brandy sauce; its vodka bar offers a whopping 220 types of vodka.

Jake's Restaurant (☎ 215-483-0444; dishes $20-27) is a pricey hotspot serving everything from pan-seared foie gras to grilled New York strip steak.

Grasshopper (☎ 215-483-1888; 4427 Main St; dishes $12-18) Has Sino-French cuisine with several vegetarian options.

An Indian Affair (☎ 215-482-8300; 4425 Main St; dishes $13-18) Serves upscale thalis and other Indian specialities.

United States Hotel Bar & Grill (☎ 215-483-9222; 4439 Main St; dishes $8-12) Serves unique light fare, like the wild-mushroom sandwich with basil mayo.

Drinking

BARS & CLUBS

Most bars stay open until 2am.

Dirty Frank's (☎ 215-732-5010; 347 S 13th St at Pine St) On Antique Row, this is a dive that's a local institution, adorned with an outdoor mural of about a dozen famous Franks; it's got cheap booze and artsy patrons.

New Deck Tavern (☎ 215-386-4600; 3408 Sansom St) In University City, students enjoy a choice of 18 draft beers.

Dock St Brewing Company (☎ 215-496-0413; 2 Logan Sq) Where more draft lines flow.

South St also has a good selection of bars and clubs.

Manny Brown's (☎ 215-627-7427; 512 South St) A down-home rib joint and beer bar.

Fluid (613 S 4th St) *The* underground nightclub, with awesome in-house and visiting DJs.

Bar Noir (☎ 215-569-9333; 112 S 18th St) In Rittenhouse Sq, Bar Noir is a long, thin bar down a long, thin stairwell where all sorts of see-and-be-seen types mush together to sip sharp cocktails and sway to the sounds of Euro-pop DJs.

Continental Martini Bar (☎ 215-923-6069; 134 Market St) Sleek and cool enough to be featured on a recent MTV series, attracts urban-chic singles for its lively cocktail bar and eclectic dinner menu.

Bijou (☎ 215-925-2623; 11 S 3rd St) In the Old City, upscale professionals flock here to sink into plush leather seats with glasses of fine chardonnay.

Cherry Street Tavern (☎ 215-561-5683; 129 N 22nd St) With wood paneling and barflies aplenty, this is where locals belly-up for cheap pitcher specials nightly. There's no need to be alarmed by the carving station just inside the door, where hot beef sandwiches are doled out all evening long.

Café Olé (☎ 215-627-2140; 147 N 3rd St) For mellowing out, this café has a funky vibe and potent java.

Last Drop Coffee House (☎ 215-893-9262; 1300 Pine St) Receives thumbs-up reviews.

Anthony's Italian Coffee House (☎ 800-833-5030; 903 S 9th St) In South Philadelphia, Anthony's serves good cakes and coffee.

Entertainment

The premier cultural destination is Broad St south of City Hall, called the 'Avenue of the Arts.' Philadelphia has a rich theater scene and something for everyone. For most entertainment, buy tickets from the following:

Ticketmaster (☎ 215-336-2000)

Upstages (☎ 215-569-9700) Offers half-price, same-day tickets.

THEATER, BALLET & ORCHESTRA

Pennsylvania Ballet (☎ 215-551-7000) Acclaimed ballet company.

Opera Company of Philadelphia (☎ 215-928-2100) A 19-year-old company known for its lavish productions.

Philadelphia Orchestra (☎ 215-893-1999) The renowned orchestra holds summer concerts at Mann Center in Fairmount Park; prices range from $23 to $58, and from $5 to $8 for lawn seats.

JAZZ & LIVE MUSIC

Jazz, blues and music clubs abound.

Zanzibar Blue (☎ 215-732-4500; 200 S Broad St) Upmarket.

Ortlieb's (847 N 3rd St) This place is a casual, long, narrow space in a former '1000-year-old' brewery.

Listen to live tunes at the following.

Khyber Pass (☎ 215-238-5888; 56 S 2nd St) Eclectic crowd and performers.

LaTazza 108 (108 Chestnut St) Cover charges vary.

SPECTATOR SPORTS

Philadelphia's two major sporting venues are in South Philadelphia on S Broad St. Major-league **Philadelphia Phillies baseball team** (☎ 215-463-1000) and **NFL Philadelphia Eagles football team** (☎ 215-463-5500) both call Veterans Stadium home.

At the indoor **CoreStates Complex** (☎ 215-336-3600) you can usually buy game-day tickets ($12 to $68) for the NBA Philadelphia 76ers basketball games and NHL Philadelphia Flyers hockey games; or call Ticketmaster.

Shopping

For upscale designer chains – Diesel, Nicole Miller, Ralph Lauren – stick to the grand **Rittenhouse Row** (Walnut St btwn Rittenhouse Sq & the Ave of the Arts). There are a few good urban malls, too.

Shops at Liberty Place (☎ 215-851-9055; 1625 Chestnut St) More than 70 stores in a wonderfully designed 60-story glass tower.

Shops at Bellevue (☎ 215-875-8350; Broad & Walnut Sts) The bottom floors of the Colonial Hotel have been turned into the upscale Shops at Bellevue.

Bourse (5th St at Market St) A late-Victorian building, and formerly the home of Philly's grain and stock exchange, Bourse now houses an airy food court and a slew of shops; and the Gallery at Market East, one of the nation's largest urban shopping centers, with 170 stores and various pushcart vendors.

Chainstore-haters should stick to the eclectic boutiques – along **South St** for clothing and accessories, along **Antique Row** for books, housewares and furniture.

The markets are best for culinary pleasures: the **Italian Market** is the place for fresh produce, fish, meats and Italian specialities, and the **Reading Terminal Market** (☎ 215-922-2317; www.readingterminalmarket.org; 12th & Arch Sts) is good for stocking up on pastries, olives, meats and Amish cheeses.

Getting There & Away

AIR

Philadelphia International Airport (☎ 215-937-6937) has direct flights from Europe, the Caribbean, Canada and more than 100 US cities.

BUS

Catch buses from the **Greyhound bus terminal** (☎ 215-931-4014; 1001 Filbert St); **New Jersey Transit** (☎ 215-569-3752) and **Capitol Trailways** (☎ 800-444-2877) buses also stop there. Daily buses run to New York ($21, two hours); Atlantic City and New Jersey ($10, 1½ hours); and Washington, DC ($19, 3½ hours). To reach Jersey City, catch a bus to Newark, then take New Jersey Transit.

TRAIN

Amtrak trains stop at 30th St Station, in University City. Philadelphia is on Amtrak's Northeast Corridor route between Richmond, Virginia and Boston, Massachusetts, via Washington, DC, and New York City. There are also trains west to Lancaster, Harrisburg, Altoona, Pittsburgh and Chicago, and south to Florida. One-way fares include New York (from $48, 1½ hours); Washington, DC ($45, two hours); and Pittsburgh ($39, eight hours). **New Jersey Transit** (☎ 800-228-8246) has a frequent rail service to Atlantic City ($10/11.50 one way/round-trip).

Getting Around

TO/FROM THE AIRPORT

The **Septa** (☎ 215-580-7800) R1 airport railway line ($5.50) and door-to-door shuttle-bus services ($8 to $10) run there. A one-way cab fare to Center City costs about $20.

CAR & MOTORCYCLE

Parking in central Philadelphia is difficult, and regulations are enforced. Hostel and hotel validation can reduce fees at some garages. The Vine St Expressway, under the city streets, is the quickest east–west route across downtown.

Philly is an inexpensive place to rent cars. Typical daily rates for a compact are $30 to $50 with unlimited mileage, less on weekends or by the week. See p1121 for car rental advice.

PUBLIC TRANSPORTATION

Septa (☎ 215-580-7800) operates the subways and buses. Its three subway routes are the Market–Frankford line, the Broad St line (servicing Veterans and CoreStates Spectrum stadiums) and the Subway-Surface line along Market St (one way $3 to $6; 50¢ to 75¢ less off-peak). Most Septa bus trips cost $2 (plus 60¢ for a transfer); a DayPass ($5.50) and weekly pass ($19) allow unlimited rides on city transit vehicles. Bus No 76 runs from Penn's Landing through Society Hill and South St, along Market St to City Hall and the Benjamin Franklin Parkway to the Philadelphia Museum of Art, Fairmount Park and zoo. Bus No 42 connects Old City with the Civic Center and University City.

The **Phlash** (☎ 215-474-5274) shuttle bus loops downtown from Logan Circle through Center City to the waterfront and South St ($2/4 one way/all day). The **Patco** (☎ 215-922-4600) subway line to Camden, New Jersey, crosses downtown ($1).

Taxi fares are $1.80 for the first sixth of a mile, then 30¢ per additional sixth of a mile, plus 20¢ per minute of waiting time. Drivers serve major hotels. Call **Quaker City Cab** (☎ 215-728-8000) or **Olde City Taxi** (☎ 215-338-0838).

AROUND PHILADELPHIA

New Hope

New Hope, which sits equidistant from Philadelphia and New York City, is a quaint, artsy town that sits on the Delaware River. It's edged with a long and peaceful towpath that's perfect for runners, cyclists and strollers, and you can walk across the water to its sister town, Lambertville, in New Jersey. The town draws a large amount of gay folk, who feel comfortable here because of the rainbow flags that hang outside of various businesses, as well as a gay anti-discrimination ordinance that was passed in 2002.

One of New Hope's most unique offerings are the mule-drawn canal boat rides in the Delaware Canal, a leftover from the canal building era of the mid-19th century. Stop by the **New Hope Canal Boat Company** (☎ 215-862-0758; 149 Main St; adult/child $10/8; tours 12:30pm & 3pm May-Oct) for tickets.

A great day trip from either Philly or NYC, New Hope has a plethora of cute B&Bs if you decide to make a weekend out of it.

Fox & Hound Bed & Breakfast (☎ 215-862-5082; www.foxhoundinn.com; 246 W Bridge St; r from $85;) One of the best, has cute rooms in an 1850 stone manor.

Porches on the Towpath (☎ 215-862-3277; www.porchesnewhope.com; 20 Fisher's Alley; r from $95;) One of several gay-owned inns, this is another relatively good deal. It features elegant quarters and is tucked away on a quiet lane fronting the canal.

Main St is filled with decent, affordable eateries.

Landing Inn (☎ 215-862-5711; 22 N Main St; dishes $8-14) A great romantic spot with a fireplace and waterfront views.

Brandywine Valley

Straddling the Pennsylvania-Delaware border, the Brandywine Valley is a patchwork of rolling, wooded countryside, historic villages, gardens, mansions and museums. The spectacular **Longwood Gardens** (☎ 800-737-5500; Rte 1; adult $12, child under 6 free, child 6-15 $2; 9am-5pm Nov-Mar, until 6pm Apr-Oct), near Kennett Sq, has 1050 acres, 20 indoor gardens and 11,000 kinds of plants, with something always in bloom. There's also a Children's Garden with a maze, illuminated fountains in summer, and festive lights at Christmas.

A showcase of American artwork, the **Brandywine River Museum** (☎ 610-388-2700; Hwy 1 & Rte 100; adult $5), at Chadd's Ford, includes the work of the 'Brandywine School' – Pyle, several Wyeths and Maxfield Parrish.

For more information on local attractions, see p341.

Valley Forge

After defeating the colonists at the Battle of Brandywine Creek and occupying Philadelphia in 1777, General Washington and 12,000 Continental troops withdrew to Valley Forge. It was here that 2000 men lost their lives in a bitter winter of cold, hunger and disease, and many others returned home. The rest were trained, drilled and organized into a disciplined force. Today, Valley Forge symbolizes Washington's endurance and its leadership. The **visitors center** (☎ 610-783-1077; cnr N Gulph Rd & Rte 23; 9am-5pm) has information and a film on the winter encampment. The **Valley Forge Historical Society Museum** (☎ 610-917-3651; 435 Devon Park Dr; admission $2; 9am-5pm) features exhibits on George Washington.

PENNSYLVANIA DUTCH COUNTRY

The core of Pennsylvania Dutch Country lies in the southeast region of Pennsylvania, in an area about 20 by 15 miles, east of Lancaster. The Amish (*ah*-mish), Mennonite and Brethren religious communities are collectively known as the 'Plain People.' The Old Order Amish, with their dark, plain clothing, live a simple, Bible-centered life but have, ironically, managed to become a major tourist attraction. Anabaptist sects, persecuted in their native Switzerland, settled in tolerant Pennsylvania starting in the early 1700s. Speaking German dialects, they became known as 'Dutch' (from 'Deutsch'). Most Pennsylvania Dutch live on farms, and their beliefs vary from sect to sect. Many do not use electricity, and most opt for horse-drawn buggies – a truly delightful sight, and sound, in the area.

The small and charmingly rural 'Dutch Country' has, unfortunately, been sullied by busloads of tourists who come to gawk and overeat at one of the area's all-you-can-eat family-style dinners. Much of the area has been overdeveloped and is plagued by strip malls and superstores. To escape the crowds and learn about the region, rent a bike, pack some food and explore the numerous back roads. You may also consider hiring a guide for a private tour, or simply visiting in winter, when tourism is down. Some farm homes rent rooms for $50 to $100 – they welcome kids and offer a unique opportunity to experience farm life. Craft shops sell quilts, wooden furniture and faceless dolls. Farmers' markets are popular for pies, preserves, fresh fruit and vegetables.

The **visitors center** (☎ 717-299-8901; www.padutchcountry.com; 9am-5pm), off Rte 30 in Lancaster, offers comprehensive information. For a true overnight experience, just ask to be directed to one of the farming families who rent rooms and offer home-cooked meals.

RRTA (☎ 717-397-4246) local buses link the main towns, but a car is better for sightseeing. **Amish Country Tours** (☎ 717-768-3600) runs 2½-hour bus tours that take back roads and visit farms (from $20). **Lancaster County Bicycle Tours** (☎ 717-768-8366) rents bikes and leads intimate tours that visit an Amish home and grocery store ($50 per half day).

There are a slew of inns in the Amish country, and you will find cheap motels along the southeast portion of Rte 462/Rte 30. In Intercourse, **Beacon Hill Camping** (☎ 717-768-8875; Rte 772; r from $24) has a range of family-friendly sites. The **Landis Guest Farm** (☎ 717-898-7028; Gochlan Rd; r from $85) in Manheim puts you up in a cozy cottage, feeds you a big country breakfast and lets you milk the cows.

The **Capitol Trailways & Greyhound terminal** (☎ 717-397-4861), located at the train station, has buses to Philadelphia ($15, two hours) and Pittsburgh ($38, five hours). The **Amtrak train station** (☎ 717-291-5080; 53 McGovern Ave) has trains to and from Philadelphia ($14, 80 minutes) and Pittsburgh ($85, six hours). Hertz (see p1122) rents cars.

Lancaster & Around

On the western edge of the Amish country, the pleasant town of Lancaster was briefly the US capital in September 1777, when Congress stopped here overnight. The downtown **chamber of commerce** (☎ 717-397-3531; 100 Queen St; 🕒 8am-5pm Mon-Fri) provides tourist information. The touristy **Central Market** (Penn Sq; 🕒 6am Tue, Fri & Sat) offers good food and crafts. Nearby, the **Heritage Center Museum** (☎ 717-299-6440; 13 W King St; admission free; 🕒 10am-5pm Tue-Sat) has a collection of 18th- and 19th-century paintings, period furniture and local craftwork.

Probably named for its crossroads location, nearby Intercourse has shops selling clothing, quilts, candles, furniture, fudge and even souvenirs with Intercourse jokes. Browse along Rte 340 or 772, northwest of Intercourse. Friendly **People's Place** (☎ 800-390-8436; Rte 340; admission $5; 🕒 10am-5pm Mon-Sat) gives a sensitive overview of Amish and Mennonite life with a *Who Are the Amish?* documentary.

Bird-in-Hand has craft stores, restaurants and a farmers market. Country Barn Quilts & Crafts, east of town, has a good selection. **Abe's Buggy Rides** (☎ 717-392-1794; adult $10) does a 2-mile tour. The **Amish Farm & House** (☎ 717-394-6185; admission $6.50) is an original farmhouse with a tour that describes Amish culture.

In Lititz, visitors come for the **Sturgis Pretzel House** (☎ 717-626-4354; www.sturgispretzel.com; Rte 772; admission $2; 🕒 9am-5pm Mon-Fri), the USA's first pretzel factory. The nearby **Ephrata Cloister** (☎ 717-733-6600; 632 W Main St; admission $6; 🕒 9am-5pm Mon-Sat, from noon Sun), a collection of medieval-style buildings, is where the Pietists lived and worked under rigorous conditions.

To sample one of the famous family-style restaurants, get prepared to rub elbows with lots of tourists. The experience is part of coming to Amish country, though – and it'll fill you with lots of delicious dishes. Two stand-outs are **Shady Maple Smorgasbord** (☎ 717-354-8222; Rte 23; mains $15) in Blue Ball, or **Willow Valley Family Restaurant** (☎ 717-464-2711; 2416 Willow St Pike; mains $18) in Lancaster. Locals, however, get their Pennsylvania Dutch grub at the family-owned **Chimney Corner Restaurant** (☎ 717-626-4707; Rte 772; mains $10) in Lititz, or Ephrata's tiny **Bright's Restaurant** (☎ 717-738-1177; Rte 272; dishes $8).

GOING DUTCH

Famous not only for its plainly clad Amish folk, the Dutch Country is also home to hearty Pennsylvania Dutch food. Author Tamar Myers, who writes mysteries set in this region and includes some of the mouth-watering recipes, helps folks bring these dishes into their homes. But it's best to sample the tastes authentically: in Amish style, you sit at a long table beside other diners sharing friendly conversation and oven-baked bread. These home-cooked, all-you-can-eat meals are not for the faint of stomach. From pepper cabbage appetizers to homemade sausage, candied sweet potatoes and farm-grown vegetables, the food keeps coming until you can't take another bite. Save room for the local favorite, shoofly pie – a sticky, sweet dessert topped with molasses and cinnamon that has been known to capture those pesky critters in the kitchen. Authentic Amish meals cost around $17 per person – go with an appetite.

Harrisburg & Around

The state capital of Harrisburg, located on the Susquehanna River, is not much to see. The **capital dome**, modeled after St Peter's Basilica in Rome, however, is impressive. The **State Museum of Pennsylvania** (☎ 717-787-4980; www.statemuseumpa.org; cnr North & 3rd Sts; admission free; 🕑 9am-5pm Tue-Sat, from noon Sun) exhibits Civil War artifacts and the huge *Battle of Gettysburg* painting.

The infamous **Three Mile Island** nuclear power plant is just 10 miles from the capital. While Unit 2 is permanently closed due to a partial meltdown in 1979, Unit 1 is back in action. But you can only get a glimpse of the controversial spot from afar, as the **visitors center** (☎ 717-948-8829) is currently closed for security reasons.

Just 12 miles from here is **Hershey**, the home of Milton S Hershey's chocolate empire, **Chocolate World** (☎ 717-534-4900). While kids might fall under its spell, it's actually a disappointing mock factory and giant candy store. Much better is **Hershey Park** (☎ 800-437-7439; www.hersheypa.com/attractions/hersheypark; adult/child $36/20; 🕑 10am-10pm Jun-Aug), an amusement park with more than 50 rides.

Gettysburg

This tranquil, compact and history-laden town, 145 west of Philadelphia, saw one of the Civil War's most decisive and bloody battles. It's also where Lincoln delivered his Gettysburg Address. The area is surrounded by the Gettysburg National Military Park, memorials and monuments. Lincoln Sq is the town center. The **Gettysburg Convention & Visitors Bureau** (☎ 717-334-6274; www.gettysburg.com; 35 Carlisle St; 🕑 8:30am-5:30pm) distributes a comprehensive list of attractions.

The 8-sq-mile National Military Park encompasses most of the area of the three-day battle. South of the visitors center along the High Water Mark Trail, **Cemetery Ridge** is the site of Pickett's Charge, where the Confederates suffered 80% casualties. Other hikes include the mile-long **Big Round Top Loop Trail**. There's also **Devil's Den**, a mass of boulders that Confederate snipers once used as a hideout. The **Cyclorama Center** (admission $2.50) is a 360-degree painting of the battle.

Other Gettysburg attractions include the **Eisenhower National Historic Site** (☎ 717-338-9114; 97 Tinytown Rd; admission $7; 🕑 9am-5pm), Ike's former home, as well as the house that served as **General Lee's Headquarters** (🕑 717-334-3141; Budford Ave; admission free; 🕑 9am-5pm mid-Mar–Nov). Lincoln prepared his Gettysburg Address in the **Wills House** (☎ 717-334-8188; Lincoln Sq; admission $3.50), now a museum. In the evening, you can mingle with the battle spirits on the Ghosts of **Gettysburg Candlelight Walking Tours** (☎ 717-337-0445; adult $6.50).

The annual **Civil War Heritage Days** (recorded information ☎ 717-334-6274) festival, taking place from the last weekend of June through the first weekend of July, features living history encampments, battle reenactments, a lecture series and book fair. Book early, as it's a popular event for history buffs.

For accommodations, which are crowded in summer, try **Battlefield Heritage Resort** (☎ 717-334-1577; Business Rte 15; campsites $17-24), southwest. **Herr Tavern & Publick House** (☎ 717-334-4332; 900 Chambersburg Rd; mains $18-25) serves upscale American lunch and dinner in a historic setting, while the **Pub & Restaurant** (☎ 717-334-7100; Lincoln Sq; mains $12) has cheap sandwiches, soups and salads.

PITTSBURGH

To most Americans, the mention of Pittsburgh conjures up stark images of steel and coal factories – if anything at all. But today's city, still somewhat of a secret even to East Coasters, is absolutely teeming with culture and beauty and universities. It's well worth a trip.

Pittsburgh's location at a major river junction made it a colonial-era trading center; iron and steel industries boomed until the 1960s and 1970s, when competition from newer, more efficient steelworks overseas devastated Pittsburgh's heavy industries and closed factories.

These days, an endearing, scrappy, blue-collar element remains, as do distinct, closely knit neighborhoods, a growing white-collar workforce and marked ethnic diversity. Air quality and civic amenity have improved greatly from the closure of many old industrial plants, with much of the city now clean and green. Proud locals focus on the city's economic future, but the powerful Pittsburgh Steelers football team is a constant reminder of its great industrial past.

Orientation

The city, spread out among a series of rivers and connected by seven picturesque bridges

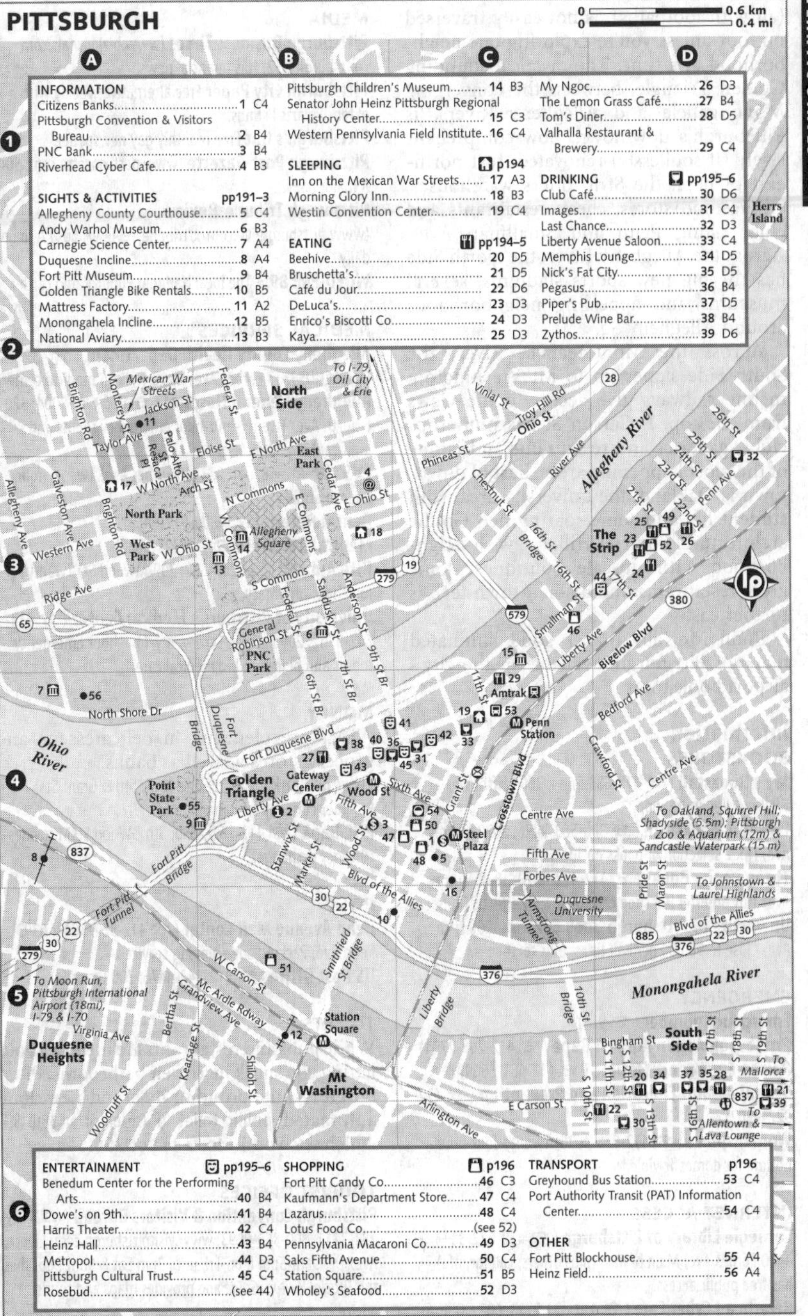
PITTSBURGH
0 0.6 km
0 0.4 mi
INFORMATION
Citizens Banks.....1 C4
Pittsburgh Convention & Visitors Bureau.....2 B4
PNC Bank.....3 B4
Riverhead Cyber Cafe.....4 B3
SIGHTS & ACTIVITIES pp191–3
Allegheny County Courthouse.....5 C4
Andy Warhol Museum.....6 B3
Carnegie Science Center.....7 A4
Duquesne Incline.....8 A4
Fort Pitt Museum.....9 B4
Golden Triangle Bike Rentals.....10 B5
Mattress Factory.....11 A2
Monongahela Incline.....12 B5
National Aviary.....13 B3
Pittsburgh Children's Museum.....14 B3
Senator John Heinz Pittsburgh Regional History Center.....15 C3
Western Pennsylvania Field Institute.....16 C4
SLEEPING p194
Inn on the Mexican War Streets.....17 A3
Morning Glory Inn.....18 B3
Westin Convention Center.....19 C4
EATING pp194–5
Beehive.....20 D5
Bruschetta's.....21 D5
Café du Jour.....22 D6
DeLuca's.....23 D3
Enrico's Biscotti Co.....24 D3
Kaya.....25 D3
My Ngoc.....26 D3
The Lemon Grass Café.....27 B4
Tom's Diner.....28 D5
Valhalla Restaurant & Brewery.....29 C4
DRINKING pp195–6
Club Café.....30 D6
Images.....31 C4
Last Chance.....32 D3
Liberty Avenue Saloon.....33 C4
Memphis Lounge.....34 D5
Nick's Fat City.....35 D5
Pegasus.....36 B4
Piper's Pub.....37 D5
Prelude Wine Bar.....38 B4
Zythos.....39 D6
ENTERTAINMENT pp195–6
Benedum Center for the Performing Arts.....40 B4
Dowe's on 9th.....41 B4
Harris Theater.....42 C4
Heinz Hall.....43 B4
Metropol.....44 D3
Pittsburgh Cultural Trust.....45 C4
Rosebud.....(see 44)
SHOPPING p196
Fort Pitt Candy Co.....46 C3
Kaufmann's Department Store.....47 C4
Lazarus.....48 C4
Lotus Food Co.....(see 52)
Pennsylvania Macaroni Co.....49 D3
Saks Fifth Avenue.....50 C4
Station Square.....51 B5
Wholey's Seafood.....52 D3
TRANSPORT p196
Greyhound Bus Station.....53 C4
Port Authority Transit (PAT) Information Center.....54 C4
OTHER
Fort Pitt Blockhouse.....55 A4
Heinz Field.....56 A4
Herrs Island
North Side
Mexican War Streets
To I-79, Oil City & Erie
East Park
North Park
West Park
Allegheny Square
Allegheny River
Ohio River
Monongahela River
The Strip
PNC Park
Golden Triangle
Point State Park
Gateway Center
Wood St
Steel Plaza
Penn Station
Amtrak
Duquesne University
Station Square
Mt Washington
Duquesne Heights
South Side
To Oakland, Squirrel Hill; Shadyside (5.5m); Pittsburgh Zoo & Aquarium (12m) & Sandcastle Waterpark (15 m)
To Johnstown & Laurel Highlands
To Moon Run, Pittsburgh International Airport (18mi), I-79 & I-70
To Mallorca
To Allentown & Lava Lounge

(all with footpaths), is not easily traversed on foot unless you're exploring one neighborhood at a time. The mystical-sounding Golden Triangle, between the converging Monongahela and Allegheny Rivers, is Pittsburgh's downtown, now comprehensively (if soullessly) renovated. Just northeast of here, the Strip offers warehouses, ethnic food stores, cheap restaurants and clubs along Penn and Smallman Aves. Across the Allegheny River, the North Side has the big new sports stadiums, several museums and appealing neighborhoods around Allegheny Sq.

Across the Monongahela River, the South Side slopes up to Mt Washington; incline railways give access to the views from the top. E Carson St has numerous clubs, galleries and restaurants and is one of the most happening areas. East of downtown is Oakland, the university area, with student life and some soaring neo-Gothic architecture. Squirrel Hill, a Jewish neighborhood with upscale boutiques, some great restaurants and a small-town feel, is further east.

Rand McNally makes good laminated maps of Pittsburgh, available in the city's airport bookstores.

Information

BOOKSTORES

Jay's Bookstall (☎ 412-683-2644; 3604 Fifth Ave) Well-stocked indie shop.
Pinskers Bookstore (☎ 800-583-2476; 2028 Murray Ave) Huge selection of books on Judaism.
Three Penny Books (☎ 412-422-5420; 1827 Murray Ave) Tiny Squirrel Hill shop crammed with eclectic finds.
University of Pittsburgh Book Center (4000 Fifth Ave) Close to 90,000 general titles, plus textbooks.

EMERGENCY

Emergency number (☎ 911)
Pittsburgh Action Against Rape (☎ 412-765-2731)
Poison Emergency Hotline (☎ 412-681-6669)
Sexual Assault Education and Prevention (☎ 412-922-9902)
Womansplace (☎ 412-678-4616) Twenty-four-hour hotline for domestic violence.

INTERNET ACCESS

Carnegie Library of Pittsburgh (☎ 412-622-3114; 4400 Forbes Ave) Main branch (plus others; call for info) has free public access.
Riverhead Cyber Cafe (☎ 412-322-2223; 607 E Ohio St)

MEDIA

Pittsburgh Business Times (www.bizjournals.com/pittsburgh/; $2) Has financial news.
Pittsburgh City Paper Free alternative weekly with extensive arts listings.
Pittsburgh's Out Free monthly gay newspaper.
Pittsburgh Post-Gazette (www.post-gazette.com; 50¢) A major daily.
Pittsburgh Tribune-Review (www.pittsburghlive.com/x/tribune-review/; 50¢) A major daily.
WQED-FM: 89.3 The local National Public Radio carrier.

MEDICAL SERVICES

Allegheny County Health Department (☎ 412-687-ACHD; 3333 Forbes Ave) Has a walk-in medical center.
Allegheny General Hospital (☎ 866-680-0004; 320 E North Ave) Twenty-four-hour emergency rooms and high-ranking medical care.
CVS (☎ 412-687-4180; 3440 Forbes Ave) Twenty-four-hour pharmacy.
Dental Referral (☎ 800-917-6453)
Medical Referral (☎ 412-321-5030)
Rite Aid (☎ 412-621-4302; 209 Atwood St) Twenty-four-hour pharmacy.
University of Pittsburgh Medical Center (☎ 412-647-8762; 200 Lothrop St) Twenty-four-hour emergency rooms and high-ranking medical care.

MONEY

ATMs are plentiful, in delicatessens and grocery stores as well as banks.
Citizens Bank (☎ 412-234-4215; 5th & Grant Sts) Provides currency exchange.
PNC Bank (☎ 412-762-2090; 5th &Wood Sts) Provides currency exchange.

POST

Penn Avenue Mail Center (☎ 412-362-3841; 6393 Penn Ave) Packing and shipping services.
US Post Office (☎ 412-642-4476; 700 Grant St)

TOILETS

While pubs and restaurants are mellow about letting you sneak in to their bathrooms, Pittsburgh is quite proud of its brand-new, lone automated **public toilet** (E Carson St at 18th St), which lets you in for a fee of 25¢.

TOURIST OFFICES

Pittsburgh Convention & Visitors Bureau (☎ 412-281-7711, 800-366-0093; www.visitpittsburgh.com; Liberty Ave; 🕘 9am-5pm Mon-Fri, until 3pm Sat & Sun) Publishes the *Official Visitors Guide* and provides maps and tourist advice.

ANDY WARHOL

Andy Warhol (1928–87) was one of the most influential US artists of the 20th century. Born in the Oakland district of Pittsburgh, Warhol was the son of Polish immigrants who turned into one of America's favorite freaky artists. He coined the phrase about everyone having '15 minutes of fame.' Warhol, though, had more than 15 years of it.

At his mother's suggestion, he studied art at the Carnegie Institute (now Carnegie Mellon University). Come graduation in 1949 he was outta there, relocating to big, bad New York City, where he became a leading freelance commercial artist. He developed his distinctive style of pop art, and by the early 1960s was exhibiting some of his now-famous works, including the large, multi-image silkscreen paintings of Marilyn Monroe, Mao Tse-tung, Campbell's soup cans and Coca-Cola bottles. In addition to painting, Warhol produced many experimental, underground movies, starring a motley crew of drag queens, dykes and models. *Sleep* (1963) was one of his first and most memorable: the silent movie showed a man sleeping for eight hours.

Warhol eventually opened the Factory, which is when the fun really started. His studio became party central for avant-garde artists, druggies, prostitutes, tricks, poor little rich girls (and boys) and various other pals and sycophants. In 1968 he was shot by angry feminist Valerie Solanis, once part of his artistic circle. A year later he started *Interview* magazine. In the 1970s and 1980s he continued to produce portraits and some of his most famous paintings, and also stayed in the public eye by cavorting with all sorts of film and music stars at the debauched Studio 54 nightclub.

After his death (following a gallbladder operation), it was decided to devote a museum to the man and his work. He had lived most of his life and achieved fame in New York City, but, despite some controversy, the museum is now firmly established in his hometown.

Pittsburgh Council for International Visitors (☎ 412-624-7800; www.pciv.org; 315 S Bellefield Ave)

UNIVERSITIES

University of Pittsburgh, Carnegie-Mellon University and Duquesne University are all large presences in town, with sprawling campuses and bustling academic crowds.

Dangers & Annoyances

While walking around within the neighborhoods covered below is safe at anytime, stretches of no-man's land that fall in between 'hoods can be isolated and creepy at night, particularly the South Side stretch between Station Sq and the bustling strip of E Carson St, as well as the North Side, once the museums have closed for the evening.

Sights

Points of interest in Pittsburgh are scattered everywhere, and its spread-out nature makes it a difficult place to cover thoroughly on foot. Stick to public buses, which are quite reliable, and you'll get to see it all, from the historic buildings of the Golden Triangle and the intellectual pockets of Oakland to the kosher delis of Squirrel Hill and the quirky mix of museums and sports on Pittsburgh's North Side.

GOLDEN TRIANGLE

Although it's been renovated into a modern, generic landscape, downtown – parts of which feel quite abandoned after weekday business hours – still has a few fine older buildings, such as Kaufmann's department store and the **Allegheny County Courthouse** (☎ 412-350-5410; 436 Grant St; admission free; ⏲ 9am-5pm Mon-Fri), a 19th-century Romanesque stone building designed by Henry Hobson Richardson. At the triangle's tip is **Point State Park**, which is popular during summer with strollers, runners and loungers. Just don't swim in the big fountain. The renovated **Fort Pitt Museum** (☎ 412-281-9284; www.fortpittmuseum.com; 101 Commonwealth Pl; admission $2.50; ⏲ 10am-5pm Wed-Sat, noon-4:30pm Sun) displays material about Native Americans and the French-British conflicts. The nicely remodeled brick warehouse that is the **Senator John Heinz Pittsburgh Regional History Center** (☎ 412-454-6000; www.pghhistory.org; 1212 Smallman Ave; admission $6; ⏲ 10am-5pm) offers a good take on the region's past. Its audiovisuals and exhibits give varied perspectives on the French and Indian War, early settlers, immigrants, steel, the glass industry, and, of course, the HJ Heinz company (Senator Heinz was a major supporter).

NORTH SIDE

While this part of town feels most populated when its PNC Park is filled with sports fans for a Pittsburgh Steelers game, the area is also a big draw for museum fans. **Andy Warhol Museum** (☎ 412-237-8300; www.warhol.org; 117 Sandusky St; $8; 10am-5pm Tue-Thu & Sat & Sun, until 10pm Fri), just over the 7th St Bridge, is one of the town's Carnegie museums. A Pittsburgh native, Warhol became famous for his pop art, avant-garde movies, celebrity connections and Velvet Underground spectaculars (see Andy Warhol p191). Exhibits include the classic Campbell's soup cans (for 20 years, he reportedly drank the soup every day), celebrity portraits and frequent film screenings. The Warhol Café downstairs has excellent snacks and coffee, and the gift shop is well stocked with Warhol paraphernalia.

Modern-art enthusiasts should also check out the **Mattress Factory** (☎ 412-231-3169; www.mattress.org; 500 Sampsonia Way; admission $8, free Thu; 10am-5pm Tue-Fri, 10am-7pm Sat, 1-5pm Sun), featuring edgy installations. **Carnegie Science Center** (☎ 412-237-3400; www.carnegiesciencecenter.org; 1 Allegheny Ave; admission $14; 10am-5pm Sun-Thu, until 7pm Fri-Sat), great for kids, is a cut above the average hands-on science museum. The Try Your Hand at Surgery exhibition simulates some high-tech medical treatments (one of Pittsburgh's cutting-edge industries). There's also a planetarium and submarine.

A major treat is the **National Aviary** (☎ 412-321-4364; www.aviary.org; W Commons, Allegheny Sq; admission $5; 9am-5pm daily), and shouldn't be missed – whether you're a big bird fan or not. You'll see over 500 exotic and endangered birds here, many of which are flying freely in high-ceilinged, climate-controlled aviaries that let you walk among the fascinating creatures. Nearby are the **Mexican War Streets**: residential neighborhoods developed in the 1860s and 1970s that were named after battles and soldiers of the 1846 Mexican War. The carefully restored row-houses, with Greek revival doorways and Gothic turrets (in the blocks just above W North Ave), are on quiet streets that make for a peaceful, post-museum stroll.

SOUTH SIDE & MT WASHINGTON

Monongahela Incline (☎ 412-442-2000; round-trip $2.20; 5:30am-12:45am Mon-Sat, 8:45am-midnight Sun) and **Duquesne Incline** (☎ 412-381-1665; 5:30am-12:45am Mon-Sat, 8:45am-midnight Sun) are the funicular railroads that run up and down Mt Washington's steep slopes. (Duquesne is pronounced doo-*kane*.) They're what remain of last century's 15 incline railroads, which served to open the South Side – featuring the bustling nighttime strip of E Carson St – to suburban development. Take the Monongahela Incline up to the aptly named Grandview Ave and walk northwest to the Duquesne Incline, which has historical railcar photos. You can ride that down and walk back to Station Sq, but it's more scenic to go back the way you came. At the start of the Duquesne Incline is **Station Sq** (☎ 412-261-9911), an over-hyped group of railway buildings that, recycled into a shopping and entertainment complex, is basically a big ol' mall.

OAKLAND AREA

The University of Pittsburgh and Carnegie Mellon University are here, surrounded by streets that are packed with cheap eateries, cafés, shops and student-packed multi-family homes.

Two Carnegie institutions, the Museum of Art and the Museum of Natural History share a site. Admission at one museum covers entrance to both. **Carnegie Museum of Art** (☎ 412-622-3131; www.cmoa.org; 4400 Forbes Ave; admission $8; 10am-5pm Tue-Sat, from noon Sun) has a terrific collection of impressionist, post-impressionist as well as modern American paintings, plus a very fine architecture exhibit. **Carnegie Museum of Natural History** (www.carnegiemuseums.org/cmnh; 4400 Forbes Ave; admission $8; 10am-5pm Tue-Sat, from noon Sun) features a complete tyrannosaurus skeleton, Pennsylvania geology and Inuit prehistory.

The unmissable **Cathedral of Learning** (☎ 412-624-6000; 157 Cathedral of Learning; admission free, tours $3; 9am-2:30pm Mon-Fri, from 9:30am Sat, from 11:30am Sun) is a grand, 42-story Gothic tower at the University of Pittsburgh campus. At 535ft, it's the second-tallest education building in the world. It houses the elegant Nationality Classrooms, each representing a different style and period, with gorgeous details such as the cherry-wood chalkboard doors in the India room and the red-velvet upholstered chairs of Austria. While a few rooms are always left open to viewers, most are accessible only with a guided tour.

GAY & LESBIAN PITTSBURGH

While Pittsburgh is still a bit behind other area cities when it comes to gay acceptance – you won't see much same-sex hand holding on the street, for example – a tight-knit LGBT (lesbian, gay, bisexual and transgender) community does exist, centered around a mixed bag of bars and cultural events. But anyone who watches Showtime's *Queer As Folk* series, which is set in Pittsburgh, should be forewarned: that sex-drenched, hottie-filled nightclub scene has *nothing* to do with the reality here!

The **Gay & Lesbian Community Center of Pittsburgh** (☎ 412-42200; 114 5808 Forward Ave; ⏲ 6:30-9:30pm Mon-Fri, 3-6pm Sat), in Squirrel Hill, organizes social events including bingo nights and dances at various spots. It also heads up the annual PrideFest, held in June. The **Inn on the Mexican War Streets** (p194) is a friendly, gay-owned place to stay.

Most gay bars, such as **Pegasus** (☎ 412-281-2131; 818 Liberty Ave), **Images** (☎ 412-391-9990; 965 Liberty Ave) and the **Liberty Avenue Saloon** (412-338-1533; 41 Liberty Ave), are in a concentrated stretch of Liberty Ave in the downtown area. The **Eagle** (☎ 412-766-7222; 1740 Eckert St), on the North Side, is a dance club that draws known DJs. In Squirrel Hill, not far from the community center, you'll find a **Pleasant Present** (☎ 412-421-7104; 2301 Murray Ave), a gay-owned gift shop, with books, videos and all-things rainbow.

Frick Art & Historical Center (☎ 412-371-0600; www.frickart.org; 7227 Reynolds St; admission $10; ⏲ 10am-5pm Tue-Sat, noon-6pm Sun), located in Point Breeze, east of Oakland, displays some of Frick's Flemish, French and Italian paintings. The **Car & Carriage Museum** includes assorted Frickmobiles like a 1914 Rolls Royce, but the highlight is **Clayton**, the restored 1872 mansion of industrialist Henry Clay Frick

SQUIRREL HILL & SHADYSIDE

These upscale neighborhoods feature wide streets and huge, beautiful homes, excellent restaurants and eclectic shops. Squirrel Hill, home to Pittsburgh's large Jewish population, has the city's best kosher eateries, butchers and Judaica shops. **Temple Sinai** (☎ 412-421-9715; www.templesinaipgh.org; 5505 Forbes Ave) is a synagogue that's housed in the architecturally stunning Elizabethan-style former mansion of John Worthington.

Activities

Riverfront trails along the north side of the Golden Triangle are perfect for strolling, running or biking. **Golden Triangle Bike Rentals** (☎ 412-655-0835; 416 Woodrift Lane; rental per hr/day $6.50/25) rents bikes. It also leads two-hour bike tours of the city for $15. The **Western Pennsylvania Field Institute** (☎ 412-255-0564; www.wpfi.org; 304 Forbes Ave) promotes outdoor recreation in the region, and sponsors bike rides and hikes in the city. The perimeter of the Golden Triangle's Point State Park is a popular short run; for a longer run, head to the 11-mile gravel-paved **Montour Trail**, accessible by crossing the 6th St bridge and catching the paved path at the Carnegie Science Center. For night runs, contact **People Who Run Downtown** (☎ 412-366-7458; www.amiscu.com/pwrd), a group of folks who organize weekly runs, followed by drinks at a neighborhood pub.

Tours

Just Ducky Tours (☎ 412-402-3825; www.justduckytours.com; Station Sq; adult $16; Apr-Oct) General city tours in a WWII amphibious vehicle.

Pittsburgh History & Landmarks Foundation (☎ 877-471-5808; www.phlg.org; Station Sq; tours from $3) Specialized historic or cultural tours by foot or motorcoach.

Unlimited Sightseeing Inc (☎ 412-897-1461; www.seepgh.com; 115 Frank Ave; adult $10) Offers a selection of neighborhood walking tours.

Festivals & Events

City of Pittsburgh Marathon Run over bridges and through city parks. Early May.

10K Another run where people run over bridges and through city parks. Early May.

Greek Food Festival Souvlakia and spanakopita draw thousands. Early May.

International Children's Festival A slew of kids' events held mid-May.

Pittsburgh Folk Festival Outdoor folkie music on Memorial Day weekend.

Three Rivers Arts Festival A series of shows. Early June.

Pittsburgh Vintage Grand Prix Car races galore. July.

Pittsburgh Three Rivers Regatta Sails soar on the three rivers. Early August.

Holidays at the Nationality Rooms University of Pittsburgh's Cathedral of Learning gets decked out in international style. Held December.

Sleeping

With a bit of searching, you can find bargain and charm all in one spot. For pure bargains, though, look 10 miles west of town at Moon Run, off the I-79 at exit 16, Steubenville Pike, where there's a predictable choice of chains with rooms averaging $45 per night.

Pittsburgh Bed & Breakfast Association (☎ 724-352-4899; www.pittsburghbnb.com) For pure charm, this association can put you in touch with the local inn that best fits your taste.

Inn on the Mexican War Streets (☎ 412-231-65434; innwarst@aol.com; 604 West North Ave; r $50-200; P ⊠ ⁜) This gay-owned mansion, with rooms for every price range, is near North Side museums and right on the bus line that takes you downtown. A hearty home-made breakfast, charming hosts, stunning antique furnishings and a brand-new four-star restaurant on the grounds – set to open in 2004 – are just a few reasons to make a beeline here.

The Priory: A City Inn (☎ 412-231-3338; www.thepriory.com; 614 Pressley St; r $122-152; P ⊠ ⁜) This elegant historic inn on the North Shore has 24 gorgeous rooms, from tiny quarters to sprawling suites. Complimentary breakfasts and evening wine, plus the tranquil library on the main floor, will make you feel right at home.

Morning Glory Inn (☎ 412-431-1707; 2119 Sarah St; r from $125; ⊠ ⁜) Head to this Italianate-style Victorian brick townhouse for a quiet and elegant room with character, right in the heart of the jumpin' South Side scene.

Westin Convention Center (☎ 412-281-3700; www.westin.com; 1000 Penn Ave; r from $100; P ⊠ ⁜ ⁂) The tallest, most imposing of the high-rise hotels in the downtown district, the Westin offers great special rates throughout the year, along with wonderfully anonymous rooms that feature Internet hook-up, comfortable beds and puffy down comforters, rather than the usual polyester spreads.

HI Pittsburgh Hostel (☎ 412-431-1267; 830 E Warrington Ave; dm $19) In South Side's Allentown neighborhood, this hostel is in a still-splendid early-20th-century building, and hosts several city bike tours each year. Its travel store is stocked with guidebooks and maps.

Eating

Downtown is not the culinary capitol of Pittsburgh by any means: bland, touristy steak houses and standard office-worker grub abounds. If you're staying in the area and are too hungry to wait till you can reach the South Side or Squirrel Hill, there are a few to try:

Lemon Grass Café (☎ 412-765-2222; 124 Sixth St; dishes $12) Really impressive Cambodian and Thai cuisine, including killer pad thai, green curry and plenty of vegetarian options.

The nearby Strip has a much more lively selection.

DeLuca's (☎ 412-566-2195; 2015 Penn Ave; dishes $4-7) Self-described (but deservingly so) home of the 'best breakfast in town.' The behemoth omelettes, strong coffee and greasy-spoon charm have crowds waiting patiently on the sidewalk each weekend.

My Ngoc (☎ 412-765-1150; 1120 Penn Ave; dishes $7-11) Cheap Vietnamese and Chinese dishes.

Kaya (☎ 412-261-6565; 2000 Smallman Ave; dishes $10-14) A cool Caribbean place with vegetarian options and funky decor.

Enrico's Biscotti Co (☎ 412-281-2602; 2022 Penn Ave; snacks $3-5) For coffee and dessert, don't skip Enrico's. Featuring an airy café infused with the bakery's scent of almond, apricot and chocolate biscotti.

For an absolute cornucopia of choices, though, hit the South Side.

Tom's Diner (1715 E Carson St; dishes $7-12) Brightly lit Tom's Diner serves up the all-American favorites, such as baked fish and tuna casserole, in a nifty 1950s setting.

Zenith Tea Room (☎ 412-481-4833; Sarah St & 26th St; dishes $8-11) A gem of a find is this high-ceilinged, antique-strewn old warehouse serving delicious and unique vegetarian meals; don't miss its brunch buffet on Sunday.

Mallorca (☎ 412-488-1818; 2228 E Carson St; dishes $13-24) An upscale Spanish restaurant boasting 'the best paella in town.'

Bruschetta's (☎ 412-431-3535; 1831 E Carson St; dishes $17-20) Takes care of the discerning Italian-loving crowd with its big plates of veal and linguini.

Café du Jour (☎ 412-488-9695; 1107 E Carson St; dishes $10-17) A fresh, seasonal menu that features creative vegetarian options.

Beehive (☎ 412-488-HIVE; 1327 E Carson St; snacks $2-5) A great place to snack on sandwiches or pastries and sip really good coffee is this café with funky decor, low lighting, a pinball machine and an intimate garden patio out back.

On and around Forbes Ave in Oakland, cheap (but not necessarily great) places cater to local students.

LuLu's Noodle Shop & YumWok Pan Asian Diner (☎ 412-687-7777; 400 S Craig St; dishes $5-8) A cute spot serving noodle bowls, great stir-fries and Thai-style salads.

Mad Mex (☎ 412-681-5656; 370 Atwood St; dishes $4-10) Popular, and with other city locations, Mad Mex has fresh and yummy burritos and salads with vegan options.

Pittsburgh's large Jewish population means there's lots of kosher food on offer. Squirrel Hill has plenty of veggie options (all closed on Saturday for the Jewish Sabbath).

Milky Way Dairy & Vegetarian Restaurant (☎ 412-421-3121; 2120 Murray Ave; dishes $5-7) Serving pizzas, falafel, vegetarian meatball hoagies and the Middle Eastern speciality, *melawach* (fried dough).

Café Asia (☎ 412-521-2080; 5833 Forbes Ave; dishes $8-12) Specializes in pan-Asian cuisine such as Vietnamese soups, Thai curries and Japanese noodles.

Rose Tea Café (☎ 412-421-2238; 5880 Forbes Ave; snacks $2-6) Don't miss this café, serving light Asian finger food and refreshing bubble-tea drinks – flavored tea drinks, with milk or without, filled with chewy, black-tapioca pearls.

For other good food options, see Shopping p196.

Drinking

Most nightlife is centered around the South Side, along the E Carson St strip.

Zythos (☎ 412-481-2234; 2108 E Carson St) A mellow, trendy pub with specialty martinis.

Memphis Lounge (☎ 412-481-2234; 2108 E Carson St) Zythos' upstairs counterpart, Memphis is a darker, sultrier lounge featuring DJs who spin hip-hop, house and deep grooves.

Club Café (☎ 412-431-4950; 56 S 12th St) Inside a retro-cool building that's all tile and neon, Club Café is a formal bar with plush booths and a live jazz and blues show.

Piper's Pub (☎ 412-381-3977; 1828 E Carson St) A tasteful, tin-ceilinged Irish pub serving creamy pints of – what else? – Guinness.

Forbes Field Tavern (☎ 412-431-9500; 2901 Sarah St) A true locals' hangout where you will find endless Pirates memorabilia, a down-to-earth crowd and cheap plates of good 'n' greasy pierogi.

Last Chance (2533 Penn Ave) A popular neighborhood pub in the strip for guys who can hold their liquor.

Prelude Wine Bar (Pittsburgh Renaissance Hotel, 107 6th St) Downtown, the fancy Prelude has a swanky vibe and offers more than 50 wines by the glass.

Hemingway's Café (3911 Forbes Ave) In Oakland, Hemingway's is a college pub that packs 'em in for cheap drinks, friendly crowds and occasional poetry and fiction readings.

Entertainment

Pittsburgh Cultural Trust (☎ 412-471-6070; www.pgharts.org; 803 Liberty Ave) Promotes all downtown arts, from dance and theater to visual art and opera; the website has links to all main arts venues.

Benedum Center for the Performing Arts (☎ 412-456-6666; 719 Liberty Ave; tickets from $15) Benedum hosts dance, ballet, opera and Broadway shows.

Byham Theater (☎ 412-456-6666; 101 6th St) This mid-sized venue hosts theater and dance performances.

Heinz Hall (☎ 412-392-4800; www.pittsburghsymphony.org; 600 Penn Ave) Where the Pittsburgh Symphony Orchestra plays from October to May.

Harris Theater (☎ 412-682-4111; 800 Liberty Ave) A wide variety of art-house films, often part of film festivals, play at this restored theater.

Andy Warhol Museum (☎ 412-237-8300; www.warhol.org; 117 Sandusky St) An eclectic venue (see p192), also used by comedy troupes, music groups and lecturers. Art-house films play here too.

BARS & NIGHTCLUBS

South Side's E Carson is the place for rock, R & B and all-round funk.

Nick's Fat City (☎ 412-481-6880; 1601 E Carson St) A local favorite for rock and alternative bands.

Lava Lounge (☎ 412-431-5282; 2204 E Carson St) Doles out rock and blues.

Metropol (☎ 412-261-2232; 1600 Smallman Ave) At the Strip. For clubbers.

Rosebud (☎ 412-261-2221) Adjacent to Metropol, Rosebud spins hip-hop, house, trance and acid jazz.

To hear good jazz, head to **Dowe's on 9th** (☎ 412-281-9225; 121 Ninth St) and **Club Café** (see p195).

SPECTATOR SPORTS

The old Three Rivers Stadium is mourned by real Pittsburghers, while the Pittsburgh promotion industry hypes the replacements.

On the North Side, just by the Allegheny River, are **PNC Park** (☎ 412-321-2827; www.pirateball.com), where the Pittsburgh Pirates major-league baseball team bases itself; and **Heinz Field** (☎ 412-323-1200; www.pittsburghsteelers.com), where the NFL Pittsburgh Steelers put their boots to the leather.

Civic Arena (☎ 412-642-1800; www.pittsburghpenguins.com), just east of downtown, is where the NHL Pittsburgh Penguins play hockey.

Shopping

CLOTHING

Traditional department-store fans should stick to downtown. The following department stores have floors and floors of clothing, accessories and housewares:

Saks Fifth Avenue (☎ 412-263-4800; 513 Smithfield St)
Kaufmann's (☎ 412- 232-2000; 400 Fifth Ave)
Lazarus (☎ 412-291-2200; 301 Fifth Ave)

Hipsters, head to E Carson St on South Side, where funky boutiques provide everything from vintage furniture to leather miniskirts.

Over in Squirrel Hill, upscale shops hawking fine lingerie, housewares and clothing line Forbes Ave.

FOOD

Wanna get your hands on some Thai fish sauce? How about a head of bok choy, bags of fresh pasta or handfuls of candy? Head to the Strip, where you'll find it all:

Lotus Food Co (☎ 412-281-3050; 1649 Penn Ave) A huge Asian market.

Pennsylvania Macaroni Co (☎ 412-471-8330; 2010-12 Penn Ave) Sells quality Italian foods.

Wholey's Seafood (☎ 412-391-2884; 1711 Penn Ave) A sprawling indoor market featuring a sea of fresh fish and produce.

Fort Pitt Candy Co (☎ 412-281-9016; 1642 Penn Ave) Has bulk candies that you've long forgotten about, from Whoppers to Mary Janes.

Getting There & Away

Pittsburgh International Airport (☎ 412-472-3500), 18 miles from downtown, has direct connections to Europe, Canada and major US cities. **Airport buses** (☎ 412-321-4990) run downtown every hour ($14).

Greyhound (☎ 412-392-6513; 11th St & Liberty Ave) has frequent buses to Philadelphia ($40, seven hours), New York ($52, 11 hours) and Chicago, Illinois ($60, eight to 12 hours). **Amtrak** (☎ 412-471-6171; 1100 Liberty Ave) is behind the magnificent original train station. Trains head to Philadelphia ($39, eight hours), New York ($65, 10 hours) and Chicago, Illinois ($57, 10 hours).

Getting Around

Port Authority Transit (PAT; ☎ 412-442-2000; 345 Sixth Ave) operates buses and a light-rail system called the 'T.' The **information center** (☎ 412-442-2000; 534 Smithfield St) is open weekdays. Bus and T fares range from free to $2.75, depending on the zone in which you're traveling. For taxis, call **Yellow Cab** (☎ 412-665-8100) or **People's Cab** (☎ 412-681-3131) – unmarked cabs may be uninsured or unsafe.

There are several car rental companies at the airport and around the city (see p1120 for more rental information).

AROUND PITTSBURGH

Ohiopyle State Park

The picturesque wooded hills of Laurel Highlands are just 40 miles southeast of Pittsburgh, making for a popular weekend destination. The little riverfront village of Ohiopyle (oh-*hi*-oh-pile), on Rte 381, in the middle of the park, is a base for rafting and canoeing on the Youghiogheny River ('Yough,' pronounced yock) and a focus for visitors to this lovely area. The **park office** (☎ 724-329-8591; ☎ 8am-4pm Apr-Oct, 8am-4pm Mon-Fri Nov-Mar) and visitors center is at the end of the old steel railway bridge.

Fallingwater & Kentuck Knob

A true Frank Lloyd Wright masterpiece, **Fallingwater** (☎ 724-329-8501; www.wpconline.org/fallingwaterhome.htm; weekday/weekend $12/15; 🕑 10am-4pm Tue-Sun Mar-Nov) is 3 miles north of the park on Rte 381. Completed in 1939 as a weekend retreat for the Kaufmanns, owners of the Pittsburgh department store, the building sports a design acclaimed for its integration with the natural setting. To see inside, you must take one of the guided tours. Reservations are recommended. A more intensive two-hour tour, with photography permitted, is offered at

8:30am ($50). The rather attractive, forested grounds open at 8:30am. Much less visited is **Kentuck Knob** (☎ 724-329-1901; www.kentuckknob.com; weekday /weekend $10/15; 10am-4pm Tue-Sun, from noon Mon), another Frank Lloyd Wright house (designed in 1953), built into the side of a rolling hill. It's noted for its natural materials, hexagonal design and honeycomb skylights. House tours last about an hour.

Country Seasons Bed & Breakfast Inn (☎ 724-455-6825; www.countryseasonbb.com; Rte 381; Mill Run; r $93-108) This nearby B&B has charming rooms, a big front porch and a main fireplace, and is near both the Frank Lloyd Wright homes and the Ohiopyle State Park.

NORTHERN PENNSYLVANIA

Allegheny National Forest

Northwestern Pennsylvania was stripped of its timber in the late 19th and early 20th centuries. Now the 797-sq-mile Allegheny National Forest, encompassing several state parks, has hemlock, maples, white ash and the valuable Allegheny black cherry. It's a really excellent place for outdoor activities, from camping through to canoeing; the region's main town of **Warren**, on the forest's northwest edge, has information at its **tourist office** (☎ 814-726-1222).

Erie

Lake Erie is named for the Eriez Indians, whom the Seneca killed in the 17th century. The city of Erie is an industrial center and a stop for travelers skirting the lake. It does have a **visitors bureau** (☎ 814-454-7191; State & W 7th Sts). During the War of 1812, Lieutenant Oliver Perry was sent here, had six ships built and went to confront the British on Lake Erie. After the battle, Perry reported 'We have met the enemy and they are ours.' A working replica of Perry's flagship, US Brig *Niagara,* is at the **Erie Maritime Museum** (☎ 814-452-2744; 150 E Front St; admission $6; 9am-5pm Mon-Sat, from noon Sun), which has exhibits on the Great Lakes' history. **Presque Isle State Park** (☎ 814-833-7424) is an attractive, curving, sandy peninsula, great for cycling, hiking, boating and watching migrating waterfowl.

Sara's Beachcomber Campground (☎ 814-833-4560; campsites/RV sites $15/20) is just outside the park. The 1960s-style **Peninsula Motel** (☎ 814-838-1938; 1002 Peninsula Dr; r $60-90) is a clean, standard motor lodge.

New England

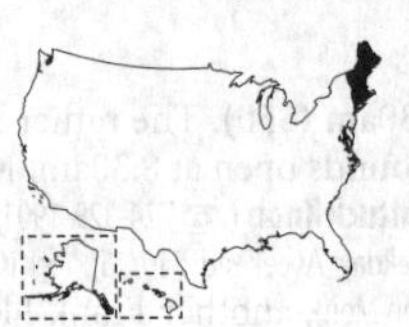

CONTENTS

With graceful colonial towns, thousands of miles of beautiful coastline, and cities filled with museums, universities and high-tech businesses, New England's six states – Massachusetts, Rhode Island, Connecticut, Vermont, New Hampshire and Maine – have preserved their character as a unique region. In addition to Boston, the self-proclaimed 'hub' of the area, New England has vibrant small cities, including revitalized Providence, Rhode Island, which has a fantastic food scene, and Portland, Maine, which is also an emerging restaurant mecca. The area's many universities add culture and funkiness to Cambridge, MA, Burlington, VT, New Haven, CT, and the 'Five College area' in western Massachusetts. And from Portsmouth, NH, to Newport, RI, to Mystic, CT – and of course, in Boston – there's culture and history aplenty.

For outdoor types, New England offers outstanding hiking, biking, rafting, kayaking and sailing. The heavily forested region is scattered with granite mountain ranges, lakes and ponds, while the coasts are lined with wide sandy beaches and secluded waterfront coves.

New Englanders are traditionally reserved – traces of this Yankee frugality still appear as a thriftiness of speech, as well as in material goods – which stands in marked contrast to the brash energy of New York City or the good-natured trendiness of California. Visitors sometimes see this reserve as unfriendliness, but it's simply a slightly more formal style.

Americans from other regions often say that New England feels almost like Europe, but its Revolutionary-era roots are all-American. And even if Bostonians tell you to 'pahk your cah in Havahd Yahd' – don't.

HIGHLIGHTS

- Exploring the mix of colonial history and contemporary culture in **Boston** (p206)
- Sunning and splashing on the beaches of **Cape Cod** (p223), **Martha's Vineyard** (p230) or **Nantucket** (p232)
- Pretending to be super-rich in the palatial **Newport mansions** (p239)
- Hiking the craggy **White Mountains** (p261) or kayaking the rugged **Maine coast** (p271)
- Dining in first-rate bistros and ethnic enclaves in cities throughout the region, particularly in **Boston** (p214), **Providence** (p238) and **Portland** (p270)
- Ogling the spectacular fall colors in the **Berkshires** (p235), **White Mountains** (p261), **Green Mountains** (p253), **interior Maine** (p276) and **Litchfield Hills** (p248)

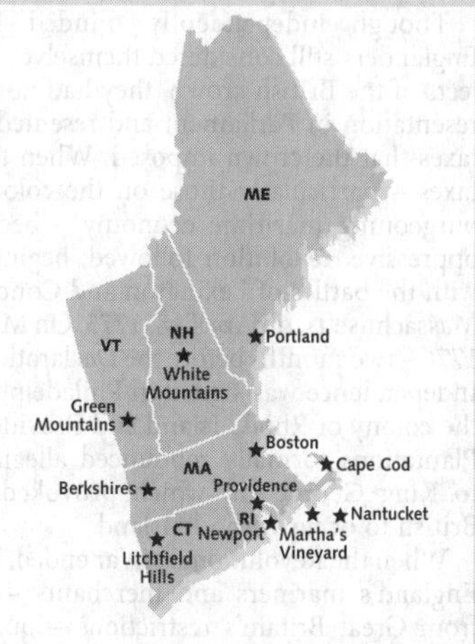

HISTORY

Algonquin peoples inhabited present-day New England when the first European settlers arrived. They lived in small, semi-agrarian tribes, raising corn, beans and other foodstuffs while hunting plentiful game and harvesting the fruits of the rich coastal waters. Intertribal warfare was common, rendering a united defense against the encroachments of European settlers impossible.

The famous explorers – Columbus, John Cabot and others – arrived in the late 15th century, but it was the second wave of mariners, including Bartholomew Gosnold, who explored the New England coast from Maine to Rhode Island in the early 1600s and opened the area to colonization. In 1614, English explorer Captain John Smith christened the land 'New England.' With the landing of the Pilgrims at Plymouth in the summer of 1620, European settlement began in earnest, and the European population grew rapidly from the 1650s to 1750s. Shipbuilding thrived along the coast, particularly in Maine, where vast stands of virgin pine were reserved as masts for royal vessels. However, while the wealth of the New England colonies grew, the region's native peoples were reduced to small, relatively powerless groups of survivors.

Though independently minded New Englanders still considered themselves subjects of the British crown, they had no representation in Parliament and resented the taxes that the crown imposed. When these taxes – particularly those on the colonies' burgeoning maritime economy – became oppressive, revolution followed, beginning with the battles of Lexington and Concord, Massachusetts, on April 18, 1775. On May 4, 1776 – two months before the Declaration of Independence was signed in Philadelphia – the colony of Rhode Island and Providence Plantations formally renounced allegiance to King George III, which provoked the British to occupy Rhode Island.

When the Revolutionary War ended, New England's mariners and merchants – free from Great Britain's restrictions – quickly built up the young nation's trade in fishing, whaling and commerce. The first water-powered cotton-spinning mill in North America was established at Pawtucket, Rhode Island, in 1793. Soon afterward, New England's many swift rivers were bordered by vast mills turning out clothing, shoes and machinery.

But no boom lasts forever. The settlement and cultivation of the Great Plains made farming New England's rocky soil even less profitable, and after the Civil War, with the emancipation of slaves and the invention of steam power, many New England industries moved south to take advantage of cheaper labor. Steel vessels replaced New England's renowned wooden clipper ships, and petroleum, gas and electricity superseded whale oil for illumination.

New England suffered greatly during the 1930s depression, but its factories and shipyards boomed during WWII, and its traditional strengths in education, commerce and medicine continued through the latter half of the 20th century and on to today. Finance, insurance, computers and software, biotechnology and tourism are mainstays of the economy.

GEOGRAPHY & CLIMATE

The Appalachian Mountains partly isolate New England from states to the west. The Atlantic Ocean defines its eastern boundary. A scant million years ago, glaciers covered New England. When they retreated (10,000 to 20,000 years ago) they left glacial deposits, such as oblong hills called 'drumlins' (Bunker Hill is one) and scooped-out holes that became glacial ponds (Thoreau's Walden Pond).

The resulting landscape has appealing variety: verdant valleys, abundant forests and a rocky coastline sculpted into coves and sprinkled with sandy beaches. The mountains lack dramatic height, which makes them all the more accessible.

Thick forests of oak, maple, hemlock, beech, pine and spruce blanket the region, making New England's colorful fall foliage world famous. Groves of sugar maple trees produce maple syrup and are busy with moose, white-tailed deer, wild turkeys, raccoons, squirrels and, in summer, mosquitoes. Though coastal waters, once rich with sea life, have been badly overfished, seafood is still widely available. Good local produce includes apples, blueberries, cranberries, peaches, plums, rhubarb and strawberries, and the region produces notable dairy products, including milk, yogurt, cheese and the famous Ben & Jerry's ice cream.

Late May through June and September are the best times to visit. Everything's open, prices are moderate, days are warm and nights are cool. The busiest, most expensive times are high summer (July and August) and foliage season (late September to mid-October). During these popular times, many lodgings have restrictions about minimum stays, children, service charges, deposit refunds and payment; be sure to ask. The winters are often snowy and quite cold.

New England's weather is famously changeable. Hot, muggy 90°F days in July may be followed by a day or two of cool 65°F weather. Precipitation averages about 3 inches per month year-round.

ACTIVITIES

New Hampshire's **White Mountains**, Vermont's **Green Mountains** and the dense forests of northern Maine offer good hiking, rock climbing, mountain biking, camping, canoeing, whitewater rafting and skiing. The Appalachian Trail spans New England, from its northern terminus at Maine's Mt Katahdin (5268ft) through all the states but Rhode Island, continuing south to Georgia; contact the **Appalachian Mountain Club** (Map pp210-12; ☎ 617-523-0636; www.outdoors.org; 5 Joy St, Boston, MA 02108).

Vermont's Long Trail is a primitive footpath that follows the crest of the Green Mountains 270 miles from Canada to Massachusetts, with 175 miles of side trails and 70 rustic cabins, lean-tos or campsites for shelter. The **Green Mountain Club** (☎ 802-244-7037; www.greenmountainclub.org; 4711 Waterbury-Stowe Rd, Waterbury Center, VT 05677) has details.

Maine's **Acadia National Park** has a good system of hiking and biking trails. Northwestern Vermont (particularly around Burlington) and Cape Cod are among the region's easiest but most rewarding biking areas.

Thousands of miles of rugged coastline are great for sailing, sea kayaking, windsurfing and whale-watching. Swimming, canoeing, boating, fishing and waterskiing are available on many of the region's lakes and ponds. Though the Atlantic's waters are quite chilly, swimming and other beach sports are popular in summer; you'll find slightly warmer, sheltered waters in Rhode Island and along Cape Cod Bay.

Once known for whaling, New England mariners now like to take visitors out on whale-watching cruises from April to October. Naturalist-guided cruises usually cost around $25 to $30 and last four to five hours. Seas can sometimes be rough; if you are prone to seasickness, powdered ginger capsules or Dramamine taken before boarding can certainly help. A warm sweater or jacket (a lined windbreaker is perfect), sun hat, sunglasses and sunscreen are essential.

In summer windjammers (sailing ships) cruise coastal Maine's protected waters. These graceful two- or three-mast sailing ships normally sleep 20 to 45 passengers, and passengers dine aboard. See p273 for more information.

ACCOMMODATIONS

New England lodging choices range from simple campsites to roadside motels to more than 1500 country inns, which vary from small B&Bs to lavish historic mansions. Hotels in major cities tend to be in the mid-price and top-end range. Unless otherwise noted, all hotel rates quoted are for doubles. Single rooms in hotels, motels and inns tend to be only about $10 less, if offered at all. Nearly all lodgings in the region have no-smoking rooms, and many – especially B&Bs – prohibit smoking altogether.

People with mobility challenges may find that more modern lodgings are better suited to their needs than historic B&Bs, since the latter tend to have many stairs and narrow doorways. Do ask, though, since some B&Bs have first-floor rooms that are more accessible.

GETTING THERE & AWAY

Except in the city of Boston, driving around New England is your best bet for flexibility and accessibility. Note that outside of major urban areas, addresses may include only a road name, but no number, so you may want to phone for directions or check with the local visitors center. If you're relying on public transportation, buses will get you almost anywhere you want to go (eventually). Train service is frequent along the coast between Boston and New York, but it's more difficult to travel the New England interior by rail. Boston is the region's hub, so you'll likely pass through on your way to somewhere else.

Air

Boston's Logan International Airport is New England's air hub. Providence, Rhode Island

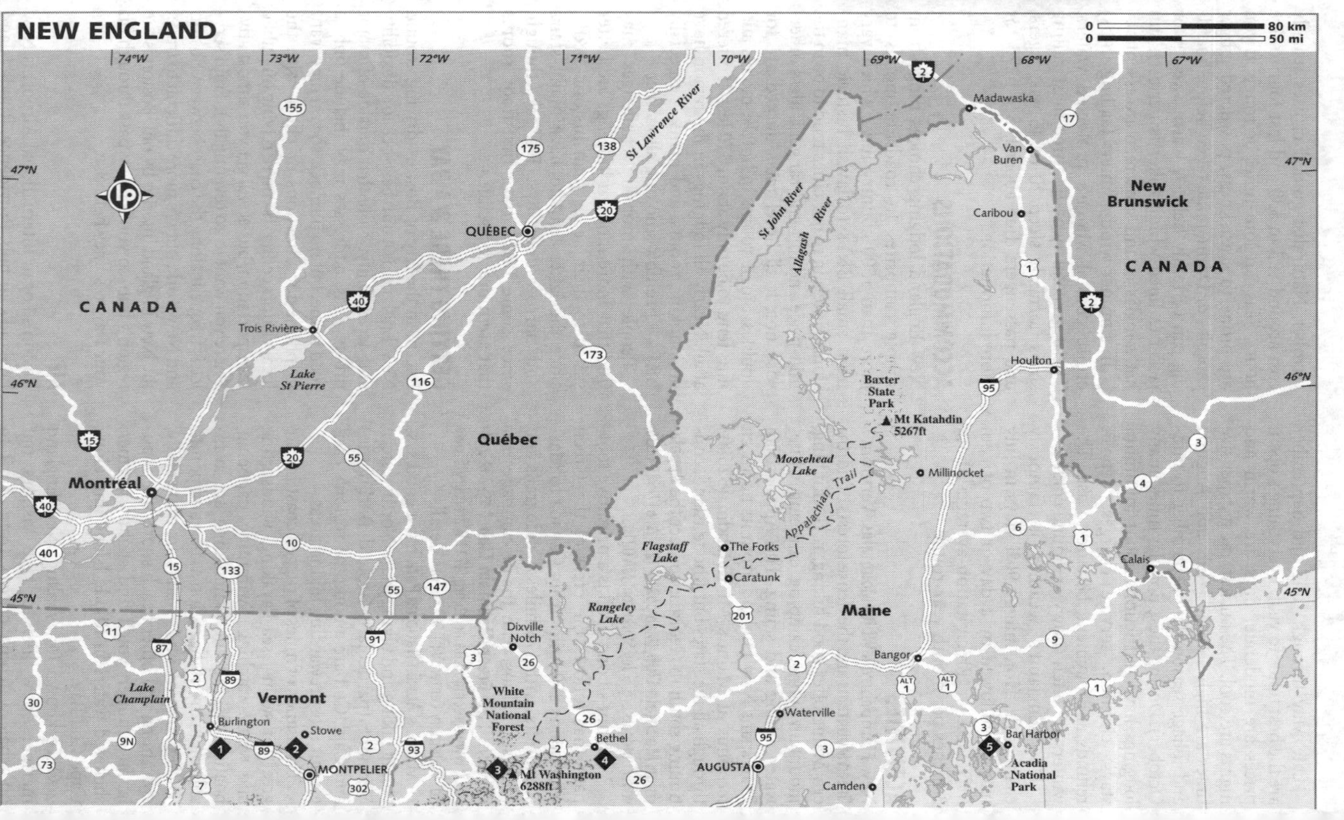
NEW ENGLAND
0 80 km
0 50 mi
74°W
73°W
72°W
71°W
70°W
69°W
68°W
67°W
47°N
46°N
45°N
CANADA
New Brunswick
CANADA
Québec
QUÉBEC
Montréal
Trois Rivières
Lake St Pierre
St Lawrence River
St John River
Allagash River
Madawaska
Van Buren
Caribou
Houlton
Baxter State Park
Mt Katahdin 5267ft
Moosehead Lake
Millinocket
Appalachian Trail
Flagstaff Lake
The Forks
Caratunk
Calais
Rangeley Lake
Maine
Dixville Notch
Bangor
Lake Champlain
Vermont
White Mountain National Forest
Waterville
Burlington
Stowe
Bethel
Bar Harbor
MONTPELIER
Mt Washington 6288ft
AUGUSTA
Acadia National Park
Camden

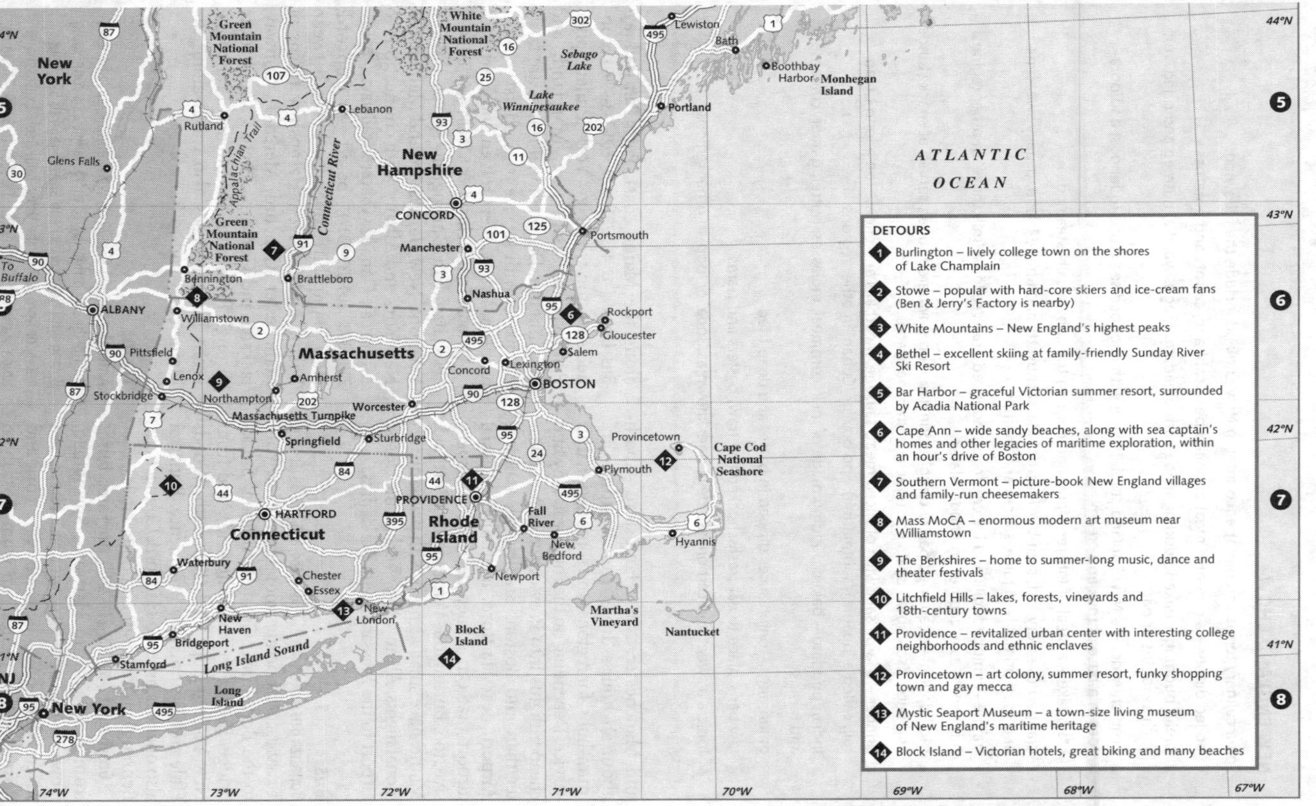
ATLANTIC OCEAN
DETOURS
1 Burlington – lively college town on the shores of Lake Champlain
2 Stowe – popular with hard-core skiers and ice-cream fans (Ben & Jerry's Factory is nearby)
3 White Mountains – New England's highest peaks
4 Bethel – excellent skiing at family-friendly Sunday River Ski Resort
5 Bar Harbor – graceful Victorian summer resort, surrounded by Acadia National Park
6 Cape Ann – wide sandy beaches, along with sea captain's homes and other legacies of maritime exploration, within an hour's drive of Boston
7 Southern Vermont – picture-book New England villages and family-run cheesemakers
8 Mass MoCA – enormous modern art museum near Williamstown
9 The Berkshires – home to summer-long music, dance and theater festivals
10 Litchfield Hills – lakes, forests, vineyards and 18th-century towns
11 Providence – revitalized urban center with interesting college neighborhoods and ethnic enclaves
12 Provincetown – art colony, summer resort, funky shopping town and gay mecca
13 Mystic Seaport Museum – a town-size living museum of New England's maritime heritage
14 Block Island – Victorian hotels, great biking and many beaches
New York
New Hampshire
Massachusetts
Connecticut
Rhode Island
NJ
Green Mountain National Forest
White Mountain National Forest
Sebago Lake
Lake Winnipesaukee
Appalachian Trail
Connecticut River
Long Island Sound
Long Island
Cape Cod National Seashore
Martha's Vineyard
Nantucket
Block Island
Monhegan Island
Massachusetts Turnpike
To Buffalo
Glens Falls
Rutland
Lebanon
CONCORD
Manchester
Nashua
Portsmouth
Portland
Lewiston
Bath
Boothbay Harbor
Bennington
Brattleboro
Williamstown
ALBANY
Pittsfield
Lenox
Stockbridge
Northampton
Amherst
Worcester
Springfield
Sturbridge
Concord
Lexington
BOSTON
Salem
Rockport
Gloucester
Provincetown
Plymouth
Hyannis
PROVIDENCE
HARTFORD
Fall River
New Bedford
Newport
Waterbury
Chester
Essex
New London
New Haven
Bridgeport
Stamford
New York
44°N
43°N
42°N
41°N
74°W
73°W
72°W
71°W
70°W
69°W
68°W
67°W

NEW ENGLAND

NEW ENGLAND CHOW

Some culinary terms you might encounter in New England include the following:

- boiled dinner – a one-dish meal of boiled beef, cabbage, carrots and potatoes
- bread pudding – baked pudding made with bread, milk, eggs, vanilla, nutmeg and dried fruit such as raisins or dates
- clam chowder – a New England staple, made with chopped sea clams (quahogs) and potatoes in a base of milk and cream
- clambake – a meal of lobster, clams and corn on the cob, usually steamed
- cranberries – very tart, sour berries from Massachusetts and Rhode Island, usually sweetened, and used primarily in juice, sauces and muffins
- frappe – whipped milk and ice cream, pronounced 'frap'; called a 'milkshake' in other regions, but known as a 'cabinet' in Rhode Island
- fried dough – deep-fried pastry dough sprinkled with powdered sugar, served at snack stands and fairs; also known by its Portuguese name: malasada
- grinder – a large sandwich of sliced meat, sausage, meatballs and cheese, on a long bread roll; called a 'hoagie,' 'sub(marine),' 'po'boy' or 'Cuban' in other regions
- Indian pudding – baked pudding made of milk, cornmeal, molasses, butter, ginger, cinnamon and raisins
- onion rings – onion slices dipped in batter and deep fried
- raw bar – place to eat fresh-shucked live (raw) oysters and clams
- tonic – a sweet and carbonated beverage; known as 'soda' or 'pop' in other regions

and Manchester, New Hampshire – both about an hour's drive from Boston – are 'mini-hubs' for regional and some national air service. Depending on the route, you may find cheaper flights into Providence or Manchester than into Boston. Bradley International Airport, near Hartford, is another regional airport that can sometimes be less expensive, too. Burlington, Vermont and Portland, Maine, have small airports with primarily regional flights; Albany, New York, is the closest airport to the Massachusetts Berkshires.

Bus

Bonanza Bus Lines (☎ 212-564-8484, 800-556-3815; www.bonanzabus.com) operates routes from New York to the Berkshires (Great Barrington, Stockbridge, Lee, Lenox and Pittsfield); and from New York to Cape Cod (Falmouth, Woods Hole and Hyannis) via Providence. Bonanza also operates buses to Hartford, Connecticut; Bennington, Vermont and other cities.

Greyhound (☎ 800-231-2222) operates buses from New York to Hartford, Springfield, New Haven and Providence. There are several daily buses between New York and Boston. Other routes run from Boston to Portsmouth, New Hampshire, and then along the Maine coast. **Peter Pan Trailways Bus Lines** (☎ 413-781-3320, 800-343-9999) connects Boston with New York; Philadelphia, Pennsylvania; Baltimore, Maryland; and Washington, DC. Regional routes are fairly extensive, with service to Amherst, Northampton, Lenox, New Haven and Hartford.

Vermont Transit Lines (☎ 802-864-6811, 800-451-3292), based in Burlington, serves Boston, Vermont, New Hampshire and Maine from New York and Albany, with connections to Montreal, Canada. **Concord Trailways** (☎ 603-228-3300, 800-639-3317), based in Concord, New Hampshire, operates buses between Boston and the New Hampshire towns of Manchester, Concord, Meredith, Conway, Jackson and Gorham. There's also a route through Plymouth, Lincoln and Franconia. From Boston, buses also travel along the Maine coast and to Bangor.

Train

Amtrak (☎ 800-872-7245; www.amtrak.com) Services the Northeast Corridor by 10 to 15 daily trains connecting Boston with New York's Penn Station ($64 to $76, four hours, or from $99 on the three-hour Acela Express) and Union Station in Washington, DC ($81 to $106, 7¾ hours, or from 6½ hours on the Acela Express, $165 to $176).

GREG GAWLOWSKI

Constantino Brumidi fresco (p289), Capitol Rotunda, Washington DC

CHRIS MELLOR

Vietnam Veterans Memorial (p291), Washington DC

RICHARD CUMMINS

Antique stores, **Georgetown** (p293), Washington DC

Fireworks above the **Washington Monument** (p291) and the **National Mall** (p289), Washington DC

DENNIS JOHNSON

ANN CECIL

Skyscrapers, **Chicago** (p355)

PETER PTSCHELI

Amish buggy, **Shipshewana** (p389), Indiana

RICK GERHARTER

Frank Lloyd Wright's **Robie House** (p366), Chicago

Mickey's Dining Car (p438), St Paul, Minnesota

RICHARD CU

Downeaster Runs several times daily between Boston and Portland, Maine.
Ethan Allen Express Runs daily from New York via Albany, New York, to Rutland, Vermont.
Northeast Corridor Inland Route Runs from Washington, DC, to Springfield, MA, with stops in New Haven and Hartford, CT.
Northeast Direct Shore Route Runs from Washington, DC, to Boston, stopping in New York, New Haven and Mystic, CT, and Providence, RI, among other places.
Vermonter Offers daily service between Washington, DC, via New York to New Haven and Hartford, CT, Springfield and Amherst, MA, and Brattleboro, Montpelier, and Essex Junction (Burlington), VT.

MASSACHUSETTS

Massachusetts, New England's most populous state, is full of appealing places. From bustling and historic Boston, you can travel back to the colonial era in Plymouth or Salem, head for the seashore on Cape Cod, Nantucket and Martha's Vineyard, or explore the scenic Five College area and Berkshire hills. Since colonial times, Boston has been the hub of the state and indeed of all New England.

History

From the earliest days of colonial settlement, Massachusetts has been the heart of New England. As shipbuilding and maritime trade developed in the 18th century, making many coastal towns wealthy, Massachusetts felt acutely the trade restrictions imposed from London. The Stamp Act (1765) and Townshend Acts (1767) preceded the Boston Massacre (1770), in which British sentries fired into a rowdy mob, killing five. The 1773 Boston Tea Party – when colonists dumped chests of taxable British tea into Boston harbor – set the stage for the 1775 battles between British troops and colonial militia at Lexington and Concord, which began the Revolutionary War.

Following the war, speedy clipper ships brought rich cargoes to Massachusetts ports from the Pacific Northwest, China and the Mediterranean. Ship captains and merchants in Boston, Salem and Marblehead built fine mansions with the proceeds. Fishing craft brought in huge hauls of cod from the Grand Banks, while whaling vessels out of Gloucester, New Bedford and Nantucket caught and rendered the leviathans for their precious oil and bone.

Before the Civil War, the Great Potato Famine sent thousands of Irish immigrants to Boston. They were later joined by waves of immigrants from French Canada, Italy and Portugal, with some staying in the port towns and others moving inland to work in the mills and factories of Fall River, Northampton, Springfield and Worcester. More recent immigrants hail from China, Vietnam, Latin America and the Caribbean.

Arts

If New England is the birthplace of US culture, then Massachusetts represents the center of the center. Scrimshaw, carved from ivory and whalebone by sailors on long voyages in the mid-19th century, remains a treasured art. Shakers (in communities in western Massachusetts, New Hampshire and Maine) were the finest furniture makers in the 19th century; their simple but artful designs still reign. Even Paul Revere, remembered for his midnight ride to warn that redcoats were coming, was a master silversmith.

James Abbott McNeill Whistler (1834–1903), of Lowell, blurred the lines of representational painting and emphasized the play of light. In the 20th century John Singer Sargent (1856–1925) painted telling portraits of Boston's upper class, while Norman Rockwell (1894–1978) painted common men for *Saturday Evening Post* covers. Daniel Chester French (1850–1931) sculpted the seated Lincoln in Washington's Lincoln Memorial; his former studio is in Lenox. In Boston, modern architect IM Pei's radical JFK Library and John Hancock Tower stand in stark contrast to traditional European works by Henry Hobson Richardson (1838–86), who designed Trinity Church, and Charles Bulfinch (1763–1844), architect of the State House in Boston. Cape Cod cottages, town greens with steepled churches and Georgian brick campuses are well known around the country.

New Englanders' passion for literature was evident as early as 1828, when Noah Webster (1758–1843) published his *American Dictionary of the English Language.* Concordian Ralph Waldo Emerson (1803–82) gained a nationwide – even worldwide – audience for his philosophical and ethical teachings, as did Henry David Thoreau (1817–62), who

MASSACHUSETTS FACTS

Nicknames Bay State, Old Colony
Population 6,427,801 (13th)
Area 10,555 sq miles (44th)
Admitted to Union February 6, 1788 (6th)
Capital city Boston (population 589,000; metro area 3 million)
Other cities Worcester (173,000), Springfield (152,000)
State insect Ladybug
State doughnut Boston cream
State's official children's book author Dr Seuss (1904–91)
Birthplace of Ben Franklin (1706–90), Paul Revere (1735–1818), John Hancock (1737–93), Ralph Waldo Emerson (1803–82), Emily Dickinson (1830–86), cotton-gin inventor Eli Whitney (1765–1825), Samuel Morse (1791–1872), heavyweight boxer Rocky Marciano (1924–69), Presidents John Adams (1735–1826), John Quincy Adams (1767–1848), John F Kennedy (1917–63) and George HW Bush (1924–)

was among the first Americans to advocate living simply in harmony with nature. *Little Women* author Louisa May Alcott (1832–88) also resided and wrote in Concord. Poet Henry Wadsworth Longfellow (1807–82) lived and worked in Cambridge for 45 years, while Henry James (1843–1916) wrote about Boston parlor society in *The Bostonians* (1886). Pulitzer prize-winning novelist Edith Wharton (1862–1937) wrote *Ethan Frome* while summering in Lenox. Sold from a slave ship in Boston, Phyllis Wheatley (1753–84) was the first African-American female poet of note. Reclusive poet Emily Dickinson (1830–86) lived quietly in Amherst.

Information

Just south of Boston Common is the **Massachusetts Office of Travel & Tourism** (Map pp210-12; ☎ 617-973-8500, 800-227-6277; www.massvacation.com; Transportation Building, 10 Park Plaza, Suite 4510, Boston, MA 02116).

BOSTON

Once called 'the hub of the solar system' by proud resident Oliver Wendell Holmes, Boston is at least the hub (and largest city) of New England. With distinctive neighborhoods, this attractive, historic city is young at heart because of the 35 colleges and universities in the metropolitan area.

History

As capital and chief port of the Massachusetts Bay Colony (established in 1630), Boston was the center of Puritan New England. The Boston Latin School (the first public school in the USA) was founded in 1635, followed by Harvard College a year later. The first newspaper in the 13 original colonies was established here in 1704. Boston was also the center of resistance to British rule during the Revolutionary War. The Boston Massacre (1770), Boston Tea Party (1773) and Battle of Bunker Hill (1775) were significant events in the colonies' fight for freedom. Prominent Bostonians such as John Hancock, Samuel Adams, James Otis and Paul Revere were among the founders of the American republic.

Today, greater Boston remains at the forefront of American education. Its education resources have spawned important industries in electronics, biotechnology, medicine and finance. The city has always been a leader in US intellectual life.

Orientation

Boston is eminently walkable: the most interesting area for travelers – radiating out from the Boston Common – is only about 1 mile wide by 3 miles long. The Park St station, the hub of the Massachusetts Bay Transportation Authority (MBTA) subway system (the 'T'), is beneath the Common's northeast corner. Harvard Sq, the heart of neighboring Cambridge (across the Charles River) is about 5 miles west of the Common. Red Line trains from Park St whisk you there in minutes.

Information

BOOKSTORES

Avenue Victor Hugo Bookshop (Map p207; ☎ 617-266-7746; 353 Newbury St) Used books.
Globe Corner Bookstore (☎ 617-497-6277; 49 Palmer St, at Church St, Cambridge) Travel books and maps.
Grolier Poetry Book Shop (☎ 617-547-4648; 6 Plympton St, Cambridge)
Harvard Book Store (☎ 617-661-1515; 1256 Massachusetts Ave, Cambridge)
Harvard Cooperative Society (☎ 617-499-2000; 1400 Massachusetts Ave, Cambridge) Known as 'the Coop,' sells books, music and Harvard memorabilia.
We Think the World of You (Map pp210-12; ☎ 617-574-5000; 540 Tremont St) Gay titles.
Wordsworth (☎ 617-354-5201; 30 Brattle St, Cambridge)

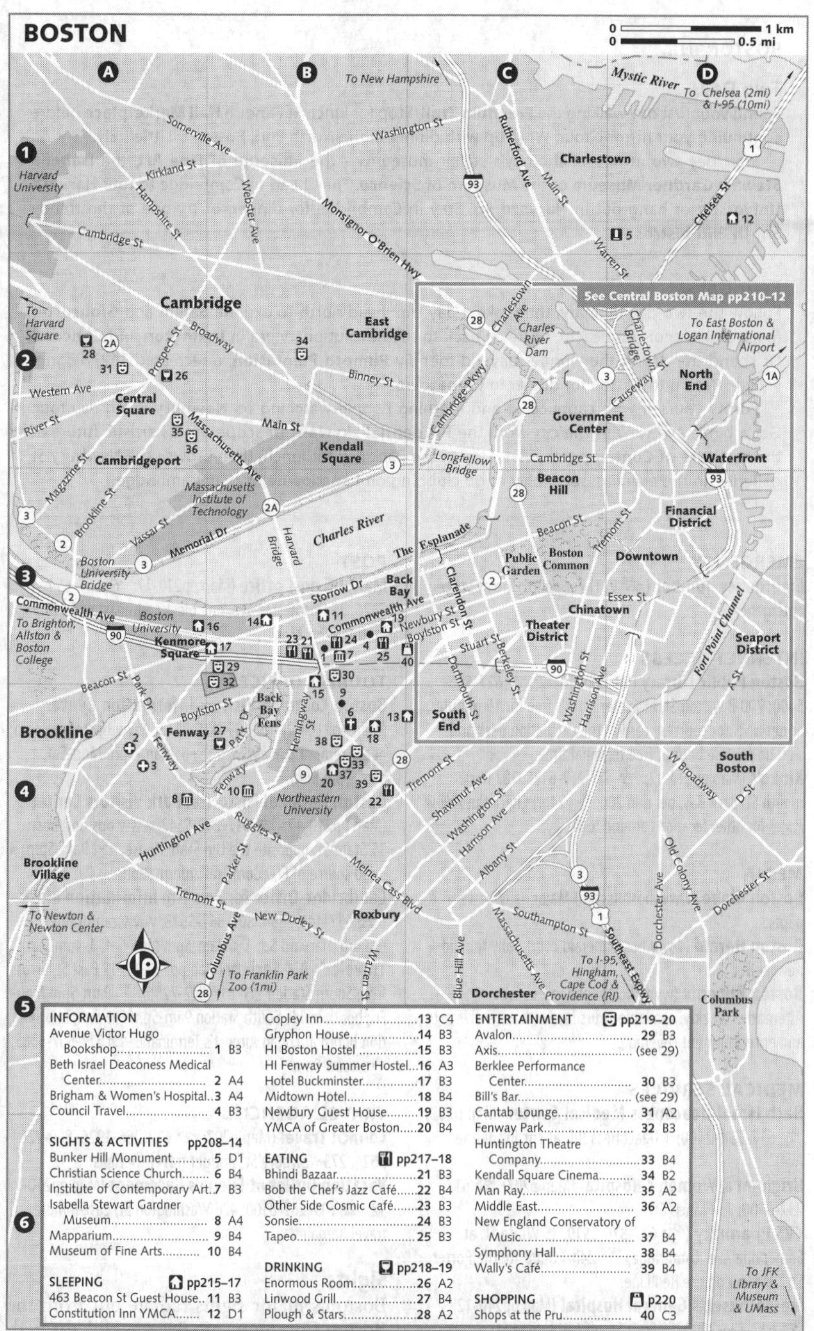
BOSTON
0 1 km
0 0.5 mi
A
B
C
D
1
2
3
4
5
6
To New Hampshire
Mystic River
To Chelsea (2mi) & I-95 (10mi)
Somerville Ave
Washington St
Harvard University
Kirkland St
Rutherford Ave
Charlestown
Main St
Hampshire St
Webster Ave
Monsignor O'Brien Hwy
Chelsea St
Cambridge St
Warren St
See Central Boston Map pp210–12
To Harvard Square
Cambridge
Broadway
Prospect St
East Cambridge
Charlestown Ave
Charles River Dam
To East Boston & Logan International Airport
Charlestown Bridge
Binney St
North End
Western Ave
Central Square
Cambridge Pkwy
Causeway St
River St
Main St
Government Center
Massachusetts Ave
Kendall Square
Longfellow Bridge
Cambridge St
Waterfront
Cambridgeport
Magazine St
Massachusetts Institute of Technology
Beacon Hill
Brookline St
Harvard Bridge
Charles River
Financial District
Vassar St
Memorial Dr
The Esplanade
Tremont St
Beacon St
Boston University Bridge
Public Garden
Boston Common
Downtown
Back Bay
Clarendon St
Storrow Dr
Essex St
Commonwealth Ave
Boston University
Newbury St
Boylston St
Chinatown
Fort Point Channel
To Brighton, Allston & Boston College
Kenmore Square
Stuart St
Theater District
Seaport District
Berkeley St
Dartmouth St
Washington St
Harrison Ave
A St
Beacon St
Park Dr
Back Bay Fens
Boylston St
Hemingway St
South End
Brookline
Fenway
South Boston
W Broadway
Tremont St
Shawmut Ave
D St
Northeastern University
Washington St
Harrison Ave
Huntington Ave
Ruggles St
Albany St
Old Colony Ave
Brookline Village
Parker St
Melnea Cass Blvd
Dorchester St
Tremont St
Roxbury
Dorchester Ave
To Newton & Newton Center
New Dudley St
Southampton St
Massachusetts Ave
Southeast Expwy
Columbus Ave
Warren St
Blue Hill Ave
To I-95, Hingham, Cape Cod & Providence (RI)
To Franklin Park Zoo (1mi)
Dorchester
Columbus Park
To JFK Library & Museum & UMass
INFORMATION
Avenue Victor Hugo Bookshop 1 B3
Beth Israel Deaconess Medical Center 2 A4
Brigham & Women's Hospital 3 A4
Council Travel 4 B3
SIGHTS & ACTIVITIES pp208–14
Bunker Hill Monument 5 D1
Christian Science Church 6 B4
Institute of Contemporary Art 7 B3
Isabella Stewart Gardner Museum 8 A4
Mapparium 9 B4
Museum of Fine Arts 10 B4
SLEEPING pp215–17
463 Beacon St Guest House 11 B3
Constitution Inn YMCA 12 D1
Copley Inn 13 C4
Gryphon House 14 B3
HI Boston Hostel 15 B3
HI Fenway Summer Hostel 16 A3
Hotel Buckminster 17 B3
Midtown Hotel 18 B4
Newbury Guest House 19 B3
YMCA of Greater Boston 20 B4
EATING pp217–18
Bhindi Bazaar 21 B3
Bob the Chef's Jazz Café 22 B4
Other Side Cosmic Café 23 B3
Sonsie 24 B3
Tapeo 25 B3
DRINKING pp218–19
Enormous Room 26 A2
Linwood Grill 27 B4
Plough & Stars 28 A2
ENTERTAINMENT pp219–20
Avalon 29 B3
Axis (see 29)
Berklee Performance Center 30 B3
Bill's Bar (see 29)
Cantab Lounge 31 A2
Fenway Park 32 B3
Huntington Theatre Company 33 B4
Kendall Square Cinema 34 B2
Man Ray 35 A2
Middle East 36 A2
New England Conservatory of Music 37 B4
Symphony Hall 38 B4
Wally's Café 39 B4
SHOPPING p220
Shops at the Pru 40 C3

BOSTON IN...

Two Days

Spend your first day walking the **Freedom Trail**. Stop for lunch at **Faneuil Hall Marketplace** before continuing your historic tour. Wrap up with dinner in the North End, Boston's 'Little Italy.'

Start day two at one of the city's stellar museums – the **Museum of Fine Art**, the **Isabella Stewart Gardner Museum** or the **Museum of Science**. Then head to Cambridge to tour **Harvard University** or hang out in **Harvard Sq**. Stay in Cambridge for dinner, or try one of the trendy **South End bistros**.

Four Days

Follow the two-day itinerary, then take a day trip: head north to explore **Salem** and **Gloucester** (pack a picnic for the beach), or travel back to the Revolutionary era in **Lexington** and **Concord**. Or spend the day at the wonderfully kid-friendly **Plimoth Plantation**, a recreated 1627 Pilgrim village. Return to Boston for dinner in **Chinatown**.

Fortify yourself with cappuccino and morning people-watching on **Newbury St** on day four. Get a bird's eye view of the city from the **Prudential skywalk**, or scope out its artistic future at the **Institute of Contemporary Art**. Stay in the Back Bay for lunch, then browse the Newbury St galleries. In the evening, see a play or go clubbing on **Lansdowne St** or in Cambridge.

EMERGENCY

Emergency number (☎ 911) For police, fire or other emergency.

INTERNET ACCESS

Boston Public Library (Map pp210-12; ☎ 617-536-5400; 700 Boylston St, at Exeter St) It's free for 15 minutes, or get a visitor courtesy card at the circulation desk and sign up for one hour of free terminal time.

Kinko's (Map pp210-12; ☎ 617-262-6188; 187 Dartmouth St, Back Bay; per min 20¢; 24hr) Check the *Yellow Pages* for other locations around town.

MEDIA

Boston Globe (www.boston.com) Major daily newspaper.

Boston Herald (www.bostonherald.com) Daily tabloid newspaper.

Boston Phoenix (www.bostonphoenix.com) Alternative weekly, available Thursday, with extensive arts and entertainment coverage.

MEDICAL SERVICES

Beth Israel Deaconess Medical Center (Map p207; ☎ 617-754-2400; 1 Deaconess Rd, at cnr Brookline Ave)

Brigham & Women's Hospital (Map p207; ☎ 617-732-5500; 75 Francis St)

CVS Pharmacy (☎ 617-876-5519; 35 White St, at Somerville Ave, Cambridge; 24hr) Opposite the Porter Sq T station on the Red Line.

Massachusetts General Hospital (Map pp210-12; ☎ 617-726-2000; 55 Fruit St, off Cambridge St)

POST

Main US post office (Map pp210-12; ☎ 617-654-5326; 25 Dorchester Ave, one block southeast of South Station; 24hr)

TOURIST OFFICES

Boston Common Visitors Information Center (Map pp210-12; ☎ 617-426-3115; www.bostonusa.com; near Tremont & West Sts; 8:30am-5pm Mon-Sat, 9am-5pm Sun)

Boston National Historical Park Visitors Center (Map pp210-12; ☎ 617-242-5642; www.nps.gov/bost; 15 State St, opposite the Old State House; 9am-5pm) A good source of Freedom Trail information.

Cambridge Office for Tourism information kiosk (☎ 617-441-2884, 800-862-5678; www.cambridge-usa.org; Harvard Sq; 9am-5pm Mon-Sat, 1-4pm Sun)

Traveler's Aid Society (Map pp210-12; 17 East St, across from South Station ☎ 617-542-7286; 9am-5pm Mon-Fri; booth inside South Station 9am-5pm Sat-Sun; information booth at Logan Airport's Terminal E ☎ 617-567-5385; noon-9pm)

TRAVEL AGENCIES

Council Travel (Map p207; ☎ 617-266-1926, 800-226-8624; 273 Newbury St) Budget travel specialist.

Vacation Outlet at Filene's Basement (Map pp210-12; ☎ 617-267-8100; 426 Washington St) Last-minute travel bargains.

Sights

Boston's major sights radiate out from the Boston Common – up Beacon Hill, through the downtown streets that take you toward Chinatown, the waterfront and the North End, and to the upscale Back Bay (full of restaurants and shops). South of the Back Bay, the gay-friendly South End is where you'll find many of the city's hip bistros. Cambridge, home to Harvard University, is across the Charles River.

BOSTON COMMON & PUBLIC GARDEN

Established in 1634, the 50-acre Boston Common (bounded by Park, Tremont, Boylston, Charles and Beacon Sts) is the country's oldest public park. In the northeast corner is the **Robert Gould Shaw Memorial** (Map pp210–12), created by sculptor Augustus Saint-Gaudens (1848–1907) and dedicated to the leader and troops of the first African-American regiment to fight for the Union in the Civil War. In winter, the Common's **Frog Pond** is a popular public ice skating rink.

Adjacent to the Common is the **Public Garden**, a 24-acre botanical oasis of cultivated flower beds, clipped grass, ancient trees and a tranquil lagoon with the kid-pleasing pedal-powered **Swan Boats** (☎ 617-522-1966; adult $2, child 5-11 $1; 10am-4pm mid-Apr–mid-Jun, 10am-5pm mid-Jun–early Sep, noon-4pm Mon-Fri & 10am-4pm Sat-Sun early Sep–mid-Sep). Historic buildings, top-end hotels and shops surround both parks.

FREEDOM TRAIL

The 2.5-mile **Freedom Trail** (☎ 617-242-5642) links 16 important colonial and Revolutionary history sites. Follow the double row of red sidewalk bricks (or red line) beginning near the Park Street T station, winding through downtown and the North End, and terminating at the **USS Constitution** (Map pp210–12) in Charlestown. Maps are available from both visitors centers (opposite). National Park Service rangers lead free tours daily.

BEACON HILL & DOWNTOWN Map pp210–12

North of Boston Common is Beacon Hill, Boston's most historic and affluent residential neighborhood. Nearby is the city's downtown.

Crowning Beacon Hill is **State House** (☎ 617-727-3676; www.state.ma.us/sec/trs/; Beacon St, at Park St; admission free; 10am-4pm Mon-Fri), the majestic 1798 golden-domed seat of Massachusetts' government. If you'd like to take a tour, call first, since tours often book up with local school groups.

The small **Museum of Afro American History** (☎ 617-725-0022; www.afroammuseum.org; 46 Joy St, at Smith Ct; admission by donation; 10am-4pm daily Jul-Aug, closed Sun Sep-Jun) illustrates the history of Boston's African-American community, which flourished on Beacon Hill in the 19th century. Next door, the **African Meeting House** (☎ 617-725-0022; 8 Smith Ct) is the country's oldest African-American meeting house, where Frederick Douglass and William Lloyd Garrison delivered passionate speeches.

Next to the historic **Park Street Church**, **Granary Burying Ground** (Tremont St, near Park St) dates to 1660; Revolutionary heroes Paul Revere, John Hancock and Samuel Adams are buried here. Just northeast is **King's Chapel** (☎ 617-227-2155; 58 Tremont St, at School St); its bell, made by Paul Revere, is still rung before services.

Colonists met at **Old South Meeting House** (☎ 617-482-6439; www.oldsouthmeetinghouse.org; 310 Washington St; adult $5, child 5-11 $1; 9:30am-5pm Apr-Oct, 10am-4pm Nov-Mar) in 1773 to protest British taxation before dumping tea from British ships into the harbor in the event that became known as the Boston Tea Party. You can listen to the audio tape ($1) that re-creates the events leading up to the tea revolt.

Originally, this 1713 structure was the colonial government house; now **Old State House** (☎ 617-720-3290; www.bostonhistory.org; 206 Washington St; adult $5, child 5-11 $1; 9am-5pm) is a comprehensive museum of Revolutionary history. The Declaration of Independence was first read to Bostonians from its balcony in 1776.

Faneuil Hall (fan-yul hall; Congress St) was constructed in 1740 as a market and public meeting place. It's a brick building topped with the grasshopper weather vane. Today, along with the granite Quincy Market and North and South Market buildings, it's part of Faneuil Hall Marketplace, a shopping and dining complex.

NORTH END & CHARLESTOWN

Follow the Freedom Trail into the North End, which has been Boston's Italian quarter since the 1920s. Historic Charlestown is across the Charlestown Bridge (off Commercial St).

Paul Revere House (Map pp210-12; ☎ 617-523-1676; www.paulreverehouse.org; 19 North Sq; adult $3, child 5-11 $1; 9:30am-5:15pm mid-Apr–Oct, 9:30am-4:15pm

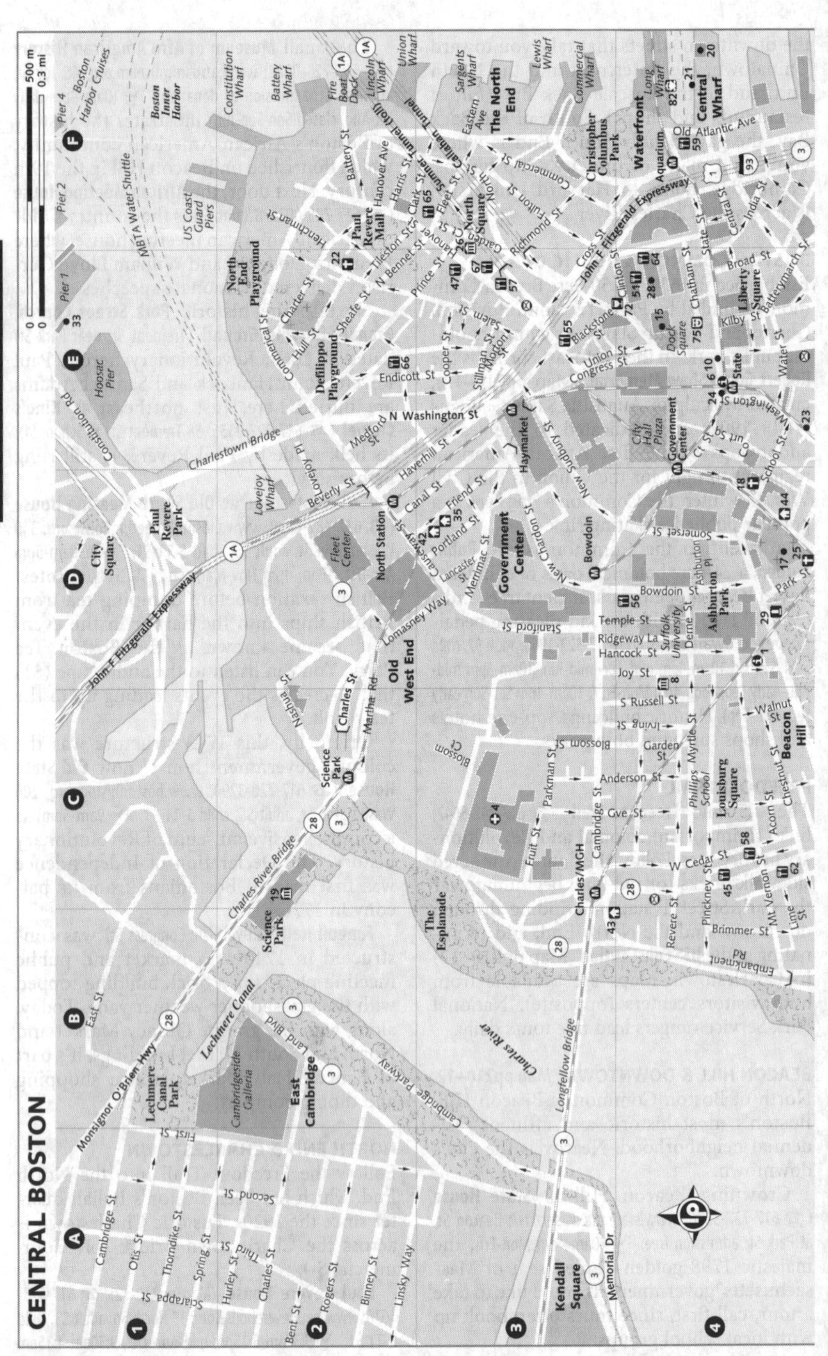
CENTRAL BOSTON
500 m
0.3 mi
Cambridge St
Otis St
Thorndike St
Spring St
Hurley St
Third St
Charles St
Rogers St
Bent St
Binney St
Linsky Way
Sciarappa St
Second St
First St
Lechmere Canal Park
Cambridgeside Galleria
East Cambridge
Monsignor O'Brien Hwy
Lechmere Canal
East St
Land Blvd
Cambridge Parkway
Science Park
Charles River Bridge
Charles River
Longfellow Bridge
Kendall Square
Memorial Dr
The Esplanade
Charles/MGH
Embankment Rd
Brimmer St
Mt Vernon St
Pinckney St
Revere St
W Cedar St
Chestnut St
Acorn St
Louisburg Square
Phillips School
Myrtle St
Beacon Hill
Walnut St
Garden St
Anderson St
Irving St
S Russell St
Joy St
Hancock St
Ridgeway La
Temple St
Suffolk University
Derne St
Ashburton Park
Bowdoin St
Park St
Somerset St
Ashburton Pl
Fruit St
Parkman St
Blossom St
Blossom Ct
Old West End
Martha Rd
Charles St
Nashua St
Lomasney Way
North Station
Fleet Center
Causeway St
Lancaster St
Merrimac St
Portland St
Friend St
Canal St
Government Center
New Chardon St
Bowdoin
Staniford St
Haymarket
New Sudbury St
Haverhill St
Beverly St
Lovejoy Pl
Lovejoy Wharf
Medford St
N Washington St
Charlestown Bridge
Constitution Rd
Hoosac Pier
City Square
Paul Revere Park
John F Fitzgerald Expressway
Defilippo Playground
Endicott St
Cooper St
Stillman St
Morton St
Salem St
Commercial St
Hull St
Charter St
Sheafe St
North End Playground
Henchman St
Paul Revere Mall
Tileston St
N Bennet St
Prince St
Hanover St
Clark St
Fleet St
North Square
Garden Ct St
North St
Richmond St
Fulton St
Cross St
Blackstone St
Union St
Congress St
Clinton St
Dock Square
Chatham St
Kilby St
Liberty Square
Batterymarch St
Broad St
State St
Central St
India St
Water St
State
Washington St
School St
Court St
City Hall Plaza
Government Center
Battery St
Harris St
Hanover Ave
Eastern Ave
The North End
Sumner Tunnel (toll)
Callahan Tunnel
Commercial St
Christopher Columbus Park
Waterfront
Aquarium
Old Atlantic Ave
Central Wharf
Long Wharf
Commercial Wharf
Lewis Wharf
Sargents Wharf
Union Wharf
Lincoln Wharf
Fire Boat Dock
Battery Wharf
Constitution Wharf
Boston Inner Harbor
US Coast Guard Piers
MBTA Water Shuttle
Pier 1
Pier 2
Pier 4
Boston Harbor Cruises

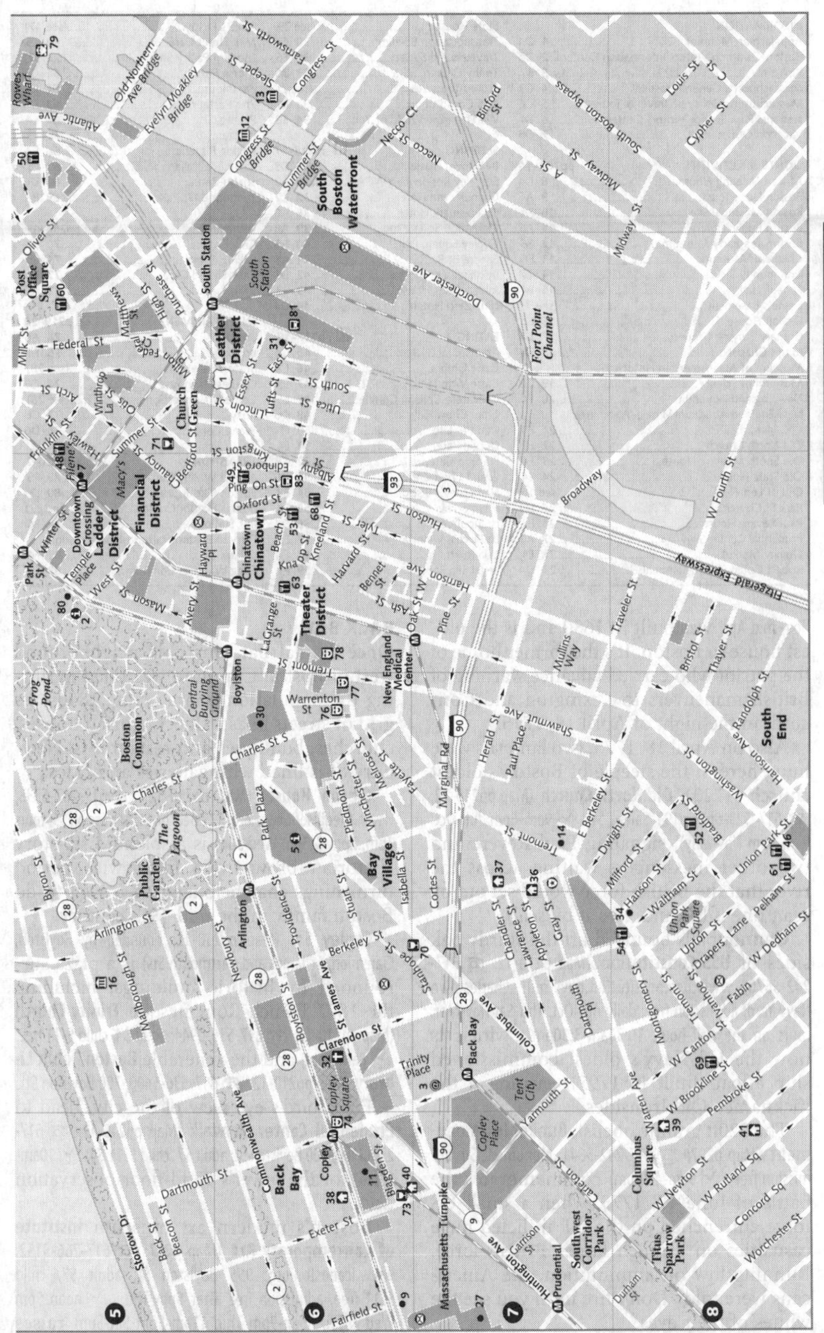

Boston Common
Frog Pond
Central Burying Ground
Public Garden
The Lagoon
Back Bay
Copley Square
Copley Place
Tent City
Bay Village
Theater District
Chinatown
Leather District
Financial District
Ladder District
Downtown Crossing
Church Green
South Station
South Boston Waterfront
Fort Point Channel
South End
Union Park Square
Columbus Square
Southwest Corridor Park
Titus Sparrow Park
Post Office Square
Rowes Wharf
New England Medical Center
Trinity Place
Massachusetts Turnpike
Fitzgerald Expressway
Storrow Dr
Commonwealth Ave
Boylston St
Newbury St
Tremont St
Washington St
Columbus Ave
Huntington Ave
Shawmut Ave
Harrison Ave
Charles St
Arlington St
Berkeley St
Clarendon St
Dartmouth St
Summer St
Congress St
Atlantic Ave
Dorchester Ave
Broadway
South Boston Bypass
Evelyn Moakley Bridge
Old Northern Ave Bridge
Congress St Bridge
Summer St Bridge

NEW ENGLAND

INFORMATION

- Appalachian Mountain Club 1 D4
- Boston Common Visitors Information Center 2 D5
- Kinko's 3 B7
- Massachusetts General Hospital 4 C3
- Massachusetts Office of Travel & Tourism 5 C6
- National Park Service Visitors Center 6 E4
- Vacation Outlet 7 D5

SIGHTS & ACTIVITIES pp208–14

- African Meeting House 8 D4
- Boston Duck Tours 9 A6
- Boston Massacre Site 10 E4
- Boston Public Library 11 A6
- Boston Tea Party Museum 12 F6
- Children's Museum 13 F6
- Community Bicycle Supply 14 C7
- Faneuil Hall 15 E4
- Filene's Basement (see 7)
- Gibson House 16 B5
- Granary Burying Ground 17 D4
- King's Chapel 18 D4
- Museum of Afro-American History (see 8)
- Museum of Science 19 C2
- New England Aquarium 20 F4
- New England Aquarium Whale-Watching Cruises 21 F4
- Old North Church 22 E2
- Old South Meeting House 23 E4
- Old State House 24 E4
- Out of Left Field (see 15)
- Park St Church 25 D4
- Paul Revere House 26 F3
- Prudential Center Skywalk 27 A7
- Quincy Market 28 E4
- Robert Gould Shaw Memorial 29 D4
- State House (see 29)
- Transportation Building 30 C6
- Travelers Aid Society 31 E6
- Trinity Church 32 B6
- Trolley Tours (see 2)
- USS Constitution 33 E1
- We Think the World of You 34 B8

SLEEPING pp215–17

- Beantown Hostel 35 D3
- Berkeley Residence YWCA 36 C7
- Chandler Inn Hotel 37 C7
- Charlesmark Hotel 38 A6
- Clarendon Square Inn 39 A8
- Copley Square Hotel 40 A6
- Encore B&B 41 A8
- Irish Embassy Hostel 42 D3
- John Jeffries House 43 B3
- Nine Zero Hotel 44 D4

EATING pp217–18

- Artu 45 C4
- Caffe Umbra 46 C8
- Caffè Vittoria 47 E3
- Chacarero Chilean Cuisine 48 E5
- Chau Chow City 49 D6
- Country Life 50 F5
- Durgin Park 51 E4
- Franklin Café 52 C8
- Grand Chau Chow 53 D6
- Hamersley's Bistro 54 B8
- Haymarket 55 E3
- Istanbul Café 56 D4
- La Piccola Venezia 57 E3
- Lala Rokh 58 C4
- Legal Sea Foods 59 F4
- Mike's Pastry (see 47)
- Milk Street Café 60 E5
- Modern Pastry Shop (see 57)
- Morse Fish 61 C8
- Paramount 62 C4
- Pho Pasteur 63 D6
- Pinang 64 E4
- Prezza 65 F3
- Regina Pizzeria 66 E2
- Salumeria Italiana 67 E3
- Shabu-Zen 68 D6
- Tremont 647 69 B8

DRINKING pp218–19

- Club Café 70 B7
- Peking Tom's 71 E5
- Rack Billiard Club 72 E4
- Saint 73 A6

ENTERTAINMENT p219–20

- Bostix 74 A6
- Bostix 75 E4
- Boston Ballet (see 78)
- Charles Playhouse 76 C6
- Comedy Connection (see 28)
- Roxy 77 C6
- Wang Center 78 D6

TRANSPORT pp220–2

- Airport Water Shuttle 79 F5
- Boston Bike Tours 80 D5
- Boston Harbor Cruises (see 82)
- Bus Station 81 E6
- Ferry to Boston Harbor Islands National Park 82 F4
- Fung Wah Bus Company 83 D6

Nov–mid-Apr) was built in 1680 and is the oldest house in Boston. It's the former home of the patriot who carried advance warning of British maneuvers to Lexington and Concord on the night of April 18, 1775.

Also on April 18, 1775, two lanterns were hung here in the steeple of Boston's oldest church (1723), **Old North Church** (Map pp210-12; ☎ 617-523-6676; 193 Salem St; 9am-6pm Jun-Oct, 9am-5pm Nov-May), signaling Paul Revere and two other messengers waiting across the river that the British force would set out by sea ('one if by land, two if by sea').

Cannonballs bounced off the sturdy oak sides of **USS Constitution** (Map p210-12; ☎ 617-242-5670; www.ussconstitution.navy.mil; Charlestown Navy Yard; admission free; daily Apr-Oct, Thu-Sat Nov-Mar, tours on the half-hour, 10:30am-3:30pm), which is now the US Navy's oldest commissioned ship afloat (built in 1797), earning it the nickname, 'Old Ironsides.'

The 220ft granite obelisk **Bunker Hill Monument** (Map p207; ☎ 617-242-5641; Monument Sq; admission free; 9am-4:30pm) commemorates the battle of June 17, 1775, when a small US force entrenched on the hill inflicted huge casualties on a much larger British force. Running low on ammunition, the Americans were told, 'Don't fire until you see the whites of their eyes.'

BACK BAY

Once a tidal flat, this chic neighborhood west of Boston Common was filled in during the population boom of the 1850s. Its grid of streets boasts fine Victorian houses, churches, boutiques and restaurants. Newbury St is lined with galleries and cafés.

Gibson House (Map pp210-12; ☎ 617-267-6338; www .thegibsonhouse.org; 137 Beacon St; admission $5; tours 1pm, 2pm & 3pm Wed-Sun) is a splendid six-story Victorian brownstone filled with period furnishings that belonged to a well-to-do Boston family in the mid-19th century.

Copley Sq (Map pp210-12; bounded by Boylston, Clarendon, St James and Dartmouth Sts) is a plaza surrounded by historic buildings, including the 1877 French-Romanesque **Trinity Church** (Map pp210-12; ☎ 617-536-0944; adult $4, child 5-11 free; 8am-6pm) and the venerable **Boston Public Library** (Map pp210-12; ☎ 617-536-5400; 700 Boylston St).

For a bird's-eye view of the city, head to **Prudential Center Skywalk** (Map pp210-12; ☎ 617-236-3100; 800 Boylston St; adult $7, child 5-11 $4; 10am-10pm) for the tower's 52nd-floor observation deck.

Boston's modern art museum **Institute of Contemporary Art** (Map p207; ☎ 617-266-5152; www.icaboston.org; 955 Boylston St; adult $7, child 5-11 free, admission free after 5pm Thu; noon-5pm Wed & Fri, noon-9pm Thu, 11am-5pm Sat-Sun) raises eyebrows now and then with its avant-garde exhibits.

The **Christian Science Church's** (Map p207; ☎ 617-450-3790; 175 Huntington Ave; admission free; 10am-4pm Mon-Sat, last tour at 3:30pm) international headquarters is open for tours. The church complex also houses the **Mapparium** (Map p207; ☎ 617-450-7000; 200 Massachusetts Ave; adult $5, child 5-11 $3; 10am-9pm Tue-Fri, 10am-6pm Sat, 11am-5pm Sun), where visitors can walk inside a three-story stained-glass globe built in 1935.

CAMBRIDGE

With a combined enrollment of almost 30,000 students from some 100 countries, Cambridge's two well-known universities – Harvard University and the Massachusetts Institute of Technology (MIT) – keep this city lively, smart and young. **Harvard Sq** overflows with cafés, bookstores and street performers. The 'square' is a triangle of brick above the Harvard T station. The epicenter is Out of Town News, the place for foreign newspapers and magazines. The gates to famed **Harvard Yard** (1636), a quadrangle of ivy-covered brick buildings, are just across Massachusetts Ave. **Harvard University tours** start from the rather modern **Holyoke Center** (☎ 617-495-1573; 1350 Massachusetts Ave; admission free; tours 10am & 2pm Mon-Fri, 2pm Sat Sep-May, 10am, 11:15am, 2pm & 3:15pm Mon-Sat mid-Jun–mid-Aug).

The **Harvard Museum of Natural History** (☎ 617-495-3045; www.hmnh.harvard.edu; 26 Oxford St; adult $6.50, child 5-11 $4, admission free 9am-noon Sun; 9am-5pm) has an amazing collection of more than 800 glass flowers. With the same admission ticket, you can visit the first-rate Native American exhibits at the adjacent **Peabody Museum of Archeology and Ethnology** (☎ 617-496-1027; www.peabody.harvard.edu; 11 Divinity Ave).

Harvard's art museum, **Fogg Art Museum** (☎ 617-495-9400; www.artmuseums.harvard.edu; 32 Quincy St; adult $6.50, child 5-11 free, admission free 10am-noon Sat; 10am-5pm Mon-Sat, 1-5pm Sun), showcases Western art from the Middle Ages through to the present. The **Busch-Reisinger Museum**, which is entered via the Fogg, specializes in Northern European artists. Across the street, the **Arthur Sackler Museum** (☎ 617-495-9400; 485 Broadway; adult $6.50, child 5-11 free, admission free 10-noon Sat; 10am-5pm Mon-Sat, 1-5pm Sun) is devoted to Asian and Islamic art. One admission ticket will admit you to the three art museums. The Harvard Hot Ticket ($10), available at any of the five Harvard museums, grants admission to them all.

The **Massachusetts Institute of Technology** (Map p207) is 2 miles southeast of Harvard Sq along Massachusetts Ave. Campus walking tours begin at the **information center** (☎ 617-253-4795; 77 Massachusetts Ave; admission free; tours 10am & 2pm Mon-Fri).

OTHER ATTRACTIONS

Purchase the discount visitor pass, **CityPass** (adult $34, child 5-11 $20), if you plan on visiting at least half of the following attractions: Museum of Fine Arts, Museum of Science, John F Kennedy Library & Museum, New England Aquarium, Harvard Museum of Natural History and the Prudential Center Skywalk. CityPass is available at each of these sights and at the Boston Common Visitors Information Center.

Museum of Fine Arts Boston (MFA; Map p207; ☎ 617-267-9300; www.mfa.org; 465 Huntington Ave; adult $15, child 5-11 $6.50, 'voluntary contribution' 4-9:45pm Wed; 10am-4:45pm Mon, Tue, Sat, Sun, 10am-9:45pm Wed-Fri) is one of the country's finest art museums. The vast galleries are especially strong in American painting, decorative arts, Asian treasures and European painting, including French impressionists. Adult tickets are good for two visits within 30 days (a handy feature, since there's so much to see); children are free on weekends and after 3pm weekdays.

Located just west of the MFA, **Isabella Stewart Gardner Museum** (Map p207; ☎ 617-566-1401; www.gardnermuseum.org; 280 The Fenway; adult $11 ($10 weekdays), child free; 11am-5pm Tue-Sun) is a magnificent Venetian-style palazzo housing almost 2000 priceless art objects, primarily European. Well-to-do arts patron Isabella Stewart Gardner assembled her vast collection in the late 19th and early 20th centuries; her will specified that the collection remain exactly as she had left it. The building itself, with its flower-filled enclosed courtyard, is worth the price of admission.

Dating to 1912, **Fenway Park** (Map p207; ☎ 617-236-6666; www.bostonredsox.com; adult $9, child 5-11 $7; tours on the hour 9am-4pm Apr-Sep, by appointment Oct-Mar) is the nation's oldest. The Boston Red Sox play major-league baseball in this historic park.

Museum of Science (Map pp210-12; ☎ 617-723-2500; www.mos.org; Science Park, on the Charles River Dam; adult $12, child 5-11 $9; 9am-5pm, 9am-9pm Fri) is an excellent museum and an educational feast of fun, especially for kids. Check out what's playing on the **Omni Theater's** (adult $8, child 5-11 $6) five-story screen.

On the waterfront at Atlantic Ave, the **New England Aquarium's** (Map pp210-12; ☎ 617-973-5200; www.neaq.org; Central Wharf; adult $16, child 5-11 $8; 9am-5pm Mon-Fri, 9am-6pm Sat-Sun) three-story-high tank holds over 700 sea creatures. There's a big-screen Imax theater (adult/child $8.50/6.50) here, too.

The **Boston Tea Party Museum** (Map pp210-12; ☎ 617-269-7150; closed for renovation until 2004) commemorates the colonial protest against the tea tax imposed from London in 1773, when locals dumped tea into the harbor.

In a modern building, **John F Kennedy Library & Museum** (☎ 617-514-1600; www.jfklibrary.org; Columbia Point, Dorchester; adult $8, child 5-11 free; 9am-5pm) is the repository for memorabilia about the 35th US president. You can watch excerpts of the Kennedy-Nixon debates; other exhibits describe Kennedy's brief term as president and the role of his wife, Jacqueline. Take the T's Red Line to JFK/UMass, then hop on a free shuttle bus.

A refuge on hot summer days, **Boston Harbor Islands National Park** (☎ 617-223-8666; www.nps.gov/boha; 9am-dusk May–early Oct) is a string of islands with great city views. **Boston Harbor Cruises** (Map pp210-12; ☎ 617-227-4320; adult $8, child 5-11 $6 round-trip) runs daily ferries from Long Wharf off Atlantic Ave, near the New England Aquarium. Pack a picnic – food concessions on the islands are very limited.

Boston for Children

Boston's relatively small scale and convenient subway system make it an easy city for families to explore. Just put on your walking shoes and head out.

TOURS

For a guided walk through the city, try **Boston by Little Feet** (☎ 617-367-3766; www.bostonbyfoot.com; tour $6; tours depart from Faneuil Hall at 10am Mon & Sat, 2pm Sun May-Oct), 60-minute walking tours for ages six to 12. Older kids may enjoy the somewhat corny **Boston Duck Tours** (p214) that cruise the downtown streets before splashing into the Charles River. Another option is **Boston by Sea** (☎ 617-350-0358; www.bostonbysea.org; Rowes Wharf; adult $19, child 5-11 $11; tours noon & 2pm Thu-Sun late Jun–Aug, 2pm Sat-Sun late May–late Jun & Sep), a musical harbor cruise where actors re-create the city's maritime history.

SIGHTS

Many of Boston's historic sites are linked along the **Freedom Trail** (p209), where kids can follow the red line on the sidewalk from place to place. Young ones may not have the stamina to complete the entire 2.5-mile walk, but you can stop and start as you please.

Little kids can play at the entertaining **Children's Museum** (Map pp210-12; ☎ 617-426-8855; www.bostonkids.org; 300 Congress St; adult $8, child 5-11 $7, 5-9pm Fri $1; 10am-5pm, 10am-9pm Fri). The interactive educational exhibits here entertain kids for an entire day (or more), while elementary-schoolers (and up) can spend hours at the **Museum of Science** (p213) and its companion planetarium and Imax theater. At the **New England Aquarium** (p214), don't miss the Animal Rescue Center, the aquarium's animal hospital, where you can observe how injured marine creatures are nursed back to health.

If you have time for a day trip, head south to **Plimoth Plantation** (p223), a restored Pilgrim village where kids can chat with 'Pilgrims' who go about their business as if it's still 1627.

In the middle of Boston Common, little ones can cool their tired toes in the **Frog Pond**; in winter, it's an ice-skating rink. In the adjacent Public Garden, fans of Robert McCloskey's classic Boston tale, 'Make Way for Ducklings,' can visit statues of the famous mallards or cruise on the crowd-pleasing **Swan Boats** (p209). For more green space, hop a ferry to the **Boston Harbor Islands National Park** (p214) to hike or picnic with views of the city skyline.

If you're traveling with baseball buffs, take a behind-the-scenes tour of the Red Sox' **Fenway Park** (p213), where the notorious 'Green Monster' wall has stopped many a home run.

EATING

When one kid wants pizza, another likes clam chowder, and a third is insisting on an ice-cream-only diet, the something-for-everyone food stalls at **Quincy Market** (p209) are a convenient grazing stop. Most Chinatown restaurants are family-friendly and can cater to both simple and sophisticated palates. Children are also welcome at most North End eateries, where plain pasta is an option for picky eaters. And what kid can resist a stop for cannoli or cookies at one of the North End's sweet shops? Wrap up your family's Boston experience with a treat from **Mike's Pastry** (Map pp210-12; ☎ 617-742-3050; 300 Hanover St) or **Modern Pastry Shop** (Map pp210-12; ☎ 617-523-3783; 257 Hanover St).

Tours

Boston Duck Tours (☎ 617-723-3825; www.bostonducktours.com; adult $23, child 5-11 $14; tours depart every half-hour, 9am-dusk Apr-Nov) offers touristy but popular land-and-water tours using WWII amphibious vehicles known as 'ducks.' Tours leave from either the Prudential Center or the Museum of Science. **Boston Harbor Cruises** (Map pp210-12; ☎ 617-227-4321; www.bostonharborcruises.com; Long Wharf; adult $17, child 5-11 $12) operates 1½-hour narrated sightseeing trips in the summer; they also offer a three-hour **whale-watch trip** (adult $29, child 5-11 $23) on a high-speed catamaran. The **New England Aquarium** (adult $29, child 5-11 $18) also runs well-regarded whale-watch excursions.

Boston is a big walking city. In addition to the Freedom Trail, there are a number of other free, self-guided specialty walking trails, including the Harbor Walk, Black Heritage Trail and Women's History Trail. If you prefer to ride, several companies run **trolley tours** (Map pp210–12) connecting major sites. Get details from the Boston Common Visitors Information Center.

If you prefer seeing the city on two wheels, arrange a ride with **Boston Bike Tours** (☎ 617-308-5902; www.bostonbiketours.com; $20-25; 2½-4½hr). Departing daily (except Tuesday) from Boston Common, they'll take you on a guided spin around town. Call or check the website for details and schedule.

Festivals & Events

Call the **visitors center** (☎ 800-888-5515) for up-to-the-minute details and lots of events. The following celebrations are always huge in Boston:

Chinese New Year Enjoy the parade in Chinatown and stop for a meal in any of the neighborhood's eateries. Late January or early February.

St Patrick's Day (www.irishmassachusetts.com) On March 17 the substantial Irish-American community in South Boston hosts a huge parade, and bars all over town serve green beer.

Patriot's Day & Boston Marathon (www.bostonusa.com) Paul Revere's ride from the North End to Lexington in 1775 is reenacted, commemorating the start of the American Revolution. On the same day, serious runners from around the world participate in the 26-mile race from Hopkinton to Boston's Copley Sq. Third Monday in April.

Gay Pride (www.bostonpride.org) Held mid-June, events include a parade, block parties, casino night and other festivities.

Boston Pops on the Esplanade (www.bso.org) This wildly popular, free, outdoor Independence Day concert culminates with fireworks over the Charles River. July 4.

Italian festivals (www.northendboston.com) During July and August the North End honors saints with weekend street fairs throughout the summer.

Head of the Charles Regatta (www.hocr.org) More than 7000 college rowers compete in this Charles River race. Third weekend in October.

First Night (www.firstnight.org) On December 31 Boston rings in the New Year with arts events and festivities all over town.

Sleeping

Hotel rates in Boston are generally higher than elsewhere in New England; expect to pay between $100 and $200 for a mid-range room in high season. Peak times include May college graduation weekends, summer and early fall. Hotels that cater to business travelers often cut their rates on weekends. And if you're visiting in winter, shop around for steep discounts.

Central Reservation Service of New England (☎ 617-569-3800, 800-332-3026; www.bostonhotels.net) Can usually secure discounts from hotels and guesthouses.

Bed & Breakfast Agency of Boston (☎ 617-720-3540, 800-248-9262; www.boston-bnbagency.com; d $90-160) Represents about 150 varied B&Bs, most downtown.

BUDGET

Reserve hostel beds a month ahead in summer, or at least phone ahead with a credit card.

Berkeley Residence YWCA (Map pp210-12; ☎ 617-375-2524; 40 Berkeley St; with breakfast s/d/tr $56/86/99) This South End facility rents small rooms to women.

YMCA of Greater Boston (Map p207; ☎ 617-536-7800; www.ymcaboston.org; 316 Huntington Ave; s/d $45/65; 🖳) Near the Museum of Fine Arts, the 'Y' rents 95 rooms to both sexes in summer. Eight rooms are available only to men the rest of the year. Reserve by mail two weeks prior to your visit or walk in after 11am.

HI Boston Hostel (Map p207; ☎ 617-536-9455; www.bostonhostel.org; 12 Hemenway St; with breakfast dm $32-38, d $69-89; 🖳) This large hostel, just off Boylston St in the Back Bay, has 208 beds as well as some private rooms.

HI Fenway Summer Hostel (Map p207; ☎ 617-267-8599; www.bostonhostel.org/fenway; 575 Commonwealth Ave; with breakfast dm $35-38, d $89-92) In a former hotel near Kenmore Sq, this hostel has rooms with three dorm beds each, as well as private rooms. It's open early June to mid-August.

Other choices include the **Irish Embassy Hostel** (Map pp210-12; ☎ 617-973-4841; 222 Friend St; dm $25), which is above its eponymous pub near North Station. Its sister hostel, **Beantown Hostel** (Map pp210-12; ☎ 617-723-0800; dm $25), is next door.

The **Boston Harbor Islands National Park** (☎ 617-223-8666) has primitive campsites open daily late June to August on Lovells and **Peddocks Islands** (☎ 617-727-7676; campsites free, but reservations required) and on Grape and Bumpkin Islands (☎ 877-422-6762; www.reserveamerica.com; campsites $5).

MID-RANGE

Charlesmark Hotel (Map pp210-12; ☎ 617-247-1212; www.charlesmarkhotel.com; 655 Boylston St; with breakfast d $120-190) Located in Copley Sq, opposite the Boston Public Library, this relative newcomer has 33 modern, smartly-appointed rooms. They're not large, but they're full of conveniences like CD players and TV/VCRs.

Newbury Guest House (Map p207; ☎ 617-437-7666, 800-437-7668; www.hagopianhotels.com; 261 Newbury St; with breakfast d $140-190; P) With a fabulous Back Bay location, this Victorian-style B&B has 32 rooms in three interconnected 1882 brownstones.

John Jeffries House (Map pp210-12; ☎ 617-367-1866; www.johnjeffrieshouse.com; 14 David G Mugar Way, at Charles St; with breakfast d $95-125, ste $150-165) The 46 simply-furnished rooms and suites – some with kitchenettes – in this solid brick building opposite the Charles St 'T' station are good value. The parlor, where breakfast is served, overlooks the Charles River.

Hotel Buckminster (Map p207; ☎ 617-236-7050, 800-727-2825; www.bostonhotelbuckminster.com; 645 Beacon St; d $109-149, ste $169-219) In Kenmore Sq, just a baseball's toss from Fenway Park, this European-style dowager has 93 rooms ranging from tiny to expansive; the larger ones easily accommodate families or groups.

Copley Inn (Map p207; ☎ 617-236-0300, 800-232-0306; www.copleyinn.com; 19 Garrison St; d $125-145) This rehabbed brownstone, in a residential neighborhood between the Back Bay and South End, houses 21 comfortable studios with kitchenettes.

Constitution Inn YMCA (Map p207; ☎ 617-241-8400; www.constitutioninn.com; 150 Second Ave, Charlestown; d $99-125; P) In the Charlestown Navy Yard, this basic modern facility has 147 rooms and a fitness center.

Other places worth considering:

463 Beacon St Guest House (Map p207; ☎ 617-536-1302; www.463beacon.com; 463 Beacon St; d $89-109; P) In a Back Bay townhouse.

Chandler Inn (Map pp210-12; ☎ 617-482-3450; www.chandlerinn.com; 26 Chandler St; d $119-139) Popular with gay travelers; the South End.

Friendly Inn (☎ 617-547-7851; www.afinow.com; 1673 Cambridge St, Cambridge; d $117-137) A 10-minute walk to Harvard Sq; 17 rooms.

The gay-friendly South End also has several upscale B&Bs, straddling the mid-range and top end, which are stylish alternatives to larger hotels. Among the best are **Clarendon Square Inn** (Map pp210-12; ☎ 617-536-2229; www.clarendonsquare.com; 198 W Brookline St; with breakfast d $159-249) and **Encore B&B** (Map pp210-12; ☎ 617-247-3425; www.encorebandb.com; 116 W Newton St; with breakfast d $170-190).

TOP END

Nine Zero (Map pp210-12; ☎ 617-772-5800; www.ninezero.com; 90 Tremont St; d $159-287; P) If chic and contemporary is your style, wear black and check into this trendy deluxe hotel downtown, one block from the Boston Common. The luxe rooms have all sorts of business-friendly high-tech gadgets, from high-speed Internet access to multi-line speaker phones.

Gryphon House (Map p207; ☎ 617-375-9003, 877-375-9003; www.gryphonhouseboston.com; 9 Bay State Rd; ste $185-265; P) A five-story brownstone near Kenmore Sq, this nattily updated inn offers eight 19th-century period suites with modern amenities including TV/VCRs, gas fireplaces and CD players.

Copley Square Hotel (Map pp210-12; ☎ 617-536-9000, 800-225-7062; www.copleysquarehotel.com; 47 Huntington Ave; d $189-229) Built in 1891, this low-key Back Bay hotel, which you'll find around the corner from Copley Sq, has 143 traditionally appointed rooms.

Midtown Hotel (Map p207; ☎ 617-262-1000, 800-343-1177; www.midtownhotel.com; 220 Huntington Ave; d $159-239; P) This low-rise motel looks like it belongs by the side of the highway, instead of in the shadow of the Prudential Center, but its 159 spacious, if plain, rooms fill up with families, businesspeople and tour groups.

Eating

Though you'll still find chowder, pot roast and other old-time New England fare, 'Beantown' (a reference to Boston's traditional baked beans) is now a top dining city. The myriad ethnic eateries are often the best bang-for-the-buck, but even at many top-end restaurants, you can get a lighter lower-priced meal by eating at the bar.

BEACON HILL — Map pp210–12

Paramount (☎ 617-720-1152; 44 Charles St; dinners $10-16) At this Beacon Hill neighborhood hangout, a rather stylish coffee shop, you can get inexpensive cafeteria-style breakfasts and lunches, as well as more upscale New American dinners.

Istanbul Café (☎ 617-227-3434; 37 Bowdoin St; mains $7-15) This cozy eatery on the back side of Beacon Hill features some of the best Turkish cuisine this side of the Izmir Peninsula.

Lala Rokh (☎ 617-720-5511; 97 Mt Vernon St; dinners $14-19) In a gracious Beacon Hill townhouse, this romantic little dining room serves intriguing Persian fare.

DOWNTOWN — Map pp210–12

Durgin Park (☎ 617-227-2038; 340 N Market St, at Faneuil Hall Marketplace; lunches $5-9, dinners $10-20) This Boston institution has been serving up chowder, chicken potpie, huge slabs of prime rib, Boston baked beans and Indian pudding at family-style tables since 1827. Sure, it's touristy, but it's good and cheap, too.

Pinang (☎ 617-227-6866; mains $7-13) Also at Faneuil Hall, this contemporary restaurant with a pretty glass-walled dining room and outdoor tables offers fresh Malaysian fare, including vegetarian choices.

Legal Sea Foods (☎ 617-227-3115; 255 State St; lunches $9-15, dinners $15-23) This local chain has built its seafood reputation on the motto 'If it isn't fresh, it isn't Legal.' In addition to this branch near the waterfront, a few blocks from Faneuil Hall, there are other locations around town, including the Prudential Center and Copley Pl.

Haymarket (Blackstone St) Near Faneuil Hall, this king of open-air produce markets sells cheap goods Friday and Saturday. Near closing time, you can get especially good deals, but check your produce for freshness before leaving.

Quincy Market (off Congress & North St) This food hall and tourist attraction has numerous take-out food shops under one roof.

If you're walking the Freedom Trail, detour to **Milk Street Café** (☎ 617-542-3663; 50 Milk St, near Post Office Sq; lunches $5-8; 🕑 7am-3pm Mon-Fri) for vegetarian-kosher soups, sandwiches and hot meals, or to **Chacarero Chilean Cuisine** (☎ 617-542-0392; 426 Franklin St; lunches $4-6; 🕑 11am-6pm Mon-Fri) for enormous hot take-out sandwiches. **Country Life** (200 High St; lunches $7; 🕑 closed Sat) boasts a vegan all-you-can-eat lunch buffet.

> **THE AUTHOR'S CHOICE**
>
> **Prezza** (Map pp210-12; ☎ 617-227-1577; 24 Fleet St; first courses & pastas $9-14, mains $24-28) Don't miss this sleek dining room if you favor modern Mediterranean cuisine. Dress up a bit and you can make a fine meal of appetizers – perhaps clam and arugula pizza or pasta with shrimp, white beans and dandelion greens – at the bar.

CHINATOWN — Map pp210–12

Pho Pasteur (☎ 617-482-7467; 682 Washington St; soups $5-8) Crowds throng this modest Vietnamese noodle shop for filling meal-in-a-bowl soups. There are other branches in the Back Bay and in Cambridge.

Chau Chow City (☎ 617-338-8158; 83 Essex St) For daily dim sum, this multi-level eatery is a favorite, while sister restaurant **Grand Chau Chow** (☎ 617-292-5166; 45 Beach St; dinners $8-12) serves excellent Hong Kong–style seafood.

Shabu-Zen (☎ 617-292-8828; 16 Tyler St; mains $10-17) Bring a gang to this fun spot for cook-it-yourself Japanese hot pots.

NORTH END — Map pp210–12

At the more than 50 Italian eateries in this neighborhood, choices range from traditional spaghetti and meatballs served on red-checkered tablecloths to chic contemporary restaurants.

Artu (☎ 617-523-3888; 6 Prince St; mains $8-12) A good-value choice for traditional Italian fare, this cozy spot serves pastas and grilled meats.

La Piccola Venezia (☎ 617-523-3888; 263 Hanover St; mains $10-14) This old-timer consistently provides great value with huge portions of old-fashioned Italian dishes.

Salumeria Italiana (☎ 617-523-8743; 151 Richmond St) This is a really atmospheric market selling prosciutto, salami, cheese, bread and olives.

Regina Pizzeria (☎ 617-227-0765; 11½ Thatcher St; large pizzas $11-17) Here you'll find some of Boston's best thin-crust pizza.

Caffè Vittoria (☎ 617-227-7606; 296 Hanover St; coffee $2-4) Serves up espresso and old-world charm.

BACK BAY Map p207

Tapeo (☎ 617-267-4799; 266 Newbury St; tapas $4-8.50, mains $16-24) This lively spot offers a wonderful list of tapas and other Spanish fare, and has prime sidewalk tables in summer.

Bhindi Bazaar (☎ 617-450-0660; 95 Massachusetts Ave; lunches $7-8, dinners $11-14) For regional dishes from across India, try this classy restaurant just off Newbury St.

Sonsie (☎ 617-351-2500; 327 Newbury St; lunches $7-15, dinners $15-24) With tables facing the street, this is one of the trendiest place to sip a cappuccino. The eclectic international cuisine is tasty, too.

Other Side Cosmic Café (☎ 617-536-9477; 407 Newbury St; lunches $5-7) This grunge café serves juices, coffee and sandwiches with a funky, Seattle-inspired style.

SOUTH END

The South End is hip restaurant central and an especially popular destination for weekend brunch.

Franklin Café (Map pp210-12; ☎ 617-350-0010; 278 Shawmut Ave; mains $13-16) In a relaxed neighborhood-bar setting, this perpetually packed hangout serves updated comfort food until 1:30am.

Tremont 647 (Map pp210-12; ☎ 617-266-4600; 647 Tremont St; brunches $7-9, dinners $17-24) You really can wear your PJs for the Sunday pajama brunch at this funky contemporary restaurant – the staff does, too.

Bob the Chef's Jazz Café (Map p207; ☎ 617-536-6204; 604 Columbus Ave; mains $9-15) This is the place for down-home soul food – barbecued ribs or fried chicken with sides of collard greens and black-eyed peas. There's a jazz brunch, too.

HOW TO EAT A LOBSTER

Eating lobster is a messy pleasure. The best place to go is an informal eatery called a lobster 'pound' or 'pool,' where you can tear them apart with your fingers. You'll get a plastic bib, a metal cracker, melted butter for dipping the meat, a dish for the shells and lots of napkins. Suck the meat out of the legs, crack the claws and eat the meat inside, then twist off the tail and fork out the meat in one piece.

Lobsters are cheapest during the summer harvest season; part of the catch is kept alive in saltwater pools for winter sale. Lobster pounds sell them cooked for about $10 apiece, restaurants for $12 to $40.

Morse Fish (Map pp210-12; ☎ 617-262-9375; 1401 Washington St; mains $6-12) This bare-bones fish market and take-out shop has been satisfying seafood seekers since 1903.

For top-notch, high-end dining ($75 to $100 for two), book a table at the contemporary French **Hamersley's Bistro** (Map pp210-12; ☎ 617-423-2700; 553 Tremont St) or the modern French-Italian **Caffe Umbra** (Map pp210-12; ☎ 617-867-0707; 1395 Washington St).

CAMBRIDGE

Garage (36 John F Kennedy St) In Harvard Sq, Garage contains a dozen fast food eateries, along with Vietnamese Pho Pasteur (see p217).

Veggie Planet (☎ 617-661-1513; 47 Palmer St, at Club Passim; mains $6-10) This place lures the earthy-crunchy crowd with vegetarian pizzas, soups and salads.

Mr & Mrs Bartley's Burger Cottage (☎ 617-354-6559; 1246 Massachusetts Ave) Harvard Sq's primo hamburger joint since the 1960s.

Café Pamplona (12 Bow St) For old-world ambience with your coffee.

Chez Henri (☎ 617-354-8980; 1 Shepard St, at Massachusetts Ave; bar menu $7-11, mains $21-27) This is a low-key but lively French-Cuban bistro; the bar is quite popular for *mojitos* (ultra-refreshing Cuban cocktails) and massive *cubano* (Cuban-style) sandwiches.

Drinking

Rack Billiard Club (Map pp210-12; ☎ 617-725-1051; 20 Clinton St) Near Faneuil Hall Marketplace, Rack Billiard Club is an upscale pool hall and bar.

Linwood Grill (Map p207; ☎ 617-247-8099; 81 Kilmarnock St) This is a Fenway mainstay for beer and BBQ.

Club Café (Map pp210-12; ☎ 617-536-0966; 209 Columbus Ave) A convivial South End bar and restaurant, Club Café caters to gays and lesbians.

Young professionals flock to upscale lounges to drink and socialize.

Dress up and try the Polynesian tiki lounge–style **Peking Tom's** (Map pp210-12; ☎ 617-482-6282; 25 Kingston St) downtown, or the New York–sophisticated **Saint** (Map pp210-12; ☎ 617-236-1134; 90 Exeter St) in the Back Bay.

Cambridge is swarming with good pubs.

John Harvard's Brew House (☎ 617-868-3585; 33 Dunster St) In Harvard Sq, this subterranean pub feels like an English pub.

Plough & Stars (Map p207; ☎ 617-441-3455; 912 Massachusetts Ave) Between Harvard and Central Sqs, this is but one of the city's friendly Irish bars.

Enormous Room (Map p207; ☎ 617-491-5550; 567 Massachusetts Ave) Decorated like a pasha's parlor, with Oriental rugs and plush pillows, this loungey bar in Central Sq is all the rage.

Burren (☎ 617-776-6896; 247 Elm St, Somerville) In trendy Davis Sq, this laid-back bar pours a good Guinness and hosts traditional Irish music.

Entertainment

Boston boasts an impressive variety of cultural attractions. For up-to-the-minute listings, buy Thursday's *Boston Globe* or Friday's *Boston Herald* or pick up the free weekly *Boston Phoenix*, the biweekly *Stuff @Night*, or its sassy biweekly competitor, the *Improper Bostonian*. Gay and lesbian travelers should check Bay Windows for up-to-the-minute information, since nights devoted to one sex or the other frequently change. Most bars close at 1am, clubs around 2am. Subway service is less frequent after 11pm and stops altogether at 12:30am.

Half-price tickets to same-day theater, dance, music, comedy and sporting events are sold for cash only (beginning at 11am) at the **Bostix** (Map pp210–12) kiosks next to **Faneuil Hall** (☎ 617-723-5181) and in **Copley Sq** (Dartmouth & Boylston Sts).

CINEMAS

Brattle Theater (☎ 617-876-6837; 40 Brattle St) In Harvard Sq; shows art and foreign films.

Harvard Film Archive (☎ 617-495-4700; 24 Quincy St) Housed in the Carpenter Center for the Visual Arts; screens a minimum of two films daily.

Kendall Square Cinema (Map p207; ☎ 617-494-9800; 1 Kendall Sq, Cambridge) Artsy films are shown on its nine screens; call for details.

Hatch Shell (☎ 617-727-9547; Charles River Esplanade; ⏲ dusk Fri late Jun-Aug) The City of Boston shows free movies under the stars here; bring a blanket and picnic.

DANCE CLUBS

Many clubs are along Lansdowne St near Kenmore Sq and the Fenway, but the Theater District (on tiny Boylston Place, between Tremont and Charles St, and on Tremont St near Stuart St) has some too. Cover varies widely, from free (if you arrive early) to around $15. Most clubs are open 10pm to 2am Friday and Saturday; call about other days.

Avalon (Map p207; ☎ 617-262-2424; 15 Lansdowne St) A huge club featuring house, techno, international and industrial dance music. Sunday night is popular with the gay crowd.

Axis (Map p207; ☎ 617-262-2437; 13 Lansdowne St) On Monday night everyone from the transgender community to drag queens converges here.

Bill's Bar (Map p207; ☎ 617-421-9678; 5½ Lansdowne St) Usually packed with students; on different nights, DJs spin classic rock, hip hop and reggae.

Roxy (Map pp210-12; ☎ 617-338-7699; 279 Tremont St) In the Theater District; plays Latin (Thursday), international (Friday), and house and Top 40 dance music (Saturday).

LIVE MUSIC

Cambridge has lots of music options.

Middle East (Map p207; ☎ 617-354-8238; 472 Massachusetts Ave) In Central Sq. Hosts emerging indie rock bands and hip-hop groups.

Man Ray (Map p207; ☎ 617-864-0400; 21 Brookline St) This is the city's most 'underground' club; kinky goth-central.

Cantab Lounge (Map p207; ☎ 617-354-2685; 738 Massachusetts Ave) Grungy and laid-back, plays good blues and bluegrass.

Club Passim (☎ 617-492-7679; 47 Palmer St) This venerable club has supported the early careers of notable folk artists such as Patty Larkin, Tracy Chapman and Jackson Browne.

Regattabar (☎ 617-661-5000; Charles Hotel, 1 Bennett St) This upscale bar hosts big-name jazz acts.

Johnny D's Uptown (☎ 617-776-2004; 17 Holland St) One of the best and most eclectic venues for rock, R & B and world music; in Somerville's Davis Sq.

Wally's Café (Map p207; ☎ 617-424-1408; 427 Massachusetts Ave) For traditional jazz, R & B, Latin and Cuban in Boston, stop by this gritty cafe.

Berklee Performance Center (Map p207; ☎ 617-747-2261; 136 Massachusetts Ave) Hosts impressive (and inexpensive) student and faculty jazz concerts.

PERFORMING ARTS

Wang Center (Map pp210-12; ☎ 617-482-9393; 270 Tremont St) This cavernous 1925 landmark hosts the Boston Ballet, modern dance, as well as opera and theater.

Charles Playhouse (Map pp210-12; 74 Warrenton St) Here you'll find the long-running comical whodunit mystery **Shear Madness** (☎ 617-426-5225) and the **Blue Man Group** (☎ 617-426-6912), mixed media performance art.

American Repertory Theater (A-R-T; ☎ 617-547-8300; 64 Brattle St, Cambridge) This prestigious company produces serious and experimental plays in Harvard Sq.

Huntington Theater Company (Map p207; ☎ 617-266-0800; 264 Huntington Ave) This professional repertory company is another source for high-quality drama.

Comedy Connection (Map pp210-12; ☎ 617-248-9700; Quincy Market) Hosts national and local comedy acts.

Symphony Hall (Map p207; ☎ 617-266-1492, tickets 266-1200; 301 Massachusetts Ave) Performing here are one of the world's best symphony orchestras and the beloved Boston Pops.

Many free summer concerts take place at the **Hatch Shell** (see p219); the Boston Pops' July 4th concert, complete with fireworks and brass cannons, is the most lavish and crowded. The **New England Conservatory of Music** (Map p207; ☎ 617-585-1122; Jordan Hall, 30 Gainsborough St) hosts free classical concerts by professors and students.

SPECTATOR SPORTS

Boston Red Sox (☎ 617-267-1700; 4 Yawkey Way; tickets $10-44) From April to September this major-league baseball team play at Fenway Park.

At the **Fleet Center** (150 Causeway St) from October to April, the NBA **Boston Celtics** (☎ 617-523-3030; tickets $10-85) play basketball and the NHL **Boston Bruins** (☎ 617-624-1000; tickets from $20) play ice hockey.

The NFL **New England Patriots** (☎ 800-543-1776) and MLS **New England Revolution** (☎ 877-438-7387) play football and soccer, respectively, in Foxboro Stadium, about 50 minutes south of Boston.

Shopping

Newbury St is chock-full of chic boutiques, upscale merchants and art galleries. But its renegade western end has used CD and clothing stores, condom shops and retro home goods. Charles St on Beacon Hill is lined with blue-blood antique stores and a smattering of intriguing newcomers. Shops in Downtown Crossing, a pedestrian zone that's enlivened with street performers and pushcart vendors, are geared to everyday needs such as shoes and music.

Filene's Basement (Map pp210-12; ☎ 617-542-2011; 426 Washington St) This bargain-hunter's paradise anchors the neighborhood. The South End, particularly along Clarendon and Tremont St, has a growing number of eclectic boutiques.

Out of Left Field (Map pp210-12; ☎ 617-722-9401) Sells local sports memorabilia.

Copley Place (100 Huntington Ave) and the **Shops at the Pru** (Map p207; 800 Boylston St), both in Back Bay, are luxe indoor malls.

Most independent Harvard Sq shops have been supplanted by the likes of the Gap and HMV, but it's still fun to walk around. For more eclectic shopping, take the Red Line two stops past Harvard to Somerville's hip Davis Sq, where cool gift shops and coffeehouses stand side-by-side with neighborhood butchers and pizza joints.

Getting There & Away

Since Boston is the region's hub, getting in and out of town is easy. The train and bus stations are adjacent, and the airport is a short subway ride away.

AIR

Logan International Airport (☎ 800-235-6426), in East Boston just across Boston Harbor from the city center, is served by all major US airlines and many foreign ones. It has currency-exchange booths, as well as a traveler's aid booth.

BOAT

Bay State Cruises (☎ 617-748-1428) operates boats from Commonwealth Pier in South Boston to Provincetown at the tip of Cape Cod.

BUS

Boston's main bus station is in **South Station** (Map pp210-12; 700 Atlantic Ave, at Summer St). **Bonanza Bus Lines** (☎ 617-720-4110) serves western Massachusetts; Hyannis and Falmouth on Cape Cod; Providence, Rhode Island; and New York and Albany, New York. **Greyhound** (☎ 617-526-1808) departs for New York throughout the day (from $20, from 4½ hours), as well as New Haven ($29, from 3½ hours) and Hartford ($23, from 2¼ hours), Connecticut; Albany, New York ($32, from 3½ hours); and Newark, New Jersey ($42, from 5½ hours). Several discount bus services operate between the Chinatowns in Boston and New York City; fares frequently dip to $20 or less each way; the largest operator is the **Fung Wah Bus Company** (Map pp210-12; ☎ 617-338-1163; www.fungwahbus.com; 68 Beach St).

Plymouth & Brockton (☎ 508-746-0378) provides frequent services to most Cape Cod towns, including Hyannis ($14, 1½ hours) and Provincetown ($23, three hours). **Peter Pan Bus Lines** (☎ 617-946-0960) serves Amherst, the Berkshires, Springfield, Hartford, New Haven and New York. **Concord Trailways** (☎ 800-639-3317) run from Boston to New Hampshire, as well as Portland and Bangor, Maine. **Vermont Transit** (☎ 800-522-8737) links Boston with Manchester and Concord in New Hampshire, Portland and Bar Harbor in Maine, and many Vermont destinations.

CAR & MOTORCYCLE

Most national car rental companies have offices at the airport, and many have locations around town as well. Check the Transport chapter (p1121) for details.

Bear in mind that driving in Boston is confusing – with many narrow, one way streets and very aggressive drivers – and that parking is difficult and expensive. It's almost always better to stick to public transportation within the city. If you're traveling onward by rental car, pick up your car at the end of your Boston visit.

TRAIN

The **Amtrak** (Map pp210-12; ☎ 617-345-7460, 800-872-7245) terminus is at South Station on Atlantic Ave and Summer St; most Amtrak trains also stop at the Back Bay Station on Dartmouth St. Trains to New York cost $64 to $76 (four hours) or from $99 on the Acela Express (three hours). **MBTA Commuter Rail** (☎ 617-222-3200) trains from Boston's North Station serve cities west and north of Boston, including Concord, Salem and Gloucester.

> **THE BIG DIG**
>
> The depression of Boston's Central Artery highway and creation of a third harbor tunnel connecting downtown to the airport is the country's biggest public works project – $14 billion and continually rising. New roadways have been opening in sections – the Ted Williams airport tunnel, the soaring Leonard P Zakim Bunker Hill Bridge linking downtown and Charlestown, and segments of the underground highway are up and running – but traffic continues to be nightmarish as roads and ramps near the waterfront are moved frequently. Officially, and perhaps optimistically, slated for completion in late 2004, the project has been likened to performing open-heart surgery on someone while they are running a marathon. When it's done, the city plans to create parklands where the raised highway currently stands. In the meantime, you can peer into stories-deep caverns near the North End, South Station and South Boston.

Getting Around

Logan Airport is reachable via the T Blue Line to the Airport station ($1). Free shuttle buses (Nos 22 and 33) connect the subway with all terminals. A water shuttle ($10) also runs between the airport and Rowes Wharf, near the Boston Harbor Hotel. A taxi to/from the city costs $17 to $25; taxis from the airport add $6 in tolls and fees to the meter fare.

The **MBTA** (☎ 617-222-3200; adult $1, child 5-11 50¢) operates the USA's oldest subway (the 'T'), begun in 1897. Four color-coded lines – Red, Blue, Green and Orange – radiate from the system hub at Park St and neighboring Downtown Crossing and Government Center stations. 'Inbound' trains are headed for these three stations, 'outbound' trains away from them. Trains operate from 5:30am to 12:30am. Tourist passes ($6 per day, $11 for three days, $22 per week) for unlimited travel are sold at Airport, North Station, South Station, Back Bay, Copley, Government Center and Hynes, as well as Bostix booths in Faneuil Hall and Copley Sq.

Taxis are plentiful; expect to pay about $7 to $9 for a short ride downtown, $15 to $20 from Back Bay to Harvard Sq. Flag taxis on the street, find them at major hotels or call **Metro Cab** (☎ 617-242-8000) or **Checker Taxi** (☎ 617-497-9000).

There are bike paths on both sides of the Charles River that extend from Beacon Hill west to suburban Watertown. If you're riding on city streets, be extra careful. **Community Bicycle Supply** (Map pp210-12; ☎ 617-542-8623; 496 Tremont St; per 2hr/day $10/20), in the South End, rents mountain and hybrid bikes. **Boston Bike Tours** (Map pp210–12, see p215) also rents bikes ($10/20 2hr/day).

AROUND BOSTON

Boston is surrounded with historic towns that are quite easily explored in a day trip.

Information

Concord Chamber of Commerce (☎ 978-369-3120; www.concordmachamber.org; 100 Main St, Concord)
Destination Plymouth (☎ 508-747-7533; www.visit-plymouth.com; 170 Water St, Plymouth)
North of Boston Convention & Visitors Bureau (☎ 978-977-7760; www.northofboston.org; 17 Peabody Sq, Peabody)

Lexington & Concord

About 15 miles northwest of Boston, the colonial town of Lexington is where the first battle of the Revolutionary War took place in April 1775. After the battle, the British redcoats marched 10 miles west to Concord where they fought the American minuteman at the town's North Bridge – the first American victory. The **Minute Man National Historic Park** (☎ 978-369-6993; www.nps.gov/mima; visitors centers, MA 2A, Lexington & 174 Liberty St, Concord; admission free; 🕑 9am-5pm mid-Apr–Sep, 9am-4pm Oct–mid-Apr) has detailed information, including a first-rate multimedia presentation, about these 1775 events.

In the 19th century, Concord was a vibrant literary community. Next to the North Bridge is the **Old Manse**, former home of author Nathaniel Hawthorne. Within a mile northeast of Concord's Monument Sq, the center of town, are the **Ralph Waldo Emerson house**, Louisa May Alcott's **Orchard House** and the **Wayside**, where Alcott's *Little Women* was set. The **Concord Museum** has informative exhibits about the town's Revolutionary and literary past. **Walden Pond**, where Henry David Thoreau lived and wrote *Walden*, is 3 miles south of Monument Sq; you can visit his cabin and swim in the pond. Contact the Concord Chamber of Commerce for details.

Salem & the North Shore

Salem, 14 miles northeast of Boston, is known for the 1692 witch hysteria, when 19 people were put to death for witchcraft (see opposite). **Destination Salem** (☎ 877-725-3662; www.salem.org; 63 Wharf St) has some information about the town's 'witchy' attractions, many of which are a bit hokey. More serious is the Salem Maritime National Historic Site, which details Salem's past as a maritime power, and the nearby House of Seven Gables, from Nathaniel Hawthorne's book of the same name. Salem also has the Peabody Essex Museum, which examines the town's maritime history and focuses on the art and furnishings these traders brought back from their expeditions to Asia.

Farther north along the coast is the region known as Cape Ann, centered around the fishing port of **Gloucester**, which was founded in 1623. Follow the Maritime Trail around town, visit the Rocky Neck Artists' Colony, explore the quirky elegance of the early-20th-century Beauport Mansion and of Hammond Castle Museum, the palatial former home of an eccentric but brilliant inventor. Several companies offer whale-watching cruises, too. Get details from the **Cape Ann Chamber of Commerce** (☎ 978-283-1601; www.capeannvacations.com; 33 Commercial St, Gloucester).

Just north of Gloucester, seaside **Rockport** is much favored by 19th-century painters and 21st-century tourists. Walk out onto Bearskin Neck for quaint shops or around Halibut Point State Park for dramatic views of the sea.

Off I-95 just south of the New Hampshire border is **Newburyport**, a pretty town with a restored downtown district (with lots of good restaurants) and streets lined with Federal-style former sea captain's homes. One of the area's nicest beaches, Plum Island, is also here. The **Greater Newburyport**

SALEM WITCH TRIALS

In the late 17th century it was widely believed that one could make a pact with the devil to gain evil powers. When a number of girls in Salem began behaving strangely in early 1692, their parents believed that the devil had come to their village. The girls accused a slave named Tituba of being a witch. Tituba 'confessed' under torture and then accused two others to save her own life. Soon accusations flew thick and fast, as the accused implicated others in attempts to save themselves.

When a special court convened to deal with the accusations, its justices accepted 'spectral evidence,' evidence of 'spirits' seen only by witnesses. With imaginations and religious passions inflamed, the situation careened out of control. By September 1692, 156 people stood accused, 55 people had pleaded guilty, and 14 women and five men who would not 'confess' to witchcraft had been hanged. Giles Corey, who refused to plead either way, was weighted down with stones and pressed to death.

The frenzy died down when the accusers began pointing at prominent merchants, clergy and the governor's wife. With the powers-that-be in jeopardy, the trials were called off and the remaining accused were released.

Chamber of Commerce (☎ 978-462-6680; www.newburyportchamber.org; 38R Merrimac St, Newburyport) has information.

Plymouth

The *Mayflower* set sail from Plymouth, England, in late summer 1620, bound for New York harbor. Carrying 102 passengers, some animals, tools, seed, household effects and foodstuffs, it was blown onto Cape Cod instead. By December the Pilgrims had found their way to Plymouth, about 40 miles south of present-day Boston, and decided to stay.

Today, travelers make the pilgrimage to **Plimoth Plantation** (☎ 508-746-1622; www.plimoth.org; Warren Ave/MA 3A; adult $22, child 5-11 $14; 🕑 9am-5pm Apr-Nov) – an authentically re-created 1627 Pilgrim village, complete with 'Pilgrims,' actors who meticulously maintain the characters of the 17th-century inhabitants. If you're traveling with kids, or if you're a history buff, don't miss it. In the center of town, about 3 miles from the Plantation, is the *Mayflower II*, a replica of the ship, and Plymouth Rock, the supposed point where the Pilgrims came ashore.

Getting There & Away

MBTA Commuter Rail (☎ 617-222-3200) trains from North Station serve Concord, Salem, Gloucester, Rockport and Newburyport. **Plymouth & Brockton buses** (☎ 508-746-0378) travel to Plymouth from Boston's South Station.

CAPE COD

This 65-mile-long peninsula and the neighboring islands of Nantucket and Martha's Vineyard are among the region's top vacation destinations. Attractions include well-preserved historic towns, fresh seafood, long beaches and good walking and biking. Summer is the most popular time to visit (and prices are highest), though the weather in late spring and early fall can be quite balmy. Many places close from November until March or April; call first. At any time of year, accommodations are cheapest midweek.

Information

The **Cape Cod Regional Chamber of Commerce** (☎ 508-759-3814, 888-332-2732; www.capecodchamber.org; MA 6 at MA 132; 🕑 9am-5pm Mon-Sat, 10am-4pm Sun) provides information on all the Cape towns; their website lists lodging availability.

Sandwich

It may be a cliché, but the Cape's oldest village is a picture-perfect New England town.

SIGHTS & ACTIVITIES

Sandwich was a glass-making center in the 1800s, a heritage that's colorfully displayed in the small **Sandwich Glass Museum** (☎ 508-888-0251; www.sandwichglassmuseum.org; 129 Main St; adult $3.50, child 5-11 $1; 🕑 9:30am-5pm Apr-Dec, 9:30am-4pm Feb-Mar, closed Jan).

Heritage Museums & Gardens (☎ 508-888-3300; www.heritagemuseumsandgardens.org; Grove St; adult $12, child 5-11 $6; 🕑 9am-6pm Fri-Wed, 9am-8pm Thu May-Oct, 10am-4pm Tue-Sun Nov-Dec, call for hr Jan-Apr) Set on a 76-acre estate, this complex of museums appeals to history buffs. One museum is devoted to American history,

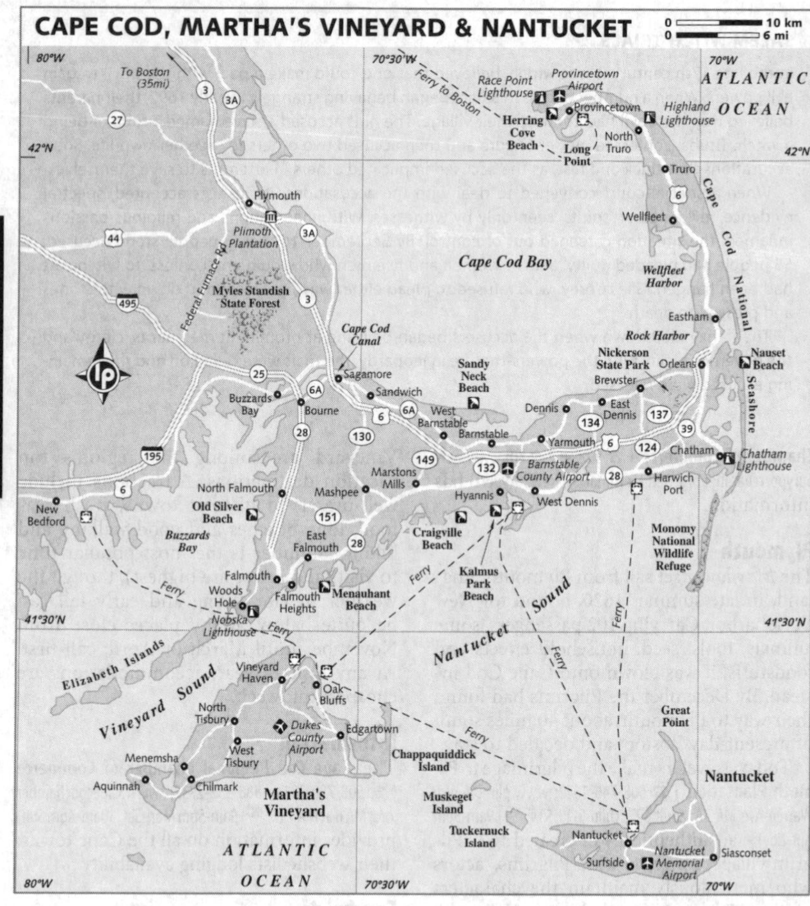

one to art and one to automobiles. The extensive gardens are a pleasant spot for a stroll or a picnic.

You can watch the miller at work at **Dexter Gristmill** (☎ 508-888-4910; Water St; adult $3, child 5-11 $1.50; 10am-4:45pm Tue-Sat late Jun–mid-Oct), constructed in 1654 (and rebuilt in 1961) by a picturesque pond in the town center.

East of town, **Green Briar Nature Center** (☎ 508-888-6870; 6 Discovery Hill Rd, off MA 6A; 10am-4pm Mon-Sat, 1-4pm Sun, closed Sun-Mon Jan-Mar) has walking trails and an old-fashioned jam kitchen.

Giving Tree (☎ 508-888-5446; 550 MA 6A, East Sandwich), about 5 miles east of the town center, this art gallery, crafts shop and nature garden is a peaceful spot to browse.

On the Sandwich–Barnstable town line, **Sandy Neck Beach** (☎ 508-362-8300; Sandy Neck Rd, off MA 6A; P $10) is a 6-mile dune-backed beach with the most beautiful stretch of sand on the Cape's bay side.

SLEEPING & EATING

Spring Garden Inn (☎ 508-888-0710, 800-303-1751; www.springgarden.com; 578 MA 6A, East Sandwich; d $89-125;) Facing a broad lawn and a salt marsh, this family-friendly motel about 5 miles east of the town center has eight knotty-pine-walled rooms and three efficiencies.

Shawme Crowell State Forest (☎ 508-888-0351, 877-422-7662; off MA 130; campsites $12), 2 miles from the center, has 285 campsites, while **Scusset Beach State Reservation** (☎ 508-888-0859,

877-422-7662; Scusset Beach Rd; campsites/RV sites $15/20), on the mainland side of the Cape Cod canal, has 98 RV sites and five campsites.

Dunbar Tea Room (☎ 508-833-2485; 1 Water St; lunches $7-10) Serves light lunches and authentic British tea in a cute little house.

Falmouth & Woods Hole

Falmouth is the Cape's second-largest town, with a quintessential village green, historic homes and nature preserves. Some sections are surprisingly suburban, too, with many year-round residents.

INFORMATION

The **Falmouth Chamber of Commerce** (☎ 508-548-8500, 800-526-8532; www.falmouth-capecod.com; 20 Academy Lane; 9am-5pm Mon-Fri, also 9am-5pm Sat late May–mid-Oct) has information.

SIGHTS & ACTIVITIES

The popular **Old Silver Beach** (off MA 28A, North Falmouth; P $10) is long and sandy. It fronts Buzzards Bay, so the water is calm. Facing Nantucket Sound in a residential East Falmouth neighborhood, another good sun-worshipping option is sandy **Menauhant Beach** (Menauhant Rd, off MA 28, East Falmouth; P $10). It's sometimes a bit less crowded than other Falmouth-area beaches.

With eventual views of the coastline and **Nobska Light**, the flat, 3.5-mile **Shining Sea Bike Path** heads south to oh-so-picturesque Woods Hole. **Corner Cycle** (☎ 508-540-4195; 115 Palmer Ave), located two blocks from the Shining Sea Trail, rents bicycles ($8/18 hour/day), including children's bikes ($5/14 hour/day).

Woods Hole is the departure point for Martha's Vineyard ferries and home of the **Woods Hole Oceanographic Institution** (☎ 508-289-2663; www.whoi.edu), one of the world's largest independent marine research facilities. You can learn about the institution's work at the kid-friendly **WHOI Exhibit Center** (☎ 508-289-2252; 15 School St; adult $2, child 5-11 free; call for hr Apr-Dec, closed Jan-Mar).

SLEEPING & EATING

Elm Arch Inn (☎ 508-548-0133; www.elmarchinn.com; 26 Elm Arch Way; d $95-135;) Though it's just off Main St, this inn has plenty of green space, with tall trees and an expansive lawn. Inside are 20 old-fashioned rooms.

Woods Hole Passage B&B (☎ 508-548-9575, 800-790-8976; www.woodsholepassage.com; 186 Woods Hole Rd, Woods Hole; with breakfast d $125-165;) Convivial owner Deb Pruitt makes this B&B a welcoming spot. On the main road from Falmouth to Woods Hole, its five rooms are in a renovated carriage house and adjacent barn.

Captain Tom Lawrence House (☎ 508-540-1445, 800-266-8139; www.captaintomlawrence.com; 75 Locust St; with breakfast d $140-175;) Close to the town center, this sea captain's home-turned-B&B has six comfortable Victorian-style rooms with frilly curtains and floral comforters. An efficiency apartment accommodates families ($195 to $210).

Sippewisset Family Campground (☎ 508-548-2542; www.sippewissett.com; 836 Palmer Ave, off MA 28; campsites/RV sites $31/33) Two miles north of the center, this campground with about 100 sites is mostly for RVs, but has some tent sites, too.

Fishmonger Café (☎ 508-540-5376; 56 Water St, Woods Hole; mains $9-23) For great waterfront seafood, head to this cool Woods Hole spot, where the international menu also treats vegetarians well.

Clam Shack (☎ 508-540-7758; 227 Clinton Ave; mains $5-12) Right on Falmouth Harbor, this in-the-rough shack serves fried clams and other traditional Cape seafood.

SHOPPING

Falmouth's Main St has lots of boutiques and shops.

Eight Cousins Children's Books (☎ 508-548-5548; 189 Main St) Browse here if you've brought kids.

Handworks (☎ 508-540-5291; 68 Water St) Check out the contemporary crafts in this Woods Hole shop.

GETTING THERE & AWAY

Bonanza Bus Lines (☎ 800-556-3815) serve Falmouth and Woods Hole from Boston (Falmouth $16, Woods Hole $17, 1½ hours), New York ($49, six hours) and Providence, Rhode Island ($20, two hours). The Steamship Authority's car and passenger **ferries** (☎ 508-477-8600) make the 45-minute sail from Woods Hole to Martha's Vineyard.

Hyannis

Cape Cod's commercial hub has lots of motels, varied restaurants and a bustling waterfront. It's also the summer home of the Kennedy clan; visit the **John F Kennedy Hyannis Museum** (☎ 508-790-3077; 397 Main St;

adult $5, child 5-11 $2.50; 9am-5pm Mon-Sat, noon-5pm Sun mid-Apr–Oct, 10am-4pm Thu-Sat, noon-4pm Sun Nov-Dec & mid-Feb–mid-Apr), which is filled with photos of the USA's 35th president and his family. To explore by water, take a sightseeing cruise with **Hyannisport Harbor Cruises** (☎ 508-778-2600; Ocean St docks; adult $12, child 5-11 $6; daily mid-Apr–Oct) or rent a kayak from **Eastern Mountain Sports** (☎ 508-362-8690; 1513 MA 132; per day $40-50). **Kalmus Park Beach** (Ocean St; P $10) is popular for sunning and windsurfing, while **Craigville Beach** (Craigville Beach Rd, off MA 28, Centerville; P $10) draws the college set and families.

SLEEPING & EATING

Sea Breeze Inn (☎ 508-771-7213; www.seabreezeinn.com; 270 Ocean Ave; with breakfast d $80-140;) With 13 cozy, quilt-bedecked rooms, this B&B is a hop, skip and a jump from the beach.

Anchor-In (☎ 508-775-0357; 1 South St; d $89-199, ste $169-349;) This family-friendly 43-room motel has a convenient harborside location near the ferry docks.

RooBar City Bistro (☎ 508-778-6515; 586 Main St; mains $10-25) Hyannis's hippest restaurant serves creative New American fusion dinners and has a happening bar scene.

Brazilian Grill (☎ 508-771-0109; 680 Main St; mains $6-15) Carnivores on a budget head for this authentic *churrascaria* (Brazilian-style barbecue) for tasty all-you-can-eat grilled meats.

Baxter's (☎ 508-775-4490; 177 Pleasant St; mains $8-20) This fish house is largely about the location (harborside) and the scene (singles), but it cooks up the standard fried and broiled seafood.

Spiritus (☎ 508-775-2955; 500 Main St; mains under $5) Serves excellent pizza, focaccia sandwiches and strong coffee.

Prodigal Son (☎ 508-771-1337; 10 Ocean St) Live folk music or blues served with microbrews and coffees at this bohemian venue.

GETTING THERE & AWAY

Plymouth & Brockton (☎ 508-778-9767; www.p-b.com) runs frequent buses to Boston ($14, 1¾ hours) as well as Provincetown ($9, 1¾ hours). **Bonanza Bus Lines** (☎ 800-556-3815) serve Providence, Rhode Island ($20, two hours) and New York ($49, six hours). Buses depart from the **Hyannis Transportation Center** (Barnstable Rd at Main St). The **Steamship Authority** (☎ 508-477-8600; South St docks) runs ferries to Nantucket.

Brewster

On the Cape's bay side, this little town is a pleasant base for outdoorsy types. The 2000-acre oasis of **Nickerson State Park** (☎ 508-896-3491; MA 6A) has it all: ponds with sandy beaches, boating, biking and walking trails. The **Cape Cod Rail Trail**, a 25-mile paved bike path, passes by the park. The trail begins in Dennis on MA 134, just south of MA 6, and continues to South Wellfleet; the Cape Cod Chamber of Commerce has maps.

The **Cape Cod Museum of Natural History** (☎ 508-896-3867; www.ccmnh.org; 869 MA 6A; adult $7, child 5-11 free; 9:30am-4:30pm Mon-Sat, 11am-4:30pm Sun) has exhibits about the area's flora and fauna, as well as several pleasant nature trails.

The 19th-century **Stony Brook Grist Mill** (☎ 508-896-6745; 830 Stony Brook Rd; admission free; 2-5pm Thu-Sat May-Jun, 2-5pm Fri Jul-Aug) still grinds corn. In the spring, thousands of herring migrate through the nearby the **Herring Run**. The old-fashioned **Brewster Store** (☎ 508-896-3744; 1935 MA 6A) has been operating since 1866.

Once a girls' school, spick-and-span **Old Sea Pines Inn** (☎ 508-896-6114, 2553 MA 6A; d $75-150, ste $135-165;) rents 24 rooms, 19 with private bath. White chenille spreads and floral wallpaper give the rooms a comfortably old-fashioned feel. The larger units accommodate families.

Nickerson State Park (☎ 877-422-6762; campsites $15) has 420 popular, wooded campsites; reserve early. Or try the 100 sites at **Shady Knoll Campground** (☎ 508-896-3002; 1709 MA 6A, at MA 137; campsites/RV sites $33/43).

Just off the Cape Cod Rail Trail, **Cobie's** (☎ 508-896-7021; 3260 MA 6A; mains $4-13) is a little place with good fried seafood and outdoor picnic tables.

Brewster Fish House (☎ 508-896-7867; 2208 MA 6A; lunches $9-14, dinners $18-28) is a frequently jammed seafooder; you might find herb-roasted monkfish, cod with lemon fettuccine, or other creative fish dishes.

Chatham

Chatham is among the Cape's prettiest towns, lined with sea captain's houses, manicured lawns, tony lodgings and lots of shoreline. Visit the 1878 **Chatham Light** (Shore Rd) and **Monomoy Island**, an offshore bird sanctuary accessible only by boat. Contact the **Monomoy Island Ferry Rip Ryder** (☎ 508-945-5450) to take you to the island and secluded beach, or take a tour run by the **Wellfleet Bay Wildlife Sanctuary** (☎ 508-349-2615).

Monomoy Theatre (☎ 508-945-1589; 776 Main St, MA 28) hosts summer productions by the Ohio University Players. Friday-night summertime band concerts in **Kate Gould Park** (Main St; admission free) are nostalgia-in-the-making.

Chatham Highlander (☎ 508-945-9038; www.realmass.com/highlander; 946 MA 28; d $115-155;) has 28 spotless rooms and two pools; this family-friendly motel is a short walk to the town center.

Port Fortune (☎ 508-945-0792, 800-750-0792; www.portfortuneinn.com; 201 Main St; with breakfast d $135-210, ste $205-250;) has 12 rooms, many outfitted with four-poster beds and mahogany armoires. It's set in two gray-shingled buildings with a prime location across from the lighthouse and the beach.

In summer, try the alfresco **Beach House Grill** (☎ 508-945-0096; Shore Rd; lunches $7-16), opposite its regal parent Chatham Bars Inn, for casual lunchtime seafood and sandwiches.

Townsfolk appreciate the low-key **Chatham Squire** (☎ 508-945-0945; 487 Main St; lunches $5-13, dinners $15-23) for its varied menu that rambles from fried fish to lobster ravioli to beef tenderloin. After dark the tavern gets boisterous.

Eastham

In 1620 the Pilgrims first encountered Native Americans at Eastham's First Encounter Beach. Most modern-day pilgrims zoom through Eastham, but a few stop to see the set of huge whalebones in front of the **Edward Penniman House** (☎ 508-255-3421; Fort Hill Rd; admission free; generally 1-4pm Jun-Aug). You can tour this former sea captain's house, too, but call ahead for the schedule.

Rent bikes at **Little Capistrano Bike Shop** (☎ 508-255-6515; 341 Salt Pond Rd; 2hr/day $10/20), opposite the Salt Pond Visitors Center (see p227), and follow the bike path across a tranquil salt marsh and forest to Coast Guard Beach. Here you can hop onto the 25-mile Cape Cod Rail Trail. Farther north, **Nauset Light Beach** (P $10) is prime.

Midway Motel & Cottages (☎ 508-255-3117, 800-755-3117; www.midwaymotel.com; MA 6, North Eastham; d $89-112) has nice, quiet motel rooms. **HI Mid-Cape Hostel** (☎ 508-255-2785, 888-901-2085; 75 Goody Hallet Dr; dm $18-24) rents 50 beds from mid-May to mid-September; reservations are essential. **Atlantic Oaks Campground** (☎ 508-255-1437; 3700 MA 6; campsites/RV sites $33/50) has 100 shady campsites.

First Encounter Coffee House (☎ 508-255-5438; 220 Samoset Rd; tickets $10-15) holds folksy concerts twice a month.

Cape Cod National Seashore

Covering more than 42 sq miles, the **Cape Cod National Seashore** (CCNS; www.nps.gov/caco) includes most of the eastern shoreline from Chatham to Provincetown. It's known for beaches, crashing waves, dunes, nature trails, ponds, salt marshes and forests. Everything of interest is on or just off MA 6, the only highway from the Orleans rotary (traffic circle) to Provincetown. The **Salt Pond Visitors Center** (☎ 508-255-3421; Nauset Rd, at MA 6, Eastham; 9am-4:30pm) has exhibits, films and nature walks explaining the Cape's history and landscape. The **Province Lands Visitors Center** (☎ 508-487-1256; Race Point Rd, Provincetown; 9am-5pm May-Oct) has similar services and information.

NEW ENGLAND

Wellfleet

Visitors dine on famous Wellfleet oysters, enjoy fine beaches and hike in the **Wellfleet Bay Wildlife Sanctuary** (☎ 508-349-2615; www.wellfleetbay.org; West Rd, off MA 6; adult $5, child 5-11 $3; 8:30am-5pm daily late May–mid-Oct, 9am-4:30pm Tue-Sun mid-Oct–mid-May), 1000 acres of tidal creeks, salt marshes, forest and beach. **Marconi Beach** (P $10), on the Atlantic within the National Seashore, is broad and seemingly unending.

More than 20 Wellfleet art galleries host receptions on summer Saturday evenings. At dusk, park at **Wellfleet Drive-In** (☎ 508-349-7176; MA 6; adult $7, child 5-11 $4), one of a dwindling number of drive-in cinemas left in the USA. The **Wellfleet Flea Market** (☎ 508-349-2520; MA 6; per car $2; 7am-4pm Wed, Thu, Sat & Sun in summer, Sat & Sun only in spring & fall), at the Wellfleet Drive-In, is the Cape's biggest trading fest. **Wellfleet Harbor Actors Theater** (☎ 508-349-6835; 1 Kendrick Ave; tickets $21) produces thoughtful experimental theater.

SLEEPING

Inn at Duck Creeke (☎ 508-349-9333; www.innatduckcreeke.com; 70 Main St; d $75-110;) Within walking distance of town, this inn has 25 simple rooms with shared or private bath.

Holden Inn (☎ 508-349-3450; www.theholdeninn.com; 140 Commercial St; s $53, d $70-80) These 26 spartan rooms, many of which have shared bath, haven't changed much since the 1920s.

Maurice's Campground (☎ 508-349-2029; 80 MA 6; campsites/RV sites/cabins $27/34/80) Just north of the Eastham–Wellfleet line, this campground allots about half of its 180 sites to tents.

EATING & DRINKING

Moby Dick's (☎ 508-349-9795; MA 6, opposite Gull Pond Rd; mains $8-20) Melville would have enjoyed the seafood at this popular spot that serves up fried clams, scallops, fish-and-chips and chowder.

Captain Higgins Seafood Restaurant (☎ 508-349-6027; Town Pier; mains $13-22) Try this seafooder for Wellfleet oysters and other fare from the deep.

Beachcomber (☎ 508-349-6055; Cahoon Hollow Beach, Ocean View Dr) This former lifesaving station currently serves as a cool bar for bronzed 20-somethings.

Truro

There are good bayside and Atlantic beaches here, as well as two noteworthy small sites. In North Truro, **Cape Cod Light** (Highland Light; ☎ 508-487-1121; off South Highland Rd; tours $3; 10am-5:45 May-Oct) shines the brightest light on the New England coastline. Next door, the old **Highland House Museum** (☎ 508-487-3397; adult $3, child 5-11 free; 10am-4:30pm Jun-Sep) is dedicated to the area's maritime and agrarian roots.

HI Truro (☎ 508-349-3889, 888-901-2085; North Pamet Rd, North Truro; dm $20-24) has 42 dorm beds in a former Coast Guard Station dramatically sited amid dunes and marshes. It's open mid-June through August and reservations are essential. High on a bluff above the sea, **Adrian's** (☎ 508-487-4360; 535 MA 6; breakfasts $5-8, dinners $10-25) excels at Italian fare, brick-oven pizzas and breakfast dishes such as *huevos rancheros*.

Provincetown

Provincetown is the funky end of the Cape – a mecca for tourists and artists, with an active gay scene. Your first impression is likely to be of the carnival atmosphere along Commercial St, the town's main drag (where you'll undoubtedly see a queen or two), but your memories may be of a walk across the dunes or a bike ride through ocean-edged forest.

Commercial St runs parallel to the shoreline. MacMillan Wharf sits in the center.

INFORMATION

The **Provincetown Chamber of Commerce** (☎ 508-487-3424; www.ptownchamber.com; 305 Commercial St, at MacMillan Wharf; 9am-5pm late Jun–early Sep, 10am-4pm May–late-Jun & early Sep–mid-Oct, call for winter hr) provides information for visitors.

SIGHTS & ACTIVITIES

Provincetown is known for its art scene. Dating from 1914, the **Provincetown Art Association & Museum** (☎ 508-487-1750; www.paam.org; 460 Commercial St; adult $5, child 5-11 free; daily late May–Sep, weekends only Oct–late May, call for hr) ranks among the country's best small museums. Galleries around town generally hold openings Friday evening.

The Pilgrims first set foot on American soil in 1620 at Provincetown, anchoring here for five weeks in search of abundant freshwater and fertile ground. Finding neither, they sailed on to Plymouth. The **Pilgrim Monument & Provincetown Museum** (☎ 508-487-1310; www.pilgrim-monument.org; High Pole Rd; adult $7, child 5-11 $3; 9am-4:15pm Apr-Nov, 9am-6:15pm Jul-Aug) commemorates their time in Provincetown. Climb the 116 stairs and 60 ramps for a panoramic view of town and sea – on a clear day you can see Boston.

Between mid-April and October, several companies offer whale-watching cruises from Macmillan Wharf. Try the 3½-hour cruise by **Dolphin Fleet Whale Watch** (☎ 508-349-1900, 800-826-9300; adult $22, child 5-11 $19). **Art's Dune Tours** (☎ 508-487-1950, 800-894-1951; Commercial and Standish Sts; adult $12, child 5-11 $8) runs hour-long 4WD tours along the beach; reservations are required for the 1½-hour sunset trip (adult $15, child five to 11 $10).

Race Point Beach has pounding surf; **Herring Cove Beach** is calmer, with spectacular sunsets. Rent a bike ($16 to $19 a day) from **Arnold's** (☎ 508-487-0844; 329 Commercial St) or **Galeforce Bicycle & Beach Market** (☎ 508-487-4849; 144 Bradford St Extension) to ride to the beach or explore the 7 miles of paved CCNS bicycling trails.

SLEEPING

Provincetown has nearly 100 inns and guesthouses. In summer most require minimum stays and fill up well in advance. If you don't have a reservation, arrive early and ask the chamber of commerce for help. Most lodgings offer steep discounts off-season, and many close for the winter; call for exact rates and dates.

Fairbanks Inn (☎ 508-487-0386; www.fairbanksinn.com; 90 Bradford St; with breakfast d $99-155; P) The 14 rooms at this antique-filled B&B are nicely furnished with 1770s details; the least expensive rooms share baths.

White Horse Inn (☎ 508-487-1790; 500 Commercial St; d $70-80, ste $125-140) Quirky and bohemian, this inn rents 12 spartan rooms, many with shared bath, and six artsy, airy studio apartments.

Windamar House (☎ 508-487-0599; 568 Commercial St; d $85-140, ste $120-140; P) This friendly place has six pretty rooms with quilt-topped beds (some share baths) and two apartments.

Masthead (☎ 508-487-0523, 800-395-5095; 31-41 Commercial St; d $86-249, cottages & apt $250-363) At the far end of town, this sprawling property offers a huge variety of charming and eccentric rooms, cottages and apartments.

Bill White's Motel (☎ 508-487-1042; www.billwhitesmotel.com; 29 Bradford St Extension; d $80; P) Perched near the dunes, this is a family-run place with 12 units.

Cape Colony Inn (☎ 508-487-1755, 800-841-6716; www.capecolonyinn.com; 280 Bradford St; d $109-122, ste $175; P) Has 57 standard rooms and two-room suites.

Surfside Hotel & Suites (☎ 508-487-1726, 800-421-1726; www.surfsideinn.cc; 543 Commercial St; d $159-259; P) Though the exterior is rather charmless, there are 84 family-friendly motel rooms in two buildings; the more expensive rooms are waterside.

Outermost Hostel (☎ 508-487-4378; 28 Winslow St; dm $19) Off Bradford St, this non-HI has 30 well-worn bunk beds in five depressing cabins.

Dune's Edge Campground (☎ 508-487-9815; www.dunes-edge.com; off MA 6; campsites/RV sites $28/34) Has about 100 pine-shaded campsites.

Coastal Acres Camping Court (☎ 508-487-1700; www.coastalacres.com; West Vine St Extension; campsites/RV sites $24/35) At the western edge of town.

EATING

Whether it's fast food or cuisine-as-high-art, Provincetown has the best dining on Cape Cod.

Mojo's (☎ 508-487-3140; Ryder St at MacMillan Wharf; mains $3-15) This classic clam shack serves up heaping portions of fried clams, onion rings and other traditional New England fare.

Karoo Café (☎ 508-487-6630; 338 Commercial St; mains $4.50-9) The menu at this tiny spot starts with basic sandwiches but quickly moves on to the intriguing fare of the owner's native South Africa. Try the spicy *peri-peri* (a hot sauce from southern Africa) or the samosas.

Tofu a Go-Go (☎ 508-487-6237; 336 Commercial St; lunches $3.50-9.50) Vegetarians climb the stairs here for sesame noodles, tofu burritos and other veggie dishes.

Lobster Pot (☎ 508-487-0842; 321 Commercial St; lunches $7-13, dinners $13-19) Tourists line up outside this venerable fish house, which serves chowder and seafood at tables overlooking the harbor.

Café Edwige (☎ 508-487-2008, 333 Commercial St; breakfasts $4-8; dinners $18-24) This second-floor café is popular for morning meals, but also serves sophisticated, creative dinners.

For more light bites, try:

Portuguese Bakery (☎ 508-487-1803; 299 Commercial St) Purveyor of malasadas – hot, sugary fried dough ($2).

Angel Foods (☎ 508-487-6666; 467 Commercial St) Gourmet market for classy picnic foods.

Spiritus (☎ 508-487-2808; 190 Commercial St) Late-night pizza hangout for those who'll be nursing hangovers.

If you're looking for a more upscale dining experience (mains from high teens to high 20s), Provincetown delivers, too. Reservations are advised at the following places:

Mews Restaurant & Café (☎ 508-487-1500; 429 Commercial St) Romantic waterfront dining on contemporary fare.

Chester (☎ 508-487-8200; 404 Commercial St) Chichi bistro food in an elegant Greek Revival-style manor.

Front Street (☎ 508-487-9715; 230 Commercial St) Fine Italian in a romantic subterranean space.

Napi's (☎ 508-487-1145; 7 Freeman St, at Bradford St) Eclectic veggie-friendly menu with a Mediterranean slant.

ENTERTAINMENT

Much of Provincetown's nightlife scene is in the bars and clubs, gay and straight.

Post Office Cabaret (☎ 508-487-2234; 303 Commercial St) Hosts impersonators and comedians.

Governor Bradford (☎ 508-487-9618; 312 Commercial St) A dark bar with big windows, this is an old-time dive.

Crown & Anchor (☎ 508-487-1430; 247 Commercial St) Offers something for everyone – a disco, four bars, cabaret and female impersonators.

Boatslip Beach Club (☎ 508-487-1669; 161 Commercial St) Hosts wildly popular afternoon tea dances.

Waterfront **Pied Piper** (☎ 508-487-1527; 193A Commercial St) is the town's women's bar. **Atlantic House** (☎ 508-487-3821; 4 Masonic Pl), more commonly referred to as 'the A-House,' is the men's equivalent.

SHOPPING

Along Commercial St you'll find everything from leather implements of torture to rubber stamps, from edgy women's clothing to artsy T-shirts, from sculpture to handcrafted jewelry.

GETTING THERE & AWAY

Cape Air (☎ 508-487-0241, 800-352-0714; www.flycapeair.com) flies from Boston (from $110 one way or $150 to $180 round-trip). **Plymouth & Brockton buses** (☎ 508-746-0378) leave MacMillan Wharf several times daily for Boston in summer ($23, 3½ hours). Also in summer, **Bay State Cruise Company** (☎ 508-487-9284, 617-748-1428; www.boston-ptown.com) runs a fast ferry (adult/child $60/50 round-trip; 1½ hours; three times a day) and a weekend-only slower ferry (adult/child $39/29 round-trip, three hours) between Boston's Commonwealth Pier and MacMillan Wharf.

MARTHA'S VINEYARD

Thought to be named after the daughter of mariner Bartholomew Gosnold, who found wild grapes on the island when exploring the coast in the 16th century, Martha's Vineyard was a prosperous haven for whaling vessels and merchant fleets until the early 20th century. After the Age of Steam, it became a popular vacation resort known for its beaches, bike paths and charming towns.

The main ports are the year-round commercial center Vineyard Haven and the honky-tonk, more diverse Oak Bluffs. The other major town, Edgartown, is the pricey grande dame, filled with whaling captain's houses separated by white picket fences. The island's other towns – West Tisbury, Chilmark, Menemsha and Aquinnah (formerly Gay Head) – are less developed and collectively referred to as 'Up-Island.'

Island Transport (☎ 508-693-1555; adult $18, child 5-11 $5) runs 2½-hour guided tours to Aquinnah, departing from the Vineyard Haven and Oak Bluffs ferry terminals approximately every hour May through mid-October.

Information

Martha's Vineyard Chamber of Commerce (☎ 508-693-0085; www.mvy.com; Beach Rd, Vineyard Haven; 🕑 9am-5pm Mon-Fri, also 10am-4pm Sat & noon-4pm Sun late May–early Sep) has visitors information.

Vineyard Haven

This hub is an appealing year-round town with as many shops catering to locals as to tourists. **West Chop Lighthouse**, outside of town at the northern end of Main St, is worth a look. A vineyard on the Vineyard? But of course: about 3.5 miles southwest of town, **Chicama Vineyards** (☎ 508-693-0309; Stoney Hill Rd, off State Rd, West Tisbury) offers free tours daily in the summer. Contact **Wind's Up** (☎ 508-693-4252; 199 Beach Rd) to rent windsurfers (from $16 per hour), sailboats (from $25 per hour), canoes (from $20 per hour) and kayaks (from $14 per hour).

SLEEPING

Crocker House Inn (☎ 508-693-1151, 800-772-0206; www.crockerhouseinn.com; 12 Crocker Ave; with breakfast d $185-385) A block from the harbor and within walking distance of town, this gray-shingled inn rents eight country-casual rooms.

Kinsman Guest House (☎ 508-693-2311; 278 Main St; d $125) At this year-round lodging in an 1880 Victorian, there are three homey rooms (two share a bath).

Vineyard Harbor Motel (☎ 508-693-3334; www.vineyardharbormotel.com; 60 Beach Rd; d $140-160) This standard motel near the harbor has about 40 simple rooms, some with small kitchens.

Martha's Vineyard Family Camping (☎ 508-693-3772; 569 Edgartown Rd; campsites/RV sites $38-42, cabins $100-120) Offering the island's only camping, this spot has sites for tents and RVs, as well as several basic cabins.

EATING

Vineyard Haven is 'dry' – no alcoholic beverages are sold in restaurants or shops. You're allowed to bring your own bottle (BYOB) to most restaurants, which will uncork it for a small fee.

Artcliff (☎ 508-693-1224; 39 Beach Rd; breakfasts $4-9, lunches $7-9) A short walk from the ferry docks, this little shingled house is popular for both traditional diner fare and more inventive dishes (perhaps almond-crusted French toast or a lamb sausage and broccoli rabe sandwich).

Black Dog Tavern (☎ 508-693-9223; 21 Beach St Extension; lunches $7-14, dinners $13-26) With its ubiquitous signature T-shirts, this tourist magnet is always crowded, particularly at breakfast.

Zephrus (☎ 508-693-3416; 9 Main St; lunches $9-14, dinners $21-28) Casually sophisticated, this Main St dining room serves contemporary bistro fare, with lots of seafood selections.

Oak Bluffs

In 1835 the Methodist Campmeeting Association began holding summer revival meetings in Oak Bluffs (OB). Participants pitched tents, but after a few years they began constructing much more substantial shelters. The result was a village of some 300 Carpenter Gothic cottages surrounding the **Trinity Park Tabernacle** (1879), where the association still holds its meetings. Since that time, OB has had a very strong African-American community. For a close look, examine the memorabilia at the **Cottage Museum** (☎ 508-693-0525; 1 Trinity Park; 🕑 10am-4pm Mon-Sat mid-Jun–mid-Oct). The **Flying Horses Carousel** (Circuit Ave, at Lake Ave; $1) is over 125 years old and still going strong. There are nice ocean views from the **East Chop Lighthouse** (c 1850), on Telegraph Hill off Vineyard Haven–Oak Bluffs Rd.

SLEEPING

Lodging and dining is generally a bit cheaper in Oak Bluffs than in other towns.

Narragansett House (☎ 508-693-3627, 888-693-3627; www.narragansetthouse.com; 46 Narragansett Ave; with breakfast d $100-165) At this rambling, restored gingerbread Victorian, the 13 rooms come in quirky shapes and sizes.

Nashua House (☎ 508-693-0043; www.nashuahouse.com; 30 Kennebec Ave; d $109) Another old-time choice, this inn has 15 shared-bath rooms.

Attleboro House (☎ 508-693-4346; 42 Lake Ave; d $85-115) This gingerbread-style house has 11 basic shared-bath rooms.

EATING & DRINKING

Linda Jean's (☎ 508-693-4093; 25 Circuit Ave; dinners $8-10) This diner-style spot on bustling Circuit Ave is the town's best all-around inexpensive restaurant, and everyone knows it.

Giordano's (☎ 508-693-0184; 107 Circuit Ave; lunches $8-14, dinners $9-18) Established in 1930, this old favorite serves large portions of home-style Italian-American fare – and fried clams, too.

Lola's Southern Seafood (☎ 508-693-5007; 15 Beach Rd; pub menu $6-14, mains $20-26) Between OB and Edgartown, lively Lola's dishes up huge helpings of down-home cookin'. The bar bounces with live music weekends (nightly in the summer).

After the sun sets, OB is the Vineyard's playground.

Atlantic Connection (☎ 508-693-7129; 19 Circuit Ave) Has live music nightly.

Ritz Café (☎ 508-693-9851; 4 Circuit Ave) Features mostly blues.

Balance (☎ 508-696-3000; 57 Circuit Ave) The beautiful people gather at this stylish bar.

Edgartown

The island's most graceful town has a patrician air and many grand 17th-, 18th- and 19th-century **historic buildings**. The **Martha's Vineyard Preservation Trust** (☎ 508-627-8619) manages several of these buildings, including the **Dr Daniel Fisher House** (99 Main St), an 1840 mansion; the **Old Whaling Church**, next door; and the island's oldest house, the **Vincent House Museum** (🕑 10:30am-3pm Mon-Sat May–mid-Oct); you can tour them with a combination ticket ($8). The **Martha's Vineyard Historical Society** (☎ 508-627-4441; 59 School St; adult $7, child 5-11 $4; 🕑 10am-4pm Tue-Sat mid-Jun–mid-Oct, call for off-season hr) operates galleries with whaling and maritime displays, as well as historic houses.

Once you've strolled through town and walked out to **Edgartown Lighthouse** at the end of North Water St, take the short **ferry ride** (☎ 508-627-9427; car & driver $6; 🕑 7am-midnight Jun–mid-Oct, call for off-season hr) to **Chappaquiddick Island** for its good beaches. The **Felix Neck Wildlife Sanctuary** (☎ 508-627-4850; Edgartown-Vineyard Haven Rd; adult $4, child 5-11 $3; 🕑 trails 7am-dusk, visitors center 8am-4pm Jun-Sep, closed Mon Oct-May) has several walking trails on its 197 acres, and the **Manuel E Correllus State Forest** (☎ 508-623-2540; off Edgartown-Vineyard Haven Rd) in the center of the island has miles and miles of walking trails, plus bike trails. **Katama Beach** (or 'South Beach'), off Katama Rd, stretches for 3 miles facing moderate surf.

SLEEPING & EATING

Edgartown Inn (☎ 508-627-4794; 56 N Water St; d $110-250) There are 20 doubles in this central former sea captain's home; the cheapest share baths.

Edgartown Commons (☎ 508-627-4671, 800-439-4671; www.edgartowncommons.com; Pease's Point Way; d $170-195, ste $245-270; 👪) Has 35 family-friendly efficiencies near the center of town.

Among the Flowers (☎ 508-627-3233, 17 Mayhew Lane, off N Water St; mains $6-12) Friendly and small; serves omelettes, soups, salads and quiches.

Newes from America (☎ 508-627-4397; 23 Kelley St; mains $8-12) Offers traditional pub grub and modern variations (like grilled salmon salad). Try the 'rack of beer,' five samples of unusual brews.

Alchemy (☎ 508-627-9999; 71 Main St; lunches $9-14, dinners $26-32) A sophisticated bistro offering innovative variations on old standbys, like a 'soft shell crab BLT'; there's a lighter bar menu, too ($10 to $13).

Up-Island

Outside the busy towns, Martha's Vineyard is rolling fields dotted with sheep and framed by stone walls. The main 'sight,' 21 miles from Edgartown, is the colorful 150ft **Clay Cliffs of Aquinnah**, formerly known as 'Gay Head Cliffs.' Formed by glaciers 100 million years ago, the cliffs are on lands owned by the Wampanoag Indians. To the south is the 5-mile **Aquinnah Beach** (P $15), where clothes seem optional in some stretches. At **Menemsha Harbor**, an authentic fishing village, you can pick up a quick bite (preferably at sunset).

The **Cedar Tree Neck Sanctuary** (☎ 508-693-5207; Indian Hill Rd, off State Rd, West Tisbury) covers over 300 acres of bogs, fields and forests, and has a few trails. The 600-acre **Long Point Wildlife Refuge** (☎ 508-693-3678; off the Edgartown-West Tisbury Rd; adult $3, child 5-11 free; 9am-5pm mid-Jun–mid-Sep, sunrise-dusk mid-Sep–mid-Jun; P $9) has just a few short trails, one of which leads to a deserted stretch of South Beach.

Reserve early for one of the 74 beds at the **HI Manter Memorial Hostel** (☎ 508-693-2665, 888-901-2087; Edgartown-West Tisbury Rd, West Tisbury; dm $18-24); it's open from mid-April to mid-October.

Getting There & Away

Cape Air (☎ 800-352-0714) flies frequently from Boston; Nantucket; Hyannis; New Bedford; and Providence, Rhode Island.

Car and passenger ferries operated by the **Steamship Authority** (☎ 508-477-8600; www.steamshipauthority.com; round-trip adult/child/bike/car $11/5.50/6/110) run from Woods Hole to Vineyard Haven (about 15 per day in summer) and to Oak Bluffs (about half that), a 45-minute voyage. The **Steamship Authority** (☎ 508-997-1688; round-trip adult/child/bike $20/10/10) also runs three boats daily from New Bedford to Oak Bluffs from May to September (1½ hours).

Two summertime ferries, which take passengers only, operate out of Falmouth. The **Island Queen** (☎ 508-548-4800; www.islandqueen.com; Falmouth Heights Rd; round-trip adult/child/bike $10/5/6) has a service to Oak Bluffs. The **Falmouth-Edgartown Ferry** (☎ 508-548-9400; 278 Scranton Ave; adult/child/bike $30/24/8) docks in Edgartown five times daily. From Hyannis, **Hy-Line Cruises** (☎ 508-778-2600; www.hy-linecruises.com; Ocean St Dock; round-trip adult/child/bike $27/13/10) runs four boats daily to Oak Bluffs (two hours). From June through to mid-September, **Hy-Line Cruises** (☎ 508-693-0112, 508-228-3949; one way adult/child/bike $14/6.80/5) also operates four boats between Oak Bluffs and Nantucket (2¼ hours).

The year-round **Martha's Vineyard Regional Transit Authority** (☎ 508-693-9440; www.vineyardtransit.com; day/weekly pass $5/15) operates a good network of buses that travel frequently between all towns. Pick up the VTA map for details.

Adventure Rentals/Thrifty (☎ 508-693-1959; 19 Beach Rd, Vineyard Haven) has convertibles, mopeds, 4WDs and regular cars. **Budget** (☎ 508-693-1911) has locations near the Oak Bluffs and Vineyard Haven ferry terminals and at the airport, while **All-Island Rent-a-Car** (☎ 508-693-6868) is based at the airport. Expect to shell out about $75 daily for car rental, $36 to $53 for a moped. Beware that Vineyarders disdain mopeds – and accidents are common.

All three main towns have plenty of bicycle rental shops that charge $20 a day.

NANTUCKET

Thirty miles south of the Cape Cod coast, Nantucket is a beautiful island of grassy moors, salt bogs, blueberry fields and sandy beaches. Its one real town, also called Nantucket, is filled with graceful old houses.

There are two ferry terminals, Steamboat Wharf and Straight Wharf, both about a block off Main St in the town center and within walking distance of most lodgings.

Information

Nantucket Visitors Services & Information Bureau (☎ 508-228-0925; 25 Federal St; 9am-6pm daily late May–early Dec, 9am-5:30pm Mon-Sat early Dec–late May) provides information about room availability, bus schedules and other details.

Sights & Activities

The **Nantucket Historical Association** (☎ 508-228-1894; www.nha.org; 15 Broad St) oversees the island's most important **historic buildings**, including the excellent **Whaling Museum** (13 Broad St) and the 1686 **Jethro Coffin House** (Sunset Hill Rd), the island's oldest. A combination ticket (adult $15, child five to 11 $8) covers all houses and includes a walking tour; call for hours. The **Atheneum** (☎ 508-228-1110; www.nantucketatheneum.org; 1 India St; admission free; 🕒 9:30am-5pm, 9:30am-8pm Tue & Thu, closed Sun, also closed Mon in winter) is filled with artwork, books and other artifacts about the island.

The island's relatively flat terrain and dedicated paths are well suited to **bicycling**. All rental shops have good, free island maps with routes highlighted. The island's only real destination is Siasconset ('Sconset), 7 miles away. On the way, stop at the **Lifesaving Museum** (☎ 508-228-1885; www.nantucketlifesavingmuseum.com; 158 Polpis Rd; adult $5, child 5-11 $2; 🕒 9:30am-4pm mid-Jun–mid-Oct) to appreciate the heroic rescue efforts made on nearby shoals. Alternatively, reserve a spot with **Gail's Tours** (☎ 508-257-6557; tour $15; departures at 10am, 1pm & 3pm) for a 1¾-hour narrated spin around the island.

Popular **Jetties Beach** (off Bathing Beach Rd from N Beach Rd) is about a 20-minute walk from town. You can reach **Surfside Beach** and **Madaket Beach** by bike or bus.

Sleeping

Lodging is expensive; minimum stays and advance reservations are de rigueur. Camping is strictly prohibited. A long day trip from Hyannis is a feasible alternative to staying overnight.

Nesbitt Inn (☎ 508-228-0156; 21 Broad St; with breakfast r $85-110) Central and delightfully old-fashioned, this guesthouse has 12 rooms with shared bath.

Martin House Inn (☎ 508-228-0678; www.martinhouseinn.net; 61 Center St; with breakfast s $80-95, d $165-245) This 1803 sea captain's house has 13 rooms furnished with canopy beds and other period pieces.

HI Nantucket Youth Hostel (☎ 508-228-0433, 888-901-2084; 31 Western Ave; dm $18-24) Three miles from town at Surfside Beach, this 49-bed hostel is open from late April through to mid-October; reservations are essential.

Eating & Drinking

There are hordes of good restaurants in the center of Nantucket. At most, though, expect big-city prices.

Even Keel Café (☎ 508-228-1979; 40 Main St; lunches $7-13, dinners $10-20) This Main St café serves three meals a day, from morning pastries and eggs, to salads and hearty soups midday, to more elaborate contemporary dinners.

Provisions (☎ 508-228-3258; 3 Harbor Sq; sandwiches $6-7) Near Straight Wharf, this shop makes great take-out sandwiches.

Arno's 41 Main (☎ 508-228-7001; 41 Main St; lunches $8-12, dinners $12-19) You can count on this Main St standby for varied American dishes – popular breakfasts, too.

Sushi by Yoshi (☎ 508-228-1801; 2 E Chestnut St; sushi $5-11, other mains $9-15) Squeeze into this teeny Japanese café for first-rate raw fish and noodle dishes.

Among the higher-end places, excellent choices are the Italian trattoria **Sfoglia** (☎ 508-325-4500; 130 Pleasant St; mains $17-27), the contemporary **Fifty-Six Union** (☎ 508-228-6135; 56 Union St; mains $19-30) and **American Seasons** (☎ 508-228-7111; 80 Centre St; mains $23-30), featuring regional fare from across the USA.

Brotherhood of Thieves (23 Broad St; mains $9-15) A dark but friendly local tavern serving chowder, burgers and beer.

Cambridge Street Victuals (☎ 508-228-7109; 12 Cambridge St) Sample microbrews, including the local Cisco.

Getting There & Away

Cape Air and **Nantucket Airlines** (☎ 800-352-0714) offer many daily flights between Nantucket and Boston, Hyannis, New Bedford and Martha's Vineyard, as well as Providence, Rhode Island.

From Hyannis, the **Steamship Authority** (☎ 508-771-4000, car reservations 508-477-8600; www.steamshipauthority.com; South St Dock; round-trip adult/child/bike/car $26/13/10/330) carries people and autos year-round. At least six ferries run daily in summer, three in winter (2¼ hours). The **Steamship Authority** (☎ reservations 508-495-3278; round-trip adult/child/bike $52/39/10) also runs a passenger-only fast ferry, which takes only an hour and makes several trips a day year-round. **Hy-Line Cruises** (☎ 508-778-2600; www.hy-linecruises.com; Ocean St Dock; round-trip adult/child/bike $58/41/10) runs a one-hour fast ferry year-round and a two-hour slower boat from

May to October (round-trip adult/child/bike $27/14/10).

Freedom Cruise Line (☎ 508-432-8999; 702 Main St, MA 28, Harwichport; round-trip adult/child/bike $46/37/10), at Saquatucket Harbor, departs for Nantucket away from Hyannis' traffic. Morning, noon and evening ferries leave mid-June through August; one boat a day in each direction travels mid-May to mid-June and from September to mid-October (1½ hours). **Hy-Line Cruises** (☎ 508-693-0112, 508-228-3949; one way adult/child/bike $14/6.80/5) operates four inter-island boats to Martha's Vineyard from June to mid-September (2¼ hours).

The **NRTA Shuttle** (☎ 508-228-7025) operates buses to popular beaches and 'Sconset. Some buses have bike racks. Pick up a full schedule and pass information at the visitors services (25 Federal St). Bicycling is the best way to get away from the summertime crowds, savor the island's natural beauty and reach much of the protected conservation land. You can rent a bike from at least half a dozen shops, including **Young's Bicycle Shop** (☎ 508-228-1151; Steamboat Wharf; per day $25).

CENTRAL MASSACHUSETTS & THE PIONEER VALLEY

A few years after the Pilgrims landed at Plymouth in 1620, fur traders and settlers began making their way up the Connecticut River, earning this region the name 'Pioneer Valley.' East of the Pioneer Valley, in Sturbridge, and also at the valley's north end, in Deerfield, you can visit restored villages that recall the area's pioneer past. Today's pioneers, though, tend to be academic ones – Hampshire County (north of Springfield) is often known as the Five College area because it's home to Amherst, Hampshire, Mount Holyoke and Smith Colleges and the University of Massachusetts.

Sturbridge

Sturbridge, 65 miles west of Boston, is home to one of the country's first living history museums. **Old Sturbridge Village** (OSV; ☎ 508-347-3362; US 20; www.osv.org; adult $20, child 5-11 $10, tickets good for 2 days; 🕒 9:30am-5pm daily Apr-Oct, 9:30am-4pm Tue-Sun mid-Feb–Mar, 9:30am-4pm Sat-Sun Jan–mid-Feb) is an authentically re-created 1830s New England town, with 40 restored, antique-filled structures and interpreters dressed in period style. The town's **tourist office** (☎ 508-347-7594, 800-628-8379; www.sturbridge.org; 380 Main St, US 20; 🕒 9am-5pm) is opposite OSV.

US 20 is lined with motels, but the grande dame option is the 1771 **Publick House Inn** (☎ 508-347-3313, 800-782-5425; www.publickhouse.com; MA 131; d $104-165;), with inn, motel and B&B rooms and traditional dining on the Common. The closest campground is mega **Yogi Bear's Sturbridge Jellystone Park** (☎ 508-347-9570; campsites $44, RV sites $42-52, cabins $73-94;), with pools, a hot tub and a water slide; take I-84 exit 2 and follow signs. At the opposite end of the spectrum, **Wells State Park** (☎ 508-347-9257, 877-422-6762; MA 49, north of I-90; campsites $12) has 60 wooded campsites near a swimming pond.

Springfield

In the 19th century, Springfield and other valley towns became important industrial centers. Today, there are several museums worth a stop. **Court Sq** is ground zero, where there's the **visitors center** (☎ 413-787-1548; www.valleyvisitor.com; 1441 Main St; 🕒 9am-5pm Mon-Fri). Two blocks northeast, the **Springfield Library & Museums** (☎ 413-263-6800; 220 State St, at Chestnut St; adult $7, child 5-11 $3; 🕒 noon-4pm Wed-Fri, 11am-4pm Sat-Sun) houses the Smith Art Museum, the Museum of Fine Arts, the Springfield Science Museum and the Connecticut Valley Historical Museum. The museums surround Museum Quadrangle, which houses the **Dr Seuss National Memorial** (admission free; 🕒 7am-8pm). Here you'll find life-size sculptures from the author's many children's books. Basketball, invented here, is enshrined at the **Basketball Hall of Fame** (☎ 413-781-6500, 877-446-6752; 1000 W Columbus Ave; adult $15, child 5-11 $10; 🕒 9am-6pm daily, until 8pm Sat mid-Jun–Aug, 10am-6pm Sun-Thu, until 8pm Fri-Sat Sep–mid-Jun), south of I-91 exit 7. Springfield also claims the invention of gasoline-powered motorcycles; find out more at the funky **Indian Motorcycle Museum** (☎ 413-737-2624; 33 Hendee St; adult $5, child 5-11 free; 🕒 10am-4pm Mar-Nov, 1-4pm Dec-Feb), off Page Blvd from I-291 exit 4.

If you need to stay overnight, a string of chain motels lines US 5 in West Springfield.

The **bus station** (☎ 413-781-2900; 1776 Main St), at Liberty St, and **train station** (☎ 800-872-7245; 66 Lyman St) are a 10-minute walk northwest of Court Sq. **Peter Pan Bus Lines** (☎ 800-343-9999; www.peterpanbus.com) has service to Boston and Amherst, MA, Bennington, VT, Hartford and New Haven, CT, and New York City.

Six daily trains connect Springfield and New York ($42, 3½ hours); there are two trains to Boston ($26, 2½ hours).

Northampton

Northampton is the region's most sophisticated town, with a surprising variety of ethnic restaurants, cafés and funky stores. This gay-friendly town has a particularly visible lesbian community. You can tour **Smith College** (☎ 413-584-2700; www.smith.edu); 10 miles south in South Hadley is **Mount Holyoke College** (☎ 413-538-2000; www.mtholyoke.edu), the USA's oldest women's college (1837). The **Greater Northampton Chamber of Commerce** (☎ 413-584-1900; www.northamptonuncommon.com; 99 Pleasant St; 9am-5pm Mon-Fri) offers lots of information.

For vegetarian food, try **Paul and Elizabeth's** (☎ 413-584-4832; 150 Main St; lunches $5-8, dinners $9-14), inside the Thorne's Marketplace minimall. For Mexican, head down to down-home **La Veracruzana** (☎ 413-586-7181; 31 Main St; mains $4-9) or hipper **La Taqueria Cha Cha Cha!** (☎ 413-586-7311; 134 Main St; mains $4-7). **Bakery Normand** (☎ 413-584-0717; 192 Main St) serves rich pastries, while **Pizzeria Paradiso** (☎ 413-586-1468; 12 Crafts Ave; mains $9-16) is a wine bar masquerading as a brick-oven pizza place. **Northampton Brewery** (☎ 413-584-9903; 11 Brewster Court) serves pub fare with its pints. Upscale **Spoleto** (☎ 413-586-6313; 50 Main St; mains $15-20) has classic Italian dishes with modern accents, while the stylish **Del Raye Bar & Grill** (☎ 413-586-2664; 1 Bridge St, off Main St; mains $21-28) concocts eclectic dinners ranging from grilled salmon with blue corn cakes to citrus-glazed duck.

Amherst

Amherst boasts three colleges and the home of poet Emily Dickinson (1830–86), the 'belle of Amherst.' You can tour the restored **Dickinson Homestead** (☎ 413-542-8161; www.dickinsonhomestead.org; 280 Main St; adult $5, child 5-11 $3; tours on the hr, 10am-5pm Wed-Sat, 1-5pm Sun Jun-Aug, call for spring & fall hr); tour reservations are recommended. Contact **Amherst College** (☎ 413-542-2000; www.amherst.edu), **Hampshire College** (☎ 413-549-4600; www.hampshire.edu) and the **University of Massachusetts** (☎ 413-545-0111; www.umass.edu) for campus tours and event information. For more details, visit the **Chamber of Commerce** (☎ 413-253-0700; www.amherstarea.com; 409 Main St; 8:30am-4:30pm Mon-Fri).

The seven rooms in the meticulously restored **Allen House B&B** (☎ 413-253-5000; www.allenhouse.com; 599 Main St; with breakfast d $75-175) are filled with antiques and Victoriana; the eight-room 1850 **Amherst Inn** (257 Main St), under the same ownership, offers similar rates. Free transportation is available to and from the train and bus stations and the area colleges.

Motels are strung out along MA 9, including **Amherst Motel** (☎ 413-256-8122; 408 Northampton Rd; d $55-70). The nearest camping is in Whatley, 8 miles away off MA 116, at **White Birch Campground** (☎ 413-665-4941; 214 North St; campsites/RV sites $24/26).

Rao's Coffee Roasting Company (☎ 413-253-9441; 17 Kellogg Ave), one block from Main St, is the local java joint. For first-rate Chinese fare, including many dishes with locally grown organic vegetables, try **Amherst Chinese Food** (☎ 413-253-7835; 62 Main St; lunches $5-10, dinners $7-13). You can pick up excellent fresh produce and picnic supplies south of town at **Atkins Farms Country Market** (☎ 413-253-9528; 1150 West St, at Bay Rd).

Deerfield

Sixteen miles northwest of Amherst on MA 5, Deerfield was settled in the 1660s. Along the noble main street of **Historic Deerfield Village** (☎ 413-774-5581; www.historic-deerfield.org; The Street, off US 5; adult $12, child 5-11 $5), you can tour a dozen well-preserved houses dating from the 18th and 19th centuries.

THE BERKSHIRES

The hills of western Massachusetts have been a summer retreat for wealthy families from Boston, Hartford and New York for more than a century, and these hill towns boast surprising cultural riches.

Information

Berkshire Visitors Bureau (☎ 413-443-9186, 800-237-5747; www.berkshires.org; Berkshire Common, Plaza Level, Pittsfield, MA 01201) has information and a lodging reservation service.

Stockbridge

This postcard-perfect New England town is straight out of a Norman Rockwell illustration. In fact, the artist lived and worked here, and the **Norman Rockwell Museum** (☎ 413-298-4100; MA 183, south of MA 102; adult $12, child 5-11 free; 10am-5pm daily May-Oct, 10am-4pm Mon-Fri &

10am-5pm Sat-Sun Nov-Apr) holds mementos and much of his art. The **Chesterwood estate and museum** (☎ 413-298-3579; Williamsville Rd, off MA 183; adult $10, child 5-11 $5; ⏲ 10am-5pm May-Oct) was the summer home of sculptor Daniel Chester French.

For lodging, try **Red Lion Inn** (☎ 413-298-5545; www.redlioninn.com; 30 Main St; d with shared bath $95-105, d with private bath $180-215), a stately c 1770 wood-frame hotel. Or ask the **Stockbridge Lodging Association** (☎ 413-298-5200, 866-626-5327; www.stockbridgechamber.org) for help; expect to spend at least $125 for an area B&B.

Lenox

Gracious Lenox is a summertime cultural capital. The town hosts one of the country's premier music series, the **Tanglewood Music Festival** (☎ 617-266-1492, in summer 413-637-5165; www.bso.org; admission $14-80), featuring the Boston Symphony Orchestra, late June to early September. **Shakespeare & Company** (☎ 413-637-3353; www.shakespeare.org; 70 Kemble St; admission $10-50) performs the Bard's work throughout the summer. The **Jacob's Pillow Dance Festival** (☎ 413-243-0745; admission $20-55), 10 miles east of Lenox in Becket, stages renowned contemporary dance from late June through August.

The **Mount** (☎ 413-637-1899; 2 Plunkett St, at US 7; adult $16, child 5-11 free; ⏲ 9am-5pm May-Oct), the former home of novelist Edith Wharton, has hour-long guided tours. The **Lenox Chamber of Commerce** (☎ 413-637-3646; www.lenox.org; 5 Walker St) helps with accommodations and other information.

Lenox lodgings consist primarily of charming, pricey inns. Vacancies are rare on summer weekends, but prices drop 20% to 35% on weekdays. Try the eight-room **Walker House** (☎ 413-637-1271, 800-235-3098; www.walkerhouse.com; 64 Walker St; with breakfast d $90-220) or the 19-room **Gables Inn** (☎ 413-637-3416, 800-382-9401; www.gableslenox.com; 81 Walker St; with breakfast d $125-250; 🏊).

Centrally situated Church St has good eateries, including the upscale **Church Street Café** (☎ 413-637-2745; 65 Church St; lunches $10-12, dinners $19-16), which offers inventive meals in its art-filled space.

Hancock Shaker Village

Just southwest of the town of Pittsfield, midway between Lenox and Williamstown, is **Hancock Shaker Village** (☎ 413-443-0188, 800-817-1137; www.hancockshakervillage.org; US 20, near MA 41; adults $15 summer-fall, $12 winter-spring, children free; ⏲ 9:30am-5pm late May–late Oct, 10am-3pm late Oct–late May), a fascinating living history museum that illustrates the lives and beliefs of the Shakers, a religious sect founded in England in 1747. The Shakers believed in communal ownership, pacifism, celibacy, gender equality and the sanctity of work. The products of their hands – including the buildings and artifacts in this community, which was an active town until 1960 – are of a very high order.

Williamstown & North Adams

Another one of western Massachusetts' lively college towns, Williamstown is the home of Williams College and of the **Clark Art Institute** (☎ 413-458-2303; www.clarkart.edu; 225 South St; adults $15 Jun-Oct, admission Nov-May free, children free; ⏲ 10am-5pm Tue-Sun Sep-Jun, 10am-5pm daily Jul-Aug). This gem of a museum is particularly strong in 19th-century European and American painting, including works by Renoir, Monet and other French impressionists.

The first-rate **Williamstown Theatre Festival** (☎ 413-597-3399; www.wtfestival.org; admission $20-53) stages contemporary and classic plays from mid-June to mid-August, often with notable casts.

In nearby North Adams, don't miss **Mass MoCA** (☎ 413-662-2111; 87 Marshall St; adult $7, child 5-11 $2; ⏲ 10am-6pm daily Jun-Oct, 11am-5pm daily except Tue Nov-May), the eclectic and truly enormous Massachusetts Museum of Contemporary Art, located in a sprawling former factory complex.

Nearby **Mt Greylock State Reservation** (☎ 413-499-4262, camping reservations 877-422-6762; Rockwell Rd, Lanesborough) includes Massachusetts' highest peak (3491ft), as well as nearly 60 miles of hiking trails.

River Bend Farm (☎ 413-458-3121; 643 Simonds Rd; d $100), a meticulously restored colonial tavern-turned-B&B, dates from 1770, with four guestrooms filled with period antiques (and shared baths). Near the Williams campus, the **Northside Motel** (☎ 413-458-8107; www.northsidemotel.com; 45 North St, US 7; d $75-105) has 30 family-friendly standard rooms. There are scenic **campsites** ($12) at Mt Greylock and in the nearby town of Florida at **Savoy Mountain State Forest** (☎ 413-663-8469, reservations 877-422-6762; Central Shaft Rd, off US 2; campsites $12).

At Mass MoCA, the restaurant **Eleven** (☎ 413-662-2004; 1111 Mass MoCA Way; lunches $7-9, dinners $15-20) serves contemporary cuisine in a chic 1950s-style space. Williamstown's Spring St is loaded with eateries; look for **Cold Spring Coffee Roasters** (☎ 413-458-5010; 47 Spring St) for java and sweets or **Arugula Cocina Latina** (☎ 413-458-2152; 25 Spring St; dishes $3-8) for empanadas, Cuban sandwiches and other light Latin fare. The white-tablecloth **Mezze** (☎ 413-458-0123; 16 Water St; mains $20-25) woos foodies with modern bistro dishes like roasted sea scallops in red wine sauce.

Getting There & Away

Peter Pan Trailways buses run to the Berkshires from Boston. Bonanza Bus Lines connects the Berkshire towns with New York and with Bennington, VT.

RHODE ISLAND

The Ocean State is the smallest of the United States, but it certainly packs a lot into a compact waterfront package. Providence is the bustling capital city, with loads of excellent restaurants, while nearby Newport, the famed 19th-century summer playground of the colossally wealthy, remains the region's yachting – and tourist – center. Block Island, a more peaceful version of Nantucket, is perfect for a day or overnight trip.

In 1636 Reverend Roger Williams (1603–83) founded Providence as a haven for freedom of conscience and separation between religion and civil government. Some 140 years later, the Colony of Rhode Island and Providence Plantations was the first American colony to declare independence from Britain.

RHODE ISLAND FACTS

Nicknames Ocean State, Little Rhody
Population 1,069,725 (43rd)
Area 1545 sq miles (50th)
Admitted to Union May 29, 1790 (13th)
Capital city Providence (population 174,000)
Other cities Newport (26,000)
Birthplace of Broadway composer George M Cohan (1878–1942)
Famous for the Rhode Island Red, a chicken that revolutionized the poultry industry
First state to declare independence from Britain (1776), abolish slavery (1784), use steam-powered mills (1848)

Rhode Island built its wealth on maritime commerce, first in slaves and then in the China trade. The state now prospers through higher education, health care, light manufacturing and tourism.

PROVIDENCE

Rhode Island's capital is pleasant, walkable and well endowed with cultural and academic institutions. Forty-five miles southwest of Boston, Providence makes a good day trip.

Information

BOOKSTORES

Brown Bookstore (☎ 401-863-3168; 244 Thayer St)
College Hill Bookstore (☎ 401-751-6404; 252 Thayer St)

EMERGENCY

Emergency number (☎ 911) For police, fire or other emergency.

INTERNET ACCESS

Kinko's (☎ 401-273-2830; 236 Meeting St, at Thayer St; per min 20¢; 🕒 24hr from noon Sun-10pm Fri, also 9am-5pm Sat) Check the *Yellow Pages* for other locations around town.
Providence Public Library (☎ 401-455-8000; 225 Washington St; free for 1 hr)

MEDIA

Providence Journal (www.projo.com) Major daily newspaper.
Providence Phoenix (www.providencephoenix.com) Alternative weekly, available on Thursdays, with extensive arts and entertainment coverage.

MEDICAL SERVICES

Brooks Pharmacy (☎ 401-272-3048; 1200 N Main St; 🕒 24hr)
Rhode Island Hospital (☎ 401-444-4000; 593 Eddy St)

POST

US post office (☎ 401-421-5214; 2 Exchange Tce; 🕒 7:30am-5:30pm Mon-Fri, 8am-2pm Sat)

TOURIST OFFICES

Providence-Warwick Convention & Visitors Bureau (☎ 401-274-1636, 800-233-1636; www.providencecvb.com; 1 W Exchange St; 🕒 8:30am-5pm Mon-Fri)
Rhode Island Tourism Division (☎ 401-222-2601, 800-556-2484; www.visitrhodeisland.com; 1 W Exchange Pl, Providence, RI 02903)

Sights & Activities

Kennedy Plaza, anchored by the Providence Biltmore Hotel, constitutes the city center. North of the plaza and Waterplace Park are the train station and, perched atop a hill, the capitol. You can take a guided tour (reserve ahead) of the marble **State Capitol** (☎ 401-222-3983; admission free; 8:30am-4pm Mon-Fri, tours 9am, 10am & 11am Mon-Fri) modeled in part on St Peter's Basilica in the Vatican City, or visit on your own.

The colorful Italian enclave of **Federal Hill**, full of cafés, restaurants and bakeries, lies on (and off) Atwells Ave, just west of the city center. On the city's east side, the College Hill neighborhood is home to the Ivy League **Brown University** (☎ 401-863-2378; www.brown.edu) and the artsy **Rhode Island School of Design** (RISD; ☎ 401-454-6300; www.risd.edu), which has a fine **art museum** (☎ 401-454-6500; 224 Benefit St; adult $6, child 5-11 $3, 10am-1pm Sun admission free; 10am-5pm Tue-Sun), showcasing everything from ancient Greek art to the French Impressionists to eclectic contemporary works. Near RISD, Benefit St – lined with colonial homes dating back to the 1700s – makes for a pleasant stroll.

If you're traveling with kids, detour south of the city to the expansive Roger Williams Park and its first-rate **Roger Williams Zoo** (☎ 401-785-3510; www.rogerwilliamsparkzoo.org; 1000 Elmwood Ave; adult $8, child 5-11 $5; 9am-5pm Mon-Fri, 9am-6pm Sat-Sun mid-May–mid-Oct, 9am-4pm daily mid-Oct–mid-May). From downtown, take I-95 south to exit 17, Elmwood Ave.

Sleeping

Old Court B&B (☎ 401-751-2002; www.oldcourt.com; 144 Benefit St; with breakfast d $115-165; P) Located near Brown and RISD, this B&B has nine antique-filled rooms in a stately 1863 brick building.

Providence Biltmore (☎ 401-421-0700, 800-294-7709; www.providencebiltmore.com; 11 Dorrance St, on Kennedy Plaza; d $179-269; P) Downtown, this is a classic grand hotel of the 1920s.

You'll find that less pricey chain motels are clustered south of town near the airport in Warwick.

Bed & Breakfast of Rhode Island (☎ 401-849-1298, 800-828-0000; www.visitri.com/bedandbreakfast; PO Box 3291, Newport, RI 02840) Has statewide listings.

Eating

The Providence restaurant scene has taken off in recent years, with first-rate dining all around town. You'll find everything from homey spots to chic city-style bistros, many started by graduates of the city's highly regarded Johnson & Wales culinary school.

Arcade (☎ 401-598-1199; 65 Weybosset St) The oldest shopping mall in the US, this 1828 structure now houses an array of inexpensive lunchtime eateries.

Geoff's (☎ 401-751-9214; 253 Thayer St; sandwiches $4-7) This funky sandwich shop near the Brown campus has been catering to students and locals for years. Sandwiches come in hundreds of combos, many named for local personalities.

XO Café (☎ 401-273-9090, 125 N Main St; mains $18-28) Wear black to this trendy spot that mixes Asian and Mediterranean flavors with New England ingredients to create eclectic modern dishes.

Good choices on Federal Hill include the following:

Casa Christine (☎ 401-453-6255; 145 Spruce St; mains $14-17) A top local choice for hearty Italian fare.

Caserta Pizzeria (☎ 401-621-3618; 121 Spruce St; pizzas $5-12) Primo pies.

L'Epicureo (☎ 401-454-8430; 238 Atwells Ave; mains $13-27) High-end Italian.

Gracie's (☎ 401-272-7811; 409 Atwells Ave; mains $17-28) Modern Mediterranean-American – for a break from the neighborhood's ubiquitous red sauce.

And more foodie favorites (with main dishes averaging $20):

Al Forno (☎ 401-273-9760; 577 S Main St) The now nationally known Italian restaurant that helped launch the city's restaurant renaissance.

Mills Tavern (☎ 401-272-3331; 101 N Main St) Hearty New American fare, including steaks and seafood from the grill and the wood-burning oven.

Neath's (☎ 401-751-3700; 262 S Water St) Modern Asian-fusion restaurant overlooking the Providence River.

Drinking

Thayer St, near Brown, is lined with laid-back bars that cater to students.

Trinity Brewhouse (☎ 401-453-2337; 186 Fountain St) Downtown, try this pub for Irish- and British-style brews; entertainment several nights a week.

Union Station Brewery (☎ 401-274-2739; 36 Exchange Terrace) On Kennedy Plaza, serving American-style beers.

Entertainment

WaterFire (☎ 401-272-3111; www.waterfire.org; Waterplace Park; admission free; call for schedules) On periodic Saturdays throughout the summer, the city sets its river on fire – it's part of an eclectic and exceedingly popular performance art work. Bonfires are set at sunset on pyres in the middle of the river and black-clad gondoliers row past to the accompaniment of eerie music.

Lupo's Heartbreak Hotel (☎ 401-272-5876; 239 Westminster St) This legendary hotel has been hosting cool national rock and R & B bands in an intimate club since the 1970s.

AS220 (☎ 401-831-9327; 115 Empire St) An alternative space open to folk singers, performance artists, offbeat films, art workshops and more; you never know what you might find.

Trinity Repertory Company (☎ 401-351-4242; 201 Washington St) One of the nation's top regional repertory theaters performs classic and contemporary plays downtown.

Getting There & Away

TF Green Airport (☎ 401-737-8222, 888-268-7222; I-95, exit 13, Warwick), about 20 minutes south of Providence, handles regional and national flights, often at lower prices than flights into Boston. Most major rental car companies have offices at the airport; see p1121 for details. **Bonanza Bus Lines** (☎ 401-751-8800) connects Providence with Boston, Cape Cod and New York; buses also run between TF Green Airport and Boston. Several daily **Amtrak** (☎ 800-872-7245) trains link Providence with Boston ($9, one hour) and New York ($56, from 3¼ hours); the **Acela Express** trains cut the Boston travel time to 35 minutes and New York to under three hours, but fares run roughly $32 to Boston and $88 to New York. The **MBTA** (☎ 617-222-3200; fare $5.80) operates weekday commuter trains between Providence and Boston.

The **Rhode Island Public Transit Authority** (RIPTA; ☎ 401-781-9400, 800-244-0444; www.ripta.com) runs buses around town from its Kennedy Plaza hub and also links Providence with Newport and other state localities. RIPTA's Providence **LINK Trolley** ($1) operates two lines from Kennedy Plaza – the Green line goes to Federal Hill and to the East Side, while the Gold goes to the train station and State Capitol. **New England Fast Ferry** (☎ 401-453-6800; www.nefastferry.com; adult $6, child 5-11 $4) runs several boats a day from Providence's Point St Landing to Newport's Perrotti Park (near the Gateway Visitors Center) from May through October (45 minutes); trolleys to the Providence ferry docks leave Kennedy Plaza 15 minutes before each ferry departure.

NEWPORT

Perfectly situated for access by sea, Newport was an important commercial port and a wealthy summer resort before becoming one of New England's busiest tourist destinations. Most people visit to ogle sumptuous Bellevue Ave mansions, admire colonial architecture or attend a big-name music festival.

Downtown Newport's main north–south commercial streets are America's Cup Ave and the harborside Thames (that's thaymz, not temz) St.

Information

The bus station and a large parking facility are at the same location as **Newport County Convention & Visitors Bureau** (☎ 401-849-8048, 800-976-5122; www.gonewport.com; 23 America's Cup Ave; 🕑 9am-5pm).

Mansions

During the 19th century, the wealthiest New York bankers and business families chose Newport as their summer resort and built elaborate 'cottages.' Many of these mansions are now managed by the **Preservation Society of Newport County** (☎ 401-847-1000; www.newportmansions.org; 424 Bellevue Ave; combination tickets for five mansions adult $31, child 5-11 $10, the Breakers plus one other mansion adult/child $22/6, the Breakers only adult/child $15/4, other mansion adult/child $10/4; 🕑 the Breakers 9am-5pm daily, other mansions 10am-5pm mid-Jun–mid-Sep, call for off-season schedules). Their combination tickets will save you money if you plan to visit more than one mansion.

Don't miss the **Breakers**, a 70-room 1895 Italian Renaissance palace built for Cornelius Vanderbilt II, which is Newport's most splendid 'cottage.' **Rosecliff** looks like the Grand Trianon at Versailles, with Newport's largest ballroom. The palace of Versailles inspired the 1892 **Marble House**, filled with Louis XIV–style furnishings. The 1841 Elizabethan-style **Kingscote** (adult $10, child five to 11 $4) was Newport's first 'cottage' strictly for summer use. The **Elms**, nearly identical to the Chateau d'Asnières near Paris, was built in 1901 for a coal magnate. Victorian Gothic **Chateau-sur-Mer**

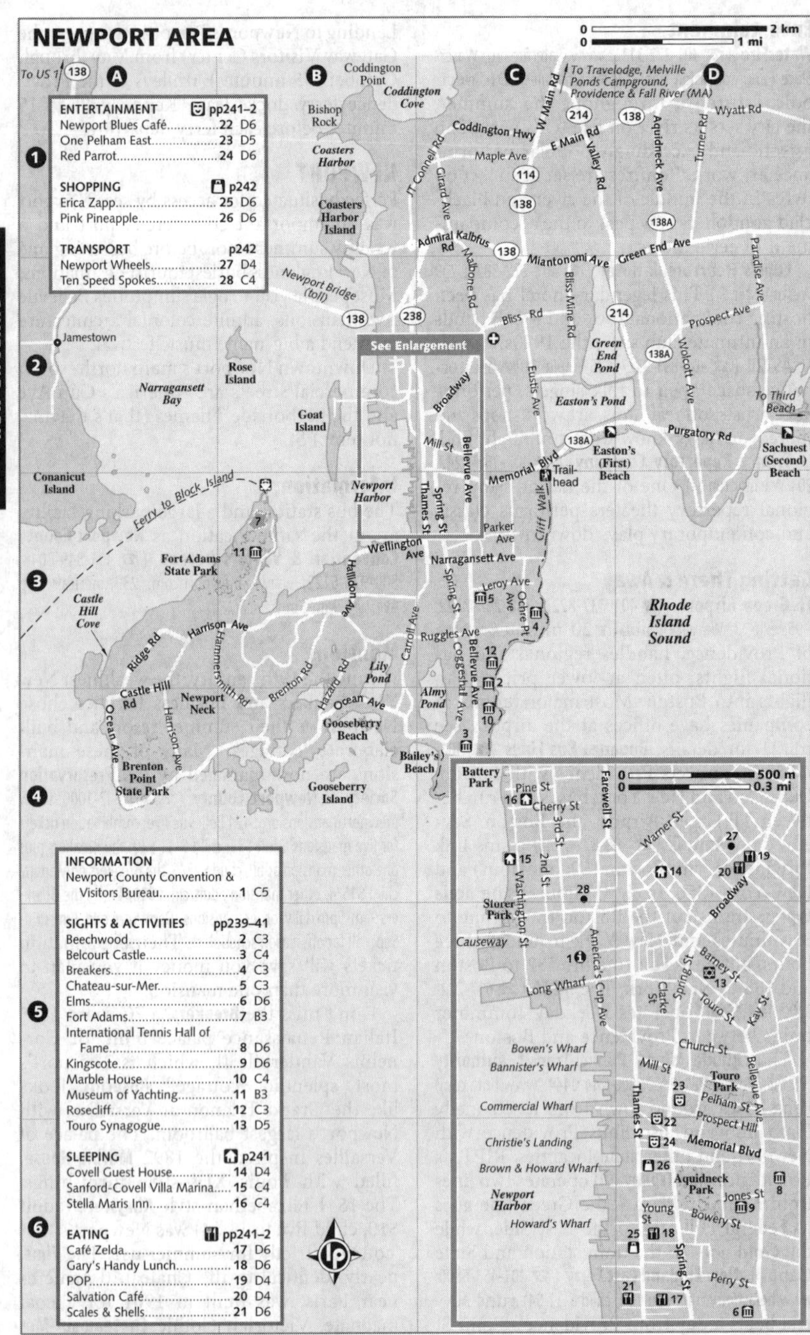
NEWPORT AREA
0 2 km
0 1 mi
To US 1
138
A
B
C
D
Coddington Point
Coddington Cove
Bishop Rock
Coasters Harbor
Coasters Harbor Island
To Travelodge, Melville Ponds Campground, Providence & Fall River (MA)
W Main Rd
214
138
Wyatt Rd
Coddington Hwy
E Main Rd
Aquidneck Ave
Turner Rd
Maple Ave
Valley Rd
JT Connell Rd
Girard Ave
114
138
138A
Admiral Kalbfus Rd
138
Miantonomi Ave
Green End Ave
Paradise Ave
Malbone Rd
Newport Bridge (toll)
138
238
Bliss Mine Rd
Bliss Rd
214
Prospect Ave
ENTERTAINMENT pp241–2
Newport Blues Café 22 D6
One Pelham East 23 D5
Red Parrot 24 D6
SHOPPING p242
Erica Zapp 25 D6
Pink Pineapple 26 D6
TRANSPORT p242
Newport Wheels 27 D4
Ten Speed Spokes 28 C4
1
2
3
4
5
6
Jamestown
See Enlargement
Green End Pond
138A
Rose Island
Narragansett Bay
Broadway
Eustis Ave
Wolcott Ave
Easton's Pond
To Third Beach
Goat Island
Mill St
Bellevue Ave
138A
Purgatory Rd
Easton's (First) Beach
Sachuest (Second) Beach
Conanicut Island
Ferry to Block Island
Memorial Blvd
Trail-head
Newport Harbor
Thames St
Spring St
Cliff Walk
7
Parker Ave
11
Wellington Ave
Narragansett Ave
Fort Adams State Park
Leroy Ave
Ochre Pt Ave
5
Halidon Ave
Castle Hill Cove
4
Rhode Island Sound
Ruggles Ave
Harrison Ave
Carroll Ave
Hammersmith Rd
12
Ridge Rd
Bellevue Ave
Coggeshall Ave
Lily Pond
Brenton Rd
Hazard Rd
2
Castle Hill Rd
Newport Neck
Almy Pond
Ocean Ave
10
Gooseberry Beach
3
Ocean Ave
Harrison Ave
Bailey's Beach
Brenton Point State Park
Gooseberry Island
INFORMATION
Newport County Convention & Visitors Bureau 1 C5
SIGHTS & ACTIVITIES pp239–41
Beechwood 2 C3
Belcourt Castle 3 C4
Breakers 4 C3
Chateau-sur-Mer 5 C3
Elms 6 D6
Fort Adams 7 B3
International Tennis Hall of Fame 8 D6
Kingscote 9 D6
Marble House 10 C4
Museum of Yachting 11 B3
Rosecliff 12 C3
Touro Synagogue 13 D5
SLEEPING p241
Covell Guest House 14 D4
Sanford-Covell Villa Marina 15 C4
Stella Maris Inn 16 C4
EATING pp241–2
Café Zelda 17 D6
Gary's Handy Lunch 18 D6
POP 19 D4
Salvation Café 20 D4
Scales & Shells 21 D6
Battery Park
Farewell St
0 500 m
0 0.3 mi
Pine St
16
Cherry St
3rd St
Warner St
27
15
2nd St
19
14
20
Washington St
28
Broadway
Storer Park
Causeway
1
America's Cup Ave
Barney St
Long Wharf
Clarke St
Spring St
13
Touro St
Kay St
Church St
Bowen's Wharf
Bannister's Wharf
Mill St
Bellevue Ave
Touro Park
23
Thames St
Pelham St
Commercial Wharf
22
Prospect Hill
Christie's Landing
24
Memorial Blvd
Brown & Howard Wharf
26
Aquidneck Park
8
Newport Harbor
Jones St
9
Young St
Bowery St
Howard's Wharf
25
18
Spring St
Perry St
21
17
6

(1852) has a decidedly more lived-in feel to it than the others.

The 1856 **Beechwood** (☎ 401-846-3772; www.astorsbeechwood.com; 580 Bellevue Ave; adult $15, child 5-11 $10; call for tour schedule), former home of the wealthy Astor family, is now a living history museum, with actors portraying the family, their staff and visitors. **Belcourt Castle** (☎ 401-846-0669; www.belcourtcastle.com; 657 Bellevue Ave; adult $10, child 5-11 $5; noon-5 Sun-Fri) was designed according to the 17th-century tastes of France's King Louis XIII.

Other Attractions

For sweeping views of the mansions and the sea, walk the walk – the **Cliff Walk**, that is, a footpath hugging the eastern edge of the peninsula. The 3.5-mile trek starts off of Memorial Blvd, just west of Easton's Beach, and ends at Bailey's Beach, although there are numerous points to start or stop en route.

Touro Synagogue (☎ 401-847-4794; 85 Touro St; admission free; call for tour schedule), built in 1763, is North America's oldest Jewish house of worship.

The historic Newport Casino building (1880) houses the **International Tennis Hall of Fame** (☎ 401-849-3990; 194 Bellevue Ave; adult $8, child 5-11 $4; 9:30am-5pm), once the wealthy Newporters' summer club.

Fort Adams (☎ 401-841-0707; Harrison Ave; adult $6, child 5-11 $3; 10am-4pm mid-May–Oct) was built in the mid-1800s; this fort crowns a rise at the peninsula's end; tours are offered on the hour. It's the centerpiece of **Fort Adams State Park** (☎ 401-847-2400), a fine place to picnic or sunbathe, which also hosts the Newport Jazz and Folk Festivals. For decades Newport was the home port for America's Cup races, which explains the park's **Museum of Yachting** (☎ 401-847-1018; adult $5, child 5-11 $4; 10am-5pm mid-May-Oct).

Easton's Beach (P $8-15), also called 'First Beach,' is the largest sweep of sand, with bathhouses, showers and a snack bar. East along Purgatory Rd is Sachuest (Second) Beach, with showers and a snack bar. Continuing east, Third Beach is a favorite with windsurfers. **Gooseberry Beach** (P Mon–Fri $10, Sat–Sun $15) is on Ocean Ave.

Festivals & Events

If you like music, visit Newport in the summer when several big-name festivals come to town.

Newport Music Festival (☎ information 401-846-1133, tickets 401-849-0700; www.newportmusic.org; admission $25-45) Two weeks of classical concerts in July at many of the mansions.

JVC Jazz Festival/Newport (☎ 401-847-3700; Fort Adams State Park; adult $49-65, child $5) National jazz acts in early August.

Newport Folk Festival (☎ 401-847-3700; adult $49-54, child $5; Fort Adams Start Park) Big-name stars and up-and-comers in mid-August.

Sleeping

Stella Maris Inn (☎ 401-849-2862; www.stellamarisinn.com; 91 Washington St; with breakfast d $125-195) This welcoming and comfortably old-fashioned inn in the residential Point neighborhood has eight large, high-ceilinged rooms, including some with water views.

Covell Guest House (☎ 401-847-8872, 800-291-9848; www.covellguesthouse.com; 43 Farewell St; with breakfast d $115-180) Close to the town center and Thames St, this B&B has five country-style rooms.

Sanford-Covell Villa Marina (☎ 401-847-0206; www.sanford-covell.com; 72 Washington St; with breakfast d $160-325;) This ornate Victorian has elaborate painted ceilings, really beautifully restored woodwork and a prime waterfront location.

Motels on the outskirts, particularly those in nearby Middletown, are a bit cheaper than in-town inns.

Travelodge (☎ 401-849-4700; 1185 W Main Rd, Middletown; d $85-130;) On the outskirts of town.

You can camp at **Melville Ponds Campground** (☎ 401-849-8212; 181 Bradford Ave, Portsmouth; campsites/RV sites $15/25) and across the Newport Bridge at **Fort Getty Campground** (☎ 401-423-7211; Conanicut Island, Jamestown; campsites/RV sites $20/30).

Eating & Drinking

Head to lower Thames St, south of America's Cup Ave, for the densest concentration of diverse eateries.

Scales & Shells (☎ 401-846-3474; 527 Thames St; mains $14-23) Seafood seekers crowd this casual spot for simple fresh fish. Expect long waits during summer prime times.

Café Zelda (☎ 401-849-4002; 528 Thames St; mains $18-21) At this cute, stylish bistro, you'll find more contemporary fare, perhaps blackened halibut with barley risotto or roast duck with tarragon sweet potatoes.

Gary's Handy Lunch (☎ 401-847-9480; 462 Thames St; breakfasts & lunches $3-6) This local coffee shop serves a rather budget-friendly menu of eggs, burgers and sandwiches.

Salvation Café (☎ 401-847-2620; 140 Broadway; mains $9-17) A short distance away from the tourist center, this funky vintage-1950s room offers up an eclectic menu with Asian, Latino and Mediterranean influences.

POP (☎ 401-846-8456; 162 Broadway; small plates $4-14) A sleek 21-plus lounge and tapas bar.

Red Parrot (☎ 401-847-3800; 348 Thames St) A Caribbean-themed club hosting live jazz most Friday evenings.

One Pelham East (☎ 401-847-9460; 1 Pelham St E) and **Newport Blues Café** (☎ 401-841-5510; 286 Thames St) both have live music most summer nights.

Shopping

Thames St has the usual range of touristy T-shirt and postcard shops, but there are some funky and upscale boutiques as well.

Erica Zap (☎ 401-849-4117; 477 Thames St) Sells contemporary jewelry, ranging from stretchy $3 bracelets to elaborate $100 necklaces.

Pink Pineapple (☎ 401-849-8181; 380 Thames St) Preppy style is alive and well at this fuchsia-hued shop.

Getting There & Away

Bonanza Bus Lines (☎ 401-846-1820, 888-751-8800), at the Convention & Visitors Bureau, runs several buses daily to Boston ($17, 1½ hours). State-run **RIPTA buses** (☎ 401-781-9400, 800-244-0444) traverse the hour-long route to Providence at least every hour ($1.25). RIPTA also runs **trolleys** (all-day pass adult/family $5/10) from late May to mid-October from the visitors bureau to the Bellevue Ave mansions and other destinations around town. **New England Fast Ferry** (☎ 401-453-6800; www.nefastferry.com; adult $6, child 5-11 $4) operates several boats a day from Providence's Point St Landing to Newport's Perrotti Park (near the visitors bureau) from May through October (45 minutes).

You can rent bicycles from **Ten Speed Spokes** (☎ 401-847-5609; 18 Elm St, at America's Cup Ave; per hour/day $5/20) near the visitors bureau, and from **Newport Wheels** (☎ 401-849-4400; 77 Dr Marcus Wheatland Blvd, off Broadway; per hour/day $5/20), which also rents scooters (per hour/day $35/150).

BLOCK ISLAND

In 1614 a mariner named Adriaen Block stopped at this 11-sq-mile island, giving it its name. For two centuries the settlement of New Shoreham was a fishing town, but in the late 19th century, Block Island became a summer resort.

The island is only 7 miles from end to end. The ferry docks at Old Harbor, the main town. The other settlement is New Harbor, on Great Salt Pond just over a mile away.

Information

Block Island Chamber of Commerce (☎ 401-466-2982, 800-383-2474; 9am-5pm daily May-Oct, 10am-3pm Mon-Sat Nov-Apr) is located in the ferry parking lot. They can help with accommodations.

Activities

Rent a bicycle at **Old Harbor Bike Shop** (☎ 401-466-2029; per hr/day $6/20) near the ferry landing, and head for Mohegan Bluffs, topped by the **Southeast Light** (house). You'll encounter 5 miles of hills while bicycling out to the 1867 **North Light**, at the island's northernmost tip. **Block Island Beach** stretches for 2 miles along the island's east coast. The southern part, closest to Old Harbor, is called 'Benson Town Beach' and offers a changing and showering pavilion.

The island has some great places for hiking. **Rodman's Hollow** (entrance off Cherry Hill Rd) is a 100-acre wildlife refuge laced with trails ending at the beach – perfect for a picnic. The **Clay Head Nature Trail**, off Corn Neck Rd, follows high clay bluffs along the beachfront, then veers inland through a maze-like series of paths cut into low vegetation that attracts dozens of bird species.

Sleeping & Eating

Camping isn't allowed, and though there are some 35 B&Bs and guesthouses, rooms aren't cheap. Book ahead.

Rose Farm Inn (☎ 401-466-2034; 1005 Roslyn Rd; with breakfast d $185-235) This 19-room B&B is convenient to Old Harbor and the beach; two less expensive rooms share baths (double $139).

Atlantic Inn (☎ 401-466-5883, 800-224-7422; www.atlanticinn.com; High St; with breakfast d $145-265) Built in 1879, this stately 21-room lodging overlooks Old Harbor from a lofty hill.

Hotel Manisses (☎ 401-466-2421, 800-626-4773; www.blockislandresorts.com; Spring St; with breakfast d $175-300) This commanding hotel with a huge front porch has 17 Victorian-style guestrooms, while its sister **1661 Inn** has nine rooms; ask about the less expensive shared-bath rooms in nearby guesthouses.

1661 Inn (☎ 401-466-2421; Spring St; brunches $13) Serves an excellent outdoor champagne buffet brunch in summer.

Harborside Inn (☎ 401-466-5504; Water St; lunches $8-15, dinners $20-30) is a good choice for seafood, as is the more casual **Finn's Seafood Restaurant** (☎ 401-466-2473; Water St; mains $14-22), which has a fish market next door.

Getting There & Away

New England Airlines (☎ 401-596-2460, 800-243-2460; round-trip $76) makes the 12-minute flight from Westerly State Airport, on Airport Rd off RI 78, to Block Island.

Ferries (☎ 401-783-4613; www.blockislandferry.com) to Block Island run from Galilee State Pier, Point Judith (adult/child/bicycle/car $17/9/52/5, one hour), year-round and from Newport's Fort Adams Dock (adult/child/bicycle $17/8/5 round-trip, two hours) from late June through August. There's also a daily car-and-passenger ferry from early June to mid-September, departing from New London, Connecticut (adult/child/bicycle/car $30/18/7/56 round-trip, two hours). There are reduced prices for same-day round-trips.

Island Hi-Speed Ferry (☎ 877-733-9425; www.islandhighspeedferry.com; round-trip adult/child/bicycle $26/12/6) makes the trip from Galilee State Pier to Block Island in only 30 minutes, from mid-May to mid-October.

CONNECTICUT

Connecticut has surprising variety – the southeastern region looks to New York, while the coast mixes historic towns and booming high-tech cities. Hartford, the capital, is an island of skyscrapers amid miles of farmers' fields. The northwestern corner is a more sedate, low-key version of the Massachusetts Berkshires. Connecticut is known for its submarine bases in New London and Groton, Yale University in New Haven and Hartford's many insurance companies.

History

In 1633, Dutch settlers built a small settlement at what is now Hartford, but it was the English who settled Connecticut in numbers. Many came from Massachusetts, such as Thomas Hooker, who founded Hartford in 1636. A year later a separate colony was set up at New Haven. Both joined the New England Confederation in 1643 and Connecticut received a royal charter in 1662.

These early colonists set up their own government and did not appreciate it when, in 1687, British governor-general Sir Edmund Andros demanded that they surrender their charter and submit to his rule. Legend has it that the charter was hidden in the hollow of an oak tree, the Charter Oak, and thus saved from forfeiture. Overall, few Revolutionary War battles took place in Connecticut, but the colony was an important source of military supplies for the Continental Army.

Because of the industrial inventiveness of the state's citizens, the Connecticut Yankee peddler became a fixture in early American society, traveling by wagon from town to town selling clocks, buttons and other manufactured goods. In 1798, Eli Whitney established a factory at New Haven that made firearms with interchangeable parts – the beginnings of modern mass production.

Among Connecticut's most famous artistic residents, Alexander Calder (1898–1976) made many of his world-famous mobiles and stabiles at his studio in Roxbury. Harriet Beecher Stowe (1811–96), who penned the enormously popular and influential tale of the abuses of slavery, *Uncle Tom's Cabin*, and Mark Twain (1835–1910), who wrote *The Adventures of Tom Sawyer*, were Hartford neighbors for 17 years.

CONNECTICUT FACTS

Nicknames Constitution State, Nutmeg State
Population 3,460,503 (28th)
Area 5544 sq miles (48th)
Capital city Hartford (population 122,000)
Admitted to Union January 9, 1788 (5th)
Other cities New Haven (124,000)
Home of the first written US constitution (1639), Webster's dictionary (1806), Colt revolver (1835), pay telephone (1889)
Birthplace of abolitionist John Brown (1800–59), Harriet Beecher Stowe (1811–96), traitor Benedict Arnold (1741–1801), circus man PT Barnum (1810–91), Katharine Hepburn (1909–2003), Ralph Nader (b 1934)

Information

Connecticut Tourism Department (☎ 860-270-8081, 800-282-6863; www.ctbound.org; 505 Hudson St, Hartford, CT 06106) has information.

HARTFORD

Connecticut's capital is a workaday city – it's a center for the insurance industry – but if you're passing through, there are several appealing historical and artistic attractions.

Information

Greater Hartford Tourism District (☎ 860-244-8181, 800-793-4480; 234 Murphy Rd) has information for visitors.

Sights & Activities

A mile west of the city center along CT 4, you can tour **Mark Twain House** (☎ 860-247-0998; www.marktwainhouse.org; 351 Farmington Ave; adult $9, child 5-11 $5; 9:30am-4pm Mon-Sat, noon-4pm Sun May-Oct & Dec, closed Tue Jan-Apr & Nov), the former home of author Samuel Langhorne Clemens – aka Mark Twain. A new visitors and education center is slated to open here in 2004.

Harriet Beecher Stowe House (☎ 860-522-9258; www.harrietbeecherstowecenter.org; 77 Forest St; adult $6.50, child 5-11 $2.75; 9:30am-4:30pm Tue-Sat, noon-4:30pm Sun) Adjacent to Mark Twain House and sharing its spacious lawn is this former home of the *Uncle Tom's Cabin* author.

Wadsworth Atheneum (☎ 860-278-2670; www.wadsworthatheneum.org; 600 Main St; adult $9, child 5-11 free, 10am-noon Sat admission free; 11am-5pm Tue-Fri, 10am-5pm Sat-Sun) is the oldest public art museum in the USA. The Atheneum is especially strong in Hudson River school paintings, old masters and contemporary art.

You can tour the imposing white marble and granite **State Capitol** (☎ 860-240-0222; 210 Capitol Ave, at Trinity St; admission free; tours hourly 9:15am-1:15pm Mon-Fri, also 10:15am-2:15pm Sat Apr-Oct), built in 1879, with neo-Gothic details and a gold-leaf dome. Adjoining the capitol grounds, 37-acre **Bushnell Park** features a working 1914 carousel as well as art exhibits and summer concerts at the **Pump House Gallery** (☎ 860-722-6536).

Sleeping & Eating

Goodwin Hotel (☎ 860-246-7500, 800-922-5006; www.goodwinhotel.com; 1 Haynes St, at Asylum Ave; d $139-269;) This elegant 1881 building across from the Civic Center has a historic facade and an updated interior. Catering largely to business travelers, it often offers discounted weekend rates.

HI Mark Twain Hostel (☎ 860-523-7255; 131 Tremont St; dm $15-18) Off Farmington Ave, this hostel is in a big Victorian-style house on a pretty residential street; reservations are advised.

Museum Café (☎ 860-728-5989; 600 Main St; mains $9-14) Inside the Wadsworth Atheneum, this café serves lunch from Tuesday to Sunday.

Mo's Midtown (☎ 860-236-7741; 25 Whitney St, at Farmington Ave; breakfasts & lunches $3-7) Grab a seat at the counter for a hearty breakfast of eggs and peppery home fries or blueberry pancakes. It's two blocks from the Mark Twain Hostel.

Tapas (☎ 860-525-5988; 126 Ann St; mains $7-17) Casual Greek-Mediterranean light bites and larger meals.

Max Downtown (☎ 860-522-2530; 185 Asylum St; lunches $9-17, dinners $18-28) For creatively prepared fusion dishes, along with steak-house classics, try this airy, all-business space opposite the Civic Center.

Getting There & Away

Bradley International Airport (☎ 860-292-2000; I-91, exit 40, Windsor Locks), north of the city, has regional and national flights. Most major rental car companies have offices at the airport; see p1121 for details.

Greyhound, Peter Pan Trailways and Bonanza Bus Lines link Hartford's **Union Station** (☎ 860-247-5329; One Union Pl, at Spruce St) to other northeast cities. Amtrak trains connect Hartford to New York ($36, 2½ hours).

LOWER CONNECTICUT RIVER VALLEY

The Lower Connecticut River Valley has several charming towns dating from the colonial era.

Essex

Established in 1635, Essex makes a good starting point for poking around the valley. It's full of Federal-period houses, the legacy of 19th-century rum and tobacco fortunes. The **Connecticut River Museum** (☎ 860-767-8269; 67 Main St, at Steamboat Dock; adult $5, child 5-11 $3; 10am-5pm Tue-Sun) depicts the area's history with exhibits including a reproduction 1776 *Turtle*, the world's first submarine. See the countryside aboard the Valley Railroad's **Essex Steam Train and Riverboat** (☎ 860-767-0103; One Railroad Ave; adult $16, child 5-11 $8, with cruise $24/12; daily late Jun-Aug, call for spring & fall schedules);

a coal-fired steam locomotive hauls the train 12 miles (one hour) to Deep River, where you can take a riverboat cruise before heading back by train.

Revolutionary War–era **Griswold Inn** (☎ 860-767-1776; www.griswoldinn.com; 36 Main St; with breakfast d $105-140, ste $165-225;), with 30 colonial-style rooms, has been a hostelry since 1776, but Sunday-morning 'hunt breakfasts' have been a tradition only since 1812.

Old Lyme

Some 60 sea captains lived here in the 19th century, but since the early 1900s it has been better known as a center for American impressionist painters. Many stayed in the mansion of local art patron Florence Griswold, decorating its walls with murals in lieu of rent. The house has been converted into the **Florence Griswold Museum** (☎ 860-434-5542; 96 Lyme St; adult $7, child 5-11 $4; 10am-5pm Tue-Sat, 1-5pm Sun); the Griswold House will be closed for renovation in 2004, but the museum's Krieble Gallery of American Art will remain open.

Bee & Thistle Inn (☎ 860-434-1667, 800-622-4946; www.beeandthistleinn.com; 100 Lyme St; d $79-189; lunches $9-16, dinners $21-30) is a 1756 Dutch Colonial farmhouse with 11 romantic rooms (some with shared baths) and very fine dining.

East Haddam

Gillette Castle (☎ 860-526-2336; 67 River Rd; adult $5, child 5-11 $3; 10am-5pm late May–mid-Oct) is a 24-room, stone-turreted 1919 mansion built by actor-director William Hooker Gillette and now set in a 117-acre state park. The 1876 **Goodspeed Opera House** (☎ 860-873-8668; CT 82; tickets $22-51) is an *American Gothic*–style confection known as 'the birthplace of the American musical'; the theater still produces several musicals each year.

Wolf's Family Den Campground (☎ 860-873-9681; 256 Town St; RV sites $32;) has 205 sites, as well as lots of sports facilities.

CONNECTICUT COAST

The southwestern coast is crowded with industrial and commercial cities, along with suburban bedroom communities within the magnetic influence of New York. The central coast, from New Haven east to the mouth of the Connecticut River, is less urban, with historic towns and villages. The southeastern coast includes New London and Groton, both important in naval history, and Mystic, where the Mystic Seaport Museum brings maritime history to life.

Information

Southeastern Connecticut Tourism District (☎ 860-444-2206, 800-863-6569; www.mysticmore.com; 470 Bank St, New London 06320) provides information for visitors.

New London & Groton

In the mid-19th century, New London was home port to some 200 whaling vessels. Today this city of 30,000 preserves its links to the sea. Across the river, the country's largest submarine base resides in Groton.

In New London, tour **Monte Cristo Cottage** (☎ 860-443-0051; 325 Pequot Ave; tours $5; 10am-5pm Tue-Sat, 1-5pm Sun late May–early Sep), the boyhood home of playwright Eugene O'Neill. The **Lyman Allyn Art Museum** (☎ 860-443-2545; 625 Williams St; adult $5, child 5-11 $4; 10am-5pm Tue-Sat, 1-5pm Sun) is a neoclassical building with exhibits that include early American silver; Far Eastern, Greco-Roman and European art; and ethnic art of many other cultures. In Groton, visit the world's first nuclear-powered submarine at the **Historic Ship Nautilus & Submarine Force Museum** (☎ 860-694-3174, 800-343-0079; CT 12; admission free; 9am-5pm Wed-Mon, 1-5pm Tue mid-May–mid-Oct, 9am-4pm Wed-Mon Nov–mid-May).

The high-Victorian 1903 **Queen Anne Inne** (☎ 860-447-2600, 800-347-8818; www.queen-anne.com; 265 Williams St; with breakfast d $115-175;) features eight antique-filled guestrooms, some with canopy beds or working fireplaces. On a private beach, **Lighthouse Inn** (☎ 860-443-8411; www.lighthouseinn-ct.com; 6 Guthrie Place; d $145-380) occupies a restored 1902 mansion and carriage house. There are also plenty of chain motels off I-95. For great, inexpensive pizza, New London has **Recovery Room** (☎ 860-443-2619; 445 Ocean Ave), a family-run place near the beach.

Connecticut Commuter Rail Service's **Shore Line East** (☎ 203-777-7433) travels from New London to New Haven. **Cross Sound Ferry** (☎ 860-443-5281, 631-323-2525; www.longislandferry.com; 2 Ferry St; adult/child/car $10/5/37) operates ferries between New London and Orient Point on Long Island year round (1½ hours). There's also a passenger-only fast ferry that cuts the travel time to 40 minutes (adult $16, child five to 11 $8).

AMISTAD

On July 2, 1839, the slave ship *Amistad* was sailing along the Cuban coast with its 'cargo' of 55 abducted Africans. During the voyage one captive managed to remove his shackles and lead a rebellion to seize control of the ship. The US Coast Guard eventually towed the ship to New London, Connecticut, where the Africans were accused of rebellion and sent to New Haven to await trial.

The case became a cause célèbre among abolitionists and made its way to the US Supreme Court, where former president John Quincy Adams was persuaded to emerge from retirement to plead their case. The court found that since the abductees had been taken illegally, they couldn't be held liable for mutiny. The victory was a powerful moral and legal victory for the antislavery forces, and the *Amistad* abductees were repatriated to Africa. The compelling tale was made into a movie by Steven Spielberg.

Mystic & Around

Long before its popular museum was built and the movie *Mystic Pizza* (starring Julia Roberts) was released, Mystic was a lovely, centuries-old seaport town.

INFORMATION

Mystic Chamber of Commerce (☎ 860-572-9578; www.mysticchamber.org; 14 Holmes St; ⏲ 9am-5pm Mon-Fri) has information for visitors.

SIGHTS & ACTIVITIES

Costumed interpreters staff many of the more than 60 historic buildings at **Mystic Seaport Museum** (☎ 860-572-5315; www.visitmysticseaport.com; CT 27; adult $17, child 5-11 $9; ⏲ 9am-5pm Apr-Oct, 10am-4pm Nov-Mar), talking with visitors about their crafts and trades. You can board the *Charles W Morgan* (1841), the last surviving wooden whaling ship in the USA; the *LA Dunton*, a three-masted fishing schooner; and the *Joseph Conrad*, a square-rigged training ship. You can also take a half-hour excursion up the Mystic River on the **Sabino** (☎ 860-572-5315; adult $5, child 5-11 $4; ⏲ 11am-4pm mid-May–mid-Oct), a 1908 steamboat.

Mystic Aquarium (☎ 860-572-5955; www.mysticaquarium.org; 55 Coogan Blvd; adult $16, child 5-11 $11; ⏲ 9am-6pm Mar-Dec, 9am-7pm Sun-Thu Jul-Aug, 10am-5pm Mon-Fri, 9am-6pm Sat-Sun Jan-Feb) has more than 6000 species of sea creatures on view.

North of Mystic near Ledyard, the **Mashantucket Pequot Museum & Research Center** (☎ 800-411-9671; www.pequotmuseum.org; 110 Pequot Trail, off CT 214, Mashantucket; adult $15, child 5-11 $10; ⏲ 9am-5pm) pays homage to an ancient people. The Mashantucket Pequot Indian tribe also run the **Foxwoods Resort & Casino** (☎ 800-752-9244; www.foxwoods.com; CT 2, Ledyard), with the standard lineup of entertainment, sports events, hotels, restaurants, shops and, of course, gambling. You can lose money just as easily at **Mohegan Sun** (☎ 888-226-7711; www.mohegansun.com; I-395 exit 79A, Uncasville), a casino run by the Mohegan tribe.

SLEEPING

Whaler's Inn (☎ 860-536-1506, 800-243-2588; www.whalersinnmystic.com; 20 E Main St; d $139-249; ⊠) This centrally located inn has an assortment of traditionally decorated rooms in an 1865 Victorian house and adjacent buildings.

Inn at Mystic (☎ 860-536-9604, 800-237-2415; www.innatmystic.com; US 1 & CT 27; d $115-295; ⊠ 🏊) Accommodations at this property overlooking the harbor range from period rooms in a 1904 mansion to simple motel-style rooms (prices vary accordingly).

Taber Inne & Suites (☎ 860-536-4904, 866-466-6978; www.taberinne.com; US 1; d $149-185, ste $195-365) Spread across seven buildings, lodgings run the gamut from motel rooms to luxurious suites.

Old Mystic Motor Lodge (☎ 860-536-9666; www.oldmysticmotorlodge.com; 251 Greenmanville Ave; d $79-179; ⊠ 🏊) Many Mystic hotels and motels are clustered at I-95 exit 90, including this basic but family-friendly one.

EATING

S&P Oyster Co (☎ 860-536-2674; 1 Holmes St; lunches $8-14, dinners $9-26) In the town center next to the drawbridge, with excellent views, this seafooder features lunchtime fish-and-chips and sandwiches. At dinner, the menu runs the seafood gamut from fried clams to shrimp scampi to clambakes.

Captain Daniel Packer Inne (☎ 860-536-3555; 32 Water Ave; dinners $17-25) With its original fireplaces, beams and mantles, this historic 1754 building is full of colonial charm. The menu leans to such classics as filet mignon, lemon peppered chicken and crab-stuffed flounder.

Abbott's Lobster in the Rough (☎ 860-536-7719; 117 Pearl St, Noank; mains $8-24) This comfortable old favorite in Noank, just west of Mystic, serves lobsters, clams and other traditional shore fare at waterfront picnic tables. The hot lobster roll – dripping-with-butter lobster meat on a hamburger bun – is a local speciality.

New Haven

Yale University, the Ivy League alma mater of presidents George W Bush, Bill Clinton, George HW Bush and Gerald Ford, is the heart of this city of about 125,000. The city is 75 miles northeast of New York City. Established in 1637, New Haven, though not without its urban problems, has a lively cultural life and dining scene. Its traditional town green, the city's spiritual center, is framed by beautiful churches.

INFORMATION

Greater New Haven Convention & Visitors Bureau (☎ 203-777-8550, 800-332-7829; www.newhavencvb.org; 59 Elm St; 8:30am-5pm Mon-Fri) provides a range of information, including an 'alternative' guide to gay-friendly locations.

SIGHTS & ACTIVITIES

Yale University is crowded with Gothic buildings. The campus is marked by Harkness Tower, from which a carillon peals at appropriate moments throughout the day. For campus tours, contact Yale University's **visitors center** (☎ 203-432-2302; www.yale.edu/visitor; 149 Elm St; 9am-4pm Mon-Fri, 10am-4pm Sat-Sun; tours 10:30am & 2pm Mon-Fri, 1:30pm Sat-Sun), on the north side of the green.

Yale Center for British Art (☎ 203-432-2800; 1080 Chapel St; admission free; 10am-5pm Tue-Sat, noon-5pm Sun) is west of the green. This museum holds the most comprehensive collection of British art outside the UK.

The **Yale University Art Gallery** (☎ 203-432-0600; 1111 Chapel St; admission free; 10am-5pm Tue-Sat, 10am-8pm Thu, 1-6pm Sun) boasts masterworks by Manet, Picasso and van Gogh, as well as other art from Africa, Asia, Europe and the Americas. Parts of the museum will be closed for renovation in 2004–05; call before visiting.

Five blocks northeast of the green along Temple St, **Peabody Museum of Natural History** (☎ 203-432-5050; 170 Whitney Ave; adult $5, child 5-11 $3; 10am-5pm Mon-Sat, noon-5pm Sun) is Yale's natural history museum, with dinosaur fossils, wildlife dioramas, meteorites and minerals.

SLEEPING

Hotel Duncan (☎ 203-787-1273; 1151 Chapel St; s/d $50/70;) The decor, facilities – and prices – of *fin de siècle* New Haven have certainly been preserved.

Colony (☎ 203-776-1234, 800-458-8810; www.colonyatyale.com; 1157 Chapel St; d $90-110; P) Modern-ish, with 86 rooms.

EATING

Louis' Lunch (☎ 203-562-5507; 261-263 Crown St; closed Sun-Mon) This self-proclaimed birthplace of the hamburger (around 1900) still uses its historic vertical grills and serves ground-beef patties on white toast for around $4. Don't even think about asking for ketchup.

Frank Pepe's (☎ 203-865-5762; 157 Wooster St) New Haven also claims the USA's first pizza, served at this old reliable.

Sally's Pizza (☎ 203-624-5271; 237 Wooster St) These days a vocal contingent prefers this pizzeria.

Roomba (☎ 203-562-7666; 1044 Chapel St; mains $19-24) Book a table at this hot spot for hip Nuevo Latino fare in a stylish setting.

Zinc (☎ 203-624-0507; 964 Chapel St; lunches $8-10, dinners $19-26) This oh-so-chic place offers up an eclectic fusion-like menu where ricotta gnocchi in an oxtail demi-glacé with dried cherries sits side-by-side with grilled tuna in wasabi oil.

Atticus Bookstore Café (☎ 203-776-4040; 1082 Chapel St; mains $3-8) Serves coffee, scones, soups, sandwiches and good books.

Claire's (☎ 203-562-3888; 1000 Chapel St; mains $5-8) Attracts health-conscious students with its veggie dishes.

ENTERTAINMENT

Attention theater buffs, New Haven has two first-rate professional repertory theaters that produce a mix of classics and new work: **Yale Repertory Theatre** (☎ 203-432-1234; www.yale.edu/yalerep; 1120 Chapel St; tickets $25-40) and **Long Wharf Theatre** (☎ 203-787-4282, 800-782-8497; www.longwharf.org; 222 Sargent Dr; tickets $15-48).

Toad's Place (☎ 203-624-8623; 300 York St; shows $5-25) Still a hot nightclub, hosting national and local rock and rollers. The Yale visitors center has details on other current happenings around town.

NEW ENGLAND

GETTING THERE & AWAY

Peter Pan Trailways (☎ 800-237-8747) buses connect New Haven to New York ($20, from 2½ hours) and other cities. For train service to New York City's Grand Central Terminal (1¾ hours), you can take **Amtrak** (☎ 800-872-7245; from $30) or **Metro North** (☎ 212-532-4900, 800-638-7646; $12-18).

LITCHFIELD HILLS

Sprinkled with lakes and dotted with state parks and forests, this rather tranquil area of northwestern Connecticut offers an excess of natural beauty but few accommodations. The historic town of Litchfield is at the region's center.

Information

Litchfield Hills Information Booth (US 202, on the Green, Litchfield; 10am-4pm Jun-Oct)

Litchfield Hills Visitors Bureau (☎ 860-567-4506; www.litchfieldhills.com; PO Box 968, Litchfield, CT 06759-0968)

Litchfield

Founded in 1719, Litchfield prospered thanks to the commerce brought by stagecoaches traveling between Hartford (34 miles away) and Albany. The town's grand 18th-century houses survive as a reminder of this era.

Stroll along North St and South St to see these fine homes, including the 1773 **Tapping Reeve House** (☎ 860-567-4501; www.litchfieldhistory.org; 82 South St; adult $5, child 5-11 free; 11am-5pm Tue-Sat, 1-5pm Sun mid-Apr-Nov). The tiny adjacent building once housed the USA's first law school (1775), which trained John C Calhoun and 130 members of Congress. Included in the admission fee, you can also visit the **Litchfield Historical Society Museum** (☎ 860-567-4501; 7 South St).

This part of Connecticut is a wine-producing area. **Haight Vineyards** (☎ 860-567-4045; 29 Chestnut Hill Rd, off CT 118; admission free; 10:30am-5pm Mon-Sat, noon-5pm Sun) offers tours and tastings.

The **White Memorial Conservation Center** (☎ 860-567-0857; US 202), 2.5 miles west of town, has 35 miles of hiking trails.

The graceful **Litchfield Inn** (☎ 860-567-4503, 800-499-3444; US 202; with breakfast d $135-225), 2 miles west of the town green, has 32 rooms; it's a modern inn in colonial clothing.

Along US 202 west of town, you'll find the simple 50-site **Looking Glass Hill Campground** (☎ 860-567-2050; US 202, Bantam; campsites/RV sites $18) and the elaborate **Hemlock Hill Camp Resort** (☎ 860-567-2267; Hemlock Hill Rd, off Milton Rd; campsites/RV sites $22/32;).

The bookstore-café **Barnidge & McEnroe** (☎ 860-567-4670; 7 West St) serves coffee and pastries. Pick up gourmet picnic supplies at the **Litchfield Grocer** (☎ 860-567-4884; 33 West St). For fine dining, try the creative New American cuisine at **West Street Grill** (☎ 860-567-3885; 43 West St; dinners $18-34).

Lake Waramaug

Of the dozens of lakes and ponds in the Litchfield Hills, Lake Waramaug, north of New Preston, is the most beautiful. As you make your way around the northern shore on North Shore Rd, stop at **Hopkins Vineyard** (☎ 860-868-7954; 25 Hopkins Rd; 10am-5pm Mon-Sat, 11am-5pm Sun May-Dec, 10am-5pm Wed-Sat, 11am-5pm Sun Mar-Apr, 10am-5pm Sat, 11am-5pm Sun Jan-Feb) for tastings. It's next to country-style **Hopkins Inn** (☎ 860-868-7295; www.thehopkinsinn.com; 22 Hopkins Rd; d $85-95), with 11 rooms. Or camp in one of the 78 scenic lakeside sites at **Lake Waramaug State Park** (☎ 860-868-0220; 30 Lake Waramaug Rd; campsites $13); book well in advance in summer.

VERMONT

Green and mountainous Vermont has far more trees than people. Known affectionately as the 'Green Mountain State', Vermont's has only one city worthy of the title: Burlington. To enjoy Vermont properly, you must drive slowly, hike in the forests or canoe down a rushing stream.

In summer the Vermont hills are alive with the sound of music – in the form of music festivals, that is. New England poet Robert Frost (1874–1963) was long associated with Vermont and New Hampshire. Anna Mary Moses (1860–1961), who was known as 'Grandma Moses,' painted lively, natural depictions of farm life around Bennington until she was 100 years old. Illustrator Norman Rockwell (1894–1978) lived and worked in the town of Arlington in addition to Lenox, Massachusetts. More recently, Annie Proulx, the award-winning author of *The Shipping News*, wrote about rural Vermont in her novel *Postcards*.

History

The French explorer Samuel de Champlain gave his name to Vermont's largest lake in 1609, but the French did not settle here until 1666. Though their settlements didn't survive, the English settlement at Fort Dummer (1724), close to present-day Brattleboro, did. Still, Vermont was something of a wilderness for years, important only to New York and New Hampshire, which disputed its ownership.

Ethan Allen organized his Green Mountain Boys to push the claim of New Hampshire against New York. But when the Revolutionary War broke out, Allen turned his efforts against the British, capturing

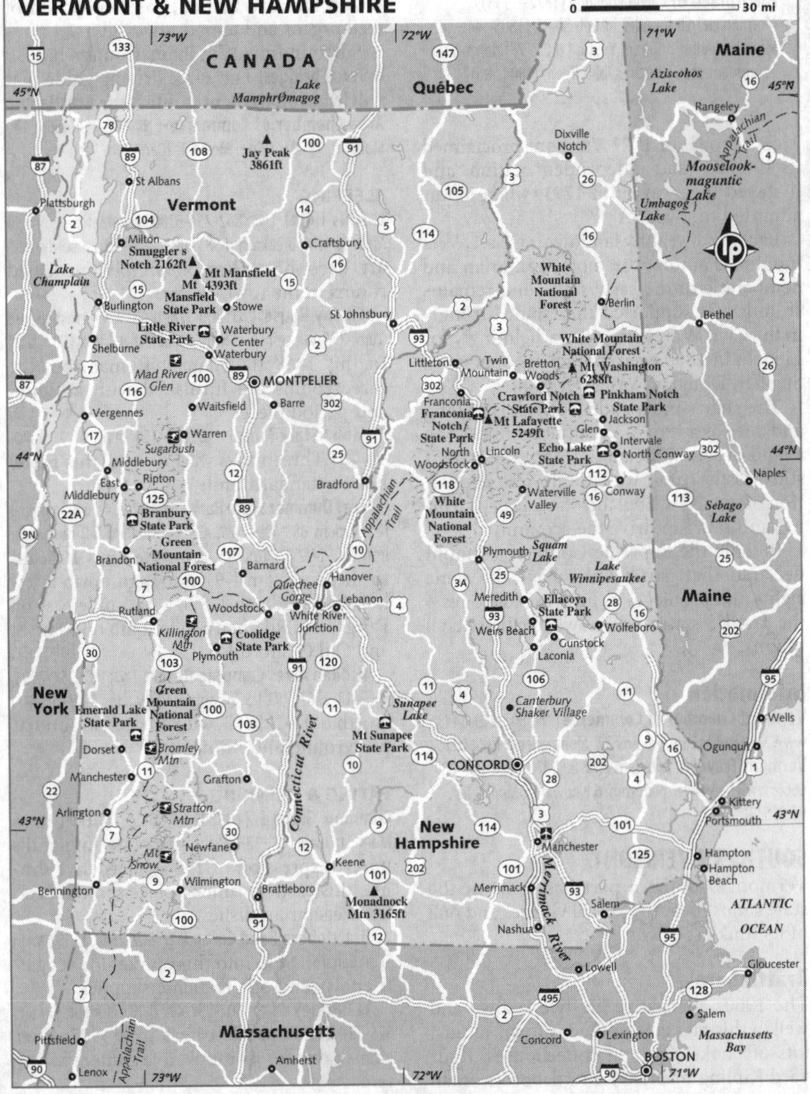

VERMONT FACTS

Nickname Green Mountain State
Population 616,592 (49th)
Area 9615 sq miles (45th)
Admitted to Union March 4, 1791 (14th)
Capital city Montpelier (population 8500)
Other cities Burlington (40,000), Bennington (16,000), Brattleboro (12,000)
Birthplace of Calvin Coolidge (1872–1933), Mormon church founder Joseph Smith (1805–44), Mormon leader Brigham Young (1801–77), farm-equipment manufacturer John Deere (1804–86)

Ticonderoga. In 1777 Vermont proclaimed itself a free and independent nation, and it stayed that way until 1791, when it was admitted to the USA.

Lacking a wealthy landowning class, Vermont was among the most egalitarian and democratic of the early states and remains so today. It supported the Union strongly in the Civil War, voting overwhelmingly for Lincoln in 1860 even though his opponent, Stephen Douglas, was a Vermonter.

The state's independent streak is as long and deep as a vein of Vermont marble. Long a land of self-sufficient farmers, the state is still mostly rural, with the lowest population of any New England state. Dairy farming and tourism drive the economy.

In 2000 the Supreme Court of Vermont declared that gay couples have the same rights and privileges as heterosexual ones – the first US state to acknowledge these civil unions.

Information

Vermont Chamber of Commerce (☎ 802-223-3443; www.vtchamber.com; PO Box 37, Montpelier, VT 05601)
Vermont Travel & Tourism (☎ 802-828-3676, 800-837-6668; www.travel-vermont.com; 6 Baldwin St, Montpelier, VT 05633)

SOUTHERN VERMONT

Vermont's southern part has some of the state's most beautiful small villages and one of its funkiest towns.

Brattleboro

The 1960s alternative lifestyle is alive and well in this pleasant workaday town, amidst lots of bookstores and coffeehouses. Rudyard Kipling married a Brattleboro woman in 1892 and lived for a time in a big Brattleboro house he named 'Naulaukha,' where he wrote *The Jungle Book*.

At the center of the town's commercial district is the art deco Latchis Building, which includes a theater, hotel, brewpub and restaurant. The **Brattleboro Museum & Art Center** (☎ 802-257-0124; www.brattleboromuseum.org; 10 Vernon St; adult $3, child 5-11 free; ⏰ noon-6pm Tue-Sun), in the Union Railroad Station, has a collection of reed organs and temporary exhibits.

Surrounding Windham County has 30 **covered bridges**. For a free driving guide that will lead you to them, contact the **Brattleboro Area Chamber of Commerce** (☎ 802-254-4565; 180 Main St; ⏰ 9am-5pm Mon-Fri, 10am-2pm Sat).

SLEEPING

Latchis Hotel (☎ 802-254-6300; www.latchis.com; 50 Main St; with breakfast d $85-105;) This restored art deco hotel has 30 simply furnished rooms in the town center.

Crosby House (☎ 800-528-1868; www.crosbyhouse.com; 175 Western Ave; with breakfast d $120-150;) In this 1868 Italianate-style mansion, the three rooms are furnished with antiques and period pieces.

Molly Stark Motel (☎ 802-254-2440; VT 9; d $70-80;) Three miles west of I-91, this motel has 14 standard units.

Fort Dummer State Park (☎ 802-254-2610, camping reservations 888-409-7579; 434 Old Guilford Rd; campsites/lean-tos $14/21) Has 51 campsites and 10 lean-to shelters; from I-91 exit 1, go north a few hundred yards on US 5, a half-mile east on Fairground Rd, then a mile south on Main St and Old Guilford Rd.

Hidden Acres Camping Resort (☎ 802-254-2098, 866-411-2267; 792 US 5; campsites/RV sites $20/26;) North of I-91 exit 3, with 40 sites, a laundry, playground and minigolf.

EATING & DRINKING

Common Ground (☎ 802-257-0855; 25 Elliot St, off Main St; mains $5-12) Perhaps New England's purest expression of 1960s alternative dining, this earthy crunchy place serves excellent vegetarian dishes.

Brattleboro Food Co-op (☎ 802-257-0236; 2 Main St, at Canal St) Stop into this market for veggie-friendly (and other) picnic supplies.

TJ Buckley's (☎ 802-257-4922; 132 Elliot St; dinners $25-32) This upscale eatery in a 1927 diner earns raves for its innovative contemporary fare.

Windham Brewery (☎ 802-254-4747; 6 Flat St) Try the Olde Guilford Porter, a dark, medium-bodied ale.

Moles Eye Café (☎ 802-257-0771; Main & High Sts) There's live music on weekends at this oak-paneled café.

Wilmington & Mount Snow

Wilmington is the gateway to **Mt Snow** (☎ 802-464-3333, 800-245-7669; www.mountsnow.com; VT100), a popular family skiing and biking area. Contact the **Mt Snow Valley Chamber of Commerce** (☎ 802-464-8092, 877-887-6884; www.visitvermont.com; 21 W Main St; 10am-5pm) for information.

The 14-room **Nutmeg Inn** (☎ 802-464-3351, 800-277-5402; www.nutmeginn.com; VT 9; with breakfast d $89-139, ste $159-199;), in an 18th-century farmhouse, is furnished with antiques; some rooms have fireplaces. **Vintage Motel** (☎ 802-464-8824, 800-899-9660; VT 9; d $95;), just west of town, has 18 tidy units.

Bennington

A mix of picture-perfect Vermont village (Old Bennington) and, a mile to the east, blue-collar town (Bennington proper), this is also home to the alternative Bennington College. The city is known for its tall obelisk commemorating the Battle of Bennington (1777), during the Revolutionary War, when Vermont troops defeated two units of British soldiers. Robert Frost, perhaps the most famous 20th-century US poet, is buried here.

US 7, VT 7A and VT 9 converge in Bennington. Most lodgings and restaurants are in the downtown area.

INFORMATION

Bennington Area Chamber of Commerce (☎ 802-447-3311, 800-229-0252; US 7; 9am-5pm Mon-Fri, also 10am-4pm Sat-Sun mid-May–mid-Oct) provides information for visitors.

SIGHTS & ACTIVITIES

The **Bennington Museum** (☎ 802-447-1571; www.benningtonmuseum.com; VT 9; adult $7, child 5-11 free; 9am-6pm Jun-Oct, 9am-5pm Nov-May) holds an outstanding collection of early Americana, as well as a rich collection of paintings by Anna Mary 'Grandma' Moses.

Towering at the center of Old Bennington, **Old First Church** (☎ 802-447-1223) is a Palladian-style church built in 1806. Its churchyard holds the bones of five Vermont governors, numerous Revolutionary War soldiers and poet Robert Frost.

Built in 1887–91, **Bennington Battle Monument** (☎ 802-447-0550; Monument Ave; adult $1.50, child 5-11 50¢; 9am-5pm mid-Apr–Oct) is the loftiest structure in Vermont. To reach the **Bennington Battlefield Historic Site**, the actual battlefield, follow the signs from the monument along back roads, through a covered bridge to North Bennington, then go west on VT 67 just over the NY state line.

BattenKill Canoe Ltd (☎ 802-362-2800, 800-421-5268; 6328 VT 7A, Arlington; canoes $45-55, kayaks $25-30) rents canoes and kayaks for self-guided paddling down the Batten Kill River.

SLEEPING & EATING

Molly Stark Inn (☎ 802-442-9631, 800-356-3076; www.mollystarkinn.com; 1067 E Main St; with breakfast d $70-125, ste $135-160, cottage $150-175) This Victorian inn has six comfortable rooms, with quilt-topped beds and antique furnishings, as well as a separate cottage and two 'sugarhouse' suites with fireplaces and whirlpool tubs.

Paradise Motor Inn (☎ 802-442-8351; www.theparadisemotorinn.com; 141 W Main St; d $75-105;) This big (76-room) place with a heated pool and tennis courts is right in the town center.

Other motel options include the **Vermonter Motor Lodge** (☎ 802-442-2529; VT 9; d $55-80;) about 2 miles west of Old Bennington and the **Mid-Town Motel** (☎ 802-447-0189; www.themidtownmotel.com; 107 W Main St; d $68-75;) in town.

HI Greenwood Lodge Hostel & Campsites (☎ 802-442-2547; VT 9; dm $19-22, d $41-47, campsites/RV sites $19/23) Eight miles east of Bennington at Prospect Mountain in Woodford, is set in a wooded area with three ponds. There are dorm and private rooms, as well as camping facilities.

Alldays & Onions (☎ 802-447-0043; 519 Main St; lunches $5-7, dinners $13-23) Create your own lunchtime sandwich.

Blue Benn Diner (☎ 802-442-5140; 314 North St; mains $5-11) Supplements breakfast-all-day; standard diner fare with Asian-inspired and veggie dishes.

Rattlesnake Café (☎ 802-447-7018; 230 North St; mains $6-16) Pair a margarita with a hefty burrito at this Tex-Mex café.

Manchester

For almost two centuries, Manchester really has been a popular summer resort. The

NEW ENGLAND

mountain scenery, the moderate summer climate and the Batten Kill River – one of Vermont's best trout streams – continue to draw crowds. Now there's also skiing, golfing and shopping.

Manchester Village is the southern part of town, a dignified, historic Vermont village centered on the posh Equinox Hotel. Manchester Center, a few miles north along VT 7A, is devoted mostly to upscale outlet stores, inns and restaurants.

INFORMATION

Manchester Regional Chamber of Commerce (☎ 802-362-2100, 800-362-4144; www.manchestervermont.net; 5046 Main St, Manchester Center; 🕐 10am-5pm, closed Sun Nov-Apr) has information for visitors.

SIGHTS & ACTIVITIES

Just south of Manchester, **Hildene** (☎ 802-362-1788; www.hildene.org; 1005 Hildene Rd/VT 7A; adult $10, child 5-11 $4; 🕐 9:30am-4pm mid-May–Oct) is a 24-room Georgian Revival mansion. It was the country estate of Robert Todd Lincoln, son of President Abraham Lincoln. Tours of the stately house and its formal gardens last about 1½ hours.

Fisher-folk appreciate the fine display of fly-fishing equipment at **American Museum of Fly Fishing** (☎ 802-362-3300; 4070 Main St; call for hr and admission). The museum expects to reopen in 2004 after a renovation.

You can drive to the summit of the 3835ft peak **Mt Equinox**. Take VT 7A south of Manchester to **Skyline Dr** (☎ 802-362-1114), a private 5-mile toll road ($8 for car and two passengers).

For bicycling, rent a road, mountain or hybrid bike from **Batten Kill Sports Bicycle Shop** (☎ 802-362-2734; US 7 & VT 11/30; per day $20-25).

Bromley Mountain (☎ 802-824-5522; www.bromley.com; VT 11, Peru), a small family ski resort, switches gears in the summer to become an adventure park, with an Alpine Slide, go-carts, trampolines, a climbing wall, a water slide and more. **Stratton Mountain** (☎ 802-297-4000, 800-787-2886; www.stratton.com; VT 30), 16 miles east of Manchester, is a larger ski area, with a vertical drop of more than 2000ft, 90 downhill trails and almost 20 miles of cross-country trails.

The **Appalachian Trail**, which overlaps the **Long Trail** in Vermont, passes just east of Manchester. There are shelters about every 10 miles. For details and maps of good area hikes, contact the chamber of commerce or the **USFS Green Mountain National Forest** (☎ 802-362-2307; 2538 Depot St, Manchester Center).

SLEEPING

Manchester has plenty of inns and motels. The chamber of commerce can usually help you find a room.

Barnstead Inn (☎ 802-362-1619, 800-331-1619; www.barnsteadinn.com; Bonnet St; d $100-210;) In Manchester Center, this renovated 1830s hay barn has 14 country-style rooms with wide-beamed ceilings.

Seth Warner Inn (☎ 802-362-3830; 2353 Main St; with breakfast d $110-120;) The five cheery rooms at this 1800s B&B have canopy beds topped with quilts.

Equinox (☎ 802-362-4700, 800-362-4747; www.equinoxresort.com; 3567 Main St; d $229-399;) Manchester's top place to stay boasts 183 rooms, its own 18-hole golf course, indoor and outdoor pools, a spa, multiple tennis courts and quite a multitude of other resort services.

The many area motels include **Chalet Motel** (☎ 802-362-1622, 800-343-9900; www.thechaletmotel.com; VT 11/30; d $60-110;), **Stamford Motel** (☎ 802-362-2342; www.stamfordmotel.com; 6458 Main St; d $60-80;) and **Aspen Motel** (☎ 802-362-2450; VT 7A; d $70-105).

Emerald Lake State Park (☎ 802-362-1655, camping reservations 888-409-7579; US 7; campsites/lean-tos $16/23) Just north of the village of East Dorset, with 69 campsites and 36 lean-tos on a wooded ridge above the lake.

EATING

Bistro Henry (☎ 802-362-4982; 1778 VT 11/30; dinners $19-24) Run by husband-and-wife chef-owners, this upscale bistro earns real kudos for its adventurous Mediterranean fare and decadent desserts; save room for the Grand Marnier crème brûlée or the flourless chocolate Chambord cake.

Perfect Wife (☎ 802-362-2817; 2594 Depot St; dinners $13-24) Chef-owner Amy Chamberlain claims that her contemporary American restaurant is 'not just another pretty place.' Sample her crab cakes, sesame-crusted tuna or turkey schnitzel and decide for yourself.

Forty Nine Forty (☎ 802-362-9839; 4940 Main St; mains $7-22) This something-for-everyone place serves omelettes, burgers and sandwiches as well as more substantial updated American fare.

Restaurant at Willow Pond (☎ 802-362-4733; VT 7A; dinners $13-24) Head to this 1770s colonial farmhouse for northern Italian cuisine, from pasta with pesto to veal *piccata*.

For lighter fare, stop into **Mrs Murphy's Donuts & Coffee Shop** (☎ 802-362-1874; VT 11/30; mains $3-5) or the **Little Rooster Café** (☎ 802-362-3496; VT 7A; breakfasts & lunches $5-9).

CENTRAL VERMONT

Vermont's midsection, bisecting the Green Mountains, features ski villages, a college town and a rarified postcard-perfect village.

Woodstock & Around

This Vermont town is the antithesis of Woodstock, New York, that symbol of 1960s hippie living. Vermont's version, chartered in 1761 and centered around a classic village green, has been the highly dignified shire town of Windsor County since 1766.

INFORMATION

Woodstock Area Chamber of Commerce (☎ 802-457-3555; www.woodstockvt.com; 18 Central St) provides information for visitors.

SIGHTS & ACTIVITIES

At the historic **Marsh-Billings-Rockefeller National Historical Park** (☎ 802-457-3368; www.nps.gov/mabi; VT 12; adult $6, child 5-11 $3; 🕑 10am-5pm late May–Oct) you can tour the property's 1805 mansion and formal gardens.

Learn about Vermont dairying, past and present, at **Billings Farm & Museum** (☎ 802-457-2355; www.billingsfarm.org; VT12 at River Rd; adult $9, child 5-11 $4.50; 🕑 10am-4pm May-Oct) – a working dairy farm and exhibit center.

Vermont Institute of Natural Sciences (☎ 802-457-2779; 27023 Church Hill Rd) is just 1.5 miles southwest of the green, this facility has a raptor center, which houses hawks, falcons, eagles and owls and has exhibits about these birds. The institute is constructing a new visitors center that is expected to open in 2004; phone for an update before visiting.

To learn about maple sugaring and cheese-making (and taste different varieties), head for the friendly **Sugarbush Farm** (☎ 802-457-1757, 800-271-1757; www.sugarbushfarm.com; 591 Sugarbush Farm Rd; admission free; 🕑 8am-5pm Mon-Fri, 9am-5pm Sat-Sun). It's just 4 miles east of town on a dirt road off US 4. The sugaring season is from March to April, although you can tour the sugarhouse year-round. Be sure to phone for directions and road conditions before visiting.

Eight miles east of Woodstock, US 4 passes over **Quechee Gorge** (*kwee*-chee, US 4), a 170ft craggy chasm cut by the Ottauquechee River. You can hike along the gorge in Quechee Gorge State Park, which also has campsites and picnic facilities.

SLEEPING

Shire Motel (☎ 802-457-2211; www.shiremotel.com; 46 Pleasant St/US 4; d $88-145; ⊠) This well-maintained motel is set right on the Ottauquechee River, within walking distance of the town center. The 33 rooms are furnished with colonial-style reproductions.

Village Inn of Woodstock (☎ 802-457-1255; www.villageinnofwoodstock.com; 41 Pleasant St/US 4; with breakfast d $85-155; ⊠) Across the street, this pastel-pink Victorian house-turned-inn has eight frilly, antique-filled rooms.

Woodstock Inn & Resort (☎ 802-457-1100, 800-448-7900; www.woodstockinn.com; 14 The Green; d $200-390; ⊠ ⊠) The town's grand dame is the stately inn with four restaurants, cross-country skiing, an indoor sports center and a host of other facilities. Off-season, rates for some rooms may drop below $130. Gourmets should inquire about the 'Chef for a Day' cooking-class program.

Quechee Gorge State Park (☎ 802-295-2990, camping reservations 888-409-7579; US 4, Quechee; campsites/lean-tos $14/21) There are 47 pine-shaded campsites and seven lean-tos.

EATING

Pane e Salute (☎ 802-457-4882; 61 Central St; lunches $5-11, dinners $12-16) At this Italian café, you can get first-rate coffees, pastries and light lunches during the day. In the evening it becomes a classic Italian dining room; a four-course prix-fixe dinner is available for $36.

Woodstock Farmers' Market (☎ 802-457-3658; 468 Woodstock Rd/US 4) Just west of town, this grocery sells organic produce, cheeses, prepared foods and breads – the perfect fixings for a picnic lunch.

Prince & the Pauper (☎ 802-457-1818; 24 Elm St; bistro $13-20, prix-fixe dinners $39) This elegant New American bistro in the town center serves a three-course prix-fixe menu that might include prosciutto-wrapped sea bass or grilled veal chops with porcini mushrooms. There's a lighter bistro menu, too, with dishes such as pizza, crab cakes or meatloaf.

Simon Pearce Restaurant (☎ 802-295-1470; 1760 Main St, Quechee; lunches $10-14, dinners $19-29) Located in the mill where Simon Pearce glass is blown by hand, this restaurant overlooks a waterfall and covered bridge. Luckily, the New American dishes rival the scenery.

Killington

Killington is Vermont's prime **ski resort** (☎ 802-422-3333; www.killington.com), with 200 runs on seven mountains, a vertical drop of more than 3000ft and 31 lifts. In the summer, the **Mountain Bike Center** (☎ 802-422-6232; Killington Rd) rents mountain bikes for $50 per day (helmet and trail map included). You and your bike can take the gondola to the 4241ft summit of Killington Mountain and ride down, finding your way among 45 miles of trails; all-day access to the trails and gondola costs $32.

There are well over a hundred lodging places in the Killington area. For help finding a bed, call the **Killington Lodging Bureau** (☎ 800-621-6867).

Middlebury

Set in the western Vermont hills, prosperous Middlebury is home of **Middlebury College** (☎ information & tours 802-443-3000; www.middlebury.edu; 131 S Main St; admission free; tours 10am & 2pm Mon-Fri, also 10am Sat Aug-Sep & Oct-Nov).

INFORMATION

Addison County Chamber of Commerce (☎ 802-388-7951; www.midvermont.com; 2 Court St; 9am-5pm Mon-Fri) provides information for visitors.

SIGHTS & ACTIVITIES

The **Middlebury College Museum of Art** (☎ 802-443-5007; S Main St; admission free; 10am-5pm Tue-Fri, noon-5pm Sat-Sun) is worth a look, particularly for its collections of 19th-century European and American sculpture, photography and contemporary prints. The **Vermont State Craft Center at Frog Hollow** (☎ 802-388-3177; 1 Mill St) showcases and sells fine works by Vermont artisans.

Morgan horses, America's first unique breed, all derive from a Thoroughbred-Arabian colt bred by Justin Morgan in the late 18th century. You can see 70 registered Morgans at the University of Vermont's **Morgan Horse Farm** (☎ 802-388-2011; Horse Farm Rd; adult $4, child 5-11 $1; 9am-4pm May-Oct), about 3 miles from Middlebury; take VT 125 west and go north on VT 23.

SLEEPING & EATING

Chipman Inn (☎ 802-388-2390, 800-890-2390; www.chipmaninn.com; VT 125, Ripton; with breakfast d $95-150) This 1828 Federal-style house 8 miles east of Middlebury, is close to the farm where poet Robert Frost spent 23 years. It has eight country-comfortable rooms.

Swift House Inn (☎ 802-338-9925; www.swifthouseinn.com; 25 Stewart Ln; with breakfast d $110-130, carriage house d $225-255) This inn has 21 rooms in three buildings – mid-priced rooms in the Main House and Gate House, and more luxurious accommodations in the Carriage House. There's even a sauna for guests.

Nearby motels include the 12-room **Sugarhouse Motel** (☎ 802-388-2770, 800-784-2746; US 7; d $55-95), 2 miles north of town, and the 22-room **Blue Spruce Motel** (☎ 802-388-4091; US 7 S; d $75-85).

Branbury State Park (☎ 802-247-5925, camping reservations 888-409-7579; VT 53, Salisbury; campsites/lean-tos $16/23) About 10 miles south of Middlebury, with campsites dotted around 69 acres near Lake Dunmore.

Tully & Marie's (☎ 802-388-4182; 5 Bakery Lane; lunches $6-10, dinners $8-19) Overlooking the creek, this spot serves up New American fare with Asian, Italian and Mexican influences – lots of vegetarian options, too.

Storm Café (☎ 802-388-1063; 3 Mill St; lunches $5-8) This café in the basement of the stone Frog Hollow Mill is popular with artists and artisans for its lunchtime soups, salads and sandwiches.

Steve's Park Diner (☎ 802-388-3297; 66 Merchants Row; mains $6-8) Cheap eats for breakfast and lunch.

Otter Creek Bakery (☎ 802-388-3371; 14 College St) Excels in take-out pastries and coffee.

Sugarbush, Warren & Waitsfield

The towns of Warren and Waitsfield boast two significant ski areas: **Sugarbush** and **Mad River Glen**, in the mountains west of VT 100. There are hordes of opportunities for bicycling, canoeing, horseback riding, kayaking, gliding and other activities. Stop at the **Sugarbush Chamber of Commerce** (☎ 802-496-3409, 800-828-4748; www.madrivervalley.com; VT 100, Waitsfield; 9am-5pm Mon-Fri) for a mountain of current details. Information, rest rooms and telephones are available 24 hours a day in the chamber of commerce's lobby.

NORTHERN VERMONT

Northern Vermont's draws are diverse: a tiny state capitol, a groovy university town on the edge of Lake Champlain and a ski mecca.

Montpelier

Montpelier (mont-*peel*-yer) would qualify as a large village in some countries. But in sparsely populated Vermont it is the capital, complete with a gold-domed **State House** (☎ 802-828-2228; admission free; tours 10am-3:30pm Mon-Fri, 11am-2:30pm Sat Jul–mid-Oct), built in 1836 of granite quarried nearby. The **Vermont Chamber of Commerce** (☎ 802-223-3443; www.vtchamber.com) can provide assistance when you're planning a visit.

Montpelier is also home to the New England Culinary Institute (NECI). Students gain prowess at the smart-casual **Main Street Grill & Bar** (☎ 802-223-3188; 118 Main St; lunches $6-8, dinners $6-17), which serves New American fare, and upstairs at the smaller, more formal **Chef's Table** (☎ 802-229-9202; 118 Main St; lunches $6-9, dinners $16-28).

Stowe & Around

Founded in 1794, Stowe was a simple, pretty backwoods farming town until 1859, when the Summit House was built as a summer resort atop Mt Mansfield (4393ft), Vermont's highest peak. Skiing was introduced around 1912, and in the late 1930s the longest and highest chairlift in the USA at the time was installed, and skiing really took off. Today the bustling town, with its Alpine architecture, draws visitors for its great ski trails. Biking and hiking are popular when the snows melt. Ice cream devotees make the pilgrimage to the Ben & Jerry's factory nearby.

Most lodgings and restaurants are along VT 108, the Mountain Rd.

INFORMATION

Stowe Area Association (☎ 802-253-7321, 877-467-8693; www.gostowe.com; 51 Main St; 🕒 9am-5pm Mon-Fri, 9am-8pm summer & fall) provides information and lodging assistance.

SIGHTS & ACTIVITIES

The two-peak **Stowe Mountain Resort** (☎ 802-253-3000; 800-253-4754; www.stowe.com; 5781 Mountain Rd) has a vertical drop of 2360ft, 11 lifts (including a gondola) and 48 ski trails, including some of New England's toughest runs.

Cross-country skiing is available at several places near Stowe, including the **Trapp Family Lodge** (☎ 802-253-8511, 800-826-7000; www.trappfamily.com; 700 Trapp Hill Rd), run by the family whose life inspired the film *The Sound of Music*. The Catamount Trail is North America's longest ski trail; it follows forest paths and old logging roads from northern to southern Vermont. For information, contact the **Catamount Trail Association** (☎ 802-864-5794; www.catamounttrail.org).

To walk, bike, or skate, follow the 5.25-mile **Stowe Recreation Path** that runs from the village toward the mountain. Rent bikes at **Mountain Sports & Bike Shop** (☎ 802-253-7919; 580 Mountain Rd; per 2hr/day $11/25). **AJ's Ski & Sports** (☎ 802-253-4593; Mountain Rd) rents bikes ($7/24 per hour/day) and in-line skates ($7/24 per hour/day).

The **Green Mountain Club** (☎ 802-244-7037; www.greenmountainclub.org; VT 100), a few miles south of Stowe, maintains the **Long Trail** (see p201) and is an excellent resource for long and short hikes.

If you visit in mild weather, take a drive through dramatic **Smuggler's Notch**, northwest of Stowe on VT 108 (the road is closed in the winter).

For canoeing and kayaking, **Umiak Outdoor Outfitters** (☎ 802-253-2317, 849 S Main St) has rentals ($18/42 per hour/day) and offers river shuttle trips ($28 to $38) and instruction for all levels.

Worked up an appetite and deserve a treat? Head 10 miles south to the **Ben & Jerry's Ice Cream Factory** (☎ 802-882-1260, 866-258-6877; www.benjerry.com; VT 100, Waterbury; adult $3, child 5-11 free; tours 9am-8 pm Jul-Aug, 9am-6pm Sep-Oct, 10am-5pm Nov-May, 9am-5pm Jun) and find out how their super-premium ice creams are made. Tours include a free sample.

SLEEPING

Auberge de Stowe (☎ 802-253-7787, 800-387-8789; www.aubergedestowe.com; 692 S Main St; with breakfast d $69-79; 🏊) Though this eight-room B&B fronts busy VT 100, the interior is homey and family-friendly – think quilt-topped beds and a cozy common room. Out back, it faces a broad lawn and woods. There's a swimming pool and hot tub, too.

Sun & Ski Inn (☎ 802-253-7159, 800-448-5223; www.stowesunandski.com; 1613 Mountain Rd; with breakfast d $85-110; 🏊) The motel-style rooms are perfectly adequate, but it's the pretty setting facing a wide lawn and a stream that make this lodging more than run of the mill. In winter, the outdoor pool is heated to 102°F. Guests can also use the indoor pool at the sister Grey Fox Inn.

Innsbruck Inn (☎ 802-253-8582, 800-225-8582; www.innsbruckinn.com; 4361 Mountain Rd; with breakfast d $90-120;) This 25-room motel is done up in Alpine style. In true Alpine fashion, there's a hot tub and sauna.

Stowehof Inn (☎ 802-253-9722, 800-932-7136; www.stowehofinn.com; 434 Edson Hill Rd; with breakfast d $110-240;) Another Alpine-style hostelry, this one is a relaxed resort set in the woods off Mountain Rd. The best of the 46 rooms have mountain views; some have vaulted ceilings, fireplaces or canopy beds.

Other lodging options include the **Stowe Motel** (☎ 802-253-7629, 800-829-7629; www.stowemotel.com; 2043 Mountain Rd; d $70-130;), which has both rooms and efficiencies (plus an outdoor hot tub), and the **Fiddler's Green Inn** (☎ 802-253-8124, 800-882-5346, 4859 Mountain Rd; d $60-90), with seven rustic but comfortable rooms.

Smugglers Notch State Park (☎ 802-253-4014; 7248 Mountain Rd; campsites/lean-tos $14/21), 8 miles northwest, has 21 campsites and 14 lean-to shelters. **Little River State Park** (☎ 802-244-7103; 3444 Little River Rd, Waterbury; campsites/lean-tos $16/23), next to the Waterbury Reservoir, also has campsites and lean-tos; from VT 100, take US 2 1.5 miles west, then go 3.5 miles north on Little River Rd.

EATING

Dutch Pancake Café (☎ 802-253-5330; 990 Mountain Rd; pancakes $6-10) Serving over 80 varieties of sweet and savory crepes the size of a dinner plate, this cheery breakfast café is a pancake-lover's dream. Try the apple-cinnamon or the potato.

McCarthy's (☎ 802-253-8626; 454 Mountain Rd; mains $3-7) Locals stop in for hearty breakfasts of French toast, apple pancakes and omelettes.

Harvest Market (☎ 802-253-3800; 1031 Mountain Rd) This upscale market sells morning coffee and pastries, as well as pâtés, cheeses, salads, fresh breads, wine and other picnic supplies.

Gracie's Restaurant (☎ 802-253-8741; Main St, in the Carlson Building; lunches $6-10, dinners $8-18) This canine-themed eatery offers a huge American menu, ranging from 'dog-gone good' burgers to Caesar salads to steaks. There's nothing doggy about the food, but purists may bark about the doggy puns and decor.

Trattoria La Festa (☎ 802-253-8480; 4080 Mountain Rd; mains $15-20) At this Tuscan-style trattoria, you can tuck into first-rate Italian dinner classics, including pasta Bolognese, chicken parmigiana and veal marsala.

Pie in the Sky (☎ 802-253-5100; 492 Mountain Rd; pizzas $9-16, pastas $7-10). Try this Mountain Rd spot for pizzas and pastas.

Burlington

With the University of Vermont's student population and a vibrant cultural and social life, Burlington, set right on Lake Champlain, has a spirited, youthful ambience.

INFORMATION

Emergency

Emergency number (☎ 911) For police, fire or other emergency.

Internet Access

Fletcher Free Library (☎ 802-8633403; 235 College St; free for 45 min per day)

Kinko's (☎ 802-658-2561; 199 Main St; per min 20¢; 24hr)

Media

Burlington Free Press (www.burlingtonfreepress.com)

Medical Services

Fletcher Allen Health Care (☎ 802-847-0000; 111 Colchester Ave) Twenty-four-hour emergency service.

Post

US post office (☎ 802-863-6033; 11 Elmwood Ave; 8am-5pm Mon-Fri, 9am-1pm Sat)

Tourist Offices

Lake Champlain Regional Chamber of Commerce (☎ 802-863-3489; www.vermont.org; 60 Main St; 8am-5pm Mon-Fri)

SIGHTS & ACTIVITIES

On a 45-acre estate 7 miles south of Burlington, **Shelburne Museum** (☎ 802-985-3346; www.shelburnemuseum.org; US 7, Shelburne; adult $18, child 5-11 $9; 10am-5pm May-Oct) holds 100,000 works of American arts and crafts in 39 exhibition buildings. There's a classic round barn (1901), a circus building, a sawmill (1786), a lighthouse (1871) and even the 1906 side-wheeler SS *Ticonderoga*.

Shelburne Farms (☎ 802-985-8686; www.shelburnefarms.org; Harbor Rd; adult $6, child 5-11 $4; 10am-4pm mid-May–mid-Oct) is a 1400-acre working farm with a 24-bedroom English country manor (see below). It was the Vermont hideaway of the wealthy Webb family. The farm still produces really good cheese, maple syrup, mustard and other comestibles you can buy. At the Children's Farmyard, kids can help with farm chores and visit with the animals.

Children also enjoy touring **Vermont Teddy Bear Factory** (☎ 802-985-3001; www.vermontteddybear.com; US 7, Shelburne; adult $2, child 5-11 free; 9:30am-5pm Mon-Sat, 10:30am-4pm Sun) to see stuffed animals being made. Although the admission fees are low, beware: it's hard to leave without purchasing a cuddly little bear (starting at $20).

Fleming Museum (☎ 802-656-2090; 61 Colchester Ave; adult $3, child 5-11 $2; 9am-4pm Tue-Fri & 1-5pm Sat-Sun early Sep–Apr, noon-4pm Tue-Fri & 1-5pm Sat-Sun May–early Sep) is the University of Vermont's art museum, which showcases works from ancient times and contemporary America.

Walk or bike along the 7.5-mile **Burlington Recreation Path**, which follows the lakeshore. Rent bikes at **Ski Rack** (☎ 802-658-3313; 85 Main St; per hr/day $10/22).

SLEEPING

Hartwell House B&B (☎ 802-658-9242, 888 658 9242; www.vermontbedandbreakfast.com; 170 Ferguson St; with breakfast d $70-75;) In a residential neighborhood south of downtown, welcoming owner Linda Hartwell rents three smartly-decorated, homey, shared-bath rooms and dispenses travel tips over breakfast.

Inn at Shelburne Farms (☎ 802-985-8498; Harbor Rd; d $100-325) This 24-bedroom country manor (1899) on the grounds of Shelburne Farms is now an upscale inn. Though the overall style is traditional, rooms vary considerably (as do the prices); the lowest-priced ones share baths.

Many budget and mid-range chain motels cluster along Shelburne Rd (US 7) in South Burlington on the way to Shelburne.

HI Mrs Farrell's Home Hostel (☎ 802-865-3730; www.hiayh.org; dm $15-17; Apr-Oct) Try this six-bed hostel for another budget option; call for reservations and directions.

North Beach Campground (☎ 802-862-0942, 800-571-1198; 60 Institute Rd; campsites/RV sites $21/29) Has 67 campsites and 69 RV sites on 45 acres fronting the lake.

EATING

A Single Pebble (☎ 802-865-5200; 133 Bank St; mains $6-16) You might not expect to find a sophisticated gourmet Chinese restaurant in northern Vermont, but the fine regional fare at this smart-casual downtowner would stand up to Asian eats most anywhere. Even if you're not a vegetarian, try Buddha's Sesame 'Beef' (made with seitan) – it's crisp, garlicky and delicious. Make reservations, especially on weekends.

Five Spice Café (☎ 802-864-4045; 175 Church St; lunches $7-9, dinners $10-18) Despite cramped quarters, this Pan-Asian eatery manages to serve contemporary creations inspired by Chinese, Thai, Vietnamese and Indonesian classics. Sunday dim sum brunch is very popular.

Penny Cluse Café (☎ 802-651-8834; 169 Cherry St; breakfasts $4-8, lunches $6-9) Innovative breakfasts (such as polenta with eggs) are a speciality at this cheerful downtown café. Expect long waits on weekends.

Stonesoup (☎ 802-862-7616; 211 College St; lunches $4-10) A godsend for vegetarians, this friendly, funky spot serves hearty soups, sandwiches and pizzas and offers a salad bar, too; it's open until 7pm.

Uncommon Grounds (☎ 802-865-6227; 482 Church St) This good-coffee mecca has prime sidewalk tables.

For simple old-time fare, try **Henry's Diner** (☎ 802-862-9010; 115 Bank St; mains $4-8) or **Oasis Diner** (☎ 802-864-5308; 189 Bank St; mains $4-6).

DRINKING

Sweetwaters (☎ 802-864-9800; 120 Church St) With nouveau-Victorian decor, this is a local watering hole for the upwardly mobile.

Vermont Pub & Brewery (☎ 802-865-0500; 144 College St) has pints made on the premises, as does **Three Needs** (☎ 802-658-0889; 207 College St).

ENTERTAINMENT

Thursday's *Burlington Free Press* has up-to-the-minute entertainment information.

Red Square (☎ 802-859-8909, 136 Church St) Mixes mean martinis and roadhouse music; stylish.

Ri-Ra The Irish Pub (☎ 802-860-9401; 123 Church St) Pours pints and hosts live music several nights a week, from acoustic to jazz to Irish.

Waiting Room (☎ 802-862-3455; 156 St Paul St) A somewhat older, cosmopolitan crowd hangs out here for live jazz, blues and international music Wednesday to Saturday.

135 Pearl (☎ 802-863-2343; 135 Pearl St) The center of northern Vermont's gay scene.

GETTING THERE & AWAY

Vermont Transit (☎ 802-864-6811, 800-451-3292; www.vermonttransit.com; 345 Pine St) serves many Vermont towns, as well as Boston, Albany, NY, and Montreal. **Greyhound** (☎ 800-231-2222) operates buses between Burlington and Montreal ($25, 2½ hours). The **Lake Champlain Transportation Co** (☎ 802-864-9804; www.ferries.com; King St Dock; adult/child/car $4/1.50/14) runs frequent car ferries from late May to mid-October across the lake to Port Kent, New York (one hour).

NEW HAMPSHIRE

Mountainous, politically conservative and naturally beautiful, New Hampshire considered its symbol to be the craggy Old Man of the Mountain (or Great Stone Face), a natural 'profile' of a man formed by a granite hillside at Franconia Notch. In 2003, the Old Man finally eroded and crumbled. Despite region-wide laments about the Old Man's demise, the state remains stoic in spirit – and just as scenic. Make a beeline for the White Mountain National Forest, which covers much of the state. Portsmouth, the state's coolest small city and gateway to its short seacoast, is also worth a visit.

History

In 1629, Captain John Mason laid claim to the area between the Piscataqua and Merrimack Rivers, coining the name 'New Hampshire.' In 1679 the region became a royal colony, governed jointly with Massachusetts by Boston's royal governor-general. Only in 1741 did New Hampshire get its own royal governor. By the mid-1750s, lumbering, flax and linen production kept the colonists busy. In 1788 New Hampshire ratified the new US Constitution and joined the union.

During the 19th-century industrialization boom, Manchester became a manufacturing powerhouse, with the great Amoskeag Mills stretching for more than a mile along the Merrimack River. Today agriculture, some manufacturing and tourism are the state's economic mainstays.

NEW HAMPSHIRE FACTS

Nicknames Granite State, White Mountain State
Population 1,275,056 (41st)
Area 9351 sq miles (46th)
Admitted to Union June 21, 1788 (9th)
Capital city Concord (population 41,000)
Other cities Manchester (108,000), Portsmouth (21,000)
State motto Live free or die
State amphibian Spotted newt
Birthplace of astronaut Alan Shepard (1923–98), teacher and *Challenger* space-shuttle astronaut Christa McAuliffe (1948–86), *New York Tribune* founder and editor Horace Greeley (1811–72), Tupperware inventor Earl Tupper (1907–83)
Famous for the 1944 Bretton Woods conference establishing the postwar economic order

Information

New Hampshire Division of Travel & Tourism (☎ 603-271-2665, 800-386-4664; www.visitnh.gov; 172 Pembroke Rd, PO Box 1856, Concord, NH 03302) provides information for visitors.

PORTSMOUTH

An hour's drive north of Boston, Portsmouth has a restored city center with good restaurants and shops housed in old brick buildings. The city was established in 1623 when a band of intrepid settlers sailed to the mouth of the Piscataqua River and scrambled up a bank covered with wild strawberries. Deciding to stay, they named the place 'Strawbery Banke' but changed it to 'Portsmouth' 30 years later. The town grew wealthy on fishing and maritime trade.

Information

Greater Portsmouth Chamber of Commerce (☎ 603-436-1118; www.portcity.org; 500 Market St; ⌚ 8:30am-5pm Mon-Fri) provides information for visitors.

Sights & Activities

Strawbery Banke Museum (☎ 603-433-1100; www.strawberybanke.org; Hancock & Marcy Sts; adult $12, child 5-11 $8; ⌚ 10am-5pm Mon-Sat, noon-5pm Sun May-Oct) is an intriguing living history enclave, set in a 10-acre park and encompassing nearly 40 buildings. It illustrates life in the Portsmouth area from the 1600s through the mid-20th century. Special events and children's programs are held frequently: call for details. From November to April, the museum is open only for 90-minute guided walking tours (tours on the hour 10am to 2pm Thursday to Saturday; closed January).

USS Albacore (☎ 603-436-3680; Market St; adult $5, child 5-11 $2; ⏲ 9:30am-4:30pm late May–mid-Oct, call for winter hr), 205ft-by-27ft submarine, was launched from the Portsmouth Naval Shipyard in 1953 and has been converted into a museum; near I-95 exit 7.

The many hands-on exhibits delight kids at **Children's Museum of Portsmouth** (☎ 603-436-3853, 280 Marcy St; admission $5; ⏲ 10am-5pm Tue-Sat, 1-5pm Sun, also 10am-5pm Mon mid-Jun–Aug).

Several of Portsmouth's grand historic houses have been beautifully preserved, including the 1758 **John Paul Jones House** (☎ 603-436-8420; 43 Middle St, at State St; adult $5, child 5-11 $2.50; ⏲ 11am-5pm mid-May–mid-Oct, closed Wed), which belonged to the man known as 'the father of the US Navy.' You can also tour the 1760 **Wentworth Gardner House** (☎ 603-436-4406; 50 Mechanic St; tours $5; 1-4pm mid-Jun–mid-Oct, closed Mon). The chamber of commerce can provide details about these and other historic homes.

Portsmouth Harbor Cruises (☎ 603-436-8084, 800-776-0915; www.portsmouthharbor.com; Ceres St Dock; adult $11-18, child $7-10; ⏲ mid-May–Oct) runs several trips in neighboring waters, including a cruise to the Isle of Shoals. **Isle of Shoals Steamship Company** (☎ 603-431-5500, 800-441-4620; www.islesofshoals.com; 315 Market St; adult $12-29, child $12-19) also runs island trips spring through fall, as well as summer music cruises.

Sleeping

Bow Street Inn (☎ 603-431-7760; www.bowstreetinn.com; 121 Bow St; with breakfast d $135-149; ✖ P) Located above a theater in a redbrick former brewery, this downtown inn has 10 rooms with brass beds; some have harbor views.

Inn at Strawbery Banke (☎ 603-436-7242, 800-428-3933; www.innatstrawberybanke.com; 314 Court St; with breakfast d $145-150; ✖ P) This inn has seven rooms with quilt-topped beds. It's near the Strawbery Banke Museum, walking distance to the city center.

Portsmouth's motels are clustered at exits 5 and 6 off I-95. Try the **Port Inn** (☎ 603-436-4378, 800-282-7678; www.theportinn.com; Rte 1 Bypass; with breakfast d $100-160; ✖ ♿), the **Anchorage Inn** (☎ 603-431-8111, 800-370-8111; www.anchorageinns.com; 417 Woodbury Ave; d $99-179; ✖ ♿) or the **Meadowbrook Inn** (☎ 603-436-2700, 800-370-2727; www.meadowbrookinn.com; Rte 1 at I-95 exit 5; d $100-120; ✖ ♿).

Eating

Jumpin' Jay's Fish Café (☎ 603-766-3474; 150 Congress St; mains $14-20) Local fish fanciers book tables at this contemporary seafooder, where the 'catch of the day' frequently comes with Asian or Mediterranean flavors.

Blue Mermaid World Grill (☎ 603-427-2583; 409 The Hill; lunches $7-13, dinners $14-20) There's more world-beat fare at this fun grill, where the eclectic dishes range from chicken quesadillas to plantain-crusted grouper to steak with papaya-pineapple salsa. Make a meal of budget-friendly small plates ($7 to $9).

Portsmouth Brewery (☎ 603-431-1115; 56 Market St; mains $6-16) This microbrewery serves several specialty beers, paired with a long pub-fare menu of appetizers, pizzas, salads and more substantial dishes.

Breaking New Grounds (☎ 603-436-9555; 16 Market St) Java purists head here.

Café Brioche (☎ 603-430-9225; 14 Market Sq; mains $3-10) Holds its own in the coffee and pastry department.

Portsmouth Gas Light Company (☎ 603-430-9122; 64 Market St; mains $8-15) This brick-oven pizza specialist runs an all-you-can-eat pizza buffet at lunch weekdays ($6).

Entertainment

Press Room (☎ 603-431-5186; 77 Daniel St) Offers varied nightly music.

Metro (☎ 603-436-0521; 20 High St) Jazz on Friday and Saturday.

Getting There & Away

Greyhound/Vermont Transit (☎ 800-231-2222) connects Boston and Portsmouth with the Maine cities of Portland, Bangor and Bar Harbor. The **Federal Cigar Store** (☎ 603-436-0163; 10 Ladd St), off Market Sq, doubles as Portsmouth's bus station.

MANCHESTER

Exploiting the abundant waterpower of the Merrimack River, Manchester became the state's manufacturing and commercial center in the 19th century. You can still see the brick **Amoskeag Mills** (1838), which stretch along the Commercial St riverbanks for almost 1.5 miles. Manchester is not much of a tourist center; the **Greater Manchester Chamber of Commerce** (☎ 603-666-6600; www.manchester-chamber.org; 889 Elm St; ⏲ 8am-5pm Mon-Fri) has much more information than you'll need.

Manchester does have a fine small art museum: the **Currier Museum of Art** (☎ 603-669-6144; www.currier.org; 201 Myrtle Way; adult $5, child 5-11 free; 🕒 11am-5pm Sun, Mon, Wed, Fri, 11am-8pm Thu, 10am-5pm Sat). The large **Anheuser-Busch Brewery** (☎ 603-595-1202; 221 Daniel Webster Hwy; tours 9:30am-5pm daily Jun-Aug, 10am-4pm daily May & Sep-Dec, 10am-4pm Thu-Mon Jan-Apr), in nearby Merrimack, offers free tours and tastings; take the Everett Turnpike (US 3) to exit 10 (Industrial Dr).

You can always get a square meal at the 24-7 **Red Arrow Diner** (☎ 603-626-1118; 61 Lowell St; mains $2-8), a downtown fixture serving all the basics – from eggs to tuna melts to hot turkey sandwiches; try a big plate of biscuits with sausage gravy.

The recently expanded **Manchester Airport** (☎ 603-624-6539; www.flymanchester.com) is served by most major carriers, as well as discounter **Southwest Airlines**. Air fares to Manchester from other eastern cities (and sometimes from further afield) are often cheaper than fares into Boston. Most major rental car companies have offices at the airport; see p1121 for details. **Vermont Transit** (☎ 800 451-3292) has several buses a day between Manchester Airport and Boston (1¼ hours).

CONCORD & AROUND

The state capital may not have a lot to draw travelers, but there are worthwhile attractions nearby. The **Greater Concord Chamber of Commerce** (☎ 603-224-2508; www.concordnhchamber.com; 40 Commercial St) has information.

The handsome 1819 **State House** (☎ 603-271-2154; 107 N Main St; admission free; 🕒 8am-5pm Mon-Fri) is open weekdays for self-guided tours. The **Museum of New Hampshire History** (☎ 603-226-3189; 6 Eagle Sq; adult $5, child 5-11 $2.50; 🕒 9:30am-5pm Mon-Sat, noon-5pm Sun Jul–mid-Oct & Dec, closed Mon Jan-Jun & Nov) chronicles the 'live free or die' ethic and history of the Granite State.

Christa McAuliffe Planetarium (☎ 603-271-7827; www.starhop.com; 2 Institute Dr; adult $8, child 5-11 $5; 🕒 10am-5pm Mon-Sat, noon-5pm Sun late Jun–Aug, closes at 2pm Mon-Wed rest of the year) honors the New Hampshire schoolteacher-astronaut who died in the Challenger explosion on January 28, 1986. Most shows last about one hour. Take exit 15 from I-93.

Well worth a visit, **Canterbury Shaker Village** (☎ 603-783-9511; www.shakers.org; 288 Shaker Rd, Canterbury; adult $12, child 5-11 $6; 🕒 10am-5pm May-Oct, 10am-4pm Sat-Sun Apr & Nov-Dec) is a traditional Shaker community – now a living history museum. It was founded in 1792 and actively occupied for two centuries. Today, interpreters in period dress demonstrate the Shakers' daily lives and tasks. The village is 15 miles north of Concord on NH 106 (or I-93 exit 18).

LAKE WINNIPESAUKEE

The euphonious Indian name of New Hampshire's largest lake means 'smile of the Great Spirit.' Winnipesaukee has 183 miles of coastline, more than 300 islands and excellent salmon fishing.

Laconia & Around

The largest population center of the lakes region, this regional gateway offers lots of services. The **Greater Laconia & Weirs Beach Chamber of Commerce** (☎ 603-524-5531; 11 Veterans Sq; 🕒 8:30am-5pm Mon-Fri) maintains an information office in the old railroad station.

Ellacoya State Beach (☎ 603-293-7821; NH 11, Gifford; adult $3, child 5-11 free; RV sites $35) has a 600ft-wide beach, as well as a picnic area and a campground with 35 unshaded RV sites. **Gunstock** (☎ 800-486-7862; www.gunstock.com; NH 11A, Gilford) has an active summer sports center, a winter ski area with a vertical drop of 1400ft, and lots of cross-country trails. The **campground** (campsites/RV sites/cabins $25/32/60) also has two sleeping cabins.

The **Belknap Point Motel** (☎ 603-293-7511, 888-454-2537; www.bpmotel.com; 107 Belknap Point Rd, Gilford; d $95-115) has rooms and efficiencies right on the lake.

Weirs Beach

Called 'Aquedoctan' by its Native American inhabitants, Weirs Beach takes its English name from the Indian fishing weirs found here by the first white settlers. Contact the **Greater Laconia & Weirs Beach Chamber of Commerce** (☎ 603-366-4770; US 3; 🕒 10am-4pm Mon-Sat, 11am-3pm Sun) for information.

Honky-tonk Weirs Beach is famous for video arcades and junk food. But there is also a nice lakefront promenade, a small state park and beach, and the **Winnipesaukee Scenic Railroad** (☎ 603-745-2135; adult $9-10, child $8-9; 🕒 late May–mid-Oct). **Mount Washington Cruises** (☎ 603-366-5531) operates several lake cruises from Weirs Beach, including a 2½-hour trip aboard the MS *Mount Washington* (adult/child $19/9), a two-hour cruise on the US mailboat MV *Sophie C* (adult/child $16/8) and a one-hour cruise (adult/child $10/5) on the MV *Doris E*.

Area motels include the 24-room **Birch Knoll Motel** (☎ 603-366-4958; www.birchknollmotel.com; 867 Weirs Blvd; d $79-129;) and the 12-room **Bay Top Motel** (☎ 603-366-2225; www.baytop.com; 1025 Weirs Blvd; d $79-119;). The chamber of commerce can supply information about campgrounds.

Weirs Beach is all about eating: burgers, hot dogs, fried dough, lobsters, ice cream, doughnuts – anything sweet or fatty. Stroll the main street for the snack shops. Try the long-standing **Weirs Beach Lobster Pound** (☎ 603-366-2255; US 3) for more substantial seafood and steaks.

Meredith

More sedate and upscale than Weirs Beach, Meredith is still a real lakes region town with a lakeside strip of restaurants, shops and places to stay. Get more information from the centrally located **Meredith Chamber of Commerce** (☎ 603-279-6121, 877-279-6121; 272 US 3; 9am-5pm).

Tuckernuck Inn (☎ 603-279-5521; 25 Red Gate Lane; with breakfast r $100-139;), a short walk from the center of town, has five cozy doubles decorated with quilts and stenciled walls. Also in town, the **Meredith Inn** (☎ 603-279-0000; www.meredithinn.com; Main St; with breakfast d $109-175;), a Victorian 'painted lady,' has eight rooms with period furnishings.

Just east of Meredith, the family-oriented **Harbor Hill Camping Area** (☎ 603-279-6910; 189 NH 25; campsites $24, RV sites $28-33, cabins $50-60;) has mostly wooded campsites, as well as a playground and recreation center with Ping-Pong and pool tables.

Wolfeboro

Named for General Wolfe, who died vanquishing Montcalm on the Plains of Abraham in Quebec, Wolfeboro claims to be 'the oldest summer resort in America.' This pleasant lakeside resort town has good examples of New England's various architectural styles, including Georgian, Federal and Greek Revival. The **Wolfeboro Chamber of Commerce** (☎ 603-569-2200, 800-516-5324; 32 Central Ave; 10am-3pm Mon-Fri, 10am-1pm Sat) is in the old railroad building.

The **Clark House Museum Complex** (☎ 603-569-4997; 233 S Main St; adult $4, child 5-11 free; 10am-4pm Mon-Fri, 10am-2pm Sat Jul-Aug) is Wolfeboro's eclectic historical museum. Three miles north of town, the **Libby Museum** (☎ 603-569-1035; NH 109, Winter Harbor; adult $2, child 5-11 $1; 10am-4pm Tue-Sat, noon-4pm Sun Jun–early Sep) contains the collections of Dr Henry Forrest Libby, a local dentist and avid amateur naturalist.

Tuc' Me Inn (☎ 603-569-5702; www.tucmeinn.com; 118 N Main St; with breakfast d $105-125) is a quaint seven-room B&B in an 1850 Federal-style building; three rooms have private baths. The 44-room **Wolfeboro Inn** (☎ 603-569-3016, 800-451-2389; www.wolfeboroinn.com: 90 N Main St; with breakfast d $180-225, ste $245-295;) has been the town's principal lodging since 1812; some of the country-style rooms have lake views.

Farther north along N Main St (NH 28) are several good motels, including the 17-room **Lakeview Inn & Motor Lodge** (☎ 603-569-1335; www.lakeviewinn.net; 200 N Main St; d $90-100;). Off NH 28 north of town, **Wolfeboro Campground** (☎ 603-569-9881; Haines Hill Rd; campsites/RV sites $18/19) has 50 wooded campsites.

For breakfast or a nice light lunch of pancakes, eggs or sandwiches, try **Strawberry Patch** (☎ 603-569-5523; 50 N Main St; mains $4-8). At the Wolfeboro Inn, **Wolfe's Tavern** (☎ 603-569-3016; 90 N Main St; mains $6-19) is an old New England pub with substantial, traditional fare; nab a terrace seat in good weather.

WHITE MOUNTAINS

New England's greatest range is one of its prime outdoor playgrounds, and the White Mountain National Forest is action central for hiking, camping, canoeing, kayaking and skiing.

Information

Appalachian Mountain Club (☎ 617-523-0636; www.outdoors.org; 5 Joy St, Boston, MA 02108) Publishes the useful *AMC White Mountain Guide*, which you can purchase from the club or from local bookstores and outfitters.

White Mountain National Forest Headquarters (☎ 603-528-8721; 719 Main St; Laconia)

White Mountains Visitors Center (☎ 603-745-8720, 800-346-3687; www.visitwhitemountains.com; 200 Kangamagus Hwy, North Woodstock; 8:30am-5pm)

Waterville Valley

In the shadow of Mt Tecumseh, on the banks of the Mad River, the valley was developed as a resort community during the latter half of the 20th century, when hotels, condominiums, golf courses, downhill and cross-country ski trails, and services were all laid out. The town's sports facilities also include hiking trails, tennis, road and mountain-bike routes, in-line skating routes and other organized family fun. The **Waterville Valley Region Chamber of Commerce** (☎ 603-726-3804, 800-237-2307; 12 Vintinner Rd, Campton; 9am-5pm), off I-93 exit 28, has details.

Like many New England ski mountains, the **Waterville Valley ski area** (☎ 800-468-2553; www.waterville.com) is open in the summer for mountain biking and hiking; the ski area's main phone number connects you to the year-round lodging reservations service.

North Woodstock & Lincoln

These towns straddle the Pemigewasset River, just south of Franconia Notch. The Kancamagus Hwy (NH 112) comes into Lincoln from Conway, about 18 miles east of Kancamagus Pass. **Loon Mountain** (☎ 603-745-8111; www.loonmtn.com; Kancamagus Hwy, Lincoln) offers winter skiing (vertical drop over 2000ft) and many summer activities.

INFORMATION

Lincoln-Woodstock Chamber of Commerce (☎ 603-745-6621, lodging reservations 800-227-4191; www.lincolnwoodstock.com; I-95, exit 32; 9am-5pm Mon-Fri) provides information for visitors.

SLEEPING

Kancamagus Motor Lodge (☎ 603-745-3365, 800-346-4205; www.kancmotorlodge.com; NH 112; d $79-119;) Many of the 34 rooms at this motel have steam-bath showers; there's an indoor pool, too.

Woodstock Inn (☎ 603-745-3951, 800-321-3985; www.woodstockinnnh.com; Main St, North Woodstock; d $105-172) The 24 rooms in these several restored houses vary in size; some can sleep four to five. There's an onsite brewpub.

Red Doors Motel (☎ 603-745-2267, 800-527-7596; www.reddoorsmotel.com; US 3; d $75-99;) Pleasant with 30 rooms.

Lost River Valley Campground (☎ 603-745-8321, 800-370-5678; 951 Lost River Rd, North Woodstock; campsites $23-28, RV sites $27-33, cabins $45-50), set near a stream just off NH 112 west of I-93 exit 32, has 125 campsites, including camping cabins. **Country Bumpkins** (☎ 603-745-8837; US 3, Lincoln; campsites/RV sites $19/25, cabins $55-95), near the Pemigewasset River, has 45 campsites, as well as six cabins with private baths; take I-93 to exit 33, then go south on US 3 for half a mile.

EATING

For food, head to Main St (US 3) in North Woodstock.

Sunny Day Diner (☎ 603-745-4833; US 3; mains $2-8) From corned beef hash, to grilled cheese sandwiches, to meatloaf, this spot dishes up classic, inexpensive diner fare.

Peg's Restaurant (☎ 603-745-2740; US 3; breakfasts $1-6, lunches $3-6; 5:30am-4pm) Locals head to this popular eatery for early breakfasts and cheap lunches.

Woodstock Inn Station & Brewery (☎ 603-745-3951; US 3; mains $6-16) This restaurant-brewpub satisfies basic food cravings with pasta, steaks, Mexican food and sandwiches.

Kancamagus Hwy

The 34.5-mile Kancamagus Hwy (NH 112) winds between Lincoln and Conway, through White Mountain National Forest and over Kancamagus Pass (2868ft). This scenic route remains unspoiled by commercial development, with many USFS campgrounds along it.

About 1684, Kancamagus (Fearless One) assumed the powers of *sagamon* (leader) of the region's Pennacook Confederacy of Native American peoples. He worked hard to keep the peace between indigenous peoples and European explorers and settlers, but after provocation by whites, he finally resorted to battle to rid the region of the explorers. By 1691, however, he and his followers were fleeing north.

White Mountain National Forest is laced with excellent hiking trails. Stop at the **Lincoln-Woodstock Chamber of Commerce** (☎ 603-745-6621) in Lincoln for details. Parking anywhere along the highway costs $3 per trailhead (honor system), $5 per week or $20 per season. Purchase passes at ranger stations or at many local businesses, including the Kancamagus Country Store on NH 112 in Lincoln (open 24 hours).

Most of the popular, heavily wooded national-forest campgrounds along the Kancamagus Hwy east of Lincoln have pit toilets; a few have flush toilets. The campgrounds, from west to east (Lincoln to Conway) are as follows:

Big Rock Campground (☎ 603-744-9165; campsites $14) Six miles east of Lincoln; 28 campsites.

Passaconaway Campground (☎ 603-447-5448; campsites $14) Fifteen miles west of Conway; 33 campsites.

NEW ENGLAND

Hancock Campground (☎ 603-744-9165; campsites $14) Twelve miles west of Conway; 56 campsites.
Jigger Johnson Campground (☎ 603-447-5448; campsites $16) Twelve miles west of Conway; 76 campsites.
Covered Bridge Campground (☎ 603-447-5448, reservations 877-444-6777; campsites $14, reservation fee $9) Six miles west of Conway; 49 campsites.
Blackberry Crossing Campground (☎ 603-447-5448; campsites $14) Six miles west of Conway; 26 campsites.

Franconia Notch State Park & Franconia

Dramatic Franconia Notch is a narrow gorge shaped over the eons by a wild stream cutting through craggy granite. The symbol of the Granite State, the natural rock formation called the 'Great Stone Face,' or more commonly, 'Old Man of the Mountain,' used to gaze across Franconia Notch; in 2003, the 40ft-tall rock crumbled and slid down the mountain. If you get a commemorative New Hampshire quarter, you'll see the state's proud but sadly passed away symbol.

The park **visitors center** (☎ 603-745-8391; I-93, exit 34A) is located 4 miles north of North Woodstock at the **Flume** (adult $8, child 5-11 $5; 9am-5pm May-Oct), a natural cleft in the granite bedrock. A 2-mile self-guided nature walk takes you to and through the opening – 12ft- to 20ft-wide – along an 800ft boardwalk. Nearby, the **Basin**, a huge glacial pothole 20ft in diameter, was carved deep into the granite 15,000 years ago by the falling water and swirling stones.

The **Cannon Mountain Aerial Tramway** (☎ 603-823-8800; I-93, exit 34B; round-trip adult $10, child 5-11 $6; 9am-5pm mid-May–mid-Oct) offers a breathtaking view of Franconia Notch and the surrounding mountains. In winter, Cannon is open for downhill skiing.

Franconia Notch State Park has a good system of hiking trails; most are relatively short, some are steep. Trail maps are available at the visitors center. The park's **Lafayette Place campground** (☎ 603-823-9513, reservations 603-271-3628; campsites $16) has 97 wooded campsites, but they fill up early in summer; half can be reserved in advance.

A few miles north of Franconia Notch, visit the **Frost Place** (☎ 603-823-5510; www.frostplace.org; Ridge Rd, Franconia; adult $3, child 5-11 $1.25; 1-5pm Sat-Sun late May–Jun, 1-5pm Wed-Mon Jul–mid-Oct), the farm that belonged to renowned mid-20th-century poet Robert Frost (1874–1963). Here, he wrote many poems describing life on this farm and the scenery surrounding it, including 'The Road Not Taken' and 'Stopping by Woods on a Snowy Evening.'

Mt Washington Valley & North Conway

The Mt Washington valley, stretching north from the eastern terminus of the Kancamagus Hwy, includes the towns of Bartlett, Conway, Glen, Intervale, Jackson and North Conway. Every conceivable outdoor activity is available here. Less energetically, North Conway is also a center for outlet shopping.

INFORMATION

Jackson Area Chamber of Commerce (☎ 603-383-9356, 800-866-3334; www.jacksonnh.com; PO Box 304, Jackson, NH 03846) Provides lodging assistance.
Mt Washington Valley Chamber of Commerce (☎ 603-356-3171, 800-367-3364; Main St, North Conway; 9am-5pm Mon-Fri)

SIGHTS & ACTIVITIES

Two miles west of North Conway off US 302, placid **Echo Lake State Park** (☎ 603-356-2672; adult $2.50, child 5-11 free; late May–early Sep) rests at the foot of a sheer rock wall called **White Horse Ledge**. There's a scenic road up to the 700ft-high **Cathedral Ledge** and panoramic views of the White Mountain Range.

The **Conway Scenic Railroad** (☎ 603-356-5251, 800-232-5251; www.conwayscenic.com; NH 16, North Conway; adult $10.50, child 5-11 $7.50; daily mid-Jun–mid-Oct, weekends mid-Apr–mid-Jun & mid-Oct–Dec) takes passengers on a one-hour, 11-mile antique steam train ride through the Mt Washington Valley. Longer trips (1¾ hours and five hours) are also offered.

Areas for skiing include **Attitash/Bear Peak** (☎ 603-374-2368, 877-677-7669, lodging reservations 888-544-1900; www.attitash.com; US 302, Bartlett), west of Glen, which also runs a summertime **Alpine Slide** ($12); **Cranmore Mountain Resort** (☎ 603-356-5543, 800-786-6754; www.cranmore.com), just outside North Conway; and **Black Mountain Ski Area** (☎ 603-383-4490, lodging reservations 800-698-4490; www.blackmt.com; NH 16B, Jackson). Jackson, 7 miles north of North Conway, is a cross-country skiing mecca, with 93 miles of trails.

For canoeing and kayaking, **Saco Bound** (☎ 603-447-2177; US 302, Conway; per day $26-31, shuttle service per boat $11-12) has rentals and they also run organized trips.

SLEEPING

Cranmore Inn (☎ 603-356-5502, 800-526-5502; www.cranmoreinn.com; Kearsarge St, North Conway; with breakfast d $59-99, kitchen units $99-139;) This traditional country inn has 18 rooms in the main building, plus three larger family units with kitchens in a converted stable.

Spruce Moose Lodge (☎ 603-356-6239, 800-600-6239; www.sprucemooselodge.com; 207 Seavey St, North Conway; with breakfast d $79-109, apt $89-109, cottages $129-159;) Run by a family of hockey fans, this inn has nine rooms in the lodge, as well as two studio apartments with whirlpool tubs and three cottages that sleep up to seven.

Cranmore Mountain Lodge (☎ 603-356-2044, 800-356-3596; www.north-conway.com; 859 Kearsarge Rd, North Conway; dm $20, d $100-130;) North of town, this old-fashioned country inn has lodge rooms and a hostel (22 beds in three bunkrooms). But there's nothing old-fashioned about the heated pool and hot tub.

Most of North Conway's motels are south of town along NH 16/US 302. Try **Yankee Clipper Motel** (☎ 603-356-5736, 800-343-5900; NH 16; d $59-109;), **Briarcliff Motel** (☎ 603-356-5584, 800-338-4291; www.briarcliffmotel.com; NH 16; d $69-128), or **Eastern Inns** (☎ 603-356-5447, 800-628-3750; www.easterninns.com; NH 16; d $95-121, ste $141-145;).

HI Albert B Lester Memorial Hostel, White Mountains (☎ 603-447-1001; www.conwayhostel.com; 36 Washington St, Conway; with breakfast dm/d $20/48;) Perched on the edge of the White Mountain National Forest, off Main St/NH 16, the 30-bed HI and 'sustainable living center' focuses on environmentally friendly practices and conservation.

Camping options include **Cove Camping Area** (☎ 603-447-6734; Cove Rd, off Stark Rd, Conway; campsites/RV sites $22-44) on Conway Lake, **Eastern Slope Camping Area** (☎ 603-447-5092; NH 16, Conway; campsites/RV sites $25/34, cabins $50-75), with long beaches on the Saco River, and **Saco River Camping Area** (☎ 603-356-3360; off NH 16, North Conway; campsites/RV sites $21/29;), also on the river.

EATING

Gunther's (☎ 603-356-5200; Main St at Seavey St, North Conway; mains $3-7) This café is the place for hearty breakfasts like corned beef hash and eggs or 'blueberry pigs in a blanket' (pancake-wrapped sausages).

Café Noche (☎ 603-447-5050; 147 Main St, Conway; lunches $5-7, dinners $7-13) For south-of-the-border fare – tacos, burritos, fajitas and the like – try this festive Tex-Mex spot. The margaritas will warm you up, too.

Horsefeathers (☎ 603-356-2687; Main St, North Conway; mains $7-17) This popular gathering place has a long, jokey menu of bar food, sandwiches and light meals. In summer, there's entertainment on weekends.

GETTING THERE & AWAY

Concord Trailways (☎ 603-228-3300, 800-639-3317) runs a daily route between Boston and Berlin, NH, stopping at Manchester, Concord, points near Lake Winnipesaukee, Conway, North Conway, Jackson and Pinkham Notch. The trip between Boston and the Mt Washington Valley takes about 3½ hours ($28).

Pinkham Notch & Crawford Notch

From Pinkham Notch (2032ft), an excellent system of trails provides access to the natural beauties of the Presidential Range, especially **Mt Washington** (6288ft), the highest mountain in the northeastern USA. For the less athletically inclined, the **Mt Washington Auto Road** (☎ 603-466-2222; www.mountwashingtonautoroad.com; car & driver $18, extra passengers adult $7, child 5-11 $4; early May–early Oct, weather permitting) offers easier summit access; rates include an audio cassette tour. If you don't want to drive yourself, take a 1½-hour guided van tour (adult $24, child five to 11 $10). Mt Washington's weather is notoriously severe and can turn on a dime. The average temperature at the summit is 45°F in summer and the wind is always blowing.

The Appalachian Mountain Club's **Pinkham Notch Visitors Center** (☎ 603-466-2727, 800-262-4455; www.outdoors.org) is the area's informational nexus and meeting ground for like-minded adventurers. The AMC runs the adjacent **Joe Dodge Lodge** (dm adult $35, child 5-11 $23, with breakfast & dinner $52/34, d $70); reserve well in advance. **Dolly Copp Campground** (☎ 603-466-3984; off NH 16; campsites $15), a USFS campground that's 6 miles north of the AMC camp, has 176 simple campsites.

US 302 heads west from Glen, then north to Crawford Notch (1773ft) through appealing mountain scenery. **Crawford Notch State Park** (☎ 603-374-2272) maintains a system of shorter hiking trails as well as trailheads for longer hikes to the Mt Washington summit.

Bretton Woods

Before 1944, Bretton Woods was known primarily among locals and wealthy summer visitors who patronized the grand

Mt Washington Hotel. When President Roosevelt chose the hotel for the historic conference to establish a new post-WWII economic order, it introduced the town to the world. The **Twin Mountain–Bretton Woods Chamber of Commerce** (☎ 800-245-8946; www.twinmountain.org; US 302 & US 3, Twin Mountain) maintains a booth several miles northwest of Bretton Woods.

The quaintest way to the summit of Mt Washington is aboard the **Mt Washington Cog Railway** (☎ 603-846-5404, 800-922-8825; www.thecog.com; adult $49, child 5-11 $35; 9am-4pm mid-Jun–Jul, 8am-5pm Aug, call for spring & fall schedule), 6 miles east of US 302. A coal-fired, steam-powered 'little engine that could' locomotive follows a 3.5-mile track along a steep trestle up the mountainside (three hours). Make reservations, and dress for chilly weather.

The **Bretton Woods ski area** (☎ 603-278-3320; www.brettonwoods.com; US 302), New Hampshire's largest, has 76 trails.

The grand **Mt Washington Hotel** (☎ 603-278-1000, 800-258-0330; www.mtwashington.com; US 302; with breakfast & dinner d $230-600), which opened in 1902, boasts more than 200 rooms and thousands of acres of grounds, 12 clay tennis courts, a golf course, an equestrian center, and indoor and outdoor heated pools. Also run by the Mt Washington resort, the more modest 50-room **Bretton Woods Motor Inn** (☎ 603-278-1000, 800-258-0330; www.mtwashington.com/motorinn.html; US 302; d $69-199;) is a modern motel. There are numerous other motels nearby. In summer, at the 70-site **Twin Mountain KOA** (☎ 603-846-5559, 800-562-9117; NH 115; campsites $26-30, RV sites $30-38, cabins $48-52;), off US 3 from US 302 north, evening activities include movies, ice cream socials and campfire sing-alongs.

HANOVER

Hanover, settled in 1765, is defined by Dartmouth College, which was chartered in 1769 primarily 'for the education and instruction of Youth of the Indian Tribes.' Smart people of all types are admitted today. To take a free **campus walking tour** (☎ 603-646-2875; www.dartmouth.edu) contact the admissions office.

INFORMATION

Chamber of Commerce information booth (☎ 603-643-3512; Dartmouth College green; 9:30am-5pm mid-Jun–Aug, 10am-5pm Sep)

Hanover Area Chamber of Commerce (☎ 603-643-3115; 216 Nugget Building, Main St; 8:30am-4:30pm Mon-Fri)

SIGHTS & ACTIVITIES

On the Dartmouth campus, **Baker-Berry Library** (☎ 603-646-2560; generally 8am-8pm) houses a series of murals by José Clemente Orozco (1883–1949), the renowned Mexican muralist who taught and painted at Dartmouth from 1932 to 1934.

The collections at **Hood Museum of Art** (☎ 603-646-2808; www.dartmouth.edu/~hood; Wheelock St; admission free; 10am-5pm Tue & Thu-Sat, 10am-9pm Wed, noon-5pm Sun) range from ancient Greece and Rome through the European Renaissance to modern times.

Hopkins Center for the Arts (☎ 603-646-2422; www.dartmouth.edu/~hop) is an outstanding performing arts venue that hosts all manner of music, dance and theater events.

SLEEPING

Chieftain Motor Inn (☎ 603-643-2550, 800-845-3557; www.chieftaininn.com; 84 Lyme Rd; with breakfast d $100-110;) This motel on NH 10 N has 22 large pine-paneled rooms.

Trumbull House B&B (☎ 603-643-2370, 800-651-5141; www.trumbullhouse.com; 40 Etna Rd; with breakfast d $120-210;) Four miles east of the Dartmouth campus, this B&B with five country-style rooms is set on 16 acres with a swimming pond.

Storrs Pond Recreation Area (☎ 603-643-2134; campsites/RV sites $15-25;) Has both a pool and the pond for swimming; from I-89 exit 18, follow NH 10 north and look for signs.

EATING

Murphy's on the Green (☎ 603-643-4075; 11 S Main St; lunches $6-10, dinners $8-17) At this pub opposite the Hanover Inn, students and faculty discuss weighty matters over pints of Catamount amber ale and hearty bar food.

Mai Thai (☎ 603-643-9980; 44 S Main St; mains $6-14) This Thai eatery serves a range of traditional dishes, from the ubiquitous pad Thai to such intriguing fare as *pla douk pad ped* (spicy catfish fillets) and *som tum* (papaya salad).

Lou's (☎ 603-643-3321; 30 S Main St; mains $4-7) This old-fashioned restaurant and bakery has been serving up typical diner fare – eggs, burgers and the like – since 1947.

GETTING THERE & AWAY

Vermont Transit (☎ 603-643-2128, 800-552-8737 in New England) runs buses from Boston and Boston's Logan Airport, and from Manchester, NH airport, to Hanover. They also serve Springfield, Massachusetts, and have connecting service from New York, Hartford and Montreal to White River Junction, Vermont, a 6-mile taxi ride to Hanover. **Dartmouth Mini Coach** (☎ 603-448-2800) operates seven shuttles daily from Hanover to Logan Airport ($35), with departures about every two hours from 5am to 5pm.

MAINE

Maine has the largest land area of the six New England states but the sparsest population of any state east of the Mississippi River. The 'rockbound coast of Maine' is about 225 miles long as the crow flies, but a tall-masted schooner sailing its tortuous course would cover almost 3500 miles.

Southern coastal Maine is thickly populated, ranging from well-preserved historic towns to miles of factory outlet malls. You'll find both genteel summer resorts and blue-collar beach towns, too. Northern, inland Maine is wilderness, with vast (for New England) areas of dense forest and thousands of lakes inhabited only by fish and fowl.

A car is by far the best means of getting around Maine, unless you're going only as far as Portland. Amtrak, as well as several bus companies, offer service between Boston and Portland.

History

French and English colonists vied to establish the first European colony in Maine in the early 17th century. In 1639, King Charles I issued a royal charter 'for the province and countie of Maine,' and settlement began, but in 1659 the province was subsumed in the colony of Massachusetts Bay. Conflict between the Wabanaki tribal confederation and colonists was savage at times in this frontier province, but by the mid-18th century the power of the indigenous peoples was broken.

During the Revolutionary War, Portland (then called 'Falmouth') was devastated by a British fleet. In the War of 1812, Maine suffered again due to inadequate defense measures, which strengthened the faction that wanted statehood apart from Massachusetts. In the Missouri Compromise of 1820, Maine was admitted to the Union as a free state, and Missouri as a slave state, preserving the political balance between North and South.

Painter Winslow Homer (1836–1910), though a Bostonian, is best known for his depictions of the Maine coast. Edna St Vincent Millay (1892–1950) wrote poetry that reflected her native Maine, while horror writer Stephen King sets many novels and stories in his home state.

Though its great stands of virgin pine forest are now gone, the 'Pine Tree State' still harvests a living out of lumbering, in addition to shipbuilding, agriculture and tourism.

MAINE FACTS

Nickname Pine Tree State
Population 1,294,464 (40th)
Area 35,387 sq miles (39th)
Admitted to Union March 15, 1820 (23rd)
Capital city Augusta (population 18,000)
Other cities Portland (64,000), Bangor (33,000)
State animal Moose
State cliché Ayuh!
Birthplace of Henry Wadsworth Longfellow (1807–82), LL Bean (1872–1967), Stephen King (b 1947)

Information

Maine Office of Tourism (☎ 888-624-6345; www.visitmaine.com; 59 State House Station, Augusta, ME 04330) provides information for visitors.

SOUTHERN MAINE COAST

The most touristy part of Maine has developed beaches, outlet shopping and resort villages that are packed in summer. The southernmost town of any size is Kittery, famous for shopping malls and outlet stores along US 1. Between Kittery and Portland, there are several popular beach towns.

Ogunquit & Around

Ogunquit ('Beautiful Place by the Sea' in the Abenaki tongue), 35 miles south of Portland, is a small town famous for its 3-mile sand beach. Swimmers here can choose either chilly, pounding surf or

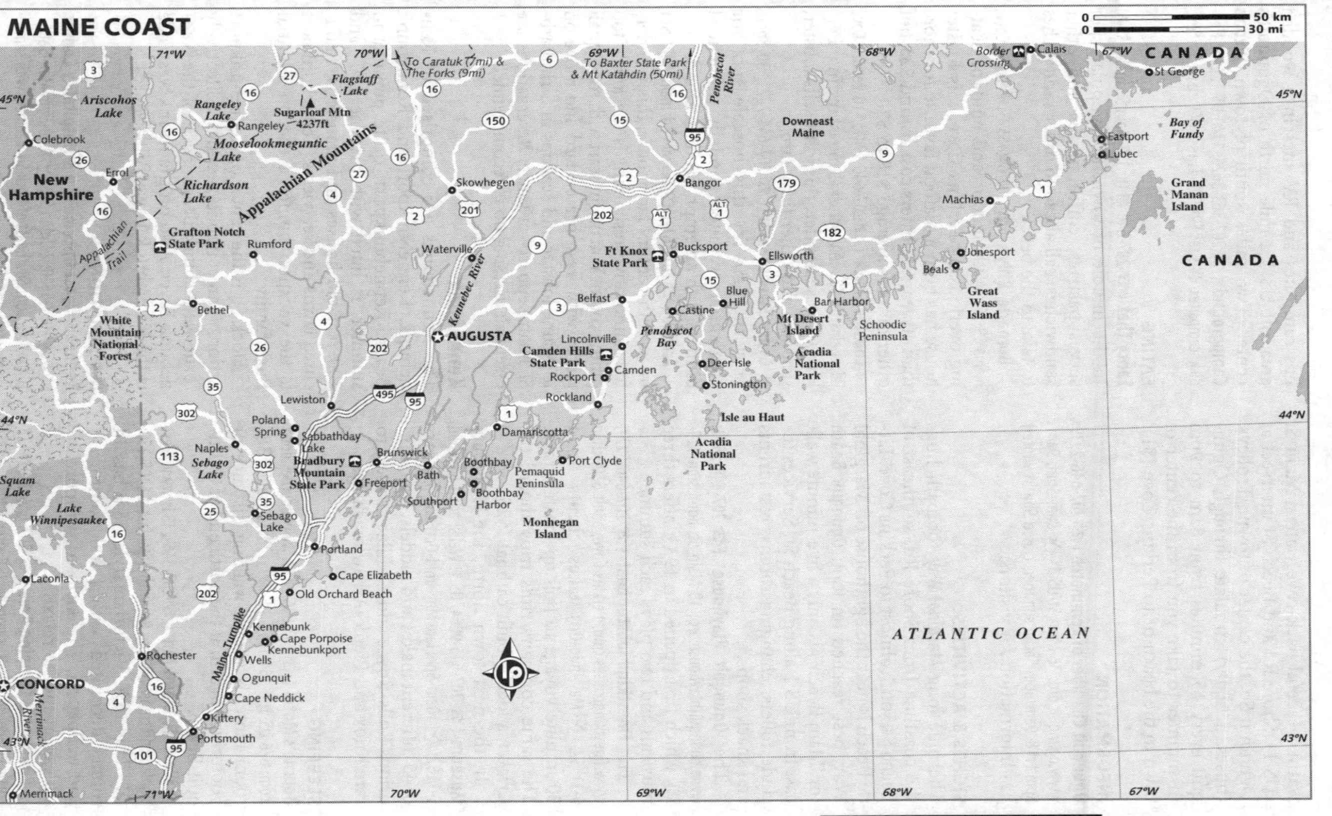
MAINE COAST
0 50 km
0 30 mi
CANADA
ATLANTIC OCEAN
New Hampshire
Colebrook
Errol
Ariscohos Lake
White Mountain National Forest
Lake Winnipesaukee
Squam Lake
Laconia
CONCORD
Merrimack River
Merrimack
Rochester
Portsmouth
Kittery
Cape Neddick
Ogunquit
Wells
Kennebunk
Cape Porpoise
Kennebunkport
Maine Turnpike
Old Orchard Beach
Cape Elizabeth
Portland
Sebago Lake
Naples
Poland Spring
Sabbathday Lake
Bradbury Mountain State Park
Freeport
Brunswick
Lewiston
Bath
Southport
Boothbay
Boothbay Harbor
Pemaquid Peninsula
Damariscotta
Port Clyde
Monhegan Island
Rockland
Rockport
Camden
Camden Hills State Park
Lincolnville
Belfast
AUGUSTA
Kennebec River
Waterville
Skowhegan
Rumford
Bethel
Grafton Notch State Park
Richardson Lake
Mooselookmeguntic Lake
Rangeley Lake
Rangeley
Sugarloaf Mtn 4237ft
Flagstaff Lake
Appalachian Mountains
Appalachian Trail
To Caratuk (7mi) & The Forks (9mi)
To Baxter State Park & Mt Katahdin (50mi)
Bangor
Penobscot River
Bucksport
Ft Knox State Park
Castine
Penobscot Bay
Deer Isle
Stonington
Blue Hill
Isle au Haut
Acadia National Park
Ellsworth
Mt Desert Island
Bar Harbor
Downeast Maine
Schoodic Peninsula
Beals
Jonesport
Great Wass Island
Machias
Border Crossing
Calais
Eastport
Lubec
St George
Bay of Fundy
Grand Manan Island

warm, peaceful back-cove waters. Main St (US 1), Shore Rd and Beach St intersect at Ogunquit Sq, the center of town. 'Trolleys' (buses, actually) circulate through Ogunquit every 15 minutes from 8am to 9pm in summer to take you from the center of town to the beach or to Perkins Cove ($1).

INFORMATION

Ogunquit Chamber of Commerce (☎ 207-646-2939; www.ogunquit.org; 36 Main St/US 1; 9am-5pm, 9am-8pm Fri & 9am-6pm Sat in summer, closed Sun in winter) has information for visitors.

SIGHTS & ACTIVITIES

The mile-long **Marginal Way** footpath hugs the coastline from Shore Rd, southeast of Beach St, south almost to Perkins Cove. Little Beach is near the lighthouse on Marginal Way, best reached on foot. **Ogunquit Beach** (or 'Main Beach') is only a five-minute walk east from US 1 along Beach St. Services include toilets, changing rooms, restaurants and snack shops.

The **Ogunquit Playhouse** (☎ 207-646-5511; www.ogunquitplayhouse.org; 10 Main St; admission $29-38), which first opened in 1933, offers three musicals and two plays each summer.

The **Finestkind lobster boat** (☎ 207-646-5227; www.finestkindcruises.com; Perkins Cove; adult $10, child 5-11 $7; May–mid-Oct) takes clients on a 50-minute voyage to pull up lobster traps. The same company runs trips aboard the *Cricket*, a locally built catboat ($25).

In the next town north, the **Wells Auto Museum** (☎ 207-646-9064; US 1, Wells; adult $5, child 5-11 $2; 10am-5pm late May–mid-Oct) has 80 cars of 45 different makes and models, from luxurious Rolls-Royce and Cadillac cruisers to rare Knox and Pierce-Arrow machines.

SLEEPING

Bourne's Motel (☎ 207-646-2823; www.bournesmotel.com; 676 US 1; d $64-115;) This basic 38-room motel is within walking distance of Footbridge Beach, at the north end of Ogunquit Beach.

West Highland Inn (☎ 207-646-2181; www.westhighlandinn.com; 38 Shore Rd; with breakfast d $105-150;) This 1890 Victorian-style B&B has 14 rooms decorated with floral comforters and wallpapers. The enclosed sun porch is a pleasant spot to relax.

Pinederosa Camping Area (☎ 207-646-2492; 128 North Village Rd, Wells; campsites/RV sites $20/25;) has campsites and RV sites in a wooded area, off US 1 a mile north of Ogunquit's center. Two miles south of town, **Dixon's Campground** (☎ 207-363-3626; 1740 US 1, Cape Neddick; campsites/RV sites $24/28) has 100 campsites.

EATING

Fancy That (☎ 207-646-4118; 138 Main St; mains $3-6) In the middle of town, this popular spot serves pastries, coffee, wraps and other sandwiches; call ahead to order sandwiches to take to the beach.

Barnacle Billy's (☎ 207-646-5575; Perkins Cove; mains $9-25) With indoor and outdoor seating overlooking Perkins Cove, this lobster house has been a seafood favorite for more than 40 years. Lobsters cost around $25, but other dinners average $18 to $20.

Lobster Shack (☎ 207-646-2941; 110 Perkins Cove Rd; mains $6-18) Another long-standing Perkins Cove seafooder, this joint sells lobster, steamers and other fishy fare.

Gypsy Sweethearts (☎ 207-646-7021; 30 Shore Rd; mains $17-25) Try this upscale spot for contemporary, internationally influenced dinners with an emphasis on seafood.

Arrows (☎ 207-361-1100; Berwick Rd; mains $40) Set in an 18th-century farmhouse, this wonderfully innovative restaurant is the area's top dining room. You might start with roast quail paired with fresh pea custard and move on to Maine lobster and scallops in a rhubarb-Sichuan peppercorn sauce. Reservations are essential; dressing up is recommended.

Kennebunks

The Kennebunks are comprised of Kennebunk, Kennebunkport and Kennebunk Beach. Kennebunkport, quite popular in summer, is lined with pristine 100- and 200-year-old houses and mansions, manicured lawns and sea views. Kennebunkport is the vacation home of the presidential Bush family.

Dock Sq is the center of Kennebunkport action. Three public beaches collectively form 'Kennebunk Beach,' west of the Kennebunk River. Also on the river's west side is the Kennebunk Lower Village area.

INFORMATION

Kennebunkport Information & Hospitality Center (☎ 207-967-8600; 2 Union Sq; 9am-5pm Mon-Sat, 10am-4pm Sun) Southeast of Dock Sq, can help with same-night accommodations.

Kennebunk-Kennebunkport Chamber of Commerce (☎ 207-967-0857; www.visitthekennebunks.com; 17 Western Ave; 🕒 9am-5pm Mon-Fri) In Kennebunk Lower Village.

SLEEPING

Beachwood Resort (☎ 207-967-2483; www.beachwoodmotel.com; 272 Millis Rd/ME 9; d $98-108;) Located a few miles northeast of Dock Sq, this basic but family-friendly motel has efficiencies with kitchenettes.

Cove House B&B (☎ 207-967-3704; www.covehouse.com; 11 S Maine St; with breakfast $110) At this 18th-century colonial farmhouse, there are four comfortably old-fashioned rooms.

Green Heron Inn (☎ 207-967-3315; www.greenheron inn.com; 126 Ocean Ave; with breakfast r $130-160;) This homey 10-room inn, with a large porch and a parlor filled with games, is a solid choice.

Salty Acres Campground (☎ 207-967-8623; ME 9; campsites/RV sites $21/28;) Opposite the Beachwood Resort, about a mile from Goose Rocks Beach, this campground has 225 campsites catering to a mix of tents and RVs.

EATING

Clam Shack (☎ 207-967-2560; 3 Western Ave; mains $3-13) One of the best places around for pints of fried clams, the Shack also has fish plates and hamburgers. It's on the west side of the bridge in Kennebunk Lower Village. You can eat standing up on its long deck, but beware of seagulls snatching your food.

Alisson's (☎ 207-967-4841; 11 Dock Sq; lunches $4-11, dinners $6-17) With a central location and decent pub food – from burgers and pizza to all sorts of seafood – Alisson's is always crowded.

Federal Jack's Restaurant & Brew Pub (☎ 207-967-4322; 8 Western Ave; mains $6-17) Above the Kennebunkport Brewing Co in the Shipyard complex, this brewpub restaurant serves bar food and heartier all-American main courses with its handcrafted ales.

White Barn Inn (☎ 207-967-2321; 37 Beach St; prix-fixe dinners $85) Considered one of the region's top restaurants, this elegant New American serves elaborate prix-fixe dinners. Make reservations and dress up (men should wear jackets) for a special evening.

PORTLAND

Maine's largest city, port and commercial center is a pleasant and relatively prosperous city. In the Old Port, the cobblestone streets inspire twilight wanderings and pub crawls. Centered on Commercial St (US 1A), the Old Port holds many of the city's good restaurants, galleries and shops. Congress St is the main thoroughfare.

Information

EMERGENCY

Emergency number (☎ 911) For police, fire or other emergency.

INTERNET ACCESS

Kinko's (☎ 207-773-3177; 50 Monument Sq; per min 20¢; 🕒 24hr from 8am Mon-9pm Fri, 8am-9pm Sat-Sun)

Portland Public Library (☎ 207-871-1700; 5 Monument Sq; free for 30min-2hr)

MEDIA

Portland Phoenix (www.portlandphoenix.com) Alternative weekly, emphasizing arts and entertainment.

Portland Press Herald (www.pressherald.com) Major daily newspaper.

MEDICAL SERVICES

Maine Medical Center (☎ 207-871-2381; 22 Bramhall St)

POST

US post office (☎ 207-871-8464; 400 Congress St; 🕒 8am-7pm Mon-Fri, 9am-1pm Sat)

TOURIST OFFICES

Greater Portland Convention & Visitors Bureau (☎ 207-772-5800; www.visitportland.com; 245 Commercial St; 🕒 8am-5pm Mon-Fri, 10am-5pm Sat, until 3pm Sat mid-Oct–mid-May)

Sights & Activities

To get your bearings, take the 90-minute **Old Port Walking Tour** (☎ 207-774-5561; adult $8, child 5-11 free; 🕒 10:30am mid-Jun–mid-Oct), which is led by Greater Portland Landmarks. Buy your tickets at the Greater Portland Convention & Visitors Bureau, where the tour begins.

The small **Portland Museum of Art** (☎ 207-775-6148; www.portlandmuseum.org; 7 Congress Sq; adult $8, child 5-11 $2; 🕒 10am-5pm Sat-Thurs, 10am-9pm Fri) is in a modern building at the intersection of Congress, High and Free Sts. It has a rich collection of works by Maine painters Winslow Homer, Edward Hopper, Rockwell Kent, Maurice Prendergast and Andrew Wyeth. Special exhibitions showcase more contemporary works of art.

PORTLAND IN...

Two Days

Fuel up with breakfast at **Becky's Diner**, then take a walking tour of the **Old Port**. After lunch nearby, check out the **Museum of Art**, or tour one of the city's **historic houses**. Set sail on a sunset **harbor cruise** before sitting down to dinner at one of the city's top-notch bistros.

On day two, stop by the Portland **Public Market** for picnic supplies. Then head for **Portland Head Light** or wander past the **stately old homes** in the city's West End. After a picnic lunch, browse the **boutiques** back in the Old Port, or go outlet hopping up in Freeport. Be sure to return to Portland in time for dinner out.

If you have kids in tow, head for **Children's Museum of Maine** (☎ 207-828-1234; www.childrensmuseumofme.org; 142 Free St; admission $6; 10am-5pm Mon-Sat, noon-5pm Sun late May–early Sep, closed Mon Sep–late May). This house of fun is next to the Portland Museum of Art. It's best suited for children under nine.

Many **historic houses** are open to the public, including the 1850s **Victoria Mansion** (☎ 207-772-4841; 109 Danforth St; adult $10, child 5-11 $4; 10am-4pm Tue-Sat, 1-5pm Sun May-Oct) and **Wadsworth-Longfellow House** (☎ 207-879-0427; 485 Congress St; adult $7, child 5-11 $3; 10am-4pm Mon-Sat, noon-4pm Sun May-Oct), the childhood home of poet Henry Wadsworth Longfellow.

Portland Head Light (☎ 207-799-2661; 1000 Shore Rd, Cape Elizabeth; adult $2, child 5-11 $1 10am-4pm late May–Oct) is the oldest of Maine's 61 lighthouses (1791). It's about 4 miles south of central Portland in **Fort Williams Park** – a pleasant picnic spot.

Mail boats operated by **Casco Bay Lines** (☎ 207-774-7871; www.cascobaylines.com; 56 Commercial St; adult $12, child 5-11 $5.50) make a three-hour tour of the Casco Bay islands delivering letters, freight and visitors; other cruises are offered, too.

The **Palawan** (☎ 207-773-2163), a 58ft racing yacht, offers cruises under full sail ($20 to $40, two to three hours). The **Olde Port Mariner Fleet** (☎ 207-775-0727, 800-437-3270; www.marinerfleet.com; Commercial St) departs Long Wharf on deep-sea fishing, whale-watching and lobstering trips, plus one-hour harbor cruises.

Sleeping

Lodging rates are quite high in July and August, but drop significantly in the off-season.

Inn at St John (☎ 207-773-6481, 800-636-9127; www.innatstjohn.com; 939 Congress St; with breakfast d $69-185;) Though the neighborhood is a little dreary, this rambling 1897 Victorian-style inn across from the bus station is pretty inside, with 39 rooms furnished with period pieces and floral wallpapers. Ten rooms share baths.

Inn at Park Spring (☎ 207-774-1059, 800-437-8511; www.innatparkspring.com; 135 Spring St; with breakfast d $145-175; P) Conveniently located near the Portland Museum of Art, this 1835 brick bowfront has six rooms that range from traditional to more modern.

Pomegranate Inn (☎ 207-772-1008, 800-356-0408; www.pomegranateinn.com; 49 Neal St; with breakfast d $175-235) In the quiet residential West End, this stately home houses an eight-room antique-filled B&B decorated in a wildly eccentric style.

There are several chain motels outside the city center at I-95, exit 8.

Eating

This is a town for serious eating.

Portland Public Market (☎ 207-228-2000; 25 Preble St) This excellent food hall features Maine products and picnic supplies – cheeses, breads, fruits and veggies, and more.

Maine Lobster & Seafood (☎ 207-228-2010; mains $6-13) In the market, you'll find good lobster rolls, other fish dishes, and lobsters to go – alive or cooked.

Breaking New Grounds Also in the market, one of Portland's many good coffee outlets.

Becky's Diner (☎ 207-773-7070; 390 Commercial St; mains $3-10) This popular diner near the waterfront fills the bellies of working fishermen (and other folks, too).

Ezo African Restaurant (☎ 207-772-1796; 51 Oak St; mains $7-8) Near the Portland Museum of Art, this tiny family-run hole-in-the-wall serves exotic African stews and grilled dishes.

Gilbert's Chowder House (92 Commercial St) A simple diner serving fish-and-chips and, of course, chowder.

Pepperclub (☎ 207-772-0531; 78 Middle St; mains $9-15) For world-beat seafood and vegetarian dishes.

For contemporary fine dining in a smart-casual setting (figure about $30 to $40 per person), top bistro choices are **Street & Company** (☎ 207-775-0887; 33 Wharf St), **Michaela's** (☎ 207-780-1818; 18 Monument Sq), and **Hugo's** (☎ 207-774-8538; 88 Middle St).

Drinking

Gritty McDuff's Brew Pub (☎ 207-772-2739; 396 Fore St) The most popular spot for locally made pints.

Brian Ború (☎ 207-780-1506; 57 Center St) A fun Irish pub.

Free Street Taverna (☎ 207-774-1114; 128 Free St) This bohemian venue often hosts local bands.

Getting There & Away

Portland International Jetport (☎ 207-774-7301) is served by several domestic carriers, but long-distance or international connections must be made through Boston or New York.

Both **Vermont Transit** (☎ 207-772-6587; 950 Congress St), inside the Greyhound Terminal off I-295, exit 5, and **Concord Trailways** (☎ 207-828-1151, Thompson Point Connector Rd), also off I-295, exit 5, run buses between Portland and Boston and also travel north along the Maine coast. Coastal Maine is much more easily explored by car, but dedicated bus travelers should call for schedules and fares.

Amtrak's *Downeaster* train runs several times a day between Portland and Boston ($21, 2¾ hours).

Prince of Fundy Cruises' **M/S Scotia Prince** (☎ 207-775-5616, 800-845-4073; www.scotiaprince.com; adult/child/car from $90/45/110) runs overnight car-and-passenger ferries to Yarmouth, Nova Scotia.

The local bus line, **Metro** (☎ 207-774-0351; fares $1), has its main terminus at Monument Sq (Elm and Congress St).

CENTRAL MAINE COAST

Midcoast Maine features long, scraggy peninsulas jutting deep into the Atlantic, friendly seaside villages, thick pine forests and lots of opportunities for biking, hiking, sailing and kayaking.

Freeport

The fame and fortune of Freeport, 16 miles northeast of Portland, began a century ago, when Leon Leonwood Bean opened a shop to sell equipment and provisions to hunters and fishers heading north into the Maine woods. LL Bean's good value earned him loyal customers, and over the years the **LL Bean store** (☎ 800-341-4341; www.llbean.com; Main St) added lots of good-quality outdoor gear. The wildly popular store is now open 24 hours a day, every day of the year.

Ironically, this former stopover for hearty outdoor types amid the natural beauty of Maine's rockbound coast is now devoted entirely to city-style shopping, with more than 100 shops selling tony luggage, perfumed soaps and trendy clothes. Freeport's mile-long Main St (US 1) is a perpetual traffic jam of cars from all over, their occupants coming with nature in their hearts but discounted urban luxuries on their shopping lists.

INFORMATION

Freeport Merchants Association (☎ 207-865-1212, 800-865-1994; www.freeportusa.com) has information centers on Main St at Mallet St and on Mill St a block south of Main St.

SLEEPING & EATING

James Place Inn (☎ 207-865-4486, 800-964-9086; www.jamesplaceinn.com; 11 Holbrook St; with breakfast d $135-165;) This Victorian-style cottage has six rooms; some have whirlpool tubs and some have kitchenettes.

Harraseeket Inn (☎ 207-865-9377, 800-342-6423; www.harraseeketinn.com; 162 Main St; with breakfast d $195-260;) The most upscale lodging in town is this traditional 84-room inn.

Casco Bay Inn (☎ 207-865-4925; www.cascobayinn.com; 107 US 1; with breakfast d $90-110;) Motels are mostly south of town on US 1 near I-95 exit 19, including this one.

Winslow Memorial Park (☎ 207-865-4198; Staples Point Rd; campsites $17-19) The choicest campground is this 100-site ground on the ocean, south of town.

Bradbury Mountain State Park (☎ 207-688-4712; ME 9, Pownal; campsites $14) To the northwest, this has 41 forested campsites; it's a good place for hiking, too.

Lobster Cooker (☎ 207-865-4349; 39 Main St; mains $5-20) A fast-food place with excellent clam chowder, coleslaw and boiled lobsters.

Harraseeket Lunch & Lobster Co (☎ 207-865-4888; 36 Main St, South Freeport; mains $8-18) For lobster, fish-and-chips and clambakes at bayside picnic tables.

Bath

In colonial times, the forested Maine coasts were thick with tall trees – just right for making masts for the king's navy. Today Bath continues the tradition by building steel frigates, cruisers and other navy craft at the **Bath Iron Works** (BIW), one of the largest shipyards in the USA. The **Maine Maritime Museum** (☎ 207-443-1316; www.bathmaine.com; 243 Washington St; adult $9.50, child 5-11 $6.50; 9:30am-5pm), which is south of the ironworks, showcases maritime art, wooden boats and historic buildings. Get more information from the **Bath-Brunswick Chamber of Commerce** (☎ 207-443-9751; www.midcoastmaine.com; 45 Front St; 8:30am-5pm Mon-Fri).

Boothbay Harbor

A beautiful little seafarers' town on a broad fjordlike harbor – that's Boothbay Harbor.

INFORMATION

Boothbay Harbor Region Chamber of Commerce (☎ 207-633-2353; www.boothbayharbor.com; 192 Townsend Ave; 8am-5pm Mon-Fri, also 10am-5pm Sat & 11am-3pm Sun May-Oct) provides information for visitors.

SIGHTS & ACTIVITIES

Balmy Days Cruises (☎ 207-633-2284, 800-298-2284; www.balmydayscruises.com; Pier 8) runs one-hour harbor tours (adult $10, child five to 11 $4.50) and takes folks out to Monhegan Island for a day (adult/child $30/18). **Cap'n Fish's Boat Trips** (☎ 207-633-3244, 800-636-3244; Pier 1) runs whale-watch trips (adult/child $28/15, 3½ hours); they also operate shorter wildlife scouting trips including puffin nature cruises (adult/child $20/10) and seal-watch trips (adult/child $14/7).

SLEEPING

Seagate Motel (☎ 207-633-3900, 800-633-1707; www.seagatemotel.com; 138 Townsend Ave; with breakfast d $105-120;) At the north entrance to Boothbay Harbor, this motel has good rooms with refrigerators.

Topside Inn (☎ 207-633-5404, 877-486-7466; www.topsideinn.com; 60 McKown St; with breakfast d $95-140) Atop McKown Hill, this lodging has nearly unparalleled views of the ocean and town. There are 21 rooms in three buildings – the main inn and two motel-like guesthouses.

Welch House Inn (☎ 207-633-3431, 800-279-7313; www.welchhouse.com; 56 McKown St; with breakfast d $125-185;) This classic hilltop inn was built in 1873. Twelve of the 14 rooms have water views.

Check out **Little Ponderosa Campground** (☎ 207-633-2700; 159 Wiscasset Rd/ME 27, Boothbay; campsites/RV sites $25-31), 6 miles north of Boothbay Harbor, with 96 wooded campsites and 36 on the water, and the oceanfront **Gray Homestead** (☎ 207-633-4612; 21 Homestead Rd, Southport; campsites $21-23, RV sites $21-29), 4 miles south of Boothbay Harbor, with 40 campsites (and kayaks to rent).

EATING

Lobstermen's Co-Op (☎ 207-633-4900; 97 Atlantic Ave; mains $9-14) On the east side of the bay, this informal spot serves lobster dinners at picnic tables on the dock.

Lobsterman's Wharf (☎ 207-633-3443; ME 96, East Boothbay; dinners $15-22) You can have a full sit-down seafood meal here away from the tourists.

Christopher's Boat House (☎ 207-633-6565; 25 Union St; dinners $22-30) This innovative bistro serves 'New World cuisine' with lots of dishes from the wood-fired grill.

Cabbage Island Clambakes (☎ 207-633-7200; Pier 6, Fisherman's Wharf; per person including boat trip $42) Take this ferry to Cabbage Island for a classic New England clambake – fish chowder, lobsters, steamers, corn, potatoes and blueberry cake.

Pemaquid Peninsula

South from Damariscotta the ME 130 goes to Pemaquid Neck, the southernmost part of the peninsula. On the west side of Pemaquid Neck are Pemaquid Beach and **Fort William Henry** (☎ 207-677-2423; adult $1, child 5-11 free; 9am-5pm late May–early Sep), a relic of the colonial period. At the southern tip of Pemaquid Neck is **Pemaquid Point**, one of the most beautiful places in Maine, with its tortured, grainy igneous rock formations pounded by restless, treacherous seas. Perched atop the rocks in **Lighthouse Park** (adult $2, child 5-11 free) is the 11,000-candlepower Pemaquid Light, built in 1827. It's one of the 61 surviving lighthouses along the Maine coast. The keeper's house is now the **Fishermen's Museum** (☎ 207-677-2494; Pemaquid Point; admission free; 9am-5pm late May–mid-Oct).

Monhegan Island

This small island (1.5 miles long by a half-mile wide), off the Maine coast due south of Port Clyde, is a popular goal for summer excursions, particularly because of its 17 miles of walking trails. It's also a favorite of artists, who admire its dramatic views and agreeable isolation.

Many island rooms are booked months in advance, so unless you have reservations, take a day excursion from Port Clyde or Boothbay Harbor, and allow four hours or more to walk the trails. Stop at the 1824 **lighthouse** for a look at the little museum set up in the former keeper's house.

Island Inn (☎ 207-596-0371; www.islandinnmonhegan.com; with breakfast s $98-110, d $120-225) is a typical Victorian mansard-roofed summer hotel overlooking the harbor. Its 33 rooms are small and simple; the less expensive ones share baths.

Some of the 33 rooms at the 1870s **Monhegan House** (☎ 207-594-7983; www.monheganhouse.com; with breakfast s $75-79, d $119-125) have ocean views.

Shining Sails (☎ 207-596-0041; www.shiningsails.com; d $105-125, apt $110-170) is a B&B with five apartments that sleep two to four, as well as two guestrooms.

Also try **Tribler Cottage** (☎ 207-594-2445), **Trailing Yew** (☎ 207-596-0440), or **Hitchcock House** (☎ 207-594-8137).

From Port Clyde, the **Monhegan Boat Line** (☎ 207-372-8848; www.monheganboat.com; round-trip adult $27, child 5-11 $14) runs three daily boats from late May to mid-October; make reservations. Boats run year-round, but much less frequently in winter. The **MV Hardy III** (☎ 207-677-2026, 800-278-3346; adult $27, child 5-11 $15) departs from New Harbor, on the east side of the Pemaquid Peninsula.

Camden

Home to Maine's large fleet of windjammers, Camden continues its historic close links with the sea. Its harbor is stunning when the fleet is in port.

INFORMATION

Camden-Rockport-Lincolnville Chamber of Commerce (☎ 207-236-4404; www.camdenme.org) provides information for visitors.

SLEEPING & EATING

Whitehall Inn (☎ 207-236-3391, 800-789-6565; www.whitehall-inn.com; 52 High St; with breakfast s $90-100, d $110-170) At this stately country inn with a broad front porch, the 50 rooms are traditionally decorated. There's a tennis court and shuffleboard, too.

Blue Harbor House (☎ 207-236-3196, 800-248-3196; www.blueharborhouse.com; 67 Elm St; with breakfast d $115-155, ste $145-205; ⊠) This cozy 1810 Cape-style house, with an adjacent carriage house, has 11 country-style rooms, including four suites.

Towne Motel (☎ 207-236-3377, 800-656-4999; www.midcoast.com/townemotel; 68 Elm St; with breakfast d $85-100) This in-town mom-and-pop-style motel has 18 standard rooms.

Camden Hills State Park (☎ 207-236-3109, reservations 207-287-3824; 280 Belfast Rd/US 1; campsites $20) has hot showers and forested campsites (no hookups), as well as good hiking trails; make summer reservations. Also try **Megunticook by the Sea** (☎ 207-594-2428, 800-884-2428; US 1, Rockport; campsites $32, RV sites $34-40; ♿), 3 miles south of Camden, with a quarter of its 100 campsites reserved for tents.

Cappy's Chowder House (☎ 207-236-2254: 1 Main St; mains $5-15) The town's old reliable serves 'wicked good' chowder and other seafood dishes.

WINDJAMMERS

These historic sailing ships – originally dubbed 'windjammers' pejoratively by sailors on steam-powered ships – take passengers out for day and overnight sails from Camden, Rockport and Rockland. Day sails cruise for two hours in Penobscot Bay from May to October ($25 to $28). Usually you can book your place the same day. On the Camden waterfront, look for **Surprise** (☎ 207-236-4687), **Appledore** (☎ 207-236-8353) and **Olad** (☎ 207-236-2323).

Some overnighters, such as Rockland's schooner **Wendameen** (☎ 207-594-1751), take passengers cruising for a day and a night ($180, all meals included). Other schooners make three- and six-day cruises, which may include stops at Stonington, Castine, various small islands offshore and points in and around Acadia National Park ($350 to $850 per person, accommodations and meals included). Reservations are a must. June is perhaps the best month to cruise, as the days are long, the harbors uncrowded, and the rates lower, though the weather can be cool, even chilly. Rates are highest July to August. Contact the **Maine Windjammer Association** (☎ 800-807-9463; www.sailmainecoast.com) for details.

Marriner's (☎ 207-236-2647; 35 Main St; mains $5-11) This old-fashioned breakfast nook and lunchroom serves bacon and eggs, big fish-and-chips plates and fried clams.

Castine

The quiet, pretty town of Castine hosts the **Maine Maritime Academy** and its big training ship, the *State of Maine* (1952), which you can board when it's in port. **Castine Inn** (☎ 207-326-4365; www.castineinn.com; 33 Main St; with breakfast d $90-215) is a 19-room Victorian summer hotel that offers outstanding gourmet dinners. Across the street, the **Pentagoet Inn** (☎ 207-326-8616, 800-845-1701; www.pentagoet.com; 26 Main St; with breakfast d $99-195), an 1890s Victorian adorned with turrets, gables and a wrap-around porch, has 16 rooms.

Blue Hill

Charming and upscale, this dignified small Maine coastal town is brimming with tall trees, old houses and lots of culture. In the center of town, the **Captain Isaac Merrill Inn** (☎ 207-374-2555, 877-374-2555; www.captainmerrillinn.com; 1 Union St; with breakfast d $105-155, ste $115-175) has traditionally decorated rooms and suites in an 1830 sea captain's home and adjacent renovated barn. **Patten Pond Camping** (☎ 207-667-8826, 877-667-7376; www.pattenpond.com; 1470 Bucksport Road, Ellsworth; campsites $23-30, RV sites $35-40), northeast of town, has over 150 campsites near a lake. For creatively prepared local seafood and other contemporary fare, make reservations at the fine-dining **Arborvine** (☎ 207-374-2119; 33 Main St; mains $16-22), set in an 1823 Cape-style house.

ACADIA NATIONAL PARK

Established in 1919, Acadia National Park boasts a large variety of plant and animal species as well as 50 miles of one-lane 'carriage roads,' excellent for hiking and biking. Dramatic scenery and a plethora of outdoor sports possibilities make it a popular summer destination. The park covers over 62 sq miles, including most of mountainous Mt Desert Island and large tracts of land on the Schoodic Peninsula, across the Frenchman Bay to the east, and on Isle au Haut, far to the southwest.

The park's main entrance and visitors center are at Hulls Cove, northwest of Bar Harbor off ME 3 ($10 per vehicle, good for seven days).

Information

Acadia Information Center (☎ 207-667-8550, 800-358-8550; www.acadiainfo.com; ME 3, Trenton; ⌚ mid-May–mid-Oct)
Acadia National Park Headquarters & Winter Information Center (ME 233; ⌚ 8am-4:30pm)
Acadia National Park Hulls Cove Visitors Center (☎ 207-288-3338; www.nps.gov/acad; ME 3; ⌚ 8am-4:30pm mid-April–Jun & Sep-Oct, 8am-6pm Jul-Aug)

Sights & Activities

Start your explorations from the Hulls Cove Visitors Center with a drive along the 20-mile **Park Loop Rd**, most of which is one way and which circumnavigates the northeastern section of the island. On the portion called Ocean Dr, stop at Thunder Hole, south of the Overlook Entrance, for a look at the surf crashing into a granite cleft (the effect is best during a strong incoming tide). Otter Cliffs, not far south of Thunder Hole, is a wall of pink granite rising right from the sea. At Jordan Pond there's a self-guided nature trail. Stop for lunch, or afternoon tea and popovers, at **Jordan Pond House** (☎ 207-276-3316; lunches $8-16). For swimming, try Sand Beach or Seal Harbor (chilly salt water) or Echo Lake (barely less chilly freshwater). Finish your first exploration with a stop at the windy summit of Cadillac Mountain (1530ft), the park's highest point. Insomniacs can drive to the summit for a stunning sunrise; they won't be alone.

See opposite for outfitters offering guided park tours as well as lessons and equipment rental.

Sleeping & Eating

See Bar Harbor (opposite) for more information about places to stay and eat.

There are two park campgrounds. The year-round **Blackwoods Campground** (☎ 800-365-2267; ME 3; campsites $20), 5 miles south of Bar Harbor, requires reservations in summer. **Seawall Campground** (ME 102A; campsites $14-20), 4 miles south of Southwest Harbor, rents sites on a first-come, first-served basis; it's open from May to September. No backcountry camping is allowed. Commercial campgrounds are along ME 3 from Ellsworth and clustered near the entrances to Acadia National Park. This stretch is also dotted with motels.

The best place for a lobster picnic is at one of the lobster pounds. Several are clustered north of Trenton Bridge on ME 3, about 6.5 miles south of Ellsworth, including **Trenton Bridge Lobster Pound** (☎ 207-667-2977; ME 3; prices vary). In Southwest Harbor, **Beal's Lobster Pier** (☎ 207-244-3202; Clark Point Rd; mains $7-14) is the best bet, and in affluent Northeast Harbor, save your appetite for **Docksider** (☎ 207-276-3965; 14 Sea St; mains $9-17).

Getting Around

The **Island Explorer** (☎ 207-667-5796; www.exploreacadia.com; admission free; mid-Jun–mid-Oct) runs seven bus routes through the park and to nearby towns, including Bar Harbor, Southwest Harbor and Northeast Harbor.

BAR HARBOR

Bar Harbor, which once rivaled Newport, Rhode Island, for the stature of its summer-colony residents, is a really pleasant town of big old houses (many of which are now inns) and a good base for exploring Acadia National Park.

Information

Bar Harbor Chamber of Commerce (☎ 207-288-5103, 800-345-4617; www.barharbormaine.com; 93 Cottage St; 8am-5pm Mon-Fri Apr-Nov, 9am-4pm Mon-Fri Dec-Mar) is where you can pick up information.

Sights & Activities

Bar Harbor Whale Watch (☎ 207-288-2386, 800-508-1499; www.whalesrus.com; 1 West St), at Main St next to the town pier, offers whale- and puffin-sighting cruises (adult/child $43/25), whale-watch trips (adult/child $39/25), lobster and seal trips (adult/child $19/15) and nature cruises (adult/child $22/15); they also run deep-sea fishing trips (adult $35 to $40, child $25 to $30). **Downeast Windjammer Cruises** (☎ 207-288-4585; 27 Main St; adult $30, child 5-11 $20) departs from the Bar Harbor Inn Pier on two-hour cruises aboard the 51ft, four-mast schooner *Margaret Todd*.

Numerous outfitters provide guide service, equipment for rent or sale, and lessons on hiking, rock climbing, mountain biking, canoeing and sea kayaking, including the following:

Acadia Bike & Coastal Kayak (☎ 207-288-9605, 800-526-8615; www.acadiafun.com; 48 Cottage St)
Acadia Mountain Guides (☎ 207-288-8186, 888-232-9559; www.acadiamountainguides.com; 198 Main St)
Acadia Outfitters (☎ 207-288-8118; 106 Cottage St)
Bar Harbor Bicycle Shop & Island Adventures (☎ 207-288-3886; www.barharborbike.com, www.islandadventureskayaking.com; 141 Cottage St)
National Park Kayak Tours (☎ 207-288-0342, 800-347-0940; www.acadiakayak.com; 39 Cottage St)

Sleeping

Villager Motel (☎ 207-288-3211, 888-383-3211; www.acadia.net/villager; 207 Main St; d $89-138;) This centrally located, family-run motel has 52 well-kept rooms.

Acadia Hotel (☎ 207-288-5721, 888-876-2463; www.acadiahotel.com; 20 Mt Desert St; d $100-160;) Originally a private home, this 1884 inn has 11 guestrooms decorated with floral wallpapers and brass beds; some have whirlpool tubs.

Stratford House Inn (☎ 207-288-5189; www.stratfordinn.com; 45 Mt Desert St; with breakfast d $85-175) The 10 rooms in this Tudor fantasy range from stately to country-cottage style; the two cheapest have a shared bath.

Ledgelawn Inn (☎ 207-288-4596, 800-274-5334; www.barharborvacations.com/welcomelli.htm; 66 Mt Desert St; d $125-245, ste $225-275;) This grand downtown inn is a vast Colonial Revival former summer 'cottage.' There are 23 traditionally appointed rooms in the main inn, 10 in the adjacent carriage house; some have whirlpool tubs, saunas or working fireplaces.

Additional motel options include the 50-room **Anchorage Motel** (☎ 207-288-3959, 800-336-3959; 51 Mt Desert St; d $89-129;) and **Aurora Inn** (☎ 207-288-3771, 800-841-8925; www.aurorainn.com; 51 Holland Ave; d $109-139;) with pool privileges nearby.

Mt Desert Island YWCA (☎ 207-288-5008; 36 Mt Desert St; dm/s/d $27/37/64) Offers lodging to women only; it's usually booked by late April for the entire summer.

Bar Harbor Youth Hostel (☎ 207-288-5587; 27 Kennebec St; dm $12) Open from mid-June through August; 20 beds.

Eating

Café This Way (☎ 207-288-4483; 14½ Main St; breakfasts $4-7, dinners $13-23) A favorite among locals for breakfasts of blueberry pancakes and omelettes, this casual book-filled spot also serves contemporary fare in the evenings, when you might find crab cakes, Thai seafood stew or ginger-spiced roasted veggies.

Lompoc Café & Brewpub (☎ 207-288-9392; 36 Rodick St; lunches $5-8, dinners $9-18) Here more than 20 beers on tap join a really eclectic international menu, which ranges from chipotle-chorizo pizza to cornmeal-crusted trout, at this casual eatery and pub. There's even live music (jazz, blues and R & B) on weekends.

Café Bluefish (☎ 207-288 3696; 122 Cottage St; mains $14-22) This intimate storefront bistro offers innovative seafood (lobster strudel, pecan-crusted salmon with Creole brown butter) and some vegetarian dishes, too.

Reel Pizza Cinerama (☎ 207-288-3828; 33B Kennebec St; pizzas $9-15) Wanna grab a pizza and movie? Lounge on the couches here, munching a slice and catching a flick ($5).

Getting There & Away

US Airways (☎ 207-667-7171, 800-428-4322) connects Bar Harbor and Boston with several flights every day. The Hancock County-Bar Harbor Airport is at Trenton off ME 3 just north of the Trenton Bridge. **Vermont Transit/Greyhound** (☎ 800-451-3292) runs an early-morning bus daily from Bar Harbor, via Bangor and Portland, to Boston and New York. Buses depart from the Villager Motel (207 Main St). Bay Ferries' high-speed car ferry **Cat** (☎ 207-288-3395, 888-249-7245; www.catferry.com; adult/child/car $55/25/95) links Bar Harbor and Yarmouth, Nova Scotia in under three hours.

DOWNEAST MAINE

The 900-plus miles of coastline east of Bar Harbor are sparsely populated, slower-paced and foggier than the Maine to the south and west. Highlights include the **Schoodic Peninsula** territory of Acadia National Park; **Jonesport** and **Beals Island**, with Maine's largest lobster-boat fleet; and **Great Wass Island**, a large nature preserve with walking paths and good bird-watching opportunities (including puffins).

Machias, with a branch of the University of Maine, is the center of commerce along this stretch of coast. **Lubec** is just across the bridge from Canada and **Roosevelt Campobello International Park** (☎ 506-752-2922; www.nps.gov/roca), where Franklin Roosevelt's father James built a palatial summer home. The future US president spent many boyhood summers here and was later given the 34-room cottage. He and his wife Eleanor made brief but well-publicized visits during his long presidential tenure.

Calais (*ka*-lus), at the northern end of US 1, is a twin town to St Stephen, in New Brunswick, Canada. St Stephen is the gateway to Atlantic Canada, covered in Lonely Planet's *Canada*.

INTERIOR MAINE

In northern and western Maine, the ski town of Bethel and the outdoor pleasures of Maine's tallest mountain are popular getaways for outdoorsy types.

Augusta & Bangor

Augusta, which became Maine's capital in 1827, is undoubtedly small. If you're passing through, take a gander at the granite **State House** (1832), then stop at the adjacent **Maine State Museum** (☎ 207-287-2301; 83 State House Station, off State St; admission free; 🕒 9am-5pm Mon-Fri, 10am-4pm Sat, 1-4pm Sun) to learn more about the state's natural, cultural and political history. The **Kennebec Valley Chamber of Commerce** (☎ 207-623-4559; www.augustamaine.com; 21 University Dr) provides information.

A boomtown during Maine's 19th-century lumbering prosperity, Bangor is now a modern, workaday town, perhaps most famous as the hometown of best-selling novelist Stephen King (look for his spooky mansion – complete with bat-and-cobweb fence – among the grand houses along Broadway).

Sebago Lake

Sebago Lake, 15 miles northwest of Portland, is among Maine's largest and most accessible lakes. At its northern end, southeast of Naples, is **Sebago Lake State Park** (☎ 207-693-6613; US 302), with camping, swimming, boating and fishing.

Sabbathday Lake

Take Maine Turnpike exit 11, then ME 26 to reach the town of Sabbathday Lake, 30 miles north of Portland. Sabbathday Lake is home to the nation's only active Shaker community. It was founded in the early 18th century and a handful of devotees keep the Shaker tradition of prayer, simple living, hard work and fine artistry alive. You can tour several of the buildings and visit the **Shaker Museum** (☎ 207-926-4597; adult $6.50, child 5-11 $2; 🕒 10am-4pm Mon-Sat late May–mid-Oct).

Bethel

For a small community nested in the Maine woods, Bethel, 63 miles northwest of

Portland on ME 26, is surprisingly refined. In winter, it's a busy ski town.

INFORMATION

Bethel Area Chamber of Commerce (☎ 207-824-2282, 800-442-5826; www.bethelmaine.com; 30 Cross St; 9am-6pm Mon-Fri, 10am-6pm Sat, noon-6pm Sun Apr-Sep, closed Sat & Sun Oct-Mar) provides information for visitors.

SIGHTS & ACTIVITIES

Sunday River Ski Area (☎ 207-824-3000, 800-430-0771; www.sundayriver.com; ME 26) is one of the best family-oriented ski centers in the eastern USA, with a 2011ft vertical drop.

Bethel Outdoor Adventure & Campground (☎ 207-824-4224, 800-533-3607; www.betheloutdooradventure.com; 121 Mayville Rd/US 2) rents canoes and kayaks and arranges guided trips, lessons and shuttles to and from the Androscoggin River. **Grafton Notch State Park** (☎ 207-824-2912; ME 26), north of Bethel, has hiking trails and pretty waterfalls, but no camping.

SLEEPING

Norseman Inn & Motel (☎ 207-824-2002, 800-824-0722; www.norsemaninn.com; Mayville Rd/US 2; d $58-148) Choose from one of the eight rooms in the 200-year-old inn or the 22 motel rooms in the converted barn.

Chapman Inn (☎ 207-824-2657, 877-359-1498; www.chapmaninn.com; Main & Broad Sts; with breakfast dm $25-33, d $69-129;) Located on the town common, this B&B has 10 country-style doubles, as well as 30 dorm beds. A sauna, billiards and ping pong add to the fun.

River View Resort (☎ 207-824-2808, 888-224-8413; www.riverviewresort.com; 357 Mayville Rd; d $93-199;) This lodging, with an indoor pool, tennis courts and games room, has 32 two-bedroom suites with kitchens that can sleep up to five.

White Mountains National Forest (☎ reservations 877-444-6777; campsites $16-18) The National Forest has five basic campgrounds near Bethel; contact the **Evans Notch Visitors Center** (☎ 207-824-2134; 18 Mayville Rd/US 2) for details.

Caratunk & the Forks

The **Kennebec River**, below the Harris Hydroelectric Station, passes through a rather dramatic 12-mile gorge that's among the country's prime rafting places. The **Kennebec Valley Tourism Council** (☎ 800-393-8629; www.kennebecvalley.org) has information.

The villages of Caratunk and The Forks, on US 201 south of Jackman, are the center of the Kennebec rafting area. Trips ($80 to $130 per person) are suitable for everyone from eight-year-olds to seniors. Operators include the following:

Crab Apple Whitewater (☎ 207-663-4491, 800-553-7238; www.crabappleinc.com)

New England Outdoor Center (☎ 207-723-5438, 800-766-7238; www.neoc.com)

Northern Outdoors (☎ 800-765-7238; www.northernoutdoors.com)

Baxter State Park

Mt Katahdin (5267ft), Maine's tallest mountain and the northern terminus of the 2160-mile Appalachian Trail, is the centerpiece of Baxter State Park, which has 46 other mountain peaks, 1200 campsites and 180 miles of hiking trails.

Arrive at the park entrance early (ie at the crack of dawn: only a certain number of visitors are allowed in per day) and come well equipped. Campsites within the park's 10 campgrounds must be reserved well in advance by mail (preferably in January or February) by contacting **Baxter State Park** (☎ 207-723-5140; www.baxterstateparkauthority.com; 64 Balsam Dr, Millinocket, ME 04462).

If you can't get a reservation at one of the park's campsites, you can usually find a site at one of the **private campgrounds** just outside the park's Togue Ponds and Matagamon gates. There are several campgrounds in Medway (just off I-95 exit 56), Millinocket and Greenville. Get more information from the **Katahdin Area Chamber of Commerce** (☎ 207-723-4443; www.katahdinmaine.com; 1029 Central St, Millinocket).

Washington DC & the Capital Region

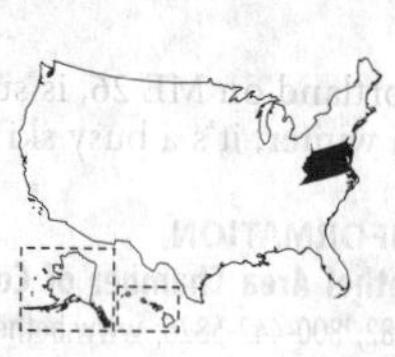

CONTENTS

Much of the USA's formative past has been played out within the Capital Region boundary. Virginia's Jamestown and Williamsburg settlements were instrumental in advancing the young colonies during the United States' infancy. Crucial Civil War battles occurred here, as well as in West Virginia (which was once part of Virginia) and Maryland.

Today, the Capital Region thrives not only on its rich, historical yarns, but its contemporary outlook on politics, outdoor pursuits and entertainment, and is a must-see for visitors looking to capture a slice of Americana.

Washington DC is constantly reinventing itself as a world-class cosmopolitan city. Home to such national symbols as the White House, Capitol and memorials honoring the country's great leaders and events, Washington DC is the nation's capital as well as a living monument to the USA itself.

The cherished maritime heritage of the Chesapeake Bay is evident in attractions such as Baltimore's Inner Harbor and traditional watermen communities on the Eastern Shore. Further inland are the bucolic Shenandoah Valley and beautiful Blue Ridge Mountains, where forests, trails and rivers provide opportunities for outdoor activities. Deeper into the Appalachian and Allegheny mountain ranges, especially in West Virginia, even more rugged adventures await.

HIGHLIGHTS

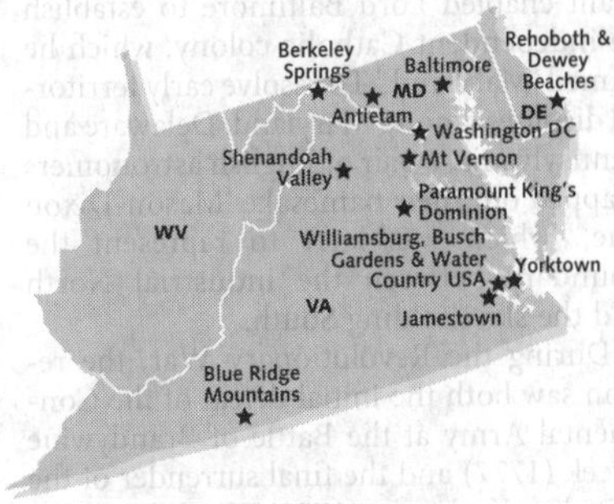

- Learning about United States history right where it happened – just off the **Mall** in Washington DC (p289)
- Picturing yourself following in George Washington's footsteps at his **Mt Vernon country estate** (p303)
- Observing history through the museums of colonial America in **Williamsburg, Jamestown** and **Yorktown** (p311)
- Learning about the 'brother-against-brother' US Civil War through evocative battlefields such as **Antietam** (p339)
- Driving through Virginia's scenic blockbusters, **Shenandoah Valley** (p319) and the **Blue Ridge Mountains** (p322)
- Strolling along the Inner Harbor promenade in the all-American city of **Baltimore** (p325)
- Getting your charkas aligned in the quirky spa town of **Berkeley Springs**, West Virginia, where George Washington used to bathe (p345)
- Partying along the **Delaware seashore** at Rehoboth and Dewey beaches (p342)
- Screaming at the top of your lungs at wild amusement parks such as **Paramount King's Dominion** (p311), **Busch Gardens** (p313) and **Water Country USA** (p313)

HISTORY

Early European settlements in the Capital Region were variously assisted and resisted by Native Americans. The Powhatan initially helped the English when they arrived at Jamestown Island in 1607, but hostility contributed to the woes of the fledgling settlement as relations deteriorated. While the tale of how a chieftain's daughter named Pocahontas saved the life of English captain John Smith is now a treasured American legend, the bulk of Native American history in the region is far less romantic.

Inhabitants of many European and Native American settlements engaged in 'Indian Wars,' though European-borne diseases proved more devastating than warfare, wiping out whole tribes. A handful of Native American communities remain on isolated reservations in Virginia today.

In 1624 the British founded the royal colony of Virginia in honor of the 'Virgin Queen' Elizabeth, liberally claiming all territory in a wide strip from the Atlantic Coast to the west. The English soon absorbed Dutch and Swedish settlements on the Delaware coast, established in 1631 and 1638, respectively. In 1634 a royal grant enabled Lord Baltimore to establish an independent Catholic colony, which he named 'Maryland.' To resolve early territorial disputes among Maryland, Delaware and Pennsylvania, a pair of English astronomers mapped out their namesake 'Mason-Dixon line,' which was later to represent the boundary between the industrial North and the slaveholding South.

During the Revolutionary War, the region saw both the initial defeat of the Continental Army at the Battle of Brandywine Creek (1777) and the final surrender of the British at Yorktown (1781). Virginians were again influential in the 1787 Constitutional Convention, and four of the new republic's first five presidents came from that state.

The site of Washington was selected as a convenient point between Northern and Southern states after a post–Revolutionary War compromise. The new capital's position proved particularly strategic during the Civil War. While Maryland and Delaware were technically 'slave states,' they chose to remain in the Union. Virginia seceded and established the capital of the Confederacy in Richmond. The mountainous western part of Virginia was admitted to the Union as a separate state in 1863 to grant Lincoln the votes needed to advance Emancipation.

After the Civil War, the region slowly recovered on the strength of new industrial growth, and the coastal urban corridor became increasingly developed. The mountain regions, particularly West Virginia, remain much less developed; boom-to-bust coal production peaked here in the early 20th century.

Today, the area is still growing professionally and economically, despite the slumping economy (particularly tourism) and the impact that September 11, 2001, had on the DC area. The main things that came out of September 11 were the reawakening of patriotic feelings and an increase in people's desire to reconnect with this country's incredible past. This region has no shortage of patriotism. DC is the birthplace of democracy, Maryland is the home of the Star-Spangled Banner, and Virginia is the home of many US presidents. This area remains resilient to conflict and struggle, and continues to grow. There are still some problems, though. The Chesapeake Bay is still trying to replenish its once abundant seafood and other marine life, and extreme weather patterns have flooded some areas and affected the farming life in Maryland and Virginia. However, a renaissance of construction projects and commitment to preserving the region's natural resources has kept it strong and will continue to remain an indicator of the nation's overall health.

GEOGRAPHY & CLIMATE

The region's coastal areas include a low, flat, 100-mile-wide coastal plain as well as the 'Delmarva' (Delaware-Maryland-Virginia) Peninsula between the Chesapeake and Delaware Bays. The Chesapeake Bay is an estuary, where some 48 navigable rivers join the sea in a geographically and culturally distinct region called the 'Tidewater.'

Further inland, the undulating Piedmont Plateau holds the region's farmlands and many of its cities and towns. The Appalachian range, which forms a barrier to the northwest, has a number of subsidiary ranges, including the Allegheny Mountains and the Blue Ridge Mountains; the fabled Shenandoah Valley lies between them. On the west side of the Alleghenies, the principal rivers of heavily forested West Virginia drain inland to the Ohio River system.

The Capital Region experiences the best (and worst) of all four seasons. It has cold, often snowy winters, and hot and humid summers with temperatures hanging around 100°F in July and August. Springtime is beautiful but a bit rainy, with comfortable temperatures. Fall in this area brings out awesome foliage backdrops and keeps temperatures cool and crisp.

With forests and gardens in bloom and comfortable temperatures, spring is a lovely time to visit the region. Summer brings crowds, heat and humidity to the Tidewater region, though this is when most businesses and attractions are open.

The mountains are a cool refuge in summer; in winter, the ski resorts open, but many other mountain businesses close.

With both northern and southern varieties, the Appalachian forests here shelter more than 130 types of trees, notably dogwood, redbud, pine, poplar, wild cherry and hemlock. In the Piedmont there's red maple, black oak, ash, elm, pine and cedar, with a transition from deciduous northern trees to the southern conifers. The coastal plains have pine and birch, while the southwest has groves of walnut, hickory and chestnut.

Many large mammals have disappeared, but black bears and white-tailed deer are still common. The coastal and tidewater areas are great for bird-watching; migratory and wintering waterfowl include snow geese, tundra swans, mallards, wigeons, killdeers, sandpipers and ospreys. Raptors include golden eagles and American bald eagles.

POPULATION & PEOPLE

Some traditional local cultures manage to survive within a short distance of cosmopolitan cities. Around Chesapeake Bay, communities of watermen speak with an accent similar to that of the Cornish fishers who migrated here generations ago. Though not as isolated as they once were, many still make a living harvesting oysters and crabs. Likewise, some communities in the Appalachians retain a distinctive culture most noted for its bluegrass music and traditional crafts.

ACTIVITIES

Though history may be the biggest draw in the Capital Region, the active traveler won't be disappointed with the wide range of outdoor activities available. Throw in the Appalachian Trail, Shenandoah National Park, the Blue Ridge Mountains for hiking, bicycling and camping; the James, Shenandoah, Maury, and Youghiogheny Rivers for rafting, tubing and kayaking; the world-class sailing center of Annapolis; endless fishing and boating possibilities on the Chesapeake Bay; bird-watching at Chincoteague and Assateague Islands; and even ski resorts with downhill and cross-country trails – just to mention a few possibilities – and you'll see the many-faceted appeal of this area.

GETTING THERE & AROUND

These are the region's three major airports:

Baltimore-Washington International Airport (BWI; ☎ 410-859-7111) Thirty-five miles north of Washington DC and 10 miles south of Baltimore.

Ronald Reagan national airport (☎ 703-417-8000) Washington DC.

Washington Dulles International Airport (☎ 703-572-2700) Twenty-six miles west of Washington.

Regional Virginia is also served by the following airports:

Newport News-Williamsburg (☎ 757-877-0221)

Richmond (☎ 804-226-3000)

Roanoke (☎ 540-362-1999)

West Virginia is served by the central **Charleston Airport** (☎ 304-344-8033), Delaware by **Philadelphia International Airport** (PIA; ☎ 215-937-6937), a 30-minute drive north of Wilmington.

Buses are the budget alternative for reaching many smaller cities not served by air or rail (though travelers should check car rental rates and packages to compare costs). Nearly every city has a **Greyhound** (www.greyhound.com) bus station or stop; **Trailways** (www.trailways.com) is another bus line that often uses the same terminals. See individual city sections for more on local and regional bus transit.

Amtrak (www.amtrak.com for fares & schedules) and the regional **MARC system** (www.mtamaryland.com) provide rail transit to Washington DC and other regional destinations. See the Washington DC section (p301) for fares from that city to other East Coast destinations.

You'll need a car for extensive exploring outside major cities.

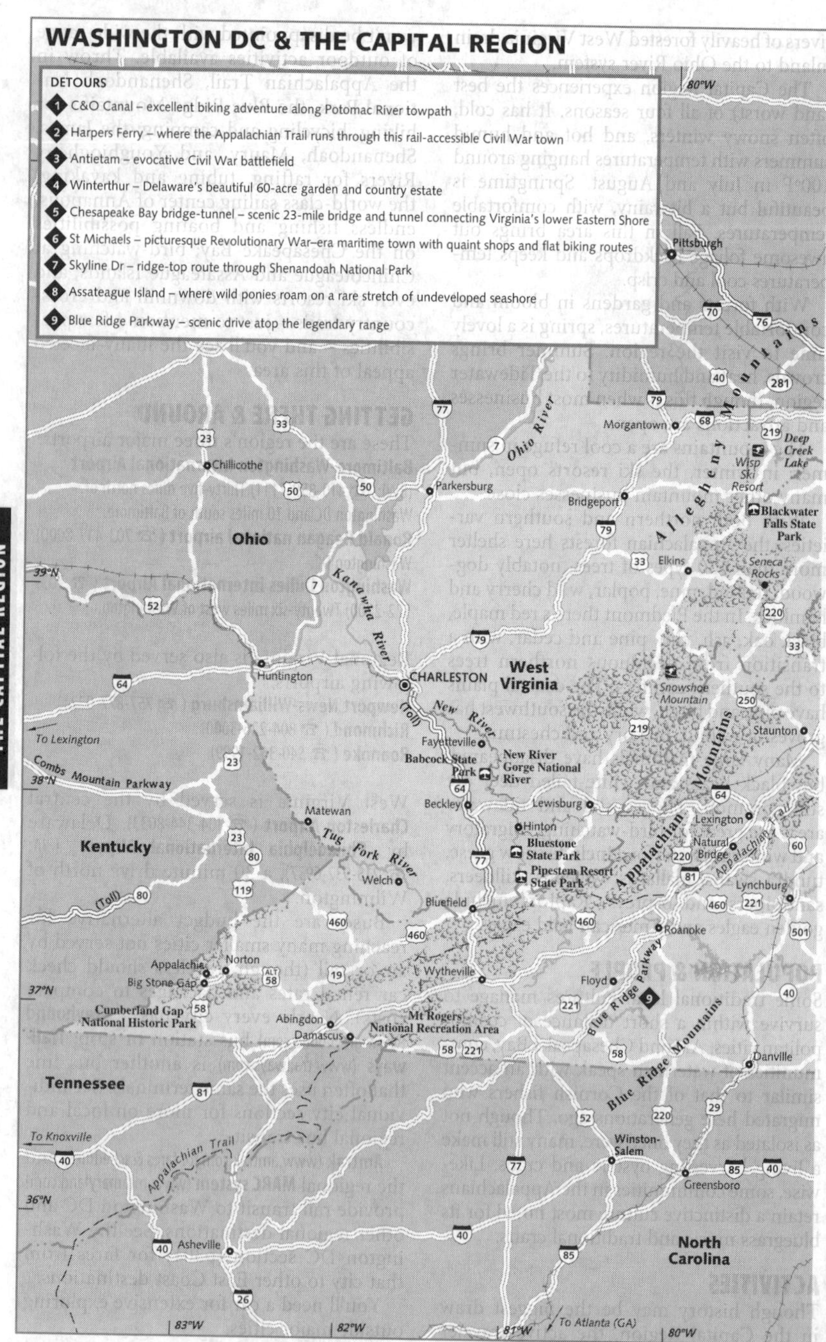

WASHINGTON DC & THE CAPITAL REGION

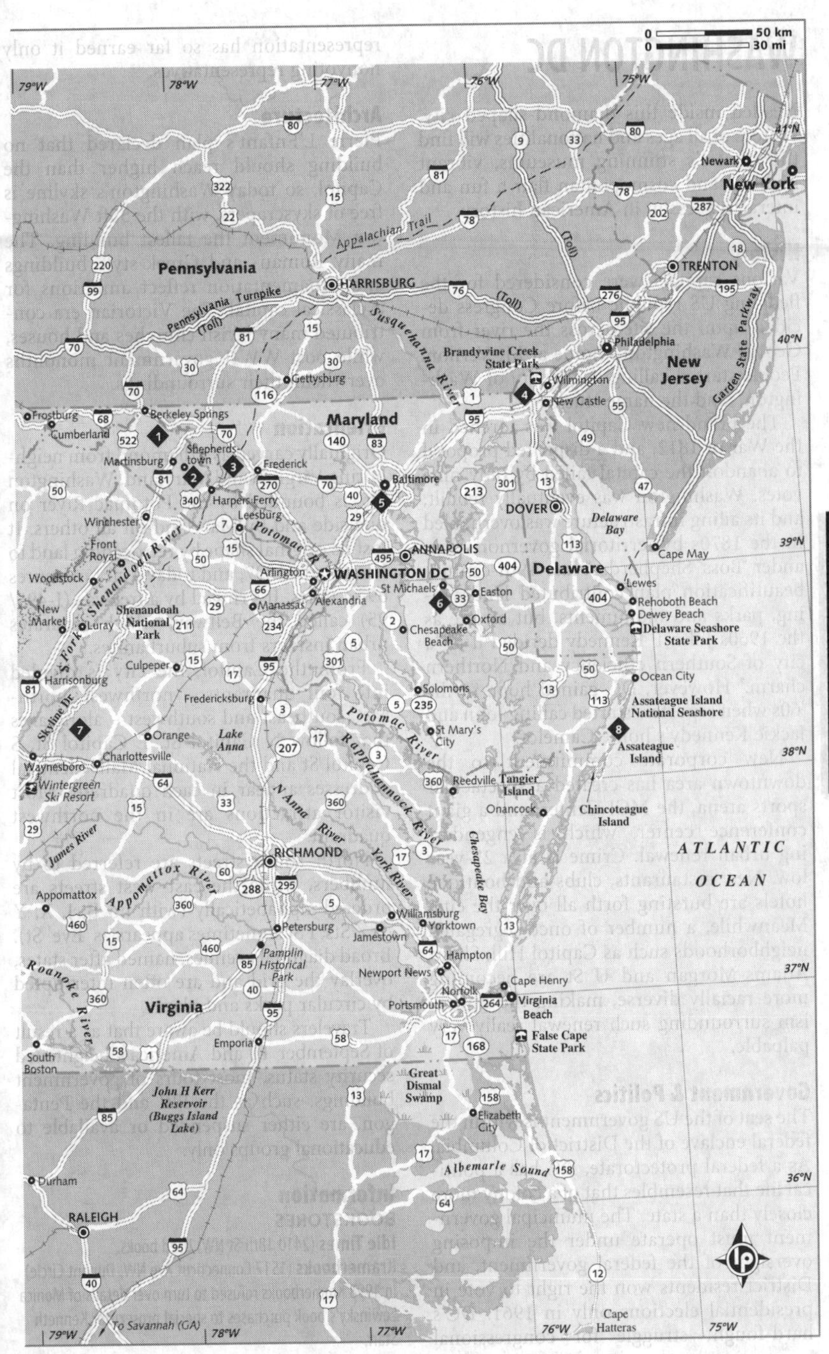
0 50 km
0 30 mi
79°W
78°W
77°W
76°W
75°W
41°N
40°N
39°N
38°N
37°N
36°N
Newark
New York
TRENTON
HARRISBURG
Pennsylvania
Appalachian Trail
Pennsylvania Turnpike (Toll)
(Toll)
Susquehanna River
Garden State Parkway
Philadelphia
New Jersey
Brandywine Creek State Park
Wilmington
New Castle
Gettysburg
Maryland
Frostburg
Cumberland
Berkeley Springs
Martinsburg
Shepherdstown
Frederick
Baltimore
Harpers Ferry
Leesburg
Winchester
Front Royal
Woodstock
New Market
Luray
Shenandoah National Park
S Fork Shenandoah River
Potomac River
ANNAPOLIS
WASHINGTON DC
Arlington
Alexandria
Manassas
St Michaels
Easton
Oxford
Chesapeake Beach
DOVER
Delaware Bay
Delaware
Cape May
Lewes
Rehoboth Beach
Dewey Beach
Delaware Seashore State Park
Ocean City
Assateague Island National Seashore
Assateague Island
Chincoteague Island
Culpeper
Harrisonburg
Skyline Dr
Fredericksburg
Solomons
St Mary's City
Orange
Lake Anna
Charlottesville
Waynesboro
Wintergreen Ski Resort
Rappahannock River
N Anna River
Reedville
Tangier Island
Onancock
Chesapeake Bay
James River
RICHMOND
York River
Appomattox River
Appomattox
Williamsburg
Yorktown
Jamestown
Petersburg
Pamplin Historical Park
Hampton
Newport News
Cape Henry
Norfolk
Virginia Beach
Portsmouth
Roanoke River
Virginia
Emporia
False Cape State Park
ATLANTIC OCEAN
South Boston
John H Kerr Reservoir (Buggs Island Lake)
Great Dismal Swamp
Elizabeth City
Albemarle Sound
Durham
RALEIGH
Cape Hatteras
To Savannah (GA)

WASHINGTON DC

Nestled inside this diamond-shaped city, visitors of all ages and nationalities will find the capital's stunning museums, vibrant nightlife and cosmopolitan flair a fun and interactive lesson in American history.

History

Various capitals were considered for the fledgling US republic before Congress decided upon the site across the river from George Washington's home at Mt Vernon. People started calling it 'the city of Washington,' and the name stuck.

The brand-new Capitol was torched in the War of 1812, and a dispirited proposal to abandon the capital failed by only nine votes. Washington was eventually rebuilt, and its ailing infrastructure was overhauled in the 1870s by territorial governor Alexander 'Boss' Shepherd. A late-19th-century beautification plan contributed landscaping, parks and monuments, but as late as the 1960s John F Kennedy derided it as 'a city of Southern efficiency and Northern charm.' However, DC gained hope in the '60s when reporters started calling John and Jackie Kennedy's home Camelot.

New corporate commitment to the downtown area has created a spectacular sports arena, the MCI Center, and a giant conference center, which is engendering urban renewal. Crime is at a 25-year low. New restaurants, clubs and boutique hotels are bursting forth all over the city. Meanwhile, a number of once-segregated neighborhoods such as Capitol Hill, Shaw, Adams-Morgan and U St are becoming more racially diverse, making the optimism surrounding such renewal really very palpable.

Government & Politics

The seat of the US government is within the federal enclave of the District of Columbia. As a federal protectorate, DC has a political life that resembles that of a colony more closely than a state. The municipal government must operate under the imposing oversight of the federal government, and District residents won the right to vote in presidential elections only in 1961. DC's hard-fought struggle for congressional representation has so far earned it only nonvoting representatives.

Architecture

Pierre L'Enfant's plan declared that no building should reach higher than the Capitol, so today Washington's skyline is free of skyscrapers, with the 55ft Washington Monument the tallest building. The many Roman- and Greek-style buildings and ornamentation reflect ambitions for a classical capital. The Victorian era contributed many lavish churches and houses, while post-WWII government monoliths overwhelm their surroundings.

Orientation

Originally carved as a diamond from neighboring Virginia and Maryland, Washington DC is bounded by the Potomac River on one side and by Maryland on all others. It lost its original shape by retroceding land to Virginia in 1837, and today's city measures 69 sq miles. It's ringed by a freeway (I-495/95) called the Beltway, which separates urban insiders from suburbanites.

From the Capitol, the city is divided into four quadrants – northwest, northeast, southeast and southwest – along axes that follow N Capitol St, E Capitol St, S Capitol St and the National Mall. Identical addresses appear in each quadrant. Most visitor attractions are in the northwest quadrant.

North–south streets are referred to by numbers, while the east–west streets are ordered alphabetically (with no B, J, X, Y or Z Sts; I St sometimes appears as 'Eye' St). Broad diagonal avenues, named after states, overlay the grid and are often interrupted by circular parks and plazas.

Travelers should be aware that as a result of September 11 and America's heightened security status, most tours of government buildings, such as the FBI and the Pentagon, are either suspended or available to educational groups only.

Information

BOOKSTORES

Idle Times (2410 18th St NW) Used books.

Kramerbooks (1517 Connecticut Ave NW, Dupont Circle) In 1998 Kramerbooks refused to turn over details of Monica Lewinsky's book purchases to special prosecutor Kenneth Starr.

Politics & Prose (5015 Connecticut Ave NW)
Travel Books & Language Center (4437 Wisconsin Ave NW)

EMERGENCY

Emergency numbers (☎ 911 for life threatened, fire, ambulance; ☎ 311 otherwise)
Poison center (☎ 202-625-3333)

INTERNET ACCESS

CyberStop Cafe (☎ 202-234-2470; 1513 17th St NW, Dupont Circle)

MEDIA

99.5 WIHT-FM Top 40.
90.9 WETA-FM NPR affiliate.
101.1 WIYY-FM and 99.1 WHFS-FM Rock and alternative.
Washington Afro-American (www.afro.com) African-American daily.
Washington City Paper (www.washingtoncitypaper.com) Free weekly paper with useful entertainment listings.
Washington Post (www.washingtonpost.com) Daily city (and national) paper.

MEDICAL SERVICES

George Washington University Hospital (☎ 202-715-4000; 901 23rd St NW)
Washington Hospital Center (☎ 202-877-3627; 110 Irving St NW)

MONEY

Currency exchange is available at the three major airports, during weekday business hours at most of the banks, and at the following locations:
American Express (1150 Connecticut Ave NW)
Thomas Cook (Union Station, Gate G booth; 🕑 Mon-Sat 9am-5pm, Sun noon-6pm)

POST

Main post office (2 Massachusetts Ave NE)

TOURIST OFFICES

Chamber of Commerce visitors center (☎ 202-328-4748; 1300 Pennsylvania Ave NW, Ronald Reagan Building)
International Visitors Information Service (☎ 202-536-4911, language bank ☎ 202-939-5538; 🕑 weekdays) At the Arrivals Terminal at Washington-Dulles Airport; its language bank answers questions in over 50 languages.
National Park Service (NPS; www.nps.gov/nama)
Online visitor information (www.dcvisit.com)
Washington Convention & Visitors Association (☎ 202-789-7000; www.washington.org; 1212 New York Ave NW, Suite 600, Washington DC 20005; 🕑 Mon-Fri 9am-5pm)
White House visitors center (☎ 202-456-7041; 1450 Pennsylvania Ave NW; 🕑 7:30am-4pm)

Travelers with disabilities can call the following numbers for information:
General information (☎ 202-789-7000) On hotels, restaurants and attractions.
Metrorail (Metro; ☎ 202-635-6434)
Smithsonian access (☎ 202-357-2700, TTY 202-357-1729)

Dangers & Annoyances

Although DC has bleak inner-city areas and one of the nation's highest murder rates, the most violent crime occurs outside tourist areas. Almost all major sights are in relatively safe areas, except for the Capitol area, which has a higher concentration than others of homeless and people asking for money.

Note that many attractions get very crowded; prepare for long, standing waits in sun or rain. Thorough security checks are common.

Sights

Historic and entertaining attractions are scattered throughout the district and within a variety of distinct neighborhoods. The Capitol Hill, downtown and National Mall areas contain the biggies like the White House, Smithsonian museums and war memorials, and are within convenient walking distances

STATE OF THE UNION POST-SEPTEMBER 11

On September 11, 2001, life changed dramatically for the US and Washington DC, when a Boeing 767 slammed into the Pentagon (home of the US Department of Defense) as part of the terrorists attacks that leveled NYC's World Trade Center. It had since been repaired, but the damage will be long-lasting, with new security measures initiated throughout the District, including limited or no access to many national buildings that the public was once free to enjoy. As a result, the Department of Homeland security created a terrorist 'threat advisory' pyramid to alert citizens and visitors of the likelihood of terrorist activity. Visitors should check www.dhs.gov/dhspublic and be aware that many buildings (the Capitol, naval bases and museums) will be closed as the threat increases.

WASHINGTON DC
Woodley Park-Zoo
Kalorama Park
ADAMS MORGAN
Meridian Hill Park
Banneker Recreation Center
Normanstone Park
To Mr Henry's (0.3mi)
Kalorama Circle
Dumbarton Oaks Park
KALORAMA
U St/ Cordozo
Mitchell Park
Montrose Park
GEORGETOWN
SHAW & THE NEW U DISTRICT
Shaw/Howard University
Oak Hill Cemetery
Sheridan Circle
To Georgetown University (1.3mi)
Dupont Circle
DUPONT CIRCLE
Logan Circle
Kennedy Playground
To Saloun (0.1mi); Georgetown Visitor Center; Restaurants (1mi)
Scott Circle
Thomas Circle
Mt Vernon Sq/UDC
Farragut North
Juarez Circle
Washington Circle
Farragut Square
McPherson Square
Franklin Square
CHINATOWN
Mt Vernon Square
Foggy Bottom/ GWU
George Washington University
Farragut West
Lafayette Square
Metro Center
Gallery Pl/ Chinatown
Theodore Roosevelt Island
WHITE HOUSE AREA & FOGGY BOTTOM
White House
South Lawn
Rawlins Park
The Ellipse
Federal Triangle
DOWNTOWN
Archives/Navy Memorial
Theodore Roosevelt Bridge
Constitution Gardens
Reflecting Pool
Rainbow Pool
National Mall
Smithsonian
West Potomac Park
Arlington Memorial Bridge
Franklin Delano Roosevelt Memorial Park
Hancock Park
Tidal Basin
L'Enfant Plaza
To Arlington (1.2mi); Alexandria (7mi); Dulles Airport (18mi)
Lady Bird Johnson Park
Potomac River
Benjamin Banneker Park
Washington Channel
To Alexandria (4mi); Ronald Reagan National Airport (15mi)
To Pentagon (2.3mi)
East Potomac Park
East Potomac Park Golf Course

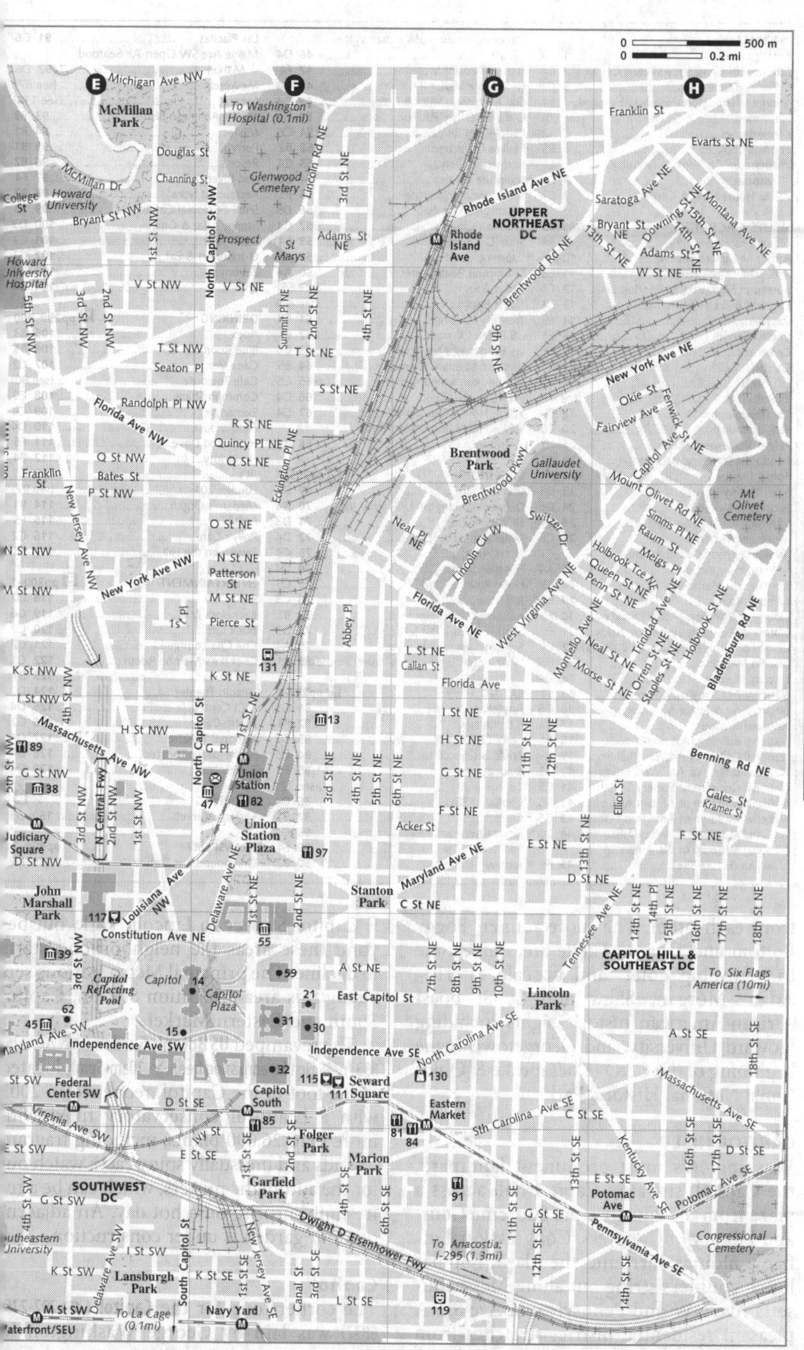
0 500 m
0 0.2 mi
E
F
G
H
Michigan Ave NW
McMillan Park
To Washington Hospital (0.1mi)
Douglas St
Channing St
Glenwood Cemetery
Lincoln Rd NE
3rd St NE
Franklin St
Evarts St NE
McMillan Dr
College St
Howard University
Bryant St NW
1st St NW
North Capitol St NW
Prospect
St Marys
Adams St NE
Rhode Island Ave NE
UPPER NORTHEAST DC
Rhode Island Ave
Saratoga Ave NE
Bryant St NE
Downing St NE
15th St NE
Montana Ave NE
13th St NE
14th St NE
Adams St
W St NE
Brentwood Rd NE
Howard University Hospital
V St NW
V St NE
5th St NW
3rd St NW
2nd St NW
Summit Pl NE
2nd St NE
4th St NE
9th St NE
T St NW
T St NE
Seaton Pl
S St NE
New York Ave NE
Okie St
Fenwick St NE
Fairview Ave
Randolph Pl NW
Florida Ave NW
R St NE
Quincy Pl NE
Eckington Pl NE
Q St NW
Q St NE
Bates St
Franklin St
P St NW
Brentwood Park
Brentwood Pkwy
Gallaudet University
Capitol Ave NE
Mount Olivet Rd NE
Mt Olivet Cemetery
New Jersey Ave NW
O St NE
Neal Pl NE
Switzer Dr
Simms Pl NE
Raum St
Meigs Pl
N St NW
N St NE
Patterson St
Lincoln Cr W
Holbrook Tce NE
Queen St NE
Penn St NE
M St NW
New York Ave NW
M St NE
Pierce St
Florida Ave NE
West Virginia Ave NE
Montello Ave NE
Trinidad Ave NE
Holbrook St NE
Bladensburg Rd NE
Abbey Pl
131
L St NE
Callan St
Neal St NE
Orren St NE
Staples St NE
Morse St NE
K St NW
4th St NW
K St NE
Florida Ave
I St NW
North Capitol St
1st St NE
13
I St NE
Massachusetts Ave NW
H St NW
H St NE
11th St NE
12th St NE
89
G Pl
Union Station
3rd St NE
4th St NE
5th St NE
6th St NE
G St NE
Benning Rd NE
G St NW
38
N Central Fwy
47
82
Elliot St
Gales St
Kramer St
3rd St NW
2nd St NW
1st St NW
F St NE
Judiciary Square
Union Station Plaza
Acker St
13th St NE
F St NE
E St NE
97
D St NW
Louisiana Ave NW
Delaware Ave NE
1st St NE
2nd St NE
Maryland Ave NE
D St NE
Stanton Park
C St NE
Tennessee Ave NE
14th St NE
14th Pl
15th St NE
16th St NE
17th St NE
18th St NE
John Marshall Park
117
Constitution Ave NE
55
39
3rd St NW
7th St NE
8th St NE
9th St NE
10th St NE
CAPITOL HILL & SOUTHEAST DC
To Six Flags America (10mi)
Capitol Reflecting Pool
Capitol
14
Capitol Plaza
59
A St NE
21
East Capitol St
Lincoln Park
62
45
15
31
30
North Carolina Ave SE
A St SE
18th St SE
Maryland Ave SW
Independence Ave SW
Independence Ave SE
32
130
Massachusetts Ave SE
D St SW
Federal Center SW
D St SE
Capitol South
115
111
Seward Square
Eastern Market
Sth Carolina Ave SE
C St SE
Virginia Ave SW
Ivy St
85
81
84
1st St SE
2nd St SE
Folger Park
Kentucky Ave SE
16th St SE
17th St SE
D St SE
E St SW
E St SE
Marion Park
13th St SE
E St SE
Potomac Ave SE
4th St SW
SOUTHWEST DC
Garfield Park
4th St SE
6th St SE
91
11th St SE
G St SE
Potomac Ave
G St SW
Dwight D Eisenhower Fwy
Pennsylvania Ave SE
Congressional Cemetery
Southeastern University
I St SW
Delaware Ave SW
South Capitol St
New Jersey Ave SE
To Anacostia; I-295 (1.3mi)
12th St SE
K St SW
Lansburgh Park
K St SE
Canal St
3rd St SE
14th St SE
L St SE
M St SW
To La Cage (0.1mi)
Navy Yard
119
Waterfront/SEU

INFORMATION
American Express 1 C3
Chamber of Commerce Visitors Center 2 C4
CyberStop Café 3 C2
George Washington University Hospital 4 B4
Idle Times (see 80)
Kramerbooks 5 B2
Thomas Cook 6 B3
Washington Convention & Visitors Association 7 D4
White House Visitors Center 8 C4

SIGHTS & ACTIVITIES pp285–95
Albert Einstein Statue 9 B4
Arthur M Sackler Gallery 10 D5
Arts & Industries Building 11 D5
Bureau of Engraving & Printing 12 C5
Capital Children's Museum 13 F4
Capitol 14 F5
Capitol Service Kiosk 15 E5
Carousel 16 D5
Corcoran Gallery 17 C4
DC Eagle 18 D3
Explorers' Hall (see 41)
FBI Headquarters 19 D4
FDR Memorial 20 B6
Folger Shakespeare Library 21 F5
Fondo del Sol Visual Arts Center 22 B2
Ford's Theatre (see 34)
Freer Gallery of Art 23 D5
Hirshhorn Museum 24 D5
International Spy Museum 25 D4
Jefferson Memorial 26 C6
John F Kennedy Center for the Performing Arts 27 A4
Korean War Memorial 28 B5
Lambda Rising 29 B2
Library of Congress (Adams Building) 30 F5
Library of Congress (Jefferson Building) 31 F5
Library of Congress (Madison Building) 32 F5
Lincoln Memorial 33 B5
Lincoln Museum 34 D4
National Academy of Sciences 35 B4
National Air & Space Museum 36 D5
National Archives 37 D4
National Building Museum 38 E4
National Gallery of Art, East Building 39 E5
National Gallery of Art, West Building 40 D5
National Geographic Society 41 C3
National Museum of African Art 42 D5
National Museum of American History 43 D5
National Museum of Natural History 44 D5
National Museum of the American Indian (Future Site) 45 E5
National Museum of Women in the Arts 46 D4
National Postal Museum 47 F4
NPS Ellipse Visitor Pavilion 48 C4
Old Executive Office Building 49 C4
Old Post Office Pavilion 50 D4
Paddleboat Rentals 51 C6
Phillips Collection 52 B2
Renwick Gallery 53 C4
Sculpture Garden 54 D5
Sewall-Belmont House 55 F5
Smithsonian Castle 56 D5
St John's Church 57 C4
State Department 58 B4
Supreme Court 59 F5
Thompson Boat Center 60 A4
Ticket Booth (see 65)
Ticket Booth (see 82)
Treasury Building 61 C4
US Botanic Garden 62 E5
US Holocaust Memorial Museum 63 C5
Vietnam Veterans Memorial 64 B5
Washington Monument 65 C5
White House 66 C4
White House Tour Main Entrance 67 C4
White House Tour Wheelchair Entrance 68 C4

SLEEPING pp295–7
Channel Inn 69 D6
George Washington University Inn 70 A4
HI Washington DC 71 D3
Hotel Harrington 72 D4
Hotel Helix 73 C3
Hotel Monaco 74 D4
Hotel Rouge 75 C3
Jefferson 76 C3
Kalorama Guest House 77 B1
Morrison-Clark Inn 78 D3
Swissôtel Watergate 79 A4
Washington International Guest House 80 B1

EATING pp297–9
Anatolia 81 G5
B Smith's 82 F4
Ben's Chili Bowl 83 D2
Bread & Chocolate 84 G5
Bullfeathers 85 F5
Cafeteria (see 32)
Capital Q BBQ 86 D4
Cities 87 B1
Florida Avenue Grill 88 D1
Full Kee 89 E4
Johnny's Half Shell 90 B2
Las Placitas 91 G6
Maine Ave SW Open-Air Seafood Market 92 D6
Meskerem (see 87)
Meze (see 114)
Mimi's American Bistro 93 B3
Mixtec 94 B1
Perry's 95 B1
Pesce's 96 B2
Red River Grill 97 F4
Restaurant Nora 98 B2
Sholl's Colonial Cafeteria 99 B3
Stoney's Bar & Grill 100 D3
Sushi Taro 101 C2
U-topia Art & Eat 102 C2
Zaytinya 103 D4
Zola 104 D4

DRINKING pp299–300
Apex 105 B3
Blue Room 106 B1
Cada Vez 107 C2
Cafe Toulouse (see 80)
Common Share 108 C2
Exchange 109 C4
Fadó 110 D4
Hawk and Dove 111 F5
Hung Jury 112 B4
JR's 113 C2
Lounge 201 (see 97)
Madam's Organ 114 B1
Politiki 115 F5
Polly's Cafe 116 C2
Tavern on the Hill 117 E5

ENTERTAINMENT pp300–1
9:30 Club 118 D2
Bachelor's Mill 119 G6
Black Cat 120 C2
Cha Cha Lounge 121 C2
Chef Ike's Mambo Room 122 C1
City Blues 123 B1
Lincoln Theater 124 D2
MCI Center 125 D4
Metro Cafe 126 C2
National Theatre 127 D4
Shakespeare Theater 128 D4
Ticketplace 129 D4

SHOPPING
Eastern Market 130 G5

TRANSPORT pp301–2
Greyhound Bus Station 131 F3

from each other. The more refined Foggy Bottom and Dupont Circle areas are home to many big hotels and upscale eateries. Adams-Morgan, Shaw and U St boast African-American historic sights including Howard University, and Georgetown is the beginning of the C&O (Chesapeake & Ohio) Canal National Historic Park.

CAPITOL HILL

Washington's most prominent landmark, the Capitol, sits atop Capitol Hill across a plaza from the equally regal Supreme Court and Library of Congress. Congressional office buildings surround the plaza. Popular lunch counters string out along Massachusetts Ave NW and Pennsylvania Ave SE. A pleasant residential district stretches from E Capitol St over to Lincoln Park, but beyond these areas the neighborhood starts to decline. The principal Metro stations servicing this area are Union Station, Capitol South and Eastern Market.

The revamped **US Botanic Garden** (☎ 202-225-8333; 245 First St; admission free; 10am-5pm), located at the foot of the Capitol, reopened in 2003 with a beautiful conservatory filled with more than 26,000 plants, including fragrant orchids and unusually spiny cacti; watch out for the automatic misters, which can be a refreshing surprise on a hot day. An adjacent outdoor garden is under construction.

Capitol

The cornerstone for the **Capitol** (☎ 202-225-6827) was laid by George Washington in

1793, and Congress moved in seven years later. Nearly destroyed in the 1814 British invasion, it was rebuilt within five years. The House (south) and Senate (north) wings were added in 1857, and the massive iron dome in 1863. A flag raised above either wing indicates that that body is in session. Be aware that construction on a new visitors center is underway.

Construction is in progress on a secure visitors center in this post–September 11 time. Visitors can only enter on a guided tour and must wait in an often very long line for free tickets at the makeshift **Capitol Service Kiosk** (cnr Independence Ave SE & S Capitol St SW; ticket distribution begins 9am Mon-Sat). Once inside the dramatic central **Rotunda**, note the Constantino Brumidi fresco inside the dome and the hallway murals and ceilings.

To watch Congress in action, call ☎ 202-225-6827 for session dates. US citizens can request visitor gallery passes from their representatives or senators; foreign visitors show their passports at the House gallery. Committee hearings (often fascinating) are open to the public; check the *Washington Post*'s 'Today in Congress' notice. Special **tours** (☎ 202-224-4048) for the disabled are available.

Library of Congress

The world's largest **library** (☎ 202-707-4604 for exhibitions; www.loc.gov) fills three buildings with over 26 million books, 36 million manuscripts, and maps, photographs, sheet music and musical instruments.

The 1897 Jefferson Building features an impressive Main Reading Room and an ornate **Great Hall** with vaulted ceilings. The Madison Building houses the visitors center and cafeteria.

The library screens classic films (free), stages concerts and has four free tours daily.

Supreme Court

This imposing 1935 marble building is home of the highest court in the land. Visitors can watch oral arguments (October to April, Monday to Wednesday) and bench sittings (mid-May to June, Mondays). Arrive early to get in line.

Union Station & Around

Washington's most impressive gateway, **Union Station** (☎ 202-371-9441) is a massive, beautifully restored 1908 beaux arts building; its great hall was modeled on the Roman baths of Diocletian. It hosts Amtrak, Metro and commuter rail stations, as well as shops, restaurants, cinemas and traveler resources.

The **National Postal Museum** (☎ 202-357-2700; admission free; 🕐 10am-5:30pm), across from Union Station, features a postal potluck including the world's largest stamp collection and Cliff Clavin's uniform worn in TV's *Cheers*.

The **Folger Shakespeare Library** (☎ 202-544-7077; 201 E Capitol St; admission free; 🕐 Mon-Sat 10am-4pm) has the world's largest collection of Shakespearean works.

Sewall-Belmont House (☎ 202-546-1210; 114 Constitution Ave NE; admission free; 🕐 Tue-Sat) honors heroines of the women's rights movement and has a vast feminist library.

NATIONAL MALL

This 400ft-wide green expanse stretching from the Potomac River to Capitol Hill is home to DC's most famous monuments and museums. It's also renowned for mass gatherings designed to influence public policy, such as anti–Vietnam War protests in the 1960s and Martin Luther King Jr's 'I Have a Dream' speech.

Pierre L'Enfant envisioned the Mall as a grand promenade lined with mansions and embassies, but it evolved in a more American way into a national lawn lined with family-friendly museums and filled with joggers and picnickers.

Smithsonian Institution

In 1826 Englishman James Smithson, without ever visiting the USA, willed $4,100,000 to the country to found an 'establishment for the increase and diffusion of knowledge.' Today's Smithsonian Institution is a world-class research center that administers more than a dozen Washington museums and galleries along the Mall, plus the National Zoo. Its collection is so large that only 1% is on display at any given point.

Admission to all museums is free.

The **Smithsonian Institution Building** (☎ 202-357-2700; www.si.edu; 🕐 10am-5pm), a turreted red-brick building on the south side of the Mall that was the original Smithsonian museum, is now the visitors center for all the museums. Be prepared for lines; your bags will be searched at all entrances due to heightened security measures.

The following museums are open daily from 10am to 5:30pm.

The **National Museum of American History** (The Mall, cnr 14th & Constitution Ave SW) is a celebration of US culture. The museum's eclectic collection includes the original American flag, first ladies' inauguration ball gowns, Archie Bunker's armchair (from TV's *All in the Family*), a whites-only Woolworth's lunch counter, and touching memorabilia left at the Vietnam Memorial; major African-American and Native American exhibits are also featured.

The **National Museum of Natural History** (The Mall, cnr 10th St & Constitution Ave SW) has such highlights as a towering 13ft elephant, the 45-carat Hope diamond, a life-size model of a blue whale, dinosaur skeletons, a live insect zoo and a state-of-the-art gem and mineral exhibit. Get timed admission passes as soon as it opens.

The cavernous halls of the **National Air & Space Museum** (cnr 6th St & Independence Ave SW), one of the world's most popular museums, holds full-size air- and spacecraft, from the Wright brothers' flyer and Charles Lindbergh's *Spirit of St Louis* to the *Apollo 11* command module. There is an Imax theater screening several movies ($5.50), plus a planetarium ($3.75), shops and a restaurant.

The **Hirshhorn Museum** (cnr 7th St & Independence Ave SW), a modern doughnut-shaped building, houses a huge collection of 20th-century sculptures, including works by Rodin, Brancusi, Calder and Henry Moore, as well as paintings by Dubuffet, O'Keeffe, Warhol, Pollock and de Kooning; a pleasant patio café opens in summer.

The **Arts & Industries Building** (900 Jefferson Dr SW), an odd little structure, displays mainly Victorian-era inventions from the 1876 Philadelphia Centennial Exposition, in a ghostly, carnival-type ambience.

The **National Museum of African Art** (950 Independence Ave SW) and **Arthur M Sackler Gallery** (1050 Independence Ave SW) are the bookends behind the Castle; they deliver visitors to vast, interconnected underground galleries. The first gallery includes masks, textiles and ceramics from the sub-Sahara, and the Sackler exhibits Asian arts, including Chinese ritual bronzes and jade ornaments. The **Freer Gallery of Art** (cnr Jefferson Dr & 12th St SW) features American art, including an extensive collection of Whistler paintings, and evocative Asian exhibits.

The **National Museum of the American Indian** is due to open in 2004; there's a temporary visitors center on the Mall that contains a small exhibition area and a window to view the construction.

Renwick & Corcoran Galleries

The regal entrance and very dignified Grand Salon of the Smithsonian's **Renwick Gallery** (☎ 202-357-2700; cnr 17th St & Pennsylvania Ave NW) are a startling contrast to the wild craftwork, whimsy and abstraction found within.

The **Corcoran Gallery** (☎ 202-639-1700; cnr 17th St & New York Ave NW; admission by donation; 🕒 9am-5pm Mon-Wed, until 9pm Thu) houses a great collection of American art – Hudson River school, Ashcan, pop, abstract expressionism. These are exhibited in a lovely beaux arts building.

National Gallery of Art

This famous **gallery** (☎ 202-737-4215; www.nga.gov; Constitution Ave btwn 3rd & 4th Sts NW) consists of two buildings connected by an underground passage. The original, neoclassical west-wing exhibits primarily European art from the Middle Ages to the early 20th century, including works by Rembrandt, Vermeer, El Greco, Renoir, Monet and Cézanne, plus a lone da Vinci. The east wing features a four-story atrium with a Calder mobile, plus various abstract and modern works. The sculpture garden outside has an ice-skating rink ($5).

US Holocaust Memorial Museum

Opened in 1993, this haunting **memorial** (☎ 202-488-0400; www.ushmm.org; 100 Raoul Wallenberg Plaza SW, formerly 15th St) to WWII Holocaust victims portrays in grim detail the events of Nazi Germany. The museum recommends that only those over 11 years of age view the main exhibit, and provides a separate children's exhibit (no ticket required) for over-eight-year-olds; parental caution is advised.

Admission is free, but crowds necessitate tickets (limit of four per person), distributed from 10am for admission at a specific time that day. Call ☎ 800-400-9373 for advance passes.

Bureau of Engraving & Printing

The **bureau** (☎ 202-874-2330; cnr 14th & C Sts SW) designs and prints US paper currency. The lines are long for what is, essentially, just a print-shop tour. In peak tourist season you'll need tickets (free) from the kiosk on Raoul Wallenberg Plaza.

Washington Monument

A 555ft-tall white obelisk, **Washington Monument** (☎ 202-426-6841; 🕑 9am-4:45pm) rises above the Mall, offering wonderful views, especially at night. Construction began in 1848 but was not completed until 37 years later; the two phases are evident in the slightly different colors of the stone. There's free admission but **tickets** (kiosk, cnr 15th St & Madison Dr; 🕑 8am-4:30pm) are required; advance tickets from **Ticketmaster** (☎ 800-505-5040; $2 service charge).

Lincoln Memorial

This imposing monument to the 16th US president resembles a Greek temple. **Lincoln Memorial** (☎ 202-426-6895) has 36 columns representing the 36 states in Lincoln's Union. The Lincoln statue's hands read 'A' and 'L' in American Sign Language. Open 24 hours, the monument provides stunning nighttime views.

War Memorials

The **Vietnam Veterans Memorial** (☎ 202-462-6842; 🕑 24hr) features two black marble walls meeting in a V shape, on which are the names of more than 58,000 Americans who were killed or disappeared during the Vietnam War. Designed by Maya Lin, a 21-year-old student, in a national competition, it's now DC's most-visited memorial. Names are inscribed chronologically from date of death; registers and volunteers aid name searches.

Across the Mall, the **Korean War Memorial** consists of an eerie troop of 19 stone soldiers. The **National World War II Memorial** is under construction between the two, scheduled to open in late 2004.

TIDAL BASIN

The scenic Tidal Basin, southwest of the Mall, is lined with cherry trees, a gift from Japan; their spring blossoming marks the beginning of DC's peak tourism season. **Paddleboat rentals** ($7 per hr for two) are available at the boathouse.

Designed to mimic the Monticello home of the third president, the domed **Jefferson Memorial** (☎ 202-426-6822) was derided as the 'Jefferson muffin' when it was built next to the basin. Inside, the walls are etched with Jefferson's writings.

Although Franklin Delano Roosevelt entreated that no memorial 'larger than his desk' be built in his honor, the 1997 **FDR Memorial** covers a 7.5-acre plaza and includes a water sculpture with stone-etched quotes and a seated statue of the 32nd president (the only president elected for four terms).

DOWNTOWN

Downtown Washington began in what is now called Federal Triangle, but it has since spread north and east. It now encompasses the area east of the White House to Judiciary Sq at 4th St, and from the Mall north to K or M St. Avoid the rough borderlands between Judiciary Sq and Capitol Hill, including 2nd, 3rd and 4th Sts NW. All the following sites are in the Federal Triangle.

On April 14, 1865, John Wilkes Booth assassinated Abraham Lincoln in his box seat at **Ford's Theatre** (☎ 202-638-2941). It still operates today, with a basement **Lincoln Museum** (🕑 9am-5pm) devoted to the assassination. Across the street, **Peterson House** (🕑 9am-5pm) is where Lincoln died – another poignant memorial.

Within **National Archives** (☎ 202-501-5000; www.nara.gov; 🕑 8:45am-5pm Mon & Wed, until 9pm Tue, Thu & Fri, until 4:45pm Sat), a grand neoclassical building, are gallery displays of blockbuster originals: the Declaration of Independence, the Constitution and the Bill of Rights. Also here is one of four remaining versions of the 1297 Magna Carta.

THE AUTHOR'S CHOICE

International Spy Museum (☎ 202-393-7798; 800 F St NW; adult $11, child over 4 $8; 10am-8pm, until 6pm Nov-Mar) Ever wanted to step into James Bond's or Ms Emma Peel's shoes, and live a glamorous spy life? Here's your chance to learn their secrets in DC's hottest attraction, plus learn all about the high-tech gadgetry, notorious spy cases, secret methods and not-so-pleasant consequences of being an international person of mystery. Get there early, as long, theme-park lines are standard, and allow at least three hours to get through this highly detailed and entertaining museum; kids (and many adults) especially love crawling through the duct-work exhibit and spying on fellow visitors.

Old Post Office Pavilion (☎ 202-298-4224; admission free) is an 1899 Romanesque revival landmark that's now the convenient Pavilion food and shopping complex; the 400ft observation tower affords great downtown panoramas.

Also recommended are the **National Museum of Women in the Arts** (☎ 202-783-5000; donations suggested), and **National Building Museum** (☎ 202-272-2448; free), the latter of which occupies an entire city block.

The **FBI headquarters** in the J Edgar Hoover building is also in this area, but the popular tours have been indefinitely closed to the public for renovations.

WHITE HOUSE AREA

An expansive park called the **Ellipse** borders the Mall. Look for the well-stocked **NPS Ellipse Visitor Pavilion** (☎ 202-485-9880) in the northeast corner – it offers the free *Welcome to Washington* map. On the Ellipse's east side is a power-broker block of Pennsylvania Ave, and Pershing Park, with an outdoor café in summer and fast-food vendors. Around Lafayette Sq, modern offices loom behind Victorian row houses and the presidential St John's Church. Federal Triangle Metro station is nearest the visitors center.

White House

Since 1800 every US president has lived at 1600 Pennsylvania Ave. Torched by the British in 1814, the White House reopened in 1818. Jacqueline Kennedy redecorated extensively in the 1960s. Additions to the White House include Franklin Roosevelt's pool, Truman's 2nd-story porch, George Bush Sr's horseshoe-throwing lane, Clinton's jogging track and George W Bush's T-ball field.

Tours are only available to school, military and veterans groups.

Executive Buildings

The 1883 Greek Revival **Treasury Building** (☎ 202-622-0896), next to the White House, is decorated with golden eagles, ornate balustrades and a two-story marble Cash Room. On the White House's other side is the **Old Executive Office Building** (☎ 202-395-5895). Designed by Alfred Mullet, this elaborate French Second Empire building contains the offices of White House staff.

FOGGY BOTTOM

DC's west end district falls roughly betwee[n] 17th St NW and Rock Creek Park, the Mall and K or M St. Foggy Bottom got its nam[e] from a smelly gasworks once sited here George Washington University was buil[t] here in 1912. The neighborhood is now [a] mix of workers, professionals and students

Tours of the diplomatic reception room of the **State Department** (☎ 202-647-3241; 220[1] C St NW) are by appointment only, and mus[t] be made at least four weeks in advance The **National Academy of Sciences** (☎ 202-334-2000; 2100 C St NW; 9am-5pm), facing the Mall features interior exhibits and a climbabl[e] statue of Albert Einstein outside to th[e] west of the building; see p295.

The **John F Kennedy Center for the Performing Arts** (☎ 202-467-4600; www.kennedy-center.or[g]; 2700 F St NW; daily) is a 'living memorial, with three theaters, a concert hall, oper[a] house and movie theater. It was long con[-]sidered an oasis in DC's cultural desert The waterfront center offers frequent fre[e] performances, festivals and other event[s] (see p300 for details).

The posh riverfront **Watergate comple[x]** (2650 Virginia Ave NW) encompasses apartments boutiques, the deluxe Swissôtel Watergate and the office towers that made 'Watergate a byword for political scandal after Presiden[t] Nixon's plumbers broke into Democrati[c] National Committee headquarters in 1972.

DUPONT CIRCLE

Once a marshland, the Dupont Circle are[a] north of the White House, became a fashion[-]able residential district at the end of the 19t[h] century and remains so today. Many man[-]sions were later converted to elegant embas[-]sies along a stretch of Massachusetts Av[e] known as Embassy Row and nearby Sheri[-]dan Circle – now the center of Washington diplomatic community. Scenic Dupont Ci[r]cle itself is at Connecticut and Massachuset[ts] Aves, though the term generally refers to th[e] entire neighborhood, which offers restau[r]ants, cafés, clubs and boutiques.

The first modern-art museum in the USA the **Phillips Collection** (☎ 202-387-2151; 1600 21st NW; admission free Tue-Fri for permanent collection, Sat Sun adult $8, child 18 and under free; 10am-5pm Tu[e]-Sat, until 8:30pm Thu summer, noon-5pm Sun) has lim[-]ited exhibits due to its extensive renovation through 2005 – call ahead. Rotating exhibi[ts]

WASHINGTON DC & THE CAPITAL REGION

n worldwide expeditions are found at the Jational Geographic Society's **Explorers Hall** (☎ 202-857-7588; 1145 17 St NW; admission free; ⌚ Mon-t 9am-5pm, from 10am Sun). The artist-run **Fondo el Sol Visual Arts Center** (☎ 202-483-2777; 2112 St NW; ⌚ Tue-Sat 12:30-5:30pm) promotes the ultural heritage of the Americas, including xhibits of pre-Columbian artifacts and folk rt exhibits. Patterned after the Mausoleum f Halicarnassus, the elaborate **Scottish Rite asonic Temple** (☎ 202-232-3579; 1733 16th St NW; lmission free; ⌚ 8am-2pm) offers weekday tours f its J Edgar Hoover Room downstairs.

DAMS-MORGAN, SHAW & U STREET

he heart of ethnic, bohemian Adams-Iorgan is 18th St between Florida Ave ıd Columbia Rd, and along Columbia Rd self. Restaurants, cafés, bookstores, bars, ubs and boutiques abound. Parking is ifficult, and it's not convenient by Metro; ıbs are best at night. To the east, Shaw is largely African-American neighborhood ıat stretches from around Thomas Circle Meridian Hill Park and from N Capitol to 15th St NW, and is best known for its emendous African-American history and thiopian restaurants.

Back in the 1930s, **Lincoln Theater** (1215 U St V) was a high point on the 'chitlin' circuit' African-American entertainment, hosting ıch celebrities as DC native Duke Elling-n. Riots following the 1968 assassination of artin Luther King Jr devastated the com-ercial district. Shaw's recent renaissance ıs followed the reopening of the historic eater, and new cafés, shops and clubs ıve popped up along U St around 14th St ongside neighborhood institutions.

Among the nation's most distinguished ıiversities, **Howard University** (☎ 202-860-2900 campus tours; 2400 6th St NW) was founded in '67 to educate African-Americans.

ORGETOWN

edating the capital, Georgetown was the ative American settlement of Tohoga ıen British fur trader Henry Fleet arrived 1632. In 1789 Georgetown University was unded, and it continues to dominate the strict today. Many 18th-century buildings ıve been converted to fashionable restaur-ts, clubs and boutiques, surrounded lovely historic residential districts (the ennedys did live here in the 1950s). The nearest Metro station, Foggy Bottom, is almost a mile away – a pleasant walk in decent weather and preferable to George-town's parking congestion.

Get a quick, historical overview from the **visitors center** (☎ 202-653-5190; 1057 Thomas Jefferson St NW; ⌚ Apr-Oct) or costumed guides, who relive history by running mule-driven barges along the towpath ($7.50).

The USA's oldest Roman Catholic college, **Georgetown University** (☎ 202-687-5055; 37th & O Sts) sits atop a hill overlooking the Potomac and retains many stately historic buildings. The inaugural director of the university was the country's first black Jesuit, and Bill Clinton is among the university's most distinguished alumnae.

Dumbarton Oaks (☎ 202-339-6401; R & 31st Sts NW) is an intimate modern gallery of Byzantine tapestries and pre-Columbian gold alongside an historic mansion with 10 acres of outstanding formal gardens ($5 afternoons from April to October, free admission other times).

The **Potomac Heritage National Scenic Trail** connects the Chesapeake Bay to the Al-legheny Highlands in a 700-mile corridor. It includes the Chesapeake & Ohio (C&O) Canal towpath, the 17-mile Mt Vernon Trail (Virginia), and the 75-mile Laurel Highlands Trail (Pennsylvania). **Big Wheel Bikes** (☎ 202-337-0254; 1034 33rd St; from $5 per hr & $25 per day), between M St and the C&O Canal towpath, is a good bike rental and outfitter.

UPPER NORTHWEST

The massive high-Gothic **Washington National Cathedral** (☎ 202-537-6200; tours daily) is an Epis-copal venue for state funerals and other high-profile events, including weekly prayers devoted to different state and religious tradi-tions. Check out the *Apollo 11* stained-glass window and tower views.

Rock Creek Park starts at the Potomac River, extends north through DC along the nar-row corridor of Rock Creek, then expands to wide parkland in the Upper Northwest district. It boasts terrific biking and hik-ing. Historic sights include the remains of two Civil War forts and the 1820 **Peirce Mill** (☎ 202-426-6908; admission free; ⌚ Wed-Sun).

WATERFRONT & ANACOSTIA

At the southwestern waterfront, a really nice promenade along the Washington

Channel has great sunsets and overrated seafood restaurants.

Stretching along the Anacostia River, the Washington Navy Yard features the **Marine Corps Museum** (☎ 202-433-3534; admission free; ⌚ 10am-4pm Mon-Fri) and **Navy Museum** (☎ 202-433-4882; admission free; ⌚ 9am-5pm Mon-Fri).

Across the river in hard-luck Anacostia, the **Frederick Douglass National Historic Site** (☎ 202-426-5960; 1411 West St SE; ⌚ 9am-4pm) opens the hilltop home of the abolitionist and former slave; the visitors center screens a biographical film. The Smithsonian's **Anacostia Museum** (☎ 202-287-3307; 1901 Fort Pl SE; ⌚ 10am-5pm) is a national resource for African-American culture and operates rotating exhibits.

Anacostia has a well-earned reputation for violent crime; take a cab from Anacostia Metro.

Activities

Outdoor enthusiasts head northwest to Rock Creek Park, with miles of trails for biking, hiking and horseback riding, and to the C&O Canal for biking along the towpath and many hiking trails in canal-side parks (see p293). **Thompson Boat Center** (☎ 202-333-9543), at the Potomac River end of Rock Creek Park, down from the Kennedy Center, rents tandem kayaks ($10 per hour) and bikes ($8 per hour).

DC for Children

The nation's capital is a virtual playground for families. Outdoor parks and gardens, and fascinating, hands-on museums around the city, will really entertain and educate children of all ages. If you do get tired of indoor attractions, however, there are quite a few **public pools** (http://dpr.dc.gov/informationswimming_pools/swimming_pools.asp?type=3) as well as playgrounds (see opposite for the Awakening, which is also a popular child magnet, and try Guy Mason Playground, at 3600 Calvert St NW just off Wisconsin Ave) open to travelers as well.

Many major hotels offer babysitting services, but here are a few independent agencies:

Bring Along the Children (☎ 202-484-0889) Offers day and evening babysitting services and kid-oriented tours.

Family & Childcare Inc (☎ 202-723-2051)

We Sit (☎ 703-764-1542)

THE MALL & SMITHSONIAN MUSEUMS

The wide-open squares of grass that make up the Mall are perfect places for outdoor family fun, whether you want to throw a Frisbee, have a picnic, ride the world's oldest **carousel** or stroll into the entertaining museums that line its borders.

At the **National Air & Space Museum** (see p290), kids can happily view moon rocks, taste freeze-dried ice cream that the astronauts eat, and learn about the solar system from a giant scale model outside. The **National Museum of Natural History** (see p290) is the most entertaining for children, where they come face-to-face with triceratops dinosaurs, and handle creepy-crawlies in the Insect Zoo. They can get their hands wet in hands-on science and history rooms at the **Museum of American History** (see p290) where they perform experiments in controlled lab settings and send messages via historic methods. If they're into art or acting, spend an afternoon at the **Hirshorn Museum** (see p290) putting on a play or creating sculptures from chocolate or putter around the eclectic sculpture garden out front. The **National Theatre** (☎ 202-783-3370; 1321 Pennsylvania Ave NW; performances 9:30am & 11:30am Sep-Apr; reservations required) offers free Saturday morning performances from puppet shows to tap dancers in the Helen Hayes Gallery.

OFF THE MALL

Capital Children's Museum (☎ 202-675-4120; 800 3rd St NE; adult $7, child under 3 free, half-price Sunday before noon; ⌚ Tue-Sun 10am-5pm, daily in summer) has three floors of inviting interactive exhibits including a TV studio, animation laboratory, Japanese schoolroom and a cityscape fire-pole slide.

A Smithsonian property, **National Zoological Park** (☎ 202-357-2700; 3000 Connecticut Ave NW; admission free; ⌚ Apr 6-Oct 25 6am-8pm, Oct 26-Apr 5 6am-6pm) was beautifully designed by Frederick Law Olmsted to follow the contour of its woodland canyon setting, with some 2000 species in natural habitats. Children especially love the famous pandas and daily monkey feedings. Parking is extremely limited.

Tucked inside the US Department of Commerce building, the **National Aquarium** (☎ 202-482-2826; cnr 14th St & Constitution Ave; adult $3.50, child 2-10 $1; ⌚ 9am-4:30pm), a small aquatic center, offers daily animal keeper talks and feedings at 2pm, and fascinating piranha shows.

Located 15 minutes from DC in Largo, MD, **Six Flags America** (☎ 301-249-1500; adult $36, child over 3 $25; ⏲ May-Oct) is Maryland's only theme park; the place for kids and adults to let loose on spiraling roller coasters and tamer kiddie rides. The most popular rides are the soaring Superman coaster, the lay-down Batwing coaster and the Penguin's Blizzard River where you'll absolutely get wet.

Quirky Washington DC

The **Albert Einstein statue**, across the street from the Vietnam and Lincoln memorials, is a little-known statue of a rather dumpy-looking Einstein, immortalized with his $E = mc^2$ equation and a generous lap where many children get their picture snapped.

Squished Penny Museum (☎ 202-986-5644; Northwest Washington; admission by appointment only) has an unusual collection of, you heard it, squished pennies, coins and other ephemera from around the world. Exhibited in the owners' living room, it gives new meaning to the term *common cents*.

The power of quirkiness compels you! See the famous exterior of the **Exorcist House** (3600 Prospect St NW, Georgetown) and its steep staircase from the *Exorcist*, which gave many people nightmares in the '70s.

The stuffed body of Owney, the unofficial postal mascot, rests behind glass at the **National Postal Museum** (cnr 1st & Massachusetts Ave NE). Adopted by the postal service in 1888, he 'worked' as a mail carrier until 1897 when he died from a mysterious gunshot wound.

Ever wonder what the world's largest hairball looks like? Wishes do come true at the **National Museum of Health and Medicine** (☎ 202-782-2200; cnr 6900 Georgia Ave & Elder St NW; admission free; ⏲ 10am-5:30pm), a fascinating display that shares the oddball category with pieces of Abraham Lincoln's skull and a touchable human stomach.

In Anacostia on V St the **world's largest chair** towers over Martin Luther King Dr; at 19ft of pure mahogany, no one is sure how it got there.

The **Awakening**, near the Jefferson Memorial in Haines Point, is a somewhat disturbing statue of a man climbing out of the ground. His jolly green giant-size hand and mouth has freaked visitors out for years; try explaining those photos to the folks back home.

Tours

Tourmobile Sightseeing (☎ 202-554-5100, 888-868-7707; www.tourmobile.com; adult/child $20/11) is an open-air trolley, which adapts to both cold and wet weather, and runs its convenient trams daily between all the major sights. Ticket booths are located at the Washington Monument and Union Station; the spectacular 'Washington by night' tour is a must for viewing the monuments by illumination and moonlight.

Gray Line (☎ 800-862-1400; Union Station, 1st parking level, 50 Massachusetts Ave NE; all-day hop on/off pass adult $28, child 3-11 $14) offers a variety of city excursions, including bilingual tours (adult/child $35/17).

Bike the Sites (☎ 202-966-8662; adult $40, child under 13 $30), the popular 'Capital sites' tour, is a favorite with families, and includes all gear and a snack on the three-hour excursion. Other tours include 'Sites at night' and 'Civil War statues.'

Scandal Tours (☎ 202-783-7212; Old Post Office Pavilion; $27; ⏲ Apr-Sep Sat at 1pm) gives you all the gossip about DC's infamous spots (expanding daily), covering George Washington to George W Bush.

Festivals & Events

National Cherry Blossom Festival (☎ 202-547-1500; www.nationalcherryblossomfestival.org) DC's chance to bloom, this internationally known event is held late March to early April when the trees blossom.

Smithsonian's Folklife Festival (☎ 202-357-2700; www.folklife.si.edu) This fun family event, held over two weekends in June and July, features distinctive regional folk art, crafts, food and music.

Independence Day Also big here, celebrated on July 4 with parades, concerts and fireworks.

Sleeping

DC is a business town, so hotel rates can drop as much as 50% on weekends and in summer; tourist season is April to September, with a heat-related August lull. Professional associations, veteran status, government or nongovernmental-organization (NGO) affiliation and even museum membership can also earn discounts. Accommodation tax is 13% plus $1.50 per night.

Washington DC Accommodations (☎ 800-554-2220) provides assistance with lodging. For B&Bs citywide, call **Bed & Breakfast Accommodations** (☎ 413-582-9888) or the **Bed & Breakfast League** (☎ 202-363-7767).

BUDGET

Kalorama Guest House (☎ 202-667-6369; fax 202-319-1262; 1854 Mintwood Pl NW; r from $60;) What a find! This charming place is an oasis in a sea of overpriced lodging. Extremely friendly innkeepers greet visitors with hot or cold beverages, depending on the season, and escort you to simple rooms with period furniture. Close to Adams-Morgan and many major sites, you'll also find a community fridge, sunroom and free local calls.

HI Washington, DC (☎ 202-737-2333; www.hiwashingtondc.org; 1009 11th St NW at K St; dm members/nonmembers $20/29; 24hr; reservations & photo ID re-quired) Newly remodeled in 2002, this 270-bed hostel is a hotspot for budget travelers, with good amenities such as a theater-style TV room and big-screen TV, Internet access, coin laundry and luggage storage.

Washington International Student Center (☎ 202-667-7681; dcstudentcentr@aol.com; 2451 18th St NW; dm $20; 24hr; P) Located in lively Adams-Morgan, this small hostel has a great, friendly atmosphere and major plusses: within walking distance of major sites, convenient to the bus and Metro, fre

GAY & LESBIAN DC

Home to more than 30 national gay and lesbian organizations and more than 300 social, athletic, religious and political support groups, DC is one of the most gay-friendly cities in the USA. The community is most visible in the Dupont Circle and Capitol Hill neighborhoods, where there are many gay-owned and gay-friendly businesses, including the Lambda Rising bookstore (see below). Washington is often the scene of huge gay-rights marches, and gay pride is an integral part of DC's character.

Dupont Circle is by far the city's most gay-friendly neighborhood, offering the bulk of the city's nightlife options, clustered on 17th NW between P and R Sts NW and along P St west of the circle. The club and bar scene on Pennsylvania Ave and around Capitol Hill is easily reached by the Eastern Market Metro station. You'll find popular male strip clubs – one of the few places in the US where full nudity is legal – in Southeast DC near the Navy Yard Metro station, but it's safer to take a cab here after dark.

Lambda Rising (1625 Connecticut Ave NW) is the landmark bi-gay bookstore in Dupont Circle, specializing in gay and lesbian titles, and free flyers on local entertainment; it's a popular community gathering place. **La Cage** (18 O St SE) is a male go-go dancing crowd; **DC Eagle** (639 New York Ave NW), near Vernon Sq, is 'leather and Levi's' with shirtless men the norm; **Apex** (1415 22nd St NW; admission $8), at P St, is a popular, steamy club; **Hung Jury** (1819 H St NW) is still the best-known lesbian bar in the city; **JR's** (1519 17th St NW) is a friendly Dupont Circle gay bar; **Bachelors Mill** 1106 Eighth St SE) is a dance club in Capitol Hill catering to gay and lesbian African-Americans; and there's also the casual, mixed crowd at Georgetown's **Mr Henry's** (4321 Wisconsin Ave NW).

Information

AIDS hotline (☎ 800-342-2437)

Gay and Lesbian Activists Alliance (GLAA; www.glaa.org)

Gay and Lesbian hotline (☎ 202-833-3234)

Gay Bazaar (www.gaybazaar.com) Online resource for gays and lesbians.

Metro Weekly (www.metroweekly.com) Free weekly gay and lesbian magazine that's available in print and online.

Washington Blade (www.washblade.com) Hometown gay and lesbian weekly paper covering local politics, information about community resources, and a slew of nightlife and meeting-place listings.

Whitman-Walker Clinic (☎ 202-797-3500; www.wwc.org; 1407 S St NW) Serves gay and lesbian DC with general health care, and HIV and AIDS care.

Women in the Life (www.womeninthelife.com) Organization for lesbians of color, sponsoring events and parties throughout DC.

Women's Monthly (WOMO; www.womo.com) Monthly lesbian magazine in print and online with a great calendar section.

WASHINGTON DC & THE CAPITAL REGION

breakfast, and free pickup from the train or bus station. You'll also find cable TV and Internet access.

MID-RANGE

Hotel Harrington (☎ 202-628-8140; www.hotel-harrington.com; 436 11th St NW at E St; r from $89;) Smack in the city center, this modest hotel boasts neighbors like the Smithsonian museums and the White House, and is a great base for exploring.

Morrison-Clark Inn (☎ 202-898-1200; www.morrisonclark.com; 1015 L St NW; s/d from $155/175;) Elegant rooms ranging from Victorian to neoclassical make for a luxurious experience at a great price. Conveniently located just steps from Mt Vernon Sq, there's also an elegant Southern dining room on-site.

George Washington University Inn (☎ 202-337-6620; www.gwuinn.com; 824 New Hampshire Ave NW; r from $120;) Located in Foggy Bottom, this all-suite boutique hotel stands out for its tasteful designs and proximity to the cultural district; families can ask for the fully equipped kitchen suites.

Channel Inn (☎ 202-554-2400; 650 Water St SW; r from $125;) An intriguing and quiet waterfront hotel away from the city hubbub, it's also convenient for drivers.

TOP END

Jefferson (☎ 202-347-2200, 800-235-6397; www.thejeffersondc.com; 1200 16th St NW; from $169; P) Unless your last name is Bush, you really can't get much closer to the White House than here. With indulgences such as putting greens set up in their rooms, this indulgent hotel dotes on a traveler's every whim, and has great family and kids programs to keep the little ones busy.

Swissôtel Watergate (☎ 202-965-2300; 2650 Virginia Ave NW; r from $175; P) One of the world's most infamous hotels because of its famous 'plumbing' convention (it was here that Nixon aides broke in to spy on the Democrats). It's nonetheless a luxurious, full-service hotel with elegant marble bathrooms, an onsite fitness center with spa, sauna and panoramic balconies on which you can plot your own scheme to uncover DC's secrets.

Eating

Dining is an adventure in DC where around every corner a different slice of the world is waiting to be discovered. Among DC's numerous ethnic enclaves, **Adams-Morgan** is known for its amazing Ethiopian restaurants and vibrant **Chinatown** for authentic homeland dishes.

BOUTIQUE HOTELS

A new wave of boutique hotels are sweeping the city, but there's a catch – they're actually affordable. Here are some of the best.

Hotel Rouge (☎ 202-667-9827; www.rougehotel.com; 1315 16th St NW; r from $129; P) Pure fun. Stylish and luxurious with a wild red decor, the rooms offer flat-screen TVs, in-room computers with high-speed Internet access and stainless steel kitchenettes. While a Bloody Mary bar and cold pizza are complimentary, ask for their special packages for more indulgent amenities.

Also recommended are **Hotel Helix** (☎ 800-706-1202; www.hotelhelix.com; 1430 Rhode Island Ave NW; r from $149; P), which has hip family suites, bunk beds and a lounge with a color scheme that morphs every few minutes; and **Hotel Monaco** (☎ 202-628-7177; www.monaco-dc.com; 700 F St NW; r from $169 in summer; P) where a complimentary goldfish is delivered to your room for the duration of your stay.

CAPITOL HILL

Eastern Market (225 7th St SE) This is a must for market eats, with an international smorgasbord of food stalls.

Bullfeathers (☎ 202-543-5005; 410 1st St SE; dishes $5) Feel like an extra from the *West Wing* TV show at this popular Capitol Hill hangout, named after Teddy Roosevelt's favorite expression, and decorated much like the time he was president.

Red River Grill (☎ 202-546-7200; 201 Massachusetts Ave NE; mains $10) A casual Tex-Mex joint that entertains sports fans with 10 TVs lining the walls and a great children's menu for family dining.

B Smith's (☎ 202-289-6188; 50 Massachusetts Ave NE; mains $10) A taste of New Orleans with hot Cajun food and soulful southern soups and desserts, in a wild, spacious room adjacent to Union Station.

Anatolia (☎ 202-544-4753; 633 Pennsylvania Ave SE; mains $5) Duck into this mysteriously lit restaurant for authentic and inexpensive

Turkish dishes, and don't forget to finish with a hit of strong, sublime coffee.

Bread & Chocolate (☎ 202-547-2875; 666 Pennsylvania Ave SE; mains $5) Primarily a pretty sinful bakery with creative chocolate concoctions, it serves equally inventive salads and sandwiches, even Hungarian goulash.

Las Placitas (☎ 202-543-3700; 517 8th St SE; dishes $5) With bright, screaming decor resembling the aftermath of a piñata explosion, you know this place is fun, and the food isn't so bad either. Great Mexican and Salvadorean dishes make for a unique and crowd-pleasing menu.

WHITE HOUSE AREA & DOWNTOWN

Zola (☎ 202-654-0999; 800 F St NW; mains $15) A classic film noir theme is carried through into the International Spy Museum's restaurant with dark corner tables, kitchen peepholes for glimpses of what really goes into your food, and declassified documents lining the glass floors and walls. There's no need to 'cover up' anything in this restaurant where the American-style food is excellent.

Capital Q BBQ (☎ 202-347-8396; 707 H St NW; dishes $4.50) A must for Texas-style BBQ lovers, with piled-high portions of smoked meat and plenty o' slaw on the side; try the brisket sandwich.

Full Kee (☎ 202-371-2233; 509 H St NW; dishes $5) Despite the dingy exterior you'd be crazy to pass up this excellent Chinese restaurant, a well-guarded secret by in-the-know locals. Expect a lengthy, cheap menu that includes savory roast pork, inventive soups and delectable dumplings – but this is definitely not service with a smile.

Zaytinya (☎ 202-638-0800; 701 9th St NW; mains $20) An expensive, exotic newcomer that mixes Greek, Lebanese and Turkish dishes against a designer all-white backdrop. Its spicy and exotic 'mezzas' (similar to tapas and dim sum) are as intriguing as the decor (check out the bathrooms!).

Sholl's Colonial Cafeteria (☎ 202-296-3065; 1990 K St NW; dishes $5) This cultural icon sells regional rock-bottom cafeteria fare such as baked chicken and mashed potatoes.

Stoney's Bar & Grill (☎ 202-347-9163; 1307 L St NW; dishes $5) Near the youth hostel, this homey dive is a dirt-cheap choice for American fare, burger-and-beer deals and half-price specials.

DUPONT CIRCLE

Connecticut Ave NW on either side of Du pont Circle is the city's upscale restauran district, with many cafés.

Mimi's American Bistro (☎ 202-464-6464; 2120 St NW; mains $7-12) From duck to roasted po lenta, this quirky eatery boasts outstandin food, but the singing waitstaff who perforn cabaret-style are the true draw.

Pesce's (☎ 202-466-3474; 2016 P St NW; mains $12 Rave reviews for this whimsical seafood bis tro, combining simple and complex dishe with flair and freshness.

Johnny's Half Shell (☎ 202-296-2021; 2002 P S NW; mains $7) A popular, casual oyster bar an café with possibly the best hot dogs arounc Grab a seat, get your bivalves raw or in be tween fresh-baked bread, and go crazy.

Sushi Taro (☎ 202-462-8999; 1503 17th St NW; mair $13) The drab exterior is an unfortunate en trance to a superb sushi bar with traditiona rolls, steaming soups and more authenti cuisine as evidenced by its dedicate Japanese clientele; beware the per-perso dining minimum.

Restaurant Nora (☎ 202-462-5143; 2132 Florida Av NW; mains $26) America's first certified organi restaurant specializes in New America cuisine, but you'll pay for it; try the fixe tasting menu for a delicious sampling.

ADAMS-MORGAN

Choose from an international smorgasbor in DC's ethnic and bohemian restaurar district along 18th St NW.

Mixtec (☎ 202-332-1011; 1792 Columbia Rd NV mains $5-10) No gimmicky taco imitatior here; this is the real deal for authenti Mexican cuisine. The grilled steak tacc and pork-stuffed tamales are big sellers.

Cities (☎ 202-328-2100; 2424 18th St NW; mains $2 This former firehouse heats up the Soh esque crowd with an innovative rotatin menu based on international cities. Dre to thrill, and be prepared for the Cinderell style transformation into a thumping clu at midnight.

Meskerem (☎ 202-462-4100; 2434 18th St N mains $10) A favorite for Ethiopian fare (which there are many) with three floo of African-themed rooms and great ope spaces to bring a group of friends.

Perry's (☎ 202-234-6218; 1811 Columbia Rd N mains $10) The sprawling rooftop deck sublime for al fresco summer dining wi teaks, seafood and even a sushi bar. The ·iews of the city are quite incredible, and ›utrageous Sunday brunches accompanied ›y singing drag queens are really a sight to ›ehold.

Meze (☎ 202-797-0017; 2437 18th St NW; mains $10) \ narrow Turkish restaurant with fabulous apas-style dishes of lamb and beef kabob ınd potato balls; an intimate upstairs lounge s great to chill after a luscious Turkish ›aklava.

HAW & U STREET

ioul-food landmarks next to avant-garde afés can be found in the energetic U dis- rict in Shaw.

U-topia Art & Eat (☎ 202-483-7669; 1418 U St W; mains $10) An artistic feast for the senses, vith creative North African–Cajun fusion uisine set among local artwork and live laily jazz; don't miss the funky bar.

One cultural institution is **Ben's Chili Bowl** ☎ 202-667-0909; 1213 U St NW; mains $7), a famous live, more so for the 'greasy diner' atmos- here than quality of food. That said, the alf-smokes and chili bowls are some of the est around – not too spicy, not too pricey. 'he nearby **Florida Avenue Grill** (☎ 202-265- 586; 1100 Florida Ave NW; dishes $5), another cul- ıral institution, serves up fried catfish and ollard greens along a well-worn counter; heck out the celebrity wall behind it.

EORGETOWN

)espite some wonderful choices lining this rea's clogged arteries, M St and Wiscon- n Ave NW, crowds and traffic make it an verrated restaurant district.

Basil Thai (☎ 202-944-8660; 1608 Wisconsin Ave; ains $10) This is a trendy Thai place for the ounger crowd, with excellent pad thai and ınky artwork on the walls for sale.

Booeymongers (☎ 202-333-4810; 3265 Prospect St V; from $5) The place with the funny name ffers crazy, stuffed deli sandwiches like the cheherazade' and the 'Great Gatsby.'

Cafe Milano (☎ 202-333-6183; 3251 Prospect St NW; ıins $25) A sleek Italian bistro, well worth ›lashing out the cash for homemade ra- oli that melts on the tongue and more elicious ways to prepare mushrooms than ›u can imagine.

Filomena (☎ 202-338-8800; 1063 Wisconsin Ave V; mains $13) Like walking into an Italian andmother's kitchen. Watch the women pull the pasta through the storefront window, then go in and *mangiare*.

DC Coast (☎ 202-216-5988; 1401 K St NW; mains $20) A little pricey but simply worth it for its innovative fusion menu with Thai calamari and Peking-style chicken with noodles.

OTHER AREAS

Open-air seafood market (Maine Ave SW) This market sells fresh seafood (crab cakes $5, seafood sandwiches from $3, fish platters $6).

Drinking

There's no shortage of great watering holes in the nation's capital. The greatest concentration is in **Adams-Morgan**; walk down 18th St NW between Florida Ave and Columbia Rd. Another good area is along M St in **Georgetown** between 29th and 33rd Sts NW.

CAPITOL HILL

Politiki (319 Pennsylvania Ave SE) A fun, three-story bar with three very different themes offering concoctions ranging from coconut rumrunners to long-neck bottles to dirty martinis. Hint: the higher you go, the more 'refined' the crowd.

Hawk and Dove (329 Pennsylvania Ave SE) A hotspot for political junkies to House pages, with free-food happy hours and intimate corner booths perfect for chilling over boutique martinis and creating the next District scandal.

Lounge 201 (201 Massachusetts Ave NE) Lounge lizards lurk at this upscale retro martini bar modeled after the 1950s. Red pool tables, plush leather chairs and a smooth jazz soundtrack transport sleek-dressed sippers away from the political scene for just a little while.

Tavern on the Hill (233 2nd St NW) It's actually at the foot of the Capitol, but don't blink or you'll miss this cozy Irish pub offering up to eight taps of microbrews and Guinness, of course; it tends to fill up fast so get there early.

WHITE HOUSE AREA & DOWNTOWN

Exchange (1719 G St NW) DC's oldest saloon and biggest sports bar, the Exchange is where it's not unusual to see the local adult kickball team and other organized sports teams throw back a few on the patio.

Fadó (808 7th St NW) In a sea of imitators, this fantastic Irish pub in Chinatown caters for sports fans and preperformance drinkers visiting the MCI Center.

DUPONT CIRCLE

Brickskeller (1523 22nd St NW) With a drink menu as thick as a bible, this is heaven for beer worshippers, and probably the best place to grab a brew in DC if you can choose from the 1100 around-the-world varieties.

ADAMS-MORGAN, SHAW & U STREET

Madam's Organ (2461 18th St NW) This is a staple in this area with nightly blues, bluegrass or jazz sessions. Red-headed women – natural or dyed – get half-price rolling rocks.

Cafe Toulouse (2431 18th St NW) An authentic French atmosphere without the attitude, this is a great place to actually hear conversations and listen to cool jazz; watch out for the tap-dancing bartender (on the bar).

Blue Room (2321 18th St NW) Blue is the word at this two-level bar and nightclub (blue velvet curtains in the bathrooms?), with the second floor mixing trippy candles and chill attitude. This place is one of the hottest venues on this crowded street.

Cada Vez (1438 U St NW) This totally wired venue is where the Beat Generation would meet up today; you can sip martinis while surfing the net.

Common Share (2003 18th St NW) Think you can't drink in DC on a budget? You've hit the mother lode here, where all drinks are $2, that's right, only $2. The only drawbacks are large and loud crowds, and standing room only.

Polly's Cafe (1342 U St NW) A similar feel to Soho watering holes, this bohemian bar lets everything hang out, and has an eclectic set of tunes on the jukebox.

GEORGETOWN

Tombs (cnr 36th & P Sts) If it looks familiar, think back to the '80s; this was the setting for *St. Elmo's Fire*. Today it's a local feel-good fave with university students and those looking to escape the yuppie-filled urban bars.

Georgetown Bar & Billiards (3251 Prospect St NW) With well-worn couches and overstuffed armchairs backing up to the dimly lit billiards tables, this is like stepping into your best friend's finished basement – with a long, wooden bar taking center stage, of course.

Mr Smith's (1218 Wisconsin Ave NW) This is a casual hangout with some great happy-hour specials and a lush back patio that hops all year long.

Georgetown Station (3125 M St NW) Restaurant by day, South Beach–style nightclub at night, this place has affordable happy hours and a VIP lounge upstairs.

Entertainment

The *Washington Post*'s 'Weekend' section and the free weekly *Washington City Paper* are useful for planning your time out. The Convention and Visitors Association issues a quarterly events calendar. Conveniently located at the Old Post Office Pavilion, **Ticketplace** (☎ 202-842-5387; 1100 Pennsylvania Ave NW; ⌚ Tue-Sat) sells same-day concert and show tickets at half price.

PERFORMING ARTS

DC's theater district (such as it is) is east of Dupont Circle around 14th St, P and Q Sts NW.

Kennedy Center (☎ 202-467-4600; www.kennedy-center.org; 2700 F St NW; ⌚ daily) The National Symphony and Washington Chamber Symphony perform here; this is also home to the **Washington Opera** (www.dc-opera.org), of which Placido Domingo is artistic director.

Wolf Trap Farm Park for the Performing Arts (☎ 703-255-1900; www.wolftrap.org; 1645 Trap Rd, Vienna, Virginia) This symphony also performs summer concerts a 40-minute drive away in Vienna, Virginia.

National Theater (☎ 202-628-6161; 1321 Pennsylvania Ave NW), which opened in 1835, is Washington's oldest continuously operating theater, though the **Shakespeare Theater** (☎ 202-547-1122; 450 7th St NW) is a more evocative venue.

LIVE MUSIC

DC, birthplace of Duke Ellington (he was born in Shaw), really excels in jazz and blues, and most bars in DC will rock out with live music on weekends. The capital boasts many music venues, ranging from intimate stages to 30,000-seat arenas where rock headliners such as U2, up-and-coming alternative acts like OKGo and even country bands satisfy various musical tastes.

9:30 Club (☎ 202-393-0930; 815 V St NW) This spacious dive, featuring two floors and a mid-size stage, is the best place to see well-known rock acts.

Black Cat (☎ 202-667-7960; 1811 14th St) Dave Grohl is part owner of this amazing club – and if you don't know who he is, you probably won't like the bands who have gigs here. More intimate than the 9:30, it boasts an equally impressive roster of bands and tends to be more adventurous in its bookings.

Blues Alley (☎ 202-337-4141; 1073 Rear Wisconsin Ave) This smoky Georgetown venue attracts well-known artists, but tickets are steep ($14 to $40).

Chi-Cha Lounge (☎ 202-234-8400; 1624 U St NW) Located in Shaw, Chi-Cha Lounge is where the Middle East comes to DC with Latin American fare and flair; enjoy jazz along with the low-cushioned seats and hookahs.

Chief Ike's Mambo Room (1725 Columbia Rd NW) This venue, in Adams-Morgan, has mambo Monday, blues Thursday, and disco and hip-hop on weekends.

MCI Center (☎ 202-628-3200; 601 F St NW) Primarily a sports arena, MCI Center hosts big-name bands. Previous concerts include the Dixie Chicks, U2, Christina Aguilera and the Eagles.

The best jazz venues in Washington DC are **Saloun** (3239 M St NW); **City Blues** (☎ 202-232-2300; 2651 Connecticut Ave NW), in Woodley Park; and the 170-plus seat **Metro Cafe** (☎ 202-518-7900; 1522 14th St NW), which is in the U St precinct.

SPECTATOR SPORTS

Washington Redskins (☎ 301-276-6060) Three-time NFL champions, the Washington Redskins, play at FedEx Field, east of DC in Maryland. Without a professional baseball team, locals tend to follow the Baltimore Orioles.

Robert F Kennedy Memorial Stadium (RFK; ☎ 202-547-9077; 2400 E Capitol St SE btwn 7th & 8th Sts) This stadium is home to DC United, winners of the inaugural US soccer championship (1996), and the women's soccer team **Washington Freedom** (☎ 202-547-3137), featuring Mia Hamm.

MCI Center mega-stadium (tickets and information ☎ 202-628-3200, 202-432-7328) The NBA Washington Wizards, the WNBA Washington Mystics, the NHL Washington Capitals ice hockey team and the Washington Power lacrosse team all play at this downtown stadium.

Getting There & Away

For air connections, see p281.

BUS

Greyhound (☎ 800-231-2222l; 1005 1st St NE)

Peter Pan Trailways (☎ 800-343-9999; 1005 1st St NE) Buses stop opposite.

Take a cab through this rough neighborhood to the nearest Metro station, Union Station, eight blocks away.

One-way coach fares and travel times from Washington DC include the following:

Baltimore, Maryland $11, one hour.
Charleston, West Virginia $60, 10 hours.
New York City $42, 4½ hours.
Philadelphia, Pennsylvania $22, four hours.
Richmond, Virginia $18, 2¼ hours.
Wilmington, Delaware $20, three hours.

TRAIN

Union Station (☎ 202-371-9441; 50 Massachusetts Ave NE), DC's major transport hub, connects directly to the Metro and Amtrak.

MARC (☎ 800-325-7245) commuter trains run weekdays to many regional cities, including Baltimore and Harpers Ferry, West Virginia. **Amtrak** (☎ 800-872-7245) services to and around the region include the Metroliner express service between DC and New York City; the Cardinal and Capitol Limited between DC and Chicago; the Carolinian, which stops in Baltimore, DC and Richmond; and Crescent, from New York City to New Orleans with stops in DC and Charlottesville, Virginia. Sample one-way fares (which vary widely) and times from DC are as follows:

Baltimore $22, 40 minutes.
Charlottesville, Virginia $44, 2½ hours.
Harpers Ferry, West Virginia $12, 1¼ hours.
New York City $68, 3½ hours.
Philadelphia $63, three hours.
Richmond $32, two hours.

Getting Around

TO/FROM THE AIRPORT

Number 5A **Metrobus** (☎ 202-962-1234; $2 express) leaves from the Dulles car hire area to central DC (L'Enfant Plaza) once an hour – a cheap transportation alternative, but not much room for baggage.

For door-to-door van service between all three airports and downtown DC, try

SuperShuttle (☎ 800-258-3826). Fares are $10 to Reagan National, $22 to Dulles and $28 to BWI (return fares do vary according to destination).

Washington Flyer (☎ 888-927-4359; $8) has a handy service from Dulles to West Falls Church, Virginia, connecting with the Metro. The bus service from Dulles to National Airport or downtown DC is $16/26 one way/round-trip.

Car rentals include the following:

Budget (Dulles ☎ 703-920-3360; Reagan ☎ 703-419-1021)
Dollar (Dulles ☎ 703-661-6888)
Thrifty (Dulles & Reagan ☎ 703-658-2200)

TRAIN

Amtrak and regional MARC commuter trains run between DC's Union Station and a rail terminal near BWI ($9 one way; a 10-minute free shuttle is provided to BWI proper).

METRO

Metrorail (☎ 202-637-7000) runs to most sights, hotel and business districts, and to the Maryland and Virginia suburbs. Trains operate 5:30pm to midnight weekdays, 8am to 1am weekends. Machines inside stations sell computerized fare cards; fares (from $1.20) depend on distance traveled and time of day. All-day excursion passes cost $5.

Metrobus (☎ 202-637-7000) operates buses throughout the city and suburbs (from $1.20). The L2, along 18th St through Adams-Morgan (connecting with Woodley Park and Foggy Bottom Metro stations) and the D5, from Union Station to Georgetown's central M St strip, are handy routes.

CAR & TAXI

Drivers beware: middle lanes of some streets change direction during rush hour. Street parking is often scarce, especially around Georgetown and the Mall. Most national car rental agencies in DC won't rent to those under 25. Taxis, which operate on a zone system, charge a base rate of $5 per zone and are plentiful in the central city. Try the following:

Capitol (☎ 202-546-2400)
Diamond (☎ 202-387-6200)
Yellow Cab (☎ 202-544-1212)

AROUND WASHINGTON DC

Arlington National Cemetery

Just across the Potomac in Virginia, the 612-acre national **cemetery** (☎ 703-692-0931; Apr 1-Sep 30 8am-7pm, until 5pm rest of year) is the burial ground for over 225,000 military personnel and their dependents, with veterans from every US war since the Revolution. **Tourmobiles** (☎ 202-554-5100, 888-868-7707) are a handy way to visit the cemetery's notable memorials; trams leave every 15 minutes from the visitors center.

Robert E Lee's 1100-acre property, and his home, **Arlington House**, were confiscated when Lee left to command northern Virginia's army. Union soldiers were buried around the house so he could never use it again. After the Civil War, the site became the national cemetery, and now the house is open to the public. The **Tomb of the Unknowns** represents unknown soldiers killed in action; military guards retain a round-the-clock vigil. One of Arlington's most impressive sights is the ritual changing of the guard (every hour or half hour). Arlington's newest sight at the main gate is a memorial to women in military service. Don't miss the famous Iwo Jima monument nearby, depicting marines raising the Stars and Stripes. An eternal flame marks the **grave of John F Kennedy**, next to those of Jacqueline Kennedy Onassis and two of her infant children. The grave of Robert Kennedy is marked with a cross nearby.

Alexandria

Along with Georgetown, Alexandria preceded the founding of the nation's capital. As in Georgetown, walkable blocks of attractive brick row houses in the historic district find modern uses as restaurants, taverns and shops. The **visitors center** (☎ 800-388-9119; www.funside.com; 221 King St; 9am-5pm) issues discount tickets to historic sights and free parking permits (know your license-plate number).

The **Torpedo Factory Art Center** (☎ 703-838-4565; 105 N Union St; 10am-5pm) heads up the waterfront and displays the work of local artists. At **Alexandria Archaeology** (☎ 703-838-4399; admission free; Mon-Sun 10am-5pm), also in the converted WWI torpedo plant, archaeologists clean and catalog artifacts from local urban digs.

Northwest of town, **Fort Ward Museum & Historic Site** (☎ 703-838-4848; 4301 W Braddock Rd; admission free; 🕑 9am-4pm Tue-Sat, noon-5pm Sun, park open 9am-dusk) preserves one of the largest of the 162 Civil War fortifications known as the Defenses of Washington.

Warehouse Bar & Grill (214 King St; mains $8-26), across from the visitors center, has simply superb seafood meals, featuring both Cajun and traditional cuisine.

DC's Metro and Amtrak service the King St station; local buses cover the mile to the visitors center.

Mt Vernon & Around

One of the most visited historic sites in the nation, George Washington's country estate of **Mt Vernon** (☎ 703-780-2000; www.mountvernon.org; admission $9; 🕑 9am-5pm) has been meticulously restored, and affords a glimpse of 18th-century farm life and the first president as a country squire. Beautifully situated on the banks of the Potomac in Virginia, the estate holds a 19-room country house, immaculate gardens, slaves' quarters, a working farm and Washington's tomb.

The Washingtons lived here from 1759 to 1775, when George assumed command of the Continental Army. After the Revolutionary War and eight years as president, he retired to Mt Vernon, living here from 1797 until his death two years later.

Mount Vernon Inn (☎ 703-780-0011; mains $10-20), at the main gate, is a casual place serving hearty colonial fare; there's an adjacent **snack bar**.

Mt Vernon is only 16 miles south of DC by road; you can take the Metro to Huntington, then bus No 11P to the estate.

VIRGINIA

Travelers to Virginia will be overwhelmed by the state's rich historic past. The Revolutionary period is nowhere better represented than in the historic triangle of Williamsburg, Jamestown and Yorktown, and the James River plantations. The bulk of the Civil War battles were fought on Virginian soil, and reminders of that cataclysm are everywhere. Jefferson, Washington and many other founders of the nation also had long associations with Virginia, the 'mother of presidents.'

Virginia is more than a vast museum, and there is much scope for outdoor activities, especially in the rugged Blue Ridge Mountains and Shenandoah National Park, and along the coastline of Chesapeake Bay and the Eastern Shore.

History

In 1607 Jamestown Island became the site of the first permanent English settlement in Virginia. The settlement was short-lived, however, as two-thirds perished in the first year alone; between 1607 and 1625, 8500 settlers arrived but only 1200 survived.

Virginia grew on the tobacco trade, and a slaveholding planter elite came to control most of the land and the colony's government. Expansionism led to conflict with the Native Americans, and Nathaniel Bacon's ragtag army took them on, then turned on the colonial elite in an abortive rebellion that destroyed much of Jamestown.

In 1699 the colony's capital moved to nearby Williamsburg, where stately public buildings echoed the English style (more than 300 years later, the restored town is a big tourist attraction). Nearby at Yorktown, George Washington's 1781 victory over the British effectively brought an end to the Revolutionary War.

In 1861 Virginia seceded from the Union, and though the brilliant general Robert E Lee of Arlington was offered command of the Northern armies, he elected to lead opposing Virginia's forces in the Civil War instead.

Virginia's colonial and plantation past is now a nostalgic memory, revived as the basis for a tourist industry that threatens to turn many parts of the state into a theme park of US history. Its major industries continue to revolve around historic themes. The state's eastern ports and naval bases were quite busy post–September 11 deploying battleships and carriers to the Middle East. The year 2003 kicked off the bicentennial of the Lewis and Clark expedition, with rotating exhibits at Monticello, and also saw the opening of a new Smithsonian air and space center at Dulles International Airport. Tourism, which is one of the top three state industries, remains strong despite the rest of the country's slumping numbers. This is surely due to Virginia's sheer number of

VIRGINIA FACTS

Nicknames The Old Dominion State, Mother of Presidents
Population 7,293,542 (12th)
Area 42,777 sq miles (35th)
Admitted to Union June 25, 1788 (10th); seceded April 1861; readmitted January 1870
Capital city Richmond (population 207,000)
Other cities Virginia Beach (425,257), Norfolk (234,403)
State motto Thus always to tyrants
Birthplace of presidents George Washington (1732–1799, first), Thomas Jefferson (1743–1826, third), James Madison (1751–1836, fourth), James Monroe (1758–1831, fifth), William Henry Harrison (1773–1841, ninth), John Tyler (1790–1862, 10th), Zachary Taylor (1784–1850, 12th) and Woodrow Wilson (1856–1924, 28th); Booker T Washington (1856–1915); Pocahontas (c 1596–1617); Robert E Lee (1807–70); Ella Fitzgerald (1917–96); Shirley MacLaine (b 1934); Arthur Ashe (1943–92)
Famous for presidents, ham, Southern aristocracy, battlefields

enduring historical sites that make a lasting impression on locals and visitors alike.

Information

Virginia's **Division of Tourism** (☎ 800-321-3244; www.virginia.org; 901 E Byrd St, Richmond, VA 23219) produces a comprehensive state guide. There are 10 welcome centers throughout the state on the interstates. State sales tax is 4.5%.

National & State Parks & Activities

The wild beauty and recreational opportunities of Virginia's more than 30 state parks are a magnet for many outdoor enthusiasts and those who just want to get away to the mountains or the shore. For a comprehensive listing of parks and detailed information, contact the **Department of Conservation and Recreation** (☎ 804-786-1712; www.dcr.state.va.us/parks; 203 Governor St, Suite 213, Richmond, VA 23219).

Northern Virginia

Across the Potomac from Washington, many of northern Virginia's sights are so closely linked with the nation's capital that they're covered in the earlier Around Washington DC section (p302). Rural retreats provide weekend refuge for stressed-out Washingtonians, such as the **Great Falls Park** (☎ 703-285-2966; Old Dominion Dr, off I-183; cyclist/vehicle $3/5; 🕒 dawn to dusk).

MANASSAS BATTLEFIELD

South of where Dulles airport now stands, major Civil War battles known collectively as the Battles of Bull Run (by the North) or Battles of Manassas (by the South) were fought in July 1861 and August 1862. The Manassas National Battlefield Park **visitors center** (☎ 703-361-1339; 🕒 daylight) is the start of a good self-guided tour ($2).

FREDERICKSBURG

On the Rappahannock River, Fredericksburg prides itself on its illustrious history. Captain John Smith visited the site as early as 1608, George Washington grew up here and James Monroe practiced law here. During the Civil War, many bloody battles were fought in the area.

Today the attractive 40-block historic district is fun to stroll through, taking in museums, shops, restaurants and B&Bs – an inviting weekend retreat, easily accessible by rail. The **visitors center** (☎ 800-678-4748; www.fredericksburgvirginia.net; 706 Caroline St; 🕒 9am-5pm) offers a pass to historic Fredericksburg for nine local sights (adult $24, child six to 18 $8) including the ones described below. Unless otherwise indicated, opening hours for the following museums are 9am to 5pm Monday to Saturday, 11am to 5pm Sunday (March 1 through November 30); 10am to 4pm Monday to Saturday, noon to 4pm Sunday (December 1 through February 28).

Rising Sun Tavern (☎ 540-371-1494; 1304 Caroline St; adult $5, child 6-18 $1.50), once patronized by the town's luminaries, is now a museum, as is the nearby **Hugh Mercer Apothecary Shop** (☎ 540-373-3362; 1020 Caroline St).

The biggest attraction in these parts is the **Fredericksburg & Spotsylvania National Military Park**, which is maintained by the NPS. This park preserves four crucial Civil War battlefields, among them Chancellorsville, where General Stonewall Jackson received his fatal wound. The main **visitors center** (☎ 540-373-6122; 1013 Lafayette Blvd) offers informative exhibits, 75-mile driving-tour maps and weeklong passes.

Area museums that highlight the town's colonial importance include the following: **Fredericksburg Area Museum** (☎ 540-371-3037; 907 Princess Anne St; adult $5, child under 7 free)

James Monroe Museum (☎ 540-654-1043; 908 Charles St; adult/child $5/1; ⌚ 10am-5pm Mon-Sat, 1-5pm Sun Mar 1–Nov 30, 10am-4pm Mon-Sat, 1-4pm Sun Dec 1–Feb 28) Honors the native son and author of the Monroe Doctrine.
Mary Washington House (☎ 540-373-1569; 1200 Charles St; adult $5, child under 7 free) Home of George Washington's mother for her last 17 years.

Fredericksburg Colonial Inn (☎ 540-371-5666; 1707 Princess Anne St; r from $65; P ⊠) is a scaled-down version of Tara, with 30 rooms exuding antebellum atmosphere.

Goolrick's (901 Caroline St; dishes $8), the oldest continually operating soda fountain in the US, serves great, inexpensive lunches and thick milkshakes. **Virginia Deli** (101 William St) is another inexpensive alternative for breakfast and lunch (Brunswick stew $2.50).

Several daily Amtrak trains operate between DC and the train station on Caroline St. Weekday **commuter trains** (☎ 800-742-3873, www.vre.org; per person $7) are cheaper. Buses come into the **Greyhound/Trailways depot** (☎ 540-373-2103; 1400 Jefferson Davis Hwy).

NORTHERN NECK & MIDDLE PENINSULA

The northern 'neck' peninsula extends east from Fredericksburg. Off its tip is **Tangier Island**, an isolated fishing community that retains it own unique Elizabethan dialect. **Tangier & Chesapeake Cruises** (☎ 804-453-2628; 468 Buzzard Point Rd; adult $22, child 6-12 $11; ⌚ May-Oct 10am) makes the six-hour round-trip to the island, with some amusing narratives along the way. Overnight lodging is available on the island or at B&Bs in Reedville.

Yes, he undeniably slept here at the **George Washington Birthplace National Monument** (☎ 804-224-1732; 1732 Popes Creek Rd; adult $3, child under 16 free; ⌚ 9am-5pm), along the way to the tip of the Northern Neck at Pope's Creek Plantation. **Stratford Hall Plantation** (☎ 804-493-8038; 485 Great House Rd; adult $8, child 6-11 $4; ⌚ 9am-5pm), to the east, is the birthplace of Robert E Lee, and the impressive mansion is open for tours; its log cabin restaurant serves Southern lunches from $10.

On the middle peninsula, outside West Point, the 100-member, 125-acre Mattaponi Indian Reservation offers a **tribal museum** (☎ 804-769-2194; ⌚ 9am-5pm) and new fish hatchery center, which is open 2pm to 5pm weekends in summer. In 1997 the Mattaponi successfully defended their opposition to a local reservoir project by citing their 1677 treaty with the British to retain a buffer zone surrounding their community.

Historic waterfront **Urbanna** offers several restaurants and places to stay. **HI Sangraal-by-the-Sea** (☎ 804-776-6500; members/nonmembers $18/21) is the nearest budget option to Williamsburg. Call for directions.

RICHMOND

Richmond was the linchpin of the Confederacy during the Civil War, and many of its historic sites relate to that time of division. Today it still exudes an air of the antebellum old South, with wide tree-lined boulevards, gracious houses and restaurants that offer home-style Southern cooking.

Orientation

The James River bisects Richmond, with most attractions to the north. Access downtown via Broad St.

Information

BOOKSTORES

Carytown Books (2930 W Cary St, Carytown)
Fountain Bookstore (1312 E Cary St, downtown)

EMERGENCY

Crisis Hotline (☎ 804-819-4100)
Police (☎ 804-780-5100, 911)
Traveler's Aid 24-hour hotline (☎ 804-643-0279)

MEDIA

88.9 FM WCVE National Public Radio affiliate.
90.1 FM WDCE University of Richmond station.
93.5 FM WBBC Country.
101.1 WDYL Alternative rock.
Richmond-Times Dispatch (www.richmondtimesdispatch.com) Daily city newspaper with weekend section on Thursday.
Style Weekly (www.styleweekly.com) Free weekly paper with listings; comes out Tuesday.

MEDICAL SERVICES

Johnston-Willis Medical Center (☎ 804-330-2273; 1401 Johnston-Willis Dr)
Richmond Community Hospital (☎ 804-225-1700; 1500 N 28th St)
St Mary's Hospital (☎ 804-285-2011; 5801 Bremo Rd)

POST

Richmond branch at Capitol Center (700 E Main St)

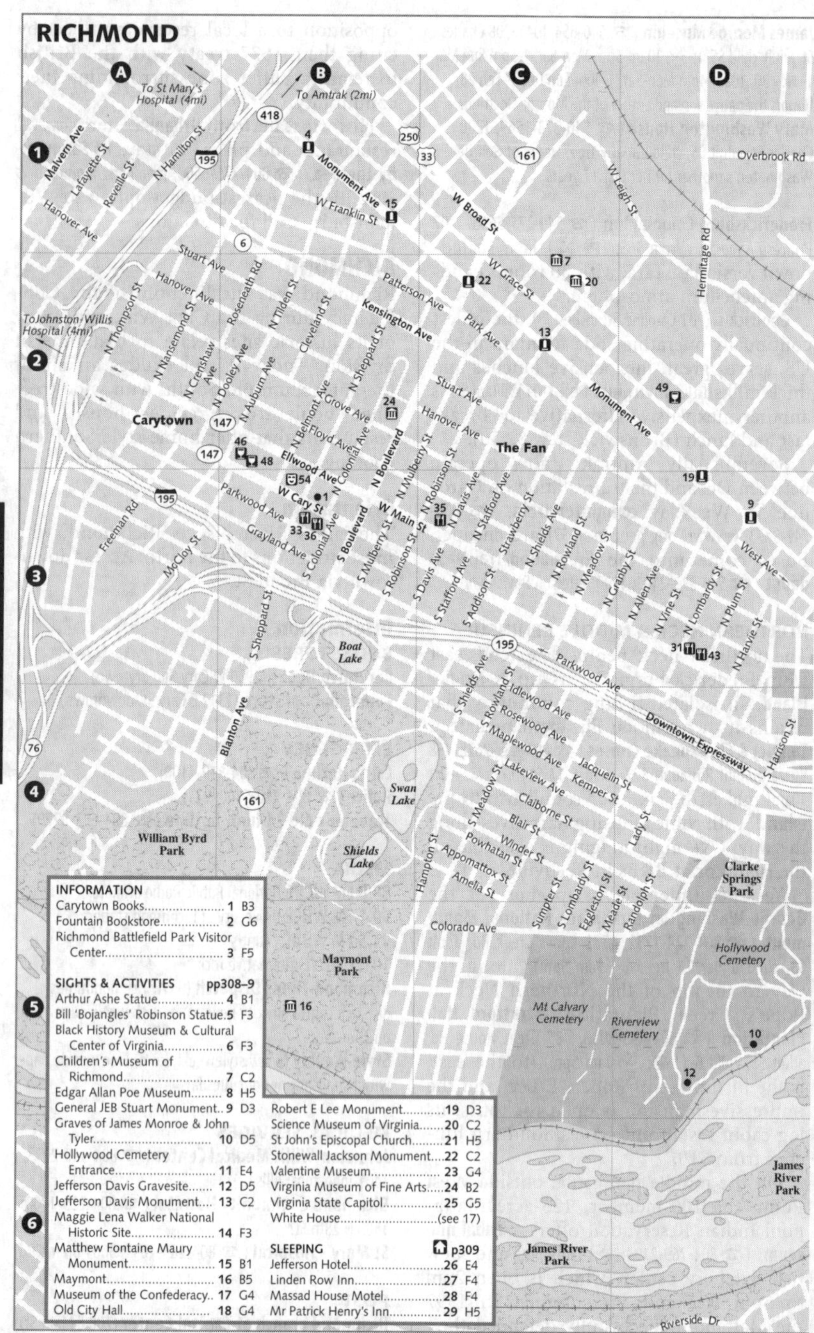
RICHMOND
A
B
C
D
1
2
3
4
5
6
To St Mary's Hospital (4mi)
To Amtrak (2mi)
ToJohnston-Willis Hospital (4mi)
Malvern Ave
Lafayette St
Reveille St
N Hamilton St
Hanover Ave
Monument Ave
W Franklin St
W Broad St
W Leigh St
Overbrook Rd
Hermitage Rd
Stuart Ave
Hanover Ave
N Thompson St
N Nansemond St
Roseneath Rd
N Crenshaw Ave
N Dooley Ave
N Auburn Ave
N Tilden St
Cleveland St
Patterson Ave
Kensington Ave
N Sheppard St
W Grace St
Park Ave
Monument Ave
Stuart Ave
Hanover Ave
Grove Ave
N Belmont Ave
Floyd Ave
Ellwood Ave
N Colonial Ave
N Boulevard
N Mulberry St
N Robinson St
N Davis Ave
N Stafford Ave
Strawberry St
N Shields Ave
N Rowland St
N Meadow St
N Granby St
N Allen Ave
N Vine St
N Lombardy St
N Plum St
N Harvie St
West Ave
Carytown
The Fan
W Cary St
W Main St
Parkwood Ave
Grayland Ave
S Colonial Ave
S Boulevard
S Mulberry St
S Robinson St
S Davis Ave
S Stafford Ave
S Addison St
Freeman Rd
McCloy St
S Sheppard St
Boat Lake
Parkwood Ave
S Shields Ave
S Rowland St
Idlewood Ave
Rosewood Ave
S Maplewood Ave
Lakeview Ave
Jacquelin St
Kemper St
Downtown Expressway
S Harrison St
Blanton Ave
Swan Lake
Shields Lake
S Meadow St
Claiborne St
Blair St
Winder St
Powhatan St
Appomattox St
Amelia St
Hampton St
Lady St
William Byrd Park
Clarke Springs Park
Colorado Ave
Sumpter St
S Lombardy St
Eggleston St
Meade St
Randolph St
Maymont Park
Hollywood Cemetery
Mt Calvary Cemetery
Riverview Cemetery
James River Park
James River Park
Riverside Dr
418
250
33
161
195
6
147
147
195
195
76
161

INFORMATION
Carytown Books........ 1 B3
Fountain Bookstore........ 2 G6
Richmond Battlefield Park Visitor Center........ 3 F5

SIGHTS & ACTIVITIES pp308–9
Arthur Ashe Statue........ 4 B1
Bill 'Bojangles' Robinson Statue. 5 F3
Black History Museum & Cultural Center of Virginia........ 6 F3
Children's Museum of Richmond........ 7 C2
Edgar Allan Poe Museum........ 8 H5
General JEB Stuart Monument.. 9 D3
Graves of James Monroe & John Tyler........ 10 D5
Hollywood Cemetery Entrance........ 11 E4
Jefferson Davis Gravesite........ 12 D5
Jefferson Davis Monument........ 13 C2
Maggie Lena Walker National Historic Site........ 14 F3
Matthew Fontaine Maury Monument........ 15 B1
Maymont........ 16 B5
Museum of the Confederacy.. 17 G4
Old City Hall........ 18 G4
Robert E Lee Monument........ 19 D3
Science Museum of Virginia........ 20 C2
St John's Episcopal Church........ 21 H5
Stonewall Jackson Monument........ 22 C2
Valentine Museum........ 23 G4
Virginia Museum of Fine Arts........ 24 B2
Virginia State Capitol........ 25 G5
White House........ (see 17)

SLEEPING p309
Jefferson Hotel........ 26 E4
Linden Row Inn........ 27 F4
Massad House Motel........ 28 F4
Mr Patrick Henry's Inn........ 29 H5

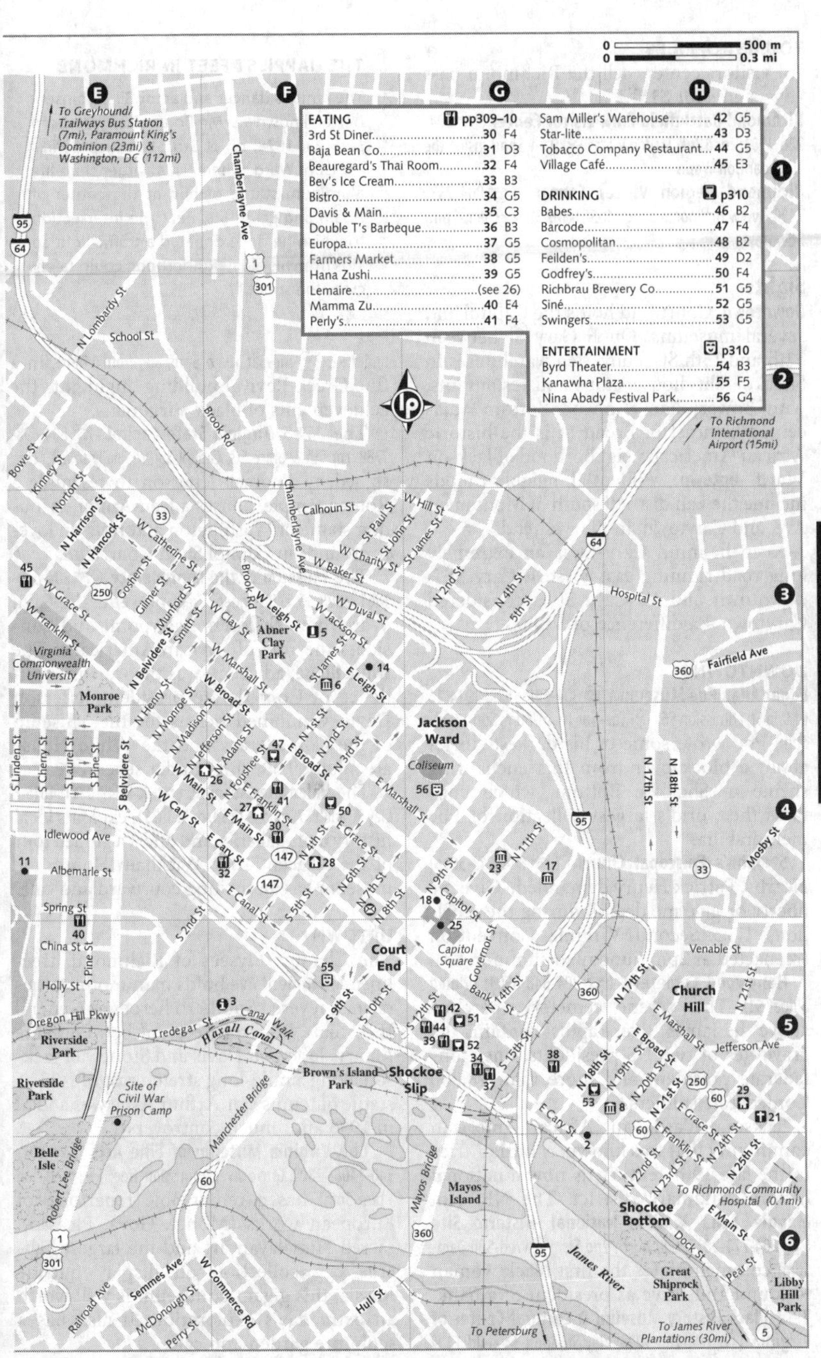
0 500 m
0 0.3 mi
EATING pp309–10
3rd St Diner 30 F4
Baja Bean Co 31 D3
Beauregard's Thai Room 32 F4
Bev's Ice Cream 33 B3
Bistro 34 G5
Davis & Main 35 C3
Double T's Barbeque 36 B3
Europa 37 G5
Farmers Market 38 G5
Hana Zushi 39 G5
Lemaire (see 26)
Mamma Zu 40 E4
Perly's 41 F4
Sam Miller's Warehouse 42 G5
Star-lite 43 D3
Tobacco Company Restaurant 44 G5
Village Café 45 E3
DRINKING p310
Babes 46 B2
Barcode 47 F4
Cosmopolitan 48 B2
Feilden's 49 D2
Godfrey's 50 F4
Richbrau Brewery Co 51 G5
Siné 52 G5
Swingers 53 G5
ENTERTAINMENT p310
Byrd Theater 54 B3
Kanawha Plaza 55 F5
Nina Abady Festival Park 56 G4
To Greyhound/ Trailways Bus Station (7mi), Paramount King's Dominion (23mi) & Washington, DC (112mi)
To Richmond International Airport (15mi)
To Richmond Community Hospital (0.1mi)
To Petersburg
To James River Plantations (30mi)
Jackson Ward
Coliseum
Court End
Capitol Square
Church Hill
Shockoe Slip
Shockoe Bottom
Abner Clay Park
Monroe Park
Virginia Commonwealth University
Riverside Park
Site of Civil War Prison Camp
Belle Isle
Brown's Island Park
Mayos Island
Great Shiprock Park
Libby Hill Park
James River
Haxall Canal
Canal Walk
Robert Lee Bridge
Manchester Bridge
Mayos Bridge
Chamberlayne Ave
N Lombardy St
School St
Brook Rd
Calhoun St
W Hill St
Hospital St
Fairfield Ave
W Grace St
W Franklin St
W Broad St
E Broad St
W Main St
E Main St
W Cary St
E Cary St
E Marshall St
E Grace St
E Franklin St
Capitol St
Bank St
Governor St
Venable St
Jefferson Ave
Mosby St
N 17th St
N 18th St
Idlewood Ave
Albemarle St
Spring St
China St
Holly St
Oregon Hill Pkwy
Tredegar St
Semmes Ave
W Commerce Rd
Hull St
Dock St
Pear St
Railroad Ave
McDonough St
Perry St

TOURIST OFFICES

All visitors centers sell the Richmond pass (five sights for $15).

Richmond Battlefield Park Visitor Center (☎ 804-226-1981; cnr 5th & Tredegar Sts; 9am-5pm) Inside the Tredegar Iron Works.

Richmond Region Visitor Center (☎ 804-783-7450; www.richmondva.org; 405 N 3rd St; 9am-5pm) Downtown.

Sights

Downtown, Court End holds the Capitol and several museums. On E Cary St between 12th and 15th Sts, converted warehouses in Shockoe Slip house shops and restaurants, with bowery-like Shockoe Bottom adjacent. Northeast of Broad St is the historic African-American neighborhood of Jackson Ward. **Uptown**, residential neighborhoods include the Fan district, south of Monument Ave, and Carytown, in the west end.

Keep in mind Cary St is an extremely long road running east–west. E Cary St is downtown and W Cary St is considered Carytown – a difference of 5 miles.

DOWNTOWN

Edgar Allan Poe Museum (☎ 804-648-5523; 1914-16 E Main St; admission $6; Tue-Sat 10am-5pm, Sun 11am-5pm) Poe wrote some of his darkest stories about a block over from this enchanting shrine in Shockoe Bottom, which contains the world's largest collection of Poe memorabilia.

St John's Episcopal Church (☎ 804-648-5015) Nearby, Patrick Henry demanded, 'Give me liberty or give me death!' during the rebellious 1775 Second Virginia Convention (reenacted at 2pm Sunday in summer; $3).

Hollywood Cemetery (☎ 804-648-8501; printed guide $1) This serene cemetery, perched above the James River rapids, contains the gravesites of two US presidents, one Confederate president and more than 18,000 Confederate soldiers.

Jackson Ward, an African-American community that was known as Little Africa in the late 19th century, is now a national historic landmark district. The NPS-run **Maggie Lena Walker National Historic Site** (☎ 804-771-2017; 600 North 2nd St; Wed-Sun 9am-5pm) commemorates the first black woman to found and serve as president of a bank. The **Black History Museum & Cultural Center of Virginia** (☎ 804-780-9093; Clay St; adult $4 child 12 & under $2; Tue-Sat 10am-5pm, Sun from 11am), in a fine Greek Revival building, highlights the achievements of black Virginians.

The 1785 **Virginia State Capitol** (☎ 804-698-1788; cnr 9th & Grace Sts, Capitol Sq; free daily tours), designed by Thomas Jefferson to resemble a Roman temple, houses a Jean-Antoine Houdon statue of Washington and rests on lovely grounds in Capitol Sq in Court End.

The **Museum of the Confederacy** (☎ 804-649-1861; adult $6, child under 7 free) presents the Civil War from the losers' viewpoint and considers the role of African-Americans. The **White House**, adjacent, was the wartime residence of Confederate president Jefferson Davis. Combined tickets for the Museum of the Confederacy and the White House are adult $9.50, child under seven free.

The **Valentine Museum** (☎ 804-649-0711; 1015 E Clay St; adult $7, child 7-12 $4, child 3-6 $1) explains local history in its galleries and offers a guided tour of the adjacent 1812 Wickham House; the museum has an inviting courtyard and café.

THE HAPPIEST FEET IN RICHMOND

The famous dancer and actor Bill Robinson, better known as Mr Bojangles, was born May 25, 1878, on N 3rd St in Richmond's Jackson Ward. There is a larger-than-life aluminum statue of him at the corner of Adam and Leigh Sts, near the intersection to which he once donated a traffic light so kids from his old neighborhood could safely cross the street.

UPTOWN

The Champs Elysées of Richmond, tree-lined **Monument Ave** holds mammoth statues of such revered Southern heroes as General JEB Stuart, Robert E Lee, Matthew Fontaine Maury, Jefferson Davis and Stonewall Jackson along a mile-long stretch east of I-95. A statue of tennis star Arthur Ashe was added in 1996 after much controversy.

The **Virginia Museum of Fine Arts** (☎ 804-340-1400; 2800 Grove Ave; admission free; Wed-Sun 11am-5pm) has a remarkable repertoire of European works (Monet, Goya, Picasso), sacred Himalayan art and the largest Fabergé egg collection on display outside Russia, this gigantic museum is well worth an extra day's exploration. It also has a sculpture garden and café.

Housed in the gargantuan 1919 Broad St Station, **Science Museum of Virginia** (☎ 804-367-0000; 2500 W Broad St; adult $7, child 4-12 $6; ⏲ Mon-Sat 9:30am-5pm, Sun 11:30am-5:30pm) is a highly entertaining museum that holds three floors of hands-on exhibits covering the galaxy of science topics. Combo tickets with Imax films are adult child $12.50/11.50. But adults sans children may find it somewhat dull. Same goes for the adjacent **Children's Museum of Richmond** (☎ 804-474-2667; 2626 W Broad St; adult $6.50, child under 2 free; ⏲ Tue-Sat 9:30am-5pm, Sun from noon), ranked 11th of the top children's museums in the country.

A former grand estate, **Maymont** (☎ 804-358-7166; 1700 Hampton St; ⏲ 10am-5pm) is now a sprawling 100-acre garden, public park and petting zoo, and the most visited attraction in Richmond – and so it should be. With an exotic mix of Japanese and Italian gardens, an arboretum and nature center, moderate grassy hills, and plenty of open areas for afternoon pick-up games of Frisbee, it's a great place to spend a warm afternoon outdoors. Admission is free, but donations are suggested for the estate tour and nature center.

CANAL WALK

The 1.5-mile Canal Walk along the James River is an ambitious redevelopment along the waterfront. There are 12 stops along the waterfront walk, and the city's history is carefully highlighted. One of the stops, Belle Isle, was a former POW camp for Union soldiers and today is a lovely outdoor excursion, with a climbing wall, hiking and biking trails, and access to the white-water rapids (up to class V) that run through downtown Richmond. The island is accessible by a wavy footbridge at the Tredegar Iron Works.

Sleeping

Budget options are rare and chain hotels the norm.

BUDGET

Massad House Motel (☎ 804-648-2893; 11 N 4th St; r from $55) Though certainly the cheapest option, it's centrally located for exploring downtown. You will find small rooms equipped with cable TV and air-con in a boarding-house-style building, with hallway vending machines and a friendly, 24-hour desk clerk with plenty of entertainment suggestions.

MID-RANGE

Linden Row Inn (☎ 804-783-7000; www.lindenrowinn.com; 100 E Franklin St; r from $100) Rumored to be the place where Poe played as a child, this intimate inn occupies antebellum row houses that are set around a balcony-lined courtyard.

Mr Patrick Henry's Inn (☎ 804-644-1322; 2300 E Broad St; r from $95) Named for the fiery American patriot, this place suffers from a slight identity problem, also housing a gourmet restaurant and an English-themed pub in the basement. A perfect cozy respite from the wild city.

TOP END

Jefferson Hotel (☎ 804-788-8000; www.jefferson-hotel.com; 101 W Franklin St; r from $120) This is the city's premier historic hotel in a grand old building. Sunday brunch is served in the Rotunda.

Eating

The happenin' eats are found in the **Fan**, **Carytown**, and E Cary St in **Shockoe Slip**.

DOWNTOWN

Forget about grabbing as much as a bagel in downtown on the weekends; it's a virtual ghost town.

Farmers market (cnr 17th & Main St) If you do find yourself downtown on the weekend, this is the place to try.

Perly's (111 E Grace St; dishes $5) This place is recommended for a quick bite.

Beauregard's Thai Room (103 E Cary St; mains $8-16) Stop here for outstanding Thai food.

Lemaire (☎ 804-788-8000; 101 W Franklin St; mains $23-34) At the Jefferson Hotel (see above), Lemaire is where you'll find upscale Virginia-inspired dishes.

THE AUTHOR'S CHOICE

3rd St Diner (☎ 804-788-4750; 218 E Main St; mains $8; ⏲ 24hr) Guns n' Roses at 8am? You bet! This hole-in-the-wall diner resembles the aftermath of a pink-and-blue explosion and attracts an eclectic crowd from truck drivers to drag queens. Bring an appetite and lose the attitude because this dive serves it up quick, no frills, 24-7. Besides, you haven't lived until you've had pork chops as a side dish.

WASHINGTON DC & THE CAPITAL REGION

SHOCKOE SLIP

Bistro (☎ 804-344-8222; 1417 E Cary St; mains $15-23) A spacious yet intimate eatery with exceptional Italian pasta dishes, Bistro serves up giant salads and a wonderful Sunday brunch featuring $9 stuffed crepes and VA-style eggs Benedict (country ham and cornbread).

Tobacco Company Restaurant (☎ 804-782-9555; 1201 E Cary St; mains $18-30) A total embodiment of the era when tobacco was king – it's a famous getup for its three-story, brothel-like restaurant and bar, but the contemporary food is only so-so and slightly overpriced.

The following are also recommended:

Hana Zushi (1309 E Cary St) For inexpensive Japanese take-away *bento* (lunch boxes).

Sam Miller's Warehouse (1210 E Cary St) A landmark for steaks and seafood.

Europa (1409 E Cary St) For trendy Mediterranean tapas.

THE FAN

Star-lite (☎ 804-254-2667; 2600 W Main St; dishes under $20) Traditionally known as a great corner bar in these parts, the food is simply too outstanding not to highlight as well – they make meatloaf a must-try! The menu ranges from simple Reubens to scallops Rockefeller, and the brunches are even better; the outdoor patio is great in summer.

Village Café (1001 W Grace St) Near Star-lite, Village Café is a funky little eatery serving cheese boards, among other things. It's been referred to as 'a counter with a culture behind it.'

The following are also recommended:

Davis & Main (2501 W Main St; mains $18) For grilled vegetable sides.

Baja Bean Co (1520 W Main St; mains $18) For California-style meals in a cantina setting.

Mamma Zu (501 S Pine St; mains $18) For authentic Italian dishes; beware the heavy garlic smell.

CARYTOWN

Double T's Barbeque (☎ 804-353-9861; 2907 W Cary St; mains $7-13) Just follow the smokehouse scent to this wooden shack and some of the best barbecue you'll ever have. Choose from six kinds of BBQ sauce and rib-stickin' sides like homemade cornbread, southern-style potato salad and fried apples.

Bev's Ice Cream (☎ 804-204-2387; 2911 W Cary St) If you have room for dessert, save it for this popular place, next door to Double T's Barbeque.

Drinking & Entertainment

You can't throw a bottle cap in the **Fan, Carytown** or **Shockoe Slip** without hitting a bar or club; E and W Cary Sts, and W Main St, have the most action.

Richbrau Brewing Co (1214 E Cary St) Despite the Wal-Mart-size megaclub and bar here, lines still wrap around the block. It's worth the wait for sheer madness on the thumping two-story dance floor, the billiards rooms and many, many bars, known for their boutique ales.

Siné (1327 E Cary St) This is a rather unusual upscale Irish pub in Shockoe Slip popular with a 20-something crowd, especially for late-night drinks.

Swingers (12 N 18th St) Here the blood-red walls and mahogany bar melt into one of the hottest watering holes downtown. Dress like a reality–TV show contestant and select your room, with live rock bands and billiards downstairs, and an *über*-hip lounge above.

Nina Abady Festival Park (btwn 6th St Marketplace and the Coliseum) Free concerts are held here Wednesday and Friday, starting at dusk.

Byrd Theater (☎ 804-353-9911; 2908 W Cary St; tickets $2) At this fabulous old theater, Wurlitzer-organ concerts precede recent movies.

The gay and lesbian scene plays out in Carytown. **Feilden's** (2033 W Broad St), **Babes** (3166 W Cary St) and **Cosmopolitan** (3156 W Cary St) are well-known gay clubs. **Godfrey's** (308 E Grace St) and **Barcode** (6 E Grace St) are part of a circle of gay bars along Grace St, affectionately known as the fruit loop. For more on the gay and lesbian scene, see www.gayrichmond.com.

Getting There & Around

The **Greyhound/Trailways** bus terminal (☎ 804-254-5938) is at 2910 N Blvd. **Greater Richmond Transit Company** (GRTC; ☎ 804-358-4782) runs local buses ($1.25 base fare, exact change only). The local GRTC bus No 27 runs to/from downtown; cab fare is about $15. **Amtrak** (☎ 800-872-7245) stops off way north of town at 7519 Staples Mill Rd.

AROUND RICHMOND

The many Civil War battlefields relating to the battles for Richmond are the main attractions in this area, but there are several other points of interest.

Paramount King's Dominion

Packed with death-defying roller coasters, soaking water rides, kiddie amusements and performance stages for concerts and dance reviews, this giant theme park kicks butt with adults and children. Kids will especially love getting their picture snapped with cartoon characters such as Bugs Bunny, and getting a bird's-eye view from the Eiffel Tower replica. **Paramount King's Dominion** (☎ 804-876-5000; www.kingsdominion.com; adult $42, child 3-6 $28; Mar-Oct) is 22 miles north of Richmond on I-95 (Doswell exit).

Petersburg & Around

At a vital junction on the Appomattox River, Petersburg fell to the British in 1781 and saw the Civil War's last great battle in April 1865. The **visitors center** (☎ 804-733-2400; 425 Cockade Alley) sells block tickets for the following city-run sites ($7 for any three).

Blandford Church (☎ 804-733-2396; 111 Rochelle Lane; 10am-5pm) is the pride of Petersburg, with a complete set of intricate Tiffany & Co windows dedicated to Confederate states and their war dead. The sprawling cemetery is said to have inspired the first Memorial Day.

The **Siege Museum** (☎ 804-733-2404; 15 W Bank St; 10am-5pm) poignantly relates the plight of civilians during the 10-month siege of 1864–65. **Petersburg National Battlefield** (vehicle/pedestrian $5/3; 9am-5pm) is the site of the siege and the huge crater. The **visitors center** (☎ 804-732-3531), off Rte 36 via I-95 exit 52, features daily living-history programs in summer.

The **Walker House B&B** (☎ 804-861-5822; www.walker-house.com; r $95-115; P) is an amazing find, boasting a lovely waterfront garden and four giant bedrooms (named for the four seasons) you could do cartwheels in. Call for directions. **Brickhouse Run** (☎ 804-862-1815; 407-409 Cockade Alley; r $5-15), next to the visitors center, is a lively British pub with zesty homemade soups and traditional pub fare.

In the nearby Pamplin Historical Park, the **Museum of the Civil War Soldier** (☎ 804-861-2408; adult $12, child 6-11 $6; 9am-6pm Jun 14–Aug 17), southwest of Petersburg, has an exceptional audio tour illustrating the privations faced by soldiers on both sides of the conflict.

HISTORIC TRIANGLE

Set on the peninsula between the York and James Rivers, Colonial Williamsburg, Jamestown and Yorktown constitute the historic triangle, collectively one of the state's most popular tourist destinations. The NPS-maintained **Colonial Parkway** links all three sites. Williamsburg is accessible by train or bus, but the other sites require a car or bicycle.

It's hard to say this area is not a compelling stop, what with its critical historic past that shaped the young United States. However, the towns today seem more theme parklike in their attractions and are typically overrun by hordes of school children. Yorktown and Jamestown can be done in a day and are often lumped onto a Williamsburg trip. The attractions are certainly worth seeing in order to understand the hardships and struggles the early settlers had to endure, but apart from Williamsburg, the other towns won't hold your attention for very long.

Williamsburg

First settled as Middle Plantation in 1632, Williamsburg was from 1699 to 1780 the capital of England's largest, richest and most populous colony and the seat of power in the new nation's most influential state. Named to honor King William III and designed by Royal Governor Francis Nicholson, Williamsburg lives intimately with its distinguished past.

After Virginia's capital moved to Richmond in 1780, Williamsburg was nearly forgotten, but it became embroiled in the Civil War. Starting in the mid-1920s, John D Rockefeller contributed some $70 million to local restoration efforts, and endowments ensured continuing restoration of the historic district now known as Colonial Williamsburg. This 220-acre restoration is now surrounded by the city of Williamsburg, which is full of visitor services and home to the College of William & Mary.

INFORMATION

The nonprofit **Colonial Williamsburg Foundation** (☎ 757-220-7645, 800-447-8679; www.colonialwilliamsburg.org) opens dozens of authentic 17th- and 18th-century buildings to ticket holders in the 173-acre restored historic district. Walking around the historic district and patronizing the shops and taverns is free, but entry to the gardens and participation in historic building tours are restricted to ticket holders. Expect crowds, lines and a

WALKING WILLIAMSBURG

Merchants Sq is a good starting point. At the head of the beautiful Palace Green, the **Governor's Palace** is one highlight, with its lavish interiors, formal gardens and boxwood maze. The **Capitol**, where the legislature reenacts the topics of the day (it might be one of four historical days from 1774 to 1776), is the highlight at the opposite end of the main thoroughfare – Duke of Gloucester St. This street also holds colonial souvenir shops and taverns as well as the landmark **Bruton Parish Church**, home to an Episcopalian congregation since 1715.

In central Market Sq, surrounding the 1770 courthouse, the magazine holds the town arsenal, stalls sell food, and a pillory and stock provide irresistible photo opportunities. Around town, house tours tell stories of colonial home life and notable families, and craft shops demonstrate coopering, smithing, wheel-making and other trades.

Chartered in 1693, the **College of William & Mary** (☎ 757-221-1540) retains the oldest college building in the USA (the Sir Christopher Wren Building) and the **Muscarelle Museum of Art** (☎ 757-221-2703; admission free). The school's esteemed alumnae include Thomas Jefferson and James Monroe.

certain unavoidable theme-park quality, particularly in summer.

To park and purchase tickets, follow signs to the futuristic main **visitors center** (☎ 757-220-7645, 800-447-8679; north of the historic district, sandwiched between Rte 132 & the Colonial Parkway; 🕑 8:30am-6pm). Parking here is free; shuttle buses run frequently to and from the historic district. Parking anywhere around the district is severely restricted. Exhibitions are open 9am to 5pm daily.

Types of passes include the following:

One Day Pass (adult $37, child 6-14 $19, for an extra day adult $40, child 6-14 $20) Covers most exhibition buildings, not including the palace, along with two museums.

Freedom Pass (adult/child $49/25) Includes all exhibition buildings and museums and is good for 12 months.

Liberty Pass (adult/child $69/35) Includes year-round access and admission to special events.

Museum-only passes are also available ($11). Disabled visitors should call ahead to arrange special vehicles (☎ 757-220-7644).

The small Merchants Sq **information booth** (🕑 9am-5pm), within the district at the west end of Duke of Gloucester St (about four blocks from the bus and train station), also sells tickets.

SLEEPING

You'll certainly find a place to stay in any price range here.

Williamsburg Hotel/Motel Association (☎ 800-446-9244; north of the historic district, sandwiched between Rte 132 & the Colonial Parkway) Located at the visitors center, this association finds accommodations at no charge.

Colonial Williamsburg Foundation lodging (CWF; ☎ 800-447-8679) Alternatively, try this central reservation line; prices are given for one night's accommodation off peak – breakfast, dinner and an attractions pass included (minimum two-night stay).

Budget

Williamsburg & Colonial KOA Resorts (☎ 800-562-1733; 5210 & 4000 Newman Rd respectively, I-64 exit 234; campsites/Kabins $29/55) With two of the best campgrounds rolled into one, here you'll find superb amenities such as a heated and kiddie pool, movies and game rooms, and free buses to area attractions; a great place to take the family.

King Guest Home (☎ 757-229-7551; 307 Cary St; r from $55) Just five blocks to Colonial Williamsburg makes this homey place a steal, with private bathrooms as well as refrigerators in all three rooms; no TV or children, though.

Mid-Range

Governor's Inn (☎ 757-229-1000; www.history.org/visit/staywithus/governorsinn; 506 N Henry St; r from $110) A hotel atmosphere at a motel price, with free continental breakfast, outdoor pool, refrigerators and a convenient three-block stroll to the historic district.

Liberty Rose B&B (☎ 757-253-1260; 1022 Jamestown Rd; r from $165) Heavily dripping in Victorian furnishings and fringed fabrics, this is like stepping back in time to complete the whole colonial experience – with the exception of a few modern inventions such as Jacuzzi tubs and satellite TV.

Top End

Williamsburg Inn (☎ 757-229-1000; www.history.org/visit/staywithus/williamsburginn; 136 E Francis St; r from $425) CWF's premier property is noted by its not-so-colonial price tag. If you can afford it, the pampering is nonstop at this beautiful property, which looks like a grand country estate; it houses indoor/outdoor pools, lavish rooms and a world-class restaurant.

EATING

Several local promotional publications include tear-out discount coupons.

Williamsburg Shopping Center (157 Monticello Ave) The place for campers to stock up with supplies.

Cheese Shop (☎ 757-220-0298; 410 Duke of Gloucester St, Merchants Sq) Locals swear by this inexpensive gourmet deli, with an eclectic assortment of sandwiches and, of course, an extensive international cheese display; watch costumed docents from the shaded outdoor patio.

College Delly & Pizza (☎ 757-229-6627; 336 Richmond Rd; mains $12; until 2am) This William & Mary College hangout has satisfied late-night, exam-cramming students as well as budget-conscious travelers for years, with their Greek, vegetarian and, of course, Italian fare.

Trellis Cafe (☎ 757-229-8610; Merchants Sq; mains from $16) This is a must in Colonial Williamsburg for the superb cuisine such as smoked bacon risotto and grilled pork tenderloin; a tad on the expensive side but simply exquisite. Reservations are suggested.

And for something completely different, four historic district taverns – **Chowning's** (Duke of Gloucester St, next to Market Sq; mains $6-15), **Christiana Campbell** (Waller St, near Capitol; mains $22), **Shield's** (☎ 800-828-3767; Duke of Gloucester St, near Capitol; mains $27; walk-up reservations only) and **King's Arms** (Duke of Gloucester St, across from Raleigh Tavern; mains $25) – serve 'ye old vittles and grog' from costumed waitstaff; there's entertainment most evenings.

ENTERTAINMENT

At night the crowds thin out and the historic district is particularly evocative as folks stroll to evening performances. Choral concerts, 18th-century dances and even witch trials are just a sample of many interesting diversions sponsored by the CWF for around $10 per ticket (see event listings in the free program available to ticket holders and at ticket booths). Highly recommended for those who don't scare easily is the chilling **Original Ghosts of Williamsburg tour** (☎ 757-253-1058; 8pm). Tickets ($9) are sold at the Williamsburg Attraction Center at the prime outlets.

GETTING THERE & AROUND

Amtrak (☎ 757-229-8750) runs to Richmond and Washington DC from the transportation center at the corner of Lafayette and N Boundary Sts. The center also houses a **Greyhound/Trailways station** (☎ 757-229-1460), with buses to the same major cities and smaller towns. Bike rentals are available from **Bikes Unlimited** (☎ 757-229-4620) and **Bikesmith** (☎ 757-229-9858).

Around Williamsburg

Three miles east of Williamsburg on Hwy 60, **Busch Gardens** (☎ 800-343-7946; www.buschgardens.com; adult $45, child 3-6 $38; Apr-Oct; P $7) is a megatheme park with many roller-coaster rides. Just down the road, **Water Country USA** (☎ 800-343-7946; www.watercountryusa.com; off Rte 199 east of Williamsburg; adult $34, child 3-6 $27; May-Sep) is a water-lovin' kids' paradise with twisty slides, raging rapids and wave pools, and a perfect place to beat the summer heat. A two-day 'Bounce' ticket for both parks is $60.

Jamestown

Founded in May 1607, the first permanent English settlement on the continent survived less than a century before succumbing to starvation, disease and Native American attacks. In 1619 the first representative assembly met, and Jamestown served as Virginia's capital until 1699, when the colonists moved inland to what is now Williamsburg. By the end of the 19th century, only an overgrown churchyard and church tower remained, and today the collection of ruins at the two Jamestown attractions, though historically important, are on the bland side and can easily be covered in a day.

Historic Jamestowne (☎ 757-253-4838; adult $6, child under 17 free; 9am-5pm, gate closes 4:30pm), run by the NPS, is the original site of the settlement, overlooking the James River. Grassy paths lead to James Citte where the story of Pocahontas, Captain John Smith and other historical activities come alive. You'll also find a 1640s church tower and several statues and monuments. The visitors center offers free living-history tours and a cheesy film. A combo ticket with Yorktown Battlefield is adult/child $9/free.

The state-run **Jamestown Settlement** (☎ 757-253-4838; adult $10.80, child 6-12 $5.80; 9am-5pm) features a reconstruction of the 1607 James Fort, a Native American village and full-scale replicas of the first ships to bring settlers to Jamestown, along with living-history fun. A combo ticket that includes the Yorktown Victory Center is adult $16, child six to 12 $7.80.

Yorktown

Founded in 1691, the busy tobacco port of Yorktown became famous in 1781 as the site of the last major Revolutionary War battle – thousands of Cornwallis' troops surrendered to George Washington after the British defeat. Today's Yorktown is dramatically different, now just a sleepy town with several intact Revolutionary and Civil War fortifications scattered between its two main attractions.

Yorktown Battlefield (adult $5, child under 17 free; 9am-5pm), run by the NPS, preserves the bluff site of the British defeat, and contains intriguing displays explaining the battle inside the **visitors center** (☎ 757-898-3400). A combo ticket with Historic Jamestowne is adult/child $9/free. Cars can tour a 7-mile battlefield drive and a 10.5-mile encampment route. The **Yorktown Victory Center** (☎ 757-253-4838; adult $8.30, child 6-12 $4; 9am-5pm) features a reconstruction of the encampment, battle scenes where full-size toy soldiers come to life, and daily canon firings. A combo ticket that includes the Jamestown Settlement is adult $16, child six to 12 $7.80.

Yorktown Pub on Water St is a friendly place with hearty daily specials (cash only).

James River Plantations

The grand homes of Virginia's slaveholding aristocracy were a clear sign of the class divisions in that era. Today, many of the restored plantation homes give a glimpse into that life complete with beautiful architecture, hand-carved staircases and magnificent views of the James River. They're located near scenic Rte 5 on the north side of the river, and it's best to see a couple in detail. **Block tickets** (www.jamesriverplantations.org; $28) are sold at each cover the four homes following.

Having hosted the first 10 presidents, **Berkeley** (☎ 804-829-6018; $8.50) is the grandest. It was used as the 1862 Civil War headquarters of Union general George McClellan, and also the site of the first American Thanksgiving. **Shirley** (☎ 800-232-1613; $9) is Virginia's oldest plantation (1660s). Its hanging staircase ascends three stories without any apparent support. **Evelynton** (☎ 804-829-5075; $7.50) has antique furnishings and gardens filled with flowers. **Sherwood Forest** (☎ 804-829-5377; $8.50) was the home of the 10th US president, John Tyler.

HAMPTON ROADS

The waterway called Hampton Roads empties the James, Nansemond and Elizabeth Rivers into the Chesapeake Bay. Europeans settled the surrounding region in the 17th century. During the Revolutionary War, Norfolk was torched by the British, but it later prospered as an international port. The Civil War battle of the ironclad ships *Monitor* and *Merrimack* was fought near here.

Norfolk later boomed as an industrial and shipbuilding area, especially during WWI and WWII. Today the region bustles with maritime activity, from its huge naval bases and seafood industry to pleasure boating. Note that I-64 can get very congested through the region, particularly at the bridge-tunnel bottleneck.

Hampton

The city of Hampton, home of the historically significant African-American Hampton University, holds several attractions along its modern harborside waterfront, with the **visitors center** (☎ 800-800-2202; 710 Settlers Landing Rd) off I-64 exit 267.

Virginia Air & Space Center (☎ 757-727-0900; 600 Settlers Landing Rd; admission $6; Mon-Sat 10am-5pm, Sun noon-5pm), at the NASA Langley Research Center, holds 110,000 sq ft of air- and spacecraft, including an Apollo command module and lunar lander, and a great assortment of Imax flicks ($6.50). **Hampton University Museum** (☎ 757-727-5308; admission free; 8am-5pm Mon-Fri, noon-4pm Sat) displays traditional African, Asian, Pacific and Native American art, as well as contemporary works by African-American artists.

Newport News

More naval history is crammed into this small city, 10 miles from Williamsburg;

check out the **visitors center** (☎ 888-222-8072; 13560 Jefferson Ave).

The fascinating **Mariner's Museum** (☎ 757-596-2222; 100 Museum Dr; adult $7, child under 6 free; ⏰ 10am-5pm), one of the largest maritime museums in the world, features carved figureheads, Captain John Smith's map of the Chesapeake Bay, and the turret from the USS *Monitor*, sunk during the Civil War. **Virginia Living Museum** (☎ 757-247-8523; 9285 Warwick Blvd, Huntington Park; adult $9, child 3-12 $7; ⏰ Mon-Sat 9am-5pm, Sun noon-5pm), nearby, guides you around a lakeside boardwalk to see wildlife in local habitats, and the **Virginia War Museum** (adult $5, child 7-18 $3), next door, is packed with military history collections, including a section of the Dachau concentration camp.

Also recommended are the grand **Lee Hall Mansion and Endview Plantation** (362 Yorktown Rd; adult $5, child 7-18 $3).

Newport News Park (☎ 757-888-3333; tent site/RV site $16/18) offers year-round camping, and boat and bike rentals, or try indoor lodging at **Mulberry Inn** (☎ 757-887-3000; 16890 Warwick Blvd; r from $90).

Norfolk

No longer just a navy town, Norfolk's dramatic renaissance welcomes all with free concerts in waterfront parks, world-class museums and an international restaurant mix. Most attractions are linked through the free Norfolk Electronic Transit (NET) shuttle, and the downtown Waterside Festival Marketplace has shops and restaurants alongside a bricked promenade.

Here's where you'll find visitors centers:

Interstate (☎ 757-441-1852; Ocean View I-64 exit 273) Near the bridge-tunnel.

Downtown (☎ 757-664-6620; 232 E Main St)

SIGHTS & ACTIVITIES

Nauticus (National Maritime Center; ☎ 757-664-1000; adult $9.50, child 4-12 $7; ⏰ May-Sep 10am-6pm, Oct-Apr Tue-Sat 10am-5pm, Sun noon-5pm), next to Town Pointe Park, is the biggest attraction here, overshadowed only by the USS *Wisconsin* battleship (a Desert Storm veteran) docked alongside. This comprehensive naval museum has ingenious interactive exhibits and entertaining shows, including submarine rides, multimedia naval battles and flight simulators.

MacArthur Memorial (☎ 757-441-2965; MacArthur Sq; admission free) houses the WWII general's military and personal artifacts, and the tombs of the general and his wife. **Chrysler Museum of Art** (☎ 757-664-6200; 245 W Olney Rd; adult $7, child 12 & under free; ⏰ Wed 10am-9pm, Tue-Sat 10am-5pm, Sun 1-5pm) is a grand place with a superb collection and well worth a detour. Exhibits include paintings by Gainsborough, Renoir, Picasso, Pollock and Warhol, and glass ranges from ancient Roman to Tiffany & Co pieces.

Also recommended are the beautiful blooms of **Norfolk Botanical Gardens** (☎ 757-441-5830; 6700 Azalea Garden Rd of I-64 exit 279B; adult $6, child 6-16 $4; ⏰ Apr 15–Oct 15 9am-7pm, until 5pm rest of year) and the **Virginia Zoo** (☎ 757-624-9937; 3500 Granby St; adult $5, child 2-11 $2; ⏰ 10am-5pm), a few minutes from downtown. At the zoo, strollers are available for $4.

The magnificent 135ft schooner **American Rover** (☎ 757-627-7245; $14) cruises Hampton Roads (two hours) April to October. The **Spirit of Norfolk** (☎ 757-625-1748; $29-43) operates narrated cruises.

SLEEPING & EATING

Page House Inn (☎ 757-625-5033; 323 Fairfax Ave; r $130-195) Uptown opposite the Chrysler Museum, this is a glamorous place. Management also operates the excellent Bianca Boat & Breakfast at the waterfront.

Doumar's (☎ 757-627-4163; 919 Monticello Ave) Since 1904, this slice of Americana has been the drive-up home of the world's original ice-cream-cone machine, plus local award-winning barbecue.

Elliott's (☎ 757-625-0259; 1421 Colley St) A local favorite in Ghent, Elliott's has built its reputation on its great hamburgers.

Dumbwaiter (117 Tazewell St; mains from $10) This is the place for Mississippi-influenced meals.

GETTING THERE & AROUND

The **Greyhound/Trailways terminal** (☎ 757-627-7500) is several blocks from the downtown waterfront at Monticello and Brambleton Aves. The Amtrak terminal in **Newport News** (☎ 800-872-7245) runs a free Thruway shuttle to downtown Norfolk. **Tidewater Regional Transit** (TRT; ☎ 757-623-7433) has buses serving Virginia Beach and Norfolk. TRT's Norfolk trolley tour runs downtown and into the shopping district of Ghent on its one-hour circuit ($3.50). The **Elizabeth River Ferry** (☎ 757-222-6100; $0.75) links Norfolk and Portsmouth.

COASTAL VIRGINIA

With the exception of neon Virginia Beach, the Virginia coastline is uncluttered, with many hidden-away places to fish, walk and relax. On the Delmarva peninsula are many remote wild refuges, including Chincoteague Island. South of the beach are the equally remote Back Bay National Wildlife Refuge and False Cape State Park.

Virginia Beach

Burgeoning Virginia Beach started with the 1791 Cape Henry Lighthouse. The first oceanfront hotel went up in 1883 and the beach developed as a holiday retreat. Now it attracts young revelers to its crowded 6-mile beach. I-264 runs straight into the beach and the **visitors center** (☎ 800-822-3224; www.vbfun.com; 2100 Parks Ave).

The area's central attraction is, of course, the beach, with its boardwalk bike path and occasional markets and exhibitions. Surfing is permitted at the beach's southern end, near Rudee Inlet, and alongside the 14th St pier.

Other activities include the following:

Lynnhaven Dive Center (☎ 757-481-7949; 1413 N Great Neck Rd) For scuba diving.

Virginia Beach Fishing Center/Cruise (☎ 757-422-5700; 200 Winston Salem Ave; $12) For summer cruises.

Tidewater Adventures (☎ 757-480-1999; 110 W Randall Ave) For kayak ecotours.

Other attractions include the **Virginia Marine Science Museum** (VMSM; ☎ 757-425-3474; 717 General Booth Blvd; adult/child $11/7; 9am-5pm) with hands-on exhibits, an otter habitat and an aviary; it runs dolphin-watching trips June to September ($12). The **Old Coast Guard Station** (☎ 757-422-1587; cnr 24th St & Atlantic Ave; admission $3; 10am-5pm Tue-Sat, noon-5pm Sun, Memorial Day–Oct 1), near the water, has displays on local shipwrecks. Kids'll love the **Ocean Breeze Water Park** (☎ 757-422-4444; 849 General Booth Blvd; adult $19, child 3-11 $15; May-Sep) with its 13 waterslides and giant wave pool.

You couldn't ask for a prettier campground than the bayfront **First Landing State Park** (☎ 757-412-2300; Cape Henry; campsites/cabins $21/80). **Angie's Guest Cottage B&B** (☎ 757-428-4690; 302 24th St; r $50) is also an **HI-AYH Hostel** (HI members/nonmembers $13/15). **Colonial Inn** (☎ 757-428-5370; 2809 Atlantic Ave at 42nd St; r from $99; P) is a clean hotel with all oceanfront rooms, plus an indoor and outdoor pool.

Jewish Mother (☎ 757-422-5430; 3108 Pacific Ave) welcomes all with blintzes, 'penicillin soup,' packed deli sandwiches and monster pies and cakes; a crude stage hosts live music nightly. Get a psychic reading with your organic sandwich at **Heritage Cafe & Deli** (☎ 757-428-0500; 314 Laskin Rd).

Among the myriad tacky clubs and bars between 17th and 23rd Sts around Pacific and Atlantic Aves, **Ocean Eddie's** (☎ 757-425-7742; 14th St Pier) has wild Friday-night bashes to the strains of a country/R & B band, and **Verizon Wireless Virginia Beach Amphitheater** (☎ 757-368-3000; 3550 Cellar Door Way) has bigger acts.

Make sure when booking bus tickets that Virginia Beach is specified as the **Greyhound** (☎ 757-422-2998) terminus. **Virginia Beach Wave** (☎ 757-222-6100; $1), which is a trolley, runs along Atlantic Ave in summer.

Around Virginia Beach

Many natural areas are within easy reach. **Back Bay National Wildlife Refuge** (☎ 757-721-2412) is a wildlife and migratory bird habitat. The 6-mile beach of **False Cape State Park** can be accessed only by bicycle, boat or foot. Primitive **camping** (☎ 757-426-7128; campsites $7)

SUNTANS AND COLONIC IRRIGATIONS?

An unlikely combination at a beach resort, **Edgar Cayce Association for Research and Enlightenment** (☎ 800-333-4499; 215 67th St) is nevertheless an unusual oceanside attraction where you can get the latter after the former. The founder Edgar Cayce was a self-proclaimed psychic of sorts who could put himself in a sleeping, meditative state and answer questions, which became known as 'readings.' Cayce's readings and work emphasized the importance of diet and exercise in treating illnesses; numerous courses of action to cure all ailments from asthma to eczema are recommended. The readings also delve into a more spiritual realm, including parapsychology, astral projection, dreams and auras. An extensive library, classes and courses, wellness therapies, massage treatments, and even a mediation garden are here for followers and curiosity seekers from all walks of life.

requires a permit; bring drinking water. The fascinating **Great Dismal Swamp National Wildlife Refuge** (☎ 757-986-3705), 30 miles southwest of Virginia Beach, is rich in flora and fauna with more than 200 bird species.

Eastern Shore

Across the impressive 17-mile Chesapeake Bay bridge-tunnel ($10) from VB, Virginia's isolated Eastern Shore offers bayside fishing villages and many natural areas on both the marshy bay and Atlantic shore.

Tucked behind windswept Assateague Island (see Maryland, p338), the town of Chincoteague (*shink*-o-teeg), on the island of the same name, is Virginia's principal Eastern Shore destination. A **Virginia Welcome Center** (☎ 757-824-5000) is nearby on US 13, south of the Maryland border. Legendary **Chincoteague Island** is famous for its July roundup, when the wild ponies that inhabit the Assateague Island refuge are led across the channel for annual herd-thinning foal auctions (see below for its most famous foal, Misty). The **chamber of commerce** (☎ 757-336-6161) has great maps for the scenic hiking and biking trails up to and into the **Chincoteague National Wildlife Refuge** (☎ 757-336-6122; $5 per person), which protects migratory waterfowl.

Waterside Motor Inn (☎ 757-336-3434; 3761 S Main St; r from $99; P) has all waterfront rooms, a heated outdoor pool and a small workout room with sauna. **Muller's Ice Cream Parlor** (4034 Main St) has soda-fountain treats, splits and malts.

MISTY OF CHINCOTEAGUE

Chincoteague's most famous attraction is its ponies (actually a breed descended from the wild horses from neighboring Assateague Island), which are auctioned off every July after their ceremonious swim across the channel. One particular pony caught the fancy of author Marguerite Henry, who came to see the famous pony swim in 1946 as part of her book research. She made friends with a Chincoteague family who purchased the beloved pony Misty – and Henry eventually acquired the pony for herself. The pony and family were immortalized in the *Misty of Chincoteague* novel, and many American schoolchildren grow up reading about Misty and her famous foal, Stormy, and their adventures on this rugged Virginian island. Misty passed away in 1976, but visitors can see her stuffed and mounted in front of Henry's former house.

To learn more about local Misty attractions and the annual pony penning (last Wednesday & Thursday in July), contact the **chamber of commerce** (☎ 757-336-6161; www.chincoteague.com), or check out your local bookstore for the Misty of Chincoteague series.

THE PIEDMONT

The Virginia plain is perhaps the least interesting part of an attraction-filled state. But if you are prepared to drive you will find several gems, especially examples of the architectural genius of Thomas Jefferson.

Charlottesville

Virginia's Cambridge, Charlottesville is a smart university town in a beautiful setting. As the home of Thomas Jefferson and the University of Virginia, C-ville draws visitors to its impressive architecture and magnolia-lined streets set against a Blue Ridge Mountain backdrop. The helpful **Charlottesville/Albemarle Convention & Visitors Bureau** (☎ 877-386-1102; www.charlottesvilletourism.org), on Rte 20S near I-64 exit 121A, features a *Thomas Jefferson at Monticello* exhibit, and sells tickets for area attractions (block passes $22).

MONTICELLO & AROUND

East of town, Thomas Jefferson's magnificent **home** (☎ 804-984-9822; adult $13, child 6-11 $6; Mar-Oct 8am-5pm, Nov-Feb 9am-4:30pm), featured on the nickel coin, embodies its resident designer: Jefferson's quirky inventions and French-inspired innovations are scattered throughout. Jefferson's tomb is downhill; its inscription, noting the author of the Declaration of Independence and Virginia's religious freedom statute, and founder of the University of Virginia, was chosen by the man himself.

Daily specialty tours include a plantation community tour exposing the complicated past of the slave owner who declared all men to be equal.

Keep in mind that Monticello (mon-ta-*chel*-o) is one of Virginia's premier historic attractions; arrive early to avoid long lines. Frequent shuttles run from the parking lot up the hill. Tours are also offered of the nearby 1784 **Michie Tavern** (☎ 804-977-1234), and James Monroe's 535-acre estate, **Ash Lawn-Highland** (☎ 804-293-9539), 2.5 miles east of Monticello. A combo ticket for all three is $24, and the Jefferson-era tavern is best known for providing luncheon buffets in the **Ordinary** (around $10).

UNIVERSITY OF VIRGINIA

At the west end of town, the grounds (never 'campus') of the **University of Virginia** (UVA), which were founded by Thomas Jefferson, revolve around the stately Rotunda, a scale replica of Rome's Pantheon. UVA's **Bayly Art Museum** (☎ 804-924-3592; 🕑 1-5pm Tue-Sun) hosts traveling exhibits featuring works by the likes of Rodin.

SLEEPING

Charlottesville KOA (☎ 434-296-9881; 3825 Red Hill Rd; campsites/Kabins $20/36) This motel is southwest on County Rd 708. Most budget chain motels are at interstate exits miles from downtown, and inbound traffic can be fierce.

English Inn (☎ 434-971-9900; 2000 Morton Dr; r from $75) This is a tidy motel with a great pool, near the Rte 29 and 250 Bypass.

Guesthouses (☎ 434-979-7264) This reservation service provides cute cottages as an alternative to lodging, and many have full kitchens.

EATING

Inexpensive student eateries crowd the Corner, the busy commercial district adjacent to UVA grounds.

Miller's (☎ 434-971-8511; 109 W Main St) An unpretentious jazz dive with smoke, junk food and character, Miller's is a wildly popular college band venue, but has grown weary of its famous ties to the Dave Matthews Band.

C&O Restaurant (☎ 434-971-7044; 515 E Water St; mains $12) Here you'll find excellent French bistro cuisine in a funky dive that was once a train workers' boardinghouse.

Hardware Store (☎ 434-977-1518; 316 E Main St; mains $18) This is a city landmark, with a great menu and heaps of memorabilia.

Farmers market (🕑 Wed & Sat) Near the Hardware Store, this market is held in the public parking lot behind the mall.

ENTERTAINMENT

There's varied and lively nightlife and performing arts in town; check the free *C-ville Weekly* for exhaustive listings. Many bars and clubs along the downtown pedestrian mall feature local bands.

GETTING THERE & AROUND

Charlottesville is easily accessible by **Amtrak** (☎ 434-296-4559; 810 W Main St) and the **Greyhound/Trailways terminal** (☎ 434-295-5131; 310 W Main St). A free trolley runs through the historic district.

Lynchburg

Founded along the James River by an enterprising Quaker ferryman in 1757, Lynchburg is a pleasant enough city with a comfortably gritty downtown and refined hilltop historic districts. It's a convenient base from which to visit Appomattox. The **visitors center** (☎ 800-732-5821; www.discoverlynchburg.org; 216 12th St) is near the Community Market.

Up 139 steep steps from Church St, the landmark **Monument Terrace** holds a war memorial to the city's Confederate soldiers. Many historic buildings line Court House Hill, one of the city's seven noted hills. **Poplar Forest** (☎ 804-525-1806; adult $7, child 6-16 $1; 🕑 Apr-Nov 10am-4pm), a few miles southwest of downtown, preserves Thomas Jefferson's summer retreat – a mini-Monticello.

A cluster of chain motels surrounds the intersection of Hwys 29 and 501. **Community Market** (1219 Main St; 7am-2pm) is the third-oldest US farmers market, and offers a variety of food stalls, including the excellent **Philippine Delight.** The **Farm Basket** (☎ 434-528-1107; 2008 Langhorne Rd; dishes $7) has a small, always-packed restaurant, and prepares lunch boxes.

Lynchburg is serviced by **Greyhound/Trailways** (☎ 434-846-6614) and **Amtrak** (☎ 434-847-8247), both located at 825 Kemper St.

Appomattox & Around

Robert E Lee surrendered the Army of Northern Virginia to Ulysses S Grant at Appomattox. Today the compact village is preserved within a 1300-acre park as **Appomattox Court House National Historic Park**, which houses a museum and NPS **visitors center** (☎ 434-352-8987; adult $4, child 16 & under free for grounds & buildings; 🕑 year-round) within the evocative pedestrian-only village. It provides maps of 27 surrounding restored buildings, including McLean House. See the boxed text opposite.

Around 25 miles east of Appomattox in Farmville, the **Robert Russa Moton Museum**

SURRENDER AT APPOMATTOX

On April 9, 1865 (Palm Sunday), in the modest house of Wilmer McLean at Appomattox Court House, Lee, resplendent in his best uniform with his sword by his side, sat down to talk with Grant, who was dressed in a private's tunic with lieutenant general's stars pinned to its shoulders. Traveller, Lee's horse, munched on the grass outside.

After a pause, Grant opened his notebook, and in straightforward fashion spelled out the terms. These were generous, and included the lines that would make it impossible for acts of vengeance to be taken against former Confederate soldiers. After an exchange of military salutes, Lee returned to Traveller and rode away.

Grant sat down in front of his tent and reminisced about the Mexican War, not outwardly savoring the moment of victory. Lee rode past his troops, many of whom had tears streaming down their faces. In the following days the once-proud army of northern Virginia stacked up its arms, formally surrendered, and wandered away to recommence their shattered lives.

(www.moton.org) tells the story of the beginnings of the Civil Rights movement within the high school that first pressed for desegregation in 1951. The **Farmville Chamber of Commerce** (☎ 434-392-3939; 116 N Main St) provides directions.

Holliday Lake State Park (☎ 804-248-6308; campsites/cabins from $14/90) near Appomattox, offers seasonal camping.

SHENANDOAH VALLEY

The beautiful Shenandoah Valley lies between the Blue Ridge and Allegheny Mountains. The Shenandoah River starts near Lexington, flowing northeast to the Potomac. The area was settled in the early 18th century by Scotch-Irish and German families. A vital Confederate troop corridor and food source, the fertile valley saw much Civil War action and is studded with historic sites.

Valley towns are accessible from I-81, and the Blue Ridge Parkway provides a scenic alternative. But the true flavor of the region lies in the wilder mountain areas, beyond the towns and the beaten-path parkway.

George Washington & Jefferson National Forests

Stretching the entire western edge of Virginia, these two mammoth **forests** (www.southernregion.fs.fed.us/gwj; campsites from $15, primitive camping free) comprise more than 1562 sq miles of mountainous terrain bordering the Shenandoah Valley, and contain challenging to easy trail networks, which include 300 miles of the **Appalachian Trail** (AT) and mountain-biking routes. Hundreds of developed campgrounds are scattered throughout. **USDA Forest Service headquarters** (☎ 540-265-5100; 5162 Valleypointe Parkway), off the Blue Ridge Parkway in Roanoke, oversees a dozen ranger stations along the ranges. You can also pick up information at the **Natural Bridge Visitor Center** (☎ 540-291-1806) across from the Natural Bridge entrance.

Shenandoah National Park

The centerpiece of this famously beautiful **park** (☎ 540-999-2243; www.nps.gov/shen; $10/5 vehicles/cyclists) is **Skyline Dr**, which crosses the spine of the Blue Ridge Mountains 105 miles from Front Royal in the north to Rockfish Gap in the south. It's spectacular in spring and fall in particular, but expensive and slow (35mph limit, congested in peak seasons).

Two visitors centers, **Dickey Ridge** (☎ 540-635-3566; Mile 4.6 in the north) and **Byrd** (☎ 540-999-3500; Mile 51 in the south), have maps, backcountry permits, and information on hiking (the AT frequently crosses Skyline), horseback riding, hang gliding, biking (only on public roads) and other recreational activities.

Camping is available at four **NPS campgrounds**: Mathews Arm at (Mile 22.1), Big Meadows (Mile 51.3), Lewis Mountain (Mile 57.5), and Loft Mountain (Mile 79.5) at $14 per day, with laundry and showers, and requires registering a free backcountry permit with a visitors center. Reservations are required only at Big Meadows May to November (☎ 800-365-CAMP). For not-so-rough lodging, try **Skyline Lodge** (☎ 703-242-0315; Mile 41.7; r from $79), and **Lewis Mountain** (☎ 800-999-4714; Mile 57.5; cabins from $60/85 weekdays/weekends).

Front Royal & Around

Once a raucous 18th-century packhorse stopover, Front Royal is today a natural

I WANT MY MOUNTAIN TV

Bo and Luke Duke may be long gone from Hazzard County, cutting albums and performing on Broadway, but the *Dukes of Hazzard* spirit lives on in a tiny town called Sperryville just off Skyline Dr. Coming down the mountain, travelers can't miss the Day-Glo orange of the General Lee parked in front of **Cooter's Place** (www.cootersplace.com). That's right, Cooter, also known as actor Ben Jones, runs this shrine to all things Dukedom, which doubles as an excellent local bluegrass venue and front for Cooter's Garage Band. Inside are thousands of photos of the TV cast, plus every imaginable gadget made in the image of Hazzard County: Uncle Jesse salt-and-pepper shakers, Daisy Duke wind sockets, Boss Hogg punching bags, Roscoe P Coltrane beverage coasters and a wide-screen TV playing a constant loop of *Dukes of Hazzard* shows. Truly a religious experience for anyone who remembers jumping through mom and dad's car windows as a kid.

Heading southeast toward Schuyler, you can almost hear the strains of 'G'night John boy' coming over Walton's Mountain, boyhood home of author Earl Hamner. Though they didn't film here, there's a small museum with sets and memorabilia from the TV show, plus a thirty-minute behind-the-scenes film about the cast members.

starting point for the Shenandoah National Park. Stop in to the extremely friendly and well-stocked **visitors center** (☎ 800-338-9758; 414 E Main St) and load up on all things Virginia.

Chester House B&B (☎ 540-635-3937, 800-621-0441; www.chesterhouse.com; 43 Chester St; r from $120; P) is a beautiful home in which to rest up before going down Skyline Dr. Otherwise, you can try the **Front Royal/Washington DC West KOA** (☎ 540-635-2741; I-81 exit 6; campsites/Kabins $28/39). **Grapes & Grains** (☎ 540-636-8379; 401 E Main St; dishes $10) serves lunch and dinner.

The **New Market Battlefield Historical Park** (☎ 540-740-3101; I-64 exit 264) has a Hall of Valor dedicated to the bravery that the Virginia Military Institute (VMI) cadets displayed during the Battle of New Market. The **Shenandoah Valley Travel Association** (☎ 540-740-3132; www.shenandoah.org; Rte 211 W, I-81 exit 264) highlights valley attractions.

Staunton & Around

At the junction of I-81 and I-64, near the junction of Blue Ridge Parkway and Skyline Dr, Staunton (*stan*-tun) is a picturesque town perched among steep hills and lovely architecture. A free **trolley** (⏲ Mon-Sat 10am-6pm) helps navigate those hills.

A unique living-history farm, **Frontier Culture Museum** (☎ 540-332-7850; overlooking I-81 exit 222; adult $8, child 6-12 $4; ⏲ mid-Mar–Nov 9am-5pm, Dec–mid-Mar 10am-4pm) is where authentic historic farm buildings from Germany, Ireland and England have been transported to compare and contrast with an American frontier farm that's also on the sprawling grounds.

Woodrow Wilson Birthplace & Museum (☎ 540-885-0897; 18-24 N Coalter St; adult $7, child 6-12 $2.50; ⏲ Mar-Nov 9am-5pm, Dec-Feb 10am-4pm) reveals the stately 1846 Greek Revival house and garden of the 28th president. **Blackfriars Playhouse** (☎ 540-885-5588; 10 S Market St; performances from $10) hosts Shenandoah Shakespeare performances in an intimate theater-in-the-round.

Walnut Hills Campground (☎ 540-337-3920; 391 Walnut Hills Rd; campsites from $17) in nearby Mint Spring, is an excellent, well-equipped site. **Thornrose House** (☎ 540-885-7026; www.thornrosehouse.com; 531 Thornrose Ave; r from $75; P) is a really beautiful B&B with a sweeping porch overlooking picturesque **Gypsy Hill Park**, which has open-air concerts in the summer.

Mrs Rowe's (☎ 540-886-1833; I-81 exit 222; mains $3-15) is a Staunton institution well-known for its rib-stickin' Southern home-cooking and sumptuous coconut-cream pies. **Wrights Dairy-Rite** (☎ 540-886-0435; 346 Greenville Ave; mains $8), another Staunton original, is straight outta *Happy Days* with its curb service drive-in, which has been operating since 1952.

Staunton is serviced by **Amtrak** (☎ 800-872-7245; 1 Middlebrook Ave) and **Greyhound/Trailways** (☎ 540-886-2424; 1211 Richmond Rd).

Ten miles north of Staunton, near Mt Solon, **Natural Chimneys Regional Park** (☎ 540-350-2510; campsites $12) features a remarkable rock formation and camping. **Wintergreen** (☎ 800-325-2200), 16 miles southeast, offers skiing (1000ft drop) and snowboarding in winter.

.exington & Around

Гhe last resting place of Stonewall Jackson ınd Robert E Lee, this graceful historic own is also renowned for two academies ıccounting for nearly half the town's popuation. The excellent **visitors center** (☎ 540-63-3777; 106 E Washington St; 9am-5pm) has free parking for day-trippers.

Virginia Military Institute (☎ 540-464-7207; etcher Ave; 9am-5pm), founded in 1839, ıouses a free museum on the school's hisory. **George C Marshall Museum** (☎ 540-463-7103; VMI Parade Ground; adult/child $3/1.50; 9am-5pm), on campus, honors the creator of the Marshall Plan for post-WWII European reconstruction. A full-dress parade takes place most Fridays at 4:30pm during the school year.

Colonnaded Washington & Lee University, founded in 1749, contains **Lee Chapel and Museum** (☎ 540-463-8768; admission free), with Lee interred downstairs and his horse Traveller buried outside. **Stonewall Jackson House** (☎ 540-463-2552; 8 E Washington St; adult/child $5/2.50; Mon-Sat 9am-5pm, Sun 1-5pm), a restored 1801 building, houses the general's possessions and period pieces. Jackson is buried in nearby Lexington Cemetery.

Overnight Guests (☎ 540-463-3075; 216 W Washington St) is Virginia's best lodging bargain, at $10 per bed. Chain motels are found at I-81 exit 195 and I-64 exit 55. **Historic Country Inns** (☎ 540-463-2044; 11 N Main St; r $90-170) operates two inns downtown and one outside town. **Blue Heron Cafe** (4 E Washington St) has creative vegetarian mains from $8.

Outside Lexington, horse shows and the Virginia Horse Festival (April) are held at the **Virginia Horse Center** (☎ 540-463-4300). Scenic Rte 39 retraces an old stagecoach trail along a stream and over **Goshen Pass** to mineral-spring resorts in Bath County, including the preeminent **Homestead** (☎ 800-838-1766; r from $230) resort in Hot Springs; contact the Hwy 220 **visitors center** (☎ 540-839-5409) for some less expensive alternatives.

discoverbath.com

Natural Bridge

Bypass the oddball museums of the tacky **Natural Bridge** resort and head straight for the awesome 215ft-high natural **arch** (☎ 540-291-2121; adult $10, child 6-15 $5), which was discovered by a young George Washington on a scouting mission (look close to see his initials carved into the side). The rushing waterfalls beyond the arch provide a scenic backdrop

VIRGINIA'S NATURAL CAVERNS

Particular to the Shenandoah Valley are a handful of cavernous attractions: chilly caves with bizarre stalactites and stalagmites, dizzying light displays and crazy rock formations like pipe organs, oriental gardens and even bacon strips. Though some push the line on tackiness and political correctness, they are nevertheless a wild way to see Virginia's rocky underbelly.

At the northern tip of Skyline Dr in Front Royal, **Skyline Caverns** (☎ 800-296-4545; www.skylinecaverns.com; Rte 340; adult $12, child 7-13 $6; Mon-Fri 9am-5pm, Sat-Sun until 6pm) boasts rare, white-spiked anthodites (mineral formations that look like prickly sea urchins) and a 37ft rainbow wall. The anthodites here are the only publicly viewable ones in the US. The spiritualness of the caverns is overshadowed by a preachy light show midway through. The granddaddy of them all is **Luray Caverns** (☎ 540-743-6551; www.luraycaverns.com; I81 exit 264; adult $16, child 7-13 $7; 9am-6pm, until 7pm in summer). **Luray Caverns Motel West** (☎ 540-743-4536; Hwy 211 Bypass; r from $60) has incredible mountain views.

Endless Caverns (☎ 800-544-2283, 540-896-2283; www.endlesscaverns.com; I81 exit 264; adult $12, child 3-12 $6; 9am-5pm, until 6pm summer) is nearby. Near Monticello, a tour of **Shenandoah Caverns** (☎ 540-477-3115; www.shenandoahcaverns.com; I81 exit 269; adult $17.50, child 6-14 $7; 9am-5pm, until 6pm in summer) begins in the only cavern elevator, leading to the odd bacon strip and Scottish castle formations. There's also an antique window display exhibit, featuring fantastical, nostalgic window dressings from prominent US stores. **Grand Caverns** (☎ 888-430-2283; 181 exit 235; adult $15, child 3-12 $8; daily Apr-Oct, weekends only Nov-Mar) is the nation's oldest show cave, steeped in Civil War history and enormous stalagmites with rippling flowstone. **Crystal Caverns** (☎ 540-465-5884; www.waysideofva.com/crystalcaverns; I81 exit 298; adult $8, child $6; 9am-5pm) leads visitors in period costume and lantern, and relates tales of Civil War skirmishes above. Admission price includes entry to the adjacent Stonewall Jackson Museum.

for a picnic lunch, and there are **caverns** (☎ 540-291-2121; adult $18, child 5-15 $10; ⌚ Mar-Dec) onsite, but you can skip the preachy 'drama of creation' light show nightly. The nearby **Yogi Bear Jellystone Park** (☎ 540-291-2727; www.campnbr.com; Natural Bridge Station; campsites/cabins/deluxe cabins $22/45/90; two-night minimum in summer) is a great camping resort for families and single travelers, with waterfront and wooded accommodation options, a swimming lake with beach and outdoor pool, a stocked trout pond, canoe and tube rentals and an air-conditioned rec room. Hotel accommodations can be found off I-81 exit 180/180A.

A **National Forest Service ranger station** (☎ 540-291-2189), across from the resort, provides information about recreation and camping in nearby forest service areas, including $10 sites at Cave Mountain Lake, 8 miles south.

BLUE RIDGE HIGHLANDS & SOUTHWEST

The southwestern tip of Virginia is the most rugged part of the state and still retains a frontier feel. It has many natural attractions, including the stunning drive along the Blue Ridge Parkway and many eclectic towns evoking quintessential small-town America, where you'll always find strains of bluegrass in the air.

Blue Ridge Parkway

The Blue Ridge Parkway traverses the southern Appalachian ridge from Shenandoah National Park at Mile 0 to North Carolina's Great Smoky Mountains National Park at Mile 469. Wildflowers bloom in spring, and fall colors are spectacular, but watch out for foggy days; no guardrails can make for mighty hairy driving. High-quality NPS campgrounds and visitors centers are open May to October. To break up the scenery, detour often.

A worthwhile detour for gritty, Friday-night bluegrass jamborees is the tiny town of **Floyd** and the famous **Floyd's Country Store** (206 S Locust St; adult $2, child under 3 free). Further south, **Mabry Mill** (☎ 540-952-2947), at Meadows of Dan, is one of the most photogenic objects in the state. Galax hosts the **Old Fiddlers' Convention** (☎ 540-238-8130), the oldest and largest event of its kind in the nation, each August.

The parkway has nine **campgrounds** (☎ 800-933-7275), four in Virginia:

Otter Creek (Mile 61) Year-round.
Peaks of Otter (Mile 86) Seasonal.
Roanoke Mountain (Mile 120) Seasonal.
Rocky Knob (Mile 167) Seasonal, plus full-facility cabins.

All sites are $9 (cabins extra). **Peaks of Otter Lodge** (☎ 540-586-4357), a very scenic spot, has year-round lakeside accommodations and buffet dining. **HI Blue Ridge Country** (☎ 540-236-4962), at Mile 214.5 on the parkway, offers hostel-style dorm lodging with a view ($14/15 members/nonmembers).

Roanoke

Illuminated by its giant star (the local equivalent of the Hollywood sign), Roanoke is the big city in these parts, with a compact set of attractions based around the great downtown **farmers market** (213 Market St; ⌚ Mon-Sat 7:30am-5pm). For maps and local information, check out the **Roanoke Valley Visitor Information Center** (☎ 540-345-8622, 800-635-5535; www.visitroanokeva.com; 114 Market St), which is across the street from the market, and the **Blue Ridge Parkway Visitor Center** (☎ 540-427-5871; Mile 115 off the Parkway; ⌚ May-Nov 9am-5pm).

Center in the Sq (☎ 540-342-5700; www.centerinthesquare.org; 1 Market Sq; ⌚ Tue-Sun) is the downtown focus, housing five attractions, including a science museum, theater, planetarium, local-history museum, and free art museum showcasing the work of folk and local artists. The nearby **Virginia Museum of Transportation** (☎ 540-342-5670; 303 Norfolk Ave SW; adult $7.50, child 3-11 $5.50; ⌚ Mon-Fri 11am-4pm, Sat 10am-5pm, Sun from 1pm) will thrill kids and train spotters alike, and the **Harrison Museum of African American Culture** (☎ 540-345-4818; 523 Harrison Ave; admission free; ⌚ Tue-Sun 1-5pm) chronicles the historical impact of African-American culture in the area.

Roanoke Appalachian Trail Club organizes hikes, Blue Ridge Bicycle Club has year-round rides, and there's cross-country skiing at Mountain Lake (☎ 540-626-7121); the visitors center has a contact list.

Roanoke Mountain Campground (☎ 540-982-9242; Blue Ridge Parkway Mile 120.4; sites $12; May-Nov), which has 74 sites, is maintained by the NPS. There's also **Sleep Inn Tanglewood** (☎ 540-772-1500; intersection of Hwy 419 & Hwy 220; r from $65). **Hotel Roanoke** (☎ 540-985-5900; 110 Shenandoah Ave NE; r from $140), downtown, has faithfully integrated 1882 features into an ultramodern convention hotel.

City Market houses local vendors offering pizza, sushi, burritos and more, with counter seating. Surrounding restaurants and cafés offer more choices, including seafood, Brazilian and vegetarian cuisine, within a block. The beloved hole-in-the-wall **Texas Tavern** (114 W Church Ave) is a must – you'll have to nab one of the few seats. The chili bowls ($3) are great.

Mill Mountain Zoo (☎ 540-343-3241; adult $6.50, child 3-12 $4.30; 10am-4:30pm) and an adjacent wildflower garden are perched on a hilltop near the Blue Ridge Parkway, and are perfect for the kids. Directly next to it is the **Roanoke Star** with a breathtaking view of the city. **Virginia's Explore Park** (☎ 540-427-1800; adult $8, child 3-11 $4.50; May-Oct Wed-Sat 10am-5pm, Sun from noon) depicts local living-history spanning three centuries.

Around Roanoke

The tiny town of Bedford suffered the most casualties per capita during the war, and hence was chosen to host this eerily moving tribute, **National D-Day Memorial** (☎ 540-586-3329; US Rte 460 & Rte 122 in Bedford; $10 per car; h 10am-5pm). Among its towering arch and English flower garden is a cast of bronze figures re-enacting the 'storming of the beach' complete with bursts of water symbolizing the hail of bullets the soldiers faced.

Twenty miles southeast of Roanoke, **Booker T Washington National Monument** (☎ 540-721-2094; Rte 122; 9am-5pm) is a re-created tobacco farm honoring the former slave who became an international and controversial African-American leader.

Twenty-five miles southeast, **Smith Mountain Lake State Park** (☎ 540-297-6066; www.state.va.us/~dcr; 1235 State Park Rd) is the state's second-largest body of water, and comes alive in summer with a plethora of biking, hiking and fishing activities, as well as cool waterfront **cabins** (☎ 800-933-PARK; from $93).

Mt Rogers National Recreation Area

You'll find ample hiking, fishing and cross-country skiing in these ancient hardwood forests surrounding Virginia's highest peaks. The **park headquarters** (☎ 540-783-5196), on Rte 16 in Marion, offers maps and recreation directories. The NPS operates five **campgrounds** in the area; contact park headquarters.

Abingdon

A lovely theater and inn are the centerpieces of this cultural oasis in southwestern Virginia. Abingdon retains fine Federal and Victorian architecture in its 20-block historic district. The **visitors center** (☎ 800-435-3440; www.abingdon.com/tourism; 335 Cummings St) has exhibit rooms on local history.

Founded during the Depression, **Barter Theatre** (☎ 540-628-3991; www.bartertheatre.com; 133 W Main St; performances from $20) earned its name from audiences trading food for performances – 'ham for Hamlet.' Since then, such actors as Gregory Peck and Ernest Borgnine have cut their teeth on Barter's stage.

The **Virginia Creeper Trail** (www.vacreepertrail.org), named for the railroad that once ran this route, travels 33 miles between Whitetop Station (3576ft), near the North Carolina border, and downtown Abingdon. Several outfitters rent bikes, organize outings and run uphill shuttles, including **Virginia Creeper Trail Bike Shop** (☎ 276-676-2552; 201 Pecan St) in Abingdon, and **Adventure Damascus** (☎ 888-595-2453; 128 W Laurel Ave), in Damascus.

Abingdon hosts the bluegrass Virginia Highlands Festival over the first two weeks in August. **Camberley's Martha Washington Inn** (☎ 540-628-3161; 150 W Main St; r from $169; P), opposite the Barter, is the region's premier historic hotel and worth a splurge. The **Tavern** (☎ 276-628-1118; 222 E Main St; mains $8; Mon-Sat), in Abingdon's oldest building, has a history as innovative as its menu. **Starving Artist Cafe** (☎ 276-628-8445; 134 Wall St; mains $5-15) is a hidden gem by the railroad tracks, with overstuffed sandwiches named for famous writers and artists, and has monster homemade pies.

Coal Country

Far beyond the interstate world, Virginia's southwest tip is rugged Appalachian territory. Big Stone Gap is a no-frills mountain town, despite some nicer homes left from its entrepreneurial coal-hauling and railroading heyday. The **Virginia Coalfield Tourism Authority** (☎ 888-798-2386; 311 Wood Ave; Mon-Fri 9am-5pm) distributes information about the 125-mile Heart of Appalachia bike route through the backcountry.

Cumberland Gap National Historical Park

This break in the Appalachian mountains is where Virginia, Tennessee and Kentucky meet. In the late 18th century some 200,000 pioneers crossed this gap along the Wilderness Rd. The **visitors center** (☎ 606-248-2482) is across the border. The 20,000-acre park contains 70 miles of hiking trails (backpacking permits required).

MARYLAND

With her beaches, Chesapeake Bay, mountains and historical firsts, Maryland is a snapshot of America and all its treasures. The central portion almost surrounds the nation's capital and acts as a dormitory and service center for DC's workforce. The west offers all forms of outdoor activities and much for history buffs to explore, such as the C&O Canal and the Civil War battlefield of Antietam. It is the Chesapeake Bay region for which the state is most famous – this water playground includes the revitalized seafaring city of Baltimore, the world-renowned sailing center of Annapolis, watermen communities along the bay's fringe, plus ample fishing, crabbing and just about every water-based pursuit imaginable.

History

George Calvert (Lord Baltimore) received a royal grant to establish a Catholic colony in what was then northern Virginia, and in 1634 he settled in St Mary's City, which prospered as the capital of the new Maryland colony until 1695, when the colony's capital was moved to the superior port of Annapolis.

In 1729 the settlement of Baltimore was founded as a tobacco and flour-milling center, with a fine harbor and access to first-rate shipbuilding timber. Baltimore developed rapidly as colonial America's shipping center, but was bombarded by British ships in the War of 1812. Soldiers kept the flag flying at Fort McHenry and resisted the attack, and the event inspired a Maryland lawyer, Francis Scott Key, to write a poem called 'The Star-Spangled Banner,' which later became the national anthem.

Maryland prospered in the early 19th century as a result of tobacco and wheat plantations, Chesapeake Bay fisheries and seaports, and railroads pushing west. During the Civil War, an 1862 Confederate invasion of Maryland was halted at the bloody battle of Antietam. Maryland abolished slavery in 1864.

After the war Maryland continued its Baltimore-based industrial development. European immigration swelled the workforce, but African-Americans continued to experience discrimination. The exponential growth of the nearby national capital, pushing its suburban population and development deep into Maryland, is a large factor in the state's present-day economy.

MARYLAND FACTS

Nicknames Old Line State, Free State
Population 5,458,137 (18th)
Area 12,407 sq miles (42nd)
Admitted to Union April 28, 1788 (7th)
Capital city Annapolis (population 35,838)
Other cities Baltimore (651,154), Frederick (52,767)
State motto Manly deeds, womanly words
Birthplace of Frederick Douglass (1817–95), Babe Ruth (1895–1948), Billie Holiday (1915–59), John Wilkes Booth (1838–65), Frank Zappa (1940–93), 'Pope of Trash' John Waters (b 1946)
Famous for Baltimore Orioles, crab cakes

Information

Maryland's **Office of Tourism Development** (☎ 410-767-3400, 800-543-1036; www.mdwelcome.org; 217 E Redwood St, Baltimore, MD 21202) has 'welcome centers' throughout the state with maps and guides. State sales tax is 5%.

National & State Parks

From sandy beaches with wild-roaming ponies, to lush forests with parts of the Appalachian Trail running through, Maryland's parks are sure to provide a memorable outdoor adventure. For a comprehensive listing of all parks, contact the **Maryland Department of Natural Resources** (☎ 877-620-8367; www.dnr.state.md.us/publiclands; 580 Taylor Ave Tawes State Office Building, Annapolis, MD 21401) or the **NPS** (www.nps.gov/parks.html).

Activities

Maryland's exceptional geography allows for a variety of activities, whether it's skiing and snow tubing at the state's only ski resort in western Maryland, sailing and fishing on the Chesapeake Bay, or jet skiing and other leisurely beach pursuits on the Atlantic Ocean. Hunting deer and waterfowl is as popular as water sports, whether it's deer or waterfowl. Extreme sports such as rock climbing, white-water rafting and challenging hiking are known throughout the western portion of the state. Central Maryland indulges in a taste of everything, from sportfishing, canoeing, and exceptional flat biking excursions along scenic paths. The Eastern Shore is the main hunting destination, but also enjoys less aerobic pursuits such as pier fishing, bay and ocean cruises, and bike trails.

BALTIMORE

Baltimore's dramatic and continuing redevelopment has transformed the gritty city into an exciting historical and modern destination worthy of a few days' exploration. The Inner Harbor's waterfront promenade is the main attraction here, along with distinct neighborhoods bursting with personality. The city's undeniable importance in shaping American history – from the birthplace of the national anthem to underground railroad hideaways – is highlighted in numerous attractions, and there's plenty of entertainment for both children and adults. It's a great hardworking, ball-playing, no-nonsense US city where blood largely runs blue, and citizens are eager to welcome visitors with a friendly 'Hey Hon.'

History

After the Revolutionary War, Baltimore's shipyards became famous for a new breed of ship – fast, two-masted schooners called Baltimore Clippers. Baltimore became the second-largest city in the USA, its ships plying trade routes to Europe, the Caribbean and South America.

Baltimore suffered no damage in the Civil War, but in 1904 a warehouse fire engulfed its business district, destroying 1500 buildings. Undaunted, Baltimore's wealthy financed a recovery that continued until the Great Depression. Thereafter Baltimore struggled with growing social problems, and following the 1968 murder of civil rights leader Martin Luther King Jr, mobs burned and looted the city. Baltimore's transformation since then into a lively, attraction-filled destination is an urban-renewal success story.

Orientation

The Inner Harbor is the heart of tourist activity. Downtown's business district is immediately north and west of the Inner Harbor, climbing uphill to the swank Mt Vernon district. East of the Inner Harbor (accessible by water taxi) are Little Italy, Fells Point and Canton. The Camden Yards Sports Complex borders the Inner Harbor to the West. Federal Hill is south of the Inner Harbor.

Information

BOOKSTORES

Barnes & Noble (Power Plant, Inner Harbor) Massive bookstore chain.
Book Thing (2645 N Charles St) Free books.

EMERGENCY

Emergency number (☎ 911) For police, ambulance, fire.
Poison Center (☎ 800-222-1222)

INTERNET ACCESS

Enoch Pratt Free Library (☎ 410-396-5430; 400 Cathedral St) This granddaddy of a library is the only venue in town with Internet access.

MEDIA

88.1 FM WYPR National Public Radio.
89.7 FM WTMD Local Towson University station; great alternative music.
103.1 FM WRNR Alternative rock.
106.5 FM WWMX Modern pop and rock.
Baltimore Gay Paper (www.bgp.org) Free biweekly.
Baltimore Sun (www.sunspot.net) Daily city newspaper.
City Paper (www.citypaper.com) Free weekly with extensive entertainment listings and restaurants.

MEDICAL SERVICES

Johns Hopkins Hospital (☎ 410-955-5000; 600 N Wolfe St)
Maryland General Hospital (☎ 800-492-5538; 22 S Greene St)
Mercy Medical Center (☎ 410-332-9000; 301 St Paul Pl)
University of Maryland Medical Center (☎ 410-328-6971; 655 W Baltimore St)

MONEY

American Express (100 E Pratt St)

POST

Baltimore main branch (900 E Fayette St; 🕒 8:30am-5pm Mon-Fri, until 4pm Sat)

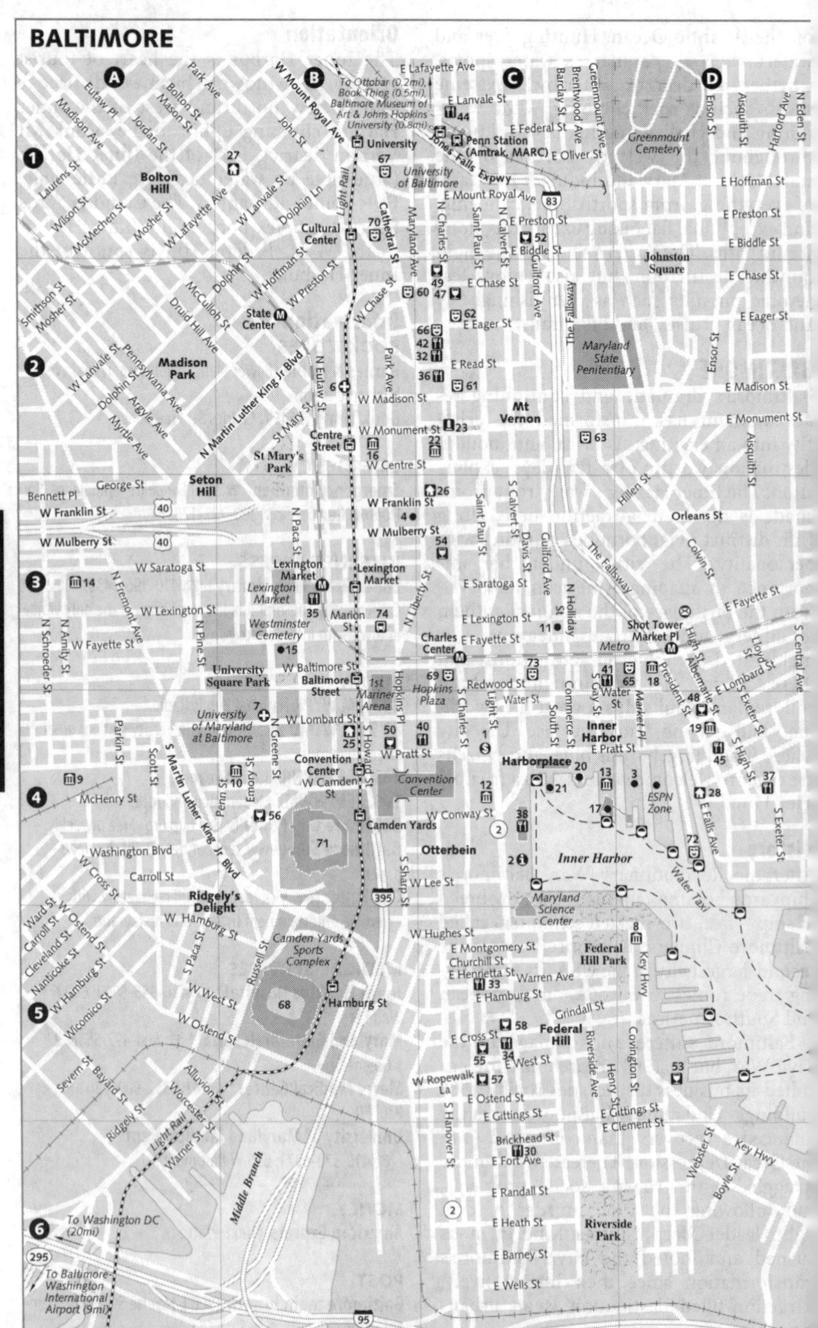
BALTIMORE
A
B
C
D
1
2
3
4
5
6
To Ottobar (0.2mi), Book Thing (0.5mi), Baltimore Museum of Art & Johns Hopkins University (0.8mi)
E Lafayette Ave
E Lanvale St
E Federal St
E Oliver St
Penn Station (Amtrak, MARC)
Jones Falls Expwy
University
University of Baltimore
E Mount Royal Ave
83
Greenmount Cemetery
Greenmount Ave
Brentwood Ave
Barclay St
Ensor St
Asquith St
Harford Ave
N Eden St
E Hoffman St
E Preston St
E Biddle St
E Chase St
E Eager St
E Read St
E Madison St
E Monument St
Johnston Square
Eutaw Pl
Madison Ave
Park Ave
Bolton St
Mason St
Jordan St
John St
W Mount Royal Ave
Laurens St
Wilson St
McMechen St
Mosher St
Bolton Hill
W Lafayette Ave
W Lanvale St
Dolphin Ln
Light Rail
Cultural Center
Cathedral St
Maryland Ave
N Charles St
Saint Paul St
N Calvert St
Guilford Ave
The Fallsway
Maryland State Penitentiary
Smithson St
W Hoffman St
W Preston St
W Chase St
State Center
McCulloh St
Druid Hill Ave
Madison Park
W Lanvale St
Dolphin St
Pennsylvania Ave
Argyle Ave
Myrtle Ave
N Martin Luther King Jr Blvd
N Eutaw St
Park Ave
W Madison St
W Monument St
Mt Vernon
St Mary St
St Mary's Park
Centre Street
W Centre St
Seton Hill
George St
Bennett Pl
W Franklin St
W Mulberry St
40
W Franklin St
W Mulberry St
Hillen St
Orleans St
Colvin St
The Fallsway
N Paca St
Saint Paul St
S Calvert St
Davis St
Guilford Ave
N Holliday St
W Saratoga St
N Fremont Ave
Lexington Market
Lexington Market
Lexington Market
N Liberty St
E Saratoga St
W Lexington St
E Lexington St
Marion St
Westminster Cemetery
Charles Center
E Fayette St
N Schroeder St
N Amity St
W Fayette St
N Pine St
University Square Park
W Baltimore St
Baltimore Street
1st Mariner Arena
Hopkins Pl
Hopkins Plaza
Redwood St
Water St
Metro
Shot Tower Market Pl
High St
E Fayette St
Lloyd St
S Central Ave
E Lombard St
Albemarle St
President St
Market Pl
S Gay St
Water St
Commerce St
South St
Light St
S Charles St
University of Maryland at Baltimore
N Greene St
W Lombard St
S Howard St
W Pratt St
E Pratt St
Inner Harbor
Exeter St
S High St
Parkin St
Scott St
S Martin Luther King Jr Blvd
Penn St
Emory St
Convention Center
W Camden St
Convention Center
Harborplace
ESPN Zone
E Falls Ave
S Exeter St
McHenry St
W Conway St
Camden Yards
Otterbein
Inner Harbor
Washington Blvd
W Cross St
Carroll St
S Sharp St
W Lee St
395
Water Taxi
Ridgely's Delight
Maryland Science Center
Ward St
Carroll St
W Ostend St
Cleveland St
Nanticoke St
W Hamburg St
W Hamburg St
S Paca St
Russell St
Camden Yards Sports Complex
W Hughes St
E Montgomery St
Churchill St
E Henrietta St
Warren Ave
E Hamburg St
Federal Hill Park
Key Hwy
Wicomico St
W West St
W Ostend St
Hamburg St
Grindall St
E Cross St
Federal Hill
E West St
Riverside Ave
Henry St
Covington St
Severn St
Bayard St
Alluvion St
Worcester St
Ridgely St
Light Rail
Warner St
W Ropewalk La
E Ostend St
E Gittings St
S Hanover St
E Gittings St
E Clement St
Brickhead St
E Fort Ave
Webster St
Key Hwy
Boyle St
Middle Branch
E Randall St
E Heath St
Riverside Park
To Washington DC (20mi)
295
To Baltimore-Washington International Airport (9mi)
E Barney St
E Wells St
95

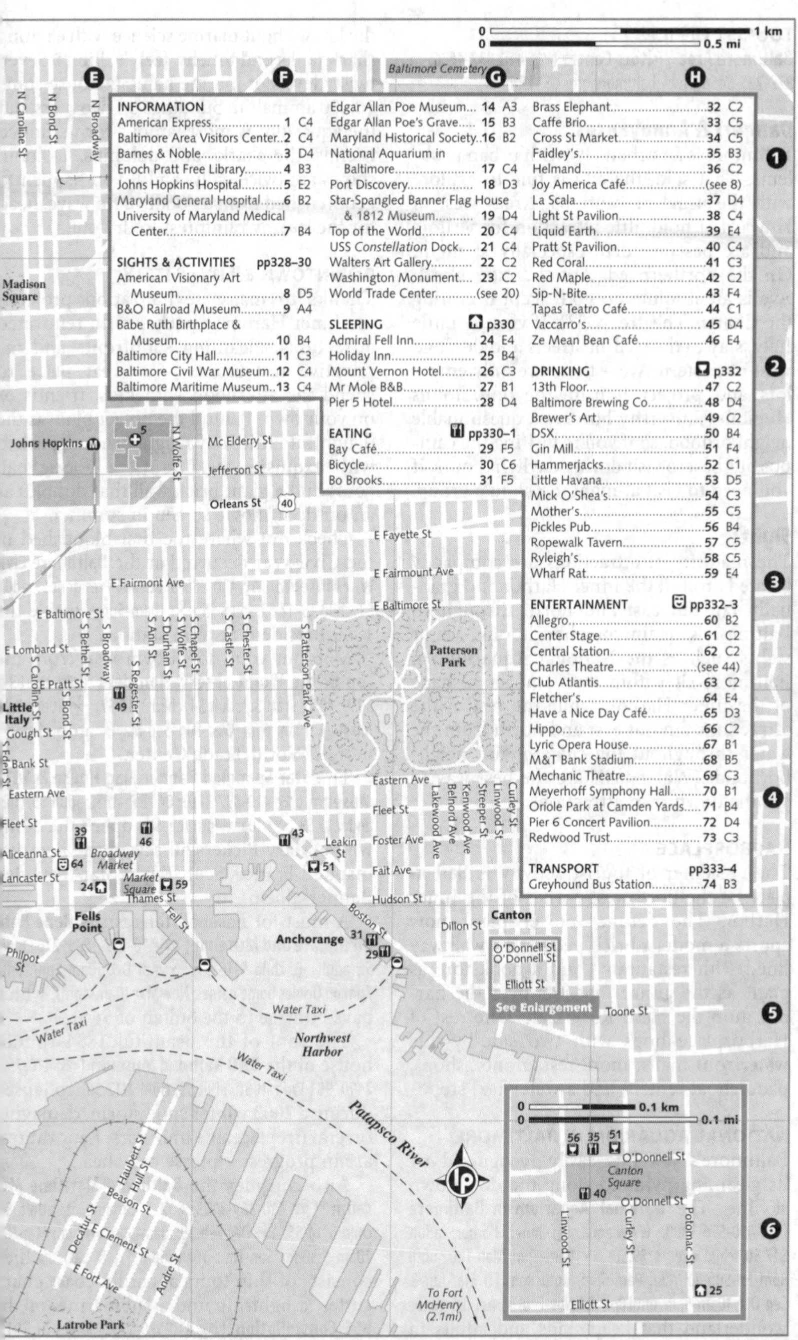
0 1 km
0 0.5 mi
E
F
G
H
1
2
3
4
5
6
INFORMATION
American Express....1 C4
Baltimore Area Visitors Center..2 C4
Barnes & Noble....3 D4
Enoch Pratt Free Library....4 B3
Johns Hopkins Hospital....5 E2
Maryland General Hospital....6 B2
University of Maryland Medical Center....7 B4
SIGHTS & ACTIVITIES pp328–30
American Visionary Art Museum....8 D5
B&O Railroad Museum....9 A4
Babe Ruth Birthplace & Museum....10 B4
Baltimore City Hall....11 C3
Baltimore Civil War Museum..12 C4
Baltimore Maritime Museum..13 C4
Edgar Allan Poe Museum....14 A3
Edgar Allan Poe's Grave....15 B3
Maryland Historical Society..16 B2
National Aquarium in Baltimore....17 C4
Port Discovery....18 D3
Star-Spangled Banner Flag House & 1812 Museum....19 D4
Top of the World....20 C4
USS Constellation Dock....21 C4
Walters Art Gallery....22 C2
Washington Monument....23 C2
World Trade Center....(see 20)
SLEEPING p330
Admiral Fell Inn....24 E4
Holiday Inn....25 B4
Mount Vernon Hotel....26 C3
Mr Mole B&B....27 B1
Pier 5 Hotel....28 D4
EATING pp330–1
Bay Café....29 F5
Bicycle....30 C6
Bo Brooks....31 F5
Brass Elephant....32 C2
Caffe Brio....33 C5
Cross St Market....34 C5
Faidley's....35 B3
Helmand....36 C2
Joy America Café....(see 8)
La Scala....37 D4
Light St Pavilion....38 C4
Liquid Earth....39 E4
Pratt St Pavilion....40 C4
Red Coral....41 C3
Red Maple....42 C2
Sip-N-Bite....43 F4
Tapas Teatro Café....44 C1
Vaccarro's....45 D4
Ze Mean Bean Café....46 E4
DRINKING p332
13th Floor....47 C2
Baltimore Brewing Co....48 D4
Brewer's Art....49 C2
DSX....50 B4
Gin Mill....51 F4
Hammerjacks....52 C1
Little Havana....53 D5
Mick O'Shea's....54 C3
Mother's....55 C5
Pickles Pub....56 B4
Ropewalk Tavern....57 C5
Ryleigh's....58 C5
Wharf Rat....59 E4
ENTERTAINMENT pp332–3
Allegro....60 B2
Center Stage....61 C2
Central Station....62 C2
Charles Theatre....(see 44)
Club Atlantis....63 C2
Fletcher's....64 E4
Have a Nice Day Café....65 D3
Hippo....66 C2
Lyric Opera House....67 B1
M&T Bank Stadium....68 B5
Mechanic Theatre....69 C3
Meyerhoff Symphony Hall....70 B1
Oriole Park at Camden Yards....71 B4
Pier 6 Concert Pavilion....72 D4
Redwood Trust....73 C3
TRANSPORT pp333–4
Greyhound Bus Station....74 B3
Baltimore Cemetery
N Caroline St
N Bond St
N Broadway
Madison Square
Johns Hopkins
N Wolfe St
Mc Elderry St
Jefferson St
Orleans St
40
E Fayette St
E Fairmount Ave
E Baltimore St
E Lombard St
E Pratt St
S Bethel St
S Broadway
S Ann St
S Durham St
S Wolfe St
S Chapel St
S Castle St
S Chester St
S Patterson Park Ave
S Regester St
S Caroline St
S Bond St
S Eden St
Little Italy
Gough St
Bank St
Eastern Ave
Fleet St
Aliceanna St
Lancaster St
Broadway Market
Market Square
Thames St
Fell St
Fells Point
Philpot St
Patterson Park
Eastern Ave
Fleet St
Foster Ave
Fait Ave
Hudson St
Lakewood Ave
Belnord Ave
Kenwood Ave
Streeper St
Linwood St
Curley St
Leakin St
Boston St
Dillon St
Canton
Anchorange
O'Donnell St
Elliott St
See Enlargement
Toone St
Water Taxi
Northwest Harbor
Patapsco River
Haubert St
Hull St
Beason St
Decatur St
E Clement St
E Fort Ave
Andre St
Latrobe Park
To Fort McHenry (2.1mi)
0 0.1 km
0 0.1 mi
O'Donnell St
Canton Square
Linwood St
Curley St
Potomac St
Elliott St

TOURIST OFFICES

Baltimore Area Visitors Center (☎ 410-837-4636, 877-225-8466; www.baltimore.org; 451 Light St)

Dangers & Annoyances

Baltimore is an urban city with urban problems. That said, the city is fine to explore with the usual precautions. Areas west of Howard St hold little attraction for visitors and are best avoided, especially at night. On the northern edge of the city, North Ave is an absolute no-go (except if visiting the Charles Theatre, p333). If visiting Little Italy, stay to the well-lit streets and don't go west of Eastern Ave – there are only empty lots and project housing beyond. Johns Hopkins University borders a questionable neighborhood, so if you're visiting the campus, it's best to visit during daylight hours. If you need to visit at night, do so in a group.

Sights

The majority of attractions are compactly located around the Inner Harbor and gradually fan out east and north throughout Baltimore's quaint neighborhoods. Major sights such as the National Aquarium in Baltimore sit within the compact L-shape of the Inner Harbor, while the rest of the attractions fan out east and north from the water throughout the city's quaint neighborhoods. Water taxis are the best way to see the downtown attractions.

HARBORPLACE

The epicenter of tourist activity is **Harborplace**, at the northwest corner of the Inner Harbor. The defunct power plant now sports a modern brick pedestrian walkway lined with restaurants and a bookstore as giant as the guitar that juts over the harbor atop the Hard Rock Café. The rest of Harborplace hops with two side-by-side waterfront malls, more restaurants, shops, paddleboat rentals, and a water-taxi stop.

NATIONAL AQUARIUM IN BALTIMORE

Baltimore's jewel is easily recognized by its gleaming pyramid along the downtown skyline. The **National Aquarium in Baltimore** (☎ 410-576-3800; www.aqua.org; Inner Harbor; adult $17.50, child over 3 $9.50; 9am-6pm Mon-Thu, until 8pm Fri-Sun Jul-Aug; 9am-5pm, until 8pm Fri Mar-Jun & Sep-Oct; 10am-5pm, until 8pm Fri, Nov-Feb) is an aquatic wonderland that keeps kids and adults in the know about marine science with excitin shark tanks and touchy-feely exhibits. Sever twisty levels of marine habitats house som 10,000 animals in buildings on two piers, bu the aquarium is most famous for its finnec friends: the sharks and dolphins. Dolphir shows are twice daily, and if you happen tc get drenched from a goodbye fin wave, heac for the steamy rainforest to dry out.

DOWNTOWN & LITTLE ITALY

Thanks to major revitalization projects the Inner Harbor is packed with renovate attractions, gleaming shopfronts and innovative restaurants – a great place tc spend the afternoon with kids, friends o on your own. Behind the power plant is th delightful Little Italy neighborhood, packe with exquisite restaurants, a boccie ba court and a giant brick wall that doubles a an outdoor movie screen in summer.

Check out where the first bloodshed o the Civil War occurred at the **Baltimore Civi War Museum** (☎ 410-385-5188; 601 President St; adul $3, child 13-17 $2, tours $5; 10am-5pm), inside th 1849 President St train station.

Map out your downtown visit from th **Top of the World observation deck** (☎ 410-837 8439; 401 E Pratt St; adult $4, child 3-16 $2; 10am-9pr Jun-Aug, 10am-6pm Wed-Sun Sep-May), atop Baltimore's World Trade Center.

The **Star-Spangled Banner Flag House & 181 Museum** (☎ 410-837-1793; 844 E Pratt St; adult $5, chil under 17 $3; 10am-4pm Tue-Sat) opens the hom where Mary Pickersgill sewed the flag tha inspired Francis Scott Key's 'Star-Spangle Banner' poem.

A must for baseball fans is the **Babe Rut Birthplace and Museum** (☎ 410-727-1539; 216 Emor St; adult $6, child 5-16 $3; Apr-Oct 10am-5pm, unt 7pm on Orioles home games; Nov-Mar 10am-4pm), whic pays homage to the Sultan of Swat.

The roof of the beautiful 1884 roundhouse of the **B&O Railroad Museum** (☎ 410-75 2490; 901 W Pratt St; adult $9, child 2-12 $6) collapse during a 2003 winter snowstorm, damagin several irreplaceable train cars. Renovation are in progress – please call ahead.

Also consider the **Baltimore Maritime Museum** (☎ 410-369-3153; 802 S Caroline St; adult $ child 6-14 $5; Dec-Feb 10:30am-5pm Fri-Sun; Mar-N 10am-5:30pm Sun-Thu, 10am-6pm Fri & Sat), whic consists of ship tours aboard a coast guar cutter, a lightship and a submarine, or th **USS Constellation** (☎ 410-539-1797; Pier 1 at 301

Pratt St; adult $5, child under 15 $2.50; ⌚ May 1–Oct 14 10am-6pm; Oct 15–April 30 10am-4pm), which is the last remaining all-sail ship of the Civil War docked in the Inner Harbor. Mystery lovers will get a thrill from the **Edgar Allan Poe Museum** (☎ 410-396-7932; 203 N Amity St; adult $3, child 12 & under $1; ⌚ noon-3:45pm Wed-Sat), where Poe penned some of his most famous works. His grave is nearby in Westminster Cemetery.

MT VERNON

Walters Art Gallery (☎ 410-547-9000; 600 N Charles St; adult $8, child under 18 $5; ⌚ 10am-5pm Tue-Sun), which overlooks the cobblestoned Mt Vernon Sq, is the city's finest museum. Its art collection spans 55 centuries, from ancient to contemporary, with excellent displays of Asian treasures, rare and ornate manuscripts and books, and a comprehensive French paintings collection; there's also a great atrium café.

Baltimore's own **Washington Monument** (☎ 410-396-7837; 699 Washington Pl; suggested donation $1; ⌚ dawn-dusk Wed-Sun) crowns the regal Mt Vernon Sq; climb 228 steps to the top of the obelisk for a city view or see the exhibits in its base.

N Charles St is known for its 'restaurant row.' The **Maryland Historical Society museum** (☎ 410-685-3750, 201 W Monument St; admission $4, free Sat morning; ⌚ 10am-5pm Wed-Fri, 9am-5pm Sat) relates state history with period rooms and many inviting, kid-friendly exhibits.

FEDERAL HILL & AROUND

On a bluff overlooking the harbor, **Federal Hill Park** lends its name to the comfortable neighborhood that's set around the Cross St Market. The avant-garde **American Visionary Art Museum** (☎ 410-244-1900; 800 Key Hwy; adult $9, child under 4 free; ⌚ 10am-6pm Tue-Sun) showcases the genius of 'outsider' artists; there's also an unusual gift shop and restaurant, Joy America Café (see p331).

The **Fort McHenry National Monument & Historic Shrine** (☎ 410-962-4290; 1 E Fort Ave; adult $5, child under 17 free; ⌚ fort & grounds 8am-7:45pm summer, 8am-4:45pm otherwise) is one of the most-visited sites in Baltimore, and was instrumental in saving Baltimore from the British attack during the War of 1812. Just offshore, prisoner Francis Scott Key saw the Star-Spangled Banner still waving over the fort, and the US national anthem was born. A new film plays in the visitors center and the scenic grounds and fort are perfect territory for kids to explore.

FELLS POINT & CANTON

Further east, cobblestones fill Market Sq (the scene of many street festivals) between the **Broadway Market** and the harbor in the historic maritime neighborhood of **Fells Point**. A number of 18th-century homes now house restaurants, bars and shops that range from funky to upscale. Further east, the slightly more sophisticated streets of **Canton** fan out, and its grassy square is surrounded by more great restaurants and bars.

NORTH BALTIMORE

The 'Hon' expression of affection, an often imitated but never quite duplicated Baltimorese peculiarity, was born from **Hampden**, an urban neighborhood just reaching its pinnacle of hipness. Spend a long afternoon browsing kitsch, antiques and eclectic clothing along the avenue (aka 36th St). Wednesday nights mean $7 lobsters at **Mamie's Café** (☎ 410-366-2996; 911 W 36th St).

Close by, **Johns Hopkins University** (☎ 410-516-8171) and a few attractions are found within this largely residential district. The **Baltimore Museum of Art** (☎ 410-396-7100; 10 Art Museum Dr; adult $7, child under 19 free; ⌚ 11am-5pm Wed-Fri, until 6pm Sat & Sun) houses the state's largest art collection. Admission is free for all on the first Thursday of the month.

Baltimore for Children

This city loves kids, and proves it with amazing museums, strollable waterfront promenades and family-friendly restaurants. Most attractions are centered on the Inner Harbor, including the famous National Aquarium (opposite), which is perfect for pint-sized visitors. Don't forget historic Fort McHenry (above), where kids can run wild o'er the ramparts.

Port Discovery (☎ 410-727-8120; 35 Market Pl, Power Plant Live complex; adult $11, child 3-12 $8.50; ⌚ Mon-Sat 10am-5pm, Sun from noon, Fri Jul-Aug until 8pm) Swinging into a three-level jungle tree house, producing a television show and solving riddles in the Mystery House are just a sample of the interactive adventures in this totally cool kids' museum where even the adults have fun; hop in the HiFlyer Balloon outside for a bird's-eye view of Baltimore. Tickets that include a balloon ride are adult $19, child three to 12 $15.

Baltimore Zoo (☎ 410-366-5466; Druid Hill Park; adult $11, child 2-11 $7; reptile house $1; ⌚ 10am-4pm)

Lily-pad hopping, adventures with Billy the Bog Turtle and grooming live animals in the KidZone are all in a day's work at the children's zoo, rated number one in the country.

Maryland Science Center (☎ 410-685-5225; 601 Light St; adult $12, child 3-12 $8; Mon-Fri 10am-5pm, Sat until 6pm, Sun from noon) Hands-on exhibits ranging from BodyLink, Dino Digs and Asteroids in the Atrium teach the little ones that science can be fun. A combo ticket with the Imax and planetarium is adult $15.50, child three 12 $10.50.

Tours

Baltimore Ducks (☎ 410-727-3825; 25 Light St, Inner Harbor; adult $22, child 3-12 $12) Amphibious WWII military vehicles nicknamed 'Ducks' show visitors the city via land and water.

Fells Point Ghost Walk (☎ 410-342-5000; 1623 Thames St, Amuse toy store; admission $12; Mar-Nov) Uncover the tawdry, playful and downright bizarre secrets of a bawdry maritime area.

Sleeping

Budget options are limited here, and although large convention-style hotels ring the Inner Harbor, stylish and affordable B&Bs are found in the downtown burbs of **Canton**, **Fells Point** and **Federal Hill**.

BUDGET

Mount Vernon Hotel (☎ 410-727-2000; www.bic.edu/mtvernon.asp; 24 W Franklin St; r from $95;) Nine floors of functional rooms in a swank neighborhood, and free shuttles.

MID-RANGE

Mr Mole B&B (☎ 410-728-1179; www.mrmolebb.com; 1601 Bolton St; r from $119; P) This beautifully restored town house in the upscale Bolton Hill area is a good choice to explore the city's cultural arts district. Garage parking makes this B&B's price a steal. Gay friendly.

Inn at 2920 (☎ 410-342-4450; www.theinnat2920.com; 2920 Elliott St; r from $155;) This is a modern B&B a few steps from Canton Sq, with gourmet breakfasts, high-speed Internet access, Jacuzzi tubs and beds to die for.

Holiday Inn (☎ 410-685-3500; www.holidayinn.com; 301 W Lombard St; r from $130; P) A mere block from the Camden Yards Sports Complex, Holiday Inn is central to downtown, and has a huge indoor pool and guest laundry facilities.

TOP END

Pier 5 Hotel (☎ 410-539-2000; www.thepier5.com; 711 Eastern Ave; r from $189; P) Within walking distance of Harborplace, the bold splashes of color in all 65 rooms will motivate you to explore the city, as you plan from your water or city view.

Admiral Fell Inn (☎ 410-522-7377, www.admiralfell.com; 888 S Broadway; r from $219; P) A guesthouse in Fells Point, Admiral Fell Inn overlooks Market Sq. Rooftop brunch is great in the summer; babysitting services and a courtesy shuttle to downtown are available. The room price includes breakfast.

Eating

Known for its outstanding steamed crabs, Baltimore's culinary options are ever expanding with Italian, Asian, Middle Eastern and comfort foods. Chain restaurants such as the sinful Cheesecake Factory and sports-lovin' ESPN Zone ring the Inner Harbor's two **pavilions** (Light and Pratt Sts), and quick take-aways are abundant. Across busy Pratt St, the Power Plant Live complex has numerous open-air options from sushi to Cuban to steakhouses. Beyond the harbor are delicious ethnic eateries that haven't changed much over the years – and that's a good thing. **Canton Sq** and **Fells Point's Broadway St** go casual, while **Federal Hill**, **Little Italy** and **Mt Vernon** swing upscale.

DOWNTOWN & LITTLE ITALY

Vaccarro's (☎ 410-685-4905; 222 Albemarle St; mains $3-10) This place is the best reason to skip dessert in nearby restaurants – the sinful cannoli, rum cakes and homemade gelati from this Italian institution are absolute heaven. Attempt all-you-can-eat Mondays if you dare (6 to 9pm, $11).

La Scala (☎ 410-783-9209; 1012 Eastern Ave; mains $14-30) Oh so worth the price for Little Italy's best. Here you'll find creamy risotto, penne and gnocchi dishes that melt on the tongue, and a wine list that'd make even the Godfather cry.

Bo Brooks (☎ 410-558-0202; 2701 Boston St; mains $10) There are only two things you need to order here for a true taste of Maryland: platters of steamed crabs by the dozen ($35), thrown ceremoniously down on newspaper-covered tables, and a cold pitcher of beer.

THE AUTHOR'S CHOICE

Red Coral (☎ 410-528-1925; 614 Water St; mains $12) Enjoy creative sushi roll combinations from three sushi bars and pan-Asian fare in this upscale, urban downtown restaurant. Outfitted in rich reds and soothing neutrals, the walls sport sleek, flat-screen TVs that play silent loops of kung-fu movies and *anime* (animated) cartoons, and thin mesh curtains divide diners between intimate tables. After dinner, tables are cleared, music is cranked up and the mild-mannered atmosphere turns into a high-energy dance club. For a quick bite, try the incredible $8 sushi box lunch special.

Faidley's (☎ 410-727-4898; Lexington Market; mains $5-15) This seatless favorite has a popular raw bar known for $1 oysters plus enormous lump crab cakes.

MT VERNON

Helmand (☎ 410-752-0311; 806 N Charles St; mains $12-18) Deservedly the best of Baltimore's handful of Afghan restaurants, Helmand's daring menu of leek-filled ravioli and pan-fried pumpkin are incredible.

Brass Elephant (☎ 410-548-8480; 924 N Charles St; mains $14-26) This elegant, tony town house, with gleaming brass and intricately carved woodwork, is a city favorite for upscale dining. Get the same flavor upstairs in the Tusk Lounge at cheaper prices. Free valet parking!

Red Maple (☎ 410-547-0149; 930 N Charles St; dishes $4-10) Here you'll find a groovy mix of exotic cocktails and Asian-inspired tapas in a gorgeous setting dripping with red satin walls. Themed evenings. No jeans.

Tapas Teatro Café (☎ 410-332-0110; 1711 N Charles St; mains $6-11) This is the place for gutsy Spanish tapas and tangy sangria; a prime outdoor dining area makes this a perfect spot if you're catching a flick at the arty Charles Theatre next door.

FEDERAL HILL

Cross St Market (1065 S Charles St) Grab some sushi at the raw bar or a burger during weekend happy hours before heading out to the plethora of area bars.

Caffe Brio (☎ 410-234-0235; 902 S Charles St; mains $4-11) This trendy vegetarian eatery is a neighborhood favorite and displays the work of local artists. It's within walking distance of Camden Yards.

Bicycle (☎ 410-234-1900; 1444 Light St; mains $12-24) Striking colored walls and a hip art-gallery-feel accent the French, South American and Asian tastes. Large parties can grab the 14-person table in the garden.

Joy America Café (☎ 410-244-6500; 800 Key Hwy; mains $15-30; ⏰ Tue-Sun) On the roof of the American Visionary Art Museum, Joy America Café's organic, gourmet fare is as eclectic as its artwork. Enjoy Sunday brunch (11am to 4pm) with a great view of the harbor.

FELLS POINT & CANTON

Broadway Market (btwn Fleet & Lancaster Sts) In two buildings, this market has a health food and herb shop, and several places to sit down and eat; the water taxi stops nearby.

Liquid Earth (☎ 410-276-6606; 1626 Aliceanna St; mains $6-11) This totally veggie menu has everything from vegan soups to organic sandwiches, all served from the juice bar made of funky 'found rocks.'

Ze Mean Bean Café (☎ 410-675-5999; 1759 Fleet St; mains $12-18) Like a cross between a mountain lodge and a European café, Ze Mean Bean Café serves up hearty Eastern European plates of pierogi, Ukrainian borscht and chicken Kiev, all dished out home style.

Bay Café (☎ 410-522-3377; 2809 Boston St; mains $12-24) This is a great place to grab jerk chicken, shrimp salad or a burger in the summer glow of an outdoor tiki torch, when the sandy beach opens onto a view of the Patapsco River.

Helene's Garden (☎ 410-276-2233; 2908 O'Donnell St; mains $18-24) Artsy and intimate, Helene's Garden has an extremely narrow entranceway – don't let it scare you off the innovative dishes, from seafood to free-range chicken. Half-price mains are available on Wednesday nights.

Nacho Mama's (☎ 410-675-0898; 2907 O'Donnell St; mains $12-18) This shrine to Elvis and Natty Bo beer, once locally brewed, serves a jumble of meals from mom's meatloaf to loaded quesadillas.

Sip-N-Bite (☎ 410-675-7077; 2200 Boston St; mains $6-11) Not much has changed at this bare-bones diner since it opened in 1940 – including prices – serving up 24-hour breakfasts and an expansive menu. Cash only.

Drinking

Baltimore's drinking scene has grown exponentially, but **Fells Point**'s reigning reputation for imbibing has been knocked out by trendy newcomers. The V-shaped Water St area teems with people in summer attending open-air block parties. The new Power Plant Live complex across from the National Aquarium has a cluster of bars and dance clubs, including a frenetic open-air patio that comes alive in summer. And a lively bunch of bars spill people into Canton Sq throughout the year.

DOWNTOWN & LITTLE ITALY

Mick O'Shea's (328 N Charles St) Baltimore's Irish mayor makes frequent stops here, playing traditional Irish music with his band.

DSX (200 W Pratt St) Grab a pint and catch an Orioles or Ravens pre-game show on any number of TVs in this always crowded but lively sports bar before heading across the street to the stadiums.

Pickles Pub (520 Washington Blvd) Directly across the street from the Camden Yards Sports Complex, fans meet here for pre-game bevies and burgers.

Hammerjacks (316 Guilford Ave) Open Thursday to Saturday only, this two-level nightclub and bar leans toward the big-hair band music of the '80s and books live bands accordingly; you'll find great happy-hour buffets and drink specials, plus plenty of parking (a rarity in Baltimore).

Baltimore Brewing Co (104 Albemarle St) This is a popular watering hole with a range of local brews.

MT VERNON

13th Floor (1 E Chase St) Atop the gothic Belvedere Hotel, 13th Floor's soothing neon lights beckon long drinking sessions to the tune of nightly live music from 9:30pm.

Owl Bar A nostalgic throwback to '50s Baltimore, first-floor Owl Bar, also in the Belvedere Hotel, has a long wooden bar – just like in the *Shining* – that attracts a big martini-sippin' university crowd.

Brewer's Art (1106 N Charles St) This is a subterranean cave that mesmerizes the senses with an overwhelming selection of beers.

FEDERAL HILL

Mother's (1113 S Charles St) Here is a classic Baltimore neighborhood bar where the drinks flow freely; you'll be called 'Hon' more than once and the Purple Patio is the meeting spot for wing specials and post-football-game discussions.

Ropewalk Tavern (1209 S Charles St) A historical and quite roomy bar, Ropewalk Tavern has exposed brick and a wood-beam ceiling. It's the kind of place where America's founding fathers would have polished off a few. Fortunately, so can you, with more than 150 superb ales to choose from.

Other recommendations follow:

Little Havana (1325A Key Hwy) Sip chilled *mojitos* (cocktails with mint, lime, rum and soda) and dance to Cuban beats in this extremely spacious waterfront bar.

Ryleigh's (32-36 E Cross St) A comfy local brew pub with a fantastic raw bar.

FELLS POINT & CANTON

Wharf Rat (801 S Ann St) The authentic maritime decorations, brass bars and dark lighting take drinkers back to a turn-of-the-20th-century pub; try the 'three for $3' local brew samples. Spirits of a non-alcoholic nature are rumored to frequent the fireplace area.

Other recommendations follow:

Gin Mill (2300 Boston St) A casual, two-level bar with pool tables and daily happy hours.

Looney's (2900 O'Donnell St) Small bar showing sports downstairs; gets rowdier on the second level, which has lots of space.

Claddagh Pub (2918 O'Donnell St) A Canton favorite which packs 'em in on weekends; great Guinness.

Entertainment

When blue-collar roots intertwine with nouveau white-collar establishments, the results are a creative, energetic crowd that works hard and plays even harder. Baltimoreans love their sports teams, dancing hotspots and historic theaters with a fervor that's contagious.

MUSIC

Redwood Trust (☎ 410-659-9500; 202 E Redwood St, admission $10) This two-level dance club is a former bank, and mimics South Beach clubs with VIP lounges and couch-sitting fees.

Have a Nice Day Café (☎ 410-385-8669; 34 Market Pl, Power Plant Live; admission $3-8) This café plays a groovy mix of '70s, '80s and electronica on a Billie Jean–style light-up dance floor.

Fletcher's (☎ 410-558-1889; 701 S Bond St; admission $5) For live music, this is downtown

Baltimore's best venue for alternative rock bands, where you can get a pint and a coke for under $5.

Ottobar (☎ 410-243-3535; 2549 N Howard St; $3-8) A little harder than Fletcher's, the roomy Ottobar rocks with punk, indie and new wave bands, some well-known, from around the country.

Pier 6 Concert Pavilion (☎ 410-625-3100; Inner Harbor) Summertime at this amphitheater sees big country and rock names.

Classical music and opera are found at the **Meyerhoff Symphony Hall** (☎ 410-783-8000; 1212 Cathedral St) and the **Lyric Opera House** (☎ 410-685-5086; 140 W Mount Royal Ave) respectively.

THEATER

Theater options include the following:

Charles Theatre (☎ 410-727-3456; 1711 N Charles St) The best art house in the city, this theater screens new releases, revivals and art films.

Center Stage (☎ 410-332-0033; 700 N Calvert St) Alternative plays.

Mechanic Theatre (☎ 410-625-4269; 25 Hopkins Plaza) For touring Broadway productions.

SPECTATOR SPORTS

Whether it's stick action, touchdowns, home runs, goals or monster-truck shows, Baltimoreans love their sports. The town plays hard and parties even harder, with tailgating parties in parking lots and bars keeping taps open and games on numerous televisions.

The Baltimore Orioles play at **Oriole Park at Camden Yards** (☎ 888-484-2473; www.theorioles.com; 333 W Camden St; Apr-Oct), while the 2000 Super Bowl champion birds of a purple feather, the Baltimore Ravens, play football at the **M&T Bank Stadium** (☎ 800-551-7328; www.baltimoreravens.com) next door.

Baltimore also boasts professional soccer and both indoor and outdoor lacrosse teams: 2003 major indoor soccer league champions, **Baltimore Blast** (www.baltimoreblast.com); the major indoor lacrosse league team, Baltimore Thunder; and the 2002 major lacrosse league champions, **Baltimore Bayhawks** (www.baltimorebayhawks.com). The Blast and Thunder play at the **1st Mariner Arena** (☎ 410-321-1908; 201 W Baltimore St), which also hosts rock concerts, motocross, circuses, and World Wrestling Entertainment (WWE) matches. The Bayhawks play north of Baltimore on the Johns Hopkins University campus, at Homewood Field.

Horse racing is big in this area, especially at **Pimlico** (www.marylandracing.com), where the second jewel of the Triple Crown, the Preakness, is held to great fanfare. **Laurel Park**, 22 miles from Baltimore, is the state's other major race track.

Though you may be more familiar with tenpin bowling, Baltimore is the birthplace of **duckpin bowling** – a popular form of entertainment for families and groups; alleys are throughout the city. Look for 'rock 'n' bowl' specials, usually beginning after league play at 11pm, where they turn down the lights and blast music to encourage your strikes.

GAY & LESBIAN VENUES

Though it does not have a huge population of gays and lesbians (most flock to DC's hot spots), Mt Vernon is the predominantly gay enclave. Check out www.bgp.org or www.outinbaltimore.com for more comprehensive listings.

Hippo (☎ 410-547-0069; 1 W Eager St) This is the city's largest gay club, with ladies' and men's tea, cabaret and outrageously themed dance nights.

Allegro (☎ 410-837-3906; 1101 Cathedral St; admission $3) Also a popular dance club, Allegro is where boywatch and lava lounge themes play out on the dance floor.

Central Station (☎ 410-752-7133; 1001 N Charles St) This energetic bar is where house diva Ms Tia gets the mixed crowd going with karaoke, drag shows and *Will & Grace* TV nights.

Club Atlantis (☎ 410-717-9099; 615 The Fallsway) John Waters' fans will recognize Club Atlantis as the Fudge Palace from the movie *Pecker*.

Getting There & Away

AIR

Baltimore-Washington International Airport (BWI) is 10 miles south of downtown via Rte 295.

BUS

The sketchy **Greyhound terminal** (☎ 410-752-1393; 210 W Fayette St) is near Lexington Market. Buses run to Philadelphia, Pennsylvania ($18, 2½ hours); New York ($37, four hours); and Washington DC ($10, one hour).

TRAIN

More respectable trains stop at Baltimore's **Penn Station** (1515 N Charles St), in a fine area bordering north Baltimore. Amtrak runs to Philadelphia ($43, 1½ hours); New York ($70, 2¼ hours); and Washington DC ($14, 40 minutes). MARC operates weekday commuter trains to and from Washington DC (one way/round-trip $5.75/11.50). This is the cheapest, most convenient way to travel between these cities.

Getting Around

TO/FROM THE AIRPORT

Check www.mtamaryland.com for all schedules and fares.

Light Rail (☎ 410-539-5000; $1.35) runs directly from BWI to downtown's Lexington Market and Penn Station.

MARC trains (☎ 800-325-7245; weekdays only) run hourly 16-minute trips between Penn Station and BWI. **SuperShuttle** (☎ 800-258-3826) runs an airport-van service to the Inner Harbor for $12 one way; buy tickets at the ground transportation desk at C Pier.

Taxis run around $20.

CAR & TAXI

Driving in the city is a catch-22: many sights require a car but parking is either scarce or overpriced. Fortunately, downtown sights are relatively compact and taxis are plentiful and inexpensive. If you are driving (and you probably are), many Inner Harbor garages charge cheaper 'In before' prices if you park there before or after rush hours.

BOAT

Seaport Taxi (☎ 410-675-2900; Inner Harbor; adult $5, child under 11 $3) and **Ed Kane's Water Taxi** (☎ 410-563-3901; Inner Harbor; adult $5, child under 11 $3) land at many of the harborside attractions and neighborhoods.

PUBLIC TRANSPORTATION

Sporadic at best, the **Maryland Transit Administration** (MTA; ☎ 410-539-5000; www.mtamaryland.com) has information on Baltimore's bus, light-rail and metro systems. Single fares within the city are $1.35 or $3 for an all-day pass (correct change required).

ANNAPOLIS

Maryland's capital, deeply rooted in its colonial past, is a lively and picturesque modern town. Annapolis retains its colonial appearance with much original 18th-century architecture and design. Narrow lanes lined with brick-row houses radiate from traffic circles drawn around the primary church and State House. From its perch on the highest hill, the State House overlooks the City Dock and harbor that established Annapolis as an important port after the area was first settled by Puritans in 1649. The US Naval Academy was established here in 1845. Today the town is also well known as America's Sailing Capital; it has 17 miles of waterfront and is home dock to more than 2500 craft.

There's a **visitors center** (☎ 410-280-0445, www.visit-annapolis.org; 26 West St; 9am-5pm) and a seasonal information booth at City Dock. A **Maryland Welcome Center** (☎ 410-974-3400; 350 Rowe Blvd; daily) is inside the State House, and runs tours of the building.

Sights & Activities

Think of the State House as a wheel hub from which most attractions will fan out, leading straight down to the **City Dock** and **historic waterfront**. Most water-based activities originate from the dock area, while tours are handled straight from the visitors center.

US NAVAL ACADEMY

The prestigious **US Naval Academy** is the undergraduate college of the US Navy. The **Armel-Leftwich Visitor Center** (☎ 410-263-6933; Gate 1 at the City Dock entrance; fee for tours; photo ID required) has a film, tours and interactive exhibits about the 338-acre yard (never 'campus'). Most visitors come to see the formation daily at 12:05pm sharp. This is when the 4000 midshipmen and midshipwomen conduct a 20-minute military marching display in the plaza around their massive dormitory – a memorable spectacle.

MARYLAND STATE HOUSE

The country's oldest state capitol in continuous legislative use, the stately 1772 **State House** (☎ 410-974-3400; 9am-5pm Mon-Fri, 10am-4pm Sat & Sun; photo ID required) also served as the fledgling national capitol for a short time from 1733 to 1734, when it housed the Continental Congress. The Senate is in action here from January to April. Note the giant acorn, which stands for wisdom, atop the dome; it's ironically upside down.

DOWNTOWN ANNAPOLIS

The **Three Centuries Walking Tour** (☎ 410-263-5401; adult $11, child under 18 $6) is a great introduction to all things Annapolis. The two-hour tour, which leaves daily at 10:30am from the visitors center, covers scandalous tales, early American political life and the country's largest concentration of 18th-century buildings, some of which housed a Declaration of Independence signer, influential African-Americans and colonial spirits who don't want to leave.

Historical buildings abound: **St John's College**, at College Ave and King George St, is one of the USA's three oldest colleges; 1735 **Old Treasury Building** (alongside the State House) is Maryland's oldest official building; and the **Banneker-Douglass Museum** (☎ 410-216-6180; 84 Franklin St; admission free; 🕑 Tue-Sat), once a church, now relates Maryland's African-American history.

Annapolis has many sailing schools, cruises and bareboat (sail-it-yourself) charters. **Watermark Cruises** (☎ 410-268-7600; City Dock) is the best, with daily cruises, sunset sails and excursions around Annapolis. The 74ft schooner **Woodwind** (☎ 410-263-7837; 80 Compromise St; day sails/sunset cruises $25/27; 🕑 May-Oct) offers two-hour cruises; or stay aboard overnight (see Sleeping, p335). The 19-mile **Baltimore & Annapolis Trail** (☎ 410-222-6244) is a popular recreational route that follows the old B&A Short Line Railroad. **Historic Annapolis Foundation** (☎ 410-268-5576; 77 Main St; tours $5) offers two self-guided walking tours from the foundation's City Dock museum.

Sleeping

The colonial capital has many cozy B&Bs but few budget options except for chain hotels outside the historic district. Call ☎ 800-848-4748 for free accommodation reservations.

Country Inn & Suites (☎ 800-456-4000, 410-571-6700; www.countryinnsdestinationguide.com; 2600 Housley Rd; r from $110; P) A surprisingly charming chain hotel that has free shuttles to the historic district and both an indoor and outdoor pool.

ScotLaur Inn (☎ 410-268-5665; www.scotlaurinn.com; 165 Main St; r from $75) The folks from Chick and Ruth's Deli offer simple B&B rooms above the deli in the heart of the historic district.

Annapolis Inn (☎ 410-295-5200; www.annapolisinn.com; 144 Prince George St; ste from $295; P) An antique-laden upscale, gay-friendly B&B absolutely worth the splurge for the breakfasts alone. Just a stone's skip from the City Dock.

Woodwind (☎ 410-263-7837; www.schoonerwoodwind.com; 80 Compromise St; $235;) For a maritime experience, you can sleep aboard a replicated 74ft schooner. The price includes a sunset sail.

Eating

Annapolis brims with an eclectic assortment of eateries where one street can serve up crab cakes, ribs, sushi and steaks. The majority of restaurants line City Dock and Main St.

Chick & Ruth's Deli (☎ 410-269-6737; 165 Main St; mains under $10) This deli is a 24-hour diner, where reciting the Pledge of Allegiance is mandatory every morning at 8:30am (9:30am weekends).

Middleton Tavern (☎ 410-263-3323; 2 Market Space; mains $19) Though dinner here can be expensive, you'd get your fill from the giant appetizers, or try the slippery $1 oyster shooters and platefuls of other catches-of-the-day in this historic waterfront tavern.

Buddy's Crabs & Ribs (☎ 410-626-1100; 100 Main St; mains $12) This is a family-friendly restaurant. Tuesday is kids' night, with hearty rib-and-seafood plates from $15.

Drinking & Entertainment

As the T-shirts proclaim, 'Annapolis is a drinking town with a sailing problem' – so there's no shortage of nightlife. Among the best is the **Rams Head Tavern** (33 West St) with the 100 World Beer Club passport for ale connoisseurs and a small stage that inexplicably attracts national bands and performers.

Getting There & Around

Greyhound runs buses to Washington DC ($11.50, one hour). **Annapolis Transit** (☎ 410-263-7964) buses and trolleys provide local transport.

SOUTHERN MARYLAND

The shores of Chesapeake Bay south of Annapolis draw weekenders to convenient sailing and sunbathing spots nestled among forests, farms and marshland that get progressively quieter (sometimes deathly quiet) further south.

Southern Calvert County

In Prince Frederick, **Calvert County Tourism** (☎ 410-535-6355), inside the courthouse, guides you to attractions, including Chesapeake Beach and popular parks further south such as seasonal **Flag Ponds Nature Park** (☎ 410-586-1477; $6 per car; swimming permitted) and **Calvert Cliffs State Park** (☎ 301-872-5688; no swimming), which is great for fossil hunting.

Jefferson Patterson Park & Museum (☎ 410-586-8500; 10515 Mackall Rd; admission free; 🕑 10am-5pm Wed-Sun Apr-Oct), along the Patuxent River, charts 12,000 years of Native American culture through its archaeological sites and museum.

Solomons

Once a sleepy waterfolk town, Solomons has been transformed to a crisp New England–like sailing center. The **visitors center** (☎ 410-326-6027; 14175 Solomons Island Rd S) is off Rte 2. Small, outboard-motor boat rentals cost around $45 for half a day.

Calvert Marine Museum (☎ 410-326-2042; adult $5, child 2-5 $2; 🕑 10am-5pm) At the end of MD Rte 2, this octagonal lighthouse holds exhibits on estuarine biology and local maritime history, and is a hit with kids, especially with a summertime waterside music series (past performers include Bob Dylan!).

With the closest camping 15 miles north, the **Solomons Victorian Inn** (☎ 410-326-4811; www.solomonsvictorianinn.com; 125 Charles St; r from $95) and **By-The-Bay** (☎ 410-326-3428; 14374 Calvert St) are tidy B&Bs. **Lighthouse Inn** (☎ 410-326-2444; 14636 Solomons Island Rd; r $17-30) has surf-and-turf buffets for $26.

St Mary's City

Historic St Mary's City (☎ 301-862-0990; adult $7.50, child 6-12 $3.50; 🕑 vary by season) is a living-history park with costumed interpreters occupying original and re-created buildings on the site of Maryland's original waterfront settlement, which dates back to 1634 – sort of a mini-Williamsburg in a now nearly deserted corner of the state.

Point Lookout State Park

At Maryland's southern tip, **Point Lookout State Park** (☎ 301-872-5688; admission $3; 🕑 May-Sep weekends & holidays) was once the site of a Civil War prison, and is supposedly haunted by lost soldiers. Today it offers swimming, canoe rentals and an excursion ferry to Smith Island in summer ($20). **Campsites** ($20 per night) are available and must be reserved in advance. Check www.dnr.state.md.us for reservations.

EASTERN SHORE

On the Delmarva Peninsula, the Eastern Shore was settled 300 years ago by shore-people (farmers) and waterfolk from England's west coast. Explore the back roads and Chesapeake waterways to discover the area's charm. The knot of villages west of Easton offer a particularly scenic bike tour, including a ferry ride and seafood stops.

Easton

Named one of America's best small towns, the quaint hamlet of Easton is a charming stopover for biking, walking and just taking it easy. The historic district holds most sights – find local maps at the **Easton Welcome Resource Center** (☎ 410-822-0345; 11 Harrison St; 🕑 9am-5pm), which also serves as a booking agent for the historic **Avalon Theatre** (www.avalontheatre.com; 40 E Dover St). Restored to its former art deco style, the 400-seat theater showcases local plays and national live music acts.

Browse the new museum at the **Historical Society of Talbot County** (☎ 410-822-0773; 25 S Washington St; 🕑 11am-3pm Tue-Fri, 10am-4pm Sat) and join a historic house **tour** ($5; 11:30am & 1:30pm Tue-Sat). Or stay in your car for the **Frederick Douglass Driving Tour**, which details the life of this famous former slave and the local sites where he grew up.

Budget sleeping options in town are slim. **Tidewater Inn** (☎ 410-822-1300; www.tidewaterinn.com; 101 E Dover St; P ✕ ☒) and the **Inn at Easton** (☎ 410-822-4910; www.theinnateaston.com; 28 S Harrison St; r from $140-350; P ✕) are the two premier inns with excellent yet pricey restaurants ($25 to $31).

For breakfast or a cheap lunch, try **Alice's Café** (☎ 410-819-8590; 22 N Harrison St; mains under $7) for her ricotta pancakes, pecan sticky buns and Cuban roast-pork sandwiches. Directly across from the courthouse, the **Washington Street Pub** (☎ 410-822-9011; 20 N Washington St; mains $6-19) serves hearty meals, giant sandwiches and Easton's famous pub chips in a casual two-story setting. **General Tanuki**'s (☎ 410-819-0707; 25 Goldsborough St; lunch $4-10, dinner $18-24) hula girls and Pacific-inspired artwork is a funky venue to enjoy 'morphing' quesadillas ($9), curry-fried oyster sandwiches ($8.95) and a delicious assortment of fresh sushi (live music Thursday nights). Splurge at upscale **Mason's** (☎ 410-822-3204; 24 S Harrison St; mains $25-31) for fine French food, or the above-mentioned Easton inns.

Trailways (☎ 410-822-3333) stops at the Texaco station on Hwy 50 N.

St Michaels & Tilghman Island

Standing beside the octagonal lighthouse that has become a symbol of Chesapeake Bay, St Michaels dates back to the 18th century. It's famous as 'the town that fooled the British': during the War of 1812, the inhabitants rigged up a system of lanterns in a nearby forest and blacked out the town. British naval gunners mistook the lanterns for the town and shelled the forest instead, allowing St Michaels to escape destruction. More notoriety followed the publication of James Michener's novel *Chesapeake*. Today this precious waterfront village attracts sailors from around the Chesapeake Bay to its marina, restaurants, B&Bs and shoppes.

In the landmark lighthouse, the **Chesapeake Bay Maritime Museum** (☎ 410-745-2916; Navy Point; adult $9, child 6-17 $4; 9am-6pm summer, until 5pm spring & fall, until 4pm winter) features a boat shop, sailboats and historic houses at its base.

Rent bikes ($4 per hr; $16 per day) and motorboats at the town dock marina. One-hour narrated historic cruises aboard the **Patriot** (☎ 410-745-3100; Navy Point; $10 per person; 11am, 12:30pm, 2:30pm & 4pm) leave from the Crab Claw dock.

Best Western St Michaels Motor Inn (☎ 410-745-3333; 1228 S Talbot St; r from $85; P) is the best budget option. In town, half a dozen exclusive B&Bs charge upward of $100 (or try a 'bed and boat' – ☎ 410-745-9701). **Carpenter St Saloon**, on Talbot St at Carpenter St, is a good old corner bar with meals. Though expensive, **208 Talbot** (☎ 410-745-3838; 208 N Talbot St; dishes $15-30) is a unique venue where, if the oysters in champagne sauce or pan-seared rockfish on the menu don't grab you, you can bring in your own waterfowl from your day's hunting excursion and have the chef cook it up.

At the end of the road over the Hwy 33 drawbridge (a great biking excursion), the tiny town of **Tilghman Island** retains its traditional waterfolk roots, and local captains take visitors out on working skipjacks from Dogwood Harbor. Try the **HM Krentz** (☎ 410-745-6080) or the **Rebecca T Ruark** (☎ 410-886-2176; www.skipjack.org; adult/child $30/15; 2hr cruises), the oldest skipjack on the Chesapeake. **Harris Creek Kayak** (☎ 410-886-2083; www.harriscreekkayak.com; 7857 Tilghman Island Rd) has custom tours and hourly rentals. If you're staying overnight here, try **Harrison's Chesapeake House** (☎ 410-886-2121; www.chesapeakehouse.com) for a bite and bed; inquire about fishing charters.

Blackwater National Wildlife Refuge

About 20 miles south of Easton, 17,000 acres of tidal marshes protect migrating waterfowl; also here are the Delmarva fox squirrel and eagles. There are trails, drives and a **visitors center** (☎ 410-228-2677; cars/cyclists $3/1). Bird-watching is best mid-October to mid-March.

Ocean City

Known as OC, Maryland's mammoth Atlantic coast resort swells from a year-round population of 7500 to a summer throng of 300,000, when Coppertone-slicked beachgoers crowd the boardwalk corn-dog stands and Skee-Ball arcades, and cruise along Coastal Hwy, lined with budget motels.

The **visitors center** (☎ 410-289-8181) and local **hotel-motel-restaurant association** (☎ 410-289-5645; www.ocvisitor.com), in the swank convention center on the Coastal Hwy at 40th St, can help you find lodging and more.

Extending 2.5 miles from the inlet to 27th St, the **boardwalk** is the center of the action. At the southern end, a museum at the Coast Guard station has exhibits on **lifesaving** (☎ 410-289-4991; admission $2), but OC is all about the beach.

Many establishments are only open during temperate months; prices plummet in the off-season. Traffic is jammed and parking scarce in summer.

Carolina Trailways (☎ 410-289-9307; cnr 2nd St & Philadelphia Ave) has regular buses to major regional cities. The **Ocean City Municipal Bus Service** (☎ 410-723-1607; day pass $1; daily) runs the length of the beach.

SLEEPING

Of the 9500 guest rooms in town, the cheapest are found around the inlet at the south end and throughout town on the bay side.

Budget

Ocean City Campground (☎ 410-524-7601; www.occamping.com; 70th St on Coastal Hwy; tent site/RV site $32/37) Just one block from the beach, this family-friendly park is surrounded by plenty of amusements, miniature golf and restaurants, as well as a convenient local bus stop out front (for more camping options see Assateague Island, below).

Surf Villa (☎ 410-289-9434, 888-333-7873; www.surfvilla.com; 705 N Baltimore Ave; r from $79/99 weekdays/weekends; P ✲) This is a comfy hotel boasting rocking chairs, ocean-view rooms, and shower and changing facilities on checkout days.

King Charles Hotel (☎ 410-289-6141; www.kingcharleshotel.com; 1209 Baltimore Ave; r from $83/101 weekdays/weekends; P ✲) This place feels like a summer cottage and is an outstanding deal for high season, centrally located half a block from the beach and in the heart of all the boardwalk action.

Mid-Range

Thunderbird Beach Motel (☎ 410-289-8136, 800-638-3244; www.purnellproperties.com/thunderbird; cnr 32nd St & Baltimore Ave; r from $135/150 weekdays/weekends; P ✲) Here you'll find a good beach bargain, with clean rooms, refrigerators and microwaves, and a heated outdoor pool.

Spinnaker Motel (☎ 410-289-5444; www.purnellproperties.com/spinnaker; cnr 18th St & Baltimore Ave; r from $195; P ✲) Thunderbird's slightly more expensive sister property, Spinnaker has oceanfront views with balconies, a huge outdoor pool and fully-equipped kitchenettes.

Hotel Monte Carlo (☎ 410-289-7101, 877-375-6537; www.montecarlo-2000.com; 3rd St & Baltimore Ave; r from $165/215 weekdays/weekends; P ✲) Here a bit of luxury accents the 77 efficiency units, with Jacuzzis, a rooftop pool and hot tub, indoor heated pool, and individual balconies overlooking the ocean or bay.

Top End

Lighthouse Club Hotel (☎ 410-524-5400, 888-371-5400; www.fagers.com/hotel; 201 60th St on the Bay; r from $204/245 weekdays/weekends; P ✲) You might never make it to the beach, when your suites are equipped with working gas fireplaces, double Jacuzzis in white-marbled bathrooms, platform beds and romantic views of the bay. All suites contain refrigerators, comfy sofas and wet bars, and continental breakfast is included.

Edge (☎ 410-524-5400, 888-371-5400; www.fagers.com/hotel; r from $299/325 weekdays/weekends; P ✲) Near the Lighthouse Club, the Edge is a new boutique hotel with Philippe Stark–like decor and the ultimate in luxury – and you'll pay for it.

Stowaway Grand Hotel (☎ 410-289-6191, 800-447-6779; www.grandhoteloceancity.com; 2100 Baltimore Ave; r from $229/259 weekdays/weekends; P ✲) This hotel has a commanding view of the ocean as well as a full-service salon and poolside bars, both indoor and out.

EATING & DRINKING

Restaurants are as plentiful as motels, and plenty of cheap eats line the **boardwalk** and **Coastal Hwy** (watch for many all-you-can-eat and early-bird deals, particularly on seafood). An influx of dance clubs cluster around the boardwalk's southern tip.

Hobbit (☎ 410-524-8100; 81st St; mains $19-27) This is one of OC's best seafood restaurants.

Fager's Island (☎ 410-524-5500; 60th St; mains $18) This place is well known for prime rib, and as the place where the 1812 Overture precedes every sunset.

Macky's Bayside Bar & Grill (☎ 410-723-5565; 53rd St; mains $18) Overlooking Assawoman Bay, this lively joint boasts Creole food, 14 TVs for sports fans, and great views.

Seacrets (117 W 49th St) A Jamaican-themed bar and club straight out of MTV's *Spring Break*, Seacrets has beach parties, spring-loaded indoor dance floors, and watery areas where you can drift in an inner tube while sipping your drinks.

Shenanigans (4th St & Boardwalk) Here you'll find live traditional music and thick Guinness pints.

Party Block (17th St & Coastal Hwy; entry free before 10pm) This combines four wild nightclubs for a slightly raunchy yet very fun clubbing experience and plenty of bikini contests.

Assateague Island

This beautiful 37-mile-long barrier island preserves a rare stretch of undeveloped seashore. Legendary herds of wild horses roam free on the island. Its lower third is in Virginia (see Chincoteague Island p317). Get maps and information at the Barrier Island **visitors center** (☎ 410-641-1441; on Rte 611; vehicle/cyclist/pedestrian $5/5/2).

Two **campgrounds** (☎ 800-365-2267) maintained by the NPS are near the access road and cost $10 ($14 peak season). There is **backcountry camping** ($5 permit plus $5 NPS entry fee), a great alternative. **Assateague State Park** (☎ 410-641-2120; with/without hookups $30/20) offers 350 campsites with bathrooms and hot showers.

WESTERN MARYLAND

This obscure region offers mountain recreation set against scenic Appalachian landscapes and significant Civil War sites, most notably Antietam.

Frederick

Halfway between the blockbuster battlefields of Gettysburg and Antietam, Frederick is certainly a popular stop along the Civil War trail. Its quiet 50-square-block historic district retains many 18th- and 19th-century buildings in various states of renovation. The **visitors center** (☎ 301-663-8687; 19 E Church St), at Market St, conducts weekend walking tours ($4.50); there's parking next door.

The **National Museum of Civil War Medicine** (☎ 301-695-1864; 48 E Patrick St; adult $6.50, child 10-16 $4.50; ⌚ 10am-5pm Mon-Sat, 11am-5pm Sun), Frederick's premier attraction, guides visitors through a personal look at the health conditions soldiers faced on the battlefields and beyond. The **Historical Society of Frederick** (☎ 301-663-1188), across from the visitors center, opens its historic mansion furnished with period antiques and local artwork ($2); inquire about other historic-house museums in town.

Gambrill State Park (☎ 301-271-7574), 5 miles northwest on Rte 40, charges campers $10/14 weekdays/weekends for sites. Chain-motel rooms at around $65 are south of town off I-270.

Taverns, a deli and an Irish pub can be found along Market St from the creek-side promenade north through the historic district. **Mudd Puddle** (124 S Carroll St) prepares tasty, inexpensive Italian sandwiches. The **Common Market** (5813 Buckeystown Pike) sells quality natural foods.

Frederick is accessible via **Greyhound** (☎ 301-663-3311; E All Saints St) and **MARC trains** (☎ 301-228-2888; 141 B&O Ave at East Ave; weekdays only).

Antietam National Battlefield

Called 'Sharpsburg' by Southerners, the Battle of Antietam (ann-*tee*-tum) was the bloodiest day of the Civil War and in US history. On September 17, 1862, General Lee's first invasion of the North was stalled in a tactical stalemate that left 23,000 dead, wounded or missing. The battlefield and surrounding area are solemn and haunting, uncluttered save for plaques and statues. Living-history demonstrations are conducted monthly from June to December.

The **visitors center** (☎ 301-432-5124; State Rd 65; 3-day pass for individuals/families $3/5; ⌚ 8:30am-6pm) offers driving-tour pamphlets and audiotapes ($5) to guide you past 8 miles of evocative landmarks; free summer talks and walks are also offered.

The neighboring town of Sharpsburg has few services; it's better to continue across the river to eat (see Shepherdstown, p345) or stay in Hagerstown to the north.

Cumberland

At the Potomac River, the frontier outpost of Fort Cumberland was the pioneer gateway across the rugged Alleghenies to Pittsburgh and the Ohio River (not to be confused with the famous Cumberland Gap between Virginia and Kentucky). It also was a vital base during the French and Indian War. At the western end of the C&O Canal and the first national pike (Alt 40 these days), Cumberland boomed in 19th-century transport and later as an industrial center serving local coalfields. Today Cumberland remains largely industrial but has begun to expand an outdoor-recreation trade to guide visitors to the region's rivers, forests, mountains and ski areas.

The **Transportation & Industrial Museum** (☎ 301-724-4398; 13 Canal St) is located in the 1913 Western Maryland Station Center, along with Allegheny County **visitors center** (☎ 301-777-5132). The terminus **NPS visitors center** (☎ 301-722-8226) for the C&O Canal National Historic Park (see section following) is in the depot on Canal St.

Outside, passengers catch steam locomotive rides aboard the **Western Maryland Scenic Railroad** (☎ 800-872-4650; www.wmsr.com), traversing forests and steep ravines to Frostburg ($16 to $18, three-hour round-trip). Nearby, **Allegheny Adventures** (☎ 301-729-9708) rents bikes seasonally; inquire about tours. Another local outfitter is **Allegheny Expeditions** (☎ 301-722-5170), on Rte 2.

C&O Canal National Historic Park

A marvel of engineering technology, the C&O Canal was designed to stretch alongside the Potomac River from Chesapeake Bay to the Ohio River – linking commercial centers in the East with the frontier resources of the West. Construction on the canal began in 1828 but was halted in 1850 in Cumberland by the rugged Appalachian Mountains. By then the first railroad had made its way to Cumberland, in time rendering the canal obsolete.

The **C&O Canal National Historic Park** (☎ 301-739-4200) commemorates the importance of river trade in eastern-seaboard history and provides recreational opportunities (such as near-level mountain-biking) within its historic setting (see also Georgetown, p293). Along its protected 185-mile corridor, the park preserves the 12ft-wide towpath as a hiking and biking trail. There are six visitors centers along the trail (Georgetown, Great Falls Tavern, Brunswick, Williamsport, Hancock and Western Maryland Station).

Deep Creek Lake

In the extreme west, Maryland's largest lake is an all-seasons playground with summer water sports and wintry ski resort adventures. The vibrant red and orange glow of the Allegany mountains attracts thousands during the annual Autumn Glory Festival (October), rivaling New England's popular leaf-turning backdrops. Contact the **visitors center** (☎ 301-387-4386; www.garrettchamber.com; 15 Visitors Center Dr) for information on all outdoor activities. **Railey Mountain Lake Vacations** (☎ 800-846-7368; rentals.deepcreek.com; 22491 Garrett Hwy) rents gorgeous lakefront homes year round.

DELAWARE

Despite some endowed museums and fantastic beaches, this region holds few attractions compelling enough to prolong a long detour. Art lovers take note that the state is well known for the homespun Brandywine School of artists of the early 20th century – Howard Pyle, NC Wyeth, Andrew Wyeth and Maxfield Parrish are highly regarded as illustrators and painters.

History

The first Dutch settlement in 1631 was wiped out by the local Nanticoke Indians. The Swedes arrived in 1638. In 1655 the flourishing settlement was claimed by the Dutch, and then taken over by the English. The Swedes and Dutch continued to farm the north, while English settlers established tobacco plantations and slavery further south.

DELAWARE FACTS

Nicknames Diamond State, First State
Population 807,385 (45th)
Area 1982 sq miles (49th)
Admitted to Union December 7, 1787 (1st)
Capital city Dover (population 33,000)
Other cities Wilmington (72,664), Newark (28,547)
State Motto Liberty and independence
Birthplace of Valerie Bertinelli (1960), nylon, Miss USA pageant (1880)
Famous for no state sales tax, du Pont fortune, liberal corporate regulations
Home of half the nation's Fortune 500 companies

When Delaware joined the Revolutionary War, English frigates blockaded Wilmington's port and 18,000 British troops landed nearby. George Washington brought 11,000 soldiers to protect the Brandywine Valley and the port, but he was outflanked and withdrew to Valley Forge while the British occupied Wilmington. Dover Green was the site of the Delaware convention that ratified the Federal Constitution. Delaware was the first state to sign the Constitution and is thus the 'first state' of the Union, giving it precedence in national ceremonial occasions.

In 1802 a French immigrant by the name of du Pont started a gunpowder factory on the Brandywine Creek, which profited greatly in the War of 1812. Despite its slave-owning farms, Delaware, like Maryland, sided with the Union in the Civil War.

In the 20th century, industrial growth in general, and du Pont's booming chemical businesses in particular, contributed to the state's prosperity. The state's low taxes (no sales tax) and liberal incorporation laws have made it a center for commerce.

Information

Delaware Tourism Office (☎ 302-739-4271, 866-284-7489; www.visitdelaware.com; 99 King's Hwy, Dover, DE 19903)

Visitors center (☎ 302-737-4059) On I-95 between exits 1 and 3. There's an 8% lodging tax but no sales tax on other goods or services.

National & State Parks

Oceanfront and inland waterways and even a zoo are among Delaware's 14 state parks. For more information contact the **Delaware**

Division of Parks and Recreation (☎ 302-739-4702; www.destateparks.com; 89 Kings Hwy, Dover, DE 19901).

Activities

This tiny state boasts a beautiful 90-mile coastline famous for its intimate beaches such as Dewey, Rehoboth and Lewes. Coming in a close second are the boating, sailing and myriad saltwater fishing opportunities along the Atlantic Ocean. Charter boats also take visitors deep-sea fishing, and kayak ecotours glide through several wildlife refuges. Inland, hunters vie for duck, red fox and white-tailed deer in season. For more information on fishing and hunting regulations, check out www.dnrec.state.de.us, and for other outdoor activities, see www.visitdelaware.com.

NORTHERN & CENTRAL DELAWARE

Northern Delaware, known as castle country, includes the great du Pont mansion Winterthur. The major urban city of Wilmington lies at the gateway to the scenic Brandywine Valley. Central Delaware, the region south of the Chesapeake and Delaware Canal, is a mosaic of neatly tended farms and marshes and home to Dover, the state capital.

Wilmington

Delaware's largest city sits at the confluence of Brandywine Creek and Christina River. The central commercial district is along Market St. The **visitors center** (☎ 302-652-4088; www.visitwilmingtonde.com; 100 W 10th St), local historical society and city history museum are close together. A mile from downtown, the **Delaware Art Museum** (☎ 302-571-9590; 800 S Madison St; adult $7, child under 7 free; Tue, Thu, Fri 10am-6pm, Wed until 9pm, Sat until 5pm, Sun 1-5pm) exhibits examples of the local Brandywine School.

Hotel du Pont (☎ 302-594-3100, doubles from $180), in the commercial district at Market and 11th Sts, is the city's premier hotel. **Deep Blue** (111 W 11th St; mains from $20) is an American fish house with live entertainment, and **Govato's** (800 N Market St; mains $8) is a fairly old-fashioned candy store and restaurant known for its amazing desserts.

Wilmington is accessible via **Greyhound/Carolina Trailways** (☎ 302-655-6111; 318 Market St) and **Amtrak** (☎ 302-658-1515), at the foot of Market St.

Brandywine Valley

The rural Brandywine Valley, straddling the Delaware-Pennsylvania border, is accessible from Wilmington or Philadelphia. The **Brandywine Valley Tourist Information Center** (☎ 610-280-6145, 800-228-9933), outside Longwood Gardens in Kennett Sq, Pennsylvania, distributes information on the region's triple crown of châteaus and gardens: Winterthur, Longwood Gardens and Nemours.

Winterthur (☎ 302-888-4600; www.winterthur.org; Rte 52 off Kennett Pike; adult/child $10/10; 10am-5pm), the valley's highlight, includes the 175-room country estate of industrialist Henry Francis du Pont, along with a decorative arts museum and gardens that can be viewed by tram. It really is a monument to American excess.

See p186 for more on the Brandywine Valley's attractions.

New Castle

Seven miles south of Wilmington, historic New Castle retains cobblestone streets and attractive blocks of 18th-century buildings. It was originally founded by the Dutch in 1651; later the English gained control, and the colony established its legislature here in 1704.

The **visitors center** (☎ 302-322-8411) arranges walking tours, or you can wander the compact old town on your own. The district is laid out in an easy grid around a small park called the Green and along Delaware St to the riverside Strand. Sights include the Old Court House (closed Mondays), the arsenal on the Green, churches and cemeteries dating back to the 17th century, and historic houses, which can be toured.

The charming **Terry House B&B** (☎ 302-322-2505; www.terryhouse.com; 130 Delaware St; r from $90; P) overlooks a lush garden and the Delaware River. Enjoy English pub fare and hearty ales at **Jessop's Tavern** (☎ 302-322-6111; 114 Delaware St) or more upscale colonial atmosphere at the sister restaurant **Arsenal at Old New Castle** (☎ 302-328-1290; 30 Market St).

Dover

Since William Penn laid out the Green on State St in 1722, the square remains the historical center of the state capital and most attractions are within walking distance. The 1792 Old State House and 1874 Court

House here are tucked in beside attractive brick-row houses shaded by tall trees.

Walk beside the State House to find the state **visitors center** (☎ 302-739-4266; www.destatemuseums.org; 406 Federal St) and history exhibits at the foot of a long plaza from the new capitol. **Johnson Victrola Museum** (☎ 302-739-5316; cnr Bank & New Sts; admission free; Tue-Sat 10am-3:30pm) honors 'talking machine' pioneer Eldridge Johnson with exhibits including the RCA trademark dog, His Master's Voice.

Dover Air Force Base, used by giant C-5 Galaxy aircraft, is also the US military morgue (shown on TV whenever the government brings home a dead American). The free **museum** (☎ 302-677-5938; Tue-Sat 9am-4pm) has an expanding collection of vintage planes and other artifacts.

There are budget motels along the tacky Hwy 13 strip, but the **Dover House B&B** (☎ 302-672-7017; 1325 State St; r from 90; P) in town is a cozy escape from the big chains.

Barking Frog (33 Loockerman St) is a good coffeehouse that features entertainment on weekends. **WT Smithers** (140 S State St) is an inviting downtown tavern with a great happy hour and a jazz brunch on Sunday. **Hollywood Diner** (☎ 302-734-7462; 123 N Dupont Hwy; mains $13) satisfies munchies 24 hours in a 1950s-style diner.

DELAWARE SEASHORE

Delaware's 28 miles of pristine, sandy Atlantic Ocean beaches (some preserved as state parks) are the best reason to linger in the tiny state. Many businesses, campgrounds and services are open only for an extended summer season when prices are highest; off-season bargains abound.

Lewes

Anchoring Cape Henlopen, Lewes (*loo*-iss) has more history than your ordinary beach town. The Dutch founded a whaling settlement here in 1631, and though the whalers were massacred by Native Americans, more Europeans were soon attracted to its natural harbor. Today the rugged cape beachscapes are the town's biggest draw.

The **visitors center** (☎ 302-645-8073; www.leweschamber.com; 120 Kings Hwy) directs you to sights such as the small **Zwaanendael Museum** (☎ 302-645-1148; 102 Kings Hwy; admission free; Tue-Sat 10am-4:30pm, Sun 1:30-4:30pm), which explains the Dutch roots of this first state settlement and houses 18th-century shipwreck treasures inside a distinctive 1931 replica of a Dutch town hall. Kids particularly enjoy hour-long steam-train excursions offered by **Queen Anne's Railroad** (☎ 302-644-1720; 730 Kings Hwy; adult/child $14/9) twice a week in summer. Rent bikes at **Lewes Cycle Sports** (☎ 302-645-4544; 525 Savannah Rd; from $4 per hour).

If you don't mind shared baths, the quaint **Savannah Inn** (☎ 302-645-5592; 330 Savannah Rd; r from $40; P) is your best budget option in a house in tiny downtown, with an incredible vegetarian breakfast included. Reminiscent of small European hotels, **Zwaanendael Inn** (☎ 302-645-6466; 142 2nd St; www.zwaanendaelinn.com; r from $90; P) has 18 antique-laden rooms that are convenient to the beaches, ferry and downtown; there's a fitness facility onsite. **Blue Plate Diner** (☎ 302-644-8400; 329 Savannah Rd; dishes $5) serves filling diner food and breakfast all day; there's occasional live entertainment. The **Buttery** (☎ 302-645-7755; cnr 2nd Ave & Savannah Rd; mains $19) is upscale and expensive but worth it; get there between 5pm and 6:30pm for the bargain prix fixe three-course dinner at $21.

The **Cape May-Lewes Ferry** (☎ 800-643-3779 for reservations, ☎ 302-644-6030 for schedule) across Delaware Bay to New Jersey, runs daily 80-minute ferries across Delaware Bay to New Jersey from the terminal a mile from downtown Lewes (fares for vehicle and driver are $20, plus $6 for additional vehicle or foot passengers, from November to March; and $25, plus $8 for additional passengers, from April to October (children under seven travel free).

Cape Henlopen State Park

East of Lewes, more than 4000 acres of tall dune bluffs, pine forests and wetlands are preserved in an attractive **state park** (☎ 302-645-8983) that's popular with bird-watchers and beachgoers ($5 per out-of-state car). You can see clear to Cape May, New Jersey. There's a nature center, well-kept bathhouses and paved bike paths. North Beach draws many gay and lesbian couples. **Camping** (☎ 302-645-2103; campsites $19-26, cabins $54-70, yurts $46) options include oceanfront or wooded.

Rehoboth Beach

Downtown Rehoboth Beach is a vibrant old seaside town tucked behind a very congested and tacky stretch of Hwy 1 (follow signs to the resort area). The main drag, Rehoboth

Ave, is lined with restaurants, food stalls and souvenir shops, from the easy-to-miss **visitors center** (☎ 302-227-2233; 501 Rehoboth Ave) to the mile-long beach boardwalk.

Each summer, the population swells to 50,000 sunseekers and has long been known as a fashionable gay resort. The crowd is diverse and by no means exclusive, as evidenced by the influx of families, older couples, students and yuppies. Poodle beach, at the southern tip of the boardwalk, is primarily gay, while lesbians congregate at north shores beach at the south end of Cape Henlopen State Park. Check out www.gayrehoboth.com for more information.

Greyhound/Carolina Trailways (☎ 919-833-3601) buses stop on Rehoboth Ave; buses run to Wilmington ($15) and Dover ($10).

SLEEPING

Big Oaks Campground (☎ 302-645-6838; www.bigoakscamping.com; Rte 1 & Rd 270; campsites $32;) Family-friendly and just three miles from the boardwalk, Big Oaks has a pool and playground; beach shuttles are available.

Homey guesthouses within two shady blocks of the beach, though pricey in season for aging accommodations without pools, are preferable to highway motels. Most include continental breakfast (the visitors center has a list).

Summer Place Hotel (☎ 302-226-0766; www.rehobothsummerplace.com; 30 Olive Ave; r weekday/weekend $80/120; P) You'll find the best budget option here, with a choice between spacious condos and comfy hotel-style rooms with refrigerators, microwaves and TV. Condos have a five-night minimum stay ($850).

Royal Rose Inn B&B (☎ 302-226-2535; www.royalroseinn.com; 41 Baltimore Ave; r from $115;) This place is a great bang for your buck, with a rooftop hot tub, screened porch and sundeck; it's just a block from the boardwalk.

Mallard Guest House (☎ 302-226-3448; 60 Baltimore Ave & 67 Lake Ave; r from $95/195 weekday/weekend;), Highly recommended for its proximity to the beach and sparkling lake, Mallard Guest House has friendly staff and a cozy atmosphere; a hot tub and outdoor showers also add a nice touch.

Rehoboth Guest House (☎ 302-227-4117; www.guesthse.com/reho; 40 Maryland Ave; r from $80/150 weekday/weekend, shared bath from $70/100;) Gay-owned and -operated, this cool guest house is wildly popular for its afternoon wine-and-cheese parties, private sunbathing decks and immaculate rooms, not to mention its five-minute walk to the boardwalk; reservations are highly recommended.

EATING & ENTERTAINMENT

The beach boardwalk and Rehoboth Ave are a smorgasbord of quick food and bars.

Corner Cupboard (☎ 302-227-8553; 50 Park Ave; mains $10) This is a standout for its tucked-away location and Eastern Shore cookin'.

Planet X (☎ 302-226-1928; 35 Wilmington Ave; from $19) This café has expensive yet incredible food combinations.

Sydney's Blues & Jazz (25 Christian St) This café has a good selection of visiting acts that supplement tasty Creole dishes.

Dogfish Head (320 Rehoboth Ave) The vast wine and beer selections here will keep you moving to the high-energy live music.

Renegade (4274 Hwy 1) The town's premier gay venue, Renegade has live music every night in season.

Blue Moon (35 Baltimore Ave) Here you'll find daily afternoon tea dances.

Dewey Beach

Further south, along Hwy 1, is Rehoboth's wild little sister, **Dewey Beach**, known for its frantic nightlife. Throngs of under-30s swarm the congested streets in search of sunburn relief at popular watering holes such as the **Rusty Rudder** (113 Dickenson St) and **Northbeach** (Dagsworthy St). **Bottle & Cork** (Dagsworthy St) is the best known, especially for excellent live bands, with the Dave Matthews Band and Joan Jett among its past repertoire.

WEST VIRGINIA

West Virginia bears the unflattering stereotypes of hillbillies, inbreeding and unsavory activities, thanks to the movie *Deliverance.* The reality is completely different. Though it remains one of the more economically depressed states, there are jewels tucked within the hills of Appalachia in the form of ruggedly beautiful terrain, churning white-water rivers and charming towns that glitter far brighter than the way it's negatively perceived.

The Appalachian highlands are known for outstanding handicrafts, including woodwork, quilts, basketry and glassmaking; it's also known for 'mountain' music.

Outstanding recreational opportunities include white-water rafting and paddling adventures along the New, Gauley and Cheat Rivers, hiking excursions, mountain biking, rock climbing, spelunking and skiing. Towns such as Berkeley Springs, Shepherdstown and Harpers Ferry are standouts for their spas, restaurants and historical importance respectively, and are easy day trips from DC or Baltimore.

History

Originally part of Virginia, the land west of the Appalachians was settled in the mid-17th century by pioneering small farmers of a different stripe than the large tobacco plantation owners in the Tidewater. This rift grew with the Civil War and the secession of old Virginia's slave owners, and the mountain region that remained aligned with the Union was declared a separate state in 1863.

After the war, timber and coal companies arrived to exploit the natural resources – and the mountaineers – of West Virginia. Despite the early development of labor unions, West Virginia was economically depressed for many years, and it remains among the nation's poorest states. West Virginia's cities continue to serve largely as industrial centers, though their quaint and quirky smaller towns like Berkeley Springs and Shepherdstown continue to fuel their tourism revenue.

Though coal, mineral and timber processed through West Virginia's industrial cities remain important to the state's economy, growing numbers of recreationists drawn to the natural beauty support a tourism industry that strives to disturb the environment less.

Information

West Virginia Division of Tourism (☎ 304-558-2200, 800-225-5982; www.callwva.com) operates Welcome Centers at interstate borders and in **Harpers Ferry** (☎ 304-535-2482). State sales tax is 6%.

National & State Parks

The **Division of Natural Resources** (www.wvparks.com; State Capitol Complex, Charleston) operates a toll-free **reservations line** (☎ 800-225-5982).

WEST VIRGINIA FACTS

Nicknames Mountain State, Switzerland of America
Population 1,801,873 (37th)
Area 24,231 sq miles (41st)
Admitted to Union June 20, 1863 (35th)
Capital city Charleston (population 57,300)
Other cities Huntington (51,475), Wheeling (31,419)
State motto Mountaineers are always free
Birthplace of General Stonewall Jackson (1824–63), aviator Charles E 'Chuck' Yeager (b 1923), gymnast Mary Lou Retton (b 1968), actor Don Knotts (b 1924), Mother's Day (1908)
Famous for Appalachian highland culture, mountain recreation

EASTERN PANHANDLE

The northeast of this rugged state is best known for the historic village of Harpers Ferry, but there are also quaint old towns where you can lose yourself in the past.

Harpers Ferry

This town packs a rich history and tremendous recreation onto a scenic spit of land where the Shenandoah and Potomac Rivers meet to form the boundaries of three states. The federal armory here was the target of abolitionist John Brown's raid in 1859, and though Brown's ambition to arm slaves and spark a national rebellion against slavery died once he was caught and hanged, the incident incited slaveholders' worst fears and helped precipitate the Civil War. Union and Confederate forces soon fought for control of the armory and town.

With little development altering the antebellum appearance of the tiny downtown, the district was declared a national historic park in 1986. Today visitors and residents alike may walk the steep cobblestone lanes and wander among the shops without charge, but staffed museum buildings are accessible to pass-holders only. Passes, parking and shuttles are available above town at the **visitors center** (☎ 304-535-2482; off Hwy 340; vehicle/pedestrian $5/3). There is no parking allowed in Harpers Ferry.

SIGHTS & ACTIVITIES

Among a score of free sites in the historic district, the 1858 **Master Armorer's House** explains how rifle technology that was developed here revolutionized the firearms industry; the **Storer College building**, long ago a teachers college for freed slaves, now traces the town's African-American history. The **John Brown Museum** (168 High St; adult $4.50, child 6-12 $2.50) tells the story of his raid in wax.

Passing through town, the 2160-mile Appalachian Trail (AT) is headquartered at the **Appalachian Trail Conference** (☎ 304-535-6331; www.atconf.org; cnr Washington & Jackson Sts; Apr-Oct), a tremendous resource for local hikers as well as backpackers. Day hikers also scale the Maryland Heights Trail past Civil War fortifications or the Loudoun Heights Trail for scenic river views.

You can rent bikes to explore the **C&O Canal** towpath (see p293); the visitors center has a list of outfitters. To arrange raft and float excursions, contact **River & Trail Outfitters** (☎ 301-695-5177; 604 Valley Rd in nearby Knoxville, MD) or **River Riders** (☎ 800-326-7238; Harpers Ferry).

SLEEPING & EATING

Harpers Ferry KOA (☎ 304-535-6895; tent site/RV site/cabin $26/32/42; year-round;) Two miles southwest on Hwy 340, Harpers Ferry KOA is a good camping option.

HI Harpers Ferry Lodge (☎ 301-834-7652; 19,123 Sandy Hook Rd; dm members/nonmembers $15/17; closed Nov–mid-Mar) You'll find this lodge 2.5 miles from the train station in Knoxville, MD; inquire about camping or shuttles.

In town are higher-priced motels and B&Bs within walking distance of the AT or train station.

Jackson Rose B&B (☎ 304-535-1528; www.bbonline.com/wv/jackson; 1141 Washington St; weekday/weekend r $95/105;) With resplendent roses and a peach orchard out back, this B&B was Stonewall Jackson's first headquarters during the Civil War.

Last Resort Inn (☎ 304-535-2812; www.bbonline.com/wv/lastresort; 280 Clay St; weekdays/weekends r $80/90;) This place boasts a magnificent view of three states and two rivers from its sweeping porch.

Anvil (☎ 304-535-2582; 1270 Washington St; mains $11-23) Here you'll find seafood and steak mains and fun happy hours.

Mountain House Cafe (179 High St; mains $5) This café serves up fresh salads and sandwiches in the backyard rose garden.

GETTING THERE & AROUND

Harpers Ferry is a rarity: a rural destination well served by rail. Daily **Amtrak** (☎ 800-872-7245) and **MARC** (☎ 800-325-7245) trains run between the historic-district station and Washington's Union Station (bikes permitted if disassembled and boxed).

Shepherdstown

An unexpected little jewel, Shepherdstown dates back to 1762 and is the oldest town in the state. Home of Shepherd College, the sophisticated town boasts several restaurants, cafés and arty shops along a short length of German St. It hosted the Israeli-Syrian peace talks in 2000. The **visitors center** (☎ 304-876-2786; www.shepherdstownvisitorscenter.com) is across from the town hall. Shepherdstown makes a great biking destination along the C&O Canal towpath 12 miles north of Harpers Ferry (see the C&O Canal, p293).

The distinct **Bavarian Inn** (☎ 304-876-2551; www.bavarianinnwv.com; off Rte 1;) towers over the Potomac River in full Alpine style. Rooms with garden views start at $85. The **Yellow Brick Bank** (☎ 304-876-2208; 201 German St; mains $16) is an unexpected culinary treat with appetizers the size of mains. Gourmet sandwiches and hot lunch specials are found at the landmark **Betty's Restaurant** (☎ 304-876-6080; 112 E German St; mains $5).

For entertainment, see movies at the restored 1909 **Opera House** (☎ 304-876-3704; 131 W German St); check out local musicians at the **Mecklenberg Inn** (☎ 304-876-2126) or call **Shepherd College** (☎ 304-876-5497) for its performing-arts schedule.

Berkeley Springs

Off scenic Hwy 9, quirkily quaint Berkeley Springs was once visited by George Washington and other founding fathers for its thermal springs. Today, it's a microcosm of spiritualism, artistic expression and soul-pampering spa centers, boasting more masseuses in town than lawyers.

Don't let the clinical appearance deter you from a soak in the Roman-style baths at **Berkeley Springs State Park** (☎ 304-258-2711; bath/bath with massage $20/38; 10am-4:30pm); it's also the cheapest spa deal in town. Alternatively, try the stone massages and tingling body scrubs at the **Bath House** (☎ 304-258-9071; 10am-5pm) directly across from the park; take home yummy lotions and aromatherapy oils from the small shop.

Country Inn (☎ 800-822-6630; www.countryinnwv.com; r $69, with shared bath from $49) also across from the park, offers its own 'renaissance' spa with mineral whirlpools for two weekend accommodation packages, which include spa treatments. Also recommended is the holistic **Coolfont Resort** (☎ 304-258-4500; camping/r/chalet $20/95/169) up the hill for a *Dirty Dancing* camplike setting.

Get a bite, buy a local piece of artwork and listen to live entertainment at the casual **Tari's** (☎ 304-258-1196; 123 N Washington St; dishes $10-25), or go gourmet at the fabulous **Lot 12 Public House** (☎ 304-258-6264; 302 Warren St; mains $19-28; Wed-Sun) atop a steep hill.

MONONGAHELA NATIONAL FOREST

This vast expanse of rugged terrain in the Allegheny Mountains is the kind that earned West Virginia the nickname 'the Colorado of the East.' Within its 1400 sq miles, the forest encompasses wild rivers, caves and the highest peak in the state (Spruce Knob). More than 850 miles of trails include the 124-mile **Allegheny Trail**, for hiking and backpacking, and the scenic 75-mile rails-to-trails **Greenbrier River Trail**, popular with cyclists.

Elkins, at the forest's western boundary, is a good base of operations. Here the **National Forest Service office** (☎ 304-636-1800; 200 Sycamore St; campsites/primitive sites $5/free, RV sites available) distributes recreation directories for hiking, biking and camping.

The **Augusta Heritage Center** (☎ 304-637-1350; Davis Elkins College, 100 Campus Dr) hosts a folk music and dance summer camp for adults that culminates in a weeklong city festival in August. **Fat Tire Cycle** (☎ 304-636-0969; 101 Randolph Ave) rents gear and sponsors excursions.

Cranberry Mountain Nature Center (☎ 304-653-4826; Rte 150 & Rte 39/55) has detailed information about Monongahela.

An 8-mile portion of the Allegheny Trail links two full-service state parks 30 miles northeast of Elkins: **Canaan Valley Resort** (☎ 304-866-4121), a downhill ski resort, and **Blackwater Falls State Park** (☎ 304-259-5216), with backcountry ski touring (restaurants, lodge rooms, cabins and campgrounds available at both). Further south, **Snowshoe Mountain** (☎ 877-441-4386; www.snowshoemtn.com) is the state's largest downhill resort and has also become a mountain-biking center from spring to fall (rentals and excursions available).

Nearby, the **Cass Scenic Railroad State Park** (☎ 304-456-4300; excursions from $13) runs steam trains from an old logging town to mountaintop overlooks daily in summer and for peak fall foliage. Accommodations include **cottages** (from $76, Jun-Feb) for four. Other highlights include the surreal landscapes at **Seneca Rocks**, 35 miles southeast of Elkins, which attract rock climbers to demanding challenges up 900ft-tall sandstone strata.

Seneca Shadows Campground (☎ 877-444-6777; basic s/d campsites $13/22), one mile east, is handy to the rocks.

SOUTHERN WEST VIRGINIA

This is one of the true getaway places close to the eastern seaboard, truly representative of the mountain state. It is a mecca for white-water rafting, hiking, mountain biking and cross-country skiing. Check the **Southern West Virginia website** (www.visitwv.com).

New River Gorge National River

A 1000ft-deep gorge is the dramatic setting for the best white-water rafting adventures in the eastern USA. The NPS protects a stretch of the New River that falls 750ft in 50 miles, with a compact set of rapids up to Class V concentrated at the northernmost end.

Canyon Rim Visitor Center (☎ 304-574-2115), in Lansing north of the impressive gorge bridge, is the only one of five NPS visitors centers along the river that is open daily year round to provide information on river outfitters, gorge climbing, hiking and mountain biking, as well as rafting on rougher white water to the north in the Gauley River National Recreation Area. Rim and gorge trails offer beautiful views. There are four free basic **camping areas**.

Nearby **Hawk's Nest State Park** (☎ 304-658-5212; from $70/75 for forest views/gorge views) offers views from its rim-top lodge; in summer it operates an aerial tram down to the river, where you can catch a cruising boat ride (tram closed Monday). **Babcock State Park** (☎ 304-438-3004; campsites/cabins $15/68) offers accommodations and boats, and 15 miles of trails.

Fayetteville

Among the many state-licensed rafting outfitters in the area, **USA Raft** (☎ 800-872-7232; www.usaraft.com; packages from $26) stands out for the thrilling white-water rafting trips.

Mountain Laurel RV Park/Campground (☎ 304-574-0188; Laurel Creek Rd at Rte 19) is a cheap camping option in town. **Elliot's Whitewater Grill** (☎ 304-574-3443; Laurel Crescent & Rte 19; mains $9) is a good place to replenish and relax after rafting.

Further south off of Hwy 19, a poignant coal-miner memorial stands outside the **county tourist office** (☎ 304-465-5617), where lodging and camping directories can be found.

Charleston

Situated just along the Kanawha (ka-*naw*) River, the state capital is a pleasant city in which to spend a few hours before moving on to more exciting outdoor destinations; the **visitors center** (☎ 304-344-5075; 200 Civic Center Dr) has maps and information.

The gold-domed **capitol** is worth a look. Within the plaza, a cultural center features state-history and mountain-heritage exhibits, and the Mountain Stage radio program broadcasts mountain music statewide to public broadcasting stations from the State Theater every Sunday.

Budget lodging is available off I-77. At the foot of Capitol St, a **farmers market** at the old depot offers quick eats along with fresh flowers and produce. The city's true cultural oasis, **Taylor Books** (226 Capitol St), two blocks from the river, has a bookstore and espresso bar with live weekend entertainment. **Allie's** (200 Lee St), in the Marriott, is a popular local watering hole.

Amtrak trains, running daily between Chicago, Illinois and Washington DC, stop at the station across the river.

Great Lakes

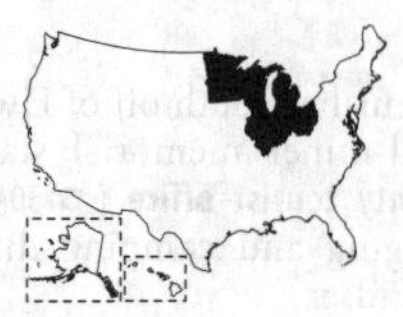

CONTENTS

The Great Lakes area – part of the Midwest – is the USA's heartland. It might not have the glitz of the East Coast or sex appeal of the West Coast, but it's where the pulse of the nation beats.

The Great Lakes themselves are huge, like inland seas, offering beaches, islands, dunes, resort towns and lots of lighthouse-dotted scenery. The soaring city of Chicago – the nation's third-largest metropolis – anchors the region. Most of the Great Lakes' larger cities – Detroit, Minneapolis and Cleveland, as well as Chicago – were founded as trading outposts or farm towns, and began developing into transport, processing and industrial centers, spurred by the lakes and waterways. Many cities became wealthy, and as tides of European immigrants arrived (Scandinavians in Minnesota and Wisconsin, Germans in southern Ohio, Eastern Europeans and Irish in Chicago), these cities also became centers of culture, with excellent art galleries, museums, orchestras and universities. Their legacy ensures much of interest for visitors to unearth.

You certainly won't go hungry while in this abundant region. Dairy farms churn out cheese and ice cream, apple and cherry orchards produce luscious pies and jams, and waterways yield fresh whitefish, lake trout and walleye. You won't go thirsty, either. The Midwest's cities have long been known for beer crafting, thanks to their German heritage, and several microbreweries maintain the tradition.

If you want an exceptional bite of America, the Great Lakes will leave you well-satisfied. Most visitors come in summer when the weather is pleasant to hike, bike, canoe and kayak around the lakes and pristine forests.

HIGHLIGHTS

- Looking up at (or down from) Chicago's steely **skyscrapers** (p357)
- Listening to **jazz and blues** in the smoky hotbed of Chicago (p376)
- Driving the rocky coastline by picturesque lighthouses in Wisconsin's **Door County** (p428)
- Paying homage to US car culture and inventiveness at the **Henry Ford Museum** and **Greenfield Village** near Detroit (p413)
- Exploring the waterfalls, rugged forests and local color of Michigan's **Upper Peninsula** (p418)
- Canoeing through the legendary **Boundary Waters** of Northeastern Minnesota (p442)

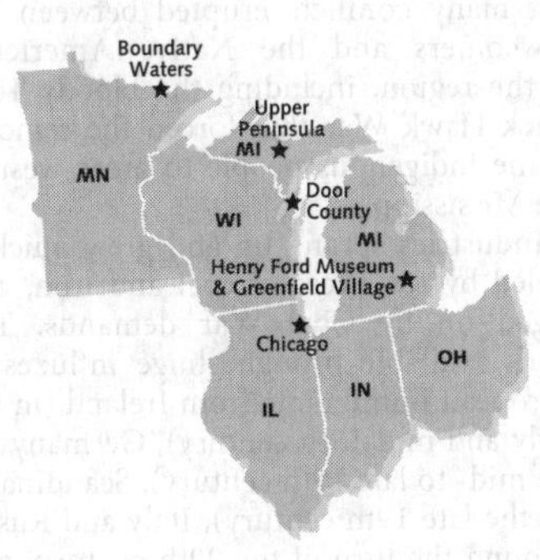

HISTORY

This fertile region has long been inhabited by advanced cultures like the Hopewell, which emerged around 200 BC, and the Mississippi River mound builders, who flourished from around AD 600. They built distinctive and mysterious mounds that were tombs for their leaders and possibly symbolic expressions of homage to their deities. The mound building cultures began to decline around AD 1000, and when the first Europeans arrived in the early 17th century, the area was home to groups like the Miami, Shawnee and Winnebago.

The first Europeans were French voyageurs, who explored, traded for furs with the indigenous people and established missions and forts. But the French soon had rivals: the Ohio Company, a group of British entrepreneurs from England and Virginia, formed in 1748 to develop trade and control the Ohio Valley. Its explorations helped precipitate the French and Indian Wars (1754–61), after which Britain gained all the lands east of the Mississippi. Following the Revolutionary War, the area south of the Great Lakes became the new USA's Northwest Territory, which soon was divided into states.

The canals linking the Great Lakes to the area's river systems, built in the 1820s and 30s, along with railroad development in the next decades, stimulated settlement. But many conflicts erupted between the newcomers and the Native Americans in the region, including the bloody 1832 Black Hawk War that forced the removal of the indigenous people to areas west of the Mississippi.

Industries sprang up and grew quickly, fueled by resources of coal and iron, and urged on by Civil War demands. The work available brought huge influxes of European immigrants from Ireland (in the early and mid-19th century), Germany (in the mid- to late 19th century), Scandinavia (in the late 19th century), Italy and Russia (around the turn of the 20th century) and southern and eastern Europe (in the early 20th century). In addition, for decades after the Civil War a great number of African-Americans migrated to the region's urban centers from the South.

The region prospered during WWII and through the 1950s. Then came 20 years of social turmoil and economic stagnation. The decline of manufacturing in the 1970s, particularly in the car industry, resulted in unemployment in many 'Rust Belt' cities; Detroit and Cleveland were especially hard hit. The 1980s brought urban revitalization and a shift away from economic reliance on industry. In the past decade, growth in the light manufacturing, service and high-tech sectors has meant better economic balance for the region. This process is continuing and the area's population has increased again, notably with newcomers from Asia and Mexico.

GEOGRAPHY & CLIMATE

Glaciers carved the Great Lakes during the last ice age. They now contain 15% of the world's fresh water. The largest by volume is Lake Superior, followed by Michigan, Huron, Ontario and Erie – all four of which Lake Superior could contain easily.

Glaciers scraped flat much of the low-lying land south of the lakes, leaving behind large areas of clay, sand and gravel called glacial till or drift. This action left some areas with huge mineral deposits close to the surface and others with thick, fertile soil. Higher land, around northwestern Illinois and the southern Wisconsin–Minnesota border, was bypassed by glaciers and now forms the 'driftless' region.

Most of the area's larger rivers run south into the major Ohio-Mississippi system. As these rivers were the main transportation and communication routes before the railways arrived, most of the region's larger cities lie along them or on the lakeshores. Lake-filled north-country forests cover much of Michigan, Minnesota and Wisconsin and hold a mix of softwood trees – pine, spruce and cedar – and hardwoods such as maple and birch. Further south, deciduous trees such as oak are dominant.

Among the mammals, the much-loved white-tailed deer is common, as are opossums, raccoons and coyotes. Moose, bears and wolves inhabit remote northern areas. Major sport fish include bass, lake trout, muskellunge, walleye and whitefish. Among birds, the loon charms visitors with its wonderful, varied cries, and bald eagle populations continue to rise, making sightings increasingly likely.

Winters are long and can last from late November well into April, with plenty of snow, icy winds and subfreezing temperatures (eg Chicago and Minneapolis each average about 20°F in January, the coldest month). Don't be intimidated – but do pack warmly. Many people visit during this time as it's prime for skiing and snowmobiling. By June the sun is out and temperatures start to rise, and by July and August it can be downright hot and sticky. Spring and autumn fit in around the edges, and are wonderful times to visit (particularly autumn, when leaves are at their peak of color).

NATIONAL PARKS

Several national parks and lakeshores are brushed across the Great Lakes region, including Voyageurs National Park (p444) in Minnesota; Isle Royale (p420), Sleeping Bear Dunes (p415), and Pictured Rocks (p419) in Michigan; the Apostle Islands (p429) in Wisconsin; and Indiana Dunes (p389). The midwest office of the **National Park Service** (NPS; ☎ 402-221-3471; www.nps.gov) can provide general information; better is the park service's website, which has direct links and phone numbers for individual parks. Make camping reservations on the website or call ☎ 800-365-2267.

Wide swathes of state park land also crisscross the Great Lakes. See individual state introductory sections for state park details.

ACTIVITIES

Hiking and **backpacking** opportunities abound in the area's numerous state and national parks and forests. Michigan's Upper Peninsula holds a long stretch of the 3000-mile North Country Trail, which extends from North Dakota to New York. Isle Royale National Park, Pictured Rocks National Lakeshore and Porcupine Mountains Wilderness State Park are also popular destinations.

In northern Minnesota, the Boundary Waters Canoe Area Wilderness (BWCAW) is world-renowned canoe country. Rivers in less wild areas throughout the Great Lakes states are suitable for **canoeing** – along many you'll find outfitters or 'canoe liveries' for rentals. Voyageurs National Park and Wisconsin's Apostle Islands provide challenging **sea kayaking**. The region's many waterways also mean there's bountiful **fishing**.

Bicycle touring opportunities are abundant as well. Resurfaced 'rail trails' traverse converted old railroad grades in numerous areas, especially in Michigan and Wisconsin. Excellent **cycling** can also be found on many islands, including Mackinac in Lake Huron and Kelleys in Lake Erie.

The area's forests are laced with trails for wintertime **cross-country skiing**. **Snowmobiling** is huge in northern Michigan, Wisconsin and Minnesota, which also offer downhill skiing.

DANGERS & ANNOYANCES

Relentless blackflies (spring) and mosquitoes (summer) can be an unfortunate reality in the northern woods. Protect yourself with a repellent, such as Muskol (not recommended for kids). Campers, make sure your tent has a fine mesh screening. Light-colored clothing also helps (sort of), as does a smoky fire. Ask rangers about deer ticks (they can transmit Lyme disease) and how to prevent bites. By late summer most bugs are gone.

In winter, thin ice is a deadly hazard for skiers and especially snowmobilers. Always err on the side of caution, and don't trust the ice-safety opinion of anyone other than police, park or forestry officials. Every year people die after crashing through supposedly frozen lake ice.

GETTING THERE & AROUND

Air

Chicago's O'Hare International Airport is the main air hub for the region. Detroit, Cleveland and Minneapolis also have busy airports.

Boat

The **SS Badger ferry** (☎ 888-337-7948; www.ssbadger.com; adult one way $47, child $21, car $49; mid-May–Oct) crosses Lake Michigan between Ludington, Michigan, and Manitowoc, Wisconsin.

Bus

Greyhound (☎ 800-231-2222), which originated in Minnesota, is the principal long-distance carrier and connects major cities and towns. The secondary bus lines do cover a few areas:

Indian Trails (☎ 800-292-3831; www.indiantrails.com) Michigan, northern Indiana and Illinois.

Jefferson Lines (☎ 800-451-5333; www.jeffersonlines.com) Southern Minnesota and Wisconsin.

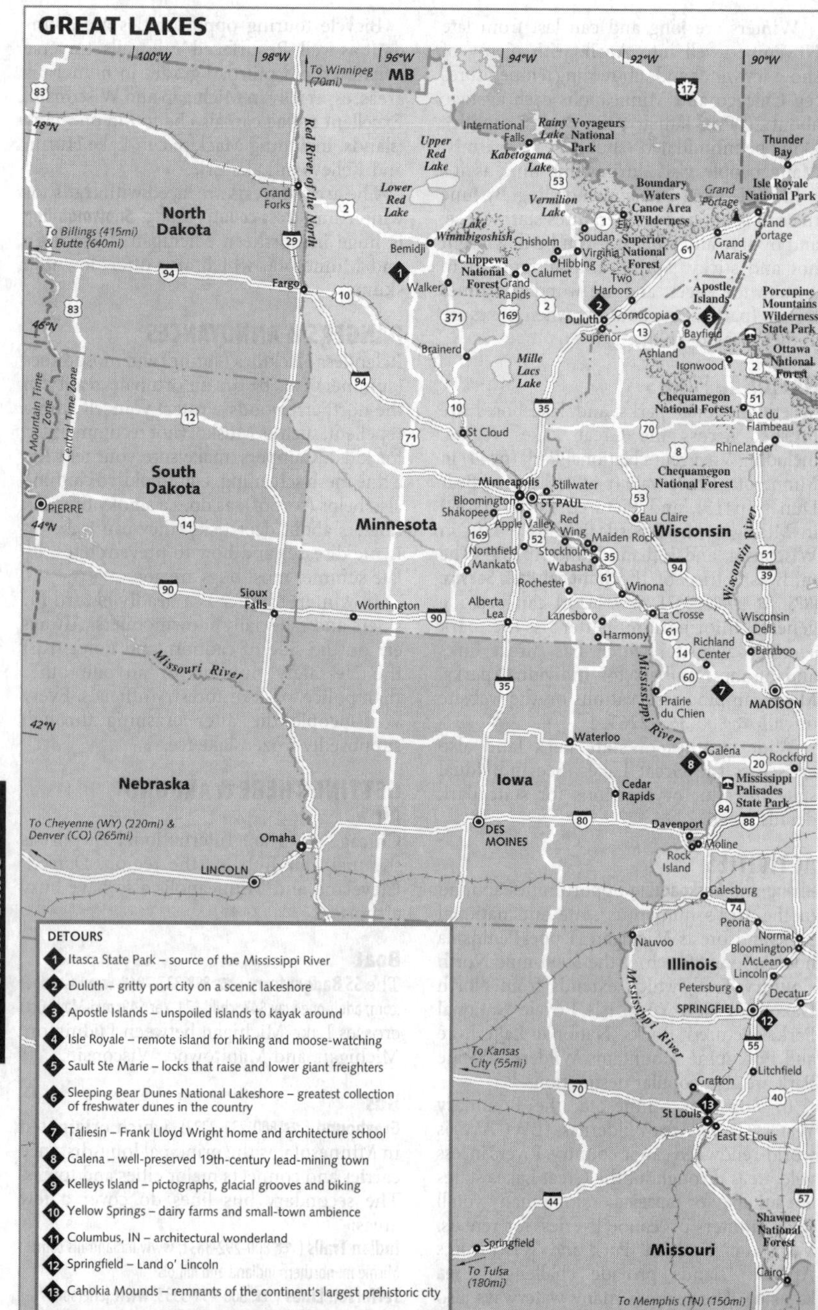
GREAT LAKES
100°W
98°W
96°W
94°W
92°W
90°W
To Winnipeg (70mi)
MB
48°N
46°N
44°N
42°N
Thunder Bay
International Falls
Rainy Lake
Voyageurs National Park
Kabetogama Lake
Upper Red Lake
Lower Red Lake
Vermilion Lake
Boundary Waters Canoe Area Wilderness
Grand Portage
Isle Royale National Park
Grand Forks
North Dakota
To Billings (415mi) & Butte (640mi)
Red River of the North
Lake Winnibigoshish
Bemidji
Chisholm
Soudan
Ely
Virginia
Hibbing
Superior National Forest
Grand Marais
Chippewa National Forest
Calumet
Grand Rapids
Two Harbors
Apostle Islands
Porcupine Mountains Wilderness State Park
Fargo
Walker
Duluth
Superior
Cornucopia
Bayfield
Ashland
Ironwood
Ottawa National Forest
Brainerd
Mille Lacs Lake
Chequamegon National Forest
Lac du Flambeau
Mountain Time Zone
Central Time Zone
St Cloud
Rhinelander
South Dakota
Minneapolis
Stillwater
ST PAUL
Bloomington
Shakopee
Apple Valley
Red Wing
Maiden Rock
Eau Claire
PIERRE
Minnesota
Wisconsin
Wisconsin River
Northfield
Stockholm
Mankato
Wabasha
Rochester
Winona
Sioux Falls
Worthington
Alberta Lea
Lanesboro
La Crosse
Wisconsin Dells
Harmony
Richland Center
Baraboo
Missouri River
Mississippi River
Prairie du Chien
MADISON
Waterloo
Galena
Rockford
Nebraska
Iowa
Cedar Rapids
Mississippi Palisades State Park
To Cheyenne (WY) (220mi) & Denver (CO) (265mi)
DES MOINES
Davenport
Moline
Rock Island
Omaha
LINCOLN
Galesburg
Peoria
Normal
Bloomington
McLean
Lincoln
Nauvoo
Illinois
Petersburg
Decatur
SPRINGFIELD
To Kansas City (55mi)
Litchfield
Grafton
St Louis
East St Louis
Shawnee National Forest
Missouri
Springfield
To Tulsa (180mi)
Cairo
To Memphis (TN) (150mi)
DETOURS
1 Itasca State Park – source of the Mississippi River
2 Duluth – gritty port city on a scenic lakeshore
3 Apostle Islands – unspoiled islands to kayak around
4 Isle Royale – remote island for hiking and moose-watching
5 Sault Ste Marie – locks that raise and lower giant freighters
6 Sleeping Bear Dunes National Lakeshore – greatest collection of freshwater dunes in the country
7 Taliesin – Frank Lloyd Wright home and architecture school
8 Galena – well-preserved 19th-century lead-mining town
9 Kelleys Island – pictographs, glacial grooves and biking
10 Yellow Springs – dairy farms and small-town ambience
11 Columbus, IN – architectural wonderland
12 Springfield – Land o' Lincoln
13 Cahokia Mounds – remnants of the continent's largest prehistoric city

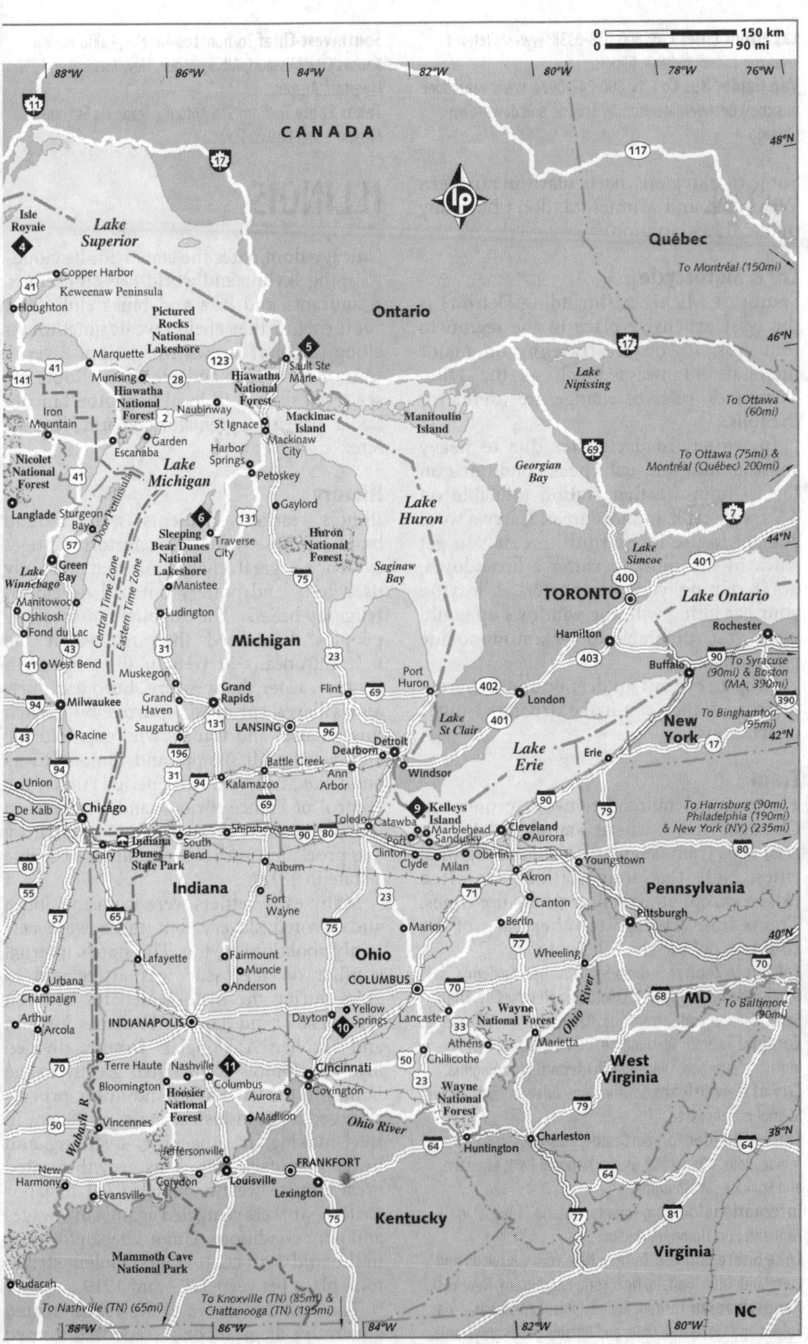

CANADA
Ontario
Québec
Lake Superior
Isle Royale
Copper Harbor
Keweenaw Peninsula
Houghton
Pictured Rocks National Lakeshore
Marquette
Munising
Hiawatha National Forest
Sault Ste Marie
Naubinway
St Ignace
Mackinac Island
Mackinaw City
Iron Mountain
Garden
Escanaba
Nicolet National Forest
Langlade
Lake Michigan
Harbor Springs
Petoskey
Gaylord
Sturgeon Bay
Door Peninsula
Sleeping Bear Dunes National Lakeshore
Traverse City
Huron National Forest
Manitoulin Island
Lake Huron
Saginaw Bay
Georgian Bay
Lake Nipissing
Lake Simcoe
TORONTO
Lake Ontario
Hamilton
Rochester
Buffalo
London
Lake Winnebago
Green Bay
Manitowoc
Oshkosh
Fond du Lac
West Bend
Milwaukee
Racine
Central Time Zone
Eastern Time Zone
Manistee
Ludington
Muskegon
Grand Haven
Grand Rapids
Saugatuck
Michigan
LANSING
Flint
Port Huron
Lake St Clair
Detroit
Dearborn
Windsor
Battle Creek
Kalamazoo
Ann Arbor
Lake Erie
Erie
New York
Union
De Kalb
Chicago
Gary
Indiana Dunes State Park
South Bend
Shipshewana
Toledo
Catawba
Kelleys Island
Marblehead
Sandusky
Port Clinton
Clyde
Milan
Oberlin
Cleveland
Aurora
Youngstown
Akron
Canton
Auburn
Fort Wayne
Indiana
Marion
Ohio
Berlin
Pennsylvania
Pittsburgh
Wheeling
Lafayette
Fairmount
Muncie
Anderson
COLUMBUS
Urbana
Champaign
Arthur
Arcola
INDIANAPOLIS
Dayton
Yellow Springs
Lancaster
Wayne National Forest
Athens
Marietta
Ohio River
MD
West Virginia
Terre Haute
Nashville
Columbus
Bloomington
Hoosier National Forest
Cincinnati
Covington
Aurora
Madison
Chillicothe
Vincennes
Wabash R
Huntington
Charleston
Jeffersonville
Louisville
FRANKFORT
Lexington
New Harmony
Corydon
Evansville
Kentucky
Virginia
Mammoth Cave National Park
Paducah
NC
To Montréal (150mi)
To Ottawa (60mi)
To Ottawa (75mi) & Montréal (Québec) 200mi)
To Syracuse (90mi) & Boston (MA, 390mi)
To Binghamton (95mi)
To Harrisburg (90mi), Philadelphia (190mi) & New York (NY) (235mi)
To Baltimore (90mi)
To Nashville (TN) (65mi)
To Knoxville (TN) (85mi) & Chattanooga (TN) (195mi)
0 150 km
0 90 mi
88°W
86°W
84°W
82°W
80°W
78°W
76°W
48°N
46°N
44°N
42°N
40°N
38°N

GREAT LAKES

Lakefront Lines (☎ 800-638-6338; www.lakefrontlines.com) Ohio, Indiana, Illinois.
Van Galder Bus Co (☎ 800-747-0994; www.vangalderbus.com) Between Madison, Wisconsin and downtown Chicago.

Some rural regions, particularly in northern Wisconsin and Minnesota, don't have any public transportation.

Car & Motorcycle

Southeast Michigan (including Detroit) is the least expensive place in the region to rent cars. If you are traveling on major interstate highways (such as the Ohio Turnpike), piles of change are useful for the tolls.

In winter, road closures due to heavy snow are not unusual; check conditions on the 24-hour weather station available on TVs with cable in most areas. Carry a wool blanket to use for warmth in case you get stuck in the snow or suffer a breakdown; don't rely on your car heater, as leaving your car idling with the windows up could make you vulnerable to carbon monoxide poisoning.

Keep an eye out for deer bounding across the road – they can make driving at night treacherous.

Train

The national railroad network centers on Chicago, from where **Amtrak** (☎ 800-872-7245) runs trains regularly to major regional cities. Note that train stations are often closed except at arrival or departure times. Trains from Chicago to other parts of the country include the following:

California Zephyr To/from San Francisco, California via Omaha, Nebraska; Denver, Colorado; Salt Lake City, Utah; Reno, Nevada; and Sacramento, California.
Cardinal To/from Washington, DC via Indianapolis, Indiana; Cincinnati, Ohio; and Charleston, West Virginia.
City of New Orleans To/from New Orleans, Louisiana via Memphis, Tennessee.
Empire Builder To/from Seattle, Washington via Minneapolis, Minnesota; Glacier National Park, Montana; and Spokane, Washington.
International To/from Toronto, Ontario (Canada) via Flint and Port Huron, Michigan.
Lake Shore Limited To/from New York via Toledo and Cleveland, Ohio; Buffalo, New York; and Albany, New York.
Pennsylvanian To/from Philadelphia, Pennsylvania via Toledo and Cleveland, Ohio; and Pittsburgh, Pennsylvania.
Southwest Chief To/from Los Angeles, California via Kansas City, Missouri; Albuquerque, New Mexico; and Flagstaff, Arizona.
Texas Eagle To/from San Antonio, Texas via St Louis, Missouri; and Dallas, Texas.

ILLINOIS

Chicago dominates the state with its cloud-scraping skyline and world-class museums, restaurants and jazz and blues clubs. But venturing further afield reveals quiet towns along the bluff-strewn Mississippi River, a trail of corn dogs and pie down Route 66, scattered shrines to local hero Abe Lincoln and a surprising prehistoric World Heritage Site.

History

Illinois' earliest residents were mound builders whose scattered prehistoric vestiges evidence a great civilization that not only used tools and pottery but had developed religious beliefs. The Algonquian-speaking peoples dominated the area when the first Europeans arrived in the early 17th century. Later that century, European forts and villages sprouted, spurred by French missionaries and traders who explored the area via the Mississippi and Illinois Rivers and Lake Michigan. After periods under the control of France, Britain and Virginia, an independently governed Illinois Territory was proclaimed in 1809, and Illinois became a state in 1818.

Many early settlers were from the South and favored slavery, but there were certainly abolitionists, too. The state's internal conflict on the issue was articulated in 1858 during the historic debates between senatorial candidates Abraham Lincoln and Stephen A Douglas. Despite divided loyalties, Illinois contributed greatly to the Union in the Civil War, and in the process emerged as an industrial state, proficient in steel-making, meatpacking, distilling and heavy manufacturing. This growth created great private wealth but also led to labor strife as workers struggled against low wages and poor conditions. Unions began forming in the mid-19th century, and violent strikes took place between 1877 and 1919.

The Prohibition era of the 1920s created a lucrative illegal alcohol trade that funded

ILLINOIS FACTS

Nicknames The Prairie State, Land of Lincoln
Population 12,600,620 (5th)
Area 57,900 sq miles (25th)
Admitted to Union December 3, 1818 (21st)
Capital city Springfield (population 111,500)
Other cities Chicago (2,896,000), Rockford (150,100), Peoria (112,900)
Birthplace of author Ernest Hemingway (1899–1961), animator Walt Disney (1901–66), jazz musician Miles Davis (1926–91), model Cindy Crawford (b 1966)
Famous for the 'Chicago Schools' of architecture, poetry, sociology and economics

gangsterism and the wholesale corruption of the state's political system. Then the Great Depression hit hard – up to half of Illinois' workers were unemployed. In the 1930s, Democratic governor Henry Horner was able to rebuild state finances and restore honest and efficient government. WWII enabled the state economy to recover.

Today the state's prairies and fertile plains help it maintain one of the country's highest agricultural outputs; pork, corn and soybeans are the most significant.

Information

Illinois Bureau of Tourism (☎ 800-226-6632; www.enjoyillinois.com; 620 E Adams St, Springfield, IL 62701)
Illinois highway conditions (☎ 800-452-4368; www.dot.state.il.us)

Illinois sales tax is 6.25%; city and county taxes add up to 3% more.

National & State Parks

Illinois state park information (☎ 217-782-6752; www.dnr.state.il.us; 1 Natural Resources Way, Springfield, IL 62702) State parks are free; some accept campsite reservations.

CHICAGO

The City of Big Shoulders has always thought big. It shaped modern architecture when it built the first skyscraper; today its sleek skyline is punctuated by several of the world's tallest buildings. Chicago is a wonderful city to roam, from downtown where you can gawk at the architecture to the 18 miles of Lake Michigan beachfront. Its 77 neighborhoods support vibrant Mexican, Polish, Indian and Vietnamese communities, among others, that offer amazing places to eat and shop. The city is an arts mecca, with a renowned blues and jazz scene, and recently has emerged as a theater hotbed, with more than 200 stages producing live works. Chicagoans tend to hibernate (often in bars) in the blustery winter, then make a greedy dash for the beaches and parks in the all-too-short summer.

History

Native Americans were fishing and canoeing in the region by AD 1000. In the late 17th century, the Potawatomi dominated the land, and it was they who gave the name 'Checaugou' – or wild onions – to the vicinity around Chicago River's mouth. By the time the area's 4170 residents incorporated as a town in 1837, the Native Americans were gone, their lands requisitioned in the Black Hawk War five years earlier.

The small settlement quickly established itself as a crossroads and grew. When new canals opened in the 1840s, shipping between the Caribbean and New York began to flow through Chicago, traveling via the Mississippi River, Great Lakes and St Lawrence Seaway. In 1851 the Illinois Central Railroad was given land to establish freight yards, and Chicago was soon the USA's railroad hub.

The first steel mill opened in 1857, and immigrants flooded in to take jobs in industry and with the railroads; the population had soared to 100,000 by 1860. The opening of the stockyards in 1865 drew even more newcomers.

On October 8, 1871, legend has it that Mrs O'Leary's cow kicked over a lantern and started the great Chicago Fire, which destroyed the whole inner city and left 90,000 people homeless. The disaster became an opportunity to replace wide areas of substandard housing and create space for modern industrial and commercial buildings, like the world's first skyscraper, which appeared on the horizon in 1885.

The Union Loop Elevated rail system was completed in 1897. More civic improvements were made in the early 20th century under the guidance of Daniel Burnham and his visionary Plan of Chicago, which called for a network of boulevards, parks and unobstructed lakefront space. The

CHICAGO IN...

Two Days

Take an architectural boat cruise and look up at the city's skyscrapers. Look down from the **John Hancock Center**, one of the world's tallest buildings. Stroll along the **Magnificent Mile** and out on festive **Navy Pier**. Hungry after all the walking? Chow down on Chicago's famous deep-dish pizza. Make the second day a cultural one: browse in the **Art Institute**, **Shedd Aquarium**, **Field Museum** and **Adler Planetarium**. Listen to live jazz in the evening at one of Chicago's many clubs.

Four Days

Follow the two-day itinerary, then on your third day rent a bicycle, dip your toes in Lake Michigan at **North Avenue Beach**, and cruise through **Lincoln Park**, making stops at the zoo and conservatory. If it's baseball season, head directly to **Wrigley Field** for a Cubs game; if it's winter, take in a Bulls (basketball), Bears (football) or Blackhawks (hockey) game. A smoky blues club is a fine way to finish the day (or start the morning).

Pick a neighborhood on your fourth day – **Hyde Park**, **Andersonville** or **Devon Ave** – and wander, eat, shop and eat some more. Then see a play at one of Chicago's 200 theaters.

population swelled to more than two million by 1910.

In the 1920s, Prohibition led almost immediately to the infamous period of gangsterism and to widespread corruption. In the middle of the devastating Depression, after the murder of Mayor Anton Cermak, the Democratic Party machine gained control of city politics and has maintained it for most of the years since.

The city's population peaked in 1950, then started to decline as residents moved to outer suburbs and other states. Despite some improvements, the postwar period was dominated by corruption scandals, civil rights protests and the fiasco of the 1968 Democratic Convention, when anti-Vietnam War demonstrators were the victims of what was later termed a 'police riot.' Starting in the 1970s, traditional industries declined severely: the stockyards and the South Shore steel mills closed, and many smaller factories moved away or went out of business.

The City That Works went to work on itself, and with classic, steely determination cleaned up its image. Today, the processing of information and ideas has taken precedence over the processing and transport of products. The city's downtown and many of its neighborhoods are thriving, though areas of great poverty remain, particularly on the south side. Mayor Richard M Daley is Chicago's popular Democratic leader, continuing the tradition started by his father, who was mayor for 21 years.

Orientation

The central downtown area is the Loop – beyond this, Chicago is a city of neighborhoods. Chicago's streets are laid out on a grid and numbered; Madison and State Sts are the grid's center. As you go north, south, east or west from here, each increase of 800 in street numbers corresponds to 1 mile. At every increase of 400, there is a major arterial street. For instance, Division St (1200 N) is followed by North Ave (1600 N) and Armitage Ave (2000 N), at which point you're 2.5 miles north of downtown. Pick up a copy of Lonely Planet's *Chicago City Map* for details.

Information

BOOKSTORES

Savvy Traveler (Map pp358-60; ☎ 312-913-9800; 310 S Michigan Ave)

Seminary Co-op Bookstore (☎ 773-752-4381; 5757 S University Ave) Beloved by scholars worldwide, located at the University of Chicago.

Women & Children First (☎ 773-769-9299; 5233 N Clark St) Women-penned fiction and other feminist tomes.

CHILD MINDING

American Childcare Services (☎ 312-644-7300; 445 E Ohio St) Professional babysitters come to your hotel. Four-hour minimum; $16.50 per hour, $10 transportation fee.

EMERGENCY

Emergency number (☎ 911) For police, fire or ambulance services.

Rape crisis (☎ 888-293-2080)

INTERNET ACCESS

Harold Washington Library Center (Map pp358-60; ☎ 312-747-4300; 400 S State St) Free access in a grand building.

Screenz Digital Universe (Map pp362-4; ☎ 773-348-9300; 2717 N Clark St; $8.40 per hr)

MEDIA

The *Chicago Tribune* and *Chicago Sun-Times* are the competing dailies. Both publish excellent Friday entertainment sections. Look for the free *Reader*, a huge weekly paper out on Thursday with comprehensive event listings. *New City* is a smaller weekly freebie out on Wednesday. Both are available at bookstores, bars and coffee shops around town. Chicago's National Public Radio (NPR) affiliate is WBEZ-FM 91.5. For alternative music tune into WXRT-FM 93.1.

MEDICAL SERVICES

Northwestern Memorial Hospital (Map pp358-60; ☎ 312-926-5188; 251 E Erie Ave)

Walgreens (Map pp358-60; ☎ 312-664-8686; 757 N Michigan Ave) Twenty-four-hour pharmacy.

MONEY

ATMs are plentiful downtown, with many concentrated near Chicago and Michigan Aves. To change money, try the currency exchange at Terminal 5 at O'Hare Airport or the following services in the Loop.

Thomas Cook Currency Services (Map pp358-60; ☎ 312-807-4940; 19 S LaSalle St)

World's Money Exchange (Map pp358-60; ☎ 312-641-2151; 203 N LaSalle St)

POST

Main post office (Map pp358-60; ☎ 312-983-8182; 433 W Harrison St) Open 24 hours.

Fort Dearborn office (Map pp358-60; ☎ 312-644-0485; 540 N Dearborn St)

TOURIST INFORMATION

Chicago's visitors centers are well-staffed and stocked.

Chicago Cultural Center Visitors Center (Map pp358-60; 77 E Randolph St; 🕑 10am-6pm Mon-Fri, 10am-5pm Sat, 11am-5pm Sun)

Chicago Office of Tourism (☎ 312-744-2400, 877-244-2246; www.cityofchicago.org/tourism or www.877chicago.org)

Illinois Market Place Visitors Center (Map pp358-60; 600 E Grand Ave; 🕑 10am, closing varies 7-10pm) At Navy Pier.

Water Works Visitors Center (Map pp358-60; 163 E Pearson St; 🕑 7:30am-7pm)

TRAVEL AGENCIES

STA Travel (Map pp362-4; ☎ 312-951-0585; 1160 N State St) Budget travel specialists.

Dangers & Annoyances

The lakefront, major parks and some neighborhoods, especially south and west of the Loop, can become bleak and forbidding places at night. Neighborhoods can change completely in just a few blocks, so be aware of your surroundings.

Most of Chicago's violent crime is committed by street gangs battling over drug turf. The most common crimes against tourists are pickpocketing, bag snatching, vehicle break-ins and bike theft.

Sights

Chicago's main attractions are in or near the city center, though visits to distant neighborhoods like Andersonville, Devon Avenue and Hyde Park are rewarding. Purchase the lump-sum **CityPass** (☎ 707-256-0490; www.citypass.net; adult $49, child 3-11 $38) and save on fees into six of Chicago's most popular attractions including the Field Museum, Art Institute, Adler Planetarium, Hancock Observatory, Museum of Science & Industry and Shedd Aquarium. Students with ID often get reduced museum admission.

THE LOOP

The city center is named for the elevated tracks that circle its streets. It's busy all day and has a burgeoning nightlife, thanks in part to the Theater District where playhouses cluster near the intersection of N State and W Randolph Sts.

Art Institute of Chicago

Chicago's premier cultural institution, the **Art Institute** (Map pp358-60; ☎ 312-443-3600; 111 S Michigan Ave; adult/child $10/6, free Tue; 🕑 10:30am-4:30pm Mon-Fri, until 8pm Tue, 10am-5pm Sat & Sun) houses treasures and masterpieces from around the globe, including a fabulous selection of both impressionist and postimpressionist paintings. Georges Seurat's pointillist *A Sunday on La Grande Jatte* is here; so is Grant Wood's *American Gothic*. Allow two hours to see the highlights, much longer for art buffs.

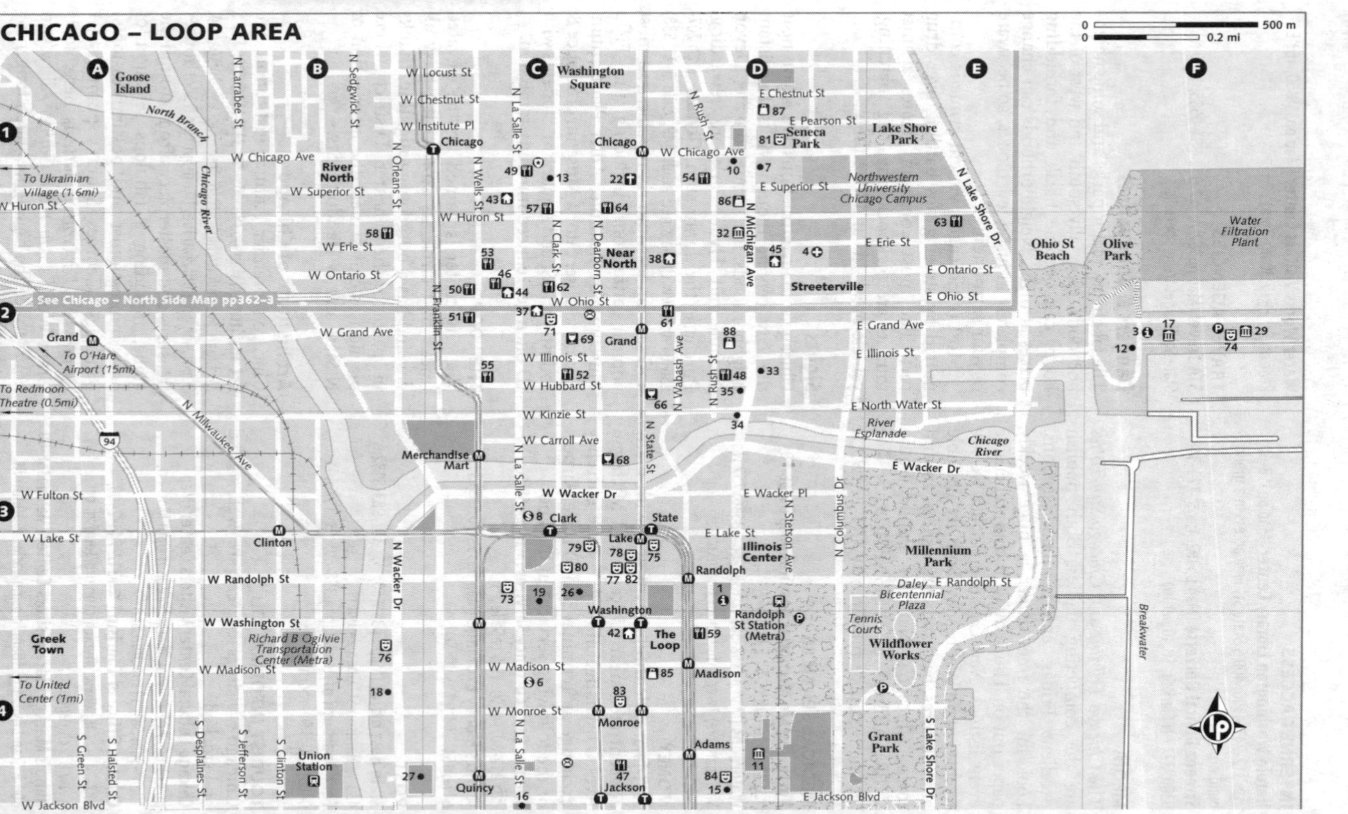
CHICAGO – LOOP AREA
0 500 m
0 0.2 mi
Goose Island
North Branch
Chicago River
W Locust St
W Chestnut St
W Institute Pl
Chicago
Washington Square
N Larrabee St
N Sedgwick St
N Orleans St
N La Salle St
N Wells St
N Rush St
E Chestnut St
E Pearson St
Seneca Park
Lake Shore Park
W Chicago Ave
River North
W Superior St
To Ukrainian Village (1.6mi)
W Huron St
E Superior St
Northwestern University Chicago Campus
N Lake Shore Dr
W Erie St
W Ontario St
N Clark St
N Dearborn St
Near North
N Michigan Ave
E Erie St
E Ontario St
E Ohio St
Streeterville
Ohio St Beach
Olive Park
Water Filtration Plant
See Chicago – North Side Map pp362-3
W Ohio St
N Franklin St
Grand
To O'Hare Airport (15mi)
W Grand Ave
W Illinois St
W Hubbard St
W Kinzie St
W Carroll Ave
N Wabash Ave
E Grand Ave
E Illinois St
To Redmoon Theatre (0.5mi)
N Milwaukee Ave
94
Merchandise Mart
N State St
E North Water St
River Esplanade
Chicago River
E Wacker Dr
W Wacker Dr
E Wacker Pl
N Stetson Ave
N Columbus Dr
W Fulton St
Clark
State
W Lake St
Clinton
Lake
E Lake St
Illinois Center
Millennium Park
W Randolph St
N Wacker Dr
Randolph
Daley Bicentennial Plaza
E Randolph St
Washington
W Washington St
Greek Town
Richard B Ogilvie Transportation Center (Metra)
The Loop
Randolph St Station (Metra)
Tennis Courts
Wildflower Works
Breakwater
W Madison St
Madison
To United Center (1mi)
W Monroe St
Monroe
Adams
Grant Park
S Lake Shore Dr
S Green St
S Halsted St
S Desplaines St
S Jefferson St
S Clinton St
Union Station
Quincy
Jackson
W Jackson Blvd
E Jackson Blvd

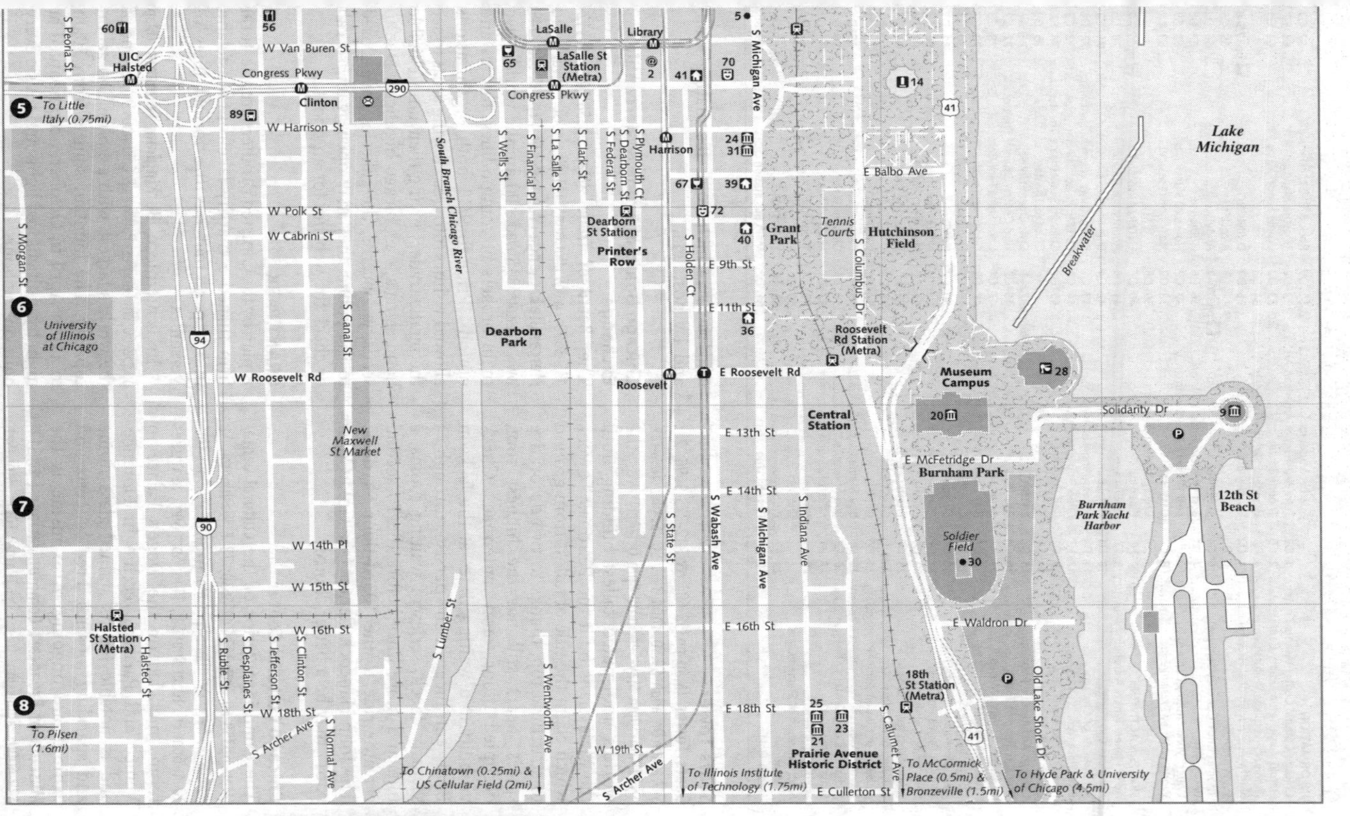
S Peoria St
UIC-Halsted
W Van Buren St
Congress Pkwy
Clinton
To Little Italy (0.75mi)
W Harrison St
LaSalle
LaSalle St Station (Metra)
Library
Congress Pkwy
S Michigan Ave
Lake Michigan
E Balbo Ave
Harrison
S Wells St
S Financial Pl
S La Salle St
S Clark St
S Federal St
S Dearborn St
S Plymouth Ct
South Branch Chicago River
W Polk St
W Cabrini St
S Morgan St
Dearborn St Station
Printer's Row
S Holden Ct
Grant Park
Tennis Courts
S Columbus Dr
Hutchinson Field
Breakwater
E 9th St
E 11th St
University of Illinois at Chicago
S Canal St
Dearborn Park
Roosevelt Rd Station (Metra)
W Roosevelt Rd
Roosevelt
E Roosevelt Rd
Museum Campus
Solidarity Dr
Central Station
E 13th St
New Maxwell St Market
E McFetridge Dr
Burnham Park
E 14th St
S State St
S Wabash Ave
S Michigan Ave
S Indiana Ave
Soldier Field
Burnham Park Yacht Harbor
12th St Beach
W 14th Pl
W 15th St
S Lumber St
W 16th St
E 16th St
E Waldron Dr
Halsted St Station (Metra)
S Halsted St
S Ruble St
S Desplaines St
S Jefferson St
S Clinton St
W 18th St
S Wentworth Ave
S State St
E 18th St
18th St Station (Metra)
Old Lake Shore Dr
To Pilsen (1.6mi)
S Archer Ave
S Normal Ave
W 19th St
S Archer Ave
Prairie Avenue Historic District
S Calumet Ave
To Chinatown (0.25mi) & US Cellular Field (2mi)
To Illinois Institute of Technology (1.75mi)
E Cullerton St
To McCormick Place (0.5mi) & Bronzeville (1.5mi)
To Hyde Park & University of Chicago (4.5mi)
GREAT LAKES

INFORMATION
- Chicago Cultural Center Visitors Center... 1 D3
- Harold Washington Library Center... 2 C5
- Illinois Marketplace Visitors Center... 3 F2
- Northwestern Memorial Hospital... 4 D2
- Savvy Traveller... 5 D5
- Thomas Cook Currency Services... 6 C4
- Walgreens... 7 D1
- Water Works Visitors Center... (see 1)
- World's Money Exchange... 8 C3

SIGHTS & ACTIVITIES pp357–70
- Adler Planetarium & Astronomy Museum... 9 F7
- American Girl Place... 10 D1
- Art Institute of Chicago... 11 D4
- Bike Chicago... 12 F2
- Blue Chicago Store... 13 C1
- Buckingham Fountain... 14 E5
- Chicago Architecture Foundation... 15 D4
- Chicago Board of Trade... 16 C4
- Chicago Children's Museum... 17 F2
- Chicago Mercantile Exchange... 18 B4
- County Building & Chicago City Hall... 19 C3
- Field Museum of Natural History... 20 E7
- Henry B Clarke House... 21 D8
- Holy Name Cathedral... 22 C1
- John J Glessner House... 23 D8
- Museum of Broadcast Communications... (see 1)
- Museum of Contemporary Photography... 24 D5
- National Vietnam Veterans Art Museum... 25 D8
- Richard J Daley Center ('The Picasso')... 26 C3
- Sears Tower... 27 B4
- Shedd Aquarium... 28 E6
- Smith Museum of Stained Glass Windows... 29 F2
- Soldier Field... 30 E7
- Spertus Museum... 31 D5
- Terra Museum of American Art... 32 D2
- Tribune Tower... 33 D2
- Wendella Sightseeing Boats... 34 D3
- Wrigley Building... 35 D2

SLEEPING pp370–2
- Best Western Grant Park Inn... 36 D6
- Best Western River North... 37 C2
- Cass Hotel... 38 D2
- Chicago Hilton & Towers... 39 D5
- Essex Inn... 40 D6
- HI Chicago... 41 D5
- Hotel Burnham... 42 C4
- Howard Johnson Inn... 43 C1
- Ohio House Motel... 44 C2
- Red Roof Inn... 45 D2

EATING pp372–4
- Al's... 46 C2
- Berghoff... 47 C4
- Billy Goat Tavern (Lower Level)... 48 D2
- Cafe Iberico... 49 C1
- Carson's... 50 C2
- Corner Bakery... (see 1)
- Cyrano's Bistrot... 51 C2
- Frontera Grill... 52 C2
- Gino's East... 53 C2
- Giordano's... 54 D1
- Lou Malnati's... 55 C2
- Lou Mitchell's... 56 B5
- Mike's Rainbow Restaurant... 57 C1
- Mr Beef... 58 B2
- Oasis... 59 D4
- Parthenon... 60 A5
- Pizzeria Uno... 61 D2
- Rock & Roll McDonald's... 62 C2
- Treasure Island... 63 E2
- Whole Foods... 64 C1

DRINKING pp375–6
- Alcock's Inn... 65 C5
- Andy's... 66 D2
- Hothouse... 67 D5
- House of Blues... 68 C3
- Jazz Showcase... 69 C2

ENTERTAINMENT pp376–7
- Auditorium Theater... 70 D5
- Blue Chicago... 71 C2
- Buddy Guy's Legends... 72 D6
- Cadillac Palace Theater... 73 C3
- Chicago Shakespeare Theater... 74 F2
- Chicago Theater... 75 D3
- Civic Opera House... 76 B4
- Ford Center/Oriental Theater... 77 C3
- Gene Siskel Film Center... 78 C3
- Goodman Theatre... 79 C3
- Hot Tix... 80 C3
- Hot Tix... 81 D1
- Noble Fool Theatre Company... 82 C3
- Shubert Theater... 83 C4
- Symphony Center... 84 D4

SHOPPING p378
- Carson Pirie Scott & Co... 85 D4
- Chicago Place... 86 D1
- Marshall Field's... 87 D1
- Shops at North Bridge... 88 D2

TRANSPORT pp378–9
- Main Bus Station... 89 B5

Sears Tower

Sears Tower (Map pp358-60; ☎ 312-875-9696; 233 S Wacker Dr; adult $9.50, child 3-11 $6.75, plus 10% tax; 10am-10pm May-Sep, until 8pm Oct-Apr) was the world's undisputed tallest building until the Malaysians built the Petronas Towers, which claim the title of tallest from ground to structural top, thanks to two decorative spires. Sears still has the highest roof, occupied floor, and antennae. Check visibility and waiting times at the Jackson Blvd entrance, then persist through a security check, series of waiting rooms, a film and more lines before the 70-second elevator ride to the 103rd-floor Skydeck. The John Hancock Center (see Gold Coast p361) may be a better choice.

Chicago Cultural Center

The exquisite interior of the **Cultural Center** (Map pp358-60; ☎ 312-744-6630; 78 E Washington St; admission free; 10am-7pm Mon-Wed, 10am-9pm Thu, 10am-6pm Fri, 10am-5pm Sat, 11am-5pm Sun) features rooms modeled on the Doge's Palace in Venice and Palazzo Vecchio in Florence, and is notable for its stained-glass dome and sparkling mosaics. Free concerts and exhibits are ongoing. Also inside is the **Museum of Broadcast Communications** (☎ 312-629-6000; admission free; 10am-4:30pm Mon-Sat, noon-5pm Sun), which holds fascinating radio and TV nostalgia.

Chicago Board of Trade & Mercantile Exchange

The **Board of Trade** (Map pp358-60; ☎ 312-435-3590; www.cbot.com; 141 W Jackson Blvd) and **Mercantile Exchange** (Map pp358-60; ☎ 312-930-8249; www.cme.com; 30 S Wacker Dr) are the world's two main brokers of commodities, futures and options. Prior to 9/11 both organizations allowed visitors into free viewing areas to see the manic traders giving their unintelligible hand signals – a Chicago highlight. Due to security concerns, the galleries have closed to the public; they may open again, so call or check the websites for an update.

GRANT PARK

A plan by the Olmsted Brothers architectural firm turned a marshy lakefront wasteland into a park that has the formal lines of Versailles.

Its centerpiece, **Buckingham Fountain** (Map pp358-60; cnr Congress Parkway & Columbus Dr), is one of the world's largest, with a 1.5 million gallon capacity. The fountain squirts from 10am to 11pm April to October, accompanied at night by multicolored lights and music every hour on the hour.

Just north, the new **Millennium Park** (Map pp358-60; along Michigan Ave, btwn Monroe & Randolph Sts) is slowly being completed. Visitors can ice skate at the outdoor rink during winter. The Frank Gehry–designed band shell is slated for completion in 2004.

SOUTH LOOP

The gentrification of Printer's Row has revived the South Loop. Stroll S Dearborn St to see the rare bookshops and great old buildings that are now luxury lofts.

The excellent **Spertus Museum** (Map p3p58-60; ☎ 312-922-9012; 618 S Michigan Ave; adult $5, child over 5 $3, Fri free; 🕑 10am-5pm Sun-Wed, until 7pm Thu, 3pm Fri) covers 5000 years of Jewish faith and culture. Kids can dig for relics at the Artifact Center.

The nearby **Museum of Contemporary Photography** (Map pp358-60 ☎ 312-663-5554; 600 S Michigan Ave; admission free; 🕑 10am-5pm Mon-Fri, until 8pm Thu, noon-5pm Sun) displays US photographs taken since 1945.

MUSEUM CAMPUS

This lakefront area south of Grant Park has three significant attractions side by side.

Shedd Aquarium

Top draws at the famous **Shedd Aquarium** (Map pp358-60; ☎ 312-939-2438; 1200 S Lake Shore Dr; adult $21, child 3-11 $15; 🕑 9am-5pm Mon-Fri Sep-May, until 6pm Mon-Fri Jun-Aug, until 6pm Sat & Sun year-round) include the Oceanarium, with its beluga whales and frolicking white-sided dolphins, and the new shark exhibit, where there's just five inches of Plexiglas between you and 30 or so fierce-looking swimmers.

Field Museum of Natural History

The mammoth **Field Museum** (Map pp358-60; ☎ 312-922-94 10; 1400 S Lake Shore Dr; adult $10, child 3-11 $5; 🕑 9am-5pm) houses everything but the kitchen sink. Highlights include 'Africa,' a walk-through exhibit that moves from city streets to Saharan sand dunes, culminating in the hold of a slave ship; and Sue, the largest *Tyrannosaurus rex* yet discovered.

Adler Planetarium & Astronomy Museum

Touch a 1000-pound meteorite in the interactive galleries at the **Adler Planetarium** (Map pp358-60; ☎ 312-922-7827; 1300 S Lake Shore Dr; adult $13, child 4-17 $11; 🕑 9:30am-4:30pm Mon-Fri, 9am-4:30pm Sat & Sun), then view the cosmos in a digital sky show controlled from your chair's armrest.

NEAR NORTH

The area north of the river to Chicago Ave encompasses several points of interest. The **Magnificent Mile** (Map pp358-60; N Michigan Ave btwn the river & Oak St) is the much-touted upscale shopping strip where Bloomingdales, Neiman's and Saks will lighten your wallet.

Navy Pier (Map pp358-60; ☎ 312-595-7437; 600 E Grand Ave; admission free; 🕑 10am, closing times vary from 7pm-midnight) was once the city's municipal wharf. Its 0.5-mile length is now covered with a Ferris wheel, an Imax theater, numerous shops and gimmicky chain restaurants. Locals groan over its commercialization, but its lakefront view and cool breezes can't be beat.

The **Chicago Children's Museum** (p369) and gorgeous **Smith Museum of Stained Glass Windows** (Map 358-60; ☎ 312-595-5024; admission free; 🕑 same as Navy Pier) are also on the Pier.

Take a close look when passing by the gothic **Tribune Tower** (Map 358-60; 435 N Michigan Ave) to see chunks of the Taj Mahal, Parthenon and other famous structures embedded in the lower walls. The white terracotta exterior of the **Wrigley Building** (Map 358-60; 400 N Michigan Ave) glows day or night.

The modest **Terra Museum of American Art** (Map 358-60; ☎ 312-664-3939; 664 N Michigan Ave; admission free; 🕑 10am-8pm Tue, 10am-6pm Wed-Sat, noon-5pm Sun) includes works by Winslow Homer, James Whistler and Mary Cassatt. The Terra will be closing in late 2004, and many of its works moved to the Art Institute (p357).

GOLD COAST

Starting in 1882, Chicago's wealthy flocked to this neighborhood flanking the lake between Chicago and North Aves. Within 40 years, most of the Gold Coast was covered with mansions.

Today the neighborhood giant is the 1127ft-tall **John Hancock Center** (Map pp362-4; ☎ 312-751-3681; 875 N Michigan Ave; adult $9.75, child 5-12 $6; 🕑 9am-11pm), which has a great 94th-floor observatory that's often less crowded than the one at Sears Tower. Better yet, skip the observatory and head straight up to the 96th-floor Signature Lounge, where the view is free if you buy a drink ($5 to $10).

The 154ft-tall, turreted **Water Tower** (Map pp362-4; cnr Chicago & Michigan Aves) is a defining

GREAT LAKES

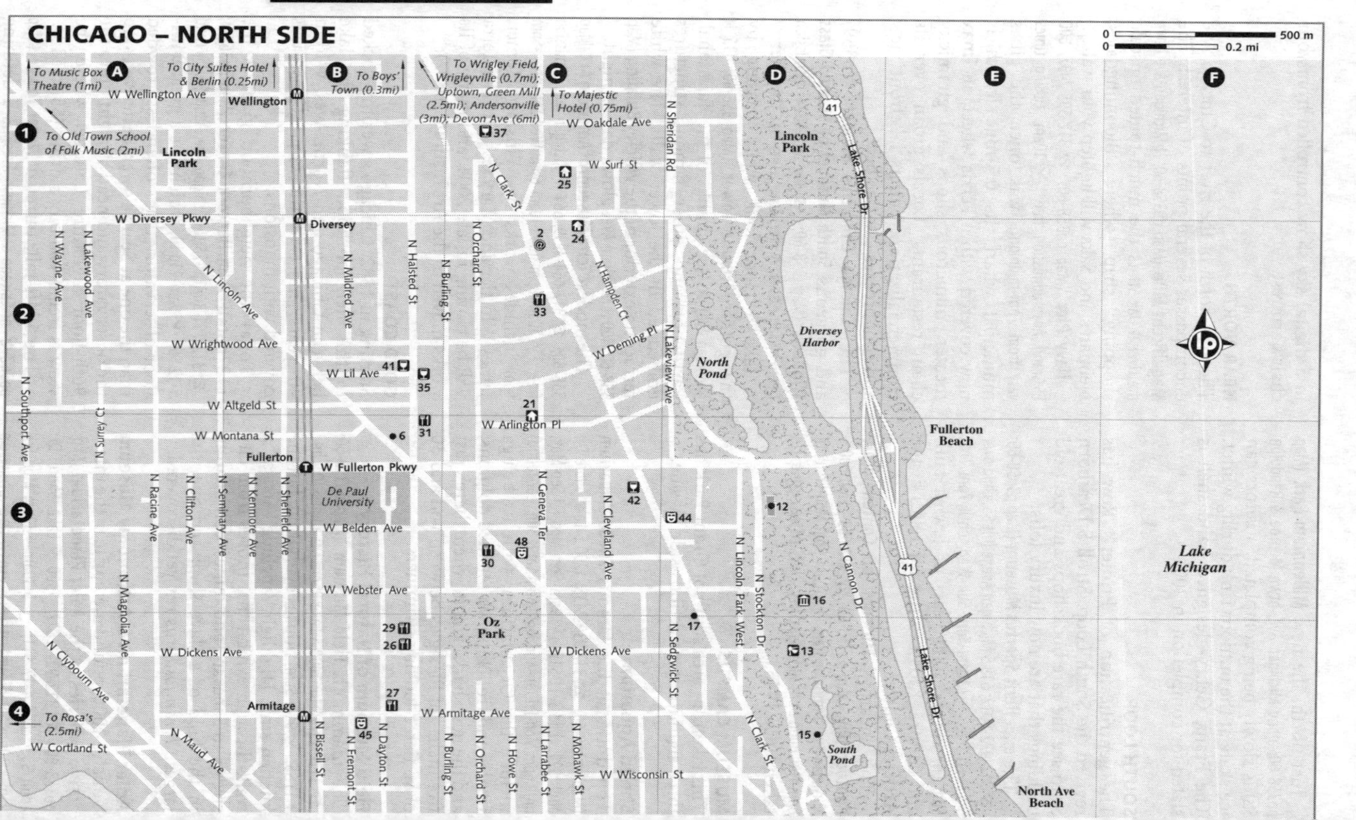

CHICAGO – NORTH SIDE
0 500 m
0 0.2 mi
To Music Box Theatre (1mi)
To City Suites Hotel & Berlin (0.25mi)
To Boys' Town (0.3mi)
To Wrigley Field, Wrigleyville (0.7mi); Uptown, Green Mill (2.5mi); Andersonville (3mi); Devon Ave (6mi)
To Majestic Hotel (0.75mi)
To Old Town School of Folk Music (2mi)
To Rosa's (2.5mi)
W Wellington Ave
Wellington
Lincoln Park
W Oakdale Ave
W Surf St
N Clark St
N Sheridan Rd
Lake Shore Dr
W Diversey Pkwy
Diversey
N Wayne Ave
N Lakewood Ave
N Lincoln Ave
N Mildred Ave
N Halsted St
N Burling St
N Orchard St
N Hampden Ct
W Deming Pl
N Lakeview Ave
North Pond
Diversey Harbor
W Wrightwood Ave
W Lil Ave
W Altgeld St
W Montana St
W Arlington Pl
N Southport Ave
N Surrey Ct
Fullerton
W Fullerton Pkwy
Fullerton Beach
N Racine Ave
N Clifton Ave
N Seminary Ave
N Kenmore Ave
N Sheffield Ave
De Paul University
W Belden Ave
N Geneva Ter
N Cleveland Ave
N Magnolia Ave
W Webster Ave
Oz Park
W Dickens Ave
N Sedgwick St
N Lincoln Park West
N Stockton Dr
N Cannon Dr
N Clybourn Ave
Armitage
W Armitage Ave
N Maud Ave
W Cortland St
N Bissell St
N Fremont St
N Dayton St
N Burling St
N Orchard St
N Howe St
N Larrabee St
N Mohawk St
W Wisconsin St
N Clark St
South Pond
North Ave Beach
Lake Michigan

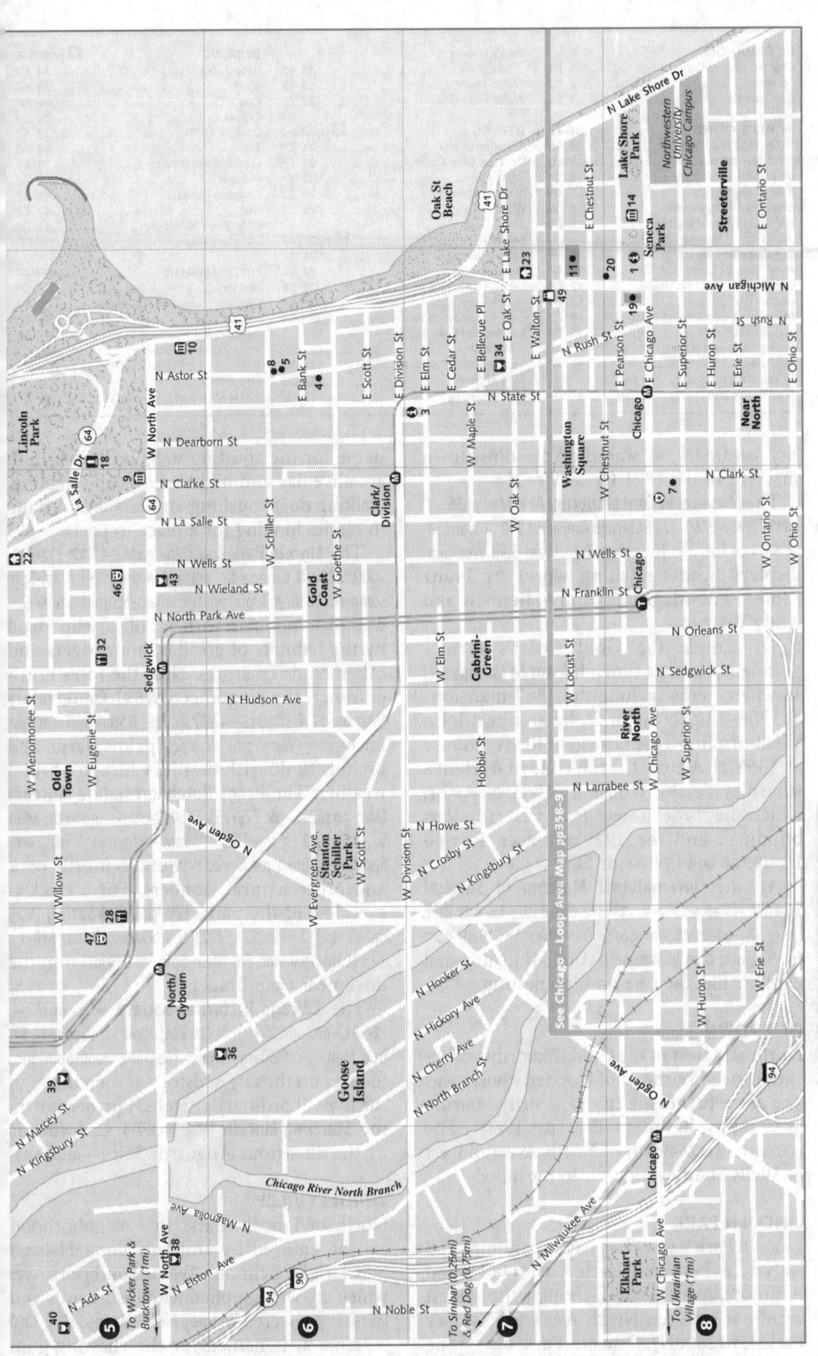
Lincoln Park
La Salle Dr
N Astor St
W North Ave
N Dearborn St
N Clarke St
N La Salle St
N Wells St
N Wieland St
N North Park Ave
Sedgwick
N Hudson Ave
W Menomonee St
W Eugenie St
Old Town
W Willow St
N Ogden Ave
North/ Clybourn
N Marcey St
N Kingsbury St
Chicago River North Branch
N Magnolia Ave
N Elston Ave
N Ada St
To Wicker Park & Bucktown (1mi)
Goose Island
N Hooker St
N Hickory Ave
N Cherry Ave
N North Branch St
N Noble St
To Sinibar (0.75mi) & Red Dog (0.75mi)
N Milwaukee Ave
Elkhart Park
W Chicago Ave
To Ukrainian Village (1mi)
Oak St Beach
E Lake Shore Dr
N Lake Shore Dr
Lake Shore Park
Northwestern University Chicago Campus
Streeterville
E Ontario St
E Chestnut St
Seneca Park
N Michigan Ave
N Rush St
E Pearson St
E Chicago Ave
E Superior St
E Huron St
E Erie St
E Ohio St
Near North
E Bank St
E Scott St
E Division St
E Elm St
E Cedar St
E Bellevue Pl
E Oak St
E Walton St
N State St
W Maple St
Washington Square
W Chestnut St
Chicago
N Clark St
W Schiller St
W Goethe St
Gold Coast
Clark/ Division
W Oak St
N Franklin St
W Ontario St
W Ohio St
N Orleans St
N Sedgwick St
W Elm St
Cabrini-Green
W Locust St
River North
W Chicago Ave
W Superior St
Hobbie St
N Larrabee St
W Evergreen Ave
Stanton Schiller Park
W Scott St
W Division St
N Howe St
N Crosby St
N Kingsbury St
See Chicago – Loop Area Map pp358–9
W Huron St
W Erie St
N Ogden Ave
GREAT LAKES

INFORMATION		
Chicago Visitors Center	1	E8
Screenz	2	C2
STA Travel	3	E7

SIGHTS & ACTIVITIES	pp357–78	
1308-1312 N Astor St	4	E6
1355 N Astor St	5	E6
Biograph Theater	6	B3
Blue Chicago Store	7	D8
Charnley-Persky House	8	E6
Chicago Historical Society	9	D5
International Museum of Surgical Science	10	E5
John Hancock Center	11	E7
Lincoln Park Conservatory	12	D3
Lincoln Park Zoo	13	D4
Museum of Contemporary Art	14	F8
Paddleboat Rental	15	D4
Peggy Notebaert Nature Museum	16	D3
St Valentine's Day Massacre Site	17	D4
Standing Lincoln Sculpture	18	E5
Water Tower	19	E8
Water Tower Place	20	E8

SLEEPING	pp370–2	
Arlington House	21	C3
Days Inn Gold Coast	22	D5
Drake Hotel	23	E7
Inn of Lincoln Park	24	C2
Willows Hotel	25	C1

EATING	pp372–4	
Cafe Bernard	26	B4
Charlie Trotter's	27	B4
Kabul House	28	B5
Nookies Too	29	B4
Potbelly Sandwich Works	30	C3
Red Rooster Cafe & Wine Bar	(see 26)	
Taco & Burrito Palace #2	31	B3
Twin Anchors	32	D5
Wiener Circle	33	C2

DRINKING	pp375–6	
Back Room	34	E7
Blues	35	B2
Coq d'Or	(see 23)	
Crobar	36	B6
Duke of Perth	37	C1
Exit	38	A5
Goose Island Brewery	39	B5
Hideout	40	A5
Kingston Mines	41	B2
Neo	42	C3
Olde Town Ale House	43	D5
Signature Lounge	(see 11)	

ENTERTAINMENT	pp376–7	
Hot Tix	44	D3
Old Town School of Folk Music	45	B4
Second City	46	D5
Steppenwolf Theatre	47	B5
Victory Gardens Theater	48	C3

SHOPPING	p378	
900 N Michigan	49	E7

city landmark; it was the sole downtown survivor of the 1871 Great Fire.

The **Museum of Contemporary Art** (Map pp362-4; ☎ 312-280-2660; 220 E Chicago Ave; adult $10, student 12-18 $6, free Tue; 10am-8pm Tue, 10am-5pm Wed-Sun) displays head-scratching works by Franz Kline, René Magritte, Cindy Sherman and Andy Warhol.

To sample the Gold Coast's former grandeur, saunter down **N Astor St** (Map pp362-4), where gems include the 1887 mansions at 1308–1312 N Astor St, by architect John Wellborn Root; the Georgian Revival house at 1355 N Astor St; Frank Lloyd Wright's Charnley-Persky House at 1365 N Astor, which he proclaimed the 'first modern building'; and the 1929 art deco Russell House at 1444 N Astor St.

At the **International Museum of Surgical Science** (Map pp362-4; ☎ 312-642-6502; 1524 N Lake Shore Dr; adult/student $6/3, free Tue; 10am-4pm Tue-Sat, also Mon in summer) you'll find unusual exhibits like the one on bloodletting.

OLD TOWN

North and west of the Gold Coast, this once-simple neighborhood of wooden houses was one of the first in the city to gentrify, starting as a hippy haven in the late 1960s. The narrow streets north of North Ave and west of Wells St are wonderful to meander.

LINCOLN PARK

Lincoln Park is an urban oasis spanning 1200 leafy acres between North Ave (1600N) and Ardmore Ave (5800N), though the widest swathe is between North Ave and Diversey Parkway (2800N). 'Lincoln Park' also is the name for the abutting neighborhood. Both are alive day and night with people skating, walking dogs, pushing strollers and driving in circles looking for a place to park.

The **Lincoln Park Zoo** (Map pp362-4; ☎ 312-742-2000; 2200 N Cannon Dr; admission free; 10am-5pm summer, 10am-4:30pm winter, 10am-6:30pm Sat & Sun summer) is popular with families who stroll by the habitats of gorillas, lions, tigers and other exotic creatures. Near the zoo's north entrance, the magnificent 1891 **Conservatory** (Map pp362-4; ☎ 312-742-7736; 2391 N Stockton Dr; admission free; 9am-5pm) coaxes palms, ferns and orchids to flourish despite Chicago's brutal weather. The **Peggy Notebaert Nature Museum** (Map pp362-4; ☎ 773-755-5100; 2430 N Cannon Dr; adult $7, child 3-12 $4, free Thu; 9am-4:30pm Mon-Fri, 10am-5pm Sat & Sun) has a year-round butterfly park and other natural wonders. For a duck's-eye view of the park, try **paddleboating** (Map pp362-4; 312-742-2038; 2021 N Stockton; 30 min $10-15; 10am-5pm Mon-Fri, 10am-6pm Sat & Sun) from the dock near Cafe Brauer.

The **Chicago Historical Society** (Map pp362-4; ☎ 312-642-4600; 1601 N Clark St; adult $5, child 6-12 $1, free Mon; 9:30am-4:30pm Mon-Sat, noon-5pm Sun) focuses on the city's history as seen through the lives of ordinary citizens. Further north, the **Standing Lincoln** (Map pp362-4) sculpture is by the illustrious Augustus Saint-Gaudens.

WRIGLEYVILLE

North of Lincoln Park, this neighborhood can be enjoyed by ambling along Halsted St, Clark St, Belmont Ave or Southport Ave, which are well supplied with restaurants and bars. Ivy-covered **Wrigley Field** (Map pp362-4; 1060 W Addison St) is named for the chewing-gum guy and is home to the adored Chicago Cubs (see Sports p377).

ANDERSONVILLE

Creative types, lesbians, gays and yuppies occupy most of this walkable neighborhood, which was once heavily Swedish. The small **Swedish-American Museum Center** (☎ 773-728-8111; 5211 N Clark St; adult/child $4/3; 10am-4pm Tue-Fri, 11am-4pm Sat & Sun) tells the story. Take the CTA Red Line to the Berwyn stop and walk west a 0.5 mile. Get off one stop south at the pagoda-like Argyle St station, and you're in the heart of New Chinatown and its abundant Chinese, Vietnamese and Thai restaurants.

FAR NORTH & DEVON AVENUE

Devon Ave, in Chicago's northernmost neighborhood, is where worlds collide – Indian women in jewel-toned saris glide by Muslim men in white skullcaps, and Nigerian women in bright print robes shop beside Orthodox men in black yarmulkes. It is one of the most diverse communities you'll see, and makes an outstanding destination for shopping and serial eating (samosas, kabobs, kosher donuts and more). Devon Ave at Western Ave is the main intersection; get there via the Western Ave 49B bus.

WICKER PARK & BUCKTOWN

West of Lincoln Park, these two neighborhoods were once havens for working-class, central European immigrants. Bucktown was yuppified in the 1980s, but Wicker Park still has a polyglot character. It's an interesting place to wander, with loads of small galleries, boutiques, trendy restaurants and hipster lounges (the kind that have velvet curtains and chocolate martinis); take the CTA Blue Line to Damen.

WEST SIDE

West of the Loop is a patchwork of ethnic neighborhoods, urban renewal, blight and gentrification. Old neighborhood names, like Greek Town and Little Italy, may not typify the current residents.

The huge **United Center** (1901 W Madison St) is home to the Bulls and Blackhawks (see Sports p378), and is a venue for various special events. **Little Italy**, between Eisenhower Expressway/I-290 and Roosevelt Rd, was a thriving community until the 1950s, when the expressway was rammed through. **Taylor St** preserves many Italian family businesses.

PILSEN

Long a first stop for immigrants, this neighborhood southwest of Little Italy is now predominantly Latino – 18th St has scores of taquerías, bakeries and small shops selling everything from devotional candles to Mexican CDs. The CTA Blue Line 18th St station is covered with Mexican murals.

The **Mexican Fine Arts Center Museum** (☎ 312-738-1503; 1852 W 19th St; admission free; 10am-5pm Tue-Sun) exhibits work by Mexican artists. It is the largest Latino arts institution in the US.

NEAR SOUTH SIDE

A century ago, the best and worst of Chicago lived side by side south of the Loop. Prairie Ave between 16th and 20th Sts was Millionaire's Row, while the Levee District, four blocks to the west, was packed with saloons, brothels and opium dens. When the millionaires moved north, the neighborhood declined, and mansions were demolished for industry. Now trendy businesses are moving in, and once-derelict warehouses are being transformed into loft apartments.

In a humble building on Michigan Ave, the Chess brothers started a recording studio in 1957. Muddy Waters, Bo Diddley and Chuck Berry cut tracks here. Now incarnated as **Willie Dixon's Blues Heaven** (☎ 312-808-1286; 2120 S Michigan Ave; admission $10; 10am-4pm Mon-Fri, 11am-3pm Sat), it holds a collection of blues memorabilia.

The moving **National Vietnam Veterans Art Museum** (Map pp362-4; ☎ 312-326-0270; 1801 S Indiana Ave; admission $5; 11am-6pm Tue-Fri, 10am-5pm Sat, noon-5pm Sun) exhibits artworks by veterans.

The Prairie Avenue Historic District has preserved a few old mansions in the area, like the 1880s **John J Glessner House** (Map pp358-60; ☎ 312-326-1480; 1800 S Prairie Ave; adult $7, child 5-12 $4; tours 1, 2 & 3pm Wed-Sun) and 1836 Greek Revival **Henry B Clarke House** (☎ 312-326-1480; 1855 S Indiana Ave; adult $7, child 5-12 $4, free Wed; tours noon, 1 & 2pm Wed-Sun). You can tour both for $11/7 per adult/child aged 5 to 12.

CHINATOWN

Chinatown's charm is best enjoyed by browsing its many small shops for herbs, tea and almond cookies and eating in its restaurants. Wentworth Ave south of Cermak is the retail heart; look for the fanciful **On Leong Building** (2216 S Wentworth Ave). Take the CTA Red Line to Cermak-Chinatown.

SOUTH SIDE

The South Side has had a tough time since WWII. Housing projects created impoverished neighborhoods where community ties were broken and gangs held sway. Whole neighborhoods vanished as crime and blight drove residents away. Some areas survived the damage, and redevelopment now aims to promote mixed-income communities.

The **Illinois Institute of Technology** is noted for its 22 campus buildings, many of them designed by Mies van der Rohe. **Crown Hall** (3360 S State St), with its wide, column-free interior and black-glass-box exterior, is the most famous.

The neighborhoods radiating from 35th St and Martin Luther King Jr Dr are unofficially named **Bronzeville** and were the center of Chicago's black culture from 1920 until 1950, comparable to Harlem in New York. After years of decline, many of the area's grand houses are being restored, especially on Calumet Ave between 31st and 33rd Sts (though visitors should still be cautious). Note the Frank Lloyd Wright row houses at 3213–3219 S Calumet. The **Pilgrim Baptist Church** (3301 S Indiana Ave) was an early home of gospel music and has a vast, opulent interior. To reach the area, take the CTA Green Line to 35th St-Bronzeville-IIT.

HYDE PARK

At the prestigious University of Chicago, the heart of the Hyde Park enclave, graduate students outnumber undergrads, and some 73 Nobel prizes have been won. The bookish residents give the place an insulated, pleasant, small-town air. The area is easily reached via Metra Electric trains from the Randolph St station to the 55th-56th-57th St station.

The **Museum of Science & Industry** (☎ 773-684-1414, cnr 57th St & S Lake Shore Dr; adult $9, child 3-11 $5; 🕑 9:30am-4pm Mon-Sat, 11am-4pm Sun) is a vast and confusing place that was the Palace of Fine Arts at the 1893 Columbian Exposition. Highlights include a WWII German submarine, replica coal mine and informative new genetics exhibit.

Of the numerous buildings that Frank Lloyd Wright designed in the Chicago area, none is more famous or influential than the **Robie House** (☎ 773-834-1847; 5757 S Woodlawn Ave; adult $9, child 7-18 $7; tours 11am, 1 & 3pm Mon-Fri, continuous 11am-3:30pm Sat & Sun). The resemblance of its horizontal lines to the flat landscape of the Midwestern prairie became known as the Prairie style. Inside are 174 art glass windows and doors.

The **DuSable Museum of African American History** (☎ 773-947-0600; 740 E 56th Pl; adult $3, child 6-12 $1, free Sun; 🕑 10am-5pm Mon-Sat, noon-5pm Sun) has good artworks and exhibits on black Americans from slavery to the civil-rights era.

The University of Chicago's small **Oriental Institute Museum** (☎ 773-702-9514; 1155 E 58th St; admission free; 🕑 10am-4pm Tue-Sat, until 8:30pm Wed, noon-4pm Sun) displays artifacts from the mighty civilizations of Egypt, Mesopotamia and the Near East; the museum is undergoing restoration until fall 2004, so some galleries are closed. The **David & Alfred Smart Museum** (☎ 773-702-0200; 5550 S Greenwood Ave; admission free; 🕑 10am-4pm Tue-Fri, until 8pm Thu, 11am-5pm Sat & Sun) has the university's fine-arts collection, with works by Henry Moore and Rodin.

PULLMAN

Millionaire railcar manufacturer George M Pullman started a model factory town here in 1880, but his dream died with a violent strike in 1894. The factory finally closed in 1981, and the southern part of Pullman (where craftsmen and managers lived) was bought up by people determined to preserve it. Metra Electric trains go from the Randolph St station to 111th St station, in the heart of Pullman, 13 miles south of the Loop. The **visitors center** (☎ 773-785-8901; 11141 S Cottage Grove Ave; 🕑 noon-2pm Mon-Fri, 11am-2pm Sat, noon-3pm Sun) offers detailed maps and walking tours (all covered in a $3 suggested donation).

Activities

Tucked away in Chicago's 552 parks are public golf courses, ice rinks, swimming pools and more. Activities are free or low-cost, and the needed equipment is available for rent in the parks. Contact the **Chicago Park District** (☎ 312-742-7529; www.chicagoparkdistrict.com); there's a separate number for golf information (☎ 312-245-0909).

BICYCLING

Bicycling is popular along the 18.5-mile lakefront path. For rentals, try **Bike Chicago**

GANGLAND CHICAGO

The city would rather not discuss its gangster past, and consequently there are no brochures or exhibits about infamous sites. So you'll need to use your imagination when visiting the following, as most are not designated as notorious.

Holy Name Cathedral (Map pp358-60; 735 N State St) Two murders took place near here. In 1924, North Side boss Dion O'Banion was gunned down in his florist shop (738 N State St) after he crossed Capone. O'Banion's replacement, Hymie Weiss, fared no better. In 1926 he was killed on his way to church by bullets flying from a window at 740 N State St.

St Valentine's Day Massacre Site (Map pp362-4; 2122 N Clark St) Capone goons dressed as cops, lined up seven members of Bugs Moran's gang against the garage wall that used to be here and sprayed them with bullets. The garage was torn down in 1967.

Biograph Theater (Map pp362-4; 2433 N Lincoln Ave) This is where the 'lady in red' betrayed John Dillinger in 1934. He was shot by the FBI outside the theater.

Green Mill (4802 N Broadway Ave) The speakeasy in the basement was a Capone favorite. Today it's a glamorous, smoky jazz bar (see the Author's Choice, p376).

Capone's Chicago Home (7244 S Prairie Ave) The south side residence was used mostly by Capone's wife, Mae, and other relatives.

(☎ 312-755-0488; www.bikechicago.com; 600 E Grand Ave, Navy Pier & North Ave Beach; bikes per hr/day $8.75/34; 🕑 9am-7pm Apr-Oct, extended hours in summer). The company provides free tours from Navy Pier at 1:30pm daily, or a free map to do it yourself. You can also rent in-line skates.

BOATING

The **Chicago Sailing Club** (☎ 773-871-7245; www.chicagosailingclub.com; 2712 N Campbell Ave) offers all levels of instruction, including five-day beginner's classes for $395, or sailboats to rent from $35/55 per hour on weekdays/weekends. Departure is from Belmont Harbor, where Belmont Ave meets Lake Michigan.

KAYAKING

For a duck's-eye view of downtown, kayak down the Chicago River with **Wateriders Adventure Agents** (☎ 312-953-9287; www.wateriders.com). Various tours take in architectural sights and ghost and gangster spots. Beginners welcome. Call for prices, schedule and departure locations.

BASEBALL BATTING CAGES

Brush up on your batting skills at **Sluggers** (☎ 773-472-9696; 3540 N Clark St), a popular bar and grill across from Wrigley Field. If you'd rather sidestep the drunk Cubs fans and giant TV screens, try the batting cages at **Warren Park** (☎ 312-742-7888; 6601 N Western Ave; 🕑 Apr-Sep). Ten pitches cost $1 at both places.

BOWLING

Diversey River Bowl (☎ 773-227-5800; 2211 W Diversey Parkway; lanes per hour $19-32, shoe rental $3; 🕑 noon-2am Sun-Fri, 9am-3am Sat) is often called the 'rock 'n bowl' for its evening fog machine, light show and loud music. Everyone from pierced punks to well-heeled ad execs to brooding artists aims for strikes here.

Walking Tour

This 3-mile tour covers tall buildings, gangster sites and more in three dawdling hours.

Start at the **Cultural Center** (**1**; p360). After examining the gorgeous interior, exit onto Washington St and head west to Dearborn St. Turn right, where you'll see the **'Picasso'** ensconced in the plaza at the **Richard J Daley Center** (**2**), created by Mr Abstract himself. Bird, dog, woman? You decide, then continue north to Randolph St. Turn east (right), where you'll pass theaters and **Marshall Field's** (**3**) en route to Michigan Ave.

Turn north (left) and soon you'll cross the Chicago River. If you go down the steps flanking the bridge, you'll find the **Wendella architectural sightseeing boats** (**4**; p370), a worthy way to view Chicago's steely overlords.

Just north of the bridge you'll pass the **Wrigley Building** (**5**), glowing as white as the Double Mint twins' teeth, followed closely by the Gothic, eye-popping **Tribune Tower** (**6**).

Carry on 1½ blocks to Grand Ave, and go down the steps. Now you've got some walking to do – it's a hearty 0.5 miles due

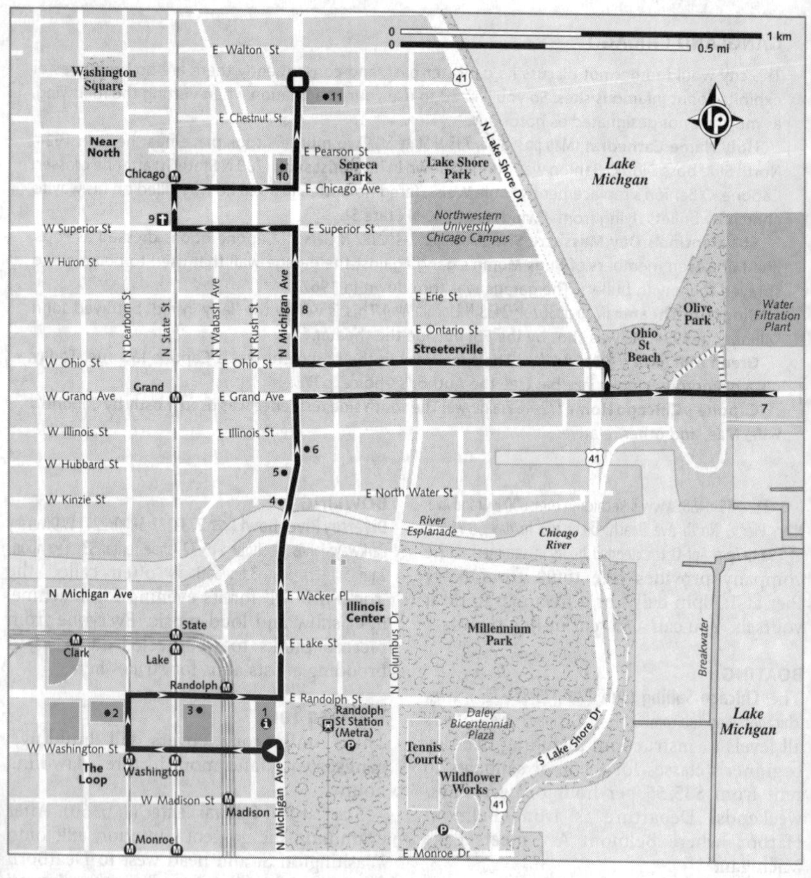

east to **Navy Pier** (7), where you can twirl on the Ferris wheel, explore the stained glass museum or just park it on a bench and watch the crowds and boats flow by.

Feeling refreshed? Return to Grand and just before Lake Shore Dr passes overhead, jog right into the park. Take the pedway up to Ohio St and follow it west until you reach Michigan Ave. You're in the heart of the **Magnificent Mile** (8) now. Shop for four blocks until you reach Superior St. Go west (left) to State St. **Holy Name Cathedral** (9), on the corner, is where Al Capone's gang murdered two North Side bosses.

Walk north on State to Chicago Ave, turn east (right) and continue to the Chicago-Michigan corner, where you'll see the **Water Tower** (10). Head north two blocks on Michigan and you've reached the **John Hancock Center** (11). Finish with a drink on the 96th floor and a spectacular view of the city you've just traversed.

Chicago for Children

Chicago is a kid's kind of town. Most museums have special areas to entertain and educate wee ones. A good resource is **Chicago Parent** (www.chicagoparent.com), a free publication available throughout the city; check at the Children's Museum or see its website.

BLUE CHICAGO STORE

Kids can listen to a live blues band perform in the smoke- and alcohol-free basement of the **Blue Chicago Store** (Map pp362-4; ☎ 312-661-1003; 534 N Clark St; adult $5, child 11 & under free;

(hourly 8-11pm Sat), next door to venue Blue Chicago (see Jazz & Blues, p377). What the kids' setting lacks in smoky atmosphere it makes up for in fret-bending music – authentic blues licks that have nothing to do with lollipops. If desired, adults can pay $7 at entry, which provides later admission to the adjoining blues club and/or the sister club at 736 N Clark St.

CHICAGO CHILDREN'S MUSEUM

The **Children's Museum** (Map pp362-4; ☎ 312-527-1000; 700 E Grand Ave; admission $7; 10am-5pm Tue-Sun, until 8pm Thu) is on Navy Pier, and features exhibits where kids can climb a schooner, excavate dinosaur bones and generate hydroelectric power (it's fun – really). Follow up with an expedition down the Pier itself, including spins on the Ferris wheel and carousel.

OTHER SIGHTS

Shedd Aquarium (p361) is drenched with whales, sharks and weird-looking fish – always young-crowd pleasers. The **Field Museum** (p361) offers lots and lots of that perennial kid favorite – dinosaurs! **Lincoln Park Zoo** (p364) has a children's area and farm where tykes can touch the animals. The **Museum of Science & Industry** (p366) has a chick hatchery and model trains running over a 3500-sq-ft track.

Other kid-friendly activities in Chicago include an **El ride** around the Loop; get on the Brown Line at Merchandise Mart and go to Clark St, which takes you on a leisurely trip through the thick of downtown's tall buildings, or try the Loop Tour Train (p370). In July and August, a lakefront swim at **North Avenue Beach** (Map pp362-4; 1600 N Lake Shore Dr) is a must, where there's soft sand, lifeguards, a snack bar and bathrooms.

The **Thomas Hughes Children's Library** (Map pp358-60; ☎ 312-747-4647; www.chipublib.org; 2nd fl, 400 S State St; admission free; 9am-7pm Mon-Thu, 9am-5pm Fri-Sat, 1-5pm Sun), located within the massive Harold Washington Library, schedules frequent story-times, puppet shows and craft projects, often on Saturdays. Call, check the web or stop by to pick up a monthly activities list.

Some stores offer special experiences for kids: in addition to purveying dolls from bygone eras, **American Girl Place** (Map pp358-60; ☎ 877-247-5223; 111 E Chicago Ave) has a theater with performances of a girl-oriented musical ($26 per ticket) and a café where dolls are seated and treated as part of the family. The **Lego Store** (Map pp358-60; ☎ 312-494-0760; shops at North Bridge, 520 N Michigan Ave) lets kids go wild in a vibrantly colored play area where they can build their own creations; use the models of Chicago skyscrapers for inspiration.

Quirky Chicago

Sure, your friends will listen politely as you describe your trip to the Sears Tower's tip. But you'll stop them mid-yawn when you unleash your knowledge of all things kinky culled from a Leather Museum visit, or show them the bruises amassed at a Jerry Springer Show fight. Chicago has a fine collection of unusual sights and activities to supplement its standard attractions.

LEATHER ARCHIVES & MUSEUM

Ben Franklin liked to be flogged? Egypt's Queen Hatshepsut cross-dressed and had a foot fetish? Learn the kinky history of leather, fetish, and S&M subcultures at the **Leather Archives & Museum** (☎ 773-761-9200; 6418 N Greenview Ave; admission free; 5-8pm Thu, noon-3pm Sat, or call for appointment). Exhibits rotate every six months; past displays have included home-crafted whips and a leather rose collection. The on-site shop sells posters, pins and other 'pervertibles.'

JERRY SPRINGER & OPRAH WINFREY TELEVISION SHOWS

On the lurid **Jerry Springer Show** (☎ 312-321-5365; 454 N Columbus Dr, 2nd fl, Chicago, IL 60611) you can bet you'll see mud-slinging, nudity, a knock-down drag-out fight or all three simultaneously. Call or write well in advance for tickets. Far more genteel is self-help queen **Oprah** (☎ 312-591-9222; 1058 W Washington Blvd). Her show is extremely popular; the phone line often is busy, but keep trying.

MUSEUM OF HOLOGRAPHY

The **Museum of Holography** (☎ 312-226-1007; 1134 W Washington Blvd; adult $4, child 6-12 $3; 12:30-4:30pm Wed-Sun) contains the world's largest collection of holograms (three-dimensional imaging), as well as an on-site school and laboratory dedicated to the science.

BUBBLY CREEK & UNION STOCKYARD GATE

Bubbly Creek (just west of the cnr 37th & Racine Sts) is a legacy of Chicago's role as 'hog butcher for the world.' The vile-looking water got its name from the bubbles that rose from its depths, emitted by the tons of waste rotting on the bottom. The packing plants that fed the murk are long gone, but you can visit the nearby **Union Stockyard Gate** (850 W Exchange Ave, near 4100 S Halsted St), which was the main entrance to the stockyards where millions of cows and hogs met their demise.

CEMETERIES

Graceland Cemetery (☎ 773-525-1105; 4001 N Clark St; admission free; 🕒 8:30am-4:30pm Mon-Sat) is the final resting place of local millionaires (including George Pullman), architects (Daniel Burnham, Louis Sullivan) and retail magnates (including Marshall Field). Pick up a free map at the office to help navigate the swirling paths.

Rosehill Cemetery (☎ 773-989-2170; 5800 N Ravenswood Ave; admission free; 🕒 8am-5pm) is Chicago's oldest and largest. WW Boyington designed the entrance gate in 1864 using the same gothic style as he used for the Water Tower. Free tours are offered at 10am on the first and third Saturday of the month, May to November.

Tours

For a choice of excellent architectural tours by foot, bus or boat, contact the **Chicago Architecture Foundation** (Map pp358-60; ☎ 312-922-3432; www.architecture.org; 875 N Michigan Ave in the John Hancock Center or 224 S Michigan Ave; tours year-round) The tours are highly recommended, especially those by boat; costs and times vary.

The 40-minute **Loop Tour Train** (Map pp358-60; Cultural Center, 1st fl visitors center, 77 E Randolph St; tours 11:35am-1:35pm Sat, May-Sep), guided by an Architecture Foundation docent, is a great way to see Chicago's buildings and learn the history of the elevated train (aka 'El'). Tickets for the free tours are first-come, first-served and must be obtained in person.

The Cultural Center (p360) sponsors **Chicago Greeter** (☎ 312-744-8000; www.chicagogreeter.com; tours year-round) is a service in which a local Chicagoan takes you on a free personal tour customized by theme (architecture, history, gay and lesbian and more) or neighborhood. It lasts two to four hours, either by foot or complimentary public transportation, and must be reserved seven business days in advance.

Mercury Chicago Skyline Cruises (Map pp358-60; ☎ 312-332-1353; cnr Michigan Ave & Wacker Dr; adult $17, child under 12 $7; 🕒 May-Sep) and **Wendella Sightseeing Boats** (Map pp358-60; ☎ 312-337-1446; 400 N Michigan Ave; adult $16, child 4-11 $8; 🕒 Apr-Nov) offer identical 90-minute tours of the river and lake. Various other lake cruises leave seasonally from Navy Pier.

Festivals & Events

Chicago has a full events calendar year-round, but the biggies are held in the summer. For exact dates and other details, call the city's **Office of Special Events** (☎ 312-744-3315; www.cityofchicago.org/specialevents). Each of the following listed events is free and held downtown on a weekend, unless noted otherwise.

JUNE

Blues Festival The biggest free blues fest in the world with four days of the music that made Chicago famous.

Country Music Festival Nashville's biggest stars come to town for a weekend of twanging.

Gospel Festival More than 35 choirs and performers sing a weekend's worth of hallelujahs.

Pride Parade A true celebration of individuality, held in late June in Wrigleyville's Boys' Town neighborhood.

Taste of Chicago This 10-day food festival in Grant Park concurs with the Independence Day celebration. Many locals think the Taste is over-rated.

JULY

Independence Day Concert Held on July 3, featuring Tchaikovsky's '1812 Overture' and big-time fireworks.

AUGUST

Air and Water Show People flock to North Avenue Beach to see daredevil displays by boats and planes.

Latin Music Festival The merengue, salsa and other Latin rhythms are as sultry as the late summer weather.

SEPTEMBER

Jazz Festival Chicago's longest-running music festival attracts big names on the national jazz scene.

Sleeping

Big conventions attract thousands of visitors, and hotel rates ratchet up fast based on occupancy. So an $80 room one day could cost $200 the next. Call ahead to avoid unpleasant surprises. The rooms listed below are normal midweek rates in summer, the high season. Taxes add 14.9% to the rates. The closest decent campgrounds are at least an hour away in any direction.

GAY & LESBIAN CHICAGO

Chicago has a flourishing gay and lesbian scene; for details, check the weekly free publications of *Chicago Free Press* (www.chicagofreepress.com) or *Windy City Times* (www.windycitymediagroup.com). The **Chicago Area Gay & Lesbian Chamber of Commerce** (☎ 773-303-0167, 888-452-4262; www.glchamber.org; 1210 W Rosedale Ave; 9:30am-6pm Mon-Fri) also provides useful visitor information.

The **Gerber/Hart Library** (☎ 773-381-8030; 1127 W Granville Ave), specializing in gay and lesbian materials, hosts book groups, art exhibits and other programs. **Chicago Greeter** (see Tours, p370) offers personalized sightseeing trips.

The biggest concentration of bars and clubs is on N Halsted St between Belmont Ave and Grace St, an area known as 'Boys' Town.' Friendly **Roscoes** (☎ 773-281-3355; 3354 N Halsted) is an excellent place to start the night, while **Closet** (☎ 773-477-8533; 3325 N Broadway), a few blocks east, attracts an active crowd until 4am.

The late-June **Pride Parade** also takes place in this neighborhood.

Andersonville is another area with many choices including the **Chicago Eagle** (☎ 773-728-0050; 5015 N Clark St), a popular leather bar, and **Big Chicks** (☎ 773-728-5511; 5024 N Sheridan Ave) which has a DJ on weekends and interesting art displays.

For B&B accommodations, contact **Chicago Bed & Breakfast** (☎ 773-549-0962, 888-271-3365; www.chicago-bed-breakfast.com; r $95-295), which represents inns and guest houses throughout the city. Many properties have two to three night minimum stays.

Hotels in The Loop are convenient to Grant Park, the museums and business district, but not very near the best nightlife.

Popular with visitors, the Near North/Gold Coast neighborhood has a plethora of places for eating, drinking, shopping and entertainment.

Hotels in Lincoln Park are often cheaper than the big ones downtown and are near hip nightlife, with the Loop a short El ride away.

Sleeping – Budget

THE LOOP

HI Chicago (Map pp358-60; ☎ 312-360-0300; www.hichicago .org; 24 E Congress Parkway; dm from $34.50, r $120; P $18) Chicago's main hostel is immaculate and has bonuses like a staffed information desk, free volunteer-led tours, discount passes to museums and shows, an attached café and luggage storage ($1 per bag). Most of the simple dorm rooms have 8 beds and an attached bath.

NEAR NORTH & GOLD COAST

Cass Hotel (Map pp358-60; ☎ 312-787-4030, 800-227-7850; www.casshotel.com; 640 N Wabash Ave; s $64-84, d $84-109; P $19) The Cass isn't much to look at, but its simple, clean rooms win the day for their reasonable prices and prime location.

LINCOLN PARK

Arlington House (☎ 773-929-5380, 800-467-8355; www.arlingtonhouse.com; 616 W Arlington Pl; dm $24, r $54-68) Arlington House has a fantastic location in the heart of Lincoln Park, but is an extremely bare-bones hostel; some readers have complained about the poor quality. Parking can be ugly.

Sleeping – Mid-Range

THE LOOP

Essex Inn (Map pp358-60; ☎ 312-939-2800, 800-621-6909; www.essexinn.com; 800 S Michigan Ave; r $89-169; P $21) The Essex has nice amenities – indoor pool, internet access and free shuttle to the Michigan Avenue shops – though the rooms have a dated '70s feel. Still, it's a pretty good deal. Ask for an 01 room for a park view.

Best Western Grant Park Inn (Map pp358-60; ☎ 312-922-2900; 1100 S Michigan Ave; s/d $119/129; P $15) One of Chicago's stock mid-rangers, this Best Western is further south than the others, but nearer to the Museum Campus.

NEAR NORTH & GOLD COAST

Ohio House Motel (Map pp358-60; ☎ 312-943-6000; 600 N LaSalle St; s/d $85/115; P) The fact that this retro 1960s motor lodge is still standing in the heart of the big city – and hasn't yet been taken over by developers – deserves applause. The rooms are just fine, if faded, and the attached coffee shop is a classic. The free parking is a considerable perk.

Howard Johnson Inn (Map pp358-60; ☎ 312-664-8100; 720 N LaSalle St; s/d $90/99; P ⌘) The HoJo looks a lot like retro 1960s motor lodge Ohio House, complete with free parking in a lot surrounded by timeless American motel rooms.

Best Western River North (Map pp358-60; ☎ 312-467-0800, 800-727-0800; 125 W Ohio St; s & d $119-149; P ⌘) Clustered near Ohio House and HoJo, the Best Western is a step up. It includes an indoor pool and ever-precious free parking.

Red Roof Inn (Map pp358-60; ☎ 312-787-3580; 162 E Ontario St; s/d $100/120; P $22 ⌘) Red Roof Inn has a great location just east of Michigan Ave and occupies a handsome 1930s building, but has the Red Roof chain's usual utilitarian rooms. Lots of tour groups stay here.

Days Inn Gold Coast (Map pp362-4; ☎ 312-664-3040; 1816 N Clark St; s/d 109/$129; P $15 ⌘) This good-value hotel is across from the zoo and in the midst of the Old Town.

LINCOLN PARK

Willows Hotel (Map pp362-4; ☎ 773-528-8400, 800-787-3108; www.cityinns.com; 555 W Surf St; s/d $99/129; P $17 ⌘) The Willows is a stylish little place with antique furnishings, and is within walking distance of the beach. The owners have two other, similar properties in the neighborhood: **City Suites Hotel** (☎ 773-404-3400, 800-248-9108; 933 W Belmont Ave; s/d $99/139; P $18 ⌘), near the CTA Red Line Belmont station, and the **Majestic Hotel** (☎ 773-404-3499, 800-727-5108; 528 W Brompton Ave; s/d $99/139; P $19 ⌘), close to Wrigley Field and the Halsted St gay scene.

Inn of Lincoln Park (Map pp362-4; ☎ 773-348-2810; 601 W Diversey Parkway; s/d $125/149; P $10 ⌘) This inn's pleasant rooms are located right on enjoyable Diversey, about five minutes' walk to the lakefront.

OTHER NEIGHBORHOODS

House of Two Urns (☎ 773-235-1408, 877-896-8767; www.twourns.com; 1239 N Greenview Ave; r $69-145; P ⌘) This excellent B&B is distinctive on several fronts: it's owned by artists and filled with antiques and original art, and it's located in Wicker Park near the vogue restaurant/bar scene. Take the CTA Blue Line to Division.

Sleeping – Top End

THE LOOP

Chicago Hilton & Towers (Map pp358-60; ☎ 312-922-4400; 720 S Michigan Ave; s/d from $179/204; P $28 ⌘) The Hilton was the largest hotel in the world in 1927, with nearly 2000 rooms. Renovated in the mid-1980s, it now has only 1543 rooms, but the public spaces and gilded ballroom are exquisitely grand, with crystal chandeliers dangling everywhere. You often can get big discounts on weekends.

Hotel Burnham (Map pp358-60; ☎ 312-782-1111, 877-294-9712; www.burnhamhotel.com; 1 W Washington St; r from $199; P $29 ⌘) The Burnham's super-cool decor is a favorite of architecture buffs. It's housed in the landmark 1890s Reliance Building, and the rooms are lavishly furnished with pieces like mahogany writing desks and chaise lounges.

NEAR NORTH & GOLD COAST

Drake Hotel (Map pp362-4; ☎ 312-787-2200, 800-553-7253; 140 E Walton St; r from $169, though usually higher; P $32 ⌘) The grand 1920s Drake is an ageless dowager that has hosted the likes of Gloria Swanson and Queen Elizabeth II. The quiet rooms have heavy doors and marble baths. Its **Coq d'Or** is one of the classiest bars around (see Drinking, p375).

Eating

The cultural hodgepodge that gives Chicago's neighborhoods their character translates into a mind-reeling, diverse restaurant scene. The hungry can fill up on anything from Afghani dumplings to Costa Rican empanadas, from $150 multicourse meals to $1 hot dogs. And where else besides Chicago will you get the real deal for deep-dish pizza? The prices listed here are for dinner mains; lunch main courses often cost less.

THE LOOP

Most Loop eateries are geared for lunch crowds of office workers, but many now cater to evening diners as well.

Berghoff (Map pp358-60; ☎ 312-427-3170; 17 W Adams St; dishes $11-19; ⏲ Mon-Sat) The first place to fling open its doors after Prohibition, the Berghoff mixes old-world classics like sauerbraten and schnitzel with modern treats like swordfish Caesar salad. The creamed spinach is a delicacy. Next door the Berghoff Cafe, aka Stand Up Bar, serves sandwiches and excellent house-brand beer.

FAMED CHICAGO FARE

You can't leave town without sampling the deep dish pizza, in which flaky crust rises an inch or two above the plate and cradles a pile of toppings. One piece is practically a meal. It's hard to say which maker is the best, as they all serve gooey slices that will leave you a few pounds heavier. A large pizza averages $15 at the following places.

Pizzeria Uno (Map pp358-60; ☎ 312-321-1000; 29 E Ohio St) Where the deep dish concept originated in 1943; sister outlet Due is one block north.

Gino's East (Map pp358-60; ☎ 312-988-4200; 633 N Wells St) Write on the walls while you wait for your pie.

Lou Malnati's (Map pp358-60; ☎ 312-828-9800; 439 N Wells St) Famous for its buttercrust.

Giordano's (Map pp358-60; ☎ 312-951-0747; 730 N Rush St) Another popular purveyor.

No less iconic is the Chicago hot dog – a wiener and bun that have been 'dragged through the garden,' (ie topped with onions, tomatoes, shredded lettuce, bell peppers, pepperoncini and sweet relish, or variations thereof). **Wrigley Field** (see Sports, p377) makes a beauty, as does the **Wiener Circle** (see Lincoln Park, p364).

Chicago is also known for its Italian beef sandwiches, with thin-sliced, slow-cooked roast beef heaped onto a hoagie roll, smothered in meat juice and giardiniera. They cost about $4 at **Mr Beef** (Map pp358-60; ☎ 312-337-8500; 666 N Orleans St) or **Al's** (Map pp358-60; ☎ 312-943-3222; 169 W Ontario St).

Oasis (Map pp358-60; ☎ 312-558-1058; 21 N Wabash Ave; dishes $3-6; ⏰ until 5pm Mon-Sat) Oasis is a diamond in the rough, like the ones they're polishing in the jeweler's mall you walk through to get here. The falafel is crisped to perfection and the hummus is the best this side of Amman. Eat in or carry out to the nearby parks.

Corner Bakery (Map pp358-60; ☎ 312-201-0805; 78 E Washington St; sandwiches $4-6) This outlet of the gourmet sandwich shop chain is in the Cultural Center (p360), so you can take your eats to the Atrium and listen to free music.

NEAR NORTH

Hundreds of eateries dot the area, from family-run snackeries to renowned restaurants and high-concept cafés.

Billy Goat Tavern (Map pp358-60; ☎ 312-222-1525; lower level, 430 N Michigan Ave; burgers $2-4) Scruffy like the titular animal, this bar and burger joint is the legendary haunt of *Tribune* and *Sun-Times* reporters. Only the dimmest of bulbs orders fries with their cheezborger (remember John Belushi's famous *Saturday Night Live* skit: 'No fries – chips!').

Frontera Grill & Topolobampo (Map pp358-60; ☎ 312-661-1434, 445 N Clark St; dishes $12-22; closed Monday) The kitchen of renowned chef Rick Bayless cooks innovative, high-end Mexican fare for both of these places; Topolobampo is the more formal establishment.

Carson's (Map pp358-60; ☎ 312-280-9200; 612 N Wells St; dishes $12-20) Billed as 'The Place for Ribs' Carson's practices what it preaches, serving tender pork ribs in a tangy sauce.

Mike's Rainbow Restaurant (Map pp358-60; ☎ 312-787-4499; 708 N Clark St; dishes $3-7; h24hr) Big portions and small prices are the hallmark at this classic diner catering to cops and cabbies craving big breakfasts.

Rock & Roll McDonald's (Map pp358-60; ☎ 312-664-7940; 600 N Clark St; burgers $2-4) Yes, it's a McD's, but it serves the schlock with rock. There's 50s memorabilia, Route 66 signs and even a 1959 Corvette inside.

Cafe Iberico (Map pp358-60; ☎ 312-573-1510; 737 N LaSalle St; dishes $4-13), proffers Spanish tapas with Mediterranean flair.

Cyrano's Bistrot (Map pp358-60; ☎ 312-467-0546; 546 N Wells St; dishes $16-26; h Tue-Sat) Cyrano's is the spot for casual French food.

Whole Foods (Map pp358-60; ☎ 312-932-9600; 50 W Huron St) and **Treasure Island** (Map pp358-60; ☎ 312-664-0400; 680 N Lake Shore Dr) are both large supermarkets with lots of organic and deli items.

OLD TOWN

Wells St north of Division St has an assortment of swank eateries.

Twin Anchors (Map pp362-4; ☎ 312-266-1616; 1655 N Sedgwick St; slab $22) This hugely popular, neon-lit place has hordes of people waiting on weekends to get at the baby back ribs.

LINCOLN PARK

Halsted and Clark Sts are the main veins teeming with restaurants and bars. Parking is frightful, but it's handy to the CTA train stops at Armitage and Fullerton.

Kabul House (Map pp362-4; ☎ 312-751-1029; 1629 N Halsted St; dishes $9-14; Tue-Sun) The walls covered with Afghan travel posters are your first hint that you're in for an exotic treat; the juicy dumplings and lamb and vegetarian dishes with pumpkin, lentils, eggplant and spinach confirm it. Live Afghan music on weekends.

Potbelly Sandwich Works (Map pp362-4; ☎ 773-528-1405; 2264 N Lincoln Ave; sandwiches $4-5) The hot submarine sandwiches here are addictive. Ex-Chicagoans returning to visit family for the first time in years have been known to stop here first before seeing mom and dad.

For fun French dishes, try **Cafe Bernard** (Map pp362-4; ☎ 773-871-2100; 2100 N Halsted St; dishes $13-22) and **Red Rooster Cafe & Wine Bar** (dishes $10-15), owned by the same folks. Red Rooster is the less formal, cheaper sibling.

Nookies Too (Map pp362-4; ☎ 773-327-1400; 2114 N Halsted St; dishes $6-9) and **Clarke's** (Map pp362-4; ☎ 773-472-3505; 2441 N Lincoln Ave; dishes $4-7; 24hr) specialize in all-day breakfast and comfort foods.

For those seeking a raucous late-night munchie, two places do it well: the **Wiener Circle** (Map pp362-4; ☎ 773-477-7444; 2622 N Clark St; items $2-4) is famous for its unruly ambience, char-dogs and heart-stopping cheddar fries. **Taco & Burrito Palace #2** (Map pp362-4; ☎ 773-248-0740; 2441 N Halsted St; items $2-4) is tiny inside, but cooks up giant, football-sized burritos.

Charlie Trotter's (Map pp358-60; ☎ 773-248-6228; 816 W Armitage Ave) At the very top end, Charlie Trotter's is a famous gourmet mecca that customers book months ahead of time and remember years afterward. Budget on around $150 per person with wine.

WRIGLEYVILLE

Clark, Halsted, Belmont and Southport are fertile streets. Parking is near impossible, so take the CTA train to the Belmont, Southport or Addison stops.

Tibet Cafe (☎ 773-281-6666; 3913 N Sheridan Ave; dishes $5-9; Tue-Sun) A group of Tibetans runs this small, humble restaurant serving generous portions of melt-in-your-mouth momos and other Himalayan dishes. Yak-butter wall sculptures, a smiling Dalai Lama picture and non-stop tea enhance the serene atmosphere.

River Kwai (☎ 773-472-1013; 1650 W Belmont Ave; dishes $5-8; 11pm-6am) Yes, it's small and scruffy and has weird hours, but these irksome details melt away with the first spoonful of seafood soup or pad thai. This is outstanding cheap food, but it can take a long time. Quit whining and wait.

Leona's (☎ 773-327-8861; 3215 N Sheffield Ave; dishes $8-17) Part of a legendary local chain, Leona's serves heaping portions of excellent pizza, sandwiches, lasagna and other Italian dishes.

Chicago Diner (☎ 773-935-6696; 3411 N Halsted; dishes $8-11) This one's for the vegetarians in the crowd: the diner serves large portions of tofu omelets, tofu stroganoff, tofu loaf and tofu everything else.

The following are also recommended:

Addis Ababa (☎ 773-929-9383; 3521 N Clark; dishes $9-12) Ethiopian legumes, grains and injera bread.

Ann Sather's (☎ 773-348-2378; 929 W Belmont Ave; dishes $7-13) Swedish potato sausages and cinnamon rolls.

Shabu-ya (☎ 773-388-9203; 3475 N Clark St; dishes $9-16) Sushi and 'cook-your-own' Japanese dishes.

Matsuya (☎ 773-248-2677; 3469 N Clark; dishes $9-15) Sushi, octopus and teriyaki-marinated grilled fish.

The area surrounding Wrigley Field is becoming a Chicago theme park with popular local eateries and bars opening outlets here to cash in on the nighttime mobs. Beware of places such as **Billy Goat Tavern** and **Goose Island Brewery** between 3500 and 3600 N Clark St; the original locations of these places (see Eating, p373, and Drinking, p375) are far better.

ANDERSONVILLE/DEVON AVENUE

These northern neighborhoods are bursting with Indian, Vietnamese, Russian and other ethnic eateries. See Andersonville, p365, and Far North, p365, for directions.

Arya Bhavan (☎ 773-274-5800; 2508 W Devon Ave; dishes $9-13) At Arya Bhavan's vegetarian Indian bonanza everything's good. Sample away at the buffet.

Udupi Palace (☎ 773-338-2152; 2543 W Devon Ave; dishes $8-13) The Indian dosai (crepes filled with potato, onion and chutney) served here are to die for.

Thai Binh (☎ 773-728-0283; 1113 W Argyle St; dishes $6-13) The owner's *über*-precocious daughter Linda will help you decide what to order from Thai Binh's huge Vietnamese selection.

Kopi Traveler's Cafe (☎ 773-989-5674; 5317 N Clark St; dishes $5-8) Kopi's has an Indonesian trekker vibe, from the pile of cushions to sit upon, to the bulletin board where travelers post flyers. And look at all those Lonely Planet books on the shelves!

WICKER PARK & BUCKTOWN

It's where the hipsters hang these days. Take the CTA Blue Line to Damen or Western.

Margies (☎ 773-384-1035; 1960 N Western Ave; dishes $3-5) Note to chocolate lovers: when the gates of heaven open, you'll be led into Margie's. Chocolates and hot fudge are made on the premises of this old fashioned parlor. Sink your spoon into an unbelievably rich sundae or attempt a foot-tall milkshake. Guaranteed to put your pancreas into blissful overdrive.

Irazu (☎ 773-252-5687; 1865 N Milwaukee Ave; dishes $4-8; Mon-Sat) The Costa Rican owners of Irazu dish up unusual items like *yuca* (cassava) with garlic, empanadas and mango milkshakes.

Cafe Laguardia (☎ 773-862-5996; 2111 W Armitage Ave; dishes $5-15) This Cuban café has great roasted pork sandwiches among its arsenal.

Soul Kitchen (☎ 773-342-9742; 1576 N Milwaukee Ave; dishes $14-22) Soul Kitchen's pecan-crusted catfish wins raves.

WEST SIDE & PILSEN

The ethnic areas are the main draw. Greek Town extends along S Halsted St, Little Italy is along Taylor St and the Mexican Pilsen enclave centers around W 18th St (the CTA Blue Line stops here, but you'll need wheels to reach the other areas easily).

Lou Mitchell's (Map p358-60; ☎ 312-939-3111; 565 W Jackson Blvd; dishes $4-9; to 3pm) There's a queue to get in for the famed breakfasts, but they give out free Milk Duds to ease the wait.

Nuevo Leon (☎ 312-421-1517; 1515 W 18th St; dishes $3-5) Tacos, tamales and enchiladas are served at peso-size prices at Nuevo Leon.

Parthenon (Map pp358-60; ☎ 312-726-2407; 314 S Halsted St; dishes $9-16) This is a long-standing Greek favorite.

CHINATOWN

From the CTA Red Line Cermak-Chinatown stop, walk one block west to Wentworth Ave.

Three Happiness (☎ 312-791-1228; 2130 S Wentworth Ave; dishes $7-11) Delicious dim sum is served from 10am to 3pm.

Emperor's Choice (☎ 312-225-8800; 2238 S Wentworth Ave; dishes $8-12) This enduring Cantonese-style restaurant is known for excellent seafood.

Drinking

During the long winters, Chicagoans seek social life indoors, and the city's many bars cater to every mood and personality. Usual closing time is 2am, but many places stay open until 4am on weekdays and 5am on Saturday. In summer many boast beer gardens and outdoor seating.

LOOP, NEAR NORTH & OLD TOWN

Signature Lounge (Map pp362-4; ☎ 312-787-7230; John Hancock Center, 875 N Michigan Ave) Have the Hancock Observatory view without the Hancock Observatory admission price. Shoot straight up to the 96th floor and order your beverage while looking out over the glittering city. Ladies: don't miss the bathroom view.

Coq d'Or (Map p362-4; ☎ 312-787-2200; 140 E Walton) This classy joint in the Drake Hotel offers a taste of old Chicago – a piano player, bejeweled women in furs sipping Manhattans, and everyone smoking with abandon.

Berghoff (Map pp358-60; ☎ 312-427-3170; 17 W Adams St) Berghoff's great German bar matches its food (p372).

Olde Towne Ale House (Map pp362-4; ☎ 312-944-7020; 219 W North Ave) There are no pretenses at this long-time favorite, across from Second City, where you'll mingle with beautiful people and not-so-beautiful people (they're the ones face down at the bar).

Alcock's Inn (Map pp358-60; ☎ 312-922-1778; 411 S Wells St) Rowdy traders lament the day's losses or celebrate their winnings at Alcock's.

LINCOLN PARK & WRIGLEYVILLE

These neighborhoods are chockablock with bars, with rich veins along Lincoln Ave, Halsted St and Clark St.

Ginger Man (☎ 773-549-2050; 3740 N Clark) The arty patrons, pool tables and good beer selection make Ginger Man joyously different from the surrounding Wrigley sports bars.

Duke of Perth (Map pp362-4; ☎ 773-477-1741; 2913 N Clark St) The Duke is endowed with a brilliant Scotch selection and all-you-can-eat fish and chips on Wednesday and Friday.

Goose Island Brewery (Map pp362-4; ☎ 312-915-0071; 1800 N Clybourn Ave) Goose brews its wildly popular beers on site and serves tasty sandwiches. What more could you want?

WICKER PARK & BUCKTOWN

Hideout (☎ 773-227-4433; 1354 W Wabansia Ave) Tucked behind a factory, Hideout is as hard to find as the name implies, but worth it for the laid-back atmosphere and excellent live music.

Rainbo Club (☎ 773-489-5999; 1150 N Damen Ave) The Rainbo has been a fertile brooding ground for generations of under-employed artists.

Also recommended for relaxed drinking are the **Charleston** (☎ 773-489-4757; 2076 N Hoyne St Ave) and **Map Room** (☎ 773-252-7636; 1949 N Hoyne St Ave).

ANDERSONVILLE

Hopleaf (☎ 773-334-9851; 5148 N Clark St) You've hit the mother lode of beer selection when you walk into this beauty – there are 200 beers available (30 on tap) and a Belgian eatery upstairs.

Carol's Pub (☎ 773-334-2402; 4659 N Clark St) The sign at the front of Carol's boasts 'Live Country Music/Hot Sandwiches' – a heavenly hillbilly combination.

Simon's (☎ 773-878-0894; 5210 N Clark St) This popular musicians' watering hole is filled with big-spectacled indie rockers.

Entertainment

Check the *Reader* and other local media (p357). **Hot Tix** (78 W Randolph St, 163 E Pearson St or 2301 N Clark St) sells same-day tickets at half the price.

CINEMAS

Music Box Theatre (☎ 773-871-6604; 3733 N Southport Ave) Patrons are treated to live organ music and clouds rolling across the ceiling prior to their art films at this theater.

Gene Siskel Film Center (Map pp358-60; ☎ 312-846-2800; 164 N State St) Offbeat films are screened here.

COMEDY

Improvisational theater began in Chicago, and the city still nurtures the best in the business.

Second City (Map pp362-4; ☎ 312-337-3992; 1616 N Wells St) The cream of the crop – the place where John Belushi, Bill Murray and many others honed their wit.

> **THE AUTHOR'S CHOICE**
>
> **Green Mill** (☎ 773-878-5552; 4802 N Broadway Ave) In the modest heart of Uptown lays a cocktail lounge with a gangster past. The Green Mill earned its notoriety as Al Capone's favorite speakeasy (the tunnels where he hid the booze are still underneath the bar), and you can feel his ghost urging you on to another martini. The lounge retains its glamorous 1920s feel, dark and smoky with curved leather booths. Oh, and there's jazz – top-flight local and national artists perform six nights per week; Sundays are for the nationally acclaimed poetry slam.

Improv Olympics (☎ 773-880-0199; 3541 N Clark St) Improv is also recommended.

DANCE CLUBS

The club scene ranges from hip snooty places to casual joints where all you do is dance. Covers range from nix to $20.

Exit (Map pp362-4; ☎ 773-395-2700; 1315 W North Ave) A thrashy, trashy punk-tinged club.

Berlin (☎ 773-348-4975; 954 W Belmont Ave) Caters to a crowd as mixed as the music.

Sinibar (☎ 773-278-7797; 1540 N Milwaukee Ave) Plays funk and soul in exotic Moroccan decor.

Neo (Map pp362-4; ☎ 773-528-2622; 2350 N Clark St) A gritty long-standing favorite.

Crobar (Map pp362-4; ☎ 312-587-8574; 1543 N Kingsbury St) and **Red Dog** (☎ 773-278-1009; 1958 W North Ave) are popular, stylish clubs, the kind you might even wait in line to enter.

FOLK

Old Town School of Folk Music (☎ 773-728-6000; 4544 N Lincoln Ave) A superb place offering an eclectic line-up of world music and yes, folk music.

JAZZ & BLUES

Blues and jazz both have deep roots in Chicago, and world-class performers appear at myriad venues nightly.

Buddy Guy's Legends (Map pp358-60; ☎ 312-427-0333; 754 S Wabash Ave) This place gets the top acts in town, including the venerable Mr Guy himself.

Noisy, hot and sweaty – as all blues bars should be – are **Blues** (Map pp362-4;

(☎ 773-528-1012; 2519 N Halsted St) and **Kingston Mines** (Map pp362-4; ☎ 773-477-4646; 2548 N Halsted St), which is conveniently located and draws the 4am crowd.

Rosa's (☎ 773-342-0452; 3420 W Armitage Ave) A well-respected club playing minor-key grooves.

Blue Chicago (Map pp358-60; ☎ 312-642-6261; 536 & 736 N Clark St) A pair of friendly clubs downtown.

House of Blues (Map pp358-60; ☎ 312-923-2000; 329 N Dearborn St) Part of a chain, House of Blues is the largest venue for the genre.

The south-side New Checkerboard Lounge, one of the city's best blues clubs, was closed recently due to building maintenance problems. It is trying to reopen in Hyde Park; check local club listings for an update.

Back Room (Map pp362-4; ☎ 312-751-2433; 1007 N Rush St) This jazz joint is so tiny it's like having a band in your bedroom.

Hothouse (Map pp358-60; ☎ 312-362-9707; 31 E Balbo St) Hothouse is a beautiful room offering esoteric jazz and world music to a stylish crowd.

Andy's (Map pp358-60; ☎ 312-642-6805; 11 E Hubbard St) This renowned club features both jazz and blues.

Jazz Showcase (Map pp358-60; ☎ 312-670-2473; 59 W Grand Ave) An upscale club.

PERFORMING ARTS

Chicago's excellent reputation for stage drama is well deserved. Below are the main companies.

Goodman Theatre (Map pp358-60; ☎ 312-443-3800; 170 N Dearborn St) Known for both new and classic works.

Steppenwolf Theatre (Map pp362-4; ☎ 312-335-1650; 1650 N Halsted St) Hollywood-friendly.

Court Theatre (☎ 773-753-4472; 5535 S Ellis Ave) At the University of Chicago, concentrating on classics.

Victory Gardens (Map pp362-4; ☎ 773-871-3000; 2257 N Lincoln Ave) Specializing in plays by Chicago authors.

Chicago Shakespeare Theater (Map pp362-4; ☎ 312-595-5600; 800 E Grand Ave) At Navy Pier.

For first-rate smaller companies try the farcical **Noble Fool Theatre Company** (Map pp358-60; ☎ 312-726-1156; 16 W Randolph St), heady **Neo-Futurists** (☎ 773-275-5255; 5153 N Ashland Ave) and puppet-oriented **Redmoon Theater** (☎ 312-850-8440; 1438 W Kinzie St).

Major venues include the following:

Auditorium Theater (Map pp358-60; ☎ 312-922-2110; 50 E Congress Parkway)

Cadillac Palace Theater (Map pp358-60; ☎ 312-977-1700; 151 W Randolph St)

Chicago Theater (Map pp358-60; ☎ 312-443-1130; 175 N State St)

Ford Center/Oriental Theater (Map pp358-60; ☎ 312-977-1700; 24 W Randolph St)

Shubert Theater (Map pp358-60; ☎ 312-977-1700; 22 W Monroe St)

Symphony Center (Map pp358-60; ☎ 312-294-3000; 220 S Michigan Ave) The Chicago Symphony Orchestra is headquartered in this superb center.

Civic Opera House (Map pp358-60; ☎ 312-332-2244; 20 N Wacker Dr) The Lyric Opera of Chicago, one of the country's best, performs in the grand old opera house.

Grant Park Orchestra (☎ 312-742-7638) In summertime, watch for free classical concerts by the Grant Park Orchestra in Millennium Park.

Joffrey Ballet of Chicago (☎ 312-739-0120) and **Hubbard Street Dance Chicago** (☎ 312-850-9744) are two local dance companies of great renown. Both perform at a variety of venues.

ROCK

Metro (☎ 773-549-3604; 3730 N Clark St, Wrigleyville) Local bands and big names play at Metro; its basement **Smart Bar** hosts dancing until dawn.

At **Double Door** (☎ 773-489-3160; 1572 N Milwaukee Ave) and **Empty Bottle** (☎ 773-276-3600; 1035 N Western Ave), the hard-edge Chicago music scene is epitomized in Wicker Park & Bucktown (p376).

SPECTATOR SPORTS

Wrigley Field (☎ 773-404-2827; 1060 W Addison St) The Chicago Cubs last won the World Series in 1908, but their fans still pack baseball's most charming and intimate stadium, dated from 1916 and known for its ivy-walled field and classic neon sign. Note the kids who stand on Waveland Ave to catch homerun balls (and throw them back if they've been slugged by the opposing team). Take the CTA Red Line to Addison. Wrigley is 4.5 miles north of the Loop.

US Cellular Field (☎ 312-674-1000; 333 W 35th St) The Chicago White Sox (1917 World Series winners) play in this antiseptic bowl of Comiskey Park, recently renamed. It's 4 miles south of the Loop and near the CTA Red Line Sox-35th station.

United Center (☎ 312-455-4000; 1901 W Madison St) The Chicago Bulls play basketball in this huge stadium, also used by the Blackhawks for hockey (☎ 312-455-7000). It's about 2 miles west of the Loop. CTA runs special buses on game days; it's not safe to walk here.

Soldier Field (Map pp358-60; ☎ 847-615-2327; 425 E McFetridge Dr) 'Da Bears,' Chicago's NFL team, tackles at this renovated field. The Chicago Fire soccer team (☎ 312-705-7200) competes here as well.

Shopping

The shoppers' siren song emanates from N Michigan Ave, along the Magnificent Mile (see Sights, Near North, p361).

Large vertical malls here include **Shops at North Bridge**, **Chicago Place**, **Water Tower Place** and **900 N Michigan**. In the Loop, the flagship **Marshall Field's** (Map pp358-60; ☎ 312-781-1000; 111 N State St) and **Carson Pirie Scott** (Map pp358-60; ☎ 312-641-7000; 1 S State St) are the biggies.

Getting There & Away

AIR

O'Hare International Airport (ORD; ☎ 800-832-6352) is the world's busiest. It's huge but user-friendly, with good signs and maps. Most non-US airlines and international flights use Terminal 5 (except Lufthansa and flights from Canada).

The smaller **Midway Airport** (MDW; ☎ 773-838-0600) has a new terminal and is used by domestic carriers like Southwest, which often have cheaper flights than airlines serving O'Hare.

BUS

The **main bus station** (Map pp358-60; ☎ 312-408-5800; 630 W Harrison St) is two blocks from the CTA Blue Line Clinton stop. Greyhound has frequent buses to Cleveland ($42 to $71, seven hours), Detroit ($32 to $63, seven hours), Indianapolis ($32 to $47, four hours), Milwaukee ($13 to $28, 2½ hours) and Minneapolis ($59 to $80, nine hours).

CAR

Car rental is subject to 18% tax. Many rental agencies – Alamo/National, Avis and others – have 24-hour desks at both airports and around town. Check rental information in the Transport chapter (p1121) for more details.

TRAIN

Chicago's classic **Union Station** (Map pp358-60; 225 S Canal St) is the hub for Amtrak's national and regional service. Three trains a day go to Detroit ($23 to $57; six hours), and seven trains per day go to Milwaukee ($20; 1½ hours). Connections to other cities include the following:

Cleveland $40 to $96, seven hours, two trains daily.
Minneapolis/St Paul $38 to $105, eight hours, one train daily.
New York $68 to $165, 19 hours, two trains daily.
St Louis $21 to $59, 5½ hours, three trains daily.
San Francisco (Emeryville) $122 to $293, 51 hours, one train daily.

Getting Around

TO/FROM THE AIRPORT

O'Hare International Airport is 17 miles northwest of the Loop. The cheapest, and often the quickest, way to/from O'Hare is by the CTA Blue Line ($1.50), but the station is a long walk from the flight terminals – a difficult haul if you have lots of luggage. At the airport, signs point variously to 'CTA,' 'Rapid Transit' and 'Trains to City.' Airport Express shuttles run between the airport and downtown ($20 per person; discount for pairs). Taxis to/from downtown cost $28 to $35, or a flat $19 per person using Share-a-Ride.

Midway Airport is 11 miles southwest of the Loop. The CTA Orange Line runs between the two airports ($1.50). Other options to and from downtown are shuttles ($15 per person), taxis ($20 to $25) and Share-a-Ride ($14 per person).

BICYCLE

There are bike lanes on some major roads, but they aren't well marked or respected. Bike racks are plentiful; lock it or lose it. See Bicycling, p366, for rental information.

CAR & MOTORCYCLE

Be warned: it's difficult to find street parking and expensive to park in a lot. Rush-hour traffic is abysmal.

PUBLIC TRANSPORTATION

The **Chicago Transit Authority** (CTA; ☎ 312-836-7000; www.transitchicago.com), operates the city bus network and train system that includes both elevated (El) and subway trains. CTA buses go everywhere from early morning until late evening. Two of the seven color-coded train lines – the Red Line, and the Blue Line to O'Hare International Airport – operate 24 hours a day. The other lines run from about 5am to 11pm daily. During the day, you shouldn't have to wait more than 15 minutes for a train. Get free maps at any train station.

The standard fare on a bus or train is $1.50; transfers cost 30¢. On buses, you can use a fare card (called a Transit Card) or pay with exact change. On the train, you must use a Transit Card, sold from vending machines at train stations. A $5 daily pass is available.

Metra commuter trains (☎ 312-836-7000; www.metrarail.com) have 12 routes serving the suburbs from four terminals ringing the Loop (LaSalle St Station, Randolph St Station, Richard B Ogilvie Transportation Center and Union Station – all on map pp358-60). Some lines run daily, while others operate only during weekday rush hours. Metra fares cost $1.75 to $5 or more. An all-weekend ticket costs $5.

PACE (☎ 312-836-7000; www.pacebus.com) runs the suburban bus system that connects with city transport.

Much of the city train system is inaccessible to people with reduced mobility, but most buses are accessible.

TAXI

Cabs are plentiful in the Loop, north to Andersonville and west to Bucktown. In other areas, call **Yellow Cab** (☎ 312-829-4222) or **Flash Cab** (☎ 773-561-1444). Flagfall is $1.90, plus $1.60 per mile; a 15% tip is expected. If you venture outside city limits, you'll pay one and a half times the fare.

AROUND CHICAGO

Evanston

Evanston, 14 miles north of the Loop and reached via the CTA Purple Line, combines sprawling old houses with a compact downtown. It's home to Northwestern University and the small **Mitchell Indian Museum** (☎ 847-475-1030; 2600 Central Park Ave; adult/child $5/2.50; 🕑 10am-5pm Tue-Sat, until 8pm Thu, noon-4pm Sun), which documents the lives of Native Americans past and present.

North Shore

Chicago's northern lakeshore suburbs became popular with the carriage set in the late 19th century. A classic 30-mile drive follows Sheridan Rd through various tony towns to the socioeconomic apex of Lake Forest. Attractions include the glistening white **Baha'i House of Worship** (☎ 847-853-2300; 100 Linden Ave, Wilmette; admission free; 🕑 10am-10pm May-Sep, until 5pm Oct-Apr) and **Chicago Botanic Garden** (☎ 847-835-5440; 1000 Lake Cook Rd, Glencoe; admission free; 🕑 8am-dusk; P $8.75).

Oak Park

From 1898 to 1908, Frank Lloyd Wright worked and lived in Oak Park, west of the Loop.

The Oak Park **visitors center** (☎ 708-848-1500; 158 Forest Ave; 🕑 10am-4pm winter, 9am-5pm summer) sells an architectural walking-tour map ($3.25). The **Frank Lloyd Wright Home & Studio** (☎ 708-848-1976; 951 Chicago Ave; adult $9, child 7-18 $7; tours 11am, 1 & 3pm Mon-Fri, continuous 11am-3:30pm Sat & Sun) provides tours of the home and other Wright-designed dwellings. The town is easily reached on the CTA Green Line.

NORTHERN ILLINOIS

The highlight of northern Illinois is the hilly northwest, which was untouched by the last ice age and is bordered by the Mississippi River. It's an easy and popular excursion from Chicago.

En route is **Union**, where the **Illinois Railway Museum** (☎ 815-923-4000; US Rte 20 to Union Rd; adult/child $6-9/4-7; 🕑 varying hours mid-Apr–late Oct) is a good stop for rail buffs. Further along US 20, the industrial city of **Rockford** features a time-warp 1950s downtown.

Galena

Though just a speck on the map, Galena is the area's main attraction. The beautiful town spreads across wooded hillsides and is perfectly preserved, despite a slew of tourist-oriented antique shops and restaurants.

Lead was mined in the upper Mississippi area as early as 1700, but industrial demands in the mid-19th century resulted in a boom. Galena (named for the lead sulfide ore) became a center for the industry, a major river port and the most important regional town, with solid businesses, hotels and mansions in Federal and Italianate styles. The boom ended abruptly after the

Civil War, and Galena was all but deserted until restoration began in the 1960s.

The main **visitors center** (☎ 815-777-4390, 800-747-9377; www.galena.org; 101 Bouthillier St; 9am-5pm Mon-Sat, 10am-5pm Sun, extended hours in summer) is on the eastern side of the Galena River, in the 1857 train depot. Get a walking guide, leave your car and explore on foot.

Elegant old Main St curves around the hillside and the historic heart of town. Among numerous sights is the **Ulysses S Grant Home** (☎ 815-777-3310; 500 Bouthillier St; adult/child $3/1; 9am-4:45pm Wed-Sun), which was a gift from local Republicans to the victorious general at the end of the Civil War. Tours are provided (sometimes conducted by a guy who pretends he 'is' Grant).

The elaborate Italianate **Belvedere Mansion** (☎ 815-777-0747; 1008 Park Ave; adult/child $10/3; 11am-4pm Mon-Fri, until 5pm Sat & Sun, late May–Oct) has the green drapes from *Gone With the Wind*, while the 1826 **Dowling House** (☎ 815-777-1250; 220 Diagonal St; adult/child $7/3.50; 10am-5pm Sun-Fri, until 6pm Sat, May-Oct; Fri-Sun only Apr, Nov, Dec) is Galena's oldest home.

Six miles north you can tour the underground **Vinegar Hill Lead Mine and Museum** (☎ 815-777-0855; 8885 N Three Pines Rd; adult $5, child over 6 $2.50; 9am-5pm in summer, 9am-5pm Sat & Sun Sep-Oct).

Good accommodation and places to eat are plentiful here. Most accommodations are B&Bs, guesthouses and inns, many of which are pricey – minimum $85. Except during winter, many places are full, especially on weekends.

Grant Hills Motel (☎ 815-777-2116; US Rte 20; s/d $63/73;) is a cozy motel 1.5 miles east of town, and has fine views.

West of town, **Triangle Motel** (☎ 815-777-2897; US Rte 20; s/d $45/60;) is a distant second choice.

Splash out like Grant and Lincoln and stay in the well-furnished rooms at **DeSoto House Hotel** (☎ 815-777-0090; 230 S Main St; r $108-200;), dating from 1855.

Clarks Again (☎ 815-777-4407; 200 N Main St; dishes $3-6) is ideal for biscuit-and-gravy breakfasts or lunchtime sandwiches.

Log Cabin (☎ 815-777-0393; 201 N Main St; dishes $10-17) is where you'll find huge dinner portions served amid Americana ambience.

Perry St Brasserie (☎ 815-777-3773; 124 N Commerce St; dishes $23-28; dinner only Tue-Sat), a pricey, dressy place, boasts a renowned European chef.

For a little grit with some locals, have a beer at the **VFW Hall** (cnr Main & Hill Sts).

Quad Cities

South of Galena along a pretty stretch of the Great River Road is scenic **Mississippi Palisades State Park** (☎ 815-273-2731). Further downstream, the Quad Cities (Moline and Rock Island in Illinois, and Davenport and Bettendorf across the river in Iowa), known as the Q-C, make a surprisingly good stop. Check in at the **Q-C visitors center** (☎ 563-322-3911; 2021 River Dr, Moline; 8:30am-5pm Mon-Fri, also 10am-4pm Sat summer).

Rock Island has an appealing downtown (based at 3rd Ave and 18th St) with a couple of cafés, restaurants, a lively pub and music scene and a paddle wheeler casino. On the edge of town, **Black Hawk State Historic Site** (☎ 309-788-0177; 1510 46th Ave; dawn-10pm) is a huge park with trails by the Rock River. Its **Hauberg Indian Museum** (☎ 309-788-9536; in Watch Tower Lodge; admission free; 9am-noon & 1-4pm Wed-Sun) outlines well the sorry story of Sauk leader Black Hawk and his people.

Out in the Mississippi River, the actual island of **Rock Island** once held a Civil War–era arsenal and POW camp. It now has two military museums and a Civil War cemetery.

Moline is the home of John Deere, the international farm machinery manufacturer, which has a museum/showroom in town.

CENTRAL ILLINOIS

Lincoln and Route 66 sights are sprinkled liberally throughout central Illinois, which is otherwise farmland plain. East of Decatur, Arthur and Arcola are centers for the Amish.

Peoria

During the 20th century's first decades, Peoria was a thriving, wealthy town built on whiskey. The phrase 'But will it play in Peoria?' originated in the '20s, when the local well-to-do spawned a vibrant vaudeville/theater scene and brought in big-name performers from New York and Europe. The phrase is still heard today, but often in a political context. The town's reinvented riverfront along Water St makes a good pit stop for a meal or beer.

Springfield

The small state capital has a serious obsession with Abraham Lincoln, who practiced law here from 1837 to 1861. Its Abe-related sights offer an in-depth look at the man and his turbulent times, which only some cynics find overdone. Many of the attractions are walkable downtown and cost little to nothing. Get your bearings with maps from the central **visitors center** (☎ 217-789-2360; www.visit-springfieldillinois.com; 109 N 7th St; 8am-5pm Mon-Fri).

SIGHTS & ACTIVITIES

To visit the top-draw Lincoln Home, you must first pick up a ticket at the **Lincoln Home Visitors Center** (☎ 217-492-4150; 426 S 7th St; admission free; 8:30am-5pm). The site is where Abraham and Mary Lincoln lived from 1844 until they moved to the White House in 1861. You'll see considerably more than just the home: the whole block has been preserved, and several structures are open to visitors.

The **Lincoln Presidential Library & Museum** (cnr Capitol & 7th Sts) will contain the most complete Lincoln collection in the world when it opens in summer 2004, with many never-before-seen items.

After his assassination, Lincoln's body was returned to Springfield, where it lies today. The impressive **Lincoln's Tomb** sits in **Oak Ridge Cemetery** (☎ 217-782-2717; admission free; 9am-4pm, until 5pm summer), north of downtown. The gleam on the nose of Lincoln's bust, created by visitors' light touches, indicates the numbers of those who pay their respects here.

Standing a block apart are the noteworthy **Lincoln-Herndon Law Offices** (☎ 217-785-7289; cnr 6th & Adams Sts; suggested donation adult/child $2/1; 9am-noon & 1-4pm Tue-Sat year-round, until 5pm summer) and **Old State Capitol** (☎ 217-785-7961; cnr 5th & Adams Sts; suggested donation adult/child $2/1; 9am-4pm Tue-Sat year-round, until 5pm summer). Both offer detailed tours covering Lincoln's early political life; the latter takes in his dramatic pre–Civil War debates with Stephen Douglas.

Lincoln-free attractions include the pristine 1904 **Dana-Thomas House** (☎ 217-782-6776; 301 E Lawrence St; adult/child $3/1; 9am-4pm Wed-Sun), one of Frank Lloyd Wright's Prairie-style masterworks, with an insightful tour; **Shea's Gas Station Museum** (☎ 217-522-0475; 2075 Peoria Rd; admission free; 7am-4pm Tue-Fri, 7am-noon Sat) with Route 66 pumps and signs; and the sumptuous **State Capitol** (☎ 217-782-2099; cnr 2nd & Capitol Sts; admission free; 8am-4pm Mon-Fri, 9am-3pm Sat & Sun) with free tours.

SLEEPING & EATING

Motel 6 (☎ 217-529-1633; 6010 S 6th St; s/d $40/46; P) This is just one of the chain hotels lining I-55 east of town where you'll find budget prices.

For good mid-range lodging downtown, try the **Carpenter Street Hotel** (☎ 217-789-9100, 888-779-9100; www.carpenterstreethotel.com; 525 N 6th St; r $69-75; P) or **Mansion View Inn** (☎ 217-544-7411, 800-252-1083; www.mansionview.com; 529 S 4th St; r from $80; P).

Inn at 835 (☎ 217-523-4466; www.innat835.com; 835 S 2nd St; s/d from $100/115; P) This fine B&B in a 1909 landmark building is worth the splurge for its historic ambience.

Cozy Dog Drive In (☎ 217-525-1992; 2935 S 6th St; corn dogs $1.50-3; Mon-Sat) Though the food tends toward the deeply fried variety, all must stop to hail the corn dog's birthplace at Cozy Dog Drive In. It's a Route 66 legend, with all sorts of memorabilia and souvenirs.

For an array of tasty meal options, cruise S 6th St between Monroe and Adams Sts. A local speciality is the 'horseshoe,' an artery-clogging fried meat sandwich covered with melted cheese; **Brewhaus** (☎ 217-525-6399; 617 E Washington; horseshoes $3-6; Mon-Sat), a popular pub, serves them.

GETTING THERE & AROUND

The **Greyhound station** (☎ 217-544-8466; 2351 S Dirkson Parkway), southeast of downtown, has frequent connections to St Louis ($24 to $32, two hours), Indianapolis ($45 to $50, eight hours) and Chicago ($36 to $42, five hours).

The downtown **Amtrak station** (☎ 217-753-2013; cnr 3rd & Washington Sts) has three daily trains to/from St Louis ($11 to $32, 2½ hours) and Chicago ($16 to $45, four hours).

Petersburg

When Lincoln first arrived in Illinois in 1831, he worked variously as a clerk, storekeeper and postmaster in the frontier village of New Salem before studying law and moving to Springfield. In Petersburg, 20 miles northwest of Springfield, **Lincoln's New Salem State Historic Site** (☎ 217-632-4000; Rte 97; adult/child $2.50/1; 9am-5pm Wed-Sun Mar-Oct, 8am-4pm Mon-Wed Nov-Feb) reconstructs the village with building replicas, historical displays and costumed performances – a pretty informative and entertaining package.

Route 66

The classic highway from Chicago to Los Angeles, known through legend, song and television, once cut diagonally across Illinois to St Louis and beyond. Though now almost totally superseded by I-55, the old route – affectionately called Main St, USA – still exists in scattered sections, and its associated Americana survives in towns bypassed by the interstate.

Burgers and fries are somehow more enticing when proffered by a 28ft fiberglass spaceman. The Gemini Giant beckons hungry travelers to the **Launching Pad Drive-In restaurant** (☎ 815-476-6535; dishes $3-4) in Wilmington, 20 miles south of Joliet.

In McLean, the modest **Route 66 Hall of Fame** display at the **Dixie Truckers Home** (☎ 309-874-2323; 24hr), a gas station/restaurant complex, is a kick for 66ers.

Further south, a good section of old Route 66 parallels I-55 through Litchfield. Grab a meal and piece of pie at time-defiant **Ariston Cafe** (☎ 217-324-2023; dishes $5-14), or see a $1 movie at the **Sky View Drive-In Theater** (☎ 217-324-4451) amidst the corn and soybean fields. Hotels are nearby on Rte 16.

Mount Olive has the classic 1926 **Soulsby Shell Station**, the route's oldest gas station; it's in the process of becoming a museum.

SOUTHERN ILLINOIS

A surprise awaits near Collinsville, 10 miles east of East St Louis: classified as a Unesco World Heritage Site with the likes of Stonehenge, the Acropolis and the Egyptian pyramids is **Cahokia Mounds State Historic Site** (☎ 618-346-5160; exit 6 off I-55/70; suggested donation adult/child $2/1; 9am-5pm Wed-Sun). Cahokia protects the remnants of North America's largest prehistoric city (20,000 people, with suburbs!), dating from AD 1200. While the 65 earthen mounds, including enormous Monk's Mound and the 'Woodhenge' sun calendar, are not overwhelmingly impressive in themselves, the whole is well worth seeing.

Not a World Heritage Site, though it should be, is the **World's Largest Catsup Bottle** (800 S Morrison Ave) near Main St in downtown Collinsville. Nearby, Hwy 157 is lined with motels and chain restaurants.

Grafton lies to the north at the confluence of the Illinois and Mississippi Rivers. The Great River Road in this area is edged with cliffs and is especially scenic.

An exception to the state's flat farmland is the green southernmost section, punctuated by rolling **Shawnee National Forest** (☎ 681-253-7114) and rocky outcroppings. The area has numerous state parks and recreation areas good for outdoor activities. **Union County**, near the state's southern tip, has wineries and orchards. At little **Cairo**, on the Kentucky border, the Mississippi and Ohio Rivers converge.

INDIANA

Just because Indiana is home to the world's oldest and most famous car race doesn't mean you have to speed through. It can make a pleasant and relaxing pit stop, as most of the state is free of mass commercialism. Columbus and Bloomington are two small towns with big culture: Columbus is one of the USA's premiere architectural meccas, with schools, banks and fire stations designed by IM Pei, Eero Saarinen and other noted designers. Bloomington is a lively university town filled with ethnic restaurants and Tibetan temples. The flourishing capital, Indianapolis, has the nifty Indy 500 museum where you can take a spin around the race track. The south is blessed with verdant hills, valleys, limestone caves and forests – choice areas for off-the-beaten path touring.

History

As was the case in neighboring Illinois and Ohio, prehistoric mound builders once occupied much of Indiana, and the Algonquian tribes had succeeded by the time the first Europeans arrived.

French fur traders were plying the state's waterways by the mid-17th century, and by 1679 had charted a water route between the Great Lakes and the Mississippi River, forging a tenuous link across their North American empire. The French established several forts to protect this route. Vincennes, on the lower Wabash River, is the era's only surviving permanent settlement.

Indiana was first settled by farmers from Kentucky (including Abraham Lincoln's family). Expanding settlement and resulting

INDIANA FACTS

Nicknames The Hoosier State, Crossroads of America
Population 6,159,068 (14th)
Area 36,420 sq miles (38th)
Admitted to Union December 11, 1816 (19th)
Capital city Indianapolis (population 791,900)
Other cities Fort Wayne (205,700), Evansville (121,600), Gary (102,700), South Bend (107,800)
Birthplace of gangster John Dillinger (1903–34), actor James Dean (1931–55), author Kurt Vonnegut (b 1922), TV host David Letterman (b 1947), singer Michael Jackson (b 1958)
Famous for Indy 500 motor race, winning basketball teams

conflicts displaced the Native Americans, with the final battle fought in 1811 at Tippecanoe. The Kentucky connection meant that Indiana had many Southern sympathizers in the Civil War, but as elsewhere around the Great Lakes, the war's main impact on the state was the growth of the northern industrial towns. In 1906, steelmaking started in Gary, using coal from Illinois and Indiana and iron ore shipped from Minnesota; the industry continues to add fuel to the state economy. Indiana also has oil refineries and is a major rail and trucking center.

Information

Indiana highway information (☎ 800-261-7623; www.in.gov/dot)
Indiana Tourism (☎ 800-289-6646; www.enjoyindiana.com; 1 N Capitol Ave, Suite 700, Indianapolis, IN 46201)

Indiana's state sales tax is 6%.

National & State Parks

Indiana state park information (☎ 800-622-4931; www.in.gov/dnr) Campground reservations accepted. Park entry requires a vehicle permit of $4/24 per day/year for residents, $5/30 for nonresidents.

INDIANAPOLIS

The location of Indiana's capital, on flat cornfields in the geographical center of the state, was the result of a legislative compromise in 1820 between agricultural and industrial regions. The city had many early carmakers but they were eclipsed by the Detroit giants. Their legacy was a 2.5-mile rectangular test track that was used in 1911 for the first Indianapolis 500 race (won at an average speed of 75mph).

Indianapolis' considerable and ongoing downtown redevelopment began in the 1980s. Today the growing, prosperous city continues positive change. Public spending – remember that? – is everywhere. The spacious, clean center offers abundant museums, memorable architecture, war memorials and major sports venues, collectively making a stopover worth planning.

Orientation

Indianapolis is geometrically laid out, much like Washington, DC, with diagonal avenues superimposed on a grid layout. Everything radiates from the massively impressive Monument Circle. Meridian St divides streets east from west; Washington St divides them north from south.

Information

BOOKSTORES

Borders Books & Music (☎ 317-972-8595; 11 S Meridian St)

EMERGENCY

Emergency number (☎ 911) Police, ambulance, fire.
Rape crisis (☎ 800-221-6311)

INTERNET ACCESS

Interim Central Library (☎ 317-269-1700; 202 N Alabama St) Temporary digs until renovation at 40 E St Clair St is completed in early 2006.

INTERNET RESOURCES

www.culturalindy.com For details on and direct links to exhibits, festivals and cultural attractions.
www.indy.org With information on lodging, restaurants and attractions, plus maps to get you there.

MEDIA

The *Indianapolis Star* is the daily newspaper. *Nuvo*, distributed free on Wednesdays, outlines Indy's arts, music and nightclub scene.

NPR can be found on the dial at WFYI-FM 90.1, while WFBQ-FM 94.7 is the main rock channel.

MEDICAL SERVICES

CVS (☎ 317-923-1491; 1744 N Illinois St) Twenty-four-hour pharmacy.
Indiana University Medical Center (☎ 317-274-4705; 550 University Blvd)

MONEY

Travelex (☎ 317-241-0440; airport) In the main terminal by Delta Airlines.

Most major banks are downtown near the Statehouse and Circle Centre Mall, along Washington, Illinois and Meridian Sts.

POST

Main post office (☎ 800-275-8777; 125 W South St)

TOURIST OFFICES

Visitors center (☎ 800-323-4639; cnr Washington & Illinois Sts in the Artsgarden building; 🕒 10am-9pm Mon-Sat, noon-6pm Sun)

Sights & Activities

INDIANAPOLIS MOTOR SPEEDWAY

The Speedway, home of the **Indianapolis 500** motor race, is Indy's super-sight and an absolute must-see. The **Hall of Fame Museum** (☎ 317-484-6747; 4790 W 16th St; adult $3, child 6-15 $1; 🕒 9am-5pm) features 75 sleek racing cars (including former Indy winners), a 500lb Tiffany trophy and a track tour ($3 extra). OK, so you're on a bus for the latter and not even beginning to burn rubber at 37 mph; it's still fun to pretend when you pass the grandstand. Tickets (☎ 317-484-6700, 800-822-4639; www.imstix.com; tickets $20-140) are hard to come by for the big event, held each year on Memorial Day weekend in May and attended by 450,000 crazed fans. Tickets for pre-race trials and practices are more likely (and cheaper). Other races at the Speedway are the Nascar **Brickyard 400** in August and Formula One **US Grand Prix** in September.

WHITE RIVER STATE PARK

Sprawling White River State Park, at the edge of downtown, contains several worthwhile sights. The adobe **Eiteljorg Museum of American Indians and Western Art** (☎ 317-636-9378; 500 W Washington St; adult $7, child 5-17 $4; 🕒 10am-5pm Tue-Sat, noon-5pm Sun, plus Mon in summer) features Native American artifacts, such as basketry, pots and masks, as well as a fabulous realistic/romantic Western painting collection with works by Frederic Remington and Georgia O'Keeffe.

The **Indiana State Museum** (☎ 317-232-1637; 650 W Washington St; adult $7, child 3-12 $4; 🕒 9am-5pm Mon-Sat, 11am-5pm Sun) includes displays on prehistory, famous Hoosiers, butter churning and African-American settlement in the region.

The **NCAA Hall of Champions** (☎ 800-735-6222; 700 W Washington St; adult/child $7/4; 🕒 10am-5pm Mon-Sat, noon-5pm Sun) reveals the country's fascination with college sports. You'll probably find most Hoosiers hovering around the basketball exhibits, as locals are renowned hoop-ball fanatics. Other park highlights include gardens, a zoo, a canal walk and a military Medal of Honor Memorial.

INDIANAPOLIS MUSEUM OF ART

The **Indianapolis Museum of Art** (☎ 317-920-2660; 4000 Michigan Rd; admission free; 🕒 10am-5pm Tue-Sat, until 8:30pm Thu, noon-5pm Sun) has an excellent collection of European art (especially Turner and some postimpressionists), African tribal art, South Pacific art and Chinese works. The museum is undergoing a massive expansion linking it to **Oldfields – Lilly House & Gardens** (☎ 317-920-2660; 4000 Michigan Rd; adult $5, child 13-18 $4), the plush, 26-acre estate of the Lilly pharmaceutical family; and **Fairbanks Art & Nature Park**, which will feature installations amid 100 acres of woodlands and wetlands when it opens in late 2004.

OTHER

At Monument Circle, the city center is marked by the jaw-dropping 284ft **Soldiers and Sailors Monument**. Beneath is the **Civil War Museum** (☎ 317-232-7615; admission free; 🕒 10am-6pm Wed-Sun), which neatly outlines the conflict and Indiana's abolition position. Also on the circle are the 1916 Circle Theatre and the 1857 Christ Church Cathedral, with Tiffany glass windows. The gorgeous, restored 1880 **Indiana Statehouse** (☎ 317-233-5239; cnr Capitol & Washington Sts; admission free; 🕒 9am-3pm) is just west.

North of downtown, the **Scottish Rite cathedral** (☎ 317-262-3100; 650 N Meridian St; admission free; 🕒 10am-3pm Mon-Fri) is a 1929 Tudor-Gothic Masonic wonder. Further north, the **Children's Museum** (☎ 317-334-3322; 3000 N Meridian St; adult $9.50, child 2-17 $4; 🕒 10am-5pm Mar-Aug, 10am-5pm Tue-Sun Sep-Feb) offers interactive exhibits, a carousel and always-adored dinosaur displays.

Sleeping

Hotels cost more and are usually full during race weeks in May, August and September.

BUDGET

Look for low-cost motels off I-465, the freeway that circles Indianapolis.

Motel 6 (☎ 317-248-1231; 5241 W Bradbury St, off I-75 at Airport Expressway; s/d $40/46; P) This is an OK option 6 miles west of town.

MID-RANGE

Nestle Inn (☎ 317-610-5200, 877-339-5200; www.nestleindy.com; 675 N East St; r $95-135; P) Each of the immaculate rooms at this B&B are painted a different bright color, and all have private baths. It's a short walk to Massachusetts Ave's restaurants and bars, or just stay put reading in one of the inn's comfy sitting rooms.

Stone Soup (☎ 317-639-9550; www.stonesoupinn.com; 1304 N Central Ave; r $85-135; P) Stone Soup is a lovely B&B in a rambling house filled with antiques and stained glass. The less-expensive rooms share a bath. Not quite as conveniently located as the Nestle Inn.

Comfort Inn (☎ 317-631-9000; 530 S Capitol Ave; r $109-169; P) This pleasant, big and bustling hotel is near the RCA Dome. It has spacious rooms and nice facilities, like an indoor pool. Breakfast included.

Days Inn (☎ 317-637-6464; 401 E Washington St; r $64-89; P) This is good value for the downtown location. The lobby is stately with a fireplace; the rooms are clean. Breakfast included.

TOP END

Canterbury (☎ 317-634-3000; 123 S Illinois St; weekend/weekday r from $160/175; P $15) Indianapolis' finest oozes class, like rooms furnished with Chippendale four-poster beds.

Eating

Central Massachusetts Avenue ('Mass Ave' to locals) is bounteous when the stomach growls. The **Broad Ripple** area, 6 miles north at College Ave and 62nd St, has pubs and eateries representing numerous nationalities. At lunch it's hard to beat the incredible range of cheap eats at the old **City Market** (on Market St, two blocks east of Monument Circle), filled with ethnic food stalls and produce vendors.

Bazbeaux (☎ 317-636-7662; 334 Massachusetts Ave; sandwiches $5-7, large pizza $18) A local favorite, Bazbeaux offers an eclectic pizza selection: the 'Tchoupitoulas' is topped with Cajun shrimp and andouille sausage, the 'Chilope' with black bean dip and salsa. If these sound too bizarre, create your own from 50-plus toppings. Muffalettas, stromboli and Belgian beer are some of the other unusual offerings. There is another outlet in Broad Ripple (811 E Westfield Blvd).

Abbey Coffeehouse (☎ 317-269-8426; 771 Massachusetts Ave; dishes $6-7) The Abbey is everything a good coffee shop should be: serene, arty, with comfy chairs and swirled clouds on the ceiling. The sandwiches, wraps and vegetarian items, like the tempeh burrito, are delicious.

India Garden (☎ 317-253-6060; 830 Broad Ripple Ave; dishes $7-13) This is a local Broad Ripple fave for curries, tandooris, thalis and the like.

St Elmo's (☎ 317-635-0636; 127 S Illinois St; dishes from $40; dinner only) Join the limos and Jaguars parked in front of this elegant seafood and steakhouse, which has been feeding the rich since 1902.

WHO'S A HOOSIER?

Since the 1830s, Indianans have been nicknamed 'Hoosiers.' But ask any local what the odd moniker means, and you'll be met with a sheepish smile and shrug of shoulders.

The word's origin has more theories about it than the Kennedy assassination. One idea is that early settlers knocking on a door were met with 'Who's here?' which soon became 'Hoosier.' Another notion is that the early rivermen were so good at pummeling or 'hushing' their adversaries that they got reputations as 'hushers.' Then there's the one about a foreman on the Louisville and Portland canal whose name was Hoosier and who preferred workers from Indiana. They became known as Hoosier's men. More likely, others say, pioneers walking into a tavern on a fight-filled Saturday night would find a torn, displaced body part and say 'Whose ear?'

Scholarly types suggest that the word derives from *hoozer,* from an early dialect in England's Cumberland District, which was used in the 19th-century South to describe woodsmen or hillbilly types. In any case, the word is now well entrenched and thought to have only honorable attributes – though the exact definition remains undefined.

Drinking

Downtown and Mass Ave have a few good watering holes; Broad Ripple has several.

Chatterbox Tavern (☎ 317-636-0584; 435 Massachusetts Ave; ⏰ Mon-Sat) Chill out with the varied clientele at this intimate bar just northeast of the center. It features live jazz Monday through Saturday and a hearty stock of beer and wine.

Rathskeller (☎ 317-636-0396; 401 E Michigan St) This is a long-established German haunt, in the Athenaeum building, with traditional and modern fare and a busy biergarten pouring imported brews.

Entertainment

GAY & LESBIAN VENUES

Check www.gayindy.org for listings.

Club Cabaret (☎ 317-951-8569; 151 W 14th St; ⏰ Thu-Sat) Features bombshell female impersonators.

Greg's Indianapolis/Our Place (☎ 317-638-8138; 231 E 16th St) Has a heated patio and live entertainment.

LIVE MUSIC

Slippery Noodle Inn (☎ 317-631-6974; 372 S Meridian St) The Noodle is the oldest bar in the state and has seen action as a whorehouse, slaughterhouse, gangster hangout and Underground Railroad station, not to mention it's one of the best blues clubs in the country. There's live music nightly, and it's cheap. Located behind Union Station.

Patio (☎ 317-253-0799; 6308 Guilford Ave, in Broad Ripple) This place gets a young crowd for local alternative bands.

PERFORMING ARTS

Madame Walker Theatre Center (☎ 317-236-2099; 617 Indiana Ave) This is a long-established venue for African-American performing arts – jazz, dance, theater. It's worth visiting just to see the unusual African-Egyptian decor.

Indianapolis Symphony Orchestra (☎ 317-639-4300), **Indiana Repertory Theatre** (☎ 317-635-5252) and **Indianapolis Opera** (☎ 317-940-6444) all perform at various venues around the town.

SPECTATOR SPORTS

The motor races are Indy's most prized spectator events (see Speedway, p384).

RCA Dome (☎ 317-262-3389; 100 S Capitol Ave) Under a vast fiberglass dome 63,000 fans watch the NFL's Indianapolis Colts play football.

Conseco Fieldhouse (☎ 317-917-2500; 125 S Pennsylvania St) The beloved NBA Pacers play basketball at this central venue.

Getting There & Around

TO/FROM THE AIRPORT

Indianapolis International Airport (☎ 317-487-7243; www.indianapolisairport.com) is 7 miles southwest of town. The No 8 Washington bus runs between the airport and downtown ($1, 30 minutes). A cab to downtown costs $20 to $22.

BUS

The **Greyhound station** (☎ 317-267-3071, 800-231-2222; 350 S Illinois St) has several buses daily to Cincinnati ($17 to $28, 2½ hours) and Chicago ($32 to $47, four hours).

CAR

Avis, Hertz and other rental agencies have offices at the airport and around town. Check rental information in the Transport chapter (p1121) for more details.

PUBLIC TRANSPORTATION

IndyGo (☎ 317-635-3344; www.indygo.net) runs the local buses; the fare is $1. Service is minimal on weekends.

TAXI

Yellow Cab (☎ 317-487-7777)

TRAIN

The **Amtrak terminal** (☎ 317-263-0550) is in the bus station and has trains to Chicago ($16 to $37, 4½ hours), Cincinnati ($17 to $38, 3½ hours) and Washington, DC ($82 to $197, 20 hours).

AROUND INDIANAPOLIS

Who would have thought there was so much here? Experience everything from bluegrass to pork tenderloins, Tibetans to rebels without a cause.

Fairmount

This small town, north on Hwy 9, is the birthplace of James Dean, one of the original icons of cool. Fans should visit the **Historical Museum** (☎ 765-948-4555; 203 E Washington St; admission $1 donation; ⏰ 10am-5pm Mon-Sat, noon-5pm Sun), the **Dean Memorial Gallery** (☎ 765-948-3326; exit

59 off I-69; admission $4.80; ☎ 9am-7pm) and his grave site.

Columbus

When you think of the USA's great architectural cities – Chicago, New York, Washington, DC – Columbus, Indiana, doesn't quite leap to mind with the others. But it should. Located 40 miles south of Indianapolis on I-65, Columbus is a remarkable gallery of physical design. Since the 1940s, the city and its leading corporations have commissioned some of the world's best architects, including Eero Saarinen, Richard Meier and IM Pei, to create both public and private buildings. Stop at the **visitors center** (☎ 812-378- 2622; 506 5th St; 9am-5pm Mon-Sat Dec-Feb, 9am-5pm Mon-Sat, 10am-4pm Sun Mar-Nov) to pick up a self-guided tour map ($2) or join a bus tour (adult $9.50, child 6-12 $3; 10am Mon-Fri, 10am & 2pm Sat, 11am Sun). Over 60 notable buildings are spread over a wide area (car required), but about 15 diverse works can be seen on foot downtown. Motels are found on the city's outskirts on I-65. To sample a pork tenderloin, an Indiana speciality, head 12 miles west to the hamlet of Gnaw Bone; the **Food & Fuel** (☎ 812-988-4575; Hwy 46; tenderloin $4.75), inside the Marathon gas station, is reputed to have the best.

Nashville

Gentrified and antique-filled, this 19th-century town west of Columbus on Rte 46 is now a bustling tourist center. It's the jump-off point to **Brown County State Park** (☎ 812-988-6406; campsites $16-22), Indiana's largest, where trails give hikers and horseback riders access to the area's lovely green hill country.

Among several B&Bs, central **Artist's Colony Inn** (☎ 812-988-0600, 800-737-0255; www.artistscolonyinn.com; 105 S Van Buren St; r $72-135; dishes $8-14;) stands out for its wonderful rooms and rooftop hot tub. The inexpensive dining room offers traditional Hoosier fare, such as catfish. **Nashville House** (☎ 812-988-4554; cnr Van Buren & Main Sts; dishes $16-20; Wed-Mon) is famous for its home-cooked meals served with fried biscuits and apple butter. Top country-music bands are featured regularly at several venues. The **Bill Monroe Museum** (☎ 812-988-6422; 5163 SR 135 N, in Bean Blossom; adult $4, child 12 & under free; 9am-5pm Mon-Sat, 1-5pm Sun) hails the bluegrass hero 5 miles north of town.

Bloomington

Lively and lovely Bloomington, 45 miles south of Indianapolis on Hwy 37, is the home of Indiana University. The town centers on Courthouse Sq, surrounded by restaurants, bars, bookshops and the historic facade of Fountain Sq Mall. The super-stocked **visitors center** (☎ 812-334-8900; www.visitbloomington.com; 2855 N Walnut St; 8am-5pm Mon-Fri, 9am-4pm Sat) is a few miles north of the center. Nearly everything else is walkable. On the lovely, expansive campus, the **Art Museum** (☎ 812-855-4826; 1133 E 7th St; admission free; 10am-5pm Tue-Sat, noon-5pm Sun), designed by IM Pei, has an excellent collection of African art as well as European and US paintings. The colorful, prayer-flag-covered **Tibetan Cultural Center** (☎ 812-331-0014; 3655 Snoddy Rd; admission free; 10am-4pm, meditation sessions 1pm Sun) and stupa, as well as the **Dagom Gaden Tensung Ling Monastery** (☎ 812-339-0857; 102 Clubhouse Dr; call for hours), indicate Bloomington's significant Tibetan presence.

Look for cheap lodgings along N Walnut St near Rte 46. The limestone **Motel 6** (☎ 812-332-0820; 1800 N Walnut St; s/d $45/51, less on weekdays;) may be the Midwest's most attractive. Ten miles south of town, Lake Monroe makes an attractive outing, and there's camping at quiet **Paynetown Recreation Center** (☎ 812-837-9546; campsites $16-22).

For a town its size, Bloomington offers a mind-blowing array of ethnic restaurants – everything from Burmese to Eritrean to Mexican. Browse Kirkwood Ave and E 4th St. Charming **Little Tibet** (☎ 812-331-0122; 415 E 4th St; dishes $6-8; Wed-Mon) offers specialities from the Himalayan homeland, as well as Thai-influenced dishes and curries. The **Scholar's Inn Bakehouse** (☎ 812-331-6029; 125 N College Ave; dishes $3-9) is excellent for coffee and sandwiches. Pubs on Kirkwood Ave close to the university cater to the student crowd.

SOUTHERN INDIANA

The pretty hills, caves, rivers and absorbing history of southern Indiana mark it as a completely different region than the flat and industrialized north.

Ohio River

The Indiana segment of the historic 981-mile-long Ohio River marks the state's southern border. From tiny Aurora, in the southeastern corner of the state, Rtes

56, 156, 62 and 66, known collectively as the **Ohio River Scenic Route**, wind through a varied landscape.

Coming from the east, a perfect place to stop is little **Madison**, a well-preserved river settlement from the mid-19th century. This clean, attractive town is lined with architectural gems and remains unsullied by ugly commercial strips. At the **visitors center** (☎ 812-265-2956; 301 E Main St; 9am-5pm Mon-Fri, 9am-3pm Sat, 10am-3pm Sun), pick up a pamphlet on the walking tour, which includes the James Lanier Mansion, a designated landmark overlooking the river.

Madison has motels around its edges, as well as several B&Bs. Large, wooded **Clifty Falls State Park** (☎ 812-265-4135; off Rte 56; campsites $10-22), a couple of miles west of town, has camping, hiking trails, views and waterfalls. Main St, with numerous antique stores, also has several places for a bite. **Cafe Camille** (☎ 812-265-5626; 149 E Main; dishes $3-6) is ideal for breakfast or lunch.

In Clarksville, **Falls of the Ohio State Park** (☎ 812-280-9970; 201 W Riverside Dr) has only rapids, no falls, but is of interest for its Lewis and Clark expedition history and its 386-million-year-old fossil beds. The **interpretive center** (adult $4, child 2-18 $1; 9am-5pm Mon-Sat, 1-5pm Sun) explains it all. The rest of town and adjacent New Albany, the largest Indiana town in the region, aren't much, with one exception: **Rich O's Public House** (☎ 812-949-2804; 3312 Plaza Dr, New Albany) and its superlative beer selection. From here head into Kentucky and catch I-64 west, which returns to Indiana with more of historical interest. The village of **Corydon** was once the capital of Indiana, and the Federal-style **capitol building** (☎ 812-738-4890; 202 E Walnut St; admission free; 9am-5pm Tue-Sat, 1-5pm Sun, call for hours late Nov–mid-Apr) is now the town's main attraction.

From Corydon, scenic Rte 62, lined with historic plaques, leads to the Lincoln Hills and southern Indiana's fascinating limestone caves. A visit to **Wyandotte Caves State Recreation Area** (☎ 812-738-2782; 7315 S Wyandotte Cave Rd), near Leavenworth, is highly recommended. Tours (adult $11-15, child 5-12 $5.50-7.50; 9am-5pm Mar-Oct) range from 30 to 90 minutes and take you through caves featuring ancient formations, bats and more. **Marengo Cave** (☎ 812-365-2705; north on Route 66; adult $12-13, child 4-12 $6-6.50; 9am-5:30pm year-round) is another stand-out. Nearby in Milltown, **Cave Country Canoes** (☎ 812-365-2705) runs good half-day, full-day or longer trips on the scenic Blue River.

To the west, **Hoosier National Forest** provides opportunities for walking, swimming, camping and other outdoor recreation. Pick up a guide at any local Chamber of Commerce.

Four miles south of Dale, off I-64, is the **Lincoln Boyhood National Memorial** (☎ 812-937-4541; adult/child $3/free; 8am-5pm) where young Abe lived from age seven to 21. The isolated but good site also includes admission to a working pioneer farm (8am-5pm Wed-Sun May-Sep). Further west, on the Ohio River, **Evansville** is one of the state's largest cities; its Riverside Historic District retains many early-19th-century mansions. Also near town is well-preserved **Angel Mounds State Historic Site** (☎ 812-853-3956; 8215 Pollack Ave; suggested donation $2; 9am-5pm Tue-Sat, 1-5pm Sun), which contains the remains of a prehistoric Native American town (AD 1100–1450) and some reconstructed buildings.

Wabash River

In southwest Indiana, the Wabash River forms the border with Illinois, and was an important route for the early French colonists.

Near the Wabash, south of I-64, captivating **New Harmony** is the site of two early communal-living experiments and is worth a visit. In the early 19th century, a German Christian sect, the Harmonists, developed a sophisticated town here while awaiting the Second Coming. Later it was acquired by the British utopian Robert Owen. Learn more at the angular **Atheneum Visitors Center** (☎ 812-682-4488; cnr North & Arthur Sts; 9:30am-5pm).

Today New Harmony retains an air of contemplation, if not otherworldliness, which you can experience at its newer attractions, such as the temple-like Roofless Church and the Labyrinth, a sort of maze symbolizing the spirit's quest. The town has a couple of guesthouses, some pleasant eateries, and camping at **Harmonie State Park** (☎ 812-682-4821; campsites $22).

NORTHERN INDIANA

The truck-laden I-80/I-90 tollways cut across Indiana's northern section. Parallel US 20 is slower and cheaper but not much more attractive. Connoisseurs of classic cars should detour south on I-69 to the town of **Auburn**, where the Cord Company produced the USA's favorite cars in the 1920s and '30s. The **Auburn Cord Duesenberg Museum** (☎ 260-925-1444; 1600 S Wayne St; adult/child $8/5; 9am-5pm) has a wonderful display of early roadsters in a beautiful art deco setting. Almost next door is the **National Automotive and Truck Museum** (☎ 260-925-9100; 1000 Gordon Buehrig Pl; adult $6, child 5-12 $3; 9am-5pm).

Further west, around Shipshewana, Middlebury and Elkhart, is one of the USA's largest **Amish communities**. The excellent **Menno-Hof Visitors Center** (☎ 260-768-4117; Rte 5 in Shipshewana; adult $5, child 6-14 $2.50; 10am-5pm Mon-Sat Apr-Dec) provides a thorough and comprehensive background. The area holds numerous Amish and Mennonite craft outlets, bakeries and restaurants – most complete with hitching posts.

The city of **South Bend** is another ex-carmaker. Stop at the **Studebaker National Museum** (☎ 574-235-9714; 525 S Main St; adult $6.50, child 8-18 $5.50; 9am-5pm Mon-Sat, noon-5pm Sun year-round, closed Mon mid-Nov–Mar), with its gorgeous 1956 Packard and many other classic beauties. South Bend is better known as the home of the University of Notre Dame, famous for its 'Fighting Irish' football team. To tour the pretty campus with its gold-domed administration building, Lourdes Grotto Replica and Touchdown Jesus painting, start at the **visitors center** (☎ 574-631-5726; 111 Eck Center; 8am-5pm Mon-Sat, 10am-5pm Sun). US residents especially will be interested in seeing the downtown **College Football Hall of Fame** (☎ 574-235-9999; 111 S St Joseph St; adult $10, child 6-14 $4; 10am-5pm).

A good outdoor respite is the popular **Indiana Dunes National Lakeshore**, which stretches along 20 miles of Lake Michigan shoreline. Sandy beaches, dunes and woodlands are crisscrossed with hiking trails, which often afford glimpses of nearby steel mills and stark, industrial structures. The lakeshore is noted for its incredible variety of plant life – everything from cactus to grasslands to hardwood forests and pine trees. Mt Baldy has spectacular sunsets and views of Chicago on a clear day. Stop at the main **visitors center** (☎ 219-926-7561; Kemil Rd at Hwy 12 near Beverly Shores; 8am-5pm year-round, until 6pm summer) for details on beaches and activities; beaches are usually open 8am to sunset daily. You can get here from Chicago via the South Shore commuter train, which stops at Beverly Shores among other park locations (see Chicago, Public Transportation, p378).

Adjacent **Indiana Dunes State Park** (☎ 219-926-1952; end of Rte 49 near Chesterton; campsites $16-22) has year-round camping and takes reservations. **Al & Sally's Motel** (☎ 219-872-9131; 3221 Rte 12; s/d $65/75) is a good option between the park and Michigan City.

Near Illinois, the steel cities of **Gary** and **East Chicago** present some of the bleakest urban landscapes anywhere. Taking the train (Amtrak or South Shore line) through here will get you up close and personal with the industrial underbelly.

OHIO

While much of the state is farmland, Ohio's three big cities – Cleveland, Columbus and Cincinnati – have some major universities and intriguing old neighborhoods, lively arts and tasty eats. Southern Ohio cradles parks amidst the rolling foothills of the Appalachian Mountains and serpent-shaped earthen works from ancient cultures. Northern Ohio is edged with Lake Erie summer resorts, peaceful Amish communities and the hip-swinging Rock & Roll Hall of Fame. Plus aren't you curious to see the only state nicknamed after a poisonous nut (the buckeye)?

History

Following the Revolutionary War, settlers streamed into the Northwest Territory. Ohio was among the first areas settled; Marietta was the earliest town, established in 1788. Following clashes with settlers, the local Indians were decisively beaten at the 1794 Battle of Fallen Timbers. Immigrants from Ireland, Switzerland and particularly Germany began arriving in the early 19th century. In 1832 the completion of the Ohio–Erie Canal between the Ohio River and Lake Erie provided transport connections that, combined with abundant local resources, enabled Ohio cities to become early centers of industry. By 1850 Ohio was the third most populous state in the nation.

Many Ohio soldiers – including Union generals Sherman and Grant – fought in the Civil War, though many in the state's south pledged allegiance to the Confederacy. Ohio's industry grew as part of the Union war machine, and after the war, many Southern blacks migrated to Cincinnati, Cleveland and Toledo.

OHIO FACTS

Nickname The Buckeye State
Population 11,421,267 (7th)
Area 44,830 sq miles (34th)
Admitted to Union March 1, 1803 (17th)
Capital city Columbus (population 711,500)
Other cities Cleveland (478,400; metro area 1,786,600), Cincinnati (331,300; metro area 1,503,300), Toledo (313,600), Akron (217,100)
Birthplace of inventor Thomas Edison (1847–1931), flight pioneers Orville Wright (1871–1948) and Wilbur Wright (1867–1912), author Toni Morrison (b 1931), entrepreneur Ted Turner (b 1938), filmmaker Steven Spielberg (b 1947)
Famous for the first airplane and traffic lights

Seven US presidents were born in Ohio, leading to the state's sometimes-heard moniker, 'Mother of Presidents.'

Information

Ohio Division of Travel and Tourism (☎ 800-282-5393; www.ohiotourism.com; 77 S High St, Columbus, OH 43215)
Ohio road conditions (www.buckeyetraffic.org)

Ohio's sales tax is 5%, with counties assessing an additional 25% to 2%.

National & State Parks

Ohio state park information (☎ 800-282-7275; www.dnr.state.oh.us) State parks are free; campground reservations accepted for day of arrival only.

CLEVELAND

Drawing from its roots as an industrious, working man's town, Cleveland has worked hard in recent years to prove it rocks. The city can wipe the sweat from its brow. Its revitalized waterfront, known as the Flats, its prominent cultural institutions and, of course, the Rock & Roll Hall of Fame render the old jokes about urban decay and the river catching fire things of the past.

History

Surveyed in 1796, Cleveland boomed after the Civil War by using iron from the upper Great Lakes and coal transported along the river to become one of the biggest US steel producers. It diversified into machinery production, textiles, clothing and chemicals and became a center of trade unionism and socially progressive policies. Industrial wealth (think Rockefeller) bankrolled cultural aspirations, and the city still surprises with its world-class museums and performing arts.

Cleveland reached its nadir in 1969 when the Cuyahoga River burned (again) and the demise of the city's traditional industries led to urban blight and severe social problems. Ongoing renewal started in the 1980s, as derelict waterfronts became bustling restaurant, bar and entertainment precincts. Three 1990s developments had major impacts – new baseball and football stadiums became the focus of local civic pride, and the Rock & Roll Hall of Fame brought international attention.

Orientation

Cleveland's center is Public Sq, dominated by the conspicuous Terminal Tower. Ontario Street is the east–west dividing line.

Most attractions are downtown or at University Circle (the area around Case Western Reserve University). Ohio City, Tremont and Coventry are good areas nearby for eating and drinking.

Information

BOOKSTORES

Mac's (☎ 216-321-2665; 1820 Coventry Rd, Coventry) Attached to Tommy's (see Eating, p394).

EMERGENCY

Emergency number (☎ 911) Police, ambulance, fire.
Rape crisis (☎ 216-619-6192)

INTERNET ACCESS

Cleveland Public Library (☎ 216-623-2800; 325 Superior Ave)

INTERNET RESOURCES

www.artsinohio.com For a detailed roundup of arts and cultural events (regional and statewide).
www.travelcleveland.com Here you'll find attraction and lodging information as well as coupons that will save you money at places throughout town.

MEDIA

The *Plain Dealer* is the city's daily newspaper with a good Friday entertainment section. *Scene* is a free weekly entertainment paper out on Wednesday.

Tune into WCPN-FM 90.3 for NPR, or WMMS-FM 100.7 for rock.

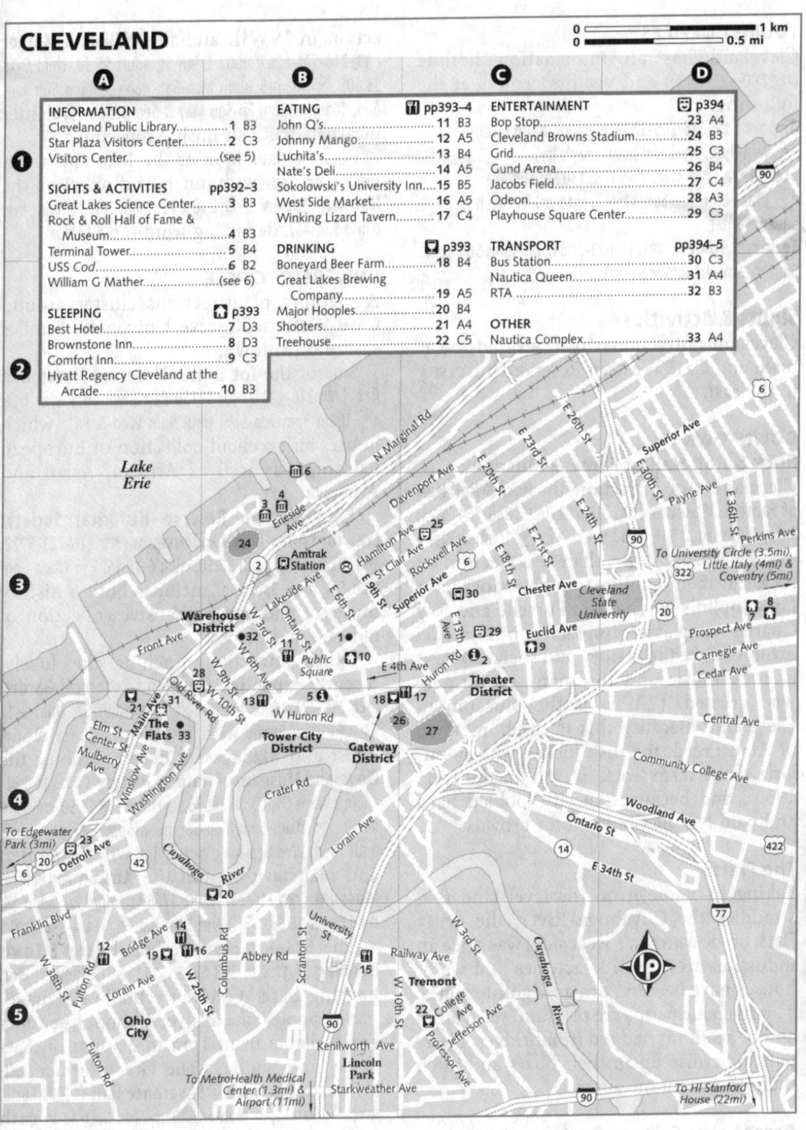

MEDICAL SERVICES

MetroHealth Medical Center Emergency Department (☎ 216-778-4152; 2500 MetroHealth Dr)

MONEY

There's not much by way of money exchanges available downtown; it's best to transact at the airport.

Cleveland Hopkins International Airport Currency Exchange (☎ 216-265-0600)

Several banks with ATMs are downtown around Public Sq.

POST

Main post office (☎ 216-861-0708; 1240 E 9th St)

TOURIST OFFICES

Cleveland has an information hotline (☎ 800-321-1004), and visitors centers at the following:

Airport (☎ 216-265-3729; baggage claim level; 9am-9pm, weekend hours may vary)

Star Plaza (☎ 216-771-9118; 1302 Euclid Ave; 11am-6pm Tue-Sat, 11am-3pm Sun) By Playhouse Square Center.

Terminal Tower (☎ 216-621-7981; 1st floor, 50 Public Sq; 9am-4:30pm Mon-Fri)

Sights & Activities

Cleveland's attractions cluster around downtown and Case Western Reserve University to the east.

DOWNTOWN

Rock & Roll Hall of Fame & Museum

Cleveland's top attraction, the **Rock & Roll Hall of Fame & Museum** (☎ 216-781-7625, 888-764-7625; 1 Key Plaza; adult $18, child 9-12 $11; 10am-5:30pm, until 9pm Wed) is more than a collection of rock star memorabilia, though it does have Janis Joplin's psychedelic Porsche and Ray Charles' sunglasses. Interactive multimedia exhibits trace the history and social context of rock music and the many performers who created it. Why is the museum in Cleveland? Because this is the hometown of Alan Freed, the disk jockey who popularized the term 'rock 'n' roll' in the early 1950s, and because the city lobbied hard and paid big. Be prepared for crowds.

The Flats

Taking its name from the level land that straddles the Cuyahoga River, the gritty **Flats**, on downtown's west side, was once an industrial area, but its factories and warehouses have been ret orn as nightlife zones. The riverside patios are pleasant, set around and beneath myriad old iron bridges. Many patrons cruise up in their boats and hitch them to restaurant docks.

Great Lakes Science Centre

The **Science Centre** (☎ 216-694-2000; 601 Erieside Ave; adult $8, child 3-17 $6; 9:30am-5:30pm), next to the Rock Hall, gives a good account of the lakes' environmental problems, with hands-on exhibits and an Omnimax theater. Berthed nearby on the waterfront are the storied submarine **USS Cod** (☎ 216-566-8770; 1089 E 9th St; adult/child $5/3; 10am-5pm May-Sep), which saw action in WWII, and the **William G Mather** (☎ 216-574-6262; 1001 E 9th St; adult $5.50, child 5-18 $3.50; 10am-5:30pm Mon-Sat, noon-5:30pm Sun Jun-Aug, 10am-5:30pm Fri-Sun May & Sep-Oct), a freighter incarnated as a steamship museum.

For a closer look at the lake and river, take a cruise (with lunch or dinner) on the **Nautica Queen** (☎ 216-696-8888; 1153 Main Ave; cruise $24-45), departing from the Flats.

UNIVERSITY CIRCLE

A plethora of attractions cluster around Case Western Reserve University, 5 miles east of downtown.

Star of the lot is the **Cleveland Museum of Art** (☎ 216-421-7340; 11150 East Blvd; admission free; 10am-5pm Tue-Sun, until 9pm Wed & Fri), which houses an excellent collection of European paintings, as well as African, Asian and American art.

The **Western Reserve Historical Society/Crawford Auto-Aviation Museum** (☎ 216-721-5722; 10825 East Blvd; adult $7.50, child 6-18 $5; 10am-5pm Mon-Sat, noon-5pm Sun) includes both a history museum and comprehensive collection of old cars and planes.

Other attractions include the lovely, recently expanded **Cleveland Botanical Garden** (☎ 216-721-1600; 11030 East Blvd; adult $7, child 3-12 $3; 10am-5pm), with its Costa Rican cloud forest and Madagascar desert exhibits; the **Cleveland Museum of Natural History** (☎ 216-231-4600; 1 Wade Oval Dr; adult $6.50, child 7-18 $4.50, child 3-6 $3.50; 10am-5pm Mon-Sat, noon-5pm Sun year-round, until 10pm Wed Sep-May) with its wildlife garden and planetarium; and the **African American Museum** (☎ 216-791-1700; 1765 Crawford Rd; adult $4, child under 18 $3; 10am-3pm Tue-Fri, 11am-3pm Sat).

The Frank Gehry–designed **Peter B Lewis Building** (☎ 216-368-6339; 11119 Bellflower Rd), housing Case Western's school of management, ripples like a silver ribbon; free tours are available from 1pm to 3:30pm on Saturday and Sunday. The Greek-influenced, art deco interior of **Severance Hall** (11001 Euclid Ave; 9am-6pm Mon-Fri, 10am-6pm Sat) is worth seeing. Beyond the circle further east, don't forget eclectic **Lake View Cemetery** (☎ 216-421-2665; 12316 Euclid Ave; admission free; 7:30am-5:30pm), the 'outdoor museum' where President Garfield and John Rockefeller rest.

ELSEWHERE IN TOWN

Coventry Village, along Coventry Rd by Mayfield Rd, is a small, relaxed neighborhood of alternative shops and restaurants. The **Museum of Contemporary Art** (☎ 216-421-8671; 8501 Carnegie Ave; adult suggested donation $4, child 12 & older $3; 11am-6pm Tue-Sat, until 8pm Thu) presents challenging exhibitions. **Edgewater Park** (☎ 216-881-8141; admission free; 6am-11pm), 3 miles west of downtown and part of Cleveland Lakefront State Park, has a beach and picnic area. Look for the Edgewater exit off Rte 2 West.

Sleeping

Prices here are for summer, which is high season; rooms can be 20% less at other times (unless there is an event or convention). Prices listed here do not include the 14.5% tax. It's best to prebook accommodation.

BUDGET

You'll have to head out of town for the cheapest digs.

HI Stanford House (☎ 330-467-8711; 6093 Stanford Rd; dm $16, sheets $3; daily Apr-Dec, Thu-Mon Jan-Mar) This hostel sits peacefully in the leafy Cuyahoga Valley National Recreation Area, 22 miles south of Cleveland in Peninsula. The fine old farmhouse is surrounded by trails, and deer often bound by. The office is open 7am to 9am and 5pm to 10pm. Call for directions; not accessible by public transportation.

MID-RANGE

Brownstone Inn (☎ 216-426-1753; 3649 Prospect Ave; r $65-125; P) Well-located between downtown and University Circle, the Brownstone is a B&B with a big personality. All five rooms in the Victorian townhouse have a private bath, and each comes equipped with comfy robes to lounge in. Breakfast is served in the morning, aperitifs in the evening.

Best Hotel (☎ 216-361-8969; 3614 Euclid Ave; s/d $80/85; P) Best Hotel's rooms are spacious and clean. Niceties include a pool, free parking, continental breakfast and friendly staff; it's located near the Brownstone Inn.

Comfort Inn (☎ 216-861-0001; 1800 Euclid Ave; s/d $90/100; P $6.50) This is the closest mid-range lodging to the center, with the bus station a short walk away. The rooms are of standard, decent quality.

There are modest motels southwest of Cleveland's center, near the airport. The W 150th exit off I-71 (exit 240) has good options for under $100, like **Baymont Inn** (☎ 216-251-8500; 4222 W 150th St; r from $74; P), with continental breakfast and near rapid transit to downtown.

TOP END

Hyatt Regency Cleveland at The Arcade (☎ 216-575-1234; 420 Superior Ave; s/d from $169/194; P $19) The historic 1890 building is a real beauty, with well-appointed rooms. The expansive interior skylight and detailing are worth seeing.

Eating

There are more hip options and ethnic range than you might expect in a Rust Belt town.

OHIO CITY & TREMONT

Ohio City and Tremont, which straddle I-90 south of downtown, are areas with lots of new establishments popping up.

Johnny Mango (☎ 216-575-1919; 3120 Bridge Ave; dishes $5-15) The Caribbean-influenced food and drinks are as flavorful as the interior is colorful. Mr Mango has a hearty vegetarian selection along with his meat dishes, all begging to be complemented by tropical drinks like sangria or Cuban *mojitos* (rum cocktail). The French fries made of plantains are mouthwatering.

Nate's Deli (☎ 216-696-7529; 1923 W 25th St; dishes $4-9; until 6pm Mon-Sat) Laid-back Nate's offers an unusual mix of Middle Eastern dishes and deli sandwiches, with choices from reubens (corned beef, swiss cheese and sauerkraut on rye) to stuffed grape-leaf platters.

Sokolowski's University Inn (☎ 216-771-9236; 1201 University Rd; dishes $8-15; Mon-Sat) The portions are huge, enough to fuel the hungriest steelworker. It's cafeteria style, so grab a tray and fill it with plump pierogi, cabbage rolls and other rib-sticking Polish fare.

The stalls at the **West Side Market** (cnr W 25th St & Lorain Ave; Mon, Wed, Fri & Sat) overflow with fresh produce and prepared foods, especially on elbow-rubbing Saturday mornings.

LITTLE ITALY & COVENTRY

Busy Little Italy is along Mayfield Rd, near the Lakeview Cemetery and University Circle (look for the Rte 322 sign).

Presti's Bakery (☎ 216-421-3060; 12101 Mayfield Rd; dishes $2-4) Try Presti's for its popular sandwiches, stromboli and divine pine nut cookies.

Food-abundant Coventry Village is a bit further east off Mayfield Rd.

Tommy's (☎ 216-321-7757; 1820 Coventry Rd; dishes $4-8) This is a neighborhood standout with a broad, veggie-heavy menu; don't miss the Mary Lynn spinach pie.

DOWNTOWN

The Warehouse District, on the west edge of downtown between W 6th and W 9th Sts, has several good restaurants.

Luchita's (☎ 216-241-8200; 740 W Superior Ave; dishes $7-15; Mon-Sat) Attached to a pool hall, Luchita's ladles out flavorsome Mexican food.

Winking Lizard Tavern (☎ 216-589-0313; 811 Huron Rd; dishes $6-15) This huge, popular branch of the local pub-grub outlet comes complete with caged iguana.

John Q's (☎ 216-861-0900; 55 Public Sq; dishes $23-38) A classic steak house.

Drinking

THE FLATS

The Flats is a prime area for lively bars. There's also food here, but you're better off in the Warehouse District.

Shooters (☎ 216-861-6900; 1148 Main Ave) Shooters, where the young and beautiful mingle, has a great waterfront location, perfect for sunset gazing. Nearby, the restored Powerhouse building in the Nautica complex contains more bars and restaurants.

Boneyard Beer Farm (☎ 216-575-0226; 748 Prospect Ave) This is a great spot to down a couple, and there are other places nearby in the downtown area.

OHIO CITY & TREMONT

Major Hooples (☎ 216-575-0483; 1930 Columbus Rd) Look over the bar for Cleveland's best skyline view from this friendly, eclectic watering hole.

Great Lakes Brewing Company (2516 Market Ave; Mon-Sat) Elliott Ness got into a shootout with criminals here; ask the bartender to show you the bullet holes.

Treehouse (☎ 216-696-2505; 820 College Ave) Treehouse caters to a young, hip crowd thronged around a giant metal tree.

UNIVERSITY CIRCLE

Barking Spider (☎ 216-421-2863; 11310 Juniper Rd) This ski-lodge-like place is the perfect spot to while away the afternoon; it's hidden, tucked behind Arabica Coffee House.

Entertainment

Check *Scene* and Friday's *Plain Dealer* (see Media, p390) for listings.

C-tix (☎ 216-771-1778; in the Star Plaza Visitors Center; 1302 Euclid Ave) Sells day-of discount tickets.

GAY & LESBIAN VENUES

The **Gay People's Chronicle** (☎ 216-631-8646; www.gaypeopleschronicle.com) is a weekly with entertainment listings and is distributed free throughout town.

Grid (☎ 216-623-0113; 1437 St Clair St) A downtown gay dance venue.

LIVE MUSIC

Odeon (☎ 216-574-2525; 1295 Old River Rd) A rock club in the Flats.

Beachland Ballroom (☎ 216-383-1124; 15711 Waterloo Rd) Hip young bands play at this venue east of downtown.

Bop Stop (☎ 216-771-6551; 2920 Detroit Ave) An excellent jazz venue.

PERFORMING ARTS

Playhouse Square Center (☎ 216-771-4444; 1501 Euclid Ave) This elegant center hosts theater, opera and ballet.

Severance Hall (☎ 216-231-1111; 11001 Euclid Ave) Near University Circle, Severance Hall is where the acclaimed Cleveland Symphony Orchestra holds its season (August to May).

SPECTATOR SPORTS

Cleveland is a serious jock town with three modern downtown venues.

Jacobs Field (☎ 866-488-7423; 2401 Ontario St) The Indians play baseball here.

Gund Arena (☎ 216-241-2121; 1 Center Ct) Nearby, the men's-league Cavaliers and women's-league Rockers play basketball at an arena which doubles as an entertainment venue.

Cleveland Browns Stadium (☎ 440-891-5000; 1085 W 3rd St) The NFL's Browns play football in the lakefront.

Getting There & Around

TO/FROM THE AIRPORT

Cleveland Hopkins International Airport (☎ 216-265-6030; www.clevelandairport.com) is 11 miles southwest of downtown and linked by the Regional Transit Authority Red Line train ($1.50).

BUS

There are frequent buses from the downtown **Greyhound station** (☎ 216-781-0520; 1465 Chester Ave) to Pittsburgh ($22 to $33, 3½ hours), Chicago ($42 to $70, 7½ hours) and New York ($73 to $88, 12½ hours).

CAR

Parking is scarce and expensive downtown during events. Avis, Hertz and other rental agencies have offices at the airport and around town. Check rental information in the Transport chapter (p1121) for more details.

PUBLIC TRANSPORTATION

The **Regional Transit Authority** (RTA; ☎ 216-621-9500; 1240 W Sixth St) operates a decent bus and train system. The useful Waterfront Line train ($1.50) connects the Flats and other attractions to Tower City Center. Day passes ($3) are valid on any bus or train for 24 hours.

TAXI

Americab (☎ 216-429-1111)

TRAIN

The **Amtrak station** (☎ 216-696-5115; 200 Cleveland Memorial Shoreway) is across from the Great Lakes Science Center. Trains leave daily for Pittsburgh ($19 to $43, three hours), Chicago ($4 to $96, seven hours) and New York ($55 to $133, 11½ hours).

AROUND CLEVELAND

Southeast of Cleveland (25 miles away off Rte 43 in Aurora) is the **Six Flags Worlds of Adventure** (☎ 330-562-7131; adult/child $40/25; 🕑 from 10am daily mid-May–Labor Day, from 10am Sat & Sun Sep-Oct, closing times vary; Ⓟ $8), which features thrill rides, a water park and a major marine-life park.

Akron, 30 miles south of Cleveland, was a small village until Dr BF Goodrich established the first rubber factory in 1869. It was also once the country's rubber capital and still produces more than half the country's tires and over 50,000 different rubber products. For an insight into US ingenuity, visit the **Inventure Place & National Inventors Hall of Fame** (☎ 330-762-4463; 221 S Broadway, Akron; adult $7.50 child 3-17 $6; 🕑 9am-5pm Tue-Sat, noon-5pm Sun).

Further south in **Canton**, birthplace of the NFL, the popular **Pro Football Hall of Fame** (☎ 330-456-8207; 2121 George Halas Dr; adult $12, child 6-14 $6; 🕑 9am-5pm) is a shrine for the gridiron-obsessed. Look for the football-shaped tower off I-77.

West of Cleveland, attractive **Oberlin** is an old-fashioned college town with noteworthy architecture by Cass Gilbert, Frank Lloyd Wright and Robert Venturi. Further west, just south of I-90, the tiny town of **Milan** is the birthplace of Thomas Edison. His home, restored to its 1847 likeness, is a small **museum** (☎ 419-499-2135; 9 Edison Dr; adult $5, child 6-12 $2; 🕑 1-4pm Wed-Sun winter, extended hours Tue-Sun in summer, closed Jan) outlining his inventions like the lightbulb and phonograph.

Still further west, on Hwy 20 and surrounded by farmland, is **Clyde**, which bills itself as the USA's most famous small town. It got that way when native son Sherwood Anderson published *Winesburg, Ohio* in 1919. It didn't take long for the unimpressed residents to figure out where the fictitious town really was. Stop at the **Clyde Museum** (☎ 419-547-9330; 124 W Buckeye St; admission free; 🕑 1-4pm Thu) in the old church for Anderson tidbits. A few doors down, the library houses memorabilia and an extensive Anderson book collection.

ERIE LAKESHORE & ISLANDS

In summer this good-time resort area is one of the busiest (and the most expensive) places in Ohio. Pre-book accommodations.

Sandusky, long a port, now mainly serves as the jump-off point to the Erie Islands. The **visitors center** (☎ 419-625-2984; www.visitohio.com; 4424 Milan Rd; 🕑 8:30am-5:30pm Mon-Fri) provides lodging and ferry information. Scads of chain motels line the roads heading into town.

For the world's tallest (420ft) and fastest (120 mph) roller coaster, head to **Cedar Point Amusement Park** (☎ 419-627-2350; adult/child $44/22; 🕑 from 10am daily mid-May–Labor Day, from 10am Sat & Sun Sep-Oct, closing times vary), 6 miles from Sandusky. If the 16 roller coasters aren't enough, the surrounding area has a nice beach, water park and slew of tacky, old-fashioned attractions.

Lake Erie Islands

The islands in Lake Erie were inhabited by hostile Iroquois when the French first arrived. In the War of 1812's Battle of Lake Erie, Admiral Perry met the enemy English fleet near South Bass Island. His victory ensured that all the lands south of the Great

Lakes became US, not Canadian territory. Today, while the nearby mainland gets congested and isn't particularly attractive, the islands remain an appealing getaway.

Access is from Sandusky, Marblehead, Catawba or Port Clinton. **Pelee Island Transportation** (☎ 800-661-2220; adult one way $14, child 6-12 $7, car $30) runs a ferry from Sandusky to Canada's **Pelee Island** and the Ontario mainland. Pelee, the largest Erie island, is a quiet, wine-producing and bird-watching destination.

KELLEYS ISLAND

Quiet and green, Kelleys is a popular weekend escape, especially for families. It has pretty 19th-century buildings, Native American pictographs, a good beach, glacial grooves...even its old limestone quarries are scenic.

The **Chamber of Commerce** (☎ 419-746-2360; www.kelleysislandchamber.com; cnr Division & Chappell Sts; 🕓 10am-4pm Mon-Sat, noon-4pm Sun summer) has accommodation information.

Kelleys Island State Park (☎ 419-746-2546; campsites $10) quickly gets full, and it doesn't take reservations. The Village, the small commercial center of the island, has places to eat, drink, shop and rent bicycles – a good way to sightsee.

Kelleys Island Ferry Boat Line (☎ 419-798-9763; adult round-trip $10, child $5, car $20) departs frequently from the Marblehead dock. **Island Rocket** (☎ 419-627-1500; adult/child one way $10/5, no cars) departs from Sandusky. Both crossings take about 20 minutes; call for schedules.

BASS ISLANDS

Forget the history and scenery – on a summer weekend, packed Put In Bay on **South Bass Island** is about drinking and carousing. But away from this party town full of restaurants and shops, you'll find a winery and opportunities for camping, fishing, walking and swimming. A singular attraction is the 352ft Doric column commemorating Perry's victory in the Battle of Lake Erie – you can climb up to the observation deck for views of the battle site and, on a good day, Canada.

The **Chamber of Commerce** (☎ 419-285-2832; www.put-in-bay.com; cnr Delaware & Toledo Aves; 🕓 10am-5pm Mon-Fri) has information on lodging, which starts at $75 in summer and often is booked up. **South Bass Island State Park** (☎ 419-285-2112; campsites $20) also fills quickly. Taxis and tour buses serve the island, but bicycling is a fine way to get around. **Jet Express** (☎ 800-245-1538; adult one way $12, child 12 & under free, no cars) leaves Port Clinton on the mainland for South Bass Island, but **Miller Boatline** (☎ 800-500-2421; adult one way $6, child 6-11 $1.50, car $15) from Catawba is cheaper.

Middle Bass Island, a good day trip by ferry from South Bass, offers nature and quiet; Miller Boatline will get you there.

AMISH COUNTRY

Wayne and Holmes Counties, between Cleveland and Columbus, have the USA's densest Amish concentration (followed by areas in Pennsylvania and Indiana). Around Millersburg and Apple Creek, horse-drawn buggies carry traditionally clothed families, and shops sell homemade crafts and foods. Near Berlin, east of Millersburg, is the **Amish & Mennonite Heritage Center** (☎ 330-893-3192; 5798 County Rd 77; adult $5.50, child 6-12 $2.50; 🕓 9am-5pm Mon-Sat year-round, until 8pm Fri-Sat Jun-Oct), which offers concise explanations of the history and life of these independent, religious people. Many places are closed Sunday.

COLUMBUS

Columbus, the state capital, is nice. Like the blind date your mom arranges, it's not the prettiest or splashiest choice, but the solid, sensible one that stays with you in the long run. So meet Columbus. Clean, spacious streets give it a prosperous air, while the 60,000 students of Ohio State University (OSU) lend it a youthful vitality. The city is easy on the wallet, with excellent opportunities to eat and drink your way through neighborhoods like German Village and the Short North.

The helpful **visitors center** (☎ 614-221-2489, 800-345-4386; www.visitcolumbus.org; 111 S 3rd St; 🕓 11am-6pm Mon-Sat, noon-6pm Sun) is on the 2nd floor of the shiny City Center Mall. For free internet access try the **main library** (☎ 614-645-2275; 96 S Grant Ave).

The *Columbus Dispatch* is the city's daily newspaper. The free, weekly *Alive* has full club listings. *Outlook News* is a weekly gay and lesbian publication.

Sights & Activities

A half mile south of downtown is the remarkably large, all-brick **German Village**, a restored 19th-century neighborhood with

GREAT LAKES

cobbled streets and Italianate and Queen Anne architecture. The **German Village Society** (☎ 614-221-8888; 588 S 3rd St; 9am-4pm Mon-Fri, 10am-2pm Sat) has self-guided tour information. Just north of downtown, **Short North** is a redeveloped strip of High St that holds contemporary art galleries, restaurants and jazz bars.

See a landscape of a painting of a landscape at the **Topiary Garden** (☎ 614-645-0197; 480 E Town St; admission free; dawn to dusk), a recreation in greenery of Georges Seurat's painting *A Sunday on La Grande Jatte*.

The **Ohio Historical Center** (☎ 614-297-2300; 1982 Velma Ave, off I-71 N at the 17th Ave exit; $6/2 adult/child; 9am-5pm Tue-Sat, noon-5pm Sun; P $3) has been made over from a fusty relic house to an interactive museum. Join the kids playing dress-ups in clothes from different eras. For those planning to tour the state's southern Hopewell Indian sites, a visit is invaluable.

Back downtown, **COSI Columbus** (☎ 614-228-2674; 333 W Broad St; adult/child $12/7; 10am-5pm Mon-Sat, noon-6pm Sun) is the popular science and industry museum.

The Greek Revival **state capitol** (☎ 614-728-2695; cnr Broad & High Sts; admission free; 7am-7pm Mon-Fri, 11am-5pm Sat & Sun) has soaring Doric columns and an inlaid marble map of Ohio; tours available.

North of downtown, the Ohio State University area has many casual storefronts. The campus' **Wexner Center for the Arts** (☎ 614-292-3535; 1871 N High St; admission $5; 10am-4pm Mon, 10am-6pm Tue-Sat, noon-6pm Sun) offers cutting-edge art exhibits, films and performances; its renovation is scheduled for completion in 2004.

Spectator Sports

The **Ohio State Buckeyes football team** (☎ 800-462-8257) packs a rabid crowd into legendary, horseshoe-shaped Ohio Stadium for its games, held on Saturdays in fall. The NHL **Columbus Blue Jackets** (☎ 614-246-2000; 200 W Nationwide Blvd) play hockey at the downtown Nationwide Arena. The popular **Columbus Crew** (☎ 614-447-2739; 2121 Velma Ave, north off I-71 & 17th Ave), Ohio's professional soccer team, play in their own stadium of the same name from March to October.

Sleeping

The 15.75% tax is not included in the following listed rates.

BUDGET

Cheap chain motels are bunched near the I-270 ring road, where the main highways intersect.

Motel 6 (☎ 614-846-9860; 1289 E Dublin–Granville Rd; s/d from $36/42; P) This Motel 6 offers the chain's standard, serviceable rooms.

MID-RANGE

German Village Inn (☎ 614-443-6506; 920 S High St; r $59; P) This super clean spot is in a great location near bars and restaurants.

Best Western Clarmont (☎ 614-228-6511; 650 S High St; r $79/99; P) The Clarmont is located near, and similar to, the German Village Inn. The adjacent restaurant serves what some say are the best steaks in town.

Red Roof Inn (☎ 614-224-6539; 111 E Nationwide Blvd; r $69-129; P $10) Located in the Arena District, it's one of the classiest-looking Red Roofs you'll ever see. Continental breakfast included.

50 Lincoln Inn (☎ 888-299-5051; www.50lincoln.com; 50 E Lincoln St; r $109-149; P) Each of this inn's eight charming rooms is themed after Picasso, Degas or other artists. It's steps away from the Short North; a full breakfast is included.

TOP END

Westin Great Southern Hotel (☎ 614-228-3800; 310 S High St; r $225; P $20) The century-old Great Southern is the classiest place in town; ask about weekend deals.

Eating & Drinking

German Village and the Short North have the top eating and drinking options.

Schmidt's (☎ 614-444-6808; 240 E Kossuth St; dishes $6-12) When they say the 'best of the wurst,' they mean it. Succulent German staples like sausage, schnitzel and potato salad. The *pièce de résistance:* half-pound cream puffs, including the 'Buckeye,' pumped up with peanut butter. The beer flows freely to the strains of an oompah band (Thursday to Saturday).

Katzinger's Deli (☎ 614-228-3354; 475 S 3rd St; dishes $7-10) Prepare for a mind-boggling array of huge, scrumptious sandwiches, from beefy to vegan.

North Market (☎ 614-463-9664; 59 Spruce St; dishes $4-7; daily, many vendors closed Mon) By the Short North, merchants at this market sell all manner of fresh foods and prepared meals, from

Middle Eastern to Indian. Elegant **Lindey's** (☎ 614-228-4343; 169 E Beck St; dishes $15-22) is well regarded for its seafood and steak.

Around OSU and along N High St from 15th Ave onward, you'll find everything from Mexican to Ethiopian to sushi, plus quality coffee and bagel shops.

Bernie's Bagels and Deli (☎ 614-291-3448; 1896 N High St; dishes $3-5) Bernie's endures as a favorite campus dive.

The **Arena District** (the area around the Nationwide Arena hockey stadium) is bursting with restaurants and bars, many of them mid-range chains and brew pubs.

You can knock back a beer in congenial German Village joints. Try the following:

High Beck (☎ 614-224-0886; 564 S High St)

Round Bar (☎ 614-461-9010; 650 S High St) A circular spot.

Short North Tavern (☎ 614-221-2432; 674 N High St)

Getting There & Around

From the **Greyhound station** (☎ 614-221-4642; 111 E Town St) buses run at least six times daily to Cincinnati ($17 to $25, two hours), Cleveland ($19, 2½ hours) and Chicago ($51, seven to nine hours). There is no Amtrak train service.

The **Central Ohio Transit Authority** (COTA; ☎ 614-228-1776; 60 E Broad St) runs the efficient local buses. Tickets cost $1.25, day passes are $3 and express buses cost extra. Pick up maps at the Broad St office. COTA's Capital City Flyer runs between the airport (10 miles east) and downtown ($5, every 20 to 30 minutes).

SOUTHEASTERN OHIO

Ohio's southeastern corner cradles most of its forested areas, as well as rolling hills and scattered farms.

Around Lancaster, southeast of Columbus, the hills lead gently into wonderful **Hocking County**, which contains more than half a dozen state parks. This region of streams and waterfalls, sandstone cliffs and cavelike formations is an excellent area to explore in any season. It has miles of trails for hiking and rivers for canoeing, as well as abundant campgrounds and cabins at **Hocking Hills State Park** (☎ 740-385-6165; 20160 Rte 664; campsites/cabins $19/33). **Old Man's Cave** is a scenic winner for hiking. This is a busy area in summer, especially on weekends.

Athens makes a lovely base for seeing the region. Situated where US 50 crosses US 33, it's set among wooded hills and built around the Ohio University campus (which comprises half the town). The **visitors center** (☎ 740-592-1819, 800-878-9767; 667 E State St; www.athensohio.com; 9am-5pm Mon-Fri year-round, plus Sat in summer) has good regional information. Inexpensive motels – including friendly **Budget Host** (☎ 740-594-2294; 100 Albany Rd at Rte 50 W; s/d from $41/48;) – dot the outskirts, and numerous student cafés and pubs line Court St, the main road. **Casa Nueva** (☎ 740-592-2016; 4 W State St; dishes $5-12) has Mexican-inspired dishes, while **Court Street Diner** (☎ 740-594-8700; 18 N Court St; dishes $4-8) serves up breakfast, lunch and dinner in '50s style.

Further south, the Ohio River marks the state boundary and flows through many scenic stretches. It's a surprisingly quiet, undeveloped area.

The area south of Columbus was a center for the fascinating prehistoric Hopewell people, who left behind huge geometric earthworks and burial mounds from around 200 BC to AD 600. For a fine introduction visit the **Hopewell Culture National Historical Park** (☎ 740-774-1126; Rte 104 north of Rte 35; admission $3; 8:30-5pm, until 6pm summer), 3 miles north of Chillicothe. The visitors center has a film and excellent interactive exhibit; then you can wander about the variously shaped ceremonial mounds spread over 13-acre **Mound City**, a mysterious city of the dead.

THE HOPEWELL & THEIR ENDURING MYSTERIES

The Hopewell Indian culture, which flourished in the Ohio Valley region between about 200 BC and AD 600, was named after the farmer's field where its remnants were first unearthed. Although relatively unknown today, the Hopewell developed a sophisticated, village-based society where successful agriculture and management allowed for complex spiritual and artistic pursuits. The Indians' most intriguing traits were their internment rites and elaborate burial mounds, many of which remain. Finely worked artifacts indicate that they had far-flung trading relationships and influence. The causes of the Hopewells' decline and the later emergence of the Mississippi mound building culture are not known.

The site is right beside two scary-looking prisons...er, correctional facilities.

In 1802 **Chillicothe** became the capital of the USA's new Northwest Territory, and later it became the first capital of Ohio. A fair selection of moderate motels is available, along with a range of eating options, especially on Rte 159. The clean **Chillicothe Inn** (☎ 740-774-2512; 24 N Bridge St; s/d $37/47) is a good deal.

West of Chillicothe, US 50 bobs pleasantly between hills, farms and woodlands. Other Hopewell sites are in the area. **Fort Hill State Memorial** (☎ 937-588-3221; 13614 Fort Hill Rd, off Rte 41 S; admission free; dawn to dusk), in a pretty Amish district, preserves a Hopewell ceremonial site in a natural area with hiking trails and a gorge. Further southwest, **Serpent Mound** (☎ 937-587-2796; 3850 Rte 73; 10am-5pm; P $6), 4 miles northwest of Locust Grove, is the most captivating site of all. The giant, uncoiling snake stretches over 0.25 mile and is the largest effigy mound in the USA.

DAYTON & YELLOW SPRINGS

Dayton has the aviation sights, but little Yellow Springs (18 miles northeast on Hwy 68) has much more personality for accommodation and places to eat.

Sights & Activities

The huge **USAF Museum** (☎ 937-255-3286; 1100 Spaatz St; admission free; 9am-5pm), at the Air Force base 6 miles northeast of Dayton, displays more than 300 aircraft and missiles. It's got everything from a Wright exhibit, a Sopwith Camel (WWI biplane) and a Stealth bomber, to astronaut ice cream, military propaganda and an Aviation Hall of Fame. Expect a visit to take three or more hours. And don't miss the annex, with its collection of presidential planes – a free shuttle bus takes you over to the hangar.

There are numerous Wright attractions. Among them, **Carillon Historical Park** (☎ 937-293-2841; 1000 Carillon Blvd; adult $5, child 3-17 $3; 9:30am-5pm Tue-Sat, noon-5pm Sun Apr-Oct) has the 1905 Wright Flyer III biplane and a replica of the Wright workshop. The **Dayton Aviation Heritage National Historical Park** (☎ 937-225-7705; 22 S Williams St; admission free; 8:30am-5pm), which includes Wright Cycle Company Complex, is where the brothers developed bikes and aviation ideas. South of town, the **Dayton-Wright Brothers Airport** (☎ 937-885-2327; 10550 Rte 741, Miamisburg; admission free; 9:30am-2:30pm Tue, Thu & Sat) has the world's only flying 'B' plane.

> **MEET ME AT THE CORNER, SMILING**
>
> Why do drivers always smile when pulling up to a certain intersection in West Chester, Ohio? Because they've reached Grinn Dr and Barret Road, which meet in this town just north of Cincinnati. 'Grin and bear it' means to tolerate something unpleasant. Remember it the next time you're stalled in a traffic jam.

Sleeping & Eating

All the following listings are in Yellow Springs, an excellent place to experience down-home Ohio.

Morgan House (☎ 937-767-7509; 120 W Limestone St; s/d $55/60;) A comfy B&B reminiscent of Grandma's house, with pink carpet and mismatched furniture.

Springs Motel (☎ 937-767-8700; www.thespringsmotel.com; 3601 Rte 68; r $45-49;) Springs Motel is a cozy mom-and-pop place.

John Bryan State Park (☎ 937-767-1274; www.johnbryan.org; 3790 Rte 370; campsites $9-15). You can fish, hike, rock climb or camp among the limestone cliffs here.

Young's Jersey Dairy (☎ 937-325-0629; 6880 Springfield–Xenia Rd) This working dairy farm has two restaurants: the **Golden Jersey Inn** (dishes $6-12; lunch & dinner Tue-Sun) serves dishes like buttermilk chicken; the **Dairy Store** (sandwiches $2-4) serves sandwiches, dreamy ice cream and Ohio's best milkshakes.

Clifton Mill (☎ 937-767-5501; 75 Water St; dishes $6-8; closed for dinner) You can watch the water wheel turn, grinding the grain for your pancakes and cornbread at Clifton Mill.

Ha Ha Pizza (☎ 937-767-2131; 108 Xenia Ave; large pizzas $9.50) Ha Ha makes its dough with organically grown whole wheat.

CINCINNATI

Stretching along the Ohio River, Cincinnati is a pretty, genteel city with a bevy of art deco buildings and an active riverfront. It's a good place to kick back, ride a paddle wheel boat, chow on the famous chili and ponder that Jerry Springer once was mayor here. The German legacy ensures you won't go thirsty.

History

With the Ohio River as a principal transport route, Cincinnati, founded in 1788, became a base for wars against the Native Americans and a center of the rich agricultural hinterland. By the mid-1800s it had become Ohio's largest city, thanks to a huge influx of German and Irish immigrants. The many meatpacking plants earned Cincinnati the nickname 'Porkopolis' and provided enough leftover lard for Messrs Procter & Gamble to become one of the world's largest soap makers.

Cincinnati became a center for the antislavery movement, an important station on the Underground Railroad and a home of abolitionist writing and publishing. The Civil War was a boost to Cincinnati's industries, but later the city suffered from corruption, maladministration and a decline in its river commerce as the railways expanded. Anti-German sentiment prevailed during WW1, and the city changed many of its street and building names to sound less Teutonic.

Cincinnati garnered bad press in 2001 for outbreaks in simmering racial tension resulting from young blacks being killed by white police. City hall continues to vow to improve relations and upgrade the central low-income neighborhoods.

Orientation

Downtown streets are laid out on a grid radiating from Fountain Sq. Vine St is the east–west dividing line; east- and west-bound streets are numbered, while north- and south-bound streets are named. The snaking Ohio River forms the city's southern boundary; Kentucky lies across the water.

Information

BOOKSTORES

Kaldi's (☎ 513-241-3070; 1204 Main St) A bookshop cum coffee shop-bar-restaurant.

EMERGENCY

Emergency number (☎ 911) Police, ambulance, fire.

INTERNET ACCESS

Cincinnati Public Library (☎ 513-369-6900; 800 Vine St)

INTERNET RESOURCES

www.artsinohio.com For a detailed roundup of arts and cultural events (regional and statewide).

www.cincyusa.com For information on everything the city has to offer – sights, hotels, restaurants – and coupons to take advantage of it all at reduced rates.

MEDIA

The *Cincinnati Enquirer* and *Cincinnati Post* are the morning and evening newspapers, respectively. *CityBeat* is a free weekly entertainment paper, out on Wednesday.

MEDICAL SERVICES

University Hospital (☎ 513-584-1000; 234 Goodman St)

MONEY

US Bank (☎ 513-632-4135; 425 Walnut St) ATM and foreign currency exchange available.

POST

Post office (☎ 800-275-8777; 525 Vine St)

TOURIST OFFICES

Visitors center (☎ 513-621-6994, 800-246-2987; 511 Walnut St; 🕒 10am-5pm Mon-Sat, noon-5pm Sun) On Fountain Sq; ask about walking tours.

Dangers & Annoyances

The area between the train station and downtown is best avoided on foot, and caution should be used at night in the Over-the-Rhine neighborhood, north of downtown.

Sights & Activities

DOWNTOWN

The elegant 1876 **Roebling Suspension Bridge** was a forerunner of John Roebling's famous Brooklyn Bridge in New York. At its foot is the **National Underground Railroad Freedom Center** (☎ 513-412-6100; north bank of the Ohio River; 🕒 opening mid-summer 2004), with exhibits on how slaves escaped to the north; Cincinnati was a prominent stop on the railroad and a center for abolitionist activities led by residents such as Harriet Beecher Stowe.

Fountain Sq (cnr 5th & Vine Sts), the city centerpiece, hosts the fancy old 'Spirit of the Waters' fountain. Just west is the **Rosenthal Center for Contemporary Arts** (☎ 513-721- 0390; 44 E 6th St; adult $6.50, child 3-13 $3.50; 🕒 11am-6pm Sun-Fri, until 9pm Thu, noon-6pm Sun), which displays all manner of modern art in a new, avant-garde building. Nearby **Carew Tower** (☎ 513-579-9735; 441 Vine St; adult $2, child 6-11 $1; 🕒 10am-3pm Mon-Fri, 10am-4:45pm Sat & Sun) has a

GREAT LAKES

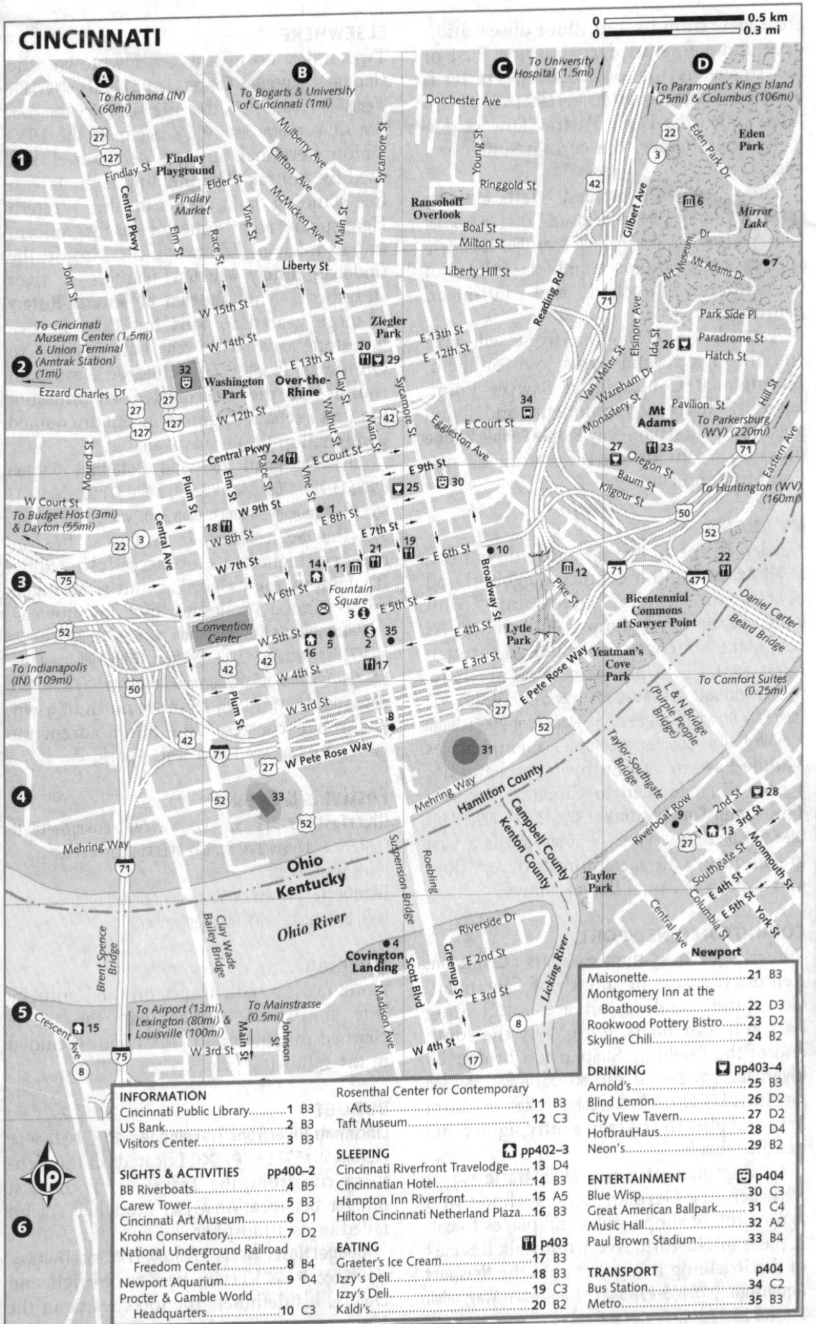
CINCINNATI
0 0.5 km
0 0.3 mi
A
B
C
D
1
2
3
4
5
6
To Richmond (IN) (60mi)
To Bogarts & University of Cincinnati (1mi)
To University Hospital (1.5mi)
To Paramount's Kings Island (25mi) & Columbus (106mi)
Dorchester Ave
Findlay Playground
Findlay St
Elder St
Findlay Market
Central Pkwy
Elm St
Race St
Vine St
Mulberry Ave
Clifton Ave
McMicken Ave
Main St
Sycamore St
Young St
Ringgold St
Ransohoff Overlook
Boal St
Milton St
Eden Park Dr
Eden Park
Mirror Lake
Gilbert Ave
Art Museum Dr
Mt Adams Dr
Liberty St
Liberty Hill St
Reading Rd
John St
W 15th St
W 14th St
Ziegler Park
E 13th St
E 12th St
Park Side Pl
Paradrome St
Hatch St
Elsinore Ave
Ida St
Van Meter St
Wareham Dr
Monastery St
Pavilion St
Hill St
Mt Adams
To Parkersburg (WV) (220mi)
To Cincinnati Museum Center (1.5mi) & Union Terminal (Amtrak Station) (1mi)
Ezzard Charles Dr
Washington Park
Over-the-Rhine
Clay St
Walnut St
W 12th St
E Court St
Eggleston Ave
Oregon St
Baum St
Kilgour St
Eastern Ave
To Huntington (WV) (160mi)
Mound St
Central Pkwy
Plum St
E 9th St
W 9th St
W Court St
To Budget Host (3mi) & Dayton (55mi)
Central Ave
E 8th St
W 8th St
E 7th St
W 7th St
E 6th St
W 6th St
Broadway St
Fountain Square
E 5th St
W 5th St
Pike St
Bicentennial Commons at Sawyer Point
Daniel Carter Beard Bridge
Convention Center
E 4th St
W 4th St
Lytle Park
E 3rd St
W 3rd St
E Pete Rose Way
Yeatman's Cove Park
To Indianapolis (IN) (109mi)
To Comfort Suites (0.25mi)
L & N Bridge (Purple People Bridge)
Taylor-Southgate Bridge
W Pete Rose Way
Mehring Way
Hamilton County
Campbell County
Kenton County
Riverboat Row
2nd St
3rd St
Monmouth St
Southgate St
E 4th St
E 5th St
York St
Columbia St
Central Ave
Newport
Taylor Park
Ohio
Kentucky
Ohio River
Suspension Bridge
Roebling
Brent Spence Bridge
Clay Wade Bailey Bridge
Covington Landing
Scott Blvd
Madison Ave
Greenup St
Riverside Dr
E 2nd St
E 3rd St
Licking River
W 4th St
Crescent Ave
To Airport (13mi), Lexington (80mi) & Louisville (100mi)
To Mainstrasse (0.5mi)
Main St
Johnson St
W 3rd St
INFORMATION
Cincinnati Public Library 1 B3
US Bank 2 B3
Visitors Center 3 B3
SIGHTS & ACTIVITIES pp400–2
BB Riverboats 4 B5
Carew Tower 5 B3
Cincinnati Art Museum 6 D1
Krohn Conservatory 7 D2
National Underground Railroad Freedom Center 8 B4
Newport Aquarium 9 D4
Procter & Gamble World Headquarters 10 C3
Rosenthal Center for Contemporary Arts 11 B3
Taft Museum 12 C3
SLEEPING pp402–3
Cincinnati Riverfront Travelodge 13 D4
Cincinnatian Hotel 14 B3
Hampton Inn Riverfront 15 A5
Hilton Cincinnati Netherland Plaza 16 B3
EATING p403
Graeter's Ice Cream 17 B3
Izzy's Deli 18 B3
Izzy's Deli 19 C3
Kaldi's 20 B2
Maisonette 21 B3
Montgomery Inn at the Boathouse 22 D3
Rookwood Pottery Bistro 23 D2
Skyline Chili 24 B2
DRINKING pp403–4
Arnold's 25 B3
Blind Lemon 26 D2
City View Tavern 27 D2
HofbrauHaus 28 D4
Neon's 29 B2
ENTERTAINMENT p404
Blue Wisp 30 C3
Great American Ballpark 31 C4
Music Hall 32 A2
Paul Brown Stadium 33 B4
TRANSPORT p404
Bus Station 34 C2
Metro 35 B3

great view from its 49th-floor observation deck and a fine art deco interior. East of the square is the postmodern **Procter & Gamble world headquarters** (cnr 6th St & Broadway), often called the Dolly Parton Towers due to its resemblance to a certain someone's chest.

The newly expanded **Taft Museum** (☎ 513-241-0343; 316 Pike St; adult $7, child 18 & under free; 11am-5pm Tue-Fri, until 8pm Thu, 10am-5pm Sat, noon-5pm Sun) holds a notable collection of Chinese porcelain and European paintings.

A stroll along the riverfront will take you through several parks; one of them, Bicentennial Commons at Sawyer Point, features whimsical monuments and flying pigs. The pedestrian-only **Purple People Bridge** provides a unique crossing from Sawyer Point to Kentucky.

MT ADAMS

Nestled in the hills high above downtown is **Mt Adams**, a 19th-century neighborhood of rail-thin, winding streets lined with galleries, bars, restaurants and views. As you make your way up, you'll go through Eden Park. Two big attractions are here: the **Cincinnati Art Museum** (☎ 513-721-5204; 953 Eden Park Dr; admission free; 11am-5pm Tue-Fri, until 9pm Wed, 10am-5pm Sat, noon-6pm Sun) emphasizes Middle Eastern and European arts and has a new wing devoted to Cincinnati works. The **Krohn Conservatory** (☎ 513-421-4086; 1501 Eden Park Dr; admission free; 10am-5pm) is a vast greenhouse with a rainforest, desert flora and superb seasonal flower shows.

COVINGTON & NEWPORT

Directly across the river is **Covington**, Kentucky, a sort of suburb of Cincinnati. Covington Landing, an area of floating bars and tour boats, is right by the south end of the Roebling Suspension Bridge. **BB Riverboats** (☎ 859-261-8500, 800-261-8586; 1 Madison Ave; tickets $13-40; call for schedules) takes off from here and plies the river in a nifty sightseeing paddle wheeler.

Covington's attractive **MainStrasse** was a 19th-century German neighborhood and is now full of shops, pubs and places to eat. A pleasant, historic riverfront walk lies east of the Roebling Bridge, as does the **Newport Aquarium** (☎ 859-491-3467; 1 Aquarium Way; adult $16, child 3-12 $10; 10am-6pm).

ELSEWHERE

Two miles northwest of downtown, the **Cincinnati Museum Center** (☎ 513-287-7000; 1301 Western Ave; adult $6.75, child 3-12 $4.75; 10am-5pm Mon-Sat, 11am-6pm Sun; P $4) occupies the 1933 Union Terminal, an art deco jewel still used by Amtrak. The building is the largest free-standing half dome in the Western Hemisphere, and its interior has magnificent murals made of Rookwood tiles. Inside, the **Cincinnati History Museum** features a river steamboat. The **Museum of Natural History** is more geared to kids but does have a limestone cave with real bats inside. An Omnimax theater and children's museum round out the offerings. Each museum requires a separate admission, but discounted combination tickets are available.

The **Cincinnati Zoo and Botanical Garden** (☎ 513-281-4700; 3400 Vine St; adult $11.50, child 2-12 $6; 8am-6pm summer, 9am-5pm winter; P $6.50), aka the 'Sexiest Zoo in America,' has the country's highest rate for successful breeding. It's famous for its gorillas and white tigers and is located 3 miles north of downtown.

Paramount's Kings Island (☎ 800-288-0808; exit 24 off I-71; adult/child $43/30; from 10am daily late May–late Aug, from 10am Sat & Sun mid-Apr to late May & Sep-Oct, closing times vary; P $9), 25 miles north of town, has roller coasters and other adrenaline generators as well as a water park.

Festivals & Events

Riverfest (☎ 513-352-4000; www.webn.com/riverfest) Concerts and fireworks; Sunday of Labor Day weekend (early September).

Oktoberfest (www.oktoberfest-zinzinnati.com) German beer, brats and mania; mid-September.

Sleeping

Hotel tax is a tad cheaper on the Kentucky side at 10.24%, rather than the 16.5% charged in Cincinnati. Tax is not included in the following prices.

BUDGET

Cincinnati Riverfront Travelodge (☎ 859-291-4434; 222 York St; r $50-59; P) Located on the Kentucky riverfront, the Travelodge is the best budget bet location-wise, though it's a bit faded in its atmosphere.

Budget Host (☎ 513-559-1600; 3356 Central Parkway; s/d $45/55; P) Trying hard to be bright and cheery, it's definitely the top cheapie in the Uptown area along Central Parkway; exit at

Hopple St, about 3 miles north of downtown on I-75, or take the No 20 bus.

MID-RANGE

Two good, similar options on the Kentucky riverfront are **Comfort Suites** (☎ 859-291-6700; 420 Riverboat Row; r $75-105; P), near the Newport attractions, and **Hampton Inn Riverfront** (☎ 859-581-7800; 200 Crescent Ave; r $99-109; P), with an indoor pool. Both include continental breakfast.

TOP END

If you feel the urge to splurge, this is an excellent city to do it, as room quality soars when you move to the top end bracket, yet prices remain reasonable. The weekend rates (especially in winter) of the downtown beauties listed here can rival those of mid-range hotels. Even if you find the price tags steep, the lobbies are worth a look.

Hilton Cincinnati Netherland Plaza (☎ 513-421-9100; 35 W 5th St; r $109-199; P $18) The 1920s-era Netherland is an art deco monument. Its Palm Court Bar is gorgeous, with fan-shaped couches, Baroque-style murals and ubiquitous palm plants. The rooms are swell, too.

Cincinnatian Hotel (☎ 513-381-3000; www.cincinnatianhotel.com; 601 Vine St; r $125-225; P $25) The Cincinnatian is in a magnificent 1882 Victorian building; the spacious rooms have fluffy towels, silk-soft sheets and huge round bathtubs.

Eating

In addition to downtown, good dining options are concentrated in Mt Adams, along the riverfront and in Clifton by the University of Cincinnati (try Calhoun, McMillan and Ludlow Sts).

Skyline Chili (☎ 513-721-4715; 1007 Vine St; dishes $3-6) Skyline has a cult-like following devoted to its version of the local speciality 'five-way chili' – ie meat sauce (spiced with chocolate and cinnamon) with spaghetti and beans, garnished with cheese and onions. You can get it three-way (minus onions and beans) or four-way (minus onions or beans), but go the whole way; life's an adventure. There are outlets throughout town; this downtown one is an experience weekdays at noon.

Kaldi's (☎ 513-241-3070; 1204 Main St; dishes $5-9) An eclectic crowd converges at Kaldi's coffee shop-bar-restaurant-bookstore in Over-the-Rhine. The hip, library-like atmosphere makes you want to linger long after you've polished off your delicious food (particularly the vegetarian 'un-burger').

Montgomery Inn at the Boathouse (☎ 513-721-7427; 925 Eastern Ave; small/large slab of ribs $12/20) Almost as renowned and addictive as Cincinnati chili are Montgomery Inn's barbecued ribs. There are a couple of outlets, but this riverside one is the most lively.

Rookwood Pottery Bistro (☎ 513-721-5456, 1077 Celestial St; dishes $7-14) Once a famous pottery factory known for its jewel-toned finishes, the Rookwood has for decades occupied a place high on the hill atop Mt Adams and high on the list of local diners. It offers a solid menu of sandwiches and inventive entrées. Ask for a table in one of the beehive-shaped kilns.

Maisonette (☎ 513-721-2260; 114 E 6th St; dishes $33-41; Mon-Sat) The elegant Maisonette, which has kept its five-star rating longer than any other US restaurant, is nationally famous for its French haute cuisine and extensive wine list. It's expensive and formal, and you'll need reservations.

For cheap eats downtown, try the food court in Carew Tower or **Izzy's Deli** (☎ 513-721-4241; 819 Elm St; also ☎ 513-241-6246; 610 Main St; dishes $5-8), where giant sandwiches and potato pancakes rule the menu.

Findlay Market (cnr Findlay & Elm Sts; morning Mon-Tue, until 6pm Wed-Sat) This is a collection of vendors in little stores and stalls offering everything from fresh fish to organic jellies to Mediterranean spices. Saturday is the biggest day.

Graeter's Ice Cream (☎ 513-381-0653; 41 E 4th St & elsewhere) Another local delicacy, this is the place for dessert.

Drinking

The city's German influence meant Cincinnati was once a beer drinkers paradise – in the 1890s there were 1800 saloons for 297,000 people, guzzling 2½ times more than the rest of the country. Mt Adams and Over-the-Rhine are still busy nightspots. Covington Landing has places on the river (in moored boats) that are refreshing on hot nights when there's a breeze.

Blind Lemon (☎ 513-241-3885; 936 Hatch St) Trains and other bric-a-brac hang from the ceiling at this gem of a bar in Mt Adams, filled with history, atmosphere and live music.

Arnold's (☎ 513-421-6234; 210 E 8th St) Arnold's is a downtown oldie but goodie dating from 1861. There's live music nightly from the front-porch-like stage – often blue grass.

City View Tavern (☎ 513-241-8439; 403 Oregon) The city sparkles out in front of you at this unassuming bar in Mt Adams.

Neon's (☎ 513-721-2919; 208 E 12th St) A cool, casual young crowd gathers to hear live music on the first floor and smoke stogies at the second-floor cigar bar.

HofbrauHaus (☎ 859-491-7200; 200 E 3rd St, Newport) The legendary Munich beer hall comes to the US.

Entertainment

Check *CityBeat* (see Media, p400) for listings. Get the free **GLBT News** (www.greatercincinnatiglbtnews.com), which has a bar and club guide.

LIVE MUSIC

Bogarts (☎ 513-281-8400; 2621 Vine St) Gets good rock bands.

Blue Wisp (☎ 513-241-9477; 318 E 8th St) This is a distinguished jazz club.

PERFORMING ARTS

Music Hall (☎ 513-721-8222; 1241 Elm St) The acoustically excellent Music Hall is the city's classical music venue, where the symphony orchestra, pops orchestra, opera and ballet hold their seasons. This is not a very good neighborhood, so be cautious and park nearby.

SPECTATOR SPORTS

Great American Ballpark (☎ 513-765-7000; 100 Main St) The Cincinnati Reds, direct descendants of the Cincinnati Red Stockings, the country's first professional baseball team, play at this new venue.

Paul Brown Stadium (☎ 513-621-3550; 1 Paul Brown Stadium) The Cincinnati Bengals pro football team scrimmage a few blocks west.

Getting There & Around

TO/FROM THE AIRPORT

Cincinnati's airport actually is in Kentucky, 13 miles south. To get downtown, take the **TANK bus** ($1) from Terminal 1 or 3, or **Airport Executive Shuttle** (☎ 800-990-8841; one way/round-trip $14/24) from their desk by baggage claim.

BUS

Buses run regularly from the **Greyhound station** (☎ 513-352-6012; 1005 Gilbert Ave) to Louisville ($20 to $30, two hours), Indianapolis ($17 to $30, three hours) and Columbus ($17 to $25, two hours).

CAR

National car rental agencies have offices at the airport and around town. Check rental information in the Transport chapter (p1121) for more details.

PUBLIC TRANSPORTATION

Metro (☎ 513-621-4455; 120 E 4th St) runs the local commuter buses and links with the **Transit Authority of Northern Kentucky** (TANK; ☎ 859-331-8265; www.tankbus.org). Fares are 80¢ during rush hour. The visitors center (p400) has route maps.

TRAIN

Amtrak (☎ 513-651-3337; 1301 Western Ave), at the Cincinnati Museum Center, has three trains a week to Indianapolis ($17 to $38, 3½ hours), Chicago ($33 to $79, eight hours) and Washington, DC ($50 to $121, 14½ hours). Trains depart at inconvenient times in the middle of the night.

MICHIGAN

Surrounded by four of the five lakes (Superior, Michigan, Huron and Erie), Michigan is a pair of peninsulas featuring 3200 miles of shoreline (second only to Alaska), the most extensive freshwater sand dunes in the country and 11,000 inland lakes. Stand anywhere in the state and you are never more than 6 miles from one of the Great Lakes, an inland lake or a blue-ribbon trout stream.

Michigan is an outdoor lover's paradise. Highlights include lazing on Lake Michigan's golden beaches; cruising the colored sandstone cliffs of Pictured Rocks; backcountry hiking on remote, wildlife-rich Isle Royale; and slowing down on car-free Mackinac Island. You want to camp? The state parks hold more than 14,000 campsites. You need a whirlpool with your bed? There are plenty of B&B's and lodges in which to soak and sleep in style.

The state's two parts consist of the larger Lower Peninsula, shaped like a mitten, and

MICHIGAN FACTS

Nickname The Great Lakes State, the Wolverine State
Population 10,050,446 (8th)
Area 96,705 sq miles (11th)
Admitted to Union January 26, 1837 (26th)
Capital city Lansing (population 119,100)
Other cities Detroit (951,300), Grand Rapids (197,800), Flint (124,900), Ann Arbor (114,000)
Birthplace of industrialists Henry Ford I (1863–1947) and II (1917–87), aviator Charles Lindbergh (1902–74), leader Malcolm X (1925–65), singer Madonna (b 1958)
Famous for cars, cornflakes, the Motown sound, the typewriter, the Model T Ford

the smaller, lightly populated Upper Peninsula, shaped like a slipper. They are linked by the awesome Mackinac Bridge, which spans the Straits of Mackinac (*mac*-in-aw; say it right and you may avoid the dreaded 'Fudgie' moniker that tourists receive; see p417).

History

Easy travel on the Great Lakes has led to a long and colorful history in Michigan. There is evidence of prehistoric copper mining in the Upper Peninsula and on Isle Royale. When the first European explorers arrived in the mid-17th century, the state already was settled by five major indigenous tribes: the Ojibwa, Ottawa, Miami, Potawatomi and Huron (or Wyandot).

The French were the first Europeans to stake a claim. Jesuit Père Jacques Marquette founded Sault Ste Marie in 1668, making it the third-oldest city in the USA. He also founded St Ignace in 1671. In 1701 the French explorer Antoine de La Mothe, Sieur de Cadillac, established Detroit in a strategic position between Lakes Erie and Huron.

In 1763 the French settlements were taken over by the British, who used Michigan as a base for instigating Indian raids against the Americans during the Revolutionary War. They also built a fort on Mackinac Island in 1780. Its location in the straits between Lake Michigan, Lake Huron and the St Marys River, which flows from Lake Superior, made it one of the most important ports in the North American fur trade, and a site the British and Americans battled over a number of times.

The Erie Canal's completion in 1825, along with the federal government's sale of Michigan land for $1.25 an acre, prompted an era of 'Michigan Fever' – its population jumped from 9000 in the early 19th century to more than 200,000 by 1840.

Prior to the mid-1970s, the car industry dominated Michigan, but the state has since worked hard to diversify its economy. Still, manufacture of passenger cars and transportation equipment accounts for about one quarter of the annual gross state product. General Motors (GM), Ford and the Chrysler Group of DaimlerChrysler all maintain their headquarters in or near Detroit. Agriculture is also important, and Michigan is a leader in a variety of commodities, including navy beans, apples and cherries.

Information

Michigan road conditions (www.michigan.gov/mdot)
Michigan Travel Bureau (☎ 800-543-2937; www.michigan.org; 4225 Miller Rd, Suite 4, Flint, MI 48507)

Michigan's sales tax is 6%.

National & State Parks

Michigan state park information (☎ 800-447-2757; www.midnrreservations.com) Campground reservations accepted. Park entry requires a vehicle permit ($4/20 per day/year).

DETROIT

Detroit is a unique, rewarding destination, where you can see the results of the American dream made, lost and in recovery. Despite the city's post-apocalyptic feel – once-grand buildings lie boarded up with trash blowing about their bases, and wide swathes of downtown are downright vacant – Detroit is home to truly top-notch sights. Motown, the Wright Museum of African American History and the Henry Ford Museum/Greenfield Village are one-of-a-kind attractions. The city's sweet and smoky soul food provides the sustenance to see them all. Remember: there's a prince beneath that toad-like exterior.

History

At the turn of the 20th century, Detroit was a medium-size city of 285,000, known as a manufacturing center for horse-drawn carriages and bicycles. Thanks in part to the massive iron and copper mines in the Upper Peninsula, cheap transport on the Great Lakes and enterprising souls such as Henry Ford, the Dodge brothers and the Fisher brothers, Detroit quickly became the motor capital of the world. Ford in particular changed the fabric of US society. He didn't invent the automobile, as so many mistakenly believe, but he did perfect the assembly line manufacturing method and became one of the first industrialists to use mass production. The result was the Model T, the first car that the USA's middle class could afford to own.

Since its 1950s heyday, when Detroit was the sophisticated home of more than 2 million people, the city has suffered through hard times. Racial tensions spurred violent riots, the worst in 1967 that left 43 dead and blocks of the city smoldering. Many residents packed up and fled to the suburbs, and the city entered an era of deep decay, with its population eventually dropping below one million.

But thanks to the car industry boom of the mid-1990s, the phoenix has been rising from the ashes. The Motor City remains a culturally rich region, and it is a national center for African-American culture.

Orientation

The glossy Renaissance Center, GM's headquarters, dominates the skyline, but the heart of Detroit is Hart Plaza, nestled alongside the Detroit River at the foot of Woodward Ave. Woodward is the city's main boulevard and heads north from the plaza all the way to Pontiac. The Mile Roads are major arteries east–west; 8 Mile (which entered the national consciousness thanks to local boy Eminem) forms the boundary between Detroit and the suburbs. Across the river lies Windsor, Canada. Detroit is a bit of a geographical oddity: it is the only US city that looks south to Canada.

Information

BOOKSTORES

Big Bookstore (☎ 313-831-8511; 5911 Cass Ave)

EMERGENCY

Crisis hotline (☎ 313-224-7000)
Emergency number (☎ 911) Police, ambulance, fire.

INTERNET ACCESS

Detroit Main Library (☎ 313-833-1000; 5201 Woodward Ave)

MEDIA

The *Detroit News* and *Detroit Free Press* are dailies. The *Metro Times*, distributed free on Wednesday, is the best guide to Detroit's arts, music and nightclub scene. Check **Between The Lines** (☎ 888-615-7003; www.pridesource.com), a free gay and lesbian weekly.

WDET-FM 101.9 is the city's NPR affiliate. WGRV-FM 105.1 plays soul music.

MEDICAL SERVICES

CVS (☎ 313-833-0201; 350 E Warren Ave) Twenty-four-hour pharmacy.
Detroit Receiving Hospital (☎ 313-745-3370; 4201 St Antoine Ave)

MONEY

Travelex (☎ 734-942-4731) In the airport's LC Smith Terminal.

ATMs are plentiful in and near the Renaissance Center.

POST

Main post office (☎ 313-226-8075; 1401 W Fort St) Open 24 hours.

TOURIST OFFICES

Affirmations Lesbian/Gay Community Center (☎ 248-398-7105; www.goaffirmations.org; 195 W 9 Mile Rd; 🕘 9am-9pm Mon-Fri, 9am-5pm Sat, 9am-1pm Sun) In Ferndale, northwest of the city center, near several gay-friendly venues.
Detroit Convention & Visitors Bureau (☎ 313-202-1800, 800-338-7648; www.visitdetroit.com; 10th fl, 211 W Fort St; 🕘 9am-5pm Mon-Fri)

Dangers & Annoyances

The main streets (Woodward Ave, Jefferson Ave, Lafayette Blvd) with office buildings, restaurants, nightclubs and attractions are as safe as any other large USA city. Travelers should avoid the areas around 12th St where the 1967 riots began.

Sights & Activities

Some of the best attractions are in nearby Dearborn (p412), 10 miles west of the town center, and other suburbs (see Classic Cars, p413). Don't overlook the kids' sights (see Detroit for Children, p409), many of which

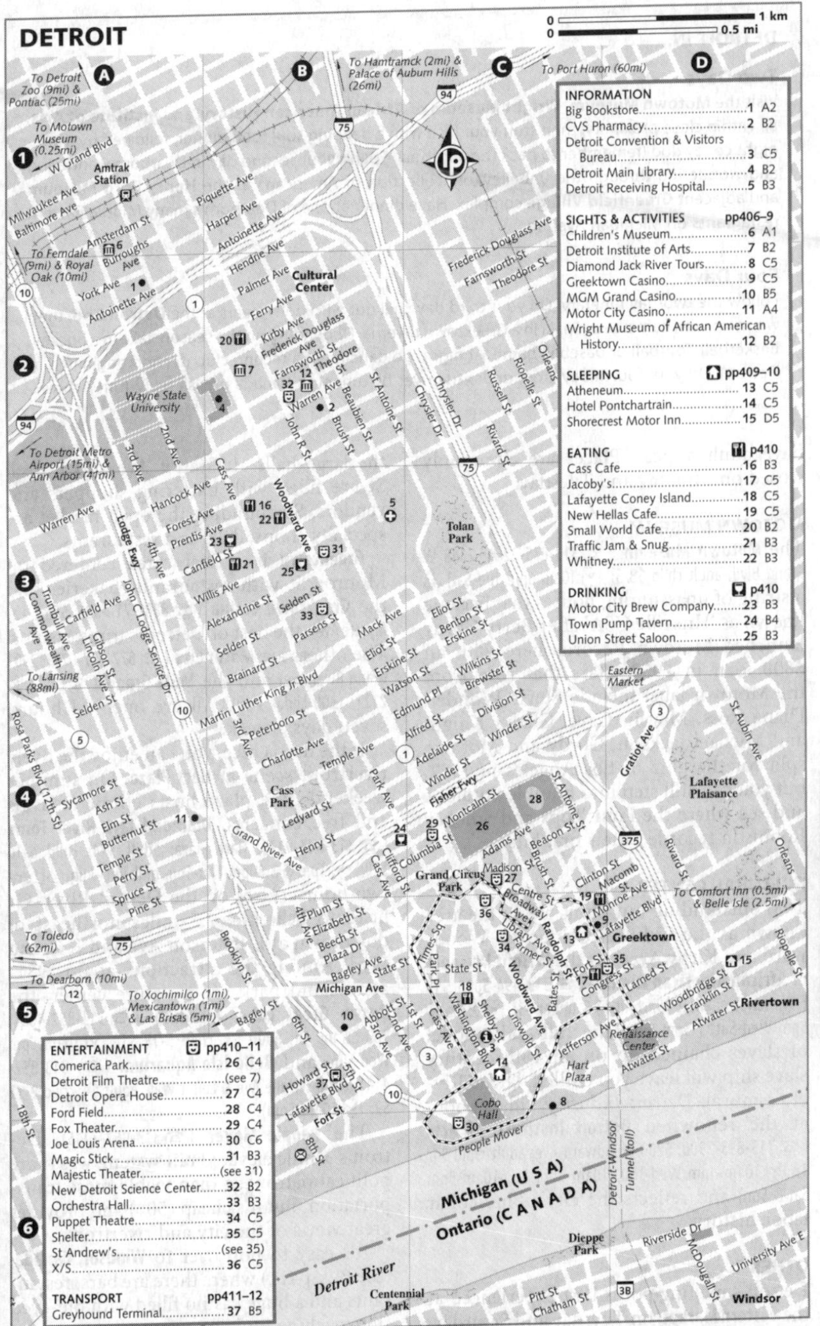
DETROIT
0 1 km
0 0.5 mi
INFORMATION
Big Bookstore 1 A2
CVS Pharmacy 2 B2
Detroit Convention & Visitors Bureau 3 C5
Detroit Main Library 4 B2
Detroit Receiving Hospital 5 B3
SIGHTS & ACTIVITIES pp406–9
Children's Museum 6 A1
Detroit Institute of Arts 7 B2
Diamond Jack River Tours 8 C5
Greektown Casino 9 C5
MGM Grand Casino 10 B5
Motor City Casino 11 A4
Wright Museum of African American History 12 B2
SLEEPING pp409–10
Atheneum 13 C5
Hotel Pontchartrain 14 C5
Shorecrest Motor Inn 15 D5
EATING p410
Cass Cafe 16 B3
Jacoby's 17 C5
Lafayette Coney Island 18 C5
New Hellas Cafe 19 C5
Small World Cafe 20 B2
Traffic Jam & Snug 21 B3
Whitney 22 B3
DRINKING p410
Motor City Brew Company 23 B3
Town Pump Tavern 24 B4
Union Street Saloon 25 B3
ENTERTAINMENT pp410–11
Comerica Park 26 C4
Detroit Film Theatre (see 7)
Detroit Opera House 27 C4
Ford Field 28 C4
Fox Theater 29 C4
Joe Louis Arena 30 C6
Magic Stick 31 B3
Majestic Theater (see 31)
New Detroit Science Center 32 B2
Orchestra Hall 33 B3
Puppet Theatre 34 C5
Shelter 35 C5
St Andrew's (see 35)
X/S 36 C5
TRANSPORT pp411–12
Greyhound Terminal 37 B5
To Detroit Zoo (9mi) & Pontiac (25mi)
To Hamtramck (2mi) & Palace of Auburn Hills (26mi)
To Port Huron (60mi)
To Motown Museum (0.25mi)
Amtrak Station
To Ferndale (9mi) & Royal Oak (10mi)
Cultural Center
Wayne State University
To Detroit Metro Airport (15mi) & Ann Arbor (41mi)
Tolan Park
To Lansing (88mi)
Eastern Market
Lafayette Plaisance
Cass Park
Grand Circus Park
Greektown
To Comfort Inn (0.5mi) & Belle Isle (2.5mi)
To Toledo (62mi)
To Dearborn (10mi)
To Xochimilco (1mi), Mexicantown (1mi) & Las Brisas (5mi)
Michigan Ave
Rivertown
Renaissance Center
Hart Plaza
Cobo Hall
People Mover
Detroit-Windsor Tunnel (toll)
Michigan (U S A)
Ontario (C A N A D A)
Dieppe Park
Detroit River
Centennial Park
Windsor

DETROIT IN...

Two Days

Visit the **Motown Museum**, **Wright Museum of African American History**, and **Institute of Arts**, all within close proximity, then stuff your face with a heaping soul food dinner, followed by a late-night coney dog (remember to pack the antacids). Spend your second day in Dearborn wandering and wondering through the unbelievable collection of Americana at the **Henry Ford Museum** and adjacent **Greenfield Village** complex. Have dinner at one of Dearborn's many Middle Eastern restaurants on Michigan Avenue.

Four Days

Follow the two-day itinerary. On your third day chill out with polar bears at the **Detroit Zoo**, then warm up with flaming saganaki in a Greektown taverna. Depending on the season, take in a hockey, basketball, football or baseball game. At night, go dancing at a techno club (techno originated in Detroit). On your fourth day cross under the river by tunnel to Canada or visit leafy **Ann Arbor**.

have adult appeal. Places are commonly closed on Monday and Tuesday.

MOTOWN MUSEUM

The **Motown Museum** (☎ 313-875-2264; 2648 W Grand Blvd; adult/child $8/5; 🕑 10am-6pm Tue-Sat) is a string of unassuming houses that became known as 'Hitsville USA' after Berry Gordy launched Motown Records here with an $800 loan in 1959. Stars that rose from the Motown label include Stevie Wonder, Diana Ross, Marvin Gaye, Gladys Knight and Michael Jackson. Gordy and Motown split for the glitz of Los Angeles in 1972, but you can still step into humble Studio A and see where the Four Tops and Smokey Robinson recorded their first hits.

CULTURAL CENTER

Two outstanding museums are in the area known as the Cultural Center, by Woodward and Kirby Aves. At the **Wright Museum of African American History** (☎ 313-494-5800; 315 E Warren Ave; adult $5, child 17 & under $3; 🕑 9:30am-5pm Wed-Sat, 1-5pm Sun), the full-scale model of slaves chained up on an 18th-century slave ship will leave you chilled. Diego Rivera's mural, *Detroit Industry*, fills a room at the renowned **Detroit Institute of Arts** (☎ 313-833-7900; 5200 Woodward Ave; adult/child $4/1; 🕑 10am-4pm Wed-Thu, 10am-9pm Fri, 10am-5pm Sat & Sun) and reflects the city's blue-collar labor history.

OTHER

Detroit's melting pot is best experienced at the **Eastern Market**; on Tuesday and Saturday, the large halls at Gratiot Ave and Russell St are filled with bartering shoppers and vendors. Surrounding the open market are specialty shops, delis and restaurants.

Greektown is a lively area centered on Monroe St with restaurants, bakeries and the **Greektown Casino** (☎ 888-771-4386; 555 E Lafayette Ave), the best of Detroit's three casinos. The others are **Motor City** (☎ 877-777-0711; 2901 Grand River Ave) and the **MGM Grand** (☎ 877-888-2121; 1300 Lodge Fwy). All are open 24 hours, seven days a week.

If the day is nice, you can enjoy the lively riverfront scene at **Hart Plaza**. On summer weekends, the plaza hosts ethnic festivals and free concerts. **Diamond Jack River Tours** (☎ 313-843-9376; Hart Plaza; adult $14, child 6-16 $10; 🕑 1pm & 3:30pm Thu-Sun, mid-Jun–Aug) offers two-hour cruises on the Detroit River. Or head to **Belle Isle**, 2.5 miles northeast of downtown at E Jefferson Ave and E Grand Blvd. Among the attractions at this 981-acre island park are a nature center, the **Dossin Great Lakes Museum** (☎ 313-852-4051; 100 Strand Dr; adult $3, child 5-18 $1; 🕑 10am-5pm Wed-Sun) and **Belle Isle Aquarium** (☎ 313-852-4141; cnr Inselruhe Ave & Loiter Way; adult $4, child 2-12 $2; 🕑 10am-5pm).

The **People Mover** (☎ 313-962-7245), Detroit's 3-mile elevated rail system, was more political patronage than viable mass transportation. But it's cheap (50¢) and provides great views of the city and riverfront.

It's easy to pop over to **Windsor, Canada**, (see Bus, p411) where there are bars, restaurants and a huge casino filled with pie-eyed slot-machine junkies.

Detroit for Children

Detroit is chock full of attractions for little ones. Purchase *Metro Parent* magazine at any bookstore, check their web site (www.metroparent.com) or pick up a free copy of their miniguide *Going Places* at the Science Center or other kid-friendly venues.

DETROIT ZOO

At the **Detroit Zoo** (☎ 248-398-0900; 8450 W 10 Mile Rd; adult $9, child 2-12 $6; 🕐 10am-5pm May-Oct, until 4pm Nov-Apr; P $5), enter the amazing Arctic Ring of Life and 'polar bear tube' where the huge white creatures swim overhead. It's the world's largest polar exhibit and has excellent displays on Inuit culture. The Penguinarium is a highlight, as is the National Amphibian Conservation Center. Located just north in Royal Oak.

DETROIT PUPPET THEATER

Puppet ART/Detroit Puppet Theater (☎ 313-961-7777; 25 E Grand River Ave; adult/child $7/5) is run by Soviet-trained puppeteers and artists who perform beautiful shows in their 70-person theater; a small museum displays puppets from different cultures. Shows are often held on Saturday afternoon; call for the schedule.

NEW DETROIT SCIENCE CENTER

The **New Detroit Science Center** (☎ 313-577-8400; 5020 John R St; adult $7, child 2-12 $6; 🕐 9am-5pm Mon-Fri, 10:30am-6pm Sat & Sun) has hands-on 'Matter & Energy' and 'Waves & Vibrations' laboratories among its arsenal, as well as an Imax cinema and planetarium. The place usually is bursting with families.

COMERICA PARK

Comerica Park (☎ 313-471-2255; 2100 Woodward Ave) is a great place to see a baseball game with kids. If there's not enough action on the field, take them for a spin on the park's Ferris wheel or clever carousel equipped with tigers. Check about promotions that allow kids to run around the bases after Sunday games.

CHILDREN'S MUSEUM

The **Children's Museum** (☎ 313-873-8100; 6134 2nd Ave; admission free; 🕐 9am-4pm Mon-Fri), run by the Detroit Public Schools, features exhibits like a horse made of automobile bumpers.

Festivals & Events

Freedom Festival (☎ 313-923-8259; www.theparade.org/freedomfest) Windsor and Detroit team up in late June for this festival that includes a huge fireworks display over the Detroit River.

Woodward Dream Cruise (☎ 888-493-2196; www.woodwarddreamcruise.com) More than 1.5 million people line Woodward Ave between Ferndale and Pontiac to watch 6,000 classic cars cruise by on the third Saturday in August.

African World Festival (www.maah-detroit.org) Ethnic music, dance and food enliven Hart Plaza on the third weekend in August.

Detroit International Jazz Festival (☎ 313-963-7622; www.detroitjazzfest.com) The Labor Day weekend freebie in Hart Plaza attracts local and international jazz artists.

Sleeping

Room rates listed here do not include the 9% hotel tax.

BUDGET

HI Country Grandma's Home Hostel (☎ 734-753-4901; 22330 Bell Rd; dm from $15; 🕐 Apr-Sep) Homey Grandma's is in New Boston, 10 miles south of Metro Airport. There are seven beds in two rooms; call in advance. Not accessible by public transportation.

Pontiac Lake Recreation Area (☎ 248-666-1020; 7800 Gale Rd; campsites $14; 🕐 May–mid-Oct) West of Pontiac on M-59 in Waterford, it's the closest state park with camping.

MID-RANGE

Shorecrest Motor Inn (☎ 313-568-3000, 800-992-9616; 1316 E Jefferson Ave; s/d $69/89; P ❄) Shorecrest is the pick of the litter with clean, comfortable rooms just six blocks northeast of Hart Plaza. Friendly, helpful staff.

Comfort Inn (☎ 313-567-8888; 1999 E Jefferson Ave; r $89-139; P ❄) Similar to the Shorecrest, though a few blocks further east, Comfort's prices reach the higher end of the spectrum when it's busy, usually in summer. Rates include a continental breakfast.

Hotel Pontchartrain (☎ 313-965-0200; 2 Washington Blvd; r $69-149; P $17 ❄ 💻) This is a historic, full-amenity hotel downtown by Cobo Hall; there are good rates if business is slow.

Affordable motels abound in the Detroit suburbs. If you're arriving from Metro Airport, follow the signs for Merriman Rd when leaving the airport and take your pick. Among the dozen motels here is a **Motel 6** (☎ 734-595-7400; 9095 Wickham Rd; s/d from $40/48; P ❄). Nearby and a step up is **Clarion**

THE AUTHOR'S CHOICE

Southern Fires (☎ 313-393-4930; 575 Bellevue Rd; dishes $8-12) Casual Southern Fires reigns supreme in this city of soul food. Choose from cornmeal-encrusted catfish, braised short ribs, fried chicken and other dishes based on old family recipes from Alabama. The best is the 3in-thick slab of meatloaf smothered in gravy, with succulent collard greens, sweet potatoes and buttered cornbread on the side. Wash it down with sweet iced tea. Huge portions, though not much here for vegetarians.

Barcelo Hotel (☎ 734-728-7900; 8600 Merriman Rd; r from $69; P).

TOP END

Atheneum (☎ 313-962-2323, 800-772-2323; www.atheneumsuites.com; 1000 Brush St; r from $145; P $18) A swanky hotel in Greektown's midst, the Atheneum has the perk of a free shuttle that will haul you around town.

Eating

Detroit restaurants reward their ethnically diverse patrons with large portions of authentic dishes at reasonable prices.

GREEKTOWN

Lafayette Coney Island (☎ 313-964-8198; 118 Lafayette Blvd; dishes $2-3; 24hr) Take care of late-night appetites at the legendary Lafayette, where the minimalist menu consists of hot dogs smothered with chili and onions (ie a 'coney'), burgers, fries, pies, donuts and beer. Cast-iron stomach required.

New Hellas Cafe (☎ 313-961-5544; 583 Monroe St; dishes $7-12) Flaming cheese and the cry of 'Opa!' are a Detroit tradition at this bustling Greektown restaurant.

CULTURAL CENTER

Small World Cafe (☎ 313-874-2233; 111 E Kirby Ave; dishes $3-6; 11am-2pm Mon-Fri) Small World offers a small but worldly menu of curries, sandwiches, Middle Eastern dishes and pizzas. It's located in the basement of the International Institute, where you can wander through the global doll collection on the first floor.

Cass Cafe (☎ 313-831-1400; 4620 Cass Ave; dishes $5-9) An artsy kind of eatery serving soups, sandwiches and vegie beauties like the lentil walnut burger.

The Whitney (☎ 313-832-5700; 4421 Woodward Ave; lunch $8-22, dinner $27-33) Silk-covered walls and Tiffany glass windows are only a few of the luxuries in former lumber baron Whitney's mansion. Even if you don't eat here, have a drink at the third floor bar.

Jacoby's (☎ 313-962-7067; 624 Brush St; dishes $6-12) Sauerbraten, Wiener schnitzel and German beer are found at Jacoby's.

Traffic Jam & Snug (☎ 313-831-9470; 511 W Canfield St; dishes $8-15; Mon-Sat) Detroit's best brew-pub food.

ELSEWHERE

Mexicantown is along Bagley St, where you'll find inexpensive, authentic Mich-Mex food.

Xochimilco (☎ 313-843-0179; 3409 Bagley St; dishes $5-12) This place has been pulling crowds for years, offering happy relief to locals in search of a margarita fix.

Las Brisas (☎ 313-842-8252; 8445 W Vernor Ave; dishes $7-9) Here you'll find a solid menu of Mexican standards in a colorful setting.

Detroit's Polish community is centered in the city of **Hamtramck**, north of downtown.

Polish Village Cafe (☎ 313-874-5726; 2990 Yemans St; dishes $4-8) You can dig into stuffed cabbage, pork goulash and pierogi at the corner of Jos Campau Ave.

The **Ferndale** area at 9 Mile Rd and Woodward Ave has many good restaurants and bars, as does **Royal Oak** just north of Ferndale on 10 Mile Rd.

Drinking

Town Pump Tavern (☎ 313-961-1929; 100 W Montcalm St) A great Euro-style decor and beer selection.

Motor City Brewing Company (☎ 313-832-2700; 470 W Canfield St; Wed-Sat) A small, intimate bar that makes its own drinks.

Union Street Saloon (☎ 313-831-3965; 4145 Woodward Ave) This place has been around since the early 1900s and attracts a mod crowd.

Entertainment

CINEMA

Detroit Film Theatre (☎ 313-833-3237; 5200 Woodward Ave; tickets $6.50) In the Detroit Institute of Arts.

LIVE MUSIC

Detroit may be Motown, but in recent years it's been rap and techno that have pushed the city to the forefront of the music scene;

GREAT LAKES

homegrown stars include Kid Rock and Eminem.

St Andrew's Hall (☎ 313-961-6358; 431 E Congress St) A legendary alternative band venue; downstairs is the **Shelter** (☎ 313-961-6358), a smaller music/dance club.

Magic Stick (☎ 313-833-9700; 4120 Woodward Ave) and larger **Majestic Theater** (☎ 313-833-9700; 4140 Woodward Ave) are side-by-side concert halls in a complex that also has bowling, billiards, a pizza joint and upscale café.

Noted blues and jazz clubs include **Baker's Keyboard Lounge** (☎ 313-345-6300; 20510 Livernois Ave, Hamtramck), with good soul food, and **Attic Bar** (☎ 313-365-4194; 11667 Jos Campau Ave, Hamtramck), a true blues bar where customers take over the piano when a band isn't around.

X/S (☎ 313-963-9797; 1500 Woodward Ave) The spot for dancing, in an old piano store that's now a techno hothouse.

PERFORMING ARTS

The revived Theater District is along Woodward Ave and anchored by the gloriously restored, 1928 **Fox Theatre** (☎ 313-983-6611; 2211 Woodward Ave).

Orchestra Hall (☎ 313-576-5111; 3663 Woodward Ave) The Detroit Symphony Orchestra plays its notes at Orchestra Hall.

Detroit Opera House (☎ 313-961-3500; 1526 Broadway) The Michigan Opera Theater lets loose high C's here.

SPECTATOR SPORTS

Palace of Auburn Hills (☎ 248-377-0100; 2 Championship Dr) The Palace hosts pro basketball – the Detroit Pistons men's team and Detroit Shock women's team.

Joe Louis Arena (☎ 313-396-7444; 600 Civic Center Dr) The much-loved Red Wings play pro hockey at this arena where, if you can wrangle tickets, you can witness the strange octopus-throwing custom.

Ford Field (☎ 800-616-7627; cnr Brush & Adams Sts) The Lions pro football team plays here.

Comerica Park (☎ 313-471-2255; 2100 Woodward Ave) Next door to Ford Field, the Tigers play pro baseball at this impressive venue.

Getting There & Around

It is best to have your own wheels to get around the Motor City; public transportation is lacking, much to the big automakers' delight.

TO/FROM THE AIRPORT

Metro Airport (☎ 734-247-7678; www.metroairport.com), 15 miles southwest of Detroit, offers direct flights to most major cities in the country. **Northwest Airlines** (☎ 800-225-2525) uses Detroit as a hub and routes many of its European flights through Metro.

Transport options from the airport to the city are few: you can take a cab for about $35, or you can take a SMART bus ($1.50), but it takes 1½ hours to get downtown. Pick up is at the lower level of LC Smith Terminal; drop off is a few blocks from the Renaissance Center.

BUS

The **Greyhound terminal** (☎ 313-961-8562; 1001 Howard St) is near Lodge Freeway. Buses travel to more than 40 cities throughout Michigan, including Grand Rapids ($23 to $29, 3½ hours), Traverse City ($44 to $46, 7½ hours) and Marquette ($59 to $91, 14½ hours).

Transit Windsor (☎ 519-944-4111) operates the Tunnel Bus to Windsor, Canada. It costs $2.60 (American or Canadian) and departs from Detroit-Windsor Tunnel (on Randolph St, across from the Renaissance Center). Bring your passport.

CAR

Southeastern Michigan is one of the cheapest places in the country to rent a car. Avis, Hertz and other rental agencies have offices at the airport (call from the courtesy phones) and around town. Check rental information in the Transport chapter (p1121) for more details.

PUBLIC TRANSPORTATION

The **Detroit Department of Transportation** (DDOT; ☎ 888-336-8287) handles the local bus service. The fare is $1.25, transfers 25¢. The **Suburban Mobility Authority for Regional Transportation** (SMART; ☎ 313-962-5515) handles the service to the 'burbs, with connections to Detroit; the fare is $1.50, transfers 25¢. The public library has schedules.

TAXI

Checker Cab (☎ 313-963-7000) Flagfall is $2.50, then $1.60 per mile.

TRAIN

From the **Amtrak station** (☎ 313-873-3442; 11 W Baltimore Ave), by Woodward Ave, trains run

MICHAEL MOORE AND MICHIGAN'S BIG BUSINESS

For insight into the relationship between the auto industry and the local communities of Eastern Michigan, watch *Roger and Me*, a documentary by Flint native Michael Moore.

The film shows the tragic and surreal consequences of General Motors pulling up its stakes from Flint – where the company was born – and moving plant operations overseas. Thousands of people lost their jobs, and the local economy was devastated, though GM continued to turn a huge profit. Moore spends the film trying to track down Roger Smith, GM's chairman at the time, to have a chat. The revelation of the corporate conscience has never been more hilarious, or more sad.

Roger and Me helped launch the career of Moore, whose works challenge big business and government and their effects on everyday Americans. His portfolio includes other films (*The Big One*), television series (*TV Nation* and *The Awful Truth*) and books (*Stupid White Men*). In 2003 his film *Bowling for Columbine*, about America's gun culture and industry, won the Academy Award for Best Documentary. Ever the social commentator, Moore used his acceptance speech to take the American government to task for its war in Iraq.

daily to Kalamazoo ($19 to $46; three hours) and Chicago ($23 to $57; six hours). You can also head east on Amtrak – to New York ($64 to $152; 16 hours) or destinations en route – but you'll first be bussed to Toledo.

AROUND DETROIT

Dearborn

Dearborn, 10 miles west of downtown Detroit, is home to one of the finest museum complexes in the country: the indoor **Henry Ford Museum** (☎ 313-271-1620; 20900 Oakwood Blvd; adult $14, child 5-12 $10; ⌚ 9am-5pm Mon-Sat, noon-5pm Sun) and the adjacent, outdoor **Greenfield Village** (☎ 313-271-1620; adult $18, child 5-12 $12; ⌚ 9am-5pm Mon-Sat, noon-5pm Sun Apr-Dec), featuring historic old buildings shipped in from all over the country, reconstructed and restored. Together the museums contain a fascinating wealth of Americana such as the chair Lincoln was sitting in when he was assassinated, Edgar Allan Poe's writing desk, Thomas Edison's laboratory from Menlo Park and the bus on which Rosa Parks refused to give up her seat, among many other items. (Don't worry: you'll get your car fix here, too.) The museum and village are separate attractions, but you can get a combination ticket for one day (adult $24, child 5-12 $18) or two (adult $36, child 5-12 $27). Tours of Ford's Rouge plant have a separate admission price.

After the hours of gawking, re-fuel at one of Dearborn's Middle Eastern restaurants. The city has a huge Arab population and a wealth of eateries from which to choose; Michigan Ave is lined with them.

Cap off the day by heading to the **Ford Wyoming Drive-In** (☎ 313-846-6910; Ford Rd), the largest drive-in theater in the Midwest with nine screens. From I-94 in Dearborn, take exit 210 and head north on Wyoming Ave.

Ann Arbor

Leafy, liberal and bookish, Ann Arbor is the affable home of the University of Michigan (the 'Harvard of the Midwest'). The university dominates the city and provides many of its top attractions, including the fine **Kelsey Museum of Archaeology** (☎ 734-764-9304; 434 S State St; admission free; ⌚ 9am-4pm Tue-Fri, 1-4pm Sat & Sun), with 100,000 well-displayed artifacts from ancient Egypt, Greece and Rome; the **University of Michigan Museum of Art** (☎ 734-763-8662; 525 S State St; admission free; ⌚ 10am-5pm Tue-Sat, until 9pm Thu, noon-5pm Sun); and the **Exhibit Museum of Natural History** (☎ 734-764-0478; 1109 Geddes Ave; admission free; ⌚ 9am-5pm Mon-Sat, noon-5pm Sun), home to the most popular dinosaur collection in the state.

Ann Arbor's biggest events are the University of Michigan football games, a fall tradition attracting 115,000 fans per game. Tickets are nearly impossible to purchase, especially when nemesis Ohio State is in town. You can try, or obtain tickets to other sporting events, by calling the **U of M Ticket Office** (☎ 734-764-0247). For theater, drama and other performing arts, call the **Campus Information Center** (☎ 734-764-4636).

Just as you would expect, Ann Arbor abounds with great restaurants and nightclubs. In fact, the city's first tavern was built in 1824, a year before residents built their first school. Grab tasty Middle Eastern dishes at **Jerusalem Garden** (☎ 734-995-5060; 307 S Fifth Ave; dishes $3-8). Live music, brewery tours and handcrafted beer are found at **Arbor Brewing Co** (☎ 734-213-1393; 114 E Washington St; dishes $7-12), while nearby **Zingerman's Delicatessen** (☎ 734-663-3354; 422 Detroit St; dishes $6-11) is regarded as one of the Midwest's finest.

Looking for a latte? There's a coffeehouse on every corner; try **Sweetwaters Cafe** (☎ 734-769-2331; 123 W Washington St; dishes $2-4). When darkness falls, head to the **Blind Pig** (☎ 734-996-8555; 208 S First St) or the **Ark** (☎ 734-761-1800; 316 S Main St), both nationally acclaimed venues for blues and more.

HEARTLAND

Michigan's heartland is a 20-county region that lies at the center of the Lower Peninsula and includes agricultural and urban areas, farm fields and suburbs.

Lansing

The state capital of Lansing makes a pleasant pit stop. Attractions are concentrated downtown and at Michigan State University (MSU; east of downtown, south of Grand River Ave). Between the two is Lansing's **River Trail**, which extends 7 miles along the shores of Michigan's longest river, the Grand. The paved path, popular with cyclists, joggers and in-line skaters, links a number of attractions, including a children's museum, zoo and salmon ladder.

Downtown the **Michigan Historical Museum** (☎ 517-373-3559; 702 W Kalamazoo St; admission free; 🕒 9am-4:30pm Mon-Fri, 10am-4pm Sat, 1-5pm Sun) features 26 permanent galleries, including a replica UP copper mine you can walk through, a 1920s street scene and a three-story relief map of the state. Nearby the **State Capitol** (☎ 517-373-2353; cnr Capitol & Michigan Aves; admission free; 🕒 9am-4pm Mon-Fri) offers tours.

The campus holds the **MSU Museum** (☎ 517-355-2370; admission free; 🕒 9am-5pm Mon-Fri, 10am-5pm Sat, 1-5pm Sun), with natural and historic displays, and the wide-ranging **Kresge Art Museum** (☎ 517-355-7631; admission free; 🕒 10am-5pm Mon-Fri, until 8pm Thu, noon-5pm Sat & Sun, closed Mon in summer). Just north, East Lansing is typical of college towns with abundant restaurants, pubs and nightclubs.

CLASSIC CARS IN MICHIGAN

More than sand dunes, Mackinac Island fudge or even the Great Lakes, Michigan is synonymous with cars the world over. You don't have to drive far to see classic cars, particularly around Detroit:

Henry Ford Museum (see opposite) This Dearborn museum is loaded with vintage cars, including the first one Henry Ford ever built. In adjacent Greenfield Village you can get a ride in a Model T that rolled off the assembly line in 1923.

Automotive Hall of Fame (☎ 313-240-4000; 21400 Oakwood Blvd, Dearborn; adult $6, child 5-18 $3; 🕒 10am-5pm May-Oct, 10am-5pm Tues-Sun Nov-Apr) Also in Dearborn, this museum is stocked with classic cars as well as a replica of the first gasoline automobile.

Motorsports Hall of Fame (☎ 800-250-7223; Novi Rd, Novi; adult $4, child under 12 $2; 🕒 10am-5pm Thu-Sun year-round, daily in summer) In the Novi Expo Center just off I-96 in Novi, the Hall of Fame has three dozen vehicles that were driven by legendary racers.

Walter P Chrysler Museum (☎ 888-456-1924; 1 Chrysler Dr, Auburn Hills; adult $6, child 6-12 $3; 🕒 10am-6pm Tue-Sat, noon-6pm Sun) This museum is in the DaimlerChrysler Technical Center Campus in Auburn Hills and has 70 vehicles on display, including rare models of Dodge, DeSoto, Nash, Hudson and Willys.

Sloan Museum (☎ 810-237-3450; 1221 E Kearsley St, Flint; adult $5, child 4-11 $3; 🕒 10am-5pm Mon-Fri, noon-5pm Sat & Sun) Flint's Sloan Museum has two buildings housing more than 60 cars, including the oldest production-model Chevrolet in existence and a 1910 Buick 'Bug' raced by Louis Chevrolet.

Gilmore-Classic Car Club of America Museum (☎ 269-671-5089; Hickory Rd at M-43, Hickory Corners; adult $7, child 7-15 $5; 🕒 9am-5pm May-Oct) North of Kalamazoo along M-43 in Hickory Corners, this museum complex is 22 barns filled with 120 vintage automobiles, including 15 Rolls Royces dating back to a 1910 Silver Ghost.

RE Olds Transportation Museum (☎ 517-372-0422; 240 Museum Dr, Lansing; admission $4; 🕒 10am-5pm Tue-Sat) In the old Lansing City Bus Garage are 20 vintage cars, from the first Oldsmobile, built in 1897, to an Indy 500 pace car.

GREAT LAKES

During the summer be sure and head to Oldsmobile Park, where you can cheer on the **Lansing Lugnuts** (☎ 517-485-4500; 505 E Michigan Ave; tickets $6.50-8), the Chicago Cubs' minor league baseball team. You've got to love the name. Go 'Nuts!

The best selection of motels is found around Cedar St, exit 104 off I-96. In this area are **Days Inn** (☎ 517-393-1650; 6501 S Pennsylvania Ave; s/d $50/60, additional $10 on weekends; P) and **Econo Lodge** (☎ 517-394-7200; 1100 Ramada Dr; r weekday/weekend $45/49; P), both with continental breakfast. The downtown hotels feed off politicians and lobbyists and are considerably more expensive.

Most of Lansing's best restaurants are clustered around the head of Michigan Ave. For dinner try **Clara's** (☎ 517-372-7120; 637 E Michigan Ave; dishes $12-18) in the historic railroad depot. For breakfast or lunch try **Kewpee's** (☎ 517-482-8049; 118 S Washington Sq; dishes $2-6; breakfast & lunch Mon-Fri), renowned for its olive burgers.

Grand Rapids

The second-largest city in Michigan, Grand Rapids is known for office-furniture manufacturing, a conservative Dutch Reform attitude and the fact that it's only 30 miles from Lake Michigan's Gold Coast. The visitors center (☎ 800-678-9859; Suite 300, 140 Monroe Center NW; 8:30am-5pm Mon-Fri) is downtown, with two outstanding museums nearby.

The **Gerald R Ford Museum** (☎ 616-451-9263; 303 Pearl St NW; adult $4, child 15 & under free; 9am-5pm) is dedicated to the country's only Michigander president. Ford stepped into the Oval Office after Richard Nixon and his vice president, Spiro Agnew, resigned in disgrace. It's an intriguing period in US history, and the museum does an excellent job of covering it, right down to displaying the burglary tools used in the Watergate break-in. Nearby is the striking **Van Andel Museum Center** (☎ 616-456-3977; 272 Pearl St NW; adult $6, child 17 & under $2.50; 9am-9pm Sun-Tue, 9am-5pm Wed-Sat), dedicated to the history of Grand Rapids (including its role as furniture-maker) and west Michigan. The 118-acre **Frederik Meijer Gardens** (☎ 616-957-1580; 1000 E Beltline NE; adult $8, child 5-13 $4; 9am-5pm Mon-Sat, noon-5pm Sun) feature the state's largest tropical conservatory, more than 100 sculptures and three indoor theme gardens.

Days Inn (☎ 616-235-7611; 310 Pearl St NW; r from $80; P), downtown, is a good option.

Affordable motels are also along 28th St on the city's south side.

Peaches B&B (☎ 866-732-2437; 29 Gay St SE; r $97; P) is a comfy lodging option and a short walk from downtown.

At night, head to **Grand Rapids Brewing Company** (☎ 616-285-5970; 3689 28th St SE; dishes $7-13) or **Cottage Bar** (☎ 616-454-9088; 18 LaGrave St SE; dishes $6-10; Mon-Sat), a hip place downtown with the city's best hamburgers and outdoor seating when it's warm.

LAKE MICHIGAN SHORE

Michigan's west coast is its Gold Coast – a 300-mile shoreline featuring sand, surf and incredible sunsets best watched while sitting atop a towering sand dune. It's lined with endless stretches of beach, and dotted with shoreline parks and small towns that boom during the summer tourist season. Note: all state parks listed here take **campsite reservations** (☎ 800-447-2752; www.midnrreservations.com) and require a vehicle permit ($4/20 per day/year), unless specified otherwise.

Saugatuck

This Lake Michigan resort town is a popular destination for gays and is known for its strong arts community and numerous B&Bs.

The best thing to do in Saugatuck is also the most affordable. Jump aboard the **Saugatuck Chain Ferry** ($1), and the operator will pull you across the Kalamazoo River. On the other side you can huff up the stairs to the grand views atop **Mt Baldhead**, a 200ft-high sand dune. Then race down the north side to beautiful **Oval Beach**.

Most of the town's B&Bs are in century-old Victorian homes and range from $100 to $180 a night per couple in the summer high season. Try the charming **Bayside Inn** (☎ 269-857-4321; www.baysideinn.net; 618 Water St; r $99-210), a former boathouse with an outdoor tub, or **Twin Gables Inn** (☎ 269-857-4346, 800-231-2185; www.twingablesinn.com; 900 Lake St; r $110-200), which overlooks Lake Michigan. Mom-and-pop motels on the edge of the city, like **The Pines Motorlodge** (☎ 269-857-5211; www.thepinesmotorlodge.com; 56 Blue Star Hwy; r weekday/weekend $85/120), have comfortable rooms.

Grand Haven & Muskegon

Clustered around these two cities are three state parks, all offering an opportunity to hike and camp on or near Lake Michigan beaches. Resort-y Grand Haven is all about silken sand, boardwalks and lighthouses. **Grand Haven State Park** (☎ 616-847-1309; 1001 Harbor Ave; campsites $16-20; ⌚ Apr-Oct) sprawls along the beach and is connected to downtown restaurants by a scenic walkway along the Grand River. Between Grand Haven and Muskegon is **PJ Hoffmaster State Park** (☎ 231-798-3711; 6585 Lake Harbor Rd; campsites $20; ⌚ mid-Apr–Oct), offering the interesting Gillette Nature Center and a 10-mile trail system with several miles along Lake Michigan. North of Muskegon is **Muskegon State Park** (☎ 231-744-3480; 3560 Memorial Dr; campsites $15; ⌚ May-Oct), with 12 miles of trails through rugged, wooded dunes.

If you're not camping, splash out at Grand Haven's Victorian-style **Harbor House Inn** (☎ 800-841-0610; 114 S Harbor Dr; r in summer/winter from $150/95; ✖) and people-watch from the huge front porch.

Ludington & Manistee

The largest state park and one of the most popular along Lake Michigan is **Ludington State Park** (☎ 231-843-8671; campsites $20; ⌚ year-round), on M-116. It has an excellent trail system, a renovated lighthouse to visit and miles of beach. To its north is **Nordhouse Dunes**, a 3000-acre federally designated wilderness with its own trail system. You enter Nordhouse Dunes through the Lake Michigan Recreation Area, a US Forest Service campground several miles south of Manistee.

One of the most unusual backpacking trips in the Lower Peninsula is the 20-mile hike from Manistee to Ludington along the undeveloped beaches of these large parks, overnighting in Nordhouse Dunes. Stop at the **Manistee Ranger Station** (☎ 231-723-2211; 412 Red Apple Rd), just south of Manistee off US 31, for maps and information.

Ludington also is where you catch the SS *Badger* ferry to Manitowoc, Wisconsin (see p351).

Sleeping Bear Dunes National Lakeshore

This national park stretches from north of Frankfort just before Leland, on the Leelanau Peninsula. Stop at the park **visitors center** (☎ 231-326-5134; www.nps.gov/slbe; 9922 Front St; ⌚ 9am-4pm winter, 9am-6pm summer) in Empire for information, trail maps and vehicle entry permits.

Attractions here include the famous **Dune Climb** along M-109, where you trudge up the 200ft-high dune and then run or roll down, and **Pierce Stocking Scenic Dr**, a 7-mile, one-lane road that passes stunning Lake Michigan vistas. The park also offers the best day hiking in the Lower Peninsula. Those seeking an overnight wilderness adventure should head to **North Manitou Island** or day-trip to **South Manitou Island** on the ferry (☎ 231-256-9061; Leland; adult $23, child 12 & under $13 round-trip; 3-7 times per week, May-Nov).

Feeling lazy? Plop your butt in an inner tube and float down the Platte River; arrange via **Riverside Canoe Trips** (☎ 231-325-5622; 5042 Scenic Hwy, Honor, MI; tube/kayak/canoe $14/22/30; ⌚ May–mid-Oct).

Traverse City

Michigan's Cherry Capital is the largest city in the northern half of the Lower Peninsula. It's got a bit of urban sprawl, but it's still beautiful, fun and a great base from which to see Sleeping Bear Dunes, the Mission Peninsula and the area's other outdoor attractions.

Two blocks from downtown along US 31 is Clinch Park, with a pretty beach, while nearby **Traverse City State Park** (☎ 231-922-5270; 1132 US 31 N; campsites $16-20) has 700ft of sugary sand. Between the two parks are dozens of resorts, motels, Jet Ski rental shops and parasail operators.

The most popular drive is to head north from Traverse City on M-37 for 20 miles to the end of **Mission Peninsula**. Stop at the Chateau Grand Traverse or Chateau Chantel wineries along the way and sample their chardonnay or pinot noir. If you purchase a bottle, you can take it out to Lighthouse Park beach, on the end of the peninsula, and enjoy it with the waves licking your toes.

Back in the city is the **Traverse Area Recreation Trail** (TART for short), an 11-mile paved path that makes its way along the bay. At **Brick Wheels** (☎ 231-947-4274; 736 E 8th St; skates/bike per day $10/25) you can rent mountain bikes or in-line skates and then jump on the trail outside.

For an indoor activity, hear rare, antique instruments played at the **Music House**

MICHIGAN'S HEMINGWAY TOUR

A number of writers have ties to northwest Michigan, but none are as famous as Ernest Hemingway, who spent the summers of his youth at his family's cottage on Walloon Lake. Hemingway buffs often tour the area to view artifacts and places that made their way into his writing.

They begin in Petoskey at the **Little Traverse History Museum** (☎ 231-347-2620; 100 Depot Ct; admission $1; 🕑 10am-4pm Mon-Fri, 1-4pm Sat summer, 1-4pm Thu-Sat May & Oct-Dec), housed in the town's historic railroad depot. Among the items on display are rare first-edition books that Hemingway autographed for a friend when he visited Petoskey in 1947.

Continue by heading south on US 31 toward Charlevoix. Just before entering that town, turn east onto Boyne City Rd, which skirts beautiful Lake Charlevoix and eventually arrives at the **Horton Bay General Store**. Built in 1876 with a high false front, the store's most prominent feature is its large front porch, with benches and stairs at either end. Hemingway idled away some youthful summers on that porch and fished nearby Horton Creek for trout. He was married in Horton Bay's Congregational Church, and the general store appeared in the opening of his short story 'Up in Michigan.'

From Horton Bay, continue the tour by heading to Boyne City, and follow the Lake Charlevoix shoreline on Ferry Rd. Just before reaching the south arm of the lake, turn north onto Sanderson Rd to reach **Hemingway Point**, originally owned by Hemingway's uncle. It's said that the young author once fled across the lake to elude a conservation officer in Horton Bay.

The tour is completed by crossing the south arm on the **Ironton ferry**, a cable-guided vessel built in 1876. Although it's now powered by a diesel engine instead of the horses used a century ago, and though cars have replaced buggies as its cargo, the ferry still makes the 100-yard crossing. It's not documented whether Hemingway himself ever took the five-minute ride, but locals, perhaps using a touch of poetic license, say he must have. It's too pleasant a crossing to pass up.

Museum (☎ 231-938-9300; 7377 US 31 N; adult $8, child 6-16 $2.50; 🕑 10am-4pm Mon-Sat, noon-4pm Sun, May-Oct).

If you arrive in mid-July, head north on US 31 to Elk Rapids and beyond for roadside stands selling cherries and pies, and farms where you can pick your own cherries.

Traverse City has plentiful lodgings, but they are often full (and more expensive) on weekends. Stop at the downtown **visitors center** (☎ 800-872-8377; www.mytraversecity.com; 101 W Grandview Parkway; 🕑 9am-5pm Mon-Fri, 9am-3pm Sat year-round, extended hours Mon-Sun in summer) for an accommodations list. **Northwestern Michigan College** (☎ 231-995-1400; 1701 E Front St; s/d $28/36) rents rooms in summer with shared bath. Motels on the other side of US 31 (away from the water) are more moderately priced, such as **Motel 6** (☎ 231-938-3002; 1582 US 31 N; r weekday/weekend $69/99;) and **Mitchell Creek Inn** (☎ 231-947-9330; www.mitchellcreek.com; 894 Munson Ave; s/d from $69/84, extra $25 on weekends;), both near the state park beach. Resorts overlooking the bay range from $100 to $190 per night.

For unique, delicious sandwiches go to **Folgarelli's** (☎ 231-941-7651; 424 W Front St; sandwiches $6-8).

GREAT LAKES

Petoskey & Harbor Springs

Tucked away inside Little Traverse Bay, Petoskey and Harbor Springs are where Michigan's upper crusters maintain summer homes. The downtown areas of both cities have gourmet restaurants and high-class shops, and the marinas are filled with yachts.

In Petoskey, **Stafford's Perry Hotel** (☎ 231-347-4000; Bay at Lewis St; r from $85) is a grand historic place to stay. Between the two cities along M-119 is **Petoskey State Park** (☎ 616-347-2311; 2475 M-119; campsites $16-20; mid-Apr–Oct), with a beautiful beach.

STRAITS OF MACKINAC

This region, between the Upper and Lower Peninsulas, features a long history of forts and fudge shops. Car-free Mackinac Island is Michigan's premier tourist draw.

One of the most spectacular sights in the area is the 5-mile-long **Mackinac Bridge** (known locally as 'Big Mac'), which spans the Straits of Mackinac. The $1.25 toll is worth every penny, as the views from the bridge, which include two Great Lakes, two peninsulas and hundreds of islands, are second to none in Michigan.

Remember: despite the spelling, it's pronounced *mac*-in-aw.

Mackinaw City

At the south end of Mackinac Bridge, bordering I-75, is Mackinaw City, a tacky tourist town with a gift shop and fudge kitchen on every corner (fudge is Northern Michigan's most famous product). Mackinaw City is best known as one of two departure points for Mackinac Island, but it does have a couple of interesting attractions of its own.

Right next to the bridge (its visitors center is actually beneath the bridge) is **Colonial Michilimackinac** (☎ 231-436-5563; adult $9, child 6-17 $5.75; 9am-4pm, May–mid-Oct, until 6pm in summer), a National Historic Landmark that features a reconstructed stockade first built in 1715 by the French. Some 3 miles southeast of the city on US 23 is **Historic Mill Creek** (☎ 231-436-4226; adult $7.50, child 6-17 $4.50; 9am-4pm, May–mid-Oct, until 5pm in summer), which has an 18th-century sawmill, historic displays and nature trails. A combination ticket for both sights, along with Fort Mackinac (see below), is available at a discount.

The only things that outnumber fudge shops in Mackinaw City are motels, which line I-75 and US 23. Thanks to the popularity of Mackinac Island and a nearby casino, it's almost impossible to find a room for less than $100 during the summer. Even **Motel 6** (☎ 231-436-8961; 206 N Nicolet St; r from $106; P) is pricey. The one exception is **Rainbow Motel** (☎ 231-436-5518, 800-888-6077; 602 S Huron St; r weekday/weekend from $63/79; P; mid-May–mid-Oct). If you have a tent, skip the high-price accommodations in favor of a scenic campsite at **Wilderness State Park** (☎ 231-436-5381; 898 Wilderness Park Dr; campsites $16-20), 9 miles west of town via County Rd 81.

St Ignace

At the north end of Mackinac Bridge is St Ignace, the second-oldest settlement in Michigan – Père Jacques Marquette founded a mission here in 1671. As soon as you've paid your bridge toll you'll pass a huge **Michigan Welcome Center** (☎ 906-643-6979; I-75N; 9am-5pm, 8am-6pm summer) with racks of brochures and lodging help.

In St Ignace, check out the **Museum of Ojibwa Culture** (☎ 906-643-9161; 566 N State St; admission $2; 11am-5pm, late May–mid-Oct, extended hours Jul-Aug) inside the **Marquette Mission Park**, where the famous Jesuit priest is buried. Look for mid-range lodging off the I-75 Business Loop and US 2 West.

Mackinac Island

From either St Ignace or Mackinaw City, you can catch a ferry to Mackinac Island, Michigan's first tourist destination. The British built a fort atop the famous limestone cliffs in 1780 and then fought with the Americans for control of it during the War of 1812.

The most important date on this 2000-acre island was 1898 – the year cars were banned to encourage tourism. Today all travel on the island is by horses or bicycles; even the police use bikes to patrol the town. The crowds of tourists (called Fudgies by the islanders) can be crushing at times, particularly on summer weekends. If at all possible, spend a night on Mackinac Island; the real charm of this historic place emerges after the last ferry leaves in the evening.

SIGHTS & ACTIVITIES

Overlooking the downtown area is **Fort Mackinac** (☎ 906-847-3328; adult $9, child 6-17 $5.75; 9:30am-4:30pm May–mid-Oct, extended hours in summer), one of the best-preserved military forts in the country. The admission price is also good for six other museums in town, including the Dr Beaumont Museum (where the doctor performed his famous digestive tract experiments) and Benjamin Blacksmith Shop. Edging the shoreline of the island is M-185, the only state highway in Michigan that doesn't permit cars. The best way to view the incredible scenery along this 8-mile road is by bicycle; bring your own on the ferry or rent one in town at any of almost a dozen bike shops for about $5 per hour plus a hefty deposit. The two best attractions – **Arch Rock** (a huge limestone arch that sits 150ft above Lake Huron) and **Fort Holmes** (the island's 'other fort') – are both free. You can also ride past the **Grand Hotel,** which boasts a veranda stretching halfway to Detroit. Unfortunately if you're not staying at the Grand (minimum $200 per night per person), then it costs $10 to stroll its long porch and step inside the lobby. Not worth it.

SLEEPING, EATING & DRINKING

Rooms are booked far in advance on summer weekends. Call or stop by the **visitors**

GREAT LAKES

center (☎ 800-454-5227; www.mackinacisland.org; Main St; 🕑 9am-5pm) for help with lodging reservations.

Camping is not permitted anywhere on Mackinac Island. That means you have to spend a wad to spend the night. Most hotels and B&Bs charge at least $150 for two people. Exceptions include the four-room **Bogan Lane Inn** (☎ 906-847-3439; Bogan Lane; r $75-95;); the 18-room **La Chance Cottage** (☎ 906-847-3526; Main St; r $95-105; 🕑 mid-May–Sept); and **Pontiac Lodge** (☎ 906-847-3364; cnr Main & Hoban Sts; r from $110-150;). All serve continental breakfast, and all are walkable to downtown.

The best-known eateries on Mackinac Island are the dozen fudge shops, which use fans to blow the tempting aroma of the freshly made confection out onto Huron St. Hamburger and sandwich shops abound downtown.

French Outpost (☎ 906-847-3772; Cadotte Ave; dishes $7-9; 🕑 mid-May–mid-Oct) A quiet spot toward the Grand Hotel from downtown. Enjoy salads or sandwiches along with a pint of beer.

Horn's Bar (☎ 906-847-6154; Main St; dishes $10-16) Horn's Bar serves good dinners and has live entertainment nightly.

Astor St Cafe (☎ 906-847-6031; Astor St; dishes $9-15; 🕑 late May–Oct) Astor St fires up midwestern lunch and dinner specials such as whitefish, roast turkey and meatloaf.

Brian's Barbeque (☎ 906-847-3526; Main St; items $2-8; 🕑 late May–early Sep) Hot dogs, bratwursts and chicken are served on the front lawn of La Chance Cottage. If you purchase a ticket to the fort, you can eat lunch at Fort Mackinac Tea Room. The outdoor tables here feature a million-dollar view of downtown and the Straits of Mackinac.

GETTING THERE & AROUND

Three ferry companies operate out of both Mackinaw City and St Ignace – **Arnold Line** (☎ 800-542-8528; www.arnoldline.com), **Shepler's** (☎ 800-828-6157; www.sheplersferry.com) and **Star Line** (☎ 800-638-9892; www.mackinacferry.com) – and charge the same rates: adult round-trip $16.50, child 5–12 $8, bicycles $6.50. The ferries run several times daily May to October; Arnold Line runs longer, weather permitting. Once you're on the island, horse-drawn taxis will take you anywhere, or rent a bicycle (p417).

UPPER PENINSULA

A third of the state lies in this rugged, wooded and isolated region. The UP has only 45 miles of interstate highway and just a handful of cities, of which Marquette is the largest and most interesting. Between the cities are miles of undeveloped shoreline (on Lakes Huron, Michigan and Superior), scenic two-lane roads, small rural towns and pasties, the local meat/vegetable pot pies brought over by Cornish miners 150 years ago.

Michigan's two best wilderness areas are both at the west end of the UP. Isle Royale National Park – famous for its populations of moose and wolves – is a 210-sq-mile island in Lake Superior. Porcupine Mountains Wilderness State Park, otherwise known as 'the Porkies,' is a rugged 94-sq-mile park 20 miles west of Ontonagon via M-64.

Lake Michigan Shoreline

From the north end of Mackinac Bridge, head 6 miles west on US 2 and stop at the Hiawatha National Forest's **St Ignace Ranger District office** (☎ 906-643-7900; 🕑 8am-4:30pm Mon-Fri), which provides a wealth of information about camping, hiking, waterfalls and scenic drives along Lake Michigan and in the eastern half of the UP. The drive continuing west along US 2 skirts the lake for several miles and is one of the most scenic in the state.

When you reach Garden Corners and County Rd 183, take it 17 miles south through the Garden Peninsula to reach **Fayette State Park** (☎ 906-644-2603; campsites $12), which has a campground, beach and preserved ghost town that was an iron-smelting center in the 19th century. North of the Garden Peninsula, via M-149, is **Kitchi-iti-kipi** (Big Spring), in Palms Book State Park, where visitors pull themselves across the state's largest spring on a wooden raft.

Iron Mountain, on the Wisconsin border 52 miles west of Escanaba via US 2, is an interesting place to visit, with lots of affordable motels and good restaurants. Here you can climb the Pine Mountain Ski Jump, where skiers set a US record of 400ft; go white-water rafting at Piers Gorge with **Kosir's Rapid Rafts** (☎ 715-757-3431; www.kosirs.com; rafting per person $44); or ride an underground train into an iron-ore mine at **Iron Mountain Iron Mine** (☎ 906-563-8077; US 2, 9 mi east of Iron Mountain; adult $7.50, child 6-12 $6.50; 🕑 9am-5pm, late May–early Oct). **Woodlands Motel** (☎ 906-774-6106,

800-394-5505; 3957 US 2; s/d $32/40;) is amiable, or rent a cabin on the Menominee River at **Edgewater Resort** (☎ 906-774-6244, 800-236-6244; 4128 US 2; s/d $71/82), which usually has a one-week minimum stay in summer.

Sault Ste Marie & Around

Founded in 1668, Sault Ste Marie (Sault is pronounced 'soo') is the oldest city in Michigan and the third-oldest in the USA. The town is best known for its locks that raise and lower 1000ft-long freighters between the different lake levels. **Soo Lock Park** is at the end of Water St in the heart of downtown. It features an interpretive center and observation decks from which you can watch the action. To get closer to the boats, go down to the adjacent walkway.

Among the handful of museums in town, check out the **SS Valley Camp** (☎ 906-632-3658; adult $8, child 6-16 $4; 10am-6pm mid-May–mid-Oct, 9am-9pm Jul-Aug), a 550ft freighter you can walk through.

An hour's drive west of Sault Ste Marie, via M-28 and M-123, is the eastern UP's (Upper Peninsula's) top attraction: **Tahquamenon Falls**. The Upper Falls in **Tahquamenon Falls State Park** (☎ 906-492-3415; campsites $15-17) are 200ft across with a 50ft drop, making them the third-largest falls east of the Mississippi River. The Lower Falls are a series of smaller cascades best viewed by renting a **boat** (☎ 906-492-3457) and rowing across the river to an island. The large state park also has camping and great hiking, and there's a brew pub in the middle of it. North of the park beyond Paradise is the fascinating **Great Lakes Shipwreck Museum** (☎ 906-635-1742; 18335 N Whitefish Point Rd; adult $8.50, child 5-18 $5.50; 10am-6pm May-Oct), dedicated to the 'Graveyard of the Great Lakes' and well worth the admission price.

Most of Sault Ste Marie's motels are along the I-75 Business Loop and Ashmun St. Try the pleasant **Plaza Motor Motel** (☎ 906-635-1881, 888-809-1881; 3901 I-75 Business; r $49-66 in summer;), which has cheaper rates from fall to spring, or go downtown to the tidy **Lockview Motel** (☎ 906-632-2491, 800-854-0745; www.lockview.com; 327 W Portage Ave; r $60-69; May-mid-Oct;), across from Soo Locks.

Cup of the Day (☎ 906-635-7272; 406 Ashmun St; dishes $5-7) This coffee shop serves breakfast and lunch.

Antlers (☎ 906-632-3571; 804 E Portage Ave; dishes $8-20) The place to head for dinner to feast on giant hamburgers and ribs and to take in the hundreds of stuffed animals on the walls (animal-rights enthusiasts beware).

Munising

Sitting roughly mid-peninsula on the Lake Superior shoreline, Munising is the gateway to **Pictured Rocks National Lakeshore**, a 110-sq-mile national park just to the east that holds the namesake colored sandstone bluffs. Most people view the 200ft-high cliffs on a 2½-hour boat tour with **Pictured Rock Boat Cruises** (☎ 906-387-2379; adult $25, child 6-12 $10; 9am-5pm, late May–mid-Oct); boats depart from downtown on the hour in summer. You also can drive to **Miners Castle Overlook** (12 miles east of Munising off M-58) for a good view. The most scenic backpacking adventure in the state is the **Lakeshore Trail**, a four- to five-day, 43-mile trek from Grand Marais to Munising through the heart of the park. Stop in at the **Hiawatha National Forest/Pictured Rocks Visitors Center** (☎ 906-387-3700; 400 E Munising Ave; 9am-4:30pm year-round, until 6pm summer) at the corner of M-28 and H-58 for maps, backcountry permits and other details.

Just offshore is **Grand Island**, part of the Hiawatha National Forest. Hop aboard the **Grand Island Ferry** (☎ 906-387-3503; round-trip adult $14, child 6-12 $8; late May–mid-Oct) to get there, and rent a mountain bike ($15) from the ferry company to zip around.

Munising has lots of motels. Recommended are the **Hillcrest Motel** (☎ 906-387-2595; M-28 E; r $60) and **Alger Falls Motel** (☎ 906-387-3536; M-28 E; s/d $58/68), across the street.

Marquette

From Munising, M-28 heads west and hugs Lake Superior. This beautiful stretch of highway has lots of beaches, roadside parks and rest areas where you can pull over and enjoy the scenery. Within 45 miles you'll reach Marquette, a city that abounds with outdoor-recreation opportunities. Stop at the **Michigan Welcome Center** (☎ 906-249-9066; US 41/M-28; 9am-5pm), in an impressive log lodge as you enter the city, and pick up brochures on hiking trails and waterfalls in the area.

Panoramic views are enjoyed on the easy **Sugarloaf Mountain Trail** or the harder, wilderness-like **Hogsback Mountain Trail**. Both are reached from County Rd 550, just north

GREAT LAKES

of Marquette. In the city, the high bluffs of **Presque Isle Park** make a great place to catch the sunset.

The most interesting museums in the area are the **Michigan Iron Industry Museum** (☎ 906-475-7857; 73 Forge Rd; admission free; 9:30am-4:30pm May-Oct), off County Rd 492, 3 miles east of Negaunee, which includes a reconstructed mine shaft; and the **National Ski Hall of Fame** (☎ 906-485-6323; US 41/M-28; admission free; 10am-5pm Mon-Sat), in Ishpeming, the birthplace of US ski jumping.

Marquette is the perfect place to stay put for a few days to explore the central UP. Good hotels include the alpine-lodge-like **Tiroler Hof Inn** (☎ 800-892-9376; 1880 US 41 S; s/d $50/66;), overlooking Lake Superior a few miles south of downtown, and **Value Host Motor Inn** (☎ 906-225-5000; 1101 US 41 W; r $50-58;), with a sauna, a few miles west of town. The city-operated **Tourist Park** (☎ 906-228-0465; Cty Rd 550; camp/RV sites $10/20) looks out over Dead River Basin.

Rice Paddy (☎ 906-225-0368; 1720 Presque Isle Ave; admission $5-7; Mon-Fri) Unbelievable but true: this tiny, one-table restaurant serves the world's best pad thai, a secret family recipe the owner would rather kill you over than reveal; don't miss it.

Sweet Water Cafe (☎ 906-226-7009; 517 N Third St; dishes $6-10) Unique breakfast, lunch and dinner dishes are served at Sweet Water. There's a large vegetarian selection.

Jean Kay's Pasties & Subs (☎ 906-228-5310; 1639 Presque Isle Ave; dishes $3) Jean Kay's is a good place to sample the local meat/veggie pie speciality.

Vierling Saloon (☎ 906-228-3533; 119 S Front St; dishes $6-15; Mon-Sat) Excellent handcrafted beer and tasty food.

Isle Royale National Park

The **Isle Royale National Park Service headquarters** (☎ 906-482-0984; www.nps.gov/isro; 800 E Lakeshore Dr; 8am-4:30pm Mon-Fri year-round, 8am-6pm Mon-Sat in summer) is in Houghton. The park charges a user fee of $4 per person per night to hike and camp in the national park.

From the dock outside the headquarters, the **Ranger III** (☎ 906-482-0984; adult round-trip $98, child 11 & under $48; 9am Tue & Fri) departs twice a week on the six-hour trip to Rock Harbor, at the east end of the island. If you're looking for a quicker trip, the **Isle Royale Seaplane Service** has operated sporadically in past years; call park headquarters to see if it's making the 20-minute flight. Or head 50 miles up the Keweenaw Peninsula to Copper Harbor (a beautiful drive) and jump on the **Isle Royale Queen** (☎ 906-289-4437; www.isleroyale.com; adult round-trip $84, child 11 & under $42). You also can access Isle Royale from Grand Portage, MN (p442). Many visitors bring their kayaks and canoes over on the ferry for an additional $42.

Isle Royale is totally free of vehicles, roads, McDonald's, rush-hour traffic – you get the picture. It is laced with 165 miles of hiking trails that connect dozens of campgrounds along Lake Superior and inland lakes. You must be totally prepared for this wilderness adventure, with a tent, camping stove, sleeping bags, food and water filter.

Porcupine Mountains Wilderness State Park

Michigan's largest state park, with 90 miles of trails, is another popular place for overnight backpacking and is a lot easier to reach than Isle Royale. The Porkies are so rugged that loggers bypassed most of the range in the early 19th century, leaving the park with the largest tract of virgin forest between the Rocky Mountains and Adirondacks.

From Silver City, head west on M-107 to reach the **Porcupine Mountains visitors center** (☎ 906-885-5275; 412 S Boundary Rd; 10am-6pm mid-May–mid-Oct), where you buy vehicle entry permits ($4/20 for day/annual) and backcountry permits ($9 per night for one to four people). Continue to the end of M-107 and climb 300ft for the stunning view of **Lake of the Clouds**.

On the road in you pass large **Union Bay Campground** (reservations ☎ 800-447-2757; M-107; campsites $15-19) on Lake Superior. Bypass it if you can and camp at the much more scenic, though rustic, **Presque Isle Campground** (☎ 800-447-2757; County Rd 519; campsites $9). For the non-campers in the group, try **Sunshine Motel** (☎ 888-988-2187; sunshine@up.net; 1442 M-64; r from $50;) in Ontonagon.

Winter is also a busy time at the Porkies, with good downhill skiing (a 640ft vertical drop) and 26 miles of cross-country trails; call the visitors center for ski conditions and costs.

WISCONSIN

When you look out the window and see lighthouses atop craggy cliffs and islands shimmering in the middle distance, it's easy to forget you're in the state of Wisconsin. Then you run into someone wearing a foam rubber cheese-wedge hat, and it all comes crashing back.

There's a definite dualism to the Dairy State. You can sea kayak around the unspoiled Apostle Islands one day, then be mobbed by families at the kitschy Wisconsin Dells the next. You can follow up beer and motorcycle tours in Milwaukee (Harley-Davidson and Miller Beer are headquartered here) with visits to the stunning art museum and nearby Frank Lloyd Wright gems. Door County's lighthouses and coastline are a draw. They sit next to Green Bay, home of the Packers, a National Football League team with legendarily rabid fans (they're the ones who sport the cheese hats).

The state's bucolic farmland is dotted with cows, while its wooded north is dotted with lakes. Lake Superior and Lake Michigan crown the north and east, respectively.

History

When Europeans arrived, Sioux-speaking Winnebago inhabited the Green Bay area, but Algonquian peoples, who lived by hunting, fishing and harvesting wild rice, occupied most of the land.

In 1634 Frenchman Jean Nicolet landed near Green Bay, where a trading post opened in 1648. Others followed on the Mississippi, though it was 25 years before the inland routes between these outposts were explored. Jesuit missions were established in the 1660s, but eventually French territorial claims passed to the British and then to the new USA.

A lead-mining boom in the 1820s spurred development. The many miners who came from nearby states were called 'badgers' for their subterranean activities. Following statehood in 1848 and the Civil War, immigrants poured in – from Germany and Scandinavia most notably. Wisconsin was soon known for its beer, butter, cheese and paper.

The state has been a consistent leader in socially progressive reforms. It was the first to legislate gay rights, and along with neighbors Michigan and Minnesota, is one of the 12 states without the death penalty.

> **WISCONSIN FACTS**
>
> **Nicknames** The Badger State, America's Dairyland
> **Population** 5,441,196 (20th)
> **Area** 65,500 sq miles (23rd)
> **Admitted to Union** May 29, 1848 (30th)
> **Capital city** Madison (population 208,100)
> **Other cities** Milwaukee (597,000), Green Bay (102,300), Racine (81,900)
> **Birthplace of** architect Frank Lloyd Wright (1867–1959), Senator Joseph McCarthy (1908–57), author Laura Ingalls Wilder (1867–1957), painter Georgia O'Keeffe (1887–1986), actor Orson Welles (1915–85)
> **Famous for** first state to legislate gay rights

Information

Wisconsin Department of Tourism (☎ 800-432-8747; www.travelwisconsin.com; 201 W Washington St, Madison, WI 53707)
Wisconsin highway information (☎ 800-762-3947; www.dot.state.wi.us)

Wisconsin's state sales tax is 5%, with many counties tacking on an additional 1%.

National & State Parks

Wisconsin state park information (☎ 888-947-2757; www.dnr.state.wi.us) Park entry requires a vehicle permit ($5/20 per day/year residents, $10/30 nonresidents). Campground reservations accepted.

MILWAUKEE

Mid-size Milwaukee is a city of charm and character smiling quietly in the shadow of Chicago. You've got to admire how it balances its Harleys and beer with world-class art and cultural festivals. Summer is a brilliant time to visit, when activity blossoms along the river and lakefront.

History

First settled by Germans in the 1840s, Milwaukee has a German character that's still evident in its architecture (the Germanic City Hall and beer-bankrolled Pabst Theater, for example) and restaurants. Later waves of Italians, Poles, Irish, African-Americans, Mexicans and others added to the varied culture.

German settlers started small breweries here in the mid-19th century, but the introduction of bulk brewing technology in the 1890s turned beer into a major Milwaukee industry. Schlitz ('the beer that made Milwaukee famous'), Pabst and Miller were all based here at one time, but among the majors, only Miller remains.

Orientation

Lake Michigan sits to the east of the city, and is rimmed by parkland. The inspired **Riverwalk** is a great system of redeveloped walking paths along both sides of the Milwaukee River downtown. Wisconsin Avenue divides streets east from west. North and south streets usually are numbered and increase as they head west from the lake.

Information

BOOKSTORES

Harry Schwartz Books (☎ 414-332-1181; 2559 N Downer Ave)

EMERGENCY

Emergency number (☎ 911) Police, ambulance, fire.
Suicide crisis (☎ 414-257-7222)

INTERNET ACCESS

Milwaukee Public Library (☎ 414-286-3000; 814 W Wisconsin Ave)
Node Coffee Shop (☎ 414-431-9278; 1504 E North Ave; $4 per hr) Open 24 hours.

INTERNET RESOURCES

www.milwaukee.org Chock-full site that includes discount coupons for hotels, theaters and more.
www.onmilwaukee.com Job listings, traffic and weather updates, and restaurant and entertainment reviews.

MEDIA

The *Milwaukee Journal Sentinel* is the local daily. *Shepherd Express* is the free weekly entertainment paper available at bookstores, coffee shops and entertainment venues.

Tune into WUWM-FM 89.7 for NPR, or WLZR-FM 102.9 for rock.

MEDICAL SERVICES

CVS (☎ 317-923-1491; 1744 N Illinois St) Twenty-four-hour pharmacy.
Froedtert Hospital (☎ 414-805-3000; 9200 W Wisconsin Ave)

MONEY

US Bank (☎ 414-765-4606; 777 E Wisconsin Ave) ATM and foreign currency exchange available.

POST

Main post office (☎ 800-275-8777; 345 W St Paul Ave)

TOURIST OFFICES

Milwaukee LGBT Community Center (☎ 414-271-2656; www.mkelgbt.org; 315 W Court St, Suite 101; ⏲ 10am-10pm Mon-Fri, 5-10pm Sat) Has information on happenings; or search www.outinmilwaukee.com.
Visitors center (☎ 414-908-6205, 800-554-1448; 400 W Wisconsin Ave; ⏲ 8am-5pm Mon-Fri, daily in summer) In the Midwest Airlines Center.

Sights & Activities

Sights are spread out, but usually accessible by public buses.

Milwaukee Art Museum

The first-rate, lakeside **Milwaukee Art Museum** (☎ 414-224-3200; 750 N Lincoln Memorial Dr; adult $6, child 13-18 $4; ⏲ 10am-5pm, until 8pm Thu) features a stunning wing-like addition by Calatrava. The museum's all-encompassing collection includes paintings from the 15th century onward, with all major schools represented. There's a permanent display on Frank Lloyd Wright and fabulous folk and outsider art galleries. Pick up the free, self-guided audio tour.

HARLEY-DAVIDSON

Kind-of-technical, one-hour tours are offered at the **Harley-Davidson** power-train plant (☎ 414-535-3666; 11700 W Capitol Dr; admission free; ⏲ usually 9:30am-1pm Mon, Wed & Fri), 20 minutes from the center. There's a film and opportunity to sit on vintage bikes. No open-toed shoes permitted; no kids under 12; and bring your ID.

BREWERIES

Connoisseurs might dismiss the bland beers churned out by the big-name national companies, but lots of drinkers line up at mega **Miller Brewing Company** (☎ 414-931-2337; 4251 W State St; admission free; ⏲ 10:30am-3:30pm Mon-Sat). The tour (children permitted) includes a slick slide show followed by visits to bottling and distribution areas that give some idea of just how much brew the public consumes. To participate in the generous tasting session, bring ID.

GREAT LAKES

For comparison purposes (and additional free swills), tour two microbreweries: **Sprecher Brewing** (☎ 414-964-2739; 701 W Glendale Ave; adult/child $3/1; 4pm Fri, 1-3pm Sat), 5 miles north of downtown, and **Lakefront Brewery** (☎ 414-372-8800; 1872 N Commerce St; admission $3; 3pm Fri, 1-3pm Sat).

OTHER

The **Eisner Museum of Advertising and Design** (☎ 414-847-3290; 208 N Water St; adult $4.50, child 13-18 $2.50; 11am-5pm Wed-Fri, until 8pm Thu, noon-5pm Sat, 1-5pm Sun) presents excellent exhibits on how the mediums influence today's culture.

Milwaukee Museum Center (800 W Wells St; 9am-5pm) is crawling with families perusing three attractions: the **Public Museum** (☎ 414-278-2700; adult $6.75, child 3-17 $4.50), the best of the lot, with exhibits on dinosaurs and Native American life; **Discovery World** (☎ 414-765-9966; adult $5.75, child 3-17 $4), with hands-on science, economics and technology displays; and an Imax cinema. Combination tickets are offered.

America's Black Holocaust Museum (☎ 414-264-2500; 2233 N 4th St; adult/student $5/3; 9am-5pm Mon-Sat) poignantly outlines the consequences of racism from slavery onward.

The 1893 **Pabst Mansion** (☎ 414-931-0808; 2000 W Wisconsin Ave; adult $7, child 6-17 $3; 10am-3:30pm Mon-Sat, noon-3:30pm Sun) is the well-appointed home of a former local brew master.

Festivals & Events

Summerfest (☎ 800-273-3378; www.summerfest.com) is the granddaddy of festivals, with 11 days of music and merriment in late June/early July.

There's also **PrideFest** (www.pridefest.com), **Polish Fest** (www.polishfest.org), **Irish Fest** (www.irishfest.com), **German Fest** (www.germanfest.com) and a host of others. Call the visitors center for details.

Sleeping

Rates listed here are for summertime; rooms can be 15% to 30% less in winter. The 14.6% tax is not included in the listed rates. Book ahead in summer.

BUDGET

HI Milwaukee Summer Hostel (☎ 414-288-3232, 414-961-2525; www.hostellingwisconsin.org; 1530 W Wisconsin Ave; dm from $17; P $3.50) Marquette University's McCormick Residence Hall serves as a hostel during June and July. It's well-located, near public transportation and has the usual amenities (kitchen, laundry) plus room phones. Office open 8am to 11pm and 5pm to 10pm.

Try Howell Ave, south near the airport, for cheap chain lodging.

MID-RANGE

Astor Hotel (☎ 800-558-0200; www.theastorhotel.com; 924 E Juneau Ave; r weekday/weekend from $99/109; P $3) The Astor, dating from 1918, has bright, spacious rooms, some with cool old furnishings, plus perks like continental breakfast, free internet and a shuttle to nearby sights.

Hotel Wisconsin (☎ 414-271-4900; 720 N Old World 3rd St; r $89;)Offering the cheapest downtown rates (usually), the Wisconsin is an old chestnut that works just fine for the price.

Best Western Inn Towne Hotel (☎ 414-224-8400; www.inntownehotel.com; 710 N Old World 3rd St s/d from $89/99; P $10) It has good-quality rooms in a vintage ambience; next door to Hotel Wisconsin.

TOP END

Pfister Hotel (☎ 414-273-8222; www.thepfisterhotel.com; 424 E Wisconsin Ave; r from $260; P $12) Built in the 19th century, the gorgeous Pfister has been meticulously restored without losing a bit of its charm. A stroll through the lobby and a peek at the Victorian painting collection emphatically declare that this ain't no chain hotel. If business is slow, rooms go for around $119.

Eating

Good places to scope for eats include **N Old World 3rd St** downtown; the fashionable **East Side** by the University of Wisconsin Milwaukee; hip, Italian-based **Brady St** by its intersection with N Farwell Ave; and the gentrified **Third Ward**, anchored along N Milwaukee St south of I-94.

Safehouse (☎ 414-271-2007; 779 N Front St; sandwiches $6-10, dishes $13-20) This downtown restaurant/bar is hidden, marked only with a door indicating an import-export business. You'll get buzzed in after giving the proper password (usually the answer to a silly trivia question that the door person will ask); then step into a spy's world filled with sliding panels and secret passageways. Fun and original, even if it is touristy.

African Hut (☎ 414-765-1110; N 1107 N Old World 3rd St; dishes $9-12; 🕒 Mon-Sat) A wonderful place to go for exotic meat and vegetarian dishes with ingredients like pounded yam, cassava and cooked-down peanuts blended with herbs, served amid leopard-print walls.

Benji's Deli (☎ 414-332-7777; 4156 N Oakland Ave; dishes $6-11) Seek out the hoppel poppel – a local speciality of eggs, potatoes, and sausage whipped together – among the many meaty offerings at the famous Jewish deli in Shorewood.

For upscale German fare, **Mader's** (☎ 414-271-3377; 1041 N Old World 3rd St; dishes $17-28) and **Karl Ratzsch's** (☎ 414-276-2720; 320 E Mason St; dishes $14-30; 🕒 Mon-Sat) both have lots of heavy wood decor, rows of beer steins and attentive service.

South of town a few blocks (over the bridge and too far to walk), around S 5th and 6th Sts, the Latin enclave of Walker's Point holds several Mexican restaurants, like **Pedrano's** (☎ 414-276-6880; 600 S 6th St; dishes $7-9). The good, inexpensive food draws crowds weekend nights.

A Milwaukee speciality is frozen custard, like ice cream only smoother and richer. **Leon's** (☎ 414-383-1784; 3131 S 27th St) and **Kopp's** (☎ 414-961-2006; 5373 N Port Washington Rd, Glendale) are popular purveyors.

Drinking

The beer legacy guarantees that a thirst-quenching array of golden nectar is available. Over a dozen bars and restaurants lie around N Water and E State Sts. More bars can be found in Walker's Point on 1st and 2nd Sts, and along Brady St between Astor and Farwell Sts.

Von Trier (☎ 414-272-1775; 2235 N Farwell Ave) The German Von Trier is a long-standing, real-deal favorite, with plenty of good stuff on tap and a biergarten.

John Hawk's (☎ 414-272-3199; 100 E Wisconsin Ave) Hawk's is a 'British' pub with a big choice of beers, fish fries, sandwiches and live Saturday jazz. It occupies a prime spot on the riverfront, marked by a red phone box.

Water Street Brewery (☎ 414-272-1195; 1101 N Water St) The emphasis here is definitely on beer: Water Street brews several fine ones that you can sip while strolling through displays of beer cans and other boozy memorabilia.

Switch (☎ 414-220-4340; 124 W National Ave) Switch is a festive gay hangout in Walker's Point, with outdoor seating when the weather's nice, and karaoke and tuneful Broadway brunches the rest of the time.

Entertainment

The city has a full cultural slate; pick up the free *Shepherd Express* (see Media, p422).

PERFORMING ARTS

Marcus Center (☎ 414-273-7206; 929 N Water St) Showcasing theater, opera and ballet.

Pabst Theater (☎ 414-286-3663; 144 E Wells St) Presents dance, opera, jazz and more.

Riverside Theater (☎ 414-290-6800; 116 W Wisconsin Ave) Wisconsin's largest theater offers Broadway stagings.

Milwaukee Repertory Theater (☎ 414-224-9490; 108 E Wells St) Produces new and classic plays.

SPECTATOR SPORTS

Milwaukee Brewers (☎ 414-902-4000; 1 Brewers Way) The National League's team, near S 46th St, play baseball in Miller Park, which has a retractable roof and real grass.

Bucks (☎ 414-227-0400; 1001 N 4th St) The NBA Bucks dribble at the Bradley Center.

Getting There & Around

TO/FROM THE AIRPORT

General Mitchell International Airport (☎ 414-747-5300; 5300 S Howell Ave) is 8 miles south of downtown. Take public bus No 80 ($1.50) or the **Airport Connection van** (☎ 800-236-5450; one way/round-trip $10/18) downtown.

BUS

Greyhound (☎ 414-272-2156; 606 N James Lovell St) is conveniently central and has frequent buses to Chicago ($13 to $28, two hours) and Minneapolis ($49 to $68, from six hours). Across the street, **Badger Bus** (☎ 414-276-7490; 635 N James Lovell St) goes to Madison ($14, 1¾ hours).

CAR

National car rental agencies have offices at the airport and around town; Hertz has one at the train station. Check rental information in the Transport chapter (p1121) for more details.

TRAIN

The downtown **Amtrak station** (☎ 414-271-0840; 433 W St Paul Ave) is served by seven trains a day to/from Chicago ($20, 1½ hours) as well as the daily Empire Builder between Chicago and Seattle.

PUBLIC TRANSPORTATION

The **Milwaukee County Transit System** (☎ 414-344-6711; www.ridemcts.com; 1942 N 17th Ave; tickets $1.50) provides efficient local bus service as well as a trolley-like bus – the 'Milwaukee Loop' – that runs downtown. The Amtrak station has route maps.

TAXI

Yellow Cab (☎ 414-271-1800)

SOUTHERN WISCONSIN

This part of Wisconsin has some of the prettiest landscapes, particularly the hilly southwest. There is whimsy for all ages in the region, from circus animals to the spaceship-like Forevertron. Madison, the laid-back capital, has great appeal, and architecture fans can be unleashed at Taliesin, the Frank Lloyd Wright *über*-sight.

Racine

Racine is an unremarkable industrial town 30 miles south of Milwaukee, but it has two key **Frank Lloyd Wright sights**, both of which offer tours that must be pre-booked. The first, **Johnson Wax Company** (☎ 262-260-2154; cnr 14th & Franklin Sts; admission free; 🕑 11am & 1:15pm Fri), dates from 1939 and is a magnificent space with tall, flared columns. The other is the lakeside **Wingspread** (☎ 262-681-3353; 33 E Four Mile Rd; admission free; 🕑 9:30am-3pm Tue-Thu), the last and largest of Wright's Prairie houses.

The new **Racine Art Museum** (☎ 262-638-8300; 441 Main St; adult $5, child 11 & under free; 🕑 10am-5pm Tue-Sat, noon-5pm Sun) houses one of the continent's most significant craft collections, focusing on ceramics, fibers, glass, metals and wood.

Madison

Wonderfully ensconced on a narrow isthmus between Mendota and Monona lakes, Madison is an irresistible combination of small state capital and lively college town.

The **visitors center** (☎ 608-255-2537; www.visitmadison.com; 615 E Washington Ave; 🕑 8am-5pm Mon-Fri) is six blocks from Capitol Sq. *Isthmus* is the local entertainment paper. The central **Greyhound station** (☎ 608-257-3050; 2 S Bedford St) is also used by the **Badger Bus** (see Milwaukee, p424) to Milwaukee ($14, 1¾ hours).

SIGHTS & ACTIVITIES

The heart of town is the grand **State Capitol** (☎ 608-266-0382; admission free; 🕑 8am-6pm Mon-Fri, 8am-4pm Sat & Sun), the largest outside Washington, DC. Tours are available on the hour most days.

Beside the square, the **Veterans Museum** (☎ 608-267-1799; 30 W Mifflin St; admission free; 🕑 9am-4:30pm Mon-Sat, noon-4pm Sun) holds thoughtful displays that outline all the country's war involvements. Across the street, the **Wisconsin Historical Museum** (☎ 608-264-6555; 30 N Carroll St; suggested donation adult/child $4/3; 🕑 9am-4pm Tue-Sat) offers solid coverage of Wisconsin's Native Americans. The nearby **Civic Center** (211 State St) is a performance venue that also houses the **Madison Art Center** (☎ 608-257-0158; admission free; 🕑 11am-5pm Tue-Thu, 11am-9pm Fri, 10am-9pm Sat, 1-5pm Sun). The venues are expanding and integrating to become the Overture Center for the Arts, scheduled to open in September 2004.

State St, the lengthy strip of student stores, bars and cafés, runs from the capitol west to the University of Wisconsin. The campus has its own attractions, including the **Elvehjem Art Museum** (☎ 608-263-2246; 800 University Ave; admission free; 🕑 9am-5pm Tue-Fri, 11am-5pm Sat & Sun) and the 1240-acre **Arboretum** (☎ 608-263-7888; 1207 Seminole Hwy; admission free; 🕑 7am-10pm), dense with lilac.

The impeccable **Monona Terrace Community and Convention Center** (☎ 608-261-4000; 1 John Nolen Dr; admission free; 🕑 8am-5pm; Ⓟ $3), two blocks from the square, has a fabulous rooftop garden overlooking Lake Monona. It finally opened in 1997, 59 years after Frank Lloyd Wright designed it. Tours ($3) are offered at 1pm daily. Take advantage of the lakes and trails when you're not relaxing in Madison's myriad coffee shops and ethnic restaurants. For rentals, try **Yellow Jersey** bicycles (☎ 608-257-4737; 419 State St; 🕑 10am-6pm Tue, Wed & Fri, 10am-8pm Mon & Thu, 9am-5pm Sat, noon-5pm Sun), which charges $9 per day, and **Carl's Paddlin' Canoe and Kayak** (☎ 608-284-0300; 110 N Thornton St; $25/half day; 🕑 10am-6pm Mon-Wed, 10am-8pm Thu & Fri, 10am-5pm Sat, noon-5pm Sun), which rents for $25 per half day. Both are near Capitol Sq.

SLEEPING & EATING

HI Madison Hostel (608-441-0144; www.madisonhostel.org; 141 S Butler St; dm from $17, r $37/40; year-round) The convenient hostel is a short walk from the capitol. The office is open from 8am to 11am and 5pm to 9pm, with extended hours in summer.

University Inn (608-285-8040; 441 N Frances St; r $69-139; P) This handy hotel is right by the State St action downtown; rates are highest during summer weekends.

Select Inn (608-249-1815, 4845 Hayes Rd; s/d from $46/51; P) Moderately priced motels such as this can be found off I-90/I-94, Hwy 12/18 and along Washington Ave 6 miles from the center.

State St holds an outstanding range of eating options and cafés, many with inviting patios.

Himal Chuli (608-251-9225; 318 State St; dishes $7-11) This cheerful and cozy place serves up homemade Nepali fare, including vegetarian dishes.

Kabul (608-256-6322; 541 State St; dishes $6-11) Head to Kabul for nicely done Afghani food.

Michelangelo's (608-251-5299; 114 State St; dishes $2-5) Try Michelangelo's coffee, sweets and sandwiches.

Cruising Williamson ('Willy') St turns up good Lao, Jamaican, Caribbean and other eateries.

For a beer, join the fun atmosphere at **Memorial Union** (608-265-3000; 800 Langdon St), by the lake at the university. State St near the university also has numerous bars.

Around Madison

FRANK LLOYD WRIGHT SIGHTS

Taliesin, 40 miles west of Madison and 3 miles south of Spring Green, was the home of Frank Lloyd Wright for most of his life and is the site of his architectural school. It's now a major pilgrimage destination for fans and followers. The house was built in 1903, the Hillside Home School in 1932, and the **visitors center** (608-588-7900; Rte 23; tours $15-75; 9-5pm May-Oct) was built in 1953. A wide range of guided tours covers various parts of the complex; reservations are required for the more lengthy ones. The two-hour walking tour ($15, no reservation needed) is a good introduction.

Spring Green has a B&B in town and half a dozen motels strung along Rte 14, north of town. Small **Usonian Inn** (877-876-6426; www.usonianinn.com; E 5116 Hwy 14; r weekday/weekend $55/75;) was designed by a Wright student; **Prairie House** (800-588-2088; E 4884 Hwy 14; r weekday/weekend $69/79;) is larger, with a whirlpool and game room. South on Rte 23, **Tower Hill State Park** (608-588-2116; campsites resident/non-resident $7/9) offers good, basic camping and walking trails.

Wright was born 27 miles northwest of Spring Green in **Richland Center**. He designed the **AD German Warehouse** (608-647-2808; 300 S Church St; admission $10; May-Nov by appointment only) in 1915, and it's the only remaining example of his work from that decade, notable for its geometric concrete decorations. (Be aware that the building is privately owned, and it can be difficult reaching the proprietor to schedule a visit.)

QUIRKY SIGHTS

Baraboo, 20 miles northwest of Madison, was once the winter home of the Ringling Brothers Circus. **Circus World Museum** (608-356-0800; 550 Water St; adult in summer $15, child 5-11 $8, winter $7/3.50; 10am-4pm Mon-Sat, 11am-4pm Sun) preserves a nostalgic collection of wagons, posters and equipment from the touring big-top heydays. In summer, admission includes clowns, animals and acrobats doing the three-ring thing. Among numerous motels, sprawling **Spinning Wheel** (608-356-3933; www.spinningwheelmotel.com; 809 8th St; r in summer from $65;) is decent.

At his **Sculpture Park** (9 mi south of Baraboo on Hwy 12; admission free; roughly 9am-5pm), Dr Evermor welds old pipes, carburetors and other salvaged metal into a hallucinatory world of futuristic creatures and structures. The crowning glory is the giant, egg-domed Forevertron, cited by Guinness as the world's largest scrap metal sculpture. The good doctor himself – aka Tom Every – is often around and happy to chat about his birds, dragons and other pieces of folk art. A visit here is highly recommended; look for sculptures along the highway marking the entrance.

The **House on the Rock** (608-935-3639; 5754 Hwy 23; adult $19.50, child 7-12 $11.50, child 4-6 $5.50; 9am-6pm daily, until 7pm summer, Wed-Sun only Nov-Dec, closed Jan-mid-Mar), south of Taliesin, is one of Wisconsin's busiest attractions. The strange 'house,' one man's obsession, was built atop a rock column and sprawled to

GREAT LAKES

become a monument of the imagination. The vast collection of objects and wonderments overwhelm. Allow three to five hours to see it all.

The **Wisconsin Dells** is a mega-center of kitschy diversions, including family theme parks, water skiing thrill shows and superminigolf courses, a jolting contrast to the natural appeal of the area with its scenic limestone formations carved by the Wisconsin River. To appreciate the original attraction, take a boat tour or walk the trails at Mirror Lake or Devil's Lake state parks; both have camping. **Gables Motel** (☎ 608-253-3831; 822 Oak St; r weekday/weekend in summer $69/98;) is a relative bargain compared to the countless garish others around town. Look for modest restaurants on Broadway Ave.

Along the Mississippi River

The Mississippi forms most of Wisconsin's western border, and alongside it run some of the most scenic sections of the Great River Road – the designated route that follows the river from Minnesota to the Gulf of Mexico.

Named for the area's prevalent prairie dogs, **Prairie du Chien** was founded in 1673 as a French fur-trading post. The sumptuous **Villa Louis mansion** (☎ 608-326-2721; 521 N Villa Louis Rd; adult $8.50, child 5-12 $4.50; 9am-5pm May-Oct) was built for a successful fur-trader in 1870 and houses an excellent collection of Victorian furnishings. Across the parkland is the intriguing **Astor Fur Trade Museum**, included in mansion admission.

Heading north, the hilly riverside, once the scene of the final battle in the bloody Black Hawk War, is eye-pleasing. Historic markers tell part of the story of the war, which finished at the Battle of Bad Ax when Native American men, women and children were massacred trying to flee across the Mississippi.

Upstream, **La Crosse** is a fine riverside town with a historic center nestling restaurants and pubs. **Grandad Bluff** offers grand views of the river. It's east of town along Main St (which becomes Bliss Rd); follow Bliss Rd up the hill and then turn right on Grandad Bluff Rd. For area information, stop by the **visitors center** (☎ 608-782-2366; Riverside Park; 8am-5pm Mon-Fri year-round, plus 10am-5pm Sat, noon-5pm Sun in summer). To bed down, try **Rode Star Inn** (☎ 608-781-3070; 2622 Rose St; s/d weekday $42/47, weekend $56/66;), with breakfast. For more on upriver attractions, see the Southeastern Minnesota, p440.

EASTERN WISCONSIN

North of Milwaukee

The 20-some **Lizard Mounds**, constructed by indigenous people between AD 500 and 1000 and laid out in geometric and zoomorphic shapes, are now part of the **Washington County Parks System** (☎ 262-335-4445; Hwy A; admission free; 7am-9pm Apr-Oct). They are located 1 mile east of Hwy 144, near West Bend. In nearby Newburg, the peaceful **HI Wellspring Center** (☎ 262-675-6755; 4382 Hickory Rd; dm from $15, s/d $50/65;) is a rustic hostel often used for retreats. It's open year-round, but call ahead.

Just north of West Bend, **Kettle Moraine State Forest** (☎ 262-626-2116; N 1765 Hwy G) is a regional highlight, and offers good walking and cross-country skiing opportunities. (Note that Kettle Moraine has two parts: this north unit, and a south unit near Whitewater).

Further north, on the west side of Lake Winnebago, **Oshkosh** is home to the **Experimental Aircraft Association AirVenture Museum** (☎ 920-426-4800; off E Frontage Rd; adult in summer $10, child 8-17 $7.50, at other times $8.50/6.50; 8:30am-5pm Mon-Sat, 10am-5pm Sun), which shows its extensive collection of weird and wonderful winged things year round. The museum is south of town on US 41. In late July the huge **Oshkosh Air Show**, featuring hundreds of historic planes and experimental aircraft, attracts some 300,000 aeronautical enthusiasts.

Green Bay

Founded in the 1660s as a fur-trading post, Green Bay boomed as a Lake Michigan port and later a terminus for Midwest railroads. Processing and packing agricultural products became a major industry and gave name to the city's legendary pro football team: the Green Bay Packers. The franchise is unique as the only community-owned non-profit in the NFL; perhaps pride in ownership is what makes the fans so die-hard (and wear cheese wedges on their head).

The **visitors center** (☎ 920-494-9507, 888-867-3342; www.greenbay.org; 1901 S Oneida St; 8am-4:30pm Mon-Fri) is by the football stadium, just off Lombardi Ave, south of downtown. The town core is on the east side of the Fox River around Walnut St.

Green Bay houses a few special-interest attractions. The **Green Bay Packer Hall of Fame**

(☎ 920-499-4281; Lambeau Field; adult $10, child 6-11 $5; ⏲ 9am-6pm, closed during home games) is indeed packed with memorabilia and has football movies and interactive exhibits, plus tours of the newly expanded stadium. The **National Railroad Museum** (☎ 920-437-7623; 2285 S Broadway; adult $7, child 4-12 $5 May-Sep, Oct-Apr $6/4; ⏲ 9am-5pm Mon-Sat, 11am-5pm Sun) features some of the biggest steam and diesel locomotives ever to haul freight into Green Bay's vast yards; train rides are offered in summer. The **Oneida Nation Museum** (☎ 920-869-2768; W 892 Cty Rd EE; adult/child $2/1; ⏲ 9am-5pm Tue-Fri, 10am-5pm Sat Jun-Aug), 7 miles west of downtown, outlines the tribe's past and present.

Motel 6 (☎ 920-494-6730; 1614 Shawano Ave; s/d $38/49;) An accessible and inexpensive motel.

Door County

With its rocky coastline, picturesque lighthouses, orchards and small 19th-century villages, Door County is often compared to New England. The county is spread across a narrow peninsula jutting out 60 miles into Lake Michigan. Despite considerable crowds in summer and increasing numbers of wealthy newcomers, development has remained essentially low-key and the atmosphere retains a certain highbrow gentility.

Visitors usually make a loop around the peninsula on its two highways. Hwy 57 runs beside Lake Michigan, and goes through Jacksonport and Bailey's Harbor. Hwy 42 borders Green Bay and passes through (from south to north) Egg Harbor, Fish Creek, Ephraim and Sister Bay. Gills Rock is perched at the peninsula's tip, decorated by a string of islands. No public buses serve the peninsula, and not much stays open from November to April.

The most attractive part of the loop begins at **Sturgeon Bay**, the peninsula's main town. As you enter it stop at the knowledgeable **Chamber of Commerce** (☎ 920-743-4456; www.doorcounty.com; 1015 Green Bay Rd; ⏲ 8:30am-5pm Mon-Thu, until 8pm Fri, 10am-4pm Sat & Sun mid-May–mid-Oct; 8:30am-4:30pm rest of year); an attached kiosk is accessible 24 hours a day with lodging information and a free phone.

The best accommodation choices are along the Green Bay shoreline. Prices listed are for July and August, the most expensive months; many places fill up early and have minimum-stay requirements. In Ephraim, **Trollhaugen Lodge** (☎ 800-854-4118; www.trollhaugenlodge.com; 10176 Hwy 42; r from $89;) is close to the action and has a hot tub. In Fish Creek, **Julie's Park Cafe and Motel** (☎ 920-868-2999; www.juliesmotel.com; 4020 Hwy 42; r $80-120; meals $7-14;) is tidy and well-run. In Sturgeon Bay, beeline to the **Chal-A-Motel** (☎ 920-743-6788; 3910 Hwy 42/57; r $59;), where you'll share the premises with 1000 Barbie dolls (including Astronaut Barbie), mechanical elves, a DeLorean car and more. Excellent camping and sunset watching are available at **Peninsula State Park** (☎ 920-868-3258; campsites weekday/weekend $8/10, additional $2 for non-Wisconsin residents) by Fish Creek.

Many restaurants have a 'fish boil,' a regional speciality started by Scandinavian lumberjacks, in which whitefish, potatoes and onions are cooked in a cauldron. It's sedate, until the chef douses the flames with kerosene, and then whoosh! A fireball creates the requisite 'boil over' (which gets rid of the fish oil), signaling dinner is ready. Finish with Door's famous cherry pie.

Attractive **Summer Kitchen** (☎ 920-854-2131; Hwy 42, Ephraim; dishes $6-17) serves tasty breakfast, lunch and dinner. At **Shipwrecked** (☎ 920-868-2767; 7791 Egg Harbor Rd; dishes $12-16) you can wash down a good dinner with the house-made brew; try the cheese curds. Also, sample the smoked fish available around Gills Rock.

From the tip of the peninsula, daily ferries (☎ 920-847-2546; Northport Pier; adult round-trip $9, child 6-11 $5, car $20, bike $4) go to **Washington Island**, which has 700 Scandinavian descendants, a couple of museums, beaches, bike rentals and carefree roads for cycling. Accommodations and camping are available. More remote is lovely **Rock Island**, a state park with no cars at all. It's a wonderful place for walking, swimming and camping. Get there via **ferry** (☎ 920-847-2252; Jackson Harbor on Washington I; adult/child round-trip $8/4).

Returning on the peninsula's quiet **east side**, secluded Newport State Park offers trails, camping and solitude. Whitefish Dunes State Park has sandscapes and a wide beach (beware of riptides). At adjacent Cave Point Park, watch the waves explode into the caves beneath the shoreline cliffs.

NORTHERN WISCONSIN

The north is a thinly populated region of forests and lakes, appreciated for camping and fishing in summer, skiing and snowmobiling in winter. Scenic Hwy 70 cuts east–west. The entire region has abundant mom-and-pop motels, resorts and rental cottages.

Northwoods & Lakelands

Nicolet National Forest is a vast, wooded district ideal for outdoor activities.

The simple crossroads of **Langlade** is a center for white-water river adventures. **Bear Paw Outdoor Resort** (☎ 715-882-3502; 3494 Hwy 55) provides trips and accommodations. Tiny **Laona**, on Hwy 8 in the middle of the forest, has a **hostel** (☎ 715-674-2615; Hwy 8; dm $15) that makes a good base for exploring; canoes are rented here.

In **Lac du Flambeau**, stop at the **Ojibwe Museum & Cultural Center** (☎ 715-588-3333; 603 Peace Pipe Rd; adult $3, child 5-15 $2; 🕑 10am-4pm Mon-Sat May-Oct, 10am-2pm Tue-Thu Nov-Apr), or, out of town on the reservation, visit **Waswagoning** (☎ 715-588-2615; adult $7, child 5-12 $5; 🕑 10am-4pm Tue-Sat, mid-Jun–Aug), a re-creation of a traditional Ojibwe village.

Apostle Islands

Wisconsin ends at the rugged, glaciated littoral of awesome Lake Superior, fringed by a sprinkling of unspoiled islands.

Access to the emerald Apostle Islands is from **Bayfield**, a humming (and growing) resort town with narrow, hilly streets, Victorian-era buildings, and lake and island vistas. The **Chamber of Commerce** (☎ 715-779-3335; www.bayfield.org; 42 Broad St; 🕑 8:30-5pm Mon-Fri) has an attached visitors center, accessible at all times, with lodging information and a free phone. Storefront outfitters renting kayaks and bikes are easily found throughout town.

Tree Top House (☎ 715-779-3293; treetop@cheqnet.net; 225 N 4th St; r $40-60) A delightful B&B.

Seagull Bay Motel (☎ 715-779-5558; www.seagullbay.com; cnr 7th St & Hwy 13; s/d $60/70, reduced mid-Oct–mid-May) Most rooms at Seagull Bay have decks.

Old Rittenhouse Inn (☎ 800-779-2129; www.rittenhouseinn.com; 301 Rittenhouse Ave; r $99-299). By far the classiest and most expensive accommodations.

The **Big Top Chautauqua** (☎ 888-244-8368; call for schedule & prices) is a major regional summer event with big-name concerts and musical theater.

Before exploring the 21 islands of **Apostle Islands National Lakeshore**, drop by the **visitors center** (☎ 715-779-3397; 410 Washington Ave; 🕑 8am-4:30pm, until 6pm summer). Campers can pick up the required camping permit here (the permit is $15 no matter how long you stay). The islands have no facilities, and walking is the only way to get around. Various companies offer seasonal charter, sailing and ferry trips to and around the islands, and kayaking is very popular. **Apostle Islands Cruise Service** (☎ 715-779-3925; adult $26, child 6-12 $15; 🕑 10am mid-May–mid-Oct), departing from Bayfield's City Dock, offers a three-hour narrated trip past sea caves and lighthouses. Other trips call at islands to drop off/pick up campers and their kayaks, which avoids the long, possibly rough paddle.

Inhabited **Madeline Island**, a fine day trip, is also reached by ferry (☎ 715-747-2051; adult round-trip $8, child 6-11 $4, car $18.50, bike $3.50) from Bayfield. Its walkable village of La Pointe has some mid-priced places to stay and varying restaurants for a nosh. There's a **visitors center** (☎ 715-747-2801, 888-475-3386; www.madelineisland.com; Middle Rd; 🕑 8am-4pm Mon-Sat mid-May–mid-Oct, 9am-3pm Mon, Wed & Fri mid-Oct–mid-May) and a **historical museum** (☎ 715-747-2415; adult $5.50, child 5-12 $2.75; 🕑 10am-5pm late May–early Oct) with fur-trade exhibits. Bus tours are available, and bikes and mopeds can be rented. **Big Bay State Park** (☎ 715-747-6425; campsites resident/non-resident $8/10) has a beach and trails.

Along Highway 13

This is a fine drive around the Lake Superior shore, past the Ojibwa community of **Red Cliff** and the mainland segment of the Apostle Islands National Lakeshore, which has a beach. Tiny **Cornucopia**, looking like a seaside village, has great sunsets. The road runs on through a timeless countryside of forest and farm reaching US 2 for the final miles into Superior.

MINNESOTA

Minnesota is known as the land of 10,000 lakes, and it offers the intrepid visitor almost as many things to do. Outdoor enthusiasts will want to wet their paddles in the spectacular wilderness of the Boundary Waters Canoe Area. Those seeking high culture will find it in the Twin Cities of Minneapolis and St Paul, where the number of performance venues per capita is second only to New York City. The pine-filled north boasts exceptional forests, fishing and the Mississippi

MINNESOTA FACTS

Nicknames The North Star State, The Gopher State
Population 5,019,720 (21st)
Area 86,943 sq miles (12th)
Admitted to Union May 11, 1858 (32nd)
Capital city St Paul (population 287,200)
Other cities Minneapolis (382,600; Twin Cities metro area 2.4 million), Duluth (86,900)
Birthplace of author F Scott Fitzgerald (1896–1940), actress Judy Garland (1922–69), cartoonist Charles Schultz (1922–2000), songwriter Bob Dylan (b 1941), filmmakers Joel Coen (b 1954) and Ethan Coen (b 1957)
Famous for the Greyhound bus line, whelped in Hibbing in the 1930s

River headwaters. It's wildly different from the sparse, raw beauty of the Iron Range or the gritty, freighter-filled port of Duluth. To see it all, give multifaceted Minnesota a lengthy stopover.

Note that in 'Minnesnowta' (as residents sometimes call it), the white stuff can fall into May.

History

The Eastern Sioux were the primary inhabitants when the first French trappers arrived in the 17th century. Starting in the early 18th century, Ojibwa bands (also called Chippewa) moved into northeast Minnesota and, armed with guns traded by the French, pushed the Sioux southwest onto the prairie.

The area east of the Mississippi River became part of the US Northwest Territory in 1787, and the area west of the Mississippi was acquired from France in the 1803 Louisiana Purchase. Timber was the territory's first boom industry, and soon water-powered sawmills arose at Minneapolis, St Paul and Stillwater. Wheat from the prairies also needed to be processed, and the first flour mills were built along the river in the 1820s.

Shortly after admission to the Union, Minnesota became the first state to send volunteers to fight the Civil War, but in 1862 an uprising of the displaced Sioux meant a series of bloody battles at home.

The population boomed in the 1880s, with mass immigration (especially from Scandinavia), development of the iron mines and expansion of the railroads. Since the 1920s, depleted forests and larger farms have meant a declining rural population, but industry and urban areas have grown steadily.

Information

Minnesota highway information (☎ 800-542-0220; www.511mn.org)
Minnesota Office of Tourism (☎ 800-657-3700; www.exploreminnesota.com; 121 E 7th Pl, St Paul, MN 55101)

Minnesota's state sales tax is 6.5%, with municipalities adding up to 1% more.

National & State Parks

Minnesota state park information (☎ 866-857-2757; www.dnr.state.mn.us/state_parks) Campground reservations accepted. Park entry requires a vehicle permit ($7/25 day/year for both residents and nonresidents).

MINNEAPOLIS-ST PAUL

The sprawling Twin Cities have distinct personalities – 'Minny' is brash and bustling, its downtown filled with tall, glassy buildings; St Paul is quiet and dignified, lorded over by the massive old Cathedral. Together they represent pure US heartland – industrious, prosperous and friendly – the kind of place where the bus drivers tell everyone to 'Have a nice day,' rain or shine (or snow). The Twin Cities are renowned for their arts scene, and are endowed with more theaters, dance companies and concert venues per person than anywhere outside New York City.

History

Belgian missionary Louis Hennepin preached to local Native Americans in 1680. Zebulon Pike explored the upper reaches of the Mississippi in 1804, a year after the USA acquired the region in the Louisiana Purchase. Fort Snelling, the most remote outpost of the USA's Northwest Territory, was built in 1820.

Power harnessed from the St Anthony waterfall in the mid-19th century enabled Minneapolis to process wheat from the prairies and timber from the north, and the city's growth spurt began. Today St Paul's German-Irish-Catholic heritage is evident, whereas Minneapolis is more Nordic.

Orientation

The Twin Cities form a metropolis on both sides of the generally hidden Mississippi River. On the west side, downtown Minneapolis – the heart of the two cities – is a modern grid of high-rise buildings, many linked by a series of enclosed overhead walkways called 'Skyways' (very welcome in winter). Downtown St Paul is 10 miles to the east on I-94.

Suburbs extend in every direction, and are interspersed with lakes and parks; to explore the outlying areas you really need a car. Downtown parking is costly and scarce.

Note that in Minneapolis, the directional street designations come after the street name (eg 7th St S). In St Paul, they come before (eg W 5th St).

Information

Greater Minneapolis-St Paul has multiple telephone area codes. To call from one to another, dial the area code and the seven-digit telephone number, without the preceding one or two.

BOOKSTORES

Booksmart (☎ 612-823-5612; 2914 Hennepin Ave S) In Uptown.

Ruminator (☎ 651-699-0587; 1648 Grand Ave) In St Paul.

EMERGENCY

Emergency number (☎ 911) Police, ambulance, fire.

Victim crisis line (☎ 612-340-5400)

INTERNET ACCESS

Minneapolis Public Library (☎ 612-630-6000; 250 Marquette Ave) Temporary quarters while a new library is being built.

PC Palace (☎ 612-378-3144; 2529 University Ave SE; $5/hr) One of many internet places near the university.

INTERNET RESOURCES

www.minneapolis.org A hip and easy-to-navigate site with maps, coupons and other goodies.

www.visitstpaul.com Along the same lines as www.minneapolis.org.

MEDIA

The *Star Tribune* is the local daily. *City Pages* and *Pulse* are weekly entertainment freebies.

KNOW-FM 91.1 broadcasts NPR, while KZNE-FM 105.3 provides pleasing sounds for alternative music listeners.

MEDICAL SERVICES

Fairview University Medical Center (☎ 612-273-6402; 2450 Riverside Ave, Minneapolis)

Walgreens (☎ 612-789-6251; 2643 Central Ave NE) Twenty-four-hour pharmacy.

MONEY

The airport and Mall of America have currency exchange facilities.

Wells Fargo Bank (☎ 612-667-7990; cnr 6th St S & Marquette Ave, Minneapolis) Has a foreign exchange as well as ATM and regular bank services.

POST

Main post office (☎ 800-275-8777; 100 1st S) In Minneapolis by the river.

MINNEAPOLIS-ST PAUL IN...

Two Days

Spend the first day in Minneapolis. Visit the **Walker Art Center** and outstanding **Sculpture Garden**. Walk the trail by **St Anthony Falls,** the power source of the timber and flour mills that gave rise to the city. Have dinner and drinks in Uptown, a hip punk-yuppie neighborhood. Still feeling frisky? Find a noisy rock club (the city is filled with them). The second day is for St Paul. The castle-like **Landmark Center** houses the **Minnesota Museum of American Art** and the **Schubert Club's** gallery of old pianos. Peek in St Paul Cathedral, then stroll by the mansions of the **Summit-Selby** neighborhood, F Scott Fitzgerald's old stomping grounds. Take a break at **Grand Avenue's** restaurants. Spend the evening at one of the Twin Cities myriad theaters.

Four Days

Follow the two-day itinerary. On your third day rent a bike and explore the city's parks and lakes, such as Calhoun, Cedar or Harriet. You can't put it off any longer: on day four, shop at the **Mall of America**, the country's largest. Pretend you only stopped there en route to historical **Ft Snelling** or the old mill city of **Stillwater**.

TOURIST OFFICES

Minneapolis visitors center (☎ 612-335-5827; cnr Nicollet Mall & 7th St S; 🕑 10am-7pm Mon-Fri, 10am-6pm Sat, noon-5pm Sun) In the city center.

St Paul visitors center (☎ 651-265-4900, 800-627-6101; 175 W Kellogg Blvd, suite 502; 🕑 8am-4:30pm Mon-Fri) In the RiverCentre.

Sights

Most attractions are closed Monday; many stay open late Thursday. **Arts & Museum Pass** (☎ 888-676-6757; adult $20, child 12 & under $16) provides discount admission to 12 museums.

MINNEAPOLIS

The 1st-class **Walker Art Center** (☎ 612-375-7622; 725 Vineland Pl; adult $6, child 12-18 $4, free Thu; 🕑 10am-5pm Tue-Sat, until 9pm Thu, 11am-5pm Sun) has a strong permanent collection of 20th-century art and photography, including big-name US painters and great US pop art. The expanding center also has performance spaces and temporary exhibitions.

Beside the Walker is the seven-acre **Minneapolis Sculpture Garden** (admission free; 🕑 6am-noon), studded with imaginative contemporary works like the oft-photographed spoon and cherry. The garden is connected to attractive Loring Park by a sculptural pedestrian bridge over I-94.

The **St Anthony Falls Heritage Trail** (on the north edge of downtown at the foot of Portland Ave) is a recommended 2-mile path that provides both interesting history (markers dot the route)

and the city's best access to the banks of the Mississippi. View the cascading falls from the car-free Stone Arch Bridge. On the north side of the river, Main St SE has a stretch of redeveloped buildings housing restaurants and bars.

The new **Mill City Museum** (☎ 612-341-7555; 704 2nd St S; adult $7, child 4-17 $4; 🕑 10am-5pm Tue-Sat, noon-5pm Sun) is a paean to the era when Minneapolis led the world in flour milling. It's housed in an old mill, and offerings include a ride inside an eight-story grain elevator ('the Flour Tower') and a baking lab.

The **Minneapolis Institute of Arts** (☎ 612-870-3131; 2400 3rd Ave S; admission free; 🕑 10am-5pm Tue-Sat, until 9pm Thu, 11am-5pm Sun) houses a veritable history of art, especially European. There's also a colorful Tibetan *thangka* gallery.

Within a mile or two of downtown, a ring of lakes circles the inner-city area. Cedar Lake, Lake of the Isles, Lake Calhoun and Lake Harriet are surrounded by parks and comfortable suburbs. Cycling paths (cross-country ski trails in winter) meander around the lakes, where you can go boating in summer or ice-skating in winter. **Wirth Park**, just west of downtown, has the full gamut. **Thomas Beach**, on Lake Calhoun, is popular for swimming; for bicycling and canoeing, see Activities, p435. Also visit **Minnehaha Park**, 6 miles south of downtown, to view the falls made famous by Longfellow's epic poem *Hiawatha*, though Longfellow

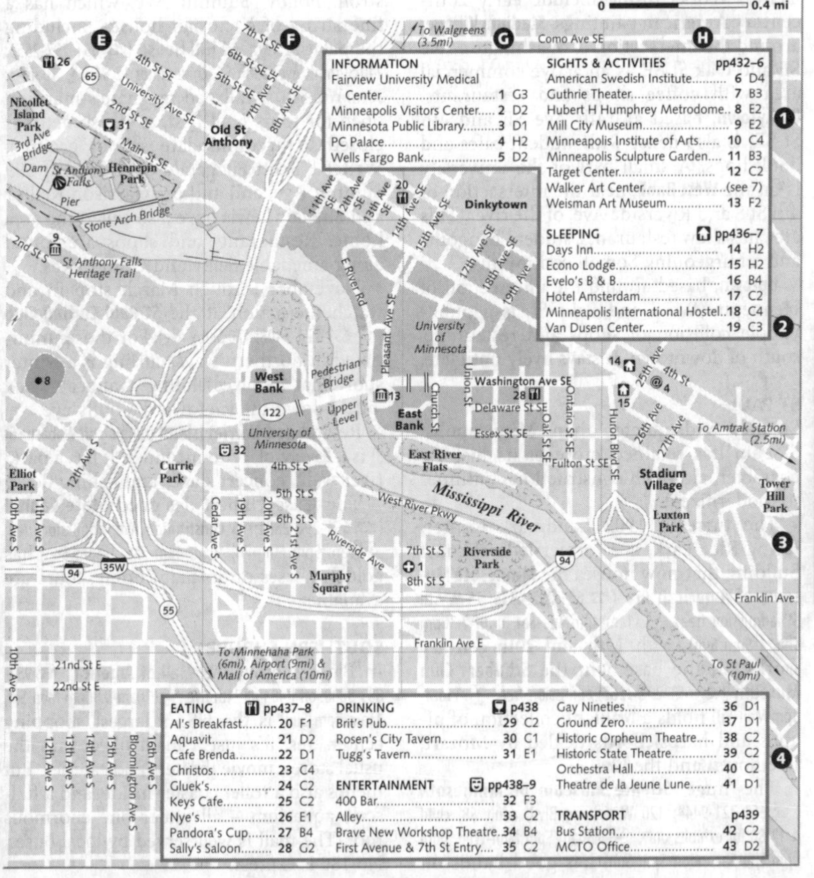

never actually visited. Call the **Parks Board** (☎ 612-661-4875) for recreation information.

The **American Swedish Institute** (☎ 612-871-4907; 2600 Park Ave S; adult $5, child 6-18 $3; noon-4pm Tue-Sat, until 8pm Wed, 1-5pm Sun) is a superb Romanesque mansion with artifacts and antiques from the time when Minneapolis had a bigger Swedish population than most cities in Sweden.

The **University of Minnesota**, by the river southeast of the center, is one of the USA's largest campuses, with over 50,000 students. Most of the campus is in the **East Bank** neighborhood. A highlight is the **Weisman Art Museum** (☎ 612-625-9494; 333 E River Rd; admission free; 10am-5pm Tue-Fri, until 9pm Thu, 11am-5pm Sat-Sun), occupying an angular, irregular, stainless-steel structure by architect Frank Gehry. Works inside include early 20th-century American paintings. **Stadium Village**, around the intersection of Washington Ave SE and Oak St SE, is an active commercial area with coffee shops and restaurants. **Dinkytown**, based at 14th Ave SE and 4th St SE, is also dense with student cafés and bookshops. A small part of the university is on the **West Bank**, near the intersection of 4th St S and Riverside Ave, of the river. This area has a few restaurants, student hangouts and a burgeoning Somali community.

Uptown, based around the intersection of Hennepin Ave S and Lake St, is a punk-yuppie collision of shops and restaurants south of downtown. It stays lively until late.

GREAT LAKES

ST PAUL

Smaller and quieter than Minneapolis, St Paul has retained more of its historic character, although construction continues to modernize it.

The turreted 1902 Landmark Center, facing Rice Park, is a former federal court building that now houses the **Minnesota Museum of American Art** (☎ 651-292-4355; 75 W 5th St; admission free; 11am-4pm Tue-Sat, until 7:30pm Thu, 1-5pm Sun), with 19th and 20th century works. In the basement the **Schubert Club Museum** (☎ 651-292-3267; admission free; 11am-3pm Mon-Fri) holds a brilliant collection of pianos and harpsichords tickled by Mozart, Beethoven and the like.

The huge **Science Museum of Minnesota** (☎ 651-221-9444; 120 W Kellogg Blvd; adult $8, child 4-12 $6 for exhibits only; 9:30am-5pm Mon-Wed, until 9pm Thu-Sat, noon-5pm Sun) has good hands-on exhibits, a Mississippi display, a laser show and the usual Omnimax theater. Best of all is the wacky quackery displayed in the 'questionable medical devices' on the fourth level.

The **Minnesota History Center** (☎ 651-296-6126; 345 W Kellogg Blvd; admission free; 10am-8pm Tue, 10am-3pm Wed-Fri, 10am-5pm Sat, noon-5pm Sun) caters to serious researchers but has excellent public exhibits on native peoples and state history. The Coolest interactive exhibit is the one where you are 'on the line' in a meat packing plant and canning plastic pigs feet.

The gorgeous **Cathedral of St Paul** (☎ 651-228-1766; 239 Selby Ave; 7am-5:30pm) presides over the city from its hilltop perch and marks the attractive **Summit-Selby neighborhood**. This wealthy 19th-century district, now ethnically mixed, is well worth a stroll. Follow Summit Ave, which has a fine string of Victorian houses, including the palatial **James J Hill House** (☎ 651-297-2555; 240 Summit Ave; adult $6, child under 12 $4; 10am-3:30pm Wed-Sat), a railroad magnate's mansion open for tours (call first, as it's sometimes closed to accommodate school groups). Writer F Scott Fitzgerald once lived at 599 Summit Ave, and authors Garrison Keillor and Sinclair Lewis have also called the area home. Restaurants and shops are found along amenable Selby and Grand Aves.

November through March stop in and watch the action at the **St Paul Curling Club** (☎ 651-224-7408; 470 Selby Ave). For those uninitiated in northern ways, curling is a winter sport that involves sliding a hubcab-sized 'puck' down the ice toward a bulls-eye.

Revitalized **Harriet Island** (running off Wabasha St S) is a lovely place to meander; it has a park, river walk, concert stages and fishing dock.

The Cass Gilbert-designed **State Capitol** (☎ 651-296-2881; 75 Constitution Ave; admission free; 9am-5pm Mon-Fri, 10am-4pm Sat, 1-4pm Sun) has golden horses on its giant dome; tours are available.

SOUTHERN SUBURBS

In Bloomington, the **Mall of America** (☎ 952-883-8800; off I-494 at 24th Ave; 10am-9:30pm Mon-Sat, 11am-7pm Sun) is the USA's largest shopping center. Yes, it's just a mall, filled with the usual stores, movie theaters and eateries. But there's also a roller coaster inside, and a full-scale aquarium – all under one enormous roof. The mall is well-served by local buses; No 180 is express.

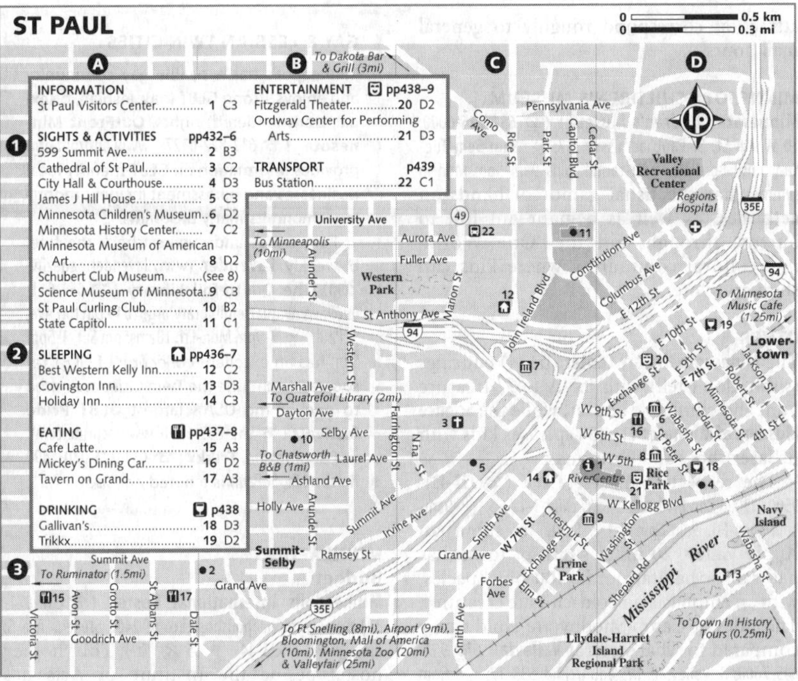

Just east of the mall, **Fort Snelling** (☎ 612-726-1171; adult/child 6-12 $8/4; ⌚ 10am-5pm Wed-Sat, noon-5pm Sun mid-Jun–early Sep, Sat & Sun only mid-Apr–mid-Jun & Sep-Oct) is the state's oldest structure, established in the early 19th century as a frontier outpost in the remote Northwest Territory. Guides in period dress show restored buildings and displays of pioneer life.

Activities

The parks around the Twin Cities and lakes offer plenty of ways to stay active, summer or winter.

BICYCLING

The parks are crisscrossed with bike paths. Get wheels at **Calhoun Rental** (☎ 612-827-8231; 1622 W Lake St; bicycle hire $7.50/hr; ⌚ 10am-7pm Apr-Oct, extended hours in summer) in Uptown; credit card and driver's license required.

CANOEING

Lake Calhoun is a wonderful place to paddle away the day, and the **Minneapolis Park and Recreation Board** (☎ 612-370-4883; 3000 E Calhoun Parkway; canoe/kayak per hour $8/8; ⌚ 11am-7pm daily late May–early Sep, 11am-6pm Sat & Sun early Sep-Oct) rents a slew of vessels.

Minneapolis-St Paul for Children

The Twin Cities have several children's attractions, some more educational than others.

MALL OF AMERICA

Prepare to spend a wad once you unleash the kids at the country's largest **Mall** (see opposite) They will want to make a beeline to **Camp Snoopy** (☎ 952-883-8555), the much-touted indoor amusement park. It has 25 rides including a little roller coaster. To walk through is free; a one-day, unlimited-ride wristband is $24, or you can pay for rides individually ($2 to $5). Also in the mall is **Cereal Adventure** (☎ 952-814-2900; admission free), compliments of local purveyor General Mills, with interactive cereal-making exhibits and the opportunity to get your picture on a box of Wheaties.

Underwater Adventures (☎ 952-883-0202; adult $14, child 13-17 $12, child 3-12 $8) is the state's largest aquarium, where children can touch sharks and stingrays. The hours for each attraction correspond roughly to general mall hours.

MINNESOTA CHILDREN'S MUSEUM

Minnesota Children's Museum (☎ 651-225-6000; 10 W 7th St, St Paul; admission $7; 🕑 9am-5pm Tue-Sun, until 8pm Thu year-round, plus 9am-5pm Mon in summer) has the usual gamut of hands-on activities, as well as a giant ant hill to burrow through and the 'One World' intercultural community where kids can shop and vote.

OTHER

The **Minnesota History Center** (p434) educates (shhh, don't tell) with its 'A to Z' treasure hunt and climbable boxcar, while the **Science Museum of Minnesota** (p434) pleases kids with its laser show and Omnimax.

The respected **Minnesota Zoo** (☎ 952-431-9500; 13000 Zoo Blvd; adult $11, child 3-12 $6; 🕑 9am-4pm Mon-Fri, 9am-6pm Sat & Sun), in suburban Apple Valley, 20 miles south of town, has naturalistic habitats for its 400-plus species, with an emphasis on cold-climate creatures. The rides at Camp Snoopy are child's play compared to what's out at **Valleyfair** (☎ 952-445-7600; 1 Valleyfair Dr; adult/child $33/17; 🕑 from 10am daily Jun-Aug, Sat & Sun May & Sep, closing times vary), a full-scale amusement park 25 miles southwest in Shakopee.

Tours

RiverCity Trolley (☎ 612-378-7000; various pick-up locations; adult $10, child 12 & under $5; tours 10am-4pm Tue-Sun, early May–late Oct) is a vintage-looking street car that tools around Minneapolis and its environs.

Down In History Tours (☎ 651-292-1220; 215 S Wabasha St; tours $5; tours 5pm Thu, 11am Sat) walks you through St Paul's underground caves that gangsters once used as a speakeasy.

Festivals & Events

St Paul Winter Carnival (☎ 651-223-4700; www.winter-carnival.com) Ten days of ice sculptures, ice skating and ice fishing in January.

Minneapolis Aquatennial (☎ 612-376-7669; www.aquatennial.org) Ten days celebrating the ubiquitous lakes in mid-July.

Sleeping

Room costs range toward the high end in summer. The 13% tax is not included in the following prices.

GAY & LESBIAN TWIN CITIES

Minneapolis has a sizable gay community and enjoys strong GLBT (gay, lesbian, bisexual, transgendered) rights. **OutFront Minnesota** (☎ 612-822-0127; www.outfront.org) provides information on GLBT-friendly local businesses and harassment incident reporting, among its many programs.

For venues and events, check the free, bi-weekly **Lavender** (www.lavendermagazine.com). The **Quatrefoil Library** (☎ 651-641-0969; www.quatrefoillibrary.org; 1619 Dayton Ave, St Paul; 🕑 7-9pm Mon-Fri, 10am-5pm Sat, 1-5pm Sun) has an excellent collection of GLBT resources. Each June the Twin Cities are home to one of the USA's largest **GLBT Pride festivals** (☎ 952-852-6100; www.tcpride.com).

For nightlife, **Trikkx** (☎ 651-224-0703; 490 N Robert St, St Paul) is a noted hot spot.

MINNEAPOLIS

Budget

Minneapolis International Hostel (☎ 612-871-3210; www.minneapolishostel.com; 2400 Stevens Ave S; dm $19-24, r $25-44; P $5 ✖ 💻) This homey hostel beside the Institute of Arts has antique furniture, wood floors and fluffy quilts on the beds. The building recently came under new management, so some things may change. Reservations recommended; $10 key deposit.

Hotel Amsterdam (☎ 612-288-0459; 828 Hennepin Ave; r $44-65; 💻) The Amsterdam is a busy, European-style, gay-friendly hotel located above a bar downtown. The rooms are utilitarian but clean, and all share a bath.

Mid-Range

Econo Lodge (☎ 612-331-6000; 2500 University Ave SE; r $55-130; P ✖) The rooms here are more than decent, and the price includes continental breakfast, making it the best value in the university area. It's located near the Washington and Oak St restaurant cluster, and a 10-minute bus ride from downtown.

Evelo's B&B (☎ 612-374-9656; sevelo@mpls.k12.mn.us; 2301 Bryant Ave; s/d $55/70; ✖) Evelo's is in a quiet neighborhood between the Walker Art Center and Uptown. The Victorian home has beautiful woodwork, lots of windows and light and comfy rooms.

Days Inn (☎ 612-623-3999; 2407 University Ave SE; r $59-119; P ✖) This is a high-end Days Inn that often caters to people in town for events (when prices move to the upper end of the spectrum).

Lots of motels lie south of town, around I-494 near the airport.

Top End

Van Dusen Center (☎ 612-874-1900; www.vandusencenter.com; 1900 LaSalle Ave; r weekday/weekend $129/149; P) The Van Dusen offers gracious rooms in an 1892 mansion, walkable to downtown.

ST PAUL

Mid-Range

Chatsworth B&B (☎ 651-227-4288; www.chatsworth-bb.com; 984 Ashland Ave; r $99-169; P) Sweetly situated in a Summit-area Victorian house dating from 1902, Chatsworth has serene gardens, cozy rooms and is near Grand Ave's restaurants.

Holiday Inn (☎ 651-225-1515; 174 W 7th St; r $79-169; P $9) Adjacent to the RiverCentre.

Best Western Kelly Inn (☎ 651-227-8711; 161 St Anthony Ave; r from $89; P) Near the capitol.

Top End

Covington Inn (☎ 651-292-1411; www.covingtoninn.com; Pier 1, Harriet Island; r Apr-Oct $150-235, less in winter; P) This charming B&B is on a tugboat floating in the Mississippi River, where you can watch the river traffic glide by while sipping your morning coffee. It's located across from St Paul's city center.

Eating

Lots of fun, good-value options exist in both cities.

MINNEAPOLIS

Areas dense with restaurants include Nicollet Mall downtown; Nicollet Ave S between 14th and 29th Sts (otherwise known as 'Eat Street') lined with Vietnamese, Mexican and other ethnic eateries; and the campus area by Washington Ave and Oak St.

Downtown

Cafe Brenda (☎ 612-342-9230; 300 1st Ave N; dishes $13-17; Mon-Sat) Brenda serves fresh seafood and gourmet vegetarian meals like mock duck tacos; beer and wine complement the menu nicely.

Keys Cafe (☎ 612-339-6399; 1007 Nicollet Mall; dishes $4-10) Bustling Keys, a local chain, dishes up luscious breakfasts and sandwiches; try the caramel rolls.

Gluek's (☎ 612-338-6621; 16 6th St N; dishes $7-16) Pot roast, walleye, macaroni-and-cheese with spaetzle and other good meals have emerged from the Gluek's German kitchen since 1902.

Aquavit (☎ 612-343-3333; 80 8th St S, in IDS Bldg; dishes $20-31) It's one of the few Swedish fine-dining restaurants this side of the fjords. The menu changes frequently, but fish, seafood and game often are the focus.

Uptown

Pandora's Cup (☎ 612-381-0700; 2516 Hennepin Ave S; sandwiches $4-6) Pandora's is situated in a big, rambling house run by pierced, pink-haired people who make damn good coffee (and sandwiches).

Chino Latino (☎ 612-824-7878; 2916 Hennepin Ave S; shared dishes $14-26; dinner daily, brunch Sun) The spangles hanging from the building's front hint at the fun inside. The food is Latin-Asian fusion, with novelties such as a satay bar and the large, shared *pupu* (Polynesian-influenced appetizer) platter.

Figlio's (☎ 612-822-1688; 3001 Hennepin Ave S; dishes $7-19) This Italian-American bistro has a constant stream of fashionable patrons, providing classic people-watching; it's open late nightly.

Other

Nye's (☎ 612-379-2021; 112 E Hennepin Ave; dishes $13-20) Nye's serves traditional Polish foods like pierogi and spare ribs, but the real draw is the dancing from Thursday through Saturday with the World's Most Dangerous Polka Band. Look out.

Christos (☎ 612-871-2111; 2632 Nicollet Ave S; dishes $10-14) Popular Christos is reminiscent of a Greek taverna, with moussaka, souvlakia

> **THE AUTHOR'S CHOICE**
>
> **Al's Breakfast** (☎ 612-331-9991; 413 14th Ave SE; dishes $3-6; until early afternoon only) It's the ultimate hole in the wall: 15 stools at a tiny counter. Whenever a customer comes in, everyone picks up their plates and scoots down to make room for the newcomer. The grease-encrusted stove tells you how much food has been lovingly cooked here; fruit-full pancakes are the big crowd-pleaser.

GREAT LAKES

and all the staples; lots of vegetarian options, too.

Sally's Saloon (☎ 612-331-3231; 712 Washington Ave SE; dishes $8-9) An East Bank campus favorite, Sally's serves burgers, spicy meats and beer inside or on the patio.

ST PAUL

Grand Ave between Dale and Victoria Sts is a worthy browse, with Ethiopian, Greek, Mexican and other eateries in close proximity.

Mickey's Dining Car (☎ 651-222-5633; 36 W 7th St; dishes $3-7) Mickey's is a downtown classic, the kind of place where the waitress calls you 'honey' and regulars line the bar with their coffee cups and newspapers. The food is timeless, too: burgers, malts and apple pie, available 24 hours a day.

Tavern on Grand (☎ 651-228-9030; 656 Grand Ave; dishes $6-17) The unpretentious Tavern is famous for its good-value walleye meals.

Cafe Latte (☎ 651-224-5687; 850 Grand Ave; dishes $5-6) This large and sleek spot is a fine place to indulge in soups, sandwiches, pastries and coffees.

Drinking

Brit's Pub (☎ 612-332-3908; 1110 Nicollet Mall) It's not every day you go to a drinking establishment with a lawn bowling green on its roof: there's a large selection of Scotch, port and beer to boot.

Rosen's City Tavern (☎ 612-338-1926; 430 1st Ave N) This is one of many busy places in Minneapolis' Warehouse District that pours a fine brew.

Tugg's Tavern (☎ 612-379-4404; 219 Main St SE) Tugg's draw is its swell outdoor patio on the Mississippi River's revitalized northside strip.

Entertainment

With its large student population and thriving performing arts scene, the Twin Cities offer an active nightlife. **TC Tix** (☎ 612-288-2060; in the Minneapolis visitors center, see p432) provides same-day discounts.

CINEMAS

Uptown Theatre (☎ 612-825-6006; 2906 Hennepin Ave S) Catch art-house flicks here.

DANCE CLUBS

Gay Nineties (☎ 612-333-7755; 408 Hennepin Ave) There's dancing, dining, drag shows and both a gay and straight clientele at Gay Nineties.

Ground Zero (☎ 612-378-5115; 15 4th St NE) This long-standing spot gets a mixed gay and straight dance crowd for recorded music. Cover charges range from nil to $5.

LIVE MUSIC

Acts such as Prince and proto-grunge bands like Hüsker Dü and the Replacements cut their chops here.

400 Bar (☎ 612-332-2903; 400 Cedar Ave S) For live rock, funk and alternative, check out 400 Bar.

First Avenue & 7th St Entry (☎ 612-338-8388; 701 1st Ave N) The Purple Rain band once featured here and it still gets top bands and big crowds.

Alley (☎ 612-333-1327; 15 N Glenwood Ave) Good blues prevails at the Alley.

Minnesota Music Cafe (☎ 651-776-4699; 499 Payne Ave, St Paul) Local musicians like this café.

Dakota Bar & Grill (☎ 651-642-1442; 1021 E Bandana Blvd, St Paul) Dakota is a well-established jazz and dinner club on the outskirts of St Paul that regularly gets name acts.

PERFORMING ARTS

The Twin Cities are applauded for their range of performing arts companies, including dozens of fine theater troupes, dance companies and classical music groups. For listings, see the local print media (p431). In particular, look for events at the following venues (all in 'Mini-Apple' unless otherwise noted):

Brave New Workshop Theatre (☎ 612-332-6620; 2605 Hennepin Ave) An established venue for musical comedy, revue and satire.

Fitzgerald Theater (☎ 651-290-1221; 10 E Exchange St, St Paul) Where Garrison Keillor tapes his *Prairie Home Companion* radio show.

Guthrie Theater (☎ 612-377-2224; 725 Vineland Place) Quality classical and contemporary performances; moving to the Mills District riverfront in spring 2005.

Historic Orpheum Theatre (☎ 612-339-7007; 910 Hennepin Ave) The usual venue for Broadway shows and touring acts.

Historic State Theatre (☎ 612-339-7007; 805 Hennepin Ave) Also hosts Broadway shows and touring acts.

Orchestra Hall (☎ 612-371-5656; 1111 Nicollet Mall) Superb acoustics, a great venue for recitals and concerts by the acclaimed Minnesota Symphony Orchestra.

Ordway Center for Performing Arts (☎ 651-224-4222; 345 Washington St, St Paul) A chamber music venue and home of the Minnesota State Opera.

TALKING MINNESOTAN

There is and isn't a Minnesota accent or dialect. Despite popular misconceptions and the influence of films such as *Fargo* (just across the border in North Dakota), you can't really define a single local speech type. But...there is a sort of in-joke language variation that residents employ for effect and humor based on the preceding generations of Swedes and Norwegians and *their* English. And there are expressions used regularly you don't hear much elsewhere such as *alrighty, doncha know, you betcha* and *hokey dokey* that add a homey, casual flavor to conversation. 'That's different' is often said to avoid disagreement, hurt or insult over an opposite opinion. Best known of all is the wonderful, all-purpose 'uff da,' a Scandinavian term heard in a variety of situations and seen on bumper stickers. It conveys consternation and disgruntlement...but politely, sort of like *oops* or *oy vey*. Give it a try the next time you find a moose sniffing your car or another bird-sized mosquito diving toward your skin.

Theatre de la Jeune Lune (☎ 612-333-6200; 105 1st St N) Features experimental French-American collaborations.

SPECTATOR SPORTS

Hubert H Humphrey Metrodome (900 5th St S), Minneapolis' metrodome, is home to the **Vikings** (☎ 612-338-4537) pro football team and the **Twins** (☎ 612-338-9467) major league baseball team. There's lots of talk about a new or renovated stadium; when it happens remains to be seen.

Target Center (☎ 612-337-3865; 600 1st Ave N) The male **Timberwolves** and female **Lynx** pro basketball teams play at the center.

Xcel Energy Center (☎ 651-222-9453; Kellogg Blvd) NHL hockey has returned with the **Wild** skating in the new in center in St Paul. Football and hockey are usually sold out, but scalpers offer tickets (illegally).

Getting There & Away

AIRPORT

Minneapolis-St Paul International Airport (☎ 612-726-5555; www.mspairport.com) is a major regional hub and home of Northwest Airlines, which operates several direct flights to/from various European cities.

BUS

Greyhound has stations in Minneapolis (☎ 612-371-3323; 950 Hawthorne Ave) and St Paul (☎ 651-222-0509; 166 W University Ave). Buses go frequently to Milwaukee ($52 to $68, 7½ hours) and Chicago ($59 to $80, nine hours).

CAR

National car rental agencies have offices at the airport and around town. Check rental information in the Transport chapter (p1121) for more details.

TRAIN

The **Amtrak station** (☎ 651-644-1127; 730 Transfer Rd), off University Ave SE, is between the Twin Cities. Trains go to Chicago and Seattle daily. The ride east to La Crosse, WI, is beautiful, skirting the Mississippi River and offering multiple eagle sightings.

Getting Around

TO/FROM THE AIRPORT

SuperShuttle (☎ 612-827-7777) links the airport with downtown Minneapolis ($13) and St Paul ($11). Public buses ply the route: No 7 goes to Minneapolis (45 minutes), while No 54D goes to St Paul (30 minutes); the fare is $1.25 to $2.25. A cab costs $25/14 to Minneapolis/St Paul.

By late 2004, a **light-rail line** (☎ 612-215-8200; www.hiawatha-ltr.org) is scheduled to run between the airport and downtown, with fares comparable to buses.

PUBLIC TRANSPORTATION

Metropolitan Council Transit Operations (MCTO; ☎ 612-373-3333) runs clean, frequent and well-used buses throughout the area (fare $1.25, plus 50¢ for express or rush hour buses). Express bus No 94 connects the Twin Cities. A day pass ($6) is available; pick it up with route maps at the downtown **MCTO office** (719 Marquette Ave; 🕑 7:30am-5:30pm Mon-Fri).

TAXI

Yellow Cab (☎ 612-824-4000) Flagfall $2, per mile $1.60.

SOUTHEASTERN MINNESOTA

Some of the scenic southeast can be seen on short drives from the Twin Cities. Better is a loop of a few days' duration, following the rivers and stopping in some of the historic towns and state parks.

A few miles east of St Paul, the **St Croix River** forms the border with Wisconsin. Northeast of the city along US 61, then east on US 8, attractive Taylors Falls marks the upper limit of navigation. Take a walk along the gorge in Interstate Park. Due east of St Paul, on Rte 36, touristy **Stillwater**, on the lower St Croix, is an old logging town with restored 19th-century buildings and river cruises. Larger **Red Wing** to the south on US 61, is a similar but less interesting restored town.

The best part of the **Mississippi Valley** area begins south of here, but on the Wisconsin side – cross the river on US 63 (see Along the Mississippi River p427).

Maiden Rock, on Wisconsin Rte 35 downstream from Red Wing, offers views from its 400ft Indian-legend namesake. A bit further south, a great stretch of Rte 35 edges beside the bluffs around **Stockholm** (population 90).

Continuing south, cross back over the river to **Wabasha**, in Minnesota, which has a historic downtown. The **Arrowhead Bluffs Museum** (☎ 651-565-3829; Hwy 60; admission free; 🕒 10am-6pm May-Dec) holds a collection of Native American artifacts and mounted wildlife. To learn more about the local bald eagles, stop at the **National Eagle Center** (☎ 651-565-4989; 152 Main St; admission free; 🕒 10am-4pm Tue-Sun year-round). Try **Rivertown Cafe** (☎ 651-565-2202; 119 Pembroke St; dinners from $7) for a taste of small-town America.

On the Wisconsin side again, Rte 35 is very scenic heading south to **Alma**, offering superlative views from Buena Vista Park. Cross the river once again further downstream at **Winona**. This former port offers historical exhibits aboard the **Wilkie Steamboat Center** (☎ 507-454-1254; foot of Main St; adult $3, child 6-12 $1; 🕒 10am-4pm Wed-Sun early Jun–early Sep), as well as river cruises from adjacent Levee Park. Landlubbers can enjoy river views from Garvin Heights Park.

Inland and south, the Bluff Country is dotted with limestone bluffs, the southeast corner's main geological feature. **Lanesboro** is a gem and acts as an activity center. Cycling and canoeing are popular. Seven miles westward on County Rd 8 (call for directions), **Old Barn Resort** (☎ 507-467-2512; www.barnresort.com; dm/s/d $18/27/37, campsite/RV site $20/27, Apr–early Nov) is a pastoral hostel cum campground/restaurant/outfitter.

Harmony, south of Lanesboro, is the center of an Amish community, and another welcoming town. Stay at **Selvig House B&B** (☎ 507-886-2200; www.selvighouse.com; 140 Center St E; r $95).

Head north on US 52 to **Rochester**, home of the famed **Mayo Clinic** (☎ 507-284-2511; 200 First St SW), which attracts medical patients and practitioners from around the world. Free morning tours (at 10am weekdays) and a film outline the Mayo brothers' story and describe how the clinic developed its cutting-edge reputation. The extensive art collection, found throughout the complex, ranges from pre-Columbian pottery to Miró and Warhol paintings.

Tiny, touristy **Mantorville**, several miles west of Rochester, was once a stagecoach stop and retains several 1850s-era buildings and its old Opera House. Toward Minneapolis, the pleasant college town of **Northfield** makes a good lunch stop. The Jesse James gang was foiled in a bank robbery here in 1876.

NORTHEASTERN MINNESOTA

Duluth

At the westernmost end of the Great Lakes, Duluth (with its neighbor, Superior, Wisconsin) is one of the busiest ports in the country, sporting over 40 miles of wharf and waterfront. Daniel Du Lhut brokered a peace agreement here in 1679 with the Ojibwa and Sioux nations, which enabled French adventurers to develop the fur trade. Duluth grew as a shipping point for timber and, later, for Minnesota's iron ore.

Duluth's dramatic location (it's built into a cliffside) is an excellent place to see changeable Lake Superior in action. It can shimmer like a cut diamond one minute, then send off ferocious, ice-capped waves the next. Attractions here naturally revolve around the water. Duluth's gritty maritime history, its ships and its shops make it an absorbing place to linger.

The **Endion Station visitors center** (☎ 218-722-4011; www.visitduluth.com; 100 Lake Place Dr; 🕒 8:30am-5pm Mon-Fri year-round) is near the clock tower. A summer **visitors center** (☎ 218-722-6024; 350 Harbor Dr; 🕒 10am-7pm mid-May–Sep, reduced hours in Oct) is in the Duluth Entertainment Convention Center (DECC) opposite the Vista dock.

SIGHTS & ACTIVITIES

The waterfront area is distinctive; mosey along the Lakewalk trail and the Canal

Park/Lake St District. Look for the Aerial Lift Bridge, which rises to let ships through to the port area. The first-rate **Maritime Visitors Center** (☎ 218-727-2497; 600 Lake Ave S; admission free; 🕑 10am-4:30pm Sun-Thu, until 6pm Fri & Sat spring & fall, until 9pm summer, 10:30am-4:30pm Fri-Sun winter) has a great view of the bridge and exhibits on Great Lakes shipping and shipwrecks. Call the **boat-watchers' hotline** (☎ 218-722-6489) to learn when the big ones come and go; 1000 ships a year pass through here.

To continue the nautical theme, walk the **William A Irvin** (☎ 218-722-7876; 350 Harbor Dr; adult $6.75, child 3-12 $4.50; 🕑 10am-4pm May-Oct, until 6pm Fri & Sat in summer), a 610ft Great Lakes freighter. The interesting hour-long tour also includes a look aboard a tug boat. The tug alone costs adult/child $3/2.

The impressive **Great Lakes Aquarium** (☎ 218-740-3474; 353 Harbor Dr; adult $11, child 3-11 $6; 🕑 10am-6pm) is America's only freshwater aquarium. It has exhibits on the Amazon and Africa's Lake Victoria in addition to Lake Superior. If you're grumpy, go look at the otters.

Back toward the city, in the fine old train station, is **The Depot** (☎ 218-727-8025; 506 Michigan St; adult $8.50, child 6-13 $5.25; 🕑 10am-5pm Mon-Sat, 1-5pm Sun year-round, 9:30am-6pm summer). It houses three museums: one for children, one on history and, perhaps of most interest, the Railroad Museum, which holds a good collection of old locomotives. Admission covers all three.

Other sights include **Stora Enso Paper Mills** (☎ 218-722-6024; 100 N Central Ave; admission free; 🕑 Mon, Wed & Fri Jun-Aug), which offers free tours (get tickets at the summer visitors center) and **Glensheen** (☎ 218-726-8910; 3300 London Rd; adult $9.50, child 12-17 $7.50, child 6-11 $4.50; 🕑 9:30am-4pm daily May-Oct, 11am-2pm Fri-Sun Nov-Apr), a grand 39-room Jacobean mansion.

Local tour excursions include lakeside **rail trips** departing The Depot (☎ 218-722-1273; 506 Michigan St; adult/child $10-18/5-12; 🕑 May-Oct, call for schedule) and **lake cruises** from Vista Fleet (☎ 218-722-6218; 323 Harbor Dr; adult/child $10/5; May-Oct, call for schedule). For a spectacular view of the city and harbor (when it's not foggy) get to First United Methodist Church, at the corner of Skyline and Mesaba Aves.

Skiing and snowboarding are the big winter activities, and **Spirit Mountain** (☎ 218-628-2891; 9500 Spirit Mountain Pl; adult per day $45, child 7-12 $35; 🕑 10am-9pm Mon-Fri, 9am-9pm Sat & Sun, mid-Nov–Mar), 10 miles south of Duluth, is the place to go; rentals available. In summer, kayak next to Duluth's freighters with the University of Minnesota Duluth's program (☎ 218-726-6533; kayaks per person $40; 🕑 Fri & Sat Jul-Aug). For swimming (if you dare brave the icy water) follow Lake Ave south across the Aerial Lift Bridge to Minnesota Point – there are 5 miles of public beach on the north side, stretching all the way to Park Point Recreation Area.

SLEEPING

This is a busy place in summer, and lodgings are often full (if so, try Superior).

Voyageur Lakewalk Inn (☎ 218-722-3911, 800-258-3911; www.voyageurlakewalkinn.com; 333 E Superior St; s/d peak weekends $63/68; ⊠) Right downtown with rooftop views, Voyageur Lakewalk Inn is a real find with cozy rooms.

London Rd, east of downtown, has a couple of inexpensive lodging options, like the **Chalet Motel** (☎ 218-728-4238, 800-235-2957; 1801 London Rd; r $45-85; ⊠).

College of St Scholastica (☎ 218-723-6000; 1200 Kenwood Ave; r $30-55) Residence hall rooms are available here in summer and there are two guest rooms all year.

Fitgers Inn (☎ 218-722-8826; www.fitgers.com; 600 E Superior St; cityside/lakeside r from $115/145; ⊠) Occupying a former brewery, Fitger's is an interesting and plush inn.

Spirit Mountain (☎ 218-628-2891; 9500 Spirit Mountain Pl; campsites/RV sites $15/25) Camping is available at Spirit Mountain, 10 miles south of town, where the best sites are the walk-ins.

EATING & DRINKING

The Canal Park waterfront area has eateries of all price ranges in restored commercial spaces. In the **DeWitt-Seitz Marketplace** (394 Lake Ave S), **Taste of Saigon** (☎ 218-727-1598; dishes $6-10) creates scrumptious Vietnamese meals, including vegetarian dishes like mock duck, while **Amazing Grace** (☎ 218-723-0075; sandwiches $3-6) serves sandwiches is a comfortable café with folk music some evenings.

Fitgers Brewhouse & Grill (☎ 218-726-1392; 600 E Superior St; dishes $7-10) Fitgers makes its own beer and has tasty pub fare.

Grandma's Saloon & Grill (☎ 218-727-4192; 522 Lake Ave S; dishes $13-17) Filling down-home favorites, many including the local wild rice, are on offer here.

Check *Ripsaw*, the local entertainment paper, for the music scene low-down.

GETTING THERE & AROUND

From the **Greyhound station** (☎ 218-722-5591; 4426 Grand Ave), several buses go to Minneapolis-St Paul ($23 to $41, three hours) and Milwaukee ($49 to $80, 11 hours).

North Shore

Heading northeast, Hwy 61 (a continuation of Skyline Dr) is a wonderfully scenic strip of pavement along Lake Superior's shore. On its way to the Canadian border, the route passes numerous spectacular state parks, hiking trails (notably the long-distance Superior Hiking Trail) and low-key towns. Lots of weekend and summer traffic makes reservations essential.

Two Harbors has a museum and lighthouse. Just beyond town is the **Houle Information Center** (☎ 218-834-4005; 1330 Hwy 61; 9am-5pm Mon-Sat, until 3pm Sun, reduced hours in winter) with area information.

Route highlights are Split Rock Lighthouse and Palisade Head. About 110 miles from Duluth, agreeable little **Grand Marais** is a good base for exploring Superior National Forest, BWCAW (see below) and the rest of the region. For information on Boundary Waters, visit the **Gunflint Ranger Station** (☎ 218-387-1750; 6am-6pm May-Sep), just south of town. Outfitters rent equipment and organize trips here. The **visitors center** (☎ 218-387-2524; www.grandmarais.com; 13 N Broadway St; 9am-5pm, reduced hours in winter) also is a good resource.

Lodging options include camping, motels and the rambling and resorty **East Bay Hotel** (☎ 800-414-2807; www.eastbayhotel.com; Wisconsin St; r $28-169). Doors away are good eating choices such as the **Gunflint Tavern** (☎ 218-387-1563; 111 Wisconsin St).

Hwy 61 continues to **Grand Portage National Monument**, beside Canada, where the early voyageurs had to carry their canoes around the Pigeon River rapids. This was the center of a far-flung trading empire, and the reconstructed 1788 trading post is well worth seeing. **Isle Royale National Park** in Lake Superior is reached by daily **ferries** (☎ 715-392-2100; www.grand-isle-royale.com; adult one way $36-58, child 11 & under $18-34) from May to October. (The park also is accessible from Michigan; see Isle Royale, p420).

Boundary Waters

From Two Harbors, Hwy 2 runs inland to the legendary BWCAW. This pristine region has more than a thousand lakes and streams in which to dip a paddle. It's possible to go just for the day, but most people opt for at least one night of camping, a wonderfully remote experience where it most likely will be you, the moose who's nuzzling the tent and a sky full of stars. Beginners are welcome, and everyone can get set up with gear from local lodges and outfitters. **Permits** (☎ 877-550-6777; www.bwcaw.org; adult $10, child 17 & under $5, plus $12 reservation fee) are required for overnight stays; day permits, though free, are also required.

Many argue the best BWCAW access is via the engaging town of **Ely**, northeast of the Iron Range area, which has accommodations, restaurants and scores of outfitters. The **Chamber of Commerce** (☎ 800-777-7281; www.ely.org; 1600 E Sheridan St; 9am-5pm Mon-Fri year-round, plus noon-3pm Sat & Sun in summer) has general information and accommodation assistance. Don't miss the **International Wolf Center** (☎ 218-365-4695; 1369 Hwy 169; adult $7, child 6-12 $3.25; 9am-5pm daily, until 7pm Jul-Aug, Sat & Sun only late Oct–mid-May), which offers intriguing exhibits and wolf-viewing trips. Also in the Wolf Center is **Kawishiwi Wilderness Station** (☎ 218-365-7561; 6am-6pm May-Sep), which offers expert camping and canoeing details, trip suggestions and required permits.

NORTH-CENTRAL MINNESOTA

Wooded and lake-filled, this area is synonymous with outdoor activities and summer fun. Campsites and cottages abound, and almost everybody is fishing-crazy. The lake land begins at large, circular Mille Lacs Lake, where an **Indian museum** (☎ 320-532-3632; Hwy 169; adult $6, child 6-12 $4; 10am-6pm daily summer, 11am-4pm Fri-Mon May & Sep-Oct) outlines local Ojibwa culture.

Nearby **Kathio State Park** (☎ 320-532-3523; campsites $15-18) is excellent, offering camping, cabins, hiking trails, canoe rentals and small lakes to explore.

Chippewa National Forest Area

The original pine forests were almost eliminated by logging in the late 19th and early 20th centuries, but natural regrowth and commercial replanting now cover a third of the state. The 1036-sq-mile

Chippewa National Forest is a mixed-use area with managed forests, water catchments, Indian reservations and recreational opportunities.

Attractive **Walker** has a beach and makes a good spot for a break. For information on hiking, canoeing and camping, check in at the **Chippewa National Forest office** either here (☎ 218-547-1044; 201 Minnesota Ave E; 🕒 7:30am-5pm), or in the town of Cass Lake, to the north.

Northwest of Walker, **Itasca State Park** (☎ 218-266-2100; off Hwy 71 N; campsites $15-18) is an area highlight. You can walk across the official headwaters of the mighty Mississippi, rent canoes or bikes, hike the trails and camp. The log **HI Mississippi Headwaters Hostel** (☎ 218-266-3415; www.himinnesota.org; dm $15-21, r $30-64; 🕒 daily in summer, Sat & Sun rest of year) is in the park. Or if you want a little rustic luxury, try the venerable **Douglas Lodge** (☎ 866-857-2757; r $57; ⊠), run by the park, which also has cabins and two good dining rooms.

On the western edge of the forest, neat and tidy **Bemidji** is an old lumber town with a well-preserved downtown and a giant statue of legendary logger Paul Bunyan and his faithful blue ox, Babe. The **visitors center** (☎ 218-751-3541; www.visitbemidji.com; 300 Bemidji Ave N; 🕒 8am-5pm Mon-Fri year-round, plus 10am-2pm Sat & Sun summer) display includes Paul's toothbrush. Among the modest motels south of town is **Midway Motel** (☎ 218-751-1180; 1000 Paul Bunyan Dr NE; r $40-55; ⊠) the **Greyhound bus** (☎ 218-751-7600) stops behind here. **Cyber Bugs Paradise Cafe** (☎ 218-444-2927; 311 3rd St NW; dishes $2-5) has fine light lunches, coffee and internet access.

North of Bemidji, the population thins, the land flattens and the vegetation becomes less lush.

On the east side of the forest, **Grand Rapids** is another old lumber town, with the enormous Blandin paper mill and some defunct open-pit mines nearby. A few attractions make it OK for a brief visit. The **Chamber of Commerce** (☎ 218-326-6619; 1 NW 3rd St; 🕒 8:30am-5pm Mon-Fri, 10am-2pm Sat), in the old railroad depot, has 24-hour accommodation information. Judy Garland was born here in 1922, and the **Itasca Heritage Center** (☎ 218-326-6431; 10 Fifth St NW; adult $4, child 6-18 $2; 🕒 9:30am-5pm Mon-Fri, 10am-4pm Sat, plus noon-4pm Sun in summer) has a collection of artifacts and photos. Also see the **Judy Garland Birthplace Historic House and Museum** (☎ 800-664-5839; 2727 Hwy 169; admission $5; 🕒 10am-5pm Mon-Sat, noon-5pm Sun). Three miles southwest of town, the **Forest History Center** (☎ 218-327-4482; 2609 Cty Rd 76; adult/child 6-12 $6/4; 🕒 10am-5pm Mon-Sat, noon-5pm Sun, early Jun-early Sep) is a reconstructed logging camp, complete with lumberjacks. Hwy 2 west of town has inexpensive local motels. For a munch, don't miss central **Pasties Plus** (☎ 218-327-2230; 20 NW 4th St; dishes $3-4; 🕒 Mon-Sat), where you can write your name on the wall.

Iron Range District

An area of red-tinged scrubby hills rather than mountains, Minnesota's Iron Range District consists of the Mesabi and Vermilion Ranges, running north and south of US 169 from roughly Grand Rapids northeast to Ely. Iron was discovered here in the 1850s, and at one time 70% of the nation's iron ore was extracted from these vast open-pit mines. Visitors can see working mines and the terrain's sparse, raw beauty all along US 169.

In **Calumet**, **Hill Annex Mine State Park** (☎ 218-247-7215; 880 Gary St; adult $7, child 5-12 $5; 🕒 9am-5:30pm late May–early Sep, until 4pm rest of year, tours Fri-Sun in summer) is a perfect introduction with its open-pit tour and exhibit center. There's an even bigger pit in **Hibbing**, where a must-see **viewpoint** (☎ 218-262-4166; admission free; 🕒 9am-6pm mid-May–mid-Sep) north of town overlooks the 3-mile-long Hull-Rust Mahoning Mine. The Greyhound bus company got its start in Hibbing, carrying miners to the pit. The **Greyhound Bus Museum** (☎ 218-263-5814; 1201 Greyhound Blvd; adult $3, child 6-12 $1; 🕒 9am-5pm Mon-Sat, 1-5pm Sun, mid-May–late Sep) tells the story with models, posters and antique buses. (Ironically, Greyhound cut its service to Hibbing a few years ago.) Bob Dylan lived at 2425 E 7th Ave as a boy and teenager; the **Hibbing Public Library** (☎ 218-262-1038; 2020 E 5th Ave; 🕒 9am-8pm Mon-Thu, until 5pm Fri & Sat) has well-done Dylan displays. For a meal or bed, try **Hibbing Park Hotel** (☎ 218-262-3481; 1402 E Howard St; s/d $73/78; ⊠ ⊠).

Chisholm has the engaging, hodgepodge **Minnesota Museum of Mining** (☎ 218-254-5543; 900 Lake St W; adult/child $3/2; 🕒 9am-5pm Mon-Sat, 1-5pm Sun) and **Ironworld Discovery Center** (☎ 218-254-7959; Hwy 169; adult $8, child 7-17 $6; 🕒 9:30am-5pm May-Sep), a theme park featuring open-pit mine tours and area ethnic displays.

Further east is **Virginia**, with more mine sites plus a giant loon, Minnesota's state bird. The **Ski View Motel** (☎ 218-741-8918; 903

BOB DYLAN'S BOYHOOD

Robert Zimmerman was born in Duluth in 1941, but his family moved to Hibbing, in the Iron Range area, when he was seven. It was an area known more for its narrow-mindedness than for its folkloric or musical traditions, and Bob never fit in. He spent much time in the music shop, and at night tuned to black radio stations from Chicago and Little Rock that nobody listened to in Hibbing. His first group, the Golden Chords, wowed the kids in a local talent quest, but the Chamber of Commerce judges gave them second prize.

He was soon making frequent trips to more cosmopolitan Minneapolis, where he hung around the student area, going to jazz joints and coffeehouses and meeting musicians. In 1959 he started college in Minneapolis, but dropped out within a year. He adopted the name Bob Dylan and told many fanciful stories about himself, typically that he was an orphan from Oklahoma, that he'd been on the road for years, and that he knew Woody Guthrie and other folk musicians. These stories were none too credible, but they were Dylan's way of disowning his mundane, middle-class origins and creating a worldly image.

Dylan hit New York's Greenwich Village folk scene in early 1961 and never looked back, though a few songs do mention 'the North Country.' His 1965 album *Highway 61 Revisited* makes obscure references to northern Minnesota's most scenic road, though it doesn't suggest happy childhood memories. God tells Abraham to kill his son on Hwy 61, and a promoter suggests where the next world war could be staged: 'We'll just put some bleachers out in the sun/And have it on Highway 61.'

N 17th St; s/d $44/48; ☒) could be the cleanest in the state.

Soudan has the area's only **underground mine** (☎ 218-753-2245; 1379 Stuntz Bay Rd; adult $7, child 5-12 $5; ⏲ 10am-4pm late May–early Sep) to visit; wear warm clothes.

International Falls & Canadian Border

North up Hwy 53, the nondescript border town of International Falls is busy in summer due to its location. Beyond, Hwy 11 leads through forest to Lake of the Woods, bordering Ontario. See the Directory (p1106) for border crossing information.

Voyageurs National Park

In the 17th century, French Canadian fur traders, or voyageurs, began exploring the Great Lakes and northern rivers by canoe. Voyageurs National Park covers part of their customary waterway, which became the border between the USA and Canada.

Twelve miles east of International Falls on Hwy 11 is **Rainy Lake visitors center** (☎ 218-286-5258; ⏲ 9am-5pm daily summer, Wed-Sun only Oct-May), the main park office. There are ranger-guided walks, and boat tours are available here. Generally, though, park access by land is limited; the park is best and most commonly explored by motorboat (the waters are mostly too wide and too rough for canoeing, though kayaks are becoming popular). A few access roads lead to campgrounds and lodges on or near Lake Superior, but these are mostly used by those putting in their own boats.

Some seasonal visitors centers can be found at **Ash River** (☎ 218-374-3221) and **Kabetogama Lake** (☎ 218-875-2111). These areas have outfitters, rentals and services, plus some smaller lakes for canoeing. At Kabetogama, **Carlson's Harmony Beach** (☎ 218-875-2811; 10002 Gappa Rd; campsites $20, cottages from $110) is a friendly, reasonably priced resort with camping, rooms and cabins.

For those seeking wildlife, canoeing or forest camping, the BWCAW is where you want to be (see Boundary Waters, p442).

GREAT LAKES

The South

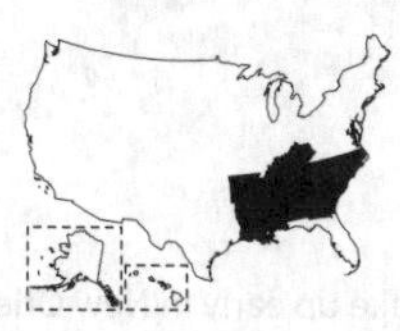

CONTENTS

Wake up early in New Orleans and sip a chicory coffee while a solo sax player plays an aching tune. Dip your paddle in the Atlantic and wonder at all those early adventurers who plied the coastal waters. Visit antebellum homes and sprawling plantations. Marvel at how cotton grows – heating in the sun until it bursts like popcorn. Gaze over the Great Smoky Mountains and let the fall colors fill your eyes like a kaleidoscope of tears. Drive through swampy bayous, lick your fingers at a crawfish boil, dance with strangers. Find heaven in a singer's voice at a Nashville bar, feel the blues of the Mississippi Delta, and listen for the high lonesome sounds in the Kentucky hills.

This is the South – North and South Carolina, Georgia, Alabama, Mississippi, Louisiana, Arkansas, Tennessee and Kentucky – where primeval swamps and coastal islands mingle with mountains and urban metropolises.

Often depicted in American literature, movies and TV as a backward region full of hillbillies, hicks and racists, the South is perhaps the most misunderstood region of the US. Though it is plagued by poverty and racial inequality, most Southerners acknowledge the problems facing their states and the majority is heartily sick of the stereotyping.

One stereotype that generally holds, however, is Southern hospitality; the gracious warmth and friendliness here exists nowhere else in the country. You'll find you can discuss everything, from race and politics to religion and economics, as long as there's enough fried chicken and Southern ice tea to go along.

HIGHLIGHTS

- Lurking alongside alligators on a **Louisiana swamp tour** (p529)
- Perusing **Savannah's historic squares** and partying in the Garden of Good & Evil (p495)
- Climbing lighthouses and beachcombing along the windswept **Outer Banks** (p459)
- Camping, hiking and taking plenty of pictures in the **Great Smoky Mountains** (p458)
- Meandering into antebellum days on a **Charleston walking tour** (p470)
- Eating sumptuous barbecue, seafood, soul food, **Cajun** and **Creole delights** (p531)
- Climbing the world's largest hunk of granite at **Atlanta's Stone Mountain Park** (p486)
- Putting on your party shoes and celebrating **Mardi Gras in New Orleans** (p522) or **Mobile** (p502)
- Paying homage to the King in **Memphis** (p545)
- Driving along the gorgeous **Blue Ridge Parkway** (p456)

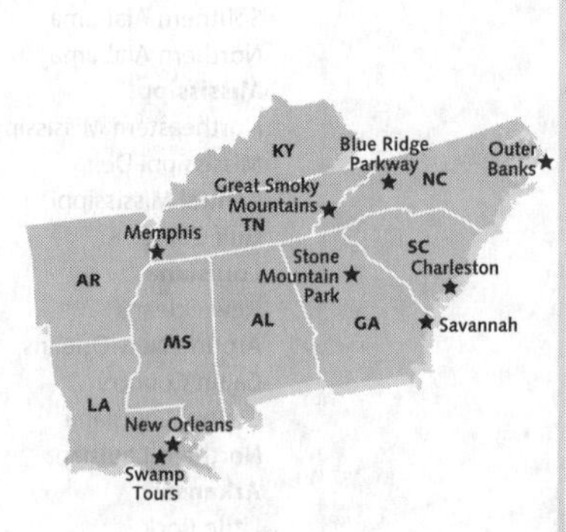

HISTORY

As early as the 16th century, European explorers started arriving along the East Coast. They came from several directions and, as elsewhere in the country, their presence wreaked havoc on the Native Indians. Immigration increased sharply in the early 18th century. The 1803 Louisiana Purchase brought the land west of the Mississippi under US control and even more settlers.

President Andrew Jackson signed the Indian Removal Act in 1830, requiring the South's 'Five Civilized Tribes' – the Cherokee, Choctaw, Chickasaw, Creek and Seminole – to relocate to 'Indian Territory' west of the Mississippi. Some 50,000 Indians were forcibly removed. In 1838, more than 15,000 Cherokee were forced west on the infamous Trail of Tears – 4000 died en route. A few isolated groups remained, but most of the South was 'cleared' for settlement.

When the invention of the cotton gin mechanized the process of removing seeds from raw cotton, large-scale cotton growing became profitable. Cotton *was* the Southern economy, but it was heavily dependent on Northern financiers who took much of the wealth back North. Increasingly, the South regarded the Northern states with resentment and mistrust.

Though small farmers and workers opposed slavery, politically strong plantation owners depended on slave labor. When Lincoln was elected US president on an antislavery platform, all nine states except Kentucky seceded and most were devastated when Union soldiers crushed Confederate dreams.

The post–Civil War 1867 Reconstruction Acts probably did more to foster hatred of Yankees than the war itself. The Confederate states were readmitted to the Union only after they had abolished slavery and provided for black suffrage. Once readmitted, however, white elites imposed 'Jim Crow' laws designed to restrict black voting. White supremacist organizations like the KKK were born and racial segregation became the norm.

In 1954, the US Supreme Court ruled that segregation of public schools was unconstitutional. Southern states did not accept this and the next 10 years saw demonstrations, protests and civil action aimed at desegregation and black political representation. Black students enrolled in Arkansas schools under armed-forces protection. Mississippi closed its public schools rather than let blacks enroll. Black students sat for days at North Carolina lunch counters waiting to be served. Segregated buses were boycotted for 13 months in Alabama. Under the leadership of Martin Luther King Jr, the protests were nonviolent, but often met with violent reaction.

The emphasis then turned from desegregation to voter registration. The Voting Rights Act in 1965 prohibited states from imposing literacy tests and other obstacles to black voting, and put an end to the threats and murder of Civil rights workers.

Today blacks hold public office in many cities across the South, and blacks and whites mix in schools, stores and public places. Yet racism and racial inequality are still a reality, and recent controversy over State and Confederate flags in Georgia, Mississippi and South Carolina are proof that the past has not been forgotten.

Educated Southerners, black and white, are quite open about these issues. They often see the rest of the country as somewhat hypocritical in its belief that racial problems are something particular to the South.

CLIMATE

You can spend a summer day in the south and wonder if somehow you stumbled into the sweaty armpit of the devil. It shore gits hot! And sticky! This is especially true in the low-lying subtropical coastal regions and in inland areas of South Carolina, Georgia, Mississippi and Louisiana, where a summer breeze is sometimes as good as a cold beer. These areas are also defined by swamplands and agricultural areas where the nutrient-rich soil depends on summer humidity and wintertime rain.

In the northern part of the region, mountains cool and dry-out the air and the mountain rivers come trickling down to seep into the fertile lands, especially in Arkansas' Ozark and Ouachita Mountains and in Tennessee's Blue Ridge Mountains, and in North Carolina where the foothills of the Appalachian Mountains thrust north into Kentucky.

Tourism in the region is at its peak from June to September. Mild weather and blossoming flowers make spring a good time, and fall colors decorate the landscape at

THE SOUTH

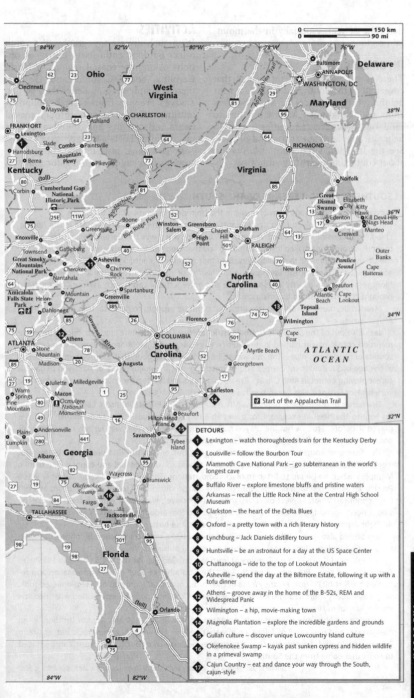

Start of the Appalachian Trail

DETOURS

1. Lexington – watch thoroughbreds train for the Kentucky Derby
2. Louisville – follow the Bourbon Tour
3. Mammoth Cave National Park – go subterranean in the world's longest cave
4. Buffalo River – explore limestone bluffs and pristine waters
5. Arkansas – recall the Little Rock Nine at the Central High School Museum
6. Clarkston – the heart of the Delta Blues
7. Oxford – a pretty town with a rich literary history
8. Lynchburg – Jack Daniels distillery tours
9. Huntsville – be an astronaut for a day at the US Space Center
10. Chattanooga – ride to the top of Lookout Mountain
11. Asheville – spend the day at the Biltmore Estate, following it up with a tofu dinner
12. Athens – groove away in the home of the B-52s, REM and Widespread Panic
13. Wilmington – a hip, movie-making town
14. Magnolia Plantation – explore the incredible gardens and grounds
15. Gullah culture – discover unique Lowcountry Island culture
16. Okefenokee Swamp – kayak past sunken cypress and hidden wildlife in a primeval swamp
17. Cajun Country – eat and dance your way through the South, cajun-style

that time of year, especially in the mountain regions.

INFORMATION

There is no central tourism agency that covers all of the South, but each state runs helpful visitors centers at state borders along major highways. Most are happy to send out brochures and information to help you preplan your trip ahead of time. See the individual states for information about contacting each state authority.

ACTIVITIES

With such diverse topography, the South offers outdoor enthusiasts plenty of options. Along the coastal regions of North Carolina, South Carolina and Georgia, there is simply nothing better than getting a wave's-eye view from a kayak. Abundant outfitters offer guided trips through coastal rivers and marshes and abundant rentals make renting boats a breeze.

In Louisiana, just slipping through the swamps in a canoe or on a gator tour will

SOUTHERN MUSIC: LEGENDS OF THE SOUTH *Scott Freeman*

Virtually every indigenous form of music in the United States was born in the South.

Country music evolved from descendants of European immigrants who settled in the Appalachian Mountains of Virginia and Tennessee. Most renowned was the Carter Family, who evolved the music from string-based instrumentals to one that emphasized vocals, and lyrics that reflected the often-hard times of their daily lives. Bill Monroe, born in Kentucky, originated the bluegrass sound. But the most notorious figure in the history of country music is Hank Williams, born in Montgomery, Alabama. His lonesome voice and unforgettable songs such as *Your Cheatin' Heart* brought country music to the mainstream.

Meanwhile, blues, gospel and jazz grew out of music brought to America from descendants of African slaves.

Jazz rose out of the Storyville brothel district of New Orleans. Some credit its origins to an unrecorded cornet player named Buddy Bolden who discovered jazz when he began to merge the sounds of gospel and blues. The mix was so powerful, legend goes, that it drove him to madness at the age of 31. Bolden influenced Louis Armstrong, the first major figure of jazz, who began his career playing cornet in King Oliver's Creole Jazz Band and formed the foundation of modern jazz with his Hot Five and Hot Seven bands.

The father of the modern blues was Mississippi guitarist Robert Johnson. Legend says he sold his soul to the devil in exchange for being able to play the blues in a way no human had ever played it before. True or not, he played guitar with a dexterity that was far advanced from his contemporaries, and brought artistry to blues songwriting.

The South, of course, was a segregated society; but one of the first places the boundaries were crossed was music. Elvis Presley grew up listening to white gospel and country as a teen in Memphis, when he began to listen to black radio stations. Those genres all came together when Presley, an aspiring singer, dropped into the tiny Sun Studio in 1954 to lay down a record as a gift for his mother. When 18-year-old Elvis, then a truck driver, was asked who he sounded like, he said, 'I don't sound like nobody!' Elvis soon began to fool around with a blues song called *That's All Right, Mama*, which was, for all practical purposes, the birth of rock 'n' roll.

Sun Studio also gave birth to rockabilly in the mid-50s, unleashing legends Johnny Cash (Arkansas), Carl Perkins (Tennessee) and Jerry Lee Lewis (Louisiana).

Little Richard (born Richard Penniman) from Macon, Georgia, hit the R & B charts in 1955 with *Tutti Frutti* and *Long Tall Sally*. James Brown, 'The Godfather of Soul' migrated to Macon and recorded his first hit, *Please, Please, Please* in the studio of a local radio station. He pioneered funk, which eventually morphed into hip-hop. Then came Otis Redding, who established what became known as soul music.

Carrying on the innovative musical tradition of Macon, in 1969 the Allman Brothers Band merged jazz and blues and rock into a genre that became known as Southern rock. But, as Gregg Allman once noted, Southern rock is a misnomer because *all* of our native music can be traced to roots that come from the South.

Author of *Otis! The Otis Redding Story* and *Midnight Riders: The Story of the Allman Brothers Band* transport you to another world. Excellent mountain biking, camping and hiking abounds in the Ozark, Blue Ridge and Great Smoky Mountains in Arkansas, Tennessee, North Carolina and Kentucky.

Horseback riding is a fun way to explore trails and green pastures, especially in Tennessee and Kentucky, where farms offer horseback riding to guests.

Hunting is wildly popular throughout the South, especially in Alabama, Mississippi and Louisiana. It's a very Southern thing for a group of 'outdoorsmen' to don their camouflage and shoot anything from grouse to deer. In some areas, hunters help control burgeoning populations of deer and wild boar. Hunting seasons are specific and heavily enforced; before you join in, be sure to obtain appropriate licenses from outfitters and obey local laws.

NATIONAL & STATE PARKS

This region is full of national parks, monuments and historic sites. Some honor people (Martin Luther King Jr in Georgia, the Wright Brothers in North Carolina), others preserve historic passages (Natchez Trace Parkway from Mississippi to Tennessee, the Cumberland Gap in Kentucky). Some sites mark significant Civil War battles (Vicksburg in Mississippi, Chickamauga in Georgia, Forts Pulaski and Sumter in South Carolina), while others honor the wilderness (Buffalo River in Arkansas, the Great Smoky Mountains in Tennessee). See the states for individual sites, or learn more at www.nps.gov.

There are hundreds of state parks throughout the region, ranging from tiny and primitive, to giant and full of amenities. If you are camping or hiking remember that insects are a feature of the Southern geography; mosquitoes can be nasty, so be sure to carry bug spray.

For an overview of each state's parks, contact the following:

Alabama (☎ 888-252-7272; www.alapark.com)
Arkansas (☎ 888-287-2757; www.arkansasstateparks.com)
Georgia (☎ 800-864-7275; www.gastateparks.org)
Kentucky (☎ 800-255-7275; www.state.ky.us/agencies/parks)
Louisiana (☎ 888-677-1400; www.lastateparks.com)
Mississippi (☎ 800-407-2575; www.mdwfp.com/parks)
North Carolina (☎ 919-733-4181; www.ncsparks.net)
South Carolina (☎ 888-887-2757; www.southcarolinaparks.com)
Tennessee (☎ 888-867-2757; www.state.tn.us/environment/parks)

GETTING THERE & AROUND

Atlanta, Georgia, is the main air gateway to the region. Charlotte and Raleigh, both in North Carolina; Memphis, in Tennessee; and New Orleans, Louisiana, have the region's largest airports.

A number of Amtrak train routes traverse the South, several conveniently converging on New Orleans:

Carolinian and Piedmont Travels inland from New York City to Charlotte, NC, via Raleigh and Durham.
City of New Orleans Travels between New Orleans and Chicago, with stops at Jackson, Mississippi; Memphis, Tennessee; and Fulton, in the western corner of Kentucky.
The Crescent Travels between New York and New Orleans, with stops including Washington, DC; Charlotte, NC; Greenville, SC; Atlanta, GA; Birmingham, AL; and Meridian, MS.
Silver Service/Palmetto Travels between New York City and Miami, FL; with stops at Columbia and Charleston, SC; and Savannah, GA.
Sunset Limited Crosses the south between Orlando, FL and Los Angeles, with stops including Mobile, AL; Biloxi, MS; New Orleans and Lafayette, LA.

The Blue Ridge Parkway, the Natchez Trace Parkway and Hwy 12 along the Outer Banks are three of the South's most scenic drives. I-10 runs along the Gulf coast from Florida to Louisiana; I-20 links South Carolina with Louisiana via Georgia, Alabama and Mississippi; and I-40 goes from North Carolina to Arkansas via Tennessee. The chief north–south routes include I-95, I-75, I-65 and I-55.

NORTH CAROLINA

Mountain folk, new South workaholics and beach bums all find solace in North Carolina. Its landscape – plains sandwiched between mountains and shore – is that of the US, but in miniature. Sweeping generalizations are out of place here. Visitors puzzle at how the climate can range from subarctic (in the highlands) to sub-Saharan (on the coast), or that politics can shift unexpectedly from New Age liberal to Stone Age fossil.

Most travelers tend to skirt through the business-oriented urban centers of the

NORTH CAROLINA FACTS

Nickname Tar Heel State
Population 8,320,146 (11th)
Area 48,711 sq miles (28th)
Admitted to Union November 21, 1789 (12th); seceded 1861; readmitted 1868
Capital city Raleigh (population 276,000)
Other cities Charlotte (541,000; metro area 1.3 million), Greensboro (224,000), Winston-Salem (185,000), Durham (187,000)
State motto To be rather than to seem
Birthplace of President James Polk (1795–1849), jazzman John Coltrane (1926–67), evangelist Billy Graham (b 1918), sportscaster Howard Cosell (1920–95), politician Jesse Helms (b 1921), boxer Sugar Ray Leonard (b 1956)
Home of the first English colony in America, powered airplane flight

central Piedmont, sticking instead to the scenic routes along the coast (via the islands of the Outer Banks) and through the Appalachian Mountains, especially along the unforgettable Blue Ridge Parkway.

History

The first enduring English settlements were established in the mid-17th century in the Albermarle region and later a series of battles defeated and displaced the Indians and made way for European colonists. The first industry was the extraction of 'naval stores' like tar, pitch and turpentine from coastal forests, followed by cultivation of tobacco and cotton.

Though well represented in the constitutional conventions, North Carolina languished as an agrarian backwater during the early years of the republic. Divided on slavery, North Carolina reluctantly seceded in 1861, and went on to provide more Confederate soldiers than any other state.

WWII brought some new industries and large military bases, and the economy has boomed with the growth of finance in Charlotte and of research and development in the Raleigh–Durham Research Triangle.

Information

North Carolina Division of Tourism (☎ 919-733-4147, 800-847-4862; www.visitnc.com; 301N N Wilmington St, Raleigh, NC 27601) Sends out good maps and information.

RESEARCH TRIANGLE

Since the 1950s research and high-tech industries have lured professionals to the Research Triangle – composed of Raleigh, Durham and Chapel Hill, each of which has its own university and is a miniuniverse.

Getting There & Around

Raleigh–Durham International Airport (☎ 919-840-2123), a significant hub, is a 25-minute drive northwest of downtown Raleigh. **Carolina Trailways/Greyhound** (Raleigh ☎ 919-834-8410; 314 W Jones Rd; Durham ☎ 919-687-4800; 820 Morgan St) serve Raleigh and Durham with limited trips to Chapel Hill.

From Raleigh, **Amtrak** (☎ 919-471-3399; 302 W Cabarrus St) runs to Washington, DC (from $44, seven hours), and Savannah, Georgia ($76, seven hours).

The **Triangle Transit Authority** (☎ 919-549-9999; www.ridetta.org; adult $1.50) operates buses linking Raleigh, Durham and Chapel Hill, and all three to the airport.

Raleigh

Named for the man John Lennon called 'a stupid git,' Raleigh, in the Triangle's southeastern corner, has a handsome old state capitol, North Carolina State University, a trendy-looking pedestrian mall and a decent cultural scene. Urban renewal has given parts of downtown a shot in the arm, and while even Sir Walter wouldn't have described it as lively, the capital city does offer a few good diversions. Downtown is bisected north to south by the pedestrian Fayetteville St Mall, with the State Capitol at the north end.

The **Capital Area Visitors Center** (☎ 919-733-3456; 301 N Blount St; 🕒 8am-5pm Mon-Fri, 9am-5pm Sat, 1-5pm Sun) has a walking-tour map of the government buildings and the old Oakwood district. Pick up other helpful information at the **Convention & Visitors Bureau** (☎ 919-834-5900; 421 Fayetteville Mall; 🕒 8:30am-5:50pm Mon-Fri).

SIGHTS

North Carolina Museum of History (☎ 919-715-0200; 5 E Edenton St; admission free; 🕒 9am-5pm Mon-Sat, noon-5pm Sun) has a good chronological exhibit, including a dugout canoe, flags, Civil War photos and a Wright Brothers plane model.

The world's only dinosaur specimen with a heart is kept at the modern, airy **North Carolina Museum of Natural Sciences** (☎ 919-733-7450;

11 W Jones St; admission free; 9am-5pm Mon-Sat, noon-5pm Sun). There's also a unique and scary Acrocanthosaurus, five habitat dioramas and lots of well-done taxidermy.

Exploris (919-834-4040; 201 E Hargett St; adult/child $8/5.50; 9am-5pm Tue-Sat, noon-5pm Sun) is a fun, hands-on museum for kids. It also has an **Imax theater** (admission adult/child $9/6.50).

North Carolina Museum of Art (919-839-6262; 2110 Blue Ridge Rd; admission free; 9am-5pm Wed-Sat, 10am-5pm Sun) is inconveniently located on the western fringe of town, but it's well worth visiting for its fine collection of antiquities and baroque and Renaissance paintings spread over several levels. They have a variety of programs, including children's films and workshops.

SLEEPING & EATING

Days Inn (828-9081; 300 N Dawson St; r $55; P) With 55 basic but clean rooms this downtown hotel is a good budget option.

Holiday Inn Brownstone Hotel (919-828-0811, 800-331-7919; www.holiday-inn.com; 1707 Hillsborough St; r $100-140; P) Near the university, this well-kept hotel has plush, renovated standard rooms, in-room amenities and an outdoor pool.

Oakwood Inn B&B (919-832-9712; www.oakwoodinnbb.com; 411 N Bloodworth St; r $100-150) There are a couple of historic accommodations in the heart of Raleigh, including this Victorian house in the pretty Oakwood district. It has six nicely furnished theme rooms (Polk, Linden etc), an afternoon tea service and full breakfast.

The Glenwood Ave area northwest of downtown has an array of good restaurants and clubs. Hillsborough St along the North Carolina State University campus is lively at night.

Big Ed's (919-836-9909; 220 Wolfe St; dishes $7-10; 7am-2pm Mon-Fri, 7am-noon Sat) Who's Ed? He's the guy in overalls, but that's not the point: all you need to know is that this barn-looking place is *the* spot for a delicious country breakfast, like cured ham and eggs, grits and gravy.

42nd St Oyster Bar (919-831-2811; cnr Jones & West Sts; lunch $7-10, dinner $12-16) This wildly popular downtown eatery has music, dancing, a raw bar and seafood restaurant.

Rathskeller (919-821-5342; 2412 Hillsborough St; meals $8-12) With a good vegetarian selection, this popular student hangout opposite the campus also serves seafood, poultry and beef dishes.

Durham

In the late 19th century, Durham's stock rose with the fortunes of the newly established American Tobacco Company, owned by Washington Duke and his sons. The Dukes had an instinct for PR as well as business, and in 1924 the founder's son, Buck, donated a wad of cash to a small college that grew into Duke University.

Durham is a lively student town at the northeast corner of the Triangle. Durham is home to the Durham Bulls, a minor-league baseball team that shot to fame after the 1988 flick *Bull Durham*. Downtown can be quiet or raucous, depending on where the students (and sports fans) are. There are two hubs of activity. **Brightleaf Sq** on the east side of downtown is a recycled tobacco warehouse with restaurants and upscale shops, and a half-mile northeast, adjacent to the Duke campus, is the student-filled **Ninth St District**.

The **visitors center** (919-687-0288, 800-446-8604; www.durham-nc.com; 101 E Morgan St; 8:30am-5pm Mon-Fri, 10am-2pm Sat) also operates a 24-hour **recording** (919-688-2855) of events and activities.

Endowed by the Duke family's cigarette fortune, **Duke University** (919-684-2572; Durham, NC 27708) has a Georgian-style East Campus and a neo-Gothic West Campus with an impressive 1930s chapel. Students juggle, play soccer and pretend to read on the front concourse.

See the humble origins of the Duke family and have an uncritical look at the tobacco industry at **Duke Homestead** (919-477-5498; 2828 Duke Homestead Rd; admission free; 10am-4pm Tue-Sat), on the north side of town.

Carolina Duke Motor Inn (919-286-0771, 800-438-1158; 2517 Guess Rd; d $36 P) You can't beat the price at this budget option off I-85. It has 182 tidy and spacious rooms, all with TVs.

Washington Duke Inn & Golf Club (919-490-0999, 800-443-3853; www.washingtondukeinn.com; 3001 Cameron Blvd; r from $150; P) On the other end of the spectrum, this four-star beauty is just off Hwy 15/501 on the Duke campus. Prices can drop dramatically during slow periods. Nicely furnished with all the amenities, including the excellent though pricey **Fairview** (mains $20-40) restaurant.

For dining, seek out the Brightleaf complex downtown and Ninth St alongside the university campus. Good eateries include the following.

Fishmongers (☎ 919-682-0128; 806 W Main St; lunch $6-9) A great seafood and crab joint. People-watch and grab a midday munch.

Taverna Nikos (☎ 919-682-0043; 905 West Main St; lunch $6-9, dinner $10-16) In the Brightleaf complex, this is the place for great Greek food, including favorites such as spanakopita, dolmas or moussaka.

Chapel Hill

An attractive university town, Chapel Hill is conspicuously more affluent than the other corners of the Triangle. The University of North Carolina (UNC), founded in 1789, was one of the nation's first state universities and has many fine old buildings. The music scene – particularly for grunge, jazz and pop – is smokin', as is the basketball; Michael Jordan rose (or rather leaped) to fame here.

Downtown lies about 2 miles northwest of the Hwy 15/501 bypass. The main drag is Franklin St, with funky clothing shops, bars and eateries on its north side and the UNC campus to the south; the same street enters Carrboro to the west. Murals are sprinkled around town, such as a big yellow No 2 pencil along the wall on Church St.

Pick up good area information from the **Chapel Hill–Orange County Visitors Bureau** (☎ 919-968-2060, 888-968-2060; www.chocvb.org; 501 W Franklin St; 8:30am-5pm Mon-Fri, 10am-2pm Sat).

Morehead Planetarium (☎ 919-549-6863; www.moreheadplanetarium.com; 250 E Franklin St; adult/child $4.50/3.50; 12:30-5pm Sun-Wed, 10am-5pm & 6:30-9:30pm Thu-Sat) features science exhibits and celestial shows under its big dome. The **visitors center** (☎ 919-962-1630), at the planetarium's west entrance, offers free walking tours of the UNC campus.

Cheap accommodations are scarce; consider staying in Durham if you're really stumped.

Red Roof Inn (☎ 919-489-9421; 5623 Chapel Hill Blvd; s/d $80/90; P) Four miles north at Hwy 15/501, this comfortable chain motel seems steep for what you get, but reasonable when compared to other area hotels.

Carolina Inn (☎ 919-933-2001, 800-962-8519; www.carolinainn.com; 211 Pittsboro St; r from $140; P) In the heart of town, this historic hotel loaded with amenities has 184 plush rooms, an elegant restaurant and oodles of charm.

You'll find that most restaurants and nightspots are along Franklin St.

Spanky's (☎ 919-967-2678; 101 E Franklin St; meals $6-10) With ceiling-high windows, live jazz and a loaded menu, this café is popular for its good, cheap meals and great upstairs view of the action.

For entertainment listings, pick up the free *Spectator* or the *Independent* weekly papers.

Local 506 (☎ 919-942-5506; 506 W Franklin St) Popular alternative bands start out at venues like this one.

Cat's Cradle (☎ 919-968-4345; 300 E Main St) In Carrboro, the renowned Cat's Cradle has live rock, reggae and big visiting acts.

THE TRIAD

The grouping of Winston-Salem, Greensboro and High Point is known locally as the Triad, an answer to its bigger and better-known rival to the southeast. The

HIS ROYAL AIRNESS

Widely considered the greatest basketball player of all time, Michael Jeffrey Jordan (b 1963) enrolled at UNC at Chapel Hill in 1981. After his junior year, the Wilmington native was drafted by the Chicago Bulls and went on to become the top NBA scorer for seven years running, averaging 32 points per game. Known for his extraordinary leaps on court, 'Air' Jordan was only the second player in NBA history ever to score 3000 points in a single season, after Wilt ('the Stilt') Chamberlain.

Much to every fan's dismay, Jordan retired in 1993. But nobody needed to worry too much cuz that basketball bug just kept on biting. Jordan returned to the Bulls in 1995, retired again in 1999, when he hung up his Nikes and became part owner of the Washington Wizards. But that darn bug kept on biting – in 2001 Jordan donned a Wizards' jersey and got back on the court. Entering the 2002–03 season, he was ranked first in NBA history in scoring average (31 points per game).

You can relive the glories of North Carolina's favorite adopted son at UNC's **Blue Heaven Basketball Museum** (www.blueheavenmuseum.com).

competition leads to headlines such as 'Triangle Tops Triad' or vice versa. Of the three Triad cities, Winston-Salem probably deserves most of your attention.

In the mid-18th century the Moravians, a group of German-speaking religious dissidents from Bohemia and Moravia, bought 100,000 acres of land in the Piedmont. The Moravians, a group sometimes compared to the Quakers or Mennonites, number about 20,000 here and have left their mark everywhere, from the quaint steepled churches to the Moravian sugar cookies sold in local shops.

Greensboro, home to the first Civil rights sit-in (1960), is noted for its early colleges for African-Americans and women. The **visitors center** (☎ 336-274-2282; 317 S Green St; 8am-5:30pm Mon-Fri) has a collection of African-American sights and area information.

Richard Joshua Reynolds built his first tobacco factory in the town of Winston in 1875, just as the railway was laid. By 1913, Winston and nearby Salem had grown to the extent that they were merged into today's **Winston–Salem**. The RJ Reynolds empire named two of its cigarettes after the city – Winstons and Salems – that dangled so carelessly from young, sophisticated fingers in the 1950s.

The **visitors center** (☎ 336-777-3796; 200 Brookstown Ave) has area information and good maps, which are useful, as sights are scattered.

CHARLOTTE

Founded at the junction of two old Indian trails, Charlotte was described as a 'hornet's nest of rebellion' against British rule in the 1770s. Miners burrowed under the town in the early 1800s, and banks were founded to handle the gold. Today, Charlotte is the second-largest US banking center after New York, complete with futuristic high-rises and elevated walkways, but its downtown isn't quite as engaging as the Big Apple's. Charlotte is primarily a business town, and its appeal consists of a few good museums, excellent restaurants and a scattered but lively music scene.

The **visitors center** (☎ 704-331-2700, 800-231-4636; www.visitcharlotte.org; 330 Tryon St; 8:30am-5pm Mon-Fri), off W 2nd St publishes maps and a visitors guide. The **public library** (☎ 704-336-2725; 301 N College St; 9am-9pm Mon-Thu, 9am-6pm Fri & Sat, 1-6pm Sun) has terminals for free Internet use.

Sights & Activities

The innovative **Levine Museum of the New South** (☎ 704-333-1887; 200 E 7th St; adult/child $6/5; 10am-5pm Tue-Sat, noon-5pm Sun) gives an excellent look at modern Southern history covering everything from sharecropping to NASCAR racing.

Mint Museum of Craft & Design (☎ 704-337-2000; 2730 Randolph Rd; adult/child $6/3; 10am-5pm Tue-Sat, noon-5pm Sun) presents pure imagination in the form of glass, metal, wood and other handcrafted materials, as well as highlights of the design world.

Afro-American Cultural Center (☎ 704-374-1565; 401 N Myers St; adult/child $3/2; 10am-6pm Tue-Sat, 1-5pm Sun) has excellent exhibits, performances and films. Check out the open-mic Slam Night on the first and third Tuesday of every month.

Discovery Place (☎ 704-372-6261; 301 N Tryon St; adult/child $6.50/5; 9am-6pm Mon-Sat, 1-6pm Sun) is a hands-on science museum with an Omnimax cinema and planetarium. You can see how astronauts work in space, peer inside a huge eyeball and sample liquid nitrogen ice cream in the chemistry lab.

Sleeping & Eating

Budget motels cluster around I-77 and I-85. Most charge about $40 to $50. Uptown hotels cater mainly to business travelers. Try **Days Inn** (☎ 704-597-8110; 1408 W Sugar Creek Rd, exit 41; r $27-40) or **La Quinta** (☎ 707-393-5306; 3100 S I-85 Service Rd, exit 33; r/ste $65/75).

Travelodge Trade St (☎ 704-377-1930, 888-515-6375; 319 W Trade St; r $60 P) Friendly and affordable, this hotel is probably the best value uptown, with cozy rooms and free continental breakfast.

Dunhill Hotel (☎ 704-332-4141, 800-252-4666; www.dunhillhotel.com; 237 N Tryon St; r from $140; P) Now dwarfed by skyscrapers, the 10-story hotel towered over the scene when it was opened in 1929. Restored to its original elegance in the 1980s, it's noted for its period furnishings as well as its original art.

Charlotte has a great selection of fine restaurants.

Mert's Heart & Soul (☎ 704-342-4222; 214 N College St; meals $7-11) The menu here is definitive Lowcountry and soul food – pork chops, Southern fried chicken thickly coated in breadcrumbs, cornbread, and fried green tomatoes.

Cosmos Cafe (☎ 704-372-3553; 300 N College St; lunch $7-10, dinner $10-15; ⏲ until 2am, closed Sun) They've got everything at this uptown café, from wood-fired pizzas to sushi and a martini bar.

Latorre's (☎ 704-377-4448; 118 W 5th St; meals $8-15; ⏲ lunch Mon-Fri, dinner Mon Sat) Ooh la la! This super-fun uptown Latin restaurant has a good selection of seafood, steak and vegetarian dishes. At weekends, experts give free salsa and meringue lessons.

Southend Brewery & Smokehouse (☎ 704-358-4677; 2100 S Blvd; meals $7-15) The decor at this South End brew house is all about the trendy converted warehouse with huge brewing vats. Smoked ribs, wood-fired pizzas and grilled seafood are the specialties; wash it all down with one of eight house beers.

Entertainment

Check out the weekly *Creative Loafing* for entertainment listings.

Blumenthal Performing Arts Center (☎ 704-372-1000; 130 North Tryon St) For theater and classical concerts, check the Blumenthal.

Mythos (☎ 704-375-8765; 300 N College St; ⏲ 10pm until late; cover charge varies) If you're looking to get your groove on, Mythos is a sizzling club, with DJs spinning house, techno and European dance music for fashion victims.

Double Door Inn (☎ 704-376-1446; 218 E Independence Blvd) Stevie Ray Vaughan and Eric Clapton played at the clapboard Double Door Inn, the place for live blues, rock and zydeco in the South End area.

SPECTATOR SPORTS

Charlotte Coliseum (☎ 704-357-0489) Off the Billy Graham Parkway. The NBA **Charlotte** and WNBA **Charlotte Sting** play professional basketball here.

Ericsson Stadium (☎ 704-358-7800; S Mint St) The NFL **Carolina Panthers** football team plays at the Ericsson Stadium.

Lowe's Motor Speedway (☎ 704-455-3200) Insanely popular NASCAR races are held at Lowe's, 12 miles northeast of town.

Getting There & Around

Charlotte-Douglas International Airport (☎ 704-359-4000; 5501 Josh Birmingham Parkway) has some direct flights to and from Europe.

The **Greyhound station** (☎ 704-375-3332; 601 W Trade St), handy to uptown, has regular connections to Atlanta, GA ($40, five hours); Charleston, SC ($45, 6½ hours); and Washington, DC ($66, nine hours).

Amtrak (☎ 704-376-4416; 1914 N Tryon St) is further out, with daily services to New York ($90, 14 hours) and New Orleans ($97, 16 hours).

Charlotte Area Transit (☎ 704-336-3366; 310 E Trade St) provides local bus services throughout the metro area.

NORTH CAROLINA MOUNTAINS

With cool summers, gentle breezes and spectacular scenery, the western mountains of North Carolina work like a shot in the arm for weary urbanites. The southern section of the Blue Ridge Mountains, which forms part of the Appalachians, has massive peaks of over 5000ft. Early European settlers took the name from the 'blue' haze caused by rising damp from the forest below.

For the plantation colonials, the mountains formed a frontier to Indian country to the west. Settlers from Ireland, Germany and England moved into the area and formed isolated farming communities that had almost no link with the African slave labor so typical in the Southeast. Cherokee Indians occupied much of the region into the early 1800s, hunting in the mountains they considered sacred.

During the 1930s, the Blue Ridge Parkway was authorized as a Depression-era public works project and gradually extended to link the Great Smoky Mountains with central Virginia.

Natural sights and options for outdoor activities abound: The Appalachian Trail roughly follows the state's western border; there's great white water around Nantahala; and the Great Smoky Mountains National Park draws thousands of hikers (and RVs) every year. Of the four ski areas south of Boone, **Sugar Mountain** (☎ 800-784-2768) has the longest runs.

Blue Ridge Parkway

This celebrated scenic drive follows the Blue Ridge Mountains from Virginia's Shenandoah National Park (Mile 0) to North Carolina's Great Smoky Mountains National Park (Mile 469). Snow causes the parkway to close in winter and it can take some time to clear. May and June are the best months for rhododendrons and wildflowers, October for the fall colors; the variation in altitude

THE SOUTH

and latitude means that some place will always be at its peak of prettiness. Check out www.blueridgeparkway.org for full information and en route attractions. Possible stops include the following:

Cumberland Knob Mile 217.5. NPS visitors center, easy walk to the knob.

Doughton Park Mile 241.1. Gas, food, trails and camping.

Bluffs Lodge (☎ 336-372-4499) Mile 241.1. Walk to the old Brinegar Cabin to feel the isolation of the old mountain life.

Blowing Rock Mile 291.8. Small tourist town, named for a craggy, commercialized cliff that offers great views, occasional updrafts and an Indian love story.

Moses H Cone Memorial Park Mile 294.1. A lovely old estate with pleasant walks and a craft shop.

Linn Cove Viaduct Mile 304.4. Graceful curves of concrete skirting the sheer domes of Grandfather Mountain.

Grandfather Mountain (☎ 800-468-7325) Mile 305.1. A picturesque, privately-run park with hiking trails.

Linville Falls Mile 316.4. Lovely hiking trails to the falls.

Little Switzerland Mile 334. Old-style mountain resort.

Mt Mitchell State Park Mile 355.5. Highest mountain east of the Mississippi (6684ft), hiking trails and tent camping.

Folk Art Center Mile 382. Traditional and contemporary local craft work.

Boone & Around

A 6-mile detour west of the Blue Ridge Parkway, Boone offers good access to the surrounding area, and the Appalachian State University (ASU) is a bonus. The **visitors center** (☎ 828-262-3516, 888-251-9867; 208 Howard St; 9am-5pm Mon-Fri) has information about canoeing outfitters, ski areas and parks.

Appalachian Cultural Museum (☎ 828-262-3117; University Hall Dr; adult/child $4/2; 10am-5pm Tue-Sat, 1-5pm Sun), off Blowing Rock Rd, is a serious attempt to present mountain life and history beyond the hillbilly stereotypes. It has first-class exhibits and thoughtful interpretive material.

Blowing Rock Stage Company (☎ 828-295-9168; 452-2 Sunset Dr) has live performances throughout the summer. Hwy 321 from Blowing Rock to Boone is studded with tourist traps. The cutesy **Tweetsie Railroad** (☎ 828-264-9061; adult/child $24/18; vary by season) is the best of them.

Boone KOA (☎ 828-264-7250; campsites $22) is 4 miles north, off Hwy 194.

Boone Trail Motel (☎ 828-264-8839; 820 E King St; r $30; P) This 22-room motel is a good budget option if you're camping and want to abandon your tent for the night.

Broyhill Inn & Conference Center (☎ 828-262-2204, 800-951-6048; www.broyhillinn.com; 775 Bodenheimer Dr; weekday/weekend $120/135; P) This great place run by ASU has a sparkling location at the top of a wooded hill above Boone. Rooms are recently renovated and the restaurant, open all day, is a treat.

Asheville

With a wonderful and surprising mix of retired rich, 1920s charm and bohemian hippy, Asheville is a beautiful place to chill for a bit. Everywhere you turn there are gorgeous, wooded Blue Ridge Mountains and sparkling blue skies. Sitting at the confluence of the Swannanoa and French Broad Rivers, Asheville sits in the middle of a loop formed by I-40/I-240. The town is relatively compact and easy to negotiate on foot.

The **visitors center** (☎ 828-258-6101, 800-257-1300; 151 Haywood St; 8:30am-5:30pm Mon-Fri, 9am-5pm Sat & Sun) is at I-240 exit 4C.

Malaprop's Bookstore & Café (☎ 828-254-6734; 55 Haywood St; 9am-9pm Mon-Thu, until 10pm Fri & Sat, until 6pm Sun) is an excellent place for regional maps and travel books; join the cappuccino-sipping bohemians.

The **public library** (☎ 828-251-4991; 67 Haywood Ave; 10am-8pm Mon-Thu, until 6pm Fri, until 5pm Sat) offers free Internet access.

Biltmore Estate (☎ 828-255-1333, 800-624-1575; adult/child $36/27; 9am-5pm), with 250 rooms, is a gorgeous, sprawling estate billed as America's largest private house and is certainly Asheville's largest tourist attraction. Built for the filthy-rich Vanderbilt family as a holiday home, the 1895 mansion is styled after a French château and is overwhelmingly sumptuous in scale and decoration. You need to spend quite a few hours viewing the estate to see everything and to justify the hefty admission charges. The estate's winery offers tastings and sales. Mid-priced meals are available at several venues, and the gift shop is the size of a small supermarket.

Thomas Wolfe Memorial (☎ 828-253-8304; 52 N Market St; 9am-5pm Tue-Sat, 1-5pm Sun) is the local literary landmark, an early-1900s boardinghouse that was the model for 'Dixieland' in Wolfe's novel *Look Homeward Angel*. The house has been undergoing extensive repairs since a 1998 arson attack, but the adjacent visitors center shows a video on the writer's life.

SLEEPING & EATING

Asheville Bed & Breakfast Association (☎ 828-252-0200, 877-262-6867; www.ashevillebba.com) Handles bookings for 21 B&Bs in the Asheville area, from Victorian mansions to mountain retreats.

Chain motels cluster north of downtown at Merrimon Ave, with rates averaging $40 to $50. East on Tunnel Rd are some independent places such as **Blue Ridge Motor Lodge** (☎ 828-254-0805; r $60) and **Townhouse Motel** (☎ 828-253-8753; 141 Tunnel Rd; r $55).

Log Cabin Motor Court (☎ 828-645-6546; 330 Weaverville Hwy; cabins $50-100) For something different, stay here in a rustic but tidy cabin. In summer, a two-day stay is required.

Grove Park Inn Resort (☎ 828-252-2711, 800-438-5800; 290 Macon Ave; r from $180; P) This sprawling resort with 510 rooms in a 1913 classic Arts and Crafts building has gorgeous rooms, a fitness center, tennis courts, spa and four restaurants. Rates fluctuate wildly, depending on the season.

Inn on Biltmore Estate (☎ 828-225-1660, 800-922-0084; P) A stunning option on Vanderbilt's property, the resort has everything, including an outdoor pool and hot tub.

Bear Creek Campground (☎ 828-253-0798; 81 S Bear Creek Rd; campsites $18-20) Southwest of town at I-40 exit 47, it has full facilities.

Downtown has many interesting eateries.

Blue Moon Bakery & Café (☎ 828-252-6063; 60 Biltmore Ave; dishes $6-10) A good stop for breakfast and sandwiches.

Beanstreets (☎ 828-255-8180; 3 Broadway Ave; pastries $2-4) Has great coffee and light meals in a fun atmosphere.

Laughing Seed Café (☎ 828-252-3445; 40 Wall St; lunch $6-10, dinner specialities $13-15; Wed-Mon) This veggie haunt offers great vegetarian dishes and organic Green Man beer.

GETTING THERE & AROUND

Greyhound (☎ 828-253-8451; 2 Tunnel Rd) has several buses daily to Knoxville, TN ($27, two hours) and Raleigh ($53, nine hours); and one to Atlanta, GA ($38, from 6¾ hours). **Asheville Transit** (☎ 828-253-5691; www.ashevilletransit.com; 60 W Haywood St; bus fare $0.75) provides a limited local bus service.

Chimney Rock Park

The photogenic 'chimney,' complete with US flag, in the heart of this private **park** (☎ 828-625-9611; adult/child $12/5.50; 8:30am-4:30pm) is a widely publicized rock spire a pleasant 20-mile drive southeast of Asheville. An elevator takes visitors 258ft up to the chimney, but the real draw is the exciting hike around the cliffs to a 404ft waterfall.

Cherokee

Some of the Cherokee people escaped removal on the Trail of Tears by hiding here in the Great Smoky Mountains. Their descendants, some 11,600 members of the Eastern Band of the Cherokee, now occupy a 56,000-acre reservation at the edge of the national park. The small town of Cherokee caters to the lowest common denominator of the tourist trade, with ersatz Indian souvenir shops, fast-food joints and **Harrah's Cherokee Casino** (☎ 800-427-7247; Hwy 19).

The best thing here is the **Museum of the Cherokee Indian** (☎ 828-497-3481; adult/child $8/5; 9am-5pm), on Drama Rd/US 441N, which has a special interpretive exhibit on the Trail of Tears.

Oconaluftee Indian Village (☎ 828-497-22315; adult/child $13/6; 9am-5:30pm mid-May–late-Oct) is a replica of an 18th-century Cherokee village where Cherokees demonstrate traditional crafts. The outdoor show **Unto These Hills** (adult/child $16/8) dramatizes the history of the Cherokee from the first European contact up to the Trail of Tears.

Great Smoky Mountains National Park

This park straddles the border with Tennessee and is noted for its biodiversity and its more than 10 million annual visitors. Near Cherokee, **Oconaluftee Visitors Center** (☎ 423-436-1200; Hwy 441) is the main access point on the southeast side of the park; the **pioneer farm** (admission free) there is worth a look. The park can be accessed at four other points on the southeast side, which may not be as crowded (p557).

Nantahala

About 25 miles southwest of Cherokee, the Appalachian Trail crosses the Nantahala River, creating a natural focus for outdoor activities. The excellent **Nantahala Outdoor Center** (☎ 828-488-2175, 800-232-7238; www.noc.com; Hwy 19/74), near Bryson City, provides equipment as well as services for **hiking**, **mountain biking**, **canoeing** and **white-water rafting**. In particular, it offers a great range of rafting trips on nearby rivers, like the Nantahala, Chatooga, Pigeon and Ocoee.

NORTH CAROLINA COAST

Barrier islands run the whole length of North Carolina's coast, with miles of sandy beaches facing the Atlantic and a series of estuaries, sounds and enclosed tidal lagoons. Many of the beaches are heavily developed as holiday resorts, but some areas are protected as national seashore.

While the Wright brothers sought sand, solitude and steady winds to get them off the ground in the Outer Banks, most seafarers hoped to avoid the islands altogether. Their common failure is noted in the 2000-plus shipwrecks that have accumulated in shoal-filled waters.

The Albermarle

The wild, swampy region around Albermarle Sound was the site of the state's first European settlement, and from the 18th century it became a focus for canals that provided protected transport routes north to the Chesapeake and south to Wilmington. Today it's popular for boating, fishing and retirement.

EDENTON

Founded in 1712, this small town at the west end of Albermarle Sound was the center of economic, social and political life in early colonial times. In the 1774 'Edenton tea party,' 50 local-society ladies swore off tea in protest at British taxes. The town provided signatories to the Declaration of Independence and the Constitution, as well as two state governors and one of the first Supreme Court justices. Within 50 years, development bypassed Edenton, leaving pretty streets of 18th-century buildings. See the **visitors center** (☎ 252-482-2637; 108 N Broad St; 9am-5pm Mon-Sat, 1-4pm Sun) for accommodations and a self-guided-tour map.

ELIZABETH CITY

At the Pasquotank River narrows, Elizabeth City became a shipping and transportation center after the Dismal Swamp Canal was completed in 1803. The **Museum of the Albermarle** (☎ 252-335-1453; 1116 Hwy 17 S; admission free; 9am-5pm Tue-Sat) gives a good account of the canals and the area's history. The town center is pleasantly old-fashioned; the **visitors center** (☎ 252-335-4365; 502 E Ehringhaus St; 9am-5pm Mon-Fri) has a walking-tour map. Motels are on the North Road St/US 17 bypass road.

Outer Banks

Hwy 12 runs along this chain of barrier islands, curving east of Albermarle and Pamlico Sounds in a 100-mile arc that's like a road across the sea. From north to south, Bodie Island, Roanoke Island, Hatteras Island and Ocracoke Island are linked by bridges and ferries. The islands are low sand dunes, with long, sandy beaches on the ocean side and lagoons and marshes on the inland side. The northern islands are heavily developed, with holiday homes, beach resorts and hordes of summer visitors. Out of season, things are very quiet and many businesses close. Much of the central islands is protected national seashore, with a few small towns and a wild, windswept beauty.

In September 2003, Hurricane Isabel unleashed her fury on the US east coast, and the Outer Banks were hit hard. High winds and massive waves toppled and flooded many buildings, wiped out parts of Hwy 12, and left many residents stranded without power or water.

Residents along this gorgeous stretch know both nature's graceful touch and her awe-inspiring might.

ORIENTATION & INFORMATION

Most of the tourist attractions and facilities are along a 16-mile strip of Bodie Island, in the virtually contiguous towns of **Kitty Hawk**, **Kill Devil Hills** and **Nags Head**. Hwy 12, also called Virginia Dare Trail, or 'the coast road,' is a two-lane road running close to the beach for the length of the strip. US 158, usually called 'the Bypass,' is a four-lane road running parallel but further inland. Locations are often given in terms of 'Mileposts,' starting from Milepost 1 at the north end of the tourist strip, where US 158 crosses to the mainland on the Wright Memorial Bridge. At the south end of the strip, just past Milepost 16, US 64/264 connects to the mainland via Roanoke Island. Roanoke has two communities: upscale, tourist-oriented Manteo and the functional fishing town of Wanchese.

The best sources of information are at the **visitors centers** (Kitty Hawk ☎ 252-261-4644;

Milepost 1½; 9am-5:30pm year-round; Manteo ☎ 252-473-2138, 800-446-6262; US 64/264; 8am-6pm Mon-Fri, noon-4pm Sat & Sun year-round). Other visitors centers in Nags Head are open April to October. Also useful is www.outerbanks.org.

SIGHTS

Wright Brothers National Monument

The dunes of Kill Devil Hills are unspectacular, but the site carries some of the excitement of the Wright brothers' historic achievement. The memorial is near Milepost 8, where there's a heavy-looking, art deco–style granite monument atop a sand dune, inscribed: 'In commemoration of the conquest of the air by the brothers Wilbur and Orville Wright. Conceived by genius, achieved by dauntless resolution and unconquerable faith.'

Exhibits at the **visitors center** (☎ 252-441-7430; admission $3; 9am-5pm) trace the Wrights' painstaking development work in Dayton, Ohio, and the experiments conducted at summer camps here over several years. See replicas of their 1902 glider and 1903 powered Flyer, with informative hourly talks. The distances of the first powered flights on December 17, 1903, are marked, from the first tentative 120ft hop to the fourth flight, which reached an impressive 852ft.

Fort Raleigh National Historic Site

This site on Roanoke Island saw the first English colonies in North America meet with total failure. The fate of the 'lost colony' remains a mystery, but the **visitors center** (☎ 252-473-5772; 9am-6pm) has exhibits, artifacts and a free film about Native Americans and English settlers that will fuel your imagination. Look for the prints based on 1585 illustrations by John White, which are now some of the best-known depictions of pre-European North America. A small mound nearby is meant to re-create the earthworks of the original fort.

The **Lost Colony Outdoor Drama** is an immensely popular and long-running show that dramatizes the debacle. It plays from mid-June through to August at 8:30pm in the **Waterside Theater** (☎ 252-473-3414, 866-468-7630; www.thelostcolony.org; adult/child $16/8).

The **Elizabethan Gardens** (☎ 252-473-3234; adult/child $6/2; daily in summer) make a pretty association with the England of 400 years ago. **Elizabeth II** is a 69ft sailing ship built in the style of an old English vessel. It gives a good feel for 16th-century sea travel, as do exhibits and a film in the **visitors center** (☎ 252-473-1144; adult/child $8/5; Apr-Oct).

Cape Hatteras National Seashore

Saving much of the Outer Banks area from overdevelopment, the fragile necklace of islands along the national seashore extends some 70 miles. Three **visitors centers** (Bodie ☎ 252-441-5711; Hatteras ☎ 252-995-4474; Ocracoke ☎ 252-928-4531; 9am-6pm) serve the park on the main islands. The visitors centers are open year round from 9am to 6pm in summer, with shorter hours during the cooler winter months. The **park headquarters** (☎ 252-473-2111; www.nps.gov/caha; 1401 National Park Drive) is in Manteo.

Natural attractions include local and migratory water birds, marshes, woodlands, dunes and miles of empty beaches.

Pea Island National Wildlife Refuge (☎ 252-473-1131; admission free; 9am-4pm daily Mar-Nov, 9am-4pm Thu-Sun rest of the year), at the northern end of Hatteras Island is a great place for watching wildlife along the nature trails and observation points.

Lighthouses are spaced all along the Outer Banks, including the horizontally striped Bodie Island Lighthouse, where the keepers' quarters are open March to September. At 208ft tall, the spirally striped Cape Hatteras Lighthouse is the tallest brick lighthouse in the US. You can climb the **268 steps** (adult/child $4/2; Apr-Oct), and check out the **visitors center** (☎ 252-995-4474; year-round).

Other things to look for include the **Chicamacomico Lifesaving Station** in the village of Rodanthe, one of seven lifesaving stations in the Outer Banks The village of Ocracoke revels in its pirate past: Edward Teach, also known as Blackbeard, used to hide out in the area.

ACTIVITIES

Popular outdoor activities include kayaking, fishing, sailing, windsurfing, hang gliding and cycling – all well catered for in the northern resort areas. Swimming is excellent offshore, though chilly outside the summer months. The usually calm coastal waters occasionally kick up, creating perfect conditions for bodysurfing.

Ocean Atlantic Rentals (☎ 252-441-7823, 800-635-9559; www.oar-nc.com; Milepost 10; bicycle/surfboard/kayak hire per day $10/15/30, per week $35/45/90) offers good

THE SOUTH

deals on rentals from everything to baby cribs, linens and water-sports equipment. Bikes, two-person kayaks and surfboards are also available.

Kitty Hawk Kites Outdoors (☎ 252-441-4124, 800-334-4777; skate/bicycle/kayak/sailboat hire $10/15/60/80), at Jockey's Ridge State Park, offers beginners' hang gliding lessons from $65. It also rents kayaks, sailboats, bikes and in-line skates and has a variety of tours and courses.

Surfing on the numerous beach breaks is best from August to October, with the East Coast championships in early September, and the hurricane season starting in October bringing the really big waves. **Whalebone Surf Shop** (☎ 252-261-8737; 4900A N Croatan Hwy) has equipment and information. **Canadian Hole**, in Pamlico Sound just south of Avon, is a serious windsurfing site.

SLEEPING

HI Outer Banks Hostel (☎ 252-261-2294, 877-453-2545; www.talking-pages.com/obhostel; 1004 W Kitty Hawk Rd; dm member/nonmember $16/19, r $31/35, campsites $17) In a pleasant but out-of-the-way location, this friendly hostel has a communal kitchen, outdoor grill and camping. The friendly management arranges kayak trips, bicycle rentals and summer campfires. No booze consumption is allowed onsite.

The area has hundreds of motels, efficiencies and B&Bs, but many close in winter and most are booked up in summer. The visitors centers can offer referrals. Listed are high-season rates; expect to pay half (or less) in the off-season.

Days Inn Mariner (☎ 252-441-2021, 800-325-2525; Milepost 7; r $130-220; P ✻ ☗) On the Beach Rd in Kill Devil Hills, it's open most of the year and has a variety of rooms and an outdoor pool.

Island Inn (☎ 252-928-4351, 877-456-3466; www.ocracokeislandinn.com; r $90-225) In Ocracoke on Hwy 12 at Point Rd, this grand old turn-of-the-century clapboard inn has Ocracoke's only heated pool. There's an excellent dining room and the front porch overlooks the ocean.

National Park Service (NPS) runs a few summer-only **campgrounds** (☎ 800-365-2267; campsites $18), with cold-water showers and flush toilets. These are **Oregon Inlet**, near the Bodie Island lighthouse, **Cape Point** and **Frisco** near the Cape Hatteras lighthouse and **Ocracoke** on Ocracoke Island. Only sites at Ocracoke can be reserved; others are first-come, first-served.

EATING

The main tourist strip on Bodie Island has the most restaurants and nightlife, but only in season. The following are all nonchain places open for lunch and dinner year-round on Beach Rd.

Black Pelican (☎ 252-261-3171; Milepost 4; mains $10-20) Good seafood dishes such as steamed oysters, blackened tuna steak, mussels and excellent wood-fired pizzas. The restaurant, in an old lifesaving station and telegraph office, opens lunch and dinner.

Awful Arthur's Oyster Bar (☎ 252-441-5955; Milepost 6; lunch $6-10, dinner $10-15) Another surefire bet for seafood and a hopping atmosphere.

Jolly Roger (☎ 252-441-6530; Milepost 6.75; meals $6-10) This small family place is good for breakfast, lunch or an inexpensive dinner. It serves hearty breakfasts, Italian meals and prime rib.

Goombays (☎ 252-441-6001; Milepost 7; meals $6-17) As well as being a friendly bar, Goombays serves seafood, good sandwiches and surprises such as coconut chicken in pineapple cream sauce. There's live music on Wednesday nights.

GETTING THERE & AWAY

If you're driving, access Hwy 12 (the main road along the cape) from Hwy 158 at Kitty Hawk or from Hwy 64-264, which leads over Roanoke Island to the park's northern entrance.

No public transport exists to or on the Outer Banks. Free car ferries between Hatteras and Ocracoke Islands run at least hourly from 5am to 10pm; bookings aren't necessary. **Ferries** (☎ 800-293-3779; per car $15) run between Ocracoke and Cedar Island (2¼ hours) every two hours or so and should be reserved, especially in summer. **Ferries** (☎ 800-773-1094) also link Ocracoke and Swan Quarter on the mainland.

Crystal Coast

The southern Outer Banks, comprising several coastal towns, sounds, islands, inlets and barrier islands, are collectively called the 'Crystal Coast,' at least for tourist offices' promotion purposes. Morehead City attracts underwater adventurers who come to explore the coast's many shipwrecks, especially June to September, when the water is warm and clear.

CAPE LOOKOUT NATIONAL SEASHORE

This 55-mile-long barrier-island system, mostly dunes and shifting sands, has virtually no visitor facilities and can be reached only by boat. The **visitors center** (☎ 252-728-2250; 8:30am-4:30pm year-round) is on Harkers Island, accessible by bridge from the mainland. The national seashore has seasonal nesting sites for turtles and shorebirds, and the picturesque abandoned village of Portsmouth is at its northern tip. With its striking diamond pattern, the **Cape Lookout Lighthouse** is arguably the most photogenic on the Atlantic coast. Day trips are possible by ferry (about $20 round-trip) from Harkers Island and the coastal towns of Atlantic, Davis and Beaufort.

BEAUFORT

One of the oldest towns in the state, Beaufort (*bow*-fort) was originally called 'Fish Town' and still trades off its maritime heritage. The **visitors center** (☎ 252-728-5225; 138 Turner St; 9:30-5pm Mon-Sat) is in the Beaufort Historic Site with several 18th-century buildings. The highlight is the **North Carolina Maritime Museum** (☎ 252-728-7317; 315 Front St; admission free; 9am-5pm Mon-Fri, 10am-5pm Sat, 1-5pm Sun), with well done displays on lifesaving, outboard motors and local fishing.

B&Bs are abundant and expensive in season. **Inlet Inn** (☎ 252-728-3600; www.inlet-inn.com; 601 Front St; r from $120) has big, comfy rooms with fireplaces and porches. On Front St are bars and eateries that can be lively on a warm evening, as well as boats and excursions to the islands.

MOREHEAD CITY

A rather unappealing industrial and commercial stretch of US 70 goes through Morehead City, but it's worth a short detour to the waterfront, where the scuba diving around shipwrecks is excellent. Get area information the from well-stocked **Crystal Coast Visitors Bureau** (☎ 252-726-8148; 3407 Arendell St/Hwy 70; 9am-5pm Mon-Fri, 10am-5pm Sat & Sun). **Olympus Dive Center** (☎ 252-726-9432; www.olymusdiving.com; 713 Shepard St) rents scuba gear and arranges dive charters starting at $60 per person.

A bridge from Morehead City crosses to Atlantic City on **Bogue Island**, a mass-market seaside resort.

Run by the Olympus Dive Center (contact it for information), **Olympus' Diver Lodge** is two blocks from the dive shop and is dedicated to hard-core divers. It has 32 bunks in five rooms with shared baths. Call ahead for rates, which vary depending on season and availability.

Best Western Buccaneer Inn (☎ 866-656-7129; 2806 Arendell; r $40-70; P) has a restaurant, huge outdoor pool and 91 rooms. It bustles with both divers and business folk.

Wilmington

Wilmington is a busy little port town with factories, a university, film studios and a neat old downtown and waterfront area. Its attractive historic district is one of the country's largest, and the oak-lined streets are fun to peruse. It is one of the best places to stop along the coast, and the surrounding area has a wealth of historic interest.

The **visitors center** (☎ 910-341-4030, 800-222-4757; 24 N 3rd St; 9am-5pm Mon-Fri, 10am-5pm Sat & Sun), in the 1892 Courthouse building, has a walking-tour map and details of several historic houses.

SIGHTS

Cameron Art Museum (☎ 910-395-5999; 3201 S 17th St; adult/child $5/2; 10am-5pm Tue-Sat, until 9pm Fri, until 4pm Sun) focuses on North Carolinian artists and is known for its exceptionally good collection of prints by impressionist Mary Cassatt. Come for the brunch on Sunday.

Cape Fear Museum (☎ 910-341-4350; 814 Market St; adult/child $5/1; 9am-5pm Tue-Sat, 1-5pm Sun) includes a model of Wilmington in the blockade-running 1860s, and a small display about local legend Michael Jordan.

Take a river taxi ($4 round-trip) or cross the Cape Fear Bridge to reach the **Battleship North Carolina** (☎ 910-251-5797; adult/child $9/4.50; year-round). This 44,000-ton monster was the epitome of sea power when she was launched. Self-guided tours take in the crew's quarters, captain's cabin, gun turrets, galleys and more.

Screen Gems Studios (☎ 910-343-3433; 1223 N 23rd St; admission $10; tour noon & 2pm Sat & Sun) offers a two-hour behind-the-scenes tour of the working studio where shows like *Dawson's Creek* and *Firestarter* were filmed. There are no Hollywood-style special effects, but the guides know their stuff and are full of anecdotes.

SLEEPING & EATING

Best Western Carolinian (☎ 910-763-4653, 800-528-1234; 2916 Market St; weekday/weekend $80/120; P) Not your average chain, the Carolinian has comfortable, spacious rooms and a friendly resort vibe.

Coastline Inn (☎ 910-763-2800, 800-617-7732; www.coastline-inn.com; 503 Nutt St; weekday/weekend $90/130; P) In a quiet spot partially overlooking the harbor, this place has spacious, comfy rooms, most with kitchenettes.

Shell Island Resort Hotel (☎ 910-256-8696, 800-689-6765; www.shellisland.com; 2700 N Lumina Ave; r from $150; P) This full-service resort complex on nearby Wrightsville Beach offers top-end luxury. There are a variety of rooms and price levels, so call ahead to see what's current.

There's a great selection of restaurants along the riverfront.

Water St Café (☎ 910-343-0042; 5 S Water St; lunch $6-10, dinner $9-15) An institution with good sandwiches, soups and more substantial fare in the evening. Bits of *Dawson's Creek* were filmed here – this was Dawson's mother's restaurant. There's sidewalk dining, and Dixieland, blues and flamenco music in the evenings.

GETTING THERE & AWAY

Greyhound (☎ 910-762-6073; 201 Hartnett St), north of downtown, sends daily buses to Raleigh ($29, 2½ hours) and Charleston, SC ($40, five hours).

Cape Fear

For a good day's detour, head south of Wilmington to the tip of Cape Fear, with possible stops at Carolina Beach, Kure Beach and **Fort Fisher State Historic Site** (☎ 910-458-5538; 9am-5pm Mon-Sat, 1-5pm Sun), where earthwork and exhibits explain the fort's vital Civil War role. You can catch a ferry across the mouth of the Cape Fear River ($5 per car) to the old fishing village of Southport, and return via **Orton Plantation**, with its exceptionally colorful gardens.

SOUTH CAROLINA

It's not hard to get off the beaten path in South Carolina – in fact, the entire state is off the beaten path. There is not a single major city, and the large population centers are really just overgrown towns. The state is most famous for the colonial port of Charleston, with its grand mansions and gracious manners. A string of islands just off the coast shelters the mainland from storms and fosters a truly unique culture called Gullah, created by former slaves who were able to retain many of their African traditions. There are diverse beaches, from tacky and crowded Myrtle Beach and golf-crazed Hilton Head to wild and undeveloped state parks. The interior of the state is dotted with small towns and miles of country roads that wind past farmlands, white clapboard churches and crumbling sharecropper shacks. Smack dab in the middle of the state is the sleepy capital of Columbia.

History

More than 28 separate tribes of Native Americans have lived in what's now South Carolina. The most influential were the Cherokee, who were eventually forcibly removed during the tragic Trail of Tears.

The English founded the Carolina colony in 1670 and built a settlement called Charles Towne, later known as Charleston. The first settlers came from Barbados and thus became a colony of a colony (Barbados was a colony of England). South Carolina's judicial system, slave code and original form of government were based on those of Barbados.

The first cash king was rice. Africans from the rice-growing regions of Sierra Leone, Senegal, The Gambia and Angola were enslaved and brought over to turn impenetrable swamps into cultivated rice fields.

By the 1730s, there existed two South Carolinas: the Lowcountry, a refined community of aristocrats and their slaves; and the Backcountry, a frontier settled by Scotch-Irish and Swiss-German farmers. This split played a major role in the Revolutionary War.

South Carolina was the first state to secede and the first battle of the Civil War (dubbed the 'late, great unpleasantness' by Charlestonians), occurred at Fort Sumter

SOUTH CAROLINA FACTS

Nickname Palmetto State
Population 4,107,183 (25th)
Area 30,109 sq miles (40th)
Admitted to Union May 23, 1788 (8th); seceded 1860; readmitted 1868
Capital city Columbia (population 100,000)
Other cities Charleston (80,000), Greenville (58,000)
State dance The shag
Birthplace of activist Mary McLeod Bethune (1875–1955), James Brown (b 1933), jazzman Dizzy Gillespie (1917–93), songstress Eartha Kitt (b 1927), political activist Jesse Jackson (b 1941), TV personality Vanna White (b 1957)
Home of the first US public library (1698), museum (1773), steam railroad (1833)

in Charleston Harbor. The fort fell to the Confederates 30 hours later.

After the fall of the Confederacy, prominent families were penniless. While white South Carolinians mourned, black South Carolinians rejoiced and racially motivated violence ensued. The KKK became extremely active. This divisiveness set the tone for South Carolina's ride through the Civil Rights movement almost a century later.

Like many Southern states, South Carolina gets media attention for white supremacy but is ignored in times of cooperation. Attitudes are changing with the passing of time and changing demographics.

NORTH COAST

South Carolina's north coast is dominated by the resort town of Myrtle Beach. Further south, sleepy villages and parks set a slower pace. A few minutes outside Charleston, grand houses remain as testaments to the state's plantation past.

Myrtle Beach

Myrtle Beach proper is the central area in the 25-mile strip of overdeveloped oceanfront called 'The Grand Strand,' which is smeared from North Myrtle Beach to Pawleys Island. College students swarm here for spring break and summer vacation, and holidaymakers come for the plethora of amusements and golf courses (there are over 100). At first, Myrtle Beach seems like a sun-bleached, whitewashed Las Vegas without the casinos. Crowds, traffic and too many tacky souvenir shops threaten anyone seeking a quiet, nature-filled vacation. Though the beach is quite pretty, it is backed by a near-continuous row of high-rises, parking lots and neon signs along Ocean Blvd. Your best bet is to get tucked into a hotel, take a long swim in the Atlantic and get into the festival spirit of it all.

The main **visitors center** (☎ 843-626-7444, 800-496-8250; www.myrtlebeachinfo.com; 1200 N Oak St; 8:30am-5pm; north 1800 Hwy 501 W in Aynor; south 3401 Hwy 17 S in Murrells Inlet) is augmented by its other offices.

The heart of the resort, historically and geographically, is the amusement park **Myrtle Beach Pavilion** (☎ 843-448-6456; www.mbpavilion.com; 9th & Ocean Blvd; day pass $24). Nearby, the **Family Kingdom** (☎ 843-626-3447; 3rd & Ocean Blvd; day/water park/combination pass $20/16/26) is cheaper and has a giant ocean-side water park. Find out about all the sights and hotels in the giant *Stay & Play* guide, available free at the visitors center.

SLEEPING

Hundreds of hotels have prices that vary by the season and day; a room might cost $30 in January and more than $150 in July. In summer, many will be all booked up, so it's helpful to prearrange or contact the visitors center for help. The following lists high-season (mid-June to mid-August) rates.

Best Western Grand Strand Motel (☎ 843-448-1461, 800-433-1461; 1804 S Ocean Blvd; weekday/weekend $80/90; P) Across the street from the beach, but with a great pool and nice rooms, this is the best value and is close to the action.

Firebird Motor Inn (☎ 843-448-7032, 800-852-7032; www.firebirdinn.com; 2007 S Ocean Blvd; d poolside/oceanfront from $95/120) Lacking in frills, this small, friendly beachfront hotel is also a great value for its beachfront location.

Compass Cove (☎ 800-326-0234, 843-448-8373; 2311 S Ocean Blvd; r $100-390; P) This sprawling oceanfront resort has quite a few amenities, including 21 pools. Rooms in three different buildings range all over the place in price and size. It's best to call ahead to see what's available.

Myrtle Beach State Park (☎ 843-238-5325; campsites $23, cabins per week $545) Most campgrounds are for RVs, but this state park 3 miles south of central Myrtle Beach has cabins that

THE SOUTH

sleep four to eight in summer, campsites and its own beach.

EATING

The 1700 or so restaurants are mostly midrange and high volume, but competition keeps prices reasonable. For Americana ambience, hit the burger bars on Ocean Blvd near the amusement parks. Seafood, ironically, is not a specialty; locals go to the nearby fishing village of Murrells Inlet.

Croissants Bakery & Café (☎ 843-448-2253; 504A 27th Ave N, at Kings Hwy; meals $2-7; 🕑 7am-2pm) Off the strip, this great little spot serves good breakfasts, wraps, sandwiches, and beautiful pies and desserts.

Cagney's Old Place Restaurant (☎ 843-449-3824; 9911 N Kings Hwy at 71st Ave; 🕑 dinner Mon-Sat) A little off the beaten track, this is a dinner favorite for surf and turf.

DRINKING & ENTERTAINMENT

Music variety shows are a Myrtle Beach standard, combining rock, country and bluegrass music with a dose of comedy, Christianity and patriotism. Some include a fixed-menu meal for around $35; reservations are recommended. Bars and clubs catering to the college crowd include:

Studebakers (☎ 843-448-9747; 2000 N Kings Hwy)

Dead Dog Saloon (☎ 843-445-6700; 404 26th Ave N) Has a great patio and hosts Saturday cookouts.

Bummz Beach Café (☎ 843-916-9111; 2002 N Ocean Blvd) Has an ocean view and a swimsuit-clad crowd.

GETTING THERE & AROUND

The traffic coming and going on Hwy 17 Business (also called Kings Hwy) can be infuriating. To avoid 'The Strand' altogether, stay on Hwy 17 bypass, or take Hwy 31 (Carolina Bays Parkway), which parallels Hwy 17 between Hwy 501 and Hwy 9.

Myrtle Beach International Airport (☎ 843-448-1589) is within the city limits. **Greyhound** (☎ 843-448-2472; 511 7th Ave N) services New York ($92, from 16 hours); Atlanta, GA ($46, from 9½ hours); and Charleston ($24, 2½ hours). **Coastal Rapid Public Transport** (☎ 843-488-0865) has frequent services up and down the resort area.

Around Myrtle Beach

At the south end of the Grand Strand, **Murrells Inlet** is a small village with charter boats for fishing trips and a choice of seafood restaurants.

The town's other restaurants are also good since all serve seafood harvested less than a mile away.

> **THE AUTHOR'S CHOICE**
>
> **Nance's Creekfront Restaurant and Oyster Roast** (☎ 843-651-2696; 4583 Hwy 17; steamed oysters $15; 🕑 dinner) During the fall and winter months, oysters are at their sweetest; they are plucked from marsh mud and steamed over a hot grill. This is the place to get 'em fresh and delicious. The hole in the middle of your table is for discarding oyster shells. Nance's sits right on the creek with a wonderful sunset view.

CHARLESTON

Whether you're an architecture connoisseur, or a person who goes, 'wow, that's cool' when you see a beautiful building, Charleston's numerous antebellum homes, churches and structures will compel you to ooh and ahh. Overflowing with history, charming streets and historic districts, Charleston is one of the most appealing urban areas in America. Blooming gardens send a sweet floral scent meandering through the streets. Whether you choose to wander on your own, or join one of many horse-drawn or walking tours, Charleston will leave its sultry kiss lingering on your skin.

History

Even well before the Revolutionary War, Charles Towne (named for Charles II) was one of the busiest ports on the eastern seaboard and the center of a prosperous rice-growing and trading colony. With influences from the West Indies and Africa, France and other European countries, it became a cosmopolitan city often compared to New Orleans.

The Charleston & Hamburg Railroad began operations in 1833, transporting cotton 136 miles from the inland area to Charleston's ports. At the time it was an engineering wonder, and it secured Charleston's position as a principal East Coast port over rival Savannah.

CHARLESTON
0 600 m
0 0.4 mi
INFORMATION
Chamber of Commerce 1 D3
Charleston Preservation Society 2 E5
Fort Sumter Visitor & Education Center 3 F3
Historic Charleston Foundation Preservation Center 4 F5
Library 5 E3
Visitors Information Center 6 E3
Waldenbooks 7 E4
SIGHTS & ACTIVITIES pp468–9
Aiken-Rhett House 8 E3
Charleston Museum 9 E3
Circular Congregational Church 10 E5
Edmonston-Alston House 11 F6
French Huguenot Church 12 F5
Gibbes Museum of Art 13 E5
Heyward-Washington House 14 F5
Joseph Manigault House 15 E3
Nathaniel Russell House 16 E6
South Carolina Aquarium 17 F3
St Michael's Episcopal Church 18 E5
The Bicycle Shoppe 19 E4
SLEEPING pp470–1
1837 Bed & Breakfast 20 D4
Andrew Pinckney Inn 21 E4
Bed, No Breakfast 22 C4
Best Western King Charles Inn 23 E4
Charleston's Historic Hostel 24 D3
Days Inn Downtown 25 E5
Hayne House 26 E6
Holiday Inn 27 E3
Market Pavilion Hotel 28 F4
Meeting Street Inn 29 E5
Mills House Hotel 30 E5
Not So Hostel 31 C3
Planters Inn 32 E4
Two Meeting St Inn 33 F6
To North Charleston (7mi), Greyhound Station (7mi), Amtrak Station (8mi), Charleston International Airport (12mi) & I-95 (49mi)
To Mount Pleasant (6.5mi), Georgetown (60mi) & Myrtle Beach (94mi)
To Fort Sumter (4mi)
To the Citadel (0.5mi)
To Lake Aire RV Park (12mi), Oak Plantation Campground (15mi) & Savannah (GA) (104mi)
Drum Island
Hampton Park
College Park
Harmon Field
Marion Square
College of Charleston
MUSC Medical Complex
Charleston Memorial Hospital
Charleston Maritime Center
Wragg Mall
Ashley River Bridge
Crosstown (Clark) Expwy

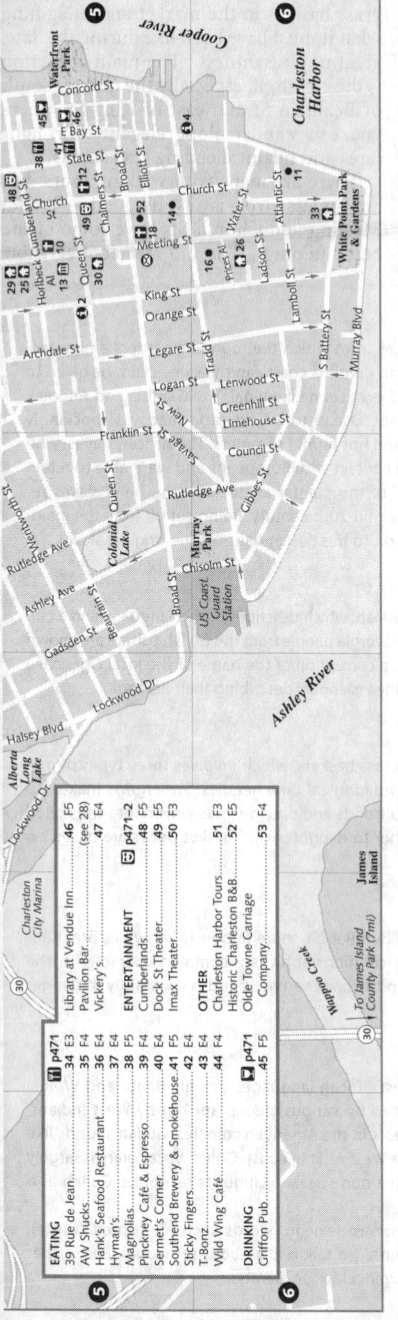

The first shots of the Civil War were fired at Fort Sumter, in Charleston's harbor, but after the war the city's importance declined, as the labor-intensive rice plantations became uneconomical without slave labor. Natural disasters wrought more damage, with a major earthquake in 1886, several fires and storms, and devastating Hurricane Hugo in 1989. It's remarkable that so much of the town's historic fabric has survived – and fortunate too, because tourism is now a major money-spinner, with close to four million visitors arriving each year.

Orientation

The Charleston metropolitan area sprawls over a broad stretch of coastal plains and islands, but the historic heart is very compact, about 4 sq miles at the southern tip of a peninsula between the Cooper and Ashley Rivers. I-26 goes to North Charleston and the airport. Hwy 17, the main coastal road, cuts across the Charleston peninsula as the Crosstown Expressway. Soaring bridges connect west to James Island and West Ashley, and east to Mount Pleasant.

Information

BOOKSTORES

Waldenbooks (☎ 843-853-1736; 120 Market St)

INTERNET ACCESS

Library (☎ 843-805-6930; 68 Calhoun St; free)

MEDIA

Charleston City Paper (www.charlestoncitypaper.com) Alternative weekly that comes out on Wednesday and has good entertainment and restaurant listings.

Post & Courier (www.charleston.net) Charleston's daily newspaper.

MEDICAL SERVICES

Charleston Memorial Hospital (☎ 843-577-0690; 83 Calhoun St)

Medical University of South Carolina (MUSC; ☎ 843-792-2300; 171 Ashley Ave)

POST

Main post office (☎ 843-577-0690; 83 Broad St)

TOURIST OFFICES

Chamber of Commerce (☎ 800-868-8000; www.charlestonsvb.com; 81 Mary St) Is also helpful.

Charleston Preservation Society (☎ 843-722-4630; 147 King St) Has local history and architecture books.

Historic Charleston Foundation Preservation Center (☎ 843-723-1623; 40 E Bay St) Has local history and architecture books.
Visitors information center (☎ 843-853-8000; 375 Meeting St; 🕑 8:30am-5pm) The well-stocked and helpful center can help with accommodations and tours. Its 23-minute *Charleston Forever* video ($2) is worth seeing.

Sights & Activities

Charleston's main tourist activities include visiting historic houses, shopping for sweetgrass baskets in the market and imagining what it must have been like during the 'late, great unpleasantness.' The main attraction is the city itself, especially the quarter south of Beaufain St and east of King St, where you can wander along elegant thoroughfares and quaint, bending backstreets.

There are maps with walking tours, but an aimless stroll is just as good – Tradd, Meeting and Church Sts have some of the best buildings. The old **Market Street** now

AMAZING GULLAH CULTURE

Many parts of the US resemble the European cities from which the founding settlers emigrated. Only in the Sea Islands along the Georgia and South Carolina coast can the same claim be given to Africa. From the region known as the Rice Coast (Sierra Leone, Senegal, The Gambia and Angola), African slaves were transported across the Atlantic Ocean to a landscape that was shockingly similar – swampy coastlines, tropical vegetation and hot humid summers. The African slaves, who were in the majority on the plantations, had little contact with Europeans and were able to retain many of their homeland traditions. After the fall of the planter aristocracy, the freed slaves remained on the islands in relative isolation until the mid-20th century. Being cut off from the mainland ensured that African traditions were passed on to the descendants of the original slaves.

Geechees & Gullahs

The result of the black sea islander's isolation was Gullah, which describes both a language and a culture that persists today in coastal South Carolina. In Georgia people from the Gullah culture are known locally as 'Geechee.' Once a pejorative term that is a corruption of the name of the local Ogeechee River, 'Geechee' is now used with pride by Georgia sea islanders describing their heritage.

Traditions

Enduring traditions include the making of sweetgrass baskets, which involves three types of materials: the marshy sweetgrass, palmetto fronds and longleaf pine needles. Sweetgrass makes up the bulk of the basket, with strips of the palmetto fronds and pine needles woven into the coiled grass. This tradition is typically passed from mother to daughter, and basket prices are based on the number of hours invested.

Gullah Storytellers

Sea island storytellers often relate the exploits of Buh Rabbit, more famously known as Brer Rabbit from the Uncle Remus books. This small yet cunning rabbit is a common character in the trickster tales of West Africa. He outwits bigger and stronger animals and is constantly in danger of retaliation.

The Gullah Language

Gullah is a Creole of Elizabethan English and West African languages (mainly Bantu and Wolof) and is spoken by about 500,000 people. Influenced by various creoles spoken by West Indians, and by English dialects used by plantation overseers in the American colonies, Gullah sounds like English, but has the grammar and melodies of the West African coast. Gullah vocabulary is largely English, but with enough African words to stump a non-speaker. Linguists recognize Gullah as a distinct language rather than a dialect.

Some Gullah words have snuck into the Southern lexicon, words such as 'cooter' (turtle), 'benne' (sesame), 'bubba' (brother) and 'bad mouth' (to talk badly about someone). For further study, look for the pamphlet *Gullah for You!* by Virginia Mixson Geraty.

has some touristy shops, craft stalls, eateries and bars, and is a good place to be at lunch or dinnertime.

Overlooking the Cooper River, **Waterfront Park** is a shady retreat; further south, White Point Park & Gardens, at the tip of the peninsula, is superb at sunset, when the South Battery mansions are beautifully illuminated. King St is full of upscale shops and eateries. West of King St are residential blocks with colorfully painted houses that are less grand but still appealing. Further north, around the College of Charleston, many smaller timber houses are somewhat timeworn, but the streets are a nice contrast from the posh neighborhoods.

North of downtown, the **Citadel** (museum ☎ 843-953-6846; www.citadel.edu; 171 Moultrie St; ⏰ 2-5pm Sun-Fri, noon-5pm Sat) is the state-sponsored military college, with a small museum and a dress parade of the cadets during the school year at 3:45pm Friday.

HISTORIC HOUSES

Quite a few fine historic houses are open to visitors. Discounted combination tickets may tempt you to see more, but one or two will be enough for most people. Most houses are open from 10am to 5pm Monday to Saturday, 1pm to 5pm Sunday and run guided tours every half hour. Admission is $7 to $9, though you can buy combination tickets to some of the houses. These are a few of the most interesting:

The 1808 **Nathaniel Russell House** (☎ 843-724-8481; 51 Meeting St) is noted for its spectacular, self-supporting spiral staircase. The only surviving urban plantation, the 1818 **Aiken-Rhett House** (☎ 843-723-1159; 48 Elizabeth St) includes well-preserved slave quarters. Wonderfully located in front of the harbor, the 1828 **Edmonston-Alston House** (☎ 843-722-7171; 21 E Bay St) has lots of portraits, porcelain and artifacts from a well-to-do family. The 1772 **Heyward-Washington House** (☎ 843-722-0354; 87 Church St) is one of the oldest, where George Washington was entertained in 1791, and has some fine examples of Charleston-made mahogany furniture. The **Joseph Manigault House** (☎ 843-723-2926; 350 Meeting St; adult/child $8/4) was on the edge of town in 1803, but the neighborhood became less classy when the railroad came in. The Adams-style house became rather run-down and was nearly demolished.

Other downtown buildings include many churches, notably **St Michael's Episcopal Church** (cnr Broad & Meeting Sts), which opened in 1752, and the **French Huguenot Church** (136 Church St), a site of French services since 1681. The Romanesque Revival Circular Congregation Church (150 Meeting St) was built in 1861 and was used as the city's first meeting place, hence the name of its street.

MUSEUMS

Charleston Museum (☎ 843-722-2996; www.charlestonmuseum.org; 360 Meeting St; adult/child $9/4; ⏰ 9am-5pm Mon-Sat, 1-5pm Sun), across Meeting St from the visitors center, offers good exhibits on the state's history. It's in a modern building, but claims to be the country's oldest museum, founded in 1773.

Gibbes Museum of Art (☎ 843-722-2706; www.gibbes.com; 135 Meeting St; admission $7; ⏰ 10am-5pm Tue-Sat, 1-5pm Sun) has many portraits and miniatures of South Carolina's aristocracy.

AQUARIUM WHARF

Fabulous **South Carolina Aquarium** (☎ 843-720-1990; www.scaquarium.com; 100 Aquarium Wharf; adult/child $14/7; ⏰ 9am-6pm, until 5pm Aug-Jun) has more than 60 incredible exhibits on fish, reptiles and other wildlife indigenous to the Carolina coast. You'll see deep-water species, along with re-created estuaries. Definitely a must-see. Next door is the Imax Theater (p471).

FORT SUMTER

Confederates fired the first shots of the Civil War at Fort Sumter, an artificial island at the entrance to Charleston Harbor, where the Union army had retreated. The Union contingent surrendered, and as a Confederate stronghold Fort Sumter was shelled by Union forces from 1863 to 1865. By the end of the war it was a pile of rubble, and some very forbidding concrete defenses were added later. A few original guns and fortifications and the obvious strategic location give a feel for the momentous history here, and there's a good little museum as well. To get here, take a boat with **Fort Sumter Tours** (☎ 843-722-1691, 800-789-3678; adult/child $12/6) from the **Fort Sumter Visitors Education Center** next to the aquarium. The tour takes about 2¼ hours.

Tours

While you're in Charleston, save some time and cash to take one of the many tours.

Listing the walking, carriage, bus and boat tours could take up this entire book. A few of the better options include the following:

Gray Line (☎ 843-722-4444; adult/child 1½hr tour $18/11, 2hr $24/16) Bus tours depart from the visitors center.

Olde Town Carriage Company (☎ 843-722-1315; 20 Anson St; adult/child $18/8) Horse-drawn carriage tours clickity-clack around town, with colorful commentary.

Charleston Harbor Tours (☎ 843-722-1315; Charleston Maritime Center; adult/child $13/8; tours 11:30am, 1:30pm, 3:30pm) A great boat trip that passes area forts and gives commentary about local history.

Walking tours Includes ghost tours, Civil War tours and black-history tours. Ask at the visitors center for the gamut.

Sleeping

Staying in the historic downtown is the most attractive option, but it's expensive, especially at weekends and during special events. All of the chain hotels are on the highways. Rates in town fluctuate wildly – a $200 room in summer could be worth $70 in winter – so call ahead to see if you can get a better deal. The rates below are for high season (spring and summer). All hotels listed have air-conditioning, offer smoking and nonsmoking rooms and have amenities including hair dryers, coffeemakers and irons.

BUDGET

Charleston's two hostels are a bit of a trek from the historic district, though both sit on CARTA lines and offer a good deal if you just need a place to crash for the night.

Charleston's Historic Hostel (☎ 843-478-1446; www.charlestonhostel.com; 194 St Philip St; dm/d $19/40;) A laid-back and friendly place with very simple but clean accommodations, free laundry, and a shared living room, kitchen and piazza.

Charleston's Not So Hostel (☎ 843-722-8383; www.notsohostel.com; dm $19, d $35-50; P) In a sort of sketchy but up-and-coming area just north of MUSC in the Canonborough neighborhood, this eco-friendly hostel is housed in two old, rambling houses.

Three campgrounds southwest of Charleston offer shuttle services downtown:

Oak Plantation Campground (☎ 843-766-5936; 3540 Savannah Hwy; campsites & RV sites $14-18)

Lake Aire RV Park & Campground (☎ 843-571-1271; at Hwy 17 & Hwy 162; campsites $11-18)

James Island County Park (☎ 843-795-9884, 800-743-7275; 871 Riverland Dr; campsites/RV sites $18/24, cabins $100) The nicest campground of the three.

MID-RANGE & TOP END

Bed, No Breakfast (☎ 843-723-4450; 16 Halsey St; r $80-100) This small, friendly *pension*-style place has just two rooms and a shared bath. It's a great option if they have rooms available. Be sure to call ahead. Cash or checks only.

Days Inn Downtown (☎ 843-722-8411; 155 Meeting St; weekday/weekend $170/190) Although way overpriced in summer, it is a good option for people with cars, as the motel style has easy access and free parking. Rooms are basic and can get noisy with traffic passing by.

Best Western King Charles Inn (☎ 843-723-7451; www.kingcharlesinn.com; 237 Meeting St; weekday/weekend $130/180;) With few frills except great location, tidy rooms and free parking, this standard hotel underwent dramatic renovations and is a pleasant place to stay. It sometimes offers heavy discounts.

Holiday Inn (☎ 843-805-7900, 877-805-7900; www.charlstonhotel.com; 125 Calhoun St; weekday/weekend $120/200;) Rooms are pretty standard here but hotel bonuses include a courtyard, pool, fitness center and restaurant.

Andrew Pinckney Inn (☎ 843-937-8800, 800-505-8983; www.andrewpinckneyinn.com; 40 Pinckney St; r weekday $129-199, weekend $170-280) With a great location near the market, a courtyard, rooftop garden and 32 rooms, the Pinckney continues to be one of the top choices in Charleston. The entire hotel is designed in a West Indies style and rooms have full amenities.

Meeting Street Inn (☎ 843-723-1882, 800-842-8022; www.meetingstreetinn.com; 173 Meeting St; r $170-250) Each room opens onto a private patio overlooking a courtyard, which has a hot tub. The 56 small rooms are furnished with 19th-century antiques. A complimentary continental breakfast is served in the morning.

Planters Inn (☎ 843-722-2345, 800-845-7082; www.plantersinn.com; 112 N Market St; r $170-225) Every spacious room here has a canopy bed and 10ft ceiling. Some rooms have fireplaces, whirlpools and verandas. There's also a restaurant and lounge. Rates fluctuate, so call to see if you can get a better deal.

Mills House Hotel (☎ 843-577-2400, 800-874-9600; 115 Meeting St; r from $140; P $16) In a great location, the Mills House is a beautiful hotel, its rooms filled with antiques. The hotel has a restaurant and lounge and the outdoor pool is in a private courtyard on the second floor.

Market Pavilion Hotel (☎ 843-723-0500, 877-440-2250; www.marketpavilion.com; 225 E Bay St; r from $275; P $15) Very swanky, baby. This luxury boutique hotel is new to Charleston, but the designers did such a fine job recreating the historic veneer and ambience that you'd never know the difference. Even if you don't stay here, stop in for cocktails at the rooftop Pavilion Bar.

One of the best ways to get to know Charleston is to stay at a small home where the owners serve up authentic Southern breakfasts and dole out great local information. Small places start at around $100 for doubles with breakfast, but many have only one or two rooms, so it helps to use an agency like **Historic Charleston B&B** (☎ 843-722-6606; 57 Broad St).

Hayne House (☎ 843-577-2633; www.haynehouse.com; 30 King St; r $150-275) Owners Brian and Jane McGreevy serve afternoon sherry in a Victorian drawing room to guests of their six rooms.

Two Meeting St Inn (☎ 843-723-7322; 2 Meeting St; r $165-325) Housed in a Queen Anne mansion that's filled with history on the Battery.

Also recommended is **1837 Bed & Breakfast** (☎ 843-723-7166; 126 Wentworth St; r $120-165), which has five rooms.

Eating

The highest concentration of restaurants and bars is at and around Market St.

T-Bonz (☎ 843-577-2511; 80 N Market St; meals $10-15) With steaks, ribs, chicken and stir-fries, this popular spot is touted with the best steaks in town.

Wild Wing Café (36 N Market St; meals $5-10) Their Chernobyl wings threaten meltdown. With 25 different wing flavors and burgers, quesadillas and other big portions, you get bang for your buck here.

AW Shucks (☎ 873-723-6000; 35 S Market St; meals $9-14) This gets major promotion around town and seems like a tourist trap, but this is a good place to go for affordable seafood, such as crab legs and oysters.

Hyman's (☎ 843-723-6000; 215 Meeting St; meals $8-20) This immensely popular seafood restaurant has everything from mussels to soft-shell crabs. We're still not convinced, however, that the line-ups are worth the wait.

Sticky Fingers (☎ 843-853-7427; 235 Meeting St; meals $6-11) They don't call it Sticky Fingers for nothing. Southern ribs and barbecue are served up here in a lively atmosphere at good prices.

Hank's Seafood Restaurant (☎ 843-723-3474; 10 Hayne St; meals $15-24; dinner) Locals come here for crab soup and other low-country dishes.

Pinckney Café & Espresso (☎ 843-577-0961; 18 Pinckney St; meals $7-12) This moderately priced place does fresh variations on Southern cuisine.

Magnolias (☎ 843-577-7771; 185 E Bay St; lunch $7-14, dinner $11-18) Offering low-country 'Down South dishes with uptown presentation,' this long-standing truly Southern spot has interesting dishes like shrimp and grits.

Sermet's Corner (☎ 843-853-7775; 276 King St; meals $7-11) Sermet, the owner, whose art decorates the walls, cooks excellent panini sandwiches and delicious grub, like crab burgers served with sweet potato fries. Upstairs, the Mezzanine has couches and a lounge-like atmosphere; it's a great place to go for drinks.

Southend Brewery & Smokehouse (☎ 843-853-0956; 161 E Bay St; meals $7-14) The wall-to-ceiling windows at this fun microbrewery open up, giving the impression you're outside but without all the pollen. The menu serves up brick-oven pizza, pasta, seafood and smoked meats.

39 Rue de Jean (☎ 843-722-8881; 39 John St; lunch $7-10, dinner $9-20) With the lively ambience of a French bistro, this is a wonderful place for coq au vin and fresh seafood prepared with a French twist.

Drinking & Entertainment

The balmy evenings are conducive to late-night dining, drinking and dancing at the various venues around Market and E Bay Sts. Check out the weekly *Charleston City Paper* (published every Wednesday) and the 'Preview' section of Friday's *Post & Courier*.

Griffon Pub (☎ 843-723-1700; 18 Vendue Range) A popular Celtic-style place with good bar food.

Library at Vendue Inn (☎ 843-723-0486; 23 Vendue Range) A nice place to catch the sunset is this rooftop bar.

Cumberlands (☎ 843-577-9469; 26 Cumberland St) Has mostly blues and regional acts.

Imax Theater (☎ 843-725-4629; www.charlestonimax.com) Call for tickets and times.

Vickery's (☎ 843-577-5300; 15 Beaufain St) The locals' watering hole of choice, Vick's has big diner-style booths, ice-cold mugs of beer, greasy burgers and a fun mixed crowd. The bar stools are always packed. It's smoky, but there's also an outdoor patio for those seeking cleaner air.

Dock St Theater (☎ 843-723-5648; at Church & Queen Sts) This historic presents classical and contemporary works from October to May.

Getting There & Around

To reach Charleston by car from the north coast or south coast, use Hwy 17. From I-95, take I-26 west for about an hour to Charleston.

The **Charleston International Airport** (☎ 843-767-7009) is 12 miles outside of town in North Charleston. Avis, Budget, Hertz and National have offices at the airport.

The **Greyhound station** (☎ 843-744-5341; 3610 Dorchester Rd) has regular buses to New York City ($85, 18 hours), Atlanta ($60, 9½ hours), Savannah ($26, three hours) and Myrtle Beach ($24, 2½ hours).

The **Amtrak train station** (☎ 843-744-8264; 4565 Gaynor Ave) is an inconvenient 8 miles north of downtown. The *Silver Meteor* and *Silver Palm* travel the coast; fares to New York are $155 (11 hours) and to Savannah, $16 (1½ hours).

The **Downtown Area Shuttle** (DASH; ☎ 843-724-7420; adult $1, day pass $3) has faux streetcars doing four loop routes from the visitors center.

The **Bicycle Shoppe** (☎ 843-722-8168; 280 Meeting St) rents single-speed bikes per hour/day from $5/20.

AROUND CHARLESTON

There's plenty to see in the surrounding area, ranging from fine old plantations and historic forts to retired superpower technology.

Patriot's Point Naval & Maritime Museum (☎ 843-884-2727; adult/child $13/6; ⏰ 9am-5pm), on the east side of the Cooper River, features the aircraft carrier USS *Yorktown*, a WWII veteran. You can also tour a submarine, a destroyer, a Coast Guard cutter and a recreated 'fire base' from Vietnam.

Popular **beaches** are Folly Island, only a 15-minute drive from downtown via Hwy 17 south to Hwy 171, and Isle of Palms, 12 miles from Charleston via Hwy 17 north to Hwy 517.

Drive south on US 17 and Hwy 703 to reach **Fort Moultrie**, where a stockade of spongy palmetto logs absorbed the shells of the British navy in one of the first American victories of the Revolutionary War.

Heading up the Ashley River on Hwy 61, **Drayton Hall** (☎ 843-769-2600; 3380 Ashley River Rd; adult/child $12/6; ⏰ 9:30am-4pm Mar-Oct) is a fine brick mansion (c 1738) still in very original condition.

The truly magnificent **Magnolia Plantation** (☎ 843-571-1266; adult/child $13/7; ⏰ 8am-5:50pm Mar-Oct) has a 50-acre garden with azaleas and camellias, and the Audubon Swamp Garden, with alligators and cypresses ($5). You can also pay extra to take boat tours, train tours and view the well-furnished Reconstruction-era house.

More educational, **Middleton Place** (☎ 843-556-6020; adult/child $30/15; ⏰ 9am-5pm) features a terraced formal garden (1741) as well as working stables, a slave house and the 1755 mansion, with interesting items from the illustrious Middleton family. It offers a variety of tours and programs.

SOUTH COAST

South of Charleston, the land is fractured into a multitude of islands separated by tidal creeks and marshes. Picturesque Beaufort is the gateway to secluded beaches and Gullah communities (p468), where descendents of African slaves maintain ancestral traditions and speak a hybridization of English and African languages. Further south is Hilton Head Island, the world-famous golf capital.

Edisto Island is only 45 minutes from Charleston but remains largely uncommercialized. Edisto (*ed*-is-tow) has luxuriant vegetation, a beautiful beach and rental houses for family holidays. Contact **Edisto Island Vacation Rentals** (☎ 800-868-5398) for short-term beach cottages.

Beaufort (pronounced *bew*-fort, not to be confused with *bow*-fort, North Carolina) began as a British colony in 1711 and became wealthy with the boom in sea-island cotton. Today the town is a tidy grid on a small peninsula, with fine 18th-century houses facing the estuary.

The **visitors center** (☎ 843-986-5400, 800-638-3525; www.beaufortsc.org; 1106 Carteret St; ⏰ 9am-5:30pm) distributes maps that tell you where scenes from *Forrest Gump* and *The Big Chill* were shot. You'll also find a satellite visitors center in the basement of the historic **John Mark Verdier House** (☎ 843-986-5400, 800-638-3525; cnr Bay & Scott Sts; ⏰ 10am-5:30pm).

Hilton Head Island

Twelve miles long and 5 miles wide, Hilton Head is South Carolina's largest barrier island, the focal point of a low-country estuary. The entire area is a veritable temple to the worship of leisure time and the game of golf. There are dozens of courses enclosed in private communities of condominiums and vacation homes called 'plantations,' and the island's great cultural events are the annual golf tournaments.

The island prides itself on being designed in concert with the natural environment, but summer traffic and miles of stoplights make it hard to see the forest (or a tree) along US Hwy 278. There are, however, some lush nature preserves. The beaches are wide, white and so hard you can ride a bike on them for miles. Right at the entrance to the island is the **visitors center** (☎ 800-523-3373; 100 William Hilton Parkway; 9:30am-5pm), which can give you information on accommodations and, well, golf.

COLUMBIA

Home to the state legislature and the University of South Carolina, Columbia is an unassuming, simple town whose pretensions were burned long ago by Sherman's troops. Trains still rumble straight through downtown like they have for a century. With broad avenues and red-brick buildings, tall scraggly pines, a funky college district, public murals and an incomparable state museum, Columbia is a pleasant stop.

The **visitors center** (☎ 803-545-0000; 801 Lady St; 9am-5pm Mon-Fri, 10am-4pm Sat) has information about four historic houses open for tours, including Woodrow Wilson's boyhood home.

Columbia's focus is the **State House** (☎ 803-734-2430; 1100 Gervais St; admission free; 9am-5pm Mon-Fri, 10am-5pm Sat); look for bronze stars on its west side, where Northern troops' cannonballs hit. Around the capitol, assorted memorials attest to the state's military history, as does the **Confederate Relic Room & Museum** (☎ 803-737-8095; 301 Gervais St; admission $3; 2-5pm Tue-Sat), two blocks southeast at Sumter and Pendleton, where Carolinians come to check the Confederate credentials of their ancestors.

The interesting **South Carolina State Museum** (☎ 803-898-4921; 301 Gervais St; adult/child $5/3; 10am-5pm Tue-Sat, 1-5pm Sun), on the west side of downtown, is housed in an 1894 textile factory building, one of the world's first electrically powered mills. Excellent exhibits over three floors cover science, technology and the state's cultural and natural history. The museum will undergo a $15 million expansion over the next couple of years, which will add a planetarium, observatory and large-format theater.

SLEEPING & EATING

There's a good collection of chain motels on the interstates just outside of town.

Best Western Governor's House Hotel (☎ 803-779-7790; 1301 Main St; r $70; P) Near the State House, this friendly place is a good value, with an outdoor pool and tidy rooms

Whitney Hotel (☎ 803-252-0845, 800-637-4008; 700 Woodrow St; r $100-160; P) In a nice tree-lined neighborhood close to trendy Five Points and upscale restaurants. All rooms are suites, some with separate sitting rooms or kitchens. In the morning you'll get a newspaper and free full breakfast.

For eating and entertainment, head to the Five Points area in the southeast corner of downtown, where Harden, Greene and Devine Sts meet Saluda Ave.

GREENVILLE

It's not on many itineraries, but aptly named Greenville is a nice little city with lots of parks and a pleasantly planned downtown. Conservative Bob Jones University, the academy of fundamentalism, has a big collection of Catholic religious art. The Greenville County Museum of Art has a good American collection, especially of Southern art. Contact the **visitors center** (☎ 864-233-0461, 800-717-0023; 206 S Main St; 8:30am-5pm Mon-Fri) for accommodations and restaurants.

GEORGIA

Georgia is the largest state east of the Mississippi River. Its northern reaches are dominated by mountains, the Cumberlands in the west, the foothills of the Blue Range in the east. Moving south the mountains give way to flat shoals, rivers, hardwood forests and fertile red soil. You'd wonder if time stood still in Southern Georgia, where the life depends on cotton, peaches, nuts and soybeans. Along the coast, the red dirt turns to

GEORGIA FACTS

Nickname Peach State, Empire State of the South
Population 8,560,310 million (10th)
Area 57,906 sq miles (24th)
Admitted to Union January 2, 1778 (4th); seceded 1861; readmitted 1870
Capital city Atlanta (population 426,600; metro area 3.6 million)
Other cites Augusta (186,000), Columbus (182,000), Savannah (130,000), Macon (111,000)
Birthplace of baseball legend Ty Cobb (1886–1961), civil rights leader Martin Luther King Jr (1929–68), president Jimmy Carter (b 1924), singer Ray Charles (b 1930), soul singer James Brown (b 1933), author Alice Walker (b 1944), country singer Trisha Yearwood (b 1964)
Famous for CNN, Coca-Cola, *Gone with the Wind*

luscious white sand, with beautiful coastal islands and Savannah, a finely preserved paean to the antebellum world. Georgia is a state of wild geographic and cultural extremes: right-leaning Republican politics pervade most of the state, but a big chunk of the population lives in the bustling and more left-leaning hub of Atlanta, a nexus of business, culture and nightlife.

Georgia's **Department of Industry, Trade & Tourism** (☎ 404-656-3590, 800-847-4842; www.georgia.org; PO Box 1776, Atlanta, GA 30301) sends out a thick travel guide. It also runs visitors centers throughout the state.

History

Permanent English settlement dates from 1733 when James Edward Oglethorpe founded Savannah. The settlement was intended as a buffer between the Spanish and English, but Oglethorpe also planned to provide refuge for the penniless released from debtors' prison. This noble goal, however, was subverted by the practical need for soldiers, farmers and merchants.

The colony grew rapidly. By the time of the Revolutionary War, almost half the population were slaves. After Eli Whitney invented the cotton gin outside Savannah in 1793, cotton farming based on slavery expanded rapidly.

In 1828, gold was discovered near Dahlonega. This sped up the dispossession of North Georgia's Cherokee population during the first half of the 19th century, culminating in their forced removal to Oklahoma along the 1838 Trail of Tears.

Though far removed from the Civil War's early phases, Georgia held two of the most important battlefronts in the latter part of the war. Union troops were defeated at Chickamauga, but fought their way to Atlanta, which they defeated and burned; they then marched through Georgia to Savannah. Atlanta, the South's major transportation hub, was rebuilt with startling speed.

Cotton farming and textile manufacturing grew. In the early 20th century, agriculture became more diversified, expanding into corn, fruit and tobacco.

In the 20th century the state vaulted to national prominence on the back of an eclectic group of events and images: the wildly popular film (and novel) *Gone With the Wind;* Rev Martin Luther King, Jr and civil rights protests; Jimmy Carter; and Atlanta's rise as a global media and business center, culminating in the 1996 Summer Olympics.

In early 2001, the Georgia state flag, which had incorporated the Confederate battle flag – to some a symbol of Southern heritage, to others a symbol of slavery and racism – was changed in an attempt to decrease racial divisions. Sonny Perdue, who in 2003 won Georgia's first Republican governorship since the Civil War, vowed to get the old flag back. The debate, which most Georgians deem a ridiculous waste of time, wages on.

ATLANTA

Like a teenager who went from cuddling dolls to drinking in bars seemingly overnight, Atlanta is still getting used to her new limbs and liberties. Between 1990 and 2000, the city's population exploded by almost 40% and Atlanta has gobbled up that growth like a kid gobbles up chocolate and Cheesies. She didn't worry about zits or extra pounds; the economic boost was too irresistible and, frankly, unstoppable.

Without natural boundaries to control growth, Atlanta keeps growing out, not up. Suburban sprawl has turned Atlanta into a seemingly endless city. Increased car dependence creates horrendous traffic, traffic creates smog, smog pollutes water, and so on. These problems keep politicians and environmental groups scratching their heads, though efforts seem somewhat futile. Recent economic downturn has slowed things a little, but the city continues to grow.

For all this suburbanization, Atlanta is a pretty city covered with trees and elegant old homes. The growth raised the roof on the restaurant and shopping scene and distinct neighborhoods are like friendly small towns. Racial tensions are minimal, but segregation persists. Atlanta's neighborhoods resemble a checkerboard of white and black.

History

Atlanta was created as a railroad junction in 1837. Because of its rail links and safe location, it became a major Confederate transportation and munitions center, like honey for General William T Sherman whose Union forces invaded Georgia in 1864.

Much of the city was destroyed in the siege, and it worsened when retreating Confederates blew up their own ammunition. Sherman's army stayed in Atlanta for about 10 weeks. When they left they burned everything; leaving more than 90% of Atlanta's buildings in ruins.

After the war, Atlanta became the epitome of the 'new South,' a concept that entailed reconciliation with the north, the promotion of industrialized agriculture, and a progressive business outlook. Atlanta's relentless boosterism led to civic improvements and energetic business partnerships. Separate black and white societies developed and segregation deepened.

Public sit-ins and demonstrations in the early 1960s led by Atlanta native Reverend Martin Luther King Jr, prompted city business leaders to sign a joint agreement to desegregate. President John F Kennedy lauded this relatively painless transition as a model for other communities facing integration.

Atlanta's century of boosterism culminated when it hosted the 1996 Summer Olympic Games. Atlanta put on her prettiest dress and CNN beamed her picture worldwide. People took notice.

Orientation

The sprawling Atlanta metropolitan area sits inside a wide circle of freeway, which is called I-285 or, locally, 'the Perimeter.' Inside the circle, I-20 travels east and west, while I-75 and I-85 run north and south. I-75 and I-85 become a single road – 'the downtown connector' – as the roads pass through the city center.

Peachtree and Piedmont Sts are the main north–south arteries, but be forewarned: you'll find that a hundred other streets, roads and avenues are also called Peachtree. Many streets also change names suddenly, so if you're driving, it's a good idea to plot your route on a map beforehand. Addresses also specify NE, SE, SW or NW. W Peachtree St divides east from west and Martin Luther King Jr Dr/Edgewood Ave divides north from south.

Downtown Atlanta is a world-class business center with a few worthwhile attractions, but for the most part, you'll have to venture into Atlanta's sprawling neighborhoods to see the best the city has to offer. East of downtown, 'Sweet Auburn' attractions pay homage to Martin Luther King Jr. Little Five Points (L5P) has bars and cafés for Atlanta's alternative set. More upscale, Virginia Highlands has great restaurants, boutique shopping and bars. Decatur – an independent city just east of Atlanta – has several good restaurants and nightspots. Turner Field and Grant Park are south and southeast of downtown.

North of downtown, Midtown is another entertainment and nightlife area, with posh Buckhead further out. The West End has a lively black community.

Information

BOOKSTORES

Borders Books Music & Cafe (☎ 404-607-7903; 650 Ponce De Leon Ave NE)

Charis Books & More (☎ 404-524-0304; 1189 Euclid Ave NE) In Little Five Points, this is a crowded, well-stocked feminist and lesbian bookstore.

Outwrite Bookstore & Coffeehouse (☎ 404-607-0082; 991 Piedmont Ave) At 10th St in Midtown, this is a cheerful gay bookstore with a full coffee bar and wonderful desserts.

INTERNET ACCESS

Maasty Computers Internet Café (☎ 404-294-8095; www.maastyinternetcafe.com; 736 Ponce de Leon Ave; 🕑 6:30am-11pm) Across from City Hall East, Maasty has laptop rentals and Internet connectivity for $10 per hour. It also has another location in **Decatur** (2968 N Decatur Rd).

Public library main branch (☎ 404-730-1700; 1 Margaret Mitchell Sq; 🕑 9am-9pm Mon-Thu, 9am-6pm Fri & Sat, 2-6pm Sun) Many branches of the public library offer free Internet, including the main branch listed here.

ATLANTA

INFORMATION		
Atlanta Medical Center	1	D6
Borders Books Music & Cafe	2	E4
Charis Books & More	3	F5
Maasty Computers Internet Cafe	4	E4
MLK Jr National Historic Site Visitors Center	5	D6
Oakland Cemetery Visitors Center	6	D7
Outwrite Bookstore & Coffeehouse	7	C3

SIGHTS & ACTIVITIES	pp479–83	
African-American Panoramic Experience Museum	8	C6
Atlanta Preservation Center	9	C8
Center for Puppetry Arts	10	B2
Children's Museum of Atlanta	11	B6
City Hall East	12	D4
CNN Center	13	B6
Ebenezer Baptist Church (new)	14	D6
Ebenezer Baptist Church (original)	15	D6
Georgia State Capitol	16	B7
High Museum of Art	17	B2
King Center for Non-Violent Social Change	18	D6
Mall at Peachtree Center	19	B6
Margaret Mitchell House & Museum	20	C3
Martin Luther King Jr Gravesite	21	D6
MLK Jr Birthplace	22	D6
Public Library	23	B6
SciTrek	24	C5
Skate Escape	25	C3
World of Coca-Cola	26	B7

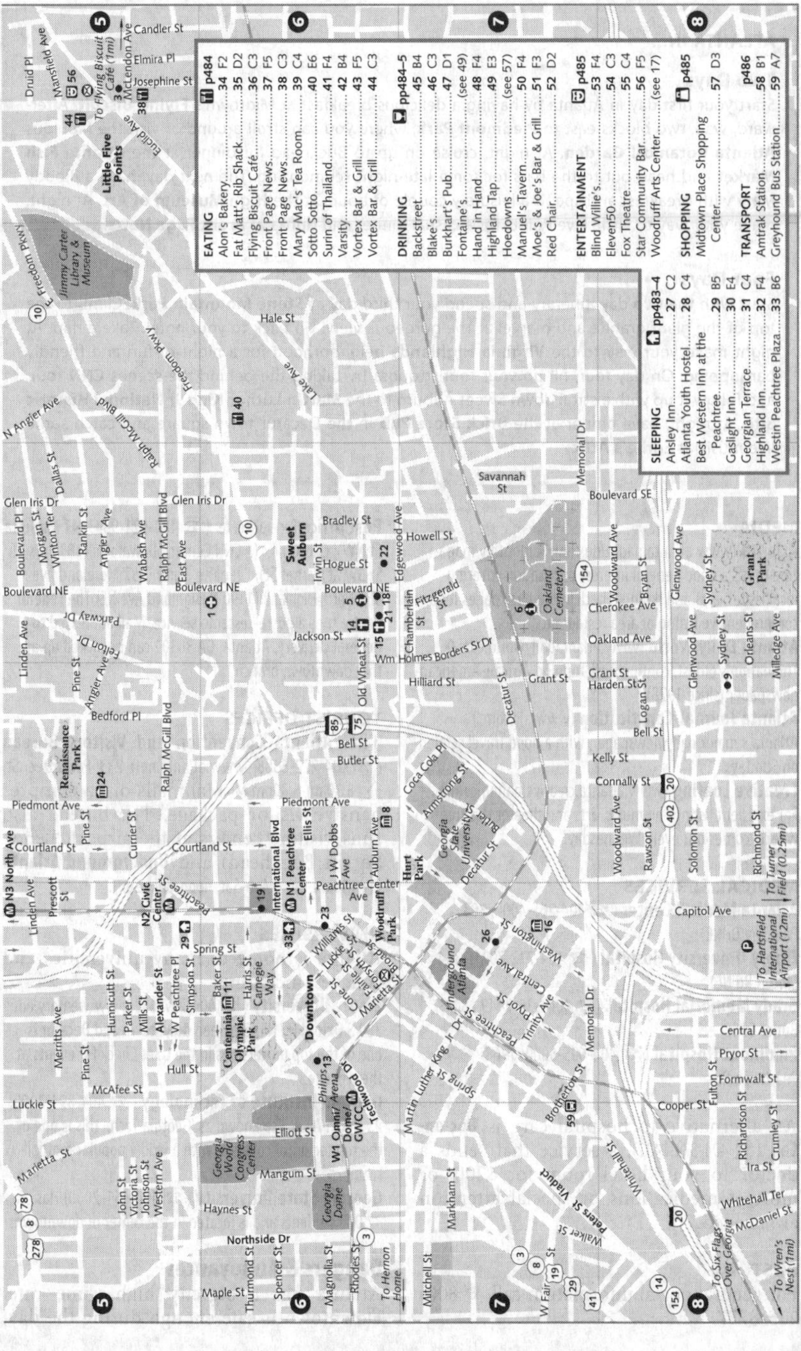

EATING p484

Alon's Bakery	34	F2
Fat Matt's Rib Shack	35	D2
Flying Biscuit Café	36	C3
Front Page News	37	F5
Front Page News	38	C3
Mary Mac's Tea Room	39	C4
Sotto Sotto	40	E6
Surin of Thailand	41	F4
Varsity	42	B4
Vortex Bar & Grill	43	F5
Vortex Bar & Grill	44	C3

DRINKING pp484–5

Backstreet	45	B4
Blake's	46	C3
Burkhart's Pub	47	D1
Fontaine's	(see 49)	
Hand in Hand	48	F4
Highland Tap	49	E3
Hoedowns	(see 57)	
Manuel's Tavern	50	F4
Moe's & Joe's Bar & Grill	51	F3
Red Chair	52	D2

ENTERTAINMENT p485

Blind Willie's	53	F4
Eleven50	54	C3
Fox Theatre	55	C4
Star Community Bar	56	F5
Woodruff Arts Center	(see 17)	

SHOPPING p485

Midtown Place Shopping Center	57	D3

TRANSPORT p486

Amtrak Station	58	B1
Greyhound Bus Station	59	A7

SLEEPING pp483–4

Ansley Inn	27	C2
Atlanta Youth Hostel	28	C4
Best Western Inn at the Peachtree	29	B5
Gaslight Inn	30	E4
Georgian Terrace	31	C4
Highland Inn	32	F4
Westin Peachtree Plaza	33	B6

ATLANTA IN...

Two Days

Start your first day in Atlanta by having a delicious breakfast at Midtown's **Flying Biscuit**. Afterward, walk two blocks east to **Piedmont Park**, where you can stroll around or visit the fabulous **Atlanta Botanical Garden**. At night, cruise on up to Buckhead for dinner at the **Atlanta Fish Market** and head out to the bars for some late-night schmoozing. The next day, have a Bloody Mary with breakfast and spend a leisurely couple of hours at the **High Museum of Art**. At night, make your way to Little Five Points for a casual dinner and drinks at **Front Page News**.

Four Days

Start with the two-day itinerary and spend your third day at **Stone Mountain Park**. Climb to the top of the giant granite and marvel at the gorgeous view. Go back to your hotel. Take a nap. At night make your way to the **Virginia Highlands** neighborhood for a night of fun and friendly barhopping. On day four, fill up your tourist quota by taking the behind-the-scenes **CNN** tour, and follow it up with a stroll down Sweet Auburn to the **Martin Luther King Jr National Historic Site**. At night, have dinner at the **Brick Store Pub** in the Decatur town square and catch some live music at **Eddie's Attic**.

MEDIA

Atlanta (www.atlantamagazine.com) A monthly magazine that's a good general interest publication covering local issues, arts and dining. Check in the back pages for a comprehensive listing of area restaurants.
Atlanta Daily World (www.atlantadailyworld.com/) The nation's oldest, continuously running African-American newspaper (since 1928).
Atlanta Journal-Constitution (www.ajc.com/) Atlanta's major daily newspaper, with a good travel section on Sundays.
Creative Loafing (www.atlanta.creativeloafing.com/) For excellent listings on music, arts and theater this free weekly comes out every Wednesday.

MEDICAL SERVICES

Atlanta Medical Center (☎ 404-265-4000; 303 Parkway Dr NE)
Emory University Hospital (☎ 404-712-7021;1364 Clifton Rd NE)
Grady Memorial Hospital (☎ 404-335-2449 ; 80 Butler St SE)
Piedmont Hospital (☎ 404-605-5000; 1968 Peachtree Rd)

An alternative to hospital care is **Doc-on-Call** (☎ 404-874-0432), a service that sends a doctor to your hotel room for $200, or more if medications or special attention are needed.

POST

For general postal information call ☎ 800-275-8777.

Post office Federal Center (☎ 404-521-9843; 41 Marietta St NW); CNN Center (1 CNN Center); Downtown (183 Forsyth St SW at Garnet St); Little Five Points (457 Moreland Ave SE); North Highland (1190 N Highland Ave NE) The Federal Centre runs a poste-restante service. Mail addressed to General Delivery, Atlanta, GA 30301 can be picked up at that downtown branch.

TOURIST OFFICES

The **Atlanta Convention and Visitors Bureau** (☎ 404-222-6688; www.atlanta.net; 233 Peachtree St; 8:30am-5:30pm Mon-Fri) mails out a comprehensive visitor package. The bureau also runs visitors centers at the airport, Lenox Sq (in Buckhead) and **Underground Atlanta** (10am-6pm Mon-Sat, noon-6pm Sun).

UNIVERSITIES

Atlanta is home to many universities and colleges, including:
Emory University (☎ 404-727-6123; www.emory.edu; 380 S Oxford Rd NE) Between downtown and Decatur is one of the top universities in the USA. Check for events at the website.
Georgia Institute of Technology (☎ 404-894-2000; 25 North Ave) Also known as 'Georgia Tech,' this is one of the top technical colleges, with a wildly popular football team.
Georgia State University (☎ 404-651-2000) Has 32,000 students and is located in the center of downtown.

Dangers & Annoyances

Atlanta has a big-city high-crime rate. Downtown is safe enough during the day, but at night the streets get eerily deserted. Atlanta is a car town; it is not pedestrian friendly, so someone walking alone somewhere at night can seem like a bit of an anomaly. Stick to the well-populated areas. Because of the car-centricity, you'll see a lot of aggressive and speedy drivers. Be kind to your blood pressure and stay off the highways during rush hour.

Sights & Activities

More intriguing and economical than the usual bus tours are walking tours of the city's older neighborhoods offered by the **Atlanta Preservation Center** (☎ 404-688-3353; www.preserveatlanta.com; 327 St Paul Ave; adult $10; ⌚ Mar-Nov).

DOWNTOWN

On weekdays, downtown Atlanta bustles with conventioneers and business folk, but on most evenings and weekends the bustle turns to a shuffle. An ongoing debate ensues in the media, in bars and in general conversation over the fate of downtown Atlanta. Some people think it should be built up into a tourism hotbed, others vie for a more livable urban core, one that doesn't shut down after five. Despite this complaint, there are a few great attractions.

Centennial Olympic Park (☎ 404-872-5338), on the west side of downtown, is a 21-acre legacy of green space from the 1996 Olympic Games.

The oldest part of the city is the area just around Alabama St. As the city grew, bridges and viaducts built over the railroad tracks made life easier for horses, pedestrians and, later, cars. Eventually an entire level of shops and storefronts vanished beneath street level. An imaginative 1960s renewal program recovered these 'lost' streets to construct **Underground Atlanta** (p485).

World of Coca-Cola (☎ 404-676-5151; www.woccatlanta.com; 55 Martin Luther King Jr Dr; admission $6; ⌚ 9am-5pm Mon-Sat, noon-6pm Sun) strives mightily to convince you that Coca-Cola is not just a soft drink, but rather one of the world's major cultural icons. Perhaps Atlanta's most overrated attraction, it features a live soda jerk bestowing the virtues of Coke, and memorabilia and historic advertising dating back to Coke's origins in 1886 Atlanta.

Next to Centennial Olympic Park, is **CNN Center** (☎ 404-827-2300, 877-266-8687; tours adult/child $8/5; ⌚ 9am-5pm), headquarters of the cable-TV news service. Every year some 240,000 people take the 50-minute CNN tour (every 20 minutes), a behind-the-scenes glance at the world's busiest news organization. Highlights include the CNN Headline News desk and a mock control room.

The gold-domed **Georgia State Capitol** (☎ 404-651-6996; www.sos.state.ga.us; 206 Washington St; ⌚ 8am-5pm Mon-Fri) is Atlanta's political hub with a small but entertaining museum. Free tours include a film about the legislative process and a glance at the government's communications facility. Call the **tour hotline** (☎ 404-656-2844) for times.

An interesting example of modern architecture is the **Mall at Peachtree Center**, a vast complex of shops, offices and restaurants built around the 73-story **Westin Peachtree Plaza** (p483). At 723ft, it is the tallest hotel in the Western Hemisphere. Its revolving restaurant is overpriced, but you can check out the excellent view by riding the elevator to the viewing deck for $7.

SWEET AUBURN

Though now dilapidated and struggling, Auburn Ave was the thumping commercial and cultural heart of African-American culture in the 1900s. It takes some imagination, but if you listen closely, you can almost here the jazz and history oozing out of the brick facades. Today, a collection of sights are associated with Sweet Auburn's most famous son: Martin Luther King Jr, who was born on Auburn and preached on Auburn and whose grave now looks onto the street.

The Martin Luther King Jr National Historic Site **visitors center** (☎ 404-331-5190; www.nps.gov/malu; 450 Auburn Ave NE; ⌚ 9am-5pm, in summer until 6pm) will help you get oriented with a map and brochure of area sites and exhibits. From here, guided tours leave for the **Martin Luther King Jr Birthplace** (501 Auburn Ave).

The historic site commemorates the life, work and legacy of the father of the Civil Rights movement. The center takes up several blocks. On Auburn Ave across from the visitors center, the **King Center for Non-Violent Social Change** (☎ 404-893-9882; 449 Auburn Ave NE) continues working toward economic and social equality. The facility has more information on King's life and work, and a few of his personal effects, including his Nobel Peace Prize. His **gravesite**, between the

IN PURSUIT OF A DREAM

Martin Luther King Jr was born 15 January 1929, in the middle-class Atlanta neighborhood of Sweet Auburn. He attended Atlanta's Morehouse College at age 15 and was ordained three years later as a Baptist minister. He attended Crozer Theological Seminary in Pennsylvania and went on to earn a PhD from Boston University.

King intended to live a quiet life as an intellectual teaching theology. Influenced by the teachings of Mahatma Gandhi, he espoused principles of nonviolence and redemption of adversaries through love. In 1955, he was chosen to lead the bus boycott in Montgomery, Alabama. After a year of boycotting, the US Supreme Court struck down the laws that enforced segregated buses. From this successful beginning, King emerged as an inspiring moral voice in civil rights.

In 1957, King and 115 other black leaders formed the Southern Christian Leadership Conference (SCLC) to expand the Montgomery success across the South. He returned to Atlanta in 1960, served as co-pastor of the Ebenezer Baptist Church (where his father was pastor), and helped form the Student Nonviolent Coordinating Committee (SNCC). King was arrested during a sit-in at a segregated snack bar and released only when Democratic presidential nominee John F Kennedy interceded (thereby winning enough black votes to carry the election).

King's strategy was to select a notoriously segregated city, mobilize the local black residents, then lead nonviolent protest marches. The demonstrations forced the white authorities to either negotiate or resort to violence; if the latter, the scenes of violence would arouse the national conscience and force the federal government to act. This worked according to plan in 1963 in Birmingham, Alabama (followed by the 1964 Civil Rights Act), and in 1965 in Selma, Alabama (followed by the 1965 Voting Rights Act). This approach failed in Albany, Georgia, in 1962 because white authorities treated the marchers with impeccable decorum and refused to resort to violence.

King's most often remembered speech, delivered in 1963 to an interracial crowd of 250,000 in Washington, DC, refers to his home state:

> I have a dream that one day on the red hills of Georgia, sons of former slaves and sons of former slave-owners will be able to sit down together at the table of brotherhood...I have a dream that my four little children will one day live in a nation where they will not be judged by the color of their skin but by the content of their character. I have a dream today!
>
> *Martin Luther King Jr*

In 1964, King was awarded the Nobel Peace Prize, at age 35 its youngest recipient in history. By 1965, King began addressing racial problems in the urban North, and he made speeches denouncing the Vietnam War. On a trip to Memphis, Tennessee, in support of sanitation workers' right to unionize, he was assassinated by James Earl Ray on April 4, 1968. Ray confessed to the crime but three days later recanted his guilty plea, claiming that he was but a pawn in a murder conspiracy. He died in prison in 1998, without ever receiving the new trial he sought.

King remains one of the most recognized and respected figures of the 20th century. In a span of 10 years, he led a movement that essentially ended a system of statutory discrimination in existence since the country's founding. His letters and speeches reflect some of the greatest American prose and a great vision still to be fulfilled. The Martin Luther King Jr National Historic Site and the King Center for Non-Violent Social Change in Atlanta are testaments to his life, his moral vision, his ability to inspire others and his lasting impact on the fundamental fabric of American society.

church and center, is surrounded by a long reflecting pool and can be viewed anytime.

Ebenezer Baptist Church (☎ 404-688-7263; 407 Auburn Ave NE; admission free; tours 9am-6pm Mon-Sat, 1:30-6pm Sun) was the preaching ground for King, his father and grandfather, who were all pastors here. This is also where King Jr's mother was murdered in 1974. You can take a free tour of the original church, but Sunday services are now held at a new Ebenezer across the street.

All of the King sites are a few blocks' walk from MARTA's King Memorial station. For more on black history, including a film about the Sweet Auburn area, visit the **African-American Panoramic Experience Museum** (APEX; ☎ 404-523-2739; 135 Auburn Ave NE; admission $4; 10am-5pm Tue-Sat), on the edge of Sweet Auburn toward downtown.

MIDTOWN

Throughout the past decade, Midtown has morphed into a minicore filled with great bars, restaurants and cultural venues.

Margaret Mitchell House & Museum (☎ 404-249-7015; www.gwtw.com; 990 Peachtree St at 10th St; adult/child $12/5; 9:30am-5pm) is a shrine to the author of *Gone With the Wind*. Mitchell wrote her epic in a small apartment in the basement of this historic house. In addition to the literary classic, Mitchell's other writings are also on display.

In the Woodruff Arts Center (p485), the highlight is the **High Museum of Art** (☎ 404-733-4400; www.high.org; 1280 Peachtree St NE; admission Mon-Fri $13, Sat & Sun $15; 10am-5pm Tue-Sat, noon-5pm Sun). Its collection includes European and American contemporary art and first-class African exhibits. The museum has special jazz nights (5pm to 10pm) on the third Friday of every month.

Piedmont Park

In the middle of Midtown, the Olmsted-designed **Piedmont Park** is a giant urban park and the setting of many cultural and music festivals. The park recently underwent a $66-million renovation that improved its playgrounds, tennis courts, dog park, bike paths and in-line skating paths. Rent bicycles for $6 per hour at **Skate Escape** (☎ 404-892-1292; 1086 Piedmont Ave NE), at 12th St. In summer, the free **Screen on the Green** (www.screenonthegreen.com) features classic movies projected onto a big screen.

In the northwest corner of Piedmont Park, the 30-acre **Atlanta Botanical Garden** (☎ 404-876-5859; www.atlantabotanicalgarden.org; 1345 Piedmont Ave NE; adult/child $10/5; 9am-6pm Tue-Sun) has a Japanese garden, a conservatory with threatened tropical and desert plants and the recently added Fuqua Orchid Center.

GRANT PARK & OAKLAND CEMETERY

Grant Park is a large oasis of green on the edge of the city center. The park is home to the **Atlanta Cyclorama** (☎ 404-658-7625; adult/child $6/4; 9:30am-4pm), one of Atlanta's most famous attractions. The Cyclorama is a circular painting 358ft around and 42ft high, depicting the 1864 Battle of Atlanta. Painted in 1886, the painting is the largest in the world and one of only three such Victorian-era circular paintings remaining in the USA. There's an accompanying Civil War museum as well.

Next door, **Zoo Atlanta** (☎ 404-624-5600; adult/child $17/12; 9:30am-5pm Mon-Fri, 9:30am-6:30pm Sat & Sun) provides natural environments, including a large gorilla exhibit. The zoo's pride and joy are Lun Lun and Yang Yang, two of only a small population of giant panda bears in captivity.

Gone With the Wind author Margaret Mitchell and golf great Bobby Jones are buried in the **Oakland Cemetery** (☎ 404-688-2107; 248 Oakland Ave; self/guided tour $1/3; 9am-5pm Mon-Fri), at Martin Luther King Jr Dr. Many very interesting Victorian and neoclassical monuments and mausoleums are scattered throughout the site. Stop at the **visitors center** for a walking tour brochure.

WEST END

Older than the city of Atlanta itself and a long-established African-American community, the West End was home to Alonzo Herndon, who was born a slave but who went on to found Atlanta Life Insurance and become one of the country's first black millionaires. The **Herndon Home** (☎ 404-581-9813; www.herndonhome.org; 587 University Place NW; admission $5; 10am-4pm Tue-Sat) is an impressive beaux arts mansion, built and decorated by black workers in 1910; tours run every hour.

South of I-20, the **Wren's Nest** (☎ 404-753-7735; 1050 Ralph David Abernathy Blvd SW; admission $7; 10am-2:30pm Tue-Sat) was the 1881–1908 home of Joel Chandler Harris, the white Atlanta journalist whose newspaper columns and Uncle Remus books retold and popularized African-American folktales.

POINTS EAST & DECATUR

Located on a hilltop overlooking downtown, the **Jimmy Carter Library & Museum** (☎ 404-331-3942; www.cartercenter.org; 441 Freedom Parkway; admission $7; 9am-4:45pm Mon-Sat, noon-4:45pm Sun, library closed Sun) is one of 11 national presidential libraries administered by the federal government. Exhibits highlight Carter's 1977–1981 presidency and include a replica of the Oval Office. The library contains 27 million pages of documents and 1.5 million photographs.

Fernbank Museum of Natural History (☎ 404-929-6300; www.fernbank.edu/museum; 767 Clifton Rd NE; adult/child $12/10; ⌚ 10am-5pm Mon-Sat, noon-5pm Sun) makes other museums seem hopelessly dull. With extensive exhibits on everything from reptiles to Egypt to seashells, and an Imax theater ($10), Fernbank is a great bet even if giant lizards don't rock your world. On **Martinis & Imax Fridays** (⌚ 6:30-10pm Friday Jan-Nov), the lobby turns into a cocktail lounge and live jazz echoes through the bones of the world's largest dinosaur. The cover charge is $5. Martinis are extra.

Atlanta for Children

Atlanta has plenty of activities to keep children entertained, delighted, thrilled and – perhaps against their will – educated. Following are some of the major sites that work at being kid-friendly.

The **Center for Puppetry Arts** (☎ 404-873-3089; 1404 Spring Street, NW; admission $12) is a wonderland for both children and adults. This fun museum and theater features puppet-making workshops, plus puppet shows for the young and young at heart (see p485).

Children's Museum of Atlanta (☎ 404-659-5437; 275 Olympic Centennial Park Dr NW; admission $11;

GAY & LESBIAN ATLANTA

Atlanta is one of the few places in Georgia – perhaps in the South – with a noticeable and active gay and lesbian population. Midtown is the center of gay life – Piedmont Park is a popular hangout, and there are several gay bars here. The town of Decatur, east of downtown Atlanta, also has a significant gay and lesbian community.

The **Atlanta Gay/Lesbian Center** (☎ 404-523-7500; 159 Ralph McGill Blvd) is a good source for organizations and information. The weekly newspaper *Southern Voice* contains regional news.

The *etcetera magazine* also has information on Atlanta's gay scene. You can view an online version, including a calendar of events, at www.etcmag.com.

The **Gay Guide to Atlanta website** (www.gayguides.com/atlanta/) has comprehensive listings of clubs and places to hang out.

The **Atlanta Pride Festival** is an annual celebration of the city's gay and lesbian community; it attracts people from all over the country and is held at the end of June around Piedmont Park in Midtown.

Outwrite Bookstore & Coffeehouse (☎ 404-607-0082; www.outwritebook.com; 991 Piedmont Ave at 10th St), in Midtown, is a cheerful gay and lesbian bookstore with a full coffee bar and wonderful desserts. Although the clientele is mostly gay men, the atmosphere is welcoming to others. **Charis Books & More** (☎ 404-524-0304; 1189 Euclid Ave NE), in Little Five Points, is a crowded, well-stocked feminist and lesbian bookstore that also sells music, cards, T-shirts and jewelry.

Backstreet (☎ 404-873-1986; 845 Peachtree St NE; cover charge $10; ⌚ 24hr) In Midtown at 6th St, gets a good mix of gay and straight. A risqué female impersonation cabaret show is always standing-room only Thursday through Sunday starting at 11pm. Several bars and a crowded dance floor with a massive sound and light show complete this complex.

Burkhart's Pub (☎ 404-872-4403; 1492 Piedmont Rd; ⌚ 4pm-4am Mon-Fri, 2pm-3am Sun) A friendly neighborhood bar, with a mainly gay male crowd. Burkhart's offers karaoke nights and the wildly popular **'The Original Gospel Girls'** (7:30pm & 10:30pm Sun).

Blake's (☎ 404-892-5786; 227 10th St NE) Near Piedmont Park is a no-cover-charge casual pub scene with no dance floor but loud dance music.

Red Chair (☎ 404-870-0532; 550 Amsterdam Ave NE) One of Atlanta's hottest upscale gay and lesbian bars. It offers a full restaurant and an adjoining bar, Red Chair, also does movie nights and a popular Sunday brunch.

Hoedowns (☎ 404-876-0001; 931 Monroe Dr; ⌚ 3pm-late Tue-Sun) Lets you practice your boot-scootin' boogie with free dance lessons. Mostly men in tight jeans and cowboy hats, it's also popular with the ladies on Thursday and Sunday.

My Sister's Room (☎ 404-370-1990; 222 E Howard St; ⌚ 8pm-1am Wed-Thu & Sun, 8pm-3am Fri & Sat) Next to the railroad tracks in Decatur, is the most popular hangout area for lesbians. A spacious covered patio, intimate garden hideaways and a stage and dance floor attract a growing clientele.

10am-5pm) is a great hands-on museum especially good for kids aged two to eight years.

In the **Fernbank Museum of Natural History** (404-929-6300; 767 Clifton Rd NE; adult/child $12/10; 10am-5pm Mon-Sat, noon-5pm Sun) the huge dinosaurs and the toddler play area are favorites (see p482).

SciTrek (404-522-5500; 395 Piedmont Ave; adult/child $9.50/7.50; 10am-5pm Mon-Sat, noon-5pm Sun) is for kids aged five to 12, and offers fun yet educational hands-on science and technology exhibits.

Six Flags Over Georgia (770-948-9290; 275 Riverside Parkway; adult/child $40/25) is located off I-20, just west of Atlanta. Spend the day at Atlanta's favorite amusement park featuring rides, shows, special events, concerts and festivals.

Introduce your little animals to much bigger ones at **Zoo Atlanta** (404-624-5600; 800 Cherokee Ave, Grant Park; adult/child $17/12; 9:30am-5pm Mon-Fri, 9:30am-6:30pm Sat & Sun) (see p481).

Sleeping

Rates at downtown hotels tend to fluctuate wildly depending on whether there is a large convention in town. Weekends are often cheaper, as are hotels away from downtown.

BUDGET

A cheap option is to stay somewhere along the MARTA line, further outside the city and take the train into the city for sightseeing. The trip by train to downtown should take 30 to 40 minutes.

Atlanta Inn (770-452-8500; 5114 Buford Hwy; r $45-50; P) A mile south of the MARTA Doraville station, this inn has worn, moderately clean rooms. Bus No 39 runs in front of the hotel to the station.

Comfort Inn (770-455-3700; 2001 Clearview Ave; r $70; P) This place offers standard chain rooms including breakfast. Shuttle service is provided to the MARTA Doraville station. The hotel is at I-285 exit 32; follow the signs to a side road.

Atlanta Youth Hostel (404-875-9449, 800-473-9449; www.hostel-atlanta.com; 223 Ponce de Leon Ave at Myrtle St; dm $17-19) In a Victorian house in Midtown, this lively hostel has 80 beds in dorm rooms and wins accolades for its cleanliness and good location. A kitchen, laundry, lockers, free morning coffee and doughnuts are available. The hostel's office is closed from noon to 5pm. It is three and a half blocks east of the MARTA North Ave station.

For camping around Atlanta see p486.

MID-RANGE & TOP END

University Inn (800-654-8591; www.univinn.com; 1767 North Decatur Rd; r $58-134; P) On the cusp of the Emory University campus, this low-key friendly inn offers rooms in four buildings. Most have kitchenettes and simple but pleasant furnishings. Breakfast and afternoon tea included.

Highland Inn (888-256-7221; www.thehighlandinn.com; 644 N Highland Ave; r $60-105; P) This European-style inn has a great location in the middle of Virginia Highland. With 100 rooms, the inn hosted the entire Japanese media crew during the 1996 Olympics. All rooms have private baths, TVs and clean, comfortable furnishings.

Gaslight Inn (404-875-1001; www.gaslightinn.com; 1001 St Charles Avenue NE; r $95-200; P) Each room is different in this charming 18th-century bed and breakfast in the heart of Virginia Highland. With homey touches like a front-porch swing, delicious breakfast and private garden, this inn makes a relaxing home away from home, just minutes from downtown.

Ansley Inn (404-872-9000, 800-446-5416; www.ansleyinn.com; 253 15th St; r $150-250; P) On a quiet residential street near Piedmont Park and within walking distance to anything in Midtown, this restored 1907 yellow-brick English Tudor mansion has 22 rooms featuring four-poster beds, period furnishings and Jacuzzis. Southern hospitality is real here. Breakfast included.

Best Western Inn at the Peachtree (404-577-6970, 800-242-4642; www.bestwestern.com; 330 W Peachtree St; r $80-150; P) Near the northern edge of downtown and within striking distance of Midtown, this well-renovated older hotel has 110 nice, comfortable rooms.

Atlanta has plenty of top-end hotels:

Westin Peachtree Plaza (404-659-1400, 888-447-8159; www.westinpeachtree.com; 210 Peachtree St NW; r $210-400; P) A towering hotel right in downtown.

Georgian Terrace (404-897-1991; www.thegeorgianterrace.com; 659 Peachtree St; r $85-400; P) A giant hotel on the National Register of Historic Places. Many of the *Gone With* *the Wind* stars stayed here during the film's debut in 1939 and the hotel, having undergone a massive facelift, is worth a wander whether you stay here or not.

Eating

BUDGET

Alon's Bakery (☎ 404-872-6000; 1394 N Highland Ave; sandwiches $6-9; 🕑 7am-7pm Mon-Fri, 8am-5pm Sat, 10am-5pm Sun; P) Consistently wins awards as the best bakery in town. You'll find an array of yummy baked goods, as well as cheeses, hearty soups and sandwiches.

The Varsity (☎ 404-881-1706; 61 North Ave at Spring St; meals $1.50-5; P) The world's largest drive-in restaurant and an Atlanta institution since 1928. A glorified fast-food joint, the place is always packed with folks ordering walk-a-dogs (hot dogs), glorified steaks (hamburgers) and bags of rags (fries).

Vortex Bar & Grill (☎ 404-688-1828; 438 Moreland Ave; burgers $6-10; P) The Vortex has arguably the best burgers in town. The bar-style atmosphere attracts a youthful, bohemian crowd who grab a burger before indulging in L5P's bar scene. Look for the giant skull and you'll find the front door. There's also a branch in **Midtown** (878 Peachtree St).

Mary Mac's Tea Room (☎ 404-846-1800; 224 Ponce de Leon Ave; meals $7-12) Three blocks east of the Fox Theatre, Mary Mac's serves authentic Southern food in a bright, cheery, grandmotherly atmosphere.

Flying Biscuit Café (☎ 404-874-8887; 1101 Piedmont Ave at 10th St; breakfasts $6-10) Yum! All-day breakfasts of omelettes, organic oatmeal pancakes, fried green tomatoes and tasty grits, all accompanied by Flying Biscuit's justifiably famous fluffy biscuits. A diverse, happy crowd enjoys the rest of the vegetarian-friendly menu of black bean quesadillas and veggie burgers. There's a second branch near L5P at 1655 McLendon Ave.

Fat Matt's Rib Shack (☎ 404-607-1622; 1811 Piedmont Rd NE; meals $7-11; P) Less than a mile north of Piedmont Park is a great place for quintessential southern barbecue. At night, up-and-coming jazz groups crank onstage from 8:30pm.

Raging Burrito (☎ 404-377-3311; 141 Sycamore St; burritos $6-10) Behind the town square in Decatur, Raging Burrito serves massive burritos in a fun, lively atmosphere. A large patio keeps folks sipping margaritas and munching nachos until the sun goes down.

MID-RANGE

Brick Store Pub (404-687-0990; 125 E Court Sq; meals $7-14) On the town square in Decatur, this pub has great atmosphere, homemade food, and a large selection of beers and single-malt scotch.

Front Page News (☎ 404-897-3500; 1104 Crescent Ave; lunch $7-11, dinner $12-22) This place has two locations, one in Midtown and another in **L5P** (☎ 404-475-7777; 351 Moreland Ave). Both have lush, roomy patios and Sunday brunch featuring live jazz and a Bloody Mary bar. The Louisiana-style menu offers sandwiches, salads and heartier fare like jambalaya. At night, the scene gets lively, especially at weekends.

Surin of Thailand (☎ 404-892-7789; 810 N Highland Ave; meals $9-15) Among the string of bars and pubs in the Virginia Highland area, it has large tables that can handle the crowds who come for the reasonable prices and large portions of tasty Thai favorites.

Café Tu Tu Tango (☎ 404-841-6222; 220 Pharr Rd; each tapas $6-8) In the heart of Buckhead's entertainment district, this tapas restaurant gets an artsy crowd. Local artists paint while you eat, while tarot card readers set up shop in the corner.

TOP END

Sotto Sotto (☎ 404-523-6678; 313 N Highland Ave NE; dishes $14-20; 🕑 dinner only, closed Sun) A lively, trendy restaurant serving authentic Italian dishes.

Bone's Restaurant (☎ 404-237-2663; 3130 Piedmont Rd NE; meals $17-40; P) All about old money and the Buckhead power set, Bone's gets top votes as Atlanta's best steakhouse. With lots of wood and brass, this old-school restaurant oozes power pheromones and serves up mouthwatering beef.

Kyma (☎ 404-262-0702; 3085 Piedmont Rd; meals $20-30; P) In Buckhead, Kyma offers high-priced though mouth-watering Greek food amid stunning decor. The service is impeccable, the clientele beautiful. If you're looking to splurge, this is a good choice.

Drinking

There's a lot of heavy partying going on in Atlanta, especially in Virginia Highland, L5P, Midtown and Buckhead.

In the heart of 'the Highlands,' (at Highland Ave & Virginia Sts) check out the following.

Fontaine's (☎ 404-872-0869; 1026 N Highland Ave) A great stop for evening cocktails.

Highland Tap (☎ 404-875-3673) Downstairs from Fontaine's, Highland has a huge array of draught beer.

Moe's & Joe's Bar & Grill (☎ 404-873-6090; 1033 N Highland Ave) A great spot for casual people-watching.

Hand in Hand (☎ 404-872-1001; 752 N Highland Ave) With a shady outdoor patio and a relaxed crowd.

Manuel's Tavern (☎ 404-521-2466; 602 N Highland Ave) A longtime political hangout, with a good, conversational beer-drinking crowd.

Fado Irish Pub Beer Bar (☎ 404-848-8433; 3035 Peachtree St) In Buckhead, this is a comfortable Irish pub with a good selection of beers.

Front Page News In Midtown, this is an L5P fave, and a restaurant (p484) that draws a big drinking crowd to its sunny patios.

Entertainment

Atlanta has big-city nightlife, with lots of live music and cultural events. Check out the free *Creative Loafing* for weekly listings.

Fox Theatre (☎ 404-881-2100; 660 Peachtree St NE) A spectacular 1929 movie palace with fanciful Moorish and Egyptian designs. It hosts Broadway shows, film festivals and concerts in a 5000-seat auditorium.

Woodruff Arts Center (☎ 404-733-4200; 1280 Peachtree St NE at 15th St) Named for Coca-Cola king Robert W Woodruff, who gave so much to local causes that he was nicknamed 'Mr Anonymous Donor.' The center includes a theater, concert hall and art school (also see p481).

Center for Puppetry Arts (☎ 404-873-3391; www.puppet.org; 1404 Spring St NW at 18th St; 🕑 9am-5pm Mon-Sat, 11am-5pm Sun) The collection consists of over 1000 puppets from around the world. Try to see one of the well-produced, full-stage puppet shows ($12).

LIVE MUSIC & NIGHTCLUBS

Cover charges at the following vary nightly, ranging from free to $10 on weekdays, to $25 on weekends or when popular live bands are playing.

Buckhead has a concentrated strip of bars and **dance clubs** in an area bounded by Peachtree, E Paces Ferry and Pharr Rds.

Eleven50 (☎ 404-874-0428; 1150 Peachtree Rd) In Midtown, this is a huge, multilevel dance club housed in an old theater.

Little Five Points serves the young college punk scene.

Star Community Bar (☎ 404-681-9018; 437 Moreland Ave) Draws a funky crowd to its live acts four nights a week.

Variety Playhouse (☎ 404-524-7354; 1099 Euclid Ave NE) A great place to see live bands.

Virginia Highland draws a more affluent yuppie crowd.

Blind Willie's (☎ 404-873-2583; 828 N Highland Ave) For serious blues, head to Blind Willie's, a well-established blues bar with local and occasional big-name acts.

On the main square in Decatur:

Eddie's Attic (☎ 404-377-4976; 515B N McDonough St) One of the city's best places to hear folk and acoustic music, in a nonsmoking atmosphere seven nights a week.

SPECTATOR SPORTS

Order tickets to sporting events through **Ticketmaster** (☎ 800-326-4000, 404-249-6400; www.ticketmaster.com).

Atlanta Braves (☎ 404-522-7630) This major-league baseball team plays at **Turner Field** (☎ 404-577-9100; tickets $1-40). Seats are available only on game days. Formerly Olympic Stadium, after the games, the stadium was reconfigured into a baseball-only facility. Turner Field is not near MARTA, but dedicated shuttle buses run between the stadium and the Five Points station during games.

Downtown, you can check out the following teams:

Atlanta Falcons NFL team (☎ 404-223-8000) Plays in the Georgia Dome; tickets start at $25.

Atlanta Hawks NBA team (☎ 404-827-3800) Plays at Philips Arena; tickets cost around $10 to $65.

Atlanta Thrashers NHL team (☎ 404-584-7825) Plays at Philips Arena; tickets cost around $10 to $55.

Shopping

Atlantans love to shop. Virginia Highland and Decatur both have a unique selection of boutique shops. Find vintage and second-hand clothes in Little Five Points.

Underground Atlanta (☎ 404-523-2311; www.underatl.com; 🕑 10am-9pm Mon-Sat, noon-6pm Sun) An enclosed, air-conditioned multilevel maze of shops and restaurants.

The two major malls that draw throngs of shoppers are adjacent to each other in Buckhead.

Lenox Sq (☎ 404-816-4001; 3393 Peachtree Rd NE; 🕑 10am-9pm Mon-Sat, noon-6pm Sun) This complex has just about anything you'd ever need.

Phipps Plaza (☎ 404-262-0992; 3500 Peachtree Rd NE; 🕑 10am-9pm Mon-Sat, noon-5:30pm Sun) Offers more upscale shops.

Getting There & Away

Atlanta's huge Hartsfield International Airport, 12 miles south of downtown, is a major regional hub and an international gateway. With nearly 80 million visitors a year, it is the busiest airport in the world in overall passenger traffic.

The **Greyhound terminal** (☎ 404-584-1728; 232 Forsyth St) is next to the MARTA Garnett station. Sample fares and journey times include: Chattanooga, Tennessee ($20, two hours); New Orleans, Louisiana ($73, 10 hours); New York ($102, 19 hours); Miami, Florida ($95, 16 hours); and Savannah ($39, 5½ hours).

The **Amtrak station** (☎ 404-881-3062, 800-872-7245; 1688 Peachtree St NW at Deering Rd) is 3 miles north of downtown. Take bus No 23 for about 0.8 miles from the MARTA Arts Center station. The *Crescent* passes through Atlanta daily between New York ($197, 19 hours) and New Orleans ($90, 11 hours).

Getting Around

A **Metropolitan Atlanta Rapid Transit Authority rail line** (MARTA; ticket $1.75; 20 minutes) travels to/from the airport to downtown. This is a great choice for getting to and from the airport. The **Atlanta Airport Shuttle** (☎ 404-524-3400, 800-842-2770; tickets $15-20) also transports passengers to hotels all over the city in a minibus. All the major car rental agencies have desks at the baggage claim level.

Driving in Atlanta can be infuriating and confusing. You'll often find yourself sitting in traffic jams, and it's easy to get disoriented – a good map really is an invaluable asset. MARTA is a good option if you are staying in town and have a lot of time (sometimes MARTA schedules leave you waiting for no apparent reason). If you're staying outside the Perimeter, you'll definitely need a car.

Because Atlanta is such a car-centric city, two-hour metered street parking is usually plentiful. Many parking garages offer reasonable rates (usually around $10 per day) for daylong parking. Parking is free at most shopping malls.

MARTA (☎ 404-848-4711; www.itsmarta.com) operates a small but efficient rail system and an extensive bus network in Atlanta and some of the surrounding communities. The rail system has only two major lines (with a couple of branches), but manages to get close to many of the major sites. All fares are $1.75.

AROUND ATLANTA

Stone Mountain Park

This 3200-acre **park** (☎ 770-498-5690; per car $7, all attractions $17), 16 miles east of downtown, is home to 825ft-high Stone Mountain, the world's largest outcrop of exposed granite. It's best known for the huge bas-relief carving of Confederate heroes Jefferson Davis, 'Stonewall' Jackson and Robert E Lee – one of the largest such sculptures in the world. There's also a sky lift, hiking trails, an antebellum plantation, a railroad, laser show, camping and ther attractions. The park is open daily and makes an excellent day trip.

Stone Mountain Family Campground (☎ 770-498-5710, 800-385-9807; www.stonemountainpark.com; campsites $23-38; P) Georgia's largest campground has 441 sites, laundry facilities, a volleyball court and is the best camping option near Atlanta.

The park is located off Hwy 78 (I-285 exit 39). Bus No 120 can take you from the MARTA Avondale station to the village of Stone Mountain, where some buses continue into the park.

Lake Sidney Lanier

About 45 miles northeast of Atlanta's urban sprawl, off I-985 in Buford, Lake Lanier was the site of the Olympic rowing competitions in 1996. The **Lake Lanier Islands Beach & Waterfront** (☎ 770-945-7201; www.laklanierislands.com; 6900 Holiday Rd; adult/child $26/17; 🕑 10am-7pm May-Sep) offers a bit of everything, including a water park, sand volleyball courts and a campground. It gets downright crowded in summer. Admission to the park is $6 per car.

NORTHERN GEORGIA

The southern end of the great Appalachian Range extends some 40 miles into Georgia's far north, providing some superb mountain scenery and wild white-water rivers. The fall colors emerge late here, peaking in October. Free brochures with directions for self-guided driving tours are available at most of the region's visitors centers.

A few days are warranted to see sites like the 1200ft-deep **Tallulah Gorge** (☎ 706-754-7970), the scenery and hiking trails at **Vogel State Park** (☎ 706-745-2628) and the interesting collection of Appalachian folk arts at the **Foxfire Museum** (☎ 706-746-5828; 9am-4:30pm Mon-Sat), near Mountain City.

The extreme northeast corner of the state also offers Georgia's lone ski area, the **Sky Valley Resort** (☎ 706-746-5305, 800-437-2416), which has one lift, five trails and a very short, weather-dependent season.

Dahlonega

In 1828 Dahlonega was the site of the first gold rush in the USA. The boom these days, though, is in tourism. It's an easy excursion from Atlanta and offers intriguing history surrounded by beautiful mountain scenery.

Walking around the historic main square is a major event itself. Many offbeat shops compete for tourist dollars. The **visitors center** (☎ 706-864-3711; www.dahlonega.org; 13 S Park St; admission free; 9am-5:30pm) has plenty of information on area sites and activities (including hiking, canoeing, kayaking, rafting and mountain biking). In the center of the square is the **Dahlonega Gold Museum** (☎ 706-864-2257; adult/child $3/1.50; 9am-5pm Mon-Sat, 10am-5pm Sun), which tells the fascinating story of gold mining in the region.

Just off the square, **Smith House** (☎ 706-867-7000, 800-852-9577; 84 S Chestatee St; meals $15, r $80-120) offers unlimited home-cooked Southern food served family-style. Smith House also operates a remodeled classic country inn decorated in 19th-century style.

Amicalola Falls State Park

The centerpiece of this gorgeous 2050-acre state park, 18 miles west of Dahlonega on Hwy 52, is 729ft Amicalola Falls, the highest waterfall in Georgia. The park is one of the most popular destinations in northern Georgia, and it's easy to see why. It offers spectacular scenery, in addition to excellent hiking and mountain-biking trails. The 57-room **Amicalola Falls Lodge** (☎ 706-265-4703, reservations 800-864-7275; campsites $15, r $80-200) offers spectacular views and camping.

Helen

Helen is the sort of town you can only find in the USA: a faux Swiss-German mountain village where the shops have names like 'Das ist Leather.' Beginning in 1968, business leaders looked for ideas to transform the dreary lumber town into a tourist attraction. Soon, the Bavarian look took hold and somehow this place has become one of northern Georgia's more popular tourist destinations.

The **visitors center** (☎ 706-878-2181, 800-858-8027; www.helenga.org; 726 Brukenstrasse; 9am-5pm Mon-Sat, 10am-5pm Sun) is on the southern side of town. **Oktoberfest**, from mid-September to early November is a popular event, with plenty of oompah bands and bratwurst. In summer, you'll see hundreds of folks **Shooting the Hooch** – going down the slow-moving Chattahoochee River on inner tubes. The best way to see Helen is on foot; just join the throngs of slow-moving tourists. If the crowds get too much, head to nearby **Unicoi State Park** (☎ 706-878-3982), a beautiful park with hiking trails, cabins, campsites and attractive mountain scenery.

SLEEPING & EATING

Hotel prices skyrocket during Oktoberfest, weekends and other popular times. There are many hotels in town with Bavarian names and decorations. These don't necessarily offer any better value than the more standard options.

Bavarian Brook Rentals (☎ 706-878-2840, 800-422-6355; www.bavarianbrookrentals.com/; 859 Edelweiss St; P) This company has a variety of options. It can arrange riverside condos ($140), standard motel accommodations ($65) or cabins ($125).

Best Western (☎ 706-878-2111, 800-435-3642; www.helengeorgiabestwestern.com; 8220 Main St; r $60-120; P) A bit south of town, Best Western has big, modern hotel rooms with a refrigerator and microwave and a nice outdoor pool and patio. Free continental breakfast.

Hofer's Bakery (☎ 706-878-8200; sandwiches $6-8) On the northern side of town between Spring and White Sts, this good restaurant lets you get into the Bavarian spirit. Specialties include bratwurst, spaetzle (noodles) and *schweinebraten* (pork roast). Hofer's also has plenty of imported beer.

Sweetwater Coffee House (☎ 706-878-1521; 2242 Hwy 17; 10am-6pm Tue-Sat, noon-6pm Sun) An excellent stop between Helen and Unicoi State Park, this hip hangout attracts patrons from the nearby arts community of Sautee. In addition to the usual lattes and espressos, they have good brownies, a great vibe and local crafts.

New Echota State Historic Site

The independent Cherokee tribe established a capital here in 1825. The Cherokee learned English, operated mills and stores, wore European dress and owned farmsteads and plantations. The **historic site** (☎ 706-624-1321; adult/child $3/2; 9am-5pm Tue-Sat, 2-5:30pm Sun) contains reconstructed buildings similar to those that populated the Cherokee town of New Echota, including a Supreme Courthouse, a tavern and print shop. A small museum contains exhibits about Cherokee history and shows a 17-minute film. From Atlanta, take I-75 north to exit 317 (GA Hwy 225) and go east 0.8 miles.

Chickamauga

During the Civil War, 58,000 Union soldiers met 66,000 Confederates in northwest Georgia and fought a bloody battle during 19–20 September 1863. The battle produced 34,000 casualties, including 4200 dead. The result was a Confederate victory, pushing the Union back to Chattanooga, Tennessee. The battle of Chickamauga also marked the beginning of the end, as the Union troops eventually won in Chattanooga, laid siege to Atlanta, then marched on to Savannah.

The battlefield is now part of the **Chickamauga & Chattanooga National Military Park** (☎ 706-866-9241; adult/child $3/1; 8am-4:45pm), designated in 1890 as the nation's first military park. More than 600 stone and bronze monuments were erected on the battlefield between 1890 and 1930. Plaques, cannons and pyramids of cannonballs show positions of fighting units, artillery batteries or where brigade commanders were killed. The park is at US Hwy 27 about 1 mile south of GA Hwy 2 at Fort Oglethorpe.

CENTRAL GEORGIA

Between the northern Georgia mountains and the southern coastal plains lies the Piedmont region. Its southern boundary is the 'fall line' – a sudden drop in elevation at the edge of a plateau. Columbus, Macon and Augusta were all established where the fall line intersects rivers. Today, most of these waterways are dammed, creating lakes popular for boating and fishing. Modern waterpower continues to operate textile mills and other manufacturing industries.

In the 18th and 19th centuries, the region grew on the promise of bountiful cotton and the slavery needed to harvest it cheaply. Though the Civil War ended slavery, and an infestation of boll weevils nearly ended cotton farming, grand antebellum homes built by wealthy planters still stand.

Atlanta lies within the Piedmont region, but native Georgians might say the true heart of the state lies beyond the gleaming office towers and sprawling interstate highways, in dozens of small towns and farming communities that populate the Piedmont's gently rolling hills.

Athens

This attractive college town, 61 miles east of Atlanta, is characterized by a vibrant nightlife and world-famous music scene. Local pop-music stars catapulted to national fame include the B-52s, REM and Widespread Panic. The University of Georgia (UGA) has almost 30,000 students. The downtown area is well supplied with music shops, bookstores, cafés, bars and clubs, which led *Rolling Stone* to call Athens the '#1 College Music Scene in America.'

Spared serious damage during the Civil War, Athens has many antebellum homes and 14 historic districts featuring a smorgasbord of architectural styles.

The **Athens Welcome Center** (☎ 706-353-1820; www.visitathensga.com; 280 E Dougherty St; 10am-6pm), housed in a historic antebellum house at the corner of Thomas St, provides good information and maps, and offers 1¼ hour bus tours of historic houses and sites ($10).

SIGHTS & ACTIVITIES

College Ave between Clayton and Broad Sts is where the college crowd hangs out; it's quite a good place for people-watching. Tours of the UGA campus depart from the **UGA visitors center** (☎ 706-542-0842; 8am-5pm Mon-Fri, 8am-4:30pm Sat, 1-5pm Sun). Call for the schedule.

State Botanical Garden of Georgia (☎ 706-542-1244; S Milledge Ave; 9am-4:30pm Mon-Sat, 11:30am-4:30pm Sun), just over a mile south of the Athens loop road, is a tranquil place away from the hubbub of the university. This 313-acre preserve contains a tropical conservatory and 5 miles of trails.

Georgia Museum of Art (☎ 706-542-4662; 90 Carlton St; admission $1; 10am-5pm Tue-Sat, until 9pm Wed, 1-5pm Sun) has an impressive array of art exhibits, as well as occasional concerts and film screenings.

Sandy Creek Nature Center (☎ 706-613-3615; 8:30am-5:30pm Tue-Sat) is about a mile past the Loop on Hwy 441/15N. The complex houses the Environment, Natural Science and Appropriate Technology (ENSAT) center, an educational building constructed using alternative building materials. It offers 6 miles of nature trails through pine forests and marshlands, and a boardwalk. Trails are open sunrise to sunset daily.

SLEEPING & EATING

Hawkes-Nest Hostel (☎ 706-769-0563; eagltavern@aol.com; 1760 McRee Mill Rd; house/cottage $10/18) On seven acres near Watkinsville, about 11 miles south of downtown Athens, the hostel is an extension of the owner's family house. The hostel has only two rooms, one inside the main house and one in a detached, rustic cottage. Guests use the kitchen and bathrooms inside the main house. Friendly owners Bonnie and Robert Murphy are helpful in planning activities around the area. Reservations are required.

Bulldog Inn (☎ 706-543-3611; 1225 Commerce Rd; s/d $35/42; P) A very no-frills budget option just north of the city.

Nicholson House (☎ 706-353-2200; 6295 Jefferson Rd; r $120-130) This place is 5 miles from downtown on US 129/Jefferson Rd. Set on large, peaceful grounds, it consists of an original structure built in the 1820s, around which a Colonial Revival house was constructed in 1947. The rate includes a delicious vegetarian breakfast.

Five Star Day Café (☎ 706-543-8552; 229 E Broad St; meals $5-7) An unpretentious little café with very reasonable prices, serving hot buttered soul chicken with Jamaican seasoning, pot roast, pesto pasta, Carolina barbecue and chicken-and-dumplings.

Grit (☎ 706-543-6592; 199 Prince Ave; meals $5-7) At lunch or dinner, this popular vegetarian place serves yummy things like hummus and falafel, Indian curried vegetables, Italian pasta dishes and Mexican quesadillas.

Bluebird Café (☎ 706-549-3663; 493 E Clayton St; meals $5-7) Another great international vegetarian restaurant with reasonable prices. It serves breakfast and lunch fare including Spanish omelettes and avocado-and-tuna sandwiches.

Harry Bissett's (☎ 706-353-7065; 279 E Broad St; lunch $7-10, dinner $10-22) A New Orleans–style restaurant and pub serving up Cajun and Creole cuisine (including a killer shrimp gumbo), Harry's is always hopping. A fun place to go for a filling lunch or dinner.

ENTERTAINMENT

40 Watt Club (☎ 706-549-7871; 285 W Washington St) The famous 40 Watt Club, where REM got its first exposure, is still one of the best places in the South to catch up-and-coming bands.

Georgia Theatre (☎ 706-549-9918; 215 N Lumpkin St) Another of the South's premiere live music halls.

GETTING THERE & AWAY

Southeastern Stages (☎ 706-549-2255; 220 W Broad St), a Greyhound connection service, has buses daily to Atlanta ($17, 1¾ hours), Augusta ($26, from three hours) and Savannah ($49, 3½ hours).

Augusta

Georgia's second-oldest and second-largest city, best known for the annual Masters golf tournament, is relatively tranquil the rest of the year. The city's **visitors center** (☎ 706-724-4067; 32 Eighth St; 9am-5pm Mon-Sat, 1-5pm Sun) in the 1886 Historic Cotton Exchange building, has many helpful maps and walking tours.

Two blocks away, the **Riverwalk** along the banks of the Savannah River links restaurants, shops and museums. It's a good place to sit and watch the river. At one end you'll find Augusta's pride and joy, the **Morris Museum of Art** (☎ 706-724-7501; 1 10th St; admission $3; 10am-5pm Tue-Sat, noon-5pm Sun), dedicated to artists of the South. At the other end is the National Science Center's child-oriented **Fort Discovery** (☎ 706-821-0200; 1 7th St; adult/child $8/6; 10am-5pm Mon-Sat, noon-5pm Sun), with more than 270 interactive science exhibits.

The Masters golf tournament is played in early April, but during the tournament the city is flooded with visitors and hotel prices skyrocket. If you don't have tickets to the tourney, don't come! Cheapie motels sit around I-20 exit 199 (Washington Rd), west of downtown.

Quality Inn (☎ 706-737-5550, 800-228-5151; 1050 Claussen Rd; r/ste $60/90; P) On a quiet side road, near the Washington Rd congestion, this hotel is convenient to restaurants and the golf course. Nice, large rooms have kitchenettes and a continental breakfast is included.

Partridge Inn (☎ 706-737-8888, 800-476-6888; 2110 Walton Way; r/ste $90/150; P) In the historic area of Summerville, the inn was restored in 1995. Its 155 rooms range from simple, to suites with kitchens. The rates include a Southern buffet breakfast, considered by locals to be one of the best in Augusta. The 5th-floor open-air penthouse offers a lovely view.

Madison & Milledgeville

Off I-20, 65 miles east of Atlanta and 30 miles south of Athens, Madison was one of the few towns that Sherman spared on his path of destruction. Part of this picturesque town is a National Historic Site; you can walk a 1.4-mile route through the historic district with a map from the **visitors center** (☎ 800-709-7406; 8:30am-5pm Mon-Fri, 10am-5pm Sat, 1-5pm Sun), on Madison's main square.

Milledgeville was the state capital from 1803 to 1868, and it retains some rather well-preserved Federal, Greek Revival, Victorian and Classic buildings, some of which are open for tours. Sherman occupied the town for two days in November 1864 on his march to the sea, burning most government buildings but sparing most residences. Pick up a walking tour from the **visitors center** (☎ 478-452-4687, 800-653-1804; 200 W Hancock St; 9am-5pm Mon-Fri, 10am-5pm Sat).

Macon

Macon is a pleasant, though often overlooked, little city with a few interesting sights. The town was established in 1823 and prospered as a cotton port on the Ocmulgee River. The area had a strong Unionist and peace movement before and during the Civil War, which left Macon mostly unscathed. Many antebellum houses remain today. In fact, it has more structures on the National Register of Historic Places (5500) than any other Georgian city. Held the third week of March, Macon's **Cherry Blossom Festival** (☎ 478-751-7429) celebrates the blossoming of 250,000 flowering Japanese Yoshino cherry trees.

The **visitors center** (☎ 478-743-3401, 800-768-3401; 200 Cherry St; 9am-5pm Mon-Sat) in the 1916 Terminal Station, has information about history tours of the city.

Georgia Music Hall of Fame (☎ 478-750-8555, 888-427-6257; www.gamusichall.com; 200 Martin Luther King Jr Blvd; adult/child $8/3.50; 9am-5pm Mon-Sat, 1-5pm Sun) showcases the multitude of musical talent that has bloomed in Georgia, from native sons and daughters to groups that got their start in the state, including REM, James Brown, Little Richard and Ray Charles. The museum is a collection of nostalgia-inducing artifacts, listening stations and hands-on exhibits. Duane Allman died in Macon while working on the Allman Brothers album *Eat a Peach*. He and fellow band-member Berry Oakley are buried in the **Rose Hill Cemetery**.

Tubman African American Museum (☎ 478-743-8544; www.tubmanmuseum.com; 340 Walnut St; adult/child $3/2; 9am-5pm Mon-Sat, 2-5pm Sun) pays homage to Harriet Tubman, the escaped slave known as 'the Black Moses' who led hundreds of slaves north to freedom before the Civil War.

Hay House (☎ 478-742-8155; 934 Georgia Ave; adult/child $8/3; 9am-5pm Mon-Sat, 1-5pm Sun) is an amazing, 24-room Italian Renaissance Revival mansion built in the 1850s. According to legend, a hidden room in a staircase stored the Confederate gold.

Die-hard Georgia sports fans will like the giant **Georgia Sports Hall of Fame** (☎ 478-752-1585; 301 Cherry St; adult/child $6/3.50; 9am-5pm Mon-Sat, 1-5pm Sun), which features live action footage, a NASCAR simulator and sports memorabilia from the state's athletes.

Ocmulgee National Monument (☎ 478-752-8257; 1207 Emery Hwy; admission free; 9am-5pm), just east of town, is an archaeological site with Indian burial mounds, artifacts and an ancient earth lodge.

SLEEPING & EATING

Most of Macon's hotels are along commercial strips on Eisenhower Parkway near I-475 and on Riverside Drive along the I-75.

1842 Inn (☎ 478-741-1842, 877-452-6599; www.the1842inn.com; 353 College St; s/d $190/290; P) This is one of the preeminent historic inns in the state. Set in an 1842 Greek Revival antebellum house and an adjoining Victorian house, the inn has 21 rooms decorated with English antiques, oriental carpets and fine paintings. Extras include complimentary hors d'oeuvres and a cash bar in the evening.

Len Berg's (☎ 478-742-9255; 240 Post Office Alley; meat & vegetable plate $6-7, vegetable plate $4.20;

11am-2:30pm Mon-Sat) Set back from the Broadway in an alley between Walnut and Mulberry Sts, it has been a Macon tradition since 1908. A conglomeration of tiny rooms, this restaurant serves Southern fried catfish and turnip greens.

GETTING THERE & AWAY

Macon is a straight 82 miles down I-75 from Atlanta, or 90 miles south of Athens on Hwy 129. **Greyhound** (479-743-2868; 65 Spring St) runs buses to Atlanta ($16, two hours), Savannah ($35, four hours) and Jacksonville, Florida ($53, from five hours).

Warm Springs

In 1928, eight years before he was elected US president, polio-stricken Franklin D Roosevelt took a curative trip to Warm Springs. Later he built a home, founded a polio treatment center and ultimately died from a stroke here in April 1945. The **Little White House State Historic Site** (706-655-5870, 800-864-7275; 401 Little White House Rd; adult/child $5/2; 9am-4:45pm) is just south of the hamlet. The site has pools (hand-dipping, no swimming), a small museum with some of FDR's personal effects and other memorabilia.

Pine Mountain

The tiny town of Pine Mountain serves as the gateway for **Callaway Gardens** (706-663-2281; www.callawaygardens.com; junction Hwys 18 & 27; adult/child $13/6.50; 9am-5pm), one of Georgia's most popular and beautiful attractions. The gardens encompass more than 14,000 acres of artificial 'nature' and attractions, including a butterfly center, a horticultural center, a famous vegetable garden, a beach, and acres upon acres of azaleas that bloom from March to May.

Columbus

Georgia's third-largest city, 100 miles southwest of Atlanta, was established at the highest navigable point on the Chattahoochee River. Waterfalls powered Columbus' early industries, and the city produced Confederate armaments in the Civil War. Shortly after the South surrendered at Appomattox, Union General James H Wilson launched a mistaken attack that badly damaged the city. Modern Columbus is still mostly industrial. Fort Benning, a huge army base that is the home of the US infantry, is just south of town. The **visitors center** (706-322-1613, 800-999-1613; 1000 Bay Ave; 8:30am-5:30pm Mon-Fri, 11am-5pm Sat, 1-5pm Sun), downtown at 10th St, has plenty of brochures and maps.

SOUTH GEORGIA

Georgia's agricultural heritage lives on in South Georgia. Though this area was once at the bottom of the sea, its predominantly sandy soil is overlain in some spots by richer soils that are good for growing cotton. Other common crops include peaches, pecans and peanuts. The world-famous Vidalia sweet onion is grown only in the South Georgia town of the same name. Pine trees throughout the region support a vibrant timber industry, and there are many textile mills and pulp and paper plants.

Plains

This tiny town is best known as the birthplace and current residence of Jimmy Carter, the 39th US president. Many Carter-related buildings are now part of the **Jimmy Carter National Historic Site**. Watch a film and get good information at the **Plains High School Museum and Visitors Center** (229-824-4104; www.nps.gov/jica; 300 N Bond St; 9am-5pm). Also part of the site, the **Carter Boyhood Home**, 2.5 miles west of downtown Plains, was renovated and opened to the public in 2000; the Carter family grew cotton, peanuts and corn here. Jimmy and Rosalynn still live in the **Carter Home**, west of downtown on Hwy 280, but it is closed to the public. Carter occasionally teaches Sunday school at **Maranatha Baptist Church** (229-824-7896). Adult visitors are welcome; call for the current schedule.

Andersonville National Historic Site

The site of the Civil War's most infamous prison lies 10 miles northeast of Americus on Georgia Hwy 49. The Andersonville prison camp was in operation only 14 months (1864–65), but in that time 12,919 of its 45,000 Union prisoners died from disease, poor sanitation, overcrowding and exposure.

National Prisoner of War Museum (229-924-0343; 496 Cemetery Rd; admission free; 8:30am-5pm) honors American POWs throughout history. The stirring film *Echoes of Captivity* presents interviews with POWs and the museum displays moving and sometimes disturbing information about the history of POWs. The

FROM PEANUTS TO PRESIDENT

Jimmy Carter served as US president for one term, from 1977 to 1981, and has since made his name as an activist for international peace. James Earl (Jimmy) Carter was born in 1924 in the rural town of Plains. His boyhood home in nearby Archery lacked plumbing and electricity. Carter attributes his values of hard work, integrity and family to his rural Georgia upbringing.

Carter attended the US Naval Academy at Annapolis, studied nuclear physics and served as a senior officer on the *Sea Wolf*, the second US nuclear-powered submarine. When his father died in 1952, Carter returned to Plains to run the family peanut business and became involved in local politics. Hampered at first by his stance in favor of Civil rights legislation, Carter served two terms as a state senator and then became Georgia's governor in 1970. His accomplishments in office included increasing government employment of African-Americans and women, opening day care and drug abuse rehabilitation centers and streamlining state agencies.

When his term as governor ended, Carter ran for president in 1976. The choice came down to the grinning populist and the recently disgraced Nixon; the public chose the populist with the wide grin.

As president, Carter brokered the Camp David peace accords between Israel and Egypt; signed the Panama Canal treaty, which scheduled the return of the canal's control to Panama; signed the Strategic Arms Limitation Treaty with the USSR; developed a comprehensive energy program; recognized human rights as a key consideration in developing foreign policy; appointed unprecedented numbers of African-Americans and women to major government positions; and pardoned Vietnam War draft evaders. His presidency was marred, though, by high inflation and unemployment, the capture of 52 American hostages by Iranian militants and problems getting his energy program through Congress. Some criticized him for being politically naive and too sincere and conscientious. He was handily defeated by Ronald Reagan in 1980.

Since 1981, Carter has continued to pursue efforts of peace and human rights around the world. *Time* magazine claimed that he has been 'the best ex-president the US has had since Herbert Hoover.' He has helped monitor elections in Haiti, Panama and Nicaragua, conferred with Middle Eastern leaders, attempted to mediate the Eritrean–Ethiopian civil war, and forged an agreement with Haiti to end military control of the government. For his work, Carter was awarded the Nobel Peace Prize in 2002.

Despite his fame, he and wife Rosalynn continue to live in Plains, population 650.

Andersonville National Cemetery contains the tightly-spaced graves of the Union soldiers who died at the camp. As a national cemetery, it continues to provide a permanent resting place for deceased veterans.

Okefenokee National Wildlife Refuge

Established in 1937, the **Okefenokee Swamp** is a national gem, encompassing 396,000 acres of bog that fills a giant saucer-shaped depression that was once part of the ocean floor. The swamp comprises islands, lakes and forests, and remains one of the oldest and best-preserved freshwater areas in the country. It's home to 234 reptile species, including an estimated 9000 to 15,000 alligators, 234 bird species, 49 types of mammal, and 60 amphibian species. The best way to see it is in a canoe or on a boat tour. The ultimate experience is a multiday canoe trip on the swamp's 120 miles of waterways. Call the US Fish & Wildlife Service's **Okefenokee National Wildlife Refuge Wilderness Canoe Guide** (☎ 912-496-7836; okefenokee.fws.gov; canoes/motor boats per hour $6/30, per day $15/60) if you're considering a trip. If you want to rent a canoe for the day or join a boat trip, you'll find outfitters at the swamp's three main entrances. Guided boat trips are also available.

The **Stephen C Foster State Park** (☎ 912-637-5274; admission per vehicle $5) western entrance is at an 18-mile drive from the tiny town of Fargo along state Hwy 177. By far the best activity here is to get out on the accessible 25 miles of day-use waterways. Alligator sightings are almost certain if you keep alert. The park also has camping and cabins. Call for details.

Okefenokee Swamp Park (☎ 912-283-0583) provides northern access to the swamp at this private concession and wildlife park 8 miles south of Waycross. The park's main attraction is a zoo of live swamp creatures, including alligators (many unfenced), black bears, otters, turtles and deer. Boat trips and rentals are also available.

Suwannee Canal Recreation Area (☎ 912-496-7836) is the eastern entrance, 11 miles southwest of Folkston, and is the most convenient for visitors who are also exploring the Georgia coast. It has some of the most comprehensive facilities (rentals and trips) and is the main US Fish & Wildlife Service entrance. The 9-mile Swamp Island Drive is suitable for exploration by car or bike.

SAVANNAH & THE COAST

It's hard not to fall under the spell of Georgia's coastline and its isles. Southeast of Savannah, the 100 miles of coastline are protected by 13 large and small barrier islands. Many of these are uninhabited and inaccessible to travelers; some are private compounds and/or nature preserves for waterfowl, migratory birds, alligators, nesting sea turtles and wild horses. At the southern end of the coast, several islands that were once retreats for America's megarich are now favorites of beachcombers, bicyclists, golfers and history buffs.

All of this variety is set amid a coastal plain of startling beauty – the omnipresent live oak trees; small streams cutting through tidal marshlands, with hundreds of fiddler crabs scurrying for hiding places and great egrets looking for their next meal; and mile after mile of cordgrass swaying with the wind.

Savannah

'This place is fantastic. It's like *Gone with the Wind* on mescaline.' Such is the description of Savannah rendered by the protagonist (John Cusack) in Clint Eastwood's film version of *Midnight in the Garden of Good and Evil.* He ain't wrong, Scarlett.

Set on the Savannah River about 18 miles from the coast amid Lowcountry moors and mammoth live oak trees dripping with Spanish moss, this city is steeped in tradition. With about 2.5 sq miles of historic mansions, cotton warehouses and public buildings, Savannah preserves its antebellum history in a way only its Lowcountry sister city Charleston can rival. Walking among the cotton wharves and urban squares, you can trace American history from Georgia's first settlement to the moment in the Civil War when the Yankee General Sherman seized the city and offered it as a Christmas present to President Abraham Lincoln.

While Charleston has always harbored its reputation as a dignified, refined and politically courageous cultural center, Savannah revels in being the bad girl. The town loves its sinful pleasures. Be they the brown sugar and hot-pepper sauce on Lowcountry shrimp or the bump and grind of a drag-queen diva.

HISTORY

Founded in 1733, Savannah was the first English settlement in the colony of Georgia. It became a wealthy shipping center, handling the export of cotton and import of slaves. In the 19th century, the railroads added to the city's wealth, bringing in ever greater volumes of plantation produce.

Savannah was the goal of General Sherman's devastating March to the Sea, and the city surrendered to him on December 21, 1864. Instead of burning the city, Sherman rested his troops there for six weeks before turning north to cut another path of destruction through South Carolina.

The collapse of cotton prices in the late 1800s sent Savannah into a severe economic decline. In the long run, this may have been a good thing; had it prospered, the elegant streets may well have been demolished in the name of development.

ORIENTATION

Savannah's Historic District is a rectangle bounded by Savannah River, Forsyth Park, E Broad St and Martin Luther King Jr Blvd. Almost everything of interest to visitors lies within or just outside this area. River St, the commercial district of bars, restaurants and shops in converted cotton warehouses along the Savannah River, is the heart of the tourist district. City Market is an equally important district of shops and restaurants along the western edge of the Historic District at W St Julian St near Franklin Sq.

Twenty-one of Savannah's original 24 squares are the pillars of the historic districts. Each marks an exquisite place to relax among flower gardens, shade trees and – usually – a monument to some notable person buried (like Georgia's first settler James Oglethorpe) in the square. Bull St, running north–south, divides the east and west branches of streets. The Historic District turns distinctly residential south of York St.

INFORMATION

Bookstores

E Shaver, Bookseller (☎ 912-234-7257; 326 Bull St)

Post

Post office Main (☎ 912-235-4653; 2 N Fahm St; 🕑 7am-6pm Mon-Fri, 9am-3pm Sat) Just west of downtown at the intersection with Bay St; Downtown (intersection of W State and Barnard Sts) The most convenient branch.

Tourist Offices

Visitors center (☎ 877-728-2662, 912-944-0455; www.savannahvisit.com; 301 Martin Luther King Jr Blvd; 🕑 10am-10pm) Excellent resources and services are available in the restored 1860s Central of Georgia train station.

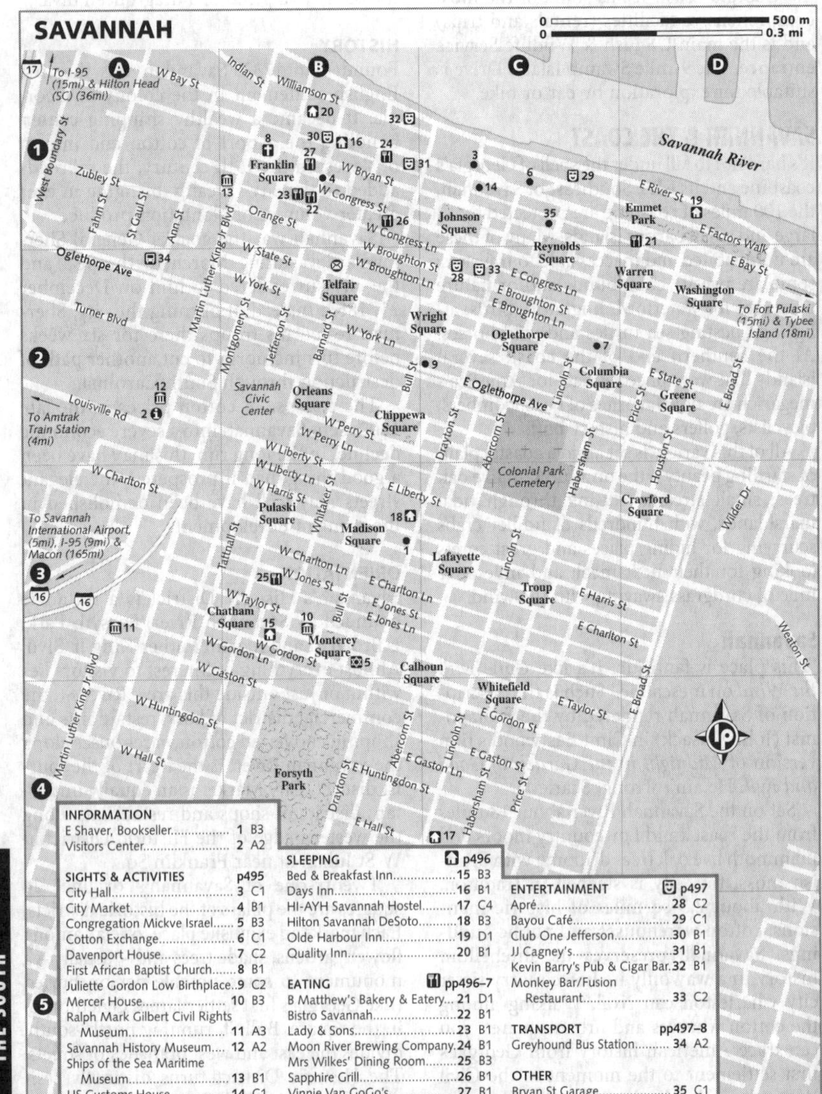

DANGERS & ANNOYANCES

The Historic District is safe during the day but desperate folks prowl the area after dark. Muggings and drug dealing are common in neighborhoods that surround the Historic District. At night, use commonsense precautions and stay in well-lit, populated areas.

SIGHTS & ACTIVITIES

The Riverfront

Along the wharves of the Savannah River, on the northern edge of the Historic District, the Riverfront is Savannah's most popular tourist attraction. The main pedestrian and auto artery is **River St**, which is home to dozens of shops, restaurants and nightspots. This brick-and-cobblestone waterside promenade along a gallery of restored cotton warehouses is a great place for strolling, shopping and people-watching. **Factor's Walk** promenade is essentially the upper level of buildings between River and Bay Sts and was the city's business center in the 19th century. Nearby are the gold-domed **City Hall** and the **Cotton Exchange** building, guarded by lion statues and once one of the world's busiest exchanges.

Museums

Just behind the visitors center, the **Savannah History Museum** (☎ 912-238-1779; 303 Martin Luther King Jr Blvd; adult/child $4/3; 🕑 8:30am-5pm Mon-Fri, 9am-5pm Sat & Sun) is a good place to start a visit to Savannah's Historic District. The film and displays here give a feel for the city's past. There's a replica of Forrest Gump's park bench (which, in the film, was in Oglethorpe Sq).

Ralph Mark Gilbert Civil Rights Museum (☎ 912-231-8900; 460 Martin Luther King Jr Blvd; adult/child $4/2; 🕑 9am-5pm Mon-Sat) just south of the I-16 overpass, tells the story of African-Americans in Savannah, focusing on the civil rights struggle. In 1964, Martin Luther King Jr called Savannah 'the most integrated city south of the Mason–Dixon line.'

The small but engaging **Ships of the Sea Maritime Museum** (☎ 912-232-1511; 41 Martin Luther King Jr Blvd; adult/child $5/4; 🕑 10am-5pm Tue-Sun) has attractive exhibits that focus on models of ships, particularly ones associated with the city, and nautical memorabilia. The SS *Savannah* was the first steamship to cross the Atlantic Ocean; much later, the NS *Savannah* was nuclear powered.

Historic Homes

Savannah is a fabulous city for long, leisurely strolls. The ambience of Spanish moss hanging from live oaks, entire streets of historic 18th- and 19th-century buildings, and the squares are Savannah's main attractions. Some of the best historic houses are Davenport, Mercer and Juliette Gordon Low Birthplace.

Davenport House (☎ 912-236-8097; Columbia Sq; adult/child $7/3.50; 🕑 10am-4pm Mon-Sat, 1-4pm Sun) was the first of Savannah's historic homes to be restored, and its 30-minute tour is exceptional for both its antique collection and the knowledge of the guides. If you have time for touring only one house, make it this one.

Mercer House (429 Bull St on Monterey Sq), the immense red-brick Italianate mansion, became the home of the extravagant socialite antique dealer Jim Williams in 'Midnight.'

Juliette Gordon Low Birthplace (☎ 912-233-4501; 10 E Oglethorpe Ave; adult/child $8/7; 🕑 10am-4pm Mon-Sat, 12:30-4:30pm Sun), at the northeastern corner of Bull and Oglethorpe Sts, is a upper-middle-class Victorian home dating from 1821 and was the childhood abode of the founder of the Girl Scouts of America.

Historic Houses of Worship

First African Baptist Church (☎ 912-233-6597; 23 Montgomery St at Franklin Sq; admission free; 🕑 10am-3pm Mon-Fri) is the oldest African-American church in North America. It was built in 1859 by slaves. There are church services on Sunday.

Congregation Mickve Israel (☎ 912-233-1547; 20 E Gordon St at Monterey Sq; admission by donation $2; 🕑 10am-noon, 2-4pm Mon-Fri) is the oldest Reform Judaism temple in the USA (the congregation formed in 1733, though the present gothic building dates from 1878). Inside you will see the oldest Torah in the USA and over 1800 articles of Judaica.

TOURS

If you have a choice, few excursions are more romantic than a carriage ride around the city at sunset on a fair, warm evening. The visitors center is the best place to book tours, whether on foot, trolley, minibus or horse-drawn carriage ($18 for 50 minutes). Most of the city's tour operators begin and end their excursions from the center's parking lot. Another fun activity is a boat cruise. **Savannah Riverboat Cruises** (☎ 912-232-6404; 9 E River St; adult/child $14/9; 🕑 9am-8pm) travel by

STARSTRUCK SAVANNAH

Books and films have glamorized Savannah as a surreal remnant of the old South, where tradition beds down with sweet decadence. Now most of the world knows Savannah through its roles in *Forrest Gump*, John Berendt's hugely successful 1994 murder-mystery travelogue *Midnight in the Garden of Good and Evil*, and the subsequent film directed by Clint Eastwood. Books like *Wise Blood* by Savannah-born Flannery O'Connor, songs like 'Moon River' by native-son composer Johnny Mercer and the 2002 hit movie the *Legend of Bagger Vance* have added to the city's mythology. These days, hardly a year goes by without another feature film being made in Savannah with a gaggle of stars moving about incognito in the city's bars, clubs and restaurants and dipping into the local real estate market to buy a little piece of this garden of good and evil.

classic paddleboat through the Lowcountry marshes. Daytime cruises take one hour.

SLEEPING

If your idea of a great escape is a plush bedroom with a window to a wild and mysterious city, you're going to love Savannah. The city has a dizzying array of accommodations for romantic getaways, about 60 options in the Historic District alone.

Though most rates start above $100 and the fancier places run well over $200, many of the historic inns and B&Bs have a wide range of rates. Rates tend to be cheaper midweek and they drop dramatically outside of spring and summer.

HI-AYH Savannah Hostel (☎ 912-236-7744; 304 E Hall St; dm/r $20/40) In a restored mansion in the Historic District this hostel comes well recommended. It offers dorm beds and one private room ($36). It's closed January and February, and sometimes December.

Days Inn (☎ 912-236-4440; 201 W Bay St; r $80-120; P ✖) The dark brick facade of this 253-room hotel dates back 160 years and fits in with the character of the surrounding architectural heirlooms. Days Inn has an excellent location within a two minute walk of all the shops, restaurants and nightlife.

Quality Inn (☎ 912-236-6321; 300 W Bay St; r $90-139; P ✖) On the edge of the Historic District, between Montgomery and Jefferson Sts, the Quality Inn is near the Riverfront and a good value if you want to be in the heart of Savannah's action. Its generic exterior belies its 52 modern rooms.

Hilton Savannah DeSoto (☎ 912-232-9000, 800-445-8667; www.desotohilton.com; 15 E Liberty St; r $120-160; P ✖ ☐) Near Madison Sq, the HSD has modern business-class rooms, an outdoor pool and convention facilities. Be careful to avoid the $50 cancellation fee for leaving before your scheduled departure date.

Bed and Breakfast Inn (☎ 912-238-0518; bedbreak fast@travelbase.com; 117 W Gordon St; r $80-150; P ✖) Among Savannah's historic inns, the B&B Inn stands out for its value. Adjacent to Chatham Sq, the inn is an 1853 Federal row house. Its 16 rooms aren't as posh as those in some other inns, but then B&B Inn is less expensive. It's decorated in antiques, period reproduction pieces and oriental carpets, and it has a relaxing private garden and deck. You get hearty breakfasts with eggs and fresh fruits.

Olde Harbour Inn (☎ 912-234-4100, 800-553-6533; www.oldharbourinn.com; 508 E Factors Walk; r $130-230; P ✖) Once a cotton warehouse on the bluff above the riverfront, this small inn rents 24 comfortable suites, each with a fully-equipped kitchen. Ask for one of the rooms with a balcony overlooking the river.

EATING

Get ready to feast! Savannah offers a legion of fine-dining experiences, from gourmet Southern food to wild fusion combos with fresh seafood. Many restaurants are concentrated along the waterfront and in City Market, on W Congress St. Restaurants are also scattered throughout the Historic District. All listed have non-smoking sections.

B Matthew's Bakery & Eatery (☎ 912-233-1319; 325 E Bay St; pastries $2-4, sandwiches $4-6) There is simply no better place to spend a lazy morning in Savannah than this sensuous café at the east end of the Historic District. The owners have converted a run-down bar (dating from 1791!) into an attractive mix of tables and window seats overlooking the river. The bakery cases tempt with spinach croissants and yummy apple tarts. Pick one, get a fresh espresso and kick back to the soft tones of Etta James seeping from the stereo.

Vinnie Van GoGo's (☎ 912-233-6394; 317 W Bryan St; pizzas $12-16) You can get a killer 14-inch New

York–style pizza here with two toppings for $12. They also sell pizza by the slice, calzones and domestic and imported beers. This hangout isn't much to look at, but the tables outside are great for people-watching. Cash only.

Lady & Sons (☎ 912-233-2600; 311 W Congress St; meals $17-21) A Savannah institution, this exceedingly popular Southern-style restaurant serves delicacies like candied sweet potatoes and fried chicken. You can go for the outstanding buffet or order off the menu. If you don't want to wait in line for dinner come at 11:30am for the lunch menu, which echoes the dinner offerings, but at half the price.

Mrs Wilkes' Dining Room (☎ 912-232-5997; 107 W Jones St; meals $12-20) A longtime favorite for sociable Southern-style breakfasts and lunches, this family-style eatery packs its guests around long tables, three meals a day. Mrs Wilkes passed away in 2002, but her cuisine lives on through her family and loyal customers who infuse the restaurant with her friendly, fun-loving spirit. No credit cards.

Moon River Brewing Company (☎ 912-447-0943; 21 W Bay St; sandwiches $5-8) You'll find this aromatic brewpub in an 1821 building a block from the Riverfront. Heavy with the scent of hops from the vats, it attracts a young crowd with its homemade brews and local artwork on the walls. The menu ranges from buffalo wings to burgers and sandwiches.

Sapphire Grill (☎ 912-443-9962; 110 W Congress St; meals $22-28) Chef Chris Nason fires up quite a feast in this converted warehouse near City Market. The menu is highly eclectic, ranging from bouillabaisse in champagne to Colorado lamb lollipops.

Bistro Savannah (☎ 912-233-6266; 309 W Congress St; meals $16-23) One of the top seafood restaurants in Georgia. The restaurant uses organically grown local and regional produce.

GAY & LESBIAN SAVANNAH

With so many gay merchants, innkeepers, college students and military personnel, Savannah has a lively gay and lesbian scene. John Berendt's book *Midnight in the Garden of Good & Evil* opened the closet doors on Savannah's gay scene a decade ago with a big ka-boom, but the city had a rich gay underground for decades. Check out www.gaysavannah.com for a complete list of gay-friendly inns, bars clubs, accommodations and businesses.

DRINKING & ENTERTAINMENT

For an up-to-date list of events at clubs and bars, check out Thursday's *Savannah Morning News* and the weeklies *Connect Savannah* and *Creative Loafing*.

Live Music & Nightclubs

Monkey Bar/Fusion Restaurant (☎ 912-232-0755; 8 E Broughton St) It rocks! Owner Wendy Snowden and her clientele ooze an authentic, artsy glam, giving the place the feel of an indie film party. The American-Asian fusion cuisine is just as far out there. Couples get up right in the middle of dinner and start dancing. Plenty of folks never eat at all.

Kevin Barry's Pub & Cigar Bar (☎ 912-233-9626; 117 W River St) Just west of the Hyatt Regency, Kevin's has live Irish music Wednesday to Sunday and food such as shepherd's pie. It's like St Paddy's Day every night here.

JJ Cagney's (☎ 912-233-2444; 17 W Bay St) Here's an excellent place to spot both up-and-coming local bands and singer-songwriter types.

Bayou Café (☎ 912-233-6411; 14 N Abercorn St) Between Bay and River Sts, across from the Hampton Inn, the Bayou is a gritty place, popular with partying students. It also has music every night, mostly alternative and country-rock.

Apré (☎ 912-238-8888; 2 E Broughton St; cover $10) Set above Il Pasticcio restaurant, Apré is the hippest club in town. The music is hard house and dance. At weekends the crowd gets fancier and older (25–35). The club gets packed, particularly between midnight and 1:30am when the booze is FREE.

Club One Jefferson (☎ 912-232-0200; www.clubone-online.com; 1 Jefferson St) Savannah's premier gay venue, Club One features drag shows, pool tables and a large dance floor. Although its clientele is mostly gay, straight party animals also come here to dance and see the most excellent drag queens.

GETTING THERE & AWAY

The **Savannah International Airport** (☎ 912-964-0514) is about 5 miles west of downtown off I-16. If you're driving, Savannah's Historic District lies an easy 15-mile drive east of I-95. I-16 is your connecting route, which brings you virtually to the doorstep of the visitors center at Martin Luther King Jr Blvd.

Greyhound (☎ 912-232-2135; 610 W Oglethorpe Ave) has connections to Atlanta ($48, 5½ hours); Charleston, South Carolina ($27, three hours); and Jacksonville, Florida ($25, 2½ hours).

The **Amtrak station** (☎ 800-872-7245, 912-234-2611) is 4 miles from City Hall and is served only by taxis. Three 'Silver Service' trains per day go south to Jacksonville, FL ($52, 2½ hours), continuing on to Miami ($130, 12 hours). Northbound, there are two trains per day to Charleston ($25, two hours).

GETTING AROUND

Coastal Transportation (☎ 912-964-5999; adult $21) provides a shuttle from the airport to downtown.

You don't need a car to enjoy Savannah. If you have one, it's best to park it and walk or take tours around town. Visitors can buy a 48-hour parking pass for $8 at the visitors center and the Bryan St Garage. The pass works at the municipal garages, River St lots and one-hour meters.

Chatham Area Transit (CAT; ☎ 912-233-5767) operates local buses, including a free shuttle that makes its way around the Historic District and stops within a couple of blocks of nearly every major site.

Around Savannah

About 15 miles east of Savannah off US Hwy 80 is **Fort Pulaski National Monument** (☎ 912-786-5787; www.nps.gov/fopu; US Hwy 80; adult/child $3/free; 9am-5pm). Laborers built this fort on Cockspur Island in 1847 to guard the mouth of the Savannah River. Military engineers thought that such a huge masonry fort, with 7½ft-thick walls, was impenetrable. The fort was seized before the state even seceded from the Union. Visitors can view the well-preserved fort, complete with moat and drawbridge.

About 18 miles east of Savannah at the end of US 80, **Tybee Island** (☎ 912-786-5444, 800-868-2322; www.tybeevisit.com; 1st St/US Hwy 80; 9:30am-5pm) is a small beach community sitting on a lot of history. The island's main attraction is the 3 miles of wide, sandy beach, good for swimming and castle building. The 154ft-tall **Tybee Island Lighthouse** (☎ 912-786-5801; adult/child $5/4; 9am-5:30pm Wed-Mon) is the oldest in Georgia and still in use. The 178 steps to the top reward you with views of the Lowcountry islands, Savannah and the ocean, which is a breeding ground during the winter for the rare and endangered Northern Atlantic right whales. The neighboring **Tybee Island Museum** is in the basement of Fort Screvens, which operated from 1897 to 1947.

Brunswick & the Golden Isles

Mainly used as a jumping-off point for nearby St Simon Island and Jekyll Island, Brunswick is worth a stop. With its large shrimp-boat fleet and downtown Historic District shaded beneath lush live oaks, this town dates from 1733 and has charms you might miss when sailing by on I-95 or the Golden Isle Parkway (US Hwy 17). During WWII, Brunswick shipyards constructed 99 Liberty transport ships for the navy. Today, a new 23ft scale model at **Mary Ross Waterfront Park** on Bay St stands as a memorial to those ships and their builders.

Brunswick-Golden Isles Visitors Bureau (☎ 912-265-0620; www.bgivb.com; Hwy 17 at St Simons Causeway; 8:30am-5pm Mon-Fri) has information about all the Golden Isles, accommodations and dining. Another good source of information is www.brunswickexperience.com.

ST SIMONS ISLAND

Famous for its golf courses, resorts and majestic live oaks, St Simons Island is the largest and most developed of the Golden Isles. It lies 75 miles south of Savannah and just 5 miles from Brunswick. While the southern half of the island is a thickly settled residential and resort area, the northern half and adjacent **Sea Island** and **Little St Simons** offer vast tracts of coastal wilderness amid a tidewater estuary. 'The Village' is a bustling center of good restaurants and shops on the southern end of the island. The **visitors center** (☎ 912-638-9014; 9am-5pm), tucked away in the library complex east of the fishing pier, has excellent maps of the island and bike routes, as well as information on lodging.

JEKYLL ISLAND

An exclusive refuge for millionaires in the late 19th and early 20th centuries, Jekyll Island is a 4000-year-old barrier island 7 miles long and 2 miles wide, with 10 miles of beaches. The **visitors center** (☎ 912-635-3636, 877-453-5955; 9am-5pm), on the causeway to the island, has maps and good brochures about activities and lodging. The 240-acre **historic**

area is a good place to just wander among the oaks and fancy cottages, although you cannot go inside the houses unless you take a tour. Jekyll Island has 20 miles of dedicated, paved **bicycle paths** around the entire island, including the Historic District, the beach and some of the natural areas.

CUMBERLAND ISLAND

Most of this southernmost barrier island is occupied by the **Cumberland Island National Seashore** (☎ 912-882-4335; www.nps.gov/cuis/; admission $4). Almost half of its 36,415 acres are marsh, mudflats and tidal creeks. On the ocean side are 16 miles of wide, sandy beach that you might have all to yourself. The island's interior is characterized by a maritime forest. Animals include deer, raccoons, feral pigs and armadillos (a recent arrival). Freshwater ponds harbor alligators. Feral horses roam the island and are a common sight around the mansion ruins, in the interdune meadows and occasionally on the beach.

The only public access to the island is via the ferry *Cumberland Queen,* which leaves from the St Marys dock. Reservations are recommended (☎ 912-882-4335; adult/child $12/7; 10am-4pm Mon-Fri). October through February, the ferry does not operate on Tuesday or Wednesday.

The only private accommodations on the island are at the **Greyfield Inn** (☎ 904-261-6408; www.greyfieldinn.com; d $250-395 meals included), a grand and graceful mansion built in 1900 as a home for Lucy and Thomas Carnegie's daughter, Margaret Ricketson. Camping is available at **Sea Camp Beach** (☎ 912-882-4335; per person $4), a pristine, developed campground set among magnificent live oaks. Each of the campsites is surrounded by palmetto stands and comes with a raccoon box (to store your food, not your raccoons). Facilities include flush toilets, cold showers and drinking water. It's a short walk to the beach or the ferry from here, and there are a few carts you can borrow to help move your equipment.

ALABAMA

Two of the most significant, culture-altering events in American history began here: the Civil War in 1861 and the crux of the Civil Rights movement in the mid-1950s. Alabama has had to conquer its reputation of rednecks, rebels, segregation, discrimination and wayward politicians. There's no denying the important events of the past; indeed they have helped Alabamians move closer toward racial harmony.

Alabama has a surprising diversity of landscapes, from the northern foothills and central farmlands to the subtropical Gulf Coast. Visitors come to see the heritage of antebellum architecture, to celebrate the country's oldest Mardi Gras in Mobile, and to learn about the struggle for black civil rights.

The **Alabama Bureau of Tourism & Travel** (☎ 334-242-4169, 800-252-2262; www.touralabama.org; PO Box 4927, Montgomery, AL 36103) sends out a vacation guide and the publication *Alabama's Black Heritage.*

History

Alabama was occupied by Choctaws, Cherokees, Chickasaws and especially Creeks until the early 1800s, when white settlers began arriving from the Carolinas, Virginia and Tennessee. By 1839 all the surviving Indians were removed to Oklahoma.

Small-scale farming dominated the early economy, and Alabama was among the first states to secede. In the Civil War, Montgomery was the first Confederate capital, Mobile was a major Confederate port and Selma was a munitions center. Alabama lost around 25,000 men in the war, and reconstruction was painful. Widespread rural poverty was partly alleviated by black agriculturist George Washington Carver, who promoted the rotation of crops and developed numerous new products that could be made from peanuts and sweet potatoes.

The boll weevil devastated cotton crops after 1914, destroying the livelihood of the sharecroppers, and many blacks left the state for good. New iron and steel factories made Birmingham the most industrialized city in the new South.

Racial segregation and Jim Crow laws survived well into the 1950s, when the Civil Rights movement campaigned for desegregation of everything from public buses to private universities. Alabama saw brutal repression and hostility, but federal civil rights and voting laws eventually prevailed. At a political level, reform has seen the election of dozens of black mayors and representatives. Still, Alabama is one of the USA's poorest states, with many blacks

ALABAMA FACTS

Nicknames Camellia State, Heart of Dixie
Population 4,486,508 (23rd)
Area 52,423 sq miles (30th)
Admitted to Union December 14, 1819 (22nd); seceded 1861; readmitted 1868
Capital city Montgomery (population 322,400)
Other cities Birmingham (933,000), Mobile (200,200), Huntsville (177,900)
Birthplace of Nat 'King' Cole (1919–65), Helen Keller (1880–1968), Olympian Jesse Owens (1913–80), author Harper Lee (b 1926), musicians Hank Williams (1923–53) and Lionel Ritchie (b 1949), actress Courteney Cox-Arquette (b 1964)
Home of the first electric streetcars (1866), 300 uses for the peanut (1880s)

among its poorest citizens, and there is abundant evidence of social inequality.

CENTRAL ALABAMA

Called the 'Black Belt,' central Alabama was named for the swath of fertile soil perfect for growing cotton. The region's treasures include several state parks and numerous Civil War and civil rights sites.

Montgomery

Alabama's capital sits on a bend in the Alabama River, a historically important port for shipping cotton. Montgomery became the capital of the Confederacy in 1861. Shortly after, Confederate president Jefferson Davis gave the word and – bang – the Civil War began.

Today, Montgomery is mostly a sleepy politics-and-government town, but in 1955, anger at segregation and Jim Crow laws came to a boil when a black woman named Rosa Parks refused to give up her seat to a white man on a city bus. For 381 days, blacks boycotted city buses until the US Supreme Court finally ordered their desegregation. Racial tensions in Montgomery boiled. In 1961, black Freedom Riders were beaten by Ku Klux Klansmen; in 1963 George Wallace won governorship on a pro-segregation platform. In 1965, Martin Luther King Jr led the Selma-to-Montgomery Civil Rights march to the capital's doorstep, and things started to change.

After surviving the Civil War and all the turmoil of the Civil Rights movement, Montgomery may be emerging from yet another struggle: the fight against boredom. For two decades, the conservative mayor routinely denied permits for nightclubs or music events; nightlife consisted of looking at the stars to the tune of chirping crickets. Things are looking up, however, as Montgomery redefines itself.

Montgomery sprawls across seven hills overlooking the Alabama River, but many attractions are downtown and can be reached on foot. The **visitors center** (☎ 334-262-0013, 800-240-9452; www.visitingmongomery.com; 300 Water St; 🕑 9am-5pm Mon-Sat, noon-4pm Sun) is in the historic Union Station.

SIGHTS

The Southern Poverty Law Center grew out of Montgomery's racial strife. It teaches tolerance and protects the rights of the poor and minorities. Outside the center, the **Civil Rights Memorial** (400 Washington Ave), designed by Maya Lin, honors 40 martyrs of the Civil Rights movement.

Rosa Parks Museum (☎ 334-241-8615; 252 Montgomery St; adult/child $5.50/3.50; 🕑 9am-5pm Mon-Fri, 9am-3pm Sat) features a bronze bust of Rosa and a sophisticated video re-creation of the bus-seat protest.

Free tours are available around the **Alabama State Capitol** (☎ 334-242-3935; 600 Dexter Ave; admission free; 🕑 10am-5pm Mon-Sat), where Jefferson Davis took the oath of office as president of the Confederacy. You can also check out the **First White House of the Confederacy** (☎ 334-242-1861; 644 Washington Ave; 🕑 9am-5pm Mon-Fri), which was moved to its current site opposite the capitol in 1919.

Hank Williams Museum (☎ 334-262-3600; 118 Commerce St; adult/child $7/2; 🕑 9am-6pm Mon-Sat, noon-4pm Sun) pays homage to the country music master. You'll see Hank's personal stuff, including the baby-blue 1952 Cadillac he died in. Other tributes to Williams include a life-size bronze statue in Lister Hill Plaza and an oversize hat where he's buried in the Oakwood Cemetery Annex.

Scott & Zelda Fitzgerald Museum (☎ 334-264-4222; 919 Felder Ave; admission free; 🕑 9am-5pm Wed-Sun) is where Montgomery-born Zelda spent most of her life. F Scott was stationed here during WWI. The writers fell in love, married and lived here from 1931 to 1932.

The superb **Alabama Shakespeare Festival** (☎ 334-271-5353, 800-841-4273; www.asf.net) shows live performances at **Blount Cultural Park** from March through July. A must-see if you're here at that time.

SLEEPING & EATING

Quality Inn (☎ 334-277-1919, 800-228-5151; 5175 Carmichael Rd; d $60; P) A good value on the eastern bypass off Hwy 85, with a sauna, outdoor pool and 108 comfortable rooms with coffeemakers.

Embassy Suites (☎ 334-269-5055; 300 Tallapoosa St; r from $110; P) Downtown right next to the visitors center, this 237-room tidy hotel gets a lot of the city's action.

Montgomery KOA (☎ 334-288-0728; 250 Fischer Rd; campsites/RV sites $20/30; P) You'll find it 4 miles south of town, at I-65 exit 164.

Chris' Hot Dog (☎ 334-265-6850; 138 Dexter Ave; hot dogs $2-5) The plump juicy dogs have made this a Montgomery institution since 1917.

Farmer's Market Cafeteria (☎ 334-262-1970; 315 N McDonough St; breakfast $5; 5:30am-2pm Mon-Fri) The homey Southern breakfast keeps the crowd coming back. At lunch there's more good country cooking and incredibly reasonable prices.

Montgomery Brewing Co (MBC; ☎ 334-834-2739; 12 W Jefferson St; dinner $10-16) A lively hub of activity, the MBC is a great place for a microbrew and salad, burger or savory steak. There's live entertainment on weekends.

Olive Room (☎ 334-262-2763; 121 Montgomery St; meals $13-19) A stylish downtown favorite for romantic but casual dinners, where the menu features hefty martinis and trendy takes on meat and pastas.

GETTING THERE & AWAY

Greyhound (☎ 334-286-0658; 950 W South Blvd) has regular buses to destinations including Atlanta, GA ($30, four hours); Birmingham, AL ($18, 1¾ hours); Jackson, MS ($50, five hours); and New Orleans, LA ($50, seven hours).

Selma

Selma thrived as a center for shipping cotton on the Alabama River and the railways. As plantations thrived, slave trading became big business. After Union soldiers defeated and burned Selma in 1865, the town built itself back, only to be devastated by the nasty boll weevil, a burrowing beetle that decimated entire fields of cotton.

On Bloody Sunday, March 7, 1965, the media captured state troopers and deputies beating and gassing African-Americans and white sympathizers near the Edmund Pettus Bridge. Led by Martin Luther King Jr, the crowd was marching to the state capital (Montgomery) to demonstrate for voting rights. This was the culmination of two years of violence, which ended when President Johnson signed the Voting Rights Act of 1965.

Despite the fact that Selma's electorate shifted from nearly all white to 65% black, Selma's pro-segregationist mayor held onto his seat until 2000, when computer consultant James Perkins became the city's first black mayor. Today, Selma is a quiet, sleepy town, and though its attractions are few, they do provide an excellent insight into the voting rights protests that were at the crux of the Civil Rights movement.

Selma's **visitors center** (☎ 334-875-7485; 2207 Broad St; 8am-8pm) has a wealth of area information about civil rights history and sights. Segregation and Bloody Sunday are remembered at the small **National Voting Rights Museum** (☎ 334-418-0800; 1012 Water Ave; admission $5; 9am-5pm Tue-Fri), near the Edmund Pettus Bridge.

Jameson Inn (☎ 334-874-8600; 2420 N Broad St/Hwy 22; s/d $60/65; P) This inn has 60 spacious rooms, a pool and free continental breakfasts.

St James Hotel (☎ 334-872-3234; 1200 Water Ave; r $75-85, ste $135; P) Overlooking the river, this historic hotel has 42 guest rooms, a good restaurant and a popular streetside lounge. Hotel guests can use the nearby YMCA pool.

Major Grumbles (☎ 334-872-2006; 1 Grumbles Alley; meals $7-11; 11am-11pm Mon-Sat) In a restored riverfront warehouse, this local favorite offers red beans, rice and chicken gumbo.

Tally Ho (☎ 332-872-1390; Mangum St at N Broad St; meals $11-15; 5-10pm) Serving up delicious steaks and seafood in a former log cabin, this is Selma's best restaurant.

Greyhound (☎ 334-874-4503; 434 Broad St) has buses to and from Birmingham ($25, three hours), Mobile ($34, four hours) and Montgomery ($13, one hour).

SOUTHERN ALABAMA

Wedged like a doorstop between Mississippi and Florida, the Southern Alabama coastline – with beaches, rivers, estuaries, bays, a delta and pine-covered barrier islands – is all of 52 miles long.

Mobile

Mobile (mo-*beel*) citizens have long grown weary of explaining to visitors how they've been celebrating Mardi Gras since before New Orleans was founded. But perhaps they're just trying to keep their city a secret. Mobile is interesting and fun in the same sense as New Orleans, only with the volume and brightness turned down.

A major seaport and shipbuilding center, Mobile has green spaces, shady boulevards and four historic districts. It's ablaze with azaleas in early spring and Mardi Gras (which begins 40 days before Easter) has been a big celebration for nearly 300 years. The Dauphin St historic district is where you'll find many bars and restaurants. It's where much of the Mardi Gras action takes place.

Pick up walking and driving tours of the historic districts at the **visitors center** (☎ 251-208-7658, 800-566-2453; 150 S Royal St; 🕑 8am-3pm Mon-Fri), part of the reconstructed **Fort Condé** (☎ 251-208-7304; admission free; 🕑 8am-5pm).

Museum of the City of Mobile (☎ 251-208-7569; 111 S Royal St; admission $5; 🕑 9am-5pm Mon-Sat, 1-5pm Sun) underwent major renovations in 2001, which bolstered its already neat collection of Mardi Gras costumes and maritime antiques with interesting interactive displays about things such as what it's like to live through a hurricane, for example.

TOURS

USS Alabama (☎ 251-433-2703, 800-426-4929; 2703 Battleship Parkway; adult/child $10/5; 🕑 8am-6pm, until 4pm Oct-Mar) Moored near Fort Condé the USS *Alabama* is famous for escaping nine major WWII battles unscathed. It's a worthwhile tour for its pure size and might.

Oakleigh (☎ 251-432-1281; 350 Oakleigh Pl; admission $6; 🕑 9am-4pm Mon-Fri) Guides in period costume lead visitors around Oakleigh, an 1833 Greek Revival mansion with a modest Creole cottage.

Antebellum architecture tours:

Bragg-Mitchell Mansion (1906 Springhill Ave) West of downtown.

Condé-Charlotte House (104 Theatre St) Beautiful house. Downtown.

Richards-DAR House (256 N Joachim St) Italianate house. Downtown.

SLEEPING & EATING

Olsson Motel (☎ 251-661-5331, 800-332-1004; 4137 Government Blvd/Hwy 90 W; s/d $30/35; Ⓟ ✖) Just 7 miles west of downtown, this good budget option is spacious, friendly and cheap.

Malaga Inn (☎ 251-438-4701, 800-235-1586; 359 Church St; r courtyard/street $80/100) Right along the parade route, this is the place to be during Mardi Gras. Nicely furnished rooms open onto balconies overlooking the courtyard or street. A recently restored wing has slightly more expensive rooms. There's also a good restaurant.

Spot of Tea (☎ 251-433-9009; 310 Dauphine St; meals $6-10) Oozing down-home Southern hospitality, here you'll find big breakfasts, thick sandwiches and hearty dinners.

Wintzell's Oyster House (☎ 251-432-4605; 605 Dauphin St; meals $7-12) Order 'em fried, baked, in a sandwich or on the shell – it's all about oysters, served up in a lively atmosphere.

Brick Pit (☎ 251-343-0001; 5456 Old Shell Rd; meals $5) East of the university campus, it offers the best barbecue for miles around.

Around Mobile

Bellingrath Gardens (☎ 251-973-2217; 12401 Bellingrath Gardens Rd; adult/child $7.50/4.50; 🕑 8am-5pm) sits on 65 acres on the west side of Mobile Bay, about 20 minutes from Mobile. The 250,000 azaleas burst alive in spring. You can join a guided tour of the **house** (adult/child $9/5.25) and **gardens** (adult/child $9/5.25). There's also a 45-minute **river cruise** (adult/child $17/11). Take I-10 west, exit 15A. Look for signs.

On the east side of Mobile Bay, the charming **Meaher State Park** (☎ 251-626-5529) features wetlands with a boardwalk for wildlife viewing. Scenic Alt Hwy 98 goes through Fairhope and Point Clear to the Gulf Coast, where **Pleasure Island** has some great beaches and 32 miles of beachfront condos and hotels. **Gulf State Park** (☎ 251-948-7275) preserves 2.5 miles of beach and dunes in a more or less natural state, and has a 468-site **campground** (campsites non-lakeside/lakeside $15/17).

NORTHERN ALABAMA

During the 1930s, the Tennessee Valley Authority brought jobs to this poorest part of the state by building dams, which created numerous lakes. Not surprisingly, the northern third of Alabama, nestled in the Appalachian foothills, has became really very popular with outdoor enthusiasts. Birmingham has big-town culture and nightlife; Huntsville offers fantasies of space travel.

Birmingham

Friends star Courtney Cox-Arquette, soul-singer Nel Carter, *Charlie's Angels* Kate Jackson, and NBA superstar Charles Barkley hail from Birmingham, by far the largest and most cosmopolitan city in Alabama. Its growth, however, wasn't so glamorous. With the discovery of coal, iron ore and limestone in the late 19th century, Birmingham, once a small farming town, grew into the South's foremost industrial center, giving it the nickname 'the Pittsburgh of the South.'

Jim Crow legislation peaked in 1915, at a time when the KKK dominated local politics. By the 1950s Birmingham became America's most segregated city. Racial tensions erupted in 1963 when police attacked students marching for civil rights and turned a blind eye to more than 50 racially motivated bombings.

Faced with disaster, newly-elected politicians forced change. Within a decade, the city council integrated, the economy diversified and a new mayor – this time black – helped stabilize both the economy and the community.

ORIENTATION

The primary attractions are downtown, in and around the Fourth Avenue Historic District, where the black community thrived despite segregation. Hipsters throng to Southside and Five Points South – off 20th St (the main north–south thoroughfare) – where art deco buildings house lively shops, restaurants and nightclubs. Also keeping things youthful is the nearby University of Alabama at Birmingham.

INFORMATION

Historical 4th Ave Visitors Center (☎ 205-328-1850; 319 17th St N; ⌚ 9am-5pm Mon-Sat) Conducts free walking tours.

Visitors center (☎ 205-458-8000, 800-458-8085; www.sweetbirmingham.com; 2200 9th Ave N; ⌚ 8:30am-5pm Mon-Fri) Downtown. Has a small gift shop and good information, including the interesting *Downtown Historic Walking Tour* brochure.

SIGHTS & ACTIVITIES

The most worthwhile sight in town is the **Birmingham Civil Rights Institute** (☎ 205-328-9696, 866-328-9696; www.bcri.bhal.al.us; 520 16th St N; adult/child $8/free; ⌚ 10am-5pm Tue-Sat, 1-5pm Sun). Audio, video, photography, art and artifacts tell the story of racial segregation from WWI to the Civil Rights movement and to racial and human-rights issues around the world today. Across the street is **Kelly Ingram Park**, where 1960s Civil rights marches are depicted in sculptures of Martin Luther King Jr and of police dogs attacking children, who at the time were jailed for their involvement in the protests.

The Carver Performing Arts Center houses the **Alabama Jazz Hall of Fame** (☎ 205-254-2731; 1631 4th Ave N; admission free; ⌚ 10am-5pm Tue-Sat, 1-5pm Sun), which celebrates jazz musicians like Dinah Washington, Nat King Cole and Duke Ellington.

16th St Baptist Church (☎ 205-251-9402; at 6th Ave N; ⌚ 10am-2pm Tue-Fri) was long the center of the black community. During Civil rights protests, it became a gathering place for meetings and protests. When KKK members bombed the church in 1963, killing four girls, the city was flung into a whirlwind of social change. Today, the rebuilt church is a memorial and a house of worship (services on Sunday at 11am).

Birmingham Museum of Art (☎ 205-254-2565; 2000 8th Ave N; admission free; ⌚ 10am-5pm Tue-Sat, noon-5pm Sun) specializes in European decorative arts (especially Wedgwood) and has works from Africa and North America.

The **McWane Center** (☎ 205-714-8300; www.mcwane.org; 200 19th St N; museum/museum & Imax $7.50/13; ⌚ 10am-6pm Mon-Sat, 1-6pm Sun), truly state of the art, houses a science center and Imax theater.

Art deco buildings in Five Points South house shops, restaurants, breweries and nightclubs. **Vulcan Park** (20th St S & Valley Ave) has the US's second-largest statue and an observation tower offering fantastic views. Twelve miles south of town, **Oak Mountain State Park** (☎ 205-620-2524; 15 miles south on I-65, exit 246; admission $2; ⌚ dawn-dusk) is Alabama's largest state park, where you can hike, bike, boat or chill out on the lakeside beach.

SLEEPING

Microtel (☎ 205-945-5550, 800-275-8047; 251 Summit Parkway; s/d $38/42; P ✻ ⊠) South of Southside and halfway between downtown and Oak Mountain State Park, this no-frills hotel is clean and cheap.

Pickwick Hotel (☎ 205-933-9555, 800-255-7304; www.pickwickhotel.com; 1023 20th St S; r from $100;) This art deco hotel sits in the middle of bustling Five Points South. Nightly wine and cheese, afternoon tea and a cheery staff make this beautiful hotel even more endearing.

Tutwiler Hotel (☎ 205-322-2100, 866-850-3053; www.wyndham.com/tutwiler; 2021 Park Place N; r from $140;) This beautiful landmark hotel downtown has a nice mix of 19th-century furnishings and modern accoutrements like a fitness center, marble baths and high-speed Internet access. Its restaurant, the **Grille**, serves up hearty meals, while its pub features good burgers and casual fare.

Oak Mountain State Park (☎ 205-620-2524; 15 miles south on 1-65, exit 246; tents $10, cabins $100) With 131 campsites open year-round and with many recreation opportunities, this makes a good spot to pitch a tent for a couple of nights.

EATING

Pete's Famous Hot Dogs (☎ 205-252-2905; 1925 2nd Ave N; hot dogs $1.50) This tiny hole-in-the-wall has been serving up yummy hot dogs since 1915.

Rib-It-Up (☎ 205-328-7427; 830 1st Ave N; meals $3-8) Diners can eat in or takeout delicious finger-licking Southern barbecue beef, pork and chicken.

La Vase (☎ 205-328-9327; 328 16th St N; meals $6-8; closed Mon) In the historic 4th avenue district, this old-timer serves cheap home-style soul food.

Bombay Cafe (☎ 205-322-1930; 2839 7th Ave S; meals $6-10) With an emphasis on fresh seafood, this restaurant is one of the best values in town.

Mill Bakery, Eatery & Brewery (☎ 205-939-3001; 1035 20th St S; meals $7-14) This fun-loving restaurant attracts students and business folks who come for the lively atmosphere, good beer and menu filled with sandwiches, salads and to-die-for crabcakes.

Highlands Bar & Grill (☎ 205-939-1400; 2011 11th Ave S; meals $12-20) One of internationally acclaimed chef Frank Sitt's trio of restaurants, and arguably Birmingham's best restaurant, the sumptuous menu features meat and seafood beautified by a flash of sophistication borrowed from traditional Southern cuisine.

ENTERTAINMENT

Check the monthly *Black & White* for listings. Most popular nightclubs are in Southside.

Garage Cafe (☎ 205-322-3220; 2304 10th Terrace S) A local favorite.

Nick (☎ 205-252-3831; 2514 10th Ave S) Has the latest bands.

22nd St Jazz Cafe (☎ 205-252-0407; 710 22nd St S) The place for live jazz and blues.

Club 21 (☎ 205-322-0469; 117 21st St N) Has a mixed straight and gay clientele.

GETTING THERE & AROUND

The **Birmingham International Airport** (☎ 205-595-0533) is about 5 miles northeast of downtown. **Greyhound** (☎ 205-251-3210, 618 19th St N), north of downtown, serves cities including Atlanta, GA ($23, three hours); Huntsville ($15, two hours); Montgomery ($18, two hours); Jackson, MS ($29, five hours); and New Orleans, LA ($68, 8½ hours).

Amtrak (☎ 205-324-3033; 1819 Morris Ave), downtown, has trains daily to New York ($165, 11 hours) and New Orleans ($24, seven hours). **Birmingham Transit Authority** (☎ 205-322-7701; adult $1.25) runs local buses.

Tuscaloosa

This mostly industrial town was the state capital from 1826 to 1846, and the University of Alabama was established in 1831. The world here revolves around its successful Crimson Tide football team – grown men cry like babies when UA loses a game.

The **visitors center** (☎ 205-391-9200, 800-538-8696; 1305 Greensboro Ave; 9am-5pm Mon-Fri) is in the historic Jemison-Van de Graaf House.

The most interesting site is 15 miles south of Tuscaloosa at the **Moundville Archaeological Park** (☎ 205-371-2234), which features 26 archaeologically important Mississippian-era Indian mounds.

Huntsville

Pioneer John Hunt settled in this area in 1805, following the removal of Creek and Chickasaw Indians. Wealthy merchants and planters built lavish houses in the Twickenham area, many of which still survive. This wealthy aerospace community had its high-tech beginnings in the 1950s when German scientists were brought in to develop rockets for the US army. The US space program took off and attracted international aerospace-related companies.

The **visitors center** (☎ 256-551-2230, 800-772-2348; www.huntsville.org; 700 Monroe St; 🕑 9am-5pm Mon-Sat, noon-5pm Sun) is in the Von Braun Civic Center. The center does free walking tours of the historic district.

US Space & Rocket Center (☎ 256-837-3400, 800-637-7223; www.ussrc.com; I-565, exit 15; adult/child museum $12/8, museum & Imax $17/12; 🕑 9am-5pm) is a combination science museum and theme park without the hype. It's a great place to take a kid, or to become one again. The center has Imax films, space demonstrations, simulators and the Space Shot ride, which takes you from four g's to weightlessness at 45 mph.

Baymont Inn (☎ 256-830-8999, 800-301-2022; 4890 University Dr; r from $60; P) With big, nicely furnished rooms, this is a great value in a superb location. The outdoor pool is ultra-refreshing after a long day at the space center.

Hampton Inn (256-830-9400, 800-426-7866; 4815 University Dr; r $65-80; P) Just a couple of miles from the Space Center, this 164-room hotel also has nice rooms and a great outdoor pool. Continental breakfast is included.

Huntsville International Airport (☎ 256-772-9395; 1000 Glen Hearn Blvd) is just west of town. **Greyhound** (☎ 256-534-1681; 601 Monroe St NW) has buses to Atlanta, GA ($29, six hours); Birmingham ($16, 2½ hours); Nashville, TN ($16, 2½ hours); and New Orleans, LA ($77, 11 hours). **Huntsville Shuttle System** (☎ 256-532-7433) runs 11 routes and an hourly tourist bus to most hotels.

The Shoals

Four cities on the Tennessee River make up the area known as 'the Shoals': Florence, Sheffield, Tuscumbia and Muscle Shoals. The Wilson Dam, completed in 1924, improved navigation on the 37-mile Muscle Shoals rapids and brought inexpensive electricity to the area. The Shoals made a name for itself in the music industry from 1966, when Fame Recording Studios and Quinvy Studio got Atlantic Records to release Percy Sledge's 'When a Man Loves a Woman.' That song was followed by hits from Wilson Pickett, Aretha Franklin, the Rolling Stones, Paul Simon and others.

Information on area sights and accommodations is available at the **visitors center** (☎ 256-383-0783, 800-344-0783; www.choals-tourism.org; 179 Hwy 72W Tuscumbia; 🕑 8:30am-5pm Mon-Fri year-round, 9am-4pm Sat & 1-4pm Sun summer).

MISSISSIPPI

Long scorned for its lamentable civil rights history and its low ranking on the list of nearly every national marker of economy and education, most people feel content to malign Mississippi without ever experiencing it firsthand. Unpack your bags for a moment and you'll see much more. While Mississippi's Gulf Coast has some wonderful coastal environments, plus the famous history and scenery of Natchez Trace Parkway, the state's principal attraction is a glimpse of the real South. It lies somewhere amid the Confederate defeat at Vicksburg, the literary legacy of William Faulkner at Oxford, the birthplace of the blues in the Mississippi Delta, and the humble origins of Elvis Presley in Tupelo.

The **Mississippi Division of Tourism** (☎ 601-875-0705, 800-927-6378; www.visitmississippi.org; PO Box 1705, Ocean City, MS 39566) has Welcome Centers at the state line.

History

There are several remnants from the ancient Mississippian culture in modern-day Mississippi; three Indian nations were here when Hernando de Soto arrived in 1540, but only one Choctaw community survives. Most others were displaced by a series of sham treaties and ultimate removal to Oklahoma in the 1830s.

Cotton dominated the economy, and by 1860 Mississippi was the country's leading cotton producer and one of the 10 wealthiest states. Cotton required slaves, the vast majority of whom were owned by a few giant plantations; most whites held no slaves at all. Nevertheless, the institution of slavery was entrenched and there was a great fear of slave rebellion. Mississippi was the second state to secede in the Civil War, which cost it more than 60,000 lives. Vicksburg was the last Confederate stronghold on the Mississippi, and its fall to General Grant after a long siege was a turning point in the conflict.

The war ruined Mississippi's economy, and Reconstruction was traumatic. The discriminatory 'Black Code' laws made racial segregation a way of life, with most blacks and many whites doomed to wretched poverty. It was not until the late 1960s that the state's schools and colleges were integrated, and the Civil rights struggle was marked by

MISSISSIPPI FACTS

Nickname Magnolia State
Population 2,871,782 (31st)
Area 49,907 sq miles (32nd)
Admitted to Union December 10, 1817 (20th); seceded 1861; readmitted 1870
Capital city Jackson (population 184,000)
Other cities Biloxi (51,000), Greenville (42,000)
Birthplace of novelist William Faulkner (1897–1962), musicians Tennessee Williams (1911–83), Elvis Presley (1935–77), BB King (b 1925) and Jimmy Buffett (b 1946), puppeteer Jim Henson (1936–90), talk-show host Oprah Winfrey (b 1954)

violence, murder and federal intervention. Despite some economic diversification and the growth of oil and natural-gas industries, Mississippi has the highest poverty rate – almost 20% – in the country.

NORTHEASTERN MISSISSIPPI

The Appalachian foothills begin in this lovely corner of the state – a gently rolling terrain of well-watered forests and cropland. Many visitors rather sensibly base themselves in Oxford, a literary and intellectual hub of the South and home to the University of Mississippi.

Tupelo & Around

Incorporated in 1870 and named after a native gum tree, Tupelo was once a railroad hub and today mass produces upholstered furniture. It's famous around the world as the birthplace of Elvis Presley, the King of Rock 'n' Roll, and everyone in town has their own story of who cut the King's hair or who taught him his first chord.

The Natchez Trace Parkway and Hwy 78 intersect northeast of downtown. Get information at the Tupelo **visitors center** (☎ 662-841-6521, 800-533-0611; 399 E Main St; ⌚ 8am-5pm Mon-Fri) and the Natchez Trace Parkway **visitors center** (☎ 662-680-4025, 800-305-7417; Milepost 266; ⌚ 8am-5pm), on the parkway north of Hwy 78. Gloster St has motels, restaurants and other services, especially at the intersection with McCullough Blvd. The older downtown area is about a mile east at 'Crosstown,' the intersection of Gloster and Main Sts, marked by an old blue-and-yellow neon arrow.

Elvis Presley's Birthplace (☎ 662-841-1245; 306 Elvis Presley Blvd; adult/child all sights $7/3.50; ⌚ 9am-5:30pm Mon-Sat, 1-4pm Sun) is east of downtown off Hwy 78. The 15-acre park complex contains the two-room shack built by Elvis' dad, a museum displaying personal items and a tiny chapel that contains Elvis' own Bible.

Brices Cross Roads National Battlefield, 12 miles northwest, has a small cemetery and a monument to the Confederate victory here in 1864. More Civil War sites are further north in **Corinth**. 'Faulkner Country' is centered around **New Albany**, 20 miles up Hwy 78, the birthplace of William Faulkner.

All American Inn (☎ 662-844-5610; 767 East Main St; r from $30; P ✲) Right downtown, this roomy, slightly aged place has a restaurant and comfortable enough rooms.

Days Inn (☎ 662-842-0088; 1015 N Gloster; r $55; P ✲ ☺) With 40 comfortable rooms, laundry services, complimentary continental breakfast and an outdoor pool, this is a good value.

Commodore Motel (☎ 662-840-0285; s/d $30/35) On Business 78, a half-mile east of Elvis' birthplace.

Two state parks on either side of town, **Tombigbee** (☎ 662-842-7669; campsites $13) southeast of town, and **Trace** (☎ 662-489-2958; campsites $13) to the west, have fishing, swimming and campsites.

Jefferson Place (☎ 662-844-8696; 823 Jefferson; meals $7-10; ⌚ 11am-midnight, closed Sun) Just a block northwest of the Crosstown arrow off Gloster St, this popular bar and grill serves steaks and sandwiches.

Greyhound (☎ 662-842-4557; 201 Commerce St), downtown, has daily buses to Memphis, TN ($26, 20½ hours), Jackson ($40, from 6½ hours) and Oxford ($12, 1½ hours).

Oxford

Cultivated, bustling and prosperous Oxford is home to the University of Mississippi ('Ole Miss'), which opened in 1848. During the Civil War, Oxford was captured and torched by Union soldiers, and only a few treasured buildings survived. Later, William Faulkner mythologized the area in his famous stories of Yoknapatawpha County: 'I discovered my little postage stamp of native soil was worth writing about, and…I would never live long enough to exhaust it.'

In 1962 ugly riots accompanied the enrollment of James Meredith, the first black student at Ole Miss. Troops were called in, and two people died. The university and

THE KING'S HUMBLE ORIGINS

Elvis and his stillborn twin, Jesse, were born in Tupelo in the front room of a 450-sq-ft shotgun shack at 4:35am on January 8, 1935. The Presleys lived there until Elvis was three, when the house was repossessed.

Elvis bought his first guitar at **Tupelo Hardware** (114 W Main St) for $12; attended grades one to five at Lawhon School; won second prize in a talent quest at the fairgrounds west of town; earned A grades in music at Milam Junior High School, Gloster and Jefferson Sts; and attended the **First Assembly of God church** (909 Berry St).

When Elvis was 13, he and his family left Tupelo for Memphis. He returned at 21 to play the Mississippi–Alabama Fair, and the National Guard was called in to contain the crowds. The following year, Elvis came back for a benefit concert, with proceeds going to help the city purchase and restore his birthplace, which now attracts nearly 100,000 visitors each year.

town are now quietly integrated, with galleries, bookstores and cafés grouped around Courthouse Sq. It's a vibrant, artsy town and well worth a stop.

INFORMATION

Bookstores

For a taste of what's happening in Oxford's lively literary scene, be sure to check out **Square Books** (☎ 662-236-2262; 111 Courthouse Sq; 9am-9pm Mon-Thu, 9am-10pm Fri & Sat, 10am-5pm Sun) next door to the visitors center. Mississippi has a strong literary history including the likes of Eudora Welty, Walker Percy and Ellen Gilchrist. Square Books continues the literary heritage.

Tourist Offices

Visitors center (☎ 662-234-4680, 800-758-9177; 111 Oxford Sq; 9am-5pm Mon-Fri)

SIGHTS

The University of Mississippi, a mile or so west of the square, has an attractive campus shaded by magnolias and dogwoods. Its **Center for the Study of Southern Culture** (☎ 662-915-5993; admission free) covers everything from Southern folklore to Elvis cults, and has the largest collection of blues recordings and publications in the world. The **University Museum** (☎ 662-915-7073; University Ave at 5th Ave; admission free) contains several collections of ancient, decorative, fine and folk arts.

From 1930 until his death in 1962, William Faulkner lived and worked in the 1840 house at **Rowan Oak** (☎ 662-234-3284; Old Taylor Rd; admission free; 10am-noon & 2-4pm Tue-Sat, 2-4pm Sun). The sparsely furnished house, set in grounds behind an arcade of oak and cedar, attracts literary pilgrims and aspiring writers.

SLEEPING & EATING

Several motel franchises are available around exits off the Hwy 6 bypass. In-town options include the following.

Ole Miss Motel (☎ 662-234-2424; 1517 University Ave; s/d $40/50; P) Budgeters will find a good option here at this family-run establishment just a few blocks away from the square.

Oliver-Britt House (☎ 662-234-8043; 512 Van Buren Ave; r $60-90; P) With five comfortably worn rooms in a 1905 Greek Revival house, this a good homey option just three blocks from the square.

Puskus Lake campground (☎ 662-252-2633; campsites $5) The USFS campground, 10 miles northeast off Hwy 30, has primitive sites.

There are several campgrounds around **Sardis Lake** (☎ 662-487-1345), northwest off Hwy 314.

Coffee Bistro (☎ 662-281-8188; 107 N 13th St; meals $3-6; 9am Mon-Sat, 11am-12pm Sun) In an artsy interior just off the square and serving pastries, sandwiches and espresso drinks, this is a great spot to chill and people-watch. Live entertainment most nights.

City Grocery (☎ 662-232-8080; 152 Courthouse Sq; lunch $8-12, dinner $15-20; closed Sun) This is the place for great nouveau Southern specialities such as shrimp and cheese grits and 'angels on horseback' (a smoked oyster dish).

Don Pancho's (☎ 662-238-0058; 512 Jackson Ave; dishes $8-16) For an affordable meal of chicken or catfish with the flavors of the Dominican Republic, try Don Pancho's, an intimate place where the daily specials are superb. Blues, bluegrass and roots rock can be heard most nights; check the free weekly *Oxford Town* for what's on.

Greyhound (☎ 662-234-0094; 2625 W Oxford Loop) runs daily to Memphis, Tennessee ($20, two hours), among others.

Holly Springs

Elvis-obsessed Paul MacLeod has turned his Holly Springs house into **Graceland Too** (200 Gholson Ave; admission $5; 24hr), a shrine wallpapered with Elvis posters and crammed with Elvisania. He sells tiny swatches of Graceland carpet ($10) and does Elvis impersonations with little encouragement.

Famous **Phillips Grocery** (☎ 662-252-4671; 541 Van Dorn Ave; dishes $6-12) serves acclaimed burgers and fried okra; it's close to the downtown square but tricky to find. To get there, follow Van Dorn Ave half a mile east from the square; at the traffic light near the gas station, veer left up the hill, and Phillips is a block up on the right.

MISSISSIPPI DELTA

The area called the Delta stretches for 250 miles along the Mississippi River from Memphis, TN to Vicksburg. Technically it's an alluvial plain rather than a river delta, and flooding was a perennial problem until the levee system was installed. With flooding under control, the railroads moved in, trees were clear-cut for timber, and cotton fields were established using black sharecroppers instead of black slaves. Towns grew rapidly until boll weevils devastated the cotton in 1914, after which many sharecroppers joined the Great Migration to cities in the north and west. Now casinos, catfish farms, soybean, rice and cotton diversify the economy, but most Delta residents remain poor and some shantytowns look positively third world.

The harsh lives of sharecroppers were reflected in their music – work chants based on African rhythms, old slave songs and spirituals. This evolved into the bittersweet sound known as the blues, and this heritage is the main attraction for visitors. Regular blues festivals occur in towns throughout the Delta, and local performers play small 'juke joints' every weekend (p508). Steve Cheseborough's *Blues Traveling: The Holy Sites of Delta Blues* is an essential guide.

Don't flaunt valuables here, and don't stop for strangers. Guns are prevalent in the region, and encounters with local law enforcement are best avoided; tent camping is not a good option. Though lacking in atmosphere, cheap chain motels are your best bet for safety and cleanliness, but book ahead during festivals. There's virtually no public transport, and visitors on foot or bike stand out like Martians. US 61 is the legendary Blues Route, but Hwy 1 makes a scenic alternative.

VISITING JUKE JOINTS

Most juke joints are African-American neighborhood clubs, and outside visitors can be a rarity. Lots are mostly male hangouts; others are frequented by men and couples. There are very few places where local women would turn up to, even in a group, without a male chaperone. Though the chances of women actually being assaulted are slim, expect a *lot* of persistent, suggestive attention. For visitors of both sexes, having a friendly local with you to make some introductions can make for a much better evening. Also consider calling ahead to find out what's going on and to say you're going to stop by. If you arrive alone and unannounced, do start talking to people to break the ice, but women might want to act like they're training to be nuns.

Clarksdale

Legend has it that bluesman Robert Johnson sold his soul to the devil at a crossroads in Clarksdale, the heart of the Delta and a good base for exploring the area. 'Downtown' is the few blocks where the railroad tracks meet the Sunflower River. Across the tracks, in a rough-looking part of town along Martin Luther King Jr Blvd, are several eateries and juke joints, with lots of people hanging out in front of boarded-up stores. The **chamber of commerce** (☎ 662-627-7337; www.clarksdale.com; 1540 DeSoto Ave/Hwy 49; 8:30am-5pm Mon-Fri) has some information, but staff know little about the other side of the tracks.

Delta Blues Museum (☎ 601-627-6820; www.deltabluesmuseum.org; 1 Blues Alley; adult/child $6/3; 9am-5pm Mon-Sat) is ground zero for blues fans or for anyone wanting to make the pilgrimage to Delta blues sites. You can get maps and charts that plot musical milestones, see an effigy of Muddy Waters, a re-created section of WC Handy's home, and a modest collection of artifacts. Specialist recordings and books are available.

Tennessee Williams spent much of his childhood in Clarksdale. The **Tennessee Williams Festival** (☎ 662-627-7337), in the second weekend of October, features scholarly presentations and popular performances. Also popular is the **Sunflower River Blues and Gospel Festival** (☎ 662-627-6805; www.sunflowerfest.org) the first weekend in August.

Shack Up Inn (☎ 662-624-8329; www.shackupinn.com; r $50-75; P) At Hopson Plantation, 2 miles south on the west side of Hwy 49, it's the best choice around. This B&B (bed & beer) in comfortably refurbished sharecropper shacks offers a totally unique experience that'll immerse you in Delta life.

Comfort Inn (☎ 662-627-5122, 800-228-5150; 818 S State St; r $65) With none of the could-be-anywhere feeling of most chains, here the managers are enthusiastic ambassadors who make homemade waffles every morning.

Abe's (☎ 662-624-9947; 616 State St; meals $3-6) Has been serving the tenderest barbecue for almost 80 years.

Chamoun's Rest Haven (☎ 662-624-8601; 419 State St; meals $7-10) Serves delicious Lebanese food.

Madidi (☎ 662-627-7770; 164 Delta Ave; meals $15-22) Co-owned by actor Morgan Freeman, well-regarded Madidi serves fancy nouveau Southern cuisine to a prosperous clientele.

Musical events are often publicized by word of mouth and on last-minute posters around town. Usually only one juke joint features live entertainment on any given night; try **Red's** (☎ 662-627-3166; 395 Sunflower Ave) or **Smitty's** (377 Yazoo Ave). **Ground Zero** (☎ 662-621-0990), in Blues Alley, is a hot music club – another Morgan Freeman venture.

Greyhound (☎ 662-627-7893; 1604 State St) buses run to several cities including Memphis, TN ($17; 1½ hours), and New Orleans, LA ($68; nine hours).

Around Clarksdale

Seventeen miles south, **Stovall Farms** is a former plantation where Muddy Waters lived and worked. In **Tutwiler**, an outdoor mural illustrates WC Handy's first exposure to the blues in 1903. Further south on Hwy 49, **Parchman Penitentiary** has been a temporary home for many bluesmen and the subject of several songs – the 'Midnight Special' was the weekend train bringing prison visitors. On Hwy 61 in Shelby, **Do-Drop Inn** (cnr 4th & Lake Sts) is a locally famed juke joint.

Barely a Podunk, **Merigold** has three draws: **McCarty's Pottery Store** (☎ 662-748-2293), with a wonderfully eccentric garden out back; **Crawdad's** (☎ 662-748-2254; dishes $6-10), a barn-sized restaurant with walls of animal heads and generous portions; and **Poor Monkey's Lounge** (☎ 662-748-2254), an old-time juke joint that's welcoming to strangers.

Greenville

The Delta's largest city has a more liberal reputation than its neighbors. The local paper was urging racial moderation in 1946 (a mere 80 years after the Civil War!). The **Mississippi Delta Blues Festival** (☎ 662-335-3523; www.deltablues.org) is held off Hwy 454, south of town, on the third Saturday in September. Stop by the **visitors center** (☎ 662-334-2711; 410 Washington Ave; 8am-5pm Mon-Fri) for information on accommodations and sights.

Leland & Indianola

A tiny visitors center in **Leland** displays photographs of Muppet man Jim Henson, his Delta childhood and early Kermit-like characters.

Indianola is home to bluesman BB King, Civil rights heroine Fannie Lou Hamer and the Citizens Council, a white-collar KKK. On the first weekend in June, BB returns to play an outdoor festival with local musicians, then retreats to sleek **Club Ebony** (☎ 601-887-9915; 404 Hannah Ave).

Greenwood & Belzoni

Greenwood Le Flore negotiated the treaty of Dancing Creek, which banished the Choctaw to Oklahoma and gave Le Flore a 15,000-acre estate with hundreds of slaves. Greenwood is now the country's second-largest cotton market. The **Mississippi Crossroads Festival** (☎ 601-254-9333; www.mudcat.org/mdbs.cfm) is held on the last Saturday in May. Find out more at the **visitors center** (☎ 800-748-9064; 1902 Leflore Ave; 8am-5pm Mon-Fri). **Cottonlandia** (☎ 662-453-0925; admission $5; 9am-5pm Mon-Fri, 2-5pm Sat & Sun), out on Hwy 82 west of town, is a quirky museum with cotton exhibits and a large collection of Indian crafts.

The self-proclaimed Catfish Capital of the World, Belzoni is surrounded by ponds of farm-raised catfish. The **Catfish Visitors Center** (☎ 800-408-4838; 111 Magnolia St; 9am-5pm Mon-Fri) will reveal all.

Vicksburg

The high bluffs overlooking the Mississippi made this place a strategic location in the Civil War. General Ulysses S Grant besieged the city for 47 days, until its surrender on July 4, 1863. The major sights are readily accessible from I-20 exit 4B (Clay St). For information head to the **visitors center** (☎ 601-636-9421, 800-221-3536; cnr Clay & Washington Sts). The old, slow downtown stretches along several cobblestone blocks of Washington St, and casinos glitter beside the river. Historic-house museums cluster in the Garden District, on Oak St south of Clay St, and also between 1st St E and Clay St.

National Military Park (☎ 601-636-0583; www.nps.gov/vick; per car $5; 8am-5pm), north of I-20 on Clay St is a huge attraction for Civil War buffs or anyone who plays with toy soldiers. A 16-mile driving tour passes historic markers explaining gun emplacements, battle scenarios and key events. Rent an audiotape tour ($5) for the whole story. The cemetery contains some 17,000 Union graves, and a museum houses the ironclad gunboat USS *Cairo*. Civil War re-enactments are held in May and July.

Battlefield Inn (☎ 601-638-5811, 800-359-9363; www.battlefieldinn.org; 4137 N Frontage Rd; s/d $65/70), at I-20 exit 4B, is an incongruously comfortable road motel, with free evening cocktails and free breakfast buffet.

Cedar Grove B&B (☎ 601-636-1000, 800-862-1300; 2300 Washington St; r $95-185) This 1840 Greek Revival mansion has gardens overlooking the river and 24 nicely decorated rooms, all with private baths.

Walnut Hills (☎ 601-638-4910; 1214 Adams St; meals $9) Serving up traditional Southern favorites. Everyday except Saturday you can have lunch 'in the round' and feast family-style at big round tables. Also open weeknights for dinner.

CENTRAL MISSISSIPPI

The rolling midlands of central Mississippi are largely agricultural, with Jackson the only sizable urban center. One of the most scenic ways to see the region is along the Natchez Trace Parkway, which is ablaze with wildflowers in springtime.

Jackson

Earlier known as 'LeFleur's Bluff,' Jackson became state capital in 1821 and was renamed after the national hero of the time, General Andrew Jackson. During the Civil War the city was burned on three separate occasions by Sherman's troops, though the capitol, governor's mansion and city hall were spared. Although Jackson is Mississippi's largest city by far, most modern development has sprawled into suburbs leaving the downtown area – essentially a short stretch of Capitol St – something of a ghost town.

The **visitors center** (☎ 601-960-1891, 800-354-7695; www.visitjackson.com; 921 N President St; 9am-5pm Mon-Fri) also has a desk at the **Agriculture & Forestry Museum** (☎ 601-713-3365; 1150 Lakeland Dr; adult/child $4/2; 9am-5pm Mon-Sat), east of I-55 exit 98B. The 'Ag Museum' looks at cultural and ecological history in displays of farm machinery, crop-dusting planes, a re-created 1920s town and an 1860s farmstead.

Old Capitol Museum (☎ 601-359-6920; 100 State St; adult/child $4/2; 8am-5pm Mon-Fri, 9:30am-4:30pm Sat, noon-4:30pm Sun), in the beautifully restored 1833 capitol building, has an excellent 20th-century exhibit on Mississippi's ignominious history, with vintage footage of civil rights clashes. A few blocks away, the new capitol, styled after the one in Washington, DC, was completed in 1903.

Mississippi Museum of Art (☎ 601-960-1515; 201 E Pascagoula St; adult/child $5/3; 10am-5pm Mon-Sat, noon-5pm Sun) displays a small, bright collection of contemporary works, including pieces by Georgia O'Keeffe and Andy Warhol.

Lovers of lit will want to check out the city's **Eudora Welty Library** (☎ 601-968-5811; 300 N State St), where a small room is dedicated to Mississippi literati.

African-American heritage sites include the excellent **Smith Robertson Museum** (☎ 601-960-1457; 528 Bloom St; admisison $1; 9am-5pm Mon-Fri, 10am-1pm Sat, 2-5pm Sun), housed in the first public school for African-American kids in Jackson. It traces black cultural history with photographs and contemporary art.

Mississippi Museum of Natural Science (☎ 601-354-7303; 2148 Riverside Dr; adult/child $4/2; 9am-5pm Mon-Sat, 1-5pm Sun), at LeFleur's Bluff State Park, has excellent exhibits on plants, animals and habitats indigenous to Mississippi, including cypress swamps and Delta bottomlands.

SLEEPING & EATING

Microtel Inn & Suites (☎ 601-352-8282, 888-771-7171; 614 Monroe St; r $45-60; P) Legislators used to stay at the famed Sun-n-Sand, which shut its doors in 2001. Now they stay here, in this comfortable motel, with fresh clean rooms.

Edison-Walthall Hotel (☎ 601-948-6161, 800-932-6161; 225 E Capitol St; r/ste $90/110; P ✖ ☒) The preeminent capital hotel has a dark wood lobby, atrium pool and comfortable, motel-like rooms. It has an excellent restaurant and offers free shuttle to the airport.

LeFleur's Bluff State Park (☎ 601-987-3985; I-55, exit 98B; campsites & RV sites $12) Offers nicely wooded tent and RV sites.

Mayflower Cafe (☎ 601-353-4122; 123 Capitol St; dishes $6-9) A local institution serving Southern plates, seafood and Greek salads.

Frank's (☎ 601-354-5357; 219 N President St; dishes $6-9) Serves up cheap and delicious hearty Southern fare.

Kiefers (☎ 601-355-6825; 705 Poplar St; dishes $6-10) Serves souvlakia, falafel and salads to a mixed crowd on its comfy patio.

GETTING THERE & AWAY

At the junction of I-20 and I-55, it's easy to get in and out of Jackson. Its **regional airport** (☎ 601-939-5631) is 10 miles east of downtown.

Greyhound (☎ 601-353-6342; 201 S Jefferson) buses serve Birmingham, AL ($29, five hours); Memphis, TN ($32, five hours); and New Orleans, LA ($29, four hours). Amtrak's *City of New Orleans* stops at the run-down **station** (☎ 601-355-6350) on Capitol St at Mill St.

Natchez

Perched on a bluff overlooking the Mississippi, this antebellum town attracts tourists with its opulent architecture, especially during the 'pilgrimage' seasons in spring and fall, when local mansions are opened to visitors. The **visitors center** (☎ 601-446-6345, 800-647-6724; www.natchez.ms.us; 640 S Canal St; ⌚ 8:30am-5pm Mon-Sat, 9am-4pm Sun) shows a film about the town's history. The staff can tell you about tours.

Over a dozen fine **historic houses** are open for tours year-round. Some of the best include the following:

House on Ellicott's Hill (☎ 601-442-2011; 211 N Canal St; admission $6; ⌚ 9am-4pm)

Longwood (☎ 601-442-5193; 140 Lower Woodville Rd; admission $6; ⌚ 9am-4:30pm)

Melrose (☎ 601-446-5790; 1 Melrose-Montebello Parkway; admission $6; ⌚ 9am-4pm)

Rosalie (☎ 601-445-4555; 100 Orleans St; admission $6; ⌚ 9am-4pm)

Stanton Hall (☎ 601-442-6282; 401 High St; admission $6; ⌚ 9am-4:30pm)

Natchez-under-the-Hill was once the commercial center of town. When the legitimate businesses moved higher up to the bluff, this cove beside the Mississippi retained its lusty riverboat activities. The present reconstruction features picturesque cafés, saloons and a number of popular family restaurants.

Natchez Museum of African American History & Culture (☎ 601-445-0728; 301 Main St; admission $5, Wed-Sat by donation; ⌚ 1-4:30pm Tue-Fri, 10am-2pm Sat) recounts local black history from the 1880s to the 1950s.

SLEEPING & EATING

The shady, 50-site **Natchez State Park** (☎ 601-442-2658; campsites $14) is 10 miles north at the start of the Natchez Trace. Motels dot the highways north and south of town.

Natchez Inn (☎ 601-442-0221; 218 John R Junkin Dr; r $35; P ✖) This no-frills budget choice offers basic but clean rooms.

Radisson Eola (☎ 601-445-6000, 866-445-3652; www.natchezeola.com; 110 Pearl St; r from $110; P ✖) Once the town's preeminent hotel with a graceful lobby and six floors of nice, comfortable rooms, this is a good value in a good location.

Get into the spirit of Natchez by staying at a B&B in one of the grand old houses or inns. Rooms start at $90 and they feature antique furnishings, elaborate breakfasts and Southern hospitality. Check the extensive list at the visitors center.

Several eateries around the old depot on Canal St offer reasonably priced, family-friendly meals in cute settings.

Cock of the Walk (☎ 601-446-8920; 200 N Broadway; meals $10-16; ⌚ dinner) At the bluff is a casual Southern restaurant serving fried catfish and skillet cornbread.

Biscuits & Blues (☎ 601-446-9922; 315 Main St; meals $6-10; ⌚ closed Mon) Open for lunch and dinner, this fun spot serves up Southern cuisine, with live blues music every weekend.

GETTING THERE & AROUND

Greyhound (☎ 601-445-5291; 103 Lower Woodville Rd) offers daily bus service to Jackson ($25, 2¾ hours). Downtown attractions are easily seen on foot, or you can catch a pseudo-trolley bus at the depot downtown. You can rent bikes at the **Natchez Bicycle Center**

(☎ 601-446-7794; 334 Main St; bicycle per half/full-day $15/20; 10am-5:30pm Mon-Fri, 10am-3pm Sat).

Natchez Trace Parkway

Early European explorers followed this Indian route, and French explorers set up trading posts at its northern and southern ends. In the late 18th century, traders coming downriver would sell their cargo, boats and timber rafts, and return north on foot. The route became a US post road and was later widened to serve as a military road. When steamboats arrived the road was supplanted by river traffic, and the trace fell into disuse until it was revived as a national historic route in the 1930s.

Today the Natchez Trace Parkway is a scenic two-lane road through woodlands and pasture from Natchez to Nashville, TN. The **parkway headquarters** (☎ 662-680-4025, 800-305-7417; Milepost 266; 8am-5pm) and visitors center are in Tupelo, and several other centers also distribute maps and information. Commercial vehicles are banned, and there are no businesses or advertising on the roadside. The parkway is popular for bicycle touring, and driving along it is pleasant but slow. Some stops and detours include the following:

Emerald Mound A turnoff about 10 miles from Natchez, this is one of the largest Indian mounds in the Southeast, constructed around AD 1400.

Port Gibson The town General Grant thought 'too pretty to burn' retains an attractive residential district and a small exhibit on the town's Civil Rights movement.

Sunken Trace This is a deeply worn stretch of the original route.

Rocky Springs This ghost town has a nicely wooded NPS campground (campsites free) and hiking trails along the original trace.

Woodville This is a little town with an attractive courthouse square; detour west to Clark Creek Nature Area, with winding trails, waterfalls and hardwood forest.

GULF COAST

The Gulf Coast is nothing like the rest of Mississippi and it never has been. The luscious white sandy beaches and the lovely breeze from the Gulf of Mexico have long attracted vacationers from nearby New Orleans. It's an interesting mix down here. The economy, traditionally based on the seafood industry, got a shot of adrenaline in the 1990s when big Vegas-style casinos muscled in alongside the sleepy fishing villages. The mix seems odd at first: you've got Southern-speaking Vietnamese and Irish fishermen playing blackjack alongside bigwigs who have jetted in from big cities. The casinos are in Biloxi and Gulfport, while Ocean Springs is a nice residential community with great beaches. Pick up dining and accommodations information at the **Mississippi Gulf Coast Convention & Visitors Bureau** (☎ 228-896-6699, 800-237-9493; www.gulfcoast.org; 135 Courthouse Rd; 8am-6pm) in Gulfport.

Biloxi & Gulfport & the Islands

A funky mix of low-scale motels and giant casino resorts line the coast from Biloxi to Gulfport. Rates at the casinos fluctuate tremendously; a room that's $150 in spring and summer can drop to $60 in the cooler months. It's best to call beforehand. Budget options include the tidy **Sun Tan Motel** (☎ 228-432-8641, 800-615-9330; 780 Beach Blvd; r Sun-Thu/Fri-Sat $50/70; P).

Beachside resort casinos with restaurants, fitness facilities, spas and a range of rooms include the following:

Palace Casino (☎ 228-432-8888, 800-725-2239; www. palacecasinoresort.com; r from $100; P)

Grand Casino Biloxi (☎ 800-354-2450; www.parkplace.com/grandcasino; 265 Beach Blvd; r from $100; P)

Grand Casino Gulfport (☎ 800-946-7777; 3215 W Beach Blvd)

Beau Rivage (☎ 228-386-7111, 888-567-6667; 875 Beach Blvd; r from $120; P)

Ole Biloxi Schooner (☎ 228-374-8071; 159 Howard Ave; breakfast $5-7, lunch $5-9, dinner $12-15) is a real longtime favorite for hearty fishermen's breakfasts, good po'boy sandwiches and seafood dinners.

McElroy's Harbor House (☎ 228-435-5001; 695 Beach Blvd; meals $7-15), a scenic and popular seafood restaurant overlooking the water, is open for breakfast, lunch and dinner.

Biloxi was the capital of French Louisiana from 1699 to 1702, and again from 1719 to 1722, when the village of New Orleans took over the role. Now Biloxi is the center of vacation action, with a **visitors center** (☎ 228-374-3105; 710 Beach Blvd/Hwy 90; 8am-4:30pm Mon-Fri, 9am-4:30pm Sat, 10am-4pm Sun) next to the town green.

A busy industrial port, Gulfport is also the jumping-off point for ferry rides out to

West Ship Island. **Pan Isles Ferries** (☎ 228-864-1014; adult round-trip $18) makes the short trip once or twice a day.

The **Gulf Islands National Seashore** comprises four barrier islands 12 miles off the Mississippi coast: West and East Ship Islands, Horn Island and Petit Bois Island. In 1965 Ship Island was split in two by Hurricane Camille, and though the two islands are now officially named West Ship and East Ship, folks still refer to a singular 'Ship Island.' It's a great place to sunbathe, swim and hike, and West Ship is also home to the Civil War–era **Fort Massachusetts**. A shop there sells snacks and drinks. **Camping** is permitted on all islands except West Ship. Boats to the other islands can be arranged via the Gulf Islands **ranger station** (☎ 228-875-3962) at Davis Bayou, on Hwy 90 just east of Ocean Springs. Horn Island is remarkable for pristine wilderness with pine and palmetto forests, lagoons and 13 miles of deserted beach.

LOUISIANA

Anticipation and excitement swirl in the Louisiana air, charged, like a summer sky minutes before a thunderous storm. You'll feel it the moment you step into this state, where clashing cultures share few traits except a seemingly undeniable urge to eat well and dance. In the rolling hills and pine forests of northern Louisiana, the mostly protestant population shares similar traits with other Southern states. Head south, however and the geography and cultural landscape change dramatically. While you watch a Creole man dip his fishing pole into a lazy river, your ears will perk at the distinct sound of zydeco music – a funky blend of jazz and blues, where accordions crash with the rolling, clicking sound of hands strumming a washboard.

The world becomes a different place amid the swampy, gator-infested bayous of southern Louisiana, where Cajun flavors tempt even the tame. All this centers on New Orleans, where jazz and Afro-Caribbean sounds color the thick sultry air with so much history and invincibility, you just can't resist the beautiful urge to let loose.

The **Louisiana Department of Culture, Recreation & Tourism** (☎ 225-342-8119, 800-633-6970; www.louisianatravel.com; PO Box 94291, Baton Rouge, LA 70804-9291) has Welcome Centers on freeways at state borders.

LOUISIANA FACTS

Nicknames Bayou State, Pelican State, Sportsman's Paradise
Population 4,482,646 (24th)
Area 42,562 sq miles (31st)
Admitted to Union: April 30, 1812 (18th); seceded 1861; readmitted 1868
Capital city Baton Rouge (population 228,000)
Other cities New Orleans (485,000; metro area 1.3 million), Shreveport (200,000), Lafayette (110,000)
Birthplace of jazz, naturalist John James Audubon (1785–1851), Louis 'Satchmo' Armstrong (1901–71), Antoine 'Fats' Domino (b 1928), author Truman Capote (1924–84), singer Jerry Lee Lewis (b 1935), singer Lucinda Williams (b 1953), pop star Britney Spears (b 1981)
Famous for Creole and Cajun cooking, Mardi Gras, Tabasco sauce

History

The lower Mississippi River area was dominated by the Mississippian Mound Building culture until around AD 1000 when Europeans arrived and disposed the Indians with the usual combination of disease, unfavorable treaties and outright hostility.

The land was passed back and forth from the Spanish to the French, to the British and back to the French. After the American Revolution and some colonial double-dealing, the whole area passed to the USA in the 1803 Louisiana Purchase, and Louisiana became a state in 1812.

Steamboats plying the river system opened a vital trade network across the continent. New Orleans became a major port, and Louisiana's slave-based plantation economy kept a flowing export of rice, livestock, tobacco, indigo, sugarcane and especially cotton. Alarmed by Abraham Lincoln's election as president, Louisiana seceded from the Union and was an independent republic for about two months before joining the Confederacy. Union forces seized control of New Orleans in 1862, occupying much of the state during the war. Some 24,000 Louisiana blacks joined Union forces, though quite a few 'free people of color' volunteered to fight for the Confederacy.

Louisiana was readmitted to the Union in 1868, after a new state constitution granted suffrage to blacks. The next 30 years saw political wrangling and economic stagnation, and in 1898 most blacks were effectively disenfranchised by the imposition of literacy tests and other impediments. In the early 20th century oil discovery gave the economy a boost, while the devastation of cotton crops by boll weevils forced some agricultural diversification. From the 1920s, autocratic governor Huey Long was able to modernize much of the state's infrastructure. Industry developed further after WWII. Tourism cashed in on the state's cultural heritage, but the tradition of unorthodox, volatile and sometimes ruthless politics continues today. Race and economics are ongoing sources of struggle – Louisiana has the second-highest per capita poverty rate in the US.

NEW ORLEANS

Naturally languid from the subtropical heat and humidity, New Orleans is a town where nothing ever goes too fast or grows too worrisome. The town's unofficial motto is *Laissez les bons temps rouler* (let the good times roll); its nicknamed 'the Big Easy' for its laid-back vibe. With jazz, zydeco and blues music oozing out of seemingly every crevice and with the succulent aromas of African, Spanish, French, Italian and Caribbean culinary influences spilling onto the streets, it's easy to get drunk on the thick, alluring air. Its rollicking history, splendid Spanish architecture and general commitment to good times make New Orleans a major attraction for some 50,000 tourists each month.

It's a great city to walk around, anchored by the beguiling French Quarter and the adjoining *faubourgs* (false towns). Though its famous month-long Mardi Gras (p522) celebration and Jazz Festival (p524 up the ante for craziness and fun, New Orleans is a blast anytime. In fact, it's the times when things are quiet – late afternoon when everyone is at the hotel getting ready to go out, early morning when the light explodes on the city and work crews come out to spray away last night's sins – that New Orleans reveals its many sober charms.

History

The town of Nouvelle Orlèans was founded in 1718. Early immigrants arrived from France, Canada and Germany, and the French imported thousands of African slaves. Many Africans earned their freedom and had an established place in the community as *les gens de couleur libres* (free people of color), regulated by the Code Noir. Unsuccessful as a mercantile economy, the colony came to rely on barter, smuggling and local trade, and the city developed a reputation for extralegal enterprises.

The 1791 slave revolt in the French colony of St Domingue (now Haiti) caused thousands of former slaves to move to New Orleans. The French resumed control in 1803, but within days Napoleon sold the city to the US, along with the rest of the state in the Louisiana Purchase. Soon Anglo Americans developed slave-based plantations similar to those in Georgia and the Carolinas. By 1840 New Orleans was the nation's fourth-largest city, with more than 100,000 people.

New Orleans survived the Civil War as the South's largest city, while new federal laws required that voting and civil rights be extended to black males. White supremacists formed the White League, which ousted the government elected by newly enfranchised black voters, and introduced the Jim Crow laws. The end of the plantation economy and the declining importance of river traffic hit New Orleans hard, and its economy languished until oil and petrochemical industries developed in the 1950s.

Though now eclipsed by Atlanta as the South's largest city, metropolitan New Orleans has over 1.3 million people, composed of a growing African-American population (62%), Anglo Americans (35%) and Latinos (3%). Despite the Civil War and the gains of the Civil Rights movement, many blacks remain impoverished, and the gap between wealthy whites and poor blacks seems as wide as ever.

Orientation

New Orleans sits wedged between the Mississippi River to the south and Lake Pontchartrain to the north. Places are referred to as either 'lakeside' or 'riverside,' 'upriver' or 'downriver.' For example, the Lower Garden District is downriver from the central Garden

NEW ORLEANS IN...

Two Days

Start your first day with a coffee and beignet at **Café du Monde** followed by a walk to Jackson Sq and the visitors center. Pick up a free map of the city. Take the leisurely **French Quarter Walking Tour**, to get your bearings and delight in the details of the Quarter. In the afternoon, hop on the **St Charles Ave streetcar** and follow it up with a cocktail at a local bar, such as the **Lafitte's Blacksmith Shop**. At night, don some good walking shoes and head back out to **Bourbon St**. Drink plenty of water before bed.

Did you drink the water? If so, your hangover is well under control. Start day two with a stroll through the **French Market** to shop for souvenirs. Walk down to the Riverwalk and take a river trip on the **Canal St Ferry**. Return to your hotel. Take a nap. At night, plan a splurge at one of the excellent restaurants, such as **Emeril's** or **K-Paul's Louisiana Kitchen**.

Four Days

Follow the two-day itinerary, and on the third day get out of the city and search for gators on a must-do swamp tour or, if gators aren't your thing, take a driving tour of the **Mississippi River plantations**. At night, stray off Bourbon St to the **Faubourg Marigny** or **Tremé** districts to listen to live music in a small local bar. The next day, savor the city's neighborhoods by hopping on the **St Charles Ave streetcar**. Get goose bumps on a cemetery tour and spend your evening dining on delicious Cajun cuisine.

District, so it's called 'lower,' even though it appears higher on maps.

The historic French Quarter (the *Vieux Carré*) consists of 80 blocks around Jackson Sq. Southwest of the French Quarter, the Central Business District (CBD) extends from Canal St to around Lee Circle. Upriver (ie, south) from the French Quarter, the old Warehouse District is an appealing arts precinct, south of which is the Lower Garden District, a ramshackle neighborhood with a bohemian enclave. This adjoins the lovely Garden District, well known for its historic homes. Uptown is further west, accessed by the venerable St Charles Ave streetcar. Further upriver, 3 miles west of the French Quarter, the Riverbend area is populated by many university students.

The Tremé district, centered on Louis Armstrong Park, west of the French Quarter, is a predominantly black residential district. Faubourg Marigny, a lively and predominantly gay district, is centered on Frenchmen St, downriver from the French Quarter. The rugged Bywater district of the city is even further downriver.

Workable maps of the city are available at the New Orleans Welcome Center (p518) in Jackson Sq. Lonely Planet's *New Orleans City Map* has all the key neighborhoods, a street index and key sights.

Information

BOOKSTORES

Beaucoup Books (☎ 504-895-2663; 5414 Magazine St)
Bookstar (☎ 504-523-6411; 414 N Peters St)
Maple Street Bookstore (☎ 504-866-4916; 7529 Maple St)
Tower Records (☎ 504-529-4411; 408 N Peters St)

INTERNET ACCESS

Bastille Computer Café (☎ 504-581-1150; e@netzero.net; 605 Toulouse St; 🕑 10am-11pm; $5 per 30min) In the French Quarter.
New Orleans Public Library (☎ 504-529-7323; 219 Loyola Ave) Near City Hall has terminals for free Web access.
Royal Blend, Royal Access (☎ 504-525-0401; 621 Royal St; $5 per 30min) Also in the French Quarter.

MEDIA

New Orleans Magazine (www.neworleansmagazine.com) A monthly glossy, tourist-oriented rag that offers good-quality writing about the city's attractions and issues.
Times-Picayune (www.timespicayune.com) New Orleans' daily newspaper. It has a daily entertainment calendar and *Lagniappe*, an extensive entertainment guide that comes out every Friday.
WWOZ (90.7 FM) Tune into this station for Louisiana music.

MEDICAL SERVICES

Emergency number (☎ 911)
Medical Center of Louisiana (☎ 504-903-2311; 1532 Tulane Ave)

NEW ORLEANS

0 — 500 m
0 — 0.3 mi

INFORMATION		
ATM	1	B8
ATM	2	C4
ATM	3	D4
Bastille Computer Café	4	D3
Bookstar	5	D4
Jean Lafitte National Historic Park Visitor Center	6	D4
Lesbian & Gay Community Center	7	E2
Tower Records	8	D4
Welcome Center	9	D3

SIGHTS & ACTIVITIES	pp518–21	
1850 House	10	D3
Aquarium of the Americas	11	D5
Beauregard-Keyes House	12	D3
Cabildo	13	D3
Civil War Museum	(see 26)	
Contemporary Arts Center	14	C6
Farmers Market	15	E3
Faulkner House Bookstore	16	D3
Flea Market	17	E3
French Market	18	E3
Historic New Orleans Collection	19	D3
Historic Voodoo Museum	20	D3
Jackson Monument	21	D3
Louis Armstrong Statue	22	C2
Louisiana Children's Museum	23	C6
Lower Pontalba Buildings	24	D3
National D-Day Museum	25	C6
Ogden Museum of Southern Art	26	C6
Old US Mint	27	E3
Presbytère	28	D3
Public Library	29	B4
Riverwalk Mall	30	D6
Robert E Lee Monument	31	B6
St Augustine's Church	32	D2
St Louis Cathedral	33	D3
Upper Pontalba Buildings	34	D3
Ursuline Convent	35	D3
World Trade Center	36	D5

SLEEPING	pp523–4	
Andrew Jackson Hotel	37	D3
Avenue Garden Hotel	38	B7
Chateau Hotel	39	D3
Cornstalk Hotel	40	D3
Fairmont Hotel	41	C4
HI Marquette House Hostel	42	A8
Hotel St Pierre	43	D2
Lafitte Guest House	44	D3
Le Pavillon	45	B5
Le Richelieu	46	E2
Omni Royal Orleans	47	D4
Prytania Park Hotel	48	B7
St Vincent's Guest House	49	B8

EATING	pp524–5	
Acme Oyster & Seafood House	50	C4
Belle Forché	51	E2
Café du Monde	52	D3
Café Sbisa	53	D3
Central Grocery	54	D3
Crescent City Brewhouse	55	D4
Emeril's	56	C6
Galatoire's	57	C4
Johnny's Po-Boys	58	D4
K-Paul's Louisiana Kitchen	59	D4
La Péniche	60	E2
NOLA	61	D4
Old Dog New Trick	62	E2
Red Eye Grill	63	D6
Rue de la Course	64	B8
Siam Café	65	E2
Trolley Stop	66	A8
Uglesich's	67	B6
Vic's Kangaroo Cafe	68	C5

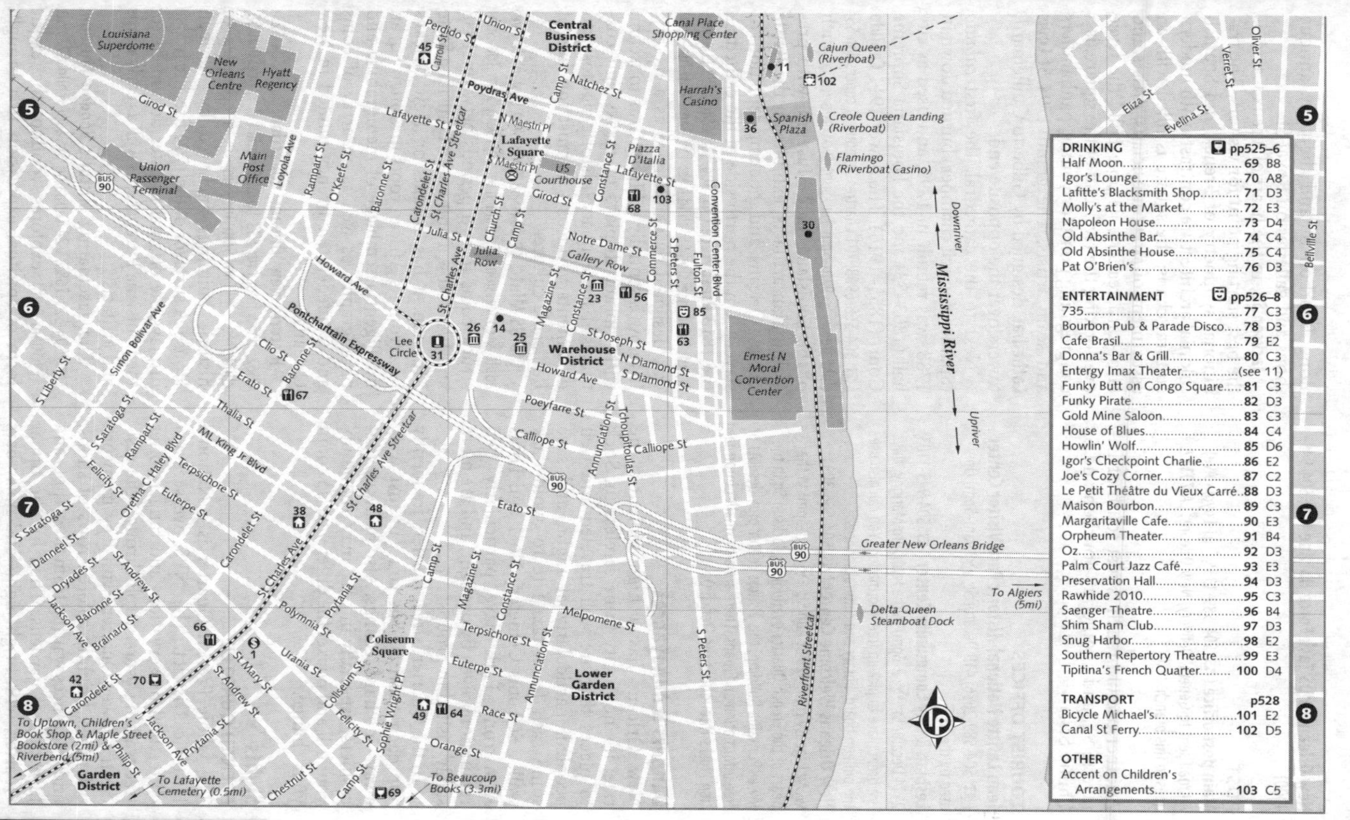
DRINKING pp525–6
Half Moon 69 B8
Igor's Lounge 70 A8
Lafitte's Blacksmith Shop 71 D3
Molly's at the Market 72 E3
Napoleon House 73 D4
Old Absinthe Bar 74 C4
Old Absinthe House 75 C4
Pat O'Brien's 76 D3
ENTERTAINMENT pp526–8
735 77 C3
Bourbon Pub & Parade Disco 78 D3
Cafe Brasil 79 E2
Donna's Bar & Grill 80 C3
Entergy Imax Theater (see 11)
Funky Butt on Congo Square 81 C3
Funky Pirate 82 D3
Gold Mine Saloon 83 C3
House of Blues 84 C4
Howlin' Wolf 85 D6
Igor's Checkpoint Charlie 86 E2
Joe's Cozy Corner 87 C2
Le Petit Théâtre du Vieux Carré 88 D3
Maison Bourbon 89 C3
Margaritaville Cafe 90 E3
Orpheum Theater 91 B4
Oz 92 D3
Palm Court Jazz Café 93 E3
Preservation Hall 94 D3
Rawhide 2010 95 C3
Saenger Theatre 96 B4
Shim Sham Club 97 D3
Snug Harbor 98 E2
Southern Repertory Theatre 99 E3
Tipitina's French Quarter 100 D4
TRANSPORT p528
Bicycle Michael's 101 E2
Canal St Ferry 102 D5
OTHER
Accent on Children's Arrangements 103 C5
Mississippi River
Downriver
Upriver
Greater New Orleans Bridge
To Algiers (5mi)
Delta Queen Steamboat Dock
Cajun Queen (Riverboat)
Creole Queen Landing (Riverboat)
Flamingo (Riverboat Casino)
Spanish Plaza
Riverfront Streetcar
Ernest N Morial Convention Center
Canal Place Shopping Center
Harrah's Casino
Piazza D'Italia
Central Business District
Lafayette Square
US Courthouse
Warehouse District
Gallery Row
Julia Row
Lee Circle
Lower Garden District
Coliseum Square
Garden District
Louisiana Superdome
New Orleans Centre
Hyatt Regency
Main Post Office
Union Passenger Terminal
Pontchartrain Expressway
St Charles Ave Streetcar
To Lafayette Cemetery (0.5mi)
To Beaucoup Books (3.3mi)
To Uptown, Children's Book Shop & Maple Street Bookstore (2mi) & Riverbend (5mi)

THE SOUTH

New Orleans/AIDS Task Force Hotline (☎ 504-945-4000)

POST

Main post office (☎ 504-589-1135; 701 Loyola Ave) All mail sent to General Delivery, New Orleans, LA 70112, goes to this branch.

Another useful branch is just south of Lafayette Sq, and another at Bourbon and St Phillip Sts.

TOURIST OFFICES

Jean Lafitte National Historic Park Visitor Center (☎ 504-589-2636; 419 Decatur St; 9am-5pm) Operated by the NPS.

Lesbian & Gay Community Center (☎ 504-945-1103; 2114 Decatur St; 2-6pm) In the Faubourg Marigny, this is a great place to pick up free information. You can also use the bulletin board, library and cultural services.

New Orleans Welcome Center (☎ 504-566-3031; www.bigeasy.com; 529 St Ann St; 9am-5pm) In the heart of the French Quarter overlooking Jackson Sq in the lower Pontalba Building, this visitors center provides lots of free information and maps. There are also smaller information kiosks throughout the French Quarter.

Dangers & Annoyances

New Orleans has a high violent-crime rate; it's not a city to be careless in. Stick to places that are well traveled and well peopled, particularly at night, and save some cash for a taxi fare to avoid dark walks. St Louis Cemetery No 1 and Louis Armstrong Park have particularly bad reputations, even by daylight, and are more safely visited in groups.

In the Quarter, street hustlers frequently approach tourists, but you can just walk away – no hard feelings. Also be aware that cashiers, especially in bars, may 'round up' your bill and pocket the difference, so count your change.

Sights

FRENCH QUARTER

The whole French Quarter is a National Historic District. The NPS oversees architectural preservation, and rangers offer free walking tours. Stroll through the residential lower Quarter, with lacy ironwork balconies, brightly colored rows of shops, and fragrances wafting from flowerpots and lush pocket gardens. Then hit the upper Quarter, with bright lights and noisy bars along Bourbon St and the tony antique shops and galleries on Royal St.

Jackson Sq, in the heart of Vieux Carré, is the best starting point for visitors. The traditional symmetry of French and Spanish colonial architecture contrasts with modern cultural chaos; the square is filled with an assortment of street musicians, artists and tarot-card readers. 'Hippie Hill,' the levee overlooking the river end of the square, is a congregating point for youths, panhandlers and scam artists. The grand 1794 **St Louis Cathedral**, designed by Gilberto Guillemard, towers over the opposite end.

Next to the cathedral, the first *cabildo* (Spanish council chamber) burned down in 1788, was rebuilt in 1799, and used as city hall (1803–53) and the Louisiana Supreme Court (1853–1910). The newer 1911 **Cabildo** (☎ 504-568-6968; 701 Chartres St; adult & concession $5, child free; 9am-5pm Tue-Sun) houses a branch of the Louisiana State Museum, with pre-Columbian artifacts, exhibits on the Battle of New Orleans, and shocking depictions of slavery. On the north side of the cathedral, the 1813 **Presbytère** (☎ 504-568-6968; 751 Chartres St; adult & concession $5, child free; 9am-5pm Tue-Sun) was designed by Guillemard as a rectory. It's now essentially a Mardi Gras museum, with vibrant displays of masks and costumes, parade floats, historic photos and documentary videos – a must for fans of Louisiana culture.

Old US Mint (☎ 504-568-6968; 400 Esplanade Ave; adult & concession $5, child free; 9am-5pm Tue-Sun) struck coins in two periods between 1838 and 1910. Now a unit of the Louisiana State Museum, it has exhibits on New Orleans jazz from its African roots in Congo Sq, an intelligent assemblage of memorabilia and photographs, as well as an array of coins and Confederate currency minted in New Orleans.

Historic New Orleans Collection (☎ 504-523-4662; www.hnoc.org; 533 Royal St; adult & concession $5, child free; 9am-5pm Tue-Sun) is a complex of historic buildings anchored by Merieult House. A survivor of the 1794 fire, the house displays the original transfer documents of the Louisiana Purchase, as well as early maps and artifacts.

The fascinating **Historic Voodoo Museum** (☎ 504-523-7685; 724 Dumaine St; adult/child $7/3.50; 10am-8pm) explores voodoo, the exotic form of spiritual expression first brought to New Orleans by West African slaves who came on ships via Haiti.

In 1728, 12 Ursuline nuns arrived in New Orleans to care for the French garrison's 'miserable little hospital' and to educate the young girls of the colony. Between 1745 and 1752, the French colonial army built the **Ursuline Convent** (☎ 504-529-3040; 1114 Chartres St; admission $5; closed Mon), now the oldest structure in the French Quarter.

A trading site since pre-Columbian times, the **French Market** (24hr) has three different markets. The open-air **Farmers Market** has a good stock of fresh fruit, vegetables, kitchen supplies, hot sauces, garlic strings and cookbooks. Cafés, such as the enjoyable Café du Monde, have occupied the Butcher's Market since 1860. A great place for souvenirs, the **Flea Market** sells inexpensive Mardi Gras masks and dolls, preserved alligator heads and CDs of dubious origin.

Also see p520 for the French Quarter walking tour.

TREMÉ

On the western edge of the French Quarter, the Tremé district was New Orleans' first suburb, traditionally populated by black Creoles. The 1824 **St Augustine's Church** (☎ 504-525-5934; 1210 Governor Nicholls St) is the second-oldest African-American Catholic church in the USA. One of its stained-glass panels depicts the Sisters of the Holy Family, the order of black Creole nuns founded in 1842. Today, the small congregation works to provide food for the needy. Many jazz funeral processions can be seen leaving the church before parading through the streets.

One of New Orleans' more macabre attractions, **St Louis Cemetery No 1** (8am-3pm) received the remains of most early Creoles. The shallow water table necessitated aboveground burials, with bodies placed in family tombs or long rows of 'oven' vaults. Don't enter the cemetery alone; if the ghosts don't get you, the muggers might.

CBD & WAREHOUSE DISTRICT

On the upriver side of Canal St, the CBD and Warehouse District comprise the American commercial section that was established after the Louisiana Purchase in 1803. Artists moved into the Warehouse District following the 1984 Louisiana World Exposition.

Extending nearly half a mile along the Mississippi, the shop-till-you-drop **Riverwalk Marketplace** (☎ 504-522-1555; 10am-9pm Mon-Thu, 10am-10pm Fri & Sat, 10am-7pm Sun) has an outdoor walkway where you can watch the paddle wheelers and freighters plying the Mississippi. When Bienville founded New Orleans in 1718, this site was underwater, but shifts in the river's course enabled land reclamation east of the old warehouses that were once on the waterfront. Today, the massive air-conditioned space is filled with shops and a food court.

Canal St Ferry (adult free; 6am-midnight) from the foot of Canal St is the best way to admire the city from the traditional river approach. **Steamboat tours** (adult $16-22) also run up and down the river.

Aquarium of the Americas (☎ 504-581-4629; Canal St; adult/child $14/7; 9am-5pm) simulates an eclectic selection of watery habitats including the Mississippi River and Delta wetlands. You can buy combination tickets to the Imax theater (p528) next door and to the excellent Audubon Zoo (p520) in uptown (boats from Woldenberg Park will take you there).

The 33-story **World Trade Center** (2 Canal St) has a revolving observation deck where the **Top of the Mart Lounge** (☎ 504-522-9795; 10am-11pm Mon-Thu, 10am-midnight Fri, 11-1am Sat, 2-11pm Sun) offers spectacular views for the price of a drink.

In a renovated warehouse, the **Contemporary Arts Center** (p527) has galleries and two performance spaces for plays, dance and concerts.

Civil War Museum (☎ 504-523-4522; 929 Camp St; adult/child $5/2; 10am-4pm Mon-Sat) humanizes the Civil War without overdoing the Southern angle, with strangely moving personal effects, guns, and artifacts of the industrial age. It's Louisiana's oldest museum, opened in 1891.

Ogden Museum of Southern Art (☎ 504-539-9600; 925 Camp St; 10am-5pm Mon-Sat) began with the stellar collection of entrepreneur Roger Houston Ogden. The museum is affiliated with the Smithsonian Institute in Washington DC, giving it access to that bottomless collection.

Half a world away from Normandy, **National D-Day Museum** (☎ 504-527-6012; www.ddaymuseum.org; 923 Magazine St; adult/child $10/5; 9am-5pm) is a worthwhile stop for its eyewitness accounts of the Allied invasion, planes, weaponry and landing craft.

GARDEN DISTRICT & UPTOWN

Following the Louisiana Purchase in 1803, subdivision of former plantation lands began in the Lower Garden District, and extended uptown following the steam railway on St Charles Ave, where the **St Charles Ave streetcar** now runs. Many elegant mansions line the route, surrounded by live oaks and palms, lawns and lush, fragrant floral gardens. In the 1850s and 1860s, the Greek Revival style was a symbol of staunch classical tastes.

Further west, Tulane and Loyola Universities occupy adjacent campuses in a more diverse area. Modest shotgun shacks sit next to multistory Arts and Crafts bungalows; Greek Revival mansions next to neo-Gothic campus buildings.

Tulane was founded in 1834 as a medical college in an attempt to control repeated cholera and yellow-fever epidemics. Its **Amistad Research Center** (☎ 504-865-5535; 6823 St Charles Ave; admission free; 🕑 9am-4:30pm Mon-Sat) is one of the nation's largest repositories of African-American history. The **Hogan Jazz Archive** (☎ 504-865-5688; 304 Freret St; 🕑 8:30am-5pm Mon-Fri, 9:30am-1pm Sat) is a must for jazz scholars.

Established in 1833, **Lafayette Cemetery No 1** has German and Irish names on its aboveground tombs. Fraternal organizations (like Jefferson Fire Company No 22) buried members and their families in large shared crypts. The gates close at 2:30pm – don't get locked in.

Among the country's best zoos, the **Audubon Zoological Gardens** (☎ 504-861-2537; 6500 Magazine St; adult/child $9/4.80; 🕑 9am-5pm) is also the headquarters of the Audubon Institute, which also maintains the Aquarium of the Americas. Its Louisiana Swamp exhibit displays flora and fauna in a Cajun cultural setting, with alligators, bobcats, red foxes, black bears and snapping turtles. The nicest way to get there is by a zoo cruise from Woldenberg Park, downtown. **Combined tickets** (adult/child $26/13) for the aquarium, riverboat and zoo are available.

CITY PARK & FAIR GROUNDS

Besides hosting the regular horseracing season, the Fair Grounds are also the site of the huge springtime New Orleans Jazz and Heritage Festival (p524). Acquired in 1850, the 1500-acre City Park is famous for its huge moss-draped live oaks and scenic bayou lagoons, especially along the narrow strip fronting City Park Ave. Unfortunately, I-610 slices through the park, so most visitors stick to the southern third of the area, where the **Botanical Garden** (☎ 504-482-4888; adult/child $3/1; 🕑 10am-4:30pm Tue-Sun) features an art deco pool and fountain.

Also in City Park, the **New Orleans Museum of Art** (☎ 504-488-2631; 1 Collins Diboll Circle; adult/child $6/3; 🕑 10am-5pm Tue-Sun) was founded in 1910. It has three floors and a collection valued at $200 million.

LAKESHORE PARK

This park stretches nearly 10 miles along a narrow shoreline strip fronting Lake Pontchartrain. It's where locals come to jog, bike, skate or check each other out – but not to swim in the polluted water.

Walking Tour

FRENCH QUARTER

The French Quarter's narrow streets and passageways feature elegant architectural vestiges of the 18th-century Spanish colony. But the Quarter also has its mysterious charms, seen best at a low, leisurely pace. This tour should take about 90 minutes.

Begin your walk at the **Presbytère** (**1**; p518) on Jackson Sq and head down Chartres St to the corner of Ursulines Ave and the **Ursuline Convent** (**2**; p519).

Directly across Chartres St, at No 1113, the 1826 **Beauregard-Keyes House** (**3**) combines Creole- and American-style design. Civil War General PGT Beauregard rented rooms here, and author Francis Parkinson Keyes lived here from 1942 to 1970.

Walk along Ursulines Ave to Royal St and take a peek inside the **Royal Pharmacy** (**4**). The soda fountain, a preserved relic from the USA's halcyon malt-shop days is no longer in use, but the owners of the pharmacy feel it's too classic to pull out.

Continue heading up Ursulines Ave and then left onto Bourbon St. The ramshackle one-story structure on the corner of St Philip St is a great little tavern and National Historic Landmark called **Lafitte's Blacksmith Shop** (**5**; p526). Head down St Phillip and back to Royal St, take a right.

When it comes to classic New Orleans postcard images, Royal St takes the prize.

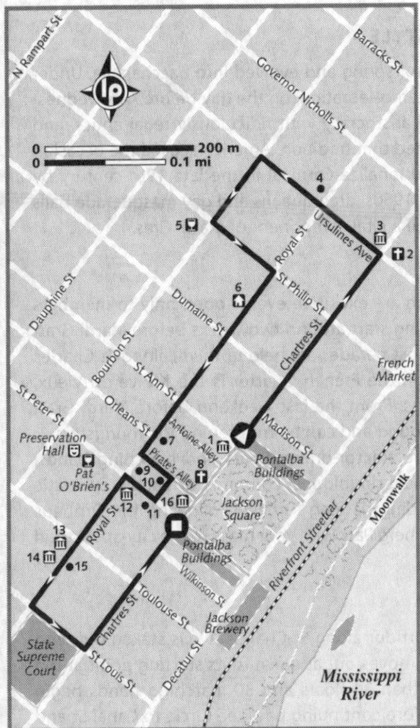

Many of the structures along the following stretch are graced by cast-iron galleries and potted plants hanging from the balconies. Take it slow and appreciate the details.

At No 915 the **Cornstalk Hotel** (6; p523) stands behind one of the most frequently photographed fences anywhere. At Orleans Ave, stately magnolia trees and lush tropical plants fill **St Anthony's Garden** (7), behind **St Louis Cathedral** (8).

Alongside the garden, **Pirate's Alley** is an inviting, shaded walkway that calls for a little detour. The first buildings to the right, Nos 622–624 Pirate's Alley, are just two of the **Labranche Buildings** (9). Note the original wrought-iron balconies, some of the finest in town, which date to the 1840s. At 624 Pirate's Alley is the small but charming **Faulkner House Bookstore** (10; ☎ 504-524-2940; 624 Pirate's Alley; 🕑 10am-6pm), so named because author William Faulkner briefly lived here in 1925.

Turn right down Cabildo Alley and then right up St Peter St, toward Royal St. At No 632 St Peter, the **Avart-Peretti House** (11) is where Tennessee Williams lived in 1946–47, when he wrote *A Streetcar Named Desire*.

When you reach the corner of Royal, take a look at **LeMonnier Mansion** (12), at No 640, which is commonly known to be New Orleans' first 'skyscraper'. If you kept going up St Peter, you'd reach Pat O'Brien's (famous for its 'Hurricane') and the rustic facade of Preservation Hall.

Turn left on Royal St. At the corner of Royal and Toulouse Sts stand a pair of houses built by Jean François Merieult in the 1790s. The **Court of Two Lions** (13), at 541 Royal St, has a gate on the Toulouse St side. Next door at 527–533 is the **Historic New Orleans Collection** (14; p518). Across the street, at No 520, a carriageway leads to the picturesque **Brulatour Courtyard** (15).

On the next block, the massive 1909 **State Supreme Court Building** was the setting for many scenes from the movie *JFK*. The white marble and terracotta facade stands in attractive contrast with the rest of the Quarter.

Head down St Louis St to Chartres St and turn left. As Jackson Sq comes into view, you'll reach the Presbytère's near-identical twin, the **Cabildo** (p518). Have a seat on the benches in front. Relax and enjoy the lively street musicians.

New Orleans for Children

Apart from the **Audubon Zoo** (see p520) and **Aquarium of the Americas** (p519), most children's activities are set apart from the city's major attractions for grown-ups. Check out the 'kid stuff' listings in the *Times-Picayune*'s Living section on Mondays.

Louisiana Children's Museum (☎ 504-523-1357; 420 Julia St; admission $6; 🕑 9:30am-4:30pm Mon-Sat, noon-4:30pm Sun) Some great hands-on exhibits. Children under 16 must be accompanied by an adult.

Children's Book Shop (☎ 504-861-2105; 7529 Maple St; 🕑 10am-6pm) Operates cozy kids storytelling out of this wonderful bookstore next door to the Maple Street Bookstore.

Accent on Children's Arrangements (☎ 504-524-1227; 938 Lafayette St) A great, trustworthy service that will give you both a break. While you tour the city, Accent will provide day-care services, which include arts and crafts, themed tours and organized activities.

Tours

Check the *New Orleans Official Visitors Guide* for a full selection of the many available tours. The Jean Lafitte National Historic Park Visitor Center (p518) offers

CARNIVAL & MARDI GRAS, NEW ORLEANS-STYLE

Mardi Gras, or 'Fat Tuesday,' began as a pagan rite of spring and evolved into bacchanalia. Under the Roman Catholic influence, it became a pre-Lenten celebration, on the day before Ash Wednesday. In Europe it was an opportunity to mock the aristocracy with ridiculously regal antics, and Creoles in New Orleans and the Caribbean maintained that tradition. Americans used the occasion to satirize Creole pretensions, and began to institutionalize Carnival in the late 19th century by establishing 'krewes' (men-only social clubs). In the 1950s, drag queens and gay masquerade balls became a popular mode of parody, and they are still a vital component of Mardi Gras.

Carnival

While most krewe balls held during Carnival season are exclusive events open only to members and guests, public celebrations, parades and partying start around two weeks before Mardi Gras, with nonstop frivolity from the Thursday before. Most parades are held uptown, along St Charles Ave to Canal St. The only krewe to parade through the French Quarter is the Krewe du Vieux, whose procession is three weeks before Mardi Gras. From the last weekend before Mardi Gras, the Quarter is full of people; it's difficult to walk around and can be frightening for youngsters.

Krewe parades usually feature a dozen or more tractor-drawn floats and marching bands. Crowds scramble for the souvenir 'throws' of beads, doubloons, condoms or candy. Dramatic nighttime parades feature flambeaux carriers wielding flaming torches. Following the Orpheus parade on Lundi Gras (Fat Monday), head for Woldenberg Park with your mask to the city-sponsored bash and fireworks display.

Mardi Gras

Before sunrise on the big day, the entire parade corridor along St Charles Ave is staked out with chairs, ladders and coolers. The Zulu Krewe parade moves out at dawn to its starting point at the statue of Martin Luther King Jr. At 8:30am, more than 30 floats and 30 marching bands begin rolling down Jackson Ave toward St Charles Ave before continuing past Lee Circle to Canal St and through the Tremé district along N Galvez St and Orleans Ave.

Rex Krewe begins its elaborate procession at about 10am further up S Claiborne Ave at Napoleon Ave, then continues along St Charles Ave from Jackson Ave to Canal St. Trucks and throws follow the parade, and by mid-afternoon it's beer and beads on Bourbon St. By the evening, a besotted mass of humanity is tightly wedged on the street. Celebrations in the lower Quarter vary from block to block. Check out the ribald costume contest in front of the Rawhide 2010 bar on Burgundy St and the festivities across from the Quarter on Esplanade Ave at Dauphine St or at Chartres and Frenchmen Sts.

free walking tours of the French Quarter at 9:30am (show up at 9am).

Carriage ride (4 people/half hr from $50; ⌚ to midnight) The tourist cliché, a carriage ride through the French Quarter is actually a great way to see the narrow streets at a gentle pace. The drivers are entertaining, if not always historically precise. Tours depart from Jackson Sq.

Friends of the Cabildo (☎ 504-523-3939; adult/child $10/8; tours 10am & 1:30pm Tue-Sun, 1:30pm Mon) Offers volunteer-led two-hour walking tours of the French Quarter. Tours start at the 1850 House Museum Store at 523 St Ann St. The cost includes admission to any two of the four Louisiana State Museums.

Historic New Orleans Walking Tours (☎ 504-947-2120; www.tourneworleans.com; adult/child $15/13) Of the many voodoo tours available, this one offers the most authenticity and humor. Call or check the website for times.

Steamboat Natchez (☎ 504-586-8777; www.steamboatnatchez.com; adult/child $18/9; departs 11:30am & 2:30pm) New Orleans' only steamboat. Taking a riverboat cruise is a neat way to see the city. Cruises take two hours; skip the on-board buffet lunch. Buy tickets at the boat dock behind JAX Brewery at the foot of Toulouse St.

Festivals & Events

Just after New Year's Eve (no slouch celebration here), New Orleans residents break out the king cakes and spirits to begin celebrating Carnival, which culminates in the Mardi Gras madness. Arthur Hardy's *Mardi Gras Guide* contains a good history along with detailed descriptions and maps of all parades. Other excuses to celebrate include:

St Patrick's Day March 17th.
New Orleans Jazz & Heritage Festival Late April and early May.
Halloween October.

Sleeping

Room rates peak during Mardi Gras and Jazz Fest, but in the hot summer months prices fall by as much as 50%. The prices below are high-season non-festival rates. Book as soon as you know you'll be going and be sure to call around for special deals. Hotel sales-tax amounts to 13%, plus $1 per person per night. Beware, too, that hotels charge $15 to $25 per day for parking.

BUDGET

St Vincent's Guest House (☎ 504-523-3411; www.stvincentsguesthouse.com; 1507 Magazine St; r $60-90; P ❄ ♒) Originally an orphanage, the house's modernized rooms still have some remnant of that institutional feel, but the place doesn't feel haunted by its former young tenants. The courtyard swimming pool is infrequently cleaned, but its mossy green waters make a pretty centerpiece in the brick courtyard. At times, St Vincent's seems poorly managed, but guests seem mostly satisfied with what they get at this price.

Prytania Park Hotel (☎ 504-524-0427, 888-498-7594; www.prytaniaparkhotel.com; 1525 Prytania St; r from $60; ❄) A block from the streetcar line in the Garden District, this modern motel is adjoined to a restored 1850s guesthouse. It has 49 small but nicely appointed rooms, with refrigerators and microwaves, and offers a free shuttle to the French Quarter.

HI Marquette House Hostel (☎ 504-523-3014; www.hiayh.org; 2253 Carondelet St; dm $18-21, r from $50; ❄ 💻) This 176-bed facility on the edge of the Garden District consists of four buildings that are kept impressively clean. Picnic tables in the backyard are an ideal place to meet fellow travelers. Internet access is available in the lobby, and there are two laundries nearby (one is in a bar). Sheet rental is an additional $2.25

Camping

Four state parks within a half hour's drive of New Orleans offer shady, well-maintained sites with toilets, hookups, hot showers and campsites for about $12.

St Bernard Parish State Park (☎ 504-682-2101; campsites $12) Most convenient of the four is this state park, about 13 miles south near the Mississippi, with lagoons, nature trails and a swimming pool. Take Hwy 46 along the east bank to Bayou Rd and turn right on Hwy 39.

The closest privately operated campgrounds are along the Chef Menteur Hwy/Hwy 90 in eastern New Orleans.

New Orleans West KOA (☎ 504-467-1792; 11129 Jefferson Hwy; campsites/RV sites $22/32) Out near the international airport West KOA offers a shuttle service to and from the French Quarter.

MID-RANGE

Le Richelieu (☎ 504-529-2492, 800-535-9653; www.lerichelieu.com; 1234 Chartres St; r $95-180; P ❄ ♒) On the quiet side of the Quarter, Le Richelieu's red brick walls once housed a macaroni factory, but extensive reconstruction in the 1960s converted it into a conservative-looking hotel with some nicely decorated rooms.

Lafitte Guest House (☎ 504-581-2678, 800-331-7971; www.lafitteguesthouse.com; 1003 Bourbon St; r $160-220; P $15 ❄) An elegant, 1849 three-story French manor house that offers 14 rooms near enough, but far enough away, from the partying part of Bourbon St. All rooms are nonsmoking.

Cornstalk Hotel (☎ 504-523-1515; www.travelguides.com/bb/cornstalk; 915 Royal St; r low season $85-135, high season $145-185; P $15 ❄) The Cornstalk's famous cast-iron fence is possibly the most-photographed fence in the USA. The old house offers smallish rooms with high ceilings and antique furnishings.

Andrew Jackson Hotel (☎ 504-561-5881, 800-654-0224; www.historicinnsneworleans.com; 919 Royal St; r $100-185; P on street) Next door to the Cornstalk, this hotel has spacious, comfortable rooms overlooking a courtyard.

Chateau Hotel (☎ 504-524-9636; www.chateauhotel.com; 1001 Chartres St; r $130-210; P ❄) Though it's more of a motel than a chateau, this convenient spot offers a quiet location in the midst of the French Quarter.

Hotel St Pierre (☎ 504-524-4401, 800-225-8040; www.historicinnsneworleans.com; 911 Burgundy St; r $80-140; P ❄ ♒) This 74-room hotel is housed in a group of historic Creole cottages with modern furnishings and two pools.

Avenue Garden Hotel (☎ 504-521-8000, 800-379-5322; www.avenuegardenhotel.com; 1509 St Charles Ave; r $80-140; P ❄ 💻) In an uncharacteristically drab block of St Charles Ave, this Garden

NEW ORLEANS JAZZ & HERITAGE FESTIVAL

New Orleans' second-biggest reason to party, 'Jazz Fest,' began as a celebration of the city's 250th birthday in 1968. It attracted famous jazz players such as Louis Armstrong, Duke Ellington, Dave Brubeck, Woody Herman, Ramsey Lewis and Pete Fountain. After struggling with poor attendance, Jazz Fest moved to the Fair Grounds in 1972. It expanded to two weekends in late April and early May and began showcasing different musical forms in addition to jazz. The event blossomed into what it is today: a musical smorgasbord served up on more than 10 stages. Whether you want to hear local zydeco, R & B, bluegrass, gospel, reggae or authentic jazz, you'll find it at the festival.

Come hungry, as vendors' food booths overflow with in-season boiled crawfish, oyster and catfish po'boys, jambalaya and barbecue galore. Bring comfortable shoes, sunscreen, a hat, some water and a blanket for chilling out between concerts.

The Jazz Fest schedule comes out in January, and it's wise to make reservations as soon as possible to ensure you get the dates you want. Daily passes cost $20 in advance or $25 at the gate. The Fair Grounds are open 11am to 7pm, but Jazz Fest continues well into the wee hours in bars and clubs throughout New Orleans (Jazz Fest tickets do not cover nighttime admission prices).

For more information, contact or write to the **New Orleans Jazz & Heritage Festival** (☎ 504-522-4786; www.nojazzfest.com; 1205 N Rampart St, New Orleans, LA 70116). Tickets are available through **TicketMaster** (☎ 504-522-5555).

District hotel is a good value, offering tidy antique furnished rooms and free continental breakfast in the inner courtyard.

TOP END

Le Pavillon (☎ 504-581-3111, 800-535-9095; www.lepavillon.com; 833 Poydras Ave; r from $180; P $25) Built in 1907, this elegant place offers a lovely marble lobby, plush, modern rooms and a rooftop pool. During slow times, you can get unbelievable deals; it's worth a call ahead.

Omni Royal Orleans (☎ 504-529-5333, 800-843-6664; www.omniroyalorleans.com; 621 St Louis St; P $23) With the best furnishings and in-room amenities anywhere in the Quarter, this upscale hotel has it all, including a rooftop observation deck, spa and an activities program devoted to kids.

Fairmont Hotel (☎ 504-529-7111, 800-257-7544; www.fairmont.com; 123 Baronne St; r & ste from $300; P $20) With its majestic block-long lobby, this elegant hotel has long been among the city's best since the 1920s. Rooms are nicely remodeled and the swanky bar is a great place to spend cocktail hour. The outdoor rooftop pool offers an impressive downtown view.

Eating

Eating is a major activity in New Orleans, with the indigenous Creole and Cajun cooking, plus flavors from Italy, Mexico and the Caribbean, and a mouthwatering selection of snack foods. With its strong French influences and a taste for liquid refreshment, this is a city that enjoys its food. You have to resort to street parking at most restaurants.

FRENCH QUARTER

Café du Monde (☎ 504-581-2914; 800 Decatur St; beignets $2.50; 24hr) This New Orleans Institution keeps its prices low despite its proximity to the French Market and Jackson Sq. It's a great place to kick off a morning with a café au lait and yummy beignets (sweet pastries dusted with powdered sugar).

Central Grocery (☎ 504-523-1620; 923 Decatur St; sandwiches $6-8; 8am-5:30pm Mon-Sat, 9am-5:30pm Sun) The *muffaletta* sandwich was invented by a Sicilian immigrant here way back in 1906. Today, it's still the best place in town to get the sandwich, a round, seeded loaf of bread filled with ham, salami and provolone and drizzled with oily olive relish.

Johnny's Po-Boys (☎ 504-524-8129; 511 St Louis St; meals $4-8; closed dinner) This is a good place for traditional po'boys and budget hot plates for breakfast and lunch.

Acme Oyster and Seafood House (☎ 504-522-5973; 724 Iberville St; mains $6-10; 11am-late) Both out-of-towners and locals alike flock to this old-school oyster bar – its reputation for shucking the city's best oysters, along with seafood gumbo and po'boys, has lasted since its inception in 1910.

Café Sbisa (☎ 504-522-5565; 1011 Decatur St) This venerable Vieux Carré institution, with an exposed-brick dining room, has a reputation for innovative Creole cuisine, including blackened redfish and pasta jambalaya.

Crescent City Brewhouse (☎ 504-522-0571; 527 Decatur St; mains $8-18) A lively microbrewery where the predominately seafood menu and in-house brews draw conventioneers and tourists. Live music nightly.

Galatoire's (☎ 504-525-2021; 209 Bourbon St; meals $15-25) Regulars here are treated regally while tourists are sometimes dished out surprisingly average food. Local devotees so love this revered establishment that to die here over a plate of, say, grilled pompano is considered a *belle mort*, or good death. Try the daily special for the freshest taste. Expect to wait outside for a table, or make reservations for the upstairs dining room.

K-Paul's Louisiana Kitchen (☎ 504-596-2530; 416 Chartres St; dinner mains $26-36) Chef Paul Prudomme started this popular restaurant in the 1980s. It skyrocketed with Louisiana Creole and Cajun favorites like jambalaya and gumbo with spicy andouille sausages.

FAUBOURG MARIGNY

Old Dog New Trick (☎ 504-943-6368; 517 Frenchmen St; meals $6-11; 🕑 11am-10pm) Really one of the few vegetarian-only restaurants in town, Old Dog has great food, including the Ben burger and delicious noodle dishes.

Siam Café (☎ 504-949-1750; 435 Esplanade Ave; dishes $7-12; 🕑 5pm-2am) This dimly lit, small restaurant serves Thai standards, with spicy curries and vegetarian dishes.

La Péniche (☎ 504-943-1460; 1940 Dauphine St; burgers $6-10; 🕑 24hr Tue-Thu) This popular late-night dinner spot serves greasy diner fare but gets interesting late at night when partiers from the Quarter start trickling in.

Belle Forché (☎ 504-940-0722; 1407 Decatur St; meals $17-24; 🕑 dinner only) A stylishly cool dining room where the lights are low and the innovative fish dishes blend with the usually beautiful crowd.

CBD & WAREHOUSE DISTRICT

Red Eye Grill (☎ 504-593-9393; 852 S Peters St; burgers $5-8) Late night munchies and night-cap cravings get satisfied here with greasy burgers and beers.

Vic's Kangaroo Cafe (☎ 504-524-4329; 636 Tchoupitoulas St; meat pie $6-8) A transplanted Aussie pub serving up savory pies washed down with Fosters.

THE AUTHOR'S CHOICE

NOLA (☎ 504-522-6652; 534 St Louis St; mains $15-25) One of popular chef Emeril Lagasse's New Orleans institutions, and the least pretentious of the three. NOLA offers impeccable service, an excellent atmosphere and delicious fish, meats and wine.

Emeril's (☎ 504-528-9393; 800 Tchoupitoulas St; mains $20-34) Built in an old warehouse space, this flagship restaurant for chef Emeril Lagasse continues to be a top spot for dining out, despite the fact the famous chef is rarely there and the noise level is deafening. The kitchen still serves up delicious Creole fare and a well-priced wine list.

GARDEN DISTRICT & UPTOWN

Rue de la Course (Garden District ☎ 504-529-1455; 1500 Magazine St; Uptown ☎ 504-899-0242; 3128 Magazine St; baked goods $2-4; 🕑 7:30am-11pm) Both locations of this comfortable coffeehouse are great for ducking out of the rain to read a magazine while sipping coffee.

Trolley Stop (☎ 504-523-0090; 1923 St Charles Ave; burgers $6-10; 🕑 24hr) An assortment of unspectacular burgers and sandwiches sustain the always interesting crowd in this former gas station cum busy local hangout.

Uglesich's (☎ 504-523-8751; 1238 Baronne St; mains $8-15; 🕑 11am-2pm Mon-Fri) A funky lunchtime institution, family run since 1924. Here you will find authentic Louisiana cuisine served without the trappings of most tourists restaurants. Try the top-notch oysters or seafood specials such as crawfish bisque.

Commander's Palace (☎ 504-899-8221; 1403 Washington Ave; lunch $14-25, dinner $22-32) The training ground for such fine New Orleans chefs as Emeril Lagasse and Paul Prodhomme, owner Ella Brennan offers outstanding old-style Creole cuisine with fresh, local ingredients. You'll need a reservation and a jacket (for men).

Drinking

It doesn't matter what time of year it is, the elasticity of your budget or how early you go to bed – New Orleans keeps its carnival atmosphere stoked round the clock year-round. Nonstop music spills out of clubs and bars, luring passersby in for one more drink. Most bars serve a 'hurricane,' with dark rum, white rum, orange juice, pineapple juice and grenadine in a hurricane-lantern shaped glass. Also common are the gin fizz and mint julep. You can get plastic 'go cups' at any bar; it's legal to drink in the streets but illegal to have open glass containers. Most bars and pubs feature live music – jazz trios or acoustic soloists.

Pat O'Brien's (☎ 504-525-4823; 718 Peter St) The sugary sweet hurricane was developed here, where a labyrinthine series of alcoves link Bourbon St and St Peter St in a continuous party.

Molly's at the Market (☎ 504-525-5169; 1107 Decatur St) The Irish cultural center of the French Quarter serves Guinness and pub grub to a diverse mix of local characters.

Lafitte's Blacksmith Shop (☎ 504-523-0066; 941 Bourbon St) This well-worn corner bar whose lighting comes strictly from candles has a sing-along piano in the rear.

Napoleon House (☎ 504-524-9752; 500 Chartres St) Having opened its doors way back in 1797, this ancient haunt has seen it all, including years of decay. Its well-worn stuccoed walls haven't seen a dab of paint in what must be decades, but the place earns respect, much like a wise old man.

The budget bars in the Garden District and uptown attract a local crowd plus visitors from nearby hostels.

Igor's Lounge (☎ 504-522-2145; 2133 St Charles Ave) A dive that never closes, Igor's has a greasy grill, pool tables and washing machines.

Half Moon (☎ 504-522-7313; 1125 St Mary St) Draws barhopping trendsetters.

Though absinthe, 'the spirit of New Orleans,' was outlawed in 1914 because of its insanity-inducing effects, a couple of local joints keep the absinthe memories alive. Today Pernod, a safe liqueur flavored with anise, is now the poison of choice. Head to the following:

Old Absinthe House (☎ 504-523-3181; 240 Bourbon St)
Old Absinthe Bar (☎ 504-525-8108; 400 Bourbon St)

Entertainment

Generations of New Orleans club owners have thrived by promoting a combination of music and booze. Look out for shows by top performers like the Iguanas, Dr John and Terence Blanchard, and the musical dynasties of Marsalises and the Neville Brothers. Also watch for brass bands like Kermit Ruffins or the Dirty Dozen Brass Band.

The free monthly *Offbeat* and weekly *Gambit* are your best sources for reviews and performances.

You can also call the **events hotline** (☎ 504-840-4040) at WWOZ (90.7 FM).

TicketMaster (☎ 504-522-5555) has several outlets in New Orleans.

CLASSICAL MUSIC

Louisiana Philharmonic Orchestra (☎ 504-523-6530; www.lpomusic.com; box office 6th fl, 305 Baronne St; tickets $10-36) New Orleans' concert-goers are proud of their orchestra, one of only two musician-owned symphonies in the world. When the former symphony collapsed in 1990, the musicians pooled their money to keep it alive. It presents concerts downtown at the richly ornamented **Orpheum Theater** (☎ 504-524-3285; www.orpheumneworleans.com; 129 University Pl) from September to May.

LIVE MUSIC

In the French Quarter, live jazz, blues, Dixieland, zydeco and Cajun music emanate from clubs along upper Bourbon St between Bienville and St Ann Sts. Below St Ann St, disco throbs in clubs with gay and lesbian crowds. Clubs on the Quarter's riverfront margin are more for mainstream crowds seeking headline acts, while smaller venues toward the Quarter's periphery offer live brass bands, Irish folk music and disco. 'Kitty' clubs provide musicians with an opportunity to jam and pass the hat, especially in the Tremé district.

Preservation Hall (☎ 504-522-2841; 726 St Peter St; cover charge $5) A historically significant place, this worn music hall attracts veteran jazz musicians. Get there early to get a seat, or stand outside and listen through the open shutters.

Donna's Bar & Grill (☎ 504-596-6914; 800 N Rampart St; cover charge $5-15) All the best jazz musicians book gigs here and when they're not booked, they'll often stop by to jam.

Funky Butt on Congo Sq (☎ 504-558-0872; 714 N Rampart St; cover charge $5-15) With a swanky, sexy atmosphere, the Funky Butt usually turns up the heat, with modern jazz and a lively crowd.

House of Blues (☎ 504-529-2583; 255 Decatur St; cover charge $7-25) Though locals grumbled when Dan Ackroyd and his gang of partners opened up this franchise, they will undoubtedly now agree that it's one of

GAY & LESBIAN NEW ORLEANS

New Orleans' gay community revolves around the lower French Quarter and the Faubourg Marigny. The **Lesbian & Gay Community Center** (LGCC; ☎ 504-945-1103; 2114 Decatu St; 2-6pm) is a great resource for travelers or anyone thinking of moving to the Big Easy. You can also find out about special events, the hottest bars and the gay-friendly businesses.

For nightlife ideas, check out *Ambush Magazine* (www.ambushmag.com) or *Centerline*, which is published by the LGCC. Gay and gay-friendly bars of note include the following.

Oz (☎ 504-593-9491; 800 Bourbon St; cover charge around $5; 24hr) Open to straights who want to dance nonstop and don't mind guys in G-strings.

Bourbon Pub & Parade Disco (☎ 504-529-2107; 801 Bourbon St; cover charge $2-5; 24hr) As with Oz, this place is open to straights who love to dance.

735 (☎ 504-581-6740; 735 Bourbon St) Flashy 735 spins industrial/house for glow-stick gay and straight groupies.

Rawhide 2010 (☎ 504-525-8106; 740 Burgundy St; 24hr) Rawhide is – surprise! – a leather bar.

Gold Mine Saloon (☎ 504-586-0745; 705 Dauphine St) A young, mixed crowd packs the dance floor at Gold Mine. Ask around here about high-energy nightspots and unadvertised rave parties.

The Faubourg Marigny has some cool gay and mixed venues.

Cafe Brasil (☎ 504-949-0851; 2100 Chartres St; cover charge $5) Where a hip, bohemian crowd dances to Caribbean influences, Latin jazz bands and brass artists.

the best live-music venues in town. The calendar fills with fine rock, country and alternative acts. The Sunday Gospel Brunch will fortify your soul.

Margaritaville Cafe (☎ 504-592-2565; 1104 Decatur St) Dependent mostly on Jimmy Buffett's cheesy appeal, the club does book first-rate blues, jazz and zydeco and runs up to three shows daily.

Shim Sham Club (☎ 504-565-5400; 615 Toulouse St; cover charge $5-15) This hip, retro nightclub features headliner punk and acid jazz groups performing in a dark, theater-like decor.

Snug Harbor (☎ 504-949-0696; 626 Frenchmen St) This club in Faubourg Marigny is the city's premier contemporary jazz venue.

Igor's Checkpoint Charlie (☎ 504-947-0979; 501 Esplanade Ave; 24hr) Loud rock and R & B groups perform at this grungy spot, where you can do your laundry and play pool while listening to the bands.

Joe's Cozy Corner (☎ 504-581-4676; 1030 N Robertson St) In down-at-heel Tremé, this local kitty club, popular for brass, soul and R & B has a regular Sunday-night show featuring Kermit Ruffins and the Rebirth Brass Band.

Howlin' Wolf (☎ 504-523-2551; 828 S Peters St; cover charge $5-15) One of the best live music venues in town, this Warehouse District club attracts local talent as well as touring rock and alt-rock bands.

Tipitina's (☎ 504-895-8477; 501 Napoleon Ave; cover charge $10-20) This legendary music club is where the Neville Brothers and the Meters regularly rocked the city until dawn in the 1970s. The bar is marked by a bust of Henry Roland Byrd (1918–80), or 'Professor Longhair,' whose 1953 hit 'Tipitina' inspired the club's name. **Tipitina's French Quarter** (☎ 504-895-8477; 233 N Peters St) doesn't match the original uptown 'Tips' but still has great music.

You can enjoy a great Dixieland set for the price of a drink at **Maison Bourbon** (☎ 504-522-8818; 641 Bourbon St) and **Palm Court Jazz Café** (☎ 504-525-0200; 1204 Decatur St). **Funky Pirate** (☎ 504-523-1960; 727 Bourbon St) regularly features Big Al Carson & the Blues Masters.

SPECTATOR SPORTS

Louisiana Superdome (☎ 504-587-3810; 1500 Poydras Ave; tickets $22-50) The 60,000-seat superdome is home to the NFL New Orleans Saints and every few years it hosts the Super Bowl. In January, the Superdome hosts the NCAA (college) Sugar Bowl.

Fair Grounds Race Track (☎ 504-944-5515; 1751 Gentilly Blvd) Horseracing is a New Orleans tradition at the Fair Grounds Race Track. The racing season lasts from November to March.

THEATER & CINEMA

Contemporary Arts Center (☎ 504-528-3800; 900 Camp St; adult/child $5/3; 11am-5pm Tue-Sun) The premier venue for New Orleans' cutting-edge performances.

Saenger Theatre (☎ 504-524-2490; 143 N Rampart St) Major touring troupes perform at this ornate and finely restored 1927 theater.

Le Petit Théâtre du Vieux Carré (☎ 504-522-2081; 616 St Peter St) One of the oldest theater groups in the US. Classic and contemporary Southern plays.

Southern Repertory Theatre (☎ 504-861-8163; 333 Canal Place) On the third floor of the Canal Place Shopping Center, it presents classic and contemporary Southern plays.

Entergy Imax Theatre (☎ 504-581-4620; Canal St; adult/child $7/5) Next to the Aquarium of the Americas Imax shows films on a 74ft by 54ft screen.

Getting There & Away

Louis Armstrong New Orleans International Airport (☎ 504-464-0831; www.flymsy.com; 900 Airline Hwy), 11 miles west of the city, handles mostly domestic flights. A departure tax of $24 is charged to all passengers traveling to foreign cities.

Greyhound (☎ 800-231-2222, in Spanish ☎ 800-531-5332) buses run from the **Union Passenger Terminal** (☎ 504-524-7571; 1001 Loyola Ave), west of the Warehouse District. Regular services go to Baton Rouge ($15, two hours); Memphis ($50, nine hours) and Nashville ($50, 15 hours), TN; and Atlanta, GA ($73, 10 hours).

Amtrak (☎ 504-528-1610, 800-872-7245) trains also operate from the Union Passenger Terminal. The *City of New Orleans* runs to Jackson, MS; Memphis, TN; and Chicago, IL. The *Crescent Route* serves Birmingham, AL; Atlanta, GA; Washington, DC; and New York City. New Orleans is also on the *Sunset Limited* route between Los Angeles, California and Miami, Florida.

To get to the French Quarter from the Union Passenger Terminal, search for the sheltered stop east of the station across broad Loyola Ave at Howard Ave and take the RTA No 17 S Claiborne Ave bus to the corner of Canal and Rampart Sts. It's not far to walk, but be wary of going through the CBD at night. A cab to the corner of Bourbon and Canal Sts costs about $7.

Getting Around

TO/FROM THE AIRPORT

There's an **information booth** at the airport's A&B concourse. **Airport Shuttle** (☎ 504-522-3500; one way per person $10) goes to downtown hotels. The **Louisiana Transit Company** (☎ 504-818-1077) runs the **Jefferson Transit Airport Express** (☎ 504-737-7433; adult $1.50), route E2, which stops along Airline Hwy (Hwy 61) on its way into town.

Taxis downtown cost $28 for one or two people, $12 more for each additional passenger.

CAR & MOTORCYCLE

Bringing a car to downtown New Orleans is often a costly proposition and may actually hinder your visit, dealing with the narrow one-way streets, congestion and parking. During daytime, street parking has a two-hour limit. Parking garages in the upper (southern) part of the Quarter charge about $5 for the first hour, or $20 for 24 hours.

PUBLIC TRANSPORTATION

The **Regional Transit Authority** (RTA; ☎ 504-248-3900) runs the local bus service. Fares are $1.50, plus 25¢ for transfers; express buses cost $1.50. Exact change is required. RTA Visitor Passes for one/three days cost $5/12.

The RTA also operates two streetcar lines. One of the best ways to see the city beyond the Quarter is to take the St Charles Ave Streetcar Tour, which links the Quarter with the CBD, the Lower Garden and Garden Districts, uptown and Riverbend. Catch the streetcar at the corner of St Charles Ave and Common St. It costs $1.55 each way and the round-trip takes about 90 minutes. The Riverfront Line has vintage red streetcars running 2 miles from the Old US Mint, past Canal St, to the upriver convention center and back.

For a taxi, call **White Fleet Cabs** (☎ 504-948-6605) or **United Cabs** (☎ 504-522-9771).

Rent bicycles at **Bicycle Michael's** (☎ 504-945-9505; 622 Frenchmen St; bicycle per day from $15), in Faubourg Marigny.

AROUND NEW ORLEANS

New Orleans is a beguiling – and exhausting – city. When you reach the point where you can't face another plate of jambalaya, and the thought of one more hurricane cocktail sets your stomach churning, head for the hinterlands. Along Lake Pontchartrain's north shore browse through the hip antique stores in cool, artsy **Covington** or take a nature retreat at **Fontainebleau State Park** (☎ 504-624-4443), a 2700-acre gem on the lakeshore near Mandeville, with nature trails, plantation ruins, a sandy beach, a swimming pool, picnic areas and campsites. Head north of Mandeville and sip a microbrew in the bucolic village of **Abita Springs**, which was popular in the late 1800s as a spot to bask in what were thought to be curative waters. Today, the spring water still flows from a fountain in the center of the village, but the primary liquid attraction here is the **Abita Brewery** (☎ 985-893-3143; 21084 Hwy 36), just a mile or so west of town. Abita was the first microbrewery in the southeast, and its popular Turbo Dog, Purple Haze and Amber beers are top sellers.

South of New Orleans, the Mississippi River flows 90 miles to the swampy environment of the 'bird's foot' delta. Go west on Hwy 90 and you'll hit **Westwego,** which has a huge open-air fish market ringed by earthy shacks, plus the intimate, family-run and excellent **Chacahoula Swamp Tours** (☎ 504-436-2640; 422 Louisiana St; with/without transportation from New Orleans $38/22).

Barataria Preserve & Lafitte

A great way to learn about swamplands is to visit this preserve, which is a unit of the Jean Lafitte National Historic Park. Set in an area originally settled by Isleños (Canary Islanders) in 1779, it offers hiking and canoe trips into the swamp and a good introduction to the wetlands environment. It is not a pristine wilderness, as canals and other structures offer evidence of human activity, but wild animals and plants are abundant. Even a brief walk on the boardwalks that wend their way through the swamp will yield sightings of gators and egrets.

Start at the **NPS Visitors Center** (☎ 504-589-2330; Hwy 3134; 🕑 9am-5pm), 1 mile west of Hwy 45, where you can pick up a map, join a ranger-led walk or watch the center's free 25-minute introductory nature film, *Jambalaya: A Delta Almanac.*

Bayou Barn (☎ 504-689-2663; canoes per 2hr $15; 🕑 Tue-Sun) rents canoes. It's on the Bayou de Familles just outside the park, and is a pleasantly funky restaurant compound of tin-topped weather-beaten buildings on the opposite side of the intersection. Cajun or zydeco bands play to lively local crowds at the **dances** (adult $5; 🕑 noon-6pm) held most Sundays.

South of the preserve, the quaint fishing village of **Lafitte** gets such frequent flooding, even the mobile homes are set on stilts. Spanish moss hangs heavy – like green streamers tossed onto the boughs of the live oak trees. Hardy commercial fishers make it home and although it has scant tourist sights, it has abundant waterside funk and **swamp tours**.

Cochiara's Marina (☎ 504-689-3701; r from $55) On the northern end of the bridge, this hardware store, grocery and bar offers scruffy motel rooms overlooking the bayou.

Victorian Inn (☎ 504-689-4757; r from $100) On the southern side of the Goose Bayou Bridge, this is the area's de facto tourism office, where the innkeepers will help you book swamp tours and offers up 14 rooms in two West Indies–style plantation homes.

Mississippi River Plantations

Elaborate plantation homes line the east and west banks of the Mississippi River between New Orleans and Baton Rouge. First indigo, then cotton, rice and sugarcane brought great wealth to these plantations, many of which are open to the public as historic sites, usually with costumed guides leading 45- to 60-minute **tours** (adult $6-8). Many present a romantic picture of plantation life, focusing on the lovely architecture, ornate gardens and genteel lifestyle of antebellum Louisiana. The tours are pleasant and historically interesting through most evade the story of plantation slaves, who lived in relative squalor and whose backbreaking labor built the houses and kept fields bountiful. Be sure to round out a plantation tour with a visit to the **River Road African-American Museum & Gallery**.

It's easy enough to explore the region by car, and organized tours are widely available from New Orleans. A full-day trip, including visits to two or three plantations and lunch, will cost you around $75. Check at the visitors centers for the range of tours. Tour prices at the plantations are mostly $10 for adults, $5 for children.

EAST BANK

Destrehan Plantation (☎ 985-764-9315; 13034 Hwy 48; 🕑 9:30am-4pm) on the east bank is the oldest plantation home remaining in the lower Mississippi Valley. Indigo was the principal crop in 1787 when the landowner hired a mulatto builder to construct a French colonial-style mansion using *bousillage* (mud- and straw-filled) walls supported by cypress timbers. Later additions added today's Greek Revival facade.

WEST BANK

Laura Plantation (☎ 225-265-7690; 2247 Hwy 18; adult/child $10/5; 🕑 9:30am-5pm) at Vacherie is an unassuming French Creole plantation built in 1905. Unlike other tours, this ever-evolving and popular plantation doesn't gloss over the role of slavery; you get a good picture of what life was like for both master and slave via accounts from the lives of the Creole women who ran the place for generations.

Oak Alley Plantation (☎ 225-265-2151; 3645 Hwy 18; adult/child $10/5; 🕑 9am-5pm) features the most dramatic approach, with a 0.25-mile canopy of 28 majestic live oaks lining the entry that leads to the grand Greek Revival–style house. The trees predate the house by about 100 years.

River Road African-American Museum & Gallery (☎ 225-474-5553; www.africanamericanmuseum.org; 406 Charles St, Donaldsonville; museum/walking tour $4/15; 🕑 9am-5pm) was founded by Louisiana native Kathe Hambrick in 1994, the original museum sat on the grounds of the Tezcuco Plantation, a popular stop on the plantation tour until it burned down in 2002. Hambrick took the opportunity to open up an expanded and vastly improved museum in the historic town of Donaldsonville, a prosperous city for blacks after the Civil War. In addition to exhibits about plantation slavery and the slaves' journey to freedom via the underground railway, Hambrick gives 45-minute walking tours of Donaldsonville.

Nottoway Plantation (☎ 225-545-2730; www.nottoway.com; Hwy 1; adult/child $10/5; 🕑 9am-5pm), closer to Baton Rouge, is the largest plantation house in the South, with 64 rooms and 53,000 sq ft. It retains its original furnishings, and tour guides shed the period garb and faux drama, but keep the tours rich in personal history. You can also stay overnight at the plantation, which is a real treat as you essentially get the run of the place at night. You can stay in the **mansion** ($200-225), in the **boy's wing** ($140-190) or in the **overseer's cottage** ($140-190). The rate includes a plantation breakfast, refreshments and a tour.

Baton Rouge

Native Americans painted cypress poles with blood, and staked them here on the east bank of the Mississippi to mark the boundaries of their hunting grounds. French explorers named the area *baton rouge* (red stick). An industrial town and the state capital, Baton Rouge has two universities, the tallest capital building in the nation, a few casinos and a riverfront entertainment complex.

Most attractions are downtown, off I-110. Louisiana State University (LSU) is in the southwest quadrant of the city. Highland Rd is the main thoroughfare, while Perkins Rd has many restaurants, bookstores and shops north and south of I-10. The **convention and visitors center** (☎ 225-346-1253, 800-527-6843; www.batonrougetour.com; 730 North Blvd; 🕑 8am-5pm Mon-Fri) has maps and brochures.

SIGHTS

The 'new' **Louisiana State Capitol** (☎ 225-342-7317; 🕑 9am-5pm) building, on State Capitol Dr, is an art deco skyscraper built at the height of the Great Depression to the tune of $5 million; it's populist governor Huey Long's most visible legacy. A tour is worthwhile, and the 27th-floor **observation deck** (admission free) has a great view. The **Old State Capitol** (☎ 225-342-0500; 100 N Blvd; 🕑 10am-4pm Tue-Sat, noon-4pm Sun) is a neo-Gothic structure overlooking the river, with exhibits and multimedia presentations about Huey Long and the state's colorful political history.

SLEEPING

Unfortunately, your best bet for accommodations in Baton Rouge are in the many moderately-priced chain hotels just off I-10 around the College Rd and Acadian Thruway exits. Cheaper chains cluster along the north side of I-12, within a mile of I-10.

Pleasant Hall (☎ 225-387-0297, 888-551-5933; cnr Dalrymple Dr & Highland Rd, LSU campus; r/ste $45/65; P ✖ 🅰) Anyone spending time at the university will find good accommodations at this 85-room campus hotel. Rooms include a continental breakfast and free airport shuttle.

Ramada Inn (☎ 225-387-1111; 1480 Nicholson Dr; r $65-120; P ✖ 🅰) Near downtown, just south of the I-10 bridge, this business hotel has 158 standard but nice rooms with amenities.

Comfort Suites (☎ 225-923-3377, 800-945-7667; 3045 Valley Creek Dr; r $70; P ✖ 🅰) In a good location between I-10 and Perkins Rd, this tidy hotel has 110 rooms with in-room refrigerators.

Embassy Suites (☎ 225-924-6566; 4914 Constitution Ave; Mon-Thu $110, Fri-Sun $130; P) One of the nicest in the city, this hotel has big standard rooms and two-room suites with galley kitchens. The indoor pool has a whirlpool and sauna. A full complimentary breakfast is served each morning.

EATING & DRINKING

Cafeteria (☎ 225-342-0371; dishes $4-7; Mon-Fri) The cafeteria in the basement of the Louisiana State Capitol building offers the best breakfast and lunch that government money can subsidize.

Phil's Oyster Bar (☎ 225-924-3045; 5162 Government St; oysters $8-12) Oyster shuckers keep up a steady banter as they slide dozens of oysters down the bar to waiting customers. Phil's also serves up seafood and Italian fare.

Arzi's Café (☎ 225-927-2111; 5219 Government St; meals $10-15) This may well be one of the only Louisiana restaurants outside New Orleans where you can get a great vegetarian meal. The Mediterranean-influenced menu features excellent falafel and dolmas. You can get lamb, chicken and beef dishes too.

Louie's Cafe (☎ 225-346-8221; 209 W State St; breakfast $6-10) Near LSU, Louie's is the best 24-hour eatery in town, with 1950s ambience, delicious omelettes and hash browns.

Bayou (☎ 225-346-1765; 124 W Chimes Rd) Scenes from the movie *Sex, Lies and Videotape* were filmed at this bar, which still hosts quality live music acts.

Varsity Theatre (☎ 225-383-7018; 3353 Highland Rd) *The* place for live music, with small and large acts like Wilco and String Cheese Incident.

Tabby's Blues Box & Heritage Hall (☎ 225-387-9715; 244 Lafayette St) An old stand-by for live blues.

GETTING THERE & AROUND

Traveling from New Orleans I-12 merges into I-10 on the eastern edge of Baton Rouge, at which point I-10 continues west toward Lafayette. Driving the 80 miles from New Orleans takes about 90 minutes.

The **Baton Rouge Metropolitan Airport** (☎ 225-355-0333), north of the city off I-110, is served by many regional airlines.

Greyhound (☎ 225-383-3811; 1253 Florida Blvd at N 12th St) has regular buses to Atlanta, GA ($88, from 11 hours); Birmingham, AL ($80, from 10 hours); Lafayette ($13, one hour); and New Orleans ($15, two hours).

Capital Transportation City Bus (☎ 225-389-8920, 225-389-8282) provides local transport Monday to Saturday from the **transfer station** (2222 Florida St).

CAJUN COUNTRY

This region encompasses a 22-parish region of southern Louisiana from the Mississippi River to the Texas border. Home to the largest French-speaking minority in the US, the region is named for French settlers who were exiled by the British in 1755 from L'Acadie (now Nova Scotia, Canada). They sought refuge in Louisiana and were shunted to the western swamplands. Houma and Chitimacha Indians taught their new neighbors to trap, fish, hunt and eat crawfish. These Indians corrupted 'Acadian' to 'Cagian,' and hence 'Cajun.'

From 1916 to 1956 the state banned French in schools, during a period called the *Heure de la Honte* (Time of Shame). In WWII, Acadian soldiers in France became valuable interpreters, and GIs returned with seeds of renewed cultural pride. In a complete reversal of earlier policies, the Council for the Development of French in Louisiana (Codofil) began fostering the local language and culture. The I-10 bridge over the Atchafalaya Basin, completed in 1973, made the area readily accessible for the first time, and interest in Cajun music and cuisine has attracted an increasing number of visitors.

The logical starting point is Lafayette, 130 miles west of New Orleans, but the real Cajun experience is found in small towns, bayous and rural back roads. Cajun and zydeco music rocks out at bars and restaurants, *fais-do-do* (Cajun dances) are mostly held on weekends, and Cajun food is available everywhere.

Lafayette

This small city isn't exceptionally attractive, with the old downtown struggling for definition somewhere between decline and renewal. The University of Louisiana at Lafayette (ULL), with 17,000 'Ragin' Cajuns,' gives Lafayette some college-town vitality. From I-10, exit 103A, the Evangeline Thruway (Hwy 167) goes to the center of town via the **visitors center** (☎ 337-232-3737, 800-346-1958; 1400 NW Evangeline Thruway; 8:30am-5pm Mon-Fri, 9am-5pm Sat & Sun).

SIGHTS & ACTIVITIES

The best NPS museum in Cajun Country is the **Acadian Cultural Center** (☎ 337-232-0789; 501 Fisher Rd; admission free; ⏰ 8am-5pm). Interactive displays – like a Cajun joke-telling booth – give life to local folkways. The rangers speak French.

Vermilionville (☎ 337-233-4077; 1600 Surrey St; adult/student $8/5) is a living history and folklife museum. Docents in period costumes guide you through a 19th-century Cajun village. Bands perform shows daily in the barn, and there are daily cooking demonstrations and tastings. **Acadian Village** (☎ 337-981-2364; 200 Greenleaf Dr; adult/child $6.50/2) is less glitzy than Vermilionville and is favored by locals. Follow a brick path around a rippling bayou to restored houses, craft shops and a church.

The **Children's Museum** (☎ 337-232-8500; 201 E Congress St; admission $5) is of the hands-on variety. Children are encouraged to explore an operating room, a TV studio and an Acadian-style cottage.

SLEEPING

Lafayette offers nearly 4000 hotel and B&B rooms. All the usual chains are present at or near exits 101 and 103, off I-10. Budget rates are around $40 to $50 for doubles.

Blue Moon Hostel (☎ 337-234-2422, 877-766-2583; www.bluemoonhostel.com; 215 E Convent St; dm $20, r $40-70; ⊠) This small, tidy hostel south of I-10 exit 103A is a great place to pick up local information from the friendly owners. It has a communal kitchen, dining room and lounge area. Five rooms are dorm-style, plus one private room.

Travelodge (☎ 337-234-7402, 800-578-7878; 1101 W Pinhook Rd; r $50; P ⊠) It's a bit south of downtown but well located for exploring the city.

Maison Mouton (☎ 337-234-4661, fax 337-235-6755; 402 Garfield St; r with/without bath $90/60; P ⊠) A centrally located B&B, this friendly 100-year-old inn has nice rooms and is close to everything, including the bus depot.

T'Frere's B&B (☎ 337-984-9347, 800-984-9347; 1905 E Verot School Rd; s/d $80/95; P ⊠) Within walking distance of the zydeco Hamilton Club, with six rooms all with private bath, in an 1880 house. Breakfast is served on the porch.

EATING

Many places offer one-stop entertainment, dancing and regional cuisine. Markets, convenience stores and even gas stations keep a pot of hot *boudin* (pork-and-rice-filled sausage) by the cash register, a sure sign you're in Cajun country.

T-Coons (☎ 337-232-3803; 740 Jefferson Blvd; meals $5-7) The local favorite for crawfish omelettes in the morning and plates of smothered rabbit or jambalaya for lunch.

Old Tyme Grocery (☎ 337-235-8165; 218 W St Mary St; po'boys $5) Excellent shrimp or roast beef po'boys at lunch or dinner.

Cedar Deli (☎ 337-233-5460; 1115 Jefferson Blvd; meals $4-6) This Syrian-owned deli serves up delicious falafels, as well as veggie and meat *muffalettas*.

Borden's (☎ 337-235-9291; 1103 Jefferson Blvd) Next door, dishes up fountain treats and milkshakes. Take a seat in a red-vinyl booth beneath Elsie the Cow's wide-eyed gaze.

Blue Dog Café (☎ 337-237-0005; 1211 W Pinhook Rd; entrées $13-21) A Cajun-fusion restaurant decorated with 'blue dog' paintings by George Rodrique, this is a good place for a splurge at dinner. The menu features authentic Cajun with creative and delicious spins. Try the Treasures of the Bayou – a stew of local seafood simmered in herbed wine. Yum!

ENTERTAINMENT

To find out who's playing in the clubs, look for the free weekly *Times*.

El Sid O's (☎ 337-237-1959; 1523 Martin Luther King Dr) For zydeco, try El Sid O's at St Antoine St, a big and welcoming cinder-block joint.

Hamilton Club (☎ 337-991-0783; 1808 Verot School Rd) For zydeco.

Grant St Dance Hall (☎ 337-237-2255; 113 W Grant St) For a more eclectic menu of musical offerings, head to Grant St, a cavernous warehouse of a place.

GETTING THERE & AWAY

Greyhound (☎ 337-235-1541) operates from a hub beside the central commercial district, making 11 runs daily to New Orleans and Baton Rouge. The decrepit Amtrak station is served by the *Sunset Limited*, which goes to New Orleans three times a week.

Cajun Wetlands

In 1755, *le Grande Dérangement*, the British expulsion of the rural French settlers from Acadia, created a homeless population of Acadians who searched for decades for a place to settle. In 1785, seven boatloads of exiles arrived in New Orleans. By the early 19th century, some 3000 to 4000 Acadians arrived to occupy the swamplands southwest of New Orleans. Here, they eked out a living based upon fishing and trapping and developed a culture substantially different from the Cajuns who settled further inland in the prairie region, where animal husbandry and farming were the primary vocations. Southwest of Lafayette, historic **Abbeville** has great seafood and the surrounding communities are well known for small-town festivals. Southeast of Lafayette, along US 90 beside the **Atchafalaya Basin**, the heart of the Cajun wetlands is a lowland area of dense vegetation, swamps, lakes and bayous.

A massive Evangeline Oak, poised along Bayou Teche just off Main St in **St Martinville**, about 15 miles southeast of Lafayette, has become a lodestar for those seeking a connection to deposed Acadians. Thanks goes, in large part, to Henry Wadsworth Longfellow's 1847 epic poem *Evangeline*, which recounts the story of star-crossed French lovers Evangeline and Gabriel.

About 20 miles southeast of Lafayette, **New Iberia** was settled by the Spanish in 1779 and makes a good base for exploring the area. The town prospered on the sugarcane of surrounding plantations. Today, the town's best-known native son may well be mystery writer James Lee Burke, whose novels often take place in and around New Iberia and feature Detective Dave Robicheaux.

A cheap place to stay with basic but clean rooms is the **Teche Motel** (☎ 337-369-3756; 1830 Main St; r $40; P ❄). On Hwy 14, chain hotels vie for traveler business, including **Best Western** (☎ 337-364-3030; 2714 Hwy 14; d $62; P ❄) and **Holiday Inn** (☎ 337-367-1201; 2915 Hwy 14; r $65; P ❄). The town has numerous B&Bs, among them the comfortable 100-year-old **Estorage-Norton House** (☎ 337-365-7603; 446 E Main St; d $70-80; P ❄), where five guest rooms have private baths and include a full breakfast.

A favorite weekday breakfast and lunch spot is the **LagniappeToo Café** (☎ 337-365-9419; 204 E Main St; dishes $5-9). It also serves dinner on Friday and Saturday. For delicious boiled seafood, locals head a few miles north of town along I-49/Hwy 90 to the simple **Guiding Star** (☎ 337-365-9113; dishes $8-12; 🕑 3-10pm). If you need crawfish-cracking lessons, this is the place to come.

A drive southwest of New Iberia along Hwy 329 through cane fields brings you to **Avery Island**, home of **McIlhenny Tabasco** (☎ tours 337-365-8173; 🕑 9am-4pm) and a wildlife sanctuary. The island is actually a salt dome that extends 8 miles below the surface. The salt mined here goes into the sauce, as does locally grown peppers. The mixture ferments in oak barrels before being mixed with vinegar, strained and bottled.

Just 60 miles southwest of New Orleans, **Thibodaux** (ti-ba-doh) sits at the confluence of two bayous. The big attraction here is the **Wetlands Cajun Cultural Center** (☎ 985-448-1375; 314 St Mary St; 🕑 9am-8pm Mon, 8am-5pm Tue-Fri, 9am-5pm Sat & Sun), a spacious museum and gallery operated by the NPS. Exhibits cover virtually every aspect of Cajun life in the wetlands, from music to the environmental impacts of trapping and oil exploration. Local musicians jam here Monday evenings from 6pm to 8pm.

Named for the Houma tribe of Native Americans, who were displaced in the mid-19th century by the Acadians, **Houma** is the economic hub of the Cajun Wetlands. The city itself offers little of interest to visitors, save functioning as a way station for travelers on their way to the docks just west of town, where some of the area's best swamp tours depart.

TOURS

If you're after a tour of Houma Swamp check out the following:

Alligator Annie Miller's Swamp Tours (☎ 985-879-3934; Hwy 90; adult/child $15/10) Eight miles west of Houma, Annie has been feeding chicken drumsticks to the gator babies for so long that they're now trained to respond to the sound of her approaching motor and rise from the muck to take a bite. No matter if you take advantage of the moment as a photo opportunity or plunge headlong for the opposite side of the boat, it's great fun.

Annie Miller's Son's Swamp and Marsh Tours (☎ 985-868-4758) More recently, this company has got into the act, and may soon be the primary family provider.

Cajun Man's Swamp Cruise (☎ 985-868-4625; Hwy 90; adult/child $15/10) Ten miles west of Houma, this is run by Black Guidry, who serenades his passengers with a bit of accordion music, while piloting them through a scenic slice of swamp, his trusty dog Gator Bait at his side.

Cajun Prairie

As the elevation climbs north out of Lafayette, the land dries out a bit, crypts in cemeteries rise only a few inches above ground and roads become more predictable than in the southern wetlands. The simple geometry of grain silos echoes those of the Midwest, and it's no surprise Midwestern farmers were some of the earliest rice growers in the region. This entire area is fertile ground for Cajun and zydeco music, fishing camps and crawfish boils.

Opelousas has a historic city center and a museum covering Indian, Acadian and Creole cultures. On the main square, **Palace Cafe** (☎ 337-942-2142; dishes $6-10) does great crawfish étoufée and bisque.

Top zydeco venues include **Slim's Y-Ki-Ki** (☎ 337-942-9980), a few miles up Washington St, and **Richard's** (☎ 337-543-8223), 8 miles west in Lawtell. **Plaisance**, northwest of Opelousas, hosts the **Southwest Louisiana Zydeco Festival** (☎ 337-942-2392; www.zydeco.org) at the end of August.

North of Opelousas, **Washington** retains its character as a historic steamboat port. To the southwest, **Church Point** is known for Cajun music.

In **Eunice**, the **Prairie Acadian Cultural Center** (☎ 337-457-8490; cnr Third St & Park Ave) is part of Jean Lafitte National Historic Park and Preserve. Displays introduce visitors to Acadian heritage and map the immigration of French men and women to Louisiana. The **Liberty Theater** (☎ 337-457-7389; cnr S Second St & Park Ave), c 1924, is best known for its **Rendez-vous des Cajuns** (adult/child $3/free), a Saturday-night performance broadcast on local radio stations. Surrounded by woods, **Cajun Campground** (☎ 337-457-5753; Hwy 190; campsites/RV sites $10/16, cabins $55) has a pool, small store, playground and small lake. The seven cabins also have kitchenettes.

The rough-and-tumble self-proclaimed 'Cajun Music Capital,' **Mamou** has a big bash of drinking and dancing starting at around 8am every Saturday morning at **Fred's Lounge** (☎ 337-468-5411; 420 6th St).

Off I-10 between Lafayette and Lake Charles, the Rice Belt sports 19th-century railroad towns like Rayne, 'Frog Capital of the World,' and Crowley, the 'Rice Capital of Louisiana.'

CENTRAL LOUISIANA

The central part of the state is a crossroads of Louisiana's distinct cultures, politics and religions. You'll find French heritage in Natchitoches, Tunica Indian traditions in Marksville, and Franco African people along the Cane River. This is also the region where bilingual French Catholic Louisiana shades into the monolingual, chiefly Protestant parishes to the north. Much of central Louisiana is a lonely place, densely forested and sparsely populated. Though logging of Southern yellow pine and hardwoods continues today, 937 sq miles of forest land is protected by the spread out Kisatchie National Forest.

Natchitoches

Despite its storied history and charming French architecture, Natchitoches (mysteriously pronounced *nak*-id-esh) remained a sleepy little backwater town until Hollywood filmmakers arrived in 1988 to film the blockbuster movie *Steel Magnolias*. Based on the play by native son Robert Harling, the film's cast – including Shirley MacLaine, Julia Roberts, Dolly Parton and Sally Field – brought a lot more than star power

After the movie, Natchitoches' attractive 33-block National Historic District, established in 1714 on the west bank of the Cane River Lake, bloomed into a tourist attraction. The busiest time of year here is December, when the town puts on its famous **City of Lights Festival** (www.christmasfestival.com). Whatever season, the best way to explore Natchitoches is on foot. Grab a map at the **visitors center** (☎ 318-352-8072, 800-259-1714; www.natchitoches.net; 781 Front St; 🕑 9am-5pm Mon-Sat, 10am-3pm Sun).

SLEEPING & EATING

Lakeview Inn (☎ 318-352-9561; 1316 Washington St; s/d $42/45; P ✖) A good budget option on the north side near the Hwy 1 bypass, this motel has clean, simple rooms, some of which overlook the river.

The town is full of charming B&Bs, most of which cost $65 to $120 a night. Three good options include the following:

Fleur de Lis (☎ 318-352-6621, 800-489-6621; 336 2nd St)
Breazeale House (☎ 318-352-5630, 800-352-5631; 926 Washington St)
Cloutier Townhouse Bed & Breakfast (☎ 318-352-5242, 877-699-8471; 416 Jefferson St)

Authentic Natchitoches meat pies are crusty, crescent-shaped little turnovers, stuffed with spicy ground beef, pork and onions and then fried.

Lasyone's Meat Pie Kitchen (☎ 318-352-3353; 229 2nd St; meals $4-10; 🕑 7am-7pm Mon-Sat) Absolutely the best place for savory meat pies.

Almost Home (☎ 318-352-2431; 729 3rd St; meals $6-10; 🕑 6am-2:30pm Sun-Thu, 6am-2:30pm & 5-8pm Fri) On Hwy 1 near Sibley Lake, locals come here for the delicious home-style breakfasts, lunch buffets and the Friday night all-you-can-eat catfish buffet.

Cane River Country

South from Natchitoches, Hwy 119 meanders alongside the Cane River. You'll pass locals dipping fishing poles into the lazy river or whiling away the day on front-porch rockers. **Melrose Plantation** (☎ 318-379-0055, 800-259-1714; exit 119 off I-49; admission $6; 🕑 noon-4pm) is a whole complex of buildings with an interesting history. In the early 20th century, hostess Cammy Henry offered lodging in the 'Yucca House' to artists and writers like William Faulkner and John Steinbeck. Africa House is done in Congo style and looks like a squat brick mushroom. Inside is a vivid 50ft mural depicting plantation life by folk artist Clementine Hunter.

Five separate units of **Kisatchie National Forest** (☎ 318-473-7160 for maps, information and ranger stations) cover 937 sq miles of northern and central Louisiana. Most have free campgrounds and extensive hiking trails.

The economic and political hub of the area, **Alexandria**, on the banks of the Red River, is primarily a crossroads town, where people from surrounding areas come to shop at Wal-Mart. Worth a stop if only for the historic **Hotel Bentley** (☎ 318-448-9600, 800-306-1074; 200 DeSoto St), dubbed the 'Biltmore of the Bayous.' The imposing neoclassical building contains a lobby with a marble fountain and stained-glass ceiling.

Southward, on the cusp of Cajun Country, **Marksville** has a proud French heritage and Native American connections and survives mostly on tourism to its casino. The **Marksville State Commemorative Area** (☎ 318-253-8954; 700 Martin Luther King Jr Dr; admission $2; 🕑 9am-5pm) was the site of a complex society believed to have lived here 2000 years ago. In the 1920s archeologists began studying the many dirt mounds here, which were used for burial ceremonies. The **Tunica–Biloxi Museum** (☎ 318-253-8174; admission $5; ☎ 8am-4pm), on Hwy 1 just south of town, has a mound built for the symbolic re-interment of 200,000 artifacts looted from Tunica graves. Many restored objects are displayed, most from the 18th-century Tunica trade with French settlers.

Terrace Inn (☎ 318-253-5274; 915 Tunica Dr W; r $40-50; P ✕ ♠) A great deal, this nice, inviting little motel has a pool and free shuttle to the casino.

Paragon Casino Resort (☎ 318-253-0777, 800-642-7777; www.paragoncasinoresort.com; 711 Paragon Place; weekday/weekend $60/110; P ✕ ♠) Run by the local Tunica–Biloxi tribe, this giant casino has restaurants, a hotel, golf course and live-concert venue.

NORTHERN LOUISIANA

Make no mistake: the rural backwaters and oil-industry towns along the Baptist Bible Belt make northern Louisiana as far removed from New Orleans as Paris, Texas is from Paris, France. Emanating from the commercial center of Shreveport, this is a region battling to find self-definition after decades of decline.

In the northwest corner of the state, Captain Henry Shreve cleared a 165-mile logjam on the Red River to found **Shreveport** as a river port in 1839. The city boomed with oil discoveries in the early 1900s, but the port declined after WWII. Many downtown businesses were closed, but big gambling dollars are now generated by the area's huge Vegas-size casinos and a riverfront entertainment complex. The city is bisected by I-49 and I-20 and encircled by I-220. The **visitors center** (☎ 318-222-9391, 800-551-8682; 629 Spring St; 🕑 8am-5pm Mon-Fri, 11am-3pm Sat) is downtown.

In northeast Louisiana, **Monroe** used to be a prosperous town that boomed with the discovery of oil and natural gas. Those prosperous times, however, are long gone. Ramshackle homes have replaced moneyed mansions; jails now occupy former schools. Greenthumbs and God-fearin' folk come to check out the **Biedenharn Museum & Garden** (☎ 318-387-5281; www.bmuseum.org; 2006 Riverside Dr; admission free; 🕑 10am-5pm Mon-Sat, 2-5pm Sun). Created by Coke father Joseph Biedenharn's daughter Emy-Lou, the complex features a bible museum, conservatory and a pretty garden filled with plants mentioned in the good book.

About 50 miles northeast of Monroe on Hwy 557 near the town of Epps, the **Poverty Point National Monument** (☎ 318-926-5492, 888-926-5492; www.crt.state.la.us; admission $2; 🕑 9am-5pm) archaeological site, has a remarkable series of earthwork and mounds along what was once the Mississippi River.

Around 1000 BC it was the hub of a civilization comprising hundreds of communities, with trading links as far north as the Great Lakes. There's a good introductory film, and a two-story observation tower gives a view of the site's six concentric ridges.

ARKANSAS

Once a jumping-off point for frontier expeditions to the west and south, Arkansas later attracted visitors with its natural hot springs. Today it promotes itself as 'the Natural State,' with camping, fishing and hunting in the Ozark and Ouachita Mountains. Unnatural attractions include sites associated with Bill Clinton, civil rights history and quirky hillbilly culture.

The **Department of Parks & Tourism** (☎ 501-682-7777, 800-628-8725; www.arkansastravel.com; 1 Capitol Mall, Little Rock, AR 72201) sends out a vacation plan kit on request.

ARKANSAS FACTS

Nickname Natural State
Population 2,710,079 (33rd)
Area 52,068 sq miles (27th)
Admitted to Union June 15, 1836 (25th); seceded May 1861; readmitted 1868
Capital city Little Rock (population 183,000)
Other cities Fort Smith (80,000), North Little Rock (60,000), Pine Bluff (55,000)
Birthplace of General Douglas MacArthur (1880–1964), musician Johnny Cash (1932–2003), editor Helen Gurley Brown (b 1922), former president Bill Clinton (b 1946), author John Grisham (b 1955), actor Billy Bob Thornton (b 1955)
Famous for electing the first female US senator, Hattie Caraway (1931)

History

Spaniard Hernando de Soto was among the early European explorers to visit here in the mid-16th century, but it was a Frenchman, Henri de Tonti, who founded the first white settlement – Arkansas Post – in 1686. Caddo, Osage and Quapaw Indians had permanent villages here when European explorers arrived, though they were often erroneously called 'Cherokee.' After the 1803 Louisiana Purchase, Arkansas became a US territory, and slaveholding planters moved into the Delta to grow cotton. Poorer immigrants from the Appalachians settled in the Ozark and Ouachita plateaus.

Arkansas was on the edge of the frontier, and problems of lawlessness persisted until the Civil War. Arkansas joined the Confederacy in 1861, but from 1863 the northern part of the state was occupied by Union troops. Reconstruction was difficult, and development did not take off until after 1870, when the expansion of railroads permitted agricultural growth. Oil and gas added to the state's wealth, but the industrial sector did not boom until the 1950s. Racial tension peaked in 1957, when the federal government intervened to enforce the integration of Arkansas schools.

The state has one of the lowest per-capita incomes in the US, with many poor blacks in the Delta area and poor whites in the Ozarks. The KKK is rumored to have a following in some rural areas, but race relations seem quite harmonious in the larger towns, and black and white students mix freely at schools that were once segregated.

LITTLE ROCK

Today, downtown Little Rock is like a sleepy small town with some great big-city characteristics. Recent redevelopment of the downtown and riverfront areas have really spruced things up, bringing a level of sophistication to the staid 19th- and 20th-century architecture. Across the river, North Little Rock is a growing enclave of shops, restaurants stretching alongside the long riverfront park, with trails that are great for walking or jogging.

Established in 1814 as an outpost on the Arkansas River, Little Rock became the capital of the Arkansas territory in 1821 and state capital in 1836, though federal troops controlled the city in the Civil War. Little Rock boomed in the late 19th century as the commercial and administrative center of a growing state, and some fine homes and public buildings went up. Development was sporadic in the 20th century, dogged by political corruption and racial segregation.

The **visitors center** (☎ 877-220-2568; www.littlerock.com; 615 E Capitol; 🕒 8am-6pm) is housed in the 1842 Curran Hall. There's also an **information kiosk** (🕒 Mon-Fri) at the convention center. Check email at the **public library** (☎ 501-918-3000; 100 Rock St; 🕒 9am-6pm Mon-Sat, 1-5pm Sun).

Sights & Activities

The best place to stroll around the city is in the **River Market District**, an area of shops and restaurants anchored on W Markham St/President Clinton Ave and along the banks of the Arkansas River. **Riverfront Park** provides a pleasant, walkable area along the riverbank. At the park's eastern end you might discern the little rock for which the city is named. Nearby, the **River Market** has a good food court and outdoor spaces overlooking the water.

The **Old State House Museum** (☎ 501-324-9685; 300 W Markham St; admission free; 9am-5pm Mon-Sat, 1-5pm Sun) was the state capitol from 1836 to 1911, with impressively restored legislative chambers, period furnishings and displays on Arkansas history.

To be completed in fall 2004, the **William J Clinton Presidential Center** (☎ 501-370-5050; www.clintonpresidentialcenter.com; 1200 E President Clinton Ave) will house the largest archival collection in presidential history, along with a museum, replica of the oval office and plenty of parkland. The project includes the restoration of a railroad bridge into a pedestrian footbridge spanning the river.

Kids will enjoy the **Museum of Discovery** (☎ 501-396-7050; www.amod.org; 500 President Clinton Ave; adult/child $5.50/6; 9am-5pm Mon-Sat, 1-5pm Sun), with interactive exhibits on dinosaurs, science and technology and history.

Perhaps the most compelling attraction in Little Rock is the NPS's **Central High Museum & Visitor Center** (☎ 501-374-1957; 2125 W Daisy L Gatson Bates Dr; admission free; 10am-4pm Mon-Sat, 1-4pm Sun). The center is housed in a restored 1950s-era Mobil gas station opposite the school where, in 1957, nine black teenagers defied the state's policy of racially segregated schooling. Despite a US Supreme Court ruling that Arkansas must integrate its schools, the state militia prevented the black students from enrolling. After about three weeks of court battles and racial tension, President Eisenhower intervened and the students enrolled under armed protection. Newspaper reprints, old photos and TV footage outline the history of segregation and the integration movement, and show what happened to the 'Little Rock Nine' after they enrolled. The school itself, now integrated, is closed to visitors.

Sleeping

Because of government and convention center traffic, it's difficult to find inexpensive hotels right in downtown, though rates can downright plummet midweek when there's no convention in town. All of the usual budget-oriented motels can be found off the interstates.

Holiday Inn (☎ 501-375-2100, 888-465-4329; 600 I-30; r $90-110; P) Next door to the visitors center, this standard business hotel offers a good value for its proximity to downtown and the River Market. It has a bar and mediocre restaurant.

Peabody Little Rock (☎ 501-906-4000, 800-723-2639; www.peabodylittlerock.com; 3 Statehouse Plaza; r from $120; P) This gorgeous hotel, sister to the famous Peabody Hotel in Memphis, TN, recently underwent a $40 million reconstruction. Its 418 rooms offer the height of luxury and run the gamut from standard rooms to deluxe suites. Amenities include in-room babysitters, a five-star restaurant and bar overlooking the river.

ROMANCE IN A BOTTLE

Who says you can't buy love? **Niagara** (www.female-viagra-alternatives.com; per bottle $4.50), touted as the natural female Viagra, is a fizzy Swedish tonic that contains a herbal recipe that reportedly makes women's – and some men's – libidos turn from a trickle into a rush. For years, Little Rock's Lari Williams was the sole American distributor who sold the liquid aphrodisiac out of a Little Rock coffeehouse. Though she no longer owns it and it now has a different name, the **Roasted Bean Coffeehouse** (☎ 501-228-4448; 10700 N Rodney Parham Rd) still stocks the mighty potion. Williams did the national talk show and radio circuit, talking about the benefits of the magical tonic, which is made from South American herbs including damiana, ginseng and schizandra. After drinking the potion, a sexy glowing rush takes over and…well, you get the picture. Order ahead, as mega-shipments of the 6oz bottles of blue can sell out in a few days, if not hours. If you get that tingly feeling, remember that this 'aphrodisiac energy drink' is loaded with caffeine. You can now buy the love juice online through a number of sources.

Capital Hotel (☎ 501-374-7474, 800-766-7666; www.thecapitalhotel.com; 111 W Markham St; r from $150; P) Dating back to 1876, this Victorian-era landmark maintains an elegant but casual air. You get the feeling more laws were made here over dinner at **Ashley's** (dinner $18-28), the hotel's excellent restaurant, than were made down the street at the real capital building. The lobby is worth a look even if you don't stay in one of the 126 charming rooms.

Eating & Drinking

The food court at **River Market** (7am-6pm Mon-Sat) is an economical place for breakfast or lunch. You'll find everything from fresh fruit and pastries, to Greek and Lebanese food, burgers and barbecue.

Sim's Bar-B-Que (☎ 501-372-1148; 109 Main St; meals $4-8; closed Sun) One of the oldest restaurants in town, where locals flock for ribs and pork sandwiches.

Tuesday USA (☎ 501-375-3287; 801 W Markham St; lunch $7-12, dinner $15-20) This is a great spot for upscale Cajun fare, such as a delicious crawfish étouffée.

Juanita's Cafe & Bar (☎ 501-372-1228; 1300 S Main St; meals $8-14) Juanita's serves up authentic Mexican food and live rock and blues music nightly, starting at about 9pm.

Margarita Mama's (☎ 501-975-7687; 300 President Clinton Ave; dishes $6-10) The limited Mexican cantina-style menu is uninspired, but this is a great spot to sip a margarita on the patio, which overlooks the river. Adjoining the restaurant, **Banana Joe's** is a hot dance bar.

Getting There & Around

Little Rock National Airport (☎ 501-372-3439), just east of downtown, is strictly domestic. The **Greyhound station** (☎ 501-372-3007; 118 E Washington St) is over the river, in North Little Rock. Regular buses go to Memphis, TN ($25, 2½ hours); New Orleans ($77, from 12½ hours); Dallas, TX ($54, from 7 hours); and St Louis, MO ($48, 8½ hours). Local buses are run by **CAT** (☎ 501-375-1163), more for commuters than visitors.

Amtrak occupies the old **Union Station** (☎ 501-372-6841; 1400 W Markham St). The *Texas Eagle* runs daily to Dallas, Texas ($53, from 7½ hours); St Louis, Missouri ($56, from 8½ hours); and Chicago, Illinois ($100, from 13 hours).

ARKANSAS RIVER VALLEY

The Arkansas River cuts right across the state from the Oklahoma border to the Mississippi. Outdoor enthusiasts fish, canoe and camp along its quiet lakes and tributaries. Downstream from Little Rock **Pine Bluff** was an early trading post. Arkansas Post, near the confluence with the Mississippi, was set up in 1686 and also became an important river port, yet it was all but abandoned by 1900.

Upstream from Little Rock, I-40 is the fast route, but **US 64** is studded with small-town Americana: **Atkins**, the 'Pickle Capital of Arkansas' (try fried dill pickle); **Russellville**, home of Jimmy Lile Custom Knives, as used in Rambo movies; **Clarksville**, a college town and capital of 'Arkansas Peach Country'; **Ozark**, where the bridge across the river is rated by the Institute of Steel Construction as 'one of the 16 most beautiful long spans in the US'; **Altus**, the center of Arkansas' Germanic wine-growing region; and **Alma**, 'Spinach Capital of the World,' with a giant can of spinach and a statue of Popeye.

In **Van Buren**, have a look at the six-block historic district, a sometime movie set left over from the town's heyday as a river port and trading outpost. Here you can catch the **Ozark Scenic Railway** (☎ 800-687-8600; www.arkmorr.com; Fri/Sat $25/30; Apr-Nov), which offers a scenic three-hour, 70-mile trip over trestles and through tunnels to **Winslow** and back, in antique railroad passenger cars.

Across the river, **Fort Smith** was set up in 1817 and became a base for anti-Indian operations and the last outpost of law and order on the Oklahoma frontier. Get information at **Fort Smith Visitors Center** (☎ 501-783-8888; 2 North B St; 8am-5pm Mon-Fri, 9am-4pm Sat, noon-4pm Sun), a century-old brothel. The **Fort Smith National Historic Site** (☎ 479-783-8888; at 3rd & Rogers Sts) includes the courtroom, jail and gallows used by Judge Isaac C Parker, 'the hanging judge,' from 1875 to 1896.

SOUTHWESTERN ARKANSAS

Hot Springs

Hot Springs National Park, 55 miles southwest of Little Rock, is almost surrounded by the city of Hot Springs. The thermal waters spout a million gallons of 143-degree water daily from 47 natural springs. A few people still come for the waters, which you can bathe in at spas or taste from fountains around town, but these days there's more interest in the Victorian architecture, the horse racing at Oaklawn and scenes from Bill Clinton's boyhood. The elaborate old bathhouses line up on Bathhouse Row, behind shady magnolias on the east side of Central Ave. Opposite is a row of restored 19th-century commercial buildings.

For city information and a map of Clinton-related sites, go to the **Convention & Visitors Bureau** (☎ 501-321-2277, 800-543-2284; www.hotsprings.org; 134 Convention Boulevard; 8am-5pm Mon-Fri). On Bathhouse Row, the **NPS visitors center** (☎ 501-624-3383; 369 Central Ave; 9am-5pm), in the 1915 Fordyce bathhouse, has a free short film about the park history as a Native American free-trade zone, a quack-cure capital, and its early 20th-century zenith imitating a European spa. The Gatsby-era marble and mosaic, hydrotherapy apparatus and chrome-plated plumbing can be viewed on a free tour.

Resort hotels and spas have private bathhouses, or you can visit the **Buckstaff Bathhouse** (☎ 501-623-2308; www.buckstaffbaths.com; thermal bath/massage $18/20; closed Sun), just south of the Fordyce, where a thermal bath and Swedish massage are on offer. A promenade runs around the hillside behind Bathhouse Row, where some springs survive in a more or less natural state. A network of trails covers **Hot Springs Mountain**, and a scenic drive goes to the top, where the 216ft **Hot Springs Mountain Tower** (☎ 501-623-6025; admission $6; 9am-6pm) affords great views of the surrounding mountains, which are all covered with dogwood, hickory, oak and pine – lovely in the spring and fall. **National Park Duck Tours** (☎ 501-321-2911; 418 Central Ave; adult/child $12/7) offers boat tours and the **Belle of Hot Springs** (☎ 501-525-4438; www.belleriverboat.com; 5200 Central Ave; tours $12-30) does cruises on Lake Hamilton.

EATING & SLEEPING

The cheap motels are on the highways around town. Ask at the visitors center for a list of lakeside rental properties and area B&Bs.

Alpine Inn (☎ 501-624-9164; 741 Park Ave/Hwy 7 N; r from $35; P) This friendly motel is a great value and less than a mile to Bathhouse Row. The 15 tidy rooms have coffeemakers and hairdryers and some have kitchenettes.

Arlington Resort Hotel & Spa (☎ 501-623-7771, 800-643-1502; www.arlingtonhotel.com; 239 Central Ave; r queen/king $90/122, ste $170-300; P) This imposing historic hotel at the top end of Bathhouse Row has 481 rooms, ranging from small and cramped to snazzier quarters like the Al Capone Suite. In addition to the grand lobby, the hotel has its own bathhouse, spa, three restaurants and two pools.

Gulpha Gorge Campground (☎ 501-624-3383; campsites $12) The NPS's attractive Gulpha Gorge campground, 2 miles northeast of downtown off Hwy 70B, has 43 campsites (no showers, hookups or reservations).

There are lots of places to grab a bite along the Central Ave tourist strip.

Granny's Kitchen (☎ 501-624-6183; 362 Central Ave; meals $5-10) Where you'll find good down-home breakfast, lunch or dinner.

Faded Rose (☎ 501-624-3200; 210 Central Ave; meals $8-12) Serves up inexpensive New Orleans cuisine.

There's a good choice further south on Central Ave.

Brick House Grill (☎ 501-321-2926; 801 Central Ave; meals $10-15) Has well-prepared seafood, steaks and chicken dishes.

McClard's (☎ 501-624-9586; 505 Albert Pike; meals $6-9) Bill Clinton's favorite boyhood barbecue was southwest of the center, where you can fill up on sweet, succulent ribs, pork, beef and slaw.

Around Hot Springs

The **Ouachita National Forest** (☎ 501-321-5202) is a wild and pretty area studded with artificial lakes and popular for hunting, fishing and boating. **Petit Jean State Park** (☎ 501-727-5441), a detour east off Rte 7, has particularly attractive scenery, walking trails, campgrounds, and rustic lodges built by the Civilian Conservation Corps (CCC).

I-30 makes a pretty straight run from Little Rock to the Texarkana and the Texas border. Clinton buffs might stop at **Hope**, where the ex-pres spent his first seven years. Check the **Hope Visitor Center & Museum** (☎ 870-722-2580, 800-233-4673; at S Main & Division Sts).

OZARK MOUNTAINS

The Ozarks still bring to mind the Al Capp comic strip Li'l Abner, which depicts a ramshackle town where the men were too lazy to work and the women were desperate enough to chase them. This is where the sitcom *Beverly Hillbillies* hailed from before the characters became oil barons in California. Although locals tend to milk the hillbilly angle, the region is also blessed with gorgeous scenery, clear river waters and good outdoor sports outfitters. The best way to explore the region is by driving the back roads. For information or driving tours of the region call ☎ 800-544-6867 or search online at www.ozarkmountainregion.org.

Mountain View

Heading north from Little Rock, detour east of US 65 to this perfectly ordinary (read: wacky) Ozark town, known for its tradition of informal weekend music-making at Courthouse Sq. Creeping commercialism is taking its toll, as the **chamber of commerce** (☎ 870-269-8068; 107 N Peabody Ave; 9am-5pm Mon-Fri, 10am-4pm Sat, 12:30-3pm Sun) promotes the place as the 'Folk Music Capital of the World.' **Cash's White River Hoe-Down** (☎ 870-269-8042) is a heavily hyped country music and comedy show. A calendar of annual events also pulls in the punters, from the **Folk Festival** (April) and **Auto Show** (April) to the **Bean Fest** (October) and **Ozark Christmas** (December). These festivals are organized by the **Ozark Folk Center** (www.ozarkfolkcenter.com).

The **Ozark Folk Center State Park** (☎ 870-269-3851, 800-264-3655), just north of town, is a sanitized but sincere attempt to preserve the crafts, traditions and music of the Ozarks. Demonstrations cover basket weaving, gunsmithing, country cooking and quilting. The theater features traditional mountain music, square dancing, clogging and jigs. About 10 miles north of town, **Blanchard Springs Recreation Area** (☎ 870-757-2211) has a cave system with spectacular formations.

There's a very nice **campground** ($10) at Blanchard Springs, with an inviting swimming hole. The usual chain motels can be found along the highway, with rates starting at $40.

Mountain View Motel (☎ 870-269-3209; E Main St; r $45; P) is a low-key and basic motel that offers clean rooms and a good location just a couple of blocks from the town square.

Dry Creek Lodge (☎ 870-269-3871, 800-264-3655; 382 Spur, off Hwy 5 N; r $60-80; P), at the Ozark Folk Center, is where every room has two double beds and sliding glass doors opening onto the forest. The lodge's **Iron Skillet Restaurant** (meals $6-12) serves up tasty Southern breakfasts, lunches and dinners.

The **Inn at Mountain View** (☎ 870-269-4200; www.innatmountainview.com; 307 W Washington St; s/d $63/78; P), an 1886 B&B near the town square, has 12 charming rooms, old-fashioned rockers on the porch and friendly owners who serve up a delicious seven-course breakfast.

Eureka Springs

Near the northwest corner of the state, Eureka Springs could easily be mistaken for an old mining village, but tourists are the only things ever mined here. It's pretty enough, with Victorian buildings lining crooked streets in a steep valley, but the combination of commercialized country

NOT A DAM IN SIGHT

Although it mightn't look like the Colorado or the Columbia, the Buffalo National River sure is purty. Administered by the NPS, the river flows beneath dramatic bluffs through unspoiled Ozark forest.

Evidence of human occupation dates back some 10,000 years to the Archaic Indians, but this wild and naturally bountiful area kept even modern Ozarks settlers self-sufficient and isolated. They developed a distinct dialect, along with unique craftsmanship and musical traits that continue today. Thanks to its National River designation in 1972, the Buffalo is one of the few remaining unpolluted, free-flowing rivers in the country. Starting as a trickle in the Boston Mountains, the river travels 150 miles along an ancient riverbed until pouring into the White River. Magnificent limestone bluffs and pristine wilderness make this a great spot for camping and hiking.

The best way to see the park is by canoe or raft. Outfitters such as **Wild Bill's** (☎ 800-554-8657; www.ozark-float.com) and **Buffalo Outdoor Center** (☎ 800-221-5514; www.buffaloriver.com) can arrange canoes or rafting trips for around $40 per person. They can also arrange hiking tours, fishing trips and horseback riding.

The **Buffalo National River** (☎ 870-741-5443; www.nps.gov/buff) has three designated wilderness areas, the most accessible is through the **Tyler Bend visitors center** (☎ 870-439-2502; 8am-5pm Sep-Jun), 11 miles north of Marshall on I-65. Other access points are at **Pruitt** (☎ 870-446-5373), 5 miles north of Jasper on Hwy 7, and **Buffalo Point** (☎ 870-449-4311), 17 miles south of Yellville Hwy 14.

music, honeymoon romance and Bible-themed attractions, including a 70ft Christ of the Ozarks statue, sends things a little over the top.

The **visitors center** (☎ 501-253-8737; www.eurekaspringschmber.com; 137 W Van Buren/Hwy 62) has information about lodging, tours and attractions. The best things to do are walk the streets, shop for tacky souvenirs and ride on the old **ES & NA Railway** (☎ 501-253-9623; www.esnarailway.com; 299 N Main St; adult $9; hourly 10am-4pm Apr-Oct), which puffs through the hills on an hour-long tour. Do the mineral-spring thing at the **Palace Hotel & Bathhouse** (☎ 479-253-7474; 135 Spring St; mineral bath $15; 8am-5pm).

Eureka Tradewinds (☎ 479-253-9774, 800-242-1615; www.eurekatradewinds.com; 141 W Van Buren; r from $50; P), right next to the visitors center, is a funky, tidy motel with a variety of theme rooms decorated in everything from tiki decor to 1950s flair. Spend an afternoon on the outdoor pool and sundeck.

Eureka Matterhorn Towers (☎ 479-253-9602, 800-426-0838; www.eurekamatterhorn.com; 130 W Van Buren; d from $60; P) has nice rooms and great rates. It is one of the best values in the Ozarks. Most rooms have two double beds, or a king size bed and Jacuzzi tub. The outdoor pool is refreshing and clean.

Eureka Springs has a couple of fabulous historic hotels with full-service spas, including the **Crescent Hotel** (☎ 479-253-9766, 800-342-9766; www.crescenthotel.com; 75 Prospect St; r from $120, ste from $180) and the **Basin Park Hotel** (☎ 479-253-7837, 800-643-4972; www.basinpark.com; 12 Spring St; r from $100, ste from $170).

Mud Street Cafe (☎ 479-253-6732; 22G S Main St; dishes $6-12; 8am-3pm Thu-Tue) is a great place to go for hearty breakfasts and good lunches of quiche and sandwiches. Excellent coffee and desserts, too.

Local Flavor Café (☎ 479-253-9522; 71 S Main St; dishes $7-16) is open every day for lunch and dinner, and Sundays for brunch. This fun spot has excellent indoor and outdoor seating. At lunch, get healthy sandwiches and salads, and at dinner taste fresh fish and meat dishes.

Fayetteville

One of Arkansas' oldest towns, dating from the 1820s, Fayetteville is home to the University of Arkansas (UA). Bill Clinton taught constitutional law at UA from 1973 to 1976, and he and Hillary were hitched here in 1975. The campus is moderately attractive, and there's a posh Victorian residential district. The **Arkansas Air Museum** (☎ 501-521-4947; 4290 South School St; admission $2; 11am-4:30pm), 5 miles south of town, specializes in pre-WWII aircraft, especially racing and aerobatic biplanes.

ARKANSAS DELTA

The Great River Rd follows the west bank of the Mississippi River through the Arkansas Delta in eastern Arkansas. With cotton and rice fields and juke joints, the Arkansas Delta is less interesting than the Mississippi side. In **Helena**, 120 miles from Little Rock on Hwy 49, the **Delta Cultural Center** (☎ 870-338-4350; www.deltaculturalcenter.com; 141 Cherry St; admission free; 9am-5pm Tue-Sat) has a comprehensive exhibit about the geography and history of the Delta.

TENNESSEE

'Far as I'm concerned, we got it all in *Tinnessay*,' says a man pumping gas at a highway gas station near Memphis. 'We got beer, fried chicken, football and Jesus. What more do ya need?' OK, so maybe you need more than the above, but the guy's point is that Tennessee has it all, and whatever 'it all' means, there's a good chance that he's right. This beautiful state – its geography as diverse as its culture – can be geographically and psychologically divided into three regions: the Great Smoky Mountains in the east, the central plateau and Middle Tennessee around Nashville, and the Mississippi bottomlands in the west around Memphis. These regions embody the musical heritage of the state, where the mountain music from the East became the country music of the West and fused with the blues of the Mississippi Delta. It's also the place where a white boy adapted black rhythms and became the King of Rock & Roll. Elvis aside, the state that gave birth to so many American musicians seems perpetually filled with music – songs so sorrowful your eyes tear, beats so original you feel rumbling in your soul. Everywhere you go, whether deep in the hills or on the streets of Nashville, you'll feel the taste of music on your lips like sweet lickable nectar.

Welcome centers at the state borders are run by the Tennessee **Department of Tourist**

TENNESSEE FACTS

Nickname Volunteer State
Population 5,797,289 (16th)
Area 41,217 sq miles (36th)
Admitted to Union June 1, 1796 (16th); seceded 1861; readmitted 1866
Capital city Nashville (population 570,000)
Other cities Memphis (650,000), Knoxville (174,000), Chattanooga (156,000)
Birthplace of frontiersman Davy Crockett (1786–1836), guitarist Chet Atkins (1924–2001), rockabilly Carl Perkins (1932–98), singer Tina Turner (b 1939), soul diva Aretha Franklin (b 1942), singer Dolly Parton (b 1946), former vice president Al Gore (b 1948)
Famous for Tennessee walking horses, the Tennessee Waltz, country music, rock 'n' roll

Development (☎ 615-741-2159, 800-462-8366; www.tnvacation.com; 320 6th Ave N, Nashville, TN 37243).

History

European encroachment on this Cherokee territory began when de Soto wandered through in 1540. Though the British crown colony of Carolina nominally extended to the Mississippi, the French were actively trading on the rivers from the late 17th century. After the French and Indian War, Virginian pioneers soon established a settlement west of the Appalachians, creating their own treaty of purchase with the Cherokee. They drafted a written constitution that asserted their independence from British Carolina and were soon active participants in the American Revolution. After independence, Tennessee alternated between North Carolina and the US government, then acquired territorial status and eventually statehood.

Treaties in 1818 displaced the Chickasaw from west Tennessee, and President Andrew Jackson (himself an early Tennessee settler) expelled the Indians to Oklahoma. While immigrants from Scotland, Ireland and the Eastern states established small farms in east Tennessee, the west was settled by planters and the state became increasingly divided between the pro-slavery west and abolitionist east. Tennessee was the last state to secede in the Civil War.

Tennessee abolished slavery by popular vote in 1865 (the only state to do so without Federal intervention), though reaction to emancipation was often hostile. The KKK became influential in 'protecting whites' and disenfranchising the state's blacks by restrictive poll-tax laws.

In the 20th century industries like chemicals, textiles and metal products overtook agriculture, moving the majority of the population to urban areas. Tennessee still produces cotton and dairy products and is one of the top tobacco-producing states but tourism, especially in Nashville and Memphis, bolsters the state's income.

MEMPHIS

Named for the ancient Egyptian capital on the Nile, Memphis on the Mississippi is best known as the capital of Elvis Presley idolatry and a musical heritage going back to the birth of the blues. Gutsy guitar riffs and heart-numbing blues belt out and travel like electricity through the streets.

A landmark of the civil rights struggle where Martin Luther King Jr was martyred in 1968, Memphis today has moved a long way from the days imbedded with racial tension. Black and whites mix to create a certain soulful grittiness borne from its history of cotton, riverboats and music.

History

Mounds on the bluffs on Mississippi River's eastern shore were built by a Mississippian civilization more than a thousand years ago. The French established Fort Assumption on the bluffs in 1739 to protect their river trade. After the US took control, a treaty in 1818 edged the Chickasaw nation out of western Tennessee, and Andrew Jackson helped found the settlement of Memphis. The city was incorporated in 1826 and prospered on the expanding cotton trade of the Mississippi Delta.

Early in the Civil War a Union fleet defeated the Confederates and occupied the city, but postwar collapse of the cotton trade was far more devastating. A yellow-fever epidemic in 1878 claimed more than 5000 lives and many white residents abandoned the city. Memphis declared bankruptcy and its city charter was revoked until 1893. The black community revived the town. A former slave named Robert Church became a prominent landowner, civic leader and millionaire, and by the

1920s Beale St was the hub of social, civic and business activity, but it was equally well known as a place of gambling, drinking and prostitution.

WC Handy's 'Beale Street Blues' established Memphis as an early center of blues music, and in the 1950s local recording company Sun Records cut tracks for blues, soul, R & B and rockabilly artists, both white and black.

The old downtown was largely abandoned by the 1970s, and Beale St was nearly demolished to make way for 'redevelopment.' Instead, a restoration program revived the entertainment district.

Orientation

Downtown Memphis runs along the east bank of the Mississippi, with Riverside Dr and a promenade parallel to the river. The principal tourist district is a bit inland, roughly the area bounded by Union Ave and Beale St, and 2nd and 4th Sts. Further east, Union Ave and Overton Sq have shops, bars and restaurants. Graceland is 3 miles south of town on US 51, also called 'Elvis Presley Blvd.'

Information

INTERNET ACCESS

Café Francisco (901-578-8002; 400 N Main St; 25¢ per min; 7am-10pm Mon-Fri, 8am-10pm Sat, 8am-6pm Sun) In the Pinch district, this café has wireless Internet and terminals for customer use.

Public library (3030 Poplar Ave; 9am-9pm Mon-Thu, 9am-6pm Fri & Sat, 1-5pm Sun)

MEDIA

Commercial Appeal (www.gomemphis.com) Daily newspaper.

Memphis Flyer (www.memphisflyer.com) Pick up the free weekly, which comes out on Thursday and is chock-full of entertainment listings.

Triangle Journal News (www.memphistrianglejournal.com) A monthly, free resource for the gay community.

MEDICAL SERVICES

St Jude's Research Hospital (901-495-3306; 332 N Lauderdale)

MONEY

ATMs are widely available around town. If you need to go into a bank, try **First Tennessee Bank** (888-382-6654; 165 Madison Ave; 8am-4pm Mon-Fri, 10am-2pm Sat).

POST

Main post office (555 South 3rd St) There's another outlet at 1 N Front St.

TOURIST OFFICES

Tennessee State Visitor Center (901-543-5333, 888-633-9099; 119 Riverside Dr; 9am-5pm) Well stocked with brochures for the whole state. The helpful staff can assist you to find hotel deals in Memphis.

Dangers & Annoyances

Memphis is a friendly city but has its share of crime. Harmless but sometimes aggressive panhandlers hang around Beale St, but a polite firm no will send them on their way. Stick to populated areas, or take cabs if you stray far at night.

Sights & Activities

BEALE STREET

The strip from 2nd to 4th Sts is filled with clubs, restaurants, souvenir shops and neon signs – a veritable theme park of the blues – though only one of the stores is an original from Beale St's heyday in the early 1900s. It's easy and safe to walk around.

The **Orpheum Theater** (p548), at Main St, is restored to its 1928 glory, and an Elvis statue stands at the corner of 2nd Ave in front of a nightclub and restaurant called 'Elvis Presley's.' In front of the Orpheum, the **Walk of Fame** features musical notes embedded in the sidewalk with the names of well-known blues artists.

The Beale St substation **Police Museum** (901-579-0887; 158 Beale St; admission free; 8am-11pm) exhibits assorted criminalia, and the original **A Schwab's** (907-523-9782; 163 Beale St; admission free; 9am-5pm Mon-Sat) dry-goods store has three floors of voodoo powders, 99-cent neckties, clerical collars and a big selection of hats. Between 3rd and 4th Sts, a statue of songwriter and composer WC Handy overlooks a park and amphitheater; Handy's old **home** is nearby on 4th St.

The **New Daisy Theater** (p549) has art deco backdrops depicting the district's honky-tonk heyday, and continues to hold concerts. The little-used **Old Daisy Theater** stands forlornly across the road.

The Smithsonian's **Rock 'n' Soul Museum** (901-543-0800; www.memphisrocknsoul.org; 145 Lt George W Lee Ave; adult/child $8.50/5; 10am-6pm), examines the social and cultural history that produced the music of the Mississippi Delta.

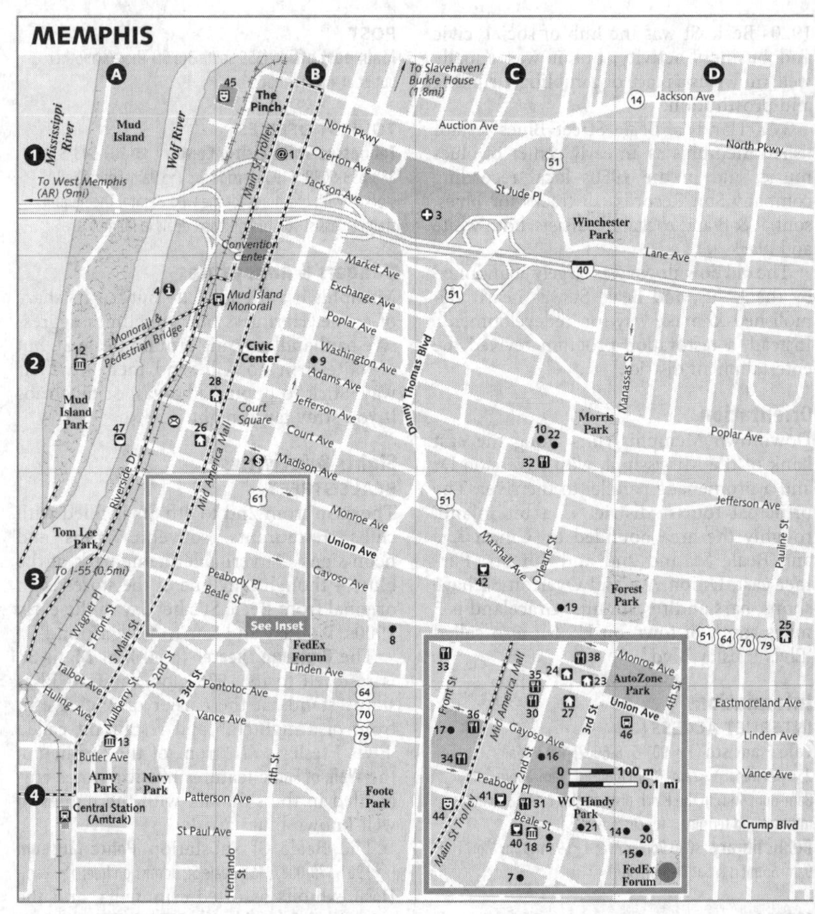

Next door (at the same address), the giant **Gibson Beale Street Showcase** (☎ 800-444-4766; admission $10; tours 1pm Sun-Wed, 11am, noon, 1pm & 2pm Thu-Sat) gives way-cool 30-minute tours of its guitar factory, where solid blocks of wood are transformed into legendary Gibson guitars.

The two-story Federal-style **Hunt-Phelan Home** (☎ 901-344-3166; 533 Beale St; admission $10; closed Sun) was headquarters for Ulysses S Grant when the city was occupied by Union forces in 1862.

NATIONAL CIVIL RIGHTS MUSEUM

Housed in the Lorraine Motel, where the Reverend Dr Martin Luther King Jr was fatally shot on April 4, 1968, is the **National Civil Rights Museum** (☎ 901-521-9699; www.civilrightsmuseum.org; 450 Mulberry St; adult/child $8.50/6.50; 9am-5pm Wed-Sat, 1-5pm Sun). Five blocks south of Beale St, this museum brings to light one of the most significant moments in modern American history. The turquoise exterior of the 1950s motel remains much as it was at the time of King's assassination. Documentary photos and audio displays chronicle key events in civil rights history.

MUD ISLAND PARK

A monorail and elevated walkway cross the Wolf River to **Mud Island Park** (☎ 901-576-7241; admission $8; 10am-8pm Jun-Sep, 10am-5pm Tue-Sat Oct-May), where there's a model of the lower Mississippi River and the Gulf, and various

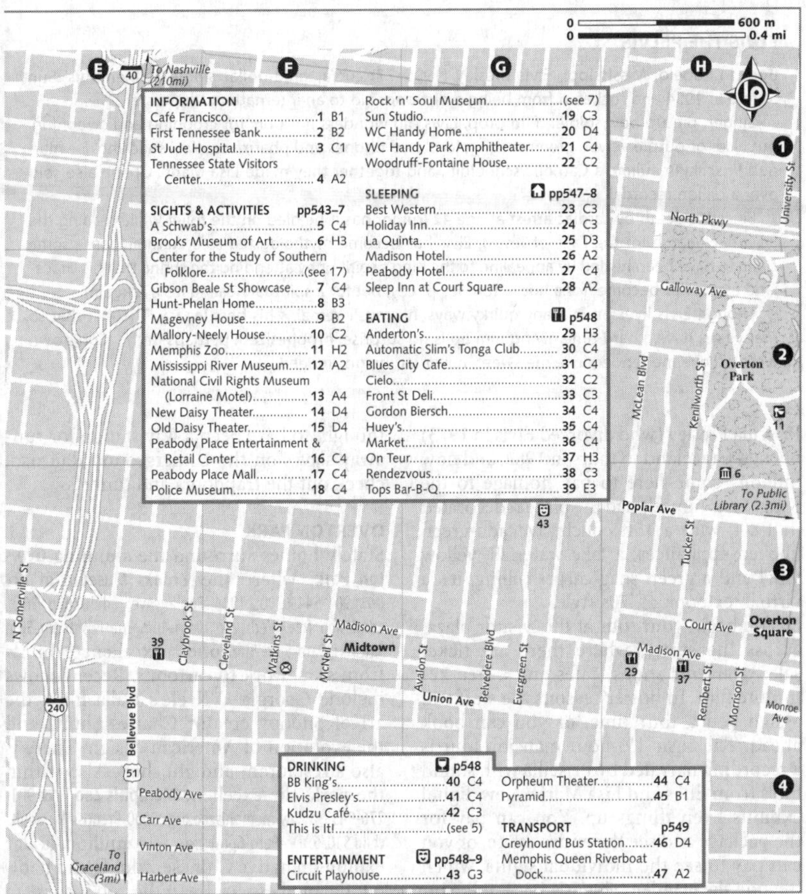

exhibits in the **Mississippi River Museum** (☎ 901-576-7230; 125 Front St; adult/child $8/5; 🕒 10am-8pm Jun-Sep, 10am-5pm Tue-Sat Oct-May).

SUN STUDIO

Any serious Elvis or country-music fan will want to pay homage to **Sun Studio** (☎ 901-521-0664, 800-441-6249; www.sunstudio.com; 706 Union Ave; admission $9.50; 🕒 10am-6pm). Starting in the early 1950s, Sun's Sam Phillips gave birth to rock 'n' roll by recording blues artists like Howlin' Wolf, BB King and Ike Turner, followed by the rockabilly dynasty of Jerry Lee Lewis, Carl Perkins, Johnny Cash, Roy Orbison and, of course, Elvis Presley (who started here in 1955). Sun Records moved on in 1959, but the studio reopened in 1987, and Ringo Starr, U2, Sheryl Crow and Matchbox 20 have all come here to record. Today the studio offers a 30-minute narrated visit to a tiny room, with warped tiles and a chance to hear the original tapes of historic recording sessions.

GRACELAND

In the spring of 1957, at age 22, Elvis spent $100,000 on this house, part of the 500-acre farm named **Graceland** (☎ 901-332-3322, 800-238-2000; www.elvis.com; Elvis Presley Blvd (US 51); adult/child all attractions $25/12; 🕒 grounds 9am-5pm Mon-Sat & 10am-4pm Sun Mar-Oct, 10am-4pm Mon, Wed-Sun Nov-Mar, mansion closed Tue Nov-Mar). He lived here until his death in 1977, and he's buried next to the swimming pool with his closest relatives.

ELVIS THE PELVIS

Born in Tupelo, Mississippi, Elvis Presley (1935–77) cut a three-dollar single at Memphis' Sun Studio in 1954 and rocketed from being a dirt-poor kid to an international superstar.

Singer, pin-up boy, soldier, film prop, Elvis did wonders not only for crooning and swooning, but also for purple velvet, green shag, gold-plated phones and pharmaceutical snacking. He married Priscilla Beaulieu, a Catholic schoolgirl, and together they made Lisa Marie. Oh, he also sold over a billion records.

Since his death by cardiac arrest at age 42 (rumor has it he died on the toilet while reading the Scientific Search for the Face of Jesus), Elvis has become mythologized as a cultural icon – some claim to have been healed by appealing to the King's spirit or by attending the shrine that his Graceland estate has become (for a house tour it's pricey, but for a spiritual healing it's a bargain).

Though Elvis lives on in many quirky ways, his music remains his best legacy. The fact that so many fans have a hard time giving him up is no surprise, prophesized, perhaps in the King's own words: 'Love me tender, love me sweet, never let me go.' Indeed.

Priscilla Presley (who divorced Elvis in 1973) opened Graceland to tours in 1982, and now millions come here to pay homage to the King. Elvis himself had the place redecorated in 1974, with a 15ft couch, avocado-green kitchen appliances, a fake waterfall, yellow vinyl and a green shag-carpet ceiling; it's a virtual textbook of '70s style.

You begin your tour at the 'visitor plaza' across the street, where there are ticket sales, souvenir shops, cafés and a free 22-minute film. In busier seasons the staff will assign you a tour time, or you can book ahead. The basic 1½-hour mansion tour is a recording narrated by Priscilla with sound bites from Elvis and Lisa Marie. New digital exhibits liven things up. You can pay for the package and see the entire estate, or you can pay to see the individual sights, which include the **mansion** (adult/child $16/6), the 'Sincerely Elvis' **memorabilia collection** (adult/child $5/2.50), the **car museum** (adult/child $7/3) and an **aircraft collection** (adult/child $6/3).

HISTORIC HOUSES

In the 'Victorian Village' district on Adams Ave, east of downtown, two rather grand houses are open for public tours: the 1870 **Woodruff-Fontaine House** (☎ 901-526-1469; 680 Adams Ave; admission $5; 🕑 10am-4pm Wed-Sat, 1-4pm Sun) and the 1852 **Mallory-Neely House** (☎ 901-523-1484; 652 Adams Ave; admission $5; 🕑 10am-4pm Tue-Sat, 1-4pm Sun). The smaller **Magevney House** (☎ 901-526-4464; 198 Adams Ave; admission free) reflects the lifestyle of a 19th-century Irish immigrant family.

The **Slavehaven/Burkle House** (☎ 901-527-3427; 826 N 2nd St; adult/child $6/4; 🕑 10am-4pm Wed-Sun) is thought to have been a way station for runaway slaves on the Underground Railroad; check out the trapdoors and tunnels.

OVERTON PARK

Stately homes surround the stunning **Overton Park**, where the **Brooks Museum of Art** (☎ 901-544-6200; 1934 Poplar Ave; adult/child $6/2, admission free Wed; 🕑 10am-4pm Tue-Fri, 10am-5pm Sat, 11:30am-5pm Sun) offers excellent exhibits from stonework to cartoons. Recent shows include Georgia O'Keefe's Calla lilies, the art of Snoopy creator Charles Shultz and the evolution of American design. There is also a restaurant and gift shop. Also within the park, the excellent **Memphis Zoo** (☎ 901-276-9453; www.memphiszoo.org; 2000 Prentiss Pl; adult/child $10/6; 🕑 9am-6pm) has a 16-million-dollar exhibit on native Chinese wildlife and habitat, devoted especially to the zoo's stars, Ya Ya and Le Le, two giant pandas who arrived from Beijing, China in 2003.

MUSEUMS

The **Pink Palace Museum & Planetarium** (☎ 901-320-6362; www.memphismuseums.org; 3050 Central Ave; adult/child $8/4.50; 🕑 9am-4pm Mon-Thu, 9am-9pm Fri & Sat, noon-6pm Sun), east of town off US 72, was built here in 1923 as a residence for Piggly Wiggly founder Clarence Saunders and reopened in 1996 as a natural- and cultural-history museum. It mixes fossils, Civil War exhibits, restored Works Projects Administration (WPA) murals and an exact replica of the original Piggly Wiggly, the world's first self-service grocery store, which opened in 1916. There is also a planetarium and Imax theater; tickets sold separately.

Also east of town, the **Dixon Gallery** (☎ 901-761-5250; 4339 Park Ave; adult/child $5/free; 10am-4pm Tue-Fri, 10am-5pm Sat, 1-5pm Sun) houses a very impressive collection of impressionist as well as post-impressionist paintings, including works by Monet, Degas, Renoir and Cézanne.

The **Center for the Study of Southern Folklore** (☎ 901-525-3655; www.southernfolklore.com; 119 S Main St; 11am-5pm Mon-Fri, noon-4pm Sat) in Pembroke Sq at Peabody Place, has a restaurant, exhibits arts and crafts and holds free music performances, local tours and film screenings.

Tours

Memphis Queen (☎ 901-527-5694, 800-221-6197; www.memphisqueen.com; Riverside Dr at Monroe Ave; adult/child sightseeing cruise $13/9.50, music cruise with/without buffet $32/18) Riverboat rides aboard the Memphis Queen depart from the foot of Monroe Ave at Riverside Dr. Tour times fluctuate monthly so call ahead.

Blues City Tours (☎ 901-522-9229; 325 Union Ave; adult from $20) Offers a wide variety of bus tours; call ahead for times.

Horse-drawn carriage (rides 30min/2 persons around $35) Departs from Beale St or outside the Peabody Hotel.

Sleeping

If you want to save on accommodations, you'll find cheaper highway-side motels across the river in West Memphis, Arkansas, where chain places cluster at I-40, exit 279. Total tax on accommodations in Memphis is a stiff 15%.

La Quinta (☎ 901-526-1050, 800-531-5900; 42 S Camilla St; s/d $62/68; P) This is a clean, friendly option just 0.5 miles east of downtown. A complimentary continental breakfast is included.

Best Western (☎ 901-527-4100, 800-380-3236; 164 Union Ave; r $70-100; P $5) Though slightly dated and run-down, this is a great choice for its location, three blocks from Beale St. Rooms have hair dryers and coffeemakers. The hotel has a great lobby and fitness center.

Sleep Inn at Court Sq (☎ 901-522-9700; 40 N Front St; s/d $80/90; P) This is about the cheapest you'll get for the location, near the river and just six blocks from Beale St.

Holiday Inn (☎ 901-525-5491, 888-300-5491; www.hisdowntownmemphis.com; 160 Union Ave; r from $140; P $6) Next door to the Best Western and across the street from the Peabody, this hotel has generous updated rooms. Added bonuses include a fitness center and restaurant and bar.

Madison Hotel (☎ 901-333-1200; www.madisonhotelmemphis.com; 79 Madison Ave; r from $190; P) If you're looking for a complete treat, check in to this swanky, ultramodern hotel that's chock full of amenities. The rooftop garden is one of the best places in town to watch a sunset. Rooms have nice touches, like Italian linens and whirlpool tubs. Even if you don't stay here, stop in for a cocktail at Madison's artsy chic bar.

Heartbreak Hotel (☎ 901-332-1000, 877-777-0606; www.heartbreakhotel.net; 3677 Elvis Presley Blvd; queen/king ste $90/109; P) OK, so it's not at the end of Lonely St but the Heartbreak Hotel, behind Graceland's parking lot, is all about Elvis. The King's movies play in every room. Other amenities include a heart-shaped outdoor pool, a refrigerator and microwave in every room and free transportation to Beale St at night.

THE AUTHOR'S CHOICE

Peabody Hotel (☎ 901-529-4000, 800-732-2639; www.peabodymemphis.com; 149 Union Ave; r from $260; P self/valet $12/17) This grand old dame has been Memphis' premiere hotel since the 1930s. With 468 rooms, the historic hotel has a variety of rooms at many prices. It's a social center in Memphis, with a spa, restaurant and the groovy Capriccio Lounge. It also boasts its own quirky (quacky?) tradition: at 11am sharp, the hotel's ducks file from the elevator across the red-carpeted lobby to cavort in the fountain until 5pm, when they return to their penthouse.

REVEREND GREEN'S GOSPEL

Some of Memphis' most soulful music isn't heard in the Beale St clubs, but rather at the Full Gospel Tabernacle presided over by '70s recording star Al Green. Reverend Green's powerful oratory is backed by electric guitar and a formidable choir. Visitors are welcome to attend the 2½-hour service. The **church** (☎ 901-396-9192; 787 Hale Rd; service 11am Sun) is in Whitehaven, four traffic lights south of Graceland off Elvis Presley Blvd.

KOA Kampground (☎ 901-396-7125; 3691 Elvis Presley Blvd; campsites from $21, cabins $36) Practically across the street from Graceland KOA has campsites (hookups extra) and cabins.

TO Fuller state park (☎ 901-543-7581; campsites $13) South of town off Hwy 61, TO Fuller state park has 53 campsites on a remote bluff.

Eating

Memphis has a great array of restaurants, with the regional focus on barbecue, specifically chopped pork shoulder served in a sandwich, or dry-rubbed ribs. Most restaurants have smoking and nonsmoking sections.

Market (☎ 900-543-8400; 119 S Main St; meals $2-7) In the Peabody Place Mall on Main St, this grocery store and deli is a healthy stop for delicious salads, sandwiches and fresh juices.

Front St Deli (☎ 901-522-8945; 77 S Front St; sandwiches $4-8; 🕑 9am-5pm Mon-Fri) This excellent deli, featured in the movie *The Firm*, makes great sandwiches.

Huey's (☎ 901-527-2700; 77 S 2nd St; meals $5-7) A long-time city favorite for having the best burger in town, Huey's is a good bet for casual pub food, right on the edge of the Beale St action.

Blues City Cafe (☎ 901-526-1724; 138 Beale St; meals $8-13) For lunch or dinner on the strip and with live music Tuesday to Sunday, this is a great choice for chowing on some good old Southern fare while listening to local bands.

Rendezvous (☎ 901-523-2746; 53 S 2nd St; meals $10-22; 🕑 dinner Tue-Sat, lunch Fri & Sat) Tucked in an alleyway off Union Ave, Rendezvous sells five tons of barbecue ribs weekly. The speciality is the dry ribs, served with friendly service in an old Memphis atmosphere.

Automatic Slim's Tonga Club (☎ 901-525-7948; 83 S 2nd St; lunch $8-14, dinner $15-25; 🕑 Mon-Sat) In an artsy atmosphere, this bistro has slow-roasted yellowfin tuna, jerk duck and a killer coconut shrimp with mango sauce.

Gordon Biersch (☎ 901-543-3330; 145 S Main St; meals $9-23) With a good streetside patio and lively bar scene, this handsome brewery-slash-bar has hearty food and sports TV.

Cielo (☎ 901-524-1886; 679 Adams Ave; meals $15-25) A long-time local favorite where creative, international cuisine is served in a Victorian manor house. Try the specials, which are usually spectacular.

MIDTOWN

Tops Bar-B-Q (☎ 901-725-7527; 1286 Union Ave) With many locations, including this one in Midtown, Tops has been a Memphis favorite for cheap barbecue since 1952.

On Teur (☎ 901-725-6059 2015; Madison Ave; dishes $10-20) An old favorite for veggie dishes and yummy munchies like halibut burgers and pecan-smoked sausages. You can sit on the patio or inside. You can also bring your own wine for a small corkage fee. On Teur also serves up a delicious brunch on weekends.

Anderton's (☎ 901-726-4010; 1901 Madison Ave; dinner $15-25; 🕑 closed Sat lunch & Sun) A Memphis institution since 1945, Anderton's serves choice steaks and succulent lobster and crab.

Entertainment

Most Memphis restaurants serve up food with a musical accompaniment, so it's easy to turn a meal into a party. For fun-lovers of all ages, Beale St is the place to go. The cool thing here is that both locals and tourists slide over to hear live blues, country, rock and jazz. On weekend nights, Beale St's two-block strip is closed to traffic, turning it into a walk-around party zone. Cover for most clubs is either free or only a few dollars.

LIVE MUSIC

Elvis Presley's (☎ 901-527-9036; 126 Beale St) Locals avoid it, but this swanky star-studded joint is a big draw for tourists. It serves passable food and has good live music.

BB King's (☎ 901-524-5464; 143 Beale St) BB's always has great live music.

This is It! (☎ 901-527-8200; 167 Beale St) Further east, This is It! is another lively option.

Kudzu Café (☎ 901-525-4924; 603 Monroe Ave) Near downtown, Kudzu has comedy and regular guitar-pickin' contests.

SPECTATOR SPORTS

Memphis Redbirds (☎ 901-721-6000) Sports fans can check out the Memphis Redbirds, a AAA minor-league baseball team that plays at the 15,000-seat AutoZone Park.

Memphis Grizzlies (☎ 901-678-2331) For basketball, the NBA's Memphis Grizzlies currently play at The Pyramid, though are moving to the new FedEx Forum in August 2004.

THEATER

Orpheum Theater (☎ 901-743-2787; www.orpheum-memphis.org; 203 S Main St) A 1928-era vaudeville palace, restored as a venue for Broadway shows and major concerts.

Circuit Playhouse (☎ 901-726-4656; 1705 Poplar Ave) In Overton Sq, the Circuit Playhouse offers alternative drama.

New Daisy Theater (☎ 901-525-8979; www.newdaisy.com; 330 Beale St; shows at 7pm) This hip, all-ages venue hosts a variety of live music shows. Call the hotline to see what's playing.

Getting There & Around

Memphis International Airport (☎ 901-922-8000; 2491 Winchester Rd) is 20 miles southeast of downtown via I-55; a taxi to or from downtown runs at about $30. The **Downtown Airport Shuttle** (DASH; ☎ 901-522-1677; one way per person $15) serves most downtown hotels.

Greyhound (☎ 901-523-1184; 203 Union Ave) runs frequent buses to Nashville ($29, four hours); Little Rock, Arkansas ($25, 2½ hours); and New Orleans, Louisiana ($45, eight to 10 hours).

Central Station (☎ 901-526-0052; 545 S Main St), the **Amtrak** terminal, has been restored to its original 1914 splendor. The *City of New Orleans* goes to Chicago, Illinois ($86, 10½ hours) and New Orleans, Louisiana ($70, nine hours).

Local **buses** are run by the **Memphis Area Transit Authority** (MATA; ☎ 901-722-7100; www.matatransit.com). And the **Main St Trolley** (☎ 901-274-6282; adult 60¢) runs vintage trolley cars on a loop from the Amtrak station to the Pyramid via Main St and Riverside Dr.

NASHVILLE

Yee haw! The country-music capital of the world, Nashville (*nash*-vul, according to locals) offers a musical experience that'll get anyone tapping toes. Though this is the town that spawned almost every Country star from Dolly Parton to Garth Brooks, in the words of one local, 'It ain't all boots and cowboy hats.' Yes, siree. In addition to traditional country and western music, Nashville is a haven for singer/songwriters of any genre. Almost every bar and many restaurants in town feature live music, and it's often a solo singer with nothing but a sweet voice and an acoustic guitar. Nashville has many attractions, from the fantastic Country Music Hall of Fame and the Grand Ole Opry House to rough blues bars, historic buildings and big-name sports. It also has friendly people, cheap food and an unrivaled assortment of tacky souvenirs.

History

Ancient Mound Builders and the wandering Shawnee occupied the Cumberland River bluffs before Europeans established Fort Nashborough in 1779. The legendary

NASHVILLE IN...

Two Days

Begin your first day in Nashville with a twang and a bang at the **Country Music Hall of Fame & Museum**. Spend a few hours gaining a new appreciation for the venues, music and artists to whom Nashville owes its legacy. At night, eat an early dinner and stroll along Broadway, listening to the new sounds of Nashville's music artists. Take in the fun-loving scene at **Tootsie's Orchid Lounge**. Clap your hands, stomp your feet – you are, after all, in Nashville.

The next day, sleep in and then head outside and walk up 5th Ave N toward the imposing **State Capitol building**. Climb over the hill and down the steps to the colorful and eclectic **Farmers Market**. Grab lunch, either from the market fruit and veggie stands or from the food court. Have a leisurely lunch on a bench at the Bicentennial Mall. Walk back to your hotel. At night, catch a show at the world-famous **Ryman Auditorium**.

Four Days

Follow the two-day itinerary. On the third day, wander down to the bus depot. Hop on an express bus to Music Valley and wander around the attractions surrounding the **Grand Ole Opry**. Come back downtown for a leisurely lunch. Follow your ears and enjoy an afternoon beer in one of the District music venues. At night, take a taxi out to the **Blue Bird Cafe** and enjoy an incredible acoustic show away from the bustle of Broadway. The next day, wander out to the outer neighborhoods or check out the action at Vanderbilt University.

Daniel Boone brought emigrants over the Appalachians from Virginia, the Carolinas and Northeastern states.

Renamed 'Nashville' around 1784, the town was an important railroad junction with a riverboat connection to the Mississippi, and a strategic point during the Civil War. It surrendered to federal troops in 1862, and Andrew Johnson (then a US senator) was appointed military governor, imposing martial law until 1865. Confederate troops were destroyed in the 1864 Battle of Nashville. Nashville survived the war intact, though its postwar recovery was hampered by two major cholera epidemics. The Tennessee Centennial Exposition in 1897 signaled the city's eventual recovery.

From 1925, Nashville became known for its live-broadcast Barn Dance, later nicknamed the 'Grand Ole Opry.' Its popularity soared, the city proclaimed itself the 'country-music capital of the world,' and recording studios sprang up in Music Row. The Fisk Jubilee Singers built on another musical tradition in the 1870s, popularizing black spirituals with benefit tours for Fisk University, a struggling black college. Ninety years later, Fisk students led sit-in demonstrations at downtown lunch counters, supported economic boycotts and marched on city hall to demand desegregated facilities.

Today, Nashville draws a wide mix of friendly locals and talented transients who play small stages and hope their dreams will come true – that they'll sign multimillion-dollar recording contracts and be the next Shania Twain or Garth Brooks. The resulting glut of excellent musicians and songwriters has created an exciting, ever-evolving music scene. Though sprawling in many directions, both geographically and culturally, Nashville is a small town at heart.

Orientation

Nashville sits on a rise beside the Cumberland River, with the capitol at the highest point. The compact downtown slopes south to Broadway, the city's central artery. Briley Parkway is the main road out of town.

Downtown, historic commercial buildings compose the entertainment area called 'the District,' from 2nd Ave to 5th Ave and along Broadway, where old dives and rib joints sit alongside slicksters like the Hard Rock Cafe. Across the river is the Coliseum where the Titans play Music Row; Elliston Place and Vanderbilt University sit west of downtown, with funky restaurants along Broadway, 21st Ave and West End Ave. Off the Briley Parkway northeast of town, Music Valley is a tourist zone of budget motels, franchise restaurants and outlet stores built around the Grand Ole Opry.

Information

BOOKSTORES

Elders Booksellers (☎ 615-327-1867; 2115 Elliston Pl; Mon-Sat) An excellent used bookstore near Music Row.

INTERNET ACCESS

Public library (Church St, btwn 6th & 7th Sts; free access)

MEDIA

Nashville Scene (www.nashscene.com) Free alternative weekly covering local entertainment and news.
Rage (www.nashvillerage.com) Another free alternative weekly covering local entertainment and news.

MEDICAL

Baptist Hospital (☎ 615-284-5555; 2000 Church St)
Vanderbilt University Medical Center (☎ 615-322-5000; 1211 22nd Ave S)

POST

Main post office (☎ 800-275-8777; 525 Royal St) All mail sent to General Delivery, Nashville, TN 3722 goes to this main branch.

Another branch is in the Frist Center for Visual Arts, or on Church St between 17th and 18th Aves N.

TOURIST OFFICES

Nashville Convention & Visitors Bureau (☎ 615-259-4700, 800-657-6910; 211 Commerce St) Maintains a 24-hour **hotline** (☎ 615-244-9393).
Nashville Visitors Information Center (☎ 615-259-4747; www.nashvillecvb.com; 8:30am-5:30pm) In the glass tower of the Gaylord Entertainment Center. Provides free city maps.

Sights & Activities

DOWNTOWN

The historic 2nd Ave N business area was the center of the cotton trade in the 1870s and 1880s, when most of the Victorian warehouses were built; note the cast iron and masonry facades. Today it's the heart of the **District**, with shops, restaurants, underground saloons and nightclubs. Two blocks

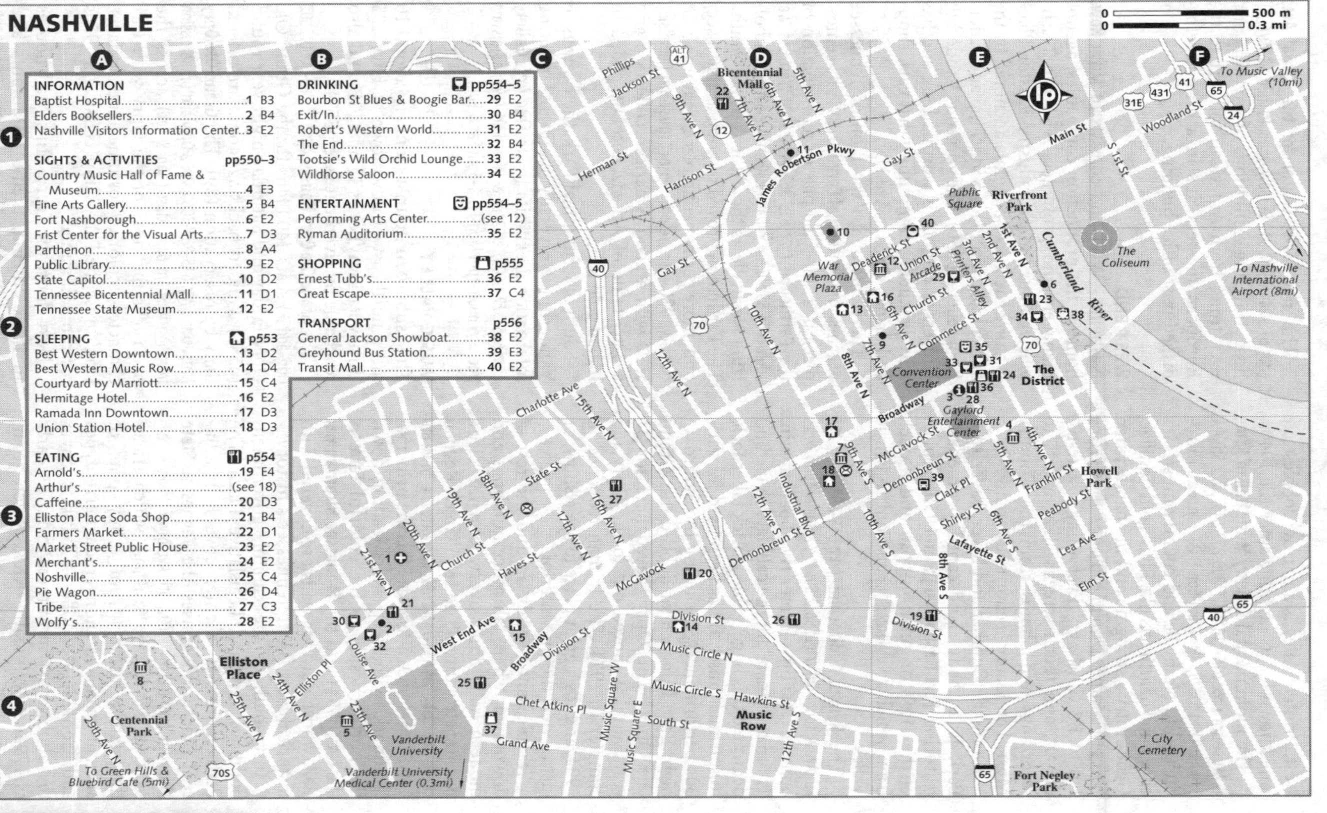
NASHVILLE
0 500 m
0 0.3 mi
INFORMATION
Baptist Hospital.....1 B3
Elders Booksellers.....2 B4
Nashville Visitors Information Center..3 E2
SIGHTS & ACTIVITIES pp550–3
Country Music Hall of Fame & Museum.....4 E3
Fine Arts Gallery.....5 B4
Fort Nashborough.....6 E2
Frist Center for the Visual Arts.....7 D3
Parthenon.....8 A4
Public Library.....9 E2
State Capitol.....10 D2
Tennessee Bicentennial Mall.....11 D1
Tennessee State Museum.....12 E2
SLEEPING p553
Best Western Downtown.....13 D2
Best Western Music Row.....14 D4
Courtyard by Marriott.....15 C4
Hermitage Hotel.....16 E2
Ramada Inn Downtown.....17 D3
Union Station Hotel.....18 D3
EATING p554
Arnold's.....19 E4
Arthur's.....(see 18)
Caffeine.....20 D3
Elliston Place Soda Shop.....21 B4
Farmers Market.....22 D1
Market Street Public House.....23 E2
Merchant's.....24 E2
Noshville.....25 C4
Pie Wagon.....26 D4
Tribe.....27 C3
Wolfy's.....28 E2
DRINKING pp554–5
Bourbon St Blues & Boogie Bar.....29 E2
Exit/In.....30 B4
Robert's Western World.....31 E2
The End.....32 B4
Tootsie's Wild Orchid Lounge.....33 E2
Wildhorse Saloon.....34 E2
ENTERTAINMENT pp554–5
Performing Arts Center.....(see 12)
Ryman Auditorium.....35 E2
SHOPPING p555
Ernest Tubb's.....36 E2
Great Escape.....37 C4
TRANSPORT p556
General Jackson Showboat.....38 E2
Greyhound Bus Station.....39 E3
Transit Mall.....40 E2
Bicentennial Mall
War Memorial Plaza
Public Square
Riverfront Park
Cumberland River
The Coliseum
To Music Valley (10mi)
To Nashville International Airport (8mi)
Convention Center
The District
Gaylord Entertainment Center
Howell Park
Music Row
Elliston Place
Centennial Park
Vanderbilt University
Vanderbilt University Medical Center (0.3mi)
To Green Hills & Bluebird Cafe (5mi)
City Cemetery
Fort Negley Park
James Robertson Pkwy
Broadway
West End Ave
Main St
Woodland St
Charlotte Ave
Church St
Commerce St
Demonbreun St
McGavock St
Division St
Lafayette St
Industrial Blvd

west, Printers Alley is a narrow cobblestone lane known for its nightlife since the 1940s.

The monumental **Country Music Hall of Fame & Museum** (☎ 615-416-2001, 800-852-6437; 222 5th Ave S; adult/child $15/8; 🕐 10am-6pm) is a great introduction to Nashville and country music. It's chock-full of artifacts like Elvis' gold Cadillac, Gene Autry's string tie and the handwritten lyrics to 'Mamas Don't Let Your Babies Grow Up to Be Cowboys.' Everything's state-of-the-art, and touch screens allow access to recordings and photos from the Country Music Foundation's enormous archives.

Along the Cumberland River, Riverfront Park is a shady, landscaped promenade featuring **Fort Nashborough**, a 1930s replica of the city's original outpost, and a dock from which river taxis cruise out to Music Valley.

The **Ryman Auditorium** (☎ 615-254-1445; 116 5th Ave N; tour adult/child $6/2.50; 🕐 8:30am-4pm) was built in 1890 by a former riverboat captain. Thomas Ryman 'got the call' late in life and dedicated this huge, gabled, brick tabernacle to spiritual music. It has been used for various performances, including the Saturday-night Barn Dance, later dubbed the 'Grand Ole Opry.' The Opry stayed here for 31 years, until it moved out to the Opryland complex in 1974. The Ryman reopened in 1994, and it's a great place to see a show, or just to view the fine interior.

It's pleasant to walk around the rest of downtown, where tall office buildings and modern halls don't overwhelm the city's historic structures. The 1845 Greek Revival **state capitol** (☎ 615-741-2692; Charlotte Ave, btwn 6th & 7th Sts; free tours 9am-4pm Mon-Fri) is the principal landmark, with steep stairs leading down the northern side to the colorful **Farmers Market** (p554) and the **Tennessee Bicentennial Mall**, whose outdoor walls are covered with historical facts about Tennessee's history.

Just south of the capitol, government buildings surround Legislative Plaza. The Performing Arts Center covers an adjacent block and houses the **Tennessee State Museum** (☎ 615-741-2692; 5th Ave btwn Union & Deaderick; admission free; 🕐 10am-4pm), which traces the state's history from effigy pots of ancient tribes to pioneer daguerreotypes and Confederate dollars. Exhibits cover the abolitionist movement from as early as 1797, as well as the KKK, which began here in 1868.

The new **Frist Center for the Visual Arts** (☎ 615-244-3340; 919 Broadway; adult/child $8.50/6.50) hosts traveling exhibitions of anything and everything from American folk art to the European masters. It's in a grand, refurbished post office building.

WEST END

Nashville's West End consists of **Music Row**, home of the production companies, agents, managers and promoters who run Nashville's country-music industry. Elliston Place is a tiny enclave of bohemia anchored by the ancient Elliston Place Soda Shop and Elders Booksellers (p550). The gorgeous Vanderbilt University campus is worth a look and has a lively student community that eats, shops and drinks on 21st Ave N.

The Centennial Exposition of Tennessee was held in **Centennial Park** in 1897; its centerpiece is a full-scale plaster reproduction of the **Parthenon** (☎ 615-862-8431; 2600 West End Ave; adult/child $3.50/2; 🕐 9am-4:30pm Tue-Sat), symbolizing Nashville as the 'Athens of the South.' The Parthenon proved so popular that a second, more permanent replacement was built in the 1930s. Inside is an **art museum** (admission $3.50) with a good American collection and a 42ft statue of Athena, recently gilded in Italian gold leaf.

South of Centennial Park, the campus of Vanderbilt University maintains rotating international exhibits in its **Fine Arts Gallery** (☎ 615-322-0605; at 23rd & West End Aves; admission free; 🕐 noon-4pm Mon-Fri, 1-5pm Sat & Sun).

MUSIC VALLEY

This suburban tourist zone is about 10 miles northeast of downtown at Hwy 155 (Briley Parkway) exits 11 and 12B, and also reachable by riverboat (see p553).

The **Grand Ole Opry House** (☎ 615-889-3060; 2802 Opryland Dr) seats 4400 fans for the Grand Ole Opry Friday and Saturday night year round (p555). Guided backstage tours are offered daily by reservation ($9). The **Grand Ole Opry Museum** (☎ 615-889-3060; 2802 Opryland Dr; admission free; 🕐 10:30am-6pm, closed Jan & Feb) across the plaza tells the story of the Opry with wax characters, colorful costumes and artifacts. Don't miss the Patsy Cline classic – a 1950s rec-room diorama.

Next door, the Opry Mills Mall houses an Imax cinema, theme restaurants and the **Gibson Bluegrass Showcase** (☎ 615-514-2200;

admission free; 10am-6pm), a working factory and concert venue where you can see banjos, mandolins and resonator guitars being made through the glass.

Exit 12B goes to the Opryland Hotel as well as several other sights, including the **Music City Wax Museum** (☎ 615-883-3612; adult/child $3.50/1.50; 9am-5pm, until 9pm May-Sep), with stacks of wax statues of costumed country stars, and the **Willie Nelson Museum** (☎ 615-885-1515; adult/child $3.50/1.50; 9am-5pm, until 9pm May-Sep), with guitars and gold records.

Tours

Ask at the visitors center for a list of the many theme tours available in Nashville.

General Jackson Showboat (☎ 615-871-5043; www.generaljackson.com; 2812 Opryland Dr) Offers trips on the Cumberland River from the Opry Land Hotel. Prices and trips vary; call for more information.

Gray Line (☎ 615-883-5555, 800-251-1864; www.graylinenashville.com) Offers a variety of bus tours from its hub at Broadway and 2nd Ave.

Nashville Trolley Tours (☎ 615-248-4437) Also based at Broadway and 2nd Ave. Runs a narrated tour to downtown tourist sites and out to Music Row.

Sleeping

There's a cluster of budget motels on all sides of downtown, on I-40 and I-65, including Motel 6, Super 8 and Hampton Inn. They all charge from around $40 to $60 for rooms. At any hotel, lower rates are available midweek, on slow weekends and during the winter. Be aware hotel tax in Nashville adds 14.25%.

DOWNTOWN

Best Western Downtown (☎ 615-242-4311, 800-627-3297; 711 Union St; r $70-120; P) With a great location near the capitol and free parking, this is one of the cheaper options. Rooms are tidy and the staff welcoming. An attached deli sells snacks.

Ramada Inn Downtown (☎ 615-244-0150, 800-251-1856; 920 Broadway; r from $80; P) This 285-room hotel, geared toward the corporate set on business at the convention center, is also convenient to the District.

Hermitage Hotel (☎ 615-244-3121, 888-888-9414; www.thehermitagehotel.com; 231 6th Ave N; r from $109; P) Oozing with elegance, this beautiful hotel has tons of marble and serves the upper-end business set, or those attending the opera. Even if you don't stay here, make sure you stop by for a drink in the lounge or a walk through the lobby.

THE AUTHOR'S CHOICE

Union Station Hotel (☎ 615-726-1001, 800-996-3426; www.wyndham.com; 1001 Broadway; starts at $125; P) Resembling a castle with its limestone fortress and buttresses, this 1900 hotel is one of the city's most beautiful. If you want to splurge a bit, this is your best bet. The 124 rooms are uniquely designed, built around the architectural integrity; 5th-floor rooms, for example, have grand 30ft ceilings. All rooms are chock full of amenities. The lobby is stunning, sitting regally under a vaulted ceiling of Tiffany stained glass.

WEST END

Best Western Music Row (☎ 615-242-1631, 800-528-1234; 1407 Division St; r from $50; P) Not far from the action, but too far to walk to the action on Broadway, this standard hotel near Music Row is a good budget option.

Courtyard by Marriott (☎ 615-327-9900, 800-245-1959; 1901 West End Ave; r from $90; P) You'll join visitors to Vanderbilt at this comfortable hotel near Music Row and on the brink of the university campus. It has large rooms (many with sleeper sofas to fit more people), an outdoor pool and laundry facilities.

MUSIC VALLEY

Fiddlers Inn North (☎ 615-885-1440; 2410 Music Valley Dr; weekday/weekend $60/64;) This family-oriented hotel is a good option if you want to see shows at the Grand Ole Opry.

Opryland Hotel (☎ 615-889-1000, 877-456-6779; www.gaylordhotels.com; 2800 Opryland Dr; r without/with balcony $200/260) This sprawling hotel recently underwent an $80 million renovation and today has, gulp, 2881 rooms. The lobby features a self-contained 'Oprysphere' with waterfalls, boat rides, magnolia trees and an elevated walkway above the rainforest.

Camping

Opryland KOA Kampground (☎ 615-889-0286, 800-562-7789; www.koa.com; 2626 Music Valley Dr; campsites $28; P) At the north end of Music Valley, and with 460 tent and RV sites and every convenience you can think of, this is the best place for tenting near Nashville.

Eating

Farmers Market (8th Ave N at Jackson St; ⏰ 9am-5pm) Here you'll find a great variety of cheap food, including gyros, empanadas, *muffalettas*, Reubens and more.

Market Street Public House (☎ 615-259-9611; 134 2nd Ave N; meals $8-20) This friendly neighborhood pub has a great selection of local microbrews, with the regular clientele's beer steins hanging on the walls. The menu has a good selection of salads, burgers, fish-and-chips, and more substantial meals like chicken and pasta.

Wolfy's (☎ 615-251-1621; 425 Broadway; meals $5-10) With pretty decent burger fare and good sandwiches like a fine veggie Reuben, Wolfy's spot right on the strip, plus free live music, makes it a good place for a bite.

Merchant's (☎ 615-254-1892; 401 Broadway; meals $20-30) Right in the heart of the District, this upscale bistro has an excellent wine list and lovely mahogany bar at which to swill. The dining room features excellent but pricey seafood, steaks and pastas.

Arthur's (☎ 615-254-1494; 1001 Broadway; fixed-price dinner $65) In the Union Station Hotel, Arthur's menu changes daily making it the only restaurant in town with 365 menu changes. The price seems high, but the delicious food, enveloping elegance and excellent service are well worth the splurge.

WEST END

The true taste of Nashville can best be found in cinder-block cabins in the industrial zone south of Broadway, where meat-and-threes come in heaping portions.

Arnold's (☎ 615-256-4455; 605 8th Ave S; meals $5-8; ⏰ 10:30am-2:30pm Mon-Fri) For locals, Arnold's has long been a favorite for the ubiquitous meat-and-three. Folks line up to get into this tiny shack for the fried green tomatoes, peppery roast beef, greens and lemon ice-box pie. Grumpy but lovable Jack Arnold has owned this place for more than 20 years.

Pie Wagon (☎ 615-256-5893; 1302 Division St; meals $5-10; ⏰ 6am-2pm Mon-Fri) The first incarnation opened in 1922 in an old trolley wagon. This location has been here since 1990 and still has a loyal local following for its homey Southern cuisine and hot chicken.

Caffeine (☎ 615-259-4993; 1516 Demonbreun St; meals $6-7; ⏰ 6am-11pm Mon-Fri, 4pm-11pm Sat, 6am-6pm Sun) Looking for a good cup o' Joe? Look no further. Caffeine is an excellent stop for a strong latte or cappuccino; it also serves light sandwiches and wraps. If you've got a laptop, it has free high-speed Internet connections, but no computers. Live music at night.

Elliston Place Soda Shop (☎ 615-327-1090; 2111 Elliston Place; meals $3-6; ⏰ closed Sun) Slurp it up, baby. This old joint serves soda fountain treats along with meat-and-three plates.

Noshville (☎ 615-329-6674; 1918 Broadway; meals $5-10) A wonderful New York–style Jewish deli specializing in pastrami sandwiches that take both hands to eat. Delicious specialties like bagels with lox are served up in the crisp chrome interior. A great place to eat in or take a snack to go.

Tribe (☎ 625-329-3912; meals $9-19; ⏰ 4pm-midnight Sun-Thu, 4pm-2am Fri & Sat) Catering to Nashville's gay community (though anyone is welcome), Tribe is a hot, groovy spot with a delicious, eclectic menu.

Drinking & Entertainment

Apart from the big venues, many talented country, folk, bluegrass, Southern-rock and blues performers play smoky honky-tonks, blues bars, seedy storefronts and organic cafés for tips. Almost anywhere you go in town, you'll hear great live music. Many places are free Monday to Friday or if you arrive early enough.

LIVE MUSIC

Connection (☎ 615-742-1166; 901 Cowan St; admission $10-20; ⏰ Wed-Mon) Three miles from the District, Connection is a massive dance complex and must-stop for gay boys and girls looking to funk out to techno. Men outnumber women by far, but all are welcome, regardless of sexual preference. In addition to the dancing, there's also an excellent drag show in the club's theater.

Wildhorse Saloon (☎ 615-902-8200; 120 2nd Ave N; cover charge $4-10) A popular spot to snap yer fingers and tap yer toes while listening to new Country music. The saloon offers free dance lessons, so you'll be doing the Rebel Slide and Cowboy Stomp before you know it.

Bourbon St Blues & Boogie Bar (☎ 615-242-5837; 220 Printers Alley; cover charge free-$10) This spot, in the tiny Printers Alley between 3rd & 4th Ave and Union and Church Sts, is the city's premier blues venue.

Robert's Western World (☎ 615-244-9552; 416 Broadway) On the strip, this longtime bar has

LIVE FROM THE BLUEBIRD CAFE

In an unassuming strip mall away from the kickin' country scene on Broadway, a 21-table restaurant bursts with atmosphere, history and the best acoustic music to come out of Nashville.

Opened in 1982 by Amy Kurland as a casual restaurant with some live music, the Bluebird Cafe has evolved into a world-renowned venue geared solely toward the singer/songwriter. If you make it at the Bluebird, you can make it anywhere, and it's likely you're pretty damn good.

Many folks got their first big break at the Bluebird. Veterans include commercial successes like Garth Brooks, Terri Clark, Bonnie Raitt, along with critically acclaimed songwriters like Lucinda Williams, Townes Van Zandt, Steve Earle and Guy Clark. There's fame in the air here, but more than that, there's just unbelievable acoustic music.

Tomorrow's hit makers can be heard on Sunday Writer's Night. Monday nights are open-mic nights, where 24 invited artists perform two original songs. On other nights four select performers share songs and inspiration while sitting together 'In the Round.'

You can reserve a table up to a week in advance and there are usually two shows nightly. There is a minimum charge of $7 per person, but it's easy to spend that on drinks or food (try the blackened catfish sandwich). The Bluebird has a pretty strict no-talking policy during shows, so if you want to get loud, this is not the place for you. If you want to see the best acoustic musicians in Nashville, well then, you should stick around.

To get here, take a cab from downtown or, if you're driving, follow Broadway away from the district. It becomes 21st Ave, passes Vanderbilt University before becoming Hillsboro. The Bluebird is on the left, across the street from the Green Hills mall.

live music starting in the afternoon and lasting through the night.

Tootsie's Wild Orchid Lounge (☎ 615-726-7937; 422 Broadway) Truly a must-visit for anyone – Tootsies is a venerated dive that sees a lot of whoopin' and hollerin' every night. Up-and-coming Country musicians play the stage here, and it's not unusual for big stars, whose photos cover the walls, to stop by for a jam.

Bluebird Cafe (☎ 615-383-1461; 4104 Hillsboro Rd; cover charge free-$10) In an unassuming strip mall in suburban Green Hills area (5 miles west of the District), the Bluebird (see boxed text, above) attracts some of the city's most talented musicians.

Exit/In (☎ 615-321-4400; 2208 Elliston Pl; cover charge varies) Good ole rock 'n' roll is the name of the game here, with everything from rock cover bands to original, usually electric, music.

End (☎ 615-321-4457; 2219 Elliston Place; cover charge varies) This tiny venue, also in the Elliston Place area, is a grunge spot for rock and alternative music.

Ryman Auditorium (tickets ☎ 615-458-8700, info 615-889-3060; 116 5th Ave; ticket prices vary) Often called the 'mother church of country music,' the Ryman was the home of the Grand Ole Opry from 1943 to 1974. The Ryman's excellent acoustics, historic charm and large seating capacity have kept it the premier venue in town. If you see a show here, it'll no doubt be a memorable experience.

Grand Ole Opry (☎ 615-871-6779; www.opry.com; 2802 Opryland Dr; adult $23.50-27.50, child 13.50-17.50; 🕑 7:30pm Fri, 6:30pm & 9:30pm Sat) Though the Opry has a variety of shows, the production Friday and Saturday evenings is a lavish tribute to classic Nashville Country music

SPECTATOR SPORTS

Tennessee Titans (☎ 615-565-4000) The NFL Tennessee Titans play in the Coliseum, across the river from downtown.

Nashville Sounds (☎ 615-242-4371) A minor-league AAA baseball team for the Pittsburgh Pirates, play at Greer Stadium, south of town.

Nashville Predators (☎ 615-770-2300) For NHL hockey, catch the Nashville Predators at Gaylord Entertainment Center.

Shopping

Nashville's music stores are numerous and well stocked.

Great Escape (☎ 615-327-0646; 1925 Broadway) For new and used CDs or records of all genres, comic books and videos.

Ernest Tubb's (☎ 615-255-7503; 417 Broadway) The legendary Ernest Tubb's has a great selection of country and bluegrass.

Getting There & Around

Nashville International Airport (☎ 615-275-1662), 8 miles east of town, is not a major air hub. MTA bus No 18 links the airport and downtown; the **Gray Line Airport Express** (☎ 615-883-5555; one-way/return $11/17; ⏰ 6am-11pm) serves major downtown and West End hotels.

Greyhound (☎ 615-255-3556; 200 8th Ave S) has frequent buses to Memphis ($29, four hours); Atlanta, GA ($36, five hours); Birmingham, AL ($28, four hours); and New Orleans ($44, 14 hours).

The **Metropolitan Transit Authority** (MTA; ☎ 615-862-5950; adult $1.45) operates city bus services based at the downtown transit mall at Deaderick St and 4th Ave N. It also has express buses that go to Music Valley and back.

AROUND NASHVILLE

About 25 miles southwest of Nashville off Hwy 100, drivers pick up the **Natchez Trace Parkway**, which leads 450 miles southwest to Natchez, Mississippi (p511). This northern section is one of the most attractive stretches of the entire route. Near the parkway entrance, look for the landmark **Loveless Cafe** (☎ 615-646-9700; 8400 Hwy 100; dishes $5-15), a 1940s roadhouse famous for its ham, jam and ample portions of Southern country cooking (reservations needed at weekends).

About 20 miles south of Nashville off I-65, the historic town of **Franklin** has a charming historic downtown area and beautiful B&Bs. About 50 miles south of Nashville on Hwys 41A and 231, **Shelbyville** is the epicenter of Tennessee walking horse activity. The town's 10-day Celebration festival in late August draws some 200,000 trainers, breeders and enthusiasts.

In nearby Lynchburg is the **Walking Horse Museum** (☎ 931-759-5747; 183 Main St; admission free; ⏰ 10am-4pm Tue-Sat).

Off Hwy 55 in Lynchburg (population 361), you'll come to the only place in the world that distills Tennessee's famous whiskey. The **Jack Daniel's Distillery** (☎ 931-759-6180; www.jackdaniels.com; tours free; ⏰ 9am-4:30pm) offers hour-long tours. Owing to the local liquor laws, they can't offer samples but you're encouraged to take long sniffs of the distilling whiskey.

EASTERN TENNESSEE

Largely a rural region with unhurried towns dotting the hills and river valleys, Eastern Tennessee boasts spectacular scenery dominated by the Great Smoky Mountains where you can spot bears, hike and camp, while the white waters of the Ocoee River are great for rafting. The region's two main urban areas, Knoxville and Chattanooga, are pleasant riverside cities with lively college populations, good restaurants and an easygoing energy.

Knoxville

Knoxville was once Tennessee's territorial capital and is now the seat of the state university. It's a good base for exploring the region, but not much of an attraction itself. The **visitors center** (☎ 865-971-4440, 800-727-8045; www.knoxtsc.com; ⏰ 9am-5pm Mon-Sat, 1-5pm Sun) is on the riverfront off I-40 exit 388A. Concerts and University of Tennessee sports teams play at the Neyland Coliseum. The city's visual centerpiece is the **Sunsphere**, the main remnant of the 1982 World Fair. Most sites are nearby.

TENNESSEE WALKING HORSES

If you didn't know they were highly trained professionals, the high-stepping, head-bobbing Tennessee walking horses might look like they're impersonating pigeons walking on hot coals. Their gaits look pretty strange to the uninitiated, but riders swear that a walking horse travels smoother than a Cadillac on fresh blacktop.

During the Civil War, Confederate Pacers bred disloyally with Union Trotters, resulting in a smooth-striding neddy that was later fused with thoroughbred standard-breed Morgan and saddle-horse to come up with the Tennessee walking horse in the late 19th century.

At the annual **Celebration** (www.twhnc.com; Shelbyville; tickets from $7; ⏰ late August), the world championship for this breed, judges look for perfect execution of the horse's three gaits: the flat walk (think of a pigeon on hot coals), running walk (now a pigeon chased by a cat) and the rocking chair canter (and a rocking chair chased by a pigeon). It's a fun place to soak up some Tennessee hospitality.

SIGHTS

Four galleries feature permanent collections of prints, drawings and photographs at the **Knoxville Museum of Art** (☎ 865-525-6101; www.knoxart.org; 1050 World's Fair Park Dr; admission $5; 10am-5pm Tue-Thu & Sat, 10am-9pm Fri, noon-5pm Sun). Rotating exhibits highlight American artists.

At the **Women's Basketball Hall of Fame** (☎ 865-633-9000; www.wbhof.com; 700 Hall of Fame Dr; adult/child $8/6; 10am-7pm Mon-Sat, 1-6pm Sun) you can't miss the massive orange basketball that marks this sleek and worthwhile museum that features memorabilia, a touring wagon owned by the All-American Redheads, and practice courts downstairs.

On the edge of downtown are two noteworthy historical sites. The 1792 **Blount Mansion** (☎ 865-525-2375; 200 W Hill Ave; admission $5; 9:30-5pm Mon-Sat) was the residence of William Blount, signer of the US Constitution and governor when Knoxville served as the capital of all US territories south of the Ohio River. A few blocks up Hill St is a replica of **James White's Fort** (☎ 865-525-6514; 205 E Hill Ave; admission $4; 9:30am-4:30pm Mon-Sat); the original, built in 1786, was the town's first house.

SLEEPING & EATING

Days Inn (☎ 865-521-5000; 1719 Lake Avenue; r from $50; P) This old but renovated hotel on the university campus is a lively place, with tidy rooms and a great location.

Hilton Knoxville (☎ 865-523-2300; 501 W Church Ave; r from $90; P) Adjacent to the convention center, the Hilton has great amenities and is right in the thick of downtown. It's got an outdoor pool, restaurant and bar.

KOA Kampground (☎ 865-933-6393; at I-40/I-75, exit 117; campsites $19-22) Your best bet for camping close to the city.

Knoxville is a town dominated by chain hotels and motels. For cheaper stays, your best bet is to go north of downtown on I-40 at exits 394 and 398, and south of the center at exits 378A and 378B.

Tomato Head (☎ 865-933-4067; Market Sq; sandwiches $5) Downtown, this is a pretty popular lunchtime hangout serving pizza and giant sandwiches.

Calhoun's (☎ 865-673-3355; 400 Neyland Dr; mains $12-20) This Tennessee-based chain serving succulent ribs and barbecue has a great location on the river between downtown and the University of Tennessee campus.

GETTING THERE & AWAY

Knoxville is at the crossroads of I-75 and I-40, about 180 miles east of Nashville. **Greyhound** (☎ 865-522-5144; 100 Magnolia Ave; 24hr) has four daily buses to Chattanooga ($15, two hours), with continuing service to Atlanta, GA ($25, 4¼ hours). A direct service goes to Nashville ($23, 3½ hours) and Memphis ($46, eight hours).

Great Smoky Mountains National Park

Eastern Tennessee's most famous attractions are its mountains, centered on the **Great Smoky Mountains National Park** (recorded info ☎ 865-436-1200, road info 865-436-1297; www.nps.gov/grsm/). The 810-sq-mile park straddles the Appalachian Mountains between Tennessee and North Carolina, the elevation rising to over 6600ft. Northern and southern ecosystems collide here, giving the park a huge variety of flora and fauna – about 100,000 species, of which only around 15% have been identified. Wildflowers are a particular delight, and there are more than 125 tree species – more than in all of Europe. Some 60 species of mammals call the park home, including the bears for which the park is famous.

Established in 1934, the park now draws over 10 million visitors a year, making it the most visited national park in the USA.

The best-known sites are **Clingman's Dome**, the highest point in the park (6643ft), and the dramatic twin summits of **Chimney Tops**. These and the popular hiking trails around Mt LeConte are all fairly close to Gatlinburg. The **Cades Cove** area features an 11-mile, one-way driving loop that's popular with cyclists. Summer is peak season and the park can be extremely crowded at any time May to September.

On the Tennessee side, the **Sugarlands Visitors Center** (☎ 865-436-1291; ☎ 8am-4:30pm) is on the main access road from Gatlinburg. This road, US 441, crosses the park for 35 scenic miles to Cherokee, NC, where there's another visitors center at Oconaluftee. Entrance to the park is free.

CAMPING

With 10 developed campgrounds offering about 1000 campsites, you'd think finding a place to pitch would be easy. Not so in the busy summer season. Your best bet is to plan ahead. You can make **reservations** (☎ 800-365-2267; www.reservations.nps.gov) up to five months in advance. Otherwise it's first-come, first-served. Camping fees are $12 to $20 per night, except for the five horse camps, which cost $20 to $25 per site. Of the park's 10 campgrounds only Cades Cove and Smokemont are open year round; others are open March through October.

Backcountry camping is an excellent option. A (free) permit is required; you can make **reservations** (☎ 865-436-1231) and get permits at the ranger stations or visitors centers.

GATEWAY TOWNS

Several gateway communities provide access to the park. The best known, and most crowded, is **Gatlinburg**. Because the small **Ober Gatlinburg Ski Area** (☎ 865-436-5423) is just outside town you'll find more services here in winter, when many of the shops, restaurants and motels at other park gateways close. The city has three **visitors centers** (☎ 865-436-0504, 800-568-4748; www.gatlinburg.com; 8am-6pm, until 8pm Fri-Sat, until 10pm summer), at the third and fifth stoplights and just north of town on US 441. They have separate information desks – one for city information (motels, restaurants) and one run by the park service (for campsite reservations, hiking routes etc) – that are all open.

Ten miles north of Gatlinburg, **Pigeon Forge** is a tacky complex of motels, outlet malls and country-music theaters and restaurants, all of which have grown up in the shadow of **Dollywood** (☎ 865-428-9488; www.dollywood.com; adult/child $35/26; closed Jan-Mar), Dolly Parton's personal theme park.

Chattanooga

Chattanooga was born of one of the great injustices of the early USA: the removal of the Cherokee along the 'Trail of Tears'. One of the trail's two starting points was Ross's Landing in what is now downtown Chattanooga. Once the Indians were gone, the city grew quickly. It was a key strategic point during the Civil War, and several important battles were fought nearby at Lookout Mountain and Chickamauga. After the war it became a major transport hub, hence the 'Chattanooga Choo-Choo,' originally a reference to the Cincinnati Southern Railroad's passenger service from Cincinnati to Chattanooga and later the title of a Glenn Miller song.

Today, Chattanooga is one of the most interesting – and most often overlooked – small cities in the South. Rather than focusing on sprawl, Chattanooga planners have focused on beautifying the city's core. An ongoing $120 million revitalization of the downtown and waterfront has transformed this already pretty city into a first-class, pedestrian-friendly community.

Most of Chattanooga's main sites are within a few blocks of the **visitors center** (☎ 423-856-8687, 800-322-3344; www.chatanoogafun.com; 2 Broad St; 8:30am-5:30pm) at the corner of 2nd and Broad Sts. The Bluff View Art District at High and E 2nd Sts has upscale shops and restaurants overlooking the river.

SIGHTS & ACTIVITIES

The local tourist industry plays quite heavily on the song 'The Most Famous Train in the World Returns to Track 29,' but those with sharp memories will remember that the musical train was going to Tennessee, and the famous Track 29 is actually at Penn Station in New York.

Absolutely a must-see, **Tennessee Aquarium** (☎ 800-262-0695; www.tnaqua.org; 1 Broad St; adult/child $14/7.50; 10am-6pm) is the world's largest freshwater aquarium. Exhibits mirror a large river system and give visitors a unique look at the interconnectedness of riparian areas. Part of the aquarium, an **Imax theater** (☎ 800-262-0695; 201 Chestnut St; adult/child $8/5.25) also has a cool environmental learning lab for kids. Nearby, **Ross's Landing** is a good place to start a riverfront stroll.

Chattanooga Regional History Museum (☎ 423-265-3247; 400 Chestnut St; 10am-5pm Mon-Fri, 11am-4pm Sat & Sun) does a good job depicting the area's history.

Chattanooga African-American Museum (☎ 423-266-8658; 200 ML King Jr Blvd; adult/child $5/2; ☎ 10am-5pm Mon-Fri, noon-4pm Sat) is also worthwhile, especially for the exhibit on Chattanooga native Bessie Smith.

Some of Chattanooga's oldest and best-known attractions are outside the city at nearby **Lookout Mountain** (☎ 423-821-4224; www.lookoutmtnattractions.com; 827 East Brow Rd; adult/child $35/17; vary by season). These include the Incline Railway, which chugs up a steep incline to the top of the mountain, underground caverns called Ruby Falls, and Rock City – a garden with a dramatic cliff top overlook and waterfall. The admission gets you into all three attractions. **Point Park**, at the mountain's summit, is part of the NPS's **Chickamauga & Chattanooga National Military Park** (admission $2) complex. Entry to the **visitors center** (☎ 423-866-9241) is free.

SLEEPING

You can find budget motels around I-24 exit 178.

Comfort Suites/Downtown (☎ 423-265-0008, 800-517-4000; 2431 Williams St; r from $70; P) Less than 2 miles south of downtown, this is a good option, where a standard but comfortable suite comes with microwave, fridge and coffeemaker.

Chattanooga Choo-Choo Holiday Inn (☎ 423-266-5000, 800-872-2529; www.choochoo.com; 1400 Market St; r from $100; P) Housed in the old railway terminal on 30 acres, the Choo-Choo is a grand hotel and a hub of activity. It has 360 rooms, including 48 in authentic railcars, ranging from nothing special to very deluxe. It has a restaurant where the waiters sing, both indoor and outdoor pools and a small railroad museum.

Chattanoogan (☎ 423-756-3400, 877-756-1684; www.chattanooganhotel.com; 1201 S Broad St; r/ste from $120/200; P) This resort hotel in the heart of downtown has excellent modern amenities, such as T-1 lines in each room, groovy decor and a slick spa. It also has a bar, restaurant, indoor pool and fitness center. Rates vary widely. Call to see if any deals are on.

There are many campgrounds around Chattanooga.

KOA Chattanooga North (☎ 423-472-8928; campsites $15-18) Fifteen miles north at I-75 exit 20.

Raccoon Mountain RV Park & Campground (☎ 423-821-9403; campsites $12) To the west at I-24 exit 174.

EATING

Sticky Fingers (☎ 423-265-7427; 420 Broad St; mains $10-15) Locals agree that this place has the best hickory-smoked ribs, chicken and barbecue in town. Try the sampler, which gives you a taste of all four varieties.

Big River Grille & Brewing Works (☎ 423-267-2739; 222 Broad St; mains $7-15) In a great location, this microbrewery offers a friendly vibe, with an extensive menu of sandwiches, pasta, steaks and Mexican food.

Greyfriar's (☎ 423-267-0376; 406B Broad St;) This coffeehouse, which has computers with Internet access, is a good stop for a light breakfast or quiet cup of coffee.

GETTING THERE & AROUND

Chattanooga's modest airport is just east of the city. Nearby, the **Greyhound station** (☎ 423-892-1277; 960 Airport Rd) has daily busses to Atlanta, GA ($20, 2½ hours); Nashville ($20, from 2½ hours); and Knoxville ($16, two hours).

With an utter lack of nostalgia, Amtrak does not serve Chattanooga.

For access to most downtown sites, ride the free electric shuttle buses that ply the center. The visitors center has a route map.

KENTUCKY

Kentucky is a wonderful combination of the South and North, the East and West. It combines mountains and forests with some of the most beautifully manicured rural landscapes imaginable. The limestone-rich pastures with green grasses that bloom blue buds in spring (earning Kentucky the moniker 'Bluegrass State') showed early pioneers the state's horse-breeding potential. Today, thoroughbred breeding is a multibillion dollar industry and Kentucky's Derby is perhaps the most famous horseracing event in the world. The state's cities are small but somehow appealing, and even the industries are engaging – a state that produces bourbon, baseball bats and Corvettes can't be all bad.

Kentucky Travel (☎ 502-564-4930, 800-225-8747; www.kentuckytourism.com; Box 2011, Frankfort, KY 40602) sends out a detailed booklet on the state's attractions. State sales tax is 6%.

The boundary between Eastern and Central time goes through the middle of Kentucky. If you go from Mammoth Cave to Lincoln's birthplace, you'll arrive an hour later than you thought.

History

The fertile lands to the west of the Appalachians were inhabited by Cherokee, Shawnee and Iroquois, who resisted the encroachment of whites. In 1775 a treaty with the Cherokee opened the way for settlers from the eastern colonies, and Daniel Boone marked a trail through the Cumberland Gap. Within 20 years, 100,000 people had migrated into

KENTUCKY FACTS

Nickname Bluegrass State
Population 4,092,891 (26th)
Area 39,728 sq miles (37th)
Admitted to Union June 1, 1792 (15th)
Capital city Frankfort (population 28,000)
Other cities Louisville (256,000), Lexington (261,000), Owensboro (54,000)
Birthplace of Confederate president Jefferson Davis (1808–89), 16th US president Abraham Lincoln (1809–65), bluegrass musician Bill Monroe (1911–96), country singer Loretta Lynn (b 1935), journalist Hunter S Thompson (b 1939), boxer Muhammad Ali (b 1942), newswoman Diane Sawyer (b 1945), actors George Clooney (b 1961) and Johnny Depp (b 1963)
Famous for Kentucky bluegrass, the Kentucky Derby, bourbon, the Louisville Slugger

the 'wilderness' that was Virginia's western territory. Kentucky became the first non-seaboard state admitted to the Union.

Kentucky became divided between its slaveholding plantation class and the workers who opposed slavery. Both the Union and Confederate presidents were Kentucky-born, but when the Civil War began, 25,000 Kentuckians fought for the Confederacy, while 75,000 others fought for the Union.

Because Kentucky did not secede, it avoided the trauma of Reconstruction, but the state became strongly pro-South after the war. Coal discovered in the Appalachians became a source of wealth and of the state's first labor movements.

LOUISVILLE

Call it Looeyville, Lewisville or Louahvul; the locals don't mind – it's an easygoing kind of place. Aristocrats flock to Churchill Downs and its world-famous Kentucky Derby in May. For the rest of the year, Louisville is a nice place to stop, and a cultural and industrial center with some classic Americana. Louisville's old downtown is a compact grid beside the Ohio River – and the I-64 freeway. A series of pretty parks (laid out by Frederick Law Olmsted in the 1890s) encircle the city, along with an inner (I-264) and outer (I-265) ring road. The **visitors center** (☎ 502-582-3732, 888-568-4784; 221 S 4th St; 🕑 9am-5pm Mon-Fri) runs an outlet in the convention center. It has maps and information, as well as the good *African American Visitors Guide*. Surf the Web free at the **public library** (301 York St) downtown.

Sights

At the **Louisville Slugger Museum** (☎ 502-588-7228; www.sluggermuseum.org; 800 W Main St; adult/child $6/3.50; 🕑 9am-5pm Mon-Sat, noon-5pm Sun Apr-Oct) look for the 120ft baseball bat leaning against the building – ya can't miss it. Since 1884, Hillerich & Bradsby Co have been making the famous Louisville Slugger baseball bat and here you can watch the wooden bats being crafted in the factory. The admission fee includes a video, baseball exhibits, a plant tour, enthusiastic guides and a collection of baseball memorabilia. Note: bat production halts on Sunday.

Speed Art Museum (☎ 502-634-2700; 2035 S 3rd St; admission free; 🕑 10:30am-4pm Tue, Wed & Fri, until 8pm Thu, until 5pm Sat & Sun) is a handsome neoclassical museum that has more than 13,000 pieces of art, including European paintings and sculptures, plus exhibits of Classical antiques and Kentucky artists.

Children enjoy the interactive exhibits at **Louisville Science Center** (☎ 502-561-6100; www.louisvillesciencecenter.org; 727 W Main St; adult/child $8.50/7.50; 🕑 9:30am-5pm Mon-Thu, 9:30am-9pm Fri-Sat, noon-6pm Sun), which also houses an Imax theater.

There are four **historic homes** (www.historichomes.org; adult per tour $4): **Farmington** (☎ 502-452-9920; 3033 Bardstown Rd) is an 1810-era house designed by Thomas Jefferson, **Locust Grove** (☎ 502-897-9845; 561 Blankenbaker Lane) was a 1790 Georgian mansion owned by the city's founder, **Whitehall** (☎ 502-897-2944; 3110 Lexington Rd) is an 1855 house remodeled in Classic Revival style, and **Thomas Edison House** (☎ 502-585-5247; 729 E Washington St) is a shotgun cottage where Edison rented a room in the 1860s while working as a telegrapher for Western Union. Hours vary; it's best to call ahead.

The **Belle of Louisville** (☎ 502-574-2355, 800-832-0011; adult $10), a 1914-era stern-wheeler, does scenic two-hour sightseeing cruises on the Ohio River, departing from the 4th St Wharf.

CHURCHILL DOWNS

Home to the Kentucky Derby (see opposite), **Churchill Downs** (☎ 502-636-4400, 800-283-3729; www.churchill downs.com; 700 Central Ave), 3 miles south of downtown, is one of the most important horse-oriented venues in the country. Most seats at the Kentucky Derby on the first Saturday in May are by invitation only or they've been reserved years in advance. On Derby Day, $40 gets you into the Paddock party scene (no seat) if you arrive by 6am, but it's so crowded you won't see much of the race. Don't fret, however. From April through to November, you can get a $2 seat at the Downs for many exciting races, often warm-ups for the big events.

On the grounds, the surprisingly interesting **Kentucky Derby Museum** (502-637-7097; Gate 1, Central Ave; adult/child $8/3; 8am-5pm Mon-Sat, noon-5pm Sun) has displays on horses, jockeys and mint juleps, a 360-degree audiovisual about the race and a tour of the track.

Sleeping & Eating

Emily Boone Home Hostel (502-585-3430; 102 Pope St; dm $10) Provides three futon beds with kitchen facilities in a private home. Space is limited, so call first. The cheapest motels are on the outskirts, especially around I-65 near the airport.

Travelodge (502-583-2629; 401 S 2nd St; r from $65; P) This downtown place has very standard rooms but the good price, location and outdoor pool make up for its lack of atmosphere.

Galt House (502-589-5200, 800-626-1814; www.galthouse.com; 140 N 4th Ave; r from $80) With 700 standard rooms and more suites, this big convention hotel offers a wide-range of rates. Amenities include a revolving restaurant and lounge with great views and a British-style pub. Ask for a room with a view of the river.

Doubletree Club (502-585-2200; 101 E Jefferson St; r from $120; P) A business-traveler hotel with a restaurant, pool and fitness room, plus attractive rooms.

Bluegrass Brewing Company (502-899-7070; 3929 Shelbyville Rd; mains $6-10) With delicious beers like Altbier, an amber ale, this microbrewery does all its brewing and bottling right here. It also serves up a good selection of salads, burgers and other pub grub. It's got a nice patio for outside dining and drinking.

Lilly's (502-451-0447; 1147 Bardstown Rd; lunch $8-14, dinner $15-25) Most of the good restaurants and bars are found at Bardstown Rd, including Lilly's, a longtime favorite for upscale lunches and dinners. Chef Kathy Cary whips together miracles featuring fresh fish, seafood, pork and beef.

Entertainment

The free weekly *Leo* lists gigs and entertainment.

Jillians (502-589-9090; 630 Barret Ave) The fun and popular Jillians is a bar, restaurant and live-music venue all rolled into one.

Kentucky Center for the Arts (502-562-0100; 5 Riverfront Plaza) This prime performance venue

RUN FOR THE ROSES

The first thoroughbred was brought to Kentucky in 1779 and by 1789 there were more horses here than people. Today, Central Kentucky has the world's greatest concentration of thoroughbred breeding farms, many of which are like equine palaces. All this horsing around pays off on the first Saturday in May, when the 'greatest two minutes in sports' takes place at Louisville's Churchill Downs. Ah, the Kentucky Derby, where the crowd wears wide-brimmed derby hats, sips mint juleps and waits to see which horse will make its owner rich, or richer.

Churchill Downs founder Colonel M Lewis Clark (grandson of William Clark of the Lewis and Clark expedition) held the first Kentucky Derby in 1875. Through Prohibition, the Great Depression and two world wars, the Kentucky Derby has never missed a race, making it the oldest uninterrupted sporting event in the world.

The first race of the year in horse-racing's prestigious Triple Crown (followed by the Preakness Stakes and the Belmont Stakes), the Derby sees up to 20 of the world's best three-year-old thoroughbreds pound through the race's 1.25-mile course. More than 250,000 fans attend each year. Though the race only lasts a couple of minutes, the festivities start about three weeks before for the **Kentucky Derby Festival** (502-584-6383; www.kdf.org). After the race, the crowd sings My Old Kentucky Home and watches as the winning horse gets covered in a blanket of roses. Later its name will be written on the racetrack wall.

Though interest in horse racing has waxed and waned through the years, the Kentucky Derby traditions (mint juleps and all) gallop on.

THE BOURBON TOUR

Named after the French royal family, bourbon whiskey was first distilled in Bourbon County, north of Lexington, in 1789. Today 90% of all bourbon is produced in Kentucky (no other state is allowed to put its own name on the bottle). A good bourbon must contain at least 51% corn, and must be stored in charred oak barrels for at least two years. Be forewarned that there are imposters. Legal versions of Kentucky moonshine, distilled from fermented corn mash, are available in some liquor stores: guaranteed less than one month old, cheap as spit and highly flammable. While in Kentucky, you must try a mint julep, the archetypical Southern drink made by adding sugar syrup and crushed mint.

The **Oscar Getz Museum of Whiskey History** (☎ 502-348-2999; 114 N 5th St), in Bardstown, tells the bourbon story pretty well. Most of Kentucky's distilleries, which are centered around Bardstown and Frankfort, offer free tours, where you come to see the drink as a delicate art form borne of long-standing tradition and integrity. You'll see it all, from the grain silos to the tubs of fermenting mash. Some offer tastings, others do not. No one gives up (or sells) the good stuff on Sundays or election days.

Distilleries

Near Bardstown (exit 112 off I-65, look for signs):

Heaven Hill (☎ 502-348-3921; 1064 Loretto Rd, Bardstown; tours 10am-5pm) The largest family-owned bourbon producers who hold the world's second-largest supply. See row upon row of aging barrels.

Jim Beam (☎ 502-543-9877; 149 Happy Hollow Rd in Clermont; tours 9am-4:30pm Mon-Sat, 1-4pm Sun) You watch a good film about the grandson of Jim Beam with some informative bourbon-making secrets thrown in.

Maker's Mark (☎ 502-865-2099; 3350 Burks Spring Rd near Loretto; tours 10:30am-3:30pm Mon-Sat, 1:30pm, 2:30pm & 3:30pm Sun) Perhaps the most attractive distillery amid pretty countryside 15 miles southeast of Bardstown. It's a National Historic Landmark where the Samuels family has been making whiskey since 1840.

Near Frankfort/Lawrenceburg:

Four Roses (☎ 502-839-3436; 1224 Bonds Mills Rd, Hwy 513 W; tours by appointment only) In a Spanish hacienda-style building, this distillery gives very detailed tours, good for bourbon connoisseurs.

Wild Turkey (☎ 502-839-4544; Hwy 62 E, Lawrenceburg; tours 9am, 10:30am, 12:30pm & 2:30pm Mon-Fri) Real wild turkeys fly through the nearby valleys. You get a good look at the industrial side of distilling.

Labrot & Graham (☎ 859-879-1939; 7855 McCracken Pike, Versailles; tours 10am, 11am, 1pm, 2pm & 3pm Mon-Sat) The historic site along a creek is restored to its 1800s glory. The small distillery is the only one still using old-fashioned copper pots.

Buffalo Trace (☎ 502-696-5926; 1001 Wilkinson Blvd near Frankfort; tours 9am-3pm Mon-Fri, 10am-2pm Sun) Named for the ancient buffalo that led early pioneers westward, this pretty distillery shows the whole process, including its special single-barrel bourbon.

has theater, ballet, opera, orchestra, modern dance and popular music. It's worth checking what's on or looking around the center, with its unusual design and sculptures.

Palace Theater (☎ 502-583-4555; 625 4th Ave) The 1928 Palace Theater is a wonderfully ornate venue for theater and concerts.

Getting There & Around

Louisville's International Airport (☎ 502-367-4636) is 5 miles south of town on I-65. Get there by cab ($15) or local bus No 2. The **Greyhound station** (☎ 502-585-3331; 720 W Muhammad Ali Blvd), just west of downtown, has buses to Chicago, IL ($44, six hours); Lexington ($9, 1¾ hours); Memphis ($66, from 6½ hours); and Nashville ($28, from three hours). Local buses are run by **TARC** (☎ 502-585-1234; 1000 W Broadway), based at the Union Station depot.

CENTRAL KENTUCKY

Following I-65 south toward Tennessee, this region holds several cultural attractions, including several whiskey distilleries. About 40 miles south of Louisville is **Bardstown**, a sleepy town with a gaggle of distilleries (see boxed text, above). It comes alive in mid-September for the **Kentucky Bourbon Festival**

(☎ 270-638-4877; www.kybourbonfestival.com). The **visitors center** (☎ 502-348-4877, 800-638-4877), just east of the square, has a walking-tour map of historic sites. Bardstown makes a good home base for exploring the area.

The most hyped attraction in Bardstown is **My Old Kentucky Home State Park** (☎ 502-348-3502; 501 E Stephen Foster Ave), supposedly the place where, in 1852, Stephen Foster wrote the song 'My Old Kentucky Home.' In fact, Foster was from Pittsburgh and spent his whole life in the North, though he may have visited his cousin's plantation here once. The state's official and much-loved song, which originally said that 'the darkies are gay,' is today rendered as 'the people.' Later verses, now rarely heard, elaborate on the not-so-gay life of the slaves. Costumed guides take tours of the house and **garden** (adult/child $4.50/2.50; 🕑 9am-5pm).

Camping ($10-13) is available at the state park. Motels include pleasant **Bardstown Inn** (☎ 502-349-0776; 510 E Stephen Foster Ave; d $60; P ❄) and the family-run **Wilson Motel** (☎ 502-348-3364; 530 N 3rd St; d $50; P ❄), north of Court Sq in the historic district. The most interesting B&B is **Jailer's Inn** (☎ 502-348-5551; 111 W Stephen Foster Ave; r $105-125), a thoroughly renovated jailhouse.

My Old Kentucky Dinner Train (☎ 502-348-7300; 602 N 3rd St; $65), runs 35 miles through the Kentucky countryside while guests enjoy dinner in vintage 1940s dining cars. The trip takes 2½ hours, leaving at 5pm. A lunch train runs at noon on Saturdays ($46). **Tom Pig's** (☎ 502-348-9404; 732 N 3rd St; dishes $4-9) serves cheap breakfasts and down-home chicken and steak dishes to locals in padded booths.

Further south, **Elizabethtown**, settled in 1779, was once home to Abe Lincoln's father. The **visitors center** (☎ 270-765-2175, 800-437-0092; 1030 N Mulberry St; 🕑 9am-5pm Mon-Fri, 10am-2pm Sat summer) has details of walking tours. It also houses **Schmidt's Museum of Coca-Cola Memorabilia** (☎ 270-765-2175; admission $2; 🕑 closed Sun), with a 100,000-piece collection highlighting 'the real thing' in American life.

Follow Hwy 61 11 miles southeast of Elizabethtown and you'll hit **Hodgenville** and the **Abraham Lincoln Birthplace National Historic Site** (☎ 270-358-3137; admission free; 🕑 8am-5pm), which features a replica of a Greek temple constructed around an old log cabin. Research has established that Lincoln was not actually born in the cabin, so it's referred to as his 'symbolic birthplace.' In front are 56 steps, one for every year of Lincoln's life, and the visitors center features a film and diorama. When Abe was 2½, his family moved to Knob Creek, 10 miles away on US 31E, where his first memory was of slaves being driven down a public road.

About 115 miles southeast of Louisville off I-65 exit 28, **Bowling Green** is home to Western Kentucky University and the Corvette. All the world's corvette sports cars are now produced at the Bowling Green **plant** (☎ 270-745-8419; tours free; 9am & 1pm Mon-Fri). Opposite, the **National Corvette Museum** (☎ 270-781-7973, 800-538-3883; www.corvettemuseum.com; 350 Corvette Dr; adult/child $8/4.50; 🕑 8am-5pm) has over 50 examples of this classic American car. Exhibits span half a century and cover racing, advertising and motorcar culture.

Mammoth Cave National Park

Between Bowling Green and Elizabethtown, **Mammoth Cave National Park** (☎ 270-758-2328; www.nps.gov/maca; exit 53 from I-65) has the most extensive cave system on earth. With some 350 miles of surveyed passageways, Mammoth is at least three times bigger than any other known cave. The caves have been used for prehistoric mineral gathering, as a source of saltpeter for gunpowder and as a tuberculosis hospital. Tourists started visiting around 1810 and guided tours have been offered since the 1830s. The area became a national park in 1926 and now brings nearly 2 million visitors each year.

To see the caves, you must take a **ranger-guided tour** (☎ 800-967-2283; adult $8-20), and it's wise to book ahead, especially in summer. Tours range from easy to strenuous; there's also a tour for those mobility impaired. Even if you don't get into caves, the aboveground attractions of the Green River, the hiking trails and the natural forest are alluring. The visitors center shows a film about the caves, books cave tours, issues permits for backcountry camping (free) and has excellent publications. The caves are in the central time zone, an hour earlier than Louisville.

Mammoth Cave Hotel (☎ 270-758-2225; r $75, d cottage/woodland cabin $65/50), near the visitors center, has an inexpensive coffee shop and restaurant. The hotel and cottages have power, but the cabins do not. Three developed **campgrounds** have campsites with water and toilets but no hookups. Call for reservation information.

PICKIN' & GRINNIN'

Early American settlers maintained oral history by singing ballads about their homelands, about the hardships and discoveries of forging life on foreign ground. Early bluegrass and country music developed from this 'mountain' music, defined by its gritty, honest storytelling about honest folks trying to eke out a life on farms or in the hills.

In the 1920s and 1930s, Bill Monroe and his brother Charlie gained attention as a duo with their combination of guitar, mandolin and sweet harmonies. Being from Kentucky where the grassy meadows sprout blue buds that give the grass a blue hue in spring, Bill went on to form Bill Monroe and the Blue Grass Boys.

The Boys created a sound like no other. Using traditional acoustic banjos, fiddles, mandolins and guitars, combined with vocal harmonies, the music incorporated songs and rhythms borrowed from gospel, blues and country. It even incorporated work songs and 'shouts' of black laborers.

In 1939, the Boys appeared at Nashville's Grand Ole Opry and soon became a wildly successful touring band. In 1946, Earl Scruggs joined the group bringing his banjo and a distinct three-finger picking style that further honed the bluegrass sound. Later, Lester Flatt brought the slide Dobro guitar, injecting bluegrass with a touch of the blues.

Bluegrass festivals popped up in the 1960s and bluegrass bands from around the south added regional flavor. In 1969, Scruggs recorded Foggy Mountain Breakdown used in the movie *Bonnie & Clyde*, and the world opened its ears.

Bluegrass music was later used in the theme song to TV's the *Beverly Hillbillies*. It's featured in the movie *Deliverance* and, more recently in *O Brother, Where Art Thou*, starring Kentucky native George Cloony.

Learn more about Bluegrass at the International Bluegrass Music Museum in Owensboro (p564), or find a scratchy LP of Bill Monroe, who is rightfully considered as the father of Bluegrass.

Greyhound buses go to nearby Cave City, I-65 exit 53, which has touristy attractions and facilities.

WESTERN KENTUCKY

The most direct route through western Kentucky is the Western Kentucky Parkway/Purchase Parkway, confusingly signposted with a blue 'P' that looks like a 'parking' sign. A better route west is along US 68. About 15 miles west of Bowling Green, at South Union, the **Shaker Museum** (☎ 270-542-4167; admission $4; ⏲ Mar-Dec) is not as extensive as the settlement near Lexington, but the 1824 Centre House is a fine Shaker building with examples of Shaker crafts and furnishings.

At Fairview, the imposing **Jefferson Davis Monument** is a 351ft obelisk marking the birthplace of the first and only president of the Confederacy. The **visitors center** (☎ 270-886-1765; ⏲ 9am-5pm May-Nov) makes a good case that Davis (1808–89) was a reluctant secessionist, an honorable man reluctantly caught up in a series of tragic events.

Further to the west, US 68 passes through the **Land Between the Lakes National Recreation Area** (☎ 270-924-2000). This pretty spot is popular for hiking, fishing and camping. Park attractions include the **Elk & Bison Prairie** (admission $3; ⏲ year-round), a habitat restoration project where the mammals roam admission free; the **Home Place** (admission $3.50; ⏲ Mar-Nov), a re-created pioneer village; Woodlands Nature Station (admission $3.50; ⏲ Mar-Nov), an environmental education center; and Planetarium (admission $3; ⏲ Mar–mid-Dec). You can buy combination tickets to all attractions for $9.50.

Along the Ohio River

No road follows the river very closely. The towns here grew on the strength of river transport. Owensboro has an International Bar-B-Q Festival in May, a bluegrass festival in October and the excellent **International Bluegrass Music Museum** (☎ 270-926-7891; www.bluegrass-museum.org; 207 E 2nd St; adult/child $8/4; ⏲ 10am-5pm Tue-Fri, 1-5pm Sat & Sun).

Henderson was for several years home to renowned ornithologist and artist John James Audubon. **John James Audubon State Park** (☎ 270-827-1893; admission free) includes a nature reserve and a museum featuring over 400 original engravings from Audubon's definitive 1839 *Birds of America*.

At the meeting of the Ohio and Tennessee Rivers, Paducah was the scene of important Civil War battles. The **Museum of the American Quilter's Society** (☎ 270-442-8856; 215 Jefferson St; adult/child $5/3; ⏲ year-round) has three galleries of antique and modern quilts and the National Quilt Show in April. Across the river in Illinois, the small town of Metropolis gets mileage from its Superman associations.

BLUEGRASS COUNTRY

Groomed pastures filled with awe-inspiring thoroughbred horses long ago replaced the herds of shaggy bison that once roamed this area's oak-ash woodlands and clover meadows. Encompassing the northeast corner of Kentucky, east of Louisville, Bluegrass Country emanates from Lexington in an undeniable and incredibly scenic ode to the horse.

Frankfort

Kentucky's diminutive capital, 26 miles west of Lexington, was a locational compromise with rival city Louisville. It's a small country town with some imposing buildings, notably the neoclassical 1910 beaux arts **capitol building** (☎ 502-564-3449; tours free; ⏲ Mon-Sat) and the nearby governor's mansion.

The older part of town is across the Kentucky River, where the **old state capitol** (☎ 502-564-1792; admission free; ⏲ 10am-5pm Tue-Fri) functioned from 1827 to 1910. Nearby is the handsome **Kentucky History Center** (☎ 502-564-1792; 100 W Broadway St; admission free; ⏲ 8am-4pm Tue-Sat), for those interested in state history.

On the east bank of the river, Frankfort Cemetery has the grave of Daniel Boone and a big war memorial. Further south, the oft-visited Kentucky Vietnam Veterans Memorial is a giant sundial engraved with 1000 names.

Lexington

With a distinctly small-town feel, Lexington is saved from parochialism by University of Kentucky (UK) students and the international jet-setting thoroughbred racehorse industry. Most of Lexington's best attractions are outside the city. On a fine day, the sublimely beautiful horse country seems like the loveliest place on earth, with gently rolling hills, brilliant green grass, handsome houses, shady trees and picturesque plank fences receding into the distance. The barns are often more imposing than the houses, and the aristocratic thoroughbreds prance around like they own the place (which, given racing purses, they probably do). A loop around Paris Pike, Iron Works Pike, Yarnallton Rd and Old Frankfort Pike will take you past many horse farms, but scenic detours are recommended. Pick up good maps and area information from the **visitors center** (☎ 859-233-7299, 800-845-3959; 301 E Vine St; ⏲ 8:30am-5pm Mon-Fri, 10am-4pm Sat).

SIGHTS & ACTIVITIES

Historic Houses

Downtown Lexington has a pleasant mix of old and new buildings and historic houses. The following offer tours for $5 to $6. You can also purchase a $10 combination ticket to visit all four – available at the visitors center or at Ashland.

The 1806 **Mary Todd-Lincoln House** (☎ 859-233-9999; 578 W Main St) home has articles from the first lady's childhood and her years as Abe's wife.

Hunt-Morgan House (☎ 859-253-0362; 201 N Mill St) is a fine Federal-style mansion (c 1814) with a small Civil War museum.

Six miles south of Main St off US 27 (Nicholasville Rd) is **Wavelan State Historic Site** (☎ 859-272-3611; 225 Waveland Museum Lane).

Ashland (☎ 859-266-8581; 120 Sycamore Rd), 1.5 miles east of downtown, was the handsome Italianate-style home and estate of Henry Clay (1777–1852), the Kentucky statesman who brokered compromises that staved off civil war for 40 years.

Kentucky Horse Park

A working horse farm, educational theme park and equestrian sports center the **Kentucky Horse Park** (☎ 859-233-4303, 800-678-8813; kyhorsepark.com; 4089 Iron Works Parkway; adult/child $16/11; ⏲ 9am-5pm mid-Mar–Nov, 9am-5pm Wed-Sun winter) sits on 1200 acres just north of Lexington. A visit to the horse farm will delight horse lovers and could convert anyone who isn't. Demonstrations of riding, horse breeds and equipment are included. Also included, the international **Museum of the Horse** follows the horse through human history, describing its role in hunting, transport, warfare and sport. Seasonal horseback riding cost $14.

The adjacent **American Saddlebred Museum** (☎ 859-259-2746, 800-829-4438; 4093 Iron Works Parkway; admission $3) focuses on America's

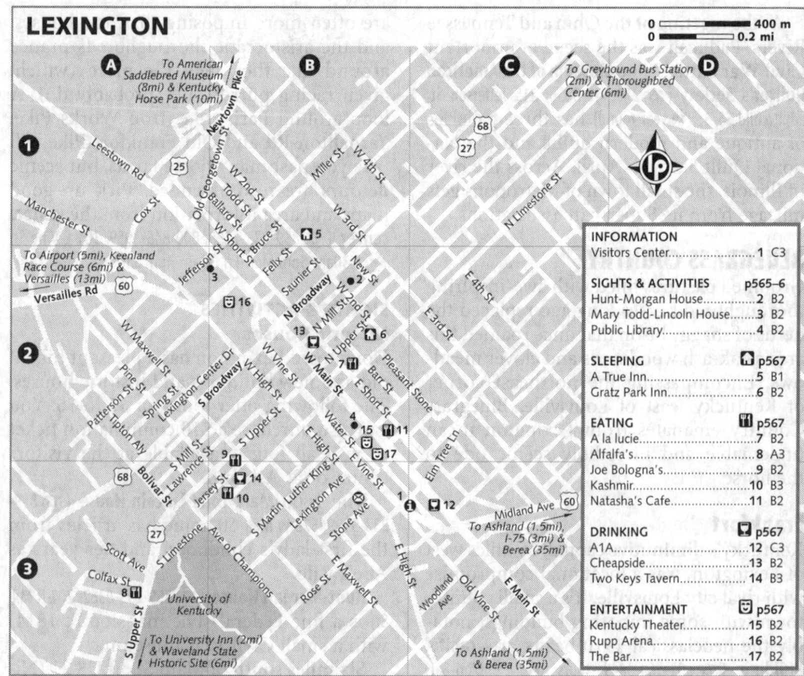

first registered horse breed – for hardcore enthusiasts only; others might get bored. Admission is free with a Kentucky Horse Park ticket.

Thoroughbred Center

Most farms are closed to the public, but you can visit the **Thoroughbred Center** (☎ 859-293-1853; 3380 Paris Pike; adult/child $10/5; tours 9am, 10:30am & 1pm Mon-Fri, 9am & 10:30am Sat Apr-Nov, by appointment Nov-Mar). Tours of this working thoroughbred training facility take in stables, practice tracks and paddocks.

Keeneland Race Course

Horses earn their living 32 days a year at this exciting **racecourse** (☎ 859-254-3412, 800-456-3412; www.keeneland.com; 4201 Versailles Rd; admission $3), west of town on US 60, Versailles Rd (that's ver-*sales*). The spring and fall racing seasons are in April and October (seats $2.50, reserved seats $7.50). When the Derby is happening in Louisville, Keeneland throws its own party with live music and a barbecue, which prompts Lexingtonians to say, 'Louisville may have the race, but we have the party!' On other days from March to November, you can watch the champions train from sunrise to 10am. Afterward, you can enjoy breakfast in the **track kitchen** (🕑 year-round).

Horseback Riding

So you're itching to get in the saddle? Several working ranches around Lexington offer **horseback riding** to both newbie and experienced riders.

Whispering Woods (☎ 859-570-9663; 265 Wright Land; 1hr/full-day trail rides $20/60; 🕑 May-Oct), in Georgetown, offers guided trail rides.

Deer Run Stables (☎ 859-527-6339), in Combs Ferry off Hwy 627, also offers guided trips. Call ahead for directions and reservation.

TOURS

Blue Grass Tours (☎ 859-252-5744; www.bluegrasstours.com; from $25) Takes visitors to Keeneland or private horse farms and will pick up downtown.

Horse Farm Tours (☎ 859-268-2906; www.horsefarmtours.com; adult $25; tours 9am & 1pm Mon-Sun) Picks up at Lexington hotels and offers two tours daily to working horse farms. Reservations required.

SLEEPING

University Inn (☎ 859-278-6625, 866-881-9676; 1229 S Limestone St; r $65; P) Across from the university, this basic but well-equipped hotel is a good value. All rooms have a fridge, which is handy if you need to chill some beer.

A True Inn (☎ 859-252-6166, 800-374-6151; 467 W 2nd Ave; r $130-189; P) Built in 1843, this lovely Greek Revival B&B has antique-decorated, homey rooms each named for a famous Lexingtonian. A delicious breakfast is served in the garden.

Gratz Park Inn (☎ 859-231-1777; 120 W 2nd St; r/ste $150/180; P) The city's grand dame hotel, Gratz Park is a charmer without the stuffiness of some fancy hotels. And the antique furnishings, four-poster beds and fresh flowers add nice touches.

Kentucky Horse Park (☎ 859-259-4257, 800-370-6416; 4089 Iron Works Parkway; paved/primitive campsites $23/15) The convenient campground with 260 paved sites on the Horse Park farm is open year-round. There's a pool, showers, laundry and more. Some 'primitive' sites are also available.

The visitors center has a listing of highway motels, most of which charge about $45.

EATING

The liveliest area in the evening is around E Main and S Limestone Sts.

Natasha's Cafe (☎ 859-259-2754; 112 Esplanade; lunch $6-8, dinner $10-14) A gem in a town this size, Natasha's serves an excellent Mediterranean-inspired buffet full of fresh, healthy ingredients including lots of vegetarian options.

A la lucie (☎ 859-252-5277; 159 N Limestone St; dinner $15-25; 6-10pm Mon-Sat) This funky bistro serves well-prepared dinners such as lobster pot pie, paella and crusted lamb.

Alfalfa's (☎ 859-253-0014; 557 S Limestone St; meals $6-12) Near the university, this vegetarian place serves up good breakfasts and sandwiches. Try the yummy buckwheat pancakes.

Kashmir (☎ 859-233-3060; 341 S Limestone St; lunch buffet $6) An excellent value for good spice-filled Indian food, though the service can be gruff and slow.

Joe Bologna's (☎ 859-252-4933; 120 W Maxwell St; meals $6-11) Housed in a former Jewish temple, Joe's is popular with the university crowd for pizza and pasta.

Billy's Hickory Pit Bar-B-Q (☎ 859-269-9593; 101 Cochran Rd; meals $6-15) A longtime institution for inexpensive Kentucky-style smoked pork, beef and mutton. Look out for 'burgoo,' which is a satisfying beef stew.

DRINKING

For beer, bourbon and bar food, try friendly watering holes like **Cheapside** (☎ 859-254-0046; 131 Cheapside St), with a tropical patio. Cheapside, **Two Keys Tavern** (☎ 859-254-5000; 333 S Limestone St) and **A1A** (☎ 859-231-7263; 367 E Main St) all have live music.

ENTERTAINMENT

Applebee's Park (☎ 859-422-7867; 1200 N Broadway) Home to Lexington's minor-league baseball team. It is also a great venue for outdoor concerts.

Rupp Arena (☎ 859-233-4567) The 23,000-seat venue on Patterson St, is the home court for the UK Wildcats and also hosts any big-name rock and country acts.

Kentucky Theater (☎ 859-231-6997; 214 E Main St) The restored 1927 theater shows movies and is an intimate venue for occasional live music.

GETTING THERE & AROUND

Lexington, at the crossroads of I-75 and I-64 is 77 miles east of Louisville. **Greyhound** (☎ 859-299-8804; 477 W New Circle Rd; 7am-11pm) is 2 miles from downtown. Regular buses go to Louisville, some by very indirect routes ($19, 1¾ hours). There are also buses to Nashville, TN ($57, from five hours) and Washington, DC ($91, from 14 hours). **Lex-Tran** (☎ 859-253-4636) runs local buses (No 6 goes to the Greyhound stop).

Around Lexington

About 10 miles north of Lexington, **Georgetown** was settled in 1776 and named after George Washington. The town's claims to fame include a historic downtown and the first bourbon whiskey. About 60 miles northeast of Lexington, **Maysville** is a late-18th-century river town. The **visitors center** (☎ 859-564-6986) has information about covered bridges in the area.

Set in bucolic farmland 16 scenic miles southwest of Lexington in Harrodsburg, the old **Shaker Village of Pleasant Hill** (☎ 800-734-5411; 3501 Lexington Rd; adult/child $10/5.50) is the site of the last western Shaker commune. Founded by Shakers from New England in 1805, it became a farming and craft-based community.

Its population peaked at about 500 in the 1830s and declined as strict celibacy took its toll. The village officially closed in 1910, but the 33 original buildings survive intact because of sound construction and recent restoration. Fine Shaker craftwork abounds, and there's a full program of events, demonstrations and craft workshops. A **communal dining room** (breakfast & lunch around $8, dinner $18) serves traditional Shaker country cooking, and you can stay overnight in old **village buildings** (s/d from $70/80). For accommodations and meals, call ☎ 800-734-5611.

About 35 miles south of Lexington off I-75, **Berea** (buh-*re*-ah) is on the edge of the Appalachians and is big on folk arts and crafts. Berea College has a long tradition of employing its own students in lieu of charging tuition fees. You might find students working at the Berea **Welcome Center** (☎ 859-986-2540, 800-598-5263) or at the college's **Appalachian Gallery** (☎ 859-985-3140), with artifacts, pictures and displays on mountain life.

Boone Tavern Hotel (☎ 859-985-3700, 800-366-9358; 100 Main St; s/d $65/75) is a handsome 1909-era building and its dining room specializes in hearty regional fare (meals around $17). It's all staffed by the college's hospitality students and has a lot more character than your average motel.

Daniel Boone National Forest

This vast area in the east of the state is noted for its rich variety of plants and wildlife and an extensive trail system. The north end, around Morehead, is popular for boating in Cave Run Lake and for the Zilpo Rd Scenic Byway. The central area, around Stanton and Slade, features the dramatically symmetrical **Natural Bridge**. The nearby Red River Gorge has excellent hiking trails as well as Class I to III white water. Ranger stations throughout the area have maps and information. The main **ranger station** (☎ 859-745-3100; 1700 Bypass Rd; 8am-4pm Mon-Fri Nov-Mar, 10am-6pm daily April-Oct) is in Winchester.

The south end of the national forest, easily accessed from I-75, has some depressed communities and old coal-mining areas around Stearns, on US 27. Within the forest, **Cumberland Falls State Resort Park** (☎ 859-528-4121; admission free; campsites $15) has a rustic lodge ($46 to $65), a swimming pool and campgrounds. Nearby Corbin is the site of the original outlet of **Kentucky Fried Chicken**. The chicken tastes like it does at any KFC, but the exhibits are nostalgic for those of us who grew up lickin' our fingers.

CUMBERLAND GAP NATIONAL HISTORIC PARK

In the southeast corner of the state, where Kentucky, Virginia and Tennessee come together, the Cumberland Gap has long been a crucial link across the mountains. Carved by wind and water, the gap forms a major break in the formidable Appalachian Mountains. Indians followed migratory buffalo, Daniel Boone followed the Indians and the pioneers followed Boone. Now a four-lane highway and a railway both tunnel under the gap. The **visitors center** (☎ 859-248-2817; www.nps.gov/cuga) is at the Kentucky end of the road tunnel, while the 100-site **Wilderness Road Campground** (campsites/RV sites $10/15) is off Hwy 58 in Virginia.

Florida

CONTENTS

There's a lot to love about Florida – 1250 miles of beach-luscious coastline, year-round warm weather, attractions galore – and lots and lots of people come every year to love it. But for all its growing pains (the state's population has tripled since the 1960s), Florida maintains its comely natural charms. In addition to its cozy snuggle between the Atlantic Ocean and the Gulf of Mexico, the state is full of watery treasures, with more than 7700 lakes, 1700 rivers and 300 gin-clear springs making it a mecca for water lovers. Canoeing, kayaking, fishing, snorkeling, scuba diving, surfing, boating, waterskiing – if you can't find a place to indulge in these pursuits then double-check your whereabouts because you aren't in Florida. Want hiking trails through piney wood forests? Got 'em. Want to camp on semitropical islands? Got them, too. Want to climb a mountain? Forget about it, but Florida's flat-as-a-pancake terrain does make it a no-brainer for bicyclists of every ability.

The state's constructed diversions are equally dazzling: the grand art deco hotels of Miami Beach, the Overseas Hwy to Key West, the technological wonders of Kennedy Space Center, the high speeds of Daytona Beach. And then there are all those central Florida theme parks, such as Walt Disney World, Universal Studios, SeaWorld, Busch Gardens. When you've had enough of the thrills and make-believe, explore the state's many museums, galleries and gardens or visit St Augustine, the nation's oldest city, for some cultural sustenance. A lot to love, a whole lot to see and do.

HIGHLIGHTS

- Snorkeling and diving around **Key Largo** (p594)
- Club-hopping in Miami's ever-trendy **South Beach** (p585)
- Taking the Mickey at Orlando's theme parks – **Walt Disney World, Universal Studios** and **Sea World** (p616)
- Paddling and slogging through the **Everglades National Park** (p591)
- Soaking up the history at the oldest European settlement in the USA – **St Augustine** (p606)
- Strolling along the glistening sands of **Canaveral National Seashore** (p602)
- Taking off to the moon in a simulated control room at **Kennedy Space Center** (p602)
- Communing with the gentle, endangered manatees in **Blue Spring State Park** (p605)
- Exploring swamp trails and spotting rare Florida panthers in **Big Cypress National Preserve** (p593)

HISTORY

Florida's earliest inhabitants – hunter-gatherer tribes that wandered south – probably appeared here around 9000 BC. By the time the first Europeans began exploring the peninsula, the principal groups were the Apalachee in the panhandle, Timucuan in the north and Calusa in the southwest.

Spanish explorer Juan Ponce de León arrived near present-day Cape Canaveral in 1513 and named the new land in honor of Pascua Florida, the Easter Feast of Flowers. In 1565, Pedro Menéndez de Avilés founded St Augustine, the USA's oldest European settlement. As a Spanish colony, Florida became a refuge for the Seminoles, a group formed by runaway African slaves and Native Americans, primarily Creeks. From 1817 to 1853, the Seminoles waged three wars against US troops. Under the Indian Removal Act in 1830, most of Florida's indigenous people were uprooted to reservations west of the Mississippi, with a few surviving Seminoles taking refuge in the Everglades.

Florida was admitted to the Union on March 3, 1845, only to secede 16 years later at the onset of the Civil War. It was readmitted in 1868. Post–Civil War construction of railroads linked Florida's east coast, Tampa and Key West to the northern states. This unlocked the state's tourism potential and led to the first real-estate boom. The 1898 Spanish-American War and WWI brought the construction of naval stations and the influx of thousands of new residents. Post-WWII Florida thrived with the first wave of retirement communities and the fledgling aerospace industry. After the 1959 Cuban revolution, anti-Castro immigrants flooded in and established a permanent Cuban community in Miami.

In the 1970s, Walt Disney World created hundreds of thousands of tourism-related jobs and launched a development boom that, except for a few bumps in the 1980s and 1990s, has continued ever since. The contentious 2000 presidential election, between Democratic US Vice President Al Gore and Republican Texas Governor George W Bush, was decided in Florida. Gore won the country's popular vote, but Bush, using Florida to take the electoral vote, won the hotly contested state and thus the election by a few hundred votes.

FLORIDA FACTS

Nickname Sunshine State
Population 16,713,149 (4th)
Area 65,755 sq miles (22nd)
Admitted to Union March 3, 1845 (27th); seceded January 10, 1861; readmitted July 4, 1868
Capital city Tallahassee (population 150,000)
Other cities Jacksonville (790,500), Miami (365,120), Tampa (304,000), Orlando (188,000)
State symbols Florida panther (animal), manatee (tropical marine animal), orange blossom (flower), *Old Folks at Home* by Stephen Foster (song)
Birthplace of Zora Neale Hurston (1891–1960), Sidney Poitier (b 1927), Pat Boone (b 1934), Janet Reno (b 1938), Faye Dunaway (b 1941), Jim Morrison (1943–71), Tom Petty (b 1950), Chris Evert (b 1954), Wesley Snipes (b 1962)
Famous for orange groves, theme parks, and beaches, beaches, beaches

GEOGRAPHY & CLIMATE

Florida's terrain is mainly flat, with coastal lowlands and low hills in the north and central regions. The south-central portion of the state is wetlands and reclaimed swampland. The coasts are protected by natural barrier islands and, in the south, coral reefs. The stretch of water between the barrier islands and mainland form the Intracoastal Waterway. In Miami and south Florida, the peak season is December through March, with warm, dry weather, big crowds and high prices. The hottest and wettest time is June through October. Orlando is hot and muggy in summer and remains popular year-round. Jacksonville, St Augustine and the panhandle can be cold in winter, and summer is their main tourist season.

INFORMATION

The state's privatized tourism agency, **Visit Florida** (☎ 850-488-5607, 888-735-2872; www.flausa.com; Suite 300, 661 E Jefferson St, Tallahassee) operates welcome centers on I-95, I-75 and I-10 at exits just inside the Florida state line. It also has an information center in Tallahassee at the plaza level of the New Capitol Building.

NATIONAL & STATE PARKS

Florida has three national parks – Biscayne National Park (p581), Dry Tortugas National Park (p601), and Everglades National Park (p591). The **Division of Recreation and**

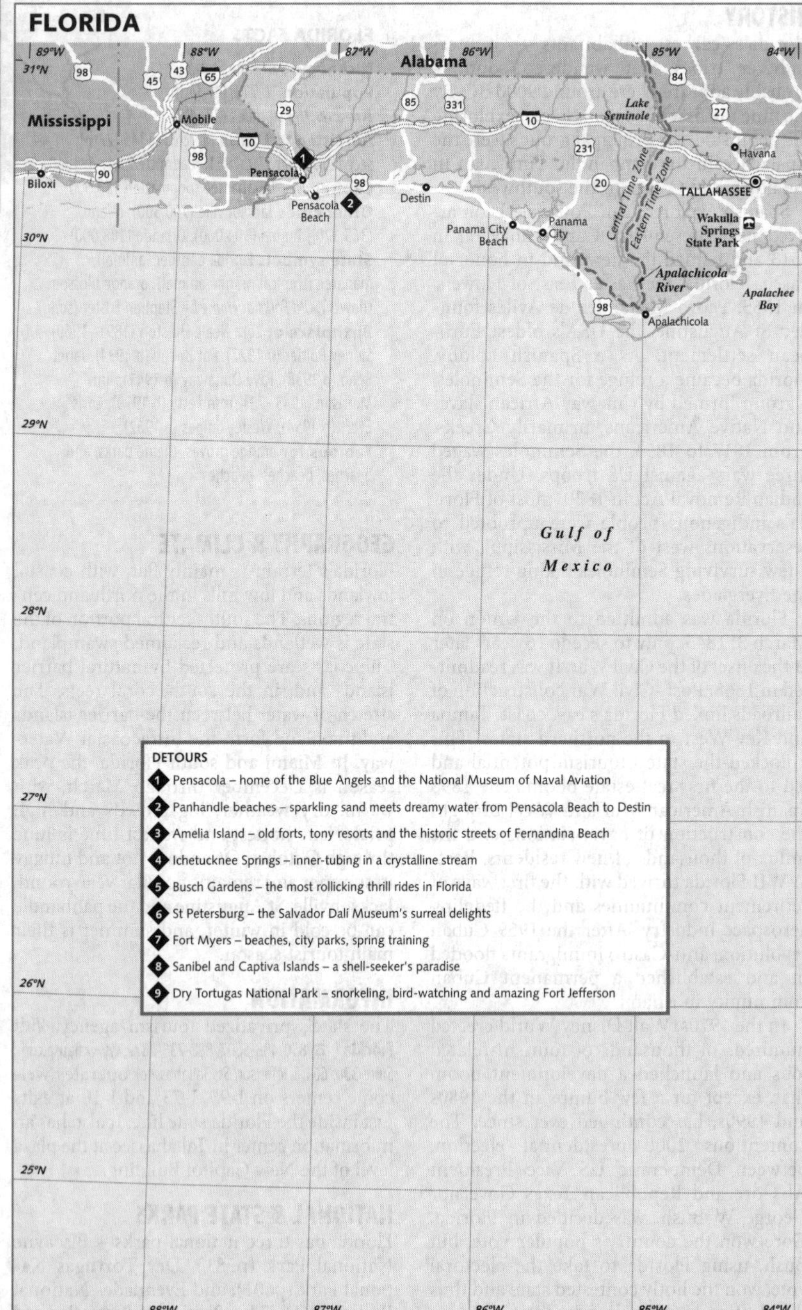
FLORIDA
89°W
88°W
87°W
86°W
85°W
84°W
31°N
30°N
29°N
28°N
27°N
26°N
25°N
Alabama
Mississippi
Mobile
Biloxi
Pensacola
Pensacola Beach
Destin
Panama City Beach
Panama City
Lake Seminole
Havana
TALLAHASSEE
Wakulla Springs State Park
Central Time Zone
Eastern Time Zone
Apalachicola River
Apalachicola
Apalachee Bay
Gulf of Mexico
98
45
43
65
29
10
90
85
331
84
27
231
20
DETOURS
1 Pensacola – home of the Blue Angels and the National Museum of Naval Aviation
2 Panhandle beaches – sparkling sand meets dreamy water from Pensacola Beach to Destin
3 Amelia Island – old forts, tony resorts and the historic streets of Fernandina Beach
4 Ichetucknee Springs – inner-tubing in a crystalline stream
5 Busch Gardens – the most rollicking thrill rides in Florida
6 St Petersburg – the Salvador Dalí Museum's surreal delights
7 Fort Myers – beaches, city parks, spring training
8 Sanibel and Captiva Islands – a shell-seeker's paradise
9 Dry Tortugas National Park – snorkeling, bird-watching and amazing Fort Jefferson

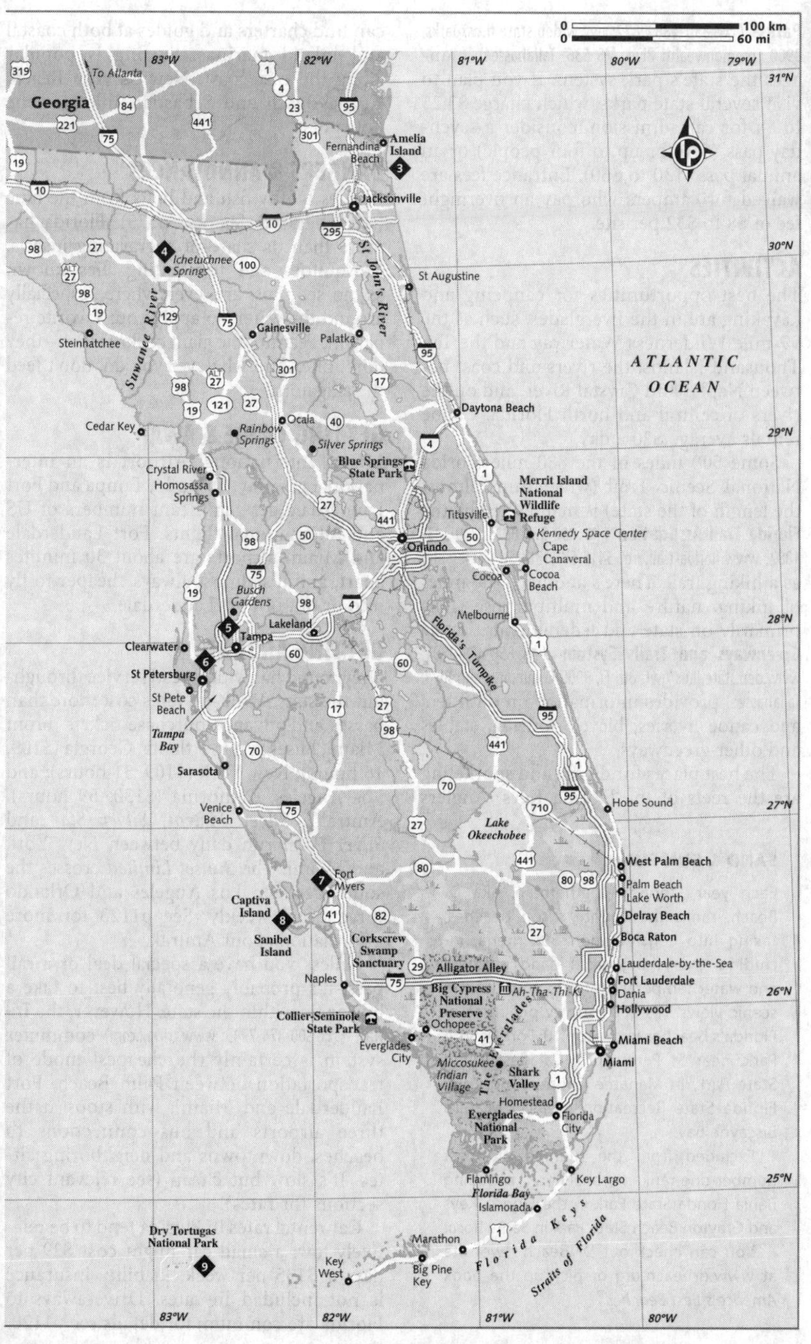
0
0
100 km
60 mi
83°W
82°W
81°W
80°W
79°W
31°N
30°N
29°N
28°N
27°N
26°N
25°N
To Atlanta
Georgia
ATLANTIC
OCEAN
Amelia
Island
Fernandina
Beach
Jacksonville
St John's River
St Augustine
Ichetuchnee
Springs
Suwanee River
Gainesville
Palatka
Steinhatchee
Daytona Beach
Cedar Key
Ocala
Rainbow
Springs
Silver Springs
Blue Springs
State Park
Crystal River
Homosassa
Springs
Merrit Island
National
Wildlife
Refuge
Titusville
Kennedy Space Center
Orlando
Cape
Canaveral
Cocoa
Cocoa
Beach
Busch
Gardens
Lakeland
Melbourne
Florida's Turnpike
Tampa
Clearwater
St Petersburg
St Pete
Beach
Tampa
Bay
Sarasota
Venice
Beach
Hobe Sound
Lake
Okeechobee
West Palm Beach
Palm Beach
Lake Worth
Delray Beach
Boca Raton
Fort
Myers
Captiva
Island
Sanibel
Island
Corkscrew
Swamp
Sanctuary
Alligator Alley
Lauderdale-by-the-Sea
Fort Lauderdale
Dania
Hollywood
Naples
Big Cypress
National
Preserve
Ah-Tha-Thi-Ki
Collier-Seminole
State Park
Ochopee
Everglades
City
The Everglades
Miami Beach
Miami
Miccosukee
Indian
Village
Shark
Valley
Homestead
Florida
City
Everglades
National
Park
Flamingo
Key Largo
Florida Bay
Islamorada
Florida Keys
Straits of Florida
Dry Tortugas
National Park
Marathon
Key
West
Big Pine
Key

Parks (☎ 850-488-9872; www.dep.state.fl.us/parks; 3900 Commonwealth Blvd, MS 536, Tallahassee) manages the state's park system. If you plan to visit several state parks, which charge $3.25 to $4 for car admission, consider a seven-day pass ($10 for up to four people) or an annual pass ($30 to $60). Entrance fees are waived for campers who pay an overnight fee of $8 to $32 per site.

ACTIVITIES

The best opportunities for canoeing and kayaking are in the Everglades, such as the 99-mile Wilderness Waterway and the Ten Thousand Islands; the rivers and coast between Naples and Crystal River; and on the rivers of central and north Florida. Canoe rentals average $20 a day.

Some 500 miles of the 880-mile Florida National Scenic Trail (which runs almost the length of the state) is maintained by the **Florida Trail Association** (☎ 352-378-8823, 800-343-1882; www.florida-trail.org; 5415 SW 13th St, Gainesville) as a hiking trail. There's another 1700 miles of hiking, nature and multipurpose trails primarily on state and federal lands. **Florida Greenways and Trails System** (☎ 850-488-3701; www.dep.state.fl.us/gwt; 8th Fl, 3900 Commonwealth Blvd, Tallahassee) provides information on outfitters and canoe liveries, bicycle touring, stables and other greenways.

The best places for diving and snorkeling are the reefs of the Florida Keys. Anglers can find charters and guides at both coastal and inland marinas. Surfing is popular along the east coast: New Smyrna Beach, Cocoa Beach and Sebastian Inlet are the hot spots.

SAND & SUN FUN

Each year Stephen Leatherman, aka Dr Beach, ranks the country's top beaches, taking into consideration 50 criteria, including everything from sand softness and water temperature to rip currents and scenic views. His 2003 survey put three of Florida's beaches in the top 10: Fort DeSoto Park, near St Petersburg; Caladesi Island State Park, in Manatee County; and Cape Florida State Recreation Area, in Miami's Biscayne Bay.

Excluded from the running are past number-one-ranked beaches, including Bahia Honda State Park in the Florida Keys and Grayton Beach State Park in Santa Rosa.

You can check out Dr Beach's website at www.drbeach.org or pick up the book *America's Best Beaches*.

DANGERS & ANNOYANCES

Besides toothy fish and bolts from the blue (see 'Sparks & Sharks,' p575), Florida has more than its share of aggravating insects. Mosquitoes and tiny biting flies known as no-see-ums are everywhere, especially around the water, so apply your favorite repellent. Fear not the giant cockroaches – they don't bite. And whatever you do, don't feed the alligators.

GETTING THERE & AWAY

Miami International Airport is an international gateway. Orlando, Tampa and Fort Lauderdale get significant numbers of US and international flights. Fort Lauderdale and Miami airports are about 30 minutes apart, and it's almost always cheaper to fly into or out of Fort Lauderdale.

GETTING AROUND

Greyhound has widespread service throughout the state. Walk-up fares cost more than passes and advance-purchase tickets. From Miami, buses run to Atlanta, Georgia ($109, 16 hours); New York ($109, 31 hours); and Los Angeles, California ($130, 59 hours). Amtrak's *Silver Meteor, Silver Star* and *Silver Palm* run daily between New York and Miami. The *Sunset Limited* crosses the south between Los Angeles and Orlando three times weekly. See p1123 for more information about Amtrak.

Unless you have a special deal or a rail pass, it's probably generally best to take a bus or fly within the state. However, the **Tri-Rail** (☎ 800-874-7245; www.tri-rail.com) commuter system is certainly the cheapest mode of transportation between Palm Beach, Fort Lauderdale and Miami, with stops at the three airports and bus connections to beaches, downtowns and neighboring cities. It's slow but cheap (see relevant city sections for rates).

Car rental rates in Florida tend to be relatively low: a small car might cost $29 per day or $135 per week. Liability insurance is not included in rates. Drive-aways to Florida are common; for details see p1120.

SPARKS & SHARKS

A couple of dubious Florida distinctions to keep you on your toes: the state ranks number one in the world for shark attacks and death-by-lightning. Of the 606 shark attacks worldwide between 1990 and 2002, 252 were in Florida, mostly on the Atlantic coast in the Daytona Beach–Cocoa Beach region. Two of the attacks resulted in fatalities. Lightning is much deadlier. Florida averages about 10 lightning deaths a year, mainly in central Florida during the summer months.

Florida beach patrols do issue warnings when sharks are spotted near beaches, so heed them, and avoid swimming near schools of small baitfish. As for dodging the lightning, head for cover well in advance of thunderstorms and make sure to stay clear of water, beaches, open high ground and isolated large trees during storms.

TOURS

Several national companies offer tours that include Florida in their itineraries (see p1102). **Gray Line Tours** (☎ 800-394-6935; www.grayline.com) offers day excursions from Orlando and Tampa.

SOUTH FLORIDA

Most visitors to this region seek the glamour, culture and hip lifestyle of Miami's South Beach. The well-heeled head north for Palm Beach and Boca Raton. And those seeking a laid-back, quasi-Caribbean holiday make tracks south to the Florida Keys, a chain of islands made famous by Jimmy Buffett, Zane Grey and Ernest Hemingway, among others. Natural diversions rank high on the must-do list, from snorkeling and diving the coral reefs of the Keys to birding, hiking and canoeing through Everglades National Park.

MIAMI & MIAMI BEACH

In just over 100 years, Miami has developed a burgeoning financial and tourist economy, and its multiethnic and multicultural metropolitan population numbers over 2.2 million. It's blessed with natural areas and tropical beaches and has cultivated six major sports teams, a 20th-century district on the National Register of Historic Places, and an image as a 'New World Center.' Across the Intracoastal Waterway lies Miami Beach. Since the restoration of Miami Beach's Deco District in the 1980s, South Beach (SoBe) has become *the* fabulous spot, perhaps the world's hippest photo backdrop and a playground for the rich and beautiful, the youthful and the retired. South Beach is also a major gay and lesbian destination.

History

The first passenger train service to Miami, in 1896, encouraged thousands of people whose livelihoods had been wiped out by the previous year's freeze in north Florida to flock to the southern region's warmer climes. Blacks were among the first settlers, coming from the Bahamas as farm laborers and railroad workers. The establishment of military training facilities during WWI and WWII encouraged many trainees to return permanently. The 1930s saw a boom and the construction of Miami Beach's art deco buildings. In the 1950s blacks were relegated to federal housing projects in Liberty City, and Miami's Cuban population swelled following the 1959 Castro coup. In 1968, blacks – displaced and disillusioned with the 'American Dream' – rioted in Liberty City.

The early 1970s brought more integration and advances in arts and education, before the 1975 recession halted yet another boom. As Miami found solutions by transforming itself into an international tourism and business center, Barbara Capitman led the revival of Miami Beach's Deco District. The 1980s brought a second wave of Cuban refugees, race riots, a burgeoning drug trade and skyrocketing crime. The 1990s unfolded with violence directed at tourists and Hurricane Andrew, one of the country's worst natural disasters. It took two years, bad northern winters and a city committed to protecting visitors to revive the tourism industry.

Today, driven by the cruise-ship industry, a glittering entertainment scene and its international business connections (not all of them wholly legitimate), Miami thrives almost as a nation unto itself.

Orientation

Greater Miami is a sprawling metropolis that includes suburbs such as Coral Gables and Coconut Grove, and neighborhoods

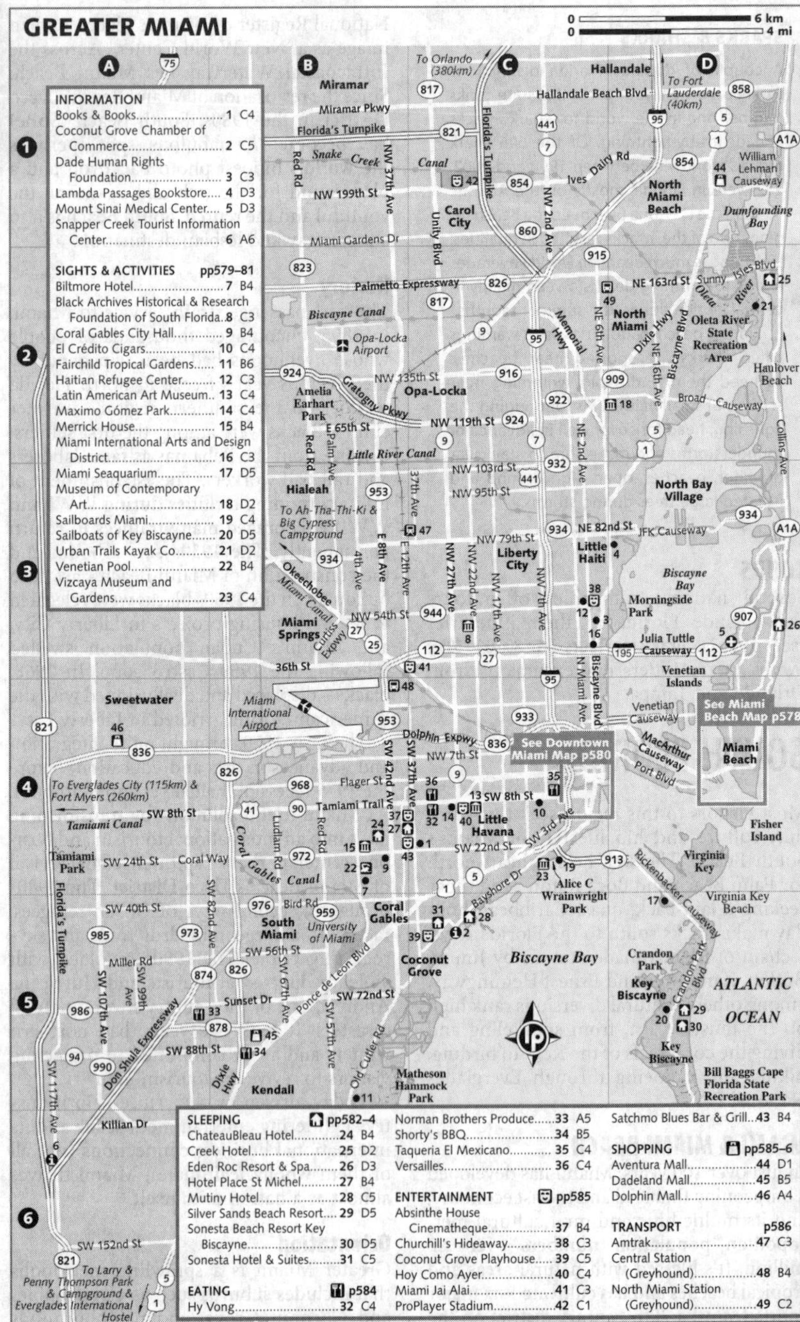
GREATER MIAMI
0 6 km
0 4 mi
A
B
C
D
1
2
3
4
5
6
INFORMATION
Books & Books 1 C4
Coconut Grove Chamber of Commerce 2 C5
Dade Human Rights Foundation 3 C3
Lambda Passages Bookstore 4 D3
Mount Sinai Medical Center 5 D3
Snapper Creek Tourist Information Center 6 A6
SIGHTS & ACTIVITIES pp579–81
Biltmore Hotel 7 B4
Black Archives Historical & Research Foundation of South Florida 8 C3
Coral Gables City Hall 9 B4
El Crédito Cigars 10 C4
Fairchild Tropical Gardens 11 B6
Haitian Refugee Center 12 C3
Latin American Art Museum 13 C4
Maximo Gómez Park 14 C4
Merrick House 15 B4
Miami International Arts and Design District 16 C3
Miami Seaquarium 17 D5
Museum of Contemporary Art 18 D2
Sailboards Miami 19 C4
Sailboats of Key Biscayne 20 D5
Urban Trails Kayak Co 21 D2
Venetian Pool 22 B4
Vizcaya Museum and Gardens 23 C4
SLEEPING pp582–4
ChateauBleau Hotel 24 B4
Creek Hotel 25 D2
Eden Roc Resort & Spa 26 D3
Hotel Place St Michel 27 B4
Mutiny Hotel 28 C5
Silver Sands Beach Resort 29 D5
Sonesta Beach Resort Key Biscayne 30 D5
Sonesta Hotel & Suites 31 C5
EATING p584
Hy Vong 32 C4
Norman Brothers Produce 33 A5
Shorty's BBQ 34 B5
Taqueria El Mexicano 35 C4
Versailles 36 C4
ENTERTAINMENT pp585
Absinthe House Cinematheque 37 B4
Churchill's Hideaway 38 C3
Coconut Grove Playhouse 39 C5
Hoy Como Ayer 40 C4
Miami Jai Alai 41 C3
ProPlayer Stadium 42 C1
Satchmo Blues Bar & Grill 43 B4
SHOPPING pp585–6
Aventura Mall 44 D1
Dadeland Mall 45 B5
Dolphin Mall 46 A4
TRANSPORT p586
Amtrak 47 C3
Central Station (Greyhound) 48 B4
North Miami Station (Greyhound) 49 C2
To Orlando (380km)
To Fort Lauderdale (40km)
Hallandale
Hallandale Beach Blvd
Miramar
Miramar Pkwy
Florida's Turnpike
Snake Creek Canal
NW 199th St
NW 37th Ave
Red Rd
Ives Dairy Rd
Carol City
Unity Blvd
NW 2nd Ave
North Miami Beach
William Lehman Causeway
Dumfounding Bay
Miami Gardens Dr
Palmetto Expressway
NE 163rd St
Sunny Isles Blvd
Oleta River
Biscayne Canal
Memorial Hwy
NE 6th Ave
North Miami
Dixie Hwy
Biscayne Blvd
NE 16th Ave
Oleta River State Recreation Area
Opa-Locka Airport
Haulover Beach
NW 135th St
Opa-Locka
Amelia Earhart Park
Gratogny Pkwy
Broad Causeway
NW 119th St
E 65th St
Palm Ave
Little River Canal
NE 2nd Ave
Collins Ave
NW 103rd St
NW 95th St
Hialeah
North Bay Village
To Ah-Tha-Thi-Ki & Big Cypress Campground
37th Ave
E 8th Ave
E 12th Ave
4th Ave
NE 82nd St
JFK Causeway
NW 79th St
Little Haiti
Liberty City
NW 27th Ave
NW 22nd Ave
NW 17th Ave
NW 7th Ave
Biscayne Bay
Okeechobee
Miami Canal
Morningside Park
Miami Springs
Curtiss Expwy
NW 54th St
Julia Tuttle Causeway
36th St
N Miami Ave
Venetian Islands
Sweetwater
Miami International Airport
Venetian Causeway
See Miami Beach Map p578
Miami Beach
Dolphin Expwy
See Downtown Miami Map p580
NW 7th St
MacArthur Causeway
Port Blvd
To Everglades City (115km) & Fort Myers (260km)
Flagler St
Tamiami Trail
SW 8th St
SW 42nd Ave
SW 37th Ave
Little Havana
Tamiami Canal
Fisher Island
Coral Gables Canal
Ludlam Rd
SW 22nd St
SW 3rd Ave
Tamiami Park
SW 24th St
Coral Way
Virginia Key
Rickenbacker Causeway
Bayshore Dr
Alice C Wainwright Park
SW 40th St
SW 82nd Ave
Bird Rd
Virginia Key Beach
South Miami
University of Miami
Coral Gables
Florida's Turnpike
Miller Rd
SW 99th Ave
SW 56th St
Biscayne Bay
Crandon Park
Coconut Grove
Ponce de Leon Blvd
SW 107th Ave
SW 67th Ave
Crandon Park Blvd
ATLANTIC OCEAN
Sunset Dr
SW 72nd St
Key Biscayne
Don Shula Expressway
SW 57th Ave
SW 88th St
Old Cutler Rd
Dixie Hwy
SW 117th Ave
Kendall
Matheson Hammock Park
Bill Baggs Cape Florida State Recreation Park
Killian Dr
SW 152nd St
To Larry & Penny Thompson Park & Campground & Everglades International Hostel

MIAMI IN...

Two Days

Stretch your legs with a morning stroll on the **Miami Beach boardwalk**, which starts at 21st St. Follow up with lunch at the always-trendy **News Cafe**, indulging in all the people-watching you can handle. Hang out on the beach in the afternoon, then grab a cocktail at the terribly fashionable **Delano Hotel**. If you're in a Caribbean mood, it's **Tap Tap** for dinner, then boogie the night away at **Crobar**. Next morning head for **Coconut Grove** to ogle all the boats in the marina, then grab lunch at a classic Cuban restaurant – **Versailles**, in Little Havana. Slide by **Bayside Marketplace** for some quick shopping before hotel-hopping on **South Beach**, checking out the art deco scene at the Edison, Cardozo and Avalon hotels.

Four Days

Follow the two-day itinerary, adding a snorkeling trip at **Biscayne National Park** on the third day and spending the fourth day in the Everglades with a naturalist-led tram tour at **Shark Valley**. Try the sidewalk cafés at pedestrian-friendly **Lincoln Road Mall** and save one evening to catch live blues and rock 'n' roll at Miami's oldest bar, **Tobacco Road**.

such as Little Havana and Little Haiti. Miami is on the mainland, while the City of Miami Beach lies 4 miles east on a stretch of white sand crowded with buildings.

Downtown Miami is divided by the Miami River. The north–south divider is Flagler St; the east–west divider is Miami Ave. It's laid out in a numerical grid, with numbers increasing away from the two dividing thoroughfares. Streets run east–west, avenues and courts run north–south. Compass prefixes are given to thoroughfares based on their position relative to the intersection of Flagler St and Miami Ave. For example, 10786 SW 40th St is on 40th St south of Flagler St, west of Miami Ave and at 107th Ave.

In Miami Beach, streets also run east–west and avenues north–south.

Information

BOOKSTORES

Books & Books Coral Gables (Map p576; ☎ 305-442-4408; 265 Aragon Ave); Miami Beach (Map p578; ☎ 305-532-3222; 933 Lincoln Rd) One of the finest independent bookstores in the US.

Downtown Book Center (Map p580; ☎ 305-377-9941; 247 SE 1st St)

Lambda Passages Bookstore (Map p576; ☎ 305-754-6900; www.lambdapassages.com; 7545 Biscayne Blvd NE) For gay and lesbian travelers.

EMERGENCY

All of these numbers operate on a 24-hour basis.

Beach Patrol (☎ 305-673-7711)

Emergency number (☎ 911)

Rape Hotline (☎ 305-585-7273)

INTERNET ACCESS

Cybr Caffe (Map p578; ☎ 305-534-0057; 1574 Washington Ave, Miami Beach)

Kafka Kafe (Map p578; ☎ 305-673-9669; 1464 Washington Ave, Miami Beach)

Miami-Dade Public Library Downtown (Map p580; ☎ 305-375-2665; 101 W Flagler St); Miami Beach (Map p578; ☎ 305-535-4219; 2100 Collins Ave) Free access on a screen-available basis.

MEDIA

El Nuevo Herald Spanish daily published by the *Miami Herald*.

Miami Herald The city's only major English-language daily. Entertainment section on Friday.

New Times Alternative weekly with good listings of restaurants, clubs, bars and theater.

Wire Free gay weekly. All about partying on Miami Beach.

MEDICAL SERVICES

Miami Beach Community Health Center (Map p578; ☎ 305-538-8835; 710 Alton Rd) Charges fees based on income.

Mount Sinai Medical Center (Map p576; ☎ 305-674-2121; 4300 Alton Rd) Area's best emergency room. Also has a medical line on ☎ 305-674-2222.

MONEY

Abbot Foreign Exchange (Map p580; ☎ 305 374 7885; 230 NE 1st St, Downtown Miami)

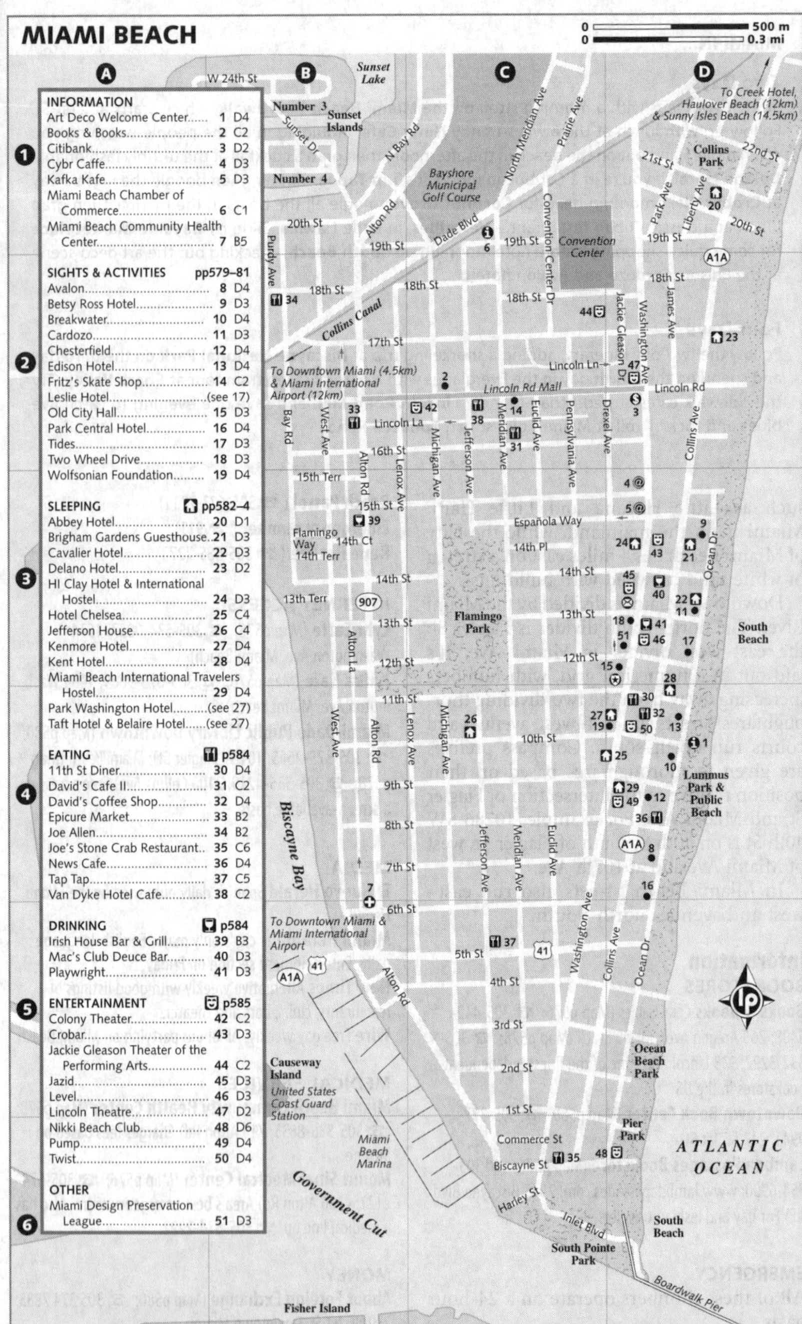
MIAMI BEACH
0 500 m
0 0.3 mi
A
B
C
D
1
2
3
4
5
6
INFORMATION
Art Deco Welcome Center......1 D4
Books & Books......2 C2
Citibank......3 D2
Cybr Caffe......4 D3
Kafka Kafe......5 D3
Miami Beach Chamber of Commerce......6 C1
Miami Beach Community Health Center......7 B5
SIGHTS & ACTIVITIES pp579–81
Avalon......8 D4
Betsy Ross Hotel......9 D3
Breakwater......10 D4
Cardozo......11 D3
Chesterfield......12 D4
Edison Hotel......13 D4
Fritz's Skate Shop......14 C2
Leslie Hotel......(see 17)
Old City Hall......15 D3
Park Central Hotel......16 D4
Tides......17 D3
Two Wheel Drive......18 D3
Wolfsonian Foundation......19 D4
SLEEPING pp582–4
Abbey Hotel......20 D1
Brigham Gardens Guesthouse......21 D3
Cavalier Hotel......22 D3
Delano Hotel......23 D2
HI Clay Hotel & International Hostel......24 D3
Hotel Chelsea......25 C4
Jefferson House......26 C4
Kenmore Hotel......27 D4
Kent Hotel......28 D4
Miami Beach International Travelers Hostel......29 D4
Park Washington Hotel......(see 27)
Taft Hotel & Belaire Hotel......(see 27)
EATING p584
11th St Diner......30 D4
David's Cafe II......31 C2
David's Coffee Shop......32 D4
Epicure Market......33 B2
Joe Allen......34 B2
Joe's Stone Crab Restaurant......35 C6
News Cafe......36 D4
Tap Tap......37 C5
Van Dyke Hotel Cafe......38 C2
DRINKING p584
Irish House Bar & Grill......39 B3
Mac's Club Deuce Bar......40 D3
Playwright......41 D3
ENTERTAINMENT p585
Colony Theater......42 C2
Crobar......43 D3
Jackie Gleason Theater of the Performing Arts......44 C2
Jazid......45 D3
Level......46 D3
Lincoln Theatre......47 D2
Nikki Beach Club......48 D6
Pump......49 D4
Twist......50 D4
OTHER
Miami Design Preservation League......51 D3
W 24th St
Sunset Lake
Number 3
Sunset Islands
Number 4
Sunset Dr
N Bay Rd
Bayshore Municipal Golf Course
North Meridian Ave
Prairie Ave
To Creek Hotel, Haulover Beach (12km) & Sunny Isles Beach (14.5km)
Collins Park
22nd St
21st St
Park Ave
Liberty Ave
20th St
Dade Blvd
Alton Rd
20th St
19th St
Convention Center Dr
Convention Center
19th St
A1A
Purdy Ave
18th St
18th St
18th St
18th St
Collins Canal
17th St
Jackie Gleason Dr
Washington Ave
James Ave
Lincoln Ln
To Downtown Miami (4.5km) & Miami International Airport (12km)
Lincoln Rd Mall
Lincoln Rd
Bay Rd
West Ave
Lincoln La
Michigan Ave
Jefferson Ave
Meridian Ave
Euclid Ave
Pennsylvania Ave
Drexel Ave
Collins Ave
16th St
Lenox Ave
Alton Rd
15th Terr
15th St
Española Way
Flamingo Way
14th Ct
14th Terr
14th Pl
14th St
14th St
Ocean Dr
13th Terr
907
13th St
13th St
Flamingo Park
South Beach
12th St
12th St
11th St
Alton La
West Ave
Lenox Ave
Michigan Ave
10th St
Alton Rd
Lummus Park & Public Beach
9th St
Biscayne Bay
8th St
A1A
Jefferson Ave
Meridian Ave
Euclid Ave
7th St
6th St
Washington Ave
Collins Ave
Ocean Dr
To Downtown Miami & Miami International Airport
41
A1A
5th St
41
4th St
Alton Rd
3rd St
2nd St
Causeway Island
United States Coast Guard Station
Ocean Beach Park
1st St
Pier Park
Commerce St
Miami Beach Marina
Biscayne St
ATLANTIC OCEAN
Harley St
Government Cut
Inlet Blvd
South Beach
South Pointe Park
Boardwalk Pier
Fisher Island

Bank of America (Map p580; ☎ 305-373-0970; 150 W Flagler St, Downtown Miami)
Citibank (Map p578; ☎ 305-673-6900; 1685 Washington Ave, Miami Beach)

POST

US Post Office main branch (Map p580; 500 NW 2nd Ave); Miami Beach (Map p578; 1300 Washington Ave)

TOURIST OFFICES

Art Deco Welcome Center (Map p578; ☎ 305-531-3484; www.mdpl.org; 1000 Ocean Dr, Miami Beach; 11am-6pm Mon-Fri, 10am-10pm Sat, 11am-10pm Sun)
Greater Miami & the Beaches Convention & Visitors Bureau (www.gmcvb.com; 8:30am-5pm Mon-Fri) main branch (Map p580; ☎ 305-539-3000; 701 Brickell Ave); Coconut Grove (2820 MacFarlane Rd); Snapper Creek Plaza (Map p580; Florida Turnpike, Mile Marker 19); Sunny Isles Beach (17100 Collins Ave); Florida City (160 Hwy 1)
Miami Beach Chamber of Commerce (Map p578; ☎ 305-674-1300; www.miamibeachchamber.com; 1920 Meridian Ave, Miami Beach)

Miami Beach Map p578

In 1979, Miami Beach's **Art Deco Historic District** was placed on the National Register of Historic Places. The district lies between the Atlantic Ocean and Lenox Ave on the east and west, and 6th St and 23rd St–Dade Blvd on the south and north. It includes examples of streamline, moderne and Mediterranean revival architecture, as well as other art deco styles.

Examples of streamline buildings include the **Avalon**, **Chesterfield**, **Leslie**, **Tides**, **Cardozo** and **Breakwater** hotels. Mediterranean highlights include most of the buildings along and near **Española Way**, plus the **HI Clay Hotel & International Hostel** (former home of Desi Arnaz and a casino run by Al Capone), the **Old City Hall**, the **Wolfsonian Foundation** building and the **Edison Hotel**. **Ocean Drive** boasts the **Park Central Hotel**. The finest example of Depression-era moderne is the 1937 **post office** on Washington Ave. The **Betsy Ross Hotel** typifies neoclassical revival.

The pedestrian-only **Lincoln Road Mall** is Miami Beach's cultural epicenter, replete with galleries, restaurants and cafés.

The **South Beach** area is the most crowded, especially on weekends. The beaches north of 21st St – especially the one at 53rd St – are more family-oriented. Latin American families tend to congregate between 5th St and South Pointe, where topless bathing is commonplace. The most popular gay beach centers on 12th St. Nude bathing is legal at Haulover Beach.

Downtown Miami Map p580

The **Metro-Dade Cultural Center Plaza** (101 W Flagler St) resembles an old Spanish fortress and includes the **Historical Museum of Southern Florida** (☎ 305-375-1492; www.historical-museum.org; adult $5, child 6-12 $2; 10am-5pm Mon-Sat, noon-5pm Sun), with an excellent series of kid-friendly exhibits, and the **Miami Art Museum** (www.miamiartmuseum.org; adult/child under 12 $5/free, admission free Sun; 10am-5pm Tue-Fri, noon-5pm Sat & Sun) showcases international contemporary art and has some beautiful works by Cuban-born artists. **Bayside Marketplace** (☎ 305-577-3344; www.baysidemarketplace.com; 401 Biscayne Blvd) near the marina is a popular shopping mall–cum-dining and entertainment center with places offering the full range, from Brazilian *feijoada* (black beans and pork stew) at SteakMasters to the poppy Americana of Hard Rock Café to the Disney Store.

Little Havana Map p576

Spanish is the predominant language in this distinctly Cuban neighborhood. The heart of Little Havana is **Calle Ocho** (*kah*-yeh *oh*-cho), SW 8th St, which is lined with Cuban shops and cafés. Elderly Cubans play dominoes at **Máximo Gómez Park**, named for the Dominican-born chief of the army that fought for Cuban independence in the 1890s. The **Latin American Art Museum** (☎ 305-644-1127; www.latinartmuseum.org; 2206 SW 8th St; admission free; 11am-5pm Tue-Fri, 11am-4pm Sat) showcases contemporary Latin American artists with special emphasis on women artists. Watch Cuban *tabaqueros* (tobacconists) hand-roll cigars at **El Crédito Cigars** (☎ 305-858-4162; 1106 SW 8th St; admission free; 7am-6pm Mon-Fri, 7am-4pm Sat).

Coral Gables Map p576

This lovely, upscale city with a Mediterranean influence was designed as a 'model suburb' by George Merrick in the early 1920s. Its crown jewel is the **Biltmore Hotel** (☎ 305-445-1926; www.biltmorehotel.com; 1200 Anastasia Ave), a Mediterranean revival edifice that once housed a speakeasy run by Al Capone. Carved from a limestone quarry in 1923 and fed by springs, the superb **Venetian Pool** (☎ 305-460-5356; www.venetianpool.com; 2701 DeSoto Blvd; adult/child $9/5; vary widely) is one of the

DOWNTOWN MIAMI
0 500 m
0 0.3 mi
A
B
C
D
1
2
3
4
5
6
To Fort Lauderdale (40km)
To Little Haiti (5km), North Miami (14km) & Fort Lauderdale (40km)
To Port of Miami (1km)
To Little Havana
To Coral Gables (6.5km), Coconut Grove (7km) & South Miami (12km)
To South Miami (12km)
Metrorail
Metromover
NW 11th St
NE 11th St
11th St
NW 10th St
NE 10th St
NW 9th St
NE 9th St
NW 8th St
NE 8th St
NE 7th St
NW 7th St
NW 6th St
NE 6th St
NE 5th St
NW 5th St
NW 4th St
NE 4th St
NW 3rd St
NE 3rd St
NW 2nd St
NE 2nd St
NW 1st St
NE 1st St
W Flagler St
E Flagler St
SW 1st St
SE 1st St
SW 2nd St
SE 2nd St
SE 3rd St
SW 5th St
SE 5th St
SW 6th St
SE 6th St
SW 7th St
Calle Ocho (SW 8th St/Tamiami Trail)
SW 9th St
SW 10th St
SW 11th St
SW 12th St
SW 13th St (Coral Way)
SW 15th Rd
SW 18th Rd
NW 4th Ave
NW 3rd Ct
NW 3rd Ave
NW 2nd Ave
NW 1st Ct
NW 1st Ave
NE 1st Ave
NE 2nd Ave
North-South Expressway
N Miami Ave
S Miami Ave
SE 1st Ave
SE 2nd Ave
SE 3rd Ave
Biscayne Blvd
Biscayne Blvd Way
Brickell Ave
SW North River Dr
SW South River Dr
SW 4th Ave
SW 3rd Ave
SW 2nd Ave
SW 1st Ave
SW 1st Ct
SE 1st Ave
Miami Arena
Overtown
Park West
Freedom Tower
Arena/ State Plaza
College North
Miami-Dade Community College-Wolfson Campus
College/ Bayside
Government Center
1st St
Miami Ave
Third St
Knight Center
Bayfront Park
Riverwalk
5th St
8th St
10th St Promenade
Brickell
Bicentennial Park
Bayside Marketplace
Marina
Bayfront Park
Pepper Fountain
Lummus Park
José Martí Park
Miami River
Biscayne Bay
Brickell Park
Brickell Key
95
5
1
41
886
968
90

SIGHTS & ACTIVITIES pp579–81
Historical Museum of Southern Florida............(see 4)
Metro-Dade Cultural Center....4 B3
Miami Art Museum..............(see 4)

SLEEPING pp582–4
Mandarin Oriental Miami........5 D5
Miami River Inn.....................6 A4

EATING p584
Perricone's.............................7 C5
Provence Grill........................8 C5

ENTERTAINMENT p585
American Airlines Arena..........9 C2
Club Space............................10 C1
Tobacco Road........................11 B4

TRANSPORT p586
Bayside Station (Greyhound)..12 B2

INFORMATION
Abbot Foreign Exchange..........1 C3
Bank of America...................(see 4)
Downtown Book Center...........2 C3
Downtown Miami Convention & Visitor's Bureau.................3 C5
Miami-Dade Public Library.....(see 4)

oldest public swimming pools in the US, a playground of waterfalls and coves in an Italianate theme; call in advance for opening hours.

Other attractions include the late-1920s **Coral Gables City Hall** (☎ 305-446-6800; 405 Biltmore Way; 8am-5pm Mon-Fri) and the 1899 **Merrick House** (☎ 305-460-5361; 907 Coral Way; adult/child $5/1; 1-4pm Mon & Wed), the boyhood home of George Merrick.

South Miami

Map p576

Site of the area's first major settlement, **Coconut Grove** is a former bohemian hangout that has evolved into a ritzy commercial hub with trendy shops, restaurants and hip nightclubs. The 10-acre **Vizcaya Museum and Gardens** (☎ 305-250-9133; 3251 S Miami Ave; adult $10, child 6-12 $5; 9:30am-4:30pm) is a garden and Italian Renaissance–style villa built in 1916 by industrialist James Deering. The lush and exotic **Fairchild Tropical Garden** (☎ 305-667-1651; 10901 Old Cutler Rd; adult $10, child 3-12 $5; 9:30am-4:30pm) is the largest tropical botanical garden in the continental USA.

Key Biscayne

Map p576

Linked to the mainland by the Rickenbacker Causeway (toll $1), Key Biscayne boasts the **Bill Baggs Cape Florida State Recreation Park** (☎ 305-361-5811; 1200 S Crandon Park Blvd; individual $2, groups 2-8 $4; 8am-dusk), which has boardwalks, trails, a café, the 1845 Cape Florida Lighthouse and a fine beach. The excellent **Miami Seaquarium** (☎ 305-361-5705; www.miamiseaquarium.com; 4400 Rickenbacker Causeway; adult $24, child 3-9 $19; 9:30am-6pm) features aquariums, marine mammal shows and a swim-with-dolphins program.

Central & North Miami

Map p576

The **Little Haiti** district is home to Miami's Haitian refugees. The **Haitian Refugee Center** (☎ 305-757-8538; 119 NE 54th St; 9am-5pm Mon-Fri) has information on Haitian culture and community events.

The 18-block neighborhood of Buena Vista, between N Miami Ave and NE 2nd Ave, from NE 36th St to NE 42nd St, is the **Miami International Arts and Design District**. It's a miracle of urban renewal and home of the interior-design industry and stunning murals. It's pegged as a 'new South Beach,' and the artsy crowd is settling here. Further north, the **Museum of Contemporary Art** (☎ 305-893-6211; www.mocanomi.com; 770 NE 125th St; admission $5; 11am-5pm Tue-Sat, noon-5pm Sun) has excellent exhibitions by national and international artists.

From the birth of Miami, blacks were relegated to the northwest quarter of downtown, called 'Colored Town,' later renamed **Overtown** (over the tracks). It was largely destroyed by freeway development. During the 1930s and '40s, music greats like Nat King Cole, Lena Horne and Billie Holiday played Overtown's clubs, which developers are renovating today. For information on Overtown, contact the **Black Archives, History & Research Foundation of South Florida** (☎ 305-636-2390; 5400 NW 22nd Ave; 9am-5pm Mon-Fri), which also owns the historic Lyric Theater and offers tours by request.

Activities

CYCLING

The best places are along the Promenade in South Beach, under the leafy canopies of Coconut Grove and Coral Gables, and on Key Biscayne.

Key Cycling (☎ 305-361-0061; 61 Harbor Dr, Key Biscayne; per hr/day $7/20; 10am-7pm Mon-Fri, 10am-6pm Sat, 10am-3pm Sun)

Two Wheel Drive (Map p578; ☎ 305-534-2177; 1260 Washington Ave; per hr/day $5/15; 10am-7pm Mon-Fri, 10am-6pm Sat, noon-5pm Sun)

IN-LINE SKATING

Fritz's Skate Shop (Map p578; ☎ 305-532-1954; 730 Lincoln Rd; per hr/half day/day $7/15/22.50; 10am-10pm)

WATER SPORTS

If you haven't gotten out on the water then you haven't visited south Florida. The best options include the following:

Sailboards Miami (Map p576; ☎ 305-361-7245; 1 Rickenbacker Causeway; per hr $20-25; 9am-6pm)

Sailboats of Key Biscayne (Map p576; ☎ 305-361-0328; 4000 Crandon Park Blvd; per hr/day $27/130; 10am-6pm)

Urban Trails Kayak Co (Map p576; ☎ 305-947-1302; 3400 NE 163rd St; per hr/day single $8/25, tandem $12/35; 9am-6pm)

Tours

In Miami Beach, the **Miami Design Preservation League** (☎ 305-672-2014; www.mdpl.org; Suite 207, 1234 Washington Ave) leads walking tours ($10) of the Deco District, 10:30am Saturday

GAY & LESBIAN SOUTH FLORIDA

Welcome to fun central, boys and girls. From the South Beach circuit parties to the clubs of Key West, south Florida is a major destination for gay and lesbian travelers, who contribute more than $100 million annually to the local economy. Yes, you're very welcome here.

A fixture in Miami ever since the 1980s, the bookstore **Lambda Passage** (p577) is a font of local knowledge. The local newspaper *Twn*, 'the weekly news,' (www.twnonline.org) focuses on community and cultural issues, and *Hotspots!* magazine (www.hotspotsmagazine.com) covers entertainment. The **Dade Human Rights Foundation** (Map p576; ☎ 305-572-1841; www.dhrf.com; 4500 Biscayne Blvd) publishes a calendar of gay and lesbian events.

The most popular sun-and-sand hangout is at 12th St on Miami Beach. Nighttime brings an ever-changing list of venues and it's best to check local listings to find the flavor of the week. Major annual events include the **White Party** (www.whiteparty.net), a 10-day November spectacle, and the **Winter Party** (www.winterparty.com), a weeklong event in early March, both of which draw big crowds in the name of local charities. The **Miami Gay & Lesbian Film Festival** (☎ 305-534-9924; www.miamigaylesbianfilm.com) takes places in late April to early May.

In Key West, the **Gay & Lesbian Community Center** (☎ 305-292-3223; www.glcckeywest.org; 1075 Duval St) and **Key West Business Guild** (☎ 305-294-4603; www.gaykeywestfl.com; 728 Duval St) offer assistance in finding gay-run accommodations and the best in nightlife.

and 6:30pm Thursday, from the Art Deco Welcome Center at 1001 Ocean Dr. Self-guided audio tours cost $5.

Sleeping

Rates in south Florida tend to be higher than the rest of the state, especially in Miami Beach and Key West. Expect to pay between $100 and $200 for a mid-range room. Beachfront rooms always fetch a premium, and travelers can typically find big savings by staying a block or two off the beach. Many hotels reduce rates by as much as 35% during summer, except for 4 July and Labor Day.

Sleeping – Budget

MIAMI BEACH

HI Clay Hotel & International Hostel (Map p578; ☎ 305-534-2988; www.clayhotel.com; 1438 Washington Ave; dm/s $15/42;) One of the loveliest hostels in the US, this 100-year-old Spanish-style complex offers everything from single-sex dorms to spacious suites with balconies. Española Way pedestrian mall is right outside the front door.

Miami Beach International Travelers Hostel (Map p578; ☎ 305-534-0268; www.sobehostel.com; 236 9th St; dm/d $17/38;) It's loud and busy, but so what? It's also smack dab in the middle of the club and art deco district.

Creek Hotel (Map p576; ☎ 305-538-1951; 2360 Collins Ave; www.thecreeksouthbeach.com; dm/d $20/69;) The so-called creek is really just a canal. No matter. The former Banana Bungalow is just a couple of blocks from the beach and attracts a party-hearty international crowd.

GREATER MIAMI

ChateauBleau Hotel (Map p576; ☎ 305-448-2634, 888-642-6442; www.hotelchateaubleau.com; 1111 Ponce de Leon Blvd, Coral Gables; s/d $89/99; P) The name's a lot fancier than the digs at this friendly place run by Best Western. Some rooms feature balconies overlooking the pool and others have kitchenettes.

Larry & Penny Thompson Park & Campground (☎ 305-232-1049; www.co.miami-dade.fl.us/parks/campgrounds.htm; 12451 SW 184 St; campsites/RV sites $10/22;) This grassy, wooded 270-acre county park features trails, paths and a small lake for fishing.

Sleeping – Mid-Range

MIAMI BEACH **Map p578**

Cavalier Hotel (☎ 305-534-2135, 800-688-7678; www.cavalierhotel.com; 1320 Ocean Dr; d $175;) Part of the hip Island Outpost collection, this 45-room hotel offers one of the best value deals on Ocean Dr. The Afro-Caribbean decor provides relief from art deco overload.

Hotel Chelsea (☎ 305-534-4069; www.thehotelchelsea.com; 944 Washington Ave; d $155;) Feng shui meets art deco at this newly renovated 1936 gem with bamboo floors and sleeping platforms in some rooms. The lobby bar serves complimentary evening cocktails for guests.

AbbeyHotel (☎ 305-531-0031; www.abbeyhotel.com; 300 21st St; d $140;) Need a break from the party crowd? This classy 50-room hotel sits across from Collins Park. The rooftop solarium offers a comely sanctuary.

Kent Hotel (☎ 305-531-6771, 800-688-7678; www.thekenthotel.com; 1131 Collins Ave; d $145;) Another winner from Island Outpost, this 54-room hotel has a retro-modern feel with blond wood floors and brushed steel accents. Plus, continental breakfast is on the house.

Brigham Gardens Guesthouse (☎ 305-531-1331; www.brighamgardens.com; 1411 Collins Ave; d/ste $100/145;) Built around a lush garden, this 23-unit charmer is one of the best deals on Miami Beach. Stretch out in a hammock by the courtyard fountain.

Jefferson House (☎ 305-534-5247; www.jeffersonhouse.com; 1018 Jefferson Ave; d $140; P) This gay and lesbian B&B has plenty of bells and whistles. There's ultracool decor, complimentary cocktails and a lushly landscaped pool area.

Best Western took over a cluster of art deco hotels, including the **Kenmore Hotel**, **Park Washington Hotel**, **Taft Hotel** and **Belaire Hotel** (☎ 305-674-1930; www.bestwesterncom; 1020-1050 Washington Ave; d $135;) in 2002, but has preserved much of their charm. The renovations are ongoing, so avoid a room near the construction.

DOWNTOWN & GREATER MIAMI

Miami River Inn (Map p580; ☎ 305-325-0045, 800-468-3589; www.miamiriverinn.com; 118 SW South River Dr; d $99; P) Who would expect a New England B&B in an otherwise dicey downtown neighborhood? This gated complex oozes charm and serves a free continental breakfast to boot.

Silver Sands Beach Resort (Map p576; ☎ 305-361-5441; www.silversandsmiami.com; 301 Ocean Dr; d $169; P) This Key Biscayne gem is hidden in a quiet neighborhood just steps from the beach. Pay a little extra for a room on the garden courtyard.

Hotel Place St Michel (Map p576; ☎ 305-444-1666, 800-848-4683; www.hotelplacestmichel.com; 162 Alcazar Ave; d $150; P) There are only 27 rooms at this European-style hotel in Coral Gables, which means great service. Continental breakfast included.

Sonesta Hotel & Suites (Map p576; ☎ 305-529-2828, 800-766-3782; www.sonesta.com; 2889 McFarlane Rd; d $199; P) This hotel is nestled near the shopping district of Coconut Grove. The pool deck offers a great view of the marina and bay.

Sleeping – Top End

MIAMI BEACH

Eden Roc Resort & Spa (Map p576; ☎ 305-531-0000, 800-228-9290; www.edenrocresort.com; 4525 Collins Ave; d $259;) You can almost envision Sinatra and the Rat Pack romping at this legendary and gloriously renovated hotel. Hang out by the Olympic-size pool or try the rock-climbing wall.

Delano Hotel (Map p578; ☎ 305-672-2000, 800-848-1775; www.ianschragerhotels.com; 1685 Collins Ave; d $325;) The rooms are minimalist and the staff a bit smug, but this is mecca for the style-conscious. The long lobby resembles a sultan's harem with its billowy-curtained cocktail cubicles. The pool is among the gardens, with great cushioned lounge chairs on the lawn.

DOWNTOWN & GREATER MIAMI Map p576

Sonesta Beach Resort Key Biscayne (☎ 305-361-2021, 800-766-3782; www.sonesta.com; 350 Ocean Dr; d $295; P) You'll be tempted not to stray from this 295-room hotel on a wide stretch of white-sand beach. Plenty of kids' activities and a great pool.

Mutiny Hotel (☎ 305-441-2100, 888-868-8469; www.mutinyhotel.com; 2951 S Bayshore Dr; ste $219 P) This small Coconut Grove

THE AUTHOR'S CHOICE

Mandarin Oriental Miami (☎ 305-913-8288, 800-526-6566; www.mandarinoriental.com; 500 Brickell Key Dr; d $575; P) When pampering is a must and money doesn't matter, the Mandarin Oriental Miami offers the ultimate life in the luxe lane. This 20-story stunner rises like a giant Chinese fan from an island just offshore from downtown Miami, offering sumptuous views of the city and the bay. The rooms are sleek and elegant with bamboo carpets and marble bathrooms. The two restaurants – overseen by chef Michelle Bernstein, a former dancer with the New York City Ballet – are among the best in this food-rich city. The 15,000-sq-ft spa is a serene escape, and even the lobby makes you feel like you're floating in your own private Zen oasis.

hotel is all suites, with balconies and an extra-attentive staff. The beds are the comfiest around.

Eating

From hole-in-the-wall Cuban joints to haute New World fusion, Miami offers something for every palate and budget. The heaviest concentration of restaurants – and the most variety – is on South Beach. Many downtown Miami eateries cater to nine-to-fivers and close on Sunday. Florida bans smoking in all establishments that serve food. Bars that don't serve food are exempt.

MIAMI BEACH Map p578

Tap Tap (☎ 305-672-2898; 819 5th St; dishes $9-15) This friendly, lively Creole delight serves wonderful fruit and vegetable salads, plus Caribbean specialties like pumpkin soup and stewed goat. The killer rum drinks are made with Barbancourt, straight from Haiti.

David's Cafe II (☎ 305-672-8707; 1654 Meridian Ave; breakfast $4-7, buffet lunch $7.50) The breakfasts are bountiful and the lunches even more so at this long-standing Cuban favorite and its second location, **David's Coffee Shop** (☎ 305-534-8736; 1058 Collins Ave). Chow down on fried plantains, black beans and rice, and various pork and chicken dishes. The take-out window is open 24 hours.

Epicure Market (☎ 305-672-1861; 1656 Alton Rd; dishes $5-9) Gourmet goodies galore. Head to the kosher deli counter for fine salads, sandwiches and pastas.

11th St Diner (☎ 305-534-6373; 1065 Washington Ave; dishes $5-15) A classic 24-hour diner with good omelettes and sandwiches.

News Cafe (☎ 305-538-6397; 800 Ocean Dr; dishes $9-12) The people-watching is great and so is the food at this 24-hour landmark. Terrific salads and bruschetta.

Joe Allen (☎ 305-531-7007; 1787 Purdy; mains $15-25) This hidden gem is off the tourist radar. It's low-key with great steaks and fish.

Van Dyke Hotel Cafe (☎ 305-534-3600; 846 Lincoln Rd; dishes $6-15) The setting is cool – lots of models preening – and the food is secondary, but decent. Good burgers and eggplant parmigiana.

Joe's Stone Crab Restaurant (☎ 305-673-0365; 227 Biscayne St; mains $12-45; closed mid-May–mid-Oct) Established in 1913 this is surely the most famous restaurant in town. Open only during stone crab season, the lines are almost always long. There's better seafood in town, but the scene is the thing here.

DOWNTOWN & GREATER MIAMI

Versailles (Map p576; ☎ 305-444-0240; 3555 SW 8th St; dishes $8-10) The name might sound French, but the food is classic Cuban. The dining room is loud and almost always crowded, which is part of the charm. Try anything with pork in it and a cup of *café con leche*.

Shorty's BBQ (Map p576; ☎ 305-670-7732; 9200 S Dixie Hwy; dishes $6-16) This local institution has been serving up baby back ribs, corn on the cob and fall-off-the-bone chicken for nearly 50 years.

Perricone's (Map p580; ☎ 305-374-9449; 15 SE 10th St; lunch $8-9, dinner $12-22) A huge Vermont barn might look a tad out of place in the semitropics, but this deli-restaurant has a winning menu. Sandwiches, pastas and grilled dishes are tops.

Provence Grill (Map p580; ☎ 305-373-1940; 1001 S Miami Ave; lunch $5-12, dinner $13-20) Across the street from Perricone's, you'll be transported across the Atlantic. Try the mussels in garlic.

Taqueria El Mexicano (Map p576; ☎ 305-858-1160; 521 SW 8th St; dishes $5-10) Hit this friendly place in Little Havana for a Mexican breakfast of champions – tortilla chips simmered in green sauce topped with scrambled eggs and lots of cheese, rice and beans.

Hy Vong (Map p576; ☎ 305-446-3674; 3458 SW 8th St; dishes $8-15) Spicy Vietnamese in the heart of Little Havana. Start with the squid salad marinated in lime juice.

Norman Brothers Produce (Map p576; ☎ 305-274-9363; 7621 SW 87th Ave; dishes $4-7) This appealing farmers market also offers delicious take-out lunches and dinners. A good place to stop on your way to the Everglades or the Florida Keys.

Drinking

Mac's Club Deuce Bar (Map p578; ☎ 305-531-6200; 222 14th St) Established in 1926, it's the oldest bar in Miami Beach. The clientele is wonderfully eclectic.

Irish House Bar & Grill (Map p578; 1430 Alton Rd) A comfy local fave with pool tables, video games and dartboards.

Playwright (Map p578; ☎ 305-534-0667; 1265 Washington Ave) An authentic Irish pub with a vast selection of imports.

Entertainment

While nightlife gets the bulk of the tourist attention, Miami and Miami Beach offer stellar theater, sports and live music. If you want to boogie until the wee hours, then head for South Beach.

CINEMAS

All the malls have cavernous multiplexes, but there are a couple of small-scale cinemas, including the following:

Bill Cosford Cinema (Map p576; ☎ 305-284-4861; University of Miami, Memorial Bldg, Coral Gables) International offerings and home to the Cuban Film Festival.

Absinthe House Cinematheque (Map p576; ☎ 305-446-7144; 235 Alcazar Ave) Independent and foreign films in Coral Gables.

LIVE MUSIC

Tobacco Road (Map p580; ☎ 305-374-1198; 626 S Miami Ave; cover $5) A venerable local hangout with jazz, blues and classic-rock bands, this place has been packing 'em in since 1912. There's a throwback roadhouse feel to the place and it's often the scene of impromptu jams by well-known rockers when they're in town.

Churchill's Hideaway (Map p576; ☎ 305-757-1807; 5501 NE 2nd Ave; cover $10-15) An English pub in Little Haiti? Yep, and it rocks.

Also recommended are **Hoy Como Ayer** (Map p576; ☎ 305-541-2631; 2212 SW 8th St; cover $5-10) for authentic Cuban music, **Jazid** (Map p580; ☎ 305-673-9372; 1342 Washington Ave; cover $10 Fri & Sat) for sophisticated jazz, soul and funk in a candlelit lounge, and **Satchmo Blues Bar & Grill** (Map p576; ☎ 305-774-1883; 60 Merrick Way), a Coral Gables institution featuring local and national acts, plus jazz and rock 'n' roll.

NIGHTCLUBS

Crobar (Map p578; ☎ 305-531-5027; 1445 Washington Ave; cover $25) The hottest scene on SoBe is in the renovated art deco Cameo Theatre. Cool sound-and-light show.

Club Space (Map p580; ☎ 305-375-0001; 142 NE 11th St; cover $20) Head to this gargantuan warehouse in downtown Miami where dancers have a chance to spread out and groove to the DJ sounds. Liquor is served until late. Club 34 is the alter ego of this popular dance spot.

Nikki Beach Club (Map p578; ☎ 305-538-1111; 1 Ocean Dr; cover $20) It's spring break year-round at this beach-blanket–bimbo themed party.

Other hip dance spots lie on Washington Ave in SoBe:

Pump (Map p578; ☎ 305-538-9478; 841 Washington Ave; cover $15-20; ⏲ opens 4am)

Twist (Map p578; ☎ 305-538-9478; 1057 Washington Ave) Gay club with a rooftop bar.

SPECTATOR SPORTS

Miami Dolphins (☎ 305-620-2578; tickets $20-54) NFL football from September to December at **ProPlayer Stadium** (Map p576; 2269 Dan Marino Blvd).

Florida Marlins (☎ 305-626-7400; adult $4-55, child $2-55) Major-league baseball April to September; also at ProPlayer Stadium.

Miami Heat (☎ 305-577-4328; tickets $18-100) NBA from November to April at the **American Airlines Arena** (Map p576; 601 Biscayne Blvd).

Florida Panthers (☎ 954-835-7000; tickets $14-67) NHL hockey October to April at the **Florida Panthers Hockey Club** (One Panther Parkway, Sunrise).

Miami Fusion (☎ 888-387-4664) Major-league soccer March to September at the **Lockhart Stadium** (5201 NW 12th Ave, Fort Lauderdale).

Miami Jai Alai (Map p576; ☎ 305-633-6400; 3500 NW 37th Ave; tickets $1-5) Watch and bet on this lightning-fast court game in the oldest fronton in the US.

THEATER

Colony Theater (Map p578; ☎ 305-674-1026; 1040 Lincoln Rd) Everything from off-Broadway productions to ballet and movies plays in this renovated 1934 deco showpiece.

Coconut Grove Playhouse (Map p576; ☎ 305-442-4000; 3500 Main Hwy) This lovely state-owned theater in Coconut Grove stages major shows in an intimate setting.

Jackie Gleason Theater of the Performing Arts (Map p578; ☎ 305-673-7300; www.gleasontheater.com; 1700 Washington Ave) Miami Beach's premier showcase for Broadway shows, headliners and the Miami City Ballet.

Lincoln Theatre (☎ 305-673-3331; 555 Lincoln Rd) The Lincoln hosts the New World Symphony and major shows.

Shopping

For quirky, one-of-a-kind and designer items head for the South Beach boutiques. Calle Ocho, Little Havana's main drag, is lined with unique shops including cigar stores with hand-rolled stogies, and dozens of botanicas, the spiritual shops of the Santeria religion, that carry everything from lotions and potions to candles and soap that will aid a prayer or ward off a hex.

There are dozens of malls, but the best are the following:

Dadeland Mall (Map p576; ☎ 305-665-6226; 7535 N Kendall Dr)

Aventura Mall (Map p576; ☎ 305-935-1110; 19501 Biscayne Blvd)

Dolphin Mall (Map p576; ☎ 305-365-7446; Florida's Turnpike & Dolphin Expressway)

Getting There & Around

AIR

Miami International Airport (MIA; Map p576; ☎ 305-876-7000, flight information ☎ 305-876-7770) is about 6 miles west of downtown and accessible by **SuperShuttle** (☎ 305-871-2000), which costs $10 to downtown or $12 to Miami Beach.

BUS

Greyhound buses go to Fort Lauderdale ($6, 45 minutes), Jacksonville ($45, seven hours), Key West ($32, four hours), Orlando ($37, five hours), Tallahassee ($67, 11 hours) and Tampa ($39, eight hours).

They have four stops in the Miami area:

Greyhound Bayside (Map p580; ☎ 305-379-7403; 100 NW 6th St)

Greyhound Central (Map p576; ☎ 305-871-1810; 4111 NW 27th St; 24hr)

Greyhound MIA (across from baggage claim in Concourse E)

Greyhound North Miami (Map p576; ☎ 305-945-0801; 16560 NE 6th Ave)

CAR

Major and minor car rental companies have booths or phones at MIA.

Alamo (☎ 800-327-9633)

Budget (☎ 800-527-0700)

Hertz (☎ 800-654-3131)

TRAIN

Amtrak (Map p576; ☎ 305-835-1222; 8303 NW 37th Ave) has a main Miami terminal.

Tri-Rail (☎ 800-874-7245) commuter system serves Miami (with a free transfer to Miami's transit system) and MIA, Fort Lauderdale and its airport ($3), plus West Palm Beach and its airport ($5.50).

Metro-Dade Transit (☎ 305-770-3131) runs the local Metrobus, Metromover (downtown) and Metrorail services. Metromovers are monorails that run on loops over the downtown region – great for orientation (25¢). The Metrorail line runs from Hialeah through downtown Miami and then south to Kendall ($1.25).

FORT LAUDERDALE

Fort Lauderdale once had an image as a raunchy spring-break haven, but the city has yanked away the welcome mat for college kids and reinvented itself as an upscale, cosmopolitan destination. While there's still plenty of partying in its clubs, bars and pubs, Fort Lauderdale is known more today as a hub of fancy yachts and boats, along with a surprising number of cultural and historical sites. It's also a major destination for gay visitors. The **visitors bureau** (☎ 954-765-4466, 800-227-8669; www.sunny.org; 1850 Eller Dr, Port Everglades; 8:30am-5pm Mon-Fri) has an **activities hot line** (☎ 954-527-5600; www.activityline.net). There's also a **Gay & Lesbian Community Center of South Florida** (☎ 954-463-9005; www.glccsf.org; 1717 N Andrews Ave).

The best features of the **Museum of Art** (☎ 954-525-5500; 1 E Las Olas Blvd; admission $10, more during special exhibits; 10am-5pm Tue-Sat, noon-6pm Sun) are works from the post-WWII CoBrA art movement (from *Co*penhagen, *Br*ussels and *A*msterdam), as well as collections of Cuban and ethnographic African and South American art.

The exciting, interactive exhibits at the **Museum of Discovery & Science** (☎ 954-467-6637; www.mods.org; 401 SW 2nd St; adult/child $14/13; 10am-5pm Mon-Sat, noon-5pm Sun) make it a must-stop – admission includes a movie at its Imax theater, which shows 3-D films.

The **Old Fort Lauderdale Village & Museum** (☎ 954-463-4431; www.oldfortlauderdale.org; 231 SW 2nd Ave; adult/child $8/3; 11am-5pm Tue-Fri, noon-5pm Sat & Sun) claims the largest historical collection in the US; it covers the history of Fort Lauderdale and Broward County, Seminole folk art and baseball.

Built in 1901, **Stranahan House** (☎ 954-524-4736; 3335 SE 6th Ave; adult/child $6/3; 10am-3pm Wed-Sat, 1-3pm Sun), at Las Olas Blvd, is one of Florida's oldest residences; interpretive tours illuminate the history of the house and area.

Bonnet House Museum & Gardens (☎ 954-563-5393; www.bonnethouse.org; 900 N Birch Rd; adult/child $10/8; 10am-4pm Tue-Sat, closes 3pm May-Nov), near Hwy A1A and Sunrise Blvd, is a beautiful historic estate near the beach with a nature trail, native and imported tropical plants, and tours.

Many of Fort Lauderdale's best sights and hangouts are near the Intracoastal Waterway and are accessible by the fun

BOP OVER TO THE BAHAMAS

Want to add some island flavor to that Florida vacation, mon? Take a day trip to the Bahamas. US residents need only a birth certificate or a passport; UK and commonwealth citizens don't even need a passport. The coolest way to get there is aboard a vintage Grumman G-73 Mallard seaplane from **Chalk's Ocean Airways** (☎ 800-424-2557, 305-371-8628; www.chalksoceanairways.com). Based in Fort Lauderdale, Chalk's is the oldest scheduled airline in the world, founded in 1919. It offers several flights daily from Fort Lauderdale–Hollywood International Airport to Bimini ($249 round-trip) and Nassau's Paradise Island (from $209 round-trip), setting gently down in the lustrous waters and pulling up near the beach.

Travelers looking for a taste of the high life should visit Nassau and hit the casino at the *über*-glitzy **Atlantis Paradise Island** (☎ 242-363-3000; www.atlantis.com; d from $325; P), then for a reality check and a tasty snack visit one of the seafood shacks at **Arawak Cay** on Nassau's W Bay St to sample conch fritters – a Bahamian specialty made from the meat of the queen conch, a large pink-shelled marine mollusk – or just bliss out on the postcard-perfect beach. To make a weekend of it, spend the night at opulent Atlantis; even the standard Beach Tower rooms have balconies with views and tasteful decor. Guests can relax at one of several bars and lounges, get a thrill on one of many water slides or slip into one of the 11 pool and lagoon areas. Tons of kids activities, too.

Tiny Bimini offers lower-key charms, including the chummy bar at the **Compleat Angler** in Alice Town, one of the haunts of Ernest Hemingway, who kept a home on the island and pursued marlin in its offshore waters. Alice Town offers a few sleeping choices, including the Compleat Angler (sort of noisy). A better choice is the **Bimini Sands Beach Club** (☎ 242-347-3500; www.biminibeachclub.com; r from $130;), which has a freshwater pool and tidy rooms with beach views.

Water Bus (☎ 954-467-6677; www.watertaxi.com; 651 Seabreeze Blvd; day pass $5), whose drivers offer a lively and sometimes offbeat narration of the passing scenery. A replica of a 19th-century riverboat, the **Carrie B** (☎ 954-768-9920; cnr SE 5th Ave & W Las Olas Blvd; adult/child under 12 $13/7; closed in summer) offers 90-minute tours (at 11am, 1pm and 3pm) of New River and the Intracoastal Waterway. Sure, it's kitschy, but the **Jungle Queen** (☎ 954-462-5596; Bahia Mar Yacht Center, 801 Sea Breeze; dinner cruises $30; sight-seeing tours adult/child $13.50/9.25; dinner 7pm, others 11am & 2pm) is a Fort Lauderdale tradition and a fun way to travel the waterway.

Sleeping

Yes, there is life on Mars, in this case the Mars area of Fort Lauderdale – from Rio Mar St at the south to Vistamar St at the north, and from Hwy A1A at the east to Bayshore Dr. It offers the highest concentration of hotels, motels and B&Bs on the beach.

BUDGET

Beach Hostel (☎ 954-567-7275; www.fortlauderdalehostel.com; 2115 N Ocean Blvd; dm $17;) This hot-pink, 61-bed hostel is just a block from the beach and about a mile north of the main beach area. Free local calls, high-speed DSL and free snorkeling gear are also included. Most beds are filled with international visitors since a passport is required to stay here.

Floyd's Youth Hostel & Crew House (☎ 954-462-0631; www.floydshostel.com; 445 SE 16th St; dm $17, d $39-59;) Very similar to the Beach Hostel, Floyd's is a backpacker institution in Fort Lauderdale. Close to most crew placement agencies.

John D Easterlin County Park (☎ 954-938-0610; 1000 NW 38th St, Oakland Park; campsites $18) This quiet 47-acre park is the closest campground to Las Olas Blvd's action. It has nature trails, a fishing lake and clean facilities, and allows pets.

Quiet Waters County Park (☎ 954-360-1315; 4015 S Powerline Rd, Deerfield Beach; campsites $25) A 427-acre tent-only park, this facility also has bike and boat rentals, hiking trails and a small aquatic park.

MID-RANGE

Caribbean Quarters Bed & Breakfast (☎ 954-523-3226; www.caribbeanquarters.com; 3012 Granada St; d/ste from $110/200; P) The spacious pastel-colored rooms have island furnishings and beds with pillow-top mattresses. Eat breakfast in the lush courtyard.

La Casa Del Mar (☎ 954-467-2037; www.lascasadelmar.com; 3003 Granada St; d/d with kitchenette $110/145;

(P) The rooms are cozy, but spiffy, at this family-owned B&B. A full breakfast – and a darn good one – is part of the deal.

A Little Inn by the Sea (☎ 954-772-2450; www.alittleinn.com; 4546 El Mar Dr; d/efficiencies $119/199; P) The cutesy name matches the decor at this older inn. But it's forgivable since most of the units face the ocean and the amenities are generous, including free bikes and free tennis.

Tropi Rock Resort (☎ 954-564-0523; www.tropirock.com; 2900 Belmar St; d from $60-100) The lush gardens surrounding this friendly place more than make up for the clean but ho-hum rooms.

A number of Fort Lauderdale hotels cater exclusively to gays and lesbians, including the **Blue Dolphin** (☎ 954-565-5000; www.bluedolphinhotel.com; 725 N Birch Rd; d $119; P), the **Flamingo – Inn Amongst the Flowers** (☎ 954-561-4568; www.theflamingoresort.com; 2727 Terramar St; d $140; P) and the **Worthington Guest House** (☎ 954-563-6819; 543 N Birch Rd; d $139; P).

TOP END

Riverside Hotel (☎ 954-467-0671; www.riversidehotel.com; 620 E Las Olas Blvd; d $209; P) Formerly known as the Riverside Inn (the recent addition of 116 rooms prompted the moniker change), this three-story charmer is far and away the best option downtown. It's Fort Lauderdale's oldest hotel, but it's not dowdy. Most of the rooms have old oak furniture and fluffy beds.

Hyatt Regency Pier 66 (☎ 954-525-6666; www.hyatt.com; 2301 SE 17th St Causeway; d $269; P) The rooms are nice, but nothing ultrafancy. The real draw is a ringside seat on your balcony to watch the mega-yachts plowing up and down the Intracoastal Waterway.

Eating

Lester's Diner (☎ 954-525-5641; 250 Hwy 84; dishes $6-8; 24hr) Lester's is proud to be a greasy-spoon kind of joint and that's what people love about it. Dine on straightforward meat-and-potatoes fare with everyone from the high-and-mighty to late-night club-hoppers and retirees.

Mark's Las Olas (☎ 954-463-1000; 1032 E Las Olas Blvd; lunch $9-22, dinner $16-38) One of the most celebrated restaurants in Florida, the kitchen here turns out Caribbean-fusion specialties that include crab-crusted grouper and cracked conch with black bean–mango salsa. The place is almost always bustling.

Ernie's Bar-B-Q (☎ 954-523-8636; 1843 S Federal Hwy; dishes $7-13) You can find everything from burgers and ribs to conch chowder and pulled pork at this blues, booze and BBQ joint that revels in its good-time squalor.

Floridian (☎ 954-463-4041; 1410 E Las Olas Blvd; dishes $5-15; 24hr) The locals flock here for basic diner fare served in huge portions. Try it at breakfast for omelettes or the pile-it-on house special known as 'the Mess.'

Blue Moon Fish Co (☎ 954-267-9888; 4405 Tradewinds Ave W; lunch $10-17, dinner $26-38) The excellent and eclectic seafood menu is rivaled only by the dazzling waterside setting. Try the peel-and-eat shrimp or the salmon strudel.

Himmarshee Bar & Grille (☎ 954-524-1818; 210 SW 2nd St; lunch $10-13, dinner $16-25) Grab an outdoor table and try one of the imaginative burgers for lunch. Salads are good, too.

Bierbrunner German Bar (☎ 954-462-1008; 425 Fort Lauderdale Beach Rd; dishes $7-15) Don't let the alley setting throw you off. This place dishes up authentic schnitzel, sauerbraten and bratwurst along with a belly-busting array of beers.

Shirttail Charlie's (☎ 954-463-3474; 400 SW 3rd Ave; dishes $9-11) As casual as its name implies, this friendly place serves excellent fried seafood along the banks of the New River.

Left Bank (☎ 954-462-5376; 214 SE 6th Ave; mains $19-32) Come here for romance and splendid Provençal-style French cooking.

Entertainment

Take advantage of a **24-hour hotline** (☎ 954-357-5700, 800-249-2787) to get the latest on events as well as info on same-day discount tickets.

Broward Center for the Performing Arts (☎ 954-462-0222; 201 SW 5th Ave) Hosts everything from Broadway musicals to pop and classical concerts.

Suntrust Sunday Jazz Brunch (☎ 954-828-5985; SW 2nd St; 11am-2pm) This event on the Riverwalk is a free outdoor jazz concert on the first Sunday of the month; bring a picnic and enjoy the music.

There's live blues and jazz nightly at **O'Hara's Pub & Jazz Cafe** (☎ 954-524-1764; 722 E Las Olas Blvd). **Beach Place** (17 S Atlantic Blvd) offers an all-in-one experience, with clubs, restaurants and shops. **Club Cathode Ray** (☎ 954-462-8611; 1307 E Las Olas Blvd) remains a hip gay and lesbian dance spot, as does **Copa** (☎ 954-463-1507; 2800 S Federal Hwy), even after 28 years.

Getting There & Around

Fort Lauderdale–Hollywood International Airport (FLL; ☎ 954-359-1200) is about 20 minutes from Las Olas Blvd. BCT Bus No 1 goes from the airport to the Broward Central Terminal. **Airport Express** (☎ 954-561-8888) runs shuttles (shared/private $8/30).

The **Greyhound station** (☎ 954-764-6551; 515 NE 3rd St at Federal Hwy) is five blocks from Broward Central Terminal. Frequent buses go to Miami ($6, 45 minutes), Orlando ($37, five hours) and Tampa ($39, six hours).

The **train station** (☎ 954-587-6692; 200 SW 21st Tce) serves Amtrak and Tri-Rail service to Miami and Palm Beach.

BCT buses (☎ 954-357-8400; fare/day pass $1/2.50) operate between downtown and the beach, Port Everglades and surrounding towns and beaches. The **Central Bus Terminal** (101 NW 1st Ave) is one block west of S Andrews Blvd. **TMAX** (☎ 954-761-3543), BCT's free downtown minibus, loops downtown every 15 minutes (Monday to Friday) and Las Olas Blvd every 30 minutes (weekends). The very cool, narrated **Water Taxis** (☎ 954-467-0008) run between Oakland Park Blvd to Las Olas Riverfront and the New River (one-way/round-trip/day-pass $7.50/14/16).

BOCA RATON

Thanks to some ecologically minded local benefactors who bought beach property for preservation rather than development, Boca Raton's waterfront remains relatively wild compared to the rest of south Florida. Combined with a couple of good museums and some decent places to dine and bunk down, it makes a stop along this section of the coast well worthwhile. The **chamber of commerce** (☎ 561-395-4433; 1800 N Dixie Hwy; 🕑 9am-5pm Mon-Fri) has plenty of pamphlets and free maps. The town is centered on Palmetto Park Rd and Old Dixie Hwy.

It's hard to miss the upscale, outdoor shopping mall **Mizner Park** (☎ 561-362-0606; www.miznerpark.org; cnr Hwy US 1 & Mizner Blvd; 🕑 10am-6pm Mon-Thu, 10am-9pm Fri-Sat, noon-6pm Sun), where you can grab a snack, catch a free concert or shop for resortwear. It's bookended by the **International Museum of Cartoon Art** (☎ 561-391-2200; 201 Plaza Real; admission free; 🕑 10am-5pm Wed-Sun), a unique tribute to the newspaper funny pages and comic books, and **Boca Raton Museum of Art** (☎ 561-392-2500; www.bocamuseum.org; 501 Plaza Real; adult/child under 12 $8/free; 🕑 10am-5pm Tue, Thu & Fri, 10am-9pm Wed, noon-5pm Sat & Sun), which has an impressive permanent collection that includes works by Picasso, Matisse and Warhol, and pre-Columbian and Mesoamerican collections. **Gumbo Limbo Nature Center** (☎ 561-338-1473; 1801 N Ocean Blvd; suggested donation $2; 🕑 9am-4pm Mon-Sat, noon-4pm Sun) is the crown jewel of the beach park system with a small but impressive natural history museum and an excellent array of events and walks.

The **Ocean Lodge** (☎ 561-395-772; 531 N Ocean Blvd; d $125; P ✗ 🏊) has big, comfortable rooms right across the street from South Beach Park. It's a good option for this price range, especially in this neighborhood. The swankiest address in town is the **Boca Raton Resort & Club** (☎ 888-0498-2622; www.bocaresort.com; 501 El Camino Real; d $260; P ✗ 💻 🏊), which is a Mediterranean-themed resort with luxurious furnishings in several different styles.

Flakowitz Bagel Inn (☎ 561-368-0666; 1999 N Federal Hwy; dishes $2-6) serves huge breakfasts and deli lunches. Also recommended are the Peruvian seafood specialties at **Inca Grill** (☎ 561-395-3553; 515 NE 20th St; mains $10-15) and the sumptuous Greek dinners at **Culinaros** (☎ 561-338-3646; 6897 SW 18th St; mains $17-30).

PALM BEACH

One of the world's most elite enclaves, Palm Beach attracts the rich, famous and downright snooty for its winter 'social season,' along with lots of elderly snowbirds. Wall-to-wall condos line the beachfront, attractions are limited and it's expensive (though the beaches are decent enough). The **chamber of commerce** (☎ 561-655-3282; www.palmbeachchamber.com; 45 Cocoanut Row) dispenses visitor information and can help arrange local tours.

With its chic boutiques and designer shops, **Worth Ave** grabs most of the fame and glamour, but **Ocean Blvd** (Hwy A1A) is glittery in its own right with some of the country's most grandiose estate homes. **Whitehall Mansion** (cnr Cocoanut Row & Whitehall Way) was built by wealthy railroad baron Henry Flagler in 1901 for $2.5 million. It now houses the **Henry Morrison Flagler Museum** (☎ 561-655-2826; www.flaglermuseum.us; 1 Whitehall Way; adult $10, child 6-12 $3; 🕑 10am-5pm Tue-Sat, noon-5pm Sun). The **Society of the Four Arts** (☎ 561-655-7227; www.fourarts.org; 2 Four Arts Plaza; admission free; 🕑 10am-5pm Mon-Fri May-Oct, 10am-5pm Mon-Sat, 2-5pm Sun Nov-Apr) throws its arms open to the public with concerts, films, lectures, recitals and documentaries November to April.

You won't find budget digs in Palm Beach (try West Palm Beach, following), and the **Palm Beach Hotel** (561-659-7665; 235 Sunrise Ave; d $125; P), with its fairly swank rooms, is what passes for a bargain. Other recommended lodgings include: the **Chesterfield** (561-659-5800; www.redcarnationhotels.com; 363 Cocoanut Row; d $225; P) with its chummy, clubby feel and small but elegant rooms; the charming **Palm Beach Historic Inn** (561-832-4009; www.palmbeachhistoricinn.com; 365 S County Rd; d $150; P), which offers tasty in-room breakfasts; and the **Brazilian Court** (561-655-7740; 301 Australian Ave; d $215; P), which cheerfully welcomes pets and even indulges them at the on-site restaurant. If you've got money to burn, the **Breakers** (561-655-6611; www.thebreakers.com; 1 S County Rd; d/ste $465/3300;) is the grand dame of Palm Beach hotels. It opened in 1861 as one of Henry Flagler's opulent domains. Wednesday afternoon tours of the property, modeled after Rome's Villa Medici, are a mere $10.

Chuck & Harold's (561-659-1440; 207 Royal Poinciana Way; mains $10-32) is a popular local haunt. Try the filet mignon and eggs for breakfast and the salmon *puttanesca* for dinner. 'New York deli goes hip' best describes **Toojay's Cafe** (561-659-7232; 313 Royal Poinciana Way; dishes $4-11). **Amoroso's Garden Cafe** (561-805-9812; 240 Worth Ave; mains $4-9) serves good sandwiches in a flowerful setting.

There is no direct public transportation to Palm Beach. However, from West Palm Beach you can take **PalmTran buses** (561-841-4200).

WEST PALM BEACH

While West Palm Beach is decidedly more middle class than its wealthy cousin to the east, the city does boast one truly stellar cultural attraction, terrific shopping and a couple of high-end sporting venues. Load up on local information at the **visitors bureau** (561-471-3995, 800-833-5733; www.palmbeachfl.com; 1555 Palm Beach Lakes Blvd; 9am-5pm Mon-Fri).

Florida's largest art museum, the **Norton Museum of Art** (561-832-5196; 1451 S Olive Ave; adult/child $8/3; 10am-5pm Tue-Sat, 1-5pm Sun) displays a superb collection of contemporary American and European art (modern masters and impressionists) alongside Chinese and pre-Columbian Mexican exhibits. One of its strengths is its wealth of Chinese jade carvings, ceramics and Buddhist statues.

Looking for something other than a bar or club at night? Visit the **South Florida Science Museum** (561-832-1988; 4801 Dreher Trail N; adult/child $7/5, planetarium extra $2; 10am-5pm Mon-Thu, 10am-10pm Fri, 10am-6pm Sat, noon-6pm Sun); its Buzz Aldrin Planetarium, named after the astronaut, has comfy high-back chairs to watch the sky shows.

Want to enjoy south Florida's great weather? Cool off at **Mid-Town Beach** (400 S Ocean Blvd) and **Phipps Ocean Park Beach** (2145 S Ocean Blvd). Watch the sport of kings at **Palm Beach Polo** (561-793-1440), Wellington, and **Royal Palm Polo** (561-994-1876), Boca Raton, from January to April.

SunFest (www.sunfest.com) is Florida's largest music and art festival. Held the first weekend in May on the Intracoastal Waterway, at five days its also the area's longest music festival.

Sleeping & Eating

The best deals are found at the south end of town where several locally owned motels, along with the usual chains, are huddled along busy S Dixie Hwy (US 1).

Apollo Motor Lodge (561-833-1222; 4201 S Dixie Hwy; d $70; P) Friendly management preside over the bright and cheerful rooms at this motel.

Old Northwood Historic District, an attractive community north of downtown, has two homey B&Bs: **Hibiscus House** (561-863-5633, 800-203-4927; www.hibiscushouse.com; 501 30th St; d $115; P) where all the rooms have private terraces, and **Royal Palm House** (561-863-9836; www.royalpalm.com; 3215 Spruce Ave; d $90; P) where the cozy rooms have a tropical feel.

Oriental Food Market & Takeout (561-588-4626; 4919 S Dixie Hwy; dishes $5-7; closed Sun) Palm Beach millionaires and Thai expats alike come here for the great Thai food.

Clematis St has several worthy bars and restaurants including **ER Bradley's Saloon** (561-833-3520; 104 Clematis St; mains $7-14) which is justly famous for its crab cakes, and the **Samba Room** (561-659-3442; 1 N Clematis St; mains $17-24) a Latino-fusion restaurant with pain-killing *mojitos* (cocktails with mint, lime, rum and soda) and table-side cigar rollers.

The CityPlace shopping/entertainment complex on Rosemary Ave at Okeechobee

Blvd boasts several stellar spots including **Mezzanotte** (☎ 561-655-3665; 700 S Rosemary Ave; mains $24-32), with the loveliest dining room in town and an osso buco to die for.

Entertainment

Check out the schedule at the **Raymond F Kravis Center for the Performing Arts** (☎ 561-832-7469, 800-572-8471; www.kravis.org; 701 Okeechobee Blvd) for cultural performances and headline acts.

Clematis Street and CityPlace are the best options for nightlife. A free trolley links the two venues. **Clematis by Night** (☎ 561-659-8007; www.clematisbynight.net; 100 Clematis St) lights up the streets with free live outdoor concerts at 5pm Thursdays. **CityPlace** (☎ 561-366-1000; www.cityplace.com; Okeechobee Blvd, just east of I-95) has theaters, movies and live entertainment nightly.

In addition to offering a variety of good eating options, CityPlace is a great place to people-watch, even if you aren't interested in browsing one of the multitude of shops. The outdoor design makes window-shopping a treat: tan while you scan.

Getting There & Around

Greyhound (☎ 561-833-8536; 205 S Tamarind Ave) operates buses to Miami ($9, two hours) and Orlando ($33, four hours). The downtown **Tri-Rail station** (☎ 800-874-7245; 201 S Tamarind Ave), which also serves as the **Amtrak station** (☎ 561-832-6169), is near Okeechobee Blvd. **PalmTran** (☎ 561-841-4200) provides local buses (fare/day pass $1.25/3).

THE EVERGLADES

The largest subtropical wilderness in the continental USA – the states of Delaware and Connecticut could fit inside it – the Everglades was called Pa-hay-okee (Grassy Water) by the Calusa Indians. Before developers came along in the early 1900s and began draining it, the Everglades was a 100-mile-long, 60-mile-wide 'river of grass' that stretched all the way from Lake Okeechobee to Florida Bay. After deadly hurricanes in the 1920s caused Lake Okeechobee to overflow and kill thousands of nearby residents, the government built an earthen dike around the lake and a network of canals through the swamp to regulate water flow. In recent years, runoff from sugarcane fields has threatened the Everglades' water quality and wildlife, particularly its wading birds, and the US government has approved a multibillion dollar, decades-long restoration plan – the largest and most expensive environmental rescue plan ever undertaken – aimed at restoring much of its hallowed habitat.

More than 3125 sq miles of the original Everglades were designated the Everglades National Park in 1947, the third largest national park in the US and the only one created not for its scenery but for its biological diversity. Even with booming Florida developments crowding in on all sides this visitor-friendly park still offers excellent opportunities for hiking, biking, canoeing, kayaking, boating, camping, fishing and wildlife observation. The area features museums, land and water tours and lectures.

Everglades National Park

There are three entrances to Everglades National Park: the main or east entrance near Homestead, the north entrance at Shark Valley on US 41, and the west or Gulf entrance at Everglades City. No roads within the park connect the entrances. The admission price – good for seven days at all three entrances – is $10 per car, $5 per pedestrian or bike. If you enter at Shark Valley ($8 per car, $4 per pedestrian or bike) you must pay the extra $2 per car or $1 per pedestrian or bike if you want to go to the other areas. For information, contact **Everglades National Park** (☎ 305-242-7700; www.nps.gov/ever; 40001 State Rd 9336, Homestead). The park's five visitors centers are open daily 8am to 5pm.

Even in winter it's almost impossible to avoid mosquitoes, but they are downright fierce during the summer months. It's a no-brainer – bring strong repellent. Never provoke or feed alligators, which are common. There's also the chance of spotting the endangered American crocodile, especially in the vicinity of Flamingo. Poisonous snakes, which you're not likely to see, include rattlesnakes, water moccasins and coral snakes. Wear long, thick socks and lace-up boots on hikes.

The main entrance, open 24 hours, leads to the **Ernest F Coe Visitors Center** (☎ 305-242-7700; 40001 State Rd 9336), a 45-minute drive from downtown Miami. It has interesting interactive exhibits, films, a bookstore and fun ranger-led activities such as slough slogs (see 'A Walk on the Squishy Side,' p593), hikes, talks and canoe trips. A few miles beyond is

IT'S THE WATER

The Sunshine State's water is what attracts many tourists – why not vacation on it? Two cost-effective ways to enjoy the water are houseboats and sailboats. You can spend your days island-hopping or anchored looking ashore rather than out to sea.

Few boating skills are needed with the houseboats, which chug along slowly. However, you're given some basics before you're given the keys. One option is Everglades National Park's **Flamingo Lodge, Marina & Outpost Resort** (☎ 239-695-3101). Two to three days with a fully equipped boat will cost about $475 to $635 in high season.

Lack of boating skills shouldn't stop you from chartering a sailboat, at least not at **Southwest Florida Yachts** (☎ 239-656-1339, 800-262-7939), which offers live onboard sailing classes. Two days of lessons, accommodation and food run to about $395 per person (two person minimum).

the **Royal Palm Visitors Center** (☎ 305-242-7700), the entryway to the short Gumbo-Limbo and Anhinga trails – favorites for wildlife viewing, especially in winter.

The road continues 38 miles to Florida Bay and the **Flamingo Visitors Center** (☎ 239-695-3101), at the southernmost point in the park. En route and at Flamingo are some of the park's best birding areas (Eco Pond, Mrazek Pond and Snake Bight), as well as short walking trails. The **Flamingo Lodge, Marina & Outpost Resort** (☎ 239-695-3101; www.flamingolodge.com) offers boat tours ($10 to $32) and fishing trips into the mangroves and Florida Bay. Serious Everglades explorers can rent fully-equipped houseboats (see 'It's the Water,' above) Day-trippers can rent canoes (half-/full-day $22/32), kayaks ($27/43), bikes ($8/14) and powerboats ($65/90). The lodge also has accommodations and dining (see below).

You'll come face-to-face with nature at **Shark Valley** (☎ 305-221-8776; US 41), 25 miles west of Florida Turnpike, when you walk or cycle ($4.50 per hour) the alligator-strewn, 15-mile paved loop road. Those with less energy or interest in getting that close to nature can take a narrated two-hour tram tour ($10.50).

The **Gulf Coast Visitors Center** (☎ 239-695-3311; Rte 29, Everglades City), is at the park's west entrance. It sits at the edge of a terrific canoe and kayak region called **Ten Thousand Islands**. You can take short trips to sandy beaches and shallow, brackish lagoons, or you can be really adventurous and tackle the mangrove- and island-studded 99-mile **Wilderness Waterway**, which runs along the park's southern edge from here to the Flamingo Visitors Center. Rangers lead canoe trips and walks. A **concessionaire** (☎ 239-695-2591) offers 90-minute boat tours ($16) and canoe rentals ($20 per day).

Tours

The best outfitter for outings and rentals is **Everglades Rentals & Eco Adventures** (☎ 239-695-3299; 107 Camellia St), at the Ivey House B&B in Everglades City (see p593). They provide rental canoes ($25 per day) and kayaks ($35), plus tours (single/multiday $40/250). The Gulf Coast Visitors Center has a few canoes, too (see below). For Flamingo area trips, use the concessionaire at the Flamingo Lodge, Marina & Outpost Resort (see below).

Sleeping & Eating

With a few exceptions, accommodations in the Everglades fall into two categories: camping or basic motels.

Flamingo Lodge, Marina & Outpost Resort (☎ 239-695-3101; d/cottage $95/135; P) This is the only motel inside the park, all of the no-frills rooms offer a view of Florida Bay. There's a grocery store, restaurant and small bar – a good thing, since the nearest other facilities are 40 miles east in Homestead. The Flamingo Lodge's developed campsites are free during the brutally hot months of June to August and $14 the rest of the year, when reservations are recommended. Camping elsewhere on the park's west side includes beach sites, ground sites and chickees (covered wooden platforms above the water) in the backcountry along the Wilderness Waterway. All require a permit ($10) from the **Gulf Coast Visitors Center** (☎ 239-695-3311) and a boat for access.

Glades Haven (☎ 239-695-2746; www.gladeshaven.com; 800 SE Copeland Ave; campsites $20) Pitch a tent at this campground in Everglades City, which also offers boating and marina facilities.

Captain's Table (☎ 239-695-4211; d $70; pais) This is a nice place with 48 spartan-but-tidy rooms.

Ivey House (☎ 239-695-3299; www.iveyhouse.com; 107 Camellia St; d $75-175; closed May-Oct; P) A fine, family-run remodeled 1928 boarding-house, Ivey House serves hearty breakfasts as part of the deal.

On the east side, the Homestead-Florida City area has a number of chain motels on US 1 and along Krome Ave. Clean, basic properties near the east park entrance include bright **Coral Roc Motel** (☎/fax 305-246-2888; 1100 N Krome Ave; d $50; P) and **Everglades Motel** (☎/fax 305-247-4117; 605 S Krome Ave; d $43; P). The anomaly in this otherwise straightforward mix is the **Miccosukee Resort & Convention Center** (☎ 305-925-2555, 877-242-6464; www.miccosukee.com; 500 SW 177th Ave; d $99; P), a 302-room resort run by the Miccosukee Indians. The big draw is the 24-hour casino which features second-tier nationally known entertainers and five restaurants.

West-side eateries are limited unless you travel all the way into Naples. Otherwise, in Everglades City try **Seafood Depot** (☎ 239-695-0075; 102 Collier Ave; mains $7-17) for fried fish and shrimp, and the **Rod & Gun Club** (☎ 239-695-2101; 200 Riverside Dr; mains $9-27), a 1920s-era lodge that once catered to wealthy sportsmen. In between park entrances, just east of Ochopee, is **Joanie's Blue Crab Cafe** (☎ 239-695-2682; 39395 Tamiami Trail; dishes $10-13), a funky, quintessential 1950s-style swamp café that serves blue crabs, burgers and chicken.

On the east side of the Everglades, try the inexpensive Homestead favorites, **El Toro Taco** (☎ 305-245-8182; 1 S Krome Ave; dishes $2-9), for authentic fajitas, burritos and other Mexican specialties, and **Farmers' Market Restaurant** (☎ 305-242-0008; 300 N Krome Ave; mains $6-14) for big breakfasts, and seafood and veggies for lunch and dinner.

A WALK ON THE SQUISHY SIDE

Most people don't voluntarily get knee-deep in muck, but for the intrepid and unsqueamish, there are slough slogs – ranger-led immersions in the swamps of the Everglades and Big Cypress. They're muddy, messy and lots of fun. Beware: those who don't shave their legs should wear long pants. Seems floating leg hairs look a lot like mosquito larvae to nip-happy minnows.

AROUND THE EVERGLADES

State and national parks occupy most of the land around Everglades National Park. In between is the Miccosukee Reservation, with Native American cultural attractions, gaming and accommodations.

Big Cypress National Preserve

Sprawling along the Tamiami Trail (Hwy 41), which crosses swamp, prairie, hammock and other ecosystems between Miami and Naples, this preserve is a 1139-sq-mile federally protected area on the north edge of Everglades National Park. It came about as a compromise for preservation among environmentalists, cattle ranchers, and oil and gas explorers.

The preserve is a major player in the Everglades' ecosystem, as the rains that flood the prairies and wetlands here slowly filter down through the 'Glades. The preserve's name comes from its sheer acreage, not the height of the occupying dwarf pond cypress trees. Try to spot alligators, snakes, wading birds, wild turkeys and red-cockaded woodpeckers. This is also the habitat of the endangered Florida panther, but chances are slim you'll catch a glimpse of the 40 or so critters still thought to survive in the wild.

At the **Big Cypress National Preserve Visitors Center** (☎ 239-695-4111; Tamiami Trail; 8:30am-4:30pm), 20 miles west of Shark Valley, you can watch a film, then sign up for ranger-led activities including bike and canoe tours, exciting swamp hikes and lectures. The preserve's Turner River is excellent for canoeing and kayaking.

Within the preserve lie 31 miles of the **Florida National Scenic Trail**, accessible by car from the Monroe or Tamiami ranger stations. Also, just off Loop Rd, there's the short **Tree Snail Hammock Nature Trail**.

The preserve's four no-fee primitive **campgrounds** (☎ 239-695-4111) are along the Tamiami Trail and Loop Road. **Monument Lake Campground** (campsites $14) has facilities. **Dona Drive Campground** (campsites $4) has a dump station and potable water. Expect bugs year-round, and in confounding quantities in summer.

FLORIDA

Ah-Tha-Thi-Ki

This excellent **Seminole museum** (☎ 863-902-1113; Big Cypress Seminole Indian Reservation, Hwy 8333; adult/child $6/4; ⏲ 9am-5pm Tue-Sun), 17 miles north of I-75 exit 14, showcases Seminole culture from ancient to modern times through interesting exhibits, films, a mile-long boardwalk and high-tech interactive videos. In Seminole, the name means 'a place to learn' or 'a place to remember,' and this is a great place to experience a bit of the area's culture as it was before Europeans arrived. The reservation's **Big Cypress Campground** (☎ 800-437-4102) has primitive sites ($15), improved camping and RV sites ($20/22) and cabins ($35).

Big Cypress Gallery

For art of the swamp, drop by the **studio of Clyde Butcher** (☎ 239-695-2428; 52388 US 41, Ochopee; ⏲ 10am-5pm). His award-winning B&W photography captures nature in the Big Cypress Swamp and the Everglades in elaborate detail.

Collier-Seminole State Park

Fresh and saltwater meet in this 6423-acre **state park** (☎ 239-394-3397; 20200 US 41/Tamiami Trail; per car $3.25), 17 miles southeast of Naples. It's home to manatees (in winter), white ibis, snowy egrets and alligators. There's a 13.5-mile canoe trail along the **Blackwater River** (rentals per hour/day $3/15). Ranger-led canoe trips ($10) on Sunday are limited to four canoes, so call in advance. You'll need reservations to canoe to the primitive **campsites** ($3) at Grocery Place. Picturesque developed sites start at $8. There's also a 6-mile hiking trail and an interpretive center near the main campsites. Mosquitoes are ferocious in summer.

FLORIDA KEYS

In 1513 Juan Ponce de León sailed around the string of islands now known as the Florida Keys, but it wasn't until the 1938 completion of the Overseas Highway (US Hwy 1) that the Keys became accessible by automobile all the way to Key West. Former home of Hemingway and other modern literary types, Key West is the end of the 126-mile string. Many addresses in the Keys are noted by their proximity to mile markers (indicated as MM) showing distances between Key West (MM 0) and the mainland at Florida City (MM 126). The string is divided into the Upper, Middle and Lower Keys. The **Florida Keys & Key West Visitors Bureau** (☎ 800-352-5397; www.fla-keys.com; 402 Wall St, Key West) has information on the entire area. The multilingual **Keys Hotline** (☎ 800-771-5397) provides information and emergency assistance.

Key Largo

Key Largo leapt to the public eye after the eponymously named 1948 film starring Humphrey Bogart and Lauren Bacall. It's best known as an absolutely fabulous place to snorkel, dive and kayak. Like much of the Upper Keys, it appears tacky from the road, but from the water it looks like paradise. For maps and brochures, check in at the **chamber of commerce** (☎ 305-451-1414, 800-822-1088; www.keylargo.org; MM 106).

John Pennekamp Coral Reef State Park (☎ 305-451-1202; MM 102.5; vehicle with 1 person $2.50, with 2 or more $4 plus $0.50 per person, pedestrian $1.50), was the first underwater park in the US. It also has a small but interesting museum and aquarium, and excellent ranger-led programs in winter ($4). The park is the most user-friendly way to get out onto the Florida reef. Snorkel trips cost $26, plus $5 for gear; dive trips are $39, plus $29 for gear. There are also reasonably priced rentals on canoes, kayaks, powerboats and personal glass-bottom boats. Glass-bottom boat tours ($18) depart regularly to **Molasses Reef**.

There are dozens of outfitters who will take visitors to the reef on half-day and day scuba trips. Among the best are **American Diving Headquarters** (☎ 305-451-0037; MM 105.5), which has predive reef and marine-life orientations, and **Quiescence Diving Service** (☎ 305-451-2440; MM 103.5), which specializes in small groups and twilight dives. Rates vary according to the destination and the amount of gear you need to rent. Figure about $70 for a two-tank dive with tank and weight rental, $85 to $90 if you need mask, fins, wet suit and other gear.

The best way to enjoy the Keys is by water. **Florida Bay Outfitters** (☎ 305-451-3018; www.kayakfloridakeys.com; MM 104) makes it happen up close and personal in kayaks and canoes from $20/35 for a half/full day. It leads kayak tours from $45, including a full-moon paddle, and will deliver the kayak to your hotel. It also rents camping equipment.

SLEEPING & EATING

In addition to a handful of luxe resorts, Key Largo has lots of clean, cheerful mom-and-pop motels and amenity-rich camping facilities.

Largo Lodge (☎/fax 305-451-0424, 800-468-4378; www.largolodge.com; MM 101.5 bayside; efficiencies $115; P ✻) At the top of the charm list comes this lovely lodge, set in a tropical hardwood forest. Children under 16 are not allowed.

Bay Harbor Lodge (☎ 305-852-5695; www.thefloridakeys.com/bayharborlodge; MM 97.7 bayside; r/efficiencies/waterfront cottages $85/105/125; P ✻) Another charmer, where guests get free use of a variety of watercraft.

Sunset Cove Resort (☎ 305-451-0705; www.sunsetcoveflorida.com; MM 99.5 bayside; efficiencies/waterfront ste $90/135; P ✻) Beyond the larger-than-life plaster-of-paris dinosaur guarding the entrance of this kitschy resort, there are tidy, well-appointed rooms and a cozy beach area.

Coconut Palm Inn (☎ 305-852-3017, 800-765-5397; www.coconutpalminn.com; MM 92, 198 Harborview Dr; d from $139; P ✻) The place to stay if you live for the water, Coconut Palm Lodge offers lovingly appointed tropical-style rooms near the bay and a variety of diving and fishing packages.

Kona Kai Resort (☎ 305-852-7200, 800-365-7829; www.konakairesort.com; MM 97.8 bayside; d $199; P ✻) A relaxed and intimate hideaway with tennis, kayaking, a white-sand beach, orchid greenhouse and comfy hammocks strung between the palms.

John Pennekamp Coral Reef State Park (☎ 305-451-1202; www.pennekamppark.com; MM 102.5; campsites $19) Those who like to sleep under the stars should make an advance booking for this campground.

Fish House (☎ 305-451-4665; MM 102.4 oceanside; lunch $8-13, dinner $15-22) Great service, tasty smoked fish specialties and conch salad.

Señor Frijoles (☎ 305-451-1592; MM 104 bayside; dishes $8-12) The tequila flows copiously and the all-you-can eat taco and burrito dinners are a bargain at this great restaurant.

Mrs Mac's Kitchen (☎ 305-451-3722; MM 99.4 bayside; breakfast & lunch $5, dinner $6-12) This casual, screened, Keys-funky place serves BBQ, seafood and burgers.

Calypso's (☎ 305-451-0600; off MM 99.5 oceanside, 1 Seagate Blvd; dinner $16-21) This very laid-back waterfront eatery features innovative dishes like seafood-and-black-bean burritos.

Ganim's (☎ 305-451-3337; MM 102 bayside; dishes $4-10) Perfect for quick, reliable American grub.

Sundowners (☎ 305-451-4502; MM 104 bayside; dishes $10-20) Grab a ringside seat for sunset along with pastas, chicken and seafood.

Islamorada

This area boasts some of the world's most diverse sea life, making for wonderful fishing and diving, as well as lots of good restaurants and an active nightlife. The **chamber of commerce** (☎ 305-664-4503, 800-322-5397; www.islamoradachamber.com; MM 82.5 bayside) distributes visitor information from an old red caboose.

Locals like to kayak out to **Indian Key State Historic Site**, a little island where only the crumbling foundations remain from a 19th-century settlement, along with an observation tower and trail. Another paddler's destination is **Lignumvitae Key State Botanical Site**, site of Matheson House, former private retreat of chemical magnate William Matheson. There are ranger-led tours on both keys. Rent kayaks from **Robbie's Marina** (☎ 305-664-9814; www.robbies.com; MM 77.5; per day $35), which also offers a powerboat shuttle service twice daily ($15 one island, $25 both). Get information on both keys from nearby **Long Key State Recreation Area** (☎ 305-664-4815; www.floridastateparks.org; MM 67.5).

Theater of the Sea (☎ 305-664-2431; www.theaterofthesea.com; MM 84.5; adult $18.50, child 3-12 $11.50) has exhibits and continuous marine mammal shows. Opportunities to swim with dolphins, stingrays and sea lions cost extra ($35 to $110). Visit the Environmental Center at **Windley Key Fossil Reef State Geologic Site** (☎ 305-664-2540; www.floridastateparks.org; MM 85.5; admission $5), then take a guided or self-guided tour to see the fossil-rich quarry walls. The village of Islamorada has good sun and sand at **Anne's Beach** (MM 73.5; admission free); **Library Beach** (MM 81.5; admission free), behind Islamorada Public Library; and **Islamorada Founder's Park** (MM 87; per car $10), which also has a dog park, Olympic-size pool and tennis courts.

SLEEPING & EATING

Key Lantern & Blue Fin Inn (☎ 305-664-4572; www.keylantern.com; MM 82; d $55; P ✻) Though this inn is neither on the water nor long on amenities, it does offer rooms with a fridge.

Drop Anchor Motel (☎/fax 305-664-4863; MM 85; d $80; P ✻) Another beachless offering, but most of the rooms have cozy screened porches under the palms.

Star of the Sea (☎/fax 306-664-2961, 800-664-2961; MM 77.5; d $75; P) Small, basic and friendly, the Star of the Sea has a small white-sand beach.

Ragged Edge Resort (☎ 305-852-5389; www.ragged-edge.com; off MM 86.5, at 243 Treasure Harbor Rd; d $129; P) Kick back and relax at this happily rough-around-the-edges resort, with its quiet setting and friendly hosts.

Lime Tree Bay Resort Motel (☎/fax 305-664-4740, 800-723-4519; MM 68.5; d $115; P) A cozy 2.5-acre waterfront hideaway with an on-site water-sports concessionaire.

Moorings (☎ 305-664-4708; www.themooringsvillage.com; off MM 81.5, at 123 Beach Rd; d $200; P) A top-of-the line place, with lovely cottages and townhouses.

Cheeca Lodge (☎ 305-664-4651; www.cheecalodge.com; MM 82; d $300; P) This ecofriendly 27-acre lodge caters to upscale anglers and features lagoons, gardens, a nice beach and a spa.

Holiday Isle Resort (☎ 305-664-2321; 800-327-7070; www.theisla.com; MM 84; d/efficiencies $130/260; P) Join party-hearty crowd at this kinetic complex of restaurants, bars and a marina.

Long Key State Recreation Area (☎ 305-664-4815; MM 68; campsites $25) The shady campsites here are oceanfront.

Lorelei (☎ 305-664-4656; MM 82 bayside; lunch $6-9) Come sunset, or any time you want to sip a cold one and enjoy a good burger or fish sandwich, you can't really beat Lorelei.

For a splurge try **Morado Bay** (☎ 305-664-0604; MM 81.6 bayside; mains $21-27) for 'Floribbean' seafood or the adjacent **Pierre's** (☎ 305-664-4959; MM 81.6 bayside; mains $25-30) for gourmet seafood specialties.

For good eatin', inexpensive perennial favorites include **Manny & Isa's** (☎ 305-664-5019; MM 81.6; lunch $5-8, dinner $11-18), for great Cuban food and award-winning key lime pie; **Islamorado Fish Company** (☎ 305-664-9271; MM 88 bayside; mains $15-24; closed Mon) for its fried fish baskets; **Time Out Barbecue** (☎ 305-664-8911; MM 81.5 oceanside; lunch $5-6, dinner $10-14) for smoked pork with fixings; and **Green Turtle Inn** (☎ 305-664-9031; MM 81.5 oceanside; lunch $4-10, dinner $13-19), which has been serving conch chowder and fine steaks since 1947.

Marathon

Midway down the chain is Marathon, base camp for numerous commercial fishing and lobster boats, along with some sizable marinas. Get detailed local information at the **visitors center** (☎ 305-743-5417; MM 53.5).

At the southwest city limit of Marathon, the graceful **Seven Mile Bridge** is the longest of the 40-plus bridges that link the island chain. On its north side stand remnants of the original Seven Mile Bridge, built in the early 1900s as part of the railroad to Key West.

Park on the Marathon side of the Seven Mile Bridge (MM 45) and walk (or take the tram) across a 2.5-mile stretch of the old bridge to **Pigeon Key National Historic District** (☎ 305-289-0025; www.pigeonkey.org; adult/child $8.50/6.50), a restored 5-acre railroad work camp that dates from 1908. Its museum and video chronicle the railroad and its baron, Henry M Flagler. You can swim and picnic here. The district runs two of its historic buildings as **guesthouses**, with prices less than $100 for four people. The **Museums and Nature Center of Crane Point Hammock** (☎ 305-743-9100; www.cranepoint.org; MM 50.5; admission $7.50; 9am-5pm Mon-Sat, noon-5pm Sun) includes the Museum of Natural History, the Florida Keys Children's Museum, restored George Adderly House – one of the state's only remaining examples of tabby construction – and a nature trail.

A sandy beach, clean bathhouse, picnic tables and kayak trails where you can see manatees and birds constitute the worthwhile **Curry Hammock State Park** (☎ 305-664-4815; MM 57; per car $3.25), on Crawl Key. The **Dolphin Research Center** (☎ 305-289-1121; MM 59; admission $12.50) on Grassy Key is a not-for-profit educational facility where you can study and swim with dolphins ($70 to $110, 30-day advance reservations recommended).

Sea Cove (☎ 305-289-0800; MM 54.5; d $99; P) is a friendly, family-owned place with efficiencies, rooms on houseboats and a floating motel. Pleasantly landscaped **Coral Lagoon Resort** (☎ 305-289-0121; www.corallagoonresort.com; MM 53.5 oceanside; d $70; P) has pastel-colored canal-front duplex cottages loaded with amenities, like free use of rods and reels for fishing. Originally built as a private estate, art-filled **Seascape Ocean Resort** (☎ 305-743-6455; 800-332-7327; www.seascaperesort.us; off MM 50.5 at 1075 75th St; d $150; P) is an upscale option with continental breakfast and afternoon wine included in the price.

Knight Key Campground (☎ 305-743-4343; MM 47; campsites/RV sites $39/47) has shaded sites near the Seven Mile Bridge.

Folks have been pulling up a chair for a square meal at the weatherworn, open-air **7 Mile Grill** (☎ 305-743-4481; MM 47; dishes $3-11; closed Wed & Thu) for almost 50 years. Grab a picnic table on the porch at **Herbie's** (☎ 305-743-6373; MM 50.5 bayside; dishes $5-10; closed Sun & Mon) for fried seafood baskets and burgers. For creative New American cuisine dinners try the stylishly casual **Barracuda Grill** (☎ 305-743-3314; MM 49.5 bayside; mains $15-20).

Lower Keys

Aside from Key West, the Lower Keys (MM 46–MM 0) are the least developed area of the island chain. The **chamber of commerce** (☎ 305-872-2411, 800-872-3722; www.lowerkeyschamber.com; MM 31) is on Big Pine Key.

Some not-to-be-missed sights include the **National Key Deer Refuge** (☎ 305-872-2239; nationalkeydeer.fws.gov; headquarters at MM 30.5 bayside; admission free) where, with a little luck, you might see the endangered dog-size deer; and the largest body of freshwater in the Keys, the **Blue Hole**, a former quarry that's home to alligators, turtles and fish along with wading birds. **Watson's Nature Trail** is a short self-guided walk through the key deer's natural habitat. On weekends November to March, there are volunteer-led guided walks of **Watson's Hammock**, a prime key-deer fawning area (closed April to May). The refuge also oversees the **Great White Heron National Wildlife Refuge**, a large wading-bird nesting area. Guided kayak nature tours ($50 to $195) are offered to both refuges through **Reflections Kayaking Tours** (☎ 305-872-2896, 877-595-2925; www.floridakeyskayaktours.com).

Looe Key is a grove reef off Ramrod Key teeming with colorful tropical fish, coral and other sea life. **Looe Key Dive Center** (☎ 305-872-2215 ext 2, 800-942-5397; MM 27.5), on Ramrod Key, provides snorkeling tours ($30, plus $9 for gear) and dive trips (from $45).

The Keys' best beach is **Bahia Honda State Park** (☎ 305-872-2353; www.floridastateparks.org; MM 37; admission $4), a 524-acre park with nature trails, ranger-led programs, bike and kayak rentals ($10 per hour), snorkeling tours ($26, plus $5 for gear). Bahia Honda State Park also offers the best place to pitch a **tent** ($19), plus cozy waterfront **cabins** ($110).

Big Pine Key has two lovely oceanside B&Bs: **Casa Grande** (☎ /fax 305-872-2878; 1619 Long Beach Dr; d $90; P ✕) and **Deer Run B&B** (☎ 305-872-2015; 1985 Long Beach Dr; d $110; P ✕). **Parmer's Place Guesthouse** (☎ 305-872-2157; www.parmersresort.com; off MM 28.5 bayside at 565 Barry Ave; d/2-bedroom efficiencies $75/140; P ✕) sits on a lush 5 acres along the waterway at Little Torch Key.

Big Pine Shopping Center (MM 30.5) has pizza and sandwich joints. **No Name Pub** (☎ 305-872-9115; MM 30; dishes $5-15), serves up lots of local color as well as the best pizza for miles. On Summerland Key, ultracasual **Montes Restaurant & Fish Market** (☎ 305-745-3731; MM 25; dishes $8-10) specializes in the Keys staple – fish sandwiches – and other seafood.

Key West

Key West exudes charm and eccentricity in equal measure. It's a small island and the city's popularity, along with exuberant development, is straining resources, not to mention the patience of old-timers. Big cruise ships dock on a daily basis, sending swarms of tourists onto Duval St. A steady procession of anything-goes festivals and street parties (see 'Key West Festivals,' p600) takes its toll on the municipal psyche. And the ongoing gentrification of old 'conch' houses has not only priced longtime residents out of the market, but launched the wholesale subdividing of several neighboring keys.

That said, Key West remains a comely destination both for its natural beauty – it's the most tropical of all US mainland cities – and its let-it-all-hang-out attitude. No wonder that ever since the Great Depression artists of every ilk have converged on the area for inspiration and recreation. Like Fort Lauderdale and South Beach, Key West is a major gay destination.

The town is divided into two parts. The historic Old Town is home to most of the preferred accommodations, sights, shops, restaurants and watering holes. The New Town is occupied by everyday businesses, quiet residential areas, the airport and the US Navy. The **chamber of commerce** (☎ 305-294-2587, 800-527-8539; www.keywestchamber.org; 402 Wall St, off Mallory Sq) provides an accommodations booking service. Two groups cater to gay and lesbian visitors: the **Key West Business Guild** (☎ 305-294-4603, 800-535-7797; www.gaykeywestfl.com; 728 Duval St) and the

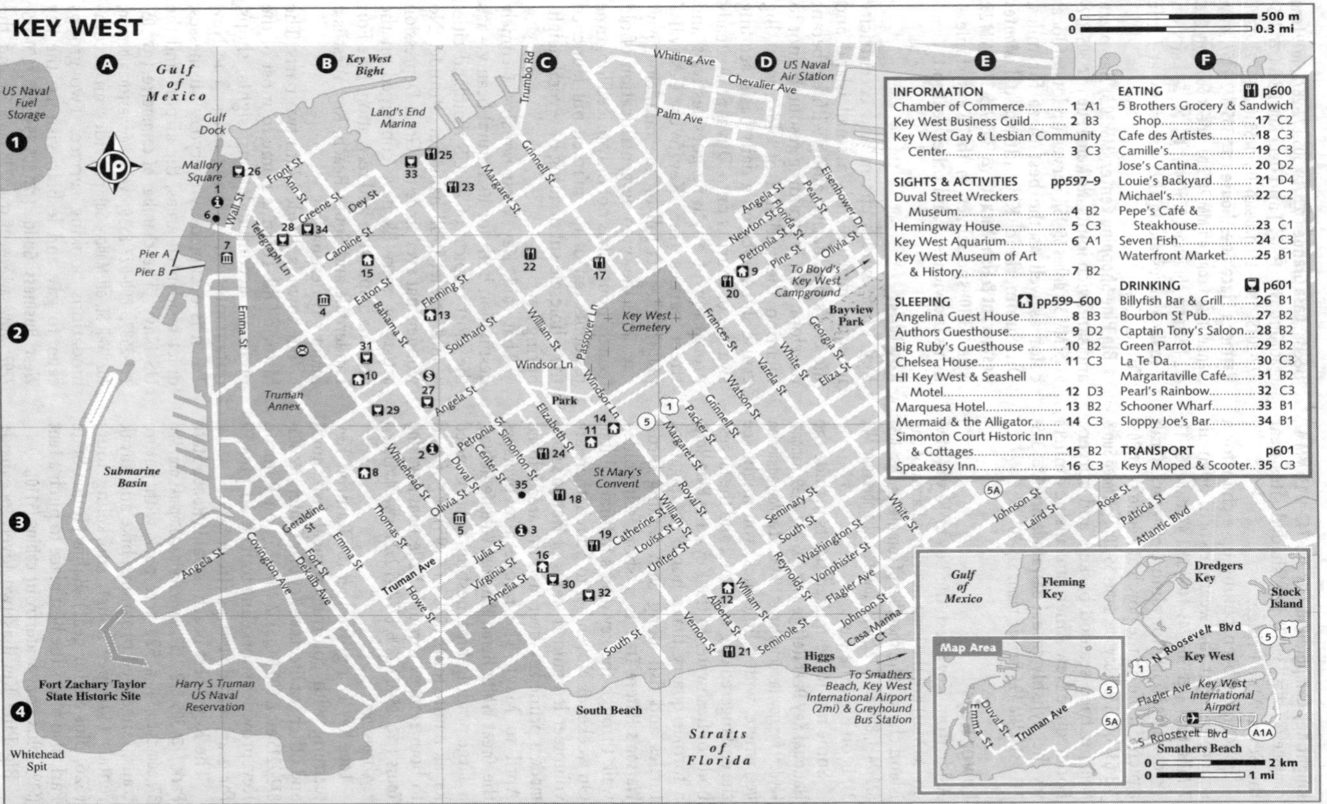
KEY WEST
0 500 m
0 0.3 mi
INFORMATION
Chamber of Commerce 1 A1
Key West Business Guild 2 B3
Key West Gay & Lesbian Community Center 3 C3
SIGHTS & ACTIVITIES pp597–9
Duval Street Wreckers Museum 4 B2
Hemingway House 5 C3
Key West Aquarium 6 A1
Key West Museum of Art & History 7 B2
SLEEPING pp599–600
Angelina Guest House 8 B3
Authors Guesthouse 9 D2
Big Ruby's Guesthouse 10 B2
Chelsea House 11 C3
HI Key West & Seashell Motel 12 D3
Marquesa Hotel 13 B2
Mermaid & the Alligator 14 C3
Simonton Court Historic Inn & Cottages 15 B2
Speakeasy Inn 16 C3
EATING p600
5 Brothers Grocery & Sandwich Shop 17 C2
Cafe des Artistes 18 C3
Camille's 19 C3
Jose's Cantina 20 D2
Louie's Backyard 21 D4
Michael's 22 C2
Pepe's Café & Steakhouse 23 C1
Seven Fish 24 C3
Waterfront Market 25 B1
DRINKING p601
Billyfish Bar & Grill 26 B1
Bourbon St Pub 27 B2
Captain Tony's Saloon 28 B2
Green Parrot 29 B2
La Te Da 30 C3
Margaritaville Café 31 B2
Pearl's Rainbow 32 C3
Schooner Wharf 33 B1
Sloppy Joe's Bar 34 B1
TRANSPORT p601
Keys Moped & Scooter 35 C3
Gulf of Mexico
US Naval Fuel Storage
Key West Bight
Land's End Marina
Gulf Dock
Mallory Square
US Naval Air Station
Whiting Ave
Chevalier Ave
Palm Ave
Trumbo Rd
Pier A
Pier B
Truman Annex
Key West Cemetery
St Mary's Convent
Park
Bayview Park
To Boyd's Key West Campground
Submarine Basin
Fort Zachary Taylor State Historic Site
Harry S Truman US Naval Reservation
Whitehead Spit
South Beach
Higgs Beach
Straits of Florida
To Smathers Beach, Key West International Airport (2mi) & Greyhound Bus Station
Map Area
Fleming Key
Dredgers Key
Stock Island
Key West
N Roosevelt Blvd
S Roosevelt Blvd
Flagler Ave
Key West International Airport
Smathers Beach
0 2 km
0 1 mi

Key West Gay & Lesbian Community Center (☎ 305-292-3223; www.glcckeywest.org; 1075 Duval St).

Cobblestoned **Mallory Sq** is the site of Key West's famous sunset celebrations – featuring jugglers and buskers – and the **Key West Aquarium** (☎ 305-296-2051; www.keywestaquarium.com; 1 Whitehead St; adult/child $8/ 4.50). **Hemingway House** (☎ 305-294-1575; www.hemingwayhome.com; 907 Whitehead St; adult/child $10/6) was home to the author from 1931 to 1940.

The **Key West Museum of Art & History** (☎ 305-295-6616; 281 Front St; adults/child $6/4) occupies the old Custom House and has revolving art exhibits, along with some interesting historical relics, like Hemingway's bloodstained army uniform. The **Duval Street Wreckers Museum** (☎ 305-294-9502; 322 Duval St; admission $5) commemorates 'wreckers' – federally licensed workers who salvaged cargo from sinking or sunken ships, which was then brought into Key West for auction.

Owned by the same company, both **Old Town Trolley** (☎ 305-296-6688) and **Conch Tour Train** (☎ 305-294-5161) offer tours (adult/child $20/10) of Old Town. They depart from various locations around town and allow you to get off and reboard in the same direction as often as you like.

For all its tropical flavor, Key West's beaches aren't nearly as sublime as others in Florida. The best one is at the **Fort Zachary Taylor State Historic Site** (☎ 305-292-6713; end of Southard St; admission $2.50). The most popular one, and the best for people-watching, is **Smathers Beach**, on S Roosevelt Blvd.

SLEEPING

While there are a number of chain motels, mostly in New Town, the most memorable accommodations will be found in the restored homes of Old Town. You'll find all are pretty much gay-friendly and many are gay-run.

SLEEPING – BUDGET

HI Key West & Seashell Motel (☎ 305-296-5719; www.keywesthostel.com; 718 South St; dm members/nonmembers $18.50/21.50, d $110; P ✻ 💻) It's the cheapest place in town and it's not a dump. The dorm rooms are spick-and-span, there's a communal kitchen, the hostel restaurant serves cheap meals, and they'll even pick you up for free at the bus station or the airport. The adjacent motel, though perfectly adequate, does not offer quite the same bargain.

Boyd's Key West Campground (☎ 305-294-1465; boydscampground@aol.com; 6401 Maloney Ave; campsites nonwaterfront/waterfront $45/55; 🏊) Located on Stock Island, about 12 miles from Old Town, Boyd's sites don't offer much shade, but the grounds are immaculate and the big swimming pool provides blessed relief from the heat.

SLEEPING – MID-RANGE

Angelina Guest House (☎ 305-294-4480; www.angelinaguesthouse.com; 302 Angela St; d without/with bath $79/99, ste $139; P ✻ 🏊) The folks who run this lovely little place are sooooo nice, they even bake hot cinnamon buns for breakfast. The dreamy lagoon-style pool is a sanctuary from nearby Duval St and the cheery rooms, with hardwood floors, are spotless.

Authors Guesthouse (☎ 305-294-7381, 800-898-6909; www.authorskeywest.com; 725 White St; d $145; P ✻ 🏊) The friendly couple who own this quiet place near the cemetery are smitten with literary types, hence rooms named for Tennessee Williams, Lillian Hellman, Thornton Wilder and other writers, and decorated in period styles.

Speakeasy Inn (☎ 305-296-2680, 800-217-4884; www.keywestcigar.com; 1117 Duval St; d/ste $85/135; P ✻) Run by the same folks who own a nearby cigar shop, the Speakeasy is in the middle of Key West's party district. The nicely restored rooms feature wood floors and contemporary accessories.

Chelsea House (☎ 305-296-2211, 800-845-8859; www.chelseahousekw.com; 707 Truman Ave; d $160; P ✻ 🏊) It looks like a staid Victorian mansion, but the atmosphere is typically rollicking at this 18-room complex. Rooms are well-appointed and there's a clothing-optional sundeck. Kids under 16 are not allowed.

Mermaid & the Alligator (☎ 305-294-1894, 800-773-1894; www.kwmermaid.com; 729 Truman Ave; d $120; P ✻ 🏊) Rooms in this Victorian-style home are individually decorated with period trimmings. Enjoy complimentary afternoon wine on the charming brick patio and pool area.

Big Ruby's Guesthouse (☎ 305-296-2323, 800-477-7829; www.bigrubys.com; 409 Applerouth Lane; d without/with bath $163/180; P ✻ 💻 🏊) This impeccable 17-room complex is high on design and comfort. There is fine linen on the comfy beds and an elegant deck around the lagoon pool.

SLEEPING – TOP END

Simonton Court Historic Inn & Cottages (☎ 305-294-6386, 800-944-2687; www.simontoncourt.com; 320 Simonton St; d/quad $209/399; P) This quiet enclave of rooms and cottages was created from a 19th-century cigar factory and dressed up in style. A brick walkway winds past several gemlike pools and a secluded hot tub.

Marquesa Hotel (☎ 305-292-1919, 800-869-4631; www.marquesa.com; 600 Fleming St; d/ste $275/410; P) Elegant and refined, the rooms in this restored 1884 Greek-revival mansion look like they were transported straight from New England, and all have marble bathrooms. The pool is divine and the concierge staff is ultra-accommodating.

EATING

As a general rule, ask if the fish is fresh (it often isn't), when in doubt order something Cuban, and don't pass up key lime pie, a sweet and tart dessert made with key limes (which are yellow, not green), sweetened condensed milk, eggs and sugar.

Jose's Cantina (☎ 305-296-4366; 800 White St; dishes $6-20) Off the tourist radar and near the cemetery, this neighborhood Cuban restaurant serves three very affordable meals a day. Specialty of the house is a crispy whole fried snapper with black beans and rice.

Pepe's Café & Steakhouse (☎ 305-294-7192; 806 Caroline St; dishes $6-20) The 'Eldest Eating Place in the Florida Keys' has been serving three meals a day since 1909. Everything is good – from the eggs and grits for breakfast to oysters, burgers and steaks for lunch and dinner.

Camille's (☎ 305-296-4811; 1202 Simonton St; dishes $3-25) While it is always packed for breakfast, the lunch salads and burgers and creative seafood dinners at Camille's are worth the visit.

Michael's (☎ 305-295-1300; 532 Margaret St; mains $16-30; dinner only) Chef Michael Wilson creates fish and pasta with a Key West flair and also offers dynamite fondue choices for those tempted to try something different.

Seven Fish (☎ 305-296-2777; 632 Olivia St; mains $12-23; closed Tue) The name says it all at this small storefront restaurant, and that includes comfort food like sautéed scallops over mashed potatoes.

Louie's Backyard (☎ 305-294-1061; 700 Waddell Ave; lunch/dinner $15/30) One of Key West's most popular restaurants, Louie's Caribbean-American cuisine is as divine as the waterfront setting.

Cafe des Artistes (☎ 305-294-7100; 1007 Simonton St; mains $25-35) Sit on the rooftop deck and enjoy a French twist on such local faves as yellowtail snapper or shrimp.

5 Brothers Grocery & Sandwich Shop (☎ 305-296-5205; 930 Southard St; dishes $1-6; closed Sun) Come and stand in line at the counter for the quintessential Cuban mix sandwich. The *bollos* (garlicky black-eyed pea fritters) are a must-have side dish.

Waterfront Market (☎ 305-296-0778; 201 William St; dishes $3-12) Yachties stock up on gourmet nibbles here and so should you. Great bagels, sandwiches and organic foods.

KEY WEST FESTIVALS

Key Westers need no encouragement to have fun. The following is *not* an exhaustive list.

Feeling Ernest? Join the 150-plus 'Papa' look-alikes converging on Sloppy Joe's Bar during the **Hemingway Days Festival** in July. Festivities strike a balance between the high- and low-brow; there's readings and short-story contests, as well as the key lime pie–eating competition and the distinctly Key Western 'running of the bulls.'

Cities don't get much prouder than Key West, where nearly 30% of locals identify themselves as gay or lesbian. **PrideFest** (www.pridefestkeywest.com) is a huge June celebration of the 'One Human Family' (the city's official motto).

The huge 10-day **Fantasy Fest** (www.fantasyfest.net), held in October, is best summed up as a cross between Carnivale and Halloween. Themes run the gamut from 'plays of Tennessee Williams' to 'secrets of the zodiac revealed.' Unless you want to field lots of questions about human anatomy, leave the young ones with a sitter.

Conch Republic Independence Day (www.conchrepublic.com) commemorates the 'secession' of the Keys from the US. Events take place the week before Mardi Gras, but the highlight is the parade in which the Conch Republic takes on US Coast Guard troops with wet bread as ammunition.

DRINKING

They call it the 'Duval Crawl,' the local version of bar-hopping. And there are way too many places to choose from, either on or within a short stumble of Key West's main drag. The following places generally don't have a cover charge.

Sloppy Joe's Bar (☎ 305-294-5717; 201 Duval St) and **Captain Tony's Saloon** (☎ 305-294-1838; 428 Greene St) both claim connections to the Hemingway era, both attract tons of tourists and both are worth at least a quick stop. Jimmy Buffett's **Margaritaville Café** (☎ 305-292-1435; 500 Duval St) appeals to die-hard fans and a college-age crowd. For the crowd that wants to gaze out across the sea, don't miss **Billyfish Bar & Grill** (☎ 305-296-7701; Ocean Key Sunset Pier, end of Duval St). If variety is the spice of life, everyone from shrimpers to socialites to wanna-be pirates hangs out at the funky waterfront **Schooner Wharf** (☎ 305-292-9520; 202 William St), one of the spiciest joints in town. Hang with the locals, but don't try to outdrink them, at the open-air and happily raunchy **Green Parrot** (☎ 305-294-6133; 601 Whitehead St). Among the more popular gay and lesbian hangouts are **Bourbon St Pub** (☎ 305-296-1992; 724 Duval St), with three bars and hot dancing, **La Te Da** (☎ 305-296-6706; 1125 Duval St) with live entertainment and several bars, and **Pearl's Rainbow** (☎ 305-292-1450; 525 United St), an outdoor patio bar within a guesthouse that caters to lesbians.

GETTING THERE & AROUND

There's service between **Key West International Airport** (☎ 305-296-5439; 3535 S Roosevelt Blvd) and Miami, Tampa, Naples, Fort Lauderdale and Orlando. **Greyhound** (☎ 305-296-9072, 800-410-5397, 800-231-2222) runs four buses daily between Miami and the Keys, stopping en route at Miami International Airport. There are designated stops, but the driver also stops on request. The Key West station ($32, four hours from Miami) is at the airport. Along the way you can get off in the Upper, Middle and Lower Keys; tickets cost $12 to $29. The **Dade–Monroe Express** (☎ 305-770-3131) runs daily buses ($1.25) from Key Largo (MM 98) to Florida City.

The best way to get around the Keys is by rental car or Greyhound. Key West is best navigated on foot, especially in Old Town, or by moped, with rates from $12 per three hours. Try **Keys Moped & Scooter** (☎ 305-294-0399; 523 Truman Ave).

DRY TORTUGAS NATIONAL PARK

The **Dry Tortugas** (www.dry.tortugas.national-park.com) is a tiny archipelago of seven islands about 70 miles west of Key West. The name means 'the turtles', for the hawksbill, green, leatherback and loggerhead sea turtles that roam the islands. The park's open for day-trips, but overnight camping allows you more time for snorkeling and diving in the sparkling waters, and the nighttime stargazing is mind-blowing.

When the US saw a need to protect and control traffic flowing into the Gulf of Mexico, they began construction on Fort Jefferson on Garden Key. A federal garrison during the Civil War, it also served as a prison for Union deserters and for at least four people arrested for complicity in the assassination of Abraham Lincoln.

Garden Key has 13 **campsites** (per person $3). Reserve early by calling the **Everglades National Park Office** (☎ 305-242-7700; www.nps.gov/dtro/index.htm). There are toilets, but no freshwater showers or drinking water; bring everything you'll need. As for food, most of the time you'll find Cuban-American fishing boats trolling the waters. Stock up on beverages to trade them for lobster, crab and shrimp. Just paddle up and start bargaining.

The experienced crew of the **Yankee Freedom II** (☎ 305-294-7009, 800-634-0939; www.yankeefleet.com) operates a fast ferry between Garden Key and the Key West Seaport. Round-trip fares cost $109/69 per adult/child. For an overnight drop-off (including gear) the cost is $130/99 per adult/child. **Seaplanes of Key West** (☎ 305-294-0709; www.seaplanesofkeywest.com) will fly you out to camp for $329/235 per adult/child, including snorkeling equipment. They also do day tours.

EAST COAST

This stretch of Florida's Atlantic shore is markedly different from south Florida – a little less affluent, a little less developed, a lot slower paced. Favored by family vacationers, the area boasts narrow barrier islands with long, wide beaches and shallow lagoons, which skirt the mainland.

SPACE COAST

Dubbed the Space Coast by its boosters, Brevard County's Melbourne–Cocoa Beach–

Titusville area is a domain where high technology and nature comfortably coexist. The highlight of the county is the Kennedy Space Center (KSC), the only spot in the US from which humans have been hurled into space. Though the US and Russia have until recently been the sole players in the space game, China and Japan are leading a growing list of nations joining them on the field.

Stiff competition aside, NASA is facing its toughest times yet in the wake of the orbiter *Columbia* disaster in February 2003, in which all seven crew members were lost when a foam tile on the wing came loose upon re-entry. Charges of mismanagement and technical carelessness are countered by NASA's insistence that such woes wouldn't be plaguing the agency if it had been properly funded – and staffed – all along. (At the height of the Cold War the space program received 4% of the federal budget; today it gets 0.7%.) Either way, NASA has vowed to comply with all the recommendations laid out by the Columbia Accident Investigation Board, and is looking to resume shuttle flights by summer 2004.

A large buffer of natural wilderness and gorgeous beaches – most of which is protected national parkland – surrounds the KSC. Birding, canoeing and kayaking opportunities abound. There is splendid camping on both beach and land, and hotel accommodations are inexpensive.

Visitor information is available through **Florida's Space Coast Office of Tourism** (☎ 800-872-1969; www.space-coast.com; No 102, 8810 Astronaut Blvd).

Sights & Activities

KENNEDY SPACE CENTER

Present NASA tribulations aside, this place is awesome, even for nontechies. Plan to spend an entire day at the **Kennedy Space Center Visitor Complex** (☎ 321-449-4444; www.kennedyspacecenter.com; maximum access pass adult $33, child 3-11 $23; 9am-6pm). The standard admission (adult/child $28/18) doesn't include a trip to the complex's most recent addition – the Astronaut Hall of Fame, which holds the motion simulator rides – so it's worth the extra dough for the full pass. With it you'll also have access to all the visitor complex exhibits, Imax films and a bus tour that stops at the Apollo/Saturn V Center; International Space Station Center; LC 39 Observation Gantry (with views of the mammoth Vehicle Assembly Building); Space Shuttle Launch Pads 39A and 39B; and the Launch Control Center.

KSC is an especially exciting place to watch any liftoff, be it a shuttle (when these resume) or an uncrewed craft like a rocket. Tickets for launch viewing (plus your maximum access pass) are $43.50/33.50 per adult/child, and can be ordered from the visitor complex, by phone or from the website. Depending on the mission, you'll either watch from KSC or be trundled out by bus to a viewing spot 6 miles away. Check out NASA's public affairs office at www-pao.ksc.nasa.gov/kscpao/schedule/schedule.htm for the most up-to-date launch schedule.

If you can't score KSC tickets or you crave a more tailgate-party atmosphere (watching a launch can be a patient business), head to the popular Jetty Park Campground ($5 per car), Cherie Down Park, Rotary Riverfront Park or Brewer Parkway bridge in Titusville. BYO beer and binoculars.

MERRITT ISLAND NATIONAL WILDLIFE REFUGE

This Titusville **refuge** (☎ 321-861-0667; SR Hwy 402; admission free) contains in its mangrove swamps, marshes and hardwood hammocks more endangered and threatened species than any other refuge in the continental USA. It is also one of the best birding spots, since it's on the migration path between North and South America. The best time to visit is October to May; the best viewing times are early morning and after 4pm. Be sure to cruise the 6-mile Black Point Wildlife Dr. The refuge is closed two days prior to shuttle launches. The visitors center is closed Sunday from April to October.

Among several outfitters offering water excursions is **Village Outfitters** (☎ 321-633-7245; www.villageoutfitters.com; 113 Brevard Ave, Cocoa; single-/double-kayak rental $25/40) which runs a variety of kayak tours to the refuge.

CANAVERAL NATIONAL SEASHORE & COCOA BEACH

These 25 miles of windswept and mainly pristine beach are favored by surfers (at the south end), vacationing families (at the north end) and campers and nature lovers (on Klondike Beach, in the center). The seashore has a **ranger station** (☎ 321-867-4077; per car $5) at the south end near Playalinda

SURF'S UP

Hawaii it ain't, but Florida has got some of the best surfing east of the Mississippi. Comprehensive, up-to-date specs of the most happenin' spots on Florida's east coast can be found at www.cflsurf.com.

Surf

Cocoa Beach South of Cape Canaveral, the Cocoa Beach pier, which extends 800ft out, gets packed with space tourists and the surf crowd, but it's a good area to find a surf school and catch some waves.

Sebastian Inlet South of Melbourne, the inlet is one of the most consistent – and powerful – breaks in the state.

New Smyrna Beach South of Daytona, this 13-mile stretch is called the 'world's safest bathing beach' because of its offshore rock ledges, which counteract the treacherous undercurrents common to the East Coast.

Reef Road Not for newbies (or out-of-towners, some elitists would maintain), this classic Palm Beach spot promises a perfect left break. A favorite with sharks, too.

Learn

Surf schools are thick on the ground, so it's wise to ask around for a recommendation. Make sure the business is licensed, insured and instructors are CPR certified. One well-established company is South Cocoa Beach's **Nex Generation Surf School** (☎ 321-591-9577; www.nexgensurf.com; 3901 North Atlantic Ave; clinic/semiprivate/private lessons $30/40/50), which runs out of Comfort Inn.

Shop

You've seen the billboards, now visit the shop. Cocoa Beach's **Ron Jon Surf Shop** (☎ 321-799-8888; www.ronjons.com; 4151 N Atlantic Ave; 24hr) is more than just a place to stock up on Sex Wax; there's live music (think Beach Boys covers), classic cars and a warehouse packed with all things surf. Plus it's open 24 hours a day, seven days a week, 365 days a year. A worthy stop even for landlubbers.

Beach at the end of Hwy 406/402; and a **visitors center** (☎ 904-428-3384) at the north end at Apollo Beach, on Hwy A1A east of New Smyrna Beach.

Greyhound has service only as close as Cocoa and Titusville. A taxi costs around $16 from Cocoa to the Kennedy Space Center.

Sleeping & Eating

Accommodations here are fairly reasonable, except during launches when the rates spike.

Randolph Inn (☎ 312-269-5945; www.nbbd.com/randolphinn; 3810 S Washington St; nonlaunch/launch $64/99; P) A friendly, cozy place to stay if you want to be near KSC in Titusville.

Best Western Space Shuttle Inn (☎ 321-269-1000; www.spaceshuttleinn.com; 3455 Cheney Hwy; nonlaunch/launch $75/112; P) This surprisingly unchainlike inn is another good choice near KSC. For a bit more green you can even sleep in your very own orbiter.

Fawlty Towers Motel (☎ 321-784-3870; www.fawlty towersresort.com; 100 E Cocoa Beach Causeway; nonlaunch/launch $60/140; P) For beachside digs, head to Cocoa Beach and this gloriously garish motel, where the rooms are prettier than the Pepto-Bismol pink exterior.

Inn at Cocoa Beach (☎ 321-799-3460; www.theinnatcocoabeach.com; 4300 Ocean Beach Blvd; nonlaunch/launch $135/295; P) Also in Cocoa Beach, this place is smack-dab on the beach and offers onsite spa treatments.

Canaveral National Seashore (☎ 386-428-3384; www.nps.gov/cana) There's free camping at the Canaveral National Seashore (except in summer when turtles are nesting and beach camping is a no-no), on Klondike Beach (November 1 to April 30 only) or on the islands that fill the north end of Mosquito Lagoon. The Canaveral National Seashore is closed to campers the night before shuttle launches.

Dixie Crossroads (☎ 321-268-5000; 1475 Garden St; mains $9-18) You'll likely have to wait in line at this Titusville eatery, which is popular with locals for all sorts of seafood, but especially the locally-caught rock shrimp.

Cocoa and Cocoa Beach have a wider variety of restaurants. Among the recommended are the following:

Crab Heaven (☎ 321-783-5001; 6910 N Atlantic Ave; mains $6-28) For all-you-can-eat blue crabs and snow crabs.

Black Tulip (☎ 321-631-1133; 207 Brevard Ave; mains $13-24) For creative New American cuisine.

Heidelberg Restaurant (☎ 321-783-6806; 7 N Orlando Ave; mains $15-20) For well-prepared German specialties and live jazz nightly.

DAYTONA BEACH

What began with men and their expensive, fast cars racing along the hard-packed sand here in 1902 has culminated in an entire city dedicated to the pursuit of speed. By 1904 the event was called the Winter Speed Carnival, and this was the place where records were made and smashed. Today Daytona Beach thrives on racing and young, party-based tourism. It has one of the last Atlantic Coast spring breaks, and during **Bike Week** (early March), hordes of Harleys roar into town. The **visitors bureau** (☎ 386-255-0415, 800-544-0415; www.daytonabeach.com; 126 E Orange Ave; 🕑 9am-5pm Mon-Fri) has a **booth in Daytona USA** (1801 W International Speedway Blvd). The **Greater Daytona Beach Business Guild** (☎ 386-322-8003; www.gaydaytona.com) can assist gay and lesbian travelers with information; phone calls or web only.

Sights & Activities

The beach is hard, flat and wide. By long-standing tradition – one that is perennially fought by environmentalists – you can drive your car ($5 per day), jog, walk or bike on most of it. There's good swimming and great waves for boogie boarding and surfing. During nesting season for sea turtles (May to October) some spots may be marked off to protect the eggs and hatchlings.

The **Daytona International Speedway** (☎ 386-254-2700, box office 386-253-7223; 1801 W International Speedway Blvd) hosts Winston, Nascar, stock and sports-car, go-cart, monster truck and motorcycle races. When there aren't any races, motorheads can get a peek of the track for free. The place goes crazy in February for the Daytona 500. The adjoining **Daytona USA** (☎ 386-947-6800; adult/child $20/14; 🕑 9am-7pm) is an excellent, but pricey, shrine to the sport with a museum, famous cars, high-tech interactive displays and two motion simulator rides. The fine **Museum of Arts & Science** (☎ 386-255-0285; 1040 Museum Blvd; adult/child $7/2) collects American, African and Cuban art, and has planetarium shows ($5). Downtown's renovated **Beach Street**, with shops, restaurants and brew pubs, is less frenetic than the beach, especially during spring break. Bus No 17A runs hourly to the **Ponce de León Inlet Lighthouse & Museum** (☎ 386-761-1821; 4931 S Peninsula Dr; adult/child $7/1; 🕑 10am-7pm) where you can climb the 203 stairs for a terrific view and some interesting exhibits. If Daytona's hedonism is getting to you, find refreshment both spiritual and gastronomic (free coffee and doughnuts!) at the **Little Chapel by the Sea** (S Atlantic Ave; 🕑 8:30am & 10am Sun) a former drive-in theater and now a drive-in Christian church.

Sleeping

There's no shortage of inexpensive and moderately priced accommodations – except during holidays, Bike Week and spring break, when prices soar. Unless you're into huge crowds, traffic jams and nonstop partying, consider staying in New Smyrna Beach or west of Daytona Beach (see p605) for quieter lodging. However, even these areas raise rates during Daytona Beach's special events. Summer is high season, but even then you can often find motel rooms for $35 or less off the beach on US 1.

Streamline Hotel (☎ 386-258-6937; www.streamline.com; d/d with kitchenette $29/49; P ✖) The best deal on the beach is the art deco hotel where Nascar was born, which now caters to a gay and lesbian crowd. Recent renovations have upgraded the rooms and added a rooftop bar.

Dream Inn (☎ 386-767-282, 800-767-9738; www.dreaminn.com; 3217 S Atlantic Ave; d nonoceanfront/oceanfront $50/80; P ✖ 🏊) A small, quiet property with big-hotel conveniences.

Coquina Inn B&B (☎ 386-254-4969; www.coquinainndaytonabeach.com; 544 S Palmetto Ave; r $90-140; P ✖ 🏊) Historic Coqunia Inn B&B has a Jacuzzi in the lush garden.

Villa B&B (☎ 386-248-2020; www.thevillabb.com; 801 N Peninsula Dr; r $100-150; P ✖) A gay-owned, grand Spanish-style manse in a garden setting.

Other beachfront lodgings include **Thunderbird Beach Motel** (☎ 386-253-2562; 500 N Atlantic Ave; d $60; P ✖ 🏊) with spacious rooms featuring balconies, and **Sun Viking Lodge** (☎ 386-252-5463; www.sunviking.com; 2441 S Atlantic Ave; d $70; P ✖ 🏊) where the big pool features a 60ft water slide.

A few miles south of Daytona, in New Smyrna Beach, the **Riverview Hotel** (☎ 386-428-5858; rvhotel@aol.com; d $85; P) and the **Night Swan Intracoastal Bed & Breakfast** (☎ 386-423-4940; www.nightswan.com; d/ste $95/145) provide charming lodgings on the river. The luxurious **Adam's Mark Beach Resort** (☎ 386-254-8200; www.adamsmark.com; 100 N Atlantic Ave; d $135; P) is perched on a section of the beach that is blessedly traffic-free.

Eating & Drinking

Lighthouse Landing (☎ 386-761-9271; 4940 S Peninsula Dr; mains $5-15) Near Ponce de León Lighthouse, this funky waterfront establishment serves good fish sandwiches and burgers.

Starlite Diner (☎ 386-255-9555; 401 N Atlantic Ave; dishes $4-8) Specializes in hearty breakfasts and good ol' American lunches and dinners.

Anna's Italian Trattoria (☎ 386-239-9624; 304 Seabreeze Blvd; mains $13-20) This friendly trattoria makes a sensational veal marsala and other Italian specialties.

Dancing Avocado Kitchen (☎ 386-947-2022; 110 S Beach St; mains $5-8; closed Sun) Vegetarians will swoon over the meatless burgers and the avocado melt sandwich here.

Pasha (☎ 386-257-7753; 919 W International Speedway Blvd; dishes $4-6) On target with authentic Middle Eastern food.

Rosario's Restaurant (☎ 386-258-6066; 444 S Beach St; mains $16-28; closed Sun & Mon) If you're looking for a place to splurge, head to Rosario's for fine steaks and a massive wine list.

For dining with a view, head to New Smyrna Beach, where the **Breakers** (☎ 386-428-2019; 518 Flagler Ave; mains $6-15) garners just praise for its burgers, and the riverfront **JB'S Fish Camp & Restaurant** (☎ 386-427-5747; 859 Pompano Ave; mains $7-19) serves oysters from its own beds, along with the full range of seafood fare.

The good thing about biker bars – and there are lots of them in Daytona – is that they provide the perfect excuse to wear leather. Rev up your engine at **Dirty Harry's Pub** (☎ 386-252-9877; 705 Main St), where there's occasional live music, or **Froggy's Saloon** (☎ 386-253-0330; 800 Main St). Check out **Razzles** (☎ 386-257-6236; 611 Seabreeze Blvd; cover $5-10), a high-energy dance club, and **Bank & Blues Club** (701 Main St) for down 'n' dirty blues.

Getting There & Around

Daytona Beach International Airport (☎ 386-248-8030) is just west of the Speedway. **Greyhound** (☎ 386-255-7076; 138 S Ridgewood Ave) offers daily routes to Florida's major cities. The nearest **Amtrak station** (☎ 386-734-2322) is in DeLand, where there is a connecting Amtrak bus. **Votran buses** (☎ 386-761-7700) run landside and beachside from Ponce Inlet (south end of Daytona Beach) to Ormond Beach ($1, exact change required). **Scooters Cycles** (☎ 386-253-4141; 2020 S Atlantic Ave) rents scooters for cruising the beach and streets.

AROUND DAYTONA BEACH

About 25 miles west of Daytona Beach you'll find two superb state parks within 5 miles of one another. They offer a rare opportunity to experience Florida 'BD' (before developers).

Near Orange City, **Blue Spring State Park** (☎ 386-775-3663; 2100 W French Ave; per car $4; 8am-dusk), is one of the best places to see manatees in Florida, especially November to March. Warm, spring-fed waters for swimming, fishing and canoeing are another attraction. Book ahead for the excellent **campsites** ($20) and air-conditioned **cabins** ($56).

The free pontoon ferry to **Hontoon Island State Park** (☎ 386-736-5309; 2309 River Ridge Rd; per person $2; 8am-dusk), in DeLand, leads to 1650 pristine acres with 12 **campsites** ($10), primitive **cabins** ($25), pontoon docks and trails, all visible from an 80ft tower.

DeLand has the most accommodations and eateries in the area. Among the choices are **Quality Inn** (☎ 386-736-3440; www.qualityinn.com; 2801 E New York Ave; d $56; P) and **Chimney Corner Motel** (☎ 386-734-3146; 1941 S Woodland Blvd; d $45; P). For a setting on the St John's River, next to the park's ferry landing, try **Hontoon Landing Resort & Marina** (☎ 386-734-2474; www.hontoon.com; 2317 River Ridge Rd; d $85; P).

Brian's Bar-B-Q (☎ 386-736-8851; 795 N Spring Garden Ave; mains $5-9), serves tangy pork and chicken. Locally grown edible flowers and homemade pasta make **Pondo's Restaurant** (☎ 386-734-1995; 1915 Old New York Ave; mains $10-17) a good dinner choice.

Greyhound (☎ 386-734-2747; 224 East Ohio Ave) buses connect DeLand to Daytona ($9, 45 minutes) and Orlando ($11, 45 minutes), among other cities. **Amtrak** (☎ 386-734-2322; 2491 Old New York Ave), in DeLand, is less than 2 miles from Blue Spring State Park. It has a connecting bus service to Daytona Beach. Taxis serve both parks.

ST AUGUSTINE

The nation's oldest city, St Augustine was settled in 1565 by Spanish explorer Don Pedro Menéndez de Avilés. After being twice attacked by the British, St Augustine built the Castillo de San Marcos in 1672. Over the next 150 years or so, the city traded hands three times between the Spanish, British and finally the USA. In the late 1880s, Henry Flagler brought his railroad through town, creating a building boom.

Today St Augustine's historic district is a charming mix of narrow cobblestone streets, European architecture and Spanish colonial flair. Across the Intracoastal Waterway is 18-mile Anastasia Island, with a state park, pier, dunes and beaches. The main **visitors information center** (☎ 904-825-1000, 800-653-2489; www.visitoldcity.com; 10 Castillo Dr; 🕑 8:30am-5:30pm) has an overwhelming abundance of brochures and pamphlets about things to see and do in the area.

Sights & Activities

While St Augustine has more than its share of cheesy tourist traps, there are a number of significant museums and exhibits. The state-operated **Spanish Quarter Living History Museum** (☎ 904-825-6830; 53 St George St; adult/child $6.50/4; 🕑 9am-5:30pm) is a re-creation of Spanish colonial St Augustine in 1740. St Augustine's City Hall Complex, the former luxury Hotel Alcazar (1888), is also home to the **Lightner Museum** (☎ 904-824-2874; 75 King St; adult/child $6/2; 🕑 9am-5pm), with 19th-century fine and decorative arts, early Americana, European art and wonderfully bizarre collections of everything from matchbox labels to buttons and salt shakers. **Government House Museum** (☎ 904-825-5033; 48 King St; adult/child $3/1.50; 🕑 9am-4:30pm) houses historical exhibits as well as archaeological artifacts.

The **Oldest Wooden School House** (☎ 904-824-0192; 14 St George St; adult/child $3/2; 🕑 9am-5pm) was built from 1750 to 1763 out of cypress and red cedar with handmade nails and joists. With continuous occupancy since the early 1600s, the restored **González-Alvarez House** (☎ 904-824-2872; 14 St Francis St; adult/child $5/3; 🕑 9am-5pm) claims to be the oldest house in America. Built in 1887, Henry Flagler's wonderfully ornate **Hotel Ponce de León** (☎ 904-823-3378; cnr King & Cordova Sts; tours adult/child $5/1; 🕑 May-Aug) was once an exclusive winter resort but is now part of Flagler College.

The Spanish began the fortress that is now called **Castillo de San Marcos National Monument** (☎ 904-829-6506; btwn San Marcos Ave & Matanzas River; adult/child $5/2; 🕑 8:45am-4:45pm) in 1627, making it the country's oldest masonry fort. One of the city's most distinctive features, the **Bridge of Lions** was built in 1926 to connect the city with St Augustine Beach. Five miles beyond it, **Anastasia State Recreation Area** (☎ 904-461-2033; 1340A Hwy A1A S; per pedestrian/car $1/3.25; 🕑 8am-dusk) has a terrific beach, a campground, a trail and bird-watching, plus rentals for windsurfing, kayaking, canoeing and sailing.

Two companies provide interesting, convenient tours on open-air trams: **St Augustine Sightseeing Trains** (☎ 904-829-6545, 800-226-6545; 170 San Marco Ave; $12) and **Old Town Trolley Tours** (☎ 904-829-3800; 167 San Marco Ave; $12). For a little evening fun, take the 90-minute **Ghostly Experience Walking Tour** (☎ 904-461-1009, 888-461-1009; $8) to learn about St Augustine's spirited past.

The nearest airport is **Jacksonville International** (☎ 904-741-4902), 50 miles north. **Greyhound** (☎ 904-829-6401; 100 Malaga St) has easy connections to Jacksonville ($9.50, 45 minutes). The closest Amtrak is off US 17 in Palatka, 25 miles west.

Sleeping

The most desirable places to stay are in the center of the Old City where there are more than two dozen B&Bs. There are plenty of mom-and-pop motels and chain establishments on Hwy US 1 and Anastasia Blvd (on Anastasia Island). Weekend getaways to St Augustine are popular and that's when rates tend to spike – often by as much as 30% – rather than by season, although summer rates are typically higher than winter. Weekend rates are quoted below.

BUDGET

Pirate Haus Hostel (☎ 904-808-1999; www.piratehaus.com; 32 Treasury St; dm/r $15/36; Ⓟ ✖ 💻) This great place has everything going for it – terrific downtown location, comfy lodgings and a really friendly staff. The 'Guess Who's Coming to Dinner' program connects guests with local families for dinner.

Anastasia State Recreation Area (☎ 904-461-2033; 1340A Hwy A1A S; campsites $18-20) This lovely waterfront campground is typically booked months ahead but if you can, try for one of the shady sites in the hardwood hammock.

MID-RANGE

Anastasia Inn (☎ 904-825-2879, 888-226-6181; www.anastasiainn.com; 218 Anastasia Blvd; d $69; P ❄ 💻 🏊) Located just over the Bridge of Lions from the Old City, this friendly place doesn't exactly ooze charm, but the rooms are immaculate and the amenities are many.

Edgewater Inn (☎ 904-825-2697; www.edgewaterinn.com; 2 St Augustine Blvd; d $95; P ❄ 🏊) Although it looks historic this inn was only built in 1998. The spotless rooms offer great views across the bridge to the city.

Southern Wind (☎ 904-825-3623; www.southernwind.com; 18 Cordova St; r $99-239; P ❄) The spacious veranda out front is comforting and so are the tastefully decorated rooms. Bounty from the backyard garden often highlights the buffet breakfast.

Kenwood Inn (☎ 904-824-2116, 800-824-8151; 38 Marine St; d $125; P ❄ 🏊) Period antiques and balconies make this venerable inn – welcoming guests since 1886 – a long-standing favorite.

Old City House Inn (☎ 904-826-0113; www.oldcityhouse.com; 115 Cordova St; d $135; P ❄) With seven rooms decorated according on the theme of famous cities and settings – Old Venice, Out of Africa – this sweet little place narrowly avoids kitsch. The garden is quite lovely and the restaurant (see below) is a winner.

Castle Garden (☎ 904-829-3839; www.castlegarden.com; 15 Shenandoah St; loft/d $79/179; P ❄) This c 1860 Moorish-revival home near the fort really does look like a little castle. Some of the rooms are doll-like, but comfortable.

Wescott House Inn (☎ 904-824-4301; www.westcotthouse.com; 146 Avenida Menendez; d $175; P ❄) You'll pay a little extra for the view at this 1880s-era Victorian home, but it's worth it. Many of the lovingly appointed rooms have fireplaces.

TOP END

La Fiesta Oceanside Inn (☎ 904-471-2220; www.lafiestainn.com; 810 Beach Blvd; d $199; P ❄ 🏊) There are many hotels on St Augustine Beach but this is the nicest. Great ocean views, and the hotel runs a free shuttle to the Old City.

Casa Monica Hotel (☎ 904-827-1888, 800-648-1888; www.casamonica.com; 95 Cordova St; d $219; P ❄ 🏊) If you're going to splurge in St Augustine, this spectacular hotel is the place to do it. Built in 1888 as the illustrious Cordova Hotel and restored in 2000, it is a showcase of Moorish-revival architecture with ornate balconies, a glistening Italianate lobby, soaring towers, the whole shebang. No two rooms are alike and all are wonderful.

Eating

Athena Restaurant (☎ 904-823-9076; 14 Cathedral Pl; dishes $2-8; 🕐 closed Sun) A classic Greek diner. There's always a line, but it's worth the wait.

Gypsy Cab Co (☎ 904-824-8244; 828 Anastasia Blvd; mains $12-20) The place to go on Anastasia Island for great seafood, pasta and weekend brunches.

Manatee Café (☎ 904-826-0210; 179A San Marco Ave; dishes $4-8) Vegetarians and vegans – in fact any one who likes good food – should try this excellent café.

Old City House Inn (☎ 904-826-0113; 115 Cordova St; mains $16-24) For a big night out make reservations for the fine restaurant at this inn and enjoy 'world cuisine' in a Mediterranean atmosphere.

95 Cordova (☎ 904-827-1888; 95 Cordova St; mains $17-32) Also worth heading to for those special occasions is Casa Monica Hotel's terrific dining room, where the chef blends Moorish, Mediterranean, Asian and American influences, and it all turns out fine.

Visit the **Spanish Bakery** (☎ 904-471-3046; 42½ St George St; dishes $1-4; 🕐 closes 3pm) for their heavenly sweet-potato turnover or **DeNoël French Pastry** (☎ 904-829-3974; 212 Charlotte St; dishes $5-7) for fresh-baked baguettes and sandwiches.

Entertainment

Get a bellyful of laughs from famous comics at the **Gypsy Comedy Club** (☎ 904-808-1305; 828 Anastasia Blvd). **TradeWinds Lounge** (☎ 904-829-9336; 124 Charlotte St) is a classic St Augustine local bar with live music. **Scarlett O'Hara's** (☎ 904-824-6535; 70 Hypolita St) is a popular neighborhood bar with entertainment from DJs to folk to rock, plus dining. **Pot Belly's Cinema 4 Plus** (☎ 904-829-3101; 36 Granada St; admission $5) offers first-run movies, comfy seats and reasonably priced burgers, beer, wine and soda.

JACKSONVILLE

The saying in Florida is that the further north you go, the more Southern it gets. That's surely true of Jacksonville, which Floridians often refer to as the capital of South Georgia. Jacksonville is a sprawling city – in terms of area, the second largest in the US (Anchorage in Alaska is the largest). It sits near the mouth of the mighty

St John's River, the only major river in the US that flows from south to north. Bypassed by most travelers in favor of the diversions that lie further south, Jacksonville is an amiable place that divides its pleasures between the art-filled downtown and the natural wonders in and around the city. The **Southbank Riverwalk** is a 1.5-mile boardwalk along the St John's River that's popular with joggers and connects downtown hotels, museums and eateries. The **visitors bureau** (☎ 904-798-9111, 800-733-2668; www.jaxcvb.com; 201 E Adams St; 8am-5pm Mon-Fri) runs three information booths:

Jacksonville Airport (2400 Yankee Clipper Dr)
Jacksonville Beach (403 Beach Blvd)
Jacksonville Landing (2 Independent Dr)

Spend an idyllic afternoon viewing European artwork and beautiful riverfront Italian-style gardens at the **Cummer Museum of Art & Gardens** (☎ 904-356-6857; www.cummer.org; 829 Riverside Ave; adult/child $6/3, admission free 4-9pm Tue; 10am-9pm Tue & Thu, 10am-5pm Wed, Fri & Sat, noon-5pm Sun). Then get to know the city through the trio of museums on the Southbank Riverwalk at 1015 Museum Circle: the **Museum of Science & History and Alexander Brest Planetarium** (☎ 904-396-6674; www.themosh.org; adult/child $7/5; 10am-5pm Mon-Fri, 10am-6pm Sat, 1-6pm Sun), with Florida history and local marine and wildlife exhibits; **Jacksonville Maritime Museum** (☎ 904-398-9011; admission free; 10am-3pm Mon-Fri, 1-5pm Sat-Sun), with model ships and local maritime photos; and the **Jacksonville Historical Center** (☎ 904-398-4301; 11am-5pm Mon-Sat), which chronicles the city's colorful history.

Miles of beaches are another reason to come to Jacksonville. They're toasty-warm late spring through fall, then cool to cold but uncrowded in winter. Take your pick of **Little Talbot Island State Park** (☎ 904-251-2320; per pedestrian/car $1/4; 8am-dusk) which sits between Jacksonville and Amelia Island to the north; **Kathryn Abbey Hanna Park** (☎ 904-249-4700; 500 Wonderwood Dr; admission $1, children under 6 free; 8am-dusk), with exceptional hiking, biking, fishing and beaches; and three community locales – **Atlantic Beach** for surfing, **Neptune Beach** for quiet beaches and **Jacksonville Beach** for swimming, biking, skating and nightlife.

Sleeping & Eating

Jacksonville's hotels are not affected by seasonal travelers, except for beach properties, where B&Bs and mom-and-pop motels charge $10 to $25 more during summer, weekends and special events.

Sea Horse Oceanfront Inn (☎ 904-246-2175; www.seahorseresort.com; 120 Atlantic Blvd; d $89; P) This beachside inn has nice rooms and a great view.

Beach Landing Inn (☎ 904-249-9778; www.beachlanding.com; d $99; P) Another beachside inn, Beach Landing has basic rooms and is near the beach bar district.

Fig Tree Inn (☎ 904-246-8855; 185 4th Ave S; d $105; P) This is a 1915 cottage with five lovely rooms.

Ruby Inn by the Sea (☎ 904-241-5551; www.rubyinnbythesea.com; 802 2nd St S; d $110; P) This cedar-shingled option offers plenty of beach chairs and beach toys.

Cleary-Dickert House (☎ 904-387-4762; www.cleary-dickert.com; 1804 Copeland St; s/d/ste $99/109/139; P) One of a couple of cheery downtown B&Bs, this is a comfy charmer in a 1914 Prairie-style home. The friendly owners bake breads and other treats.

House on Cherry St (☎ 904-384-1999; houseoncherry@bellsouth.com; 1844 Cherry St; d $85; P) An exquisitely decorated Colonial-style home near the river, this is another of the cheery B&Bs downtown.

Kathryn Abbey Hanna Park (☎ 904-249-4700; 500 Wonderwood Dr; campsites/cabins $14/34) In Atlantic Beach, this park offers shady camping just 200 yards from the ocean.

Two big, amenity-rich hotels that tower over downtown are the **Jacksonville Hilton** (☎ 904-398-8800; www.hilton.com; 1201 Riverplace Blvd; d $99; P) and the **Omni Jacksonville Hotel** (☎ 904-355-6664, 800-843-6664; www.omnihotels.com; 245 Water St; d $155) which has acres of marble, a fitness room and free video rentals.

First Street Grille (☎ 904-246-6555; 807 N 1st St; mains $9-22) For eats near the beach, go for fancy with some Cajun and seafood specialities.

Beachside Seafood & Sandwich Co (☎ 904-241-4880; 120 3rd St S; dishes $4-8; 11am-6:30pm Mon-Sat, 11am-5pm Sun) This world-class hole-in-the-wall with a seafood market offers a more casual beachside dining experience.

In the downtown and Riverwalk areas, try **Da Real Ting Café** (☎ 904-633-9738; 45 W Monroe St; mains $5-10; lunch Tue-Sun, open until late Fri-Sun), for spicy, authentic Caribbean fare (and weekend reggae), popular **Akel's Delicatessen** (☎ 904-356-5628; 130 N Hogan St; dishes $1-5; 7am-4pm) for huge sandwiches, and

Southern Paradise Restaurant (☎ 904-358-1082; 229 W Forsyth St; dishes $5-7) for heaped helpings of southern specialities such as chicken 'n' dumplings with lots of veggie sides.

Entertainment

Jacksonville boasts a fine performing arts venue, **Times-Union Center** (☎ 904-633-6110; 300 Water St), where the Jacksonville Symphony Orchestra performs, plus touring rock and pop groups. The smaller **Florida Theatre** (☎ 904-355-2787; www.floridatheatre.com; 128 E Forsyth St) features headline artists, as does the **Marquee Theatre** (☎ 904-356-5555; www.marqueetheatre.com; 1028 Park St).

The NFL **Jacksonville Jaguars** (☎ 904-633-2000; www.jaguars.com) play professional football at AllTel Stadium.

Getting There & Around

North of the city, **Jacksonville International Airport** (☎ 904-741-4902) has rental cars, taxis and buses. **Greyhound** (☎ 904-356-9976; 10 Pearl St) operates buses to Miami ($60, seven hours), Orlando ($32, three hours) and Tallahassee ($30, three hours), among many other cities. Jacksonville is a hub for **Amtrak** (☎ 904-766-5110; 3570 Clifford Lane). **Jacksonville Transit** (☎ 904-630-3100; fare/week pass $1/10) runs the not particularly efficient municipal bus system.

AMELIA ISLAND

The French landed on this island, 30 miles northeast of Jacksonville, in 1562. Eventually the Spanish, British, Confederates, Union and various renegade groups claimed dominion over it. After the Civil War, hotels popped up and resorts rose on the beach. The main town and restored historic district is Fernandina Beach, where you'll find the **visitors center** (☎ 904-261-3248, 800-226-3542; 102 Centre St; closed Sun) in an old railroad depot.

Displays of Spanish artifacts are found at the **Amelia Island Museum of History** (☎ 904-261-7378; 233 S 3rd St; adult/child $4/2; 10am-5pm Mon-Fri, 10am-4pm Sat), which conducts 90-minute walking tours through the historic district. **Fort Clinch State Park** (☎ 904-277-7274; 2601 Atlantic Ave; per pedestrian/car $1/3.25; 9am-5pm), begun in 1847 but never completed, is now a super state park with 19th-century military relics, reenactments, good facilities and lots for nature lovers and active outdoor types.

Head east on Atlantic Ave for the excellent, broad beaches. **American Beach** was founded in the 1930s for African-American beachgoers at a time when beaches were segregated. It remains an interesting – but run-down – area and a popular vacation spot, especially (but not exclusively) for middle-class African-Americans. It's easily the most tranquil spot on the island.

Ocean View Inn (☎ 904-261-0193; www.oceanviewamelia.com; 2801 Atlantic Ave; d winter $85, higher in summer; P) has basic rooms right on the beach. In downtown Fernandina Beach, **Florida House Inn** (☎ 904-261-3300, 800-258-3301; www.floridahouse.com; 22 S 3rd St; r $80-180), built in 1857, claims to be Florida's oldest hotel and offers wonderfully restored rooms with beautiful artwork. The very upscale **Ritz-Carlton Resort** (☎ 904-277-1100, 800-241-3333; www.ritzcarlton.com; 4750 Amelia Island Parkway; r winter/summer $150/225; P) pampers its guests with a gorgeous pool area and a dreamy spa. You can find shaded riverfront and sandy beachfront campsites at **Fort Clinch State Park** (☎ 904-277-7274, 800-326-3521; 2601 Atlantic Ave; campsites/RV sites $19/21).

It's just a take-out joint on the pier but **Fernandina Seafood Market** (☎ 904-491-0476; 315 N Front St; dishes $6-8; lunch) serves some of the freshest fried seafood imaginable. There's innovative cooking at the **Beech Street Grill** (☎ 904-277-3662; 801 Beech St; mains $21-30; dinner), located in a historic house. Enjoy traditional Southern family fare at **Florida House Inn** (☎ 904-261-3300; 22 S 3rd St; dishes $7-12). The boardinghouse-style meals come with platters of fried catfish, collard greens, mashed potatoes and other fare.

Hwy A1A links the island to the mainland, but there's no public transportation. Rent bikes to cruise the island at **Fernandina Beach Bike & Fitness** (☎ 904-277-3227; 115 8th St; per hour/day $5/14; Mon & Wed-Sat).

WEST COAST

From culture to nature, the Gulf Coast's diversity offers visitors an almost endless palette of opportunity. It has the biggest, baddest roller coaster at Busch Gardens, world-class arts in Sarasota and St Petersburg, a party-hearty nightlife with a Latin beat in Tampa's Ybor City, clear springs that attract manatees, and parks with canoe trails that meander through miles of unspoiled landscape.

SPRING TRAINING *Robert D Hershey Jr*

Even if you're a disenchanted baseball fan – suffering overly long games and increasingly remote players flitting between teams for exorbitantly high pay – spring training is likely to prove a tonic. From mid-February through March each year, 18 of the 30 major league teams prepare in Florida for their grueling seasons and appraise new talent in one of the most cherished rituals of spring.

The atmosphere at the 17 sites – the St Louis Cardinals and Florida Marlins both train at Roger Dean Stadium in Jupiter – is far more relaxed than during the regular season, with players often accessible for autographs (and sometimes conversation) and engaging in personality-revealing byplay. Stadiums are small, so while games in recent years have gained popularity, the average crowd for the games in 2003 was just 5200. This means you get to see and hear things you'd miss when wins and losses start to count.

Prices are up on past years, too, with the New York Yankees, the biggest draw by far, commanding up to $16 for their games at Legends Field in Tampa. But while sellouts are common, you can buy tickets in advance and usually at the gate so long as you don't count on sitting in the shade. A big plus is the fact that these 'grapefruit league' teams are situated in four main pockets – areas around Orlando, Tampa Bay, Fort Myers and the state's east coast – so that even casual fans can see a half dozen teams with little strain.

Contact the **Florida Sports Foundation** (☎ 850-488-8347) for a copy of their annual guide to spring training or visit www.floridaspringtraining.com.

FORT MYERS

Home at one time to Thomas Edison and Henry Ford, palm-luscious Fort Myers is best known for its beach and excellent parks. The downtown sits several miles inland from the Gulf of Mexico, along the Caloosahatchee River.

Get information from the **visitors bureau** (☎ 239-338-3500; 2180 W 1st St) and **chamber of commerce** (☎ 239-332-3624; www.fortmyers.org; 2310 Edwards Dr).

Sights & Activities

Visitors are drawn to the **Edison Estate, Laboratory & Museum** (☎ 239-334-3614; www.edison-ford-estate.com; 2350 McGregor Blvd; adult/child/family $14/7.50/32) to see the great inventor's winter home, a museum housing hundreds of his inventions and possessions, and the gardens. Tours of the estate include a visit to **Henry Ford's winter home**, next door.

The **Fort Myers Historical Museum** (☎ 239-332-5955; 2300 Peck St; adult/child $6/3; closed Sun & Mon) has exhibits on southwest Florida and the city's history, including some Calusa and Seminole artifacts.

Two state parks are worth a visit. **Koreshan State Historic Site** (☎ 239-992-0311; Corkscrew Rd at US 41; pedestrian or cyclist $1, car $3.50; 8am-dusk) is the intact former community of a 19th-century religious sect that boasts furnished historical structures and canoe rentals ($4/20 per hour/day). Between Fort Myers Beach and Bonita Beach, **Lover's Key State Recreation Area** (☎ 239-597-6196; pedestrian or cyclist $1, car $4; 8am-dusk) is a four-island park with good beaches and bird watching.

Babcock Wilderness Adventure (☎ 239-489-3911, 800-500-5583; adult/child $18/10) offers airboat rides and swamp-buggy excursions through a variety of ecosystems north of Fort Myers.

Fort Myers Beach is on Estero Island, about 40 minutes southwest of downtown. It manages to be both a party town (at Times Square) and a quiet beach resort (at the south end). Many people make this their base for exploring the area. Look for blue, white and yellow flags marking beach access between houses. There are loads of hotels and condos and a few energetic bars. To get around, try **Fun Rentals** (☎ 239-463-8844; 1901 Estero Blvd) for bikes ($10 per day), scooters ($40 per day) and skates ($10 per day).

Sleeping & Eating

Fort Myers Beach has scores of small motels, each with their unique charms.

Lighthouse Island Resort (☎ 239-463-9392; www.lighthouseislandresort.com; 1051 5th St; d $95;) A lovely family-owned resort in Fort Myers Beach, with lots of amenities, including an on-site bar and restaurant, and laundry facilities.

Silver Sands Villas (☎ 239-463-6554; www.silversandsvillas.com; 1207 Estero Blvd; efficiencies $107) Canal-front villas in Fort Myers Beach, just '58 steps from the sand.'

Ta Ki-Ki Riverfront Inn (☎ 239-334-2135; www.takikimotel.com; 2631 1st St; d $70; P ✻ ♿) In downtown Fort Myers, Ta Ki-Ki is a 1950s throwback with good, clean rooms.

Red Coconut RV Resort & Campground (☎ 239-463-7200; www.redcoconut.com; 3001 Estero Blvd; campsites $48) You can pitch a tent under the stars at this beachfront resort in Fort Myers Beach.

Mel's Diner (☎ 239-267-2468; 19050 S Tamiamia Trail; mains $4-10) Join locals in their three-square-meals-a-day pilgrimage to Mel's Diner. A throwback to Happy Days of meat, mashed potatoes, fruit pies and smiling waitresses.

Veranda (☎ 239-332-2065; 2122 2nd St; mains $15-33) In downtown Fort Myers, this Southern haute cuisine in a 19th-century house is an extravagance well worth your indulgence.

State Farmers Market (☎ 239-332-6910; 2744 Edison Ave; mains $5-12) Serves Southern favorites like fried chicken, grits and barbecue.

Split Rail (☎ 239-466-3400; 17493 San Carlos Blvd; dishes $4-10) Situated just landside of Fort Myers Beach, this place has a weird but tasty mix of food, from Mexican and Greek to American.

Snug Harbor (☎ 239-463-4343645; San Carlos Blvd; mains $7-22) A popular seafood spot with picturesque views of Fort Myers Beach.

Getting There & Around

Southwest Florida International Airport (☎ 239-768-1000) has regional, national and international services and car rentals. **Greyhound** (☎ 239-334-1011; 2250 Peck St) goes to Miami ($25, four hours), Tampa ($25, four hours) and Orlando ($31, four hours). **Lee Trans'** (☎ 239-275-8726) Orange bus No 50 leaves downtown at Daniels Rd and Hwy 41 for Fort Myers Beach ($1) every hour on the hour. The Beach Connection runs from pickup points on the mainland in Fort Myers to Bonita Beach all day for just 25¢.

AROUND FORT MYERS

Across a 2-mile causeway (toll $3) from Fort Myers lie charming Sanibel and Captiva Islands. They offer restaurants, hotels and shops along a maze of tree-lined streets that lead to beaches where shell collecting is nonpareil. The lagoons and mangroves teem with wildlife and are ideal for kayaking and canoeing. A little further south, back on the mainland, is one of the most idyllic spots in Florida, Audubon's Corkscrew Swamp Sanctuary.

Sanibel & Captiva Islands

Despite residential and commercial development, Sanibel and Captiva retain much natural appeal. They're ideally suited for biking and hiking, with trails all over the islands and a wide bike path running most of the length of the islands. The **chamber of commerce** (☎ 239-472-1080; www.sanibel-captiva.org; 1159 Causeway Rd) has mountains of tourist info.

The 6300-acre **JN 'Ding' Darling National Wildlife Refuge** (☎ 239-472-1100; 1 Wildlife Dr; pedestrian & cyclist $1, car $5; 🕑 7:30am-7:30pm cars, sunrise-dusk pedestrians & cyclists, wildlife drive closed Fri) has a marvelous 5-mile wildlife drive that's as popular with drivers as it is with hikers and bikers. When it's closed, other trails are open. **Tarpon Bay Recreation** (☎ 239-472-8900), the refuge's concessionaire in Tarpon Bay Marina, supplies canoes, kayaks and bikes and gives darn good guided paddle tours ($25) at 10:30am daily through the refuge waters. You can also rent kayaks at **Wildside Adventures/Captiva Kayak Co** (☎ 239-395-2925; McCarthy's Marina; 15041 Captiva Dr; hour/half-day $15/35).

You can identify beach shells you pick up by visiting the fascinating **Bailey-Matthews Shell Museum** (☎ 239-395-2233; www.shellmuseum.org; 3075 Sanibel-Captiva Rd; adult/child $5/3; 🕑 10am-4pm Tue-Sun).

When it comes to lodgings, there's nothing cheap on these upscale barrier islands, with Christmas and February to April the peak times. Visit outside that period for big savings. The rooms are bright with cool tile floors at the adult-only **Seahorse Cottages** (☎ 239-472-4262; www.seahorsecottages.com; 1223 Buttonwood Lane; d $95; P ✻ ♿), in a quiet residential area near the lighthouse. It's just a short walk to the beach from **Buttonwood Cottages** (☎ 239-395-9061; www.buttonwoodcottages.com; d $125; P ✻). For a real splurge visit **Casa Ybel Resort** (☎ 239-472-3145; www.casaybelresort.com; 2255 W Gulf Dr; quad $400; P ✻ ♿), a luxury condo/rental community with a gorgeous beach and manicured grounds.

With its old-fashioned bubbling Christmas lights and antiques, the fun, fun, fun **Bubble Room** (☎ 239-472-5558; 15001 Captiva Dr; mains $15-25) has become something of an attraction as well as a place that serves excellent steaks and seafood along with incredible desserts.

Other spots to stop and fill up include the following:

Bean (☎ 239-395-1919; 2240 Periwinkle Way; dishes $5-7) Light meals such as panini sandwiches, salads, coffees and desserts.

Lazy Flamingo (dishes $6-13) Sanibel (☎ 239-472-6939; 1036 Periwinkle Way) Captiva (☎ 239-472-5353; 6520 Pine Ave) Great grouper sandwiches and smoked fish.

McT's Shrimp House & Tavern (☎ 239-472-3161; 1523 Periwinkle Way; mains $15-23) All kinds of scrumptious crustaceans.

Corkscrew Swamp Sanctuary

This 11,000-acre National Audubon Society **preserve** (☎ 239-348-9151; 375 Sanctuary Rd; adult/child $8/3.50; 7am-5:30pm Oct–mid Apr, 7am-7:30pm mid-Apr–Sept), off Hwy 846 east of Naples, is the crown jewel of the environmental group's national holdings. The 2-mile **boardwalk** passes under a canopy of the world's largest subtropical old-growth bald-cypress forest and offers a chance to see all kinds of wildlife, from alligators, otters and turtles to more than 200 species of birds, including the wood storks that nest here. Knowledgeable trail volunteers answer questions and point out wildlife your untrained eyes miss. The **Blair Audubon Center** features exhibits, theater and interactive productions.

SARASOTA

The largest city between Fort Myers and Tampa–St Petersburg, Sarasota is an affluent community that is big on the arts. The **visitors bureau** (☎ 941-957-1877, 800-522-9799; 655 N Tamiami Trail) has reams of good local information.

The former winter retreat of railroad, real-estate and circus baron John Ringling, the **Ringling Museum Complex** (☎ 941-359-5700; www.ringling.org; 5401 Bayshore Rd; adult/child under 12 $15/free) encompasses museums, tropical gardens, a café and a 30-room mansion. The Ringlings were avid art collectors, and the John and Mable Ringling Museum of Art has a first-rate collection. Ca d'Zan was the Ringling's lavish winter home, a combination of architectural styles. The fascinating **Museum of the Circus** has circus wagons, costumes, paraphernalia and memorabilia.

Towles Court Art Colony (☎ 941-362-0960; www.towlescourt.com; 1945 Morrill St; admission free) is an art colony where dozens of creative folks have galleries and studios. Equally refreshing is the **Marie Selby Botanical Gardens** (☎ 941-366-5731; www.selby.org; 811 S Palm Ave; adult $12, child 6-11 $6; 10am-5pm), a green respite in an urban landscape.

The **Pelican Man's Bird Sanctuary** (☎ 941-388-4444; www.pelicanman.org; 1708 Ken Thompson Parkway, City Island; adult $6, child 4-17 $2) rehabilitates injured wildlife. View sea life next door at the **Mote Marine Laboratory** (☎ 941-388-4441; 1600 Ken Thompson Parkway; adult $12, child 4-12 $8), a research center and marine rehabilitation facility with a 135,000-gallon shark tank.

Beaches abound on the barrier islands. Local favorites are South Lido Beach, at the end of Ben Franklin Dr on Lido Key; Turtle and Siesta Key Beaches, on Siesta Key; and Coquina Beach, on Longboat Key.

Greyhound (☎ 941-955-5735; 575 N Washington Blvd) runs to Miami ($38, six hours), Tampa ($11, two hours) and Fort Myers ($13, two hours). **Sarasota County Area Transit** (☎ 941-316-1234) operates buses (75¢) through most of the area.

Sleeping & Eating

Sarasota has some of the priciest hotels around.

Sunsets on the Key (☎ 941-312-9797; www.sunsetsonthekey.com; 459 Beach Rd; d $129; P) This hotel on Siesta Key has only eight rooms but they are all tip-top.

Harrington House (☎ 941-778-5444; www.harringtonhouse.com; 5626 Gulf Dr; d $189; P) An enormous, first-rate B&B on Anna Maria Island with large rooms, many with balconies

Resort at Longboat Key Club (☎ 941-383-8821; www.longboatkeyclub.com; d $315; P) For luxe digs head for this resort, which has a big marina, plus tennis and golf.

Gulf Beach Campground (☎ 941-349-3839; 8862 Midnight Pass Rd; campsites $37) If you like the beach and don't mind tight spaces, try this campground on Siesta Key.

Between the airport and downtown Sarasota on N Tamiami Trail is a slew of small, economical motels. Weekly rates are considerably better value. Some recommendations:

Sunset Terrace Resort (☎ 941-355-8489; 4644 N Tamiami Trail; d $75; P)

Cadillac Motel (☎ 941-355-7108; 4021 N Tamiami Trail; d $55; P)

Sundial Motor Inn (☎ 941-351-4919; 4801 N Tamiami Trail; d $65; P) Friendly and family-run.

Morton's Gourmet Market (☎ 941-955-9866; 1924 S Osprey Ave; dishes $3-12) Located in downtown Sarasota, Morton's can fix you up for a picnic with great sandwiches and deli items.

Alley Cat Cafe (☎ 941-954-1228; 1558 Fourth St; mains $19-29) Hidden away in a ramshackle garden, this rustic yet romantic offering boasts a sophisticated menu and live music.

Marina Jack's (☎ 941-365-4232; at the Marina at Central Ave; mains $8-32) You can get everything from good burgers to gourmet seafood at this popular waterfront eatery.

Broken Egg (☎ 941-346-2750; 210 Avenida Madera, Siesta Key; dishes $5-8) Head down to this beachside spot, which serves Paul Bunyan–size pancakes at breakfast and killer meat loaf at lunch.

Lobster Pot (☎ 941-349-2323; 5157 Ocean Blvd, Siesta Key; mains $6-30) Home of enormous lobster rolls and all sorts of crustacean fare.

Hemingway's (☎ 941-388-3948; 325 John Ringling Blvd; mains $10-22) Near trendy St Armand's Circle, Hemingway's offers a tasty range of salads and grilled items, plus a good seat for people watching.

Entertainment

The **Sarasota County Arts Council** (☎ 941-365-5118; www.sarasota-arts.org; 506 Burns Ct) has schedules for theater and ballet performances, jazz clubs, orchestras and film groups. The Sarasota Film Society's **Burns Court Cinema** (☎ 941-955-3456; 506 Burns Ct) shows foreign and independent films.

Patrick's (1400 Main St), a popular sports bar, attracts large crowds for drinks, games and breaking bread. **Gator Club** (1490 Main St) has live rock, blues or alternative music nightly.

ST PETERSBURG

Perched on a peninsula along the west side of Tampa Bay, St Petersburg has all the beaches that its sister city of Tampa lacks, along with the best cultural venues. The **visitors bureau** (☎ 727-464-7200, 877-352-3224; www.floridasbeach.com; No 108, 14450 46th St N, Clearwater) has satellite offices at 2001 Ulmberton Rd, I-275 exit 18, and on the **St Petersburg Pier** (☎ 727-821-4715; 800 2nd Ave N).

The **Salvador Dalí Museum** (☎ 727-823-3767; www.salvadordalimuseum.org; 1000 3rd St S; adult $12.50, child 5-9 $3, after 5pm Thu $5; 🕑 9:30am-5:30pm Mon-Sat, until 8pm Thu, noon-5:30pm Sun) houses the largest collection of works by the artist outside Spain. **St Petersburg Museum of Fine Arts** (☎ 727-896-2667; 255 Beach Dr NE; adult/child $6/2; 🕑 10am-5pm Tue-Sat, 1-5pm Sun) includes Asian, Indian and African art, and pre-Columbian sculpture. The **Florida International Museum** (☎ 727-822-3693, 800-777-9882; 100 2nd St N; adult/child $12/6; 🕑 10am-5pm Mon-Sat) features blockbuster international exhibitions. At the foot of the pier, the **St Petersburg Museum of History** (☎ 727-894-1052; 335 2nd Ave NE; adult/child $5/2; 🕑 10am-5pm Mon-Sat, 1-5pm Sun) covers the city, Pinellas Peninsula and the early days of commercial aviation.

The **Pinellas Trail** (☎ 727-464-4751) is an awesome 34-mile urban biking, skating and walking trail that's oh so popular. It starts north of downtown at 34th St and Fairfield Ave and ends at US 19 in Tarpon Springs. The free *Guidebook to the Pinellas Trail*, with mile-by-mile details, is available at visitors centers. The crown jewel of the county park system, **Fort DeSoto Park** (☎ 727-582-2267; www.fortdesoto.com; 3500 Pinellas Bayway S; admission free; 🕑 dawn-dusk) has a fort, fishing pier, historic trail, concessions, camping and one of Florida's best beaches.

The area's major-league baseball franchise is the Tampa Bay Devil Rays, who play at **Tropicana Field** (☎ 727-825-3333; 1 Stadium Dr; tickets $2-24).

Sleeping & Eating

Bayboro House B&B (☎ 727-823-4955; www.bayborohousebandb.com; 1719 Beach Dr SE; d $150; P) One of numerous cheery B&Bs in the area, Bayboro House is situated on the bay and has lots of Victorian charm.

Mansion House B&B (☎ 727-821-9391; www.mansionbandb.com; d $150; P) Another cheery B&B, featuring rooms overlooking a tranquil garden.

Lamara Motel Apartments (☎ 727-360-7521; www.lamara.com; 520 73rd Ave; d $65; P) Just a short walk to St Pete Beach.

Pasa Tiempo B&B (☎ 727-367-9907; www.pasatiempo.com; 7141 Bay St; r/ste $110/150; P) Also on St Pete Beach, this B&B features a lush courtyard overlooking the Intracoastal Waterway.

Alden Beach Resort (☎ 727-360-7081; www.alden beachresort.com; 5900 Gulf Blvd; d/ste $125/250; P) This lovely family-run resort manages to provide all the amenities of the big chain resorts, and a lot more personal touches.

There are lots of accommodations near downtown St Pete attractions, including the no-frills digs at **Tops Motel & Apartments** (☎ 727-526-9071, 727-209-0252; 7141 4th St N; d/d with kitchenette $40/50; P) and the dated but spotless rooms at **Beach Park Motel** (☎ 727-898-632; 300 Beach Dr NE; d $75; P).

Fort DeSoto Park Campground (☎ 727-582-2267, 866-2484; 3500 Pinellas Bayway S; campsites $30) One of the very best views of the elegant Sunshine Skyway Bridge is from this waterfront campground, but be advised that reservations are typically necessary several weeks in advance.

Lots of low-priced rustic restaurants serve good seafood in St Petersburg.

Ted Peter's Famous Smoked Fish (☎ 727-381-7931; 1350 Pasadena Ave; dishes $10-15; 11:30am-7:30pm, closed Tue) Don't miss this venerable institution, which smokes salmon, mackerel and mullet and serves them with cold beer and German potato salad.

Garden (☎ 727-896-3800; 217 Central Ave; dishes $5-15; 11:30am-2am) The oldest restaurant in town, the Garden has Mediterranean influenced entrees and fine tapas.

Maritana Grill (☎ 727-360-1882; 3400 Gulf Blvd; mains $27-32; dinner) Serves creative American-Caribbean fare on the beach.

Other longtime favorites:

Fourth Street Shrimp Store (☎ 727-822-0325; 1006 4th St N; dishes $7-26; lunch & dinner)

Crabby Bill's (☎ 727-360-8858; 5100 Gulf Blvd; dishes $10-29; lunch & dinner)

Hurricane's Seafood Restaurant (☎ 727-360-9558; 807 Gulf Way; mains $8-20; 8am-1am) Justly famous for its grouper sandwiches and its sunset views.

Getting There & Around

St Petersburg–Clearwater International Airport (☎ 727-535-7600) has car rentals. **Greyhound** (☎ 727-898-1496; 180 9th St N) goes to Miami ($39, eight hours), Tampa ($7, 30 minutes) and Orlando ($18, three hours). Amtrak has a bus link from Tampa's station to St Petersburg, where it stops at the **Pinellas Sq Mall** (7200 Hwy 19 N).

Pinellas Suncoast Transit Authority (☎ 727-530-9911; www.psta.net) operates buses (fare/day pass $1.25/3). **The Looper trolley** links the museums and pier on a 30-minute narrated loop running from 11am to 5pm, starting at the St Petersburg Pier (fare/day pass 50¢/$2.50).

TAMPA

Located on the grittier side of the bay, Tampa is a bustling port city with a couple of notable attractions. Revitalized and renovated Ybor City, the historic heart of the old cigar industry, nurtures its Cuban-Spanish heritage while embracing a lively nighttime scene. Another major draw is Busch Gardens, which combines an excellent zoo with great roller coasters.

Travelers can find assistance at the **visitors bureau** (☎ 813-223-1111, 800-448-2672; www.visittampa bay.com; Suite 2800, 400 N Tampa St) or the **Ybor City Chamber of Commerce** (☎ 813-248-3712; www.ybor.org; Suite 104, 1600 E 8th Ave). **Tampa Bay Business Guild** (☎ 813-237-3751; www.tbbg.org;

MAD ABOUT MANATEES

The little nose barely breaks the surface of the water; you hear a 'pfft' as it sprays water and air. Then you see the creature itself – a huge gray mass with a walruslike body that tapers to a beaverlike tail.

For all their mass, West Indian manatees *(Trichechus manatus)* are shy and elusive – so much so that early explorers thought they were mermaids. Later, as they watched them graze on underwater vegetation, they called them sea cows.

These slow, nearly blind mammals are an endangered species, protected by federal and state laws. They have no natural enemies, but their numbers are threatened by loss of habitat, careless anglers and increasing boat traffic.

Some 3000 manatees are thought to live in Florida waters, and among the best places to see them are Blue Spring State Park and Homosassa Springs State Wildlife Park, and along the Crystal River. They spend November to March in the parks' 72°F springs. If you're in a boat, you can catch them warming themselves in the heated water discharged by power plants, near Sanibel Island and Fort Myers, and in the canals and marinas of the Florida Keys. In warmer periods, they also swim in St John's River.

If you've dreamed of snorkeling with the manatees, choose a tour company that keeps the number of guests low – around six. Also, most have a 'Manatee awareness program,' but go with an outfit that incorporates this educational lecture into the tour itself and doesn't treat it as an optional, extra-cost feature.

1222 S Dale Mabry) provides information for gay and lesbian visitors.

Downtown

The **Tampa Museum of Art** (☎ 813-274-8130; 600 N Ashley St; adult/child $5/3; 10am-5pm Tue, Wed, Fri & Sat, 10am-8pm Thu, 1-5pm Sun) has exhibits from the avant-garde to old masters, sculpture, photography and works by emerging Florida artists. At the **Florida Aquarium** (☎ 813-273-4000; 701 Channelside Dr; adult/child $15/10; 9:30am-5pm), you can experience coral reefs, marshes, bays, wetlands and beaches, not to mention the critters that thrive within them.

Would-be scientists explore the heavens, hurricanes and human body at the excellent **Museum of Science & Industry** (☎ 813-987-6000; 4801 E Fowler Ave; adult/child $14/10; 9am-5pm Mon-Fri, 9am-7pm Sat & Sun) before sitting down to view a feature in the Imax Dome theater.

Ybor City

A national historic district in the northeast of Tampa, Ybor (*ee*-bore) City began in the late 1800s as a community of Cuban and Spanish cigar makers and Italian immigrants. It's now a lively area for day and evening historic tours, entertainment, shopping and dining.

The **Ybor City Museum State Park** (☎ 813-247-6323; 1818 E 9th Ave; admission $2; 9am-5pm), in the former Ferlita Bakery building, chronicles the history of cigar making. Historic **walking tours** ($4 including museum admission) depart at 10:30am Saturday. Dramatic, actor-led one-hour **Ybor City Ghost Walk tours** (☎ 813-242-9255, 813-242-4660; 1600 E 8th Ave; $10; tours depart 7pm Thu, 4pm Fri-Sun) lend a spicy touch to history and architecture. A number of cigar shops line Ybor City's main drag and some of them, including **Gonzalez y Martinez Cigar Company** (☎ 813-248-8210; www.gonzalezymartinez.com; 2103 E 17th Ave) offer free cigar-rolling demonstrations.

Busch Gardens & Adventure Island

Thrills, spills and exotic animals await you at **Busch Gardens** (☎ 813-987-5082; www.buschgardens.com; 3000 E Busch Blvd; adult/child $50/41; 9:30am-7pm with seasonal variations), an African-themed amusement park and world-class zoo that features two of the country's most thrilling roller coasters. Next door is **Adventure Island** (☎ 813-987-5600; www.adventureisland.com; 10001 McKinley Dr; adult $30, child 3-9 $28; 10am-5pm with seasonal variations), a 25-acre water park with rides, slides and pools. Combination tickets for one day at each park are available for $59 per person.

Sleeping

Don Vicente de Ybor Historic Inn (☎ 813-241-4545; www.donvicenteinn.com; 1915 Republica de Cuba; d $129; P) This truly historic inn was built in 1895 by the founder of Ybor City.

Casita de Verdad (☎ 813-654-6087; www.yborguesthouse.com; weekday/weekend $180/250; P) If you're feeling like a little time to yourself, rent out this entire two-room 1908 cigar maker's house with four-poster bed and claw foot bathtub.

Economical choices abound near Busch Gardens, along Fowler Ave/Morris Bridge Rd (Hwy 582) and Busch Blvd (Hwy 580). Chains include **Red Roof Inn** (☎ 813-932-0073; 2307 E Busch Blvd; d $55; P), **Best Economy Inn** (☎ 813-933-7831; 11414 N Central Ave; r $40; P) and the excellent **Best Western All Suites** (☎ 813-971-8930; www.thatparrotplace.com; 3001 University Center Dr; d $119; P) with plenty of extra perks in the rooms like VCR, microwave and boom boxes.

Hillsborough River State Park (☎ 813-987-6771; 15402 N Hwy 301; campsites $13) North of the city, camping doesn't get any better than at this 3400-acre park, where shady sites are grouped in separate loops to create a feeling of privacy.

Eating

Bern's Steak House (☎ 813-251-2421; www.bernssteakhouse.com; 1208 S Howard Ave; mains $18-35; 5-11pm) Wine connoisseurs and steak lovers come from around the country to this Tampa landmark. Reservations are recommended.

SideBern's (☎ 813-258-2233; 2208 W Morrison Ave; from 6pm Mon-Sat) Bern's Steak House slightly cheaper sister, SideBern's features world cuisine and indoor/outdoor seating.

Hyde Park Historic District has two excellent, surprisingly inexpensive choices: **Cactus Club** (☎ 813-251-4089; www.cactusclub.com; 1601 Snow Ave; dishes from $7 11am-10:30pm Mon-Thu, 11am-11:30pm Fri & Sat, 11am-10pm Sun), for fine Southwestern fare; and **Mise En Place Bistro** (☎ 813-839-3939; 2616 MacDill Ave; dishes from $7; closed Sun), one of Tampa's best restaurants, serving Floribbean cuisine.

Worth a try in Ybor City:

La Tropicana (☎ 813-247-4040; 1822 E 7th Ave) Grab a traditional Cuban breakfast of toast and gear-revving coffee.

La Segunda Central Bakery (☎ 813-248-1531; 2512 N 15th St) Also serves great Cuban breakfasts and coffee guaranteed to wake you up.
Carmine's (☎ 813-248-3834; 1802 E 7th Ave) For tasty Cuban sandwiches.
Little Sicily (☎ 813-248-2940; 1724 E 8th Ave) Serves up yummy calzones.
Café Creole & Oyster Bar (☎ 813-247-6283; 1330 E 9th Ave) Moderately priced gumbos, crawfish and andouille.
Sushi on 7th (☎ 813-247-8744; 1919 E 7th Ave) The place to go for sushi and sashimi.

Entertainment

Find out what's happening from the *Weekly Planet*, *Tampa Tribune*'s 'Friday Extra,' the *Times*'s 'Friday Weekend,' or the **arts hotline** (☎ 813-229-2787). Gay and lesbian publications include the monthly *Gazette*.

The **Tampa Bay Performing Arts Center** (☎ 813-229-7827; www.tbpac.org; 1010 N MacInnes Place) has four stages for concerts and theatrical productions. The artsy crowd flocks to the renovated 1926 **Tampa Theatre** (☎ 813-274-8286; www.tampatheatre.org; 711 N Franklin St) to sit in red fabric chairs and watch independent and classic films and special events ($6.25).

When it comes to nightlife, head for Ybor City's 7th Ave and pick your pleasure.

Spectator Sports

The NFL Tampa Bay Buccaneers play football at **Raymond James Stadium** (☎ 813-870-2700; 4201 Dale Mabry Hwy; tickets $22-75) August to December, but most seats are grabbed by season ticket holders and you'll pay dearly for tickets on the street. The NHL Tampa Bay Lightning play hockey October to April at the **Ice Palace** (☎ 813-301-6600; 401 Channelside Dr; tickets $15-60).

Getting There & Around

There's commuter, national and international service into **Tampa International Airport** (☎ 813-870-8700). Major car rental agencies have counters inside. **Greyhound** (☎ 813-229-2174; 610 E Polk St) has buses to Miami ($39, eight hours), Orlando ($18, two hours) and St Petersburg ($7, 30 minutes). You can catch a train south to Miami or north through Jacksonville at the **Amtrak station** (☎ 813-221-7600; 601 Nebraska Ave N). Amtrak also runs shuttle buses to and from Orlando. The **HARTline** (☎ 813-254-4278; fare/day pass $1.25/3) stops at all the major sites and has bike racks. Electric streetcars run between downtown Tampa and Ybor City ($1).

CENTRAL FLORIDA

As the story goes, in 1964 Walt Disney flew over central Florida seeking a site for his new theme park. He looked out the window, saw vast parcels of undeveloped land near the confluence of two major highways – I-4 and US 27 – and said, 'This is it.' Within 10 years, what had been thousands of acres of scrub forest, swamp and citrus groves became the theme-park capital of the world. Beyond all the glitter are charming small towns, chains of lakes, cypress-shrouded rivers and cool, clear swimming springs.

Orientation

I-4 is the main north–south connector, though it's labeled east–west: to go north, take I-4 east (toward Daytona); to go south, hop on I-4 west (toward Tampa).

The main east–west roads are Hwy 50 and Hwy 528 (the Bee Line Expressway, a toll road), which connect Orlando to the Space Coast. Orlando International Airport is accessible from the Bee Line Expressway.

ORLANDO

Contrary to widespread rumor, there was an Orlando before Disney came along. The city, which was named after a US soldier – Orlando Reeves – who was killed near here during the Seminole Wars of the 1830s, has been, successively, a railroad, real-estate, citrus and space-technology boomtown. While the 1971 opening of Walt Disney World, 20 miles southwest, placed the city firmly on the tourist map as a theme-park paradise, it is also home to first-rate museums, beautiful parks and neighborhoods, and a thriving nighttime scene. The **visitors bureau** (☎ 407-363-5872, 800-551-0181; www.orlandoinfo.com; 8723 International Dr; 🕒 8am-7pm) publishes multilingual guides and maps. Gay visitors should also check the **Gay, Lesbian and Bisexual Community Center** (☎ 407-228-8272; www.glbcc.org; 946 N Mills Ave; 🕒 noon-9pm Mon-Thu, noon-5pm Sat). Beware of unofficial tourist information centers, which offer discount tickets to theme parks in exchange for a hard-sell visit to various real-estate properties.

Discovery Cove & SeaWorld

If you yearn for an up-close-and-personal marine experience then head to **Discovery**

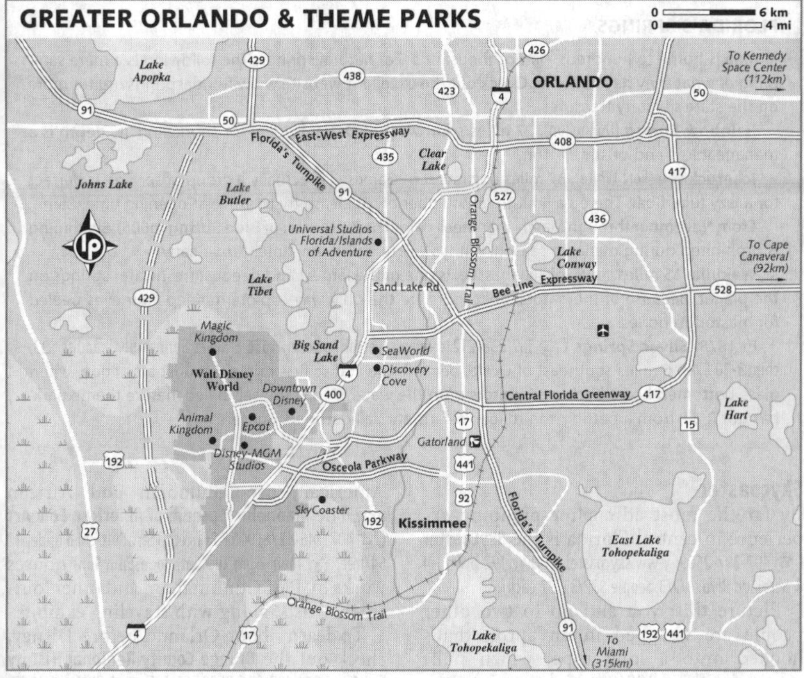

Cove (☎ 877-434-7268; www.discoverycove.com; 6000 Discovery Cove Way; without/with dolphin encounter $129/229; P $7), a faux tropical island where you can snorkel on a saltwater coral reef face-to-face with denizens of the deep – separated by a Plexiglas window, of course. Admission is limited to 800 to 1000 guests a day, so it's not crowded. Plus, the admission price includes lunch, swim gear and a seven-day pass to SeaWorld.

SeaWorld (☎ 407-351-3600; www.seaworld.com; 7007 SeaWorld Dr; adult $52, child 3-9 $43; P $7) has entertaining and educational marine-theme exhibits, including Kraken, the tallest and fastest roller coaster in Orlando; Journey to Atlantis, a thrilling water-coaster ride; killer-whale and sea-lion shows; and polar bears. There are also interaction programs such as swims with dolphins and touch tanks.

Universal Studios & Islands of Adventure

A combination working movie lot and theme park, **Universal Studios** (☎ 407-363-8000; www.universalstudios.com; 1000 Universal Studios Plaza, I-4 at Kirkman Rd; adult $52, child 3-9 $43; P $8) has many rides based on popular films, like Men in Black Alien Attack, Terminator 2 3-D, Back to the Future and others. Its sister park, **Islands of Adventure** (same prices) features roller coasters, thrill rides and shows that include the Amazing Adventures of Spider-Man, Incredible Hulk Coaster, and Jurassic Park River Adventure. Both parks offer a third-day free ticket with two-day/two-park tickets (adult/child $97/86), which are good over a seven-day period.

Gatorland

You're in Florida, so you've got to see gators. And **Gatorland** (☎ 407-855-5496, 800-393-5297; www.gatorland.com; 14501 S Orange Blossom Trail; adult $20, child 3-12 $10; 9am-dusk) is a fine place to do it. A warning though: this place probably isn't approved by PETA (People for the Ethical Treatment of Animals) and the **Wrestlin' Gator Show** may have more empathic folks squirming. If you can handle it, however, try to catch Babs Steorts, Gatorland's first female wrestler, take on one of the toothy critters.

FLORIDA'S SPRINGS

Florida is home to hundreds – if not thousands – of natural springs. The following is a mere sampling of what they have to offer. Check out the excellent website www.floridasprings.org for more on the state's watery treasures.

Rainbow Spring (Dunnellon), 27 miles southwest of Ocala, is ideal for snorkeling. Its depth is a manageable – and pristine – 16ft.

Ichetucknee (Fort White), 37 miles northwest of Gainesville, actually a group of springs, is perfect for a lazy tube float. There's a limit to the number of tubers, so try to arrive at opening time (8am).

From November through March, manatees enjoy the 72°F water of **Blue Spring** (p605). Swimming is prohibited during manatee season, but it's worth a visit any time. Arrive early.

Wakulla, 15 miles south of Tallahassee, is one of the largest and deepest freshwater springs on the planet. Because of the gators, boat tours are the only way explore it. Keep your eyes peeled for mastodon bones.

In 1878, **Silver Springs** (☎ 352-236-2121; www.silversprings.com; 5656 E Silver Springs Blvd; adults $33, child 3-10 $24), 6 miles southeast of Ocala, became the state's first original tourist attraction, when glass-bottomed boats beckoned visitors onto the water. Today the self-billed 'nature theme park' has got it all; from a petting zoo to jeep safaris and 'alligator encounters.'

Skycoaster

By far the most adrenaline-pumping experience in central Florida is the **SkyCoaster** (☎ 407-397-2509; www.skycoaster.cc; Hwy 192 btwn I-4 & Seralago Blvd; 1/2/3 people $37/32/27 each).

Picture this: you and up to two other people are wrapped in an apron that's hooked onto a long rope, which pulls you more than 300ft straight up into the air. You dangle helplessly for a few moments, and then a voice counts down, and someone yanks the release. Then you shoot down, straight toward the pond below, head first, at speeds of up to 85mph. At the last second before impact, you're suddenly soaring above the water, and now you can enjoy a minute of swinging to and fro over the water while you catch your breath. It's over fast, but worth every penny.

Other Attractions

Leave the thrills and make-believe behind and head to downtown Orlando to find cultural sustenance at Loch Haven Park, home to three museums. The **Orlando Science Center & John Young Planetarium** (☎ 407-514-2000; 777 E Princeton St; adult $15, child 3-9 $10; 🕑 9am-5pm Tue-Thu, 9am-9pm Fri & Sat, noon-5pm Sun) is the largest science center in the southeast, with exhibits like 'Wired Science' and 'Dino Digs,' large-format films, and planetarium and laser-light shows. The **Orlando Museum of Art** (☎ 407-896-4231; 2416 N Mills Ave; adult $6, child 4-11 $3; 🕑 10am-4pm Tue-Fri, noon-4pm Sat & Sun) presents blockbuster touring exhibits and American, pre-Columbian and African art. The **Mennello Museum of American Folk Art** (☎ 407-246-4278; 900 E Princeton St; adult/child under 12 $4/free; 🕑 11am-5pm Tue-Sat, noon-5pm Sun) houses works by Earl Cunningham and other 'outsider' artists, along with traveling exhibits.

To learn about Orlando before Disney, check out the **Orange County Regional History Center** (☎ 407-836-8500; 65 E Central Blvd; adult $7, child 3-12 $3.50; 🕑 10am-5pm Mon-Sat, noon-5pm Sun) with exhibits and interactive displays in a renovated 1927 courthouse.

Sleeping

There are hundreds of accommodations options, with the bulk of them located along International Dr, US 192 in Kissimmee and off I-4. The **Central Reservation Service** (☎ 800-548-3311) works with the visitors bureau to assist in making hotel reservations. The service is free.

Peabody Hotel (☎ 407-352-4000; www.peabodyorlando.com; 9801 International Dr; d/ste $350/850; P ✕ 💻 ♿) If you feel like a splurge, check yourself in here. The rooms are luscious and there's a daily 'duck parade,' featuring the hotel's mallard mascots.

Prices for the mostly chain establishments near International Dr tend to be a bit steeper.

Howard Johnson (☎ 407-351-2000; www.howardjohnsonhotelorlando.com; 7050 S Kirkman Rd; r $49-79; P ✕ ♿) Has a miniature golf course.

Quality Inn Plaza Orlando (☎ 407-996-8585, 800-999-8585; 9000 International Dr; r $89; P ✕ ♿)

Sheraton Studio City Hotel (☎ 407-351-2100, 800-327-1366; www.sheratonstudiocity.com; 5905 International Dr; r $89-165; P) Fairly swank rooms and lots of amenities.

Kissimmee boasts dozens of reasonably priced chains and simple, clean budget motels just outside the Disney domain. Each of the following has free shuttle buses to the theme parks:

Gator Motel (☎ 407-396-0127; www.gatormotel.com; 4576 W Hwy 192; d $39; P)

Magic Castle Inn & Suites (☎ 407-396-1212; www.magicorlando.com; 4559 W Hwy 192; s $23-33, d $29-39, ste $35-45; P)

Casa Rosa Motel (☎ 407-396-2020; 4600 W Hwy 192; d without/with fridge & microwave $25/30)

Sevilla Inn (☎ 800-367-1363; www.sevillainn.com; 4640 W Hwy 192; d $32-60; P)

Campers should try for shaded sites under the tall pines at **KOA Orlando** (☎ 407-277-5075; 12345 Narcoossee Rd; campsites $25-30, RV sites $35-47, cabins $45-51).

Eating

Emeril's Orlando (☎ 407-224-2424; Universal Studios CityWalk; dishes $18-32) Prices tend to be higher at theme parks than at restaurants outside, and the best blow-it-out option is Emeril Lagasse's noisy and popular restaurant, where the New Orleans–inspired creations are wonderfully inventive.

Cafe Tu Tu Tango (☎ 407-248-2222; 8625 International Dr; dishes $5-9) A fun, multiethnic café, featuring lots of creative tapas.

Pebbles (dishes $9-20; W Hwy 434 ☎ 407-774-7111; 2110 W Hwy 434; Hwy 534 ☎ 407-827-1111; 2551 Hwy 534; Aloma Ave ☎ 407-678-7001; 2516 Aloma Ave) This upscale local chain specializes in everything from fancy salads and gourmet burgers to good fish and pasta.

Le Coq au Vin (☎ 407-851-6980; 4800 S Orange Ave; mains $15-27; closed Mon) For haute cuisine at bistro prices, you can't do better than Le Coq au Vin, where the namesake chicken dish is always a treat.

Downtown Orlando boasts a number of good, reasonably priced Vietnamese restaurants like **Little Saigon** (☎ 407-423-8539; 1106 E Colonial Dr; dishes $7-8.50) and **Pho 88** (☎ 407-897-3488; 730 N Mill Av; dishes $4-8) both of which offer great spring rolls and soups of every description.

Entertainment

Universal Studio's **CityWalk** features movies, clubs and restaurants galore including **Margaritaville** (☎ 407-224-2155; cover after 10pm $5; 11am-2am) with steel band and reggae, and **Hard Rock Live** (☎ 407-351-5483; tickets $20-30), a 2800-seat auditorium that features big-name musical acts. Downtown Orlando showcases its thriving music scene along with touring acts at bars and clubs like **Bar BQ Bar** (☎ 407-648-5441; 64 N Orange Ave; no cover), **Back Booth** (☎ 407-999-2570; 37 W Pin St; cover $3-10) and the delightfully grungy **Will's Pub** (☎ 407-898-5070; 1850 N Mills Ave; cover $3-10). **Parliament House** (☎ 407-425-7571; 410 N Orange Blossom Trail; cover varies), with six clubs and bars, is the biggest, baddest gay hangout in town. The daily **Orlando Sentinel** is the best source for entertainment options.

Getting There & Around

Orlando International Airport (☎ 407-825-2001) has easy connections to the major tourist areas via the Lynx Bus System. Taxis to International Dr and the theme-park corridor cost about $25 to $30, shuttle vans $15 to $20.

Greyhound (☎ 407-292-3440; 555 N John Young Parkway) serves Miami ($37, six hours), Jacksonville ($25, three hours), Tampa ($18, two hours) and other cities. **Amtrak** (☎ 407-843-7611; 1400 Sligh Blvd) offers daily trains south to Miami and north to New York City.

City buses are operated by the **Lynx Bus System** (☎ 407-841-8240; fare/week pass $1.25/10).

WALT DISNEY WORLD

The mother of all theme parks, Walt Disney World (WDW) covers nearly 43 sq miles. It's a conglomeration of four parks, the Magic Kingdom, Disney-MGM Studios, Animal Kingdom and Epcot, plus several water parks, a sports complex and a shopping, dining and evening entertainment park, Downtown Disney. It's an amazing place with something for everyone.

WDW is least crowded in January, February (except Presidents' Day weekend), September (after Labor Day), October and early December. Curiously, weekends are less busy than early in the week. For inexpensive accommodations, the best time is August to December; prices climb during the holidays. June, July and August are very hot and humid, with frequent downpours. Weather-wise, late fall tends to be best. The immensely popular annual **Gay Day** (www.gayday.com) at Disney World kicks off the first weekend in June.

From Orlando's Lynx Bus Center, bus No 50 leaves hourly for WDW. Many hotels provide scheduled shuttles to the parks.

Orientation & Information

WDW is 20 miles southwest of downtown Orlando, 4 miles northwest of Kissimmee. For reservations at Disney resorts and WDW information, call ☎ 407-934-7639.

Ticket lines can be long, so buy your tickets in advance from a Disney store, online at www.waltdisneyworld.com, through American Automobile Association (multi-day only) or by mail from **WDW Guest Communications** (PO Box 10040, Lake Buena Vista, FL 32830). There are numerous ticket options, ranging from the **One-Day One-Park ticket** (adult $50, child 3-9 $40) to the **Four-Day Park-Hopper** (adult $192, child 3-9 $152) for unlimited admission to the four parks; discounts are offered if you buy in advance. Parking costs $7.

Crowds are horrific in summer, but entertainment for those in the lines makes waiting less painful. Pick up a free FastPass to get confirmed times on certain rides. Bring drinking water (refills free at Disney restaurants) and sunscreen. Food from outside is not permitted.

Sights & Activities

The centerpiece of WDW is the **Magic Kingdom**, home of Cinderella's Castle, Splash Mountain (a thrilling 50ft drop) and the wild Big Thunder Mountain Railroad ride. The kid in everyone will also like: Extra-TERRORestrial Alien Encounter, where mad scientists experiment on cute, cuddly aliens; Buzz Lightyear's Space Ranger Spin, which spins you into outer space and lets you defend the galaxy; and the Many Adventures of Winnie the Pooh, a kids' ride through the characters' storybook pages. The fireworks show goes off daily at 10pm.

The rides and attractions at the **Disney-MGM Studios** theme park are absolutely first-rate. You can go for a wild ride on the Rock 'n' Roller Coaster (starring Aerosmith), chill at Jim Henson's Muppet Vision 3D, or watch Mickey Mouse square off against an assortment of Disney villains at *Fantasmic!* (which is much better than it sounds).

Epcot Center is broken into two main sections. Future World offers corporate-sponsored journeys through the history of technology, with bold predictions about the future. The park's longest, fastest ride, the Test Track, mimics an automotive testing ground. The excellent Living Seas offers one of the largest aquariums in the world. The new Mission Space is Disney's most technically advanced ride and offers a thrilling simulation of a rocket trip to Mars.

At Disney's 500-acre **Animal Kingdom**, visitors go on safaris, riverboat rides and trails to see wild animals up close in re-created 'natural' environments. There are shows like **Tarzan Rocks!** with stunts, and live music and rides like Kali River Rapids.

Disney also has several water parks, including **Blizzard Beach** (adult $33, child 3-9 $26.50), where you can free-fall down a 100ft slide, and **Typhoon Lagoon** (adult $33, child 3-9 $26.50), with a huge wave pool and a fish observatory.

Sleeping

There are over 25 places to stay on Disney property, with more in the works. Disney-owned lodging is designed with families in mind, so rooms usually accommodate four or more. Guests at Disney-owned properties can enter the parks 1½ hours early and whiz through all the best rides and shows before the crowds arrive. A central reservation line handles bookings and information for all Disney hotels (☎ 407-934-7639).

Wilderness Lodge (r $370-753; P ⛝ ⛝) A top-of-the-line resort with easy access to the Magic Kingdom.

Animal Kingdom Lodge (r $337-615; P ⛝ ⛝ ⛝) The best rooms in this lush lodge offer views of zebras, giraffes and other critters from the animal kingdom.

Grand Floridian Resort & Spa (r $579-899; P ⛝ ⛝ ⛝) Relive the luxury of times past at the Grand Floridian Resort & Spa, which hearkens to the era of Henry Flagler's lush resorts.

Fort Wilderness Resort & Campground (☎ 407-824-2900; campsites $35-82, cabins $387-504) At the other end of the price scale, try camping at this Disney-owned site in a shady preserve. Programs here include hayrides and sing-alongs around the campfire.

The four themed resorts – **All-Star Sports Resort**, **All-Star Music Resort**, **All-Star Movies Resort** and **Pop Century Resort** (r $129-187; P ⛝ ⛝ ⛝) – have thousands of small and somewhat garish rooms between them.

RICHARD CUMMINS

Oak Alley Plantation (p530), Louisiana

Art deco lifeguard's hut, **South Beach** (p579), Miami

NEIL SETCHFIELD

THOMAS DOWNS

Mardi Gras reveler (p522), New Orleans

Diving above *Christ of the Deep* statue, **Key Largo** (p594), Florida

WILLIAM HARRIGAN

RICHARD CUMMINS

Windmill at the **American Wind Power Center** (p672), Lubbock, Texas

JOHN NE

Jamming at **Joe's Generic Bar** (p646), Austin, Texas

JOHN ELK III

Signage, Route 66, **Clinton** (p698)

Burning fields on the **Great Plains** (p675)

JIM

Port Orleans (r $227-329; P) has the charm of New Orleans' French Quarter; the **Caribbean Beach Resort** (r $227-329; P) takes you away to the islands; and **Coronado Springs Resort** (r $227-329; P) features rooms with a Mexican-Southwestern flair.

Eating & Drinking

To dine at a restaurant inside WDW, you'll need a ticket for whichever park the restaurant's in. There's a central reservation and information number for all the restaurants, ☎ 407-939-3463. Character restaurants, where you dine with Mickey Mouse or his colleagues, require reservations up to 60 days in advance (especially for breakfast). These restaurants offer buffet meals at fixed prices.

California Grill (Contemporary Resort; dishes $18-35; dinner only) Disney's most acclaimed restaurant, where the menu changes nightly (but the grilled pork tenderloin is always a good bet).

Crystal Palace (buffet for adult $16-20, child $9-11) Located in the Magic Kingdom, this place has a pretty good buffet with salad, pasta and dessert bars. The meals are enlivened by Disney characters.

Tony's Town Square (mains $10-24) Also in the Magic Kingdom, Tony's serves generous portions of Italian fare with a Lady and the Tramp motif.

The international food at the Epcot Center is somewhat pricey, but you usually get your money's worth.

Coral Reef (mains $17-24) Derives its name from the dining room's giant aquarium, as well as the bounty found on it.

Bistro de Paris Extend your holiday with a quick trip to France – Bistro de Paris serves excellent French dinners at Parisian prices.

Yakitori House Next stop is Japan. Prices here are more reasonable than at Bistro de Paris.

Marrakesh Restaurant (lunch/dinner from $11/19) Fill up on some tasty couscous in this re-created palace, which serves excellent Moroccan food.

Prime Time Cafe (mains $11-17) Go retro at Disney-MGM's Prime Time Cafe, which serves diner grub like meat loaf with mashed potatoes.

Commissary (mains $6-12) Just the place to grab a quick lunch from an international menu.

Hollywood Brown Derby (dishes $13-25) Pretend you're at the LA original, while enjoying the killer Cobb salad.

Jiko, the Cooking Place (mains $16-28) Jiko, in the Animal Kingdom, is one of those rare pleasures – an African restaurant. Specialties include flavorful soups and pan-roasted monkfish with stuffed papaya.

Disney offers late-night fun at Downtown Disney, an entertainment, dining and shopping complex that features **Pleasure Island** (☎ 407-934-7781; admission $21), where the ticket price gets you entry to more than half a dozen themed nightclubs and an outdoor stage show. You'll also find the **House of Blues** (☎ 407-934-2583; cover $10-20), where big-name artists perform just about everything from gospel to rock 'n' roll.

THE PANHANDLE

Culturally, Florida's panhandle is more in tune with neighboring Georgia and Alabama than it is with the kinetic melting pot that is the rest of the state. It is a place of sprawling pine forests and broad muddy rivers. The main attraction is miles and miles of white-sand beaches – among the best in all of Florida – dubbed the 'Redneck Riviera.' Its coastal area aside, the panhandle is the state's least-traveled region, although it boasts some of the most beautiful natural areas. It's also home to the state capital, Tallahassee.

TALLAHASSEE

This lovely little city with its oak-lined streets was named the capital of the Florida territories in 1824 because it was midway between St Augustine and Pensacola, which nowadays leaves the booming urban centers of Orlando, Tampa and Miami to constantly gripe about Tallahassee's relatively remote location. Tallahassee is home to the state legislature, Florida State University (FSU) and the Florida Agricultural and Mechanical University (FAMU), but offers little of real interest to visitors. If you're driving between Pensacola and St Augustine, it's worth a stop, but given the state's other attractions, it's not worth a special trip. You can check in at the **visitors bureau** (☎ 850-413-9200; 106 E Jefferson St).

The stately **Old Capitol** (☎ 850-487-1902; 400 S Monroe St; admission free; 9am-4:30pm Mon-Fri, 10am-4:30pm Sat, noon-4:30pm Sun), is now a museum devoted to the state's political and social history. The 25-story monolithic **New Capitol** (☎ 850-488-6167; Pensacola and Duval Sts; admission free; 🕑 8am-5pm Mon-Fri) is where the Florida legislature meets 60 days a year, starting in March, and an observation deck affords a panoramic view of the city.

The **Black Archives Research Center & Museum** (☎ 850-599-3020; Martin Luther King Jr Blvd & Gamble St, FAMU campus; admission free; 🕑 8am-5pm Mon-Fri) showcases one of the country's largest collections of African-American and African artifacts. The **Museum of Florida History** (☎ 850-488-1484; 500 S Bronough St; admission free; 🕑 9am-4:30pm Mon-Fri, 10am-4:30pm Sat, noon-4:30pm Sun) chronicles Florida through its art, artifacts, military weapons and clothing.

The 16-mile **Tallahassee–St Marks Historic Railroad State Trail** (☎ 850-922-6007; trailhead along Woodville Hwy near Hwy 319; admission free; 🕑 8am-dusk) follows the abandoned rail line of the same name and is popular with bicyclists, joggers, skaters and horseback riders.

Sleeping & Eating

Note that accommodations rates skyrocket during football-game weekends, when there might be a two-night minimum, and the busy March through May legislative session. Most accommodations are uninspiring and are clumped at exits along I-10 and along Monroe St between I-10 and downtown. Here a few exceptions to that rule.

Calhoun Street Inn (☎ 850-425-5095; 525 N Calhoun St; r $65-95; 🕑 closed Aug; P ✖) A pleasant B&B with antiques and handmade quilts in a quiet residential neighborhood.

Quality Inn & Suites (☎ 850-877-4437; www.qualityinn.com; 2020 Apalachee Parkway; d $65; P ✖ 🏊) You get a lot of room and plenty of extras for your money here.

Wakulla Springs Lodge (☎ 850-224-5950; 550 Wakulla Park Dr; r $79-99; P ✖) Fifteen miles south of the capital, in Wakulla Springs State Park, you can stay in this refreshing lodge, where the comfortable marble-floored rooms hearken to their 1930s heritage by not having TV (there's one in the immense lobby, along with a big fireplace and a giant, stuffed alligator).

Governor's Inn (☎ 850-681-6855; www.thegovinn.com; 209 S Adams St; d $139-159, ste $169-229; P ✖ 💻 🏊). The poshest place in Tallahassee, the Gov is a favorite with the political heavyweights.

Tallahassee is Florida's Bible Belt, so many restaurants are closed Sunday.

International House of Food (☎ 850-386-3433; 2013 N Monroe St; dishes $2.50-7; 🕑 8am-10 pm Mon-Fri, 10am-6pm Sat) A Middle Eastern food market with a deli, this place is worth a visit for good, cheap meal.

Uptown Café (☎ 850-222-3253; 111 E College Ave; mains $1-6; 🕑 breakfast & lunch Mon-Fri) Ease the pain of getting out of bed by heading straight for the heavenly breakfasts at the Uptown Café. Good sandwiches, too.

Hopkin's Eatery (☎ 850-386-4258; 1700 N Monroe St; lunch $4-6; 🕑 lunch Mon-Sat) This place bustles through the day with government workers and students, who come for the excellent grilled subs and Cuban sandwiches.

Andrew's 228 (☎ 850-222-3444; 228 S Adams St; dishes $7-24) A chummy hangout with good fish and pasta dishes for the city's movers and shakers.

Chez Pierre (☎ 850-222-0936; 1215 Thomasville Rd; mains $15-23) A top-rated, cozy French place in a historic house, this is just the ticket for a big night out.

Getting There & Around

Greyhound (☎ 850-222-4249; 112 W Tennessee St) serves Pensacola ($24, four hours), Jacksonville ($28, three hours), Miami ($67, 11 hours) and other locales. **Amtrak** (☎ 850-224-2779; 918½ Railroad Ave) connects to New Orleans and Jacksonville. **TalTran** (☎ 850-891-5200; fare/day pass $1/2.50) loops through the university campuses and downtown. Take the free downtown **Old Town Trolley** (🕑 7am-6:30pm Mon-Fri).

PANAMA CITY BEACH

During spring break, students flock to the white, Appalachian-quartz sand beaches of Panama City Beach, a 27-mile-long gulf barrier island almost due west of the separate municipality of Panama City. It extends east from St Andrews State Recreation Area, one of the country's finest beaches, to the Philips Inlet Bridge at the west. Front Beach Rd is garishly lined with fast-food joints, motels, hotels, condos and minigolf and amusement parks that seem to scream, 'Give me your money!' Check in at the **visitors bureau** (☎ 850-233-6503, 800-722-3224; 17001 Panama City Beach Parkway, intersection of Hwys 98 & 79; 🕑 8am-5pm).

Thankfully, the state created **St Andrews State Recreation Area** (☎ 850-233-5140; 4607 State Park Lane; carload $4, single occupancy car $2, pedestrian or cyclist $1; dawn-dusk), or this region too would be overbuilt. It has dunes with tall grasses, a jetty, a lagoon safe for small kids to swim in, nature trails, swimming, hiking, kayaking and lots of wildlife. The **Museum of Man in the Sea** (850-235-4101; 17314 Panama City Beach Parkway; adult/child $5/2.50; 9am-5pm) gives a thorough and fascinating look at diving, from the old-time hard-hat suits to modern scuba diving. More than 300 animals, including 20 endangered species are on display at **Zoo World Zoological & Botanical Park** (850-230-1243; 9008 Front Beach Rd; adult/child $12/7; 9am-6:30pm).

Sleeping, Eating & Entertainment

Summer is definitely the high season for panhandle beaches.

Sea Witch Motel (850-234-5722; www.seawitchmotel.com; 21905 Front Beach Rd; r $35-60, apt $59-125; P) Many of the beach hotels show the wear and tear of spring break, but you can bask pleasurably in the sun on the deck of this family-oriented motel.

Island Breeze (850-234-8841, 800-874-6617; www.islandbreezemotel.com; 17281 Front Beach Rd; r $49-119, ste $83-175; P) Enjoy a host of amenities, like hot tubs and full kitchens, at this lovely motel with immaculate rooms.

Sugar Sands Beach Resort (850-234-8802, 800-367-9221; www.sugarsands.com; 20723 Front Beach Rd; d $50-115, ste $70-145; P) Another prime beachfront location, this friendly resort offers perks like a BBQ area and a playground.

Marriott Bay Point Resort Village (850-236-6000; www.marriottbaypoint.com; 4200 Marriott Dr; d/ste $119/229; P) This fancy resort is definitely at the top end of the scale and offers spacious, comfy rooms and gorgeous Gulf views.

Capt Anderson's (850-234-2225; 5551 N Lagoon Dr; dishes $12-35; closed Sun) Probably the area's most popular restaurant for dinner, serving steaks, seafood and pasta. There's also an adjacent seafood market.

Panama City Brewery (850-230-2739; 11040 Hutchinson Blvd; lunch $10-14, dinner $15-18) Kick back at this brewery and enjoy some high-class pub-grub and handcrafted beers.

All-American Diner (850-233-6007; 15406 Front Beach Rd; dishes $3-11; 6am-12am) and **Sunnyside Grill** (850-233-0729; 21828 Front Beach Rd; dishes $2-11) both serve home-style meals for breakfast, lunch and dinner.

Entertainment is geared to the MTV crowd at two adjacent beachfront nightclubs: **Club La Vela** (850-234-3866; 8813 Thomas Dr; cover $5-15) and **Spinnaker** (850-234-7892; 8795 Thomas Dr; cover varies), which serve up food, fun and nightly entertainment, including national touring acts. **Harpoon Harry's** (850-234-6060; 12627 Front Beach Rd) offers a beachside bar and a big dance floor.

Getting There & Around

Panama City Bay County International Airport (850-763-6751) is served by major airlines and regional commuters. Car rentals and taxis are available, but there is no local bus service. **Greyhound** (850-785-6111; 917 Harrison Ave) runs buses to Tallahassee ($14, two hours), Pensacola ($21, three hours) and Miami ($79, 14 hours). The closest Amtrak service is in Chipley, 57 miles away. There are bike racks on the **Bay Town Trolley** (850-769-0557; fare 50¢), which runs weekdays along the beach to St Andrews State Recreation Area and into Panama City.

PENSACOLA

Founded as a permanent settlement in 1568, when it was an outpost of Spanish colonialism, much of Pensacola's downtown area today dates from the 19th century. Its three historic districts have undergone extensive reconstruction and renovation. Gently curving Pensacola Beach features white sand, clear gulf water and spectacular sunsets. There's a large military population here thanks to two big bases – Pensacola Naval Air Station and Eglin Air Force Base.

The city is a typical Florida sprawler – it's difficult to get around without a car. For directions, stop by the **visitors bureau** (850-434-1234, 800-874-1234; 1401 E Gregory St; 8am-5pm).

Sights & Activities

The **Historic Pensacola Village** (850-595-5985; Tivoli House, 205 E Zaragoza St; adult/child $6/2.50; 10am-4pm Mon-Fri) is an interesting collection of early homes and museums through which costumed guides give entertaining walking tours. The enormous **Pensacola Naval Air Station** is home to the Blue Angels, the navy's amazing precision-flying outfit, and one of the world's best air museums, the **National Museum of Naval Aviation** (850-452-3604; 1750 Radford Blvd; admission free; 9am-5pm). Exhibits such as the prisoner-of-war artifacts are enlightening, and the museum's Imax theater ($6.50) shows thrilling, G-pulling aviation films.

Gulf Islands National Seashore (☎ 850-934-2600; www.nps.gov/guis; pedestrian or cyclist $3, vehicle $8; ⏰ dawn-dusk) covers many of the barrier islands for 150 miles between West Ship Island, Mississippi, and Santa Rosa Island, Florida. Within the park is **Fort Pickens** (☎ 850-934-2635), built between 1829 and 1834, the site of Geronimo's 1886–7 incarceration. There's swimming and nature and bike trails. The park's other fort, **Fort Barrancas** (☎ 850-934-2600), has been built, destroyed, remodeled and occupied by Spanish, French, British, Confederate and US forces.

Sleeping & Eating

There are plenty of chain options on the I-10 corridor through Pensacola.

Five Flags Inn (☎ 850-932-3586; www.fiveflagsinn.com; 299 Fort Pickens Rd; r $55-99; P ✖ 🏊) On the beach, try this two-story beachfront inn, where all rooms face the gulf.

Bay Beach Inn (☎ 850-932-2214, 866-932-2214; 51 Gulf Breeze Parkway; r $99; P ✖ 🏊) A family-friendly, beachfront place with almost a mile of Pensacola Bay beach outside the door.

Seville Inn (☎ 850-433-8331, 800-277-7275; www.sevilleinn.com; 223 E Garden St; d/ste $75/119; P ✖ 💻 🏊) Those who want to stay downtown should check out the clean rooms on offer at the Seville Inn, located near Pensacola's historic district.

New World Inn (☎ 850-432-4111; www.newworldlanding.com; 600 S Palofax Rd; d/ste $75/125; P ✖) Also downtown, New World Inn is a former 19th-century box factory with cozy accommodations and a very helpful staff.

Crown Plaza Pensacola Grand Hotel (☎ 850-433-3336, 800-348-3336; www.pensacolagrandhotel.com; 200 E Gregory St; d/tr/quad $135/145/155; P ✖ 💻 🏊) After all that lazing on the beach, you should really spoil yourself with a night at the luxe Crown Plaza, which occupies part of a restored early-1900s railroad depot.

Ever'man Natural Foods (☎ 850-438-0402; 315 W Garden St; dishes $4-9) One of a number of eateries in the historic district, this natural food market has a deli that serves terrific sandwiches.

Dharma Blue (☎ 850-433-1275; www.dharmablue.com; 300 S Alcaniz St; mains $8-18; ⏰ lunch & dinner Mon-Sat, dinner Sun) Creative pasta and seafood dishes are served up in this funky old house.

McGuire's Irish Pub (☎ 850-433-6789; 600 E Gregory St; dishes $4-19) Good beer and burgers – plus some Irish specialties – keep them coming back to this Irish pub.

Peg Leg Pete's (☎ 850-932-4139; 1010 Fort Pickens Rd; mains $14-16) Sit outside on Pensacola Beach (or inside if it's nippy), and feast on oysters any way you like them, plus seafood dishes with a Louisiana flavor.

Getting There & Around

Pensacola Regional Airport (☎ 850-436-5000) has commuter and jet service, taxis, rental cars and local bus service. **Greyhound** (☎ 850-476-4800; 505 W Burgess Rd) has buses to New Orleans ($28, four hours), Panama City ($21, three hours) and Miami ($79, 15 hours), among others. *Sunset Limited* stops at the **Amtrak station** (☎ 850-433-4966; 980 E Heinburg St) on its way from Los Angeles, California, to Jacksonville.

Escambia County Area Transit (☎ 850-436-9383) has a very efficient system of trolleys (25¢) and buses ($1, 10¢ transfers) that run to major attractions, the airport, the visitors bureau, downtown and the beaches.

Texas

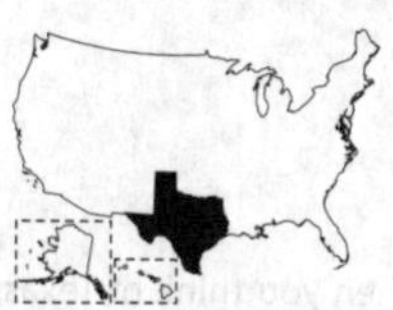

CONTENTS

When you think of Texas, it's hard not to imagine a land of longhorn cows, oil derricks and lonesome cowboys. After all, it's the only state in the Union to have been its own country. But Texas is more than cows, oil and cowboys. From Austin's blues bars to Big Bend's natural splendor to Amarillo's old Route 66, Texas is full of surprises. It's a film capital and a music powerhouse. It offers great rock climbing, kayaking, river running and backpacking. And the country's booming wine industry didn't start in California but right here in the Lone Star State. Of course, if you want a taste of the old West, you'll find that too – just mosey on over to Fort Worth's stockyards or Amarillo's cattle auction.

The Texas border with Mexico has created an entire Tex-Mex subculture, blending the best from each side of the Rio Grande into a uniquely Texan stew. Down in laid-back San Antonio, for example, you can listen to Dixieland jazz on Saturday night and go to mariachi mass Sunday morning. Further west on the Mexican border is the wild and enchanting Big Bend National Park where the Texas flatlands soar skyward on 8000ft mountains.

More surprising is the legacy left by early European settlers in central Texas. When you see a region of Czech bakeries, German breweries and French bistros, where else could you be but the Texas Hill Country – a polyglot place where *Wilkommen* appears on as many signs as 'Welcome.'

HIGHLIGHTS

- Spending a night in the **Terlingua Ghost Town** sipping margaritas at the Starlight Theatre (p667)
- Listening to the auctioneer sell cattle to the cowboys at the **Amarillo Stockyards** (p673)
- Eating cotton candy and corny dogs at the **State Fair** in Dallas (p635)
- Seeing the **Congress Avenue bats** (p644) before heading out for a night of **live music** in Austin (p646)
- Checking out the art and the coffee shops in Houston's **Montrose District** (p656)

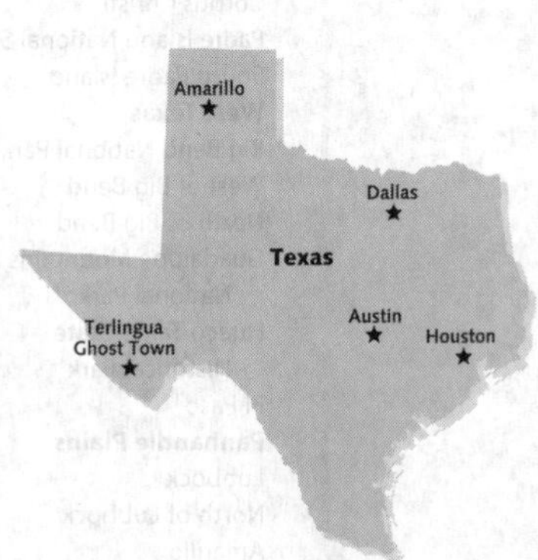

HISTORY

The area's earliest-known human society hunted bison on the panhandle plains over 10,000 years ago. The first Europeans to encounter the territory were the Spanish, who mapped the coast in 1519 before unceremoniously wrecking on what is now Galveston Island. The Spaniards named their new territory *tejas* (*tay*-has), a corruption of the Caddo Indian word for 'friend.'

In 1821 Texas became a state of the newly formed country of Mexico, an agreement that never sat well with the independent-minded Texans.

The Texas War for Independence (1835–6) started when William B Travis led a group of armed, hotheaded Texans against Mexican troops defending a customs office in the south Texas town of Gonzales. Texan troops (comprising Americans, Mexicans and a fair number of English, Irish, Scots, Germans and other Europeans) then captured San Antonio and the Alamo. After Mexicans sacked the Alamo, Sam Houston and his Texan army trounced Mexican troops at San Jacinto, and the Republic of Texas was born. Nine years later Texas was annexed as the 28th state of the Union.

Texas' early economic boom came from free-range cattle ranching until the invention of barbed-wire fencing. That and the discovery of oil in east Texas changed everything. WWII brought more prosperity to Texas in the form of military bases, and the energy crisis of the 1970s brought the state unadulterated Sultan-of-Bruneian wealth. Petroleum prices tripled, gasoline prices quadrupled, and Texans – the biggest domestic oil suppliers – laughed all the way to the bank.

The bubble burst in the 1980s, when a worldwide glut devastated the Texas oil industry.

The early 1990s saw an explosion of technology businesses, turning south-central Texas into a high-tech corridor that rivals Silicon Valley. The 1994 North American Free Trade Agreement (Nafta), loosening trade restrictions between the US, Mexico and Canada, was a huge economic shot in the arm for Texas, which does a booming business with Mexico.

In 2001 former Texas oilman and Republican governor George W Bush followed in his daddy's footsteps to become the 43rd president of the United States.

TEXAS FACTS

Nickname The Lone Star State
Population 21,779,893 (2nd)
Area 261,797 sq miles (2nd)
Admitted to Union December 29, 1845 (28th); seceded 1861; readmitted 1870
Capital city Austin (population 680,899)
Other cities Houston (1.9 million), Dallas-Fort Worth (1.7 million), San Antonio (1.1 million)
State small mammal armadillo
State large mammal longhorn steer
State flying mammal Mexican free-tailed bat
Birthplace of Buddy Holly (1936–59), Howard Hughes (1905–76), Ima Hogg (1882–1975), Janis Joplin (1943–70), Roy Orbison (1936–88), Dwight D Eisenhower (1890–1969), Lyndon B Johnson (1908–73), Steve Martin (b 1945), Renee Zellweger (b 1969), Mathew McConaughey (b 1969)
Famous for the Alamo; the Bushes; the 'Six Flags' – French, Spanish, Mexican, Texas Republic, USA and Confederate States – that have flown over Texas

GEOGRAPHY & CLIMATE

Texas, as any Texan will say, is big. Though less than half the size of Alaska, it's larger than Germany, England, Scotland, Ireland, Northern Ireland, Belgium and the Netherlands combined.

The state gets a bad reputation for being flatter than a bookkeeper's butt and Texas does have its share of pancake-flat views west of Dallas, though there's plenty of other scenery to take in as well – the eastern part of the state is covered by pine forests; the Gulf Coast has over 600 miles of beaches and bird sanctuaries; the panhandle (p670), in the far north west of the state wedged between Oklahoma and New Mexico, is cut with deep canyons; west Texas has a few peaks over 8000ft (Guadalupe Peak at 8749ft is the highest); and the central Texas Hill Country offers a gently rolling landscape crisscrossed with clear-running rivers and streams.

In July and August, Texas gets Africa-hot with temperatures routinely hovering around 100°F. August and September is hurricane season along the coast, bringing plenty of tropical rain to Houston and surrounds. In the spring and fall you can

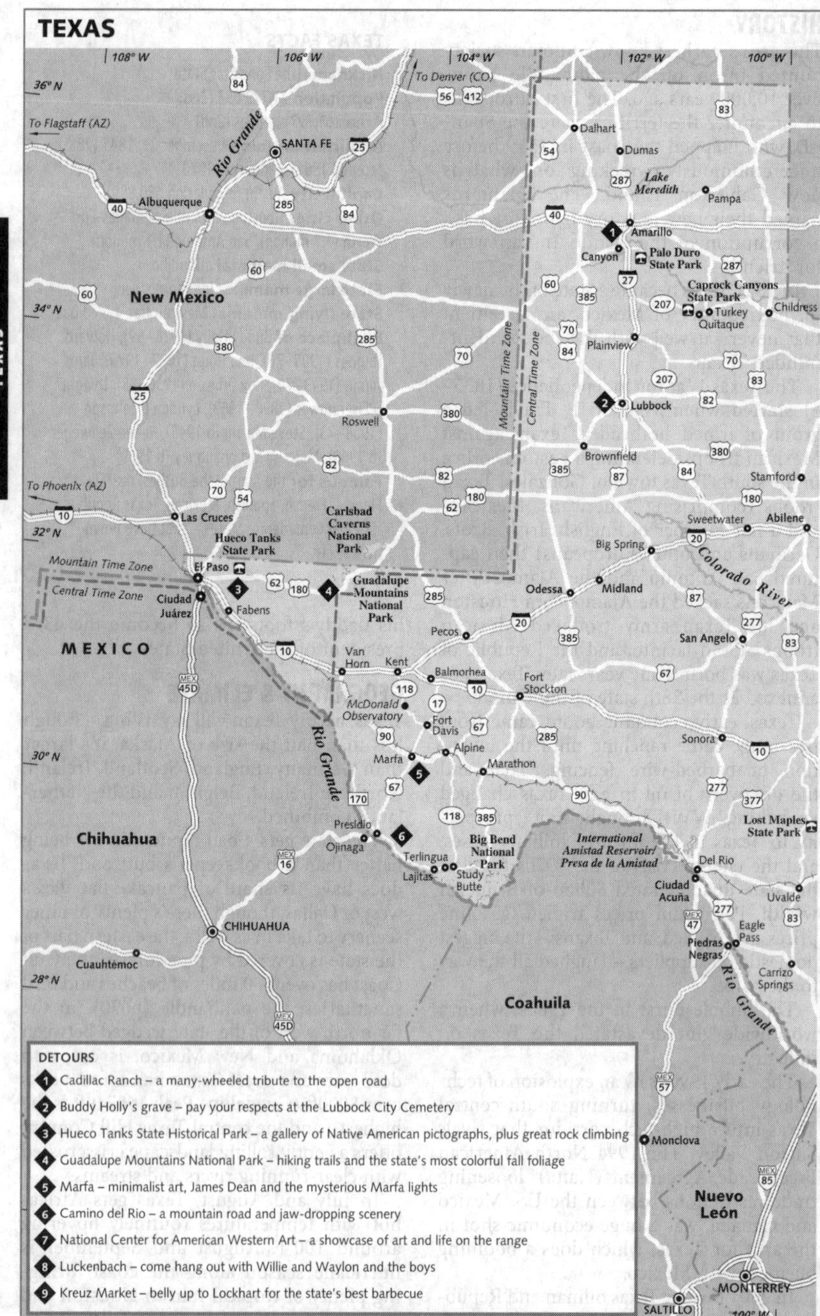
TEXAS
108° W
106° W
104° W
102° W
100° W
36° N
34° N
32° N
30° N
28° N
To Denver (CO)
To Flagstaff (AZ)
To Phoenix (AZ)
SANTA FE
Albuquerque
Rio Grande
New Mexico
Roswell
Las Cruces
Carlsbad Caverns National Park
Hueco Tanks State Park
Guadalupe Mountains National Park
Mountain Time Zone
Central Time Zone
El Paso
Ciudad Juárez
Fabens
MEXICO
Van Horn
Kent
Balmorhea
Fort Stockton
McDonald Observatory
Fort Davis
Alpine
Marfa
Marathon
Presidio
Ojinaga
Terlingua
Lajitas
Study Butte
Big Bend National Park
Chihuahua
CHIHUAHUA
Cuauhtémoc
Coahuila
Dalhart
Dumas
Lake Meredith
Pampa
Amarillo
Canyon
Palo Duro State Park
Caprock Canyons State Park
Turkey
Quitaque
Childress
Plainview
Lubbock
Brownfield
Stamford
Sweetwater
Abilene
Big Spring
Colorado River
Odessa
Midland
Pecos
San Angelo
Sonora
Lost Maples State Park
International Amistad Reservoir/ Presa de la Amistad
Del Rio
Ciudad Acuña
Uvalde
Eagle Pass
Piedras Negras
Carrizo Springs
Monclova
Nuevo León
MONTERREY
SALTILLO
DETOURS
1 Cadillac Ranch – a many-wheeled tribute to the open road
2 Buddy Holly's grave – pay your respects at the Lubbock City Cemetery
3 Hueco Tanks State Historical Park – a gallery of Native American pictographs, plus great rock climbing
4 Guadalupe Mountains National Park – hiking trails and the state's most colorful fall foliage
5 Marfa – minimalist art, James Dean and the mysterious Marfa lights
6 Camino del Rio – a mountain road and jaw-dropping scenery
7 National Center for American Western Art – a showcase of art and life on the range
8 Luckenbach – come hang out with Willie and Waylon and the boys
9 Kreuz Market – belly up to Lockhart for the state's best barbecue

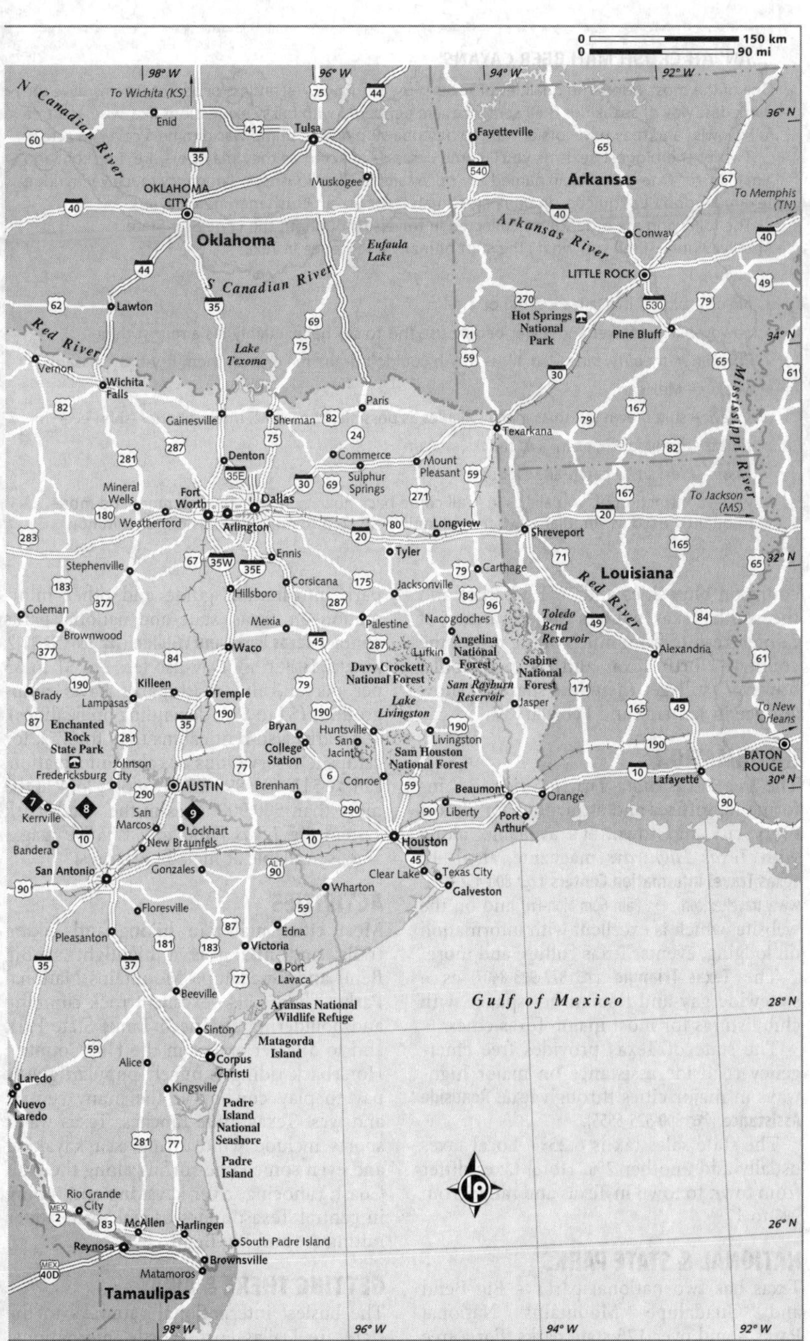
0 150 km
0 90 mi
98° W
96° W
94° W
92° W
36° N
34° N
32° N
30° N
28° N
26° N
N Canadian River
To Wichita (KS)
Enid
Tulsa
Fayetteville
Muskogee
Arkansas
OKLAHOMA CITY
Oklahoma
To Memphis (TN)
Eufaula Lake
Arkansas River
Conway
LITTLE ROCK
S Canadian River
Lawton
Hot Springs National Park
Pine Bluff
Red River
Lake Texoma
Vernon
Wichita Falls
Mississippi River
Paris
Gainesville
Sherman
Texarkana
Denton
Commerce
Mount Pleasant
Sulphur Springs
Mineral Wells
Fort Worth
Dallas
To Jackson (MS)
Weatherford
Arlington
Longview
Shreveport
Ennis
Tyler
Stephenville
Carthage
Louisiana
Corsicana
Jacksonville
Hillsboro
Red River
Coleman
Mexia
Palestine
Nacogdoches
Toledo Bend Reservoir
Brownwood
Angelina National Forest
Waco
Lufkin
Alexandria
Davy Crockett National Forest
Sabine National Forest
Killeen
Sam Rayburn Reservoir
Brady
Temple
Lampasas
Jasper
Lake Livingston
To New Orleans
Enchanted Rock State Park
Bryan
Huntsville
Livingston
San Jacinto
College Station
Sam Houston National Forest
BATON ROUGE
Johnson City
Fredericksburg
Conroe
AUSTIN
Brenham
Beaumont
Lafayette
Orange
Kerrville
San Marcos
Liberty
Port Arthur
Lockhart
New Braunfels
Houston
Bandera
San Antonio
Gonzales
Clear Lake
Texas City
Galveston
Wharton
Floresville
Edna
Pleasanton
Victoria
Port Lavaca
Beeville
Aransas National Wildlife Refuge
Gulf of Mexico
Sinton
Matagorda Island
Corpus Christi
Alice
Laredo
Kingsville
Nuevo Laredo
Padre Island National Seashore
Padre Island
Rio Grande City
McAllen
Harlingen
South Padre Island
Reynosa
Brownsville
Matamoros
Tamaulipas

TEXAS

'...AN' AH CRUSH MAH BEER CAYANS'

One of the most wonderful qualities of Texas is the language. Regardless of accent, Texans have the darnedest way of speaking. Their sentences are peppered with folksy expressions like 'wise as a tree full o' owls,' and they have lots of ways to describe stupidity ('If dumb was dirt, he'd cover an acre').

Two of the biggest Texisms you'll come across – affected as they may be – are 'I reckon' and 'I'm fixin' to.' One great Texan named Tim once said, in all seriousness, 'I'm pretty much yer avridge Texan. Ah don't eat quiche, ah *don't* cross mah laygz an' ah crush mah beer cayans.'

The following are other gems collected in travels throughout the Lone Star State:
Ahtellyawhut – 'I tell you what'; the start of many a sentence in Texas

- *awl* – oil
- *big ol'* – big, as in 'Dallas is a big ol' city'
- *howdy; hidey* – fewer and fewer people use this to say hello; mainly it's a tourist thing
- *little bitty; itty-bitty; bitty* – small, as in 'Ah couldn't drahv me one uh them itty-bitty Nissans'
- *Meskin* – Mexican
- *sheeyit* – shit, drawn out to as many syllables as possible: two is fine, three is better (shhh-eee-yit)
- *shucks* – golly, gosh, as in 'aw, shucks, ma'am'
- *yassir* – 'Yes, sir,' a catch-all response
- *y'all* – contraction of 'you all,' as in 'y'all come back now, ya hear?,' though more and more frequently used as singular – 'where y'all goin'?' spoken to one person is not uncommon

count on blue skies and 70°F weather and the south Texas winters are a warmer, if rainier, respite from much of the rest of the country. North Texas and the panhandle, however, still get their fair share of snow and ice in January and February.

INFORMATION

The free *Texas State Travel Guide* lists information offices and attractions for almost every city and town. It's available, along with *Texas Highways* magazine, at all 12 **Texas Travel Information Centers** (☎ 800-452-9292; www.traveltex.com; 8am-6pm Mon-Fri) and on the website, which is excellent with information on lodging, events, Texas culture and more.

The **Texas Triangle** (☎ 877-903-8407) is a statewide gay-and-lesbian newspaper with club listings for most major Texas cities.

The state of Texas provides free emergency roadside assistance on major highways in major cities through **Texas Roadside Assistance** (☎ 800-525-5555).

The state sales tax is 6.25%. Local taxes usually add another 2%. Hotel taxes differ from town to town in Texas and range from 9% to 17%.

NATIONAL & STATE PARKS

Texas has two national parks – Big Bend and Guadalupe Mountains National Parks – and over 125 state parks. For a free park information guide and other information on Texas' state and national parks contact **Texas Parks and Wildlife** (☎ 800-792-1112; www.tpwd.state.tx.us). Day-use fees are $1 to $5 per person, and most parks have campgrounds ($4 to $16, depending on facilities). Ten parks also rent cabins ($40 to $75); for campsite reservations or cabin information, call ☎ 512-389-8900. For a glossy look at the more than 500,000 acres in the state's park system the *Texas Parks and Wildlife* magazine is available at most bookstores.

ACTIVITIES

Most cities maintain hiking and biking trails, and hiking is a highlight at Big Bend and Guadalupe Mountains National Parks. There's also excellent rock climbing and bouldering at Hueco Tanks State Park and to a lesser extent in the Hill Country. Horseback riding is hugely popular; guests pay to play cowboy at the many central and west Texas dude ranches. Texas water sports include windsurfing, sea kayaking and even some lame surfing along the Gulf Coast; canoeing, river kayaking and tubing in central Texas; and seasonal white-water rafting around Big Bend.

GETTING THERE & AWAY

The busiest international gateways to the state are Dallas-Fort Worth International

Airport (DFW) and Houston's George Bush Intercontinental Airport (IAH). Austin, San Antonio and El Paso also have major airports.

Amtrak (☎ 800-872-7245; www.amtrak.com) offers two routes through Texas. The *Sunset Limited* runs between Orlando, Florida and Los Angeles three times a week, with stops in Houston, San Antonio, Del Rio, Alpine (near Big Bend National Park) and El Paso. The *Texas Eagle* runs between Chicago and San Antonio daily, with stops in Texarkana, Dallas-Fort Worth, Austin and San Marcos.

GETTING AROUND

The best way to see Texas is by car. Unfortunately, most car rental companies slap you with a huge fee for one-way drop-off rentals or if you exceed a certain number of miles (rental agencies in El Paso do not allow you to go outside a 300-mile perimeter of town; how they figure out if you cross that line is a mystery). Nevertheless, it's possible to rent cars in all the big towns and make short overnight trips around the area (see p1161 for details).

Southwest and other major airlines service the major airports in Texas including Lubbock and Amarillo. Amtrak has decent fares but limited schedules outside the Dallas–Houston and San Antonio–El Paso corridors.

Greyhound (☎ 800-231-2222; www.greyhound.com) and its small Hill Country partner Kerrville Bus Co serve all but the tiniest towns in the state, meaning you'll be able to get anywhere you want, even though it may take twice as long as it would by car.

TOURS

For those looking to see the majority of the highlights while but are limited to a tight schedule, **Gray Line** (www.grayline.com) organizes a variety of coach tours in Dallas, Austin, San Antonio and Houston. Several groups and vineyards in the Hill Country offer wine tours, including **Texas Wine Cellars** (☎ 877-839-9463; $75) in Fredericksburg, which goes to five different vineyards over a five-hour stretch. TravelTex.com, the state's online visitor's guide, has an excellent selection of self-guided driving tours that you can download before getting behind the wheel.

DALLAS-FORT WORTH

Just 30 miles apart, Dallas and Fort Worth anchor a gigantic megalopolis known as the Metroplex. The two cities offer distinct takes on the Texas experience. Dallas lives up to the state's exported image: big and flashy, rich and prosperous. It's driven, a city preoccupied with growth and status. Fort Worth is going places, too, but doesn't seem as concerned with how its image plays outside the city limits. Combining lots to see and do with an easy-to-manage layout, Fort Worth might be the state's best-kept secret.

DALLAS

The 'Big D' is famous for its contributions to popular culture – everything from the Dallas Cowboys football team and its balloon-breasted cheerleaders to *Dallas,* the long-running TV series that became a worldwide symbol for the US. It's a city known for its business acumen, especially in banking, along with its restaurants and shopping. In the materially minded US, Dallas stands tall as a paragon of conspicuous consumption. The city's biggest event is the annual Texas State Fair in October.

History

Dallas was founded in 1839 and became a major railroad junction in the 1870s, sparking a boom that ensured the city's preeminence as a trade center. When the nearby East Texas Oil Field struck black gold in 1930, Dallas became the oil industry's financial center.

The city's image took a dive after President Kennedy was assassinated there in November 1963. It reclaimed its Texas swagger through Larry Hagman's portrayal of scheming oil tycoon JR Ewing on *Dallas* and the Dallas Cowboys, who have won the Super Bowl five times. Since then, Dallas has become a technology and telecommunications center and a cosmopolitan place with a population of over one million people, a thriving nightlife and gay scene, world-class cuisine and some of the best shopping west of the Mississippi.

Orientation

Downtown Dallas is just east of the junction of I-30 and I-35 E; take Commerce

DALLAS
0 0.6 km
0 0.4 mi
INFORMATION
Bank of America 1 B2
Central Library 2 C3
Chase Bank of Texas 3 C1
Dallas CVB Visitor Center 4 A3
SIGHTS & ACTIVITIES pp633–4
Conspiracy Museum 5 B3
Dallas Museum of Art 6 B1
Dallas World Aquarium 7 B2
Kennedy Memorial 8 A3
Morton H Meyerson Symphony Center 9 C1
Sixth Floor Museum 10 A3
SLEEPING pp635–6
Hotel Adolphus 11 B3
Hotel Lawrence 12 A3
EATING 636–7
Deep Sushi 13 D2
Green Room 14 D2
DRINKING p637
Club Dada 15 E2
ENTERTAINMENT p637
Adair's Saloon 16 D2
Club Clearview 17 E2
Dallas Alley 18 A2
Gypsy Tea Room 19 D2
Majestic Theatre 20 C2
Sambuca 21 D2
SHOPPING pp637–8
Neiman Marcus 22 C2
TRANSPORT p638
American Airlines Center 23 A1
DART Store 24 C2
Greyhound Bus Terminal 25 B3
To Dallas-Fort Worth International Airport (16mi)
To Dallas Market Center (2mi) & Love Field (5mi)
To Inwood Rd (4mi)
To Restaurants, Maple Ave, Turtle Creek Blvd & Oak Lawn Ave (1 mi)
To Greenville Ave (3.5mi)
To Uptown (1mi)
To Fitzhugh Ave (1mi)
To Fair Park (0.75mi)
To Texas Stadium (8mi)
To Fort Worth (24mi)
To I-20 (9mi)
To Arlington (17 mi)
Woodall Rodgers Fwy
N Central Expy
N Good Latimer Expy
S Good Latimer Expy
Central Square Park
Heritage Way Park
Carpenter Plaza
Plaza of the Americas
Thanksgiving Square
Aston Park
West End Marketplace
Founders Square Park
Lubben Plaza Park
Ferris Plaza
Dealey Plaza
Founders Plaza
Marilla Triangle Park
City Hall Plaza
Dallas Convention Center
Old City Park
Samuel Beaumont Park
Reunion Park
Amtrak Union Station
Union Station
Convention Center
West End
Akard
St Paul
Pearl

St exit off I-35. The West End in downtown is a developed tourist area with restaurants, shops and nightclubs. The Arts District, on downtown's north edge, holds the city's art museum, symphony center and other cultural-arts venues. North up McKinney Ave is Uptown, with a concentration of art galleries, clubs and posh restaurants.

Northeast of downtown, Greenville Ave is lined with hip restaurants and nightclubs. It's one of the city's two premier entertainment districts, the other one being Deep Ellum, at the east end of Elm St – a former warehouse district and now the nucleus of Dallas' energized live-music scene.

Information

BOOKSTORES

Bookstop (☎ 214-357-2697; 5550 W Lovers Lane, Inwood Village shopping center) Part of the Barnes & Noble empire.

Crossroads Market (☎ 214-521-8919; 3930 Cedar Springs Rd) Carries gay and lesbian titles.

Half Price Books (☎ 214-379-8000; 5803 E Northwest Hwy) Several locations in town for this longtime favorite used-book store.

EMERGENCY

Dallas County Rape Crisis Center (☎ 214-653-8740)

Emergency number (☎ 911)

INTERNET ACCESS

Central Library (☎ 214-670-1700; 1515 Young St) There are twelve work stations, and it's free.

MEDIA

90.1 KERA NPR (National Public Radio) and other public broadcasting.

92.5 KZPS Classic rock.

99.5 The Wolf Country music.

102.1 The Edge A popular alt-rock station.

Dallas Morning News The city's only daily.

Dallas Observer Free alternative weekly with art, music and other listings.

Dallas Voice Gay-and-lesbian newspaper.

MEDICAL SERVICES

Children's Medical Center (☎ 214-456-7000; 1935 Motor Street) Near Market Center.

Parkland Memorial Hospital (☎ 214-590-8000; 5201 Harry Hines Blvd) Near Market Center.

Walgreens (☎ 214-922-9233; 3418 McKinney Ave, uptown) This Uptown location has a 24-hour pharmacy.

MONEY

Bank of America (☎ 214-508-6881; 1401 Elm St; 🕑 8am-4pm Mon-Fri) Currency exchange at downtown location only.

Chase Bank of Texas (☎ 214-965-2925; 2200 Ross Ave; 🕑 9am-4pm Mon-Thu, 9am-5pm Fri) Every location in town can exchange money.

POST

Main Place Station (☎ 214-752-5654;1201 Main St; 🕑 12-5pm Mon-Fri)

TOURIST OFFICES

Dallas CVB Visitor Center (☎ 214-571-1300; 100 S Houston St; 🕑 8am-5pm Mon-Fri) Occupies the Old Red Courthouse.

Sights

Many of Dallas' sites are downtown, close to the visitors center and the West End historic district. Fair Park is a few miles east of there off I-30. It has a big collection of museums and art deco architecture that'll keep you busy for an afternoon.

JFK SITES

Dallas will forever be known as the city where President John F Kennedy was assassinated. At Dealey Plaza, walk down the Elm St sidewalk beside the infamous grassy knoll and look for the white 'X' in the road that marks the exact spot Kennedy was shot. From there turn around and look up at the top floor of the Texas School Book Depository for an eerily clear view of the corner window where Oswald supposedly pulled the trigger.

The **Sixth Floor Museum** (☎ 214-747-6660; 411 Elm St; adult $10, child 6-18 $9; 🕑 9am-6pm), in the old Book Depository, explains in minute-by-minute detail the events leading up to, during and right after the assassination.

Those who don't believe Oswald acted alone can head to the **Conspiracy Museum** (☎ 214-741-3040; 110 S Market St; adult/student $7/6; 🕑 10am-6pm). Across the street in the JFK Memorial Plaza is the **Kennedy Memorial**, a simple but profound sculpture by the architect Phillip Johnson.

Dallas' DART light-rail drops visitors at the West End or Union Station stops (see p638).

FAIR PARK

Created in 1936 for the Texas Centennial Exposition, **Fair Park** (☎ 214-421-9600; 1300

DALLAS IN...

Two Days

Start your day downtown at **Dealey Plaza** and the JFK sites before strolling up to the **Arts District** and catching a McKinney Ave Trolley Uptown for a cup of tea and a pastry at **Bread Winners Cafe**. That night treat yourself to dinner at the **Green Room** before cabbing it back to the fun and fancy **Hotel Za Za**.

For day two, visit the original **Neiman Marcus** store downtown and shop till you drop at **Northpark Mall, Highland Park Village** and **West Village**. Then put on your new duds for a night out on the town in **Deep Ellum**.

Four Days

Follow the two-day itinerary then check out the architecture and museums at **Fair Park**. That night, catch a foreign film at the **Lakewood Theatre** before hitting the nightlife on **Lower Greenville**.

On day four, have lunch at **Sonny Bryan's Smokehouse** before making the short drive to see the gun that shot JR at **Southfork Ranch**. That night, head over to **Adairs Saloon** for a burger and some live country music.

Cullum Blvd) is a 277-acre National Historic Landmark full of art deco architecture and a dozen museums. It's also home of the Cotton Bowl stadium and the Texas State Fair, which draws over three million visitors each October.

Sights in Fair Park include the **Dallas Museum of Natural History** (☎ 214-421-3466; adult $6.50, child 3-12 $4; 10am-5pm Mon-Sat, 12-5pm Sun); **Science Place** (☎ 214-428-5555; adult $7.50, child 3-12 $4; 9:30am-4:30pm Tue-Fri, 9:30am-5:30pm Sat, 11:30am-5:30pm Sun), which has an Imax cinema and planetarium; and the **Texas Discovery Gardens** (☎ 214-428-7476; adult $3, child 3-11 $1.50; 10am-5pm Tue-Sat, 1-5pm Sun), featuring 7 acres of gardens, including a rather prickly Texas native plant collection.

OTHER ATTRACTIONS

Southfork Ranch (☎ 972-442-7800; 3700 Hogge Rd, FM 2551, at Parker road; adult $8, child 4-12 $6; 9am-5pm), about 30 miles northeast of downtown, is the location of *Dallas*, one of television's longest-running dramas (it lasted 13 years). See the gun that shot JR, the 1978 Lincoln Continental that Jock drove and a little deli called Miss Elie's Place, where you can 'eat like the Ewings used to.'

The **Dallas World Aquarium** (☎ 214-720-2224; 1801 N Griffin St; adult $13, child 3-12 $6; 10am-5pm) features a magnificent rainforest exhibit with howler monkeys, toucans and crocs, along with an unusual collection of underwater critters. The **Dallas Museum of Art** (☎ 214-922-1200; 1717 N Harwood St; adult/child over 12 $6/4; 11am-5pm Tue-Sun, 11am-9pm Thu) has a decent ancient and Native American collection.

Between Dallas and Fort Worth in nearby Arlington you'll find the two huge amusement parks **Six Flags Over Texas** (☎ 817-530-6000; www.sixflags.com/parks/overtexas; on I-30 at Hwy 360; adult/child under 48in tall $40/25; hours vary), famous for its scary coasters, and **Hurricane Harbor Six Flags** (☎ 817-265-3356; www.sixflags.com/parks/hurricaneharbordallas; adult/child under 48in tall $29/19; hours vary), a humongous water park. Opening times and large discounts can be found through their websites.

Walking Tours

A great self-guided tour through downtown starts at the Dallas CVB Visitor Center in the Old Red Courthouse. From there walk north up Houston St past Dealey Plaza and the Sixth Floor Museum until the street curves around to the right, at which point Houston St becomes Ross Ave. Follow Ross Ave past the edge of the West End and walk 10 minutes to St Paul St and the Arts District. At that point you can plan to take part in the **Arts District Stroll** (10:30am first Sat of each month; meet at 2010 Flora St), a free hour-long guided walking tour, or you can hop on the free McKinney Ave Trolley for a 15-minute ride to the restaurants and cafés in Uptown and the shopping in the West Village shopping center.

Tours

Gray Line Dallas (☎ 866-767-9849; www.grayline.com; $30-45) is a countrywide chain, offering combination walking and bus tours of the major sites in Dallas, including one to Southfork Ranch. Children under 12 are about half price.

The **Dallas Historical Society** (☎ 214-421-4500; www.dallashistory.org; $45 including lunch) offers several excellent bus and walking tours including a blues and heritage tour of Deep Ellum and a tour that follows Lee Harvey Oswald's footsteps before he was caught at the Texas Theatre in Oak Cliff.

Festivals & Events

Fair Park holds events year-round, including antique expositions, car shows, rodeos and the granddaddy of all Texas events: the **State Fair of Texas** (☎ 214-565-9931; www.bigtex.com), held from late September through October. Come eat corny dogs and fried Twinkies, browse the blue-ribbon jelly winners and ride the Texas Star, the tallest Ferris wheel in North America.

On May 5 every year, Dallas, like much of the rest of the state, celebrates **Cinco de Mayo**, a Mexican fiesta in remembrance of May 5, 1862, the date of the Battle of Puebla in which Mexico defeated Napoleon III's occupying French army.

In March Dallas hosts the **North Texas Irish Fest** (☎ 214-823-4370; www.ntif.org), a celebration of all things Celtic, including music, crafts and Guinness – lots of it.

Sleeping

If you're looking for dirt cheapies you may be tempted to brave the dives on Fort Worth Ave, but steer clear – we couldn't find a clean or friendly spot in the bunch. The best areas to stay are downtown and Uptown, but these are also among the most expensive. Moderate prices in Dallas are between $50 and $110 and are mostly standard chain hotels. After that prices go to $160 and up. The hotel tax is 15%.

BUDGET

Welcome Inn (☎ 214-826-3510; 3243 Merrifield Ave; s/d $35/40; P ✣) This friendly spot at I-30's Dolphin Rd exit has acceptable rooms at good value.

Super 8 Dallas Market Center (☎ 214-631-6633; 9229 Carpenter Fwy; s/d $50/60; P ✣ ♿) This is a good deal near Market Center.

MID-RANGE

Hotel Lawrence (☎ 214-761-9090; 302 South Houston St; r from $90; P $15; ✣) Formerly the Paramount Hotel, this thoroughly updated downtown spot has smallish rooms but the location and the views are unbeatable.

Days Inn Market Center (☎ 214-522-6650; 4500 Harry Hines Blvd; s/d $52/65; P ✣) Rooms here aren't anything unexpected but the staff is friendly and the location puts you about 15 minutes from downtown by light-rail.

Some other recommendations include the following:

Fairfield Inn Regal Row (☎ 214-638-6100; 1575 Regal Row off Stemmons Fwy; r $50-70; P ✣ ♿)

La Quinta Inn – City Place (☎ 214-821-4220; 4440 N Central Expressway; r $90-110; P ✣ ♿) Near Knox-Henderson shopping district.

Best Western Market Center (☎ 214-741-9000; 2023 Market Center Blvd; r from $80; P ✣ ♿ 💻) This is one of a slew of moderately priced chains in Market Center.

GAY & LESBIAN DALLAS

In a city (and state) that would seem to be hostile toward gays, the gay and lesbian scene in Dallas is thriving and generally accepted. That's not to say most Dallasites won't gawk or even be offended at public displays of affection between two men or women. Nevertheless, gays enjoy lots of support and freedoms in Dallas that much of the rest of the state – with the exception of Houston – would not tolerate. And the recent historic Supreme Court decision that nullifies a Texas sodomy law, effectively backing a gay man or woman's right to privacy, has emboldened gay groups in Dallas as well as around the state and the country.

Dallas' gay and lesbian scene is centered on Cedar Springs Rd in Uptown. Look for **JR's** (☎ 214-528-1004; 3923 Cedar Springs Rd), a fun place with darts and pool, or catch the Tuesday-night mixer at the **Crew's Inn** (☎ 214-526-9510; 3215 N Fitzhugh Ave). For more meat and buns try **Hunky's** (☎ 214-522-1212; 4000 Cedar Springs Rd), a burger joint across the street from JR's. **Sue Ellen's** (☎ 214-559-0650; 3903 Cedar Springs Rd) is Dallas' biggest lesbian bar. For more info contact the **Dallas Gay & Lesbian Alliance** (☎ 214-528-4233; 2701 Reagan Ave; ⏲ 10am-1pm Mon-Fri).

TEXAS

TEXAS

TOP END

Mansion on Turtle Creek (☎ 214-559-2100; 2821 Turtle Creek Blvd; r from $195; P) This gorgeous spot is really worth a look, even if you decide no to make the splurge. Mansion on Turtle Creek sits on a beautiful 4½-acre estate and represents the ultimate in opulence.

Hotel Adolphus (☎ 214-742-8200, 800-221-9083; 1321 Commerce St; r from $200 P) This historic hotel epitomizes old Dallas: rich and refined.

THE AUTHOR'S CHOICE

Hotel Za Za (☎ 800-597-8399; 2332 Leonard St; r $195-290; P) Visitors looking for a quiet night away from the spotlight should think twice about staying at this Soho-style boutique hotel; Za Za is a place to see and be seen. The fun starts with the various themed rooms. On top of that you'll find enormous outdoor balconies, 12ft ceilings and an eye-popping collection of east Asian and African art and antiques. Guests will also be tempted to put on their best cabana attire and sip piña coladas at the poolside bar. At night, the extravagantly decorated Dragonfly restaurant packs in an Uptown crowd dressed to the nines.

Eating

With about 5000 restaurants, Dallas really does have something for every taste and budget. You'll find that the highest concentration of restaurants is in Uptown and Deep Ellum.

UPTOWN

Bread Winners (☎ 214-754-4940; 3301 McKinney Ave; mains $8-11) The laid-back ambience, a vine covered outdoor patio and great food make this bakery/café a favorite breakfast spot as well as a fine place to perk yourself up with afternoon tea.

Cosmic Cafe (☎ 214-521-6157; 2912 Oak Lawn Ave; mains $6-9) Listen to the enlightening drone of sitar music and eat monstrous portions of Indian curry, stir-fry, hummus and falafel at this colorful, easy-going veggie restaurant. Drinks include smoothies, lassies and chai.

Taco Diner (☎ 214-521-3669; 3699 McKinney Ave; mains $8-14) The slick atmosphere inside this cool 21st-century diner is as fresh as the Mexican food.

DEEP ELLUM

Green Room (☎ 214-748-7666; 2715 Elm St; mains $19-34) Part nightclub and part restaurant, this spot features chef Marc Cassel's superb four-course prix-fixe mystery meals created from the menu ($36).

Deep Sushi (☎ 214-651-1177; 2624 Elm St; mains $5-15) On the weekends this cool sushi spot is packed with Deep Ellum-bound hipsters. Alas, the people-watching may be better than the food.

LOWER GREENVILLE

Blue Goose Cantina (☎ 214-823-8339; 2905 Greenville Ave; mains $10-20) Mexican food and margaritas are the specialities at this indoor-outdoor local hangout where on any given weekend night you're likely to find a wild crowd of sorority girls, CEOs and bikers. Sunday brunch gets rowdy with the Harley-Davidson set.

Campisi's Egyptian (☎ 214-827-0355; 5610 East Mockingbird; mains $6-16) Don't be fooled by the name or the shabby exterior: Campisi's Egyptian serves pizza – dang good pizza – as it has for at least the past 45 years. The rumors vary but most claim that Jack Ruby ate here the night before he shot Oswald. One has it that Ruby ate *with* Oswald. Go figure.

Other recommendations:

Grape (☎ 214-828-1981; 2802 Greenville Ave; mains $15-25) A very romantic wine bistro with a changing menu.

Aw Shucks Oyster Bar (☎ 214-821-9449; 3601 Greenville Ave; mains $6-13) Casual Gulf-coast seafood and beer.

Cafe Izmir (☎ 214-826-7788; 3711 Greenville Ave; mains $2-5) Middle Eastern tapas with good people-watching.

DOWNTOWN

Houston St (☎ 214-742-6860; 302 S Houston Street; mains $18-32) Attached to Hotel Lawrence, this lively bar and restaurant near Dealey Plaza has creative West Coast American fare and a stylish but comfy interior. On Friday nights there's jazzy live piano.

INWOOD

Sonny Bryan's Smokehouse (☎ 214-357-7120; 2202 Inwood Rd; mains $5-9; lunch only) There are several locations around town but 'The Original' blows the rest away, both with the food and the atmosphere, which is vintage 1958.

KNOX-HENDERSON

Momos (☎ 214-521-3009; 312 Knox St; mains $7-17) This family-run restaurant has a few locations around town and with good reason: it is the most authentic Italian food in Dallas. Try the *Conchiglie a Modo Mio*, a dish of homemade shell-shaped pasta, meats and cheeses in a heart-breakingly creamy tomato sauce.

Drinking

Dubliner (☎ 214-818-0911; 2818 Greenville Ave) This is a great local Irish pub in Lower Greenville with dart boards, good pints of Guinness and the best jukebox in town.

Inwood Bar (☎ 214-350-7834; 5458 Lovers Lane) Talk movies or hatch your own plot at this hip spot located inside the old Inwood arthouse movie theater.

Nikita (☎ 214-520-6454; 3699 McKinney Ave) Located in the oh-so trendy West Village in Uptown, this ultrahip underground vodka bar has over 65 vodkas to choose from along with a respectable selection of wine and Belgian ales. Weekend nights bring long waits to get in.

Club Dada (☎ 214-744-3232; 2720 Elm St) For Deep Ellum drinks with the occasional live-music jam try this hip spot.

Entertainment

Check the *Dallas Observer* for complete entertainment listings. Deep Ellum is live-music central.

NIGHTCLUBS

Club Clearview (☎ 214-939-0077; 2806 Elm St) This grubby, artsy, labyrinthine spot has been churning out dance music and live bands for decades.

Dallas Alley (☎ 214-720-0170; 2019 N Lamar St) At West End Marketplace, this multiclub venue offers varied musical styles.

LIVE MUSIC

Gypsy Tea Room (☎ 214-744-9779; 2548 Elm St) Both local and big-name touring bands in all styles play this beloved spot.

Adairs Saloon (☎ 214-939-9900; 2624 Commerce St) Located in Deep Ellum, this boot-scootin' honky-tonkin' dive is the best place to see local country music (and they've got a dang good burger to boot).

Sambuca (☎ 214-744-0820; 2618 Elm St) Head here for your jazz fix.

Muddy Waters (☎ 214-823-1518; 1518 Greenville Ave) This place books blues, rockabilly and more.

The **Dallas Symphony Orchestra** (☎ 214-692-0203; 2301 Flora St) performs at the IM Pei-designed Morton H Meyerson Symphony Center and the **Dallas Opera** (☎ 214-443-1000) plays at Fair Park Music Hall.

CINEMAS

Lakewood Theatre (☎ 214-821-9084; 1825 Abrams Parkway) This renovated 1938 art deco cinema is off the lower end of Lower Greenville and shows indie films along with lectures, film festivals and other fun events.

Magnolia Theatre (☎ 214-520-0098; Suite 100, 3699 McKinney Ave, West Village) This is Dallas' newest cinema showing first run, indie and foreign shows.

THEATER

Majestic Theatre (☎ 214-880-0137; 1925 Elm St) Music, dance and drama are all presented at this exquisitely restored 1921 theater in Deep Ellum.

Granada Theatre (☎ 214-824-9933; 3524 Greenville Ave) This old movie theater on Greenville presents plays, musicals and live music.

SPECTATOR SPORTS

Dallas Cowboys (☎ 972-579-5000) The Cowboys play NFL football at Texas Stadium in Irving, about 20 minutes from downtown Dallas.

Texas Rangers (☎ 817-273-5100) The Rangers play pro baseball at the Ballpark in Arlington, between Dallas and Fort Worth.

Dallas Mavericks (☎ 972-988-3865) This NBA basketball team play at the new American Airlines Center, between the Woodall Rodgers Fwy and I-35 E, just north of the West End district.

Dallas Stars (☎ 214-467-8277) This NHL hockey team also plays at the American Airlines Center.

Dallas Burn (☎ 214-979-0303) This team play pro soccer at the Cotton Bowl.

Shopping

Dallas is the region's shopping mecca where you can find pretty much anything you might want or need from dime-store crafts to the highest-end designer clothes.

Neiman Marcus (☎ 214-741-6911, 800-937-9146; 1 Marcus Sq on Ervay St between Main & Commerce Sts)

A downtown landmark, this is the original Neiman Marcus store.

Malls include the centrally located **Northpark Mall** (☎ 214-361-6345; 1030 Northpark Center, Northwest Hwy at Central Expressway) and further north the **Galleria** (☎ 972-702-7100; 13355 Noel Rd at I-635 & Dallas North Tollway). **Highland Park Village** (cnr Mockingbird Lane & Preston Rd) is where you'll find Prada, Chanel and other high-end boutique stores. Uptown's **West Village** (3699 McKinney Ave at Lemmon) is the newest and trendiest shopping area in town.

For antique and home furnishing stores head to Knox and Henderson Sts (Knox St is west of Central Expressway and Henderson is the same street only east of the freeway).

Getting There & Away

AIR

Dallas is the main domestic and international gateway to Texas. **Dallas-Fort Worth International Airport** (DFW; ☎ 972-574-4420) is 16 miles northwest of the city via I-35 E, Hwy 183 and Hwy 121. Southwest Airlines uses smaller, more convenient **Love Field**, just northwest of downtown (take Inwood Rd northeast from Harry Hines Blvd and turn left on Cedar Springs).

BUS & LIGHT-RAIL

Greyhound buses make runs all over the country from the **Greyhound bus terminal** (☎ 214-655-7085; 205 S Lamar St).

CAR & MOTORCYCLE

Every major rental car company has an office at DFW and around town. See p1121 for details.

TRAIN

Amtrak's *Texas Eagle* stops at downtown's **Union Station** (☎ 214-653-1101; 401 S Houston St).

Getting Around

TO/FROM THE AIRPORT

Bus No 202 ($2) runs downtown from DFW; bus No 39 ($1) heads downtown from Love Field. The faster option is to catch the Trinity Railway Express train to downtown's Union Station ($2). **Yellow Checker Shuttle** (☎ 817-267-5150) and **SuperShuttle** (☎ 817-329-2000) run shuttles from DFW to downtown for around $15 to $18, and from Love Field for $15 to $19. A taxi between DFW and central Dallas will cost $40 to $45.

CAR & MOTORCYCLE

If you do rent a car be warned that rush-hour traffic is bad and there's little free parking in downtown Dallas, particularly at night in Deep Ellum; take a cab (about $5 from downtown).

PUBLIC TRANSPORTATION

Dallas Area Rapid Transit (DART; ☎ 214-979-1111; store at Elm & Ervay Sts) operates buses, trolley buses and light-rail trains throughout downtown and the outlying areas. Pick up a route map downtown at the store, or call for route and schedule information. Fares are 50¢ around downtown, $1 to $2 elsewhere.

Uptown and downtown Dallas are connected by the free **McKinney Ave Trolleys** (☎ 214-855-0006), which run daily between the Dallas Museum of Art and Hall St.

TAXI

Yellow Cab (☎ 214-426-6262) and **Checker Cab** (☎ 214-469-1111) have an initial $2 for each person that gets into the cab and 40¢ every quarter mile after that.

FORT WORTH

This city is proud of its nickname, 'Cowtown,' but the livestock industry is just a small part of what's happening here. It's far more user-friendly than Dallas and offers lots of attractions, all easily accessible by public transportation.

The town's biggest event is the Southwestern Stock Show and Rodeo, held late January or early February each year at Will Rogers Coliseum. Fort Worth is also home to the prestigious two-week Van Cliburn International Piano Competition, held every four years in spring (the next is in 2005).

History

In 1849 Camp Worth was one of a string of US forts on the Texas frontier. By 1853 the army had withdrawn, and settlers took over the old post buildings.

Fort Worth became famous during the great open-range cattle drives of the late 19th century. More than 10 million head of cattle were trooped through the city on the Chisholm Trail, from Texas north to Kansas.

The late 19th and early 20th centuries saw rampant lawlessness. Robert Leroy Parker and Harry Longbaugh – better known as

Butch Cassidy and the Sundance Kid – hid out in town, as did Great Depression–era hold-up artists Bonnie Parker and Clyde Barrow.

The cattle business remained king here throughout the 1920s, even as major finds in nearby oil fields turned the city into an important petroleum-industry operations center. Amon Carter, oilman and early publisher of the *Star-Telegram*, put the city on the arts map.

Orientation & Information

The three areas most interesting to visitors – downtown, the Cultural District and the Stockyards – form a lopsided triangle. North Main St runs between downtown and the Stockyards, Lancaster Ave connects downtown to the Cultural District, and University Ave and Northside Dr connect the Cultural District to North Main St near the Stockyards. All these areas are north of and easily accessed from I-30.

The **Fort Worth Convention and Visitors Bureau** (☎ 817-336-8791; 415 Throckmorton St; 8:30am-5pm Mon-Fri, 10am-4pm Sat) has visitors centers in the **Stockyards** (☎ 817-624-4741; 130 E Exchange Ave; 9am-6pm Mon-Fri, 9am-7pm Sat, noon-5pm Sun) and in the **Cultural District** (☎ 817-882-8588; 3401 W Lancaster Ave; 9am-5pm Mon-Thu, 9am-5pm Fri-Sat, noon-4pm Sun). Internet access is available at the palatial (if sterile) downtown **library** (☎ 817-871-7323; 500 W 3rd St).

Sights & Activities

Most people come to Fort Worth to check out the stockyards or take in a museum or two, but the renovated and bustling downtown offers some great architecture, good eats and a lively night scene.

DOWNTOWN

The highlight here is the vibrant 14-block **Sundance Sq**, full of colorful architecture, public art and a host of bars and restaurants. The area is safe to explore on foot day or night – it's crawling with cops on mountain bikes. (They're friendly and low-key.)

Museums here include the **Sid Richardson Collection of Western Art** (☎ 817-332-6554; 309 Main St; admission free; 10am-5pm Tue & Wed, 10am-8pm Thu & Fri, 11am-8pm Sat, 1-5pm Sun), featuring Wild West landscapes and bronzes by Frederic Remington and Charles Russell, and the **Modern at Sundance Square** (☎ 817-335-9215; 410 Houston St; admission free; 10am-5pm), the Modern Art Museum's downtown gallery.

CULTURAL DISTRICT

The city's impressive Cultural District is a museum-lover's nirvana. Within easy walking distance from one another are the following world-class museums, each trying to outdo the next in architectural merit. In the **Kimbell Art Museum** (☎ 817-332-8451; 3333 Camp Bowie Blvd; admission free; 10am-5pm Tue-Thu & Sat, noon-8pm Fri, noon-5pm Sun), you'll find a small but comprehensive collection of paintings from the Renaissance to the mid-20th century. The brand new **Modern Art Museum of Fort Worth** (☎ 817-738-9215; 3200 Darnell St; 10am-8pm Tue, 10am-5pm Wed-Thu & Sat, noon-8pm Fri, noon-5pm Sun) houses an impressive collection of paintings and sculpture from Picasso to Mark Rothko. The recently rebuilt **Amon Carter Museum** (☎ 817-738-1933; 3501 Camp Bowie Blvd; 10am-5pm Mon-Fri) holds 19th- and 20th-century American painting and sculpture as well as an extensive photography collection.

The **Museum of Science & History** (☎ 817-255-9300; 1501 Montgomery St; adult $7, child 3-12 $5; 9am-5:30pm Mon-Thu, 9am-8pm Fri & Sat, 11:30-5:30 Sun) is full of fossils, dinosaurs and kid-friendly interactive stuff. It also has a planetarium and an Omni Imax theater.

STOCKYARDS NATIONAL HISTORIC DISTRICT

Once the livestock industry's trading center, the Stockyards are now a tourist-oriented entertainment and shopping district.

The former sheep and hog pens of **Stockyards Station** (140 E Exchange Ave) now houses Western-wear shops and the depot of **Tarantula Railroad** (☎ 817-625-7245), a tourist excursion train.

Next door, the visitors bureau (see above) is the departure point for walking tours of the district. Across the street, the small **Stockyards Museum** (☎ 817-625-5087; 131 E Exchange Ave; admission free; 10am-5pm Mon-Sat) displays photos and memorabilia from the heyday of Fort Worth's cattle industry.

City-paid cowboys on horseback roam the district, answering tourist questions and posing for photos. Twice a day, at 10am and 4pm, they drive a small herd of Texas longhorns around the block. It's a goll-dang Kodak moment, pardner.

Pay parking lots are numerous; two lots straddling the easternmost end of Exchange Ave are free.

Sleeping

Like Dallas, Fort Worth has a 15% hotel tax.

BUDGET

Sims Motel (☎ 817-332-2078; 901 N Henderson Rd; s/d $35/40; P) The rooms at this friendly spot are small and a little dark but the place is clean enough and the price is right.

MID-RANGE

Park Central Hotel (☎ 817-336-2011; 1010 Houston St; r from $80; P) This independently owned former '60s-era chain motel has some of the cheapest rooms downtown and is a good choice for the money. There's also an outdoor deck with complimentary BBQ grill next to the pool.

Texas Hotel (☎ 817-624-2224; 2415 Ellis Ave at Exchange St; r Mon-Fri $50-100, Sat & Sun $80-150; P) Located right in the Stockyards, this neat old 1939 building has 21 small, surprisingly standard rooms, though you have to hand it to the management for their unusual Western decorating themes.

Two more downtown spots with great locations but not much character are the **Courtyard by Mariot** (☎ 817-885-8700; 601 Main St; r from $100; P) and the **Clarion Hotel** (☎ 817-332-6900; 600 Commerce St; r from $90; P).

TOP END

Etta's Place (☎ 817-654-0267; 200 W 3rd St; r $125-165; P) Named for Etta Place, the Sundance Kid's gorgeous girlfriend, this 10-room boutique hotel/B&B is a worthwhile splurge, even though it has some unfortunate decorating schemes in the rooms.

THE AUTHOR'S CHOICE

Stockyards Hotel (☎ 817-625-6427; 109 E Exchange Place; r $140-190; P) Located in the heart of the Fort Worth Stockyards, this historic hotel exists in a Wild West time warp. The longleaf-pine floors creak with every step, cow hides cover the beds and thick wooden shutters – some pockmarked with holes as though they were shot up in an old West gunfight – close out the dusty light on the trail outside. Ask for a quiet room away from the front if the nighttime rabble-rousing on Exchange St is going to bother you.

Eating

Steak is big in Fort Worth, but so is Mexican. The Cultural District is hurting for good eats but you'll find a few spots on 7th Ave and a great Italian spot on University Blvd.

DOWNTOWN

Reata (☎ 817-336-1009; 310 Houston St; mains $15-39) Located in new digs in Sundance Sq, this spot serves steak with a Southwestern flare and a lively atmosphere. The rooftop patio here is a great place to have drinks.

Del Frisco's Double Eagle Steak House (☎ 817-877-3999; 812 Main St; mains $25-47) The atmosphere here is serious and clubby and the slabs of steer could be some of the best-prepared cuts in the state.

Angeluna (☎ 817-334-0080; 215 E 4th St; mains $14-29) The trendy spot in Sundance Sq offers a wide-ranging international menu and Fort Worth's most beautiful clientele; make reservations and dress appropriately.

La Madeleine (☎ 817-332-3639; 305 Main St; mains $3-9) This casual French-inspired bistro has good breakfasts.

STOCKYARDS

Joe T Garcia's (☎ 817-626-4356; 2201 N Commerce St; mains $6-12) This beloved Tex-Mex spot takes up nearly an entire city block with beautiful outdoor dining amid fountains and pools.

CULTURAL DISTRICT

Sardines Ristorante Italiano (☎ 817-332-9937; 509 N University Dr; mains $15-25) This romantic Italian restaurant and jazz spot is still going strong, and there's jazz nightly at 7pm along with some pretty dang good pasta.

Four Star Coffee Bar (☎ 817-336-5555; 3324 W 7th St; mains $3-7). This is a great place to get wired on coffee and stuff in a muffin or pastry before hitting the museums. Also serves veggie burgers, soups and salads.

Drinking

Flying Saucer Emporium (☎ 817-336-7470; 111 E 4th St) Pretty young barmaids pull pints from 77 taps at this vast pub.

8.0 (☎ 817-336-0880; 111 E 3rd St) The staff, like the clientele, are a little snooty but the massive outdoor red-brick patio makes for good evening cocktails.

White Elephant Saloon (☎ 817-624-1887; 106 E Exchange Ave) This quintessential cowboy bar has live country music nightly.

Magnolia St Station (☎ 817-332-0415; 600 W Magnolia St) This is certainly the city's most popular gay bar.

Entertainment

Downtown's Sundance Sq becomes a hot spot after dark but the Stockyards and Billy Bob's honky-tonk are a hootin' and hollerin' good time too.

NIGHTCLUBS

Billy Bob's Texas (☎ 817-624-7117; 2520 Rodeo Plaza) This cavernous club in the Stockyards features top country-and-western stars as well as live bull-riding, country dance lessons, pool tables and games. Though it touts itself as the world's largest honky-tonk, Billy Bob's feels more like Las Vegas.

LIVE MUSIC

Bass Performance Hall (☎ 817-212-4325, 888-597-7827; 555 Commerce St) This hall is the exquisite home to the **Fort Worth Symphony** (☎ 817-665-6000), the **Fort Worth Opera** (☎ 817-731-0833) and the **Fort Worth-Dallas Ballet** (☎ 817-377-9988).

Blues venues in town include **J&J Blues Bar** (937 Woodward Ave), **Bad to the Bone** (702 N Henderson St) and the **Thirsty Armadillo** (2467 N Main St). For alternative rock, go to the **Wreck Room** (3208 W 7th St), near the Cultural District, or check the schedule at the popular **Ridglea Theater** (☎ 817-738-9500; 6025 Camp Bowie Blvd).

Getting There & Around

BUS

From the **Greyhound station** (☎ 817-429-3089; 901 Commerce St) buses travel all over the state. Call for fares and schedules.

TRAIN

Amtrak's *Texas Eagle* stops at the depot (☎ 817-332-2931; 1501 Jones St). **Longhorn Trolley** (☎ 817-215-8600) connects the three major tourist areas. Trolleys run every 20 minutes from 11am to 6pm (Cultural District) or 11pm (Stockyards and downtown). The fare is $2 one way, $5 all day.

SOUTH-CENTRAL TEXAS

If you've only got a short time in Texas, this would be a good place to head. Here you'll find Austin, the state's capital and music scene epicenter; San Antonio, home of the Alamo; and the Hill Country, an undulating, unhurried place a world away from the rat race. Perhaps you've heard of the Heart of Texas? Well, here it is.

AUSTIN

Though it is the state capital, Austin is better known for musicians than politicians.

In the early 1960s, Wednesday-night jam sessions at Threadgill's gas station and beer joint attracted musicians from around Texas, including Port Arthur's soon-to-be-famous rock diva, Janis Joplin. In 1970 Eddie Wilson opened his legendary Armadillo World Headquarters here, and for the next decade the Armadillo was ground zero for the Cosmic Cowboy movement – *the* musical hangout for guys like Willie Nelson and Kinky Friedman and for seminal acts like the Clash and Van Morrison. Later Austin performers and bands that would make their mark include the Butthole Surfers and Stevie Ray Vaughan. These days Austin seems to be waiting for the next big name to play his or her way up through the ranks while the town coasts on its folk, country and rockabilly roots. Austin acts that may not have garnered much national attention but who have a committed local following include Alejandro Escovedo, Don Walser, Toni Price and Dale Watson. These excellent musicians play out regularly.

Orientation & Information

Guadalupe (*gwad*-ah-loop) St runs west parallel to Congress Ave and becomes, alongside the University of Texas (UT) campus, the Drag. Just north of campus is the tony Hyde Park neighborhood. East 6th St, between Congress Ave and I-35, harbors a dizzying collection of nightclubs packed with 20-somethings and West 6th St at the intersection of Lamar Blvd is an up-and-coming shopping district surrounded by restaurants. Walking distance from East 6th St, the Warehouse District draws a slightly older, mellower crowd to generally more upscale restaurants and clubs. Town

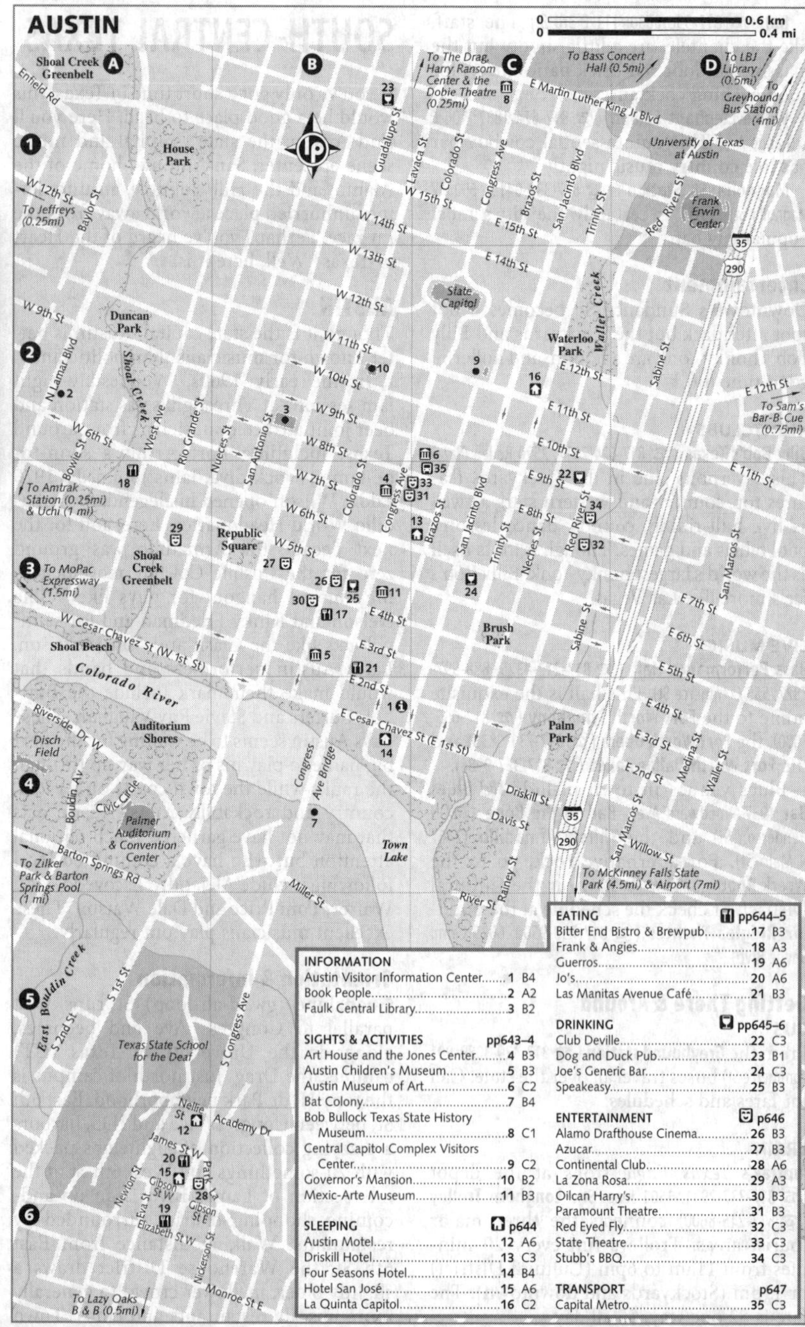

INFORMATION

Austin Visitor Information Center 1 B4
Book People 2 A2
Faulk Central Library 3 B2

SIGHTS & ACTIVITIES pp643–4

Art House and the Jones Center 4 B3
Austin Children's Museum 5 B3
Austin Museum of Art 6 C2
Bat Colony 7 B4
Bob Bullock Texas State History Museum 8 C1
Central Capitol Complex Visitors Center 9 C2
Governor's Mansion 10 B2
Mexic-Arte Museum 11 B3

SLEEPING p644

Austin Motel 12 A6
Driskill Hotel 13 C3
Four Seasons Hotel 14 B4
Hotel San José 15 A6
La Quinta Capitol 16 C2

EATING pp644–5

Bitter End Bistro & Brewpub 17 B3
Frank & Angies 18 A3
Guerros 19 A6
Jo's 20 A6
Las Manitas Avenue Café 21 B3

DRINKING pp645–6

Club Deville 22 C3
Dog and Duck Pub 23 B1
Joe's Generic Bar 24 C3
Speakeasy 25 B3

ENTERTAINMENT p646

Alamo Drafthouse Cinema 26 B3
Azucar 27 B3
Continental Club 28 A6
La Zona Rosa 29 A3
Oilcan Harry's 30 B3
Paramount Theatre 31 B3
Red Eyed Fly 32 C3
State Theatre 33 C3
Stubb's BBQ 34 C3

TRANSPORT p647

Capital Metro 35 C3

Lake, which is really a dammed stretch of the Colorado River, is where downtown ends and South Austin begins. Here you'll find Zilker Park, a new performing arts center, and SoCo, a length of S Congress Ave that's home to art galleries, antique stores and several good restaurants.

For more info check out the local **Austin Visitor Information Center** (☎ 512-583-7235, 800-926-2282; www.austintexas.org; 201 E 2nd St; 9am-5pm, later in summer). It sponsors free **walking tours** (☎ 512-454-1545). Free Internet access is available at Austin's **Faulk Central Library** (☎ 512-499-7300; 800 Guadalupe St; 10am-9pm Mon-Thu, 10am-6pm Fri & Sat, noon-6pm Sun). **The Austin Gay & Lesbian Chamber of Commerce** (☎ 512-472-8299; 3004 Medical Arts St) is near the university. **Book People Inc** (☎ 512-472-4288; 603 N Lamar Blvd) sells, of all things, books!

Sights & Activities

Austin has a budding art scene due to UT's deep pockets, and the capitol complex is the beneficiary of one of the country's wealthiest states. Otherwise, Austinites spend a lot of time outside.

CAPITOL COMPLEX

The 1888 **Texas State Capitol** (☎ 512-463-0063; 11th St at Congress Ave; admission free; 7am-10pm Mon-Fri, 9am-8pm Sat & Sun) appears like a pink mirage downtown. Nearby is the Greek revival–style 1856 **Governor's Mansion** (☎ 512-463-5516; 1010 Colorado St; admission free; tours 10am-noon); tours last 20 minutes. **The Capitol Complex Visitors Center** (☎ 512-305-8400; 112 E 11th St) has information on capitol tours.

UNIVERSITY OF TEXAS AT AUSTIN

The **Lyndon B Johnson Library & Museum** (☎ 512-721-0200; 2313 Red River St at MLK Blvd; admission free; 9am-5pm) is a good overview of LBJ's political life and contains solid exhibitions on JFK, the Bay of Pigs, the Civil Rights movement and the Vietnam War.

UT's **Jack S Blanton Museum of Art** (☎ 512-471-7324; Art Building at 23rd & San Jacinto; admission free; 9am-5pm Mon-Fri, 9am-9pm Thu, 1pm-5pm Sat & Sun) is one of the premier University art collections in the country with important holdings of 20th century and Latin American art. Nearby, the **Harry Ransom Humanities Research Center** (☎ 512-471-8944; www.hrc.utexas.edu; 21st & Guadalupe; 10am-5pm Tue-Fri, 10am-7pm Thu, noon-5pm Sat & Sun) is the resting place for some of the world's most important manuscripts, memorabilia and art, including an original copy of the Gutenberg Bible and the first photograph ever taken.

The three-year-old **Bob Bullock Texas State History Museum** (☎ 512-936-8746; MLK Blvd at N Congress Ave; adult/under 18 $5/free; 9am-6pm Mon-Sat, noon-6pm Sun) has an impressive interactive exhibit on 'The Story of Texas.' There's also a 400-seat Imax theater.

SLACKERVILLE

When Austin local Richard Linklater released the movie *Slacker* in 1992 a movement was born...sort of. The movie is about a collection of fun-loving good-for-nothings wandering through Austin's sleepy streets and coffee shops. Philosophically, it's about not working, at least not working at something you don't love to do. It's a classic because of its depiction of a long gone pre-high-tech–boom Austin and also because it helped define a generation of misfits trying to find their way.

DOWNTOWN MUSEUMS

Austin's excellent **Mexic-Arte Museum** (☎ 512-480-9373; 419 Congress Ave; admission $5; 10am-6pm Mon-Thu, 10am-5pm Fri & Sat, noon-5pm Sun) has rotating exhibitions by Mexican artists. The **Austin Museum of Art** (☎ 512-495-9224; 823 Congress Ave; admission $5; 10am-6pm Tue-Sat, 10am-8pm Thu, noon-5pm Sun) features traveling shows and offers $1 admission on Tuesdays. Half way between the two, the **Art House at the Jones Center** (☎ 512-453-5312; 700 Congress Ave; admission free; 11am-7pm Tue-Fri, 11am-9pm Thu, 10am-5pm Sat, 1pm-5pm Sun) shows fresh contemporary art. And nearby, kids will love the **Austin Children's Museum** (☎ 512-472-2499; 210 Colorado St; adult/children under 2 $4.50/2.50; 10am-5pm Tue-Sat, noon-5pm Sun), which lets young Willie Nelsons-to-be perform on 'Austin Kiddie Limits' (a childlike re-creation of the well-known music TV show *Austin City Limits*, where kids can stand on a 'stage' under lights and play toy guitars to videos of past performers). Wednesdays evenings are free.

PARKS

Just south of the Colorado River, 351-acre **Zilker Park** (☎ 512-472-4914; 2201 Barton Springs Rd; admission free; 5am-10pm) has a nature center,

AUSTIN'S BATS

Up to 1.5 million Mexican free-tailed bats make their home upon a platform beneath the Congress Ave Bridge from March to November. It's become an Austin tradition to watch around sunset as the bats swarm out to feed on an estimated 10,000 to 30,000 pounds of insects. The best viewing is in August. **Capitol Cruises** (☎ 512-480-9264), behind the Hyatt Hotel, offers bat-watching cruises on Town Lake below the bridge ($8). Bat Conservation International runs a **Bat Hotline** (☎ 512-416-5700 category 3636).

botanical gardens and a sculpture garden. The park is also home to **Barton Springs Pool** (☎ 512-476-9044; adult $2.50, child 12-17 $1, child under 12 50¢; 5am-10pm, except 5am-9am & 7pm-10pm Thu) a locally beloved spring-fed swimming hole with chilly, sparkling clear waters and lots of bathing beauties. It's 25¢ extra on the weekends.

Festivals & Events

First Thursdays on South Congress (www.firstthursday.info/vedorguide.php) Local shops and restaurants host live music and give away free beer on the first Thursday of each month.

Mardi Gras 6th St turns into a breast-baring and bead-groveling mini New Orleans; February.

South by Southwest (SXSW; ☎ 512-467-7979; www.sxsw.com) One of the American music industry's biggest gatherings; March.

Sleeping

Chain places line the interstate; avoid the seedy motels on S Congress Ave south of Olforf St. Hotel tax is 15%.

BUDGET

HI Austin (☎ 512-444-2294; 2200 S Lakeshore Blvd; dm members/nonmembers $16.50/19.50; P) This cheerful place on Town Lake includes a kitchen, common area, laundry and Internet access, plus bike, canoe and kayak rentals. There are no private rooms.

MID-RANGE

Austin Motel (☎ 512-441-1157; 1220 S Congress Ave; r $60-125; P) With a sign that reads 'So close, yet so far out,' these classic digs have friendly service in a great south Congress location.

Lazy Oaks B&B (☎ 512-447-8873, 877-947-8873; 211 W Live Oak St; r $100-120; P) This laid-back South Austin spot is in a beautiful old home run by a pair of aging hippies who will read your palms and feed you the best brownies this side of the Mississippi.

La Quinta Capitol (☎ 512-476-1166; 300 E 11th St; r $90-110; P $10) Right by the capitol, has clean and comfortable rooms for around $95 to $110.

TOP END

Driskill Hotel (☎ 512-474-5911; 604 Brazos St; r from $160) Many a visitor chooses to splurge at this famous downtown spot known for its colorful history.

Four Seasons (☎ 512-478-4500; 98 San Jacinto Blvd at Cesar Chavez Blvd; r from $195 P) Located on the shores of Town Lake, this swanky hotel takes care of all the details.

Eating

Austin has some great restaurants all over town.

DOWNTOWN & WAREHOUSE DISTRICT

Las Manitas Avenue Café (☎ 512-472-9357; 211 Congress Ave; mains $6-12) For breakfast and lunch only in deep red booths, head to this inexpensive and *sabroso* (tasty) Mexican eatery.

Bitter End Bistro & Brewpub (☎ 512-478-2337; 311 Colorado St; mains $16-26) Located in the Ware-

THE AUTHOR'S CHOICE

Hotel San José (☎ 512-444-7322, 800-574-8897; 1316 S Congress Ave; r with shared bath $75, with private bath $120-150; P) Just up the street from the Austin Motel and right next to the hip South Congress Ave antique stores, this old roadside dive was renovated four years ago into a modern boutique hotel that has become a mirror for life in Austin. Its Zen-inspired rooms and bungalow-like cabanas are a model of sleek functionality and simple comfort. The front desk has complimentary movie and CD lending as well as the *New York Times* and room service breakfasts of granola, fruit and fresh juice. At nights, the outdoor patio of the hotel becomes a casual hangout for hip young Austinites who come to drink beer and wine from the small hotel bar.

MARCH MADNESS

For five nights in mid-March music executives and record label reps from around the country and the world descend on Austin with the hope of signing the next great band at the **South by Southwest music festival** (SXSW; ☎ 512-467-7979; www.sxsw.com). The festival brings in an overwhelming thousand-some groups and solo artists from around the world to 50 different Austin venues, and almost every popular musical style is represented. The San Antonio *Express-News* called it 'an alt-rock, hip-hop, Tejano thing,' and as one music-loving wag put it, 'It's like a mile-long buffet where your stomach is ready to burst after 20ft!' Unfortunately, some of the lines to get in to a lot of the music clubs are a mile long as well. Even so, for every official band and location in one place there's an unofficial band and location elsewhere, ensuring visitors and locals alike an around-the-clock music marathon. Hotels, of course, are booked solid for up to a year in advance.

During the day, when the bands are sleeping, industry buffs head to the Austin Convention Center to talk shop and pick up free earplugs in a trade show. In addition to the music side to things, SXSW also hosts a film festival and interactive Internet conference the weekend before. The convergence of these three media outlets makes for good happy-hour conversation.

Entry to the festivities is sold in a variety of ways from a Platinum Badge ($475 to $775, depending how far ahead you buy it), which gets you all three trade shows, conferences, screenings, clubs and VIP lounges, to a Music Badge ($325 to $525), which gets you into the music conference, trade show and the nightly gigs. The cheapest way to get into the clubs during SXSW is to buy a wrist band ($115), but be forewarned; those who paid top dollar for a badge will gain entrance before those with wrist bands, which means you're not guaranteed entry as all clubs have maximum capacities determined by the city's fire department. If you're set on seeing someone, go early and sit through a couple of acts first. Either that or go somewhere else. There's music and dancing around every corner.

house District, this upscale Mediterranean-influenced eatery produces excellent beer. The place can get loud on the weekends.

6TH & LAMAR

Jeffrey's (☎ 512-477-5584; 1204 W Lynn at 12th St; mains $24-26) Located on a quiet neighborhood street, upscale romantic Jeffrey's is one of Austin's finest. It offers a cozy, dark atmosphere and a daily-changing menu of exquisite French-inspired Southwest regional cuisine, including a heavenly foie gras.

Frank & Angies (☎ 512-472-3534; 508 West Ave; mains $6-17) This spot just off W 6th St near downtown has awesome pizza, red-checkered tablecloths and a family friendly atmosphere.

SOUTH AUSTIN

Guerros (☎ 512-447-7688; 1412 S Congress Ave; mains $6-15) This popular south Austin Tex-Mex restaurant serves great margaritas and tacos *al pastor.*

Uchi (☎ 512-916-4808; 801 S Lamar Blvd; mains $8-18) This is Austin's newest and hippest restaurant with a fabulous atmosphere and the best sushi in town.

For people-watching and a hot cup o' Joe, don't miss **Jo's** (☎ 512-444-3800; 1300 S Congress Ave) or **Flipnotics** (☎ 512-482-8533; 1601 Barton Springs Rd).

OTHER LOCATIONS

East Side Cafe (☎ 512-476-5858; 2113 Manor Rd; mains $8-25) For moderately priced fine dining in a bright and cheery old house, this spot on Austin's East Side is both healthy and hearty with meals ranging from artichoke manicotti to jalapeño-pecan cornbread.

Sam's Bar-B-Cue (☎ 512-478-0378; 2000 E 12th St; mains $4-8) For a delicious artery-clogging 'cue, try this homespun ramshackle joint that's a favorite for some of Austin's local musicians.

Drinking

You won't go thirsty in Austin, a town with more bars per capita than any other in the US.

Club DeVille (☎ 512-457-0900; 900 Red River St) This place has a huge outdoor patio, a cool retro-'60s interior and a very hip crowd.

Dog and Duck Pub (☎ 512-479-0598; 406 W 17th St) This is an English-style pub with a nice outdoor patio.

Speakeasy (☎ 512-476-8017; 412 Congress Ave) This place is dressy and martini-esque, and gets the atmosphere award for its sneaky

THE AUTHOR'S CHOICE

There are scads of Mexican restaurants in Austin, but none come anywhere close to **Fonda San Miguel** (☎ 512-459-41212; 2330 W North Loop Blvd at Hancock; mains $14-30). Its unique collection of Mexican antiques, original artwork and exquisite architecture combines with a lush atmosphere to create the perfect setting for chef Miguel Ravago's transcendent interior Mexican cuisine. Make reservations for a table in the open but intimate dining room or come for appetizers in the rain forest–like bar. For dinner, try the grilled Carne Asada a la Tampiqueña (marinated steak from Tampico). And whatever you do, don't miss the stupendous fresh mango margaritas.

alley entrance and cool rooftop deck in the Warehouse District.

Entertainment

For club listings, check the free weekly *Austin Chronicle,* available citywide.

NIGHTCLUBS

Broken Spoke (☎ 512-442-6189; 3201 S Lamar Blvd) For country-and-western two-stepping and a fun, authentic scene, head to this legendary honky-tonk in South Austin.

Azucar (☎ 512-478-5650; 400 Lavaca St) This is a great place to salsa the night away.

Oilcan Harry's (☎ 512-320-8823; 211 W 4th St) This popular gay club in the Warehouse District has a dance floor, a DJ and a nice back patio. It regularly packs them in.

LIVE MUSIC

On any Friday night, hundreds of bands will be playing at more than 100 venues all over town. What's below is just the tip of the iceberg.

Stubb's BBQ (☎ 512-480-8341; 801 Red River St) Stubbs' backyard amphitheater is one of the better spots to see music in town. They regularly get big names as well as lots of insurgent country acts plus blues and more.

Backyard/Live Oak Amphitheatre (☎ 512-263-4146) When Willie and Lyle are in town they play at this excellent outdoor stage on Hwy 71 at Hwy 620, about 30 or 40 minutes west of town.

Continental Club (☎ 512-441-2444; 1315 S Congress Ave) The venerable Continental Club, located south of the river across from the Hotel San José, is a well-respected venue offering consistently good blues, rockabilly and country.

La Zona Rosa (☎ 512-472-2293; 612 W 4th St) This is a perfectly sized venue, neither too big nor too small, that offers most of the city's world-beat acts, including a healthy share of Cuban and other Latino fare.

Hole in the Wall (☎ 512-477-4747; 2538 Guadalupe St at 26th St) This legendary college dive bar near the university recently closed down to much local protest and is now up and running once again under new ownership. Local acts play roots and country on perhaps the smallest stage in town.

Joe's Generic Bar (☎ 512-480-8171; 315 E 6th St) Head to this 6th Street stalwart for down-home dirty blues.

Saxon Pub (☎ 512-448-2552; 1320 S Lamar Blvd) The Saxon has live music seven nights a week ranging from folk to blues-rock.

Red Eyed Fly (☎ 512-474-1084; 715 Red River St) Serving up local rock and punk on two stages, this spot is one of the newer, louder music venues to open its doors in town.

CLASSICAL PERFORMANCE

Austin Symphony Orchestra (☎ 512-476-6064) This is the state's oldest symphony (but the geezers can still play). Its venue is Bass Concert Hall, on the UT campus near the intersection of 23rd and Trinity Sts.

Bass Hall is also home to the **Austin Lyric Opera** (☎ 512-472-5927).

CINEMAS

Dobie (☎ 512-472-3456; 2025 Guadalupe St in Dobie Mall) Located on the Drag, this is a small but beloved Austin art house.

Alamo Drafthouse Cinema (☎ 512-867-1839; 409 Colorado St) At this old-time theater in the Warehouse District you can eat dinner and watch a movie at the same time. You must be 18 or older to enter.

THEATER

The **Austin Theatre Alliance** (www.austintheatrealliance.org) stages plays and musicals at the **Paramount Theatre** (☎ 512-472-5470; 713 Congress Ave), a refurbished grande dame that also hosts big screen classics, and the **State Theatre** (☎ 512-472-5470), located right next door.

Getting There & Around

AIR

Austin Bergstrom International Airport (☎ 512-530-2242) is off Hwy 71 southeast of downtown. Bus No 100 (50¢) runs hourly between the airport and downtown. **SuperShuttle** (☎ 512-258-3826, 800-258-3826) runs when needed and charges $10 to downtown. A taxi between the airport and downtown costs $17 to $21.

BUS

The station for **Greyhound** and the **Kerrville Bus Co** (☎ 512-458-4463 for both; www.greyhound.com; 916 E Koenig Lane) is on the north side of town off I-35; take bus No 7/Duval to downtown. Call the station or check the website for fares and schedules.

Bus company **Capital Metro** (☎ 512-474-1200; www.capmetro.org; 106 E 8th St) runs Austin's public transit. In addition to regular city buses (standard fare 50¢), the company operates the 'Dillo Lines,' a free shuttle service with five routes blanketing downtown and running up to UT.

CAR & MOTORCYCLE

Most major car rental agencies can be found at Austin Bergstrom airport and around town. See p1121 for details.

TAXI

Roy's Taxi (☎ 512-482-0000) and the **Austin Cab Company** (☎ 512-478-2222) charge $1.75 at flag fall and $1.75 for every mile after that.

TRAIN

Austin's **Amtrak station** (☎ 512-476-5684; 250 N Lamar Blvd) is served by the *Texas Eagle* and *Sunset Limited* trains.

AROUND AUSTIN

Northwest of Austin along the Colorado River, **Lake Travis** and **Lake Austin** are popular recreation areas, while **Lake Buchanan** is more serene.

You must be over 18 to enter **Hippie Hollow**, Texas' only official clothing-optional beach and a popular gay hangout. It has excellent lake views, swimming and hiking trails. From RR 620 at FM 2222, take RR 620 south 1.3 miles to Comanche Trail and turn right. The entrance is 2 miles ahead on the left.

The best reason to come to the little town of **Lockhart**, about 20 minutes south of Austin on US 183, is to stuff yourself silly on the barbecue at **Kreuz Market** (☎ 512-398-2361; 619 N Colorado St; mains per pound $8-14) – by far the best in Texas.

HILL COUNTRY

West of I-35 between Austin and San Antonio lies the Hill Country, an area filled with peaceful little towns, cactus-speckled cattle ranches, gently rolling hills and valleys and clear-running rivers. German and Czech settlers established roots here, and the area still has a European flavor, most obvious in Fredericksburg, a good-sized town that's cashed in on the tourism business. The best of the Hill Country, however, is found on its back roads where most visitors stop for a night or two at one of the many small towns to browse the multitude of antique stores, check into a dude ranch for a taste of the cowboy life or simply relax with friendly locals over a beer.

Fredericksburg

Center of the Hill Country, Fredericksburg was founded by German immigrants in 1846. Today the picturesque town has taken on the unfortunate air of a souvenir shop at Disney World. Nevertheless, there is beautiful Victorian architecture along with good German food and, during the first weekend in October, the best **Oktoberfest** in Texas. Check out the **Fredericksburg Convention and Visitors Bureau** (☎ 830-997-6523; www.fredericksburg-texas.com; 302 E Austin St; 🕑 8:20am-5pm Mon-Fri, 9am-noon & 1-5pm Sat, noon-4pm Sun). From Austin, **Greyhound** (☎ 800-231-2222) will get you to San Antonio where you transfer to a bus run by the **Kerrville Bus Co** (☎ 210-227-5669). The trip lasts 3½ hours and costs $26.

The visitors bureau has a free self-guided walking map of town and guided walking tours are led by **K&K Historic Tours of Fredericksburg** (☎ 830-990-0155; $10).

SLEEPING & EATING

Nearly 300 B&Bs do business in the county. To narrow your search and find a room ($65 to $180), use one of the city's reliable and efficient booking services, among them **Bed & Breakfast of Fredericksburg** (☎ 830-997-4712) and **Gastehaus Schmidt Reservation Service** (☎ 830-997-5612). The **Deluxe Inn Budget Host Hotel** (☎ 830-997-3344; 901 E Main St; r $42-70; P ✕) has friendly staff and a continental breakfast.

Popular for breakfast is the family-run **Dietz Bakery** (218 E Main St). Be sure and get there before noon, when they run out of goodies.

Altdorf Biergarten Restaurant (301 W Main St; mains $10-12) is the town's best German place, with a sunny patio, big mugs of beer, German music and typical Bavarian specialties. **Fredericksburg Brewing Company** (☎ 830-997-1646; 245 E Main St; mains $8-22) makes superb beers and serves good food.

The best dining experience in town is really out of town, 10 miles north on US 87 at the **Hill Top Café** (☎ 830-997-8922; 10661 US 87 N; mains $8-18), a converted old 1950s-era gas station where you can get Cajun seafood, Greek salads and good ol' chicken-fried steak. Reservations are recommended.

Luckenbach

With a population of three, Luckenbach is less a town than a state of mind. Its 'downtown' consists solely of a creaky old general store/beer joint and an adjacent dance hall, sitting on 10 creekside acres in the bucolic countryside. But Luckenbach has been a mecca for country music fans ever since Waylon Jennings sang about it in 1977. Pilgrims and devotees have left their hand-scrawled howdies on the walls.

The **store** (☎ 830-997-3224, 888-311-8990) hosts Sunday afternoon acoustic jam sessions and regular weekend concerts. You can count on a crowd on the Labor Day and Fourth of July weekends, when Jennings and Nelson often perform, along with dozens of country music's finest. Country-style B&B lodging is available just down the road at **Full Moon Inn** (☎ 830-997-2205, 800-997-1124; 3234 Luckenbach Rd; r $125-150; P).

From Fredericksburg, take Hwy 290 east to FM 1376 and go south about 3 miles.

Kerrville

Central, friendly Kerrville, a large workaday town on the Guadalupe River, has accommodations and restaurants in all price ranges. The extra-friendly **Kerrville Convention and Visitors Bureau** (☎ 830-792-3535, 800-221-7958; www.kerrvilletexas.cc; 2108 Sidney Baker Rd; 8:30am-5pm Mon-Fri, 9am-3pm Sat, 10am-3pm Sun) has information about local horseback riding, dude ranches and the big **Kerrville Folk Festival**, an 18-day musical extravaganza around Memorial Day weekend.

The biggest draw here is the **National Center for American Western Art** (☎ 830-896-2553; 1550 Bandera Hwy; adult $5, child 6-18 $1; 9am-5pm Tue-Sat, 1-5pm Sun), a first-rate showcase of artwork about cowboys, Indians and that proverbial home on the range. From downtown, take Hwy 16 south to Hwy 173 (Bandera Hwy) and turn left; it's half a mile ahead on the right.

There is a bevy of chain hotels on Hwy 16 from Fredericksburg. The **YO Ranch Resort** (☎ 830-257-4440; 2033 Sidney Baker Rd; r $55-120; P) is a fun, rustic place with big rooms and a lobby filled with antlers, deer heads and other old west gear. The **Kerrville-Schreiner State Park** (☎ 830-257-5392; 2385 Bandera Hwy; day use $3, campsites $9-15), past the museum about 1.5 miles down Hwy 173, is fun for hiking, biking, swimming, tubing and camping.

Buses arrive and depart from the **Kerrville Bus Co station** (☎ 830-257-7454; 701 Sidney Baker St) with a daily route to Austin and Fredericksburg and three times a day to San Antonio.

Bandera

South of Kerrville on Hwy 173, Bandera has the look and feel of an old Western movie set. The little town is the self-proclaimed 'Cowboy Capital of the World,' and wanna-be cowpokes can saddle up at one of the many **dude ranches** dotting the surrounding hills. The **Dixie Dude Ranch** (☎ 830-796-4481, 800-375-9255; RR 1077), 8 miles west of town, and **LH7 Ranch and Resort** (☎ 830-796-4314; off FM 3240), 3.5 miles northwest of town, are two of the nearest. Visitors with less horse sense will find Bandera a good base for **kayaking** or **tubing** the Medina River. Nearby, Lake Medina and the Hill Country State Natural Area are pleasant diversions. The friendly **Bandera County Visitors Bureau** (☎ 830-796-3045, 800-364-3833; www.tourtexas.com/bandera; 1206 Hackberry St; 9am-5pm Mon-Fri, 9am-2pm Sat) can provide information on these attractions.

The best food in town is at **Fool Moon Cafe** (☎ 830-460-8434; 204 Main St; mains $6; closed Mon), a casual and cozy eatery/coffeehouse with fresh gourmet fare. Bandera also has more than its share of drinking establishments. Two local bars with friendly folks are the **11th St Cowboy Bar** (301 N 11th St), which has two pool tables and occasional guitar playing, and Arky Blue's **Silver Dollar Bar** (☎ 830-796-8826; 308 Main St), a dance hall where you can cotton-eyed-Joe with the

THE COWBOYS

Perhaps no other figure in literary or cinematic history has been so romanticized as the cowboy, who has come to symbolize the freedom of the plains and the industrious and untamable nature of the American people themselves.

The origins of the American cowboy go back to 16th-century Spain, where cattle were allowed to graze freely and were herded by ranch hands on horseback. The Spaniards brought this practice to Mexico, and Mexican *vaqueros* (wranglers) later passed on their methods to settlers in Texas. The Americans mispronounced *vaquero*, corrupting it to 'buckaroo.'

With westward expansion and the capture of new lands from the Indians, cattle drives became common. Cowboys, under the direction of a foreman, would herd together thousands of cattle to be driven north. The cowboys caught calves using a lariat (from the Spanish *la reata*) and marked them for identification using the heated-iron design that comprised the owner's brand.

The cattle drive was led by a scout and chuck wagon, which would prepare food in advance of the herd's arrival. Cowboys would ride in packs at the front, sides and, if they were unlucky, the rear of the herd, eating dust the whole way. To filter the dust, cowboys used bandana handkerchiefs tied over their noses and mouths.

Though horses would be changed in relays along the trail, the cowboy always kept his own saddle. Masterfully crafted and as comfortable as possible for rides that were often 24 hours or more, a cowboy's saddle was his most important tool and the last thing he sold in hard times.

The lives of cowboys changed drastically after the fencing of the range. With smaller areas for grazing cows, the duties of a cowboy are far different today, though there are still cowboys throughout the western USA.

But the cowboy culture lives on. One spectacular place to gain insights into the life of a cowboy is at the remarkable National Center for American Western Art at Kerrville (see opposite).

best of them. Ask to see the table where Hank Williams Sr carved his signature several decades ago.

SAN ANTONIO

San Antonio is the nation's ninth-largest city, but its Tex-Mex culture gives it a laid-back feel. Locals joke that everyone's on 'San Antonio Standard Time.' The city's eminently walkable downtown holds that legendary monument to American courage, the Alamo, as well as Riverwalk, the gentrified renovation of a once-seedy flood-control canal. It's this feature that has given San Antonio the nickname River City.

Although the city is very spread out, much of what there is to see in San Antonio is centered around downtown and the Riverwalk, so taking in the sites and feel shouldn't take more than two or three days. The city is also in a fairly central location in the state, so if you're looking for more Tex than Mex in your visit to the region, it's not far away: Austin and the Hill Country are an hour's drive northeast, while Houston is a straight three-hour jaunt along I-10 to the east.

History

The Spanish established San Antonio as a military garrison in 1718 and built missions in the area. In 1731 Spanish settlers from the Canary Islands founded a town here; by 1791 the area was attracting Mexican and American settlers.

During the Texas War for Independence (1835–6), the legendary Battle of the Alamo was fought here. After the state's independence from Mexico, San Antonio, at the southern end of the Chisholm Trail, boomed as a cattle town.

The city's growth in the 20th-century was largely military. Fort Sam Houston (1879) was later joined by Kelly, Lackland, Randolph and Brooks Air Force Bases. Today's economy revolves around the tourism, oil, livestock and technology industries.

Orientation & Information

The intersection of Commerce and Losoya Sts is the very heart of both downtown and the Riverwalk. The Alamo is several blocks east and north of this intersection. Major arteries include Broadway, St Mary's St and Fredericksburg Rd.

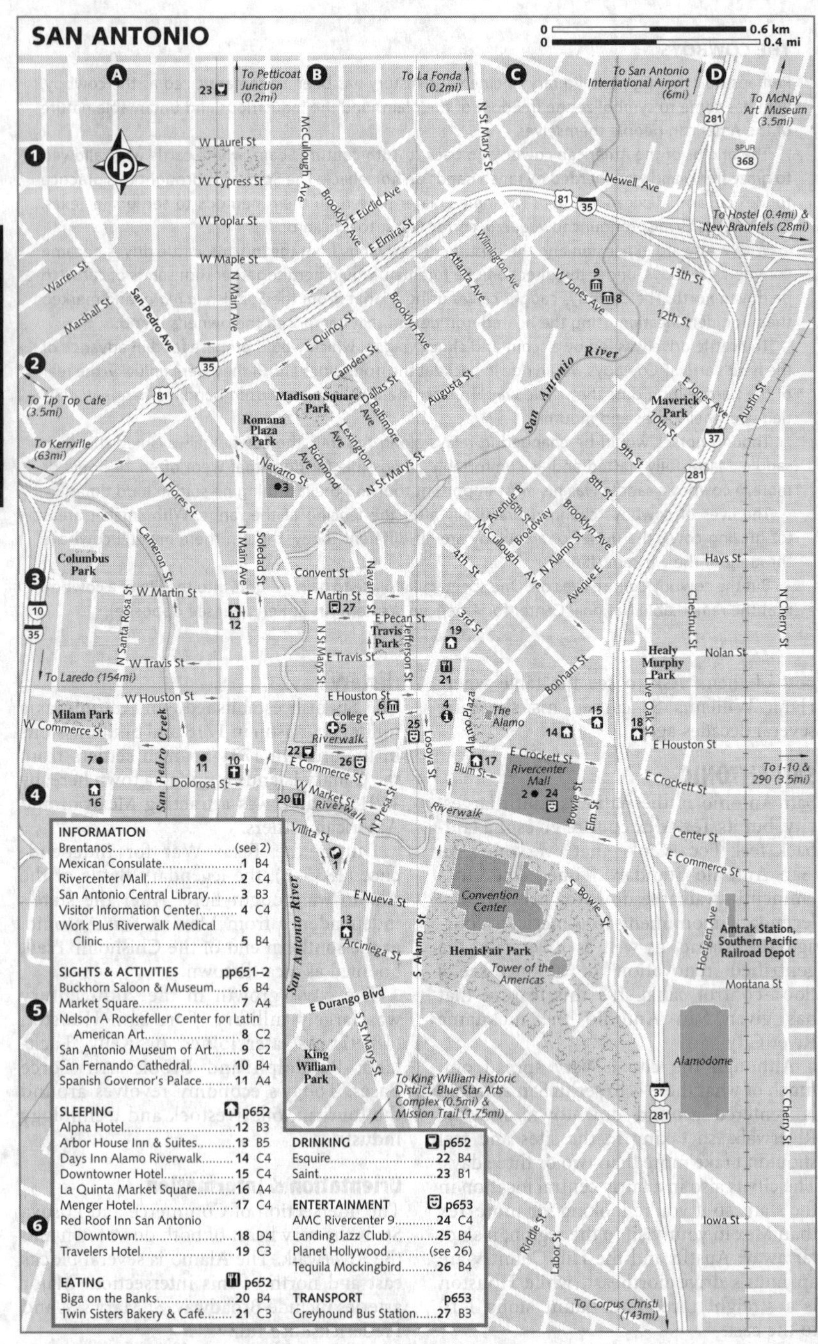
SAN ANTONIO
0.6 km
0.4 mi
To Petticoat Junction (0.2mi)
To La Fonda (0.2mi)
To San Antonio International Airport (6mi)
To McNay Art Museum (3.5mi)
To Hostel (0.4mi) & New Braunfels (28mi)
To Tip Top Cafe (3.5mi)
To Kerrville (63mi)
To Laredo (154mi)
To I-10 & 290 (3.5mi)
To King William Historic District, Blue Star Arts Complex (0.5mi) & Mission Trail (1.75mi)
To Corpus Christi (143mi)
Madison Square Park
Romana Plaza Park
Maverick Park
Columbus Park
Travis Park
Healy Murphy Park
Milam Park
The Alamo
Rivercenter Mall
Convention Center
HemisFair Park
Tower of the Americas
King William Park
Amtrak Station, Southern Pacific Railroad Depot
Alamodome
San Antonio River
Riverwalk
San Pedro Creek
INFORMATION
Brentanos.....(see 2)
Mexican Consulate.....1 B4
Rivercenter Mall.....2 C4
San Antonio Central Library.....3 B3
Visitor Information Center.....4 C4
Work Plus Riverwalk Medical Clinic.....5 B4
SIGHTS & ACTIVITIES pp651–2
Buckhorn Saloon & Museum.....6 B4
Market Square.....7 A4
Nelson A Rockefeller Center for Latin American Art.....8 C2
San Antonio Museum of Art.....9 C2
San Fernando Cathedral.....10 B4
Spanish Governor's Palace.....11 A4
SLEEPING p652
Alpha Hotel.....12 B3
Arbor House Inn & Suites.....13 B5
Days Inn Alamo Riverwalk.....14 C4
Downtowner Hotel.....15 C4
La Quinta Market Square.....16 A4
Menger Hotel.....17 C4
Red Roof Inn San Antonio Downtown.....18 D4
Travelers Hotel.....19 C3
EATING p652
Biga on the Banks.....20 B4
Twin Sisters Bakery & Café.....21 C3
DRINKING p652
Esquire.....22 B4
Saint.....23 B1
ENTERTAINMENT p653
AMC Rivercenter 9.....24 C4
Landing Jazz Club.....25 B4
Planet Hollywood.....(see 26)
Tequila Mockingbird.....26 B4
TRANSPORT p653
Greyhound Bus Station.....27 B3

The **Visitors Information Center** (☎ 210-207-6748; 317 Alamo Plaza; 8:30am-6pm), across from the Alamo, has loads of good info. Nearby, the **Rivercenter Mall** has a **Brentanos bookstore** (☎ 210-223-3938; Commerce at Crocket Sts), along with a movie theater and other shops. **Work Plus River Walk Medical Clinic** (☎ 210-272-1741; 408 Navarro St) is a 24-hour clinic and the **San Antonio Central Library** (☎ 210-207-2500; 600 Soledad St; 9am-9pm Mon-Thu, 9am-5pm Fri & Sat, 11am-5pm Sun) has free Internet access.

Sights & Activities

THE ALAMO

In the early 18th century, the Spanish constructed five San Antonio–area missions as way stations for colonial expansion. Mission San Antonio de Valero, better known as the **Alamo** (☎ 210-225-1391; 300 Alamo Plaza; admission free; 9am-5:30pm Mon-Sat, 10am-5:30pm Sun) is the most famous.

In December 1835, Texan troops captured San Antonio and occupied and fortified the Alamo throughout the winter. On February 23, 1836, Mexican general Antonio López de Santa Anna led 2500 Mexican troops in an attack against it. Santa Anna's troops pounded the Alamo for 13 days before retaking it and executing almost all of the surviving defenders, including James Bowie, William Travis and Davy Crockett. Bowie's and Travis' black slaves (Sam and Joe, respectively) fought alongside their masters during the battle and survived the attack.

RIVERWALK

Though touristy with cantinas and restaurants at every turn, the Riverwalk is still a pleasant strolling ground. Even hard-boiled visitors will probably enjoy a cruise along it with **Yanaguana River Cruises** (☎ 210-244-5700; adult/child under 6 $6/1.25; 9am-10pm Sun-Thu, 9am-11pm Fri & Sat). Get tickets at Rivercenter Mall, Holiday Inn Riverwalk or on the Riverwalk opposite Hilton Palacio del Rio. Signs throughout downtown point out stairways down to the Riverwalk, which is well below street level.

MISSION TRAIL

South of the Alamo lie the other four missions, including (from north to south): Concepción (1731), San José (1720), San Juan (1731) and Espada (1745–56). Together, these four missions make up **San Antonio Missions National Historical Park** (☎ 210-932-1001; 2202 Roosevelt Ave; admission free; 9am-5pm). Mission San José, the most beautiful, is the site of the national-park visitors center. From the Alamo, take S St Mary's St south until it becomes Mission Rd, which leads to all the missions. Parts of the Mission Trail are served by VIA (the city's bus system) and local tour companies.

MUSEUMS

The **McNay Art Museum** (☎ 210-824-5368; 6000 N New Braunfels Ave; admission free; 10am-5pm Tue-Sat, noon-5pm Sun) exhibits an outstanding collection of European and American modern art, including works by Van Gogh, Toulouse-Lautrec, Chagall, Cézanne, Hopper, Dali and Matisse.

San Antonio Museum of Art (SAMA; ☎ 210-978-8100; 200 W Jones Ave; adult $6, child 4-11 $1.75; 10am-9pm Tue, 10am-5pm Wed-Sat, noon-5pm Sun) houses rotating exhibitions and a core collection of Asian, Egyptian and ancient art. Admission is free on Tuesdays from 3pm to 9pm. Included in the admission price is SAMA's impressive collection of Spanish Colonial, Mexican and pre-Columbian works housed next door in the **Nelson A Rockefeller Center for Latin American Art**.

Buckhorn Saloon & Museum (☎ 210-247-4000; 318 E Houston St; adult $10, child 3-11 $7.50; 10am-5pm, 10am-6pm in the summer) houses big-game taxidermy, cheezoid Americana and a camp wax museum.

OTHER ATTRACTIONS

Just east of I-35, touristy **Market Sq** (☎ 210-207-8600; 514 W Commerce St; 10am-6pm, 10am-8pm summer) re-creates a Mexican marketplace, with shops selling fabrics, craftwork and clothing, plus restaurants and food kiosks serving decent Mexican food. The **Museo Americano**, a Smithsonian-affiliated museum exhibiting Latino art, history and culture in America, is scheduled to open here in September 2004.

Other downtown attractions include the 1749 **Spanish Governor's Palace** (☎ 210-224-0601; 105 Plaza de Armas; adult $1.50, child 7-13 75¢; 9am-5pm Mon-Sat, 10am-5pm Sun), behind city hall, and **San Fernando Cathedral** (☎ 210-227-1297; 115 Main Plaza; admission free; 6:15am-7pm), on N Main Ave just south of E Commerce St, which was established by the Canary Islanders (see p649) and is the nation's oldest surviving cathedral.

TEXAS

Off the outer loop (Loop 1604), **SeaWorld San Antonio** (☎ 210-523-3611; 105000 SeaWorld Dr; adult/child $40/30) features marine-life shows along with water slides and a kick-ass roller coaster. **Six Flags Fiesta Texas** (☎ 210-697-5050; Loop 1604 at I-10; adult/child under 48in tall $37/23; P $7) offers more gravity-defying coasters, a water park and other entertainment.

Festivals & Events

The biggest festival in the city is the **Fiesta San Antonio** (☎ 210-227-5191; www.fiesta-sa.org), a nine-day, citywide, multicultural party that takes place in mid- to late April. Fiesta's far-reaching events include a 10km run, traditional *conjunto* music and, of course, food – lots of it.

December brings **Las Posadas**, a candlelight procession along the Riverwalk to celebrate Christmas. Mexican chocolate, piñatas and other goodies are part of the fun.

In mid-February the **San Antonio Stock Show and Rodeo** (www.sarodeo.com) heads in to town and takes place at the downtown SBC center.

Sleeping

Everything's booked solid during major college sporting events, festivals and large conventions, so call ahead. Hotel tax is 16.75%.

BUDGET

HI San Antonio Hostel (☎ 210-223-9426; 621 Pierce St; dm members/nonmembers $16/19, s/d $40/44; P) Located 2 miles north of the city center, this place is a good budget choice with a kitchen and common area. From downtown, head north to I-35 exit 159A, turn left, go to Grayson, turn left again and go two blocks to Pierce St.

Spartan (with a capital S) lodgings downtown include **Travelers Hotel** (☎ 210-226-4381; 220 N Broadway; s/d without bath $26/37, with bath $36/43), with cleanish rooms and the **Alpha Hotel** (☎ 210-223-7644; 315 N Main Ave; s/d $35/40 P), with worn rooms.

MID-RANGE

Arbor House Inn & Suites (☎ 210-472-2005, 888-272-6700; 540 S St Marys St; r from $125; P) With a great location near Riverwalk and the Alamo, this quirky-artsy piece of property has intimate rooms in four historic houses.

Red Roof Inn San Antonio Downtown (☎ 210-229-9973; 1011 E Houston St; r $60-95; P) This place is within walking distance of the Riverwalk.

Other recommendations:

La Quinta Market Sq (☎ 210-271-0001; 900 Dolorosa St; r from $90; P) Friendly atmosphere and continental breakfast is included.

Days Inn Alamo Riverwalk (☎ 210-227-6233; 902 E Houston St; r $75-95; P)

Downtowner Hotel (☎ 210-227-6233; 100 Starr St; r $65-85; P) Managed by the Days Inn, which is across the street.

TOP END

Menger Hotel (☎ 210-223-4361, 800-345-9285; 204 Alamo Plaza; r from $135; P) Downtown has several top-end hotels with historic style, but this old beauty, built in 1859, is the most famous. Legend has it that General Robert E Lee once rode his horse into the lobby.

Eating

Tip Top Cafe (☎ 210-732-0191; 2814 Fredericksburg Rd; mains $4-10) Low-budget gourmands will love this place between West Ave and Babcock Rd. The colossal chicken-fried steak is enough to make you weep, and the heaving plates of crunchy and enormous onion rings are just as spectacular.

Twin Sisters Bakery and Cafe (☎ 210-354-1559; 124 Broadway; mains $4-10) This healthy spot offers a large selection of vegetarian dishes for breakfast and lunch

La Fonda (☎ 210-733-0621; 2415 N Main Ave; mains $7-12) For authentic and lively Mexican food, head to this local institution in the beautiful Monte Vista Historic District.

Other recommendations:

Liberty Bar (☎ 210-227-1187; 328 E Josephine St; mains $5-10)

Josephine Street (☎ 210-224-6169; 400 E Josephine St; mains $8-14)

Biga on the Banks (☎ 210-225-0722; 203 S St Marys St; mains $17-35)

Drinking

Esquire (☎ 210-222-2521; 155 E Commerce St) Come here for cheap drinks, colorful regulars and the longest bar in Texas (or so they claim).

Menger Hotel Bar (☎ 210-223-4361; 204 Alamo Plaza) The bar is little but it's a great rainy-day hideaway with dark wood and subdued lighting.

Saint (☎ 210-225-7330; 1430 N Main St) This is the city's most popular gay bar.

CLEM LINDENMAYER

Lake McDonald, **Glacier National Park** (p780), Montana

Thermal activity, **Yellowstone National Park** (p765), Wyoming

CAROL POLICH

CAROL POLICH

Bighorn sheep, **Glacier National Park** (p780), Montana

Evening snow, **Jackson Hole** (p770), Wyoming

CHEYENNE ROUSE

RICHARD CUMMINS

Frozen stream, **Zion National Park** (p857), Utah

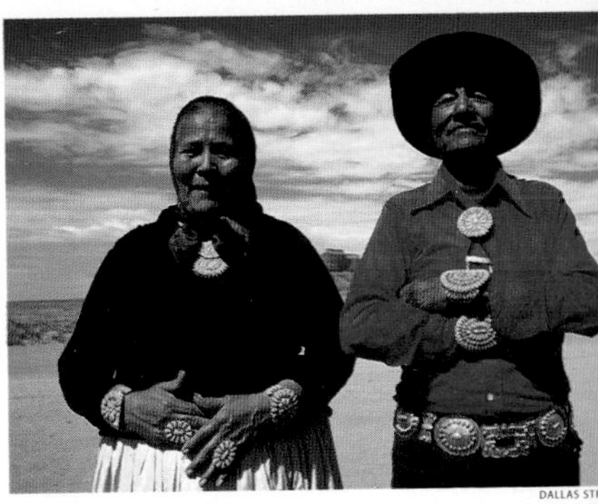

DALLAS ST

Navajo tribe members with **traditional jewelry** (p72)

ANDREW LEANNE WALKER

Adobe building (p70), Taos, Santa Fe

Las Vegas (p857), Nevada

RICHARD CU

Entertainment

Check the *Current* or the *Express-News* for listings of clubs, local music and cultural events.

LIVE MUSIC

Far West Rodeo (☎ 210-646-9378; 3030 NE Loop 410) This live music venue at the I-35/Loop 410 intersection has a huge country-music dance hall attracting big-name performers. It also features a mechanical bull and indoor pro rodeo.

Tequila Mockingbird (☎ 210-226-2473; 245 E Commerce St) This place is downtown, behind and underneath Planet Hollywood.

Landing Jazz Club (☎ 210-223-7266; 123 Losoya St) For a San Antonio tradition visit this jazz spot on the Riverwalk at the Hyatt Regency.

CINEMAS

AMC Rivercenter 9 (☎ 210-558-9988; 849 E Commerce St) Here you'll find mainstream movies in the center of downtown.

Regal Crossroads (☎ 210-333-3456; 4522 Fredericksburg Rd at Loop 410) Old and well worn, this is San Antonio's only theater showing foreign and indie films.

SPECTATOR SPORTS

The **San Antonio Spurs** (☎ 210-554-7787), the city's NBA basketball franchise, plays at the **SBC Center** (☎ 210-444-5000; SBC Center Parkway at Walters St off I-35). Tickets can be bought through **Ticketmaster** (☎ 210-224-9600; www.ticketmaster.com).

Getting There & Around

AIR

San Antonio International Airport (☎ 210-207-3411) is about 10 miles north of downtown, just north of the Loop 410/US 281 intersection. City buses (75¢) run to downtown San Antonio about every 45 minutes at peak times and far less frequently at other times. **SATrans** (☎ 210-281-9900) runs shuttle buses to downtown ($8). A cab to downtown will cost $15 to $17.

BUS

Greyhound (☎ 210-270-5824) and **Kerrville Bus Lines** (☎ 210-227-5669) share a terminal at 500 N St Mary's St downtown. Call for fares and schedules.

VIA (☎ 210-362-2020), San Antonio's city bus system, has a downtown information center at 260 E Houston St, where you can pick up a systemwide route map ($2). The company runs four handy streetcar routes across downtown (50¢ one way, $2 all day) about every 10 minutes.

CAR & MOTORCYCLE

San Antonio is a driving nightmare, and then you have to park, which is nearly impossible. Many downtown-area lodgings offer free guest parking. Otherwise, the metered spaces around Travis Park would be a good place to start looking. Major car rental agencies have offices at the airport and around town. Check p1121 for details.

TAXI

Taxi rates are $1.60 flag fall ($2.60 after 9pm) plus $1.50 per mile. The biggest company in town is **Yellow-Checker Taxi** (☎ 210-222-2222).

TRAIN

Amtrak's *Sunset Limited* and *Texas Eagle* trains stop at the beautiful **depot** (☎ 210-223-3226; 350 Hoefgen Ave), just east of I-37 north of the Alamodome.

HOUSTON & THE GULF COAST

America's 'Third Coast,' as folks there like to call it, is home to one of the country's most diverse cities (which is also one of its busiest) as well as a collection of pretty and relaxed small towns far from the rat race. If it's world-class dining or an exciting art scene you're after, head to Houston. A short drive from there is the Johnson Space Center, where all astronaut fantasies can be filled for a small fee. Further afield are country towns and long stretches of almost untouched beaches, islands and surf interspersed with coves, bayous, rivers and bays. Those wanting to pitch a tent on the beach, spot migrating birds and other wildlife, or simply relax at an ocean-front hotel could spend an eternity wandering these sands.

HOUSTON

Sprawling, congested and vibrant, the state's largest city, and the nation's fourth-largest, can be both maddening and exhilarating for the visitor. The traffic (and its attendant pollution) is some of the worst in the country

HOUSTON IN...

Two Days

Kick off the day with a hot cup o' Joe at one of the **Montrose District's** cool coffee shops, then head to the nearby **Museum District** to take a peek at the **Menil Collection** and the **Museum of Fine Arts**.

For dinner, splurge at the illuminating **Cafe Annie** and see a Broadway play in the **Theater District** before spoiling yourself for a night at the luscious chateaulike mansion **La Colombe d'Or**.

Day two should include a drive through the old money **River Oaks** neighborhood, followed by shopping and a stroll around **Rice Village**, lunch at **Goode Co Barbecue** on Kirby, dinner at Montrose's **La Mexicana**, drinks downtown at **Market Sq** and some live music at one of Houston's many clubs.

Four Days

Follow the two day itinerary, then on your third day head 30 minutes south to Clear Lake and the **Johnson Space Center** for a gander at the Apollo rockets and the nation's space program. On the fourth day, take a trip to the **Cockrell Butterfly Center** and the **Museum of Natural Science** before having a relaxing stroll through the Central Park–like **Hermann Park**.

and in the summer the heat and humidity can be downright oppressive. But Houston has air conditioning aplenty along with a youthful and ebullient population, one of the best art collections in the country and the most accomplished culinary scene in Texas.

History

Houston was founded in 1836 by shipping merchants Augustus and John Allen. In 1914 construction on the Houston Ship Channel was completed and the city became the state's oil export capital. US government contracts helped develop Houston's petrochemical and petroleum industries, making the city one of the wealthiest energy exporters in the world by the 1970s. A glut on the world market sent oil prices plummeting and by the mid-'80s the economy hit rock bottom, turning downtown Houston into a veritable ghost town. Since then, Houston's economy has diversified into medical services and high-tech industries (including aerospace and computer-related industries), and the city is again oozing big bucks from every pore.

Orientation

Houston's street names can be very confusing. Most have no official suffix such as St, Rd, Ave etc and many can have several different names all together. Furthermore, there is no official boundary between north and south or east and west designations on streets. You're going to need a good map.

In general, the most interesting areas of town are within a rectangle in the city center. Westheimer is the main east–west artery and heading east it will take you from I-610 West and shopping paradise at the Galleria mall, past wealthy River Oaks, on through the shop-heavy Upper Kirby District, past eclectic Montrose and (as Elgin St) on to Main St. The distance is roughly 6 miles.

Main St starts downtown near Market Sq, where there's an up-and-coming collection of bars, nightclubs and restaurants, and heads south to the Museum District, Hermann Park, the Texas Medical Center and on to the behemoth Reliant Stadium. This is also the route for the brand new Houston Metro light-rail line (see p662).

Information

Much of central Houston uses the original ☎713 area code. Other local area codes currently include ☎281 and ☎832. New phone numbers may be assigned any one of these area codes without regard to geography, so you always have to dial all ten digits.

BOOKSTORES

Bookstop (Map p655; ☎713-529-2345; 2922 South Shepherd Dr) A biggie located in the beautiful old Alabama movie theater.

Brazos Bookstore (Map p655; ☎713-523-0701; 2421 Bissonnet) Indie store with occasional poetry readings and book signings.

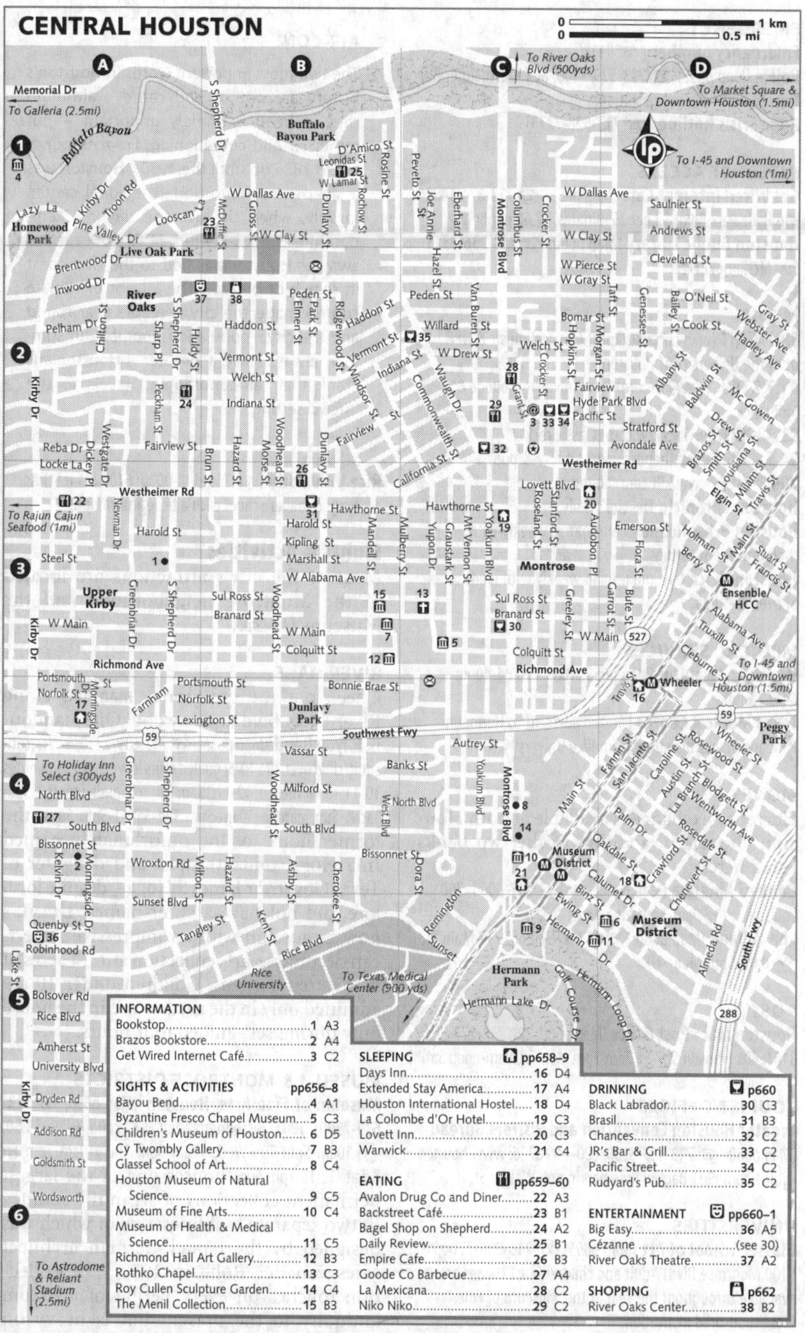
CENTRAL HOUSTON
0 1 km
0 0.5 mi
To River Oaks Blvd (500yds)
To Market Square & Downtown Houston (1.5mi)
To I-45 and Downtown Houston (1mi)
Memorial Dr
To Galleria (2.5mi)
Buffalo Bayou
Buffalo Bayou Park
Homewood Park
Live Oak Park
River Oaks
To Rajun Cajun Seafood (1mi)
Upper Kirby
Montrose
Ensemble/HCC
Wheeler
To I-45 and Downtown Houston (1.5mi)
Dunlavy Park
Southwest Fwy
Peggy Park
To Holiday Inn Select (300yds)
Museum District
Hermann Park
Rice University
To Texas Medical Center (900 yds)
To Astrodome & Reliant Stadium (2.5mi)
INFORMATION
Bookstop....................1 A3
Brazos Bookstore....................2 A4
Get Wired Internet Café....................3 C2
SIGHTS & ACTIVITIES pp656–8
Bayou Bend....................4 A1
Byzantine Fresco Chapel Museum....5 C3
Children's Museum of Houston....... 6 D5
Cy Twombly Gallery....................7 B3
Glassel School of Art....................8 C4
Houston Museum of Natural Science....................9 C5
Museum of Fine Arts.................... 10 C4
Museum of Health & Medical Science....................11 C5
Richmond Hall Art Gallery....................12 B3
Rothko Chapel....................13 C3
Roy Cullen Sculpture Garden....................14 C4
The Menil Collection....................15 B3
SLEEPING pp658–9
Days Inn....................16 D4
Extended Stay America....................17 A4
Houston International Hostel....................18 D4
La Colombe d'Or Hotel....................19 C3
Lovett Inn....................20 C3
Warwick....................21 C4
EATING pp659–60
Avalon Drug Co and Diner....................22 A3
Backstreet Café....................23 B1
Bagel Shop on Shepherd....................24 A2
Daily Review....................25 B1
Empire Cafe....................26 B3
Goode Co Barbecue....................27 A4
La Mexicana....................28 C2
Niko Niko....................29 C2
DRINKING p660
Black Labrador....................30 C3
Brasil....................31 B3
Chances....................32 C2
JR's Bar & Grill....................33 C2
Pacific Street....................34 C2
Rudyard's Pub....................35 C2
ENTERTAINMENT pp660–1
Big Easy....................36 A5
Cézanne....................(see 30)
River Oaks Theatre....................37 A2
SHOPPING p662
River Oaks Center....................38 B2

TEXAS

EMERGENCY

Emergency number (☎ 911)
Police (Map p655; ☎ 713-529-3100; 802 Westheimer Rd) Twenty-four-hour police station.
Rape crisis hotline (☎ 713-528-7273)

INTERNET ACCESS

Get Wired Internet Cafe (Map p655; ☎ 713-874-1482; 816 Hyde Park Blvd) $2 per 15 minutes, $7.50 per hour.
Houston Public Library (Map p660; ☎ 713-236-1313; 500 McKinney) Free.

MEDIA

88.7 KUHT (www.uh.edu/kuht) Classical music & NPR from the University of Houston.
91.7 KTRU (www.ktru.org) Rice University college & indie rock.
93.7 KKRW (www.kkrw.com) Classic rock.
94.5 KTBZ (www.thebuzz.com) Alt rock & pop.
100.3 KILT (www.kilt.com) Country.
Houston Chronicle The city's daily.
Houston Press Houston's alternative weekly with thorough event listings.
Houston Voice Gay and lesbian weekly with loads of event listings.

MEDICAL SERVICES

Hermann Hospital (Map p655; ☎ 713-704-4000; 6411 Fanin)
Texas Medical Center Located adjacent to Hermann Park and across the street from Rice University.

MONEY

Currency exchange is available at both Houston airports in addition to the two banks listed here.

Bank of America (Map p660; ☎ 713-247-6000; 700 Louisiana; ⏲ 9am-5pm Mon-Fri)
Chase Bank (Map p660; ☎ 713-216-4865; 712 Main St; ⏲ 8am-5pm Mon-Fri)

POST

Houston Main Post Office (Map p660; ☎ 713-226-3161; 401 Franklin St; ⏲ 7am-7pm Mon-Fri, 8am-noon Sat)

TOURIST OFFICES

Greater Houston Convention and Visitors Bureau (Map p660; ☎ 713-437-5200, 800-446-8786; www.houston-guide.com; 901 Bagby) Free parking on Walker St.

UNIVERSITIES

Glassel School of Art (Map p655; ☎ 713-639-7700; 5100 Montrose Blvd) Adult and children's art classes are available throughout the year at this Museum of Fine Arts–sponsored institution.

> **AIR-CON**
>
> The two most important words in Houston's history are not oil and cattle – although they've been extremely important – but rather 'air' and 'conditioning.' From its founding in 1836 up until the 1930s, Houston was a sleepy, mosquito-ridden regional center. In July, when the average daytime temperature is a sweltering 94°F, work melted away as Houstonians fled to the Gulf coast in search of breezes. The advent of climate control made the city bearable year round and the city's population boomed. (In summer, always carry a sweater – Houstonians crank their air-conditioning levels to the 'Arctic' setting.)

Rice University (☎ 713-348-0000; 6100 Main St) An ivy-league caliber school with a beautiful campus.

Sights & Activities

Most of the city's attractions are located in the Montrose neighborhood and the Museum District.

RIVER OAKS

Check out the old-money **mansions** along River Oaks Blvd and Inwood. One standout is **Bayou Bend** (Map p655; ☎ 713-639-7750; 1 Westcott; adult/child over 10 $10/5; guided tours leave every 15 minutes 10-11:30am Tue-Fri, 10-11:15am Sat; self guided tours 1-5pm Sat & Sun; garden 10am-5pm Tue-Sat, 1-5pm Sun), the former home of the unfortunately named Ima Hogg, philanthropist and daughter of Texas Governor James S Hogg – despite local lore, did not have a sister named Ura. It's now a museum with an impressive American decorative-arts collection and 14 acres of manicured gardens. Children under 10 are admitted only in the garden and in the house only during self-guided tour hours.

MUSEUM & MONTROSE DISTRICTS

Museum of Fine Arts, Houston (Map p655; ☎ 713-639-7300; 1001 Bissonnet; adult $7, child 6-18 $3.50; ⏲ 10am-5pm Tue-Wed, 10am-9pm Thu, 10am-7pm Fri & Sat, 12:15-7pm Sun) houses one of the largest permanent collections of art in the country in two separate buildings, one of which was designed by the famed German architect Mies van der Rohe in 1958. The collection touches on every period of art from antiquity to the present but is heavy on

French Impressionism, photography, and post-1945 European and American paintings and sculpture. Admission is free every Thursday. Across the street, the excellent **Roy Cullen Sculpture Garden** (Map p655) holds works by Rodin, Matisse and others.

If you're looking for dinosaur skeletons and other wonders of the natural world, check out the **Houston Museum of Natural Science** (HMNS; Map p655; ☎ 713-639-4629; 1 Hermann Circle; adult $6, child 3-11 $3.50; 9am-6pm Mon-Sat, 11am-6pm Sun), another fine museum located in Hermann Park next to the equestrian statue of Sam Houston. In addition to the permanent exhibits (which are free after 2pm on Tuesdays), the HMNS also has a **planetarium** (adult $5, child 3-11 $3.50; noon-5:30pm); an **Imax theater** (adult $7, child 3-11 $3.50; 10am-6pm Mon-Thu, 10am-8pm Fri & Sat, 11am-6pm Sun); and the **Cockrell Butterfly Center** (adult $5, child 3-11 $3.50; 9am-6pm Mon-Sat, 11am-6pm Sun), a three-story dome where you can walk among thousands of butterflies.

In Montrose, the outstanding **Menil Collection** (Map p655; ☎ 713-525-9400; 1515 Sul Ross St; admission free; 11am-7pm Wed-Sun) contains several rooms devoted to surrealists, including René Magritte and Max Ernst. Nearby, two annexes – the **Cy Twombly Gallery** (Map p655; ☎ 713-525-9450; 1501 Branard St; admission free; 11am-7pm Wed-Sun) and **Richmond Hall** (Map p655; ☎ 713-525-8512; 1500 Richmond Ave; admission free; 11am-7pm Wed-Sun) – house permanent works by the abstract artist Cy Twombly and the minimalist fluorescent-light sculptor Dan Flavin.

Also, a block east of the main museum, the Menil has created two meditative sanctuaries in the **Rothko Chapel** (Map p655 ☎ 713-524-9839; 3900 Yupon St; admission free; 10am-6pm) and the **Byzantine Fresco Chapel Museum** (Map p655; ☎ 713-521-3990; 4011 Yupon St; admission free; 11am-6pm Fri-Sun). The first holds 14 large paintings by the American abstract expressionist Mark Rothko and the second contains stunning 13th-century frescoes that arrived from Cyprus under Maltese Falcon-esque circumstances.

OTHER ATTRACTIONS

The aging **Astrodome** (8400 Kirby), built in 1963 and once billed as the eighth wonder of the world, now sits in a state of limbo after its last big tenant – the Houston Livestock Show and Rodeo – moved out in 2003. Many Houstonians fear the dome may not be much longer for this world. To get an idea of how far sports stadiums have come since 1963, look next door at **Reliant Park**. It's the home field for the new Houston Texans NFL-football franchise and, at the time of writing, was slated to play host to Super Bowl XXVIII in 2004. Opposite, the theme park **Six Flags AstroWorld** (☎ 713-799-1234; 9001 Kirby; adult/child under 48in tall $39/24; 10am-10pm Sat-Sun) features killer coasters and thrill rides, while affiliated **WaterWorld** (☎ 713-799-1234; 9001 Kirby; adult/child under 48in tall $39/24; 11am-6pm Sat & Sun) provides slides, pools, beaches and other watery pleasures. A two-day ticket good for both parks costs $47.

Houston for Children

Finding something for the youngsters to do is not hard to do in **Hermann Park** (Map p655; ☎ 713-524-5876; www.hermannpark.org; 600 Fanin), which has playgrounds, an 8 acre lake, train and boat rides and the revitalized **Houston Zoo** (☎ 713-533-6500; 1513 N MacGregor, in Hermann Park; adult $5, child 3-12 $2; 10am-6pm). Out front of the zoo is the **Herman Park Miniature Train** (☎ 713-529-5216; $2; 10am-5pm), which leaves the station every 30 minutes, and the **Hermann Park Pedal Boats** (☎ 713-524-5876; half-hour hire $7; 1pm-dusk Tue-Fri, 10am-dusk Sat & Sun), which can be used to explore the 8 acre **McGovern Lake**.

Nearby, kids will love the hands-on exhibits at the **Children's Museum of Houston** (Map p655; ☎ 713-522-1138; 1500 Binz; admission $5; 9am-5pm Tue-Sat, 9am-8pm Thu, noon-5pm Sun), which is free after 5pm on Thursdays. A block away at the **Museum of Health and Medical Science** (Map p655; ☎ 713-521-1515; 1515 Hermann; adult $5, child 4-12 $2; 9am-5pm Tue-Sat, noon-5pm Sun) kids will love the huge interactive models of human innards, including a giant walk-through heart, lung and, yes, colon...'eww, gross!'

If that doesn't cool them down, head to the indoor **Galleria Ice Skating Center** (☎ 713-621-1500; 5015 Westheimer Rd; admission $6, skate rental $3; noon-5pm & 8pm-10pm Mon-Thu, noon-10pm Fri, 12:30pm-10pm Sat, noon-6pm & 8pm-10pm Sun), which is located inside the Galleria shopping mall (see p662).

Quirky Houston

Evidence of Houston's endearing eccentricity is apparent in several ways around town, none more so than at the **Orange Show Foundation** (☎ 713-926-6368; 2402 Munger St;

GAY & LESBIAN HOUSTON

Houston, and specifically Montrose, has been the region's gathering place for gay men and women for decades. Today, the gay community is involved with many aspects of city life from the local art scene to state and national politics. Every June the **Pride Committee of Houston** (☎ 713-529-6979; www.pridehouston.org) hosts a gay pride parade, the pinnacle of gay and lesbian celebration in Texas, with visitors arriving from all over the state.

Gay-friendly B&Bs include the **Lovett Inn** (Map p655; ☎ 713-522-5224; www.lovettinn.com; 501 Lovett Blvd; r $75-175;), which occupies a large, stately home in Montrose.

Montrose-area gay-and-lesbian clubs include the popular **Pacific Street** (Map p655; ☎ 713-523-0213; 710 Pacific St) and **JR's Bar & Grill** (Map p655; ☎ 713-521-2519; 808 Pacific St), where 'happy hour' lasts almost all day. **Chances** (Map p655; ☎ 713-523-7217; 1100 Westheimer Rd) is a popular lesbian bar with dancing until 2am.

admission free; Mar-Dec noon-5pm Sat-Sun, Memorial Day–Labor Day 9am-1pm Wed-Fri, noon-5pm Sat-Sun), an outrageously creative folk-art gallery south of downtown that was hand built by the late postal worker Jeff McKissack over a span of 22 years. In addition to putting on films, lectures, workshops and performances, the foundation also curates the **Beer Can House** (222 Malone St), a house and folk-art sculpture made out of 50,000 beer cans, and the **Flower Man House** (3311 Sampson St), another paean to the folk-art gods. The Orange Show also sponsors the **Art Car Weekend**, two days when hundreds of painted, altered, augmented and plain wacky automobiles from around the country descend Sturgis-style upon Houston. The annual weekend culminates in the truly magnificent **Art Car Parade** on the second Sunday in May. If you miss the festivities, head to the **Art Car Museum** (☎ 713-861-5526; 140 Heights Blvd; admission free; 11am-6pm Wed-Sun), an unaffiliated repository for more zany art on wheels.

Tours

Gray Line (☎ 866-767-9850; www.grayline.com; adult $25-75, child $12-35) has bus tours hitting all the major districts in town as well as tours that will take you to the Johnson Space Center and Galveston.

Festivals & Events

February in Houston is rodeo time when the **Houston Livestock Show & Rodeo** rolls into Reliant Stadium. It bills itself as 'The World's Largest Rodeo' and draws more than a million visitors every year.

May brings the **Orange Show Art Car Weekend**, a wild and wonderful parade of dolled up autos (see above) while in June it's time for the **Westheimer Street Festival**, a weekend gathering of artisans, parades and superb people-watching along Westheimer St in the heart of Montrose.

Sleeping

Houston's hotel tax is a whopping 17%.

BUDGET

Houston International Hostel (Map p655; ☎ 713-523-1009; 5302 Crawford; dm $14;) As comfortable as a favorite old slipper gently chewed by the dog, this hostel is near the Museum District.

Low-budget digs with good locations near downtown and Montrose are also available at the **YMCA** (☎ 713-659-8501; 1600 Louisiana; r $23-32; P) and at **Days Inn** (Map p655; ☎ 713-523-3777; 4640 S Main St; s/d $54/60; P). Be advised, however, that the Days Inn is right next to US59 and it can be loud.

MID-RANGE

Holiday Inn Select (☎ 713-523-8448; 2712 Southwest Fwy; r Mon-Fri $140, r Sat & Sun $70; P) This upscale version of the chain hotel is a refreshing change from the normal roadside stop. It's right next to Upper Kirby and not far from the Museum District.

Close by are **La Quinta Inn Astrodome** (☎ 713-668-8082; 9911 Buffalo Speedway; r $77-87; P), with big rooms, and **Extended Stay America** (Map p655; ☎ 713-521-0060; 2330 Southwest Fwy; s/d $60/80, weekly $320/370; P). You won't be surprised by either but the staff in both are friendly and the locations are right on.

The following are also recommended:

Crowne Plaza Hotel – Medical Center (☎ 713-797-1110; 6701 S Main St; r from $130; P) 128 rooms in a great location near Hermann Park and the museums.

JW Marriott Hotel (☎ 713-961-1500; 5150 Westheimer; r from $100; P ✕ 💻 ♿) Shopping and dropping distance from the Galleria.

TOP END

Warwick (Map p655; ☎ 713-526-1991, 800-670-7275; 5701 Main St; Mon-Fri r from $160, Sat & Sun r from $130 P ✕ 💻 ♿) This elegant 1920s-era hotel behind the Museum of Fine Arts has large rooms with comfy beds, complimentary robes and good-sized bathtubs. The standard weekend rates are great value.

Eating

You could gain some serious weight on a gastronome's tour of Houston, home to the largest and most varied collection of restaurants in the state. Cooks from every corner of the world prepare their home-country recipes here. The local favorites listed here are the first course.

MUSEUM DISTRICT & MONTROSE

Daily Review (Map p655; ☎ 713-520-9217; 3412 West Lamar St; dishes $9-15) There's charming and abundant outdoor seating and a cozy indoors at this artsy back-street bistro. The healthy home cooking (it's true) is progressive and creative. Try the chicken pot pie.

La Mexicana (Map p655; ☎ 713-521-0963; 1018 Fairview; dishes $6-17) The frozen margaritas in this neighborhood favorite could very well be the best in town and the quesadillas in homemade flour tortillas, with or without the marinated fajita meat, are absolute heaven.

THE AUTHOR'S CHOICE

La Colombe d'Or (Map p655; ☎ 713-524-7999; 3410 Montrose Blvd; r $195-275; P ✕) Stepping into this charming old-world mansion is like stepping into a chateau in the middle of Provence. Each of the six suitelike rooms are large and luscious and draped in museum-quality antiques and rare oil paintings. There are sitting areas, spacious bathrooms and private dining rooms in each, and the staff is warm and attentive to every detail. Downstairs is a cozy and elegant walnut-paneled bar, a stately library and a gourmet restaurant serving superb southern French cuisine.

The following are also recommended:

Niko Niko (Map p655; ☎ 713-528-1308; 2520 Montrose; dishes $5-13) Houstonians regularly line up for kabobs and falafel here.

Empire Cafe (Map p655; ☎ 713-528-5282; 1732 Westheimer; dishes $6-11) Hip urban coffee shop and good people-watching.

Brasil (Map p655; ☎ 713-528-1993; 2604 Dunlavy; dishes $5-8) Another great place for coffee.

UPPER KIRBY

Goode Co Barbecue (Map p655; ☎ 713-522-2530; 5109 Kirby Dr; dishes $4-10) For the best 'cue in town follow the sound of Bob Wills' high-pitched croon and the smoky smell of burning mesquite wood to this Houston favorite.

Avalon Drug Co and Diner (Map p655; ☎ 713-527-8900; 2417 Westheimer Rd; dishes $3-7) This throwback soda shop and breakfast diner has been a morning favorite for River Oaks families since 1938.

RIVER OAKS

Backstreet Cafe (Map p655; ☎ 713-521-2239; 1103 S Shepherd) This longtime favorite in River Oaks was voted 'Best Alfresco Dining' in a *Houston Press* readers' poll. It serves excellent soups, salads and sandwiches on a flower-filled patio.

Bagel Shop On Shepherd (Map p655; ☎ 713-520-0340; 2009 S Shepherd Dr; dishes $2.50-4; cash only) This small and simple local shop serves a dozen different kinds of fresh bagels every morning to a regularly packed house.

DOWNTOWN

Solero (Map p660; ☎ 713-227-2665; 910 Prairie Ave; dishes $4-19) At 10:30pm Friday and Saturday nights at this stylish tapas restaurant, the staff push the tables aside, crank up the merengue and salsa dancers sweat into the wee hours.

Kaveh Kanes Coffee (Map p660; ☎ 713-236-0411; 912 Prairie Ave; 💻) Next door to Solero, this eclectic coffee shop serves a big selection of coffee and tea drinks along with regular poetry readings and the occasional live jazz band.

CHINATOWN

Kim Son (Map p660; ☎ 713-222-2461; 2001 Jefferson St & 300 Milam; dishes $6-19) This legendary restaurant is run by the La family, who escaped in a boat from Vietnam in 1979. The 280-item menu ranges from rice-noodle soup to jellyfish and lotus root.

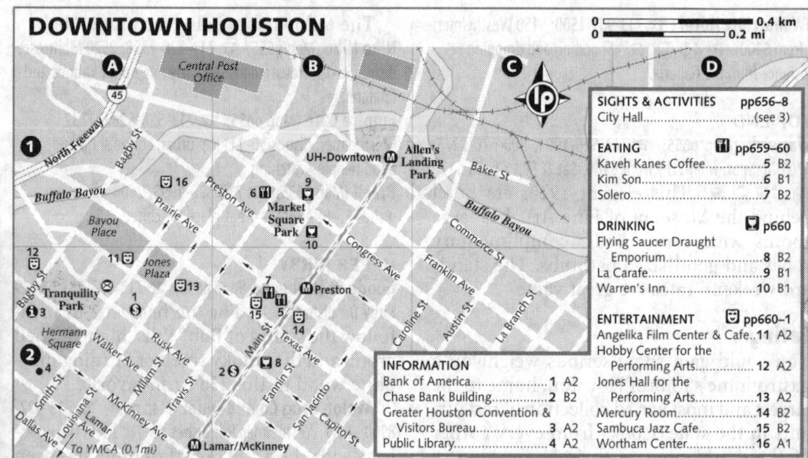

RICHMOND & THE GALLERIA

Rajun Cajun Seafood (☎ 713-623-6321; 4302 Richmond; dishes $6-14) For a big, fun time eatin' gumbo, étouffée or a big pile of boiled crawfish, come here to rub elbows with the locals at the long community tables.

Hunan (☎ 713-965-0808; 1800 Post Oak Blvd; dishes $13-19) Former president George Bush (Dubya's dad) and wife Barbara are regulars here, where they rave about their dim sum.

Drinking

La Carafe (Map p660; ☎ 713-229-9399; 813 Congress Ave) Housed in Houston's oldest building right on Market Sq, this narrow candlelit wine bar is one of the city's most beloved hideaways.

Warren's Inn (Map p660; ☎ 713-247-9207; 307 Travis St) Also on Market Sq is this spot whose now-deceased original owner – Warren – was a boyfriend of the late great Liberace. Evidence of Warren's flamboyant tastes remains in the blood-red paint, the Louis XIV–style floor-to-ceiling mirrors and the stiff cocktails.

Ginger Man (☎ 713-526-2770; 5607 Morningside) Popular with beer connoisseurs, this Rice Village pub has 69 beers on tap, and has been a favorite for Rice University students for at least two decades. It has a festive beer garden out back and the jukebox is a winner.

Black Labrador (Map p655; ☎ 713-529-1199; 4100 Montrose St) This European-style pub has an upscale atmosphere, British pub fare and the requisite pints of Guinness and Bass.

The following are also recommended:

Harp (☎ 713-528-7827; 1625 Richmond Ave) A lovely low-key neighborhood Irish pub between Montrose and Upper Kirby.

Flying Saucer Draught Emporium (Map p660; ☎ 713-228-9472; 705 Main St) An enormous place with 85 taps.

Entertainment

Houston has never been a town with an entertainment district like Dallas' Deep Ellum or Austin's 6th Street, but the area around Market Sq in downtown – easily accessible by the Main St light-rail line – is definitely headed that way. But no matter where you are, Houston's nightlife is happening and whatever your style, the city has someplace for you to step out at night. Check out the weekly *Houston Press* or the alternative *Houston's Other* for comprehensive club listings.

NIGHTCLUBS

Mercury Room (Map p660; ☎ 713-225-6372; 1008 Prairie) Downtown's upscale art deco hangout with a trendy crowd, DJs and live entertainment.

Blanco's (☎ 713-439-0072; 3406 W Alabama) There's Lone Star and two-steppin' at this authentic country bar.

Elvia's International (☎ 713-266-9631; 2727 Fondren) This spot offers live music and dancing to wild Latin rhythms.

LIVE MUSIC

Continental Club (☎ 713-529-9899; 3700 Main St)

This is the number two location of Austin's famed live-music venue, and it hasn't missed a beat with top-notch blues, swing and rockabilly at least five nights a week.

Cézanne (☎ 713-522-9621; 4100 Montrose St) This cozy spot, located above the Black Labrador (see Drinking, opposite), offers really superb live jazz.

Sambuca Jazz Cafe (Map p660; ☎ 713-224-5299; 900 Texas Ave) Downtown in the Rice Hotel, this suave spot is a supper club serving Mediterranean cuisine and live jazz nightly.

For down-and-out 12-bar blues, try the **Big Easy** (Map p655; ☎ 713-523-9999; 5731 Kirby), the **Shakespeare Pub** (☎ 281-497-4625; 14129 Memorial) or **Dan Electro's Guitar Bar** (☎ 713-862-8707; 1031 E 24th St), which hosts a Thursday-night blues jam.

The following are also recommended:

Rudyard's Pub (Map p655; ☎ 713-521-0521; 2010 Waugh Dr) A local institution with live local music five nights a week.

Engine Room (☎ 713-654-7846; 1515 Pease) A great place to catch local rock acts.

Fitzgerald's (☎ 713-862-3838; 2706 White Oak) Alternative live bands.

Fabulous Satellite Lounge (☎ 713-869-2665; 3616 Washington Ave) Regularly has a big name bill.

CLASSICAL PERFORMANCE

Houston Symphony (Map p660; ☎ 713-224-7575; 615 Louisiana) For live classical music see the symphony at Jones Hall.

The **Houston Grand Opera** and **Houston Ballet** (Map p660; ☎ 713-227-2787, 800-828-2787 for both; 500 Texas Ave) both play at the beautiful Wortham Center.

> **THE AUTHOR'S CHOICE**
>
> **Cafe Annie** (☎ 713-840-1111; 1728 Post Oak Blvd; mains $27-40) Ranked as one of the country's top 50 restaurants by *Gourmet* magazine, this romantic fine-dining spot near the Galleria has all the makings of a special night out. Not only is the Southwestern cuisine out of this world, but the atmosphere is elegant and fun. Menu highlights include a Muscovy duck confit crepe appetizer drizzled with a smoked black chili and raisin sauce followed by a watercress salad tossed with pears and Roquefort cheese and topped off with a cinnamon roasted pheasant in a red chili pecan sauce. Need we say more?

CINEMAS

River Oaks Theatre (Map p655; ☎ 713-524-2175; 2009 West Gray St) This landmark theater is one of Houston's long-favorite art houses.

Angelika Film Center (Map p660; ☎ 713-225-5232; 510 Texas St) Head downtown for a mix of first-run, foreign and indie films.

THEATER

Downtown is home to the **Theater District**, centered around the **Bayou Place entertainment complex** (Map p660; Texas Ave at Smith). The complex holds clubs, restaurants, and the Aerial Theater, a prime concert venue. Several other theaters and the impressive new **Hobby Center for the Performing Arts** are nearby.

Aerial Theater (☎ 713-230-1600; 520 Texas Ave) This is a major venue for popular music and entertainment.

Alley Theatre (☎ 713-228-8421; 615 Texas Ave) The Alley, as it's known locally, presents first-rate drama with many first-run Broadway and off-Broadway shows making their way here.

Society for the Performing Arts (☎ 713-227-4772) Located in the spiffy new Hobby Center for the Performing Arts, on Bagby, this group produces Broadway musicals.

Theatre Under the Stars (☎ 800-678-5440) This acclaimed theater also claims the Hobby Center as its home venue.

Miller Outdoor Theatre (☎ 713-284-8350; 100 Concert Dr) For more drama alfresco, Hermann Park's outdoor theater is a great place to lay out a blanket on a summer night and take in a free performance.

SPECTATOR SPORTS

Houston Astros (☎ 713-259-8000) The Astros play pro baseball downtown at Minute Maid Park, 501 Crawford.

Houston Rockets (☎ 713-627-3865) This men's basketball team bounced into a new $200 million arena at Bell Ave and La Branch St for the 2003–4 season.

Houston Comets (☎ 713-627-9622) The women's basketball team also bounced into the new arena for the 2003–4 season.

Houston Aeros (☎ 713-627-2376) The IHL hockey team has its home ice at Compaq Center, Greenway Plaza, just off the Southwest Fwy.

Houston Texans (☎ 877-635-2002) This NFL franchise calls Reliant Park home.

Shopping

The biggest collection of shops in Houston are located in and around the **Galleria** (5075 Westheimer Rd) at the corner of Westheimer and Post Oak just off Loop 610. There you'll find everything from Baby Gap to Tiffany's along with a bevy of restaurants, two hotels and an ice-skating rink.

For smaller crowds (and easier parking) head to the **River Oaks Shopping Center** (Map p655), located along West Gray between Shepherd and Woodhead or make your way south down Kirby Dr near Rice University to **Rice Village**, known locally as simply 'the Village,' a good place to explore on foot.

A dense collection of **antique stores** can be found on Westheimer Rd at Woodhead.

Getting There & Away

AIR

George Bush Intercontinental Airport (IAH; ☎ 281-230-3100), 22 miles north of city center, is served by major domestic and inter national airlines. **William P Hobby Airport** (HOU; ☎ 713-640-3000) is a major domestic hub.

BUS

Greyhound buses arrive at the **Houston Bus Terminal** (☎ 713-759-6565, 2121 Main St), located between downtown and the Museum District. Call for fares and schedules.

TRAIN

Amtrak's *Sunset Limited,* which serves New Orleans (from $71) and Orlando (from $150) to the east and San Antonio (from $45), El Paso (from $138), Tucson (from $227) and Los Angeles (from $258) to the west, stops at the **downtown depot** (☎ 713-224-1577; 902 Washington Ave).

Getting Around

Getting around sprawling Houston is not for the weak at heart. The bus system is unreliable at best and driving even the shortest distances once the bus arrives can take up a lot of time as you sit in traffic. A good option is the new traffic-free (and therefore reliable) light-rail line. However, its service is limited to Main St between downtown and Reliant Park. For those on a short time schedule, it's almost essential to rent a car, even though the city's seven-lane freeways will test the will of anyone who doesn't have Nascar racing credentials.

BUS

Houston's Metropolitan Transit Authority or **Metro** (☎ 713-635-4000; www.ridemetro.org) runs a network of bus lines throughout Houston. Weekend service is sketchy. Standard fare is $1 or $2 for a day pass. A free trolley system serves downtown. Bus No 102 ($1.50) runs between IAH airport and downtown daily. Bus No 88 ($1) serves HOU airport twice in the morning and twice in late afternoon (weekdays only).

Express Shuttle USA (☎ 713-523-8888) offers van service from both IAH ($19) and HOU ($14) airports.

CAR & MOTORCYCLE

Every major rental agency can be found at either airport and at offices throughout town. Check p1121 for details.

TAXI

Cab rates are $3 flag fall and $1.50 for each additional mile. Note that given Houston's sprawl, your cab tab can quickly surpass car rental rates. You must call for a cab; companies include **United** (☎ 713-699-0000) and **Yellow** (☎ 713-236-1111). A taxi to IAH/HOU airports from downtown runs about $35/20.

TRAIN

Metro is Houston's brand new **MetroRail** light-rail line, which runs 7.5 miles along Main St from Reliant Park to downtown's University of Houston campus. Trains run about every 10 minutes and cost $1.

AROUND HOUSTON

One site you don't want to miss on a trip to Houston is NASA's world-famous Johnson Space Center, 25 minutes south of town on I-45. While you're in the area there are a few other attractions that make for a good day trip.

San Jacinto

The Texas War for Independence was won at the Battle of San Jacinto, where General Sam Houston finally defeated Mexican general Antonio López de Santa Anna in 1836. At **San Jacinto Battleground State Historical Complex** (☎ 281-479-2421; 3523 State Hwy 134, La Porte; admission free; 🕑 8am-7pm) more than 1000 acres of the battleground are preserved. The complex includes the 570ft **San Jacinto Monument** (admission free; 🕑 8am-6pm), which has an observation deck (adult/child $3/2); the **San Jacinto Museum of History** (admission free; 8am-6pm); and the vintage 1914 **Battleship Texas** (adult $5, child 6-18 $3; 10am-5pm), a veteran of both World Wars.

Johnson Space Center

One of the state's most popular tourist destinations, the space center is 25 miles southeast of downtown Houston. To check out the interesting, if overly-sponsored and overly-hyped history of the nation's space program, head to the official NASA visitors center: the **Space Center Houston** (☎ 281-244-2100; 1601 NASA Rd 1; adult $17, child 4-11 $13; 10am-5pm Mon-Fri, 10am-6pm Sat & Sun, later Jun-Aug), where you will find lunar landers, moon buggies, space suits and all the rest of it. To see the actual Johnson Space Center and its shuttle training facilities, zero-gravity labs, mission control and the NASA hardware at **Rocket Park**; you have to take a tram tour, which is included in the admission fee and leaves every 20 minutes. Parking at the Space Center costs $4. It is possible to drive yourself to Rocket Park for free, but because of the heightened security after September 11 the fence line is as close as you'll get. Take I-45 to the NASA Rd 1 exit and drive east.

Clear Lake

Restaurants galore overlook the water and the parades of billowing sails at this happy-go-lucky spot while margarita bars play Jimmy Buffet into the wee hours for the perennially shorts-clad crowd. The **NASA/Clear Lake Convention and Visitors Bureau** (☎ 281-338-0333, 800-844-5253; www.nasaclearlaketexas.com; Suite 40, 20710 I-45, Webster; 9am-5pm Mon-Fri) has a great website with information about the area, including event and festival listings.

Also interesting is **Armand Bayou Nature Center** (☎ 281-474-2551; 8500 Bay Area Blvd; admission $3; 9am-5pm Tue-Sat, noon-5pm Sun), a pristine 2500-acre nature preserve with trails, exhibits and guided canoe trips. Out on Galveston Bay, touristy **Kemah Boardwalk** (☎ 877-285-3624; Bradford at 2nd Sts) beckons with shops, restaurants and amusement-park rides.

GALVESTON

Sultry, genteel Galveston is as close as you'll get in Texas to the Deep South. The city has an odd mix of beautifully restored Victorian mansions in historic neighborhoods side by side with crumbling row houses. Even so, this town has a sensuality found nowhere else in the state.

Memories of the 1900 hurricane that took 6000 lives, the country's worst natural disaster ever, run deep. But Galveston knows how to party, and its Mardi Gras festivities are the state's biggest.

Orientation & Information

Galveston Island is 30 miles long and no more than 3 miles wide. Seawall Blvd (also known as simply 'the seawall') follows the gulf shore for more than 10 miles; the Strand centers the city's historic downtown along the ship channel. Both areas are usually safe, but be wary west of 25th St and a block or two north of Seawall.

The local **Galveston Island Visitors Center** (☎ 409-763-4311, 888-425-4753; www.galvestoncvb.com; 2428 Seawall) provides visitor information. **Rosenberg Library** (☎ 409-763-8854; 2310 Sealy) offers public Internet access.

Sights & Activities

Incorporating multimedia attractions, an Imax theater, artificial beach, paddlewheeler and high-tech aquarium, glitzy and over-hyped **Moody Gardens** (☎ 409-744-4673, 800-582-4673; 1 Hope Blvd; $6-12 per attraction, day pass $30; 10am-6pm Sun-Fri, 10am-8pm Sat) is Galveston's top tourist draw. The best component is the aquarium, which holds more than 8,000 sea creatures, including kid-aweing sharks, in some two million gallons of tank space.

The historic Strand district is bounded by 20th and 25th Sts, Mechanic St and Harborside Dr. Museums here include the **Galveston County Historical Museum** (☎ 409-766-2340; 2219 Market; admission free; 10am-4pm Mon-Sat, noon-4pm Sun, later in summer).

North of Harborside Dr at 21st St, **Pier 21** holds shops, restaurants and museums around a converted old dock. Here the **Texas Seaport Museum** (☎ 409-763-1877; adult $6, child 7-18 $4; 10am-5pm) details Galveston's seaport life during its 19th-century heyday. It's home to the tall ship *Elissa*, a beautiful 1877 Scottish bark. At nearby Pier 20, the **Ocean Star** (☎ 409-766-7827; adult/child $6/4; 10am-5pm) is a retired offshore rig with excellent exploration exhibits.

For sand and surf head to **Stewart Beach Park** on the east end of Seawall Blvd at Broadway. There's even a fair bit of surfing done in the coffee-colored waves (if you can call them that) just off the seawall in front of the visitors center.

Festivals & Events

Mardis Gras The biggest and the best in Texas with accompanying beads, floats and debauchery.

Dickens on the Strand Residents dress up in 19th-century English gear for this two-day Christmas festival.

Sleeping

Galveston is incredibly seasonal with hotel rates all over the island fluctuating by as much as $100 between the off season (September to March) and the high season (March to August). Prices border on extortion during peak weekends.

On the quiet east end of Seawall Blvd is the **HI Galveston Hostel** (☎ 409-765-9431; 201 E Seawall Blvd; dm members/nonmembers $18.50/21.50, r $45-120; P), right on the beach in the Sandpiper Motel. It's old but hasn't thoroughly gone to seed, and the hostel section has a nice common room with a TV, small library and Internet access.

Also on the east end is the new, moderately priced **Holiday Inn Express** (☎ 409-766-7070; 102 E Seawall Blvd; r $70-210; P), a nice choice for this chain.

For mid-range spots west of the visitors center on the seawall, try **Gaidos Seaside Inn** (☎ 409-762-9625, 800-525-0064; 3828 Seawall Blvd; r $50-145; P). The rooms here are a little bunker-like but clean.

The nicest place to stay in Galveston is the historic **Hotel Galvez** (☎ 409-765-7721; 2024 Seawall Blvd; r $110-245; P), a handsome landmark near the beach with a beautiful, sweeping lobby, a classy bar and fine-dining restaurant and spacious, comfy rooms. The private, lagoonlike pool has a hot tub and wading pool for the kids. During the off season, this is a great value.

Eating & Drinking

Start your day at **Mosquito Cafe** (☎ 409-763-1010; 628 14th; mains $6-14), where the sophisticated menu includes frittatas, quiches, fresh-baked muffins and even granola with yogurt and fresh fruit.

The best seafood in town is at **Gaido's** (☎ 409-762-9625; 3800 Seawall; mains $13-30), one of Galveston's oldest restaurants. Try one of the 'Famous Complete Dinners.' More low key is **Bennos on the Beach** (☎ 409-762-3666; 112 28th St; mains $5-12), a locally popular spot serving awesome fried shrimp and oyster po-boys. Near the Strand on Pier 21, there's a slew of seafood chains as well as the **Fisherman's Wharf** (☎ 409-765-7074; Harborside Dr at Pier 22; mains $8-16), a huge restaurant over the water that started out as a one room shack.

For something other than fish, the **Original Mexican Cafe** (☎ 409-762-6001; 1401 Market; mains $5-13) has served tacos, tamales and enchiladas since 1916. Five bucks will get you a good barbecued-beef sandwich at either **Leon's World's Finest In & Out B-B-Q House** (☎ 409-744-0070; 5427 Broadway) or **Queen's Barbecue** (☎ 409-762-3151; 3428 Ave S), near the seawall.

Good coffee, sidewalk tables and a hip atmosphere can be had near the Strand at **Mod Coffee and Tea House** (☎ 409-765-5659; 2126 Postoffice St). On Friday nights this spot shows indie films 'living room style' on a big screen TV upstairs.

Nearby, **Molly's Pub** (☎ 409-763-4466; 2013 Postoffice St), an English-style establishment, has 62 beers on tap, dart boards and a jovial atmosphere.

Getting There & Around

Kerrville Bus Co (☎ 409-765-7731; 714 25th St) runs four buses a day to Houston. The **Galveston Island Rail Trolley** (☎ 409-763-4311) links the Strand with Seawall via 25th St (60¢). A small Strand loop is free. The city also operates a fleet of electric shuttle buses serving many hotels and visitor attractions. The shuttles operate Thursday to Sunday ($1).

ARANSAS NATIONAL WILDLIFE REFUGE

This 70,504-acre **refuge** (☎ 361-286-3559; $5 per car) is the Texas coast's premier bird-watching site. The birding frenzy peaks in March and November. Most watched are the whooping cranes (one of the continent's rarest creatures) who winter here. You also might see wild boars, alligators, armadillos, white-tailed deer and many other species. The refuge is 35 miles northeast of Rockport; take Hwy 35 to FM 774 and follow the signs.

CORPUS CHRISTI

Corpus is a pleasant enough port town, but you wouldn't book your honeymoon here. For a good traveler's resource head to the **Corpus Christi Convention and Visitors Bureau** (☎ 361-881-1888, 800-678-6232; 1823 N Shoreline; 8:30am-5pm Mon-Fri). Downtown are **Heritage Park**, with restored old buildings, and the

THE BORDER

The borderlands are where the third world runs smack dab into the first, and it's this easily-accessible bicultural experience that is a highlight for many visitors to Texas. There are more than a dozen major crossings on the border, including El Paso, Presidio, Del Rio, Eagle Pass, Laredo, Falcon Reservoir, Roma, McAllen and Brownsville, all open 24 hours. Spanish is spoken in these towns at least as much as English and 'Spanglish,' the commonly used name for the local linguistic mixture, is really the speech of choice.

Los Dos Laredos, or the two towns of Laredo (US) and Nuevo Laredo (Mexico), comprise the border's most popular tourist crossing. More than 90% of the Laredo population is Latino, and most are bilingual.

Since September 11, crossing the Tex-Mex border is not as hassle free as it used to be, and there is an increased US Border Patrol presence all along the border. For this reason you should heed these regulations and restrictions: US citizens should carry proof of citizenship; Canadians should carry a passport or birth certificate, other foreign nationals must have a passport and appropriate visas both before entering Mexico and returning to the USA.

With that in mind, you can walk across the border from Laredo into Mexico for 25¢ on **International Bridge No 1** (IB1), which leads you right onto the north end of Av Guerrero, Nuevo Laredo's main street and seven blocks from the main plaza. Most of Nuevo Laredo's *casas de cambio* (exchange offices) won't change traveler's checks, but most businesses will accept them for purchases. Avoid dark streets and watch for pickpockets on both sides of the border.

For tourist info on the US side head to the friendly **Laredo Convention and Visitors Bureau** (☎ 956-795-2200; 501 San Augustín; ⌚ 8am-5pm Mon-Fri, 8am-3pm Sat) and on the Mexican side to the **Nuevo Laredo tourist office** (☎ 8-712-73-97; Calle Herrera at Av Juárez; ⌚ 9am-3pm Mon-Sat, noon-3pm Sun).

Laredo's cobblestoned and oak-lined **San Augustín Plaza** dates to 1767; at its east is the Gothic Revival **San Augustín Church**.

Nuevo Laredo has an interesting market and many restaurants, bars and souvenir shops catering to US day-trippers – most accept US currency and quote prices in dollars.

Most of Laredo's lodgings are along I-35. **Motel 6** (☎ 956-722-8133; 5920 San Bernardo Ave off I-35, exit 4; s/d $45/50; P) has rooms that are better than the chain's usual standard. In Nuevo Laredo, **Hotel Romanos** (☎ 8-172-23-91; Calle Dr Mier 2420; r from $34; P), just east of the plaza, has clean rooms.

For good food try **907 Zaragoza** (☎ 956-712-9825; 907 Zaragoza; mains $15-28), Laredo's fine-dining spot. In Nuevo Laredo, **Victoria 3020** (☎ 8-713-30-20; Victoria 3020; mains $13-27), two blocks south and one block west of IB1, is the town's nicest restaurant. The bars in town get rowdy at night – tequila's cheap and so are the crowds.

Buses arrive and depart Laredo from the **Greyhound bus terminal** (☎ 956-723-4324; 610 Salinas).

Museum of Science & History (☎ 361-883-2862; 1900 N Chaparral St; adult $9, child 5-12 $5; ⌚ 10am-5pm Tue-Sat, noon-5pm Sun), which is located in the shadow of the harbor bridge and has on display artifacts from the Padre Island Shipwreck Collection that date to 1554, as well as replicas of two of Columbus' three ships (the third, the *Niña*, is moored in the Corpus Christi Marina, downtown).

Just across the harbor bridge from downtown you'll find the good **Texas State Aquarium** (☎ 361-881-1200; 2710 N Shoreline; adult $9.25, child 4-12 $5.50; ⌚ 9am-5pm Mon-Sat, 10am-5pm Sun, 1 hr later in summer) with exhibits focusing on the Gulf of Mexico. Permanently docked in front of the aquarium is the 900ft aircraft carrier **USS Lexington** (☎ 361-888-4873; 2914 N Shoreline Blvd; adult $10, child 4-12 $5; ⌚ 9am-5pm).

Several budget motels on the beach provide basic accommodations in the $35 to $50 range. At night, grab dinner at **Padre Island Brewing Company** (☎ 361-884-6533; 405 Chaparral; mains $10-18), then walk down to **Dr Rockit's Blues Bar** (☎ 361-884-7634; 709 Chaparral), which features live music nightly.

PADRE ISLAND NATIONAL SEASHORE

One of the longest stretches of undeveloped seashore in the US, Padre Island has 70 miles of white-sand beaches backed by grassy dunes (admission $10 per vehicle). It's home to all the wildlife found elsewhere along the coast and then some.

The **visitors center** (☎ 361-949-8068; 🕑 8:30am-4:30pm, later in summer) is on the beach just before the end of the paved road. A small grocery store has mainly convenience foods and drinking water, which is unavailable further south. Hikers and campers who trek south on the island need 1 gallon of water per person per day, sunscreen, insect repellent and good shady hats.

The developed campground near the entrance costs $8 and has campsites and RV sites (no hookups). Camping on the beaches is free with a permit.

SOUTH PADRE ISLAND

Don't confuse the national seashore with South Padre Island, a condo-crammed resort comprising the island's southern 5 miles. South Padre Island is developed, but its beaches are clean, its water warm for much of the year and the locals ready to make your acquaintance. South Padre Island is also the state's prime spring-break destination; it's infested with partying college students most of March (when all motels are booked solid at inflated prices).

For more information, contact the **South Padre Island Visitor Center** (☎ 956-761-6433, 800-767-2373; 600 Padre Blvd).

WEST TEXAS

The western reaches of the state are to many native Texans the quintessential Texas experience. Desert sands, dry heat and craggy mountains introduce the visitor to the frontier spirit and leather-tough cowboys the state is known for. Here is where you'll find Guadalupe Mountains National Park, home to the state's tallest mountain (Guadalupe Peak at 8749ft) and Big Bend National Park, a moonlike landscape of desert mountains, deep canyons and big sky. It's a river-running, mountain-biking and hiking paradise and it's also one of the least visited national parks in the country. For that reason it's all the more surprising to discover that the area around the park is home to a collection of artist retreats, historic hotels and quaint mountain villages far away from the stress of city life.

West Texas is also home to El Paso, a city that's in many ways more like New Mexico and old Mexico than the rest of Texas. The town is closer to Santa Fe than to Austin, and Spanish is spoken here as often as English – as is the case in much of this part of the state. El Paso is as close as you can get to Mexico without actually being there, though going south of the border is a walk away.

Note that El Paso and the rest of far-west Texas are in the mountain time zone, one hour behind the rest of the state.

BIG BEND NATIONAL PARK

This park is vast enough for a lifetime of discovery but has enough roads and trails to permit short-term visitors to see a lot in two to three days. Its diverse geography makes for an amazing variety of critters: mountain lions, black bears, collared peccaries and white-tailed deer, as well as 56 species of reptiles and amphibians and more than 100 bird species. **Big Bend Birding Expeditions** (☎ 915-371-2356) offers bird-watching trips. Spring and fall are the best times to visit. Summer is scorching. Spring means moderate temperatures and lots of wildflowers (and crowds), while fall is a great time for river-running. Winter storms bring snow and freezing temperatures.

The main **visitors center** (☎ 915-477-2251; 🕑 8am-6pm) is along the main park road, 29 miles from the Persimmon Gap entrance south of Marathon and 26 miles from the Maverick entrance at Study Butte. Admission is $10 per car, $5 for bicyclists and pedestrians.

The park's 110 miles of paved road and 150 miles of dirt road make scenic driving the most popular activity. But 150 miles of **hiking trails** also web the park; the Chisos Mountains have the most. Free backcountry permits, available at all visitors centers, are required for **backpacking** and **camping**.

Several companies located west of the park offer guided **river trips** in and around Big Bend (see West of Big Bend, opposite). Undeveloped **campgrounds** at Rio Grande Village, Chisos Basin and Cottonwood, near Castolon, have campsites for $7. Rio Grande Village has RV sites for $14.50. **Chisos Mountain Lodge** (☎ 915-477-2291; cottages $84) is good for accommodations and so-so for food. Its cottages sleep three; No 103 has the best view in Texas. It's best to bring in your own food from outside the park and during peak season like spring break (April to March) it's essential to book these spots well in advance.

No public transportation serves the park but you can get as far as Alpine where the **Trans-Pecos Transport** (☎ 915-837-0100, 877-388-1776) offers shuttles to the park.

WEST OF BIG BEND

West of the park, the atmosphere has more in common with a Mexican beach town than with the rough-and-tumble desert frontier nearby.

In **Terlingua** travelers and artists passing through tend to stay a bit longer, some for good. There are several excellent restaurants, a live-music scene, a radio station (101.1) and a bar that would make Austin proud. It's also one of the main jumping-off points into the national park where you can resupply, hire horses or arrange river-rafting trips. **Big Bend Stables** (☎ 432-371-2212; junction Hwys 118 & 170; hour rides $28, half day with lunch $70) and **Far Flung Adventures** (☎ 915-371-2489, 800-359-4138) will set you up. Both companies are 6 miles west of the junction of Highways 118 and 170.

The **El Dorado Hotel** (☎ 915-371-2111; Hwy 170 at Ivey St; r $90-150) is the friendliest and the best as well as the only place to stay in **Terlingua Ghost Town**, a long-gone mining village that's now home to the **Starlight Theatre** (☎ 915-371-2326; Ivey St, Terlingua Ghost Town; mains $9-23). This former movie theater has been resurrected and turned into a lively restaurant, watering hole and music venue serving up hand-cut filet mignon, tart margaritas and a dang good time. For drinks only don't miss **La Kiva** (☎ 432-371-2250; Hwy 170), located in the Big Bend Travel Park, a funky underground bar with a fully stocked well and a cool jukebox.

The only thing **Lajitas** (☎ 877-525-4827; www.lajitas.com) has in common with Terlingua is the scenery. This playground resort for wealthy Texans situated on the shores of the Rio Grande was bought by billionaire Steve Smith, who promptly spent $50 million sprucing the place up. There's a private landing strip, a fine-dining restaurant, a spa, a golf course, shops and handsome condos that rent for about $200 a night.

West of Lajitas, FM 170 hugs the Rio Grande through some of the most spectacular and remote scenery in the country.

GIANT

Giant, filmed in 1955 in Marfa, Texas and starring James Dean, Elizabeth Taylor and Rock Hudson, is required viewing for anyone venturing west of Junction. The story is an epic tale about heartbreak, oil and the transformation of west Texas from a land of cattle ranches to a land of black gold. Dean, as the troubled oil baron Jett Rink, is at his methodical best and Taylor, as the pretty Leslie Lynnton Benedict, is a knockout. There's even an appearance by a very young and innocent Dennis Hopper.

Known as the **Camino del Rio** (River Road) it takes you through a lunar landscape of low desert arroyos, sweeping vistas and rugged mountains (at one point there's a 15% grade, the maximum allowable) as it winds its way for 50 miles to **Presidio**, a dreary border town with not much else to do other than cross into Mexico. From there US67 heads north to Marfa (see following).

NORTH OF BIG BEND

Several interesting towns lie between Big Bend and I-10. **Marfa** is home to the **Chinati Foundation** (☎ 432-729-4362; adult/child $10/5; 10am & 2pm, tours only), a sprawling complex of minimalist art founded by New York artist Donald Judd in 1986. The town's original fame, however, came after James Dean, Elizabeth Taylor and Rock Hudson filmed *Giant* here in 1955. The cast and crew stayed a block off the main square at the 1930s-era **Hotel Paisano** (☎ 866-729-3669, 866-729-3669; N Highland & West Sts; r $90-170; ⊠), which has recently reopened after a thorough remodel. Marfa is also known for the unexplained 'Marfa lights,' which flash across the desert sky on random nights; no one yet has been able to figure out where they come from.

Fort Davis (elevation 5000ft) is the highest town in Texas. Sixteen miles north of town is the **McDonald Observatory** (☎ 432-426-3640; Hwy 118; 🕑 9am-5pm), which hosts occasional public star parties and other tours of the universe. Also nearby is **Prude Guest Ranch** (☎ 915-426-3202, 800-458-6232; Hwy 118; r $50-75; P ⊠), 6 miles north of Fort Davis, a children's summer camp and dude ranch high in the Fort Davis Mountains. **Balmorhea**, up on I-10, has a small state park around a huge spring-fed pool that's the best swimming hole in the state.

East of Marfa is **Marathon**, an artsy hamlet home to art galleries, an Internet coffee shop, a bookstore, several great eateries and the best place to spend the night in all of Texas, the **Gage Hotel** (☎ 432-386-4205, 800-884-4243; 101 Hwy 90; r $70-190; P). The rooms here are straight out of a Wild West pulp novel, with wide wooden blinds on the windows, saddles in the rooms and cowhides on the beds. The nicest rooms are the cabana-style suites next door that surround a lush courtyard and feature antique wooden doors, Mexican tile floors, fireplaces and outdoor patios.

GUADALUPE MOUNTAINS NATIONAL PARK

At 8749ft, remote Guadalupe Peak is the highest point in Texas. Elsewhere in the park, McKittrick Canyon has the state's best fall foliage. If you seek high-desert splendor, this place is a must. The park headquarters and **visitors center** (☎ 915-828-3251; admission free; 8am-4:30pm, later in summer) are at Pine Springs, off US 62/180. No gasoline, food or beverages are available.

The park has more than 80 miles of trails, from short nature walks to strenuous treks. The most popular day hike is McKittrick Canyon Trail, especially scenic in fall, when the hardwoods change color. The strenuous trail to Guadalupe Peak is an 8.5-mile round-trip and gains 3000ft in elevation.

Ten backcountry campsites dot the park. Overnight hikers must get a free permit at either Pine Springs visitors center or Dog Canyon ranger station on the park's north side, reached via New Mexico Hwy 137; both places have primitive campgrounds ($8). No water is available in the backcountry. **Silver Stage Lines** (☎ 915-778-0162) runs a shuttle past the park.

HUECO TANKS STATE HISTORICAL PARK

About 32 miles east of El Paso off US 62/180, the Hueco Tanks have attracted humans and animals for thousands of years. Three small granite mountains here are pocked with depressions (*hueco* is Spanish for 'hollow') that hold rainwater, creating an oasis in the barren desert. Wildlife is abundant, and so is evidence of human habitation in the form of pictographs, potsherds and bits of worked flint. The 860-acre **park** (☎ 915-857-1135) is also a magnet for rock climbers. Free guided pictograph tours are offered, as are bouldering tours and bird-watching tours.

To minimize human impact on the fragile park, a daily visitor quota is enforced; call ahead to check status. Day-use fee is $4. Twenty campsites are available for $9 to $11 and reservations are suggested. You can also camp down the road at Pete's Country Store, a longstanding climbers' haven. **Silver Stage Lines** (☎ 915-778-0162) runs a shuttle from El Paso to the park for $20 each way per person.

EL PASO

Isolated at the state's far-western tip – further west than most of New Mexico – El Paso has little in common with the rest of Texas. Without the bounties of big oil or high-tech, El Paso seems disproportionately poor for a city its size. Nevertheless, most El Pasoans seem content and proud with what they do have: an unpretentious, bicultural society with a strong independent streak.

Across the Rio Grande lies Ciudad Juárez (population approaching two million), Mexico's fourth-largest city. Though the US Border Patrol tries to keep the two countries neatly separated, Mexican culture has always been dominant in El Paso and Spanish is the default language. You don't find Tex-Mex food here – it's Mexican.

History

For centuries, the broad pass for which the city is named has been traversed by an anthropologist's laundry list of peoples.

The years between 1881 (when the railroad arrived) and 1920 might well be called the city's glory days. El Paso became a major rail hub, bringing wealth and urban sophistication. One noted architect of the era, Henry C Trost, designed and built many exceptional structures downtown, most of which still stand. The railroads also brought some of the Wild West's most colorful characters to town: gunfighter John Wesley Hardin lived and died here, and Mexican revolutionary Pancho Villa holed up in El Paso for a time.

Orientation & Information

The Franklin Mountains pin the downtown area against the border and cleave the rest of the city into eastern and western sides. The airport is on the east side, while the

University of Texas at El Paso (UTEP) and the New Mexico border lie on the west. The two sides are connected by I-10, which squeezes between the mountains and downtown, and by scenic Transmountain Rd, which traverses the Franklins further north. The soul of El Paso lies right downtown by the border.

The **El Paso Visitors Center** (☎ 915-534-0601, 800-351-6024; www.visitelpaso.com; Santa Fe St; 8am-5pm Mon-Fri), at the Civic Center, has basic information and an OK tourist map. **El Paso Public Library** (☎ 915-544-6772; 501 N Oregon; 8:30am-8:30pm Mon-Thu, 8:30am-5:30pm Fri & Sat, 1pm-5pm Sun) offers free Internet access. **Adelante** (☎ 915-533-9875) is a bilingual gay-and-lesbian information line. **StantonStreet.com** is an excellent online magazine about El Paso.

Sights & Activities

The historic heart of El Paso is **San Jacinto Plaza**, which could easily be in Mexico with its food vendors and its groups of elderly men sitting on park benches watching the afternoon go by. Local history has it that the park once held a pond containing live alligators. Today, the critters are memorialized with a sculpture by El Paso native Luis Jimenez. For a more extensive, **self-guided walking tour** of historic downtown, grab the free pamphlet at the visitors center.

Die-hard history buffs might enjoy the lower valley's Mission Trail, a driving route southeast of town that connects several early Spanish missions. **Mission Ysleta** (originally built in 1691) is on the Tigua reservation (take I-10 east to the Zaragoza exit, turn right and continue 3 miles). Also here, the **Tigua Cultural Center** (☎ 915-859-5287; 305 Yaya Lane; 9am-3pm Wed-Sun) explains tribal history and hosts traditional dance performances on weekends. Follow signs east to **Socorro Mission** (1691) and **San Elizario Chapel** (1877). For information on the missions, call the **Mission Trail Association** (☎ 915-534-0677).

For a sweeping panorama of El Paso and sprawling Juárez that the whole family can enjoy, head to the top of 5632ft Ranger Peak on the **Wyler Aerial Tramway** (☎ 915-566-6622; 1700 McKinley; adult $7, child 4-12 $4; noon-6pm Mon, Thu & Sun, noon-8pm Fri-Sat). Acrophobes get a comparable view from the turnout along **Scenic Dr**, right above downtown. Go at night when the sea of lights is breathtaking.

When you've finished exploring El Paso, cross the border to **Ciudad Juárez,** Mexico. The **El Paso-Juárez Trolley Co** (☎ 915-544-0061; 1 Civic Center Plaza; adult $12.50, child 4-12 $9; 10am-4pm) operates the Border Jumper, a trolley looping hourly from El Paso Civic Center through Juárez and back, making 11 stops en route (you get off and on at will). The early trolley can fill up so it's best to call for reservations. Or you can just walk across the Santa Fe St bridge (25¢ for pedestrians) into Mexico. The bridge leads right onto Av Juárez, the city's main tourist strip. Stroll down Juárez to the vibrant cathedral area and back, passing restaurants and shops galore. Don't forget your passport.

Sleeping

Compared to the rest of the state, lodging in El Paso is very affordable. Look to spend between $50 and $100 for a good mid-range spot. Hotel tax is 15.5%.

Budget digs downtown include the vintage 1922 **Gardner Hotel/El Paso International Hostel** (☎ 915-532-3661; www.gardnerhotel.com; 311 E Franklin Ave; dm $15, r $20-40). A short drive from downtown near the airport, the western-style **Coral Motel** (☎ 915-772-3263; 6308 Montana Ave; s/d $34/38) is an excellent value.

Mid-range hotels include the **Cliff Inn** (☎ 915-533-6700; 1600 Cliff Dr; r $55-90; P), a worn but friendly spot with big clean rooms and a **Best Western** (☎ 915-587-4900; 1045 Sunland Park Dr; s/d $60/65; P), which is off I-10, three exits west of downtown.

To pamper yourself, head to the historic but modern **Hilton Camino Real** (☎ 915-534-3000; 101 S El Paso St; r Mon-Fri $120-150, Sat & Sun $80-100). Ask for the corner room 1315, a queen deluxe standard with views on two sides.

Eating & Drinking

Start your day at **H&H Car Wash** (☎ 915-533-1144; 701 E Yandell Ave; mains $3-7) a beloved hole-in-the-wall diner where you can eat a Mexican breakfast while getting your car washed (yes, it's a real car wash).

More traditional is **Kiki's** (☎ 915-565-6713; 2719 N Piedras Ave; mains $5-10), which perennially wins Best of El Paso awards.

If you need a break from Mexican, try **Ardovino's Pizza** (☎ 915-760-6000; 206 Cincinnati St; mains $5-15), a fixture in El Paso for 50 years that serves up delicious stone oven gourmet pizzas on red-checkered tablecloths.

THE AUTHOR'S CHOICE

Ardovino's Desert Crossing (☎ 505-589-0653; 1 Ardovino Dr, Sunland Park, New Mexico; 🕑 5pm-1am Thu-Sat; mains $7-13) A short drive across the state border high up in the New Mexican desert, you will find the best entertainment spot in El Paso. Ardovino's is a former casino from the early-'60s turned retro jazz lounge. Kick back at a table in the upscale dining room or head into the **Mecca Lounge** to hear a jazz quartet kick out Sinatra tunes. Top it off with a martini on the outdoor stone patio while you take in the stars and watch the Amtrak trains whistle by towards the lights of El Paso in the valley below. On Saturdays there's a farmers market on the grounds and the owner has future plans to renovate and rent several adobe-walled cabins on the grounds. Dean Martin and the rest of the Rat Pack would be proud.

Fine-dining honors go to the opulent **Dome Restaurant** (☎ 915-534-3000; 101 S El Paso St; mains $19-29). Located inside the Hotel Camino Real, the 25ft ceilings, glass chandeliers and white tablecloths set the stage for the inventive Southwestern cuisine made with a spicy Latin American flare. Next door the elegant **Dome Bar** was named for the stunning glass domed ceiling, 30ft above the circular granite bar. Across the street (behind the Fray Garcia statue), **Cafe Central** (☎ 915-545-2233; 1 Texas Ct; mains $16-35) has a lovely European-bistro setting and a creative nouvelle menu with regional accents (reservations suggested).

Entertainment

For extensive entertainment listings, pick up the free weekly *What's Up,* the free monthly *El Paso Scene* or the Friday Tiempo supplement to the *El Paso Times.*

The closest thing El Paso has to an entertainment district is a single block of restaurants and bars on Cincinnati St between Mesa and Stanton, near UTEP. **Dolce Vita Cafe** (☎ 915-533-8482; 205 Cincinnati Ave; mains $5-7) is El Paso's coolest coffeehouse with an alternative crowd and lots of students. Next door the **Cincinnati Club** (☎ 915-532-5592; 207 Cincinnati Ave; mains $5-10) is a well-worn favorite that serves cheap chili, burgers, fries and beer. Down the street, **Fellini's Film Cafe** (☎ 915-544-5420; 220 Cincinnati Ave; 🕑 2pm-10pm Mon-Sat, noon-3pm Sun) rents and screens art films and serves sandwiches and coffee drinks.

Getting There & Around

El Paso International Airport (☎ 915-772-4271) is 8 miles northeast of downtown. Bus No 33 ($1) runs between the airport and downtown. A cab to downtown costs $15 to $17. Try **United Independent Cab** (☎ 915-590-8294). Car rental companies at the airport include **Budget** (☎ 915-778-5287) and **Dollar** (☎ 915-778-5445).

The **Greyhound Bus station** (☎ 915-532-2365; 200 W San Antonio Ave) sends buses to all points beyond. Call for fares and schedules.

Sun Metro (☎ 915-533-3333) is the citywide bus service. Incredibly, the company offers no systemwide route map. Get individual route schedules at the bus information booth, across from San Jacinto Plaza on the corner of Oregon and Main Ave, or inside the Jack in the Box across the street. Standard fare is $1. Two trolley routes transport folks around downtown's historic areas (25¢).

Amtrak's *Sunset Limited* stops at **Union Depot** (☎ 915-545-2247; 700 San Francisco Ave).

PANHANDLE PLAINS

The northwest Texas panhandle is a land of sprawling cattle ranches, where people can still make a living on the back of a horse. Its landscape seems endlessly flat, punctuated only by utility poles and windmills, until a vast canyon materializes almost miragelike to play tricks on the horizon. The canyonlands, formed by eroding caprock (the layer of caliche, marl, chalk and gravel that lies beneath the plains), make for classic Western scenery, which continues once you get into the region's two cities: Lubbock, where you'll find all things Buddy Holly, and Amarillo, home to the old Route 66 and a fast-disappearing Texas.

LUBBOCK

Situated on the high plains between a few cotton farms, some ranches and a whole lot of nothing, Lubbock has a heart made of music – rock 'n' roll to be exact – as the hometown of horn-rimmed rocker himself,

Buddy Holly. It's also home to Texas Tech University, which gives the place a fun college-town atmosphere. There are a few good restaurants, an abundance of bars and nightclubs, several performing-arts venues and two excellent museums. There's even a vineyard or two (you heard right) that outsells anything bottled in the Hill Country.

Information

Lubbock, also known as 'Hub City,' is at the intersection of several main highways, including I-27 from the north, US 82 from the east, US 84 from the southeast and northwest, US 87 from the south and US 62 from the southwest. Loop 289 circles the city. The Texas Tech campus is bordered by 4th and 19th Sts on the north and south and Quaker and University Sts on the east and west. The city's main night life happens in the Depot District, located on Buddy Holly Ave (formerly Ave H) and 19th St.

For loads more tourist info check out the **Lubbock Convention and Visitor's Bureau** (☎ 806-747-5232, 800-692-4053; www.lubbocklegends.org; Ste 200, 1301 Broadway; 9am-5pm Mon-Fri). Event listings and other goings-on around town are listed in the free monthly **Caprock Chronicle**. Free Internet access is available when you apply for a free library card at the **Lubbock Public Library** (☎ 806-775-2840; 1306 9th St; 9am-9pm Mon-Wed, 9am-6pm Thu-Sat, 1-5pm Sun). Radio stations include Texas Tech's **KTXT 88.1**, which plays alt college rock and NPR and **96.3 KLLL**, a country station where Waylon Jennings was a DJ in the 1950s. In September, music fans flock to the **Crossroads of Texas Music Festival** to hear musicians from around the world pay tribute to Buddy Holly

THE FLATLANDERS: NOW AGAIN

In 1971, three Lubbock school mates – Joe Ely, Jimmie Dale Gilmore and Butch Hancock – used to swap guitar licks and dream of making the big time, which they did, but in very different solo careers in Austin and Nashville. Now, however, the school mates have gotten back together as the Flatlanders (named after their hometown geography) and in 2002 recorded *Now Again*, a rock/folk/country CD that borrows from each of the band mates musical skills. It's a winner.

Sights & Activities

The main event in Lubbock is the excellent **Buddy Holly Center** (☎ 806-767-2686; 1801 Ave G; adult/child $5/3; 10am-5pm Mon, 10am-6pm Tue-Fri, 11am-6pm Sat), a homage to the hometown rocker whose plane went down in an Iowa snow storm in 1959. Among the exhibits are a couple of Holly's guitars, photos of Holly and his band the Crickets and Holly's trademark glasses, which were recovered from the crash site.

More Holly attractions include the **Buddy Holly Statue & Walk of Fame** (8th St at Ave Q), found toward the back of Buddy Holly Plaza, on a small strip of grass and concrete. Visitors still leave guitar picks at **Buddy Holly's grave** in Lubbock City Cemetery (31st and Teak Ave). Take a right when you get in the cemetery and the modest headstone will be on your left just by the side of the road.

On Texas Tech's north side are two outstanding university-affiliated museums. The **National Ranching Heritage Center** (☎ 806-742-0498; 3121 4th St; admission free; 10am-5pm Mon-Sat, 1-5pm Sun) details ranch life on the high plains since the late 18th century including 36 historic structures – everything from an opulent 1909 Queen Anne ranch house to a rickety sticks-and-sod pioneer cabin. Keep your eyes peeled for roaming jackrabbits.

Next door is the **Museum of Texas Tech University** (☎ 806-742-2490; 4th St & Indiana Ave; admission free; 10am-5pm Tue-Sat, 1-5pm Sun), which has expertly presented art from the American west as well as life-size castings of dinosaur skeletons.

Just south of town are the **Llano Estacado Winery** (☎ 806-745-2258; FM 1585 east of US 87; 10am-5pm Mon-Sat, noon-5pm Sun) and Mission-style **Cap Rock Winery** (☎ 806-863-2704; Woodrow Rd, east of 87; 10am-5pm, noon-5pm Sun). Both offer free tours and tastings every day.

Sleeping

On busy weekends – and in Lubbock that means whenever there's a home football game – it's hard to find a hotel room anywhere and when you do prices are at a premium. Book ahead to get the best rates. Hotel tax is a stiff 17%.

Most of the low-budget hotels along Ave Q are pretty seedy but tolerable in a pinch. **Travelers Inn** (☎ 806-765-8847; 714 Ave Q; s/d $35/40; P) is the cheapest of the bunch and has

TEXAS

QUIRKY LUBBOCK

The high plains of Texas are notoriously windy so it should come as no surprise to discover the one-of-a-kind **American Wind Power Center** (☎ 806 747-8734; 1701 Canyon Lake Dr; admission free; 🕑 10am-5pm Tues-Sat & 2-5pm Sun May-Aug only), a sprawling antique windmill repository that was conceived by the late Texas Tech professor Billie Wolfe. Located a mile east of the Buddy Holly Center, this park and warehouse holds nearly 100 different types of windmill including three that were bought out from under the Smithsonian Institute. Don't miss the rare double-sectional metal Centennial Power Mill built in the 1880s in the United States; the South African-made Southern Cross – which at 55ft high with a 25ft wheel diameter is one of the largest windmills made in the world – will blow you away.

the friendliest staff but the rooms are tiny and musty.

For mid-range options the recently remodeled **Lubbock Inn** (☎ 806-792-5181; 3901 19th St; r $70-120; P) is one of the better places to stay in town even though its exterior seems to be stuck in modular '70s hell. Room prices include a breakfast of bacon, eggs and hash browns. Another excellent option is the **Country Inn** (☎ 806-795-5271; 4105 19th; r $50-70; P), a sneaker's throw away from the Lubbock Inn. Owned by a Texas Tech professor, this comfortable hotel has a bright helpful staff and the big rooms are immaculate.

Eating

On the southern border of Texas Tech is **Café J** (☎ 806-743-5400; 2605 19th St; mains $14-20), a hip, upscale spot serving Italian cuisine with a Southwestern flair. Downstairs is **J's Cocktail Lounge**, a refreshingly alternative drinking establishment with a young, professional and stylish clientele. Nearby, **Jazz** (☎ 806-799-2124; 3703 C 19th St; mains $8-14), serves up fried and blackened Louisiana Cajun cuisine along with New Orleans–style jazz.

In the Depot District, **Hub City Brewery** (☎ 806-747-1535; 1807 Buddy Holly Ave; mains $6-12) offers wood-fired pizzas and homebrew in an exposed brick dining room. The best Mexican food in town is at **Abuelos Mexican Embassy** (☎ 806-794-1762; 4401 82nd St; mains $9-18). For a splurge, visitors can cancan over to **Chez Suzette** (☎ 806-795-6796; 4423 50th St; mains $12-23) for romantic French and Italian fare.

Drinking & Entertainment

The neon lined Depot District is the town's premier nightlife center with a collection of restaurants, bars and nightclubs. Here you'll find a sports bar, a daiquiri bar, a martini bar, a brewpub, a mellow cocktail lounge, several big dance clubs and plenty of live music. There's also the **Cactus** (☎ 806-762-3233; 1812 Buddy Holly Ave), a renovated movie house now showing plays, musicals and other family entertainment.

Getting There & Away

From the unlucky **bus depot** (☎ 806-765-6641) at 1313 13th St, buses depart to the rest of the state and beyond. The optimistically named **Lubbock International Airport** (☎ 806-775-3126; 5401 N Martin Luther King Blvd) is 7 miles north of town.

NORTH OF LUBBOCK

Almost to Amarillo, in Canyon, the huge and superb **Panhandle Plains Historical Museum** (☎ 806-651-2244; 2401 4th Ave; adult $4, child 4-12 $3; 🕑 9am-5pm Mon-Sat, 1-6pm Sun, later in the summer) features exhibits on the petroleum industry, pioneer life and the cultural history of the southern Great Plains.

Twelve miles east of Canyon on Hwy 217, at **Palo Duro Canyon State Park** (☎ 806-488-2227; campsites $9-14, cabins $75, day pass $3), the Prairie Dog Town Fork of the Red River has carved its way spectacularly through the caprock to create the second largest canyon in the US. A paved road leads down into the canyon to great camping, horseback riding (rentals available), hiking and mountain biking – though it's dang hot in summer.

For more of the same beautiful scenery with a lake, bison herd and a 64-mile hike/bike trail along an abandoned railroad right-of-way go to **Caprock Canyons State Park** (☎ 806-455-1492; campsites $7-14; day pass $2) near Quitaque. In nearby Turkey, the **Bob Wills Museum** (☎ 806-423-1253; admission free) is a shrine to the King of Western Swing.

AMARILLO

In the 1950s Amarillo was a happening stop for cross-country drivers on the fabled Route 66, a fact that ended with the building of I-40. Now the chain restaurants and hotels alongside the freeway have blurred the town's rich history, leaving travelers passing through with the impression that this is one big truck stop. Those who stop will find an intact link to a rapidly disappearing past.

Information

Downtown is north of I-40 and west of US 87, the main north–south road through town. The **Visitors Information Center** (☎ 806-374-8474; www.amarillo-cvb.org; Suite 101, 401 S Buchanan St; 9am-6pm Mon-Fri, 10am-4pm Sat & Sun) is in the Civic Center. Internet access is available at the **Amarillo Public Library** (☎ 806-378-3054; 413 E 4th Ave; 9am-9pm Mon-Thu, 9am-6pm Fri & Sat, 2-6pm Sun). **Barnes & Noble** (☎ 806-352-2300; 2415 Soncy Rd off I-40) carries the *New York Times* and the *Wall Street Journal.*

Sights & Activities

Fifteen minutes west of town off I-40 in a rather plain wheat field is the **Cadillac Ranch** (Exit 60, Arnot Rd), a sculptural salute to Route 66 by local eccentric Stanley Marsh. Park along the feeder road and walk the well-worn path to pay your respects to these 10 Cadillacs buried hood first into the ground.

The old Route 66 in Amarillo may be gone but it's certainly not forgotten along **West 6th Ave**, also known as the San Jacinto District. This stretch of road is a character-filled collection of old shop front buildings from the 1920s selling everything from burgers and beer to books, hardware and antiques.

For a slice of Texas' past, head to the **Amarillo Stockyards** where every Tuesday at 10am cowboys from around the region come to bid for steers, bulls and heifers. Visitors are welcome.

Sleeping & Eating

Amarillo has every chain hotel you can think of, and then some, along I-40. To get the best deals, however, you have to venture elsewhere. Hotel tax is 15%.

For good value, the **Amarillo Motel** (☎ 806-353-9193; 4051 Canyon Dr; s/d $28/32; P) located on US 87 south of downtown is a friendly, family-run place with large, clean rooms, king size beds, microwaves and minifridges.

Mid-range options in Amarillo don't include much other than the chains. On Coulter St, just off I-40 close to Northwest Texas Hospital, the **La Quinta Inn Medical Center** (☎ 806-352-6311; 2108 S Coulter St; r $70-75; P) and the **Best Western Amarillo Inn** (☎ 806-358-7861; 1610 Coulter Dr; r $70-100; P) are both fine choices.

For breakfast, mosey over to the Amarillo Stockyards and the **Amarillo Stockyard Café** (☎ 806-342-941; mains $2-10; 6:30am-2:30pm), which serves a hearty breakfast of biscuits and gravy, fried eggs and rib eyes. On auction days the crowd is particularly colorful.

I-40 has a host of chain restaurants with the exception of the infamous **Big Texan Steak Ranch** (☎ 800-657-7177; north side of I-40 at Lakeside Exit; mains $10-28), home of the 'free' 72oz steak dinner. (By 'free' they mean you have to eat the meat along with the shrimp cocktail, baked potato, dinner salad and dinner roll that come with it all in under an hour. Otherwise it costs $50.)

In the San Jacinto District, the tiny **Golden Light Café** (☎ 806-374-0097; 2908 W 6th Ave; mains $4-7), has been serving burgers, home-cut fries and cold beer to crowds on Route 66 since 1956. It's a classic. Down the street, the **Shack** (☎ 806-374-6522; 3020 W 6th Ave; mains $8-14) is a 'tropical barbecue hut' serving up jerk chicken and other Jamaican favorites in a festive atmosphere.

Drinking & Entertainment

The San Jacinto District is the only area in town with a pulse after 8pm and there's live music on the weekends.

For after lunch drinks head to the **Circus Room Cocktail Lounge** (2305 6th Street), a dive bar extraordinaire with red carpet, and statues of camels and elephants on the walls. Next door to the Golden Light Café you'll find live music most every night at the **Golden Light Cantina** (☎ 806-374-0097; 2908 W 6th Ave). Across the street, there's live music at the **Blue Gator Bar and Grill** (☎ 806-372-7750; 2903 W 6th Ave) where you can sit on picnic tables, drink dollar beer and watch the Harleys go by.

Getting There & Away

Greyhound coaches leave from the **bus terminal** (☎ 806-374-5371; 700 S Tyler St). Several major airliners fly to **Amarillo International Airport**, located on the east edge of town north of I-40 via exit 76.

Great Plains

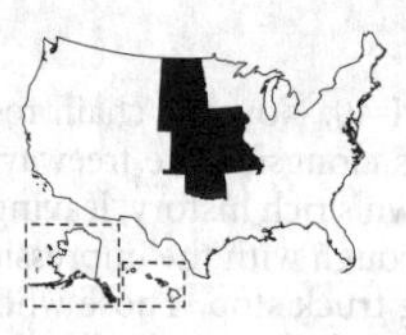

CONTENTS

Ridiculed as a flat fly-over zone and raced through by travelers heading elsewhere, the Great Plains is likely the USA's least understood (or thought-about) region. Those who do venture off the interstates find that there's more than meets the eye at 75mph. Each of the Great Plains' seven states – Missouri, Oklahoma, Kansas, Iowa, Nebraska, South Dakota and North Dakota – is home to diverse bumps in the landscape: forested Ozarks, rugged Wichitas, grass-bearded Sand Hills, rock-solid canyons, soft loess hills, badlands and Black Hills.

Along Kansas' wheat-lined I-70, the Plains quickly roll into something new. If a horizon seems short, detour toward it and discover a canyon dropping out of nowhere. This is where cowboys became cowboys, 60 million buffalo ran wild, pioneers blazed trails west and the heroic Plains Indians fought overpowering forces.

It's also the land of plugged oil wells and abandoned farmhouses. In recent years, falling populations have brought back the 'frontier' to some areas of the western Plains. Those proud folk who stuck it out have faced droughts, dust bowls, tornadoes, insects, battles, reservations and – for family farmers – corporations.

Most visitors to the region will stop for St Louis' Arch, Kansas City's barbecue or South Dakota's Mt Rushmore. Others are curious to see the great Mississippi and Missouri Rivers, or the spots where movies such as *Field of Dreams* were filmed. Some travelers stop in 'corn towns' to chat with ball-cap-wearing diners or watch a rodeo in the land where it was created.

But the Great Plains' greatest gift to travelers isn't in the destination, it's in the discoveries made when traveling without one.

HIGHLIGHTS

- Indulging in **St Louis'** Cajun grub and free beer, all under one tall arch (p685)
- Experiencing the world's greatest barbecue and the world's largest shuttlecock in **Kansas City** (p691)
- Soaking in the history at **Mt Rushmore**, **Crazy Horse Memorial** and **Custer State Park** (p718)
- Driving up Scotts Bluff and spending the night with Crazy Horse's ghost in the **Nebraska panhandle** (p711)
- Canoeing, camping and old-mine scuba diving in the **Ozarks** (p688)

HISTORY

Paleo-Indian nomadic groups hunted mammoths here 10,000 years ago. Spaniards introduced the horse around AD 1630, and its use reached the far ends of the Plains by the mid-18th century.

French explorers, following the Mississippi and Missouri Rivers, claimed a huge region west of the Mississippi for France. It passed to Spain in 1763, was returned to France in 1800, and was sold to the USA in the 1803 Louisiana Purchase, which included the seven states in this chapter. The next year President Thomas Jefferson sent Meriwether Lewis and William Clark to explore the new lands.

The prairie west of the Mississippi River was later settled in waves. The settlers' hunger for land pushed the Native American tribes westward, often forcibly, as in the infamous resettlement of the Five Civilized Tribes along the 1838–39 'Trail of Tears' (see History, p692).

Meanwhile a new mythology was in the making – that of the cowboy. Among the many contributing factors were: the cattle drives along the Chisholm Trail (1867–80); wild towns such as Dodge City, Deadwood and Abilene; the Range Wars of the 1880s; gamblers and gunfighters; train robberies; and the very practical means of dress required for long-distance horseback riding.

At the same time, the railroad expanded the possibilities for agriculture and the movement of produce, and open prairie was transformed into farms and towns, surrounded by barbed-wire fences, barns and windmills. Slowly the Plains were incorporated into the USA, first as territories, then as states.

The early 20th century was witness to an oil boom, but by the mid-1930s the neglect and mismanagement of the prairies resulted in a lot of topsoil being blown away during the dust bowl, especially in Oklahoma. Improved land management and environmental controls have enabled the evolution of thriving agribusiness throughout the Plains and industrial growth in the larger cities. Today the Plains is the breadbasket of the country, but vast, remote areas in its west are dying off, evident in Kansas' 6000 ghost towns and falling populations in 70% of the region.

GEOGRAPHY & CLIMATE

The Plains are not completely flat but rise gradually from the Mississippi River to the Rocky Mountains. Much of the terrain is low, rolling hills, such as the Ozark Plateau and Oklahoma's Ouachitas in the southeast, and the Black Hills in western South Dakota. One aberration is the convoluted, below-the-plains badlands of the Dakotas.

Thunderstorms, drought, blizzards and hailstorms all contribute to the wild weather that brews in these parts. And don't be surprised to find yourself running for the root cellar, as the Great Plains are smack dab in the heart of what is known as 'tornado alley.'

Summer can be hot and humid (about 90°F) and is the peak tourist season with accommodations heavily booked and attractions choked. Spring and fall are mild in the central Plains area, with an average maximum of about 50°F, so these are good seasons to visit. Harsh winters cause many attractions to close and make travel difficult.

NATIONAL & STATE PARKS

Despite the fact that the region has so much open land and is home to relatively few people, the Plains is home to only three national parks, all of which are found in North or South Dakota. These gems are the Wind Cave, Badlands and Theodore Roosevelt National Parks. Most of the prairie grasslands, which once dominated the Great Plains, have succumbed to the plow and alien crops. Only 0.1% of the original tallgrass prairie survives. It can be seen in the Oglala (Nebraska), Buffalo Gap (South Dakota) and Little Missouri (North Dakota) National Grasslands and the Tallgrass Prairie National Preserve in Kansas.

In the mid-19th century, the wanton slaughter of bison (usually called buffalo) nearly killed all 60 million; mere thousands survived. Recent conservation efforts, however, have brought more than 150,000 bison back to the Plains, where they can be viewed in many places. The best place to see them is at North Dakota's Theodore Roosevelt National Park.

State tourist offices can provide information about parks, and the National Park Service's trail pamphlets are indispensable. Check the National Park Service website (www.nps.gov) for more information.

ACTIVITIES

Adventurous travelers can hike, bike, rock climb and spelunk in the spectacular landscapes of South Dakota's Badlands National Park and Black Hills National Forest as well as Oklahoma's Wichita Mountains Wildlife Refuge. Missouri's water-filled Bonne Terre mine is open for scuba diving, and canoeists will be giddy on Nebraska's Niobrara River.

The 3700-mile-long Lewis and Clark National Historic Trail follows the original path of these two great explorers, passing through portions of every Great Plains state except for Oklahoma.

GETTING THERE & AROUND

Air

The region's main airport is **Lambert–St Louis International** (☎ 314-426-8000), but it has few direct international flights. Visitors from abroad may be better off getting a connection from O'Hare Airport in Chicago.

Bus

The carless brave won't be able to see much of the Plains beyond the major highways. **Greyhound** (☎ 800-229-9424) buses work the interstates except for South Dakota's I-90, which is served by **Jefferson Lines** (☎ 605-348-3300, 800-451-5333), and I-29 between Sioux Falls, South Dakota, and Fargo, North Dakota.

Car & Motorcycle

For traveling in the Plains states, driving sure beats public transport. Six east–west interstate highways cross the Plains states; north–south routes are less developed and less direct. I-44 has been built over and around the original Route 66 across Missouri and Oklahoma, but substantial stretches survive and are covered in the Oklahoma section (p696). US 50, the last surviving transcontinental route that is not a modern interstate, crosses Kansas and Missouri. The Great River Rd is a well-signed network of roads and highways that runs along the Mississippi River.

Train

A few **Amtrak** (☎ 800-872-7245) routes cross the Plains states (mostly at night).

Ann Rutledge Daily between Chicago and Kansas City (including St Louis).

California Zephyr Between Chicago and San Francisco via Iowa (including Osceola, south of Des Moines) and Nebraska (including Omaha and Lincoln).

Empire Builder Between Chicago and Seattle via North Dakota (including Fargo).

Heartland Flyer Daily between Fort Worth and Oklahoma City.

Kansas City Mule Daily between St Louis and Kansas City.

Southwest Chief Between Chicago and Los Angeles via Missouri (including St Louis and Kansas City) and Kansas (including Newton, north of Wichita).

Texas Eagle & State House Daily between Chicago and St Louis.

MISSOURI

Missouri is the Great Plains' most consistently scenic state, as it has a mix of urban attractions, wilderness areas, the Mississippi and Missouri Rivers and Branson – the Ozarks' answer to Nashville.

Historically the 'Gateway to the West,' St Louis is known for its Arch and its blues. A number of music legends – Chuck Berry, Tina Turner and Miles Davis – got their start here in the 'Home of the Blues.' Kansas City is known for its barbecue, fountains and jazz. It was an important launching pad for many great jazz performers, including Count Basie and Charlie Parker.

The plateaus, hills and valleys of the Ozarks are great recreational areas. Historic river towns possess their own charm. There have been many jokes about Missouri's nickname, the 'Show Me State'; it's based on the legendary skepticism, not willful flashers.

MISSOURI FACTS

Nickname Show Me State

Population 5,672,600 (17th)

Area 69,710 sq miles (21st)

Admitted to Union August 10, 1821 (24th)

Capital city Jefferson City (population 39,000)

Other cities Kansas City (443,500), St Louis (338,400), Springfield (151,000)

Birthplace of Samuel Clemens (Mark Twain), Jesse James, George Washington Carver, Harry S Truman, TS Eliot, singer Sheryl Crow, author Maya Angelou

Famous for Gateway Arch, Budweiser, the first ice-cream cone, hot dog and iced tea

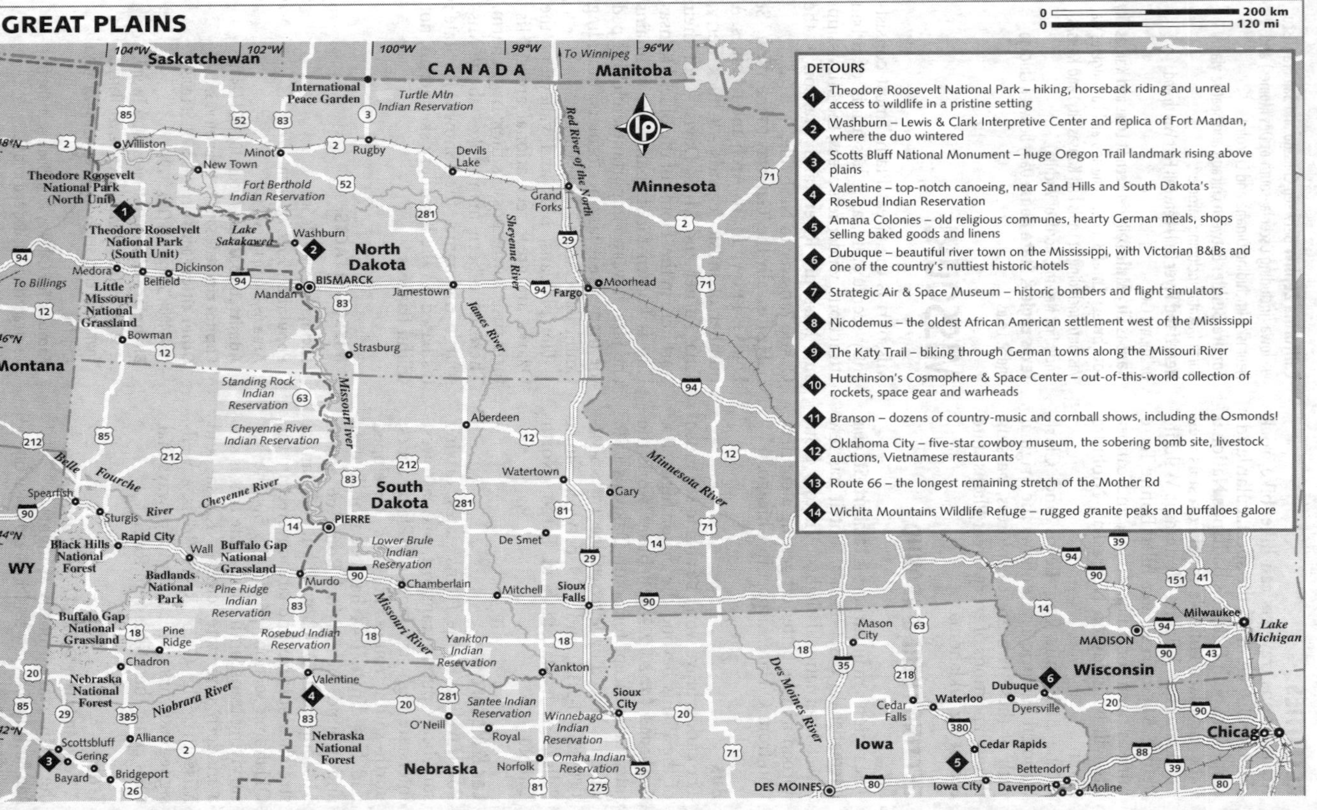

GREAT PLAINS
0 200 km
0 120 mi
DETOURS
1 Theodore Roosevelt National Park – hiking, horseback riding and unreal access to wildlife in a pristine setting
2 Washburn – Lewis & Clark Interpretive Center and replica of Fort Mandan, where the duo wintered
3 Scotts Bluff National Monument – huge Oregon Trail landmark rising above plains
4 Valentine – top-notch canoeing, near Sand Hills and South Dakota's Rosebud Indian Reservation
5 Amana Colonies – old religious communes, hearty German meals, shops selling baked goods and linens
6 Dubuque – beautiful river town on the Mississippi, with Victorian B&Bs and one of the country's nuttiest historic hotels
7 Strategic Air & Space Museum – historic bombers and flight simulators
8 Nicodemus – the oldest African American settlement west of the Mississippi
9 The Katy Trail – biking through German towns along the Missouri River
10 Hutchinson's Cosmophere & Space Center – out-of-this-world collection of rockets, space gear and warheads
11 Branson – dozens of country-music and cornball shows, including the Osmonds!
12 Oklahoma City – five-star cowboy museum, the sobering bomb site, livestock auctions, Vietnamese restaurants
13 Route 66 – the longest remaining stretch of the Mother Rd
14 Wichita Mountains Wildlife Refuge – rugged granite peaks and buffaloes galore
104°W
102°W
100°W
98°W
96°W
48°N
46°N
44°N
42°N
Saskatchewan
CANADA
Manitoba
To Winnipeg
International Peace Garden
Turtle Mtn Indian Reservation
Rugby
Minot
Williston
New Town
Devils Lake
Theodore Roosevelt National Park (North Unit)
Fort Berthold Indian Reservation
Red River of the North
Grand Forks
Minnesota
Theodore Roosevelt National Park (South Unit)
Lake Sakakawea
Washburn
North Dakota
To Billings
Medora
Belfield
Dickinson
BISMARCK
Mandan
Jamestown
Sheyenne River
Fargo
Moorhead
Little Missouri National Grassland
Bowman
James River
Strasburg
Montana
Standing Rock Indian Reservation
Missouri iver
Aberdeen
Cheyenne River Indian Reservation
Minnesota River
Belle Fourche River
Cheyenne River
Watertown
Gary
Spearfish
Sturgis
South Dakota
PIERRE
Rapid City
Black Hills National Forest
Wall
Buffalo Gap National Grassland
Lower Brule Indian Reservation
De Smet
WY
Badlands National Park
Murdo
Chamberlain
Mitchell
Sioux Falls
Pine Ridge Indian Reservation
Missouri River
Buffalo Gap National Grassland
Pine Ridge
Rosebud Indian Reservation
Yankton Indian Reservation
Mason City
Chadron
Valentine
Yankton
Des Moines River
Nebraska National Forest
Niobrara River
Santee Indian Reservation
Sioux City
Winnebago Indian Reservation
Cedar Falls
Waterloo
Dubuque
Dyersville
Wisconsin
MADISON
Milwaukee
Lake Michigan
O'Neill
Royal
Omaha Indian Reservation
Iowa
Cedar Rapids
Chicago
Scottsbluff
Gering
Bayard
Alliance
Bridgeport
Nebraska National Forest
Nebraska
Norfolk
DES MOINES
Iowa City
Davenport
Bettendorf
Moline

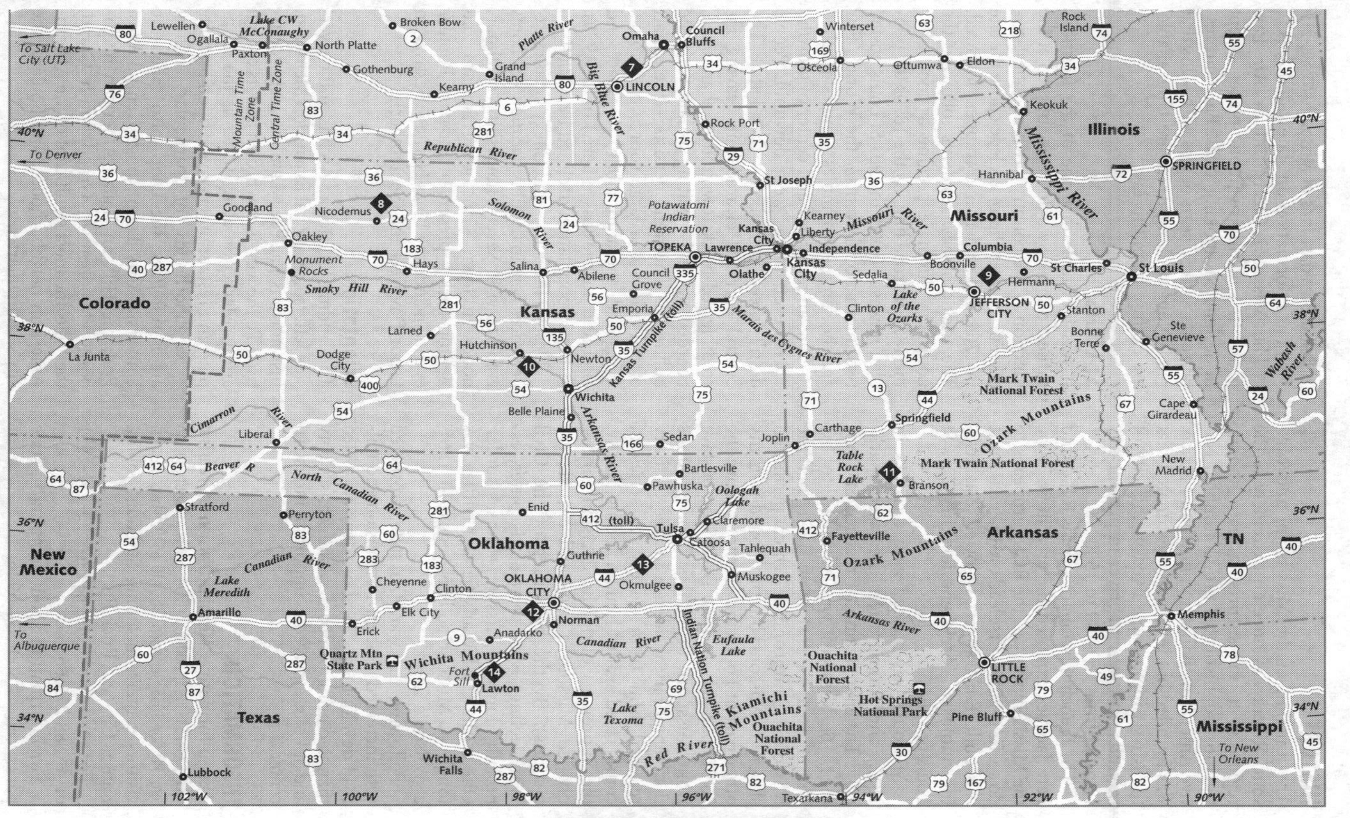

GREAT PLAINS

HISTORY

The junction of the Mississippi and Missouri Rivers was once an extremely fertile region, so it isn't surprising that Cahokia, the most sophisticated pre-Columbian Native American civilization north of Mexico, was founded in the area. It is estimated that the Mississippi people lived in this city of mounds (just over the river in present-day Illinois) from AD 700 to 1500.

The French missionaries Louis Jolliet and Pere Jacques explored the area in 1673 via the Mississippi River, the first Europeans to do so. In 1720 the first lead ore (galena) mine was built. Fur trappers followed, establishing outposts – Ste Genevieve in 1725, St Louis in 1764.

Missouri was created as a territory in 1812, and immigration increased markedly. The first steamboat reached St Louis in 1816. Missouri was admitted to the Union as a slave state in 1821, per the Missouri Compromise (which permitted slavery in Missouri but prohibited it in any other part of Louisiana Territory above the 36°30' parallel). In 1846 Dred Scott, a slave from Missouri, brought suit on grounds that temporary residence in free territory released him from slavery. A series of courts ruled against him, including, finally, the Supreme Court (the decision further divided Missouri's pro- and anti-slavery factions). By the beginning of the Civil War, feelings were particularly bitter, especially along the Missouri–Kansas border. One of the Civil War's fiercest battles was fought on Missouri soil on August 10, 1861, at Wilson's Creek.

Following the war, the state prospered with increased westward expansion and railroad development. Local ore deposits fueled manufacturing companies, and Kansas City and St Louis emerged as important industrial centers.

INFORMATION

The informative **Missouri Division of Tourism** (☎ 573-751-4133, 800-877-1234; www.missouritourism.org; PO Box 1055, Jefferson City, MO 65102) has seven visitors centers, including St Louis, Joplin, Kansas City and Rock Port.

For road conditions, call ☎ 573-751-2551 or ☎ 888-275-6636.

For information about camping in state parks, call ☎ 800-334-6946.

Bed & Breakfast Inns of Missouri (☎ 800-213-5642) has information on statewide B&Bs.

The Missouri Clean Indoor Air Law prohibits smoking in public places except in designated smoking areas. Bars and restaurants with 50 seats or less with signs that read 'Non-smoking Areas are Unavailable' are exempt from this law.

ST LOUIS

It was inevitable that one of the frontier's earliest outposts would be established at the junction of the country's two mightiest rivers. Fur-trapper Pierre Laclede chose the site in 1764, and settlers and trappers followed. The trickle of new residents following the Louisiana Purchase became a flood after the 1857 railroad link. By the 1870s the population was 300,000. In 1904 St Louis hosted two international events – the World's Fair and the Summer Olympics – and established itself as an innovator and center of growth.

However, things went downhill. People didn't 'meet' in St Louis; they left it. The central corridor cleared out, leaving incredible red-brick townhouses abandoned, boarded up and awaiting a date with the bulldozer. (The trend persists – the export of red bricks is a large source of income, along with the automobile, aerospace and aircraft industries based here.) In the 1990s, St Louis' population declined by 50,000.

Despite the stats – and Chevy Chase's experiences here in the film *Vacation* – St Louis is fun to visit. Several flourishing neighborhoods in town – including Soulard and Benton Park – preserve their past. Popular events include the Blues Heritage Festival on Labor Day weekend (September).

Orientation

The landmark Gateway Arch is in the riverside Jefferson National Expansion Memorial. Just north is Laclede's Landing historic district. To the west is downtown and its central artery, Market St, along which is the shopping and restaurant enclave, Union Station.

Neighborhoods of particular interest are Forest Park; the Loop (also called the University City Loop); posh Central West End; the Hill, an Italian-American neighborhood; bohemian Grand South Grand; the Ville, the most significant of the African-American neighborhoods; and Soulard, the city's Latin quarter.

East St Louis, in Illinois, is not a pleasant place after dark.

Information

BOOKSTORES

Hammond's Books & Antiques (Map p681; ☎ 314-776-4737, 800-776-4732; 1939 Cherokee St) Used and out-of-print books with espresso.

Left Bank Books (Map p681; ☎ 314-367-6731; 399 North Euclid, Central West End) New and used indie books.

Rand McNally (☎ 314-863-3555; 2423 St Louis, Galleria) Travel books galore.

EMERGENCY

Aid for Victims of Crime (☎ 314-652-3623)

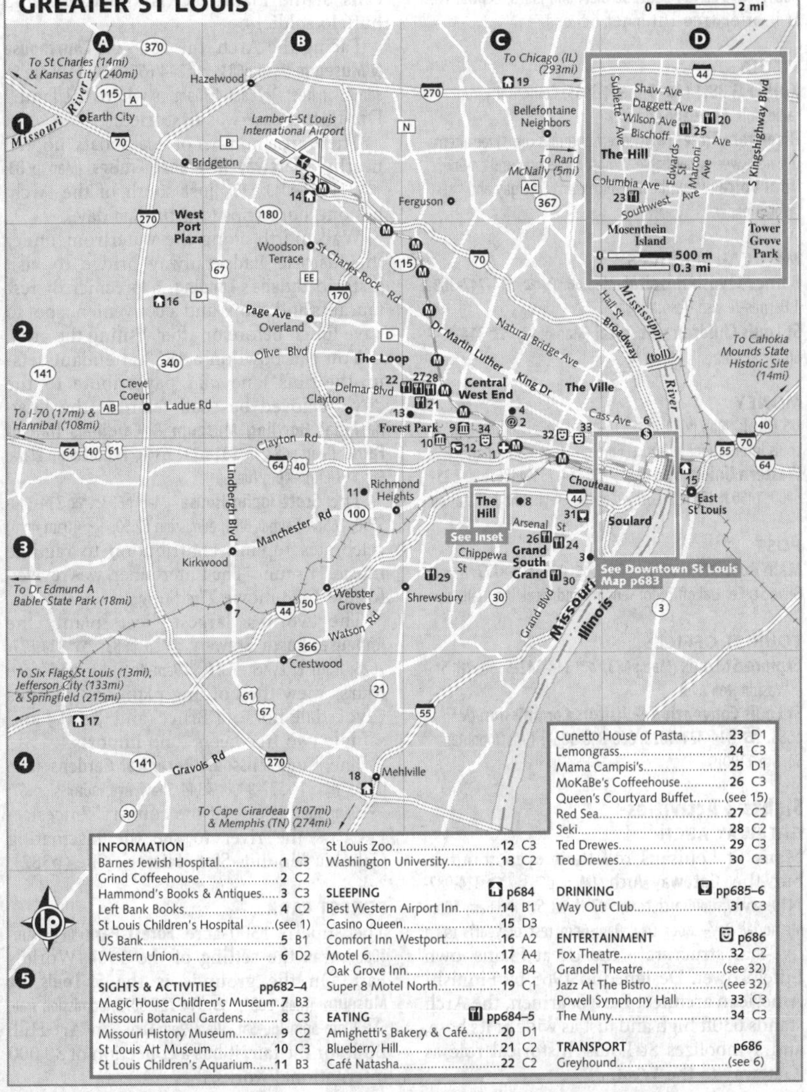

Emergency number (☎ 911) For police, fire or ambulance service.
St Louis Police (☎ 314-444-0100)
Sexual Assault (☎ 314-726-6665)
Travelers Aid Society (☎ 314-241-5820)

INTERNET ACCESS

The **St Louis Public Library** (Map p683; ☎ 314-241-2288; 1301 Olive St) and the **Grind Coffeehouse** (Map p681; ☎ 314-454-0202; 56 Maryland Plaza, Central West End) offer free Internet access.

MEDIA

KDHX FM 88.1 (☎ 314-664-3955) Community-run radio; folk, blues and odd rock.
Riverfront Times (www.riverfronttimes.com) Free alternative newsweekly; available at most bookstores and on-line.
Vital Voice (www.thevitalvoice.com) Free gay and lesbian paper.

MEDICAL SERVICES

Barnes Jewish Hospital (Map p681; ☎ 314-747-3000; 1 Barnes-Jewish Hospital Plaza)
St Louis Children's Hospital (Map p681; ☎ 314-454-6000; 1 Children's Place)

MONEY

US Bank (Map p681; ☎ 314-429-1248; Lambert–St Louis International Airport) Foreign-currency exchange.
Western Union (Map p681; ☎ 314-231-4485, 800-325-6000; 1450 N 13th St) Located at the Greyhound bus station.

POST

Main Post Office (Map p683; ☎ 800-275-8777; 815 Olive St) Central office for sending and receiving mail.

TOURIST OFFICES

Explore St Louis (Map p683; ☎ 314-342-5160; 7th St & Washington Ave)
St Louis Convention & Visitors Commission (Map p683; ☎ 314-421-1023, 800-888-3861; 1 Metropolitan Sq, Ste 1100)

Sights & Activities

GATEWAY ARCH

Many St Louisans roll their eyes about it, but the **Gateway Arch** (Map p683; ☎ 314-982-1410; www.stlouisarch.com; 707 N 1st St; 8am-10pm Memorial Day–Labor Day, 9am-6pm rest of year) is a five-star structure – the Great Plains' own Eiffel Tower. Designed in 1965 by Finnish-American architect Eero Saarinen, the Arch stands 630ft high and just as wide at its base, and symbolizes St Louis' historical role as 'Gateway to the West.'

Unless you're particularly claustrophobic or faint from heights, take the four-minute **tram ride** (adult/child under 12 $8/3.50) to the observatory – it's wise to buy tickets in advance from the website.

The subterranean **Museum of Westward Expansion** (Map p683; admission free; 8am-10pm Memorial Day–Labor Day, 9am-6pm rest of year), under the Arch, has coverage of the Native Americans of the Plains, Lewis and Clark, and buffalo soldiers.

Facing the Arch, the 1845 **Old Courthouse & Museum** (Map p683; ☎ 314-655-1600; 11 N 4th St; admission free; 8am-4:30pm) is where the famed Dred Scott case was first tried.

There are a number of steamboats moored nearby. **Gateway Riverboat Cruises** (Map p683; ☎ 314-621-4040; $10), just south of the Arch, has one-hour trips four times a day.

Walk north along the waterfront under the historic Eads railway bridge to visit historic **Laclede's Landing**, a precinct of restaurants and shops and a convenient spot to have lunch before or after visiting the arch.

You can bowl on a 1922 attendant-sets-up-the-pins lane *and* pay tribute to the city's beloved baseball team at the **International Bowling Museum & Cardinals Hall of Fame** (Map p683; ☎ 314-231-6340; 111 Stadium Plaza; $6; 11am-4pm Tue-Sat).

The **Scott Joplin House** (Map p683; ☎ 314-340-5790; 2658A Delmar Blvd; admission $2.50; 10am-4pm) celebrates Joplin's contribution to ragtime music. His tune 'The Entertainer' was revived for the 1973 movie *The Sting*.

The world's largest beer plant, the **Anheuser-Busch Brewery** (Map p683; ☎ 314-577-2626; 12th & Lynch Sts; 9am-4pm), gives free tours. View the bottling plant and famous Clydesdale horses ('Bruce' and 'Scott') and sample two free beers – no imports.

The huge **Missouri Botanical Gardens** (Map p681; ☎ 314-577-9400; 4344 Shaw Ave; admission $7; 9am-5pm) is one of the country's nicest.

Cross the river to see the fascinating Cahokia Mounds State Historic Site (p382).

FOREST PARK

The superb 1300-acre **Forest Park** (6am-10pm) was the setting of the 1904 World's Fair. On the grounds is the **St Louis Art Museum** (Map p681; ☎ 314-721-0072; admission free; 10am-5pm Tue-Sat, 10am-9pm Sun), on Art Hill. Built for the fair, it has a collection of 30,000 international works.

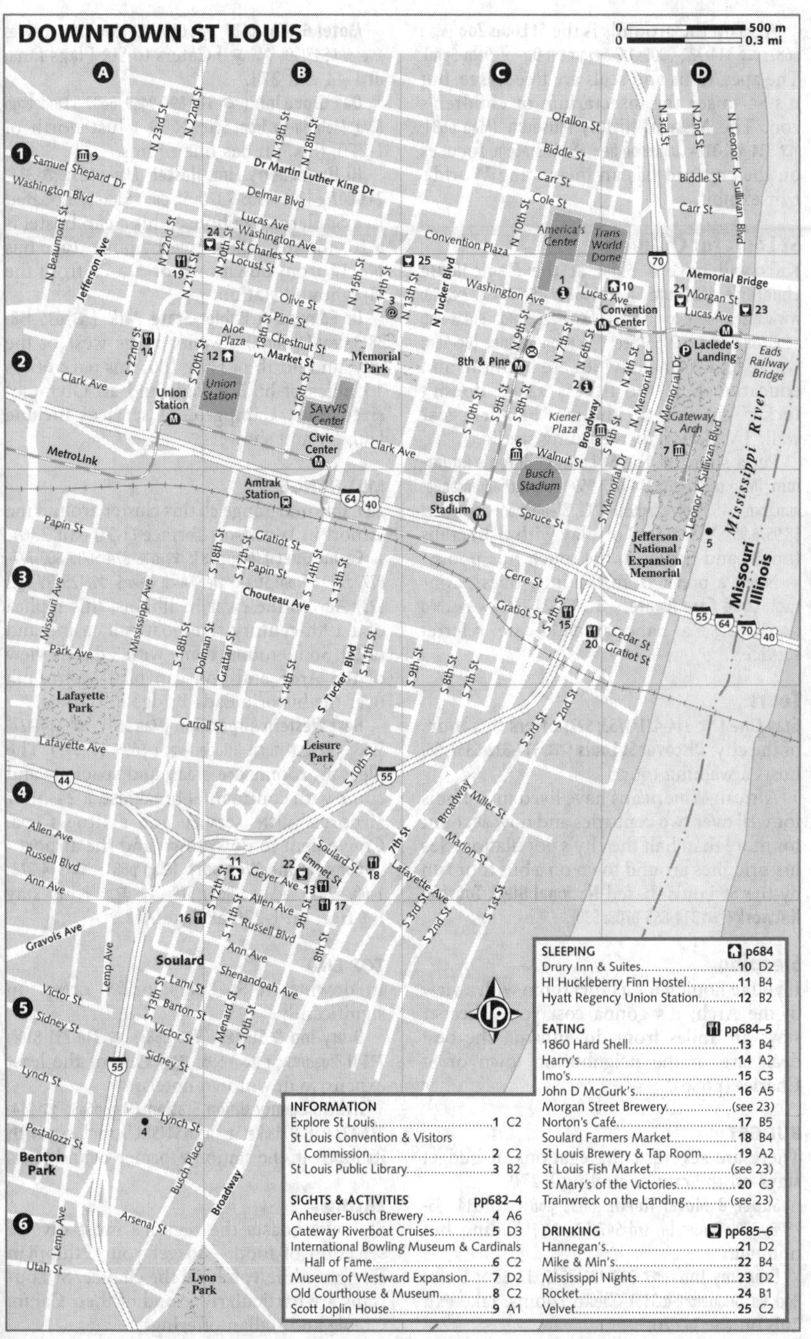
DOWNTOWN ST LOUIS
0 500 m
0 0.3 mi
A
B
C
D
1
2
3
4
5
6
Samuel Shepard Dr
Washington Blvd
N Beaumont St
Jefferson Ave
N 23rd St
N 22nd St
N 19th St
N 18th St
Dr Martin Luther King Dr
Delmar Blvd
Lucas Ave
Washington Ave
St Charles St
Locust St
N 22nd St
N 21st St
N 20th St
Convention Plaza
N 15th St
N 14th St
N 13th St
N Tucker Blvd
Olive St
Pine St
Chestnut St
Market St
Aloe Plaza
S 22nd St
S 20th St
S 18th St
S 16th St
Memorial Park
Union Station
SAVVIS Center
Civic Center
Clark Ave
MetroLink
Amtrak Station
Busch Stadium
Ofallon St
Biddle St
Carr St
Cole St
N 10th St
America's Center
Trans World Dome
Washington Ave
Lucas Ave
Convention Center
N 9th St
8th & Pine
N 7th St
N 6th St
N 4th St
N Memorial Dr
N 3rd St
N 2nd St
N Leonor K Sullivan Blvd
Biddle St
Carr St
Memorial Bridge
Morgan St
Lucas Ave
Laclede's Landing
Eads Railway Bridge
S 10th St
S 9th St
S 8th St
Kiener Plaza
Broadway
S 4th St
S Memorial Dr
Gateway Arch
S Leonor K Sullivan Blvd
Mississippi River
Walnut St
Spruce St
Jefferson National Expansion Memorial
Missouri
Illinois
Papin St
Gratiot St
Papin St
Chouteau Ave
S 18th St
S 17th St
S 14th St
S 13th St
Cerre St
Gratiot St
S 4th St
Cedar St
Gratiot St
Missouri Ave
Mississippi Ave
Park Ave
S 18th St
Dolman St
Grattan St
S 14th St
S Tucker Blvd
S 11th St
S 9th St
S 8th St
S 7th St
S 3rd St
S 2nd St
Lafayette Park
Carroll St
Lafayette Ave
Leisure Park
S 10th St
Broadway
Miller St
Marion St
Allen Ave
Russell Blvd
Ann Ave
Soulard St
Emmet St
7th St
Lafayette Ave
S 3rd St
S 2nd St
S 1st St
Geyer Ave
Allen Ave
Russell Blvd
S 12th St
S 11th St
9th St
8th St
Gravois Ave
Lemp Ave
Soulard
Ann Ave
Shenandoah Ave
Lami St
Barton St
Victor St
Sidney St
S 13th St
Menard St
S 10th St
Victor St
Sidney St
Lynch St
Lynch St
Pestalozzi St
Benton Park
Busch Place
Broadway
Arsenal St
Lemp Ave
Utah St
Lyon Park
SLEEPING p684
Drury Inn & Suites 10 D2
HI Huckleberry Finn Hostel 11 B4
Hyatt Regency Union Station 12 B2
EATING pp684–5
1860 Hard Shell 13 B4
Harry's 14 A2
Imo's 15 C3
John D McGurk's 16 A5
Morgan Street Brewery (see 23)
Norton's Café 17 B5
Soulard Farmers Market 18 B4
St Louis Brewery & Tap Room 19 A2
St Louis Fish Market (see 23)
St Mary's of the Victories 20 C3
Trainwreck on the Landing (see 23)
DRINKING pp685–6
Hannegan's 21 D2
Mike & Min's 22 B4
Mississippi Nights 23 D2
Rocket 24 B1
Velvet 25 C2
INFORMATION
Explore St Louis 1 C2
St Louis Convention & Visitors Commission 2 C2
St Louis Public Library 3 B2
SIGHTS & ACTIVITIES pp682–4
Anheuser-Busch Brewery 4 A6
Gateway Riverboat Cruises 5 D3
International Bowling Museum & Cardinals Hall of Fame 6 C2
Museum of Westward Expansion 7 D2
Old Courthouse & Museum 8 C2
Scott Joplin House 9 A1

Also on the grounds is the **St Louis Zoo** (Map p681; ☎ 314-781-0900; 1 Government Dr; 9am-5pm). The apes, lions and seals are free to see, but it's $4 to see the insectarium or children's zoo. The **Missouri History Museum** (Map p681; ☎ 314-454-3124; admission free; 10am-6pm) focuses on the city and has an interesting World's Fair exhibit.

St Louis for Children

Kids will have a blast at the **Magic House Children's Museum** (Map p681; ☎ 314-822-8900; www.magichouse.com; 516 S Kirkwood Rd, Kirkwood; adult/child under 2 $6/free; noon-5:30pm Tue-Sun) where hands-on activities are both fun and educational. If the fitness safari doesn't tucker 'em out, try the face blender, gear wall, TV station or recording studio.

Pet a shark at the **St Louis Children's Aquarium** (Map p681; ☎ 314-647-9594; www.childrensaquarium.com; 416 Hanley Industrial Ct, Brentwood; adult/child $8.95/6.95; 9am-5pm) or play with fish, crabs (ouch) and turtles in the touch tide pools.

Need a break from the little ones? Contact **Child Care Aware** (☎ 800-424-2246; www.childcareaware.org), a national child-care referral service.

GREAT PLAINS

Tours

Gray Line (☎ 314-421-4753; $22) offers bus tours of the city. **Discover St Louis** (☎ 314-522-6367; $8) hosts a walking tour.

African-Americans have lived in St Louis for well over two centuries and now account for more than half the city's population. See historic sites around town on a bus tour run by the St Louis–based **National Black Tourism Network** (☎ 314-865-0708; $30).

Sleeping

If you're hoping for a hotel room with a view of the Arch, it's gonna cost you. Cheaper stays are miles from downtown. The best deals are in the neighboring town of St Charles (p686).

BUDGET

There are several congregations of budget stays off the city-encircling I-270.

Super 8 Motel North (Map p681; ☎ 314-355-7808; 2790 Target Dr; s/d $47/52) Fading but not bad.

Economy Inn (☎ 314-291-8545, 12433 St Charles Rock Rd, Bridgeton; d $35) Clean rooms; take exit 20B on the I-270.

Motel 6 (Map p681; ☎ 636-349-1800; 1860 Bowles Ave; s/d $45/50) Caters to Six Flags fans; at I-44 exit 274.

Oak Grove Inn (☎ 314-894-9449, 6602 S Lindbergh Blvd, Mehlville; r from $60) Just north of I-270, this inn has fine rooms.

HI Huckleberry Finn Hostel (Map p683; ☎ 314-241-0076; 1904–1908 S 12th St; dm/r $18/40) Located in a Soulard townhouse, this clean hostel is a 10-minute walk to nearby pubs. Take bus No 17 from downtown or No 73 from the Greyhound station.

Dr Edmund A Babler State Park (☎ 636-458-3813; tent/RV $8/14) Twenty miles west of the city, and north of Hwy 100, this park offers 13 miles of hiking trails and an Olympic-sized pool. Campground services include laundry and showers.

MID-RANGE

Reliable mid-range chains cluster around the airport in Woodson Terrace (I-70 exit 236).

Casino Queen (Map p681; ☎ 618-874-5000, 800-777-0777; 200 S Front St; city view/Arch view $104/125, RV sites $23) Across the river in Illinois, this replica of a 19th-century riverboat is a casino and hotel. Some rooms come with a dandy view of the Arch and you can take MetroLink over the historic Eads Bridge into town.

Best Western Airport Inn (Map p681; ☎ 314-427-5955; 10232 Natural Bridge Ave; r $69) The pleasant rooms are clean and spacious and come with continental breakfast, a 24-hour airport shuttle service and a fitness spa. Convenient to downtown and the airport.

Comfort Inn Westport (Map p681; ☎ 314-878-1400; 12031 Lackland Rd; r $79) Kids stay for free; off I-270 at Page Ave.

TOP END

In downtown St Louis, prices creep up significantly.

Drury Inn & Suites (Map p683; ☎ 314-231-8100; 711 N Broadway; r from $95) One of the least expensive downtown hotels.

Hyatt Regency Union Station (Map p683; ☎ 314-231-1234; 1820 Market St; r from $115) Ultraclassy with its lobby in the station's former Grand Hall.

Eating

St Louis boasts the region's most diverse selection of food – so get your Ethiopian fix here while you have the chance. St Louisans are particularly proud of their Cajun, Creole and Italian offerings.

RIVERFRONT & DOWNTOWN

At **Laclede's Landing** are all manner of American eateries, most in restored warehouses. **Union Station** (18th & Market) once housed trains and now is also home to shops and fine eateries.

Hannegan's (Map p683; ☎ 314-241-8877; 719 N 2nd St; mains $14-20) Prime rib and live jazz.

St Louis Fish Market (Map p683; ☎ 314-621-4612; 901 N 1st St) Fish fillets and sushi.

Trainwreck on the Landing (Map p683; ☎ 314-436-1006; 720 N 1st St; mains $7) Try the yummy ostrich burgers.

Morgan Street Brewery (Map p683; ☎ 314-231-9970; 721 N 2nd St; mains $15-25) Microbrews and pasta.

Imo's (Map p683; ☎ 314-421-4667; 742 S 4th St; $7) St Louis' own tasty style of pizza – square-shaped and thin-crusted – ready to eat under the Arch.

Queen's Courtyard Buffet (Map p681; ☎ 618-874-5000, 800-777-0777; 200 S Front St) In the Casino Queen with buffets all day.

Harry's (Map p683; 2144 Market St) Upscale and next to the FBI, Harry's attracts a well-dressed after-work crowd.

St Louis Brewery & Tap Room (Map p683; ☎ 314-241-2337; 2100 Locust St) Offers alternatives to Budweiser, as well as innovative pub grub.

SOULARD

If you will only eat one dinner in St Louis, head to this leafy 'hood. There are restaurants and pubs on most corners.

John D McGurk's (Map p683; ☎ 314-776-8309; 1200 Russell Blvd; mains $7-19) The city's favorite pub has traditional Irish dishes and Irish bands play most nights.

For Cajun and Creole food, try **Norton's Café** (Map p683; ☎ 314-436-0828; 808 Geyer Ave; mains $10-20) for jambalaya or crawdad specials, or go to **1860 Hard Shell** (Map p683; ☎ 314-231-1860; 1860 S 9th St; mains $7-20), a three-part restaurant-bar with delicious broiled cod and live blues every night.

You can buy vittles at the **Soulard Farmers Market** (Map p683; Lafayette Ave & 7th St; ⌚ Tue-Sat).

THE HILL

This neighborhood – marked with 'Italian-flag' fire hydrants – features some of the best Italian food this side of the Mississippi.

Cunetto House of Pasta (Map p681; ☎ 314-781-1135; 5453 Magnolia Ave; mains $9-17) Veal dishes and low-salt pastas.

Amighetti's Bakery & Café (Map p681; ☎ 314-776-2855; 5141 Wilson Ave; mains $5) A traditional place.

Mama Campisi's (Map p681; ☎ 314-771-1797; 2132 Edwards St; $8-24) Delicious toasted ravioli.

GRAND SOUTH GRAND

Running along South Grand Blvd, this area thrives with a youthful lot and is a good area to find vegetarian fare.

MoKaBe's Coffeehouse (Map p681; ☎ 314-865-2009; 3606 Arsenal St) Famous for its grilled veggie sandwich ($5) and the huge sprawling all-vegetarian Sunday brunch ($10).

Lemongrass (Map p681; ☎ 314-664-6702; 3216 S Grand Blvd; mains $5-10) This is a cheap, authentic Vietnamese restaurant, with many meatless dishes.

Ted Drewes (Map p681; ☎ 314-481-2652; 4224 S Grand Blvd; ⌚ year-round) Do not leave St Louis without gorging on the frozen custard here. On a warm evening, bring a book; lines get long. There's another branch at 6726 Chippewa St, which is open in summer.

CENTRAL WEST END & THE LOOP

Near Washington University, 'the Loop' runs along Delmar Blvd with many international eateries catering to a younger crowd.

Red Sea (Map p681; ☎ 314-863-0099; 6511 Delmar Blvd; mains $6-12) Ethiopian specialities.

Seki (Map p681; ☎ 314-726-6477; 6335 Delmar Blvd; mains $16) Tasty Japanese box lunches.

Café Natasha (Map p681; ☎ 314-727-0419; 6623 Delmar Blvd; mains $11.50-16.50) Upscale, with good Persian dinners.

Blueberry Hill (Map p681; ☎ 314-727-0880; 6504 Delmar Blvd; mains $5-9) Heaps of rock memorabilia and good burgers.

Drinking

Most bars around town close at 1am, when the action moves to '3am licensed' downtown clubs (centered on Washington Ave, west of Tucker Blvd).

Rocket (Map p683; 2001 Locust St) A good bar on the indie-rock circuit.

Velvet (Map p683; 1301 Washington Ave; $5 cover; ⌚ until 3am) DJ-blasting trance, house and techno and laser-lit dance floor.

Most of the Laclede's Landing and Soulard pubs are archetypal drinking holes with live music on weekends.

In the Landing, **Mississippi Nights** (Map p683; 914 N 1st St) is a club hosting big-name acts, while in Soulard, go to **Mike & Min's** (Map p683;

(🕑 Wed-Sat; 925 Geyer Ave) to sit side-by-side with Soulardians chugging Bud Light and listening to blues bands. Further west, **Way Out Club** (2525 S Jefferson Ave) is another worthy rock venue.

Entertainment

St Louis' best show is held once a month (on the third Thursday) when St Louis native Chuck Berry rocks the small basement bar at **Blueberry Hill** (see Eating, p685). The $22 tickets sell out quickly.

Fox Theatre (Map p681; ☎ 314-534-1111, tours 314-534-1678; 527 N Grand Blvd) Catch a concert, dance performance or Broadway show at this 1929 theater in the heart of the Grand Center, St Louis' arts district. Seeing the Fox's ornate interior alone is worth the price of admission.

Powell Symphony Hall (Map p681; ☎ 314-534-1700; 718 N Grand Blvd) The St Louis Symphony Orchestra raises its bows and tubas here.

The **Muny** (Map p681; ☎ 314-361-1900) Otherwise known as the Municipal Opera Association, it hosts nightly summer shows in Forest Park (some of the 12,000 seats are free).

Jazz at the Bistro (Map p681; ☎ 314-531-1012; 3536 Washington Ave) Straight-up jazz across from the Fox Theatre.

Grandel Theatre (Map p681; ☎ 314-534-3807; www.stlouisblackrep.com; 3610 Grandel Sq; $30) The St Louis Black Repertory Company puts on plays by African-American playwrights at this Grand Center Theater.

For listings, grab the free weekly *Riverfront Times*.

SPECTATOR SPORTS

They're sports mad in St Louis.

Busch Stadium (Map p683; ☎ 314-421-2400; 250 Stadium Plaza) A baseball shrine to the Cardinals, whose fortunes rose with the exploits of slugger Mark McGwire, interim heir to Roger Maris' home-run record (Barry Bonds passed him just a couple of years later).

NFL team the Rams play downtown at Trans World Dome (Map p683; ☎ 314-425-8830; 901 N Broadway) at America's Center, while the St Louis Blues play NHL hockey at the Savvis Center (Map p683; ☎ 314-622-2500; 1401 Clark Ave).

Getting There & Away

Lambert–St Louis International Airport (Map p681; ☎ 314-426-8000) has services to all major US cities as well as Omaha (Nebraska), Des Moines (Iowa), and Oklahoma City (Oklahoma). The airport is 12 miles northwest of downtown, connected by bus, light-rail system, taxi (about $30) or the shuttle service **Exit Express** (☎ 314-646-1166; $30). If you can gather other travelers destined for the same part of town the group rate is considerably less at $11 a person.

The **Greyhound bus station** (Map p681; ☎ 314-231-4485; 1450 N 13th St) is just north of downtown, though some buses stop at the airport. Several buses leave daily for Chicago ($31, 6½ hours), Indianapolis ($23, 4½ hours), Memphis ($41, seven hours) and Oklahoma City ($79, 12½ hours).

The **Amtrak station** (Map p683; ☎ 314-331-3300, 550 S 16th St) is a couple of blocks southeast of Union Station. Three trains travel to Chicago daily ($27 to $58, 5½ hours); there are also trains bound for Kansas City ($26 to $52, 5½ hours) and, with bus connection, Memphis ($69 to $100, 7½ hours).

Getting Around

The **Bi-State Transit System** (BSTS; ☎ 314-231-2345; $1.25, day pass $4) runs local buses as well as the excellent MetroLink light-rail. The Levee Line is a free rail service between Union Station and Laclede's Landing (weekdays only). **Yellow Cabs** (☎ 314-361-2345) charges $1.50 a mile.

RIVER TOWNS

Interesting towns that make popular weekend excursions for St Louisans lie north and south of St Louis on the Mississippi River and just west on the Missouri.

St Charles

This historic river town, founded in 1769 by the French, is on the Missouri River 20 miles northwest of St Louis, and is now almost a suburb. The **St Charles Convention & Visitors Center** (☎ 636-946-7776; 230 S Main St) has information.

The picturesque, historic nine-block downtown is a few miles off the interstate and features the first **state capitol** (S Main St). The historic 26-block **Frenchtown neighborhood** (N Main St) is just north.

Lewis and Clark heritage days are reenacted in the third week of May, and the **Lewis & Clark Center** (☎ 636-947-3199; 1050 Riverside Dr; $2; 🕑 10am-5pm) has exhibits.

For cyclists, St Charles is the eastern gateway to the Katy Trail State Park (p688).

GREAT PLAINS

Near the small town of Defiance, on Hwy 94, 20 miles southwest of St Charles, the **Daniel Boone Home** (☎ 636-798-2005; $7; closed in winter) is where the frontier legend lived from 1803 until his death in 1820.

Along St Charles' three I-70 exits are newer, better-value motels than those in St Louis. The reliable **Red Roof Inn** (☎ 636-947-7770; 2010 Zumbehl Rd; s/d $40/43) has clean rooms. St Charles has several good B&Bs, including **Boone's Lick Trail B&B** (☎ 636-947-7000; www.booneslick.com; 1000 S Main St; r from $120; P), a class act with claw-foot bathtubs and four-poster beds.

Hannibal

From the look of things in the weary birthplace of Mark Twain, 105 miles north of St Louis, the author's appeal to travelers began to wane around the time MTV got rolling. No new motels have been built since around then, and most attractions are dated.

Still, for big-time fans, the scenes of Tom Sawyer and Huck Finn's great adventures are irresistible. You can see the white fence Tom didn't paint and the cave where he and Becky Thatcher got lost. The large **Mark Twain Boyhood Home & Museum** (☎ 573-221-9010; 208 Hill St; $6; 8am-6pm) features four replica buildings, two films and three gift shops. Get a new copy of *Life of Mississippi* stamped with the museum logo. Float down the Mississippi on the **Mark Twain Riverboat** (☎ 573-221-3222; Center St; $10; 11am, 1:30pm, 4pm & 6:30pm). The Saturday and Sunday dinner cruises offer a live Dixieland band.

The **Hannibal Inn** (☎ 573-221-6610; 4141 Market St; s/d $65/75; P), off Hwy 61, boasts a large, heated cloverleaf pool (with additional whirlpool and sauna) and a playground.

Ste Genevieve

This little town, 60 miles south of St Louis, was the first permanent settlement in Missouri (1725). French influences are evident in many buildings; several can be toured, including the **Bolduc-Le Meilleur House** (admission $4; Apr-Oct) and **Bolduc House** (☎ 573-883-3105; 125 S Main St; admission $4; 10am-4pm Apr-Oct). The **Ste Genevieve Museum** (☎ 573-883-3461; Merchant & Duborg; $2; 9am-4pm) has many relics relating to the town's heyday. The **Great River Road Interpretive Center** (☎ 573-883-7097; 66 S Main St; 9am-5pm) has exhibits on the Mississippi River and information on B&Bs.

Cape Girardeau

Another pleasant river town, 115 miles downstream from St Louis, Cape Girardeau was a steamboat stop as early as 1835. Drop by the **visitors center** (☎ 573-335-1631; 100 Broadway; 8am-5:30pm) for brochures. The **Cape Heritage Museum** (☎ 573-334-0405; 538 Independence St; $2; 11am-4pm) tells the story of the town. Downtown's **Water St** and the nearby **riverfront** are fine places for a stroll.

About 10 miles north, on Hwy 177, is **Trail of Tears State Park** (☎ 573-334-1711), a beautiful region that belies its sad past as part of the Cherokees' forced march to Oklahoma. There are trails, Mississippi overlooks and **camping** (tent/RV $8/15).

ALONG I-70

The fastest route between St Louis and Kansas City is I-70, but it's not particularly interesting. Halfway across the state, **Columbia** is a nice college town, home to the University of Missouri – the oldest university west of the Mississippi.

Boone's Lick State Historic Park (admission free), northwest of Boonville on Hwy 87, is where Daniel Boone's sons manufactured salt from the 'licks,' natural saltwater springs. Just across the Missouri, and reached by Hwy 41, tiny **Arrow Rock State Historic Site** (☎ 660-837-3330) was first settled in 1810 and was later an important stopover on the Santa Fe Trail. It has more than a dozen historic buildings and a superb **visitors center** (admission free; 10am-4pm) which has information about the Boone's Lick region. Arrow Rock has good, developed **campsites** (campsites/RV sites $8/14).

ALONG US 50, HWY 94 & HWY 100

A slower alternative from St Louis to Kansas City is US 50 but, frankly, it's not much more attractive. Better drives between St Louis and Jefferson City hug the banks of the Missouri: to the north, Hwy 94 runs alongside the Katy Trail; to the south, Hwy 100 passes through the pretty German town of **Hermann**, home to wineries and the cozy rooms of **Acorn Bunk & Bagel** (☎ 573-486-4003; 236 W 4th St; r $39-49).

So little is going on in the small state capital, **Jefferson City** ('Jeff City'), on US 50, that a law had to be passed requiring state officials to live here. The state capitol does, however, have impressive **murals**.

Ragtime immortal Scott Joplin once lived in **Sedalia**, 75 miles east of Kansas City. The town hosts a **Ragtime Festival** in June and the **Missouri State Fair** in August. The **chamber of commerce** (☎ 816-826-2222; 113 E 4th St) provides information.

Katy Trail State Park

The **Katy Trail State Park** (☎ 800-334-6946; www.katytrailstatepark.com) boasts a superb 225-mile biking and hiking trail that connects St Charles and Clinton, 65 miles southeast of Kansas City. Open since 1986, the trail runs along the former Missouri–Kansas–Texas railroad (the 'Katy'). Along its eastern end, the trail snakes between high bluffs and the Missouri River. Some of its most scenic sections are west of Defiance, where wee German towns make up 'Missouri's Rhineland,' including hilltop Hermann. Another highlight is the stretch between Jefferson City and New Franklin, including areas inaccessible to cars. Amtrak stops in Hermann, Jeff City and Sedalia, and bike rentals and accommodations are available in each (and also in Defiance).

ALONG I-44

Between St Louis and the state's southwest border with Oklahoma, I-44 is built over Route 66, and derelict gas stations, diners and motels dot the roadside. Just south of Stanton, the **Meramac Caverns** (☎ 800-676-6105; adult/child $14/7; 9am-7pm) are as interesting for their Civil War history and hokey charm as for their stalactites. Watch for **Route 66 relics** toward Springfield, which is the turnoff to the Ozarks (see below).

West of Springfield a 40-mile stretch of Route 66 survives as Hwy 96, and 19th-century **Carthage** provides serious nostalgia appeal. South of Joplin, on Hwy 71, the **George Washington Carver National Monument** (☎ 417-325-4151; 5646 Carver Rd, Diamond; admission free; 9am-5pm) has displays on the African-American scientist, known for developing 105 ways to prepare the peanut.

OZARK MOUNTAINS

Most of the Ozarks are in Arkansas, but the charming hill country extends into the southern quarter of Missouri and into eastern Oklahoma. Much of the Missouri Ozarks were stripped of timber in the late 19th century, and many rivers have been dammed to create a network of lakes.

The **Ozark Trail** (☎ 573-751-2479) is a 300-mile hiking trail through parts of the Mark Twain National Forest. One day it will run 500 miles from St Louis to Arkansas' Ozark Highland Trail.

North of US 60, midway between Cape Girardeau and Springfield, the **Ozark Scenic Riverways** (☎ 573-323-4236) – Current River and Jack's Fork – boast 134 miles of splendid canoeing and tubing. There are six **campgrounds** along the Riverways. **Van Buren**, on Hwy 60, has motels and canoe rentals. Take the fun car ferry across the river, off Hwy KK near Rector.

About 70 miles southwest of St Louis, **Bonne Terre Mine** (☎ 314-731-5003; walking tour/boat tour $12.50/17.50; 10:30am-3:30pm) is near the intersection of Hwys 47 and 67. The water-filled, 80-sq-mile mine, built in 1864 to mine lead, is open for scuba diving on weekends only and requires a two-dive minimum. Dives start at $65.

Branson

This love-it-or-hate-it tourist town (population 6050) is to country music what Disney is to history. The main attractions are the 47 theaters hosting 70 country music and corny comedy shows. During peak season – June and July, and Labor Day to Christmas – the population swells to 150,000.

The neon-lit '76 Strip' (Hwy 76) looks like an Ozark Vegas, with several miles of hotels, theaters, restaurants and wax museums. When shows let out, traffic crawls. Watch for the color-coded routes that bypass it.

The **visitors center** (☎ 417-334-4136; Hwy 248), just west of the US 65 junction, has town and lodging information. The scores of 'Visitor Information' centers around town offer free tickets to shows if you'll sit through a 90-minute time-share plug.

Many **theater shows** are associated with particular performers (often performing in peak season only), such as Wayne Newton, Andy Williams, Glen Campbell, the Osmond Brothers (but not Tito, he's a Jackson), Bobby Vinton, Yakov Smirnoff and Mel Tillis. Other shows include the long-running, hokey 'Baldknobbers Jamboree.' Show prices are $20 to $53 a head; theaters usually run afternoon and evening shows. For tickets, call **Ozark Ticket & Travel** (☎ 417-336-3432, 888-998-4253). Reserve a week in advance during peak season.

Two outdoor attractions, open since 1959, spurred the Branson boom. Huge **Silver Dollar**

City (☎ 417-336-7180, 800-831-4386; adult/child $39/28; 🕒 9:30am-6pm), west of town, is a popular amusement park that relives the Mark Twain era with music shows, replica buildings and craft shops. The **Shepherd of the Hills** (☎ 417-334-4191; 5586 W Hwy 76; $35 with dinner) is a show based on a homespun novel of Ozark life.

Around popular Table Rock Lake, southwest of town, are tons of **campsites** (most geared to RVs). Branson fills up with package-tour visitors during peak times. To snare any of the overpriced accommodations, you might have to use a reservation service: **Branson Hotline** (☎ 800-523-7589) books rooms for $50 and up, and **Branson Vacation Reservations** (☎ 800-221-5692) has package deals (three shows and two nights for $229).

Shady Lane Resort (☎ 417-334-3823; 404 N Sycamore St; $45-55) has clean cabins with kitchenettes.

KANSAS CITY

It's said that St Louis looks east and Kansas City (KC) looks west. This bustling farm-distribution and industrial center was, for generations, a serious 'cow town.' Its giant stockyards closed in 1991.

KC started life in 1821 as a trading post and expanded rapidly after the arrival of the steamboats and, later, westward expansion (it was then called Westport). Prior to the Civil War, KC was caught up in the maelstrom of 'Bleeding Kansas,' a conflict between pro- and anti-slavery groups. During KC's roaring gangster days of the 1930s, rabble-rousing mayor Tom Pendergast built lovely buildings and winding Brush Creek, profiting his own cement company.

Today, Kansas City – including its smaller neighbor Kansas City, Kansas – is a very livable (and large) metropolis. Within its sprawl is more space than any other large US city: each person gets 85,842 sq ft. That extra elbow room comes in handy when chowing down at one of the 90-plus establishments devoted to KC's famous barbecue.

Orientation

I-70 is the main east–west route into the city, and it connects the two halves of KC across the Kansas River. In downtown, I-70 meets I-35, which runs northeast–southwest (crossing the Missouri River), as well as I-29, which heads north to the airport. The encircling I-435 takes in all of KC's sprawl, from the airport in the north, to near Independence in the east, and the suburb of Overland Park in the southwest.

State Line Rd, running north–south, divides KC Missouri and KC Kansas (which has little to offer travelers). KC Missouri has some distinct areas, including the historic River Market (also called City Market), centered on 5th St and Walnut St, north of downtown; the historic African-American 18th & Vine District; the historic Westport District, based on Westport Rd near Broadway; and the huge Country Club Plaza shopping and dining precinct, based on Broadway between 46th and 48th Sts.

Information

The Greater Kansas City **visitors center** (☎ 816-221-5242, 800-767-7700; www.gointokansascity.com; 25th fl, 1100 Main St) is in City Center Sq. A good resource is the **Missouri Visitors Center** (☎ 816-889-3330; 4010 Blue Ridge Cutoff), off I-70, east of I-435.

Kansas City's **Main Library** (☎ 816-701-3400, 311 E 12th St) and **Westport Library** (☎ 816-701-3635; 118 Westport Rd) have free Internet access.

Sights & Activities

The outdoor deck observatory at **City Hall** (414 12th St) has great views and is free. The **Hallmark Visitors Center** (☎ 816-274-5672; 2450 Grand Blvd; admission free; 🕒 9am-5pm Mon-Sat), in Crown Center, is a celebration of the syrupy sentimentality of greeting cards. Kids can design their own cards.

The **Kansas City Zoo** (☎ 816-513-5701; Swope Pk, 63rd St & Swope Parkway; adult/child $7.50/4.50; 🕒 9am-5pm), southeast of the Country Club Plaza, is popular for its gibbons and rhinos. Another kid favorite, the amusement park **Worlds of Fun** (☎ 816-454-4545; adult/child $36/15) and adjoining water-park **Oceans of Fun** (☎ 816-454-4545; adult/child $25/15) are a few miles northeast of downtown (I-435 exit 54).

The recently reopened 1914 **Union Station** (Main St & Pershing Rd) has a restaurant, small historical museum, several giant-screen movie theaters and the new **Science City** (☎ 816-460-2000; adult/child $9/7; 🕒 10am-5pm Mon-Sat, noon-5pm Sun), which is a metropolis with kid-friendly exhibits, including an astronaut-training program and a foamy floored 'sewer.' Across Pershing Rd is the towering **Liberty Memorial**, built for WWI veterans.

Take an eerie drive through the 800-acre **SubTropolis**, just east of I-435 on Hwy 210

GREAT PLAINS

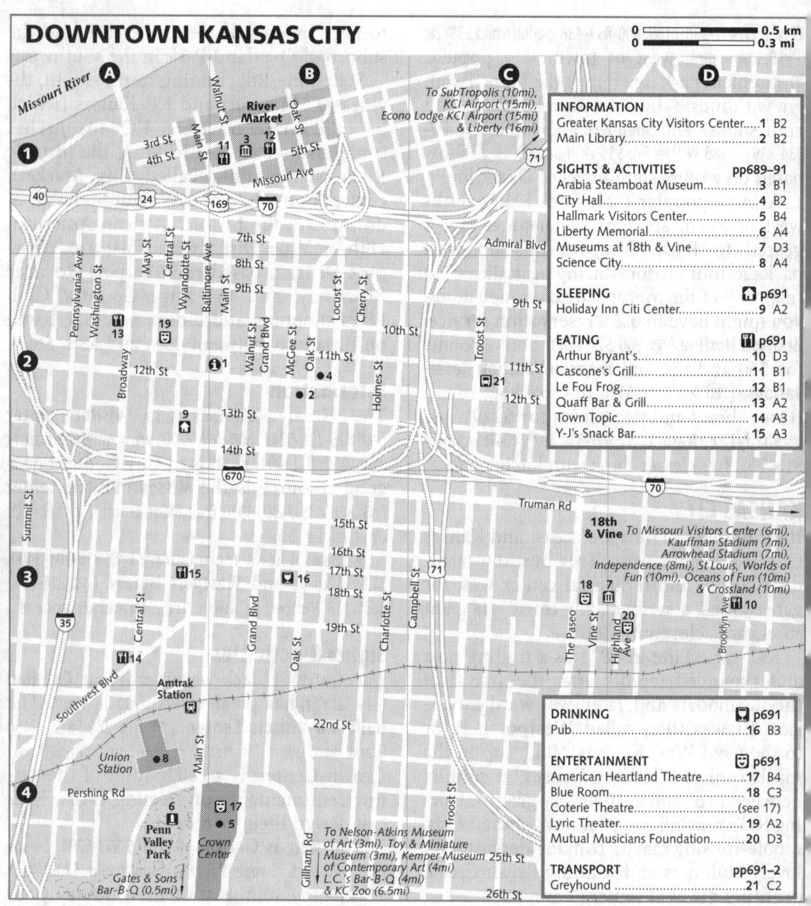

(northeast of downtown), a subterranean free-trade zone built in limestone.

MUSEUMS

The **Museums at 18th & Vine** (☎ 816-474-8463; 1616 E 18th St; one/two museums $6/8; 🕘 9am-6pm Tue-Sat, noon-6pm Sun) are well worth visiting. You can play drums to Sonny Rollins at the interactive **American Jazz Museum**, which also has displays on key musicians, including KC Kansas native Charlie Parker. Visit the **Negro Leagues Baseball Museum** to learn about African-American teams (eg the KC Monarchs and New York Black Yankees) that flourished until baseball became fully integrated in 1959. Displays cover stars such as Satchel Paige and Jackie Robinson.

Home to 200 tons of salvaged 'treasure' from a riverboat that was snagged and then sunk in 1856, the **Arabia Steamboat Museum** (☎ 816-471-4030; 400 Grand Blvd; $9.75; 🕘 10am-6pm Mon-Sat, noon-5pm Sun), located in River Market, offers insight to the crafty Missouri River, which claimed 289 steamboats.

The grand **Nelson-Atkins Museum of Art** (☎ 816-561-4000; 4525 Oak St; $5) has giant shuttlecocks on its lawn (courtesy of Claes Oldenburg) and an excellent collection of Asian, American and European art. Be sure to see the 14th-century Chinese temple and Duane Hanson's Museum Guard, which amazes school kids. Nearby is the **Kemper Museum of Contemporary Art** (☎ 816-753-5784; 4420 Warwick Blvd; free).

The **Toy & Miniature Museum** (☎ 816-333-2055; 5235 Oak St; adult/child $4/2; 10am-4pm Mon-Sat, 1-4pm Sun) draws an older crowd for its detailed dollhouses and antique toys.

Sleeping

Cheap motels are way outside the city center. You'll find some near the KC airport to the north (I-29 exits 12 and 13), around the city at I-435 exits and in Independence (p692).

Econo Lodge KCI Airport (☎ 816-464-5082; 11300 NW Prairie View Rd; s/d $45/55;) Comfortable rooms, off I-29 exit 12.

Crossland (☎ 816-413-0060; 4301 N Garrington Ave; s/d $45/55;) Clean rooms and across the street from Worlds of Fun. Off I-435 in Overland Park (about 12 miles southwest of downtown).

Downtown accommodations are all costly; try the historic **Holiday Inn Citi Centre** (☎ 816-471-1333; 1215 Wyandotte St; r from $ 129), within walking distance of the theater district.

Eating & Drinking

Cascone's Grill (☎ 816-471-1018; 20 E 5th St; mains $5.50) An old River Market favorite for cheap breakfasts, sandwiches and minestrone soup.

Le Fou Frog (☎ 816-474-6060; 400 E 5th St; lunch $8-14, dinner mains $18-32) An exquisite Provence-inspired bistro with a menu changing daily. On Sunday nights there's live music.

Quaff Bar & Grill (☎ 816-842-4745; 1010 Broadway; mains $6) Downtown workers laze in Quaff's vinyl booths; tuna melts are served on plastic plates.

Town Topic (☎ 816-842-2298; 2021 Broadway; mains $3) Burgers sizzle on Town Topic's grill all night long.

Y-J's Snack Bar (☎ 816-472-5533; 128 W 18th St; mains $6) Tiny but crammed with 1950s whatnots. It's good for coffee and sandwiches, and is near many art galleries.

A diverse crowd meets at the friendly downtown bar the **Pub** (1721 McGee St). The bubbling grease fry drowns out the jukebox.

'CUEING IT UP

Savoring hickory-and-oak smoked brisket, pork or ribs at one of the classic barbecue joints around town is a must for any meat eater. KC's own style of barbecue is pit-smoked and slathered with a really thick, sweet, tomato-based sauce. **Arthur Bryant's** (☎ 816-231-1123; 1727 Brooklyn Ave) flops two handfuls of meat between outmatched slices of bread. Arguably the city's most famous barbecue is at **Gates & Sons Bar-B-Q** (☎ 816-753-0272; 3201 Main St), where it is assumed you'll want a frosted mug of beer with your brisket or turkey. Hole-in-the-wall **LC's Bar-B-Q** (☎ 816-923-4484; 5800 Blue Parkway) is a modest joint that serves up some immodest ribs.

Entertainment

Pick up the free *Pitch Weekly* for entertainment listings.

CLUBS

There are live-music venues in Westport and the River Market.

Blue Room (☎ 816-474-2929; 18th & Vine; $5) In the heart of the Jazz District, this slick club hosts jazz shows on Monday, Thursday, Friday and Saturday nights.

Mutual Musicians Foundation (☎ 816-471-5212; 1823 Highland Ave) One of a kind, this historic place is home to all musicians. Saturday night jam sessions roll from midnight, when the musicians show up after other gigs, well into the morning hours.

PERFORMING ARTS

Coterie Theatre (☎ 816-474-6552; Crown Center; adult/child $8/6) Kids dig the plays staged here. Recent hits include *Schoolhouse Rock Live Too!*

American Heartland Theatre (☎ 816-842-9999; www.ahtkc.com; Crown Center; $15-25) Broadway-style productions.

The **Lyric Opera of Kansas City** (☎ 816-471-7344) and the **Kansas City Symphony** (☎ 816-471-0400) perform downtown at the **Lyric Theater** (1029 Central St).

SPECTATOR SPORTS

The Chiefs NFL and Wizards pro soccer teams play at **Arrowhead Stadium** (☎ 816-920-9300), east of downtown at I-70 and the Blue Ridge Cutoff. The city's baseball team, the **Kansas City Royals** (☎ 800-676-9257; $5-22), play at **Kauffman Stadium** (I-70 & Blue Ridge Cutoff).

Getting There & Around

KC International Airport (KCI; ☎ 816-243-5237) is 17 miles northwest of downtown. A taxi into town costs about $42; call **Yellow Cab** (☎ 816-471-5000). The **KCI Shuttle** (☎ 816-243-5000; $14) is cheaper.

Greyhound (☎ 816-221-2885; 12th & Troost Sts) sends buses daily to Omaha ($30; four hours), Chicago ($50; 13 hours) and St Louis ($32; five hours), among others. **Amtrak** (☎ 816-421-3622) is just behind Union Station.

Local transport is with **Metro buses** (☎ 816-221-0660; $1).

AROUND KANSAS CITY

Independence

East of Kansas City, Independence was the home of Harry S Truman, US president from 1945 to 1953. The **Truman Presidential Library & Museum** (☎ 816-833-1400; 500 W US 24; adult $7, child 6-18 $3; 9am-5pm Mon-Sat, noon-5pm Sun) exhibits more than 30,000 objects, from political cartoons to the presidential piano. See how Harry and Bess lived at the **Truman Home** (219 N Delaware St; $3), packed with unmoved, original belongings. Tour tickets are sold at the **visitors center** (☎ 816-254-9929; 223 N Main St). All the Truman sites are open daily in summer; after Labor Day they're closed. The courthouse where Harry began his political career is in nearby Independence Sq.

There are a number of motels around the junction of I-70 and Noland Rd (exit 12). **Serendipity B&B** (☎ 816-833-4719; 116 S Pleasant Ave; s/d from $45/85), near Truman's home, is great value with six antique-like Victorian rooms and great breakfasts. **Shoney's Inn** (☎ 816-254-0100; 4048 S Lynn Ct; r $50;) accommodates wheelchair users and was recently renovated.

St Joseph

As the western terminus of the railways before the Missouri River was bridged, St Joseph was the departure point for many pioneers traveling west. In 1860 the first Pony Express carried messages from 'St Jo' 1900 miles west to California, a service that lasted just 18 months before going bust. The **Pony Express Memorial** (☎ 816-279-5059; 914 Penn St) tells the story of the Express and its riders: 'skinny, wiry fellows' recruited to face death daily – 'orphans preferred.'

St Jo was also home to Jesse James (his last) and jazz great Coleman Hawkins, the namesake of a mid-June festival. Pick up a downtown walking-tour map at the **visitors center** (☎ 816-233-6688, 800-785-0360; 109 S 4th St).

Housed in a former mental hospital, the large **Glore Psychiatric Museum** (☎ 816-387-2310; 3406 Frederick Ave; admission free; 9am-5pm Mon-Sat, 1-5pm Sun) is fascinating. Simple displays show how lobotomies accidentally began and how 'treatment' has advanced from the 'bath of surprise' to occupational therapy, such as painting.

Several chain motels are near I-29 exit 47.

OKLAHOMA

Oklahoma rightly touts itself as 'Native America' – referring to both its natural beauty and its Native American roots (it still has the country's biggest Native American population). Oklahoma also has surprisingly diverse scenery – lush Green Country in the northeast, the pine-covered Ouachita and Kiamichi Mountains in the southeast and rugged Wichita Mountains in the southwest.

Oklahoma has more miles of Route 66 than any other state (400 miles). While on the roads, look out for old 'Oklahoma is OK' license plates – a much-maligned slogan that adorned the state's vehicles for many years.

HISTORY

Evidence has been found of Native American settlement 10,000 years ago in the Oklahoma area. Much later, Wichita, Comanche and Osage occupied the area. In 1834 Oklahoma was declared an Indian Territory, and thousands of Choctaw, Creek, Cherokee, Chickasaw and eventually Seminole (collectively, the Five Civilized Tribes) were forced here from their homelands in the southeastern states. During the winter of 1838–39 more than 15,000 Cherokee were marched along the infamous 'Trail of Tears'; 4000 perished of cold and hunger before they reached Oklahoma.

In the 1880s eager homesteaders ('Sooners') crossed territory lines to stake claims before the US gave the go-ahead to parcel out former Native American lands. That's right: the Sooner State is named for law-breakers.

Following statehood in 1907, Oklahoma struck it rich during an oil boom in the 1920s, but the Depression, dust bowl and the plunge of oil prices affected the state badly. Thousands of disillusioned 'Okies' – mostly farmers – migrated west to states offering a better future. The state's agricultural industry rebounded, due largely to improved conservation techniques and greater care for the fragile Plains environment.

OKLAHOMA FACTS

Nickname Sooner State
Population 3,493,714 (28th)
Area 69,900 sq miles (20th)
Admitted to Union November 16, 1907 (46th)
Capital city Oklahoma City (population 506,132)
Other cities Tulsa (392,000), Norman (97,800)
State song 'Oklahoma!' (Rodgers & Hammerstein)
Birthplace of Woody Guthrie, athlete Jim Thorpe, parking meters (1935), Will Rogers, Boy Scouts of America, Garth Brooks, Brad Pitt, bands Flaming Lips and Hanson
Famous for 1930s dust bowl, tornadoes, football, 1995 Oklahoma City bombing

INFORMATION

The state has 12 conveniently positioned, state-operated visitors centers, including one at either end of I-40. The **Oklahoma Tourism & Recreation Department** (☎ 405-521-2406, 800-652-6552; www.travelok.com) provides an information pack.

For highway conditions, call ☎ 405-425-2385.

OKLAHOMA CITY

Oklahoma's capital is like a four-door 1976 Coup de Ville with a broken bumper and bullhorns on the front: It's big and ugly but oozes a style all its own. Its fistful of attractions transform the flat, fairly treeless city into a pretty good place to spend a day or two.

Oklahoma City (OKC) sprang up on April 22, 1889, as 10,000 legitimate land claimants staked out land around the Santa Fe railroad station. The city yanked capital honors from Guthrie in 1910 and was catapulted into wealth in 1928 when OKC's first gusher erupted above a vast oil field.

Amid all the fun, OKC forgot to think much about city planning, and IM Pei gave the city a much-needed makeover in 1965; the skywalks and gardens did help downtown's looks. In 1993 city voters passed a landmark $310 million tax for another downtown building spree. The results included a canal and baseball park in the historic Bricktown district – both big hits. In 2003 OKC got a new convention center, library, capitol dome and 7 miles of trails and parks along North Canadian River.

Orientation

Oklahoma's main interstates (I-44, I-35, I-40 and Route 66) pass through OKC. Downtown is bordered by I-40 to the south, 5th St to the north, Shartel Ave to the west and the Santa Fe train track to the east. The Bricktown District is just east of downtown.

Information

BOOKSTORES

Full Circle Bookstore (☎ 405-842-2900; 50 Penn Pl)

EMERGENCY

Emergency number (☎ 911) For police, fire and ambulance service.

INTERNET ACCESS

Library (☎ 405-231-8650; 131 McGee Ave)

MEDIA

Daily Oklahoman (www.dailyoklahoman.com) Daily newspaper.
King Country 93.3 FM Gives OKC a steel-guitar soundtrack.
Oklahoma Gazette Independent weekly.

MEDICAL SERVICES

Deaconess Hospital (☎ 405-604-6000, emergencies 405-604-6106; 5501 N Portland Ave) Has a 24-hour emergency room.

POST

Main Post Office (☎ 800-275-8777; 320 SW 5th St)

TOURIST OFFICES

Oklahoma City visitors center (☎ 405-297-8912, 800-225-5652; www.visitokc.com; 189 W Sheridan Ave)

Sights

The city's most worthwhile attraction is the huge **National Cowboy & Western Heritage Museum** (☎ 405-478-2250; 1700 NE 63rd St; adult $8.50, child over 5 $4; 🕑 9am-5pm), formerly the Cowboy Hall of Fame. Highlights include cowboy art by Charles M Russell and Frederic Remington, James Earle Fraser's 18ft statue *The End of the Trail*, Native American artifacts and a rodeo room with an exhibit on African-American bulldogger Bill Pickett. The Children's Cowboy Corral is a hit with the young'uns. Sadly, the museum's focus leaves most cowgirls in the dust.

The **Oklahoma City Art Museum** (☎ 405-236-3100; 415 Couch Dr; adult/child $7/5; 🕑 10am-5pm Tue-Sat, 1-5pm Sun, until 10pm Thu) opened to acclaim

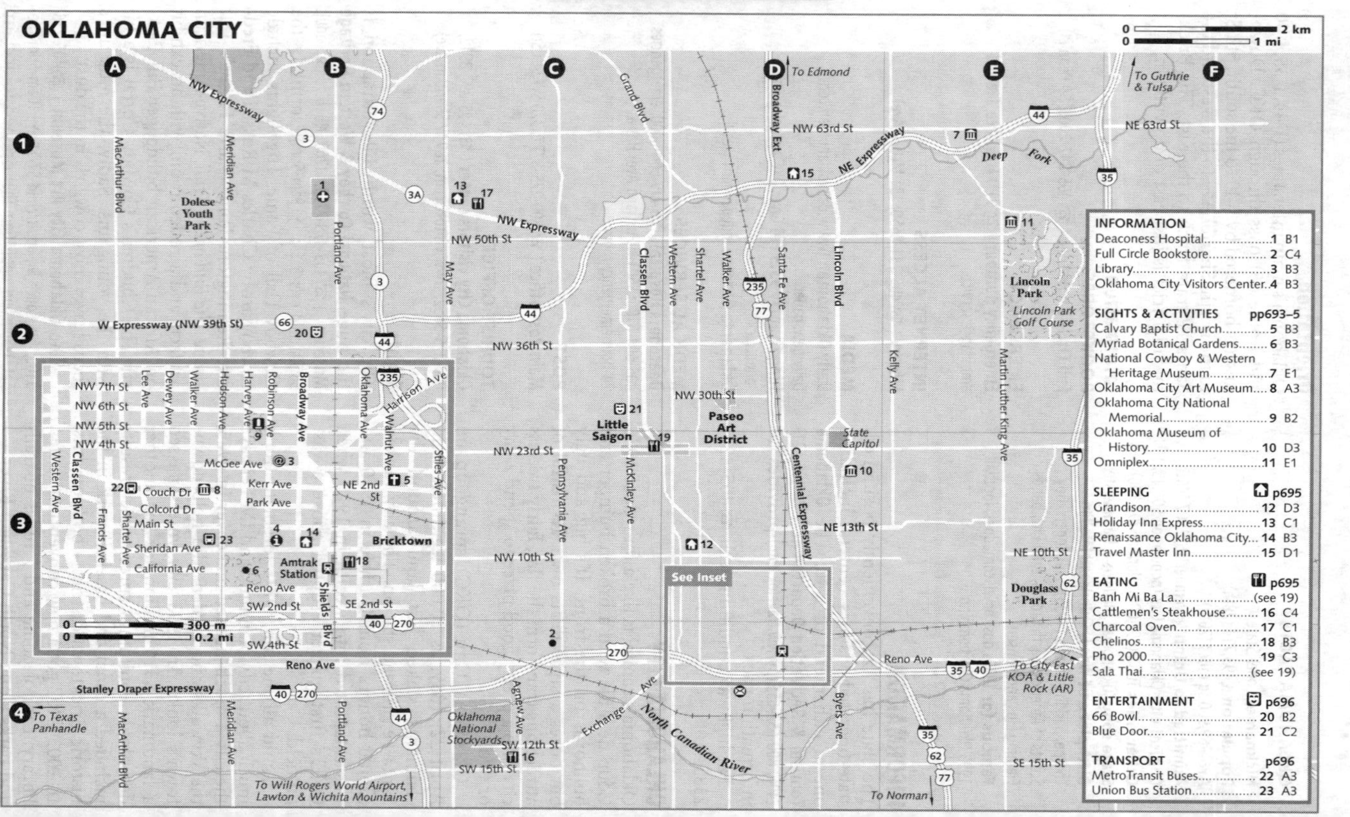
OKLAHOMA CITY
0 2 km
0 1 mi
To Edmond
To Guthrie & Tulsa
To Texas Panhandle
To Will Rogers World Airport, Lawton & Wichita Mountains
To Norman
To City East KOA & Little Rock (AR)
NW Expressway
NE Expressway
NW 63rd St
NE 63rd St
NW 50th St
W Expressway (NW 39th St)
NW 36th St
NW 30th St
NW 23rd St
NE 13th St
NW 10th St
NE 10th St
Reno Ave
Stanley Draper Expressway
SW 12th St
SW 15th St
SE 15th St
MacArthur Blvd
Meridian Ave
Portland Ave
May Ave
Pennsylvania Ave
McKinley Ave
Classen Blvd
Western Ave
Shartel Ave
Walker Ave
Santa Fe Ave
Broadway Ext
Lincoln Blvd
Kelly Ave
Martin Luther King Ave
Grand Blvd
Centennial Expressway
Agnew Ave
Exchange Ave
Byers Ave
North Canadian River
Deep Fork
Dolese Youth Park
Lincoln Park
Lincoln Park Golf Course
Little Saigon
Paseo Art District
State Capitol
Douglass Park
Oklahoma National Stockyards
See Inset
NW 7th St
NW 6th St
NW 5th St
NW 4th St
Lee Ave
Dewey Ave
Hudson Ave
Harvey Ave
Robinson Ave
Broadway Ave
Oklahoma Ave
Harrison Ave
Walnut Ave
Stiles Ave
McGee Ave
Kerr Ave
Park Ave
NE 2nd St
Couch Dr
Colcord Dr
Main St
Sheridan Ave
California Ave
Francis Ave
Bricktown
Amtrak Station
SW 2nd St
SE 2nd St
SW 4th St
Shields Blvd
0 300 m
0 0.2 mi
INFORMATION
Deaconess Hospital 1 B1
Full Circle Bookstore 2 C4
Library 3 B3
Oklahoma City Visitors Center 4 B3
SIGHTS & ACTIVITIES pp693–5
Calvary Baptist Church 5 B3
Myriad Botanical Gardens 6 B3
National Cowboy & Western Heritage Museum 7 E1
Oklahoma City Art Museum 8 A3
Oklahoma City National Memorial 9 B2
Oklahoma Museum of History 10 D3
Omniplex 11 E1
SLEEPING p695
Grandison 12 D3
Holiday Inn Express 13 C1
Renaissance Oklahoma City 14 B3
Travel Master Inn 15 D1
EATING p695
Banh Mi Ba La (see 19)
Cattlemen's Steakhouse 16 C4
Charcoal Oven 17 C1
Chelinos 18 B3
Pho 2000 19 C3
Sala Thai (see 19)
ENTERTAINMENT p696
66 Bowl 20 B2
Blue Door 21 C2
TRANSPORT p696
MetroTransit Buses 22 A3
Union Bus Station 23 A3

THE OKLAHOMA CITY BOMBING

On April 19, 1995, OKC's security and self-confidence were destroyed in moments with the tragic bombing of the Alfred P Murrah Federal Building by American right-wing extremists. In the bombing 168 lives were lost, including those of 16 preschoolers. The devastated city block now called the **Oklahoma City National Memorial** (5th St & Harvey Ave) immediately became a macabre attraction, with many visitors pinning mementos to a chain-link fence.

Today there are two memorials. The chilling **Outdoor Symbolic Memorial** (admission free; 24hr) has walls marked '9:01' and '9:03' to frame the time of the blast; 168 empty chairs represent each of the victims and are illuminated at night. The **Memorial Center Museum** (☎ 405-235-3313; 620 N Harvey Ave; www.oklahomacitynationalmemorial.org; adult/child $7/5; 9am-6pm Mon-Sat, 1-6pm Sun) has comprehensive and sometimes graphic exhibits. It starts in a 'conference room' where an actual recording of the blast is played.

in 2003; its three stories house world-class art – some permanent and some traveling exhibits, with a focus on American art of the mid-20th century.

In the seven-story Crystal Bridge at the 17-acre **Myriad Botanical Gardens** (☎ 405-297-3995; Reno & Robinson Aves; adult $5, child $3.50; 10am-6pm Mon-Sat, noon-6pm Sun), you can witness three ecosystems that include a waterfall and myriad fauna. The **Calvary Baptist Church** (☎ 405-523-0754; 300 N Walnut Ave) played a big role in Oklahoma's Civil Rights movement.

The **Oklahoma Museum of History** (☎ 405-522-5248; 2100 N Lincoln Blvd; admission free; 9am-5pm Mon-Sat) has an interesting Civil War exhibit on Native American and African-American soldiers.

The **Omniplex** (☎ 405-602-6664; NE 52nd St & Martin Luther King Ave; adult/child $6.50/5; 9am-5pm Mon-Fri, 9am-6pm Sat, 11am-6pm Sun) is a huge complex featuring a planetarium and air-and-space museum, plus interactive exhibits ranging from the *Titanic* to a Tesla coil.

Festivals & Events

Festival of the Arts (www.artscouncilokc.com/festival) OKC's own 'rite of spring' festival takes place in April.

Red Earth Native American Cultural Festival (☎ 405-427-5228) North America's largest gathering of American Indian tribes. Held in June.

Charlie Christian Jazz Festival Held the first week in June.

World Championship Quarter Horse Show (☎ 405-297-8938) More than 3000 horses and $1 million in prize money spread over 15 days in November.

Sleeping

Many budget motels (including some rough ones) are along I-35 south of town.

Travel Master Inn (☎ 405-840-1824; 33 NE Expressway; s/d $28/38; P) The best buck-saver in town, with tidy rooms.

The **Holiday Inn Express** (☎ 405-848-1500; 2811 NW Expressway; r $94; P) Centrally located, offers free continental breakfast and caters well for kids.

Renaissance Oklahoma City (☎ 405-228-8000, 800-468-3571; 10 N Broadway Ave; r from $139; P) offers some of the city's more luxurious rooms, but the real pampering is at the **Grandison** (☎ 405-232-8778; www.bbonline.com/ok/grandison; 1200 N Shartel Ave; r $75-145; P), where you can opt for flower petals in your Jacuzzi or champagne delivered to your tasteful room.

Eating

Bricktown has a herd of tasty eateries.

Chelinos (15 E California Ave; mains from $7) Right on the mile-long canal, this beloved three-story restaurant leisurely serves good Mexican meals.

Cattlemen's Steakhouse (1309 S Agnew Ave) Great steaks in the Stockyards City District. If you're not up for a whole strip sirloin ($17), try the lamb fries with baked potato ($11).

The Little Saigon neighborhood, centered on 23rd St and Classen Blvd, ain't quaint, but it has many authentic Vietnamese restaurants. Try **Pho 2000** (1400 NW 23rd St) for beef noodle soup, or **Banh Mi Ba La** (2426 N Classen Blvd; sandwiches $2), under the huge milk bottle, for quick Vietnamese sandwiches.

Sala Thai (1614 NW 23rd St; mains from $8) Many good Thai vegetarian dishes.

Charcoal Oven (2701 NW Expressway) This timeless drive-in has served hickory burgers since 1958 – ask for the sauce.

Entertainment

For listings, pick up the free *Oklahoma Gazette*. Bricktown usually has some action in the evenings.

66 Bowl (☎ 405-946-3966; 3810 NW 39th St) This Route 66 bowling alley often hosts rockabilly and punk shows.

Blue Door (☎ 405-524-0738; 2805 N McKinley Ave) Bring your own beer or wine to its low-key concerts

Getting There & Around

Will Rogers World Airport is several miles southwest of downtown. Take I-44 south from I-40, or I-240 west from I-35. Getting downtown from the airport in a **Yellow Cab** (☎ 405-232-6161) costs $17; the **Blue Vans Shuttle** (☎ 405-681-3311) charges $13.

Greyhound buses depart from the **Union Bus Station** (☎ 405-235-6425; 427 W Sheridan Ave). Daily buses leave for Dallas ($41, four hours), Tulsa ($16, two hours), Kansas City ($70, seven hours), Little Rock ($70, seven hours) and Albuquerque ($61, 12 hours). **Jefferson Lines** (☎ 405-239-6831) also runs buses out of the station.

Daily **Amtrak** (100 S EK Gaylord Blvd) trains go to Fort Worth ($26 to $50, 4½ hours).

Fares on **MetroTransit city buses** (☎ 405-235-7433; 200 N Shartel Ave) are $1.

GUTHRIE

Oklahoma's first capital, 20 miles north of Oklahoma City, is one of the Great Plains' best-preserved towns. Its 12-square-block downtown, lined with 100-year-old buildings, teems with life on summer weekends and during April's '89er Celebration, which commemorates the beginning of the Great Land Rush.

The **visitors center** (☎ 405-282-1947; 212 W Oklahoma Ave) has brochures.

At the excellent **Oklahoma Territorial Museum** (☎ 405-282-1889; 402 E Oklahoma Ave; admission $1; ⌚ 9am-5pm Tue-Fri, 10am-4pm Sat, 1-4pm Sun), see a copy of the state's first flag, changed in 1922 for looking 'too communist.' The Texas-sized **Scottish Rite Temple** (☎ 405-282-1281; 900 E Oklahoma Ave; tours $5; ⌚ 10am & 2pm Mon-Fri, 10am Sat) is the largest such temple in the world.

Guthrie has a dozen historic B&Bs, including **Harrison House** (☎ 405-282-1000; www.machtolff.com/harrison/index.html; 124 W Harrison; r $80-125), with rooms spread over five buildings. No TV.

NORMAN

Oklahoma's third-largest city is the home of the University of Oklahoma (OU) and its worshipped Sooners football team. The **OU Visitor Center** (☎ 405-325-2151; Jacobson Hall, Boyd & Parrington Oval) can arrange tours. The wee campus corner is nearby, centered on Boyd and Asp Sts. OU's best attraction is the dinosaur-packed **Sam Noble Oklahoma Museum of Natural History** (☎ 405-325-4712; 2401 S Chautauqua Ave; adult $4, child $2; ⌚ 10am-5pm Mon-Sat, 1-5pm Sun), a mile south of Lindsey St.

ROUTE 66 – OKLAHOMA CITY TO TULSA

Route 66 between Oklahoma's two biggest cities is the country's longest remaining continuous stretch of the Mother Road. Take it for fun (and to save the $3.50 toll required for the I-44, which Route 66 snakes around).

In **Arcadia**, stop at the famed **Round Barn** (☎ 406-396-2761; admission free; ⌚ 10am-5pm Tue-Sun). About halfway to Tulsa, **Chandler** is the route's nicest town and has old Route 66 filling stations and the **Lincoln Motel** (☎ 405-258-0200; 740 E First St; r $35), with a US flag hanging outside each of its rooms. In Stroud, 14 miles east, **Rock Cafe** serves some intense peach cobbler.

TULSA

Seen from the highways, Tulsa's downtown pops out of a sea of oaks that give the area its 'Green Country' nickname. Tulsa's name comes from the Creek Indians: Their word 'Tallahassee' (Old Town) evolved to 'Tulsey Town' and finally 'Tulsa.' Known as the 'Oil Capital of the World' in the early to mid-20th century, Tulsa actually didn't have much oil – just heaps of oil companies that reaped the rewards of statewide wells.

I-44 rolls through town, and I-244, US 75 and US 64 conveniently lead from it into downtown.

The **visitors center** (☎ 918-477-1000; 616 S Boston St, Ste 100) has brochures. The nearest state **visitors center** (☎ 918-439-3212) is east of town on I-44 in Catoosa. Radio station KVOO 1170 AM has given Tulsa its country twang since 1926.

Sights

The **Thomas Gilcrease Museum** (☎ 918-596-2700; 1400 Gilcrease Museum Rd; admission $3; ⌚ Tue-Sun), northwest of downtown off US 64, has a tremendous art collection depicting the

American West, Native American art and a detailed Las Artes de Mexico exhibit.

The **Philbrook Museum of Art** (☎ 918-749-7941; 2727 S Rockford Rd; admission $5.50; Tue-Sun), east of Peoria Ave, is housed in a villa of Italian Renaissance style with surrounding gardens. The collection is superb – Asian, Native American and European.

The Historic Greenwood District is a few blocks northeast of downtown. The area thrived as the entrepreneurial center of the black community in the early 20th century. Legal segregation forced African-Americans to start and patronize their own businesses and thus the area earned the moniker 'Black Wall Street.' The **Greenwood Cultural Center** (☎ 918-596-1030; 322 N Greenwood Ave) displays photos of the area before and after the 1921 Tulsa Race Riot, and houses the **Oklahoma Jazz Hall of Fame** (admission free; Mon-Sat).

Named for the TV evangelist, **Oral Roberts University** (ORU; ☎ 918-495-7910; 7777 S Lewis Ave) flaunts a retro-futuristic campus that looks like the Jetsons meet Jesus. To prompt funds, Oral once camped out in the 200ft glass Prayer Tower east of the huge praying hands. Climb it for a view (free).

Tulsa is famed for its **art deco buildings**, though most are spaced apart. The 1931 **Tulsa Union Depot** (1st St) is closed to the public, but you can view the outside. Downtown's most distinctive building is the skyscraper **United Methodist Church** (1301 S Boston Ave).

Western swing hero Bob Wills was taken back to Tulsa after his death in 1975. Visit **Bob Wills' grave** (☎ 918- 627-0220; 5111 S Memorial Dr) at Memorial Park.

Sleeping

Tulsa isn't a mecca for unique places to stay. A number of chains can be found along the city's busy (if uninspired) commercial district of E 71st St. West of the Arkansas River, on I-44, are some old-timer motels, some a bit haggard.

Victorian Inn (☎ 918-743-2009; 114 E Skelly Dr; s/d $43/48) Off I-44 exit 226, it has clean rooms with mini-kitchenettes.

Ramada Inn (☎ 918-743-9811; 3131 E 51st St; r from $69; P) Central and easy to find, right off I-44 at the Harvard Ave exit.

McBirney Mansion (☎ 918-585-3234; www.mcbirneymansion.com; 1414 S Galveston; r $119-225; P) South of downtown, this historic place is Tulsa's best B&B. Built in 1927, it's set on three leafy acres on a hillside overlooking the Arkansas River. Joggers can take advantage of the 12 miles of river paths nearby. Book ahead to enjoy one of these antique-filled rooms. Great bathrooms (en suite).

Eating

There's good dining in the Brookside neighborhood, on **Peoria Ave**, between 31st and 51st Sts. **Cherry Street**, along 15th St just east of Peoria, has several tasty options. Northeast of Brookside, at 21st St, **Utica Sq** is a long-running well-to-do shopping area with several eating places.

Brookside By Day (☎ 918-745-9989; 3313 Peoria Ave; breakfast $3) Busy at breakfast.

Ron's Hamburgers & Chili (☎ 918-686-7667; 3239 E 15th St; cheeseburger $3.25) Many locals swear that Ron's grills Tulsa's best burger.

India Palace (☎ 918-492-8040; 6963 S Lewis Ave; lunch buffet $7) Some of the best Indian food this side of Punjab. The lunch buffet is huge and the cups of chai are bottomless.

Ri Le (☎ 918-747-3205; 4932 E 91st St; mains $7) Run by a Vietnamese monk, Ri Le is tiny and simple, but serves Tulsa's favorite Vietnamese meals. Try the tasty, all-vegetarian pineapple soy with fake beef – you'll have to ask, it's not on the menu.

Entertainment

Check the *Urban Tulsa Weekly* for what's going on. Brookside bars are a good place to start. **Caravan Cattle Company** (☎ 918-663-5468; 7901 E 41st St) gives free two-step lessons on Tuesday nights, and there's a dandy production of Oklahoma! at **Discoveryland!** (☎ 918-742-5255; 5529 S Lewis Ave, Sand Springs; $15; 8pm summer), 5 miles northwest of Tulsa.

Getting There & Around

Tulsa International Airport (☎ 918-838-5046), off Hwy 11, is northeast of downtown. **Greyhound** (☎ 918-584-4428; 317 S Detroit Ave) has daily buses bound for **Oklahoma City** ($17, two hours) and **Kansas City** ($57, five hours). Tulsa Transit **metro buses** (☎ 918-582-2100) run limited routes.

GREEN COUNTRY

Full of lakes and subtle, forested hills, Oklahoma's northeast corner (including Tulsa) is called 'Green Country.' Drivers heading to Missouri can go along segments of Route 66.

Bartlesville

North of Tulsa, the oil town Bartlesville is noted for Frank Lloyd Wright's tallest skyscraper, **Price Tower Arts Center** (☎ 918-336-4949; 510 Dewey Ave; adult/child $3/free; 🕑 10am-5pm Tue-Sat, 12:30-5pm Sun), which is filled with original Wright-designed furnishings from the 1950s. (It was originally intended to be a New York City apartment building.) Tours are at 11am and 2pm (adult/child $5/3). You can stay here too: the **Inn at Price Tower** (☎ 918-336-1000, 877-424-2424; www.pricetower.org/hotel/index-7.html; s/d from $125/145;) offers 21 Wright-inspired rooms. Free breakfast, tour and gallery admission.

Kids love **Woolaroc** (☎ 918-336-0307; adult/child $5/free; 🕑 10am-5pm, closed Mon in winter), 12 miles southwest on SR 123, one of the state's best-loved attractions. Frank Phillips, the founder of Phillips Oil, poured a good deal of his fortune into this eclectic collection of Native American and Wild West artifacts. You can tour Phillips' lodge, a Native American center and an oil site, and see scores of buffalo. If you touch the stuffed buffalo, next to the buffalo burger stand, it'll scold you.

Claremore

Many folks no longer know who Will Rogers was, but don't say this in his home town of Claremore, on Route 66 northeast of Tulsa. Born in 1879, Will was a Cherokee cowboy, movie star, comedian and homespun philosopher. Two hours at the smashing **Will Rogers Memorial Museum** (☎ 918-341-0719; 1720 W Will Rogers Blvd; 🕑 8am-5pm), a mile west of Route 66, will give you a sense of his importance; admission is by donation.

Trail of Tears Country

The Five Civilized Tribes (Cherokee, Choctaw, Chickasaw, Creek and Seminole) were moved into this region, southeast of present-day Tulsa, in the late 1830s. Anyone interested in learning about Native American culture should stop here for a few days.

Known from the Merle Haggard song 'Okie from Muskogee,' Muskogee (49 miles southwest of Tulsa) is home to the **Five Civilized Tribes Museum** (☎ 918-683-1701; Agency Hill, Honor Heights Dr; adult/student $3/1.50; 🕑 10am-5pm Mon-Sat, 1-5pm Sun), near the US 62 and 69 junction, which is housed in the 1875 Union Indian Agency building.

West on US 62, **Tahlequah** has been the Cherokee capital since 1839. The **Cherokee Heritage Center** (☎ 918-456-6007; Keeler Rd; adult $8.50, child $5; 🕑 10am-5pm Mon-Sat, 1-5pm Sun), south of town, has good displays of the Trail of Tears forced march. In July and August see **Tsa-La-Gi** (adult/student/child $20/18/10; 🕑 8pm Thu-Sat), a great outdoor production of the Trail of Tears drama. The nearby **Illinois River** is popular for canoe trips in spring and summer.

Downtown **Okmulgee** looks like the set of a 1950s film, with shops such as Boy Howdy Variety Store going strong. The **Creek Council House Museum** (☎ 918-756-2324; 106 W 6th St; admission free; 🕑 10am-4:30pm Tue-Sat) is in the former capital of the Muscogee (Creek) Nation, built in 1878.

In August, Okmulgee hosts a few **African-American rodeos**, as does the African-American historic town of Boley on Memorial Day weekend. It's great fun.

WESTERN OKLAHOMA

West of Oklahoma City, on I-40, Oklahoma opens into the 'real West.' Amid expansive fields of prairie and the jarring Wichita Mountains, you'll find much evidence of Native American and pioneer heritages, plus heaps of worthy Route 66 sites.

Oklahoma City to Texas Panhandle

West of Oklahoma City, I-40 runs to Texola, on the state's western border. Route 66 frequently twists on and off the interstate; get the free Official Oklahoma Route 66 Association Trip Guide to help locate its many landmarks.

In Clinton, at the junction of US 183, the neon-lit **Route 66 Museum** (☎ 580-323-7866; 2229 W Gary Blvd; adult/child $3/1; 🕑 9am-5pm Mon-Sat, 1-5pm Sun) has six decades of 'Mother Road' memorabilia. Revel in more of the lore further west in Elk City at the **National Route 66 Museum** (☎ 580-225-6266; $5; 🕑 9am-5pm Mon-Sat, 2-5pm Sun).

Cheyenne, 24 miles north of I-40, is worth a detour. Its **Washita Battlefield Site** is where George Custer's troops launched the 1868 attack on the slumbering (and peaceful) village of Chief Black Kettle. Learn more at the **Black Kettle Museum** (☎ 580-497-3929; US Hwy 283 & State Hwy 47; admission free; 🕑 9am-5pm Tue-Sat). **Coyote Hills Guest Ranch** (☎ 580-497-3931; www.coyotehillsguestranch.com; Hwy 47; per person $135), west of the battlefield, offers horseback riding and mountain biking, cook-outs and a 'Social Barn,' which should help you forget there's no phone or TV.

Anadarko

West of I-44 via US9, Anadarko and the surrounding area is home to 64 tribes and calls itself the 'Indian Capital of the Nation.' Anadarko hosts powwows and rodeos most months; get information from the **chamber of commerce** (☎ 405-247-6651), inside the **National Hall of Fame for Famous American Indians** (☎ 405-247-5555; Hwy 9; admission free; 🕒 9am-5pm Mon-Sat, 1-5pm Sun), a 40-acre park with 43 bronze busts. The **post office** (SR 8 & Oklahoma St) has 16 impressive murals.

Indian City USA (☎ 405-247-5661; tours adult/child $7.50/4; 🕒 9am-5pm), 2 miles south on SR 8, is worth visiting for the guided tour of seven authentic Native American villages scattered along a hilltop trail. Ask about Tonkawa ghosts seen in the area.

Oklahoma's best barbecue is at **Jake's Rib** (☎ 405-222-2825; 100 Ponderosa Dr; dinner from $7.50), 19 miles east in Chickasha.

Lawton

The last of the land-rush cities, Lawton ain't too lovely, but the **Museum of the Great Plains** (☎ 580-581-3460; 601 NW Ferris St; adult/child $4/2.50; 🕒 10am-5pm Mon-Sat, 1-5pm Sun, call ahead in winter) has magnificent collections of Plains Native American artifacts and prairie dogs outside.

North of town, **Fort Sill**, established in 1869 as a fighting outpost against Native Americans, is an active base with a frontier flavor. Follow signs from the fort to **Geronimo's grave**. The **Fort Sill Museum** (☎ 580-442-5123; 435 Quanah Rd; admission free; 🕒 8:30am-4:30pm Mon-Sat, 12:30-4:30pm Sun) has photos and a film of the African-American troop that built the fort.

Lawton has plenty of chain hotels

Wichita Mountains

In of the Great Plains' most beautiful settings, the **Wichita Mountains Wildlife Refuge** (SR 49), west of I-44 (northwest of Fort Sill), is a mixed-grass prairie superb for hiking and wildlife viewing (more than 600 buffalo roam the refuge). The Wichitas' granite peaks are ideal for rock climbing; check with the **Wichita Mountains Climbers Coalition** (www.wichitamountains.org) for tips.

The **visitors center** (☎ 580-429-3222; 🕒 8am-4:30pm Mon-Fri) shows a good film on buffalo. Drive up Mt Scott or, if you're feeling energetic, hike up Elk Mountain for incredible views. Pets are welcome at **Doris Campground** (campsites/RV sites $6/12).

Nearby **Medicine Park** is an amazing cobblestone village unknown to most Oklahomans. For generations, Native Americans used the water from the area's creek for healing purposes. Hollywood stars and gangsters splashed in it in the early 20th century.

Another extension of the Wichitas is 51 miles west at the gorgeous 4500-acre **Quartz Mountain State Park**, on Lake Altus-Lugert. There are mountain trails and developed **campsites** (☎ 580-563-2238; $7). The **Quartz Mountain Resort** (☎ 580-563-2424, 877-999-5567; www.quartzmountainresort.com; r from $109; P ✕ 🏊) is a great place to get some rest and relaxation, play some golf, paddle a boat or go for a hike. Good for families, too.

KANSAS

The vast, rolling prairies of Kansas are blanketed with wheat and occasionally battered by tornadoes – such as the mythical one that whisked Dorothy and Toto away in the *Wizard of Oz*. Though the state's tourist attractions are few, the Kansas Plains dwellers are some of the friendliest folks you could hope to meet.

HISTORY

Kansas has historically been a place people passed through – Coronado seeking Quivira, cowboys driving cattle, pioneers following the Santa Fe Trail, the Pony Express delivering mail, railroads transporting people and goods, and carloads of college kids heading to Colorado ski slopes.

The Kansas-Nebraska Act of 1854, which allowed settlers in Kansas and Nebraska to vote for or against slavery, triggered 'Bleeding Kansas,' a conflict between the pro- and anti-slavery settlers that hastened the Civil War. In 1856 the town of Lawrence was ransacked by pro-slavery border 'Ruffians'; retaliatory raids by anti-slavery forces followed, including one led by the abolitionist John Brown. Kansas was admitted as a free state shortly after the Southern states seceded from the Union in 1860.

The buffalo were wiped out, the Native Americans pushed off (even the state's

KANSAS FACTS

Nickname Sunflower State
Population 2,715,900 (32nd)
Area 82,280 sq miles (15th)
Admitted to Union January 29, 1861 (34th)
Capital city Topeka (population 122,100)
Other cities Wichita (355,100), Lawrence (81,600)
State song 'Home on the Range'
Birthplace of Amelia Earhart, Charlie Parker, Annette Bening, Melissa Etheridge, Buster Keaton
Famous for Turkey Red wheat, starting prohibition, fictional residents Dorothy and Toto (of *Wizard of Oz* fame)

namesake Kansa, who were relocated to Oklahoma in 1873) and the settlers moved in, after which Kansas changed quickly from rip-roaring open range to some of the most productive wheat lands in the world. Aviation industries, based in Wichita, have also been big moneymakers.

INFORMATION

Kansas runs four information centers – in Kansas City on I-70, in Olathe at I-35 exit 220, in Belle Plaine on the I-35 (south of Wichita) and way out west in Goodland on I-70. Ask for information from **Kansas Travel & Tourism** (☎ 785-296-2009, 800-252-6727; www.kansascommerce.com).

All **state parks** (☎ 620-672-5911) require a daily vehicle permit ($5). For road conditions, call ☎ 800-585-7623.

WICHITA

This now-prosperous city on the confluence of the Big and Little Arkansas Rivers had a humble beginning in the 1860s as a cow-town on the Chisholm Trail. The railroad's arrival in 1872 triggered a boom, and burgeoning wheat and oil industries fanned its growth. Following WWI, Wichita began producing heaps of airplanes. Boeing, Beech and Cessna have manufacturing plants near the city.

Ongoing riverfront development is helping transform a ho-hum downtown into something special (as a guide said, 'even folks from Kansas City are starting to visit'). Wichita's McConnell Air Force Base treats the town with an air show in June, and the city hosts the Mid-America All Indian Center Inter-Tribal Powwow in July.

Incidentally, Wichitans have bickered over the pronunciation of the Arkansas River for well over 100 years. Most locals continue to refer to it as are-*kan*-sus. Conform or be cast out. (And never pronounce the city as wa-*chee*-tuh.)

The **Boathouse Visitors Center** (☎ 316-337-9088; 335 W Lewis; 🕘 9am-5pm Mon-Sat, noon-4pm Sun) also houses an America's Cup-class yacht. Tune in to KFDI 1070 AM for old-time country tunes and a lost-dog report.

Sights

Across the Arkansas from downtown are several quite interesting museums. The stylish and modern **Exploration Place** (☎ 316-263-3373; 300 N McLean Blvd; adult $8, child 5-15 $6; 🕘 9am-5pm Tue-Fri, 10am-8pm Sat, 10am-5pm Sun) has lots of kid-friendly science exhibits, including a touchable tornado ($5).

The **Indian Center Museum** (☎ 316-262-5221; 650 N Seneca St; admission $6; 🕘 10am-5pm Tue-Sat, 1-5pm Sun) has a Native American flag collection, plus a new grass house (the traditional Wichita dwelling). Events are scheduled here year-round. For a hokier version of the Wild West, visit **Old Cowtown** (☎ 316-264-6398; 1871 Sim Park Dr; adult/child $7/4; 🕘 10am-5pm Mon-Sat, noon-5pm Sun Apr-Oct), featuring pioneer-era buildings and gunfights. The **Wichita Art Museum** (☎ 316-268-4921; www.wichitaartmuseum.org; 1400 Museum Blvd; adult/child $5/2, admission free Sat; 🕘 10am-5pm Tue, Wed & Sat, 11am-8pm Thu, noon-5pm Sun) was revamped in 2003 to add a new wing.

The prairie-style **Allen-Lambe House** (☎ 316-687-1027; 255 N Roosevelt St; $8; 🕘 by appointment) was designed by Frank Lloyd Wright in 1915; Wright ranked it among his best. No one under the age of 16 allowed.

In a fascinatingly unrestored 1935 art deco building, the **Kansas Aviation Museum** (☎ 316-683-9242; 3350 George Washington Blvd; adult/child $5/1; 🕘 9am-4pm Tue-Fri, 1-5pm Sat) has a bunch of (small) planes inside and a view of the air force base from the tower.

Sleeping

La Quinta Inn Wichita Towne East Mall (☎ 866-665-9330; 7700 E Kellogg; r from $86; P ✿) One of piles of motels on the East Corridor just west of US 54 and I-35.

Mark 8 Lodge (☎ 316-685-9415, 888-860-7268; 8136 E Kellogg; d from $33; P) Well kept, with kitchenettes in the tidy rooms.

Another concentration of motels is near the airport, around US 54 and I-235.

Hotel at Oldtown (☎ 316-267-4800, 877-265-3269; www.hotelatoldtown.com; 830 1st St; d from $92; P) Steps away from restaurants and bars, the location can't be beaten. The lobby and piano bar are elegant in a turn-of-the-century (19th!) sort of way.

Eating & Drinking

Though Wichita is home of Pizza Hut (there are 21 outlets here), Wichitans' favorite eateries are in Old Town, the eight-block historic district just east of downtown. You're likely to have to wait for a seat at dinner.

Larkspur Restaurant (☎ 316-262-LARK; 904 E Douglas, Old Town; dinner mains $16-22) On sunny days, locals crowd the outside patio for pastas and steaks. Children's menu available.

Knolla's Pizza (☎ 316-942-0344; 3817 W 13th St; medium pizza $8-11) Some say Knolla's Pizza has the best slices and pies in town.

Nu Way (☎ 316-267-1131; 1416 W Douglas; meals $3) A local chain, west of the museums, serving unique shredded-beef burgers and homemade root beer ('made from a ton of sugar').

River City Brewing Co (☎ 316-263-2739; www.rivercitybrewingco.com; 150 N Mosley, Old Town; burgers $7.50) Pairs its six different microbrews with tasty chow: buffalo steaks, a good veggie burger, homemade soup. Check the website for live music listings.

Getting There & Around

The Mid-Continent Airport is 5 miles southwest of downtown on US 54 (Kellogg Dr).

The **Greyhound station** (☎ 316-265-7711; 312 S Broadway) sends buses to Kansas City ($32, three hours), Oklahoma City ($31, two hours) and Denver ($72, 12 hours).

The nearest **Amtrak station** (☎ 316-283-7533) is 27 miles north in Newton on I-135. It has trains leaving around 3am, on their way to Kansas City and Albuquerque; a local bus connects to Wichita.

Wichita Metro Transit Authority (WMTA; ☎ 316-265-7221; 214 S Topeka St) buses run a few routes around town ($1). For a taxi, call **Best Cabs** (☎ 316-838-2233).

ALONG I-70

This is Kansas' 'main street,' running east-west across the state, from Kansas City to the Colorado border. Most of Kansas City and its points of interest are in Missouri (see Kansas City, p689).

Lawrence

The nicest city in Kansas, Lawrence was founded in 1854 by abolitionists and was often a hotbed for clashing forces. The city was an important stop on the Underground Railroad, but it suffered for its anti-slavery zeal in 1863 when the Confederate Quantrill's Raiders swooped down, killing around 150 civilians.

Today Lawrence is home to **Kansas University** (KU), which has a few free museums worth seeing, and **Haskell Indian Nations University**, the country's only intertribal university (where Olympian Jim Thorpe studied). Best of all is Lawrence's active downtown, perhaps one of the country's nicest. Stroll down **Massachusetts St** to get that hometown vibe. Pick up brochures at the **visitors center** (☎ 785-865-4499; N 2nd & Locust Sts). Lawrence is a great spot for **golf**, with more than a dozen public courses within 30 minutes' drive.

Downtown, the historic rooms at **Eldridge Hotel** (☎ 785-749-5011; 7th & Massachusetts Sts; r from $89; P) are well-appointed; treat yourself to room service, as it's hard to come by in these parts.

A few blocks west, **Halcyon House B&B** (☎ 785-841-0314; www.thehalcyonhouse.com; 1000 Ohio St; r with shared bath from $49, cottage from $129) has pretty landscaping, cozy rooms and homemade baked goods for breakfast.

Dining is a good reason to stop in Lawrence; head to 'Mass St,' downtown's chainless strip. Transformed from a bank, **Teller's Restaurant** (☎ 785-843-4111; 746 Massachusetts St; mains from $12) has good pastas, a gay-friendly atmosphere and a 'vault' bathroom. **Rudy's Pizzeria** (☎ 785-749-0055; 704 Massachusetts St; $2) is famous for spicy slices. Nearby, the appropriately named **Wheatfields** (☎ 785-841-5553; 904 Vermont St) serves excellent breads and is a local fave for breakfast.

Grab a pint or two at the first legal brewery in Kansas, **Free State Brewing Co** (☎ 785-843-4555; 636 Massachusetts St). Next door, see a live show or movie at historic **Liberty Hall** (☎ 785-749-1972; 644 Massachusetts St).

Call **Kansas Transportation Services** (☎ 877-942-0544) for a shuttle to or from the KCI airport ($29).

Topeka

Kansas' rather grim capital has a few attractions worth seeing. The **visitors center** (☎ 785-234-1030; 1275 SW Topeka Blvd) has brochures.

The **Brown vs Board of Education National Historic Site** (☎ 785-354-4273; 15th & Monroe; admission free; 9am-5pm), at the Monroe Elementary School, shows a compelling video on the landmark 1954 Supreme Court case that banned segregation in US schools.

The impressively domed **State Capitol** (☎ 785-276-8681; 6425 SW 6th Ave) houses a famous mural of John Brown. Free tours are offered weekdays.

Abilene

Driving into Abilene from I-70 is like a summer rain rinsing a muddy face. This friendly town, tucked away south of the interstate, is one of Kansas' highlights, with a priceless **visitors center** (☎ 785-263-2231; 800-569-5915; 201 NW 2nd St; 8am-5pm Mon-Sat, 1-4pm Sun) that provides coffee, cookies and smiles to go with your information.

In the late 19th century, however, Abilene was a pretty damn rowdy cow-town at the end of the Chisholm Trail. Today Abilene prefers to celebrate onetime resident and former president Dwight D Eisenhower. The **Eisenhower Center** (☎ 785-263-4751; 200 SE 4th St) includes his boyhood home (admission free), museum ($3.50), library (free) and grave. Dog lovers should go across the street to the **Greyhound Hall of Fame** (☎ 785-263-3000; 409 S Buckeye; admission free; 9am-5pm), where retired racers 'Abby', 'Douglas' and 'Chig' greet visitors.

Diamond Motel (☎ 785-263-2360; 1407 NW 3rd St; s $29, d $34-45, ste $55;) offers well-maintained rooms, most equipped with microwaves.

Western Kansas

West of Abilene, I-70 opens up into rolling, wide-open plains, where winds can knock over 18-wheelers and monotonous scenery can send the perpetually curious into a freefall of boredom. But there are a few interesting detours.

Hays sprang to life in the 1860s when Fort Hays was built to protect railroad workers. Today, some original buildings stand at the **Fort Hays Historical Site** (☎ 785-625-6812; admission free), 4 miles south of I-70 on US 83. The domed **Sternberg Museum of Natural History** (☎ 877-332-1165; 3000 Sternberg Dr; adult/child $6/4; 9am-7pm Tue-Sat, 1-7pm Sun) has an unusual fish-within-a-fish fossil and animated dinosaurs.

Founded in 1877 by African-American settlers seeking a promised land, lonely but friendly **Nicodemus** (population 25), 59 miles northwest of Hays, is one of the oldest surviving towns of its kind in the US. There are five historic buildings (and a lone parking meter). The **visitors center** (☎ 785-839-4233) has a film and gives free guided tours. Nicodemus' Homecoming, in late July, is a big event.

Back on I-70, Oakley has a **fossil museum** (admission free) with heaps of prehistoric shark teeth. South, on US 83, are the surprising **Monument Rocks**, 80ft chalk formations that look like a Jawa hangout (think *Star Wars*).

ALONG US 50 & US 56

More attractive alternatives to taking I-70 across Kansas are US 50 and US 56. Both pass through the Flint Hills in the east, then meet out west and enter Dodge City arm-in-arm.

Fabled US 50 pairs up with I-35 southwest from Kansas City; after crossing I-135, it heads out on its own as it passes through Chase County, which William Least Heat-Moon examined in his book *Prairyerth*. Just west, **Jones Sheep Farm B&B** (☎ 620-983-2815; 1556 E 59th St, Peabody; r from $55) is a private rustic farmhouse. If you can't fall asleep, count the sheep.

Hutchinson, on US 50 west of I-135, is the unlikely home of the amazing **Cosmosphere & Space Center** (☎ 620-662-2305, 800-397-0330; 1100 N Plum Ave; admission $5; 9am-9pm Mon-Sat; noon-9pm Sun), where you can see the original Apollo 13, cool Soviet cosmonaut outfits and a nuclear warhead found rotting in an Alabama warehouse.

Another route is US 56 southwest, which follows the old Santa Fe Trail (a little north of US 50). Council Grove used to be a good place to fix the Conestoga wagon. The **Cottage House Hotel** (☎ 620-767-6828; www.cottagehousehotel.com; 25 N Neosho; r from $68-155) has inviting, squeaky-floored rooms.

The large Mennonite communities around **Hillsboro**, on US 56 west of Marion, are descendants of Russian immigrants who brought the Turkey Red strain of wheat to the Plains, where it thrived despite harsh conditions. Cute **Lindsborg**, about 15 miles north of US 56, on SR 4 west of I-135, flaunts its Swedish roots.

Back on US 56, continue west to Great Bend, then southwest to Larned, where you can see the **Santa Fe Trail Center Museum** (☎ 620-285-2054; adult/child $4/1.50; 9am-5pm) and, just west of this, the restored **Fort Larned National Historic Site** (☎ 620-285-6911; admission $2; 8am-6pm most days), the only fort along the Santa Fe Trail.

Dodge City

Modern Dodge, on US 50/56 southwest of Larned, revels in its infamous Wild West past, but today's humming grain elevators all but drown out the distant echo of the hell-raisin' days. For brochures, saunter into the **visitors center** (☎ 620-225-8186; 400 W Wyatt Earp Blvd; 8am-6:30pm summer, 8am-5pm Mon-Fri rest of the year).

The **Boot Hill Museum & Front Street** (☎ 620-227-8188; adult/child $8/free; 9am-5pm Mon-Sat, 1-5pm Sun) includes a cemetery, jail and saloon, where reenactments invoke the memory of Wyatt Earp. Take your very own stagecoach ride for $5 more.

More fetching is **Fort Dodge** (☎ 620-227-2121; US 154; admission free; 10am-4pm). This mix of old and new buildings is home to retired soldiers, who tend to wave at visitors. There's a museum and a house where General Custer once spent a night. About 9 miles west of town on US 50 are Santa Fe Trail wagon-wheel ruts, most visible at dusk.

Thunderbird Motel (☎ 620-225-4143; 2300 W Wyatt Earp Blvd; s $35, d $40-45;) has friendly staff and good-value rooms, each decked out with a microwave and fridge.

IOWA

This predominately agricultural state is a pleasant destination. Most visitors are keen to see the Madison County bridges or pose in front of Grant Wood's American Gothic house. More rewarding detours can be found, too, particularly the drives along the Mississippi valley in the east, or through the Loess Hills in the west. Iowa's 13 well-signed scenic drives negate any notion that growing crops makes for ugly scenery.

Author Bill Bryson jokes that he's from Iowa because 'someone has to be,' but actually Iowans burst with as much state pride as Texans.

IOWA FACTS

Nickname Hawkeye State
Population 2,936,800 (30th)
Area 56,275 sq miles (26th)
Admitted to Union December 28, 1846 (29th)
Capital city Des Moines (population 198,100)
Other cities Cedar Rapids (122,500), Davenport (97,800)
Birthplace of John Wayne, author Bill Bryson, bandleader Glen Miller, Herbert Hoover, 'Buffalo Bill' Cody, Capt James T Kirk of *Star Trek*
Famous for *American Gothic,* Madison County's bridges, John Deere tractors, hogs (No 1 in US pork production)

HISTORY

Iowa was long traversed by Native Americans crossing to the main arteries of the Missouri, Big Sioux and Mississippi Rivers. Their burial and ceremonial mounds, dating from 500 BC to AD 1300, can still be seen near the western banks of the Mississippi (such as the Effigy Mounds, north of Dubuque).

Iowa was part of the Louisiana Purchase of 1803 but was not settled by whites until the 1830s. When the Black Hawk War against local Native Americans ended in 1832, the US government traded salt and tobacco for Iowa's fertile Mississippi valley region. Soon afterward, dragoons (lightly armed cavalry) 'pacified' the region and established a string of forts north of Des Moines. Immigrants then flooded in from all parts of the world, some of whom established experimental farming communities. Of these, only the Amana Colonies (p706) remain.

Today Iowa is a patchwork quilt of carefully tended farms (95% of the land is fertile). Iowa – the 'food capital of the world' – leads the US in hog, corn and soybean production.

INFORMATION

You can't throw a hog in Iowa without it landing on a visitors center – there are 23 in all. The handiest are near the borders, just off the interstates, in Council Bluffs (I-80 exit 1B), Lamoni (I-35 exit 4), Le Claire (off I-80 in the Mississippi valley) and Northwood (I-35 exit 214).

Contact the **Iowa Division of Tourism** (☎ 515-242-4705, 800-345-4692; www.traveliowa.com).

For highway conditions, call ☎ 515-288-1047 or 800-288-1047.

DES MOINES

Sometimes chided as 'Dead Moans' by locals, Iowa's capital city's few attractions are really good ones, but the downtown is struggling for a little life. The city's name comes from 'La Rivière des Moines' (River of the Monks), bestowed by early French voyageurs.

I-80 and I-35 skirt Des Moines to the north; I-235 cuts through its center. The Des Moines **visitors center** (☎ 515-286-4960, 800-451-2625; 405 6th Ave) provides city information.

Sights & Activities

The **State Capitol** (☎ 515-281-5591; E 9th St & Grand Ave; 8am-4:30pm Mon-Fri, 9am-4pm Sat) must have been Liberace's favorite government building. Its every detail – from the sparkling gold dome to the smell of fried chicken wafting from the basement cafeteria – seems to strive to outdo the other. On no account miss the collection of first-ladies-of-Iowa dolls. The ambitious **Iowa Historical Building** (☎ 515-281-6412; 600 E Locust St; admission free; 9am-4:30pm Tue-Fri, noon-4:30pm Sat) has a 'favorite things of the 20th century' exhibit, which includes pacemakers and miniskirts.

The **Des Moines Art Center** (☎ 515-277-4405; 4700 Grand Ave; admission free; 11am-4pm Tue & Wed, 11am-9pm Thu, noon-4pm Sat & Sun), south of I-235 42nd St exit, is worth a look for both its interesting architecture and modern-art collection. Best is IM Pei's sculpture garden, featuring Red Grooms' Germanic 'butter cow.'

The amazing, 600-acre **Living History Farms** (☎ 515-278-5286; 2600 111th St, Urbandale; adult/child $10/6; 9am-6pm May-Oct), off I-80/I-35 at Hickman Rd, west of town, has four re-created villages ranging from a 1700 Ioway village to a 1900 big-red-barn farm – and kids will love the piglets. Learn how the introduction of livestock and new tools revolutionized farming. Dedicated historians farm here with period tools all year.

Sleeping

Kirkwood Civic Center Hotel (☎ 515-244-9191, 800-798-9191; www.kirkwoodcchotel.com; 400 Walnut St; r $54-79;) A great downtown place, this 1930s art deco hotel has 13 murals decorating its handsome interior and features a meat-and-potatoes café.

There are several chain motels at I-80/I-35 exit 131 in Urbandale, such as **Best Inn** (☎ 515-270-1111; 5050 Merle Hay Rd; s/d $59/71;), where you can enjoy a continental breakfast.

Motel 6 (☎ 515-287-6364; 4817 Fleur Dr; s/d $42/48;) Good rooms across from the airport.

Fairfield Inn by Marriott (☎ 515-226-1600; 1600 114th St, Clive; r $69;) At the I-80/I-35 exit 124, this inn offers continental breakfast where you can make your own waffles. Mmm, waffles.

Eating

The food is good in Des Moines, but don't ask Ozzy Osbourne about it. He bit the head off a bat here in 1982. Downtown's Court Ave has several lively restaurants.

Machine Shed Restaurant (☎ 515-270-6818; 11151 Hickman Rd; mains $5-10) Next to Living History Farms, it has some fine country cooking, with weekend buffets for $8.

Drake Diner (☎ 515-277-1111; 1111 25th St; mains $5-10) In 1950s style and popular with students of nearby Drake University. The meatloaf comes recommended.

Tasty Tacos (☎ 515-266-4242; 5847 SE 14th St; $2.25-2.75) This beloved local chain has served fried-flour steak, chicken and bean tacos since 1961.

A Dong (☎ 515-284-5632; 1905 Cottage Grove Ave; mains $6-12) Carnivores and vegetarians alike will find happiness at this excellent Vietnamese/Chinese restaurant, just south of the Martin Luther King Jr exit off I-235. Try the phenomenal noodle soup.

Getting There & Around

There are limited air services to Des Moines International Airport, southwest of downtown. **Greyhound** (☎ 515-243-1773; 1107 Keosauqua Way) has buses leaving daily for Chicago ($38, seven hours) and Omaha ($24, 2½ hours). Amtrak's nearest stop is in Osceola, Iowa, 39 miles south.

MTA metro buses (☎ 515-283-8100; 6th & Walnut Sts) run several routes.

AROUND DES MOINES

Madison County

This sleepy county, about 30 miles southwest of the capital, slumbered for half a century until Robert James Waller's blockbusting, tear-jerking novel *The Bridges of Madison County* and its movie version brought in scores of fans to check out the sites. The covered bridges where Robert and Francesca fueled their affair are here. Pick up a map at the Madison County **chamber of commerce** (☎ 515-462-1185, 800-298-6119; 73 Jefferson St, Winterset). The best bridge – Cedar Bridge, northeast of town – was destroyed by arson in 2002, and funds are being raised for reconstruction. The Covered Bridges Festival is held in mid-October.

The **birthplace of John Wayne** (☎ 515-462-1044; 216 S 2nd St, Winterset; admission $2.50; ⏲ 10am-4:30pm), aka Marion Robert Morrison, is in a humble dwelling.

Neal Smith National Wildlife Refuge

About 20 miles east of Des Moines, near Prairie City, this wonderful, 5000-acre wildlife refuge is the site of an unprecedented tallgrass reconstruction project. See the film and displays at the **Prairie Learning Center** (☎ 515-994-3400; Hwy 163; admission free; ⏲ 9am-4pm Mon-Sat, noon-5pm Sun) to learn about the ecosystems that began to vanish with the arrival of pioneers, farming, livestock, cities and interstates. Outside are herds of buffalo and elk, plus a 5-mile auto tour and 2-mile hiking trail.

Eldon

About 90 miles southeast of Des Moines, on Hwy 16, tiny Eldon lives in infamy as the source of Grant Wood's iconic (and often parodied) *American Gothic* (1930). You can see the house, on the subsequently named American Gothic St, and strike your own grimacing pose with whatever 'tool' you have on you. The actual painting is in the Art Institute of Chicago.

ALONG I-80

Most of Iowa's attractions are within an easy drive of I-80, which runs east–west across the center of the state. Des Moines (see p704) is about midway along the road.

Iowa City

The former capital is a busy student town that has outgrown its infrastructure. The University of Iowa campus spills across both sides of the Iowa River; on the east side (at Iowa Ave and Clinton St) it mingles with riverfront parks and downtown restaurants and bars. A lot goes on. In summer (when the student-to-townie ratio evens out) bands often play at the pedestrian mall. The Iowa City/Coralville **visitors center** (☎ 319-337-6592, 800-283-6592; 408 1st Ave; ⏲ 8am-5pm Mon-Fri, 10am-4pm Sat & Sun), in neighboring Coralville, has information.

> **ON THE RAGBRAI** *by Alex Hershey*
>
> Described as a rolling Mardi Gras and held the last week in July, Ragbrai (Register's Annual Great Bike Ride Across Iowa) started in 1973 when a few guys from the *Des Moines Register* up and biked across the state – and then opened up the invitation to all and sundry. From the moment I ceremoniously dipped my back wheel into the Missouri River until my front wheel hit the ol' Mississip', I was part of a rolling mass of 8500 riders – young, old, in and out of shape, camping in small host towns, inhaling the down-home grub and, above all, absorbing the landscape and people-scape of Iowa in a way that just can't be done from inside a car. To submit a rider application, head to www.ragbrai.org.

The university has a few good, free museums, including the **old capitol**, a **natural history museum** (with a huge sloth) and the newly renovated **University of Iowa Museum of Art** (☎ 319-335-1727; 150 N Riverside Dr; ⏲ noon-5pm Wed-Sat, noon-10pm Thu & Fri) with a particularly good African collection. The **Iowa Children's Museum** (☎ 319-625-6255; 1451 Coral Ridge Ave; admission $4.50; ⏲ 10am-6pm Tue-Thu, 10am-8pm Fri, 10am-6pm Sat, 11am-6pm Sun), near I-80 exit 240, is chock-full of hands-on activities and exhibits.

Near Coralville Lake, the **Devonian Fossil Gorge** (Dubuque St; free), 2.5 miles north of I-80 exit 244, is a Devonian-era seafloor with countless fossils, all exposed by the 1993 floods.

In West Branch, 11 miles east on I-80, is the worthwhile **Herbert Hoover Birthplace & Library** (☎ 319-643-2541; adult/child $3/free; ⏲ 9am-5pm). Hoover served as president from 1928 to 1932 and was a famous relief administrator, but he's more remembered (deservedly or not) as the namesake of Depression-era 'Hoovervilles.' The site includes the tiny cottage where lil' Herbie was born.

Take I-80 exit 242 to get to comfortable **Big Ten Inn** (☎ 319-351-6131; 707 1st Ave; s/d $34/46; ⊠). At the riverside **Iowa House Hotel** (☎ 319-335-3513; Madison & Jefferson Sts; r $60-108; ⊠) all rooms have two double beds and a fridge, and some rooms are wheelchair accessible. The reception room of the 1908 Edwardian **Haverkamps Linn Street B&B Homestay** (☎ 319-337-4363; 619 N Linn St; r $35-50) is crammed with antique hats and other sartorial paraphernalia, which you're welcome to borrow when hitting the town.

It's food and beer galore around downtown. **Masala** (☎ 319-338-6199; 9 Dubuque St; mains $3-9) serves yummy vegetarian curries; you'll be spoiled for choice at the busy lunch buffet ($6.25).

Grab a bus out of town from the **Greyhound bus station** (☎ 319-337-2127; 404 E College St).

Amana Colonies

These seven villages, 18 miles northwest of Iowa City, are stretched along a 15-mile loop. All were established as German religious communes in the 1850s by Inspirationists, who follow a belief in *Werkzeuge*, the divine revelation of inspired prophets. Unlike the Amish and Mennonite religions, Inspirationists embrace modern technology, evident in their booming refrigerator business (note the plant in Middle Amana).

Today the well-preserved villages offer a glimpse at this unique culture, and there are lots of arts, crafts, cheeses, baked goods and wines to buy. Stop at the Amana Colonies **visitors center** (☎ 319-622-7622; I-80; 8am-4:30pm Mon-Sat, 10am-5pm Sun), at exit 225, for the indispensable guide map.

There's a handful of museums around the villages open daily from April through October. Popular stops include the **Amana Woolen Mill** (☎ 800-222-6430; exit 225 off I-80; 8am-6pm Mon-Sat, 11am-5pm Sun) and the **Barn Museum** (☎ 319-622-3058; admission $3; 9am-5pm) in South Amana, which has Henry Moore's collection of miniature replicas.

A $6 combo ticket ($2 for kids) gets you into the insightful **Museum of Amana History** (☎ 319-622-3567; 10am-5pm Mon-Sat, noon-5pm Sun) in Amana, the **Communal Kitchen & Cooper Shop Museum** (☎ 319-622-3567; 1003 26th Ave; 9am-5pm Mon-Sat, noon-5pm Sun), Middle Amana, the agricultural museum (South Amana), the church museum and the newly restored general store museum (both in Homestead). Get your ticket at any of these sites. Individually all are $3 for adults and $1 for kids.

The villages are home to a campsite and many good-value B&Bs, including Homestead's timeless **Die Heimat** (☎ 319-622-3937; 4434 V St; r $69-89;), with its simple, elegant rooms.

One of the Amanas' top draws is the hefty-portioned, home-cooked German cuisine. Closest to I-80 is **Zuber's Restaurant** (☎ 319-622-3911; 2206 44th Ave, Homestead), which serves great pork chop and spaetzle meals.

Council Bluffs

At Iowa's western end of I-80 is Council Bluffs, known for its casinos and budget motels, which make it a good base for exploring its big brother across the Missouri River – Omaha, Nebraska.

The **Iowa visitors center** (☎ 712-366-4900; 3434 Downing Ave), off I-80 exit 1B, has displays on Lewis and Clark.

Off I-80/I-29 exit 3 there are many budget motels, including the reliable **Motel 6** (☎ 712-366-2405; 3032 S Expressway; s/d $50/56;).

Loess Hills Byway

The well-signed Loess Hills Byway – an inviting 200-mile network of roads that run along Iowa's western edge parallel to I-29 – is named for the rare loess (rhymes with Gus), a windblown glacier-ground soil that began piling up into unique formations about 18,000 years ago. Dramatic (and soft) 'catwalk' slopes step down steep hills. Nowhere else but China do loess hills reach these heights.

The hills' most dramatic scenery is off I-29 (north of Council Bluffs), in Harrison and Monona Counties; exit I-29 at Hwy 183 and head north. In Moorhead, stop at the **Loess Hills Hospitality Association** (☎ 712-886-5441; 119 Oak St; 9am-4:30pm Mon-Sat, 1-4:30pm Sun) for route maps and tips on hikes. Pick up the helpful Iowa's Loess Hills Scenic Byway booklet at any Iowa visitors center.

ALONG US 20

Most scenery along US 20, Iowa's northern passage from Dubuque on the Mississippi River to Sioux City on the Missouri River, is brick-smacked flat. But detours along the Mississippi valley pass implausibly farmed lands that ripple like lime-green waves.

Dubuque

One of the Mississippi's nicest towns, Dubuque makes for a great stop: 19th-century Victorian homes line its narrow, and surprisingly urban, streets between the river and seven steep hills. Those seeking action can canoe on the area's rivers, cycle the 26-mile Heritage Trail or square dance.

Get information from the **visitors center** (☎ 563-556-4372; 300 Main St) near the river.

The **4th Street Elevator** (☎ 563-582-6496; 4th St & Fenelon; round-trip $1.50; 🕑 8am-10pm Apr-Nov) at the Fenelon Place Elevator Company climbs a steep hill for huge views. Ring the bell to begin the ride. Learn about 300 years of life on the Mississippi at the impressive **National Mississippi River Museum & Aquarium** (☎ 563-557-9545, 800-226-3369; 350 E 3rd St; adult /child $9/7; 🕑 10am-6pm). Nearby, the **Spirit of Dubuque** (☎ 563-583-8093; 3rd Street, at Ice Harbor; adult/child $12.50/7.50) offers Mississippi cruises. Bird-watchers may see the national bird at **Eagle Point Park**, north of downtown (take Rhomberg to Shiras).

The historic **Julien Inn** (☎ 563-556-4200, 800-798-7098; 200 Main St; s $49-59, d $59-69) is pure fun. The lobby flaunts its 1960s makeover; fleur-de-lis signs hang over carpeted doors; a little bedside bulb lights up when guests have a message. Dubuque has great Victorian B&Bs too, including the lovely **Richards House** (☎ 563-557-1492; 1492 Locust St; r with shared bath $40-50, r with private bath $50-65). If you want to camp, head to **Miller Riverview Park** (☎ 563-589-4238; Admiral Sheehy Dr; $8) on Schmidt Island.

Try to make it to **Breitbach's Country Dining** (☎ 563-552-2220; 563 Balltown Rd, Balltown; mains $8-15, weekend buffet $9), a rewarding 17-mile drive north of Dubuque. Breitbach's has been serving gut-busting cod and chicken dinners since 1852. Don't miss the Depression-era gypsy-drawn mural.

Greyhound buses (☎ 563-583-3397) leave from the Julien Inn.

Dyersville & Around

An otherwise quiet farm town, Dyersville attracts thousands of visitors each year for two reasons: baseball and toys. Run around the bases at the **Field of Dreams baseball diamond** (☎ 888-875-8404; 28963 Lansing Rd; admission free; 🕑 9am-6pm Apr-Nov), as seen in the 1989 film.

Dyersville's farm-toy show in November attracts more than 20,000 fans, and four farm-toy manufacturers are here. Plus there's the surprising **National Farm Toy Museum** (☎ 563-875-2727; 1110 16th Ave; adult/child $4/1; 🕑 8am-7pm) with a fun film and 30,000 historic toy tractors and barns.

Waterloo & Around

Home of four John Deere tractor plants, Waterloo is the place to get one of those prized green-and-yellow caps that you've seen all over middle America. Fun tractor-driven tours of the **John Deere Tractor Assembly** (☎ 319-292-7697; 3500 E Donald St; tours free; 8am, 10am & 1pm) show how these monstrously sized vehicles are made ('with pride'). Minimum age is 12, and reservations are required.

You can sleep at the **Twister House Movie Site** (☎ 641-858-5133; 26302 Y Ave; r $25), southwest of Waterloo, where the final tornado showdown in the movie *Twister* was shot.

About 40 miles east of Waterloo, stop to see the lovely Frank Lloyd Wright–designed **Cedar Rock** (☎ 319-934-3572; admission $3; 🕑 11am-5pm Tue-Sun May-Oct), near Quasqueton. The 1950 house, overlooking the Wapsipinicon River, is an example of Frank's 'simplified residential architecture.'

Sioux City

The Missouri and Big Sioux Rivers meet here – also called Siouxland – a city known for its tasty Sue Bee Honey (and its cute logo) and the site of a 1989 United plane crash. The **visitors center** (☎ 712-279-4800; 801 4th St) has some brochures.

The **Sgt Floyd Monument**, off I-29 south of town, marks the burial site of the only explorer to die during the Lewis and Clark expedition. North and south of town are drives along the Loess Hills Byway (see p706).

Across the river in Nebraska, **Marina Inn** (☎ 402-494-4000, 800-798-7980; 4th & B Sts; r $84-119) has riverfront rooms.

You won't need to live on bread alone at the popular **Bread Basket** (☎ 712-252-5040; 1101 4th St). Create your custom sandwich from a choice of eight breads and eight meats. There are also – surprise – eight delicious daily soups, and live music on weekends.

NEBRASKA

Apart from the cities of Omaha and Lincoln in the east, Nebraska is a vast, scantily inhabited prairie grassland that rises imperceptibly to the foothills of the Rockies. Crossing this expanse makes for an interesting journey – following in the footsteps of the Pony Express and the pioneers in their Conestoga wagons ('prairie schooners') who blazed

NEBRASKA FACTS

Nickname Cornhusker State
Population 1,729,200 (38th)
Area 77,360 sq miles (16th)
Admitted to Union March 1, 1867 (37th)
State tree Cottonwood
Capital city Lincoln (population 232,300)
Other cities Omaha (399,400), Grand Island (43,000)
Birthplace of Lakota leader Red Cloud, Malcolm X, Gerald Ford, author Willa Cather, Johnny Carson, Marlon Brando, Nick Nolte, Kool-Aid
Famous for first rodeo (1882), only unicameral state legislature (1934), Chimney Rock, football

the Oregon, Mormon and California Trails. The chubby panhandle is a particularly worthwhile detour. There are also rewarding wildlife refuges, forests, sand hills, canoeable rivers (such as the Niobrara) and recreational lakes.

I-80 is the state's major east–west artery, although much of its length is boring. Those traveling to South Dakota's Black Hills may prefer the more scenic US 275 and US 20 northwest of Omaha, or Hwy 2 through the Sand Hills.

HISTORY

Lewis and Clark followed the Missouri along Nebraska's eastern fringe and met with Native Americans here in 1804. It took another 20 years before the Platte River was used by trappers.

The trickle of white visitors turned to a flood after 1841, when the first covered wagon passed through on its way to Oregon. The Platte Valley was soon swarming with settlers – around 400,000 hopefuls – looking for a new start in the mythical West.

The arrival of transcontinental railroads such as the Union Pacific made covered wagons unnecessary, and the trail ruts succumbed to pasture as settlers rushed in after the 1862 Homestead Act. Settlers took advantage of the rich soils and abundant grasslands, and Nebraska developed into a productive agricultural state.

INFORMATION

Nebraska has about 30 state visitors centers (half of which are staffed), especially along I-80 between Omaha and Kimball. You can get information in advance from the **Nebraska Travel & Tourism Division** (☎ 402-471-3796; www.visitnebraska.org). Visitors to Nebraska state parks must purchase a vehicle sticker (daily $2.50, annual $14), which is good at any park. For more information, contact the **Nebraska Game & Parks Commission** (☎ 800-826-7275; www.ngpc.state.ne.us).

For highway information, call ☎ 800-906-9069; if you're out of the state, dial ☎ 402-471-4533.

OMAHA

Nebraska's largest city is not its prettiest, but Omaha has a rich history as a prairie outpost. Its location on the Missouri River and its proximity to the Platte made it a favored jumping-off point for the Oregon and Mormon Trails. Fort Omaha was built in 1868 as a staging post for troops fighting in the Indian Wars. These days Omaha is home to more millionaires per capita than any other US city. (Leading Omaha's list is Warren Buffet.)

Omaha has a strained relationship with its Iowan neighbor, Council Bluffs. An Omaha mayor once called Council Bluffs 'the 000 city' because of its casinos and adult novelty shops.

The Omaha **visitors center** (☎ 402-444-4660; 6800 Mercy Rd, Ste 202), in the Ak-Sar-Ben complex, is tough to find (take I-80 exit 449). More convenient is the **Nebraska I-80 Information Center** (☎ 402-595-3990; 212 Bob Gibson Blvd). The **W Dale Clark Library** (☎ 402-444-4800; 215 S 15th St) has free Internet access.

Sights & Activities

The grand **Old Market**, between 10th and 13th Sts and Farnam and Jackson Sts, has century-old warehouses, cobblestone streets and nightlife to enjoy. A few blocks west, the art deco **Joslyn Art Museum** (☎ 402-342-3300; 2200 Dodge St; admission $6; 🕒 10am-4pm Tue-Sat, noon-4pm Sun) houses a great collection of Renaissance and 19th- and 20th-century American and European art. It's open late on Thursday.

The ever-growing **Henry Doorly Zoo** (☎ 402-733-8401; 3701 S 10th St; adult/child $9/5.25; 🕒 9:30am-5pm), off I-80 exit 454, has a giant cat complex and the world's largest nocturnal exhibit, plus up-close looks at Plains animals.

Omaha was the birthplace of an unlikely pair, 38th president Gerald Ford and civil-rights leader Malcolm X. One proved that it was difficult to 'walk and chew gum at the same time'; the other swayed crowds of African-Americans with his eloquence. The swank **Gerald R Ford birth site** (☎ 402-444-5955; 32nd St & Woolworth Ave; admission free; 7:30am-dusk) commemorates the nation's 38th president (born Leslie King) and is adjacent to the Gerald R Ford Conservation Center. The **Malcolm X birth site** (3448 Pinkney St; admission free; 7:30am-dusk) was closed for restoration at the time of research. The **Great Plains Black Museum** (☎ 402-345-6817; 2213 Lake St; admission free; 10am-2pm Tue-Sun) recounts the role of African-Americans in the West.

One of Nebraska's top attractions owes its fortune to the state's smack-dab location in the center of the USA, which helped it become the headquarters of the Strategic Air Command (SAC). Midway between Omaha and Lincoln, the fascinating **Strategic Air & Space Museum** (☎ 402-827-3100, 800-358-5029; 28210 West Park Hwy; adult/child $7/3; 9am-5pm), at I-80 exit 426, boasts two massive hangars housing more than 30 aircraft (including the bomb-dropping B-36 Peacemaker) and 20 missiles. Take a jolting ride on the real 'Desert Storm' flight simulator – if you can handle waiting for Boy Scouts to finish their turn.

Sleeping

Motels abound along I-80 and I-680 N exits. (The best deals, however, are over in Council Bluffs.)

Motel 6 (☎ 402-331-3161, 10708 M St; s/d $52/58;) At I-80 exit 445.

Travelodge Cornhusker Inn & Suites (☎ 402-391-5757; 7101 Grover St; r from $60;) At I-80 exit 449, it has continental breakfasts and a hot tub to go with the decent rooms.

Best Western Redick Tower Hotel (☎ 402-342-1500; 1504 Harney St; r from $89; P) A comfortable downtown hotel near Old Market.

Louisville State Recreation Area (☎ 402-234-6855; south of I-80 exit 440; campsites/RV sites $8/11) Sites clustered around five artificial lakes west of town.

Platte River State Park (☎ 402-234-2217; tepees $15, cabins $30-90) Good cabins and plenty of wild turkeys 25 miles south of I-80.

Eating

Omaha's huge stockyards closed in 1998, but you still can't swing a stick in town without hitting a great steakhouse. One of the best is **Johnny's Café** (☎ 402-731-4774; 4702 S 27th St; mains $13-25), next to the former stockyards. Its iron cow-sculpture doors open to meat-eating bliss.

Bohemian Café (☎ 402-342-9838; 1406 S 13th St; lunch $6, dinner mains $9-11) Sprightly place a few blocks south of Old Market, serving belt-busting Czech meals.

McFoster's Natural Kind Café (☎ 401-345-7477; 302 S 38th St; $5-10) Give your arteries a break at this mostly vegetarian joint which also offers free-range fish and chicken.

Getting There & Around

Omaha's **Eppley Airfield** (☎ 402-422-6817), northeast of downtown, has links to a number of other nearby cities. One major carrier is **Midwest Express** (☎ 800-452-2022). A ride downtown with **Happy Cab** (☎ 402-339-8294) costs about $12.

Greyhound (☎ 402-341-1906; 1601 Jackson St) has daily buses bound for Lincoln ($12, one hour), Kansas City ($30, three hours), Rapid City ($90, 13 hours) and Denver ($75, 11 hours).

Amtrak (☎ 402-342-6699; 1003 9th St) has daily train service to Lincoln (from $14, one hour), Chicago (from $148, 9½ hours) and Denver (from $132, nine hours).

LINCOLN

Nebraska's capital ('Star City') is a good place for an overnight stop. The downtown and historic Haymarket District are within easy walking distance of several museums, the University of Nebraska campus and the state capitol. Named for honest Abe (former US president), Lincoln has a low crime rate, as well as low cost of living and more city parks per capita than any other US city. Get information from the helpful **visitors center** (☎ 402-434-5348; 201 N 7th St; 9am-8pm Mon-Fri, 8am-4pm Sat, noon-4pm Sun) in Lincoln Station in the Haymarket.

Sights & Activities

The remarkable 400ft-high **State Capitol** (☎ 402-471-0448; 14th & M Sts; tours free; 9am-4pm Mon-Fri, 10am-4pm Sat, 1-4pm Sun) represents the best in phallic capitol buildings. The outside view will be marred until 2007, when a restoration will be complete, but a tour is worthwhile for the lovely 1932 art deco interior.

Museum of Nebraska History (☎ 402-471-4754; P & 15th St; admission free; 9am-4:30pm Tue-Sun) has a worthwhile First Nebraskans exhibit.

Nearby, the **Lincoln Children's Museum** (☎ 402-477-4000; 1420 P St; admission $4; 🕓 8am-5pm Mon-Fri) has a whole indoor, whippersnapper-sized town. Another good diversion is the **University of Nebraska State Museum** (☎ 402-472-2642; Morrill Hall; admission $2; 🕓 9:30am-4:30pm Mon-Sat, 1:30-4:30pm Sun), which has mammoth bones supposedly dug up by a chicken.

The prized Nebraska Cornhuskers football team plays home games here in fall. On most weekdays, you can tour the team's field and hall of fame at **Memorial Stadium** (☎ 402-472-1905).

Sleeping

There are budget motels aplenty on W '0' St, near I-80 (exits 395, 396 and 397), including **Welcome Home Inn & Suites** (☎ 402-474-7666; 2231 W '0' St; r $47-99;), with a fridge and HBO in all the rooms. Pickings are slightly better off I-80 at the Cornhusker Hwy (NW 12th St) exit; **Horizon Inn** (☎ 402-474-5252; 2901 NW 12th St; r from $40;) has tidy rooms with a VCR in each.

The **Embassy Suites Hotel** (☎ 402-474-1111; 1040 P St; r from $129; P) Luxurious rooms, Jacuzzi and a nine-story open atrium featuring two waterfalls. Included is a cooked-to-order breakfast.

HI Cornerstone Hostel (☎ 402-476-0926; 640 N 16th St; member/nonmember $10/13) In a church between two fraternity houses, it has a few basic dorm rooms with beds, and no lock-out time.

Eating

Lincoln's Haymarket District, a rejuvenated six-block warehouse area dating from the early 20th century, has a good variety of grub.

Oven (☎ 402-475-6118; 201 N 8th St; mains $10-18) An upscale Indian restaurant with more than a dozen vegetarian dishes on the menu.

Maggie's Vegetarian Vittles (☎ 402-477-3959; 311 N 8th St; $4-6) Serves vegan wraps, soups and baked goodies.

Mill (☎ 402-475-5522; 800 P St; $1-5) University students and downtown workers soak in the afternoon sun on the dock, which serves coffees and snacks and offers Internet access.

Getting There & Around

Greyhound (☎ 402-474-1071; 940 P St) has four daily buses to Omaha ($12, one hour).

Amtrak (☎ 402-476-1295; 201 N 7th St) arrives in the wee hours; trains head west to Denver (from $130, eight hours) and east to Omaha (from $14, one hour).

A ride with **Husker Cabs** (☎ 402-477-4111) from either station to the budget hotels is about $14.

ALONG I-80

The shortest route across the Plains, I-80 (also called the Great Platte River Rd) is also the least interesting, but there are a few diversions.

West of Lincoln, in Grand Island, near the junction of US 281, is the modern **Stuhr Museum of the Prairie Pioneer** (☎ 308-385-5316; adult/child $8/6; 🕓 9am-5pm Mon-Sat, noon-5pm Sun), which has the building where Henry Fonda was born, plus a well-interpreted collection of artifacts.

At Grand Island, Hwy 2 branches northwest through Broken Bow to Alliance in the panhandle. Hwy 2 is slow but scenic. It passes through Sand Hills – 20,000 sq miles of sand dunes covered in grass – one of the country's most isolated areas. Keep your gas tank full.

Fort Kearny State Historical Park (☎ 308-865-5305; admission per car $2.50; 🕓 9am-5pm), near I-80 & Hwy 44, west of Grand Island, is a partial reconstruction of the Oregon Trail outpost built here in 1848. The small museum has an exhibit on Moses Sydenham, the nutty pioneer who fought to move the nation's capital to Kearny.

There's no missing the **Great Platte River Road Archway Monument** (☎ 877-511-2724; adult $8.25, child $3-6; 🕓 9am-7pm), which hangs perilously over I-80 a few miles east of Kearney. The gadget-heavy museum traces Nebraska's history.

Further west at Gothenburg is an original **Pony Express station** (☎ 308-537-2143; Ehmen Park, 15th & Lake Sts; admission free; 🕓 8am-8pm Jun-Aug, 9am-6pm May & Sep), which was used from 1860 to 1861.

North Platte is home to the **Buffalo Bill Ranch State Historic Park** (☎ 308-535-8035; Scouts Rest Ranch Rd; admission free; 🕓 9am-5pm summer, 10am-4pm Mon-Fri until Nov), six miles north of town, which celebrates Bill Cody, the father of rodeo and the famed Wild West Show. His house and big red barn are packed with memorabilia. To the west, near Paxton, Central Time changes to Mountain Time. You can spend the extra hour at **Ole's Steakhouse & Big Game Lounge** (☎ 308-239-4500; I-80 exit 145;

mains $5-15) looking at stuffed versions of what you are probably eating.

ALONG US 26 (OREGON TRAIL)

Branch off I-80 at Ogallala, and follow the Oregon Trail (basically the North Platte River) along US 26 to the huge landmarks of Nebraska's panhandle. At **Ash Hollow State Historical Park** (☎ 308-778-5651), near Lewellen, you can see wagon ruts on Windlass Hill made in the 19th century. Near Bridgeport, 56 miles northwest, stands the **Courthouse & Jail Rocks**, the first of the major landmarks. From Bridgeport, take a detour 40 miles north on US 385 to rural Alliance, the quiet, somewhat reluctant home to **Carhenge**, in a field two miles north. This Stonehenge replica is made from 34 discarded car bodies to 'surprise people.' You might bump into a few happy teens drinking brewskis here.

Continuing west on US 26, you'll find **Chimney Rock**, the most frequently mentioned trail landmark in pioneer diaries – and the model for the artwork on many Nebraska license plates. The excellent **visitors center** (☎ 308-586-2581; adult/child $3/free; 9am-5pm) interprets the pioneer trails. Dirt roads surround the center and allow for some exploring.

Relive pioneer days on an overnight prairie schooner trip by **Oregon Trail Wagon Train** (☎ 308-586-1850), just northwest of Chimney Rock; trips start at $175, including meals and bedding. There are also chuck wagon cookouts, canoes and cabins.

Visible for miles, the most impressive Trail landmark, **Scotts Bluff National Monument** (☎ 308-436-4340; Hwy 92; admission per car $5) is three miles west of Gering. The Sioux called it *me-a-pa-te* ('hill that is hard to go around') millennia ago. Today you can drive up it in a flash, or take the 1.5-mile hike. The views of Wyoming's Laramie Peak 90 miles west and North Platte River 800ft below are outstanding.

ALONG US 20

This route is a nice (if lonesome) road across Nebraska. The further west you go, the more space you'll see between towns, trees and pickup trucks. Be sure to snare the free *Highway to Adventure: US 20* brochure, available at visitors centers.

Running on converted railroad lines, the ongoing **Cowboy Trail** (☎ 402-370-3374) is a network of good cycling, hiking and horseback-riding trails. When completed, the route will run nearly 200 miles and connect Norfolk with Valentine.

At **Ashfall Fossil Beds State Historical Park** (☎ 402-893-2000; $3/2 adult/child; 9am-5pm Mon-Sat, 11am-5pm Sun), off US 20 north of Royal, you can see unearthed prehistoric skeletons of more than 200 critters, buried 10 million years ago by ash from a Pompeii-like explosion in what is now Idaho.

HALF A MILLION SANDHILL CRANES CAN'T BE WRONG

The area along I-80 may be dullsville to many travelers, but for nine million years and counting, it's had very devoted fans in sandhill cranes. In February and March, more than 500,000 of these 4ft-tall, reddish-brown birds stop in the North Platte River valley between Grand Island and Kearney to roost and dine before heading north for a Canadian summer. Endangered whooping cranes also roost here.

Any time of year, stop by **Crane Meadows Nature Center** (☎ 308-382-1820; I-80 exit 305) to hike 7 miles of trails through prairie land and along the Platte River.

Valentine

On the northern edge of the Sand Hills, the 'Cupid Capital of Nebraska' is the hub for remarkable canoeing, kayaking and inner-tubing in the Niobrara River. The **visitors center** (☎ 402-376-2969; US 20 & US 83; 9am-8pm Mon-Sat) has information on the dozen outfitters in town. River routes east of town are the most rewarding, but you'll see fewer folks floating to the west.

A tidy cheapie in town, the red-brick **Valentine Motel** (☎ 402-376-2450; Main St; s/d $35/40) has cute rooms and a 1953 Ford parked out front.

About 12 miles east, on Hwy 12, an impressive waterfall can be seen at **Smith Falls State Park** (☎ 402-376-1306), which is also an enjoyable place for **camping** (campsites per person $3, vehicle pass $2.50).

Northern Panhandle

Many interesting attractions – and solitude – make this area a rewarding place to visit. The **Museum of the Fur Trade** (☎ 308-432-3843;

adult/child $2.50/free; 8am-5pm summer), 3 miles east of Chadron, has many displays and the restored Bordeaux Trading Post, which was shut down for trading guns with the Native Americans who wiped out Custer.

Northwest of Crawford are a few paleontological wonders. **Toadstool Geological Park** is a mini-badlands with a wide variety of fossils and a hiking trail. The nearby **Hudson-Meng Bison Bonebed** (☎ 308-665-3900; adult/child $4/1; 9am-5pm May-Sep) displays the site where 1000 bison enigmatically perished more than 10,000 years ago.

Beautiful **Fort Robinson State Park** (☎ 308-665-2900; admission per $2.50; sunrise-sunset), 4 miles west of Crawford, is where Crazy Horse was killed in 1877 while in captivity – a plaque marks the spot. The **Fort Robinson Museum** (☎ 308-665-2919; adult/child $2/free; 10am-5pm Tue-Sun summer, Mon-Fri rest of the year) gives a disappointingly one-sided version of the Sioux Wars but has good displays on the fort's reputation as the 'country club of the army.' From April to November, there's cozy lodging in the 1909 barracks ($40 to $45) and 1874 quarters ($85). In summer the **Post Playhouse** (☎ 308-665-1976; adult/child $12/8) puts on a play six nights a week.

Further west on US 20, at Harrison, drive 23 miles south on Hwy 29 to reach **Agate Fossil Beds National Monument** (☎ 308-668-2211; adult /car $3/5; 8am-6pm summer, 8am-5pm rest of the year), a rich source of unusual fossils dating back 10 to 20 million years. The most interesting is the Daemonelix, a fossilized corkscrew tunnel dug by prehistoric beavers. Don't skip a walk on one of the two short trails.

SOUTH DAKOTA

South Dakota is the highlight of a visit to the Plains states, offering excellent introductions to Native American culture and the Old West, as well as the region's most beautiful natural attractions, including the rugged Badlands and the beautiful Black Hills. No visitor should miss the giant Mt Rushmore and Crazy Horse sculptures.

I-90 gives good access to the state's premier attractions, crossing the state from Sioux Falls in the east to Spearfish in the west. Get off the interstate to enjoy South Dakota's unique 'pink' two-lane highways, made from the state's abundant reddish quartzite.

SOUTH DAKOTA FACTS

Nicknames Sunshine State, Mt Rushmore State
Population 761,063 (46th)
Area 77,125 sq miles (17th)
Admitted to Union November 2, 1889 (40th)
Capital city Pierre (population 14,000)
Other cities Sioux Falls (130,500), Rapid City (60,300)
State tree Black Hills spruce
State fossil Triceratops
Birthplace of Sitting Bull, Crazy Horse, Black Elk, Calamity Jane, news anchor and author Tom Brokaw, Catherine 'Daisy Duke' Bach, quarterback Josh Heupel
Famous for Mt Rushmore, Black Hills, the Sioux, *Little House on the Prairie*

HISTORY

Best remembered for the Great Sioux Nation's struggle to retain its traditional lands in the late 19th century, South Dakota has a long history of settlement, reaching back to warrior-hunters around 8000 BC. By AD 900 large settlements had been established by the Arikara. The Sioux arrived in the mid-18th century.

When the USA acquired South Dakota with the 1803 Louisiana Purchase, the region was very much the domain of the Sioux and a few brave fur trappers.

It wasn't until the 1850s that the rich Dakota soil attracted the interest of settlers. The 1868 Fort Laramie Treaty between the USA and the Sioux promised the Sioux large tracts of land on which to roam freely.

The treaty was irrevocably broken in 1874 when Lieutenant Colonel George Custer led an expedition into the Black Hills in search of gold – unfortunately, he was successful. Miners and settlers soon streamed in illegally, and the Sioux retaliated in the biggest of the Indian Wars.

By the late 1870s, it became obvious to the emergent USA that there was one remaining obstacle to the unfettered development of the Plains: the independent Plains Indians. In 1876 the army supremo General Sherman, responding to the Native Americans' decision not to return to their reservations, planned to eliminate all opposition in a three-pronged attack. The Sioux and other tribes gathered at Rosebud, South Dakota, for their last great year on the Plains, a last taste of the old way of life. Thousands of warriors came – including chiefs Crazy Horse, Sitting Bull, Red Cloud, Little Big Man and Two Moons. Sitting Bull entered a trance and foresaw the death of white soldiers.

The three forces then converged on the Sioux and their allies. The charismatic chief Crazy Horse and 1500 bedecked braves held off the southern force at Rosebud, killing 90. Shortly after, Crazy Horse led the charge that annihilated Custer and the 7th Cavalry at the Battle of Little Big Horn.

It was to be the Plains Indians' last real victory over the invaders. Faced with overwhelming force, the tribes split up. Sitting Bull fled to Canada, Crazy Horse turned in his gun in 1877, and the railroads and settlers inched forward. The final decimation of Sioux resistance came at Wounded Knee in 1890, when the army reacted to a revival of the Ghost Dance religion and ruthlessly massacred around 300 men, women and children. (Much later, in 1973, Oglala Sioux loyal to the American Indian Movement occupied Wounded Knee and kept federal officers at bay for 70 days.)

After the captured Plains lands were 'freed,' settlers flooded in to face drought, dust storms and depression in their efforts to establish a viable agricultural base. Today South Dakota is one of the poorest states in the USA, but it has a vibrant tourism industry.

INFORMATION

The **South Dakota Department of Tourism** (☎ 800-732-5682; www.state.sd.us/tourism; 711 E Wells Ave, Pierre, SD 57501) publishes a good information pack. Most state information centers, along I-90 and I-29, are staffed only in summer. Good brochures include the *South Dakota Guide to Indian Reservation & Art* and *Lewis and Clark: the South Dakota Adventure*.

In the center of the state, roughly along the Missouri River, Central Time changes to Mountain Time.

Call ☎ 800-710-2267 for state park campground information or reservations. For winter road conditions, call ☎ 605-394-2255; for details on road construction (and there is plenty), call ☎ 605-773-3571.

SIOUX FALLS

South Dakota's biggest city, at the intersection of I-90 and I-29, is a regional center for marketing, banking and agriculture – not to mention lottery 'casinos', of which Sioux Falls has 64. The Sioux Falls **visitors center** (☎ 605-336-1620; 200 N Phillips Ave) can provide information.

See the Big Sioux River splash over quartzite rocks at **Falls Park** off Weber Ave north of downtown; the park has a good **visitors center** (☎ 605-367-7430; 9am-9pm Apr-Sep, 9am-5pm Sat & Sun rest of the year), with an observatory. The restored **Old Courthouse Museum** (☎ 605-367-4210; 6th St & Main Ave; admission free; 9am-5pm Mon-Sat, noon-5pm Sun) has a good display on Plains Indians. It also hosts free concerts on Friday in summer.

At I-29 exit 77, in the city's southwest, is the slightly aged **Empire Inn** (☎ 605-361-2345; 4208 W 41st St; s/d $45/66;). The best mid-range deal is at **Country Inn & Suites** (☎ 605-373-0153; 200 E 8th St;), with rooms near the falls. Continental breakfast included.

Around Sioux Falls

About 80 miles southwest of Sioux Falls, **Yankton** is a well-preserved town at the east end of Lewis and Clark Lake, a boaters' paradise. The **visitors center** (☎ 605-665-3636; 218 W 4th St) has brochures. **Lewis & Clark Resort** (☎ 605-665-2680; 43496 Lake Shore Dr; r $65-75;) offers basic motel units and cabins lakeside. Camp in one of 400 sites at the **Lewis & Clark Recreation Area** (☎ 605-668-2985; campsites & RV sites $10-15, cabins $37).

Little House on the Prairie fans (only) should head to Laura Ingalls Wilder's former home in De Smet. There are two original **Wilder homes** (☎ 605-854-3383; adult/child $6/3; 9am-5:30pm summer, closed Sat & Sun rest of the year), a drive-by tour of sites featured in her books and an **outdoor play** (☎ 605-692-2108; adult/child $7/4) performed weekends in June and July.

The remote **HI Pleasant Valley Hostel** (☎ 605-272-5614; SR 22; dm $15), west of I-29, is on the Minnesota border near Gary, and is near some good hikes and a swimming hole.

ALONG I-90

From Sioux Falls to Rapid City is a straight, boring stretch, but north and south of it lie some of the state's most scenic parts.

Mitchell

This city, 66 miles west of Sioux Falls, is the home of the overwhelmingly kitschy,

Moorish-style **Corn Palace** (☎ 605-996-5031; 6th & Main Sts; admission free; 8am-9pm summer, 8am-5pm May & Sep, 8am-5pm Mon-Fri rest of the year), which is redecorated each year with 275,000 ears of corn. It serves as Mitchell's civic center, active all year. Stop by for a basketball game in winter.

The domed **Mitchell Prehistoric Indian Village Museum** (☎ 605-996-5473; adult/child $6/4; 8am-6pm summer, call for times rest of the year), north of the palace, contains two unearthed 11th-century Mandan lodges. Archaeologists dig up relics on most days.

Motel rates go way up in summer. Try the **Corn Palace Motel** (☎ 605-996-5559; 902 S Burr; s/d $43/46;).

Chamberlain

I-90 crosses the Missouri River at Chamberlain, where you can see the excellent **Akta Lakota Museum & Cultural Center** (☎ 605-734-3452, 800-798-3452; admission free; 8am-6pm Mon-Sat, 1-5pm Sun May-Sep, 8:30am-4:30pm Mon-Fri rest of the year), at St Joseph's Indian School, with Sioux and other Native American artifacts. History buffs should pop into the hilltop visitors center, east of town, where the **Lewis & Clark Information Center** (☎ 605-734-4562; 8am-8pm summer only) has exhibits on the duo.

Pierre

South Dakota's pleasant capital is 30 miles north of I-90 on US 83 but is more rewardingly approached from Chamberlain via Hwys 50 and 34, an 87-mile drive through the Crow Creek Indian Reservation. The area north of Pierre (pronounced peer – no one is sure why) was the setting for many scenes in *Dances with Wolves*. The Pierre **visitors center** (☎ 605-224-7361; 800 W Dakota Ave; 8am-5pm Mon-Fri, 10am-5pm Sat, 1-5pm Sun) has brochures.

The photogenic **State Capitol** (☎ 605-773-3765; 500 E Capitol Ave; 8am-10pm) has a self-guided tour available; search the capitol's tile floors for 11 never-found 'signature stones' set in 1910 (no reward). Don't blame legislators for the faint stench outside; it's natural gas flowing into nearby Capitol Lake. Exhibits at the **South Dakota Cultural Heritage Center** (☎ 605-773-3458; 900 Governor's Dr; adult/child $3/free; 9am-4:30pm Mon-Fri, 1-4:30pm Sat & Sun) include a bloody ghost dance shirt from Wounded Knee. On the Missouri River, **Framboise Island** (where Lewis and Clark had a rough encounter with the Sioux) has hiking trails.

The **Budget Host Inn/State Motel** (☎ 605-224-5896; 640 N Euclid St; s/d from $39/52) has a recliner in each single room.

Rosebud Indian Reservation

At Murdo, detour 40 miles south on US 83 to **Rosebud Indian Reservation** (☎ 605-856-2538), the home of the Sicangu Lakota Oyate. Workers at the **Buechel Memorial Lakota Museum** (☎ 605-747-2745) in St Francis (7 miles southwest of Rosebud town) may talk you through the displays, including some Crazy Horse belongings. In Rosebud, **Salt Camp Cabins & B&B** (☎ 605-747-2206; BIA Hwy 7; r/cabin from $50/100) overlooks the lovely Crazy Horse Canyon, which has a nice lake for a dip. If you stay as a guest of the B&B (not the cabins), you'll be treated to three hearty meals a day.

Back in Murdo, Elvis' Harley-Davidson can be seen at the **Pioneer Auto Show** (☎ 605-669-2691; I-90 & US 83; adult/child $7/4; 8am-8pm).

Pine Ridge Indian Reservation

The home of the Lakota Oglala Sioux, south of the Badlands, is the nation's poorest 'county' and makes for a sobering experience for visitors, as wrecked cars dot the yards of run-down homes and carless residents walk along dusty roads. The Sioux have rejected government compensation offers for the Black Hills because taking money for their traditional home would bring them 'spiritual poverty.'

Wounded Knee Massacre Site, 20 miles northeast of Pine Ridge town, is the reservation's top attraction, but it is not a feted part of South Dakota. Tourist literature neglects it, and the site has little more than a ramshackle cemetery, a roadside sign and a few souvenir sellers in summer.

In Pine Ridge town, stop at the **Red Cloud Indian School** (☎ 605-867-5491) to visit Chief Red Cloud's grave and the Heritage Center, which has a shop selling art and Lakota flash cards. In town, the heroic youth center Visions of SuAnne Big Crow includes the '50s-themed Happytown USA diner. At the farmhouse **Wakpamni B&B** (☎ 605-288-1800; s/d $60/75;), 20 miles east of Pine Ridge, guests can enjoy a sweat-lodge ceremony, horseback-riding ($50) and may get a chance to talk with an Oglala guide.

Look for the locally produced *Welcome to the Oglala Lakota Nation* brochure, which includes listings of the area's frequent powwows.

Wall

If you don't know about Wall before you arrive in South Dakota, you soon will. Billboards for its famous 'drugstore' infest the state. The block-long **Wall Drug** (☎ 605-279-2275; 510 Main St; 6am-10pm, 6:30am-6pm in winter) is pretty much what it advertises: 5¢ coffee, 1970s Wild West toys, Black Hills gold, moccasins, fudge, leather, books on Wall Drug, 'Wall Drug' bumper stickers, singing cowboy machines and big gorillas. Go crazy.

Welsh's Motel (☎ 605-279-2271; 312 South Blvd; r from $60;) is one of several decent motels in town.

Badlands National Park

The desolate lunar landscape of this region was referred to as *mako sica* ('badland') by Native Americans. The views from the corrugated 'walls' surrounding the Badlands are spectacular – colorful eroded spires, pinnacles and canyons stretch into the distance. The setting was perfect for a frightening battle scene in the sci-fi film *Starship Troopers*. Today the Badlands National Park protects a remnant of one of the world's greatest prairie grasslands, several species of Plains mammals and golden eagles. Plus there's rattlers.

The park's north unit is the most developed; the Hwy 240 loop road is easily reached from I-90 – seen in a couple of hours if you're in a hurry. The gravel Sage Creek Rim Rd goes west of the loop, above the Badlands Wilderness Area, which is open for backcountry hiking and camping. The less-accessible south units are in Pine Ridge Indian Reservation.

The **Ben Reifel visitors center** (☎ 605-433-5361; Cedar Pass; 9am-4pm) is open all year, but **White River visitors center** (☎ 605-455-2878; 10am-4pm), in the southern section, is open in summer. If you visit in winter, watch for snowdrifts. A seven-day pass costs $10 for cars and $5 for hikers and cyclists.

The **Badlands Circle 10 Campground** (☎ 605-433-5451; campsites $15, RV sites $15-23) is half a mile south of I-90 exit 131. Motels can be found on I-90 in Kadoka and Wall (see above), or in the park at the Oglala Sioux–operated **Cedar Pass Lodge** (☎ 605-433-5460; cabin $47-61), which is open April to October. Drop by its **Buffalo Dining Room** for Indian tacos.

BLACK HILLS

This 8000-sq-mile mountainous region on the Wyoming–South Dakota border boasts 7000ft 'hills' (the ironic highlight of the Plains states). The region's name – the 'Black' comes from the dark Ponderosa pine-covered slopes – was conferred by the Lakota Sioux, to whom the hills were a sacred, spiritual and ancestral home. In the 1868 Fort Laramie Treaty, they were assured that the hills would be theirs for eternity, but the discovery of gold changed that, and the Sioux were pushed north, and later into reservations. Today, the Sioux continue their struggle to reclaim the lands.

You'll need several days (at least) to explore the area, which covers more ground than Rocky Mountain, Grand Canyon or Yosemite National Parks. Throughout are incredible back-road drives, rock climbing, mines, caves, Custer State Park, Mt Rushmore and Crazy Horse monuments, the Black Hills National Forest, myriad activities (ballooning, cycling, boating, hiking, skiing and panning for gold) and heaps of kitsch sandwiched in between.

About half the 4½ million annual visitors choose one place as a base; others split their stay between the North Hills (Spearfish, Deadwood, Sturgis) and the more visited South Hills (Custer, Keystone, Hot Springs). At the cusp of the hills stand the 'gateway' towns on I-90 (Rapid City, Sturgis, Spearfish). Between Memorial Day and Labor Day, room rates skyrocket – sometimes even 300% above off-season rates – and reservations are essential.

Each of the main attractions and towns has an information office or visitors center. The best is Rapid City's **Black Hills Visitors Center** (☎ 605-355-3700; 1851 Discovery Circle; 8am-8pm summer). **Black Hills Central Reservations** (☎ 800-529-0105; 68 Sherman St, Deadwood) will find last-minute motel and cabin vacancies around the Black Hills.

I-90 skirts the north of the Black Hills, and three major access roads head into the hills: US 14A, which loops from Spearfish to Sturgis via Deadwood; the US 385 Black Hills Parkway (initially US 85), which runs north–south the length of the hills; and US 16 (and US 16A), running east–west from Rapid City to the Jewel Cave National Monument via Mt Rushmore. **Gray Line** (☎ 605-342-4461; adult/child 12 & under $38/19), in

Rapid City, offers a nine-hour, greatest-hits bus tour.

Just south of Wall is the **Buffalo Gap National Grassland**, an area of prairie and badlands. The **National Grassland visitors center** (☎ 605-279-2125; 708 Main St; 🕑 8am-6pm summer) interprets the history, flora and fauna of the region.

Black Hills National Forest

The majority of the Black Hills' attractions lie within this 1875-sq-mile mixture of protected and logged forest, perforated by pockets of private land along most roads. The forest stretches from Spearfish in the north to Angostura State Recreation Area in the south.

The best way to explore is on any of the 353 miles of hiking trails or along the many scenic byways and gravel 'fire roads.' The Peter Norbeck Byway is a 70-mile loop from Keystone via the Needles Hwy, Iron Mountain Rd (with tunnels offering perfectly framed glimpses of Mt Rushmore) and Custer State Park. Spearfish Canyon Scenic Byway (US 14A) follows Spearfish Creek. Black Hills Parkway runs north–south from I-90 to Hot Springs via Deadwood and Custer.

Many side roads are mapped poorly in the free and otherwise helpful *Black Hills National Forest Recreation Guide*; if you're planning to explore the area, pick up the widely available *Black Hills National Forest* map ($6).

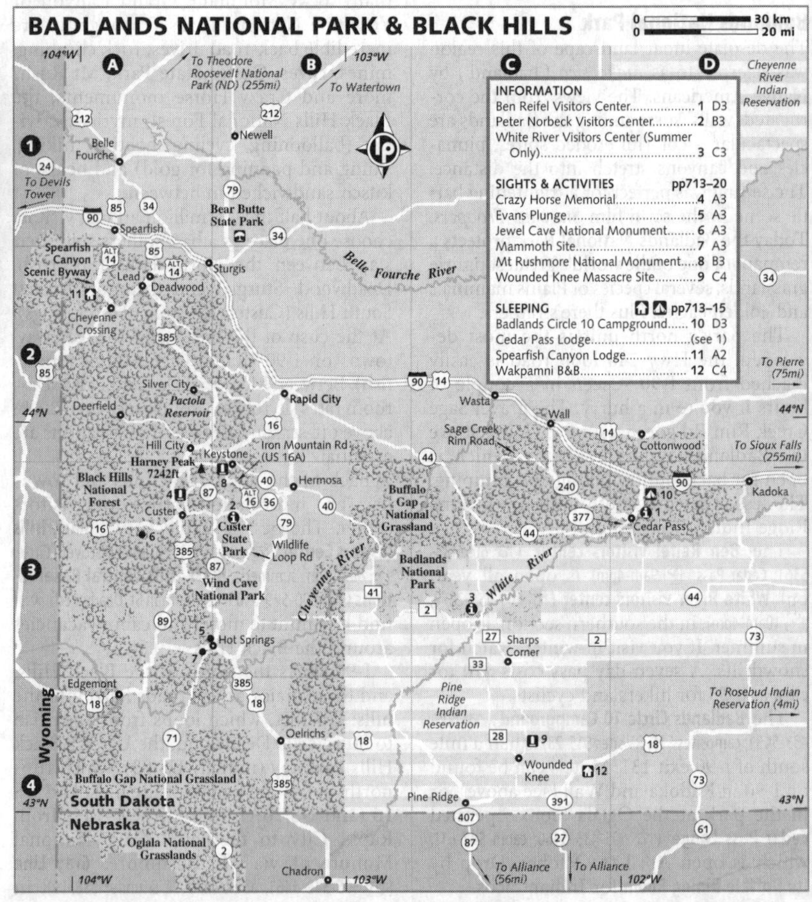

For cycling, the 114-mile George S Mickelson Trail cuts through much of the forest, running from Lead through Hill City and Custer to Edgemont. Deadwood's Penny Motel (see Deadwood & Lead, p718) runs a shuttle to pick up or drop off bikers at various points on the trail.

There are six ranger stations around the forest and a **visitors center** (near US 385 & Hwy 44; May 15–Oct 1) at Pactola Reservoir. The **Black Hills National Forest office** (☎ 605-673-9200; 7:30am-5pm Mon-Fri, 8am-4:30pm Sat & Sun) is in Custer.

Good camping abounds in the forest. There are 30 basic **campgrounds** (☎ 877-444-6777; $9-18), and backcountry camping is allowed anywhere (free; no open fires). Reservations are recommended for the campgrounds for summer weekends.

Rapid City

This is where the plains and the Black Hills meet. Rapid City ('Rapid') is the main gateway town to the hills, and it has accommodations, restaurants, tour services and a junk pile of kitschy attractions. The **visitors center** (☎ 605-343-1744; 444 Mt Rushmore Rd) has city information.

If it's raining, visit the **Journey Museum** (☎ 605-394-6923; 222 New York St; adult/child $6/4; 9am-5pm) for a trip through 2½ billion years of the history of the Black Hills, focusing on the Lakota Sioux.

Many chain motels linger at interstate exits, and older motels line Hwy 79 (St Joseph St), east of downtown. **Lamplighter Inn** (☎ 605-342-3385; www.lamplighterinn.net; 27 St Joseph St; s/d $59/69;) has simple but spacious lodgings. South of Rapid, on US 16, the hilltop **Big Sky Motel** (☎ 605-348-3200; 4080 Tower Rd; s/d $48/64) has clean and quiet rooms.

The **Rapid City Regional Airport** (☎ 605-393-9924; Hwy 44) is southeast of town. The **Airport Express Shuttle** (☎ 605-399-9999, 800-357-9998) charges $12 to downtown and $60 to Deadwood or Custer. Greyhound buses don't serve the Black Hills; **Jefferson Lines** (☎ 605-348-3300, 800-451-5333; 333 6th St) connects Rapid with Denver ($84) and Sioux Falls ($93). The orange **Rapid Taxi** (☎ 605-348-8080) cabs charge $1.60 per mile.

Sturgis

Poky little Sturgis is known the world over as the annual gathering ground of up to 500,000 'hog' (Harley-Davidson motorcycle) lovers, at the **Sturgis Rally & Races** (☎ 605-347-9190; www.sturgismotorcyclerally.com) in early August. During the rally, temporary campsites are set up around town, and motels boost rates to hundreds of dollars a night. Check the rally website for vacancies.

The **chamber of commerce** (☎ 605-347-2556; 2040 Junction Ave) has town information.

At the new **Sturgis Motorcycle Museum & Hall of Fame** (☎ 605-347-2001; 1344 Main St; adult/child $3/free; 8am-4pm Mon-Fri, 9am-4pm Sat & Sun) fans who missed the rally can ogle at 38 Harleys. Pick up a rally T-shirt for your hog-lovin' chums back home.

Standing stoically apart from the Black Hills, the namesake mountain of **Bear Butte State Park** (☎ 605-347-5240), 12 miles north of Sturgis on Hwy 79, juts 1400ft above the plains. Once the stronghold of Crazy Horse, it remains of great spiritual significance to the Plains Indians, evident in hundreds of prayer cloths strung along the 1.7-mile drive to the summit (person/car $3/5). Bear Butte is the northern end of the **Centennial Trail**, a 111-mile riding/hiking trail to Wind Cave National Park (p720). There are basic **campsites** ($6).

Unless you're a 'rider,' you'll likely not linger long in Sturgis but there are a few chain motels around I-90 exit 32 and cheaper places along Junction Ave. **Super 8 Motel** (☎ 605-347-4447; I-90 exit 30; s/d $71/80;) is a safe choice.

One-Eyed Jack's Saloon (1304 Main St) is a biker bar with burgers and a happy hour (4pm to 7pm) most nights.

Spearfish

Another base on I-90 is Spearfish, near Wyoming and at the mouth of scenic **Spearfish Canyon Scenic Byway** (US 14A). The **chamber of commerce** (☎ 605-642-2626; 106 W Kansas) has regional information, and its foyer – stocked with all sorts of brochures – is open 24/7. The outdoor **Black Hills Passion Play** (☎ 605-642-2646; $14-20) is staged three times a week in summer. In winter, many skiers come to hit nearby downhill slopes and cross-country trails.

There are motels around I-90 exit 14, including **Howard Johnson Express Inn** (☎ 605-642-8105; 323 S 27th St; r/ste from $80/110;), with continental breakfast and heated pool. The **Spearfish Canyon Lodge** (☎ 605-584-3435; 10619 Roughlock Falls Rd; r from $109;),

13 miles south of Spearfish, sits triumphantly in its namesake, near trails, streams and a *Dances with Wolves* film site. There are four nearby campgrounds. **Spearfish KOA** (☎ 605-642-4633; campsites $21, RV sites $28-37, Kabins $40) is southwest of I-90 exit 10.

Deadwood & Lead

Settled illegally by anxious gold rushers in the 1870s, Deadwood is now a proud (and respectable) National Historic Landmark. Its Main St is lined with many fine, restored (if a bit contrived) gold-rush-era buildings. The town's hell-raisin' days are long gone, replaced by a gentler crowd of poker players taking advantage of legalized limited-stakes gambling, which jump-started the town's tourist appeal in the 1990s.

Deadwood plays up its pioneer days, and some famous names crop up repeatedly: Wild Bill Hickok, shot in the back here in 1876; Jack McCall, the drifter who shot Hickok; Calamity Jane (also known as Martha Canary); gunslingers Doc Holliday and Wyatt Earp; the prospector Potato Creek Johnny; and brothel owner Poker Alice Tubbs. Hickok and Jane now rest side by side, up in Boot Hill at **Mt Moriah Cemetery** (admission $1; ⌚ sunrise-sunset).

The Deadwood **visitors center** (☎ 605-578-1876, 800-999-1876; 735 Main St) has brochures, as does the more helpful **History & Information Center** (☎ 605-578-2507; Pine St & USA 85/14A; ⌚ 8am-7pm), a block west of Main St.

In nearby Lead (pronounced *leed*), peek at the 944ft-deep open cut of the **Homestake gold mine** (☎ 605-584-3110; 160 W Main St; admission /van tour free/$5.25) to see what mining will do to a mountain.

Budget motels in Deadwood, all on Main St, include the clean **HI Penny Motel** (☎ 605-578-1842, 877-565-8140; 818 Upper Main St; dm $13-16, s $49-59). It also rents bikes ($16 to $24 per day) and offers a shuttle service for the Mickelson Trail (see Black Hills National Forest, p716). In downtown, you can't beat the **Historic Franklin Hotel** (☎ 605-578-2241; 700 Main St; r from $95). Many rooms are named for celebrities who've stayed in them, though the frenzy of slots in the lobby takes away from the step back in time.

There are six campgrounds near Deadwood. **Deadwood KOA** (☎ 605-578-3830, campsites $20, Kabins $40) is a mile west of town on US 14A. The bald 'mountain' across US 14A was made from dug-up rock from the Homestake mine. **Wild Bill's Campground** (☎ 605-578-2800; US 385; campsites/RV sites $13/19, cabins $58) is 5.5 miles south.

Nearly all gambling houses have a menu of sorts – mostly greasy buffets. If you prefer eating without slot machines at your elbow, your best bet is the **Deadwood Social Club** (657 Main St), above Saloon No 10, where Hickok got rubbed out.

Mt Rushmore National Monument

The 60ft faces of George Washington, Thomas Jefferson, Abraham Lincoln and Theodore Roosevelt – carved in the granite of a Black Hills outcrop – are one of the most famous images in the USA (the monument gets three million visitors each year). You can't help but be overwhelmed by its sheer scale and the massive physical effort of the team (led by sculptor Gutzon Borglum) that created it. If Washington were depicted from head to toe, he would be 465ft high. The site was dedicated in 1927, and 14 years of work commenced – Washington emerged in 1930, Jefferson in 1936, Lincoln in 1937 and Roosevelt in 1939. Borglum died in March 1941, and his son Lincoln supervised the completion in October 1941.

The monument is 3 miles south of Keystone (see below) via US 16A, and 25 miles southwest of Rapid City (p717) via US 16. The **visitors center** (☎ 605-574-2523; ⌚ 8am-10pm summer, 8am-5pm rest of the year) plays a good film. You pass through an avenue of all 50 state flags before reaching the Grand View Terrace. The **Presidential Trail** (admission free) loop leads near the monument – and offers some fine nostril views. There's a 9pm **light show** in summer. You can park near the center ($8 annual permit) or at a free lot just 400yd away.

Keystone

The nearest lodging and restaurants to Mt Rushmore are in Keystone, a one-time mining town now solely devoted to the monument. You can learn more about Mt Rushmore's enigmatic creator by visiting the touristy **Rushmore-Borglum Story** (☎ 605-666-4448; US 16A; admission $7; ⌚ 8am-7pm Mon-Sat, 9am-7pm Sun summer, call for hours rest of the year).

There are several chain motels in town, but better stays are just north on US 16A: the bush-clad **Powder House** (☎ 605-666-4646;

24125 Hwy 16A; cabins $65-160) and the **Holy Smoke Resort** (☎ 605-666-4616, 866-530-5696; cabins $50-135;), with lovely, rustic log cabins featuring modern amenities such as satellite TV and full bath. Reserve early. If you must sleep under the gaze of stone men, **Mt Rushmore's Presidents View Resort** (☎ 605-666-4212; 290 Speck Rd; s/d $50/129;), in town, has exactly one room with a view, the $160 Jacuzzi suite. It also has several wheelchair-accessible rooms.

Crazy Horse Memorial

The world's largest monument, 4 miles north of Custer, **Crazy Horse Memorial** (person/car $8/19) is, as author Ian Frazier describes, 'a ruin, only in reverse.' Onlookers at the 563ft work-in-progress can gawk at what will be – the Sioux leader astride his horse, pointing to the horizon saying, 'My lands are where my dead lie buried'.

Never photographed, defeated in battle or his signature found on the dotted line of a meaningless treaty, the great Crazy Horse was the obvious choice for a 'monument for all Native Americans.' Lakota Sioux elders hoped a monument would balance the presidential focus of Mt Rushmore, and in 1948 they asked Boston-born sculptor Korczak Ziolkowski to build it. He blasted at the mountain until his death in 1982. Often mountain goats were his only companions.

Crazy Horse's head and torso and his horse's front section were finished at the time of research. No one can guess when it will be complete. Depending on weather, you can see (and hear) blasts on most days.

The huge **visitors center** (☎ 605-673-4681; 8am-9pm) charts the progress, exhibits scale models and has a viewing deck. During the Volksmarch, held the first weekend of June, there are trips up to the mountain, which is lit nightly. Adjacent to the center is the impressive **Indian Museum & Cultural Center** and Ziolkowski's studio. Blasted-off pieces of the monument are available as free (but heavy) souvenirs.

Offers of federal funding have been refused. Ziolkowski felt the 'American people' – not the government – should finance such a work. Do go.

You can stay in a tepee at the **Heritage Village** (☎ 605-673-4761; tepee/tent $22/14), 1 mile south.

Custer

Named for the enigmatic general who found gold in the hills in 1874 (and death from the Sioux in 1876), Custer isn't too much to look at, but it has a great location near Custer State Park. The **chamber of commerce** (☎ 605-673-2244; 615 Washington St; 9am-6pm Mon-Sat, 9am-2pm Sun) can dole out more information.

Chief Motel (☎ 605-673-2318; 120 Mt Rushmore Rd; s/d $65/87;) has a hot tub and cable TV. Comfier are the yellow-and-red 1930s cottages at **Shady Rest Motel** (☎ 605-673-4478, 800-567-8259; 238 Gordon St; cabin $55-165;), two blocks south of Mt Rushmore Rd, and across the street from where the kids can pan for gold.

There are 17 campgrounds in the region. The popular **Flintstones Bedrock City** (☎ 605-673-4664; US 385; campsites $18, RV sites $21-23), 1 mile south of town, is rather treeless, but there's a wealth of activities for the kids.

Custer State Park

This superb 114-sq-mile park is one of the state's highlights. The only reason it isn't a national park is the state grabbed it first. It boasts one of the largest free-roaming buffalo herds in the world (about 1500), the famous 'begging burros' (donkeys seeking handouts) and more than 200 species of bird. Elk, whitetail and mule deer, pronghorns, mountain goats, bighorn sheep, coyotes, mountain lions and bobcats may also be seen along the 18-mile **Wildlife Loop Rd**, **Iron Mountain Rd** and the incredible, 14-mile **Needles Hwy**.

Every year in October there is a roundup of the park's buffalo, and 500 are sold at the November auction (get one for $500 to $1000).

The **Peter Norbeck Visitors Center** (☎ 605-255-4464; US 16A; person/car $5/10 summer, $2/5 rest of the year; 8am-8pm summer, call for hours rest of the year), 15 miles east of Custer in the center of the park, has exhibits and offers activities.

Hiking through the prairie grassland and pine-covered hills gives you a great opportunity to observe wildlife. Trails such as Sylvan Lake Shore, Cathedral Spires, French Creek Natural Area and Centennial allow visitors to explore a variety of habitats. A popular hike is up the state's tallest mountain, Harney Peak; the trailhead is at Sylvan Lake. Swimming, fishing and boating on the park's lakes – as well as climbing on its jagged rock spires – are also very popular.

You can pitch a tent in eight developed **campgrounds** (☎ 800-710-2267; $15) around the park. Reservations are recommended in summer.

The park has four impressive **resorts** (☎ 800-658-3530; www.custerresorts.com), each with cabins and campsites: the State Game Lodge, Sylvan Lake, the Blue Bell and the Legion Lodge. Summer rates for a lodge room or cabin start at $80. Book well ahead.

Wind Cave National Park

This park filled with grassland and forest, just south of Custer State Park, covers nearly 47 sq miles. The **visitors center** (☎ 605-745-4600; 8am-7pm summer, 8am-5pm rest of the year) has displays and conducts interpretive walks.

The central (but hidden) feature is, of course, the cave, which is 98 miles long and growing (new tunnels are frequently discovered). The cave's foremost feature is its 'boxwork' formations – calcite 'fins' which look like honeycomb and date back 60 to 100 million years. The strong gusts – felt at the entrance, not inside –give the cave its name (these are caused by changes in atmospheric pressure, not a snoring cave demon). The five tours range from one to four hours (from $6 to the $20 down-and-dirty spelunking tour). Children are half-price, but there are age restrictions on some of the tours. Call ahead to check.

Hiking is a popular activity in the park, where you will find the southern end of the 111-mile **Centennial Trail**. There's first come, first served primitive **camping** ($12) in summer.

Jewel Cave National Monument

The best of the Black Hills' many caves is 125-mile-long Jewel Cave, 13 miles west of Custer on US 16. It's known for the nailhead calcite crystals that line its walls. Tours range in length and difficulty, from $4 to $20. Arrange your tour at the **visitors center** (☎ 605-673-2288; 8am-7:30pm summer, 8am-5pm rest of the year).

Hot Springs

This attractive town, south of the main Black Hills circuit, boasts beautiful 1890s sandstone buildings and warm mineral springs. The **visitors center** (☎ 605-745-6974; North River St; 9am-7pm Mon-Fri, 9am-6pm Sat, noon-4pm Sun May-Sep) is in the old train depot.

The water at **Evans Plunge** (☎ 605-745-5165, 1145 N River St; adult/child $8/6; 5:30am-9pm Mon-Fri, 8am-9pm Sat & Sun summer, 5:30am-8pm Mon-Fri, 10am-8pm Sat & Sun rest of the year), a giant indoor geothermal springs pool, is 87°F all year. Locals like to wade in **Fall River Park**, off S River St, or swim at **Cascade Falls** (warm all year), 10 miles south on US 71.

The remarkable **Mammoth Site** (☎ 605-745-6017; 1800 US 18; adult/child $7/5; 8am-8pm May 15–Aug 15, call for hours rest of the year) is the country's only left-as-found mammoth fossil display. Hundreds of animals perished in a sinkhole here over several centuries about 27,000 years ago. Most of the 52 mammoths found so far are adolescents (and all are male!); in July you can cheer on paleontologists digging for more bones.

The fun, hilltop **Historic Log Cabin Motel** (☎ 605-745-5166; US 385; cabins $48-98), north of town, has a petting zoo, hot tub, basketball court and bikes.

NORTH DAKOTA

Travelers crossing the USA's least-visited state on I-94, US 2 or Amtrak's *Empire Builder* should be ready for 300 miles of uninterrupted rolling plains. Theodore Roosevelt National Park is North Dakota's highlight, with an amazing amount of wildlife.

Though linked by name with South Dakota, North Dakota tends to be more chummy with its eastern neighbor, Minnesota, which locals like to point out is colder. So concerned are some North Dakotans over perception of their state as a frozen, lifeless land that, in 1947 and 1989, legislation nearly passed to drop the 'North' in the state name. The drama resurfaced in 2001, as the name-change proposal was once again put forth. (Governor Ed Schafer said it would be 'fun' to change the name.)

HISTORY

During their epic trip, Lewis and Clark spent more time in present-day North Dakota than any other state, meeting up with Shoshone guide Sacagawea on their way west. In the mid-19th century, smallpox epidemics came up the Missouri River, decimating the Arikara, Mandan and Hidatsa tribes, who affiliated and established the Like-a-Fishhook Village in

GREAT PLAINS

NORTH DAKOTA FACTS

Nicknames Peace Garden State, Roughrider State, Flickertail State
Population 634,100 (48th)
Area 70,705 sq miles (19th)
Admitted to Union November 2, 1889 (39th)
Capital city Bismarck (population 56,200)
Other cities Fargo (91,200), Grand Forks (48,500)
Birthplace of singer Peggy Lee, actress Angie Dickinson, homerun hero Roger Maris, cream of wheat
Famous for 2063ft TV tower in Blanchard, world's largest buffalo and Holstein statues, Teddy Roosevelt's retreat, Mandan villages

the mid-19th century. The Like-a-Fishhook Village was fated to be the last earth lodge settlement in the Northern Plains. The site now lies underwater, thanks to the Garrison Dam and Reservoir project.

When the railroad arrived in North Dakota in the 1870s, thousands of settlers flocked in to take up allotments under the Homestead Acts. As farmers adopted new machines and techniques, the state's grain farms became so productive they were called 'Bonanza Farms.' By 1889 the state population was more than 250,000, half foreign-born (one in eight were from Norway).

North Dakota has been good to its people. The young Theodore Roosevelt came here to hoop, holler and work the 'dogies,' and later became the president who created the first national parks. In the early 20th century, farmers were being exploited by monopolized grain-elevator companies, so North Dakota set up state-owned banks and a state-run grain elevator that paid fair prices.

Mining of coal, oil, natural gas and uranium has increased in recent years. Many family farms have been taken over by big agricultural companies, but the state population continues to grow slightly.

INFORMATION

The helpful state **Tourism Department** (☎ 701-328-2525, 800-435-5663; www.ndtourism.com) has information. **North Dakota Parks and Recreation** (☎ 701-328-5357) is in Bismarck. Visitors to state parks will need to purchase a $4 daily vehicle permit. For information on park campsites or to make reservations, call ☎ 800-807-4723.

For highway conditions, especially in the harsh winters, call ☎ 701-328-7623.

ALONG I-94

The quickest route across North Dakota, I-94 also provides easy access to most of the state's top attractions.

Fargo

North Dakota's biggest city sits along the north-running Red River, across from Moorhead, Minnesota. Fargo has been a fur-trading post, a frontier town, a quick-divorce capital and a frequent destination for folks in the Federal Witness Protection Program. But Fargo is best known from the wacky characters in the film *Fargo*, still a source of debate in town (though it was filmed in Minnesota).

Housed in a humongous grain elevator, the Fargo-Moorhead **visitors center** (☎ 701-282-3653, 800-235-7654; 2001 44th St; 🕑 7:30am-7pm Mon-Fri, 9am-6pm Sat, 10am-5pm Sun in summer, call for hours rest of the year), off I-94 exit 348, showers visitors with free popcorn, coffee and brochures.

The **Walk of Fame** outside the visitors center includes George W Bush and Def Leppard. In the historic downtown, the 1926 art deco **Fargo Theatre** (☎ 701-235-4152; 314 Broadway) has an old Wurlitzer organ and screens independent films. Across the river in Moorhead, the **Heritage Hjemkomst Interpretive Center** (☎ 218-299-5511; 202 1st Ave; adult/child $6/4; 🕑 9am-5pm Mon-Sat, noon-5pm Sun) tells the gripping story of how a high school guidance counselor named Robert Asp single-handedly built a 76ft replica of a 9th-century Viking ship in Hawley, MN, and how his family, after his death, sailed it to Norway in 1982.

C'mon Inn (☎ 701-277-9944; 4338 20th Ave; r $59), near the visitors center, beckons guests with nice rooms, an indoor pool and a Jacuzzi. **Motel 6** (☎ 701-232-9251; 1202 36th St; s/d $40/46) is just north of I-29 13th St exit. You can camp right in town on the riverfront **Linwood Park Campground** (☎ 701-232-3987; 17th Ave & 5th St; campsites/RV sites $8/15), near I-94 exit 351.

Downtown, the **Dakota Soda** (☎ 701-239-4729; 420 Broadway; $3-7), located in the Zandbrõz Variety shop, has nice pasta salads, soups and sandwiches. You'll want a malt with that. Students and musicians hang out at **Trentino** (☎ 701-293-3115; 315 Broadway), a café with snacks.

GETTING THERE & AROUND

There are stations for **Greyhound** (☎ 701-293-1222; 402 Northern Pacific Ave) and **Amtrak** (☎ 701-232-2197; 420 4th St N). For a cab, call **Doyle's** (☎ 701-235-5535).

Bismarck & Mandan

Most of Bismarck, North Dakota's capital, is a victim to commercial sprawl, but a handful of sights (plus great side trips) make it a nice stopover. There are pleasant beaches and trails along the Missouri River. Mandan, named after the area's original riverside dwellers, is a somewhat run-down railway town across the river.

The Bismarck-Mandan **visitors center** (☎ 701-222-4308, 800-767-3555; 1600 Burnt Boat Dr, Bismarck) has brochures.

The impressive 1930s art deco **State Capitol** (☎ 701-328-2480; N 7th St, Bismarck) is often referred to as the 'skyscraper of the prairie' and looks something like a Stalinist school of dentistry. There's an observatory deck on the 18th floor. Behind the Sacagawea statue, the huge **North Dakota Heritage Center** (☎ 701-328-2666; Capitol Hill; admission free; 8am-5pm most days) offers comprehensive displays of the state's history. By all means listen to the recording of the State March. The **Bank of North Dakota** (BND; ☎ 701-328-5700; 9th & Main Sts) is the country's only state-owned bank; ask for a tour.

Some 7 miles south of Mandan on SR 1806, **Fort Abraham Lincoln State Park** (☎ 701-663-9571) is well worth the detour. Its **On-A-Slant Indian Village** has three re-created Mandan earthlodges. Nearby you can tour full-scale replicas of the fort's cavalry post. Up the hill, the **infantry blockhouses** (admission $5, vehicle permit $5) have top-notch views. The park has **campsites** (campsites/RV sites/cabins $7/12/30).

In Bismarck, there is a congregation of motels around I-94 exit 159 and State St. **Select Inn** (☎ 701-223-8060; 505 Interchange Ave; s/d $40/54; P) has free breakfast. Bismarck's action – amid malls and megastores – is centered on Bismarck Expressway Ave and S Washington St. Here you'll find **Expressway Inn** (☎ 701-222-2900; 200 Bismarck Expressway Ave; r from $50;), which provides transport to the airport and is also close to several chain restaurants. If you can't face another steak, try the **Rice Bowl** (☎ 701-663-1986; 609 W Main St, Mandan; mains $6-12).

AROUND BISMARCK

North of Bismarck are several worthwhile attractions near the spot where Lewis and Clark wintered with the Mandan in 1804–05. The best is the **North Dakota Lewis & Clark Interpretive Center** (☎ 701-462-8535; adult/child $5/3; 9am-7pm summer, 9am-5pm rest of the year) in Washburn, where you can learn about the duo's epic expedition and the Native Americans who helped them. There's an interesting new exhibit on Fort Clark, a trading post established nearby in 1830. **Fort Mandan** (CR 17), a replica of the 30-acre fort built by Lewis and Clark, is 2.5 miles west (10 miles downstream from the flooded original site). Just north of Stanton, the **Knife River Indian Villages** (☎ 701-745-3309; CR 37; admission free; 7:30am-6pm summer, 8am-4:30pm rest of the year) feature the sites of three Hidatsa and Mandan villages that were occupied for 900 years. Sacagawea joined Lewis and Clark from here. The visitors center runs a great video.

West of Bismarck on I-94, stop and see **Sue, the World's Largest Holstein Cow** (New Salem). The view (not the udders) is the highlight. In Dickinson, 65 miles west of Sue, the **Dakota Dinosaur Museum** (☎ 701-225-3466; adult/child $6/3; 9am-6pm Mon-Sat, 11am-4pm Sun summer, call for hours rest of the year) has 10 dinosaur reconstructions and a risky evolutionary skulls display. Ask to speak with the friendly fossil finder, who is usually around.

South of Bismarck, scenic SR 24/1806 goes through Standing Rock Indian Reservation. The **burial site of Sitting Bull** is at Fort Yates, not far from Lake Oahe.

Theodore Roosevelt National Park

Undoubtedly North Dakota's highlight, the superb **Theodore Roosevelt National Park** (person/car $5/10) near the state's western border has two very different units. The South Unit, near I-94 at Medora, has rolling badlands and a 36-mile scenic loop. The remote North Unit, 68 miles north on US 85, offers a 14-mile drive – as well as fewer visitors. An extensive area around the units is protected as the Little Missouri National Grassland.

Wildlife is everywhere – around 200 species of bird, mule and whitetail deer, wild horses, bighorn sheep, elk and herds of bison. And there's no missing the squeaking prairie dogs watching out from their sprawling subterranean 'towns.'

There are opportunities for hiking on 85 miles of backcountry trails (a permit is required) as well as many horseback-riding trails. You can hike, ride or cycle the 110-mile **Maah Daah Hey Trail** (☎ 701-225-5151) between the park units.

The park has three visitors centers, including the Medora **visitors center** (☎ 701-623-4466; 8am-8pm in summer, call for hours rest of the year), with Theodore Roosevelt's old cabin out back. Theodore credited his rise to presidency to his experiences in North Dakota. He described this area as 'a land of vast, silent spaces, of lonely rivers, and of plains, where the wild game stared at the passing horsemen,' which still rings pretty true today.

The park has two developed **campgrounds** ($10). Free backcountry camping is allowed throughout the park. There are some accommodations and restaurants in Medora (see below), Belfield and Dickinson.

Medora

This partially restored frontier town cashes in on its proximity to one of the country's best parks. The **Medora Musical** (☎ 800-633-6721; adult/child $23/14), a downright unabashed Teddy dedication, is staged in the Burning Hills Badlands Amphitheater from mid-June to Labor Day.

Badlands Motel (☎ 701-623-4444, 800-633-6721; 501 Pacific Ave; r $89 in summer;), a rustic-lodge style motel, is only a block from downtown.

All eating places are privately run. **Cowboy Café** (☎ 701-623-4343; 4th St & 3rd Ave; 7am-2pm) has great breakfasts and a talkative cook. **Iron Horse Saloon** (☎ 701-623-9894; Pacific Ave & 3rd St; mains $8-15; 6:30am-1am in summer, opens at 10am rest of the year) serves good pan-fried pike with potatoes.

Greyhound buses stop in town.

ALONG US 2

Once the Great Northern Rd, US 2 offers more of a prairie feel than I-94. The route goes by many **missile silos** buried in the prairie, particularly between Grand Forks and Devils Lake and around Minot – watch for a parking garage or small field surrounded by a chain-link fence. These are not open to the public.

Grand Forks

An island of suburbia in a sea of prairie, Grand Forks is home to the University of North Dakota (UND) and an air force base. The town was hit hard by the Red River flood in 1997 but has recovered well. Get brochures at **Greater Grand Forks Visitors Center** (☎ 701-746-0444, 800-866-4566; 4251 Gateway Dr; 9am-6pm in summer, 9am-5pm rest of the year).

UND, near DeMers Ave east of I-29, is a civilizing influence on the town, and its **Museum of Art** (☎ 701-777-4195; Centennial Dr; admission free; 9am-5pm Mon-Fri, 1-5pm Sat & Sun) is worth seeing. Pick up a cool $1 flour bag from the state-owned **North Dakota State Mill** (Mill Rd), north of Gateway Dr.

Rooms at the **Budget Inn** (☎ 701-775-5341; 3400 Gateway Dr; r from $41), east of I-29 exit 141, have comfy beds and old-style phones.

Grand Forks is the birthplace of cream of wheat; get a $2 bowl of it at **2-29 Café** (☎ 701-772-1273; 4720 Gateway Dr), a friendly truck stop open all day. The natural grocery store co-op **Amazing Grains** (☎ 701-775-4542; 214 Demers Ave) has ready-made sandwiches, baked goods and organic produce.

Devils Lake

This nice town shares its name with the popular lake. There's a restored 19th-century downtown and inexpensive lodgings along the highway. The **visitors center** (☎ 701-662-4903, 800-233-8048) has information.

The lake was called Miniwakan ('Spirit Water') by the Sioux and later misinterpreted as 'Evil Spirits' by settlers. Today it's surrounded by campgrounds and a few state parks.

The Spirit Lake Sioux Indian Reservation includes **Fort Totten** (☎ 701-766-4441; admission $4; 8am-5pm May-Sep), south of town.

Minot

The main interests in Minot (rhymes with 'Thai Baht') are the big state fair in July and the October **Norsk Hostfest**, a Scandinavian shindig in which *lefse* (potato flatbread) predominates. The **visitors center** (☎ 701-857-8206; 1020 S Broadway) has information. The infrequent tours of the **Minot Air Force Base** (☎ 701-723-6212; US 83), 15 miles north of town, include a visit to a missile silo used to train military folk.

New Town

About 15 miles south of Stanley (on US 2), in the Fort Berthold Indian Reservation, New Town is worth a detour. Drive up Crow Flies High Butte, 4 miles west of town, for views of Lake Sakakawea. Across the bridge, the splendid **Three Tribes Museum** (☎ 701-627-4477; admission $3; 10am-6pm Apr-Aug) explains why the Mandan, Hidatsa and Arikara peoples affiliated in the 19th century. The reservation is host to several summer powwows.

West to Montana

Small prairie towns are spaced along US 2 west of Minot, some picturesquely decrepit, all dotted with empty buildings. West of Williston, **Fort Buford** (☎ 701-572-9034; SR 1804; admission free; 9am-6pm Mon-Fri) was the army outpost where Sitting Bull surrendered; note the causes of death marked on tombstones at the cemetery. A bit further is the **Fort Union Trading Post** (☎ 701-572-9083; 8am-8pm summer, 9am-5:30pm rest of the year), a reconstruction of the American Fur Company post built in 1828. Its colorful walls look like a clown palace from a distance.

Rocky Mountains

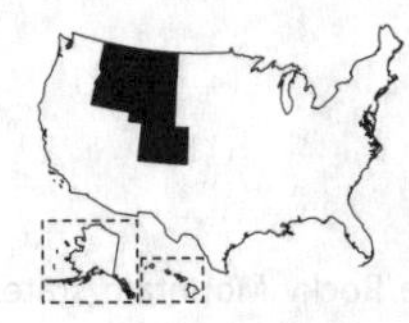

CONTENTS

Rocky Mountains

The Rocky Mountain states are home to some of the country's most stunning wilderness. What Paris is for art lovers and New York is for theatergoers, this region is for outdoor enthusiasts. Hiking, biking, climbing, fishing, rafting, kayaking and even llama-trekking – it's here for all levels, from beginner to brawny, under a limitless sky that humbles and astonishes.

Road trips were invented for places like this. The byways of Colorado, Wyoming, Montana and Idaho provide endless, riveting natural scenery. Routes ease you through alpine valleys, windswept prairies and undulating landscapes – and before long, you're winding your way past lofty peaks once considered impassable by humans.

National parks are the region's most popular draws, and Rocky Mountain in Colorado, Yellowstone in Wyoming and Glacier in Montana are all caretakers of true natural wonders. In less-trodden National Forests and other wilderness areas, as much beauty can be viewed in more solitude. Wildlife, though increasingly encroached upon by urban sprawl, may be spotted on your travels. Bisons and bald eagles, grizzlies and gray wolves, and even the ultraelusive river otter, roam the region.

Even with ever-more urban development, it's easy to see some of the old West born in this region – the one where Lewis and Clark became pioneers, Custer stood his last at Little Bighorn and many people of various backgrounds seized the reins on a new life. Frontier towns like Telluride, Leadville and Laramie – amid their pleasant shops and restaurants – still wear a hint of those difficult and boisterous bygone days.

HIGHLIGHTS

- Gallivanting in **Denver**, from rivers to roller coasters (p732)
- Hiking then partying in the progressive bubble of **Boulder** (p740)
- Lapping up lake vistas in **Rocky Mountain National Park** (p742)
- Speeding down slopes in ever-friendly **Crested Butte** (p755)
- Exploring ancient cliff dwellings at **Mesa Verde National Park** (p759)
- Viewing gushing geysers and wondrous wildlife in **Yellowstone National Park** (p765)
- Adventuring among the jagged granite spires of the **Grand Tetons** (p768)
- Living it up in lively **Missoula**, then meeting its raftable, hikeable, skiable outdoors (p775)
- Hiking to sublime glacial lakes at **Glacier National Park** (p780)
- Skiing on the celebrity slopes of **Sun Valley** (p785)

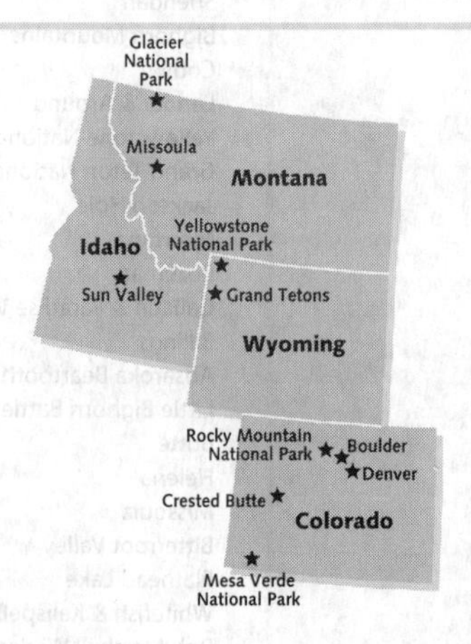

HISTORY

Before the late-18th century when French trappers and Spaniards stepped in, the Rocky Mountain area was a land of many tribes, including the Nez Percé, the Shoshone, the Crow, the Lakota and the Utes.

Meriwether Lewis and William Clark claimed their enduring fame after the USA bought almost all of present-day Montana, Wyoming and eastern Colorado in the Louisiana Purchase in 1803. The two explorers set out to survey the land, covering 8000 miles in three years. Their success urged on other adventurers, and soon the migration was in motion. Wagon trains voyaged to the mountainous lands into the 20th century, only temporarily slowed by the completion of the Transcontinental Railroad across southern Wyoming in the late 1860s.

To accommodate settlers, the USA purged the western frontier of the Spanish, British and, in a truly shameful era, most of the Native American population. The government signed endless treaties to defuse Native American objections to increasing settlement, but always reneged and shunted tribes onto smaller reservations. Gold miners' incursions into Native American territory in Montana and the building of US Army forts along the Bozeman Trail ignited a series of wars with the Lakota, Cheyenne, Arapaho and others.

Gold and silver mania preceded Colorado's entry to statehood in 1876. Statehood soon followed for Montana (1889), Wyoming (1890) and Idaho (1890). Along with miners, white farmers and ranchers were the people with power in the late 19th century.

Mining, grazing and timber played major roles in the area's economic development, sparking the growth of cities and towns to provide financial and industrial support. They also subjected the region to boom-and-bust cycles by unsustainable use of resources, and left a legacy of environmental disruption.

After the economy boomed post-WWII, the national parks started attracting vacationers. Tourism is now a leading industry in all four states.

GEOGRAPHY & CLIMATE

While complex, the physical geography of the region divides conveniently into two principal features: the Rocky Mountains proper and the Great Plains. Extending from Alaska's Brooks Range and Canada's Yukon Territory all the way to Mexico, the Rockies sprawl northwest to southeast, from the steep escarpment of Colorado's Front Range westward to Nevada's Great Basin. Their towering peaks and ridges form the Continental Divide: To the west, waters flow to the Pacific; to the east, toward the Atlantic and the Gulf of Mexico.

For many travelers, the Rockies are a summer destination, and it starts to feel summery around June. The warm weather lasts until about mid-September. The winter, which brings in packs of powder hounds, doesn't usually hit until late November, though snowstorms can start in the mountains as early as September. Winter usually lasts until March or early April. In the mountains, the weather is constantly changing (snow in summer is not uncommon), so always be prepared.

Summer (usually Memorial Day weekend, the last in May, to Labor Day, the first Monday in September) is the high season, which means crowds and increased lodging rates. At ski resorts, peak-season rates and conditions also apply in winter. Accommodation prices can increase by up to 30% during peak seasons, depending on where you are. The best off-season time is mid-September through October, as the weather usually stays warm and services aren't totally shut down yet. Fall, when the aspens flaunt their autumn gold, or spring, when wildflowers bloom, are wonderful times to visit.

INFORMATION

Tourism-information organizations, which provide free state-highway maps and statewide travel information, are as follows:

Colorado Travel & Tourism Authority (☎ 800-265-6723; www.colorado.com; PO Box 3524, Englewood, CO 80155)

Idaho Travel Council (☎ 208-334-2470, 800-635-7820; www.visitid.org; PO Box 83720, Boise, ID 83720)

Travel Montana (☎ 406-444-2654, 800-847-4868; www.visitmt.com; PO Box 200533, Helena, MT 59620)

Wyoming Travel & Tourism (☎ 307-777-7777, 800-225-5996; www.wyomingtourism.org; I-25 at College Dr, Cheyenne, WY 82002)

For details on road conditions:

Colorado (☎ 877-315-7623; www.state.wy.us)

Idaho (☎ 208-336-6600, within Idaho ☎ 888-432-7623)

ROCKY MOUNTAINS

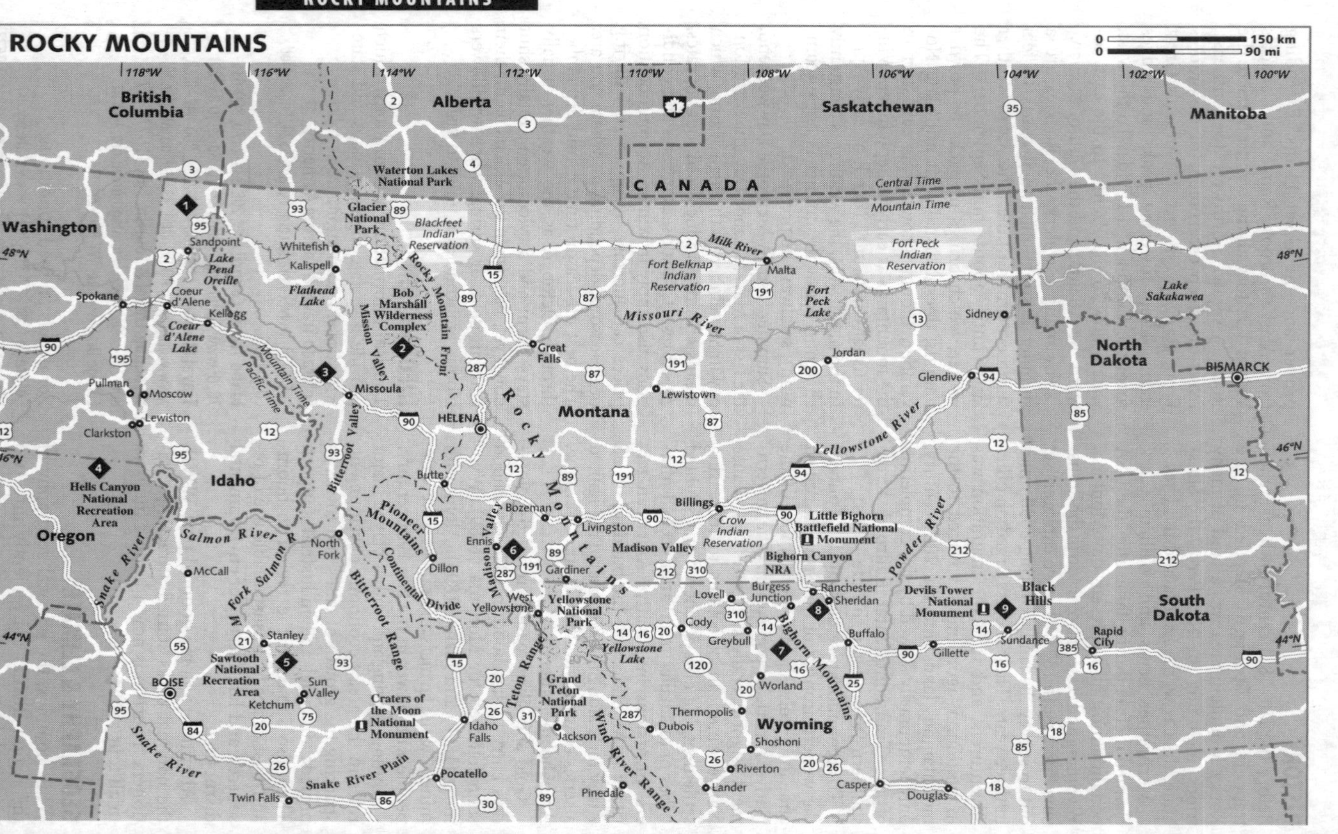

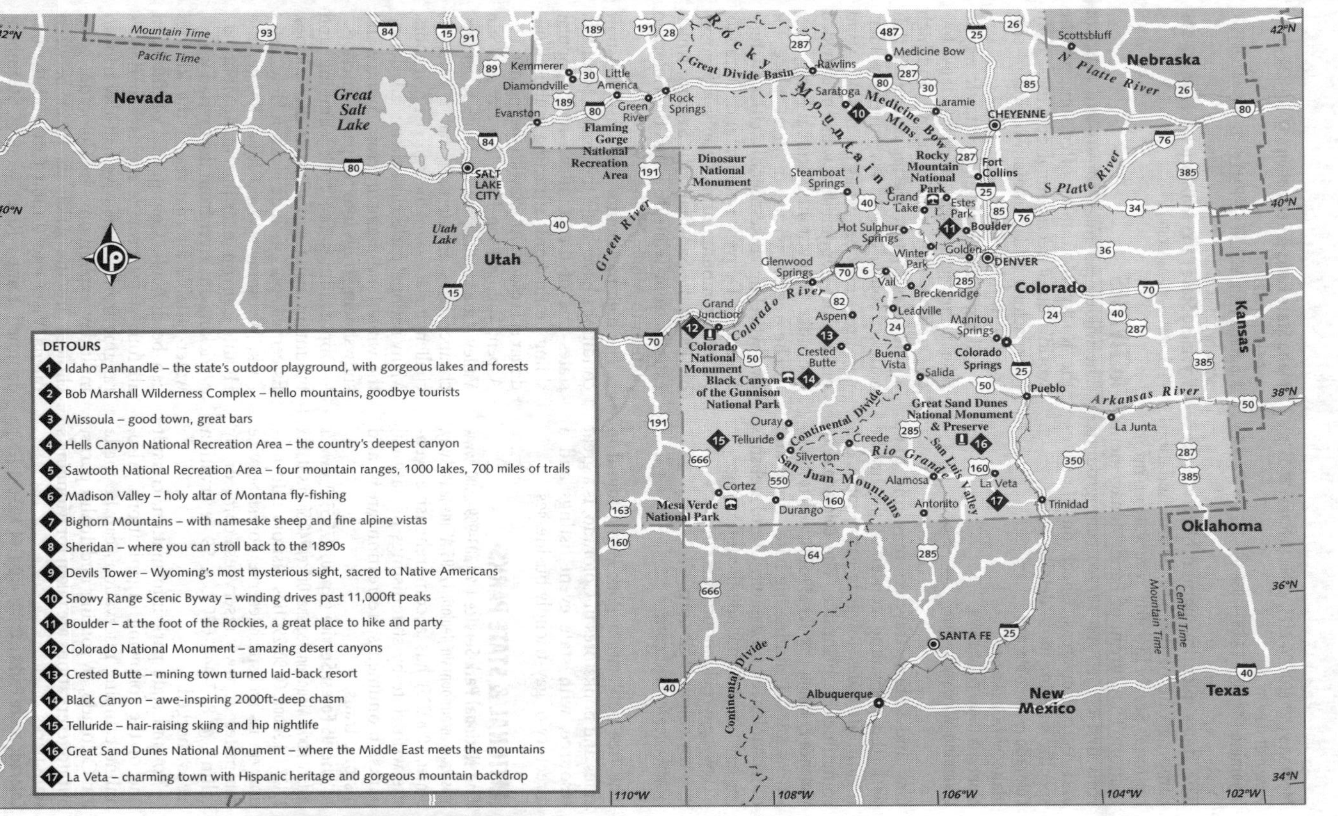

ROCKY MOUNTAINS

Montana (☎ 800-226-7623, within Montana ☎ 511; www.mdt.state.mt.us)
Wyoming (☎ 307-772-0824, 888-996-7623)

The states' plentiful natural beauty makes camping one of the best accommodation options. See below for reservation information. The Bureau of Land Management runs first-come, first-served campgrounds and recreation areas. Check out its state-specific sites for more details:
Colorado (www.co.blm.gov)
Idaho (www.id.blm.gov)
Montana (www.mt.blm.gov)
Wyoming (www.wy.blm.gov)

Gay and lesbian travelers may find that, with the prevailing conservatism in the region, attitudes towards gay people can sometimes be primitive. The **Colorado Anti-Violence Program** (☎ 303-839-5204; www.coavp.org) works toward eliminating hate crimes and other violence and assault. Useful websites for gay travelers include the following:

- www.gayrockymountains.com
- www.coloradoglbt.org
- www.cafevivid.com

The free publication *Pink Pages*, found in cafés and bookstores in Colorado, is a great resource, with state event listings and a directory of gay-friendly businesses.

NATIONAL & STATE PARKS

The **National Park Service** (☎ 303-969-2500; www.nps.gov; Intermountain Region, 12795 Alameda Parkway, Denver, CO 80225) has a comprehensive website with state-by-state listings of national parks, monuments, recreation areas and historic trails.

The **US Forest Service** (☎ 303-275-5350; www.fs.fed.us; Rocky Mountain Regional Office, 740 Simms St, Box 25127 Lakewood, CO 80225) has visitors information on its website. Reserve Forest Service campsites at www.reserveusa.com, or by calling ☎ 877-444-6777. A $9 reservation fee is charged.

To find state park information, consult one of the following organizations. Also, online camping reservations can be made for Colorado, Wyoming and Idaho parks, but no reservations are taken for Montana's state parks.
Colorado State Parks (☎ 303-470-1144, 800-678-2267; www.parks.state.co.us)
Idaho State Parks & Recreation (☎ 208-334-4199; www.idahoparks.org)
Montana Fish, Wildlife & Parks (☎ 406-444-2535; www.fwp.state.mt.us)
Wyoming State Parks & Historic Sites (☎ 877-996-7275; www.wyo-park.com)

ACTIVITIES

The wilderness areas, forests and parks of the Rocky Mountains offer some of the world's finest recreational activities, from backpacking and mountain biking to caving and windsurfing.

Hiking is an all-around fantastic way to take in the region's glacial peaks, dense forests, remote mountain meadows and high alpine lakes. Worth bearing in mind is that a trek through one of Wyoming's wilderness areas may be just as breathtaking and much more tranquil than walks in crowded spots like Yellowstone National Park.

The region is also a great place for two-wheeling. Bike-friendly cities include Missoula, Denver, Boulder and Durango. Multiday mountain-bike tours are possible using the San Juan Hut System, which extends from Telluride across the Colorado Plateau to Moab, Utah.

The high mountains and consistent snow conditions have made the Rocky Mountain states one of the country's most popular skiing destinations, attracting multimillion-dollar ski resorts. Along with the big names – Aspen, Vail, Jackson Hole, Big Sky and Sun Valley – are small operations with fewer lifts, cheaper rates and terrain that is often as challenging as that of their glitzier neighbors. Many national parks close their roads during the winter and maintain cross-country and snowshoeing trails into the parks' interiors.

Opportunities for rock climbing and mountaineering run high in the Rockies. Esteemed spots include Jackson Hole, Estes Park, Wyoming's Wind River Range, and Hyalite Canyon, near Bozeman, Montana.

Picking one river from the myriad whitewater-raftable alternatives in the Rockies can be difficult. Commercial outfitters in all four states provide rapids experiences ranging from inexpensive half-day trips to multiday expeditions. In Colorado, good choices are the Arkansas River between Buena Vista and Cañon City and the undammed Yampa River west of Steamboat Springs. Acclaimed Wyoming spots include

TOP FIVE SKI SPOTS

Aspen, CO A range of mountains for the glitzy and humble, pro and novice (p753).
Crested Butte, CO So little pretension, such gorgeous slopes (p755).
Jackson Hole, WY A vertical rise that will make your jaw drop (p770).
Telluride, CO Superb skiing and a happening, historic town (p757).
Vail, CO One of the world's favorites; offers reams of top terrain (p750).

the Snake River between Hoback Junction and Alpine, and the Shoshone River west of Cody. Near Gardiner, Montana, the Yellowstone River is the longest free-flowing river in the country. The stretch of the Clark Fork River through Alberton Gorge, west of Missoula, is considered western Montana's best white water. In Idaho, rivers include the Lower Salmon River, the Snake River, the Payette River and, in the Panhandle, St Joe National Wild & Scenic River. Many raft-laden rivers are just as remarkable for canoeing or more sedate float or tube trips.

GETTING THERE & AROUND

Denver International Airport (DIA) is the region's main hub. From here you can fly to the small airports dotting the area (see Denver p738). Salt Lake City (see p845) also has connections with destinations in all four states.

Greyhound (☎ 800-231-2222; www.greyhound.com) has fixed routes throughout the Rockies. **TNM&O** (☎ 719-635-1505; www.greyhound.com) is affiliated with Greyhound and serves the same lines through Colorado and parts of Wyoming. **Powder River Coach USA** (☎ 800-442-3682) primarily serves eastern Wyoming, but it also goes to Denver, Billings and Rapid City, South Dakota. **Rimrock Stages** (☎ 800-255-7655; www.rimrocktrailways.com) also serves Montana destinations.

Amtrak (☎ 800-872-7245; www.amtrak.com) services that run to and around the region are as follows:

Empire Builder Daily from Seattle or Portland to Chicago, with 12 stops in Montana (including Whitefish and East and West Glacier) and one stop in Idaho at Sandpoint.
California Zephyr Daily between Emeryville, California (in San Francisco Bay Area) and Chicago, with six stops in Colorado, including Denver, Fraser-Winter Park, Glenwood Springs and Grand Junction.
Southwest Chief Links Los Angeles with Chicago with stops in the southern Colorado towns of Trinidad, La Junta and Lamar.

The Rockies are vast and public transport is limited, so it's most convenient to have your own wheels. The cheapest place to rent or buy a car is Denver (p739).

The scenic drives in this region could justify a separate book. Along with famous ones like Rocky Mountain National Park's Trail Ridge Rd and Glacier National Park's Going-to-the-Sun Rd, great drives can be found throughout most of central and western Colorado, western Wyoming and Montana and the central Idaho Rockies. Others include Colorado's Million Dollar and Peak to Peak Hwys.

TOURS

Econnections (☎ 303-444-2555; www.earthnet.net/~eco) Ecological tours.
Freedom Tours (☎ 303-823-5731; www.twisty-roads.com) Mountain passes by motorcycle.
World Outdoors (☎ 800-488-8483; www.theworldoutdoors.com) Adventure tours in the Rockies region and elsewhere.

COLORADO

The diva of the Rocky Mountain states, Colorado owes its fame to its mountains – they soar majestically skyward, creating unrivaled views. The state boasts 54 'fourteeners' (peaks over 14,000ft above sea level), more than the rest of the USA combined, and a wealth of alpine scenery. Everyone from endurance-driven backpackers to families with little 'uns could spend weeks happily immersed in the state's recreational opportunities. Even during the peak summer season, there is a remote mountain lake or craggy summit free somewhere to ponder life's riches.

The populated Front Range, on the eastern edge of the Rockies, sees the most visitors, largely because of Rocky Mountain National Park, Pikes Peak and Colorado Springs. Head further south toward La Veta for miles of sedate scenery.

The alpine Mountain Region is home to incredible, world-class ski resorts, some of which offer exceptional hiking and biking

COLORADO FACTS

Nickname The Centennial State
Population 4,506,542 (22th)
Area 104,247 sq miles (8th)
Admitted to Union August 1, 1876 (38th)
Capital city Denver (population 2,581,500)
Other cities Colorado Springs (360,900), Boulder (94,700), Grand Junction (42,000)
State insect Colorado Hairstreak Butterfly
Birthplace of Paul Whiteman (1890–1967), the 'King of Jazz'; Florence Sabin (1871–1953), one of the first prominent female scientists; Douglas Fairbanks (1883–1939), star of silent films
Home of ski slopes, hot springs, bighorn sheep, breweries

when the snow melts, and outdoor fiends can fish, raft, kayak and holler. Western Colorado is, apart from Grand Junction, a lone land of desert canyons and mesas. Colorado National Monument and Mesa Verde National Park are gems worth a good, long look.

History

Six bands of Utes once resided in a vast area stretching between the Yampa and San Juan Rivers. When white miners entered their lands, the Utes did not give in so easily. Chief Ouray (1833–80), remembered for paving the way to peace between the two parties, actually had little choice but to eventually give up most of the Ute territory.

The mining era was launched with the discovery of gold west of Denver in 1859, but by the 1870s silver took center stage. Mountain smelter sites like Leadville and Aspen turned into thriving population centers almost overnight.

The state relied heavily on its abundant natural resources, and the 20th century was economically topsy-turvy. Tourism, as well as the high-tech industry, have come to the rescue and made Colorado the most prosperous of the Rocky Mountain states.

Getting There & Around

See p731 for bus and train lines that run through Colorado. Denver is the main transportation hub (see p738). Car rentals are available in all larger cities and at most airports; (see p1121) for rental agencies' contact information.

DENVER

The 'Mile High City' shows little of its erstwhile cow-town days. It's a friendly and burgeoning place with multiple cultural attractions, top-notch restaurants and diverse bars and clubs. Denver is the only urban metropolis in the region – it's not huge by US standards, which is nice for those who prefer touring by foot. It has ample city parks, and once through the web of freeways hugging the city, you'll have choices galore for more outdoor recreation.

History

The allied tribes of Arapaho and Cheyenne hunted buffalo in their home of the South Platte River Valley long before the first fur traders and trappers started trickling in during the early 19th century.

In 1858, General William Larimer shamelessly proposed to the Kansas territorial governor, James W Denver, that he grant Larimer and his party a township at the confluence of Cherry Creek and the South Platte River – if they named it 'Denver.' The plan worked a charm, and thus arose the Denver City Township Company. The same year, gold struck west of Denver prompted a rush of settlers, and then a boom in transport and finance. These new white settlements didn't bode well for the natural resources that the Arapaho and Cheyenne tribes depended upon, and the newcomers bore little concern for the tribes' welfare.

Denver Pacific and Kansas Pacific railroads laid down their tracks in 1870, connecting the city to Wyoming and Kansas. Before the turn of the century, the city saw dramatic booms and then downturns resulting from a volatile mining industry.

The 20th century saw economic ups and downs. With WWII came a plethora of jobs at munitions and chemical-warfare plants. In the 1970s and '80s, though, plummeting oil prices halted growth. The city underwent a face-lift in the 1990s, with the success of telecommunications and high-tech firms and providers, but it has not been unaffected by the woes of a wavering national economy in the start of the 21st century.

Orientation

Most of Denver's sights are in the downtown district, which roughly comprises a square defined to the south and east by

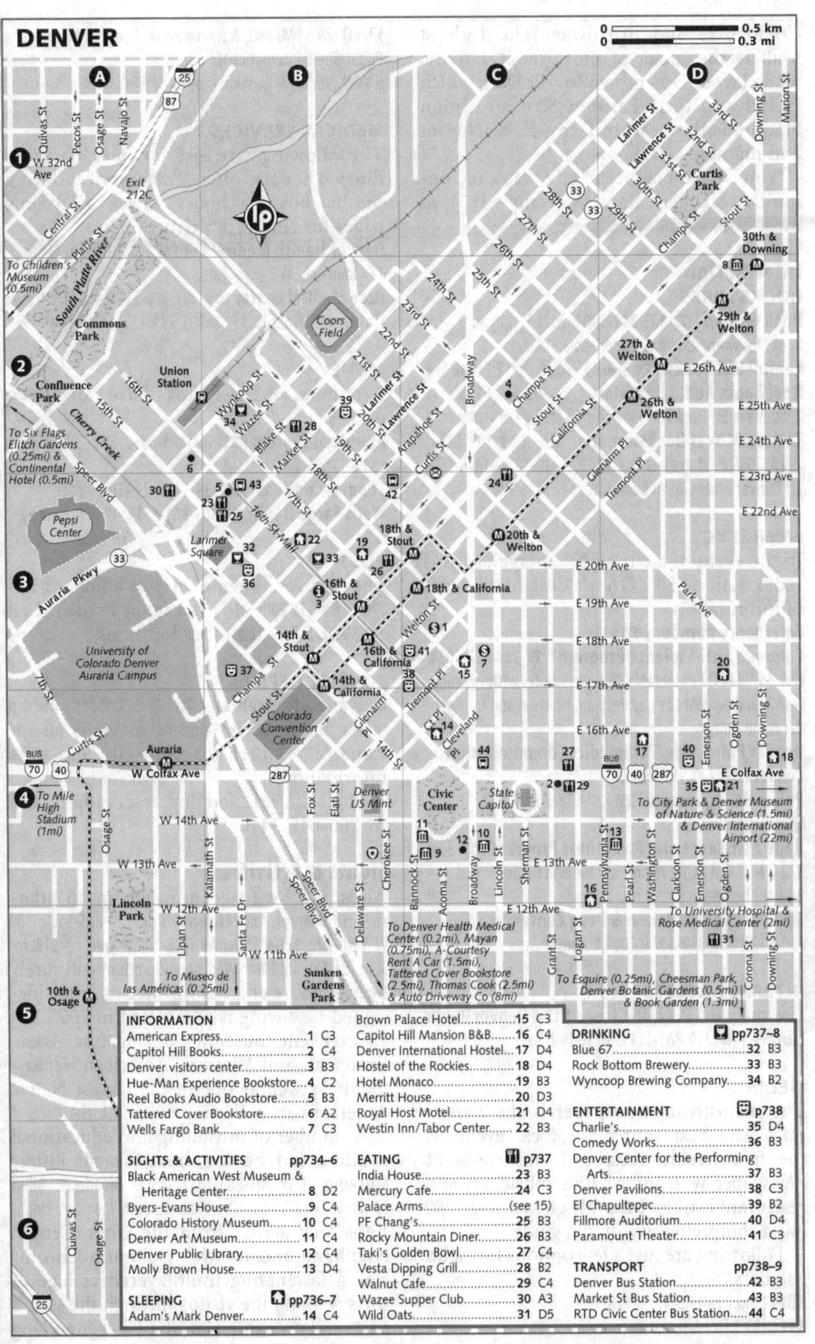

ROCKY MOUNTAINS

Colfax Ave and Broadway. The 16th St Mall is the focus of most retail activity, while Lower Downtown (or 'LoDo'), which includes historic Larimer Sq near Union Station, is the heart of Denver's restaurant and nightlife scene.

You'll have a choice of city maps, including the excellent Rand McNally's ($5), at most bookshops.

Information

BOOKSTORES

Book Garden (☎ 303-399-2004; 2625 E 12th Ave) Books for women, and gay and lesbian readers.
Capitol Hill Books (☎ 303-837-0700; 300 E Colfax Ave)
Reel Books Audio Bookstore (☎ 303-629-5528; 1580 Blake St) Books on tape and CD for sale or rental.
Tattered Cover Bookstore Cherry Creek (☎ 303-322-7727; 2955 E 1st Ave); LoDo (☎ 303-436-1070; 1628 16th St) Denver's most loved bookstore.

EMERGENCY

In the event of a city-wide emergency, AM radio station 850 KOA is a designated point of information.

Emergency number (☎ 911)
Colorado Anti-Violence Program (☎ 303-852-5094, 888-557-4441) Contactable 24 hours; works with violence within and against the gay, lesbian, bisexual and transgender community.
Denver Police/Fire/Paramedics Communications Center (☎ 720-913-2000)
Police Headquarters (☎ 720-913-2000; 1331 Cherokee St)
Rape Assistance and Awareness Program (☎ 303-322-7273) Can assist victims of rape and domestic violence; 24-hour hotline.
Rocky Mountain Poison & Drug Center (☎ 303-739-1123, 800-332-3073; 1001 Yosemite St)

INTERNET ACCESS

Use the wild Web for free at the **Denver Public Library** (☎ 720-865-1111; 10 W 14th Ave).

MEDIA

The mainstream newspaper is the *Denver Post*. The best source for local events is the free weekly *Westword*, an irreverent newspaper with informative music, art and restaurant listings. Monthly glossy-mag *5280* has a comprehensive dining guide.

Following are just a few options for radio listeners:

KBPI (106.7 FM) Rock.
KTCL (93.3 FM) Alternative rock.
KUVO (89.3 FM) Jazz, National Public Radio (NPR) and Public Radio International.
KVOD (90.1 FM) Classical music and NPR.

MEDICAL SERVICES

The following have 24-hour emergency facilities. They also offer dental services during normal business hours. Check the yellow pages for emergency dental help.

Denver Health Medical Center (☎ 303-436-6000; 777 Bannock St)
Rose Medical Center (☎ 303-320-2121; 4567 E 9th Ave)
University Hospital (☎ 303-399-1211; 4200 E 9th Ave)

MONEY

A number of large banks have downtown offices.

American Express (☎ 303-383-5050, 800-291-9598; 555 S 17th St)
Thomas Cook (☎ 303-333-5713; 299 Detroit St)
Wells Fargo Bank (☎ 303-861-8811; 1740 Broadway)

POST

The Denver downtown **post office** (☎ 303-296-4692; 951 20th St) is the main branch. Call ☎ 800-275-8777 for other locations.

TOURIST OFFICES

Denver visitors center (☎ 303-892-1505; www.denver.org; 918 16th St; 9am-5pm Mon-Fri) is an invaluable resource for both city and state information.

For statewide lodging reservations, call ☎ 800-645-3446.

Sights & Activities

Already a lot to get through in an afternoon, **Denver Art Museum** (☎ 720-865-5000; 100 W 14th Ave; adult $6, child 12 & under free; 10am-5pm Tue-Sat, until 9pm Wed, noon-5pm Sun) will surely be even more engrossing once its boldly designed new wing is completed in 2005. It's an excellent museum housing fine Asian, European and Western American departments as well as one of the largest Native American art collections in the USA.

A number of intriguing and educational exhibits can be found at **Colorado History Museum** (☎ 303-866-3682; 1300 Broadway; adult $5, child 6-12 $3.50; 10am-4:30pm Mon-Sat, noon-4:30pm Sun), across from the Civic Center. Highlights include the 'Colorado Chronicle,' a fascinating multilayered collage of sorts walking the visitor through the state's past, and an exhibit on the Cheyenne Dog

THE BLACK & WHITE OF THE AMERICAN WEST

The subject of 19th-century exploration of the American West usually conjures up images of gold rushes and white pioneers like Lewis and Clark and Kit Carson. But old Western flicks and even history books have long skipped over the significant contributions that African-Americans made in the development of the West after the Homestead Act of 1862. There were escaped or newly freed black slaves from the South who set westward for land and a new life, though many found that discrimination and ensuing difficulties weren't so easy to shake off. And there were black cowboys and rodeo riders, like Bill Pickett, who rode throughout the country exhibiting his techniques like 'bulldogging' – which involved biting a steer on its lip.

In Denver, you can find out more about notable African-Americans of local history at the **Black American West Museum & Heritage Center** (☎ 303-292-2566; 3091 California St; adult $5, child 5-12 $4; 🕒 10am-2pm Mon-Fri, 10am-5pm Sat & Sun, closed Mon-Tue winter), which claims to 'tell it like it was.' In the former residence of Justina L Ford, a black doctor who delivered thousands of babies from her home, the worthwhile museum introduces many intriguing figures deserving of more recognition.

For more in-depth study of African-American Western history, try the following books: *Black, Red and Deadly: Black and Indian Gunfighters of the Indian Territory, 1870–1907* by Arthur T Burton and *Black People Who Made the Old West* by William Loren Katz. The bookshop **Hue-man Experience** (☎ 303-293-2665; 911 Park Ave W) stocks these and other titles about/by African-American authors.

Soldiers, which is a division of the Cheyenne nation.

Denver Museum of Nature & Science (☎ 303-322-7009; 2001 Colorado Blvd; museum only adult/child $9/6, museum & Imax $13/9; 🕒 9am-5pm), in spacious City Park, east of downtown, is one of the country's premier natural-history museums, featuring excellent wildlife and geological and dinosaur exhibits. Also housed in the complex is a giant-screen (four and a half stories high) Imax theater.

Restored historic homes worth a tour are **Byers-Evans House** (☎ 303-620-4933; cnr 13th Ave & Bannock St; admission free with ticket to Colorado History Museum; 🕒 11am-3pm Tue-Sun) and the **Molly Brown House Museum** (☎ 303-832-4092; 1340 Pennsylvania St; adult $6.50, child 6-12 $2.50; 🕒 10am-3:30pm Mon-Sat, closed Mon Sep-May).

Southeast of downtown, **Museo de las Américas** (☎ 303-571-4401; 861 Santa Fe Dr; adult $4, child 10 & under free; 🕒 10am-5pm Tue-Sat) focuses on Latino art, history and contributions to the Southwest.

The Black American West Museum & Heritage Center shows another side to the myth of the old West. See the boxed text (above) for details.

Popular **cycling trails** follow the S Platte River and Cherry Creek from Confluence Park.

Denver for Children

Children have no reason to be bored in Denver, unless, of course, their adults poop out on them. The **Children's Museum** (☎ 303-433-7444; 2121 Children's Museum Dr; $6; 🕒 9am-4pm Mon-Fri, 10am-5pm Sat & Sun) is full of excellent exhibits that allow parents to interact with their children. A particularly well-regarded section is the kid-size grocery store, where your little consumerists can push a shopping cart of their very own while learning about food and health. In the 'Arts à la carte' section kids can get creative with crafts that they can take home – all use recycled materials.

Older children are unlikely to frown upon a day at **Six Flags Elitch Gardens** (☎ 303-595-4386; 2000 Elitch Circle; adult $34, child under 4ft $21). This amusement park is packed with nearly 50 rides, with a varying range of fright-inducement. Opening times can vary; call for the season's schedule.

For something a little more traditionally educational, the **Colorado History Museum** (☎ 303-866-3682; 1300 Broadway; adult $5, child 6-12 $3.50; 🕒 10am-4:30pm Mon-Sat, noon-4:30pm Sun) is an enriching experience for people of all ages, but particularly for children who are old enough to read.

The **Denver Museum of Nature & Science** (☎ 303-322-7009; 2001 Colorado Blvd; museum only adult/child $9/6, museum & Imax $13/9; 🕒 9am-5pm) also provides absorbing exhibits for all ages in its extraordinary collection. Check in with the information desk to receive age-specific supplemental materials.

For greenery, the 23-acre **Denver Botanic Gardens** (☎ 720-865-3500; 1005 York St; adult $6.50, child 4-15 $4) are worth exploring with your botanists-to-be. Other green spaces to stroll, play or settle down with a picnic include **City Park** (home of the Denver Zoo and Denver Museum of Nature & Science) and **Cheesman Park**, west of the Botanic Gardens.

At bookstores and sites around the city, you can find useful free publications. *Colorado Parent* publishes monthly event listings for families. *Family Phone Book & Destination Guide* is a great resource for child-care services, recreation centers, children's classes and more. *Get Up & Go* is geared toward grandparents and provides suggestions for day trips with the grandkids.

So it's a good time for quiet time? The **Tattered Cover Bookstore** (☎ 303-322-7727; 2955 E 1st Ave, Cherry Creek) has an excellent children's section, with desks and chairs of all sizes – as well as couches for the bigger among us who need a bit of a break.

Tours

From Memorial Day to Labor Day, **Gray Line Tours** (☎ 303-289-2841, 800-348-6877; www.coloradograyline.com; adult $16, child 12 & under $8; 2 hr) runs the Cultural Connection Trolley, a tour of numerous Denver sights. The trolley leaves the Denver Pavilion and Cherry Creek Shopping Center. The rest of the year a longer city tour (adult/child $25/13, 3½ hours) is offered.

Festivals & Events

These are just a few highlights of Denver's festival-laden year. Ask the visitors center for a complete schedule.

Cinco de Mayo (☎ 303-534-8342; www.newsed.org) Food, drink, entertainment and family fun; held in May.

Denver March Pow Wow (☎ 303-934-8045; www.denvermarchpowwow.org) Music, dance, storytelling and more by 70 tribes; held in March.

Great American Beer Festival (☎ 303-447-0816; www.beertown.org) A whole gamut of brew; held in September.

Sleeping

BUDGET

Royal Host Motel (☎ 303-831-7200; 930 E Colfax Ave; s/d $45/55; P) On the busy Colfax Ave, this secure motel offers basic rooms. Though roomy enough for wheelchair users, the bath may be too snug. Some rooms don't have a phone, so request one if needed.

Both the following hostels' dorms have their own bath, TV and kitchenette, and both are fairly convenient to downtown.

Denver International Hostel (☎ 303-832-9996; fax 303-861-1376; 630 E 16th Ave; dm $8.60; P) With the cheapest beds in town, this hostel is very fine value. The same-sex rooms are a little cramped but cheerful, and there are rarely more than five people in a dorm.

Hostel of the Rockies (☎ 303-861-7777; 1530 Downing St; dm $16/19 HI member/nonmember, r $40; P) It's the busiest hostel in town, offering same-sex dorms that are a little more spacious, with just four beds to a room. A free, basic breakfast is available daily.

MID-RANGE

Generally, hotels in the mid-range and top-end brackets that cater toward business travelers, offer much cheaper rates on the weekends.

Capitol Hill Mansion B&B (☎ 303-839-5221, 800-839-9329; www.capitolhillmansion.com; 1207 Pennsylvania St; r from $95; P) With beautifully decorated, not-too-frilly rooms and a welcoming air, this is one of the country's top-rated B&Bs. Some of the special features, which vary by room, include a solarium, a canopy bed and whirlpool tubs.

Continental Hotel (☎ 303-433-6677; fax 455-1530; 2601 Zuni St; s/d $55/65; P) The exterior may lack pizzazz, but its rooms are comfortable. The hotel is a big complex northwest of the river, so those without car may find the location a tad inconvenient.

Adam's Mark Denver (☎ 303-893-3333; www.adams mark.com; 1550 Court Place; r Sun-Thu from $80, Fri & Sat $120; P $15-22;) This huge hotel boasts a great downtown location and amenities like a fitness room and sauna. It's well set up for business travelers, though others can reap the rewards of discounted weekends.

Merritt House (☎ 303-861-5230, 877-861-5230; fax 861-9009; 941 E 17th Ave; r $90-150; P) You'll be greeted by a jar of cookies upon entering this lovely 1889 Victorian mansion, now an accommodating B&B. A full breakfast is served in the nice dining area.

Westin Inn/Tabor Center (☎ 303-572-9100; www.westin.com/taborcenter; 1672 Lawrence St; r from $110; P $12-24) Part of an international chain, this modern hotel is a good bet for decor, service, location and facilities including a heated indoor/outdoor pool. The rooms are well stocked, with bonus items like a personal safe and speaker phone with voicemail.

TOP END

Hotel Monaco (☎ 303-296-1717, 800-397-5380; www.monaco-denver.com; 1717 Champa St; r from $210; P $7-21 ✻) A very smart option, this bright, modern place boasts great rooms with feather beds and sees to all the details (including free shoe-shining!). Sizable rooms and an elevator make it accommodating for wheelchair users. Discounts are routinely offered.

Brown Palace Hotel (☎ 303-297-3111, 800-321-2599; www.brownpalace.com; 321 17th St; r from $170; P $22 ✻) The famous historic landmark hasn't missed a day of operation since 1892. It's an atmospheric hotel, a highly graceful Victorian-styled bastion of character and charm. All rooms are spacious.

Eating

Wild Oats (☎ 303-832-7701; 900 E 11th Ave; deli items $3-6) This national natural-foods grocery store of favorable repute stocks juices, organic produce and meats, vitamins and all manner of healthy edibles. It's a perfect stop prepicnic, and there's a café and good deli counter.

Walnut Cafe (☎ 303-832-5108; 338 E Colfax Ave; meals $5-7; 7am-2pm) This is *the* breakfast spot in the 'hood, with a diverse range of offerings, from American standards like waffles and egg variations to breakfast burritos; healthy lunches are also served. Get there early, or be patient.

Taki's Golden Bowl (☎ 303-832-8440; 341 E Colfax Ave; meals $4-6) In this casual space, you can slurp down healthful Japanese noodles, scarf down big bowls of rice and drink down miso-ginger soup (aka 'flu killer soup'). It's a good-value option with plenty for the vegetarian.

Rocky Mountain Diner (☎ 303-293-8383; 1800 Stout St; mains $8-15) If 'old-fashioned,' 'chicken-fried' and 'yuppie-I-O' are adjectives you like preceding your meal, then yee-haw yourself to this comfy-boothed, family-friendly restaurant for sandwiches, salads and hearty American fare.

Wazee Supper Club (☎ 303-623-9518; 1600 15th St; mains $7-9, pizzas $10-18; 11am-1am Mon-Sat, noon-midnight Sun) Once you step into Wazee, there's little chance that you'll turn around – it smells that delicious. Known for some of the best pizza in the city, this longtime local favorite is a friendly, buzzing place.

Vesta Dipping Grill (☎ 303-296-1970; 1822 Blake St; mains $15-25; 5-10pm Sun-Thu, until 11pm Fri-Sat) The menu item 'brown-sugar-smoked roasted duck' should give you an idea of the possibilities here. In the restaurant's fabulous interior, creative dishes – many Asian-inspired – are given more intrigue with accompanying sauces.

Palace Arms (☎ 303-297-3111; 321 17th St; mains $30-50) In the Brown Palace Hotel, the Palace Arms is said to be Denver's finest restaurant. Continental cuisine à la steaks, veal or even caviar are for the choosing, as are hundreds of wines. Reservations are essential; men must don jackets.

Other good eateries include the following:

India House (☎ 303-595-0680; 1514 Blake St; mains $13-16) Mouthwatering North Indian fare.

PF Chang's (☎ 303-260-7222; 1415 15th St; mains $8-13) Popular place for Chinese and Southeast Asian fusion.

THE AUTHOR'S CHOICE

Mercury Cafe (☎ 303-294-9281; 2199 California St; mains $7-14) Leave your iodine and refined flour at the door because here sea salt and whole grains rule. Most of the ingredients used are organic, including produce, dairy and beans. From protein-packed salads to hearty stroganoff, lots is on offer for vegetarians – though carnivores will do fine, too. Its deep-red art-covered walls and cool lamp-shades lend a relaxed feel to the dining area. In the next lounge-like room, music and spoken-word performances often take stage.

Drinking

Denver locals love a good brewery, and the city has numerous ones offering fine beer and tasty food. Most other bars and night-spots are in LoDo, though you'll also find action on the grittier E Colfax Ave, east of the State Capitol.

Wyncoop Brewing Company (☎ 303-297-2700; 1634 18th St) The big Wyncoop is arguably the city's most rocking brewery. It offers an interesting selection of beers. There are over 20 pool tables upstairs – you can reserve yours in advance by phone.

Rock Bottom Brewery (☎ 303-534-7616; 1001 16th St) On the pedestrian mall, this place has people-packed booths, a bustling bar, sports-screening TVs and an outdoor patio prime for sunny afternoons with a pitcher.

Blue 67 (☎ 303-260-7505; 1475 Lawrence St) The true-blue draw at this suave bar and restaurant is the drink – it offers over 60 styles of martini. Flavors include chocolate strawberry, Japanese pear and a token 'cowboy martini.' Live jazz plays nightly from about 9:30pm.

Entertainment

To find out what's happening with music, theater and other performing arts, pick up a free copy of *Westword*. The biweekly gay newspaper *Out Front*, found in coffee shops and bars, has entertainment listings.

NIGHTCLUBS & LIVE MUSIC

Charlie's (☎ 303-839-8890; 900 E Colfax) Who says Colorado's a straight state? There are masses – predominantly male – here who would happily contest that. Shoot some pool, croon a tune in the karaoke lounge, jabber around one of the bars or get on down to some music on the roomy dance floor.

El Chapultepec (☎ 303-295-9126; 1962 Market St) Near the ballpark, this smoky little old-school joint hears some good tunes. Local jazz bands take flight from the tiny stage nightly (starting at 9pm), where they're sometimes joined by a big name who has just happened to drop by.

In town, the main venues for national acts are **Paramount Theater** (☎ 303-534-8336; 1621 Glenarm Pl) and **Fillmore Auditorium** (☎ 303-837-0360; 1510 Clarkson St).

CINEMAS

For independent and foreign films, check the schedule at the **Mayan** (☎ 303-744-6796; 110 Broadway; adult $8.30, child 12 & under $6) or **Esquire** (☎ 303-733-5757; 590 Downing St; adult $8.30, child 12 & under $6). For a mainstream number, you'll have at least 15 to choose from at **Denver Pavilions** (☎ 303-454-9032; 500 16th St; adult $8.50, child 3-11 $5.50).

THEATER

Denver Center for the Performing Arts (☎ 303-893-4100; www.denvercenter.org; 1245 Champa St) Occupying almost four city blocks, this complex is the world's second-largest performing-arts center. It hosts resident Colorado Symphony Orchestra, Opera Colorado, Denver Center Theater Company, Colorado Ballet and touring Broadway shows.

Comedy Works (☎ 303-595-3637; www.comedyworks.com; 1226 15th St) For some merriment, head to this top-rated comedy club, which snickers and snorts with world-class stand-up acts.

SPECTATOR SPORTS

Denver is a city known for manic sports fans and boasts five pro teams. The **Colorado Rockies** (☎ 303-762-5437, 800-388-7625) play baseball at the highly rated Coors Field. The **Pepsi Center** (☎ 303-405-1111) hosts the Denver Nuggets basketball team and the Colorado Avalanche hockey team. The much-lauded **Denver Broncos football team** (☎ 720-258-3333) and the **Colorado Rapids soccer team** (☎ 303-299-1599, 800-844-7777) play at **Mile High Stadium** (☎ 720-258-3000).

Getting There & Away

AIR

Denver International Airport (DIA; www.flydenver.com; 8500 Peña Blvd) is served by around 20 airlines and offers flights to nearly every major US city. Located 24 miles from downtown, DIA is connected with I-70 exit 238 by the 12-mile-long Peña Blvd.

Tourist and airport information is available at a **booth** (☎ 303-342-2000, 800-247-2336) in the terminal's central hall.

BUS

Greyhound buses stop at the **Denver Bus Station** (☎ 303-293-6555; 1055 19th St), which runs services to Cheyenne ($19, three hours) and Billings ($95, 14 hours). **Powder River Coach USA** (☎ 800-442-3682) and **TNM&O** (☎ 806-763-5389) also stop here.

TRAIN

Amtrak's *California Zephyr* runs daily between Chicago and San Francisco via Denver. Trains arrive and depart from **Union Station** (☎ 303-825-2583; 17th & Wynkoop Sts). For recorded information on arrival and departure times, call ☎ 303-534-2812. **Amtrak** (☎ 800-872-7245) can also provide schedule information and train reservations.

Denver's **Ski Train** (☎ 303-296-4754; www.skitrain.com; same-day round-trip $45) to Winter Park operates on weekends throughout the ski season as well as in July and August; discounted tickets for children ($20) are available for Sunday trips only.

Getting Around

TO/FROM THE AIRPORT

All transportation companies have booths near the baggage claim. **Public Regional Transit District** (RTD; ☎ 303-299-6000, 800-366-7433; www.rtd-denver.com) buses runs a SkyRide service to the airport from downtown Denver hourly ($8, one hour). RTD also goes to Boulder ($10, 1½ hours).

Front Range cities and towns that have airport shuttles to Denver include Estes Park and Grand Lake. Mountain Region areas with shuttle services to Denver include Winter Park, Breckenridge, Leadville, Vail, Glenwood Springs and Aspen. Taxis to downtown Denver charge a flat $45, excluding tip.

The following offer van services from downtown Denver and around to the airport, and vice versa:

Denver Mountain Express (☎ 303-333-4000; $16-18)
Shuttle King (☎ 303-363-8000; $20-35)
Super Shuttle (☎ 303-370-1300, 800-258-3826; from $18)

CAR & MOTORCYCLE

Street parking can be a pain, but there are slews of pay garages in downtown and LoDo. Nearly all the major car rental firms have counters at DIA, though a few have offices in downtown Denver; check the yellow pages.

For those lacking a credit card, **A-Courtesy Rent A Car** (☎ 303-733-2218, 800-441-1816; 270 S Broadway; 7:30am-5pm Mon-Fri) accepts cash deposits, but its vehicles cannot be driven outside the state.

For drive-aways (rented from vehicle transport companies that need drivers to move cars from one place to another), try **Auto Driveaway Co** (☎ 303-757-1211; autodriveaway@quest.net; 5777 E Evans Ave; 9am-5pm Mon-Fri).

PUBLIC TRANSPORTATION

RTD provides public transportation throughout the Denver and Boulder area. Local buses cost $1.15 for local services, $2.50 for express services. Useful free shuttle buses run along the 16th St Mall.

RTD also operates a light-rail line serving 16 stations on a 12-mile route through downtown. Fares are the same as for local buses.

TAXI

Freedom Cab (☎ 303-292-8900; 24hr)
Metro Taxi (☎ 303-333-3333; 24hr)
Yellow Cab (☎ 303-777-7777; 24hr)

AROUND DENVER

Golden

A city with a small historic district and a few engaging sites, Golden is one seen by the masses largely for the **Coors Brewing Company** (☎ 303-277-2337; cnr 13th & Ford Sts; tours 10am-4pm Mon-Sat). Touring the vat-laden facilities is a bit like volunteering to step into a Coors ad, but there are free samples (three glasses worth!) at the end. Kids and train-spotters will get a better buzz from the **Colorado Railroad Museum** (☎ 303-279-4591; 17155 W 44th Ave; adult $7, child 2-16 $4; 9am-5pm), with its 50 locomotives and train cars on display.

Interesting historical sites include the 1867 late-Victorian **Astor House Hotel Museum** (☎ 303-278-3557; 822 12th St; adult/child $3/2; 10am-4:30pm Tue-Sat), **Clear Creek History Park** (☎ 303-278-3557; cnr Arapahoe & 11th Sts; adult $3, child 12 & under $2; tours 11am-4pm May-Oct) and **Golden Pioneer Museum** (☎ 303-278-7151; 923 10th St; adult $3, child 6-18 $2; 10am-4:30pm Mon-Sat).

About 5 miles west of Golden, **Lookout Mountain Park**, the gateway to the Denver Mountain Parks system, has – no surprise – great views. Fun **mountain-bike trails** are in Matthews/Winters Park, south of I-70 along Hwy 26, and the White Ranch Open Space Park, a few miles north of town.

The **Golden visitors center** (☎ 303-279-3113, 800-590-3113; www.goldencochamber.org; 1010 Washington Ave; 8:30am-5pm Mon-Fri, 10am-4pm Sat & Sun) has the lowdown on sites and accommodations.

RTD (☎ 303-299-6000, 800-366-7433; www.rtd-denver.com) buses No 14, 16 and 16L run between Golden, from the corner of Washington and 10th Sts, and downtown Denver (corner of California and 15th Sts).

Mountain Parks

Denver's outdoor playground, this system of 27 parks stretches from 15 to 60 miles west of the city. One of the more memorable spots is **Red Rocks Park** (☎ 303-640-2637; www.redrocksonline.com), home of a wonderful natural amphitheater used for summer concerts. It's just north of the tiny town of **Morrison**, a National Historic District 32 miles southwest of Denver. Park maps and information are available from the Denver visitors center.

Idaho Springs & Georgetown

These two small towns west of Denver have a historical air born from their 19th-century mining pasts. West of Denver along I-70, Idaho Springs and Georgetown sit pretty with antique shops, galleries and restaurants against the dramatic backdrop of the rising Rockies. From late May to early October hop aboard the steam train around the **Georgetown Loop Railroad** (☎ 303-569-2403,

800-691-4386; adult $16, child 3-15 $10) through the mountains between Devil's Gate (Georgetown) and Silver Plume.

Relaxation is for sale at the inviting **Indian Springs Resort** (☎ 303-989-6666; 302 Soda Creek Rd; www.indianspringsresort.com; campsite $18, r $55-95) in Idaho Springs. The geothermal caves ($15), pool ($10) and 'Club Mud' ($10) are open to day-trippers.

Late-May to mid-September, drive to the 14,264ft summit of **Mt Evans** via the Mt Evans Hwy, off I-70 exit 240 at Idaho Springs. Near the exit, the **USFS Clear Creek Ranger Station** (☎ 303-567-3000; 8am-5:30pm) has information on campgrounds.

Loveland Ski Area

About 55 miles west of Denver, **Loveland Ski Area** (☎ 303-571-5580, 800-736-3754; www.skiloveland.com; lift tickets adult $45, child 6-14 $20), on the Continental Divide off I-70, is appealing for its proximity to the city, good snow conditions, unassuming atmosphere and great rates.

BOULDER

Attractive Boulder is a long ways away from the conservative mind-set found in much of Colorado. A fun and lively city, it's also an intellectual and cultural oasis, mainly due to the 30,000-student strong University of Colorado. Though not filled with sights per se, Boulder is great for hanging out a while and boasts an extensive mountain-parks system.

Orientation & Information

Boulder's two areas to see and be seen are the downtown Pearl St Mall and the University Hill district (next to campus). Overlooking the city from the west are the Flatirons, an eye-catching rock formation.

The **Boulder visitors center** (☎ 303-442-2911; www.bouldercoloradousa.com; 2440 Pearl St, 8:30am-5pm Mon-Thu, 8:30am-4pm Fri) offers information and Internet access. For details on the Arapaho and Roosevelt National Forests, contact the **USFS Boulder Ranger District** (☎ 303-541-2503; 2140 Yarmouth Ave; Mon-Fri 8am-4:30pm). For books, try **Boulder Bookstore** (☎ 303-447-2074; 1107 Pearl St).

Downtown

The main feature of downtown Boulder is the **Pearl St Mall**, a vibrant and oft-offbeat pedestrian zone filled with shops, bars, galleries and restaurants. Nearby is **Mapleton Hill**, home to Boulder's oldest and most magnificent homes.

Because of a small but significant south Asian population in Boulder, you will see Himalayan handicrafts for sale downtown – mural paintings, clothing and other art and goods from Nepal, Tibet and India.

Activities

From the popular Chautauqua Park, at the west end of Baseline Rd, **hiking** trails head in many directions, including up to the Flatirons. Other nice hikes head up Gregory Canyon and Flagstaff Mountain. The easy Mesa Trail runs north 7 miles from Chautauqua to Eldorado Canyon and offers access to more difficult routes, such as Shadow Canyon, Fern Canyon and Bear Canyon, which leads up to Bear Peak (elevation 8461ft). The **Boulder Open Space & Mountain Parks Ranger Cottage** (☎ 303-441-3440; off Baseline Rd; 10am-4pm) at Chautauqua offers maps. Visitors are charged a $3 parking fee at most of the area trailheads.

The 16-mile Boulder Creek Trail is the main **cycling** route in town and leads west to an unpaved streamside path to Four Mile Canyon. Challenge-seekers can also ride 4 miles up Flagstaff Rd to the top of Flagstaff Mountain.

Most Boulder Mountain Parks trails are off-limits to mountain bikes. Exceptions include Doudy Draw, near Eldorado Springs; Marshall Mesa, off Marshall Rd; and the challenging 10-mile loop at Walker Ranch, 10 miles west of Boulder.

Bike rentals, maps and information are available from **University Bicycles** (☎ 303-444-4196; 839 Pearl St) and **Full Cycle** (☎ 303-440-7771; 1211 13th St).

Eldorado Canyon State Park (☎ 303-494-3943; visitors center 9am-5pm) is one of the country's most favored **rock-climbing** areas, offering Class 5.5 to 5.12 climbs. The park entrance is on Eldorado Springs Dr, west of Hwy 93. Information is available from **Boulder Rock Club** (☎ 303-447-2804; 2829 Mapleton Ave).

Sleeping

Hotel Boulderado (☎ 303-442-4344, 800-433-4344; www.boulderado.com; 2115 13th St; r winter/summer from $120/170; P) The charming Boulderado is in an exquisitely restored 1909 brick building with antique-furnished rooms. Choose between one of the small but quaint historic rooms and one of the modern rooms, which are more spacious and wheelchair-friendly.

Colorado Chautauqua Association (☎ 303-442-3282; www.chautauqua.com; apartments/cottages from $65/95; P) This 26-acre historic district at the base of the Flatirons offers lovely accommodations year-round (apartments available June-August only), including one fully wheelchair-accessible cottage. Nearby trailheads make it a great home base for hikers.

Foot of the Mountain Motel (☎ 303-442-5688; www.footofthemountainmotel.com; 200 Arapahoe Ave; r winter/summer from $60/70; P) For both remoteness and convenience to the city, this attractive motel may be ideal. Near the entrance to Boulder Canyon, it has cozy wood-paneled rooms. There's a playground across the road for the youngsters.

Boulder International Youth Hostel (☎ 303-442-0522; www.boulderhostel.com; 1107 12th St; dm $17, s/d $39/45; P) This hostel near the university offers tidy shared-bath accommodations, a kitchen and laundry facilities. There's a three-day limit on the dorms, and room rates are reduced after the first night.

University Inn (☎ 303-442-3830, 800-258-7917; www.u-inn.com; 1632 Broadway; r winter/summer from $70/85; P) The basic rooms here are comfortable, and it's hard to beat the location if you're looking to explore both University Hill and Pearl St Mall – it's a short walk to both.

Boulder Mountain Lodge (☎ 303-444-0882; www.bouldermountainlodge.com; 91 Four Mile Canyon Rd; campsites $14, r winter/summer from $60/70 ; P) Just west of town on Hwy 119, this lodge gorgeously set amid nature offers shady camping, as well as clean, uncrowded motel-style rooms.

Eating

Boulder Co-op Market (☎ 303-447-2667; 1906 Pearl St) Boulder's community-owned grocery store has bulk bins galore, fresh and joyful produce, beauty products and even organic cotton-hemp socks. Its busy café serves sandwiches and soups ($4 to $6) and organic juice ($3 to $5).

Sherpa's Adventurers Restaurant & Bar (☎ 303-440-7151; 825 Walnut St; lunch $7-10, dinner $8-14) The steamed momos are a superb start at the delightfully warm Sherpa's, where the menu consists of bits of Tibet, pieces of Nepal and a few pinches of India. Most mains can be made meatless.

Dot's Diner (☎ 303-447-9184; 1333 Broadway; meals $4-6; 7am-2pm) Students and locals talk love and politics over hearty omelets and espresso drinks at this busy eatery. Early birds should beeline for the before-8am special: eggs, hash browns and toast for $3.

Boulder Dushanbe Teahouse (☎ 303-442-4993; 1770 13th St; mains $8-14) Incredible Tajik craftsmanship envelops the phenomenal interior of this teahouse presented by Boulder's Russian sister city, Dushanbe. The international fare served ranges from Amazonian to Mediterranean and, of course, Tajik.

Illegal Pete's (☎ 303-444-3055; 1320 College Ave; mains $4-6; 11am-10pm Mon-Wed & Sun, 11am-2:30am Thu-Sat) On University Hill, Illegal Pete's is a little place that sees lots of action. Students line up for its burly burritos.

Flagstaff House (☎ 303-442-4640; 1138 Flagstaff Rd; mains $30-60) Get high on elegance, outstanding views, fine wines and top-shelf continental cuisine at this much-lauded restaurant perched on the north side of Flagstaff Mountain. Reservations are advised.

Drinking

Mountain Sun Pub & Brewery (☎ 303-546-0886; 1535 Pearl St) A rainbow of brews is available in this tapestry-lined pub, including fruity beers and a 'Colorado Kind Ale.' The place manages to feel relaxed even when busy with its usual eclectic mix of students and locals.

Walnut Brewery (☎ 303-447-1345; 1123 Walnut St) The crowds that flock here to drink locally brewed beer are quite diverse – except when there's a game on TV, when everyone is cheerfully Coloradan, even if they're not.

Other recommended bars:

Library Pub (☎ 303-444-2330; 1718 Broadway) Very few are studying here!

West End Tavern (☎ 303-444-3535; 926 Pearl St) Great rooftop deck.

Getting There & Around

RTD (☎ 303-299-6000, 800-366-7433; www.rtd-denver.com) buses provide frequent service in and around Boulder; maps are available at **Boulder Station** (14th & Walnut Sts). RTD buses (route B) operate between Boulder Station and Denver's Market St Station ($3.50, one hour). RTD's Skyride bus (route AB) heads

GAY & LESBIAN BOULDER

In the social bubble of Boulder, attitudes are much more relaxed than you'll find in most of Colorado with regards to lesbian and gay culture. The city offers domestic-partner registration, and city-government employees can take advantage of domestic-partner benefits. The gay traveler will have no problem accessing resources, advice and a fine time.

A great starting place, particularly for women, is the **Word is Out Women's Bookstore** (☎ 303-449-1415; 1731 15th St), which has books, magazines and a helpful staff. It also stocks free queer publications from Denver and other parts of the state.

Organizations worth noting include **Boulder Pride** (☎ 303-499-5777; 2132 14th St) and, at the university, the **GLBTQ Resource Center** (☎ 303-492-1377; room 227 Willard Hall). Or call the **Gay Info Line** (☎ 303-939-8588).

And for some F-U-N? **Billy D's** (☎ 303-417-0090; 2690 28th St, No C) is *the* gay and lesbian bar in Boulder. It's a welcoming spot, with pool tables and room to dance. DJs set up from 9pm on Friday and Saturday nights, and karaoke brings in the crowds on Wednesday. **Walnut Cafe** (☎ 303-447-2315; 3073 Walnut St; dishes $5-7; 🕑 7am-4pm) is an upbeat eatery known to be a gay hangout. But the straight folks can't help but come in droves, too. It has an extensive breakfast menu, as well as sandwiches at lunch.

hourly to DIA ($10, 1½ hours). **Super Shuttle** (☎ 303-444-0808) provides hotel ($19) and door-to-door ($25) shuttle service.

ROCKY MOUNTAIN NATIONAL PARK

Rocky Mountain National Park teems with stunning natural beauty and creatures such as elk, bighorn sheep, moose and beaver. It's so alluring, in fact, that over three million visitors mosey in annually. Most stay near **Trail Ridge Rd** (open Memorial Day, the last Monday in May to mid-October), which winds through spectacular alpine tundra environments. Those who prefer communing with nonhuman nature should venture on foot away from the road corridor; the reward is quiet, superlative scenery.

Late 19th-century hotel and road construction in the settlement of Estes Park prompted naturalist Enos Mills to campaign in 1909 to protect the area. He faced opposition from private grazing and timber interests, but in early 1915, Congress approved the bill creating Rocky Mountain National Park.

Orientation

Trail Ridge Rd (US 34) is the only east–west route through the park; the US 34 eastern approach from I-25 and Loveland follows the Big Thompson River Canyon. The most direct route from Boulder follows US 36 through Lyons to the east entrances. Another approach from the south, mountainous Hwy 7, provides access to campsites and trailheads (including Longs Peak) on the east side of the Continental Divide. Winter closure of US 34 through the park makes access to the west side dependent on US 40 at Granby.

Two entrance stations are on the east side: at Fall River (US 34) and Beaver Meadows (US 36). The Grand Lake Station (US 34) is the sole entry on the west side.

Information

Three of the park's five visitors centers are actually outside the park's entrances: **Beaver Meadows visitors center/Park Headquarters** (☎ 970-586-1206; US 36; 🕑 8am-5pm, until 6pm summer), **Kawuneeche visitors center** (☎ 970-627-3471; US 34; 🕑 8am-4:30pm, until 5:30pm summer), a mile north of Grand Lake, and **Lily Lake visitors center** (☎ 970-586-5128; Hwy 7; 🕑 9am-4:30pm May-Nov), south of Estes Park. Within the park are **Fall River visitors center** (☎ 970-586-1415; 🕑 9am-5pm summer, Sat & Sun winter) and **Alpine visitors center** (🕑 10:30am-4:30pm May-Oct). General park information is broadcast on 1610 AM; for road and weather information, call ☎ 970-586-1333.

Entry to the park (vehicles $15, hikers and cyclists $5) is valid for seven days. Backcountry permits ($15) are required for overnight trips. The **Backcountry Office** (☎ 970-586-1242; Rocky Mountain National Park, Estes Park, CO 80517; 🕑 7am-7pm) is east of the Park Headquarters. Reservations can be made by mail or in person from March to the end of December, or by phone from March to mid-May and November to April.

Hiking

The bustling Bear Lake Trailhead offers easy hikes to several lakes and beyond. Another busy area is Glacier Gorge Junction Trailhead. Both are serviced by the free Glacier Basin–Bear Lake shuttle.

Due to planned construction on Bear Lake Rd, you'll have to catch a shuttle if you're traveling between Sprague Lake and Bear Lake from May to October 2004.

Forested Fern Lake, 4 miles from the Moraine Park Trailhead, is dominated by craggy Notchtop Peak. You can complete a loop to the Bear Lake shuttle stop in 8.5 miles for a rewarding day hike, or head into the upper fern creek drainage to explore the backcountry. The strenuous **Flattop Mountain Trail** is the only cross-park trail, linking Bear Creek on the east side with either Tonahutu Creek Trail or the North Inlet Trail on the west side.

Families might consider the moderate hikes to **Calypso Cascades** in the Wild Basin or to **Gem Lake** in the Lumpy Ridge area.

One of the easiest peak climbs in the area is the 1.5-mile trail up **Lily Mountain** (great views), 6 miles south of Estes Park on Hwy 7. At the other extreme is the strenuous hike to the 14,255ft summit of **Longs Peak**, which usually doesn't open till July. An easier option near here is the hike to Chasm Lake (11,800ft).

Trail Ridge Rd crosses the Continental Divide at **Milner Pass** (10,759ft), where trails head 4 miles (and up 2000ft!) southeast to Mt Ida, which offers fantastic views.

Trails on the west side of the park are quieter and less trodden than those on the east side. Try the short and easy East Inlet Trail to **Adams Falls** (0.3 miles) or the more moderate 3.7-mile Colorado River Trail to the **Lulu City site**.

Before July, many of the trails are snowbound, and high water runoff makes passage difficult.

Other Activities

All **cycling** is restricted to paved surfaces like Trail Ridge Rd and the Horseshoe Park/Estes Park Loop. The only exception is the 9-mile, 3000ft climb up Fall River Rd (head back down on Trail Ridge Rd).

On the east side, the Bear Lake and the Glacier Gorge Junction Trailheads offer good routes for **cross-country skiing** and **snowshoeing**. Backcountry skiing is also possible; check with the visitors centers.

Sleeping

The only overnight accommodations in the park are at campgrounds; the majority of motel or hotel accommodations are around Estes Park (see p744) or Grand Lake (see p744).

The park has five formal campgrounds, listed following. All have a seven-day limit during summer; all but Longs Peak take RVs (no hookups). Fees are $18 ($10 in winter, when the water supply is off).

Aspenglen (54 sites) 5 miles west of Estes Park on US 34.
Glacier Basin (150 sites) 7 miles west of Beaver Meadows visitors center.
Longs Peak (26 sites) 12 miles south of Estes Park on Hwy 7; provides Longs Peak hikers with an early trail start.
Moraine Park (247 sites) 2.5 miles from Beaver Meadows visitors center.
Timber Creek (100 sites) 7 miles north of Grand Lake.

The Moraine Park, Longs Peak and Timber Creek campgrounds are open year round. Moraine Park and Glacier Basin accept credit-card reservations up to five months in advance through the **National Park Reservation Center** (☎ 800-365-2267; http://reservations.nps.gov; PO Box 85705, San Diego, CA 92186-5705). Both these campgrounds are served by the shuttle buses on Bear Lake Rd. The other three campgrounds are first-come, first served. You will need a permit to stay in backcountry campgrounds (see p742).

At the southeast boundary of the park near Wild Basin, the USFS **Olive Ridge Campground** (campsites $12 to $16) has 56 sites, 29 of which are reservable; it's open May to October.

Getting Around

A free shuttle bus provides frequent summer service from the Glacier Basin parking area to Bear Lake. Another shuttle operates between Moraine Park campground and the Glacier Basin parking area. Shuttles run daily from mid-June to early September, and thereafter on weekends only until mid-October.

FRONT RANGE

Estes Park

Because it's the more popular gateway to the loved Rocky Mountain National Park, Estes Park's population can skyrocket on summer weekends. To cater to visitors, the town has countless motels and a surfeit of places to buy outdoor equipment, as well as souvenir T-shirts, ice-cream cones and taffy. Estes Park can be charming in the off-season, and it does offer nearly any convenience a traveler might need.

Try the **Estes Park visitors center** (☎ 970-586-4431, 800-443-7837; www.estesparkresort.com; 500 Big Thompson Ave; 9am-8pm summer, 8am-5pm Mon-Fri, 9am-5pm Sat, 10am-4pm Sun winter), just east of the US 36 junction, for help with lodging; note that many places close in winter.

Most of the budget motels are east of town along US 34 or Hwy 7.

Black Canyon Inn (☎ 970-586-8113, 800-897-3730; www.blackcanyoninn.com; 800 MacGregor Ave; cabin/ste from $125/185;), on a lovely 14 acres, offers cabins with kitchenette and fireplace – and some with Jacuzzi. The entire place is non-smoking, even its outdoors. Its restaurant is known for quality steak dinners.

Hobby House Motor Lodge (☎ 970-586-3336, 800-354-8253; 800 Big Thompson Ave; www.hobbyhorselodge.com; s/d $50/60), Hwy 34, is one of the more likable ones. It has a playground, fishing pond and plenty of green lawn, so it's a particularly nice choice for those journeying with kids.

In town, the dorms at **Colorado Mountain School** (☎ 970-586-5758, 888-267-7783; www.cmschool.com; 351 Moraine Ave; dm $25), which runs climbing courses and guide services, are a great choice if there's space. Reservations are advised.

YMCA of the Rockies (☎ 970-586-3341, 800-777-9622; www.ymcarockies.org; 2515 Tunnel Rd; quad cabin/lodge from $75/100;), on the town outskirts, offers abundant accommodations within its 860-acre grounds, a space massive enough to feel peaceful. The roomy cabins work especially well for families, and there are a few fully wheelchair-accessible cabins and lodge rooms.

Also recommended are the quiet **Triple R Cottages** (☎ 970-586-5552; www.triplercottages.com; 1000 Riverside Dr; d/quad from $55/80) and riverside **Telemark Resort** (☎ 970-586-4343; 650 Moraine Ave; d/tr from $65/80).

Mary's Lake Campground (☎ 970-586-4411, 800-445-6279; maryslake@aol.com; 2120 Mary's Lake Rd; campsites/RV sites $24/33-36;) is a good camping choice.

One of the best spots in town for tasty and healthy meals is **Notchtop Bakery & Cafe** (☎ 970-586-0272; 457 E Wonderview Ave; meals $4-7; 7am-6pm), in the Stanley Village shopping center. Fill up on fair-trade coffee, breakfast and lunch, and scrumptious baked goods.

THE AUTHOR'S CHOICE

Stanley Hotel (☎ 970-586-3371, 800-976-1377; www.thestanleyhotelestescolorado.com; 333 Wonderview Ave; winter/summer r from $150/180;) This, the grand dame of northern Colorado's historic resort hotels, has great mountain views, splendid dining and ghost tours of the building on weekend nights. Speaking of which, you should book room No 401 if you want to increase your chance of a ghost-spotting – staff consider it the 'most haunted.' If you simply fancy some comfortable (fright-free) digs, room No 234 is an excellent deluxe choice.

Mama Rosa's (☎ 970-586-3330; 338 E Elkhorn Ave; mains $8-14; 4-8pm Mon-Sat, 11am-8pm Sun) is the place for the likes of lasagna and veal parmesan. It offers pleasant indoor and outdoor seating and family-style Italian dinners.

From Denver's airport, **Estes Park Shuttle** (☎ 970-586-5151; www.estesparkshuttle.com) runs four times daily to Estes Park ($39, 1¾ hours).

Grand Lake

The other gateway to Rocky Mountain National Park, Grand Lake is true enough to its name with a handsome body of water, plus an enjoyable downtown area. Like Estes Park, it is brimful with humans and activity during the summer and quiet in the off-season. The **Grand Lake visitors center** (☎ 970-627-3402, 800-531-1019; www.grandlakechamber.com; 9am-5pm summer, closed Tue & Wed winter) is at the junction of US 34 and W Portal Rd.

The Arapaho National Forest, to the west of town, has some good **mountain-biking** trails; get a map from the **Grand Lake Metro Recreation District** (☎ 970-627-8328; 928 Grand Ave, Suite 204; 8am-5pm Mon-Fri). **Rocky Mountain Sports** (☎ 970-627-8124; 900 Grand Ave) rents and sells outdoor equipment. Several Rocky Mountain Park **hiking** trailheads are just outside the town limits, including those to the Tonahutu Creek Trail and the Cascade Falls/North Inlet Trail, both near Shadowcliff Lodge.

Overlooking Grand Lake, the nonprofit **HI Shadowcliff Lodge** (☎ 970-627-9220; 405 Summerland Park Rd; www.shadowcliff.org; dm members/nonmembers $14/18, r/cabin $45/100), open June through September, boasts a beautiful setting. Cabins, which accommodate six to eight, have

ROCKY MOUNTAINS

kitchen, fireplace and porch. Reservations are essential.

Peacefully situated under the trees next to the Tonahutu River, **Historic Rapids Lodge** (☎ 970-627-3707; www.rapidslodge.com; 209 Rapids Lane; r & condos from $75), with lovely if slightly frilly rooms and simply decorated, functional condos for larger groups, is a place where you'll feel at home. The lodge rooms cater to adults only.

For camping, head to **Elk Creek Campground** (☎ 970-627-8502, 800-355-2733; elkcreek@rkymtnhi.com; Golf Course Rd; campsites $20, RV sites $23-25, cabins $44), just west of US 34 and south of the park entrance, or the **Winding River Resort** (☎ 970-627-3215; off Grand County Rd 491; www.windingriverresort.com; campsites/RV sites $20/25).

EG's Garden Grill (☎ 970-627-8404; 1000 Grand Ave; mains $6-12) serves good grub from salads to seafood; their fish tacos make for a very satisfying lunch. Nearby, the big and casual **Pancho & Lefty's** (☎ 970-627-8773; 1120 Grand Ave; mains $7-12) dishes up a commendable mix of American and Mexican classics and offers a small kids' menu.

Home James Transportation Services (☎ 970-726-5060, 800-359-7535; www.homejamestransportation.com; 9am-5pm) runs door-to-door shuttles to Denver's airport ($58, 2½ hours); reservations are a must.

Colorado Springs

Colorado's second-largest city, Colorado Springs sits below the famous Pikes Peak. With a runaway train of listed attractions, the city is really bustling with visitors in the summer months, when the sun is at its strongest and accommodation rates are at their highest. Spring, fall and – since Colorado Springs is not a skiing destination – winter are pleasant times to visit attractions like Garden of the Gods.

Pick up a copy of the free weekly *Independent* for interesting local news and articles and for the scoop on local music and cultural events.

ORIENTATION & INFORMATION

I-25 bisects the metropolitan area; to the east is the central business district and to the west are Old Colorado City, Garden of the Gods and Manitou Springs.

The following are useful resources:

Colorado Springs visitors center (☎ 719-635-7506, 800-888-4748; www.coloradosprings-travel.com; 515 S Cascade Ave; 8:30am-5pm summer, closed Sat & Sun winter)

USFS Pikes Peak Ranger District (☎ 719-636-1602; 601 S Weber St; 8am-4:30pm Mon-Fri)

Pikes Peak Gay & Lesbian Community Center (☎ 719-471-4429; www.ppglcc.org; 716½ North Tejon St)

SIGHTS & ACTIVITIES

The bizarre and bewitching red sandstone formations at the **Garden of the Gods** draw around two million visitors each year to see highlights like Balanced Rock, High Point and Central Garden. Soak up the beauty on one of the park trails, if you can, as most visitors prefer the windshield tour. The **visitors center** (☎ 719-634-6666; 1805 N 30th St; 8am-8pm summer, 9am-5pm winter) is an excellent starting point.

The **US Air Force Academy** (☎ 719-333-2025), off I-25 exit 156B, has long been one of Colorado Springs' star attractions, but at time of writing, it was closed to visitors due to security reasons. Call for current status.

Since 1891 travelers have been making the trip on **Pikes Peak Cog Railway** up to the summit of Pikes Peak (14,110ft). Katherine Lee Bates was inspired to write 'America the Beautiful' after her 1893 journey up the mountain. Now Swiss-built trains smoothly make the round-trip in 3¼ hours, which includes 40 minutes at the top. Trains leave the **Manitou Springs depot** (☎ 719-685-5401; www.cograilway.com; 515 Ruxton Ave, Manitou Springs; adult/child $26/14) from April to the beginning of January. Reservations are essential. The depot is 6 miles from downtown Colorado Springs. Take US 24 west to Manitou Ave; head westward on Manitou Ave, from where you'll make a left onto Ruxton Ave. The small town of **Manitou Springs** is known for its nine soda-water springs and historic downtown area.

From the town of Divide, west of Manitou Springs on US 24, you can drive the **Pikes Peak Toll Rd** (person/car $10/35) to the summit. For road conditions and directions, call ☎ 719-385-7325 or ☎ 800-318-9505. The road is open 9am to 3pm (7am to 7pm in summer). Due to weather, it's sometimes closed in winter.

SLEEPING

Garden of the Gods Motel (☎ 719-636-5271; 2922 W Colorado Ave; r winter/summer from $45/80; P) With spacious rooms, an indoor pool and a sauna, this motel is good value. Conveniently situated within walking distance of

Old Colorado shops and restaurants, it's family-run and happy to host families.

Old Town Guesthouse (☎ 719-632-9194, 888-375-4210; oldtown@databahn.net; r $100-200; P) This inviting B&B has lovely rooms – the 'African Orchid' room is fully wheelchair-accessible. Gay travelers are very welcome, but families with little ones are not encouraged to stay.

Husted House (☎ 719-632-7569; www.avenetmkt.com/husted; 3001 W Kiowa St; s & d $75-110; P) This 1884 Victorian Gothic belle is an easy stroll from shops and amenities. After breakfast or evening wine, you can relax on a porch swing – or in the hot tub.

El Colorado Lodge (☎ 719-685-5485, 800-782-2246; www.pikes-peak.com/elcolorado; 23 Manitou Ave; d/quad from $60/95; P) You may start hallucinating tumbleweeds if you spend too much time in the comfortable Southwest-style adobe abodes here. Most of the cabins have a fireplace, and the larger ones (for up to six people) are split-level.

Closer to downtown is **Dale Downtown Motel** (☎ 719-636-3721; 620 W Colorado Ave; r from $40; P).

For camping close to town, try the **Garden of the Gods Campground** (☎ 719-475-9450, 800-248-9451; www.coloradocampground.com; 3704 W Colorado Ave; campsites & RV sites $28-38, cabins $40;).

EATING

Poor Richard's (☎ 719-632-7721; 324 N Tejon St; dishes $6-8, pizzas $12-14) Since the mid-1970s, this colorful low-key space has served great vegetarian meals, pizza and beer. If you've forgotten what tofu is, you can remedy that here. There's a kids' room in the back with a small play area.

Howard's Bar-B-Q Pit (☎ 719-473-7427; 114 S Sierra Madre St; breakfast $2-5, lunch & dinner $5-9; 7am-8pm Mon-Thu, 7am-9pm Fri-Sat) You don't get much more old-school barbecue than this rib-cooking eatery, sweetly cluttered with antiques, photos and even a flying pig. On the outside patio, lick your fingers while the trains go by.

Warehouse Restaurant & Art Gallery (☎ 719-475-8880; 25 W Cimarron St; lunch $8-15, dinner mains $12-20; 11am-midnight Mon-Fri, 6pm-midnight Sat) The exterior murals of this restaurant-gallery-brewery make it the hippest thing on the block. It offers a diverse selection of food, from pasta to pork burritos. The adjoining gallery has a pool table and lots of art.

32 Bleu (☎ 719-955-5664; 32 S Tejon St; lunch $7-9, dinner mains $13-24) This snazzy place makes 32 different glasses of wine available to accompany its internationally influenced nosh. After swallowing down your three courses, shake it off in the nightclub upstairs, where bands perform from 9pm nightly (admission $3 to $20).

Also recommended is **Bon Ton's Cafe** (☎ 719-634-1007; 2601 W Colorado Ave; meals $4-7; 6:30am-3pm Mon-Sat, 7am-3pm Sun), for breakfast and lunch.

GETTING THERE & AROUND

The **Colorado Springs Municipal Airport** (☎ 719-550-1900; 7770 Drennan Rd) offers a viable alternative to DIA. The **Yellow Cab** (☎ 719-634-5000) fare from the airport to the city center is between $20 and $25.

TNM&O buses between Cheyenne, Wyoming, and Pueblo stop daily at the **depot** (☎ 719-635-1505; 120 Weber St; 5am-10pm). The **transportation center** (☎ 719-385-7433; 127 E Kiowa St; 8am-5pm Mon-Fri) offers schedule information and route maps for all 31 city bus lines.

La Veta

Little La Veta is the gateway to the Cuchara Valley and the Great Dikes of the Spanish Peaks. Artists and writers have been drawn to La Veta's splendor, and the town makes a lovely base from which to explore the beautiful surrounding countryside.

Go to the **La Veta visitors center** (☎ 719-742-3676; 117 W Grand Ave; www.lavetacucharachamber.com; 10am-4pm Thu-Sat, 10am-2pm Sun) for information on the few motels and restaurants in town. The **USFS San Isabel National Forest Ranger Station** (☎ 719-742-3681; 103 E Field St; 9am-4:30pm Mon-Fri) has information on hiking and mountain biking in the area.

In town, visit galleries for local artworks or explore La Veta's history and Hispanic culture at **Francisco Fort Museum** (☎ 719-742-5501; 306 Main; adult $4, child 9-18 $3; 10am-4pm Wed-Sat, 1pm-4pm Sun).

MOUNTAIN REGION

Steamboat Springs

Steamboat Springs has everything a good ski town should have but with more character and charm than other high-end resorts. Its great outdoors provide abounding options in the summer months, as well.

Steamboat Springs' two major areas are Old Town and, 5 miles south, the newer

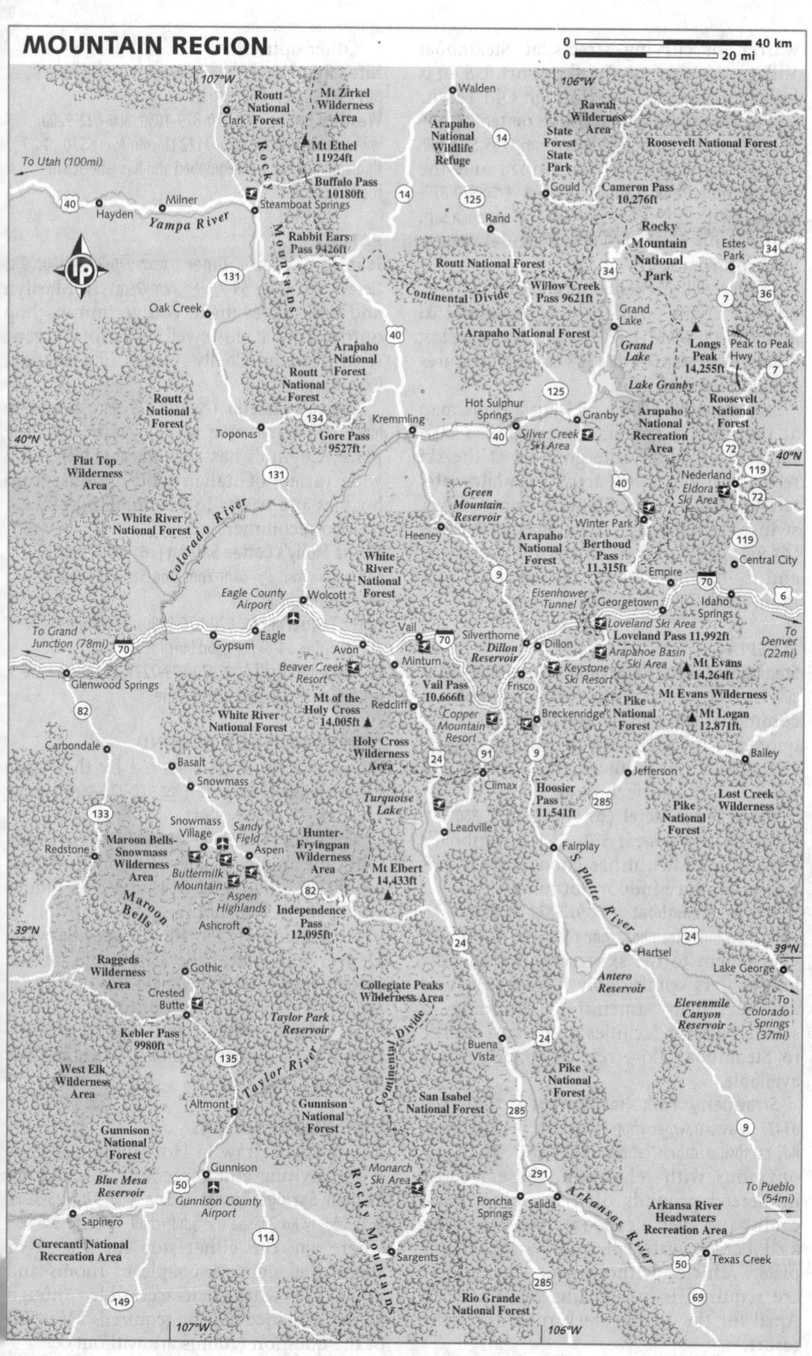
MOUNTAIN REGION
0 40 km
0 20 mi
107°W
106°W
Walden
Routt National Forest
Clark
Mt Zirkel Wilderness Area
Mt Ethel 11924ft
Arapaho National Wildlife Refuge
Rawah Wilderness Area
State Forest State Park
Roosevelt National Forest
To Utah (100mi)
Rocky Mountains
Buffalo Pass 10180ft
Gould
Cameron Pass 10,276ft
Milner
Hayden
Steamboat Springs
Yampa River
Rand
Rabbit Ears Pass 9426ft
Rocky Mountain National Park
Estes Park
Routt National Forest
Continental Divide
Willow Creek Pass 9621ft
Oak Creek
Grand Lake
Arapaho National Forest
Longs Peak 14,255ft
Peak to Peak Hwy
Arapaho National Forest
Routt National Forest
Lake Granby
Routt National Forest
Hot Sulphur Springs
Granby
Arapaho National Recreation Area
Roosevelt National Forest
Toponas
Kremmling
Gore Pass 9527ft
Silver Creek Ski Area
40°N
Flat Top Wilderness Area
Nederland
Eldora Ski Area
Green Mountain Reservoir
White River National Forest
Colorado River
Heeney
Winter Park
Arapaho National Forest
Berthoud Pass 11,315ft
Central City
White River National Forest
Empire
Eagle County Airport
Wolcott
Eisenhower Tunnel
Georgetown
Idaho Springs
To Grand Junction (78mi)
Gypsum
Eagle
Vail
Silverthorne
Loveland Ski Area
Loveland Pass 11,992ft
To Denver (22mi)
Avon
Dillon Reservoir
Dillon
Arapahoe Basin Ski Area
Glenwood Springs
Beaver Creek Resort
Minturn
Keystone Ski Resort
Mt Evans 14,264ft
Vail Pass 10,666ft
Frisco
Mt Evans Wilderness
Mt of the Holy Cross 14,005ft
Redcliff
Copper Mountain Resort
Breckenridge
Pike National Forest
Mt Logan 12,871ft
White River National Forest
Holy Cross Wilderness Area
Carbondale
Bailey
Basalt
Jefferson
Snowmass
Climax
Hoosier Pass 11,541ft
Lost Creek Wilderness
Turquoise Lake
Pike National Forest
Snowmass Village
Sandy Field
Hunter-Fryingpan Wilderness Area
Leadville
Redstone
Maroon Bells-Snowmass Wilderness Area
Aspen
Fairplay
Buttermilk Mountain
Mt Elbert 14,433ft
S Platte River
Aspen Highlands
Maroon Bells
Independence Pass 12,095ft
39°N
Ashcroft
Hartsel
Lake George
Raggeds Wilderness Area
Gothic
Antero Reservoir
Crested Butte
Collegiate Peaks Wilderness Area
Elevenmile Canyon Reservoir
To Colorado Springs (37mi)
Taylor Park Reservoir
Kebler Pass 9980ft
Buena Vista
Taylor River
West Elk Wilderness Area
Pike National Forest
Altmont
Gunnison National Forest
San Isabel National Forest
Gunnison National Forest
Gunnison
Monarch Ski Area
Blue Mesa Reservoir
Gunnison County Airport
Poncha Springs
Salida
Arkansas River
To Pueblo (54mi)
Sapinero
Arkansa River Headwaters Recreation Area
Curecanti National Recreation Area
Sargents
Texas Creek
Rio Grande National Forest
ROCKY MOUNTAINS

warren of curving streets at Steamboat Village, centered on the ski resort. US 40 is known as Lincoln Ave through Old Town.

The **Steamboat Springs visitors center** (970-879-0880; www.steamboat-chamber.com; 1255 S Lincoln Ave; 8am-5pm Mon-Fri, 10am-3pm Sat) and the **USFS Hahn's Peak Ranger District** (970-879-1870; 925 Weiss Dr; 8am-5pm Mon-Fri, 9am-noon Sat), at the southeast end of town, can set you up with information.

With a well-earned reputation for consistently satisfying powder skiing, **Steamboat Ski Area** (970-879-6111, 800-922-2722; www.steamboat.com; lift tickets adult $64, child 12 & under $39) features a 3600ft vertical drop.

For **mountain biking**, pick up a trails map at the visitors center; there are also bike trails accessible by the gondola at the ski resort. A popular area activity is **white-water rafting**. In fact, a stretch of the Yampa River swings right through town. **Bucking Rainbow** (970-879-8747; 402 Lincoln Ave) offers rafting and fly-fishing trips on the Yampa, Colorado, Eagle and Arkansas Rivers.

SLEEPING

Steamboat Central Reservations (970-879-0740, 800-922-2722; www.steamboat.com) helps book accommodations and ski-stay packages. Rates quoted below are for winter; summer prices are usually a little lower, while spring and fall rates can be much lower.

Nordic Lodge Motel (970-879-0531, 800-364-0331; 1036 Lincoln Ave; r $80) Steamboat's best-value motel, it has good, large rooms and a very nice indoor hot tub.

Inn at Steamboat (970-879-2600, 800-872-2601; www.innatsteamboat.com; r $90-150) Convenient to the ski resort, this friendly lodge offers comfortably furnished rooms and excellent amenities, including a sauna, laundry facilities and a free shuttle to Steamboat Ski Area. Ski packages are available.

Strawberry Park Hot Springs (970-879-0342; www.strawberryhotsprings.com; 44200 County Rd; campsites/cabins/caboose $40/50/80) Synonymous with relaxation, these woods-immersed grounds offer camping, basic cabins and even a caboose, plus hot pools, a cool creek, waterfalls and massage therapists. Vehicles without four-wheel drive are required to use chains November to April for the 3-mile steep road up to the resort.

Other options:

Nite's Rest Motel (970-879-1212, 800-828-1780; 601 Lincoln Ave; r $80) Attractive.

Western Lodge (970-879-1050, 800-622-9200; www.western-lodge.com; 1122 Lincoln Ave; r $70) Unglamorous but well-equipped and has wheelchair-friendly rooms.

EATING

Johnny B Good's Diner (970-870-8400; 738 Lincoln Ave; mains $5-7; 7am-9pm) If Marilyn and milkshakes make you go 'mmm,' hop onto a stool at this swell diner for burgers, sandwiches and 'belly stuffers' like meatloaf and spaghetti.

Cugino's Pizzeria (970-879-5805; 825 Oak St; lunch $5-6, dinner mains $11-15) A pretty little place, Cugino's has an amiable staff and a wide variety of Italian-food options, from hoagies and pastas to calzones and pizza.

Also recommended:

Mocha Molly's Coffee Saloon (970-879-0587; 635 Lincoln Ave; 6am-7pm Mon-Sat, 7am-6pm Sun) For a caffeine boost.

Aztec Taqueria (970-870-9980; cnr Lincoln Ave & 4th St; dishes $4-6) For good burritos.

Cottonwood Grill (970-879-2229; 701 Yampa Ave; mains $20-28) For Asian-Pacific fare.

GETTING THERE & AROUND

Steamboat Springs is served by the **Yampa Valley Regional Airport** (970-276-3669), near Hayden, 22 miles west.

Alpine Taxi (970-879-8294, 800-343-7433) serves both the Yampa Valley Regional Airport (adult $27, child 6-12 $14) and DIA (adult/child $70/35, four hours).

Greyhound's US 40 service between Denver and Salt Lake City stops at the **Stockbridge Center** (970-870-0504; 1505 Lincoln Ave), about 0.5 miles west of town.

Steamboat Springs Transit (970-879-3717) runs free buses between Old Town and the ski resort year round.

Hot Sulphur Springs

The primary draw in Hot Sulphur Springs is the inviting and gorgeously situated **Hot Sulphur Springs Resort & Spa** (970-725-3306, 5617 County Rd 20; spa use adult/child $15/12; r $88-98), where you can either stop for a soak or spend the night. A couple of rooms and pools are wheelchair-accessible, though some assistance may be required. TV is out of the question (rooms are without).

Winter Park

Less than a two-hour drive from Denver, Winter Park is one of Colorado's more enjoyable and least pretentious ski resorts, and the congenial town is a wonderful base for summertime romping. Most services are along US 40 (the main drag), including the **visitors center** (☎ 970-726-4118, 800-903-7275; www.winterpark-info.com; 78841 Hwy 40; 🕑 8am-5pm Mon-Fri, 9am-5pm Sat & Sun).

South of town, **Winter Park Resort** (☎ 970-726-5514; www.skiwinterpark.com; lift tickets adult $63, child 6-13 $31) covers four mountains and has a vertical drop of over 2600ft. It also has 45 miles of lift-accessible **mountain-biking** trails connecting to a 600-mile trail system running through the valley. Other fine rides in the area include the road up to **Rollins Pass**.

Winter Park Central Reservations (☎ 970-726-5587, 800-453-2525) is the area's booking agent.

Cozy **Arapahoe Ski Lodge** (☎ 970-726-8222; www.arapahoeskilodge.com; 78594 Hwy 40; s/d winter $75/95, summer $55/70;), just north of Lions Gate Rd, offers an indoor sauna, spa, games and fireplace-warmed lounge areas. Rates include breakfast, though ski-season rates (from $140) also include dinner and transportation to ski resort. Also good is **Viking Lodge** (☎ 970-726-8885, 800-421-4013; Hwy 40 near Vasquez Rd; s/d from $65/70 winter, from $35/40 summer).

Rocky Mountain Inn & Hostel (☎ 970-726-8256, 866-467-8351; www.therockymountaininn.com; Hwy 40; dm/r from $19/50;), 2 miles from Winter Park in Fraser, is a clean and well-maintained hostel-inn, stocked with a kitchen, laundry facilities and common space.

A pleasant B&B within walking distance of the ski resort, **Pines Inn** (☎ 970-726-5416, 800-824-9127; www.winter-park-lodging.com; 115 Timber House Rd; s/d $75/130) serves afternoon snacks as well as breakfast. The rooms don't come with TV or telephone. Rates for doubles are cheaper outside of ski season.

The USFS **Idlewild Campground** (campsites $10), at the south end of Winter Park, offers 24 first-come, first-served sites.

Higher Grounds (☎ 970-726-0447; Hwy 40; dishes $8-12), a café and martini lounge, starts with breakfast and brunch (think Belgian waffles and bloody Marys) and ends with fresh tapas; it hosts a weekly gay night. **Pepe Osaka's** (☎ 970-726-0455; Hwy 40; mains $10-20) comes recommended by locals for its sushi. If you don't do raw, fear not – they also whip up Mexican and Thai dishes, as well as steak.

Other restaurants worth your while include **Carver's Bakery Cafe** (☎ 970-726-8202; 93 Cooper Creek Way; dishes $6-9) and **Deno's Mountain Bistro** (☎ 970-726-5332; Hwy 40; lunch $6-8, dinner mains $13-23).

Home James Transportation Services (☎ 970-726-5060, 800-359-7535) runs shuttles to DIA ($40, two hours).

Amtrak's *California Zephyr* stops daily in Fraser (near Winter Park), while the scenic **Ski Train** (☎ 303-296-4754; 🕑 9am-4pm Tue-Fri) links Denver with Winter Park (see Denver p738).

Greyhound buses stop at the Winter Park visitors center and at the Amtrak station in Fraser.

Breckenridge

In the mountain playground of Summit County, pleasurable Breckenridge retains a 19th-century mining feel. Stop by the **visitors center** (☎ 970-453-6018, 800-221-1091; www.gobreck.com; 309 N Main St; 🕑 9am-5pm) and **activity center** (☎ 970-453-5579; 137 S Main St; 🕑 9am-5pm) for information on accommodations, restaurants and the great **hiking** and **mountain biking** to be had. The **Summit Historical Society** (☎ 970-453-7798; 309 Main St) sells tickets for guided tours ($5) of the Edwin Carter Museum, Lomax Placer Mine, Washington Mine and the Breckenridge Historic District.

The ski resort at **Breckenridge** (☎ 800-789-7669; http://breckenridge.snow.com; lift tickets adult $63, child 5-12 $31), spanning 600 acres over four mountains, has a lot for experts, much less for beginners.

Breckenridge Resort Central Reservations (☎ 970-453-2918; 311 S Ridge St) can help book condos, the main form of accommodations in town.

The following two B&Bs are within a close walk to a ski-resort shuttle stop.

The welcoming **Fireside Inn B&B and Hostel** (☎ 970-453-6456; www.firesideinn.com; 114 N French St; dm $30, r summer/winter from $65/100;) offers a very comfortable stay, ski and bike storage and a hot tub. Breakfast is free for private-room guests, $3 for dorm guests.

The well-run **Abbett Placer B&B** (☎ 970-453-6489, 888-794-7750; www.abbettplacerbnb.com; 205 S French St; r $85-130), in a restored Victorian home, is also a personable choice. It has a hot tub, and most of the rooms have a fireplace.

Healthy options like whole-wheat pancakes and multigrain French toast make

Blue Moose (☎ 970-453-4859; 540 S Main St; dishes $5-8; 🕑 7am-1pm) one of the town's favorite morning stops. The positively colorful **Rasta Pasta** (☎ 970-453-7467; 411 S Main St; mains $7-12) serves massive portions of innovative pastas in busy environs. The ones with garlic are very garlicked. For gourmet, try **Hearthstone** (☎ 970-453-1148; 130 S Ridge St; mains $20-30).

The **Free Ride Transit System** (☎ 970-547-3140) runs buses around town. Also free, **Summit Stages** (☎ 970-668-0999) buses, which carry skis and bikes, connect to the rest of Summit County, hitting Copper Mountain, Keystone, Frisco, Dillon and Silverthorne. **Resort Express** (☎ 970-468-7600, 800-334-7433; www.resort-express.com) offers service to DIA ($53, two hours).

Around Breckenridge

The aptly named Summit County is home to three ski mountains in addition to Breckenridge. **Arapahoe Basin Ski Area** (☎ 970-468-0718, 888-272-7246; www.arapahoebasin.com; lift tickets adult $50, child 14 & under $20) is a high-altitude spot favored by expert skiers and is often open until June. **Keystone Ski Resort** (☎ 970-496-2316, 877-625-1556; www.keystoneresort.com; lift tickets adult $61, child 5-12 $31) is great for families, as the mountain has terrain for all ability levels, as well as night skiing.

Copper Mountain Resort (☎ 970-968-2882, 866-841-2481; www.coppercolorado.com; lift tickets adult /child $60/30), like Keystone, is a modern, self-contained resort; the terrain is mainly suited to intermediate skiers.

Leadville

The air is thin in the 10,200ft Leadville, aka 'Cloud City.' It's a wonderfully scenic town with a dramatic mining legacy, and it's well suited for ambling.

For area advice, head to the **visitors center** (☎ 719-486-3900, 800-933-3901; www.leadvilleusa.com; 809 Harrison Ave; 🕑 9am-5pm summer, 9:30am-3:30pm winter) and the **USFS Leadville Ranger Station** (☎ 719-486-0749; 2015 Poplar St; 🕑 8am-4:30pm Mon-Fri), on the north end of town.

The town's **historic buildings** include the Tabor Opera House and National Mining Hall of Fame & Museum. Historic **mining areas** are a short drive away and can also be viewed via a 2½-hour ride on the scenery-scoping **Leadville, Colorado & Southern Railroad** (☎ 719-486-3936; 326 E 7th St; adult $24, child 4-12 $13; 🕑 8:30am-5pm Jun-Sep).

For **hiking**, the stunning mountains surrounding Leadville include two 14,000ft peaks, Mt Massive and Mt Elbert, the latter being Colorado's highest (14,433ft). There's also good **mountain biking** – rent bikes at **Bill's Sport Shop** (☎ 719-486-0739; 225 Harrison Ave). **Ski Cooper** (☎ 719-486-2277; www.skicooper.com; lift tickets adult $33, child 6-14 $17), 9 miles north of Leadville, is a small mountain with 26 trails. The resort offers day care.

Right downtown, **Delaware Hotel** (☎ 719-486-1418, 800-748-2004; www.delawarehotel.com; 700 Harrison Ave; r from $80), is a carefully restored building with Victorian rooms, attentive service and a locally lauded restaurant.

Leadville Hostel & Inn (☎ 719-486-9334; www.leadvillehostel.com; 500 E 7th St; dm $15, r from $20; 💻) is a great-value, low-key choice with no curfew, laundry, pool table and loads of common space.

In town, pitch your tent at **Leadville RV Corral** (☎ 719-486-3111; 135 W 2nd St; campsites $18-24, RV sites $28).

For pastas, pizza, seafood and even a few Thai dishes, head to the cheerful and spotless **Tennessee Pass Café** (☎ 719-486-8101; 222 Harrison Ave; mains $8-12). Vegetarians should find plenty of fresh and savory fare to keep their appetites stimulated here.

Some other busy eateries include **Quincy's** (☎ 719-486-9765; 416 Harrison; mains $7-15) for filet mignon and prime ribs and **Casa Blanca** (☎ 719-486-9969; 118 E 2nd St; meals $5-8; 🕑 11:30am-8:30pm Mon-Sat) for no-frills Mexican food.

Dee Hive Tours & Transportation (☎ 719-486-2339; 506 Harrison Ave) provides service to DIA ($135, additional passenger $68).

Vail

One of the Elk Mountains' two shining stars, Vail (its glittering counterpart is Aspen), is internationally famous for its incredible skiing. It's a resort town in every sense of the word – the compact Vail Village offers restaurants, bars and boutiques of high standard. Those not shopping and skiing can hike, bike and explore the surrounding alpine country.

ORIENTATION & INFORMATION

Vail Village is the principal center of activity. Motorists must park at the Vail Transportation Center & Public Parking garage before entering the pedestrian mall area near the chairlifts. About 0.5 miles to the west, Lionshead is a secondary center and lift.

You'll find guidance at the following:

Vail visitors center (☎ 970-479-1385; www.visitvailvalley.com; Transportation Center; 9am-5pm, 8am-6pm winter)

Visitors information booth (☎ 970-479-1385; S Frontage Rd, Lionshead Village; 9am-5pm)

White River National Forest Holy Cross Ranger District (☎ 970-827-5715; I-70 exit 176 & US 24; 8am-5pm Mon-Fri)

SKIING & SNOWBOARDING

Vail Mountain (☎ 970-476-9090; vail.snow.com; lift tickets adult $70, child 5-12 $40), with over 5200 skiable acres, has 193 trails. Experts will go gaga, but other ability levels are well taken care of, too.

Cross-country skiers can head to the **Nordic Center** (☎ 970-476-8366) at the Vail golf course or the larger **Cordillera Nordic Center** (☎ 970-926-5100; www.cordillera-vail.com; 650 Clubhouse Dr, Edwards), 15 miles west of Vail. Check with the USFS Holy Cross Ranger District (see Orientation & Information p750) for details on nearby backcountry ski routes like Shrine Pass.

OTHER ACTIVITIES

The Holy Cross Wilderness Area is rich with **hiking** opportunities like the strenuous Notch Mountain Trail, affording great views of Mt of the Holy Cross. The Half Moon Pass Trail leads up Mt of the Holy Cross. The Eagles Nest Wilderness Area – in particular, Booth Falls, Gore Lake and Two Elk Pass – is a sensible reason to lace up those boots.

On the south side of I-70, a paved **cycling** route extends through Vail and continues east to the Ten Mile Canyon Trail over Vail Pass to Frisco, the hub of Summit County bike trails. Another popular but demanding ride climbs over Tennessee Pass to Leadville on the narrow shoulders of US 24. Vail Mountain has over 20 well-marked mountain-bike trails crisscrossing the ski runs.

Otherwise, why not spend a day **horseback riding** (ponies are generally available), **rafting** or **snowshoeing**? Or even, **llama trekking** or **hot-air ballooning**? Find reputable operators for these activities in the seasonal guides to Vail available at the visitors center.

VAIL FOR CHILDREN

So the kids don't want yet another day of ski school, while you sparkle down your black diamonds? Fret not. There are plenty of other things to keep children busy in Vail – and not just in winter but year round.

At mountaintop **Adventure Ridge** (☎ 970-476-9090), youth can enjoy mountain biking, disc golf, volleyball and trampolining in the summer, and tubing, ice skating, snowshoeing and laser tag in winter. 'Kids Night Owl' ($60) is for people age 7-14 years who desire a parent-free evening of dinner and activities.

In summer, **Gore Range Natural Science School** (☎ 970-827-9725; www.gorerange.org; courses $230-350) hosts various multiday and overnight educational programs in wildlife, ecology and environmental sciences for students from 1st to 12th grades. See its website for a schedule.

Vail Recreation District (☎ 970-479-2279; www.vailrec.com; 395 E Lionshead Circle) runs many active activities year-round for all ages, including basketball, gymnastics, ice-skating and junior golf. Teens might want to disappear into the '20 Below Club' for its pool tables, movies and skateboarding. The Rec District's **Gold Peak Children's Center** (☎ 970-479-2290; E Meadow Dr) runs the summer Pre-Kamp Vail ($60 daily) for 2½- to 5-year-olds.

SLEEPING

Don't expect any budget lodgings near Vail. **Vail Valley Central Reservations** (☎ 970-476-1000, 800-525-3875; 100 E Meadow Dr) handles most of the properties.

Tivoli Lodge (☎ 970-476-5615, 800-451-4756; www.tivolilodge.com; 386 Hanson Rd; winter/summer from $150/70;) A friendly European-style place, it's just one block from four lifts in Vail Village. The lodge offers cozy rooms, most with balcony, as well as a hot tub and sauna.

Roost Lodge (☎ 970-476-5451, 800-873-3065; www.roostlodge.com; 1783 N Frontage Rd; s/d winter $100/110, summer $60/70;) This lodge in West Vail provides a very clean and comfortable stay, though the rooms are on the small side. Rates include continental breakfast and the use of a hot tub and sauna.

The forested USFS **Gore Creek Campground** (campsites $13), 6 miles from Vail Village at the east end of Bighorn Rd, has 25 first-come, first-served campsites June to September.

EATING

Joe's Famous Deli (☎ 970-479-7580; 288 Bridge St; dishes $5-8; 7am-10pm) A casual, counter-service joint, Joe's does a great sandwich – if you don't like one of the 20 grilled and cold varieties, create your own. Kids will delight in the ice-cream possibilities.

Billy's Island Bar & Grill (☎ 970-476-8811; Lionshead Mall; mains $15-25) This restaurant, with a great deck for cocktail sipping, brings the ocean to the mountains with a handsome-looking selection of seafood, plus steaks, chicken, pizza and a couple of vegetarian options. For anything from schnitzel to green eggs and ham, try **Blu's** (☎ 970-476-3113; 193 E Gore Creek Dr; mains $8-15).

GETTING THERE & AROUND

From December to early April only, the **Eagle County Airport** (☎ 970-524-9490), 35 miles west of Vail, has direct jet services to destinations across the country.

Colorado Mountain Express (☎ 970-926-9800, 800-525-6363; www.cmex.com) shuttles to/from DIA ($62, 2½ hours). Greyhound buses stop at the **Vail Transportation Center** (☎ 970-476-5137; 241 S Frontage Rd) en route to Denver ($23, 2¼ hours) or Grand Junction ($18, 3¼ hours).

Vail's free **buses** (☎ 970-477-3456; http://vailgov.com/transit) stop in West Vail, East Vail and Sandstone; most have bike racks.

Glenwood Springs

Glenwood Springs is a pleasurable place to kick up your heels. Aside from its world-famous hot springs, it offers palatable food and lodging as well as sites ranging from the adventurous to soothing. It's a sensible base for day-trippers to Aspen and Vail, both 45 minutes away.

For area information, hit the **visitors center** (☎ 970-945-6589; 1102 Grand Ave; www.glenwoodchamber.com; 🕑 9am-5pm Mon-Fri, 10am-5pm Sat & Sun) and the **USFS White River National Forest Headquarters** (☎ 970-945-2521; 900 Grand Ave; 🕑 8am-5pm Mon-Fri).

The **Hot Springs Lodge & Pool** (☎ 970-947-2955; 401 N River St; www.hotspringspool.com; adult $10, child 3-12 $6.80; 🕑 7:30am-10pm summer, opens 9am winter) is one of Colorado's favorite vacation spots. It's not a secluded retreat, but there is lots to keep families happy – ample shallow areas, deeper areas with diving boards, water-slides and mini-golf.

There's tiptop road and mountain **biking** as well as tons of **hiking** around Glenwood Springs; pick up a free trails guide at the visitors center and USFS. Rent bikes at **BSR Sports** (☎ 970-945-7317; 210 7th St).

Glenwood Canyon offers Class III and IV **white-water rafting** below the Shoshone Dam, 7.5 miles east of town. For guided tours, try **Rock Gardens Rafting** (☎ 970-945-6737, 800-958-6737; trips $20-64). For something deeper, arrange a three- to four-hour guided caving venture in the **Glenwood Caverns** (☎ 970-945-4228, 800-530-1635; www.glenwoodcaverns.com; adult $12, child 3-12 $7). The caves are a bit different (read: more relaxing) at **Yampah Spa and Vapor Caves** (☎ 970-945-0667; 709 E 6th St; 🕑 9am-9pm; cave admission $10), which has sauna-like caves once used by the Utes; massages, hot tubs and spa treatments are also on offer.

Glenwood Springs Hotel Reservations (☎ 888-445-3696) can help arrange accommodations.

About 20 motels and hotels are in the Glenwood area, and those closest to the city center fill up quickly in summer. There is also a string of mildly cheaper motels in West Glenwood, 1 to 2 miles from town on Hwy 6.

Glenwood Motor Inn (☎ 970-945-5438, 800-543-5906; www.glenwoodmotorinn.com; 141 W 6th St; s/d $65/80; ❄) is good value, with spacious, decent rooms, plus a hot tub and sauna.

Glenwood Springs Hostel (☎ 970-945-8545, 800-946-7835; 1021 Grand Ave; dm $12-14, r $19-26; 💻) is a welcoming and relaxed place with kitchens, common lounges and over 3000 records for your listening pleasure. Discounts for hostel guests are available at some area restaurants and sites.

Hotel Denver (☎ 970-945-6565, 800-826-8820; www.thehoteldenver.com; 402 7th St; r from $75; ❄) is a modern hotel with spacious rooms; it has two wheelchair-friendly rooms, one with roll-in shower. It's an easy stroll to the hot springs and the town center.

Fuel up before hitting the slopes or trails at **Glenwood Cafe** (☎ 970-945-2639; 311 8th St; meals $4-8). Breakfast is of the eggs, hash browns and hotcakes variety, and you won't feel comatose after your meal.

Spagnolo's (☎ 970-945-8440; 812 Grand Ave; mains $9-14), with its red-and-white checkered tablecloths and festive lighting, is a cheerful place to tuck into huge portions of pasta, accompanied by salad and tasty garlic bread. It makes great vegetarian dishes.

Colorado Mountain Express (☎ 970-926-9800, 800-525-6363; www.cmex.com) offers shuttle service to and from Denver's airport ($75, four hours). Amtrak's *California Zephyr* stops daily at the **train depot** (☎ 970-945-9563; 413 7th St). Buses between Grand Junction and Denver stop at the Greyhound **bus station**

(☎ 970-945-8501; 118 W 6th St; 🕑 6am-7pm Mon-Sat, 8:30am-6:30pm Sun).

Roaring Fork Transit Authority (☎ 970-920-1905; www.rfta.com; 🕑 8am-5pm Mon-Fri) has buses that connect the Glenwood Mall with Aspen.

Aspen

Home to great skiing and beautiful alpine scenery, Aspen is a truly unique resort known for hosting some of the wealthiest skiers in the world. Though watching the parade of personalities strutting about can provide for an entertaining afternoon in itself, its natural draws and really fun outdoor recreation are more rewarding ventures.

INFORMATION

Aspen visitors center (☎ 970-925-1940; 888-290-1324; www.aspenchamber.org; 425 Rio Grande Pl; 🕑 8am-5pm Mon-Fri)

Visitors center at Wheeler Opera House (☎ 970-920-7149; 320 E Hyman Ave; 🕑 10am-6pm)

White River National Forest Aspen Ranger District (☎ 970-925-3445; 806 W Hallam; 🕑 8am-4:30pm Mon-Fri winter, also 8am-4:30pm Sat summer)

SKIING & SNOWBOARDING

Four ski areas are operated by Aspen Skiing Company. **Aspen** (or Ajax), overlooking the town, is an athlete's mountain, offering more than 3000ft of steep vertical drop. **Aspen Highlands**, about 1 mile west of town, has outstanding extreme skiing and breathtaking views. **Buttermilk Mountain**, 2 miles west of Aspen, provides gentle slopes for beginners and intermediate skiers. **Snowmass**, 12 miles northwest of Aspen on Hwy 82, offers a nice mix of intermediate and extreme expert terrain, plus it boasts the longest vertical drop in the USA (4400ft). Contact **Aspen Skiing Company** (☎ 970-925-1220, 800-308-6935; www.aspensnowmass.com) for information on lift tickets, resort hotels or rentals.

The best cross-country skiing in the area is at **Ashcroft** (☎ 970-925-1971), in the beautiful Castle Creek Valley, with 20 miles of groomed trails passing through a ghost town. For backcountry skiing, the **10th Mountain Division Hut Association** (☎ 970-925-5775; www.huts.org; 1280 Ute Ave, Aspen) offers nearly 300 miles of trails connecting 22 overnight cabins. Getting to the cabins requires both skill and advance reservations. The office also handles bookings for the Braun Hut System, which covers Aspen, Vail, Leadville and Hunter Creek.

OTHER ACTIVITIES

The three wilderness areas surrounding Aspen offer bountiful **hiking** trails in summer and early fall. The Hunter Valley Trail leads through wildflower meadows and into the Hunter-Fryingpan Wilderness Area. Hot springs are the reward after 8.5 miles of moderate climbing on the Conundrum Creek Trail. Other trails in the Hunter-Fryingpan or Collegiate Peaks Wilderness Areas, east of Aspen, tend to be less used than the popular Maroon Bells-Snowmass Wilderness Area.

Plenty of heavily used **mountain biking** routes ply Aspen Mountain and Smuggler Mountain. Hunter Valley and the Sunnyside trails provide a challenging single-track loop north of town. The Montezuma Basin and Pearl Pass rides offer extreme cycling experiences, well above timberline, south of town from Castle Creek Rd. The **Hub** (☎ 970-925-7970; 315 E Hyman Ave) rents mountain bikes.

ASPEN FOR CHILDREN

Aspen offers a myriad of organized activities for the younger set year round, as well as heaps for teens who might prefer less structured activities like swimming or ice-skating.

A summertime site to consider is **Anderson Ranch Arts Center** (☎ 970-923-3181; www.andersonranch.org; Snowmass Village), a nonprofit arts institution recommended for its wonderful array of five-day summer courses (from $165) focusing in crafts and creativity.

Aspen Club & Spa (☎ 970-925-8900; www.aspenclub.com; 1450 Crystal Lake Rd) runs Camp Aspen Club ($70 per day) in the summer, keeping kids busy all day with hiking, sports and crafts like kite-making.

The **Aspen Center for Environmental Studies** (ACES; ☎ 970-925-5756; www.aspennature.org; 100 Puppy Smith St) runs great day programs in the summer for children aged five to 10, which can include hiking, storytelling, playing and even some learning; rates vary. Summer evenings here feature a free Sunset Beaver Walk – splendid for families.

The city is proud of the new **Aspen Recreation Center** (☎ 970-544-4100; www.aspenrecreation.com; 0895 Maroon Creek Rd), loaded with facilities, including pools and hot tubs, an ice rink and climbing wall. Its **Aspen Youth Center** (☎ 970-925-7091) runs activities, such as crafts sessions and parties, for children aged eight to 18; summer fun includes roller hockey and skateboarding.

In winter, ski-school kids at Buttermilk and Snowmass can take part in the Winter Wild Things program to learn about our animal friends; contact the ACES for information. The **Aspen Ice Garden** (☎ 970-5141; 223 W Hyman Ave; adult $4, child 6-17 $3) has public skating and hosts local hockey-league games.

Childcare is available in Aspen year-round. Contact the Aspen Recreation Center (see earlier) for referrals to services in the area.

SLEEPING

Stay Aspen Snowmass Central Reservations (☎ 970-925-9000, 800-262-7736; www.stayaspensnowmass.com; 425 Rio Grande Pl) Can book B&Bs, hotels and condos.

St Moritz Lodge (☎ 970-925-3220; 334 W Hyman Ave; www.stmoritzlodge.com; dm summer/winter $30/39; r summer/winter from $60/95;) Neat and congenial, this European-style lodge offers a wide variety of options, from nice dorms to two-bedroom condos. Continental breakfast is served, and pool and steam room are for all guests.

Mountain Chalet (☎ 970-925-7797, 800-321-7813; 333 E Durant Ave; r from $85;) Stay here for convenience to both the lifts and town center. Some rooms have a mountain view, and the lounge is well suited for lounging. Amenities include a hot tub and sauna.

The **USFS White River National Forest's Aspen Ranger District** (☎ 970-925-3445; 806 W Hallam; 8am-4:30pm Mon-Fri winter, also 8am-4:30pm Sat summer) operates nine **campgrounds** (campsites $14).

Also recommended:

L'Auberge d' Aspen (☎ 970-925-8297, 877-282-3743; lauberge@aspenpreferred.com; 435 W Main St; cottages summer/winter from $75/175;) Cozy cottages.

Molly Gibson Lodge (☎ 970-925-3434, 800-356-6559; www.mollygibson.com; r summer/winter from $95/160;) Friendly.

EATING & DRINKING

Main St Bakery (☎ 970-925-6446; 201 E Main St; meals $6-10; 7am-9:30pm Mon-Sat, 7am-4:30pm Sun) It's a hit, especially at breakfast time, for its gamut of sweet and savory goods – granola and pancakes to chicken pot pie – in its convivial room and outdoor patio.

Mother Lode (☎ 970-925-7700; 314 E Hyman Ave; mains $15-25; 5:30pm-10pm) This highly praised longtimer has been serving innovative Italian cuisine to the masses since 1959. The menu is equal parts salad, pasta, and meat- and seafood-focused specialty dishes.

THE AUTHOR'S CHOICE

Explore Booksellers & Bistro (bookstore ☎ 970-925-5336, bistro ☎ 970-925-5338; 221 E Main St; mains $10-14) Two of life's greatest joys – good books and good grub – join forces at this great spot. The upper-floor bistro is suited for slow dining, deep conversing and cups of tea. And if you've traveled too many miles on the chuck-wagon trail, this is where you can boost yourself up on nutritious delights. Everything is vegan, save for the eggs, which are free-range.

After dining, explore further through the bookstore's nooks, stocked with regional and Western titles, literature, music and an excellent kids' section.

Friendly places for drink and accompanying food include the **Red Onion** (☎ 970-925-9043; 420 E Cooper Ave; dishes $8-12) and **Cooper St Bar** (☎ 970-925-7758; 508 E Cooper Ave; dishes $7-12).

ENTERTAINMENT

Double Diamond (☎ 970-920-6905; 450 S Galena St; admission from $5) When live music acts – from rock and blues to salsa and reggae – come into town, they play at this spacious club. It's seen George Clinton, G-Love and many others. Shows generally get rocking at 10pm.

GETTING THERE & AROUND

Sardy Field (☎ 970-920-5380), 4 miles north of Aspen on Hwy 82, has commuter flights from Denver and nonstops to Phoenix, Los Angeles, San Francisco, Minneapolis and Memphis. **Colorado Mountain Express** (☎ 970-947-0506, 800-525-6363; www.cmex.com) offers frequent services to DIA ($100, four hours).

Roaring Fork Transit Agency (☎ 970-920-1905; www.rfta.com) buses connect Aspen with the ski mountains and Glenwood Springs.

Buena Vista & Salida

South of Leadville on US 24, Buena Vista and Salida offer fantastic **white-water rafting** in the Arkansas River Headwaters Recreation Area, a 148-mile stretch of state-run recreation facilities and wildlife areas. Narrow Brown's Canyon, south of Buena Vista, is the most popular stretch of the river in Colorado. For maps and information, check out **Arkansas**

Headwaters Recreation (☎ 719-539-7289; 307 W Sackett St; ⏲ 8am-5pm summer, Mon-Fri winter) in Salida. The alpine country around both towns offers awesome **hiking**, **mountain biking** and **fishing**.

For lodging advice, contact the **Buena Vista visitors center** (☎ 719-395-6612; www.buenavistacolorado.org; 343 S US 24; ⏲ 9am-5pm Mon-Sat, 11am-3pm Sun summer, 9am-5pm Mon-Fri winter) and the **Salida visitors center** (☎ 719-539-2068; www.salidachamber.org; 406 W US 50; ⏲ 9am-5pm summer, closed Sun winter). Motels aplenty dot both towns, though they fill up in summer.

Soaking aficionados should try the beautifully situated **Mt Princeton Hot Springs Resort** (☎ 719-395-2447, 888-395-7799; www.mtprinceton.com; springs adult $8, child 12 & under $5; r winter/summer from $60/70), 12 miles southwest of Buena Vista, where you can dip or stay the night.

Great Sand Dunes National Monument & Preserve

In the vast San Luis Valley, between the jagged 14,000ft peaks of the Sangre de Cristo Range to the east and the San Juan Mountains to the west, the **Great Sand Dunes National Monument & Preserve** (adult $3, child 16 & under free) is a standout. It's a surreal 30-sq-mile sea of sand dunes, the tallest of which rise 700ft from the valley floor. For information on camping and hiking in the dunes or the surrounding alpine forests, stop by the **visitors center** (☎ 719-378-2312; ⏲ 8:30am-6pm summer, 9am-4:30pm winter), 3 miles north of the entry gate. The main campground in the monument is **Pinyon Flats** (campsites $12), open year-round.

Outside the monument's entrance, the **Great Sand Dunes Lodge** (☎ 719-378-2900; www.gsdlodge.com; 7900 Hwy 150 N; r from $80; ⛝) is a peaceful motel-style place; rooms have back-porch areas for dune-gazing.

Crested Butte

There is very little cookie-cutter about the remote and beautiful Crested Butte, which feels more relaxed and less glossy than other resort towns. Though the terrain on Crested Butte Mountain, arguably Colorado's best ski resort, is aimed mainly at expert skiers, the unpretentious atmosphere of the area and wealth of summer outdoor activities welcome everyone. Most everything in town is on Elk Ave, including the **visitors center** (☎ 970-349-6438, 800-545-4505; www.crestedbuttechamber.com; 601 Elk Ave; ⏲ 9am-5pm). The best way to keep the friendly locals friendly is to stick to the posted 15mph speed limit through town (or forget the car altogether).

Crested Butte Mountain Resort (☎ 970-349-2333, 800-544-8448; www.skicb.com; lift tickets adult $60, child 16 & under $27) sits 2 miles north of the town at the base of the impressive mountain of the same name. The area is surrounded by forests, rugged mountain peaks and the West Elk, Raggeds and Maroon Bells-Snowmass Wilderness Areas.

Crested Butte is also a **mountain-biking** mecca, full of excellent high-altitude singletrack trails. For maps, information and mountain-bike rentals visit the **Alpineer** (☎ 970-349-5210; 419 6th St).

SLEEPING

Crested Butte International Hostel (☎ 970-349-0588, 888-389-0588; www.crestedbuttehostel.com; 615 Teocalli Ave; dm $20-27, r $60-75;) This hostel is a smooth operation, offering dorm beds, rooms with

FROM COLORADO TO OUTER SPACE

On Hwy 17, en route to the Great Sand Dunes National Monument & Preserve, signs alert travelers to the **UFO Watchtower** (☎ 719-378-2271; www.ufowatchtower.com; 2.5 miles north of Hooper; admission by donation; ⏲ 11am-10pm) ahead. The mind begins to conjure up images of a biblical Babel, a tower kissing the stars. Surprise is a logical reaction upon seeing this 'watchtower,' founded in 2000 after farmers in the area allegedly reported strange sightings. It's a humble dome with a small second-story viewing deck. A sign in the tiny shop assumes no responsibility for injuries or abductions.

Curiosity seekers drop in for a visit, buy a light-up alien pen and often brush off the whole extraterrestrial business as a silly hoax. Others who visit – some of them brave souls who **camp on-site** ($10) – are true believers. One visitor claims she has been alien-abducted several times; she says that government agencies are in cahoots with the space folk.

This place is pegged locally as totally loony or interesting and inspiring, depending upon who you ask. Whatever you make of it, the UFO Watchtower is nonetheless a unique stopover for a half-hour, or dare we say it, a night…

THE AUTHOR'S CHOICE

Claim Jumper (☎ 970-349-6471; fax 970-349-7757; 704 Whiterock Ave; r $100-140) The only drawback to staying in this zany place is that you may never muster the motivation to get outdoors. It's an extraordinarily decorated B&B – living testament to the owner's lifelong collection of kitsch and knickknacks. Road signs lead to nowhere, furniture is constructed of car parts, and the six rooms are worlds unto themselves. Stay in 'Soda Creek' if you have an affinity for pop bottles. 'Ethyl's' is a mishmash of old oil cans and license plates, and the sports-themed room boasts its own little putting green.

shared and private bath, a kitchen, laundry, library, fireplace and more. One wheelchair-accessible room is available. Reservations are advised.

Inn at Crested Butte (☎ 970-349-1225, 800-949-4828; www.innatcrestedbutte.com; 510 Whiterock Ave; r winter/summer from $70/95) An attractive cedar-built inn, it has comfy doubles and triples, an outdoor hot tub, free continental breakfast and a free shuttle bus to the ski resort. There's a wheelchair-accessible room on the ground floor.

Another option is the **Old Town Inn** (☎ 970-349-6184; fax 970-349-1946; 708 6th St; r from $68/78 winter/summer; ❄) – not ultracharming, but its rooms are decent and spacious.

Mt Crested Butte is a small village of hotels, shops and restaurants at the base of the ski resort. **Crested Butte Vacations** (☎ 800-810-7669) can help book rooms and condos there.

The closest large campground to Crested Butte is the reservable USFS **Lake Irwin** (campsites $12), west of town before Kebler Pass.

EATING

Secret Stash (☎ 970-349-6245; 21 Elk Ave; pizzas $13-17; ⏲ from 5pm) Certainly not a secret, this enticing pizza place offers its pies to go, but you'd miss out on the joyful interior. Sit on the floor upstairs, or park yourself in a velvety chair.

Le Bosquet (☎ 970-349-5808; cnr 6th St & Belleview Ave; mains $17-25) Fine-food offerings and an admirable range of French and California wines make this elegant restaurant a safe bet for a lovely evening out.

Other recommendations:

Buckaroo Beanery (☎ 970-349-5252; 601 6th St; dishes $2-5; 💻) For pastries and coffee.

Paradise Cafe (☎ 970-349-6233; cnr 4th St & Elk Ave; meals $4-7) For breakfast and lunch.

Ginger Cafe (☎ 970-349-7291; 313 3rd St; mains $8-12) For Thai and Vietnamese fare.

ENTERTAINMENT

Eldo (☎ 970-349-6125; 215 Elk Ave) Crested Butte has an interesting music scene year round, and this lively bar is where most out-of-town bands play. From the great outdoor deck here, you can peep at street life below.

Princess Wine Bar (☎ 970-349-0210; 218 Elk St) This intimate bar, perfect for sitting and chatting a while, knows its grape (glasses from $5). First-rate live music of the local singer/songwriter flavor is on show nightly.

GETTING THERE & AROUND

Crested Butte's air link to the outside world is **Gunnison County Airport** (☎ 970-641-2304), located 28 miles south. **Alpine Express** (☎ 970-641-5074, 800-822-4844) meets all commercial flights in winter but requires reservations in summer. The fare to Crested Butte is $25.

The free **Mountain Express** (☎ 970-349-7318) connects Crested Butte with Mt Crested Butte every 15 minutes in winter, less often in other seasons; check departure times at bus stops.

Ouray

Getting there is half the fun if you reach Ouray, in the lush San Juan Mountains, via the breathtaking stretch of US 550 from Silverton known as the **Million Dollar Hwy**. The route – scary when raining or snowing – passes many old mine head-frames and extraordinary Alpine scenery. Spectacular peaks leave barely a quarter mile of valley floor for Ouray.

The **visitors center** (☎ 970-325-4746, 800-228-1876; www.ouraycolorado.com; ⏲ 10am-4pm Mon-Fri, noon-3pm Sat & Sun summer, 9am-5pm Mon-Fri, 10am-4pm Sat, noon-4pm Sun winter) at the hot springs has information on lodging and recreation in the nearby Mt Sneffels and Uncompahgre Wilderness Areas.

Ouray is known for the **Ouray Hot Springs** (☎ 970-325-4638; pool admission adult $8, child 7-17 $6) and **Ouray Ice Park** (☎ 970-325-4061; www.ourayicepark.com), the world's first dedicated ice-climbing area.

Don't miss **Cascade Falls**, a short walk east up 8th Ave. Good **hiking** trails with views are Cascade Trail and the more strenuous Horsethief Trail. There's also good **mountain biking** around.

Some of Ouray's lodges are destinations within themselves.

Box Canyon Lodge and Hot Springs (☎ 970-325-4931, 800-327-5080; www.boxcanyonouray.com; 45 3rd Ave; s/d from $70/80) offers geothermally heated rooms that are spacious and accommodating, but the real treats here are the four wooden, springs-fed hot tubs for guests – perfect for a stargazing soak.

The **Wiesbaden** (☎ 970-325-4347; cnr 6th Ave & 5th St; www.wiesbadenhotsprings.com; r from $120;) is another cozy spot where you can take advantage of hot springs just outside your door; this hotel's star lure is a natural indoor vapor cave, free for guests.

Camp at the reservable USFS **Amphitheatre Campground** (campsites $12), a mile from the south end of town on US 550, or the **4J + 1 + 1 RV Park** (☎ 970-325-4418; 790 Oak St; campsites $18; RV sites $18-24).

Find appetizing steaks and seafood at the **Outlaw** (☎ 970-325-4366; 610 Main St; mains $14-22; 5pm-9pm), New Orleans-style fare at **La Papillon Bakery & Cafe** (☎ 970-325-0644; 207 7th Ave; dishes $5-8) and filling Mexican food at **Buen Tiempo Restaurant & Cantina** (☎ 970-325-4544; 515 Main St; mains $5-8).

Telluride

It's been a hunting ground for the Utes, a saloon-swinging mining mecca and a ghost town in its past. But nowadays, folks flock to Telluride for its white slopes rather than its red lights and golden roads. With a well-preserved Victorian downtown and wonderful outdoors offerings, this small walkable town is a sure-fire nice time. The **visitors center** (☎ 970-728-3041, 800-525-3455; 398 W Colorado Ave; 10am-7pm summer, 9am-5pm Mon-Fri winter) will be happy to assist, and **Telluride Reservations Center** (☎ 888-376-9770; www.telluride.com) handles accommodations. Book festival tickets at www.tellurideticket.com.

Covering three distinct areas, **Telluride Ski Resort** (☎ 970-728-6900, 866-287-5015; www.tellurideskiresort.com; lift tickets adult $70, child 6-12 $40) is served by 16 lifts. Much of the terrain is for advanced and intermediate skiers, but there's still ample choice for beginners. Families with youngsters should check out www.telluridekids.com.

Surrounding mountains offer great **mountain biking** and **hiking**. **San Juan Hut Systems** (☎ 970-626-3033; www.sanjuanhuts.com) is a series of huts accessible to mountain bikers along a 206-mile route from Telluride to Moab, Utah.

Easy Rider (☎ 970-728-4734; 101 W Colorado Ave) rents out bikes, and **Telluride Sports** (☎ 970-728-4477; 150 W Colorado Ave) has topo and USFS Uncompahgre Forest maps.

Telluride does not boast much budget lodging. Its exterior doesn't look very Victorian, but the **Victorian Inn** (☎ 970-728-6601, 800-611-9893; www.tellurideinn.com; r summer/winter from $80/88) has comfortable rooms (some with kitchenettes) with a hint of the era. Continental breakfast is served, and there's a hot tub and sauna outside.

Hotel Columbia (☎ 970-728-0660, 800-201-9505; www.columbiatelluride.com; r summer/winter from $135/165;) is a real gem. All rooms have fireplace, TV/VCR and larger than average bath. Breakfast is included and so is use of the rooftop-Jacuzzi, library and fitness room.

In town, **Telluride Town Park Campground** (☎ 970-728-2173; 500 W Colorado Ave; campsites/RV sites $10/12), open mid-May to mid-September, has 20 unreservable sites with shower access ($1.50 for hot shower) but no hookups.

For a fill-up on pizza, sandwiches, salads and calzones, head to the counter at **Baked in Telluride** (☎ 970-728-4775; 127 S Fir St; dishes $6-10); it's a very casual place with a front deck that's all the rage. Free in-town delivery is available.

Other recommended places for your dining pleasure include low-key **Fat Alley** (☎ 970-728-3985; 128 S Oak St; mains $6-9) for barbecue, atmospheric **Tellurice** (☎ 970-728-8787; 142 E Colorado Ave; meals $9-16) for Asian cuisine, and classy **221 S Oak** (☎ 970-728-9507; 221 S Oak; mains $22).

Commuter aircraft serve the mesa-top **Telluride Airport** (☎ 970-728-5051; www.tellurideairport .com), 5 miles east of town, weather permitting. At other times, planes fly into Montrose, 65 miles north. **Telluride Express** (☎ 970-728-6000, 888-212-8294; www.tellurideexpress.com) shuttles to Montrose airport (adult $42, child two to 10 $20).

Durango

The **visitors center** (☎ 800-525-8855; www.durango.org; 111 S Camino del Rio; 8am-6pm summer, 8am-5pm Mon-Fri winter) is south of town at the Santa Rita exit from US 550. **San Juan-Rio Grande National Forest Headquarters & BLM** (☎ 970-247-4874; 15 Burnett Ct; 8am-5pm Mon-Fri) gives information and maps.

In summer all head to Durango to climb aboard the steam-driven **Durango & Silverton Narrow Gauge Railroad** (☎ 970-247-2733, 888-872-4607; round-trip adult from $55, child 5-11 from $27), which makes a scenic 45-mile trip north to Silverton, a National Historic Landmark. Another service (adult/child from $45/22) heads to Cascade Canyon, 26 miles north of Durango, in September and again from November to May. The atmospheric town's other main draw is **Durango Mountain Resort** (☎ 970-247-9000, 800-693-0175; www.durangomountainresort.com; lift ticket adult $52, child 6-12 $25), 25 miles north on US 550, which offers mountain biking, rafting and more in summer and skiing during winter.

Gateway Reservations (☎ 866-294-5187) handles reservations for lodgings in town. **Durango Central Reservations** (☎ 970-247-8900, 800-525-0892) deals in lodging as well, plus train reservations and lift tickets.

The family owned **Siesta Motel** (☎ 970-247-0741; fax 247-0971; 3475 N Main Ave; s/d from $45/55;) is a welcoming place offering spacious and comfortable rooms. There's a little courtyard on-site with a barbecue grill.

A Victorian hotel dating to 1898, the graceful **General Palmer Hotel** (☎ 970-247-4747, 800-523-3358; 567 Main Ave; r winter/summer from $75/100;) is downtown. Attentive details like bathrobes and chocolates in rooms make it all the more charming.

The nicest camping option near town is the riverside **United Campground** (☎ 970-247-3853; 1322 Animas View Dr; camp & RV sites $20-33;). The city trolley makes a stop here.

The relaxed **Carver Brewing Co** (☎ 970-259-2545; 1022 Main Ave; lunch $5-7, dinner $10-15) churns out 1000 barrels a year of brew; enjoy a pint, with burgers and sandwiches in the outdoor beer garden (open in summer). If you're lucky, you'll show up on an all-you-can-eat barbecue night.

Caffeine up at **Steaming Bean Coffee Co** (☎ 970-385-7901; 915 Main Ave;); sushi up at **East by Southwest** (☎ 970-247-5533; 160 E College Dr; mains $12-20).

Durango-La Plata County Airport (☎ 970-247-8143), 18 miles southeast of Durango via US 160 and Hwy 172, offers commuter flights to and from Denver, Phoenix and Albuquerque – get there via a **Durango Transportation** (☎ 970-259-4818; 24hr) shuttle ($15, 20 minutes). Greyhound/TNM&O buses run daily from **Durango Bus Center** (☎ 970-259-2755; 275 E 8th Ave) north to Grand Junction and south to Albuquerque, New Mexico.

The **Durango LIFT** (☎ 970-259-5438; 7:30am-4:30pm Mon-Fri) operates a frequent trolley minibus service ($1) along Main Ave.

WESTERN COLORADO

Grand Junction

Western Colorado's main urban hub, Grand Junction has a pleasant downtown district, but is frequented by most travelers for its proximity to nearby scenic wonders Colorado National Monument and the Grand Mesa.

Obtain tourist information at the following offices:

Visitors center (☎ 970-244-1480, 800-962-2547; 740 Horizon Dr; www.visitgrandjunction.com; 8:30am-8pm summer, until 5pm winter)

USFS Grand Junction (☎ 970-242-8211; 2777 Crossroad Blvd; 8am-5pm Mon-Fri)

BLM Grand Junction Area (☎ 970-244-3000; 2815 H Rd; 7:30am-4:30pm Mon-Fri)

Some of Colorado's finest **mountain biking** can be found around Grand Junction, particularly near Fruita, 13 miles west. **Ruby Canyon Cycles** (☎ 970-241-0141; 301 Main St), **Bicycle Outfitters** (☎ 970-245-2699; 437 Colorado Ave) and, in Fruita, **Over the Edge Sports** (☎ 970-858-7220; 202 E Aspen Ave) rent bikes. Rentals cost $20 to $35 per day.

The historic **Hotel Melrose** (☎ 970-242-9636; www.hotelmelrose.com; 337 Colorado Ave; dm $20, r $33-45) is close to downtown, Greyhound and Amtrak. The place has character and good-value accommodations.

Two Rivers Inn (☎ 970-245-8585; 141 N 1st St; s/d $50/55;), along a traffic-heavy street, is a basic motel with comfortable enough rooms. It's convenient to downtown and has a hot tub and pool.

North Ave, northwest of downtown, and Horizon Dr, near the airport, play host to stacks of chain motels and hotels of varying price range.

The innocently attractive **Crystal Cafe & Bake Shop** (☎ 970-242-8843; 314 Main St; dishes $4-8), with low muzak playing and wine glasses on the table, is where locals come for their sweets injection; it also serves excellent breakfasts and lunches. Visit **Rockslide Brewery** (☎ 970-245-2111; 401 Main St; mains $9-15) for food and beer or the **Winery** (☎ 970-242-4100; 642 Main St; mains $15-25) for upscale steak-and-seafood nosh.

Walker Field (☎ 970-244-9100; www.walkerfield.com), Grand Junction's commercial airport, is 8 miles northeast of downtown (I-70 exit 31) and offers daily flights to Denver, Phoenix and Salt Lake City. Buses leave the **Greyhound depot** (☎ 970-242-6012; 230 S 5th St) for Denver ($40, 5½ hours), Durango, Salida and more. Amtrak's daily *California Zephyr* stops at the **train depot** (☎ 970-241-2733; 339 S 1st St).

Around Grand Junction

An 'island in the sky,' **Grand Mesa** is a lava-capped plateau rising more than 11,000ft above sea level at its highest point. Its broad summit offers a refresher from the Grand Valley's summer heat, as well as beautiful alpine scenery and an interesting four-hour loop drive from Grand Junction (via I-70, Hwy 65 and US 50). Get maps and information at the Grand Junction visitors center; the **Grand Mesa Byway Welcome Center** (☎ 970-856-3100; 9am-4pm Mon-Sat, 1-4pm Sun mid-May–mid-Oct), on Hwy 65 in Cedaredge; or several smaller information stations atop the mesa. In winter test the fine powder and intermediate runs of **Powderhorn Ski Area** (☎ 970-268-5700, 800-241-6997; www.powderhorn.com; lift tickets adult $38, child 7-18 $28), on the mesa's northern slope.

Grand Mesa National Forest holds 12 USFS campgrounds (campsites $8 to $12). Lodges at **Alexander Lake** (☎ 970-856-2539; www.alexanderlakelodge.com), **Grand Mesa** (☎ 970-856-3250, 800-551-6372; www.coloradodirectory.com/grand mesalodge) and **Powderhorn** (☎ 970-268-5700) have rooms (from $45) and cabins ($65 to $125). Alexander Lake Lodge has a wheelchair-accessible cabin.

The 32-sq-mile scenic wonder called **Colorado National Monument** (hiker/car $3/5) is one of the most rewarding side trips possible off an interstate highway – well worth a driving detour year round but more stellar for backcountry exploration. With about half a dozen accessible colorful sandstone canyons precipitously descending to the flatlands, this beauty is exceptional for hiking and camping, as well as biking on Rim Rock Rd, which links the eastern and western entrances.

The monument is 4 miles west of Grand Junction, though its western entrance is closer to Fruita. The **visitors center** (☎ 970-858-3617; 9am-5pm winter, 8am-6pm summer) is 7 miles south of Fruita, on the plateau at the north end of the park. **Saddlehorn Campground** (campsites $10), near the visitors center, has the only formal sites within the park. Backcountry camping is free (permits required).

Black Canyon of the Gunnison National Park

Awe and vertigo are natural reactions to this dark, 2000ft-deep chasm over the Gunnison River. The 7-mile S Rim Rd winds along the canyon edge and past 10 overlooks (some reached by short trails). More information can be had at the **visitors center** (☎ 970-249-1914; S Rim Dr; 8am-6pm, until 4pm winter), 2 miles from the entrance point. Entry to the park (bicycle or motorcycle $4 per person, car or RV $7 per vehicle) is good for seven days.

South Rim Campground (campsites $10) has 88 campsites. **North Rim Campground** (campsites $10), closed in winter, offers 13 sites.

Mesa Verde National Park

For its focus on preserving cultural relics of the fascinating Ancestral Puebloan culture, **Mesa Verde** (7-day pass hiker/car $5/10) – on a high plateau south of US 160 – is unique. Magnificent sites dot the canyons and mesa tops. Hiking and biking opportunities are slim, but immersion into the past is readily on offer.

Ancestral Puebloan dwellings here first evolved from simple natural structures in AD 450 to great cliff cities that were inhabited around 1200 and were then mysteriously abandoned in 1300. Their disappearance after only a century still defies explanation. The cliff dwellings remained undisturbed until 1849, when a US Army lieutenant stumbled upon them. Congress established Mesa Verde National Park in 1906.

From the entrance, it's 21 miles to the **Chief Ranger's Office** (☎ 970-529-4461; 8am-4:30pm Mon-Fri winter, summer), which has road information and the word on park closures (many portions are closed in winter). The **Chapin Mesa Museum** (☎ 970-529-4631; admission free; 8am-6:30pm, until 5pm winter) is near the Chief Ranger's Office. Along the way are panoramic **Park Point** (10 miles from the entrance) and the **Far View visitors center** (☎ 970-529-5034; 8am-5pm), 15 miles from the entrance, where visitors must stop for required tickets ($2.50) for tours of the magnificent Cliff Palace or Balcony House.

The largest concentration of Ancestral Puebloan sites in the area is at **Chapin Mesa**, including the densely clustered Far View Site and the large Spruce Tree House. At **Wetherill Mesa**, the second-largest concentration, visitors may enter stabilized surface sites and two cliff dwellings, including the Long House, open late May through August. South from Park Headquarters, the 6-mile **Mesa Top Rd** connects excavated mesa-top sites, accessible cliff dwellings and vantages of inaccessible cliff dwellings from the mesa rim.

Aramark Mesa Verde (☎ 970-529-4421, 800-449-2288; adult $34, child 5-17 from $23) offers guided tours from April to October.

Morefield Campground (☎ 970-533-1944, 800-449-2288; campsites/RV sites $19/25) is open April to October. **Far View Lodge** (☎ 970-533-1944, 800-449-2288; www.visitmesaverde.com; r off-peak/peak from $80/110), 15 miles from the park entrance, offers small Southwestern-style rooms with no phone or TV – just appealing views of the park from your deck.

There are also motels aplenty in Cortez and a few places in the towns of Dolores and Mancos, including the charming and gay-friendly **Old Mancos Inn** (☎ 970-533-9019; fax 970-533-7138; 200 W Grand Ave; shared-bath s/d $30/35, s & d private-bath $50).

WYOMING

Much of the beauty of Wyoming lies in a romantic emptiness: Miles of forested mountains; untrodden, empty, arid basins; acres of cattle-strewn fields; and lonely landscapes dotted with dilapidated barns. The sparsely populated state feels vast, and the people who reside here are an independent and unhurried lot, adamantly tied to the land. Outdoor-enthusiasts are spoiled for choice: excellent hiking, backcountry camping, fishing, climbing and skiing are all possible, perhaps near pronghorn herds in the desert or moose, elk and bear in the mountains.

The most popular destinations, by far, lie in the northwest, such as geyser-filled Yellowstone, the majestic Grand Tetons and slick Jackson Hole. The Bighorn Mountains and Devils Tower National Monument also see a number of visitors. Lander is an interesting jump-off point for the outdoors while Laramie is good for some culture – both are more politically diverse than the rest of the conservative state.

Wyoming's vibrant tales of a pioneer past tend to overlay the enduring presence of the Shoshone and Arapaho people, who today live on the Wind River Indian Reservation. Galloping with rodeos and pageants, the Wild West image in the 'Cowboy State' can be a lot of fun – but it does not always align with actual history.

History

Home to native tribes, including the Arapaho and Shoshone who now reside on the 1.7 million-acre Wind River Indian Reservation, Wyoming was opened up to settlers in the 1860s after the construction of the Transcontinental Railroad.

In 1869 legislators granted women 21 years and older the right to vote and hold office, and Wyoming was later known as the Equality State. Some of the law-makers thought it a clever way to attract much-needed female settlers – in 1870, adult men outnumbered women six to one.

In the late 19th century, disputes that sometimes erupted in shoot-outs arose between big cattle barons and the small-time ranchers on the frontier. The Johnson County Cattle War of 1892 remains one of the most contemplated events in the region's history. In 1903, infamous range detective Tom Horn (who worked for the cattle companies) was hanged in Cheyenne, for a murder that many still say he did not commit.

The 20th century saw economic development for the state based largely on extractive industries such as mining. Uranium was discovered in 1918; trona was found in 1939. An economic mainstay for Wyoming and its surrounding states, however, has long been Yellowstone National Park, which has lured large wads of tourist dollars since the end of WWII.

Getting There & Around

Towns with airports include Casper, Cheyenne, Cody, Gillette, Jackson Hole, Laramie, Riverton, Rock Springs and Sheridan. Most are not linked to each other by air, but have service to Denver or Salt Lake City. There is no passenger train service in Wyoming, and bus routes are limited. As in other Rockies states, a car is the easiest way to go.

> **WYOMING FACTS**
>
> **Nicknames** The Equality State, The Cowboy State
> **Population** 498,700 (50th)
> **Area** 97,914 sq miles (9th)
> **Admitted to Union** July 10, 1890 (44th)
> **Capital city** Cheyenne (population 53,000)
> **Other cities** Casper (49,700), Laramie (27,200)
> **State mammal** bison
> **Birthplace of** abstract expressionist artist Jackson Pollock (1912–56)
> **Famous for** Yellowstone, homes where buffalo roam, agriculture, dude ranches

CHEYENNE

State capital Cheyenne, Wyoming's largest city, is on the brink of the Great Plains and still carries some spirit of its former cattle-town days. Visitors here don't tend to linger long, but the city does present a few good sites and events.

Information

The **Cheyenne visitors center** (☎ 307-778-3133, 800-426-5009; www.cheyenne.org; 1 Depot Sq; 🕑 8am-5pm Mon-Fri, 9am-5pm Sat, 11am-5pm Sun, closed Sat & Sun winter) is a great resource, while **City News** (☎ 307-638-8671; 1722 Carey Ave) stocks a fair range of publications, including regional titles.

Sights & Activities

In the summer, you can tour the historic downtown by **horse-drawn carriage** (☎ 307-778-3133). Though a sign warns those likely offended by taxidermy and hunting trophies not to enter **Nelson Museum of the West** (☎ 307-635-7670; 1714 Carey Ave; adult $3, child 18 & under free; 🕑 8am-5pm Mon-Sat summer, closed Sat winter), others may want to check out this unique private collection à la the Old West, from train gangs to movie posters.

Frontier Days Old West Museum (☎ 307-778-7290; 4601 N Carey Ave; adult $5, child 12 & under free; 🕑 8am-6pm Mon-Fri, 9am-5pm Sat & Sun summer, 9am-5pm Mon-Fri, 10am-5pm Sat & Sun winter), at I-25 exit 12, takes a lively look at early Cheyenne; there's a diverse collection of Western wagons on display.

Festivals

Beginning late July, the city stages Wyoming's largest celebration, **Cheyenne Frontier Days** (☎ 307-778-7222, 800-227-6336; 4501 N Carey Ave): it's 10 days of rodeos (admission $10 to $22), concerts, dances, air shows, chili cook-offs and other shindigs.

Sleeping

Reservations are a must during Frontier Days, when rates double and everything within 50 miles is booked. If you're reserving ahead for that time, the visitors center's website can tell you which hotels in the area still have availability. Rates drop during winter.

Plains Hotel (☎ 307-638-3311, 866-275-2467; r $100-200; P ⊠) With a convenient downtown location and a dose of the new Old West, this hotel has personality. It offers eye-catching well-equipped rooms, including one that's wheelchair-friendly, and an on-site restaurant.

Lincoln Court (☎ 307-638-3302; 1720 W Lincolnway; s/d from $45/50; P ⊠ 🏊) It has decent rooms and is the best-value motel in the summer, when it shares facilities with the pricier Best Western next door, including an indoor pool, fitness room and Jacuzzi. A string of other motels lines noisy Lincolnway (I-25 exit 9).

Little America Hotel (☎ 307-775-8400, 888-709-8384; www.littleamerica.com; 2800 W Lincolnway; s/d $75/85; P ⊠ 🏊) This sprawling chain hotel west of I-25 has a golf course and large rooms with extras like bigger-than-standard TVs and hair dryers. Wheelchair-accessible rooms are available.

For camping, head to tidy **AB Camping** (☎ 307-634-7035; abcamping@juno.com; 1503 W College Dr; campsites $13, RV sites $14-23), I-25 exit 7, open March to October. The closest public camping is 25 miles west, in scenic Curt Gowdy St Park.

Eating

Whalen's Deli (☎ 307-637-7400; 318 W 17th St; 6am-3pm Mon-Wed, 6am-8pm Thu-Sat; dishes $3-6) Run by a lovely couple, this is an attractive café and deli with quality coffee and great deals on healthy sandwiches, soup, bagels, waffles and more.

Sanford's Grub & Pub (☎ 307-634-3381; 115 E 17th St; mains $7-16) Walls aflutter with sports bric-a-brac and road signs, the fun Sanford's has a novella-length menu of tasty eats, including burgers, chicken and even a range of 'porker' dishes. Beer is served in ice-cold glasses.

Shopping

Wrangler (☎ 307-634-3048; 1518 Capitol Ave) This huge Western-wear emporium has hundreds of boots, hats for every head and silver belt buckles that will glisten just so at sunset.

Getting There & Around

Cheyenne Airport (☎ 307-634-7071; www.cheyenneairport.com; 200 E 8th Ave) has daily flights to Denver, but at time of writing, Cheyenne had no shuttle service to this airport or to DIA. The **bus depot** (☎ 307-634-7744; 222 E Deming Dr) sends Powder River and Greyhound services daily to Billings ($80, 11 hours), Denver ($19, three hours), Chicago and San Francisco.

On weekdays, the **Cheyenne Transit Program** (CTP; ☎ 307-637-6253; 8am-5pm Mon-Fri) operates six local bus routes ($1). It also runs a door-to-door service ($3) Monday to Saturday by appointment.

LARAMIE

Wyoming's only four-year university injects a healthy vibrance into Laramie. It's the state's cultural capital, with museums and a thriving historic downtown that is not short on eats, drinks and nightlife.

Area resources include the following:

Laramie Events Hot Line (☎ 307-721-7345)

Laramie visitors center (☎ 307-745-7339, 866-876-1012; 800 S 3rd St; 8am-5pm Mon-Fri)

USFS Medicine Bow-Routt National Forest & Thunder Basin National Grassland Headquarters (☎ 307-745-2300; 2468 Jackson St; 8am-5pm Mon-Fri)

Spend an afternoon wandering Laramie's interesting 1860s-era **historic district**. The **University of Wyoming** (UW; ☎ 307-766-4075) has a myriad of museums, including the **University of Wyoming Art Museum** (☎ 307-766-6622; 2111 Willett Dr; admission free; 10am-5pm Mon-Sat). It has an interesting range of paintings, sculptures and other rotating works from the 17th to 21st centuries, including some by internationally renowned artists. **Wyoming Territorial Prison & Old West Park** (☎ 307-745-6161, 800-845-2287; www.wyoprisonpark.org; 975 Snowy Range Rd; adult $11, child 12 & under free), open mid-May to September, is a curious restoration of an early prison and frontier town.

Lodging reservations are recommended (and rates are much higher) for UW graduation (mid-May), Fourth of July, Cheyenne Frontier Days (see p761) and fall UW football weekends.

Numerous budget options sit off I-80 exit 313. A sensible choice is **Sunset Inn** (☎ 307-742-3741, 800-308-3744; 1104 S 3rd St; s/d $50/65;) for its very comfortable and roomy rooms, pool and hot tub. It has a few wheelchair-friendly rooms available.

1st Inn Gold (☎ 307-742-3721, 800-462-4667; 421 Boswell Dr; s/d $60/75;), from which you can gaze longingly at the freeway off-ramp, offers quite spacious and comfortable rooms. Rates include continental breakfast.

The best camping options are **USFS sites** (campsites $10) in the Pole Mountain area, just 10 miles east of town.

Laramie has some of Wyoming's better restaurants, including **Jeffrey's Bistro** (☎ 307-742-7046; 123 Ivinson Ave; mains $6-14), which boasts a zesty menu of fresh and innovative salads, sandwiches and pastas. Various international influences come into play here (eg Thai).

Students like **Sweet Melissa's Vegetarian Cafe** (☎ 307-742-9607; 213 S 1st St; meals $4-6), a mellow and comforting place with nonmeaty foods for protein intake: fakin' BLT and even Italian-sausage lasagna. Fill up on coffee or chai and a hunk of yummy dessert, too.

For a drink or two, try smoky **Old Buckhorn Bar** (☎ 307-742-3554; 114 Ivinson St) or quieter **3rd St Bar & Grill** (☎ 307-742-5522; 220 Grand Ave).

Laramie Regional Airport (☎ 307-742-4164), located 4 miles west of town via I-80 exit 311, has daily flights to Denver. At time of writing, Laramie had no airport-shuttle service. **Greyhound** (☎ 307-742-5188) and **Powder River** (☎ 800-442-3682) buses stop at the **Tumbleweed Express gas station** (4700 Bluebird Lane) at the east end of town (I-80 exit 316).

THE AUTHOR'S CHOICE

Gas Lite Motel (☎/fax 307-742-6616, 800-942-6610; 960 N 3rd St; s/d $50/63;) This motel's rooms are decorated with playful renditions of the Old West; cowboy murals wall the indoor pool and caricatures color the parking lot. On a more practical note, the spic-and-span rooms are well equipped with fridge, microwave and iron. Pets are welcome.

MEDICINE BOW MOUNTAINS & SNOWY RANGE

The Snowy Range's lovely, lofty summits cap the rugged Medicine Bow Mountains west of Laramie. Southwest are the Sierra Madre and the Continental Divide – the Medicine Bow National Forest stretches across both.

ROCKY MOUNTAINS

The 29-mile **Snowy Range Scenic Byway** (Hwy 130) traverses Snowy Range Pass (10,830ft; open Memorial Day to mid-October) between Centennial and Saratoga. Wildflowers and wildlife are abundant, as are overlooks, trails, rafting, fishing areas and campgrounds. Pick up a map at the **Centennial visitors center** (☎ 307-742-6023; ⌚ 9am-4pm summer, Sat & Sun winter), a mile west of Centennial on Hwy 130.

DEVILS TOWER NATIONAL MONUMENT

Known as Bears Lodge by some of the 20-plus Native American tribes who consider it sacred, the **Devils Tower National Monument** (hiker/car $3/8) rises dramatically above the Belle Fourche Valley. A must-see for those traveling between the Black Hills (on the Wyoming–South Dakota border), and western Wyoming's parks, it has a unique history: It was the nation's first national monument, established in 1906, and drew international curiosity in 1941 when parachutist George Hopkins was stuck atop the monument for six days. And in 1977, it was the point of alien contact in Spielberg's *Close Encounters of the Third Kind*. Covering only about 2 sq miles, the park offers hiking, bird-watching, picnicking and camping. Rock-climbing is also popular, though climbers are asked to not to indulge in June, a time of Native American ceremonies.

The **visitors center** (☎ 307-467-5283; ⌚ 8am-8pm Jun-Aug, 8:30am-4:30pm Apr & May, 9am-5pm Sep & Oct), which is 3 miles beyond the entrance, is open April through mid-October. The **Belle Fourche Campground** (campsites $12), open April to October, can fill early. You can also camp in the Bearlodge Mountains, Black Hills and in the pleasant town of Sundance. The nearest motels are in Hulett (Wyoming), Sundance and Moorcroft.

SHERIDAN

A smart base for excursions up to the Bighorn Mountains, Sheridan has one of Wyoming's more interesting **historic districts**, which includes the 1893 Sheridan Inn, occasional home to Buffalo Bill Cody.

Get information at the **Sheridan visitors center** (☎ 307-672-2485, 800-453-3650; www.sheridanwyomingchamber.org; E 5th St at I-90 exit 23; ⌚ 8am-7pm summer, 8am-5pm Mon-Fri winter).

Most motels are along Main St north of 5th St, and along Coffeen Ave.

You'll notice **Apple Tree Inn** (☎ 307-672-2428, 800-670-2428; 1552 Coffeen Ave; s/quad $45/65; ✖) from a distance, thanks to its cheerful 'Prussian green' paint job. The single rooms are snug, but unsurprisingly, the quads are much more spacious.

An erstwhile flourmill, **Mill Inn** (☎ 307-672-6401; 2161 Coffeen Ave; s/d $90/100; ✖) has nice well-equipped rooms and affable staff. It's a better option for wheelchair users than the Apple Tree Inn, though its rooms are not 100% accessible.

Sheridan/Big Horn Mountains KOA (☎ 307-674-8766, 800-562-7621; 63 Decker Rd; campsites $17, RV sites $22-29), north of town off I-90 exit 20, is open May through September. The closest public camping is in the Bighorn National Forest.

Hungry yet? The pretty **Paolo's** (☎ 307-672-3853; 123 N Main St; mains $7-14) knows its dough, and it makes for scrumptious pizza. Also on offer are authentic pastas and olive oil–drizzled salads.

The **Sheridan County Airport** (☎ 307-672-8861), at the south end of town via Big Horn Ave (Hwy 332), has daily flights to Denver. Northbound and southbound **Powder River** (☎ 800-442-3682) buses stop twice daily at **Boogie's Texaco** (588 E 5th St).

BIGHORN MOUNTAINS

Bighorn Mountains are an awe-inspiring range, home to large grassy meadows, seas of wildflowers, conifer forests, waterfalls and wildlife. Three scenic east–west roads cross the mountains. US 16 (Cloud Peak Skyway), between Buffalo and Worland via Powder River Pass (9666ft), skirts the pristine Cloud Peak Wilderness Area. US 14 (Bighorn Scenic Byway), between Ranchester and Greybull, conquers Granite Pass (8950ft). US 14 Alternate (Medicine Wheel Passage) connects Burgess Junction and Lovell via Baldy Pass (9430ft). The latter passes Medicine Wheel National Historic Landmark, a mysterious sacred site that may represent a lunar month or a likeness of the Sun Dance Lodge of Crow legend. The surrounding grounds are thought to have been used by tribes for 7,000 years.

All three routes urge you to explore trailheads, picnic areas and scenic vistas, and campers can choose from dozens of inviting USFS and BLM campgrounds. A few private lodges offer basic stays, campsites and services. Both Sheridan and Buffalo have a good range of accommodation. Detailed information is available from the following offices:

Buffalo Area BLM (☎ 307-684-1100; 1425 Fort St; 8am-4:30pm Mon-Fri)

Bighorn National Forest Buffalo Ranger District (1415 Fort St; 8am-4:30pm Mon-Fri)

Bighorn National Forest Headquarters (☎ 307-674-2600; 2013 Eastside 2nd St; 8am-5pm Mon-Fri)

CODY

Summer is peak season for the boisterous Cody, which draws in visitors – to or from Yellowstone National Park – who want a romp in the Wild West. With a streak of yeehaw, the town happily relays stories (not always the whole story, mind you) of the past. The **visitors center** (☎ 307-587-2777; 836 Sheridan Ave; 8am-6pm Mon-Sat, 10am-3pm Sun summer, 8am-5pm Mon-Fri winter) and the **USFS Shoshone National Forest Wapiti Ranger District** (☎ 307-527-6921; 203A Yellowstone Ave; 8am-4:30pm Mon-Fri) are logical starting points.

Cody's major tourist attraction is the **Buffalo Bill Historical Center** (☎ 307-587-4771; 720 Sheridan Ave; adult $15, child 6-17 $4; 7am-8pm summer, 10am-3pm Tue-Sun winter). Its newest wing is the Draper Museum of Natural History, which explores the Yellowstone region's ecosystem. The other museums are dedicated to Buffalo Bill, Western art, Plains Indians and American firearms. Also popular is the **Cody Nite Rodeo** (☎ 307-587-2992, 800-207-0744; Stampede Park, 421 W Yellowstone Ave; adult/child from $12/6), which giddyups nightly June to August.

Accessed 20 miles west of Cody, the North Fork Shoshone River is a favorite among **white-water rafting** fans. A variety of wildlife, including elk and moose, are often seen from the river.

Try **Cody Area Central Reservations** (☎ 307-587-0200, 888-468-6996) for accommodation bookings. Built by ol' Mr Bill in 1902, **Irma Hotel** (☎ 307-587-4221, 800-745-4762; www.irmahotel.com; s/d from $70/75;) offers historic rooms in the main building and newer, more modern and less expensive motel-style rooms. A couple of the latter are wheelchair-accessible.

Pleasing **Gateway Campground** (☎ 307-587-2561; gateway@gatewaycamp.com; 203 Yellowstone Ave; campsites/RV sites $12/19, r & cabins $55-65;) has a nice range of accommodations: shady sites for camping, cozy cabins and motel rooms.

Maxwell's Fine Food & Spirits (☎ 307-527-7749; 937 Sheridan Ave; lunch $5-8, dinner mains $10-17; 11am-9pm Mon-Sat) has a comfortable interior devoid of trophy animal heads and a good selection of sandwiches, pasta, pizza and more; the vegetarians will do just fine here.

Yellowstone Regional Airport (☎ 307-587-5096; www.flyyra.com), 1 mile east of Cody, offers daily flights to Salt Lake City and Denver. **Powder River** (☎ 800-442-3682) buses stop at **Palmer's Outpost** (1521 Rumsey Ave) en route to Casper or Billings, Montana.

LANDER & AROUND

The small town of Lander, a stone's throw from the Wind River Indian Reservation, is a mixed bag of culture and people, from longtime ranchers to outdoors enthusiasts. The presence of the reputable National Outdoor Leadership School (NOLS) lends an interesting flavor and a college-town feel.

Explore your options at the **Lander visitors center** (☎ 307-332-3892, 800-433-0662; www.landerchamber.org; 160 N First St; 9am-5pm Mon-Fri) and the **USFS Shoshone National Forest Washakie District Ranger Station** (☎ 307-332-5460; 333 E Main St; 8am-4:30pm Mon-Fri), which has useful information on the **Popo Agie** (pah-*poh*-za) **Wilderness Area** and other backcountry.

Lander's location at the foot of the glaciated Wind River Range (comprising Wyoming's highest mountains) makes it a perfect base for **rock climbing** and **mountaineering**. The rugged areas around Lander are also reputed for **mountain biking**, **hiking** and **fishing**.

Wild Iris Mountain Sports (☎ 307-332-4541; 333 Main St) is the climbers' mecca, while cyclists and powder hounds head to **Freewheel Ski & Cycle** (☎ 307-332-6616; 378 W Main St).

Sinks Canyon State Park, 6 miles south of Lander on Sinks Canyon Rd (Hwy 131), is a beautiful park with perplexing natural features. The Middle Fork of the Popo Agie River flows through the narrow canyon, disappears into the soluble Madison limestone called the Sinks, and pops up faster and warmer 0.25 miles downstream in a pool called the Rise – what the water does underground is up for debate. The summer-only **visitors center** (☎ 307-332-3077; 3079 Sinks Canyon Rd; 9am-6pm summer) is near two scenic **campgrounds** (campsites $8).

For lodging, one of the better returns for your money is **Pronghorn Lodge** (☎ 307-332-3940; www.pronghornlodge.com; 150 Main St; s/d from $55/60;), a Budget Host hotel; it has faultless and spacious rooms and a hot tub. Its wheelchair-friendly room has a roll-in shower.

RESERVATION RADIO

In central Wyoming, home of the Wind River Indian Reservation, tune in to KWRR (89.5 FM) for music and talk-radio revolving around Native American issues. You might drop in on some Arapahoe music or even Shoshone-language lessons. The program **Native American Calling** (NAC; www.nativecalling.org) is a central feature that focuses on preserving and celebrating Native culture – its diverse topics touch upon activism, politics, current events, literature and music. Started by Native Koahnic Broadcast Corporation in Alaska, NAC is broadcast on over 60 stations on the continent, mostly in the western half of the USA. KWRR also broadcasts local news and National Public Radio (NPR) programs.

For something a little more personal, try B&B **Blue Spruce Inn** (☎ 307-332-8253; www.bluespruceinn.com; 677 S 3rd St; s/d $70/85;).

Camping is free (three-night maximum) at **Lander City Park** (☎ 307-332-4647; 405 Fremont St), but you can shower and use a hot tub if you tent up on the riverfront spots at **Holiday Lodge** (☎ 307-332-2511, 800-624-1974; 210 McFarlane Dr; campsites per person $8).

Pizza, sandwiches and salads go down well on the outdoor deck at **Gannett Grill** (☎ 307-332-8228; 126 Main St; meals $5-8), especially when the sun is out. Special kids' meals ($4.50) come with a toy.

Cowfish (☎ 307-333-8227; 148 Main St; mains $10-17) is a Western restaurant for the new millennium, serving a range of innovatively seasoned 'cows, pigs and chickens'; interesting seafood selections are also on offer.

For espresso, smoothies and truffles, chomp your sweet tooth into **Chocolates for Breakfast** (☎ 307-332-9273; 329 Main St).

Wind River Transportation Authority (☎ 307-856-7118, 800-439-7118; www.wrtabuslines.com) provides scheduled weekday service between Lander, Riverton, Dubois, Rock Springs and Riverton Regional Airport ($15).

YELLOWSTONE NATIONAL PARK

In addition to housing half the world's geysers, Yellowstone is also home to the highest concentration of wildlife in the lower mainland USA, and its copious alpine lakes, rivers and waterfalls have celebrity status. This natural cornucopia attracts up to 30,000 visitors daily and millions each year, and the park's extreme popularity is the single greatest threat to its environment. If you want to part ways with the friendly hordes, you're going to have to hike.

The park was established to preserve Yellowstone's spectacular and unique geography: the geothermal phenomena, the fossil forests and Yellowstone Lake. In 1807, when John Colter became the first white man to visit the area, the only inhabitants were Tukudikas, a Shoshone-Bannock people who hunted bighorn sheep. Colter's reports of the soaring geysers and boiling mud holes (at first dismissed as tall tales) brought in expeditions and interests, and it was designated the nation's first national park in 1872.

Orientation

Five distinct regions comprise the 3472-sq-mile park. Clockwise from the north, they include Mammoth Country, Roosevelt Country, Canyon Country, Lake Country and Geyser Country.

Of the park's five entrance stations, only the historic arched North Entrance, near Gardiner, Montana, is open year-round. The others, typically open May to October, are the Northeast Entrance (Cooke City, Montana), the East Entrance (Cody), the South Entrance (north of Grand Teton National Park) and the West Entrance (West Yellowstone, Montana). The park's main road is the 142-mile Grand Loop Rd scenic drive .

Information

Albright visitors center (☎ 307-344-2263; 8am-7pm summer, 9am-5pm winter)
National Park Service (www.nps.gov/yell; Visitor Services, Box 168, Yellowstone National Park, WY 82190)
Old Faithful visitors center (☎ 307-545-2750; 9am-7pm Apr-Oct & Dec-Mar)
Park headquarters (☎ 307-344-7381; Fort Yellowstone; 9am-6pm)
Xanterra Parks & Resorts (☎ 307-344-7311; www.travelyellowstone.com; Box 165, Yellowstone National Park, WY 82190) Concessionaire for activities, camping and accommodations.

The park is open year round, although some roads and entrances close during winter. Park entrance permits (hiker or cyclist $10, vehicle $20) are valid for seven

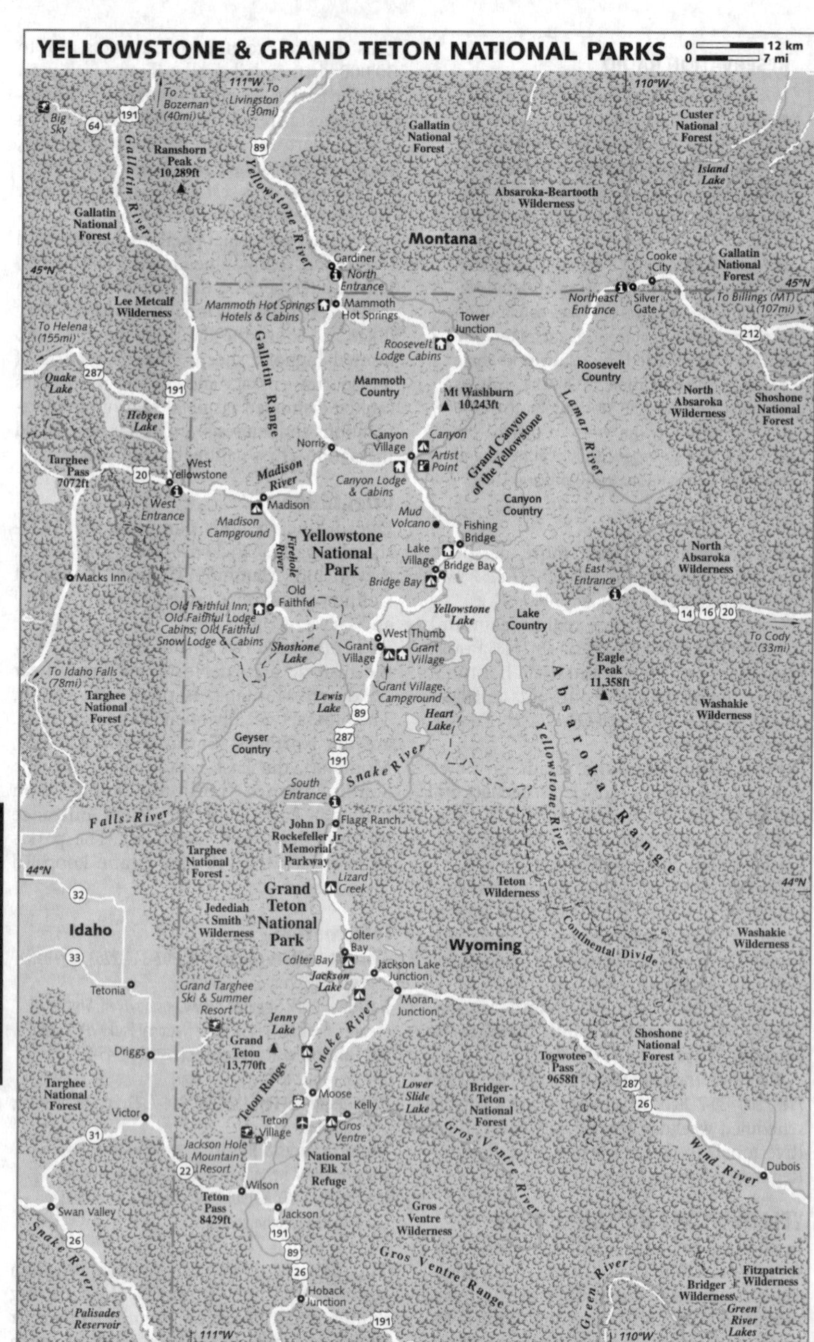
YELLOWSTONE & GRAND TETON NATIONAL PARKS
0 12 km
0 7 mi
Montana
Wyoming
Idaho
Yellowstone National Park
Grand Teton National Park
Gardiner
North Entrance
Mammoth Hot Springs
Mammoth Hot Springs Hotels & Cabins
Tower Junction
Roosevelt Lodge Cabins
Mt Washburn 10,243ft
Norris
Canyon Village
Canyon
Artist Point
Canyon Lodge & Cabins
Grand Canyon of the Yellowstone
West Yellowstone
West Entrance
Madison
Madison Campground
Mud Volcano
Fishing Bridge
Lake Village
Bridge Bay
Old Faithful
Old Faithful Inn; Old Faithful Lodge Cabins; Old Faithful Snow Lodge & Cabins
West Thumb
Grant Village
Grant Village Campground
Yellowstone Lake
East Entrance
Northeast Entrance
Silver Gate
Cooke City
South Entrance
Flagg Ranch
John D Rockefeller Jr Memorial Parkway
Lizard Creek
Colter Bay
Jackson Lake
Jackson Lake Junction
Moran Junction
Jenny Lake
Grand Teton 13,770ft
Moose
Kelly
Teton Village
Gros Ventre
Jackson Hole Mountain Resort
National Elk Refuge
Wilson
Jackson
Hoback Junction
Teton Pass 8429ft
Togwotee Pass 9658ft
Dubois
Macks Inn
Tetonia
Driggs
Victor
Swan Valley
Grand Targhee Ski & Summer Resort
Big Sky
Ramshorn Peak 10,289ft
Eagle Peak 11,358ft
Targhee Pass 7072ft
To Bozeman (40mi)
To Livingston (30mi)
To Helena (155mi)
To Billings (MT) (107mi)
To Cody (33mi)
To Idaho Falls (78mi)
Gallatin National Forest
Custer National Forest
Absaroka-Beartooth Wilderness
Lee Metcalf Wilderness
Targhee National Forest
Shoshone National Forest
North Absaroka Wilderness
Washakie Wilderness
Teton Wilderness
Jedediah Smith Wilderness
Bridger-Teton National Forest
Gros Ventre Wilderness
Bridger Wilderness
Fitzpatrick Wilderness
Mammoth Country
Roosevelt Country
Canyon Country
Lake Country
Geyser Country
Gallatin Range
Absaroka Range
Teton Range
Gros Ventre Range
Continental Divide
Gallatin River
Yellowstone River
Madison River
Firehole River
Lamar River
Snake River
Falls River
Gros Ventre River
Wind River
Green River
Quake Lake
Hebgen Lake
Island Lake
Shoshone Lake
Lewis Lake
Heart Lake
Lower Slide Lake
Palisades Reservoir
Green River Lakes
45°N
44°N
111°W
110°W

days for entry into both Yellowstone and Grand Teton National Parks.

A series of summer-only visitors centers are evenly spaced every 20 to 30 miles along Grand Loop Rd. Dial ☎ 307-344-2114 for current road and weather conditions.

Sights & Activities

Known for its fossil forests and geothermal areas at Mammoth Hot Springs and Norris Geyser Basin, **Mammoth Country** is North America's most volatile and oldest-known continuously active (115,000 years) geothermal area. The peaks of the Gallatin Range rise to the northwest, towering above the lakes, creeks and the area's numerous hiking trails.

Fossil forests, the commanding Lamar River Valley and its tributary trout streams, Tower Falls and the Absaroka Mountains' craggy peaks are the highlights of **Roosevelt Country**, the park's most remote, scenic and undeveloped region. Several good hikes begin near the Tower Junction.

A series of scenic overlooks and a network of the Grand Canyon of the Yellowstone rim trails highlight the beauty of **Canyon Country**. S Rim Dr leads to the canyon's most spectacular overlook, at Artist Point. Mud Volcano is Canyon Country's primary geothermal area. Notable trails include the Seven Mile Hole Trail, which descends from the north rim into the canyon and tracks up Mt Washburn, the park's highest peak (10,243ft).

Yellowstone Lake, the centerpiece of **Lake Country** and one of the world's largest alpine lakes, is also home to the country's largest inland population of cutthroat trout. The often-snowcapped Absaroka Mountains rise east and southeast of the lake.

Geyser Country has the most geothermal features in the park. Upper Geyser Basin contains 180 of the park's 200 to 250 geysers. The most famous is **Old Faithful**, which spews from 3700 to 8400 gallons of water 100ft to 180ft into the air every 1½ hours or so. The Firehole and Madison Rivers offer superb fishing and wildlife viewing.

Hikers can explore Yellowstone's backcountry from over 85 trailheads that give access to 1200 miles of **hiking** trails. A free backcountry use permit, available at visitors centers and ranger stations, is required for overnight trips. Backcountry camping is allowed in 300 designated sites, 60% of which can be reserved in advance by mail; a $20 fee applies regardless of the number of nights.

Cycling is best April to October, when the roads are usually snow-free. Cyclists can ride on public roads and a few designated service roads, but not on the backcountry trails.

Most park trails are not groomed, but unplowed roads and trails are open for **cross-country skiing**. The rapids of Yankee Jim Canyon on the Yellowstone River host **white-water-rafting** trippers. **Yellowstone Raft Company** (☎ 800-858-7781; www.yellowstoneraft.com) offers a range of guided adventures.

Sleeping & Eating

National Park Service (NPS) and private campgrounds, cabins, lodges and hotels are in the park. Reservations are strongly advised in summer. Contact park concessionaire Xanterra (see Info p765) to reserve a spot at its campsites, cabins or lodges.

Xanterra operates the five reservable campgrounds; campsites/RV sites are $17/23, except where noted:

Bridge Bay Campground (Lake Country) 431 sites.
Canyon Campground (Canyon Country) 272 sites.
Fishing Bridge RV Park (Lake Country; $31) 346 sites for hard-shell RVs.
Grant Village Campground (Lake Country) 425 sites.
Madison Campground (Geyser Country) 280 sites.

Seven other campgrounds, in Mammoth, Roosevelt and Geyser Countries, are operated by the National Park Service on a first-come, first-served basis (campsites $10 to $12, RV sites $23).

Most hotels and cabins that are operated by Xanterra are open May to October. Note that all rooms are nonsmoking and none have air-conditioning.

Canyon Lodge & Cabins (Canyon Country; cabins $40-115, r $135) ADA-compliant, including a roll-in shower.
Grant Village (Lake Country; r $95-110) ADA-compliant, including a roll-in shower.
Lake Lodge Cabins (Lake Country; cabins $55-115)
Lake Yellowstone Hotel & Cabins (Lake Country; cabins $85-115, r $170-410) Historic hotel with comfortable cabins and rooms in a stylish lodge. ADA-compliant, including a roll-in shower.
Mammoth Hot Springs Hotel & Cabins (Mammoth Country; cabins $60-90, r $70-280) Usefully located with a good variety of rooms.
Old Faithful Inn (Geyser Country; $75-350) Good variety of rooms.

Old Faithful Lodge Cabins (Geyser Country; $55-75) ADA-compliant, including a roll-in shower.
Old Faithful Snow Lodge & Cabins (Geyser Country; r $75-150)
Roosevelt Lodge Cabins (Roosevelt Country; $55-90) Pleasant cabins, good for families. ADA-compliant, including a roll-in shower.

Plentiful accommodations can be found in the gateway towns of Gardiner and West Yellowstone. For advice, contact the **West Yellowstone visitors center** (☎ 406-646-7701; www.westyellowstonechamber.com; Yellowstone Ave & Canyon St; 🕑 8am-5pm summer) or the **Gardiner visitors center** (☎ 406-848-7971; www.gardinerchamber.com; 222 Park St; 🕑 9am-5pm Mon-Fri summer).

In West Yellowstone, historic **Madison Motel** (☎ 406-646-7745, 800-838-7745; 139 Yellowstone Ave; dm $20, r $50-75;), open May to October, has rooms with or without bath; hostel rooms are on its 2nd floor, but there's no kitchen. A real gem, **Sleepy Hollow Lodge** (☎ 406-646-7707; www.sleepyhollowlodge.com; 124 Electric St; cabins $70-86) has small log cabins with kitchens; it has barbecue grills and picnic tables for use.

In Gardiner, a very good choice is **Hillcrest Cottages** (☎ 406-848-7353, 800-970-7353; www.hillcrestcottages.com; 200 Scott St; cottages $60-100;). The lovely little cottages come with kitchenettes, and one is wheelchair accessible with roll-in shower.

Snack bars, delis and grocery stores are scattered around the park. At Canyon Lodge, Lake Lodge, Old Faithful Lodge, Grant Village Lake House Restaurant, Mammoth Hot Springs Hotel and Roosevelt Lodge Dining Room, lunch is reasonably good value. Dinners are more upscale and require reservations at **Lake Yellowstone Hotel** (☎ 307-242-3899), **Old Faithful Inn** (☎ 307-545-4999) and **Grant Village** (☎ 307-242-3499).

Getting There & Away

Year-round airports are: Cody Airport (52 miles); Jackson Hole Airport (56 miles); Gallatin Field Airport (Bozeman, 65 miles); and Idaho Falls Regional Airport (107 miles) in Idaho. The airport in West Yellowstone, Montana, is usually open June to September. It's usually more affordable to fly into Salt Lake City, Utah (390 miles), or Denver, Colorado (563 miles) and rent a car.

No public transport exists to or within Yellowstone National Park. During the summer, commercial buses operate from Jackson and Cody. Buses operate to West Yellowstone and Gardiner from Bozeman year round.

GRAND TETON NATIONAL PARK

South of Yellowstone, the Teton Range's jagged granite spires are the marvel of spectacular Grand Teton National Park. Twelve glacier-carved summits rise above 12,000ft, crowned by the singular Grand Teton (13,770ft). This 40-mile-long range towers above Jackson Hole, where lakes and streams, including the nascent Snake River, mirror the soaring peaks.

Orientation & Information

The park has two entrance stations: Moose (south), on Teton Park Rd west of Moose Junction; and Moran (east), on US 89/191/287 north of Moran Junction.

The **Park headquarters** (☎ 307-739-3600; www.nps.gov/grte; Box 170, Moose, WY 83012; 🕑 8am-5pm, until 7pm summer) shares a building and hours with **Moose visitors center** (☎ 307-739-3399, for backcountry permits ☎ 307-739-3309; Teton Park Rd), half a mile west of Moose Junction. Summer-only visitors centers are at Jenny Lake and Colter Bay.

Three concessionaires operate accommodations, restaurants and activities:
Dornan's (☎ 307-733-2522; www.dornans.com)
Grand Teton Lodge Company (☎ 307-543-2811, 800-628-9988; www.gtlc.com)
Signal Mountain Lodge (☎ 307-543-2831, 800-672-6012; www.signalmtnlodge.com)

The park is open year round, although some roads and entrances close from around November to May 1, including part of Moose–Wilson Rd, restricting access to the park from Teton Village. Park entrance permits (hiker or cyclist $10, vehicle $20) are valid for seven days for entry into both Yellowstone and Grand Teton National Parks.

Sights & Activities

Interesting **historic buildings** can be found at Menor's Ferry, half a mile north of Moose Village, and along Mormon Row, east of Blacktail Butte.

The 5-mile **Signal Mountain Summit Rd**, east of Teton Park Rd, goes to Signal Mountain's summit; it's generally closed to vehicles in winter. Another nice route is the **Jenny Lake Scenic Loop Rd**, which abuts Grand Teton.

BRIGHTER DAYS FOR WOLVES

Gray wolves *(Canis lupus)*, the ultimate symbol of wilderness, have been making a comeback. Once strongly protected in Yellowstone Park, they were then deliberately eradicated, and then reintroduced in 1995 under considerable controversy. Since then, in a reintroduction program that the US Fish and Wildlife Service has deemed extremely successful, wolves have multiplied and, at time of writing, totaled over 120 in Yellowstone and Grand Teton Parks. In the Rocky Mountains, there are over 650 wolves in more than 40 packs.

Getting to this point wasn't easy. The reintroduction – using Canadian wolves – began when the National Park Service (NPS) recognized the need for a natural sustainable control regime. Ranchers in the surrounding area were predictably suspicious of reintroduction, claiming that the carnivore would attack livestock. The NPS and other authorities compromised: they revised the wolves' status from 'endangered' to 'threatened,' thereby giving ranchers the right to shoot any wolves attacking their livestock.

Biodiversity-focused **Defenders of Wildlife** (www.defenders.org), a self-proclaimed 'champion of wolves,' has worked extensively for the cause. It continues to reimburse ranchers for livestock depredation and rewards those who allow wolves to give birth and raise pups on their land.

The park has 200 miles of **hiking trails**; pick up maps at the visitors centers. A free backcountry use permit, available at visitors centers, is required for overnight trips, though reservations can be made by mail January to May by writing to park headquarters (see Orientation p768). The north-south **Teton Crest Trail**, which runs just west of the main summits, can be accessed from trailheads that wind up steep canyons. Several paths in the park are wheelchair accessible, including ones at Jenny Lake, Menor's Ferry and String Lake.

The Tetons offer great **rock climbing**. Excellent short routes abound, as well as classic longer summits like Grand Teton, Mt Moran and Mt Owen. The **Jenny Lake Ranger Station** (☎ 307-739-3343; 8am-6pm summer) is ground zero for climbing information. For instruction and guided climbs, contact **Exum Mountain Guides** (☎ 307-733-2297; www.exumguides.com) or **Jackson Hole Mountain Guides** (☎ 307-733-4979, 800-239-7642; www.jhmg.com).

Adventure Sports (☎ 307-733-3307), located at Dornan's Market in Moose Village, has maps, rents bikes and can suggest road- and mountain-biking routes.

Fishing is also a draw – whitefish and cutthroat, lake and brown trout thrive in park rivers and lakes. Get a license at the Moose Village store, Signal Mountain Lodge or Colter Bay Marina.

Cross-country skiing and **snowshoeing** are the best ways to take advantage of winter in the park. Pick up a brochure at Moose visitors center detailing routes.

Sleeping & Eating

The park features NPS campgrounds and private cabins, lodges and motels. Most campgrounds and accommodations are open May to October, weather depending.

The **NPS** (recorded information ☎ 307-739-3603) operates the park's only five **campgrounds** (campsites $12), all first-come, first-served:

Colter Bay Campground (Near Jackson Lake Junction) 350 sites.

Gros Ventre Campground (Near Gros Ventre Junction) 360 sites, 100 tent-only.

Jenny Lake Campground (Near Moose Junction) 49 tent-only sites.

Lizard Creek Campground (Near Colter Bay Junction) 60 sites.

Signal Mountain Campground (Near Jackson Lake Junction) 86 sites.

Demand for sites is high early July to Labor Day. Most campgrounds fill by 11am (Jenny Lake fills much earlier; Gros Ventre rarely fills up). Colter Bay and Jenny Lake have tent-only sites reserved for backpackers and cyclists.

Grand Teton Lodge Company runs **Colter Bay Village** (canvas tents $36, cabins $35-110), **Jackson Lake Lodge** (r $160-240) and the exclusive **Jenny Lake Lodge** (packages from $450).

Signal Mountain Lodge (cabins $95-140, r $120) sits along Jackson Lake, and Dornan's **Spur Ranch Log Cabins** (cabins $140-170, $40 less in winter) is in Moose. Contact the appropriate concessionaire (see p768) for reservations.

Several reasonably priced restaurants are in and around Colter Bay Village, Jackson

Lake Lodge and Moose Village. Jackson Lake Lodge's upscale **Mural Room** (☎ 307-543-1911; mains $20-30) and the **Jenny Lake Lodge Dining Room** (☎ 307-543-3352; 5-course meal per person $50) require dinner reservations and advise men to wear jackets.

JACKSON HOLE

Recreation generates the buzz of handsome Jackson Hole, Wyoming's most upscale destination. Though world-class downhill skiing dominates, summer visitors can hike, bike, raft and roam outdoors up the wazoo. Moose, elk and bison cruise the valley floor, set against the backdrop of the stellar Tetons.

For information, head to the **visitors center** (☎ 307-733-3316; www.jacksonholechamber.com; 532 N Cache Dr; 🕑 9am-5pm) and the **USFS Bridger-Teton National Forest Headquarters** (☎ 307-739-5500; 340 N Cache Dr; 🕑 8am-4:30pm Mon-Fri). A good website for area information is www.jacksonholenet.com. **Valley Bookstore** (☎ 307-733-4533; 125 N Cache St) has a superb selection of books as well as regional maps.

Orientation

The region known as Jackson Hole is a valley bounded by the Gros Ventre and Teton Ranges to the east and west, respectively. Most of the area's amenities are concentrated in the town of Jackson. Teton Village, 12 miles northwest of Jackson, is home to the wintertime mecca of Jackson Hole Mountain Resort.

Sights & Activities

From the 6311ft base at Teton Village to the summit of Rendezvous Mountain (10,450ft), **Jackson Hole Mountain Resort** (☎ 307-733-2292, 888-333-7766; www.jacksonhole.com; lift tickets adult $61, child 14 & under $31), known as 'the Village,' boasts the USA's greatest continuous vertical rise and is one of the country's top ski destinations, with mostly advanced terrain. The resort also offers hiking, aerial tram rides ($15), mountain biking and horseback riding.

Right in town, the year-round 400-acre **Snow King Resort** (☎ 307-733-5200, 800-522-5464; www.snowking.com; lift tickets adult/child $32/22) offers a two-hour ski lift ticket for $15. In winter you can also go **tubing** (☎ 307-734-8823) and **ice skating** (☎ 307-734-3000). And when the snow melts, you can ride horses, mountain bike or ride the summer scenic chairlift.

Downtown Jackson has a handful of **historic buildings** and, in summer, a re-enactment of a **Town Square shoot-out** from Monday to Saturday starting at 6:15pm. For more substance, visit the **National Elk Refuge** (☎ 307-733-9212), northeast of Jackson via Elk Refuge Rd, which offers winter sleigh rides, or the **National Museum of Wildlife Art** (☎ 307-733-5771; www.wildlifeart.org; 2820 Rungius Rd; adult $8, child 6-18 $7; 🕑 9am-5pm), 3 miles north of town.

Sleeping

Reservations are essential in summer and winter. Cheap weekly rates are available October 1 until the first big snowfall, and from the beginning of April to Memorial Day weekend, though some hotels shut down at this time. **Jackson Hole Central Reservations** (☎ 800-443-6931) is the one-stop shop for lodgings.

Bunkhouse (☎ 307-733-3668; www.anvilmotel.com/bunkhouse; 215 N Cache Dr; dm $22) This basement-level hostel has clean dorm beds and a common kitchen. Hostelers can use the hot tub in the attached motel, and nonguests can use showers for $5.

Virginian Lodge (☎ 307-733-2792, 800-262-4999; 750 W Broadway; r winter/summer $55/95;) Sprawling but welcoming, it has orderly rooms, a pool, hot tub, a smoky saloon as swinging as its doors and a liquor store with a drive-up window. Its wheelchair-friendly rooms have roll-in shower.

Also recommended is **Sundance Inn** (☎ 307-733-3444, 888-478-6326; www.sundanceinnjackson.com; 135 W Broadway; r winter/summer from $50/95).

Wagon Wheel Village (☎ 307-733-4588; www.wagonwheelvillage.com; 435 N Cache Dr; campsites/RV sites $24/45) Wagon Wheel has tight creekside campsites that encourage getting to know your neighbor. The closest USFS campground is first-come, first-served **Curtis Canyon** (campsites $12), just east of the Elk Refuge off USFS Rd 30440.

Hostel X (☎ 307-733-3415; www.hostelx.com; d/quad $50/63) Teton Village's only budget option is this relaxed place, which has basic rooms with bath and a common room loaded with entertainment. There's a five-night minimum in winter; reservations are advised.

Snake River Lodge (☎ 307-732-6000, 800-445-4655; www.snakeriverlodge.com; 7710 Granite Loop Rd; r summer/winter from $170/200;) Gorgeously situated at the bottom of Jackson Hole Mountain Resort, it has beautiful pool and spa facilities, a fitness room with a view and fully stocked comfortable rooms.

Eating

Jackson is home to Wyoming's most sophisticated grub.

Harvest Bakery & Cafe (☎ 307-733-5418; 130 W Broadway; dishes $3-7) This natural foods store – filled with organic produce, fresh breads and baked goods – serves up wholesome soups, sandwiches and smoothies from its café.

Bubba's Bar-B-Que (☎ 307-733-2288; 515 W Broadway; meals $5-12) The biggest, fluffiest biscuits for miles are served for breakfast at this friendly and energetic eatery. Later in the day, it serves a range of ribs and racks.

Snake River Grill (☎ 307-733-0557; 84 E Broadway; mains $18-28; 🕑 from 6pm) Locally adored for its gourmet offerings, this place isn't afraid to get creative. There's much seafood on offer, and the chicken is free-range – little for the vegetarian, though.

Rendevous Bistro (☎ 307-739-1100; 380 S Broadway; mains $13-18) Near the Albertson's center, this bustling bistro hosts lots of chattering locals in its smart interior. It's made slicker with flavorful fare that spans the continents.

Also good is **Nora's Fish Creek Inn** (☎ 307-733-8288; breakfast $5-9, mains $8-16) in Wilson.

Drinking

Like all resort towns with a gleaming bunch of seasonal workers and play-hard visitors, Jackson has an animated nightlife revolving around many rounds of drink.

Stagecoach Bar (☎ 307-733-4407; 5755 W Hwy 22, Wilson) This bar is worth the 5-mile drive from Jackson, particularly on Sunday nights when the famous Stagecoach Band recites country favorites. Herb tokers and cowpokers mingle here more than any other place in the Wild West. Horse parking is available outside.

Visitors should at least drop in (if briefly) to the entertaining landmark **Million Dollar Cowboy Bar** (☎ 307-733-2207; 25 N Cache Dr) and the **Silver Dollar Bar** (☎ 307-732-3939; cnr Glenwood St & Broadway); a bluegrass band plays at the latter most nights. The beer's better than the grub at **Snake River Brewing Co** (☎ 307-739-2337; 265 S Millward St), popular with the local ski crowd.

Getting There & Around

Jackson Hole Airport (☎ 307-733-7682) is 7 miles north of Jackson off US 26/89/191 within Grand Teton National Park. Daily flights serve Denver, Salt Lake City, Dallas and Houston, while weekend flights connect Jackson with Chicago. **Jackson Hole Express** (☎ 307-733-1719, 800-652-9510; www.jacksonholebus.com) buses shuttle daily between Salt Lake City and Jackson, via Idaho Falls ($55, 5½ hours). The Jackson depot is the Country Store/Exxon Station on the corner of Hwy 89 S and S Park Loop Rd. **Southern Teton Area Rapid Transit** (☎ 307-733-4521; www.startbus.com) runs between Jackson and Teton Village.

MONTANA

With its feet firmly planted on mountains and plains, and its head in the clouds of a big sky, Montana is the kind of place that, once you've visited, remains alive in nostalgia. The 'live and let live' state, immersed in beautiful wilds, has a sparsely populated countryside, though those bitten by the bug – artists, writers, real-estate developers, students and movie stars – have been trickling in ever more rapidly.

Visitors to the state will find that even the biggest draws, Glacier National Park and Flathead Lake, offer quiet beauty and opportunities for remote exploration. Montana – from *montaña* (Spanish for 'mountain') – has ranges aplenty that beckon backcountry adventurers, and anglers will be keen on the trout-filled rivers, including those outside Yellowstone Park.

Once you've seen more forest than you can shake a ponderosa pine at, the state's interesting towns will provide amusement and education. Old mining hotspots like Butte are chock full of history, as are sites like Battle of the Little Bighorn, where Custer made his infamous last stand.

History

If these lands could talk: Montana has seen many a historical conflict between white settlers and Native American tribes, including battles of the Big Hole and Rosebud. The gold frenzy hit in 1863, with a discovery near Bannack. Marcus Daly struck the world's largest and purest copper vein in Butte, which was mined for the next 100 years.

In 1889, Montana became the 41st state of the Union. Though tourism began to sweep through the Rockies in the late 19th century, the boom didn't really hit Montana

MONTANA FACTS

Nickname The Treasure State
Population 909,500 (44th)
Area 147,045 sq miles (4th)
Admitted to Union November 8, 1889 (41st)
Capital city Helena (population 29,100)
Other cities Billings (92,300), Missoula (58,500)
State fossil Duck-billed dinosaur
Birthplace of Evel Knieval (b 1938), legendary motorcycle daredevil; Gary Cooper (1901-1961), Hollywood star of 1930s to '50s
Famous for big sky, fly-fishable rivers, snow, rodeos, bears

until the 1980s. Now, the state's attractions support the economy. The tourism industry has yet to prove completely reliable, though, as was shown by the forest fires of summer 2003. The blazes in northwest Montana affected thousands of acres as well as the local economy.

Getting There & Around

See p731 for bus and train lines that run through Montana. There are airports in Bozeman, Billings, Helena, Missoula and near Glacier Park. Cars can be rented at airports and in larger cities.

BOZEMAN

Bozeman's small-town agricultural roots have sprouted a vibrant, fast growing hub, where farmers and ranchers pass hip college students and boutique shops on the sidewalks lining Main St. At the foot of the Bridger Mountains, Bozeman is also a natural beauty. The **visitors center** (☎ 406-586-5421, 800-228-4224; www.bozemanchamber.com; 1003 N 7th Ave; 8am-5pm Mon-Fri) has information on sites.

Montana State University's **Museum of the Rockies** (☎ 406-994-2251; www.museumoftherockies.org; 600 W Kagy Blvd; adult/child museum $7/4, with planetarium $9/6.50; 8am-8pm summer, 9am-5pm Mon-Sat, 12:30pm-5pm Sun winter) is the most entertaining natural-history museum in Montana, with dinosaur exhibits, early Native American art and laser shows. The planetarium shows can be fascinating for adults and children, and there are special summer programs for kids.

South of town, Hyalite Canyon is great for **climbing**, **trail running** and **mountain biking**. North of town, the Bridger Mountains offer excellent hiking and skiing at **Bridger Bowl Ski Area** (☎ 406-587-2111; 15795 Bridger Canyon Rd; www.bridgerbowl.com) and **Bohart Ranch Cross-Country Ski Center** (☎ 406-586-9070; 16621 Bridger Canyon Rd).

Barrel Mountaineering (☎ 406-582-1335; 240 E Main St) has maps, trail guides and gear rentals.

Sleeping & Eating

The full gamut of chain motels lies north of downtown on 7th Ave, near I-90. There are also a few options east of downtown on Main St.

Voss Inn (☎ 406-587-0982; www.bozeman-vossinn.com; 319 S Wilson; d/tr from $105/125) This restored brick mansion circa 1883 has six pretty rooms. The 1st-floor room is large enough for visitors in wheelchairs, but assistance would be needed to get into the house.

Bozeman Backpacker's Hostel (☎ 406-586-4659; 405 W Olive St; dm/r $14/32) This independent hostel's casual approach means a relaxed ambience, friendly folk and no lockout – but also wavering cleanliness and uncomfortable beds. It's *the* place to meet active international travelers.

Lewis & Clark Motel (☎/fax 406-586-3341, 800-332-7666; www.lewisandclarkmotel.net; 824 W Main St; s/d $60/70) For a drop of Vegas in your Montana, stay at this flashy motel with casino games and cold beers in the lobby. The large rooms have floor-to-ceiling front windows, and there's a pool, Jacuzzi and sauna on-site.

Bear Canyon Campground (☎ 800-438-1575; www.bearcanyoncampground.com; campsites $15, RV sites $20-25) Three miles east of Bozeman off I-90 exit 313, Bear Canyon Campground is open May through October.

Community Food Co-Op (☎ 406-587-4039; 908 W Main St) The co-op has all the fixings for a splendid meal, plus a deli ($3 to $6). Head to the second floor café for gorgeous desserts, accompanied by fair-trade coffee and mountain views. Some nights live music is on.

Cateye Café (☎ 406-587-8844; 23 N Tracy Ave; meals $5-8; 7am-2:30pm Wed-Mon, 7:30am-2pm Sat & Sun) Many heaping hot plates of eggs and more are served up here in the morning, though vegans can chew happily, too. And why not try a mimosa ($2.75)?

Other goodies are the **Montana Ale Works** (☎ 406-587-7700; 611 E Main St; mains $7-17) and **John Bozeman's Bistro** (☎ 406-537-4100; 125 W Main St; lunch $10-12, dinner mains $15-25).

Getting There & Away

The **Gallatin Airport** (☎ 406-388-6632), 8 miles northwest of downtown, has flights to Salt Lake City, Seattle, Denver and Minneapolis. Greyhound and Rimrock Trailways depart from the **bus depot** (☎ 406-587-3110; 1205 E Main St), half a mile from downtown, and service all Montana towns along I-90. **Karst Stage** (☎ 406-388-2293, 800-287-4759; www.karststage.com) runs buses daily, December to April, from the airport to Big Sky ($27, one hour) and West Yellowstone ($37, two hours); summer service is by reservation only.

GALLATIN & PARADISE VALLEYS

Within the expanse of beauty around the Gallatin River, hikers and skiers can explore for days. **Big Sky** (☎ 800-548-4486; www.bigskyresort.com; lift tickets adult $60, child 11-17 $45), with three mountains, is the valley's foremost destination for skiing; it has the longest vertical drop in Montana (4350ft). In summer, it offers gondola-served hiking and mountain biking. For backpacking and backcountry skiing, head to the **Lee Metcalf Wilderness Complex**, which covers 389 sq miles of Gallatin and Beaverhead National Forest land west of US 191. Numerous scenic USFS campgrounds snuggle up to the Gallatin Range on the east side of US 191.

Fisherfolk will prefer to tie their blue ribbon round Paradise Valley, full of **fishing** access sites to the river's edge. Rafts, kayaks and canoes take to the river June to August.

Twenty miles south of Livingston, **Chico Hot Springs** (☎ 406-333-4933; www.chicohotsprings.com; r from $50, pool for nonguests $6;) was established in 1900. The place is unpretentiously suave and restored with great attention to rustic detail; it has one large pool for soaking. Its restaurant (mains $20 to $30) is renowned the region over for fine steak and seafood fare.

BILLINGS

Montana's largest city is a friendly ranching and oil center with city conveniences but little stress. Though it's not an absolute must-see in and of itself, it's a worthwhile place to break your journey. Cultural sites worth visiting include the **Yellowstone Art Museum** (☎ 406-256-6804; 401 N 27th St; adult/child $7/5; 10am-5pm Tue-Sat), which has the largest publicly held Will James collection, as well as a diverse range of Western art, and the small but interesting **Western Heritage Center** (☎ 406-256-6809; 2822 Montana Ave; admission free; 10am-5pm Tue-Sat).

Fun Adventures Tours (☎ 406-254-7180, 888-618-4386; www.montanafunadventures.com) runs 1½-hour **historic tours** (adult/child $20/8) of Billings by trolley in the summer.

Ask the **visitors center** (☎ 406-245-4111, 800-735-2635; www.billingscvb.visitmt.com; 8:30am-6pm Mon-Sat, 10am-4pm Sun summer, 8:30am-5pm Mon-Fri winter) about **hiking trails** in the area.

For budget accommodations, the welcoming **Big 5 Motel** (☎ 406-245-6646, 888-544-9358; s/d $31/36; P) is a good bet – it has a convenient location and tidy rooms.

Billings Inn (☎ 406-252-6800, 800-231-7782; www.billingsinn.com; s/d from $55/60; P) has comfortable rooms with a continental breakfast in the morning and popcorn at night. Request one with fridge and microwave, if you want those amenities. There's one fully wheelchair-accessible room.

Wake up at the chipper **McCormick Cafe** (☎ 406-255-9555; 2419 Montana Ave; meals $4-7; 7am-4pm Mon-Fri, 8am-3pm Sat;), where you can get your coffee and hot and cold breakfasts. Soups, salads and pizza are on at lunch.

Finally, Guinness on tap (!) at **Pug Mahon's** (☎ 406-259-4190; 3011 1st Ave N; lunch & brunch $6-8, dinner $9-15), a friendly Irish pub with good food, great beer, and a Sunday champagne brunch that brings in the crowds.

Logan International Airport (☎ 406-238-3420), 2 miles north of downtown, is served by direct flights to Salt Lake City, Denver, Minneapolis, Seattle, Phoenix and destinations within Montana. The **bus depot** (☎ 406-245-5116; 2502 1st Ave N; 24hr) has services to Bozeman ($27, three hours), Butte ($40, five hours), Missoula ($53, eight hours), Denver, Portland and Seattle. **Billings Metropolitan Transit System** (☎ 406-657-8218; 75 cents; 8am-5pm Mon-Fri) provides service in the city Monday to Saturday. **Billings Area City Cab** (☎ 406-252-8700) and **Billings Area Yellow Cab** (☎ 406-245-3033) run 24 hours.

ABSAROKA BEARTOOTH WILDERNESS

The vista-packed Absaroka Beartooth Wilderness – stretching over 943,377 acres – saddles up next to Paradise Valley in the west and Yellowstone National Park in the south. The thickly forested Absaroka Range dominates the area's west half and is most easily reached from Paradise Valley or the Boulder River Corridor. The Beartooth Range's jagged peaks and Alpine tundra are best reached from Hwy 78 and US 212 near Red Lodge. Because of its proximity to Yellowstone, the Beartooth portion gets two-thirds of the area's traffic. But there is a plethora of uncrowded alpine wonder to be experience in the rugged interior.

A picturesque old mining town with fun bars and restaurants and a good range of places to stay, **Red Lodge** is rich with options for day hiking, backpacking and, in winter, skiing right near town. The **Red Lodge visitors center** (☎ 406-446-1718; 601 N Broadway Ave; 🕑 9am-5pm summer, 9:30am-4:30pm Mon-Fri winter) has accommodation information, while the **Beartooth Ranger Station** (☎ 406-446-2103; 6811 Hwy 212 S; 🕑 8am-4:30pm Mon-Fri), about a mile south of Red Lodge, has maps and information.

The **Beartooth Highway** (US 212; open June to mid-October) connects Red Lodge to Cooke City and Yellowstone's north entrance by an incredible 68-mile journey that passes soaring peaks and the wildflower-sprinkled tundra. Within 12 miles of Red Lodge along the highway are six USFS campgrounds; five are reservable.

LITTLE BIGHORN BATTLEFIELD

Ensconced within the boundless prairies and pine-covered hills of Montana's southwest Plains, the Crow Indian Reservation holds the famous **Little Bighorn Battlefield National Monument** ($10 per car; 🕑 8am-6pm). This is where General George Custer made his infamous 'last stand' and where many other clashes between Native Americans and the US Cavalry occurred. At time of writing, a long-awaited Indian Memorial was to be dedicated.

The monument's **visitors center** (☎ 406-638-3224) is worth visiting for its intriguing displays, videos, books and maps. Beyond the visitors center, the battlefield is best visited by car, though there are also three short walking trails. The entrance is 1 mile east of I-90 on US 212. **Hardin**, the area's hub and the only major service center around, has a few motels and restaurants.

BUTTE

With a skyline of massive mining headframes and a plethora of vacant ornate buildings, Butte feels almost lost in time. Though more staid nowadays than in its late-19th-century boom times, fascinating Butte still carries an air of historical and political intrigue that is significant beyond the development of Montana's other cities. Get a walking tour map of Uptown Butte, one of the USA's largest **historic districts**, from the **visitors center** (☎ 406-723-3177, 800-735-6814; www.butteinfo.org; 1000 George St; 🕑 8am-8pm summer, 9am-5pm Mon-Fri winter), north of I-15/I-90, or just stroll along Granite, Broadway and Park Sts and read the National Register of Historic Places plaques.

The **Mineral Museum** (☎ 406-496-4414; 1300 W Park St; free; 🕑 9am-6pm summer, 9am-4pm winter), on the Montana Tech campus, is more than just a bunch of rocks. It has extensive and impressive displays of minerals, including 'Big Daddy,' the largest quartz crystal ever found in Montana. Nearby, the **World Museum of Mining** (☎ 406-723-7211; 155 Museum Way; adult/child $7/5; 🕑 9am-5:30pm Apr-Oct) will keep you exploring its interesting exhibits and replica of an old mining town for a good hour or two.

Historic **Finlen Hotel & Motor Inn** (☎ 406-723-5461, 800-729-5461; www.finlen.com; 100 E Broadway; s/d $50/60) has a friendly staff and big, well-maintained rooms (request one with a view) in its hotel. It also has an elevator and a couple of rooms with wheelchair-accessible bath. They do offer motel rooms.

Another fine place to rest your sleepy head is the **Scott Inn** (☎ 406-723-7030, 800-844-2952; www.scottinn.com; 15 W Copper; r $75-85), once a boarding house for local miners. It's now a friendly B&B with seven snug rooms and a balcony with pleasing views of town.

Butte KOA (☎ 406-782-8080; campsites $18, RV sites $20-30) is near I-90 exit 126.

The lingering aroma and intimate yet festive atmosphere at **Spaghettini's** (☎ 406-782-8855; 26 N Main; mains $10-17) will transport you from Butte into a quaint Italian trattoria. A diverse range of pastas, polenta etc is served, and there's oodles for the vegetarian.

Dining 'institutions' include **Gamer's** (☎ 406-723-5453; 15 W Park St; dishes $4-7), with OK American fare, and **Pekin Noodle Parlor** (☎ 406-782-2217; 117 S Main St; dishes $5-10), whose garish pink walls and dining cabins are more interesting than its food.

Rimrock Bus and Greyhound use Butte's **bus depot** (☎ 406-723-3287; 103 E Front St; 🕑 8am-8pm Mon-Fri, 8am-noon & 5-8pm Sat & Sun) en route to Bozeman, Dillon, Missoula and Helena.

HELENA

The state capital Helena is an agreeable city with a hint of hustle-bustle due to its businessfolk and politicians.

For information, visit the following:

Helena visitors center (☎ 406-442-4120, 800-743-5362; www.helenachamber.com; 225 Cruse Ave; ⏲ 8am-5pm Mon-Fri)

Summer-only visitors center (☎ 406-447-1540; 2003 Cedar St; ⏲ 9am-5pm)

Helena National Forest Ranger District (☎ 406-449-5490; 2001 Poplar St; ⏲ 7:30am-6pm Mon-Fri, 8:30am-5pm Sat summer, 7:30am-5pm Mon-Fri winter)

Aunt Bonnie's Books (☎ 406-443-3093; 419 N Last Chance Gulch) has a good range of new and used books, particularly with regard to Western and Native American titles, though kids will prefer the **Montana Book & Toy Co** (☎ 406-443-0260; 331 N Last Chance Gulch), which has a whole floor of books (and toys) for the younger set.

Many of Helena's sites of interest to visitors are free, including the neoclassical **State Capitol** (☎ 406-444-4789; ⏲ 8am-6pm Mon-Fri), the elegant old buildings along Last Chance Gulch (Helena's pedestrian shopping district) and the **Holter Museum of Art** (☎ 406-442-6400; 12 E Lawrence; ⏲ 10am-5pm Mon-Sat summer, 11:30am-5pm Tue-Fri, noon-5pm Sat & Sun winter) which exhibits modern pieces by Montana artists and usually has some excellent temporary exhibits.

For something perhaps unexpected, visit **Kumamoto Plaza** (☎ 406-449-7904; 34 N Last Chance Gulch; admission free; ⏲ 9am-5pm), a small Japanese-arts gallery and cultural center born of links between Montana and its sister state, Kumamoto, Japan. Self-guided tours can be taken during the day of the **Archie Bray Foundation** (☎ 406-443-3502; 2915 Country Club Ave; admission free), one of the nation's top training grounds for ceramics and pottery artists. In summer a **tour train** (☎ 406-442-1023; adult $5, child under 13 $4) leaves from the Montana Historical Society, near the capitol, and circles the Last Chance Gulch area.

Mt Helena City Park has **hiking** and **mountain biking** trails that wind around the base and to a 5460ft-high summit with great views.

East of downtown near I-15 is a string of chain motels – most have free continental breakfast, pool and Jacuzzi for $60-85.

Jorgenson's Inn & Suites (☎ 406-442-1770, 800-277-1770; 1714 11th Ave; s/d $70/80; P ❄ ✕), though it may not ooze with personality, is a good mid-range choice with modern, well-equipped rooms and a restaurant/lounge. One fully wheelchair-accessible room is on the first floor.

Conveniently located to downtown, **Helena Inn** (☎ 406-442-6080, 877-387-0102; fax 449-4131; 910 Last Chance Gulch; s/d $36/45; P ❄ ✕) is cheaper.

A beautiful B&B, **The Sanders** (☎ 406-442-3309; 328 N Ewing St; www.sandersbb.com; s/d from $85/95; P ❄) boasts exquisite vintage furnishings, much of it from the original owners in the late 19th century. The thoughtfully decorated rooms make it a real gem.

Fire Tower Coffee House (☎ 406-495-8840; 422 Last Chance Gulch; 💻) is where to get coffee, light meals and sometimes live music on Friday evenings. **No Sweat Café** (☎ 406-442-6954; 427 N Last Chance Gulch; meals $4-7; ⏲ 7am-2pm Tue-Fri, 8am-2pm Sat & Sun) is a feel-good spot with art-lined walls and mostly organic hearty egg dishes, sandwiches and Mexican fare; the juice is very fresh.

Also good, but for beer and food, is **Bert & Ernie's** (☎ 406-443-5680; 361 N Last Chance Gulch; lunch $6-8, dinner $13-16).

Helena Regional Airport (☎ 406-442-2821; www.helenaairport.com), 2 miles north of downtown, operates flights to most other airports in Montana, Salt Lake City, Spokane and Minneapolis. Rimrock Stages services Helena's **bus depot** (☎ 406-442-5860; 3100 E Hwy 12; ⏲ 7:30am-8:30pm Mon-Fri, 7:30am-9am & 4-8:30pm Sat & Sun), 7 miles east of town on US 12, where buses go to Missoula ($21, 2¼ hours), Billings ($37, 4¾ hours), Bozeman ($18, two hours), as well as Butte and Great Falls. **Taxis** (☎ 406-449-5525) run from the depot to downtown ($7).

MISSOULA

Locals joke that Missoula has ten months of winter and two months of relatives. Its climate is actually milder than that of the much of Montana, but visitors do thrive in this very enjoyable town. It boasts a few good local sites, and the University of Montana adds a cultural vein. And it's an outdoor playland: The Rattlesnake Recreation Area is spittin' distance from town, the Bitterroot Range spans its western edge and the Clark Fork River courses right through it.

For maps and information, contact:

Visitors center (☎ 406-532-3250, 800-526-3465; www.missoulacvb.org; 1121 E Broadway; ⏲ 8am-5pm Mon-Fri)

Trail Head (☎ 406-543-6966; 110 E Pine St) Also rents out camping, rafting and kayaking gear.

USFS Northern Region Headquarters (☎ 406-329-3511; 200 E Broadway; 🕑 8:30am-4:30pm Mon-Fri)

Radio listeners can tune to University of Montana stations KUFM (89.1 FM) and KUKL (89.9 FM) for National Public Radio (NPR) and Public Radio International (PRI) broadcasts. Both also feature local news and a variety of nonmainstream music.

Sights & Activities

One of the most accessible **hikes** around is along the south side of Clark Fork from McCormick Park (west of the Orange St bridge) back into Hellgate Canyon. Ascend the steep Mt Sentinel Trail (about a mile past the university) to reach Mt Sentinel's 5158ft summit.

Advanced skiers like **Snowbowl Ski Area** (☎ 406-549-9777; www.montanasnowbowl.com; lift tickets adult $31, child 6-12 $14), 17 miles north of Missoula, for its 2600ft vertical drop. **10,000 Waves** (☎ 406-549-6670, 800-537-8315) offers a range of **rafting** and **kayaking** trips on the Class III and IV rapids of Alberton Gorge (of the Clark Fork River) or on the gentler Blackfoot River; they also run scenic trips on the Blackfoot and Bitterroot Rivers.

In town, the **Art Museum of Missoula** (☎ 406-728-0447; 335 N Pattee St; admission free; 🕑 10am-7pm Tue, 10am-6pm Wed-Fri, 10am-4pm Sat) is well worth a visit for its contemporary exhibits and installations that tend toward fascinating. Children will be delighted with **A Carousel for Missoula** (☎ 406-549-8382; 1 Caras Park; adult/child $1/50 cents; 🕑 11am-7pm summer, until 5:30pm winter), near the river, a hand-carved carousel aflutter with people on ponyback.

Sleeping & Eating

Most lodging is on Broadway between Van Buren and Orange Sts, within walking distance to the campus and downtown.

Goldsmith's Bed & Breakfast (☎ 406-728-1585, 866-666-9945; www.goldsmithsinn.com; 809 E Front St; s/d from $70/80; P ⊠) This delightful B&B, with comfy rooms, is a pebble's toss from the river – absorbing a novel from the overlooking deck will take you leap years from Missoula's traffic. It's also just a footbridge away from the university.

Campus Inn (☎ 406-549-5134, 800-232-8013; www.campusinnmissoula.com; 744 E Broadway; s/d $60/70; P ⊠ ♿) A great choice in this price range, it has pleasant spacious rooms with ample amenities. Some rooms are inside the main building, while others are motel-style, and one room is fully wheelchair-accessible.

City Center Motel (☎ 406-543-3193; 338 E Broadway; s/d $38/42; P ⊠) With a subtle Western touch, ie a swinging wooden door to the bath, this motel is good value. Its comfortable rooms come with fridge and microwave. **Creekside Inn** (☎ 406-549-2387, 800-551-2387; 630 E Broadway; s/d $45/55; P ⊠ ♿) is also recommended.

Tipu's (☎ 406-542-0622; 1151/2 S 4th St; mains $6-12) Missoula's only all-vegetarian restaurant makes one rich and flavorful chai (dairy or soy). Its food is tasty and filling – pick out one of their fresh chutneys for accompaniment. The lunch buffet is $7.

Hob Nob (☎ 406-542-3188; 208 E Main St; mains $7-14) In the back of the busy Union Club bar, this softly lit restaurant serves comforting foods like meatloaf and seafood stew, as well as some interesting twists à la penne spiked with vodka.

Go to **Bernice's Bakery** (☎ 406-728-1358; 190 S 3rd St; 🕑 6am-10pm Sun-Thu, 6am-11pm Fri-Sat) for coffee and toothsome sweets and **Food For Thought** (☎ 406-721-6033; 540 Daly Ave; mains $4-7), across from University of Montana, for good-value healthy food.

Drinking & Entertainment

Missoula's barstools are warm with beer-guzzlers nightly. For live music, see the *Independent* or the Entertainment section of Friday's *Missoulian* for what's on.

Iron Horse Brewpub (☎ 406-728-8866; 501 N Higgins) Near the north end of Higgins Ave, this upbeat pub favored by the student crowd offers plenty of places to sit and sip, including outdoor patio seats.

Top Hat (☎ 406-728-9865; 134 W Front St) Fun bluegrass, blues and rock bands get this big, open space moving at night. Pool and table tennis are available for amusement as well.

Old Post (☎ 406-721-7399; 103 W Spruce St) This cozy wood-walled number draws in crowds for its drink and food (including sandwiches and Southwestern fare). Jazz and blues bands saunter in on Thursday and Friday nights.

Jay's Bar (☎ 406-728-9915; 119 W Main St) A smoky venue that has punk bands.

Sean Kelly's (☎ 406-542-1471; 130 W Pine St) Often packed and has sports on the TV.

For recent cinema releases, check the schedule at **Carmike Cinemas** (☎ 406-541-7469; 3640 Mullan Rd; adult $7, child under 12 $4.50) and

Village 6 (☎ 406-541-7469; 3804 S Reserve; adult $6.50, child under 12 $4). The **Wilma Theatre** (☎ 406-728-2521; 131 S Higgins; adult $7, child under 15 $4) screens independent, art-house and foreign films.

Getting There & Around

Missoula County International Airport (☎ 406-728-4381), 5 miles west of Missoula on US 12 W, has flights to Kalispell, Seattle, Portland, Salt Lake City, Boise, Denver and Minneapolis.

Greyhound buses arrive and depart from the **bus depot** (☎ 406-549-2339; 1660 W Broadway), 1 mile west of town. Daily departures include Kalispell, Whitefish, Helena, Bozeman, Butte and Billings.

The free **Emerald Line Trolley** makes a full loop downtown every 20 minutes, weekdays until 4pm. Mountain Line Buses depart from the **transfer center** (☎ 406-721-3333; 200 W Pine St); bus No 10 goes to the Greyhound station and, upon request, the airport.

BITTERROOT VALLEY

Contoured with dramatic canyons the Bitterroot Range is full of wonderful hiking, fishing and skiing. East Side Rd – the scenic route known as the 'back road' – is parallel to Hwy 93 and offers a glimpse of the Bitterroot's agricultural soul and leads to a few historical sites, including **St Mary's Mission** (☎ 406-777-5734; 315 Charlos St, Stevensville; adult/child $3/1; 🕑 10am-5pm summer, 10am-4pm Mon-Sat, 10am-2pm Sun winter) and the 24-bedroom **Marcus Daly Mansion** (☎ 406-363-6004; 251 East Side Rd, Hamilton; adult $6, child over 4 $3; 🕑 10am-5pm mid-Apr–mid-Oct).

About halfway down the valley in Hamilton, the **Bitterroot visitors center** (☎ 406-363-2400; 105 E Main; 🕑 8am-6pm Mon-Fri summer, 8am-5pm winter) can provide information on accommodations, and the **Forest Supervisor's Office** (☎ 406-363-7117; 🕑 8:30am-4:30pm Mon-Fri) has maps for surrounding wilderness areas.

Sula's **Lost Trails Hot Springs Resort** (☎ 406-821-3574; www.losttrailhotsprings.com; adult/child pool $5.50/3.50, cabin & r $55-95;) has a hot outdoor pool and overnight accommodations.

FLATHEAD LAKE

It will come as no surprise that the beautiful fish-filled Flathead Lake is one of Montana's most favored attractions. Its 128 miles of wooded shoreline and picture-pretty bays are ripe for exploring. The **Flathead Lake Marine Trail** makes paddling from one access point to another a fun way to venture; two marine **campsites** (☎ 406-751-4577 for reservations; $8) are available. You can easily drive around the lake in four hours, but lingering along the way is a must.

At the south end, **Polson** is the area's service center, with the biggest concentration of motels, restaurants and gas stations. The **Polson visitors center** (☎ 406-883-5969; www.polsonchamber.com; 4 2nd Ave E; 🕑 8am-4pm Mon-Fri, 9am-4pm Sat, 10am-3pm Sun summer, Mon-Fri 10am-2pm winter) has information about accommodations.

At the lake's opposite end, **Bigfork** is a quaint village with artsy shops, good restaurants and an excellent live performance theater on Electric Ave, its main drag. The **Bigfork visitors center** (☎ 406-837-5888; www.bigfork.org; 8155 Hwy 35; 🕑 9am-5pm summer, 10am-2pm Mon-Fri winter) has local information. The **Swan Lake Ranger District Station** (☎ 406-837-5081; 200 Ranger Station Rd; 🕑 8am-4:30pm Mon-Fri), west of Bigfork, has maps and campground details.

Between Polson and Bigfork are campgrounds, summer-camp-style resorts, and, on the lake's east side, orchards adorned with plump cherries. In either town you can catch a boat tour to visit **Wild Horse Island**, where wild horses thought to be descendants of Pend d'Oreille and Flathead horses roam, and the pictographs at **Painted Rock**. Keep on alert for Flathead Nessie, a distant cousin to the Loch Ness Monster who has been lurking in the lake since the 1930s. **Flathead Raft Co** (☎ 406-883-5838, 800-654-4359; www.flatheadraftco.com) runs **kayaking** trips on the lake, **river-rafting** trips on the Flathead River and Native American–led **history trips**.

WHITEFISH & KALISPELL

A fine gateway to Glacier National Park, Old West Whitefish wears a new West coat of restaurants, shops and bars. It sits in the shadow of **Big Mountain** (☎ 406-862-2900; www.bigmtn.com;

THE AUTHOR'S CHOICE

Miracle of America Museum (☎ 406-883-6804; 58176 Hwy 93; adult $3, child 3-12 $1; 🕑 8am-8pm summer, 8:30am-5pm Mon-Sat, 1:30pm-5pm Sun winter) This mind-boggling museum, just 2 miles south of Polson on US 93, is definitely worth seeing. By turns random and fascinating, its cluttered Americana includes motorcycles, military displays and the largest buffalo ever recorded in the state.

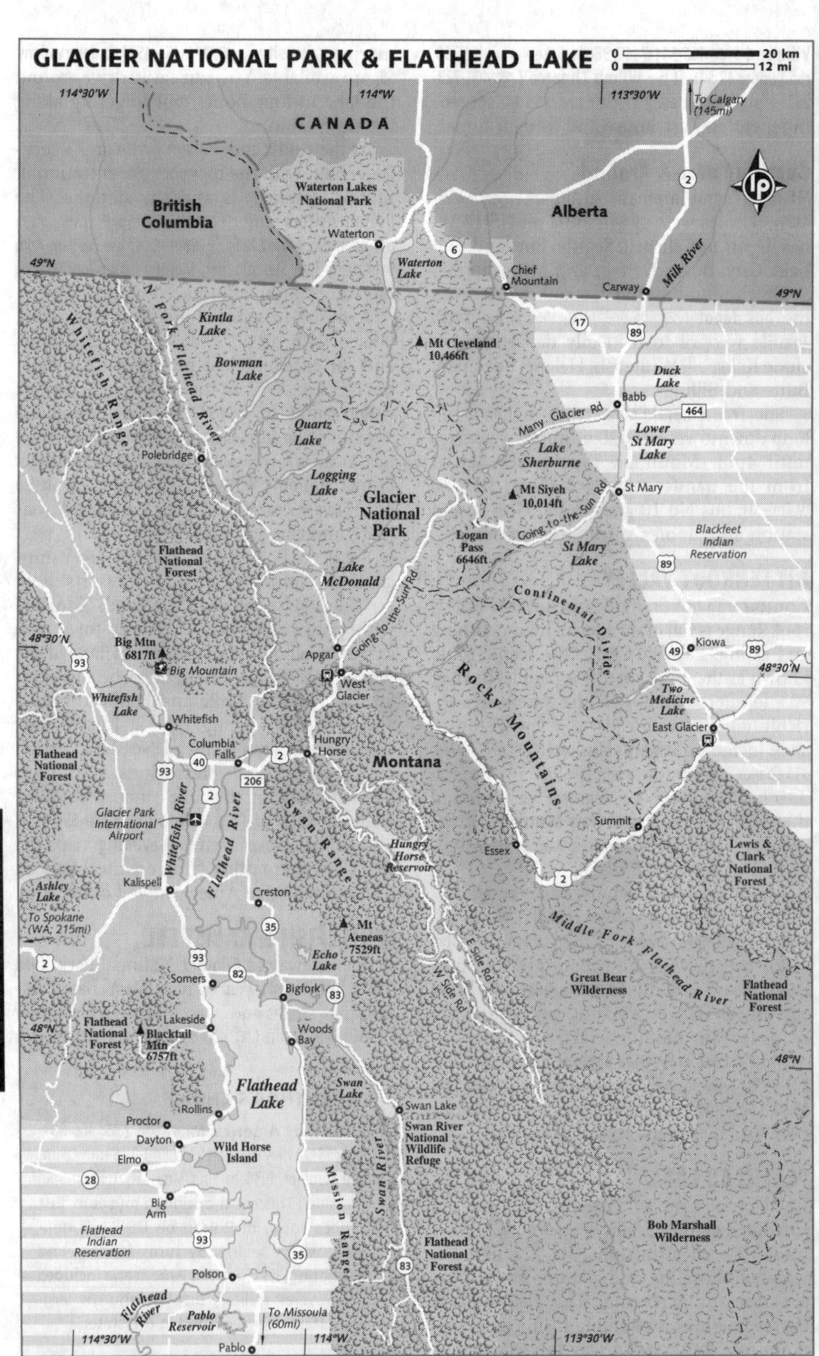
GLACIER NATIONAL PARK & FLATHEAD LAKE
0 20 km
0 12 mi
114°30'W
114°W
113°30'W
To Calgary (145mi)
CANADA
British Columbia
Alberta
Waterton Lakes National Park
Waterton
Waterton Lake
Chief Mountain
Carway
Milk River
49°N
Kintla Lake
Bowman Lake
Mt Cleveland 10,466ft
Duck Lake
Babb
Many Glacier Rd
Lower St Mary Lake
Lake Sherburne
Quartz Lake
Polebridge
Whitefish Range
N Fork Flathead River
Logging Lake
Glacier National Park
Mt Siyeh 10,014ft
St Mary
Going-to-the-Sun Rd
Logan Pass 6646ft
St Mary Lake
Blackfeet Indian Reservation
Flathead National Forest
Lake McDonald
Continental Divide
48°30'N
Big Mtn 6817ft
Big Mountain
Apgar
West Glacier
Kiowa
Rocky Mountains
Whitefish Lake
Whitefish
Two Medicine Lake
East Glacier
Columbia Falls
Hungry Horse
Montana
Glacier Park International Airport
Whitefish River
Flathead River
Swan Range
Summit
Hungry Horse Reservoir
Essex
Lewis & Clark National Forest
Ashley Lake
Kalispell
To Spokane (WA; 215mi)
Creston
Mt Aeneas 7529ft
Middle Fork Flathead River
Echo Lake
E Side Rd
W Side Rd
Somers
Bigfork
Great Bear Wilderness
48°N
Lakeside
Blacktail Mtn 6757ft
Woods Bay
Flathead Lake
Swan Lake
Rollins
Proctor
Dayton
Wild Horse Island
Swan River National Wildlife Refuge
Elmo
Big Arm
Mission Range
Swan River
Bob Marshall Wilderness
Flathead Indian Reservation
Polson
Pablo Reservoir
To Missoula (60mi)
Pablo
93
40
2
206
35
82
83
28
6
17
89
464
49

adult $50, child 7-18 $36), one of Montana's premier year-round resorts, with downhill skiing plus gondola-served hiking and mountain biking in summer. **Glacier Cyclery** (☎ 406-862-6446; 326 2nd St) has maps and rents bikes.

Kalispell, 13 miles south of Whitefish, is Flathead Valley's commercial hub. Though not as charming as Whitefish, it's a pleasant enough place to refuel on supplies. It's also home to the restored 1895 Norman-style **Conrad Mansion** (☎ 406-755-2166; Woodland Ave & 3rd St E; adult $7, child under 13 $2; 10am-6pm) is open mid-May to mid-October. Glacier National Park (see p780) is about an hour's drive from either city.

Check out www.whitefishmt.com for local weather and a variety of useful links. Following are area resources:

Kalispell Area visitors center (☎ 406-758-2800; 15 Depot Park; 8am-5pm Mon-Fri)
Tally Lake Ranger Station (☎ 406-862-2508; 1335 Hwy 93 N; 8am-4:30pm Mon-Fri)
Whitefish visitors center (☎ 406-862-3501, 877-862-3548; 520 E 2nd St; 9am-5:30pm Mon-Sat summer, 9am-5pm Mon-Fri winter)

Motel reservations are necessary in summer and winter. South of Whitefish on US 93 you'll find chain motels as well as **Chalet Motel** (☎ 406-862-5581, 800-543-8064; www.whitefishlodging.com; 6430 Hwy 93 S; s/d $70/75;), about a mile from town. It offers cheerful, spacious rooms, including two that are mostly accessible for wheelchairs. And it has a hot tub. The peaceful **Duck Inn** (☎ 406-862-3825, 800-344-2377; r $80;), a lovely wooden lodge overlooking the Whitefish River, has rooms with TV, phone, fireplace and balcony.

In a quiet residential area of Whitefish, **Bunkhouse Travelers Inn & Hostel** (☎ 406-862-3377; 217 Railway St; dm/r $15/34) advises reservations for its private rooms. There's a $3 fee for linen.

For satisfying shady campsites, try **Whitefish RV Park** (☎ 406-862-7275; www.whitefishrvpark.com; 6404 Hwy 93 S; campsites $16, RV sites $24-27), a mile south of town.

A good choice in Kalispell is **Kalispell Grand Hotel** (☎ 406-755-8100, 800-858-7422; www.kalispellgrand.com; 100 Main St; s/d from $75/80 summer, $60/70 winter;). It has smallish modern rooms with all the usual amenities, plus high-speed Internet for those with laptop in tow. Rates include continental breakfast.

Glacier Park International Airport (☎ 406-257-5994; 4170 Hwy 2), halfway between Whitefish and Kalispell on US 2, has flights to Missoula, Salt Lake City, Seattle and Minneapolis. The **Airport Shuttle Service** (☎ 406-752-2842) can get you there from Whitefish (adult $18, child six to 12 $9) or Kalispell ($7.50/3.80).

Amtrak's Empire Builder stops at Whitefish's **railroad depot** (☎ 406-862-2268; 500 Depot St; 6am-2pm & 4-11pm Mon-Fri, 6am-1pm Sat & Sun), at the north end of Central Ave. To West Glacier one-way costs $10, East Glacier $24. Intermountain Transport connects the **Kalispell bus station** (☎ 406-755-4011; 1301 S Main St; 9am-5pm Mon-Fri, 9am-noon Sat & Sun) to Whitefish (railroad depot); buses also run to Missoula, Helena, Bozeman and Seattle.

The free **Shuttle Network of Whitefish** (SNOW) runs between Whitefish and Big Mountain during ski season. **Eagle Transit** (☎ 406-758-5728; 8am-5pm Mon-Fri) provides bus service around Whitefish ($1), and to and from Kalispell ($3).

BOB MARSHALL WILDERNESS COMPLEX

The essence of Montana's wilds can be well sampled in the vast Bob Marshall Wilderness Complex, which runs roughly from the southern boundary of Glacier National Park in the north to Rogers Pass (on Hwy 200) in the south. Within the complex, three designated wilderness areas hum with a medley of geology, plants and wildlife: Great Bear, Bob Marshall and Scapegoat. National Forest lands begirding the complex offer campgrounds, road access to trailheads and quieter country when 'the Bob' hosts hunters in autumn. The core lands encompass 2344 sq miles, 3200 miles of trails and sections that are over 40 miles from the nearest road.

Access the Bob from the Seeley-Swan Valley in the west, Hungry Horse Reservoir in the north, the Rocky Mountain Front in the east or off Hwy 200 in the south. The easiest (and busiest) access routes are from the Benchmark and Gibson Reservoir trailheads in the Rocky Mountain Front.

Other good points of entry are the Holland Lake and Pyramid Pass trailheads on the Seeley-Swan side. Trails generally start steep, reaching the wilderness boundary after about 7 miles. It takes another 10 miles or so to really get into the heart of the Bob. Good day hikes run from all sides. Numerous visitors prefer to explore on horseback.

Ranger stations that tend to the Bob include the following:

Augusta Information Station (☎ 406-562-3247; 405 Manix St, Augusta; 🕑 8am-5pm, winter hours vary)

Flathead National Forest Headquarters (☎ 406-758-5204; 1935 3rd Ave E, Kalispell; 🕑 8am-4:30pm Mon-Fri)

Lewis & Clark National Forest Supervisors (☎ 406-791-7700; 1101 15th St N, Great Falls; 🕑 8am-4:30pm Mon-Fri)

Rocky Mountain Ranger District (☎ 406-466-5341; 1102 Main Ave NW, Choteau; 8am-5pm Mon-Fri)

Seeley Lake Ranger Station (☎ 406-677-2233; Hwy 83 N; 🕑 8am-4:30pm Mon-Fri) 3 miles north of Seeley Lake.

Spotted Bear Ranger District (☎ 406-758-5376; 8975 Hwy 2 E; 🕑 8am-4:30pm mid-May–Nov) Fifty-five miles south of Hungry Horse.

Swan Lake Ranger District (☎ 406-837-5081; 200 Ranger Station Rd, Bigfork; 🕑 8am-4:30pm Mon-Fri)

GLACIER NATIONAL PARK

A stunner, Glacier National Park is a veritable body of natural wonders and holds the throne as Montana's most revered attraction. Most of July and August's visitors stick to developed areas and short hiking trails. If you venture into the backcountry, you may get some one-on-one time with nature.

Those who don't have the time to explore the remote reaches can still get a dose of divine scenery by driving Going-to-the-Sun Rd, which displays tremendous examples of glacial activity and often mountain goats and bighorn sheep. In winter, when Going-to-the-Sun Rd is closed but surrounding access roads lead to snowshoe and cross-country ski trails, the park is left to wildlife and adventurous souls.

The less crowded Waterton Lakes National Park extends north into Canada. Together the two parks are a designated International Peace Park, signifying harmonious relations between the countries. In 1995 the parks were declared a World Heritage Site for their vast cross section of plant and animal species.

At the time of writing, Glacier's summerscapes were raging with a series of large fires, and forests near many trails were affected. Please check in with a visitors center or ranger station for current trail information.

Orientation

Glacier's 1562 sq miles are divided into five regions, each centred on a ranger station: Polebridge (northwest); Lake McDonald, including the West Entrance and Apgar Village (southwest); Two Medicine (southeast); St Mary (east); and Many Glacier (northeast). The 50-mile Going-to-the-Sun Rd is the only paved road that cuts across the park.

Information

Visit www.nps.gov/glac before your trip for park information. Visitors centers and ranger stations in the park sell field guides and hand out hiking maps. Those at Apgar and St Mary are open daily from May to October; the center at Logan Pass is open when Going-to-the-Sun Rd is open. The Many Glacier, Two Medicine and Polebridge Ranger Stations close at the end of September. **Park headquarters** (☎ 406-888-7800; 🕑 8am-4:30pm Mon-Fri), in West Glacier between US 2 and Apgar, is open year round.

Entry to the park (vehicles/hikers and cyclists $10/5) is valid for seven days; this does not include entrance to Waterton Lakes National Park. Day hikers don't need permits, but backpackers staying overnight in the park do (May to October only). Half of the permits ($4 per person per day) are available on a first-come, first-served basis from the Apgar Backcountry Permit Center, St Mary's Visitor Center and the Many Glacier, Two Medicine and Polebridge Ranger Stations. The other half can be reserved at the Apgar Backcountry Permit Center (open May 1 to October 31), St Mary and Many Glacier visitors centers, and Two Medicine and Polebridge Ranger Stations. Advance reservations (made more than a day before your trip) cost $20 and can be made at the permit centers or by writing to; Backcountry Reservations, Glacier National Park, West Glacier, MT 59936.

Sights & Activities

Beginning at Apgar, **Going-to-the-Sun Road** skirts shimmering Lake McDonald before angling sharply to the Garden Wall – the main dividing line between the west and east sides of the park. As the road ascends it offers phenomenal views. At Logan Pass, from the visitors center, you can stroll 1.5 miles to **Hidden Lake Overlook**; heartier hikers can try the 7.5-mile **Highline Trail**. About halfway between the pass and St Mary's Lake, the **Continental Divide Trail** crosses the road at Siyeh Bend, a good starting point for multiday hikes.

GET GLACIAL

The five- to six-hour, 9-mile day hike to Iceberg Lake is justifiably a big favorite in Glacier Park. Enclosed by stunning 3000ft vertical headwalls on three sides, it is one of the most impressive glacial lakes anywhere in the Rockies. The 1200ft ascent is gentle and the approach is mostly at or above tree line, affording awesome views. Wildflower lovers will delight in the meadows near the lake.

Iceberg Lake was named in 1905 by George Grinnell, who saw icebergs calving from the glacier at the foot of the headwalls. The glacier is no longer active, but surface ice and avalanche debris still provide sizeable flotillas of bergs as the lake melts out in early summer. The trail was built in 1914 and the Great Northern Railway (which was promoting tourism in the park at the time) tried to attract visitors to the lake with fabricated stories of the 'furred' trout that could be caught in its frigid waters.

The hike begins and finishes at Iceberg Lake Trailhead near Many Glacier.

The hiking maps provided by visitors centers cover six to 14 hikes each. Busier routes include the 5-mile **Grinnell Glacier Trail**, which climbs 1600ft to the base of the park's most visible glacier, and the 6-mile **Cracker Lake Trail**, a 1400ft climb to some of the park's most dramatic scenery. For more solitude, try trails in the North Fork or Two Medicine areas. North of the Canadian border, the approaches to spectacular hikes are much shorter.

Glacier offers two short and scenic wheelchair-accessible trails: the 0.8-mile **Trail of the Cedars** loop in Lake McDonald Valley and the 0.6-mile **Running Eagle Falls Trail** in Two Medicine Valley.

Mountain bikes are prohibited on park trails. Road bikes can ply the park's pavement but are banned from parts of Going-to-the-Sun Rd from 11am-4pm in summer.

Glacier Park Boat Co (☎ 406-257-2426; www.montanaweb.com/gpboats) runs popular guided **boat tours** (about one hour; adult/child $12/6), with departures from Many Glacier, St Mary Lake, Lake McDonald and Two Medicine. It also rents out kayaks and canoes at Apgar, Lake McDonald, Two Medicine and Many Glacier. For **rafting** trips in and around the park and guided day hikes and backpacking trips, try **Glacier Wilderness Guides** (☎ 406-387-5555, 800-521-7238; www.glacierguides.com).

For your young naturalists (ages six to 12), request the *Junior Ranger Newspaper* at the Apgar or St Mary visitors centers or the Many Glacier or Two Medicine Ranger Stations.

Sleeping

Campgrounds and lodges within the park are generally open mid-May to the end of September. East Glacier and West Glacier offer year-round accommodations and overflow space when the park fills up.

The **NPS** (☎ 406-888-7800) maintains 13 campgrounds in the park. Sites at **Fish Creek** and **St Mary campgrounds** (☎ 800-365-2267; reservations.nps.gov; campsites $17) can be reserved up to five months in advance. All other sites ($15) are first-come, first-served. Sites fill up by midmorning, particularly July to August. Only Apgar Picnic Area and St Mary campground offer winter camping.

Hike 6.5 miles from Lake McDonald Lodge to stay at historic **Sperry Chalet** (☎ 406-387-5654, 888-345-2649; www.sperrychalet.com; $155 first person, $100 each additional) for a bed, dinner, breakfast and lunch.

Dating from the early 19th century, Glacier's historic lodges are now operated by **Glacier Park, Inc** (☎ 406-892-2525 for reservations; www.glacierparkinc.com; 774 Railroad St, Columbia Falls). All are completely nonsmoking, and rooms do not have air-conditioning or television.

Glacier Park Lodge (☎ 406-226-5600; www.bigtreehotel.com; East Glacier; r $135-400)

Lake McDonald Lodge (☎ 406-888-5431; www.lakemcdonaldlodge.com; Lake McDonald Valley; cottage $95-140, r $100-140)

Many Glacier Hotel (☎ 406-732-4411; www.manyglacierhotel.com; Many Glacier Valley; r $110-220)

Prince of Wales Hotel (☎ 403-859-2231; www.princeofwaleswaterton.com; Prince of Wales Rd, Waterton Townsite, Waterton Lakes National Park; r $260-800 Canadian)

Rising Sun Motor Inn (☎ 406-732-5523; www.risingsunmotorinn.com; St Mary Valley; r $92-100)

Swiftcurrent Motor Inn (☎ 406-732-5531; www.swiftcurrentmotorinn.com; Many Glacier Valley; cabin $45-75, r $90-100)

Village Inn (☎ 406-888-5632; www.villageinnatapgar.com; Apgar; r $105-170)

The flagship Glacier Park Lodge, with interior balconies supported by Douglas fur timbers, is the first to open for summer – generally in mid-May. Many Glacier Hotel doesn't open until mid-June. Lake McDonald Complex has a cozy hunting-lodge atmosphere, and in Waterton, majestic Prince of Wales Hotel sits on a pile of glacial till overlooking icy-blue Waterton Lake.

In East Glacier, the friendly **AYH Brownie's** (☎ 406-226-4426, 727-4448; Hwy 49; dm $16, s/d $21/29; 💻), above Brownie's Grocery & Deli, is always in demand when it's open – May to September. It offers dorm rooms, private rooms and a kitchen.

The ultra-rustic (no electricity) **Northfork Hostel & Squarepeg Ranch** (☎ 406-888-5241; www.nfhostel.com; dm $15, cabins $30-65), in Polebridge, is open year round and has bunks, cabins and a kitchen. Guests can use the hostel's mountain bikes, cross-country skis, snowshoes and kayaks free of charge; nonguests can rent equipment. A ride from the Amtrak station in West Glacier is $30.

In West Glacier, **Glacier Highland Resort Motel** (☎ 406-888-5427, 800-766-0811; s/d from $65/75; ❄), opposite the train station, has 33 units and a hot tub; there's one wheelchair-friendly room. One mile west of West Glacier, **Glacier Campground** (☎ 406-387-5689; off Hwy 2; campsites $18, RV sites $19-24, cabin $30-40) has sites spanning 40 acres of lovely wooded grounds as well as a cute cluster of basic wooden cabins.

Eating

In summer there are grocery stores with an array of camping supplies in Apgar, Lake McDonald Lodge, Rising Sun and at the Swiftcurrent Motor Inn.

In East Glacier, **Serrano's Mexican Restaurant** (☎ 406-226-9392; 29 Dawson Ave; mains $7-12) is open year round and serves up good Mexican food in casual environs both inside and outside on its deck. **Brownie's Grocery & Deli** (Hwy 49) has a well-rounded grocery supply and makes its own breads. Dining options in West Glacier are unexciting; if you can, head to Whitefish.

Getting There & Around

Glacier International Airport (☎ 406-257-5994; 4170 Hwy 2) is 20 miles southeast of the park's west entrance (see p777). Amtrak's Empire Builder stops at East Glacier (Glacier Park Station) and West Glacier (Belton Station). **Glacier Park, Inc** (see p781) runs shuttles over Going-to-the-Sun Rd, including the unreservable Hiker's Shuttle ($8-24), which originates in West Glacier or Many Glacier.

IDAHO

Idaho sets a lot of records: it's second only to Alaska for most national forests and wilderness areas; it contains the deepest gorge on the continent (Hells Canyon); and its northern region boasts the densest lake population of any state in the West. Additionally, Idaho has heaps of mountains. Anybody who loves to frolic in the wilds can happily hike, bike, raft, fish, ski, sled and ride on horseback until, literally, the cows come home.

The woods of central and northern Idaho attract legions of adventurers, as surely as the Salmon and Snake Rivers are virtually flooded by river rats from the world over. Still, the state's longitudinal stretch – taking in diverse geography from arid plains to bursting-green forests – makes finding a tranquil nook quite easy to do. Get off the I-84 or US 95 and you'll find byways, vistas and loads of tantalizing territory.

The Panhandle resort towns, as well as the glitzy Sun Valley and Ketchum, offer ranges of amenities for those who prefer comfort to rustic accommodation. Visitors looking for guides and classes will find ample facilities, and those who like to forge their own way will be left in peace. Whether you're headed 'up a crick,' through the rapids or down the slopes, the scenery is spectacular and can feel boundless.

History

Idaho was not really settled until gold was struck at Pierce in 1860. Miners rushed to Idaho's mountains, establishing gold camps and trade centers like Boise and Lewiston. Rich silver and lead veins spurred further growth, and by the late 19th century a homesteading boom had begun.

The Shoshone were once the West's dominant Indian group. Some Shoshone peoples, along with the Bannock, now live on the Fort Hall Indian Reservation in the southeast.

Getting There & Around

Idaho's main airport is in Boise, which has links to Hailey, Lewiston, McCall and

IDAHO FACTS

Nickname The Gem State
Population 1,341,131 (39th)
Area 83,575 sq miles (13th)
Admitted to Union July 3, 1890 (43rd)
Capital city Boise (population 185,800)
Other cities Pocatello (51,500), Idaho Falls (50,700)
State motto Esto perpetua (Let it be perpetual)
Birthplace of Sacagawea, Shoshone woman on Lewis & Clark expedition; Gutzon Borglum (1867–1941), sculptor of Mt Rushmore; Picabo Street (b 1971), Olympic skiing medalist
Famous for spuds, wilderness, white water, hunting

Salmon as well as national flights (see Boise p785). The Idaho Falls, Pocatello and Twin Falls airports have flights to Denver and Salt Lake City. At time of writing, efforts were underway to start air services from Sandpoint to Boise and Seattle. Amtrak's daily Empire Builder stops in Sandpoint.

BOISE

Idaho's capital, largest city and home to its state university, Boise is more than a gateway to Idaho's wilder climes. As a hip place with an outdoors slant and a hassle-free feel, the city holds its own as a destination. Much of the city's late-19th-century architectural core remains. Cafés and restaurants stay open late, and on hot summer evenings crowds from nightspots spill out into the streets. It has an active gay and lesbian community, and locals consider Boise a gay-friendly city.

Information & Orientation

Boise visitors center (☎ 208-344-5338, 800-635-5240; www.boise.org; 850 Front St; 10am-5pm Mon-Fri, 10am-2pm Sat summer, 9am-4pm Mon-Fri winter)
Boise Parks & Recreation (☎ 208-384-4240; 1104 Royal Blvd; 8am-5pm Mon-Fri)
USFS Boise National Forest & Idaho State BLM (☎ 208-373-4007; 1387 S Vinnell Way; 7:45am-4:30pm Mon-Fri)

The main business district is bounded by State, Grove, 4th and 9th Sts. Restaurants and nightspots are found downtown in the brick-lined pedestrian plaza of the **Grove**, the gentrified former warehouse district at 8th St Marketplace and Old Boise, just east of downtown. Along Grove St between 6th St and Capitol Blvd, the **Basque Block** has sites commemorating Idaho's Basque pioneers.

Sights & Activities

Worthwhile sights include the impressive **state capitol**. Riverfront Julia Davis Park holds the **Idaho Historical Museum** (☎ 208-334-2120; 610 N Julia Davis Dr; 9am-5pm Mon-Sat, 1-5pm Sun; adult $2, child 6-18 $1), full of tales of the olden days, and **Boise Art Museum** (☎ 208-345-8330; 670 Julia Davis Dr; adult $8, child 6-18 $4; 10am-5pm Tue-Wed & Fri-Sat, 10am-8pm Thu, noon-5pm Sun), which has a permanent collection colored with 19th-century pieces by American artists and temporary exhibits that run international.

East of Broadway Ave off Warm Springs Rd, the **Old Idaho Penitentiary** (☎ 208-368-6080; 2445 Old Penitentiary Rd; noon-5pm winter, 10am-5pm summer; adult $4, child 6-12 $3) is fascinating, in a chilling way.

Northeast of Boise, **hiking** trails span the mountains of the Boise Front. **Bogus Basin Resort** (☎ 208-332-5100, 800-367-4397; www.bogusbasin.com; 2405 Bogus Basin Rd), 16 miles north of Boise, offers downhill and cross-country skiing during winter (full-day lift tickets adult $37, child seven to 11 $10) and hiking and mountain biking in summer. **Childcare** (☎ 208-332-5343) is available on the mountain.

The closest **white-water rafting** opportunities to Boise lie on the Payette River, an hour's drive from the city. Local outfitters offer day and multiday trips on the rapids; **kayaking** ventures can also be arranged. **Headwaters River Company** (☎ 800-800-7238; www.idahorivertours.com) has a good reputation.

Festivals & Events

Get more details about the season's events at the visitors center (see above).
Art in the Park (☎ 208-345-8330) Outdoor art fest held the weekend after Labor Day.
Boise River Festival (☎ 208-338-8887; www.boiseriverfestival.org) Parades, sporty fun and lots for kids; held the last weekend in June.
Gene Harris Jazz Festival (www.geneharris.org) Smooth jazz by masters; held the first week in April.
Snake River Stampede (☎ 208-466-8497; www.snake riverstampede.com) Action-packed pro rodeo in Nampa; held in June.

Sleeping & Eating

Cabana Inn (☎ 208-343-6000; cabanainn@interplus.net; 1600 Main St; s/d $40/45; P) A few hops west

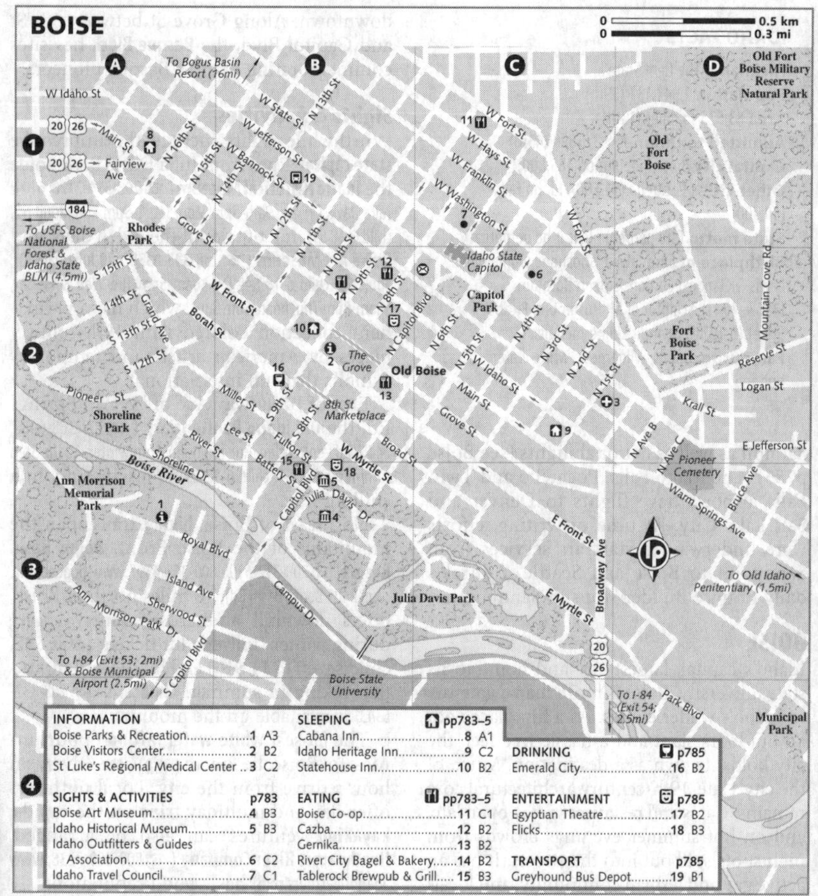

of downtown, this motel run by helpful folk offers well-kept rooms equipped with microwave, TV and a place to rest your head. You'll find other budget-range accommodations along Capitol Blvd near the university.

Idaho Heritage Inn (☎ 208-342-8066, 800-342-3445; www.idheritageinn.com; 109 W Idaho St; r $75-110) You may be welcomed with a purr from the housecats at this wonderfully charming, family-run B&B. Six cozy rooms come with varying amenities. The private baths run geothermally heated water.

Statehouse Inn (☎ 208-342-4622, 800-243-4622; www.statehouse-inn.com; 981 Grove St; s/d $95/105; P ⊠) This big modern hotel in the midst of downtown is well equipped for business travelers and those who desire convenience, professional service and extras like an on-site fitness room.

River City Bagel & Bakery (☎ 208-338-1299; 908 Main St; food $2-6) A good place for morning fuel, this amiable eatery offers a range of bagels and sandwiches, plus espresso, chai and more. It has sidewalk seating and an attached bookstore.

Cazba (☎ 208-381-0222; 211 N 8th St; mains $12-20) The popular Cazba is a fine place to catch up on missed meals. Its large platefuls of delightful food – ie gyros bigger than the Med – will leave everyone (including vegetarians) satisfied and very full.

Gernika (☎ 208-344-2175; 202 S Capitol Blvd; meals $6-8) This friendly bar on the Basque Block is where to head for the likes of pork tenderloin sandwiches and chorizo, as well as draft beers and Basque wine. 'Beef tongue Saturday' commences at 11:30am.

Other good places are the hopping **Tablerock Brewpub & Grill** (☎ 208-342-0944; 705 Fulton St; 11am-11pm Mon-Sat, 11am-10pm Sun; meals $7-16) which, of course, also offers liquid meals; and natural-foods stop **Boise Co-op** (☎ 208-472-4500; 888 W Fort St).

Entertainment

Emerald City (☎ 208-342-5446; 415 S 9th St) Proud to be 'straight friendly,' this gay bar and nightclub is a convivial spot to swill some drinks and live a little on the dance floor. DJs spin every night except Saturday, when a show gets the spotlight.

For cinema, head to Old Boise's **Egyptian Theatre** (☎ 208-342-1441; 700 W Main St; adult $8, child under 12 $5) for mainstream new releases or the **Flicks** (☎ 208-342-4222; 646 Fulton St; adult/child $7.50/5.50) for independent and foreign films.

Getting There & Around

Boise Municipal Airport (☎ 208-383-3110; I-84 exit 53) has daily flights to Denver, Las Vegas, Phoenix, Portland, Salt Lake City, Seattle and Spokane. Greyhound and Northwestern Trailway services depart from the **bus station** (☎ 208-343-3681; 1212 W Bannock St) and travel along three main routes: I-84, US 95 and I-15/20/287/91.

Boise Urban Stages (BUS; ☎ 208-336-1010) operates local buses, including an airport route (No 13).

KETCHUM & SUN VALLEY

Largely due to the highly rated Sun Valley ski resort, Ketchum and Sun Valley are Idaho's premier destinations. The area has long buzzed with high flyers: the truly wealthy live in their 'trophy homes,' and it's not uncommon to see a shining Hollywood face cruising down a slope. But this is no LA: the year-round destinations of Ketchum and Sun Valley, nestled among resplendent natural beauty, are places to get away from it all.

Ketchum began in the 1880s as a mining center, while Sun Valley – 1 mile northeast – sprang to life in 1936 after an Austrian count was hired by the Union Pacific (UP) to select a site for a European-style ski resort. Ketchum is the main commercial hub, with an abundance of restaurants, hotels and boutiques. Twelve miles south on Hwy 75, Hailey is where most seasonal workers and ski bums live.

Nobel-prize winning author (and avid sportsman) Ernest Hemingway (1899–1961) was a frequent visitor to the area, and spent his last years in Ketchum, where he's buried. *Hemingway: The Final Years* by Michael Reynolds chronicles the period that the great writer spent in Idaho.

Information

Sun Valley/Ketchum visitors center (☎ 208-726-3423, 800-634-3347; www.visitsunvalley.com; 411 Main St; 9am-5:30pm) and **USFS Sawtooth National Forest Ketchum Ranger Station** (☎ 208-622-5371; 206 Sun Valley Rd; 8:30am-5pm Mon-Fri) are happy to offer area advice.

Sun Valley Resort

Sun Valley Resort (☎ 800-786-8259; www.sunvalley.com) is famous for its prime powder and excellent slopes. West of Ketchum, world-class **Bald Mountain** (full-day lift tickets adult/child under 13 $65/36) has mostly advanced terrain, while older **Dollar Mountain** ($25/20), on Elkhorn Rd south of Old Dollar Rd, offers easier runs. In summer, both offer **hiking** and **mountain biking**.

Hiking & Mountain Biking

The well-maintained Wood River Trail System (WRTS) winds 20 miles through Ketchum and Sun Valley. The 10-mile Sun Valley Trail connects to the WRTS. Several other excellent hiking trails near Ketchum also permit mountain biking, including the 5.5-mile Adams Gulch loop and Fox Creek, a 5-mile loop with mountain views that connects with three other trails.

Sleeping

The visitors center provides a useful free reservation service. Budget accommodation is hard to come by.

Tamarack Lodge (☎ 208-726-3344, 800-521-5379; www.tamaracksunvalley.com; 500 E Sun Valley Rd; r $110;) This well-maintained lodge boasts tasteful rooms with fireplace, balcony and many amenities, including hair dryer. The Jacuzzi and indoor pool are definite assets. Discounts are often available mid-week and off-season.

Lift Tower Lodge (☎ 208-726-5163, 800-462-8646; ltowerl@micron.net; 703 S Main St; r $65-90) This friendly small motel in downtown Ketchum offers free continental breakfasts and a hot tub. It sits next to a landmark exhibition chairlift circa 1939.

Sun Valley Lodge (☎ 208-622-2001, 800-786-8259; www.sunvalley.com; r from $180;) Hemingway completed *For Whom the Bell Tolls* in this lodge, which offers comfy rooms, the cheapest of which are smallish in size. Amenities include a fitness facility, games room, a bowling alley and sauna.

Camp relatively close to town at **Meadows RV Park** (☎ 208-726-5445; 13 Broadway Run, Hwy 75; campsites/RV sites $15/27), 2 miles south of Ketchum, or the unreservable USFS **Boundary Campground** (campsites $11), off Trail Creek Rd, 3 miles east of the USFS Ketchum Ranger Station.

Eating & Drinking

Bigwood Bread (☎ 208-726-2034; 270 Northwood Way; food $4-8; 7am-5pm Mon-Fri) With a cheery and upbeat atmosphere, this art-lined café has hearty breads, baked goods, sandwiches, salads and healthy-start offerings like organic muesli ($2.50).

Desperado's (☎ 208-726-3068; 211 4th St; mains $7-9; 11:30am-10pm Mon-Sat) Despo's is a bright, busy and colorful eatery specializing in reasonably priced Mexican food. Fill up on burritos, chimichangas, tacos and quesadillas. A pitcher of margaritas is $17.

Ketchum Grill (☎ 208-726-4660; 520 East Ave; mains $10-17; from 5:30pm) A local favorite, Ketchum Grill offers a creative menu bursting with fresh fare. It throws together – elegantly, of course – lauded seafood, and doesn't scrimp on options for the vegetarian.

Grumpy's (860 Warm Springs Rd; meals $4-8) Decorated with old beer cans, this small place is big in personality. It sizzles a damn fine burger, and on clear days locals flock to the decks to down schooners in the sun.

Whiskey Jacques (☎ 208-726-5297; 251 Main St) You can do it all at this spacious and no-frills local institution: catch the game on TV or play a round of pool or foosball, let loose to live bands and DJs, and drink till the wee hours.

Getting There & Around

Hailey's **Friedman Memorial Airport** (☎ 208-788-4956), 12 miles south of Ketchum, has daily flights to Salt Lake City, Seattle, LA and, in summer and winter, Boise. **A-1 Taxi** (☎ 208-726-9351; 5:30am-2:30am) offers rides to the airport from Ketchum ($19).

Ketchum Area Rapid Transit (KART; ☎ 208-726-7576; 8am-6pm Mon-Fri) operates free daily bus service between Ketchum and Sun Valley. Door-to-door van services are available for seniors and those with disabilities.

AROUND KETCHUM

A one-hour drive southeast of Ketchum, **Craters of the Moon National Monument** (☎ 208-527-3257; vehicle/hiker or biker $4/2, 8am-4:30pm winter, until 6pm summer) is an 83-sq-mile volcanic showcase. Lava flows, cinder cones and lava tubes lie along the 7-mile **Crater Loop Rd**, which is accessible by car or bicycle from April to November; it's traversed by skiers and snowshoers in winter. Short trails lead from Crater Loop Rd to crater edges, onto cinder cones and into tunnels and lava caves. A surreal **campground** ($10) near the entrance station has running water only in the summer.

Drive 30 miles north of Ketchum on Hwy 75, which winds past timbered slopes and along the Salmon River, and you will ascend Galena Summit (8701ft), with truly breathtaking views. The 1180-sq-mile **Sawtooth National Recreation Area** spans the Sawtooth, Smoky, Boulder and Salmon River mountains and has 40 peaks over 10,000ft, over 300 high-alpine lakes, 100 miles of streams and 750 miles of trails. The adjacent 340-sq-mile Sawtooth Wilderness Area centers on the rugged Sawtooth Range.

The area sees its most visitors in July, August and the winter months. Recreation is possible year-round, but it can snow anytime. Summer activities include hiking, fishing, rafting, horseback riding, boating and camping. Snowmobiling, hunting and cross-country skiing are the most popular winter activities. The **area headquarters** (☎ 208-727-5000, 800-847-4843; Hwy 75; 8am-4:30pm winter, 8am-5pm summer), 8.5 miles north of Ketchum, can refer you to guides for climbing, fishing and backcountry skiing, and has information on yurt rentals and camping. This is also where you must buy your Trailhead Parking Pass ($5 for three days, $15 per year).

MCCALL

At the northern end of Long Valley, the wonderfully scenic McCall sits along Payette Lake's southern shore. It's a year-round community with an air of seclusion and, thankfully, minimal glitz. Residents enjoy a relaxing pace of life, and visitors take advantage of water sports, great skiing at nearby **Brundage Mountain** (☎ 208-634-4151, 800-888-7544; www.brundage.com; full-day lift tickets adult $34, child 7-11 $18), mountain biking, and good restaurants and lodgings. The **McCall visitors center** (☎ 208-634-7631; 102 N 3rd St; 8am-5pm Mon-Fri) is one block south of W Lake St. Detailed recreation information is available from the USFS Payette National Forest offices: **McCall Ranger District** (☎ 208-634-0400; 102 W Lake St; 7:30am-4:30pm Mon-Fri) and **Forest Krassel Ranger District** (☎ 208-634-0600; 500 N Mission St; 7:30am-4:30pm Mon-Fri).

HELLS CANYON NATIONAL RECREATION AREA

North America's deepest gorge, Hells Canyon is thousands of feet deeper than the Grand Canyon, plunging 8913ft from Mt Oore's He Devil Peak on the east rim to the Snake River at Granite Creek. The remote 652,488-acre Hells Canyon National Recreation Area offers fishing, swimming, camping and dramatic views of the gorge and surrounding mountains. The **Snake National Wild & Scenic River** through Hells Canyon is a favorite spot for rafting and jet-boat trips. These activities can provide ideal gazes at the skyward basaltic cliffs of the canyon. Nearly 900 miles of **hiking** trails take in a diverse range of scenery, from river banks and mountain peaks to canyon walls animated with ancient petroglyphs. Wildflowers color area meadows, and much wildlife resides here.

The Hells Canyon NRA spans the Idaho-Oregon state line, but the Oregon section is not readily accessible from Idaho. US 95 parallels its eastern boundary; a few unpaved roads lead from US 95 between the tiny towns of Riggins (a big rafting center) and White Bird into the NRA. Only one road leads from US 95 to the Snake River itself, at Pittsburg Landing.

The **Hells Canyon NRA Riggins** (☎ 208-628-3916; 8am-5pm Mon-Fri) has maps and information on campgrounds, roads, trails and fishing. The unstaffed **Salmon River visitors center** (☎ 208-628-3778; www.rigginsidaho.com; Riggins City Park, Hwy 95) has brochures on the area's numerous outfitters; the narrow strip of land called Riggins prides itself on being Idaho's white-water capital and is the base for rafting on the Lower Salmon River.

Travelers with time (and high-clearance vehicles) can drive to the canyon rim on unpaved roads for dramatic views: USFS Rd 517 (open July to October), a quarter-mile south of the Hells Canyon Riggins office on US 95, climbs 17 miles to the rim and ends 2 miles later at the breathtaking **Heaven's Gate Lookout**.

IDAHO PANHANDLE

A handle tipped up toward Canada, this alluring region is speckled with resorts, lakes and mining days gone by. **Coeur d'Alene**, **Kellogg** and **Sandpoint** are prime destinations for skiers, anglers and water-sports enthusiasts, while the old silver-mining town of **Wallace** preserves the Western flavor of its historic town center. Sixty lakes lie within 60 miles of Coeur d'Alene, including Hayden, Priest and Pend Oreille, all surrounded by campgrounds. Outdoor activities are ubiquitous, from white-water rafting the Class III run of the St Joe National Wild & Scenic River to jet-skiing on Lake Coeur d'Alene to backpacking through the primeval forest around Priest Lake.

The Panhandle has a reputation – often inflated by the media – as a base for neo-Nazi, white-supremacist groups. However, you're far more likely to meet wildlife than wildly irrational people.

The following are good starting points for visits to the region:

Coeur d'Alene visitors center (☎ 208-665-2350, 800-292-2553; 115 Northwest Blvd; 10am-3pm Tue-Sat, 10am-5pm summer)
Sandpoint visitors center (☎ 208-263-2161, 800-800-2106; 900 N 5th Ave; 9am-5pm Mon-Fri)
USFS Idaho Panhandle National Forest Sandpoint (☎ 208-263-5111; 1500 US 2; 7:30am-4:30pm Mon-Fri)

A centrally located Coeur d'Alene lodging option is the **Flamingo Motel** (☎ 208-664-2159, 800-955-2159; 718 Sherman Ave; r $70-85), a pink-doored darling with spotless, charming rooms. Travelers with wheelchairs will be much more comfortable in the specially equipped room at nearby **Resort City Inn** (☎ 208-676-1225; www.resortcityinn.com; 621 Sherman Ave; r Mon-Fri $70, Sat & Sun $80;).

In Sandpoint, **Lakeside Inn** (☎ 208-263-3717, 800-543-8126; lakeside@televar.com; 106 Bridge St; r $65-95) has, unsurprisingly, a good waterfront location, plus a Jacuzzi and comfortable rooms, some of which have balcony. One wheelchair-friendly room is available.

Southwest

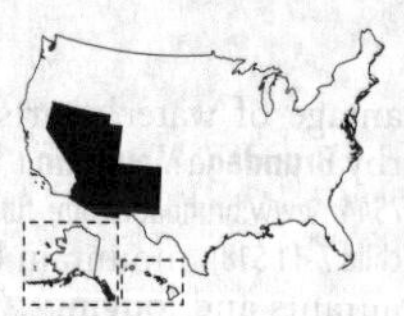

CONTENTS

America's Southwest is a mythic land, much of it an immense desert that is at once beautiful, awe-inspiring and packed full of a rich, cultural history. It includes the dramatic canyons carved by the mighty Colorado River, the mighty saguaro cacti of the Sonoran Desert, the colorful cliffs and maze-like canyons of southern Utah, and some very tall and inhospitable mountain ranges. It's a land full of contrasts, too. In summer the heat is often stifling, the air intensely dry and the ground severely parched; at the same time, however, tall green trees offer a cool refuge for those traveling in the higher elevations, and some of the highest peaks retain snow all year round.

Cities have sprouted throughout the region, some becoming as much a part of the Southwest's draw as the landscape. At the same time, the most rugged portions of the Southwest appear virtually untouched, with seemingly endless miles of eroded rock, blue sky and blazing sunshine.

The people who have chosen to live in this harsh environment have also acquired the patina of myth: the ancestral Indians and their modern descendants; the Spanish explorers and missionaries; the persecuted Mormons who settled Utah; rough-and-ready miners, cowboys, outlaws and trappers; artists drawn to the wild, surreal landscapes; and the US military, which closed off vast, uninhabited stretches of land for nuclear and other weapons testing.

In addition to experiencing this fabled terrain, visitors to the Southwest today can enjoy the chic restaurants and galleries of Santa Fe and Sedona, the buzz of Las Vegas' neon-lit casinos and the world-class skiing in Utah and northern New Mexico.

HIGHLIGHTS

- Staring into the **Grand Canyon**, a mile-deep chasm of almost incomprehensible wonder (p826)
- Wandering around 400-year-old **Santa Fe**, surrounded by rugged, beautiful scenery (p800)
- Witnessing living history in the verdant valley of **Canyon de Chelly** (p831)
- Gasping at multicolored 'hoodoos' during a **Bryce Canyon sunset** (p856)
- Being thrilled by architecturally surreal **Las Vegas** (p859)

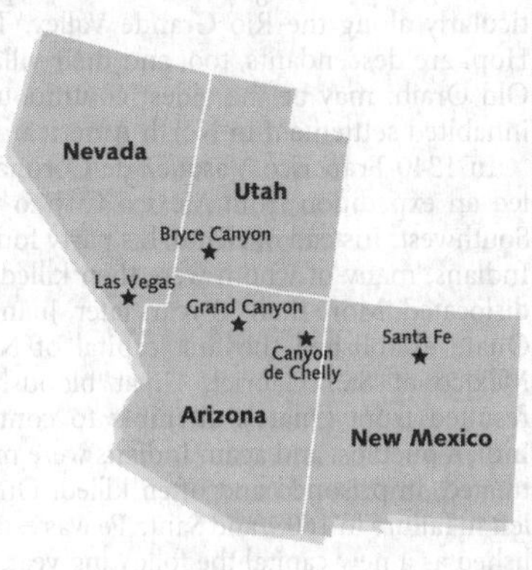

HISTORY

The history of human habitation in the Southwest is huge, dating 12,500 years. However, by AD 100, three dominant cultures had emerged: the Hohokam, the Mogollon, and the Ancestral Puebloans (formerly known as the Anasazi). And these are pretty fascinating people.

The Hohokam existed in the Arizona deserts from 300 BC to AD 1450. Amazingly adapted to desert life, they created an incredible canal irrigation system, as well as earthen pyramids and a rich heritage of pottery. Their sophisticated adaptability makes their mysterious disappearance in the mid-15th century especially haunting. Today's Pima and Tohano O'oodham Indians appear to be descendents. Visit a Hokoham site at the Pueblo Grande Museum in Phoenix.

From 200 BC to AD 1450, the Mogollon people lived in the central mountains and valleys of the Southwest, generally residing in simple pit dwellings on isolated mesas or ridge tops. Peacefully incorporated into the Ancestral Puebloans, the Mogollons left behind historic sites such as Gila Cliff Dwellings National Monument in New Mexico.

The Ancestral Puebloans left behind the richest heritage of archaeological sites, such as those at Mesa Verde in Colorado and Chaco Culture National Historic Park in New Mexico. Today, descendants of the Ancestral Puebloans are found in the Pueblo Indian groups throughout New Mexico, particularly along the Rio Grande Valley. The Hopi are descendants, too, and their village Old Oraibi may be the oldest continuously inhabited settlement in North America.

In 1540 Francisco Vásquez de Coronado led an expedition from Mexico City to the Southwest. Instead of riches, his party found Indians, many of whom were then killed or dislocated. More than 50 years later, Juan de Onate established the first capital of New Mexico at San Gabriel. Great bloodshed resulted from Onate's attempts to control Indian pueblos, and again Indians were mistreated, imprisoned and often killed. Onate left in failure in 1608, and Santa Fe was established as a new capital the following year.

Development in the Southwest expanded rapidly during the 19th century, mainly due to railroad and geological surveys. As the US pushed west, the army forcibly removed whole tribes of Native Americans in often horrifyingly brutal Indian Wars. Gold and silver mines drew fortune-seekers, and practically overnight the lawless mining towns of the Wild West mushroomed. Capitalizing on the development, the Fred Harvey Company (which built hotels and restaurants) joined forces with the Atchison, Topeka and Santa Fe Railroad to lure to the area an ocean of tourists, who were fascinated by the West's rugged beauty and Indian culture.

Modern settlement in the Southwest is closely linked to the development of water use. Following the Reclamation Act of 1902, huge federally funded dams were built to control rivers, irrigate the desert and encourage development. Constant disagreements and rancorous debates over water rights continue today. Marc Resiner's book, *Cadillac Desert*, details the fascinating history of this struggle.

GEOGRAPHY & CLIMATE

The central part of the Southwest is the Colorado Plateau, a series of plateaus between 5000ft and 8000ft in elevation and separated by deep canyons, among them the world-famous Grand Canyon. Four major deserts are in the Southwest: the Great Basin Desert, covering much of Nevada; the Mojave Desert of northwestern Arizona, southern Nevada, southeastern Utah and southern California; the Chihuahuan Desert in southern New Mexico and southeastern Arizona; and the Sonoran Desert in southern Arizona. Several mountain ranges run from north to south throughout the region, in some areas alternating with deep desert basins (forming the 'Basin and Range' country).

While mountains are capped with snow during the winter, most of the Southwest receives little annual rainfall. During the summer, temperatures can soar into the 90s and 100s; locals often boast 'it's a dry heat,' but it's still uncomfortable. Nights are usually cooler, and spring and fall can be downright pleasant.

INFORMATION

The offices listed here provide information regarding activities on US Forest Service land. For general regional guidance, see the individual state entries.

USFS Intermountain Regional Office (☎ 801-625-5306; www.fs.fed.us/r4; 324 25th St, Ogden, UT 84401)

SOUTHWEST

WHERE'S THE FIRE?

Thousands of fires occur naturally (and unnaturally) throughout the West every year. Travelers have little to fear, but it's worth checking for regional closures – forest fires often shut down roads, campgrounds and other facilities. For updates, contact the **forest service hotline** (☎ 877-864-6985; www.fs.fed.us/r3/fire), which also provides fire information for the National Park Service (NPS), the Bureau of Land Management (BLM), and tribal and other federal lands in the region. Information is updated daily during fire season (usually summer and fall).

Provides information on national forest land in Utah, Nevada and parts of Wyoming, Idaho, California and Colorado.

USFS Southwest Regional Office (☎ 505-842-3292; www.fs.fed.us/r3; 333 Broadway SE, Albuquerque, NM 87102) The central USFS office for New Mexico and Arizona. It sells maps, and fields general questions regarding camping, hiking and other activities.

NATIONAL PARKS

There are so many national parks throughout the Southwest it's practically impossible to list them all. Visit the **National Park Service** (NPS; www.nps.gov/parks.html) website for general information on the region's parks.

One of the national park system's most popular destinations is the Grand Canyon in Arizona. Other parks in Arizona include remote Organ Pipe Cactus National Monument and Canyon de Chelly National Monument, run in conjunction with the Navajo Nation.

In Utah, most national parks are in the red-rock canyon country in the south, including Arches and Canyonlands. Cedar Breaks National Monument sees far fewer visitors than nearby Zion and Bryce national parks, and Grand Staircase-Escalante National Monument is a mighty region of undeveloped desert for those adventurous travelers.

New Mexico has impressive Carlsbad Caverns National Park and mysterious Chaco Culture National Historic Park, once a major center for Indian trade. Nevada's only national park is Great Basin, a rugged mountain oasis in a remote desert area on the state's eastern edge.

DANGERS & ANNOYANCES

Many people traveling to desert regions are worried about snakes and scorpions, and while they do exist here, chances are you'll never see one. Far more common and often overlooked, however, are the dangers of heat exhaustion and dehydration. Summer heat can be intense, even for experienced travelers and outdoor enthusiasts. Do not attempt any hike, *however short*, without carrying plenty of water. A minimum is 4 quarts (3.8 liters) per person per day, though this is a bare minimum – carry more on hot days. And keep several extra gallons in the car.

Summer rainstorms, often with lightning, can come out of nowhere, and flash floods occur regularly, sometimes from a storm many miles away. In minutes, a dry riverbed or wash can become a raging torrent. Never camp in washes, and always inquire about conditions before entering canyons or driving into remote areas.

ACTIVITIES

The mountains around Salt Lake City and Taos offer unbeatable skiing, and smaller ski resorts can be found all over. In the summer, white-water rafting is popular on the Colorado River and Rio Grande in southern Utah and northern New Mexico. Throughout the region, in such varied terrain as Red Rock Canyon in Nevada and the Wasatch Cache National Forest of Utah, there is plenty of opportunity for hiking, camping, rock climbing, horseback riding, mountain biking and fishing. One of the most distinctive features of the American Southwest is the variety of landscapes. Thus, while the low-lying deserts broil in summer, you can often hike or quickly drive into cooler nearby mountains, with fly-fishing streams, alpine forests and meadows of wildflowers.

GETTING THERE & AROUND

Air

Phoenix International Airport (Sky Harbor) and McCarran International Airport, in Las Vegas, are the region's busiest airports, followed by Salt Lake City, Albuquerque and Tucson. America West, Southwest and Delta are the main carriers here.

Bus

Greyhound buses run several times a day along major highways (including I-40, I-25,

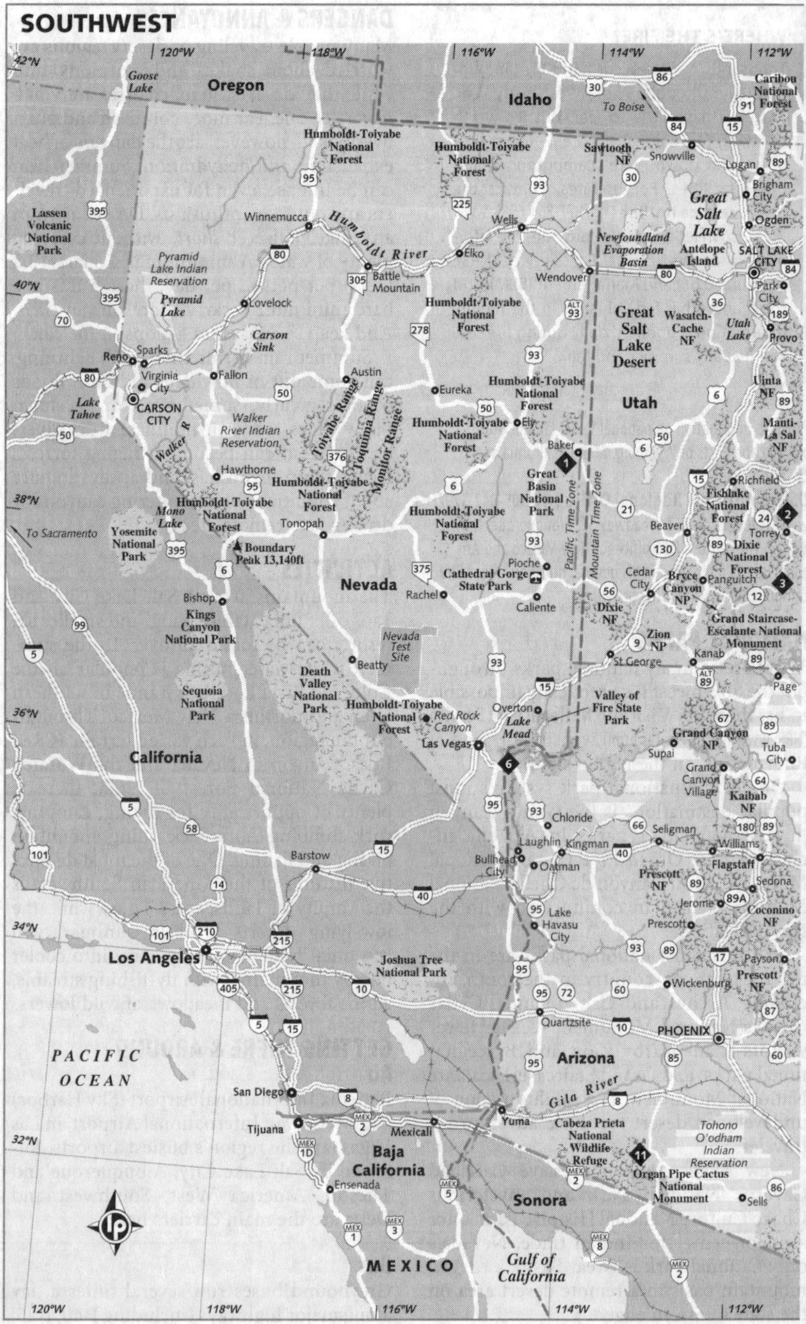

SOUTHWEST

120°W
118°W
116°W
114°W
112°W
42°N
40°N
38°N
36°N
34°N
32°N

Goose Lake
Oregon
Idaho
To Boise
Caribou National Forest
Humboldt-Toiyabe National Forest
Humboldt-Toiyabe National Forest
Sawtooth NF
Snowville
Logan
Brigham City
Great Salt Lake
Ogden
Lassen Volcanic National Park
Winnemucca
Humboldt River
Elko
Wells
Newfoundland Evaporation Basin
Antelope Island
SALT LAKE CITY
Pyramid Lake Indian Reservation
Battle Mountain
Wendover
Park City
Pyramid Lake
Lovelock
Humboldt-Toiyabe National Forest
Great Salt Lake Desert
Wasatch-Cache NF
Utah Lake
Provo
Carson Sink
Reno
Sparks
Virginia City
Fallon
Austin
Humboldt-Toiyabe National Forest
Uinta NF
Lake Tahoe
CARSON CITY
Eureka
Utah
Walker River Indian Reservation
Toiyabe Range
Toquima Range
Monitor Range
Humboldt-Toiyabe National Forest
Ely
Manti-La Sal NF
Walker R
Baker
Hawthorne
Great Basin National Park
Richfield
Humboldt-Toiyabe National Forest
Fishlake National Forest
Pacific Time Zone
Mountain Time Zone
Humboldt-Toiyabe National Forest
Mono Lake
Humboldt-Toiyabe National Forest
To Sacramento
Yosemite National Park
Tonopah
Beaver
Torrey
Boundary Peak 13,140ft
Dixie National Forest
Pioche
Cathedral Gorge State Park
Cedar City
Bryce Canyon NP
Panguitch
Nevada
Rachel
Caliente
Bishop
Dixie NF
Grand Staircase-Escalante National Monument
Kings Canyon National Park
Zion NP
Nevada Test Site
Kanab
St George
Beatty
Page
Death Valley National Park
Sequoia National Park
Valley of Fire State Park
Overton
Humboldt-Toiyabe National Forest
Red Rock Canyon
Lake Mead
Las Vegas
Grand Canyon NP
Supai
Tuba City
California
Grand Canyon Village
Kaibab NF
Chloride
Seligman
Laughlin
Kingman
Williams
Flagstaff
Barstow
Bullhead City
Oatman
Prescott NF
Sedona
Jerome
Coconino NF
Lake Havasu City
Prescott
Los Angeles
Joshua Tree National Park
Payson
Prescott NF
Wickenburg
Quartzsite
PHOENIX
PACIFIC OCEAN
Arizona
San Diego
Gila River
Yuma
Tijuana
Mexicali
Cabeza Prieta National Wildlife Refuge
Tohono O'odham Indian Reservation
Baja California
Organ Pipe Cactus National Monument
Ensenada
Sonora
Sells
MEXICO
Gulf of California

SOUTHWEST

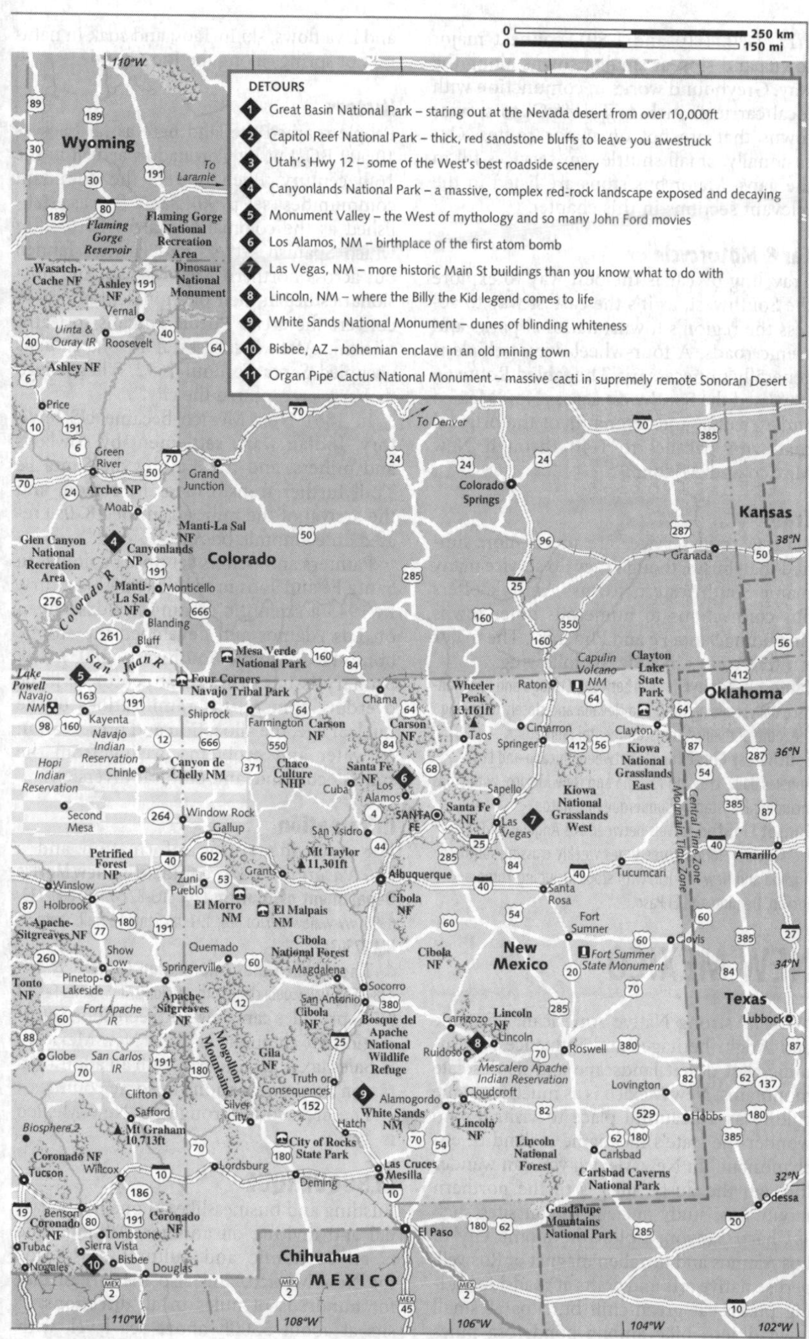
0 250 km
0 150 mi
DETOURS
1 Great Basin National Park – staring out at the Nevada desert from over 10,000ft
2 Capitol Reef National Park – thick, red sandstone bluffs to leave you awestruck
3 Utah's Hwy 12 – some of the West's best roadside scenery
4 Canyonlands National Park – a massive, complex red-rock landscape exposed and decaying
5 Monument Valley – the West of mythology and so many John Ford movies
6 Los Alamos, NM – birthplace of the first atom bomb
7 Las Vegas, NM – more historic Main St buildings than you know what to do with
8 Lincoln, NM – where the Billy the Kid legend comes to life
9 White Sands National Monument – dunes of blinding whiteness
10 Bisbee, AZ – bohemian enclave in an old mining town
11 Organ Pipe Cactus National Monument – massive cacti in supremely remote Sonoran Desert
Wyoming
To Laramie
Flaming Gorge Reservoir
Flaming Gorge National Recreation Area
Wasatch-Cache NF
Ashley NF
Dinosaur National Monument
Vernal
Uinta & Ouray IR
Roosevelt
Ashley NF
Price
Green River
Grand Junction
Arches NP
Moab
Manti-La Sal NF
Glen Canyon National Recreation Area
Canyonlands NP
Colorado
Colorado R
Manti-La Sal NF
Monticello
Blanding
Bluff
San Juan R
Lake Powell
Navajo NM
Mesa Verde National Park
Four Corners Navajo Tribal Park
Kayenta
Shiprock
Navajo Indian Reservation
Farmington
Hopi Indian Reservation
Chinle
Canyon de Chelly NM
Chaco Culture NHP
Second Mesa
Window Rock
Gallup
Petrified Forest NP
Winslow
Holbrook
Zuni Pueblo
El Morro NM
El Malpais NM
Apache-Sitgreaves NF
Show Low
Pinetop-Lakeside
Tonto NF
Fort Apache IR
Apache-Sitgreaves NF
Springerville
Quemado
Globe
San Carlos IR
Mogollon Mountains
Clifton
Safford
Mt Graham 10,713ft
Biosphere 2
Coronado NF
Tucson
Willcox
Lordsburg
Benson
Coronado NF
Tombstone
Coronado NF
Tubac
Sierra Vista
Bisbee
Nogales
Douglas
Chihuahua
MEXICO
To Denver
Colorado Springs
Kansas
Granada
Chama
Carson NF
Carson NF
Wheeler Peak 13,161ft
Taos
Raton
Capulin Volcano NM
Clayton Lake State Park
Oklahoma
Cimarron
Springer
Clayton
Kiowa National Grasslands East
Santa Fe NF
Cuba
Los Alamos
SANTA FE
Santa Fe NF
Sapello
Las Vegas
Kiowa National Grasslands West
Central Time Zone
Mountain Time Zone
San Ysidro
Mt Taylor 11,301ft
Grants
Albuquerque
Cibola NF
Tucumcari
Santa Rosa
Amarillo
Fort Sumner
Fort Sumner State Monument
Clovis
Cibola National Forest
Magdalena
Cibola NF
New Mexico
Socorro
San Antonio
Cibola NF
Bosque del Apache National Wildlife Refuge
Carrizozo
Lincoln NF
Lincoln
Ruidoso
Roswell
Mescalero Apache Indian Reservation
Texas
Lubbock
Gila NF
Truth or Consequences
Silver City
Cloudcroft
Alamogordo
White Sands NM
Lovington
Hatch
Lincoln NF
Lincoln National Forest
Hobbs
City of Rocks State Park
Carlsbad
Deming
Las Cruces
Mesilla
Carlsbad Caverns National Park
El Paso
Guadalupe Mountains National Park
Odessa
110°W
108°W
106°W
104°W
102°W
38°N
36°N
34°N
32°N

I-17, I-70, I-10 and I-80), connect major towns and stop at smaller towns along the way. Greyhound works in conjunction with local carriers, such as TNM&O, to service towns that are not on major routes. Occasionally, small shuttle van services fill in the gaps. Major bus stops are listed in the relevant sections in this chapter.

Car & Motorcycle

Traveling by car is the best way to explore the Southwest, as it's the easiest way to access the region's towns, national parks and scenic roads. A four-wheel-drive vehicle is generally unnecessary. The fabled Route 66 traversed the Southwest across New Mexico and Arizona, and remnants of the original road run parallel to I-40 through New Mexico and Arizona.

Train

Amtrak train services are much more limited than buses, though they do service many major Southwestern towns. Amtrak offers bus connections to numerous other towns (including Santa Fe and Phoenix). The major Amtrak routes include the following:

California Zephyr Travels between Chicago and San Francisco daily, crossing Utah and Nevada and closely following the route of the first transcontinental railroad.
Southwest Chief Travels between Chicago and Los Angeles daily, crossing Arizona and New Mexico, with stops including Flagstaff, Albuquerque and Raton.
Sunset Limited Travels between Los Angeles and Jacksonville, Florida, three times weekly crossing southern Arizona and New Mexico, with stops including Yuma, Tucson, Deming and El Paso.

NEW MEXICO

With its strong Native American, Hispanic and Anglo heritages and influences, its luminescent desert landscape and its desolate mountains, New Mexico is as much a unique culture as a beautiful place to visit. It's no wonder the state's nickname is 'land of enchantment.' In New Mexico you can wander through the dusty villages of the northern mountains; study ancient Indian sites such as Chaco Canyon; explore the 'atomic city' of Los Alamos and the alien magnet of Roswell; peruse native arts and crafts at roadside trading posts; eat green-chili burritos at small town diners; hike among ponderosa pines and lava flows; ski in Taos; and soak in natural hot springs along the Rio Grande.

History

People roamed the land here as far back as 10,500 BC, but by Coronado's arrival in the 16th century, Pueblos were the dominant communities (see p790). Santa Fe was established as the colonial capital in 1610, after which Spanish settlers and farmers fanned out across northern New Mexico, and missionaries began their often violent efforts to convert the area's Pueblo Indians to Catholicism. After a successful revolt, Indians occupied Santa Fe until 1692, when Diego de Vargas recaptured the city.

In 1851 New Mexico became US territory. Indian wars, settlement by cowboys and miners, and trade along the Santa Fe Trail further transformed the region, and the arrival of the railroad in the 1870s created an economic boom.

Painters and writers set up art colonies in Santa Fe and Taos in the early 20th century. In 1943 a scientific community descended on Los Alamos and developed the atomic bomb (see 'Atomic Southwest,' p805). The primary issues of the 21st century will be overdevelopment, the ramifications of the nuclear age, the allocation and preservation of water and problems arising from the state's economic and cultural diversity.

Information

For statewide visitor information and a free *Vacation Guide*, contact the **New Mexico Department of Tourism** (☎ 505-827-7400, 800-733-6396; www.newmexico.org; 491 Old Santa Fe Trail, Santa Fe, NM 87503).

The **Public Lands Information Center** (☎ 505-438-7542; www.publiclands.org; PO Box 27115, Santa Fe, NM 87502) provides camping and recreation information for all public lands in New Mexico.

Sales tax is around 6%, with an additional tax on accommodations in some counties.

The area code throughout New Mexico is ☎ 505.

ALBUQUERQUE

Bustling and businesslike on one hand, casual and inviting on another, Albuquerque is an economic and cultural crossroads for New Mexico, and also the largest city for hundreds of miles in all directions. It sits at about 5300ft above sea level, with

NEW MEXICO FACTS

Nickname Land of Enchantment
Population 1,855,059 (36th)
Area 121,356 sq miles (5th)
Admitted to Union January 6, 1912 (47th)
Capital city Santa Fe (population 62,200)
Other cities Albuquerque (448,607), Las Cruces (74,267)
State bird Roadrunner
Birthplace of outlaw William Bonney, aka Billy the Kid (1859–81); Smokey Bear
Famous for chilies, ancient pueblos, the first atomic bomb (1945)
Home of the USA's oldest road (the Camino Real), public building (Santa Fe Governors' Palace, 1610)

surrounding mountains topping 10,000ft. Like many western cities, its suburbs sprawl across the desert, though its core is built around a historic plaza that was founded in 1706. Albuquerque is a favorite of Route 66 junkies, who cruise the 'Mother Road' as it winds through downtown, seeking out the many historic businesses lining the streets. The students at the University of New Mexico (UNM), founded in 1889, bring the city a healthy dose of youthful energy and plenty of cultural events. Though Albuquerque is not as quaint as Santa Fe, just 63 miles north, it definitely has its own charms, and plenty of historic sites. It also has inexpensive accommodations and makes a comfortable, convenient base for exploring nearby mountains, deserts and pueblos.

Orientation

Albuquerque's major boundaries are Paseo del Norte Dr to the north, Central Ave to the south, Rio Grande Blvd to the west and Tramway Blvd to the east. Central Ave is the city's main artery; also known as old Route 66, it passes through Old Town, downtown, the university and Nob Hill. From the I-25 take exit 224B or from the I-40 take exit 167. The city is divided into four quadrants (NW, NE, SW and SE). The intersection of Central Ave and the railroad tracks just east of downtown serves as the center point of the city.

Information

BOOKSTORES

Page One (☎ 505-294-2026, 800-521-4122; 11018 Montgomery Blvd NE) Huge bookstore about 5 miles east of I-25. Used-book branch Page One Too! is across the street.

EMERGENCY

Albuquerque Police Department (☎ 505-242-2677; 400 Roma St NW) The number translates to 242-COPS.
Emergency number (☎ 911)

INTERNET ACCESS

Main Library (☎ 505-768-5140; 501 Copper Ave NW) Computer use fee is $3; call for branch locations.

MEDIA

Alibi (☎ 505-346-0660; www.alibi.com) Free weekly with good entertainment listings available in coffee shops and bookstores around town.

MEDICAL SERVICES

Presbyterian Hospital (☎ 505-841-1234; 1100 Central Ave SE)
University Hospital (☎ 505-272-2111; 2111 Lomas Blvd NE) On the UNM campus.

POST

Downtown Station (☎ 505-346-1674; 201 5th St SW)

TOURIST OFFICES

Albuquerque Convention & Visitors Bureau (☎ 505-842-9918, 800-733-9918; www.abqcvb.org; cnr 2nd St & Martin Luther King Jr Ave; 🕑 9am-5pm Mon-Fri) In the east wing of the Convention Center downtown.
Cibola National Forest Supervisor's Office (☎ 505-346-3900; www.fs.fed.us/r3/cibola; 2113 Osuna Rd NE; 🕑 8am-4:30pm Mon-Fri) About 1 mile west of I-25; covers Sandia mountains.
Old Town Information Center (303 Romero Street; 9am-5pm summer, 9:30am-4:30pm winter) Branch CVB office in Old Town's Dom Luis Plaza.

Sights

OLD TOWN

From its foundation in 1706 until the arrival of the railroad in 1880, Old Town Plaza was the hub of Albuquerque; today it's the city's most popular tourist area. Many original structures are still standing, along with galleries, gift shops and museums.

The **Albuquerque Museum** (☎ 505-243-7255; 2000 Mountain Rd NW; adult/child $3/1; 🕑 9am-5pm Tue-Sun) gives an excellent overview of the city's history, and has exhibits focusing on New Mexican artists, and a children's gallery.

North of Old Town is the must-see **Indian Pueblo Cultural Center** (☎ 505-843-7270, 800-766-4405; www.indianpueblo.org; 2401 12th St NW;

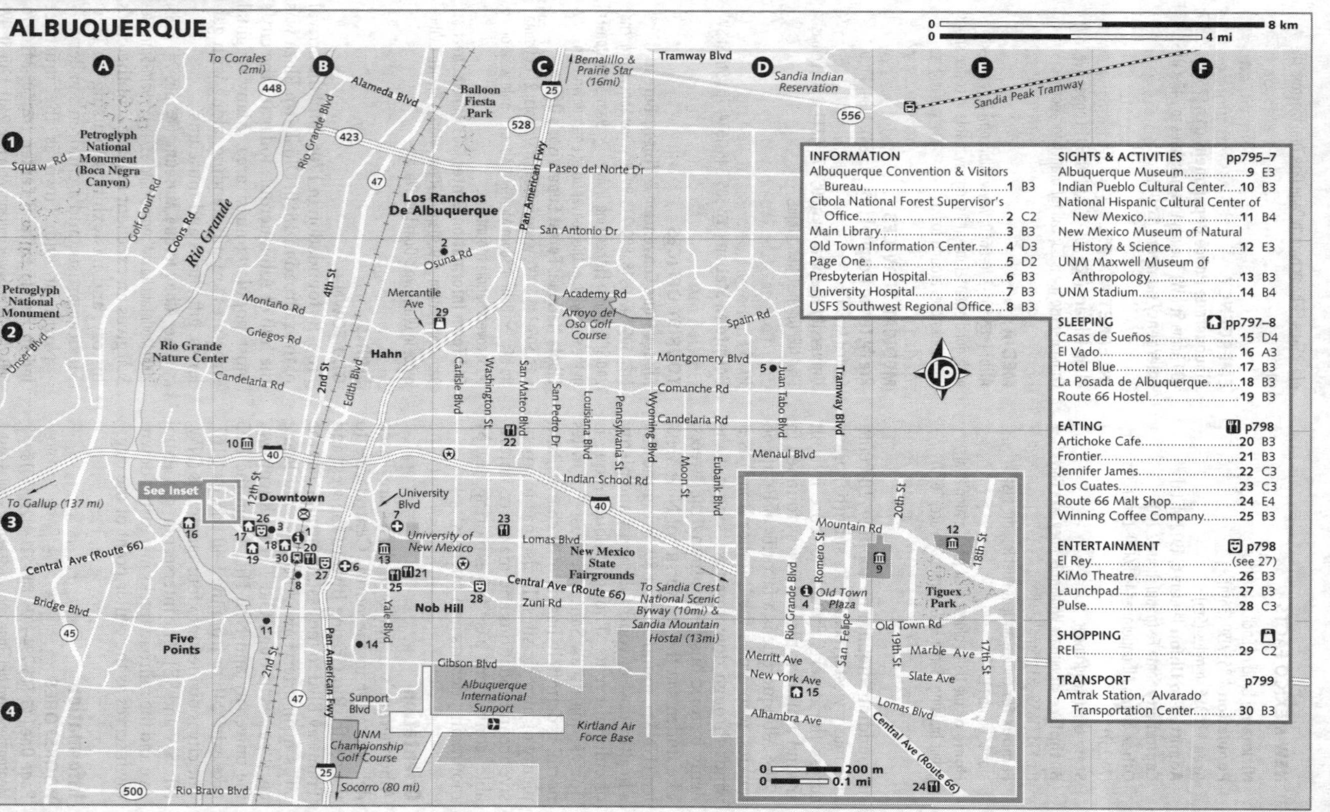
SOUTHWEST
ALBUQUERQUE
0 8 km
0 4 mi
INFORMATION
Albuquerque Convention & Visitors Bureau....1 B3
Cibola National Forest Supervisor's Office....2 C2
Main Library....3 B3
Old Town Information Center....4 D3
Page One....5 D2
Presbyterian Hospital....6 B3
University Hospital....7 B3
USFS Southwest Regional Office....8 B3
SIGHTS & ACTIVITIES pp795–7
Albuquerque Museum....9 E3
Indian Pueblo Cultural Center....10 B3
National Hispanic Cultural Center of New Mexico....11 B4
New Mexico Museum of Natural History & Science....12 E3
UNM Maxwell Museum of Anthropology....13 B3
UNM Stadium....14 B4
SLEEPING pp797–8
Casas de Sueños....15 D4
El Vado....16 A3
Hotel Blue....17 B3
La Posada de Albuquerque....18 B3
Route 66 Hostel....19 B3
EATING p798
Artichoke Cafe....20 B3
Frontier....21 B3
Jennifer James....22 C3
Los Cuates....23 C3
Route 66 Malt Shop....24 E4
Winning Coffee Company....25 B3
ENTERTAINMENT p798
El Rey....(see 27)
KiMo Theatre....26 B3
Launchpad....27 B3
Pulse....28 C3
SHOPPING
REI....29 C2
TRANSPORT p799
Amtrak Station, Alvarado Transportation Center....30 B3
To Corrales (2mi)
Alameda Blvd
Balloon Fiesta Park
Bernalillo & Prairie Star (16mi)
Tramway Blvd
Sandia Indian Reservation
Sandia Peak Tramway
Petroglyph National Monument (Boca Negra Canyon)
Squaw Rd
Rio Grande Blvd
Paseo del Norte Dr
Los Ranchos De Albuquerque
Pan American Fwy
Golf Court Rd
Coors Rd
Rio Grande
San Antonio Dr
Osuna Rd
Petroglyph National Monument
Unser Blvd
Montaño Rd
4th St
Mercantile Ave
Academy Rd
Arroyo del Oso Golf Course
Spain Rd
Griegos Rd
Rio Grande Nature Center
Hahn
Montgomery Blvd
Candelaria Rd
2nd St
Edith Blvd
Carlisle Blvd
Washington St
San Mateo Blvd
San Pedro Dr
Louisiana Blvd
Pennsylvania St
Wyoming Blvd
Comanche Rd
Juan Tabo Blvd
Menaul Blvd
Moon St
Eubank Blvd
Indian School Rd
To Gallup (137 mi)
See Inset
12th St
Downtown
University Blvd
University of New Mexico
Lomas Blvd
New Mexico State Fairgrounds
Central Ave (Route 66)
To Sandia Crest National Scenic Byway (10mi) & Sandia Mountain Hostal (13mi)
Bridge Blvd
Yale Blvd
Nob Hill
Zuni Rd
Five Points
Gibson Blvd
Sunport Blvd
Albuquerque International Sunport
Kirtland Air Force Base
UNM Championship Golf Course
Socorro (80 mi)
Rio Bravo Blvd
Mountain Rd
20th St
18th St
Romero St
Rio Grande Blvd
Old Town Plaza
Tiguex Park
San Felipe
Old Town Rd
19th St
Marble Ave
17th St
Merritt Ave
New York Ave
Slate Ave
Lomas Blvd
Alhambra Ave
0 200 m
0 0.1 mi

adult/student $4/1; 9am-4:30pm). Owned and run by an association of New Mexico's 19 Indian pueblos, it explores the history of the people, and it's a great starting point for those planning to visit the state's pueblos.

The **New Mexico Museum of Natural History and Science** (505-841-2800; 1801 Mountain Rd NW; adult/child $5/2; 9am-5pm) features an interactive walk through 4.6 billion years of history, with a focus on the Southwest. It's great for kids and dinosaur fans.

UNM & NOB HILL

The University of New Mexico area has loads of popular restaurants, casual bars, offbeat shops and hip college hangouts. The main drag is Central Ave between University and Carlisle Blvds. The university's **Maxwell Museum of Anthropology** (505-277-4405; admission free; 9am-4pm Tue-Fri, 10am-4pm Sat), on the UNM campus near Las Lomas Rd, examines 4 million years of human history, with one section focusing on the Southwest.

OTHER

The **National Hispanic Cultural Center of New Mexico** (505-246-2261; www.nhccnm.org; 1701 4th St SW; adult/child $3/free; 10am-5pm Tue-Sun) is a huge, new complex that includes a research library, performing arts center and exhibition galleries geared toward identifying, preserving and celebrating Hispanic arts. It's south of downtown and well worth a trip.

Sandia Peak Tramway (505-856-7325; adult /child $15/10; 9am-8pm Thu-Tue, also 5-8pm Wed) is a 2.7-mile ride that starts in the desert realm of cholla cactus and soars to the pines atop 10,678ft Sandia Peak. The High Finance Restaurant & Tavern is a popular destination at the top. Take I-25 north and turn east at Tramway Blvd (exit 234).

Northwest of downtown, along Albuquerque's West Mesa, **Petroglyph National Monument** (505-899-0205; weekdays/weekends $1/2; 8am-5pm) protects volcanic cones and archeological sites, including 25,000 rock etchings dating from AD 1300. You can explore the area on three trails with varying degrees of difficulty. From I-40, exit onto Unser Blvd and head north for 3 miles.

Activities

The omnipresent Sandia Mountains and the less crowded Manzano Mountains offer outdoor activities including **hiking**, **skiing** (downhill and cross-country), **mountain biking** and **camping**. The **Sandia Ranger Station** (505-281-3304; 11776 Hwy 337; 8am-5pm Mon-Fri, 8:30am-5pm Sat & Sun), off I-40 exit 175 south, has maps and information. For equipment, try **REI** (505-247-1191; 1550 Mercantile Ave NE), just west of I-25 at the Montagno Rd exit.

Reach the top of the Sandias via the eastern slope along the lovely **Sandia Crest National Scenic Byway** (I-40 exit 175 north), which passes several trailheads; or take the Sandia Peak Tramway up the western side (see Metropolitan Albuquerque earlier). An alternative is to take NM 165 from Placitas (I-25 exit 242), a dirt road through Las Huertas Canyon that passes the prehistoric dwelling of Sandia Man Cave.

The 8-mile (one way) **La Luz Trail** takes you to the top of the Sandias. To reach the trailhead, take I-25 north to Tramway Blvd, head east, then left onto USFS Rd 333.

The **Sandia Peak Ski Area** (505-242-9133; adult/child $38/29) is at the top of the Sandia Peak Tramway. On summer weekends and holidays (May to October), one lift remains open for mountain bikers, and combination bike rental and lift packages are available.

Festivals & Events

Hundreds of hot-air-balloon pilots attract almost a million spectators to **International Balloon Fiesta** (www.aibf.org) in early October. For balloon rides during the festival, contact **Rainbow Ryders** (800-725-2477).

The **New Mexico Gay Rodeo Association** (505-980-2612; www.nmgra.com) hosts the **Zia Regional Rodeo** on the second weekend of August.

Sleeping

Central Ave is the former Route 66, and it's lined with vintage motels. Look for accommodation west of downtown along Central Ave near Rio Grande Blvd, or along Central Ave in the UNM district.

BUDGET

El Vado (505-243-4594; elvado@comcast.net; 2500 Central Ave SW; r $32; P) Built in 1936, it claims to be the 'purest' surviving Route 66 motel in town – meaning it hasn't been overly modernized. Cute and clean, it's definitely a roadside gem, with guests staying in duplex-type buildings, each with its own carport.

Route 66 Hostel (505-247-1813; www.members.aol.com/route66hos/htmlRT66; 1012 Central SW; dm/d

$15/30; P) This friendly place sits between downtown and the Old Town.

Sandia Mountain Hostel (☎ 505-281-4117; dm/d $14/32; P) This rural hostel 20 miles east of the city (I-40 exit 175 north) affords easy access to mountains.

MID-RANGE & TOP END

La Posada de Albuquerque (☎ 505-242-9090, 800-777-5732; www.laposada-abq.com; 125 2nd St NW; r $120; P) Conrad Hilton, who hailed from Socorro, opened this downtown beauty in 1939. Original rooms are beautifully maintained and the fine tile, wood, stucco and leather lobby is stunning – be sure to pop your head in, even if you're not staying. The bar has weekend jazz and is great for a casual evening cocktail.

Nora Dixon Place (☎ 505-898-3662, 888-667-2349; www.noradixon.com; 312 Dixon Rd; r from $95; P) In Corrales, a farming village 8 miles north of town, this friendly B&B has three beautiful rooms nestled in the Rio Grande Bosque, all facing a lovely courtyard with Sandia Mountain views.

Casas de Sueños (☎ 505-247-4560; www.casasdesuenos.com; 310 Rio Grande Blvd SW; r from $85; P) Located near Old Town, this B&B has 22 quaint little *casitas* (cottages) among 1.5 acres of gardens; each is decorated with hand-crafted furniture and local artwork.

Hotel Blue (☎ 505-924-2400, 877-878-4868; www.thehotelblue.com; 717 Central Ave NW; r $69; P) This stylish boutique hotel is in a big white building close to downtown. It has 145 rooms and suites on six floors.

Eating

Albuquerque offers plenty of good, cheap meals, particularly if you like Southwestern cuisine. On the fine-dining side, the restaurant scene isn't as trendy and upscale (or expensive) as in Santa Fe, but it's definitely expanding, and there are some excellent choices.

Route 66 Malt Shop (☎ 505-242-7866; 1720 Central Ave SW; dishes $4-6) The original vintage interior of this tiny diner is worth a look on its own, but if you're hungry, pull up to a stool and dig into a great green-chili cheeseburger (their signature) and a chocolate malt.

Winning Coffee Company (☎ 505-266-0000; 111 Harvard St NE; dishes $4-6) Flavorful, strong coffee is the key draw at this large, laid-back coffeehouse which is a favorite with locals and students, due to its proximity to UNM. It serves breakfast and lunch, and there's often poetry or acoustic music at night.

THE AUTHOR'S CHOICE

Los Cuates (☎ 505-255-5079; 4901 Lomas Blvd NE; dishes $8-15) This spacious, unpretentious family restaurant is an Albuquerque favorite and is an excellent place to indulge in Southwestern specialties like blue-corn enchiladas, seriously cheesy and loaded with flavor. You can't eat food like this every day, but it's worth the splurge here.

Artichoke Cafe (☎ 505-243-0200; 424 Central Ave SE; dishes $14-24) A perennial Albuquerque favorite, this comfortable, elegant restaurant serves a mix of French, Italian and American cuisine in an attractive, unpretentious setting. A rotating selection of local artwork adorns the walls.

Prairie Star (☎ 505-867-3327; 288 Prairie Star Rd; dishes $17-30; Tue-Sun) Located at the Santa Ana Pueblo golf resort in Bernalillo, 16 miles north of Albuquerque, the amazing Southwestern-influenced cuisine here makes this one of the finest restaurants in New Mexico. Views of the Sandia Mountains are stellar.

Jennifer James (☎ 505-884-3665; 2813 San Mateo NE; dishes $16-30; Tue-Sat) An elegant restaurant run by one of Albuquerque's star chefs.

Frontier (☎ 505-266-0550; 2400 Central Ave SE; dishes $3-8) Inexpensive meals served 24 hours per day near UNM.

Entertainment

The free weekly *Alibi* has reviews and listings. **Ticketmaster** (☎ 505-883-7800) handles many major concerts and sports events.

KiMo Theatre (☎ 505-768-3544, 505-768-3522; 423 Central Ave NW) A pride and joy of downtown, this restored 1927 place was designed with a mixture of pueblo and Art Deco stylings. It hosts various theater, art and music events.

Several music clubs and bars line Central Ave downtown and in the UNM/Nob Hill area, including **Launchpad** (☎ 505-764-8887; 618 Central Ave SW), which has a full roster of good indie-rock and roots bands, and **El Rey** (☎ 505-242-2353; 624 Central Ave SW), in an old movie theater.

Pulse (☎ 505-255-3334; 4100 Central Ave SE) This popular gay-friendly nightclub is just east of Nob Hill.

Getting There & Around

AIR

The **Albuquerque International Sunport** (☎ 505-244-7733) airport is about 4 miles south of downtown, just east of I-25. Most major US airlines service Albuquerque, though **Southwest** (☎ 800-435-9792) has the largest presence.

SunTran Route 50 connects the airport with downtown (no Sunday or evening service). Cabs between the airport and downtown run about $13.

BUS

Greyhound (☎ 505-243-4435, 800-231-2222; 300 2nd St SW) runs buses to Santa Fe ($10, one hour), Taos ($26, three hours), Roswell ($36, 3½ hours), Carlsbad ($42, 5½ hours) and beyond.

Sandia Shuttle (☎ 888-775-5696) runs from the Albuquerque airport to Santa Fe ($23, 70 minutes) multiple times daily.

Twin Hearts (☎ 800-654-9456) has shuttles from the airport to Taos ($40, three hours).

PUBLIC TRANSPORTATION

The **Alvarado Transportation Center** (cnr 1st St & Central Ave) is the hub for all local **SunTran** (☎ 505-843-9200) buses serving metropolitan Albuquerque. The fare is $1.

National car rental agencies have offices at the airport and around town; check p1121 for details.

Yellow Cab (☎ 505-247-8888, 800-657-6232) operates 24 hours per day.

TRAIN

The Southwest Chief stops daily at Albuquerque's **Amtrak station** (☎ 505-842-9650; 214 1st St SW), heading east to Kansas City, Missouri (from $115, 18 hours) and beyond, or west through Flagstaff, Arizona (from $60, four hours) to Los Angeles (from $68, 15 hours). Service to Santa Fe ($32, 2½ hours) involves transferring to a bus in Lamy, 18 miles south of Santa Fe.

EAST ALONG I-40

Sections of old Route 66 parallel I-40 throughout New Mexico.

In **Santa Rosa**, 114 miles east of Albuquerque, the **Route 66 Auto Museum** (☎ 505-472-1966; 2766 Old Rte 66; adult/child $5/free; 🕒 7:30am-7pm) pays homage to this mother of all cross-country roads.

In **Tucumcari**, 173 miles east of Albuquerque, the **Blue Swallow Motel** (☎ 505-461-9849; www.blueswallowmotel.com; 815 E Tucumcari Blvd; s/d from $30/35; P ✕) is a lovingly restored original Route 66 motor court dating from 1939, with a stucco exterior and 11 clean, cozy rooms.

WEST ALONG I-40

Although you can zip between Albuquerque and Flagstaff, Arizona, in less than five hours, the national monuments and pueblos along the way are well worth a visit. For a **scenic loop**, take Hwy 53 southwest from Grants, which leads to all the following sights except Acoma. Hwy 602 brings you north to Gallup.

Acoma Pueblo

Known as 'Sky City' because of its fantastic mesa-top location 7000ft above sea level and 367ft above the surrounding plateau, Acoma has been populated since the 12th century, making it one of the oldest continuously inhabited settlements in North America. The famous Acoma pottery is sold by individual artists on the mesa. To reach Sky City, you must take a guided tour (adult/child $10/7) from the **visitors center** (☎ 505-469-1052, 800-747-0181; 🕒 8am-7pm summer, 8am-4pm winter). There's a photography charge of $10. From I-40 take exit 108, about 50 miles west of Albuquerque.

El Malpais National Monument

Meaning 'bad land' in Spanish, El Malpais is an eerie landscape of almost 200 sq miles of lava flows. The **El Malpais Information Center** (☎ 505-783-4774; 🕒 8:30am-4:30pm), 22 miles southwest of Grants on Hwy 53, has details on hikes and primitive (free) camping.

El Morro National Monument

The 200ft sandstone outcropping at this **monument** (☎ 505-783-4226; admission $3; 🕒 9am-5pm), also known as 'Inscription Rock,' has been a travelers' oasis for millennia. Thousands of carvings – from petroglyphs in the pueblo at the top (circa 1250) to elaborate inscriptions by the Spanish conquistadors and the Anglo pioneers – offer a unique means of tracing history. It's located about 38 miles southwest of Grants via Hwy 53.

Zuni Pueblo

The Zuni are known worldwide for their delicately inlaid silverwork which is sold in stores lining Hwy 53. Walk past stone houses and beehive-shaped mud ovens to the massive **Our Lady of Guadalupe Mission**, featuring impressive murals. The **A:shiwi A:wan Museum & Heritage Center** (☎ 505-782-4403; 02E Oho Caliente Rd; adult/child $7/3.50; ⏲ 9am-6pm Mon-Fri) displays early photos and other tribal artifacts.

The only place to stay is the small, pleasant **Inn at Halona** (☎ 505-782-4547, 800-752-3278; www.halona.com; r $79;), off Halona Plaza in Zuni Pueblo. Rate includes breakfast.

Gallup

The town of Gallup functions as the Navajo and Zuni peoples' major trading center, and the many trading posts, pawn shops, and galleries attract those seeking affordable jewelry, rugs, and other arts and crafts. Gallup is another classic Route 66 town, with loads of vintage motels and businesses. Next to the Amtrak station on Hwy 66 is the **Gallup Cultural Center** (☎ 505-863-4131; admission free; ⏲ 8:30am-4pm Mon-Fri), with an excellent collection of kachina dolls and a tiny theater. Contact the **visitors center** (☎ 505-863-4909, 800-242-4282; www.gallupnm.org; 701 Montoya Blvd; ⏲ 8am-5pm) for details.

The town's true lodging jewel is **El Rancho** (☎ 505-863-9311; www.elranchohotel.com; 1000 E Rte 66; s/d from $66/72;), which dates from 1937. It has a beautiful, spacious Southwestern lobby, an eclectic selection of rooms and a nice bar.

El Metate Tamale Factory (☎ 505-722-7000; 610 W Mesa Ave; dishes $4-7) This small, casual restaurant in a residential section, makes incredibly flavorful (and affordable) tamales and other specialties. Take-out is available, too.

SANTA FE

It's no secret that Santa Fe, the capital of New Mexico, is one of the most popular tourist destinations in the US. Yet no matter how many people may flock here, this richly historic town retains its magnetism as one of the Southwest's most fascinating places.

Initially established in 1610, Santa Fe is the oldest European community west of the Mississippi. At 7000ft, it's also the highest US capital, lying at the base of the Sangre de Cristo Mountains. It gets about 300 sunny days a year, though summer rains can be sudden and nights often get cool.

Tourism focuses on the small downtown plaza, which at any given time may be teeming with artists, craftspeople, wealthy travelers, healthy outdoor enthusiasts and a few off-the-grid hippies.

The city and its surrounding areas are loaded with fantastic museums, historic sites, colorful festivals and often surreal landscapes. Santa Fe offers a golden opportunity to dig deep into Hispanic and Native American traditions, but it's also a fantastic place to indulge in top-notch cuisine, kick back in a local café to watch a fascinating parade of people pass by, and wander Canyon Rd galleries.

Orientation

The downtown plaza lies within walking distance of many historic buildings and museums. Guadalupe St is the main north–south road through downtown and the state Capitol sits on Paseo de Peralta, which circles the center of town. Cerrillos Rd (I-25 exit 278) enters town from the south. St Francis Dr (I-25 exit 282) forms the western border of downtown and turns into US 285, which heads north toward Los Alamos and Taos.

Information

BOOKSTORES

Collected Works (☎ 505-988-4226; 208B W San Francisco St) Small downtown store with no periodicals.

Travel Bug (☎ 505-992-0418; 328 S Guadalupe St) Specializes in travel books.

EMERGENCY

Emergency number (☎ 911)

Police (☎ 505-955-5010; 2515 Camio Entrada)

INTERNET ACCESS

Santa Fe Public Library (☎ 505-955-6780; 145 Washington Ave)

MEDIA

Santa Fe Reporter (☎ 505-988-5541; www.sfreporter.com) Free alternative weekly.

MEDICAL SERVICES

St Vincent Hospital (☎ 505-820-5247; 455 St Michael's Dr)

POST

Main Post Office (☎ 505-988-6351; 120 S Federal Place)

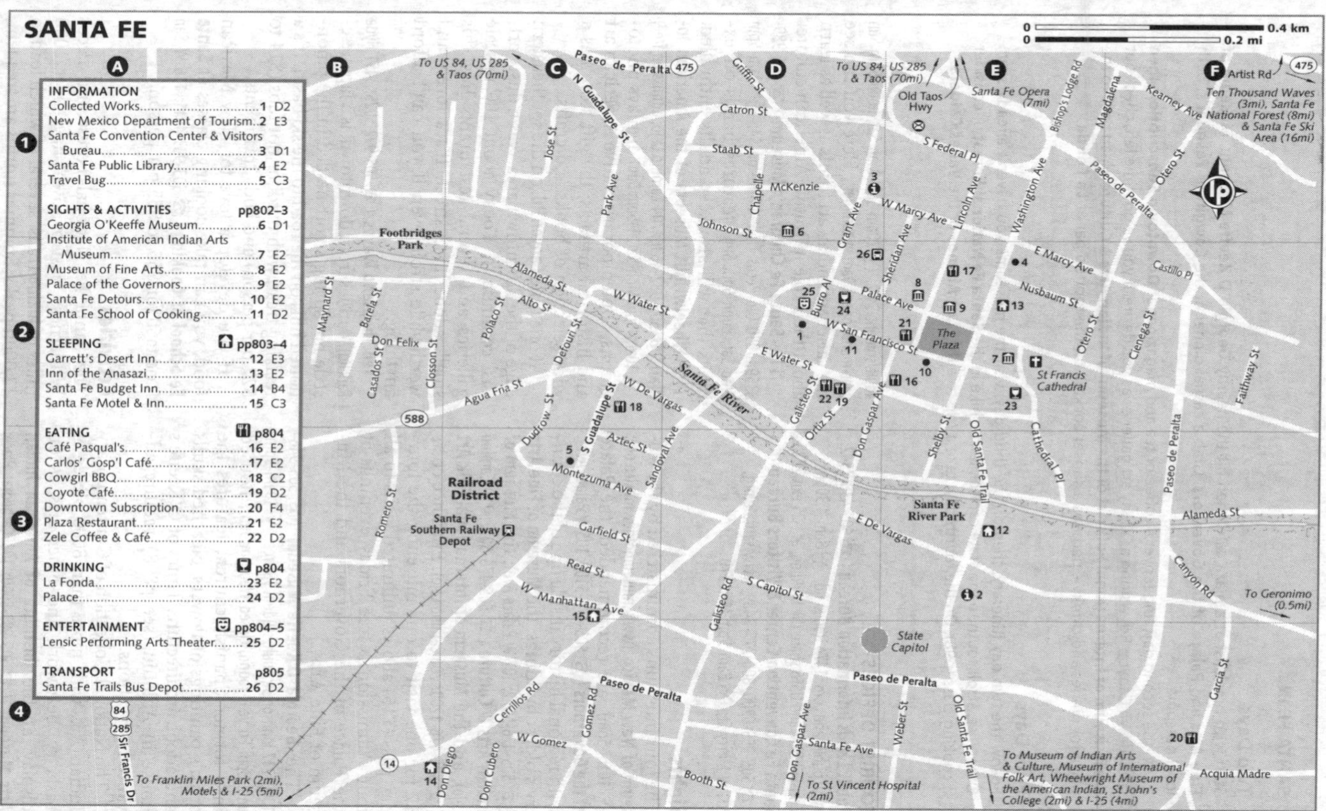
SANTA FE
0 0.4 km
0 0.2 mi
INFORMATION
Collected Works 1 D2
New Mexico Department of Tourism 2 E3
Santa Fe Convention Center & Visitors Bureau 3 D1
Santa Fe Public Library 4 E2
Travel Bug 5 C3
SIGHTS & ACTIVITIES pp802–3
Georgia O'Keeffe Museum 6 D1
Institute of American Indian Arts Museum 7 E2
Museum of Fine Arts 8 E2
Palace of the Governors 9 E2
Santa Fe Detours 10 E2
Santa Fe School of Cooking 11 D2
SLEEPING pp803–4
Garrett's Desert Inn 12 E3
Inn of the Anasazi 13 E2
Santa Fe Budget Inn 14 B4
Santa Fe Motel & Inn 15 C3
EATING p804
Café Pasqual's 16 E2
Carlos' Gosp'l Café 17 E2
Cowgirl BBQ 18 C2
Coyote Café 19 D2
Downtown Subscription 20 F4
Plaza Restaurant 21 E2
Zele Coffee & Café 22 D2
DRINKING p804
La Fonda 23 E2
Palace 24 D2
ENTERTAINMENT pp804–5
Lensic Performing Arts Theater 25 D2
TRANSPORT p805
Santa Fe Trails Bus Depot 26 D2
To US 84, US 285 & Taos (70mi)
Paseo de Peralta
475
N Guadalupe St
Griffin St
Catron St
Staab St
Jose St
Park Ave
Chapelle
McKenzie
Johnson St
Footbridges Park
Old Taos Hwy
Santa Fe Opera (7mi)
S Federal Pl
Bishop's Lodge Rd
Magdalena
Kearney Ave
Artist Rd
Ten Thousand Waves (3mi), Santa Fe National Forest (8mi) & Santa Fe Ski Area (16mi)
W Marcy Ave
Lincoln Ave
Washington Ave
Grant Ave
Sheridan Ave
E Marcy Ave
Castillo Pl
Otero St
Nusbaum St
Palace Ave
Burro Al
W San Francisco St
The Plaza
St Francis Cathedral
Cienega St
Faithway St
Maynard St
Barela St
Don Felix
Casados St
Closson St
Polaco St
Alto St
Alameda St
W Water St
Defouri St
E Water St
Santa Fe River
Galisteo St
Ortiz St
Don Gaspar Ave
Shelby St
Old Santa Fe Trail
Cathedral Pl
Agua Fria St
588
W De Vargas
S Guadalupe St
Aztec St
Dudrow St
Montezuma Ave
Sandoval Ave
Railroad District
Santa Fe Southern Railway Depot
Romero St
Garfield St
Read St
W Manhattan Ave
Santa Fe River Park
E De Vargas
Canyon Rd
To Geronimo (0.5mi)
Galisteo Rd
S Capitol St
State Capitol
Paseo de Peralta
Cerrillos Rd
Gomez Rd
W Gomez
Don Cubero
Don Diego
14
84
285
Sir Francis Dr
To Franklin Miles Park (2mi), Motels & I-25 (5mi)
Santa Fe Ave
Weber St
Booth St
To St Vincent Hospital (2mi)
Garcia St
Acquia Madre
To Museum of Indian Arts & Culture, Museum of International Folk Art, Wheelwright Museum of the American Indian, St John's College (2mi) & I-25 (4mi)

SOUTHWEST

SANTA FE IN...

Two Days

Start with breakfast at a plaza café, then hit the nearby **Georgia O'Keeffe Museum**, **Museum of Fine Arts** and **Palace of the Governors**. Grab a casual dinner at the **Cowgirl** or **Pasqual's**, both local hotspots.

On the second day, linger over a coffee or tea and magazines at **Downtown Subscription**, then stroll down Canyon Rd, visiting as many art galleries as you desire. If you've got time left, check out the **Museum of International Folk Art** or the **Museum of Indian Arts & Culture**. Head back to the plaza for dinner and drinks – perhaps a sunset cocktail on the rooftop bar at **La Fonda**.

Four Days

Follow the two-day itinerary, then on the third day, visit the museums you haven't already seen. Otherwise, stroll south to the state capitol, take a hike in the **Santa Fe National Forest** or consider a cooking class (p98). On the fourth day, take a trip to either **Los Alamos** or the **Valles Caldera**.

TOURIST OFFICES

Public Lands Information Bureau (☎ 505-438-7542; www.publiclands.org; 1474 Rodeo Rd; 🕑 8am-4:30pm Mon-Fri) BLM and USFS share the building, at I-25 exit 282B.

Santa Fe Convention Center & Visitors Bureau (☎ 505-955-6200, 800-777-2489; www.santafe.org; 201 W Marcy St; 🕑 8am-5pm Mon-Fri)

Sights

The four museums administered by the **Museum of New Mexico** (www.museumofnewmexico.org; 🕑 10am-5pm), are recommended: the **Palace of the Governors** (☎ 505-476-5100; 105 W Palace Ave), with regional history inside one of the country's oldest buildings; the **Museum of Fine Arts** (☎ 505-476-5072; 107 W Palace Ave); the **Museum of Indian Arts & Culture** (☎ 505-476-5072; 710 Camino Lejo); and the **Museum of International Folk Art** (☎ 505-476-1200; 706 Camino Lejo). Entrance costs $7 for one visit to one museum; the four-day pass ($15) allows unlimited visits to all four. Admission is free Friday evenings at the Palace of the Governors and the Museum of Fine Arts.

The **Georgia O'Keeffe Museum** (☎ 505-946-1000; 217 Johnson St; adult/student $8/free; 🕑 10am-5pm, until 8pm Fri year-round, closed Wed Nov-Jun), housed in a former Spanish church, features the artist's paintings of flowers, bleached skulls and adobe architecture. Tours of O'Keeffe's house in Abiquiu (see p808) require advance reservations.

The National Collection of Contemporary Indian Art, with more than 8000 pieces of basketry, beadwork and other arts, is on display at the **Institute of American Indian Arts Museum** (☎ 505-983-8900; 108 Cathedral Place; adult/student $4/2; 🕑 10am-5pm Mon-Sat, noon-5pm Sun year-round, opens 9am in summer). Here you can see the variety of Indian art forms as well as learn about their role in Native American culture.

The **Santa Fe Children's Museum** (☎ 505-989-8359; 1050 Old Pecos Trail; admission $4; 🕑 10am-5pm Wed-Sat, noon-5pm Sun) features hands-on exhibits that will also keep adults enthralled. The **Wheelwright Museum of the American Indian** (☎ 505-982-4636; 704 Camino Lejo; admission free; 🕑 10am-5pm Mon-Sat, 1-5pm Sun) displays photographs, contemporary Native American art and historical artifacts; the gift store has a wide selection of books and crafts.

At one time **Canyon Rd**, on the southeastern edge of the downtown area, was a dusty artists' community. Today about 100 upscale galleries and several restaurants hug this small, adobe-lined street. It's a lovely and worthwhile stroll, even if you can't afford anything.

Ten Thousand Waves (☎ 505-992-5025; 3451 Hyde Park Rd), 4 miles from downtown, is a Japanese-style hot spring resort nestled in the piñon-dotted hills on the road to the ski basin. It's a relaxing treat, with outdoor hot tubs ($14 to $27 per person) and body treatments.

If you develop a love for New Mexican food, you can take cooking classes at **Santa Fe School of Cooking** (☎ 505-983-4511; 116 W San Francisco St) for $55 to $65 per person.

Activities

The Santa Fe National Forest and Pecos Wilderness, east of town, have over 1000 miles of **hiking** trails, several of which lead to 12,000ft peaks. Summer storms are frequent, so prepare well for hikes and check weather reports. For maps and details, contact the Public Lands Information Center (p802).

Mountain biking opportunities are also abundant. Call or stop by **Bike and Sport** (☎ 505-820-0809; 1829 Cerillos Rd) for maps and advice on rides, or **Santa Fe Mountain Sports** (☎ 505-988-3337; 607 Cerrillos Rd). Both rent mountain bikes from about $35/day.

The **Santa Fe Ski Area** (☎ 505-982-4429; adult /child $44/36, beginners $22), 16 miles northeast of Santa Fe on Hwy 475, offers downhill skiing in winter, hiking in summer.

Tours

Santa Fe's rich history is evidenced in the town's buildings. To learn more, take a two-hour walking tour from any of several local companies, including **Historic Walks of Santa Fe** (☎ 505-986-8388), **Afoot in Santa Fe** (☎ 505-983-3701) and **Aboot About Santa Fe** (☎ 505-988-2774). Tours cost $10 for adults, free for children.

Many companies also offer guided outdoor trips around Santa Fe and throughout northern New Mexico, including **Santa Fe Detours** (☎ 505-983-6565, 800-338-6877; www.sfdetours.com; 54½ E San Francisco St) and **Outback Tours** (☎ 505-820-6101, 888-772-3274; www.outbacktours.com; PO Box 961, Santa Fe, NM 87504).

Santa Fe for Children

With its colorful atmosphere, numerous museums, and the fact it's so easy to walk around, Santa Fe is an excellent destination for families. New Mexico gets hot in the summer, but Santa Fe is at a high elevation and remains somewhat cooler, and the city has many cool spots to tuck inside if you need a rest.

The **Santa Fe Children's Museum** (p802) is a great first stop, with numerous hands-on exhibits and other kid-friendly activities. The **Santa Fe Public Library** (p800) has a regular summer reading series. A highlight every September is **Santa Fe Fiesta** (see below), when kids can watch the children's pet parade and then see 'Old Man Gloom' go up in flames. For recreation or a family picnic, **Fort Marcy Field Complex** (490 Washington Ave) is close to the plaza; a few miles west, **Franklin Miles Park** (cnr Camino Carlos Rey & Siringo Rd) has a large skateboard facility.

The excellent free quarterly publication *New Mexico Kids* has further resources and activity ideas.

If you're traveling throughout New Mexico with children, consider visiting **Bear Historical State Park** (p813), **Bandelier National Monument** (p805) and the **New Mexico Museum of Space History** (p812).

Referrals for child-care services can be obtained by calling the **Santa Fe Community College** (☎ 505-428-1344).

Festivals & Events

On the third weekend in August, upwards of 100,000 collectors and nonaficionados alike deluge Santa Fe for the **Indian Market** (☎ 505-983-5220; www.swaia.org), a juried show featuring the work of 1200 artists from some 100 tribes. Book hotels far in advance.

Santa Fe Fiesta (☎ 505-988-7575; www.santafefiesta.org), celebrated here since 1712, commemorates the peaceful return of the Spanish to Santa Fe in 1692. It's been modified over the years from a straightforward religious festival to an arts celebration, with music, dancing and oddball parades. Events take place the weekend following Labor Day, kicking off with the burning of Zozobra, a 50ft marionette also known as 'Old Man Gloom.'

Sleeping

Rates in Santa Fe are sometimes excruciatingly high, especially during the high season (June to August). Prices drop the further you get from downtown. The visitors center website (www.santafe.org) lists reservation services, which can be helpful.

BUDGET & MID-RANGE

Cerrillos Rd is lined with *lots* of chains and independent motels, the best place to look if you're on a budget.

Western Scene Motel (☎ 505-983-7484; 1608 Cerrillos Rd; r $40; P ✖) This humble motel is about as basic as they come, but it's also as inexpensive as almost anything you'll find in Santa Fe outside a hostel. It's an attractive adobe structure with a cool neon sign that can't help but turn your head; a charming spot for those into old roadside motels.

El Rey Inn (☎ 505-982-1931, 800-521-1349; www.elreyinnsantafe.com; 1862 Cerrillos Rd; r $89; P ✖ 🏊) For the money, this may be the nicest place to stay in Santa Fe. Located 2 miles south of the plaza, it sits on three grassy, nicely landscaped acres that are so pleasant, you may not want to leave. Rooms are tastefully appointed in Southwestern style.

Santa Fe Motel & Inn (☎ 505-982-1039, 800-930-5002; www.santafemotelinn.com; 510 Cerrillos Rd; r $99; P) This motel has just 23 rooms, but they're well put together and attractive, many detailed in Southwestern style in what once were historic residences.

Santa Fe Budget Inn (☎ 505-982-5952, 800-288-7600; www.santafebudgetinn.com; 725 Cerrillos Rd; r $82; P) Just a standard, modern hotel, the rooms here are not exactly a thrill in themselves, but they're crisp and clean. The prices are decent and the location is great, only a half-dozen blocks from the plaza.

Garrett's Desert Inn (☎ 505-982-1851, 800-888-2145; www.garrettsdesertinn.com; 311 Old Santa Fe Trail; r $111; P) This 1970s motel is just a few minutes' walk from the plaza.

Stage Coach Motor Inn (☎ 505-471-0707; 3360 Cerrillos Rd; r $89; P) Stage Coach is another reliable property, though it's about 4 miles southwest of the plaza.

TOP END

Inn of the Anasazi (☎ 505-988-3030, 800-688-8100; www.innoftheanasazi.com; 113 Washington Ave; summer/winter r from $289/199; P) If you're looking for the top of the heap of local hotels, this sumptuous inn right off the plaza will treat you right. The building and its common rooms are tastefully modeled after ancient puebloan architectural styles, and it works. The service is casual yet professional, and the rooms are impeccably appointed with Southwestern details and earthy tones, from the ceiling beams to the sink tops. Some rooms have balconies and all have kiva fireplaces.

Eating

With an overwhelming selection of excellent restaurants, many of them incredibly expensive, choosing a place to eat can be a daunting task.

Café Pasqual's (☎ 505-983-9340; 121 Don Gaspar Ave; dishes $16-24) Don't miss this popular downtown spot, deservedly famous for its creative takes on simple, hearty comfort food – breakfast, lunch or dinner. Sunday brunch is especially satisfying, and the inevitable long wait is worth it.

Downtown Subscription (☎ 505-983-3085; 376 Garcia St; dishes $3-6) Make the short trek out to this Santa Fe favorite for excellent coffee, unusual teas, pastries, desserts and an excellent array of newspapers and magazines (for sale).

Geronimo (☎ 505-982-1500; 724 Canyon Rd; dishes $25-35) A meal here is a gourmet splurge you won't soon forget, as it's among the finest restaurants in town – not to mention one of the most romantic, housed in a 1756 adobe building.

Coyote Café (☎ 505-983-1615; 132 Water St; dishes $12-18) Celebrity chef Mark Miller opened this original Coyote Café in 1987, fueling what would become a Southwestern food craze – overhyped, yes, but still delicious. The casual rooftop cantina (open from April to October only) is the place to head, though, as it offers great meals at about half the price of the dining room.

Other recommendations:

Carlos' Gosp'l Café (☎ 505-983-1841; 125 Lincoln Ave; dishes $5-8) Where locals go for lunch.

Zele Coffee & Café (☎ 505-982-7835; 201 Galisteo St; dishes $6-8) Breakfast, lunch & great coffee anytime.

Plaza Restaurant (☎ 505-982-1664; 54 Lincoln Ave; dishes $8-12)

THE AUTHOR'S CHOICE

Cowgirl BBQ (☎ 505-982-2565; 319 S Guadalupe St; dishes $7-14) Sporting iron-saddle bar chairs, a comfortably rustic interior and service that's friendly and genuine, the Cowgirl is an easy favorite. The food is affordably priced, fresh and a thrill to eat – try the salmon tacos, the buffalo burger, BBQ items or the vegetarian dishes. There's lots of good beer on tap in the bar, and it's kid-friendly, too. Reservations are worthwhile as it's quite popular.

Drinking

La Fonda (☎ 505-982-5511; 100 E San Francisco St) For a sunset drink, try the rooftop bar at La Fonda, one of the city's most historic hotels, dating from 1922.

Palace (☎ 505-982-9891; 142 W Palace Ave) The service can be terrible at the Palace, but the old bar – with its red-all-over lighting, old West atmosphere and strange Indian princess oil painting – is wacky enough to still be worth a stop.

Entertainment

Check the free *Santa Fe Reporter* for thorough arts and entertainment listings.

Lensic Performing Arts Center (☎ 505-988-1234; 211 W San Francisco Ave) Catch a concert, film or performance at this renovated arts center dating from 1931.

Santa Fe Opera (☎ 505-986-5900, 800-280-4654; www.santafeopera.org) Even if you're not an opera fan, try to see a summer performance at the open-air opera. Tailgate dinners in the parking lot are a Santa Fe tradition.

Shopping

From carved howling coyotes to turquoise jewelry to fine art, Santa Fe attracts shoppers of all budgets.

Tesuque Pueblo Flea Market (☎ 505-995-8626; Feb-Dec) On weekends, check out the flea market on US 285, north of town.

Getting There & Around

Greyhound (☎ 505-471-0008; 858 St Michael's Dr) runs daily buses to Albuquerque ($10, one hour), Taos ($15, 90 minutes) and beyond. **Sandia Shuttle** (☎ 505-474-5696, 888-775-5696) runs multiple times daily between Santa Fe hotels and the Albuquerque airport ($23, 70 minutes). **Twin Hearts** (☎ 505-751-1201, 800-654-9456) services Taos ($25, 90 minutes).

Amtrak (☎ 800-872-7245) stops at Lamy, 18 miles south of Santa Fe; the **Lamy Shuttle** (☎ 505-982-8829) brings you back and forth by reservation ($16).

Santa Fe Trails (☎ 505-955-2001; fares $1) provides local bus service. Call **Capital City Cab** (☎ 505-438-0000) for a taxi.

PAJARITO PLATEAU & JEMEZ MOUNTAINS

North and east of Santa Fe, the red rocks, pine forest and streams of this region offer a wealth of hiking, natural hot springs and fishing. Within miles of each other, Valles Caldera National Preserve, Bandelier National Monument and Los Alamos evidence the iconographic geological, human and atomic history of the American West.

Los Alamos

Perched among thick green trees atop a series of narrow, fingerlike mesas, Los Alamos is a surprisingly beautiful place – ironic, actually, since it's most famous as the home of the atomic bomb, developed in secret here as the 'Manhattan Project' during WWII.

Atomic popular-culture artifacts and exhibits on the social history of life 'on the hill' during the project are on display at the tiny **Los Alamos Historical Museum** (☎ 505-662-4493; 1921 Juniper St; admission free; 10am-4pm Mon-Sat, 1-4pm Sun), behind historic Fuller Lodge (circa 1928).

The well-designed **Bradbury Science Museum** (☎ 505-667-4444; cnr Central Ave & 15th St; admission free; 9am-5pm Tue-Fri, 1-5pm Sat-Mon) gives a detailed account of US atomic history; kids will dig the interactive science exhibits. However, it's disturbing to find only the tiniest mention of the destruction of Hiroshima and Nagasaki (seek out the guest book for interesting personal reactions).

Los Alamos has a very small commercial center and after sunset the town clears out. Visit as a day trip, or as a stopover on your way to see Bandelier, the spectacular **Valles Caldera National Preserve** (a former volcano, viewable from Hwy 4) and other areas in the Jemez Mountains.

Bandelier National Monument

Rio Grande Puebloans lived here until the mid-16th century. Today several sites (none restored), a convenient location and a spectacular landscape make **Bandelier** (☎ 505-672-3861; admission $10; campsites $10; dawn-dusk) a good choice for those interested in ancient

ATOMIC SOUTHWEST

In 1943 Los Alamos, then a boys school perched on a 7400ft mesa, was chosen as the top-secret headquarters of the Manhattan Project – the code name for research and development of the atomic bomb. Accessed by two dirt roads, the site had no gas or oil lines, only one wire service, and was surrounded by thick forest. Many of those who lived on 'the hill' – including scientists' spouses, army personnel and local Latinos and Native Americans recruited to work in the labs and homes – had no idea what kind of work was being done.

On July 16, 1945, Manhattan Project scientists first detonated an atomic bomb at the Trinity Site in southern New Mexico, now part of White Sands Missile Range. After atomic bombs destroyed Hiroshima and Nagasaki, Los Alamos was finally exposed to the public. Today the lab is still the backbone of the town, and tourism embraces the town's atomic history.

pueblos. A **campground** is open usually spring to fall.

Jemez Springs

Jemez Springs is squeezed into a narrow valley along the incredible 132-mile **Jemez Mountain Trail National Scenic Byway**, which follows Hwys 4, 44 and 126 past Cuba and San Ysidro. This town along Hwy 4 offers several small B&Bs and restaurants, a bathhouse with body treatments, a few monasteries and a Zen Buddhist center. Ask about natural **hot springs** and camping at the **Santa Fe National Forest Ranger Station** (☎ 505-829-3535).

Cuba

An old adobe lodge set in 330 acres of the Nacimiento Mountains, the friendly and beautiful **Circle A Ranch Hostel** (☎ 505-289-3350; www.circlearanch.info; PO Box 2142, Cuba, NM 87013; dm/d $18/38; May-Oct; P) is a sworn favorite among those looking for a quiet retreat. There are also some motels in town.

TAOS

Once a small, laid-back outpost for hippies, artists and other back-to-the-land bohemians, Taos has grown to become one of the state's most popular destinations, with numerous hotels, restaurants and even resorts. The town's biggest attraction, however – and justifiably so – is the Taos Pueblo, built in the 15th century and still home to many pueblos.

At 6967ft and set amid some spectacular landscape bordered by the Rio Grande and the Taos Plateau to the west and the Sangre de Cristo Mountains to the north, Taos offers a seemingly endless array of year-round outdoor activities.

Orientation & Information

Entering from the south, Hwy 68 turns into Paseo del Pueblo Sur, lined with motels and shopping centers. It turns into Paseo del Pueblo Norte at Kit Carson Rd (Hwy 64), the intersection of which marks the center of town. Taos Plaza is directly east. At the traffic signal several miles north of town, Hwy 150 leads northeast to Taos Ski Valley, and Hwy 64 heads west toward the Rio Grande Gorge Bridge. Kit Carson Rd (Hwy 64) runs east to Eagle Nest and Cimarron.

The **visitors center** (☎ 505-758-3873, 800-732-8267; www.taosguide.com; cnr Paseo del Pueblo Sur & Paseo del Cañon; 9am-5pm) can help you get your bearings.

Sights

Built around AD 1450 and continuously inhabited ever since, **Taos Pueblo** (☎ 505-758-1028; adult/student $10/5; 8am-5pm Mon-Sat, from 8:30am Sun), about 3 miles north of the plaza, is the largest existing multistory pueblo structure in the USA and one of the best surviving examples of traditional adobe construction. It's well worth a visit. An informal tour is offered daily (no fee, but tip the guide); there's a photography fee of $5. The pueblo may be closed for sacred ceremonial dances in February, March and August.

Taos Historic Museums (☎ 505-758-0505; 1/2/3 homes adult $5/7.50/10, child $3/5/7; 10am-5pm Apr-Oct, until 4pm in winter) run three houses: the **Kit Carson Home** (Kit Carson Rd), one block from the plaza; the **Blumenschein Home** (222 Ledoux St); and the **Martínez Hacienda** (Ranchitos Rd), a colonial trader's former home.

The **Millicent Rogers Museum** (☎ 505-758-2462; 1504 Millicent Rogers Museum Rd; adult/child $6/1; 10am-5pm year-round, closed Mon Nov-Mar), filled with pottery, jewelry, baskets and textiles, is considered one of the best collections of Indian and Spanish colonial art in the USA. It's about 4 miles north of the plaza.

At 650ft above the Rio Grande, the steel **Rio Grande Gorge Bridge** is the second-highest suspension bridge in the USA; it's 11 miles northwest of the plaza, and the view down is eye-popping. Just west of the bridge is a fascinating community of **Earthships** (☎ 505-751-0462; www.earthship.org), which are solid, self-sustaining, environmentally savvy houses built with recycled materials, that survive completely off the grid. Self-guided tours ($5) are worthwhile; ask about overnight accommodations.

Activities

During the summer, **white-water rafting** is popular in the Taos Box, the steep-sided cliffs that frame the Rio Grande. Day-long trips begin at around $90 per person; contact the visitors center for local outfitters. **Hiking** is plentiful here, and trailheads line the road to the ski valley.

With a peak elevation of 11,819ft and a 2612ft vertical drop, **Taos Ski Valley** (☎ 800-347-7414; adult/child $51/31) offers some of the

QUIRKY NEW MEXICO

There are some places in New Mexico you just won't find anywhere else:

- UFO Museum & Research Center, Roswell – revisit the Roswell Crash of 1947
- Lightning Field, Quemado – stay overnight among 400 lightning rods
- Earthships, Taos – learn how to live 'off the grid'
- Bisti Badlands and De-Na-Zin Wilderness – a trippy, surreal landscape of colorful rock formations
- Montezuma's Castle, Las Vegas – an eye-popping structure with hot springs bubbling at its feet

most challenging **skiing** in the US and yet remains low-key and relaxed.

ENCHANTED CIRCLE

For a scenic driving tour, an 84-mile loop known as the **Enchanted Circle** takes you north and east of Taos through barren windswept high desert, alpine forests and mountain streams. Follow Hwy 522 north to Questa; head east on Hwy 38 through Red River to Eagle Nest; then return on Hwy 64. West of Questa is the spectacular **Wild Rivers Recreation Area** (☎ 505-770-1600; admission $3), at the confluence of the Rio Grande and Red River, which have cut 800ft canyons into the plateau.

Sleeping

Adobe Wall Motel (☎ 505-758-3972; fax 505-758-3972; 227 E Kit Carson Rd; r $56; P) This cute little motel is in a lovely, tree-shaded courtyard just a short walk or drive east of the plaza. Many of the adobe rooms have their own fireplace, and while not luxurious, they're definitely cozy and homey. A sweet place you'll want to come back to.

Laughing Horse Inn (☎ 505-758-8350, 800-776-0161; www.laughinghorseinn.com; 729 Paseo del Pueblo Norte; r from $80; P) A travelers' hangout with free use of bikes and a whole lot of heart and soul, this quirky inn is a treat. The property is over a century old and the 10 rooms are in a comfy structure that feels more like an Earthship than a standard crackerbox motel. Rooms all share baths, except for two additional suites.

Taos Inn (☎ 505-758-2233; www.taosinn.com; 125 Paseo del Pueblo Norte; r from $105; P) Listed on the National Register of Historic Places, this comfortable hotel actually consists of several adobe houses. It boasts a wide variety of rooms, many with unique Southwestern decor and personality. Prices vary with room size. It's also got a great bar with live music.

Taos Creek Cabins (☎ 505-758-4715; www.taoscreekcabins.com; Hwy 64; cabins $90; P) Tucked in the woods along Hwy 64 about 6 miles east of the plaza, this company rents five cabins, each with a deck overlooking the river. Cabins have full kitchens, wood stoves and one or two bedrooms.

HI Taos Snow Mansion (☎ 505-776-8298; snowman@newmex.com; 476 Taos Ski Valley Rd; dm/teepee/d $22/34/42; P) Ten minutes north of Taos in the tiny town of Arroyo Seco, this is a friendly place with lodging options from a simple bunk to a campsite, teepee, cabin or private room. It has a pleasant, communal atmosphere that's laid-back and inviting; folks of all ages stay here.

Eating

Old Blinking Light (☎ 505-776-8787; Ski Valley Rd; dishes $9-25) A spacious, friendly restaurant that's great for families, the Old Blinking Light is found several miles north of the plaza, just east of the traffic signal on the way to the ski valley (Hwy 150). The intersection used to have a blinking caution light, hence the name. Dinner plates (fish, fajitas, steaks) are huge – consider splitting them.

Apple Tree (☎ 505-758-1900; 123 Bent St; dishes $13-18) Housed in a historic 1903 adobe home with a pleasant patio, this comfortable gourmet restaurant offers Southwestern-styled items such as duck fajitas and mango-chicken enchiladas as well as, when available, fresh rainbow trout. It has some vegetarian choices, uses local organic produce and offers brunch on Sunday.

Bean (☎ 505-758-5123; 900 Paseo del Pueblo Norte; dishes $4-6) The Bean roasts its own great coffee and also serves breakfast and lunch daily until 2pm.

Orlando's New Mexican Cafe (☎ 505-751-1450; 1114 Don Juan Valdez Lane; dishes $6-10) This homey, family-owned restaurant, 1.8 miles north of the plaza along Paseo del Pueblo Norte, serves affordable Southwestern meals.

Getting There & Around

From Santa Fe, take either the scenic 'high road' along Hwy 76 and Hwy 518, with galleries, villages and sites worth exploring, or follow the Rio Grande on straightforward Hwy 68.

Greyhound (☎ 505-758-1144; 1384 D Paseo del Pueblo Sur) has daily services from Taos to Santa Fe ($15, 90 minutes), Albuquerque ($26, three hours) and Raton ($41, five hours). **Twin Hearts** (☎ 505-751-1201, 800-654-9456) runs shuttles to Albuquerque airport ($40, three hours) and Santa Fe ($25, 1½ hours); call for other shuttle destinations.

NORTHWESTERN NEW MEXICO

In addition to some knockout scenery, this remote corner of New Mexico offers important ancient Indian monuments as well as a historic railroad at Chama, the luscious hot springs of Ojo Caliente and, in Abiquiu, Georgia O'Keefe's New Mexican home.

Abiquiu & Around

A tiny farming valley on Hwy 84, about 45 minutes northwest of Santa Fe, Abiquiu is famous as the home of artist Georgia O'Keeffe, who bought the property in 1945 and moved here permanently in 1949. The **Georgia O'Keeffe Foundation** (☎ 505-685-4539) offers tours of O'Keeffe's home and studio ($22) by reservation only on Tuesday, Thursday and Friday from April to November. Call at least one month ahead.

One of the oldest health resorts in the US, **Ojo Caliente Mineral Springs and Resort** (☎ 505-583-2233, 800-222-9162; www.ojocalientespa.com; 50 Los Baños Dr; s/d from $75/100;) is a quiet bathhouse spa, with horseback riding, a pool, body treatments and rooms in a historic hotel. It's on Hwy 285 between Taos and Abiquiu.

Chama

Nine miles south of the Colorado border, Chama is famous for the **Cumbres & Toltec Scenic Railroad** (☎ 888-286-2737; www.cumbresandtoltec.com; adult/child $60/30; Jun-Oct), both the longest (64 miles) and highest (over the 10,015ft-high Cumbres Pass) narrow-gauge steam railroad in the USA. Views are spectacular from the open-air observation car. The train departs Chama on Saturday and Tuesday, and returns from Antonito, Colorado on Sunday and Wednesday; the other leg of the journey is by bus. There are several modest motels in town.

Farmington & Around

The largest town in New Mexico's northwestern region, Farmington has plenty of facilities and makes a good base from which to explore the Four Corners area.

Contact the **visitors center** (☎ 505-326-7602, 800-448-1240; www.farmingtonnm.org; 3041 E Main St; 9am-5pm Mon-Sat) for information. It also has a small museum showcasing local history.

Reliable trading posts, with a variety of Indian crafts, are found along Hwy 64 west of town. Founded in 1875, the **Fifth Generation Trading Company** (☎ 505-326-3211; 232 W Broadway) has a big selection.

Shiprock, a 1700ft-high volcanic plug that rises eerily over the landscape to the west, was a landmark for the Anglo pioneers and is a sacred site to the Navajo. The Navajo community of Shiprock hosts an annual **Navajo Fair** with a rodeo, powwow and traditional dancing (in late September or early October).

About 35 miles south of Farmington along Hwy 371, the **Bisti Badlands and De-Na-Zin Wilderness**, an undeveloped BLM area, is a trippy, surreal landscape of strange, colorful rock formations – it's like stepping onto a science-fiction film set; desert enthusiasts shouldn't miss it. The Farmington **BLM office** (☎ 505-599-8900; 1235 La Plata Hwy; 7:45am-4:30pm Mon-Fri) dispenses information.

Three miles from downtown, **Silver River Adobe B&B** (☎ 505-325-8219, 800-382-9251; www.cyberport.com/silveradobe; 3151 W Main St; r from $105;) offers a peaceful, eco-friendly respite among the trees, overlooking the confluence of the San Juan and La Plata rivers.

Friendly and low-key, **Three Rivers Eatery & Brewhouse** (☎ 505- 324-2187; 101 E Main St; dishes $8-15) brews its own and bustles with locals for lunch and dinner.

Greyhound (☎ 505-325-1009; 101 E Animas St) runs buses to Albuquerque ($33, four hours) and other locales. **Navajo Transit System** (☎ 520-729-4111) offers a weekday bus to Window Rock; for information on visiting the Navajo Indian Reservation, see p830.

Chaco Culture National Historic Park

Featuring massive Ancestral Puebloan buildings set in an isolated high-desert environment, the intriguing **Chaco Culture National Historic Park** (admission per vehicle $8; dawn to dusk) contains evidence of 5000 years of human occupation. At its prime, the community at Chaco Canyon was a major trading and ceremonial hub for the region – and the city the Pueblan people created here was masterful in its layout and design. Pueblo Bonito is four stories tall and may have had 600 to 800 rooms and kivas. Sites have been stabilized but not reconstructed. Apart from taking the self-guided loop tour, you can hike various **backcountry trails**.

The **visitors center** (505-786-7014; 8am-5pm) is in a remote area approximately 80 miles south of Farmington. The park is open year-round, but all routes involve driving on rough dirt roads, which are sometimes impassable after heavy rains or snow. **Gallo Campground** (campsites $10, no RV sites) is 1.5 miles from the visitors center.

NORTHEASTERN NEW MEXICO

Travelers on the Santa Fe Trail (roughly paralleled today by I-25) passed through this section of New Mexico on their way from Missouri to Santa Fe, and there's plenty of Western heritage to be found in towns like Las Vegas and Cimarron. Dinosaurs walked the land here, too, adding to the stark allure of these high plains.

Las Vegas

Las Vegas has one of the most amazingly well-preserved downtown districts in the western US; more than 900 buildings are listed on the National Register of Historic Places. It's no surprise, then, that Hollywood loves the place, and films are shot here regularly. The town is about 64 miles east of Santa Fe on I-25.

The Old Town Plaza marks the initial town settlement, a major stop on the Santa Fe Trail; when the railroad arrived, however, it bypassed the plaza, creating a second 'new' town about a mile east. Today, Las Vegas is a mix of Southwestern and Victorian architecture. Ask for a walking-tour brochure from the **chamber of commerce** (505-425-8631, 800-832-5947; www.lasvegasnewmexico.com; 701 Grand Ave; 9am-5pm Mon-Fri).

From the plaza, Hot Springs Blvd leads 5 miles north to Gallinas Canyon and the massive **Montezuma's Castle**, an eye-popping structure on the flanks of the Sangre de Cristo Mountains; once a hotel, it's now the United World College of the West. Along the road are a series of **hot spring pools** (admission free; 5am-midnight).

Built in 1882, the renovated **Plaza Hotel** (505-425-3591, 800-328-1882; www.plazahotel-nm.com; 230 Old Town Plaza; r from $79; P), right on the downtown plaza, is the nicest accommodation in town, with an impressive lobby and well-preserved Victorian detailing. Check the website for special rates.

Indulge in a good New Mexican meal at **Estellas** (505-454-0048; 1148 Bridge St; dishes $4-14).

In tiny **Sapello**, 13 miles north along Hwy 518, budding astronomers will go nuts for the **Star Hill Inn** (505-425-5605; www.starhillinn.com; r $165; P). The room price includes a telescope or a one-hour guided star tour, and there's 200 private acres on which to relax.

Cimarron

Cimarron was a Wild West town following Anglo settlement; today it's very quiet. If you're driving here to or from Taos, you'll pass through gorgeous **Cimarron Canyon State Park**, a steep-walled canyon with several hiking trails, excellent trout fishing and camping.

The **St James Hotel** (505-376-2664; www.stjamescimarron.com; Rte 1; r $60-120; P) was originally a saloon in 1873, as evidenced by the bullet holes in the ceiling. Famous gunfighters stayed here, and some rooms are preserved in tribute. It's a working hotel, though, with restored 19th-century rooms (and some newer ones, too), a dining room and a bar.

Raton

Situated just south of the Colorado border and 7834ft Raton Pass, this community is today somewhat sleepy but has an attractive downtown.

The **visitors center** (505-445-3689, 800-638-6161; www.raton-nm.com; 100 Clayton Rd; 8am-5pm) has statewide information and a walking tour that takes in New Deal murals and nicely preserved 19th-century buildings from the town's mining and railroad days. There are numerous motels in town.

Capulin Volcano National Monument

Rising 1300ft above the surrounding plains, **Capulin Volcano** (☎ 505-278-2201; suggested donation $5; 7:30am-6:30pm summer, 8am-4pm winter) is the easiest to visit of several volcanoes in the area. From the visitors center, a 2-mile road spirals up the mountain to a parking lot at the crater rim (8182ft), where trails lead around and into the crater. The entrance is 3 miles north of the village of Capulin, which itself is 30 miles east of Raton on Hwy 87.

Clayton Lake State Park

Twelve miles northwest of **Clayton**, a ranch town near the Texas and Oklahoma borders, this **State Park** (☎ 505-374-8808; admission $4; campsites/RV sites $7/11; 6am-9pm) contains more than 500 footprints of eight **dinosaur** species. Clayton has chain motels and the historic **Eklund Dining Room & Saloon** (☎ 505-374-2551; 15 Main St; dishes $9-16).

SOUTHWESTERN NEW MEXICO

The Rio Grande Valley runs south from Albuquerque to El Paso, Texas, paralleled today by I-25. Much of the region is arid, sparsely populated ranchland, dominated by the Chihuahuan Desert. Along the western border of New Mexico, the Continental Divide runs through the high country of the Gila National Forest near Silver City. The landscape here is rugged, woodsy and wild, offering loads of hiking, camping and fishing opportunities. It's a good place to get away from it all.

Socorro & Around

Socorro, believe it or not, was for a short time during the 19th century, New Mexico's biggest town, thanks to gold and silver mining. Today, its Victorian buildings are testament to that brief boom period.

The **chamber of commerce** (☎ 505-835-0424; www.socorro-nm.com; 101 Plaza; 9am-5pm Mon-Fri), on the plaza, has information on the area. Thousands of minerals, fossils and other geological exhibits are displayed at the **Mineral Museum** (☎ 505-835-5420; admission free; 8am-5pm Mon-Fri, 10am-3pm Sat & Sun), on the campus of the New Mexico Institute of Mining & Technology.

Economy Inn (☎ 505-835-0276; fax 505-835-4142; 1009 California St; r $27; P) This is a decent place with clean rooms.

Martha's Black Dog Coffeehouse (☎ 505-838-0311; 110 E Manzanares St; dishes $4-10) On the east side of the plaza, this friendly place serves tasty coffees, breakfasts, lunch plates (including vegan options) and desserts.

Socorro Springs Brewing Company (☎ 505-838-0650; 113 Abeyta Ave; dishes $6-8) Good wood-fired pizzas, lasagna and microbrews are served here.

Greyhound (☎ 505-835-1767; 1007 S California St) stops in town on its way to Albuquerque ($14, 95 minutes) and other cities.

Endangered whooping cranes winter in the 90 sq miles of fields and marshes at **Bosque del Apache National Wildlife Refuge** (☎ 505-835-1828; admission $3), south of Socorro near San Antonio. There's a visitors center and driving tour. On the way from I-25, stop at **Owl Bar Cafe** (☎ 505-835-9946; Hwy 380; dishes under $5; Mon-Sat) in San Antonio for amazing green-chili cheeseburgers.

For those heading west into Arizona from Socorro, Hwy 60 makes a remote, scenic alternative to I-40. Past the town of Magdalena, and 47 miles west of Socorro, is the **Very Large Array** radio telescope facility, a complex of 27 huge antenna dishes sprouting like giant mushrooms in the high plains. Near Quemado, the **Lightning Field** (☎ 505-898-3335; www.lightningfield.org; cabins per adult/child $135/85; May-Oct) is a 1977 art installation built by Walter De Maria, consisting of 400 stainless-steel poles in a remote desert location. The only way to visit is to spend the night in a six-person cabin on site; advance reservations required.

Truth or Consequences

Built on the site of natural hot springs in the 1880s, this funky little town south of Socorro, formerly known as Hot Springs, was renamed Truth or Consequences (or 'T or C') in 1950, after a popular radio program of the same name. Wander around the little hole-in-the-wall cafés, check out the junk shops and definitely take a dip in one of the town's hot spring spas.

The **chamber of commerce** (☎ 505-894-3536; www.truthorconsequencesnm.net; 201 N Foch St; 9am-5pm Mon-Sat, 9am-1pm Sun) has listings.

Many local motels double as spas. **Riverbend Hot Springs** (☎ 505-894-6183; www.nmhotsprings.com; 100 Austin Ave; dm/d $18/42; P) is a friendly hostel with dorms, private rooms (in trailers), camping and – the main attraction – mineral baths in outdoor tubs by the river, which are free to guests. The **Charles Motel & Bath House** (☎ 505-894-7154; www.charlesspa.com; 601 Broadway; s/d $40/45; P) has various body treatments as well as remodeled, 1940s-style motel rooms.

Las Cruces & Around

The second-largest city in New Mexico, Las Cruces is a farming center for chilies, pecans and apples. The village of **Hatch**, 40 miles north, is considered New Mexico's chili capital. New Mexico State University (NMSU), with some 15,000 students, adds a collegiate flavor to some parts of Las Cruces, which is otherwise rather utilitarian. The city is at 3900ft, between the Rio Grande and the strangely fluted Organ Mountains, rising to the east. The **visitors center** (☎ 505-541-2444; www.lascrucescvb.org; 211 N Water St) has local and regional information.

Three miles southwest of downtown Las Cruces is **Mesilla**, established in 1850 for Mexican settlers who wished to avoid becoming part of the USA after the Mexican-American War. Souvenir shops and tourist-oriented restaurants dominate historic Mesilla Plaza.

White Sands Missile Range Museum (☎ 505-678-8824; admission free; 8am-4pm Mon-Fri, 10am-3pm Sat & Sun) is 25 miles east of Las Cruces on Hwy 70. It's on the military base, a major testing range and also home to the 'Trinity Site,' where the first atomic blast took place. The outdoor 'missile park' is an odd little place. At the entrance gate, be prepared to show the guard your driver's license and car registration. (For White Sands National Monument, see p812)

Of the several local B&Bs, **Lundeen Inn of the Arts** (☎ 505-526-3326, 888-526-3326; www.innofthearts.com; 618 S Alameda Blvd; s/d from $58/74; P) stands out. It's a large, turn-of-the-19th-century adobe house with 20 guest rooms and an art gallery. For budget motels, try the **Day's End Lodge** (☎ 505-524-7753; 755 N Valley Dr; $34; P), which doesn't take reservations – 'just come by.'

The university crowd hangs out at **Spirit Winds Coffee Bar** (☎ 505-521-1222; 2260 S Locust St; dishes $4-6), a comfortable place with salads, sandwiches and pastries. **Nellie's Café** (☎ 505-524-9982; 1226 W Hadley Ave; dishes $5-7; 8am-4pm Mon-Sat) has good Mexican meals. Nearby, **High Desert Brewing Company** (☎ 505-525-6752; 1201 W Hadley Ave; dishes $5-8) offers craft-brewed beer, basic pub food and live music.

Greyhound (☎ 505-524-8518; 490 N Valley Dr) runs buses to Albuquerque ($38, 4½ hours) and other cities. **Las Cruces Shuttle** (☎ 505-525-1784, 800-288-1784) has vans from Las Cruces to El Paso Airport ($30), Silver City ($33) and other regional destinations.

Silver City & Around

The Gila National Forest and Gila Wilderness is rugged country suitable for remote cross-country skiing, backpacking, camping, fishing, and other activities. On the southern edge of this mountainous region lies the comfortable, attractive old West mining town of Silver City.

The **chamber of commerce** (☎ 505-538-3785, 800-548-9378; www.silvercity.org; 201 N Hudson St; 9am-5pm Mon-Fri) and **USFS office** (☎ 505-388-8201; www.fs.fed.us/r3/gila; 3005 E Camino del Bosque; 8am-4:30pm Mon-Fri) have information on the area.

Up a winding 42-mile road north of Silver City, the recommended **Gila Cliff Dwellings National Monument** (☎ 505-536-9461; admission $3; 8am-6pm summer, 9am-4pm winter) was occupied in the 13th century by Mogollon Indians.

Strangely rounded volcanic towers make up **City of Rocks State Park** (☎ 505-536-2800; campsites/RV sites $10/14; 7am-9pm), southeast of Silver City on Hwy 61; there's secluded camping among the towers. Nearby, lovely **Faywood Hot Springs** (☎ 505-536-9663; www.faywood.com; 165 Hwy 61; adult/child per day $10/5; campsites $24, cabins $80; 10am-10pm) has both public and private pools, as well as camping and private cabins.

Silver City's restored **Palace Hotel** (☎ 505-388-1811; www.zianet.com/palacehotel; 106 W Broadway; r $47-57) dates from 1882. Built in 1928 and surrounded by 178 acres of trails, **Bear Mountain Lodge** (☎ 505-538-2538, 877-620-2327; www.bearmountainlodge.com; r from $200;) is operated by the Nature Conservancy and has a resident naturalist. A menu of pastas and creative meat dishes are served at elegant **Diane's Restaurant** (☎ 505-538-8722; 510 N Bullard St; dishes $10-16; Tue-Sun).

Las Cruces Shuttle (☎ 800-288-1784) has daily vans to El Paso Airport ($40).

SOUTHEASTERN NEW MEXICO

Often overlooked for the tourist mecca of the north, some unusual and highly recommended sites dot the southeast's varied landscape of desert, mountains, ranch and military towns – including White Sands, Carlsbad Caverns and the historic Western town of Lincoln, where Billy the Kid's life changed forever.

Alamogordo & Around

Alamogordo was founded as a railroad town and later became home to Holloman Air Force Base. It lies at 4350ft in the Tularosa Basin, though it's not as picturesque as nearby Cloudcroft or Ruidoso. White Sands Blvd (WSB) is the main north-south road.

One worthy attraction is the **New Mexico Museum of Space History** (☎ 505-437-2840, 877-333-6589; adult/child $2.50/2; 9am-5pm), a five-story glass cube at the east end of Indian Wells Rd. Inside are exhibits about space research and flight and a huge wraparound Imax theater (tickets $6; call for schedule).

Sixteen miles southwest of Alamogordo, gypsum covers 275 sq miles to create a dazzling white landscape at crisp, stark **White Sands National Monument** (☎ 505-679-2599; admission $3; 7am-sunset). A 16-mile loop leads into the heart of the park. Feel free to climb and play in the dunes; there are picnic sites and hiking trails, but no car camping (backcountry only, apply at the visitors center).

Numerous motels stretch along White Sands Blvd, including **Best Western Desert Aire** (☎ 505-437-2110, 800-528-1234; 1021 S WSB; r $57;). Stop by **Plaza Pub** (☎ 505-437-9495; cnr WSB & 10th St; dishes $4-6) for decent pub food and microbrewed beer.

About 45 miles north of Alamogordo on Hwy 54 is the **Oscuro High Desert Hostel** (☎ 505-648-4007; www.oscurohostel.com; dm/d $14/27;), a working ranch on 240 acres.

Greyhound (☎ 505-437-3050; 601 N WSB) has buses heading north to Albuquerque ($34, 4½ hours) and east to Carlsbad ($34, five hours). **Shuttle Ruidoso** (☎ 505-336-1683) services Ruidoso by reservation only.

Cloudcroft

From Alamogordo, Hwy 82 climbs from 4315ft to 9000ft within 16 miles to pleasant, forested Cloudcroft, a welcome relief from the desert heat.

The **chamber of commerce** (☎ 505-682-2733; www.cloudcroft.net; 1001 James Canyon Hwy; 10am-5pm Mon-Sat) is on Hwy 82.

The **Lodge** (☎ 505-682-2566, 800-395-6343; www.thelodge-nm.com; r from $89; P), built in 1911, is an upscale destination and one of the finest historic hotels in the state. The popular **Western Bar & Café** (☎ 505-682-2445; Burro St; dishes $6-14), just off Hwy 82, is straight out of a Wild West movie.

Ruidoso

Surrounded by thick forest at 7000ft in the Sacramento Mountains, this resort town has seen its share of commercial development, including lots of vacation homes, but it's still an attractive place. It's spread out along Hwy 48 (known as Mechem Dr or Sudderth Dr), the main drag. The **chamber of commerce** (☎ 505-257-7395, 877-784-3676; www.ruidoso.net; 720 Sudderth Dr; 8:30am-5pm Mon-Fri, 9am-3pm Sat, 9am-noon Sun) can help you get oriented.

Serious horse racing happens at **Ruidoso Downs** (☎ 505-378-4431), near the intersection of Hwys 48 and 70. Western and cowboy enthusiasts will enjoy the more than 10,000 items in the **Hubbard Museum of the American West** (☎ 505-378-4142; adult/child $6/2; 10am-5pm), just east of Ruidoso Downs on Hwy 70. North of Ruidoso is the downhill resort **Ski Apache** (☎ 505-336-4356; adult/child $45/29).

Numerous motels, hotels and cute little cabin complexes line the streets. **Ruidoso Lodge Cabins** (☎ 505-257-2510, 800-950-2510; www.ruidosolodge.com; 300 Main Rd; cabins from $119;) is attractively set along the river. The **Sitzmark Chalet** (☎ 505-257-4140, 800-658-9694; www.sitzmark-chalet.com; 627 Sudderth Dr; r from $65;) has simple but nice rooms.

Great for kids, the **Flying J Ranch** (☎ 505-336-4330; adult/child $18/9; Jun-Sep), on Hwy 48 north of Ruidoso near Alto, is a 'Western village' offering gunfights, chuckwagon dinners and stage shows each evening except Sunday. Lively **Casa Blanca** (☎ 505-257-2495; 501 Mechem Dr; dishes $7-15) serves Mexican food in a renovated Spanish-style house.

Greyhound (☎ 505-257-2660; 138 Service Rd) has daily buses to Roswell ($14, 90 minutes) and beyond.

Lincoln & Capitan

For fans of Western history, a visit to tiny **Lincoln** – where a gun battle turned Billy the Kid into a legend – is a must. The whole town is beautifully preserved in close to original form; modern influences (neon-lit motel signs, souvenir stands, fast-food joints) are not allowed. Main St is designated as **Lincoln State Monument** (☎ 505-653-4372; adult/child $6/free; 8:30am-4:30pm), and a

SOUTHWEST

TRAGEDY AT BOSQUE REDONDO

With the Union victory at Glorietta Pass in March 1862, the threat of Confederate control of the Southwest ended and the troops turned all their force on the Native Americans. The battles that followed were cruel and bloody, involving broken treaties and several massacres.

Brigadier General James H Carleton directed Kit Carson, of the New Mexico volunteers, to invade the Mescalero Apache and Navajo. Despite his initial reluctance, Carson eventually followed orders, marching in 1863 into Canyon de Chelly (see p831), the Navajo stronghold, destroying crops, orchards and livestock. Six thousand Navajo surrendered, and so began the nearly 400-mile 'Long Walk' from Canyon de Chelly to Bosque Redondo, a desolate scrap of land in eastern New Mexico near Fort Sumner. Hundreds of Navajo died before reaching the reservation.

Several chiefs hid in the mountains with their people. Others escaped the reservation. For years, Carleton hunted Navajos, but by 1866, the last of the chiefs had surrendered.

Carleton had hoped to convert the defeated Indians to Christian farmers, but the land was harsh and unsuitable for agriculture, and brackish water spurred disease. Carleton was finally removed from command in New Mexico, and officials from Washington, DC, came to assess the situation. In 1868, under the direction of General William Sherman and after four years of starvation and deprivation, the surviving Indians were allowed to return to their homelands. About 3000, however, had died since their imprisonment at Bosque Redondo.

single ticket admits you to the museum and historic buildings. For overnighters, **Casa de Patrón B&B** (☎ 505-653-4676, 800-524-5202; Main St; www.casapatron.com; r $87; P) is recommended.

Like nearby Lincoln, cozy **Capitan** is surrounded by the beautiful mountains of **Lincoln National Forest**. The main reason to come is for the kids, who'll be curious to visit **Smokey Bear Historical State Park** (☎ 505-354-2748; admission $1; 9am-5pm), where Smokey (yes, there actually was a real Smokey Bear) is buried.

Fort Sumner State Monument

Famous for the atrocious Bosque Redondo Indian Reservation disaster (see boxed text 'Tragedy at Bosque Redondo') and Billy the Kid's last showdown with Sheriff Pat Garrett (Billy's gravesite is near the town of Fort Sumner), the area here is full of Indian and outlaw history. The **monument** (☎ 505-355-2573; admission $3; 8:30am-5pm Wed-Mon) interprets the Bosque Redondo tragedy; camping and inexpensive accommodations are nearby.

Roswell

Though on the surface an assuming ranch community, this is one odd little town that's full of surprises. Much of its quirky personality comes thanks entirely to a single event – the crash of a mysterious 'spacecraft' in a field near here in 1947, and the alleged recovery of alien bodies. The 'Roswell Incident' claimed national headlines at the time, and debates still rage today about what *really* happened. The army officially says it was a weather balloon; we, of course, know differently.

All kinds of people now flock to this out-of-the-way town to try and figure it out for themselves. Roswellians, though, seem to be having fun with the concept, creating an entire tourist industry around the crash – downtown street lights are adorned with alien eyes, for instance.

Stop by the **visitors bureau** (☎ 505-624-7704, 888-767-9355; www.roswellcvb.com; 426 N Main St; 8:30am-5:30pm Mon-Fri, 10am-3pm Sat & Sun) to get oriented.

Believers and skeptics alike will want to head immediately to the **International UFO Museum & Research Center** (☎ 505-625-9495; www.iufomrc.com; 114 N Main St; admission free; 9am-5pm), the town's chief attraction. Displays are wordy and sometimes difficult to follow, but they explore the history of UFO encounters worldwide. Informative, yet still good, wacky fun.

The annual **Roswell UFO Festival** happens over the July 4 weekend. Contact the UFO Museum for details.

Roswell has a surprising number of alien-free museums, too. Make time for the **Roswell Museum & Art Center** (☎ 505-624-6744; 100 W 11th St; free admission; 9am-5pm Mon-Sat, 1-5pm Sun), which includes exhibits on Robert Goddard, who researched liquid-fuelled rockets in Roswell.

Hotels and cheap motels line Main St north of downtown (the best place to look), and 2nd St heading west. Decent choices include the **Frontier Motel** (☎ 505-622-1400; www.frontiermotelroswell.com; 3010 N Main St; s/d from $32/36; P) and the **Best Western El Rancho** (☎ 505-622-2721; www.bestwestern.com; 2205 N Main St; r from $55; P).

Scotty's Pit BBQ (☎ 505-622-9550; 109 E Deming; dishes $5-9; breakfast & lunch) Maybe it's Roswell's proximity to Texas, but the beef brisket is great at Scotty's, which also has an old jukebox of vintage 45s.

Nuthin' Fancy Café (☎ 505-623-4098; 2103 N Main St; dishes $4-8) This place features standard diner fare, but it also has espresso and an impressive 14 beers on tap.

Crash Down Diner (☎ 505-627-5533, 866-264-9107; 106 W 1st St; dishes $4-8) Head here for delights like the Galactic Gobbler and Space Burger.

If you've had enough, **Greyhound** (☎ 505-622-2510; 1100 N Virginia Ave) buses leave daily for Albuquerque ($34, four hours) and Carlsbad ($16, 1½ hours).

Carlsbad

Travelers use Carlsbad as a base for visits to nearby Carlsbad Caverns National Park and the Guadalupe Mountains (see the Texas chapter, p668). The **chamber of commerce** (☎ 505-887-6516, 800-221-1224; www.chambercaverns.com; 302 S Canal St; 9am-5pm Mon, 8am-5pm Tue-Fri) has information on both.

The **Living Desert State Park** (☎ 505-887-5516; admission $4), spread out over the Ocotillo Hills on the northwestern outskirts of town (on Miehls Dr, off US 285), exhibits the wildlife of the Chihuahuan Desert.

Many motels line Canal St, including the **Economy Inn** (☎ 505-885-4914; 1621 S Canal St; r from $35; P). Locals and visitors crowd **Lucy's** (☎ 505-887-7714; 701 S Canal St; dishes $6-12) for cheap, tasty New Mexican meals.

Greyhound (☎ 505-887-1108; 1000 S Canyon St) leaves daily for Albuquerque ($44, six hours) and El Paso ($37, three hours).

Carlsbad Caverns National Park

Established initially as a national monument in 1923, and as a World Heritage Site in 1995, this truly impressive **Carlsbad Caverns National Park** (☎ 505-785-2232, 800-967-2283; www.nps.gov/cave; admission $6; 8am-7pm summer, until 5pm winter) covers 73 sq miles and includes more than 100 known caves, including the 60-mile **Lechugilla Cave** and the justly famous **Big Room** (it's one of two free self-guided tours, and it's wheelchair accessible). Additional guided cave tours ($8 to $20) vary from moderate walks to difficult climbs; call for reservations. Another major park attraction is the Mexican free-tail **bat colony** that roosts here (April to October). Backpacking trips into the desert backcountry are allowed by permit (free).

ARIZONA

Large, looming saguaro cacti are a popular symbol of the American West, and nowhere are they more prevalent than Arizona. The state has a reputation for hot weather, and the Sonoran Desert dominates much of its southern half. But the terrain here is surprisingly varied. Tall, thickly forested mountains ring some of the state's hottest, driest cities and line the famous Grand Canyon up north. There's even skiing. Arizona is popular with American tourists, some of whom come during the winter to enjoy sunshine, often kicking back at posh resorts. Others are eager to hike deep into canyon country, explore Hopi villages or visit laid-back bohemian communities like Bisbee. There's a huge variety of activities, cultures and people here. You can chow down on steak 'n' beans at a cowboy saloon; learn about Indian history at the Navajo National Monument or Canyon de Chelly; poke around old mining towns like Jerome; and enjoy outdoor activities all year round.

History

By the time Europeans arrived in Arizona, the area had long been home to many Indian tribes. Spanish explorer Francisco Vásquez de Coronado traversed the area, bringing settlers and missionaries in his wake. By the mid-19th century, the US controlled Arizona. The Indian Wars, in which the US Army battled Indians to 'protect' settlers and claim land for the government, officially ended in 1886 with the surrender of Apache warrior Geronimo. Railroad and mining expansion grew. In 1912, President Theodore Roosevelt's support for damming the territory's rivers led to Arizona becoming the 48th state. After WWII air conditioning became widely available and growth was phenomenal.

ARIZONA FACTS

Nickname Grand Canyon State
Population 5,456,453 (19th)
Area 114,006 sq miles (6th)
Admitted to Union February 14, 1912 (48th)
Capital city Phoenix (population 1.3 million)
Other cities Tucson (487,000), Mesa (396,400), Yuma (77,500)
State reptile Arizona ridge-nosed rattlesnake
State neckwear Bolo tie
Famous for the Grand Canyon, saguaro cacti
Home of Apache chief Geronimo (1829–1909); Cesar Chavez (b 1927); first US rodeo (Prescott, 1888)

Scarcity of water resources remains among the foremost issues in Arizona. Today the state continues desperately searching for water for its burgeoning desert cities.

Information

Write to the **Arizona Office of Tourism** (☎ 602-230-7733, 800-842-8257; www.arizonaguide.com; 2702 N 3rd St, Suite 4015, Phoenix, AZ 85004) for free state information. The **Arizona Public Lands Information Center** (☎ 602-417-9300; www.publiclands.org; 222 N Central Ave, Phoenix, AZ 85004) provides information about USFS, NPS, BLM and state lands and parks.

Arizona's state sales tax is 5.6%, though the actual rate fluctuates from city to city. Arizona is on Mountain Standard Time but is the only western state that does not observe daylight saving time from spring to early fall. The exception is the Navajo Reservation, which *does* observe daylight saving time.

Generally speaking, lodging rates in southern Arizona (including Phoenix, Tucson and Yuma) are much higher in winter and spring, which is considered the state's 'high' season.

PHOENIX

Phoenix is one of those towns that makes some people swoon and leaves others scratching their heads. Its biggest draw is eternally warm weather – baking hot in summer, but amazingly pleasant in other seasons, especially during spring when the orange blossoms lend the air a sensual aroma. The downside is that the city practically defines the concept of urban sprawl, with some 2.8 million people (1.3 million in Phoenix alone) spread out across a massive 2000-sq-mile metropolitan area that, without irrigation, would normally be dry as a bone. Yet with more than 300 days of sunshine a year, Phoenix, the country's sixth-largest city, remains a prime vacation destination, its multitude of both chic resorts and RV parks magnets for 'snow birds' seeking refuge from northern winters.

Phoenix has grown at a rapid pace, with surrounding towns such as Scottsdale, Tempe, Glendale and Mesa now absorbed into the greater metropolitan area, collectively known as the 'Valley of the Sun' ('the Valley'). The whole region is connected by a maze of highways and a seemingly endless array of strip malls and subdivisions. Though many visitors complain that Phoenix lacks character and 'soul,' you'll still find worthwhile places to visit. The Desert Botanical Garden and the Heard Museum are good starting points.

Phoenix is on the northern edge of the Sonoran desert, and daytime temperatures average 66°F in December and 105°F in July. As you'd expect with so many manicured lawns, pools and golf courses (nearly 200 of them), water conservation remains an ongoing struggle in Phoenix.

The Phoenix metropolitan area has three telephone area codes: ☎ 602 is central Phoenix, ☎ 480 is the east valley (including Tempe and Scottsdale) and ☎ 423 is west Phoenix. Sales tax in Phoenix is about 8%, and hotel tax is about 11%.

All addresses listed here are in Phoenix proper unless otherwise noted.

History

Until the completion of Theodore Roosevelt Dam in 1911, northeast of town on the Salt River, modern Phoenix didn't amount to much more than a desert outpost. The Hohokam people lived here as early as 300 BC and developed a complex system of irrigation canals, only to mysteriously abandon them around AD 1450. The US Army built Fort McDowell northeast of Phoenix in the mid-1860s, and the railway arrived in 1887. Once Roosevelt Dam was built, however, the region began to boom. The Central Arizona Project (CAP), a $4 billion project completed in the early 1990s amid much controversy, brought more water to the region from the Colorado River via a series of canals and pipelines that run 336 miles from Lake Havasu to Tucson.

PHEONIX

INFORMATION

- Arizona Office of Tourism....... 1 C7
- Arizona Public Lands Information Center....... 2 E2
- Banner Good Samaritan Medical Center....... 3 C7
- Biltmore Visitor Information Center....... (see 41)
- Bookstore....... 4 C6
- Central Phoenix Library....... 5 E1
- Downtown Phoenix Visitor Information Center....... 6 E2
- Scottsdale Convention & Visitors Bureau....... 7 F6
- Wide World of Maps....... 8 B6

SIGHTS & ACTIVITIES pp818–9

- America West Arena....... 9 E3
- Arizona Science Center....... 10 E2
- Bank One Ballpark....... 11 E3
- Desert Botanical Garden....... 12 E7
- Hall of Flame....... 13 E7
- Heard Museum....... 14 C7
- Heritage Square....... (see 34)
- Phoenix Art Museum....... 15 C7
- Phoenix Museum of History....... 16 E2
- Phoenix Zoo....... 17 E7
- Pueblo Grande Museum....... 18 E7
- State Capitol....... 19 C2
- Sun Devil Stadium....... 20 F8

SLEEPING pp819–20

- Arizona Biltmore....... 21 D6
- Best Western Executive Park....... 22 E1
- Country Inn & Suites....... 23 F7
- HI Phoenix, Metcalf House....... 24 F1
- Motel 6 on Camelback....... 25 F6
- Royal Palms....... 26 E6
- San Carlos Hotel....... 27 E2

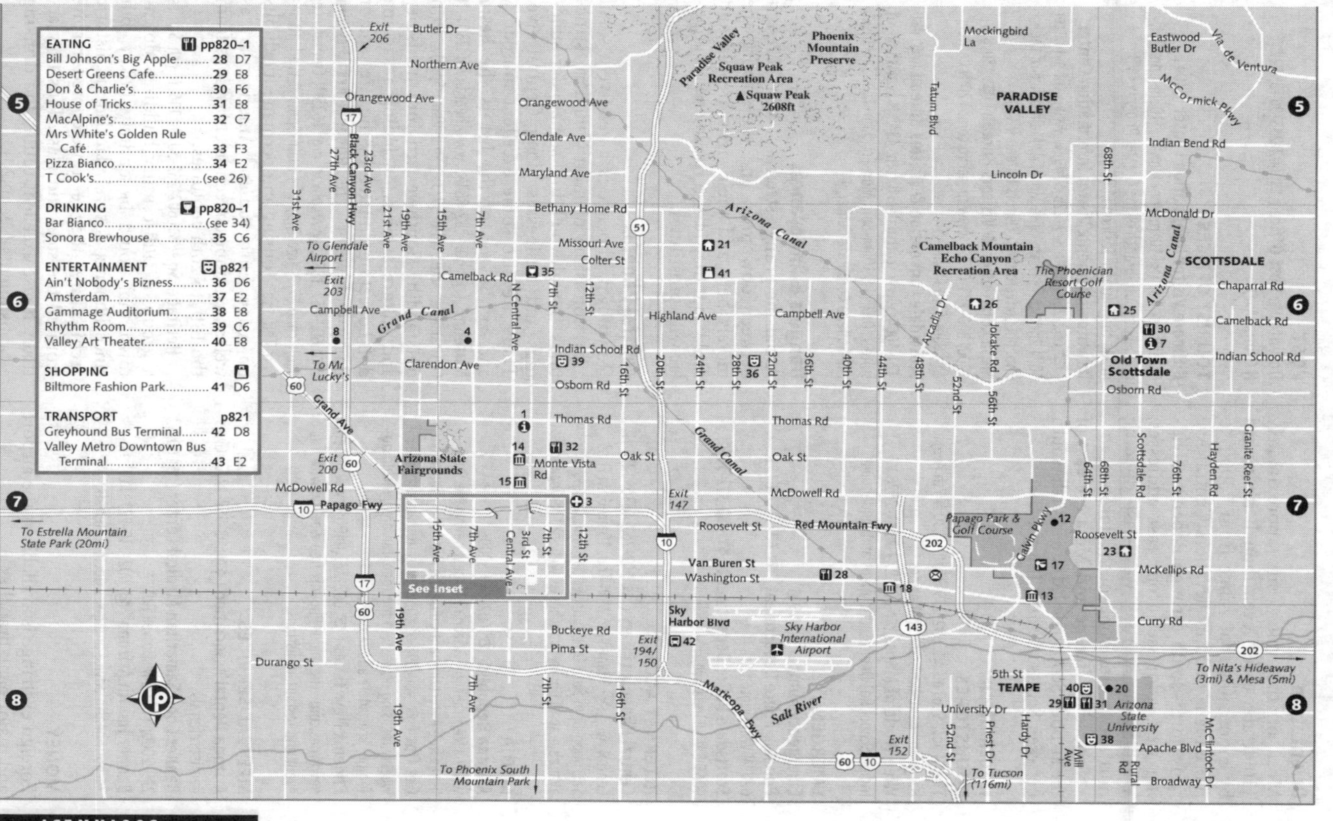
EATING pp820–1
Bill Johnson's Big Apple......28 D7
Desert Greens Cafe......29 E8
Don & Charlie's......30 F6
House of Tricks......31 E8
MacAlpine's......32 C7
Mrs White's Golden Rule Café......33 F3
Pizza Bianco......34 E2
T Cook's......(see 26)
DRINKING pp820–1
Bar Bianco......(see 34)
Sonora Brewhouse......35 C6
ENTERTAINMENT p821
Ain't Nobody's Bizness......36 D6
Amsterdam......37 E2
Gammage Auditorium......38 E8
Rhythm Room......39 C6
Valley Art Theater......40 E8
SHOPPING
Biltmore Fashion Park......41 D6
TRANSPORT p821
Greyhound Bus Terminal......42 D8
Valley Metro Downtown Bus Terminal......43 E2
SCOTTSDALE
PARADISE VALLEY
Old Town Scottsdale
TEMPE
Arizona State University
Phoenix Mountain Preserve
Squaw Peak Recreation Area
Squaw Peak 2608ft
Camelback Mountain Echo Canyon Recreation Area
The Phoenician Resort Golf Course
Papago Park & Golf Course
Sky Harbor International Airport
Arizona State Fairgrounds
Salt River
Arizona Canal
Grand Canal
Black Canyon Hwy
Red Mountain Fwy
Maricopa Fwy
Papago Fwy
See Inset
To Nita's Hideaway (3mi) & Mesa (5mi)
To Tucson (116mi)
To Phoenix South Mountain Park
To Estrella Mountain State Park (20mi)
To Glendale Airport
To Mr Lucky's

Orientation

Most of the valley sits approximately 1100ft above sea level, though it's ringed by mountains that range from 2500ft to more than 7000ft in elevation. Central Ave runs north–south through Phoenix, dividing west addresses from east addresses; Washington St runs west–east dividing north addresses from south addresses.

Scottsdale, Tempe and Mesa are east of the airport. Scottsdale Rd runs north–south between Scottsdale and Tempe.

Information

BOOKSTORES

The Book Store (☎ 602-279-3910; 4230 N 7th Ave) Has many periodicals and magazines.

Wide World of Maps (☎ 602-279-2323; 2626 W Indian School Rd) Dedicated to maps and guidebooks.

EMERGENCY

Emergency number (☎ 911)

Phoenix Police Department (☎ 602-262-6151; 620 W Washington St)

Scottsdale Police Department (☎ 480-312-5000; 9065 E Via Linda Ave)

INTERNET ACCESS

Central Phoenix Library (☎ 602-262-4636; 1221 N Central Ave; 🕑 10am-9pm Mon-Thu, 10am-6pm Fri & Sat, noon-6pm Sun) One hour per day limit; access is available at all library branches as well; call for locations.

MEDIA

Arizona Republic (☎ 602-444-8000; www.azcentral.com) Arizona's largest newspaper; publishes free entertainment guide the *Rep* every Thursday.

Get Out (☎ 480-898-5680; www.getoutaz.com) Free weekly focusing on eastern metropolitan area, including Tempe, Scottsdale and Mesa.

Phoenix New Times (☎ 602-271-0400; www.phoenixnewtimes.com) The major Phoenix free weekly, with lots of event and restaurant listings.

MEDICAL SERVICES

Arizona Dental Association (☎ 602-957-4777) Gives dentist referrals.

Banner Good Samaritan Medical Center (☎ 602-239-2000; 1111 E McDowell Rd)

Banner Health Arizona (☎ 602-230-2273) Offers 24-hour health advice and gives doctor referrals.

MONEY

Foreign exchange is available at the airport and major bank branches.

POST

Downtown Post Office (☎ 602-253-9648; 522 N Central Ave)

TOURIST OFFICES

Biltmore Visitor Information Center (2404 E Camelback Rd; 🕑 10am-8pm Mon-Fri, 10am-6pm Sat, noon-6pm Sun) Branch of the Greater Phoenix CVB inside the Biltmore Fashion Mall.

Downtown Phoenix Visitor Information Center (☎ 602-254-6500, 877-225-5749; www.visitphoenix.com; 50 N 2nd St; 🕑 8am-5pm Mon-Fri) Main office of the Phoenix Convention & Visitors Bureau (CVB).

Mesa Convention & Visitors Bureau (☎ 480-827-4700, 800-283-6372; www.mesacvb.com; 120 N Center; 🕑 8am-5pm Mon-Fri)

Scottsdale Convention & Visitors Bureau (☎ 480-421-1004; www.scottsdalecvb.com; 4343 N Scottsdale Rd, suite 170; 🕑 8:30am-6pm Mon-Fri, 9am-1pm Sat) Inside the Galleria Corporate Center.

Dangers & Annoyances

Avoid the grungy stretch of Van Buren St between downtown and the airport; the motels here and their signs are old and funky, but they're also rundown and popular with prostitutes.

Central Phoenix

Downtown Phoenix is a relatively small area, consisting of mostly modern structures, though you'll find some older buildings and businesses along Central Ave. There are also some excellent museums, and at the top of the list is the **Heard Museum** (☎ 602-252-8848; www.heard.org; 2301 N Central Ave; adult/child $7/3; 🕑 9:30am-5pm), with outstanding Southwestern Indian history and culture exhibits, including a kachina doll collection donated by the late senator Barry Goldwater. The **Phoenix Art Museum** (☎ 602-257-1880; www.phxart.org; 1625 N Central Ave; adult/child $7/2, free Thu; 🕑 10am-5pm Fri-Wed, 10am-9pm Thu) has touring and permanent exhibits on Asian, European and American art, as well as a unique collection of fashions from the 18th to 20th centuries.

Heritage Sq (☎ 602-262-5029; 115 N 6th St) is a group of 19th-century buildings downtown that could be entirely hokey, but since Phoenix is sorely lacking in historic architecture, they're a welcomed respite from all the steel and glass. Plus they actually house excellent eating and drinking establishments (see p820).

Adjoining the square is the **Arizona Science Center** (☎ 602-716-2000; www.azscience.org; 600 E Washington St; adult/child $9/7; ⏰ 10am-5pm), with 350 exhibits that encourage hands-on experimentation. Displays at the nearby **Phoenix Museum of History** (☎ 602-253-2734; www.pmoh.org; 105 N 5th St; adult/child $5/2.50; ⏰ 10am-5pm Tue-Sat) range from 2000-year-old archeological artifacts to an exhibit about the sinking of the USS *Arizona* at Pearl Harbor.

Outer Phoenix

The 145-acre **Desert Botanical Garden** (☎ 480-941-1225; www.dbg.org; 1201 N Galvin Parkway; adult/student $7.50/4; ⏰ 8am-8pm Oct-Apr, 7am-8pm May-Sep), with thousands of arid-land plants, makes for a beautiful, worthwhile urban getaway, while also providing insight into the desert ecosystem. The surrounding **Papago Park** has biking and equestrian trails. Opposite Papago Park, the **Hall of Flame** (☎ 602-275-3473; 6101 E Van Buren St; adult/student $5.50/3.50; ⏰ 9am-5pm Mon-Sat, noon-4pm Sun) exhibits more than 90 firefighting machines dating from 1725. At the **Pueblo Grande Museum** (☎ 602-495-0900, 4619 E Washington St; adult/child $2/1, free Sun; ⏰ 9am-4:45pm Mon-Sat, 1-4:45pm Sun), parts of an excavated Hohokam village remain exposed for the visitor.

Scottsdale

Most visitors come to Scottsdale to wander through its popular downtown shopping district, known as **Old Town** for its early 20th century buildings (and others built to *look* old). Basically, though, it's home to a lot of upscale galleries and gift stores.

During the mid-20th century, architect Frank Lloyd Wright built, lived in and taught at **Taliesin West** (☎ 480-860-2700; www.franklloydwright.org; 12621 Frank Lloyd Wright Blvd), a complex of mesmerizing, environmentally organic buildings set on 600 acres at the eastern edge of Scottsdale's many subdivisions. To see the complex, you must take a guided tour, and several varieties are given daily (adult/child from $18/5).

Tempe

At the center of Tempe is the main campus of **Arizona State University** (ASU), founded in 1885 and home to some 46,000 students. Mill Ave is Tempe's main drag, packed with restaurants, bars and other collegiate hangouts. There are free tours of the Frank Lloyd Wright–designed **Gammage Auditorium** (☎ 480-965-4050; cnr Mill Ave & Apache Blvd) offered on weekdays.

Activities

Several large parks in the mountains ringing the valley offer lots of hiking and cycling opportunities. Always carry plenty of water. Phoenix also has a handful of **wheelchair-accessible trails** (☎ 602-262-6862; www.phoenix.gov/parks/hikeacce.html) in some regional parks.

North of town, **Squaw Peak Recreation Area** has numerous trails including a popular route to the 2608ft summit of Squaw Peak. Enter on Squaw Peak Dr, northeast of Lincoln Dr between 22nd and 24th Sts.

Near Mesa, **Salt River Tubing** (☎ 480-984-3305; tubes $12) rents inner-tubes and provides van shuttles for **floats** down the Salt River from mid-April to September. It's 15 miles northeast of Hwy 60; from Mesa, take Power Rd north, which turns into Bush Hwy.

Sleeping

Finding cool independent motels isn't easy in Phoenix, as chains clearly dominate the scene; all the usual brands are spread throughout the region. The area along Van Buren St between downtown and the airport has what once might have been fun older motels, but now they're crummy and rundown. Your cheapest motel options, sadly, are chains along the freeway exits. Of the major freeways leaving Phoenix, you'll find most motels along I-17 north of downtown.

Quoted rates are for Phoenix's high season, generally late winter and spring. During summer, prices are often dramatically slashed.

BUDGET

Motel 6 on Camelback (☎ 480-946-2280; www.motel6.com; 6848 E Camelback Rd; r $52; P ☒) Yes, it's just a standard chain, but it's conveniently located smack dab in the middle of upscale Scottsdale, only a quick drive from Old Town.

HI Phoenix, Metcalf House (☎ 602-254-9803; 1026 N 9th St; dm/d $17/35) This friendly hostel occupies a nondescript house in a working-class residential neighborhood north of downtown (too far to walk). Check-in is 5pm to 10:30pm.

MID-RANGE

San Carlos Hotel (☎ 800-528-5446, 602-253-4121; www.hotelsancarlos.com; 202 N Central Ave; high/low season from

$140/79; P ✈ ♿) Unlike the majority of Phoenix hotels, this 1928 downtown property has loads of character. It's an Italian Renaissance-inspired beauty that's been nicely restored with early fixtures, wood trim and atmosphere intact. If you're trying to avoid a chain (and can't afford a resort), it's easily your best choice.

Best Western Executive Park (☎ 602-252-2100; www.bwexecutiveparkhotel.com; 1100 N Central Ave; r from $99; P ✈ 💻 ♿) This modern, clean-cut business-oriented hotel north of downtown includes a complimentary shuttle to the airport and other locations.

Country Inn & Suites (☎ 480-858-9898; www.countryinns.com; 808 N Scottsdale Rd, Tempe; r $129; P ✈ 💻 ♿) Clean, modern chain hotel conveniently located between Tempe and Scottsdale. Guests receive free shuttle service within a 5-mile radius, which includes Arizona State University, Old Town Scottsdale and the airport.

TOP END

Phoenix is known for its numerous lavish resorts which are basically vacation destinations in themselves, complete with restaurants, pools, spas and golf courses. Many of Phoenix's resorts are situated just off Camelback Rd north of downtown. Note that room rates can drop dramatically during the summer, making these plush, luxurious properties almost a bargain.

Arizona Biltmore (☎ 602-955-6600, 800-950-0086; www.arizonabiltmore.com; cnr 24th St & E Missouri Ave; r from $200; P ✈ ♿) This is Phoenix's oldest resort, a large spread built in 1929 and sporting architecture 'inspired' (but not actually 'designed') by Frank Lloyd Wright. It's a beautiful property, worth a stop even if you can't afford to stay (grab a drink at the bar, marvel at the magnificent lobby and take a stroll out back). The massive grounds (39 acres) contain more than 700 rooms, two golf courses, several pools, a spa, restaurants, shops and even private residences. While presidents, celebrities and assorted blue-bloods are regulars, the Biltmore's also family oriented.

Royal Palms (☎ 602-840-3610, 800-672-6011; www.royalpalmsresortandspa.com; 5200 E Camelback Rd; r from $375; P ✈ 💻 ♿) This fab Spanish-Mediterranean property was originally built in 1929 as a private estate, and with only 117 rooms and casitas, it's a more intimate choice than some of the valley's larger resorts. There's a luxurious spa, nice bar and the top-rated T Cook's restaurant (see below). The accommodations have individual character, too, as they were put together by a host of top designers. There's nothing stuffy about the place – if you can afford it, you'll adore it.

Eating

As it is with motels, many of the area's places to eat are chains. There are, however, some real gems, worthwhile whether you're staying the night or just passing through – from hole-in-the-wall lunch spots to serious gourmet restaurants.

PHOENIX

T Cook's (☎ 602-808-0766; 5200 E Camelback Rd; dishes $26-30) When you are ready to splurge, this lovely top-rated, Mediterranean-inspired restaurant at the Royal Palms resort is one of the valley's finest. The interior is spacious and colorful, the service friendly and warm, and the dinners – grilled lamb, spit-roasted chicken, fresh Maine lobster – absolutely fabulous. The adjacent bar is a cozy hideaway, too, and there's even a cigar room.

Pizza Bianco (☎ 602-258-8300; 623 E Adams St; dinner from $10; 🕐 5-10pm Tue-Sat, 5-9pm Sun) This restaurant is lovingly set inside a small brick building in the middle downtown's Heritage Sq. The wood-fired pizza here might be the best you've had in ages, which is not surprising from a restaurant that grows some of its own vegetables and even makes its own mozzarella. It's well worth the often long wait for seating, which isn't bad if you grab a beer or glass of wine at charming, atmospheric Bar Bianco next door.

Bill Johnson's Big Apple (☎ 602-275-2107; 3757 E Van Buren St; dishes $6-15) This western-themed classic dates from 1956 and is the flagship of a local chain. If you like cowboy kitsch (not to mention hearty steaks and pulled pork sandwiches), get your butt over here – and never mind the shabby neighborhood, as the restaurant is clean, inviting and family friendly.

Mrs White's Golden Rule Café (☎ 602-262-9256; 808 E Jefferson St; dishes $9; 🕐 11am-5pm Mon-Fri) Conveniently close to downtown, this no-frills lunch spot offers inexpensive, well-prepared soul food.

THE AUTHOR'S CHOICE

MacAlpine's (☎ 602-262-5545; 2303 N 7th St; dishes $17) Though it normally serves burgers, malts and phosphates at lunch only, MacAlpine's opens its doors every Friday from 6pm onward to host a lively swing dance party, complete with dance lessons and buffet dinner. The action happens inside the city's oldest soda fountain, founded in 1928, which is almost a museum in itself, lovingly holding on to its decades-old decor; the surroundings lend the festivities a vintage atmosphere that's otherwise hard to find in modern Phoenix.

SCOTTSDALE & TEMPE

House of Tricks (☎ 480-968-1114; 114 E 7th St, Tempe; dishes $15-28; Tue-Sun) Two blocks from the Mill Ave student hangouts, this charming spot boasts a changing menu of 'New American' cuisine. Meals are served in two charming wooden houses fronted by a serene patio surrounded by trees.

Don & Charlie's (☎ 480-990-7427; 7501 E Camelback Rd, Scottsdale; dinner from $20) Baseball fans (especially the carnivorous kind) will find themselves in heaven here, as the place is crammed full of autographed balls, jerseys, photographs and other memorabilia. Dishes focus on beef, seafood and barbecue, and the place is often busy, so advance reservations are recommended.

Desert Greens Cafe (☎ 480-968-4831; 234 W University Dr, Tempe; meals under $10) Vegans can find solace at this small café inside the Gentle Strength Co-op, a good natural food grocery.

Entertainment

Gammage Auditorium (☎ 480-965-3434; cnr Mill Ave & Apache Blvd) On the ASU campus in Tempe, this Frank Lloyd Wright-designed auditorium hosts concerts, plays and other events.

Mill Ave between 3rd and 7th Sts in Tempe is the heart of ASU bars and nightclubs.

Valley Art Theater (☎ 602-222-4275 ext 027; 509 S Mill Ave) Alternative film is featured at Tempe's theatre.

Good venues for live rock and blues include the **Rhythm Room** (☎ 602-265-4842; 1019 E Indian School Rd) and **Nita's Hideaway** (☎ 480-966-7715; 3300 S Price Rd, Tempe).

Ain't Nobody's Bizness (☎ 602-224-9977; 3031 E Indian School Rd) A friendly lesbian bar.

Amsterdam (☎ 602-258-6122; 718 N Central Ave) Gay men dance at this swanky place.

Spectator Sports

The men's basketball team **Phoenix Suns** (☎ 602-379-7867) and the women's team **Phoenix Mercury** (☎ 602-252-9622) play at Phoenix's America West Arena. Football team the **Arizona Cardinals** (☎ 602-379-0102) plays at Sun Devil Stadium in Tempe, though a new stadium is planned for Glendale. The **Arizona Diamondbacks** (☎ 602-514-8400) play baseball at the Bank One Ballpark downtown.

Each spring, the Cactus League Baseball Association hosts multiple major league teams for their annual **spring training** at ballparks throughout the valley. For schedule and ticket information contact the Mesa, Phoenix or Scottsdale visitors bureaus (see p818).

Getting There & Around

Phoenix's **Sky Harbor International Airport** (☎ 602-273-3300) is 3 miles southeast of downtown. Valley Metro's Red Line operates buses from the airport to Tempe, Mesa and downtown Phoenix ($1.25).

Greyhound (☎ 602-389-4200; 2115 E Buckeye Rd) runs regular buses to Tucson ($16, two hours), Flagstaff ($23, 3½ hours), Los Angeles ($37, seven hours) and other destinations.

Valley Metro (☎ 602-253-5000; www.valleymetro.org; fares $1.25) operates buses all over the valley; on weekdays they also run the free Flash service around the ASU area and free Dash service around downtown Phoenix.

National car rental agencies have offices at the airport and around town. Check p1121 for details.

EAST-CENTRAL ARIZONA

East of Phoenix, along the Mogollon Rim dividing the high desert of northeastern Arizona and the low Sonoran Desert, lies an area of mainly mountains and woods dotted here and there with small towns. It's popular with Phoenix residents, offering a cooling escape from the desert heat along with hiking, biking and cross-country skiing opportunities.

There's also downhill skiing at **Sunrise Park Resort** (☎ 800-772-7669, 928-735-7669; www.sunriseskipark.com; adult/child $38/22), owned and operated by the White Mountain Apache Tribe. The resort lies south of Hwy 260 in the White Mountains, between woodsy **Pinetop-Lakeside** and, to the east, the adjoining towns of **Springerville** and **Eagar**.

Coronado Trail

As you head south from Springerville on Hwys 180 and 191, ascending to 9000ft before dropping to Clifton at 3500ft, you run roughly parallel to the 1540 route of Francisco Vásquez de Coronado. The region offers campgrounds, a few motels and access to pristine wilderness. Expect the 120-mile drive to take about four hours; the south end of the trail is particularly slow, with many hairpin bends; trailers over 20ft are not recommended. Camping, fishing and hiking opportunities abound in the Apache-Sitgreaves National Forest, and fall colors can be especially mesmerizing.

Globe

Located 80 miles east of Phoenix, this town makes a good rural alternative and offers budget accommodations such as **El Rey Motel** (☎ 928-425-4427; 1201 E Ash St; r $28; P ❄), an old-fashioned American motor-court with basic, clean rooms. Several other chain and nonchain motels are spread out along Hwy 60. Contact the **Globe-Miami Chamber of Commerce** (☎ 928-425-4495; www.globemiamichamber.com; 1360 N Broad St; 🕑 8am-5pm Mon-Fri) for further local information.

Apache Trail

The steep and winding Apache Trail (Hwy 88) loops northwest from Globe, past a few campgrounds and motels, and on to Roosevelt Dam; there it veers southwest into the greater Phoenix area, passing through tiny **Tortilla Flat**, whose Wild West appearance makes it a popular stop. The 22 miles west of the dam are unpaved.

Constructed of bricks in 1911, **Theodore Roosevelt Dam** was the earliest of the large dams in the Southwest and, at 280ft, is the world's highest masonry dam. Nearby, **Tonto National Monument** (☎ 928-467-2241; admission $3; 🕑 8am-5pm) protects Salado cliff dwellings.

CENTRAL ARIZONA

From Phoenix you can take I-17 137 miles north to Flagstaff, or you could spend some quality time wandering through the mountains and intriguing small towns of the region. It's a rewarding chance to visit Indian sites, cowboy and mining towns, and perhaps even a few New Age vortexes. Hwy 89A between Prescott and Flagstaff, passing through Jerome and Sedona, is one of the most dramatic scenic drives in the state.

> **THE AUTHOR'S CHOICE**
>
> **Hassayampa Inn** (☎ 928-778-9434, 800-322-1927; www.hassayampainn.com; 122 E Gurley St; r from $119; ❄) When Hassayampa Inn opened in 1927, it was one of Arizona's most elegant hotels; today it's a true gem. The 68 restored rooms retain their original character yet are completely comfortable, and meals (breakfast, lunch and dinner) in the downstairs dining room are fabulous. The bar and lobby, too, are easy to settle into.

Prescott

The first territorial capital, Prescott has a Wild West pedigree that's clearly visible in the well-preserved old buildings surrounding Courthouse Plaza downtown. Along the plaza is **Whiskey Row**, an infamous strip of old saloons that still serve plenty of booze today. Contemporary residents are an intriguing mix of hippies, retirees and cowboy-style conservatives, with artsy types and outdoor enthusiasts contributing further to the multifaceted bohemian quality of this intriguing town.

The **chamber of commerce** (☎ 928-445-2000, 800-266-7534; www.prescott.org; 117 W Goodwin St) has walking and driving tour brochures ($1 each), and the office of the **Prescott National Forest** (☎ 928-443-8000; www.fs.fed.us/r3/prescott; 344 S Cortez St 🕑 8am-4:30pm Mon-Fri) has information on hiking, camping and fishing.

A cozy overnight spot is the 1917 **Hotel Vendome** (☎ 928-776-0900, 888-468-3583; www.vendomehotel.com; 230 S Cortez St; midweek/weekends r from $80/119; ❄), on a quiet side street just a block from the plaza.

Most of Prescott's Whiskey Row bars are great spots to catch a drink in old West style. A standout is the 1877 **Palace Restaurant & Bar** (☎ 928-541-1996; 120 S Montezuma St; dishes $13-20), which serves lunch and dinner. Nearby, the family-friendly **Prescott Brewing Company** (☎ 928-771-2795; 130 Gurley St; dishes $8-12) works well for burgers and local brews.

For eggs, salads, sandwiches and excellent fresh coffee, head straight to **Prescott Coffee Roasters** (☎ 928-717-0190; 318 W Gurley St; dishes $3-5; 🕑 breakfast & lunch), a cozy local hangout in yet another historic, beautifully rustic space.

Greyhound (☎ 928-445-5470; 820 E Sheldon St) has bus services to Phoenix ($20, 2½ hours). Locally owned **Shuttle U** (☎ 800-304-6114; www.shuttleu.com; 1505 W Gurley St) runs vans several times daily to the Phoenix airport ($25).

Jerome

A thriving copper-mining town during the 19th century, Jerome's mines shut down in 1953 and it's now a national historic district. A huge part of its appeal is certainly its extraordinary setting – perched on a mountainside, each block sits below its predecessor, and the entire town feels like it's about to slide away (indeed, many buildings have done just that). Artists have replaced miners, and today antique shops and galleries line the winding streets, which are worth a wander.

The **Jerome Chamber of Commerce** (☎ 928-634-2900; www.jeromechamber.com) lists local hotels and restaurants. **Jerome State Historic Park** (☎ 928-634-5381; adult/child $4/1; 🕑 8am-5pm), housed in a 1916 mansion, presents the town's mining history. It's 2 miles east of Jerome off Hwy 89A.

Cottonwood

This small town has several motels, but the chief excitement for visitors is the popular **Verde Canyon Railroad** (☎ 800-320-0718; www.verdecanyonrr.com; adult/child from $25/40). Vintage engines pull indoor and open-air coaches on a four-hour round-trip ride through splendid countryside – definitely Arizona's most scenic private train ride. Trains leave several times a week; reservations are required.

Sedona

The surrounding red-rock landscape here is among the most awe-striking in the state. Though Sedona was founded in the 19th century, the discovery of energy 'vortexes' here in the 1980s have turned this once-modest settlement into a bustling New Age destination. More than four million visitors now flock annually to its upscale resorts, restaurants and art galleries, many keen to soak up some of that electromagnetic energy allegedly emanating from Sedona's rocks, cliffs and rivers. Mountain bikers, hikers and scenery nuts love the place, too.

In the middle of town is the 'Y,' the junction of Hwys 179 and 89A. The **chamber of commerce** (☎ 928-282-7722, 800-288-7336; www.visitsedona.com; 331 Forest Rd; 🕑 8:30am-5pm Mon-Sat, 9am-3pm Sun), Sedona's official tourist center, is just north of the junction. It has masses of information, including vortex maps. If you're looking to cycle the hills, the **Bike & Bean Shoppe** (☎ 928-284-0210; 6020 Hwy 179; bicycles under $5) offers bike rentals, sales and repairs along with strong coffee.

Got a car? If so, definitely take the gorgeous 27-mile drive north toward Flagstaff through **Oak Creek Canyon** (Hwy 89A), which follows Oak Creek through red, orange and white cliffs before ascending into ponderosa forest. Be sure, too, to stop at **Slide Rock State Park** (☎ 928-282-3034; admission $8; 🕑 8am-7pm summer, 8am-5pm winter), 7 miles north of Sedona on Hwy 89A, where the creek sweeps swimmers past placid pools and through a natural rock chute, a favorite with kids.

IN SEARCH OF THE NEW AGE

Sedona is one of the most important New Age centers anywhere. The term 'New Age' refers to a trend toward seeking alternative explanations or interpretations of health, religion, the psyche and enlightenment. Drawing upon new and old factual and mystical traditions from around the world, New Agers often seek to transform themselves psychologically and spiritually in the hopes that such personal efforts will eventually transform the world at large.

Along with mainstream services like massage, nutrition counseling and yoga classes – not to mention luxurious resorts and fine restaurants – Sedona also offers such esoteric practices as psychic channeling, aura photography, past-life regressions and crystal healing.

The four best-known vortexes in the Sedona area are on the local red-rock mountains, which make nice hikes even for nonbelievers. For information and guided tours – not to mention a huge selection of crystals – visit the **Center for the New Age** (☎ 928-282-2085; 341 Hwy 179).

Sedona is a relatively expensive place to stay, and budget travelers may be happier in Flagstaff. Modest properties include the **Sedona Motel** (☎ 928-282-7187; 218 Hwy 179; r $70; P ✕).

Sky Ranch Lodge (☎ 929-282-6400, 888-708-6400; www.skyranchlodge.com; top of Airport Rd; d from $75; P ✕) One of the prettiest locations in Sedona, on a hilltop near the airport overlooking town. The popular Airport Mesa Vortex trail is nearby.

Grab a sandwich or fixings for your own meal from **New Frontiers Natural Foods & Deli** (☎ 928-282-6311; 1420 W Hwy 89A; admission $4-6). For a serious sit-down meal, **René at Tlaquepaque** (☎ 928-282-9225; 336 Hwy 179; dishes $20-28) serves lunch and dinner inside Tlaquepaque Village, an upscale shopping complex. Items include trout, venison and a seitan-tofu Wellington.

Flagstaff

Set among cool ponderosas on the southern flanks of the San Francisco Peaks, Flagstaff is northern Arizona's biggest town, yet it's worlds away from the urban angst (and heat) of Phoenix, three hours to the south. The Grand Canyon is just a 90-minute drive, making Flagstaff a good base for day trippers. Historic buildings sit alongside old Route 66 (Santa Fe Ave), which roughly parallels I-40. And as home to Northern Arizona University (NAU), Flagstaff's got a respectable degree of collegiate culture.

The **visitors center** (☎ 928-774-9541, 800-842-7293; www.flagstaffarizona.org; 1 E Rte 66; 🕑 9am-5pm) is in the historic railway depot downtown. Free weekly *Flagstaff Live* has entertainment listings.

SIGHTS & ACTIVITIES

A Hopi kiva is one of several excellent exhibits at the **Museum of Northern Arizona** (☎ 928-774-5213; www.musnaz.org; 3001 N Fort Valley Rd; adult/child $5/2 ; 🕑 9am-5pm), 3 miles north of Flagstaff on Hwy 180. Ask about museum-led tours of local mountains, mesas and canyons. Of many important observations made at **Lowell Observatory** (☎ 928-774-2096; www.lowell.edu; 1400 W Mars Hill Rd; adult/child $4/2; 🕑 9am-5pm summer, noon-5pm winter), the most famous was the discovery of the planet Pluto in 1930. Call for nighttime viewing hours.

The 1000ft-tall volcano cone at the **Sunset Crater National Monument** (☎ 928-526-0502; admission $5; 🕑 8am-6pm summer, closes 5pm winter), located on a loop road 12 miles north of Flagstaff along Hwy 89, was formed by volcanic eruptions in AD 1064–65. Climbing is prohibited, but trails give great views. Follow the loop road past the crater to **Wupatki National Monument** (☎ 928-679-2365; admission $5; 🕑 8am-6pm summer, closes 5pm winter), with hundreds of Ancestral Puebloan sites, five of which are easily accessible. The entrance fee covers both monuments.

East of Flagstaff near I-40 exit 204, the Sinagua buildings at **Walnut Canyon National Monument** (☎ 928-526-3367; admission $5; 🕑 8am-6pm summer, 9am-5pm winter) are eerily set in caves within near-vertical walls of a butte jutting splendidly from a wooded canyon. Camping is not allowed.

The mountains and forests around Flagstaff offer scores of hiking, fishing, camping and mountain-biking options in the **Coconino National Forest** (☎ 928-527-3600; www.fs.fed.us/r3/coconino; 2323 E Greenlaw Lane; 🕑 8am-4:30pm Mon-Fri), as well as skiing at **Arizona Snow Bowl** (☎ 928-779-1951; $40). Good sources for equipment and maps are **Peace Surplus** (☎ 928-779-4521; 14 W Rte 66), **Babbitt's Backcountry Outfitters** (☎ 928-774-4775; 12 E Aspen Ave), **Absolute Bikes** (☎ 928-779-5969; 18 N San Francisco St) and **Cosmic Cycles** (☎ 928-779-1092; 901 N Beaver St).

SLEEPING

Flagstaff has loads of affordable motels, and for that reason it works well as a base when exploring the region. The downside, though, is that a busy railroad line cuts right through the middle of town, and most accommodations are either right next to it or within easy earshot of train whistles. Light sleepers beware. If that's you, then head south on Milton Rd toward I-40, where several chain hotels are removed from the racket.

Hotel Monte Vista (☎ 928-779-6971, 800-545-3068; www.hotelmontevista.com; 100 N San Francisco St; midweek/weekends r from $70/80; P) This downtown gem dating from 1927 has 55 funky old rooms and suites on four floors, all with modern amenities (including cable TV). A classic old bar downstairs hosts bands on the weekend.

Weatherford Hotel (☎ 928-779-1919; www.weatherfordhotel.com; 23 N Leroux St; midweek/weekends r from $50/55) Also downtown, this friendly hotel dates from 1898, when it was northern Arizona's finest hotel. Eight old-fashioned rooms have no TV or phone. Trains

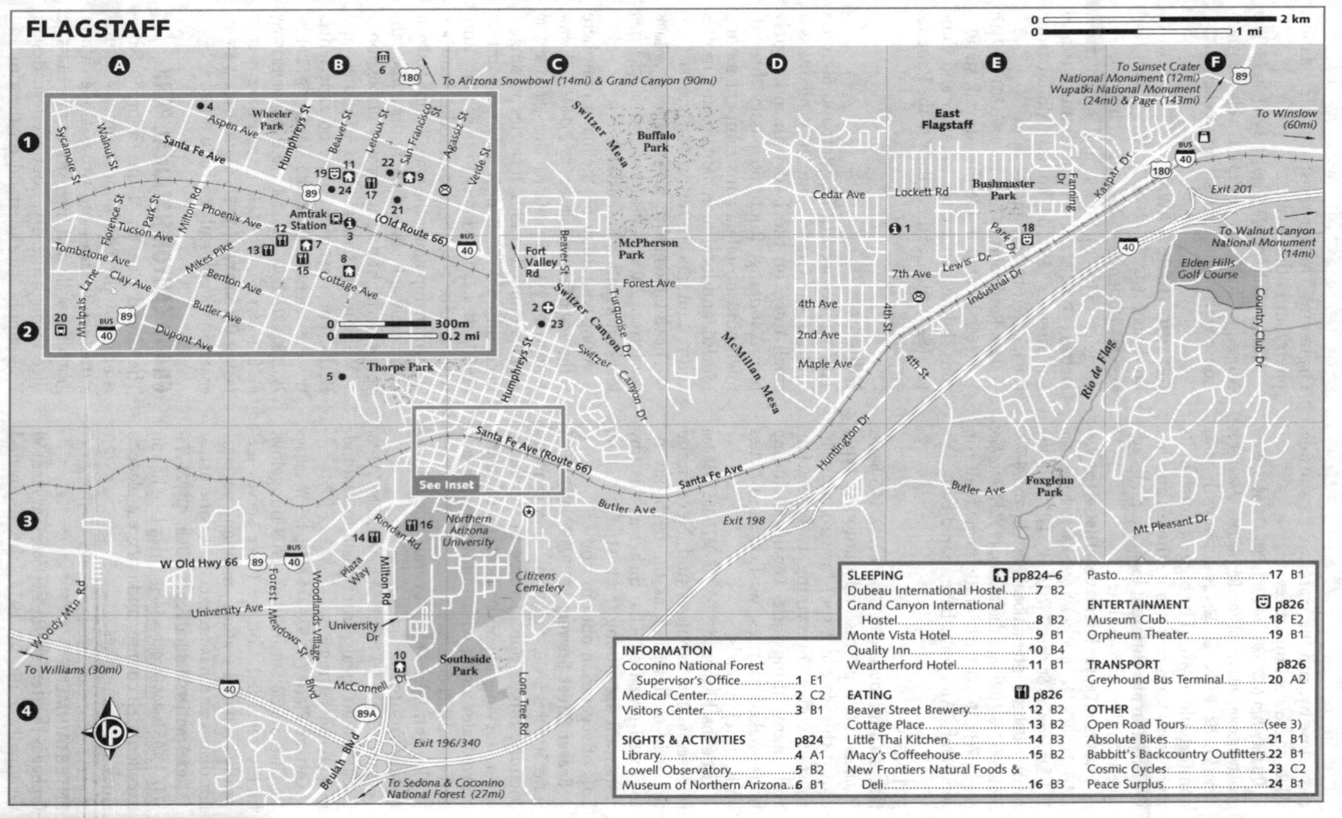
FLAGSTAFF
0 2 km
0 1 mi
To Arizona Snowbowl (14mi) & Grand Canyon (90mi)
To Sunset Crater National Monument (12mi) Wupatki National Monument (24mi) & Page (143mi)
To Winslow (60mi)
To Walnut Canyon National Monument (14mi)
To Williams (30mi)
To Sedona & Coconino National Forest (27mi)
East Flagstaff
Switzer Mesa
Buffalo Park
McPherson Park
McMillan Mesa
Bushmaster Park
Elden Hills Golf Course
Foxglenn Park
Thorpe Park
Northern Arizona University
Citizens Cemetery
Southside Park
Rio de Flag
Santa Fe Ave (Route 66)
Santa Fe Ave
Butler Ave
Huntington Dr
Industrial Dr
Kaspar Dr
Fanning Dr
Lockett Rd
Cedar Ave
Park Dr
Lewis Dr
7th Ave
4th Ave
2nd Ave
Maple Ave
4th St
Forest Ave
Turquoise Dr
Switzer Canyon Dr
Beaver St
Fort Valley Rd
Humphreys St
Country Club Dr
Mt Pleasant Dr
Lone Tree Rd
Riordan Rd
Milton Rd
Plaza Way
University Dr
McConnell Dr
W Old Hwy 66
University Ave
Forest Meadows St
Woodlands Village Blvd
Woody Mtn Rd
Beulah Blvd
Exit 201
Exit 198
Exit 196/340
See Inset
Sycamore St
Walnut St
Aspen Ave
Wheeler Park
Santa Fe Ave
Humphreys St
Beaver St
Leroux St
San Francisco St
Agassiz St
Verde St
Park St
Florence St
Milton Rd
Phoenix Ave
Tucson Ave
Tombstone Ave
Malpais Lane
Clay Ave
Mikes Pike
Benton Ave
Butler Ave
Dupont Ave
Cottage Ave
Amtrak Station
(Old Route 66)
0 300m
0 0.2 mi
INFORMATION
Coconino National Forest Supervisor's Office.....1 E1
Medical Center.....2 C2
Visitors Center.....3 B1
SIGHTS & ACTIVITIES p824
Library.....4 A1
Lowell Observatory.....5 B2
Museum of Northern Arizona..6 B1
SLEEPING pp824–6
Dubeau International Hostel.....7 B2
Grand Canyon International Hostel.....8 B2
Monte Vista Hotel.....9 B1
Quality Inn.....10 B4
Weartherford Hotel.....11 B1
EATING p826
Beaver Street Brewery.....12 B2
Cottage Place.....13 B2
Little Thai Kitchen.....14 B3
Macy's Coffeehouse.....15 B2
New Frontiers Natural Foods & Deli.....16 B3
Pasto.....17 B1
ENTERTAINMENT p826
Museum Club.....18 E2
Orpheum Theater.....19 B1
TRANSPORT p826
Greyhound Bus Terminal.....20 A2
OTHER
Open Road Tours.....(see 3)
Absolute Bikes.....21 B1
Babbitt's Backcountry Outfitters.22 B1
Cosmic Cycles.....23 C2
Peace Surplus.....24 B1

pass close by, and there are two bars inside. Also, there's a 1am curfew.

Quality Inn (☎ 928-774-8771, 800-424-6423; www.qualityinn.com; 2000 S Milton Rd; midweek/weekends r from $59/79; P ✻ 💻 ♿) A chain with basic comfortable rooms. The biggest notch in its favor is no train noise (note there's another Quality Inn at a different location that's adjacent to the railroad line).

The **Grand Canyon International Hostel** (☎ 928-774-9421, 888-442-2696; www.grandcanyonhostel.com; 19 S San Francisco St; dm/d $17/33; P 💻) and the nearby **Dubeau International Hostel** (☎ 928-774-6731, 800-398-7112; www.dubeau.com; 19 W Phoenix Ave; dm/d $17/39; P 💻) are jointly owned but run separately. All rooms have shared bath.

EATING

Macy's Coffeehouse (☎ 928-774-2242; 14 S Beaver St; dishes $3-6) Students and outdoorsy types crowd this excellent spot for strong, fresh-roasted coffee. Everything is vegetarian, and many things are vegan, including house-baked pastries, waffles, sandwiches and dinner specials.

Little Thai Kitchen (☎ 928-226-9422; 1051 S Milton Rd; dishes $6-10) A fabulous find. Never mind the strip-mall setting, as the fresh, inventive, well-prepared Thai dishes at this tiny restaurant are among the best in the state. Lots of vegetarian options, too.

Beaver Street Brewery (☎ 928-779-0079; 11 S Beaver St; dishes $7-10) Spacious, modern and friendly, this is one of three brewpubs in town, serving a good selection of craft-brewed ales along with sandwiches, salads and wood-fired pizzas.

Flagstaff also has several fine dining restaurants, too.

Pasto (☎ 928-779-1937; 19 E Aspen Ave; dishes $12-18) Great Italian meals, from pasta to seafood, in a stylish setting.

Cottage Place (☎ 928-774-8431; 126 W Cottage Ave; dishes $16-26) Set inside a 1909 bungalow, highly regarded Cottage Place serves elegantly prepared seafood, meat and vegetarian dishes and has an excellent wine list.

New Frontiers Natural Foods & Deli (☎ 928-774-5747; 1000 S Milton Rd; dishes $4-6) This place has an excellent deli counter and is a great place to stock up on supplies.

ENTERTAINMENT

Orpheum Theater (☎ 928-556-1580; 15 W Aspen St) Originally built in 1911, the renovated Orpheum Theater hosts music, dance, poetry and other events.

Museum Club (☎ 928-526-9434; 3404 E Rte 66) The Museum Club, built in 1931, is a classic roadhouse with country music on weekends.

GETTING THERE & AWAY

Greyhound (☎ 928-774-4573; 399 S Malpais Lane) serves Phoenix ($23, three hours), Los Angeles ($45, 10 hours) and other cities. **Amtrak** (☎ 800-872-7245; 1 E Rte 66) trains run to Los Angeles ($91, 11 hours), Albuquerque ($84, seven hours) and beyond.

Open Road Tours (☎ 928-226-8060, 800-776-7117; 1 E Rte 66), located inside the Amtrak station, runs shuttles twice daily to the Grand Canyon ($20) and five times daily to the Phoenix airport ($31).

Williams

Thirty miles west of Flagstaff and 60 miles south of the Grand Canyon, Williams is a small town on the I-40 with moderately priced lodging. Route 66 passes through town, and nostalgia runs rampant among tourists and local merchants; many motels and restaurants are restored originals.

The **visitors center** (☎ 928-635-1418; www.williamschamber.com; 200 W Railroad Ave; 🕑 8am-5pm) has local information and exhibits.

Along with Route 66, the major draw here is the **Grand Canyon Railway** (☎ 800-843-8724; www.thetrain.com; 233 N Grand Canyon Blvd; adult/child from $58/25). Founded in 1901, it carries passengers in century-old steam locomotives in summer (1950s diesels in winter) to the South Rim, with a mock robbery and other cowboy showmanship along the way. Trains leave at 10am daily and allow three hours at the canyon. Overnight packages are available, too.

Williams has more than 40 motels and B&Bs. For a genuine Route 66 experience, try the friendly **El Rancho Motel** (☎ 520-635-2552, 800-228-2370; www.thegrandcanyon.com/elrancho; 617 E Rte 66; r $57; P ✻ ♿), then have breakfast at **Old Smoky's** (☎ 928-635-2091; 624 W Rte 66; dishes $5-10) a colorful roadside diner.

GRAND CANYON NATIONAL PARK

The Grand Canyon of the Colorado River is arguably the USA's most famous natural attraction. Pictures and words alone cannot grasp the scale and intensity of this massive slice through the dry, Southwestern desert. You simply have to stand on the rim and

SAFE CANYON HIKING

Hundreds of people a day may enter the Grand Canyon in the heat of summer, and many don't realize the importance of a few simple rules. First, water is vital. If you're out for the day, carry at least four liters (quarts) of water per person per day; on super hot days, double that figure. Yes, water is heavy, but *don't skimp* on this part. Even if you're just going for a 'short jaunt' down 'a little way' on the Bright Angel Trail, take water. Other items to bring include a full-brimmed hat and waterproof sunscreen. For more hiking tips, see Lonely Planet's *Hiking in the USA*.

peer down into it yourself, allowing your eyes and mind to slowly soak up the multilayered, multicolored rocks, cliffs and crevices; the river rushing so far below; the pale blue of the hot sky; and all that space in between.

The canyon is some 277 miles long and about a mile deep, with most visitor services on the busy South Rim and the more sedate North Rim. Although only about 10 miles apart as the crow flies, it's 220 miles on narrow roads from the South Rim visitors center to the North Rim visitors center, which is why travelers usually explore the park one rim at a time. The South Rim is by far the most popular, packed every summer with camera-draped tourists, most only staying long enough to ogle from the designated scenic view points, which are accessible by shuttle buses, short walks and roadside pull-outs. The North Rim is better for those looking to escape the crowds; or you can visit the South Rim during autumn and winter. Of course, hiking down into the canyon is the most breathtaking (in both senses of the word) of all Grand Canyon experiences – just make sure you're prepared.

Information

The park's most developed area is Grand Canyon Village, about 6 miles north of the South Entrance Station. Here you'll find hotels, camping, restaurants, stores, showers, rim trails, a train depot, a clinic, a bank, a post office, a shuttle bus system, and lots and lots of people. The main visitors center is **Canyon View Information Plaza** (8am-6pm), at the northeast end of the village, with extensive visitor information, much of it displayed outside (viewable 24 hours) and seasonally updated. There are also displays on the local environment and a good book /map store. You can't drive directly here, though: the center is instead reached by a quick 0.25-mile walk, or via a free **shuttle bus**. Since parking is a pain, especially in summer, these buses are the best way to get around the South Rim; leave your car at one of the large central lots.

The main telephone number for the **Grand Canyon National Park** (☎ 928-638-7888; www.nps.gov/grca; PO Box 129, AZ 86023) offers general information. You can also write for the free Grand Canyon Trip Planner, or peruse the comprehensive website.

Entrance to the park is $20 per private vehicle; $10 for bicyclists and pedestrians (valid for seven days). One **rim-to-rim shuttle** (☎ 928-638-2820; one way/round-trip $65/110; May-Oct) runs each way daily; reservations required. Permits are required for all activities (backpacking, boating, horseback riding, fishing) except day hikes.

Entering the park you'll get a free map and *Visitor's Guide*, giving helpful information on what to see in the park, and how to get around it. It also lists free **ranger-led walks** and talks, given daily at various locations – and, for kids, the popular Junior Ranger Program.

The private, nonprofit **Grand Canyon Association** (☎ 928-638-2481; www.grandcanyon.org; PO Box 399, AZ 86023) sells more than 350 different books, maps, trail guides and informational videos, and will send out a mail-order catalog.

WHEN TO GO

June is the driest month; July and August are the wettest. January has average overnight lows of 13°F to 20°F and daytime highs of around 40°F. Summer temperatures inside the canyon rise above 100°F almost every day. While the South Rim is open all year, most visitors come between Memorial Day (late May) and Labor Day (early September), when it's very crowded. Some services, though, including hotels and restaurants, may close in winter. The North Rim is open from mid-May to mid-October only.

BACKCOUNTRY PERMITS

The **Backcountry Information Center** (☎ 928-638-7875; fax 928-638-2125; www.nps.gov/grca/backcountry;

PO Box 129, Grand Canyon, AZ 86023; 8am-noon, 1-5pm) accepts faxed applications for backpacking permits for the current month and the next four months only. Permits cost $10 plus $5 per person per night. Applications can be sent or faxed (but not emailed). Your chances are decent if you apply early and provide alternative hiking itineraries. If you arrive without a backcountry permit, don't despair. Head to the Backcountry Information Center, by the Maswik Lodge, and get on the waiting list for cancellations. You'll likely get a permit within one to six days, depending on season and itinerary.

River Running

Every year more than 20,000 people run the canyon's white-water rapids in a variety of boats. Most are commercial trips that get fully booked many months in advance, although occasional cancellations allow clients to pick up a trip with just a few weeks' notice. Expect to get soaked, to spend nights camping on beaches and to pay about $200 per person per day (including meals). Trips last from three to 15 days and run between April and October. Sixteen companies have permits to run the river; contact the park for a complete list.

One-day trips can be made outside the park from Page or with **Hualapai Tours** (888-255-9550; www.hualapaitours.com), on the Hualapai Indian Reservation west of the park; tours cost $265.

South Rim

The South Rim, at an elevation of 7000ft and much more accessible than the North Rim, gets 90% of park visitors. To reach the Grand Canyon at Grand Canyon Village take Hwy 64 north from Williams (60 miles) or west from the junction of Hwy 89 (53 miles); from Flagstaff (79 miles) follow Hwy 180 north.

The **Yavapai Observation Station** (8am-6pm, closes 7pm summer) has geology exhibits and a great indoor viewing area. The **Tusayan Museum** (9am-5pm), near the park's East Entrance Station, showcases Ancestral Puebloan history.

SCENIC DRIVES

East of Grand Canyon Village, Hwy 64 follows Desert View Dr with numerous scenic overlooks en route to the East Entrance Station. West of the village, the Hermit's Rest Rte also passes many overlooks but is closed to private vehicles. Take one of the frequent free shuttles, which stop at every overlook.

HIKING & BACKPACKING

There are lots of trails in and around the canyon. The popular and recommended 12.2-mile round-trip hike along **Bright Angel Trail** from the South Rim (6900ft) to Plateau Point (3800ft) is a strenuous all-day trek. There are rest houses after 1.5 miles (1130ft elevation drop) and 3 miles (2110ft elevation drop). From Indian Gardens, a campground 4.5 miles from the rim, you can continue to the Colorado River; at the bottom is Bright Angel Campground, 9.5 miles from the rim, and Phantom Ranch (see p829), with water, food and a ranger station. Note: you *must* have reservations to stay at these facilities; otherwise, rangers will make you hike right back out.

Carry plenty of water, and don't overdo it: the NPS recommends rim-to-river hikes be done as at least an overnight trip, because climbing out after a long descent is extremely strenuous. See 'Safe Canyon Hiking,' p827, for further information.

TOURS

Within the park, most tours are operated by **Xanterra** (303-297-2757, 888-297-2757; www.grandcanyonlodges.com). Various bus tours are offered several times a day.

Mule trips require advance reservation. A one-day mule trip to Plateau Point ($130) takes about seven hours round-trip. Overnight mule trips to Phantom Ranch (one/two persons $350/623, including meals and dormitory accommodations) are offered daily. Keep in mind this is no carnival ride – these journeys are hot, dusty and bumpy. Riders must weigh less than 200lb clothed (75kg), be in good physical condition and stand at least 4ft, 7in (142cm) tall.

Air tours have been much criticized for ruining the canyon's natural quiet, and while still hugely popular, they're restricted from many regions of the park.

SLEEPING & EATING

If you can't find accommodations in the national park, try Tusayan (at South Entrance Station), Valle (31 miles south), Cameron (53 miles east), Williams (about 60 miles south) or Flagstaff (79 miles south).

Xanterra (☎ 303-297-2757, 888-297-2757, same-day inquiries ☎ 928-638-2631; www.grandcanyonlodges.com) Operates all park hotels, lodges and restaurants, including Phantom Ranch.

El Tovar Hotel (r from $124-286) The park's most famous accommodation is the 1905 El Tovar Hotel, which has a glorious lobby and remodeled rooms, only a few with canyon views.

El Tovar Dining Room (☎ 928-638-2631, ext 6432; dishes $18-25) This is a well-deserved splurge. Reservations are usually required one month ahead; there's also a nice bar.

Bright Angel Lodge (r from $50) Bright Angel Lodge, dating from 1935, is full of character and slightly more rustic. Lodge rooms share baths, while cabins have their own. There's also a restaurant, bar and small **museum**, with displays on the Fred Harvey Company and architect Mary Colter, who designed Bright Angel Lodge, Phantom Ranch and other park buildings.

The South Rim's four other lodges have standard motel rooms (from $76 to $126).

Mather Campground (☎ 301-722-1257, 800-365-2267; www.nps.gov/grca; summer/winter campsites $15/10) This is the South Rim's main campground, at Grand Canyon Village; make reservations up to five months in advance (none needed December to March).

Trailer Village (☎ 303-297-2757; RV sites $25) Next door to Mather Campground and run by Xanterra, Trailer Village has RV sites.

Desert View Campground (campsites $10; 🕐 Oct-May) Sites at this campground near the east entrance are on a first-come, first-served basis only.

Phantom Ranch (dm $26, cabins $65; dinner $18-28) This small oasis at the bottom of the canyon along the Colorado River has 11 rustic cabins, usually full with mule riders, and two segregated 10-bunk dorms. Remember to plan ahead: all accommodations are by advance reservation only, as are the steak and stew dinners. Snacks, beer and wine are available daily.

The **Village Marketplace**, near the visitors center, has a deli, grocery store, ATM and post office.

GETTING THERE & AWAY

Most people drive, or arrive on a bus tour. The only regularly scheduled bus service into the park is **Open Road Tours** (☎ 928-226-8060, 800-776-7117; 1 E Rte 66), which run twice-daily shuttles to the Grand Canyon ($20) from Flagstaff. See the Williams section for the Grand Canyon Railway.

North Rim

The differences between the North and South Rims of the Grand Canyon are elevation, accessibility and the number of visitors. The North Rim is more than 8000ft above sea level. Summers are cooler, winters are colder, the climate is wetter and the spruce-fir forest above the rim is much thicker than the forests of the South Rim.

ORIENTATION & INFORMATION

The **North Rim Visitors Center** (☎ 928-638-7864; 🕐 8am-6pm), by the Grand Canyon Lodge, is 44 miles on Hwy 67 from Alt Hwy 89. The Backcountry Information Center is in the ranger station near the campground. Other services at the North Rim include a restaurant, gas station, bookshop, general store, coin laundry and showers, medical clinic and tours. From mid-October to mid-May, all services are closed except the campground, which stays open as weather permits (no later than December 1). In winter, you can ski in and camp (with a backcountry camping permit). It takes about three days to ski in from where the road is closed, so this trip is only for highly experienced winter campers/skiers.

SCENIC DRIVES

From the visitors center, about 20 miles of roads lead to several scenic overlooks with picnic areas, including Point Imperial (elevation 8803ft), the highest overlook in the park.

The remote Toroweap Overlook has primitive camping. To get there, drive 9 miles west of Fredonia on Hwy 389 and take a rough unpaved road 55 miles southwest to the Tuweep Ranger Station, which is staffed year round. (An alternative route is a 90-mile dirt road from St George, Utah.) It is five more miles from Tuweep to the overlook. (Note that you must leave and re-enter the national park to reach Toroweap.)

HIKING & BACKPACKING

The North Kaibab Trail plunges down to the Colorado River, 5750ft below and 14 miles away, connecting with trails to the South Rim. The first 4.7 miles drop well over 3000ft to **Roaring Springs**, a popular all-day hike and mule-ride destination. If you prefer a shorter day hike below the rim, you can walk just 0.75 miles down to **Coconino Overlook** or 1 mile to the **Supai Tunnel**, 1400ft below the rim.

Cottonwood campground is 7 miles and 4200ft below the rim and is the only campground between the North Rim and the river. Phantom Ranch (see South Rim p828) is 7 miles below Cottonwood. Because it's twice as far from the North Rim to the river as from the South Rim, rangers suggest three nights as a minimum to enjoy a rim-to-river and return hike. Backcountry permits are required (see p827).

TOURS

Canyon Trail Rides (☎ 435-679-8665, 435-834-5500; www.canyonrides.com) offers mule rides into the Grand Canyon (one hour/all-day tours from $20/95), though not down to the river. Children are welcome, but age limits apply. Advance reservations are recommended, or stop by its desk in the Grand Canyon Lodge.

SLEEPING & EATING

Grand Canyon Lodge (☎ 303-297-2757, 888-297-2757; www.grandcanyonnorthrim.com; r $91-116) The North Rim's only hotel is this stately lodge perched on the rim and rebuilt in 1937 after fire destroyed the original. It has over 200 cabins and rooms, plus a gorgeous **Dining Room** (☎ 928-638-2611; dinner $15-25) with glorious canyon views (dinner reservations required). There's also a cafeteria, coffee shop and saloon.

North Rim Campground (☎ 301-722-1257, 800-365-2267; www.nps.gov/grca; campsites $15) This campground is 1.5 miles north of the Grand Canyon Lodge. Make reservations up to five months in advance.

Dispersed camping is allowed north of the park borders in **Kaibab National Forest** (☎ 928-643-7298).

NORTHEASTERN ARIZONA

This section of the state is dominated by the Navajo and Hopi Indian reservations. Here Navajo *hogans* (octagonal homes made of wood and earth, with the door facing east) and Hopi kivas nestle against some of the most spectacular landscape in North America. Equally impressive are the ancient pueblos in the Canyon de Chelly and Navajo National Monuments.

Lake Powell

Originally, Glen Canyon offered wild, intricate terrain at the heart of the largest 'roadless' area in continental USA. The growing thirst of western cities, however, led to the construction of the Glen Canyon Dam during the late 1950s; environmentalists fought hard against the project but ultimately lost. The dam backs up the Colorado River and its tributaries for 186 miles, creating almost 2000 miles of shoreline.

Lake Powell is part of the **Glen Canyon National Recreation Area** (GCNRA), which stretches between Utah and Arizona. It's hugely popular with boaters. The **Carl Hayden Visitors Center** (☎ 928-608-6404; 7am-7pm summer, 8am-5pm fall-spring) is at the dam, 2 miles north of Page. Free 45-minute tours are given daily and take you inside the dam.

Wahweap Marina (☎ 928-645-2433; www.visitlakepowell.com), 5 miles north of the visitors center, has lodging, restaurants and boat rentals. On the south shore of Lake Powell is **Rainbow Bridge National Monument**, the world's largest natural bridge and a site of religious importance to the Navajo. The monument is 50 miles by boat from Wahweap, and tours are available from the marina (adult/child from $87/61).

Five miles from Lake Powell is the small town of **Page**, originally just a community of Glen Canyon Dam workers and now popular with travelers. You'll find plenty of motels, including the endearing **Bashful Bob's Motel** (☎ 928-645-3919; www.bashfulbobsmotel.com; 750 S Navajo Dr; r $39; P), which has a kitchen in every room. Rates are high in summer; reservations are recommended.

Navajo Indian Reservation

After the infamous 'Long Walk' (see 'Tragedy at Bosque Redondo,' p813), the surviving Navajo returned to their homeland in 1868 under a treaty that created a reservation of about 5500 sq miles. Today, the **Navajo Nation**, as the Navajo prefer to call it, is more than 25,000 sq miles of high desert and forest. It's the largest reservation in the US, covering parts of Arizona, New Mexico and Utah. Though some areas of the reservation are unmistakably poor, Navajo heritage is alive and vital. Tune in to the Navaho radio station (KTNN AM 660/KWRK 96.1) to catch music and commentary in both Navajo and English. Get a feel for Navajo heritage at the annual **Navajo Nation Fair** (www.navajonationfair.com), the biggest Native American event in the country held over Labor Day weekend in Window Rock.

The **Navajo Tourism Office** (☎ 928-871-7371; www.navajo.org) provides a free tourist information magazine, available on the reservation and nearby towns. All backcountry activities require a permit ($5, camping fee extra) from the **Navajo Parks & Recreation Department** (☎ 928-871-6647; www.navajonationparks.org; cnr Hwys 264 & 12; 8am-5pm Mon-Fri).

WINDOW ROCK

Straddling the border between Arizona and New Mexico, Window Rock is both the tribal capital and the most commercially developed town in the Navajo Nation. You can visit the **Navajo Council Chambers** (☎ 928-871-6417; 200 Parkway Administration; 8am-5pm Mon-Fri), which are off Hwy 12 about 2 miles north of Hwy 264.

HUBBELL TRADING POST NATIONAL HISTORIC SITE

Thirty miles west of Window Rock in the town of Ganado, **Hubbel Trading Post** (☎ 928-755-3475; admission free; 8am-5pm), now a National Historic Site, looks much as it would have soon after it was established by John Lorenzo Hubbell in 1878. There's a small museum and bookstore here alongside the trading post itself, which still sells local rugs and crafts.

CANYON DE CHELLY NATIONAL MONUMENT

The many-fingered Canyon De Chelly (pronounced *duh*-shay) is one of the most spectacular spots in the state, a unique world unto itself that contains several Ancestral Puebloan pit dwellings (circa AD 350) and some large cliff dwellings (circa 1200), all within steep canyon walls that add to the monument's mystique – entering the canyon is like stepping back in time. There are two scenic rim drives, each taking about three hours to appreciate, but to truly get a feel for the place you've got to head inside; for this you need a Navajo guide. The **visitors center** (☎ 928-674-5500; 8am-5pm) can provide details on guided hikes ($15, four hours), 4WD trips ($40 for a half day) and horseback rides ($10 per hour plus $10 for a guide).

Near the visitors center is **Thunderbird Lodge** (☎ 928-674-5841, 800-679-2473; www.tbirdlodge.com; queen/king r from $106/145; P), an attractive property with standard, clean rooms. Pleasant, modest **Cottonwood Campground** (free) is located here.

FOUR CORNERS NAVAJO TRIBAL PARK

You can put a foot into Arizona, another into New Mexico, a hand into Utah and another into Colorado at the Four Corners Navajo Tribal Park ($2.50) – the only place in the USA where four states come together. Navajo food stands and dozens of the inevitable crafts stalls surround the site, which is off Hwy 160.

MONUMENT VALLEY NAVAJO TRIBAL PARK

The magnificent mesas and buttes of Monument Valley, immortalized through westerns like John Ford's 1939 *Stagecoach*, sits on the Arizona–Utah border, 24 miles north of Kayenta on Hwy 163. You get great views along the highway, but from the **visitors center** (☎ 435-727-5870; 6am-8pm summer, 8am-5pm winter), you can get closer by taking a 17-mile driving tour ($5) or, in summer, arranging 4WD and horseback tours. **Mitten View Campground** has campsites ($10). The closest hotel is in Utah (see p854).

NAVAJO NATIONAL MONUMENT

The Ancestral Puebloan sites of Betatakin and Keet Seel are open for public visitation and are both exceptionally well preserved, extensive and impressive. Because you need to hike 5 miles round-trip to Betatakin and 17 miles round-trip to Keet Seel, this is a good place to check out pueblo sites away from crowds. Daily hiking permits are free but limited, so call for reservations up to two months in advance. The **visitors center** (☎ 928-672-2700; 8am-5pm) is 9 miles north of Hwy 160 along paved Hwy 564. Free **camping** is on a first-come, first-served basis.

SLEEPING

In Window Rock, try **Navajo Nation Inn** (☎ 928-871-4108, 800-662-6189; www.navajonationinn.com; 48 W Hwy 264; r $67; P), a Navajo-owned chain. Many visitors also stay in Gallup, New Mexico.

GETTING THERE & AWAY

The **Navajo Transit System** (☎ 928-729-4002; www.navajotransitsystem.com) runs buses from Window Rock to Gallup, New Mexico ($2.50, one hour), Tuba City ($13, four hours) – with stops along Hwy 264 via the Hopi Reservation – and other locations.

Hopi Indian Reservation

The oldest, most traditional and religious tribe in Arizona (if not the entire continent), the Hopi are a private people who have received less outside influence than most other tribes. Villages, many built between AD 1400 and AD 1700, dot the isolated mesas. **Old Oraibi**, inhabited since the early 12th century, vies with Acoma Pueblo in New Mexico for the title of the oldest continuously inhabited town in North America.

Hwy 264 runs past the three mesas (First, Second and Third Mesa) that form the heart of the reservation. There are no banks, and cash is preferred for most transactions. Photographs, sketching and recording are not allowed – *don't even ask.*

At the end of First Mesa, the tiny village of **Walpi** (circa 1200) juts out into space from the top of a spectacularly narrow mesa; it's the most dramatic of the Hopi villages. The friendly **tourist office** (☎ 928-737-2262) can arrange guided walking tours (adult/child $8/5), given several times daily. To reach Walpi, look for signs to First Mesa from Hwy 264 (around mile marker 392), and follow the road to the parking area at top of the mesa.

The Hopi are known for their kachina dolls, and these and other crafts can be purchased from individual artists in the villages and at roadside galleries.

The **Hopi Cultural Center Restaurant & Inn** (☎ 928-734-2401; www.hopiculturalcenter.com; r $90-95; dishes $6-8; P ⊠), in Second Mesa, is the reservation's only hotel. The restaurant serves burgers, salads and Hopi dishes such as *noqkwivi* (lamb and hominy stew). The Cultural Center's **museum** (☎ 728-734-6650; ⏰ 8am-5pm Mon-Fri) is a good first stop, with informative exhibits on Hopi history, including many historical photographs.

Winslow

Located along I-40, Winslow provides the closest off-reservation accommodations to the Hopi mesas. Several old Route 66 motels line 2nd and 3rd Sts, but the most memorable place to stay is the recently restored **La Posada** (☎ 928-289-4366; www.laposada.org; 303 E 2nd St; r from $79; ⊠), designed by Mary Colter.

Petrified Forest National Park

Conifers from the Triassic (225 million years ago) make up the 'forest' on the ground at this **national park** (www.nps.gov/pefo; admission per vehicle $10; ⏰ 8am-5pm). Apart from the petrified logs, visitors see a few small ancient Indian sites, some petroglyphs and the otherworldly scenery of the **Painted Desert**, a colorful, picturesque landscape. A road cuts 28 miles north–south through the park, passing short trails, signed pullouts and the **Painted Desert Visitors Center** (☎ 928-524-6228; ⏰ 8am-5pm).

WESTERN ARIZONA

Along the state's western border, the Colorado River is alive with sun-worshippers at Lake Havasu City, while Route 66 nuts enjoy well-preserved stretches of that classic highway near Kingman. South of I-10 toward Yuma, the wild, empty landscape is among the most rugged in the West.

Kingman & Around

Founded by Lewis Kingman in 1880 as a railway stop, Kingman is the biggest town along I-40 between California and Flagstaff. The **visitors center** (☎ 928-753-6106, 866-427-7866; www.kingmantourism.org; 120 W Andy Devine Ave; ⏰ 9am-6pm) is also home to the **Route 66 Museum** (☎ 928-753-9889; admission $3).

Budget motels line Andy Devine Ave (between I-40 exits 48 and 53), and while some are best avoided, others are just fine. The **Lido Motel** (☎ 928-753-4515; 3133 E Andy Divine Ave; r $25; P ⊠) is a reliable choice.

The longest extant stretch of Route 66, once called the 'Main Street of America,' winds 160 miles through empty northwestern Arizona countryside, from Seligman west to Kingman, then on through Oatman to the Arizona–California border. A former gold-mining town, **Oatman** is now a hokey but spirited tourist town, with gunfights at high noon and wild burros roaming the street. At the century-old **Oatman Hotel** (☎ 928-768-4408; r $35-55), on Route 66, the simple rooms remain almost unchanged since Clarke Gable and Carole Lombard honeymooned here in the 1930s. All rooms share baths and have ceiling fans.

The quiet town of **Chloride** is Arizona's oldest mining town, founded in 1862. From Kingman, head northwest on Hwy 93 for 19 miles; turn right and drive 3.5 miles into town.

SOUTHWESTERN SOUNDTRACKS

A half-dozen albums that make perfect sense on a long Southwestern desert drive:

- Calexico, *Black Light* – Warm, groovy and haunting, this Tucson band brings the hot Sonoran Desert to life
- Bob Dylan, *Pat Garrett & Billy the Kid* – A perfect listen when passing through Lincoln, New Mexico
- Buddy Holly, *The Buddy Holly Collection* – Bop to these classic rockabilly tracks, many cut at a small studio in Clovis, New Mexico
- Waylon Jennings, *Live at JD's* – Document of the late Country & Western singer's early years, when he was cutting his teeth at Phoenix nightclub JD's
- Little Feat, *Sailin' Shoes* – The laid-back 'Willin' is a highway classic for those driving 'from Tucson to Tucumcari' and beyond

Lake Havasu City

When the city of London auctioned off its 1831 bridge in the late 1960s, developer Robert McCulloch bought it for $2.5 million, disassembled it into 10,276 granite slabs, transported the 10,000 tons of stone and reassembled it at Lake Havasu City, which sits along a dammed-up portion of the Colorado River. Now the place is crawling with camera-toting visitors ogling for angles of the fairly unspectacular bridge, which is surrounded by an 'English Village' of pseudo-British pubs and gift shops (it's more drab than wacky). The place attracts hordes of young spring breakers and weekend warriors, too, who come to play in the water and party hard. Beyond that, the town is a growing mass of sprawling subdivisions and other commercial development.

If all that sounds like a nightmare, steer clear. For those dying to see the bridge or frolic in the hot Lake Havasu sunshine, however, you can overnight at the **Island Inn** (☎ 928-680-0606; www.havasumotels.com; 1300 McCulloch Blvd; summer/winter r from $80/60; P ⊠ ⊠) a pleasant, well-kept property 0.25 miles west of the bridge.

Yuma

Though it's not on the average tourist's Arizona agenda, this town is Arizona's third-largest metropolitan area. And being one of the state's sunniest and driest regions, it actually,attracts crowds of snowbirds every winter – it's sort of a 'poor man's Palm Springs,' as one local described it.

The top tourist attraction in town is the gruesome and offbeat **Yuma Territorial Prison State Historic Park** (☎ 928-783-4771; adult/child $4/2; ⏰ 8am-5pm), where you can visit buildings that housed more than 3000 of Arizona's most feared criminals between 1876 and 1909. Take exit 1 from I-8. The **visitors center** (☎ 928-783-0071; www.visityuma.com; 377 S Main St) has information on this and other sights.

Yuma offers several chain motels by I-8 exit 2, but even more independent accommodations line 4th Ave. Winter and spring constitute the high season.

Yuma Cabaña (☎ 928-783-8311, 800-874-0811; www.yumacabana.com; 2151 S 4th Ave; winter/summer r from $58/29; P ⊠ ⊠) Yuma is one of the town's best and most interesting budget motels.

La Fuente Inn & Suites (☎ 928-329-1814, 800-841-1814; lafuenteinn.com; 1513 E 16th St; r $83-104; P ⊠ ⊠ ⊠) At this modern Spanish-colonial-style building around a landscaped garden, guests receive coupons for free drinks.

Lutes Casino (☎ 928-782-2192; 221 Main St; dishes $3-5) Eclectic Lutes Casino serves burgers and claims to be Arizona's oldest pool hall.

Red's Bird Cage Saloon (☎ 928-783-1050; 231 Main St) While a little funky, this place has a lot of history and is a worthwhile pit stop.

Greyhound (☎ 928-783-4403; 170 E 17th Place) has buses to Phoenix ($25, four hours) and other destinations.

TUCSON

Rich in Latino roots and home to the University of Arizona (U of A), Tucson, Arizona's second-largest city, is one of the most culturally invigorating places in the Southwest. For travelers looking to get the flavor of the region, it makes a *much* more fun and satisfying base than Phoenix, 116 miles north.

The city is set in a Sonoran Desert valley at 2500ft, surrounded by mountains, some reaching more than 9000ft. Like Phoenix, Tucson has sprawled; luckily the areas most travelers will want to explore (downtown and the university district) are within easy walking and biking distance. One exception is the Arizona-Sonora Desert Museum; west of town in beautiful Saguaro National Park, it's a highlight for visitors of all ages.

Temperatures in Tucson often hover in between 70°F and 80°F degrees during the winter, but they can rise to well over 100°F in the summer.

Orientation

Downtown Tucson and the historic district are east of I-10 exit 258. Stone Ave, at its intersection with Congress St, forms the zero point for Tucson addresses. About a mile northeast of downtown is the U of A campus; 4th Ave is the main drag here and is packed with cafés, bars and funky shops.

Information

BOOKSTORES

Bookman's (☎ 520- 325-5767; 1930 E Grant Rd) Original store in a small Arizona chain with great selections of used books, music and magazines.

EMERGENCY

Emergency number (☎ 911)
Tucson Police Department (☎ 520-791-4444; 270 S Stone Ave)

INTERNET ACCESS

Main library (☎ 520-791-4393; 101 N Stone Ave) Offers free Internet access.

MEDIA

Tucson Weekly (☎ 520-792-3630; www.tucsonweekly.com) Free alternative weekly with great entertainment and restaurant listings.

MEDICAL SERVICES

Tucson Medical Center (☎ 520-327-5461; 5301 E Grant Rd)

POST

Downtown Station (☎ 520-903-1958; 141 S 6th Ave)

TOURIST OFFICES

Coronado National Forest Supervisor's Office (☎ 520-670-4552; www.fs.fed.us/r3/coronado; 300 W Congress St; 8am-4:30pm Mon-Fri)
Tucson Convention & Visitors Bureau (☎ 520-624-1817, 800-638-8350; www.visittucson.org; 110 S Church Ave; 8am-5pm Mon-Fri, 9am-4pm Sat & Sun)

Sights

In downtown Tucson, you can stroll through the 19th-century buildings and craft stores in the **Presidio Historic District**, between Court and Main Aves and Franklin and Alameda Sts. The **Tucson Museum of Art** (☎ 520-624-2333; 140 N Main Ave; adult/student $5/2, free Sun; 10am-4pm Mon-Sat, noon-4pm Sun) houses a small collection of pre-Columbian artifacts from South America as well as various works of 20th-century Western art.

The **University of Arizona** campus houses some excellent museums and several notable outdoor sculptures. At the top of the heap is the internationally renowned **Center for Creative Photography** (☎ 520-621-7968; 1030 N Olive Rd; admission free; 9am-5pm Mon-Fri, noon-5pm Sat & Sun). It houses a nice collection of works by American photographers, interesting gallery shows and a remarkable archive (including most of Ansel Adams' and Edward Weston's work), and is a must for anyone interested in photography. Opposite is the **UA Museum of Art** (☎ 520-621-7567; near Park Ave & Speedway Blvd; admission free; 9am-5pm Mon-Fri, noon-4pm Sun), another worthwhile stop.

The **Tucson Botanical Gardens** (☎ 520-326-9686; 2150 N Alvernon Way; adult/child $5/2.50; 8:30am-4:30pm) cover 5.5 acres and focus on native dry-land plants.

The extensive **Pima Air & Space Museum** (☎ 520-574-0462; 6000 E Valencia Rd; admission $10; 9am-5pm) has more than 200 aircraft. That's fascinating enough, but the nearby Davis-Monthan Air Force Base is home to an astonishing **5000 mothballed aircraft**, a strange sight indeed; see them along Kolb Rd near Escalante Rd.

Activities

Tucson may be hot in the summer, but the surrounding mountains offer year-round respite. **Sabino Canyon** (day/week pass $5/10), 15 miles northeast of downtown Tucson, is one of Tucson's most popular getaways; the USFS **ranger station** (☎ 520-749-8700; 5700 N Sabino Canyon Rd) has information on the numerous hikes here in the Santa Catalina Mountains. **Mt Lemmon** (admission $5), at 9157ft, is another popular destination. You can spend a couple of days hiking to its summit, or head east on

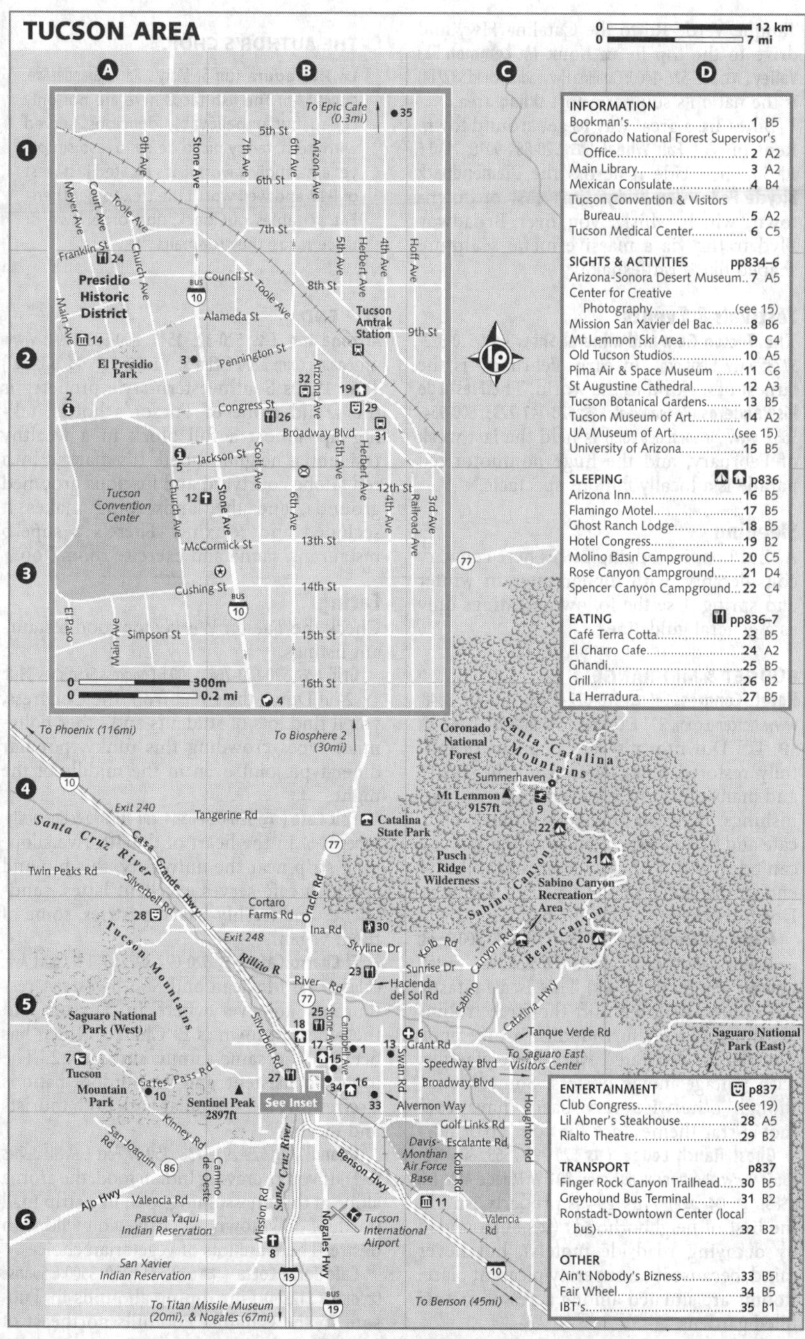
TUCSON AREA
0 12 km
0 7 mi
INFORMATION
Bookman's 1 B5
Coronado National Forest Supervisor's Office 2 A2
Main Library 3 A2
Mexican Consulate 4 B4
Tucson Convention & Visitors Bureau 5 A2
Tucson Medical Center 6 C5
SIGHTS & ACTIVITIES pp834–6
Arizona-Sonora Desert Museum 7 A5
Center for Creative Photography (see 15)
Mission San Xavier del Bac 8 B6
Mt Lemmon Ski Area 9 C4
Old Tucson Studios 10 A5
Pima Air & Space Museum 11 C6
St Augustine Cathedral 12 A3
Tucson Botanical Gardens 13 B5
Tucson Museum of Art 14 A2
UA Museum of Art (see 15)
University of Arizona 15 B5
SLEEPING p836
Arizona Inn 16 B5
Flamingo Motel 17 B5
Ghost Ranch Lodge 18 B5
Hotel Congress 19 B2
Molino Basin Campground 20 C5
Rose Canyon Campground 21 D4
Spencer Canyon Campground 22 C4
EATING pp836–7
Café Terra Cotta 23 B5
El Charro Cafe 24 A2
Ghandi 25 B5
Grill 26 B2
La Herradura 27 B5
ENTERTAINMENT p837
Club Congress (see 19)
Lil Abner's Steakhouse 28 A5
Rialto Theatre 29 B2
TRANSPORT p837
Finger Rock Canyon Trailhead 30 B5
Greyhound Bus Terminal 31 B2
Ronstadt-Downtown Center (local bus) 32 B2
OTHER
Ain't Nobody's Bizness 33 B5
Fair Wheel 34 B5
IBT's 35 B1
To Epic Cafe (0.3mi)
5th St
6th St
7th St
8th St
9th St
12th St
13th St
14th St
15th St
16th St
9th Ave
Stone Ave
7th Ave
6th Ave
Arizona Ave
5th Ave
Herbert Ave
4th Ave
Hoff Ave
3rd Ave
Railroad Ave
Meyer Ave
Court Ave
Toole Ave
Franklin St
Church Ave
Main Ave
Council St
Alameda St
Pennington St
Congress St
Broadway Blvd
Jackson St
Scott Ave
McCormick St
Cushing St
Simpson St
El Paso
Presidio Historic District
El Presidio Park
Tucson Amtrak Station
Tucson Convention Center
0 300m
0 0.2 mi
To Phoenix (116mi)
To Biosphere 2 (30mi)
Exit 240
Exit 248
Tangerine Rd
Twin Peaks Rd
Santa Cruz River
Casa Grande Hwy
Silverbell Rd
Cortaro Farms Rd
Oracle Rd
Ina Rd
Skyline Dr
Sunrise Dr
Kolb Rd
River Rd
Rillito R
Hacienda del Sol Rd
Tucson Mountains
Saguaro National Park (West)
Tucson Mountain Park
Gates Pass Rd
Sentinel Peak 2897ft
See Inset
Kinney Rd
San Joaquin Rd
Camino de Oeste
Ajo Hwy
Valencia Rd
Pascua Yaqui Indian Reservation
San Xavier Indian Reservation
Mission Rd
Nogales Hwy
Tucson International Airport
To Titan Missile Museum (20mi), & Nogales (67mi)
Stone Ave
Campbell Ave
Grant Rd
Speedway Blvd
Broadway Blvd
Swan Rd
Alvernon Way
Golf Links Rd
Escalante Rd
Davis-Monthan Air Force Base
Kolb Rd
Houghton Rd
Valencia Rd
Benson Hwy
To Benson (45mi)
Coronado National Forest
Santa Catalina Mountains
Summerhaven
Mt Lemmon 9157ft
Catalina State Park
Pusch Ridge Wilderness
Sabino Canyon
Sabino Canyon Recreation Area
Sabino Canyon Rd
Bear Canyon
Catalina Hwy
Tanque Verde Rd
To Saguaro East Visitors Center
Saguaro National Park (East)

Tanque Verde Rd to the Catalina Hwy and drive to the top in an hour. **Mt Lemmon Ski Valley** (☎ 520-576-1400; Catalina Hwy; adult/child $32/14) is the nation's southernmost **skiing** area.

Bikes are a great way to get around town. Rent one at **Fair Wheel** (☎ 520-884-9018; 1110 E 6th St), then ride it across the **Diamondback Bicycle Pedestrian Bridge**, just east of downtown, which whisks you over Broadway Blvd traffic via a massive metal sculpture shaped like a rattlesnake.

Festivals & Events

The **Tucson Gem and Mineral Show** (☎ 520-322-5773; www.tgms.org), in early February, is the largest of its kind in the world. The **Fiesta de los Vaqueros** (Rodeo Week; ☎ 520-741-2233, 800-964-5662; www.tucsonrodeo.com) is held the last week of February, and the huge nonmotorized parade is a locally famous spectacle.

Sleeping

As in Phoenix, lodging prices here can vary considerably, with higher rates in winter and spring. Use the following listings only as a general guideline.

BUDGET & MID-RANGE

Hotel Congress (☎ 520-622-8848, 800-722-8848; www.hotcong.com; 311 E Congress St; dm/s/d $24/62/72; P) Downtown's very popular, beautifully restored hotel dates from the 1920s, and many of its fine rooms have period furnishings. Downstairs there's a music club, café and bar, so expect noise at night; if you can't deal with that, ask for a room at the far end of the hotel, or for a pair of earplugs. Dorm rooms are above the bar.

Flamingo Motel (☎ 520-770-1910, 800-300-3533; www.flamingohoteltucson.com; 1300 N Stone Ave; winter/summer r $74/49; P) This is a fantastic old courtyard motel; off-the-street rooms are quiet and set surrounding a nice pool. The place is decorated everywhere you turn with vintage movie posters. Some rooms, though otherwise very basic, have cool movie-star themes (ask for your favorite).

Ghost Ranch Lodge (☎ 520-791-7565, 800-456-7565; www.ghostranchlodge.com; 801 W Miracle Mile Rd; r $83; P) This 1940s property isn't in the best of neighborhoods (it's surrounded by decaying roadside motels), but never mind, because it's a superbly pleasant place. Rooms are situated among acres of cactus-filled gardens.

THE AUTHOR'S CHOICE

La Herradura (cnr St Mary's Rd & Grande Ave; dishes $4-6) The fish tacos here are not only cheap but unbelievably delicious, served with fresh, tangy picco de gallo – so simple yet amazingly flavorful. It's located just west of I-17 and well worth the trek to get there. Eat at tables out back, and order two or three tacos; they're small.

TOP END

Arizona Inn (☎ 520-325-1541, 800-933-1093; www.arizonainn.com; 2200 E Elm St; r $239; P) This 1930s Southwestern-style property is the grand dame of Tucson's hotels, taking up almost a full block in a wealthy residential neighborhood. It's marked by a red adobe courtyard and luscious groomed grounds, and the landscaping makes it secluded and relaxing. There's a superb restaurant, sauna and exercise room, too.

Eating

Check the *Tucson Weekly* for good restaurant listings.

Grill (☎ 520-623-7621; 100 E Congress St; dishes $3-8; 24hr) Down the street from the Congress, you'll find lots of students and other bohemian types crowding this funky, popular diner-type joint even in the middle of the night.

Epic Cafe (☎ 520-624-6844; cnr 4th Ave & University; dishes $4-6) In the heart of the 4th Ave shopping strip near the university, this hip and spacious café serves excellent lattes, sandwiches and freshly-baked pastries, some of them vegan.

El Charro Cafe (☎ 520-622-1922; 311 N Court Ave; dishes $7-15) Mexican and Southwestern restaurants are everywhere in Tucson, but the oldest in town is El Charro, which has been in the same family since 1922. The food is consistent, and the outdoor patio is a refreshing treat popular with both tourists and locals.

Ghandi (☎ 520-292-1738; 150 W Fort Lowell; dishes $6-11) If you're craving Indian food, the aroma alone at this unassuming spot, in a strip mall north of downtown, will drive you wild with desire. There are lots of vegetarian choices.

Café Terra Cotta (☎ 520-577-8100, 3500 E Sunrise Dr; dishes $12-24) Fine dining abounds in Tucson. In the Catalina Foothills northeast of downtown, this restaurant gets consistently high ratings for its wood-fired pizzas, spicy pork tenderloin and other upscale Southwestern fare.

Entertainment

The *Tucson Weekly*, once again, is the place to look for entertainment listings.

Club Congress (☎ 520-622-8848; 311 E Congress St) In the Hotel Congress, Club Congress consistently has the most interesting gigs in town. From DJ dance nights to touring rock and roots bands, there's something almost every night – not to mention a great, laid-back bar for drinking.

Rialto Theatre (☎ 520-798-3333; 318 E Congress St) This restored theatre, across the street from Club Congress, hosts bigger music shows.

Octogenarian western swing bandleader Dean Armstrong and his Arizona Dancehands have been tearing it up on the outdoor stage at **Lil Abner's Steakhouse** (☎ 520-744-2800; 8501 N Silverbell Rd) on Friday and Saturday nights for years.

Getting There & Around

Tucson International Airport (☎ 520-573-8000) is 9 miles south of downtown. **Arizona Stagecoach** (☎ 520-889-1000; transfers $8-35) offers door-to-door, 24-hour airport service to points throughout Tucson.

Amtrak (☎ 800-872-7245; 400 E Toole Ave) has trains to Los Angeles three times weekly ($32, 9½ hours), and **Greyhound** (☎ 520-792-3475; 2 S 4th Ave) runs buses to Phoenix ($16, two hours) and elsewhere.

The **Ronstadt-Downtown Center** (cnr Congress St & 6th Ave) is a major local transit center. From there, **Sun Tran** (☎ 520-792-9222) buses serve metropolitan Tucson ($1).

National car rental agencies have offices at the airport and around town. Check p1121 for details.

AROUND TUCSON

Arizona-Sonora Desert Museum

Coyotes, javelinas, bobcats, snakes, hummingbirds, scorpions and just about any other local desert animals you can think of are displayed in natural-looking outdoor settings at this excellent living **museum** (☎ 520-883-2702; 2021 N Kinney Rd; adult/child $10/2; 🕐 8:30am-5pm) off Hwy 86 about 12 miles west of Tucson. A perennial local favorite, it's one of Tucson's crown jewels.

Saguaro National Park

With two separate units, east and west of Tucson, this park's main purpose is to preserve large stands of the giant saguaro cactus and their associated habitat and wildlife. The **Saguaro East Visitors Center** (☎ 520-733-5153; www.nps.gov/sagu; permits $6; 🕐 8:30am-5pm), 15 miles east of downtown along Old Spanish Trail (take E Broadway Blvd), has information regarding day hikes, horseback riding and park camping (free permits must be obtained by noon on the day of your hike). The park boasts about 130 miles of trails, including the Tanque Verde Ridge Trail, which climbs to Mica Mountain (8666ft).

Two miles northwest of the Arizona-Sonora Desert Museum is the **Saguaro West Visitors Center** (☎ 520-733-5158; admission free; 🕐 8:30am-5pm). Although night hiking is permitted, camping is not.

Mission San Xavier del Bac

Founded by the Jesuit Padre Kino in 1700, the **San Xavier mission** (☎ 520-294-2624) is Arizona's oldest European building still in use. Catholic masses are held daily. To get there, drive south on I-19 to exit 92.

Old Tucson Studios

Once an actual film set, **Old Tucson** (☎ 520-883-0100; 201 S Kinney Rd; adult/child $15/10; 🕐 10am-6pm), a few miles southeast of the Arizona-Sonora Desert Museum, is now a Western theme park with Wild West shootouts and other craziness.

Biosphere 2

Built to be completely sealed off from Biosphere 1 (that would be earth), **Biosphere 2** (☎ 520-896-6200; www.bio2.edu; adult/child $13/9; 🕐 8:30am-5pm) is a 3-acre glassed dome housing seven separate microhabitats and designed to be self-sustaining. In 1991 eight 'bionauts' entered Biosphere 2 for a two-year tour of duty, during which they were physically cut off from the outside world. They emerged thinner but in pretty fair shape. Although this experiment could be used as a prototype for future space stations, it was a privately funded endeavor and was engulfed in controversy. Now, there are various ongoing research projects. Biosphere 2 is about 30 miles north of Tucson on Hwy 77.

WEST OF TUCSON

Hwy 86 heads west from Tucson toward some of the driest (and emptiest) parts of the Sonoran Desert.

West of Sells on Hwy 86, **Kitt Peak National Optical Observatory** (☎ 520-318-8726; 🕑 9am-3:45pm) is the largest optical observatory in the world. Guided tours ($2) are available daily, as are nightly three-hour viewing sessions ($36), booked weeks in advance.

If you want solitude in stark, quiet and beautiful desert surroundings, seek out the undisturbed Sonoran Desert habitat at **Organ Pipe Cactus National Monument** (☎ 520-387-6849; admission $5). Two unpaved loop drives (21 and 53 miles) and six hiking trails take you through the park, which has three types of large columnar cacti and an excellent variety of other desert flora and fauna. The **visitors center** (🕑 8am-5pm) is 22 miles south of the Hwy 86 junction at Why. Camping ($6 to $10) is available.

SOUTH OF TUCSON

South of Tucson, I-19 is the main route to Nogales, Arizona and Mexico. Along the way are several interesting stops.

The **Titan Missile Museum** (☎ 520-625-7736; 1580 W Duval Mine Rd; adult/child $7.50/4; 🕑 9am-5pm winter, Wed-Sun summer), at I-19 exit 69, features an underground launch site for Cold War–era intercontinental ballistic missiles.

If history and/or shopping for crafts interest you, visit the small village of **Tubac** (I-19 exit 34), with more than 80 galleries.

At exit 29, **Tumacácori National Historic Park** (☎ 520-398-2341; www.nps.gov/tuma; admission $3; 🕑 8am-5pm) is the well-preserved ruin of a never-completed Franciscan church started in 1800. Facilities include a visitors center, museum and gift shop.

Nogales

Arizona's most important gateway to Mexico, Nogales is bustling with activity and tourists buying Mexican goods (keep in mind there's a Nogales on each side of the border).

The **chamber of commerce** (☎ 520-287-3685; 123 W Kino Park Way; 🕑 8am-5pm Mon-Fri) is in Kino Park off Grand Ave. The **Mexican Consulate** (☎ 520-287-2521; 571 Grand Ave) is in town if you need it.

Chain **motels** are clustered at I-19 exit 4 and along Business Hwy 19.

Greyhound (☎ 520-287-5628; 35 N Terrace St) has regular services to Tucson ($8, two hours). From the bus terminal about 3 miles south of the border, there are frequent bus departures further into Mexico and a train to Guadalajara and Mexico City.

Drivers into Mexico can obtain car insurance from friendly, helpful **Sanborn's** (☎ 520-281-1873; www.sanbornsinsurance.com; 2921 N Grand Ave; 🕑 8am-5pm Mon-Fri, 8am-4pm Sat & Sun). The cost is determined by the value of the car and length of your stay, but there's a $22 minimum. Insurance is available either on the spot or in advance. Sanborn's has a **second office** (☎ 520-281-1865; 850 W Shell Rd; 🕑 8am-5pm Mon-Fri, 8am-4pm Sat & Sun) in the lobby of Holiday Inn Express, conveniently located off exit 4 (Mariposa Rd).

SOUTHEASTERN CORNER

Cochise County is a land rich with cowboys, Indians, ranchers, miners, gunslingers and all manner of Western lore. It's also an area of rugged, scenic beauty, highlighted by the Huachuca and Chiricahua Mountains.

Rural **Benson** is a quiet travelers' stop with a few motels. The best reason to come here, though, is to visit fantastic **Kartchner Caverns State Park** (☎ 520-486-4100; admission $10), a 2.5-mile-long wet limestone cave, touted as one of the world's best 'living' caves. It's 9 miles south of Benson on Hwy 90. Guided **tours** (☎ 520-586-2283; adult/child $14/6) are hugely popular, and advance reservations are required. However, each morning some same-day tour tickets are sold, and travelers often wait from before dawn to snag one in the busy winter high season.

Small and remote **Chiricahua National Monument** (☎ 520-824-3560; admission $5), in the Chiricahua Mountains, offers strangely eroded volcanic geology and abundant wildlife. The **Bonita Canyon Scenic Dr** takes you 8 miles to Massai Point at 6870ft, and there are numerous hiking trails. The monument is 40 miles southeast of Willcox off Hwy 186.

At 5500ft, in the Huachuca Mountains 10 miles south of **Sierra Vista**, the Nature Conservancy's **Ramsey Canyon Preserve** (☎ 520-378-2640; admission $5; 🕑 8am-5pm) is famous for some 170 bird species, including up to 14 types of hummingbirds. Large RVs can't make it up the road here.

Tombstone is a formerly rip-roaring, 19th-century silver-mining town, and the site of the famous 1881 shootout at the OK Corral. Now a National Historic Landmark that attracts crowds of tourists with its old Western buildings, stagecoach rides, and gunfight reenactments, it's hokey, sure, but it's also a fun place to grab a beer in an old saloon. The **Visitor & Information Center** (☎ 520-457-3929, 888-457-3929; www.tombstone.org; cnr 4th & Allen Sts; 9am-1pm Mon-Fri) will get you oriented.

Bisbee

Many buildings in charming **Bisbee** date from the heyday of the early-20th-century copper-mining boom. The town has more of a Victorian feel to it than any other in Arizona, as well as an intriguing mix of aging miners, gallery owners, hippies and artists.

Stop by the **chamber of commerce** (☎ 520-432-5421, 866-224-7233; www.bisbeearizona.com; 31 Subway St; 9am-5pm Mon-Fri, 10am-4pm Sat & Sun) for information on local attractions. A big one is the old **Queen Mine** (☎ 520-432-2071), with tours five times daily (adult/child $13/5).

Copper Queen Hotel (☎ 520-432-2216, 800-247-5829; www.copperqueen.com; 11 Howell St; r $107;) This hotel, dating from 1902, is one of Bisbee's top accommodations.

Shady Dell RV Park (☎ 520-432-3567; www.theshadydell.com; 1 Douglas Rd; trailers $38-83; P) At funky, one-of-a-kind Shady Dell, at the Lowell traffic circle, you can spend the night in your choice of several restored 1950s trailers, each decorated with vintage items. Sorry, no children under 10.

UTAH

With its vast expanses of undeveloped mountains, red-rock canyons, lonely deserts and wild rivers, rugged Utah is certainly one of the nation's most popular recreation spots. Four-wheel-drive vehicles, loaded down with mountain bikes, river rafts or skis, are a common sight almost anywhere you go in Utah, be it an urban center like Salt Lake City or small towns like Moab, Boulder and Bluff, which dot the red-rock canyon country in the state's southern half.

Utah has two defining cultures – the ancestral Indians who left petroglyphs and remnants of early dwellings in the rocks, cliffs and canyons, and the modern Mormons, whose social and political influence reverberates throughout Utah and surrounding states. Southern Utah contains an incredible wealth of national parks and desert wilderness, while the state's northern half is marked by forested mountains, many boasting world-class skiing worthy of the Olympic Winter Games, which were held here in 2002.

UTAH FACTS

Nicknames Beehive State, Mormon State
Population 2,316,256 (34th)
Population under 18 years old 32.2% (1st)
Area 82,144 sq miles (13th)
Admitted to Union January 4, 1896 (45th)
Capital city Salt Lake City (population 181,800; metro area 1.7 million)
State insect Honeybee
Birthplace of Donny (b 1957) and Marie (b 1959) Osmond; beloved bandit Butch Cassidy (1866–1908)
Famous for Mormons, red-rock canyons, Winter Olympic Games 2002

History

Utah gets its name from the nomadic Ute people who, along with the Paiute and Shoshone, lived in the Great Basin desert more than 8000 years ago. Europeans arrived as early as 1776, but Indians inhabited the region freely until the mid-19th century. Led by Brigham Young, the Mormons fled religious persecution to Utah, establishing Salt Lake City on July 24, 1847. They called their state Deseret, meaning 'honeybee,' according to the Book of Mormon.

After the US acquired the Utah Territory from Mexico, the Mormons petitioned Congress for statehood six times. Their petitions were consistently rejected because of Mormon polygamy (the practice of having more than one spouse at the same time), which was outlawed by the US government. Tensions grew between the Mormons and the federal government until 1890, when Mormon Church President Wilford Woodruff announced that God had told him that Mormons should abide by US law. Polygamy was discontinued, and soon afterward, Utah became the 45th state in 1896. Today, Mormons remain in the majority in Utah and continue to exert a powerful conservative influence on life in the state.

DRINKING IN UTAH

Can you get a drink in Utah? Absolutely. If you're hankering for a cocktail, simply head for one of the state's so-called 'private clubs,' and become a temporary 'member.' It costs $5 for two weeks and entitles you to bring up to 5 guests. You can also get 'sponsored' by another member; don't worry, it's common practice, and anyway, there's usually a watchful doorman or bartender who'll do the asking for you.

Private clubs are full bars selling all manner of alcoholic drinks, and they stop serving nightly at 1am. Restaurants can serve wine, beer or liquor with food. 'Taverns' sell low-alcohol (3.2%) beer only. This same 3.2% beer can be purchased at grocery and convenience stores, while hard alcohol and wine can only be purchased at state liquor stores.

For the most part, you won't even notice these laws. That's because Utah has a huge range of bars, taverns and brewpubs – and no shortage of folks to keep the doors swinging and the stools warm.

Religion

The members of the Church of Jesus Christ of Latter-Day Saints (LDS) – or Mormons – prize family above all else, and Mormon families tend to be large. Hard work and strict obedience to church leaders are very important. Smoking and drinking alcohol, tea or coffee are forbidden. Women are forbidden to take leadership roles, as were African-Americans until 1978. The faith considers missionary service important, and many young adults go on missions to spread the faith around the world. Women are called Sisters during their service, and the men are called Elders. There are now around 11 million Mormons worldwide. You can find some additional background on the church at www.lds.org or www.mormon.org.

Information

The **Utah Travel Council Information Center** (☎ 801-538-1030, 800-200-1160; www.utah.com; Council Hall, Capitol Hill, Salt Lake City, UT 84114) is run by the Utah Travel Council. For information on skiing, ask for the Utah Winter Vacation Planner or visit the **Ski Utah** (www.skiutah.com) website.

Utah State Parks & Recreation Office (☎ 801-538-7220, 800-322-3770; www.stateparks.utah.gov; 1594 W North Temple, suite 116, Salt Lake City, UT 84114) sells annual multiple-park permits ($70) and arranges camping reservations.

The helpful **Gay & Lesbian Community Center of Utah** (☎ 801-539-8800, 888-874-2743; www.glccu.com; 355 N 300 West, 1st Floor, Salt Lake City, UT 84103) offers advice, activities and classes.

Call Utah's **travel information service** (☎ 800-492-2400) for updates on road conditions and traffic. The sales tax rate is 6.6%. The state's two area codes are ☎ 801 (covering Salt Lake City, Provo and Ogdon) and ☎ 435 (the rest of the state). Utah is in the Mountain Time Zone.

Utah Pioneer Day (July 24) celebrates the day Brigham Young and company first entered the Salt Lake valley in 1847. Especially in smaller Mormon towns, businesses may be closed.

Orientation

Figuring out the street names in Utah takes a little getting used to. Major streets in many Utah towns are laid out in a grid and are numbered; these numbered streets then move in all *four* directions from a '00' center point. The result reads like some sort of algebra equation: E 400 North, or S 300 West (every '100' is equivalent to one city block). Add in a building address and you wind up with '211 W 300 South,' which doesn't exactly roll off the tongue. But the idea is to show how far you are at any point from the town center (which is often the temple). So '211 W 300 South' means it's two blocks west of the town center and three blocks south of it. Ask for a local address, though, and you may get an answer along the lines of '211 west, and 300 south.' And just to keep things interesting, some locals may also refer to their streets in more traditional terms – 'South Third,' for instance. It's a little confusing, yes, but once you get the hang of it, you'll always know, more or less, where you are.

SALT LAKE CITY

It's certainly true that Salt Lake City (often abbreviated as SLC) is the headquarters of the LDS (Mormon) Church. The church's presence is certainly felt – most notably in the state's archaic drinking laws – but Salt Lake is, at the same time, a vibrant, fun city with a bohemian underground and a thriving arts and cultural scene. Not to mention the fact it's quite a beautiful place, being set spectacularly at the foot of the towering Wasatch Mountains, with the Oquirrh (pronounced 'oaker') Mountains across the valley to the west.

While the Great Salt Lake and the impressive architecture and historic Mormon Sq are the city's most famous attractions, many travelers also come to have fun skiing, hiking, camping and boating – which is how many of the city's outdoorsy residents choose to spend their weekends. Salt Lake and surrounding towns hosted the Olympics, and you'll find remnants of this event (stadiums and winter sports parks) throughout the region, including on the University of Utah campus, just east of downtown.

Orientation

Salt Lake City is laid out in a grid, with major streets aligned north-south and east-west and assigned numbers (for an explanation see p840). The city's zero point is Temple Sq. Streets immediately around the temple are North Temple, South Temple, West Temple and Main St.

North Temple is a busy, utilitarian road running west from downtown to the airport. State St (which takes the place of 100 East) is a busy north–south route. The main artery east from downtown to the university is 400 South.

Ski resorts are located east of town in the Wasatch Mountains.

Information

BOOKSTORES

Sam Weller's Bookstore (☎ 801-328-2586, 800-333-7269; 254 S Main St) Huge independent downtown bookstore, with outdoor guides and maps.

EMERGENCY

Emergency number (☎ 911)
Police Department (☎ 801-799-3000; 315 E 200 South)

INTERNET ACCESS

Main library (☎ 801-524-8200; 210 E 400 South) Offers free Internet access.

MEDIA

City Weekly (☎ 801-573-7003; www.slweekly.com) Free alternative weekly with good restaurant and entertainment listings; publishes the free, useful *City Guide* three times annually.

MEDICAL SERVICES

Salt Lake Regional Medical Center (☎ 801-350-4111; 1050 E South Temple)
University Hospital (☎ 801-581-2121; 50 N Medical Dr)

MONEY

Wells Fargo (☎ 801-246-2677; 79 S Main St; 🕑 9am-4:30pm Mon-Fri) Offers foreign currency exchange.

POST

Downtown Station (☎ 801-978-3001; 230 W 200 South)

TOURIST OFFICES

Public Lands Information Center (☎ 801-466-6411; plic@xmission.com; 3285 E 3300 South; 🕑 10:30am-7pm Tue-Sat) Multi-agency information desk inside REI.

SALT LAKE CITY IN...

Two Days

Focus your first day on the sights, monuments and museums in and around **Mormon Sq** – take your time and let one of the tour guides explain things (it's free). Stroll up **Capitol Hill** for nice views, then grab a meal downtown.

The next day, head north to **Antelope Island State Park** for a swim in the lake and maybe a picnic. In the evening, check out the hip restaurants and clubs along 200 South and 300 South.

Four Days

Follow the two day itinerary, then consider a hike in one of the nearby canyons, or a trip to **Park City**. If the **Mormon Tabernacle Choir** is rehearsing, don't miss it. Those with more time can head north to **Golden Spike National Historic Site** to see the surreal Spiral Jetty.

SALT LAKE CITY

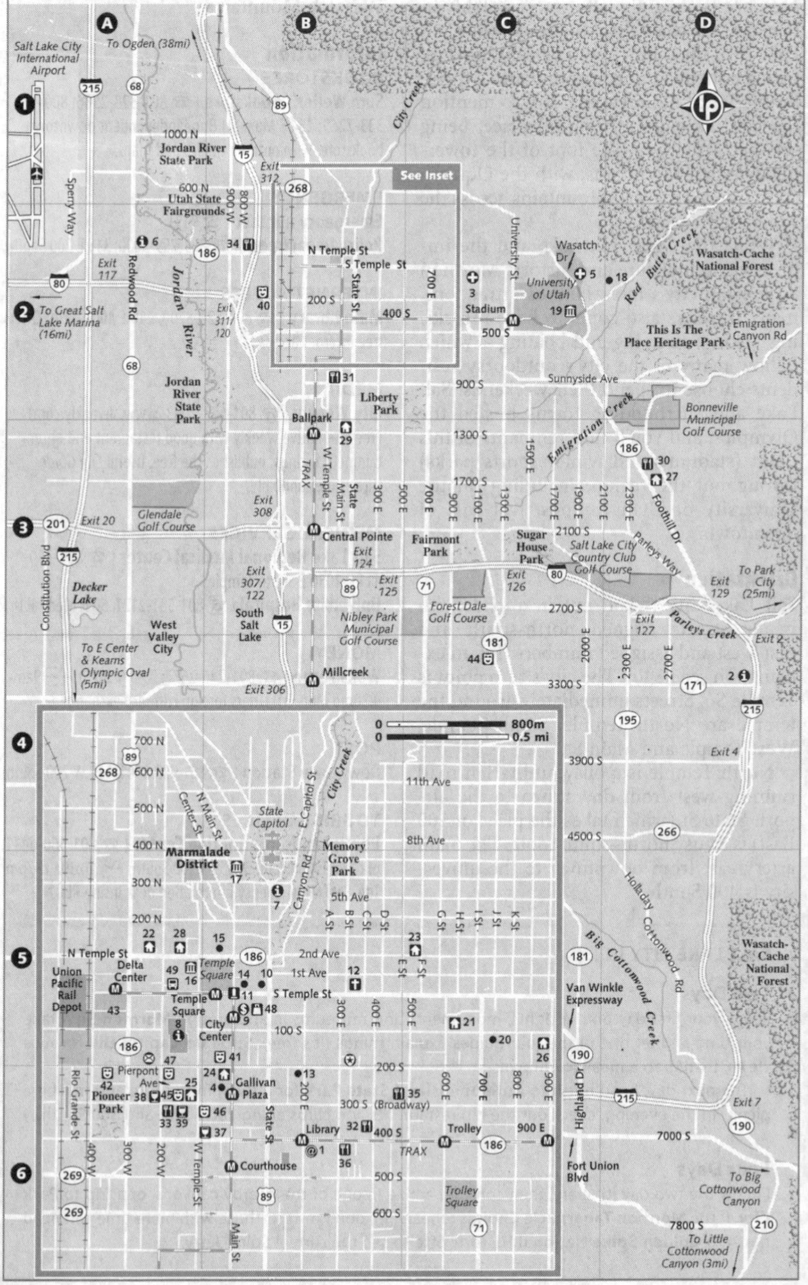

0 2 km
0 1 mi

A B C D
1 2 3 4 5 6

Salt Lake City International Airport
To Ogden (38mi)
1000 N
Jordan River State Park
600 N
Utah State Fairgrounds
Sperry Way
900 W
800 W
Exit 312
See Inset
N Temple St
S Temple St
200 S
State St
400 S
700 E
Stadium
500 S
University St
Wasatch Dr
University of Utah
Red Butte Creek
Wasatch-Cache National Forest
City Creek
To Great Salt Lake Marina (16mi)
Exit 117
Redwood Rd
Jordan River
Exit 311/120
This Is The Place Heritage Park
Emigration Canyon Rd
Sunnyside Ave
900 S
Liberty Park
Ballpark
1300 S
Emigration Creek
Bonneville Municipal Golf Course
Jordan River State Park
W Temple St
TRAX
Main St
State
300 E
500 E
700 E
900 E
1100 E
1300 E
1500 E
1700 S
1700 E
1900 E
2100 E
2300 E
Foothill Dr
Exit 308
Glendale Golf Course
Exit 20
Central Pointe
Fairmont Park
Sugar House Park
2100 S
Salt Lake City Country Club Golf Course
Parleys Way
Constitution Blvd
Decker Lake
Exit 124
Exit 307/122
Exit 125
Exit 126
Forest Dale Golf Course
Exit 129
To Park City (25mi)
South Salt Lake
West Valley City
Nibley Park Municipal Golf Course
2700 S
Exit 127
Parleys Creek
Exit 2
To E Center & Kearns Olympic Oval (5mi)
Millcreek
Exit 306
2000 E
2300 E
2700 E
3300 S
3900 S
Exit 4
4500 S
Holladay
Cottonwood Rd
Big Cottonwood Creek
Wasatch-Cache National Forest
Van Winkle Expressway
Highland Dr
Exit 7
7000 S
Fort Union Blvd
To Big Cottonwood Canyon
7800 S
To Little Cottonwood Canyon (3mi)

0 800m
0 0.5 mi

700 N
600 N
500 N
400 N
300 N
200 N
N Main St
Center St
State Capitol
E Capitol St
Canyon Rd
City Creek
11th Ave
8th Ave
Marmalade District
Memory Grove Park
5th Ave
A St
B St
C St
D St
G St
H St
I St
J St
K St
N Temple St
Delta Center
Temple Square
2nd Ave
1st Ave
E St
F St
Union Pacific Rail Depot
S Temple St
Temple Square
City Center
100 S
300 E
400 E
500 E
Pierpont Ave
Gallivan Plaza
200 S
200 E
Pioneer Park
300 S (Broadway)
600 E
700 E
800 E
900 E
Rio Grande St
400 W
300 W
200 W
W Temple St
State St
Library
400 S
Trolley
900 E
TRAX
Courthouse
500 S
Trolley Square
600 S
Main St

INFORMATION
Main Library 1 B6
Public Lands Information Center 2 D4
Salt Lake Regional Medical Center 3 C2
Salt Palace Convention Center (see 8)
Sam Weller's Bookstore 4 B6
University Hospital 5 C2
Utah State Parks & Recreation Office 6 A2
Utah Travel Council Information Center 7 B5
Visitor Information Center 8 A5
Wells Fargo 9 B5

SIGHTS & ACTIVITIES pp843–4
Beehive House 10 B5
Brigham Young Monument/Meridian Marker 11 B5
Cathedral of the Madeleine 12 B5
Guthrie Bicycle 13 B6
Joseph Smith Memorial Building 14 B5
LDS Conference Center 15 B5
Museum of Church History & Art 16 A5
Pioneer Memorial Museum 17 B5
Red Butte Gardens and Arboretum 18 D2
Utah Museum of Fine Arts 19 C2
Wasatch Touring 20 C5

SLEEPING pp844–5
Anton Boxrud 21 C5
City Creek Inn 22 A5
HI The Avenues 23 C5
Hotel Monaco 24 B6
Peery Hotel 25 A6
Saltair 26 C5
Skyline Inn 27 D3
Travelodge Temple Square 28 A5
Ute Hostel 29 B3

EATING p845
Bombay House 30 D3
Cafe Trang 31 B2
Ichiban Sushi 32 B6
Metropolitan 33 A6
Red Iguana 34 B2
Sage's Cafe 35 B6
Salt Lake Roasting Company 36 B6

DRINKING p845
Port O' Call 37 B6
Red Rock Brewing Company 38 A6
Squatter's Pub Brewery 39 A6

ENTERTAINMENT p845
Bricks 40 B2
Capitol Theater 41 B5
Cup of Joe 42 A6
Delta Center 43 A5
Liquid Joe's 44 C4
Rose Wagner Performing Arts Center 45 A6
Zephyr 46 B6
Zipperz 47 A6

SHOPPING
ZCMI Shopping Center 48 B5

TRANSPORT pp845–6
Greyhound Bus Depot 49 A5

tah Travel Council Information Center (☎ 801-38-1030, 800-200-1160; www.utah.com; 300 N State t; 8am-5pm Mon-Fri) Statewide information center, Council Hall on Capitol Hill, with a large selection of uidebooks and maps.

isitor Information Center (☎ 801-521-2822, 00-541-4955; www.visitsaltlake.com; 90 S West Temple t; 8:30am-5pm Mon-Fri, 9am-5pm Sat & Sun) In the nodern Salt Palace Convention Center.

ights

OWNTOWN

Enclosed by 15ft-high walls at the center f town, **Temple Sq** (☎ 801-240-2534; www.lds.org; 9am-9pm) features 19th-century Mormon uildings, history exhibits and the towerng **Salt Lake Temple**. Information booths re inside the north and south gates. LDS locents give free 30-minute tours every 0 minutes; meet at the flagpoles in front of he **Tabernacle**. The famous **Mormon Tabernacle hoir** performs there Sunday mornings (get here by 9am) and rehearses on Thursday venings at 8pm.

Adjoining Temple Sq, the **Museum of Church listory and Art** (☎ 801-240-3310; 45 N West Temple St; dmission free; 9am-9pm Mon-Fri, 10am-7pm Sat & Sun) as impressive exhibits of pioneer history. You can research your family's genealogy at he **Joseph Smith Memorial Building** (☎ 801-240-266; 15 E South Temple St; admission free; 9am-9pm Mon-Sat), an elegant hotel from 1911 to 1987; lso here are daily screenings of Testament, n hour-long film about Mormon beliefs. Brigham Young's home, the **Beehive House** ☎ 801-240-2671; 67 E South Temple St; admission free; 9:30am-4:30pm Mon-Sat, 10am-1pm Sun & holidays), circa 1854, has been meticulously maintained. The **LDS Conference Center** (☎ 801-240-0075; 60 W North Temple St; 9am-9pm) has great views from its rooftop gardens.

You'll find many Daughters of Utah Pioneers (DUP) museums throughout the state, but the **Pioneer Memorial Museum** (☎ 801-538-1050, 300 N Main St; admission free; 9am-5pm Mon-Sat) is by far the best. It's a vast treasure trove of pioneer artifacts. The walls of the impressive **Utah State Capitol** (☎ 801-538-1563; 8am-8pm), just north of Temple Sq, are covered with historical murals.

AROUND DOWNTOWN

Site of the Olympic Village in 2002, the **University of Utah** (☎ 801-581-7200) has several museums, including the **Utah Museum of Fine Arts** (☎ 801-581-7332; 410 Campus Center Dr; admission free; 10am-5pm Mon-Fri, noon-5pm Sat & Sun).

In the Wasatch foothills, the lovely **Red Butte Gardens and Arboretum** (☎ 801-581-4747; 300 Wakara Way; adult/child $5/3; 9am-8pm summer, 10am-5pm winter) spreads over a very relaxing 25 acres with terrific city views.

On the grounds of **This Is The Place Heritage Park** (☎ 801-582-2483; admission free; dawn-dusk), at the mouth of Emigration Canyon east of downtown, a monument marks the place where Brigham Young first entered the valley in 1847. The park's also home to **Old Deseret Village**, a village of historic Mormon pioneer buildings. From Memorial Day to Labor Day, actors in period dress work among buildings and tickets cost adult /child $7/5; during the rest of the year, self-guided tours ($2) are available.

Activities

Millcreek, Big Cottonwood and Little Cottonwood canyons, all on the east side of the Wasatch Mountains and within easy reach of Salt Lake City, offer abundant opportunities for hiking, mountain biking, camping and cross-country skiing. Inside **REI** (☎ 801-486-2100; 3285 E 3300 South) is the helpful Public Lands Information Center desk (p841), a great place to gather advice (and brochures) on exploring the area. Mountain bike rentals are about $30 a day at **Wasatch Touring** (☎ 801-359-9361; 702 E 100 South) or **Guthrie Bicycle** (☎ 801-363-3727; 156 E 200 South).

Sleeping

Salt Lake City is dominated by chain hotels and motels, especially those in the mid-range category. Many are clustered on W North Temple St near the airport; others are along S 200 West near 500 South and 600 South. Both summer and winter are the high seasons here; during late spring and fall prices may be lower than the figures below.

BUDGET

The cheapest independent motels are along W North Temple St between the airport and downtown, though some are a little grungy. Other choices are scattered throughout the city.

Skyline Inn (☎ 801-582-5350; www.skylineinn.com; 2475 E 1700 South; s/d $54/64; P) Located south of the university on a hill overlooking downtown, this modest, well-maintained hotel is a great choice for those who prefer sleeping somewhat removed from the city center. It also works well for skiers who don't want the expense of a slopeside hotel, as it affords easy access to Big and Little Cottonwood Canyons. There's a year-round pool and hot tub, and some rooms have spas.

City Creek Inn (☎ 801-533-9100, 866-533-4898; www.citycreekinn.com; 230 W North Temple St; s/d $48/58; P) This is one of Salt Lake's best budget choices, located right downtown. Family-owned for three generations, it's a simple but attractive property within walking distance of Temple Sq.

HI The Avenues (☎ 801-359-3855, 888-884-4752; www.hostel.com/slchostel; 107 F St; dm/d $17/36; P) The no-frills place is a big brick building in a pleasant, tree-lined residential neighborhood full of nice older homes.

THE AUTHOR'S CHOICE

Hotel Monaco (☎ 801-595-0000, 877-294-9710; www.monaco-saltlakecity.com; 15 W 200 South; r from $129; P) If you're going to splurge on a hotel, Hotel Monaco is a great place to do it. This is an arty boutique hotel full of contemporary character, located in a sturdy, remodeled historic building smack in the center of downtown. Rooms sport a funky, tastefully coordinated design aesthetic and are supremely comfortable; service is superb and never snooty. Be sure to ask for your companion goldfish, a little friend brought to your room free of charge.

Ute Hostel (☎ 801-595-1645; www.infobytes.com/ute hostel; 21 E Kelsey Ave; dm/d $15/35; P) South of downtown, Ute Hostel is smaller and homier than HI The Avenues and is clustered among some attractive Craftsman houses.

USFS campgrounds (☎ 801-524-3900; campsites $14) There are four basic, seasonal USFS campgrounds in Big Cottonwood and Little Cottonwood canyons, in the Wasatch Mountains.

MID-RANGE

Peery Hotel (☎ 801-521-4300, 800-331-0073; www.peery hotel.com; 110 W 300 South; r $119; P) Built during the early 1900s, when a mining boom was in full swing, this stately, historic hotel is one of the city's most elegant and charming. Rooms boast period furnishings and old-world character, yet at the same time they've been remodeled to meet contemporary tastes – it's a pretty luxurious place, and the lobby alone is worth a peek.

Anton Boxrud (☎ 801-363-8035, 800-524-5511; www.antonboxrud.com; 57 S 600 East; r $98-140; P) Close to both downtown and the university, this B&B is on a quiet, tree-lined residential street full of interesting older homes. It's named after a Scandinavian man, who built it as his home in 1901, and it's been meticulously restored to its original condition.

Saltair (☎ 801-533-8184, 800-733-8184; www.salt lakebandb.com; 164 S 900 East; r from $99; P) Housed in an old Victorian on a pretty (although busy) residential street, this bed and breakfast offers a large range of rooms and cottages. B&B rooms feature a full breakfast, while cottages are equipped with kitchens.

Travelodge Temple Square (☎ 801-533-8200; fax 801-596-0332; 144 W North Temple; r $63; P) Though not the most exciting accommodations, this standard chain hotel is located right downtown, making it supremely convenient to Temple Sq and other attractions.

Eating

The food scene here is vast and varied, with a huge, impressive assortment of ethnic restaurants. Pick up a *City Weekly* for local listings and reviews.

Red Iguana (☎ 801-322-1489; 736 W North Temple; dishes $7-12) Savvy locals head here for great, unpretentious Mexican food that many consider the tastiest in town. Try a smothered burrito, or one of their rich mole dishes, then forget about eating for the rest of the day.

Metropolitan (☎ 801-364-3472; 173 W Broadway; bistro meals $10-16, dishes $16-28; Mon-Sat) Contemporary, cosmopolitan and definitely among SLC's best restaurants, this attractive, industrial-styled space has a bistro up front along with a more upscale dining room. It's urban-elegant but not terribly formal – and the bistro menu is quite affordable, offering items such as a flank steak sandwich and Thai noodles. There's a nice bar, too.

Sage's Cafe (☎ 801-322-3790; 473 E 300 South; $6-10; Wed-Sun) Everything is made in-house, mostly organic and entirely vegan at this comfortable restaurant, where dinner items include fajitas, pesto and wild mushroom stroganoff. There is a small kids menu, too, and brunch is available on weekends. Beer and wine are served, as is house-made root beer and ginger ale.

Salt Lake Roasting Company (☎ 801-363-7572; 320 E 400 South; dishes under $5; Mon-Sat) Roasting its own beans since 1981, the coffee at Salt Lake Roasting Company is among the best in town – strong and flavorful. They serve salads, sandwiches and good pastries, and the open, two-story space allows plenty of room to think.

Bombay House (☎ 801-581-0222; 1615 S Foothill Dr; dishes $8-16) In a mini-mall east of downtown, Bombay House has a full range of vibrant Indian dishes.

Cafe Trang (☎ 801-539-1638; 818 S Main St; dishes $6-12) Cafe Trang is a well-regarded Vietnamese place.

Ichiban Sushi (☎ 801-532-7522; 336 S 400 East; dishes $8-16) Try the inventive sushi in this nontraditional space – a renovated Lutheran church.

Drinking

Squatter's Pub Brewery (☎ 801-363-2739; 147 W Broadway) Squatter's has some great microbrews to choose from; try the smooth Vienna Lager or their lighter St Provo Girl.

Red Rock Brewing Company (☎ 801-521-7446; 254 S 200 West) Around the corner from Squatter's, this is another popular, reliable brewpub.

Port O' Call (☎ 801-521-0589; 78 W 400 South) If it's liquor you're after, Port O' Call is a large, full-service bar that spreads across four floors in a cool 1912 building. It's quiet during the day, but at night crowds can pack in for DJs and bands.

Entertainment

The **Salt Lake City Arts Council** (☎ 801-596-5000) has information about various local cultural events, including theater, dance, opera and symphony. The **Capitol Theater** (50 W 200 South) and the **Rose Wagner Performing Arts Center** (138 W 300 South) are two main venues; call **ArtTix** (☎ 801-355-2787, 888-451-2787; www.arttix.org) for tickets at either venue.

Salt Lake has an active gay and lesbian scene, and a good place to get acquainted with it is at friendly gay club **Zipperz** (☎ 801-521-8300; 155 W 200 South).

Cup of Joe (☎ 801-363-8322; 353 W 200 South) Acoustic music and Saturday poetry slams take place at this cool, artsy coffeehouse in an old brick warehouse (with Internet access, too).

Good live-music venues include the following:

Bricks (☎ 801-328-0255; 579 W 200 South)
Liquid Joe's (☎ 801-467-5637; 1249 E 3300 South)
Zephyr (☎ 801-355-2582; 301 S West Temple)

SPECTATOR SPORTS

The men's professional basketball team, the Utah Jazz, and the women's professional basketball team, the Utah Starzz, play at the **Delta Center** (☎ 801-355-3865). The International Hockey League's **Utah Grizzlies** (☎ 801-988-7825) play at the **E Center** (☎ 801-988-8888; 3200 South Decker Lake Dr, West Valley City), which hosted most of the men's ice hockey competitions during the Olympics.

Getting There & Around

AIR

Salt Lake City International Airport (☎ 801-575-2400) is about 6 miles west of downtown.

Numerous door-to-door **shuttle vans** are available at the airport; a trip downtown costs $10 to $15. Call the airport's **transportation desk** (☎ 801-575-2477) for details.

BUS

Greyhound (☎ 801-355-9579; 160 W South Temple St) has several buses a day heading south through Provo and St George to Las Vegas, Nevada ($49, 8½ hours); west to San Francisco ($75, 16 hours); east to Denver ($56, 13 hours); and north to Seattle ($85, 23 hours).

PUBLIC TRANSPORTATION

UTA (☎ 801-743-3882, 888-743-3882; single/day tickets $1.25/2.50) buses serve Salt Lake City and the Wasatch Front area until about midnight (limited service on Sundays). TRAX, UTA's light-rail system, runs east from the Delta Center to the university ($1.25); a second suburban line runs south to Sandy. The center of downtown Salt Lake is a free-fare zone.

UTA buses also go to Provo, Tooele, Ogden and other Wasatch Front towns and suburbs ($1.25); and during ski season they serve the four local ski areas ($2.50).

Yellow Cab (☎ 801-521-2100) offers 24-hour taxi service.

National car rental agencies have offices at the airport and around town. See p1121 for details.

TRAIN

Amtrak's *California Zephyr* stops daily at the **Rio Grande Depot** (☎ 801-322-3510, 800-872-7245; 340 S 600 West) going east to Chicago ($199, 36 hours) and west to Oakland, California ($135, 17 hours).

AROUND SALT LAKE CITY

Once part of prehistoric Lake Bonneville, the **Great Salt Lake** today covers 2000 sq miles and is far saltier than the ocean; you can easily float on its surface.

The pretty, 15-mile-long **Antelope Island State Park** (☎ 801-773-2941; I-15 exit 335; admission $8; 🕑 7am-10pm), 40 miles northwest of Salt Lake City, has the best beaches for lake swimming, as well as nice hiking. It's also famous as the home to one of the largest bison herds in the country, and the fall corralling of these animals is one of the area's most famous wildlife spectacles. A basic **campground** (☎ 800-322-3770; campsites $10) is open year round.

Century-old **Bingham Canyon Copper Mine** (☎ 801-252-3234; I-15 exit 301; admission $4; 🕑 8am-8pm Apr-Oct) is reportedly the world's largest factitious excavation and, still operational, it's only getting bigger. The 2.5-mile-wide and 0.75-mile-deep gash, in the Oquirrh Mountains west of Salt Lake City, can be seen from space and also from a stunning overlook.

Within 40 minutes of Salt Lake City are four world-class ski resorts in Little Cottonwood and Big Cottonwood Canyons, famous for getting some 500in of powdery snow each year. **Snowbird Ski Area** (☎ 801-742-2222, 800-232-9542; www.snowbird.com; ski pass $56) has excellent snowboarding, while laid-back **Alta Ski Area** (☎ 801-742-3333; www.alta.com; ski pass $40) is the skier's choice. Two further choices are **Brighton Ski Area** (☎ 801-532-4731; www.skibrighton.com; ski pass $40) and **Solitude Ski Area** (☎ 801-534-1400; www.skisolitude.com; ski pass $44). There are plenty of accommodations at the resorts, but they can be expensive.

WASATCH MOUNTAINS REGION

Salt Lake City, Ogden and Provo sit along the Wasatch Front. The mountains are home to 11 ski resorts within 55 miles of Salt Lake City, and offer abundant hiking, camping, fly-fishing and mountain biking.

Ogden

After the completion of the first transcontinental railway in 1869, Ogden became an important railway town. Today its restored, mid-19th-century downtown is a major draw. During its heyday, historic 25th St between Union Station and Grant Ave was lined with brothels and raucous saloons; now it has the city's nicest selection of restaurants and bars. Ogden lies about 38 miles north of Salt Lake City.

The restored **Union Station** contains the **visitors center** (☎ 801-627-8288, 800-255-8824; www.ogdencvb.org; 25th St & Wall Ave; 🕑 8am-5pm Mon-Fri); it's also home to several worthy **museums** (☎ 801-629-8535; adult/child $4/3; 🕑 10am-5pm Mon-Sat) covering vintage trains, firearms, cars and more. Also in Union Station is the **National Forest Information Center** (☎ 385-625-5306; 🕑 8am-5pm Mon-Fri), with maps and information on area hiking, biking and kayaking on the Ogden and Weber Rivers.

The steep-walled **Ogden Canyon** heads 40 miles northeast through the Wasatch

Mountains to Monte Cristo Summit (9148ft), passing the following ski areas: **Nordic Valley Ski Area** (☎ 801-392-0900; ski pass $20), a tiny 85-acre resort with the cheapest skiing in the state; **Snowbasin Ski Area** (☎ 801-620-1000, 888-437-5488; www.snowbasin.com; ski pass $52), a 3200-acre resort that hosted downhill and super-G skiing events in the Olympics; and the appropriately named **Powder Mountain Ski Area** (☎ 801-745-3722; www.powdermountain.net; ski pass $39).

Millstream Motel (☎ 801-394-9425; fax 801-392-9145; 1450 Washington Blvd; r $40; P) retains the flavor of its 1940s heyday.

Park City

About 30 miles east from Salt Lake City via I-80, Park City (elevation 6900ft) is the Southwest's largest ski town and a hub of outdoor activity in the summer. A silver-mining community during the 19th century, its attractive Main St is remarkably well-preserved and lined with galleries, shops, hotels, restaurants and bars. And despite the sea of pre-fab housing that has spread across the valley and surrounding hills, the town remains relatively charming.

Park City is also famous for hosting the **Sundance Film Festival** (☎ 801-328-3456; www.sundance.org) every January, which brings independent films and their makers, stars and fans to Park City for two weeks. Tickets often sell out in advance.

Get local information from the main **Visitor Information Center** (☎ 435-658-4541; www.parkcityinfo.com; 750 Kearns Blvd; 9am-6pm); information is also available at the **Park City Historic Museum** (☎ 435-649-6104; 528 Main St; 9am-7pm Mon-Sat, noon-6pm Sun), which has mining and history exhibits.

ACTIVITIES

Park City is home to three of Utah's preeminent ski resorts. A chairlift right in town can take you to **Park City Mountain Resort** (☎ 435-649-8111; www.parkcitymountain.com; adult lift ticket $45), which hosted the Olympic giant slalom and snowboarding events. Posh **Deer Valley Resort** (☎ 435-649-1000; www.deervalley.com; adult lift ticket $67) is for skiers only, and the **Canyons** (☎ 435-649-5400; www.thecanyons.com; adult lift ticket $62) is Utah's largest resort. All host **summer activities** as well, including mountain biking and hiking via chairlift, gondola rides at the Canyons (adult/child $12/6) and, at Park City Resort, the ZipRider ($15).

At the **Utah Olympic Park** (☎ 435-658-4200; www.utaholympicpark.com; adult/child $7/5), on Hwy 224 outside Park City, the Olympians are gone, but you can tour the facilities where it all happened and, if you're lucky, watch the pros practice (call for rates, schedules and reservations). Daring souls can test their nerve by **bobsledding** (☎ 435-658-4206; summer/winter $65/200), or take classes in **ski jumping** and **luge riding.**

SLEEPING

There are more than 100 condo complexes, upscale hotels and B&Bs in Park City, and while winter rates quoted here are very high, prices drop in summer. Some places may also have minimum stay requirements of two or more days.

Chateau Après Lodge (☎ 435-649-9372, 800-357-3556; www.chateauapres.com; 1299 Norfolk Ave; dm/d $30/85; P) Well located near ski lifts, this lodge has been in business since 1963 and is popular with budget travelers as rates are among the area's most reasonable. Rooms are basic and sleep from one to four people.

Park Ave runs parallel to Main St and has a rugged Western feel; there are several interesting lodging choices in restored buildings here.

Washington School Inn (☎ 435-649-3800, 800-824-1672; www.washingtonschoolinn.com; 543 Park Ave; summer/winter r from $95/245; P) Sumptuous rooms are in a restored schoolhouse that survived a major Park City fire in 1898.

Edelweiss Haus (☎ 435-649-5100, 800-245-6417; www.pclodge.com; 1482 Empire Ave; summer/winter r from $59/70; P) This modern condominium complex offers standard hotel rooms as well as one- and two-bedroom apartments.

EATING

Park City has more than enough dining options to suit any palette.

Morning Ray Café & Bakery (☎ 435-649-5686; 268 Main St; dishes $3-8) Open early and closing late, this place is hugely popular for its New York–style bagels, breakfast plates and sandwiches.

Alpine Internet Coffeehouse (☎ 435-649-0051; 728 Main St; dishes under $5) This place not only has good coffee and pastries but easy Internet access ($10 per hour).

Wasatch Brew Pub (☎ 435-649-0900; 250 Main St; dishes $8-16) A fine microbrewery with excellent pub grub and a couple dozen drafts.

Eating Establishment (☎ 435-649-8284; 317 Main St; dishes $5-9) This establishment is famous for its filling breakfasts, served into late afternoon.

Chimayo (☎ 435-649-6222; 368 Main St; dishes $20-30) The more upscale Chimayo brilliantly captures the Southwest (reduced hours in summer).

Grappa (☎ 435-645-0636; 151 Main St; dishes $20-30) Grappa focuses on regional Italian dishes.

ENTERTAINMENT

A half dozen crowded private clubs, most with live music, line Main St.

Harry O's (☎ 435-647-9494; 427 Main St) Harry O's has interesting bands and dancing most nights.

Egyptian Theatre Company (☎ 435-649-9371, 888-243-5779; 328 Main St) This nicely restored place has plays in summer.

GETTING THERE & AROUND

Neither Greyhound nor Amtrak serve Park City. **Lewis Bros Stages** (in Park City ☎ 435-649-2256, in Salt Lake City ☎ 801-359-8677) offers daily year-round shuttles to and from Salt Lake City ($27); reserve a day ahead.

Park City Transit runs frequent, free buses around town and to the ski resorts (7:30am to 10:30pm daily), making it easy not to rent a car.

Heber City & Around

About 18 miles south of Park City and 45 miles east of Salt Lake City, this town is fairly utilitarian, but it does make an affordable base for exploring the Wasatch Mountains. Most businesses are along Hwy 40 (Main St).

A popular attraction is the **Heber Valley Historic Railroad** (☎ 435-654-5601; 450 S 600 West; adult/child from $24/14), which has Provo Canyon sight-seeing trips and other excursions from May to October; call for schedule.

Approximately 15 miles southwest of Heber City, scenic Hwy 189 squeezes through the steep-walled **Provo Canyon** on its way to Provo, home to clean-cut Brigham Young University but not really worth a stop. For information on camping and hiking in the Uinta National Forest, contact the Heber City **Ranger Station** (☎ 435-654-0470; 2460 S Hwy 40; 🕑 8am-5pm Mon-Fri).

Another attractive drive is **Alpine Loop Rd**. From Hwy 189, head north onto narrow and twisting Hwy 92. This leads to Robert Redford's **Sundance Resort** (☎ 385-225-4107, 800-892-1600; www.sundanceresort.com), an elegant, rustic, environmentally conscious getaway in a wilderness setting with excellent skiing, a year-round arts program, a spa, and summer hiking and mountain biking. The three beautiful caves in **Timpanogos Cave National Monument** (☎ 385-756-5238; admission $3; 🕑 7am-5:30pm May-Oct) can be seen only as part of a ranger-led tour (adult/child $6/5).

You can camp in the surrounding national forest and nearby state parks. Heber City motels are all basic but far cheaper than accommodations in Park City.

Swiss Alps Inn (☎ 435-654-0722; www.swissalpsinn.com; 167 S Main St; r $63; ⊠ ⊡) This inn is quainter and nicer than most of the motels.

In addition to a few greasy spoons, Heber has one local standout, the **Snake Creek Grill** (☎ 435-654-2133; 650 W 100 South; dishes $19-19; 🕑 Wed-Sun), which prepares excellent gourmet dinners in a comfortable environment.

NORTHERN UTAH

North of Ogden, the mountains get smaller but no less beautiful. In sharp contrast, north and northwest of the Great Salt Lake, the land is very arid, saline and extremely barren. Aside from Golden Spike National Historic Site, few people visit Utah's desolate northwest corner.

Golden Spike National Historic Site

On May 10, 1869, the westward Union Pacific Railroad and eastward Central Pacific Railroad met at Promontory Summit. With the completion of the transcontinental railroad, the face of the American West changed forever. This **National Historic Site** (☎ 435-471-2209; admission $7; 🕑 9am-5:30pm daily, closed Mon-Tue in winter), 32 miles west of Brigham City on Hwy 83, has auto tours, walks and demonstrations using replicas of the original steam engines.

At the end of a dirt road 15 miles west of the Golden Spike visitors center is one of the country's most unique outdoor art projects, the **Spiral Jetty** (www.spiraljetty.org). Created by Robert Smithson in 1970, it's a 1500ft coil of rock and earth spinning out into the water. Often submerged, it became visible recently due to low water level; contact Golden Spike or the **BLM** (☎ 801-977-4300) for directions and a map.

Logan & Around

Logan is a quintessential old-fashioned American community with strong Mormon ties. Situated in bucolic Cache Valley, it offers year-round outdoor activities, particularly hiking, camping, snowmobiling and cross-country skiing. It was founded in 1859 and is home to Utah State University. You can get oriented at the **Cache Valley Tourist Council** (☎ 435-752-2161, 800-882-4433; www.tourcachevalley.com; 160 N Main St; 9am-5pm Mon-Fri).

The **Wellsville Mountain range** is reputedly one of the highest in the world rising from such a narrow base. Get information and maps from the **Logan Ranger Station** (☎ 435-755-3620; 1500 E Hwy 89; 8am-4:30pm Mon-Fri).

The 40-mile drive through **Logan Canyon** (Hwy 89 to Garden City) is beautiful any time of year, but in fall it is jaw-dropping. Enjoy hiking and biking trails, rock climbing, fishing spots and seasonal campgrounds.

Perhaps the best of its kind, the **American West Heritage Center** (☎ 435-245-6050; adult/child/family $6/4/20; 10am-5pm Mon-Sat Memorial Day–Labor Day), on Hwy 89 south of town, offers authentic re-creations of frontier communities with plenty of hands-on activities. It also hosts the popular weeklong **Festival of the American West** in July, a must for frontier buffs.

For accommodation, mid-range chains are your best choice.

Beaver Creek Lodge (☎ 435-946-3400, 800-946-4485; www.beavercreeklodge.com; summer/winter r $89/129;) This lodge in Logan Canyon has 11 rooms and offers good horseback riding and snowmobiling packages.

Bluebird Restaurant (☎ 435-752-3155; 19 N Main St; dishes $4-8) For a meal, try the 1920s-style Bluebird.

Caffé Ibis (☎ 435-753-4777; 52 Federal Ave; dishes under $6) Popular with the university crowd, this place serves gourmet coffees and healthy sandwiches.

NORTHEASTERN UTAH

Despite being hyped as 'Utah's Dinosaurland,' the main attraction is actually the high wilderness terrain. All towns are a mile above sea level and the rugged Uinta Mountains make for gorgeous outdoor trips.

Mirror Lake Highway

This alpine route (Hwy 150) begins in **Kamas**, about 12 miles east of Park City, and covers 65 miles as it climbs to elevations of more than 10,000ft into Wyoming. The road provides some beautiful vistas of the western Uintas and passes by scores of lakes, campgrounds and trailheads. Contact the **Kamas Ranger Station** (☎ 435-783-4338; 50 E Center; 8am-4:30pm Mon-Fri) for information on the Wasatch-Cache National Forest.

Uinta Mountains

The only way to access the 800-sq-mile High Uintas Wilderness Area is by foot or horse – tough going, but the rewards are great. The high country has hundreds of lakes, most of which are stocked annually with trout and whitefish. Come for the excellent fishing and the rare experience of wild, remote wilderness. The Ashley National Forest's **Roosevelt Ranger Station** (☎ 435-722-5018; 244 W Hwy 40, Roosevelt; 8am-5pm Mon-Fri) has information.

Basic **campgrounds** (campsites $8-10) are in the national forest surrounding the wilderness area, and there are several interesting lodging options, too. On Hwy 35 in Hanna, **Defa's Dude Ranch** (☎ 435-848-5590; www.defasduderanch.com; cabins $30-40; May-Oct; P) has rustic cabins in a beautiful, remote setting; bring your own bedding. There's also a café, saloon and horseback riding ($20 per hour).

Flaming Gorge National Recreation Area

Named for its fiery red sandstone, Flaming Gorge offers 375 miles of shoreline around Flaming Gorge Reservoir. Along with fantastic scenery, there's fly-fishing and rafting upon the Green River, fishing for massive trout in the reservoir, hiking and cross-country skiing. Information is available from the USFS **Flaming Gorge Headquarters** (☎ 435-784-3445; PO Box 278, Manila, UT 84046), the **Flaming Gorge Visitors Center** (☎ 435-885-3135; US 191; 9am-5pm) at Flaming Gorge Dam; or the **Red Canyon Visitors Center** (☎ 435-889-3713; 10am-5pm May-Oct), 4 miles west of Greendale Junction. The day-use fee is $2.

Sheep Creek Canyon, a dramatic 13-mile paved loop through the Sheep Creek Canyon Geological Area, leaves Hwy 44 about 15 miles west of Greendale Junction.

The **campgrounds** (☎ 877-444-6777; campsites $13-18) in and around Flaming Gorge are mostly open from May to October. **Red Canyon Lodge** (☎ 435-889-3759; www.redcanyonlodge.com; 790 Red Canyon Rd; cabins from $95) provides rustic and luxury cabins, while **Flaming Gorge Lodge** (☎ 435-889-3773; www.fglodge.com; r/condo $73/117;

SOUTHWEST

) offers motel rooms and modern condominiums – both are open year-round.

Vernal

This town is the region's largest and has plenty of motels and area information. The local **visitors center** (435-789-7894; www.dinoland.com; 235 E Main St; 9am-5pm) includes a good **natural history museum** (with a garden full of life-size dinosaurs) and has brochures on **driving tours**; the Red Cloud Loop & Petroglyphs tour is a highlight. The **Vernal Ranger Station** (435-789-1181; 355 N Vernal Ave; 8am-5pm Mon-Fri) has information on area camping and hiking.

Red Fleet State Park (435-789-4432; admission $5), 12 miles northeast of Vernal on Hwy 191, has boating, camping ($11) and an easy hike to a series of fossilized dinosaur tracks.

The Green and Yampa Rivers are the main waterways in the area and both have rapids to satisfy the white-water enthusiast, as well as calmer areas for gentler float trips. Trips run from $65 to $800 for one to five days; the visitors center has a list of outfitters.

Sage Motel (435-789-1442, 800-760-1442; www.vernalmotels.com; 54 W Main St; s/d $49/55; P) is a simple, but friendly and welcoming place to stay.

Greyhound (435-789-0404; 72 S 100 West) runs buses to Salt Lake City ($37, five hours).

Dinosaur National Monument

One of the largest dinosaur fossil beds in North America was discovered here in 1909. The quarry was enclosed and hundreds of bones were exposed but left in the rock. Visitors can now come to marvel at the find. Apart from visiting the quarry, you can drive, hike, backpack and raft through the starkly eroded, dramatic canyons of the national monument.

The **monument** straddles the Utah–Colorado state line. The headquarters are in tiny Dinosaur, Colorado, while the **dinosaur quarry** (435-789-2115; admission $10; 8am-6pm summer, 8am-4:30pm Mon-Fri winter) is in Utah, about 15 miles east of Vernal via Hwys 40 and 149. There are several basic, summer-only **campgrounds** (campsites free-$12).

WESTERN UTAH

Grim names on local maps describe western Utah: Snake Valley, Skull Valley, Blood Mountain, Disappointment Hills, Confusion Range. This is harsh desert country, much of it BLM land or used for military testing (as well as destroying banned chemical weapons). Thousands of acres in the **Bonneville Salt Flats** (the remnants of ancient Lake Bonneville, which once covered northern Utah) provide a super-smooth surface for car racing and setting speed records. After marveling at the endless salt, you can gamble in the casinos at nearby **Wendover**, along I-80 on the Utah–Nevada state line.

An excellent way to experience Utah's remote Great Basin is to drive the original **Pony Express Trail**, a good dirt road (passable only in dry weather) running more than 130 miles from Fairfield (on Hwy 73) to the village of Ibapah near Nevada (allow five to seven hours). The **Salt Lake City BLM** (801-977-4300) has information; primitive camping is allowed. Along the trail, Fish Springs is a literal oasis in the desert and an important migratory bird refuge.

CENTRAL UTAH

Most folks speed through central Utah on one of the north–south highways (I-15, Hwy 89 and Hwy 6), but the mountains and valleys contain some pretty driving detours, hiking, camping and interesting Mormon towns.

Along Hwy 89

The towns along Hwy 89, with their late-19th-century Main St architecture, magnificent temples and traditional, clean-living inhabitants, have a definite early-Mormon feel. The route is a much more pleasant, slightly slower alternative to the parallel I-15.

The entirety of sleepy **Spring City** is on the National Historic Register; it's a model of Mormon town planning. **Manti**, one of Utah's earliest towns (1849), is famous for its summer **Mormon Miracle Pageant** (435-835-3000).

Richfield is the largest town for 100 road miles and it has the best selection of restaurants and motels, including the pleasant **Romanico Inn** (435-896-8471, 800-948-0001; 1170 S Main St; r from $38;).

In the conservative Mormon farming community of **Monroe** is the very unconservative **Mystic Hot Springs** (435-527-3286; www.mystichotsprings.com; 475 E 100 North; campsites per person $10, cabins per person $25;), a serene, laid-back hippie oasis. Long-hairs and crew cuts alike – and their kids – will dig soaking in the natural hot springs (day use $5) or catching one of the outdoor concerts.

On Hwy 89 near **Marysvale** is **Big Rock Candy Mountain Resort** (☎ 435-326-2000; www.marysvale.org/brcm; r/cabins from $59/49; P), a decades-old getaway tucked beneath a colorful mountain immortalized in song (Harry McClintock) and novel (Wallace Stegner).

Skyline Dr

One of Utah's most spectacular wilderness roads, this dirt road parallels Hwy 89, traversing 90 miles along the crest of the Wasatch Plateau at elevations in excess of 10,000ft. Four-wheel-drive vehicles are needed to complete the drive (open summer and fall only), although easier sections can be accessed from towns along Hwy 89 (such as Fairview and Ephraim) or Hwy 10 (such as Huntington and Castle Dale).

Most of the drive is within the **Manti-La Sal National Forest**; ranger stations in **Price** (see below) and **Ephraim** (☎ 435-283-4151; 540 N Main St; 8am-4:30pm Mon-Fri) have information.

Carbon County & Castle Valley

The imposing buttes and austere eroded formations of 'Castle Country' dominate this colorful but dry region, traversed by Hwys 6 and 10. The discovery of coal and the arrival of the railway in 1883 attracted immigrants from diverse backgrounds to Carbon County, diluting the Mormon heritage that predominates in the valleys west of here.

The mining town of **Price** has the best range of motels and restaurants. The USFS **Price Ranger Station** (☎ 435-637-2817; 599 W Price River Dr; 8am-4:30pm Mon-Fri) and the **Castle Country Travel Office** (☎ 435-637-3009; www.castlecountry.com; 90 N 100 East; 8am-5pm Mon-Fri) have information on regional attractions, driving tours and activities. The excellent **College of Eastern Utah Prehistoric Museum** (☎ 435-613-5111; 155 E Main St; suggested donation $3; 9am-6pm, closed Sun in winter) has eight full-size dinosaur skeletons, Indian artifacts and prehistoric mammal displays.

In the 19th century, outlaws used the remote **San Rafael River and Swell** region as a hideout. Dirt roads, most accessible by 4WD only, crisscross the area, and backcountry camping is allowed. The best road, which passes both a spur to the Buckhorn Wash Pictographs and the awesome **Wedge Overlook**, leaves Hwy 10, 2 miles north of Castle Dale; the entire route is more than 60 miles (allow three hours). The area is extremely hot and dry in summer, so carry water and proceed with safety.

DESERT DRIVING

When exploring in Utah's remote desert backcountry always ask about current local road conditions, let someone know where you're going, and carry *lots* of water (several gallons at least). Flash floods can happen without warning because of rain many miles away. And after a rainstorm some dirt roads become dangerously slick – even with a 4WD. If you see a sign reading 'road impassable when wet,' believe it. As a rule, check with a ranger or local authorities about travel conditions.

SOUTHEASTERN UTAH

This portion of Utah contains some of the most inhospitable and beautiful terrain in the world. Over millennia, the Colorado, Green and San Juan Rivers have carved a landscape of such sheer-walled majesty and otherworldly desolation that it can challenge one's capacity for wonder. Every year, millions come to experience this country by foot, horseback, bicycle, car, 4WD, helicopter, raft and other means. You can camp alone in the silent desert or be catered to in exclusive lodges. However you visit, though, remember to tread lightly; millions of footsteps are taking their toll on this deceptively fragile environment.

This section is organized roughly north to south, beginning with Green River, on I-70, and following US 191 into the southeast corner of the state.

Green River

The 'world's watermelon capital,' Green River offers a good base for river running on the Green and Colorado Rivers, or exploring the nearby San Rafael Swell.

The **Green River Information Center** (☎ 435-564-3526; 885 E Main St; 8am-8pm, closes 5pm winter) is located inside the **John Wesley Powell Museum** (☎ 435-564-3427; adult/child $2/1), which has exhibits on Powell's life, the history of river running and Colorado Plateau geology. **Moki Mac River Expeditions** (☎ 800-284-7280) and **Holiday River Expeditions** (☎ 435-564-3273) offer river trips.

For basic budget rooms try family-friendly **Book Cliff Lodge** (☎ 435-564-3406; www.beattie1.com/bookclifflodge; 365 E Main St; r from $35; P ✕ ☒). River rafters go to **Ray's Tavern** (☎ 435-564-3511; 25 S Broadway; dishes $6-15), which serves microbrews and great hamburgers and steaks.

Greyhound (☎ 435-564-3421; 525 E Main St) stops at the West Winds Truck Stop on its way to Salt Lake City ($37, four hours) and beyond. **Amtrak** (☎ 800-872-7245; 250 S Broadway) carries passengers to Salt Lake City ($33, 5½ hours) and Denver ($50, 11 hours).

Moab

Moab is the major center point for outdoor adventure and sight-seeing in southeastern Utah, including some of the West's most spectacular parks. The town first gained attention during the 1950s uranium boom; after the boom slowed in the 1960s, however, tourists began arriving in Moab, word having spread about the area's striking landscape. It wasn't until mountain biking took off in the mid-1980s that Moab grew to its present size. Today Moab is a sprawling but still-trendy commercial center, home to chic restaurants, art galleries and more than 50 adventure companies offering tours and rentals.

INFORMATION

The large, multiagency **Moab Information Center** (☎ 435-259-8825, 800-635-6622; www.discovermoab.com; cnr Center & Main Sts; 8am-9pm summer, 9am-5pm winter), in the center of town, is the place to head with questions about Moab and its surrounding public lands, parks and forests; they also post weather and road information and sell books and maps.

The free, opinionated newspaper *Canyon Country Zephyr* is published six times annually. Look for it at **Back of Beyond** (☎ 435-259-5154; 83 N Main St), an excellent downtown bookstore. Most businesses are along Hwy 191, also called Main St.

ACTIVITIES

The Moab Area Travel Council's website (www.discovermoab.com/tour.htm) has a long list of rafting, biking, hiking and 4WD outfitters. Among them are the following:

Adrift Adventures (☎ 435-259-8594, 800-874-4483; www.adrift.net; 378 N Main St)

Canyon Voyages (☎ 435-259-6007, 800-733-6007; www.canyonvoyages.com; 211 N Main St)

Canyonlands Field Institute (☎ 435-259-7750, 800-860-5262; www.canyonlandsfieldinst.org; 1320 S Hwy 191)

Rim Tours (☎ 435-259-5223, 800-626-7335; www.rimtours.com; 1233 S Hwy 191)

Tex's Riverways (☎ 435-259-5101; www.texsriverways.com; 691 N 500 West)

THE AUTHOR'S CHOICE

Buck's Grill (☎ 435-259-5201; 1393 N Hwy 191; dishes $12-21) Without question, Buck's Grill is among Moab's best restaurants, serving incredibly flavorful (and affordable) dinners in a rustic, lodge-style room (the building dates to 1967). Wild game is the main focus – try elk stew or the buffalo meat loaf with black onion gravy, filling and fabulous. It also has Southwestern dishes, a couple vegetarian items and grilled 'cowboy' steaks, not to mention great desserts.

SLEEPING

Despite a ton of hotels, B&Bs and campgrounds, the town is packed with visitors from spring to fall, and reservations are advised.

Hotel Off Center (☎ 435-259-4244; www.moab-utah.com/hotel/offcenter.html; 96 E Center St; s/d $39/49; ✕ ☐) This is one of the town's most charming accommodations. The eight rooms are meticulously decorated with vintage furniture, radios, lamps and other accoutrements, and each has its own unique personality. Bathrooms are shared but clean and the atmosphere is about as friendly as it gets.

Apache Motel (☎ 435-259-5727, 800-228-6882; 166 S 400 East; r $52; P ✕ ☒) Located east of Main St, this attractive two-story motel boasts that John Wayne was a regular customer (there's a suite with his name on it, too).

Gonzo Inn (☎ 435-259-2515, 800-791-4044; www.gonzoinn.com; 100 W 200 South; summer/winter r from $129/59; P ✕ ☒) The hip Gonzo Inn has a wacky lizard as its homing symbol, which offsets its otherwise modern appearance. Rooms are large, clean, comfortable and have either balconies or patios.

Lazy Lizard International Hostel (☎ 435-259-6057; www.lazylizardhostel.com; 1213 S Hwy 191; dm/d/cabin $9/24/29; P ☐) Speaking of reptiles, this lazy lizard is a quiet, easygoing place south of downtown. There are kitchen and laundry facilities, and nonguests can shower for $2.

Of course, there's all sorts of **camping** to be done around here. The visitors center and the **BLM** (☎ 435-259-2100; www.blm.gov/utah/moab; 82 E Dogwood; 7:45am-4:30pm Mon-Fri) have information on area campgrounds.

EATING

There's no shortage of restaurants in Moab, from backpacker coffeehouses to proud gourmet dining rooms.

Center Cafe (☎ 435-259-4295; 60 N 100 West; dishes $20-32) Consistently one of Moab's finest, Center Cafe is where top-notch, beautifully prepared dishes (salmon, dry-aged beef) are served in warm, elegant surroundings. Reservations are recommended.

Eddie McStiff's (57 S Main; dishes $6-14) This popular microbrewery and restaurant serves the town's best pizza, along with burgers, salads and some genuinely tasty beers. It's a lively, at times rowdy, place but always friendly; a separate 'tavern' upstairs allows you to smoke and drink without having to order food.

Breakfast at Tiffany's (☎ 435-259-2553; 90 E Center St; dishes $5-7) This homey restaurant has a funky, thrift-shop decor and delicious, creative breakfast dishes; service can be slow but the wait is worth it.

Red Rock Bakery and Net Cafe (☎ 435-259-5941; 74 S Main St; dishes $3-6) Another good morning choice, Red Rock is where the coffee is organic and strong, the pastries and sandwiches delicious, and you can enjoy them all while surfing the Internet ($9 per hour with purchase).

GETTING THERE & AROUND

Amtrak and Greyhound serve Green River, 53 miles north (see p851). Both **Bighorn Express** (☎ 888-655-7433; www.bighornshuttle.com) and **Roadrunner Shuttle** (☎ 435-259-9402; www.roadrunnershuttle.com) have daily van service from Moab to Green River ($26 to $30) and Salt Lake City ($54). Roadrunner also shuttles passengers from Grand Junction, Colorado ($165 for one to four people) and around town. Another local bike and rafting shuttle service is **Coyote Shuttle** (☎ 435-259-8656; www.coyoteshuttle.com).

Arches National Park

The Southwest has a wealth of stunning parkland and this popular **national park** (☎ 435-719-2299; admission $10) is a remarkable gem, as it boasts the greatest concentration of sandstone arches in the world. Of course, that means that Arches, 5 quick miles north of Moab on Hwy 191, is often very crowded. Even so, a visit is always worthwhile (try it under moonlight, when the rocks are spooky and the place eerily empty). Many of the most spectacular arches are easily reached by paved roads and relatively short hiking trails. Highlights are Balanced Rock, the oft-photographed Delicate Arch, the spectacularly elongated Landscape Arch and popular, twice-daily ranger-led trips into the Fiery Furnace (adult/child $8/4; reservations recommended). Because of the heat and scarcity of water, few visitors backpack, though this is allowed with free permits (available from the visitors center). The scenic **Devils Garden campground** (campsites $10) is open year round.

Dead Horse Point State Park

Whatever you do, don't pass by this tiny **state park** (☎ 435-259-2614; admission $7), which has spectacular, sweeping views of southeastern Utah's canyon country – encompassing the Colorado River, Canyonlands National Park and the distant La Sal Mountains. It's found just off Hwy 313 (the road to Canyonlands), and it's absolutely worthwhile. If you only have time for one major viewpoint, this is it. There's **camping** (campsites $14), too.

Canyonlands National Park

Covering 527 sq miles, **Canyonlands** (☎ 435-719-2313; admission $10) is the largest and wildest national park in Utah. Indeed, parts of it are as rugged as almost anywhere on the planet. Need proof? Just check the view from Dead Horse Point, and witness canyons tipped with white cliffs tumbling to the river 2000ft below. Arches, bridges, needles, spires, craters, mesas, buttes – Canyonlands is a crumbling, decaying beauty, a vision of ancient earth.

You can hike, raft and 4WD (Cataract Canyon offers some of the wildest white water in the West), but be sure that you have plenty of gas, food and water before leaving Moab. The difficult terrain and lack of water make this the least developed and least visited of the major Southwestern national parks.

The canyons of the Colorado and Green Rivers divide the park into three districts.

Island in the Sky is most easily reached and, like Dead Horse Point, it offers amazing views. There's also a helpful **visitors center** (☎ 435-259-4712) and some excellent short hikes (the mile-long trail to Grand View Overlook takes you right along the canyon's edge). This section is 32 miles from Moab; head north along Hwy 191 then west on Hwy 313.

The **Needles** is on Rte 211, which heads west from US 191, 40 miles south of Moab; you'll find more great views here and a smaller **visitors center** (☎ 435-259-4711). And then there's the **Maze**, one of the wildest and most remote areas in the Southwest, accessible by 4WD only. In **Horseshoe Canyon,** along the 32-mile-long road from Hwy 24 to the maze, is the Great Gallery, with superb life-size rock art left by prehistoric Indians.

Permits are required for all activities except day trips. You can make reservations in writing or by fax (at least two weeks in advance) through the **Canyonlands National Park Reservation Office** (☎ 435-259-4351; fax 435-259-4285; www.nps.gov/cany; 2282 S West Resource Blvd, Moab, UT 84532); the website has more information. Or you can just show up, though reservations are recommended in the busy spring and fall.

Natural Bridges National Monument

Forty miles west of Blanding via Hwy 95, this **monument** (☎ 435-692-1234; admission $6; 🕒 7am-sunset) became Utah's first NPS land in 1908. The highlight is a dark-stained, white sandstone canyon containing three easily accessible natural bridges. The oldest, the Owachomo Bridge, spans 180ft but is only 9ft thick. Basic **camping** (campsites $10) is available.

Hovenweep National Monument

Beautiful, little-visited **Hovenweep** (☎ 970-560-4282; admission $6), meaning 'deserted valley' in the Ute language, contains six sets of prehistoric ancestral Puebloan Indian sites, five of which require long hikes to reach. There is a visitors center, ranger station and basic **campground** (campsite $10), but no facilities. The main access is east of Hwy 191 on Hwy 262 via Hatch Trading Post, more than 40 miles from Bluff or Blanding.

Bluff

Surrounded by red rock, tiny Bluff, founded by Mormon pioneers in 1880, makes a comfortable, laid-back base for exploring the region. It sits at the junction of Hwys 191 and 163, along the San Juan River. **Wild Rivers Expeditions** (☎ 435-672-2244; www.riversandruins.com) has been guiding educational river trips since 1957 (day trips $120). **Far Out Expeditions** (☎ 435-672-2294; www.faroutexpeditions.com) arranges off-the-beaten-track trips to Monument Valley ($100) and other locations; ask about their fabulous bunkhouse and cookouts.

Bluff has a good selection of lodgings, from budget places to B&Bs. A favorite is the hospitable **Recapture Lodge** (☎ 435-672-2281; www.bluffutah.org/recapturelodge; Hwy 191; r $46-60; P ✱ 🏊), a rustic, cozy property pleasantly shaded behind trees between the highway and the San Juan River.

Be sure to stop by the fun, friendly **Cow Canyon Trading Post** (☎ 435-672-2208; cnr Hwys 191 & 163; dishes $10-16; 🕒 Thu-Mon), which serves a rotating menu of fabulous gourmet dinners (April to October), including vegetarian options; the trading post, open all year, has an excellent book selection.

Moki Dugway & Mule Point

The **Moki Dugway** (Hwy 261) heads south from Hwy 95 to connect with Hwy 163 at Mexican Hat. Along the way is a turnoff to **Mule Point Overlook** – don't miss this cliff-edge viewpoint as it's one of the country's most sweeping and spectacular, encompassing Monument Valley and other landmarks.

Back on Hwy 261, the pavement ends and the Moki Dugway suddenly descends a whopping 1100ft along a series of fist-clenching hairpin turns. At the bottom, a dirt road heads east into the **Valley of the Gods**, a 17-mile drive through monoliths of sandstone; again, it's mind-blowing scenery. Near the southern end of Hwy 261, a 4-mile paved road heads west to **Goosenecks State Park**, a small lookout with memorable views of the San Juan River, 1100ft below.

Monument Valley

From the village of **Mexican Hat**, Hwy 163 winds southwest and enters the Navajo Indian Reservation and, after about 30 miles, Monument Valley Navajo Tribal Park (see p831). Just inside the Utah border, **Goulding's Lodge** (☎ 435-727-3231; www.gouldings.com; r $160; P ✱ 💻 🏊) is the only hotel near Monument Valley; each room has a balcony with a million-dollar view of the colossal red buttes.

Goulding's also has a museum, tours, store, gas and **campground**.

SOUTH-CENTRAL & SOUTHWESTERN UTAH

This section is organized roughly northeast to southwest: from Hanksville, along Hwy 24 through Capitol Reef National Park and southwest along Hwy 12, which passes the Grand Staircase-Escalante National Monument and Bryce Canyon and is one of the most scenic roads in the country. From Hwy 12, US 89 goes south to Kanab (and continues to the North Rim of the Grand Canyon). Further west lie the towns of Cedar City and St George and gorgeous Zion National Park.

Hanksville

A couple of cheap motels dot this convenient stopping place at the junction of Hwys 95 and 24. The **BLM** (☎ 435-542-3461; 406 S 100 West) has information on the **Henry Mountains**, a remote, 11,000ft-high range. North along Hwy 24 is **Goblin Valley State Park** (☎ 435-564-3633; admission $5), full of delightful, alien rock formations and a **campground** (campsites $14). About 20 miles west near Caineville, look for **Luna Mesa Oasis** (☎ 435-456-9122; dishes $5-15), a friendly spot to grab a meal.

Capitol Reef National Park

Not as crowded as Utah's other national parks, but equally scenic, **Capitol Reef** contains much of the 100-mile **Waterpocket Fold**, created 65 million years ago when the earth's surface buckled up and folded, exposing a cross-section of geologic history that is almost painterly in its intensity of color. Hwy 24 through here is full of grand scenery, but a worthwhile diversion is the park's own scenic drive ($5), starting from the **visitors center** (☎ 435-425-3791); there's also a grassy, basic **campground** (campsites $10). Backcountry camping is free with a permit, but this is a desert wilderness, so be prepared. For more information, contact Capitol Reef National Park, HC 70, Box 15, Torrey, UT 84775.

Torrey

At the junction of Hwys 12 and 24, this little village is a good stopping point for lodging and surprisingly great meals. The **Capital Reef Country Visitors Center** (☎ 435-425-3365, 800-858-7951; www.capitolreef.org) is a summer-only information booth at the junction of Hwys 24 and 12.

Capitol Reef Inn & Café (☎ 435-425-3271; www.capitolreefinn.com; 360 W Main; r $52; dishes $10-15; Ⓟ ⊠) This funky, inviting place has simple rooms and home-cooked meals, including vegetarian dishes.

Rim Rock Inn (☎ 435-425-3388, 888-447-4676; www.therimrockcom; r $55; dishes $12-24; ⏲ Mar-Nov; Ⓟ ⊠) A couple miles east along Hwy 24, Rim Rock Inn has rooms with stellar views and a highly regarded restaurant.

Café Diablo (☎ 435-425-3070; 599 W Main St; dishes $16-24) Back in town, Café Diablo prepares first-rate Southwestern cuisine.

Most Torrey businesses, including those listed here, are open in summer only.

Boulder

Tiny Boulder is 32 miles south of Torrey on Hwy 12. From here, the attractive **Burr Trail** heads east as a paved road across the northeastern corner of the Grand Staircase-Escalante National Monument, winding up at Bullfrog Marina on Lake Powell (see p830). If you're interested in exploring the park, definitely stop by one of the visitors centers listed here for advice. Better yet, take a daylong, child-friendly excursion with knowledgeable **Earth Tours** (☎ 435-691-1241; www.earth-tours.com); or perhaps consider a multiday backcountry trek with **Escalante Canyon Outfitters** (☎ 435-335-7311; www.ecohike.com). Both are based in Boulder and are highly recommended.

The comfortable, modern rooms at **Boulder Mountain Lodge** (☎ 800-556-3446; Hwy 12; www.boulder-utah.com; r $85-153; Ⓟ ⊠ 💻) are among the nicest accommodations along Hwy 12. Next door, **Hell's Backbone Grill** (☎ 435-335-7464; Hwy 12; dishes $10-19) serves elegantly prepared regional cuisine made with locally raised meat and organic vegetables.

Escalante

The **Escalante Interagency Office** (☎ 435-826-5499; 755 W Main St; ⏲ 7:30am-5:30pm Mar-Oct) is a superb resource center with complete information on all area public lands. Fifteen miles east on Hwy 12, **Calf Creek Recreation Area** (☎ 435-826-5499; campsites $7) has a nice basic campground and a recommended 3-mile hike to Lower Calf Creek Falls.

Escalante Outfitters, Inc (☎ 435-826-4266; 310 W Main St; ⏲ Mon-Sat) is a great travelers' oasis, selling maps, books, camping supplies, liquor, espresso and the best homemade pizza (from $10) you'll find anywhere in the state, no kidding. Overnighters stay in cute, cozy, clean **cabins** (cabins $25; closed winter) out back.

Grand Staircase-Escalante National Monument

This 2656-sq-mile monument, established in 1996, fits in between Bryce Canyon National Park, Capitol Reef National Park and Glen Canyon National Recreation Area. Tourist infrastructure is minimal, leaving a vast, remote desert for adventurous travelers who have the time and necessary outdoor equipment to explore.

Three unpaved roads – Skutumpah /Johnson Canyon Rd (the least used and most westerly route), Cottonwood Canyon Rd and Smoky Mountain Rd – cross the monument roughly north to south between Hwys 12 and 89. A fourth unpaved road (the Hole-in-the-Rock Rd) begins from Hwy 12 and dead-ends at the Glen Canyon National Recreation Area. Roads get slick and impassable when wet. Wilderness camping is allowed with a required permit. Before any excursions, obtain current road and travel information from the Escalante Interagency Office, or from the new monument visitors centers in Kanab (see p857), Big Water or **Cannonville** (435-679-8981; 8am-4:30pm Mar-Nov). Also check the park's website (www.ut.blm.gov/monument).

Kodachrome Basin State Park

Dozens of red, pink and white sandstone chimneys highlight this colorful **state park** (435-679-8562; admission $5). There's a **campground** (800-322-3770; campsites $14; year-round) and several **cabins** (435-679-8536; www.brycecanyoninn.com; cabins $65) are available during summer, as are horseback rides ($16 per hour).

Bryce Canyon National Park

The Grand Staircase, a series of steplike uplifted rock layers stretching north from the Grand Canyon, culminates at this very popular park (435-834-5322; www.nps.gov/brca; individual/car $10/20) in the Pink Cliffs formation, full of wondrous pinnacles and points, steeples and spires, and odd formations called 'hoodoos.' The 'canyon' is actually an amphitheater eroded from the cliffs.

From Hwy 12, Hwy 63 heads 4 miles south to Rim Rd Dr (8000ft), an 18-mile dead-end road that follows the rim of the canyon, passing the visitors center, lodge, viewpoints (don't miss Inspiration Point) and trailheads, ending at Rainbow Point at 9115ft elevation. You can whisk in and out in a few hours, but for a richer experience, numerous trails will take you out among the spires and deeper into the heart of the landscape. There is a free (voluntary) shuttle system from Hwy 12.

Canyon Trail Rides (435-679-8665) operates short and long horseback trips ($30, two hours). Rangers lead new- and full-moon stargazing evenings in summer. The park's a lovely sight in winter, too, and certain trails are open to cross-country skiing and snowshoeing.

The park's two **campgrounds** (campsites $10) fill by noon in summer. With a permit ($5), you can camp at 10 designated backcountry sites below the rim.

Historic **Bryce Canyon Lodge** (303-297-2757; www.brycecanyonlodge.com; r $102-130; Apr-Oct; P), a rustic beauty dating from the 1920s, has both cabins and rooms; two rooms are wheelchair accessible. There's also a general store and restaurant.

A couple of standard motels sit at the junction of Hwys 63 and 12, including **Bryce View Lodge** (435-834-5180; www.bryceviewlodge.com; 991 S Highway 63; r $60-66; P). More basic motels are found in **Tropic**, about 8 miles east of Bryce along Hwy 12.

Panguitch & Around

Simple little Panguitch is a popular stop on Hwy 89, as it's surrounded by knockout scenic drives, has several good motels and is convenient to both Bryce Canyon (24 miles) and Zion (70 miles). **Garfield County Travel Council** (800-444-6689; 55 S Main St; 9am-6pm Mon-Fri) has regional information.

Panguitch Lake is southwest on Hwy 143. Farther west, **Brian Head Ski Resort** (435-677-2035; www.brianhead.com; adult/child $38/25) offers winter skiing geared toward families. In summer, you can hike 11,307ft Brian Head Summit.

Cedar Breaks National Monument (435-586-9451; admission $3), at 10,400ft, is usually open May to October. Its absolutely stunning amphitheater features wonderfully eroded, almost neon-colored spires. South of the

SOUTHWEST

park is **Hwy 14**, a scenic drive crossing the beautiful Markagunt Plateau between I-15 and Hwy 89.

In Panguitch, attractive budget motels line Main St; some only open seasonally. The cute little **Blue Pine Motel** (☎ 435-676-8197; 130 N Main St; r $40; P ❄), though, is open year-round.

Kanab

Surrounded by desert wilderness on all sides, Kanab was an isolated Mormon community until the advent of roads. In the 1930s, the film industry 'discovered' the area, and almost 100 movies have been filmed here. Paved roads lead to the area's famous national parks: Zion (40 miles), Bryce Canyon (80 miles), the north rim of the Grand Canyon (80 miles) and Glen Canyon National Recreation Area (74 miles) Hwy 89 snakes through town, and a good selection of motels and restaurants lie along it, making it a popular travelers' stopover.

The Grand Staircase-Escalante National Monument's brand-new **Kanab Visitors Center** (☎ 435-644-4680; 745 E Hwy 89; 7:30am-5:30pm) has information on the monument (see p856). The county **visitors center** (☎ 435-644-5033; www.kaneutah.com; 78 S 100 East; 8am-8pm Mon-Fri, 9am-5pm Sat, 9am-1pm Sun, reduced hours in winter) and the **BLM** (☎ 435-644-4600; 318 N 100 East; 7:45am-4:30pm Mon-Fri) have further information on the area.

The finest accommodations in Kanab are at **Parry Lodge** (☎ 435-644-2601; fax 435-644-2605; 89 E Center St; r $51; P ❄ 🏊), an eye-catching, historic property on a beautifully landscaped plot in the center of town. It has a restaurant and bar on site.

Cedar City

Less than an hour's drive northeast of Zion on I-15, Cedar City is a natural stopping place. For area information, head to the helpful **Iron County Tourism Bureau** (☎ 435-586-5124; www.scenicsouthernutah.com; 585 N Main St; 8am-7pm Mon-Fri, 9am-1pm Sat). From June to September, the nationally renowned **Shakespearean Festival** (☎ 435-586-7878; www.bard.org) keeps the town buzzing.

For basic accommodations, **Cedar Rest Motel** (☎ 435-586-9471; 479 S Main St; r $45; P ❄) is clean, simple and a cut above the average budget motel.

St George

A spacious Mormon town with wide streets, an eye-catching temple and pioneer buildings, St George is popular with retirees and visitors to Zion and other nearby parks. The **chamber of commerce** (☎ 435-628-1658; www.stgeorgechamber.com; 97E St George Blvd; 9am-5pm Mon-Fri, 10am-3pm Sat) has information on walking tours and where to see dinosaur tracks. The 1877 St George Temple has a **visitors center** (☎ 435-673-5181; 490 S 300 East; 9am-9pm) next door.

Nine miles north on Hwy 18, **Snow Canyon State Park** (☎ 435-628-2255; admission $5; 6am-10pm) has volcanic landscapes, petroglyphs and hiking trails to lava caves.

St George has the biggest selection of accommodations in southern Utah; most are chains, and many line St George Blvd. Try **Sun Time Inn** (☎ 435-673-6181; www.econostgeorge.com; 420 E St George Blvd; r $49; P ❄ 🏊) or **Sullivan's Rococo Inn & Steak House** (☎ 435-628-3671; www.rococo.net; 511 S Airport Rd; r $45; P ❄ 🏊).

Budget travelers may wish to drive the 17 miles east to the tiny town of **Hurricane** (on Hwy 9 to Zion National Park) and the clean, well-run **HI Hurricane Dixie Hostel** (☎ 435-635-8202; www.dixiehostel.com; 73 S Main St; dm/d $15/35; P 💻); all rooms share bath.

Greyhound (☎ 435-673-2933; 1235 S Bluff), found inside a local McDonalds, heads daily to Las Vegas ($27, two hours) and Salt Lake City ($51, 6½ hours).

Springdale

Many travelers pass through this town on their way to Zion National Park, as it sits along Hwy 9 just outside the park's southern entrance. It's a pleasant, relaxed community, catering mostly to park visitors; the **visitors bureau** (☎ 888-518-7070; www.zionpark.com) can answer questions and has a helpful website.

Springdale also has an abundance of good restaurants and nice lodging options, many of them surprisingly charming. Try friendly **Terrace Brook Lodge** (☎ 435-772-3932; fax 435-772-3596; r $49; P ❄ 🏊). **Zion Pizza & Noodle** (☎ 435-772-3815; 868 Zion Park Blvd; dishes $8-14), attractively set inside a 1930 Mormon church, has a large selection of microbrews, a nice beer garden and, as the name implies, plenty of pizza and pasta dishes. The popular **Bit & Spur Restaurant & Saloon** (☎ 435-772-3498; 1212 Zion Park Blvd; dishes $8-18) serves tasty Mexican and Southwestern cuisine and has a lively bar.

Zion National Park

The white, pink and red rocks of **Zion National Park** (☎ 435-772-3256; www.nps.gov/zion) are huge, overpowering and magnificent – you're guaranteed to be awed upon your first glimpse of the place. For most visitors, the main attraction is the 6-mile drive into Zion Canyon, a half-mile-deep slash formed by the Virgin River. Because it's so popular, the park now shuts the road to cars each summer (April to October) and runs a free shuttle bus. This has resulted in a much quieter park, but it's still very crowded. To find some solitude, come in late spring or fall (the weather's better, too), or escape by taking a hike into the spectacularly wild country beyond the scenic pullouts.

The most popular road into the park is the Zion–Mt Carmel Hwy (Hwy 9). From the south entrance at Springdale, the road leads Zion Canyon (only those staying at Zion Lodge can enter it in summer), then climbs hairpin turns to meet a very narrow tunnel; most RVs and buses require an escort to get through ($10 fee). East of the tunnel is dramatic, colorful slickrock country.

Entrance from either end of the Zion–Mt Carmel Hwy is $20/10 per car/individual. Near the south entrance is the **Zion Canyon Visitors Center** (🕑 8am-5pm) and the new **Zion Human History Museum** (🕑 8am-5pm). Park in the lot near the visitors center for the shuttle bus, which comes every six minutes during summer days. One bus loops north into Zion Canyon; the other heads south into Springdale (where there are further lots to leave your car, often a better bet).

It costs nothing to enter the park along Kolob Terrace Rd (closed November to May), which leaves Hwy 9 at the village of Virgin and climbs more than 4000ft to Lava Point. However, there are no facilities, only a ranger station and primitive campground.

At the park's northwestern corner (I-15 exit 40), you can enter via Kolob Canyons Rd ($10 per car), which leads to the much smaller **Kolob Canyons Visitors Center** (☎ 435-586-9548; 🕑 8am-5pm) and wonderful views and hikes.

More than 100 miles of trails offer everything from leisurely strolls to wilderness **backpacking** and camping. The most famous backpacking trip is through the **Narrows**, a 16-mile journey through dramatic canyons along the Virgin River (June to September). Overnight permits ($5) from the visitors centers are issued only the day of or the day before your hike.

At the south gate, two basic **campgrounds** (campsites $14) have more than 300 first-come, first-served sites, but come early. A few sites can be reserved; call ☎ 800-365-2267 to book.

Zion Lodge (☎ 303-297-2757; www.zionlodge.com; r/cabins from $120/128; P ✖ 💻), beautifully set in the middle of Zion Canyon, offers good motel rooms and family-friendly cabins, most with private porches and canyon views. A restaurant and café are also here.

NEVADA

You know you're in Nevada when you start seeing slot machines in grocery stores and gas stations, or when the waitress at a 24-hour coffee shop asks if you want a keno ticket with your eggs. For many travelers, this is the Nevada they know and love – a land of luxury hotels, uninhibited nights out and a few hours or minutes of pure adrenaline at the gaming tables.

For others, however, Nevada – from a Spanish word meaning 'snow-clad' – has a lot more to offer than just blackjack tables and nickel slot machines. The state spreads across more than 110,000 sq miles (a massive 86% of it federally owned), and there's lots of rugged, beautiful terrain to explore, from the mountains of Great Basin National Park to near-empty highways such as Hwy 50 (dubbed 'the loneliest highway in the world') and a seemingly endless number of sweeping, breathtaking desert valleys in between. You can also immerse yourself in Western history in towns like Virginia City and Elko, or just pitch a tent and spend the evening under the vast, star-dotted sky. Rarely will you have heard such absolute quiet.

History

Though claimed by Spain, Nevada was scarcely touched by Europeans until the 1820s, when trappers ventured into the Humboldt River Valley. Before that, ancient Nevada was initially inhabited by the northern Paiute people, as well as ancestral Puebloans in the southeast.

Most 19th-century emigrants passed straight through Nevada to the California

NEVADA FACTS

Nicknames Silver State, Sagebrush State
Population 2,173,491 (35th)
Area 109,826 sq miles (7th)
Admitted to Union October 31, 1864 (36th)
Capital city Carson City (population 52,500)
Other cities Las Vegas (478,400; metro area 1,425,700), Reno (180,500)
State flower Sagebrush
Birthplace of first lady Thelma 'Pat' Nixon (1912–93); Andre Agassi (b 1970)
Famous for Las Vegas, the Comstock Lode at Virginia City, UFOs, legal prostitution

gold fields. But in 1859 the Comstock Lode – the largest silver deposit ever mined – was discovered south of Reno.

As the Comstock Lode was mined out, Nevada's population declined. In the early 20th century, new mineral discoveries temporarily revived the state's fortunes, but the Great Depression brought an end to those dreams. So, in 1931, the state government legalized gambling and created agencies to tax it, turning an illegal activity into a revenue source and tourist attraction.

Since WWII, Nevada's wide-open spaces have been used to test nuclear weapons and military aircraft; its next controversial industry may be nuclear-waste storage.

Gambling

Except for poker, all gambling pits the player against the house, and the house always has a statistical edge. Some casinos offer introductory lessons in blackjack, roulette and craps. To enter a gambling area, you must be at least 18 years old. To gamble and/or drink alcohol in the casino, you must be 21 years old.

Information

The **Nevada Commission on Tourism** (☎ 800-638-2328; www.travelnevada.com; 401 N Carson St, Carson City, NV 89701) sends free books, maps and information on accommodations, campgrounds and events.

The **Las Vegas Convention and Visitors Authority** (☎ 702-892-0711; www.lasvegas24hours.com; 3150 Paradise Rd, Las Vegas, NV 89109) is another helpful organization, as is the **Nevada Division of State Parks** (☎ 775-687-4384; parks.nv.gov; 1300 South Curry St, Carson City, NV 89703-5202).

Contact the **Nevada Department of Transport** (☎ 877-687-6237; www.nvroads.com) for road conditions.

Note that prostitution is definitely illegal in Clark County (which includes Las Vegas) and Washoe County (which includes Reno), though there are legal brothels in many smaller counties.

Nevada is on pacific standard time, and it has two areas codes: Las Vegas and vicinity is ☎ 702, while the rest of the state is ☎ 775.

LAS VEGAS

Most people are dazzled by their first sight of Las Vegas, and justifiably so. The scale of the place is staggering, with eye-catching buildings rising unrepentantly out of the hot Mojave sand, looking as if several gargantuan movie facades (palaces, pyramids, New York skyscrapers) had been crammed together into one amazing playland. Which is pretty much what has happened. Sure, it's an exciting place – if you like gambling and glitter, you'll adore it.

A onetime remote railroad town, Las Vegas has grown into one of the country's top destinations, a city full of hotels built so people can come and see...those very hotels. Today, it's a popular playland, with 'sin' still, after all these years, a major selling point. Gambling and sex dominate many visitors' agendas (strip clubs are more popular than ever). Others are looking simply to kick back and be pampered, as modern Vegas brings a luxurious lifestyle within easy reach of just about anyone. It's not unusual, for instance, to spend the day by a wave pool, get an afternoon massage, shop at Gucci, eat at Le Cirque, take in a show and then retire to your 700-sq-ft suite.

History

Believe it or not, Las Vegas does possess some genuine history. The town began as a way station for travelers, thanks to a small spring north of downtown. After that, the area became known to overland travelers as *las vegas* (the meadows), with reliable water and feed for horses. It was a regular stop on the Spanish Trail. Mormons built the first structure in 1855, a small mission and fort abandoned by 1858. Remnants of the buildings have been preserved as Old Las Vegas Mormon Fort State Historic Park, near downtown.

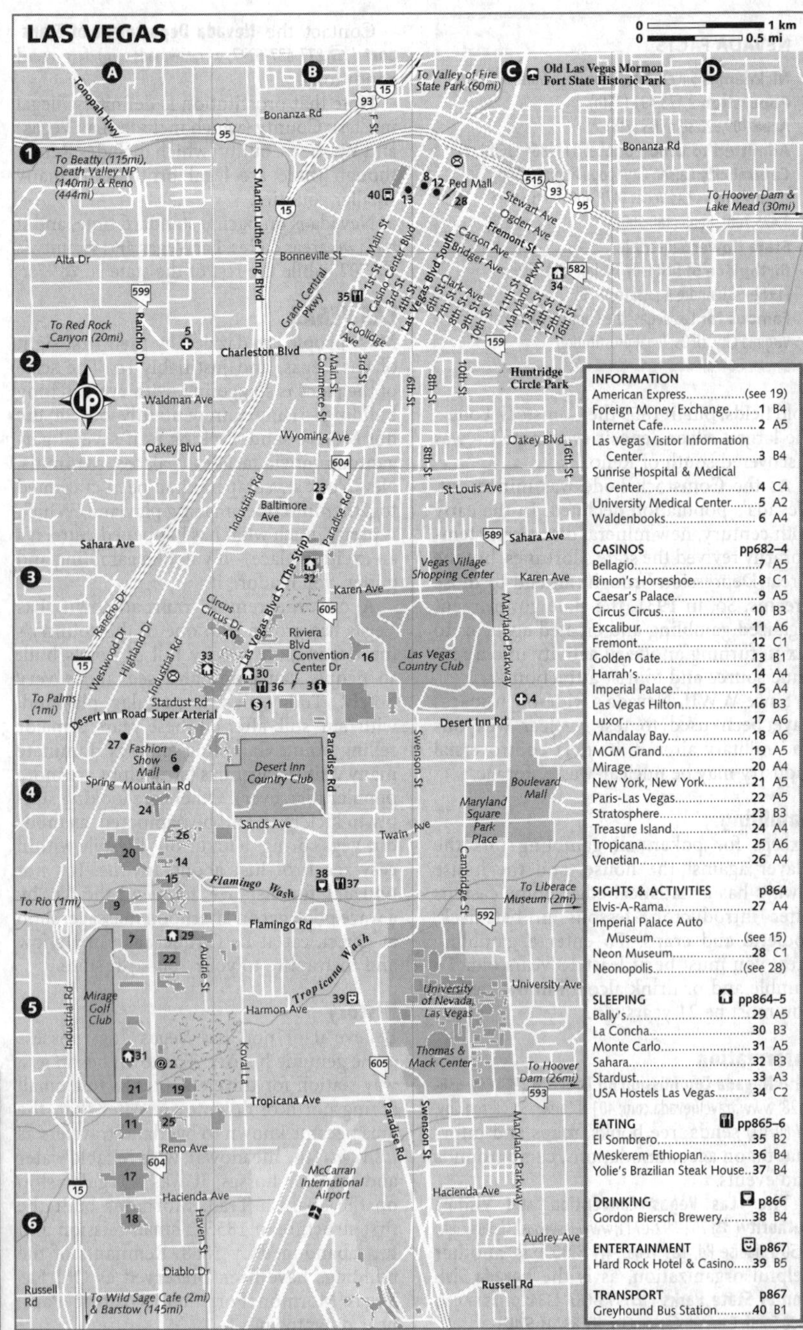
LAS VEGAS
0 1 km
0 0.5 mi
A
B
C
D
1
2
3
4
5
6
Old Las Vegas Mormon Fort State Historic Park
To Valley of Fire State Park (60mi)
To Beatty (115mi), Death Valley NP (140mi) & Reno (444mi)
To Hoover Dam & Lake Mead (30mi)
To Red Rock Canyon (20mi)
To Palms (1mi)
To Rio (1mi)
To Liberace Museum (2mi)
To Hoover Dam (26mi)
To Wild Sage Cafe (2mi) & Barstow (145mi)
Tonopah Hwy
Bonanza Rd
S Martin Luther King Blvd
Alta Dr
Bonneville St
Grand Central Pkwy
Main St
1st St
Casino Center Blvd
3rd St
4th St
Las Vegas Blvd South
6th St
7th St
8th St
9th St
10th St
11th St
Maryland Pkwy
13th St
14th St
15th St
16th St
Ped Mall
Stewart Ave
Ogden Ave
Fremont St
Carson Ave
Bridger Ave
Clark Ave
Coolidge Ave
Rancho Dr
Charleston Blvd
Huntridge Circle Park
Waldman Ave
Oakey Blvd
Wyoming Ave
Commerce St
Industrial Rd
Baltimore Ave
Paradise Rd
St Louis Ave
Sahara Ave
Las Vegas Blvd S (The Strip)
Vegas Village Shopping Center
Karen Ave
Circus Circus Dr
Riviera Blvd
Convention Center Dr
Las Vegas Country Club
Westwood Dr
Highland Dr
Stardust Rd
Desert Inn Road Super Arterial
Desert Inn Rd
Fashion Show Mall
Spring Mountain Rd
Desert Inn Country Club
Swenson St
Maryland Parkway
Boulevard Mall
Maryland Square Park Place
Sands Ave
Twain Ave
Flamingo Wash
Cambridge St
Flamingo Rd
Audrie St
Tropicana Wash
University Ave
Mirage Golf Club
Harmon Ave
University of Nevada, Las Vegas
Koval La
Thomas & Mack Center
Tropicana Ave
Reno Ave
McCarran International Airport
Hacienda Ave
Haven St
Audrey Ave
Diablo Dr
Russell Rd
INFORMATION
American Express....(see 19)
Foreign Money Exchange....1 B4
Internet Cafe....2 A5
Las Vegas Visitor Information Center....3 B4
Sunrise Hospital & Medical Center....4 C4
University Medical Center....5 A2
Waldenbooks....6 A4
CASINOS pp682–4
Bellagio....7 A5
Binion's Horseshoe....8 C1
Caesar's Palace....9 A5
Circus Circus....10 B3
Excalibur....11 A6
Fremont....12 C1
Golden Gate....13 B1
Harrah's....14 A4
Imperial Palace....15 A4
Las Vegas Hilton....16 B3
Luxor....17 A6
Mandalay Bay....18 A6
MGM Grand....19 A5
Mirage....20 A4
New York, New York....21 A5
Paris-Las Vegas....22 A5
Stratosphere....23 B3
Treasure Island....24 A4
Tropicana....25 A6
Venetian....26 A4
SIGHTS & ACTIVITIES p864
Elvis-A-Rama....27 A4
Imperial Palace Auto Museum....(see 15)
Neon Museum....28 C1
Neonopolis....(see 28)
SLEEPING pp864–5
Bally's....29 A5
La Concha....30 B3
Monte Carlo....31 A5
Sahara....32 B3
Stardust....33 A3
USA Hostels Las Vegas....34 C2
EATING pp865–6
El Sombrero....35 B2
Meskerem Ethiopian....36 B4
Yolie's Brazilian Steak House....37 B4
DRINKING p866
Gordon Biersch Brewery....38 B4
ENTERTAINMENT p867
Hard Rock Hotel & Casino....39 B5
TRANSPORT p867
Greyhound Bus Station....40 B1

LAS VEGAS IN...

Two Days

To begin, explore the **Strip**. Wander to the **Imperial Palace Auto Museum**, keeping your eyes out for people offering free passes. Catch a lunch buffet at **Paris-Las Vegas** or **Bellagio**, then head to the pool for a lazy afternoon. Come nightfall, wander the Strip casinos and gawk at the volcanic eruptions and sizzling fountain shows.

The next day, indulge your glitzy side with a trip to the **Liberace Museum** and **Elvis-A-Rama**. Then head downtown to see the **Neon Museum** and the **Fremont Street Experience**, catching a drink afterwards – or trying your luck – in vintage casinos like **Binion's Horseshoe** or the **Golden Gate**.

Four Days

Follow the itinerary for two days, then explore **Hoover Dam**, drive along Lake Mead's North Shore Rd up to **Valley of Fire State Park**; you can also take a short hike at **Red Rock Canyon**. Check out the **Guggenheim Hermitage Museum**, and maybe indulge in a gourmet meal or a **Cirque du Soleil** performance.

In 1902 most of the city's land was sold to a railroad company. Union Pacific subdivided what is now downtown Las Vegas and 1200 lots were auctioned off in a single day, May 15, 1905, now celebrated as the city's birthday. The building of nearby Hoover Dam, which began in 1931, provided not only jobs but the water and power necessary for the city's long-term growth.

The first true Strip resort was the Western-themed El Rancho Vegas, opened south of the city limits in 1941 (it burned down in 1960). Hotel Last Frontier followed soon after in 1942. Soon, Los Angeles developers and Mafia associates started building the large, flashy Strip casinos we've all come to associate with Las Vegas, beginning in 1946 with Bugsy Siegel's Flamingo. The Rat Pack (Frank Sinatra, Dean Martin, Sammy Davis Jr, Joey Bishop and Peter Lawford) held sway at the Sands, bringing the city an aura of black-tie cool. During the 1960s, billionaire Howard Hughes bought numerous casinos, and his presence helped wean the city of its unsavory mob influences. Only a few of the old Strip casinos still exist, and survivors such as the Frontier, Sahara and Stardust have undergone numerous facelifts. A new growth spurt began in the mid-1980s and led to the theme-park-like casinos now gracing the Strip's southern reaches. Since then the city's population has nearly doubled.

Orientation

Downtown Las Vegas is the original town center and home to the city's oldest hotels and casinos. The main drag is Fremont St, four blocks of which is now a covered pedestrian mall. Heading east, Fremont St turns into the Boulder Hwy, the old main route to Hoover Dam.

Las Vegas Blvd is the main north–south drag, running from North Las Vegas south toward the airport. South of the city limits, this boulevard is famously known as 'the Strip,' where you'll find most of the gargantuan hotel-casinos. Smaller motels, souvenir stands and a surprising number of vacant lots are slotted in between the big casinos, occupying sites still awaiting a fate of yet-to-be-determined grandness. More casinos are found east of the Strip along Paradise Rd, and just west of I-15 near the intersection of Flamingo Rd and Valley View Blvd. The Greyhound station is downtown.

Information

BOOKSTORES

Borders Book Shop (☎ 702-258-0999; 2323 S Decatur Blvd) West of the Strip.

Waldenbooks (☎ 702-733-1049; 3200 Las Vegas Blvd) Inside the Fashion Show Mall.

EMERGENCY

Emergency number (☎ 911)

Gamblers Anonymous (☎ 702-385-7732) May help with gambling concerns.

Police Department (☎ 702-229-3111)

INTERNET ACCESS

Internet Cafe (☎ 702-736-4782; www.cyberstopinc.com; 3763 Las Vegas Blvd S; half/full hour $8/12; 🕑 9am-midnight)

> **TIPS ON TIPPING**
>
> Las Vegas is one of the service-job capitals of the world and most of the staff depend on tips to supplement their meager wages. Drinks are usually complimentary while you're playing the tables, but tip the waitress $1 per round (more may mean better service). Dealers expect to be tipped only by winning players. Maids appreciate $2 a day and while valet parking is generally free, tip the valets a couple of bucks, too.

MEDIA

Las Vegas Bugle (☎ 702-650-0636; www.lvbugle.com) Weekly gay publication.
Las Vegas Review-Journal (☎ 702-383-0211; www.lvrj.com) Daily paper with a weekend guide on Friday.
Las Vegas Weekly (☎ 702-990-2400; www.lasvegasweekly.com) Free weekly with good entertainment and restaurant listings.

MEDICAL SERVICES

Sunrise Hospital & Medical Center (☎ 702-731-8000; 3186 S Maryland Parkway)
University Medical Center (☎ 702-383-2000; 1800 W Charleston Blvd)

MONEY

Casino cashiers, open 24 hours, exchange traveler's checks and major foreign currencies, but banks may give better rates. All casinos have ATMS.
American Express (☎ 702-739-8474; 3799 Las Vegas Blvd S) Inside MGM Grand.
Foreign Money Exchange (☎ 702-791-3301; 101 Convention Center Dr) Opposite Stardust.

POST

Downtown Station (☎ 702-385-3837; 301 Stewart Ave; 🕑 8:30am-5pm Mon-Fri)
Strip Station (☎ 702-735-8519; 3100 S Industrial Rd; 🕑 8:30am-5pm Mon-Fri) Located behind Circus Circus.

TOURIST OFFICES

Las Vegas Visitor Information Center (☎ 702-892-7575; www.lasvegas24hours.com; 3150 Paradise Rd; 🕑 8am-5pm) In the parking lot across the street from the convention center; enter from Convention Center Dr.

Dangers & Annoyances

The major tourist areas are safe. However, Las Vegas Blvd between downtown and the Strip gets pretty shabby, and Fremont Street east of downtown is definitely unsavory – it's lined with great old neon signs and fleabag motels. If you're staying at the hostel, which is east of downtown, avoid walking alone or at night.

SCAMS

Beware businesses along the Strip advertising themselves as 'Official Tourist Bureaus'; they're basically low-rent agencies pushing overpriced helicopter and Grand Canyon tours. If you want to see the canyon, the Las Vegas Visitor Information Center offers real advice.

Casinos

At the Strip's massive hotel-casinos, you can get your fill of free booze, cheap food and glitzy entertainment, though luxury accommodations, soothing spas and high-end shopping malls are now real draws. Most casino floors are windowless and deliberately disorienting; to find your way around ask an attendant, or look for overhead signs pointing to restaurants, shops or the hotel lobby.

The flashiest casinos are on the southern half of the Strip. The town's oldest hotel /casinos are downtown and while somewhat rumpled, they retain a surprising degree of Western character. Below is a selected list of Vegas casinos, running from north to south.

Golden Gate (☎ 702-385-1906, 800-426-1906; www.goldengatecasino.net; 1 Fremont St) For those curious what Vegas might have been like a century ago, this charming hotel and casino is the place to head. It dates back to 1906 (amazing that this town has let anything survive that long), when it opened as the Hotel Nevada. The casino retains the feel of an old West saloon, complete with ceiling fans and a honky-tonk pianist nightly. The 99¢ shrimp cocktails have been famous since 1959.

Binion's Horseshoe (☎ 702-382-1600, 800-237-6537; www.binions.com; 128 E Fremont St) Another venerable downtown casino, the Horseshoe was founded by Benny Binion in 1951. The 'World Series of Poker' has been held here each April and May for over 30 years, and the gambling hall has old Vegas charm in its pressed-tin ceiling and red-velvet wallpaper.

Stratosphere (☎ 702-380-7777, 800-998-6937; 2000 Las Vegas Blvd S) On the north end of the Strip this casino's 1149ft tower (down from the originally planned 1800ft) has a restaurant, lounge and observation deck on top. There are also a couple of thrill rides up there: the coaster High Roller and free-fall Big Shot, which moves up and down the tower's very tip (combo pass $17).

Las Vegas Hilton (☎ 702-732-5111, 800-732-7117; www.lv-hilton.com; 3000 Paradise Rd) Just east of the Strip, this hulking complex once hosted Elvis for 837 consecutive shows (a statue in the lobby commemorates the feat) and now attracts both suit-and-tied conventioneers and Trekkies, the latter for the thrill ride Star Trek: The Experience ($25).

Circus Circus (☎ 702-734-0410, 800-634-3450; www.circuscircus.com; 2880 Las Vegas Blvd S) One of the original casino-cum-theme parks, dating to 1968, Circus Circus has a variety of free circus acts in the tentlike interior. Under the 'Adventuredome' are a double-loop roller coaster and 15 other rides (adult/child day pass $20/14).

Treasure Island (☎ 702-894-7111, 800-944-7444; www.treasureisland.com; 3300 Las Vegas Blvd S) A swashbuckling sea battle in this casino's lagoon was a hit with kids for nearly a decade; today, the casino has rebranded itself as 'TI,' erasing much of its pirate theme. A new, sexier lagoon battle, dubbed the 'Sirens of TI,' was due to take its place – better scope it out first before bringing junior. Shows (free) take place nightly.

Mirage (☎ 702-791-7111, 800-627-6667; www.themirage.com; 3400 Las Vegas Blvd S) This casino was the first of the ridiculously theatrical flash palaces that today define modern Las Vegas. A fake volcano erupts every 15 minutes after dusk, with flames rising out of orange-colored water and a deep rumble threatening to break windows. **Siegfried & Roy** performed here for 13 years until a white tiger unexpectedly mauled Roy during a live performance, critically wounding him and bringing their iconic show to an indefinite halt. At press time, the Mirage had no alternate acts planned.

Venetian (☎ 702-414-1000, 888-283-6423; www.venetian.com; 3355 Las Vegas Blvd S) Opened in 1999 on land formerly occupied by the Sands, this massive property is beautifully appointed (it better be for costing $1.5 billion) and features numerous nods to its namesake city. Upstairs, shops line canals that are much cleaner than the Italian originals. Take a **gondola ride** (adult/child $13.50/8), or scope some serious artwork in the **Guggenheim Hermitage Museum** (adult/child $15/7; 🕑 9:30am-8:30pm).

Caesar's Palace (☎ 702-731-7110, 800-634-6001; www.parkplace.com/caesars/lasvegas; 3570 Las Vegas Blvd S) Founded by Vegas pioneer Bob Sarno (who also gave us Circus Circus), this plush hotel-casino dates back to 1966. Wander the Forum Shops past talking statues, and marvel at the painted sky that changes from dawn to dusk every three hours.

Bellagio (☎ 702-693-7111, 888-987-7111; www.bellagiolasvegas.com; 3600 Las Vegas Blvd S) The lake in front of this glam palace comes alive nightly every 15 minutes with more than 1000 water jets dancing to Pavarotti, Sinatra and (gulp) Lionel Richie. Inside is the **Bellagio Gallery of Fine Art** (adult/child $15/12; 🕑 9am-9pm), along with numerous upscale shops and restaurants.

Paris-Las Vegas (☎ 702-946-7000, 888-266-5687; www.parkplace.com/paris/lasvegas; 3655 Las Vegas Blvd S) Play the slots under the huge legs of a 50-story mock **Eiffel Tower** (adult/child $9/7; 🕑 10am-1am) or take a ride to the top. The interior is like a Parisian square and it feels surprisingly spacious and moody.

MGM Grand (☎ 702-891-7777, 800-929-1111; www.mgmgrand.com; 3799 Las Vegas Blvd S) With over 5000 rooms, this massive, green-striped hotel is the Strip's biggest. Inside are major concert venues and a **Lion Habitat** (admission free; 🕑 11am-10pm).

New York-New York (☎ 702-740-6969, 800-693-6763; www.nynyhotelcasino.com; 3790 Las Vegas Blvd S) The hotel's facade re-creates the Manhattan skyline, while inside are Park Ave shops, a Greenwich Village street scene with restaurants and false storefronts and a Coney Island midway. The **Manhattan Express roller coaster** (rides $12) is a major rush.

Excalibur (☎ 702-597-7777, 800-937-7777; www.excalibur.com; 3850 Las Vegas Blvd S) Opened in 1990, this huge property consists of a Disney-like medieval castle situated between two massive hotel towers that together boast some 4000 rooms. It's got a family-fun attitude and is popular with kids. For adults, however, unless the idea of a 24-hour Renaissance Faire is your little slice of heaven, you may want to steer clear.

Luxor (☎ 702-262-4000, 888-777-0188; www.luxor.com; 3900 Las Vegas Blvd S) The 30-story steel-and-glass pyramid has become a modern Vegas landmark since opening in 1993. A sphinx and obelisk sit out front and, at night, a beam of light points straight up from the pyramid's apex for apparently no reason other than because it can. At the pyramid's hollow center is the world's largest atrium, staggering in its vastness. Attractions here include an **Imax theater** (admission $9) and **King Tut's Museum** (admission $5).

Mandalay Bay (☎ 702-632-7777, 877-632-7000; 3950 Las Vegas Blvd S) This tropically themed resort offers an 11-acre garden complete with an artificial beach. There are also major concert venues and **Shark Reef** (adult/child $15/10) offering undersea sights and a 'touch tank' for those who dare.

Sights

Downtown is a covered pedestrian mall known as the **Fremont Street Experience**, a sound-and-light extravaganza that erupts hourly each evening (dusk to midnight). It was devised to inject new life into the area and while totally weird (not to mention loud), you can't help but stand captivated.

At the east end of the Experience is the **Neon Museum**, an outdoor exhibit showcasing vintage signs retrieved from leveled hotels. Some are also within **Neonopolis**, an adjacent shopping and entertainment complex. All are viewable 24 hours daily.

For those who are tired of pulling slot machines, a few museums are worth visiting. A Vegas favorite is the campy **Liberace Museum** (☎ 702-798-5595; 1775 E Tropicana Ave; 10am-5pm Mon-Sat, noon-4pm Sun; adult/student $12/8, child 5 & under free), complete with sequined capes, rhinestone jewelry, flashy cars and fabulous candelabra.

If the King's your thing, check out **Elvis-A-Rama** (☎ 702-309-7200; www.elvisarama.com; 3401 Industrial Rd; admission $10; 10am-6pm), which boasts a couple of thousand pieces of Elvis memorabilia.

The **Imperial Palace Auto Museum** (☎ 702-731-3311; www.autocollections.com; 3535 Las Vegas Blvd S; admission $7; 9:30am-9:30pm), at the Imperial Palace casino, has an excellent collection of some 350 exotic vehicles owned by the likes of Marilyn Monroe, Liberace and even Hitler. Free tickets are often handed out in front of the hotel or available on the museum's website.

Sleeping

If you're after a room in a Strip casino the best room deals are midweek, when doubles sometimes sink as low as $35 or $40. Prices are based on demand and they can fluctuate tremendously. Consider the prices listed here as loose guidelines, not gospel, and be sure to call ahead. Check casino websites for specials or try booking services such as the excellent, free **reservation line** (☎ 800-332-5333) at the Las Vegas Convention and Visitors Authority, which gives current prices at local casinos and hotels (name your price range and see what's available). You can stop in and use their phone (see p862) or call the service yourself.

Downtown casinos are generally cheaper than those on the Strip, though don't expect luxury. Las Vegas also has plenty of motels, where prices don't vary as drastically.

BUDGET

Sahara (☎ 702-737-2111, 800-634-6666; www.saharavegas.com; 2535 Las Vegas Blvd S; midweek/weekend r from $43/80; P) The last of the Strip casinos with a desert theme, this aging complex doesn't churn up a whole lot of excitement inside, but it does contain simple, comfortable rooms that are often among the city's better bargains. Rooms in the 'old' tower are slightly cheaper and just fine.

USA Hostels Las Vegas (☎ 702-385-1150, 800-550-8958; 1322 Fremont St; dm/s/d from $15/45/47; P) Though it's in an unsavory section of downtown, the facilities are clean and hospitable at this lively, party-friendly hostel and include a Jacuzzi, bar and 24-hour information desk. They also run regional tours and offer free pickup from the Greyhound station.

Other recommendations:

Circus Circus (☎ 702-734-0410, 800-634-3450; www.circuscircus.com; 2880 Las Vegas Blvd S; midweek/weekend r from $45/85; P)

La Concha (☎ 800-331-2431, 702-735-1255; 2955 Las Vegas Blvd S; fax 702-369-0862; midweek/weekend r $48/68; P) Classic 1950s-era motel unmistakable for its huge arched entryway.

Stardust (☎ 702-732-6111, 800-634-6757; www.stardustlv.com; 3000 Las Vegas Blvd S; midweek/weekend r from $49/75; P) Lowest rates may mean a room out back.

MID-RANGE

Monte Carlo (☎ 702-730-7000, 800-311-8999; www.montecarlo.com; 3770 Las Vegas Blvd S; midweek/weekend r from $69/$149; P) Though less overtly flashy than some of its fancy-pants Strip neighbors, the 3000 rooms here are nonetheless clean, solid and comfortable. Often a great value, too, as the price can drop during off-peak times. There's a nice spa inside (passes are sometimes 'comped,' so it's worth asking) and a wave pool.

Luxor (☎ 702-262-4000, 800-288-1000; www.luxor.com; 3900 Las Vegas Blvd S; midweek/weekend r from $69/199; P) The rooms inside this hulking black pyramid are lined around a massive atrium (vertigo sufferers beware), but save for the angled windows, they're fairly standard and only mildly reflect the casino's Egyptian theme. Further rooms are in a tower out the back. The spa is superb, so try to get passes.

Paris-Las Vegas (☎ 702-946-7000, 888-266-5687; fax 702-946-4405; www.parislasvegas.com; 3655 Las Vegas Blvd S; midweek/weekend r from $95/279; P) The elegantly appointed rooms are in a 34-story tower modeled after the famous Hotel de Ville. There are nearly 3000 rooms, each at least 450 sq ft. Room quality (and rates) rise as you climb the tower, and better views command higher prices.

Other recommendations:

Bally's (☎ 702-739-4111, 800-634-3434; www.ballyslv.com; 3645 Las Vegas Blvd S; midweek/weekend r from $89/220; P)

MGM Grand (☎ 702-891-1111, 800-929-1111; www.mgmgrand.com; 3799 Las Vegas Blvd S; midweek/weekend r from $89/139; P)

New York-New York (☎ 702-740-6969, 800-693-6763; www.nynyhotelcasino.com; 3790 Las Vegas Blvd; midweek/weekend r from $69/179; P)

TOP END

Many travelers now come to Las Vegas for the luxury, and hotels accommodate with spacious, finely appointed rooms. Properties listed here are the city's finest.

Venetian (☎ 702-414-1000, 877-857-1861; www.venetian.com; 3355 Las Vegas Blvd S; midweek/weekend r from $159/299; P) Every room is at least a 700-sq-ft suite in this Italian-flavored hotel, *the* place to head for those craving lots of space – the most of any 'standard' Vegas hotel room – and plenty of opulent appointments. With a recent expansion, there are now more than 4000 of these indulgent accommodations to choose from.

Bellagio (☎ 702-693-7111, 888-987-6667; www.bellagiolasvegas.com; 3600 Las Vegas Blvd S; midweek/weekend r from $159/259; P) The 510-sq-ft standard guest rooms include marble bathrooms, European furnishings and oversized closets. The spa is over-the-top luxury, too, of course.

A couple of other high-comfort zones are longtime veteran **Caesar's Palace** (☎ 800-634-6661, 702-731-7110; www.caesars.com; 3570 Las Vegas Blvd S; midweek/weekend r from $149/239; P) and relative newcomer **Mandalay Bay** (☎ 702-632-7777, 877-632-7000; www.mandalaybay.com; 3950 Las Vegas Blvd S; midweek/weekend r from $149/239; P), whose deluxe pool area includes an 11-acre beach.

Eating

Casinos have multiple restaurants ranging from 24-hour coffee shops to nationally renowned gourmet restaurants, the latter a recent Vegas trend. For dinner ideas, peruse the free *Las Vegas Weekly*, which has good opinionated reviews and listings. Other free publications like *Today in Las Vegas* and *What's On* also contain restaurant listings. Bargain hunters take note that most casinos advertise specially priced meals served in their various restaurants and cafés; keep your eyes on billboards and marquees, especially on the North Strip and downtown. For buffets, see 'Eating It All,' p866.

BUDGET & MID-RANGE

Monte Carlo Pub & Brewery (☎ 702-730-7777; 3770 Las Vegas Blvd S; meals from $10) Tucked inside the Monte Carlo is this spacious brewpub, serving typical but decently constructed pub sandwiches and pizzas alongside a half-dozen craft-brewed beers like the tasty Jackpot Ale.

Quark Bar & Restaurant (☎ 702-697-8725; 3000 Paradise Rd; meals from $10) *Star Trek* fans and other geek-pretenders need to head immediately to the Las Vegas Hilton, home to this surprisingly cool and moody eatery. Amid a futuristic setting you can indulge in 'Little Green Salads,' 'Hamborgers' and other 'exotic' dishes, perhaps with Klingons in a nearby booth.

Binion's Horseshoe Coffee Shop (☎ 702-382-1600; 128 E Fremont St; meals under $10) Found in the basement of Binion's Horseshoe, this 24-hour coffee shop serves typical diner meals, including a massive ham-and-egg breakfast special, the thick meat slab flopping off the edge of the plate.

Meskerem Ethiopian (☎ 702-732-4250; 252 Convention Center Dr; meals under $10) In the Somerset Shopping Center just east of the Strip, this small, pleasant spot serves Ethiopian meals in unassuming but relatively relaxed

EATING IT ALL

The all-you-can-eat buffet is a Las Vegas institution, where gluttonous gamblers pile plate after plate with wide and heavy loads of bulky food items. They aren't always the bargains they once were, but price shouldn't be a major consideration, as you definitely get what you pay for at the cheaper places. Traditionally, the food quality at these troughs has been substandard. However, a handful of hotels have recently classed-up the buffet concept, laying out spreads that are actually impressive. It's not Spago or Le Cirque, but at least the fish is fresh and the vegetables haven't been lingering under a heat lamp since daybreak. You may even find sushi, fresh pasta and assorted grilled meats. Expect prices of around $12 for breakfast, $15 for lunch and $25 for dinner. Weekend brunches are often served and weekend dinners sometimes feature special menus (and special prices). A good strategy, and value, is to hit the buffet for lunch. It's considerably cheaper than dinner, and since most casinos serve until 3pm or 4pm, all that shrimp, pork and pasta you just stuffed down your gullet will likely keep you full well past suppertime. Among the town's best buffets are those at **Bellagio**, **Paris** and **Rio** (renowned for its seafood buffet, served evenings only), along with the 'Sterling Brunch' every Sunday at **Bally's** (which costs a whopping $53 but is the spread of a lifetime).

surroundings. Some dishes are vegetarian, and they even serve breakfast, which includes Ethiopian-style egg dishes and espresso.

El Sombrero (☎ 702-382-9234; 807 S Main St; dinner from $9) For Mexican food, check out this unassuming restaurant, in business since 1951.

Yolie's Brazilian Steak House (☎ 702-794-0700; 3900 Paradise Rd; dinner $27) East of the Strip at Yolie's, out-of-towners pile in for the popular marinated steaks.

TOP END

Seemingly overnight, Las Vegas went from buffet capital to a magnet for top-end dining and celebrity chefs (Wolfgang Puck, Emeril Lagasse and Mark Miller are among those who've attached themselves to various Vegas eateries). The following hot spots are well worth your bucks, if you haven't already blown them at the craps table, and reservations are essential.

Renoir (☎ 702-791-7223; 3400 Las Vegas Blvd S; dinner $75) Though you're dining on haute New French cuisine in a room hung with original Renoirs, this elegant, romantic restaurant inside the Mirage is much more than an upmarket gimmick. The inventive dishes are among the city's finest.

Wild Sage Cafe (☎ 702-944-7243; 600 E Warm Springs Rd; dishes $12-27) This top-rated New American–cum-Californian south of the Strip area is, refreshingly, *not* found inside a casino and *doesn't* sport the gleaming face of a celebrity chef – though founders Stan Carroll and Laurie Kendrick are both veterans of Spago. The tasteful, low-key atmosphere and satisfying dishes make this a pleasant escape. The entire restaurant is nonsmoking.

Inside Bellagio, **Le Cirque** (☎ 702-693-8100; 3600 Las Vegas Blvd S; dinner $75) is a satellite of New York City's famed French restaurant; jacket required. Bellagio is also home to **Aqua** (☎ 702-693-8199; 3600 Las Vegas Blvd S; dishes $28-32), a branch of the highly regarded San Francisco seafood palace, and **Picasso** (☎ 702-693-7223; 3600 Las Vegas Blvd S; dinner from $80), featuring Julian Serrano's superb Spanish- and French-inspired cuisine and a collection of original Picassos.

Drinking

Most booze consumption in Vegas takes place while staring down slot machines and gaming tables. Sometimes, though, you just need to step away and take solace in what the country singer Dick Curless called a 'loser's cocktail.'

Houdini's Lounge (3770 Las Vegas Blvd S) Inside the Monte Carlo, next to the baccarat area, Houdini's offers a dark and comfy respite.

Lagoon Saloon (3400 Las Vegas Blvd S) Inside the Mirage, the Lagoon Saloon feels like the inside a terrarium.

Golden Gate (1 Fremont St) The old-fashioned bar at the Golden Gate is a good spot to watch the downtown gamblers get worked up.

Gordon Biersch Brewery (3987 Paradise Rd) The Vegas branch of a clean-cut microbrewery chain originating in Palo Alto, California, is found east of the Strip and offers good German-style lagers and live music.

Entertainment

Las Vegas has no shortage of entertainment on any given night, from major rock concerts to flashy, complex stage production. Lounge acts are often free, and can be kitschy fun or unbearable, depending on your attitude (or alcohol consumption). For tickets to many major concerts and sports events (including fights), contact **Ticketmaster** (☎ 702-474-4000).

Some of the town's hottest shows are quite expensive, and often sell out, so be prepared. Perpetually popular is **Cirque du Soleil's** aquatic show, **O** (☎ 702-796-9999, 888-488-7111; tickets $94-121), performed at the Bellagio. Cirque du Soleil also presents **Mystère** (☎ 702-796-9999, 800-392-1999; tickets $80) at Treasure Island (aka TI) and the new adult-themed **Zumanity** (☎ 866-606-7111; tickets $55-195) at New York-New York. Celine Dion stars in **A New Day...** (☎ 888-995-1555; tickets $83-200) at Caesar's.

Wayne Newton Theatre (☎ 702-617-5577, 888-217-9565; tickets $55) For a classic Vegas experience, stop by the Stardust's own theatre, where Mr Las Vegas himself performs regularly in all his glittery glory.

Rock concert venues include the **Events Center** (☎ 702-632-7580) and **House of Blues** (☎ 702-632-7600) at Mandalay Bay, the **Grand Garden Arena** (☎ 702-891-7777) at the MGM Grand, the **Joint** (☎ 702-693-5066; 4455 Paradise Rd) at the Hard Rock Hotel & Casino and **Rain in the Desert** (☎ 702-940-7246; 4321 W Flamingo Rd) at the Palms, west of the Strip.

Ra (☎ 702-262-4949; entry $10-20) Among the favorite dance clubs in Las Vegas is Ra, at the Luxor.

Ghost Bar (☎ 702-938-2666; $10-20) For a sky-high club experience, check out Ghost Bar, a space-age lounge on the 55th floor of the Palms.

Getting There & Around

McCarran International Airport (☎ 702-261-5743) is just south of the major Strip casinos and easily accessible from I-15. It has direct flights from most US cities and some from Canada and Europe. Shuttle service between the airport and the Strip is available from **Bell Trans** (☎ 702-739-7990; transfers $4.25) and **Gray Line** (☎ 702-384-1234; transfers $4). Downtown destinations are slightly higher.

The **Greyhound Station** (☎ 702-384-9561; 200 S Main St), downtown, has regular buses to and from Los Angeles ($37, six hours), San Diego ($47, eight hours) and San Francisco ($70, 15 hours). **Amtrak** (☎ 800-872-7245) does not run trains to Las Vegas, although they do offer connecting bus service from Los Angeles ($35, six hours).

Local bus service is provided by **Citizens Area Transport** (☎ 702-228-7433) for $1.25 to $2. Bus No 301 runs frequently 24 hours daily between the Strip and downtown, an excellent and easy transportation option.

The **Strip Trolley** (☎ 702-382-1404) does a loop from Mandalay Bay to the Stratosphere and out to the Las Vegas Hilton every 25 minutes until 2am. The fare costs $1.65.

Free **monorails** run between several Strip casinos. However, a more extensive system running from the MGM Grand to the Sahara (stopping at the convention center) is under construction and scheduled to open in 2004.

Dozens of agencies rent cars for competitive prices, including **Brooks** (☎ 702-735-3344) and **Dollar** (☎ 800-800-4000); the latter has windows in numerous Strip casinos. For further national car rental agencies, see p1121).

AROUND LAS VEGAS

Red Rock Canyon

The contrast between the artificial brightness of Las Vegas and the natural splendor of this dramatic **park** (☎ 702-363-1921; admission $5; ⏲ 8am-dusk), a 20-mile drive west of the Strip, couldn't be greater. The canyon is actually more like a valley, with the steep, rugged Red Rock escarpment rising 3000ft on its western edge. There's a 13-mile, one-way scenic loop with access to hiking trails and **camping** (campsites $10) 2 miles east of the visitors center.

Lake Mead & Hoover Dam

Lake Mead and Hoover Dam are the most-visited sites within the **Lake Mead National Recreation Area** (☎ 702-293-8907), which encompasses 110-mile-long Lake Mead, 67-mile-long Lake Mohave and many miles of desert around the lakes. The excellent **Alan Bible Visitors Center** (☎ 702-293-8990; ⏲ 8:30am-4:30pm), on Hwy 93 halfway between Boulder City and Hoover Dam, has information on recreation and natural history exhibits that are well done and interesting. From there, North Shore Rd winds north around the lake and makes a great scenic drive.

The graceful curve and art-deco style of the 726ft **Hoover Dam** contrasts superbly with the stark landscape. Originally called Boulder Dam, this New Deal project was completed in 1935 at a cost of $175 million. It's original intent was flood control, but it now helps supply Colorado River water (and hydroelectric power) to thirsty cities, including Las Vegas. Visitors are limited to surface tours (adult/child $10/4), and tickets are sold at the **visitors center** (☎ 702-294-3517; 9am-4:30pm). Note that commercial trucks and buses are not allowed to cross the dam.

Valley of Fire State Park

Near the north end of Lake Mead NRA, easily accessible from Las Vegas, Valley of Fire is a masterpiece of desert scenery, with psychedelically shaped sandstone. Hwy 169 runs through the **park** (admission $5), right past the **visitors center** (☎ 702-397-2088; 8:30am-4:30pm), which has hiking information and excellent desert-life exhibits. The winding side road to **White Domes** is especially scenic. The valley is at its most fiery at dawn and dusk, so consider staying overnight in one of the park's two year-round **campgrounds** (campsites $8).

Laughlin

Just south of Hoover Dam on Hwy 163, close to the California–Arizona–Nevada border, Laughlin is a resort town consisting pretty much entirely of a string of hulking casinos lining the west bank of the Colorado River – a strange sight indeed. Its sister city, across the river in Arizona, is utilitarian **Bullhead City**, established as the bedroom community for Davis Dam workers. One reason Laughlin has become so popular is that it boasts some of the cheapest hotel rates in the West – and while fairly straightforward rooms, these are no fleabags. Try the **Flamingo Laughlin** (☎ 702-298-5111; r from $22;) or the **Colorado Belle** (☎ 702-298-4000; www.coloradobelle.com; r from $25;), the latter shaped like a riverboat. Note that, as in Vegas, rates can fluctuate greatly.

WESTERN NEVADA

The western corner of the state is where modern Nevada got its start. It was the site of the state's first trading post, first farms and the famous Comstock silver lode in and around Virginia City, which spawned towns, financed the Union side in the Civil War and earned Nevada its statehood. For information about the Nevada side of Lake Tahoe, see p967.

Reno

Reno is a long way from Las Vegas. Not just in distance (445 miles) and climate (temperatures are consistently below those of Vegas), but in overall spirit. Both cities are home to 24-hour casinos, high-rise hotel towers, a huge service industry and many thousands of visitors with dreams of a debt-free lifestyle. But unlike Las Vegas, which is defined more by its fake cityscapes, blue-collar Reno feels more gritty and 'real.' Lately, the city has been trying to upgrade its image with a handful of flashier casinos and an impressive new art museum. Reno repeatedly reminds you that it's 'The Biggest Little City in the World' – most notably on the famous arch over N Virginia St – and as hokey as that slogan will always be, there's something refreshing about it, too.

In the 1850s, travelers on the Humboldt Trail to California needed to cross the Truckee River. Toll bridges, hotels and saloons soon sprang up, followed by a railroad depot that helped Reno cash in on the mining boom. When the mines played out, Reno made an economic virtue of gambling and prostitution, which were suppressed enterprises in increasingly respectable California. Agriculture, light industry and tourism have since helped diversify the economy.

ORIENTATION & INFORMATION

Reno's downtown is north of the Truckee River and south of I-80. Most of the action is along Virginia St, between 1st and 6th Sts. You'll also find a **visitors center** (☎ 775-827-7600, 800-443-1482; www.renolaketahoe.com; 300 N Center St; 8am-5pm Mon-Fri).

CASINOS

Few casinos have the flash of Vegas, though some do try. The attention-grabbing **Silver Legacy** (☎ 775-329-4777; 407 N Virginia St) shows off with a 19th-century streetscape plus sound-and-light shows inside a 120ft dome. One of the city's newest, and nicest, casinos is the **Siena** (☎ 775-337-6260; 1 S Lake St), just south of the Truckee River, which has Tuscan styling and a more subdued atmosphere. Veteran downtown establishments include

Fitzgeralds (☎ 800-535-5825; 255 N Virginia St), with its silly and outdated 'lucky leprachaun' theme, the nearby **Eldorado** (☎ 775-786-5700; 345 N Virginia St) and **Club Cal Neva** (☎ 877-777-7303; cnr 2nd & N Virginia Sts), which opened in 1962.

Away from downtown are the flashy **Peppermill** (☎ 775-826-2121; 2707 S Virginia St); the huge **Reno Hilton** (☎ 775-789-2000; 2500 E 2nd St), east of downtown near Hwy 395; and **John Ascuaga's Nugget** (☎ 775-356-3300; 1100 Nugget Ave), off I-80 in nearby Sparks.

SIGHTS

You'll find a mix of contemporary art and historical exhibitions at the **Nevada Museum of Art** (☎ 775-329-3333; 160 W Liberty St; adult/students $7/5; 11am-6pm Tue-Sun, until 8pm Thu), founded in 1931. The museum moved into a new building in 2003, an eye-catching black structure allegedly inspired by the Black Rock Desert that takes Reno architecture (and local art exhibition) to new, intriguing levels.

The **National Automobile Museum** (☎ 775-333-9300; 10 Lake St; adult/child $8/3; 9:30am-5:30pm Mon-Sat, 10am-4pm Sun) is an impressive collection of one-of-a-kind vehicles, including James Dean's 1949 Mercury and a 1938 Phantom Corsair. The state's oldest museum is the **Nevada Historical Society Museum** (☎ 775-688-1190; 1650 N Virginia St; adult/child $2/free; 10am-5pm Mon-Sat), on the University of Nevada campus, which has a good account of the region's indigenous cultures.

Reno's **National Bowling Stadium** (☎ 775-334-2695; 300 N Center St; admission free; 6am-2:30am) has a mind-boggling 78 lanes and a 450ft scoreboard – a sight you can take in from a spectator stage.

SLEEPING

The casinos are cheapest Sunday through Thursday, with doubles beginning around $30. Weekends, especially Saturday and during special events, can be much higher, and hotels do sell out, so phone ahead. Reno has many motels, too, and they're often much more affordable during weekends.

Siena (☎ 775-337-6260; 1 S Lake St; www.sienareno.com; midweek/weekend r from $59/99; P) Reno's newest hotel is also one of its most luxurious, with cozy, nicely appointed rooms. Midweek prices can be surprisingly affordable, too, making it one of Reno's best bargains.

Silver Legacy (☎ 775-329-4777; 407 N Virginia St; www.silverlegacyreno.com; midweek/weekend r from $59/109; P) Situated directly in the center of downtown, this large hotel-casino is newer than some of Reno's casinos, and the Victorian-themed rooms, while basic, are very clean and comfortable. If you like a view, ask for a room high in the tower facing the mountains.

Sundowner (☎ 775-786-7050, 800-648-5490; 450 N Arlington St; www.sundowner-casino.com; midweek/weekend r from $35/70; P) This aging tower west of Virginia St is consistently one of Reno's cheapest hotel options. Rooms are adequate but hardly exciting.

Seasons Inn (☎ 775-322-6000, 800-322-8588; www.seasonsinn.com; 495 West St; midweek/weekend r from $42/99; P) This reliable motel has clean, fairly quiet rooms close to the casino action.

EATING

Most casinos have all-you-can-eat buffets, but keep in mind they're less about high-quality items and more about stuffing your face. Keep your eyes out for dining deals in the casino coffee shops and restaurants, too. Steak dinners can run under $10, and if cheap's what you want, the Top Deck coffee shop in the **Cal Neva** (☎ 877-777-7303; cnr 2nd & N Virginia Sts; meals from $1) offers a 99¢ breakfast.

Lexie's (☎ 775-337-6260; dishes $10-20) Elegant Lexie's, inside the Siena, faces the Truckee River and offers gourmet beef, seafood and other dishes with Italian overtones; they also have a huge selection of wines, and the downstairs wine bar, **Enoteca**, frequently hosts special wine dinners. Reservations recommended.

Brew Brothers (☎ 775-786-5700; 345 N Virginia St; dishes $6-12) In the Eldorado, this slightly hipper-than-average casino eatery serves good pizzas and several truly tasty microbrews. The place gets packed and loud, though, when the nightly bands kick in.

Deux Gros Nez (☎ 775-786-9400; 249 California Ave; dishes $4-7) For healthier fare, abandon the casinos for the quirky Deux Gros Nez, found upstairs behind the Cheese Board; in business since 1985, it's a cycling-oriented café that serves strong coffee, excellent smoothies, sandwiches, breakfast egg dishes and vegetarian pasta dinners.

Louis' Basque Corner (☎ 775-323-7203; 301 E 4th St; dinner $18) You can taste Nevada's Basque culture at this very long-standing, popular restaurant. The six-course meal includes wine as well as dessert, and it'll definitely fill you up.

GETTING THERE & AROUND

Reno-Tahoe International Airport (☎ 775-328-6870) is a few miles southeast of downtown. **Greyhound** (☎ 775-322-8801; 155 Stevenson St) has frequent buses to San Francisco ($33, six hours) and Los Angeles ($62, 12 hours), and one daily to Las Vegas ($72, 10 hours). **Amtrak** (☎ 775-329-8638, 800-872-7245; 135 E Commercial Row) has daily service to Sacramento ($65, five hours) and Oakland ($71, 9½ hours).

Many hotels offer free shuttles to and from the airport. Local bus system **Citifare** (☎ 775-348-7433; adult/child $1.50/1.25) covers the metropolitan area; the main transfer station is at E 4th and Center Sts.

Pyramid Lake

Beautiful blue Pyramid Lake is 25 miles north of Reno on the Paiute Indian Reservation – a stunning sight in the otherwise barren landscape. Permits for **camping** ($9 per night) and **fishing** ($7 per person) are available at the **ranger station** (☎ 775-476-1155; 8am-6pm Mon-Wed, 7am-5pm Thu-Sun), on Hwy 446 in Sutcliffe. The shores are lined with beaches, and there are also interesting tufa formations (a porous rock formed by water deposits). Anaho Island, near the eastern shore, is a bird sanctuary for the American white pelican.

Carson City

Nevada's state capital is a small but fast-growing town, with pleasant tree-lined streets and some handsome old buildings downtown. It was named after the Carson River, which itself was named after frontiersman Kit Carson. The casinos are small, but there are a couple of worthwhile historical museums. Far quieter than Reno, Carson is also a great base from which to explore nearby mountains and deserts.

Hwy 395 (Carson St) is the main drag. The **visitors center** (☎ 775-882-1565; www.carsoncitychamber.com; 1900 S Carson St; 8am-5pm Mon-Fri), a mile south of downtown, gives out a local map with interesting historical walking and driving tours. For hiking and camping information, stop by the USFS's **Carson Ranger District Office** (☎ 775-882-2766; 1536 S Carson St; 8am-4:30pm Mon-Fri).

The **Nevada State Capitol** (101 N Carson St), downtown, was completed in 1871 with local sandstone from a prison-run quarry. There's an interesting free **museum** on the 2nd floor. Housed inside the 1869 US Mint building, the excellent **Nevada State Museum** (☎ 775-687-4810; 600 N Carson St; adult/child $3/free; 8:30am-4:30pm) has dioramas showing Indian life and, in the basement, a re-created gold mine.

On downtown's northern fringe, you can't miss the neon cowboy outside the **Frontier Motel** (☎ 775-882-1377; 1718 N Carson St; r from $35; P), a classic roadside spot with clean, basic rooms. Just south of downtown is the pleasant, nicely maintained **Desert Hills Motel** (☎ 775-882-1932, 800-652-7785; www.deserthillsmotel.com; 1010 S Carson St; weekday/weekend r from $55/69; P).

Carson Nugget (☎ 775-882-1626; 507 N Carson St; dishes $5-15) Hungry bargain hunters will enjoy the prime rib and other discounted dinners at the Carson Nugget.

Greyhound (☎ 775-882-3375; 1718 N Carson St) buses stop at the Frontier Motel on the way to and from Reno ($12, one hour) and Las Vegas ($72, nine hours).

Virginia City

As early as the 1860s, this mining boomtown had gas lines, a sewer system, the West Coast's first elevator and a population of 15,000 (including newspaperman Samuel Clemens, alias Mark Twain). A mining technique developed here, square-set timbering, kept the 750 miles of tunnels from collapsing. The population peaked at 30,000 in 1875, when a fire swept through and destroyed more than 2000 buildings. Virginia City (named after miner James 'Old Virginny' Finney) was miraculously rebuilt within a year, but it never again achieved its former rough-and-tumble glory.

Today the town is a National Historic Landmark, with a main street of Victorian buildings, wooden sidewalks and some hokey but fun 'museums.' The main drag is C St, with the **visitors center** (☎ 775-847-0311; 86 S C St; 9am-5pm Mon-Fri) in the historic Crystal Bar.

Many of the town's attractions are seriously silly, though some are true gems, such as the **Fourth Ward School** (☎ 775-847-0975; 537 C St; adult/child $2/1; 10am-4:30pm), a monumental four-story building that once housed 1025 students. The quirky **Way It Was Museum**

(☎ 775-847-0766; 113 N C St; admission $3; ⏰ 10am-6pm) is a fun, old-fashioned place offering good background information on mining the lode; same goes for the half-hour tour of the **Chollar Mine** (☎ 775-847-0155; adult/child $5/2; ⏰ noon-5pm summer), at the south end of F St (hours vary, call to confirm). To see how the mining elite lived, stop by the **Mackay Mansion** (D St) and the **Castle** (B St). Dozens of played-out miners are buried at the picturesque **Silver Terrace Cemetery**, off Carson St.

While not as cheap, Virginia City is a more peaceful and pleasant place to spend the night than Carson City or Reno.

Gold Hill Hotel (☎ 775-847-0111; www.goldhillhotel.net; weekdays/weekend r from $75/130; ❄) This great choice is a mile south of town on Hwy 342, which has restored original rooms in what they claim is the state's oldest hotel.

Mandarin Garden (☎ 775-847-9288; 30 B St; dishes $4-8) For dinner, noodle and rice plates as affordable as they are delicious, try Mandarin Garden; the restaurant is vegetarian friendly.

If you're thirsty, C St offers a number of creaky but cool taverns. Psychedelic-rock pioneers the Charlatans were the house band in 1965 at the crusty **Red Dog Saloon**; the **Delta Saloon** is where you can literally 'read the walls,' which are covered with articles and photographs.

NEVADA GREAT BASIN

Much of Nevada is 'basin and range' country, its landscape almost entirely textured with range after range of mountains and arid valleys. Outside the major cities, the land is largely empty, save the occasional grazing cow or buzzing military jet. The highways, though, are dotted with fascinating historic towns, quirky diversions and quite a bit of gorgeous desert scenery. For adventurous types, cool detours lead to some deeply remote territory.

Along I-80

This is the old fur trappers' route, which followed the Humboldt River from northeast Nevada to Lovelock, near Reno. The same route was used by the early Emigrant Trail and the Central Pacific Railroad.

Heading east from Reno, **Lovelock** has motels, but most people press on to **Winnemucca**, which has a vintage downtown, shops and numerous motels and restaurants. Some 50 miles north, the Santa Rosa Mountains offer rugged scenery and ghost towns. For information, stop by the **Chamber of Commerce** (☎ 775-623-2225; 30 W Winnemucca Blvd), which sells books on the local area, or the USFS **Santa Rosa Ranger Station** (☎ 775-623-5025; 1200 E Winnemucca Blvd; ⏰ 8:30am-4:30pm Mon-Fri).

Southwest of Winnemucca is the folk-art sculpture garden **Thunder Mountain**, directly off I-80 in Imlay. Built by WWII veteran Chief Rolling Mountain Thunder as a monument to the injustices against Native Americans, it's full of curious figures, buildings and other structures that are in fragile condition but currently being restored. Self-guided tours are available anytime.

The culture of the cowboy and the American West is most diligently cultivated in **Elko**. There, all aspiring cowboys and cowgirls need to check out the **Western Folklife Center** (☎ 775-738-7508; 501 Railroad St; admission free; ⏰ 9pm-5pm Mon-Fri), which offers art and history exhibits and also hosts the popular **Cowboy Poetry Gathering** each January. At the town center, **Stockmen's Casino & Hotel** (☎ 800-648-2345; www.fh-inc.com; 340 Commercial St; r $40; ❄ 🅿) is a fine place to stay, with clean, remodeled rooms.

For information about the Elko backcountry, visit the **USFS Office** (☎ 775-738-5171; 2035 Last Chance Rd; ⏰ 7:30am-4:30pm Mon-Fri). North of Elko are old mining towns like **Jarbridge** and **Tuscarora**. To the south, the **Ruby Mountains** are a superbly rugged range. The picture-perfect village of **Lamoille** has food and lodging and one of the most-photographed rural churches in the USA.

Along Hwy 50

'The loneliest road in America' crosses picturesque Great Basin terrain – desert mountains and wide, see-for-miles valleys – and towns are few. Once part of the Lincoln Hwy, lonesome Hwy 50 follows the route of the Overland Stagecoach, the Pony Express and the first transcontinental telegraph line. It's a wonderful desert drive.

Fallon is an agricultural and military town, home to a naval air base where top gunners streak through the skies. Fallon also has grocery stores, restaurants and a few good motels, such as the **Lariat** (☎ 775-423-3181; 850 W Williams St; r $44; ❄ 🅿). Three miles west on Hwy 50 is **Bob's Root Beer** (4150 Reno Hwy; ⏰ closed winter), a vintage drive-in with tasty root-beer floats ($2 to $5).

Heading east, the next substantial town is **Austin**, rundown since its 1880s heyday but still interesting. The mountainous area around it is beautiful, too, and Austin's **USFS office** (☎ 775-964-2671; 100 Midas Rd; 8am-4:30pm Mon-Fri), just off Hwy 50, can recommend good hiking and driving loops. **Mountain biking** is also popular, and the friendly shop **Tyrannosaurus-Rex** (☎ 775-964-1212; 270 Maine St), just east of town, has maps, frozen yogurt and bikes for rent (from about $25 a day).

To the southwest of Austin, the **Berlin-Ichthyosaur State Park** (☎ 775-964-2440, 702-867-3001; admission $3) features the ghost town of Berlin and the fossil remains of half a dozen ichthyosaurs (carnivorous marine reptiles that lived here 225 million years ago). Daily fossil tours are offered in summer (adult/child $2/1), and there's a good year-round **campground** (campsites $11).

During the late 19th century, $40 million worth of silver was extracted from the hills near **Eureka**. The town is now fairly well preserved, possessing a handsome courthouse, the interesting **Eureka Sentinal Museum** (☎ 775-237-5010; 10 N Monroe St; admission free; 10am-6pm), a beautifully restored 1880 opera house and a few well-kept motels.

Larger **Ely**, another silver- and copper-mining town, had its own railroad; today the **Nevada Northern Railway Museum** (☎ 775-289-2085; 1100 Ave A; admission $3; closed winter) includes the old station, depot and workshops. Downtown also has beautiful historic murals and great old neon signs, along with some decent motels.

Near the Nevada–Utah border is the awesome, uncrowded **Great Basin National Park**. It encompasses 13,063ft Wheeler Peak, rising abruptly from the desert. Hiking trails near the summit take in superb country with glacial lakes, ancient bristlecone pines and even a permanent ice field. Admission is free; the park **visitors center** (☎ 775-234-7331) arranges guided tours of **Lehman Caves** (admission $2-8), which are richly decorated with rare limestone formations. There are four developed **campgrounds** (campsites $10) within the park, and one is open year-round.

Nearby **Baker** has a couple motels and restaurants.

Along Hwy 95

Hwy 95 goes roughly north–south through the western part of the state via Winnemucca, Hawthorne, Tonopah and Goldfield. The southern section of Hwy 95 is starkly scenic as it passes the Nevada Test Site (where more than 720 nuclear weapons were exploded in the 1950s). Side roads head west to California and Death Valley. In Beatty, the gracious **HI Happy Burro Hostel** (☎ 775-553-9130; happyburro@pcweb.net; dm/d $18/35; P 💻) is a real gem, located inside a beautiful refurbished antique motel.

Along Hwys 375 & 93

Hwy 375, dubbed the 'Extraterrestrial Hwy,' intersects Hwy 93 near top-secret **Area 51**, part of Nellis Air Force Base and a supposed holding area for captured UFOs. In the tiny town of **Rachel**, on Hwy 375, **Little A'Le'Inn** (☎ 775-729-2515; www.aleinn.com; r $42) accommodates earthlings and aliens alike, sells extraterrestrial souvenirs and has a fun website.

Continuing east, Hwy 93 passes through a gorgeous Joshua-tree grove before arriving in **Caliente**, a former railroad town with a mission-style 1923 depot. Area attractions include the Rainbow Canyon scenic drive and nearby **Cathedral Gorge State Park**, with campsites amid badlands-style cliffs. Two dozen miles north is **Pioche**, an attractive hillside mining town overlooking beautiful Lake Valley.

California

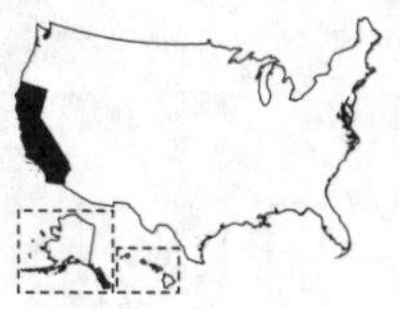

CONTENTS

'Go west, young man.'

What is California if not the American Dream incarnate? Since the 1850s, many millions have followed newspaperman Horace Greeley's advice and found, if not their dreams manifest, then at least a place that was fertile and free enough to realize them. Internet gurus, religious cults, counterculture hippies, surf gods and goddesses, radical environmentalists, stock market kingpins, world-class winemakers, defense industry behemoths, biotech wizards: the state is large enough and crazy enough to embrace them all.

California is a country all to itself. It is the nation's most populous state and its most diverse; over a quarter of residents are foreign-born (9.1 million), which is nearly a third of the nation's immigrants. California's economy (a $1.34 trillion GDP in 2001) would rank sixth in the world if it were a nation, and it has the largest agricultural output of any state. It is the home of Hollywood – the epicenter and arbiter of American pop culture – and a bottomless well of invention, spawning everything from Mickey Mouse to the personal computer.

Nevertheless, for the traveler, all that might mean little if it weren't also a land of unparalleled natural beauty. The Pacific coast, the nonnegotiable edge of westward migration, is by turns dramatically rugged and soporifically mild, bordered by an ocean of magnificent diversity. The state has ancient forests to dwarf your imagination, granite mountains and brutal, awesome deserts.

HIGHLIGHTS

- Imbibing **Los Angeles**: the hype, the horror, the hip and Hollywood (p879)
- Surviving the dizzying, dazzling original 'house of mouse': **Disneyland** (p903)
- Walking the **Golden Gate Bridge**, spectacular symbol of stylish San Francisco (p940)
- Being one of the million raucous celebrants in San Francisco's **Gay Pride Parade** (p944)
- Contemplating the **coast redwoods**, the moody, towering elders of our world (p961)
- Raising a glass to sun, food, wine and art in **Wine Country** (p955)
- Skiing the snow-clad mountains near the sapphire jewel of **Lake Tahoe** (p967)
- Hiking among **Joshua Tree National Park's** twisted trees, capricious cacti and rugged rocks (p917)
- Tackling the granite walls and waterfalls of the majestic and sublime **Yosemite National Park** (p969)
- Seeking desert solitude in the salt flats and sand dunes of **Death Valley National Park** (p919)

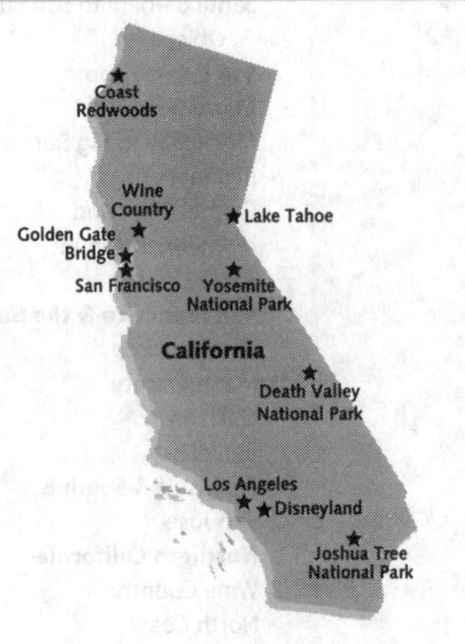

HISTORY

By the time the first European explorers arrived in the 16th century, California was home to about 300,000 indigenous people, with more than 20 language groups and 100 dialects. Conflict between the groups was almost nonexistent, and they had no class of warriors and no tradition of warfare.

The Spanish, who conquered Mexico back in the early 1500s, explored California through the 1540s in search of a fabled 'city of gold,' then, when they didn't find it, left the territory virtually alone. It wasn't until the Mission Period, from 1769 to 1810, that Spain made a serious attempt to settle the land, establishing 21 Catholic missions, to convert the natives, and several military forts (presidios) to protect the territory from British and Russian interests.

Mexico won independence from Spain in 1821, but its rule over California was short-lived. The young United States of America, filled with dreams of Manifest Destiny, defeated Mexico during the 1846–47 Mexican-American War; with the signing of the 1848 Treaty of Guadalupe Hidalgo, the USA took possession of California, New Mexico and Arizona. By coincidence, gold was discovered in northern California only days later. With the gold rush drawing people from all over the country and the world, the state population exploded from 14,000 to 90,000 by the end of 1849. Wealth and lawlessness combined most famously in San Francisco, a hotbed of gambling, prostitution and chicanery. In 1850, California gained admittance to the USA as a non-slave state.

In the mid-19th century, the effort to build the transcontinental railroad (whose eastern terminus was Sacramento) led to the arrival of some 15,000 Chinese laborers, who would then suffer under a wave of anti-Chinese legislation once the railroad was completed in 1869.

Despite the bad omen of the 1906 San Francisco earthquake, which destroyed most of the city, the 20th century resulted in California growing exponentially in size, diversity and importance. From 1910 to 1960, the population steadily rose from 2.3 to 15.8 million people. Mexican immigrants arrived during the 1910–21 Mexican Revolution and again during WWII to fill labor shortages. During WWII, important new industries developed, and some anti-Asian sentiments resurfaced, leading to widespread internment of Japanese Americans. African-Americans arrived during the postwar boom.

CALIFORNIA FACTS

Nicknames Golden State, Bear Flag Republic
Population 35,116,000 (1st)
Area 155,959 sq miles (3rd)
Admitted to Union September 9, 1850 (31st)
Capital city Sacramento (population 433,400)
Other cities Los Angeles (3,864,400), San Diego (1,275,100), San Jose (925,000), San Francisco (791,600)
Birthplace of writer John Steinbeck (1902–68), photographer Ansel Adams (1902–84), chef Julia Child (1912–), actress Marilyn Monroe (1926–62), president Richard Nixon (1913–94)
Famous for Disneyland, protests and earthquakes, Hollywood, hippie tree-huggers, Silicon Valley, surfing

This confluence of wealth, size, heavy immigration and lack of tradition is probably why California remains at the forefront of social trends. Since the 1930s, the Hollywood film industry has mesmerized the nation (and the world) with its dreams and fashions, while San Francisco has reacted against the banal complacency of post-WWII suburbia. The 1950s literary Beat movement began there, as did the hippie counterculture of the 1960s, and then the Gay Pride movement of the 1970s and 1980s. The Internet revolution, driven by the high-tech giants in Silicon Valley, rewired the country and led to a 1990s gold rush in overspeculated stocks.

The stock bubble burst at the turn of the 21st century, and the good times are over. Unprecedented state deficits have rolled back incomes and jobs. And in 2003, Californians acted on their growing displeasure in stunning fashion: they voted to recall their elected governor, Gray Davis, in the middle of his second term and to replace him with actor-turned-politician Arnold Schwarzenegger. And that's California, nutshell and all: revolutionary one minute, certifiably loony the next, and only a fool would try to tell the difference until the final credits roll.

GEOGRAPHY & CLIMATE

The main geographical regions of California are the Coastal Range (Ventura to Crescent

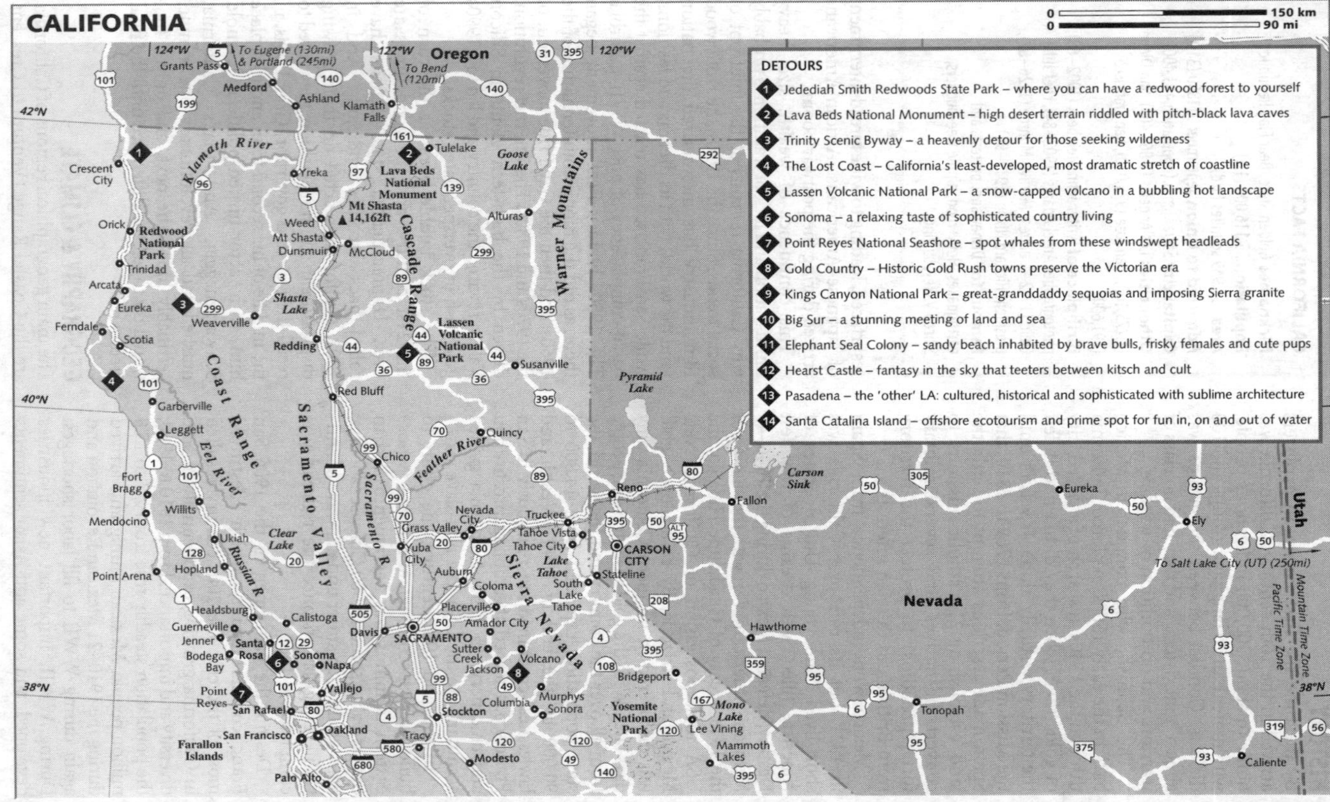
CALIFORNIA
0 150 km
0 90 mi
DETOURS
1 Jedediah Smith Redwoods State Park – where you can have a redwood forest to yourself
2 Lava Beds National Monument – high desert terrain riddled with pitch-black lava caves
3 Trinity Scenic Byway – a heavenly detour for those seeking wilderness
4 The Lost Coast – California's least-developed, most dramatic stretch of coastline
5 Lassen Volcanic National Park – a snow-capped volcano in a bubbling hot landscape
6 Sonoma – a relaxing taste of sophisticated country living
7 Point Reyes National Seashore – spot whales from these windswept headleads
8 Gold Country – Historic Gold Rush towns preserve the Victorian era
9 Kings Canyon National Park – great-granddaddy sequoias and imposing Sierra granite
10 Big Sur – a stunning meeting of land and sea
11 Elephant Seal Colony – sandy beach inhabited by brave bulls, frisky females and cute pups
12 Hearst Castle – fantasy in the sky that teeters between kitsch and cult
13 Pasadena – the 'other' LA: cultured, historical and sophisticated with sublime architecture
14 Santa Catalina Island – offshore ecotourism and prime spot for fun in, on and out of water
124°W
122°W
120°W
42°N
40°N
38°N
Oregon
Nevada
Utah
To Eugene (130mi) & Portland (245mi)
To Bend (120mi)
To Salt Lake City (UT) (250mi)
Mountain Time Zone
Pacific Time Zone
Grants Pass
Medford
Ashland
Klamath Falls
Crescent City
Klamath River
Yreka
Tulelake
Lava Beds National Monument
Mt Shasta 14,162ft
Goose Lake
Warner Mountains
Orick
Redwood National Park
Trinidad
Arcata
Eureka
Ferndale
Scotia
Weaverville
Weed
Mt Shasta
Dunsmuir
McCloud
Cascade Range
Alturas
Shasta Lake
Redding
Lassen Volcanic National Park
Susanville
Red Bluff
Coast Range
Sacramento Valley
Garberville
Leggett
Eel River
Fort Bragg
Willits
Mendocino
Ukiah
Russian R
Clear Lake
Hopland
Point Arena
Healdsburg
Calistoga
Guerneville
Jenner
Santa Rosa
Bodega Bay
Sonoma
Napa
Point Reyes
San Rafael
Vallejo
San Francisco
Oakland
Farallon Islands
Palo Alto
Chico
Feather River
Quincy
Sacramento R
Yuba City
Grass Valley
Nevada City
Auburn
Coloma
Placerville
Amador City
Sutter Creek
Jackson
Volcano
Davis
SACRAMENTO
Stockton
Tracy
Modesto
Columbia
Sonora
Murphys
Sierra Nevada
Truckee
Tahoe Vista
Tahoe City
Lake Tahoe
South Lake Tahoe
Stateline
CARSON CITY
Reno
Pyramid Lake
Bridgeport
Yosemite National Park
Mono Lake
Lee Vining
Mammoth Lakes
Fallon
Carson Sink
Hawthorne
Tonopah
Eureka
Ely
Caliente

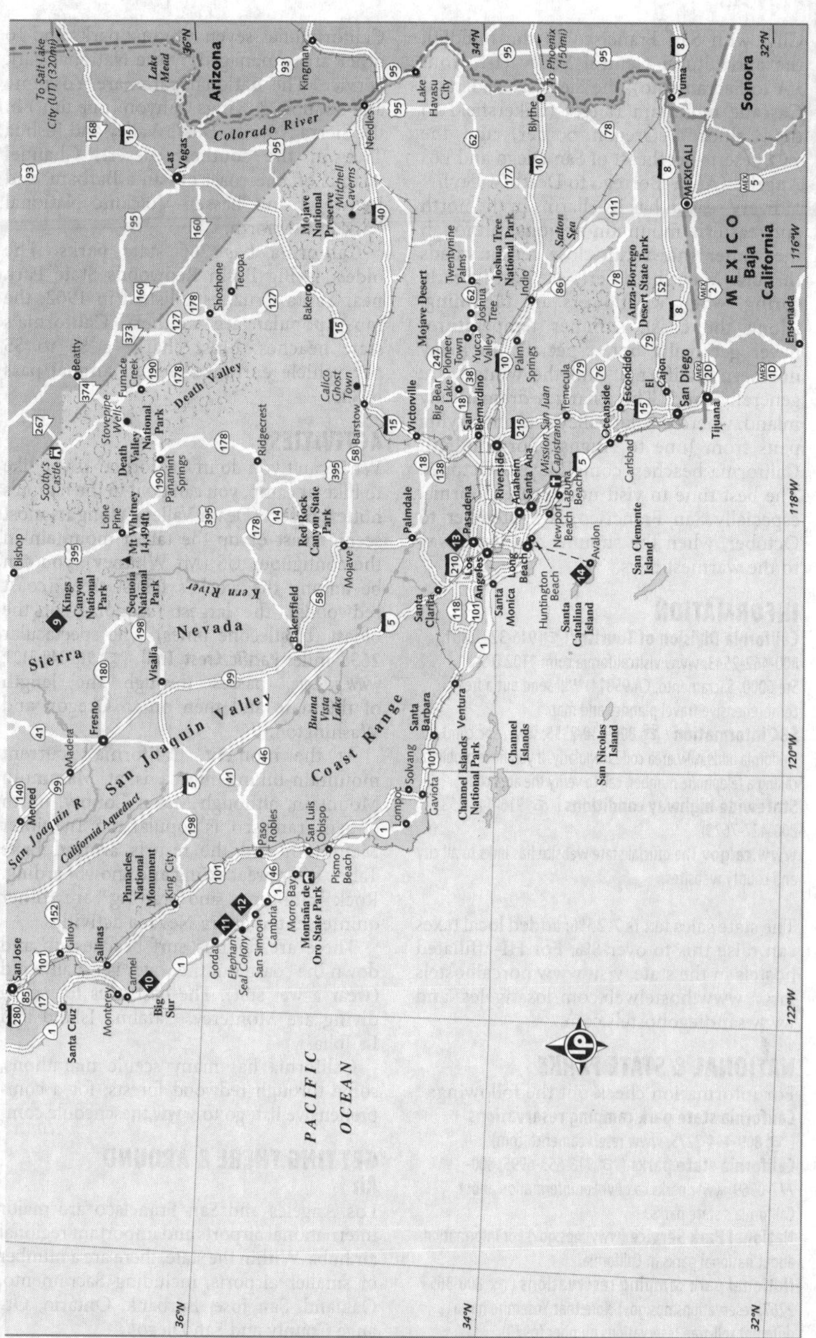
To Salt Lake City (UT) (320mi)
Lake Mead
Arizona
36°N
Kingman
Colorado River
Las Vegas
Lake Havasu City
Needles
34°N
To Phoenix (150mi)
Blythe
Yuma
Sonora
32°N
MEXICALI
MEXICO
Baja California
116°W
Ensenada
Mojave National Preserve
Mitchell Caverns
Shoshone
Tecopa
Baker
Twentynine Palms
Joshua Tree National Park
Salton Sea
Anza-Borrego Desert State Park
Mojave Desert
Beatty
Furnace Creek
Death Valley
Calico Ghost Town
Big Bear Lake
Pioneer Town
Yucca Valley
Joshua Tree
Indio
Palm Springs
Victorville
Barstow
San Bernardino
Temecula
Escondido
El Cajon
San Diego
Tijuana
Oceanside
Carlsbad
Mission San Juan Capistrano
Scotty's Castle
Stovepipe Wells
Death Valley National Park
Ridgecrest
Panamint Springs
Riverside
Anaheim
Santa Ana
Newport Beach
Laguna Beach
Bishop
Lone Pine
Mt Whitney 14,494ft
Red Rock Canyon State Park
Palmdale
Pasadena
Los Angeles
Long Beach
Huntington Beach
Avalon
San Clemente Island
Santa Monica
118°W
Kings Canyon National Park
Sequoia National Park
Kern River
Mojave
Bakersfield
Santa Clarita
Santa Catalina Island
Sierra Nevada
Visalia
Ventura
Channel Islands
San Nicolas Island
Fresno
San Joaquin Valley
Buena Vista Lake
Santa Barbara
Coast Range
Madera
Solvang
Gaviota
Channel Islands National Park
120°W
Merced
San Joaquin R
California Aqueduct
Lompoc
Paso Robles
San Luis Obispo
Pismo Beach
Morro Bay
Montaña de Oro State Park
Cambria
San Simeon
Pinnacles National Monument
King City
Elephant Seal Colony
Gorda
Salinas
Gilroy
San Jose
Carmel
Monterey
Big Sur
Santa Cruz
122°W
PACIFIC OCEAN

City, with San Francisco in the middle), the agricultural Central Valley (I-5 from LA to Sacramento), the Sierra Nevada and Cascade mountain ranges (Bakersfield to the California–Oregon border) and the vast deserts northeast of San Diego and Los Angeles (Anza–Borrego to Death Valley).

Every season has its charms in the north and eastern mountain regions, although the winter snows can close certain roads through May; the deserts are best in early spring, when wildflowers are blooming. Along the coast, summer temperatures never get really hot, especially in foggy northern California, and the winters are generally mild. This changes dramatically inland, where the flat valleys become frying pans from June to August. For southern California beaches, come May to October. The best time to visit northern California, especially San Francisco, is September to October, when the summer fog gives way to the warmest days.

INFORMATION

California Division of Tourism (☎ 916-322-2881, 800-462-2543; www.visitcalifornia.com; 1102 Q St, Ste 6000, Sacramento, CA 95814) Will send out a free, comprehensive travel planner and map.

SBC information (☎ 800-310-2355; www.sbc.com) California adds new area codes regularly. If you have problems calling a telephone number, call to verify the area code.

Statewide highway conditions (☎ 916-445-1534, 800-427-7623)

www.ca.gov The official state website has links to all city and county websites.

The state sales tax is 7.25%; added local taxes can raise this to over 8%. For HI-affiliated hostels in the state, visit www.norcalhostels.org, www.hostelweb.com/losangeles and www.sandiegohostels.com.

NATIONAL & STATE PARKS

For information check out the following:

California state park camping reservations (☎ 800-444-7275; www.reserveamerica.com)

California state parks (☎ 916-653-6995, 800-777-0369; www.parks.ca.gov) For information about California's state parks.

National Park Service (www.nps.gov) For information about national parks in California.

National park camping reservations (☎ 800-365-2267; reservations.nps.gov) Note that Yosemite has a different toll-free reservations number (p970).

California has seven national parks and 16 other areas managed by the National Park Service. The national parks are Yosemite and Sequoia & Kings Canyon (one unit) in the Sierra Nevada, Death Valley and Joshua Tree in the southern desert, Channel Islands off the coast of Santa Barbara, and Redwood and Lassen Volcanic National Park in the north.

California has 266 state parks. The oldest is Big Basin Redwoods State Park near Santa Cruz, established in 1902; the most popular are southern California's state beaches. Most charge a $3 to $5 per vehicle entrance fee; an annual pass is $35.

ACTIVITIES

What can't you do in California? If you like to hike or camp, you can do it in the nation's hottest desert (Death Valley), along its most scenic coast or up the tallest mountain in the contiguous US (Mt Whitney); you can be among the world's tallest trees (coast redwoods), the largest (sequoias) or the oldest (bristlecone pines). The spectacular 2638-mile **Pacific Crest Trail** (☎ 916-349-2109; www.pcta.org) passes through the length of the state and then on to Oregon and Washington.

At the moment, California's current mountain-biking mecca is at Mammoth Mountain, although Marin County, north of San Francisco, is popular too. In winter Mammoth and the resorts around Lake Tahoe offer great skiing and snowboarding. Rock climbing and rafting are other quintessential Sierra Nevada activities.

There are famous surf beaches up and down the coast, but the water is usually cold (wear a wet suit). The best sites for scuba diving are Monterey, Catalina Island and La Jolla.

California has many scenic marathons, some through redwood forests; for a comprehensive list, go to www.theschedule.com.

GETTING THERE & AROUND

Air

Los Angeles and San Francisco are major international airports and important regional air hubs. Within the state, there are a number of smaller airports, including Sacramento, Oakland, San Jose, Burbank, Ontario, Orange County and San Diego.

Bus

The state's cities and major towns are served by **Greyhound** (☎ 800-231-2222).

Car & Motorcycle

Los Angeles, San Diego and San Francisco are probably the best places to rent a car, with many national and local operators. See p1121.

Train

There are four main **Amtrak** (☎ 800-872-7245; www.amtrak.com) routes connecting California with the rest of the USA:

California Zephyr Daily service between Chicago and San Francisco (Emeryville), with stops in Denver, Colorado; Salt Lake City, Utah; and Reno, Nevada.

Coast Starlight Daily service along the West Coast, from Seattle, Washington, to San Diego, via Portland, Oregon; Sacramento; Oakland; Santa Barbara; and Los Angeles.

Southwest Chief Daily service between Chicago and Los Angeles via Kansas City, Missouri; Albuquerque, New Mexico; and Flagstaff, Arizona.

Sunset Limited Service three times a week between Jacksonville, Florida, and Los Angeles, via New Orleans, Louisiana; San Antonio, Texas; and Tucson, Arizona.

Within the state, useful rail routes include the *Pacific Surfliner*, which links San Diego and Los Angeles, continuing on to San Luis Obispo; the *Capitol Corridor*, between San Jose and Sacramento, with connections to South Lake Tahoe; and the *San Joaquin*, connecting the Bay Area to Bakersfield and southern California.

TOURS

Gray Line (☎ 800-826-0202; www.grayline.com) This standard tour company has something for everyone.

Green Tortoise (☎ 800-867-8647; www.greentortoise.com) Budget adventures for independent travelers.

Trek America (☎ 800-221-0596; www.trekamerica.com) Specializes in outdoor activities.

LOS ANGELES

Ah, Los Angeles. Everyone knows what to expect, right? Perpetual sunshine. Beaches full of hard bodies. Surfers shredding the perfect waves. Palatial hilltop mansions. Palm trees swaying in the breeze. And, of course, movie stars…everywhere.

You'll probably find all that and then some in one of the world's most intriguing and complex cities. Sure, cruising the Sunset Strip in a convertible, finding your favorite celebrity's star on the Walk of Fame and window-shopping on Rodeo Drive are all part of the LA experience. But once you've starred in the movie of your imagination, move on and transcend the clichés. Explore the 'other' LA with its superb art museums, cutting-edge architecture, beautiful parks and gardens and fun shopping. Pick from a United Nations of culinary experiences – Afghani to Zambian – then take in some world-class jazz or Beethoven.

What makes LA so fascinating is its wealth of human experience, its near-utopian mosaic of cultures living side by side in relative peace, and its beautiful setting by the sea. Not even earthquakes, traffic gridlock and smog can stop LA from thriving. Reality here is never far from the myth, and vice versa. And that's just what makes LA so unique. And fun.

History

LA's human history begins with the Gabrielino and Chumash Native Americans who roamed the area as early as 6000 BC. Their hunter-gatherer existence ended in the late 18th century when Spanish missionaries, led by Junípero Serra, founded two missions in the area. The first civilian settlement followed a few years later, in 1781, when 44 volunteers from Mexico became the first inhabitants of El Pueblo de la Reina de Los Angeles. The village soon became a thriving farming community but would remain a far-flung outpost for decades.

The first American to arrive in El Pueblo, in 1818, was a shipwrecked Boston millwright named Joseph Chapman. Others slowly followed until about the mid-1830s, when a book by Richard Henry Dana (*Two Years Before the Mast*), in which he extolled the virtues of the West, spurred interest among Easterners. During the Mexican–American War (1846–48), American soldiers encountered some resistance from General Andrés Pico and other commanders, but eventually LA, as with the rest of California, came under US rule. The city was incorporated on April 4, 1850.

Over the next decades a series of seminal events caused LA's population to soar from 1200 at the time of Dana's account to two million by 1930: the collapse of the Northern California gold rush in the 1850s, the arrival

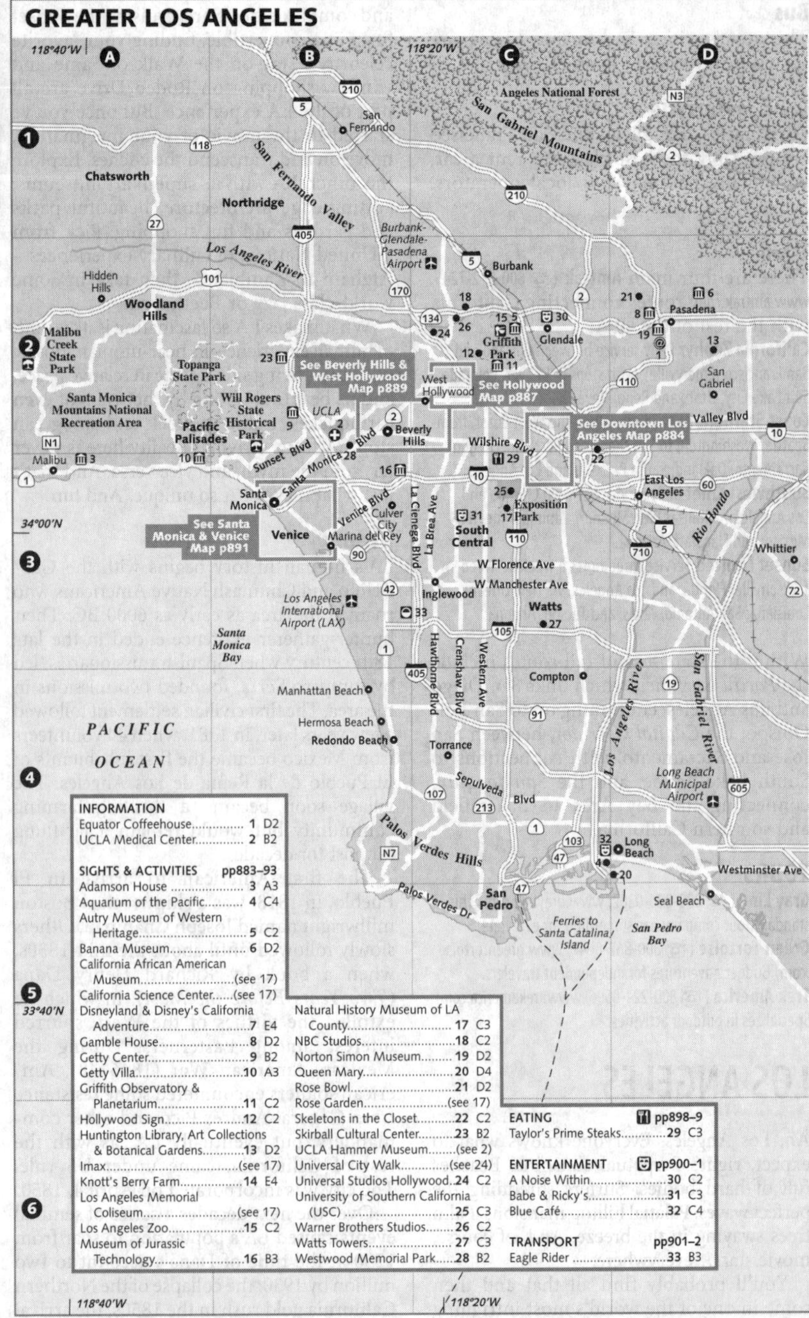
GREATER LOS ANGELES
118°40'W
118°20'W
A
B
C
D
1
2
3
4
5
6
34°00'N
33°40'N
Angeles National Forest
San Gabriel Mountains
San Fernando
San Fernando Valley
Chatsworth
Northridge
Burbank-Glendale-Pasadena Airport
Burbank
Los Angeles River
Hidden Hills
Woodland Hills
Malibu Creek State Park
Topanga State Park
Santa Monica Mountains National Recreation Area
Will Rogers State Historical Park
Pacific Palisades
Malibu
Griffith Park
Glendale
Pasadena
San Gabriel
See Beverly Hills & West Hollywood Map p889
West Hollywood
See Hollywood Map p887
See Downtown Los Angeles Map p884
UCLA
Beverly Hills
Sunset Blvd
Santa Monica Blvd
Wilshire Blvd
Valley Blvd
East Los Angeles
Rio Hondo
Santa Monica
See Santa Monica & Venice Map p891
Venice
Venice Blvd
Culver City
Marina del Rey
La Cienega Blvd
La Brea Ave
Exposition Park
South Central
Whittier
W Florence Ave
W Manchester Ave
Inglewood
Los Angeles International Airport (LAX)
Watts
Santa Monica Bay
Hawthorne Blvd
Crenshaw Blvd
Western Ave
Compton
Manhattan Beach
Hermosa Beach
Redondo Beach
PACIFIC OCEAN
Torrance
Sepulveda Blvd
San Gabriel River
Long Beach Municipal Airport
Palos Verdes Hills
Long Beach
Westminster Ave
Palos Verdes Dr
San Pedro
Ferries to Santa Catalina Island
San Pedro Bay
Seal Beach
INFORMATION
Equator Coffeehouse 1 D2
UCLA Medical Center 2 B2
SIGHTS & ACTIVITIES pp883–93
Adamson House 3 A3
Aquarium of the Pacific 4 C4
Autry Museum of Western Heritage 5 C2
Banana Museum 6 D2
California African American Museum (see 17)
California Science Center (see 17)
Disneyland & Disney's California Adventure 7 E4
Gamble House 8 D2
Getty Center 9 B2
Getty Villa 10 A3
Griffith Observatory & Planetarium 11 C2
Hollywood Sign 12 C2
Huntington Library, Art Collections & Botanical Gardens 13 D2
Imax (see 17)
Knott's Berry Farm 14 E4
Los Angeles Memorial Coliseum (see 17)
Los Angeles Zoo 15 C2
Museum of Jurassic Technology 16 B3
Natural History Museum of LA County 17 C3
NBC Studios 18 C2
Norton Simon Museum 19 D2
Queen Mary 20 D4
Rose Bowl 21 D2
Rose Garden (see 17)
Skeletons in the Closet 22 C2
Skirball Cultural Center 23 B2
UCLA Hammer Museum (see 2)
Universal City Walk (see 24)
Universal Studios Hollywood 24 C2
University of Southern California (USC) 25 C3
Warner Brothers Studios 26 C2
Watts Towers 27 C3
Westwood Memorial Park 28 B2
EATING pp898–9
Taylor's Prime Steaks 29 C3
ENTERTAINMENT pp900–1
A Noise Within 30 C2
Babe & Ricky's 31 C3
Blue Café 32 C4
TRANSPORT pp901–2
Eagle Rider 33 B3

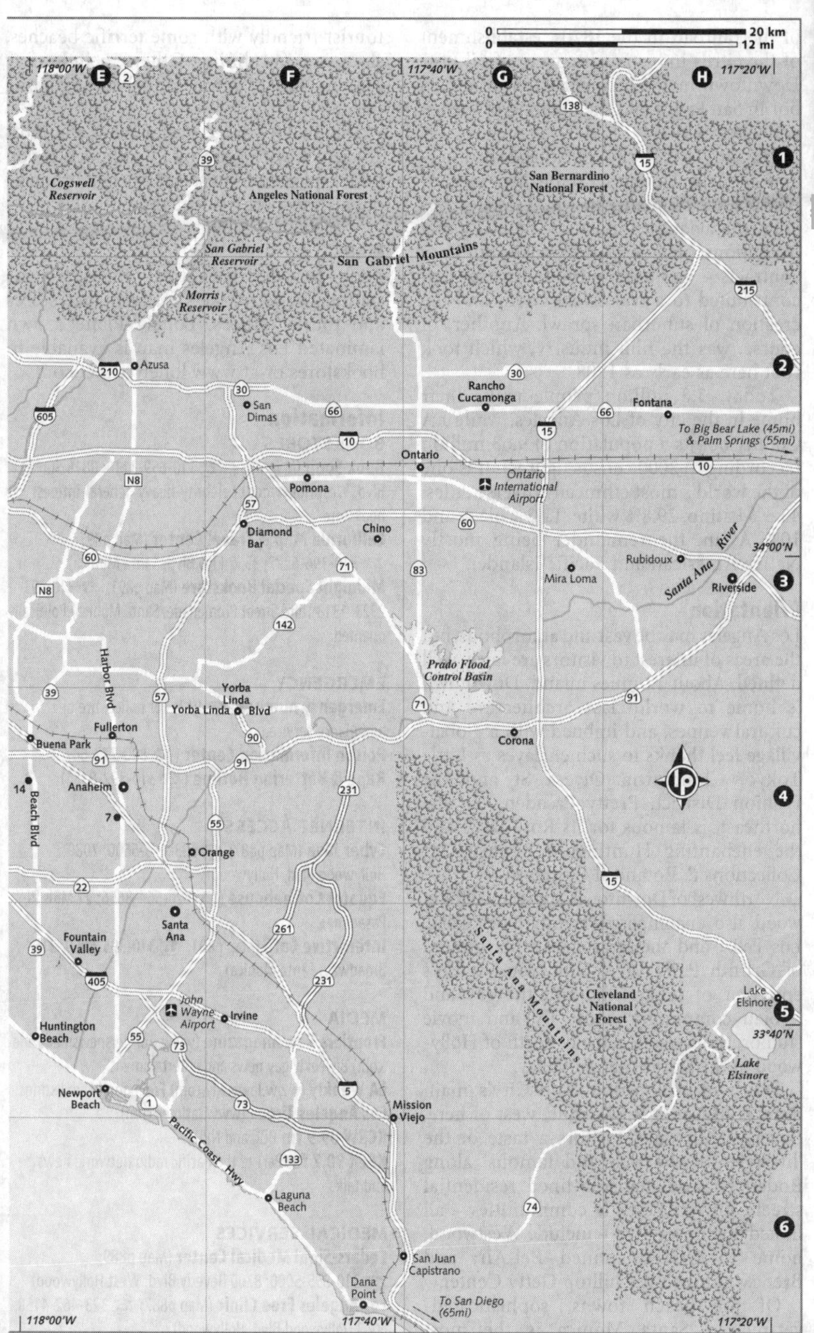

0 20 km
0 12 mi
118°00'W
117°40'W
117°20'W
E
F
G
H
1
2
3
4
5
6
Cogswell Reservoir
Angeles National Forest
San Bernardino National Forest
San Gabriel Reservoir
San Gabriel Mountains
Morris Reservoir
Azusa
Rancho Cucamonga
Fontana
San Dimas
To Big Bear Lake (45mi) & Palm Springs (55mi)
Ontario
Pomona
Ontario International Airport
Diamond Bar
Chino
34°00'N
Rubidoux
Santa Ana River
Mira Loma
Riverside
Harbor Blvd
Prado Flood Control Basin
Yorba Linda
Yorba Linda Blvd
Fullerton
Buena Park
Corona
Anaheim
Beach Blvd
Orange
Santa Ana
Fountain Valley
Santa Ana Mountains
Cleveland National Forest
Lake Elsinore
33°40'N
John Wayne Airport
Irvine
Huntington Beach
Newport Beach
Mission Viejo
Pacific Coast Hwy
Laguna Beach
San Juan Capistrano
Dana Point
To San Diego (65mi)

of the railroad in the 1870s, establishment of the citrus industry, discovery of oil near Downtown in 1892, construction of a harbor in San Pedro and the opening of the LA aqueduct in 1913.

During WWI, the Lockheed brothers and Donald Douglas established aircraft manufacturing plants in LA. Two decades later, the aviation industry – helped along by billions of federal dollars for military contracts – was among the industries that contributed to a real estate boom and the creation of suburban sprawl. Another, of course, was the film industry, which took root here as early as 1908.

Today, 3.8 million people make their home in the city of Los Angeles, while LA County boasts a population of 9.63 million (according to 2000 census figures). It is one of the world's most ethnically diverse cities: 45.6% Latino, 29.8% white, 11.2% black and 10% Asian, the remainder being mostly Native American and Pacific Islander.

Orientation

Los Angeles may be vast and amorphous, but the areas of interest to visitors are fairly well defined. About 12 miles inland, Downtown is home to world-class architecture and cultural venues, and imbued with a global-village feel thanks to such enclaves as Little Tokyo, Chinatown, Olvera St and the Fashion District. Pretty Pasadena, to the northeast, is famous for its Rose Bowl and the enchanting Huntington Library, Art Collections & Botanical Gardens.

Northwest of Downtown, sprawling Hollywood also encompasses trendy Silver Lake, Los Feliz, and the large urban playground of Griffith Park. West Hollywood is LA's epicenter of urban chic and the gay and lesbian community. Most TV and movie studios, though, are actually north of Hollywood in the San Fernando Valley.

South of Hollywood, Mid-City's main draw is Museum Row, while, west of here, Beverly Hills gives visitors a taste of the 'lifestyles of the rich and famous' along Rodeo Dr and mansion-lined residential streets. Other Westside communities – all linked by Sunset Blvd – include Westwood, home to UCLA; refined Bel-Air; and Brentwood with the hilltop Getty Center.

Of the beach towns, sophisticated-yet-relaxed Santa Monica is the most tourist-friendly with some terrific beaches, shopping and dining. Others include ritzy Malibu, funky Venice and bustling Long Beach.

Due to LA's huge size, a car is the most efficient way to get around, although if you limit explorations to specific neighborhoods, public transport is adequate.

MAPS

Look for detailed street maps at gas stations, supermarkets, convenience stores and tourist offices. Lonely Planet's own laminated Los Angeles map is available in bookstores or at www.lonelyplanet.com.

Information

BOOKSTORES

Book Soup (Map p889; ☎ 310-659-3110; 8818 Sunset Blvd, West Hollywood) Celebrity-heavy general-interest bookstore.

California Map & Travel Center (Map p891; ☎ 310-396-6277; 3312 Pico Blvd, Santa Monica)

Midnight Special Bookstore (Map p891; ☎ 310-393-2923; 1318 Third Street Promenade, Santa Monica) Politically oriented.

EMERGENCY

Emergency number (☎ 911) For police, fire or ambulance service.

Poison Information Center (☎ 800-777-6476)

Rape & Battering Hotline (☎ 310-392-8381)

INTERNET ACCESS

Cyber Java (Map p887; ☎ 323-466-5600; 7080 Hollywood Blvd, Hollywood)

Equator Coffeehouse (☎ 626-564-8656; 22 Mills Pl, Pasadena)

Interactive Café (Map p891; ☎ 310-395-5009; 215 Broadway, Santa Monica)

MEDIA

Frontiers Newsmagazine (www.frontiersnewsmagazine.com) Biweekly gay news and entertainment.

LA Weekly (www.laweekly.com) Free; good club listings.

Los Angeles Times (www.latimes.com)

KCRW 89.9 fm BBC and NPR.

KPFK 90.7 fm Part of the Pacific radio network; news and talk.

MEDICAL SERVICES

Cedars-Sinai Medical Center (Map p889; ☎ 310-855-5000; 8700 Beverly Blvd, West Hollywood)

Los Angeles Free Clinic (Map p887; ☎ 323-462-4158; 6043 Hollywood Blvd, Hollywood)

LOS ANGELES IN...

Two Days

Start your day with breakfast at the **Rose Café** in Venice, then head east to Hollywood for a stroll along the **Walk of Fame**. After lunch it's off to Beverly Hills and **Rodeo Dr** via mansion-lined **Sunset Blvd**. From here, make a beeline to the **Getty Center** before concluding the day with dinner in **Santa Monica** and people-watching on **Third Street Promenade**.

On the second day, weather permitting, spend the morning frolicking on the beach in Venice and checking the mad scene along the **Venice Boardwalk**, then hit the road for Downtown. Check out **Olvera St**, the new **Cathedral of Our Lady of the Angels** and **Walt Disney Hall** and get your cultural fix at the **Museum of Contemporary Art**. Enjoy pre-dinner drinks in the **Standard Hotel's** trendy rooftop bar, then indulge in a seafood feast at the **Water Grill**.

Four Days

Make **Universal Studios** the focus of your third day. Then try to spot real movie stars over dinner at **Spago Beverly Hills** in Beverly Hills. For a change of pace on your final day, head to Pasadena and the amazing **Huntington Library, Art Collections & Gardens**. After dinner in Old Pasadena, head to the **Sunset Strip** for one last wild night on the town.

UCLA Medical Center (Map pp880-1; ☎ 310-825-9111; 10833 LeConte Ave, Westwood)

MONEY

American Express West Hollywood (Map p889; ☎ 310-659-1682; 8493 W 3rd St) Pasadena (☎ 626-449-2281; 269 S Lake Ave)

Thomas Cook (all branches ☎ 800-287-7362) West Hollywood (Map p889; 806 Hilldale Ave, West Hollywood); Beverly Hills (Map p889; 421 N Rodeo Dr, Beverly Hills)

POST

Post offices abound in Los Angeles. Call ☎ 800-275-8777 for the nearest branch.

TOURIST OFFICES

California Welcome Center (Map p889; ☎ 310-854-7616; 8500 Beverly Blvd, West Hollywood; 🕑 10am-6pm Mon-Sat, 11am-6pm Sun)

Downtown Visitors Center (Map p884; ☎ 213-689-8822; www.lacvb.com; 685 S Figueroa St; 🕑 9am-4pm Mon-Fri)

Hollywood Visitors Center (Map p887; Hollywood & Highland complex, Hollywood; 🕑 10am-10pm daily, closes 7pm Sun)

Santa Monica Visitors Center (Map p891; ☎ 310-393-7593; www.santamonica.com; 2nd floor, Santa Monica Place Mall; 🕑 10am-6pm)

Dangers & Annoyances

Walking around LA in the daytime is generally no problem, although extra caution should be exercised in East LA, Compton and Watts, sections of which are plagued by gang activity, drugs and prostitution. Stay away from these areas after dark. Hollywood also yields dangers, especially in poorly lit side streets; ditto for Venice. Crime rates are lower in Westside communities such as Westwood and Beverly Hills, as well as in the beach towns (except Venice) and Pasadena.

Sights

Each of LA's neighborhoods has its own unique appeal and where you concentrate your sightseeing largely depends on your personal interests. Classic sights such as museums and great architecture cluster in Downtown, Pasadena and Hollywood, while the beach towns are great for soaking up the SoCal vibe.

DOWNTOWN

Few LA neighborhoods have as much to offer per square mile as Downtown, which is rich in history, architecture, restaurants and cultural institutions. It's easily explored on foot or by DASH minibuses. Downtown is also served by Metro Rail's Red and Blue Lines (see p902).

Civic Center — Map p884

The cluster of city, county and federal office buildings at the heart of Downtown are collectively known as the Civic Center.

City Hall (200 N Spring St) is a gleaming white tower that soars skyward for 28 stories. It stood in as the Daily Planet in *Superman*

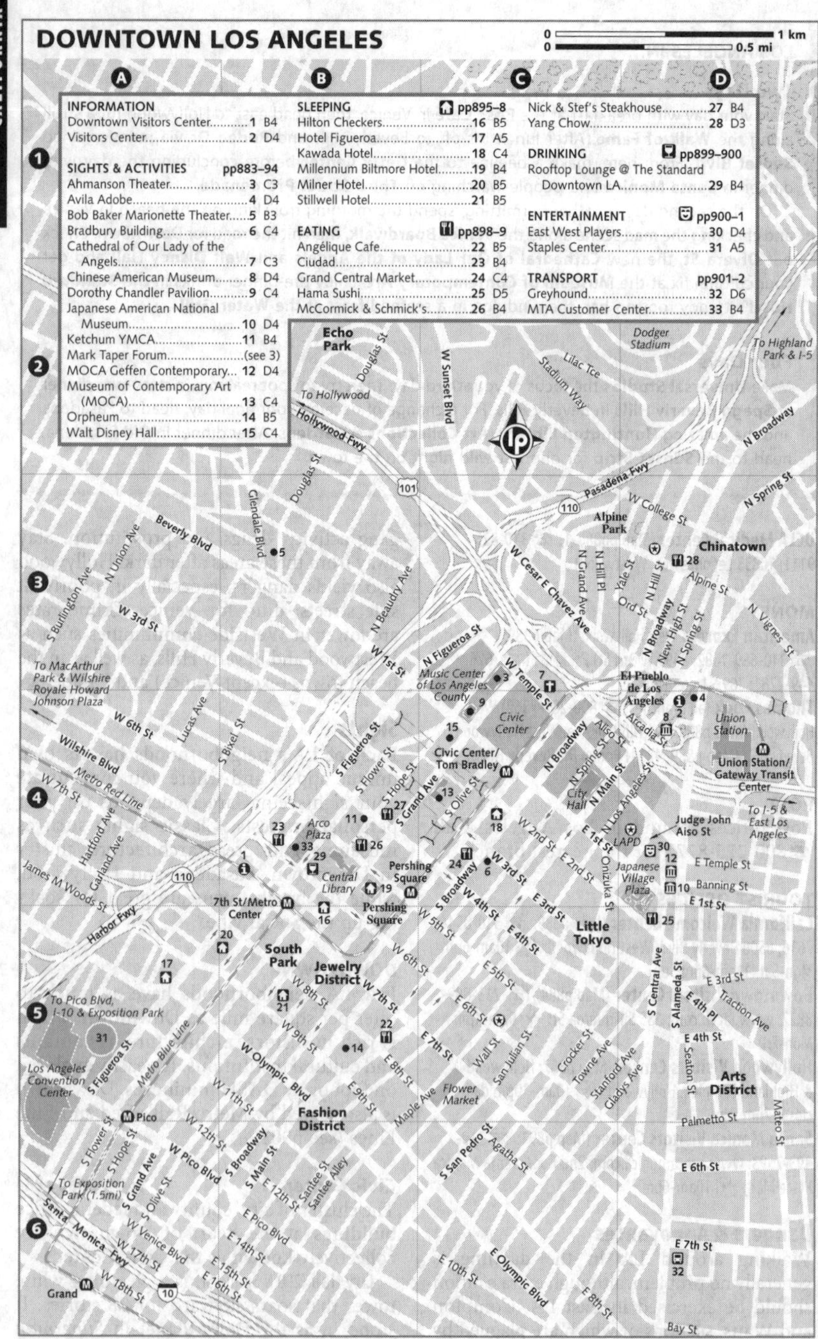

DOWNTOWN LOS ANGELES
0 1 km
0 0.5 mi
A
B
C
D
1
2
3
4
5
6
INFORMATION
Downtown Visitors Center 1 B4
Visitors Center 2 D4
SIGHTS & ACTIVITIES pp883–94
Ahmanson Theater 3 C3
Avila Adobe 4 D4
Bob Baker Marionette Theater 5 B3
Bradbury Building 6 C4
Cathedral of Our Lady of the Angels 7 C3
Chinese American Museum 8 D4
Dorothy Chandler Pavilion 9 C4
Japanese American National Museum 10 D4
Ketchum YMCA 11 B4
Mark Taper Forum (see 3)
MOCA Geffen Contemporary 12 D4
Museum of Contemporary Art (MOCA) 13 C4
Orpheum 14 B5
Walt Disney Hall 15 C4
SLEEPING pp895–8
Hilton Checkers 16 B5
Hotel Figueroa 17 A5
Kawada Hotel 18 C4
Millennium Biltmore Hotel 19 B4
Milner Hotel 20 B5
Stillwell Hotel 21 B5
EATING pp898–9
Angélique Cafe 22 B5
Ciudad 23 B4
Grand Central Market 24 C4
Hama Sushi 25 D5
McCormick & Schmick's 26 B4
Nick & Stef's Steakhouse 27 B4
Yang Chow 28 D3
DRINKING pp899–900
Rooftop Lounge @ The Standard Downtown LA 29 B4
ENTERTAINMENT pp900–1
East West Players 30 D4
Staples Center 31 A5
TRANSPORT pp901–2
Greyhound 32 D6
MTA Customer Center 33 B4
Echo Park
Dodger Stadium
To Highland Park & I-5
To Hollywood
Hollywood Fwy
Pasadena Fwy
Alpine Park
Chinatown
To MacArthur Park & Wilshire Royale Howard Johnson Plaza
Music Center of Los Angeles County
Civic Center
Civic Center/ Tom Bradley
El Pueblo de Los Angeles
Union Station
Union Station/ Gateway Transit Center
To I-5 & East Los Angeles
Judge John Aiso St
City Hall
LAPD
Japanese Village Plaza
Little Tokyo
Arco Plaza
Central Library
Pershing Square
7th St/Metro Center
South Park
Jewelry District
Harbor Fwy
To Pico Blvd, I-10 & Exposition Park
Los Angeles Convention Center
Metro Blue Line
Metro Red Line
Pico
Fashion District
Flower Market
Arts District
To Exposition Park (1.5mi)
Santa Monica Fwy
Grand

and got blown to bits in *War of the Worlds*, but in real life it serves as the nerve center of LA politics. Following an extensive restoration from 1998 to 2001 and seismic retrofitting, it opened again to the public.

In 2003, City Hall's landmark status got competition from the stunning **Walt Disney Hall** (111 S Grand Ave), the new home of LA's Philharmonic Orchestra. Designed by Frank Gehry, it is an architectural symphony of curving and billowing stainless-steel walls that seems like an abstract interpretation of a ship caught in a rough sea. The orchestra's old home, the **Dorothy Chandler Pavilion**, is just east of here. Along with the **Mark Taper Forum** (p900) and the **Ahmanson Theater**, it forms the **Music Center of LA County** (☎ 213-972-7483; 135 N Grand Ave; tours 10am-1:30pm Tue-Sun).

Also on Grand Avenue's 'cultural corridor' is the world-renowned **Museum of Contemporary Art** (MOCA; ☎ 213-626-6222; www.moca-la.org; 250 S Grand Ave; adult $8, senior & student $5; 🕑 11am-5pm Tue-Sun, closes 8pm Thu). In a building by Japanese architect Arata Isozaki, it presents paintings, sculptures and photographs from the 1940s to the present. Tickets are also good for same-day admission to the MOCA Geffen Contemporary (p886) and within 30 days at the MOCA branch at the Pacific Design Center (p888).

A short stroll northeast is another new Downtown landmark: the **Cathedral of Our Lady of the Angels** (☎ 213-680-5200; 550 W Temple St; 🕑 6:30am-7pm Mon-Fri, 9am-5pm Sat, 7am-5pm Sun). Behind its austere, ochre mantle awaits a room of worship bathed in friendly, soft light filtering through milky, alabaster windows. Spanish architect Rafael Moneo and a host of artists collaborated on the project. The cathedral runs free tours at 1pm weekdays.

El Pueblo de Los Angeles & Around — Map p884

Pick up a self-guided tour brochure of El Pueblo from the **visitors center** (☎ 213-625-3800; Olvera St; 🕑 10am-3pm) in the 1877 Sepulveda House.

This 44-acre state historic park commemorates LA's founding and preserves many of its earliest buildings, including the 1818 **Avila Adobe** on **Olvera St**, a narrow, block-long passageway that's been an open-air Mexican marketplace since 1930.

Near El Pueblo, **Union Station** is a classic 1939 Spanish Mission-style beauty that was the last of the USA's grand railroad stations. To make room for its construction, LA's original Chinatown was razed and relocated to an area just north of El Pueblo. The new **Chinatown** is still a vibrant cultural and social hub for LA's 200,000 Chinese Americans, although most now reside in communities east of Downtown. Come for authentic Cantonese or Szechuan delicacies, browse the stores for silk clothing and boxed tea, or have a herbalist whip you up a magical potion. A new **Chinese American Museum** (423-425 N Los Angeles St) should open in 2004.

Historic Core — Map p884

A stroll southwest of the Civic Center is like a trip back in time as you enter Downtown's historic core. Make your way to **Pershing Sq**, LA's oldest public park (1866), filled with public art and flanked on its north side by the grand old **Millennium Biltmore Hotel** (☎ 213-624-1011; 506 S Grand Ave). Its palatial interior boasts carved and gilded ceilings, marble floors, grand staircases and ballrooms. Just north of the hotel is LA's modern business district, easily recognized by its many futuristic high-rises.

Southwest of Pershing Sq, along Hill St, gold and diamonds are the main currency in the **Jewelry District**. But for dazzling architecture head one block northeast to Broadway, where the 1893 **Bradbury Building** (☎ 213-626-1893; 304 S Broadway; admission free; 🕑 9am-5pm) is the undisputed crown jewel. Its drab façade conceals a light-flooded, galleried atrium that has starred in many movies, most famously in *Blade Runner*.

Broadway also earned a spot on the National Register of Historic Places for its 11 spectacular **movie palaces**, built between 1913 and 1931 in a marvelous hodgepodge of styles, from Spanish Gothic to French baroque. Some, such as the **Orpheum** (842 Broadway), have been gloriously restored and are now used for special screenings, parties and other events.

Serious shoppers should head to the Fashion District, a 56-square-block area south of 7th St that's more Arabic bazaar than American mall. Bargains abound, and haggling is accepted in most places.

Little Tokyo — Map p884

This is the Japanese counterpart to Chinatown, with an attractive mix of sushi bars, traditional gardens, outdoor shopping malls, cultural centers and Buddhist temples. The **Japanese American National Museum** (☎ 213-625-0414; www.janm.org; 369 E 1st St; adult $6, senior $5, student & child $3; 🕑 10am-5pm Tue-Sun, closes 8pm Thu) exhibits objects of work and worship, photographs and art. Together, they relate the history of Japanese emigration to, and life in, the USA during the past 130 years, including the painful chapter of the WWII internment camps.

Next door, the **MOCA Geffen Contemporary** (☎ 213-626-6222; 152 N Central Ave; adult $8, senior & student $5, free Thu; 🕑 11am-5pm Tue-Sun, closes 8pm Thu), situated in a Frank Gehry warehouse, is a subsidiary of the main museum on S Grand Ave (see Civic Center, p927).

EXPOSITION PARK & AROUND

Map pp880–1

A couple of miles south of Downtown, Exposition Park is easily reached by DASH minibuses and is a great place to come with kids. What began as an agricultural fairground in 1872 now contains a trio of quality museums, a lovely **Rose Garden** (🕑 9am-sunset mid-Mar-Dec), which is at its best from April to August, and the 1923 **Los Angeles Memorial Coliseum**. The latter hosted the 1932 and 1984 Summer Olympic Games, the 1959 baseball World Series and two Super Bowls. The **University of Southern California** (USC) campus is just north of the park.

The **Natural History Museum of LA County** (☎ 213-763-3466; www.nhm.org; adult $8, senior & student $5.50, child $2; 🕑 9:30am-5pm Mon-Fri, 10am-5pm Sat & Sun) presents an in-depth journey of discovery into the world of animals – alive and extinct. Crowd pleasers include the Dinosaur Hall, stuffed mammals from Africa and North America, and the butterfly exhibit.

Another winner is the **California Science Center** (☎ 323-724-3623; www.casciencectr.org; admission free; 🕑 10am-5pm), a warren of interactive exhibits that demystify scientific concepts. Don't miss the techno-doll named Tess billed as '50ft of brains, beauty and biology.' The adjacent **Imax** (☎ 213-744-7400; adult $7.50, senior & student $5.50, child $4.50) presents nature-themed 2D and 3D movies.

The third museum is the **California African American Museum** (☎ 213-744-7432; www.caam.ca.gov; admission free; 🕑 10am-4pm Wed-Sat), which presents a range of African-American art and artifacts, with an emphasis on western states.

The district south of Exposition Park, along both sides of the I-110 (Harbor Fwy), is commonly known as South Central and plagued by gangs, drugs, poverty and crime. The main reason to visit is the **Watts Towers** (☎ 213-847-4646; 1765 E 107th St; adult $2, senior & student $1.50, child under 17 free; tours 11am-2:30pm Tue-Fri, 10:30am-2:30pm Sat, 12:30-3pm Sun), one of the world's finest examples of folk art. The intricate towers are the life's work of Italian immigrant Simon Rodia who rendered concrete and glass bottles, mirrors, sea shells, rocks, ceramic tile, pottery and other materials into his amazing free-form sculpture.

HOLLYWOOD

Aging movie stars know that a facelift can do wonders to pump up a drooping career, and it seems the same is true of Hollywood neighborhoods. Millions of dollars have been invested to rejuvenate the legendary central Hollywood district in recent years. If it's still not all that glamorous, it's at least ready for its 'close-up.' Historic movie palaces bask in restored glory, Metro Rail's Red Line makes access easy, and even 'Oscar' has found a permanent home in the Kodak Theatre, part of a vast new shopping and entertainment complex called Hollywood & Highland. Lording above the bustle in its dignified hillside perch is the city's most recognizable landmark, the **Hollywood Sign**, built in 1923 as an advertising gimmick for a real estate development called Hollywoodland. East of Hwy 101 (Hollywood Fwy), the neighborhoods of **Los Feliz** and **Silver Lake** have evolved into bohemian-chic enclaves with fun and funky shopping, nightlife and a hopping cuisine scene.

Griffith Park

Map pp880–1

Sprawling Griffith Park is a thick spread of California oak, wild sage and manzanita and is a great escape from urban velocity and stress, especially for families. At five times the size of New York's Central Park, it embraces an outdoor theater, the city zoo, an observatory, two museums, golf courses, tennis courts, playgrounds, bridle paths, hiking trails and even the Hollywood Sign. Access is easiest via the Griffith Park Dr or Zoo Dr exits off I-5 (Golden State Fwy).

The **Los Angeles Zoo** (☎ 323-644-6400; www.lazoo.org; 5333 Zoo Dr; adult/senior/child $8.25/5.25/3.25;

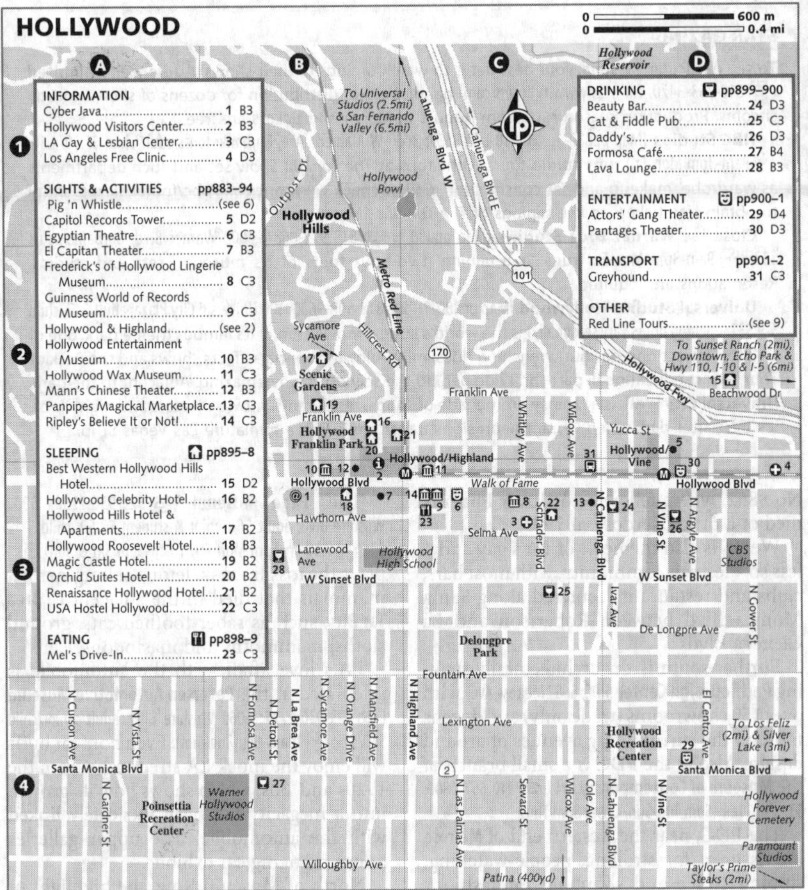

(10am-5pm), on the northern perimeter, is home to around 1200 animals representing 350 species. Highlights include the chimpanzees in the Mahale Mountains exhibit, the Koala House, the Komodo dragons and interactive Adventure Island.

Those keen on the history of the American West will hit the mother lode at the **Autry Museum of Western Heritage** (☎ 323-667-2000; 4700 Western Heritage Way; adult $7.50, senior & student $5, child 2-12 $3; 10am-5pm Tue-Sun, closes 8pm Thu). Its 10 galleries skillfully combine scholarship and showmanship to reveal how the West was 'discovered' again and again, by everyone from prehistoric tribes to missionaries.

On the upper slopes of Mt Hollywood, the landmark 1935 **Griffith Observatory & Planetarium** (☎ 323-664-1191; 2800 E Observatory Rd) is closed for renovation until at least 2005.

WEST HOLLYWOOD

Map p889

West Hollywood (WeHo) is one of LA's hippest neighborhoods, teeming with clubs, restaurants and elegant hotels. Most of the action concentrates along the (in)famous **Sunset Strip** (Sunset Blvd between Laurel Canyon Blvd and Doheny Dr), easily recognized by its giant billboards. This is where you'll find the **House of Blues**, at No 8430; the **Whisky-a-Gogo**, where The Doors were the house band in 1966, at No 8901; the **Mondrian Hotel** with its *über*-trendy Sky Bar, at No 8840; and Johnny Depp's **Viper Room**, at

STAR GAZING

To see particular TV stars, your best bet is to watch tapings of their shows. **Audiences Unlimited** (☎ 818-753-3470, ext 812; www.tvtickets.com) handles ticket distribution for dozens of shows, mostly sitcoms. Production season runs from August to March and tickets are free.

NBC Studios (Map pp880-1; ☎ 818-840-3537; 3000 W Alameda Ave, Burbank; tours adult/child $7.50/4.50; 9am-3pm Mon-Fri) runs studio tours with stops at *The Tonight Show* set and such departments as wardrobe, makeup and set construction. Call or check www.nbc.com/nbc/footer/tickets.shtml to obtain free tickets to live tapings of *The Tonight Show*.

Close by, **Warner Bros Studios** (Map pp880-1; ☎ 818-972-8687; 4000 Warner Blvd, Burbank; tours $32; 9am-3pm Mon-Fri) runs 'edu-taining' two-hour tours of its museum, sets and studios. Reservations are required.

Universal Studios Hollywood (Map pp880-1; ☎ 818-508-9600; 100 Universal City Plaza; adult $47, child 3-9 $37; opening hours vary seasonally) is the world's largest movie studio. Its famous theme park, one of LA's top attractions, has gut-wrenching rides, mind-blowing special-effects shows and the Backlot Tour, a part-educational, part-thrill ride behind the scenes of moviemaking. Adjacent to the park, **Universal City Walk** is a fantasy promenade of shops, restaurants, movie theaters and nightclubs. It's best after dark when vibrant neon signs transform it into a miniature Las Vegas Strip.

No 8852, where fellow actor River Phoenix died of a drug overdose in 1993.

WeHo is also the heart of LA's gay and – less so – lesbian community, with most bars, clubs and restaurants centered along Santa Monica Blvd between Robertson and La Cienega Blvds.

Further south is the architecturally striking **Pacific Design Center** (PDC; 8687 Melrose Ave) with over 150 showrooms (trade only) and dozens more in the surrounding avenues of art and design. Also at the PDC is a small branch of the **Museum of Contemporary Art** (☎ 310-657-0800; $3; 11am-5pm Tue-Sun, closes 8pm Thu).

The PDC, near the western end of **Melrose Ave**, is great for strolling, people-watching, sipping coffee and shopping for fashionable attire, vintage clothing and unique items. The most interesting stretch starts about 1.25 miles east of the PDC along Fairfax Ave.

MID-CITY Map p889

South of Hollywood, Mid-City is home to Museum Row, a cluster of three museums along Wilshire Blvd, just east of Fairfax Ave.

The **Los Angeles County Museum of Art** (Lacma; ☎ 323-857-6000; www.lacma.org; 5901 Wilshire Blvd; adult $7, senior & student $5, child $1; noon-8pm Mon, Tue & Thu, noon-9pm Fri, 11am-8pm Sat & Sun) is one of the country's leading art museums. Its vast collection incorporates fine art, sculpture and decorative arts from Europe, Asia and America, as well as ancient and Islamic art.

The **Page Museum** (☎ 323-936-2230; 5801 Wilshire Blvd; adult $6, senior & student $3.50, child 5-12 $2; 9:30am-5pm Mon-Fri, 10am-5pm Sat & Sun) displays the fossilized skeletons of long-extinct mammals that died in the adjacent **La Brea Tar Pits**, such as saber-toothed cats, ground sloths, mammoths and mastodons.

LA's love affair with the automobile is celebrated at the **Petersen Automotive Museum** (☎ 323-930-2277; 6060 Wilshire Blvd; adult/senior/child $10/5/3; 10am-6pm Tue-Sun). Even non-car buffs will enjoy the mock LA streetscape from the 1920s and '30s, which shows how its growth into a megacity has been intricately linked with the automobile. The upper galleries house changing car exhibits.

North of Museum Row, the highlight of the Fairfax District is the **Original Farmers Market** (6333 W 3rd St) and the adjacent **Grove**, a new and attractively designed open-air shopping mall.

BEVERLY HILLS Map p889

The mere mention of Beverly Hills conjures images of fame and wealth, reinforced by film and TV. Fact is, the reality is not so different from the myth. Stylish and sophisticated, this is indeed where the well-heeled frolic. Opulent mansions flank manicured grounds on tree-shaded avenues, especially north of Sunset Blvd. You can get maps to the stars' homes at tourist stores or from street-corner vendors, although there's no telling how current they might be. The **Beverly Hills Hotel** (☎ 310-276-2251; 9641 Sunset Blvd) is

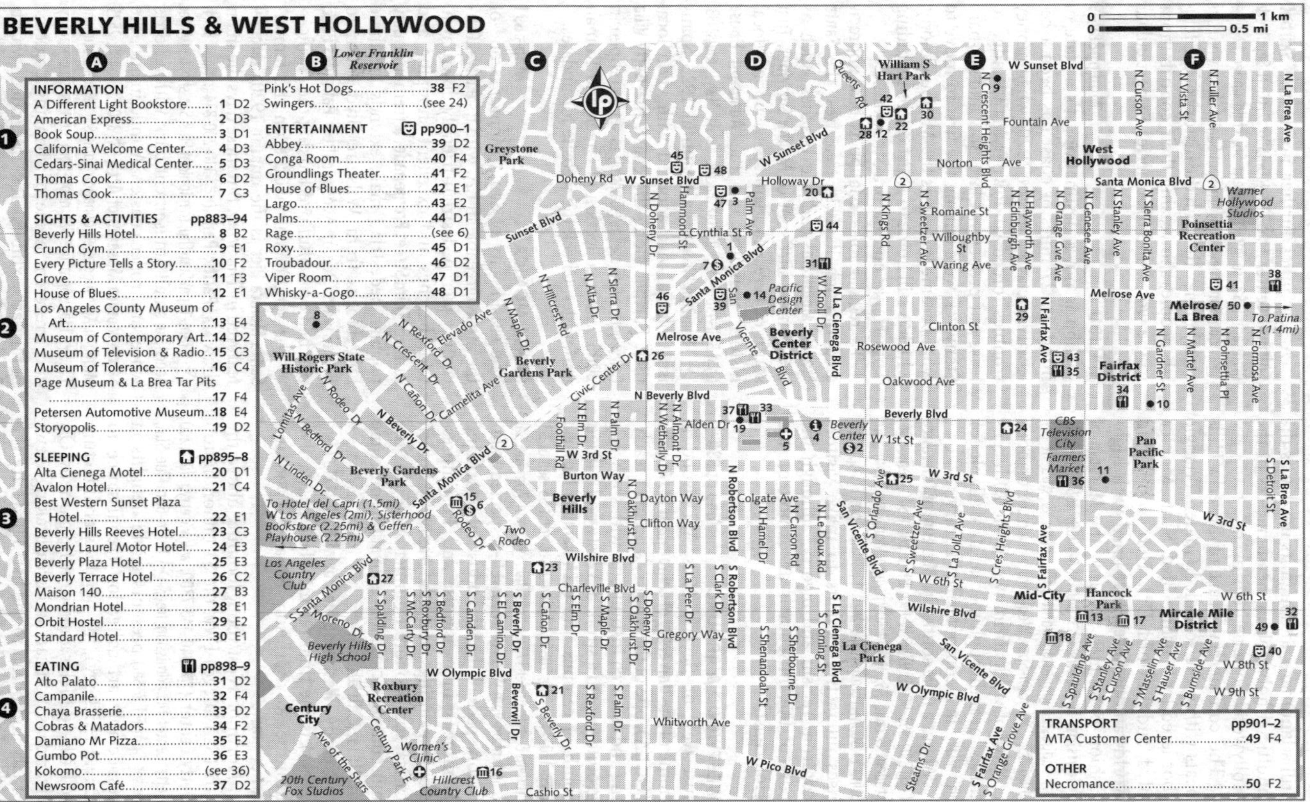
BEVERLY HILLS & WEST HOLLYWOOD
0 1 km
0 0.5 mi
INFORMATION
A Different Light Bookstore 1 D2
American Express 2 D3
Book Soup 3 D1
California Welcome Center 4 D3
Cedars-Sinai Medical Center 5 D3
Thomas Cook 6 D2
Thomas Cook 7 C3
SIGHTS & ACTIVITIES pp883–94
Beverly Hills Hotel 8 B2
Crunch Gym 9 E1
Every Picture Tells a Story 10 F2
Grove 11 F3
House of Blues 12 E1
Los Angeles County Museum of Art 13 E4
Museum of Contemporary Art 14 D2
Museum of Television & Radio 15 C3
Museum of Tolerance 16 C4
Page Museum & La Brea Tar Pits 17 F4
Petersen Automotive Museum 18 E4
Storyopolis 19 D2
SLEEPING pp895–8
Alta Cienega Motel 20 D1
Avalon Hotel 21 C4
Best Western Sunset Plaza Hotel 22 E1
Beverly Hills Reeves Hotel 23 C3
Beverly Laurel Motor Hotel 24 E3
Beverly Plaza Hotel 25 E3
Beverly Terrace Hotel 26 C2
Maison 140 27 B3
Mondrian Hotel 28 E1
Orbit Hostel 29 E2
Standard Hotel 30 E1
EATING pp898–9
Alto Palato 31 D2
Campanile 32 F4
Chaya Brasserie 33 D2
Cobras & Matadors 34 F2
Damiano Mr Pizza 35 E2
Gumbo Pot 36 E3
Kokomo (see 36)
Newsroom Café 37 D2
Pink's Hot Dogs 38 F2
Swingers (see 24)
ENTERTAINMENT pp900–1
Abbey 39 D2
Conga Room 40 F4
Groundlings Theater 41 F2
House of Blues 42 E1
Largo 43 E2
Palms 44 D1
Rage (see 6)
Roxy 45 D1
Troubadour 46 D2
Viper Room 47 D1
Whisky-a-Gogo 48 D1
TRANSPORT pp901–2
MTA Customer Center 49 F4
OTHER
Necromance 50 F2
Lower Franklin Reservoir
Greystone Park
William S Hart Park
West Hollywood
Warner Hollywood Studios
Poinsettia Recreation Center
Melrose/ La Brea
To Patina (1.4mi)
Will Rogers State Historic Park
Beverly Gardens Park
Pacific Design Center
Beverly Center District
Fairfax District
Beverly Center
CBS Television City
Farmers Market
Pan Pacific Park
Beverly Hills
Two Rodeo
To Hotel del Capri (1.5mi), W Los Angeles (2mi), Sisterhood Bookstore (2.25mi) & Geffen Playhouse (2.25mi)
Los Angeles Country Club
Beverly Hills High School
Roxbury Recreation Center
Century City
20th Century Fox Studios
Women's Clinic
Hillcrest Country Club
La Cienega Park
Mid-City
Hancock Park
Mircale Mile District
W Sunset Blvd
Santa Monica Blvd
Melrose Ave
Beverly Blvd
W 3rd St
Wilshire Blvd
W Olympic Blvd
W Pico Blvd
San Vicente Blvd
N La Cienega Blvd
N Fairfax Ave
N La Brea Ave

still a landmark, although its heyday as the unofficial hobnobbing headquarters of the Hollywood power elite is over.

The commercial heart of Beverly Hills beats within the so-called Golden Triangle (bordered by Wilshire Blvd, Santa Monica Blvd and Rexford Dr). Here you'll find world-famous **Rodeo Drive** lined with high-fashion boutiques. Nearby, the **Museum of Television & Radio** (☎ 310-786-1000; 465 N Beverly Dr; suggested donation adult $10, senior & student $8, child $5; noon-5pm Wed-Sun) is an enormous archive of works from two of the 20th century's breakthrough media, all available for viewing in a computerized library.

About a mile south, the **Museum of Tolerance** (☎ 310-553-9036; 9786 W Pico Blvd; adult $10, senior $8, student & child $6; 11:30am-4pm Mon-Thu, 11am-5pm Sun, 11:30am-1pm Fri Nov-Mar, 11:30am-3pm Fri Apr-Oct) uses interactive exhibits to make visitors confront racism and bigotry, although the core of the museum is an exhibit on the Holocaust.

WESTWOOD & AROUND — Map pp880–9

Just west of Beverly Hills, Westwood is home of the **University of California at Los Angeles** (UCLA), one of the country's premier teaching and research institutions, with sprawling grounds worth a stroll. In Westwood Village, south of campus, the **UCLA Hammer Museum** (☎ 310-443-7000; 10899 Wilshire Blvd; adult $5, senior $3, student & child under 17 free, free Thu; noon-7pm Tue, Sat & Sun, noon-9pm Wed-Fri) is a well-respected exhibition space of the late industrialist Armand Hammer's impressionist and Postimpressionist paintings, and lithographs by French caricaturist Honoré Daumier. Note that the museum may close for renovation sometime in 2004. Call ahead.

Nearby, **Westwood Memorial Park** (1218 Glendon Ave) is the final resting place of Marilyn Monroe, Roy Orbison, Natalie Wood and other stars.

North of Westwood, looming above the 405 (San Diego) Fwy, the $1 billion hilltop **Getty Center** (☎ 310-440-7300; www.getty.edu; 1200 Getty Center Dr; admission free; 10am-6pm Tue-Sun, closes 9pm Fri & Sat) presents triple delights: a respectable art collection (renaissance to David Hockney), the fabulous architecture of Richard Meier and beautiful gardens. On clear days, you can add breathtaking views of city and ocean to the list. The Getty is a highlight of any LA visit.

A few miles further north, the **Skirball Cultural Center** (☎ 310-440-4500; 2701 N Sepulveda Blvd; adult $8, senior & student $6, child under 12 free; noon-5pm Tue-Sat, 11am-5pm Sun) takes visitors on a journey through the history of the Jewish people, showcasing their contributions to the world and to America in particular.

MALIBU — Map pp880–9

Malibu is not a destination, it's a state of mind. Its 27 miles of coast has been a celebrity enclave since the 1920s when money troubles forced landowner May Rindge to lease out property. Clara Bow and Barbara Stanwyck were among the first to move to what became known as the Malibu Colony, which is still home to A-list celebs including Tom Hanks and Barbra Streisand.

To regular folks, Malibu is best appreciated through its twin treasures: the **Santa Monica Mountains** and the beaches, such as the famous surf spot of **Malibu Surfrider**. Just south of here, sea foam spews upon a local history museum and the **Adamson House** (☎ 310-456-8432; 23200 Pacific Coast Hwy; tours $3; 11am-2pm Wed-Sat), a beautiful 1928 Spanish Colonial villa adorned with vivid local tiles. Further along the coast, the **Getty Villa** (www.getty.edu/museum/villa.html) is set to reopen in 2005 with a collection of Greek and Roman antiquities. Check the website for updates.

SANTA MONICA — Map p891

The seaside city of Santa Monica is one of the most agreeable in LA, with its early-20th-century pier, pedestrian-friendly downtown, wide beaches and excellent shopping and dining. **Third Street Promenade**, a tremendously popular pedestrian mall, extends for three long blocks from Wilshire Blvd south to Broadway. Ocean Ave parallels **Palisades Park**, perched on a bluff overlooking the Pacific.

The sentimental favorite on the famous **Santa Monica Pier** is the quaint 1920s **carousel** featured in *The Sting*. But these days the main draw is **Pacific Park** (☎ 310-260-8744; rides $2-4; 11am-11pm Sun-Thu, to midnight Fri & Sat, shorter winter hours), a small amusement park with a Ferris wheel and roller coaster. A mile inland, the **Santa Monica Museum of Art** (☎ 310-586-6488; 2525 Michigan Ave; suggested donation adult $3, senior & student $2; 11am-6pm Tue-Sat, noon-5pm Sun) is the saucy and irreverent home of changing contemporary-art exhibits. It's integrated within **Bergamot Station**, a former trolley stop that's

been converted into a nexus of the LA art scene with around 40 galleries.

LONG BEACH **Map pp880–1**

Long Beach, LA's southernmost beach town, has a small but vibrant downtown, with most of the action centered on Pine Ave. It also has a pleasant shoreline where the elegant British ocean liner **Queen Mary** (☎ 562-435-3511; www.queenmary.com; 1126 Queens Hwy; adult/senior/child $25/23/13; 10am-6pm) has been moored since 1967. Larger and more luxurious than even the *Titanic*, it transported royals, dignitaries and immigrants during its 1001 Atlantic crossings between 1934 and 1964.

Long Beach's other flagship attraction is the fabulous **Aquarium of the Pacific** (☎ 562-590-3100; 100 Aquarium Way; adult/senior/child $19/15/10; 9am-6pm). It's home to around 10,000 fish, mammals and birds from three Pacific Rim regions: Southern California and Baja California, Northern Pacific, and Tropical Pacific. You can touch small sharks, meditate over the gyrations of jellyfish and be awed by cleverly camouflaged sea dragons.

Long Beach is easily reached from Downtown via the Metro Rail Blue Line.

PASADENA **Map pp880–1**

Resting beneath the lofty San Gabriel Mountains, northeast of Downtown, Pasadena is a leafy city with impressive mansions, superb Craftsman architecture and fine art museums. Every New Year's Day,

QUIRKY, WACKY, WILD: VENICE

If aliens landed on Venice's famous **Ocean Front Walk** (known locally as Venice Boardwalk), they'd probably blend right into the human zoo of bikini-clad cyclists, chainsaw-juggling entertainers, wannabe Schwarzeneggers, a roller-skating Sikh minstrel and zealous 'meat is murder' activists. This is the place to get your hair braided, your skin tattooed or your aura adjusted. It's a freak show that must be seen to be believed, preferably on hot summer weekends when the scene is at its most surreal.

It's appropriate that this quintessential bohemian playground was the brainchild of eccentric and dreamer *extraordinaire*, cigarette heir Abbot Kinney (1850–1920). Kinney's vision was to create a cultural theme park he dubbed 'Venice of America' on marshy land just south of Santa Monica, complete with canals and imported gondoliers to pole people around his beachfront paradise. The park declined soon after Kinney's death, but 3 miles of the original canals were recently restored and are now flanked by flower-festooned villas. The **Venice Canal Walk** threads through this idyllic neighborhood, best accessed from either Venice or Washington Blvds, near Dell Ave.

Kinney may have been a little kooky, but he unwittingly set the trend for 20th-century Venice, California. Such counterculture royalty as Beatniks Lawrence Lipton and Stuart Perkoff, and *über*-hippie Jim Morrison made their homes here. It's still a cauldron of creativity peopled by karmically correct New Agers, eternal hippies, cool-conscious musicians, and artists and architects of all stripes. Galleries, studios and public art abound, much of it with an unsurprisingly surreal bent. Case in point: Jonathan Borofsky's tutu-clad *Ballerina Clown* at Rose Ave and Main St. Nearby stands star architect Frank Gehry's **Chiat/Day Building** (Map p891; 340 Main St), another famous Venice landmark, fronted by a pair of four-story binoculars by Claes Oldenburg.

Abbot Kinney would probably be delighted that one of LA's most individualistic streets bears his name. Sort of a seaside Melrose Ave with a Venetian flavor, the mile-long stretch of **Abbot Kinney Blvd** between Venice Blvd and Main St is chockablock with unique boutiques, galleries, vintage clothing stores and interesting restaurants.

When you require 'quirk,' Venice definitely provides your quota.

the country turns its attention to Pasadena as it stages the Tournament of Roses Parade (p895), a tradition dating back to 1890. This is followed by a football game at the famous **Rose Bowl** (1922), which seats nearly 100,000 spectators.

Old Pasadena is a 20-block historic shopping and entertainment district stretching along Colorado Blvd, between Arroyo Parkway and Pasadena Ave. A short walk west is the **Norton Simon Museum** (☎ 626-449-6840; www.nortonsimon.org; 411 W Colorado Blvd; adult $6, senior $3, child under 18 & student free; ⏰ noon-6pm Wed-Mon, closes 9pm Fri), with an outstanding collection of European art from renaissance to the 20th century, as well as a sampling of 2000 years of Asian sculpture.

Northwest of here, the 1908 **Gamble House** (☎ 626-793-3334; 4 Westmoreland Pl; adult $8, senior & student $5, child under 12 free; tours noon-3pm Thu-Sun), designed by Charles and Henry Greene, is a premier example of Craftsman architecture. More Greene and Greene houses can be seen on Arroyo Tce, just south of Gamble House.

LA does feel a world away at the rarefied **Huntington Library, Art Collections & Botanical Gardens** (☎ 626-405-2100; www.huntington.org; 1151 Oxford Rd; adult $10, senior $8.50, student $7, child 5-11 $4; ⏰ noon-4:30pm Tue-Fri, 10:30am-4:30pm Sat & Sun), the former estate of railroad tycoon Henry Huntington. The sprawling gardens alone are a sensorial treat, especially the **Japanese Garden** and the **Desert Garden**. The library's prized collection of rare maps, manuscripts and books includes a 1455 Gutenberg Bible, while the art gallery focuses mainly on 18th-century British and French paintings.

Activities

CYCLING & INLINE SKATING

Los Angeles has more than 200 miles of designated bike trails, and one of the most popular stretches for skating or riding is along the beach. The paved trail travels 22 miles from Temescal Canyon Rd north of Santa Monica to Torrance Beach, with a detour around the yacht harbor at Marina del Rey. Rental outfits are plentiful in all beach towns. Mountain bikers should head to the

Santa Monica Mountains. For a good Web resource, go to www.labikepaths.com. For guided tours, try LA Bike Tours (p894).

GYMS

LA has pioneered many popular fitness movements, such as aerobics, spinning and Bikram yoga (held in a heated room). Most top-end hotels have small fitness centers, but for classes or a full-fledged workout, try one of these places:

Crunch Gym (Map p889; ☎ 323-654-4550; 8000 Sunset Blvd, West Hollywood; day pass $24) Cutting-edge classes such as cardio striptease and disco yoga.

Gold's Gym (Map p891; ☎ 310-392-6004; 360 Hampton Dr, Venice; day pass $20) Arnold's old stomping ground before he became governor.

Ketchum YMCA (Map p884; ☎ 213-624-2348; 401 S Hope St, Downtown; day pass $25) Good all-round gym for men and women.

HIKING

There's excellent hiking in the Santa Monica Mountains, the outer fringes of which reach all the way to Sunset Blvd and the Pacific Coast Hwy. **Will Rogers State Historic Park**, **Topanga State Park** and **Malibu Creek State Park** are among the gateways to a variety of hikes – one-hour to all-day, easy to strenuous – through beautiful terrain. Maps are usually available at park entrances.

HORSEBACK RIDING

Leave the urban sprawl behind on the forested bridle trails of Griffith Park. Riding stables on the park's northern periphery include **Circle K** (☎ 818-843-9890; 914 S Mariposa St, Burbank), which hires out horses for about $18 the first hour and $12 each subsequent hour. **Sunset Ranch** (☎ 323-469-5450; 3400 N Beachwood Dr, Hollywood) has guided tours, including popular Friday-night rides to Burbank for dinner at a Mexican restaurant ($45, plus $10 to $20 for dinner).

SWIMMING & SURFING

Beaches beckon all along LA's coastline, with Santa Monica, Venice, Hermosa and Manhattan the most popular. Water temperatures become tolerable by late spring and are highest (about 70°F or 21°C) in August and September. The water quality is mostly good, although the ocean is usually off-limits for three days after a storm because of untreated runoff. The local, nonprofit **Heal the Bay** (☎ 310-453-0395; www.healthebay.org) constantly evaluates the water quality and posts its findings on its website. There's good surfing at Malibu Lagoon State Beach, aka Surfrider Beach, and at the Manhattan Beach pier.

Walking Tour

Map p887

HOLLYWOOD BOULEVARD

Whether it's Hollywood history, architecture or just silly fun you're after, you'll find it on a stroll along Hollywood Blvd. This tour takes in the most interesting stretch between La Brea Blvd and Vine St and covers about 1 mile. To get an even better understanding of the historic significance of the area, look for the red historic signs set up along this route, or join a guided walking tour (see Tours, p894).

La Brea Blvd marks the beginning of the **Walk of Fame**, which honors more than 2000 celebrities of film, recording, television, radio and live performance with brass stars framed in marble and embedded in the sidewalk. Soon, on your left, is the **Hollywood Entertainment Museum** (☎ 323-465-7900; 7021 Hollywood Blvd; adult/student/child $8.75/4.50/4; 🕑 10am-6pm Tue-Sun), which uses state-of-the-art technology to unravel the history and mystery of movie-making. The next block is ground zero of Hollywood revitalization in the form of **Hollywood & Highland**. This humongous complex is anchored by **Babylon Court**, where a triumphal arch inspired by DW Griffith's 1916 movie *Intolerance* frames views of the Hollywood Sign. The structure dwarfs the **Mann's Chinese Theater** (☎ 323-464-6266; 6925 Hollywood Blvd) with its famous façade and forecourt. More than 150 screen legends have left their imprint here: shoes, hands and – in the case of Jimmy Durante – a famous nose. Across the street, the beautifully restored **El Capitan Theater** (☎ 323-467-7674; 6838 Hollywood Blvd) charms with its flamboyant Spanish Colonial façade and East Indian interior.

The next block starts with a trio of time-worn tourist traps: **Ripley's Believe It or Not!**, the **Guinness World of Records Museum** and the **Hollywood Wax Museum**. All are open from about 10am to midnight and admission is around $11 per person. A throwback to Hollywood's golden age is the **Egyptian Theatre**, now home of the American Cinematheque, a nonprofit film organization. Also given a new lease on life was the **Pig 'n Whistle** (☎ 323-463-0000;

LOONY LOS ANGELES

Anything goes and anything sells in LA, a city that acts as a magnet for the wacky, the outlandish and the eccentric. Take, for instance, **Angelyne**, a self-styled Hollywood bombshell of indeterminable age famous for nothing but tooling around town in a convertible pink Corvette and erecting huge billboards of her scantly-clad self. The Venice Boardwalk, no slouch in the strangeness department, has **Harry Perry**, a turbaned, roller-skating 'Karmakosmickrusader' (his word) who showers unsuspecting tourists with some pretty, shall we say, 'unique' guitar riffs. Both, of course, have their own Web pages (www.angelyne.com and www.venicebeachcalifornia.com, if you must know).

LA also has some pretty weird stores. **Necromance** (☎ 323-934-8684; 7220 Melrose Ave, Hollywood) is, of course, in love with the dead and sells animal and human bones, frogs pickled in formaldehyde and vampire repellent kits. Up the street, at **Panpipes Magickal Marketplace** (☎ 323-462-7078; 1641 Cahuenga Blvd, Hollywood), potion-master George Hiram Derby mixes more than 10,000 metaphysical blends to solve whatever problem's ailing you. And where else than LA would you find a county-operated gift shop in the coroner's office called **Skeletons in the Closet** (☎ 323-343-0760; 1104 N Mission Rd, Downtown) selling personalized toe tags and beach blankets with corpse outlines?

Even museums get into the bizarro business in LA. The **Banana Museum** (☎ 626-798-2272; $5; 🕒 by appointment), near Pasadena, brims with 17,000 items revolving around the ubiquitous 'monkey steaks.' And if that isn't strange enough for you, head to the **Museum of Jurassic Technology** (☎ 310-836-6131; www.mjt.org; 9341 Venice Blvd, Culver City; $4; 🕒 2-8pm Thu, noon-6pm Fri-Sun). Exhibits here have nothing to do with dinosaurs and even less with technology but are simply, seductively mind-bending. And please! Let us know if you figure out what it's *really* all about.

6714 Hollywood Blvd), a restaurant and celebrity hangout in the 1930s and '40s.

If the stars' undies get you all excited, drop into **Frederick's of Hollywood Lingerie Museum** (☎ 323-466-8506; admission free; 🕒 10am-9pm Mon-Sat, 11am-6:30pm Sun) in the back of the saucy store, before continuing to the fabled corner of Hollywood and Vine, which looks pretty drab in reality. Exceptions are the art deco **Pantages Theater**, which hosts Broadway blockbusters, and the **Capitol Records Tower** (1956), the world's first circular office building, which resembles a stack of records.

Los Angeles for Children

Traveling to LA with the tots in tow is not a problem. Besides such perennial favorites as Disneyland, Knott's Berry Farm and Universal Studios, there's plenty to explore on the beach, in the mountains and even in the urban core.

Museums suitable for the younger set include the Aquarium of the Pacific (p891), the Autry Museum of Western Heritage (p887), the California Science Center (p886), the Natural History Museum of LA County (p886) and the Page Museum (p888). The Los Angeles Zoo (p886) is a reliable standby, while older kids will probably get a kick out of Hollywood Blvd (p893) and the *Queen Mary* (p891).

LA also has a number of galleries that are dedicated to children, usually with an active schedule of storytelling, reading and workshops. **Every Picture Tells a Story** (Map p889; ☎ 323-932-6070; 7525 Beverly Blvd, Mid-City) and **Storyopolis** (Map p889; ☎ 310-358-2500; 116 N Robertson Blvd, West Hollywood) are both good places to check out.

Generations of Angelenos have grown up with the **Bob Baker Marionette Theater** (Map p884; ☎ 213-250-9995; 1345 W 1st St), north of Downtown. Since 1963, it has enthralled kids with its adorable singing and dancing marionettes and stuffed animals that interact with their young audiences. It's pure magic.

In Santa Monica, the **Puppet & Magic Center** (Map p884; ☎ 310-656-0483; 1255 2nd St) is a 40-seat theater with regularly scheduled performances as well as puppet workshops and a puppet museum.

The Calendar supplement of the *Los Angeles Times'* Thursday and Sunday editions has a special section dedicated to children's activities.

Tours

LA Bike Tours (☎ 323-466-5890; www.labiketours.com) Half-day and day-long tours of LA neighborhoods; bike and helmet provided.

Los Angeles Conservancy (☎ 213-623-2489; www.laconservancy.org) Thematic walking tours of Downtown with an architectural focus.

Red Line Tours (Map p887; ☎ 323-402-1074; www.redlinetours.com; 6773 Hollywood Blvd) Fun and informative guided walking tours of Hollywood and Downtown using headsets that cut out traffic noise so you can hear your guide perfectly.

Starline Tours (☎ 800-959-3131) Bus tours of the city, stars' homes and theme parks.

Festivals & Events

LA has a packed calendar of annual festivals and special events. Here are some of the blockbusters:

Rose Parade (☎ 626-449-4100; www.tournamentofroses.com) An enormous cavalcade of flower-festooned floats along Pasadena's Colorado Blvd on New Year's Day, followed by the Rose Bowl football game.

Cinco de Mayo (☎ 213-625-5045) Celebrated with bands and parades in Downtown's El Pueblo in early May.

LA Film Festival (www.lafilmfest.com) Ten days in June.

Los Angeles County Fair (☎ 909-623-3111) The world's largest fair takes place in Pomona, in eastern LA County, every September.

West Hollywood's Halloween Party (☎ 310-289-2525) A rambunctious street fair with eccentric costumes along Santa Monica Blvd on October 31.

Doo Dah Parade (☎ 626-440-7379) A wacky Pasadena parody of the traditional Rose Parade on the Saturday after Thanksgiving.

Hollywood Christmas Parade (☎ 323-469-2337; www.hollywoodchristmas.com) Held in late November it features film and TV celebrities on flashy floats, along with horses, classic cars, marching bands and, of course, Santa Claus.

Sleeping

When choosing where to stay in sprawling Los Angeles, think about what type of experience you most want. For the beach life, base yourself in **Santa Monica** or **Venice**. Urban explorers will want to be close to **West Hollywood** and its nightlife, shopping and dining. **Downtown** is great for fans of history and architecture. **Hollywood**, with its easy access to the Metro Rail Red Line, is convenient if you don't have transportation, while staying in posh **Beverly Hills** is certain to impress friends back home. Some bargains notwithstanding, hotel rates in Los Angeles are higher than the national average. Expect to pay between $100 and $175 for a mid-range room. Note that a tax of 12% to 14% is added to all room rates.

DOWNTOWN

Map p884

Hotel Figueroa (☎ 213-627-8971, 800-421-9092; www.figueroahotel.com; 939 S Figueroa St; s $100-120, d $115-140; P ⛶ 💻 ♿) A striking lobby welcomes guests to this Downtown favorite, steps from the Staples Center. The theme continues

GAY & LESBIAN LOS ANGELES

West Hollywood (WeHo) is the heart of LA's gay and lesbian scene, and there's practically 24/seven action in the bars, restaurants, clubs, coffeehouses and gyms along Santa Monica Blvd. Most focus primarily on gay men, although a few cater to lesbian and mixed audiences. Beauty reigns supreme in 'Boyz Town' and the intimidation factor can be high unless you're buff, bronzed and styled. A more low-key vibe pervades Silver Lake, where bars are far more mixed. The beach towns, historically havens of queerness, now have relaxed, neighborly scenes, especially in Venice and Long Beach. For updates and specifics about the various scenes, check out the free magazines available in bars, restaurants and gay-friendly establishments.

A Different Light Bookstore (Map p889; ☎ 310-854-6601; 8853 Santa Monica Blvd, West Hollywood) is the city's number-one gay bookstore, while **Sisterhood Bookstore** (☎ 310-477-7300; 1351 Westwood Blvd, Westwood) caters to women, though not exclusively to lesbians. The **LA Gay & Lesbian Center** (Map p887; ☎ 323-993-7400; www.laglc.org; 1625 N Schrader Blvd, Hollywood) is a one-stop service and health agency.

Good places to party include **Rage** (Map p889; ☎ 310-652-7055; 8911 Santa Monica Blvd), one of West Hollywood's top dance clubs, with plenty of posing, preening and cruising going on. The nearby **Abbey** (Map p889; ☎ 310-657-1176; 8857 Santa Monica Blvd) goes for the laid-back breakfast and lunch crowd by day but seriously turns up the heat at night, especially in the back bar with its semiprivate alcoves. The **Palms** (Map p889; ☎ 310-652-6188; 8572 Santa Monica Blvd), WeHo's oldest lesbian bar, is still going strong after three decades and even gets the occasional celebrity drop-in (eg Melissa Etheridge).

THE AUTHOR'S CHOICE

Maison 140 (Map p889; 310-281-4000, 800-432-5444; www.maison140.com; 140 S Lasky Dr, Beverly Hills; r $170-200; P) This stylish gem, housed in what was once the Beverly Hills abode of silent-movie star Lillian Gish, is as sexy as hotels can get without being risqué. Designer Kelly Wearstler has created a sumptuous fantasy setting by cleverly marrying French frivolity and Asian simplicity of line. Each of the 43 rooms is sheathed in boldly patterned and colored wallpaper. Eclectic artwork and vintage furnishings combine with Chenille throws, Frette bed linens and other luxury touches to create ultimate comfort. Finish a day of seeing the sights with complimentary wine at the evening reception or retire to the intimate Bar Noir to kick off a night on the town with the signature French Kiss champagne cocktail. Rates include breakfast.

in more subdued fashion in the comfortable rooms. The pool and outdoor bar are perfect for post-sightseeing relaxation.

Hilton Checkers (213-624-0000, 800-423-5798; www.checkershotel.com; 535 S Grand Ave; r $300-350; P) Radiant rooms in soothing natural colors form a relaxing antidote to busy days on the tourist track at this 1927 boutique hotel. Other places to unwind include the rooftop pool and the elegant restaurant.

Stillwell Hotel (213-627-1151, 800-553-4774; 838 S Grand Ave; r $60; P) Nearly a century old, the Stillwell offers clean and no-nonsense rooms, good security, an excellent Indian restaurant and a bar so noir it seems to have leapt off the pages of a Raymond Chandler novel.

Kawada Hotel (213-621-4455, 800-752-9232; www.kawadahotel.com; 200 S Hill St; r $90-130; P) Close to most Downtown attractions, the Kawada caters mostly to business clients, meaning rates often drop on weekends. Conveniences include in-room VCRs and two on-site eateries.

Also recommended:

Millennium Biltmore Hotel (213-624-1011, 800-245-8673; 506 S Grand Ave; r $175-300; P) A historic landmark.

Wilshire Royale Howard Johnson Plaza (213-387-5311, 800-421-8072; www.hojola.com; 2619 Wilshire Blvd; r $130-180; P) Family-friendly.

Milner Hotel (213-627-6981, 877-645-6377; www.milner-hotels.com; 813 S Flower St; r $80-100) A solid budget choice.

HOLLYWOOD Map p887

Hollywood Roosevelt Hotel (323-466-7000, 800-950-7667; www.hollywoodroosevelt.com; 7000 Hollywood Blvd; r $200-400; P) This history-making hotel (the first Academy Awards were held here in 1929) has completely reinvented itself with most rooms now sporting a sleek Asian contempo look. The handsome lobby and pool area, though, retain the original Spanish flair.

Hollywood Celebrity Hotel (323-850-6464, 800-222-7017; www.hotelcelebrity.com; 1775 Orchid Ave; r $65-75, family ste $125; P) A touch of glam survives in the lobby of this value-priced 1930s art deco gem with its large and clean, if fairly basic, rooms. The central location is great, as is the free breakfast and newspaper.

Best Western Hollywood Hills Hotel (323-464-5181, 800-528-1234; 6141 Franklin Ave; r $90-130; P) Spacious, well-lit rooms wrap around a central courtyard with an inviting pool. Murals are everywhere, and the popular coffee shop is open until 3am.

Orchid Suites Hotel (323-874-9678, 800-537-3052; www.orchidsuites.com; 1753 N Orchid Ave; r $90-200; P) Self-caterers can whip up gourmet meals in the fully-equipped kitchens in this old-fashioned, all-suite establishment in the shadow of Hollywood & Highland. During downtime, catch some rays poolside or on the rooftop patio.

Hollywood Hills Hotel & Apartments (323-874-5089, 800-615-2224; www.hollywoodhillshotel.com; 1999 N Sycamore Ave; r $90-120; P) Panoramic views, a tree-fringed curvy pool, and studios and suites with plenty of elbow room and kitchens are among the assets here. It's a bit remote and thus better suited for drivers.

Also recommended:

Magic Castle Hotel (323-851-0800, 800-741-4915; www.magiccastlehotel.com; 7025 Franklin Ave; studio & ste $70-170; P) Good-value standby, guests have access to the Magic Castle, a fabled private magic club nearby.

USA Hostel Hollywood (323-462-3777, 800-524-6783; www.usahostels.com; 1624 Schrader Blvd; dm $17-19, r $41-48) A well-run and central hostel.

Renaissance Hollywood Hotel (323-856-1200, 888-236-2427; www.renaissancehollywood.com; 1755 N Highland Ave; r $200-250; P) Part of the Hollywood & Highland complex.

WEST HOLLYWOOD & MID-CITY **Map p889**

Standard Hotel (☎ 323-650-9090; www.standardhotel.com; 8300 Sunset Blvd, West Hollywood; r $100-225; P ✹ ☸) This *über*-hip retro hotel has boundary-pushing surprises, including a Smurf-blue Astroturf by the pool, a barber who also does tattoos, and condoms in the minibar. So LA! The lobby-lounge and 24-hour coffee shop are a scene as well.

Beverly Laurel Motor Hotel (☎ 323-651-2441, 800-962-3824; 8018 Beverly Blvd, Mid-City; s/d $80/84; P ✹ ☸) Those wanting to ride the retro wave on a slim budget should check into one of the arty rooms at this venerable 1950s motel. The attached **Swingers** diner crawls with hipsters until the wee hours.

Best Western Sunset Plaza Hotel (☎ 323-654-0750, 800-421-3652; www.sunsetplazahotel.com; 8400 Sunset Blvd, West Hollywood; r $130-200; P ✹ ☸) Walk to clubs and restaurants from this high-energy, cosmopolitan hotel. Rooms are nicely decorated and spacious and some have kitchenettes. Rates include breakfast.

Beverly Plaza Hotel (☎ 323-658-6600, 800-624-6835; www.beverlyplazahotel.com; 8384 W 3rd St, West Hollywood; r $145-275; P ✹ ☸) One of those exceptional hotels that dazzle with class not glitz, the Beverly Plaza has oversized French-flavored rooms, gracious surroundings and a bustling location next to the Beverly Center.

Good budget options include the well-run **Orbit Hostel** (☎ 323-655-1510; 7950 Melrose Ave, Mid-City; dm/s/d $18/50/60; ✹ 💻) and the zero-frills **Alta Cienega Motel** (☎ 310-652-5797; 1005 N La Cienega Blvd, West Hollywood; r $60; P ✹ 💻), where Jim Morrison used to stay (in room 32).

BEVERLY HILLS & WESTWOOD

Beverly Terrace Hotel (Map p889; ☎ 310-274-8141, 800-421-7223; www.beverlyterracehotel.com; 469 N Doheny Dr, Beverly Hills; r $105-145; P ✹ ☸) Steps from the Sunset Strip, this good-value hotel offers snug but comfortable rooms and a free poolside breakfast in a faintly tropical setting. The on-site Italian restaurant, Trattoria Amici, attracts its share of Hollywood types.

Hotel del Capri (☎ 310-474-3511; www.hoteldelcapri.com; 10587 Wilshire Blvd, Westwood; r $120-145, ste $145-175; P ✹ 💻 ☸) A flowery island in Westwood's concrete jungle, the Capri has brightly decorated rooms and suites, some with kitchenettes and whirlpool tubs. Stays include free room-service breakfasts.

Beverly Hills Reeves Hotel (Map p889; ☎ 310-271-3006; 120 S Reeves Dr, Beverly Hills; r $45-85; P ✹) Budget and Beverly Hills don't usually mix, except at this old but clean property on a quiet side street. Rooms come with kitchenette and include a small breakfast.

Luxury abodes naturally abound in this part of town, including the mid-century, modern **Avalon Hotel** (Map p889; ☎ 310-277-5221, 800-535-4715; www.avalonbeverlyhills.com; 9400 W Olympic Blvd, Beverly Hills; r $200-230; P ✹ 💻 ☸) and the sleek and all-suite **W Los Angeles** (☎ 310-208-8765, 877-946-8357; www.whotels.com; 930 Hilgard Ave, Westwood; ste from $320; P ✹ 💻 ☸).

SANTA MONICA & VENICE **Map p891**

Hotel California (☎ 310-393-2363, 866-571-0000; www.hotelca.com; 1670 Ocean Ave, Santa Monica; r $170-300; 💻) Everything's just peachy at this beachy abode, a Frisbee throw from the sand. Most rooms are breezy and light-flooded, and larger ones have patios and kitchenettes.

Inn at Venice Beach (☎ 310-821-2557, 800-828-0688; www.innatvenicebeach.com; 327 Washington Blvd, Venice; r $110-180; P ✹) Close to the beach, the Venice canals and bars and restaurants, this pleasant inn sports fresh and cheerful decor and a good range of amenities, including refrigerators and hair dryers.

Sea Shore Motel (☎ 310-392-2787; www.seashoremotel.com; 2637 Main St, Santa Monica; r $75-95; P) Right on boutique- and restaurant-filled Main St, assets at the newly slicked-up Sea Shore include a good range of creature comforts and beach proximity.

Venice Beach House (☎ 310-823-1966; www.venicebeachhouse.com; 15 30th Ave, Venice; r $130-195; P) A block from the beach, this B&B in a 1911 Craftsman bungalow is a welcoming old-California retreat with nine cozy, antique-filled rooms, some of them with shared baths.

Cadillac Hotel (☎ 310-399-8876; www.thecadillachotel.com; 8 Dudley Ave, Venice; r $90-110, ste $130-150; P 💻) Charlie Chaplin used to spend summers at this beachfront art deco landmark. Rooms are sparse but all have ocean views, and the sundeck is conducive to striking up friendships. The area, alas, gets a bit unsavory after dark.

HI Los Angeles-Santa Monica (☎ 310-393-9913, 800-909-4776; 1436 2nd St, Santa Monica; dm/r $30/75; 💻) If money is tight, this place is a good option.

Hotel Casa del Mar (☎ 310-581-5533, 800-898-6999; www.hotelcasadelmar.com; 1910 Ocean Front Walk, Santa Monica; r $380-620; P ✹ 💻 ☸) The historic and beachfront Casa del Mar should fit the bill if money is no object.

Eating

One of the great delights of cosmopolitan LA is eating out in one of the cities that, back in the 1980s, gave birth to California cuisine. While healthily prepared dishes revolving around fresh, seasonal ingredients are still in vogue, other recent trends have included Nuevo Latino, which draws from various Latin-American food cultures, and the good old-fashioned steakhouse. West Hollywood, Beverly Hills and Santa Monica have the most innovative restaurants, but there's plenty of tasty cooking going on beyond the culinary temples. After all, LA's motley mélange of ethnicities allows for authentic and often excellent food from around the world. Be it Mexican, Thai, Japanese, French or Italian, you're rarely far from a great restaurant. Reservations are a good idea at dinnertime.

DOWNTOWN Map p884

Ciudad (☎ 213-486-5171; 445 S Figueroa St; lunch $9-19, dinner $15-26; ⏲ lunch Mon-Fri, dinner nightly) For inventive takes on Nuevo Latino fare, head to this boldly colored and high-ceilinged restaurant, where even the desserts are worth the hip-expanding indulgence.

McCormick & Schmick's (☎ 213-629-1929; 633 W 5th St; lunch $8-15, dinner $10-20) Ultra-fresh fish prepared in umpteen ways and served in an elegant and traditional setting at reasonable prices – no wonder this place is popular. Hot tip for bargain gourmets: show up for Happy Hour (3pm to 7pm Monday to Thursday and 3pm to 10:30pm Friday) and choose from the extensive $1.95 menu.

Nick & Stef's Steakhouse (☎ 213-680-0330; 330 S Hope St; lunch $12-20, dinner $19-32; ⏲ lunch Mon-Fri, dinner nightly) You'll have a fine time sending your cholesterol count through the roof with the flavorful, melt-in-your-mouth meats served in this *très moderne* dining shrine. And, damn the torpedoes, finish with the lemon meringue pie.

Hama Sushi (☎ 213-680-3454; 347 E 2nd St; meals from $12) Sublime sushi and sashimi is all that's ever served at this pocket-sized bar, which draws raw-fish connoisseurs from all over town.

Yang Chow (☎ 213-625-0811; 819 N Broadway; mains $8-15) The menu is as long as the Wall of China, but most patrons have their mind set on a plate of the famous slippery shrimp. The moo shoo pancakes are good too.

Downtown is a great place for the cash-strapped, at least for breakfast and lunch. Maria's Pescado Frito (central aisle) and China Café (upper level) at the **Grand Central Market** (317 Broadway) are recommended, as is French-flavored **Angélique Cafe** (☎ 213-623-8698; 840 S Spring St; mains $6-11).

HOLLYWOOD

Patina (☎ 323-467-1108; 5955 Melrose Ave; mains $29-39) At his strikingly handsome flagship restaurant, star chef Joachim Splichal cleverly twists French fare with California cuisine. Foodies in the know have Patina's reservation line on speed dial.

Madame Matisse (☎ 323-662-4862; 3536 Sunset Blvd; lunch $6-9, dinner $10-18) This bustling, pocket-sized French bistro wouldn't be out of place in Provence or Paris, but here it is in hip Silver Lake. Chef Olivier Bouillot's repertoire ranges from classics like coq au vin to creative takes like eggs benedict with salmon. BYOB at dinner (no corkage).

Mel's Drive-in (Map p887; ☎ 323-465-2111; 1660 N Highland Ave; mains $7-10) Catch that *American Graffiti* vibe at this fun '50s diner in the historic Max Factor Building in central Hollywood. The epic menu features all the classics.

Taylor's Prime Steaks (☎ 213-382-8449; 3361 W 8th St, Koreatown; mains $12-26) This landmark steakhouse was retro long before retro became hip. Expect perfectly prepared meats at honest-to-goodness prices.

El Conquistador (☎ 323-666-5136; 3701 Sunset Blvd; mains $10-14) This popular Mexican cantina in Silver Lake has a bar lifted straight from a Mexican fishing village. The food's delicious and the service is friendly.

Other options include **Palermo** (☎ 323-663-1178; 1858 Vermont Ave; mains $8-13; ⏲ closed Tue) for delicious pizza, and the take-out only **Yuca's** (☎ 323-662-1214; 2056 Hillhurst Ave, Los Feliz; dishes $3-6) for habit-forming Yucatan-style burritos, tacos and *tortas* (sandwiches).

BEVERLY HILLS, WEST HOLLYWOOD & MID-CITY Map p889

Alto Palato (☎ 310-657-9271; 755 N La Cienega Blvd, West Hollywood; pizzas $11-14, mains $14-27; ⏲ dinner) Alto Palato celebrates Italy's rich culinary heritage with flavorful, authentic dishes from throughout the Boot. The thin-crust pizza is a perennial favorite.

Chaya Brasserie (☎ 310-859-8833; 8741 Alden Dr; mains $14-28) Chaya's menu is as creative as the crowd and the Zen-meets-industrial dining room. The chef performs miracles with Cal-French cuisine complemented by Asian inflections.

Spago Beverly Hills (☎ 310-385-0880; 176 N Cañon Dr; mains $17-32) Wolfgang Puck's flagship restaurant has a seasonal menu that's best enjoyed on the romantic patio anchored by ancient olive trees. Make reservations early or hope for no-shows.

Cobras & Matadors (☎ 323-932-6178; 7615 W Beverly Blvd; tapas $4-12) Tables are squished together as tight as lovers at this trendy tapas bar. If you pick up a bottle of vino at the shop next door, you'll pay no corkage fee.

Campanile (☎ 323-938-1447; 624 S La Brea Ave; lunch $12-18, dinner $24-38; lunch Mon-Fri, dinner Mon-Sat) At this stellar urban-rustic food emporium, chef Marc Peel keeps the menu constantly in flux by using only farm-fresh, seasonal ingredients. His partner, Nancy Silverton, reigns as the dessert goddess.

Put together a picnic at the **Original Farmers Market** or have a sit-down meal right amid the bustle. Good choices include the New Orleans–style **Gumbo Pot** (☎ 323-933-0358; mains $5-9) and the hip, art deco **Kokomo** (☎ 323-933-0773; lunch $5-9, dinner $11-13).

Not only night owls like to refuel at **Damiano Mr Pizza** (☎ 323-658-7611; 412 N Fairfax Ave; meals less than $6) and **Pink's Hot Dogs** (☎ 323-931-4223; 709 La Brea Ave; meals less than $5), a legendary 'doggeria.' The **Newsroom Café** (☎ 310-652-4444; 120 N Robertson Blvd; mains $5-13) is great for healthy food and star spotting.

SANTA MONICA & VENICE Map p891

Border Grill (☎ 310-451-1655; 1445 4th St, Santa Monica; lunch $7.50-15, dinner $14-25) It may look as if it's designed by six-year-olds but the Border Grill has a decidedly grown-up menu of boldly flavored south-of-the-border dishes.

JiRaffe (☎ 310-917-6671; 502 Santa Monica Blvd, Santa Monica; lunch $10-12.50, dinner $18-28) The chef is an avid surfer who learned his culinary craft in Paris and now regales diners with caramelized pork chops, the signature roast-beet salad and other expertly prepared dishes. Walnut furniture, crystal chandeliers and original art give the dining room a private-mansion feel.

Rose Café (☎ 310-399-0711; 220 Rose Ave, Venice; café less than $4, restaurant $9-16) This popular standby has two tree-fringed patios, one for the self-service café serving yummy baked goods, the other for the restaurant, where the accent is on fresh salads, light pastas and seafood.

Sidewalk Café (☎ 310-399-5547; 1401 Ocean Front Walk, Venice; mains $9-13) Come here for old-fashioned American fare and front-row seats for the stream of bizarre humanity parading along the Ocean Front Walk.

Also recommended:

Real Food Daily (☎ 310-451-7544; 514 Santa Monica Blvd; mains $6-12) Excellent organic and vegan food.

Wolfgang Puck Express (☎ 310-576-4770; 1315 Third Street Promenade; mains $7-10) Try the pizza or Chinese chicken salad.

Ye Olde King's Head (☎ 310-451-1402; 116 Santa Monica Blvd; mains $7.50-14) Great fish and chips.

Drinking

Formosa Café (Map p887; ☎ 323-850-9050; 7156 Santa Monica Blvd, Hollywood) The one-time watering hole of Bogart, Monroe and Gable is a cool place to sop up some Hollywood nostalgia along with your cocktail. Mai tais and martinis are beverages of choice.

Cat & Fiddle Pub (Map p887; 6530 Sunset Blvd, Hollywood) Order up a pint, grab an outdoor table and enjoy Sunday twilight jazz radio broadcasts at this ever-popular pub, a favorite among expat Brits.

Beauty Bar (Map p887; ☎ 323-468-3800; 1638 N Cahuenga Blvd, Hollywood) At this pint-sized cocktail bar, decorated with hair-salon paraphernalia from the Kennedy era, you can sip your martini, get your nails done or peruse the scenester crowd while seated in swivel chairs beneath plastic hair dryers.

Good Luck Bar (☎ 323-666-3524; 1514 Hillhurst Ave, Los Feliz) The clientele is cool, the jukebox loud and the drinks seductively strong at this cultish watering hole decked out in Chinese opium den-inspired carmine red.

Toppers (Map p891; ☎ 310-393-8080; 1111 2nd St, Santa Monica) Get a buzz from the margaritas, fill yourself up at one of LA's best happy hours (4:30pm to 7:30pm daily) and watch the sun drop into the ocean at this buzzing bar atop the Radisson Huntley Hotel.

Also recommended:

Daddy's (Map p887; ☎ 323-463-7777; 1610 N Vine St, Hollywood) Pick-up joint with sensuously curved booths (and hips).

Lava Lounge (Map p887; ☎ 323-876-6612; 1533 N La Brea Ave, Hollywood) Tiki-themed bar, often with live music.
Circle Bar (Map p891; ☎ 310-450-0508; 2926 Main St, Santa Monica) Strong drinks and DJ dancing.
Rooftop Lounge @ The Standard Downtown LA (Map p884; ☎ 213-892-8080; 550 S Flower St, Downtown) Trendy party joint with skyline views.

Entertainment

To keep your finger on what's hot in LA, your best sources of information are the Calendar section of the *Los Angeles Times* and the free *LA Weekly*, available at restaurants, shops and pubs. Tickets, where necessary, are available from each venue's box office or through **Ticketmaster** (☎ 213-480-3232; www.ticketmaster.com).

LIVE MUSIC & NIGHTCLUBS

Babe & Ricky's (☎ 323-295-9112; 4339 Leimert Blvd, Leimert Park) Mama Laura has presided over LA's oldest blues club for nearly four decades. The Monday-night jam session, with free food, often brings the house down.

Blue Café (☎ 562-983-7111; 210 Promenade, Long Beach) This local institution is a regular stop for local and touring jazz and blues talent. Good drinks and food are best consumed on the nice, large patio.

Conga Room (Map p889; ☎ 323-549-9765; 5364 Wilshire Blvd, Mid-City) This gorgeous Latin dance club with the heady feel of pre-revolution Havana regularly vibrates with hip-shaking gents and twirling ladies in spiky heels. Dress nicely.

House of Blues (Map p889; ☎ 323-848-5100; 8430 Sunset Blvd, West Hollywood) Top talent of all stripes, not just the blues, performs at this faux–Mississippi Delta shack that helped revitalize the Sunset Strip in the '90s. The Sunday Gospel Brunch (seatings at 10am and 1pm; adult/child $35/18.50) is an institution.

Roxy (Map p889; ☎ 310-276-2222; 9009 Sunset Blvd, West Hollywood) A Sunset fixture since 1973, the Roxy still serves as a launch pad for bands on the verge of stardom. Big names, including Bruce Springsteen, have been known to pop in for impromptu concerts.

Temple Bar (Map p891; ☎ 310-393-6611; 1026 Wilshire Blvd, Santa Monica) At one of the more happening hangouts west of Hollywood the bands are hit-or-miss, but the drinks are strong, the crowd's heavy on the eye candy and the ambience fairly relaxed.

The Derby (☎ 323-663-8979; 4500 Los Feliz Blvd, Los Feliz) Some of the best swing dancers in town jump 'n' jive around the pint-size dance floor, while stylish retro bands play on. Call about free dance lessons.

Also recommended are the following:
Largo (Map p889; ☎ 323-852-1073; 432 N Fairfax Ave, Mid-City) Supper club serving up an eclectic musical schedule.
Troubadour (Map p889; ☎ 310-276-6168; 9081 Santa Monica Blvd, West Hollywood) Old-time good timer.
Viper Room (Map p889; ☎ 310-358-1880; 8852 Sunset Blvd, West Hollywood) Johnny Depp–owned, celebrity-heavy crowd.

SPECTATOR SPORTS

Dodger Stadium (Map p884; ☎ 323-224-1448; 1000 Elysian Park Ave) LA's Major League Baseball team plays from April to September in this legendary stadium.

Staples Center (Map p884; ☎ 213-742-7340; 1111 S Figueroa St, Downtown) This state-of-the-art venue is home base for all three of LA's professional basketball teams: the LA Lakers; the LA Sparks, the city's successful women's team; and the LA Clippers, its secondary men's team. The LA Kings professional ice hockey team also plays here.

THEATER

Live theater thrives in Los Angeles thanks to a seemingly endless talent pool. Half-price theater tickets for shows taking place that week are sold on-line by **Theatre LA** (www.theatrela.org).

A Noise Within (☎ 323-953-7795; 234 S Brand Blvd, Glendale) Founded by alumni of the American Conservatory Theater in San Francisco, this troupe puts the 'class' into 'classical.' The repertory ranges from Shakespeare to Noel Coward.

Actors' Gang Theatre (Map p887; ☎ 323-465-0566; 6209 Santa Monica Blvd, Hollywood) Co-founded by Tim Robbins, this socially mindful troupe presents daring and off-beat interpretations of classics and new works pulled from ensemble workshops.

Geffen Playhouse (☎ 310-208-5454; 10886 Le Conte Ave, Westwood) Come here for cutting-edge productions by leading American playwrights, often featuring a star-studded cast.

Mark Taper Forum (Map p884; ☎ 213-628-2772; 135 N Grand Ave, Downtown) Part of the Music Center of LA County complex, the well-respected Mark Taper is known for its high-caliber premieres, often with celebrity casts. Rush tickets ($12) start selling 10 minutes before curtain.

Also recommended are the following:

East West Players (Map p884; ☎ 213-625-4397; 120 N Judge John Aiso St, Downtown) Pioneering Asian Pacific American ensemble.

Groundlings Theater (Map p889; ☎ 323-934-9700; 7307 Melrose Ave, Mid-City) First-rate improv school and comedy ensemble.

Pantages Theatre (Map p887; ☎ 213-480-3232; 6233 Hollywood Blvd, Hollywood) Historic art deco venue for blockbuster musicals.

CLASSICAL MUSIC & OPERA

LA Philharmonic Orchestra (☎ 323-850-2000; tickets $15-175) Led by Esa Pekka-Salonen, the world-class LA Phil moved into the new Walt Disney Hall in the fall 2003 season. The repertory ranges from works by obscure composers to obscure works by famous composers.

LA Opera (☎ 213-972-8001; tickets $30-170) Under the stewardship of Plácido Domingo, the LA Opera has fine-tuned its mostly high-caliber repertory. Performances with English subtitles take place in the Music Center's **Dorothy Chandler Pavilion** (135 N Grand Ave, Downtown).

LA Master Chorale (☎ 213-626-0624) This critically acclaimed 120-voice choir presents stand-alone recitals around town and also serves as the chorus for the LA Phil and the LA Opera.

Hollywood Bowl (Map p887; ☎ 323-850-2000; 2301 N Highland Ave, Hollywood; tickets $1-105) From late June through September the sounds of Mozart, Gershwin, The Who and other music greats ring out at this historic outdoor venue. Bring wine and a picnic to enjoy before the show.

Getting There & Away

AIR

Los Angeles International Airport (LAX; Map pp880-1; ☎ 310-646-5252; www.lawa.org), about 17 miles southwest of Downtown, has eight terminals situated around a two-level, central traffic loop. Ticketing and check-in are on the upper (departure) level, while baggage-claim areas are on the lower (arrival) level. The hub for most international airlines is the Tom Bradley International Terminal.

To travel between terminals, board the free Shuttle A beneath the 'Shuttle' sign outside each terminal on the lower level. Hotel courtesy shuttles stop here as well. A free minibus for the disabled can be ordered by calling ☎ 310-646-6402.

Regional airports are the **Burbank-Glendale-Pasadena**, 14 miles northwest of Downtown, and **Long Beach Airport**, 22 miles south.

BUS

Greyhound (Map p884; ☎ 213-629-8421; 1716 E 7th St) is located in a fairly rough part of Downtown, so try not to arrive after dark. Bus No 58 goes to the transit plaza at Union Station with onward service around town, including Metro Rail's Red Line to Hollywood. Some Greyhound buses go directly to the **Hollywood bus terminal** (Map p887; ☎ 323-466-6381; 1715 N Cahuenga Blvd).

CAR

If you're driving into Los Angeles, there are several routes by which you might enter the metropolitan area.

From San Francisco and Northern California, the fastest route to LA is on the I-5 through the San Joaquin Valley. Hwy 101 is slower but more picturesque, while the most scenic – and slowest – route is the Pacific Coast Hwy (Hwy 1).

From San Diego and other points south, I-5 is the obvious route. Near Irvine, I-405 branches off I-5 and takes a westerly route to Long Beach and Santa Monica, bypassing Downtown LA entirely and rejoining I-5 near San Fernando.

From Las Vegas or the Grand Canyon, you'd take I-15 south to I-10, then head west into LA. I-10 is the main east-west artery through LA and continues on to Santa Monica.

TRAIN

Downtown's historic Union Station is the home of **Amtrak** (Map p884; ☎ 800-872-7245; 800 N Alameda St). Interstate trains stopping in LA are the *Coast Starlight* to Seattle, the *Southwest Chief* to Chicago and the *Sunset Limited* to Orlando. The *Pacific Surfliner* regularly travels to San Diego ($27, three hours), Santa Barbara ($20, 2¾ hours) and San Luis Obispo ($31, 5½ hours).

Getting Around

TO/FROM LAX

Door-to-door shuttles operate from the lower level of all terminals beneath the signs marked 'Shuttle.' Three companies dominate: **Prime Time** (☎ 800-473-3743), **Super Shuttle** (☎ 310-782-6600) and **Xpress Shuttle** (☎ 800-427-7483). You can expect to pay $12 to Downtown, $19 to Hollywood and $14 to Santa Monica. Practically all hostels and airport-area hotels have arrangements with shuttle companies for free or discounted pick-ups.

Curbside dispatchers will summon a taxi for you. Fares average $20 to $25 to Santa Monica, $25 to $35 to Downtown or Hollywood and up to $80 to Disneyland, plus a $2.50 airport surcharge.

CAR & MOTORCYCLE

All the major international car-rental agencies have branches at LAX and throughout Los Angeles (see p1121, for toll-free reservation numbers). Use the courtesy phones in the arrival areas at LAX to phone car-rental companies for quotes or reservations. Their offices and car lots are some distance from the terminal, but each company has free shuttles to take you there.

For Harley rentals, go to **Eagle Rider** (Map pp880-1; ☎ 310-536-6777; 11860 S La Cienega Blvd; 🕑 9am-5pm), 2 miles south of LAX, or **Route 66** (Map p891; ☎ 310-578-0112, 888-434-4473; 4161 Lincoln Blvd, Marina del Rey; 🕑 9am-6pm Tue-Sat, 10am-5pm Sun & Mon). Rates range from $75 to $135 a day, with discounts for longer rentals.

PUBLIC TRANSPORTATION

The **Metropolitan Transportation Authority** (MTA; ☎ 800-266-6883; www.mta.net) operates a very extensive bus and rail system. The fare is $1.35 and transfers are 25¢ each; weekly passes are $11 (valid Sunday to Saturday). To find out how to get from point A to point B, call MTA's toll-free number, use its website's trip planner or pick up a network map from a **customer center**. Branches are in **Downtown** (Map p884; Level C, Arco Plaza, 515 S Flower St; 🕑 7:30am-3:30pm) and near Museum Row in **Mid-City** (Map p889; 5301 Wilshire Blvd; 🕑 9am-5pm).

The fastest way across town is aboard Metro Rapid bus No 720, which travels along Wilshire Blvd from Santa Monica to Downtown and into East LA via Westwood, Beverly Hills, Fairfax and Mid-City.

Downtown and some neighborhoods, including Hollywood and Mid-City, are also served by **DASH minibuses** (☎ 213-808-2273; www.ladottransit.com; ticket 25¢; 🕑 7am-7pm Mon-Sat). Santa Monica-based **Big Blue Bus** (☎ 310-451-5444; www.bigbluebus.com) serves much of western LA, including Santa Monica, Venice, Westwood and LAX (75¢). Express bus No 10 runs from Santa Monica to Downtown ($1.75).

MTA-operated Metro Rail is a network of three rail lines: the Blue Line (Downtown to Long Beach), the Red Line (Downtown's Union Station to North Hollywood, via central Hollywood and Universal Studios) and the Green Line (Norwalk to Redondo Beach). A fourth line, the Gold Line from Downtown to Pasadena, was scheduled to open in late 2003. Tickets are dispensed by coin-operated machines ($1.35).

TAXI

Except for those lined up outside airports, train stations, bus stations and major hotels, cabbies will only respond to phone calls. Fares are metered: $2 at flagfall plus $1.80 a mile. Companies include **Checker** (☎ 800-300-5007), **Independent** (☎ 800-521-8294) and **Yellow Cab** (☎ 800-200-1085).

AROUND LOS ANGELES

Catalina Island

Mediterranean-flavored Catalina Island is a world removed from the bustle of Los Angeles. It is part of the Channel Islands, a chain of semisubmerged mountains off the coast of Southern California. Nearly all tourist activity concentrates in the tiny port town of **Avalon**. The only other settlement is remote **Two Harbors** in Catalina's largely undeveloped interior of sun-baked hillsides, valleys and canyons. A curiosity here is the herd of bison, left behind from a 1924 movie shoot. The interior is protected and may only be explored on foot or mountain bike (permits required, call ☎ 310-510-1421) or on an organized tour (from $30), such as those offered by **Discovery Tours** (☎ 310-510-8687) or **Jeep Eco-Tours** (☎ 310-510-2595).

For most people, the best way to experience Catalina's charms is in or on the water. Snorkeling and diving are both excellent, or you could rent a kayak to explore the rugged coast. Most outfitters have booths on the Green Pier in Avalon.

Room rates fluctuate enormously, soaring in summer when two-night minimum stays are often the norm.

Catalina Beach House (☎ 310-510-1078, 800-974-6835; 200 Marilla Ave; r in summer $75-195, in winter

$35-105;), up on the hill, is a flowery, diver-friendly place with accommodating staff and cute, if smallish, rooms. **Hotel St Lauren** (☎ 310-510-0322, 800-645-2496; www.stlauren.com; 231 Beacon St; r $40-345;), sitting pretty in pink, is a neo-Victorian property with upscale motel furnishings and a wide variety of rooms. **Hermit Gulch Campground** (☎ 310-510-8368; adult/child $12/6) is a 1.5-mile hike or bus ride away in scenic Avalon Canyon. For information on camping in the interior, go to the website www.scico.com/camping.

Catalina Express (☎ 310-519-1212) runs up to 30 ferries daily from San Pedro and Long Beach ($40 round trip, one hour).

Big Bear Lake

Surrounded by the San Bernardino National Forest, 110 miles east of LA, this year-round, family-friendly mountain resort gets its biggest crowds in winter when the ski slopes of Bear Mountain and Snow Mountain issue their frosty siren call. As soon as the snow melts, hikers and mountain bikers take over the terrain, while the lake itself attracts water-sport aficionados. The **visitors center** (☎ 800-4-244-2327; www.bigbearinfo.com; 630 Bartlett Rd; 8am-5pm Mon-Fri, 9am-5pm Sat & Sun) is in 'the Village' on the lake's southern shore, where most tourist activity is concentrated.

Mountain Area Regional Transit Authority (Marta; ☎ 909-584-1111) buses connect Big Bear with the Greyhound station in San Bernardino ($5). Drivers should take the I-10 to the Hwy 30 turnoff in Redlands and follow it to Hwy 330 then Hwy 18.

SOUTHERN CALIFORNIA COAST

ORANGE COUNTY

Wedged between Los Angeles to the north and San Diego to the south, Orange County is home to Southern California's most popular attraction – Disneyland in Anaheim – but is also justly famous for its 42 miles of wonderful coastline.

Disneyland Resort

Ever since Walt Disney opened the original **Disneyland** (☎ 714-781-4000; www.disneyland.com; 1313 Harbor Blvd, Anaheim; adult $45, child 3-9 $35) in 1955, the mother of all theme parks has captured the heart, minds and pocketbooks of millions of visitors. It is divided into seven thematic 'lands,' including the space-age Tomorrowland, the jungle-themed Adventureland, and Fantasyland, where classic Disney characters make their home. The most popular thrill rides include the Indiana Jones Adventure, Space Mountain and Pirates of the Caribbean.

In February 2001, a second, smaller park called **Disney's California Adventure** opened adjacent to the original, and Disneyland became the Disneyland Resort. It celebrates the natural and cultural glories of the Golden State and features such not-to-be-missed experiences as Soarin' over California, a virtual hang-gliding ride, and California Screamin', a roller coaster built around a Mickey Mouse silhouette.

Also part of Disneyland Resort are three Disney hotels and **Downtown Disney**, a walking mall teeming with dining, shopping and entertainment venues.

You can see either park in a day, but it requires at least two days to go on all the rides (three if visiting both parks), especially in summer when lines are long – visit midweek and arrive when the gates open. When getting to the parks, familiarize yourself with the FastPass system, which gives you pre-assigned time slots for faster boarding.

A variety of multi-day passes good at both parks are available. Check the website to buy tickets or check park hours. These vary daily, although in peak season the parks are usually open from 8am to midnight.

The area around Disneyland – especially along Harbor Blvd and Katella Ave – has plenty of lodging options, mostly of the chain hotel/motel variety. Recommended independent properties are **Candy Cane Inn** (☎ 714-774-5284, 800-345-7057; 1747 S Harbor Blvd; r $92-144; P) and the **Anabella** (☎ 714-905-1050; www.anabellahotel.com; 1030 Katella Ave; r $79-149; P).

Knott's Berry Farm

Just 4 miles northwest of Disneyland, **Knott's Berry Farm** (☎ 714-220-5200; www.knotts.com; 8039 Beach Blvd; adult $40, child 3-11 $30) is essentially a high-tech amusement park with an Old West theme. Tame experiences such as gold-panning demonstrations and staged gun fights contrast with such gut-wrenching roller coasters like the wooden Ghost Rider and the

A NOT-SO-SERIOUS LOOK AT MOUSE KINGDOM

'The House the Mouse Built' is a total blast, if an exhausting and over-stimulating one. And it's as tightly run a kingdom as anything this side of Spain. Nothing is left to chance and you may occasionally feel that invisible 'Imagineers' are pulling your strings. All of Main Street USA is built to a cutesy 5:8 scale and the sidewalks are all steam-cleaned nightly, for goodness sake.

After opening in 1955 it took the Mouse just one week to greet his millionth visitor. And since that time hundreds of millions have trekked to Mouse Mecca in smooth and orderly fashion. But along the way, there has been the odd grain of sand in the Vaseline. That fun-loving commie, Nikita Khrushchev, was refused entrance in 1959. The Jungle Cruise was planned to showcase live tigers, lions and snakes until some spoilsport realized that they'd sleep all day and possibly munch a Mouseketeer or two. And the Urban Legends website abounds with stories of rides gone awry resulting in projectile vomiting, thrombosis and even that most un-Disney-like of states – death!

Still and all, Disney doles out its four million hamburgers a year and a good time is had by all. Disneyland may be easy to poke fun at, but please, don't get mad with us, Mr Mouse. We're just taking the mickey out of you.

'50s-themed Xcelerator. Many people wrap up a visit with a fried-chicken dinner at **Mrs Knott's Chicken Dinner Restaurant** (mains $15-20).

Orange County Beaches

Surfers, artists and retirees give Orange County's beach towns their distinct vibe. South of Long Beach, **Seal Beach** is refreshingly noncommercial with a pleasantly walkable downtown, while relaxed **Huntington Beach** (aka Surf City, USA) further south epitomizes the California surfing lifestyle. Next up is sophisticated **Newport Beach** with good shopping and a huge pleasure-craft harbor. The main tourist area, south of Hwy 1 via Balboa Blvd, has beaches, the 1905 Balboa Pier and a family-oriented amusement center.

Secluded beaches, glassy waves and eucalyptus-covered hillsides imbue **Laguna Beach** with a Riviera-like feel. Crowds are thick on summer weekends. Laguna has a strong artistic tradition and each July hosts three art festivals as well as the Pageant of the Masters, where human models are blended seamlessly into huge re-creations of famous paintings.

Mission San Juan Capistrano (☎ 949-234-1300; 31882 Camino Capistrano; adult $6, senior & child $5; 🕒 8:30am-5pm), about 10 miles south and inland from Laguna, is one of California's most beautiful missions, featuring lush gardens and the charming Serra Chapel.

SAN DIEGO

It's easy to fall in love with San Diego, home of one of the world's great natural harbors, a historic downtown brimming with nightlife and dining, the country's largest urban cultural park and such first-rate attractions as SeaWorld and the San Diego Zoo. Not surprisingly, San Diegans are fiercely proud of their city and shamelessly, yet endearingly, promote it as 'America's Finest City.' After a few days of exploration, you may well agree.

History

San Diego's history largely mirrors that of most other California towns. The area was originally inhabited by the indigenous Kumeyaay until the arrival in 1769 of Padre Junípero Serra, who founded the first of 21 California missions here. After the breakup of the mission system around 1833, San Diego became a civilian *pueblo* but largely remained a ramshackle village until William Heath Davis erected homes, a wharf and warehouses by the waterfront in 1850. Dubbed 'Davis' Folly', the development was ahead of its time. In 1867 Alonzo Horton, another speculator and developer, had greater success when he acquired 960 acres of land in today's downtown and promoted it as 'New Town.'

Despite such efforts, San Diego continued to be a backwater until the early 20th century. Some impetus came from hosting the Panama-California Exposition of 1915–16, but it was the aviation industry that gave the city its first industrial base in the 1920s. In the wake of the Pearl Harbor attack in 1941, the US Pacific Fleet was moved from Hawaii to San Diego. Its wartime role, more

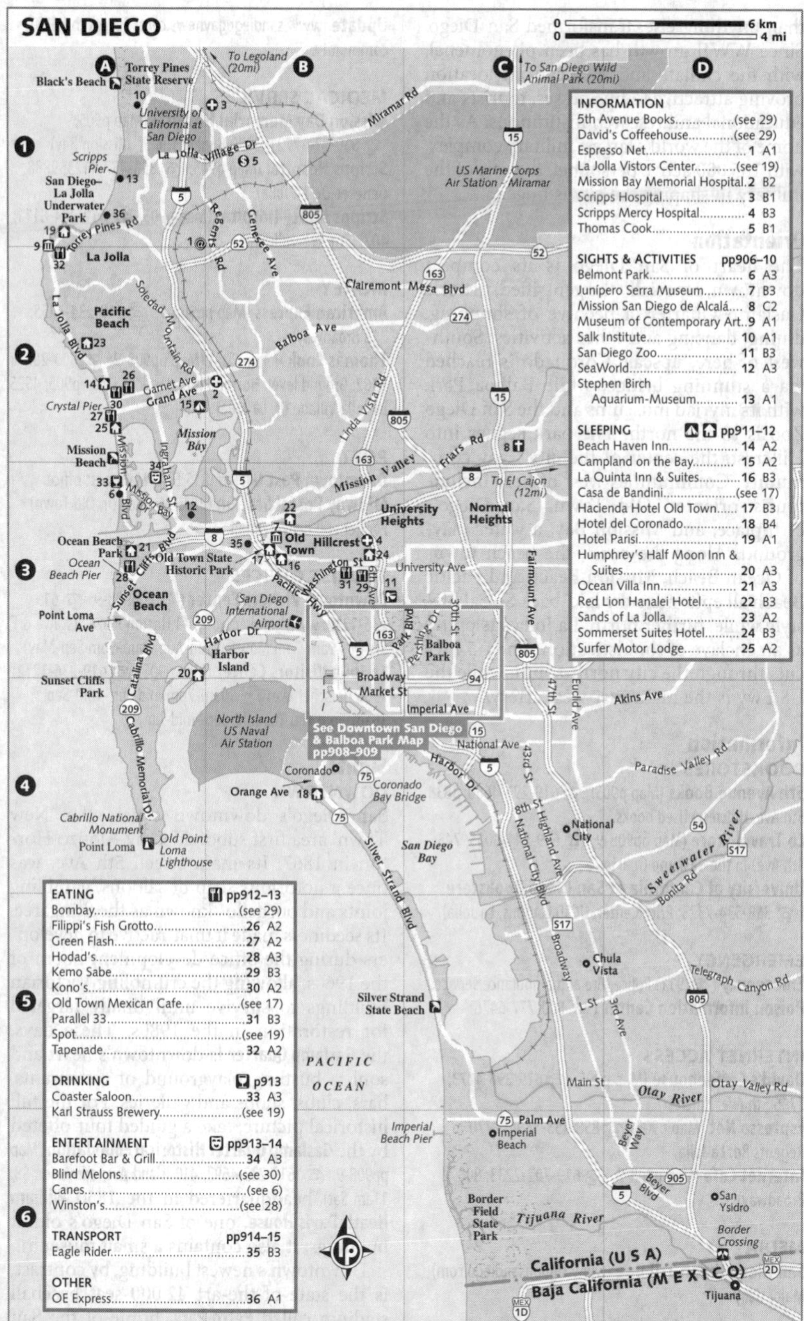
SAN DIEGO
0 6 km
0 4 mi
INFORMATION
5th Avenue Books....................(see 29)
David's Coffeehouse..................(see 29)
Espresso Net............................1 A1
La Jolla Vistors Center..............(see 19)
Mission Bay Memorial Hospital.2 B2
Scripps Hospital.........................3 B1
Scripps Mercy Hospital...............4 B3
Thomas Cook..............................5 B1
SIGHTS & ACTIVITIES pp906–10
Belmont Park..............................6 A3
Junípero Serra Museum...............7 B3
Mission San Diego de Alcalá.........8 C2
Museum of Contemporary Art...9 A1
Salk Institute..............................10 A1
San Diego Zoo.............................11 B3
SeaWorld....................................12 A3
Stephen Birch Aquarium-Museum............13 A1
SLEEPING pp911–12
Beach Haven Inn.........................14 A2
Campland on the Bay....................15 A2
La Quinta Inn & Suites.................16 B3
Casa de Bandini.......................(see 17)
Hacienda Hotel Old Town.............17 B3
Hotel del Coronado.....................18 B4
Hotel Parisi................................19 A1
Humphrey's Half Moon Inn & Suites.........................20 A3
Ocean Villa Inn............................21 A3
Red Lion Hanalei Hotel................22 B3
Sands of La Jolla.........................23 A2
Sommerset Suites Hotel...............24 B3
Surfer Motor Lodge.....................25 A2
EATING pp912–13
Bombay.....................................(see 29)
Filippi's Fish Grotto....................26 A2
Green Flash................................27 A2
Hodad's......................................28 A3
Kemo Sabe.................................29 B3
Kono's..30 A2
Old Town Mexican Cafe.............(see 17)
Parallel 33..................................31 B3
Spot..(see 19)
Tapenade....................................32 A2
DRINKING p913
Coaster Saloon............................33 A3
Karl Strauss Brewery..................(see 19)
ENTERTAINMENT pp913–14
Barefoot Bar & Grill....................34 A3
Blind Melons..............................(see 30)
Canes...(see 6)
Winston's....................................(see 28)
TRANSPORT pp914–15
Eagle Rider.................................35 B3
OTHER
OE Express.................................36 A1
To Legoland (20mi)
To San Diego Wild Animal Park (20mi)
To El Cajon (12mi)
Torrey Pines State Reserve
Black's Beach
University of California at San Diego
Scripps Pier
San Diego–La Jolla Underwater Park
La Jolla
Pacific Beach
Crystal Pier
Mission Beach
Mission Bay
Ocean Beach Park
Ocean Beach Pier
Ocean Beach
Old Town State Historic Park
Old Town
Hillcrest
University Heights
Normal Heights
San Diego International Airport
Point Loma Ave
Harbor Island
Sunset Cliffs Park
Balboa Park
North Island US Naval Air Station
See Downtown San Diego & Balboa Park Map pp908–909
Coronado
Coronado Bay Bridge
Cabrillo National Monument
Point Loma
Old Point Loma Lighthouse
San Diego Bay
National City
Chula Vista
Silver Strand State Beach
PACIFIC OCEAN
Imperial Beach Pier
Imperial Beach
Border Field State Park
Tijuana River
San Ysidro
Border Crossing
California (U S A)
Baja California (M E X I C O)
Tijuana
US Marine Corps Air Station - Miramar
Miramar Rd
La Jolla Village Dr
Torrey Pines Rd
Regents Rd
Genesee Ave
Soledad Mountain Rd
La Jolla Blvd
Clairemont Mesa Blvd
Balboa Ave
Garnet Ave
Grand Ave
Linda Vista Rd
Mission Valley
Friars Rd
Ingraham St
Mission Blvd
Mission Bay Dr
Sunset Cliffs Blvd
Washington St
Pacific Hwy
University Ave
Harbor Dr
Catalina Blvd
Cabrillo Memorial Dr
Park Blvd
Pershing Dr
30th St
Fairmount Ave
47th St
Euclid Ave
Broadway
Market St
Imperial Ave
Akins Ave
National Ave
43rd St
8th St
Highland Ave
National City Blvd
Paradise Valley Rd
Sweetwater River
Bonita Rd
Orange Ave
Silver Strand Blvd
Telegraph Canyon Rd
L St
3rd Ave
Main St
Otay River
Otay Valley Rd
Palm Ave
Beyer Way
Beyer Blvd

than anything else, transformed San Diego. Since WWII growth has been phenomenal, with the climate and the seafront location proving attractive to businesses, tourists and educational and research institutions. As the home of the world's largest military complex, with 165,000 active personnel, the role of the military in shaping the city is huge.

Orientation

The heart of San Diego is its compact downtown, especially the gentrified, historic Gaslamp Quarter, a beehive of shopping, dining, dancing and other activities. Southwest of here, upscale Coronado is reached via a stunning bridge, while Balboa Park with its myriad museums and the San Diego Zoo is to the north. The park segues into Hillcrest, the center of the city's gay community. Communities west of here include tourist-oriented Old Town, San Diego's birthplace; and Mission Bay, a water playground. Along the coast, the beach towns of Ocean Beach, Mission Beach and Pacific Beach all epitomize the laid-back SoCal lifestyle while, further north, La Jolla sits pretty as an enclave of sophistication. The I-5 Fwy cuts through the city north-south, while the I-8 Fwy is the main east-west artery.

Information

BOOKSTORES

5th Avenue Books (Map p905; ☎ 619-291-4660; 3838 5th Ave, Hillcrest) Used books.
Le Travel Store (Map pp908-9; ☎ 619-544-0005; 745 4th Ave) In the Gaslamp Quarter.
University of California at San Diego Bookstore (☎ 858-534-7323; Price Center, UCSD campus, La Jolla)

EMERGENCY

Emergency (☎ 911) Police, fire and ambulance service.
Poison Information Center (☎ 800-777-6476)

INTERNET ACCESS

David's Coffeehouse (Map p905; ☎ 619-296-4173; 3766 5th Ave, Hillcrest)
Espresso Net (Map p905; ☎ 858-453-5896; 7770 Regents Rd, La Jolla)
Internet Cafe (Map p908-9; ☎ 619-702-2233; 800 Broadway)

MEDIA

San Diego Union-Tribune (www.signonsandiego.com) Major daily.
Update (www.sandiegogaynews.com) Serves the GLBT community.

MEDICAL SERVICES

Mission Bay Memorial Hospital (Map p905; ☎ 619-274-7721; 3030 Bunker Hill St, Mission Bay)
Scripps Hospital (Map p905; ☎ 858-457-4123; 9888 Genesee Dr, La Jolla)
Scripps Mercy Hospital (Map p905; ☎ 619-294-8111; 4077 5th Ave, Hillcrest)

MONEY

American Express (Map pp908-9; ☎ 619-234-4455; 258 Broadway)
Thomas Cook Horton Plaza (Map pp908-9; ☎ 800-287-7362; Ground level, Horton Plaza); La Jolla (Map p905; 4525 La Jolla Village Dr, La Jolla)

POST

Downtown Post Office (815 E St) Main post office.
Midway Postal Station (2535 Midway Dr, Old Town) For general delivery mail.

TOURIST OFFICES

Downtown Visitors Center (Map pp908-9; ☎ 619-236-1212; www.sandiego.org; 11 Horton Plaza, 1st Ave & F St; 🕑 9am-7pm Mon-Sat Jun-Aug, 9am-5pm Sep-May)
La Jolla Visitors Center (Map p905; ☎ 619-236-1212; 7966 Herschel Ave; 🕑 10am-7pm mid-Jun–mid-Sep, 10am-5pm Thu-Tue mid-Sep–mid-Jun)

Sights

DOWNTOWN

San Diego's downtown covers the 'New Town' area first subdivided by Alonzo Horton in 1867. Its main street, 5th Ave, was once a notorious strip of saloons, gambling joints and bordellos known as the Stingaree. Its seediness made it unattractive to developers during the office-development boom of the 1960s, allowing the crumbling Victorian buildings to survive until finally targeted for restoration in the 1980s. These days, the **Gaslamp Quarter** is downtown's heart and soul, a bustling playground of restaurants, bars, clubs, shops and galleries. For the full historical picture, take a guided tour offered by the **Gaslamp Quarter Historical Foundation** (Map pp908-9; ☎ 619-233-4692; 410 Island Ave; admission $8; 11am Sat), headquartered in the 1850 **William Heath Davis House**, one of San Diego's oldest buildings; it also contains a small museum.

Downtown's newest building, by contrast, is the state-of-the-art 42,000-seat baseball stadium called **Petco Park**, home of the San

Diego Padres, and set to open in 2004. It's located adjacent to the Gaslamp Quarter, bounded by 7th and 10th Aves and K and Park Sts.

The initial spark plug for downtown's redevelopment in the 1980s was a giant shopping mall, the postmodern **Horton Plaza** (Map pp908-9; Broadway). West of here, the **Museum of Contemporary Art** (Map p884; ☎ 619-234-1001; 1001 Kettner Blvd; free; ⌚ 11am-5pm Thu-Tue) has changing exhibitions of post-1960s painting and sculpture. Families might prefer the interactive **San Diego Children's Museum** (Map pp908-9; ☎ 619-233-8792; 200 Island Ave; adult $6, child under 3 free; ⌚ 10am-4pm Tue-Sat), which keeps kids entertained with giant construction toys, craft activities, storytelling and music.

Further west, the **Embarcadero** is San Diego's well-manicured waterfront geared toward pedestrian pleasure seekers. A harborside stroll might start at the **Maritime Museum** (Map pp908-9; ☎ 619-234-9153; 1492 N Harbor Dr; adult $6, senior & child $4; ⌚ 9am-8pm) with its three historic sailing vessels, including the square-rigger 1863 *Star of India*. Head south past the piers for cruise ships and harbor ferries, and the fishing boat harbor, to **Seaport Village** (☎ 619-235-4014; ⌚ 10am-9pm), a collection of novelty shops, restaurants and snack outlets.

North of the Gaslamp Quarter, **Little Italy** is another interesting – and increasingly hip – neighborhood, with good dining options, antique stores, new condominiums and trendy hotels. India St is the main drag.

CORONADO

Joined to the mainland by a spectacularly curved bridge, Coronado is also attached by a long, narrow sand spit, the Silver Strand, which runs south to Imperial Beach. Worthwhile sights include the **Hotel del Coronado** (p912), famous for its whimsical architecture and illustrious guest book, which includes Marilyn Monroe, Frank Sinatra and Ronald Reagan. Hourly ferries to Coronado leave from Broadway Pier ($4 round trip, 15 minutes). The ferry landing has bicycle rental outlets. North Island Naval Air Station occupies most of northern Coronado.

BALBOA PARK

With its museums, gardens and famous zoo, Balboa Park tops the list of what to see in San Diego. Its landscaping reflects the skill and vision of horticulturalist Kate Sessions, while many of the ornate Beaux Arts and Spanish Colonial buildings are replicas of those constructed for the 1915–16 Panama-California Exposition and the 1935 Pacific-California Exposition. Most are grouped around plazas connected by the central east-west El Prado promenade. You can stroll around the park anytime, but be cautious after dark. Balboa Park is easily reached from downtown on bus Nos 7, 7A and 7B.

The **Balboa Park Information Center** (Map pp908-9; ☎ 619-239-0512; www.balboapark.org; 1549 El Prado; ⌚ 9am-4pm), in the House of Hospitality, sells park maps and the Balboa Passport ($30), which allows one-time entry to 13 of the park's museums for one week. Museums offer free admission Tuesday on a rotating schedule.

Entering Balboa Park from the west across Cabrillo Bridge (the most scenic approach) takes you to the Plaza de California, anchored by the spectacular **California Building**. Inside, the **Museum of Man** (Map pp908-9; ☎ 619-239-2001; www.museumofman.org; adult/senior/child $6/5/3; ⌚ 10am-4:30pm) has a world-class collection of artifacts (pottery, jewelry, baskets etc) representing a journey through the cultural history of humankind. Behind the museum, the **Simon Edison Centre for the Performing Arts** (Map p908-9; ☎ 619-239-2255) has three venues, including the Old Globe Theatre, a replica of Shakespeare's original London theater.

Further east, the Plaza de Panama is ringed by a trio of museums, including the well-respected **San Diego Museum of Art** (Map pp908-9; ☎ 619-232-7931; www.sdmart.org; adult $8, senior & student $6; ⌚ 10am-6pm Tue-Sun, closes 9pm Thu), which is especially known for its old European masters but also has good collections of American and Asian art. Also here are the **Mingei International Museum** (Map pp908-9; ☎ 619-239-0003; adult/student $5/2; ⌚ 10am-4pm Tue-Sun) with folk art from around the globe, and the **Timken Museum of Art** (Map pp908-9; ☎ 619-239-5548; 1500 El Prado; admission free; ⌚ 10am-4:30pm Tue-Sat, 1:30-4:30pm Sun) with its small but fine selection of paintings by Rembrandt, Rubens, El Greco, Cézanne and Pissarro, plus some appealing Russian icons.

East along El Prado, the **Museum of Photographic Arts** (Map pp908-9; ☎ 619-238-7559; adult $6, senior & student $4; ⌚ 10am-5pm, closes 9pm Thu) exhibits fine art photography and hosts an ongoing film series. Next up is Plaza de Balboa, flanked by the **Reuben H Fleet Science Center**

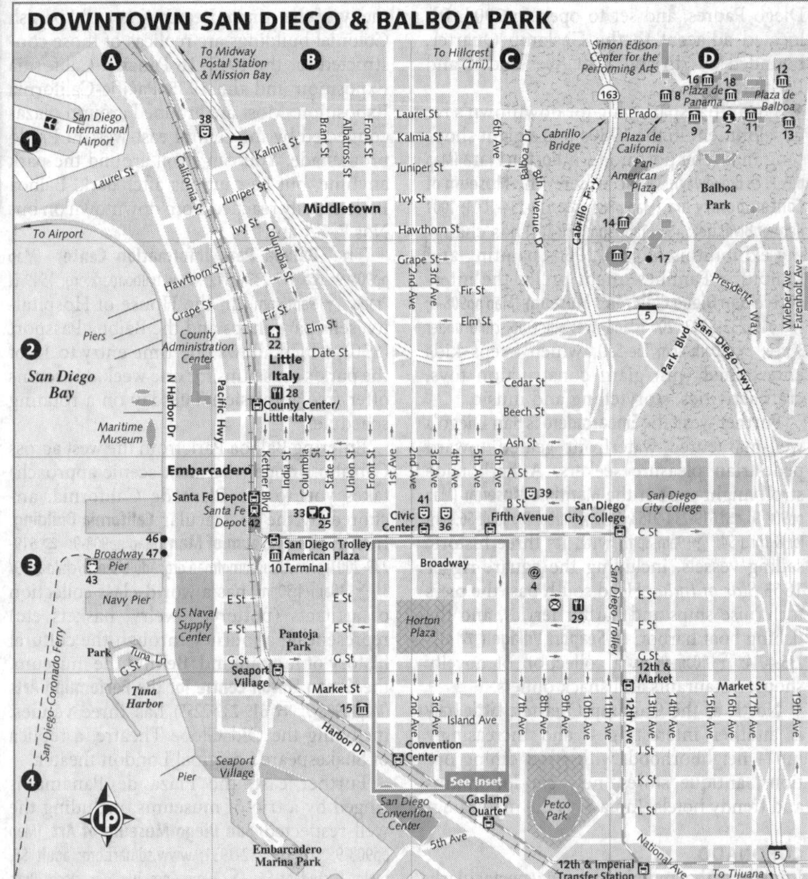

(Map pp908-9; ☎ 619-238-1233; www.rhfleet.org; adult/senior/child $6.75/6/5.50; ⏲ 9:30am-5pm Mon, Tue & Thu, 9:30am-7pm Wed, 9:30am-9:30pm Fri, 9:30am-8pm Sat, 9:30am-6pm Sun), a family-oriented hands-on science museum plus **Imax theater** (extra admission). Opposite is the **Natural History Museum** (Map pp908-9; ☎ 619-232-3821; www.sdnhm.org; adult/senior/child $8/6/5; ⏲ 9:30am-4:30pm), which has fossils, stuffed animals, dinosaur skeletons and the country's largest rattlesnake collection. A large-screen movie theater is the newest attraction.

Buildings around Pan-American Plaza in the park's southern section date from the 1935 Pacific-California Exposition. Car buffs will gravitate to the fleet of vintage vehicles at the **San Diego Automotive Museum** (Map pp908-9; ☎ 619-231-2886; www.sdautomuseum.org; adult/senior/child $7/6/3; ⏲ 10am-5pm), although the highlight in the plaza is the **Aerospace Museum** (Map pp908-9; ☎ 619-234-8291; www.aerospacemuseum.org; adult $8, senior & student $6; ⏲ 10am-4:30pm), which captures the mystique of flight in an entertaining and enlightening way. Displays of original aircraft include the Blackbird SR-71 spy plane as well as such replicas as Charles Lindbergh's *Spirit of St Louis*.

The northern section of Balboa Park is occupied by the world-class **San Diego Zoo** (Map pp908-9; ☎ 619-234-3153; www.sandiegozoo.org; adult/child $20/12, with guided bus tour & aerial tram ride $32/20; ⏲ 9am-4pm, closes 10pm Jun-Sep), one of the city's key attractions. More than 4000 animals call the zoo home, including such crowd

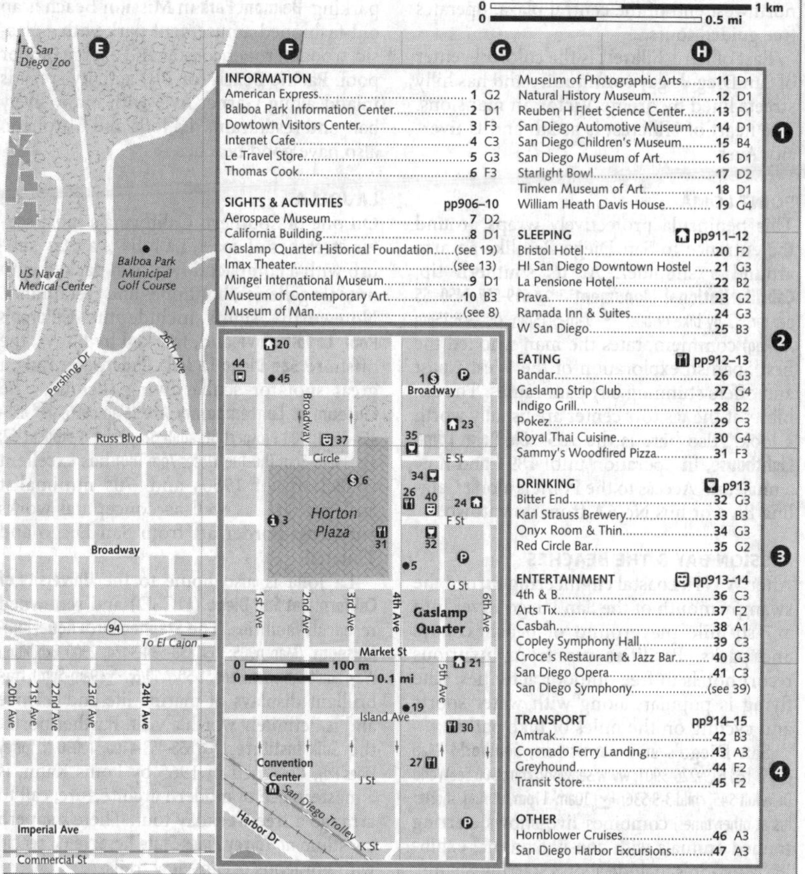

pleasers as koalas, giant pandas and forest buffalo. There are around 800 species living in beautifully re-created natural habitats. Arrive early, when the animals are most active. Combination tickets to the zoo and San Diego Wild Animal Park (p915) cost $56/36.

PRESIDIO HILL & OLD TOWN

Presidio Hill is the birthplace of San Diego and, by extension, of California. It was here in 1769 that Junípero Serra established the original Mission San Diego de Alcalá. The attractive site is now occupied by the **Junípero Serra Museum** (Map p905; ☎ 619-297-3258; adult/senior/child $5/4/2; ⏲ 10am-4:30pm Fri-Sun), a Spanish colonial building containing artifacts and pictures from the mission and rancho periods.

In 1773, Serra decided to move the mission a few miles upriver, closer to a better water supply and land. These days, **Mission San Diego de Alcalá** (☎ 619-281-8449; Friars Rd; adult/child $3/2; ⏲ 9am-5pm), rebuilt several times after Native American attacks, earthquakes and deterioration, is a modest rectangle opening up to a lovely garden.

Starting in 1821, under Mexican rule, the land around Presidio Hill was laid out with a plaza, and by the 1830s Pueblo de San Diego had 40 huts and a few large adobe houses. Many of the original buildings have been reconstructed in what is now the **Old Town State Historic Park**, a pleasant, tourist-oriented precinct with shops and restaurants. The **visitors center** (☎ 619-220-5422; ⏲ 10am-5pm), at the northwest end of the central plaza, operates free guided tours.

East of here, **Hillcrest** is the colorful center of San Diego's gay community and has hilly streets lined by ornate Victorian mansions. The heart of Hillcrest is at 5th and University Aves.

POINT LOMA

This peninsula protectively wraps around the entrance to San Diego Bay like an arm around a shoulder. At its southern tip, **Cabrillo National Monument** (☎ 619-557-5450; $5 per car, $3 by bike or bus; 🕑 9am-5:15pm, closes 6:15pm Jul-Aug) commemorates the man who led the first Spanish exploration of the West Coast and offers stunning bay panoramas. The exhibits at the visitors center are usually worth a look. Also here is the 1854 **Old Point Loma Lighthouse**, in operation until 1891 and now a museum. Access to the Point is along Catalina Blvd or bus No 6A from downtown.

MISSION BAY & THE BEACHES

After WWII, coastal engineering turned the swampy mouth of the San Diego River into a 7-sq-mile playground of beaches, bays and parks. Facilities run from luxurious resort hotels to free outdoor activities. Kite flying is popular, along with water sports and cycling on the miles of bike paths.

San Diego's star attraction, **SeaWorld** (Map p905; ☎ 619-226-3901; www.seaworld.com; 500 SeaWorld Dr; adult $45, child 3-9 $36; 🕑 10am-11pm Jul-Aug, shorter hrs at other times) combines live shows starring trained animals with zoo-like animal exhibits. Must-do's include shows starring Shamu, the killer whale, and the sea lions, Clyde and Seamore, as well as the Wild Arctic motion-simulator ride. Lines can get long in summer. Look for discount coupons in hotels and tourist offices.

San Diego has three main beaches. South of Mission Bay is bohemian **Ocean Beach**, which has a long fishing pier, beach volleyball, sunset barbecues and good surf. Newport Ave is chockablock with bars, eateries and shops selling beachwear and surf gear. West of Mission Bay, **Mission Beach** and its northern neighbor, **Pacific Beach**, are connected by the paved **Ocean Front Walk**, which attracts skaters, joggers and cyclists year-round. In summer it's 3 miles of *Baywatch* beach scene, with end-to-end bodies, cafés, beach bars, surf rental shops and impossible parking. **Belmont Park** in Mission Beach is an old-fashioned amusement park with a classic, wooden roller coaster and a large indoor pool. Pacific Beach (or PB) activity spreads inland along Garnet Ave, with many lively bars and restaurants. La Jolla and Coronado also have good beaches.

LA JOLLA

On one of Southern California's most scenic stretches of coast, La Jolla is a ritzy suburb with a compact downtown packed with upscale galleries, boutiques and restaurants. Noteworthy sights include the **Children's Pool**, **La Jolla Cove** and, marked by buoys, the offshore **San Diego-La Jolla Underwater Park**, a great spot for scuba diving (below). The **Museum of Contemporary Art** (Map p905; ☎ 858-454-3541; 700 Prospect St; adult $6, senior & student $2; 🕑 11am-5pm Thu-Tue, closes 7pm Thu) has excellent collections of 1960s and '70s minimalist and pop art, as well as conceptual works and cross-border art from San Diego and Tijuana.

La Jolla is also home to the **University of California at San Diego** (UCSD) and renowned research facilities. The **Stephen Birch Aquarium-Museum** (Map p905; ☎ 858-534-3474; 2300 Exhibition Way; adult/senior/student $8.50/7.50/6; 🕑 9am-5pm) has brilliant displays of marine life and science and is definitely worth a visit. Further north, the **Salk Institute** (☎ 858-453-4100; 10010 N Torrey Pines Rd), designed in 1965 by Louis Kahn, is a masterpiece of modern architecture; call to arrange a free weekday tour. There's superb coastline at **Torrey Pines State Reserve** ($2 per car) with gorgeous ocean-view trails.

Activities

San Diego has good surfing and windsurfing, but the water can get crowded. For surf reports call ☎ 619-221-8824. First-timers might try **Pacific Surf School** (☎ 619-742-2267; two-day camp $110) in Mission Beach. The best scuba diving is in the **San Diego-La Jolla Underwater Park**, with giant kelp forests and the 100ft-deep La Jolla Canyon; local outfitters include **OE Express** (Map p905; ☎ 858-454-6195; 2158 Avenida de la Playa, La Jolla).

Tours

Hornblower Cruises (☎ 619-686-8700; Broadway Pier) A variety of harbor cruises.

Old Town Trolley Tours (☎ 619-298-8687; adult/child $24/12; 🕑 9am-4pm, to 5pm in summer) Hop-on, hop-off loop tours around the main attractions; land-and-water SEAL tours with military emphasis.

San Diego Harbor Excursions (☎ 619-234-4111; Broadway Pier)

Sleeping

One factor in determining where to stay in San Diego should be the kind of experience you envision. Those who like to be central and close to plentiful dining and entertainment options should opt for a downtown hotel, while sun worshippers might prefer to hang their hat in one of the beach towns. Prices are generally lower in Old Town, Hillcrest and especially in the chain hotels and motels lining the aptly named Hotel Circle Rd which parallels the I-8 Fwy. Note that in summer (late May to early September) rooms book-up early and rates skyrocket, especially in the beach towns. Rates shown don't include the 10.5% room tax.

BUDGET

La Pensione Hotel (Map pp908-9; ☎ 619-236-8000, 800-232-4683; www.lapensionehotel.com; 606 W Date St; r $75; P) One of the top bargains in town, this Little Italy gem brings European flair to the West Coast, complete with black marble lobby and well-equipped rooms.

La Quinta Inn & Suites (Map p905; ☎ 619-291-9100, 800-531-5900; 2380 Moore St, Old Town; r $70-100; P) Clean, freshly spruced-up rooms with kitchenette wrap around a secluded pool at this friendly, if freeway-adjacent, motel. Rates include continental breakfast.

Sands of La Jolla (Map p905; ☎ 858-459-3336, 800-643-0530; www.sandsoflajolla.com; 5417 La Jolla Blvd, La Jolla; r $70-100; P) This excellent budget option is about 2.5 miles south of central La Jolla but only a couple of blocks away from a nice beach. Enjoy ocean views from your private balcony or whip up a meal in your kitchen (suites only).

HI San Diego Downtown Hostel (Map pp908-9; ☎ 619-525-1531, 800-909-4776; www.sandiegohostels.com; 521 Market St; dm $18-25, r $46-56) Popular Gaslamp Quarter hostel that counts a big kitchen among its assets.

Campland on the Bay (Map p905; ☎ 858-581-4200, 800-422-9386; www.campland.com; 2211 Pacific Beach Dr, Mission Bay; campsites $53-101 late May–early Sep, $40-75 rest of year, RV sites $57-277 in summer, $42-173 rest of year; P) Nicely situated right on Mission Bay, Campland caters mainly to RVs but also has a shady area for tent camping. Facilities include a market, restaurant, bike and boat rentals.

MID-RANGE

The **Bristol Hotel** (Map pp908-9; ☎ 619-232-6141, 800-662-4477; www.thebistrolsandiego.com; 1055 1st Ave; r $120-200; P) Fresh flowers, original pop art and a bold, primary-color scheme throughout gives this property an upbeat, jazzy feel. The good-sized rooms are comfortable and outfitted with a full range of communication devices.

Prava (Map pp908-9; ☎ 619-233-3300; www.pravahotel.com; 911 5th Ave; r $140-180; P) This classy boutique hotel has sparkling suites in soothing colors with kitchens and wonderful beds with sumptuous Egyptian cotton linens. Rates include access to the sauna, steam room and fitness room. Step out the door and you're in the heart of the Gaslamp Quarter.

Ramada Inn & Suites (Map pp908-9; ☎ 619-234-0155, 800-664-4400; 830 6th Ave; ste $170-290; P) Historic-meets-high-tech

Hacienda Hotel Old Town (Map p905; ☎ 619-298-4707, 800-888-1991; www.haciendahotel-oldtown.com; 4041 Harney St, Old Town; r $165-185; P) Brightly-colored tiles, bougainvillea and gurgling fountains give this sprawling complex a relaxed, Spanish-style ambience. Rooms in the upper buildings overlook the city and Old Town.

Red Lion Hanalei Hotel (Map p905; ☎ 619-297-1101, 800-882-0858; www.hanaleihotel.com; 2270 Hotel Circle N, Old Town; r $120-160; P) Sip your mai tai while lounging poolside at this full-service resort with understated tropical-island decor. Rooms are large and come with balconies overlooking a golf course or the gardens.

Sommerset Suites Hotel (Map p905; ☎ 619-692-5200, 800-962-9665; www.sommersetsuites.com; 606 Washington St, Hillcrest; ste $140-150; P) A value option for self-caterers, featuring full-kitchen suites.

Beach Haven Inn (Map p905; ☎ 858-272-3812, 800-831-6323; www.beachhaveninn.com; 4740 Mission Blvd, Pacific Beach; r $130-170; P) Although slightly worn around the edges, this little inn is only a block from the ocean and three blocks from the restaurants and nightlife of Garnet Ave. The suites with kitchen and separate sitting room are the best deal.

Also recommended:

Ocean Villa Inn (Map p905; ☎ 619-224-3481, 800-759-0012; www.oceanvillainn.com; 5142 W Point Loma

Blvd, Ocean Beach; r $120-190; (P) (pets)) Generic, but pet-friendly, quiet and right on the ocean.

Surfer Motor Lodge (Map p905; ☎ 858-483-7070, 800-787-3373; www.surfermotorlodge.com; 711 Pacific Beach Dr, Pacific Beach; r $100-160; (P) (pets)) Low-key motel with restaurant and family units.

TOP END

W San Diego (Map pp908-9; ☎ 619-231-8220; 877-946-8357; www.starwood.com/whotels; 421 W B St; r $230-360; (P) (pool) (internet) (pets)) San Diego's latest hot spot goes for sophisticated, urban sensibilities with its cool decor, sleek rooms boasting luxurious beds and amenities, and *über*-hip rooftop beach lounge complete with heated sand floor. A place to see and be seen.

Humphrey's Half Moon Inn & Suites (Map p905; ☎ 619-224-3411, 800-345-9995; 2303 Shelter Island Dr, Shelter Island; r $149-259, ste $230-500; (P) (pool) (pets)) Fans of boating, jazz and Polynesian architecture will feel at home in this waterfront resort anchored by a giant pool. Rooms, many with marina-view balconies, lack nothing in comforts, and live bands keep the popular bar hopping nightly.

Hotel del Coronado (Map p905; ☎ 619-435-6611; www.hoteldel.com; 1500 Orange Ave, Coronado; r $270-490; (P) (pool) (internet) (pets)) The red turrets of this historic hotel welcome guests to the lobby, lounges and corridors frequented by presidents, royalty and celebrities. Rooms have a surprisingly modern feel and a full range of amenities. Half of them are in a separate seven-story building.

Hotel Parisi (Map p905; ☎ 858-454-1511, 877-472-7474; www.hotelparisi.com; 1111 Prospect Ave, La Jolla; ste $280-500; (P) (pool)) Ultra-chic, all-suite retreat popular with millionaires and celebrities.

Eating

With more than 6000 restaurants, San Diego's dining scene is as diverse as its population. You can enjoy Mexican *huevos rancheros* (fried eggs on tortillas, covered in salsa) for breakfast, an Indian curry for lunch and wrap up the day with steamed lobster. Although eating out tends toward the casual, in recent years a handful of creative chefs has emerged to give the city a respectable range of gourmet options.

DOWNTOWN Map pp908-9

Gaslamp Strip Club (☎ 619-231-3140; 340 5th Ave; meals $13-25) The name refers to strip steak and not to what you were thinking! Meat's the thing here, which patrons must personally prepare on a communal grill. The decor toys with decadence (black leather booths, Vargas prints), but it's all really quite tame.

> **THE AUTHOR'S CHOICE**
>
> **Indigo Grill** (Map p884; ☎ 619-234-6802; 1536 India St; lunch $7-14, dinner $17-28) This Little Italy jewel is not only a winner in the looks department but also wows adventurous diners with boundary-pushing cuisine. Chef Deborah Scott fearlessly blends the flavors and ingredients of Alaska, the American Southwest and Mexico into perky dishes that, quite literally, tease all the senses. For extra kicks, try the Oaxaca Fire, a margarita made with spicy Serrano jelly.

Sammy's Woodfired Pizza (☎ 619-230-8888; 770 4th Ave; meals $8-15) Creative pizzas are the star of the show at this cafeteria-style eatery, although the appetizers and big salads have their fans as well.

Royal Thai Cuisine (☎ 619-230-8424; 467 5th Ave; mains $9-13) Dining at this excellent eatery, one of the city's best for Thai, takes place in a spacious dining room sprinkled with classic statues and artwork.

Other good Gaslamp choices include the following:

Pokéz (☎ 619-702-7160; 947 E St; mains less than $6) For healthy and vegetarian Mexican.

Bandar (☎ 619-238-0101; 825 4th Ave; mains $12-21) A first-rate Persian restaurant.

OLD TOWN & HILLCREST Map p905

Kemo Sabe (☎ 619-220-6902; 3958 5th Ave, Hillcrest; mains $13-26; (open) dinner) The fanciful decor blends motifs from the Far East and the American Southwest, an approach also reflected in the eclectic menu at this popular Hillcrest place.

Parallel 33 (☎ 619-260-0033; 741 W Washington St, Hillcrest; mains $18-27; (open) dinner) What do India, Morocco, Japan, China and San Diego have in common? All are located 33-degrees north of the equator and their cuisines inspired the menu at this trendy restaurant.

Bombay (☎ 619-298-3155; 3975 5th Ave, Hillcrest; mains $11-16) Big chandeliers and subdued decor create the relaxed ambience at this restaurant where the cleverly spiced curries are sure to tantalize your taste buds.

Old Town is the place for Mexican food. The no-nonsense **Old Town Mexican Café**

(☎ 619-297-4330; 2489 San Diego Ave, Old Town; mains $4-11) is a favorite with locals, while tourists gravitate to the adobe rooms and flowery patio of **Casa de Bandini** (☎ 619-297-8211; 2660 Calhoun St, Old Town; mains $9-16).

BEACHES **Map p905**

Tapenade (☎ 858-551-7500; 7612 Fay Ave, La Jolla; mains $24-32) Consistently voted one of San Diego's top restaurants, Tapenade dazzles diners with its inspired French cuisine, based on seasonal ingredients, and killer desserts. Gourmets on a budget should try the two-course lunch for $15 or the sunset dinner for $25 (5:30pm to 6:30pm).

Kono's (☎ 858-483-1669; 704 Garnet Ave, Pacific Beach; meals less than $5) Right where Garnet spills into the ocean, this quintessential surf shack draws long lines for its tasty breakfasts, burgers and sandwiches served until the early afternoon.

Spot (☎ 858-459-0800; 1005 Prospect St, La Jolla; mains $9-16) Settle into a chocolate-colored booth and sink your teeth into a juicy angus beef burger at this unpretentious tavern in the heart of La Jolla.

Also recommended:

Filippi's Fish Grotto (☎ 858-483-6222; 962 Garnet Ave, Pacific Beach; pizzas from $10) The classics: pizza, chianti and Sinatra.

Hodad's (☎ 619-224-4623; 5010 Newport Ave, Ocean Beach; meals less than $5) The ultimate burger joint.

Green Flash (☎ 858-270-7715; 701 Thomas Ave, Pacific Beach; mains $10-17) Beachside fish restaurant, often packed to the gills.

Drinking

Onyx Room & Thin (Map pp908-9; ☎ 619-235-6699; 852 5th Ave) Come for cocktails and conversations at the ultra-cool, industrial-look Thin or the plushier, candle-lit Onyx in the basement. The latter also has a dance floor.

Red Circle Bar (Map pp908-9; ☎ 619-234-9211; 420 E St) Order a martini, raise your pinkie and peruse the Soviet-era memorabilia and lissome crowd bathed in sexy red lighting at this trendy Russian-themed boîte. The bar serves more than 100 varieties of vodka.

Bitter End (Map pp908-9; ☎ 619-338-9300; 770 5th Ave) On busy nights, all three levels of this fabulous bar bustle with people of all ages. There's dancing in the basement, beer at street-level and martinis (including its signature Black Martini, made with Kahlua) in the upstairs lounge.

Coaster Saloon (Map p905; ☎ 858-488-4438; 744 Ventura Pl, Mission Beach) This old-fashioned neighborhood bar has front-row views of the Belmont Park roller coaster and draws an unpretentious crowd. Good margaritas.

An excellent stand-by for smooth, homemade brews is **Karl Strauss Brewery** Downtown (Map pp908-9; ☎ 619-234-2739; 1157 Columbia St) La Jolla (Map p905; ☎ 858-551-2739; 1044 Wall St).

Entertainment

Your best sources for what's hot in San Diego are the free weeklies, *San Diego Reader* and *San Diego City Beat*. **Arts Tix** (🕑 11am-6pm Tue-Thu, 10am-6pm Fri & Sat, 10am-5pm Sun), in a kiosk on Broadway outside Horton Plaza, has half-price tickets for same-day evening or next-day matinee performances and full-price tickets to other events.

LIVE MUSIC & NIGHTCLUBS

Casbah (Map pp908-9; ☎ 619-232-4355; 2501 Kettner Blvd) Nirvana and the Smashing Pumpkins cut their teeth at this alternative music venue where couches, pinball machines and dimly lit alcoves form the backdrop to the music.

Croce's Restaurant & Jazz Bar (Map pp908-9; ☎ 619-233-4355; 802 5th Ave) Run by Ingrid Croce, widow of bluesman Jim Croce ('Bad, Bad Leroy Brown'), this place hosts local and national jazz talent nightly. The $5 cover charge is waived for dining guests.

4th & B (Map pp908-9; ☎ 619-231-4343; 345 B St) It's mostly local bands at this popular venue with a huge dance floor, energetic crowd and eclectic music schedule – soul to Latin to alternative rock.

Barefoot Bar & Grill (Map p905; ☎ 858-274-4630; 1404 W Vacation Rd, Mission Bay) The time to be at Barefoot, in the Paradise Point Resort, is on summer Sundays for the wild all-day weekend wrap-up parties. Things cool down a bit on other days.

Other fun places to party include the following:

Blind Melons (Map p905; ☎ 858-483-7844; 710 Garnet Ave, Pacific Beach) Edgy.

Canes (Map p905; ☎ 858-488-1780; 3105 Ocean Front Walk, Mission Beach) Tropical.

Winston's (Map p905; ☎ 619-222-6822; 1921 Bacon St, Ocean Beach) Reggae-infused.

CLASSICAL MUSIC

San Diego Symphony (Map pp908-9; ☎ 619-235-0804; 750 B St) For serious music lovers, there's no

TIJUANA: CHAOS, CLASS & CULTURE CLASH

Rita Hayworth was discovered here. Carlos Santana began his career in its nightclubs. And one of the world's great culinary inventions, the Caesar salad, hails from nowhere other than…drum roll please…yes, Tijuana, that grubby, noisy, frenzied, yet oddly tantalizing city of two million right across the border from San Diego.

During Prohibition in the 1920s, Tijuana (TJ, for short) was the darling of the Hollywood crowd. These days, tequila and beer exert their siren song to college students, sailors and other revelers who each weekend descend upon the rollicking bars and nightclubs of Avenida Revolución (La Revo), the main tourist strip. By day, it's the shops that bring in bargain hunters for everything from liquor to shoes to pharmaceuticals. Alas, competition is fierce and the constant hustle from storefront vendors is rather annoying. Nearly all businesses accept US dollars. A good place for quality crafts is **Bazar de Mexico** (La Revo & Calle 7a), inside the **Frontón Palacio Jai Alai**. This TJ landmark used to host jai alai, a fast-paced game of Basque origin, until the late 1990s.

Once you've 'done' La Revo, be sure to venture beyond for a more interesting and often surprisingly sophisticated side of Tijuana. Pick up a map from a **visitors center** (☎ 664-683-1405; www.tijuanaonline.org) that shows the precise locations of all places mentioned below. There are branches right by the pedestrian and car border crossings as well as on La Revo between Calles 3a and 4a.

Wine aficionados should head to **Vinícola LA Cetto** (☎ 664-685-3031; Avenida Cañon Johnson 2108) for a chance to sample vintages from the nearby Valle de Guadalupe rarely available outside of Mexico. Architecture fans may want to visit the **Catedral de Nuestra Señora de Guadalupe** (Avenida Niños Héroes & Calle 2a), Tijuana's oldest church. For a cultural fix, make a beeline to the excellent **Museo de las Californias** (☎ 664-687-9600; Paseo de los Héroes & Miña; admission $2; 🕑 10am-6pm Tue-Fri, closes 7pm Sat & Sun), which has engaging exhibits chronicling the intriguing history of Baja California from prehistoric times to the present. The museum is part of the **Centro Cultural de Tijuana**, which has a schedule of classical concerts, theater and dance recitals that goes a long way towards undermining the city's image as a cultural wasteland. Nearby, **Mercado Hidalgo** is a fun indoor/outdoor market where the locals stock up on such basics as rice, beans and powdered chili from pussycat mild to hellishly hot.

TJ also has an interesting dining scene. Good choices on La Revo include the old-timey **Café La Especial** (☎ 664-685-6654; Avenida Revolucíon 18; breakfast & lunch $5, dinner $10-15), in a shopping arcade below Hotel Lafayette, where you can enjoy Mexican classics in the cavernous, woodsy setting. **Chiki Jai** (☎ 664-685-4955; Avenida Revolucíon & Calle 7a; mains around $10), in business since 1947, used to be the hangout of jai alai players and specializes in Spanish food. Beyond the tourist strip, excellent choices include the classy **La Espadaña** (☎ 664-634-1488; Boulevard Sánchez Taboada 10813; mains $8-20) and the gourmet-level **Cien Años** (☎ 664-634-7262; Avenida Josè María Velasco 1407; mains from $15; 🕑 dinner) which has more than 100 tequilas and recipes going back to the Aztecs and Mayans. It's dressy and requires reservations.

The easiest way to get to Tijuana from San Diego is by taking the San Diego Trolley and walking across the border. Due to heightened security, expect long lines when returning to the US. See Visas (p1103) and Customs (p1089) for border requirements.

finer place than the **Copley Symphony Hall** where this accomplished orchestra presents classical and family concerts. In summer, it moves to **Navy Pier** (960 N Harbor Dr) for more light-hearted musical fare.

San Diego Opera (Map pp908-9; ☎ 619-570-1100; Civic Theatre, 401 B St) High-quality, eclectic programming are the hallmarks of the city's opera ensemble, which occasionally draws international guest stars such as Plácido Domingo.

Starlight Musical Theatre (Map p905; ☎ 619-544-7827; Starlight Bowl, Balboa Park) In summer, musicals produced by the San Diego Civic Light Opera, the nation's oldest continuous musical theater company (since 1945), take place.

Getting There & Away

San Diego International Airport (☎ 619-231-2100) is about 3 miles west of Downtown.

Greyhound (Map pp908-9; ☎ 619-239-8082; 120 W Broadway) has frequent buses to Los Angeles,

Phoenix, Las Vegas and other US cities. *Pacific Surfliner* trains, operated by **Amtrak** (Map pp908-9; ☎ 619-239-9021; Santa Fe Depot, 1055 Kettner Blvd), make several trips daily to Los Angeles and Santa Barbara.

All major **car rental** companies have desks at the airport; or call the national toll-free numbers listed in the Transport chapter (p1121). For motorcycle rentals contact **Eagle Rider** (☎ 877-437-4337; 3655 Camino del Rio W), near the airport.

Getting Around

Bus No 992, also known as the **Flyer** ($2.25; 5-1am), operates at 10- to 15-minute intervals between the airport and Downtown, with stops along Broadway. Airport shuttle services include **Cloud 9 Shuttle** (☎ 858-505-4900) and **Xpress Shuttle** (☎ 619-222-5800). A taxi to Downtown from the airport is $8 to $13.

Local buses and the San Diego Trolley are both operated by **Metropolitan Transit Service** (MTS; ☎ 800-266-6883; www.sdcommute.com). The **Transit Store** (☎ 619-234-1060; Broadway & 1st Ave) also has maps, tickets and one/two/three day passes for $5/8/10.

Buses cover most of the metropolitan area, while the Trolley's main route travels south to the Mexican border from Old Town.

Coaster commuter trains serve communities in northern San Diego county from the **Santa Fe Depot** (1055 Kettner Blvd).

AROUND SAN DIEGO

San Diego Wild Animal Park

Go on safari at this 1800-acre **animal park** (☎ 760-747-8702; www.sandiegozoo.org; 15500 San Pasqual Valley Rd, Escondido; adult/senior/child $27/24/20; 9am-6pm May-Sep, closes 4pm other times) that lets its denizens roam freely on the open valley floor. You'll encounter herds of giraffes, zebras, rhinos and other animals while riding the Wgasa Bush Line Railway or touring the Heart of Africa and other habitats. Combination tickets with the San Diego Zoo are $56/36.

Escondido is about 30 miles north of central San Diego. Take the I-15 Fwy to the Via Rancho Park exit, then follow the signs.

Legoland

About 32 miles north of central San Diego, **Legoland** (☎ 760-918-5346; www.lego.com/legoland; 1 Legoland Dr, Carlsbad; adult $42, senior & child $35; 10am-8pm Jul-Aug, closes 5pm or 6pm other times) is an enchanting fantasy environment built entirely of those little colored plastic building blocks that many of us grew up with. It's a great place for families, especially those with kids aged 10 and under. Visually the most stunning area is **Miniland**, which recreates such American landmarks as the White House and the Golden Gate Bridge at a twentieth of their actual size. Youngsters love the rides, including the Sky Cycle where guests pedal – ET-like – above the park, and the chance to build their own Lego structures. To get there from central San Diego, take the I-5 Fwy north to the Cannon Rd East exit, then follow the signs.

CALIFORNIA DESERTS

Forget about green. After a while the starkness of the desert landscape, the clarity of the light and the spaciousness are beautiful in their own way. Be warned that the deserts present real dangers from extreme weather: hot days (120°F and up), freezing, windy nights and the potential for flash floods. Don't enter or explore abandoned mine shafts. And bring lots of water; being stranded without it is the biggest danger in the desert.

ANZA-BORREGO DESERT STATE PARK

This enormous state park – the largest in the USA outside of Alaska – is fairly undeveloped and perfect for people seeking the quintessential desert experience: quiet, solitude, remote camping and exploring, stargazing, meditating, what have you. You'll need a car to get around and several trips may be necessary to discover the three main areas around Borrego Springs, Blair Valley and Split Mountain. The park can be absolutely brilliant in wildflower season, usually February to mid-April; for recorded wildflower updates, call ☎ 760-767-4684.

If you're short on time, or if it's your first visit, head for **Borrego Springs**, a small township with a market, restaurants and motels. Stop in at the excellent **visitors center** (☎ 760-767-5311; 200 Palm Canyon Dr; 9am-5pm Oct-May, weekends only other times), 2 miles west of here for maps, information and a free permit for overnight camping and off-highway driving.

Borrego Springs is the gateway to several easy-to-reach sights, including **Font's Point**, which overlooks the Borrego Badlands, and **Borrego Palm Canyon**, where a self-guided nature trail leads to a palm grove and waterfall.

The park's southernmost region, south of and including **Blair Valley**, is the least visited and – aside from those in Blair Valley – has few developed trails and facilities. Attractions here include **Goat Trestle** and the **Carrizo Badlands**. The **Split Mountain** area, in the southeast, is popular with 4WD vehicles, but also contains interesting geology and spectacular **wind caves**.

Backcountry camping is free and permitted anywhere except within 200yd of a road or water source. Open ground fires and gathering vegetation (dead or alive) are prohibited. Developed campgrounds are **Borrego Palm Canyon** (☎ 800-444-7275; sites $13), about 2.5 miles west of the visitors center, and **Tamarisk Grove** (☎ 800-444-7275; Hwy S3; sites $13), near Hwy 78.

In Borrego Springs, the **Palm Canyon Resort** (☎ 760-767-5341, 800-242-0044; 221 Palm Canyon Dr; r $70-195; P) has a nice pool and spa, manicured grounds and a good restaurant. Considerably more upscale, the adult-oriented **Borrego Valley Inn** (☎ 760-767-0311, 800-333-5810; 405 Palm Canyon Dr; r $130-175 Jun-Sep, $140-215 Oct-May; P) has an intimate spa-resort feel. Rates include breakfast, afternoon lemonade and evening cocktails.

PALM SPRINGS

Hemmed in by the austere Colorado Desert and lorded over by the rugged San Jacinto Mountains, Palm Springs is a pretty pastiche of swaying palm trees, a profusion of flowers, emerald golf courses and immaculately kept neighborhoods. It's the oldest and ritziest of the string of desert resorts in the Coachella Valley, which also includes Rancho Mirage, Palm Desert and Indian Wells. Its pedigree as a posh playground goes back to the 1920s when Hollywood stars retreated here for privacy, parties and indiscretions. Today, a new generation of celebrities does its best to uphold the tradition.

There's plenty to do in Palm Springs besides sipping mai tais poolside or hitting the greens. You can hike palm-studded canyons or shop on Palm Canyon Blvd; explore museums or modernist architecture. In recent years, Palm Springs has also become a popular gay and lesbian getaway, with the scene centered on Arenas Rd.

Most visitors come in the cooler months (October to April), but lower prices assure that Palm Springs stays reasonably busy even in summer, when temperatures rarely drop below 100°F (38°C).

Palm Springs' compact downtown flanks Palm Canyon Dr (the continuation of Hwy 111), which runs north–south. The parallel Indian Canyon Dr runs one-way south to north.

Information

Main Visitors Center (☎ 760-778-8418, 800-347-7746; www.palm-springs.org; 9am-6pm) North of town, at the tramway turnoff.

Uptown Visitors Center (☎ 760-327-2828; 777 N Palm Canyon Dr, Suite 101; 10am-6pm)

Sights & Activities

Escape the summer heat by riding the rotating cars of the **Aerial Tramway** (☎ 760-325-1391; adult $21, child 3-12 $14; 10am-10pm Mon-Fri, 8am-10pm Sat & Sun) up Mt San Jacinto to the mountain station at 8516ft, an eight-minute journey through five vegetation zones equivalent to a trip from Mexico to Alaska. Besides awesome desert views, around 54 miles of hiking trails beckon in **Mt Jacinto State Park**, including a 5.5-mile trek to the summit. In winter, explore the forest on snowshoes or cross-country skis, available for rent at the mountain station.

Another cool place is **Knott's Soak City** (☎ 760-327-0499; 1500 S Gene Autry Trail; adult $23, child 5-11 $17, after 3pm $14 for all; 10am-6pm mid-Mar-Aug, Sat & Sun Oct). Kids especially love the slides, tube rides and wave pools at this water park.

The **Palm Springs Desert Museum** (☎ 760-325-7186; 101 Museum Dr; adult $7.50, senior & child $3.50; 10am-5pm Tue-Sat, noon-5pm Sun) in downtown has a small but choice modern-art collection as well as Native American art and objects. At the airport, the **Palm Springs Air Museum** (☎ 760-778-6262; 745 N Gene Autry Trail; adult $8, child 6-12 $3.50; 10am-5pm) will quicken the pulse of any WWII and vintage-plane aficionado. All aircraft, including the amazing B-17 (the 'Flying Fortress') are in flying condition.

In the cooler months, especially during the spring wildflower season, a hike through the scenic **Indian Canyons** (adult $6, child 6-12 $2; 8am-5pm), about 2 miles south of downtown, is a delight. These canyon oases, shaded by fan palms, were home to Cahuilla people for centuries and are now part of the Agua Caliente Indian Reservation. Tribe members also lead tours of sacred **Tahquitz Canyon** (☎ 760-416-7044; adult/child $12.50/6; closed Jun-Sep), famous for its 60ft waterfall and ancient rock art.

Golf is huge in Palm Springs, with around 100 public, semiprivate and private courses. The tourist offices and most hotels can help you arrange tee times, or try **Stand-by Golf** (☎ 760-321-2665, 800-224-2665), which can provide guaranteed tee times, at a discount, for same-day or next-day play at 35 area courses.

Tours

Celebrity Tours (☎ 760-770-2700; Rimrock Shopping Center, 4751 E Palm Dr; adult $20, child under 14 $10) Pick up on Palm Springs gossip and glamour.

Desert Adventures (☎ 760-324-5337; $59-99) Snappily narrated and information-packed jeep tours through shake, rattle 'n roll country right atop the San Andreas Fault.

PS Modern Tours (☎ 760-318-6118; $40-55) For fans of Albert Frey, Richard Neutra and other mid-century modern architects (alternatively, pick up *A Map of Palm Springs Modern* at the tourist office for $5 and do your own tour).

Windmill Tours (☎ 760-251-1997; adult/child $22/10; reservations required at least 24 hours ahead) Learn all about the grove of whirring windmills surrounding Palm Springs.

Sleeping

Both visitors centers make room reservations for free.

Villa Royale (☎ 760-327-2314, 800-245-2314; www.villaroyale.com; 1620 Indian Trail; r $119-199, villas $229-299) Towering palm trees stand sentinel over this delightful, flower-draped hideaway wrapped around three courtyards. The Mediterranean aesthetic continues in the rooms, no two decorated alike, but all featuring antiques and upscale amenities. Days begin with a cooked breakfast served poolside.

Estrella (☎ 760-320-4117, 800-237-3687; www.estrellapalmsprings.com; 415 S Belardo Rd; r $89-239, ste $139-309) Crisp white, jet black and citrus yellow form the fresh color palette at this sprawling, historic abode that's been completely made over in a glamorous modern-meets-classic style. Luxury touches abound here, including down comforters and flat-screen TVs.

Casa Cody (☎ 760-320-9346; www.casacody.com; 175 S Cahuilla Rd; studio $89-149, ste $99-349) Tucked behind a lush curtain of bougainvillea, this lovely country inn was built in the 1920s by a cousin of Buffalo Bill. It now features rooms with eclectic 'deserts of the world' decor and full kitchens. Breakfast is included.

Other good choices include the following:

Orbit In (☎ 760-323-3585, 877-996-7248; www.orbitin.com; 562 W Arenas; r $159-269) Hip, stylish and retro.

Alpine Gardens Hotel (☎ 760-323-2231, 888-299-7455; www.alpinegardens.com; 1586 E Palm Canyon Dr; r $60-85) Budget-priced.

Eating

Blue Coyote Grill (☎ 760-327-1196; 445 N Palm Canyon Dr; mains $14-25) The courtyard tables are the most coveted at this lively cantina serving Mexican and Southwestern favorites. The Wild Coyote margarita is legendary.

Europa (☎ 760-327-2314, 800-245-2314; 1620 Indian Trail; mains $18-34) In the Villa Royale, this well-respected restaurant has an intimate dining room where patrons indulge in creative takes on continental classics.

Rock Garden Café (☎ 760-327-8840; 777 S Palm Canyon Dr; mains $8-17) Come for any meal to this casual eatery with its large patio and extensive menu offering everything from roast-beef sandwiches to vegetarian quiche.

St James at the Vineyard (☎ 760-864-9335; 265 S Palm Canyon Dr; mains $23-29) St James' exotic, drop-dead-gorgeous decor matches the eclectic gourmet menu featuring culinary creations from around the world. Check out the mask collection in the bar.

Also recommended:

Bit of Country (☎ 760-325-5154; 418 S Indian Canyon Dr; breakfast $4-9) For fans of big, hearty breakfasts.

Native Foods (☎ 760-416-0070; 1775 E Palm Canyon Dr; mains $9-13) Great vegan fare.

Getting There & Around

Palm Springs International Airport (☎ 760-318-3800; www.palmspringsairport.com) is served directly from major US cities, including Houston, Atlanta and Chicago. **Greyhound** (☎ 760-325-2053; 311 N Indian Canyon Dr; 8am-6pm) has buses to Los Angeles ($20, three hours, seven daily). Local service is provided by **SunBus** (☎ 760-343-3451; $1, day pass $3).

JOSHUA TREE NATIONAL PARK

Like figments from a Dr Seuss book, the whimsical Joshua trees welcome visitors to this sprawling park popular with rock climbers and day hikers, especially in spring when many trees dramatically send up a huge single white flower.

Park highlights include the **Hidden Valley** area with its dramatic rock formations, **Keys View**, with vistas as far as Mexico (best at sunset) and the **Cholla Cactus Garden**. An excellent short hike is the 1.1-mile **Barker Dam loop trail**, which takes in all that makes Joshua Tree special: weathered rock piles, a historic dam, Indian petroglyphs and, of course, the trees themselves.

Park admission is $10 per vehicle, good for seven days and comes with a map and the useful *Joshua Tree Guide* newspaper. Note that aside from restrooms the park has no facilities, so bring food and plenty of water.

Near the park's northern entrance is the Twentynine Palms **visitors center** (☎ 760-337-5500; www.nps.gov/jotr; National Monument Rd; 🕑 8am-5pm), with the Cottonwood Springs **visitors center** (🕑 8am-4pm) just inside the south entrance.

Of the park's nine campgrounds only **Black Rock Canyon campground** (☎ 800-365-2267; sites $10) and **Indian Cove campground** (☎ 800-365-2267; sites $10) have reservable sites. **Cottonwood campground** also costs $10, while the other six are free. Only Black Rock Canyon and Cottonwood have water. Backcountry camping is permitted as long as it's 1 mile from the road and 500ft from any trail; registration is required.

Around Joshua Tree

Joshua Tree National Park is a popular day trip for people staying in Palm Springs, about an hour's drive away. If you want to be closer, base yourself in Twentynine Palms, Joshua Tree or Yucca Valley along the park's northern perimeter. None of these towns are particularly attractive but they do the trick if all you want is a motel and a bite to eat.

Near the visitors center, the **Twentynine Palms Inn** (☎ 760-367-3505; www.29palmsinn.com; 73950 Inn Ave; cabins $75-185, less in summer; 🅟) is a historic cluster of old adobe-and-wood cabins, with a restaurant, built around the Oasis of Mara. In Joshua Tree, the **Joshua Tree Inn** (☎ 760-366-1188; www.joshuatreeinn.com; 61259 29 Palms Hwy; r $75-95; 🅟) has hosted the Eagles and Emmylou Harris. Rates include a continental breakfast. If you need a more substantial feed, try **Crossroads Café** (☎ 760-366-5414; 61715 29 Palms Hwy, Joshua Tree; dishes $5-9).

For a total retreat, head to **Rimrock Ranch Cabins** (☎ 760-228-1297; www.rimrockranchcabins.com; 50857 Burns Canyon Rd; cabins $85-140, 2-night minimum), four lovingly decorated cabins from the 1940s, each with full kitchen. Reservations are required. It's about a 20-minute drive north of the town of Yucca Valley. En route you'll pass **Pioneertown**, built in 1946 as a Western movie set and now home to the legendary **Pappy's & Harriet's Pioneertown Palace** (☎ 760-365-5956; meals $6-15), a happening honky-tonk with live music, cheap beer and great barbecue.

THE MOJAVE DESERT

The vast Mojave (mo-*ha*-vee) Desert stretches from the northern edge of LA County to the Nevadan border. Most people quickly pass through this parched desert basin on route to/from Death Valley or Las Vegas, but those with time and transportation will find a lot worth stopping for.

Mojave National Preserve

This preserve in the eastern Mojave Desert contains 1.6 million acres of sand dunes, Joshua trees, volcanic outcrops and fabulous rock formations. The National Park Service maintains the Baker **visitors center** (☎ 760-733-4040; www.nps.gov/moja; 72157 Baker Blvd; 🕑 9am-5pm) and the Needles **visitors center** (☎ 760-326-6322; 707 Broadway; 🕑 8am-4pm Tue-Sun). There are no services or facilities within the preserve, so make sure you have enough gasoline, water and food. Strong winds are the norm.

Kelbaker Rd, the main route across the preserve, connects Baker with the I-40 freeway. It skirts the **Cinder Cones National Natural Landmark**, where volcanic activity has resulted in a cluster of about three dozen cinder cones. Access is via Aiken's Mine Rd.

Next up are the **Kelso Dunes**, intriguing rose-colored sand dunes that rise up to 600ft and are fun to explore on foot. North of Kelso, Cima Rd goes to **Cima Dome**, a 1500ft hunk of granite spiked with volcanic cinder cones and crusty basalt outcrops left by ancient lava flows.

Southeast of Kelso, and reached via Essex Rd off I-40, **Mitchell Caverns** (☎ 760-928-2586; adult/child $3/1; 🕑 vary, call ahead) feature whimsical formations that can be explored on guided tours. North of the caverns, at the end of unpaved Black Canyon Rd, the fascinating volcanic **Hole-in-the-Wall** rock formation is riddled with holes, many of which have eroded into larger caves. There's first-come, first-served camping ($12) here and at Mid Hills.

Elsewhere in the Mojave Desert

The I-15 freeway cuts right through the Mojave Desert. About halfway between Los Angeles and Las Vegas, it reaches **Barstow**, treated as little more than a pit stop by most travelers. The Barstow Rd exit leads to the **California Desert Information Center** (☎ 760-255-8760; 831 Barstow Rd; 9am-5pm). A few miles east is **Calico Ghost Town** (☎ 760-254-2122; adult/child $6/3; 9am-5pm), rebuilt by Walter Knott (of Knott's Berry Farm fame) and only marginally more authentic than Disney's Frontierland. It's still a fun place to stop and take a break.

Driving west from Barstow along Hwy 58, you'll eventually skirt the northern edge of **Edwards Air Force Base**, a flight-test facility for NASA and the US Air Force. It was here that Chuck Yeager flew the Bell X-1 on the world's first supersonic flight in 1947, and the first shuttles glided in after their space missions. The base is closed to the public until further notice.

The nearby town of **Mojave** is good for refueling and stocking up on supplies and little else. Driving through, you might think Mojave had a huge international airport, but all those airliners are actually in storage, because deterioration is minimal in the dry desert air.

About 25 miles north of Mojave, along Hwy 14, is **Red Rock Canyon State Park** (☎ 661-942-0662; day-use fee $3). Its dramatically eroded sandstone cliffs are especially spectacular at sunrise and sunset and featured in the opening scenes of *Jurassic Park*. For front-row stargazing, pitch a tent at **Ricardo Campground** (campsites $9).

DEATH VALLEY NATIONAL PARK

The name itself evokes all that is harsh and hellish – a lifeless place hotter than Satan's hoof. True, but not the whole truth. Death Valley is a mesmerizing medley of rugged canyons, sand dunes, ghost towns, oases and colorful mountains. It holds the US records for hottest temperature (134°F, or 56°C, measured in 1913), lowest point (Badwater, 282ft below sea level) and largest national park outside Alaska (4687 sq miles). Bring plenty of water for you and your car. There's no public transport to or within the park.

Orientation & Information

Centrally located Furnace Creek has the most facilities, including a general store, restaurants, lodging, public showers, a golf course and a **visitors center** (☎ 760-786-3200; www.nps.gov/deva; 8am-6pm) that doubles as a museum. Stovepipe Wells, about 24 miles northwest, has a store, gas station, motel/restaurant and ranger station. Gas and sustenance are also available at Scotty's Castle, in the north, and Panamint Springs, on the park's western edge. The entrance fee ($10 a vehicle; valid for seven days) comes with a free map and newspaper and must be paid at the visitors center or a ranger station.

Driving Tour

This tour can be done in a single day (even starting from outside the valley), if you begin early. Start off by catching the sunrise at either **Zabriskie Point** or **Dante's View**. From the latter, it's possible to see both Mt Whitney and Badwater, the highest and lowest points respectively in the contiguous USA. Head down to Furnace Creek, then drive about 24 miles northwest to Stovepipe Wells, where you can enjoy the interplay of light and shadow while clambering around the **Sand Dunes**.

Another 36 miles north is **Scotty's Castle** (☎ 760-786-2392; adult/child $8/4; 9am-5pm), nearly 3000ft above sea level and noticeably cooler. There's a snack bar here, if hunger strikes. Scotty's Castle was the desert home of Chicago insurance magnate Albert Johnson. It's named for Walter Scott, a local prospector and flamboyant character who lured people, including Johnson, out west with promises of gold. Although there was no gold to be found, Johnson seriously fell in love with the place and even developed a close friendship with Scotty. His fully and richly furnished home is now open to the public.

About 8 miles west, **Ubehebe Crater** – 900yd wide and 800ft deep – is the result of a massive volcanic eruption. Hiking to the bottom and back takes about 30 minutes. Backtrack south for about 60 miles past Furnace Creek to **Badwater**, where you can walk onto the constantly evaporating bed of salty, mineralized water. A few miles back north, the valley floor is filled with lumps of crystallized salt in what is called the **Devil's Golf Course**. Conclude your day on **Artists Drive** by watching the mountains erupt in a riot of color in the late afternoon sun.

Sleeping & Eating

During the peak months of March and April (wildflower season) accommodations are often booked solid and campgrounds fill by mid-morning. Crowds thin considerably from June to September.

Furnace Creek Ranch (☎ 760-786-2345; www.furnacecreekresort.com; r $105-164;) Unpretentious and family-friendly, the Ranch has the greatest number of facilities in the park, including the world's lowest golf course and several restaurants. The **Wrangler Restaurant** (breakfast/lunch $8.50/10, dinner mains $21-33) does buffet-style breakfasts and lunches and turns into a steakhouse at night. Next door, the casual **Forty-Niner Café** ($6-18) offers up a good range of belly-filling fare, although for the best burgers you should mosey over to the **19th Hole** ($6; lunch).

Furnace Creek Inn (☎ 760-786-2345; www.furnacecreekresort; r $160-355;) If you'd like to play queen or king of the desert, head uphill to this majestic mission-style abode. It's a relaxing spot where you can unwind in a spring-fed pool, count the colors of the desert from the deck or sample a fine meal in the gourmet **restaurant** (mains $19-29), which has a dinner dress code.

Less exalted lodging awaits at **Stove Pipe Wells Village** (☎ 760-786-2331; r $54-96;), with basic motel rooms of various sizes, and at the pet- and group-friendly **Panamint Springs Resort** (☎ 775-482-7680; www.deathvalley.com; r $65-94;), on the park's western edge. Both have restaurants and campgrounds.

The summer heat makes camping at the lower levels intolerable, while winter nights can be surprisingly cold. Death Valley has nine other campgrounds, but none are particularly attractive. Only **Furnace Creek** (☎ 800-365-2267; www.reservations.nps.gov; campsites $10-16), the most pleasant and shady campground, accepts reservations. Nearby is the 1000-site, RV-oriented **Sunset** (sites $10) and the much nicer, hillside **Texas Spring** (sites $12). Both are open October to April. For details about other campgrounds, check www.nps.gov/deva. For free backcountry camping, pick up a permit from the visitors center or ranger station.

OUTSIDE THE PARK

More lodging options are available within a one- to two-hour drive from Furnace Creek. The towns of Ridgecrest and Beatty, Nevada are your best bet for budget and mid-range motels. Shoestringers might steer towards the **HI Desertaire Hostel** (☎ 760-852-4580; 2000 Old Spanish Trail Hwy; dm/r $15/50;), near some hot springs in Tecopa, about 60 miles southeast near Shoshone.

CENTRAL COAST

California's Central Coast, stretching from Ventura north to Monterey Bay, covers nearly 300 miles of prime shoreline. Hwy 101 is the region's main artery, though for outstanding coastal views travel along the Pacific Coast Hwy (Hwy 1) between San Luis Obispo and Monterey.

VENTURA & THE CHANNEL ISLANDS

Ventura, an agricultural town and gateway to the Channel Islands National Park, has a charming downtown with an assortment of cafés, restaurants and antique and thrift shops. Worth a look is the beautiful 1782 **Mission San Buenaventura** (☎ 805-643-4318; 211 E Main St; admission $1; 10am-5pm Mon-Sat, 10am-4pm Sun).

Ventura Harbor, southwest of Hwy 101, is where boats depart for the Channel Islands, whose unique flora and fauna has garnered them the nickname 'California's Galápagos.' Five of the eight islands in the chain, which stretches from Newport Beach to Santa Barbara, comprise Channel Islands National Park. The National Park Service operates a **visitors center** (☎ 805-658-5730; www.nps.gov/chis; 1901 Spinnaker Dr; 8:30am-5pm) in Ventura Harbor. Anacapa is the closest island to the mainland and thus gets the most visitors. Santa Cruz is the largest and the best suited for independent explorations. San Miguel, the remotest island, offers solitude and wilderness but is often shrouded in fog. Santa Barbara supports a sizable elephant seal colony, and Santa Rosa, with its many bird species and sandy beaches, is the best island for longer trips. Swimming, snorkeling, diving, kayaking and bird-watching are popular activities on the islands, all of which have primitive **campgrounds** (☎ 800-365-2267; sites $10); bring food and water.

Two boat and one air operator offer camper transportation, and a variety of day trips and packages. Expect to pay about $37/20 per adult/child for an eight-hour boat trip to Anacapa Island.

Islands Packers (☎ 805-642-7688; www.islandpackers.com; 1867 Spinnaker Dr, Ventura) Next to the NPS visitors center.

Truth Aquatics (☎ 805-962-1127; www.truthaquatics.com; 301 W Cabrillo Blvd, Santa Barbara)

Channel Islands Aviation (☎ 805-987-1301; 305 Durley Ave, Camarillo; adult/child $106/84) Flights to Santa Rosa Island from airports in Camarillo and Santa Barbara.

SANTA BARBARA

A Central Coast highlight, Santa Barbara sits prettily and affluently between the Pacific Ocean and the Santa Ynez Mountains, its red-tile roofs and gleaming white stucco visible from afar. The downtown area has outstanding architectural integrity, a masterpiece of a courthouse and noteworthy art and history museums. Five colleges, including the University of California at Santa Barbara (UCSB), give the town a youthful vivacity and balance its yachting and retirement communities.

State St is downtown's main artery. Lower State St (south of Ortega St) is bar central, while upper State St has most of the pretty shops and museums.

Information

Visitors Center (☎ 805-965-3021; www.santabarbaraca.com; 1 Garden St; 🕑 9am-5pm Mon-Sat, 10am-5pm Sun Sep-Jun, closes 6pm Jul & Aug, closes 4pm Nov-Jan)

Visitors Center – Maritime Museum branch (☎ 805-884-1475; 4th floor, 113 Harbor Way; 🕑 11am-5pm, closes 6pm Jul & Aug) Focused on information about outdoor activities.

Sights & Activities

Ask at the visitors centers for the free **Red Tile Tour** pamphlet for self-guided tours of the downtown area.

Start your explorations at the exquisite **Santa Barbara County Courthouse** (☎ 805-962-6464; 1100 Anacapa St; 🕑 8am-5pm Mon-Fri, 10am-5pm Sat & Sun). Built in Spanish–Moorish Revival style, it features hand-painted ceilings, tiles from Tunisia and Spain and wrought-iron chandeliers. Look around on your own or take a free docent-led tour (Monday to Saturday), but don't miss the panoramic view from the clock tower. The nearby **Santa Barbara Museum of Art** (☎ 805-963-4364; 1130 State St; adult/senior/student $7/5/4, free Thu; 🕑 11am-5pm Tue-Sat, closes 9pm Fri, noon-5pm Sun) presents American and European hot shots – as in Hopper, O'Keefe, Monet and Matisse – plus Asian art, photography and classical sculpture. For a trip into the past, head to the **Santa Barbara Historical Museum** (☎ 805-966-1601; 136 E De La Guerra St; free; 🕑 10am-5pm Tue-Sat, noon-5pm Sun), in an 1817 adobe complex. Its collections range from the mundane, such as antique furniture, to the intriguing, such as Padre Serra's personal coffer.

Serra stopped in Santa Barbara in 1786 to found **Mission Santa Barbara** (☎ 805-682-4713; 2201 Laguna St; adult $4, child under 11 free; 🕑 9am-5pm), the 10th in the series and nicknamed 'Queen of the Missions.' Chumash decorations adorn the church, which abuts a large cemetery with 4000 Chumash graves and fancy mausoleums of early settlers. Two blocks north, the **Museum of Natural History** (☎ 805-682-4711; 2559 Puesta del Sol Rd; adult $7, senior & teen $6, child $4; 🕑 10am-5pm) is worth a visit, if only for its beautiful architecture and landscaping. Another mile north, **Santa Barbara Botanic Garden** (☎ 805-682-4726; 1212 Mission Canyon Rd; adult $5, senior & student $3; 🕑 9am-5pm Mon-Fri, 9am-6pm Sat & Sun) has 5.5 miles of trails devoted to California's native flora, including cacti, redwoods and wildflowers.

Back on the waterfront, stroll **Stearns Wharf**, a rough wooden pier first built in 1872, then sample the town's briny history at the **Santa Barbara Maritime Museum** (☎ 805-962-8404; 113 Harbor Way; adult $5, senior & student $3, child $1; 🕑 11am-5pm Thu-Tue, closes 6pm Jul & Aug).

Sea Landing (☎ 805-882-0088), on the beach at the foot of Bath St, rents kayaks, jet skis and jet boats and operates whale-watching excursions to the Channel Islands ($70/40 per adult/child). Near the beach end of State St, several outfits rent bikes and inline skates for about $7 an hour.

Sleeping

Santa Barbara is not known for its budget accommodations, and those seeking shelter near downtown or the beaches will have to pay accordingly. Cheaper chain motels cluster along upper State St, near Las Positas Rd, several miles north of downtown (bus Nos 6 or 11).

Hotel Oceana (☎ 805-965-4577; 202 W Cabrillo Blvd; r $175-350; Ⓟ) The rooms are breezy and beautifully appointed in this stylish oceanfront refuge in a Mediterranean garden setting. If beachin' isn't bitchin', relax in the two pools or Jacuzzi. Rooms in the back are quieter.

Cabrillo Inn (☎ 805-966-1641; www.cabrillo-inn.com; 931 E Cabrillo Blvd; r $90-170; P) Watch the sun drop into the ocean from your room at this motel-style establishment. Though not much in the looks department, its location right across from a glorious beach is definitely an asset.

Also recommended:

Hotel State Street (☎ 805-966-6586; ewtrade@ix.net com.com; 121 State St; r $40-80) Popular place with spacious rooms next to the Amtrak station (bring ear plugs). Shared bath.

Haley Cottages (☎ 805-963-3586, 800-346-7835; www.haleycottages.com; 227 E Haley St; dm $20-22, r $54; P) Brand-new hostel with dorms and two-person cottages.

Villa Rosa (☎ 805-966-0851; www.villarosainnsb.com; 15 Chapala St; r $145-280; P) Intimate inn, rates include afternoon wine hour.

Eating & Drinking

La Super Rica (☎ 805-963-4940; 622 N Milpas St; dishes less than $7) The best Mexican food in town comes out of this unassuming little shack, a favorite of food guru Julia Child. The chilaquiles and sopes are standouts. Self-service.

Brophy Brothers (☎ 805-966-4418; Breakwater; mains $7-18) Brophy's draws loyal locals with its salty setting, superbly fresh seafood and bubbly atmosphere. The clam chowder, served with chewy sourdough bread, is outstanding.

Paradise Café (☎ 805-962-4416; 702 Anacapa St; lunch $5-12, dinner $9-20) Grab a chair on the non-smoking patio at this quintessential California café and pick from a fine selection of burgers, salads, light pastas, seafood and steak.

Wine Cask (☎ 805-966-9463; 813 Anacapa St; lunch $10-15, dinner $20-35) Dine beneath a gold-leafed, beamed ceiling at this local dining shrine dedicated to classic American cuisine. Stellar wine list, too.

Drinking establishments cluster along lower State St, where **Santa Barbara Brewing Co** (☎ 805-730-1040; 501 State St) has a dozen homemade brews on tap.

Entertainment

James Joyce (☎ 805-962-2688; 513 State St) This Old World place has plenty of character and comes alive with live Dixieland jazz on Saturday nights.

Wild Cat (☎ 805-962-7970; 15 W Ortega St) A funky revival lounge that looks something like a cross between a warehouse and a love shack.

For highbrow entertainment, the **Granada Theatre** (☎ 805-966-2324; 1216 State St) has musicals and operettas, while the **Arlington Center for the Performing Arts** (☎ 805-963-4408; 1317 State St) doubles as the home of the Santa Barbara Symphony and a movie theater.

Getting There & Around

Greyhound (☎ 805-965-7551; 34 W Carrillo St) has daily buses to Los Angeles and San Francisco, while **Amtrak** (☎ 805-963-1015; State St) has a direct train and coach service to Los Angeles and San Luis Obispo.

The **Downtown-Waterfront Shuttle Bus** (25¢; 10am-6pm) runs two routes: along State St to Stearns Wharf, and along Cabrillo Blvd from the yacht harbor to the zoo.

SANTA BARBARA TO SAN LUIS OBISPO

North of Santa Barbara, Hwy 101 snakes along the coast and turns inland at Gaviota, continuing past the turnoff for Solvang, a mock-Danish village. Hwys 101 and 1 rejoin 75 miles later at Pismo Beach, which is really a dog-eared tourist town known for clams and sand dunes. Back at Gaviota, Hwy 1 swings northwest past Vandenberg Air Force Base and endless patches of sugar beets and lettuce. The largest town along this not-so-scenic stretch is Lompoc, a quiet military community.

SAN LUIS OBISPO

San Luis Obispo, known as SLO, is lively yet low-key with a high quality of life and community spirit. Just like so many other California towns, it grew up around a mission, founded in 1772 by Junípero Serra. The 17,000 students of the California Polytechnic State University inject a rather healthy dose of hubbub into the city streets, pubs and cafés. The **visitors center** (☎ 805-543-1255; www.visitslo.com; 1039 Chorro St), off Higuera St, has plenty of printed matter, maps and a phone for free hotel bookings. The best day to visit is Thursday, which is when the famous **farmers market** turns Higuera St into a fantastic giant street party from 6pm to 9pm.

Sights

SLO's attractions cluster around **Mission Plaza**, a shady oasis with restored adobes overlooking San Luis Creek. The plaza is lorded over by the **Mission San Luis Obispo De Toloso** (☎ 805-543-6850; church free, museum $2; 9am-5pm Apr-Oct, 9am-4pm Nov-Mar), with an endearingly old-fashioned museum about the Chumash and mission periods. For a more in-depth look at local history, visit the **San Luis Obispo County Historical Museum** (☎ 805-543-0430; 696 Monterey St; admission free; 10am-4pm Wed-Sun), next to the mission in the 1904 Carnegie Library building. **San Luis Obispo Art Center** (☎ 805-543-8562; 1010 Broad St; admission free; 11am-5pm Tue-Sun), on the plaza's south end, showcases local artists. One block southwest, the **Children's Museum** (☎ 805-544-5437; 1010 Nipomo St; admission $5; 11am-5pm Tue-Sat, noon-4pm Sun) has interactive displays teetering between educational and fun. The quirkiest SLO attraction is **Bubblegum Alley**, a narrow passageway accessed between 733 and 737 Higuera St covered with wads of discarded chewing gum.

Sleeping

Peach Tree Inn (☎ 805-543-3170, 800-227-6396; www.peachtreeinn.com; 2001 Monterey St; r $90-150; P) A flowery lobby welcomes guests to this friendly and folksy inn. Rates include a hearty breakfast with homemade breads. The creekside rooms are the nicest.

Quality Suites (☎ 805-541-5001, 800-424-6423; www.qualitysuites.com; 1631 Monterey St; r $119-185; P) This hacienda-style, all-suite place, with its flower-filled courtyard, is especially suited to families. Rates include a full American breakfast and a happy hour with free drinks and snacks.

HI Hostel Obispo (☎ 805-544-4678; 1617 Santa Rosa St; dm $18-20, r $50-55; closed 10am-4:30pm) This well-kept, clean hostel in a homey Victorian has a bit of a B&B feel and is close to downtown and the Amtrak station.

Many of the major chains are represented on SLO's motel row along Monterey St, north of downtown.

Eating

Big Sky Café (☎ 805-545-5401; 1121 Broad St; dishes $6-12) This hip and friendly spot serves New Millennium cuisine with a down-home touch in an artsy setting. Excellent breakfasts, too.

Mother's Tavern (☎ 805-541-8733; 725 Higuera St; dishes $4-7) Thumbs up for Mother's upscale pub-grub menu (burgers, nachos and the like) and fun decor with historical flair. At night, the college crowd invades, not least for the live entertainment.

Café Roma (☎ 805-541-6800; 1020 Railroad Ave; mains $11-17) This SLO classic near the Amtrak station serves rustic Italian cooking in a refined white-linen setting. The wine list features lots of locally produced vintages.

Getting There & Away

Greyhound (☎ 805-543-2121; 150 South St) has frequent buses to Los Angeles, Santa Barbara and San Francisco. **Amtrak's** *Pacific Surfliner* has daily service to Santa Barbara, LA and San Diego. The *Coast Starlight* between Seattle and LA also stops at the train station at the southern end of Santa Rosa St.

MORRO BAY

North of San Luis Obispo begins one of the most dramatic stretches of Hwy 1. The first town you reach is Morro Bay, still home to a large commercial fishing fleet but whose biggest claim to fame is its namesake **Morro Rock**, a 578ft volcanic peak jutting dramatically from the ocean floor. Leading south from the rock is the Embarcadero, a fairly scruffy waterfront walkway lined with tourist shops and restaurants. It's the launching area for boat tours and also home to the **Morro Bay Aquarium** (☎ 805-772-7647; admission $2; 9:30am-5:30pm), where the cramped tanks are an animal lover's nightmare.

For a nicer experience, head south to **Morro Bay State Park**, which has a natural history museum and a heron rookery reserve. Even further south is the wonderful and largely undeveloped **Montaña de Oro State Park**, featuring coastal bluffs, sand dunes and a 4-mile-long sand spit separating Morro Bay from the Pacific.

A good place to stay is the **Embarcadero Inn** (☎ 805-772-2700, 800-292-7625; 456 Embarcadero; r $115-225; P). Most rooms have balconies with views of 'the Rock' and all feature VCRs and refrigerators. There's camping at **Morro Strand State Beach** (☎ 805-772-8812; campsites $12), **Morro Bay State Park** (☎ 805-772-7434; campsites/RV sites $12/18) and at **Montaña de Oro State Park** (☎ 805-528-0513; campsites $7). For eats, try **Dorn's** (☎ 805-772-4415; 801 Market Ave; mains $10-18), famous for its clam chowder and fresh fish.

MORRO BAY TO BIG SUR

About 20 miles north of Morro Bay, the self-proclaimed artists' village of **Cambria** features a most unusual roadside attraction: **Nit Wit Ridge** (☎ 805-927-2690; 881 Hillcrest Dr), a house built entirely from recycled materials – abalone shells to beer cans to toilet seats.

Lodging options in Cambria include the **Bridge Street Inn** (☎ 805-927-7653; 4314 Bridge St; dm $20, r $40-70; P), a B&B/ hostel with character, charm and considerable comfort, and the **Bluebird** (☎ 805-927-4634, 800-552-5434; 1880 Main St; r $50-180; P) with imaginatively appointed rooms and a creekside garden. **Linn's** (☎ 805-927-0371; 2277 Main St; dishes $6-14) is a casual eatery known for its pot pies and outlandish desserts. At dinnertime, try the **Sow's Ear Café** (☎ 805-927-4865; 2248 Main St; mains $13-23) with its classic continental fare.

The main attraction along the highway, though, is **Hearst Castle** (☎ 800-444-4445; www.hearstcastle.org; 8:20am-3:20pm, later in summer; tour 1 adult/child $18/9, tours 2, 3, 4 $12/7). Overlooking the Pacific, it is California's most famous monument to wealth and ambition. William Randolph Hearst, the newspaper magnate, created an estate that sprawls over 127 acres of lushly landscaped gardens, accentuated by shimmering pools and statues from ancient Greece and Moorish Spain. The visit is worthwhile, if only to see something so ostentatious. Four estate tours are offered; tour one is best for first-time visitors. All tours last about 1½ hours, including the ride up to the castle and back to the visitors center. Reservations are recommended in summer.

The coastline north of Hearst Castle is home to California's largest **elephant seal colony**, which comes here to breed, molt and sleep. There's a viewpoint about 5 miles from the castle with interpretative panels and friendly docents. The seals are here year-round but are at their most plentiful between December and February.

As you continue north, Hwy 1 leaves civilization far behind, hugging the rugged Pacific shore and traversing vast stretches of coast where services – let alone towns – are few and far between. After about 30 miles you hit tiny **Gorda**, with an expensive gas station, deli and café. Next stop is the Central Coast's blockbuster attraction – Big Sur.

CCAT (☎ 805-541-2228) operates a bus service between San Luis Obispo, Morro Bay and San Simeon/Hearst Castle.

BIG SUR

Big Sur is an awe-inspiring symphony of nature. At times, Hwy 1 clutches at the cliffs as if in desperation, providing vista-point junkies with a steady fix. This sparsely populated region consists mainly of three state parks (Julia Pfeiffer Burns State Park, Pfeiffer Big Sur State Park and Andrew Molera State Park) and a slurry of restaurants and lodgings along the highway.

The **USFS Big Sur Ranger Station** (☎ 831-667-2315; 8am-4:30pm, until 6pm summer), 0.5 miles south of Pfeiffer Big Sur State Park, has information on all the parks and issues backcountry permits. Each park's $5 entrance fee is also valid on the same day at the other two parks. The following description is oriented from south to north.

Appropriately, the physical and spiritual beginning to Big Sur is the **Esalen Institute** (☎ 831-667-3000; www.esalen.org), a renowned New Age resort offering expensive workshops and classes. To experience Esalen without enrolling, you must either apply three days in advance for 'room and board' (if available, $115-170) or make a same-day reservation for either a massage ($120), which includes time in the sumptuous hot springs, or for 'night bathing' ($20; 1-3am).

Julia Pfeiffer Burns State Park, several miles north of Esalen, has two highlights: the first is the easy 0.25-mile hike to 50ft McWay Falls, which drops straight into the sea. The second is Julia Pfeiffer's sole pair of environmental campsites, secluded high above the surging waves; you can, and should, reserve them up to seven months in advance (p926).

Seven miles north, the **Henry Miller Memorial Library** (☎ 831-667-2574; www.henrymiller.org; 11am-6pm Wed-Mon) is, in essence, a sophisticated bookstore emphasizing Miller's works, but, more importantly, it strives to keep the author's iconoclastic spirit alive amid a gale of 21st-century conservatism.

Big Sur Center, 2 miles north, contains the first clutch of traveler services: the post office, a general store and deli, a restaurant and gas station.

A further mile, immediately north of the USFS Big Sur Ranger Station, **Pfeiffer Big Sur State Park** occupies 680 acres and has plenty of coastal hiking trails; the 1.4-mile round trip to Pfeiffer Falls is a fine experience of redwoods. Ask at the ranger station for directions to the rugged, wheelchair-accessible

SYKES HOT SPRINGS *Jeff Campbell*

Not long after I moved to California, a friend and I decided to spend Thanksgiving weekend hiking to Sykes Hot Springs in the Ventana Wilderness, then as now the most popular backpacker's destination in Big Sur.

The springs are 10 miles and five hours in from the Big Sur Ranger Station. While the crush of summer hikers is over by late November, we still had plenty of company along the trail, which begins broad and clear and narrows to a well-worn footpath. It's not the route-finding but the relentless ups and downs that make the springs feel earned.

By afternoon, we had set up camp by the Big Sur River where it is more of a creek and had found the springs – a couple of unassuming hillside pools. During our nighttime dip, an addled, autumnal wind picked up high overhead, and the towering redwoods began to sway and creak precipitously. Every now and then a lingering, faraway groan was followed by the unmistakable rending crash of a tree falling, sending goose bumps of fear-tinged wonder racing over our skin.

I quickly determined to wait out every last backpacker. I wanted, no I *needed* to be alone to soak up this magical night in silence. When at last the final person said goodnight, I slipped deeper into the delicious pool and stayed like that, listening, for hours.

In the morning, I awoke in the tent in excruciating pain, as if a team of paleontologists had spent the night scraping at my skull. I was furiously dehydrated, and no amount of water would help. Why hadn't someone warned me? Suddenly, we had no choice but to return. My neophyte's incapacitation and the specter of Thanksgiving feasts past were too much.

The hike back was grueling. Then, with despair, we realized that the sun was going to beat us to the end of the trail. But Big Sur is nothing if not radiant and forgiving. Framed by the darkening V of the hills, the sky transformed into a freakish display of color – neon orange and fuchsia, fiery magenta, and finally a jewel-toned and royal purple dotted with a mantle of stars.

Thus awed, we hustled the last mile, drove to the nearest restaurant and ordered a bottle of wine and two thick steaks. It was a sumptuous meal, and we gave a humbled and heartfelt thanks.

Pfeiffer Beach (additional fee to park entry $5); locals keep taking the sign down.

Ventana Wilderness is extremely popular with backpackers; get overnight parking permits ($4), free backcountry permits and trail information from the rangers.

Andrew Molera State Park, about 4.5 miles north of Pfeiffer Big Sur, features a gentle mile-long trail that leads to a beautiful beach. **Molera Horseback Tours** (☎ 831-625-5486; www.molerahorsebacktours.com; adult $48) runs guided horseback rides that take two hours.

Point Sur, 3 miles north, is that compelling hump of volcanic rock jutting into the ocean. The only way to visit is to take the three-hour tour of the 1899 **Point Sur Light Station** (☎ 831-625-4419; adult $5; Sat & Sun year-round, additional days in summer) on top of it.

Sleeping & Eating

Big Sur accommodations fill up at weekends, so make reservations and keep any secluded river fantasies in check. Also, bring a full cooler; groceries are expensive.

Deetjen's Big Sur Inn (☎ 831-667-2377; www.deetjens.com; r with/without bath from $110/90, meals $17-29) Cozy Deetjen's, just south of Henry Miller Library, occupies a historic homestead with bona fide rustic credentials. The atmospheric **restaurant** serves breakfast and dinner.

Nepenthe (☎ 831-667-2345; meals $26-33) Outstanding ocean views distinguish Nepenthe, about 0.6 miles north of Deetjen's. It serves expensive grilled fish and steaks. Just below the restaurant, an inexpensive café enjoys the same vistas.

Big Sur Lodge (☎ 800-424-4787; r from $179;) In Pfeiffer Big Sur State Park, this is a quiet complex of single-story attached buildings. Lovely quilts provide a cozy feel.

Ripplewood Resort (☎ 831-667-2242; www.ripplewoodresort.com; r $80-125) About 2 miles north of Big Sur Center, Ripplewood has comfortable country cabins, some perched on the riverbank, and most with kitchens. The **coffee shop** (meals $6-8.50) serves breakfast and lunch, and it has a general store.

Glen Oaks Motel (☎ 831-667-2105; www.glenoaksbigsur.com; r $70-110) Next door to Ripplewood Resort is this clean and simple motel.

Big Sur River Inn (☎ 831-667-2700; www.bigsurriverinn.com; s/ste $125/225) The motel rooms are plain, the family suites are delightful and neither have TV nor phones. Its popular restaurant is open all day and has a deck overlooking the river – or take your sandwich and claim one of the river chairs.

Camping at **Julia Pfeiffer Burns** (campsites $13-17) and 218-site **Pfeiffer Big Sur State Park** (campsites $13-17) can be reserved through **ParkNet** (☎ 800-444-7275; www.reserveamerica.com). **Andrew Molena State Park** (campsites per person $2) has 24 first-come, first-served sites. A good private campground is **Big Sur Campground & Cabins** (☎ 831-667-2322; campsites $30, tent cabins $60, deluxe cabins from $100), near Big Sur River Inn.

If you arrive without camping reservations in summer, you may find every site taken, but don't camp illegally. This ongoing problem damages the forest.

CARMEL & AROUND

Carmel-by-the-Sea became a bohemian retreat after San Francisco's 1906 earthquake forced artists to find a cheaper place to live. Today, it remains a quintessential example of a self-ordered California community, one driven by the dreams of a sophisticated upper class. Local bylaws ensure that it remains rustic and modestly picturesque – there are no streetlights, sidewalks or mail delivery service – even as refinement and wealth drips from every awning and abode. Ocean Ave is the main thoroughfare, sloping down past tony shops, galleries and eateries to a pristine beach.

The **San Carlos Borromeo del Rio Carmelo Mission** (☎ 831-624-1271; www.carmelmission.org; 3080 Rio Rd; adult/child $4/1; 9:30am-4:30pm) was founded by Padre Junípero Serra in 1769. An oasis of calm and solemnity, the mission is one of the most complete in California, and the museum is full of dusty surprises. Mass is held in the gorgeous vaulted basilica at weekends.

Poet Robinson Jeffers – one of the creators of the Carmel ethos – built his unique granite-stone home, **Tor House** (☎ 831-624-1813; www.torhouse.org; 26304 Ocean View Ave), a few blocks from Carmel Bay. You can visit only on a one-hour **tour** (adult $7; Fri & Sat), so it's wise to book in advance.

Point Lobos State Reserve (☎ 831-624-4909; http://ptlobos.org; per car $6; 9am-5pm, until 7pm summer), 3.5 miles south of Carmel, is a scenic jewel of the state park system. Its rocky coastline encompasses 554 aboveground acres and 750 submerged acres that are ideal for scuba diving. Gorgeous, easy hikes crisscross the point, from where you can spot whales, sea lions and otters. A small whaling museum pays homage to this once-vital industry.

Carmel and Monterey are linked by Hwy 1 and by the spectacularly scenic **17-Mile Drive**. Though this road is justifiably famous, you can get the same views for free – minus the signature Lone Cypress, the exclusive mansions and the Pebble Beach golf courses – by driving the coast around Pacific Grove. There are five entry gates to **Pebble Beach** (per car/bicycle $8/free). At weekends bicycles can use only the Pacific Grove gate.

See Monterey for a general description of peninsula lodging (p928). Near Carmel's town center, the **Carmel Sands Lodge** (☎ 831-624-1255; www.carmelsandslodge.com; San Carlos St & 5th Ave; r midweek/weekend from $98/159; P) is a reasonable, affordable option.

Four miles south of Carmel, **Tickle Pink Inn** (☎ 831-624-1244, 800-635-4774; www.ticklepinkinn.com; 155 Highlands Dr; r $230-330) provides succulent love nests for a special occasion. Its cliff-side perch frames the coast perfectly from the rooms, wind-protected deck and outdoor hot tub. Breakfast is included.

MONTEREY & AROUND

Monterey enjoys an envious position at the edge of the uniquely diverse Monterey Bay, now protected as the nation's largest marine sanctuary. In addition, the city's rich Latino heritage – dating back to the 18th century – is well preserved in numerous museums and restored adobe buildings from California's Spanish and Mexican periods. Most of these are concentrated in downtown 'Old Monterey,' while the world-famous aquarium and Cannery Row are just northwest in 'New Monterey.' Nothing could be finer than Monterey on a sunny day and two sturdy feet to guide you.

Among the many special events that manage to send hotel rates skyrocketing are February's AT&T Pebble Beach Pro-Am **golf tournament** (☎ 831-649-1533), August's Concours d'Elegence **car show** (☎ 831-659-0663) and September's **Monterey Jazz Festival** (☎ 831-373-3366).

The helpful **visitors center** (☎ 831-649-1770; www.montereyinfo.org; 10am-5pm Mon-Fri, 11am-4pm Sat & Sun), at Camino El Estero and Franklin

St, provides peninsula-wide information and lodging availability.

Sights

MONTEREY STATE HISTORIC PARK

Located downtown, this park is a collection of Monterey's finest historical buildings. The delightful **Pacific House Museum** (☎ 831-649-7118; admission free; ⌚ 10am-5pm), at Custom House Plaza near the wharf, contains the park's headquarters, offers free guided tours and has exhibits on the region's history and environment. Hours vary for other park buildings, so call to verify.

In 1822 the newly independent Mexico stipulated that any cargo brought to Alta California would have to be unloaded at **Monterey Custom House**, which now displays a collection of these antique goods. Thomas Larkin became the US consul in Monterey when the US Army annexed California in 1846; his 1834 home, **Larkin House**, is a prime example of 'Monterey colonial' architecture, a combination of New England design and adobe construction. Robert Louis Stevenson came to Monterey in 1879, and the **Stevenson House,** now housing a superb collection of his memorabilia, is where he stayed and reputedly wrote *Treasure Island.*

Also at Custom House Plaza, the **Maritime Museum of Monterey** (☎ 831-372-2608; admission $5; ⌚ 10am-5pm Mon & Wed-Sun) features a great ship-in-a-bottle collection plus displays about the rise and rapid fall of the local sardine industry. A short walk from the state historic park, **Fisherman's Wharf** is a low-key tourist trap with plenty of restaurants, gift shops and seafood stands.

MONTEREY BAY AQUARIUM

If the peninsula contained nothing else, it would still be worth visiting for the mighty **Monterey Bay Aquarium** (☎ 831-648-4888; www.montereybayaquarium.org; 886 Cannery Row; adult $18, child 3-12 $9; ⌚ 10am-6pm). Don't miss this temple to Monterey's underwater universe. Highlights include the two-story Kelp Forest tank, the million-gallon Outer Bay tank where sea turtles and ponderous sunfish glide by, the kid-friendly Splash Zone, feeding time with the sea otters and the new-in-2004 shark exhibit (yikes!). The aquarium receives nearly two million visitors a year. To avoid queues, reserve **tickets** (☎ 800-756-3737; transaction fee $3) in advance.

MONTEREY MUSEUM OF ART

The **Monterey Museum of Art** (☎ 831-372-5477; admission $5; ⌚ 11am-5pm Wed-Sat, 1-4pm Sun) has two downtown branches. The small but satisfying **Civic Center** (559 Pacific St) collection emphasizes Californian artists and photographers (including Ansel Adams and Edward Weston), while the branch of **La Mirada** (720 Via Mirada) explores Monterey life in the early 20th century.

CANNERY ROW

In its heyday Cannery Row was a hectic and very smelly place, and John Steinbeck's eponymous novel made it famous. Sardine canning operations began here in 1926, expanding until the peak in 1945, when the annual sardine catch reached 250,000 tons. By 1950, overfishing and climate changes caused the industry to crash in a hurry. Nowadays Cannery Row nets only tourists in its seven blocks of restaurants and souvenir shops.

MONARCH GROVE SANCTUARY

In Pacific Grove, follow signs from Lighthouse Ave to find the sanctuary, an October-to-March overwintering site for Monarch butterflies on their amazing north-south migration. They cluster in the pine trees like dead leaves, only opening as the sun warms them. Volunteer docents are often on hand, or call ☎ 831-648-3116 for information.

NATIONAL STEINBECK CENTER

The **National Steinbeck Center museum** (☎ 831-796-3828; www.steinbeck.org; 1 Main St, Salinas; adult $11, child 6-12 $6; ⌚ 10am-5pm) is well worth the 20-mile inland detour to Salinas, through the flat, fertile valley that was Steinbeck's home and passion. The interactive exhibits, displays and short movie bring together all the strands of the author's life, whose Pulitzer- and Nobel-prize-winning work captured the troubled spirit of rural and working-class America. The attached Valley of the World center explores the region's agricultural heritage.

Activities

From Cannery Row, you can walk or bike a path that follows the ragged, scenic coastline.

Adventures by the Sea (☎ 831-372-1807; 201 Alvarado St & 299 Cannery Row) rents bikes ($18 for four hours) and kayaks ($30 per day).

Knowledgeable and friendly **Monterey Bay Kayaks** (☎ 831-373-5357; 693 Del Monte Ave; kayaks full-day $30) can also get you afloat.

For surfing gear and board rentals, head to **On the Beach** (☎ 831-646-9283; 711 Cannery Row; surf gear full-day $20).

Guided scuba dives cost $50, equipment extra, at the **Aquarius Dive Shop** (☎ 831-375-1933; 2040 Del Monte Ave & 32 Cannery Row); they also rent snorkel gear with wetsuits.

Several outfits run whale-watching trips year-round from the wharf, but only the recommended **Monterey Bay Whale Watch** (☎ 831-375-4658; www.gowhales.com; 3-6hr $25-40) has marine biologists for guides; reservations required.

For an affordable taste of the peninsula's world-famous golf, try the **Pacific Grove Municipal Golf Course** (☎ 831-648-5777; 77 Asilomar Blvd; 18 holes $40); reserve one week ahead.

Sleeping & Eating

High-season rates listed here can drop by a third or more in winter, while at any time special-event weekends might be half again as much. Make sure to call ahead to know what you're in for! Many places have a two-night minimum stay at summer weekends.

HI Monterey Hostel (☎ 831-649-0375; www.montereyhostel.org; 778 Hawthorne St; dm $22-25; P) Only four blocks from Cannery Row, this hostel has plain and simple dorm rooms, and is a model of water conservation. Reservations are required June through September.

For a relatively economical motel, try downtown's Munras Ave or N Fremont St, 2.5 miles from downtown and east of Hwy 1 (Casa Verde exit). Dependable **chains** include Best Western, Comfort Inn, Econo Lodge and Travelodge. Among independents, the **Cypress Gardens Resort Inn** (☎ 831-373-2761, 877-922-1150; www.cypressgardensinn.com; 1150 Munras Ave; r from $99; P) is reliable, and the **Lone Oak Lodge** (☎ 831-372-4924, 800-283-5663; www.loneoaklodge.com; 2221 N Fremont; midweek/weekend from $80/100; P) is consistently friendly and comfortable. The latter has a nice Jacuzzi.

Located in the heart of downtown, **Monterey Hotel** (☎ 831-375-3184, 800-727-0960; 406 Alvarado St; www.montereyhotel.com; 406 Alvarado St; midweek/weekend from $139/169; P $15) is a historic hotel with reproduction antiques, ornate carved headboards and marble bathrooms. Ask about packages. There are wheelchair-accessible rooms and breakfast is included.

Lighthouse Ave above Cannery Row is the place to go for an affordable meal, while the *only* place to go for breakfast is downtown's **Old Monterey Cafe** (☎ 831-646-1021; 489 Alvarado St; 7am-2:30pm; meals $6-12): lumberjack portions, and pancakes as big as hubcaps.

The touristy restaurants at Cannery Row and Fisherman's Wharf serve fresh but overpriced seafood. Instead, just out of town is **Monterey's Fish House** (☎ 831-373-4647; 2114 Del Monte Ave; meals $13-17; lunch Mon-Fri, dinner nightly), which packs them in like, well, sardines. The divine crab cakes, *cioppino* and seafood pastas are scrumptiously rich and surprisingly affordable. Make reservations and still expect to wait.

Getting There & Around

Greyhound buses traveling between Los Angeles ($40) and San Francisco ($18) stop at the **gas station** (1024 Del Monte Ave), just east of El Estero Lake. **Monterey-Salinas Transit** (MST; ☎ 831-899-2555; www.mst.org) operates buses around the peninsula to Carmel and Pacific Grove, and south to Big Sur. The Monterey Transit Plaza, at the south end of Alvarado St, is the main MST terminal.

SANTA CRUZ

Santa Cruz is where southern California beach culture meets northern California counterculture. As the home of the University of California at Santa Cruz (UCSC) and its 13,000 left-of-center students, it is far more youthful, hip and political than touristy Monterey, and with over one-sixth of the county composed of state parks, it offers ample opportunities to walk among the redwoods.

Orientation & Information

Restaurants and shops line parallel Pacific Ave and Front St, the unofficial main drags. For the beach and Boardwalk, head south on Front St and turn left on Beach St. The helpful **visitors center** (☎ 831-425-1234, 800-833-3494; www.santacruz.org; 1211 Ocean St; 9am-5pm Mon-Sat, 10am-4pm Sun) has accommodation availability; book online through their website.

Bookshop Santa Cruz (☎ 831-423-0900; 1520 Pacific Ave) is as busy on a Friday night as any bar. **Logos** (☎ 831-427-5100; 1117 Pacific Ave) is another book-lover's paradise.

Sights

The classic 1906 **Boardwalk** (☎ 831-426-7433; www.beachboardwalk.com; 400 Beach St; individual rides $2-4, all-day ticket $25; ⌚ daily mid-April–mid-Nov, Sat & Sun mid-Nov–mid-April) is the oldest beachfront amusement park on the West Coast, with a 1923 Giant Dipper coaster and a 1911 Looff carousel – both National Historic Landmarks; call for hours, which vary weekly.

The small **Museum of Art & History** (☎ 831-429-1964; 705 Front St; admission $4; ⌚ 11am-5pm Tue-Sun) is smart and worth a gander.

The **Surfing Museum** (☎ 831-420-6289; admission free; ⌚ noon-4pm Mon & Wed-Sun, closed Wed in winter) is a teeny-tiny paean to the history and art of wave riding. It's at Lighthouse Point on W Cliff Dr and overlooks Steamer's Lane, Santa Cruz' most popular surfing break

Natural Bridges State Beach (☎ 831-423-4609; 2531 W Cliff Dr; admission $5; ⌚ sunrise–sunset), just north of Santa Cruz, has a good beach, tidal pools and trees where monarch butterflies hibernate from October to March.

Established in 1902, **Big Basin Redwoods State Park** (☎ 831-338-8860; www.bigbasin.org; per car $5; ⌚ 6am-10pm), 23 miles north of Santa Cruz via Hwys 9 and 236, is the birthplace of California's conservation movement. It contains 18,000 acres of redwood forest and over 80 miles of trails, one of which drops to the Pacific Ocean.

Santa Cruz has two scenic, historic **train rides** (☎ 831-335-4400; www.roaringcamp.com). From the Boardwalk, the Santa Cruz, Big Trees & Pacific Railway makes a three-hour round trip (adult $19, child three to 12 $15) to Roaring Camp, a re-created 1880s logging town. From Roaring Camp, narrow-gauge steam locomotives make a 75-minute round trip (adult/child $17/12) to Big Trees Redwood Forest. Call for schedules.

The **Mystery Spot** (☎ 831-423-8897; www.mysteryspot.com; adult/child $5/3; ⌚ 9am-7pm summer, until 4:30pm winter), 3 miles north of Santa Cruz on Branciforte Dr, is a classic bit of odd-ball Americana: objects defy gravity by rolling uphill, and buildings lean at unexplained angles. It really is mysterious. Don't forget your bumper sticker.

It wouldn't be Santa Cruz without meditative, holistic, therapeutic **spas**. The **Well Within** (☎ 831-458-9355; 417 Cedar St) and **Kiva House** (☎ 831-429-1142; 702 Water St) are local institutions; hourly tub rates range from $10 to $30.

Activities

Hiking or **biking** on the beautiful W Cliff Dr is satisfying anytime, but particularly at sunset. Check Beach St for bike-rental shops and **Kayak Connection** (☎ 831-479-1121; 413 Lake Ave; kayak 4hr $27) has kayak rentals.

SURFING

Recommended beginner breaks are Cowell's and 38th Ave. If all you need is a board, try **Go Skate** (☎ 831-425-8578; 601 Beach St; skateboard full-day $10). Wahines should make waves for the women-owned **Paradise Surf Shop** (☎ 831-462-3880; www.paradisesurf.com; 3961 Portola Dr), which has board sales, rentals and knowledgeable staff.

For lessons, try the venerable **Richard Schmidt Surf School** (☎ 831-423-0928; www.richardschmidt.com; 849 Almar Ave, Box 192; 2hr group lesson $80).

Sleeping & Eating

HI Carmelita Cottages Hostel (☎ 831-423-8304; 321 Main St; dm $18-21) This is one of the busiest hostels on the coast, which is perhaps why rooms and attitudes get a little frayed.

For dependable motels, try Riverside Ave and Ocean St; **chains** include Super 8, Travelodge and Best Western.

Brookdale Lodge (☎ 831-338-6433; www.brookdalelodge.com; 11570 Hwy 9; midweek/weekend from $79/99; P) Escape to the redwoods at Brookdale Lodge, 14 miles north in the Santa Cruz Mountains. Extensive facilities make it great for families (children under 12 stay free). Rooms are plain but clean. In its locally famous Brook Room restaurant you can dine next to a burbling stream.

Carousel Motel (☎ 831-425-7090, 800-214-7400; www.santacruzmotels.com; 110 Riverside Ave; midweek/weekend from $109/139; P) Another family-oriented place is Carousel, where children under 16 stay free, and they offer Boardwalk packages.

Camping (☎ 800-444-7275; campsites $12) You can camp among the redwoods in nearby Henry Cowell and Big Basin State Parks, north of town off Hwy 9, and at New Brighton State Beach, about 4 miles south of Santa Cruz near Capitola. Reservations are advised.

Downtown Santa Cruz, especially Pacific Ave and Front St, is chock-a-block with eateries of all stripes.

Seabright Brewery (☎ 831-426-2739; 519 Seabright Ave; dishes $8-15) The only true brewpub in town serves pub grub and great beer to a loud, lively crowd.

Mobo Sushi (☎ 831-425-1700; 105 S River St, San Lorenzo Park Plaza; dishes $3-5.50; ⌚ lunch Mon-Fri, dinner nightly) This place is known for inventive, especially vegetarian, sushi: try 'Mad Dog,' 'Crop Burning,' and the UCSC favorite, 'Banana Slug.'

Saturn Cafe (☎ 831-429-8505; 145 Laurel St; meals $5.50-8.50; ⌚ 11:30-4am) A Santa Cruz classic, the late-night, vegetarian Saturn Cafe is a pop-culture fever dream: flame-painted walls, thatched tiki awnings and whacked-out dioramas beneath every booth table. Don't pass on their 'chocolate madness.'

Entertainment

Check the weekly *Metro Santa Cruz* for schedules of top-name jazz musicians, which appear regularly at the excellent **Kuumbwa Jazz Center** (☎ 831-427-2227; www.kuumbwajazz.org; 320 Cedar St) and **Catalyst** (☎ 831-423-1338; 1011 Pacific Ave).

Club Dakota (☎ 831-335-5882; 1209 Pacific Ave) is a popular gay and lesbian bar with dancing till all hours.

Getting There & Away

Santa Cruz Metropolitan Transit (☎ 831-425-8600; www.scmtd.com) operates from the **Santa Cruz Metro Transit Center** (920 Pacific Ave; fare $1, day pass $3) and serves the greater Santa Cruz region. At the Transit Center, **Greyhound** (☎ 831-423-1800) runs daily buses to/from San Francisco ($11) and Los Angeles ($42). There are regular bus connections to/from the **CalTrain/Amtrak station** (☎ 800-66-4287; 65 Cahill St) in San Jose ($6).

SAN FRANCISCO & THE BAY AREA

SAN FRANCISCO

Like the roguish glance of a playful rebel, San Francisco charms both visitors and residents alike. It often begins with the views: of the ruffled bay, of majestic bridges, of pristine Victorians marching up impossible hills, of the crowded spit of land itself from across the tousled water. But as you walk – and walking is the way to explore this town – it becomes the diversity, the vibrant ethnic neighborhoods, the unhesitant embrace of eccentricity and misfits, and the abiding devotion to creativity that steal your heart and cause you to fall in love. No other American city can make you swoon like San Francisco.

History

The San Francisco peninsula was inhabited for nearly five centuries (lastly by Ohlone Indians) before the first Europeans arrived. In 1769 Gaspar de Portolá and Father Junípero Serra were exploring the California coast for Spain when they encountered the spectacular bay. By 1776 they had established a mission and presidio here, though neither prospered. As for the Ohlone, introduced diseases eventually cut their numbers significantly.

However, 1848 marks the true birth of the city. That year it received its current name (after Mexico had ceded California to the USA) and its first rush of citizens (after the almost concurrent discovery of gold in the Sierra Nevada). During 1849 the city's population exploded from 800 to 25,000.

In the following decades, entertaining free-spending miners turned San Francisco into a notorious place, full of casinos, saloons, brothels and opium dens. The 'Barbary Coast' (now Chinatown and Jackson Sq) was a place of reckless criminality, where sailors were routinely knocked out, robbed and 'Shanghai'd' – awaking to find themselves indentured to a ship that was already out to sea.

The 1906 earthquake and fire leveled most of the city, and frantic years of construction followed. This continued through the 1930s, when large-scale public works projects gave the region a lift during the Great Depression – the most outstanding examples being the San Francisco–Oakland Bay Bridge (1936) and the Golden Gate Bridge (1937).

During WWII the Bay Area became a major launching pad for military operations in the Pacific, and gigantic shipyards sprang up around the bay. Although military spending continued to drive the local economy, the postwar years were distinguished by the city's colorful countercultures: the Beats spearheaded the '50s poetry movement, and the hippies brought flower power and free love in the '60s. During this same period, San Francisco's nascent gay community coalesced and, despite resistance, established itself.

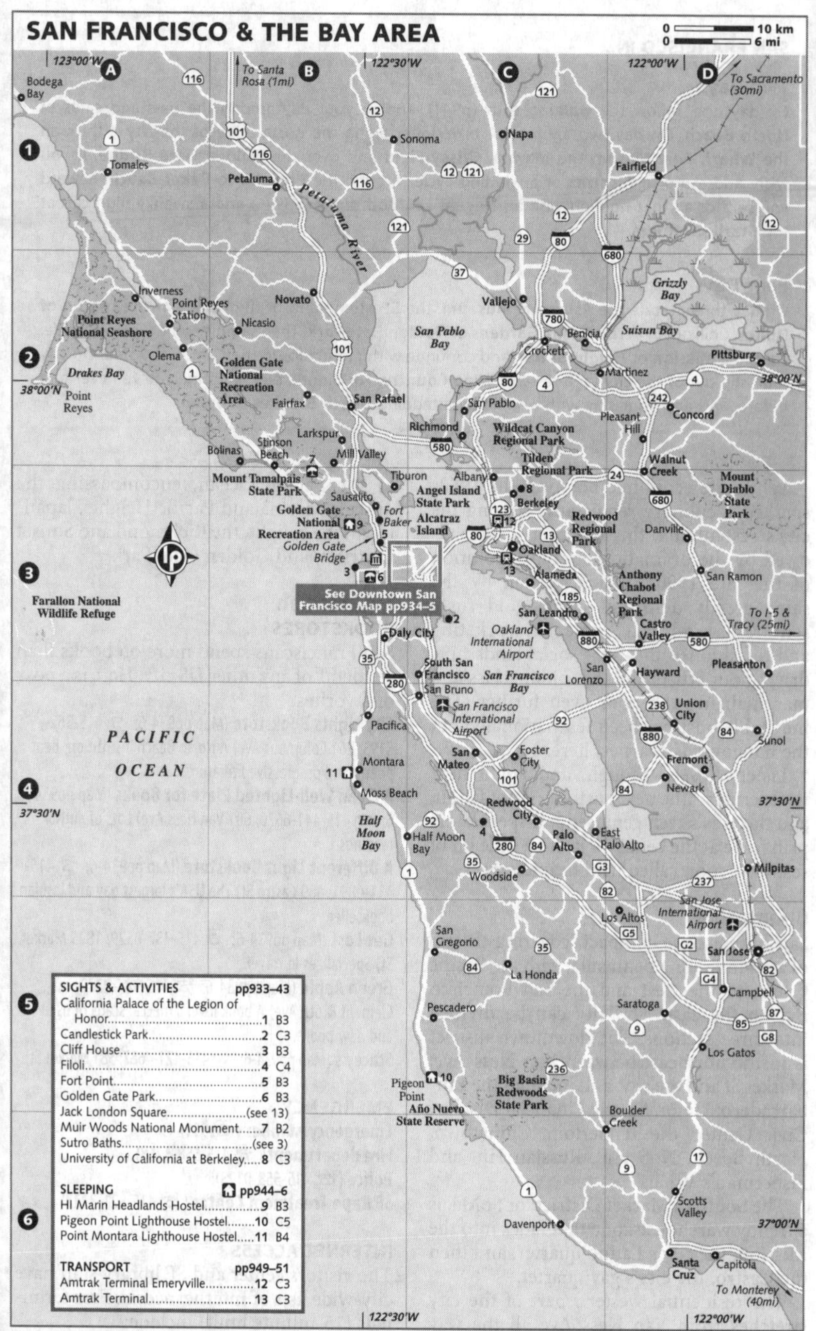
SAN FRANCISCO & THE BAY AREA
0 10 km
0 6 mi
123°00'W
A
B
C
D
122°30'W
122°00'W
To Santa Rosa (1mi)
To Sacramento (30mi)
Bodega Bay
Tomales
Petaluma
Petaluma River
Sonoma
Napa
Fairfield
Grizzly Bay
Suisun Bay
Vallejo
Benicia
Crockett
Martinez
Pittsburg
Inverness
Point Reyes Station
Point Reyes National Seashore
Nicasio
Novato
Olema
Drakes Bay
Point Reyes
38°00'N
Golden Gate National Recreation Area
Fairfax
San Rafael
San Pablo Bay
San Pablo
Richmond
Wildcat Canyon Regional Park
Pleasant Hill
Concord
Larkspur
Mill Valley
Stinson Beach
Bolinas
Mount Tamalpais State Park
Tiburon
Albany
Tilden Regional Park
Walnut Creek
Mount Diablo State Park
Sausalito
Angel Island State Park
Berkeley
Fort Baker
Alcatraz Island
Golden Gate Bridge
Oakland
Redwood Regional Park
Danville
Alameda
San Ramon
Anthony Chabot Regional Park
Farallon National Wildlife Refuge
See Downtown San Francisco Map pp934–5
San Leandro
Oakland International Airport
Castro Valley
To I-5 & Tracy (25mi)
Daly City
South San Francisco
San Francisco Bay
San Lorenzo
Hayward
Pleasanton
San Bruno
San Francisco International Airport
Union City
Pacifica
PACIFIC OCEAN
Sunol
Montara
San Mateo
Foster City
Fremont
Moss Beach
Newark
Redwood City
37°30'N
Half Moon Bay
Palo Alto
East Palo Alto
Woodside
Milpitas
San Jose International Airport
Los Altos
San Gregorio
San Jose
La Honda
Campbell
Saratoga
Pescadero
Los Gatos
Big Basin Redwoods State Park
Pigeon Point
Año Nuevo State Reserve
Boulder Creek
Scotts Valley
Davenport
37°00'N
Santa Cruz
Capitola
To Monterey (40mi)
SIGHTS & ACTIVITIES pp933–43
California Palace of the Legion of Honor 1 B3
Candlestick Park 2 C3
Cliff House 3 B3
Filoli 4 C4
Fort Point 5 B3
Golden Gate Park 6 B3
Jack London Square (see 13)
Muir Woods National Monument 7 B2
Sutro Baths (see 3)
University of California at Berkeley 8 C3
SLEEPING pp944–6
HI Marin Headlands Hostel 9 B3
Pigeon Point Lighthouse Hostel 10 C5
Point Montara Lighthouse Hostel 11 B4
TRANSPORT pp949–51
Amtrak Terminal Emeryville 12 C3
Amtrak Terminal 13 C3

SAN FRANCISCO IN...

Two Days

On day one, follow the **walking tour** (p941), ending your day among the bars and cafés of **North Beach**. On day two, by foot or bike, loiter along the north edge of the city – through the **Wharf, Fort Mason, the Marina, Crissy Field** and over the **Golden Gate Bridge**. If you wish, add a trip to **Alcatraz** or a winding cycle through the **Presidio** to **Baker Beach**. Reward yourself for all that hoofing with an elegant **seafood dinner** (p946) and a swanky nightcap at the **Starlight Room**.

Four Days

On day three, tackle the **Asian Art Museum**, the **SF Moma** and/or the **Palace of the Legion of Honor**. Chill out in **Yerba Buena Gardens** or **Golden Gate Park**. Then sample some funky nightlife: start in a **Mission** or **Haight St bar**, and continue with nightclubs in the **Castro** or **SoMa**. On day four, slip out of the city for a taste of **Wine Country**. For dinner, pick a cuisine you've never had before, and end your stay with a smile by attending **Beach Blanket Babylon**.

While the economic boom of the 1980s sparked a culinary renaissance among the city's restaurants, this has been overshadowed by the dramatic dot-com revolution of the late 1990s, which, driven by the same greedy delirium of the gold rush, sent rents and real estate sky-rocketing and refashioned the city's social landscape, driving out artists and the middle class and marginalizing the poor even further. The inevitable bust has been felt nationally, but the hangover is sharpest here.

Listen closely, though, and you'll hear whisperings – the next big thing is not far off, and the area's tech geniuses and speculators plan to be at the center of it. It's a little bit of science-fiction called nanotechnology.

Orientation

San Francisco is compact, covering the tip of a 30-mile-long peninsula, with the Pacific Ocean to the west and the San Francisco Bay to the east. The city can be divided into three sections. The downtown district is in the northeast between Van Ness Ave, Market St and the bay, and includes the Embarcadero, Union Sq, the Financial District, Civic Center, the Tenderloin, Chinatown, North Beach, Nob Hill, Russian Hill and Fisherman's Wharf.

The South of Market District, or SoMa, is a trendy warehouse zone that fades into the Mission, the city's Latino quarter, and then the Castro, the city's gay quarter.

The residential western part of the city stretches from Van Ness Ave all the way to the Pacific Ocean, encompassing the upscale Marina and Pacific Heights, Japantown, the Haight, the Richmond and Sunset Districts, and Golden Gate Park.

Information

BOOKSTORES

San Franciscans spend more on books than residents of any other US city. Here is a posy of favorites:

City Lights Bookstore (Map pp934-6; ☎ 415-362-8193; 261 Columbus Ave) A North Beach institution; Beat poetry and progressive literature.

A Clean Well-Lighted Place for Books (Map pp934-6; ☎ 415-441-6670; 601 Van Ness Ave) Lots of author readings.

A Different Light Bookstore (Map pp934-6; ☎ 415-431-0891; 489 Castro St) The USA's largest gay and lesbian bookseller.

Get Lost (Map pp934-6; ☎ 415-437-0529; 1825 Market St) Specializes in travel.

Green Apple (Map pp934-6; ☎ 415-387-2272; cnr Clement & 6th Ave) A book lover's mecca: scads of used and new books.

Stacey's (Map pp934-6; ☎ 415-421-4687; 581 Market St)

EMERGENCY

Emergency number (☎ 911)
Fire department (☎ 415-558-3268)
Police (☎ 415-553-0123)
SF Rape Treatment Center (☎ 415-821-3222)

INTERNET ACCESS

The visitors center and SF library staff have city-wide lists of Internet access. Free terminals (15-minute limit) include:

CompUSA (Map pp934-6; ☎ 415-391-9778; 750 Market St)
Main Library (Map pp934-6; ☎ 415-557-4400; www.sfpl.org; cnr Larkin & Grove Sts)

MEDIA

San Francisco Bay Guardian (www.sfbg.com) Free weekly; alternative news and entertainment.
San Francisco Chronicle (www.sfgate.com) The main daily newspaper; website is a great resource.
San Francisco Examiner (www.examiner.com) Free daily tabloid.
SF Weekly (www.sfweekly.com) Free weekly; alternative news and entertainment.
KPFA 94.1 FM Alternative news and music.
KQED 88.5 FM Local NPR affiliate.

MEDICAL SERVICES

San Francisco General Hospital (Map pp934-6; ☎ 415-206-8000; 1001 Potrero Ave)
Haight Ashbury Free Clinic (Map pp934-6; ☎ 415-487-5632; 558 Clayton St) Appointments required, but free treatment.

MONEY

For your banking needs head to **Bank of America** (Map pp934-6; ☎ 650-615-4700; www.bankamerica.com; 1 Powell St).

POST

To have mail sent to you, mark it General Delivery, along with the name and address of the particular post office.

Civic Center branch (Map pp934-6; ☎ 415-563-7284, 800-725-2161; www.usps.com; 101 Hyde St, San Francisco, CA 94142) is centrally located.

TOURIST OFFICES

San Francisco's Visitor Information Center (Map pp934-6; ☎ 415-391-2000; www.sfvisitor.org; Market & Powell Sts; 🕑 9am-5pm Mon-Fri, 9am-3pm Sat & Sun), on the lower level of Hallidie Plaza, offers comprehensive information and access to an online reservation service.

Dangers & Annoyances

Beyond the usual city smarts, be wary in the rough Tenderloin at any time, and after dark in SoMa and the areas around the 16th St and 24th St BART (Bay Area Rapid Transit) stations in the Mission.

Sights

For reasons only die-hard shoppers truly know, most visitors choose Union Sq as their home base; indeed, from here you can walk to most of the popular neighborhoods and sights: the Civic Center and SoMa museums, Chinatown, North Beach, Nob Hill and the Embarcadero. Easy public transit can get you to attractions further away: the Wharf and Marina, the Haight, the Castro, the Mission and Golden Gate Park.

UNION SQ & CIVIC CENTER Map pp934–6

The heart of Union Sq is a granite plaza – now sparkling after a $25-million facelift – surrounded by glitzy department stores, high-end boutiques and a wide range of hotels. The square is dominated by the 97ft-high **Dewey Monument** (Geary St), erected in 1903 to commemorate the Spanish–American War. On the east side, on Maiden Lane, stop by **Folk Art International Building** (140 Maiden Lane), the city's only Frank Lloyd Wright building (now a gallery; closed Sunday). Powell St is quite a scene at weekends – a crush of shoppers, buskers, hustlers, chess matches and tourists lined up at the **cable car turnaround**.

San Francisco's compact Theater District lies immediately southwest of Union Sq, crumbling from there into the blighted hotels and 'massage' parlors of the downtrodden Tenderloin District. The rose in the briar here is **Glide Memorial Cathedral** (☎ 415-674-6000; 330 Ellis St), famous for its gospel Sunday services at 9am and 11am, to which the public is warmly welcome.

A few blocks south, the Civic Center area is a study in contrasts, as the city's high culture collides with its pressing homelessness problem. San Francisco's newest belle is the reincarnated **Asian Art Museum** (☎ 415-581-3500; www.asianart.org; 200 Larkin St; adult $10, child 12-17 $6; 🕑 10am-5pm Tue-Sun, until 9pm Thu). Housed in the former main library, the museum is a stunning architectural blend of old and new, while the Asian art collection itself – which is one of the world's largest – is smartly and dramatically laid out. And encountering the 18th-century Buddhist goddess Simhavaktra Dakini is now a heart-stopping moment.

Next door, the stylish and modern new **Main Library** (☎ 415-557-4400; www.sfpl.org; cnr Larkin & Grove Sts) is worth a gander, as is its interesting, top-floor History Center. Across the way, the 1915 beaux arts–style **City Hall** (☎ 415-554-4000; 400 Van Ness Ave; 🕑 8am-8pm Mon-Fri, noon-4pm Sat & Sun) sports a grand foyer and staircase and some cute exhibits on the city's history.

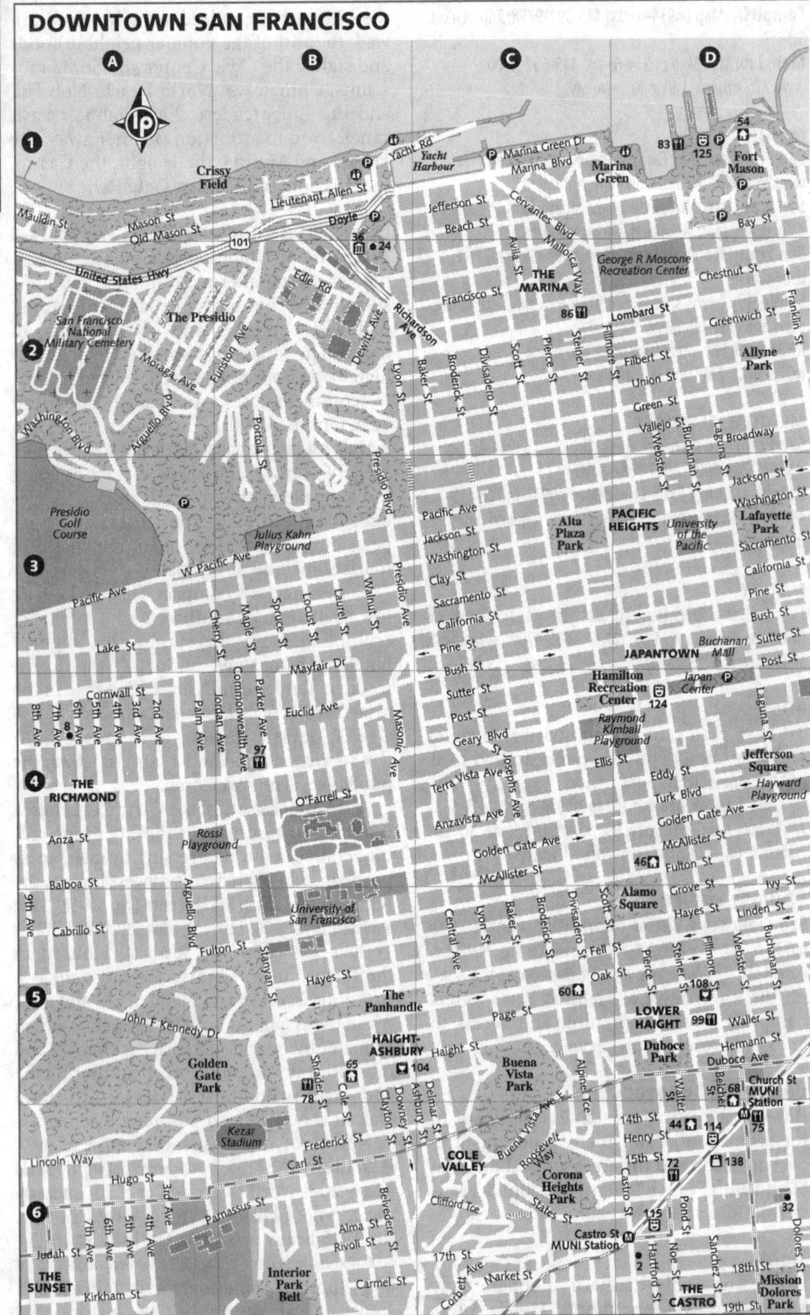
DOWNTOWN SAN FRANCISCO
A
B
C
D
1
2
3
4
5
6
Crissy Field
Yacht Rd
Yacht Harbour
Marina Green Dr
Marina Blvd
Marina Green
Fort Mason
Lieutenant Allen St
Mauldin St
Mason St
Old Mason St
Doyle
101
United States Hwy
Edie Rd
Jefferson St
Beach St
Cervantes Blvd
Mallorca Way
Bay St
George R Moscone Recreation Center
Chestnut St
Francisco St
THE MARINA
Lombard St
Greenwich St
Franklin St
Allyne Park
San Francisco National Military Cemetery
The Presidio
Moraga Ave
Funston Ave
Dewitt Ave
Richardson Ave
Lyon St
Baker St
Broderick St
Divisadero St
Scott St
Pierce St
Steiner St
Fillmore St
Filbert St
Union St
Green St
Vallejo St
Webster St
Buchanan St
Laguna St
Broadway
Washington Blvd
Arguello Blvd
Portola St
Presidio Blvd
Presidio Golf Course
Jackson St
Washington St
Lafayette Park
Pacific Ave
Alta Plaza Park
PACIFIC HEIGHTS
University of the Pacific
Sacramento St
California St
Julius Kahn Playground
W Pacific Ave
Clay St
Pine St
Bush St
Sutter St
Post St
Lake St
Cherry St
Maple St
Spruce St
Locust St
Laurel St
Walnut St
Presidio Ave
Buchanan Mall
JAPANTOWN
Mayfair Dr
Hamilton Recreation Center
Japan Center
Cornwall St
8th Ave
7th Ave
6th Ave
5th Ave
4th Ave
3rd Ave
2nd Ave
Palm Ave
Jordan Ave
Commonwealth Ave
Parker Ave
Euclid Ave
Masonic Ave
Geary Blvd
Raymond Kimball Playground
St Josephs Ave
Ellis St
Jefferson Square
Eddy St
Hayward Playground
Turk Blvd
THE RICHMOND
O'Farrell St
Terra Vista Ave
Anzavista Ave
Golden Gate Ave
McAllister St
Anza St
Rossi Playground
Fulton St
Balboa St
Arguello Blvd
University of San Francisco
Central Ave
Alamo Square
Grove St
Ivy St
Hayes St
Linden St
9th Ave
Cabrillo St
Stanyan St
Fell St
Oak St
The Panhandle
Page St
LOWER HAIGHT
Waller St
John F Kennedy Dr
HAIGHT-ASHBURY
Haight St
Buena Vista Park
Duboce Park
Hermann St
Duboce Ave
Golden Gate Park
Shrader St
Cole St
Clayton St
Downey St
Ashbury St
Delmar St
Alpine Tce
Walter St
Belcher St
Church St MUNI Station
Buena Vista Ave E
14th St
Henry St
15th St
Kezar Stadium
Frederick St
Lincoln Way
Carl St
COLE VALLEY
Roosevelt Way
Corona Heights Park
Castro St
Hugo St
Clifford Tce
States St
Pond St
Parnassus St
Alma St
Rivoli St
Belvedere St
Castro St MUNI Station
Judah St
7th Ave
6th Ave
5th Ave
4th Ave
3rd Ave
17th St
Hartford St
Noe St
Sanchez St
Dolores St
18th St
THE SUNSET
Kirkham St
Interior Park Belt
Carmel St
Corbett Ave
Market St
THE CASTRO
19th St
Mission Dolores Park
2
8
24
32
36
44
46
54
60
65
68
72
75
78
83
86
97
99
104
108
114
115
124
125
138

Fisherman's Wharf
Pier 43½
Pier 43
Pier 41
Pier 45
Pier 39
Pier 35
Pier 33
Pier 31
Pier 29
Pier 27
Pier 23
Pier 19
Pier 17
Pier 15
Pier 9
Pier 7
Pier 3
Pier 1
Pier 2
Aquatic Park
Pier 47
FISHERMAN'S WHARF
Victoria Park
Russian Hill Park
RUSSIAN HILL
North Beach Playground
Pioneer Park/ Telegraph Hill
Levi's Plaza
Farmers' Market
Washington Square
NORTH BEACH
Walton Park
Embarcadero Center
Ferry Terminal Plaza
Ferries to Tiburon & Vallejo
Ferries to Sausalito
Ferries to Larkspur
Ferries to Oakland & Alameda
San Francisco Bay
The Embarcadero (Herb Caen Way...)
The Embarcadero
Broadway Tunnel
Mini Park
CHINATOWN
NOB HILL
Huntington Park
California St Cable Car Line
Powell-Hyde St Cable Car Line
Powell-Mason Cable Car
FINANCIAL DISTRICT
Embacadero BART & MUNI Station
Folsom St MUNI Station
Bay Bridge
Pier 22½
Pier 24
Pier 26
Pier 28
Pier 30
Pier 32
Pier 34
Pier 36
Pier 38
Pier 40
Breakwater
Montgomery BART & MUNI Station
UNION SQUARE
THE TENDERLOIN
Hallidie Plaza
Powell St BART & MUNI Station
CIVIC CENTER
United Nations Plaza
Civic Center Plaza
Civic Center BART & MUNI Station
Brannan St MUNI Station
South Park
2nd & King St MUNI Station
Mission Creek Marina
Pier 46B
CalTrain Depot
4th & King St MUNI Station
SOUTH OF MARKET (SOMA)
HAYES VALLEY
Van Ness MUNI Station
Pier 48
Pier 50
Pier 52
Pier 54
Clinton Park
THE MISSION
16th St Mission BART Station
Franklin Square
Jackson Playground
To San Francisco General Hospital
Agua Vista Park
Pier 68
Pier 70
0 400 m
0 0.2 mi

INFORMATION

A Clean Well-Lighted Place for Books 1 E4
A Different Light Bookstore 2 D6
Bank of America 3 F4
City Lights Bookstore 4 F2
Civic Center Post Office 5 E4
CompUSA 6 F3
Get Lost 7 E5
Green Apple Books 8 A4
Main Library 9 E4
San Francisco's Visitor Information Center 10 F4
Stacey's 11 G3

SIGHTS & ACTIVITIES pp933–43

826 Valencia 12 E6
Asian Art Museum 13 E4
Bank of America Building 14 G3
Basic Brown Bear Factory 15 G6
Cable Car Barn & Museum 16 F2
Cannery 17 E1
Cartoon Art Museum 18 G3
Chinatown Gate 19 F3
Chinese Culture Center 20 F2
City Hall 21 E4
Coit Tower 22 F2
Dewey Monument 23 F3
Exploratorium 24 B2
Ferry Building 25 G2
George R Moscone Convention Center 26 G4
Ghirardelli Square 27 E1
Glide Memorial Cathedral 28 F4
Grace Cathedral 29 F3
Historic Ships at Hyde St Pier 30 E1
Metreon 31 G4
Mission Dolores 32 D6
Musée Mécanique 33 E1
Old St Mary's Church 34 F3
Pacific Bell Park 35 H4
Palace of Fine Arts 36 B2
Portsmouth Square 37 F2
Saints Peter & Paul Church 38 F2
San Francisco Maritime National Historic Park Museum 39 E1
San Francisco Museum of Modern Art (SFMOMA) 40 G3
Transamerica Pyramid 41 G2
Wells Fargo Bank Building 42 G3
Yerba Buena Gardens 43 G4

SLEEPING pp944–6

24 Henry 44 D6
Adelaide Hostel & Hotel 45 F3
Archbishop's Mansion 46 D4
Astoria Hotel 47 F3
Edwardian San Francisco Hotel 48 E5
Fairmont Hotel 49 F3
Globe Hostel 50 F5
Golden Gate Hotel 51 F3
Halcyon Hotel 52 F3
HI San Francisco City Center 53 E4
HI San Francisco Fisherman's Wharf 54 D1
Hotel Bijou 55 F4
Hotel Bohème 56 F2
Hotel Monaco 57 F3
Hotel Triton 58 F3
Maxwell Hotel 59 F3
Metro Hotel 60 C5
Mosser 61 F4
Pacific Tradewinds Guest House 62 F3
Palace Hotel 63 G3
Phoenix Motel 64 E4
Red Victorian B&B 65 B5
San Remo Hotel 66 F1
Sheehan Hotel 67 F3
Willows Inn 68 D5

EATING pp946–8

Aqua 69 G3
Armani Cafe 70 F3
Asia SF 71 F5
Cafe Flore 72 D6
Cafe Neibaum-Coppola 73 F2
Caffé Macaroni 74 F2
Caffe Museo ..... (see 40)
Café Cuvée 75 D6
Café de la Presse 76 F3
California Culinary Academy 77 E4
Cha Cha Cha 78 B5
Delfina 79 E6
Farallon 80 F3
Gary Danko 81 E1
Golden Boy Pizza 82 F2
Greens 83 D1
Helmund 84 F2
House of Nanking 85 F2
Isa 86 C2
Jeanty at Jack's 87 G3
Kokkari 88 G2
L'Osteria del Forno 89 F2
La Cumbre 90 E6
Limón 91 E6
Lucky Creation 92 F2
Mama's 93 F2
McCormick & Kuleto's ..... (see 27)
Pied Piper Bar 94 G3
R&G Lounge 95 F3
Slanted Door 96 E6
Straits Cafe 97 B4
Taquería Pancho Villa 98 E6
Thep Phanom 99 D5
Ti Couz 100 E6
Yank Sing 101 H3
Zuni Café 102 E5

DRINKING p948

Buena Vista Café 103 E1
Club Deluxe 104 B5
Edinburgh Castle 105 E3
Lexington Club 106 E6
Lone Star Saloon 107 F5
Mad Dog in the Fog 108 D5
Tosca Cafe 109 F2
Vesuvio Cafe 110 F2
Zeitgeist 111 E5

ENTERTAINMENT pp948–9

1015 Folsom 112 F4
Bottom of the Hill 113 G6
Cafe du Nord 114 D6
Café 115 D6
Castro Theatre ..... (see 2)
Club Fugazi 116 F2
Curran Theatre 117 F3
Davies Symphony Hall 118 E4
Elbo Room 119 E6
Endup 120 G4
Geary Theater ..... (see 117)
Golden Gate Theatre 121 F4
Harry Denton's Starlight Room 122 F3
Jezabel's Joint Microcinema 123 E4
John Lee Hooker's Boom Boom Room 124 D4
Magic Theatre 125 D1
Orpheum Theatre 126 F4
Paradise Lounge 127 F5
Roxie Cinema 128 E6
Screening Room 129 G4
Slim's 130 F5
Stud 131 F5
Theatre Rhinoceros 132 E6
Tonga Room 133 F3
Up & Down Club 134 F5
War Memorial Opera House 135 E4
Yerba Buena Center for the Arts 136 G4

SHOPPING p949

Good Vibrations 137 E3
Image Leather 138 D6

TRANSPORT pp949–51

Blue & Gold Ferries 139 G2
Transbay Terminal 140 G3

On the opposite side of City Hall, the 1932 **War Memorial Opera House** is where the city's acclaimed opera and ballet companies perform (p949). Nearby **Hayes Valley**, along Hayes St between Franklin and Laguna Sts, is a mix of trendy restaurants and hip clothing boutiques.

SOMA

Map pp934–6

South of Market, or SoMa, refers to a vast area that includes the busy George R Moscone Convention Center and a plethora of hot clubs and nightspots.

Yerba Buena Gardens (Mission St), between 3rd and 4th Sts, is a relaxing urban green space bordered by cultural institutions and containing a wealth of activities for children and families (p942). From May to October it hosts hundreds of free outdoor concerts and **events** (☎ 415-543-1718; www.ybgf.org).

San Francisco Museum of Modern Art (SFMOMA; ☎ 415-357-4000; www.sfmoma.org; 151 3rd St; adult $10, child under 12 free; 11am-6pm Mon & Tue & Thu-Sun, until 9pm Thu) This rakish red-brick landmark (designed by Swiss architect Mario Botta) is one of the nation's premier modern art showcases. The museum's strength is American abstract expressionism, but all the great American and European modern artists are represented, and it has a distinguished collection of American photography, which includes Ansel Adams, Edward Weston and Dorothea Lange.

The **Yerba Buena Center for the Arts** (☎ 415-978-2787; www.yerbabuenaarts.org; 701 Mission St) has an excellent modern **art gallery** (admission

$6; 11am-5pm Tue-Sun, until 8pm Thu) and a theater hosting a full range of performances. Also here, the **Metreon** (☎ 415-369-6000; www.metreon.com; 101 4th St; 10am-10pm) is an up-to-the-minute entertainment complex and shopping center.

Not just for kids, the nearby **Cartoon Art Museum** (☎ 415-227-8666; www.cartoonart.org; 655 Mission St; adult $6, child 6-12 $2; 11am-5pm Tue-Sun) takes the funnies seriously, spanning the gamut from Disney to Doonesbury to R Crumb.

FINANCIAL DISTRICT — Map pp934–6

Visiting the financial district, densely concentrated in the blocks from Union Sq to the bay, is essentially an architectural experience. When it was completed in 1969, the 761ft **Bank of America building** (555 California St) ushered in a new era for San Francisco's previously low-rise skyline, and its top-floor **Carnelian Room** (☎ 415-433-7500) provides amazing views. San Francisco's tallest building, the 8530ft **Transamerica Pyramid** (600 Montgomery St), was completed in 1972.

The **Wells Fargo bank building** (420 Montgomery St) has a surprisingly good **museum** (☎ 415-396-2619; admission free; 9am-5pm Mon-Fri) chronicling the gold rush, the Pony Express and Wells Fargo's own colorful history.

The refurbished **Ferry Building**, where the Embarcadero meets Market St, hosts an outstanding **farmers market** (8am-2pm Sat & Sun, 10am-2pm Tue, 3-7pm Thu) that may become a daily event; some shops are permanent. As the name suggests, ferries also run from here to points around the bay.

CHINATOWN — Map pp934–6

A steady stream of Chinese immigrants has kept this the city's most vibrant, crowded and authentic ethnic neighborhood. Cantonese remains the first language for many. **Grant Ave**, between Bush and Jackson Sts, is the main thoroughfare catering to tourists, but Chinatown is best experienced by wandering its side streets and alleys – many of which, in the late 1800s, were notorious for brothels, opium dens and gambling parlors; see p941 for more sites.

The **Chinese Historical Society of America Museum** (☎ 415-391-1188; www.chsa.org; 965 Clay St; adult $3, child 6-17 $1; 11am-4pm Tue-Fri, noon-4pm Sat & Sun) has the largest collection of Chinese American artifacts in the US, but can display only a fraction. The well-thought-out exhibits make this the best place to get a feel for the Chinese American experience, both then and now.

Portsmouth Sq, at Kearny and Washington Sts, was the heart of San Francisco during the gold rush, and to neighborhood residents it's still Chinatown's 'living room.' Children romp in the park's playground and older folks gamble on the benches. Cross the stone overpass to reach the **Chinese Culture Center** (☎ 415-986-1822; www.c-c-c.org; 750 Kearny St; admission free; 10am-4pm Tue-Sat) on the third floor of the Holiday Inn. The center has displays and a small art gallery.

NORTH BEACH — Map pp934–6

Like Chinatown, the city's Italian quarter is best experienced by wandering, soaking up the atmosphere and sampling the many delicacies on offer (p941). The adopted home of writers Jack Kerouac and Allen Ginsberg, North Beach was the birthplace of the '50s Beat movement, and it remains a center for progressive poetry and politics. Along Broadway, touts and neon signs keep alive another North Beach tradition from the early 1960s, that of the golden age of nude dancing.

Washington Sq, North Beach's playground, is a green swatch perfect for lounging, while nearby, atop Telegraph Hill, is the 210ft **Coit Tower** (☎ 415-362-0808; admission free; 10am-6pm), one of San Francisco's most prominent landmarks. The tower's lobby is adorned with superb WPA murals illustrating San Francisco industry, commerce and life. **Elevator rides** (adult $3.75) to the top are worth it.

RUSSIAN HILL & NOB HILL — Map pp934–6

West of North Beach, the steep streets of Russian Hill offer some scenic stairway gardens and the oft-photographed 1000 block of **Lombard Street**, between Hyde and Leavenworth Sts, which is famously billed as 'the world's crookedest street.'

The cable car was invented by Andrew Hallidie for the most part to make it safer for the city's ruthless 19th-century 'Silver Kings' – Mark Hopkins, Collis P Huntington, James Grantham Fair and Leland Stanford – to reach their stately homes on the summit of Nob Hill. This effort is recounted in the tidy **Cable Car Barn & Museum** (☎ 415-474-1887; www.cablecarmuseum.com; 1201 Mason St; admission free; 10am-5pm, until 6pm summer), which also showcases the noisy meeting of the cables themselves as they power the vehicles over the hills.

Wrapping its ecumenical modernism in a cloak of grand antiquity, the **Grace Cathedral** (☎ 415-749-6300; 1100 California St) is a 20th-century building of soaring Gothic proportions. The bronze doors are casts of Ghiberti's Gates of Paradise of the Baptistry in Florence, Italy, and the AIDS Interfaith Memorial Chapel contains a triptych by Keith Haring. A popular time to visit is during **choral vespers** (🕓 3pm Sun & 5:15pm Thu).

FISHERMAN'S WHARF — Map pp934–6

San Francisco's famous wharf is now the epitome of a tourist trap, a jumble of chowder stalls, overpriced restaurants, tacky shops, silly museums, amped-up kids and dull accommodations – but there's fun to be had if you can give yourself up to it.

The Hyde St cable car is the arrival method of choice, dropping you between **Ghirardelli Sq**, a former chocolate factory, and the **Cannery**, a former fruit-canning factory. Both are now essentially nostalgia-tinted shopping malls. Walk east along hectic Jefferson St to reach **Pier 39**, the epicenter of manufactured tourism. Years ago a herd of barking sea lions took over the boat docks here, and they have yet to give them back.

Of genuine interest is the **San Francisco Maritime National Historical Park**, which contains a **museum** (☎ 415-561-7100; 900 Beach St; admission free; 🕓 10am-4:30pm) on the lip of Aquatic Park and five late-19th-century ships moored nearby at Hyde St Pier ($5 boarding pass). The strikingly designed museum recounts the Bay Area's nautical history with a remarkable collection of model ships, and the historic vessels themselves bring it all to marvelous life.

THE MARINA & PRESIDIO — Map pp934–6

The northwestern edge of the peninsula, rimmed with parks, beaches, museums and one singular bridge, makes for dreamy strolling and biking.

Adjoining Aquatic Park, **Fort Mason** (☎ 415-345-7544; www.fortmason.org) was at one time a Spanish and then US military fort. It is now a hive of artistic and progressive civilian activity, housing nonprofits, art galleries, theaters and several small but excellent cultural museums.

The Marina was born in time for the 1915 Panama-Pacific International Exposition, when waterfront marshland was reclaimed to create the exhibition grounds. One of the few surviving Expo structures is Bernard Maybeck's stately **Palace of Fine Arts**, off Baker St bordering the Presidio. A great hands-on science museum, the **Exploratorium** (☎ 415-561-0360; www.exploratorium.edu; 3601 Lyon St; adult $10, child 5-17 $6; 🕓 10am-5pm Tue-Sun), is here.

The **Presidio** (☎ 415-561-4323) is also a former Spanish and US military fort, occupying acres of parkland. Windsurfers launch from the **Crissy Field** beaches, which lead to **Fort Point** (Map p931) and the view of the Golden Gate Bridge Alfred Hitchcock made famous in *Vertigo*. Along the park's west side, picturesque **Baker Beach** is popular with sunbathers, but tricky tides make swimming risky.

THE MISSION — Map pp934–6

This is the city's Latino district, by turns gritty, family-oriented, hip and political. Some of the best cheap meals and evening bar-hopping are found here, particularly around 16th St between Mission and Guerrero and along the 'Valencia St Corridor,' between 20th and 24th Sts.

The 1782 adobe **Mission Dolores** (☎ 415-621-8203; Dolores & 16th Sts; admission $3; 🕓 9am-4pm) was the sixth California mission founded by Father Junípero Serra, and is the oldest building in the city. The adjoining 1913 basilica is a must-visit for its stained glass and tilework, and the historic cemetery is also interesting. The grassy slopes of **Mission Dolores Park**, a couple of blocks south, are popular sunning grounds and a gathering spot of choice for rallies and soccer games.

The neighborhood is noted for its bounty of colorful murals depicting everything from San Francisco's labor history to Central American independence. Narrow **Balmy Alley**, off 24th St near Folsom, is resplendent with them.

THE CASTRO — Map pp934–6

The compact Castro, the gay center of San Francisco, is great for strolling, people-watching, shopping and dining – as well as for satisfying any and all transgressive urges. The magnificent **Castro Theatre** (p949), where the city's most important film festivals are held, is the primary landmark on busy Castro St. See Entertainment for a

GAY SAN FRANCISCO: YESTERDAY AND TODAY

In the early 1950s, a chapter of the Mattachine Society, the first serious homosexual-rights organization in the USA, sprang up in San Francisco, and in 1955 the Daughters of Bilitis (DOB), the nation's first lesbian organization, was founded here. During the 1959 mayoral campaign, challenger Russell Wolden accused incumbent mayor George Christopher of turning San Francisco into 'the national headquarters of the organized homosexuals in the United States.' Christopher was reelected, but was not about to be accused of being soft on queers. He responded with a massive police crackdown on gay male cruising areas, raids that resulted in a public blacklist of gay citizens.

Resistance to this persecution did not come out of the homophile movement but out of bars, and one in particular: the Black Cat, dubbed by Allen Ginsberg as 'the greatest gay bar in America.' (José Sarria, a drag performer at the Black Cat, ran for city supervisor in 1961, becoming the first openly gay person to run for public office in the USA.)

The age of tolerance had not yet arrived, however. In 1965 a dance sponsored by the Council on Religion and the Homosexual was raided by the police, and everyone in attendance was arrested and photographed. The city was outraged, and even the media denounced the police behavior. This event helped to turn the tide in the city's perception of the gay community. The crackdown on gay bars stopped, and a gay person was appointed to sit on the police community-relations board.

Another watershed moment occurred in the late 1970s. In 1977 gay activist Harvey Milk was elected to the Board of Supervisors, and recognition of the gay-rights movement reached a new peak. Then, the following year, Milk and Mayor George Moscone were assassinated by Dan White, an avowedly antigay former police officer. This tragedy, which was soon followed in the 1980s by the devastating AIDS epidemic, brought an increasing level of public sympathy and awareness, and it forever solidified the city's gay community.

Today, San Francisco is indeed the unofficial 'national headquarters of the organized homosexuals,' and proudly so. Gay politicians have not only been elected numerous times to the Board of Supervisors, but gone on to hold major state offices. The Castro has become a popular tourist destination, and gay life is everywhere: displayed, exuberant, diverse and accepted.

Here are a few ways to experience it.

If you want to cruise the bars, check out what's happening in the *Bay Area Reporter* and the *Bay Times*, and see p948.

Theatre Rhinoceros (☎ 415-861-5079; www.therhino.org; 2926 16th St) is the nation's longest-running gay-and-lesbian theater company. For more guerrilla antics, see what the **Sisters of Perpetual Indulgence** (☎ 415-552-0220; www.thesisters.org) are up to. This charitable organization is a San Francisco institution.

Kicking off Gay Pride Week at the end of June is the **San Francisco Gay & Lesbian Film Festival** (☎ 415-703-8650; www.frameline.org), an intensely scheduled two weeks of international queer cinema.

And there are other queer-ific events beyond the Pride Parade and Halloween. Check out the **Folsom St Fair** (☎ 415-861-3247; www.folsomstreetfair.com) in late September, which is known for nudity, chaps and chains and draws half a million people, and the **Castro St Fair** (☎ 415-841-1824; www.castrostreetfair.org) in early October, which attracts a milder, sweaters-and-shopping crowd.

sampling of the neighborhood's never-dull nightlife.

THE HAIGHT **Map pp934–6**

San Francisco's Summer of Love, ushered in by Golden Gate Park's Human Be-In in 1967, was a short, sweet, idealistic moment that crumbled under the weight of drug abuse and increasing violence, a legacy that still haunts this neighborhood. It was also here that San Francisco's psychedelic sound emerged, epitomized by bands like the Grateful Dead and Jefferson Airplane. Today, Haight St is more about fashion and nightlife than free love, but it maintains a unique aura.

The **Upper Haight**, also known as Haight-Ashbury, stretches from Golden Gate Park to Buena Vista Park and is lined with funky clothing shops, cafés and cheap restaurants.

Deadheads will want to snap a photo at **710 Ashbury St**, the onetime communal home of the Grateful Dead (now a private residence). On Haight St east of Divisadero St, the **Lower Haight** is a scruffy few blocks of music clubs, cafés and top-notch dive bars.

GOLDEN GATE PARK & AROUND

San Francisco's biggest park was designed in 1871 by 24-year-old William Hammond Hall, who transformed 1017 acres of windswept sand dunes into the largest developed city park in the world. Currently, several park institutions are undergoing changes; for updates on hours and admissions, contact the **McLaren Lodge office** (☎ 415-831-2700; 🕑 8am-5pm Mon-Fri), near the park's Fell St entrance.

The park's oldest building is the **Conservatory of Flowers**, an 1879 Victorian glasshouse with gorgeous plant exhibits. It was due to reopen in fall 2003 after a $25-million restoration. The **California Academy of Sciences** (☎ 415-750-7145; www.calacademy.org) – a large, kid-friendly natural-history museum, aquarium and planetarium – will move to long-term temporary digs at 875 Howard St in 2004, to await the completion of a Renzo Piano–designed building in its old spot. The **De Young Fine Arts Museum**, across from the Academy, is also being rebuilt (to open in 2005). Nearby and unchanged is the **Japanese Tea Garden** (☎ 415-752-1171; admission $3.50; 🕑 8:30am-5pm), an immaculate garden with a stylized pagoda and a horseshoe-shaped footbridge.

The park is packed with sporting facilities, including 7.5 miles of bicycle trails, 12 miles of bridle trails, a challenging nine-hole golf course and 21 tennis courts. Rowboats and pedal boats can be rented on **Stow Lake** (☎ 415-752-0347; boats per hr $12-18), along with surreys ($15 per hour), bikes ($8 per hour) and inline skates ($7 per hour).

Standing just north of Golden Gate Park, along the Great Hwy, is the landmark **Cliff House** (Map p931; ☎ 415-386-3330; www.cliffhouse.com), which is under renovation (to reopen in summer 2004). The original Cliff House, built in 1863, was turned into a stunning palace by Adolph Sutro in 1896, but it burned down in 1909; the adjacent Sutro Baths burned down in 1966. The current building's restaurant is very popular for its sunset views. The easy path around Lands End from the Sutro Baths includes photogenic views of the Golden Gate Bridge.

The **California Palace of the Legion of Honor** (Map p931; ☎ 415-863-3330; www.thinker.org; adult $8, child 12-17 $5, free Tue; 🕑 9:30am-5pm Tue-Sun), in Lincoln Park north of Golden Gate Park, is one of San Francisco's premier art museums, with a world-class collection of European art from medieval times to the 20th century.

SAN FRANCISCO BAY

Designed by Joseph Strauss and constructed between 1933 and 1937, the beautiful **Golden Gate Bridge** (☎ 415-921-5858), 2 miles in length with a main span of 4200ft, links San Francisco with Marin County. At the time of completion it was the longest suspension bridge in the world. Painting the bridge is a never-ending job – a team of 25 painters adds another 1000 orange gallons every week. A prime starting point for bridge gazing is **Fort Point Lookout**, on Marine Dr at the bridge's southern end. Cars pay a $5 toll for southbound (Marin to San Francisco) travel; pedestrians and cyclists can cross for free via the sidewalk along the bridge's east side.

From 1933 to 1963, the 12-acre rocky island located in the middle of San Francisco Bay was the nation's most famous penitentiary, supposedly escape-proof and home to such notorious convicts as Al Capone, 'Machine Gun' Kelly and Robert Stroud (the 'birdman of Alcatraz'). However, **Alcatraz** did 'lose' a few inmates, though it's never been established if any made it to land alive. **Blue & Gold Ferries** (Map pp934-6; ☎ 415-773-1188, reservations 705-5555; adult $13.25) runs to the island from Pier 41; tickets include the ferry trip and an audio tour, and must be booked in advance.

Activities

For bicycle rentals, try **Avenue Cyclery** (Map pp934-6; ☎ 415-387-3155; 756 Stanyan St; bicycles per hr/day $5/25), on the eastern edge of Golden Gate Park. Inline skates can be rented at **Skates on Haight** (Map pp934-6; ☎ 415-752-8375; 1818 Haight St), also near the park. For sailing lessons, try **Spinnaker Sailing** (Map pp934-6; ☎ 415-543-7333; Pier 40; lessons from $295, tours $25), which also runs two-hour sunset tours aboard large schooners.

Ocean Beach is a popular but very challenging place to surf, with cold swells rising 12ft or higher. Never surf alone; there are no lifeguards and the riptide is extremely dangerous. You'll also want at least a 3mm full-length wetsuit. The folks at **Wise Surfboards** (☎ 415-750-9473; 800 Great Hwy) are very knowledgeable and maintain an updated **surf report** (☎ 415-273-1618).

Walking Tour

SAN FRANCISCO

San Francisco is a walker's paradise, and this tour takes in two of its most famous neighborhoods – Chinatown and North Beach – and ends with one of the best up-and-downs the city offers. Done leisurely, this makes a good day.

At Grant Ave and Bush St, the stone dragons and jade-green awnings of the **Chinatown Gate** (**1**) announce the official entrance to Chinatown. Walk north on bustling Grant Ave, which was originally called Dupont St ('Du Pon Gai' to the Chinese), but was renamed in 1885 in honor of president and Civil War hero Ulysses S Grant.

At Sacramento St, turn left and then right onto Waverly Pl, an atmospheric alley lined with medicinal ginseng displays and filigreed open balconies. The 'real' Chinatown is often hidden behind bright façades above street level – don't forget to look up.

At Clay St, turn west uphill. At the corner of Stockton St are two notable sites. The **Kong Chow Temple** (**2**; 4th fl, 855 Stockton St) is open to respectful visitors. Redolent with burning incense, its fantastical altar is supposed to be the oldest in the USA. Next door, the dramatic **Chinese Consolidated Benevolent Building** (**3**; 843 Stockton St) is Chinatown's 'city hall' (closed to the public).

One block west up Clay St is the **Chinese Historical Society of America Museum** (**4**; p937), which is housed in the historic Chinese YWCA building.

Return east on Clay St and continue north along Waverly Pl. At Washington St, jog left and enter Ross Alley, a hidden pedestrian walkway. That delicious smell will be coming from the **Golden Gate Fortune Cookies** (**5**; 56 Ross Alley), an unadorned 'factory' where you can watch Chinese women at two old-fashioned machines churning out fortune cookies, a San Francisco invention. Try a hot sample and buy a bag!

Return to Washington St and walk east to **Portsmouth Sq** (**6**; p937), then turn north on Kearny St to Columbus Ave. Here, Chinatown and North Beach meet. If it's lunchtime, choose between the **House of Nanking** (**7**; p947) and **Cafe Niebaum-Coppola** (**8**; p947), which is on the first floor of the

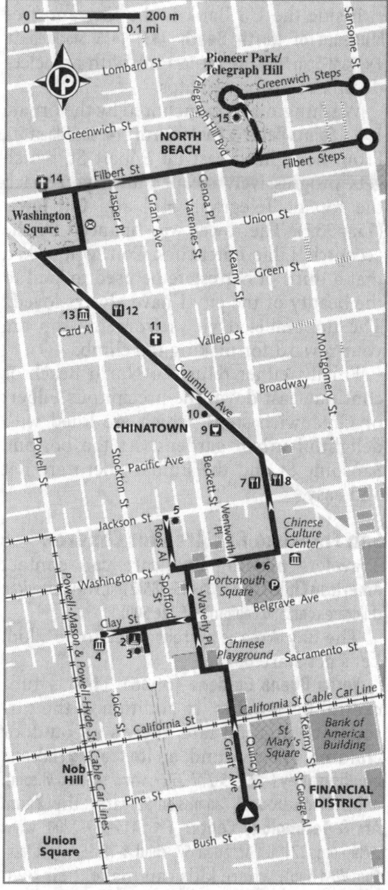

striking 1905 Sentinel Building, owned by filmmaker Francis Ford Coppola.

Columbus Ave leads into the heart of North Beach. **Vesuvio** (**9**; p948) is an old Beat bar, and next door, **City Lights Bookstore** (**10**; p932) is still owned by poet Lawrence Ferlinghetti, who opened the store in 1953. A publisher, as well as a bookseller, City Lights remains a vital and passionate San Francisco countercultural institution.

The beautiful **National Shrine of St Francis of Assisi** (**11**; 610 Vallejo St) is one of California's first churches (free concerts 4pm Sunday).

Make sure to rejuvenate with a cappuccino and a cannoli at the truly wonderful **Stella Pastry** (**12**; ☎ 415-986-2914; 446 Columbus Ave; pastries $2-5).

Inside the US Bank is the tiny and free **Museum of North Beach** (**13**; 1435 Stockton St; 9am-5pm Mon-Fri, 9am-1pm Sat), with an eclectic mix of historic photos.

Washington Sq is anchored by the ornate 1924 **Saints Peter & Paul Church** (**14**; 666 Filbert St). From here, head east up Filbert St, which gets progressively steeper until you reach the top of Telegraph Hill and **Coit Tower** (**15**; p937). The tower was financed by the eccentric Lillie Hitchcock Coit, who asked that a third of her estate be used to 'add to the beauty of the city I have always loved.' The unparalleled views from the top are your reward for making the climb.

Finally, either return to North Beach or continue east down the precipitous Filbert or Greenwich steps, which are lined with delightful urban gardens. At the bottom, Sansome St and the Embarcadero are flat and easy.

San Francisco Bay Area for Children

Travelers needing childcare can contact **American Child Care** (☎ 415-285-2300; www.americanchildcare.com; 580 California St, Ste 500).

The Bay Area is a great place to be a kid. Let's get started.

Yerba Buena Gardens (p936) This is fun-central for families. In addition to the surrounding cultural fare, there's an outdoor children's playground, an **ice skating rink and bowling alley** (☎ 415-777-3727; www.skatebowl.com), a **historic carousel** (admission $2) and the **Zeum Art & Technology Center** (☎ 415-777-2800; www.zeum.org; 221 4th St; adult $7, child 4-18 $5; 11am-5pm Wed-Sun), where kids can make their own clay-animation and music videos, among other creative activities.

Metreon (p937) This place has movies, a video arcade and restaurants, plus **Where the Wild Things Are** (child $6, under 4 free; 10am-5pm summer, closed Tue-Thu winter), a play space for the seven-and-under set that's as inspired as Maurice Sendak himself.

Exploratorium (p938) All ages will enjoy this large, interactive and rather thought-provoking museum of art, science and human perception.

Golden Gate Park (p940) Here you will find buffaloes, a carousel and a playground, some sports fields and pedal boats on Stow Lake: the possibilities are endless.

San Francisco Zoo (☎ 415-753-7080; www.sfzoo.org; Sloat Blvd at 47th Ave; adult $10, child 3-11 $4, concession $7; 10am-5pm) This above-average city zoo has all your favorites.

Basic Brown Bear Factory (Map pp934-6; ☎ 415-626-0781, 800-554-1910; 444 De Haro; 10am-5pm, noon-5pm Sun) This working teddy bear factory has a short, free, kid-friendly tour, at the end of which you get to stuff your own bear ($12 to $50). A delight for little ones.

826 Valencia (☎ 415-642-5905; www.826valencia.org; store noon-7pm Tue-Sun) Novelist David Eggers' delightful 'pirate shop' is a humorous come-on for his real purpose: providing free and fun writing workshops for kids aged eight to 18. One- to four-session classes range from comics to rock reviews, to how to be a spy.

Precita Eyes Mural Arts Center (☎ 415-285-2287; www.precitaeyes.org; 2981 24th St; store 10am-5pm Mon-Fri, noon-4pm Sat & Sun) Bring your budding urban artist here for an education in real street art and mural painting by experts; the little ones can simply explore. One- to two-hour classes are $8.

Fire Engine Tours (☎ 415-333-7077; www.fireenginetours.com; the Cannery; adult $30, youth 13-17 $25, child 12 & under $15; 1pm Wed-Mon) Tours on a 1955 open-air Mack fire engine leave from the Wharf and go over Golden Gate Bridge. For some, heaven is a big red truck.

MARIN

Bay Area Discovery Museum (p951) Currently expanding, this wonderful interactive 'museum' has an art studio, indoor and outdoor play spaces and a hands-on marine science lab. It's part of Fort Baker.

THE EAST BAY

Tilden Park (☎ 510-562-7275) This park in the Berkeley hills has a historic carousel, pony rides, a children's farm, swimming at Lake Anza, a steam train, hiking trails and picnic areas. Most activities charge a small fee.

Chabot Space & Science Center (☎ 510-336-7300; www.chabotspace.org; 10000 Skyline Blvd; adult $9, child 4-12 $7; 10am-5pm Tue-Sun) Deep in Oakland's Joaquin Miller Park, the futuristic building has exhibits to please young scientists, including great telescopes, a planetarium (open 7pm to 9pm Friday and Saturday) and a truly far-out movie theater.

THE PENINSULA

Paramount's Great America (☎ 408-988-1776; www.pgathrills.com; 1776 Great America Parkway, Santa Clara;

SAN FRANCISCO: WEIRD, WACKY, WONDERFUL

San Francisco's reputation precedes it. 'Baghdad by the Bay' still earns its hedonistic, unconventional stripes every day.

Good Vibrations (Map pp934-6; ☎ 415-345-0400; 1620 Polk St at Sacramento) This women-owned, sex-positive shop is as bright, clean and good-natured as a cable-car ride for nudists. Its humorous antique vibrator 'museum' is almost as fascinating as the displays for sale, which include a Hello Kitty version!

Image Leather (Map pp934-6; ☎ 415-621-7551; 2199 Market St) This Castro shopfront has everything for the hard-core leather fetishist. You can't miss the sign leading to the 'dungeon' – but do you dare? The faint-of-heart can simply buy a leather-clad teddy bear.

Asia SF (Map pp934-6; ☎ 415-255-2742; 201 9th St; mains $10-18; 🕓 dinner nightly) At this lively restaurant, the bawdy, short-skirted, transgender servers, or 'gender illusionists,' lip-synch songs between courses on the spaghetti-strap-thin bar. The inventive Asian-fusion menu can't quite compete with the atmosphere.

Exotic Erotic Ball (☎ 415-567-2255; www.exoticeroticball.com) When you're done window-shopping, slip into your secret fantasy and join the anything-goes crowd at this mid-October event, now over 20 years old.

Golden Gate Park drumming circle The hippie beat lives on at Sharon Meadow, near the park's Haight St entrance, where urban primitives and other assorted Deadheads gather informally on most weekends. BYOD (Bring Your Own Drum).

Jezebel's Joint Microcinema (☎ 415-345-9832; www.jezebelsjointsf.com; 510 Larkin St; admission free; 🕓 8pm Mon-Fri) Grab a cocktail at the bar to properly enjoy this 50-seat 'microcinema.' The very eclectic film series (run by SF Indie Fest) includes everything from Charlie Chaplin and *Re-Animator* to world premieres of independent films.

Galería de la Raza (☎ 415-826-8009; 2857 24th St; www.galeriadelaraza.org; admission free; 🕓 noon-6pm Wed-Sat) This small gallery hosts diverse exhibits of traditional, political and urban Latino art. It's never less than provocative, and has the pulse on Mission district events.

San Francisco Mime Troupe (☎ 415-285-1717; www.sfmt.org; admission free) It's not what you think. This Tony-award-winning theater troupe has perfected its own brand of satirical political musical theater, whereby it wallops all the contemporary hot topics with a big, absurd, commedia dell'arte stick. The traditional opening day is July 4, and free performances continue at outdoor venues at weekends throughout the summer.

Musée Méchanique (☎ 415-346-2000; Pier 45; admission free; 🕓 11am-7pm Mon-Fri, 10am-8pm Sat & Sun) Once located at the Cliff House, this is a sure-fire tourist hit. The collection of over 300 antique 'penny arcade' machines, many saved from SF's historic Playland and old Sutro Baths, includes player pianos, turn-of-the-century zoetropes and fortune-telling gypsies (who now mesmerize you for a quarter).

Bay to Breakers (☎ 415-359-2800; www.baytobreakers.com; race registration $30) Since 1912, this 12km foot race has never failed to bring out San Francisco's adorably strange side, giving ordinary citizens all the excuse they need to don elaborate costumes – or dispense with clothes entirely – and run through the city. The May event draws upwards of 70,000 participants and untold numbers of onlookers.

Grace Cathedral labyrinth (p938) For nondenominational spiritual renewal at the top of San Francisco, walk one of this church's two labyrinths, either the one on the carpet inside or in granite outside.

day pass $44; 🕓 10am-8pm daily Jun-Aug, Sat & Sun spring & fall, closed winter) No kid can resist the ultimate in theme park roller coasters, plus it has Nickelodeon Central. Look for signs off Hwy 101.

Children's Discovery Museum (☎ 408-298-5437; www.cdm.org; 180 Woz Way, San Jose; admission $7; 🕓 10am-5pm Tue-Sat, noon-5pm Sun) This may be as good as it gets for the 10-and-under set: life-size fire engines, water play and tons of hands-on activities.

Technology Museum of Innovation (p955) Make sure you don't forget San Jose's awesome Tech Museum.

Tours

San Francisco's Visitor Information Center (p933) offers an excellent line of self-guided walking-tour leaflets. Other tours include the following:

Chinese Culture Center (☎ 415-986-1822; www.c-c-c.org) Conducts a Chinese Heritage Walk ($15) and a Chinese Culinary Walk and Luncheon ($30).

Cruisin' the Castro (☎ 415-550-8110; adult $40) Tours emphasize gay history and culture, and include brunch.

Haight-Ashbury Tours (☎ 415-863-1621; adult $15; Tue & Sat)

Mission Trail Mural Walk (☎ 415-285-2287; www.precitaeyes.org; adult $10-12; weekends) Takes in dozens of fantastical Mission murals.

Public Library City Guides (☎ 415-557-4266; www.sfcityguides.org) Offers a wide range of free walking tours led by local historians.

Festivals & Events

Chinese New Year Parade (☎ 415-982-3000; www.chineseparade.com) One of the nation's largest, this winds through Chinatown in January or early February. The famous 200ft Golden Dragon ends the parade to the explosions of 600,000 firecrackers.

SF International Film Festival (☎ 415-561-5000; www.sffs.org) The nation's oldest film festival occurs in late April.

SF Gay Pride Month June begins with the Gay & Lesbian Film Festival, and the last Sunday of the month sees the **Lesbian, Gay, Bisexual & Transgender Pride Parade** (☎ 415-864-3733; www.sfpride.org), which makes a spectacle of itself along Market St in front of a million people. The Saturday before is the **Dyke March** (☎ 415-241-8882; www.dykemarch.org).

SF AIDS Walk (☎ 415-615-9255; www.aidswalk.net) This 10km walk, the state's largest AIDS fundraising event, occurs in mid-July.

Halloween (☎ 415-826-1401; www.latinbayarea.com) While this October 31 holiday is tailor-made for San Francisco (costumes and transgressions encouraged!), the famous parties on Castro St and at Civic Center have gotten too big for their own good.

SF Jazz Festival (☎ 415-788-7353; www.sfjazz.org) This renowned two weeks of great jazz begins in late October. Other sponsored events happen year-round.

Also see p939 and p943 for more events.

Sleeping

Foggy summer is the high season in expensive San Francisco; doubles from $100 to $180 are considered 'mid-range'. The **San Francisco Visitor Information Center** (p933) runs a **reservation line** (☎ 888-782-9673; www.sfvisitor.org) or you can book online. At a pinch, Fisherman's Wharf and Lombard St (Hwy 101) are packed with chains and run-of-the-mill motels. The city's hotel tax is 14%.

THE AUTHOR'S CHOICE:

San Remo Hotel (☎ 415-776-8688, 800-352-7366; www.sanremohotel.com; 2237 Mason St; s/d $85/95; P $14) This greenery-festooned jewel at the top of North Beach is one of the city's best deals. The San Remo has unfussy antique decor and an egregiously nice staff, drawing Europeans by the bucket load. Lending libraries crowd rambling hallways, and all rooms use the shared facilities, which are impeccable vintage morsels: claw-foot tubs, heated towel racks, leaded-glass windows and Old World pull-chain toilets.

UNION SQ & CIVIC CENTER — Map pp934–6

Phoenix Motel (☎ 415-776-1380, 800-248-9466; www.thephoenixhotel.com; 601 Eddy St; r from $130; P) This renovated motor court is a Civic Center oasis that takes its rock 'n' roll pretensions seriously, with tropical hues, leopard prints, an arty mosaic-lined pool, Pop Tarts for breakfast (included in rates) and on-call stylists.

Hotel Triton (☎ 415-394-0500, 800-433-6611; www.hotel-tritonsf.com; 342 Grant Ave; r $160-190; P $30) This funky designer hotel celebrates its cheeky sense of humor: from mod upholstered headboards, crushed velvet spreads and blown-glass chandeliers to feather-boa rentals and a rubber-duck mascot.

Halcyon Hotel (☎ 415-929-8033, 800-627-2396; www.halcyonsf.com; 649 Jones St; d nightly/weekly from $85/550) These 25 crisp little efficiencies (with microwaves and wet bars) retain attractive touches of the 1912 building, like exposed brick and claw-foot tubs. No elevator (four floors) might be an issue.

Hotel Bijou (☎ 415-771-1200, 800-771-1022; www.hotelbijou.com; 111 Mason St; r $110; P $20) Dedicated to movies, Hotel Bijou has a pleasing but not lavish personality. Black-and-white photos of San Francisco's historic movie houses are a nice touch, as could be the extras casting hotline. Continental breakfast is included.

Hotel Monaco (☎ 415-292-0100, 800-214-4220; www.monaco-sf.com; 501 Geary St; r from $230; P $35) Oversized, overstuffed, over-the-top: Hotel Monaco overwhelms with plush extravagance. Its Grand Cafe restaurant and bar downstairs are also highly recommended.

Maxwell Hotel (☎ 415-986-2000, 888-734-6299; www.maxwellhotel.com; 386 Geary St; r $155-165; P $24) The 1908 building has art deco stylings and paintings to inspire theatrical musings. Rooms are attractive, and the location can't be beat.

Mosser (☎ 415-986-4400, 800-227-3804; www.themosser.com; 54 4th St; r with bath $160-180, without bath $80-90; P $25) The small rooms with shared bath are the best deal: public facilities are sparkling, and the crisp modern decor is the same throughout. Double-paned windows keep out the street noise.

HI San Francisco City Center (☎ 415-474-5721; 685 Ellis St; dm $25, d $66-69; P $11) The city's newest HI hostel is a comfy gem in the rough Tenderloin. Come for the vintage 1920 hotel, and stay for the small four-bed dorms with baths private to each room.

Adelaide Hostel & Hotel (☎ 415-359-1915; www.adelaidehostel.com; 5 Isadora Duncan Lane; dm/d from $20/55;) New owners are refurbishing and expanding this dependable, well-used hostel, adding a new kitchen, lounge, satellite TVs and some rooms with private bath.

Also recommended:

Edwardian San Francisco Hotel (☎ 415-864-1271, 888-864-8070; www.edwardiansfhotel.com; 1668 Market St; r with/without bath $130/90; P $10) Rooms with private bath are best.

Golden Gate Hotel (☎ 415-392-3702, 800-835-1118; www.goldengatehotel.com; 775 Bush St; r with/without bath $130/85; P $15) Cozy Old World ambience, and good romance-to-dollar ratio.

Sheehan Hotel (☎ 415-775-6500, 800-848-1529; www.sheehanhotel.com; 620 Sutter St; r from $110;) Scuffed but roomy and the city's largest hotel pool.

CHINATOWN & NORTH BEACH — Map pp934–6

Hotel Bohème (☎ 415-433-9111; www.hotelboheme.com; 444 Columbus Ave; r $165-175; P $12) Iron bed frames, gauzy netting and ceiling lights covered by Oriental paper umbrellas create a moody atmosphere that lovingly recalls the Beat era – minus the cigarette smoke, of course.

Pacific Tradewinds Guest House (☎ 415-433-7970; 680 Sacramento St; dm $18-24) The city's smallest hostel (32 beds) is also its most intimate and friendly. Travel-savvy staff cater to Europeans. Convenient to public transport.

Astoria Hotel (☎ 415-434-8889, 800-666-6696; 510 Bush St; s/d $63/75; P $20) The great location next to Chinatown Gate can be noisy. Rooms show wear but are acceptably clean.

FISHERMAN'S WHARF

HI San Francisco Fisherman's Wharf (Map pp934-6; ☎ 415-771-7277; Fort Mason Bldg 240; dm/d $25/74; P) Twelve-bed dorms and large shared facilities lack privacy, but otherwise this top-notch hostel has it all: a bucolic setting in a national park, great public rooms, tons of activities and a café.

SOMA

Globe Hostel (Map pp934-6; ☎ 415-431-0540; 10 Hallam Pl; dm $16-18, d $46;) In the thick of SoMa nightlife, this large, worn hostel attracts a party-happy international crowd. No real kitchen, but baths are private to each dorm room. US citizens need to show a passport to stay.

HAIGHT-ASHBURY

Red Victorian (☎ 415-864-1978; www.redvic.com; 1665 Haight St; r with bath $120-130, without bath $90-110) The Summer of Love is alive and well at owner Sami Sunchild's truly remarkable B&B, which fulfills then transcends every '60s cliché. Each comfortable room is an unruly, inspirational, authentic work of art, and shared facilities are wild. Breakfast is included.

Metro Hotel (Map pp934-6; ☎ 415-861-5364; 319 Divisadero St; d $66-77; P) Plain but clean, this hotel is close to lots of public transit, and its pretty courtyard is relaxing. Avoid street-side rooms.

Archbishop's Mansion (Map pp934-6; ☎ 415-563-7872, 800-543-5820; www.thearchbishopsmansion.com; 1000 Fulton St; r $195-265; P) A memorable stay is guaranteed at this lavish historic mansion on Alamo Sq (north of the Lower Haight), which is full of museum-quality antiques. Splurge on the Presidential Suite ($425) and marvel at the bathroom's seven-head shower. Breakfast and afternoon wine reception included.

CASTRO — Map pp934–6

Willows Inn (☎ 415-431-4770; www.willowssf.com; 710 14th St; r $110-130; P $12) Gay friendly, this relaxed B&B draws an international crowd. Summery bent-willow furniture gives the inn its name. Breakfast and afternoon cocktails included; check for Web specials.

24 Henry (☎ 415-864-5686, 800-900-5686; www.24henry.com; 24 Henry St; r with bath $110, without bath

THE AUTHOR'S CHOICE

San Francisco is a nightmare for 'best of' lists, but here is an attempt at the top five seafood picks:

Aqua (Map pp934-6; ☎ 415-956-9662; 252 California St; mains $28-38; 🕑 dinner nightly, lunch Mon-Fri) By any measure, this is one of San Francisco's premier destinations for dressed-up dining. You'll dream about the smoked salmon terrine and the medallions of rare ahi tuna and fois gras.

Farallon (Map pp934-6; ☎ 415-956-6969; 450 Post St; mains $27-33; 🕑 lunch Tue-Sat, dinner nightly) You gotta love the whole package: exceedingly rich, innovative seafood creations served in Pat Kuleto's underwater fantasia of a dining room. Here, you are the fish tank.

Kabuto (☎ 415-752-5652; 5121 Geary Blvd at 15th Ave; sushi $4-10; 🕑 dinner only, closed Mon) San Francisco is a sushi-lover's town, and few feel the love more than tiny Kabuto. It's exquisite, authentic and always crowded.

McCormick & Kuleto's (☎ 415-929-1730; 900 North Point St; seafood $18-24) There are so many ways to go wrong at the Wharf, but not here. Even locals suffer the tourist hordes for the huge, intriguing menu of fresh fish and arguably the best views of the bay.

R&G Lounge (Map pp934-6; ☎ 415-982-7877; 631 Kearny St; mains $9-13) This above-average, unpretentious Cantonese place makes the list because of one dish: the salt-and-pepper crab ($25). You'll remember this addictive mess long after fancier meals have faded.

$65-85; 💻) Catering to same-sex couples, this tiny, intimate hotel is like having your own city apartment.

THE MISSION

Inn San Francisco (☎ 415-641-0188, 800-359-0913; www.innsf.com; 943 S Van Ness Ave; r $135-195; Ⓟ $12) Serious romantics can nestle into featherbeds at this gorgeous, antique-filled Victorian B&B, which also boasts a generous breakfast and gracious staff. The quiet garden includes an outdoor hot tub. Consider splurging on a deluxe room ($215-265).

Eating

The dot-com revolution has sputtered, and the papers say excess is out, but you'll hardly notice: San Francisco's culinary grande dames remain as elegant and expensive as ever, and no economic downturn can blunt the city's real strength, its smorgasbord of international cuisines. You'll find ethereal Asian, Latin American, Italian and French cooking – all cross-pollinated with the fresh approach of California cuisine.

UNION SQ & THE FINANCIAL DISTRICT Map pp934–6

The heart of downtown is a mix of the mediocre and the sublime. Tiny Belden St, between Pine and Bush Sts, is lined with smart bistros with outdoor seating; it's a good destination for lunch or dinner.

Jeanty at Jack's (☎ 415-693-0941; 615 Sacramento St; mains $18-28) Acclaimed Yountville chef Philippe Jeanty has resurrected the gorgeous, historic Jack's bistro, serving the same traditional French fare, such as exquisite steak frites, cassoulet and a divine tomato soup in a puff pastry.

Kokkari (☎ 415-981-0983; 200 Jackson St; mains $19-23; 🕑 closed Sun) California cuisine meets the Mediterranean: Kokkari's menu of updated Greek classics is popular with the expense-account set. Standing lamps and cushioned chairs make for a cozy experience.

Yank Sing (☎ 415-957-9300; 101 Spear St; dishes $10-15; ☎ lunch daily) In the Rincon Center, Yank Sing serves maybe the city's best dim sum in a more formal atmosphere.

For a lunchtime escape from the Union Sq madness, try the French **Café de la Presse** (352 Grant Ave), the stylish **Armani Cafe** (1 Grant Ave) or the regal **Pied Piper Bar** (Market & New Montgomery Sts) in the Palace Hotel.

CIVIC CENTER Map pp934–6

Zuni Café (☎ 415-552-2522; 1658 Market St; mains $11-26) This casually chic city institution is a perfect slice of San Francisco dining – rustic gourmet food, trendy cocktails and top-notch people-watching.

California Culinary Academy (☎ 415-292-8229; 625 Polk St; set-price lunch $14-20, dinner $20-36; 🕑 closed Sat-Mon) Place yourself in the hands of tomorrow's great chefs. Don't miss Friday's 'grand buffet.'

CHINATOWN **Map pp934–6**

House of Nanking (☎ 415-421-1429; 919 Kearny St; meals $4-8) It's cramped, crowded, rushed and sometimes rude, but all is forgotten and forgiven once the plates hit the table.

Lucky Creation (☎ 854 Washington St; meals $5-7) This unpretentious, simple Buddhist vegetarian restaurant is a star in the heart of Chinatown.

NORTH BEACH **Map pp934–6**

L'Osteria del Forno (☎ 415-982-1124; 519 Columbus Ave; mains $11-17; closed Tue) The place and menu are small, but you can't miss with the fresh, handmade raviolis and pizzas.

Caffè Macaroni (☎ 415-956-9737; 59 Columbus Ave; mains $10-15; dinner only, closed Sun & Mon) It's not atmospheric, but it's very Italian, and its sister restaurant across the street serves lunch.

Helmund (☎ 415-362-0641; 430 Broadway; mains $11-15; dinner only) Delicious Afghan food is served by a gracious staff at this old favorite – try the lamb and the aromatic pumpkin dishes.

Also recommended:

Cafe Niebaum-Coppola (☎ 415-291-1700; 916 Kearny St; pizza & pasta $8-15; closed Mon) As theatrical as the famous owner.

Golden Boy Pizza (☎ 415-982-9738; 542 Green St; pizza $22) Too hip, but oh, the pizza!

Mama's (☎ 415-362-6421; 1701 Stockton St; omelets $7-10; 8am-3pm Tue-Sun) Legendary brunch spot.

FISHERMAN'S WHARF

It's easy enough to troll the takeout stalls for cheap chowder and fresh crab. The older Italian American establishments over the water hold no surprises. Instead, see The Author's Choice for the top five seafood picks, opposite.

Gary Danko (Map pp934-6; ☎ 415-749-2060; 800 North Point St; set-price menu $55-74; dinner nightly) Oddly enough, one of the city's most-heralded restaurants is here. Gary Danko's New French/American cuisine deservedly tops most gourmet dance cards. Discerning palates have been known to weep over the cheese cart, which is a don't-miss event. Service is impeccable without being snooty. It's just one night – why not splurge?

THE MARINA & FORT MASON **Map pp934–6**

Chestnut St is the main drag for the affluent Marina; it's lined with numerous cafés, delis and restaurants.

Isa (☎ 415-567-9588; 3324 Steiner St at Chestnut St; plates $8-15; dinner Mon-Sat) 'Small plates' are all the rage, and the inventive morsels of French cuisine here are prepared by one of the nation's up-and-coming chefs, Luke Sung. Head for the relaxed back patio.

Greens (☎ 415-771-6222; Fort Mason, Bldg A; mains $12-25) The city's best-known vegetarian restaurant has an elegant dining room, fantastic views and a takeout lunch café.

THE MISSION

The funky Mission is a mecca for international cuisines; most of the action clusters around 16th St and along the Valencia St Corridor.

Slanted Door (Map pp934-6; ☎ 415-861-8032; 584 Valencia St; mains $10-22) This is a perennial favorite for its innovative approach to Vietnamese cuisine. Call for reservations and to make sure they've reopened their expanded Valencia address.

Delfina (Map pp934-6; ☎ 415-552-4055; 3621 18th St; mains $10-19; dinner nightly) While the dining room can be as deafening as the buzz of the hip-arazzi, Delfina's rustic Italian cooking melts all worries and rates with the city's best.

Limón (Map pp934-6; ☎ 415-252-0918; 3316 17th St; mains $10-15; closed Mon) This newcomer serves excellent modern renditions of Peruvian classics like *ceviche* and *lomo saltado*.

Ti Couz (Map pp934-6; ☎ 415-252-7373; 3108 16th St; crepes $4-8) The sweet and savory crepes make this a delicious trip to Brittany.

Hunting the perfect Mexican burrito is a San Francisco pastime; start yours at one of the following:

La Cumbre (Map pp934-6; ☎ 415-863-8205; 515 Valencia St; burritos $4-6)

La Taquería (☎ 415-285-7117; 2889 Mission St at 25th; burritos $4-6) Where nirvana is often found.

Pancho Villa Taquería (Map pp934-6; ☎ 415-864-8840; 3071 16th St; burritos $4-6)

THE CASTRO **Map pp934–6**

The Castro has several round-the-clock diners.

Cafe Flore (☎ 415-621-8579; 2298 Market St at Noe; dishes $10-13) This relaxed café, aka 'Cafe Hairdo,' is a classic Castro meeting place where the food is second to the moving scenery.

Cafe Cuvée (☎ 415-621-7488; 2073 Market St; mains $16-19; dinner Tue-Sat, brunch Sat & Sun) The owner/chef of this tiny, family-style bistro infuses each dish with love and creativity. Brunch is a highlight.

THE HAIGHT

Thep Phanom (Map pp934-6; ☎ 415-431-2526; 400 Waller St; mains $9-12; ⌚ dinner nightly) This dependable, atmospheric Lower Haight favorite serves some of San Francisco's best Thai food – focus on the specials.

Cha Cha Cha (☎ 415-386-5758; 1801 Haight St; tapas $4.50-6.50) At night, waits are long because they don't take reservations, but for pure voodoo kitsch it's hard to beat. The Caribbean-influenced tapas are even pretty good.

THE RICHMOND

Straits Cafe (☎ 415-668-1783; 3300 Geary Blvd at Parker Ave; mains $10-18) The sweet tropical drinks will put you in the right mood for the interesting Singapore cuisine, which is a mix of Chinese, Thai, Malaysian and Indian.

Aziza (☎ 415-752-2222; 5800 Geary Blvd at 22nd Ave; mains $15-20; ⌚ dinner only, closed Tue) This is that rare Moroccan restaurant where the requisite belly dancer is not meant as a distraction from mediocre food, which here is fresh and wonderful.

Drinking

The Mission, the Haight and North Beach are famous for their bars and pubs.

Buena Vista Café (☎ 415-474-5044; 2765 Hyde St) Start (or end) your night with an Irish coffee. It must be good; they serve 2000 per day.

Vesuvio (☎ 415-362-3370; 255 Columbus Ave) It doesn't just live off its Beat past; Vesuvio is still a popular North Beach bar.

Tosca Cafe (☎ 415-986-9651; 242 Columbus Ave) Politicos and local celebrities gather at this North Beach institution.

Edinburgh Castle (☎ 415-885-4074; 950 Geary St) British beers, single-malt whiskies, the occasional live bagpiper and an upstairs performance space: what's not to like?

Zeitgeist (☎ 415-255-7505; 199 Valencia St) The back beer garden is the in spot for city bikers and punk hipsters.

Lone Star Saloon (☎ 415-863-9999; 1354 Harrison St) Bears, daddies and leathermen sidle up to this gay bar.

Lexington Club (☎ 415-863-2052; 3464 19th St) This is *the* lesbian hangout in the Mission.

Mad Dog in the Fog (☎ 415-626-7279; 530 Haight St) Lower Haight denizens gather here for darts, draft Guinness and hearty pub grub.

Entertainment

Extensive entertainment listings can be found in the city's free weeklies – the *San Francisco Bay Guardian* and *SF Weekly* – and at www.sfarts.com, which also lists free events. For tickets to the theater, big music acts and other shows, call **BASS** (☎ 415-776-1999; www.tickets.com). **TIX Bay Area** (☎ 415-433-7827; www.theatrebayarea.org; ⌚ closed Mon), at Union Sq, also sells half-price tickets to opera, dance and theater events.

NIGHTCLUBS

The Mission and the Castro have tons of action, but don't forget the swanky, Union Sq hotel lounges and their great views.

Harry Denton's Starlight Room (☎ 415-395-8595; 450 Powell St) On the top floor of the Sir Francis Drake Hotel, Harry Denton's has the views and nightly dancing.

Tonga Room (☎ 415-772-5278; California & Mason Sts) In the Fairmont Hotel, this is the swizzle stick for any evening: Polynesian kitsch, tropical drinks, cover bands on a raft and a twice hourly 'monsoon.'

Elbo Room (☎ 415-552-7788; 647 Valencia St) You'll wish for more elbow room yourself at this always-packed Mission spot, whether around the bar, pool tables or upstairs dance floor.

Make-Out Room (☎ 415-647-2888; 3225 22nd St) A lesson in Mission hip, this casually cool place features alternative music most nights.

El Rio (☎ 415-282-3325; 3158 Mission St at Cesar Chavez) World beat and salsa get their due at this diverse Mission club with an outdoor patio.

Café (☎ 415-861-3846; 2367 Market St) This lively, multifaceted Castro club draws a mixed gay and lesbian crowd onto its dance floor and large street-view deck.

Club Deluxe (☎ 415-552-6949; 1511 Haight St) The crowd dresses the part at this retro Haight spot, which spins the appropriate swing and big-band tunes.

LIVE MUSIC

SoMa has the greatest concentration of live music and dance clubs.

Slim's (☎ 415-621-3330; 333 11th St) Get along here for sometimes-edgy rock and R & B artists.

Paradise Lounge (☎ 415-861-6906; 11th & Folsom Sts) It has three stages and two floors, so something's always on, from punk to poetry.

Bottom of the Hill (☎ 415-621-4455; 1233 17th St) It's worth the trek to this small, jazzy, folksy, punky spot.

Cafe du Nord (☎ 415-861-5016; 2170 Market St at Sanchez St) This former speakeasy books jazz and salsa, and patrons dance like they know how.

John Lee Hooker's Boom Boom Room (☎ 415-673-8000; 1601 Fillmore St) Live blues and funk occur nightly at this refurbished, historic Fillmore haunt.

DANCE CLUBS

Up & Down Club (☎ 415-626-2388; 1151 Folsom St) Go up for DJ-spun hip hop and down for live jazz.

EndUp (☎ 415-357-0827; 401 6th St) It's one of the city's most popular dance clubs. 'Fag Fridays' start the weekend, which finishes with Sunday's day-long tea dance.

Stud (☎ 415-252-7883; 399 9th St) This legendary gay dance club hosts numerous theme nights for all persuasions.

1015 Folsom (☎ 415-431-1200; 1015 Folsom St) This multilevel club hosts very happening parties.

PERFORMING ARTS

Yerba Buena Center for the Arts (☎ 415-978-2787; www.yerbabuenaarts.org; 700 Howard St) Yerba Buena hosts first-class modern music, dance and theater.

Davies Symphony Hall (☎ 415-864-6000; 201 Van Ness Ave) The San Francisco Symphony performs here from September to May.

War Memorial Opera House (☎ 415-864-3330; 301 Van Ness Ave) Both the acclaimed San Francisco Opera and the **San Francisco Ballet** (☎ 415-865-2000) perform here.

THEATER

San Francisco has numerous small theater companies and one major company, the American Conservatory Theater (ACT).

Geary Theater (☎ 415-749-2228; 415 Geary St) ACT performs primarily here.

Magic Theatre (Map pp934-6; ☎ 415-441-8822; Fort Mason, Bldg D) Made famous by Sam Shepard, this is an important breeding ground for new playwrights.

Club Fugazi (Map pp934-6; ☎ 415-421-4222; 678 Green St) The ribald *Beach Blanket Babylon* plays here – San Francisco's longest-running theater-comedy extravaganza.

Catch touring Broadway productions at:

Curran Theatre (☎ 415-551-2000; 445 Geary St)
Golden Gate Theatre (☎ 415-551-2000; 1 Taylor St)
Orpheum Theatre (☎ 415-551-2000; 1192 Market St)

CINEMA

Castro Theatre (Map pp934-6; ☎ 415-621-6120; 429 Castro St) This grand old-style cinema has the city's best calendar of art, independent and foreign films.

Other independent and just plain weird films can be seen at:

Red Victorian (☎ 415-668-3994; 1727 Haight St)
Roxie Cinema (☎ 415-863-1087; 3117 16th St)
Screening Room (☎ 415-978-2787) At Yerba Buena Center for the Arts (p936).

SPECTATOR SPORTS

Tickets for the local pro teams are difficult but not impossible to come by.

San Francisco 49ers (☎ 415-468-2249; www.sf49ers.com) The city's NFL football team plays at windy **Candlestick Park** (Map p931), off Hwy 101 in the southern part of the city.

San Francisco Giants (Map pp934-6; ☎ 415-467-8000; sanfrancisco.giants.mlb.com) The major-league baseball club plays at the stunning Pacific Bell Park, along the Embarcadero near downtown.

Shopping

Besides eating, there's nothing a San Francisco visitor likes more than shopping, and the city does not disappoint.

For major department stores and international designers, head for Union Sq. Other places for hip clothing boutiques include Union and Chestnut Sts in the Marina and Fillmore St north of Geary Blvd. Youth culture and vintage vultures are served in the Haight and the Mission. Polk St north of Broadway is a fun, eclectic shopping destination. And only New York has a better range of bookstores and vinyl record shops; they're everywhere.

Getting There & Away

AIR

San Francisco International Airport (SFO; ☎ 650-821-8211; www.flysfo.com) is situated 14 miles south of downtown off Hwy 101. Most domestic and international carriers fly in and out of SFO. Regular flights include New York (about $350 round trip), Los Angeles ($150) and Seattle ($200). SFO's new AirTrain, an automated people mover, connects the terminals, parking garages, rental car center and BART station.

BUS

The **Transbay Terminal** (425 Mission St), at 1st St in SoMa, is the city's major bus station. If you're heading out to neighboring communities, you can take **AC Transit** (☎ 510-817-1717; www.actransit.org) buses to the East Bay, **Golden Gate Transit** (☎ 415-923-2000; www.goldengate.org) buses north into Marin and Sonoma Counties, and **SamTrans** (☎ 800-660-4287; www.samtrans.com) buses south to Palo Alto and along the Pacific Coast.

Greyhound (☎ 415-495-1569, 800-229-9424; www.greyhound.com) has several buses daily to Los Angeles ($35 to $42, from eight hours), Lake Tahoe ($45 to $70 round trip, from five hours) and other destinations. Buses leave from the Transbay Terminal.

TRAIN

CalTrain (☎ 800-660-4287; www.caltrain.com) operates down the Peninsula. From the depot at 4th and Townsend Sts in San Francisco, it links to Millbrae (connecting to BART and SFO, 30 minutes), Palo Alto (one hour) and San Jose (1½ hours). **Amtrak** (☎ 800-872-7245; www.amtrakcalifornia.com) runs free shuttle buses to San Francisco's Ferry Building and CalTrain station from its terminals in Emeryville and Oakland's Jack London Sq. Trains arriving from the north connect with the bus at Emeryville; those from the south connect with the bus at Oakland.

Getting Around

Operated by the Metropolitan Transportation Commission, www.transitinfo.org is an excellent resource, covering transit options for the entire nine-county Bay Area. You can also call ☎ 511, an automated Bay Area transit information service.

TO/FROM THE AIRPORT

In 2003 **BART** (Bay Area Rapid Transit; ☎ 510-465-2278; www.bart.gov) opened its long-awaited SFO extension, which connects directly to downtown San Francisco ($4.70). Or, take **SamTrans** (☎ 800-660-4287) bus No KX ($3.50), which takes about half an hour to reach San Francisco's Transbay Terminal.

The **SFO Airporter** (☎ 415-246-8942; adult $12.50) bus departs from the baggage claim areas and stops at major hotels. Door-to-door shuttles typically cost around $14 to $17; try **SuperShuttle** (☎ 415-558-8500) or **Lorrie's** (☎ 415-334-9000).

Taxis to downtown San Francisco cost $35 to $45.

BOAT

Blue & Gold Ferries (Map pp934-6; ☎ information 415-773-1188, sales 415-705-5555; www.blueandgoldfleet.com) runs the Alameda–Oakland ferry from Pier 41 and the Ferry Building. It also serves Alcatraz Island. **Golden Gate Ferry** (☎ 415-923-2000; www.goldengate.org) has regular service from the Ferry Building to Larkspur and Sausalito in Marin County.

CAR & MOTORCYCLE

Avoid driving a car in San Francisco: street parking is notoriously competitive, tickets expensive and the hills daunting. Between buses, cable cars and BART, you can get around the city comprehensively and relatively easily.

However, convenient downtown parking lots are at the Embarcadero Center, at 5th and Mission Sts and at Sutter and Stockton Sts.

National car rental agencies have 24-hour offices at the airport and regular offices downtown. See p1121 for toll-free contact information.

PUBLIC TRANSPORTATION

San Francisco's **Municipal Transit Agency** (Muni; ☎ 415-673-6864; www.sfmuni.com) operates comprehensive bus and streetcar lines and three cable car lines; two cable car lines leave from Powell and Market Sts, and one leaves from California and Markets Sts. A detailed Muni Street & Transit Map ($2) is available at **San Francisco's Visitor Information Center** (p933). The general fare for buses or streetcars is $1.25; cable car fare is $3. A Muni Passport, available in one-day ($9), three-day ($15) or seven-day ($20) versions, allows unlimited travel on all Muni transport, including cable cars; it's sold at **San Francisco's Visitor Information Center** (p933) and at the TIX Bay Area kiosk at Union Sq.

The **Bay Area Rapid Transit system** (BART; ☎ 415-989-2278; www.bart.gov) is the commuter train system linking San Francisco with the

East Bay. In the city, BART runs beneath Market St, down Mission St and south to SFO and Millbrae, where it connects with CalTrain. Fares are $1.25 to $7. Most ticket machines won't make change, so it's best to have change in hand.

TAXI

Fares run about $2.25 per mile. Some of the major cab companies are:

DeSoto Cab (☎ 415-970-1300)
Veteran's Taxicab (☎ 415-552-1300)
Yellow Cab (☎ 415-626-2345)

MARIN COUNTY

Just across the Golden Gate Bridge, wealthy, laid-back **Marin County** (www.visitmarin.org) is as warm and green as San Francisco is foggy and urban. **Sausalito** (Map p931), the first town you encounter coming from San Francisco, is a pleasant but expensive bayside community; it makes a good destination for bike trips over the bridge (take the ferry back). At the harbor, the **San Francisco Bay-Delta Model** (☎ 415-332-3871; www.baymodel.org; 2100 Bridgeway Blvd; admission free; 9am-4pm Tue-Fri, 10am-5pm Sat & Sun, closed Sun winter) is a very cool, 1.5-acre hydraulic re-creation of the entire bay and delta. A day goes by every 14 minutes.

Occupying a 740-acre island in San Francisco Bay, **Angel Island State Park** (Map p931; ☎ 415-435-1915; www.angelisland.org; 8am-sunset) is a delightful place for walking and biking, and it contains the partially restored, historic Immigration Station (open weekends). **Blue & Gold Ferries** (Map pp934-6; ☎ 415-705-5555; adult round trip $12) departs daily from Pier 41 at Fisherman's Wharf (weekends only off-season).

Marin Headlands

These hilly, windswept headlands are interlaced with prime hiking trails and offer spectacular views of San Francisco. To reach the **visitors center** (☎ 415-331-1540; 9:30am-4:30pm), take the Alexander Ave exit from the Golden Gate Bridge, go past Fort Baker and head west on Conzelman Rd. Attractions include the Point Bonita lighthouse, a mammal center and the Cold War–era Nike missile site, plus there's free walk-in camping. At Fort Baker is the **Bay Area Discovery Museum** (☎ 415-487-4398; www.baykidsmuseum.org; 557 McReynolds Rd, Sausalito; admission $7; 9am-4pm Tue-Fri, 10am-5pm Sat & Sun).

Near the visitors center, the **HI Marin Headlands Hostel** (Map p931; ☎ 415-331-2777, 800-909-4776; dm/r $18/55; P) occupies two historic 1907 buildings. The private rooms in the commanding officer's house feel like hosteling in name only.

Mt Tamalpais State Park

Majestic 2571ft Mt Tamalpais, or Mt Tam, has breathtaking views of the ocean, bay and hills rolling into the distance. **Mt Tamalpais State Park** (Map p931; ☎ 415-388-2070; per car $4) was formed in 1930 and encompasses 6300 acres of wilderness plus over 200 miles of hiking and biking trails. Panoramic Hwy climbs from the quiet town of Mill Valley through the park to Stinson Beach. **Park headquarters** are at **Pantoll Station** (801 Panoramic Hwy; campsites $12), where there are trailheads and a first-come, first-served campground. Steep Ravine Trail follows a wooded creek to the coast (about 2 miles each way), where there are six magnificent **campsites** (reservations ☎ 800-444-7275).

Muir Woods National Monument

The slopes of Mt Tam were once carpeted with mighty redwoods. The only surviving remnant is 550-acre **Muir Woods** (☎ 415-388-2595; per car $3), a national monument since 1908, which was named after Sierra Club founder John Muir. The easy 1-mile Main Trail Loop leads past the splendor of the 1000-year-old trees at Cathedral Grove and returns via Bohemian Grove. Muir Woods is 12 miles north of the Golden Gate Bridge via Hwy 101 (take the Hwy 1 exit and follow the signs). Arrive early or stay late to avoid the crowds. There's a ranger station, but no camping or picnicking.

In the town of Muir Beach on Hwy 1, the **Pelican Inn** (☎ 415-383-6000; www.pelicaninn.com; 10 Pacific Way; r $200-240, meals $11-19) is an Old English–style country inn that makes a nice stop for a hearty British meal and a pint; the overpriced rooms are nevertheless very popular.

Point Reyes National Seashore

The triangle-shaped peninsula of **Point Reyes National Seashore** (Map p931) comprises 110 sq miles of windswept beaches, lagoons and forested cliffs. The westernmost point of the peninsula, Point Reyes Headlands, is crowned by the **Point Reyes Lighthouse**, the best spot in

THE AUTHOR'S CHOICE

Manka's Inverness Lodge (☎ 415-669-1034; www.mankas.com; r $185-465, extra $50 Fri & Sat) This place, tucked in the hills off Sir Francis Drake Blvd north of Inverness (look for signs), could only exist in Marin: it is a once-ratty 1917 hunting lodge that has been painstakingly refashioned into a wry, artful dream. Its now-sumptuous cabins are a memorable indulgence, but owner Margaret Grade's true love is food. A friend and disciple of Alice Waters, Grade gets nearly all of her ingredients from the Point Reyes area, a commitment that requires 50 or so local producers. What arrives on the plate is never less than exquisite. Five-or-more-course **dinner** (set-price meal per person $58-88; 7pm Thu-Sat, 4pm Sun) is available and lodge guests have the option of **breakfast** ($12-17).

the Bay Area for onshore whale-watching, while the peninsula's northern tip is home to a herd of tule elk. The **Bear Valley Visitors Center** (☎ 415-464-5100) is the park headquarters and has trail maps and park displays. Point Reyes has four hike-in **campsites** (☎ reservations 415-663-8054; campsites $12), two near the beach.

The **West Marin chamber of commerce** (☎ 415-663-9232; www.pointreyes.org) can lead you to one of the numerous cozy inns and cottages in the area. The economy-minded can head for the simple **HI Point Reyes Hostel** (☎ 415-663-8811; dm $14), off Limantour Rd, 8 miles from the Bear Valley Visitors Center. It offers a solid roof over 16-bed dorms in an idyllic location. Nearby, Point Reyes Station is a pleasant small town for a meal or picnic supplies.

OAKLAND

Oakland is a city of remarkable racial and economic diversity that in recent years has been refurbishing and polishing its downtown area. Parts of the nation's fifth-busiest port still suffer from urban decay, but the city and its rich history make for pleasant exploring.

For maps and self-guided walking tours, head to the **Oakland Convention and Visitors Bureau** (☎ 510-839-9000; www.oaklandcvb.com; 475 14th St, ste 120; 8:30am-5pm Mon-Fri); it is part of the pedestrianized City Center, which also contains the 12th St BART station and the 1914 **City Hall**, at 14th and Washington Sts.

A few blocks south, along 9th St, Old Oakland's **Victorian Row** has prime examples of architecture from the 1860s. Oakland's **Chinatown**, a less touristy version of the one in San Francisco, is east of Broadway between Franklin and Webster Sts. The 1931 **Paramount Theatre** (☎ 510-465-6400; www.paramounttheatre.com; 2025 Broadway at 21st St) is a gorgeous art deco movie theater that screens a variety of films and hosts performances by the Oakland Ballet and Oakland East Bay Symphony.

Oakland's premier museum is the state-focused **Oakland Museum of California** (☎ 510-238-2200; www.museumca.org; 1000 Oak St at 10th St; adult $6, child 6-17 $4; 10am-5pm Wed-Sat, noon-5pm Sun). The entirety of California history, culture, ecology and art are encapsulated in three floors of first-rate exhibits.

The **African American Museum and Library** (☎ 510-637-0198; www.aamlo.com; 659 14th St; noon-5:30pm Tue-Sat) has a free gallery with changing exhibits on the African-American experience in northern California. Its extensive archives, including oral histories, are available by appointment.

The waterfront **Jack London Sq** (Map p931), at the south end of Broadway, is a low-key tourist zone filled with restaurants and shops. The square is named for local hero Jack London (1876–1916), who supposedly wrote portions of the *Sea Wolf* and *Call of the Wild* in the tiny 1880 watering hole **Heinhold's First & Last Chance Saloon** (☎ 510-839-6761; 56 Jack London Sq). This National Literary Landmark is open daily for inspirational drinking.

Oakland's visual centerpiece is **Lake Merritt**, which in the late 19th century was lined with fine homes; today, however, there is just one survivor, the **Camron-Stanford House** (☎ 510-444-1876; 1418 Lakeside Dr; adult $4, child 12-18 $2; 11am-4pm Wed, 1-5pm Sun), with four meticulously restored rooms.

Nicely situated in Old Oakland, the **Washington Inn** (☎ 510-452-1776; www.thewashingtoninn.com; 495 10th St; r from $110) is attractive and charming.

Quality, inexpensive Asian restaurants abound. Try the *pho* soup at the Vietnamese **Pho Hoa Lao II** (☎ 510-763-8296; 333 10th St; meals $5), or opt for a broader Vietnamese menu at the more refined **Le Cheval** (☎ 510-763-8495; 1007 Clay St; meals $7-10). **Battambang** (☎ 510-839-8815; 850 Broadway; meals $5-9) is a less-hectic choice for

Cambodian. Also downtown, **Pacific Coast Brewing Co** (☎ 510-836-2739; 906 Washington; meals $8-10) is a fun place for American pub grub or pizza and a microbrew.

For a small offering of Oakland's once-thriving blues scene, visit gritty **Eli's Mile High Club** (☎ 510-655-6661; 3629 Martin Luther King Jr Way); a taxi is safest late at night. At the other end of the spectrum, elegant and intimate **Yoshi's** (☎ 510-238-9200; www.yoshis.com; 510 Embarcadero West; meals $15-20), at Jack London Sq, is one of the country's top jazz clubs, and it has an attached Japanese restaurant.

For comprehensive Bay Area transit information, visit www.transitinfo.org. From **Oakland International Airport** (Map p931; ☎ 510-563-2984), shuttle buses ($2) to the Coliseum BART station run about every 15 minutes until midnight daily. **SuperShuttle** (☎ 415-558-8500, 800-258-3826) offers door-to-door service to Oakland ($18) and San Francisco ($25). A taxi to downtown Oakland costs about $25, to San Francisco costs about $50.

Oakland's **Greyhound station** (☎ 800-229-9424; 2103 San Pablo Ave) is rather seedy. **AC Transit** (☎ 510-817-1717; www.actransit.org) operates local buses between San Francisco and Oakland ($3); bus No O is the most convenient. There is an **Amtrak station** (☎ 800-872-7245) at Jack London Sq. From San Francisco, take BART to the 12th St station in downtown Oakland ($2.35). Far more pleasant is the **Alameda-Oakland ferry** (☎ 510-522-3300), which operates from two locations in San Francisco (Pier 39 and the Ferry Building) to Jack London Sq up to 12 times daily ($5 one way).

BERKELEY

The entire Bay Area is a liberal enclave, but its radical core is **Berkeley** (www.visitberkeley.com). Though it has mellowed since the 1960s heyday of the student-led free speech movement and anti–Vietnam War protests, it remains an iconoclastic fiefdom. Its unofficial moniker, the 'People's Republic of Berkeley,' was originally meant as a red-baiting disparagement but has instead been embraced as a rallying cry.

Founded in 1868, the **University of California at Berkeley** (Map p931) – 'Cal' to students and locals – is one of the country's top universities and home to 33,000 ethnically diverse, politically conscious students. The university's **Visitor Services center** (☎ 510-642-5215; www.berkeley.edu; 101 University Hall, 2200 University Ave at Oxford St; 🕓 8:30am-4:30pm Mon-Fri) has information and leads free **tours** (🕓 10am Mon-Sat, 1pm Sun) of the pretty campus. Cal's landmark is the 1914 Sather Tower (also called the 'Campanile'), which was modeled on St Mark's Campanile in Venice; **rides** (adult $2) to the top are available. The Bancroft Library displays the surprisingly small gold nugget that started the California gold rush in 1848.

Other campus sights include the **Berkeley Art Museum** (☎ 510-642-0808; www.bampfa.berkeley.edu; 2626 Bancroft Way; admission $8; 🕓 11am-7pm Wed-Sun), east of Telegraph Ave. Resembling a concrete bunker, it houses several galleries of Asian and interesting cutting-edge modern art. The museum also houses the highly respected **Pacific Film Archive** (☎ 510-642-1124), which screens little-known independent, avant-garde and international films.

Leading directly to the campus's main south gate, **Telegraph Avenue** is a prime student hangout packed with cafés, cheap eateries, record stores and bookstores – including the enormous and acclaimed **Cody's Books** (☎ 510-845-7852; 2454 Telegraph Ave).

Popular with parents, close to campus and attractively old-fashioned, the 22-room **Bancroft Hotel** (☎ 510-549-1000, 800-549-1002; www.bancrofthotel.com; 2680 Bancroft Way; r $129; Ⓟ $10) is on three floors but has no elevator, while the fancier 140-room **Hotel Durant** (☎ 510-845-8981, 800-238-7268; www.hoteldurant.com; 2600 Durant Ave; r $150-195; Ⓟ $10) offers handicapped facilities and a ground-floor restaurant and bar. Basic and mid-range motels are clustered west of campus along University Ave.

A prime student pick is **Café Intermezzo** (2442 Telegraph Ave; meals $4-6), with huge fresh salads. Meanwhile, the **Gourmet Ghetto**, on Shattuck Ave north of University Ave, is home to many highly regarded restaurants, such as **Cha-am** (☎ 510-848-9664; 1543 Shattuck Ave; meals $6-10), a plant-draped hothouse of Thai food. Nearby is the birthplace of California cuisine, Alice Waters' **Chez Panisse** (☎ 510-548-5525; www.chezpanisse.com; 1517 Shattuck Ave; set-price menu $45-75; 🕓 closed Sun). The formal restaurant downstairs is open only for set-price dinners; the number of courses and price rise as the week progresses. Upstairs, a more relaxed **café** (mains $15-18) serves lunch and dinner. If you're still wondering what all the fuss is about, reserve a table (up to a month ahead).

AC Transit (☎ 510-817-1717) runs local buses in Berkeley as well as between Berkeley/Oakland ($1.50) and San Francisco ($3). From San Francisco, it's a short trip on BART to the Downtown Berkeley station ($2.75), which is four blocks from the main UCB campus gate.

PENINSULA & SOUTH BAY

San Francisco is the tip of a 30-mile-long peninsula sandwiched between the Pacific Ocean and San Francisco Bay. Heading south along Hwy 101 or the more scenic I-280 leads to suburban **Colma**, San Francisco's graveyard ever since cemeteries were banned within the city limits.

Further south, **Filoli** (Map p931; ☎ 650-364-8300; www.filoli.org; adult $10, child 7-12 $1; 10am-3:30pm Tue-Sat, closed Nov–mid-Feb) is a very grand 1915 mansion and country estate, near the small town of Woodside. The house and gardens are sufficiently opulent to warrant the two-hour tours. Exit I-280 at Edgewood, head west to Cañada Rd, then turn right.

Along Hwy 1

Far more scenic than either freeway is narrow, coastal Hwy 1. Just north of Montara, **Gray Whale Cove State Beach** is a popular, unsigned clothing-optional strand.

Close by, the **HI Point Montara Lighthouse Hostel** (Map p931; ☎ 650-728-7177; dm $16-19), on Hwy 1 at 16th St, is a scuffed, clean and very popular hostel with a private beach. Just south, **Moss Beach Distillery** (☎ 650-728-5595; Beach Way & Ocean Blvd) is a former prohibition-era speakeasy with an ocean-view deck.

South of quiet **Half Moon Bay** (Map p931), public beaches are strung like pearls. For a romantic getaway, sink into the featherbeds at **Cypress Inn** (☎ 650-726-6002, 800-832-3224; www.cypressinn.com; 407 Mirada Rd; r from $215-350), at Miramar Beach. Full breakfast and afternoon wine are included.

Tiny **San Gregorio**, 10 miles south at the Hwy 84 junction, is worth a stop for one reason: its general store-café, which maintains a distinctive northern California ambience.

Five miles south, **Pescadero** is a good stop for sandwiches and supplies, and it's home to the locally renowned **Duarte's Tavern** (☎ 650-879-0464) and its famous artichoke soup.

Another 5 miles south, **HI Pigeon Point Lighthouse Hostel** (Map p931; ☎ 650-879-0633; dm $17-20) is one of the busiest hostels in the US. It occupies a quiet, wind-swept coastal perch next to the historic lighthouse.

Año Nuevo State Reserve (☎ 650-879-0227; 8am-sunset, closed Dec 1-14), 5 miles south of Pigeon Point off Hwy 1, is highly recommended for its resident elephant seal colony. During the mating and birthing season (15 December to March), visitors are allowed only on heavily booked guided **tours** (☎ reservations 800-444-4445; per person $4; P $4), otherwise, reservations are not required.

Palo Alto

Palo Alto is the northern edge of Silicon Valley, the epicenter of the country's high-tech industry, and the home to Stanford University. Affluent and conservative, Palo Alto is still a college town at heart. At Moffett Field off Hwy 101, the **NASA-Ames Research Center** (☎ 650-604-6274; admission free; 8am-4:30 Mon-Fri) has a small public exhibit (including a moon rock and prototype spacesuit). **Tours** (☎ 650-604-6497) are in transition and no longer include the world-famous wind tunnels; call for reservations and times.

Stanford University opened in 1891, just two years before founder Leland Stanford's death. The lovely campus was built on the Stanford family homestead and, as a result, is still called 'the farm.' From downtown Palo Alto, University Ave spears straight into the heart of the spacious campus. The **Stanford University Information Booth** (☎ 650-723-2560) is in Memorial Hall, across from Hoover Tower, which you can climb for $2. The **Cantor Arts Center** (☎ 650-723-4177; admission free; 11am-5pm Wed-Sun), on Museum Way, has classical and contemporary art in a gorgeous building.

A few blocks from campus, the **Cardinal Hotel** (☎ 650-323-5101; www.cardinalhotel.com; 235 Hamilton Ave; r with bath $125-145, without bath weekend/midweek from $65/85) offers its guests graciously old-fashioned lodgings Shared facilities are spotless, making the bathless rooms an excellent deal.

University Ave, the main drag, has every café, restaurant and bookstore an Ivy League university town requires.

SAN JOSE

Perpetually in the shadow of its more eccentric neighbors, San Jose suffers a reputation of dull, sprawling conformity, but really, it's not so bad. In fact, as the undisputed 'capital' of Silicon Valley, it has grown astonishingly fast in recent decades and is California's third largest city. Especially if you have kids, San Jose's handful of stellar sites are worth an excursion from San Francisco or even an overnight stop (see also p942).

Downtown San Jose is at the junction of Hwy 87 and I-280. The helpful **visitors center** (☎ 888-726-5673; www.sanjose.org; 150 W San Carlos St; ⏲ 8am-5:30pm Mon-Fri, 11am-5pm Sat & Sun) is inside the convention center.

You don't know the meaning of interactive until you've been to the **Technology Museum of Innovation** (☎ 408-294-8324; www.thetech.org; 201 S Market St; adult $9, child 3-12 $7; ⏲ 10am-5pm, closed Mon winter), maybe the hippest museum on the planet. Exploring inventions and creativity of all kinds, it's like being dunked in a neon-bright, Nickelodeon-inspired pool of Silicon Valley genius. Caution: May induce vertigo in technophobic adults!

The underappreciated **San Jose Museum of Art** (☎ 408-294-2787; www.sanjosemuseumofart.org; 110 S Market St; admission free; ⏲ 11am-5pm Tue-Sun, until 10pm Fri) has a small collection focused on Bay Area and West Coast modern artists.

An anachronism in this high-tech town, the **Rosicrucian Egyptian Museum** (☎ 408-947-3636; www.egyptianmuseum.org; Naglee & Park Aves; adult $9, child 5-10 $5; ⏲ 10am-5pm Tue-Fri, 11am-6pm Sat & Sun) has the largest collection of Egyptian artifacts on display west of the Mississippi River. Highlights include an authentic, life-size re-creation of an Egyptian tomb and several 3000-year-old mummies.

History Park (☎ 408-287-2290; www.historysj.org; 1650 Senter Rd; adult $6, child 6-17 $4 Sat & Sun, admission free Tue-Fri; ⏲ noon-5pm Tue-Sun), in Kelley Park, is a notable collection of 27 historic buildings gathered from all over San Jose. Docents staff buildings and exhibits at weekends; otherwise, you just look from the outside.

Just west of downtown San Jose, the **Arena Hotel** (☎ 408-294-6500, 800-954-6835; 817 The Alameda; r weekend/midweek $80/90; P 💻 ✠) offers spacious, amenity-laden rooms, every bath is a Jacuzzi, and a buffet breakfast and dinner are included. It's a great deal.

Agenda (☎ 408-287-3991; www.agendalounge.com; 399 S 1st St; mains $12-20; ⏲ restaurant closed Sun & Mon) is a popular three-level spot: the first floor is a nice restaurant, the top floor is a lounge and bar with live music, and the cellar is a dance club with DJs spinning retro tunes.

Waves Smokehouse (☎ 408-885-9283; 65 Post St; sandwiches & platters $8-13; ⏲ until 1:30am, closed Sun) is a vintage bar and barbecue place with eclectic music nightly.

NORTHERN CALIFORNIA

The top half of California is markedly different from the bottom half. The Sierra Nevada and the Pacific Coast increase in drama, while the valleys in-between contain one of the nation's breadbaskets, including California's world-famous wine region.

WINE COUNTRY

Blanketed by vineyards, warmed by the sun, dotted with chateaus and gourmet restaurants: Wine Country simply puts a smile on your face. According to local lore, Hungarian Count Agoston Haraszthy started it all in 1857 when he purchased a defunct vineyard in Sonoma. The area is now home to well over 300 wineries, most in parallel Sonoma and Napa Valleys, that account for nearly 10% of California sales, which in turn account for over 50% of the US wine market. But it's not volume that sets Wine Country apart; it's quality.

Wine Country is an easy day trip from San Francisco, but an overnight stay is recommended; the heavy afternoon traffic is a buzz-kill. The days when tastings were free and you invariably met vintners are just about over; most tastings include a 'flight' of several varieties and cost from $3 to $10. Many wineries scale down their tours and tastings in winter; call ahead. A deluxe way to explore the Wine Country is by rail on the **Napa Valley Wine Train** (☎ 707-253-2111, 800-427-4124; www.winetrain.com; lunch $70-105, dinner $80-110), which offers three-hour lunch and dinner trips daily.

Napa Valley

There are over 200 wineries crowding the 30-mile-long Napa Valley along two main arteries: busy St Helena Hwy (Hwy 29) and the more scenic Silverado Trail, a mile or two east. Napa is known for cabernet sauvignon; search out the boutique wineries for the best. Most wineries are open for tours and tastings 10am to 4pm or 5pm daily. The following sites and wineries are listed south to north.

Napa, at the valley's southern end, is itself decidedly plain. Follow signs for the **Napa Valley Visitors Bureau** (☎ 707-226-7459;

www.napavalley.com; 1310 Napa Town Center; 9am-5pm), which has oodles of brochures, lodging updates and the informative free tabloid *Inside Napa Valley*, which contains a comprehensive winery map and guide.

Near the Napa wine train station, **Copia** (707-259-1600; www.copia.org; 500 1st St; adult $13, child 6-12 $8; 10am-5pm Wed-Mon) is a new cultural center that brings together all that is Wine Country in one smart, heady package. From the fun interactive exhibits about America's culinary contributions to symposiums on wine, to the fine art galleries, to the first-rate restaurant, to the wine-tasting station, to the movie and concert nights: a visit here will leave you surfeit and satisfied.

Wine and art also merge at the classy **Hess Collection** (707-255-1144; 4411 Redwood Rd), several miles west of Napa. Good modern works by Francis Bacon, Louis Soutter and others are spread over three floors, with the tasting room downstairs.

In Yountville, **Domaine Chandon** (707-944-2280), west off Hwy 29, makes excellent 'sparkling wines' (it ain't champagne unless it's grown in Champagne, France) and has an exquisite restaurant.

On the St Helena Hwy in Oakville, **Robert Mondavi** (707-226-1335, 888-766-6328; tour $10) is a big commercial winery with a good tour about the wine-making process.

In Rutherford the modern **St Supéry** (707-963-4507, 800-942-0809; 8440 St Helena Hwy) has very informative and free exhibits also illustrating the wine-making process.

Across the highway, the **Niebaum-Coppola Winery** (707-968-1100; tour $20) is owned by filmmaker Francis Ford Coppola. The tour focuses on the dramatic and imposing 1887 Inglenook chateau, while a free movie 'museum' includes such memorabilia as a Tucker car and Coppola's *Godfather* Oscars.

St Helena is a charming historic town. Just north of it is **Beringer** (707-963-7115; 2000 Main St), with an atmospheric manse and an interesting tour.

Culinary Institute of America (707-967-2320; www.ciachef.edu/greystone; 2555 Main St; cooking demonstration $10; 10am-5pm), a graduate school for chefs, occupies the Christian Brothers historic 1889 chateau. Interesting winery exhibits include a collection of 1500 corkscrews, and twice-daily cooking demonstrations are like being on a TV cooking show. The attached **Greystone restaurant** (707-967-1010; mains $15-25) is the well-regarded flagship of *Wine Spectator* magazine.

Near Calistoga, architecture, art and wine harmonize at the Michael Graves-designed **Clos Pegase** (707-942-4981; 1060 Dunaweal Lane), which is awash in modern sculpture.

Calistoga is the best town for lingering, particularly in one of its famous **thermal spas**. **Indian Springs** (707-942-4913; 1712 Lincoln Ave) and Golden Haven (opposite) are both well regarded; spa packages last about an hour and start at around $50, not including extras like massages and facials. For the complete northern California, clothing-optional experience, head for **Harbin Hot Springs** (707-987-2477; www.harbin.org; day use midweek/weekend $20/25), 4 miles north of Middletown, which is 12 miles north of Calistoga. There's a vegetarian restaurant and dorms ($35/50 midweek/weekends; bring your own linen).

SLEEPING & EATING

Napa has a selection of mid-range **chain hotels** – Discovery Inn, Budget Inn, Travelodge – but otherwise valley lodgings are expensive, particularly at weekends.

Yountville & Oakville

French Laundry (707-944-2380; 6640 Washington St; fixed-price menu $115-135) In Yountville, French Laundry is one of the best restaurants in the entire country, and priced accordingly. Call 60 days in advance at the stroke of 10am, and you might get a table.

Gordon's Cafe and Wine Bar (707-944-8246; 6770 Washington St; sandwiches & salads $5-10; until 3pm) Also in Yountville, Gordon's makes a nice, unpretentious mid-valley lunch stop.

Oakville Grocery (707-944-8802) On Hwy 29 in minuscule Oakville, the lovely Oakville Grocery sells gourmet picnic fixings and deli sandwiches.

Sugarloaf Ridge State Park

The **Sugarloaf Ridge State Park** (707-833-5712, reservations 800-444-7275; campsites $15) North of Kenwood on Adobe Canyon Rd is Sugarloaf Ridge, where you can camp.

Calistoga

Your best bet for sleeping is Calistoga.

Calistoga Inn (707-942-4101; www.calistogainn.com; 1250 Lincoln Ave; r midweek/weekend $75/100) The local institution. All rooms share a bath, and none have TVs or phones, but just amble downstairs to the friendly restaurant and bar, a popular watering hole.

Golden Haven (☎ 707-942-6793; 1713 Lake St; www.goldenhaven.com; r midweek/weekend from $69/85) Very reasonable rooms.

Catahoula (☎ 707-942-2275; 1457 Lincoln Ave; mains $18-25) In Calistoga, Catahoula is upscale Cajun; the gumbo is the real deal and the fat steaks are wood-grilled.

Sonoma Valley

Seventeen-mile-long Sonoma Valley is less commercial than Napa and has far fewer wineries (40 or so), most on or just off Hwy 12.

Sophisticated country living is the rule in **Sonoma**, at the valley's southern end. The **visitors center** (☎ 707-996-1090, 800-576-6662; www.sonomavalley.com; 453 1st St E; 9am-5pm) is on historic Sonoma Plaza, which is surrounded by nice restaurants and shops. The **Sonoma State Historical Park** (☎ 707-938-1519; per person $2; 10am-5pm) includes the nearby 1823 Sonoma Mission, the Sonoma Barracks, the Vallejo home 0.5 miles away and the Petaluma Adobe, 15 miles west near suburban Petaluma, itself a pleasant slice of small-town California.

Down a quiet country road in Sonoma, **Gundlach-Bundschu** (☎ 707-938-5277; 2000 Denmark St) has the feel of a private estate, with its own lake, picnic area and hiking trails.

Sonoma's historic **Buena Vista** (☎ 707-938-1266, 800-926-1266; 18000 Old Winery Rd) is the winery that was purchased by pioneering Hungarian vintner Count Agoston Haraszthy in 1857.

In Glen Ellen, the small, relaxed **Valley of the Moon** (☎ 707-996-6941; 777 Madrone Rd) is far enough off busy Hwy 12 to escape the crowds.

On the road to Jack London State Historic Park, **Benziger** (☎ 707-935-3000, 888-490-2739) is a highly educational winery with do-it-yourself vineyard walks and tractor-driven tours of the whole winery.

In Kenwood, **Chateau St Jean** (☎ 707-833-4134; 8555 Sonoma Hwy) has pleasant grounds for picnicking and bottles top-notch cabernets.

You won't be charmed by sprawling **Santa Rosa**, at the valley's northern end, but it's very convenient and affordable. However, charming is just the word for the new **Charles M Schulz Museum** (☎ 707-579-4452; www.schulzmuseum.org; 2301 Hardies Lane; adult/child $8/5; noon-5:30pm Mon & Wed-Fri, from 10am Sat & Sun), dedicated to Santa Rosa's native son and his enduring creation, Charlie Brown and the Peanuts gang. Warm-hearted exhibits remind you why 'Sparky' was without peer among cartoonists, and the original ice-skating rink is next door.

SLEEPING & EATING

Sonoma

The town of Sonoma is the most comfortable base for exploring the valley.

Sonoma Hotel (☎ 707-996-2996, 800-468-6016; www.sonomahotel.com; 110 W Spain St; r midweek/weekend from $160/195;) Located on Sonoma Plaza, this is an attractive historic hotel. A few smaller rooms are cheaper, and breakfast is included.

El Pueblo Inn (☎ 800-900-8844; www.elpuebloinn.com; 896 W Napa St; r new midweek/weekend $165/185, old $95/155; P) One mile west of downtown Sonoma, El Pueblo has passable older rooms and very nice newer ones. It's a quiet location.

Cafe La Haye (☎ 707-935-5994; 140 E Napa St; mains $14-22; dinner only Tue-Sat, brunch Sun) Attached to an arts center, Cafe La Haye serves big-city gourmet in a small-town atmosphere.

Artisan Bakers (☎ 707-939-1765; 750 W Napa St; sandwiches $5-8) In Sonoma, it's worth tracking down Artisan Bakers, which sells pastries, sandwiches and award-winning breads.

Santa Rosa

If you're conserving your cash, Santa Rosa's Cleveland Ave has several decent chain motels. Also try **Sandman Hotel** (☎ 707-544-8570; 3421 Cleveland Ave; s/d $80/85; P), which is dependably neat and clean

Getting There & Around

Public transportation can get you to the valleys but is not ideal for vineyard hopping. **Greyhound buses** (☎ 800-231-2222) run daily from San Francisco up Napa Valley to Calistoga ($16). **Golden Gate Transit** (☎ 415-923-2000, 707-541-2000) has buses from San Francisco to Sonoma ($6.30), Petaluma and Santa Rosa. **Sonoma County Transit** (☎ 707-576-7433; www.sctransit.com) serves Sonoma Valley.

The Wine Country is about an hour's drive north from San Francisco via Hwy 101 or I-80.

Rent bicycles in Napa at **Napa Bike Tours** (☎ 707-255-3377; bikes full-day $25-30), in Calistoga at **Getaway Adventures** (☎ 707-942-0332)

and in Sonoma at **Sonoma Valley Cyclery** (☎ 707-935-3377).

NORTH COAST

As you head north from San Francisco, California's Pacific edge continues its dramatic aria of lush forests, rocky beaches and fog-shrouded cliffs. The Pacific Coast Hwy (Hwy 1) winds leisurely along the coast, while the Redwood Hwy (Hwy 101) zips less scenically through fertile inland valleys. The two highways rejoin at Leggett, north of which old-growth redwoods predominate.

Bodega Bay to Fort Bragg

Like a panther, this famous stretch of coastline is irresistible to look at but unpredictable and even dangerous – weather is mildest in spring and fall, but cool fog and cold rain can hit anytime. Frigid ocean water and rip tides make swimming a cautious enterprise; surfing is only for the hardy. From November to April, California gray whales migrate down the coast, and whale-watching trips are popular. Overall, this stretch of Hwy 1 can take five hours without stops.

Bodega Bay is a small fishing town; from here, a series of great state beaches extends north to Jenner. Along with its inland sister city, endearing little Bodega, it was a location for Hitchcock's 1963 thriller *The Birds*. **Bodega Bay Sportfishing** (☎ 707-875-3495; adult $25) runs whale-watching trips. **Bodega Bay Surf Shack** (☎ 707-875-3944; www.bodegabaysurf.com; surfboards full-day $13, kayaks 4hr $45) rents surfboards and kayaks.

Jenner is perched on the picturesque coastal hills at the mouth of the Russian River, where there is a resident harbor seal colony; look for them from Hwy 1 turnouts north of town.

The centerpiece of **Fort Ross State Park** (☎ 707-847-3286; per car $4, campsites $10) is a reconstructed 1812 Russian trading post and interesting historical exhibits. It also has first-come, first-served camping.

Salt Point State Park (☎ 707-847-3221; per car $4, campsites $12) has hiking trails, tide pools, two campgrounds and the Gerstle Cove Marine Reserve and the Kruse Rhododendron State Reserve, where pink blooms spot the green, wet woods in springtime.

Gualala (wah-*la*-la), founded in 1858 as a lumber mill, has a breathtaking coastal location. A mile south of town, **Gualala Point Regional Park** (☎ 707-785-2377; campsites $16) has an attractive campground, hiking trails and a windswept beach.

Charming **Point Arena** has interesting old buildings and a fishing pier. A few miles north, the 1908 **Point Arena Lighthouse & Museum** (☎ 707-882-2777; admission $4) offers knockout coastal views and worthwhile tours.

Eight miles north of Elk, **Van Damme State Park** (☎ 707-937-5804; per car $4, campsites $16) has the very popular Fern Canyon Trail, passing through an unusual pygmy forest, and good camping.

Upscale, photogenic **Mendocino** puts the 'Q' in quaint. Perched on a scenic headland perfect for strolling, it's noted for its Cape Cod–style architecture and a plethora of art galleries, fine restaurants and tourist shops. The **visitors center** (☎ 707-937-5397; www.gomendo.com; 🕐 11am-4pm) is in the Ford House on Main St. The **Mendocino Art Center** (☎ 707-937-5818; 45200 Little Lake St; 🕐 10am-5pm) is a hub of artistic efforts.

Fort Bragg is more of a blue-collar town; it has a nice, unpretentious old town section, and food and lodging are cheaper. Fort Bragg's pride and joy is the 1885 **Skunk Train** (☎ 704-964-6371; 800-777-5865; www.skunktrain.com; half-/full-day $39/45; 🕐 some winter closings), with historic engines running east daily to Willits. You can join fishing and whale-watching trips at Noyo Harbor, at the south end of town.

SLEEPING & EATING

The **Bodega Harbor Inn** (☎ 707-875-3594; www.bodegaharborinn.com; r $60-82), on Hwy 1 in Bodega Bay, has plain but affordable cottage-style rooms.

The historic **Gualala Hotel** (☎ 707-884-3441; www.thegualalahotel.com; r with shared/private bath $65/95), on Hwy 1 in Gualala, is getting a sprucing up by new owners. Also in Gualala, **St Orres** (☎ 707-884-3303; www.saintorres.com; r $80-95, cottages from $210) has a gorgeous, Russian-style main hotel (where rooms have shared bath) and secluded cottages. Its gourmet restaurant is highly recommended.

Mendocino is an expensive, if stylish, place to stay. The visitors center website is a good resource. **Sweetwater Spa & Inn** (☎ 800-300-4140; www.sweetwaterspa.com; 44840 Main St; r $80-175) runs over a baker's dozen of attractive lodgings, and rates include use of the spa, which can also be enjoyed on its own.

Independent, unfussy travelers will want to head for the big-hearted **Jug Handle Farm & Nature Center** (☎ 707-964-4630; r/cabins per person $27/35), in Caspar opposite Jug Handle State Reserve. Hostel-like private rooms and cabins share a bath (linens provided, but bring a blanket); the nice farmhouse has a full kitchen. Hiking trails connect to the reserve, and a one-hour stewardship on the farm nets you a $5 discount.

Fort Bragg has a number of nondescript mid-range motels and eateries. A notable exception is the craftsman-style, 1912 **Colonial Inn** (☎ 707-964-1384, 877-964-1384; www.colonialinnfortbragg.com; 533 Fir St; d $90-150), several blocks from busy Hwy 1. Parts of the building are stunning, and the 10 more-plain rooms are spacious. Buffet breakfast is included. Fort Bragg also boasts the **North Coast Brewing Co** (☎ 707-964-3300; 444 N Main St), which serves its award-winning brews in its pub and attached restaurant, and the **Headlands Coffeehouse** (☎ 707-964-1987; 120 Lamel St), where local musicians play.

GETTING THERE & AWAY

The **Mendocino Transit Authority** (MTA; ☎ 800-696-4682) sends bus No 65 every morning from Fort Bragg south to Santa Rosa via Willits and Ukiah ($16, three hours); at Santa Rosa you can catch a San Francisco–bound bus No 80 ($6.30) operated by **Golden Gate Transit** (☎ 415-923-2000). Greyhound and Amtrak do not serve towns along Hwy 1.

Russian River

North of San Francisco, about two hours by car via Hwys 101 and 116, the lower Russian River courses through redwoods, vineyards and a few tiny towns; canoeing the river is popular in summer, when the area is crazy-busy. **Guerneville** is the region's biggest town, with plenty of hotels and restaurants. It's also a popular gay-and-lesbian vacation destination. The local **visitors center** (☎ 707-869-3533; www.russianriver.com; 16209 1st St) has maps and lodging updates.

Korbel Cellars (☎ 707-887-2294; 13250 River Rd), a picturesque 1886 winery noted for its sparkling wines, gives free tours daily.

Armstrong Redwoods State Reserve (☎ 707-869-2015; per car $4, campsites $12), about 2 miles north of Guerneville, has a magnificent stand of old-growth redwood trees. Camping is at nearby Austin Creek.

Nine miles west from Guerneville, tiny, *über*-quaint **Duncans Mills** has kayak rentals and the friendly **Blue Heron** (☎ 707-865-9135; mains $15-20) restaurant.

The **Bohemian Hwy**, south of Guerneville, is a relaxing scenic drive leading to quiet discoveries in **Occidental** and **Freestone**.

Burke's Canoe Trips (☎ 707-887-1222; www.burkescanoetrips.com; 8600 River Rd), 1 mile due north of Forestville, is *the* place to rent do-it-yourself canoes ($42) for lazy Russian River paddles.

Healdsburg to Scotia

Small, quiet **Healdsburg** is centered on a green Spanish-style plaza. The Russian River – and over 60 wineries within a 30-mile radius – attracts more than a million visitors each year to this area. Grab a Wine Country map from the **Healdsburg Visitors Center** (☎ 707-433-6935, 800-648-9922; www.healdsburg.org; 217 Healdsburg Ave; 🕑 9am-5pm Mon-Fri, 10am-2pm Sat & Sun). Taste local vintages at the attractive **Hop Kiln Winery** (☎ 707-433-6491; 6050 Westside Rd).

A detour to **Anderson Valley**, which is studded with vineyards and apple orchards, is far prettier than the equivalent stretch of Hwy 101; take Hwy 128 west to tiny Boonville, then Hwy 253 northeast to Ukiah. In some ways, **Hopland**, 15 miles south of Ukiah on Hwy 101, is the ideal small town to aim for, with historic buildings and a sophisticated country feel. For instance, on the edge of town is the **Real Goods Solar Living Center** (☎ 707-744-2017; www.solarliving.org; 13771 S Hwy 101; admission free; 🕑 10am-6pm), where the very attractive, inviting grounds are actually a rather compelling 12-acre demonstration site for permaculture, environmentally friendly building methods and alternative energy sources. The **Fetzer winery** (☎ 800-846-8637; 13601 East Side Rd) is also here.

Ukiah is the largest town for miles. It's a good refueling stop, but has few tourist attractions. The **visitors center** (☎ 707-462-7417; www.gomendo.com; 525 S Main St) has county-wide information. **Orr Hot Springs** (☎ 707-462-6277; springs day use $22, dm $40-45, r & cottages $115-185; 🕑 10am-10pm), 15 miles west of Ukiah (Hwy 101 to N State St exit), is a small, clothing-optional hot springs (reservations are required). Facilities include hot tubs, dorm rooms, private rooms and cottages and a communal kitchen.

After the highways meet up at tiny **Leggett**, keep going north on Hwy 101 to **Richardson**

Grove State Park (☎ 707-247-3318; per car $4, campsites $15) for a full immersion in a giant redwood forest. Rangers are here year-round, and the summer-only **visitors center** (🕑 9am-5pm) has good exhibits. The campground is spread beneath towering redwoods next to the S Fork Eel River.

Garberville, along with its more ragged sister town of Redway 2 miles away, became famous in the 1970s for the sinsemilla marijuana grown in the surrounding hills. Today Garberville is a quiet town with basic services, cheap motels and a few places to eat.

The **Lost Coast** became 'lost' when the state's highway system bypassed the rugged mountains of the King Range, which rises to around 4000ft only a few miles from the ocean. Today the region is mostly untouched and undeveloped and affords stunning scenery. From Garberville it's 23 miles on a rough road to Shelter Cove, a seaside resort with a deli and hotels. Other roads crossing the mountains are equally slow.

On Hwy 101, 80-sq-mile **Humboldt Redwoods State Park** (campsites $12) has some of the world's oldest redwood trees. The park's awe-inspiring Avenue of the Giants, a 32-mile stretch of two-lane road winding through wonderful old-growth forests, runs parallel to Hwy 101 and the Eel River. Near the informative **visitors center** (☎ 707-946-2409; 🕑 9am-5pm), campsites are magnificent, so book ahead.

Ferndale, at the northern tip of the Lost Coast, has beautifully restored Victorian buildings and a funky rural sensibility, epitomized by the Kinetic Sculpture Race every Memorial Day weekend. If you can't make it then, visit the **Kinetic Sculpture Museum** (☎ 707-786-9259; 580 Main St; admission free; 🕑 10am-5pm Mon-Sat, noon-4pm Sun).

Scotia is a rarity in the modern world: a 'company town' entirely owned and operated by the Pacific Lumber Company. It's a wholesome little place, and free self-guided mill **tours** (🕑 8am-2pm Mon-Fri) are offered; contact the **Scotia Museum & Visitors Center** (☎ 707-764-2222, ext 247; www.palco.com; admission free; 🕑 8am-4:30pm Mon-Fri summer only), on Main St. In winter, follow signs straight to the mill.

SLEEPING & EATING

Healdsburg has several decent motels, including the **L&M Motel** (☎ 707-433-6528; 70 Healdsburg Ave; r $110; ✤ Ⓟ). Folks drive from miles around to enjoy the gourmet California cuisine at **Dry Creek Kitchen** (☎ 707-431-0330; 317 Healdsburg Ave; $15-25). **Bear Republic** (☎ 707-433-2337; 345 Healdsburg Ave; mains $6-10) is a youthful brewpub.

In Hopland, the **Hopland Inn** (☎ 707-744-1890, 800-266-1891; www.hoplandinn.com; 13401 Hwy 101; r $110-135; 💻 ✤) is a restored 1890 Victorian hotel. High ceilings, pretty wallpapers, iron bed frames and huge baths make this a great choice. Continental breakfast is included. Nearby, the **Hopland Brewery Tavern** (☎ 707-744-1015) is the nation's oldest brewpub, and it serves some of the nation's best beer (by the Mendocino Brewing Company).

In Ukiah, **chain motels** such as Motel 6, Super 8 and Rodeway Inn line S State St.

The rather fancy Tudor-style **Benbow Inn** (☎ 707-923-2124, 800-355-3301; www.benbowinn.com; r $135-205), just south of Garberville off Hwy 101, indulges guests with complimentary decanted sherry in each lovely room; consider a riverside room if you're splurging. The atmospheric, well-regarded restaurant and bar are particularly warming on foggy evenings.

Along the Avenue of the Giants, tiny Miranda has gas and a few places to eat, as well as the **Miranda Gardens Resort** (☎ 707-943-3011; www.mirandagardens.com; cottages with kitchen $125-175, without kitchen $95; 🏊). Stand-alone, roomy cottages are perfect for families and long stays.

In Ferndale, the four rooms at the restored **Hotel Ivanhoe** (☎ 707-786-9000; www.hotel-ivanhoe.com; 315 Main St; r $95-135) are done to the Victorian nines. It also has a decent Italian restaurant and a lively saloon.

GETTING THERE & AROUND

Greyhound (☎ 800-231-2222) has frequent services from San Francisco to many towns along Hwy 101, including Ukiah ($23). The **Redwood Transit System** (☎ 707-443-0826) operates buses Monday through Saturday between Scotia and Trinidad ($1.95, one hour).

Eureka to Crescent City

From Hwy 101, **Eureka**, the largest town before Oregon, seems like nothing but a thunder of traffic, motels and strip malls. However, venture to Eureka's old town, and you'll find a pleasing, relaxing mix of historic Victorian buildings, interesting shops and good eateries. The **Eureka visitors center** (☎ 707-442-3738, 800-356-6381; www.eurekachamber.com; 2112

Broadway; 8:30am-5pm Mon-Fri, 10am-4pm Sat & Sun) has maps and information. In old town, **Going Places** (☎ 707-443-4145; 328 2nd St) is a great travel bookstore.

The **Clarke Memorial Museum** (☎ 707-443-1947; 3rd & E Sts; admission by donation; 11am-4pm Tue-Sat) has an impressive American Indian collection. One of only eight of its kind in the nation, **Blue Ox Millworks** (☎ 707-444-3437, 800-248-4289; www.blueoxmill.com; adult $7.50, child 6-12 $3.50; 9am-4pm Mon-Sat), at the ocean end of X St, hand-mills Victorian detailing using traditional carpentry and authentic 19th-century equipment. Fascinating, self-guided tours let you watch the craftsmen work. Also consider a harbor cruise on the 1910 **Madaket** (☎ 707-445-1910; adult $11; May-Oct), which departs from the foot of L St.

Nine miles north of Eureka, **Arcata** is a laid-back university town that has the same alternative bent and cast of characters as San Francisco's Haight St. Downtown's Arcata Plaza is the center of the action. On the northeast side of town, **Humboldt State University** (☎ 707-826-3011) has an attractive campus and a good art gallery. The blissful **Finnish Country Sauna & Tubs** (☎ 707-822-2228; 5th & J Sts; per hr $15) has a café and a secluded, outdoor complex.

At the junction of Hwys 299 and 101 is a **California Welcome Center** (☎ 707-822-3619, 800-346-3482; 9am-5pm), with tons of area information. See p966 for more on Hwy 299, the Trinity Scenic Byway.

Trinidad, about 12 miles north of Arcata, is a working fishing town on an almost idyllic bay. Follow Edward St to the harbor, where there is a wonderful beach and short hikes on dramatic Trinidad Head. Nearby Luffenholtz Beach is a popular surf spot, and north of town, Patrick's Point Rd is dotted with lodging and campgrounds tucked into the forest.

On Hwy 101 about a mile south of tiny **Orick** is the visitors center for the **Redwood National & State Parks** (☎ 707-464-6101, ext 5265; 9am-5pm). Together, Redwood National Park and Prairie Creek, Del Norte and Jedediah Smith State Parks are a designated World Heritage Site, as they contain almost half of the remaining old-growth redwood forests in California. The national park is free, and the state parks have a reciprocal $4 day-use fee; only the state parks have developed **campsites** ($15), which are highly recommended. The visitor center has trail maps and information about all the parks and issues free permits for backcountry camping and to visit Tall Trees Grove.

The highlights at **Redwood National Park** are the **Lady Bird Johnson Grove** and **Tall Trees Grove**, home to several of the world's tallest trees, as well as the roaming herds of Roosevelt elk.

Prairie Creek Redwoods State Park (☎ 707-464-6101, ext 5301) is famous for Fern Canyon, a sheer 60ft fissure overgrown with ferns. Plus, it's free to drive the 8-mile Newton B Drury Scenic Parkway, which passes through virgin redwood forests and runs parallel to Hwy 101.

There's not much in **Klamath** except a giant redwood carving of Paul Bunyan and Babe the Blue Ox at the entrance to the silly **Trees of Mystery** (☎ 800-638-3389; admission $17; 9am-5pm, later in summer), though its **End of the Trail Museum** (admission free) has a good collection of American Indian artifacts. A few miles north, **Del Norte Coast Redwoods State Park** (☎ 707-464-6101, ext 5120) contains beautiful redwood groves and 8 miles of unspoiled coastline.

On a crescent-shaped bay, **Crescent City** is the only sizable coastal town north of Arcata. It has few old buildings, as over half the town was destroyed by a tidal wave in 1964. The 1865 **Battery Point Lighthouse** (☎ 707-464-3089; admission $2; Apr-Sep), at the south end of A St, is accessible whenever the tide is out.

Jedediah Smith Redwoods State Park, 5 miles northeast of Crescent City, is less crowded than the other redwood parks but no less beautiful and lush. Its **Hiouchi Information Center** (☎ 707-464-6101, ext 5112; summer only) is on Hwy 199 in Hiouchi, 5 miles east of Hwy 101.

SLEEPING & EATING

Dozens of plain-Jane motels line Hwy 101 in Eureka. On a hill above the busy road is the family-run **Bayview Motel** (☎ 707-442-1673, 866-725-6813; 2844 Fairfield St; r from $80), a bright and very clean mid-range choice. Rooms are spacious and well cared for. In Eureka's old town, luxurious **Hotel Carter** (☎ 707-444-8062, 800-404-1390; www.carterhouse.com; 301 L St; r $190-330) runs a Tuscan-inspired hotel and several Victorian properties across the street. Full breakfast is included. Its classy **Restaurant 301** is famous for its new French cuisine and magnificent wine list.

On the nearby Samoa Peninsula, the popular **Samoa Cookhouse** (☎ 707-442-1659; all-you-can-eat meals $9-14) is the dining hall of an 1893 lumber camp. It's a fun, atmospheric place where grub with all the fixin's is served on long, oil-cloth-covered tables.

In Arcata, the restored 1915 **Hotel Arcata** (☎ 707-826-0217, 800-344-1221; 708 9th St; r $80-100) isn't ornate, but the rooms are comfortable and attractive. Scores of restaurants are nearby on the square.

The highly recommended **HI Redwood Hostel** (☎ 707-482-8265; 14480 Hwy 101; dm $16), 8 miles north of Klamath, occupies an enviable spot on the coast and is extremely popular.

Half a mile south of Crescent City is the modest but charming **Curly Redwood Lodge** (☎ 707-464-2137; www.curlyredwoodlodge.com; 701 Hwy 101 S; r from $60), with spacious rooms.

GETTING THERE & AROUND

Greyhound (☎ 800-231-2222) hits most major towns along Hwy 101 from San Francisco to Crescent City ($60, nine hours). **Redwood Transit System buses** (☎ 707-443-0826) stop in Arcata on their weekday Trinidad–Scotia and Eureka–Blue Lake routes.

SACRAMENTO

Sacramento sits in a flat agricultural landscape surrounded by suburbs, and as such, the state capital is often casually dismissed by Californians. However, the city has a good deal of history, tracing back to gold rush days, and – with two universities, a busy riverfront harbor and several top-notch museums and restaurants – it is the energetic urban center of the primarily rural Central Valley.

In 1839 Swiss immigrant John Sutter proposed building an outpost north of San Francisco at the confluence of the Sacramento and American Rivers. When James Marshall discovered gold at Sutter's lumber mill near Coloma in 1848, thousands of people flocked to California, most of whom traveled through Sutter's Fort. In 1854, after several years of legislative indecision, the riverfront settlement became California's permanent capital.

The **visitors center** (☎ 916-442-7644; www.discovergold.org; 1101 2nd St; 🕒 10am-5pm), in Old Sacramento, has free maps and can recommend hotels.

Sights

The 19th-century **California state capitol** is at 10th St and Capitol Mall. On the ground floor, the interesting **Capitol Museum** (☎ 916-324-0333; admission free; 🕒 9am-5pm) contains furniture, photographs and documents from various periods. The Assembly and Senate rooms are open to the public whenever they're in session.

A few blocks west next to the river, **Old Sacramento** (Old Sac; www.oldsacramento.com) contains California's largest concentration of buildings on the National Register of Historic Places, and is now a lively Old West tourist attraction à la San Francisco's Fisherman's Wharf. The **Spirit of Sacramento** (☎ 916-552-2933; adult $10), an 1842 paddlewheeler, makes one-hour narrated tours of the Sacramento River.

In Old Sac, the **California State Railroad Museum** (☎ 916-323-9280, 916-445-6645; www.csrmf.org; 125 I St; admission $4; 🕒 10am-5pm) is the largest and perhaps finest railroad museum in North America. The impressive building houses 21 equally grand locomotives and cars, and a steam train operates on summer weekends. Next door, the **Discovery Museum** (☎ 916-264-7057; www.thediscovery.org; admission $5; 🕒 10am-5pm, closed Mon in winter) has hands-on science exhibits and displays of gold-rush-era artifacts.

Housed in Judge Edwin B Crocker's Victorian home – a jaw-dropping piece of art in itself – the outstanding **Crocker Art Museum** (☎ 916-264-5423; www.crockerartmuseum.org; 3rd & O Sts; admission $6; 🕒 10am-5pm Tue-Sun, until 9pm Thu) displays Crocker's visionary collection of 19th-century American landscapes and paintings, plus modern art.

Get two sides of California history in one place: restored to its 1850s appearance, **Sutter's Fort** (☎ 916-445-4422; cnr 27th & L Sts; admission $2; 🕒 10am-5pm) was the area's first European settlement. Adjacent, the popular **California State Indian Museum** (☎ 916-324-0971; admission $2; 🕒 10am-5pm) has loving, informative displays of Native American life.

Sleeping & Eating

HI Sacramento Hostel (☎ 916-443-1691; 925 H St; dm $21, r $46-56) Convenient to Old Sac, the hostel occupies a restored 1885 Victorian mansion that makes it one of the nicest hostels in the HI network. Public areas are B&B quality, and dorm rooms are clean and spacious.

Mid-range **chain hotels** close to downtown include Quality Inn, Holiday Inn, Travelodge and Best Western.

Delta King (☎ 916-444-5464, 800-825-5464; www.deltaking.com; r midweek/weekend from $119/169) For a memorable splurge, there's this beautifully refurbished 1927 paddlewheeler docked on the river in Old Sac. It's worth the extra $15 for a riverside room. Breakfast is included; ask about packages.

Old Sac is packed with good restaurants, cheap lunch spots and bars, but it's a scene.

Cafe Bernardo (☎ 916-443-1180; 2726 Capitol Ave at 28th St; meals $6-10) To escape the scene, head for Bernardo. It's casual, inexpensive and good, with an attached bar.

Paragary's (☎ 457-5737; at 28th and N Sts; mains $14-18) Serves fancier, more formal dinners of pastas and grilled meat; they also do lunch.

Getting There & Around

Sacramento is 91 miles east of San Francisco via I-80, and 386 miles north of LA via I-5. It's also served by Hwy 99. **Sacramento International Airport** (☎ 916-929-5411; www.sacairports.org), 15 miles north of downtown off I-5, is serviced by most major airlines.

Greyhound (☎ 816-444-6858; 7th & L Sts) serves San Francisco ($14, two hours), Los Angeles ($45, nine hours), Seattle ($66, 19 hours) and other major towns.

Sacramento's **Amtrak** (☎ 800-872-7245; at 5th & I Sts) depot is near downtown. Trains leave daily for Oakland ($17, two hours), Los Angeles ($52, eight hours), Reno ($65, 4½ hours) and Seattle ($112, 8½ hours).

Sacramento Regional Transit (☎ 916-321-2877; www.sacrt.com) runs a bus system and a light-rail line, the latter mostly serving commuters. The fare is $1.50.

GOLD COUNTRY

Hugging the foothills of the western Sierra Nevada, California's Gold Country winds 300 miles north to south along Hwy 49; the most interesting stretch is from Nevada City to Sonora, which boasts a wealth of restored mining towns and historic hotels soaked in Old West atmosphere, not to mention great scenery and lots of outdoor adventure.

The gold rush started on 24 January 1848, when James Marshall was inspecting the lumber mill he was building for John Sutter, near present-day Coloma. From the mill's tailrace water Marshall pulled out a gold nugget 'roughly half the size of a pea' – an inauspicious beginning to a legendary era.

The first true rush came from San Francisco in the spring of 1848. During this wave, men found gold so easily that they thought nothing of spending (or gambling) all they had in one night. News quickly spread, and by the end of 1848 over 30,000 people had come. By 1849 the real gold rush was on, with an additional 60,000 people (known as the 49ers) migrating to California in search of the 'Mother Lode.'

Gold Country is the start for many popular **rafting trips** on the American, Tuolumne, Kings and Stanislaus Rivers. **Whitewater Connection** (☎ 800-336-7238; www.whitewaterconnection.com) and **Zephyr Whitewater Expeditions** (☎ 800-431-3636, 209-532-6249; www.zrafting.com) offer half-day trips (midweek/weekend from $90/110) and longer excursions.

Outside of Auburn off I-80, exit 121, is a **California Welcome Center** (☎ 530-887-2111; 13411 Lincoln Way; www.auburncwc.com; 9am-5pm summer, closed Sun winter), with plenty of regional and state information. Or, contact the **Gold Country Visitors Association** (☎ 209-736-0049, 800-225-3764; www.calgold.org).

Northern Mines

Hwy 50 is the dividing line between the Southern and Northern Mines, which stretch from Nevada City to Placerville.

Bright as a new coat of paint, **Nevada City** is a busy tourist town full of fancy cafés, nice accommodations, well-preserved Victorian buildings and small museums tracing the area's mining and immigrant history. For self-guided walking tours, visit the **chamber of commerce** (☎ 530-265-2692, 800-655-6569; www.nevadacitychamber.com; 132 Main St; 9am-5pm Mon-Fri, 10am-4pm Sat, 11am-3pm Sun). The **Tahoe National Forest Headquarters** (☎ 530-265-4531; 8am-4:30pm Mon-Fri, also Sat in summer), on Hwy 49 at the north end of Coyote St, has hiking and backcountry information.

About 5 miles southwest, **Grass Valley** is where many disaffected Bay Area artists and hippies have moved to, creating an interesting mix of funky sophistication and rural conservatism. Together, Grass Valley and Nevada City are a designated 'book town,' with 23 bookstores between them; **Booktown Books** (☎ 530-273-4002; 11671 Malman Dr #2) is a cooperative of nine. The area's blockbuster site is the **Empire Mine State**

Historic Park (☎ 530-273-8522; www.empiremine.org; admission $2; 🕑 9am-6pm summer, 10am-5pm winter), 2 miles east of town off Hwy 49. The park sits atop 367 miles of mine shafts that, from 1850 to 1956, produced six million ounces of gold (about two billion dollars' worth). Time your visit for a free tour partway into the shafts.

Auburn is one of Gold Country's most visited – though not picturesque – towns, perhaps because its historic center is right off I-80. Within walking distance is the fine **Placer County Museum** (☎ 530-889-6500; Maple St; admission $1; 🕑 10am-4pm Tue-Sun) in the stately Placer County Courthouse; they can point you to several other nearby gold-rush era sights.

In summer, stop for a **swim** at the confluence of the North and South Forks of the American River, 3 miles south of Auburn on Hwy 49. Ask around for the best swimming holes.

Modern-day **Coloma** is now almost completely taken up by the **Marshall Gold Discovery State Historic Park** (☎ 530-622-3470; per car $4; 🕑 8am-5pm), which contains the state's first gold discovery site, a replica of Sutter's Mill, numerous restored buildings (staffed by costumed docents Thursday to Friday in summer), a museum and short hikes. It's one of the better places to get a feel for the gold rush, and picnicking by the river is delightful. A few private campgrounds and places to eat line the highway nearby.

Once an important point along the California–Nevada stagecoach route, **Placerville** – or 'Old Hangtown' – is now chiefly a gas and food stop for travelers at the junction of Hwys 49 and 50.

Southern Mines

The Southern Mines extend from Placerville south to Sonora and are bordered by the Stanislaus National Forest and Yosemite National Park. Here, the quieter towns and bucolic rolling foothills make for slower driving.

Tiny **Amador City**, once an important gold mining center, was on the verge of ghost town status until a Sacramento family converted the dilapidated buildings into antiques shops in the 1950s.

Sutter Creek is a less-polished, more endearing version of Nevada City, with its high-balconied buildings free of modern additions. It gets quite busy on weekends.

Scruffy **Jackson** contains the dusty **Amador County Museum** (☎ 209-223-6386; 225 Church St; admission free; 🕑 10am-4pm Wed-Sun), which in addition to history displays has unique 'model mine' **tours** (adult $1) at weekends. These are worth seeing before visiting the nearby **Kennedy Gold Mine** (☎ 209-223-9542; www.kennedygoldmine.com; adult $9, child 6-12 $5; 🕑 10am-3pm Sat & Sun Mar-Oct), on Hwy 49.

For an antidote to gold rush fever, take Hwy 88 north to **Chaw'Se Indian Grinding Rock State Historic Park** (per car $3, campsites $12; 🕑 sunrise-sunset), which remains sacred ground for the local Miwok Indians. The 'grinding rock' is covered with ancient petroglyphs and mortar holes called chaw'Ses, used for grinding acorns into meal. The park's **Regional Indian Museum** (☎ 209-296-7488; 🕑 11am-3pm Mon-Fri, 10am-4pm Sat & Sun) is excellent, and camping is available. About a mile away, tiny, quiet **Volcano** is refreshingly off the tourist track.

In Cave City, 9 miles east of San Andreas, the spectacular **California Cavern** (☎ 209-736-2708, 888-818-7462; www.caverntours.com; admission $10; 🕑 10am-4pm mid-April–Nov) was described by John Muir as 'graceful flowing folds deeply pleated like stiff silken drapery.' Tours run 60 to 90 minutes.

Cross the gold rush with Napa Valley and you get **Murphys,** a sophisticated rural town abundant in wineries and fine art galleries. Intriguing **Mercer Caverns** (☎ 209-728-2101; admission $10; 🕑 10:30am-4:30pm) are 1 mile north of town via a well-marked road from the east end of Main St; tours are less than an hour. Fifteen miles north of Murphys on Hwy 4, **Calaveras Big Trees State Park** (☎ 209-795-2334; per car $2, campsites $12) has giant sequoia groves and nice campsites. Hwy 4 itself is a scenic alternate route into the mountains and to Tahoe.

Columbia is now a state **historic park** (☎ 209-536-1672; www.columbiacalifornia.com), with four full blocks of authentic 1850s buildings and concessionaires in period costumes. It provides a real flavor of the Old West (without the smelly miners) and is a great place to let the kids run loose. The park itself doesn't close, but most businesses are open from 10am to 5pm.

In its heyday **Sonora** was a cosmopolitan center, and today it's still bustling as the Tuolumne County seat, though it lacks the ambience of other towns. Sonora is a good place to rest and refuel. The **visitors center** (☎ 209-533-4420, 800-446-1333; www.thegreatunfenced.com; 542 S Stockton Rd; 9am-7pm Mon-Fri, 10am-6pm Sat) will help with Gold Country accommodations.

Nearby **Jamestown** has a restored Main St and **Railtown 1897** (☎ 209-984-3953; admission free; 9:30am-4:30pm), with steam-train **rides** (adult $6; Sat & Sun summer).

Sleeping & Eating

Don't be penny-wise and pound-foolish in Gold Country. Staying in a historic inn is one of the attractions.

However, in Nevada City, your best bet may be the **Outside Inn** (☎ 530-265-2233; www.outsideinn.com; 575 E Broad St; r $65-120), a revamped motor court that caters to outdoor enthusiasts with lots of maps and advice. Comfy rooms are now attractively rustic.

In Grass Valley, the 1852 **Holbrooke Hotel** (☎ 530-273-1353; www.holbrooke.com; 212 W Main St; r from $85 to 95) has 28 elegant but not overbearingly Victorian rooms, with exposed brick and lovely antiques. Right downtown, it has an attached restaurant and delightful bar.

Also in Grass Valley, artist-owners have made a modern-art gallery of the four-room **Swan Levine House** (☎ 530-272-1873; www.swanlevinehouse.com; 328 S Church St; r $90-100;), once a rambling 19th-century hospital. The decor is offbeat, and the welcome is warm; an attached printmaking studio is open to artistically inclined guests, professional or amateur.

If you're in a pinch there are numerous no-surprise **chain motels** along the I-80 exits near Auburn.

In Sutter Creek, the very romantic **Sutter Creek Inn** (☎ 209-267-5606; www.suttercreekinn.com; 75 Main St; r $100-165;) has 17 cozy, secluded rooms, some with swinging beds and most with fireplaces. Trim gardens are perfect for croquet. Full country breakfast is included.

Sutter Creek is also home to the **Sutter Creek Coffee Roasting Co** (☎ 209-267-5550; 20 Eureka St), a friendly coffeehouse, and across the street, **Susan's Place** (☎ 209-267-0945; 15 Eureka St; mains $18-25), a pretty wine bar and restaurant that serves lunch and dinner.

The historic 1862 **St George Hotel** (☎ 209-296-4458; www.stgeorgehotel.com; r from $80-100) is reason enough to drive to Volcano. Attractive rooms in the grand main hotel have shared baths, while six bungalows have private baths. Gourmet breakfast is included. It has a renowned dinner-only restaurant and a vintage **bar** (Thu-Sun) that's a local gathering spot.

The local choice for hospitality in Murphys is **Murphys Historic Hotel and Lodge** (☎ 209-728-3444, 800-532-7684; www.murphyshotel.com; 457 Main St; room with/without bath from $100/85). Choose between the hotel's plain-spun Victorian rooms with shared bath or the modern, bath-equipped motel rooms. Its restaurant is known for steaks, and don't miss the historic antler-festooned saloon.

In Columbia, the **City Hotel and Fallon Hotel** (☎ 209-532-1479, 800-532-1479; www.cityhotel.com; City Hotel from $105, Fallon Hotel from $70-85) are run together. Both are stunning restorations of authentic Victoriana, with particularly amazing wallpapers. All rooms share showers but have private toilets; buffet breakfast is included. The City Hotel's acclaimed **restaurant** (meals $18-25; dinner only) is a training ground for Columbia College's Culinary Arts Program, and Fallon Hotel hosts a repertory theater. Ask about packages.

Sonora's lovely **Gunn House Hotel** (☎ 209-532-3421; 286 S Washington St; r $70-100;) provides old-fashioned romance with ornate antiques and fancy bedspreads. Continental breakfast is included. If you'd rather forego quaint, **Sonora Gold Lodge** (☎ 209-532-3952; 480 W Stockton St; r $70;) is a respectably neat, tidy and affordable motel.

Getting There & Around

About 26 miles northeast of Sacramento, Hwy 49 intersects I-80 in the town of Auburn. **Greyhound** (☎ 916-922-2795) runs buses from Sacramento to Auburn ($9), Placerville ($11) and Stockton ($11).

Local bus systems include **Gold Country Stage** (☎ 530-477-0103), which charges $1 between Grass Valley and Auburn, and **Placer County Transit** (☎ 530-889-7570).

NORTHERN MOUNTAINS

North of Redding are some of California's most beautiful – and least visited – features, including majestic Mt Shasta, Lassen Volcanic National Park and Lava Beds National Monument.

Redding to Yreka

At the north end of the Sacramento Valley, **Redding** is an unremarkable but highly convenient stopover. Maps and backcountry permits for northern California's national forests are available at the **Shasta-Trinity National Forest Headquarters** (☎ 530-244-2978; 2400 Washington Ave; 7:30am-4:30pm Mon-Fri, until 5pm summer). Comprehensive public lands and tourist information is also available 10 miles south of Redding at the **California Welcome Center** (☎ 530-365-1180, 800-474-2782; www.shastacascade.org; 9am-5pm Mon-Fri, 10am-3pm Sat & Sun), off Hwy 5 in Anderson at the south end of Prime Outlets Mall.

A highly recommended detour is Hwy 299, the **Trinity Scenic Byway**, which courses through the **Trinity Alps**, where fog catches the trees like tufts of cotton; there's loads of camping, backpacking and river-running. The drive is three hours between Redding and Arcata. **Weaverville**, a pleasant mountain town, has an interesting Chinese temple museum and several decent budget motels and restaurants. **Weaverville Ranger Station** (☎ 530-623-2121; 210 N Main St; 8am-4:30pm Mon-Fri) has outdoor information and can issue backcountry permits.

North of Redding along I-5, **Shasta Lake** is the state's largest reservoir; it has numerous hiking trails, campgrounds and boat rentals along its shores. The lake exists because of the massive **Shasta Dam** (☎ 530-275-4463; www.shastalake.com; 8:30am-4:30pm), at the southern end. At the time of research, free dam tours were suspended for national security reasons; call for current status. Tours of **Lake Shasta Caverns** (☎ 530-238-2341; adult $17) include a catamaran ride across Shasta Lake.

An excellent base for area explorations, the town of **Mt Shasta** is dwarfed by its neighboring namesake mountain. The **Mt Shasta Visitor Center** (☎ 530-926-4865, 800-926-4865; www.mtshastachamber.com; 300 Pine St; 9am-5:30pm Mon-Sat, 9am-4pm Sun) provides regional information. The **Sisson Museum** (☎ 530-926-5508; admission free; 1-4pm Apr-Sep, from 10am Jun-Sep, closed Jan-Mar) is a well-done small-town museum, and next to it is the large **Mt Shasta Fish Hatchery** (☎ 530-926-2215; 8am-sunset), at 1 N Old Stage Rd.

Mt Shasta itself, which is California's sixth-highest mountain (14,162ft), seems especially magnificent because it rises alone on the landscape. Everitt Memorial Hwy goes up the mountain to 7900ft; to access it, simply head east from town on Lake St and keep going. Rangers can suggest a number of good hiking trails, depending on what the weather conditions are. To climb higher than 10,000ft, obtain a $15 permit from the **Mt Shasta Ranger Station** (☎ 530-926-4511; 204 W Alma St; 8am-4:30pm Mon-Sat, 9am-3pm Sun). On the south slope, off Hwy 89, **Mt Shasta Ski Park** (☎ 530-926-8610, 800-754-7427; www.skipark.com) offers skiing in winter, and mountain biking and chairlift rides in summer. Note that camping on Mt Shasta can be cold and mosquito-plagued.

McCloud, an atmospheric, historic mill town, is 10 miles east of I-5 on Hwy 89 at the foot of Shasta's southern slope. Hiking is good in the area, especially the Squaw Valley Creek Trail, an easy 5-mile loop south of town.

Yreka (y-*ree*-kuh), which is inland California's northernmost city, is a pleasant spot to stay and eat. Locals are proud of the **Yreka Western Railroad** (☎ 530-842-4146, 800-973-5277; www.yrekawesternrr.com; adult $14, child 3-12 $7), a 1915 Baldwin steam engine that chugs to the tiny town of Montague in summer.

SLEEPING & EATING

Redding has several older budget motels downtown on Pine St, such as the acceptably average **Thunderbird Lodge** (☎ 530-243-5422; 1350 Pine St; d $45; P). Several modest restaurants are around the Downtown Mall, also off Pine St.

In the quiet railroad town of Dunsmuir, **Dunsmuir Bed & Breakfast Inn** (☎ 530-235-4543, 888-386-7684; 5423 Dunsmuir Ave; r $75-85) is very comfortable, plain-spoken and nice, just like its owners. The area's most unusual place to stay is in one of the 23 vintage railroad cabooses at **Railroad Park Resort** (☎ 530-235-4440, 800-974-7245; www.rrpark.com; r from $85;), off I-5 just south of Dunsmuir.

Mt Shasta's lovely **Strawberry Valley Inn** (☎ 530-926-2052; 1142 S Mt Shasta Blvd; r $75-85;) has lovely rooms with lace coverlets on the beds; continental breakfast is included.

McCloud has several nice lodgings and eateries. **McCloud Hotel** (☎ 530-964-2822, 800-964-2823; www.mccloudhotel.com; 408 Main St; r from $110) is a delightful Victorian property; an on-site restaurant serves dinner Sunday to Thursday. For a romantic experience, locals board the three-hour **Shasta Sunset Dinner Train** (☎ 800-733-2141; www.shastasunset.com; set-price meals $80) on weekends from McCloud.

Several comfortable motels line Yreka's Main St, including the **Klamath Motor Lodge**

(☎ 530-842-2751, 800-551-7255; 1111 S Main St; r from $60;).

GETTING THERE & AROUND

Amtrak services Redding and Dunsmuir; Greyhounds serves those towns plus Yreka. By car, San Francisco to Redding is 215 miles (four hours); Redding to Portland, Oregon, is 420 miles (seven hours). **Stage buses** (☎ 530-842-8295) run from Dunsmuir to Yreka ($3.50, two hours). For road conditions call **Siskiyou County** (☎ 530-842-4438).

Northeast Corner

Surrounded by high desert country that recalls the Southwest, **Lava Beds National Monument** takes you back to an age when rock flowed like water. This 9-by-8-mile volcanic park features lava flows, craters, cones and over 500 amazing lava tubes, which can be explored on your own (rangers provide free flashlights). The area was also home to Modoc Indians and contains petroglyphs and historic sites pertaining to the Modoc War. The **visitors center** (☎ 530-667-2282; Hill Rd; day use $5; 8am-5pm), off Hwy 161 on the park's south side, has nice exhibits and a nearby **campsite** ($10), which is lovely on a clear summer night.

Just north, the **Klamath Basin National Wildlife Refuges** lie along the Pacific Flyway, providing safe havens for migrating birds; it's an important wintering site for bald eagles. The **visitors center** (☎ 530-667-2231; www.klamathnwr.org; 4009 Hill Rd; 8am-4:30pm Mon-Fri, 10am-4pm Sat & Sun) is along the road to Lava Beds Monument from Hwy 161. Scenic, 10-mile auto **tours** (per car $3) go through Lower Klamath and Tule Lakes.

Overall, this area has few commercial services, though there is the friendly, very tidy **Ellis Motel** (☎ 530-667-5242; r $40-45, with kitchen extra $5), 1 mile north of Tulelake on Hwy 139. **Tulelake** itself boasts an excellent Mexican restaurant, and 5 miles south on Hwy 139 is **Captain Jack's Stronghold** (☎ 530-664-5566; mains $6-12; closed Mon), with solid country fare.

Modoc National Forest covers almost 3125 sq miles of California's northeast corner. **Medicine Lake**, 14 miles south of Lava Beds Monument on Hwy 49, is a beautiful crater lake surrounded by pine forest, volcanic formations and campgrounds.

Alturas, at the junction of Hwys 299 and 395, is the Modoc County seat and primarily serves local ranchers; it has affordable accommodations. The Modoc National Forest **Supervisor's Headquarters** (☎ 530-233-5811; 800 W 12th St; 8am-5pm Mon-Fri) has hiking information and maps. The **Modoc National Wildlife Refuge**, 3 miles southeast of Alturas, is another birding site with an auto tour. Just 24 miles east of Alturas, on the California-Nevada border, is beautiful Surprise Valley, which provides access to the wild **Warner Mountains**.

Further south, **Lassen Volcanic National Park** (per car $10, campsites $8-16) is another astounding natural attraction. In addition to spectacular Lassen Peak (10,457ft), the world's largest plug-dome volcano, the park contains all the steaming geothermal sulfur pools and cauldrons of Yellowstone, only without the geyser; good hikes include a 17-mile portion of the Pacific Crest Trail. The park has two entrances, both with visitor centers: the smaller is on Hwy 44 at Manzanita Lake, and the main one is in the south off Hwy 89, via a turnoff 5 miles east of Mineral, where the **park headquarters** (☎ 530-595-4444) are located. Hwy 89 through the park is only open June through October. All camping ($8-16) is first-come, first-served, and various lodges and cabins line Hwy 89 leading to the southern entrance.

SIERRA NEVADA

The mighty Sierra Nevada mountain range is a glacier-scarred granite world interwoven with ancient forests, azure lakes and alpine meadows. Stretching 400 miles along the California-Nevada border, its highest peaks, including 14,494ft Mt Whitney, are along the Sierra Nevada Crest in the east, while Yosemite, Sequoia and Kings Canyon National Parks are mostly accessible from the west.

LAKE TAHOE

Brilliantly blue Lake Tahoe is a stunning natural wonder nestled among rugged peaks. In summer, vacationers flock to its shores and abundant parks, and in winter, skiers attack its famous slopes, which are mainly on the north side. Because it straddles the California-Nevada state border, Lake Tahoe also offers gaudy casinos, particularly along the south shore (via Hwy 50).

In winter, Hwy 89 (Emerald Bay Rd) is usually closed, and tire chains are often required on I-80 and Hwy 50; for winter road information, call ☎ 800-427-7623.

North & East Shores

On I-80 northwest of Tahoe, **Truckee** (www.truckee.com) is a onetime mining and railroad town with restaurants, shops and hotels. Adjacent **Donner Lake** is surrounded by small, woodsy resorts and is a low-key alternative to the Tahoe action. At the east end of Donner Lake, the **Emigrant Trail Museum** (☎ 530-582-7892; admission $2; 9am-4pm, until 5pm summer) does a great job chronicling the Donner Party's fateful 1846 journey, when a combination of winter storms and poor planning wiped out half of the 87-person party, and survivors were forced to eat human flesh to avoid starvation.

Tahoe City is the north shore's largest town. The **North Lake Tahoe Chamber of Commerce** (☎ 530-581-6900; 380 N Lake Tahoe; 9am-5pm Mon-Fri, 9am-4pm Sat & Sun), near the fire station on Hwy 89, has lodging, dining, hiking and skiing information. A popular activity, especially with kids, is crowding onto Fanny Bridge and watching the fish swim by underneath.

Heading northeast on Hwy 28, Tahoe Vista and Kings Beach have attractive lodgings convenient to the slopes and sandy beaches. Hiking, biking and cross-country skiing can be enjoyed at North Tahoe Regional Park, north of Hwy 28 at the end of National St.

Tahoe's northeastern shore is dominated by **Lake Tahoe-Nevada State Park** (☎ 775-831-0494; per car $6), which has cross-country skiing in winter and a nice, often-crowded beach at Sand Harbor. Crystal Bay is an aging casino town, while affluent Incline Village is home to touristy **Ponderosa Ranch** (☎ 775-831-0691; www.ponderosaranch.com; admission $9.50; 9:30am-6pm mid-Apr–Oct), where the TV Western *Bonanza* was filmed.

West & South Shores

DL Bliss State Park (☎ 530-525-7277; per car $5, campsites $12) is an ideal summer destination: clear turquoise water, white-sand beaches, lots of camping and access to unspoiled hiking trails. The 6-mile Rubicon Trail rims narrow Emerald Bay – containing the lake's only island and waters that truly justify its name – and leads to **Vikingsholm Castle** (admission $3; 10:15am-4pm Jun-Sep), a 1928 Scandinavian mansion at the lake's edge. The castle and **Emerald Bay State Park** (☎ 530-541-6498; per car $5) are also accessible via Hwy 89.

About 3 miles southeast on Emerald Bay Rd, the **Tallac Historic Site** (☎ 530-541-5227; admission free; 10am-4pm Jun-Sep) encompasses three historic estates and a museum.

Few people, even locals, have good things to say about South Lake Tahoe and its parade of cheap motels and shopping malls. It does, though, have a **visitors center** (☎ 530-541-5255; 9am-5pm Mon-Sat). Immediately across the Nevada border is **Stateline**, where you can engage in the Old West tradition of gambling all your money away at Caesar's Tahoe, Harrah's and Harvey's.

Activities

The lake is surrounded by skiing areas, including the following:

Alpine Meadows (☎ 530-583-0963, 800-441-4423; www.skialpine.com; 13 lifts $56) Large, popular, family-friendly resort; off Hwy 89 near Tahoe City.

Heavenly (☎ 775-586-7000, 800-243-2826; www.skiheavenly.com; 29 lifts $49) Best all-around resort, massive new upgrade; near Stateline in South Lake Tahoe.

Kirkwood (☎ 209-258-6000, 877-547-5966; www.kirkwood.com; 12 lifts $54) Locals' choice and popular with snowboarders; 35 miles south of Lake Tahoe on Hwy 88.

Squaw Valley USA (☎ 530-583-6985, 800-403-0206; www.squaw.com; 33 lifts $58) World-class resort, host of 1960 Winter Olympics; off Hwy 89, 10 miles north of Tahoe City.

Near Donner Pass on I-80, the Sierra Club's **Clair Tappaan Lodge** (☎ 530-426-3632) has 7.5 miles of cross-country ski trails and rentals, and **Alpine Skills International** (☎ 530-426-9108; www.alpineskills.com) has rentals and runs backcountry programs. On Hwy 89 a few miles north of South Lake Tahoe, **Camp Richardson** (☎ 530-542-6584) has marked cross-country trails, and they can point you to more, but they really excel in summer with a full-service **marina** (☎ 530-542-6570) and bike rentals.

Summer or winter, the **cable car ride** (adult $17) to **High Camp** at Squaw Valley is a true Tahoe experience: you'll find an ice-skating rink, heated swimming pool, Olympic museum and restaurants and bars, all at 8200ft.

In summer, **Ski Run Marina** (☎ 530-544-0200; www.tahoesports.com; 2½hr cruise $23), in South

Lake Tahoe, has all sorts of water sports – kayaks, powerboats, parasailing, jet skiing – and runs Emerald Bay Cruises.

Hikers have oodles of choices. A favorite trek is the strenuous 5-mile climb up Mt Tallac in the **Desolation Wilderness**. Pick up maps and permits at the **USFS Visitor Center** (☎ 530-573-2674; summer only) near the Tallac Historic Site. Another highlight is the 150-mile **Tahoe Rim Trail**, which can be divided into good one-day sections and is open to hikers and bikers. For details, contact the **Tahoe Rim Trail Association** (☎ 775-588-0686; www.tahoerimtrail.org).

Sleeping & Eating

Lake Tahoe Central Reservations (☎ 530-583-3494, 888-434-1262; www.mytahoevacation.com) can reserve rooms and organize packages around the entire lake.

Note that high-season rates are quoted below (which may mean summer, winter or both); off-season rates can be 30% less.

There is lots of camping at the state parks and at **USFS sites** (☎ reservations 877-444-6777; campsites $12). Open year-round is **Sugar Pine Point State Park** (☎ reservations 530-525-7982, 800-444-7275; campsites $12), on the western shore.

If you're bargain-hunting, check out South Lake Tahoe's cheap hotels and mid-range chains along Hwy 50 west of Hwy 89 (the 'Y'); midweek deals can go below $30. The casinos only offer good deals when it's slow. Independent travelers will find more of their kind at **Doug's Mellow Mountain Retreat** (☎ 530-544-8065; 3787 Forest Ave; dm $15), an independent hostel in a suburban house.

On the west shore, **Camp Richardson** (☎ 530-541-1801, 800-544-1801; www.camprichardson.com; campsites $19-26, r midweek/weekend from $90/125) contains several campgrounds and a very comfortable hotel where pine log bed frames set the rustic tone. Cabins are rented nightly in winter ($100 to $190), weekly in summer ($650 to $1500).

In Tahoe City, **Tahoe City Inn** (☎ 530-581-3333, 800-800-8246; 790 N Lake Blvd; r midweek/weekend $85/105) is a good mid-range choice.

In Kings Beach, the family-run **North Lake Lodge** (☎ 530-546-2731, 888-923-5253; www.northlakelodge.com; 8716 N Lake Blvd; studios midweek/weekend from $70/80) has affordable efficiencies, and is pet friendly.

In Tahoe Vista, the **Franciscan Lakeside Lodge** (☎ 530-546-6300; 6944 N Lake Blvd; studios midweek/weekend from $95/115) has delightful studios and one- and two-bedroom apartments, all with spiffy kitchenettes.

Dining choices are abundant, and the resorts have good options. In Tahoe City, the **Bridgetender** (☎ 530-583-3342; 65 West Lake Blvd; hamburgers $8) is a classic Tahoe brew-and-burger joint that draws the young après-ski crowd.

For romantic fine dining, many locals swear by **Soule Domain** (☎ 530-546-7529; 9983 Cove Ave) in an atmospheric log cabin at the North Shore's Crystal Bay.

Getting There & Around

Major commercial airlines fly out of the **Reno-Tahoe International Airport** (☎ 775-328-6400). The **Tahoe Casino Express** (☎ 800-446-6128; adult $19) runs shuttles between the airport and South Lake Tahoe casinos and hotels.

Greyhound buses (☎ 800-231-2222) run daily between Truckee and Sacramento ($26) and San Francisco ($42); they no longer have a Stateline stop.

Tahoe Area Rapid Transit (TART; ☎ 530-550-1212; www.laketahoetransit.com; adult $1.25) buses connect Tahoe City, Truckee, Tahoe Vista and other towns. In summer service is extended down the west shore to Meeks Bay Resort, where you can transfer to the **South Lake Tahoe Stage** (☎ 530-542-6077) network. In winter, some ski resorts have free shuttles, as do larger casinos.

YOSEMITE NATIONAL PARK

Few places on earth pack as much ravishing natural beauty, tranquil serenity and cliff-hanging drama as Yosemite. Despite the crowds – annual visitation swings between three and four million people – it's impossible to arrive and not find you heart touched by the area's regal grandeur and its untamed wildness and wilderness. Even a day is memorable, and a week's explorations could be the highlight of a lifetime. Come any season but summer and there's even a chance to enjoy that sublime commodity – solitude.

In 1864 President Abraham Lincoln signed a bill preserving the park under the Yosemite Grant to California. Thanks to the passionate campaigning of naturalist John Muir, the area was established as Yosemite National Park in 1890, and today it is also a World Heritage Site. Balancing tourists' needs with those of the environment is an ongoing battle in Yosemite, though the ultimate 'radical' solution –

banning or limiting cars – is unlikely to be adopted soon.

Orientation & Information

Yosemite's entrance fee ($20 per vehicle, $10 for those on bicycle or foot) is valid for seven days. There are four primary entrances to **Yosemite National Park**: South Entrance (Hwy 41), Arch Rock (Hwy 140), Big Oak Flat (Hwy 120 west) and Tioga Pass (Hwy 120 east). Hwy 120 traverses the park as Tioga Rd (which is closed in winter), connecting the valley with Mono Lake via 9945ft Tioga Pass. Yosemite Valley, located on the southwest side of the park, is the foremost destination and home to most visitor facilities. Tuolumne Meadows, on the east end of Tioga Rd, is a hub for backpackers as well as climbers. Wawona, located at the southern entrance, has a hotel, store, pioneer museum and Mariposa Grove of giant sequoias.

The visitor center in **Yosemite Valley** (☎ 209-372-0299; www.nps.gov/yose; 🕒 9am-5pm, longer hours summer) is the park's main information source, though there are ranger stations with maps and posted campground availability at all park entrances. For recorded Yosemite information and road/weather conditions, call ☎ 209-372-0200.

Free wilderness permits are required year-round for overnight trips. A quota system limits the number of people leaving from each trailhead. About 60% of permits can be reserved between six months and two days in advance through the **Yosemite Wilderness Center** (☎ 209-372-0740; reservation fee $5; 🕒 closed in winter), which is a wonderful resource for planning excursions once you're here. To reserve a permit, you must first provide the number of people in your party, entry and exit dates, starting and finishing trailheads and then your principal destination.

There is no gas in Yosemite Valley itself, but gas stations are in Wawona, El Portal, Crane Flat (Tioga Rd junction) and Tuolumne Meadows (closed in winter). In Yosemite Village, there is a 24-hour ATM near the Village Store and a 24-hour **medical clinic** (☎ 209-372-4637).

In winter, Yosemite Valley is a magical place, and accommodations are cheaper. Valley roads are plowed, and Hwys 41, 120 and 140 are kept open, but buy snow chains before approaching the park.

IMPASSABLE TIOGA PASS

Hwy 120 is the only road that connects Yosemite National Park with the Eastern Sierra, and it climbs through the mountains' highest pass, Tioga Pass at 9945ft. Most California maps mark this road 'closed in winter,' which while literally true is also misleading. Tioga Rd is usually closed from the first heavy snowfall in October until sometime in May or even June. If you are planning a trip through Tioga Pass in the spring, you're likely to be out of luck. According to the park's official policy, the earliest date that the road through the pass will be plowed is April 15, yet the pass has only been open in April once since 1980. So call ahead (☎ 209-372-0200) for road and weather conditions before heading for Tioga Pass.

Yosemite Valley

Seven-mile-long Yosemite Valley is the thrilling center of the national park, with all facilities, campgrounds, lodges and trailheads connected by a mostly one-way loop road. The hub is **Yosemite Village**, with the main visitors center, a post office, the Wilderness Center, an Indian museum, gift shops, a grocery store and basic eateries.

West of the village, world-famous **Yosemite Falls** is actually a three-tiered affair cascading 2425ft – considered the tallest waterfall in North America. An easy hike leads to the base. While in spring the falls – and the entire valley – gush beautifully, they can actually dry up by late summer. At the valley's southeast end, the well-done **Happy Isles Nature Centure** (admission free; 🕒 9am-noon & 1-4pm May-Sep) is a popular spot for Merced River swims, picnics and leisurely strolls, and it's the starting point for the strenuous hike to ever-watchful **Half Dome**.

Mirror Lake, at the valley's northeast end, is an unforgettable, wheelchair-accessible destination, particularly in spring.

Words fail when one is met with the view from **Glacier Point**, a 3200ft sheer cliff overlooking the entire valley. Glacier Point Rd (closed in winter), off Hwy 41, leads right to it, or reach it by cross-country skis or on foot via the steep, highly recommended Panorama or Four Mile Trails.

Another 'classic' Yosemite Valley view – encompassing majestic El Capitan, Half

Dome and Bridalveil Falls – is from **Tunnel View**, on the east side of the Wawona Rd tunnel. The steep, aptly named Inspiration Point Trail starts from here.

Just north of the valley, near the west end of Tioga Rd, are two giant sequoia groves: **Merced Grove** and **Tuolumne Grove**, both reached by 2- to 3-mile round-trip hikes.

Tuolumne Meadows

Situated about 55 miles from Yosemite Valley, Tuolumne (*twol*-uh-mee) Meadows, at 8600ft, is the largest subalpine meadow in the Sierra. It provides a dazzling contrast to the valley, with lush open fields, clear blue lakes, ragged granite peaks and domes, and cooler temperatures. Hikers and climbers will find a paradise of options, and campgrounds are somewhat less crowded. Tioga Rd (Hwy 120) provides access to Tuolumne and is the only road to traverse the park from east to west. The road and all facilities are open only in summer. At the meadow's west end, **Tuolumne Meadows Visitor Center** (☎ 209-372-0263; 🕑 9am-5pm) has a large selection of maps and guidebooks. About a mile east, the **Tuolumne Meadows Store** (☎ 209-372-8428) sells groceries and camping supplies. A ranger kiosk, off the road near Tuolumne Meadows Lodge, issues wilderness permits.

Activities

With over 800 miles of **hiking** trails, Yosemite is a delight for trekkers of all abilities. Easy valley-bottom trails will obviously be the most crowded, sometimes distressingly so, but simply continue up any of the steep walls to escape the hubbub. In addition to the trails mentioned above, the **Mist** and **John Muir Trails** are exceedingly and justifiably popular. They leave from Happy Isles Nature Center and lead around Vernal and Nevada Falls and up into idyllic Little Yosemite Valley.

The main stop for **rock climbing** and camping supplies is the **Curry Village Mountain Shop** (☎ 209-372-8396), in Yosemite Valley; the **Tuolumne Meadows Mountain Shop** (☎ 209-372-8435; 🕑 closed winter) is smaller. Novice and intermediate climbers might want to take an all-day class (gear included; shoe rental extra) or guided climb with the excellent **Yosemite Mountaineering School** (☎ 209-372-8344; www.yosemitemountaineering.com; full-day class from $70), in Curry Village. They also have skiing, backpacking and hiking programs.

In winter, downhill **skiing** is available at **Badger Pass** (☎ 209-372-1000; www.badgerpass.com), and cross-country skiing at Badger Pass and Crane Flat. Two backcountry ski huts – with beds, cooking facilities and water – are available for overnight stays (reservations required). Contact the **Yosemite Association** (☎ 209-372-0740) and **Yosemite Cross-country Ski School** (☎ 209-372-8444).

Bike rentals are available at **Yosemite Lodge** and **Curry Village**, where there's also a winter-only ice-skating rink.

Sleeping & Eating

INSIDE YOSEMITE NATIONAL PARK

All cabin and hotel room reservations are made through **Yosemite Concession Services** (YCS; ☎ 559-252-4848; www.yosemitepark.com; 5410 E Home Ave, Fresno, CA 93727). Wherever you stay, make reservations as early as possible, even a year in advance. Most rates decrease in the off-season. Unless otherwise noted, all lodging listed here is in the valley.

Housekeeping Camp (tents $60) is a compound with a grocery store, laundry, pay showers, outdoor grills and three-sided concrete structures with plastic roofs that are like permanent tents. It's great for families who want to settle in.

Curry Village (tent cabins $60, cabins with/without bath $95/80, r $110) could double as a labor camp, with its long lines of tightly spaced cabins. There are rough-and-simple tent cabins, nicer wooden cabins with/without bath and standard motel rooms. The Curry Village **Dining Pavilion** (meals $6-12) has an all-day self-service cafeteria, a pizza window and in the evening, a convivial, backpackers' après-hike atmosphere.

In the High Sierra, **Tuolumne Meadows Lodge** (tent cabins $65) has spartan tent cabins with four beds, a woodstove and candles (no electricity). A mile north of Tioga Rd, **White Wolf Lodge** (tent/wooden cabins $60/90) has similar tent cabins and a few wooden ones. Both have dining halls.

Character-lacking **Yosemite Lodge** (hotel/lodge r $110/145, mains $18-25) gets large tour groups and has 'standard' hotel rooms and modern, slightly larger 'lodge' rooms. There's an all-day food court, a buffet restaurant and a pricier, dinner-only restaurant with a popular bar.

Near the park's south entrance, the 1879, New England-style **Wawona Hotel** (r with/without bath $170/115) has relaxing lawns and pleasing Victorian rooms. The restaurant is a top choice.

At the historic **Ahwahnee Hotel** (r $360) rooms and cottages don't quite live up to the radiant splendor of the hotel itself, but they are worth serious consideration, especially off-season. Book far, far in advance. It's definitely worth splurging on a gourmet meal in the soaring dining room (dress-code for dinner) or a drink in the bar.

Yosemite campgrounds (☎ 310-722-1257, 800-436-7275; http://reservations.nps.gov; campsites $18) fill up fast, and not just in summer. For many, reservations are required; you can and should make them up to five months in advance. Don't expect a wilderness experience: Valley camping is sometimes like living in a beehive. Campsites on the reservation system, including all in Yosemite Valley, have flush toilets, picnic tables, fire rings and food-storage boxes.

First-come, first-served campgrounds include those with water and flush toilets, such as **Bridalveil Creek** (campsites $12) and **White Wolf** (campsites $12), and those without, including **Tamarack Flat** (campsites $8) and **Yosemite Creek** (campsites $8), which are more secluded. The only first-come, first-served camping in the valley is the ever-popular, 35-site **Camp 4** (campsites per person $5). The 304-site (half first-come, first-served) **Tuolumne Meadows Campground** (campsites $18; summer only) is more pleasant than its size suggests.

In Yosemite Village, the **Village Store** is hands-down the park's best grocery, while nearby, **Degnan's Deli** is just that, and **Degnan's Loft** serves pizza.

OUTSIDE YOSEMITE NATIONAL PARK

Each road leading to the park has lodging options.

On Hwy 140 in El Portal, only 2 miles from the park, **Yosemite View Lodge** (☎ 209-379-2681; d $140-170;) is a ranging complex of above-average hotel rooms, all with kitchenettes.

About 20 miles from the park on Hwy 140, in Midpines, the friendly **Yosemite Bug Lodge & HI Hostel** (☎ 209-966-6666; www.yosemitebug.com; dm $16, r with/without bath $75/50, campsite $17;) is the region's best budget option. Hostel rooms are very clean, the nice cabins have rustic charm and the café is a relaxing hangout. The Yarts bus stops here.

On Hwy 41 in Fish Camp, 4 miles south of the park, **Narrow Gauge Inn** (☎ 559-683-7720, 888-644-9050; www.narrowgaugeinn.com; d from $130;) offers plush rusticity at a very competitive rate. The expensive dinner-only restaurant (closed Monday and Tuesday) is well regarded.

Getting There & Around

Amtrak (☎ 209-722-6862, 800-872-7245) runs a train/bus system from cities like San Francisco ($31) and Los Angeles ($32) into Yosemite Valley via its Merced depot. The **Yosemite Area Region Transportation** (Yarts; ☎ 877-989-2787; www.yarts.com) runs daily buses to the valley from Merced ($20) and other towns along Hwy 140. Another Yarts **bus** (☎ 800-626-6684) runs in summer only from Mammoth ($20), stopping in Tuolumne Meadows.

A free **shuttle bus** (☎ 209-372-1240) is available year-round for getting to points within Yosemite Valley itself.

SEQUOIA & KINGS CANYON NATIONAL PARKS

It's both a blessing and a curse that the adjacent Sequoia and Kings Canyon National Parks are tucked in relatively remote terrain south of preeminent Yosemite. These parks receive only a quarter to a third the number of visitors, even though they encompass some of California's finest alpine scenery and superlative groves of giant sequoia trees. If Yosemite's crowds are making you crazy, come here.

Orientation & Information

Sequoia was designated a national park in 1890 (the second in the USA), Kings Canyon in 1940. The two parks, though distinct, are operated as one unit with a single admission of $10 per car, $5 for people on bicycle or foot. Admission is valid for seven days.

Enter the parks via Grant Grove (Hwy 180) or Ash Mountain (Hwy 198), the latter a series of narrow switchbacks.

The parks are connected by the 48-mile, north–south Generals Hwy. **Grant Grove Village** (☎ 559-565-4307), in Kings Canyon, and **Lodgepole** (☎ 559-565-3782), in Sequoia, are the two hubs. Each has a year-round **visitors center** (9am-4:30pm, longer hr in summer), a market, showers, a post office and ATMs. Also open all year is **Foothills Visitors Center** (☎ 559-565-3135;

(⌚ 8am-5pm), at the southern Ash Mountain entrance. There's also **Cedar Grove Visitors Center** (☎ 559-565-3793; ⌚ summer only) and the **rangers station** at remote **Mineral King** (☎ 559-565-3768; ⌚ summer only). For 24-hour recorded information, call ☎ 559-565-3341.

The parks do not sell gas, but Kings Canyon Lodge and Hume Lake, both north of Grant Grove, have private stations.

Sequoia National Park

The prime destination for first-time visitors is the **Giant Forest**. Park in the lot for the General Sherman Tree, the world's largest; it's hardly 20 paces from the road. Continue from here along the popular Congress Trail, a 2-mile pathway among awesome sequoias; other trails lead further into the forest.

Two miles south, the **Giant Forest Museum** (☎ 559-565-4480; admission free; ⌚ 9am-4:30pm) has exhibits about sequoia ecology and history, and accesses more good trails, one wheelchair accessible. For mind-boggling views of the Great Western Divide, climb the steep 0.25-mile staircase up **Moro Rock**.

Discovered in 1918, 3-mile-long **Crystal Cave** has formations estimated to be 10,000 years old. Forty-five-minute **cave tours** (adult $9; ⌚ summer only) cover 0.5 miles of chambers; tickets are available at the Lodgepole and Foothills visitors centers, not at the cave.

Kings Canyon National Park

Just north of Grant Grove Village, **General Grant Grove** contains numerous majestic giants. North of here, Hwy 180 descends into **Kings Canyon,** a spectacular, winding 36-mile drive (closed in winter) that includes sweeping mountain vistas, a surging river, waterfalls and dramatic granite cliffs. The canyon itself, plunging 8200ft, is the deepest in the contiguous 48 states. Far into the canyon is **Cedar Grove**, with seasonal campgrounds, lodging and a visitors center. It's worth the hour it takes to get to **Roads End,** if only for a short hike and picnic at beautiful Zumwalt Meadow. A ranger kiosk here issues wilderness permits for overnight backpacks.

Activities

With trail mileage 10 times greater than road mileage, the parks are a **backpacking** heaven. Kings Canyon, Lodgepole and Mineral King, in Sequoia, provide backcountry access; the Jennie Lakes Wilderness Area, in the adjacent Sequoia National Forest, has pristine meadows and lakes at lower elevations. Trails are usually open by mid-May. Wilderness permits ($15) are required for all overnight trips; since quotas have recently been instituted, reservations, particularly for midsummer, are advised. You can make a **reservation** (☎ 559-565-3766; fax 559-565-4239; Wilderness Permit Reservations, Sequoia and Kings Canyon NP, HCR 89, Box 60, Three Rivers, CA 93271; processing fee $15) by fax or post no earlier than 1 March.

In winter, Grant Grove Village and Wuksachi Lodge near Lodgepole rent equipment for **cross-country skiing**; both parks have marked trails.

GIANT SEQUOIAS

In the same family as the California coast redwood and Dawn sequoia (recently discovered in China), the giant sequoia *(Sequoiadendron giganteum)* grows only on the Sierra's western slope, between 5000ft and 7000ft. Giant sequoias are the largest living things on earth in terms of volume. They can grow over 300ft tall and up to 40ft in diameter, and live over 3000 years. Their bark alone can be over 2ft thick. Major sequoia groves are found in Yosemite, Sequoia and Kings Canyon National Parks. But giant sequoias are not the world's tallest tree. Instead, California coast redwoods *(Sequoia sempervirens)* hold this honor, growing over 350ft tall, and the very tallest are found in Redwood National Park on the Pacific Coast.

Sleeping & Eating

Most Kings Canyon lodging uses the same **reservation service** (☎ 559-335-5500, 866-522-6966; www.sequoia-kingscanyon.com). In Grant Grove Village (which has a grocery store and restaurant) is **John Muir Lodge** (tent cabins $45-60, cabins with bath from $105, r $140; ⌚ year-round), with nice hotel rooms, and some cabins with private bath. Other rustic and tent cabins, with shared bath, are seasonal.

In the canyon itself are two mediocre, seasonal options. **Cedar Grove Lodge** (r $100) has motel-style rooms. About halfway down, the privately run **Kings Canyon Lodge** (☎ 559-335-2405; r/cabins $90/180) has plain accommodations, though its café and gas pumps have nostalgic appeal.

Near Lodgepole is upscale **Wuksachi Lodge** (☎ 559-253-2199, 888-252-5757; www.visitsequoia.com; d from $160; year-round). It has three newer lodge buildings with comfortable rooms and good views; their pretty, fine-dining restaurant is open for breakfast, lunch and dinner.

At Lodgepole, the busy **Lodgepole and Dorst campgrounds** (☎ 800-365-2267; campsites with flush toilet $18-20, without $12) can be reserved ahead. All others are first-come, first-served; those at Grant Grove are particularly nice. Most have water and flush toilets, while a few have vault or pit toilets. **Lodgepole**, **Azalea**, **Potwisha** and **South Fork** campgrounds are open year-round; the rest, including the four inside Kings Canyon, are usually open May to October. Call ☎ 559-565-3341 for updates.

Tired of roughing it? Consider staying at **Bearpaw Meadow Camp** (☎ 888-252-5757; cabins $320), an 11.5-mile hike along the stunning High Sierra Trail in Sequoia. The camp has tent cabins, hot showers, linens and two meals; reservations are required.

Three Rivers, 6 miles south of Sequoia, is the best place outside the parks to stock up on food and supplies; it also has about a dozen mid-range **independent** and **chain motels** along Hwy 198.

EASTERN SIERRA

The eastern side of the Sierra Nevada mountains is a captivating region where granite peaks abruptly plunge into the Great Basin desert. At the center of the region is sun-blasted Owens Valley, but gain a few thousand feet and you're soon surrounded by high-altitude lakes and breezy alpine meadows.

Hwy 395 runs the length of the range, with turnoffs offering side trips to the region's lakes and mountains, where hikers, bikers, fishers and skiers all have a ball. The main towns are Bridgeport, Lee Vining, Mammoth Lakes and Bishop.

A worthwhile detour is **Bodie State Historic Park**, on Hwy 270, which intersects Hwy 395 about 7 miles south of Bridgeport. The drive is 13 miles, the last three unpaved and often closed in winter. Bodie, founded in 1859, is one of the West's most picturesque ghost towns, with a large number of well-maintained gold-rush-era buildings. The **visitors center** (☎ 760-647-6445; admission $2; 10am-4pm late May-Sep) is excellent.

Mono Lake is an Ice Age remnant formed more than 700,000 years ago. Appearing like drip sand castles, Mono's ancient tufa towers form when calcium-bearing freshwater bubbles up through the alkaline lake. The most photogenic concentration is at the **South Tufa Reserve** (admission $3), on the lake's southern rim. Nearby, Lee Vining is a gateway town with two helpful information centers. Immediately north of town, the USFS runs the **Mono Basin Scenic Area Visitors Center** (☎ 760-647-3044; 9am-4:30pm), which also has camping information. In town, the **Mono Lake Committee Information Center** (☎ 760-647-6595; www.monolake.org; Hwy 395 & 3rd St; 9am-5pm) is a good source for regional travel information.

A pleasing dawdle is to drive the 16-mile **June Lake Loop**. The scenic road, signposted midway between Mono Lake and Mammoth, follows Hwy 158 west into the mountains, passing Grant, Silver, Gull and June Lakes. The town of June Lake is a small resort community with grocery stores and motels.

Mammoth Lakes is a laid-back resort town amid stellar mountain surroundings, which offer great hiking. Though mainly an unattractive conglomeration of shopping centers and condominiums, the town now also boasts the brand-new, pedestrian-friendly Mammoth Village, with upscale shopping, eating, lodges and a 1-mile gondola ride directly to the area's main attraction, **Mammoth Mountain** (☎ 760-934-0745, 800-626-6684; www.mammothmountain.com; ski-lift tickets $57). This four-season resort has world-class skiing and a very popular summertime **mountain-bike park** (lift tickets $28; bike rental packages $34-63). The **Mammoth Lakes Ranger Station** (☎ 760-924-5500) and **Mammoth Lakes Visitor Bureau** (☎ 760-934-2712, 888-466-2666; www.visitmammoth.com; 8am-5pm) share a building on the north side of Rte 203, just before Old Mammoth Rd. This one-stop information center issues wilderness permits, has campground listings and offers a 24-hour courtesy phone to local hotels.

Bishop, the largest town south of Mammoth Lakes, is a major stop for hikers, since it provides access to the John Muir Wilderness. The central district has some character, with covered sidewalks, 1950s neon signs and hunting and fishing stores, and there is an interesting railroad museum and a Paiute Shoshone cultural center. Restaurants, motels and gas stations line the highway at either end of town.

For stunning views, take the hour-long drive up to the **Ancient Bristlecone Pine Forest** (☎ 760-873-2500). From Bishop drive 15 miles south to Big Pine, then head east on Hwy 168 another 13 miles to the marked turnoff. Above 10,000ft in the White Mountains, these gnarled, picturesque trees are Earth's oldest living things, some dating back 4000 years. The road (closed in winter) is paved to the top, where there are hikes of varying length, primitive camping and a visitors center. Wear sunscreen and a hat.

At 14,494ft, **Mt Whitney** is the highest point in the lower 48, and the climb to its peak is perhaps the most popular in the country. To get there, drive 13 miles east of Lone Pine to Whitney Portal, where there is a store, café, campgrounds and access to the main trail, which leads 10.7 miles to the mountaintop. The **Lone Pine Ranger Station** (☎ 760-876-6200; 7am-4:30pm May-Oct), on Main St, has trail information and issues wilderness permits. However, trail quotas apply from 1 May to 1 November, and **reservations** (per person $15) are awarded by lottery. To enter, overnight and day hikers should fax or mail applications to the **Wilderness Permit Office Inyo National Forest** (fax 760-873-2485; 873 N Main St, Bishop, CA 93514). Applications can be submitted only in February; check **USFS** (www.fs.fed.us/r5/inyo) for printable applications and tons of good hiking advice.

Sleeping & Eating

Campgrounds abound in the Eastern Sierras. On public land outside developed campgrounds, however, you'll need a free fire permit, even for a camp stove. They're obtainable at any ranger station.

In Bridgeport, two clean and friendly motels are the **Silver Maple** (☎ 760-932-7383; 310 Main St; d from $75) and **Redwood Motel** (☎ 760-932-7060, 888-932-3292; www.redwoodmotel.net; 425 Main St; d from $73;).

In Lee Vining, an unexpected delight is the **Whoa Nellie Deli** (☎ 760-647-1088; steak dinner $15-18), inside the Mobil gas station minimart on Hwy 120 near the Hwy 395 junction; it serves great sandwiches and steak dinners.

Charming June Lake is fronted by various unpretentious but nice cabins, most with kitchens. Try **Lake Front Cabins** (☎ 760-648-7527; d $85-95) and **Fern Creek Lodge** (☎ 760-648-7722, 800-621-9146; d from $60).

Mammoth Lakes' excellent **Davison St Guest House Hostel** (☎ reservations 760-924-2188, 619-544-9093; www.mammoth-guest.com; 19 Davison St; dm $32) has five tidy rooms and 22 beds – book ahead. **Swiss Chalet** (☎ 760-934-2403, 800-937-9477; 3776 Viewpoint Rd; d from $80-95) is nice and clean, and has a relaxing whirlpool and sauna. If you want a condo, contact **Mammoth Reservations Bureau** (☎ 760-934-2528, 800-462-5571; www.mammothvacations.com).

Bishop has a number of dependable chain motels – such as Comfort Inn, Motel 6 and Best Western. The plain but cozy **Elms Motel** (☎ 760-873-8118, 800-848-9226; 233 E Elm St; d $48) is a good budget choice.

Getting There & Around

Greyhound (☎ 775-882-3375; Carson City) buses travel Hwy 395 between Los Angeles and Carson City, Nevada, stopping in most towns. Free Mammoth Mountain shuttle buses make loops through Mammoth during ski season.

Pacific Northwest

CONTENTS

Some of the country's wildest and most diverse landscapes are found in Oregon and Washington. The ever-misty, moss-laden rain forests of the Olympic Peninsula and the vast, painted deserts of the John Day Fossil Beds could be on two different planets, yet it's easy to explore both in a few days' time. Add to that the rugged Oregon coast, the peaceful islands of Puget Sound, the volcanic peaks of the Cascade Range and the winding Columbia River Gorge and you have a nature lover's paradise. But these evocative landscapes aren't just for looking at. In the Northwest, you're expected to get outdoors and enjoy yourself – even if it's raining. The forests and coastlines are webbed with hiking trails, the rivers churn with white water for rafting and kayaking, and every mountain peak beckons rock climbers and mountaineers.

All this natural wonder is anchored by two of the country's most entertaining cities to visit. Seattle buzzes with a coffeehouse culture that provides innumerable retreats from inclement weather; the city's rich musical history, from jazz to grunge, has fostered an active club scene that makes it a fun destination for nightlife. Portland's riverside setting, between Mt Hood and the coast, is ideal for exploring its surroundings; the city's bookstores and microbreweries likewise reward exploration. And although the Northwest is in the far corner of mainland USA, it offers plenty of options for onward travel into Canada, north to Alaska and east to the Rocky Mountains.

HIGHLIGHTS

- Gazing into the deep blue eye of **Crater Lake** (p994)
- Counting starfish in a tidal pool at **Haystack Rock** on the Oregon coast (p1001)
- Hunting for hops in Portland's many **microbreweries** (p990)
- Chasing the perfect **cappuccino** in Seattle (p1013)
- Reenacting scenes from *Lord of the Rings* in the ancient **Hoh River Rain Forest** (p1019)

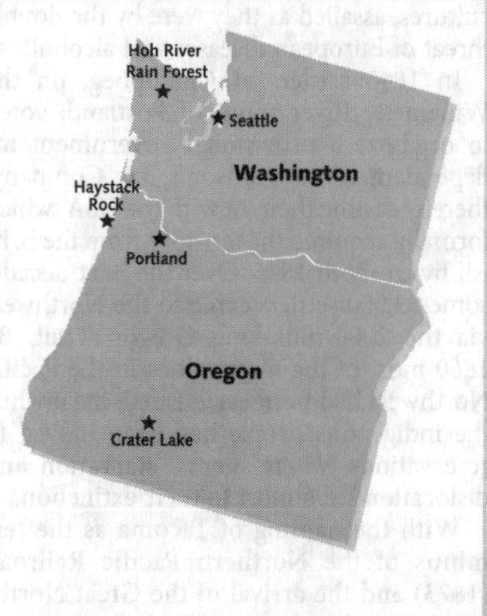

HISTORY

If the ancestors of the Native Americans did arrive via a land bridge from Russia to Alaska, the coasts, islands and river valleys of the Pacific Northwest must have been among the continent's first populated areas. When Europeans arrived in the 18th century, societies such as the Chinook and the Salish already had well-established, prosperous communities based on the rich supply of seafood. Inland, on the arid plateaus between the Cascades and the Rocky Mountains, cultures such as the Nez Percé and Spokane thrived on seasonal migration between river valleys and temperate uplands.

Three hundred years after Columbus landed in the New World, Spanish and British explorers were probing the northern Pacific coast, still seeking the fabled Northwest Passage. Captain George Vancouver was, in 1792, the first explorer to sail the waters of Puget Sound, claiming British sovereignty over the entire region. At the same time, an American, Captain Robert Gray, found the mouth of the Columbia River. In 1805 the explorers Lewis and Clark crossed the Rockies and made their way down the Columbia to the Pacific Ocean, extending the US claim on the territory.

In 1824 the British Hudson's Bay Company established Fort Vancouver in Washington as headquarters for the Columbia region. This opened the door to waves of settlers but had a devastating impact on the indigenous cultures, assailed as they were by the double threat of European diseases and alcohol.

In 1843 settlers at Champoeg, on the Willamette River south of Portland, voted to organize a provisional government independent of the Hudson's Bay Company, thereby casting their lot with the USA, which formally acquired the territory from the British by treaty in 1846. Over the next decade, some 53,000 settlers came to the Northwest via the 2000-mile-long Oregon Trail. By 1860 most of the major cities in the Pacific Northwest had been established; meanwhile the indigenous people had been moved to reservations, where illness, starvation and dislocation led almost to their extinction.

With the naming of Tacoma as the terminus of the Northern Pacific Railroad (1873) and the arrival of the Great Northern Railroad in Seattle (1893), the future of the region was set. Agriculture and lumber became the pillars of the regional economy until 1914, when the opening of the Panama Canal and WWI brought increased trade to Pacific ports. Shipyards opened along Puget Sound, and the Boeing aircraft company set up shop near Seattle.

Big dam projects in the 1930s and '40s provided cheap hydroelectricity and irrigation. WWII offered another boost for aircraft manufacturing and shipbuilding, and agriculture continued to thrive. In the postwar period Washington's population, especially around Puget Sound, grew to twice that of Oregon. But hydroelectricity production and the massive irrigation projects along the Columbia have nearly destroyed the river's ecosystem beyond repair. Logging has also left its scars, especially in Oregon. The environment remains a contentious issue in the Northwest; flash points are the logging of old-growth forests and the destruction of salmon runs in streams and rivers.

In the 1980s and '90s, the economic emphasis shifted again as the high-tech industry, embodied by Microsoft in Seattle and Intel in Portland, took hold in the region.

More recently, the tech industry has suffered the slings and arrows of a troubled national economy, and unemployment in the Northwest has soared.

GEOGRAPHY & CLIMATE

The major geographical regions are the coastal mountains and islands, the Cascade Range, and the plateaus stretching from east of the Cascades to the Rocky Mountain foothills. The mighty Columbia River drains nearly all of Oregon, Washington and Idaho. West of the Cascades, forests are fast-growing and dense. Wild berries proliferate in the undergrowth, alongside ferns, rhododendrons and Oregon grape. This area is the domain of mule deer, elk and black bear, and birds including Steller's jays, crows, ravens, rufous hummingbirds and woodpeckers; along streams dwell herons, kingfishers, ducks and loons. At the coast, sea lions and whales can be spotted in spring, and gulls, puffins, cormorants and pelicans take flight.

East of the Cascades, forests are dominated by ponderosa and lodgepole pines, with western juniper and silver sage in the savannas. Birds include the western meadowlark, nighthawk, falcon, osprey and bald eagle. Coyote, elk, mule deer and pronghorn antelope roam. Bighorn sheep have been reintroduced on mountain peaks and in canyons.

Most travelers visit in summer and fall, the period of least rainfall. In eastern Oregon and Washington, spring brings beautiful days and wildflowers. West of the Cascades, the precipitation doesn't subside until after May.

INFORMATION

For highway conditions in Oregon, call ☎ 800-977-6368, or ☎ 503-588-2941 from out of state. In Washington, call ☎ 206-368-4499 in Seattle or ☎ 800-695-7623 elsewhere in the state.

Oregon and western Washington have a 10-digit dialing system for local calls. To make a local call within the ☎ 206, ☎ 253, ☎ 425, ☎ 360 and ☎ 564 area codes in Washington, and throughout Oregon, you must dial the area code first (without a 1).

Oregon has no state sales tax, but most towns have a local 'lodging tax' of 6% to 11% on accommodations. Washington sales tax is 6.5%, but county and city taxes can bring it up to 8% or more.

The following are good sources for visitor information:

Nature of the Northwest (☎ 503-872-2750, 800-270-7504; www.naturenw.org/forest-directory.htm; Suite 177, 800 NE Oregon St, Portland, OR 97232; 9am-5pm Mon-Fri) Recreational information on national forests and state parks of the region; sells the Northwest Forest Pass (per day/year $5/30), required at many parks, trailheads, visitors centers and boat launches.

Oregon Tourism Commission (☎ 503-986-0000, 800-547-7842; www.traveloregon.com; 775 Summer St NE, Salem, OR 97301; 8am-5pm Mon-Fri) Sends out information and brochures on accommodations, camping, state parks and recreation outfitters.

Washington State Tourism Office (☎ 360-725-5052; www.tourism.wa.gov; 7am-7pm) Useful website; 'travel counselors' give advice by phone.

NATIONAL & STATE PARKS

Oregon has one national park, Crater Lake; Washington has three – Olympic, North Cascades and Mt Rainier. Nature of the Northwest (see Information) has information, maps and passes. There are 240 state parks in Oregon and 215 in Washington.

National Park Service (☎ 202-208-6843; www.nps.gov/parks.html; 1849 C St NW, Washington, DC 20240)

Oregon State Parks & Recreation Dept (☎ 503-378-6305, 800-551-6949; www.oregonstateparks.org; 1115 Commercial St NE, Salem, OR 97310)

Washington State Parks & Recreation Commission (☎ 360-902-8844, 800-233-0321; www.parks.wa.gov; PO Box 42650, Olympia, WA 98504)

ACTIVITIES

The 2638-mile Pacific Crest Trail passes through some of the most beautiful **hiking** areas in the Northwest. In Oregon, the 40-mile Timberline Trail circles Mt Hood, and a series of long **beach walks** line the coast. In Washington, Olympic National Park is wild and remote, most of it accessible only by foot. The Hoh River Trail is one of the park's most popular, traversing North America's only temperate rain forest and climbing Mt Olympus. Wonderland Trail, in Mt Rainier National Park, is a 93-mile loop.

Favorite destinations for **cycling** include the San Juan Islands in Washington and the Oregon Coast Bike Route, which follows Hwy 101 from Astoria to the California border.

Crystal Mountain, Snoqualmie Pass and Stevens Pass are the best **downhill ski resorts** in Washington; Mt Baker is great for **snowboarders** (see www.skiwashington.com for links to resort websites.). In Oregon, Timberline at Mt Hood offers downhill skiing and **snowshoeing** nearly year-round, and Mt Bachelor is famous for powder. For spectacular **cross-country skiing**, try Mt St Helens, Mt Rainier, the Methow area and Olympic National Park in Washington, and Rim Dr around Crater Lake in Oregon.

The Skagit and Wenatchee Rivers in Washington offer good **white-water rafting**. **Sea kayaking** is excellent in Puget Sound, especially with **whale-watching**. In Oregon, the Deschutes and the Rogue Rivers offer good **paddling**.

GETTING THERE & AWAY

AIR

Sea-Tac (Seattle-Tacoma) is the main airport in the Northwest, with daily service to Europe, Asia and points throughout the USA and Canada. Portland International Airport (PDX) serves the US, Canada and has nonstop flights to Frankfurt, Germany and Guadalajara, Mexico. See p1109 for a listing of major airlines.

PACIFIC NORTHWEST

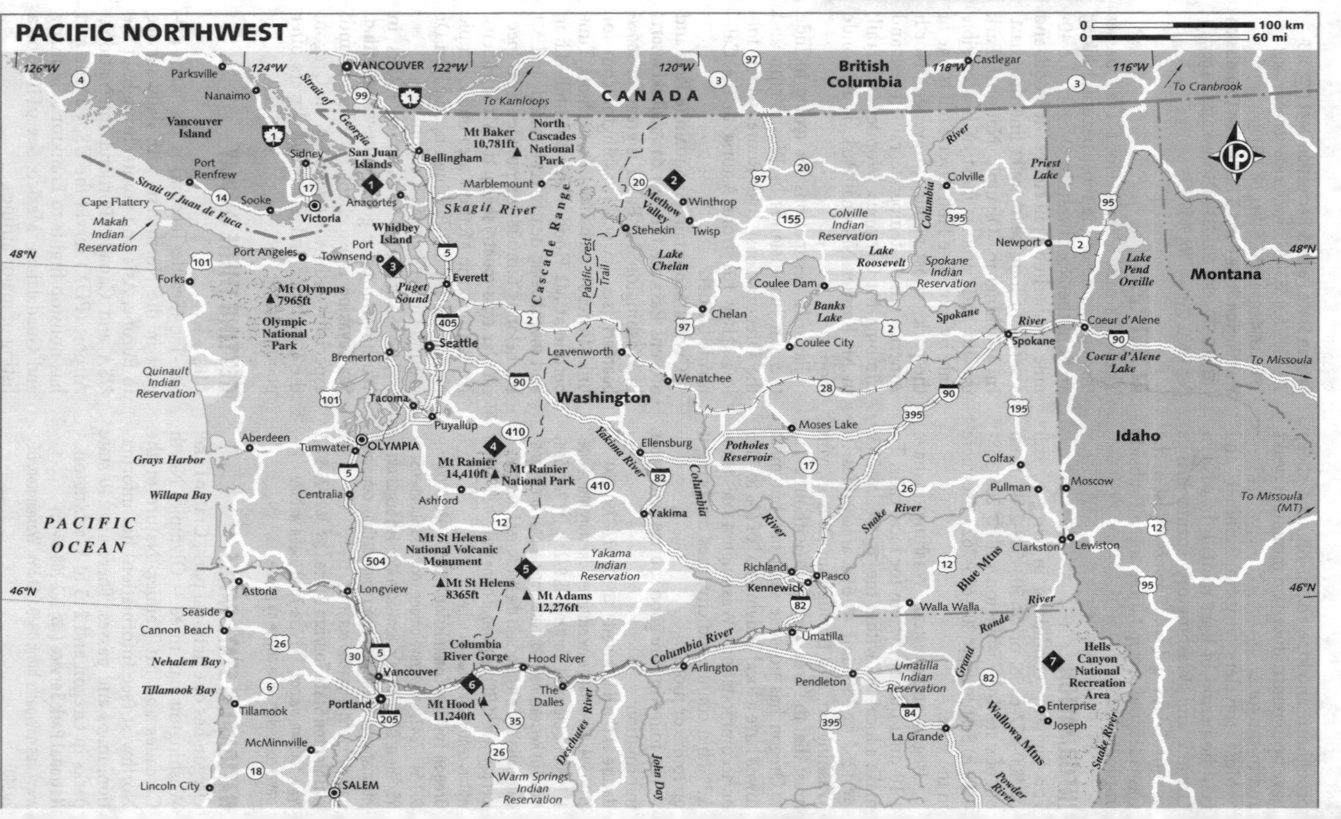
PACIFIC NORTHWEST
0 100 km
0 60 mi
CANADA
British Columbia
Washington
Idaho
Montana
Vancouver Island
PACIFIC OCEAN
To Cranbrook
To Missoula
To Missoula (MT)
To Kamloops
126°W
124°W
122°W
120°W
118°W
116°W
48°N
46°N
Parksville
Nanaimo
Port Renfrew
Sooke
Victoria
Sidney
VANCOUVER
Strait of Georgia
Strait of Juan de Fuca
San Juan Islands
Anacortes
Whidbey Island
Port Townsend
Port Angeles
Cape Flattery
Makah Indian Reservation
Forks
Mt Olympus 7965ft
Olympic National Park
Quinault Indian Reservation
Aberdeen
Grays Harbor
Willapa Bay
Bellingham
Mt Baker 10,781ft
North Cascades National Park
Marblemount
Skagit River
Cascade Range
Pacific Crest Trail
Stehekin
Methow Valley
Winthrop
Twisp
Lake Chelan
Chelan
Everett
Seattle
Puget Sound
Bremerton
Tacoma
OLYMPIA
Tumwater
Puyallup
Centralia
Leavenworth
Wenatchee
Ellensburg
Yakima River
Yakima
Mt Rainier 14,410ft
Mt Rainier National Park
Ashford
Mt St Helens National Volcanic Monument
Mt St Helens 8365ft
Mt Adams 12,276ft
Yakama Indian Reservation
Longview
Astoria
Seaside
Cannon Beach
Nehalem Bay
Tillamook Bay
Tillamook
McMinnville
Lincoln City
SALEM
Portland
Vancouver
Columbia River Gorge
Hood River
The Dalles
Mt Hood 11,240ft
Warm Springs Indian Reservation
Deschutes River
John Day
Arlington
Columbia River
Umatilla
Pendleton
Umatilla Indian Reservation
La Grande
Grand Ronde River
Wallowa Mtns
Powder River
Enterprise
Joseph
Hells Canyon National Recreation Area
Snake River
Lewiston
Clarkston
Walla Walla
Blue Mtns
Kennewick
Richland
Pasco
Potholes Reservoir
Moses Lake
Columbia River
Coulee Dam
Banks Lake
Coulee City
Colville Indian Reservation
Lake Roosevelt
Spokane Indian Reservation
Spokane
Spokane River
Colville
Columbia River
Castlegar
Newport
Priest Lake
Lake Pend Oreille
Coeur d'Alene
Coeur d'Alene Lake
Colfax
Pullman
Moscow
1
2
3
4
5
6
7

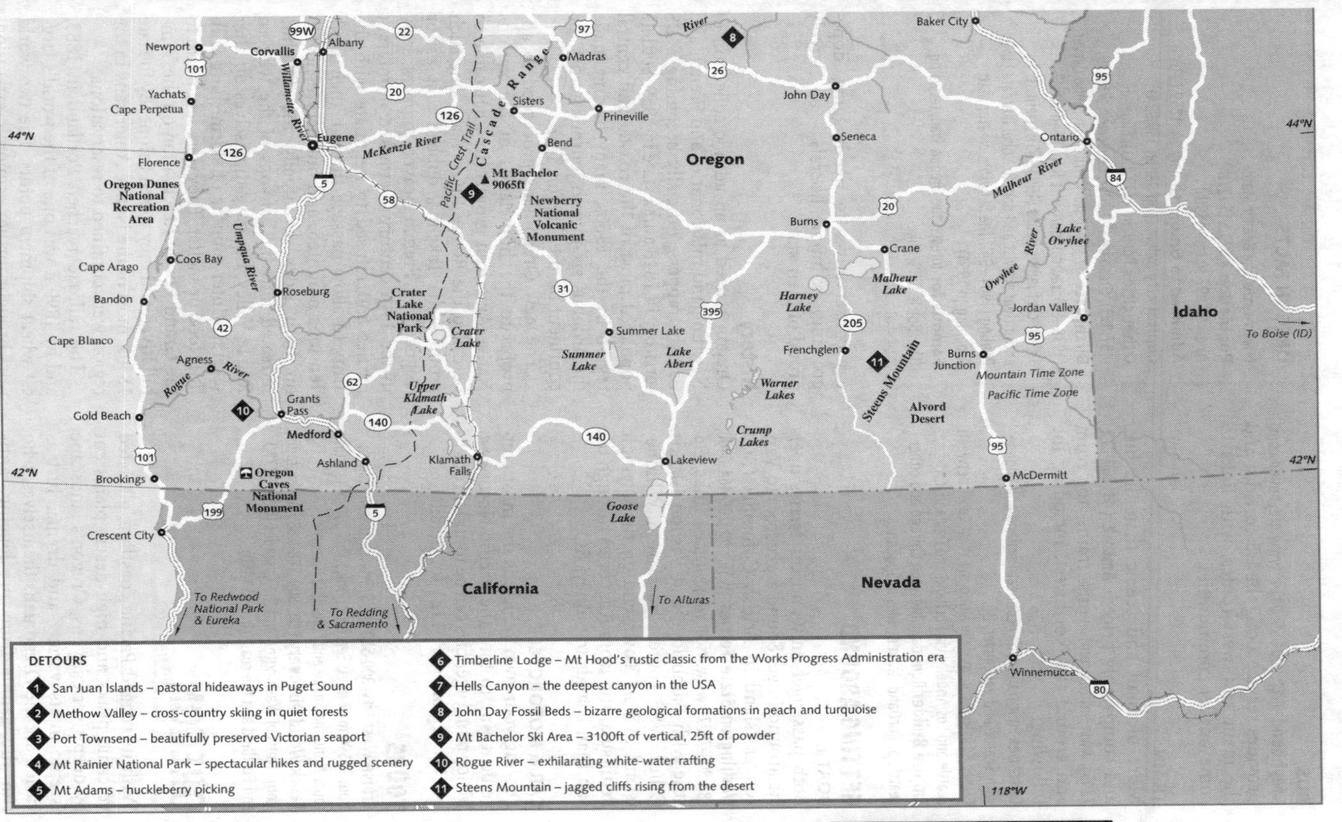

PACIFIC NORTHWEST

BUS

Greyhound (☎ 800-229-9424; www.greyhound.com) provides service along the I-5 corridor and the main east–west routes, with links to some smaller communities.

TRAIN

More pleasant and scenic than the bus, and comparably priced, **Amtrak** (☎ 800-872-7245; www.amtrak.com) runs trains to, from and around the Northwest, including the following:

Cascades Four trains a day connect Portland and Eugene with Seattle and Vancouver, BC.

Coast Starlight Runs daily along the West Coast between Seattle and Los Angeles via Portland and Oakland, CA.

Empire Builder Runs daily between Chicago and either Seattle or Portland; train divides in Spokane.

GETTING AROUND

BOAT

Both passenger-only and car ferries operate around Puget Sound and across to Vancouver Island in British Columbia (BC). **Washington State Ferries** (WSF; ☎ 206-464-6400, 888-808-7977; www.wsdot.wa.gov/ferries) links Seattle with Bainbridge and Vashon Islands. Other WSF routes cross from Whidbey Island to Port Townsend on the Olympic Peninsula, and from Anacortes through the San Juan Islands to Sidney, BC.

CAR & MOTORCYCLE

Driving your own vehicle is the most convenient way to tour the Pacific Northwest. Major rental agencies can be found throughout the region; see p1121 for details.

TOURS

Cruise West (☎ 800-580-0072; www.cruisewest.com; from $2599 for 7 days; Sep & Oct only) This 800-mile cruise tours along the Snake and Columbia Rivers.

Tauck World Discovery (☎ 800-788-7885; www.tauck.com) Tours of Washington and the Cascades (from $1770) and Portland and the coast (from $1850).

OREGON

With its rugged Pacific coastline, glaciated volcanic peaks and high-desert plains cut by deep river canyons, Oregon's landscape is epic in its variety and drama. Just as varied are the Oregonians themselves, who run the gamut from pro-logging, anti-gay conservatives to tree-hugging, dope-growing, ex-hippie liberals – all fiercely proud of their state.

OREGON FACTS

Nickname The Beaver State
Population 3,521,515 (27th)
Area 95,997 sq miles (9th)
Admitted to Union February 14, 1859 (33rd)
Capital city Salem (population 139,924)
Other cities Portland (529,121), Eugene (137,893), Gresham (90,205), Beaverton (76,129)
Birthplace of short-story writer Raymond Carver (1938–88); radical journalist John Reed (1887-1920); chef James Beard (1903–85); scientist, antinuclear activist and double Nobel laureate Linus Pauling (1901–94); *The Simpsons* creator Matt Groening (b 1954)
Famous for forests, the Oregon Trail, recycling (the 'Bottle Bill'), Nike

History

Oregon started as an ad hoc collection of New England missionaries and French and British trappers, officially becoming a US territory in 1848 and a state in 1859. Settlers populated most of the coastal and central region by the 1860s, many having made the arduous six-month journey across the continent on the Oregon Trail.

The new Oregonians proceeded to appropriate the homelands of the various Native American groups. In what came to be called the Rogue River Wars, one such group – the Takelma, dubbed *coquins*, or 'rogues,' by French beaver trappers early in the 19th century – attacked immigrant parties and refused to negotiate with the army to allow passage through their land. Tensions mounted, and butchery escalated on both sides. Eventually the Takelma retreated into the canyons of the western Rogue Valley, but gave themselves up after several winter months of skirmishing with little food or shelter. They were sent north to the Grand Ronde Reservation on the Yamhill River, and they weren't alone. By the late 1850s, most of the Native Americans in the region were confined to reservations.

The railroad reached Portland in 1883, and by 1890 it was one of the world's largest wheat-shipment points. The two world wars brought further economic expansion, much of it from logging. In the postwar era, idealistic baby boomers flooded into Oregon from California and the eastern states, seeking alternative lifestyles and natural surroundings. These arrivals brought pace-setting policies on many environmental and social issues. Oregon continues to be one of the faster-growing states in the country.

Since the 1960s, Portland and western Oregon have been particularly influenced by the new, politically progressive settlers, while small towns and rural areas have remained conservative. Its ballot-initiative system gives Oregonians the opportunity to advance citizen-proposed laws to the ballot box, and Oregon has become a stage for political dramas on divisive issues – such as physician-assisted suicide – in which the whole country has an interest.

PORTLAND

Portland is a beautiful city, especially in springtime when those infamous rains turn its many parks a supernatural green, and vivid pink rhododendrons grace every street. Nestled at the crux of the Columbia and Willamette Rivers, the city is spanned by nine bridges. Portlanders, generally a left-leaning bunch who tend to read and recycle with equal devotion, are justifiably enamored of their city's oft-praised planning and livability.

History

The Portland region was initially settled by retired trappers from the fur-trading post at nearby Fort Vancouver; the first building was erected in 1829. It was named by the flip of a coin (the other choice was 'Boston'). The city soon became the shipping center for much of the Northwest. During the 20th century it enjoyed steady growth, with a shipbuilding boom from WWII.

The port and shipping operations have since moved north of downtown, and much of the city's rough-and-tumble waterfront feel went with it. The Old Town has been substantially revitalized, and the once-industrial Pearl District now brims with expensive lofts. These days high-tech firms such as Intel and outdoor-gear companies such as Columbia Sportswear fuel economic growth, and they do so primarily from the suburbs (both Intel and Nike headquarters are west of the city).

Orientation

The Willamette River divides the city into east and west sides; Burnside St divides north from south, giving rise to the city's four quadrants. Downtown is in Southwest Portland; the historic Old Town and trendy shopping areas are in Northwest Portland. The Portland Streetcar connects Northwest and the Pearl with downtown, while

PORTLAND IN...

Two days

Breakfast at the **Bijou**, then grab the **MAX** to **Pioneer Courthouse Sq** for prime people-watching. Hit the museums on the **South Park Blocks** (they're small), then catch a streetcar down SW 10th Ave to the literary buffet of **Powell's City of Books, Reading Frenzy** and **CounterMedia**. Nestle into the dungeon of **Ringlers Annex** with your new treasures and sip a scotch or a pint of local brew. See who's playing at the **Crystal Ballroom**, or walk down Burnside St to **Berbati's Pan**. Next day, get a postcard view of Portland from the **Washington Park Rose Garden**; visit the **Zoo** or **Japanese Garden**; squeeze in some shopping along **NW 23rd** or catch an art film at **Cinema 21**; and relax with dinner at **Higgins**.

Four days

Follow the two-day itinerary then, next morning, stroll along **Tom McCall Waterfront Park** (through Saturday Market if it's a weekend) and across the Steel Bridge to the **Eastbank Esplanade**. Take the kids to **OMSI**, where they can explore the scientific world while you watch Everest in **Omnimax**. Catch the No 14 bus to **Hawthorne Blvd** for shopping, snacks, microbrews and patchouli-scented people-watching.

On day four, take a hike in **Forest Park**, then cross the river to have lunch or dinner in a stylish little winebar on **NE 28th Ave**.

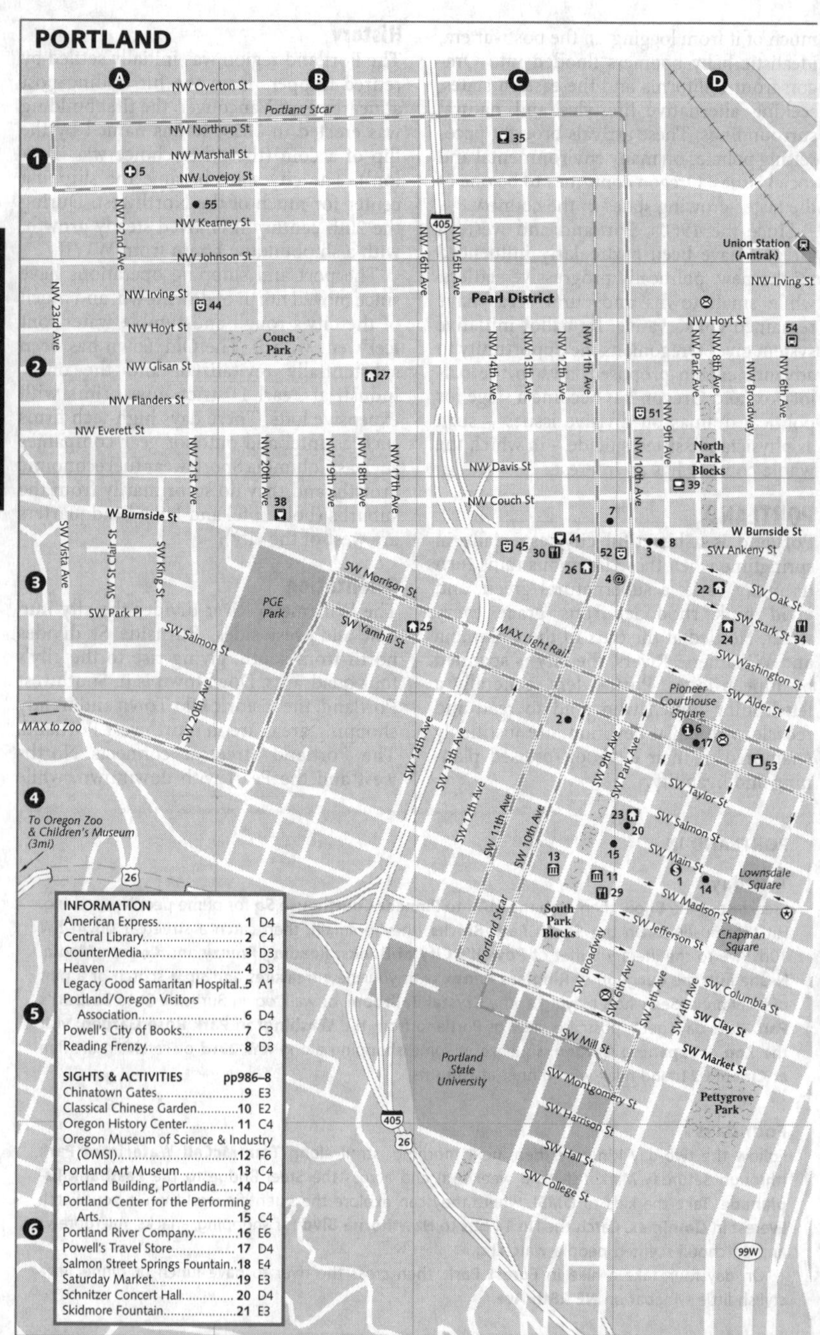
PORTLAND
A
B
C
D
1
2
3
4
5
6
NW Overton St
Portland Stcar
NW Northrup St
NW Marshall St
NW Lovejoy St
NW Kearney St
NW Johnson St
NW Irving St
NW Hoyt St
NW Glisan St
NW Flanders St
NW Everett St
NW Davis St
NW Couch St
W Burnside St
NW 23rd Ave
NW 22nd Ave
NW 21st Ave
NW 20th Ave
NW 19th Ave
NW 18th Ave
NW 17th Ave
NW 16th Ave
NW 15th Ave
NW 14th Ave
NW 13th Ave
NW 12th Ave
NW 11th Ave
NW 10th Ave
NW 9th Ave
NW Park Ave
NW 8th Ave
NW Broadway
NW 6th Ave
Union Station (Amtrak)
Pearl District
Couch Park
North Park Blocks
405
SW Vista Ave
SW St Clair St
SW King St
SW Park Pl
SW Salmon St
SW 20th Ave
PGE Park
SW Morrison St
SW Yamhill St
MAX Light Rail
SW Ankeny St
SW Oak St
SW Stark St
SW Washington St
SW Alder St
Pioneer Courthouse Square
SW Taylor St
SW Salmon St
SW Main St
SW Madison St
SW Jefferson St
SW Columbia St
SW Clay St
SW Market St
SW Mill St
SW Montgomery St
SW Harrison St
SW Hall St
SW College St
SW 14th Ave
SW 13th Ave
SW 12th Ave
SW 11th Ave
SW 10th Ave
SW 9th Ave
SW Park Ave
SW Broadway
SW 6th Ave
SW 5th Ave
SW 4th Ave
Portland Stcar
South Park Blocks
Lownsdale Square
Chapman Square
Pettygrove Park
Portland State University
MAX to Zoo
To Oregon Zoo & Children's Museum (3mi)
26
405
99W
INFORMATION
American Express....................1 D4
Central Library....................2 C4
CounterMedia....................3 D3
Heaven....................4 D3
Legacy Good Samaritan Hospital..5 A1
Portland/Oregon Visitors Association....................6 D4
Powell's City of Books....................7 C3
Reading Frenzy....................8 D3
SIGHTS & ACTIVITIES pp986–8
Chinatown Gates....................9 E3
Classical Chinese Garden....................10 E2
Oregon History Center....................11 C4
Oregon Museum of Science & Industry (OMSI)....................12 F6
Portland Art Museum....................13 C4
Portland Building, Portlandia....................14 D4
Portland Center for the Performing Arts....................15 C4
Portland River Company....................16 E6
Powell's Travel Store....................17 D4
Salmon Street Springs Fountain..18 E4
Saturday Market....................19 E3
Schnitzer Concert Hall....................20 D4
Skidmore Fountain....................21 E3

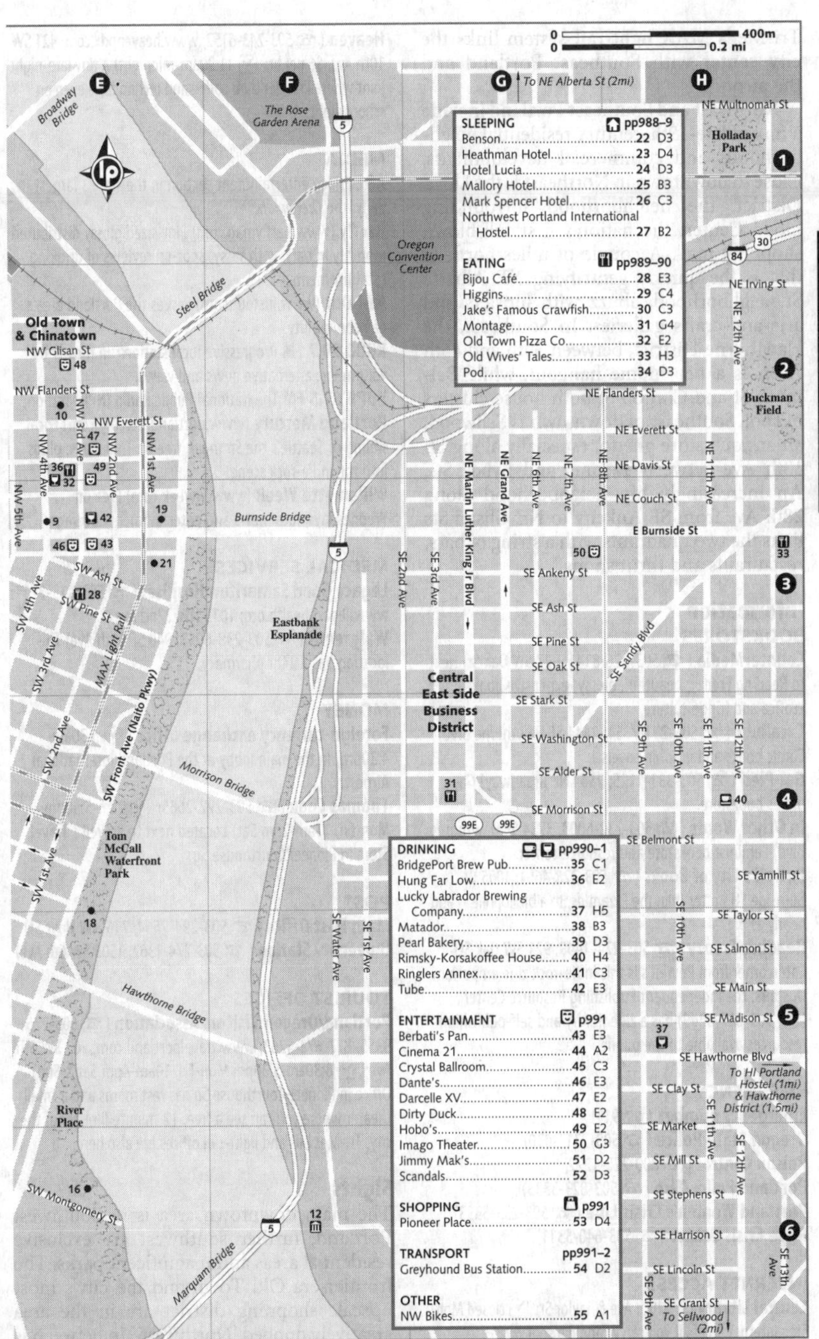
0 400m
0 0.2 mi
E
F
G
H
To NE Alberta St (2mi)
Broadway Bridge
The Rose Garden Arena
NE Multnomah St
Holladay Park
Oregon Convention Center
Steel Bridge
NE Irving St
NE 12th Ave
Old Town & Chinatown
NW Glisan St
NW Flanders St
NW Everett St
NW 3rd Ave
NW 2nd Ave
NW 1st Ave
NW 4th Ave
NW 5th Ave
Burnside Bridge
NE Flanders St
Buckman Field
NE Everett St
NE Davis St
NE Couch St
E Burnside St
NE Martin Luther King Jr Blvd
NE Grand Ave
NE 6th Ave
NE 7th Ave
NE 8th Ave
NE 11th Ave
SW Ash St
SW Pine St
SW 4th Ave
SW 3rd Ave
MAX Light Rail
SE 2nd Ave
SE 3rd Ave
SE Ankeny St
SE Ash St
SE Pine St
SE Oak St
SE Stark St
SE Sandy Blvd
Eastbank Esplanade
Central East Side Business District
SW Front Ave (Naito Pkwy)
SW 2nd Ave
Morrison Bridge
SE Washington St
SE Alder St
SE Morrison St
SE Belmont St
SE 9th Ave
SE 10th Ave
SE 11th Ave
SE 12th Ave
SE Yamhill St
SE Taylor St
SE Salmon St
SE Main St
SE Madison St
SE Hawthorne Blvd
To HI Portland Hostel (1mi) & Hawthorne District (1.5mi)
SE Clay St
SE Market
SE Mill St
SE Stephens St
SE Harrison St
SE Lincoln St
SE Grant St
To Sellwood (2mi)
SE 13th Ave
SW 1st Ave
Tom McCall Waterfront Park
Hawthorne Bridge
SE Water Ave
SE 1st Ave
River Place
SW Montgomery St
Marquam Bridge
SLEEPING pp988–9
Benson........22 D3
Heathman Hotel........23 D4
Hotel Lucia........24 D3
Mallory Hotel........25 B3
Mark Spencer Hotel........26 C3
Northwest Portland International Hostel........27 B2
EATING pp989–90
Bijou Café........28 E3
Higgins........29 C4
Jake's Famous Crawfish........30 C3
Montage........31 G4
Old Town Pizza Co........32 E2
Old Wives' Tales........33 H3
Pod........34 D3
DRINKING pp990–1
BridgePort Brew Pub........35 C1
Hung Far Low........36 E2
Lucky Labrador Brewing Company........37 H5
Matador........38 B3
Pearl Bakery........39 D3
Rimsky-Korsakoffee House........40 H4
Ringlers Annex........41 C3
Tube........42 E3
ENTERTAINMENT p991
Berbati's Pan........43 E3
Cinema 21........44 A2
Crystal Ballroom........45 C3
Dante's........46 E3
Darcelle XV........47 E2
Dirty Duck........48 E2
Hobo's........49 E2
Imago Theater........50 G3
Jimmy Mak's........51 D2
Scandals........52 D3
SHOPPING p991
Pioneer Place........53 D4
TRANSPORT pp991–2
Greyhound Bus Station........54 D2
OTHER
NW Bikes........55 A1
PACIFIC NORTHWEST

Tri-Met's MAX light-rail system links the city center with Southeast Portland and the airport.

Northeast and Southeast Portland include a mix of late-19th-century residential neighborhoods and commercial developments. Close to downtown in Northeast is the Lloyd District, the neighborhood surrounding Lloyd Center, the nation's first full-blown shopping mall. A couple of miles north of that is the quickly gentrifying NE Alberta St neighborhood, abuzz with hipsters and arts-and-crafts galleries. In Southeast, the Hawthorne District, between 30th and 45th Aves, is a neo-hippie hangout, while Belmont St and Clinton St both house clusters of cool. Southeast of downtown is Sellwood, an antique-store ghetto, especially along SE 13th Ave between Tacoma and Bybee Sts. An increasingly hip neighborhood along 28th Ave from SE Ankeny to NE Glisan Sts links the two quadrants with a string of bars, restaurants and thrift shops.

Information

BOOKSTORES

CounterMedia (☎ 503-226-8141; 927 SW Oak St) Next to Reading Frenzy; beautiful, glossy, expensive books of erotica and fringe culture.
Excalibur (☎ 503-231-7351; 2444 SE Hawthorne Blvd) Comic books and graphic novels.
Gai-Pied (☎ 503-331-1125; 2544 NE Broadway) Gay men's bookstore.
In Other Words (☎ 503-232-6003; 3734 SE Hawthorne Blvd) Feminist bookstore and resource center.
Powell's City of Books (☎ 503-228-4651; 1005 W Burnside St) Better than the Pyramids, to a bibliophile – and nearly as big.
Reading Frenzy (☎ 503-274-1449; 921 SW Oak St) Catercorner from Powell's is this indie-rock zine emporium. Upstairs, the Independent Publishing Resource Center (☎ 503-827-0249) has a zine library and self-publishing resources available to the public.

EMERGENCY

Emergency number (☎ 911)
Oregon State Police (☎ 503-731-3030)
Poison Control (☎ 800-222-1222)
Portland Police/Fire (☎ 503-823-3333)
Portland Women's Crisis Line (☎ 503-235-5333)
Rape Crisis Center (☎ 503-640-5311)

INTERNET ACCESS

Central Library (SW 10th Ave & Taylor St; 🕒 closed Mon) Free Internet access if you can wrangle a spot.
Heaven (☎ 503-243-6152; www.heavenpdx.com; 421 SW 10th Ave; $6 per hr; 🕒 11:30am-midnight) A tiny late-night joint where kids get their coffee and techno fix – even on school nights.

MEDIA

A&E Friday entertainment section in the state's largest daily, the *Oregonian*.
Barfly (www.barflymag.com) Pint-sized glossy distributed monthly in bars, with sassy, spot-on reviews of drinking establishments.
Just Out (www.justout.com) Serves the Portland area's gay community.
KBOO 90.7 FM Progressive local station run mostly by volunteers; alternative news and views.
KOPB 91.5 FM The National Public Radio (NPR) station.
Portland Mercury (www.portlandmercury.com) Local sibling of Seattle's the *Stranger*, free on Thursdays; plugs into the indie-rock scene.
Willamette Week (www.wweek.com) Free on Wednesdays, local news and entertainment coverage.

MEDICAL SERVICES

Legacy Good Samaritan Hospital (☎ 503-413-7711; www.legacyhealth.org; 1015 NW 22nd Ave)
Walgreens (☎ 503-238-6053; 940 SE 39th Ave) This location has a 24hr pharmacy.

MONEY

Foreign-currency exchange office (🕒 5:30am-4:30pm) In the main lobby at the Portland International Airport.
Thomas Cook (☎ 503-222-2665; 🕒 9am-5:30pm Mon-Fri, 11am-2pm Sat) Located next to Powell's Travel Store in Pioneer Courthouse Sq.

POST

Main Post Office (☎ 503-294-2564; 715 NW Hoyt St)
University Station (☎ 503-274-1362; 1505 SW 6th Ave)

TOURIST OFFICES

Portland/Oregon Visitors Association (☎ 503-275-8355, 877-678-5263; www.travelportland.com; 701 SW 6th Ave; 🕒 8:30am-5:30pm Mon-Fri, 10am-4pm Sat & Sun) Office in Pioneer Courthouse Sq has rest rooms and a small theater where you can see a free, 12-minute film about the city. Tri-Met bus and light-rail offices are also here.

Sights

The main downtown area is in Southwest Portland; further southwest are exclusive residential areas and magnificent parks. The frontier-era Old Town and the city's most upscale shopping district are in the area creatively dubbed 'Northwest.' In between is the Pearl District, an old warehouse precinct that's now a chic neighborhood full of lofts.

DOWNTOWN

Known as 'Portland's living room,' **Pioneer Courthouse Sq** (☎ 503-223-1613; SW 6th Ave & Morrison St) was once the regal Hotel Portland (1890–1950) and later a parking garage; it may soon hold an ice-skating rink. When it isn't full of hackeysack players, the space hosts concerts, festivals and rallies almost daily, especially during summer when downtown office workers enjoy their lunches on its steps. At night, the northwest corner is overtaken by street kids, but they won't bother you except to ask for change. Across 6th Ave is the square's namesake Pioneer Courthouse (1875).

Built in 1980, the **Portland Building** (SW 5th Ave & Main St) was designed by Michael Graves – on one of his off days, many would argue. Though derided by those who have to work in its windowless gloom, and often ridiculed for its flamboyant exterior, the building holds the distinction of being the world's first major postmodern structure. It's also one of Portland's few examples of ambitious architecture. Above its main doors crouches **Portlandia**, an immense statue representing the Goddess of Commerce.

Housed along the tree-shaded **South Park Blocks** (an ideal lunch spot, especially in summer when Pioneer Sq gets crowded and hot), the newly expanded and renovated **Oregon History Center** (OHS; ☎ 503-222-1741; www.ohs.org; 1200 SW Park Ave; adult/child $6/1.50; 🕑 10am-5pm Tue-Wed & Fri-Sat, 10am-8pm Thu, noon-5pm Sun) is the state's premier museum of history. It holds an impressive archive of photos and documents and has an excellent book- and gift-shop.

Across the park from OHS, the **Portland Art Museum** (☎ 503-226-2811; www.pam.org; 1219 SW Park Ave; adult/child $10/6; 🕑 10am-5pm Tue, Wed, Sat, 10am-8pm Thu & Fri, noon-5pm Sun) seems a bit skimpy for the price, unless a nationally touring show is in town. The museum did score a coup in acquiring the 152-piece Clement Greenberg collection of American art (though it's usually on tour), and its exhibit of Northwest Native American carvings is excellent. A planned expansion is in the works.

Two big performing-arts venues, the **Schnitzer Concert Hall** and the **Portland Center for the Performing Arts**, face each other across SW Main St at Broadway.

OLD TOWN & CHINATOWN

The core of 1890s Portland, **Old Town** once felt dodgy but, thanks to a number of new clubs, is now among the most lively sections of town after dark. Running beneath it are the **shanghai tunnels** (☎ 503-622-4798; adult/child $11/6), a series of underground corridors through which nefarious ship captains used to shanghai drunken sailors, dragging them aboard as indentured workers. Tours are by appointment.

The ornate gates on Burnside St at SW 4th Ave welcome visitors to Chinatown. The authentic Suzhou-style **Classical Chinese Garden** (☎ 503-228-8131; NW 3rd Ave & Everett St; adult/child $7/5; 🕑 summer 9am-6pm, winter 10am-5pm; wheelchair accessible) is a one-block haven of tranquility with a teahouse in the 'Tower of Cosmic Reflections.' Tours (free with admission) leave at noon and 1pm daily.

A preserve of Victorian-era architecture, the district that surrounds **Skidmore Fountain** (SW 1st Ave & Ankeny St) bustles from March to December with **Saturday Market** (🕑 10am-5pm Sat, 11am-4:30pm Sun), complete with buskers, food carts and tie-dye T-shirts.

Two-mile-long **Tom McCall Waterfront Park**, which flanks the west bank of the Willamette River from SW Clay St to the Steel Bridge, was a freeway until 1974, when it was torn up and replaced with a grassy riverside promenade. The park is now a venue for summer festivals and concerts. In warm weather, the computer-controlled **Salmon Street Springs** fountain swarms with frolicking kids. The walking/bicycling/skating/jogging route along the waterfront was extended in 2002 across the Steel Bridge to the **Eastbank Esplanade**, a 1-mile walkway with good views of downtown occasionally dampened by freeway noise.

WEST HILLS & WASHINGTON PARK

Behind downtown Portland are the West Hills, a ridge of ancient volcanic peaks that divide the city from its westerly suburbs. The huge Washington Park complex contains the **International Rose Test Gardens** (☎ 503-823-3636; admission free; 🕑 dawn to dusk) with 400 types of rose, including many rare varieties. Farther uphill is the lush **Japanese Garden** (☎ 503-223-1321; www.japanesegarden.com; adult/child $6.50/4; 🕑 10am-4pm Oct-Mar, 10am-7pm Apr-Sep; Ⓟ), closed until noon on Mondays. A real treat in fall, **Hoyt Arboretum** (☎ 503-228-8733; 4000

Fairview Blvd; admission free; trails 5am-10pm, visitors center 9am-4pm; wheelchair accessible; P) has 10 miles of hiking trails that wind through 900 species of tree.

You can feel like old-money Portland without even paying admission at **Pittock Mansion** (☎ 503-823-3624; www.pittockmansion.com; 3229 NW Pittock Dr; adult/child $5.25/2.50; 11am-4pm Jun-Aug, noon-4pm Sep-May, closed Jan; P). You can stroll the grounds and pretend you're king of all you survey.

Activities

Hikers will find more than 50 miles of **hiking** trails in Forest Park. Pick up a map of the park at the Hoyt Arboretum Visitor Center. The Wildwood Trail starts in the zoo/Children's Museum complex at the arboretum and winds through 30 miles of forest. Another easily accessible entry point is in Macleay Park at NW Thurman St and 26th Ave.

For good **mountain biking**, head uphill to the western end of NW Thurman St and continue past the gate onto Leif Erikson Dr, an old dirt logging road leading 11 miles into Forest Park (don't bike on the hiking trails!). For maps, contact the **Oregon Department of Transportation** (☎ 503-986-3602; www.odot.state.or.us/techserv/bikewalk/mapsinfo.htm).

Portland for Children

Kids and their parents both love **Oregon Museum of Science & Industry** (OMSI; ☎ 503-797-4000; www.omsi.edu; 1945 SE Water Ave; adult/child $8/6 for museum or theater, $4 planetarium or submarine, $17/13 all-museum pass; 9:30am-5pm Tue-Sun), which has hands-on science exhibits, an Omnimax theater, planetarium shows and the USS *Blueback* submarine.

In summer, the Zoo Train connects the Washington Park Rose Garden with the **Oregon Zoo** (☎ 503-226-1561; www.oregonzoo.org; 4001 SW Canyon Rd; adult/child $8/5; 9am-4pm Oct-Mar, 9am-6pm Apr-Sep), which has one of the world's most successful elephant breeding programs; inquire about summer concerts on the zoo's lawns.

Parents simply rave about the **Children's Museum** (☎ 503-223-6500; www.portlandcm2.org; 4015 SW Canyon Rd; admission $5.50; 9am-5pm Mon-Thu & Sat, 9am-8pm Fri, 11am-5pm Sun; P) near the zoo, with hands-on learning activities and exhibits. To get here, take the MAX or bus No 63.

Tours

Ecotours of Oregon (☎ 503-245-1428, 888-868-7733; www.ecotours-of-oregon.com; 3127 SE 23rd Ave; $40-60; scheduled on demand) Naturalist tours of northwest Oregon.

Portland River Company (☎ 503-229-0551; www.portlandrivercompany.com; $39-69; 315 SW Montgomery St) Year-round kayak tours of the Willamette River.

Portland Walking Tours (☎ 503-774-4522; www.portlandwalkingtours.com; adult/child $15/12) The 'A Walk Through Time' tour highlighting Old Town leaves at 3pm from Pioneer Sq every Friday, Saturday and Sunday.

Festivals & Events

Watch locals and suburbanites stake out prime parade-viewing territory by chaining lawn chairs to downtown sidewalks days in advance for the **Portland Rose Festival** (☎ 503-227-2681; www.rosefestival.org) which runs from late May to June. Other highlights of the city's biggest celebration include a seedy riverfront carnival in Tom McCall Waterfront Park, roaming packs of wild-eyed sailors, beauty queens and blooming roses.

Other festivals include the following:

Gay Pride Parade (☎ 503-295-9788; www.pridenw.org) Late June. March through downtown with dykes on bikes, the chief of police and 10,000 others.

Waterfront Blues Festival (☎ 503-282-0555; www.waterfrontbluesfest.com) July 4 weekend. Blues music of questionable authenticity but perennial appeal in Waterfront Park; proceeds go to the Oregon Food Bank.

Waterfront Park Oregon Brewers Festival (☎ 503-778-5917; www.oregonbrewfest.com) July. Quaff spring and summer microbrews from Oregon and elsewhere.

Sleeping

Most of central Portland's hotels are downtown or in Northeast, near the Lloyd District and convention center. On NE Airport Way, at I-205 exit 24, are several chain motels. Freeway exits around the outskirts of town are good places for budget options. The best place to camp near Portland is Oxbow Park in Gresham, just east of town. Downtown hotels generally have valet parking only, at $10 to $20 a night. Make summer reservations well in advance. An 11.5% bed tax will be added to the room rate listed, which, unless noted, is for high season.

BUDGET

White Eagle (☎ 503-335-8900, 866-271-3377; 836 N Russel St; dm $30, r $40-50) Opened in 1905, this musicians' hangout in an oft-ignored industrial corner of town is supposedly haunted. The

THE AUTHOR'S CHOICE

McMenamins Edgefield (☎ 503-669-8610; www.mcmenamins.com; 2126 SW Halsey St, Troutdale; dm/s $22/50, d $85-105, ste $115-130, f $200; golf from $10; movies $2-3) How many golf courses have a watering hole at every hole? At McMenamins Edgefield, a former county poor farm restored by Portland's McMenamin Brothers, you can do a multi-bar pub crawl amid squirrels and bunnies, enjoy some pitch-and-putt golf, taste the local wine, watch a movie and then collapse in your own bed mere steps away. The best spot here for sampling a scrumptious microbrew (whether or not you're in the midst of your round of golf) is the Little Red Shed, perhaps the single most adorable drinking establishment ever created. Only a handful of people fit inside the Beatrix Potter-ish hut, and those who do tend to curl up by the fire with a cigar and a glass of scotch, so plan ahead. But you won't miss out: there are half a dozen other bars on the complex, and if you're staying the night here, there's no reason not to try them all! To get here, drive east on Hwy 84 to the Troutdale exit, then take a right onto Halsey.

11 recently restored European-style rooms with shared baths are upstairs from a tavern where live acoustic music plays nightly, so it's best for night owls. But it's a great bargain and a piece of Portland music history.

HI Portland Hostel (☎ 503-236-3380, 866-447-3031; www.portlandhostel.org; 3031 SE Hawthorne Blvd; dm $18-21, f $38-48) This popular hostel is in a fun area and has good facilities and decent dorm beds. Check out the ecofriendly 'living roof.' Guests traveling by bicycle get a $3 discount. Take bus No 14 from downtown.

Northwest Portland International Hostel (☎ 503-241-2783; www.2oregonhostels.com; 1818 NW Glisan St; dm/s/d $18/46/52) Quieter and more adult-friendly than the Hawthorne location, this hostel in a tree-lined residential area is another good base, right between the Pearl District and Northwest Portland.

MID-RANGE

Mallory Hotel (☎ 503-223-6311; www.malloryhotel.com; 729 SW 15th Ave; r $95-155; Ⓟ) A local favorite, this classic boutique hotel has an understated charm. It's handy to the city center and has free parking. The adorable mirrored lounge has free popcorn.

Mark Spencer Hotel (☎ 503-224-3293; www.markspencer.com; 409 SW 11th Ave; r/ste from $99/119) This is a great deal for anyone staying several days, as all the well-furnished rooms have kitchenettes. It's smack in the middle of the Stark St nightlife action, always fun to watch.

McMenamins Kennedy School (☎ 503-249-3983; 5736 NE 33rd Ave; r $99-109) Finally, your chance to spend the night in a classroom! The former grade school is now a B&B/restaurant/bar complex, where you can drink and smoke in detention or the principal's office.

Hotel Lucia (☎ 503-225-1717, 877-225-1717; www.hotellucia.com; 400 SW Broadway; r from $125) The service entrance bears a lofty 'mission statement' and the lobby feels like a sleek techno nightclub, but the rooms in this newly face-lifted hotel, though smallish, have old-world elegance, and the service is tops.

TOP END

Heathman Hotel (☎ 503-241-4100; www.heathmanhotel.com; 1001 SW Broadway; r $139-209, ste $305-775) A Portland institution, the Heathman has top-notch service and one of the best restaurants in the city. The hotel has its own librarian who stocks its lending library with books signed by authors who have stayed here. There's high tea in the afternoons, jazz in the evenings, and each simple, spacious room is decorated with original Northwest art.

Lion & the Rose (☎ 503-287-9245, 800-955-1647; www.lionrose.com; 1810 NE 15th Ave; r $130-140) This adorable, turreted Queen Anne–style mansion in the upscale residential Irvington neighborhood of Northeast Portland has six B&B rooms, all with private baths.

Benson (☎ 503-228-2000, 888-523-6766; www.bensonhotel.com; 309 SW Broadway; r from $220) Extreme decadence is the theme here. Built in 1912 by a lumber tycoon, the Benson hosts celebrities, rock stars and high-level politicians; some of the rooms have pianos and whirlpool tubs. Even if you can't afford to stay, check out the classy bar in the lobby.

Eating

Portland has a vast selection of upscale, gourmet places and super-cheap dives, but not much in the mid-range. Self-catering is easy, though, with multiple options for organic grocery shopping (try Nature's Fresh Northwest or New Seasons, both with good delis). Most of the upscale joints are in Northwest and the Pearl District, and even at the snootiest of them, you can wear jeans and tennis shoes. Downtown, the **food carts** on SW 5th Ave at Stark St (locals call this cluster **'the Pod'**) offer cheap lunches.

Higgins (☎ 503-222-9070; 1239 SW Broadway; mains $10-25) If you spring for one fancy meal, do it here. Chef Greg Higgins consistently wins restaurant-of-the-year honors for his innovative preparation of fresh, locally grown organic ingredients. The cheaper bar menu includes downtown's best burger.

Montage (☎ 503-234-1324; 301 SE Morrison St; mains $4-10) The beloved Creole nightspot under the Morrison Bridge has long, white-clothed community tables, an aggressively oddball wait staff, oyster shooters, streetwine cocktails and legendary macaroni and cheese.

Old Wives' Tales (☎ 503-238-0470; 1300 E Burnside St; breakfast $5-8, dinner $8-12) This cornerstone of progressive Portland serves upscale organic comfort food, such as tofu scrambles and parchment-baked halibut with wild rice. There's a children's playroom off to the side.

Other recommendations:

Bijou Café (☎ 503-222-3187; 132 SW 3rd Ave; omelettes $6-8) Slightly pretentious, but the best place for breakfast downtown.

Bread & Ink Café (☎ 503-239-4756; 3610 SE Hawthorne Blvd; breakfast or lunch $6-12) A Portland standby; try blintzes, oysters or the salmon sandwich.

Jake's Famous Crawfish (☎ 503-226-1419; 401 SW 12th Ave; mains $8-18; 🕑 11:30 am-10 pm Sun-Thu, until midnight Fri & Sat) The best reason to visit this old-school seafood and steak establishment is the cheap happy-hour menu (snacks $2-4, 🕑 3-6pm Mon-Fri); arrive early for a table.

Old Town Pizza Co. (☎ 503- 222-9999; 226 NW Davis St; pies $7-10) Antique lamps, brick walls, low lights and velvet couches give away this rambling pizza parlor's past life as a bordello.

Vita Cafe (☎ 503- 335-8233; 3024 NE Alberta St; lunch $3-6) A vegan joint that serves burgers!

Drinking

Portland is rightly famous for its microbrews and brewpubs, but recently there's been a jump in the number of classy wine bars, with several near the corner of NE 28th Ave and Burnside St.

BARS

Alibi (☎ 503-287-5335; 4024 N Interstate Ave) Vehemently tiki-themed, this karaoke favorite has peppy servers and absurdly complicated tropical drinks. Show up before 9pm or hide in a black-lit corner to avoid the karaoke.

Hung Far Low (☎ 503-223-8686; 112 NW 4th Ave) Beyond the cruelly fluorescent-lit Chinese restaurant is a dark and cozy hideout, blessed by Buddha and a bartender who knows that quantity trumps quality. This is where your liver wants to go when it dies.

Other recommendations:

Horse Brass (☎ 503-232-2202; 4534 SE Belmont St) An authentic English pub, complete with football matches. Very smoky.

Matador (☎ 503-222-5822; 1967 W Burnside St) Smoke-choked old dive given new life by its hipster/rock 'n' roll clientele; absurdly cheap drinks and gross bathrooms.

Noble Rot (☎ 503-233-1999; 2724 SE Ankeny St) Sleek wine bar with excellent food in a very cool neo-industrial building.

Ringlers Annex (☎ 503-525-0520; 1223 SW Stark St) A multi-tiered bar in a triangle building, with a candlelit crypt in the basement.

Space Room (☎ 503-235-8303; 4800 SE Hawthorne Blvd) Flying saucers hang over the bar at this black hole in Hawthorne's 'Stumbling Zone'; killer Bloody Marys.

Tube (☎ 503-241-8823; 18 NW 3rd Ave) Are you sleek enough to be seen in a faux-*Space Odyssey* mint-green cylindrical bar?

BREW PUBS

Hair of the Dog (☎ 503-232-6585; 4509 SE 23rd Ave) The best local microbrewery, Hair of the Dog doesn't have its own brewpub, but it gives tours by appointment.

BridgePort Brew Pub (☎ 503-241-7179; www.bridgeportbrew.com; 1313 NW Marshall St), Portland's oldest microbrewery, BridgePort is a vast gathering place in a red-brick warehouse and is popular with groups. The beer is top-notch (try the great Black Strap Stout or the flagship Blue Heron) and the pizza's good too.

Lucky Labrador Brewing Company (☎ 503-236-3555; 915 SE Hawthorne Blvd) Quintessentially Portland, this is a friendly brewhall in industrial Southeast with a cool patio out back that invites people to bring their dogs.

Portland Brewing Company (☎ 503-228-5269; 2730 NW 31st Ave) The taproom at the Portland Brewing Company, which is in the outer industrial section of Northwest, has a nice patio and good food.

COFFEEHOUSES

Pearl Bakery (☎ 503-827-0910; 102 NW 9th Ave; pastries $3-5) Check out this bakery for delicious pastries and lunch for under $5; it's located near Powell's City of Books.

Pied Cow (☎ 503-230-4866; 3244 SE Belmont St; coffee, snacks $3-9) This elegant historic mansion has loads of atmosphere, gourmet munchies (try the lox plate) and an excellent patio.

Rimsky-Korsakoffee House (☎ 503-232-2640; 707 SE 12th Ave; coffee, snacks $3-5) This eccentric place has an unmarked facade that looks like a private home and blasts classical music like it's thrash metal. Rotating tabletops!

Entertainment

Check the *Mercury* or *Willamette Week* for listings and cover charges.

LIVE MUSIC

Dante's (☎ 503-226-6630; 1 SW 3rd Ave) National acts and vaudeville shows heat up this red, velvety bar, with an intimate stage, toasty fire pit and frosty barmaids.

Other venues include the following:

Berbati's Pan (☎ 503-248-4579; 10 SW 3rd Ave) Big and buzzing with the sound of chatter, this place features pricey drinks and eclectic billing.

Crystal Ballroom (☎ 503-778-5625; 1332 W Burnside St) Major touring bands play at this (usually all-ages) historic ballroom; the 'floating' dance floor bounces at the slightest provocation.

Jimmy Mak's (☎ 503-295-6542; 300 NW 10th Ave) Lively jazz venue.

GAY & LESBIAN VENUES

Scandals (☎ 503-227-5887; 1038 SW Stark St) This large-windowed, energetic club is a lynchpin of Portland's gay nightlife, which centers on SW Stark St at 11th Ave.

Egyptian Club (☎ 503-236-8689; 3701 SE Division St) Lesbians of all stripes gather at this Southeast Portland bar for dancing, pool and karaoke.

Other recommendations:

Darcelle XV (☎ 503-222-5338; 208 NW 3rd Ave) Portland's landmark drag club.

Dirty Duck (☎ 503-224-8446; 439 NW 3rd Ave) Working-class bear den, with pool tables.

Hobo's (☎ 503-224-3285; 120 NW 3rd Ave) Stylish piano bar.

CINEMAS

Bagdad Theater (☎ 503-232-6676; 3702 SE Hawthorne Blvd; admission $2-3) Visit this gorgeous old faux-Moorish theater for second-run films, with beer and pizza.

Cinema 21 (☎ 503-223-4515; 616 NW 21st Ave; admission $4-6) Go to the flicks at this long-standing art-house cinema.

THEATER & PERFORMING ARTS

Chamber Music Northwest (☎ 503-223-3202; www.cmnw.org; tickets $20-40) Check out the summer series of chamber music concerts.

Imago Theater (☎ 503-231-9581; 17 SE 8th Ave; adult/child $24/14) This theatre company is well-regarded for its innovative puppet theater, including the long-running 'Frogz, Lizards, Orbs and Slinkys.'

Oregon Ballet Theatre (☎ 503-222-5538; www.obt.org) Looking for a night at the ballet? Portland's resident dance troupe, performs classical and contemporary programs.

SPECTATOR SPORTS

Portland Timbers (☎ 503-553-5400; admission $8) This minor-league soccer team plays in PGE Park; head for Section 107, where beer and testosterone flow freely and local boys practice their British hooligan accents.

Portland Trail Blazers (☎ 503-231-8000) This pro basketball team plays at the Rose Garden Arena, but tickets are expensive and often sold out.

Portland Winter Hawks (☎ 503-238-6366; adult/child $14.25/5) For hockey, check out this pro hockey team, which also plays in the Rose Garden.

Shopping

The city's high-end mecca for shopping is Northwest, the neighborhood north of Burnside St bisected by NW 21st and 23rd Aves. NW 23rd is lined with clothing stores, expensive gift shops, home decor boutiques and other trendy businesses. Parking is a pain, but buses and streetcars run regularly from downtown. The Pearl District is crammed with galleries and chic, expensive interior-design shops. Hawthorne is the place to find quirky gifts, while the quickly yuppifying Sellwood is lined with antique stores. NE Alberta St is lined with galleries from 14th to 33rd Aves.

Getting There & Away

AIR

Horizon Air (☎ 800-547-9308) flies several times a day between **Portland International Airport**

(PDX; ☎ 877-739-4636; www.flypdx.com) and Seattle, and there are frequent flights to and from San Francisco and Seattle on **United** (☎ 800-241-6522) and **Alaska** (☎ 800-426-0333). **Lufthansa** (☎ 800-645-3880) offers direct flights to Frankfurt, Germany, with connections to other European cities.

BUS

Greyhound (☎ 503-243-2310; 550 NW 6th Ave) connects Portland with cities along I-5 and I-84. Regular service includes the following destinations: San Francisco ($64, 17 to 20 hours); Seattle ($20, three to four hours); Vancouver, BC ($44, eight to 10 hours).

TRAIN

Amtrak (☎ 503-241-4290) serves Union Station, NW 6th Ave at Hoyt St. Trains run regularly to and from the following destinations: Seattle ($23, four hours, four daily), Los Angeles ($96, 30 hours, one daily) and Chicago ($181, two days, two daily, one nonstop). Amtrak's fun *Coast Starlight* train leaves Portland daily for Seattle and Vancouver at 4:05pm, and for San Francisco and LA at 2:25pm.

Getting Around

TO/FROM THE AIRPORT

Tri-Met's MAX light-rail train runs between the airport lobby and downtown ($1.55, 40 minutes); in the reverse direction, catch it northbound along SW Yamhill St. Taxis cost about $30.

BICYCLE

Rent a bike at **NW Bikes** (☎ 503-248-9142; 916 NW 21st Ave; first day $25, additional day $10; closed Sun) or **Fat Tire Farm** (☎ 503-222-3276; 2714 NW Thurman St; per day $20-40). A map of metro-area bike routes is available from bike shops or **Powell's Travel Store** (☎ 503-226-4849; 701 SW 6th Ave).

CAR & MOTORCYCLE

Major car-rental agencies have outlets at PDX airport and around town. Check p1121 for details. Oregon law prohibits you from pumping your own gas. Most of downtown is metered parking; a free option is to park along an inner-Southeast street and walk across a bridge to the city center. If you use a SmartPark garage, remember to move your car after four hours (even if you just drive around the block and back in), or your costs will double.

PUBLIC TRANSPORTATION

Local buses and the MAX light-rail system are run by Tri-Met, which has an **information bureau** (☎ 503-238-7433; www.trimet.org; 8:30am-5:30pm Mon-Fri) at Pioneer Courthouse Sq. A streetcar runs from Portland State University, south of downtown, through the Pearl District to NW 23rd Ave. Within the downtown core, public transportation is free; outside downtown, fares run from $1.30 to $1.60. Bus services stop running at around 1:30am, so make alternate plans to get home if you're staying out late.

TAXI

To get a cab in Portland, you have to order it by phone; you can't hail them from the street.

Broadway Cab (☎ 503-227-1234)
Radio Cab (☎ 503-227-1212)

SOUTHERN OREGON

The valleys of the Rogue and Umpqua Rivers and the Klamath Basin hold some of Oregon's most incredible sights, including Crater Lake. The city of Ashland hosts a renowned Shakespeare festival. Siskiyou Pass, on I-5 between Oregon and California, is known for treacherous winter driving; call ☎ 800-977-6368 for a road report.

Oregon Caves National Monument

In the Illinois River valley, the 'Oregon Caves' (there's actually only one) feature 3 miles of chambers with a fast-moving stream, the River Styx, running the length of the cave. Guided tours (adult/child $7.50/5, 90 minutes) leave hourly from March to November; dress warmly and be prepared to get a little wet. In summer, guides have offered a four-hour 'off-trail' cave tour ($25); however, these might not continue if studies show they have a negative environmental impact on the caves. Call the **Illinois Valley Visitor Information Center** (☎ 541-592-4076; 201 Caves Hwy) in Cave Junction for updates.

From Grants Pass, take US 199 south 28 miles to Cave Junction, then travel 20 miles east on Hwy 46. The road to the caves is steep and narrow; ask about road conditions at the visitors center.

Ashland

The cultural center of southern Oregon, Ashland is famous for its Oregon Shakespeare

Festival, held from February to October, but it's an attractive town for sidewalk strolling even without a theater ticket. Downtown has been dolled up convincingly to echo the era of the Bard. Swans glide across the pond at Lithia Park, which serves as a venue for summer concerts and events; a trail along the creek leads to picnic spots.

INFORMATION

Southern Oregon Reservation Center (☎ 541-488-1011, 800-547-8052; www.sorc.com) Room reservations, tickets and recreation packages.

Visitors center (☎ 541-482-3486; www.ashlandchamber.com; 110 E Main St; 9am-5pm)

SIGHTS & ACTIVITIES

Though the core of the **Oregon Shakespeare Festival** repertoire is Shakespearean and Elizabethan drama, it also features contemporary theater from around the world. There are three festival theaters: the outdoor Elizabethan Theatre, the Angus Bowmer Theatre and the intimate New Theatre. To get last-minute tickets, wait at the **box office** (☎ 541-482-4331; www.osfashland.org; 15 S Pioneer St) for unclaimed tickets ($22 to $53), released at 9:30am and 6pm daily (noon for matinees).

SLEEPING

Ashland is loaded with quaint Victorian B&Bs, though they're rather expensive and booked solid in summer. Rates drop dramatically in the off season. The **Ashland B&B Clearinghouse** (☎ 541-488-0338, 800-588-0338; www.bbclearinghouse.com) can help locate a B&B. If you get stuck for accommodations, try Medford, just 12 miles north.

Ashland Hostel (☎ 541-482-9217; www.ashlandhostel.com; 150 N Main St; dm/s $20/50) Mere blocks from downtown, this convivial hostel has a fireplace in the common room, a spacious kitchen, clean dorms and attractive family rooms with shared baths. The front porch looks out to a street lined with Victorian houses.

Columbia Hotel (☎ 541-482-3726, 800-718-2530; www.columbiahotel.com; 262½ E Main St; r $64-110) This small, European-style hotel is a block from the theaters.

Timbers Motel (☎ 541-482-4242; www.ashlandtimberslodging.com; 1450 Ashland St; s/d/ste $68/78/96; 🅿) This friendly, functional, modern motel has family suites and some rooms with a refrigerator and microwave.

Grape Vine Inn (☎ 541-482-7944; www.thegrapevineinn.com; 486 Siskiyou Blvd; r $122-174) This intimate, well-regarded B&B home, just outside of downtown, has three guest rooms and a trellised garden.

EATING & DRINKING

Ashland is the only place in Oregon with a restaurant tax (5%).

Thai Pepper (☎ 541-482-8058; 84 N Main St; mains $11-15) This creekside Asian restaurant is a favorite for giant portions of spicy cuisine.

Black Sheep (☎ 541-482-6414; 51 N Main St; mains $8-15) Stick to the Stratford-upon-Avon theme at this atmosphere-drenched English pub, where you can get a proper pint of Guinness, check your email, play board games or curl up by the fire and watch the city through giant second-story windows. It's nonsmoking until 11pm and serves food until 1am nightly.

Cheap eats downtown include:

Ashland Bakery & Cafe (☎ 541-482-2117; 38 E Main St; lunch $5)

Siskiyou Brew Pub (☎ 541-482-7718; 31 Water St) Serves local brews on a comfy outdoor patio, with slightly upscale pub food and live music most nights.

Ashland Creek Bar & Grill (☎ 541-482-4131; 92½ N Main St) Ninety percent deck, an ideal spot for sipping a microbrew by the creek.

GETTING THERE & AROUND

Ashland is 350 miles north of San Francisco and 285 miles south of Portland off I-5. Greyhound runs daily to Eugene ($20, 4½ hours) and Portland ($46, seven hours) from **Mr C's Market** (☎ 541-482-8803; 2073 Hwy 99 N).

Wild Rogue Wilderness Area

Just northwest of Ashland, the Wild Rogue Wilderness lives up to its name, with the turbulent Rogue River cutting through 40 miles of untamed, roadless canyon. The area is known for hardcore white-water rafting (classes III and IV) and long-distance hikes.

Grants Pass is the gateway to adventure along the Rogue. The **visitors center** (☎ 541-476-7717; 1995 NW Vine St; 🕑 8am-5pm Mon-Fri, 9am-5pm Sat), near I-5 exit 58, and the **Siskiyou National Forest supervisor's office** (☎ 541-471-6500; 200 Greenfield Dr) have information on recreational activities. For raft permits and backpacking advice, head to the Bureau of Land Management's **Rand Visitor Center** (☎ 541-479-3735; www.or.blm.gov/rogueriver; 14335 Galice Rd, Merlin; 🕑 7am-4pm); take the Merlin exit off I-5 and drive 14 miles west on Merlin-Galice Road.

Rafting the Rogue is not for the faint of heart; a typical trip takes three days and costs upward of $500. Outfitters include **Rogue River Raft Trips** (☎ 541-476-3825, 800-826-1963; www.rogueriverraft.com), **Rogue Wilderness Inc** (☎ 541-479-9554, 800-336-1647; www.wildrogue.com) and **Sundance River Center** (☎ 541-479-8508, 888-777-7557; www.sundanceriver.com).

The 40-mile **Rogue River Trail** was once a supply route from Gold Beach. The full hike takes about five days; day hikers might aim for Whiskey Creek Cabin, a 7-mile round-trip from the Grave Creek trailhead. The trail is dotted with rustic lodges; advance reservations are required. Lodging averages $75 per person, usually including dinner and a packed lunch. Try **Black Bar Lodge** (☎ 541-479-6507) or **Marial Lodge** (☎ 541-474-2057). There are also primitive campgrounds along the way.

Greyhound and Amtrak Thruway buses run daily to Portland and elsewhere from the **station** (☎ 541-476-4513; 460 NE Agness Ave).

Crater Lake National Park

Eerily symmetrical and uncannily blue, **Crater Lake National Park** offers unbelievable vistas, hiking and cross-country skiing trails, a boat ride to a rugged island and scenic drives around the lip of the crater. The park can be reached from Medford (72 miles) or Klamath Falls (73 miles) on Hwy 62. The popular south entrance is open year-round, although it can be rough going in winter; chains are advised.

Most facilities are closed from October to late May, but people still come for cross-country skiing. In summer, a $10 vehicle fee is charged to enter the park. For information, contact **park headquarters** (☎ 541-594-2211; PO Box 7, Crater Lake, OR 97604).

Most travelers do a day trip from Medford, Roseburg or Klamath Falls. In the park choose between **Mazama Village Motor Inn** (south entrance off Hwy 62; s/d $103; ⌚ Jun-Oct) and, perched on the lake's rim, the majestic old **Crater Lake Lodge** (r from $123; ⌚ late May–Oct). For reservations at either place, or to find out about cruises, call ☎ 541-830-8700 or visit www.crater-lake.com. If park lodging is booked up, try lodges and United States Forest Service (USFS) campgrounds around Union Creek and Prospect, west on Hwy 62. **Mazama Village Campground** (☎ 541-830-8700; campsites/RV sites $14.75/15.75), near the park's south entrance, has 200 first-come, first-served sites.

Steens Mountain

Steens Mountain, the highest peak in southeastern Oregon (9670ft), is part of a massive, 30-mile fault-block range. On the west slope of the range, Ice Age glaciers bulldozed massive U-shaped valleys into the flanks of the mountain. To the east, delicate alpine meadows and lakes flank 'the Steens,' dropping off dizzyingly into the Alvord Desert 5000ft below.

Beginning in Frenchglen, the 66-mile gravel **Steens Mountain Loop Rd** offers access to Steens Mountain Recreation Area; it's open from late June to November, depending on the weather; call the **Bureau of Land Management** (☎ 541-573-4557, 541-573-4400; ⌚ 7:45am-4:30pm Mon-Fri) for information.

The tiny **Fish Lake campground** (☎ 541-573-4400; campsites $8) is 20 miles from **Frenchglen**; 2 miles further is the 36-site **Jackman Park** (campsites $6). The old-fashioned **Frenchglen Hotel** (☎ 541-493-2825; s/d with shared bath $63; ⌚ Apr-Nov) has small, austere rooms but friendly service, and is certainly popular with birdwatchers.

WILLAMETTE VALLEY

The incredibly fertile Willamette Valley, between Portland and Eugene, was the destination of the Oregon Trail pioneers. Historic sites in the northern valley and the Yamhill County vineyards are within easy reach of Portland for day trips. In the mid-valley is Salem, the state capital. The small college cities of Corvallis and Eugene, in the southern valley, are both dynamic and engaging.

Eugene

Eugene is decidedly a college town; its whole atmosphere is colored by the University of Oregon, the state's largest university. And it's still a hotbed of countercultural activity. Many of the city's successful businesses are owned by former radicals, and activism is de rigueur among the students here. Eugene is also the birthplace of Nike.

INFORMATION

Lane County Convention & Visitors Association (☎ 541-484-5307, 800-547-5445; www.cvalco.org; Suite 190, 115 W 8th Ave; ⌚ 8am-5pm Mon-Fri)

Sip & Surf Cybercafe (☎ 541-343-9607; Olive St & 10th Ave; $6 per hr; ⏰ 7:30am-6pm Mon-Fri, noon-5pm Sat) Fifteen minutes of computer time free with a $1 purchase.

SIGHTS & ACTIVITIES

At E 5th Ave between Pearl and High Sts, **Fifth St Public Market** is the heart of a small but lively shopping and café district. The famous **waffle iron** used to make the first Nike soles is displayed at the **Nike Factory Store** (☎ 541-342-5155; 296 E 5th Ave).

Housed in a replica of a Native American longhouse, the University of Oregon's **Museum of Natural History** (☎ 541-346-3024; 1680 E 15th Ave; admission $2; ⏰ noon-5pm Wed-Sun) has an impressive display of Native American artifacts, including the country's oldest pair of shoes and an interesting analysis of early architecture.

The **Oregon Country Fair** (☎ 541-343-4298), in July, is a riotous three-day celebration of Eugene's folksy, hippie past and present. It's held on a farm 13 miles west of Eugene on Hwy 126, near Veneta.

SLEEPING

Eugene International Hostel (☎ 541-349-0589; 2352 Willamette St; dm/s/d $16/30/36; ⏰ closed 11am-5pm) More friendly than tidy, this extremely casual hostel is just outside of downtown in a quiet residential neighborhood; take bus Nos 24 or 25. The kitchen is vegetarian-only.

Downtown Motel (☎ 541-345-8739, 800-648-4366; 361 W 7th Ave; s/d $35/45) A great bargain, the Downtown is much nicer than you might think at first glance, with spacious rooms, helpful staff who can recommend restaurants, and a good location.

Courtesy Inn (☎ 541-345-3391; 345 W 6th Ave; r $45-55) The friendly managers and great location make this a good choice; rooms have a refrigerator and microwave.

EATING & DRINKING

Fifth Street Market has a great bakery and a number of small restaurants, and there's a string of small, cheap cafés along 13th Ave by the university.

Ring of Fire (☎ 541-344-6475; 1099 Chambers St; appetizers $8.50, mains $11-16) Guard your tongue at this Thai place, or order one of the fancy cocktails to counteract the heat on your heaped plate of pineapple seafood red curry; lounge serves food until 1am on weekends.

Cafe Zenon (☎ 541-343-3005; 898 Pearl St; lunch $7-10, dinner $8-15) Zenon's rather uppity French-influenced cuisine keeps it packed at lunch and dinner.

Two of Eugene's best bets for live music also have great food: **Sam Bond's Garage** (☎ 541-431-6603; 407 Blair Blvd; mains $6-8) serves great vegetarian fare, and **Cafe Paradiso** (☎ 541-484-9933; 115 W Broadway; sandwiches $3.75-6), home to Eugene's longest-running open-mic night (8pm Tuesday), has good coffee, sandwiches and pasta.

GETTING THERE & AROUND

From the **Amtrak station** (☎ 541-687-1383; E 4th Ave & Willamette St), trains run to Vancouver, BC ($66, 12 hours) and San Francisco ($85, 16 hours).

From the **bus station** (☎ 541-344-6265; 987 Pearl St) you can catch a connection to Portland ($14.50, three hours), San Francisco ($59, 15 hours) and Bend ($22, five hours).

McKenzie River Valley

One of the most stunning natural areas in the state, the McKenzie River Valley is also one of the easiest to visit. The town of McKenzie Bridge, a cluster of campgrounds and cabins 50 miles east of Eugene on Hwy 126, is the gateway. There's great fishing, easy hikes and fun rafting trips to be had; for details, contact the **visitors center** (☎ 541-896-3330; 44643 Hwy 126) in Leaburg.

In summer, take the historic and hair-raising **Old McKenzie Hwy** (Hwy 242) over the 5325ft, lava-laden mountain pass to the **Dee Wright Observatory** for spectacular views of volcanoes in the adjoining Three Sisters Wilderness. The scenic, 26-mile **McKenzie National Recreation Trail** follows the river north from McKenzie Bridge to Fish Lake and is dotted with campgrounds. The old highway and pass are closed November to June, but you can access the trail year-round from Hwy 126.

From Eugene, take bus No 91 ($1) to reach the trailhead across from the **McKenzie River Ranger Station** (☎ 541-822-3381; 57600 Hwy 126). The aptly named but often crowded **Paradise Campground** (☎ 877-444-6777; campsites $10), 4 miles east of McKenzie Bridge on Hwy 126, has campsites in an old-growth forest.

Corvallis

Corvallis, 43 miles from Eugene, is a pleasant base for exploring the Willamette Valley.

Oregon State University anchors the west side of town. The tree-lined downtown district along the Willamette River has cafés, bookstores, bars and nice restaurants. Corvallis also has a **visitors center** (☎ 541-757-1544; 420 NW 2nd St; ⏲ 9am-5pm Mon-Fri).

Several inexpensive chain motels line SW 4th and 2nd Sts downtown. **Towne House Motor Inn** (☎ 541-753-4496; 350 SW 4th St; s/d $41/47) is close to everything and has a funky lounge.

The upscale, quasi-rustic waterfront **Big River Restaurant** (☎ 541-757-0694; 101 NW Jackson St; mains $16-22) has an eclectic menu that changes nightly. Near the university, **Nearly Normal's Gonzo Cuisine** (☎ 541-753-0791; 109 NW 15th; breakfast $3-5, mains $7; ⏲ closed Sun) serves veggie burritos, tofu scrambles and meatless burgers. **Interzone** (☎ 541-754-5965; 1563 NW Monroe) is a funky, arty coffee shop.

From the **bus station** (☎ 541-757-1797; 153 NW 4th St), Greyhound connects to Portland ($14, two hours) and Eugene ($8, one hour); Amtrak Thruway goes to Newport ($12, four hours).

Salem

Beyond the capitol building, there's not much reason to linger in Salem, a sprawling city of gray buildings and bureaucrats. But it is the nearest base for exploring Silver Falls State Park and the Oregon Garden. Find information at the **visitors center** (☎ 503-581-4325; 1313 Mill St SE).

The 1938 **Oregon State Capitol** (☎ 503-986-1388; 900 Court St NE; admission free; tours 9am-3pm on the hour in summer) looks like a sci-fi film director's vision of an Orwellian White House. Rambling 19th-century **Bush House** (☎ 503-363-4714; 600 Mission St SE; adult/child $4/2; ⏲ noon-5pm Tue-Sun) is an Italianate mansion now preserved as a museum within a nice public garden.

Silver Falls State Park (☎ 503-873-8681; car $3 per day) is 26 miles east of Salem on Hwy 214 (via Hwy 22). The South Falls, a 177ft waterfall you can hike behind, provides instant gratification just a few feet from the main parking lot. You can also hike a 7-mile loop and see all 10 falls on the site, or ride the 4-mile paved bike path. Camping and swimming are available. Horse riding can be organized through the **Adaptive Riding Institute** (☎ 503-873-3890; www.open.org/horses88/; ⏲ May-Sep), which offers riding for people with disabilities.

Fifteen miles northeast of Salem on Hwy 213 (Silverton Road) is the **Oregon Garden** (☎ 503-874-8100; www.oregongarden.org; 879 W Main St; adult/child/family $6/3/20; ⏲ 9am-6pm in summer, 9am-3pm winter). The garden, prettiest in late May, nurtures vast numbers of rare and native plant species, and its wetlands act as a natural water-filtration system that recycles the city of Silverton's waste water. It's also home to Oregon's only building designed by architect Frank Lloyd Wright; the **Gordon House** was set to be demolished by a wealthy but oblivious Portland-area homeowner when the Wright Conservancy intervened and moved it to its current site.

The **Marquee House** (☎ 503-391-0837, 800-949-0837; www.marqueehouse.com; 333 Wyatt Ct NE, off Center St; r $65-95) is an adorable creekside B&B with five movie-themed rooms.

The **Arbor Cafe** (☎ 503-588-1330; 380 High St NE; lunch/dinner $5/13) is Salem's best lunch spot, with pasta, pastries, soups and sandwiches.

Yamhill County Wine Country

Meandering through plush green hills on winding country roads from one wine tasting room to another is a delightful way to spend an afternoon (just make sure you designate a driver). More than 30 wineries are dotted along Hwys 99W and 18; blue signs point the way to each. If you only have time for a quick sampling, head for the **Oregon Wine Tasting Room** (☎ 503-843-3787; ⏲ 11am-6pm), 9 miles south of McMinnville on Hwy 18, where you'll find many of the area's wineries represented. The **Grape Escape** (☎ 503-282-4262) specializes in wine-country tours departing from Portland. For some more information contact the **Yamhill County Wineries Association** (☎ 503-646-2985; PO Box 871, McMinnville, OR 97218).

Also nearby, infamous eccentric Howard Hughes' **Spruce Goose**, the world's largest wood-framed airplane, is housed in the **Evergreen Aviation Museum** (☎ 503-434-4180; www.sprucegoose.com; 3850 SW Three Mile Lane; adult/child $9.50/5.50; ⏲ 9am-5pm).

CENTRAL & EASTERN OREGON

Volcanic eruptions and persistent erosion have turned central and eastern Oregon into an eerie moonscape, from the pastel ribbons of rock at the John Day Fossil Beds to the dramatic gouging of Hells Canyon and the gentle hills around Warm Springs.

Bend & Mt Bachelor

A sporty city in the midst of a rapid growth spurt, Bend has tons of outdoor fun right in its backyard. Don't let the Hwy 97 strip fool you – downtown is lined with pleasant cafés, shops and bars. The **visitors center** (☎ 541-389-8799; 63085 N US 97; 8am-5pm Mon-Fri) is in a huge building at the north end of town.

Perhaps the best museum in the state, Bend's **High Desert Museum** (☎ 541-382-4754; www.highdesert.org; 59800 S Hwy 97; adult/child $8.50/4; 9am-5pm; P) has impeccable exhibits on early cultural life and the fascinating natural history of the High Desert. Get an up-close glimpse of the famous Spotted Owl at the raptor center. Tickets are good for two days.

Lava Lands Visitor Center (☎ 541-593-2421; admission free; 9am-5pm May-Sep), on US 97 about 11 miles south of Bend, has exhibits revealing the geology, wildlife and archeology of the **Newberry National Volcanic Monument**. Nearby is Lava Butte, rising 500ft above the surrounding lava flows.

Twenty-two miles southwest of Bend, 9065ft **Mt Bachelor** (☎ 541-382-2442, 800-829-2442; www.mtbachelor.com; adult/child $44/26; 9am-4pm Mon-Fri, 8am-4pm Sat & Sun) has Oregon's best skiing, with 3100ft of vertical and more than 300 inches of snow per year; it's known for fine dry powder. The season begins in November and can last until June.

Central Oregon Reservation Center (☎ 541-382-8334; 8am-5pm Mon-Fri) can help with accommodations. There's a motel strip along US 97 (here called 3rd St), where both **Sonoma Lodge** (☎ 541-382-4891; 450 SE 3rd St; d from $35) and the **Chalet Motel** (☎ 541-382-6124; 510 SE 3rd St; d from $35) are clean and friendly; doubles have in-room microwaves and refrigerators.

For good food, try Wall or Bond Sts downtown, home to inexpensive eateries such as **Baja Norte** (☎ 541-385-0611; 801 NW Wall St; burritos $6-7), or squeeze into the **Deschutes Brewery & Public House** (☎ 541-382-9242; 1044 NW Bond St; sandwiches $8). It's crowded, so grab a pint of its signature Mirror Pond ale at the bar while you wait.

Warm Springs Indian Reservation

Home to three groups, the Wasco, the Tenino and the Northern Paiute (the Confederated Tribes), Warm Springs Reservation stretches east and west from the banks of the **Deschutes River** to the peaks of the Cascades. Contact the **Confederated Tribes of the Warm Springs Reservation** (☎ 541-553-1161; www.warmsprings.com) if you want to learn more about the reservation's residents and events. For information on **rafting** the Deschutes, stop at the north end of the eye-blink-long town of Maupin, at the **chamber of commerce** (☎ 541-395-2599; www.maupinoregon.com; PO Box 220, Maupin, OR 97037).

The **Warm Springs Museum** (☎ 541-553-3331; adult/child $6/3; 10am-5pm), on Hwy 26 just west of Warm Springs, evokes traditional Native American life and culture with artifacts, audiovisuals and re-created villages. The **Kah-Nee-Ta Resort** (☎ 541-553-1112; r from $145), 11 miles north of Warm Springs on Simnasho Rd, has a giant hot-springs-fed **swimming pool** (day passes adult/child $8/4; P $4) as well as a casino, spa, restaurant and lodgings in hotel rooms or teepees.

John Day Fossil Beds National Monument

You can't help feeling a bit like an alien visitor in the otherworldly landscape surrounding the John Day Fossil Beds. Within this vast, beautifully desolate section of the state, the monument encompasses 22 sq miles with three entry points. Services are few and far between, so fill your gas tank and have plenty of water on hand.

Only the Sheep Rock Unit has a staffed **visitors center** (☎ 541-987-2333; 9am-6pm, closed Sat & Sun in winter), 10 miles northwest of Dayville on Hwy 19, with maps, pamphlets and displays of fossils found in the area. Be sure to take the short hike up the **Blue Basin trail**, which will make you feel like you've just landed on the sunny side of the moon. The Painted Hills Unit, near the town of Mitchell, consists of low-slung, colorfully banded hills formed about 30 million years ago. The Clarno Unit exposes mud flows that washed over an Eocene-era forest and eroded into distinctive, sheer-white cliffs topped with spires and turrets of stone.

Two nice campgrounds, **Lone Pine** (☎ 541-416-6700; campsites $5) and **Big Bend** (☎ 541-416-6700; campsites $5), are on the North Fork John Day River near the Sheep Rock Unit. **Service Creek Stage Stop B&B** (☎ 541-468-3331; www.servicecreekstagestop.com; 38686 Hwy 19; s/d $40/60) has a general store, a friendly greasy-spoon and raft rentals in case you want to float the placid John Day.

Hells Canyon & the Wallowa Mountains

The **Wallowa Mountains** are among the most beautiful natural areas in Oregon, with their glacier-hewn peaks and crystalline lakes; the only drawback is the huge number of visitors who flock here in summer. Escape the hordes on one of several remote, overnight hikes into the **Eagle Cap Wilderness Area**, accessible from Wallowa Lake. Just north of the mountains, in the Wallowa Valley, Enterprise and Joseph are two small towns off Hwy 82 with lodging and food. Joseph is a miniature arts-and-crafts mecca known for its bronze galleries.

Wilder adventures and an even more dramatic landscape are found at **Hells Canyon**, where the Snake River has been carving out an 8000ft-deep trench for about 13 million years. The white-water action starts just below Hells Canyon Dam, 28 miles north (downriver) from the small campground community of Copperfield, a nexus of activity on the river. **Hells Canyon Adventures** (☎ 541-785-3352, 800-422-3568; www.hellscanyonadventures.com; 4200 Hells Canyon Dam Rd), in Oxbow, runs daylong **raft trips** ($150 per person) as well as less expensive, but noisy, **jet-boat tours** (adult/child $30/10). For perspective, drive up to the spectacular lookout at **Hat Point** (USFS Rd 4240), 23 miles from Imnaha, with views of the Wallowa Mountains, Idaho's Seven Devils, the Imnaha River and the wilds of Hells Canyon. The road is open from late May until snowfall; allow two hours and call ☎ 541-426-5546 first for conditions.

The **Wallowa Mountains Visitor Center** (☎ 541-426-5546; 88401 Hwy 82; 🕑 8am-5pm Mon-Sat, noon-5pm Sun in summer), in Enterprise, has information on both areas and is a good source for trail maps and backcountry hiking tips.

Copperfield Park Campground (☎ 541-785-3323; www.idahopower.com/riversreccopperfield.htm; Hwy 86; campsites/RV sites $6/10), just below Oxbow Dam at the beginning of Hells Canyon, has 62 riverside campsites. Or stay in Joseph at the popular **Indian Lodge Motel** (☎ 541-432-2651, 888-286-5484; 201 S Main; s/d $37/46).

MT HOOD

The state's highest peak, 11,240ft Mt Hood is visible on a sunny day from much of northern Oregon. It is accessible year-round via US 26 from Portland and via Hwy 35 from Hood River; call ☎ 800-977-6368 to check road conditions. Together with the Columbia River Hwy, these routes constitute the **Mt Hood Loop**, one of the finest scenic-road excursions in the USA.

Barely-there **Government Camp**, 56 miles from Portland and 44 miles from Hood River at the pass, has some food and lodging. The **Mt Hood Information Center** (☎ 503-622-4822, 888-622-4822; 65000 E Hwy 26; 🕑 8am-6pm in summer, 8am-4:30pm in winter) is in Welches next to Mt Hood Village.

A masterpiece of the Works Progress Administration (WPA) era, the 1930s **Timberline Lodge** was built and decorated in grand rustic style as a hotel, ski resort and restaurant. It's 5 miles north of US 26 from Government Camp. The horror movie *The Shining* was partly filmed here. The **ski area** (☎ 503-622-0717) is open almost year-round. **Mt Hood Meadows** (☎ 503-337-2222; lift tickets adult/child $44/25), 76 miles from Portland, is the largest ski area on Mt Hood and often has the best conditions. **Ski-Bowl** (☎ 503-272-3206; lift tickets adult/child $32/20), off US 26 just west of Government Camp, has night skiing.

Hikers should get the free USFS pamphlet *Day Hikes Around Mt Hood*. After Japan's Mt Fuji, Mt Hood is the world's most-climbed peak over 10,000ft, with a typical route from Timberline Lodge taking about 10 to 12 hours round-trip (for experienced climbers). **Timberline Mountain Guides** (☎ 541-312-9242; www.timberlinemtguides.com; 2 days from $385) is a well-established guide service and climbing school. Climbing is best from May to mid-July.

Huckleberry Inn (☎ 503-272-3325; 88611 E Government Camp Loop; r from $65) has standard rooms and an adjoining folksy café. For rustic decadence, treat yourself to a room at the **Timberline Lodge** (☎ 503-231-5400, 800-547-1406; www.timberlinelodge.com; dm $80, r from $120). There's feverish competition for campsites around Mt Hood; try **Still Creek** (☎ 503-622-7674; campsites $14), 1 mile east of Government Camp on Hwy 26, or the postcard-perfect **Trillium Lake** (☎ 503-622-4822, campsites $14), turn right 1 mile east of Government Camp on Hwy 26, drive 2 miles south to entrance. **Mt Hood RV Village** (☎ 503-622-4011; www.mthoodvillage.com; 65000 E Hwy 26; RV sites $34-39) is a huge resort complex near Brightwood.

COLUMBIA RIVER GORGE

The enormous canyon of the Columbia River, which divides Washington and Oregon, is one of the Pacific Northwest's most dramatic and scenic destinations. On the Oregon side, river-level I-84 is the quickest that provides access to the most popular sites. A slower but more scenic route is the historic Columbia River Hwy (US 30), from Troutdale to Warrendale. Washington's Hwy 14, though again slower going than I-84, offers spectacular vistas. Campers will find state parks on both sides of the river, although campsite places are scarce on summer weekends and traffic noise can be bothersome.

Historic Columbia River Highway

The first paved road in the Northwest and America's first scenic highway, this lushly forested, winding highway between Troutdale, just east of Portland, and Hood River opened in 1915. To reach it, take exit 17 or 35 off I-84. Famous as the western entry to the gorge, the **Vista House at Crown Point** (☎ 503-695-2230; admission free; 🕑 9am-6pm) interpretive center sits atop a craggy cliff of basalt.

Bike, walk or jog along two stretches of the old highway that have been renovated for nonautomotive use. The western section of the trail runs between Tanner Creek (at the Bonneville Dam exit from I-84) and Eagle Creek; another, longer stretch runs 4.5 miles from Hood River to Mosier (the parking lots in this section require a $3 day-use fee).

Waterfalls and hiking trails line the Oregon side of the gorge. Stop at **Multnomah Falls** to ogle the 642ft, two-tiered falls and hike to the top (about one hour). The **Forest Service visitors center** (☎ 503-695-2372; 🕑 9am-5pm) next door to the gift shop is a good place to get information on other gorge hikes.

Hood River & Around

The town of Hood River, 63 miles east of Portland on I-84, is a slender wedge of bike and ski shops, cafés and a few hotels. The Columbia River here is famous as a windsurfing hot spot, and there's great mountain biking south of town off Hwy 35 and Forest Rd 44.

The **visitors center** (☎ 541-386-2000; 405 Portway Ave; 🕑 9am-5pm Mon-Fri) is across I-84 from the city center; there's also a small information office downtown at 2nd Ave and Oak St, open daily.

The **Bingen School Inn** (☎ 509-493-3363; cnr Cedar and Humbolt Sts; dm/r $14/35, linens $3), across the Columbia in Bingen, Washington, has lodging in an old schoolhouse. The **Vagabond Lodge** (☎ 541-386-2992; www.vagabondlodge.com; 4070 Westcliffe Dr; r from $46), next to the huge, swanky Columbia Gorge Hotel, has river-view motel rooms. **Viento State Park** (☎ 541-374-8811; campsites/RV sites $14/16), 8 miles west of Hood River, is popular with windsurfers.

The **Full Sail Brewery** (☎ 541-386-2247; 506 Columbia St; burgers $5-6) has a tasting room with a small pub menu. Free 20-minute brewery tours leave on the hour from noon to 5pm daily in summer, and Thursday to Sunday in winter. **Holstein's Coffee Co** (☎ 541-386-4115; 12 Oak Ave; sandwiches $3-6) is great for coffee and sandwiches.

OREGON COAST

Oregon's most famous beach resorts are between the Columbia River and Newport. Much of the southern coast, from Florence to the California border, approaches pristine wilderness. Oregon's beaches are open to the public, even in developed areas, and the coastline is dotted with state parks.

Brookings & Gold Beach

Some 6 miles north of the California line on US 101 is the balmy harbor town of Brookings. There's not much to it beyond the **visitors center** (☎ 541-469-3181, 800-535-9469; www.brookingsor.com; 16330 Lower Harbor Rd; 🕑 9am-5pm Mon-Fri), but it's minutes from rugged coastline and redwood forest.

Roads along the Chetco River lead inland from Brookings to the western edge of remote **Kalmiopsis Wilderness Area**, the state's largest. Oregon's only redwood forests, as well as old-growth myrtle, are found here, notably in **Alfred A Loeb State Park** (☎ 541-469-2021, 800-551-6949; campsites/cabins $16/35), 10 miles east of Brookings on N Bank Chetco Rd. North of town is **Samuel H Boardman State Park**, with 11 miles of Oregon's most beautiful coastline.

Zip up the Rogue River to the Wild Rogue Wilderness Area in a **jet boat** from Gold Beach, 27 miles north of Brookings. **Jerry's Rogue Jets** (☎ 541-247-4571, 800-451-3645; www.roguejets.com) offers scenic trips (adult/child $34/14) and white-water adventures ($75/35). For about the same price you can ride to the town of Agness on a **mail boat** (☎ 541-247-7033, 800-458-3511; www.mailboat.com). The visitors center is at the **Gold Beach Ranger Station** (☎ 541-247-7526, 800-525-2334; www.goldbeach.org; 29279 S Ellensburg Ave; 🕑 9am-5pm Mon-Fri).

Gold Beach Resort (☎ 541-247-7066, 800-541-0947; 29232 Ellensburg, Hwy 101; r $109-139; P) has 39 deluxe beachfront rooms, all with ocean views, in-room refrigerator and microwave. There are also campgrounds upriver.

Bandon

Old Town Bandon is a small hub of cafés, gift shops and taverns. The **visitors center** (☎ 541-347-9616; www.bandon.com; 9am-5pm) is at 300 2nd St. Beach Loop Dr leads south of town to Bandon's best beaches, with towering sea-stacks (coastal rock pillars that have resisted the surrounding erosion) and monoliths that host large numbers of seabirds. **Coquille Point**, at the end of 11th St, is a popular place to spot migrating whales in winter and spring.

The **HI Sea Star Hostel** (☎ 541-347-9632; 375 2nd St; dm $16, r $35-75), in Old Town, has an adjoining café with heavenly coffee and a great breakfast. **Table Rock Motel** (☎ 541-347-2700, 800-457-9141; www.tablerockmotel.com; 840 Beach Loop Rd; r from $45, with view from $70), on a shrubby bluff, has rooms and apartment-style quarters with kitchenettes (from $85).

Harp's (☎ 541-347-9057; 130 Chicago Ave; seafood $14-17; closed Sun & Mon) is recommended for bay-view dining.

Oregon Dunes

Fifty miles of shifting sand between Florence and Coos Bay form the largest expanse of coastal dunes in the USA. Hiking trails, bridle paths, and boating and swimming areas have been established, and the entire region has abundant wildlife, especially birds. Unfortunately, dune buggies and dirt bikes scream up and down the dunes, especially the stretch south of Reedsport (see the boxed text 'Dune Buggy Danger'). The northern stretch has the most hiking trails. **Oregon Dunes National Recreation Area headquarters** (☎ 541-271-3611; 855 Highway Ave; 8am-4:30pm Mon-Fri) is based in logged-out Reedsport. This town hosts chainsaw carving championships in June.

Popular **Jessie M Honeyman State Park** (☎ 541-997-3641, 800-452-5687; campsites/RV sites $17/21), 3 miles south of Florence on US 101, is handy for recreation in the dunes. **Umpqua Lighthouse State Park** (☎ 503-271-4118, 800-452-5687; campsites/cabins/yurts $12/35/45) has deluxe yurts with TV/VCR and refrigerators a mile south of Winchester Bay. USFS campgrounds like **Eel Creek** (☎ 541-759-4462, 800-452-5687; campsites $13), 10 miles south of Reedsport, offer the best dune access.

DUNE BUGGY DANGER

Designated off-road vehicle (ORV) and non-ORV areas are set up to restrict ORVs, not hikers (who have full freedom to explore any public areas of the dunes). However, hikers venturing into ORV territory need to remain keen to the direction of ORV traffic. Climbing toward the crest of a high dune is an especially bad place to be when a dune buggy comes flying over the top. Red (sometimes orange) flags waving above the dunes indicate oncoming ORVs.

Yachats

Volcanic intrusions south of Yachats form some of Oregon's most beautiful shoreline. Surf explodes against the shore to create dramatic features like the Devil's Churn and the Spouting Horn at **Cape Perpetua**, where visitors can prowl among intertidal rocks and sandy inlets or hike or drive up to a fantastic viewpoint. Ten miles south of Yachats the **Heceta Head Lighthouse**, built in 1894, perches above the churning ocean; a trail leads there from enchanting Devil's Elbow State Park. Taking the elevator down to the **Sea Lion Caves** (☎ 541-547-3111; www.sealioncaves.com; 91560 Hwy 101; adult/child $7/4.50), filled with glossy, wriggling Steller sea lions, is a highlight of the central Oregon coast.

Try camping at **Cape Perpetua Campground** (☎ 541-547-3289, 800-452-5687; campsites $12). Six miles south of Yachats is the **See Vue Motel** (☎ 541-547-3227; www.seevue.com; 95590 Hwy 101; r from $70), an old charmer with ocean-view rooms. There's good food and a friendly atmosphere at the **Drift Inn** (☎ 541-547-4477; mains $8-10), a wood-lined watering hole along Hwy 101.

Newport

It's hard not to like Newport. This scruffy little port town has lively, old-fashioned seafood markets facing Yaquina Bay, some excellent marine-life museums and the picturesque and historic Nye Beach. Grab a map at the **visitors center** (☎ 541-265-8801, 800-262-7844; 555 SW Coast Hwy; 8:30am-5pm Mon-Fri, 10am-4pm Sat during May).

The **Oregon Coast Aquarium** (☎ 541-867-3474; 2820 SE Ferry Slip Rd; adult/child $10.75/6.50; 10am-5pm in winter, 9am-6pm in summer) has arresting marine exhibits such as an enormous

Plexiglas tunnel through a shark tank. Less glamorous, but also interesting, is the **Hatfield Marine Science Center** (☎ 541-867-0271; 2030 S Marine Science Dr; suggested donation $2; ⏰ 10am-5pm in summer, 10am-4pm Thu-Mon in winter), with a touch pool and exhibits.

The **Sylvia Beach Hotel** (☎ 541-265-5428; www.sylviabeachhotel.com; 267 NW Cliff St; dm $27, d $83-173), named for the proprietor of Paris' Shakespeare & Co bookstore, has rooms decorated after famous writers; the Edgar Allan Poe is inspired, with a raven in the corner and a pendulum swinging over the bed. Next door, the **Nye Beach Hotel** (☎ 541-265-3334; www.nyebeach.com; 219 NW Cliff St; r from $70) is a faux-historic inn built in 1992; it has ocean-view rooms and a good café. For camping, **South Beach State Park** (☎ 541-867-4715, 800-452-5687; campsites $21), 2 miles south of Newport on US 101, is right on the beach.

The **Rogue Ales Brewery** (☎ 541-265-3188; 748 SW Bay Blvd; sandwiches $6-8) makes two of the best beers on the planet, the award-winning Shakespeare Stout and the decadent Chocolate Stout (available only at the brewery). If you fall in love with either and can't bear to leave, you're in luck: there are a few **guest rooms** (s/d $80/120) over the pub. For seafood, drop anchor at the over-the-top nautically themed **Whale's Tale** (452 SW Bay Blvd; seafood $8-18).

Cannon Beach

Miles of sandy beaches, broken by immense basalt promontories and rocky tide pools, stretch north and south of Cannon Beach, 9 miles south of Seaside. For information try the **visitors center** (☎ 503-436-2623; 2nd St; ⏰ 10am-5pm Mon-Sat, 11am-4pm Sun). The town itself is attractive but very touristy, especially along Hemlock St; all those souvenir shops will be hard-pressed to coax you off the beautiful beach.

Park free at Tolovana Beach (take the third Cannon Beach exit off Hwy 101) for access to the deservedly much-photographed **Haystack Rock**. Stunning views grace the Oregon Coast Trail over Tillamook Head between Cannon Beach and Seaside in Ecola State Park. On the renowned Sandcastle Day, held in June, teams compete for originality and execution in sand sculpture.

Blue Gull Inn Motel (☎ 503-436-2714, 800-507-2714; 632 S Hemlock St; r from $75) is pleasant. Budget travelers can stay in Seaside, 10 minutes south on Hwy 101, at the **Seaside International Hostel** (☎ 503-738-7911; 930 N Holladay Dr; dm/ r $17/36).

At **Oswald West State Park** (☎ 503-368-5154; campsites $10-14), 10 miles south of Cannon Beach on Hwy 101, wheelbarrows are provided for hauling gear to walk-in campsites.

Dining options tend to be upscale. For fresh seafood, try **Dooger's** (☎ 503-436-2225; 1371 S Hemlock; lunch $5-10, dinner $14-18). **Pizza a Fetta** (☎ 503-436-0333; 231 N Hemlock; slice $2-3, pie $18-28) is a good budget option – provided you go for one of the huge slices, rather than a less economical whole pie.

Astoria

Astoria sits at the mouth of the Columbia River, where the 4.1-mile **Astoria Bridge** crosses over to Washington. John Jacob Astor and his Pacific Fur Trading Company established a small fort here in the spring of 1811, making this the first US settlement in the West. Find information at the **visitors center** (☎ 503-325-6311; 111 W Marine Dr; ⏰ 9am-5pm).

Astoria has some of the most lovingly restored and precipitously poised Victorian homes outside of San Francisco. Tour the ornate **Flavel House** (☎ 503-325-2203; 441 8th St; adult/child $5/2; ⏰ 11am-4pm) to get a feel for these magnificent residences, dating back to the 1880s. Cult-film fans can check out the **'Goonies house'** (368 38th St), from Spielberg's 1984 pirate-kids movie.

Reconstructed **Fort Clatsop** (☎ 503-861-2471; admission $3; ⏰ 8am-5pm), 8 miles south of Astoria off US 101, is worth a stop. The Lewis and Clark party spent a miserable winter here in 1805–06. The fort was named after a local Native American community who befriended them.

On Clatsop Spit and close to the beaches in Hammond is **Fort Stevens State Park** (☎ 503-861-1671, 800-452-5687; campsites/RV sites/yurts $13/17/29); don't miss the photogenic wreck of an English sailing ship on the beach.

Clementine's B&B (☎ 503-325-2005, 800-521-6801; www.clementines-bb.com; 847 Exchange St; r $85-150) occupies an 1888 Italianate mansion right across from Flavel House; rooms have featherbeds and balconies. Or act like Astorian royalty for a day at the downtown **Hotel Elliott** (☎ 503-325-2222, 877-378-1924; www.hotelelliott.com; 357 12th St; r $105-135, ste $165-275), built in 1924 and recently given a $4 million renovation.

Big ships float by the cannery-turned-sophisticated seafood restaurant **Gunderson's**

Cannery Cafe (☎ 503-325-8642; 1 6th St; lunch $8-10, dinner $12-25), which overlooks the river. **Brown Baggers Deli** (☎ 503-325-0325; 1269 Commercial St; sandwiches $3-5) and the next-door **Rusty Cup** are both good for sandwiches, coffee and snacks.

Amtrak Thruway buses leave for Portland ($22) at 8am daily from the **MiniMart** (95 W Marine Dr).

WASHINGTON

Washington has a postindustrial, trendsetting status in everything from wilderness values to high-tech innovation. Culturally, it runs the gamut from indigenous art all the way to bleeding-edge music. The landscape is equally varied, with glaciated peaks overlooking dynamic cities and misty harbors. To the east, the arid uplands get 300 days of sunshine a year and offer all-season recreation.

History

The first US settlement in Washington was at Tumwater, on the southern edge of Puget Sound, in 1845. Both Seattle and Port Townsend were established in 1851 and quickly became logging centers. Lumber was shipped at great profit to San Francisco, the boomtown of the California gold rush.

In 1853, Washington separated from the Oregon territory. Congress reduced the amount of land open to native hunting and fishing and opened up the eastern part of the state to settlement. The arrival of rail links in the last decades of the century created a readily accessible market for the products of the Pacific Northwest and brought in floods of settlers.

Washington was admitted to the union in 1889, and Seattle began to flourish in 1897, when it became the principal port en route to the Alaska and Yukon goldfields. The construction of the Bonneville Dam (1937) and Grand Coulee Dam (1947) accelerated the region's industrial and agricultural development by providing cheap hydroelectric power and irrigation.

The rapid postwar urbanization of the Puget Sound region created an enormous metropolitan area linked by jammed-up freeways that mar the waterfront vistas. Seattle in particular has become larger and more affluent. Boeing, the world's largest aircraft manufacturer, remains the chief economic force of western Washington despite its decision in 2001 to relocate its corporate headquarters to Chicago. The presence of Microsoft has spawned the growth of other large high-tech firms.

WASHINGTON FACTS

Nicknames Evergreen State, Chinook State
Population 6,068,996 (15th)
Area 66,544 sq miles (18th)
Admitted to Union November 11, 1889 (42nd)
Capital city Olympia (population 42,514)
Other cities Seattle (563,374; metro area 3.55 million), Spokane (195,629), Tacoma (193,556), Vancouver (143,560), Bellevue (109,569)
Birthplace of novelist and social critic Mary McCarthy (1912–89); Jimi Hendrix (1942–70); *Far Side* cartoonist Gary Larson (b 1950); Kurt Cobain (1967–94); Bill Gates (b 1955)
Famous for Lumber, Microsoft, grunge rock, Starbucks

SEATTLE

Washington's largest city sits on a slim isthmus between two bodies of water, Puget Sound to the west and Lake Washington to the east. This once tranquil town is now a vibrant trade, manufacturing and high-tech center. One of the fastest-growing metropolitan areas in the USA, the 'Emerald City' has become an exporter of trends. Seattle has made coffee a national obsession; its homegrown grunge rock swept the nation in the 1990s; and TV series and movies often base themselves here for the city's hip, quirky cultural and social life. The coastal mountains and the many islands and fingers of land and water that make up the complex geography of Puget Sound give Seattle one of the most beautiful settings of any US city.

History

Named 'Seattle' for the chief of the Duwamish tribe who originally inhabited the Lake Washington area, Washington's largest city was first settled by David Denny in 1851. In 1893 Seattle was linked to the rest of the country by rail. During this decade the city became the provisioning point for prospectors headed to the Yukon gold territory, and the banking center for the fortunes made there. The boom continued through WWI, when Northwest lumber was in great demand and the Puget Sound area prospered as a shipbuilding center. In 1916 William Boeing founded the aircraft manufacturing business that would become one of the largest employers in Seattle, attracting tens of thousands of newcomers to the region during WWII.

In more recent years, the growth of Microsoft and other software developers has made it increasingly difficult to find someone who isn't a contractor, caterer or car dealer for the Microsoft crowd.

A series of calamitous events around the turn of the millennium seemed to deflate the confidence of even the most upbeat Seattleites. In November 1999, the city drew attention as protesters and police clashed violently outside a World Trade Organization summit. In June 2000 a federal judge ruled that Microsoft should be split up as a result of its monopolistic business practices (the decision was later overturned). Then, on February 28, 2001, a 6.8-magnitude earthquake near the state capital caused billions of dollars' worth of damages (though, miraculously, little loss of life). Just a few weeks later came the ultimate kick in the teeth: Boeing announced its intention to relocate its headquarters to Chicago.

Orientation

Seattle's Sea-Tac Airport is some 13 miles (21km) south of the city. Amtrak trains use the King St Station, north of the new Seahawks stadium, just south of Pioneer Sq. Greyhound's bus terminal is at 8th Ave and Stewart St, on the north edge of downtown.

Seattle is very neighborhood-oriented; locals give directions in terms of Capitol Hill, Belltown, Fremont etc, which can be confusing if you don't know the layout. Basically, heading north from downtown, Capitol Hill and the U District lie to the east of I-5, while the historic downtown core, Seattle Center, Fremont and Ballard lie to the west. Aurora Ave (Hwy 99) is a major north–south artery. To reach Fremont from downtown, take 4th Ave to the Fremont Bridge; from here, hang a left on NW 36th Ave (which becomes Leary) to reach Ballard. Eastlake Ave goes from downtown to the U District.

Information

BOOKSTORES

Bailey/Coy Books (☎ 206-323-8842; 414 Broadway E)

Beyond the Closet Books (☎ 206-322-4609; 518 E Pike St) Gay-focused bookstore.

Bulldog News & Espresso (☎ 206-632-6397; 4208 University Way NE)

Elliott Bay Book Company (☎ 206-624-6600; 101 S Main St) Labyrinthine store in historic Pioneer Sq has readings almost nightly.

Left Bank Books (☎ 206-622-0195; 92 Pike Pl) Socialist intellectual heaven.

Metsker Maps (☎ 206-623-8747; 702 1st Ave)

University Bookstore (☎ 206-634-3400; 4326 University Way NE)

EMERGENCY

Community Info Line (☎ 206-461-3200) Information on emergency services, housing, legal advice etc.

SEATTLE IN...

Two days

Start with a leisurely latte at **Zeitgeist**. Then explore historic **Pioneer Sq** and the totem poles in **Occidental Park**. Don't miss the chance to duck into **Elliott Bay Book Company**, Seattle's best bookstore. Nosh at the café downstairs, or follow your nose to a tasty meal in the **International District**. That evening, catch a **Mariners** or **Seahawks** game or – if you have wheels – cruise over to **Ballard** for nightlife. The next day, hit **Pike Place Market**, then take the monorail over to **Seattle Center** for a close-up view of the **Space Needle**. Stop into the **EMP's Liquid Lounge** during happy hour, or go bar-hopping in **Belltown**.

Four days

Follow the two-day itinerary, then, the next morning, catch a ferry to **Bainbridge Island** and breathe in the salt air. Enjoy a tasting at the **Bainbridge Island Winery** before your return trip. In the evening, head to **Capitol Hill**. The next day, explore quirky **Fremont** or the **U District** (or both), then take a walk or rent a bicycle and ride along the nearby **Burke-Gilman Trail**.

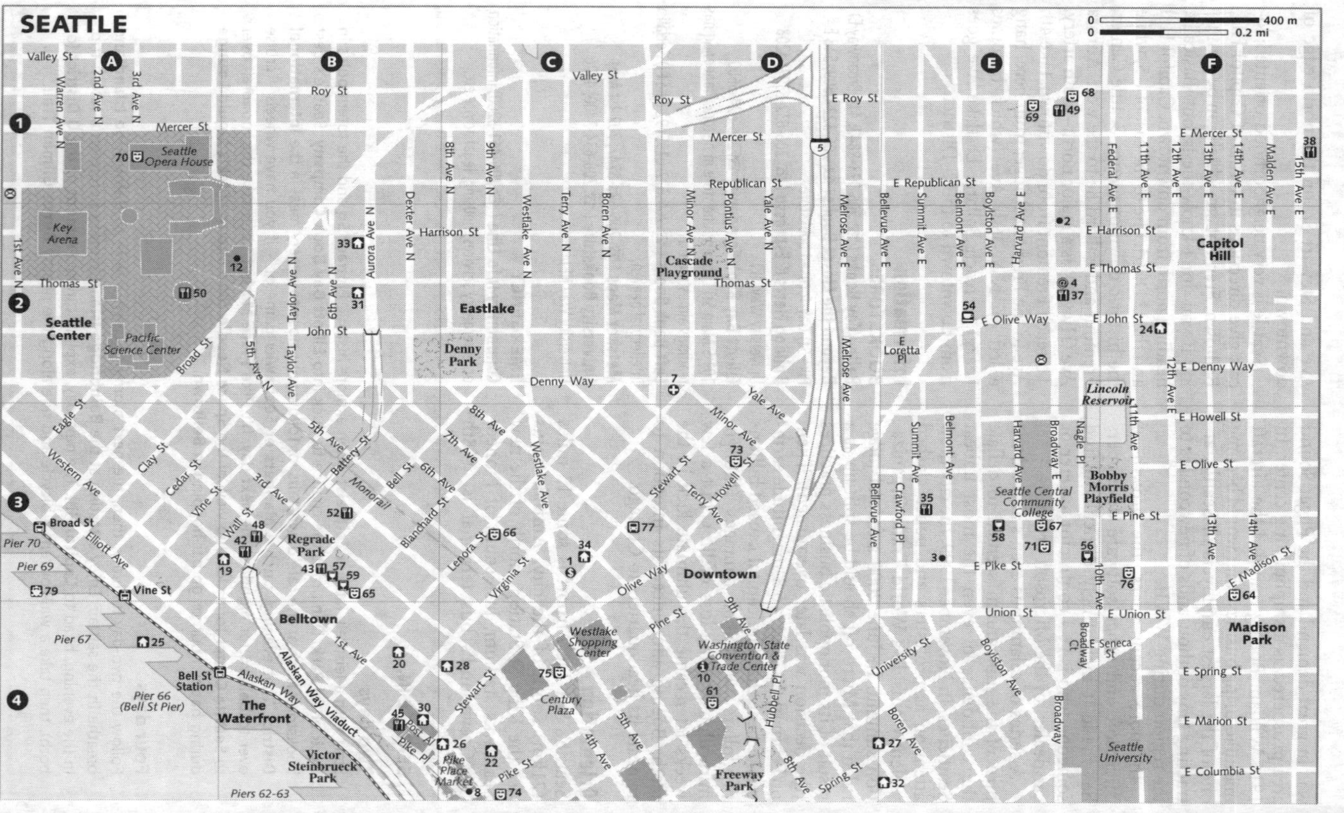
SEATTLE
0 400 m
0 0.2 mi
Seattle Center
Key Arena
Seattle Opera House
Pacific Science Center
Eastlake
Denny Park
Cascade Playground
Capitol Hill
Lincoln Reservoir
Bobby Morris Playfield
Seattle Central Community College
Madison Park
Seattle University
Downtown
Washington State Convention & Trade Center
Freeway Park
Westlake Shopping Center
Century Plaza
Pike Place Market
Regrade Park
Belltown
Victor Steinbrueck Park
The Waterfront
Alaskan Way Viaduct
Alaskan Way
Bell St Station
Broad St
Vine St
Piers 62-63
Pier 66 (Bell St Pier)
Pier 67
Pier 69
Pier 70
Valley St
Roy St
Mercer St
Republican St
Harrison St
Thomas St
John St
Denny Way
E Roy St
E Mercer St
E Republican St
E Harrison St
E Thomas St
E John St
E Olive Way
E Denny Way
E Howell St
E Olive St
E Pine St
E Pike St
E Union St
E Madison St
E Seneca St
E Spring St
E Marion St
E Columbia St
Warren Ave N
2nd Ave N
3rd Ave N
1st Ave N
Taylor Ave N
6th Ave N
Aurora Ave N
Dexter Ave N
8th Ave N
9th Ave N
Westlake Ave N
Terry Ave N
Boren Ave N
Minor Ave N
Pontius Ave N
Yale Ave N
Melrose Ave E
Bellevue Ave E
Summit Ave E
Belmont Ave E
Boylston Ave E
Harvard Ave E
Federal Ave E
11th Ave E
12th Ave E
13th Ave E
14th Ave E
Malden Ave E
15th Ave E
E Loretta Pl
Melrose Ave
Bellevue Ave
Crawford Pl
Summit Ave
Belmont Ave
Harvard Ave
Broadway E
Nagle Pl
11th Ave
12th Ave E
10th Ave
13th Ave
14th Ave
Broadway Ct
Broadway
Union St
University St
Boylston Ave
Boren Ave
Spring St
8th Ave
Hubbell Pl
9th Ave
Pine St
Olive Way
Howell St
Terry Ave
Stewart St
Minor Ave
Yale Ave
Westlake Ave
Virginia St
Lenora St
Blanchard St
Bell St
6th Ave
7th Ave
8th Ave
5th Ave
4th Ave
Pike St
Monorail
Battery St
5th Ave N
Taylor Ave
Broad St
Eagle St
Western Ave
Clay St
Cedar St
Vine St
3rd Ave
Wall St
Elliott Ave
1st Ave
Post Al
Pike Pl

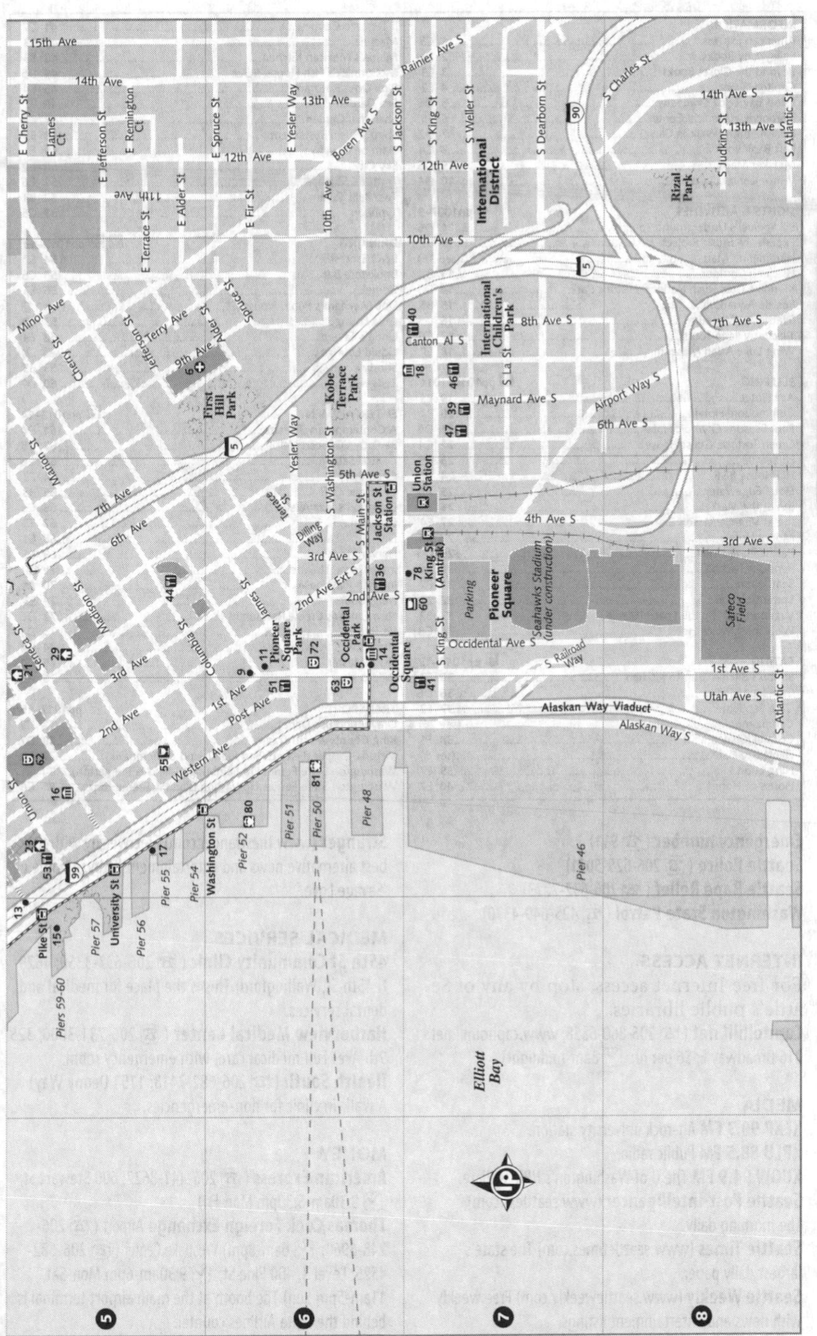
15th Ave
14th Ave
13th Ave
12th Ave
11th Ave
10th Ave
E Cherry St
E James Ct
E Jefferson St
E Remington Ct
E Terrace St
E Alder St
E Spruce St
E Fir St
E Yesler Way
Boren Ave S
Rainier Ave S
S Jackson St
S King St
S Weller St
12th Ave
International District
10th Ave S
S Dearborn St
S Charles St
14th Ave S
13th Ave S
S Judkins St
S Atlantic St
Rizal Park
Minor Ave
Cherry St
Jefferson St
Terry Ave
Alder St
Spruce St
9th Ave
First Hill Park
Marion St
7th Ave
6th Ave
Yesler Way
Kobe Terrace Park
S Washington St
Terrace St
5th Ave S
Canton Al S
International Children's Park
8th Ave S
7th Ave S
S La St
Maynard Ave S
Airport Way S
6th Ave S
Union Station
Jackson St Station
S Main St
Dilling Way
3rd Ave S
4th Ave S
3rd Ave S
Madison St
Seneca St
2nd Ave Ext S
2nd Ave S
King St (Amtrak)
Parking
Pioneer Square
Seahawks Stadium (under construction)
Safeco Field
James St
Columbia St
3rd Ave
Pioneer Square Park
Occidental Park
Occidental Square
S King St
Occidental Ave S
S Railroad Way
1st Ave S
Utah Ave S
S Atlantic St
1st Ave
Post Ave
2nd Ave
Western Ave
Alaskan Way Viaduct
Alaskan Way S
Union St
Washington St
Pier 52
Pier 51
Pier 50
Pier 48
Pier 46
Pier 55
Pier 54
Pier 57
Pier 56
University St
Pike St
Piers 59-60
Elliott Bay
PACIFIC NORTHWEST

INFORMATION

Name	No.	Grid
American Express	1	C3
Bailey/Coy Books	2	E2
Beyond the Closet Books	3	E3
CapitolHill.net	4	E2
Elliott Bay Book Company	5	D6
Harborview Medical Center	6	E5
Health South (Walk-in Clinic)	7	D2
Left Bank Books	8	C4
Metsker Maps	9	D6
Visitor Center	10	D4

SIGHTS & ACTIVITIES pp1007–9

Name	No.	Grid
Bill Speidel's Underground Tour	11	D6
Experience Music Project	12	B2
Hammering Man	(see 16)	
Hillclimb Corridor	13	B5
Klondike Gold Rush National Historic Park	14	D6
Seattle Aquarium	15	B5
Seattle Art Museum	16	C5
Tillicum Village Tours	17	C5
Wing Luke Asian Museum	18	E7

SLEEPING pp1010–1011

Name	No.	Grid
Ace Hotel	19	B3
Commodore Hotel	20	B4
Four Seasons Olympic Hotel	21	D5
Green Tortoise Guest House	22	C4
HI Seattle	23	C5
Hill House B&B	24	F2
Hotel Edgewater	25	A4
Inn at the Market	26	C4
Inn at Virginia Mason	27	E4
Moore Hotel	28	C4
Pacific Plaza Hotel	29	D5
Pensione Nichols	30	B4
Seattle Inn	31	B2
Sorrento Hotel	32	E4
Vagabond Inn by the Space Needle	33	B2
WestCoast Vance Hotel	34	C3

EATING pp1011–12

Name	No.	Grid
Bimbo's Bitchin' Burrito Kitchen	35	E3
Cafe Hue	36	D6
Café Septieme	37	E2
Campagne	(see 26)	
Coastal Kitchen	38	F1
Elliott Bay Café	(see 5)	
Hing Loon	39	E7
House of Hong	40	E7
Il Terrazzo Carmine	41	C7
Macrina	42	B3
Mama's Mexican Kitchen	43	B3
McCormick's Fish House & Bar	44	D5
Pink Door Ristorante	45	B4
Sea Garden	46	E7
Shanghai Garden	47	E7
Shiro's Sushi Restaurant	48	B3
Siam on Broadway	49	E1
Sky City	50	A2
Trattoria Mitchelli	51	C6
Two Bells Tavern	52	B3
Typhoon	53	C5

DRINKING pp1012–13

Name	No.	Grid
B&O Espresso	54	E2
Bookstore Bar	55	C5
Comet	56	E3
Doc Maynard's Public House	(see 11)	
Lava Lounge	57	B3
Linda's Tavern	58	E3
Liquid Lounge	(see 12)	
Shorty's	59	B3
Zeitgeist	60	D7

ENTERTAINMENT pp1013–14

Name	No.	Grid
A Contemporary Theatre	61	D4
Benaroya Concert Hall	62	C5
Central Saloon	63	C6
Chop Suey	64	F3
Crocodile Café	65	B3
Dimitriou's Jazz Alley	66	C3
Egyptian	67	E3
Elite	68	E1
Harvard Exit	69	E1
Imax Dome Theatre	(see 15)	
Intiman Playhouse	70	A1
Neighbours	71	E3
New Orleans Creole Restaurant	72	D6
Re-Bar	73	D3
Showbox	74	C4
TicketMaster	75	C4
Wildrose	76	F3

TRANSPORT pp1017–15

Name	No.	Grid
Greyhound Bus Depot	77	C3
King County Metro Transit	78	D7
Victoria Clipper (Ferry to San Juan Island & Victoria)	79	A3
Washington State Ferries (To Bainbridge Island & Bremerton)	80	C6
Washington State Ferries (To Vashon Island & Bremerton)	81	C6

Emergency number (☎ 911)
Seattle Police (☎ 206-625-5011)
Seattle Rape Relief (☎ 206-632-7273)
Washington State Patrol (☎ 425-649-4370)

INTERNET ACCESS

For free Internet access, stop by any of Seattle's public libraries.

Capitolhill.net (☎ 206-860-6858; www.capitolhill.net; 216 Broadway E; $6 per hr; 8am-midnight)

MEDIA

KEXP 90.3 FM Alt-rock university station.
KPLU 88.5 FM Public radio.
KUOW 94.9 FM The U of Washington's NPR affiliate.
Seattle Post-Intelligencer (www.seattlepi.com) The morning daily.
Seattle Times (www.seattletimes.com) The state's largest daily paper.
Seattle Weekly (www.seattleweekly.com) Free weekly with news and entertainment listings.
Stranger (www.thestranger.com) Free weekly with the best alternative news and entertainment listings; home of 'Savage Love.'

MEDICAL SERVICES

45th St Community Clinic (☎ 206-633-3350; 1629 N 45th St, Wallingford) This is the place for medical and dental services.
Harborview Medical Center (☎ 206-731-3000; 325 9th Ave) Full medical care, with emergency room.
Health South (☎ 206-682-7418; 1151 Denny Way) A walk-in clinic for non-emergencies.

MONEY

American Express (☎ 206-441-8622; 600 Stewart St; 8:30am-5:30pm Mon-Fri)
Thomas Cook Foreign Exchange Airport (☎ 206-248-6960; 6am-8pm) Westlake Center (☎ 206-682-4525; Level 3, 400 Pine St; 9:30am-6pm Mon-Sat, 11am-5pm Sun) The booth at the main airport terminal is behind the Delta Airlines counter.

POST

Broadway Station (☎ 206-324-5474; 101 Broadway E)
Main post office (☎ 206-748-5417; 301 Union St)
University Station (☎ 206-675-8114 ; 4244 NE University Way)

TOURIST OFFICES

Washington State Convention & Trade Center (☎ 206-461-5840; www.seeseattle.org; 7th Ave and Pike St; 8:30am-5pm Mon-Fri, 10am-4pm Sat & Sun in peak season)

Sights

The historic downtown area, Pioneer Sq, includes the area between Cherry and S King Sts, along 1st to 3rd Ave. The main shopping area is along 4th and 5th Aves from Olive Way down to University St. Just north of downtown is Seattle Center, with many of the city's cultural and sporting facilities, as well as the Space Needle. Alaskan Way is the Waterfront's main drag; the Waterfront Streetcar runs the length of it.

DOWNTOWN

The fishy-smelling, tourist-thronged heart of downtown Seattle is **Pike Place Market**, on Pike Street between Western and 1st Aves. It's good theater, though claustrophobically crowded. The Main and North Arcades are the most popular areas, with bellowing fishmongers, stacks of gem-like fruits and vegetables, and arts and crafts. Tiny shops of all descriptions fill the labyrinthine lower levels of the market. Go on a weekday morning to avoid the crush.

Jonathan Borofsky's 48ft-high mechanized sculpture *Hammering Man* welcomes visitors to the **Seattle Art Museum** (☎ 206-654-3100; www.seattleartmuseum.org; 100 University St; adult/child $7/free; 10am-5pm Tue-Sat, 10am-9pm Sun). The museum's John H Hauberg Collection is an excellent display of masks, canoes, totems and other pieces from Northwest coastal tribes.

North of Pike Place Market is **Belltown**, the cradle of grunge. The famous clubs are still here, but the area has gone seriously upscale, with fancy restaurants and designer boutiques in converted lofts. Still, it remains one of the best parts of town for nightlife.

PIONEER SQ

The birthplace of Seattle, this enclave of red-brick buildings languished for years until cheap rents and Historic Register status brought in art galleries, antique shops and cafés. Today the Waterfront Streetcar will drop you right in the heart of the district. The area's Yesler Way was the original 'skid road' – in Seattle's early days timber would skid down the road from a logging camp above town to Henry Yesler's pierside mill. With the decline of the area, the street became a haven for homeless people. The nickname Skid Road (or 'Skid Row') eventually came to mean the opposite of 'Easy Street' in cities across the US.

Just south of Pioneer Sq, on Occidental Ave S, **Occidental Park** has totem poles carved by Chinookan artist Duane Pasco. Between S Main and Jackson Sts, the park turns into a tree-lined pedestrian mall bordered by galleries, sculptures and coffee shops.

At the **Klondike Gold Rush National Historic Park** (☎ 206-553-7220; 117 S Main St; admission free; 9am-5pm), one of the few *indoor* national parks in the country, learn what kind of provisions you would've needed were you to stake a claim in the Yukon territory.

INTERNATIONAL DISTRICT

East of Pioneer Sq (take S Jackson St), Asian groceries and restaurants line the streets. The **Wing Luke Asian Museum** (☎ 206-623-5124; www.wingluke.org; 407 7th Ave S; adult/child $4/2; 11am-4:30 pm Tue-Fri, noon-4pm Sat & Sun) documents the often difficult and violent meeting of Asian and Western cultures in Seattle with artwork, special exhibits, historic photographs, a replica of a World War II Japanese-American internment camp and recorded interviews with internees.

The district's **Jackson St** was once home to a thriving jazz scene. As teens in the late '40s and early '50s, Quincy Jones and Ray Charles used to hustle their way into jazz clubs here and play into the wee hours of the morning.

SEATTLE CENTER

In 1962, Seattle hosted a World's Fair, a summer-long exhibition that enticed nearly 10 million visitors to view the future, Seattle style. The vestiges, which 40 years later look simultaneously futuristic and retro, are on view at the **Seattle Center** (☎ 206-684-8582; www.seattlecenter.com; 400 Broad St). **Space Needle** (☎ 206-905-2100; adult/child $12.50/5; 10am-10pm Sun-Thu, 10am-midnight Fri & Sat) is a 605ft-high observation station with a revolving restaurant (p1011). The **monorail** ($1.50), a 1.5-mile

BILL GATES: SUGAR DADDY?

What does it mean when Bill Gates, the richest man on earth, says on national television that poverty is a 'failure of capitalism'? The cofounder of Microsoft, William Gates III, born October 28, 1955, has publicly pledged to give away 95% of his wealth – that's $34.26 billion as of September 2003. And he seems to be following through, having shown a sincere interest in global health issues (he recently gave $28 million to benefit an AIDS program in Africa, for example). However pervasive the Windows operating system may be, the man behind it seems more interested in leaving a different kind of legacy.

Gates grew up in Seattle's upper-class Laurelhurst neighborhood and began developing software at the age of 13. In college at Harvard, he hung out in the computer lab and whipped up programming language for the world's first microcomputer. Eventually he dropped out of Harvard and hooked up with his buddy Paul Allen; the two went on to develop DOS, then the Windows operating systems.

At age 37, Gates became the second-richest man in the USA and, soon after, the richest man in the world, with a fortune estimated at $48 billion. From Luther Burbank Park on the northeast corner of Mercer Island, you can see his mansion across the lake if you know where to look. But you'd better get a glimpse while you can – he might just give it away.

experiment in mass transit, runs every 10 minutes daily from downtown's Westlake Center right through a crumple in the smashed-guitar hull of the Experience Music Project.

It's hard not to be astounded by Microsoft cofounder Paul Allen's **Experience Music Project** (EMP; ☎ 206-367-5483; www.emplive.com; 325 5th Ave N; adult/child $20/15; 9am-6pm Sun-Thu, 9am-9pm Fri & Sat in summer; 10am-5pm Sun-Thu, 10am-9pm Fri & Sat in winter). The lovechild of a fat wallet and a rock 'n' roll heart, the EMP is worth a look for the architecture alone; whether it's worth the admission price is another story. The shimmering, abstract building, designed by Frank Gehry, houses 80,000 music artifacts, including handwritten lyrics by Nirvana's Kurt Cobain and a Fender Stratocaster demolished by Jimi Hendrix. Kids will love the chance to record and mix their own song or make a video. To serious music fans, the exhibits may seem a little basic, although the video archive is excellent. The Sky Church theater, Liquid Lounge bar and Turntable restaurant are accessible free of charge.

CAPITOL HILL

This area has long been a countercultural oasis, and as the principal gay and lesbian neighborhood, it has an unmatched vitality. Capitol Hill is about 1.5 miles northeast of downtown. Take bus No 7 or 10 and get off at **Broadway**. The junction of Broadway and E John St (the continuation of Olive Way) is the core of activity. Continue north to stately **Volunteer Park**, on E Prospect St, originally Seattle's cemetery. The **Seattle Asian Art Museum** (☎ 206-654-3100; 1400 E Prospect St; adult/child $3/free; 10am-5pm Wed-Sun, 10am-9pm Thu; P), in Volunteer Park, houses an extensive collection of paintings, sculptures, ceramics and textiles of Japan, China and Korea; the cost of admission will be discounted off the admission price to Seattle Art Museum if you visit it within seven days of visiting here. Also in Volunteer Park is the glass-sided Victorian **conservatory** (admission free), filled with palms, cacti and tropical plants.

If you're driving, there is also a pay parking lot on Harvard Ave E, behind the Broadway Market.

FREMONT

Fun-loving Fremont, about 2 miles north of the Seattle Center, is known for its unorthodox public sculpture, junk stores, summer outdoor film festival and general high spirits. **Fremont Ave N** is the main strip. Probably the most discussed piece of public art in the city, *Waiting for the Interurban* (N 34th St at Fremont) is a cast aluminum statue of people awaiting a train that never comes; the Interurban linking Seattle and Everett stopped running in the 1930s (it started up again in 2001 but the line no longer passes this way). Check out the human face on the dog; it's Armen Stepanian, once Fremont's honorary mayor, who made the mistake of objecting to the sculpture. Beware the scary-eyed *Fremont Troll*, a mammoth cement figure devouring a VW bug beneath the Aurora Bridge at 36th St.

THE U DISTRICT

The 700-acre University of Washington campus sits at the edge of Lake Union in a busy commercial area about 3 miles northeast of downtown. The main streets are University Way, known as the '**Ave**,' and NE 45th St, both lined with surprisingly upscale coffee shops, restaurants and bars, cinemas and bookstores. The core of campus is **Central Plaza**, known as Red Sq because of its brick base. Get information and a campus map at the **visitors center** (☎ 206-543-9198; 4014 University Way; 8am-5pm Mon-Fri).

Near the junction of NE 45th St and 16th Ave is the **Burke Museum** (☎ 206-543-5590; adult/child $6.50/3; 10am-5pm), with an excellent collection of Northwest coast Indian artifacts. At the corner of NE 41st St and 15th Ave is the **Henry Art Gallery** (☎ 206-543-2280; adult/children under 14 $8/free, admission free 5-8pm Thu; 11am-5pm Tue-Sun, 11am-8pm Thu), the sophisticated, brainy child in Seattle's museum family.

BALLARD

The community of Ballard, settled by Scandinavian fishermen in the early 20th century, feels like your average lutefisk-flavored blue-collar neighborhood – until you turn down Ballard Ave, where a row of hip bars, restaurants and brewpubs appears. This cobbled street has suddenly become a hotbed of nightlife worth exploring.

Northwest of Seattle, the waters of Lake Washington and Lake Union flow through the 8-mile-long Lake Washington Ship Canal and into Puget Sound. Construction of the canal began in 1911; today 100,000 boats a year pass through the **Hiram M Chittenden Locks** (☎ 206-783-7059; 3015 NW 54th St; admission free; 10am-4pm Thu-Mon in winter, 10am-6pm in summer), about a half mile west of Ballard off NW Market St. Free guided tours are provided March through November. On the southern side of the locks, you can watch from underwater glass tanks or from above as salmon struggle up a **fish ladder** on their way to spawning grounds in the Cascade headwaters of the Sammamish River, which feeds Lake Washington.

Activities

You can hike through old-growth forest at Seward Park, which dominates the Bailey Peninsula that juts into Lake Washington, or on longer trails in 534-acre Discovery Park, northwest of Seattle at the mouth of Chittenden Locks. The **Sierra Club** (☎ 206-523-2019) leads day-hiking and car-camping trips on weekends; most day trips are free.

Circling Green Lake on foot or wheels is a popular weekend activity. Rent a bicycle at **Gregg's Greenlake Cycle** (☎ 206-523-1822; 7007 Woodlawn Ave NE; $20-30 per day) or, near the University of Washington campus, **Al Young Bike and Ski** (☎ 206-524-2642; 3615 NE 45th St; $20-25 per day).

Hikers and bikers use the 16.5 mile **Burke-Gilman Trail**, an abandoned railroad corridor that starts at the impressive industrial skeleton of Gas Works Park on Lake Union and ends up at the north side of Lake Washington.

Northwest Outdoor Center Inc (☎ 206-281-9694, 800-683-0637; www.nwoc.com; 2100 Westlake Ave N; kayaks $10-15 per hr), on Lake Union, rents kayaks and offers tours and instruction in sea and whitewater kayaking. The **UW Waterfront Activities Center** (☎ 206-543-9433), at the southeast corner of the Husky Stadium parking lot off Montake Blvd NE, rents canoes and rowboats for $7.50 per hour. Bring ID or a passport.

Green Lake and Lake Washington are popular for windsurfing. **Greenlake Boat Rentals** (☎ 206-527-0171; 7351 E Green Lake Dr) provides lessons and rentals.

Seattle for Children

The whole of Seattle Center will fascinate youngsters, but they'll get the most out of the **Pacific Science Center** (☎ 206-443-2001; 200 2nd Ave N; adult/child $14.50/12; 10am-6pm in summer, 10am-5pm Mon-Fri in winter; P $5-10). It entertains and educates with virtual-reality exhibits, laser shows, holograms, an Imax theater and a planetarium – parents won't be bored either.

Downtown on Pier 59 is the **Seattle Aquarium** (☎ 206-386-4320; www.seattleaquarium.org; adult/child $11/5; 10am-5pm), another fun way to learn about the natural world of the Pacific Northwest. Its centerpiece is the Dome, a spherical underwater room where you can see deepwater denizens from all angles; don't miss the daily feeding frenzy at 1:30pm.

Next door is the **Imax Dome** (☎ 206-622-1868; www.seattleimaxdome.com; combined aquarium/Imax ticket adult/child $16.50/5), a 180-degree surround-screen theater, where you can see *The Eruption of Mt St Helens* as if you were sitting on top when it blew; call for film schedule.

Tours

Bill Speidel's Underground Tour (☎ 206-682-4646; tours leave daily from Doc Maynard's Public House, 610 1st Ave, adult/child $9/5) Explores a network of subterranean chambers that predate the Great Fire and subsequent rebuilding of the district above the tide flats; reservations advised.

Gray Line of Seattle (☎ 206-626-5208, 800-426-7505; www.graylineofseattle.com; 800 Convention Place; tour $29) City Sights Tour runs year-round.

Show Me Seattle Tours (☎ 206-633-2489; www.showmeseattle.com; adult/child $33/22) Daily shuttle tours in small groups.

Festivals & Events

Bumbershoot (☎ 206-281-8111; www.bumbershoot.com) Labor Day weekend in September. A major arts and cultural event at Seattle Center.

Chinese New Year (☎ 206-382-1197; www.internationaldistrict.org) January or late February. Celebrated with parades, fireworks and food in the International District.

Northwest Folklife Festival (☎ 206-684-7300; www.nwfolklife.org) Memorial Day weekend in May. International music, dance, crafts, food and family activities at the Seattle Center.

Seafair (☎ 206-728-0123; www.seafair.com) Late July and August. Hydroplane races, a torchlight parade, an air show, music and a carnival.

Sleeping

The **Seattle Hotel Hotline** (☎ 206-461-5882, 800-535-7071) has a free reservation service with winter Super Saver Packages. For a list of bed-and-breakfast inns, try the **Seattle B&B Association** (☎ 206-547-1020, 800-348-5630; www.lodginginseattle.com; PO Box 31772, Seattle, WA 98103-1772). The prices listed below are average high-season rates, subject to a variable room tax; rates fall on weekends and plummet in winter.

BUDGET

Downtown & Pike Place Market

HI Seattle (☎ 206-622-5443, 888-622-5443; www.hiseattle.org; 84 Union St; dm $24-26, r from $54) This gigantic hostel is clean, friendly, open 24 hours, and central to the Waterfront and Pike Place Market. The dining room has a great view.

Green Tortoise Guest House (☎ 206-340-1222, 888-424-6783; www.greentortoise.com; 1525 2nd Ave; dm/s $20/50) A slightly grungier option, but personable, this backpacker's hostel is also right in the middle of the action. It has six- and eight-bed dorms and free breakfast.

Belltown & Seattle Center

Moore Hotel (☎ 206-448-4851; www.moorehotel.com; 1926 2nd Ave; r with shared bath $39, s/d with private bath $59/67) Rooms at this once-grand hotel are nothing fancy, but they're clean and unfussily elegant, and you can hardly beat the price. Don't miss the adjoining Limelight, an unpretentiously retro lounge.

Commodore Hotel (☎ 206-448-8868, 800-714-8868; www.commodorehotel.com; 2013 2nd Ave; s/d with shared bath $49/55, with private bath $59/69, ste $124-144) Rates at this newly renovated and very friendly hotel include a continental breakfast.

MID-RANGE

Downtown & Pike Place Market

Pensione Nichols (☎ 206-441-7125, 800-440-7125; www.seattle-bed-breakfast.com; 1923 1st Ave; s/d/ste $90/110/195) Ideally situated between Pike Place Market and Belltown, this charming haven has 10 European-style rooms and a common room overlooking the market.

Inn at Virginia Mason (☎ 206-583-6453, 800-283-6453; 1006 Spring St; r $85-135) This hotel on First Hill just above downtown is part of the Virginia Mason hospital complex. It has quiet rooms and a nice rooftop garden with views.

Also recommended are the business-oriented **Pacific Plaza Hotel** (☎ 206-623-3900, 800-426-1165; 400 Spring St; s/d $104/119) and the **WestCoast Vance Hotel** (☎ 206-441-4200; www.westcoasthotels.com/vance; 620 Stewart St; r from $109).

Belltown & Seattle Center

Ace Hotel (☎ 206-448-4721; www.theacehotel.com; 2423 1st Ave; s/d with shared bath $65/85, with private bath $130/175) Hands-down Seattle's hippest hotel, the Ace sports minimal, futuristic decor (everything's white and stainless steel, even the TV), antique French army blankets, condoms instead of pillow mints and a Kama Sutra in place of the Bible.

Vagabond Inn by the Space Needle (☎ 206-441-0400, 800-522-1555; www.vagabondinn.com; 325 Aurora Ave N; r from $99; P) Kids under 18 stay free with their parents at this functional chain hotel near Seattle Center.

Seattle Inn (☎ 206-728-7666, 800-255-7932; 225 Aurora Ave N; r from $79; P) This hotel has clean, spacious and disconcertingly pastel rooms, and a complimentary breakfast.

THE AUTHOR'S CHOICE

College Inn (☎ 206-633-4441; www.collegeinnseattle.com; 4000 University Way NE; s $50, d $60-80; 💻) Built in 1909 for the Alaska-Yukon Exposition, the College Inn is like an extra-classy hostel at the end of a bustling U District strip, near the Henry Art Gallery. With loads of atmosphere, a hearty breakfast and Internet access, it's a great bargain, although keep in mind there's no elevator and the rooms aren't wheelchair-accessible.

Capitol Hill & The U District

Gaslight Inn B&B (☎ 206-325-3654; 1727 15th Ave E; r with shared/private bath $78/98, ste $128-178) This Capitol Hill B&B is a restored turn-of-the-century house with a warm, dark-wood atmosphere, 15 rooms, a pool and a hot tub. The owners have amassed an impressive art collection over the years.

Also in Capitol Hill is the **Hill House B&B** (☎ 206-720-7161, 800-720-7161; www.seattlebnb.com; 1113 E John St; r $105-165), in a restored 1903 home. Off I-5 exit 169 are a number of moderately priced motels near the University of Washington. For rooms between $70 and $105, try **University Plaza Hotel** (☎ 206-634-0100, 800-343-7040; 400 NE 45th St) or **University Inn** (☎ 206-632-5055, 800-695-8284; 4140 Roosevelt Way NE; P ♿).

TOP END

Inn at the Market (☎ 206-443-3600, 800-446-4484; 86 Pine St; r from $195) A luxuriously serene little enclave right in the thick of Pike Place but insulated from the street noise by wads of cash. A suite can run you up to $600. The ivy-beribboned courtyard is precious and most rooms have views over Puget Sound.

Fairmont Olympic Hotel (☎ 206-621-1700, 800-223-8772; 411 University St; r from $275) Huge and imposing, this opulent 1924 hotel looks more like a government building or a European bank from the outside. Its 450 rooms don't come cheap, but guests are treated like movie stars.

Sorrento Hotel (☎ 206-622-6400, 800-426-1265; www.hotelsorrento.com; 900 Madison St; r $250, ste $320-608) For atmospheric lodging in the center of town, check out the city's oldest ultraswank hotel. The Italian Renaissance–style building was renovated to its present decadence in 1980.

Hotel Edgewater (☎ 206-728-7000, 800-624-0670; www.edgewaterhotel.com; 2411 Alaskan Way; r from $219) This luxury hotel on Pier 67 is the only one that faces onto Elliott Bay. You're no longer allowed to fish from the windows, but you can sit by the fireplace and reel in the salty air and views of Puget Sound. Rates vary greatly depending on views, amenities and season.

Eating

DOWNTOWN & PIKE PLACE MARKET

Campagne (☎ 206-728-2800; 86 Pine St; mains $25-35) In the courtyard at the Inn at the Market, this is Seattle's best traditional French restaurant; for a more casual option, try the **café** (mains $12-16) downstairs.

Pink Door Ristorante (☎ 206-443-3241; 1919 Post Alley; lunch $8-12, mains $14-20) There's no sign on this alley café, but you'll find pasta lunch dishes for $8.

Recommended for seafood is **McCormick's Fish House & Bar** (☎ 206-682-3900; 722 4th Ave; mains $15-23), an old-fashioned oyster bar with fresh daily specials. On the street just below the market is **Typhoon** (☎ 206-262-9797; 1400 Western Ave; lunch/dinner $8/13), a massively popular Thai restaurant; try the cheap appetizers in the bar. Or head to **Pike Place Market** to forage for fresh produce, baked goods, deli items and take-out ethnic foods.

BELLTOWN & SEATTLE CENTER

Mama's Mexican Kitchen (☎ 206-728-6262; 2234 2nd Ave; mains $5-8) Mama's is always enjoyably packed, thanks to huge combo plates, cheap burritos and some great happy-hour margaritas.

Two Bells Tavern (☎ 206-441-3050; 2313 4th Ave; burgers $6-7) This venerable nonsmoking pub is a comfortable, welcoming place to enjoy one of Seattle's best burgers.

Shiro's Sushi Restaurant (☎ 206-443-9844; 2401 2nd Ave; mains $16-20) has excellent, well-priced rolls, and head to **Macrina** (☎ 206-448-4032; 1st Ave at Battery St; lunch $8-14) for artisan bread, panini sandwiches and light lunches.

If you're planning on dinner in the Space Needle's rotating restaurant, **Sky City** (☎ 206-443-2111; appetizers $10, mains $30-45), be aware that although the ride up is free if you have reservations, and the views are spectacular if it's clear, the menu prices might make your head spin in tandem with the restaurant.

PIONEER SQ

Elliott Bay Café (☎ 206-682-6664; 101 S Main St; snacks $5-6) Beneath Elliott Bay Book Company is this cozy place for soup, salad and sandwiches. It also serves the beloved Top Pot handcrafted doughnuts.

Trattoria Mitchelli (☎ 206-623-3883; 84 Yesler Way; dishes from $10) The claim-to-fame of this homey Italian place is that it satisfies hungry club-goers with pasta dishes and salads until 4am.

Also recommended are **Cafe Hue** (☎ 206-625-9833; 312 2nd Ave S; mains $5-8), a cute Vietnamese café with colonial French influences and, at the upper end, **Il Terrazzo Carmine** (☎ 206-467-7797; 411 1st Ave S; mains $30-60), noted for its luxurious, multicourse Italian meals.

INTERNATIONAL DISTRICT

Shanghai Garden (☎ 206-625-1688; 624 6th Ave S; mains from $13) This is known as the best place in town for inventive Chinese cuisine.

House of Hong (☎ 206-622-7997; 409 8th Ave S; dinner $10-15) Some of the best dim sum in the city is served here from 10am to 5pm daily, so you don't even have to rush out of bed to get your fix.

Hing Loon (☎ 206-682-2828; 628 S Weller St; garlic prawns $9.25) specializes in seafood dishes, and the slightly more upscale **Sea Garden** (☎ 206-623-2100; 509 7th Ave S; mains $7-14) serves hot pots and huge bowls of noodle soup until 1am nightly.

CAPITOL HILL & THE U DISTRICT

Bimbo's Bitchin' Burrito Kitchen (☎ 206-329-9978; 506 E Pine St; $4.25-7.95) It looks like a hipster exploded in here, with over-the-top Mexikitsch decor covering every inch of the tiny space. The food is cheap, fresh and massive, and served until 2am on weekends. Don't miss **happy hour** ($2.50 drinks; 🕓 4-7pm) at the adjoining **Cha-Cha Lounge**, a cool, comfortable tiki bar.

Café Septieme (☎ 206-860-8858; 214 E Broadway; mains $8-14) This trendy, modern French-inspired space serves fancy drinks, gourmet salads and light meals.

Other recommendations:

Coastal Kitchen (☎ 206-322-1145; 429 15th Ave E; from $8) Eclectic mix of Mediterranean and Mexican inspirations.

Schultzy's Sausages (☎ 206-548-9461; 4142 University Way NE) A good lunch option among the many restaurants along University Way (most not as cheap and casual as you might expect for a student mecca).

Siam on Broadway (☎ 206-324-0892; 616 E Broadway; lunch/dinner $7/10) A Thai-food favorite.

BALLARD

Madame K's (☎ 206-783-9710; 5327 Ballard Ave NW; pizzas from $12) An elegant, red-and-black pizza parlor with an old bordello feel (the building was once a brothel), this small, chic place is packed at dinner. It's also popular for drinks, and the desserts are sinful.

Old Town Ale House (☎ 206-782-8323; 5233 Ballard Ave NW; sandwiches $7.95, appetizers $3-6) This cavernous, warmly lit, red-brick pub serves giant sandwich 'wedges,' massive stacks of delicious fries and microbrewed beer.

Drinking

For late-night action, head to Capitol Hill's Pike-Pine Corridor, extending from Broadway to about 12th Ave, home to a plethora of arty live-music clubs and taverns. For a less-vigorous but still very busy bar scene, check out the pubs along Ballard Ave. For a good overview of the club scene in Pioneer Sq, spring for the $5 **joint cover** ($10 Friday and Saturday) that lets you in to eight clubs, most with live music. Pay the cover and pick up a list of participating clubs at the Central Saloon or New Orleans Creole Restaurant (opposite). Most of the participating clubs are on 1st Ave S.

BARS

Liquid Lounge (☎ 206-770-2777; 325 5th Ave N) Located upstairs at the Experience Music Project (EMP), the Liquid Lounge – with its sleek high-tech atmosphere – is perhaps the best way to experience the EMP. The Lounge has DJs or live music most nights, and happy hour bargains on food and drink. Don't worry, it's not your gin and tonic that's making the ceiling go all wonky.

Shorty's (☎ 206-441-5449; 2222 2nd Ave) A totally unpretentious oasis in a block of tres-chic lounges, Shorty's has cheap beer and hotdogs, and the back room is pinball heaven.

Other good nightlife options include:

Bookstore Bar (☎ 206-382-1506; 1007 1st Ave) Cool book-nook bar adjoining the rather pretentious Library Bistro in the Alexis Hotel.

Comet (☎ 206-323-9853; 922 E Pike St) A no-frills institution with cheap beer and loyal locals; occasional bands.

Lava Lounge (☎ 206-441-5660; 2226 2nd Ave) Fiery den with massive hipster cachet.

Linda's Tavern (☎ 206-325-1220; 707 E Pine St) Amazingly popular hipster hangout with a tiki-themed patio and $1.50 cans of Black Label.
Lock & Keel Tavern (☎ 206-781-9092; 5144 Ballard Ave NW) A long, skinny saloon with a seafaring feel, popular for after-work drinks.
Monkey Pub (☎ 206-523-6457; 5303 Roosevelt Way NE) Off the beaten track, between the U District and Green Lake, this friendly punk-rock bar has a great jukebox, pool tables and occasional bands.

BREW PUBS

Jolly Roger Taproom (☎ 206-782-6181; 1514 NW Leary Way; lunch $4-7, dinner $10-12) A secret treasure tucked away off busy Leary, the Jolly Roger's a tiny, pirate-themed bar with a nautical chart painted onto the floor. Best of all, its delicious handcrafted beer comes in real, 20-ounce pints ($3.75), or you can try a sampler of five types ($7). Most of the food has beer in it and the menu pairs each meal with a suggested brew.

Hale's Ales Brewery (☎ 206-706-1544; www.halesales.com; 4301 Leary Way NW) Though short on atmosphere, the Hale's Brewery offers a self-guided tour, friendly service and, of course, great beer. Get an imperial pint for $4 or tasters for $1 each.

COFFEEHOUSES

This is the city that birthed Starbucks; and the homegrown chain now also owns Seattle's Best Coffee and Torrefazione Italia, making it rather difficult to avoid. But small coffeehouses still abound.
B&O Espresso (☎ 206-322-5028; 204 Belmont Ave E) A pleasant spot for some postcard scribbling on Capitol Hill.
Café Allegro (☎ 206-633-3030; 4214 University Way NE) Supposedly the city's first espresso bar.
Still Life in Fremont (☎ 206-547-9850; 709 N 35th St) A hippie/boho hangout with vegan food and organic coffee.
Zeitgeist (☎ 206-583-0497; 171 S Jackson St) This high-ceilinged, brick-walled café has great coffee and pastries, plus data ports for the 'working artist' crowd.

Entertainment

Consult the *Stranger*, *Seattle Weekly* or the daily papers for listings. Tickets for big events are available at **TicketMaster** (☎ 206-628-0888), which operates a **discount ticket booth** (☎ 206-233-1111) at Westlake Center.

LIVE MUSIC

Crocodile Cafe (☎ 206-441-5611; 2200 2nd Ave) This beloved institution in Belltown is one of the places that launched the whole grunge movement. It still hosts local and touring bands.

Chop Suey (☎ 206-324-8000; 1325 E Madison St) A dark, high-ceilinged space with ramshackle faux-Chinese motif, this venue currently has some of the best live rock shows in town.

Other recommendations:
Central Saloon (☎ 206-622-0209; 207 1st Ave S) The city's premier blues club.
Dimitriou's Jazz Alley (☎ 206-441-9729; 2033 6th Ave) Prestigious jazz club.
Graceland (☎ 206-381-3094; 109 Eastlake Ave) A gritty gem for lovers of sweat, booze and rock 'n' roll; formerly the Off Ramp.
New Orleans Creole Restaurant (☎ 206-622-2563; 114 1st Ave S) Jazz club near Pioneer Sq.
Showbox (☎ 206-628-3151; 1426 1st Ave) Big rock venue for touring bands.
Tractor Tavern (☎ 206-789-3599; 5213 Ballard Ave NW) An atmospheric venue mainly for folk/acoustic acts.

CINEMAS

At opposite ends of Capitol Hill are two of the city's best art cinemas, the **Egyptian** (☎ 206-323-4978; 805 E Pine St) and the **Harvard Exit** (☎ 206-323-8986; 807 E Roy St). Both are key venues during the three-week **Seattle International Film Festival** (☎ 206-464-5830), in late May and early June.

THEATER/PERFORMING ARTS

Seattle boasts one of the most vibrant theater scenes on the West Coast.

A Contemporary Theatre (ACT; ☎ 206-292-7676; 700 Union St) Located at Kreielsheimer Pl, this theater produces excellent performances year-round.

Bagley Wright Theatre (☎ 206-443-2222) The Seattle Repertory Theatre performs at the Bagley. Both the Bagley and the Intiman Playhouse front on Mercer St, the north side of Seattle Center.

Intiman Playhouse (☎ 206-269-1900) The Intiman Theatre Company, Seattle's oldest, takes the stage at this theater.

Seattle Symphony (☎ 206-215-4747) The symphony has risen to prominence as a major regional ensemble; it plays at the Benaroya Concert Hall, downtown at 2nd Ave and University St.

Seattle Opera (☎ 206-389-7676) The Seattle Opera isn't afraid to tackle weighty or nontraditional works. Performances are at the Opera House in Seattle Center.

Pacific Northwest Ballet (☎ 206-441-9411) The ballet is also based at the Opera House.

SPECTATOR SPORTS

Tickets for most of the following sports are sold through **TicketMaster** (☎ 206-628-0888).

Seattle Mariners (☎ 206-628-3555) Check out this baseball team, which plays in Safeco Field just south of downtown.

Seattle Seahawks (☎ 206-827-9777) Watch the Seahawks play pro football in the avant-garde new Seahawks Stadium.

Supersonics (☎ 206-283-3865) Seattle's National Basketball Association franchise, Supersonics draws huge crowds at Seattle Center's Key Arena.

Huskies (☎ 206-543-2200) The Huskies are the enormously popular University of Washington football team.

GAY & LESBIAN VENUES

Re-bar (☎ 206-233-9873; 1114 Howell St) This storied dance club, where many of Seattle's defining cultural events happened (Nirvana album releases etc), welcomes gay, straight, bi or undecided revelers to its dance floor nightly.

Wildrose (☎ 206-324-9210; 1021 E Pike St) This comfortable lesbian bar invites lingering and quiet conversation.

For a mostly gay male disco scene, check out **Neighbours** (☎ 206-324-5358; 1509 Broadway Ave E) or **Elite** (☎ 206-324-4470; 622 Broadway Ave E).

Shopping

The main shopping area is downtown from 3rd to 6th Aves and University to Stewart Sts. The streets around Pike Place Market are a maze of arts-and-crafts stalls, galleries and small shops. Pioneer Sq and Capitol Hill also have some interesting, locally owned gift shops. For bookstores, see p1003.

Getting There & Away

AIR

Seattle's airport, **Seattle-Tacoma International Airport** (Sea-Tac; ☎ 206-433-5388; www.portseattle.org), 13 miles south of Seattle on I-5, has daily service to Europe, Asia, Mexico and points throughout the USA and Canada, with frequent inexpensive flights to and from Portland and Vancouver, BC. Small commuter airlines link Seattle to the San Juan Islands, Bellingham, Wenatchee, Yakima and Spokane.

BOAT

Clipper Navigation (☎ 206-448-5000) runs the passenger-only *Victoria Clipper*, which departs Pier 69 for Victoria (one way/round-trip $66/109, three hours, four times daily in summer); first departure stops at San Juan Island.

Washington State Ferries (☎ 206-464-6400, in Washington ☎ 888-808-7977; www.wsdot.wa.gov/ferries) runs ferries from Seattle to Bremerton (adult/child/car and driver $6.10/4.60/11.25, 60 minutes, daily) and to Bainbridge Island ($5.10/3.60/11.25, 35 minutes, daily); both ferries leave from Pier 52, at Alaskan Way and Marion St. It also runs a passenger-only ferry from Seattle to Vashon Island (adult/child $7.10/5.60, 25 minutes), leaving from Pier 50.

BUS

Greyhound (☎ 206-628-5526; 8th Ave and Stewart St) has daily connections to Portland ($20, 4½ hours) as well as points east.

Quick Shuttle (☎ 800-665-2122; www.quickcoach.com) runs five daily express buses between Seattle and Vancouver, BC (4½ hours). Pickup is at Sea-Tac Airport ($41) or the downtown Travelodge at 2213 8th Ave ($33).

TRAIN

Amtrak (☎ 800-872-7245, 303 S Jackson St) serves the following locations (fares vary; these are average):

Chicago $217, two days, one daily.
Portland $23, 3½ hours, four daily.
Oakland $94, 23 hours, one daily.
Vancouver, BC $23, four hours, one daily.

Getting Around

TO/FROM THE AIRPORT

Gray Line runs an **Airport Express** (☎ 206-626-6088, 800-426-7532) between Sea-Tac and major downtown hotels every 30 minutes from 5am to 11pm (one way/round-trip $8.50/14). Or, catch Metro Transit bus No 174 or 194 ($1.75, 30 minutes) outside the baggage claim area. Cabs cost about $35.

CAR & MOTORCYCLE

Seattle traffic is among the worst in the country. Add to that the steep one-way streets, expensive parking and high taxes on rental cars, and you might consider relying on public transit. If you do drive, take a friend. Some Seattle freeways have High-Occupancy

PACIFIC NORTHWEST

Vehicle (HOV) lanes for vehicles carrying two or more people. National rental agencies have offices at the airport and around town. See p1121 for details.

PUBLIC TRANSPORTATION

Metro Transit (☎ 206-553-3000, in Washington ☎ 800-542-7876) serves the greater Seattle metropolitan area. All bus rides are free from 6am to 7pm in the area between 6th Ave and the Waterfront, and between Pioneer Sq and Battery St in Belltown (note that Seattle Center is not within the ride-free zone). Fares are $1.50 during peak hours (6am to 9am and 3pm to 6pm) and $1.25 off-peak. Buy tickets in advance and get a system map at the **King County Metro Transit office** (☎ 206-553-3000; transit.metrokc.gov; 201 S Jackson St) or at the Westlake Center bus tunnel station.

Vintage Australian streetcars run along the waterfront from Broad Street (a 10-minute walk from Seattle Center) to South Main and branch east to the International District. Fares are the same as for Metro buses.

TAXI

Farwest Taxi (☎ 206-622-1717)
Yellow Cabs (☎ 206-622-6500)

AROUND SEATTLE

The Washington State Ferry to Winslow, the primary town of **Bainbridge Island**, is popular for the great views of Seattle it offers as it crosses Elliott Bay. The **Bainbridge Island Winery** (☎ 206-842-9463; Hwy 305; ⌚ noon-5pm), north of Winslow, is popular with cyclists and wine lovers. Ferries leave from Pier 52 (adult/child/car and driver $5.40/4.40/12, 35 minutes, hourly).

Another outing is the four-hour tour of the waterfront and **Blake Island** operated by **Tillicum Village Tours** (☎ 206-933-8600, 800-426-1205; adult/child $65/25). Boats depart from Pier 55 in Seattle for the island's Northwest Coast Indian Cultural Center & Restaurant. The package includes a traditional Indian salmon bake, dancing and a film about Northwest Native Americans. There's time for a short hike after the meal.

SOUTH CASCADES

Mighty peaks, spectacular hikes and rugged scenery make the mountains of the Cascade Range an outdoor enthusiast's heaven. Summer days can turn blustery in an instant, so pack a warm sweater and rain gear.

Mt Adams

Mt Adams (12,276ft) is one of the most beautiful of the Cascade peaks, with enchanting hikes and an easy summit ascent. A unique activity in the area is huckleberry picking (permits required). For information on hiking or climbing, inquire at the **Trout Lake ranger station** (☎ 509-395-3400; 2455 Hwy 141; ⌚ 8am-4:30pm Mon-Fri, plus Sat & Sun in summer). There are numerous campgrounds around Mt Adams, and B&Bs on Trout Lake. Maps cost $4.25 at the ranger station.

The eastern slope is part of the Yakama Indian Reservation and mostly closed to nontribal members. A notable exception is the 3-mile **Bird Creek Meadow Trail**, one of the best-loved hikes in the Northwest, which gently climbs to an alpine meadow showered by waterfalls and ablaze with wildflowers. It begins in a small, western portion of the reservation that is open to non-Yakamas ($10 vehicle fee). Near Bird Creek Meadows are three lakeside **campgrounds** (☎ 509-865-2405).

The easiest access to Mt Adams is from the Columbia River Gorge, from either I-84 or Hwy 14. Take Hwy 141 to Trout Lake, the focal point of recreation in the area.

Mt St Helens National Volcanic Monument

On May 18, 1980, Mt St Helens erupted with the force of a 24-megaton blast, leveling hundreds of square miles of forest and blowing 1300ft off its peak. Slowly recovering from the devastation, the 171 sq miles of volcano-wracked wilderness can be visited as a day trip from Portland or Seattle.

The **Mt St Helens Visitor Center** (☎ 360-274-2100; ⌚ 9am-5pm), just off I-5 exit 49 near Castle Rock, presents an overview of the site's history and geology. At the end of state Hwy 504, in the heart of the blast zone, the **Johnston Ridge Visitors Center** (☎ 360-274-2131; ⌚ 10am-6pm) provides views directly into the mouth of Mt St Helens' north-facing crater. A more remote vista point, with good views of the lava dome inside the crater, is on the northeastern side of the mountain along **Windy Ridge**, the terminus of USFS Rd 99 (closed in winter). Admission for a single/multiple-site pass is $3/6 ($1/2 for kids).

WHEN MT ST HELENS ERUPTED

In March 1980 the Mt St Helens eruption was heralded by small steam clouds building above the mountain and earthquakes that rocked the area. Initially, geologists thought the pyrotechnics were simply the result of groundwater reaching the molten core of the mountain and didn't realize until quite late that a major eruption was imminent.

Molten rock was rising toward the surface, heavily infused with water pressurized at temperatures of more than 660°F. As the piston of lava and its explosive charge of superheated steam pushed closer and closer to the surface, a bulge formed on the north side of the peak, growing larger and more unstable every day.

On May 18, the mountain gave way and a mass of rock, ash, steam and gas blasted 15 miles into the air. The entire north face of Mt St Helens disintegrated and collapsed in what geologists believe was the largest landslide in recorded history. A 200mph rush of mud, snow, ice and rock consumed Spirit Lake and engulfed 17 miles of the North Fork Toutle River valley. Poisonous gases exploded north of the crater, leveling 150 sq miles of forest in an instant.

Huge deposits of mud and ash closed shipping channels on the Columbia River for weeks, and several inches of ash settled between Yakima and Spokane. Many years later, drifts of ash left by the region's snowplows were still visible along the roadsides. You can see 100-foot banks of dredged white ash, now covered with gorse, along the Toutle River near I-5 exit 52.

Nearby residents were given ample warning – perhaps too much, as quite a few returned to their homes when the volcano did not erupt on cue. Some 59 people were killed when it finally blew. The most famous casualty was Harry Truman – not the US president but the proprietor of a resort on Spirit Lake – who had lived in the area for many years and simply refused to leave. His lodge and all of Spirit Lake were buried beneath 200ft of mud, ash and debris. Mt St Helens has remained calm since 1980, but geologists concur that another explosion is only a matter of time.

Mt Rainier National Park

At 14,410ft Mt Rainier, 95 miles southeast of Seattle, is the highest peak in the Cascades. The park has four entrances: Nisqually, on Hwy 706 via Ashford, near the park's southwest corner; Ohanapecosh, via Hwy 123; White River, off Hwy 410; and Carbon River, the most remote entryway, at the northwest corner. Only the Nisqually entrance is open in winter, when it's used by cross-country skiers. Call ☎ 800-695-7623 for road conditions.

For some detailed information about the park, contact the **superintendent's office** (☎ 360-569-2211 ext 3314; www.nps.gov/mora). Maps and trail descriptions can be downloaded from the website. Park entry is $10/5 per car/pedestrian (free for those under 17). For overnight trips, get a wilderness camping permit (free) from ranger stations or visitors centers. The six campgrounds in the park have running water and toilets, but no RV hookups. **Reservations** (☎ 800-365-2267; www.mount.rainier.national-park.com/camping.htm; reserved campsites summer/off-season $15/12, unreserved campsites $10) are strongly advised during summer months and can be made up to two months in advance by phone or online.

The most popular route up to the summit of Mt Rainier starts in Paradise, near the Nisqually entrance. **Rainier Mountaineering** (☎ 253-627-6242, summer only ☎ 360-569-2227; www.rmiguides.com; 2-day climb $551) has guided summit climbs. Get trail information and backcountry permits at the **Longmire Hiker Information Center** (☎ 360-569-2211 ext 3317; summer only) and the **Jackson Visitor Center** (☎ 360-569-2211 ext 2328; May-Oct) at Paradise.

In addition to several campgrounds, **Longmire National Park Inn** (year-round) and **Paradise Inn** (late May–early Oct) have rooms from $82; for reservations, call ☎ 360-569-2275 or go to www.guestservices.com/rainier.

Packwood (on US 12) is the closest town to the **White River** and **Ohanapecosh** entrances, both of which have campsites ($15). The **Packwood Ranger Station** (☎ 360-494-0600) is near the east end of town. **Hotel Packwood** (☎ 360-494-5431; 104 Main St; s/d $29/39) has clean, charming rooms and a mountain-view veranda.

The remote **Carbon River** entrance gives access to the park's inland rain forest. The **ranger station** (☎ 360-829-9639), just inside the entrance, is open daily in summer.

The **Rainier Shuttle** (☎ 360-569-2331) runs between Sea-Tac Airport and Ashford ($37, three times daily) or Paradise ($46, daily). **Gray Line** (☎ 206-624-5077; www.graylineseattle.com) runs tours from Seattle ($54, 10 hours).

SOUTHEASTERN & CENTRAL WASHINGTON

The wide-open farmlands around Walla Walla, southeastern Washington's financial center, are speckled with farmhouses. Just outside of town is the site of the 1847 Whitman Mission massacre. In central Washington, the Yakima Valley Hwy (old US 12) parallels the freeway east of Yakima city, providing a pastoral alternative to I-82 and giving access to the region's wineries.

Walla Walla

Home of Whitman College and one of the most significant enclaves of historic architecture in eastern Washington, Walla Walla has a small downtown core that's cute enough to take home. More than 30 wineries grace the Walla Walla valley; sample their chardonnays at several tasting rooms on Main St. For information try the **chamber of commerce** (☎ 509-525-0850; www.wwchamber.com; 29 E Sumach St; 8:30am-5pm Mon-Fri, 9am-5pm Sat & Sun). **Coffee Connection Cafe** (☎ 509-529-9999; 226 E Main St) serves as a community center with Internet access ($5 per hour), games and magazines.

The remains of the 1836 **Whitman Mission** are 7 miles west of Walla Walla off US 12. Marcus Whitman and 14 other missionaries died when, in 1847, after a measles epidemic killed half the tribe, a band of Cayuse Indians attacked the 11-year-old mission. When news of the uprising reached Washington, DC, Congress established the Oregon Territories, the first formal government west of the Rockies. The **visitors center** (☎ 509-522-6357; adult/family $3/5; 8am-4:30pm) has exhibits and maps.

The **Capri Motel** (☎ 509-525-1130, 800-451-1139; 2003 Melrose St; s/d $36/46), at the east end of town, has spacious basic rooms.

The **Mill Creek Brew Pub** (☎ 509-522-2440; 11 S Palouse; pub food $6-8) has seven microbrews, good burgers and a nice patio. The more upscale **Backstage Bistro** (☎ 509-526-0690; 230 E Main St; mains $6-18) is a sophisticated dinner hotspot.

Yakima & Around

Yakima, the trading center of an immense and rather bleak agricultural area, holds scant charm for the visitor. The main reason to stop is the excellent **Yakima Valley Museum** (☎ 509-248-0747; 2105 Tieton Dr; adult $6; 11am-5pm Tue-Sun), with exhibits on native Yakama culture, tons of artifacts and a hands-on learning center for kids.

Numerous wineries lie between Yakima and Benton City; pick up a map at the **visitors center** (☎ 509-248-2021; www.yakima.org; 10 N 9th St; 8:30am-5pm Mon-Fri).

This valley is home to the Yakama Indian Reservation, the state's largest. The huge **Yakama Indian Nation Cultural Center** (☎ 509-865-2800; adult/child $4/1; 8am-5pm), off Hwy 97 at Toppenish, has displays on traditional daily life. Toppenish is also known for its murals depicting events from Yakama and Northwest history.

OLYMPIA

The state capital, Olympia has an outsized reputation as a hub of the indie-rock/hipster universe that belies its diminutive size. This is where riot grrrl, Sleater-Kinney and K Records were born. Downtown rings with the countercultural tone of Evergreen State College, an innovative liberal arts school – *The Simpsons* creator Matt Groening studied there. Situated at the southern end of Puget Sound, Olympia and the neighboring towns of Lacey and Tumwater constitute an urban entity known as the South Sound.

The **State Capitol Visitors Center** (☎ 360-586-3460; 14th Ave & Capitol Way; 8am-5pm Mon-Fri, plus 10am-4pm Sat & Sun in summer) provides information on the capitol campus and the Olympia area.

At the **Washington State Capitol** campus is the vast, domed 1927 Legislative Building. Due to damage from the March 2001 earthquake, the building will be closed for renovation until at least 2004. Visitors can still tour the **campus** (admission free; 1:30pm Jun-Aug) and visit the Temple of Justice and Capitol Conservatory, housing a large collection of tropical plants.

The **State Capital Museum** (☎ 360-753-2580; 211 W 21st Ave; admission $2; 10am-4pm Tue-Fri, noon-4pm Sat) has exhibits on the Nisqually Indians. The fun **Olympia Farmers Market** (☎ 360-352-9096; 10am-3pm Thu-Sun Apr-Oct, Sat & Sun Nov-Dec), at the north end of Capitol Way, has fresh local produce, crafts and food booths.

Golden Gavel Motor Hotel (☎ 360-352-8533, 800-407-7734; 909 Capitol Way S; r from $49) is a carefully maintained downtown motel. Also try the

Carriage Inn Motel (☎ 360-943-4710; 1211 Quince St SE; s/d $50/60), off I-5 exit 105.

The **Urban Onion** (☎ 360-943-9242; 116 Legion Way E; lunch $7), a classy vegetarian haunt in an old hotel, serves cheap breakfast and affordable lunch (salads and quiche), but prices soar for dinner. The **Spar Bar** (☎ 360-357-6444; 114 4th Ave E; breakfast $4-5, lunch $5-8) is a stylish old café/cigar store with a cool facade and a cozy back-room bar, the Highclimber. For a quick fix, hit **Oldschool Pizzeria** (☎ 360-786-9640; 108 Franklin St; pizzas $8.50-19).

Catch live local bands at the **4th Ave Tavern** (☎ 360-786-1444; 210 4th Ave E). **Fishbowl Brewpub** (☎ 360-943-3650; 515 Jefferson St SE) has home-brewed English-style ales and fine pub fare.

Amtrak (☎ 360-923-4602) links Olympia daily to Seattle ($13) and Portland ($16); bus No 64 shuttles between the station and downtown Olympia.

TACOMA

Tacoma gets a bad rap as a beleaguered mill town known mostly for its distinctive 'Tacom-aroma,' a product of the nearby paper mills. Its nickname, 'City of Destiny' – because it was the Puget Sound's railroad terminus – once seemed like a grim joke. But these days destiny is coming through for Tacoma. Downtown revitalization makes it a worthy destination on the Portland–Seattle route. The city's setting – backed up against the foothills of Mt Rainier and facing onto the fjords of Puget Sound and the jagged peaks of the Olympic Mountains – isn't half-bad either.

Find information at the **visitors center** (☎ 253-305-1000, 800-272-2662; www.traveltacoma.com; 1001 Pacific Ave; 🕑 8:30am-5pm Mon-Fri). For an Internet connection, visit the **Tacoma Public Library** (1102 Tacoma Ave S; Internet use $2 per day).

Tacoma's new **Museum of Glass** (☎ 253-396-1768; 1801 E Dock St; adult/child $10/4; 🕑 10am-5pm Tue-Sat, noon-5pm Sun, 10am-8pm Thu in summer), with its slanted tower called the Hot Shop Amphitheater, has art exhibits and glassblowing demonstrations. The **Bridge of Glass** walkway, created by love-him-or-hate-him Tacoma artist Dale Chihuly, connects the museum with downtown's enormous copper-domed neobaroque **Union Station** (1911), designed by the folks who built New York's Grand Central Station. Renovated in the early 1990s, the station now houses the federal courts (and more bizarre Chihuly pieces).

Next door is the **Washington State History Museum** (☎ 888-238-4373; 1911 Pacific Ave; admission $7; 🕑 10am-5pm Tue-Sat, noon-5pm Sun), with good exhibits on the tribes of the Northwest Coast.

The **Tacoma Art Museum** (☎ 253-272-4258; 1701 Pacific Ave; adult/child under 6 $6.50/free; 🕑 10am-5pm Mon-Sat, noon-5pm Sun, closed Mon in winter) has moved to new quarters and strengthened its collection of regional art; you won't see a lot of big names here, but you'll get a well-chosen cross-section of work by significant Pacific Northwest artists. The ornate **Pantages Theater** (☎ 253-591-5894; 901 Broadway), once an elaborate vaudeville hall, is Tacoma's premier performance stage. Directly north of 9th St on Broadway is **Antique Row**, a maze of collectibles shops.

Take Ruston Way out to **Point Defiance** (☎ 253-591-5337; zoo admission adult/child $7.75/6; 🕑 9:30am-5pm, 9:30am-6pm in summer), a 700-acre park complex with free-roaming bison and mountain goats, a logging museum, zoo and aquarium, and miles of forested trails.

For bed-and-breakfast inns, call the **Greater Tacoma B&B Reservation Service** (☎ 253-759-4088, 800-406-4088). About the least expensive lodging near the center is **Travel Inn Motel** (☎ 253-383-8853; 2512 Pacific Ave; r from $40). Other moderately priced options are scattered south of the center between I-5 exits 128 and 129.

Harmon Pub & Brewery (☎ 253-383-2739; 1938 Pacific Ave S; mains $9-14), opposite the history museum, draws its own homemade ales, some of which go into hearty dishes. The bayside **Harbor Lights** (☎ 253-752-8600; 2761 Ruston Way; dinner $9-17) is a longstanding favorite for seafood. **Antique Sandwich Company** (☎ 253-752-4069; 5102 N Pearl St; lunch & snacks $4-7) is a funky luncheonette and coffee shop beloved by locals.

Sound Transit bus routes 590 and 594, which use the station behind the **Tacoma Dome** (510 Puyallup Ave), are a cheap way to reach Seattle ($2.50). The free Downtown Connector service makes a loop between the station and Seattle city center every 15 minutes. **Amtrak** (☎ 253-627-8141; 1001 Puyallup Ave) links Tacoma to Seattle and Portland. **Ferry rides** (☎ 800-843-3779) from Point Defiance to Vashon Island are $3.30/14.70 per passenger/car. For a taxi, call **Yellow Cab** (☎ 253-472-3303).

OLYMPIC PENINSULA

The Olympic Peninsula is a rugged, remote area characterized by wild coastlines, deep old-growth forests and craggy mountains. Seafaring Native Americans have lived here for thousands of years. Only one road, US 101, rings the peninsula. Although the highway is in excellent condition, distances are great, and visitors often find it takes a lot longer than expected to get where they're going. From Seattle, the fastest access to the peninsula is by ferry and bus via Bainbridge Island or on Washington State Ferries from Keystone, Whidbey Island.

Olympic National Park

One of the most popular US national parks, Olympic is noted for its wilderness hiking, dramatic scenery and widely varying ecosystems. The heavily glaciated Olympic Mountains rise to nearly 8000ft. Few roads penetrate more than a few miles into the park proper, but visitors willing to hike a bit will find magnificent waterfalls, wide-open alpine meadows, moss-bearded forests and remote lakes. Most lower valley trails are passable year-round, but expect rain, or at least clouds, at any time.

INFORMATION

Park entry fee is $5/10 per person/vehicle, valid for one week, payable at park entrances. Many park visitors centers double as USFS ranger stations, where you can pick up permits for wilderness camping ($5 per group, valid up to 14 days, plus $2 per person per night).

Forks Visitor Information Center (☎ 360-374-2531, 800-443-6757; 1411 S Forks Ave; ⌚ 10am-4pm) Suggested itineraries and seasonal information.

Olympic National Park Visitor Center (☎ 360-565-3130; 3002 Mt Angeles Rd; ⌚ 9am-5pm) Very helpful center at the Hurricane Ridge gateway, a mile off Hwy 101 in Port Angeles.

Wilderness Information Center (☎ 360-565-3100; ⌚ 7:30am-6pm Sun-Thu, 7:30am-8pm Fri & Sat in summer, 8am-4:30pm in winter) Directly behind the visitors centers, you'll find maps, permits and trail information.

EASTERN ENTRANCES

The graveled Dosewallips River Rd follows the river from US 101 for 15 miles to **Dosewallips Ranger Station**, where the trails begin; call ☎ 360-565-3130 for road conditions. Even hiking smaller portions of the two long-distance paths – with increasingly impressive views of heavily glaciated **Mt Anderson** – is reason enough to visit the valley. Another eastern entry for hikers is the **Staircase Ranger Station** (☎ 360-877-5569, summer only), just inside the national park boundary, 15 miles from Hoodsport on US 101. Two state parks along the eastern edge of the national park are popular with campers: **Dosewallips State Park** and **Lake Cushman State Park** (☎ 888-226-7688; campsites/RV sites $15/21). Both have running water, flush toilets and some RV hookups.

WESTERN ENTRANCES

Isolated by distance and inclement weather, and facing the Olympic Coast National Marine Sanctuary, the Pacific side of the Olympics remains its wildest. Only US 101 offers access to its noted temperate rain forests and wild coastline. The **Hoh River Rain Forest** can get 12ft to 14ft of annual precipitation. Trails from the **visitors center and campground** (☎ 360-374-6925; ⌚ 9am-4:30pm, 9am-6pm Jul & Aug), at the end of 19-mile Hoh River Rd, plunge into thick clusters of old-growth trees wearing furry green sweaters of moss. If you want to reenact *The Lord of the Rings*, this is the place.

The **Queets River Valley** is the most remote, and hence pristine, part of the park. A gentle, 3-mile day hike starts at primitive **Queets Campground and Ranger Station** (☎ 360-962-2283; campsites $8).

Lake Quinault is a beautiful glacial lake surrounded by forested peaks; it's popular for fishing, boating and swimming. A number of short trails begin just below **Lake Quinault Lodge** (☎ 360-288-2900; www.visitlakequinault.com; r from $110) on South Shore Rd, an antique hideaway with heated pool and sauna, fireplace rooms and lake-view dining. Or try **Rain Forest Resort Village** (☎ 360-288-2535; www.rfrv.com; 516 South Shore Rd; r/cabins $92/135).

The **Enchanted Valley Trail** climbs up to a large meadow (a former glacial lakebed) that's resplendent with wildflowers and copses of alder trees. The 13-mile hike to the aptly named valley begins from the Graves Creek Ranger Station at the end of the South Shore Rd, 19 miles from US 101.

NORTHERN ENTRANCES

The higher you go along the 18-mile road toward the dizzying vistas at **Hurricane Ridge**, the smaller you feel. At the top, there's an interpretive center in a flower-strewn meadow from which you can see Mt Olympus and dozens of other peaks (on a clear day). The road begins at the visitors center in Port Angeles. The closest campground is **Heart O' the Hills** (☎ 360-956-2300; campsites $10), 5 miles south of Port Angeles on Hurricane Ridge Rd.

Popular for boating and fishing is **Lake Crescent**. From **Storm King Information Station** (☎ 360-928-3380; summer only) on the lake's south shore, a 1-mile hike climbs through old-growth forest to Marymere Falls. Along the Sol Duc River, the **Sol Duc Hot Springs Resort** (☎ 360-327-3583; www.northolympic.com/solduc; campsites/RV sites/cabins $12/20/112; closed Oct-Mar) has lodging, dining, massage ($60) and, of course, hot-spring pools (adult/child $10/7.50), as well as great day hikes.

Port Angeles

Despite the prevalence of stripmalls, Port Angeles makes an excellent base for exploring the Olympic Peninsula. The **visitors center** (☎ 360-452-2363; 121 E Railroad Ave; 8am-8pm May-Oct, 10am-4pm in winter) is adjacent to the ferry terminal. Rent outdoor gear at **Olympic Mountaineering** (☎ 360-452-0240; 140 W Front St).

Pitch a tent at **Salt Creek County Park** (☎ 360-928-3441; www.clallam.net; campsites $14), 16 miles west on Hwy 112, with stunning views of the Strait of Juan de Fuca. The amiably managed **Thor Town Hostel** (☎ 360-452-0931; www.thortown.com; 316 N Race St; dm/r $12/28) has lodging in a homey, casual setting. Or try the **Tudor Inn B&B** (☎ 360-452-3138; www.tudorinn.com; 1108 S Oak St; r from $85).

First Street Haven (☎ 360-457-0352; 107 E 1st St; breakfast $5-7) is the place for hearty country breakfasts. **Thai Peppers** (☎ 360-452-4897; 222 N Lincoln St; mains $8) offers an array of vegetarian dishes.

Two ferries run from Port Angeles to Victoria, BC: the **Coho Vehicle Ferry** (☎ 360-457-4491; passenger/car $8.50/32.50, 1½hr) and the passenger-only **Victoria Express** (☎ 360-452-8088; adult/child $12.50/7.50; May-Sep).

Olympic Bus Lines (☎ 360-417-0700) runs twice daily to Seattle from the public transit center at the corner of Oak and Front Sts (one way/round-trip $29/49). **Clallam Transit buses** (☎ 360-452-4511) go to Forks and Sequim. **Budget Rent-a-Car** (☎ 360-457-4246) is at Fairchild International Airport and across from the ferry terminal; Horizon Air flies to Fairchild daily. For a taxi, call **Blue Top** (☎ 360-452-2223).

Northwest Peninsula

Several Indian reservations cling to this corner of the continent and they welcome respectful visitors. On Hwy 112, 75 miles west of Port Angeles, is **Neah Bay**, the center of the Makah Indian Reservation. The **Makah Cultural & Research Center** (☎ 360-645-2711; adult/child under 6 $4/free; 10am-5pm in summer, closed Mon & Tue in winter) is the sole repository of artifacts from nearby Ozette; the museum's exhibits document the day-to-day life of the ancient Makah. Seven miles beyond, a short boardwalk trail leads to Cape Flattery, a 300ft promontory that marks the most northwesterly point in the lower 48 states.

Convenient to the Hoh Rain Forest and the Olympic coastline is **Forks**, 57 miles from Neah Bay. Stay at the Waltons-esque **Hoh Humm Ranch** (☎ 360-374-5337; 171763 Hwy 101; r from $35), a B&B in a working farmhouse where balconies gaze over riverside herds of sheep, cattle and llamas. Or crash at the remote **Rain Forest Hostel** (☎ 360-374-2270; www.rainforesthostel.com; dm/d $12/25), on US 101 8 miles south of the turnoff for the Hoh Rain Forest.

Port Townsend

Ferrying in to Port Townsend, one of the best-preserved Victorian-era seaports in the USA, is like sailing into a sepia-toned old photograph. The city experienced a building boom in 1890 followed by an immediate bust, leaving its architectural splendor largely intact. For information try the **visitors center** (☎ 360-385-2722; www.ptchamber.org; 2437 E Sims Way; 9am-5pm Mon-Fri, 9am-4pm Sat & Sun). Internet access is available uptown at **Port Townsend Library** (1220 Lawrence St).

Historic **Fort Worden** (☎ 360-385-4730), 2 miles north of the ferry landing (take Cherry St from uptown), was featured in the film *An Officer and a Gentleman*. Within the complex are the Commanding Officer's Quarters, a restored **Victorian-era home** (☎ 360-385-4730; admission $1; 10am-5pm Jun-Aug, 1-4pm Sat & Sun only Mar-May & Sep-Oct), and the **Coast Artillery Museum** (☎ 360-385-0373; admission $2; 11am-4pm Jun-Aug, Sat & Sun only Mar-May & Sep-Oct).

Within **Fort Worden State Park**, the **HI Olympic Hostel** (☎ 360-385-0655; olyhost@olympus.net; 272 Battery Way; dm $14-17) has impeccable if spartan quarters in a former barracks; it's up the hill behind the park office. The **Waterstreet Hotel** (☎ 360-385-5467, 800-735-9810; 635 Water St; r with shared/private bath from $55/75), in the center of town, offers old-world charm at reasonable rates. The turreted, Prussian-style **Manresa Castle** (☎ 360-385-5750, 800-732-1281;

www.manresacastle.com; 7th & Sheridan Sts; r from $85), built in 1892, was later expanded to house Jesuit priests. Even if you don't stay here, it's worth taking a self-guided tour; note the former chapel, truncated to form a breakfast room and banquet room.

The center of Port Townsend is packed with trendy cafés and restaurants. For no-nonsense breakfast, join the local marina folk at **Landfall Restaurant** (☎ 360-385-5814; 412 Water St; breakfast $5-7). **Sirens** (☎ 360-379-1100; 832 Water St) is a dimly lit, romantic upstairs bar with a balcony overlooking the port.

To reach Port Townsend, take the ferry from downtown Seattle to Bainbridge Island ($5.10). At the ferry dock catch the No 90 bus to Poulsbo ($1, 20 minutes), then pick up a No 7 bus to Port Townsend ($1, one hour). **Washington State Ferries** (☎ 206-464-6400) goes to and from Keystone, on Whidbey Island (car and driver/passenger $8.75/2, 35 minutes). For a cab, call **Peninsula Taxi** (☎ 360-385-1872).

NORTHWEST WASHINGTON

The San Juans, accessible only by ferry and air, pepper the northern Puget Sound. Simpler to reach, Whidbey Island contains beautiful Deception Pass State Park and the quaint, oyster-rich village of Coupeville. Back on the mainland is the lively university town of Bellingham.

Whidbey Island

Green, low-lying Whidbey Island snakes 41 miles along the Washington mainland from the northern suburbs of Seattle to Deception Pass – so named because, on discovering the treacherous chasm that separates Whidbey from Fidalgo Island to the north, Captain George Vancouver realized he had been 'deceived' in thinking Whidbey was attached to the mainland. **Deception Pass State Park**, with forest trails, lakes and more than 17 miles of shoreline, encompasses the narrow channel traversed by a dramatic bridge that links the two islands.

Historic **Coupeville**, 10 miles south of Whidbey's main town, Oak Harbor, has an attractive seafront, antique stores and old inns. For information try the **visitors center** (☎ 360-678-5434; 107 S Main St; 10am-5pm). The Victorian-era **Inn at Penn Cove** (☎ 360-678-8000; 702 N Main St; r from $60) has B&B-style rooms. Sample local oysters and mussels at the **Captain's Galley** (☎ 360-678-0241; 10 Front St).

Harbor Airlines (☎ 800-359-3220; www.harborair.com) has daily links from Oak Harbor Airport to Sea-Tac Airport and the San Juan Islands. **Washington State Ferries** link Clinton to Mukilteo (car and driver/passenger $7/3.10, 20 minutes, every 30 minutes) and Keystone to Port Townsend (car and driver/passenger $8.75/2, 30 minutes, every 45 minutes). **Island Transit buses** (☎ 360-678-7771, 800-240-8747) run the length of Whidbey every hour daily except Sun, from the Clinton ferry dock.

Anacortes

Pleasant Anacortes, on Fidalgo Island, is noted principally as the departure point for the San Juan Island ferries. For information try the **chamber of commerce** (☎ 360-293-3832; 819 Commercial Ave; 9am-5pm Mon-Fri, noon-5pm Sat & Sun).

Various lodgings line Hwy 20. Downtown is **Cap Sante Inn** (☎ 360-293-0602, 800-852-0846; 906 9th St; s/d $70/74), cozy and close to the eponymous marina. The similarly priced **Anacortes Inn** (☎ 360-293-3153; 3006 Commercial Ave; s/d $72/77) is also friendly. **Rockfish Grill/Anacortes Brewery** (☎ 360-588-1720; 320 Commercial Ave; pizza $7-10) has good wood-fired pizzas.

The **Bellair Airporter Shuttle** (☎ 800-423-4219; www.airporter.com) links Anacortes to the I-5 corridor at Mount Vernon ($10) and to connections for Bellingham and Sea-Tac airport. **Skagit Transit** (☎ 360-757-4433) bus No 410 travels hourly between Anacortes (10th St and Commercial Ave) and the San Juan ferry terminal.

Bellingham

The handsome port city of Bellingham, 18 miles south of the US–Canadian border, is home to Western Washington University, a busy nightlife scene and plenty of good restaurants. Its action is divided between the downtown, grouped around Commercial and Holly Sts, and Fairhaven, a cluster of red-brick buildings 3 miles to the south. Find information at the **visitors center** (☎ 360-671-3990, 800-487-2032; www.bellingham.org; 904 Potter St; 8:30am-5:30 pm), off I-5 exit 253.

Victoria/San Juan Cruises (☎ 360-738-8099, 800-443-4552) has whale-watching trips to Victoria, BC, via the San Juan Islands (adult/child $69/29, three hours). Boats leave from the Bellingham Cruise Terminal in Fairhaven.

Most of the inexpensive motels are on Samish Way, off I-5 exit 252. Downtown are the remodeled **Shangri-La Downtown Motel** (☎ 360-733-7050; 611 E Holly St; r from $45) and **Bellingham Inn** (☎ 360-734-1900; 202 E Holly St; r from $45).

For organic produce, go to the **Community Food Co-op** (☎ 360-734-0542; 1220 N Forest St). **Old Town Cafe** (☎ 360-671-4431; 316 W Holly St; breakfast $3-6) has cheap breakfast until 3pm. For Tex-Mex, try **Pepper Sisters** (☎ 360-671-3414; 1055 N State St; specials $7-9; closed Mon). In Fairhaven, **Colophon Cafe** (☎ 360-647-0092; 1208 11th St; sandwiches $6-8), at Village Books, has scrumptious pastries and big sandwiches.

Three Bs Tavern (☎ 360-734-1881; 1226 N State St) is a raucous student hangout with live music on the weekends ($5 cover). In Fairhaven, the **Archer Ale House** (☎ 360-647-7002; 1212 10th St; snacks $5-8) is a smoke-free pub with tempting seafood specials and a wide selection of draft beer.

San Juan Islands Shuttle Express (☎ 360-671-1137, 888-373-8522) offers daily summer service to Orcas and the San Juan Islands. **Alaska Marine Highway Ferries** (☎ 360-676-0212, 800-642-0066; www.state.ak.us/ferry/) go to Skagway and other southeast Alaskan ports. The **Bellair Airporter Shuttle** (☎ 800-423-4219; www.airporter.com) runs to Sea-Tac airport with connections en route to Anacortes and Whidbey Island.

SAN JUAN ISLANDS

The San Juan archipelago sprawls across 750 sq miles of Pacific waters where Puget Sound and the Straits of Juan de Fuca and Georgia meet. Long considered an inaccessible backwater of farmers and fishers, the islands today are economically dependent on tourism. Even so, they retain their bucolic charm. Late May to September is the best time to go.

For information on the islands, contact the San Juan Islands **visitors center** (☎ 360-468-3663; www.guidetosanjuans.com). During July and August, accommodation reservations are essential; try **All Island Reservations** (☎ 360-378-6977).

Sea kayaks, a popular means of exploring the shores of the San Juans, are available for rent on Lopez, Orcas and San Juan Islands. Expect a guided half-day trip to cost $30-45. Note that most beach access is barred by private property, except at state or county parks.

Airlines serving the San Juan Islands include **Harbor Air Lines** (☎ 800-359-3220; www.harborair.com), **Kenmore Air** (☎ 800-543-9595) and **West Isle Air** (☎ 800-874-4434). Public transport is pretty much nonexistent, but most motels will pick up guests at the ferry landing with advance notice, and bike rentals are available.

Washington State Ferries (☎ 206-464-6400, in Washington ☎ 800-843-3779; www.wsdot.wa.gov/ferries) leave Anacortes for the San Juans; some continue to Sidney, BC, near Victoria. Ferries run to Lopez Island (car and driver/passenger $23/8.20, 45 minutes) and to Friday Harbor on San Juan Island (car and driver/passenger $22.50/6.80, 1¼ hours). Fares are round-trip and collected on westbound journeys only (except those returning from Sidney, BC). To visit all the islands, it's cheapest to go to Friday Harbor first and work your way back through the other islands.

Lopez Island

The most agricultural of the San Juan Islands, Lopez is also the closest to the mainland. For pastoral charm, it's a hard place to beat. South of the ferry landing (1.3 miles) is **Odlin County Park** (☎ 360-468-2496; campsites from $15).

San Juan Island

San Juan offers the most hospitable blend of sophisticated amenities and rural landscapes. The main settlement is **Friday Harbor**, where the **visitors center** (☎ 360-378-5240; 9:30am-4:30pm Mon-Fri, noon-4:30pm Sat & Sun) is at Front and Spring Sts. **San Juan Island National Historical Park** (☎ 360-378-2240; 8:30am-4pm), commemorating a mid-19th-century British–US territorial conflict, consists of two former military camps on opposite ends of the island. Both of these day-use sites contain remnants of the old officers' quarters; the American Camp, on the island's southeast end, features a splendid hike up Mt Finlayson, from which three mountain ranges can be glimpsed on a clear day. On the western shore, **Lime Kiln Point State Park** (8am-5pm Oct-Mar, 6:30am-10pm Apr 1–Oct 15) is devoted to whale-watching.

Wayfarer's Rest (☎ 360-378-6428; www.rockisland.com/~wayfarersrest; 35 Malcolm St; dm/cabins $20/45) in Friday Harbor is a backpackers' hostel. **Roche Harbor Resort** (☎ 360-378-2155, 800-451-8910; www.rocheharbor.com; r from $85) is a splendid seaside village on the island's northwest corner. Friday Harbor has several great places to eat near the ferry landing.

THE MYSTERY OF THE ORCAS

Every summer a community of orcas migrates down from Vancouver Island to feed on the millions of salmon that make their way into Puget Sound. The orcas, also called killer whales (they're actually very large carnivorous dolphins), are a seasonal draw for tourists and cruise operators on the sound. But it appears this whale community is dwindling, and no one knows why.

Researchers keeping a close watch on the 'southern residents' orca community (another group resides in the waters around the northern half of Vancouver Island) have noted a steady population decline since 1992. As of 2001 there were 78 whales in the community, 21% fewer than six years earlier. The worrisome reduction could be due to the concurrent drop in salmon stocks, or it could be the result of the high level of toxic PCBs in the waters of the sound, which have been detected in the bloodstreams of the whales. Another possibility is that the numerous whale watch tours operating around the San Juan Islands are somehow disturbing the orcas' ability to communicate with one another, a requirement for team foraging. Though evidence to support any of these theories remains sparse, it's safe to say that if the orca population continues its waning trend, there won't be any left to watch by next century.

Orcas Island

Ruggedly beautiful Orcas Island is the largest of the San Juans. The ferry terminal is at Orcas Landing, 13.5 miles south of the main population center, Eastsound. On the island's eastern lobe is **Moran State Park** (☎ 360-376-2326), dominated by Mt Constitution (2409ft), with 40 miles of trails; get a map at headquarters.

For help with accommodations, call the **Orcas lodging hotline** (☎ 360-376-8888; www.orcas-island.com/lodging.html). The romantic **Turtleback Farm Inn** (☎ 360-376-4914, 800-376-4914; 1981 Crow Valley Road; d $90-225) is a restored farmhouse on a secluded 80 acres. The backwoods hippie hangout **Doe Bay Village Resort & Retreat** (☎ 360-376-2291; www.doebay.com; $25-140), on the island's easternmost shore, has cabins with or without kitchens, yurts and hostel beds, plus hot tubs, guided tours and other fringe benefits.

NORTH CASCADES

The North Cascades offer some of the most dramatic points in the state, from the visitor-friendly faux-German village of Leavenworth through to the rocky, glacier-topped crests of mountain ridges and the trails that wind among them. Only one road, Hwy 20, cuts through the 781-sq-mile North Cascades National Park, and the route is usually closed from late November to April. Pick up maps and backcountry permits at **park headquarters** (☎ 360-856-5700; 2105 Hwy 20; ⏲ 8am-4:30pm) in Sedro Woolley, well to the west of the mountains.

Leavenworth

Cuter than a Nutcracker's button nose, little Leavenworth, notched into the mountains along the Wenatchee River, would be a worthy stop even without its Bavarian schtick. Schlager music blares in the streets, and even the gas stations are dressed up like Tyrolean cottages. There's not much going on here after dark, but you'll need the rest anyway for hiking or rafting in neighboring Wenatchee National Forest.

Find information at the **visitors center** (☎ 509-548-5807; www.leavenworth.org; 220 9th St; ⏲ 8am-5pm Mon-Fri, 10am-5pm Sat, 10am-4pm Sun). For information on hiking or white-water rafting, contact the **US Forest Service office** (☎ 509-548-6977; 600 Sherbourne St; ⏲ 7:45am-4:30pm).

Mrs Anderson's Lodging House (☎ 509-548-6173, 800-253-8990; www.quiltersheaven.com; 917 Commercial St; r from $51), with antique-decorated B&B rooms above a quilt shop, is so comfortable it's almost womblike. The **Blackbird Lodge** (☎ 509-548-5800, 800-446-0240; www.blackbirdlodge.com; d from $99) does a more upscale version of the German inn theme, with fireplaces and complimentary room-service breakfast.

For the obligatory brats-and-beer, head to **King Ludwig's** (☎ 509-548-6625; 921 Front St; sausages $8) or, for a more casual take, **Gustav's** (☎ 509-548-4509; 617 Hwy 2; burgers/brats $3/4).

Lake Chelan

Long, slender Lake Chelan is central Washington's playground. **Lake Chelan State Park** (☎ 509-687-3710), on South Shore Rd, has 144 campsites; a number of lakeshore campgrounds are accessible only by boat. The town of Chelan, at the lake's southeastern tip, is the primary base for accommodation and services. It has a **USFS ranger station** (☎ 509-682-2549; 428 Woodin Ave). **Link Transit buses** (☎ 509-662-1155; www.linktransit.com) connect Chelan with Wenatchee and Leavenworth ($1).

Beautiful **Stehekin**, on the northern tip of Lake Chelan, is accessible only by **boat** (☎ 509-682-4584; www.ladyofthelake.com; one way/round-trip $16/25), **seaplane** (☎ 509-682-5555; round-trip from Chelan $120) or a long hike across Cascade Pass, 28 miles from the lake. Most facilities are open mid-June to mid-September.

Methow Valley

The Methow (*met*-how) River valley has hiking, biking, rafting and fishing, but it's best known for cross-country skiing. Snows block Hwy 20 between Marblemount and Mazama from mid-November to mid-April (call ☎ 888-766-4636 for updates), so Methow-bound skiers approach from western Washington by taking US 2 to Wenatchee, then heading north to Twisp. Three USFS campgrounds are just off Hwy 20 on Early Winters Creek. Inquire at the **USFS visitors center** (☎ 509-996-4000; 9am-5pm), west of Winthrop, about conditions. For other lodgings, call **Methow Valley Central Reservations** (☎ 509-996-2148; www.methow.com/lodging).

North Cascades National Park

Hundreds of great backcountry hikes crisscross this park. Campgrounds abound, with 19 facilities accessible from Hwy 20, but bring food and supplies. **Newhalem**, a dam-worker' town, is the jumping-off point for recreation; the **visitors center** (☎ 206-386-4495; 9am-5pm) has information on trails and camping as well as rafting on the Skagit River. The National Park Service website, www.nps.gov/noca, is another good resource.

Upper Skagit River Valley

Hwy 20 makes its subtle ascent east along this pretty Cascade river valley from Sedro Woolley toward North Cascades National Park. **Concrete**, 23 miles east of Sedro Woolley, has motels and is a base for exploring 10,781ft Mt Baker. **Rockport**, at the junction of Hwys 20 and 530, is a prime bald eagle viewing site. Stop for gas and snacks at Marblemount, where the **Wilderness Information Center** (☎ 360-873-4500 ext 39; 8am-4:30pm Mon-Fri) issues backcountry permits.

NORTHEASTERN WASHINGTON

The far-western foothills of the Rockies and the rugged landscape of the Columbia Basin afford a dramatic backdrop for the massive Grand Coulee Dam hydroelectric project. Spokane, just inside the border with Idaho, is a bustling metropolitan center.

Grand Coulee Dam

Construction of the Grand Coulee Dam, 225 miles from Seattle, started in 1933 as a WPA project. The dam disrupted the Columbia River's ecology and displaced the Colville Confederated Tribes from their riverfront land; it now provides irrigation to farmland and is the world's third-largest hydropower producer. The town of Coulee Dam is the best bet for a motel room.

The **Grand Coulee Visitor Arrival Center** (☎ 509-633-9265; 9am-5pm Sep-Nov, 8:30am-10:30pm summer, closed Dec), has historical exhibits and films on the dam's construction and regional geology. Tours of the generator and power plants have been canceled temporarily due to national security concerns; inquire at the visitors center. Also ask about nighttime laser shows, screened on the dam's smooth, angled slope.

Spokane

The largest city between Seattle and Minneapolis, Spokane feels closer in spirit to the latter than the former. As the prosperous trade center of the Inland Northwest, it's the only place hereabouts where you have a chance of seeing the opera.

Find information at the **visitors center** (☎ 509-747-3230; www.visitspokane.com; 201 W Main St; 8:30am-5pm Mon-Fri, 9am-5pm Sat, 10am-4pm Sun). Internet access is free at the Spokane **Public Library**, downtown at the corner of Lincoln and Main Sts.

Developed for the 1974 World's Fair and Exposition, **Riverfront Park** features gardens, playgrounds and a vintage carousel. A gondola at the park's west end glides over the multi-tiered **Spokane Falls** (closed until 2004), but it's almost as vertiginously thrilling to cross the river on a footbridge. For a lesson in creative recycling, check out **Steam Plant Sq**, a 1916 steam generator newly converted into an industrial-chic space with offices, shops, cafés and the **Steam Plant Grill** (☎ 509-777-3900; 159 S Lincoln St). Peer up into one of the plant's 225ft-tall smokestacks.

Spokane's **wineries** produce renowned merlots; the visitors center has a map of the top spots.

Chain motels line both Division St and Sunset Blvd. The crescent-shaped **Trade Winds Motel** (☎ 509-838-2091; 907 W 3rd Ave; r from $45) is tacky-cool, with a retro feel and big, balconied rooms. The **Budget Inn** (☎ 509-838-6101; 110 E 4th Ave; s/d from $50/55; P), off exit 281, is a roadside mammoth handy to downtown. For camping try **Riverside State Park** (☎ 509-465-5064; 9711 W Charles Rd; campsites $14), 6 miles northwest off Hwy 291.

Frank's Diner (☎ 509-747-8798; 1516 W 2nd Ave; 6am-8pm; breakfast $6-8), inside a vintage railway car, is a must for breakfast. **Europa Pizzaria & Bakery** (☎ 509-455-4051; 125 S Wall St; pasta $9-15, pizza $10-20) serves Italian comfort food until midnight in an exposed-brick salon.

The bathroom graffiti in the comfortably grubby rock bar, the **B-Side** (☎ 509-624-7638; 230 W Riverside) testifies to some of Spokane's less-glorious cultural history. There's live music most nights; a cover charge applies. Follow the locals to **Mootsy's** (☎ 509-838-1570; 406 W Sprague Ave) for happy hour, where pints of Pabst cost $1.

Buses and trains depart from the **Spokane Intermodal Transportation Station** (221 W 1st Ave). **Amtrak** (☎ 509-624-5144) has daily service to Seattle ($36, 7½ hours), Portland ($36, 9½ hours) and Chicago ($284, 14½ hours).

Alaska

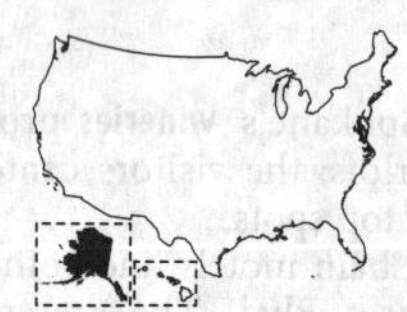

CONTENTS

It isn't just the mountains, sparkling lakes or glaciers that draw travelers to Alaska but the magic in the land, an irresistible force that tugs on those who dream about the North Country. No area in the USA possesses a more mystical pull. The lure inherent in its moniker as the Final Frontier is as strong today as it was in the past, when Alaska's promise of adventure and quick wealth brought the first invasion of miners. Today they have been replaced by travelers and backpackers, but the spirit of exploration is still the same.

Drawn to Alaska by its colorful reputation, travelers are stunned by the grandeur of what they encounter. There are mountains, glaciers and rivers in other parts of North America, but few are on the same scale or as overpowering as those in Alaska. To see a brown bear rambling up the side of a mountain valley or to sit in a kayak and watch a 5-mile-wide glacier continually calve ice off its terminus are natural experiences that can permanently change your way of thinking.

Alaska is a major side trip for most visitors to the USA, but it's worth it. Allow yourself at least three weeks. Take a flight from Seattle to Southcentral Alaska, where you can take in Prince William Sound and the Kenai Peninsula, then head north to Denali National Park and Mt McKinley. Once you're in Alaska, you will find it a difficult land to leave.

HIGHLIGHTS

- Cruising up the **Inside Passage** past islands, fjords, glaciers and isolated towns (p1033)
- **Whale-watching, bear-spotting** and **salmon-fishing** all over the state (p1032)
- Gazing upon **Mt McKinley**, the tallest peak in North America, from Flattop Peak in Anchorage (p1043)
- Exploring the **Kennicott copper mine** runs near the funky town of McCarthy (p1054)
- Chugging along the historic narrow-gauge track of **White Pass & Yukon Railroad** from Skagway (p1032)

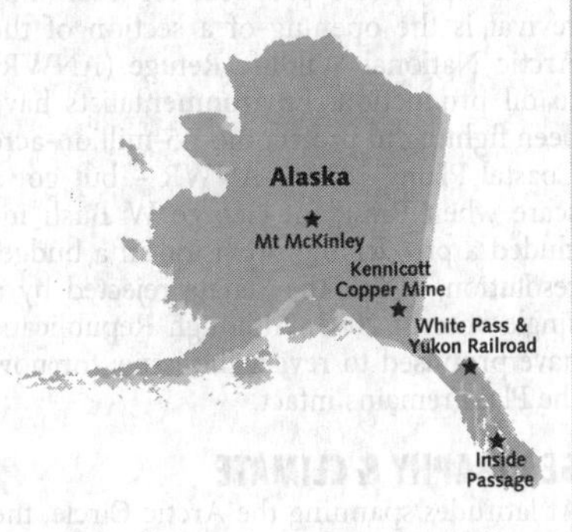

HISTORY

Indigenous Alaskans are descended from people who migrated over the Bering Strait land bridge around 35,000 years ago. In the 18th century the first large wave of Europeans, who were mostly fur traders and whalers, descended upon the area, and introduced guns, alcohol and new diseases to the Native Alaskans.

By the mid-1800s the merchants were ready to call it quits, and in 1867 US Secretary of State William H Seward signed a treaty with Russia to purchase the territory for $7.2 million, less than 2¢ an acre. There was uproar over 'Seward's Folly,' but the land's riches soon revealed themselves.

After Japan attacked some Alaskan islands in WWII, the military built the famous Alcan (Alaska–Canada) Hwy, which linked the territory with the rest of the USA and contributed greatly to the post-war development of Alaska, which became a state in 1959.

An earthquake in 1964 left Alaska in shambles, but recovery was boosted when oil deposits were discovered under Prudhoe Bay. Soon construction was underway of a 789-mile pipeline to the port of Valdez.

The party ended in 1986 when oil prices plummeted. The hangover came in 1989 when the *Exxon Valdez* fuel tanker spilled 11 million gallons of crude oil into Prince William Sound.

Alaska is now considering implementing state sales and income taxes, and recent years have seen fees at parks and campgrounds rise sharply. One proposal for economic revival is the opening of a section of the Arctic National Wildlife Refuge (ANWR) to oil production. Environmentalists have been fighting to protect the 1.5-million-acre Coastal Plain – 8% of ANWR – but got a scare when President George W Bush included a pro-drilling provision in a budget resolution, which the Senate rejected by a single vote in 2003. Although Republicans have promised to revisit the issue, for now the Plain remains intact.

ALASKA FACTS

Nickname The Last Frontier
Population 643,786 (47th)
Area 591,004 sq miles (1st)
Admitted to Union January 3, 1959 (49th)
Capital city Juneau (population 30,700)
Other cities Anchorage (261,000), Fairbanks (84,500), Ketchikan (8000), Kodiak (6330)
State flower Forget-me-not
State motto North to the future
State sport Mushing
Birthplace of singer and poet Jewel (1974–), cartoonist Virgil F Partch (1916–84)
Famous for its size (if split in half, Alaska would still be the largest two states in the USA), Eskimos (Inuit)

GEOGRAPHY & CLIMATE

At latitudes spanning the Arctic Circle, the main body of Alaska is about 800 sq miles, with the arc of the Aleutian Island chain stretching some 1600 miles south and west, and a 'panhandle' strip running 600 miles southeast down the North American coast.

Alaska's flora is diverse. The coastal regions have lush coniferous forests, while the Interior is dominated by boreal forest of white spruce, cottonwood and birch. Further north is a taiga zone – a moist subarctic forest characterized by muskeg, willow thickets and stunted spruce – then the treeless Arctic tundra, with grass, mosses and a variety of tiny flowers thriving briefly in summer.

A great variety of wildlife can be easily seen, notably moose, deer and bears. Harder to spot are caribou, which inhabit the Interior in large herds; mountain goats and Dall sheep, which also live in remote areas; and wolves, which are reclusive by nature. Marine life includes seals, porpoises, whales, sea otters and walruses. During summer, millions of spawning salmon fill rivers and streams.

Alaska has an extremely variable climate and daily weather that is famous for being unpredictable. The Interior can top 90°F during the summer. For the most part, a good summer week in Southcentral and Southeast Alaska will include three sunny days (with average temperatures 55°F to 70°F), two overcast ones and two when you need to pull your rain gear out or duck for cover. In winter expect long nights, minus-50°F temperatures and the fantastic northern lights.

The peak tourist season is early July to mid-August, when the best-known parks are packed and it's essential to make reservations for ferries, other transport and accommodations. May and September still have mild weather, less crowds, and prices are lower.

INFORMATION

The **Alaskan Center** (www.alaskan.com) has background tourist information as well as bus, ferry, air and train schedules. There are several Alaskan Internet travel sites, including **Alaska One** (www.alaskaone.com) and **Alaska Guidebook** (www.alaskaguidebook.com). The **Alaska Division of Tourism** (☎ 907-465-2010; www.travelalaska.com; Dept 901, PO Box 110801, Juneau, AK 99811-0801) distributes the free, annual *Alaska State Vacation Planner*, state maps and schedules for the Alaska Marine Hwy and Alaska Railroad. For road conditions, call the **Alaska Department of Transportation** (☎ 907-273-6037).

The best place for information on national parks before your trip is the **Alaska Public Lands Information Center** (☎ 907-271-2737; www.nps.gov/aplic/center; 605 W 4th Ave, Suite 105, Anchorage, AK 99501). There's also the **NPS Alaska Regional Office** (☎ 907-644-3501; www.nps.gov/parks.html; 240 W 5th Ave, Room 114, Anchorage, AK 99501). All national parks in Alaska have pages on the Web and can be reached through www.nps.gov.

Mass tourism and proud individualism are powerful, if sometimes conflicting, forces in Alaska. As a result, business hours are often closely linked to both the cruise ship schedules and the proprietor's personal caprice. It's a good idea to call in advance to confirm. Hours and prices in this chapter are for the summer high season unless otherwise noted.

NATIONAL & STATE PARKS

One of the main attractions of Alaska is the 54 million acres administered by the National Park Service (NPS) as national parks, preserves and monuments. State parks account for another three million acres. More than two million people visit Alaska's national parks annually, the most popular being Klondike Gold Rush National Historical Park. Other popular parks include Denali and Kenai Fjords. Most parks experienced a jump in visitors in the 1990s, due primarily to an increased number of large cruise ships into Southeast Alaska.

Elsewhere, state parks often pale against national parks, but not so in Alaska. Chugach State Park near Anchorage, and Chena River State Recreational Area both possess the wow factor of the more well-known national parks, with a fraction of the crowds. For more information on state parks, check out www.dnr.state.ak.us/parks.

DANGERS & ANNOYANCES

Alaska is notorious for its biting insects. In the cities and towns you'll have few problems, but out in the woods you'll have to contend with a variety of flying pests. The most effective protection is an insect repellant containing a high percentage of Deet (diethyltoluamide). Unfortunately, repellants are more effective against mosquitoes

ALASKA'S FOREST SERVICE CABINS

The US Forest Service (USFS) cabin program offers more than shelter in the mountains or cheap lodging in this land of high prices. When you rent a USFS cabin ($35 to $50 a night), you're renting your own slice of wilderness.

Although some cabins can be reached on foot or by boat, the vast majority require a flight on a floatplane, ensuring that your party will be the only one in the area until the next group is flown in. The fishing can be outstanding, the chances of seeing wildlife are excellent and your wilderness solitude is guaranteed.

This is Alaskan wilderness at its easiest and cheapest; but remember that a USFS cabin is not a suite at the Hilton. The cabin provides security from the weather, a wood-burning stove, an outhouse and, often, a small rowboat, but you need to pack sleeping bags, food, a water filter and a cooking stove.

Of the 190 USFS cabins, 150 are in Tongass National Forest, which covers most of Southeast Alaska, and the other 40 are in Chugach National Forest, in the Prince William Sound area. For a list, call the **Alaska Public Lands Information Center** (☎ 907-271-2737). Cabins can be reserved 180 days in advance through the **National Recreation Reservation Service** (☎ 877-444-6777; www.reserveusa.com).

In addition to the nightly fee, you need to budget the cost of the floatplane, paying a bush pilot for both a drop-off and a pickup. For cabins within 15 to 20 minutes of major towns such as Juneau or Ketchikan, expect to pay $300 to $400 for a party of two or three.

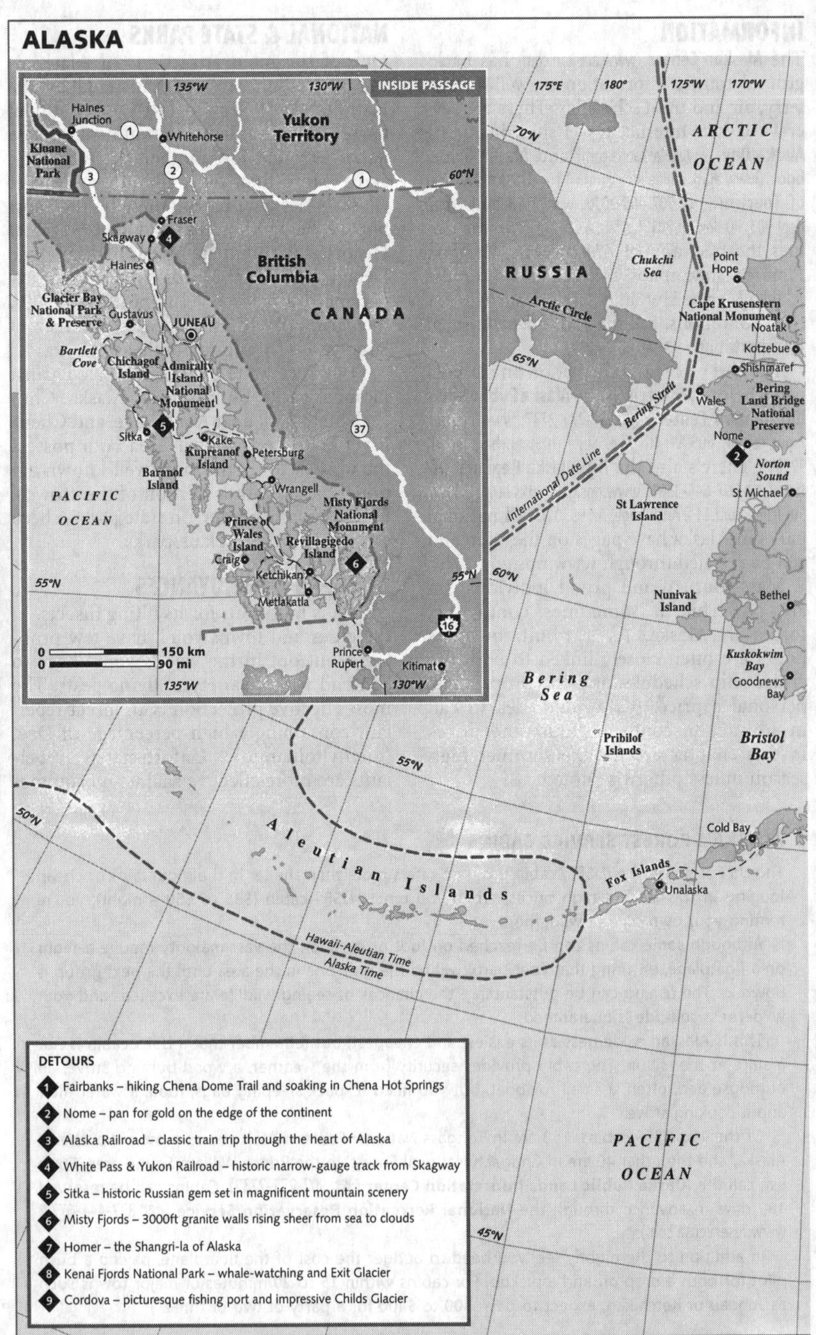
ALASKA
INSIDE PASSAGE
135°W
130°W
Haines Junction
Kluane National Park
Whitehorse
Yukon Territory
60°N
Fraser
Skagway
Haines
British Columbia
Glacier Bay National Park & Preserve
Gustavus
JUNEAU
CANADA
Bartlett Cove
Chichagof Island
Admiralty Island National Monument
Sitka
Kake
Kupreanof Island
Petersburg
Baranof Island
Wrangell
PACIFIC OCEAN
Misty Fjords National Monument
Prince of Wales Island
Revillagigedo Island
Craig
Ketchikan
55°N
Metlakatla
150 km
90 mi
Prince Rupert
Kitimat
175°E
180°
175°W
170°W
70°N
ARCTIC OCEAN
RUSSIA
Chukchi Sea
Point Hope
Arctic Circle
Cape Krusenstern National Monument
Noatak
Kotzebue
65°N
Shishmaref
Bering Strait
Wales
Bering Land Bridge National Preserve
Nome
Norton Sound
International Date Line
St Michael
St Lawrence Island
60°N
Nunivak Island
Bethel
Kuskokwim Bay
Goodnews Bay
Bering Sea
Pribilof Islands
Bristol Bay
55°N
50°N
Aleutian Islands
Cold Bay
Fox Islands
Unalaska
Hawaii-Aleutian Time
Alaska Time
PACIFIC OCEAN
45°N
DETOURS
1 Fairbanks – hiking Chena Dome Trail and soaking in Chena Hot Springs
2 Nome – pan for gold on the edge of the continent
3 Alaska Railroad – classic train trip through the heart of Alaska
4 White Pass & Yukon Railroad – historic narrow-gauge track from Skagway
5 Sitka – historic Russian gem set in magnificent mountain scenery
6 Misty Fjords – 3000ft granite walls rising sheer from sea to clouds
7 Homer – the Shangri-la of Alaska
8 Kenai Fjords National Park – whale-watching and Exit Glacier
9 Cordova – picturesque fishing port and impressive Childs Glacier

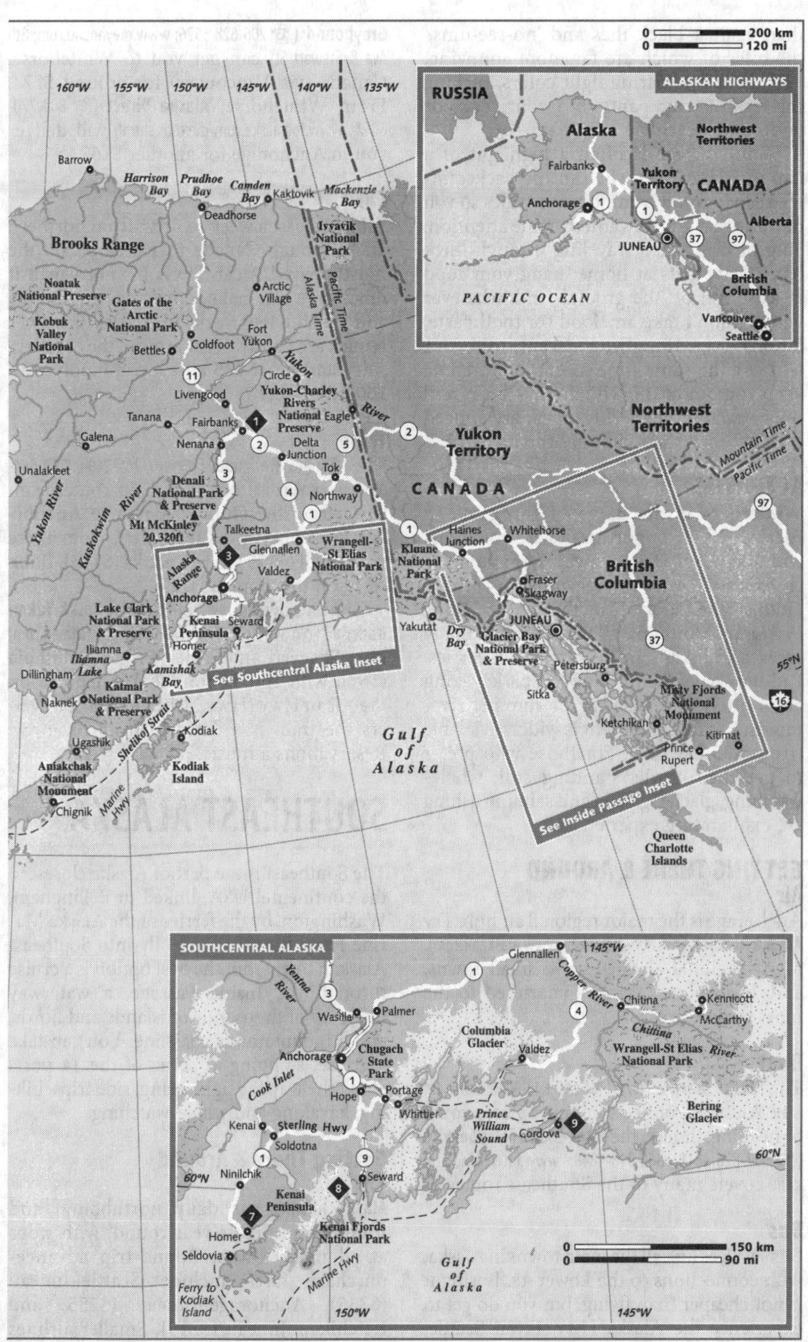

ALASKAN HIGHWAYS
RUSSIA
Alaska
Northwest Territories
Fairbanks
Yukon Territory
CANADA
Anchorage
Alberta
JUNEAU
British Columbia
PACIFIC OCEAN
Vancouver
Seattle
Barrow
Harrison Bay
Prudhoe Bay
Camden Bay
Kaktovik
Mackenzie Bay
Deadhorse
Brooks Range
Ivvavik National Park
Noatak National Preserve
Gates of the Arctic National Park
Kobuk Valley National Park
Arctic Village
Alaska Time
Pacific Time
Fort Yukon
Bettles
Coldfoot
Yukon
Circle
Livengood
Yukon-Charley Rivers National Preserve
Eagle
River
Tanana
Fairbanks
Galena
Nenana
Delta Junction
Yukon Territory
Northwest Territories
Unalakleet
Tok
Denali National Park & Preserve
Northway
CANADA
Mountain Time
Pacific Time
Yukon River
Kuskokwim River
Mt McKinley 20,320ft
Talkeetna
Glennallen
Wrangell-St Elias National Park
Kluane National Park
Haines Junction
Whitehorse
British Columbia
Alaska Range
Valdez
Anchorage
Fraser
Skagway
Lake Clark National Park & Preserve
Kenai Peninsula
Seward
Yakutat
Dry Bay
JUNEAU
Glacier Bay National Park & Preserve
Homer
Iliamna
Iliamna Lake
Kamishak Bay
See Southcentral Alaska Inset
Petersburg
55°N
Dillingham
Katmai National Park & Preserve
Sitka
Misty Fjords National Monument
Naknek
Shelikof Strait
Kodiak
Ketchikan
Kitimat
Ugashik
Gulf of Alaska
Prince Rupert
Aniakchak National Monument
Kodiak Island
Chignik
Marine Hwy
See Inside Passage Inset
Queen Charlotte Islands
160°W
155°W
150°W
145°W
140°W
135°W
0 200 km
0 120 mi
SOUTHCENTRAL ALASKA
Glennallen
145°W
Yentna River
Copper River
Chitina
Kennicott
Wasilla
Palmer
McCarthy
Columbia Glacier
Chittina River
Anchorage
Chugach State Park
Valdez
Wrangell-St Elias National Park
Cook Inlet
Hope
Portage
Whittier
Bering Glacier
Prince William Sound
Kenai
Sterling Hwy
Cordova
Soldotna
60°N
Ninilchik
Seward
Kenai Peninsula
Homer
Kenai Fjords National Park
Seldovia
Gulf of Alaska
Marine Hwy
Ferry to Kodiak Island
150°W
145°W
0 150 km
0 90 mi

ALASKA

than against black flies and 'no-see-ums,' the bites of which are far more annoying. Foil them by wearing light colors, tucking the legs of your pants into your socks or boots and wearing a snug hat.

Seeing a bear is often a highlight of a trip to Alaska, but when in the backcountry keep in mind commonsense rules so you don't attract any unwanted ursine attention: Sing or clap when traveling through thick bush; leave pets at home; hang your food at least 10ft off the ground; and, whatever you do, don't take any food (or toothpaste, lotions or anything with a scent) into your tent. At the same time, don't let paranoia keep you out of the wilderness – bears will only attack if they feel trapped, are enticed by food, or if their cubs are threatened.

ACTIVITIES

Wilderness is the name of the game in Alaska. Hiking opportunities are boundless and a sure way to get away from summer crowds and closer to the wildlife. For more on this, take a look at Lonely Planet's *Hiking in Alaska*. Mountain biking is great in many areas and bikes can be carried on ferries. Paddlers have a choice of coastal kayaking amid otters and icebergs, or running river rapids. Rental equipment is widely available (from $35 per day). For those who prefer to get their thrills standing still, whale-watching, glacier-gazing and salmon-fishing are exhilarating experiences.

GETTING THERE & AROUND

Air

Anchorage is the major regional air hub. Try **Alaska Airlines** (☎ 800-252-7522; www.alaskaair.com). Many regional airlines serve small towns, and 'bush planes' can be chartered to the most remote areas.

Boat

The **Alaska Marine Hwy** (☎ 800-642-0066; www.dot.state.ak.us/amhs) connects up most places you'll be heading, though the **Inter-Island Ferry Service** (☎ 907-826-4848, 866-308-4848; www.interislandferry.com) covers many of the Southeast routes.

Bus

Bus services link all the main towns in Alaska, with connections to the Lower 48. Busing it is not cheaper than flying, but you do get to experience the Alaska Hwy. From Seattle, **Greyhound** (☎ 206-628-5526; www.greyhound.com; 8th Ave & Stewart St) can get you to Whitehorse, Canada (via Vancouver) for around $274. From Whitehorse, **Alaska Direct** (☎ 800-770-6652; www.tokalaska.com/dirctbus.shtml) will deliver you to Anchorage for another $165.

Car

Allow at least a week to drive from northern USA through Canada to Fairbanks on the mostly paved Alcan Hwy. It's not worth it unless you can make some stops on the way and spend a few weeks in Alaska. Local car rentals are handy to get around the countryside, starting at $35 a day, commonly with 100 miles free.

Train

The **Alaska Railroad** (☎ 907-265-2494, 800-544-0552; www.akrr.com) has one main route, from Seward on the Gulf of Alaska to Anchorage ($59 one-way), and north from there via Denali ($125) to Fairbanks ($175). Book early on this popular train.

The narrow-gauge 1890s **White Pass & Yukon Railroad** (☎ 800-343-7373; www.whitepassrailroad.com) links Skagway and Fraser, British Columbia ($67), with connections to Whitehorse on the Alcan Hwy (Hwy 2), but for most travelers the train is a day trip from Skagway. Reservations a must.

SOUTHEAST ALASKA

The Southeast is the part of Alaska closest to the continental USA, linked to Bellingham, Washington, by the ferries of the Alaska Marine Hwy. It's possible to fly into Southeast Alaskan towns, but the best option is a cruise through the Inside Passage, a waterway made up of thousands of islands and fjords, and a mountainous coastline. You can take a cruise, stopping at some of the 14 ports along the way for sightseeing, side trips, hiking, kayaking and whale-watching.

Getting There & Around

AIR

Alaska Airlines has daily northbound and southbound flights year-round, with stops at all main towns. Round-trip advance-purchase fares include Seattle–Juneau ($335), Anchorage–Juneau ($255) and Ketchikan–Juneau ($215). Smaller airlines serving the region include **LAB** (☎ 907-766-2222, 800-426-0543; www.labflying.com), **Taquan Air** (☎ 907-225-8800, 800-770-8800; www.taquanair.com) and **Wings of Alaska** (☎ 907-789-0790; www.wingsofalaska.com).

BOAT

Alaska Marine Hwy (☎ 800-642-0066) runs ferries north and south along the Inside Passage, calling at the main towns almost daily in summer. Smaller boats make less frequent calls to minor settlements. The complete trip, from Bellingham, Washington, to Juneau costs $266 per person, not including berth or meals; this permits stops at ports on the way if you arrange it in advance. Fares for trips within the Inside Passage include Prince Rupert–Haines ($143), Ketchikan–Petersburg ($45), Petersburg–Sitka ($32), Sitka–Juneau ($32) and Juneau–Haines ($27). It's possible to take a car on the Alaska Marine Hwy ferries, but it costs a bundle and space must be reserved months ahead.

If you can't get on a ferry in Bellingham, take alternative transport to Prince Rupert, British Columbia, which has more departures.

You can also take a **ferry** (☎ 800-382-9229) across the Gulf of Alaska from Juneau to Seward on the Kenai Peninsula (adult/child $177/89 one-way). Book well in advance.

TRAIN

The scenic **White Pass & Yukon Railroad** (☎ 800-343-7373) runs between Skagway and Fraser (adult/child $67/34 one-way), with connections to Whitehorse on the Alcan Hwy (adult/child $95/48).

KETCHIKAN

The Alaska Marine Hwy's first Alaskan stop is Ketchikan (meaning 'thundering wings of the eagle'), a fishing and timber town with frontier character. The **visitors center** (☎ 907-225-6166, 800-770-3300; www.visit-ketchikan.com; 131 Front St; 7am-5pm) arranges tours, gives out a walking-tour map and has city bus information. For details of trails, cabins and outdoor activities, visit the **Southeast Alaska Discovery Center** (☎ 907-228-6220; 50 Main St; admission $5; 8am-5pm), which houses an impressive theater and exhibit hall. Access the Internet at **Surf City** (☎ 907-225-5475; 425 Water St; 20min/1hr/100min $5/8/10).

THE RISE AND FALL OF TOTEMS

Ironically, Europeans both stimulated and then almost ended the Native Alaskan art of carving totems in the Southeast region. Totems first flourished in the late 18th century, after clans had acquired steel knives, axes and other cutting tools through the fur trade with white explorers.

Between 1880 and the 1950s, the art form was almost wiped out when a law forbidding potlatches took effect, banning the ceremony for which most totems were carved. When the law was repealed in 1951, a revival of totem carving took place and still continues.

Generally, the oldest totems are 50 to 60 years old. Once they reach this age, the heavy precipitation and acidic muskeg soil of Southeast Alaska takes its toll on the cedar pole, until the wood rots and the totem finally tumbles.

Sights & Activities

Learn about all things salmon from the observation decks of the **Deer Mountain Tribal Hatchery & Eagle Center** (☎ 907-225-9533; 1158 Salmon Rd; admission $8; 8am-4:30pm). The fascinating eagle center is the country's only eagle feeding ground where the birds hunt for themselves.

The star of the former red-light district of Creek St is **Dolly's House** (☎ 907-225-2279; 24 Creek St; admission $4), the parlor of Ketchikan's most famous madam. The **Totem Heritage Center** (☎ 907-225-5900; 601 Deermont St; admission $4; 8am-5pm) features a collection of priceless 18th-century totem poles.

A $10 combo ticket gets you into both the Heritage Center and the hatchery.

The 3-mile **Deer Mountain Trail** begins near the city center, providing access to a **USFS cabin** for $25 a night (see p1029). More trails are in the Ward Lake Recreation Area. **Southeast Exposure** (☎ 907-225-8829; 515 Water St) rents kayaks (from $30) and runs tours (from $40).

Sleeping

Ketchikan Reservation Service (☎ 907-247-5337, 800-987-5337; www.ketchkikan-lodging.com) This service books B&B rooms (from $75). Many lodgings provide a free van service from the ferries. There's an 11.5% city and bed tax charge.

Gilmore Hotel (☎ 907-225-9423, 800-275-9423; 326 Front St; s/d from $80; ☒) Grandly perched downtown on the waterfront, the Gilmore offers a continental breakfast and a Laundromat, and allows pets in some rooms. The attached restaurant, Annabelle's, provides room service.

New York Hotel & Café (☎ 907-225-0246, 866-225-0246; www.thenewyorkhotel.com; 207 Stedman St; s/d $94/104, $5 less for multiple nights; ☒) A historic, family-owned inn in the heart of town, rooms here have cable TV, and complimentary tea and coffee is served in the lively café.

Blueberry B&B (☎ 907-247-2583, 877-449-2583; www.blueberryhillbb.com; 500 Front St; r $110-145; ☒) Four pastel-themed rooms, each with private bath. Handmade quilts adorn the queen beds.

HI-AYH Ketchikan Hostel (☎ 907-225-3319; 400 Main St; members/nonmembers $12/15; ☒) Bustling but basic, with lockout 9am-6pm.

The closest camping is available at three USFS campgrounds 10 miles north of Ketchikan, in the Ward Lake Recreation Area on Ward Lake Rd. The rustic campgrounds are **Signal Creek**, **Last Chance** and **Three C** ($10). There are 30 **USFS cabins** in the area, most involving air charter for access (see p1029).

ALASKA

Eating & Drinking

Annabelle's Famous Keg and Chowder House (☎ 907-225-6009; 326 Front St; lunch $12-20, dinner $20-35; ☒) Situated in Gilmore Mall, this place serves up elegant fare amid dark-wood, white-tablecloth decor. The brandy peppercorn filet gets rave reviews. Packed when the cruise ships arrive.

New York Café (☎ 907-225-0246; 207 Stedman St; breakfast $5-9, lunch $12-19; ☒) This is the place to savor the best pancakes in town while looking out onto the Thomas Basin.

Chico's (☎ 907-225-2833; 435 Dock St; $5-12; ☒) Here you'll find family-oriented, affordable Mexican fare and pizza.

Streamers on the Dock (☎ 907-225-1600; 76 Front St; dinner mains $20-25; ☒) This is the place for local seafood and waterfront dining.

Carr's (2417 Tongass Ave) Next to the Plaza Mall, Carr's is a 24-hour supermarket.

First City Saloon (830 Water St) This is a sprawling place with giant-screen TVs, 20 beers on tap, pool tables and live music.

The fishing crowd frequents **Potlatch Bar** (126 Thomas St), but **Eagles Club** (Creek St) serves cheaper beer.

Getting There & Around

Alaska Airlines and Alaska Marine Hwy ferries service Ketchikan (see Getting There & Around, p1033).

The **MV Prince of Wales** (☎ 907-826-4848, 866-308-4848) sails to Hollis on Prince of Wales Island twice a day June through August (adult/child $29/17). For wheels, try **Alaska Car Rental** (☎ 907-225-5123, 800-662-0007; 2828 Tongass Ave; ⏲ 8am-5pm). There's another location at the airport that's open whenever flights come in.

Around Ketchikan

Some 2 miles south of Ketchikan, **Saxman Native Village** (☎ 907-225-4421; www.capefoxtours.com; free to Totem Park, village tour $35; ⏲ 9am-5pm) is an incorporated village of the indigenous Tlingit people. Its **Totem Park** has the world's largest standing collection of totem poles, as well as a cultural center. Ten miles north of Ketchikan, **Totem Bight State Historical Park** (free; ⏲ 6am-10pm) contains 14 restored totem poles and a historic **longhouse** (free; ⏲ 8am-8pm).

If the tourist hordes are driving you mad, escape to the **Hole in the Wall Bar & Marina** (7500 S Tongass Hwy), run by the affable John Jackson for more than 40 years.

Misty Fjords National Monument begins 22 miles east of Ketchikan, offering wildlife and spectacular views of 3000ft granite walls rising sheer from the ocean. It's also a popular kayaking spot. **Alaska Cruises** (☎ 907-225-6044, 800-228-1905; $150) runs a six-hour trip; alternatively, try a two-hour sightseeing flight with **Island Wings** (☎ 907-225-2444, 888-854-2444; www.islandwings.com; $189).

PRINCE OF WALES ISLAND

The third-largest island in the USA, Prince of Wales Island features native Alaskan villages, logging camps, 900 miles of coast and the Southeast's most extensive road network (mostly unpaved). The island's **chamber of commerce** (☎ 907-826-3870; www.princeofwalescoc.org; 300A Easy St; ⏲ 9am-3pm Tue-Fri) is in Craig. The **USFS** has offices in Craig (☎ 907-826-3271; 900 9th St; ⏲ 8am-5pm Mon-Fri) and Thorne Bay (☎ 907-828-3304; 1312 Federal Way; ⏲ 8am-4:30pm Mon-Fri). Two USFS cabins are accessible from the road.

Ferries arrive at Hollis, and the fishing and timber community of Craig is 31 miles southwest. Try **Ruthann's Hotel** (☎ 907-826-3378; Main & Water Sts; r from $90; ☒) or **TLC Laundry**

& Rooms (☎ 907-826-2488; 333 Cold Storage Rd; s/d $43/53), or you can camp in the city park.

The ferry **MV Prince of Wales** (☎ 866-308-4848) visits Hollis most days from Ketchikan (adult/child $29/17). **Sea Otter Taxi** (☎ 907-755-2362) will meet the ferry in Hollis ($25). Rental cars are available in Craig and Klawock or can be brought from Ketchikan on the ferry (from $36).

WRANGELL

Founded by Russians, leased to the British and then taken over by Americans with the purchase of Alaska, the town of Redoubt St Dionysius was renamed Fort Wrangell in 1868. It thrived as a fur-trading and then a gold-mining supply center. The **visitors center** (☎ 907-874-3901, 800-367-9745; www.wrangell.com; 10am-4pm Mon-Fri) is in front of the city hall, and is also open on weekends when cruise ships are in town. There's a local **USFS office** (☎ 907-874-2323; 525 Bennett St; 8am-4:30pm Mon-Fri) and **Practical Rent-A-Car** (☎ 907-874-3975), at the airport, is open when flights arrive.

Displays of indigenous artifacts, petroglyphs and a collection of Alaskan art are at the **Wrangell Museum** (☎ 907-874-3770; 318 Church St; admission $3; 10am-5pm Tue-Fri). By midsummer 2004, it will be at its new location behind Bob's Supermarket.

Wrangell levies a 7% city sales tax and a flat $4 per-room bed tax.

Local B&Bs include **Rooney's Roost** (☎ 907-874-2026; www.rooneysroost.com; 206 McKinnon St; s/d $75/95; ☒) and **Fennimore's by the Ferry** (☎ 907-874-3012; www.fennimoresbbb.com; 321 Stikine Ave; s/d $65/70; ☒).

Hardings Old Sourdough Lodge (☎ 907-874-3613, 800-874-3613; 1104 Peninsula St; s/d $85/95; ☒), a mile south of town, has a sauna and Jacuzzi, home-style meals and free ferry/airport transport.

Stikine Inn (☎ 907-874-3388, 888-874-3388; 107 Stikine Ave; r $95-100; ☒) is a popular inn with 33 rooms, one of which can accommodate pets. For a view of the water, tack on another $10.

Wrangell Hostel (☎ 907-874-3534; 220 Church St; r $15; ☒) is in the Presbyterian church, while the free **City Park Campground** (Zimovia Hwy), 1.75 miles south of the ferry terminal, is for tents only. Three miles further south, the **Shoemaker Bay Recreation Area** is free for tents, but RV sites are from $10. There are 20 **USFS cabins** (☎ 877-444-6777, www.reserveusa.com) around Wrangell. The six on the Stikine River flats, 12 to 15 miles from Wrangell, are only accessible by canoe or bush plane.

Waterfront Grill (☎ 907-874-2353; 107 Stikine Ave; lunch $6-10, dinner $15-20; ☒) specializes in local seafood, but it will custom-make any dish with available ingredients. The panoramic view can't be beat.

Diamond C Café (☎ 907-874-3677; 223 Front St; mains $6-10; 6am-3pm; ☒) is a cheap spot to grab a bite, while **J&W's** (☎ 907-874-2120; 120 Front St; $5-8; ☒), at the City Dock, is the place for fast food. And locals still call **Bob's Supermarket** (223 Brueger St) by its old name, Benjamin's.

Mingle with locals at **Totem Bar** (116 Front St) or the **Marine Bar** (Shakes St) or boogie with them at **Stikine Inn Lounge** (107 Stikine Ave), featuring Wrangell's only dance floor.

Alaska Marine Hwy ferries stop at Wrangell (see p1033).

PETERSBURG

At the north end of spectacular Wrangell Narrows lies the picturesque community of Petersburg, a town known for its Norwegian roots and home to Alaska's largest halibut fleet.

The **visitors center** (☎ 907-772-4636; www.petersburg.org; Fram & 1st Sts; 9am-5pm Mon-Fri, noon-4pm Sat) has USFS information, or you can visit the **USFS office** (☎ 907-772-3871; Federal Building, Nordic Dr; 8am-5pm Mon-Fri).

The center of old Petersburg was **Sing Lee Alley**, which winds past weathered homes and boathouses perched on pilings above the water. The **Clausen Memorial Museum** (☎ 907-772-3598; 203 Fram St; admission $2; 10am-5pm Mon-Sat) features local artifacts and fishing relics and a small but excellent museum store.

There are kayaking opportunities, from day paddles to week-long blue-water adventures. **Tongass Kayak Adventures** (☎ 907-772-4600; www.alaska.net/~tonkayak; 106 N Nordic Dr) offers rentals and drop-off transportation, as well as several guided paddles, including one to LeConte Glacier ($790).

Petersburg has several B&Bs priced at around $75/85 single/double; ask at the visitors center.

Tides Inn (☎ 907-772-4288, 800-665-8433; 307 1st St; s/d $70/85; ☒) This place has friendly staff, offers a continental breakfast and has one wheelchair-accessible room.

Petersburg Bunk & Breakfast Hostel (☎ 907-772-3632, 907-723-5340; www.bunkandbreakfast.com; 805

ALASKA

Gjoa St; dm $25; ⊠ 🖳) is in a cozy spot 1.5 miles from the ferry terminal; it offers four-person dorm rooms and free breakfast. Call in advance for directions.

Camping options include the central **LeConte RV Park** (☎ 907-772-4680; 4th St & Haugen Dr; tents $7) and **Tent City** (☎ 907-772-4224; Haugen Dr; $5), 0.5 miles from the airport.

Alaskafe (☎ 907-772-5282; Nordic Dr; breakfast & lunch $6-8, dinner $10-15; ⊠) is the hippest restaurant in town. Mostly a coffee house serving espresso drinks and baked goods, it also offers creative breakfasts and grilled sandwiches, and Wednesday through Friday it serves up gourmet dinners, usually with a vegetarian option.

Joan Mei (☎ 907-772-4222; 1103 Nordic Dr; mains $10-14; ⊠), near the ferry terminal, whips up Chinese, American and Mexican dishes. Also try **Helse Health Foods & Deli** (17 Sing Lee Alley), which is cheap and wholesome, and **Coastal Cold Storage** (306 Nordic Dr) for great seafood.

Locals shoot pool at **Harbor Bar** (310 Nordic Dr), while **Kito's Kave** (11 Sing Lee Alley) has live music and dancing, and can get wild at times.

LeConte ferry (☎ 907-465-3941) heads off for Juneau on Tuesday ($50 one-way), stopping at Kake, Sitka, Angoon, Tenakee and Hoonah. **Tides Inn** (☎ 907-772-4288, 800-665-8433; 307 1st St) rents midsize cars from $65 a day.

SITKA

Russians established Southeast Alaska's first nonindigenous settlement here in 1799, and the town flourished on fur. A gem in a beautiful setting, Sitka sees itself as the cultural center of the Southeast.

The **visitors center** (☎ 907-747-5940; www.sitka.org; 330 Harbor Dr; 🕘 8am-5pm Mon-Fri) is in the Centennial Building. The **USFS office** (☎ 907-747-6671; 204 Siginaka Way; 🕘 8am-4:30pm Mon-Fri) provides hiking and kayaking information.

Sights & Activities

Sitka National Historical Park (☎ 907-747-6281; Lincoln St; admission free) leads you on a gorgeous trail that winds past 15 totem poles, while the visitors center shows Russian and indigenous artifacts and presents traditional carving demonstrations. **St Michael's Cathedral** (☎ 907-747-8120; 240 Lincoln St; admission $2; 🕘 9am-4pm most days) is a replica of the original 1840s Russian Orthodox cathedral destroyed by fire in 1966; priceless treasures were salvaged by residents. Castle Hill is the site of **Baranof's Castle**, where Alaska was officially transferred from Russia to the USA. Built in 1842, the **Russian Bishop's House** (☎ 907-747-6281; Lincoln St; admission $3; 🕘 9am-1pm, 2pm-5pm) is Sitka's oldest intact Russian building. **Sheldon Jackson Museum** (☎ 907-747-8981; 104 College Dr; admission $4; 🕘 9am-5pm), on the college campus, houses an excellent indigenous-culture collection. The colorful **Katlian St fishing quarter**, at the west end of town, is a photographer's delight.

SITKA SUMMER MUSIC FESTIVAL

Sitka sponsors the three-week Sitka Summer Music Festival every June. The festival brings together professional musicians for chamber music concerts and workshops. The highly acclaimed event is popular, so scoring tickets to the evening concerts can be tough. Rehearsals, however, are open to the public, easier to attend and usually free.

Sitka has superb hiking, and the Gaven Hill Trail into the mountains is accessible from the downtown area. There are also many kayaking trips around Baranof and Chichagof Islands. **Baidarka Boats** (☎ 907-747-8996; www.kayaksite.com; 320 Seward St; $60-85 per day) rents kayaks and runs guided trips. **Sitka Tours** (☎ 907-747-8443; $12) runs short trips for ferry passengers waiting for tide changes in Sitka, which includes admission to St Michael's Cathedral.

Sleeping

The Sitka area has about two dozen B&Bs; the visitors center keeps an updated list.

Karras B&B (☎ 907-747-3978; 230 Kogwanton St; s/d $62/89; ⊠) Four cozy rooms with shared bath in a private home, a few blocks from downtown and the harbor views are excellent.

Rockwell Lighthouse (☎ 907-747-3056; r $150-200; ⊠) Have the whole place to yourself. A three-minute skiff ride from town, it's worth the recommended year's advance booking.

HI-AYH Sitka Youth Hostel (☎ 907-747-8661; 303 Kimsham St; member/nonmember $13/16; ⊠) Basic and can rent you a sleeping bag, but it's best to bring your own.

There are two USFS campgrounds, **Starrigavan** (Halibut Point Rd; $8), just less than a mile north of the ferry terminal, and **Sawmill Creek** (Blue Lake Rd; free), 6 miles east of Sitka. Several **USFS cabins** (see p1029) are accessible by air in 30 minutes or less.

DAVID PEEVERS

Fake Hollywood sign at **Universal Studios Hollywood** (p888), Los Angeles

DAVID PEEVERS

Bodybuilders, **Los Angeles** (p879)

STEPHEN SAKS

Golden Gate Bridge (p940), San Francisco

Hidden Valley (p918), Joshua Tree National Park, California

RICHARD CUMMINS

JIM WARK

Crater Lake (p994), Oregon

RICHARD CUMMINS

Native American **totem pole** (p72)

RICHARD CUMMINS

Signage, **Pike Place Market** (p1011), Seattle

Space Needle (p1007), Seattle

TOM BOYD

Eating & Drinking

Back Door Café (☎ 907-747-8856; 104 Barracks St; meals under $5; ⊠) This is a calm eye in the cruise-ship storm.

Highliner Coffee (☎ 907-747-4924; 327 Seward St, in Seward St Mall; ⏲ 5:30am-5pm Mon-Sat, 8am-4pm Sun; ⊠ 💻) Good coffee, espresso drinks, fresh bagels and Internet access by the hour or half-hour.

Bayview Restaurant (☎ 907-747-5440; 407 Lincoln St; breakfast $4-10, lunch $8-11, dinner $17-19; ⏲ 5am-9pm Mon-Sat, closes 3pm Sun; ⊠) Serves a variety of hamburgers, sandwiches, pastas, steaks and seafood dinners.

Sheldon Jackson's cafeteria (☎ 907-747-2506; Sweetland Hall; breakfast/lunch/dinner $5/7/10; 6:30am-8am, 11:30am-1pm & 4:45pm-6pm; ⊠) A budget find on campus.

Lakeside Grocery (705 Halibut Point Rd) Near the hostel, it has sandwiches, soups and a salad bar.

Evergreen Natural Foods (2A-1 Lincoln St) Near the municipal building, it stocks healthy goodies.

Pioneer Bar (☎ 907-747-3456; 212 Katlian St) Grab a beer and a hot dog with the loggers and fishermen at this historic bar.

Getting There & Away

Allstar Rental (☎ 907-966-2552; Sitka airport; ⏲ 7:30am-6pm) has compact vehicles for $50 per day with unlimited mileage. **Alaska Marine Hwy ferries** (☎ 907-747-8737, 800-642-0066) stop almost at the terminal, which is 7 miles north of town. **Ferry Transit Bus** (☎ 907-747-8443) will take you the rest of the way into town for $6.

SECONDARY PORTS

Between Sitka and Juneau, the **LeConte ferry** (☎ 907-465-3941) services small ports, offering a chance to experience untouristed Alaska. **Wings of Alaska** (☎ 907-789-0790) and **LAB Flying Service** (☎ 907-766-2222) also fly to these places.

On Kupreanof Island, the Indian beachfront community of **Kake** boasts Alaska's tallest totem pole and serves as the departure point for Tebenkof Bay kayaking trips. Rustic **Tenakee Springs** (population 105) is known for its relaxed pace, alternative lifestyle and 108°F hot springs. Twice monthly, *LeConte* travels to the lively fishing town of **Pelican**, on Chichagof Island, a unique day trip from Juneau ($70). Built on pilings over tidelands, Pelican's main street is a mile-long wooden boardwalk.

JUNEAU

Alaska's scenic capital has narrow streets, a bustling waterfront and snowcapped mountains. It's also the gateway to Glacier Bay National Park (p1039) and Admiralty Island National Monument (p1039).

Site of Alaska's first major gold strike, the town became the territory capital in 1906. Downtown Juneau clings to a mountainside; the rest of the city is spread north into the Mendenhall Valley.

The main visitors center is **Davis Log Cabin** (☎ 907-586-2201, 800-587-2201; www.traveljuneau.com; 101 Egan Dr; ⏲ 8:30am-5pm Mon-Fri, 9am-5pm Sat & Sun). The **Juneau ranger's station** (☎ 907-586-8751, 907-586-8800; 8461 Old Dairy Rd; ⏲ 8am-4:30pm Mon-Fri) is in Centennial Hall and has details on cabins, hiking, Glacier Bay, Admiralty Island and Tongass National Forest. The Juneau **public library** (☎ 907-586-5249; 292 Marine Way) provides Internet access. The **information kiosk** (Marine Park), at the southern end of Egan Dr, has walking-tour maps.

Buy topographic maps at the **Foggy Mountain Shop** (☎ 907-586-6780; 134 N Franklin St).

Sights & Activities

Historic **South Franklin St** is lined with shops, bars and restaurants and bustles with tourists. **St Nicholas Russian Orthodox Church** (☎ 907-586-1023; 326 5th St; donation requested; ⏲ 9am-5pm Mon-Fri) is the Southeast's oldest church, dating from 1894.

The **Juneau-Douglas City Museum** (☎ 907-586-3572; 114 W 4th St; adult/child $3/free; ⏲ 9am-5pm Mon-Fri, 10am-5pm Sat & Sun) highlights the area's gold-mining history. Pick up the Perseverance Trail booklet and Treadwell Mine Historic Trail brochure for self-guided walks. The **Last Chance Mining Museum** (☎ 907-586-5338; 1001 Basin Rd; admission $3; ⏲ 9:30am-12:30pm & 3:30-6:30pm) is an impressive complex of railroad lines, ore cars and repair sheds. The short hike to **Treadwell Mine ruins**, near Douglas, is also interesting.

The **Alaska State Museum** (☎ 907-465-2901; 395 Whittier St; adult/child $5/free; ⏲ 8:30am-5:30pm) has historical displays and indigenous artifacts, plus a full-size eagle's nest atop a two-story tree.

About three miles north of downtown, the **Macaulay Salmon Hatchery Visitors center**

(☎ 907-463-4810, 877-463-2468; 2697 Channel Dr; adult/child $3/1.50; 🕑 10am-6pm Mon-Fri, 10am-5pm Sat & Sun) has underwater viewing windows that allow you to see fish spawning and climbing ladders. Displays explain the salmon life cycle and hatchery operations.

The area's numerous glaciers include **Mendenhall**, the famous 'drive-in' glacier; the informative **visitors center** (☎ 907-789-0097; Glacier Spur Rd; admission $3; 🕑 8am-6:30pm) is 13 miles from the city. **Capital Transit buses** from the city center cost $1.25. City tours on **Mendenhall Glacier Transport** (☎ 907-789-5460; adult/child $20/free) include the glacier.

Hiking is the most popular activity, and some trails access USFS cabins. The most stunning scenery is along the **West Glacier Trail**, which sidles along the Mendenhall Glacier. The **Mt Roberts Trail** is the most popular hike to the alpine country above Juneau. Or you can skip the hike and just jump on the **Mt Roberts Tram** (☎ 907-463-3412, 888-461-8726; 490 S Franklin St; adult/child $22/13), which takes passengers from the dock to treeline. **Juneau Parks & Recreation** (☎ 907-586-5226; 155 S Seward St) offers organized hikes.

ALASKA

The area is wonderful for kayaking day trips and longer paddles. **Alaska Boat & Kayak** (☎ 907-586-8220; 11521 Glacier Hwy) rents boats, and **Alaska Discovery** (☎ 800-586-1911; www.akdiscovery.com; 5310 Glacier Hwy; 2 people/3 or more $595/495) runs three-day paddles in Berners Bay.

The steep-sided Tracy Arm fjord, 50 miles southeast of Juneau, makes an excellent day trip. Check **Goldbelt Tours** (☎ 907-586-8687, 800-820-2628; 76 Egan Dr; $123) or **Adventure Bound Alaska** (☎ 907-463-2509, 800-228-3875; 215 Ferry Way; $105).

Sleeping

Downtown accommodations are heavily booked during summer, and they stick you with a 12% tax. Juneau has more than 50 B&Bs; stop at the visitors center to find one or call the **Alaska B&B Association** (☎ 907-586-2959). There are also several decent motels near the airport.

Alaska Capital Inn (☎ 907-586-6507, 888-588-6507; www.alaskacapitalinn.com; 113 W 5th St; r $135-225; ⊠) A stay in this gorgeously restored 1906 mansion is a real treat. Soak away your cares in the clothing-optional deck hot tub. There's a two-night minimum, and all guests should be over 11 years of age. The attic suite, complete with double whirlpool tub and fireplace, is $274.

Alaskan Hotel (☎ 907-586-1000, 800-327-9347; www.alaskanhotel-juneau.com; 167 S Franklin St; with/without bath $60/80, studio $91; ⊠) This lovely historic hotel is located in the heart of the Franklin St nightlife district – great news if you want to party, less so if you're a light sleeper. Although all the furniture is original, it welcomes (well-behaved) pets.

Driftwood Lodge (☎ 907-586-2280, 800-544-2239; www.driftwoodalaska.com; 435 Willoughby Ave; r $85-115; ⊠ 💻) Most of the rooms in this no-frills downtown motel have kitchenettes. There's a courtesy airport/ferry van and a coin laundry. Cough up an extra $5 for pets.

Also recommended:

Silverbow Inn (☎ 907-586-4146; www.silverbowinn.com; 120 2nd St; r $108-138; ⊠) An artsy downtown inn.
Inn at the Waterfront (☎ 907-586-2050; 455 S Franklin St; r from $55)
Juneau International Hostel (☎ 907-586-9559; www.juneauhostel.org; 614 Harris St; dm adult/child $10/5; ⊠ 💻) Has one private room for families or handicapped individuals.
Auke Village (☎ 907-586-8800; Glacier Hwy; $8) Camping 1.5 miles from the ferry terminal. Reservations necessary.

Eating & Drinking

Thane Ore House (☎ 907-586-3442; 4400 Thane Rd; mains $7-20; ⊠) Juneau's best salmon bake, 4 miles south of town. The all-you-can-eat buffet is reasonable at $20.

Fiddlehead Restaurant (☎ 907-586-3150; 429 W Willoughby Ave; mains $8-24; ⊠) serves seafood and Juneau's best vegetarian cuisine – try the yummy hot brown rice salad. Upstairs – and more upscale – is the Italian dining room **Di Sopra** (mains $15-25; ⊠).

Rainbow Foods (☎ 907-586-6476; 224 4th St; ⊠) A cool natural-foods store with a deli that makes a happening lunch spot.

Silverbow Inn Bakery (☎ 907-586-4146; 120 2nd St; $3-7; ⊠) Fresh-baked bagels and sandwiches.

Heritage Coffee Company (☎ 907-586-1088; 625 W 7th St; ⊠) Good espresso and atmosphere.

Cookhouse (☎ 907-463-3658; 200 Admiral Way; ⊠) Boasts Alaska's largest hamburgers.

Bullwinkle's Pizza Parlor (☎ 907-586-8988; 318 Willoughby Ave; from $12; ⊠) Cheap pizza downtown; open until midnight Fridays and Saturdays.

Carr's supermarket (Vintage Blvd & Egan Hwy) Open 24 hours, with some prepared foods available.

South Franklin St is Juneau's drinking sector. The (in)famous **Red Dog Saloon** (278

S Franklin St) has a sawdust floor and relic-covered walls. Hidden in **Alaskan Hotel** (see opposite) is a unique bar with historic ambience and folk or jazz music. Southeast Alaska's largest selection of microbrew beers and waterfront views are at **Hangar on the Wharf** (2 Marine Way, Merchant's Wharf).

Getting There & Around

The main airlines serving Juneau are **Alaska Air** (☎ 907-789-0600, 800-252-7522; www.alaskaair.com; 127 N Franklin St) and **Air North Canada** (☎ 907-789-2007). Smaller companies like **Wings of Alaska** (☎ 907-789-0790; www.wingsofalaska.com; 8421 Livingston Way) provide service to isolated communities.

The ferry terminal is 14 miles from downtown; **LeConte** (☎ 907-465-3941) runs to Hoonah, Angoon, Kake and Tenakee Springs. There are no state ferries to Gustavus (and neighboring Glacier Bay), but **Goldbelt Tours** (☎ 907-586-8687, 800-820-2628; 79 Egan Dr) runs a catamaran ($138 round-trip). Bring your kayak for an extra $40.

Juneau's public bus system, **Capital Transit** (☎ 907-789-6901), can take you from the airport to the city center for $1.50 (8am to 5pm Monday to Friday), despite the airport information center encouraging people to take taxis instead. Numerous car rental places offer pickup/drop-off and unlimited mileage. Compacts at **Rent-A-Wreck** (☎ 907-789-4111; 2450 C Industrial Blvd) go for $35, while **Evergreen Ford** (☎ 907-789-9386; 8895 Mallard St) rents them for $45.

ADMIRALTY ISLAND NATIONAL MONUMENT

Fifteen miles southeast of Juneau, this island has 1406 sq miles of designated wilderness, featuring bears, eagles, humpback whales, harbor seals, porpoises and sea lions. Stock up on supplies in Juneau and information from the **USFS office** (☎ 907-586-8751; 101 Egan Dr; 🕑 8am-5pm Mon-Fri) or the **Juneau Ranger District/Admiralty Island National Monument office** (☎ 907-586-8790; 8465 Old Dairy Rd; 🕑 8am-5pm Mon-Fri) in Mendenhall Valley.

The single settlement on Admiralty Island, **Angoon**, is the starting point for paddling trips, including the 32-mile Cross Admiralty Canoe Rte to Mole Harbor.

Favorite Bay Inn (☎ 907-788-3123, 800-423-3123; www.favoritebayinn.com; s/d $99/139; ☒) has rooms with shared bath, and will drive you the 2 miles from the ferry terminal to the inn, while **Kootznahoo Inlet Lodge** (☎ 907-788-3501; Kootznahoo Rd, at Floatlane Dock; r from $85; ☒) is also 2 miles from the ferry terminal. Angoon is a dry community with only one café.

The best bear-viewing area in Southeast Alaska is at **Pack Creek**, on the eastern side of Admiralty Island. The bears are most abundant July to August, when the salmon are running, and visitors watch them feed from a sand spit or an observation tower along the creek reached by a mile-long trail. Most people reach Pack Creek with guiding companies. **Alaska Discovery** (☎ 800-586-1911; www.akdiscovery.com; 5310 Glacier Hwy, Juneau) offers a one-day tour from Juneau ($495 per person, three-person minimum) and a three-day trip ($950, two-person minimum).

GLACIER BAY NATIONAL PARK

Sixteen tidewater glaciers spill from the mountains and fill the sea with icebergs around the famous wilderness of **Glacier Bay National Park & Preserve**. To see the glaciers, most visitors join **Goldbelt Tours** (☎ 907-586-8687, 800-820-2628; 76 Egan Dr, Juneau; $159) for an eight-hour cruise up the West Arm of Glacier Bay.

The only developed hiking trails are in Bartlett Cove, but there is excellent kayaking; rent equipment from **Glacier Bay Sea Kayaks** (☎ 907-697-2257; www.he.net/~kayakak). **Alaska Discovery** (☎ 800-586-1911; www.akdiscovery.com) runs guided day paddles from Bartlett Cove for $125. **Spirit Walker Expeditions** (☎ 907-697-2266, 800-529-2937; www.seakayakalaska.com) offers a day paddle to Pleasant Island for $125.

The park is served by the settlement of **Gustavus**. The **visitors center** (☎ 907-697-2627; at the dock; 🕑 7am-9pm) provides backcountry permits, maps and information.

Bear's Nest B&B (☎ 907-697-2440; www.gustavus.com/bearsnest; 2 White Dr; cabins $85-99; ☒), where you can stay in the Round House or A-frame cabin, is a delightful experience. Prepare breakfast in your cabin from the organic food of your choice.

Gourmet meals are included with your stay at **Gustavus Inn** (☎ 907-697-2254, 800-649-5220; www.gustavusinn.com; 1 Mile Gustavus Rd; $150; ☒). **Puffin B&B** (☎ 907-697-2260; www.puffintravel.com; Wilson Rd; r from $100; ☒) is the place for rental cabins, while **Glacier Bay Lodge** (☎ 800-451-5952; 199 Bartlett Cove Rd; dm/s/d $30/160/170; ☒) is the only overnight accommodation within the park.

Site of the **park headquarters** (☎ 907-697-2230; 1 Park Rd; 🕑 8am-4:30pm Mon-Fri), **Bartlett Cove** has a restaurant and free campground.

A quarter-mile south of the Salmon River Bridge is **Strawberry Point Café** (☎ 907-697-2227; ☒). Next door, **Beartrack Mercantile** sells groceries at outrageous prices. You'd be wise to bring your own food from Juneau.

Air Excursions (☎ 907-697-2375) has daily flights between Gustavus and Juneau ($130 round-trip). The Glacier Bay Lodge bus meets flights for $12. **Goldbelt Tours** (☎ 907-586-8687, 800-820-2628; 76 Egan Dr, Juneau) runs boats from Juneau ($138 round-trip). **Glacier Bay Cruiseline** (☎ 800-451-5952; www.glacierbaytours.com) offers three-day, two-night package tours from Juneau with accommodations at Glacier Bay Lodge for $478. Tack on another $76 for whale-watching.

HAINES

Providing access to Canada's Yukon Territory and Interior Alaska, Haines is surrounded by mountains. The Northwest Trading Company arrived in 1878, followed by missionaries and gold prospectors. WWII saw construction of the Haines Hwy, linking the city to the Alcan Hwy.

Collect information from the **visitors center** (☎ 907-766-2234; www.haines.ak.us; 2nd Ave & Willard St; 🕑 8am-7pm Mon-Fri, 9am-6pm Sat & Sun).

Sights & Activities

The **Sheldon Museum** (☎ 907-766-2366; 11 Main St; adult/child $3/free; 🕑 11am-6pm Mon-Fri, 2pm-6pm Sat & Sun) features indigenous artifacts and gold-rush relics, and is open longer hours when cruise ships are in dock. The **American Bald Eagle Foundation** (☎ 907-766-3094; 113 Haines Hwy; adult/child $3/1; 🕑 10am-5pm most days) displays more than 100 species in their natural habitat. For something quirky, hit the **Hammer Museum** (☎ 907-776-2374; 108 Main St; admission $3; 🕑 10am-noon & 1pm-5pm Mon-Fri, 1-5pm Sat & Sun), a monument to owner Dave Pahl's obsession with the tools.

Get walking-tour maps of the **Fort Seward** national historical site from Hotel Hälsingland. Also within the fort, the **Alaska Indian Arts Center** (☎ 907-766-2160; Historical Bldg 13; free; 🕑 9am-5pm Mon-Fri) has carving and weaving demonstrations.

Haines offers two major hiking trail systems (the visitors center has details) and numerous rafting trips. **Chilkat Guides** (☎ 907-766-2491; www.raftalaska.com; adult/child $79/63) run a four-hour Chilkat River float, while it and **Alaska Discovery** (☎ 907-586-1911; www.akdiscovery.com) offer pretty thrilling 10-day Tatshenshinin/Alsek River raft trips that cost between $2175 and $2900.

Sleeping

There are several B&Bs in the fort.

Hotel Hälsingland (☎ 907-766-2000, 800-542-6363; 13 Fort Seward Dr; r $69-109; ☒) Housed in a classic, recently renovated building with a pleasant restaurant and bar. Some rooms have fireplaces and claw-foot bathtubs.

Fort Seward Lodge (☎ 800-478-7772; www.ftsewardlodge.com; 39 Mud Bay Rd; s/d with shared bath $50/60, with bath $70/80, with kitchenette $85/95; ☒) Features a large restaurant and cocktail lounge. Pets are allowed for $5 a night.

Chilkat Eagle B&B (☎ 907-766-2763; 67 Soap Suds Alley; s/d/tr $70/80/100; ☒ 💻) Guests are welcome to use the kitchen.

Thunderbird Motel (☎ 907-766-2131, 800-327-2556; www.thunderbird-motel.com; 216 Dalton St; s/d $70/80; ☒) Wheelchair accessible and located in the downtown.

Mountain View Motel (☎ 907-766-2900, 800-478-2902; www.mtnviewmotel.com; 57 Mud Bay Rd; s/d $79/89; ☒) Basic rooms with kitchenettes, near the fort entrance.

Bear Creek Cabins & Hostel (☎ 907-766-2259; www.kcd.com/hostel; Small Tract Rd; tent/dm/cabin $14/16/42; ☒) is 2.5 miles south of town, while **Port Chilkoot Camper Park** (☎ 907-766-2000, 800-542-6363; Mud Bay Rd; tents $10, RV sites $16-23) is next to Fort Seward behind Hotel Hälsingland.

Eating & Drinking

Bamboo Room (☎ 907-766-2800; 11 2nd Ave; breakfast $6-8, lunch $7-8, dinner mains $10-20; ☒) Standard breakfasts with yummy blueberry pancakes.

Fireweed Restaurant (☎ 907-766-3838; Blacksmith St; dinner mains $11-19; ☒) A bright, laid-back organic bistro that comes highly recommended. Some of the produce comes straight from the restaurant's own garden.

Grizzly Greg's Pizzeria (☎ 907-766-3622; 2nd & Main; from $12; ☒) The best pizza in town but no alcohol is served.

Port Chilkoot Salmon Bake & Barbeque (☎ 907-766-2000; $25; ☒) Stuff yourself silly.

Haines is a hard-drinking town: **Fogcutter Bar** (Main St) and **Pioneer Bar** (13 2nd Ave) get lively at night, while Fort Seward has the more serene **Hotel Hälsingland Pub** (13 Fort Seward Dr).

ALASKA

Getting There & Away

Several air-charter companies service Haines, the cheapest being **Wings of Alaska** (☎ 907-789-0790; www.wingsofalaska.com). Also check with **LAB Flying Service** (☎ 907-766-2222, 800-426-0543; www.labflying.com), which also offers Glacier Bay National Park sightseeing flights for $280 for two people.

Alaska Direct Bus Line (☎ 800-770-6652; www.tokalaska.com/dirctbus.shtml) plies the Fairbanks–Haines route three times a week ($185 one-way).

Chilkat Cruises (☎ 907-766-3395, 888-766-2103; round-trip adult/child $44/22, one-way adult/child $22/12) will get you to and from Skagway.

Eagle Nest Car Rentals (☎ 907-766-2891, 800-354-6009; 1183 Haines Hwy; 8am-10pm), in the Eagle Nest Motel, has cars for as low as $45 with 100 miles included. There are also rentals at **Captain's Choice Motel** (☎ 907-766-3111; 108 2nd Ave N; 24hr) from $69 with unlimited mileage.

Around Haines

The 75-sq-mile **Alaska Chilkat Bald Eagle Preserve**, along the Chilkat River, protects the world's largest-known gathering of bald eagles. The greatest numbers of birds are spotted in December and January, but you can see eagles here any time during summer. Lookouts on the Haines Hwy, particularly between Miles 18 and 22, allow motorists to glimpse the birds. **Alaska Nature Tours** (☎ 907-766-2876; www.kcd.com/aknature; 103 2nd Ave S; tours $50) offers a three-hour tour of the preserve.

SKAGWAY

The northern terminus of the Alaska Marine Hwy, Skagway was a gold-rush town infamous for its lawlessness. In 1887 the population was two; 10 years later it was Alaska's largest city, with 20,000 residents. Today, Skagway survives almost entirely on tourism and gets packed when the cruise ships pull in.

The Skagway **visitors center** (☎ 907-983-2854; www.skagway.org; Broadway & 2nd St; 8am-6pm) is in the Arctic Brotherhood Hall – just look for the thousands of driftwood pieces tacked on to its front. The **Klondike Gold Rush National Historical Park Visitors Center** (☎ 907-983-2921; Broadway & 2nd St; 8am-6pm) provides information on the Chilkoot Trail (Alaska's most famous hiking trail), local trails and camping. (Watch the excellent 30-minute movie on the gold-rush days.)

Sights & Activities

A seven-block corridor along Broadway St, part of the historic district, features the restored buildings, false fronts and wooden sidewalks of Skagway's golden era.

The **Skagway Museum** (☎ 907-983-2420; 7th Ave & Spring St; admission $2; 9am-5pm Mon-Fri, 1-4pm Sat & Sun), jammed with gold-rush relics, is in the Skagway City Hall. **Moore's Cabin** (5th Ave & Spring St) is the town's oldest building, while **Mascot Saloon** (290 Broadway St) is now a museum devoted to Skagway's heyday as the 'roughest place in the world.' The best tour is a three-hour Summit Excursion on the **White Pass & Yukon Railroad** (☎ 907-983-2217; 800-343-7373; www.whitepassrailroad.com; 2nd Ave; adult/child $82/41), which climbs the high White Pass in a historic narrow-gauge train.

Sleeping

Golden North Hotel (☎ 907-983-2451, 888-222-1898; Broadway St & 3rd Ave; s $65-110, d $75-120; ☒) Alaska's oldest hotel has recently been restored but maintains its slightly kitschy character. Rooms 23 and 14 are said to be haunted.

Skagway Inn B&B (☎ 907-983-2289, 888-752-4929; www.skagwayinn.com; Broadway St & 7th Ave; r with shared bath $109-129, r with bath $149; ☒). Originally one of the town's brothels, this 12-room B&B provides a full hot breakfast buffet in the gourmet on-site restaurant, Olivia's.

Sgt Preston's Lodge (☎ 907-983-2521; 370 6th Ave; s $75-85, d $80-90; ☒ 💻) All rooms have ground-floor entrances, and pets are allowed in certain rooms.

Near the ferry terminal is **Pullen Creek RV Park** (☎ 907-983-2768, 800-936-3731; www.pullencreekrv.com; tent/RV sites $14/24), while **Skagway Mountain View RV Park** (☎ 907-983-3333; 1450 Broadway St; tents $14, RVs $14-25) has laundry facilities. Nine miles north of Skagway is **Dyea Camping Area** (☎ 907-983-2921; free), but bring your own water.

Eating & Drinking

For breakfast, try **Sweet Tooth Café** (☎ 907-983-2405; Broadway St & 3rd Ave; $4-8; 6am-2pm; ☒) or **Corner Café** (☎ 907-983-2155; State St & 4th Ave; 6am-8pm; $5-15; ☒), which also serves satisfying seafood dinners.

Stowaway Café (☎ 907-983-3463; 205 Congress Way; lunch mains $7-12, dinner mains $16-21) Funky and fantastic, near the Harbor Master's office.

Olivia's (☎ 907-983-2289; www.skagwayinn.com; 8am-3pm; $4-11; ☒) This bistro at the Skagway Inn serves tasty snacks and lunches.

The seafood bisque is a popular choice, and the white chocolate bread pudding with rum sauce is heavenly.

Red Onion Saloon (205 Broadway St) This former brothel is now Skagway's liveliest bar.

Skagway Brewing Company (Broadway & 3rd Ave) Handcrafted beer at the Golden North Hotel.

Getting There & Away

LAB Flying Service (☎ 907-983-2471; www.labflying.com), **Wings of Alaska** (☎ 907-983-2442; www.wingsofalaska.com) and **Skagway Air** (☎ 907-983-2218; www.skagwayair.com) have regular flights between Skagway and Juneau, Haines and Glacier Bay; Skagway Air is generally cheapest, at $85, $45 and $100 respectively.

Alaska Marine Hwy ferries (☎ 907-983-2941, 800-642-0066; www.dot.state.ak.us/amhs) depart every day in summer. **Chilkat Cruises & Tours** (☎ 907-983-3277, 888-766-2103; adult/child $44/24) run twice daily to Haines.

Sourdough Car Rentals (☎ 907-983-2523; rental@aptalaska.net; Broadway & 6th Ave; 🕑 8am-5pm) charges from $50 a day.

Northbound, **Gray Line buses** (☎ 907-983-2241) depart at 8:45am daily for Whitehorse ($46).

White Pass & Yukon Railroad (☎ 800-343-7373; www.whitepassrailroad.com) goes to Fraser, British Columbia ($67), where there's a bus connection to Whitehorse ($95 for the whole trip).

SOUTHCENTRAL ALASKA

One feature that sets spectacular Southcentral Alaska apart is a road system linking many of the towns, making it one of the cheapest, most accessible and most popular areas in the state.

ANCHORAGE

Anchorage offers the comforts (and challenges) of a large US city within 30 minutes' drive of the Alaskan wilderness. Founded in 1914 as a work camp for the Alaska Railroad, the city was devastated by a 1964 earthquake. The oil boom made it an industry headquarters, and oil money has paid for the most modern amenities.

Orientation

The pedestrian-friendly downtown is arranged in a regular grid: Numbered avenues run east–west and lettered streets north–south. East of A St, street names continue alphabetically, beginning with Barrow. Many streets are irritatingly one way.

MAPS

The best city map is Rand McNally's *Anchorage* ($4), while *Anchorage's Best Trails* ($4) shows hiking, biking and ski trails through the city. The **Maps Place** (☎ 907-563-6277; 601 W 36th Ave) has topos and road maps.

Information

BOOKSTORES

Barnes & Noble (☎ 907-279-7327; 200 E Northern Lights Blvd) It'll have anything you can't find at Title Wave.

Cook Inlet Book Company (☎ 907-258-4544; 415 W 5th Ave) Downtown indie bookstore with one of the best selections of Alaska-related titles anywhere.

Title Wave Books (☎ 907-277-5127; Northern Lights Center, 1360 W Northern Lights Blvd) Huge and well-organized, specializing in used, new and bargain books.

EMERGENCY

Anchorage Police (☎ 907-786-8500; 4501 S Bragaw St) For non-emergencies.

Crisis hotline (☎ 907-276-7273) In the rare event of sexual assault, contact this 24-hour line.

Emergency number (☎ 911)

INTERNET ACCESS

Cyber Bean Internet Café (☎ 907-272-2470; 601 E Northern Lights Blvd; $6 per hour)

ZJ Loussac Public Library (☎ 907-343-2975; 3600 Denali St; free)

MEDIA

Anchorage Daily News This top-rate paper has the largest daily circulation in the state.

Anchorage Press The city's free weekly newspaper is your source for events listings and social commentary.

KRUA 88.1 For local news.

KNBA 90.3 For Native Alaskan music and current events.

MEDICAL SERVICES

Alaska Regional Hospital (☎ 907-276-1131; 2801 DeBarr Rd) For emergency care.

Physician referral service (☎ 800-265-8624) Free.

Providence Alaska Medical Center (☎ 907-562-2211; 3200 Providence Dr)

MONEY

Key Bank (☎ 907-257-5500, 800-539-2968; 601 W 5th Ave; 🕑 10am-5pm Mon-Fri) Only exchanges Canadian dollars.

ANCHORAGE IN...

Two Days

After a stick-to-yer-ribs breakfast at **Blondie's** or **Snow City Café**, hike up **Flattop Mountain** to get a lay of the land. Then let yourself wander for hours in the excellent **Anchorage Museum of History & Art**. Enjoy an evening stroll to the monuments and parks on downtown's west side before settling into one of many nearby gourmet and ethnic eating spots. Finally, join Alaskans making fun of themselves in the 'Whale-Fat Follies' at **Mr Whitekeys Fly by Nite Club**.

On the second day pack a picnic lunch, rent a bike and enjoy the views of Cook Inlet from the **Tony Knowles Coastal Trail**. Then take in the haunting ancient Alaskan songs performed at the **Alaska Native Heritage Center**. If you've got kids in tow, or even if you don't, head to either the **Imaginarium Science Discovery Center** or the outrageous **$H_2$0asis Waterpark**. Take your pick of the bars in the Spenard neighborhood for after-hours people-watching.

Wells Fargo (☎ 800-869-3557; 301 W Northern Lights Blvd; 🕒 7am-6pm Mon-Fri, closes 4pm Sat) Can exchange the most common foreign currencies.

POST

Post office (344 W 3rd Ave) This downtown post office is located at Ship Creek Center.

TOURIST OFFICES

Alaska Public Lands Information Center (☎ 907-271-2737; 605 W 4th Ave, Suite 105; 🕒 9am-5pm) Has park, trail and cabin information as well as excellent displays.

Log Cabin Visitors Center (☎ 907-274-3531, for recorded event information ☎ 907-276-3200; www.anchorage.net; 524 W 4th Ave; 🕒 7:30am-7pm) Distributes a visitor guide and walking-tour map, and lists events.

NPS Alaska Regional Office (☎ 907-644-3501; www.nps.gov/parks.html; 240 W 5th Ave, Room 114)

Sights & Activities

The **Alaska Native Heritage Center** (☎ 800-315-6608; 8800 Heritage Center Dr; adult/child $21/16; 🕒 9am-6pm) has a theater and exhibition space devoted to the history, lifestyle and arts of Native Alaskans, as well as open studios where artists carve baleen or sew skinboats. A short trail leads past a smokehouse, covered carving shed and other traditional village structures. Around the lake, in five replica village settings – Athabascan, Yupik, Inupiat, Aleut and Tlingit/Haida – people are involved in such traditional activities as splitting and drying salmon, tanning hides or building kayaks.

The impressive **Anchorage Museum of History & Art** (☎ 907-343-4326; 121 W 7th Ave; adult/child $6.50/2 🕒 9am-6pm) features Alaskan history and indigenous culture, and the **Heritage Library Museum** (☎ 907-265-2834; 301 W Northern Lights Blvd; free; 🕒 noon-5pm Mon-Fri) displays Native Alaskan costumes, weapons and artwork.

Another excellent Native Alaskan culture experience is at the **Alaska Native Medical Center** (☎ 907-563-2662; 4315 Diplomace Dr), near Tudor Rd and Boniface Parkway, which has a simply fantastic collection of art and artifacts. The 1st-floor **craft shop** (☎ 907-729-1122; 🕒 10am-2pm Mon-Fri) sells fine pieces on consignment, and most of the money goes back to the person who carved the ivory earrings, wove the baleen basket or sewed the sealskin slippers.

The **Cadastral Survey Monument** (E St & W 2nd Ave) traces Anchorage's development as a city. The **Last Blue Whale** (K St) is a very eye-catching statue. Nearby, **Captain Cook Monument** (Resolution Park) marks the 200th anniversary of Cook's visit to Cook Inlet and offers great views of the water. The wood-framed **Oscar Anderson House** (☎ 907-274-2336; Elderberry Park; adult/child $3/1; 🕒 noon-4pm) is Anchorage's only home museum.

Beautiful city parks include Earthquake Park, Russian Jack Springs Park (the Municipal Greenhouse) and the 4000-acre Far North Bi-Centennial Park, where the Hilltop Ski Area becomes a mountain biking oasis in the summer. See Anchorage for Children (p1046) for more parks.

The city is a cyclist's dream, with 122 miles of paved paths; the 11-mile Tony Knowles Coastal Trail, which begins at the west end of 2nd Ave, is the most scenic. Rent bikes at **Downtown Bicycle Rental** (☎ 907-279-5293; W 4th Ave & C St; $29 a day). Alaska's most-climbed peak is **Flattop Mountain**, a three- to five-hour hike from a trailhead on the outskirts of Anchorage. Maps are available at the Alaska Public Lands Information Center (see above).

ANCHORAGE

A B C D

1 2 3 4 5 6

INFORMATION

Alaska Public Lands Information Center.......1 B5
Alaska Regional Hospital.......2 F2
Barnes & Noble.......3 E2
Cook Inlet Book Company.......4 B6
Cyber Bean Internet Café.......5 E2
Gay & Lesbian Community Center.......6 F2
Key Bank.......7 B6
Log Cabin Visitors Center.......8 B6
NPS Alaska Regional Office.......9 C6
Providence Alaska Medical Center.......10 F2
Title Wave Books.......11 E2
Wells Fargo.......(see 21)
ZJ Loussac Public Library.......12 E3

SIGHTS & ACTIVITIES pp1043–6

Alaska Native Heritage Center.......13 H1
Alaska Native Medical Center.......14 F3
Alaska Zoo.......15 G5
Anchorage Museum of History & Art.......16 C6
Cadastral Survey Monument.......17 B5
Captain Cook Monument.......18 A5
Downtown Bicycle Rental.......19 B5
Gray Line.......20 B5
Heritage Library Museum.......21 E2
H_2Oasis Indoor Waterpark.......22 F4
Imaginarium Science Discovery Center.......(see 48)
Last Blue Whale.......23 A5
Old City Hall.......24 B6
Oscar Anderson House.......25 A5

SLEEPING pp1046–7

Anchorage Guest House.......26 E2
Aurora Winds B&B & Resort.......27 G5
B&B on the Park.......28 B6
Caribou Inn.......29 A6
Centennial Park Campground.......30 H1
Cheney Lake B&B.......31 G2
Copper Whale Inn.......32 A6
Eagle Nest Hotel.......33 D3
HI-AYH Anchorage International Hostel.......34 B6
Hotel Captain Cook.......35 A6
Lakeshore Motor Inn.......36 D3
Lion's Camper Park.......37 G2
Mahogany Manor.......38 E2
Millennium Hotel.......39 D3
Oscar Gill House.......40 A6
Snow Shoe Inn.......41 A6
Spenard Hostel.......42 D3

EATING pp1047–8

Blondie's Café.......43 B5
Cold Stone Creamery.......44 E2
Cyrano's Books & Café.......45 B6
Downtown Deli.......46 B5
Fred Meyer Supermarket.......47 F2
Glacier Brew House.......48 B6
Hogg Brothers Café.......49 E2
Jen's Restaurant.......50 E3
Marx Bros Cafe.......51 B5
Moose's Tooth Pub & Pizzeria.......52 E2
New Sagaya's City Market.......53 E2
Sack's Café.......54 B5
Snow City Café.......55 A6
Sweet Basil Café.......56 B5
Thai Kitchen.......57 F3
Twin Dragon.......58 E2

DRINKING pp1048–9

Cheechako Bar.......59 E2
Darwin's Theory.......60 B6
Humpy's.......61 B6
Mad Myrna's.......62 C6
Raven.......63 D5

ENTERTAINMENT p1049

Alley.......64 A6
Chilkoot Charlie's.......65 E2
Mr Whitekeys Fly by Nite Club.......66 E2

SHOPPING p1049

Dimond Center Mall.......67 E4
Nenana Creative Arts.......68 B6
REI.......(see 11)
Saturday Market.......69 B5

TRANSPORT p1049

Affordable Car Rental.......70 D3
Denali Car Rental.......71 E2
Transit Center.......72 B6

OTHER

Maps Place.......73 E2
University of Alaska.......74 F2

Point Woronzof
Earthquake Park
Turnagain
W Northern Lights Blvd
Lake Hood
Lake Spenard
International Airport Rd
Anchorage International Airport
Connors Lake
Raspberry Rd
Sand Lake
Point Campbell
Kincaid/Point Campbell Park
Sand Lake Rd
Jewel Lake Rd
Jewel Lake
W Dimond Blvd
Campbell Lake

0 — 400m
0 — 0.2 mi

Ship Creek
Knik Arm
Alaska Railroad
Port Access Rd
W 1st Ave
Trailhead
W 2nd Ave
Quvana Park
E 1st Ave
E 2nd Ave
E 2nd Ct
Ben Crawford Memorial Park
W 3rd Ave
E 3rd Ave
W 4th Ave
E 4th Ave
Elderberry Park
W 5th Ave
E 5th Ave
W 6th Ave
E 6th Ave
Tony Knowles Coastal Trail
W 7th Ave
City Hall
Anchorage Memorial Park Cemetery
W 8th Ave
E 8th Ave
W 9th Ave
E 9th Ave
W 10th Ave
E 10th Ave
W 11th Ave
Delaney Park
Frontierland Park
O St
N St
M St
L St
K St
I St
H St
G St
F St
E St
D St
C St
B St
A St
Barrow St
Cordova St
Fairbanks St
Gambell St
Ingra St

ALASKA

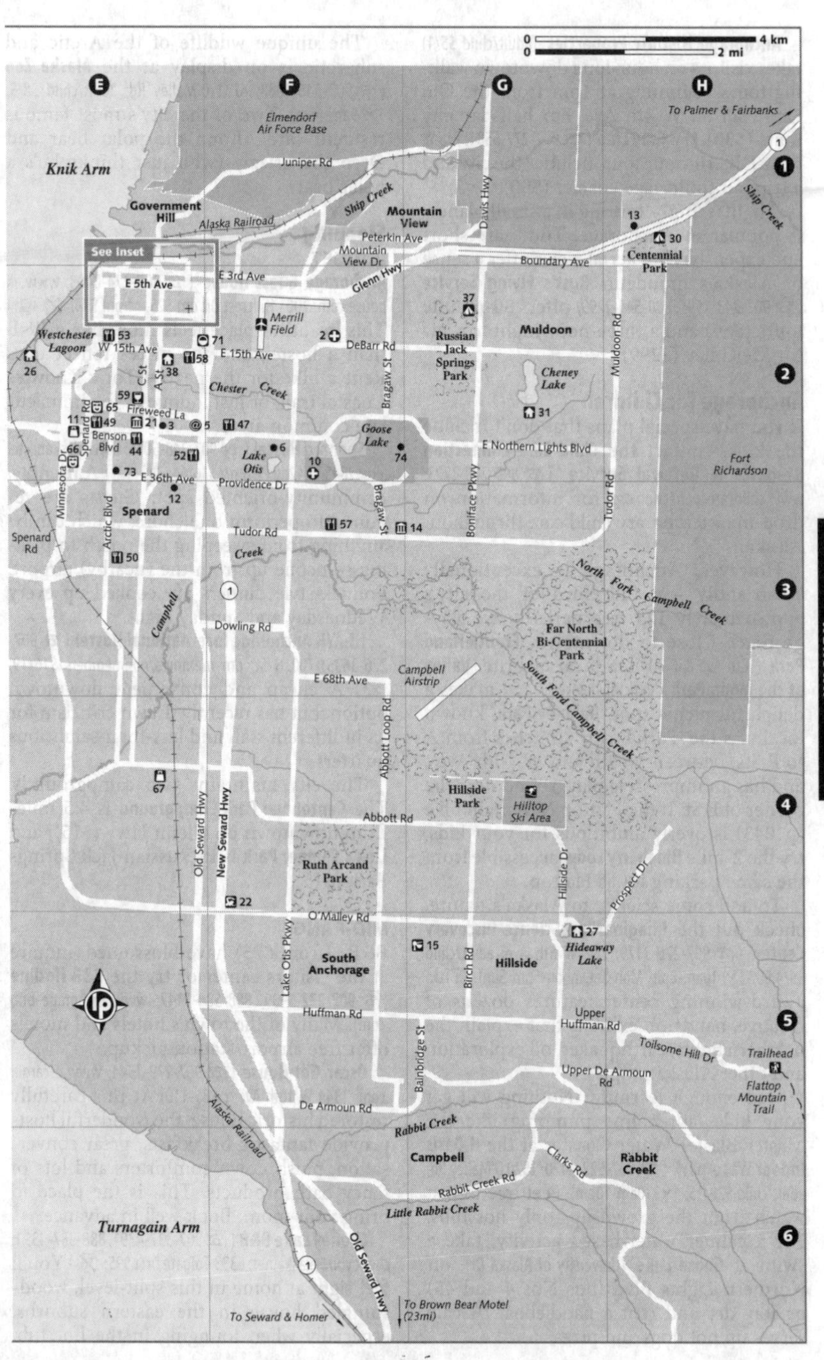

0 4 km
0 2 mi
E
F
G
H
Elmendorf Air Force Base
To Palmer & Fairbanks
Knik Arm
Juniper Rd
Ship Creek
Government Hill
Alaska Railroad
Mountain View
Davis Hwy
13
30
Centennial Park
Peterkin Ave
Mountain View Dr
See Inset
E 5th Ave
E 3rd Ave
Glenn Hwy
Boundary Ave
37
Merrill Field
Westchester Lagoon
53
W 15th Ave
71
2
DeBarr Rd
Russian Jack Springs Park
Muldoon
Muldoon Rd
E 15th Ave
38
58
26
Chester Creek
Cheney Lake
C St
A St
Spenard Rd
59
65
Fireweed La
11
49
21
3
5
47
31
Bragaw St
Benson Blvd
44
Goose Lake
Minnesota Dr
66
6
52
Lake Otis
74
E Northern Lights Blvd
Fort Richardson
73
10
E 36th Ave
Providence Dr
12
Spenard
Arctic Blvd
Boniface Pkwy
Tudor Rd
Spenard Rd
57
14
Tudor Rd
50
Creek
North Fork Campbell Creek
1
Campbell
Dowling Rd
Far North Bi-Centennial Park
South Ford Campbell Creek
E 68th Ave
Campbell Airstrip
Abbott Loop Rd
67
Hillside Park
Hilltop Ski Area
Abbott Rd
Old Seward Hwy
New Seward Hwy
Ruth Arcand Park
Hillside Dr
Prospect Dr
22
O'Malley Rd
27
Hideaway Lake
15
South Anchorage
Lake Otis Pkwy
Birch Rd
Hillside
Huffman Rd
Upper Huffman Rd
Toilsome Hill Dr
Trailhead
Flattop Mountain Trail
Bainbridge St
Upper De Armoun Rd
De Armoun Rd
Rabbit Creek
Alaska Railroad
Campbell
Clarks Rd
Rabbit Creek
Rabbit Creek Rd
Little Rabbit Creek
Turnagain Arm
Old Seward Hwy
To Brown Bear Motel (23mi)
To Seward & Homer
1
2
3
4
5
6
ALASKA

Anchorage Historic Properties (adult/child $5/1) takes visitors on hour-long downtown walking tours beginning at 1pm from the Old City Hall on W 4th Ave. For half-day city tours ($30), try **Gray Line** (☎ 907-277-5581; 745 W 4th Ave). Its 10-hour tour includes the city and a trip out to Portage Glacier ($90).

'Flightseeing' – touring in a small plane – is popular in Anchorage. Tours are short and expensive, but aerial views offer a sense of Alaska's grandeur. **Rust's Flying Service** (☎ 907-243-1595, 800-544-2299) offers 30-minute tours ($89) and a three-hour flight to view Mt McKinley ($299).

Anchorage for Children

If you have special plans that don't include the kids, contact the **Child Care Connection Resource & Referral Service** (☎ 800-278-3723; www.childcareconnection.org) for information on drop-in or temporary child care throughout Alaska.

However, Anchorage is exceptionally kid-friendly – a full third of the city's approximately 125 free parks boast playgrounds. Close to downtown, **Frontierland Park** (10th Ave & E St) is a local favorite. **Valley of the Moon Park** (Arctic Blvd & W 17th St) makes a delightful picnic spot. **Delaney Park**, known locally as the 'Park Strip,' stretches from A to P Sts, between W 9th and W 10th Aves, and has an impressive playground near the corner of E St. If the Flattop Mountain hike (p1043) is overly ambitious for your kids, try the 2-mile **Blueberry Loop**, accessible from the same parking lot as Flattop.

To add some science to Alaska's nature, check out the **Imaginarium Science Discovery Center** (☎ 907-276-3179; 737 W 5th Ave; adult/child $5/4.50; 🕓 10am-8pm Mon-Sat, noon-5pm Sun). This award-winning center features dozens of creative, hands-on exhibits that explain the northern lights, earthquakes, oil exploration and other Alaskan topics.

Had enough learning? Nothing will get your kids' adrenaline pumping like the Master Blaster Water Coaster at the **H_2Oasis Indoor Waterpark** (☎ 907-522-4420; 1520 O'Malley Rd; adult/child $20/15; 🕓 10am-10pm). Feel free to just watch from the grown-ups-only hot tubs. For a calmer water-based activity, take a swim at **Goose Lake** (University of Alaska Dr), off Northern Lights Blvd (bus Nos 4 and 45) or stay dry and rent a paddleboat. A café serves up hot dogs and pizza.

The unique wildlife of the Arctic and subarctic is on display at the **Alaska Zoo** (☎ 907-346-1088; 4731 O'Malley Rd; adult/child $8/5; 🕓 9am-6pm). Two of the city's most famous residents are Ahpun the polar bear and Oreo the grizzly (who just thinks he's a polar bear).

Sleeping

BUDGET

Anchorage Guest House (☎ 907-274-0408; www.akhouse.com; 2001 Hillcrest Dr; dm $25, r from $74; ⊠ 💻) This beautiful place feels more like a B&B than a hostel, and the prices reflect that. Rent a bike for the nearby Tony Knowles Coastal trail, or just lounge in the immaculate common areas.

Spenard Hostel (☎ 907-248-5036; www.alaskahostel.org; 2845 W 42nd Pl; dm/r $16/64; ⊠ 💻) A friendly, community-oriented spot. Guests are required to perform one chore, which can be anything from sweeping the porch to picking someone up from the (nearby) airport. Potluck-style dinners are cooked up every Wednesday and Sunday night.

HI-AYH Anchorage International Hostel (☎ 907-276-3635; 700 H St; dm members/nonmembers $16/19; ⊠) A cheap and convenient downtown option, but has recently drawn criticism for its indifferent staff and less-than-salubrious quarters.

The city maintains two campgrounds. The **Centennial Park Campground** is 4.5 miles from downtown on Glenn Hwy ($15), and **Lion's Camper Park** is in Russian Jack Springs Park ($15).

MID-RANGE

B&Bs (from $75) have blossomed; inquire at the visitors center or try the **B&B Hotline** (☎ 907-272-5909, 888-584-5147; www.anchorage-bnb.com). Many of the town's hotels and motels offer free airport/station pickup.

Oscar Gill House (☎ 907-279-1344; www.oscargill.com; 1344 W 10th Ave; r $85-110) At this carefully restored historic house, the wonderful hosts provide fantastic breakfasts, great conversation, plush down comforters and lots of fancy bath products. This is the place to bring your mom. Book well in advance.

Cheney Lake B&B (☎ 907-337-4391, 888-337-4391; cheneybb@alaska.net; 6333 Colgate Dr; r $95; ⊠) You'll feel right at home in this split-level, wood-shingled house in the eastern suburbs, especially when lounging in the hot tub.

GAY & LESBIAN ANCHORAGE

West Hollywood it ain't, but Anchorage does have a handful of gay- and lesbian-friendly bars and resources. Anchorage overall isn't particularly queer-friendly, so consider the situation carefully before revealing your sexual orientation.

The **Gay & Lesbian Community Center of Anchorage** (☎ 907-929-4528; 2110 E Northern Lights Blvd; 3-9pm Mon-Fri, noon-9pm Sat, noon-5pm Sun) has a community bulletin board and doles out lots of personal advice. It also helps organize **Anchorage Pridefest**, held in June, which includes a Queer Film Festival, Drag Queen Bingo, a parade through downtown and a party at Delaney Park. The community center also carries two good newsletters, *North View*, an Anchorage-based monthly, and the *Klondyke Kontact*, a bimonthly women's journal. Another great resource is the **Gay & Lesbian Helpline** (☎ 907-258-4777, 888-901-9876; 6pm-11pm)

Several straight bars are considered gay- and lesbian-friendly: try Cheechako Bar, the Raven (p1048), the Moose's Tooth (p1048), Mad Myrna's and the Alley (p1049).

The hosts have a small dog, but you can't bring your own.

B&B on the Park (☎ 907-277-0878, 800-353-0878; 602 W 10th Ave; r $100-111; ⊠) All five rooms in this popular 1946 restored log church have their own private bath. Family-style breakfast is served at 8am sharp, so no lollygagging in bed!

Caribou Inn (☎ 907-272-0444, 800-272-5878; 501 L St; r without/with bath $89/99; ⊠ P) Ideal downtown location, and rooms, though small and a bit worn around the edges, are definitely acceptable. Full breakfast is included.

Brown Bear Motel (☎ 907-653-7000; Mile 103 Seward Hwy; r from $48; ⊠) Well out of town, the rooms are clean, but get noisy when the adjacent Brown Bear Saloon is hopping. But they don't come any cheaper than this, folks.

Also recommended:

Eagle Nest Hotel (☎ 907-243-3433, 866-344-6835; 4110 Spenard Rd; s/d $120/160; ⊠) Two-bedroom suite with hot tub is $185.

Lakeshore Motor Inn (☎ 907-248-3485, 800-770-3000; www.lakeshoremotorinn.com; 3009 Lakeshore Dr; r $129-154; ⊠ P) Laundry facilities available. Rooms with kitchenettes $149.

Snow Shoe Inn (☎ 907-258-7669; 826 K St; r $139-169; ⊠ P) Continental breakfast included.

TOP END

Copper Whale Inn (☎ 907-258-7999; W 5th Ave & L St; r $125-185; ⊠) Just blocks from the city center, the rooms are no-frills but tidy, and the view of Cook Inlet's beluga whales is phenomenal. The innkeeper – a marine biologist – will fill you in on the inn's storied past and the area's wildlife treasures. Breakfast included.

Aurora Winds B&B & Resort (☎ 907-346-2533; www.aurorawinds.com; 7501 Upper O'Malley Rd; d $125-170; ⊠) Next to Chugach State Park, a stay here makes for a decadent reward after finishing that four-day hike. The well-run property has a theater, gourmet dining, hot tub and beautiful antique-packed rooms.

Mahogany Manor (☎ 907-278-1111, 888-777-0346; www.mahoganymanor.com; 204 E 15th Ave; d $199-249, ste $249-339; ⊠) Perched above the city, the manor is surrounded by woods that obscure the city's skyline in summer. The common areas – replete with floor-to-ceiling windows, numerous decks, huge fireplaces and 19ft whirlpool – are a tad more impressive than the rooms themselves.

Millennium Hotel (☎ 907-243-2300, 800-544-0553; 4800 Spenard Rd; r $255-270; ⊠) Four miles from downtown and right on Lake Spenard, this sprawling hotel has rustic-chic rooms and a lobby filled with stuffed bears. Babysitting service, wheelchair-accessible rooms and 24-hour room service are a few of the countless perks.

Hotel Captain Cook (☎ 907-276-6000, 800-843-1950; www.captaincook.com; W 4th Ave & K St; r $250-350) The swanky grand dame of Anchorage pampers guests with hot tubs, fitness clubs, beauty salon, Web TV and the famed **Crow's Nest Bar**. The standard rooms aren't all that amazing, though.

Eating

Anchorage boasts a variety of international cuisines you'll be hard-pressed to find in the Bush. Fill up while you can!

BUDGET

Hogg Brothers Café (☎ 907-276-9649; 1049 W Northern Lights Blvd; 6:30am-4pm; breakfast & lunch $6-8; ⊠) This bizarre, pig-obsessed joint serves

ALASKA

THE AUTHOR'S CHOICE

Snow City Café (☎ 907-272-2489; 1034 W 4th Ave; mains $4-9; 7am-9:30pm Mon-Fri, 8am-9:30pm Sat & Sun;) Serving up wholesome, slightly trendy grub, and you can get breakfast all day. The clientele is often tattooed young 'uns, but folks of all ages feel comfortable hanging out here. The bread is crusty and homemade and the cups of coffee are generous. Live music, with a $2 cover, happens most Wednesday evenings, and Sunday is open mike night.

all-day breakfasts, including 20 kinds of omelettes.

Cyrano's Books & Café (☎ 907-274-2591; 413 D St; noon-10pm Tue-Sun; meals $4-8;) Having recently expanded into Cyrano's Bookstore, Café, Cinema and Off-Center Playhouse, this is the place to lose yourself in a paperback over tempting French and Mediterranean sweets, soups, salads and wraps. Come back in the evening for entertainment of the eclectic sort.

Sweet Basil Café (☎ 907-274-0070; 335 E St; 8am-3pm Mon-Fri, 9am-4pm Sat; meals $3-10;) Inexpensive, healthy cuisine (as well as decidedly unhealthy but recommended desserts), fruit smoothies and coffee in the heart of the tourist quarter.

ALASKA

Downtown Deli (☎ 907-276-7226; 425 W 4th Ave; $5-13) This fabulous spot, owned by former governor Tony Knowles, is famed for its reindeer stew and Philly cheesesteak.

Cold Stone Creamery (2813 Dawson St) Deliciously explains why Alaskans eat more ice cream per capita than anyone else in the USA.

New Sagaya's City Market (3900 W 13th Ave) Specializing in Asian fare, this eclectic upscale grocery store stocks lots of organic goodies and has a great deli. There's another location at 3700 Old Seward Hwy.

Fred Meyer supermarket (1000 E Northern Lights Blvd) The widest selection and best prices in town.

MID-RANGE

Blondie's Café (☎ 907-279-0968; 333 W 4th Ave; breakfast $5-8, lunch & dinner mains $8-18;) Has an Iditarod theme, huge breakfasts (served till 5pm) and a liquor license. Open around the clock.

Sack's Café (☎ 907-276-3546; 328 G St; 11am-3pm & 5pm-10pm; lunch $9-13, dinner mains $18-31;) Call it Asian/Mediterranean/Alaskan fusion. Lunch items include the vegetarian marinated-olive sandwich, Thai chicken sandwich and chicken or halibut curry. For dinner try the popular chicken and Alaskan scallops with shiitake mushrooms and Asian black bean salsa.

Moose's Tooth Pub & Pizzeria (☎ 907-258-2537; 3300 Old Seward Hwy; $6-20;) Take your pick from the impressive menu of veg, meat or seafood pizzas. Wash your pizza down with one of the award-winning brews on tap.

Twin Dragon (☎ 907-276-7535; 612 E 15th Ave;) The all-you-can-eat Mongolian barbeque buffet is a bargain at $8 and $12 for lunch and dinner respectively. The Chinese food is tasty, too.

Thai Kitchen (☎ 907-561-0082; 3405 Tudor Rd; 11am-3pm & 5pm-9pm; mains $7-10;) This kid-friendly place comes highly recommended, with more than 100 items on the menu, dozens of which are vegetarian. The Thai platter is an excellent sampler.

TOP END

Marx Bros Cafe (☎ 907-278-2133; 627 W 3rd Ave; mains $27-50; dinner;) Soak up the views of Cook Inlet while enjoying fine dining with all the trimmings: white tablecloths; stemware filled with your choice of 500 vintages; macadamia-crusted halibut; and Van's justly famous Caesar salad.

Jen's Restaurant (☎ 907-561-5367; 701 W 36th Ave; lunch $10-17, dinner $20-30;) Innovative, Scandinavian-accented cuisine emphasizing fresh ingredients and elaborate presentation. There's also a tapas bar. Closed Sunday, no dinner Monday, no lunch Saturday.

Glacier Brew House (☎ 907-274-2739; 737 W 5th Ave; dinner $16-22;) Sample handcrafted beers, slurp down seafood pastas and gnaw on wood-grilled chops and ribs.

Drinking

Raven (☎ 907-276-9672; 708 E 4th Ave) At this well-lit but smoky neighborhood hangout, mingle with the locals over a game of pool. The perfect place to kick off your evening.

Cheechako Bar (☎ 907-274-6132; 317 W Fireweed Lane) This Irish-themed pub has pool tables and the occasional jam session in the evening.

Darwin's Theory (426 G St) People-watching is the activity of choice at this favorite local bar, with free popcorn and a good mixed crowd. Women can ask about discounts on souvenir T-shirts.

Entertainment

Check the *Anchorage Press* and Friday's *Anchorage Daily News* for the latest entertainment listings.

Mr Whitekeys Fly by Nite Club (☎ 907-279-7726; 3300 Spenard Rd; ⊠) Best known for the lowbrow but uproarious 'Whale-Fat Follies' musical act ($12 to $18, reservations required). It also features jazz, blues and rock.

Mad Myrna's (☎ 907-276-9762; 530 E 5th Ave; $3 cover on weekends; ⊠) A fun, cruisy bar with line dancing Thursday, drag shows on Friday and dance music most other nights after 9pm.

Chilkoot Charlie's (2435 Spenard Rd) 'Koots', as locals call this beloved landmark, is big and brash, with multiple bars and dance floors. It claims to sell more Red Bull than any other venue in the country.

Alley (☎ 907-646-2222; 900 W 5th Ave; $3 cover) Has a dance floor presided over by Anchorage DJs spinning techno, trance and hip-hop.

Humpy's (☎ 907-276-2337; 610 W 6th Ave) Fronts live music nightly around 9pm, running the gamut from acoustic folk to ska to disco retrospective. It has more than 40 beers on tap.

Shopping

Dimond Center Mall (☎ 907-344-2581; 800 E Dimond Blvd; ⏲ 10am-9pm Mon-Fri, 10am-7pm Sat, noon-8pm Sun) Pretty much every consumer item you'd need. Take bus No 1, 2 or 9.

Saturday Market (☎ 907-272-5634; www.anchoragemarkets.com; W 3rd Ave & E St; ⏲ 10am-6pm Sat) A fantastic place for souvenir shopping and cheap food.

Nenana Creative Arts (☎ 907-278-6748; 610 C St) A Native Alaskan cooperative where you can watch artists work on ivory, soapstone and other materials.

There are scores of wilderness outfitters, but **REI** (☎ 907-272-4565; 1200 W Northern Lights Blvd) has a huge selection of backpacking, kayaking and camping gear. For clothes, avoid the gift shops and head for the **University of Alaska Bookstore** (☎ 907-786-1151; 2905 Providence Dr), which has an interesting selection you won't find anywhere else.

Getting There & Around

Anchorage International Airport has frequent inter- and intrastate flights. **Alaska Airlines** (☎ 800-252-7522; www.alaskaair.com) flies to 19 Alaskan towns, including Fairbanks, Juneau, Nome and Barrow. **Era Aviation** (☎ 800-866-8394; www.flyera.com) flies to Cordova, Valdez, Kodiak and Homer. **Pen Air** (☎ 800-448-4226) serves southwest Alaska.

Downtown Connection (☎ 907-344-6667) runs between the airport and downtown ($6) and between the railroad station and downtown ($3). At the time of research, the railroad spur to connect the airport with the Alaska Railroad system was under construction but not yet complete.

Affordable Car Rental (☎ 907-243-3370, 800-248-3765; 4707 Spenard Rd) advertises economy-size cars from $39 per day. **Denali Car Rental** (☎ 907-276-1230; 1209 Gambell St; ⏲ 8am-6pm Mon-Fri, 9am-5pm Sat, 10am-4pm Sun) also has subcompacts for $37 with 150 miles included. Summer rentals are heavily booked.

Parks Hwy Express (☎ 888-600-6001) goes to Fairbanks ($79) via Denali ($59), Dawson City in Canada ($219), Valdez ($163) and Tok ($133). **Seward Bus Lines** (☎ 907-563-0800; www.sewardbuslines.com) goes to Seward ($40), while **Homer Stage Lines** (☎ 907-868-3914) will take you to Homer ($50).

Alaska Railroad (☎ 907-265-2494, 800-544-0552) goes south to Whittier ($45) and Seward ($59), and north to Denali ($125) and Fairbanks ($175).

People Mover (☎ 907-343-6543) is the local bus service; its main terminal is at the **Transit Center** (W 6th Ave & G St).

Around Anchorage

Seward Hwy runs south of Anchorage, carved into the mountainside beside the water and passing numerous scenic lookouts. At Portage, a short railroad/toll road runs to Whittier for the ferry to Valdez. South of Portage, Portage Glacier Access Rd leads 5 miles to a **visitors center** (☎ 907-783-2326) overlooking the magnificent **Portage Glacier**. **Gray Line** (☎ 907-277-5581) offers hour-long cruises near the glacier ($25). There are two USFS campgrounds along Portage Glacier Rd: **Black Bear Campground** (sites $10) and **Williwaw Campground** (1/2 people $12/18).

North of Anchorage, Glenn Hwy runs 13 miles to Eagle River Rd, a beautiful mountainside trip. The **Eagle River Nature Center** (☎ 907-694-2108; 32750 Eagle River Rd; Ⓟ $5; ⏲ 10am-5pm) offers wildlife displays and scenic hiking. Near Palmer, 35 miles north, Hatcher Pass is an alpine paradise, with hiking, parasailing, gold-rush artifacts and panoramas of the Takeetna Mountains. Stay at **Hatcher Pass Lodge** (☎ 907-745-5897; www.hatcherpasslodge.com; Mile 17.5 Hatcher Pass Rd; r $95, cabin $115-125; ☒) or **Motherlode Lodge** (☎ 907-745-6171, 877-745-6171; www.motherlodelodge.com; Mile 14 Hatcher Pass Rd; r $99; ☒). Both have restaurants.

KENAI PENINSULA

With its diverse terrain and accessibility to Anchorage, Kenai is a top recreational area and can get incredibly crowded, especially in the fishing season. In fact, some say the tourism board has been overselling the salmon experience, and visitors would be better off taking advantage of the endless backpacking, hiking and kayaking opportunities.

Seward

This scenic town is flanked by rugged mountains and overlooks salmon-filled Resurrection Bay. Founded in 1903 as an ice-free port at the southern end of the Alaska Railroad, Seward prospered as the beginning of the gold-rush trail to Nome.

The downtown **visitors center** (www.seward.net/chamber; Jefferson St & 3rd Ave; 🕑 9am-5pm) is in a Pullman railroad car. There's also a **USFS office** (☎ 907-224-3374; 4th Ave & Jefferson St; 🕑 8am-5pm Mon-Fri) The **Seward Library** (☎ 907-224-3646; 238 5th Ave) offers free Internet access. The **Kenai Fjords National Park Visitors center** (☎ 907-224-3175; 1212 4th Ave; 🕑 8am-7pm) has information on hiking and paddling.

SIGHTS & ACTIVITIES

Alaska SeaLife Center (☎ 907-224-3080, 800-224-2525; 301 Railway Ave; adult/child $13/10; 🕑 8am-8pm) is the only cold-water marine-science facility in the western hemisphere, and ranks as one of the top attractions on the Kenai Peninsula. Watch puffins, otters and 1000-pound Stellar sea lions glide past viewing windows. Plan to spend the better part of one of your best afternoons here.

Seavey's Iditaride (☎ 907-224-8607, 800-478-3139; Exit Glacier Rd; adult/child $40/20; 🕑 8:30am-7pm) is cheesy but, hey, this is where the Iditarod started. After touring the kennels, you'll be taken on a 20-minute training run – in summer, in a wheeled cart – with the dogs. Beforehand, junior mushers discuss their experiences with subzero sleep depravation and delicate doggy feet.

There's great hiking close to town. The **Mt Marathon Trail** is a 3-mile round-trip to spectacular views on the mountain overlooking Seward. The trail for **Caines Head State Recreation Area** is just south of town and leads to a military base left over from WWII.

Rent kayaks at **Kayak & Custom Adventures** (☎ 907-224-3960, 800-288-3134; 328 3rd Ave).

SLEEPING

Van Gilder Hotel (☎ 800-204-6835; www.vangilderhotel.com; 308 Adams St; d with shared/private bath $105/$135, ste $185; ☒) A historic (1916) hotel, which means two things: tiny rooms and lots of ghosts. Gossips say poltergeists haunt the 1st floor and some employees won't go in the laundry room at night; on-the-clock staff refused to confirm either way.

Farm B&B (☎ 907-224-5691; www.alaskan.com/thefarm; Mile 0.3 Salmon Creek Rd; r $75-100, cottages $90; ☒) Indulge your sylvan fantasies in this sprawling family farmhouse, just off Exit Glacier Rd. Choose a room in the house, rent the top two rooms together as an incredible suite ($170), or curl up in one of the cottages nestled on the wooded property.

Whistle Stop Lodging (☎ 907-224-5050; www.sewardak.net/ws; 411 Port Ave; d $115; ☒). This may be your only chance to sleep in a WWII-era railroad car. The rooms are lackluster, but offer excellent views of the bustling marina and Mt Marathon. A kitchenette costs $10 extra.

Motels in the Small Boat Harbor area include **Murphy's Motel** (☎ 907-224-8090; 911 4th Ave; r $100-140; ☒) and better **Breeze Inn** (☎ 907-224-5237; 1306 Seward Hwy; s/d from $120/130; ☒).

Also recommended:

Moby Dick Hostel (☎ 907-224-7072; 432 3rd Ave; dm $17, r $45-60; ☒) Friendly staff, well located and clean enough for seasoned budget travelers.

Snow River Hostel (☎ 907-440-1907; Mile 16 Seward Hwy; dm/d $15/40; ☒) Out of town but highly recommended for its sauna and wood-fired stove.

Waterfront Campground (☎ 907-224-3331; Ballaine Blvd; tent/RV sites $8/12; ☒) Between downtown and the boat harbor.

EATING & DRINKING

Terry's Fish & Chips (☎ 907-224-8807; 1210 4th Ave; $3-9; ☒) Rated the best cheapie fish stand at the harbor; open 24 hours.

Ray's Waterfront (☎ 907-224-5606; 1316 4th Ave; 🕑 6:30am-10:30pm; breakfast & lunch $6-15, dinner mains $17-24; ☒) The best seafood in town,

SPRUCE BARK BEETLES: SCOURGE OF THE KENAI PENINSULA *Paige R Penland*

The spruce bark beetle (*Dendroctonus rufipennis Kirby*) has been part of the Alaskan ecosystem for thousands of years, raising clutches of 1500 eggs apiece inside trees long past their prime. It was part of the great cycle, and survival meant flooding the nests with thick sap, forcing the eggs to the surface, an investment of water and energy some simply could not muster.

Infected trees weaken in the first year, their needles becoming brittle and red as growing larvae devour their soft vascular tissues, denying them sustenance. By the second summer, they are reduced to gray skeletons, allowing light to reach tender saplings on the forest floor. And so it was, by the efforts of this tiny beetle, that the forest remained healthy and green.

Then, in the late 1980s, something went terribly awry in the far southwestern corner of the Kenai Peninsula. Some blame fire suppression, while others point to global warming: long, dry summers unlike any this land has seen since the last ice age. The official line, halfheartedly repeated by USFS rangers, is that even this horror is part of the natural cycle.

Every 250 years, they say (though evidence is sketchy at best), the beetles receive some cosmic mandate to take down Alaska's spruce forests entirely. Their maturation period shortens, their numbers grow, and on that one day every spring when untold millions take flight simultaneously, another 50,000 acres will fall. And so the spruce trees have been making room for alder and birch, beloved by moose, ptarmigan and Arctic hare: 'Nature is not being destroyed,' explained one park ranger, 'it is simply changing.'

Dead trees cannot decay quickly here – it is simply too cold for termites and their ilk. Thus, thousands of acres of kindling surround villages and homes. When the fire comes – no one says 'if' – it will be enormous.

Be careful, then, with your campfires and cigarettes. Do not transport wood outside the hot zones.

also boasting legendary breakfast casseroles and a picture-perfect view.

Sue's Teriyaki (☎ 907-224-4593; 303 S Harbor St; $6-13; ⊠) It may not look like much, but the kim chee is great and the sushi even better.

Yukon Bar (☎ 907-224-3063; 4th Ave & Washington St) and **Tony's Bar** (☎ 907-224-3045; 135 4th Ave) have live music and can get loud at night. Head to **Resurrect Art Gallery & Coffee House** (☎ 907-224-7161; 320 3rd Ave; ⊠) for a latte and a quieter atmosphere, though Tuesday is acoustic night.

GETTING THERE & AWAY

From the **ferry terminal** (☎ 907-224-5485), ferries go to Kodiak ($64), Valdez ($68) and Homer ($113) every few days. **Seward Bus Lines** (☎ 907-224-3608; www.sewardbuslines.com) runs daily to Anchorage ($40). **Alaska Railroad** (☎ 800-544-0552) takes a spectacular daily route to Anchorage ($59).

Kenai Fjords National Park

South of Seward is Kenai Fjords National Park. The park's main features are the 917-sq-mile Harding Icefield and the tidewater glaciers that calve into the sea. **Exit Glacier**, at the end of Exit Glacier Rd, is the most popular attraction. There's a visitors center and a paved, 0.25-mile trail to a glacier overlook. Hikers can climb a difficult 5 miles to the edge of the ice field – worth it for spectacular views. The best marine-wildlife cruises in the state are the tour boats that run into Kenai Fjords past calving glaciers. The park visitors center is in Seward (opposite).

Major Marine Tours (☎ 907-224-8030, 800-764-7300; www.alaskaone.com/mmt) offers a half-day Resurrection Bay tour (adult/child $69/34) and a full-day tour viewing Holgate Arm ($109/54), both of which include a national park ranger on every boat. The latter tour is a local favorite.

Sterling Hwy

This paved route (Hwy 1) makes an arc around the peninsula, and a side road heads north to the quaint old mining town of **Hope**. The main road goes east, past the Kenai National Wildlife Refuge, where you might see wildlife and a plague of anglers. Turn north to **Kenai**, with good views and some Russian history, and continue to Captain Cook Strait Recreation Area, which is off the fishing circuit. South of Soldotna, the scenic highway hugs the coastline, passing through small villages with campgrounds and great clamming beaches. Scenic **Ninilchik** has a Russian accent, and **HI Eagle Watch Hostel** (☎ 907-567-3905; Mile 3 Oil Well Rd; members/nonmembers $10/13 with own sleeping bag; ⊠) is 3 miles east in a gorgeous rural setting.

Homer

Charming, colorful Homer, at the end of Sterling Hwy, sits on beautiful Kachemak Bay amid awe-inspiring mountains. The town attracted alternative types, starting in the 1960s, and is now home to artists and aging hippies. The **visitors center** (☎ 907-235-7740; www.homeralaska.org; 135 Sterling Hwy; 9am-7pm Mon-Fri, 10am-6pm Sat & Sun) has courtesy phones to book rooms or tours. The **library** (☎ 907-235-3180; 141 W Pioneer Ave) has Internet access.

SIGHTS & ACTIVITIES

The **Pratt Museum** (☎ 907-235-8635; 3779 Bartlett St; adult/child $6/3; 10am-6pm) features the best display anywhere on the *Exxon Valdez* oil spill, plus Native Alaskan artifacts and marine-life exhibits.

Homer Spit is a 4.5-mile sand bar with clamming, beach camping and a small boat harbor. The best hiking is along the beaches, particularly the Shoreline Rte west of Main St, and across Kachemak Bay at Kachemak Bay State Park.

SLEEPING

B&Bs have mushroomed all over town. Call **Homer's Finest B&B Network** (☎ 907-235-4983, 800-764-3211; www.homeraccommodations.com) or **Cabins & Cottages Network** (☎ 907-235-0191; www.cabinsinhomer.com).

Old Town B&B (☎ 907-235-7558; www.xyz.net/~oldtown; 106 W Bunnell St; r $70-85; ⊠) A classy and friendly number with a trippy staircase and beautiful rooms with great views to boot.

Driftwood Inn (☎ 907-235-8019, 800-478-8019; 435 W Bunnell Ave; tent/RV sites $15/29, s $55-100, d $65-130; ⊠) Quiet yet centrally located, it has rooms from tiny 'ship quarters' to large, lovely rooms with all the amenities. Fall asleep to the sound of the waves.

Room at the Harbor (☎ 907-235-1359; 235-8480; Homer Spit Rd; s/d $70/80; ⊠) Contains one beautiful room at the heart of the Spit.

Skyline B&B (☎ 907-235-3832; 60855 Skyline Dr; r $85-115) Features beautiful views of Grewingk Glacier.

Chocolate Drop Inn (☎ 907-235-3668, 800-530-6015; www.chocolatedropinn.com; r from $130) A stunning log cabin with an outdoor hot tub and inside sauna.

Seaside Farms (☎ 907-235-7850; 40904 Seaside Farms Rd; dm $15, r $40-50, cabin $55) This hostel, 5 miles east of E End Rd, is more like Burning Man than a regulation youth hostel. Staying here can be an experience.

There's (often rowdy) beach camping at **Homer Spit Public Campground** (Homer Spit Rd; tent/RV sites $6/10) but **Karen Hornaday Memorial Campground** (Bartlett St; tent/RV sites $6/10) is a better bet for families.

EATING & DRINKING

Two Sisters Bakery (☎ 907-235-2280; 106 W Bunnell Ave; light meals $4-9; ⊠) One of Homer's many excellent coffee houses, with tables on a porch overlooking the bay.

Smoky Bay Natural Foods (☎ 907-235-7252; 248 W Pioneer Ave) A co-op with organic veggies, groceries, herbs, a great bulk-foods selection and a **deli** ($3-9; 11am-3pm) with soups, quiche and healthy mains daily.

Glacier Drive-In (☎ 907-235-7148; Homer Spit Rd; $2-9; ⊠) is one of the better cheap eateries, while nearby is the **Salty Dawg Saloon** (Homer Spit Rd), Homer's best-known watering hole.

Café Cups (☎ 907-235-8330; 162 W Pioneer Ave; lunch $7-10; dinner $16-20) With a bizarre coffee-cup exterior and pleasant interior, it does creative fine dining – silver salmon with strawberry pico de gallo, for instance – served with scores of different wines and 23 types of hot sauce.

Homestead (☎ 907-235-8723; Mile 8.2 E End Rd; dinner mains $21-40; 5pm-10pm; ⊠) The finest restaurant in Homer. You must make a reservation to enjoy the steaks, king crab and Sonoran seafood stew, alongside any brilliant choice from the eclectic wine list.

GETTING THERE & AWAY

Era Aviation (☎ 907-235-7565, 800-866-8394) flies frequently from Anchorage ($110). The ferry **Tustumena** (☎ 907-235-8449) goes twice weekly to Seldovia ($21) and Kodiak ($54). **Polar Car Rental** (☎ 800-876-6417; 455 Sterling Hwy; 24hr) rents subcompacts for $75 a day. It also has a desk at the airport. **Kachemak Bay Transit** (☎ 877-235-9101) and **Homer Stage Lines** (☎ 907-235-2252) provide bus service to Anchorage ($50).

ALASKA

PRINCE WILLIAM SOUND

Prince William Sound is the northern extent of the Gulf of Alaska, flanked by mountains and featuring abundant wildlife, including whales, sea lions, harbor seals, otters, eagles and bears. Bring your raincoat – annual rainfall averages more than 100 inches. Alaska Marine Hwy ferries link Cordova, Valdez, Whittier and Seward.

Whittier

At the western end of Prince William Sound, Whittier was built by the military as a WWII warm-water port. Rail tunnels were drilled west through solid rock to connect with the main line of the Alaska Railroad. In 2000 the tunnel was converted to handle vehicles also, and many see Whittier booming with visitors and tour groups in the future. At the time of research, the proposed full-service visitors center had yet to begin construction.

Anchor Inn (☎ 907-472-2354; 100 Whittier St; r $83; ⊠) and **Sportsman Inn** (☎ 907-472-2352; 888 Frontier St; d $75) offer food and drink. Camp at **Glacier View Campground** ($5).

A train leaves Whittier daily for Anchorage ($45). The MV *Bartlett* ferry goes east to Valdez and Cordova six times weekly.

Valdez

Just 25 miles east of Columbia Glacier, the ice-free port of Valdez is the southern terminus of the Trans-Alaska Pipeline. Bustling Small Boat Harbor has a pleasant boardwalk and scenic mountain backdrop – excellent at night.

Valdez first boomed when 4000 gold seekers passed through, heading for the Klondike. After the 1964 earthquake the city was rebuilt 4 miles further east. The **visitors center** (☎ 907-835-4636, 800-770-5954; www.valdezalaska.org; 200 Fairbanks Dr; ⏲ 8am-7pm Mon-Fri, 9am-6pm Sat, noon-5pm Sun) has area information and courtesy phones to book accommodations. The **library** (☎ 907-835-4632; 212 Fairbanks St) has Internet access.

SIGHTS & ACTIVITIES

Though the *Exxon Valdez* oil spill was an environmental disaster, the cleanup created a cash bonanza, especially for opportunists who became known as the 'spillionaires.' The **Valdez Museum** (☎ 907-835-2764; 217 Egan Dr; adult/child $3/2; ⏲ 9am-6pm Mon-Sat, 8am-5pm Sun) is packed with displays, including oil-spill exhibits and a model of the pipeline.

The magnificent **Columbia Glacier** is retreating, but its 3-mile-wide face can be seen from Alaska Marine Hwy ferries going to or from Whittier. For a longer and much closer look, contact **Prince William Sound Cruises & Tours** (☎ 907-265-4500, 800-992-1297; www.princewilliamsound.com; 101 N Harbor Dr; adult/child $109/54), the town's largest tour operator, which runs six-hour boat tours.

Eight miles from town, along Richardson Hwy, Dayville Rd and scenic Solomon Gulch is the remarkable **Trans-Alaska Pipeline terminal**. It once welcomed visitors, but since September 11, 2001, all access is closed to the public. Drat.

There are few developed hiking trails in the area and no USFS office. Paddling, however, has more potential. **Keystone Raft & Kayak Adventures** (☎ 907-835-2606, 800-328-8460; www.alaskawhitewater.com; $75) runs 1½-hour Lowe River raft trips. Shoup Bay offers a popular overnight kayak trip amid icebergs, seals and other sea life; **Anadyr Adventures** (☎ 907-835-2814, 800-865-2925; www.anadyradventures.com; 225 Harbor Dr; s/d $45/65 per day) rents kayaks and offers guided day trips.

SLEEPING

There are more than 30 B&Bs around town, charging about $60/75 single/double; the visitors center has listings and a speed-dial phone.

Downtown Inn (☎ 800-835-2791; 113 Galina Dr; r with shared bath from $85; ⊠) Rooms are clean and basic and breakfast is included.

Headhunters Inn (☎ 907-835-2900; 328 Egan Dr; r with shared bath $75-159; ⊠) Perfect downtown location.

Bear Paw RV Campground (☎ 907-835-2530; 101 N Harbor Dr; tent/RV sites $17/22) Cute wooded campsites near Small Boat Harbor.

EATING

Totem Inn Restaurant (☎ 907-835-4443; 144 E Egan Dr; breakfast & lunch $4-9, dinner $15-30; ⊠) The best breakfast in town; you can find decent burgers and seafood the rest of the day.

Alaskan Halibut House (☎ 907-835-2788; 208 Meals Ave; $2-9; ⊠) has halibut, chips and salad, **Mike's Palace** (☎ 907-835-2365; 201 N Harbor Dr; $4-16; ⊠) specializes in pasta and seafood, while **Fu Kung** (☎ 907-835-5255; 207 Kobuk St; $7-15; ⊠) has killer Chinese.

GETTING THERE & AWAY

Era Aviation (☎ 907-266-8394, 800-866-8394; www.flyera.com) flies daily to Anchorage for between $130 and $165, depending on when you book. **Alaska Marine Hwy ferries** (☎ 907-835-4436) sail regularly to Whittier ($65), Seward ($65), Homer ($155) and Cordova ($34).

Cordova

At the eastern end of the sound, this beautiful little town's population of 2600 doubles in summer as fishing and cannery workers arrive.

First settled by the nomadic Eyak, who lived on the enormous salmon runs, Cordova became a fish-packing center in 1889. The **chamber of commerce** (☎ 907-424-7260; www.cordovachamber.com; 1st Ave; 10am-5pm Tue-Fri, 10am-2pm Sat & Mon) has pamphlets and tips, but the **library** (☎ 907-424-6667; 622 1st Ave; 1-8pm Tue-Fri, 1-5pm Sat) has the most useful visitor information, including B&B listings. The **USFS office** (☎ 907-424-7661; 612 2nd St; 8am-5pm Mon-Fri) has free maps to hiking trails accessible from the road.

The interesting **Cordova Museum** (☎ 907-424-6666; 622 1st Ave; admission $1; 10am-6pm Mon-Sat, 2-4pm Sun), in the Centennial Building, offers cassettes for self-guided town tours and will store your pack during the day. It has displays on history, marine life and mining.

Activity centers on the small boat harbor during summer. **Mt Eyak ski area** (☎ 907-424-7766; 6th St), east of town, has a vintage chairlift ($7) to a wonderful panorama. The most stunning scenery, which includes **Childs Glacier** calving into the Copper River, is along the 50-mile Copper River Hwy. **Alaska River Rafters** (☎ 907-424-7238, 800-776-1864; www.alaskarafters.com) operate rafting and kayaking trips in the area; guided half-day trips are from $75.

Prince William Sound Motel (☎ 907-424-3201, 888-796-6835; 502 2nd St; s/d $80/90; ☒) has huge, clean rooms, while **Reluctant Fisherman Inn** (☎ 907-424-3272, 800-770-3272; r $95-135; ☒) is as close to luxurious as Cordova gets.

Alaskan Hotel & Bar (☎ 907-424-3288; 600 1st St; r with shared/private bath $40/60; ☒) is a bit tattered but a decent choice.

You'll find **Odiak Camper Park** (☎ 907-424-6200; Whitshed Rd; tent/RV sites $5/18) half a mile east of town, but it can be dismal.

Don't pass up **Baja Taco Wagon** (☎ 907-424-5599; Harbor Loop; $6-11), a funky, converted school bus across from the harbor; this is the place to enjoy some of the best tacos north of San Diego.

Killer Whale Café (☎ 907-424-7733; 507 1st St; $7-10; ☒) has sandwiches with a view, and the **Cookhouse Café** (1 Cannery Row), formerly a cannery canteen, serves pancakes, pastries and $13 seafood dinners. **Powder House Bar** (Mile 1.5 Copper River Hwy) features folk and country music along with its grub and drinks.

Alaska Airlines (☎ 907-424-7151, 800-252-7522) flies daily from Anchorage ($120). In summer, the MV *Bartlett* ferry arrives every couple of days from Valdez ($34) or Whittier ($65). Rent a car at **Reluctant Fisherman Inn** (☎ 907-424-3272, 800-770-3272) for $75.

Wrangell-St Elias National Park

Part of a 31,250-sq-mile wilderness area, this park is a crossroads of mountain ranges: Wrangell, Chugach and St Elias. Extensive ice fields and 100 major glaciers spill from the peaks.

From Valdez, the Richardson Hwy is a jaw-droppingly scenic route to Glennallen, past canyons, mountain passes and glaciers. The Wrangell-St Elias National Park **visitors center** (☎ 907-822-7440; www.nps.gov/wrst; Mile 106.8 Richardson Hwy; 8am-6pm) is in Copper Center.

A side road at Tonsina goes east to Chitina, which has the last place to fill up your tank. Nearby are a gas station, grocery store, two restaurants and some campgrounds. From there, the rugged Mt McCarthy Rd follows former railroad tracks 60 miles east through the stunning Chugach Mountains and across the mighty Copper River to historic McCarthy. You can park a mile before McCarthy and cross the Kennicott River footbridge to the abandoned copper-mining town of Kennicott, in the national park.

McCarthy & Kennicott

Scenic and funky little McCarthy was the Wild West counterpart to the Kennicott company town.

In 1900 miners discovered the rich Kennicott copper deposit, and a syndicate built 196 miles of railroad through the wilderness to take the ore to Cordova. For 30 years Kennicott worked around the clock but in 1938 management closed the mine, giving workers two hours to catch the last train out. Despite some pilferage, Kennicott remains a remarkably preserved piece of US mining history.

Pick up a copy of the walking-tour map ($1) at the NPS visitors center on the main road.

There's some good hiking around the glaciers, peaks and mines, as well as rafting on the Kennicott River. **St Elias Alpine Guides** (☎ 907-345-9048; www.steliasguides.com) offers day trips from McCarthy. **Wrangell Mountain Air** (☎ 907-554-4411, 800-478-1160; www.wrangellmountainair.com) offers a variety of scenic flight tours, the cheapest of which is $60. **McCarthy Air** (☎ 907-544-4440; www.mccarthyair.com) can also fly you into McCarthy from Chitina.

Kennicott River Lodge & Hostel (☎ 907-554-4441; www.ptialaska.net/~grosswlr; dm/cabin/ste $28/100/150; ⊠) sports a 12-person sauna on the river's west bank. **Ma Johnson's Hotel** (☎ 907-554-4402; s/d $100/140; ⊠), in a renovated 1916 building, offers round-trip transport from the footbridges and a wholesome breakfast. There's also **Kennicott Glacier Lodge** (within Alaska ☎ 800-478-2350, outside the state ☎ 800-582-5128; s/d $149/169). **McCarthy Lodge** (☎ 907-554-4402; breakfast $10, lunch $5-9, dinner $20-25; ⊠) is run by the same folks as Ma Johnson's, offering outstanding meals, showers ($5) and cold beer ($4).

Backcountry Connections (☎ 907-822-5292, 866-582-5292; www.alaska-backcountry-tours.com) buses leave Glennallen most days for McCarthy via Chitina ($70). In McCarthy there's a five-hour layover to visit Kennicott; this long day trip costs $99.

KODIAK ISLAND

Southwest of Kenai Peninsula, Kodiak Island is most famous for Kodiak brown bears, which grow huge gorging on salmon. Accommodations and transport are expensive, but camping gear and a mountain bike can make Kodiak affordable.

The **visitors center** (☎ 907-486-4782, 800-789-4782; www.kodiak.org; 100 Marine Way; ⏲ 8am-5pm Mon-Fri, 10am-4pm Sat & Sun) has lists of accommodations (including 20 B&Bs). The **Homes Johnson Library** (☎ 907-486-8686; 319 Lower Mill Rd) has free Internet access.

Bear watching is best July to September but usually involves a charter flight to a remote salmon stream ($300 to 500 a person). **Mythos Expeditions Kodiak** (☎ 907-486-5536; www.ptialaska.net/~mythosdk/mythos) rents kayaks (from $65) and offers superb guided day trips.

Kodiak B&B (☎ 907-486-5367; www.ptialaskanet/~monroe; 308 Cope St; s/d $80/90; ⊠) Convenient to downtown with two clean rooms, a friendly owner and pleasant views.

Alaska Airlines (☎ 800-426-0333) has two flights and **Era** (☎ 907-487-4363, 800-866-8394) has five flights daily from Anchorage. The ferry **MV Tustumena** (☎ 907-486-3800) connects Kodiak three times weekly with Homer ($54) and Seward ($64).

THE INTERIOR

The great big broad land of Alaska's Interior is a central plateau drained by great rivers and bordered by the rugged Alaska Range to the south and the Brooks Range to the north. Alaska's major highways (rarely more than two-lane roads) crisscross the region.

The main route is George Parks Hwy (Hwy 3), which winds 358 miles from Anchorage to Fairbanks, passing Denali National Park. The Alaska Hwy (Hwy 2) extends southeast from Fairbanks via Delta Junction and Tok to become the Alcan Hwy, connecting to Haines Junction and Whitehorse. All the Interior roads are lined with turnoffs, campgrounds, hiking trails and wildlife-spotting possibilities. Towns are small service centers with gas stations, motels and cafés, but a few have retained their rustic gold-rush frontier flavor.

GEORGE PARKS HWY

North of Anchorage, George Parks Hwy passes through the dormitory suburb of Wasilla, just past the Glenn Hwy (Hwy 1) turn-off. A dramatic detour, the Fishook-Willow Rd between Palmer and Willow, goes through **Hatcher Pass** (see Around Anchorage, p1050), an alpine paradise with foot trails, gold-mining artifacts and panoramas of the Talkeetna Mountains.

Talkeetna

At Mile 98.7, a side road heads north to this interesting town. It was a miners' supply center in 1901 and later a riverboat station and railroad-construction headquarters. Since the 1950s, Mt McKinley mountaineers have made Talkeetna their staging post. The **Talkeetna-Denali Visitors Center** (☎ 907-733-2688, 800-660-2688; George Parks Hwy; ⏲ 7am-8pm) has information about the area.

The **Mountaineering Ranger Station** (☎ 907-733-2231; 1st & B Sts; ⏲ 9am-6pm) handles expeditions to Mt McKinley and has videos and displays for non-climbers. The four

ALASKA

restored buildings of the **Talkeetna Historical Society Museum** (☎ 907-733-2487; admission $3; 🕑 10:30am-6:30pm) are a block south of Main St and house exhibits on bush pilots and McKinley climbs.

For scenic flights to view Mt McKinley ($120 to $240), check out **Doug Geeting Aviation** (☎ 907-733-2366, 800-770-2366; www.alaskaairtours.com), **Hudson Air Service** (☎ 907-733-2321, 800-478-2321; www.hudsonair.com) or **K2 Aviation** (☎ 907-733-2291, 800-764-2291; www.flyk2.com). If the day is clear, be prepared for a long wait and an unforgettable flight.

Fairview Inn (☎ 907-733-2423; 101 Main St; s/d with shared bath $53/63) is a classic choice, though the band in the bar below plays until 2:30am on weekends. **Latitude 62 Lodge/Motel** (☎ 907-733-2262; Mile 13.5 Talkeetna Spur Rd; s/d $63/74) is more upscale and quieter, with an attached restaurant, while **Talkeetna Hostel International** (☎ 907-733-4678; I St; dm/s/d $25/50/60; ⊠ 💻), a wonderful hostel, is 10-minutes' stroll from Main St. The **River Park Campground** (Main St; $12) has tent sites near the river.

Talkeetna Roadhouse (☎ 907-733-1351; Main St; breakfast $9, dinner $10-15; ⊠) is the best spot for a hearty meal. Across the street, **McKinley Deli & Espresso Bar** serves sandwiches (from $7) and pizza (from $13) until 11pm.

Café Michele (☎ 907-733-5300; Talkeetna Spur Rd & 2nd St; dinner mains $17-25; ⊠) serves up the town's best food and has the most upscale atmosphere. Try the superb, signature soy-ginger salmon.

The **Alaska Railroad** (☎ 800-544-0552) from Anchorage stops daily in summer ($78) and heads north to Denali National Park ($73) and Fairbanks ($100). **Talkeetna Shuttle Service** (☎ 907-733-1725, 888-288-6008) runs between Anchorage and Talkeetna ($50).

Denali National Park

This breathtakingly brilliant wilderness area, which includes North America's highest mountain, attracts one million visitors a year. A single road curves 91 miles through the heart of the park, lined with campsites, trailheads, wildlife and stunning panoramas. This road can be used only by official shuttle buses, which have limited seating. Numbers in the campsites and wilderness zones are also strictly limited. This means Disneyland-like crowds at the entrance but relative solitude once you're inside.

Wildlife, including mammals, such as marmot and moose, is easy to spot. Caribou, wolves and brown bears are crowd favorites. However, the main attraction is magnificent Mt McKinley, a high pyramid of rock, snow and glaciers rising from the valley floor. Clouds will obscure McKinley more often than not, so be prepared to wait for the big view.

INFORMATION

The park entrance is at Mile 237.3 George Parks Hwy. Entry costs $5/10 a person/family, good for a week. The highway north and south of the park entrance is a touristy strip of private campgrounds, lodges, restaurants and facilities. The **Visitor Access Center** (VAC; ☎ 907-683-1266, 683-2294; www.nps.gov/dena; 🕑 7am-8pm) is the place to organize your trip into the park, pick up permits and purchase maps. If possible, plan the exact days you will be in the park, and reserve bus seats and campsites through the **Denali National Park Reservation Service** (☎ 907-272-7275, 800-622-7275).

Shuttle buses provide access for day hiking and sightseeing, and can be reserved beginning in late February for that summer. In the backcountry you can get on or off buses at any point along their routes. Buses leave the VAC regularly (6:30am–2pm) for Eielson Visitors Center ($23) and Wonder Lake ($30). Special camper shuttle buses, with space for backpacks and mountain bikes, charge $19 to any point on the road.

ACTIVITIES

For day hiking, get off the shuttle bus at any valley, riverbed or ridge that takes your fancy (no permit needed). For a guided walk, book at the VAC one or two days ahead.

For backcountry camping, you must get a backcountry permit from the VAC one day in advance. The park is divided into 43 zones, each with a regulated number of visitors. Some are more popular than others. Watch the Backcountry Simulator Program video at the VAC, covering bears, rivers and backcountry safety, and check the quota board for an area you can access. You then go to the counter to book a camper shuttle bus and buy your maps.

Most cyclists book campsites at the VAC and then carry their bikes on the camper shuttle. Cycling is permitted only on roads. Rent bikes from **Denali Outdoor Center**

(☎ 907-638-1925, 888-303-1925; www.denalioutdoorcenter.com; Mile 238.5 Parks Hwy; $37 a day).

Several rafting companies offer daily floats on the Nenana River. **Denali Raft Adventures** (☎ 907-683-2234, 800-683-2234; Mile 238 Parks Hwy) offers a canyon run through the gorge, as well as a milder Mt McKinley run ($65).

SLEEPING

Campsites inside the park cost $6 to $16, and most can be reserved for a $4 fee. It can be difficult to get a place in the campground of your choice, so take anything available and change campgrounds later.

Carlo Creek Lodge (☎ 907-683-2576; Mile 224 George Parks Hwy; tent/cabin $15/from $90) About 13 miles south of the park entrance, this lodge offers a variety of creek-side accommodations.

Denali Mountain Morning Hostel (☎ 907-683-7503; Mile 224 George Parks Hwy; dm/r $23/65, cabins $75-100; ⊠ 💻) Recommended accommodation where you can stash your gear (or rent you some) and you can shuttle between the park entrance and hostel for $3 round-trip. Make reservations!

Denali River Cabins (☎ 907-683-8000, 800-230-7275; www.denalirivercabins.com; Mile 231 George Parks Hwy, Denali Village; cabins $139-159; ⊠) Modern cabins and a restaurant/bar, but no TV or phone.

Denali Grizzly Bear Campground (☎ 907-683-2696; Mile 231 George Parks Hwy; tent sites $18, tent cabins $22-24, cabins $49-66) Has a hot shower and laundry services.

Riley Creek (tent sites $12) At the park entrance, it can be overrun by RVs, but tenters rarely feel overwhelmed.

Denali Sourdough Cabins (☎ 907-683-2773, 800-544-0970; www.denalisourdoughcabins.com; Mile 238.8 George Parks Hwy; cabins $145; ⊠) Small, cozy cabins near the park entrance.

Other campgrounds are spaced along the park road, the most lovely being **Wonder Lake** (Mile 85 Park Rd; tent sites $12), with 26 spots looking onto Mt McKinley. **Sanctuary River** (Mile 23 Park Rd; tent sites $6) is for tents only, but makes a great day-hike area. Spots can't be reserved.

Otto Lake RV Park (☎ 907-683-2100; Mile 0.5 Otto Lake Rd, Healy; tent/RV sites $17/20). Twelve miles north of the park entrance; camping and some cabins available.

EATING

The only food inside the park entrance area is at **McKinley Mercantile**, which sells fresh, dried and canned food. It's better to stock up on supplies in Fairbanks, Anchorage or Wasilla. Outside the park, **Lynx Creek Pizza & Pub** (☎ 907-683-2547; Mile 238.6 George Parks Hwy; $14-25) has excellent offerings, including beer on tap and huge pizzas, while **McKinley/Denali Steak & Salmon Bake** (Mile 238.5 George Parks Hwy) offers Alaskan salmon dinners ($20).

Bub's Subs (☎ 907-683-7827; Mile 238.5 George Parks Hwy; $7-13; ⊠) Has freshly made sandwiches.

Overlook Bar & Grill (☎ 907-683-2723; Mile 238.5 George Parks Hwy; $9-27; ⊠) This cozy and comfortable place for a meal of steak, seafood or pasta at the Crow's Nest Inn is also the best bar in the greater Denali area.

GETTING THERE & AWAY

From the VAC, **Parks Hwy Express** (☎ 888-600-6001) makes the run to Anchorage ($54) and Fairbanks ($39).

The **Alaska Railroad** (☎ 907-456-4155, 800-544-0552) departs from a depot near Riley Creek campground and is expensive but very scenic. The trip to Fairbanks is $50 and to Anchorage, $125. It also has interesting packages out of Anchorage for $349.

FAIRBANKS

A spread-out, low-rise city, Fairbanks features log cabins, sled dogs and extremes of climate. Summer days average 70°F and can reach 90°F. Downtown is roughly centered on Golden Heart Park, and Cushman St is more or less the main street. Downtown motels, B&Bs and restaurants are 15 minutes' walk from the train station.

Fairbanks was founded in 1901, when a trader could get his riverboat no further up the Chena River. A gold strike made Fairbanks a boom town, with 18,000 residents by 1908, but by 1920 it had slumped to 1000. WWII, the Alcan Hwy and military bases produced minor booms, but the town took off as a construction base for the Trans-Alaska Pipeline and still serves as a gateway to the North Slope.

Information

The **Log Cabin Visitors Center** (☎ 907-456-5774, for recording 907-456-4636; www.explorefairbanks.com; 550 1st Ave; ⏲ 8am-7pm) overlooks the Chena River and has courtesy phones to motels and B&Bs. The recording lists daily events and attractions. The **Alaska Public Lands Information Center** (☎ 907-456-0531; 250 Cushman St; ⏲ 9am-6pm) has maps, information and displays on parks, wildlife refuges and recreation areas. Log on at **Café Latte** (☎ 907-455-4898; 519 6th Ave).

Sights & Activities

Pioneer Park (☎ 907-459-1087; Airport Way & Peger Rd; admission free; 🕑 11am-9pm) is a 44-acre park and the city's biggest attraction. Formerly known as Alaskaland, it has historical displays such as an old sternwheeler, the railroad car that carried President Warren Harding to the golden spike ceremony in 1923 and a century-old working carousel.

University Museum (☎ 907-474-7505; 907 Yukon Dr; adult/child $5/3; 🕑 9am-7pm) has an excellent collection with sections on geology and history, including Blue Babe, a 36,000-year-old bison found preserved in the permafrost. An expansion that will double its size is slated for completion in the fall of 2005.

For hiking, head out to Chena River State Recreational Area, which has short walks, or the 29-mile Chena Dome Trail. At **Chena Hot Springs Resort** (☎ 907-451-8104, 800-478-4681; www.chenahotsprings.com; Mile 56.5 Chena Hot Springs Rd; adult/child $10/7) you can soak those mosquito bites all day or get ambitious and do a guided activity such as horse-back riding. Canoeing options range from afternoon paddles to overnight trips; ask at **7 Bridges Boats & Bikes** (☎ 907-479-0751; www.7gablesinn.com; 4312 Birch Lane), at 7 Gables Inn. Alternatively, cruise the calm Chena River on the historic sternwheeler **Riverboat Discovery** (☎ 907-479-6673; 1975 Discovery Dr; $40).

Sleeping

See the visitors center brochure for Fairbanks' 100-plus B&Bs, mostly priced from $65/75 single/double. The city exacts an 8% tax on hotels, and most of those with reasonable rates are either less than desirable or quite far from downtown.

Fairbanks Hotel (☎ 907-456-6411, 888-329-4685; www.fbxhotl.com; 517 3rd Ave; r with shared bath $55-90, with private bath $85-109; ⊠) This downtown art deco wonder is the exception to the rule stated above. Rates include transport from the airport or train station, and you can rent bikes for $27 a day.

Eleanor's Northern Lights Hotel (☎ 907-452-2598; 360 State St; s $70, d $80-90; ⊠) All seven rooms have cable, phone and fridge, and four have private bath. Rates include transport to/from the train station and a hot, all-you-can-eat breakfast.

Also recommended:

North Woods Lodge (☎ 907-479-5300, 800-478-5305; Chena Hills Dr; tent sites $12-15, cabins $45-55) Has a Jacuzzi, kitchen and laundry facilities.

Golden North Motel (☎ 907-479-6201, 800-447-1910; 4888 Old Airport Rd; s/d $69/74) Smallish rooms with private bath and cable TV.

Eating & Drinking

Co-op Diner (☎ 907-474-3463; 535 2nd Ave; breakfast & lunch $6-8, dinner $10-20; ⊠) Hamburgers, sandwiches and Thai specials in 1950s style.

Soapy Smith's (☎ 907-451-8380; 543 2nd Ave) Good burgers, salads, sandwiches and chowder in a saloon atmosphere.

Chef Tuan's Dog House (☎ 907-474-4004; 3400 College Rd; dinner mains $10-21; ⊠) A small Sri Lankan restaurant with an outdoor patio. The chef will make your curry as hot as you want. Burgers, sandwiches and seafood are also available. No dog, though.

Gambardella's Pasta Bella (☎ 907-457-4992; 706 2nd Ave; $10-17; ⊠) Some of the best homemade pizzas in the Interior, in a delightful outdoor setting.

Walk south on Cushman St to find more restaurants, including the veg-friendly **Thai House** (☎ 907-452-6123; 526 5th Ave; dinner mains $9-12; ⊠).

Palace Theatre & Saloon (☎ 907-456-5960; Pioneer Park; adult/child $14/7) Honky-tonk piano and cancan dancers in its Golden Heart Revue show.

Getting There & Around

Alaska Airlines (☎ 907-474-0481, 800-252-7522) has eight daily flights to Anchorage ($125 to $150), with occasional bargains. For travel into Arctic Alaska, contact **Frontier Flying Service** (☎ 907-474-0014, 800-478-6779).

Affordable Car Rental (☎ 907-452-7341, 800-471-3101; 3101 S Cushman St; 🕑 7:30am-7pm Mon-Fri, 11am-5pm Sat, noon-5pm Sun) offers cheap rentals ($34). There's also **Rent-A-Wreck** (☎ 907-452-1606, 800-478-1606; 2105 S Cushman St; 🕑 8am-5:30pm Mon-Fri, 9am-noon Sat).

Alaska Direct Bus Lines (☎ 800-770-6652) makes a Fairbanks–Whitehorse run for $140, with buses stopping at Tok ($45) and Beaver Creek ($68). Skagway to Fairbanks is $185, and Fairbanks to Anchorage is $70. **Parks Hwy Express** (☎ 888-600-6001) offers daily connections to Denali National Park ($39) and Anchorage ($79). It also services Dawson City ($155).

The **Alaska Railroad** (☎ 907-456-4155, 800-544-0552) departs at 8:30am daily for Denali National Park ($50) and Anchorage ($175).

The **Metropolitan Area Commuter Service** (☎ 907-459-1011) provides local, weekday bus service (day passes $3).

THE BUSH

The Bush is the vast area of Alaska that is not readily accessible by road or ferry. It includes Arctic Alaska, the Brooks Range, the Alaska Peninsula–Aleutian Islands chain and the Bering Sea coast. Traveling to the Bush usually involves small, expensive chartered aircraft. Facilities for travelers are also pricey and very limited. If you're planning to visit small, isolated communities, it's best to be accompanied by a local contact or tour guide.

To visit **Arctic Alaska**, take the Dalton Hwy, a rough, gravel road that goes 490 miles north from Fairbanks to Deadhorse, near Prudhoe Bay. You can tour the oil complex at Prudhoe, but you can't stay on the shores of the Arctic Ocean. It's not really worth going north of **Atigun Pass**, 300 miles from Fairbanks, where there's a good view of the North Slope. **Dalton Hwy Express** (☎ 907-452-2031; www.daltonhighwayexpress.com) makes the run to Prudhoe Bay three times a week. It's $100 round-trip from Fairbanks to the Arctic Circle.

The Dalton Hwy passes the remote **Gates of the Arctic National Park**, with great hiking and paddling, but the park is best accessed from the town of Bettles, which can be reached only by air. For information, contact the **National Park Ranger Station** (☎ 907-692-5494) or call **Sourdough Outfitters** (☎ 907-692-5252).

On the Bering Sea coast, the storied gold-rush town of **Nome** is friendly and interesting. The **visitors center** (☎ 907-443-6624; www.nomealaska.org; 9am-9pm) has information about accommodations and trips in the surrounding area. You can camp on **Golden Sands Beach** (free), where gold is still being panned. An advance-purchase Air Alaska ticket costs $350 to $400 round-trip from Anchorage.

Isolated settlements on the **Aleutian Islands** can be reached by the ferry **MV Tustumena** (☎ 800-526-6731; www.akferry.com), which makes a monthly trip along the archipelago every summer. It's a superbly scenic trip when the weather is clear, and the ferry stops at five ports beyond Kodiak, for just long enough to look around. It costs $570 from Homer to Dutch Harbor and back. If you want to stay longer on the islands, you'll probably have to fly.

Hawaii

CONTENTS

Those who haven't experienced the magic of Hawaii cannot fully comprehend the allure of the islands. Tourist brochures paint a glossy portrait of the picturesque beaches and colorful *luaus* (Hawaiian feasts), but they fail to capture Hawaii's impossibly beautiful landscapes, its exciting cultural diversity, and the spirit of hospitality that ties it all together. Critics point to the state's mass tourism, high-rise hotels and crowded beaches – and indeed, overdevelopment and cultural erosion are legitimate threats to the Hawaiian way of life. But anyone who truly dislikes Hawaii probably hasn't been there. Those who come looking for hula dancers and steel guitars won't be disappointed, but they will soon find that this is only a thin slice of the Hawaiian experience.

Naturally, the great outdoors is a huge draw. The islands are amazingly varied – from spectacular gorges and lush valleys, and stunning beaches ranging from alabaster white to jet black, to the world's most active volcano. The weather is excellent year round, and the state boasts some of the planet's top spots for surfing, windsurfing, snorkeling, swimming and kayaking.

Finally, to generalize to an unconscionable degree, Hawaiians are some of the friendliest folks you'll ever encounter. They love to 'talk story,' and it's not unusual for someone you've just met to strike up a conversation as if you were old friends.

For all these reasons, the 50th state remains first in the hearts of its lucky inhabitants and those travelers fortunate enough to visit. Aloha, indeed.

HIGHLIGHTS

- Riding the killer surf; winter waves reach 35ft high on **Oahu's North Shore** (p1073)
- Experiencing the fiery lava of **Hawaii Volcanoes National Park**, where the Big Island gets bigger (p1076)
- Being dwarfed by majestic humpback whales off **Maui's coast** (p1077)
- Sea-cliff hiking on Kauai's spectacular **Na Pali Coast** (p1080)
- Getting away from it all in the slow lane, on **Molokai** (p1080)

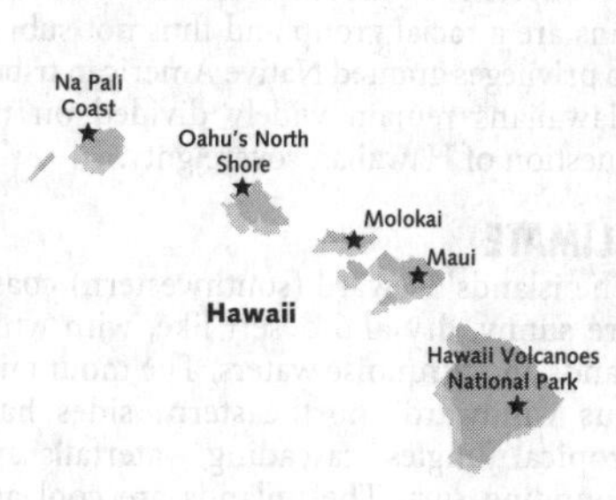

HISTORY

Hawaii's first inhabitants were Polynesians who arrived from the Marquesas Islands between AD 500 and 700. Tahitians conquered the islands around 1000, introducing human sacrifice and *kapu*, a practice of taboos regulating social interaction.

British explorer Captain James Cook spotted the archipelago in 1778. He was met warmly by the islanders but was killed in a melee on a later visit. The islands' separate warring chiefdoms were united in 1810 by King Kamehameha the Great, chief of the Big Island. Following his death in 1819, his wife, Queen Kaahumanu dismantled the *kapu* system.

During the 1820s Christian missionaries arrived. Foreigners gained control of vast tracts of land and established a sugar industry. In 1852 American plantation owners began recruiting laborers from overseas. Immigrants soon outnumbered native Hawaiians, but together they created modern Hawaii's multiethnic culture. Within a few decades, westerners owned 80% of Hawaii's privately held lands.

Hawaii was annexed in 1898, and soon became home to huge US naval and army bases. The surprise Japanese attack on Pearl Harbor in 1941 jolted the USA into WWII. In 1959 Hawaiians voted overwhelmingly to become a US state.

In 1993 President Clinton formally apologized to native Hawaiians 'for the overthrow of the Kingdom of Hawaii,' while in 2000 the US Supreme Court ruled that native Hawaiians are a racial group and thus not subject to privileges granted Native American tribes. Hawaiians remain widely divided on the question of Hawaiian sovereignty.

HAWAII FACTS

Nickname Aloha State
Population 1,244,898 (42nd)
Area 10,930 sq miles (43rd)
Admitted to Union August 21, 1959 (50th)
Capital city Honolulu (population 876,000)
Other cities Pearl City (31,000), Kailua (40,000)
State fish Humuhumunukunukuapuaa (rectangular triggerfish)
Birthplace of surfing, Olympic gold medalist and 'father of modern surfing' Duke Kahanamoku (1890–1968), the ukulele ('flea' in Hawaiian)

CLIMATE

The islands' leeward (southwestern) coasts are sunny, dry and desert like, with white sands and turquoise waters. The mountainous windward (northeastern) sides have tropical jungles, cascading waterfalls and pounding surf. The uplands are cool and green, with rolling pastures, small farms and ranches.

Hawaii enjoys warm weather year round, with average temperatures differing only 7°F from winter to summer. Near the coast the daily temperatures average a high of 83°F and a low of 68°F. Summer and fall are the driest seasons, winter the wettest. December to March is also the busiest tourist season, so that's when you can expect the most competition for affordable rooms. Fall and spring are slow seasons and offer better discounts.

NATIONAL & STATE PARKS

Hawaii's national parks are both volcano intensive. On the Big Island, **Hawaii Volcanoes National Park** (p1076) is a jaw-dropping mélange of wilderness environments ranging from tropical beaches to sub-arctic mountaintops, centered on two active volcanoes. On Maui, **Haleakala National Park** (p1079) focuses on the dormant Haleakala Crater, which could envelop a large city. For more information, see the National Parks Services website at www.nps.gov.

The islands' state parks range from well developed, with plenty of campsites and facilities, to completely wild. For information on state parks and to make camping reservations, contact the **Division of State Parks** (☎ 808-587-0400).

LANGUAGE

English and Hawaiian are the official state languages. About 9000 people speak Hawaiian, and Hawaiian words and phrases pepper the speech of most Hawaiian residents. A non-English language is spoken in one out of four homes.

GETTING THERE & AWAY

Honolulu is a major Pacific hub and an intermediate stop on many flights between the US mainland and Asia, Australia, New Zealand and the South Pacific. Passengers on any of these routes can often make a free stopover. From Europe, ask about an add-on fare from the US West Coast or perhaps a round-the-world ticket. From the US mainland, the cheapest fares generally start at $600 to $900 (depending on the season) from the East Coast, $300 to $500 from California.

GETTING AROUND

Most flights arrive in Honolulu; travelers to other islands must then make the short hop to their final destination. Interisland travel is inexpensive; fares between the main islands are $55 to $95. Ask about discount coupons and air passes. The largest airlines, **Hawaiian Airlines** (☎ 808-838-1555; www.hawaiianair.com) and **Aloha Airlines** (☎ 808-484-1111; www.alohaair.com), have frequent flights.

The only ferry services in the state are between Maui and Lanai and between Maui and Molokai. See those sections, later, for details.

An excellent bus service goes around Oahu, but the Big Island and Kauai have limited public buses. Some scenic mountain routes can be narrow and winding, but main roads are generally good. Rental cars are available on all the main islands and cost $30 to $50 a day, $150 to $200 a week. It's wise to book a car before you arrive. Phone a few companies to find the best price. You might find some companies have a minimum-age requirement of 25.

Each island offers half- and full-day sightseeing bus tours that are advertised in the free tourist booklets. Specialized tours include whale-watching cruises, bicycle tours, snorkel trips, overnight tours and helicopter tours. All can be booked after arrival in Hawaii.

HANGIN' UMI

Hawaiian surfer lingo approaches the status of a separate language. Here are some of the terms you might hear out among the waves:

- *brah* – friend, surfing buddy
- *da kine* – a great wave, top quality
- *goofy-footing* – surfing with the right foot forward
- *kaha* – traditional Hawaiian term for board surfing
- *kaha nalu* – body surfing
- *keiki waves* – small, gentle waves suitable for kids
- *macker* – huge wave, big enough to drive a Mack truck through
- *malihini* – newcomer, tenderfoot
- *pau* – quitting time
- *snake* – to steal ('That dude's snaking my wave!')
- *stick* – surfboard
- *umi* – ten
- *wahine* – female surfer
- *wipeout* – get knocked down by a big wave

TOURS

Roberts Hawaii (☎ 800-831-5541; www.robertshawaii.com) offers tours of Oahu, Hawaii, Maui and Kauai, starting at $75.

OAHU

The most developed Hawaiian island also boasts the state's most famous locales: Waikiki, Pearl Harbor, Sunset Beach. Around Honolulu it's an urban scene, with highways, high-rises and crowds, but these quickly give way to pineapple fields and mountains. Oahu also has excellent beaches and offers a full range of activities, from water sports to hiking and horseback riding.

Getting Around

Oahu's extensive public bus system, **TheBus** (☎ 808-848-5555; www.thebus.org), has some 80 routes that collectively cover most of Oahu. The one-way fare for all rides is $1.75, with free transfers to connecting routes (ask when you board). The *Honolulu & Oahu by TheBus* map ($6) shows bus routes and major attractions with bus stops and numbers. TheBus also distributes a simple, free schematic route map. Bus Nos 52 and 55 can be combined for a cheap circle-island tour (four hours).

The State Department of Transportation's *Bike Oahu* map can be found at the Hawaii Visitors & Convention Bureau (HVCB) in Waikiki and at bike shops. The **Hawaii Bicycling League** (☎ 808-735-5756; www.hbl.org) holds a variety of free bike rides around Oahu nearly every weekend. Most public buses have bike racks.

HAWAII

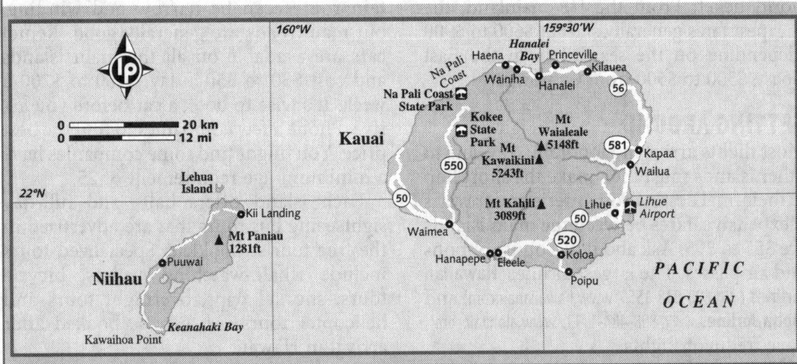
160°W
159°30'W
0 20 km
0 12 mi
22°N
Kauai
Haena
Hanalei Bay
Princeville
Na Pali Coast
Wainiha
Hanalei
Kilauea
56
Na Pali Coast State Park
Kokee State Park
Mt Waialeale 5148ft
Mt Kawaikini 5243ft
581
Kapaa
Wailua
550
Lehua Island
50
Mt Kahili 3089ft
Lihue
Lihue Airport
Kii Landing
Waimea
50
Mt Paniau 1281ft
520
Puuwai
Hanapepe
Eleele
Koloa
Niihau
Poipu
PACIFIC OCEAN
Keanahaki Bay
Kawaihoa Point

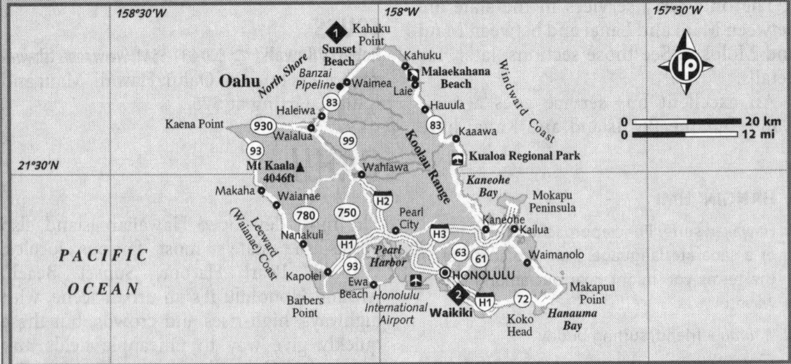
158°30'W
158°W
157°30'W
1
Kahuku Point
Sunset Beach
Kahuku
Malaekahana Beach
Windward Coast
Oahu
North Shore
Banzai Pipeline
Waimea
Laie
83
Haleiwa
Hauula
Kaena Point
930
Waialua
83
Kaaawa
0 20 km
0 12 mi
99
93
Koolau Range
Kualoa Regional Park
21°30'N
Mt Kaala 4046ft
Wahiawa
Kaneohe Bay
Makaha
Waianae
H2
Mokapu Peninsula
780
750
Pearl City
Leeward (Waianae) Coast
Nanakuli
H3
Kaneohe
Kailua
H1
PACIFIC OCEAN
63
61
Pearl Harbor
Waimanolo
93
Kapolei
Ewa Beach
HONOLULU
Makapuu Point
Barbers Point
Honolulu International Airport
2
Waikiki
H1
72
Koko Head
Hanauma Bay

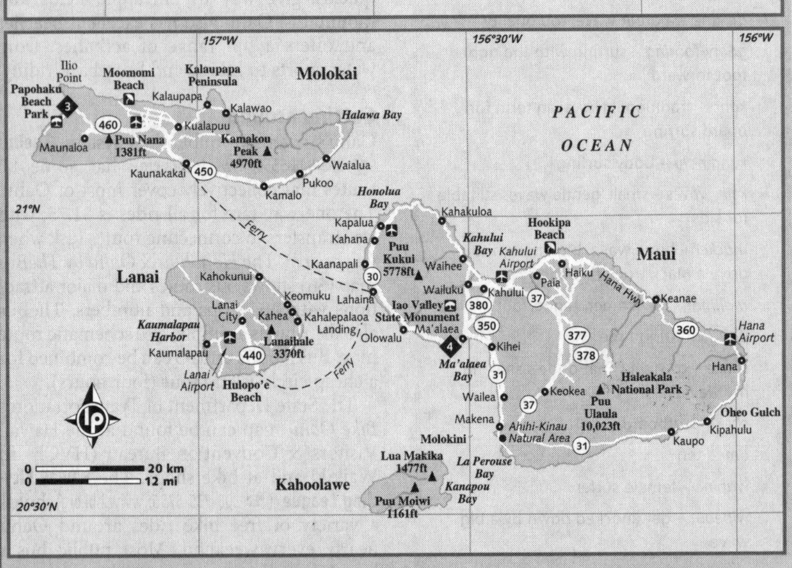
157°W
156°30'W
156°W
Ilio Point
Moomomi Beach
Kalaupapa Peninsula
Molokai
Papohaku Beach Park
3
Kalaupapa
Kalawao
Halawa Bay
460
Kualapuu
PACIFIC OCEAN
Maunaloa
Puu Nana 1381ft
Kamakou Peak 4970ft
Waialua
Kaunakakai
450
Pukoo
Kamalo
21°N
Honolua Bay
Kahakuloa
Ferry
Kapalua
Hookipa Beach
Kahana
Puu Kukui 5778ft
Kahului Bay
Kahului Airport
Maui
Kaanapali
Waihee
Haiku
Lanai
Kahokunui
30
Paia
Hana Hwy
Wailuku
Kahului
Keomuku
Lahaina
Iao Valley State Monument
380
37
Keanae
Lanai City
Kahea
Kahalepalaoa Landing
Olowalu
Ma'alaea
350
360
Hana Airport
Kaumalapau Harbor
Lanaihale 3370ft
4
Kihei
377
Kaumalapau
440
Ferry
Ma'alaea Bay
378
Hana
Lanai Airport
Hulopo'e Beach
31
Keokea
Haleakala National Park
Wailea
37
Puu Ulaula 10,023ft
Makena
Oheo Gulch
Ahihi-Kinau Natural Area
Kipahulu
Molokini
31
Kaupo
0 20 km
0 12 mi
Lua Makika 1477ft
La Perouse Bay
Kahoolawe
Kanapou Bay
Puu Moiwi 1161ft
20°30'N

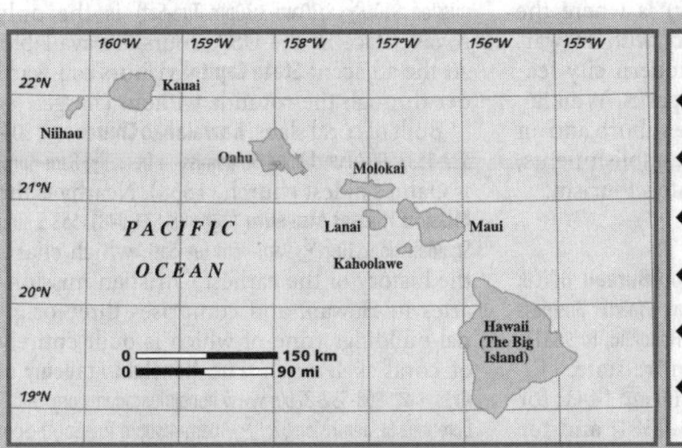

DETOURS

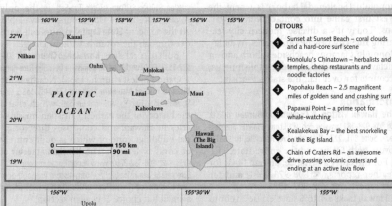

1. Sunset at Sunset Beach – coral clouds and a hard-core surf scene
2. Honolulu's Chinatown – herbalists and temples, cheap restaurants and noodle factories
3. Papohaku Beach – 2.5 magnificent miles of golden sand and crashing surf
4. Papawai Point – a prime spot for whale-watching
5. Kealakekua Bay – the best snorkeling on the Big Island
6. Chain of Craters Rd – an awesome drive passing volcanic craters and ending at an active lava flow

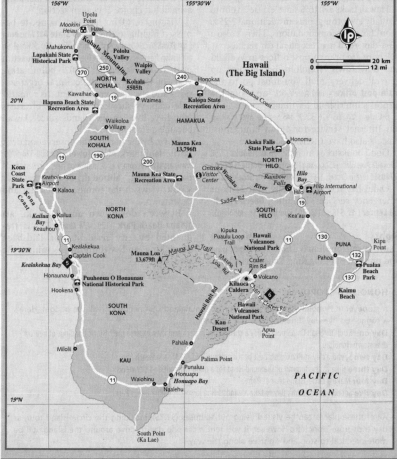

Hawaii (The Big Island)

0 20 km
0 12 mi

156°W
155°30'W
155°W
20°N
19°30'N
19°N

Upolu Point
Mookini Heiau
Hawi
Mahukona
Lapakahi State Historical Park
Kohala Mountains
Pololu Valley
Waipio Valley
NORTH KOHALA
Kohala 5505ft
Honokaa
Hamakua Coast
Kawaihae
Waimea
Hapuna Beach State Recreation Area
Kalopa State Recreation Area
HAMAKUA
Waikoloa Village
SOUTH KOHALA
Mauna Kea 13,796ft
Akaka Falls State Park
Honomu
NORTH HILO
Kona Coast State Park
Keahole-Kona Airport
Kalaoa
Mauna Kea State Recreation Area
Onizuka Visitor Center
Wailuku River
Rainbow Falls
Hilo Bay
Hilo
Hilo International Airport
Kona Coast
Saddle Rd
NORTH KONA
SOUTH HILO
Kailua Bay
Kailua
Keauhou
Kea'au
Kipuka Puaulu Loop Trail
Hawaii Volcanoes National Park
PUNA
Kipu Point
Kealakekua
Captain Cook
Kealakekua Bay
Mauna Loa 13,679ft
Mauna Loa Trail
Mauna Loa Rd
Crater Rim Rd
Pahoa
Pualaa Beach Park
Honaunau
Puuhonua O Honaunau National Historical Park
Volcano
Kilauea Caldera
Chain of Craters Rd
Hookena
Hawaii Belt Rd
Kaimu Beach
SOUTH KONA
Hawaii Volcanoes National Park
Kau Desert
Apua Point
Pahala
Milolii
Palima Point
KAU
Punaluu
Honuapu
Honuapo Bay
Waiohinu
Naalehu
PACIFIC OCEAN
South Point (Ka Lae)

HAWAII

HONOLULU & WAIKIKI

Honolulu (Sheltered Harbor) is where the West first came into contact with Hawaiians. Today it's a diverse, modern city featuring fine city beaches and parks. Waikiki, Honolulu's famous beachside suburb and an enclave of traveler-geared establishments, accounts for over half the state's tourism.

Information

The **Hawaii Visitors & Convention Bureau** (HVCB; ☎ 808-923-1811; www.gohawaii.com; Waikiki Business Plaza, Suite 801, 2270 Kalakaua Ave, Honolulu, HI 96815) covers both Oahu and the entire state.

For directory assistance, dial ☎ 1441; for weather reports, ☎ 808-973-4381; and for surf reports, ☎ 808-973-4383.

Hawaii tacks a 4.16% state 'excise' tax onto virtually everything, plus an additional 7.25% room tax on accommodations. There's also a $2-a-day 'road use' tax on all car rentals.

There are branch post offices in Waikiki and downtown Honolulu, but to pick up general-delivery mail you must go to the **main post office** (3600 Aolele St), opposite the airport's interisland terminal.

E-Cafe (☎ 808-926-3299; 445 Seaside Ave, Waikiki) has Internet service for $6 an hour; most hostels also have Internet access.

Good bookstores include **Waldenbooks** (2250 Kalakaua Ave, Waikiki Shopping Plaza) and **Borders Books & Music** (Ward Center, 1200 Ala Moana Blvd, Honolulu).

Oahu has several hospitals with 24-hour emergency services, including **Queen's Medical Center** (☎ 538-9011; 1301 Punchbowl St, Honolulu).

Sights

Map p1062

Downtown Honolulu is a hodgepodge of past and present. Built for King Kalakaua in 1882, **Iolani Palace** (☎ 808-522-0832; S King & Richard Sts; admission $10; 8:30am-3:30pm Tue-Sat) is the only royal palace in the USA; tours are available. At the adjacent **State Capitol** visitors can wander through the rotunda without charge.

Built of coral slabs, **Kawaiahao Church** (☎ 808-522-1333; 957 Punchbowl St; admission free; 8am-4pm) is Oahu's oldest church (1838). Nearby is the **Mission Houses Museum** (☎ 808-531-0481; 553 S King St; admission $10; 9am-4pm Tue-Sat), which charts the history of the earliest Christian missionaries in Hawaii, and comprises three original buildings (one of which is built entirely of coral skeletons). The **Honolulu Academy of Arts** (☎ 808-532-8700; www.honoluluacademy.org; 900 S Beretania St; admission $7; 10am-4:30pm Tue-Sat, 1-5pm Sun) has exceptional art collections, including a small but choice Hawaiian section.

Visitors to Oahu have a new not-to-be-missed highlight: the **Hawaii State Art Museum** (☎ 808-586-0900; www.state.hi.us/sfca; 250 S Hotel St; admission free; 10am-4pm Tue-Sat). The museum opened in November 2002, culminating years of work by artists, cultural organizations and the state government. Its remarkable displays showcase the work of artists who have lived in the islands since Hawaii became a state in 1959.

Down by the harbor, the observation deck of the landmark **Aloha Tower** (☎ 808-528-5700; www.alohatower.com; Pier 9; admission free; 9am-dusk) has sweeping, although not particularly scenic, views of the commercial harbor and downtown.

Between downtown and Waikiki, **Ala Moana Beach Park** (1201 Ala Moana Blvd) is frequented by city residents for laid-back picnicking and swimming – minus the tourists.

HONOLULU STOPOVER

A stopover in Honolulu on your way to or from mainland USA needn't break the budget. Here's a suggested five-day itinerary for a stay on Oahu:

Day one Stroll through Chinatown, enjoy a cheap ethnic lunch and then explore the historic buildings of nearby downtown Honolulu.

Day two Spend a day at Honolulu's best beach, untouristed Ala Moana Beach Park.

Day three Hike to the summit of Diamond Head for a good workout and city views.

Day four Make a circle-island tour of Oahu.

Day five Snorkel at Hanauma Bay or take a windsurfing lesson at Kailua Beach Park.

All of these places can be visited using public buses ($1.75), including the circle-island tour, as day trips from Honolulu. However, if you rent a car one day to drive around the island, it'll be more practical to stop and sightsee along the way.

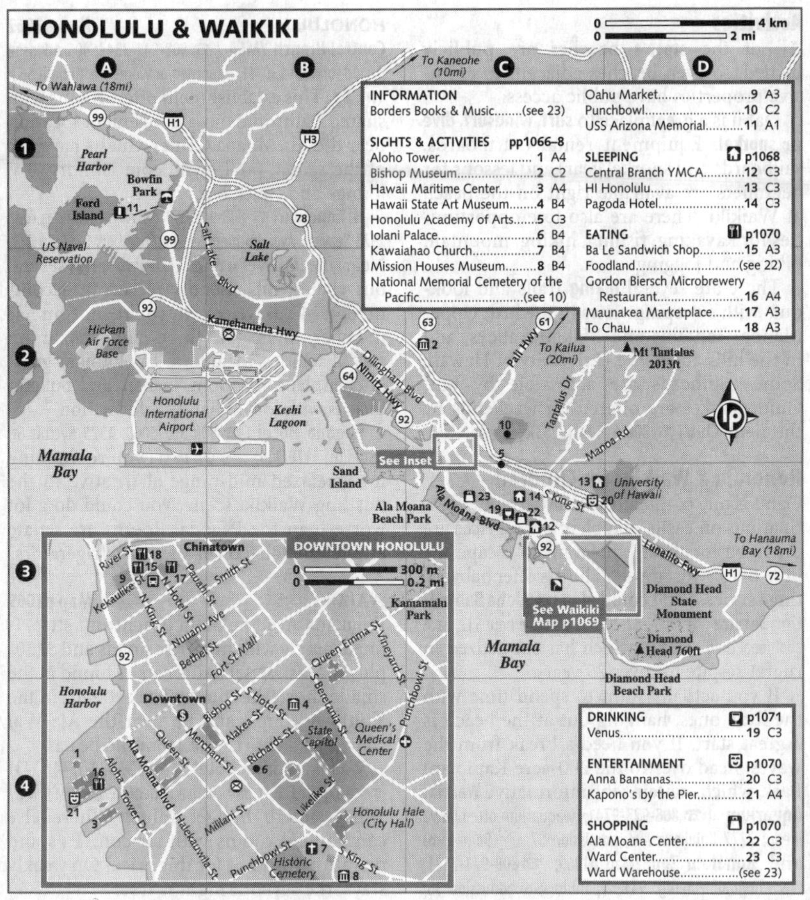

The busy and colorful **Chinatown** district, immediately north of downtown Honolulu, was settled around 1860 by Chinese immigrants who had worked off their sugarcane plantation contracts. Its bustling heart is the 1904 **Oahu Market** (Kekaulike & N King Sts). You can get tattooed, consult with an herbalist, explore the temples and antique shops or eat at inexpensive restaurants. While Chinatown is a fun place to explore during the day, walking around at night is not recommended due to drug and gang activity.

Bustling 2-mile **Waikiki Beach** is good for swimming, boogie boarding, surfing, sailing and other beach activities. (Some of the stretches of Waikiki Beach are also known by other names, such as Kahanamoku Beach, Fort DeRussy Beach and Gray's Beach.)

Bishop Museum (☎ 808-847-3591; www.bishopmuseum.org; 1525 Bernice St; admission $15; 9am-5pm) is possibly the world's best Polynesian anthropological museum. It covers the cultural history of Hawaii and also has a planetarium, daily hula shows and special exhibits for children.

Perched above downtown Honolulu is **Punchbowl**, the bowl-shaped remains of a long-extinct volcanic crater, with a panoramic view of the city. This is the site of the **National Memorial Cemetery of the Pacific**, where over 25,000 US servicepeople are buried.

Activities

All of the state's beaches are publicly owned, so even beaches adjacent to exclusive properties have public access.

Oahu is a great place to **surf**, **windsurf**, **dive** or **snorkel**. Equipment rental (surfboards, sailboards and snorkel gear) and lessons for beginners are available right on the beach at Waikiki. There are also fine opportunities for kayaking, fishing, hiking, mountain biking and jogging.

There are several **hiking** trails and lookouts with sweeping views in the lush Upper Manoa, Tantalus and Makiki Valleys, and in the hills above the University of Hawaii. Some trailheads are accessible by bus. Guided hikes are offered on weekends by the **Sierra Club** (☎ 808-538-6616; $3).

Honolulu & Waikiki for Children

Oahu is one of the most family-friendly destinations on earth, and plenty of services are provided for those who want to escape the little ones. Most top-end hotels offer babysitting services. You could also try **Aloha Babysitting Service** (☎ 808-732-2029; 1 child per hour $12, each additional child extra $1), which has specialized in rugrat respite for over 25 years.

If you actually want to spend time with the little ones, hanging out at the beach is a great start. If you need a break from the waves, head over to the 200-acre Kapiolani Park, which contains the informative **Waikiki Aquarium** (☎ 808-923-9741; waquarium.otted.hawaii.edu; 2777 Kalakaua Ave; admission $7; 9am-4pm) and **Honolulu Zoo** (Map p1069; ☎ 808-971-7171; www.honoluluzoo.org; 941 Kapahulu Ave; admission $6; 9am-4:30pm). The park is also the venue for many community events, including the famous, if touristy, **Kodak Hula Show** (admission free; 10am Tue-Thu). When it's raining, you can take the tykes in to explore the **Hawaii Maritime Center's Museum** (Map p1062; ☎ 808-536-6373; holoholo.org/maritime; Pier 7; admission $7.50; 8:30am-5pm), which boasts a good whaling-era section and the berth for the double-hulled canoe *Hokulea*, which has made several voyages retracing the routes of early Polynesian seafarers.

Sleeping

Although Oahu isn't known for its low prices, it's usually not too difficult to find a good-value place to stay in the Honolulu area.

HONOLULU Map p1062

Central Branch YMCA (☎ 808-941-3344; 401 Atkinson Dr; s/d for men $30/41, d for men or women with bath $53; P) This establishment offers rooms with shared bathrooms in a convenient location near the Ala Moana Center. Guests have use of the sauna, pool, gym, coin laundry, TV lounge and snack bar.

HI Honolulu (☎ 808-946-0591; www.hostelsaloha.com; 2323 Seaview Ave; dm members/nonmembers $14/17; P) Near the University of Hawaii and several bus routes, this friendly place can accommodate 42 travelers. If you're not an HI member, there's a three-night-maximum stay. Facilities include a TV lounge, guest kitchen, laundry room, lockers and bulletin boards with lots of handy information.

Pagoda Hotel (☎ 800-367-6060; 1525 Rycroft St; r/studios $110/115; P) If you're looking for a relaxed mid-range alternative to the bustling Waikiki scene, you could do a lot worse than the Pagoda. Rooms are sedate and feature air-con, TVs and refrigerators.

WAIKIKI Map p1069

Kalakaua Ave, the main beachfront strip, is lined largely with high-rise hotels and $150-plus rooms. Better value can be found at the smaller hostelries on the back streets, in the Kuhio Ave area, and up near the Ala Wai Canal, all a short walk from the beach.

Waikiki Prince Hotel (☎ 808-922-1544; 2431 Prince Edward St; r $50, with kitchenette $60; P) What superb budget value! Where else can you get rooms with air-con, TVs and private bathrooms for this price? On weekly stays, the seventh night is free.

Outrigger/Ohana (☎ 808-921-6870, 800-462-6262; www.outrigger.com; d from $90; P) This chain incorporates 20 mid-range hotels, comprising a quarter of the hotel rooms in Waikiki. Its lower-priced hotels have 'Ohana' in their names and start at $90, but ask about discount schemes, free rental car offers and the like. Five of them are marked on the Waikiki map.

InterClub Hostel Waikiki (☎ 808-924-2636; 2413 Kuhio Ave; dm/r $18/55; P) This long-established spot offers free Internet access and airport pickup. There's no curfew, so feel free to party the night away.

HI Waikiki (☎ 808-926-8313; ayhaloha@lava.net; 2417 Prince Edward St; dm members/nonmembers $17/20, r $42-48; P) Like other Waikiki hostels, this central establishment is in an older,

MARK NEWMAN

Cruise ship, **Alaska** (p1053)

MARK NEWMAN

Full moon over glacier, **Alaska** (p1027)

MARK NEWMAN

Brown bears (p1039), Alaska

Traditional caribou masks, **Alaska** (p1027)

LEE FOSTER

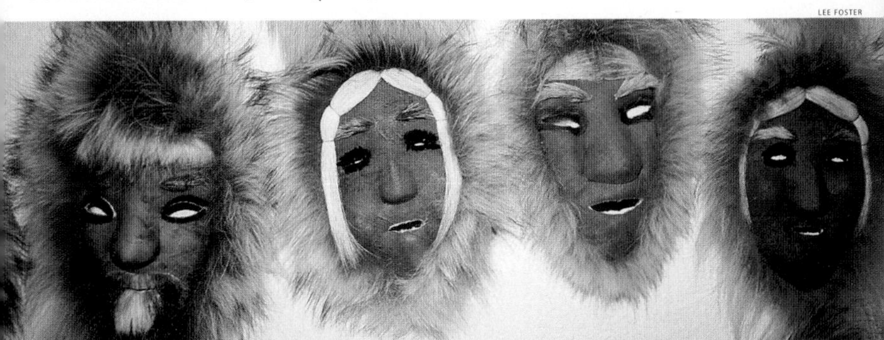

ANN CECIL

Sunset Beach Park (p1073), Oahu

CASEY MAHANEY

Snorkeler and green sea turtle, **Oahu** (p1063)

ANN CECIL

Orchids, **Lihue** (p1079), Kauai

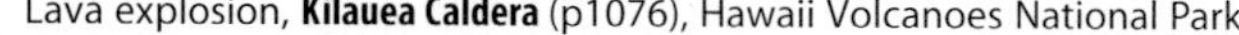

Lava explosion, **Kilauea Caldera** (p1076), Hawaii Volcanoes National Park

MARK NEWM

WAIKIKI

INFORMATION
- E-Cafe.......1 D2
- Hawaii Visitors & Convention Bureau.......2 C2
- Waldenbooks.......3 C2

SIGHTS & ACTIVITIES pp1068–71
- Duke's Canoe Club.......4 C3
- Honolulu Zoo.......5 E4
- Kodak Hula Show.......6 E4
- Waikiki-Kapahulu Library.......7 E3

SLEEPING pp1068–71
- HI Waikiki.......8 D3
- InterClub Hostel Waikiki.......9 D3
- Island Hostel.......10 B1
- Ohana Coral Seas.......11 C2
- Ohana Royal Islander.......12 B2
- Ohana Waikiki Hobron.......13 A1
- Ohana Waikiki Malia.......14 C2
- Ohana Waikiki Surf.......15 C2
- Sheraton Moana Surfrider.......16 D3
- Waikiki Prince Hotel.......17 D3

EATING pp1070–1
- Banyan Veranda.......(see 16)
- Ezogiku.......18 D4
- Fatty's Chinese Kitchen.......19 D2
- Food Pantry.......20 D2
- International Market Place.......21 C2
- Irifune's.......22 F3
- Moose McGillycuddy's.......23 C2
- Ono Hawaiian Food.......24 F2
- Patisserie.......25 B2
- Patisserie.......26 D2
- Perry's Smorgy.......27 D2
- Perry's Smorgy.......(see 11)
- Shore Bird Broiler.......28 B2

DRINKING p1071
- Angles Waikiki.......29 C2
- Fusion Waikiki.......(see 29)
- Hula's Bar & Lei Stand.......30 D4
- In-Between.......31 C2

TRANSPORT p1071
- Blue Sky Rentals.......32 B1
- Diamond Head Rentals.......33 C2

low-rise apartment complex. It can accommodate 60 travelers. The maximum stay is seven nights. Reserve two to three weeks in advance at busy times.

Island Hostel (☎ 808-942-8748; 1946 Ala Moana Blvd; dm/r $17/50; Ⓟ) Although the rooms aren't particularly huge here, they do have TVs, hot plates and private bathrooms. In addition, the hostel inhabits a relatively sedate area of the beach.

Sheraton Moana Surfrider (☎ 808-922-3111, 800-325-3535; www.moana-surfrider.com; 2365 Kalakaua Ave; d from $270; Ⓟ) Built in 1901, this grand establishment was Hawaii's first beachfront hotel. Despite the modern wings attached to the hotel's flanks, the Moana has survived with much of its original character intact. The lobby is open and airy, with high ceilings and Hawaiian artwork.

Eating & Drinking

Ethnic eateries are your best bet for value in Honolulu and Waikiki. By law every restaurant and bar is required to provide a nonsmoking section.

HONOLULU Map p1062

There are some excellent restaurants near the University of Hawaii, along S King St, S Beretania St and University Ave. Prices range from $4 to $10. You'll find other good eating options in the Ala Moana Center food court and nearby Ward Center and Ward Warehouse shopping complexes on Ala Moana Blvd.

Maunakea Marketplace In Chinatown a fun local dining option is the food court in on N Hotel St.

Ba Le Sandwich Shop (☎ 808-521-3973; 150 N King St) Near Maunakea Marketplace, this place has good snacks for breakfast and lunch.

To Chau (☎ 808-533-4549; 1007 River St) Highly recommended for its rich, noodly *pho* (Vietnamese beef or chicken noodle soup; $4).

Gordon Biersch Microbrewery Restaurant (☎ 808-599-4877; 1 Aloha Tower Dr) Beside the Aloha Tower on Ala Moana Blvd, this waterfront restaurant specializes in bistro fare and fresh brew.

Foodland In the Ala Moana Center, this supermarket is easily accessible by bus.

WAIKIKI Map p1069

Patisserie (Kuhio Ave; ☎ 808- 922-9752; 2330 Kuhio Ave; Kalia Rd; ☎ 808-922-4974; 2168 Kalia Rd) Offering pastries and coffee, Patisserie has two locations.

Fatty's Chinese Kitchen (☎ 808-922-9600; 2345 Kuhio Ave) This hole-in-the-wall eatery serves good meals for just $4.

International Market Place Waikiki's largest food court, adjacent to Fatty's.

Moose McGillycuddy's (☎ 808-923-0751; 310 Lewers St) Known for its omelettes and burgers.

Perry's Smorgy (Ohana Coral Seas ☎ 808-922-8814; 250 Lewers St; buffets $5-10; Kuhio Ave ☎ 808-926-0184; 2380 Kuhio Ave) There are two Perry's Smorgys: one at the Ohana Coral Seas hotel and the more attractive version at Kuhio Ave. Both offer all-you-can-eat buffets that go up in price as the day progresses.

Ezogiku (☎ 808-923-2013; 2546 Lemon Rd) A Japanese noodle shop with cheap food and long hours.

Shore Bird Broiler (☎ 808-922-2887; 2169 Kalia Rd) At the Outrigger Reef Hotel, this is the place for decent beachfront dining that won't break your budget.

Food Pantry (☎ 808-923-9821; 2370 Kuhio Ave; 24hr) The best place to get groceries.

There's a run of neighborhood ethnic restaurants along Kapahulu Ave, at the eastern side of Waikiki, including popular **Ono Hawaiian Foods** (☎ 808-737-2275; 726 Kapahulu Ave; dinner platters $9), with good Hawaiian meals, and **Irifune's** (☎ 808-737-1141; 563 Kapahulu Ave), with excellent Japanese fare for around $10.

For an atmospheric night out, **Banyan Veranda** (☎ 808-922-3111; 2365 Kalakaua Ave; buffet $30), at the Sheraton Moana Surfrider, has an international sunset buffet with live Hawaiian music.

Entertainment

Honolulu and Waikiki rock, gyrate, jam, croon, romance and mellow out. The free *Honolulu Weekly* has full details on what's happening in Honolulu. For information on free city-sponsored music and dance shows, held in various locales around Honolulu, call ☎ 808-527-5666.

Anna Bannanas (Map p1062; ☎ 808-946-5190, 2440 S Beretania St) Near the university, Anna Bannanas is a good weekend dance spot with rock and reggae bands.

Kapono's by the Pier (Map p1062; ☎ 808-536-2100) Next to the Aloha Tower, Kapono's has nightly live music, often including top-name Hawaiian acts.

GAY HONOLULU & WAIKIKI

Honolulu and Waikiki have well-developed gay scenes, and there are plenty of venues for folk to be queer. A fun resource with stories and links to events is www.outinhonolulu.com. For listings of gay-friendly establishments around the island and state, check out www.gayhawaii.com.

Venus (Map p1062; ☎ 808-951-8671; 1349 Kapiolani Blvd), northwest of the Ala Moana Center, is a popular gay bar with dancing, DJs and male revues. On the second floor of the Waikiki Grand hotel, **Hula's Bar & Lei Stand** (Map p1069; ☎ 808-923-0669, 134 Kapahulu Ave; 10am-2am) is Waikiki's number-one gay venue. It's a popular place to meet, dance, drink and watch the waves. Other good spots are **Angles Waikiki** (Map p1069; ☎ 808-926-9766; 2256 Kuhio Ave), with dancing, pool and video games; **Fusion Waikiki** (Map p1069; ☎ 808-924-2422; 2260 Kuhio Ave), which features karaoke and female impersonator shows; and **In-Between** (Map p1069; ☎ 808-926-7060; 2155 Lauula St), a gay karaoke bar.

Waikiki has lots of Hawaiian-style entertainment and Polynesian shows. Many beachfront hotels have events that people strolling along the shore can enjoy for free: two venues are the beachside courtyards at **Sheraton Moana Surfrider** (opposite) and **Duke's Canoe Club** (Map p1069; ☎ 922-2268; 2335 Kalakaua Ave) at the Outrigger Waikiki. **Moose McGillycuddy's** (opposite) has live music and dancing to about 1am nightly except Sunday.

Getting Around

From Honolulu International Airport, you can get to Waikiki by local bus Nos 19 and 20 ($1.75, one hour), airport shuttle ($6, 45 minutes, 6am to 10pm), taxi ($25) or rental car. The main car rental agencies all have desks at the airport.

All rides on **TheBus** (☎ 808-848-5555) cost $1.75. Nos 8, 19, 20 and 58 run between Waikiki and the Ala Moana Center, Honolulu's central transfer point. Nos 2, 19 and 20 run between Waikiki and downtown Honolulu.

Blue Sky Rentals (☎ 808-947-0101; 1920 Ala Moana Blvd), in Waikiki, rents mopeds for $30 per day and mountain bikes for $20. **Diamond Head Rentals** (☎ 808-921-2899), on Kuhio Ave, offers similar rates.

PEARL HARBOR & AROUND

Over 1.5 million people each year remember the 1941 Japanese bombing of Pearl Harbor with a visit to the **USS Arizona Memorial**. The surprise attack cost some 2500 American lives.

From the memorial, which sits directly over the sunken *Arizona*, visitors can look down on the wreck that became the tomb for 1177 sailors (whose average age was 19). The **visitors center** (☎ 808-422-2771, 24hr information 808-422-0561; 7:30am-5pm) runs free 1¼-hour tours that include an interesting documentary on the attack and a boat ride out to the memorial and back. Tours run on a first-come, first-served basis. Arrive early to beat the queues.

The nearby **Bowfin Park** (☎ 808-423-1341; admission free; 8am-5pm) contains a moored WWII submarine and the **Pacific Submarine Museum** (admission $8). Bowfin Park is also the departure point for the **USS Missouri** (☎ 808-973-2494; admission $14; 9am-5pm), whose deck hosted the Japanese surrender that ended WWII.

Following September 11, 2001, no one is allowed to bring any bags or large cameras into the sites at all, and there are no lockers.

Take bus No 42 to Pearl Harbor ($1.75, one hour from Waikiki) or the **Arizona Memorial Shuttle Bus** (☎ 808-839-0911), which picks up from Waikiki hotels ($3/5 one way/round-trip, reservations required).

North of Pearl Harbor in Aiea, **Keaiwa Heiau State Park** (☎ 808-483-2511; Aiea Heights Dr; 7am-dusk) has **camping** (☎ 808-587-0300 for a permit; campsites $5) Friday to Tuesday and a 4.5-mile scenic trail.

SOUTHEAST OAHU

Some of Oahu's finest scenery is along the southeast coast, which curves around the tip of the Koolau Range. To make the loop around southeast Oahu from Waikiki, take the BeachBus No 22 to Sea Life Park, at Makapuu Point, and then No 57 up to Kailua and back into Honolulu.

Diamond Head State Monument

Visitors can climb this extinct volcano (760ft) along a fairly steep **hiking** trail to the crater rim ($1 entry, open 6am-6pm). The trail (1.5 miles round-trip) goes through some of the tunnels built by the US Army early in the 20th century. At the top are sweeping views of Waikiki. Take bus No 22 or 58 from Waikiki.

Koko Head Regional Park

The entire Koko Head area is a county regional park, featuring volcanic tuff cones and other curious rock formations, Sandy Beach (a top spot for experienced bodysurfers) and a blowhole that gushes during incoming tides. A splendid upmarket area restaurant is **Roy's** (☎ 808-396-7697; Hawaii Kai Corporate Plaza, Hwy 72; mains $20-30), with spectacular Pacific Rim cuisine.

Hanauma Bay Beach Park

This very popular **park** (☎ 808-396-4229; admission $3; ⌚ Wed-Mon 6am-6pm, 6am-7pm in summer) encircles a wide, sheltered bay of sapphire and turquoise waters set in a rugged volcanic ring. There's excellent snorkeling and diving year round, though heavy use of the bay has damaged the coral on the shallow reef. A concession stand rents out snorkel gear. Take bus No 22 from Waikiki.

Makapuu Point

North of Sandy Beach, 647ft Makapuu Point and its lighthouse mark the easternmost point of Oahu. **Makapuu Beach** is one of the island's top winter spots for experienced bodysurfers. Opposite the beach is **Sea Life Park** (☎ 808-259-7933; 41-202 Hwy 72; adults/children $25/12.50; ⌚ 9:30am-5pm), Hawaii's only marine park, with aquariums and dolphin shows; there's no charge for the adjacent Whaling Museum. Take bus Nos 22 or 57 'Kailua/Sea Life Park.'

WINDWARD COAST

Scenic Pali Hwy (Hwy 61) runs between Honolulu and Kailua, cutting through the spectacular Koolau Range. **Nuuanu Pali Lookout** (1200ft) is where Kamehameha the Great's invading troops, in 1795, forced hundreds of Oahu warriors over the cliff (some hundred years later, more than 500 skulls were discovered at the base of the cliffs).

Windward Oahu, the island's eastern side, follows the Koolau Range along its entire length, from Kahuku Point in the north to Makapuu Point in the south. The coast is exposed to the northeast trade winds, creating ideal conditions for windsurfing.

Kailua

This ordinary middle-class community shelters lovely **Kailua Beach**, the island's top **windsurfing** spot (gear rental and lessons available weekdays on the beach). Popoia Island, an offshore bird sanctuary, is a popular destination for kayakers. **Naish Hawaii** (☎ 808-262-6068, 800-767-6068; 155A Hamakua Dr) books windsurfing vacations.

Kailua has no hotels, but there are many furnished beachfront cottages, studios and B&B-style rooms in private homes. For reservations, contact **Affordable Paradise Bed & Breakfast** (☎ 808-261-1693; www.affordable-paradise.com; 332 Kuukama St; r from $45).

Kaneohe

Kaneohe Bay is the state's largest bay and reef-sheltered lagoon. The near-constant trade winds are ideal for sailing. Free weekend camping (some of the island's safest) is allowed in **Hoomaluhia Park**, in the uplands of Kaneohe. This 400-acre park contains a lush botanical garden. To get a permit, call ☎ 808-233-7323 or visit the park between 9am and 4pm any day.

Off the Kahekili Hwy, 1.5 miles north of Haiku Rd, is the **Valley of the Temples** (☎ 808-239-8811; admission $2; ⌚ 8am-5pm), an interdenominational cemetery. The main attraction here is the Japanese Buddhist **Byodo-In**, the 'Temple of Equality,' which sits against the scenic Koolau Range.

Kualoa Regional Park

This is a nice beach park in a scenic setting just south of Kaaawa. Apua Pond, a brackish salt marsh on the point, is a nesting area for the endangered *aeo* (Hawaiian stilt). Camping is free Friday to Tuesday (permit required, ☎ 808-523-4525).

Laie

Laie is the site of a stately 1919 **Mormon Temple**, the first built outside the mainland USA (the temple interior is off-limits to tourists). The Mormon-run **Polynesian Cultural Center** (☎ 808-293-3333; admission $35; ⌚ 8:30am-4pm Mon-Thu, 8:30am-6pm Fri), Oahu's second-most-visited attraction, re-creates seven theme villages representing Samoa, New Zealand, Fiji, Tahiti, Tonga, the Marquesas and Hawaii. **Laie Inn**

(☎ 808-293-9282, 800-526-4562; laieinn@hawaii.rr.com; 55-109 Laniloa St; r $90;), outside the Polynesian Cultural Center, offers comfortable rooms with continental breakfast included.

Malaekahana Beach

Attractive Malaekahana Beach, between Laie and Kahuku, is good for swimming, bodysurfing, board surfing and windsurfing. Mokuauia, a state bird sanctuary just offshore, has a nice sandy cove with good snorkeling.

Malaekahana State Recreation Area, at the beach, has the best campgrounds on this end of the windward coast. You can camp in the park's main **Kalanai Point section** (☎ 808-587-0300; campsites $5) with a permit, or rent a rustic cabin in the **Makahoa Point section** (☎ 808-293-1736; cabins $70), which is privately operated.

NORTH SHORE

Oahu's North Shore is synonymous with surfing and prime winter waves. Sunset Beach, the Banzai Pipeline and Waimea Bay are among the world's top surf spots and attract some of the best international surfers.

Waikiki surfers started taking on North Shore breakers in the late 1950s, and big-time surf competitions followed a few years later. Each December the North Shore hosts three major surf competitions, collectively known as the Triple Crown, with prize purses reaching six figures.

Haleiwa

This is the gateway to the North Shore, with a picturesque boat harbor bounded by beach parks. It was also the main setting for the TV show *Baywatch Hawaii*. **Haleiwa Alii Beach Park** is the site of several surfing tournaments in the winter, when northern swells can bring waves as high as 20ft. The county gives free **surfing lessons** (☎ 808-637-5051) here on weekend mornings in winter. **Surf-N-Sea** (☎ 808-637-9887) rents boards and equipment for other water sports and also offers lessons.

Camping with a permit is allowed in **Kaiaka Beach Park** (☎ 808-523-4525), about a mile west of town, and **Mokuleia Beach Park**, further west. In town, the casual **Surfhouse Hawaii** (☎ 808-637-7146; www.surfhouse.com; 62-203 Lokoea Pl; s/d campsite $9/15, dm $15, bungalow $45) is a backpacker's heaven. Other people occasionally rent out rooms in their homes; check the bulletin boards at Coffee Gallery, Celestial Natural Foods and Haleiwa Super Market.

Most Haleiwa restaurants, including the famous surfer haunt **Cafe Haleiwa** (☎ 808-637-5516; 66-460 Kamehameha Ave; meals $3-8), are lined up along Kamehameha Ave, the main drag.

Waimea

The **Waimea Bay Beach Park** is the North Shore's most popular beach. Winter belongs to surfers. Summer is usually the only time the water is calm enough for swimming and snorkeling. Across the highway, **Waimea Falls Park** (☎ 808-638-8511; 59-864 Kamehameha Hwy; admission $24; 10am-5:30pm) is a botanical garden, cultural preserve and tourist park all in one.

Along the highway, **Pupukea Beach Park** is a long beach that includes the Three Tables area (so named for stone ledges) on the left and Shark's Cove on the right. Both have good snorkeling and diving in summer only, and Shark's Cove has Oahu's most popular cavern dive. In the middle is Old Quarry, where a wonderful array of jagged rock formations and tidal pools are exposed at low tide.

The main reason people come to Ekuhai Beach Park is to watch the pros surf the world-famous **Banzai Pipeline**, a few hundred feet to the left of the park. Just south of mile marker 9, **Sunset Beach Park** is Oahu's classic winter surf spot, with incredible waves and challenging breaks. Backyards, the surf break off Sunset Point at the northern end of the beach, draws a lot of top windsurfers.

KILLER WAVES

Hawaii lies smack in the path of all the major swells that run unimpeded across the Pacific, and they hit hardest in winter, breaking along the North Shore. Waimea Bay holds the record for the highest waves ever ridden in international competition. When the surf's up, crowds of spectators throng to watch Waimea surfers perform their near-suicidal feats on winter waves reaching up to 35ft.

'The Quiksilver in Memory of Eddi Aikau' contest, which attracts the world's top surfers, is named for a local surfing legend who died in a rescue attempt in 1978. The current record holder is Noah Johnson, who rode a 25ft wave to victory in 1999.

Opposite Three Tables, **Backpackers** (☎ 808-638-7838; www.backpackers-hawaii.com; 59-788 Kamehameha Hwy; dm from $15, r from $45;) is pretty much a surfers' hangout. You can get fast food and plate lunches at **Sunset Pizza** (☎ 808-638-8497; 39-176 Kamehameha Hwy; pizza $9-18), opposite Sunset Beach Park.

LEEWARD (WAIANAE) COAST

The road doesn't connect around the far western tip of the island (Kaena Point). It's a big detour to the leeward (west) coast, which has few attractions other than watching surfers or hitting the waves yourself at **Makaha Beach Park**. The Waianae Coast remains the island's least-touristed side, and the area has a history of resisting development and a reputation for being unreceptive to outsiders.

HAWAII (THE BIG ISLAND)

The island of Hawaii is suitably dubbed the 'Big Island,' as it's larger than all the other Hawaiian islands combined. It encompasses an amazingly varied geography that includes active volcanoes, coastal deserts, lush rainforests and snowy mountaintops. The prime attraction is Hawaii Volcanoes National Park, but dozens of beaches and historic sites provide stiff competition.

Getting There & Around

The airports in Kailua and Hilo both have car rental booths and taxi stands. Most flights into these airports are from other islands, but United Airlines offers a few nonstop flights to Kailua from California.

Hele-On (☎ 808-961-8744), the county public bus system, connects Hilo and Kailua ($5.25), Kailua and Waimea ($3), and Waimea and Hilo ($4.50). There are four other routes: Pahoa to Hilo, Honokaa to Hilo, Waiohinu to Hilo via Volcano, and Hilo to the Waikoloa hotels in the South Kohala district. Service is infrequent, so call ahead for schedules.

KAILUA

The Kona Coast is the dry, sunny west coast of the Big Island, but the name 'Kona' is also used to refer to this coast's largest town, Kailua. You don't even have to choose between the two, as the town is often called 'Kailua-Kona.'

The largest vacation destination on the Big Island, Kailua has good weather year-round and outdoor activities ranging from world-class deep-sea fishing to snorkeling cruises. Every October 1500 athletes from 50 countries descend on the city to compete in the Ironman Triathlon.

The grounds of King Kamehameha's Kona Beach Hotel at **Kamakahonu** beach were once the site of Kamehameha the Great's royal residence. They include the **Ahuena Heiau**, a temple once used for human sacrifice.

A few minutes away on Alii Dr is the lava-rock **Mokuaikaua Church** (☎ 808-329-0655; Alii Dr; admission free; 7:30am-5:30pm), built in 1836. The 1838 **Hulihee Palace** (☎ 808-329-1877; 75-5718 Alii Dr; admission $5; 9am-4pm), opposite, is a museum with good Hawaiian artifacts. **Kahaluu Beach**, on Alii Dr in Keauhou at the south side of Kailua, has the island's best easy-access snorkeling; gear rental ($8) is available from an on-site vendor.

Kiwi Gardens (☎ 808-326-1559; www.kiwigardens.com; 74-4920 Kiwi St; d from $85) is an amiable B&B that boasts a common room complete with jukebox and old-school soda fountain. It's 3 miles northeast of the town center. Reasonable hotels include the popular, vintage **Kona Tiki Hotel** (☎ 808-329-1425; 75-5968 Alii Dr; r from $60) and **Kona Bay Hotel** (☎ 808-329-1393, 800-367-5102; unclebillys@aloha.net; 75-5739 Alii Dr; r $90-100;), with several conveniences but not much charm. Hostel-like **Patey's Place** (☎ 808-326-7018; patey@mail.gte.net; 75-195 Ala-Ona Ona St; dm/s/d $20/35/46;) is cheap, with worn but clean rooms.

Unassuming **Ocean View Inn** (☎ 808-329-9998; 75-5683 Alii Dr; mains from $5; Tue-Sun), in the town center, has good, inexpensive Chinese, American and Hawaiian food. **Quinn's** (☎ 808-329-3822; 75-5655 Palani Rd; mains $9-20), a bar opposite King Kamehameha's Kona Beach Hotel, serves Kona's best fresh fish. **Island Lava Java** (☎ 808-327-2161; 75-5799 Alii Dr; snacks from $4), at Alii Sunset Plaza, is a great little coffee and sandwich shop and often has music in the evenings.

Happy-hour specials abound in the open-air restaurants along Alii Dr. You can dance nightly to reggae, Top 40 or Hawaiian music at **Huggo's** (☎ 808-329-1493; 75-5828 Kahakai Rd), next to the Royal Kona Resort.

The **Alii Shuttle** (☎ 808-775-7121) runs between Kailua and Keauhou ($2 one way, day pass $5). Bike rentals are available from **Hawaiian Pedals** (☎ 808-329-2294; 75-5744 Alii Dr).

SOUTH KONA COAST

Aquatic explorations and Hawaiian history are the highlights of this area.

A side road off Hwy 11 leads to the mile-wide Kealakekua Bay. **Kealakekua Bay State Historical Park** is at the bay's south end, and an obelisk at its north end marks the spot where Captain Cook was killed. The bay's north end has some of the best **snorkeling** on the Big Island, but can be reached only by sea or by hiking along a dirt trail (1½ hours). **Fairwind** (☎ 808-322-2788, 800-677-9461; www.fair-wind.com; 3½hr cruise $50) offers snorkeling trips from Keauhou.

Manago Hotel (☎ 808-323-2642; 82-6155 Mamalahoa Hwy; s/d from $25/28), on Hwy 11 in the town of Captain Cook, offers simple rooms with shared bath and the town's favorite restaurant (closed Monday).

Four miles south of Kealakekua Bay, incredible **Puuhonua O Honaunau National Historical Park** (☎ 808-328-2288; www.nps.gov/puho; week pass adult/family $3/5; 7:30am-8pm Sun-Thu, 6am-11pm Fri & Sat), also called the 'Place of Refuge,' includes ancient temples, royal grounds and a *puuhonua* (sanctuary). There's terrific snorkeling and diving near the small boat ramp immediately north of the park.

NORTH KONA COAST

Beautiful secluded beaches, most accessible only by foot, lie on the north Kona Coast, but cars can reach undeveloped **Kona Coast State Park** (Hwy 19; admission free; closed Wed). Most of the Big Island's fanciest resorts are further north, in the Waikoloa area of the South Kohala district. South Kohala was an important area in Hawaiian history, and it shelters *heiau* (ancient stone temples), fishponds, petroglyphs and ancient trails that can be fun to explore. The popular **Hapuna Beach State Recreation Park** has a snack bar and A-frame cabins ($20 for up to four); make reservations at any state park office (☎ 808-974-6200 on the Big Island).

NORTH KOHALA

The northwest tip of the Big Island is dominated by a central ridge, the Kohala Mountains. Off Hwy 270, just south of mile marker 14, are the remains of a 600-year-old deserted fishing village, now **Lapakahi State Historical Park** (admission free; 8am-4pm except holidays). **Mookini Heiau**, on the desolate northern tip of the Big Island, is one of the oldest and most historically significant temples in Hawaii. A stone enclosure nearby marks the birth site of Kamehameha the Great. Hwy 270 ends at a viewpoint that overlooks secluded **Pololu Valley** and the trailhead for a 20-minute walk down to the valley.

DORMANT DOMESTIC DISHARMONY

Just below Mauna Kea's summit is the Puu Poliahu, home of the goddess of snow. According to legend, Poliahu is far more beautiful than her sister Pele. Occasionally, Pele would get catty and erupt Mauna Kea, forcing Poliahu to pack it over with ice and snow. Further angered, Pele would cause the mountain to erupt again.

Interestingly, the legend has roots in geological fact: as recently as 10,000 years ago, there were volcanic eruptions up through glacial ice caps here.

SADDLE RD

The 50-mile Saddle Rd (Hwy 200), Hawaii's most remote thoroughfare, cuts across the 'saddle' between the two highest points on the island, Mauna Kea and Mauna Loa. Although the road is paved, most car rental contracts prohibit travel on it, and there are no gas stations or other facilities along the way.

Hawaii's highest mountain, **Mauna Kea** (13,796ft) is topped with a cluster of world-class astronomical observatories. The **Onizuka Center for International Astronomy** (☎ 808-961-2180; admission free; 9am-10pm, with breaks) offers displays, free astronomy presentations, stargazing and summit tours. A rugged 6-mile hiking trail from the visitors center to the summit begins at 9300ft and takes four to five hours; start early in the day, bring warm clothing and be prepared for severe weather conditions.

HAMAKUA COAST

The Hamakua Coast offers some of the Big Island's most gorgeous scenery.

At the end of Hwy 240, the large, lush, spectacular amphitheater of **Waipio Valley** is a mix of tangled jungle, flowering plants, taro patches and waterfalls, fronted by a black-sand beach. The 45-minute hike down from the lookout to the valley floor is steep, so expect a good workout. **Waipio Valley Shuttle & Tours** (☎ 808-775-7121; 48-5416 Government Main Rd, Honokaa; $40; tours 9am-3pm Mon-Sat) runs 90-minute 4WD taxi tours, while **Waipio Valley Wagon Tours** (☎ 808-775-9518; 45-3620 Mamane St, Honokaa; $40; tours 9:30am, 11:30am, 1:30pm & 3:30pm Mon-Sat) offers one-hour jaunts in open mule-drawn wagons.

In Honokaa, 8 miles east of Waipio, is **Hotel Honokaa Club** (☎ 808-775-0678, 800-808-0678; http://home1.gte.net/honokaac; 45-3480 Mamane St; dm/s/d $15/20/30; 💻). It may be basic, but it's the only game in town.

Akaka Falls State Park has the Big Island's most impressive accessible waterfall, with a couple of stunning lookouts along a short rainforest loop trail. Between Honomu and Hilo is the delightful 4-mile **Pepeekeo Scenic Dr** off Hwy 19 through lush tropical jungle.

HILO

In terms of lush natural beauty, Hilo, the county capital, beats Kailua any day – the only catch is finding a dry one. Not only is the city the wettest in the country (residents say, 'In Hilo, people don't tan: they rust'), but it has a habit of being slammed by tsunamis – two in the last 50 years. This soggy reputation keeps the tourists away and allows the city to remain affordable, attracting an ethnically diverse alternative community of back-to-the-earth folks.

The **Big Island Visitors Bureau** (☎ 808-961-5797; 250 Keawe St at Haili St; 🕑 8am-4:30pm Mon-Fri) offers an informative free walking-tour brochure.

Downtown Hilo is an intriguing mishmash of classic old buildings and aging wooden storefronts. The excellent **Lyman House Memorial Museum** (☎ 808-935-5021; www.lymanmuseum.org; 276 Haili St; admission $7; 🕑 9am-4:30pm Mon-Sat) offers insight into Hawaii's history. Morning is the best time to see rainbows at **Rainbow Falls**, off Waianuenue Ave. Another 1.5 miles up the avenue, **Peepee Falls** drop from a sheer rock face into bubbling pools known as the Boiling Pots.

A great place to meet other travelers is **Arnott's Lodge** (☎ 808-969-7097; www.arnottslodge.com; 98 Apapane Rd; campsites $9, dm/s/d $17/37/47; 💻), which also offers a host of activities and tours. In downtown Hilo, convenient **Wild Ginger Inn** (☎ 808-935-5556; www.wildgingerinn.com; 100 Puueo St; d from $70; 💻) boasts colorful, exuberant garden decor and includes breakfast in the price. Popular **Dolphin Bay Hotel** (☎ 808-935-1466; www.dolphinbayhilo.com; 333 Iliahi St; s/d from $66/69) is on a hill just above downtown.

For a thoroughly local dining experience, head to inexpensive **Cafe 100** (☎ 808-935-8683; 969 Kilauea Ave; sandwiches from $2). **Hawaiian Jungle** (☎ 808-934-0700; 110 Kalakaua St; mains $5-16) boasts tiki torches, lazy ceiling fans, large windows and wholesome Latin American food.

HAWAII VOLCANOES NATIONAL PARK

Unique among American parks, **Hawaii Volcanoes National Park** (☎ 24hr hotline 808-985-6000; www.nps.gov/havo; week pass per person/car $5/10) contains two active volcanoes and terrain ranging from tropical beaches to the sub-arctic summit of Mauna Loa (13,679ft). The centerpiece is Kilauea Caldera, the still-steaming sunken center of Kilauea Volcano.

Rangers at the Kilauea Visitors Center, near the park entrance, can provide the lowdown on guided walks, trail conditions and the like.

The park experiences a wide range of climatic conditions, so layering clothing is advisable. Stay on marked trails and heed warning signs.

Crater Rim Dr

This amazing 11-mile loop road skirts the rim of Kilauea Caldera with marked stops at steam vents and crater lookouts. Short trails and trailheads provide starting points for longer hikes into and around the caldera. **Jaggar Museum** (☎ 808-985-6049; admission free; 🕑 8:30am-5pm) is worth a visit for its displays and fine view of Halemaumau Crater.

The Halemaumau Overlook, perched on the crater rim, is at the start of the **Halemaumau Trail**, which runs 3 miles across Kilauea Caldera. Crater Rim Rd continues across the barren Kau Desert and then through the fallout area of the 1959 eruption of Kilauea Iki Crater. **Devastation Trail** is a fascinating 0.5-mile walk across a former rainforest devastated by cinder and pumice from that eruption. The tunnel-like **Thurston Lava Tube** is almost big enough to run a train through.

Chain of Craters Rd

Once a through route to Puna, this road, which winds 20 miles down the slopes of

Kilauea Volcano, now ends abruptly near the coast, where recent eruptions have buried it in lava. At the road's end you can see steam plumes shooting up as the molten lava flows into the sea, and if you wait till dark the hillside glows a fiery red. It's a good, paved two-lane road, but there are no services, so bring water and check the gas tank before striking out.

Mauna Loa Rd

About 1.5 miles up this road you'll find the **Kipuka Puaulu Loop Trail**, which runs through a curious sanctuary of native Hawaiian forest. The rugged 18-mile **Mauna Loa Trail**, which ascends 6600ft up the slopes of Mauna Loa, begins at the end of the road.

Sleeping & Eating

Hiking shelters and simple cabins are available at no charge along some of the park's longer backcountry trails. There are two primitive camping areas, at **Apua Point** and the **Napau Crater**. Overnight hikers must register no more than one day ahead and obtain a free permit at the visitors center before heading out. Camping is also free at two roadside campgrounds: **Namakani Paio**, which is 3 miles north off Hwy 11 and 5 miles west of the Volcanoes National Park entrance, and **Kulanaokuaiki**, about 5 miles down Hilina Pali Rd, off Chain of Craters Rd; there's no registration or reservation system.

Volcano House (☎ 808-967-7321; r from $85), opposite the visitors center, offers comfortable, heated rooms. It also manages the 10 dreary **Namakani Paio Cabins** ($40 for up to 4 people) in the park. In addition, it maintains a pricey restaurant with ordinary fare and a small snack bar.

Another option is to stay in the nondescript village of Volcano, just east of the park. **HI Holo Holo In** (☎ 808-967-7950, 800-671-2999; 19-4036 Kalani Honua Rd; dm/d $15/40) is a friendly little hostel. Also in Volcano, comfortable **Kilauea Lodge** (☎ 808-967-7366; www.kilauealodge.com; d from $125; 💻 🚭) offers a variety of solid, upmarket options.

Volcano village has some decent eating options. **Lava Rock Cafe** (☎ 808-967-8526; Old Volcano Rd; mains $6-12) offers good breakfasts and lunches, while **Thai Thai Restaurant** (19-4084 Old Volcano Rd; dishes $9-13) serves up tangy curries and noodles with plenty of vegetarian choices.

Getting There & Away

The public bus (☎ 808-961-8744) between Hilo and Waiohinu stops at the visitors center (and at Volcano village) once in each direction weekdays ($2.25, one hour).

MAUI

Maui is the paradigmatic island destination. It lures visitors with the promise of tranquil, lethargic days, free from any cares, and then bombards them with a surprising arsenal of delights. You may have your heart set on lounging in a hammock, but it's difficult to resist Maui's superb scenery and diverse landscapes, and eventually you'll have to jump into the water for a bout of world-class swimming, snorkeling, surfing or windsurfing. As if all that weren't enough, the island's warm coastal waters are the main wintering grounds for North Pacific humpback whales, making for wonderful whale-watching. Not surprisingly, Maui has become the most visited and developed of the Neighbor Islands (the main Hawaiian islands other than Oahu).

The main airport is in Kahului, with two smaller ones at Kapalua and Hana. All the major car rental companies have booths at Kahului's airport. Shuttles run from the airport to the major towns ($16 to $46 for two people).

If you fall into health trouble in paradise, head to **Maui Memorial Hospital** (☎ 808-244-9056; 221 Mahalani St, Kahului), which has 24-hour emergency services.

LAHAINA & KAANAPALI

The former whaling port of Lahaina buzzes with commercial activity and shelters plenty of historic buildings that can be fun to poke around. The main drag and tourist strip is

THE ONE THAT DIDN'T GET AWAY

According to legend, the Polynesian demigod Maui was wandering the Pacific on a fishing expedition when his fishhook snagged the sea floor. He tugged with such force that the islands of Hawaii were yanked to the surface. He then claimed the conveniently monikered island of Maui and made it his home.

HAWAII

Front St, with its bustling harbor backed by the whaling-era **Pioneer Inn** and a park boasting the largest **banyan tree** in the USA. In winter, Papawai Point, a roadside area between Lahaina and Maalaea, is a prime **whale-watching** spot.

You couldn't be closer to the action than at the harborside **Best Western Pioneer Inn** (☎ 808-661-3636, 800-457-5457; d from $120;). Lahaina has lots of restaurants and fast-food outlets in its malls. **Westside Natural Foods & Deli** (193 Lahainaluna Rd) sells organic vegetarian dishes by weight. **Lahaina Coolers** (☎ 808-661-7082; 180 Dickenson St; breakfasts & lunches $5-11, dinners $11-18) is where local dive masters hang out, enjoying burgers, salads and sandwiches. **Pacific'O** (☎ 808-667-4341; 505 Front St; lunches $10-15, dinners $20-30) is Lahaina's top fine-dining spot, with beachside tables, impeccable service and imaginative contemporary Pacific cuisine.

To the north, Kaanapali is a high-rise resort community with 3 miles of sandy beach open to the public. Kaanapali's main attractions are the snorkeling at Black Rock and the **Whaling Museum** (☎ 808-661-4567; 2345 Kaanapali Parkway; admission free; 9:30am-10pm) in the Whalers Village mall. The West Maui Shopping Express runs shuttles between Lahaina and Kaanapali ($1).

KIHEI, WAILEA & MAKENA

Maui's fastest-growing community, **Kihei** is fringed with sandy beaches and has long attracted sunbathers, boogie boarders and windsurfers. **Two Mermaids on the Sunny Side of Maui B&B** (☎ 808-874-8687, 800-598-9550; www.twomermaids.com; 2840 Umalu Pl; studio/apt $95/125;) has cheerful rooms, all with private baths, kitchenettes and acoustic guitars. Guests rave about the hospitality of the owners.

Wailana Kai (☎ 808-891-1626, 866-891-1626; www.wailanakai.com; 34 Wailana Pl; 1-bedroom units $75-90, 2-bedroom units $90-110;) has 10 pleasant condo units. **Hapa's Brew Haus** (☎ 808-879-9001; 41 E Lipoa St) is a restaurant-bar-nightclub that serves sushi and dance tunes.

The manicured lava-rock coastline around upmarket **Wailea** is broken by attractive gold-sand beaches, with really good swimming and snorkeling, and superb shoreline whale-watching in winter. **Makena** has two knockout undeveloped beaches – **Big Beach** and the secluded **Little Beach**. After Big Beach, Makena Rd goes through the **Ahihi-Kinau Natural Area Reserve**, with its lava tide pools, before ending just short of La Perouse Bay.

KAHULUI-WAILUKU & AROUND

Kahului and Wailuku, which are Maui's two largest communities, flow together in one urban sprawl. The more historic Wailuku makes for a good stroll, especially along Market St. Three miles out of Wailuku, **Iao Valley State Monument** (Iao Valley Rd; admission free; 7am-7pm) is nestled in the mountains and centers on the stunning Iao Needle rock pinnacle, which rises 1200ft from the valley floor.

In Wailuku, **Northshore Hostel** (☎ 808-242-8999; 2080 Vineyard St; dm/s/d $16/29/38;) is popular with European travelers. Nearby **Banana Bungalow** (☎ 808-244-5090, 800-846-7835; www.mauihostel.com; 310 N Market St; dm/s/d $18/32/40;) offers free Internet access, a backyard Jacuzzi and hammocks, and a shuttle to the beach.

Wailuku has a range of reasonably priced ethnic restaurants near the intersection of Vineyard and Market Sts.

PAIA

This old sugar town has a more international flavor than any other small town in Hawaii. In the 1980s, windsurfers began discovering nearby **Hookipa Beach**, and Paia was dubbed the 'Windsurfing Capital of the World.' **Mana Foods** (☎ 808-579-8078; 49 Baldwin Ave), a top-notch health-food store, has a bulletin board with rental ads. **Picnics** (☎ 808-579-8021; 30 Baldwin Ave; dishes $5-8) prepares box lunches for the road to Hana. **Jacques North Shore & Sushi** (☎ 808-579-8844; 120 Hana Hwy) has the island's longest monkeypod bar and is the most popular place in town for a drink.

HANA HWY

The Hana Hwy (Hwy 360) is Hawaii's most spectacular coastal drive. It's a cliff-hugger, winding its way deep into lush valleys and back out above a rugged coastline. **YMCA Camp Keanae** (☎ 808-242-9007; ymcacampkeanae@aol.com; 13375 Hana Hwy; campsites & dm $15) offers hostel-style beds in guest cabins, but advance reservations are required. You can also set up your tent here. **Waianapanapa State Park**, just north of Hana, shelters two impressive lava-tube caves with clear mineral waters. Tent **camping** (☎ 808-984-8109) is allowed with a permit.

HANA & AROUND

Hana's isolation has protected it from development. Surfers head to Waikoloa Beach, while nude sunbathers favor gorgeous Kaihalulu (Red Sand) Beach, reached by trail from the end of Uakea Rd. There's free tent camping (no permit necessary) at **Oheo Gulch**, 10 miles south of Hana. **Joe's Place** (☎ 808-248-7033; www.joesrentals.com; 4870 Uakea Rd; d from $45) has clean, comfortable and basic rooms, while **Aloha Cottages** (☎ 808-248-8420; 83 Keawa Pl; studios from $62) provides twin beds, a hot plate, a toaster and a fridge. **Tutu's** (☎ 808-248-8224; 174 Hana Bay; dishes under $5; Mon-Thu), a grill at Hana Beach Park, has the best food value in Hana.

The road south from Hana is also incredibly beautiful. Oheo Stream dramatically cuts its way through **Oheo Gulch** as a lovely series of wide pools and waterfalls, each tumbling into the one below. Just past the gulch is Kipahulu, burial site of aviator Charles Lindbergh.

HALEAKALA NATIONAL PARK

Haleakala Crater, in the middle of the world's largest dormant volcano, resembles the surface of the moon, with a seemingly lifeless floor dotted with high, majestic cinder cones. It's so big that the island of Manhattan could fit inside. **Haleakala National Park** (☎ 808-572-4400; www.nps.gov/hale; week pass per person/car $5/10; 8am-4pm) centers on the crater, offering impressive views from its rim and several hikes across the crater floor. For the best crater views, arrive for sunrise – Mark Twain called the experience the 'sublimest spectacle' he'd ever seen.

Check on weather conditions and sunrise times (☎ 808-871-5054) before heading up to the park. Park headquarters provides permits for camping in the crater and can give you details on free guided hikes and nature talks.

Free tent camping is allowed at **Hosmer Grove**, near the main entrance (three-night maximum), but permits (first-come, first-served, from the park headquarters) are required for the two **backcountry campgrounds** inside Haleakala Crater. The park also has primitive cabins, but demand for these is so high they hold a monthly lottery (write to Cabin Lottery Request, Haleakala National Park, Box 369, Makawao, HI 96768 two months in advance).

IT'S BEEN THE RUIN OF MANY A POOR DEMIGOD

In Hawaiian, *haleakala* means 'house of the sun.' According to legend, atop this very volcano that prankster Maui lassoed the sun with ropes braided from his sister's hair and refused to let go, even as the sun begged for mercy. Not until the celestial body agreed to slow its daily race across the sky, and thereby bathe the islands in more hours of glorious sunlight, did Maui release his hold.

KAUAI

Kauai, the least developed of Hawaii's four major islands, offers stunning natural beauty. Its central volcanic peak, Mt Waialeale, is one of the rainiest places on earth, feeding scores of scenic waterfalls and a unique rainforest. On the northwest coast of Kauai are the spectacular Na Pali cliffs, Hawaii's foremost hiking destination.

Kauai's main airport is in Lihue. All the major car rental companies maintain booths there, and taxis line up outside the arrival area. Kauai has rather a limited public bus service (☎ 808-241-6410, $1.50 all routes, no service Sunday), which does not serve the airport.

LIHUE

Lihue is the island's capital. Seek information at the **Kauai Visitors Bureau** (☎ 808-245-3971; 4334 Rice St; 8am-4:30pm Mon-Fri). The **Kauai Museum** (☎ 808-245-6931; 4428 Rice St; admission $5; 9am-4pm Mon-Fri, 10am-4pm Sat) traces Kauai's history.

Garden Island Inn (☎ 808-245-7227, 800-648-0154; 3445 Wilcox Rd; d from $75) is only a few minutes from the beach. **Tip Top Motel** (☎ 808-245-2333; tiptop@aloha.net; 3173 Akahi St; d $45;) offers basic rooms. **Motel Lani** (☎ 808-245-2965; 4240 Rice St; d from $35;) is Lihue's best budget choice.

Hamura Saimin (☎ 808-245-3271; 2956 Kress St; noodle soups $3.50) is a local favorite, serving quick Japanese fare. **Fish Express** (☎ 808-245-9918; 3343 Kuhio Hwy; fish dishes $7), on Hwy 50 near the hospital, has unbeatable fresh fish dishes.

NA PALI COAST & NORTH SHORE

Kauai's lush and mountainous North Shore features incredible scenery and good water-sports options. At Kilauea Point are a picturesque lighthouse and a thriving seabird sanctuary.

Hanalei, on a magnificent bay, has sports shops renting out kayaks for paddling up the Hanalei River. Camping is allowed on weekends at **Hanalei Beach Park** (☎ 808-241-6660; campsites $3) with a permit. **Historic B&B** (☎ 808-826-4622, 877-229-8205; www.historicbnb.com; 5-5067 Kuhio Hwy; d from $85) occupies the oldest Buddhist temple on Kauai. Serene rooms feature Japanese-style sliding doors and tatami mats.

At the western end of Hwy 56 is lovely **Kee Beach**, with some excellent snorkeling possibilities. Camping is allowed with a permit at nearby **Haena Beach Park** (☎ 808-241-6660; campsites $3), which is close to the Kalalau trailhead.

The awesome 11-mile **Kalalau Trail** runs along the high Na Pali cliffs and winds up and down a series of lush valleys. The scenery is breathtaking, with sheer green cliffs dropping into brilliant turquoise waters. You need a permit (☎ 808-274-3444) for hiking beyond the first valley (Hanakapiai) and for camping ($10), which is allowed in three valleys. This is rugged backcountry – give yourself three or four days to do it without rushing.

SOUTH SHORE

Kauai's main beach-resort area is **Poipu**. It's typically sunny, good for swimming and snorkeling year round and for surfing in summer. **Koloa Landing Cottages** (☎ 808-742-1470, 800-779-8773; 2704B Hoonani Rd; d from $60) offers basic studios. In nearby Koloa, **Kahili Mountain Park** (☎ 808-742-9921; 4035 Kaumualii Hwy; cabins from $45) offers a variety of accommodations. For an unforgettable meal, book a table at **Roy's Poipu Bar and Grill** (☎ 808-742-5000; 2360 Kiahuna Plantation Dr); chef Roy Yamaguchi is famous for blending impeccably fresh island ingredients with classic European techniques.

WEST SIDE

The top destinations here are adjacent **Waimea Canyon**, with its 2785ft-deep river-cut gorge, and **Kokee State Park**. Both feature spectacular views and a vast network of hiking trails. Waimea Canyon Dr (Hwy 550) starts in Waimea and boasts plenty of scenic lookouts along the way to the park.

At Kokee, pick up information on trail conditions at the **Kokee Museum** (☎ 808-335-9975; 3600 Kokee Rd; donation $1; 10am-4pm).

OTHER ISLANDS

MOLOKAI

As you come from the airport you'll see a casually written sign that says it all: 'Slow Down – This is Molokai.' If you're itching to get off the trodden tourist track, Molokai's a good choice. In population and atmosphere, Molokai is the most Hawaiian of any island (except Niihau, which isn't open to visitors). It's sparsely populated, has only a few small resorts, and offers quiet hikes and deserted beaches. Molokai's impenetrable North Shore, from Kalaupapa to Halawa, features the world's highest sea cliffs (3300ft).

In the center of the island, Molokai Airport (also called Hoolehua Airport) has limited car rentals, so book early. The ferry *Molokai Princess* (☎ 808-662-3355, $40, daily) runs between Kaunakakai and Lahaina, Maui.

Molokai's biggest town, **Kaunakakai**, hasn't changed its face at all for tourism. Most of its businesses are along broad Ala Malama St. Waterfront **Hotel Molokai** (☎ 808-553-5347, 800-367-5004; www.hotelmolokai.com; Kamehameha Hwy; d $85-135;) has a Polynesian design and a laid-back atmosphere. Come on Friday evening for the informal ukulele performance by the area's aunties.

The 28-mile south-coast drive from Kaunakakai to Halawa Valley takes about 1½ hours one way and rewards you with a delightful glimpse of rural Hawaii. The last part of the road is very narrow, with lots of hairpin bends and coastal views, winding up to a great panorama of **Halawa Valley**. The road then runs down to a popular surfing spot, **Halawa Beach Park**.

Central Molokai takes in the Hoolehua Plains, which stretch from windswept Moomomi Beach in the west to the former plantation town of Kualapuu. The central part of the island includes **Kamakou Preserve**, with rainforests and the island's highest point, Kamakou Peak (4970ft).

Set at the base of majestic and formidable cliffs (the highest sea cliffs in the world), the **Kalaupapa Peninsula** has been a settlement for people with Hansen's disease for more than

REMEMBERING THE FATHER

The trip to the Kalaupapa peninsula is a pilgrimage of sorts for admirers of Father Damien (Joseph de Veuster), the Belgian priest who devoted much of his life to helping people with Hansen's disease (then called leprosy). He nursed the sick, buried the dead and built 300 homes and a church, before dying in 1889 of the disease himself.

a century. Today fewer than 100 patients live here. To minimize the impact on residents, the park requires all visitors to join a guided tour – and everyone ends up with **Damien Tours** (☎ 808-567-6171; www.muleride.com; $150; tours Mon-Sat), which takes visitors down the steep trail to the settlement on a mule ride.

LANAI

A former pineapple plantation, Lanai is now pushing for the luxury-resort market and can be quite expensive. It shelters some obscure archaeological sites and petroglyphs, as well as Hawaii's last native dry land forest, the Kanepuu Preserve. Many of the sights are a good distance from **Lanai City**, the island's only town, along rutted dirt roads that require a 4WD vehicle.

KAHOOLAWE

This uninhabited island, 7 miles off the southwest coast of Maui, was used exclusively by the US military as a bombing target from WWII until 1990, and continues to be off-limits.

NIIHAU

The smallest of the inhabited Hawaiian Islands and a native Hawaiian preserve, Niihau (population 230) has long been closed to outsiders, earning it the nickname 'The Forbidden Island.' No other place in Hawaii has more successfully turned its back on change: There are no paved roads, no airport, no island wide electricity and no telephones.

NORTHWESTERN HAWAIIAN ISLANDS

These 10 island clusters, also known as the Leeward Islands, stretch from Kauai nearly 1300 miles across the Pacific in an almost straight northwesterly line. Volcanic in origin, the islands are slowly slipping back into the sea as a result of a sagging of the ocean floor and the ongoing forces of erosion.

Directory

CONTENTS

ACCOMMODATIONS

This guide emphasizes mid-range accommodations, but it also includes a good sample of budget and top-end recommendations. Hotels can be expensive in the USA: 'budget' is considered under $75, 'mid-range' $75 to $130 and 'top end' over $130. Where noted in large cities, these price ranges are sometimes adjusted upward.

In the text, accommodation rates are based on standard double-occupancy in high season. However, these rates are a general guide only. Special events, busy weekends, conventions and holidays can drive prices higher, and in most places, off-season rates will be lower, sometimes significantly. And prices do not include hotel tax, which can add 10% to 15% to your bill.

For all but the cheapest places, it is usually advisable to make reservations. For the most popular places and times, it's not unusual for every room to be booked months ahead. On the other hand, if it's slow, you

PRACTICALITIES

News & Entertainment

- National newspapers: *New York Times, USA Today, Wall Street Journal*
- Mainstream news magazines: *Time, Newsweek, US News & World Report*
- Alternative news magazines: *Mother Jones*, the *Nation, Atlantic Monthly*
- Radio news: National Public Radio (NPR), call numbers vary, lower end of FM dial
- Broadcast TV: ABC, CBS, NBC, FOX and PBS (public broadcasting)
- Major cable channels: CNN (news), ESPN (sports), HBO (movies) and the Weather Channel

Video System

- NTSC standard (not compatible with PAL or SECAM)

Electricity

- AC 110V is standard; must buy AC adapters to run most non-US electronics

Weights & Measures

- Weight: ounces (oz), pounds (lb), tons (16oz = 1lb, 2000lb = 1 ton)
- Liquid: oz, pints, quarts, gallons (16 fluid oz = 1 pint, 2 pints = 1 quart, 4 quarts = 1 gallon)
- Distance: feet (ft), yards, miles (3 ft = 1 yard, 1760 yards = 1 mile)
- To convert weights, liquid measures and distances to the metric system, see the inside front cover.

can sometimes get the best deals walking in off the street.

Some good websites for discounts include www.priceline.com, www.hotels.com, www.travelocity.com, www.orbitz.com and www.hotwire.com.

B&Bs

In the USA, B&Bs are usually high-end accommodations geared for romantics, though some appeal to the tastes and expectations of Europeans. They are often restored historic homes with lovely furnishings run by personable, independent innkeepers, and they include delicious breakfasts. Most have a theme – Victorian, rustic, Cape Cod and so on – and amenities range from merely comfortable to hopelessly indulgent. Rates usually top $100, and the best run $150 to $300 and up a night; some have minimum-night-stay requirements on weekends.

Outside of tourist hot spots, B&Bs may be plainer and geared more toward average folks or families. These may be rooms in someone's home, and rates are often lower.

B&Bs often close out of season and may require reservations. Note that reservations are essential for top-end places. Baths may be shared or private; always ask to make sure. Many towns have a local B&B agency that can recommend properties. General guides include *Bed & Breakfast USA* and the *Complete Guide to American Bed & Breakfasts*. On the Internet, check out **Select Registry** (www.selectregistry.com) and bnbfinder.com.

Camping

There are abundant opportunities to camp in the USA. Public lands usually offer the widest range of experiences; private campgrounds are most often geared toward RVs, particularly near cities.

PUBLIC LANDS

Most national forests, state and national parks, and Bureau of Land Management (BLM) lands offer some kind of campground, and 'dispersed' camping in the backcountry is usually possible. It's prudent to call rangers or the parks for details before arriving; in the backcountry, free permits are often necessary. In national forests and BLM lands, it's also sometimes permissible to simply park by the road to camp, but there are obviously no facilities.

In this book, 'primitive' campsites offer no facilities at all and usually cost $5 to $8 a night, first-come, first-served. 'Basic' campsites usually provide toilets (flush or pit), drinking water, fire pits and picnic benches; they run $5 to $15 a night, and some or all may be reserved in advance. 'Developed' campsites, usually in national or state parks, will have nicer facilities and more amenities: hot showers, barbecues, RV sites, coin laundry and so on. These run $12 to $25 a night, and most can be reserved in advance.

You can reserve a national park campsite through the **National Park Service** (NPS; ☎ 800-365-2267, outside the USA ☎ 301-722-1257; http://reservations.nps.gov) up to five months ahead. For reservations at other NPS lands, see the listing in this book or visit the **NPS website** (www.nps.gov).

National forest reservations can be made up to four months in advance through the **National Recreation Reservation Service** (NRRS; ☎ 877-444-6777, outside the USA ☎ 518-885-3639; http://reserveusa.com). The cost is $10 for each reservation.

PRIVATE CAMPGROUNDS

Private RV parks can be the equivalent of a parking lot, but many private campgrounds also provide grassy or shaded tent areas. In addition to all the facilities listed for developed campgrounds above, private campgrounds frequently provide playgrounds, convenience stores, swimming pools and other activities and supplies. Many also have some sort of camping cabin, which may be tent cabins with canvas walls and a wooden floor, hard-sided cabins with screened windows and cots or plank beds, or fully equipped cabins with proper beds, heating and private bathrooms.

Kampgrounds of America (KOA) is a national network of private campgrounds with a full range of facilities. You can order KOA's free annual **directory** (☎ 406-248-7444; http://koa.com; PO Box 30558, Billings, MT 59114). You'll be charged $8 for shipping.

Hostels

The USA has independent hostels as well as those affiliated with Hostelling International (HI), but overall the country is not well served with them. Most are clustered in the Northeast, the Northwest, California and the Rocky Mountains. Most big cities have a few choices, but across some states it's hard to find even one.

Hostelling International-American Youth Hostels (HI-AYH) runs about 125 hostels in the US. Facilities and quality vary. Most have segregated dorms, a few private rooms, provide linen free or for a small fee (sleeping bags not allowed), have shared bathrooms and a communal kitchen, prohibit alcohol, and organize activities. In big cities, hostels may be open 24 hours and forgo 'chores,' while others close in the afternoon (usually 10am to 5pm) and ask guests to do some cleaning. Dorm prices also vary; in rural areas they can be as low as $10, while in cities they can run $25 to $35.

Reservations are accepted and advised during the high season, when there may be a maximum stay of three nights. Contact HI-AYH for the **handbook** (☎ 202-783-6161; www.hiayh.org; 733 15th St NW, Suite 840, Washington, DC 20005). If you're in the US, you can reserve most affiliated hostels through the central **booking service** (☎ 800-909-4776); you need the hostel's access code, which is listed online and in the HI-AYH handbook.

For comprehensive lists of all types of hostels in the US, check out www.hostels.com, or get the **Hostel Handbook** (www.hostelhandbook.com; $5), which you'll find at many hostels and online; the website has good hosteling advice and links for other budget accommodations.

Hotels & Motels

Hotels differ from motels in that they do not surround a parking lot and usually have some sort of a lobby. Hotels may offer extra services such as laundry, but these can be very expensive. Long-distance phone calls can also be very expensive.

Prices vary tremendously from season to season. A hotel charging $80 for a double in high season may drop to $40 in the off-season or raise its rates to over $150 for a special event. Advertised prices (or 'rack rates') can be negotiable, particularly for longer stays; sometimes just asking about any 'specials' can save money. See p1093 for more details.

The cheapest budget motels will be found near interstate exits, along the highways near small towns, and in cities along motel strips outside of downtown. Most are independently owned, but standards vary widely. Most are adequately clean, with laundered sheets, but suffer from wear and tear. Rooms may not have a telephone or TV, but most have private bathrooms. Always ask to see your room before accepting it. You can't always tell from the outside or from advertising if a low-end budget place is actually, in rare cases, a 'no-tell motel' catering to transients and hourly guests.

Better budget and even some mid-range motels may offer rooms with a kitchenette. These may be simple affairs – two small burners, a tiny refrigerator and a sink – but they allow for modest food preparation.

Independent mid-range motels and hotels provide a basic level of amenities that matches the chains: private bathrooms, table and chairs, heating/air-con (depending on the region), telephone, cable TV, data ports and often morning coffee or a light continental breakfast. As they get more expensive, they may also offer refrigerators, coffee machines, irons, VCRs, guest Internet terminals, swimming pools and more. Cleanliness is rarely an issue, and wear and tear should be minimal. Independents may distinguish themselves from chains with more personalized service or special decor.

CHAINS

Chain hotels and motels predominate in the USA. They are thoroughly standardized; when you've experienced one, you pretty much know what to expect from the entire chain. In this guide, unless chain hotels are the only or the best option, they have not been mentioned, but you can count on nearly every town of any size having at least a couple. Cities will have dozens.

There are a few budget chains – Motel 6 is the cheapest – but most chains are mid-range places. Decor is usually deliberately nondescript. In better chains, you may find restaurants, bars, spas, fitness centers and indoor swimming pools. Top-end, full-service chain hotels cater to business clients and offer all the amenities you would expect.

Every chain has a toll-free central reservation number, though central reservations might not know about special local discount rates. Budget and mid-range chains include the following:

Best Western (☎ 800-780-7234; www.bestwestern.com)
Budget Host (☎ 800-283-4678; www.budgethost.com)

Clarion Hotel (☎ 877-424-6423; www.clarionhotel.com)
Comfort Inn (☎ 877-424-6423; www.comfortinn.com)
Days Inn (☎ 800-329-7466; www.daysinn.com)
Econo Lodge (☎ 877-424-6423; www.econolodge.com)
Fairfield Inn (☎ 800-228-2800; www.fairfieldinn.com)
Hampton Inn (☎ 800-426-7866; www.hamptoninn.com)
Holiday Inn (☎ 800-465-4329; www.holiday-inn.com)
Howard Johnson (☎ 800-446-4656; www.hojo.com)
La Quinta (☎ 800-531-5900; www.lq.com)
Motel 6 (☎ 800-466-8356; www.motel6.com)
Quality Inn (☎ 877-424-6423; www.qualityinn.com)
Red Roof Inn (☎ 800-733-7663; www.redroof.com)
Rodeway Inn (☎ 877-424-6423; www.rodewayinn.com)
Sleep Inn (☎ 877-424-6423; www.sleepinn.com)
Super 8 Motel (☎ 800-800-8000; www.super8.com)
Travelodge (☎ 800-578-7878; www.travelodge.com)

Top-end chains include the following:
Hilton (☎ 800-445-8667; www.hilton.com)
Hyatt (☎ 800-233-1234; www.hyatt.com)
Marriott (☎ 800-228-9290; www.marriott.com)
Radisson (☎ 800-333-3333; www.radisson.com)
Ramada (☎ 800-272-6232; www.ramada.com)
Sheraton (☎ 800-325-3535; www.starwood.com/sheraton)

Resorts & Lodges

Luxury resorts are often destinations in themselves. They are very expensive, and only a few are mentioned in the text.

Ski resorts usually have a central reservations hotline, and the accommodations can range from plain motel rooms to plush condos. Midwinter prices will be high – up to $200 or more per night/per bed – while summer prices might be half that.

Lodges in attractive scenic areas typically affect a rustic style (lots of logs and stonework) but are usually very comfortable inside. They often have restaurants and excellent services, but can be very expensive. National park lodges are usually quite nice but can be overpriced for the quality; still, make reservations months ahead.

University Accommodations

During vacations, some universities and colleges offer accommodations in student dormitories. This is generally a service for those doing summer courses on campus, and is not a popular option for independent travelers. Dorm accommodations are not well publicized, services are minimal, booking conditions can be restrictive and campuses are not very lively places during vacations.

NO SMOKING IN THE USA

Nonsmokers have never had it better in the USA. Whether because of law or custom, nearly every hotel and restaurant has nonsmoking facilities. And some cities – such as San Francisco and New York – have even banned smoking entirely from most public places.

As such, Lonely Planet's nonsmoking icon (⊠), which is meant to indicate nonsmoking facilities, hasn't been used in this book, since it would appear with nearly every entry. The three exceptions are Alaska, Pennsylvania and New Jersey. These are the only states where travelers might run across smoking-only facilities.

YMCAs

The **Young Men's Christian Association** (YMCA; www.ymca.net) runs exercise and inexpensive accommodation facilities in or near downtown in most cities. However, accommodations – ranging from same-sex dorms to private rooms – are geared mainly for temporary residents rather than travelers. 'Y's have a lot of differing restrictions for overnight guests, and they vary greatly in quality; some are seedy and located in run-down neighborhoods. Always check out the facilities in person first. YWCAs are much less common and are mostly for women only.

ACTIVITIES

It would be hard to name an outdoor activity that isn't pursued in the USA. Whether you prefer daredevil adventure or gentle hikes, you can find perfect places for it, and organizations and outfitters eager to set you up. This section focuses on the main types of activities, where they predominate and where to get more information.

Perhaps the best all-around Internet resource is the Great Outdoor Recreation Pages (GORP): www.gorp.com.

The USA's public lands contain a wealth of recreational opportunities. Here are the agencies to contact if you're looking for general information:
Bureau of Land Management (www.blm.gov)
National Park Service (www.nps.gov)
US Fish & Wildlife Service (www.fws.gov)
US Forest Service (www.fs.fed.us)

Caving

Experienced spelunkers can explore caves in several areas, and a number of caves have guided interpretive tours. Mammoth Cave National Park (p563) in Kentucky is one of the world's largest cave systems. Other highlights are Carlsbad Caverns National Park (p814) in New Mexico and Lehman Caves (p872) in Nevada's Great Basin National Park.

Contact the **National Speleological Society** (☎ 256-852-1300; www.caves.org; 2813 Cave Ave, Huntsville, AL 35810) for general information.

Courses

For comprehensive instruction in a range of outdoor skills, contact the **National Outdoor Leadership School** (NOLS; ☎ 800-710-6657; www.nols.edu; 284 Lincoln St, Lander, WY 82520). **Outward Bound** (☎ 866-467-7651; www.outwardbound.org; 100 Mystery Point Rd, Garrison, NY 10524) is also famous for its courses emphasizing wilderness skills and personal growth.

Cycling & Mountain Biking

Touring and mountain biking are very popular across the country, American cities are increasingly bike-friendly, and bike rentals are widely available. See p1116 for national cycling organizations and advice on traveling by bike.

Bikes are often banned from designated wilderness areas and national park trails, but can generally be used on national forest and BLM single-track trails. Trail etiquette requires that cyclists yield to other users.

Regions ideal for cycle touring include the forests of New England (p201), the islands of the Atlantic coast – from Nantucket off Massachusetts (p223) to Amelia off Florida (p609) – Virginia's Shenandoah Valley (p319), the islands in the Great Lakes (p417), Colorado's Summit County (p751) and California's Wine Country and coast (p957).

Marin County (p951), near San Francisco, and Crested Butte (p755), Colorado, both claim to be the birthplace of mountain biking. In summer, many ski areas open their trails and chairlifts to mountain bikes. California's Mammoth Mountain (p974) is hugely popular. The red rock desert near Moab (p852), Utah, is also a mecca.

If you're riding your own bike, bring a heavy-duty bicycle lock, as bicycle theft is a big business.

Hiking & Backpacking

The USA has so many top-notch places that reward the hiker – the choices seem almost limitless.

All national parks, as well as most state parks, have a really wide range of excellent well-marked trails, from easy, short, wheelchair-accessible paths to day- and weeklong wilderness journeys. Federal wilderness areas and forests also have trails, but they may be less well maintained or lack interpretive markers. The best way to escape national park crowds is to start hiking, though in peak periods even multiday hikes don't guarantee solitude.

For day hikes in national parks, the free park trail maps are usually all you need. For longer or other trips, topographic maps may be useful and even necessary; see p1097 for information. Always ask at a ranger station or visitors center for suitable trails and current conditions.

Most national parks require overnight hikers to carry backcountry permits, which must be obtained 24 hours in advance and require you to follow a specific itinerary. Always call the visitors center or ranger station before you start an overnight hike. *How to Stay Alive in the Woods* (1956/2001) by Bradford Angier is a classic wilderness survival guide.

For advice on low-impact camping and wilderness etiquette, see p88. The **Leave No Trace Center** (☎ 800-332-4100; www.lnt.org) dispenses lots of information for hikers. The 'Tread Lightly' program, run by the US Forest Service (USFS), emphasizes vehicular etiquette in the wilderness (☎ 800-966-9900; www.treadlightly.org).

The **Rails-to-Trails Conservancy** (☎ 202-331-9696; www.railtrails.org/content.html; 1100 17th St, 10th floor, NW, Washington DC, 20036) is a nationwide movement to convert abandoned railroad corridors into public biking and hiking trails. They also maintain a website (www.traillink.com) with descriptions of over 1200 trails nationwide.

The continental USA's three mountain systems are traversed by legendary, epic trails, which can be broken up into smaller segments. Here's where to get more information:

Appalachian Trail Appalachian Trail Conference (☎ 304-535-6331; www.appalachiantrail.org; PO Box 807, Harpers Ferry, WV 25425)

Continental Divide Trail Continental Divide Trail Alliance (☎ 888-909-2382; www.cdtrail.org; PO Box 628, Pine,

CO 80470); Continental Divide Trail Society (☎ 410-235-9610; www.cdtsociety.org; 3704 N Charles St, Suite 601, Baltimore, MD 21218)

Pacific Crest Trail Pacific Crest Trail Association (☎ 888-728-7245, 916-349-2109; www.pcta.org; 5325 Elkhorn Blvd, Suite 256, Sacramento, CA 95842)

Horseback Riding

Equestrian activities and horses in general are hugely popular in the USA. Stables offering horseback riding can be found all throughout the country. Guided back-country pack trips are popular in and near mountain parks, while dude ranches cater to would-be cowboys in Texas (particularly Hill Country, p647), the Southwest (p791) and Wyoming (p760). However, the heart of American horse country is in Kentucky (especially Bluegrass Country, p566), home of the Thoroughbred, and Tennessee, home of walking horses.

Rafting, Kayaking & Canoeing

The best rivers for white-water canoeing and rafting are in the Appalachians (p346), Rocky Mountains (p730), Sierra Nevada (p963) and Southwest desert (p806). Commercial trips range from short, inexpensive morning or afternoon trips to three- or four-day expeditions. 'Tubing' in old inner tubes is popular on smaller streams. Outfitters using rivers in publicly managed parks and forests operate with permits from the appropriate agency. Individuals and groups with their own or rented equipment sometimes also need a permit.

Lakes throughout the Northeast (p162) and the Great Lakes states are ideal for summer canoeing. Canoes are also great for exploring the wetland areas of Georgia (p492), Louisiana and Florida (p574). Sea kayaking is excellent in the Pacific Northwest (p979), the Maine coast (p275) and Alaska's Inside Passage. Canoe rentals are widely available at popular paddling places.

The **American Canoe Association** (☎ 703-451-0141; www.acanet.org/acanet.htm; 7432 Alban Station Blvd, Suite B-232, Springfield, VA 22150) publishes *Paddler* magazine and is a great resource, as is **American Whitewater** (☎ 866-262-8429; www.americanwhitewater.org; 1424 Fenwick Lane, Silver Spring, MD 20910).

Rock Climbing & Mountaineering

Rock climbing and mountaineering are especially popular pursuits in the Sierra Nevada (p971) and the Rockies (p730); rock climbing is also popular in Utah's southeast deserts (p852). In particular Yosemite National Park (p971) is legendary for rock climbing. Mt Whitney (p975), on the east side of the Sierra Nevada, is the most popular mountaineering spot in the lower 48, while Alaska's parks (p1029) have the most challenging mountaineering possibilities of all.

Scuba Diving & Snorkeling

Diving is done all over the states, even in the Great Lakes, but the best locations are the Florida Keys (p594), California's Channel Islands (p920) and Monterey Peninsula (p927), and Hawaii. Off the North Carolina coast, there's unlimited wreck diving in the 'graveyard of the Atlantic.'

If you want to try diving for the first time, some dive operations offer a short beginner's course (usually under $100) that includes a brief lesson followed by a shallow beach or boat dive. To dive with an operator, or to have tanks filled, the minimum qualification required is an open-water certificate from PADI, NAUI or another recognized organization such as BSAC. An open-water certificate course will cost from $300 to $400, equipment included, and take three days to a week.

Skiing & Snowboarding

There are ski resorts all over the USA, and most allow snowboarding and have half-pipes. All have lessons and equipment rental, and most have kids' programs and day care. Ski season is normally mid-December to April, though some resorts have longer seasons. Ski packages (including airfare, hotel and lift tickets) are easy to find through resorts and tourist agencies; they can be a good deal if your main goal is to ski.

Skiing America by Charles Leocha has information on all of North America's big ski resorts. Worthwhile magazines are *Ski*, *Skiing* and *Snow Country*. Virtually every ski area has a website. A good community website for snowboarders is www.snowboard.com, with lots of unvarnished advice.

See the regional chapters for more information about the following acclaimed areas.

Colorado is a prime ski destination with numerous famous resorts, like Vail (p751), Aspen (p753), Telluride (p757), Breckenridge (p749) and Steamboat Springs (p746).

Other premier Rocky Mountain resorts include Wyoming's Jackson Hole (p770), Montana's Big Sky (p773), and Idaho's Sun Valley (p785).

Utah's Wasatch Range (p846) has several top ski areas. Park City (p847) is the headquarters of the US Ski Team and was the site for the 2002 Winter Olympics.

In California's Sierra Nevada, Lake Tahoe (p968), which includes Squaw Valley and Heavenly, is the main destination, though further south is the aptly named Mammoth Mountain (p974).

New England's best skiing is in Vermont, at Killington (p254), Mt Snow (p251), Stratton (p252) and Stowe (p255), and in New Hampshire's White Mountains (p261). In upstate New York, Whiteface Mountain, near Lake Placid in the Adirondacks, has twice hosted the Winter Olympics.

CROSS-COUNTRY SKIING

Cross-country skiing (sometimes called Nordic skiing) is even more widespread than downhill. Most downhill ski resorts have cross-country trails, and in winter, many national park and forest hiking trails, city parks and golf courses also become cross-country ski areas. There are also specialized cross-country ski resorts. The **Cross-Country Ski Areas Association** (www.xcski.org) provides comprehensive information for North America.

In California, check out Lake Tahoe, Yosemite (p971) and Kings Canyon (p973) National Parks. In New England, elaborate trail systems exist near North Conway (p263), New Hampshire, as well as Stowe (p255), in Vermont. Other highlights are New York's Finger Lakes region (p163) and Pennsylvania's Allegheny National Forest (p197) and Laurel Highlands (p196). In the Great Lakes, Wisconsin (p427), Michigan and Minnesota (p440) are all notable.

In the Rocky Mountains, there are popular hut systems for backcountry touring. The **Colorado Cross Country Ski Association** (www.colorado-xc.org) has information on regional cross-country ski centers. Grand Teton (p768) and Yellowstone (p765) National Parks also provide excellent backcountry access.

Surfing

Hawaii and southern California are both famous for surfing and surf culture, but just about every stretch of US coastline now supports avid wave riders. Board rentals and surf lessons are common. Overall, the number of US surfers has doubled in the last decade.

Surfer magazine's travel reports cover just about every break; order copies by phone (☎ 949-661-5147) or on the net (www.surfermag.com/travel). *Stormrider Guide North America* is also recommended.

Hawaii has good surfing throughout the year. The biggest waves hit the north shores from November to February; Oahu's North Shore (p1073) is legendary. Maui (p1077) and Kauai (p1079) islands also have some excellent surfing spots.

In southern California, the 'big three' surf spots are Rincon, just south of Santa Barbara (p921), Malibu (p890) and Trestles, just south of the Orange County beaches (p904). Huntington Beach (p904) hosts the state's biggest pro surfing contest (in August/September). Further south, San Clemente, just south of the Orange County beaches (p904) and San Diego's Black's Beach (p910) are good. Northern California has its own surf culture, with colder water and bigger waves. There are breaks for all skill levels in Santa Cruz (p929), but only experts should attempt the big waves at Maverick's (p954), near Half Moon Bay. *Maverick's* by Matt Warshaw is a great account of this legendary break.

On the east coast, North Carolina's Cape Hatteras (p460) is the best bet, particularly in fall, which is when most of the east coast surf breaks.

Note that at all of these places, crowding and competition for waves can be intense, and local surfers can be territorial. On busy weekends, look for smaller, lesser-known breaks, and show respect.

Windsurfing

Windsurfing is popular on lakes and coasts throughout the country. There are many windsurfing shops, but rentals are found only at the most popular spots and resorts. Beaches in Hawaii and southern California (p910) are very popular windsurfing areas, and the Columbia River Gorge (p999) in Oregon, near the town of Hood River, and Canadian Hole (p460), in North Carolina's Outer Banks, have noted windsurfing scenes.

BUSINESS HOURS

In general, businesses are open weekdays from 9am to 5pm, but there are lots of individual variations. Some banks and many post offices are also open on Saturday from 9am to around 2pm.

Large cities will have a few 24-hour supermarkets, restaurants and a post office. In most places, retail stores and shopping malls will stay open until about 9pm Monday to Saturday, and be open for shorter hours on Sunday (typically noon to 5pm). However, in some parts of the country, everything closes on Sunday.

Restaurants, bars and pubs follow no standard hours. In general, kitchens will close around 10pm or 11pm, and bars will stay open at least until midnight or 1am. Always call ahead to confirm the hours if you're counting on a particular place.

CHILDREN

You couldn't ask for a better destination to bring the family than the USA. In practical terms, it's one of the easiest, safest and most convenient places to travel with kids. And in terms of activities, it's like a toy box full of surprises. However, most important, Americans love children, and in most places they are quick to help, and even bond with, traveling families.

Most facilities can accommodate a child's needs. You'll find that nearly all restaurants have high chairs, and if they don't have a specific children's menu, they can make a kid-tailored meal. Many chain restaurants also break out paper placemats and crayons for drawing. Most public toilets – in airports, stores, malls, movie theaters and so on – have a baby changing table, even in the men's toilet.

Motels commonly have rooms with two double beds, which are ideal for families. They also have 'roll-away beds' or 'cots' that can be brought into the room for an extra charge. Some have 'kids stay free' programs, which range up to 12, and sometimes 18, years old.

Every car rental agency should be able to provide an appropriate child seat or restraint, since these are required in every state. Make sure to ask when you book your car. Airlines also sometimes offer 'kids fly free' promotions, and they usually offer steep discounts for traveling infants.

In addition, most tourist bureaus can lead you to local resources for children's programs, childcare facilities and so on.

In this guide, nearly every large city has a City for Children section that describes the area's best children's activities. The USA is full to bursting with hands-on science museums, playgrounds, theme parks and fun centers. Many outfitters and sports centers have dedicated kids' programs, and most national and state parks make a special effort to assist families.

For all-around information and advice, check out Lonely Planet's *Travel with Children* by Cathy Lanigan. *Kids in the Wild: A Family Guide to Outdoor Recreation* (2000) by Cindy Ross and Todd Gladfelter will help ensure successful family camping trips.

CLIMATE CHARTS

For general advice on climate and when to travel in the USA, see p13. Every regional chapter also has a When to Go section with more specific regional information. The following climate charts (pp1090–1) provide a snapshot of the USA's weather patterns.

CUSTOMS

US Customs allows each person to bring 1L of liquor (provided you are 21 years old or older), 100 cigars and 200 cigarettes duty-free into the USA. US citizens are allowed to import, duty-free, $800 worth of gifts and purchases from abroad, while non-US citizens are allowed to bring in $100 worth.

US law permits you to bring in, or take out, as much as $10,000 in US or foreign currency, traveler's checks or letters of credit without formality. There's no maximum limit, but larger amounts of money must be declared to customs.

There are heavy penalties for attempting to import illegal drugs. It's also forbidden to bring in to the US drug paraphernalia, lottery tickets, items with fake brand names, and goods made in Cuba or Iraq. Any fruit, vegetables, or other food or plant material must be declared or left in the bins in the arrival area. Most food items are prohibited to prevent the introduction of pests or diseases.

The USA, like 140 other countries, is a signatory to Cites, the Convention on

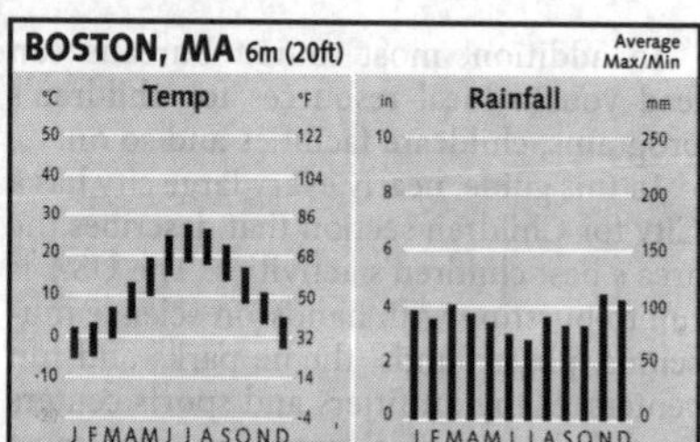
BOSTON, MA 6m (20ft)
Average Max/Min
Temp
Rainfall
°C 50 40 30 20 10 0 -10 -20
°F 122 104 86 68 50 32 14 -4
in 10 8 6 4 2 0
mm 250 200 150 100 50 0
J F M A M J J A S O N D

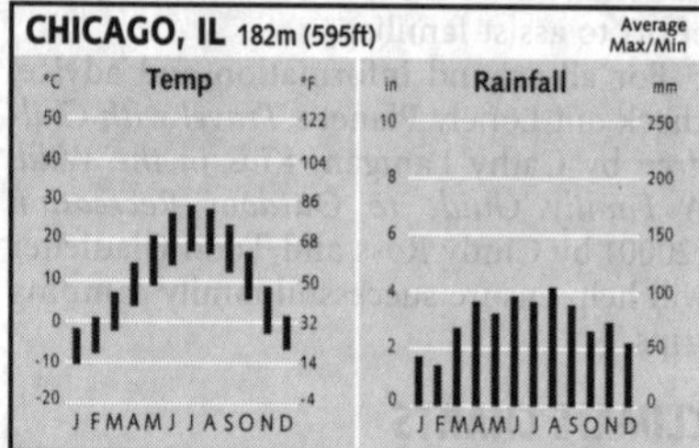
CHICAGO, IL 182m (595ft)
Average Max/Min
Temp
Rainfall
°C 50 40 30 20 10 0 -10 -20
°F 122 104 86 68 50 32 14 -4
in 10 8 6 4 2 0
mm 250 200 150 100 50 0
J F M A M J J A S O N D

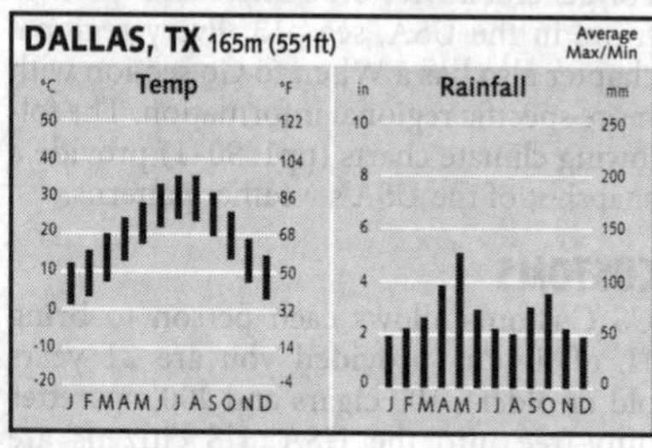
DALLAS, TX 165m (551ft)
Average Max/Min
Temp
Rainfall
°C 50 40 30 20 10 0 -10 -20
°F 122 104 86 68 50 32 14 -4
in 10 8 6 4 2 0
mm 250 200 150 100 50 0
J F M A M J J A S O N D

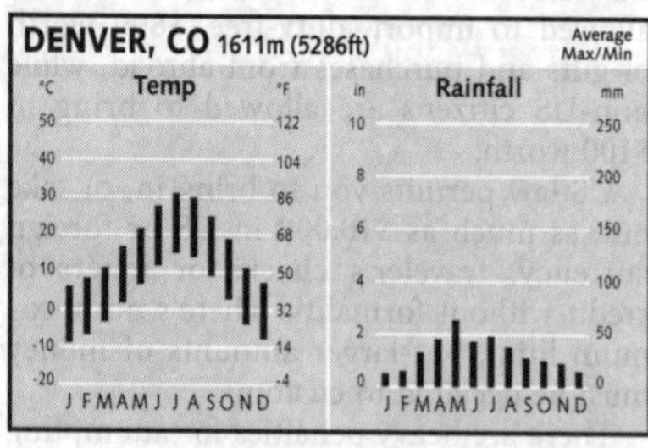
DENVER, CO 1611m (5286ft)
Average Max/Min
Temp
Rainfall
°C 50 40 30 20 10 0 -10 -20
°F 122 104 86 68 50 32 14 -4
in 10 8 6 4 2 0
mm 250 200 150 100 50 0
J F M A M J J A S O N D

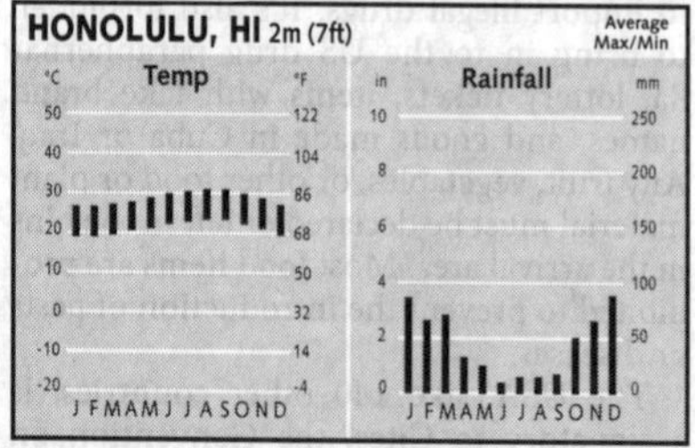
HONOLULU, HI 2m (7ft)
Average Max/Min
Temp
Rainfall
°C 50 40 30 20 10 0 -10 -20
°F 122 104 86 68 50 32 14 -4
in 10 8 6 4 2 0
mm 250 200 150 100 50 0
J F M A M J J A S O N D

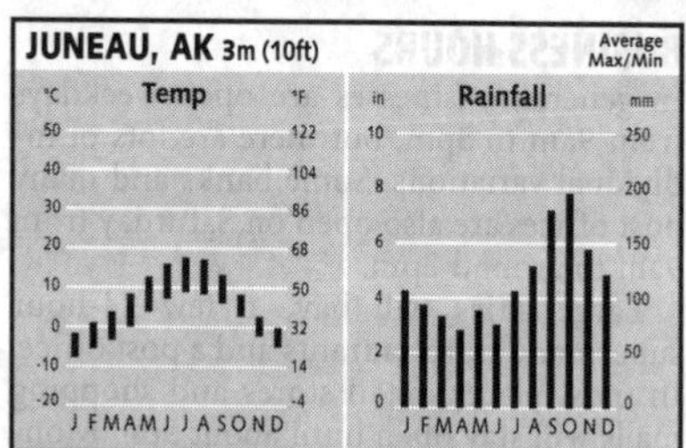
JUNEAU, AK 3m (10ft)
Average Max/Min
Temp
Rainfall
°C 50 40 30 20 10 0 -10 -20
°F 122 104 86 68 50 32 14 -4
in 10 8 6 4 2 0
mm 250 200 150 100 50 0
J F M A M J J A S O N D

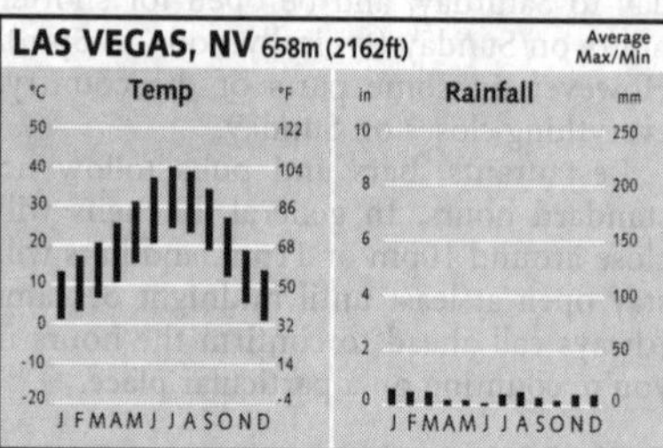
LAS VEGAS, NV 658m (2162ft)
Average Max/Min
Temp
Rainfall
°C 50 40 30 20 10 0 -10 -20
°F 122 104 86 68 50 32 14 -4
in 10 8 6 4 2 0
mm 250 200 150 100 50 0
J F M A M J J A S O N D

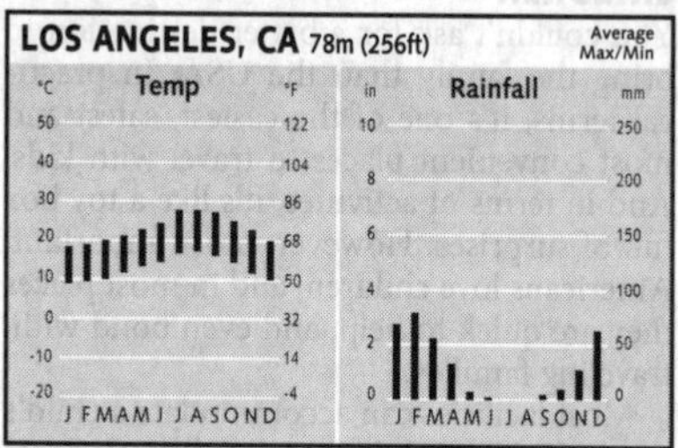
LOS ANGELES, CA 78m (256ft)
Average Max/Min
Temp
Rainfall
°C 50 40 30 20 10 0 -10 -20
°F 122 104 86 68 50 32 14 -4
in 10 8 6 4 2 0
mm 250 200 150 100 50 0
J F M A M J J A S O N D

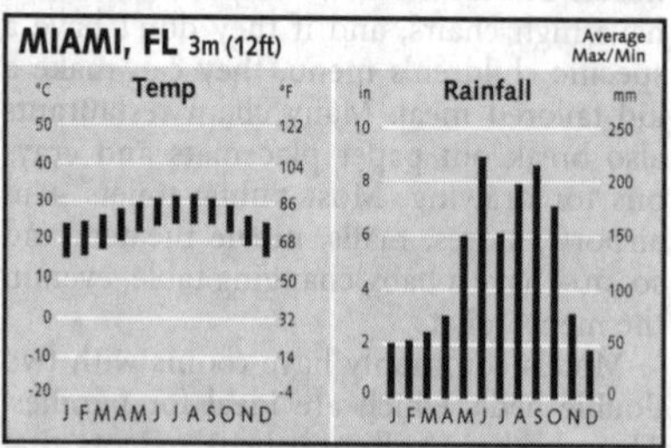
MIAMI, FL 3m (12ft)
Average Max/Min
Temp
Rainfall
°C 50 40 30 20 10 0 -10 -20
°F 122 104 86 68 50 32 14 -4
in 10 8 6 4 2 0
mm 250 200 150 100 50 0
J F M A M J J A S O N D

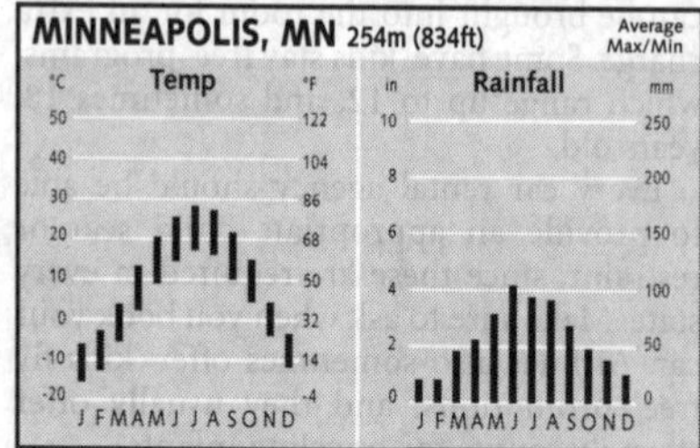
MINNEAPOLIS, MN 254m (834ft)
Average Max/Min
Temp
Rainfall
°C 50 40 30 20 10 0 -10 -20
°F 122 104 86 68 50 32 14 -4
in 10 8 6 4 2 0
mm 250 200 150 100 50 0
J F M A M J J A S O N D

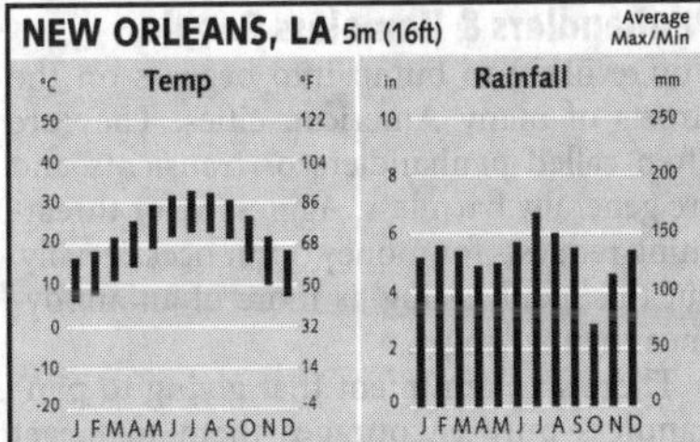

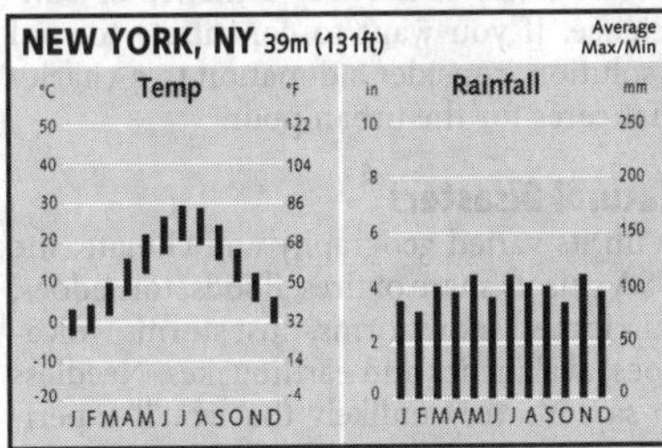

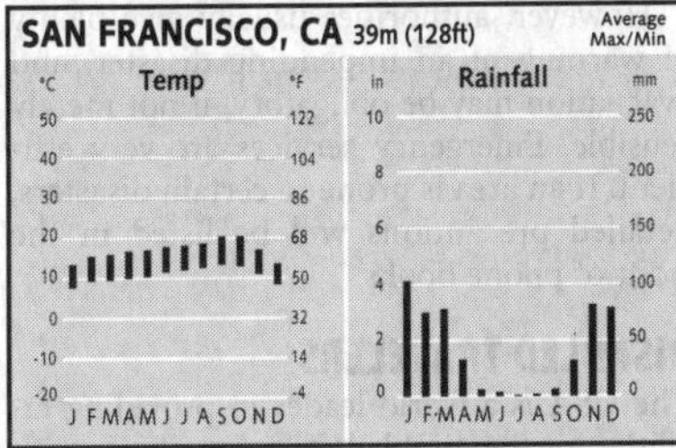

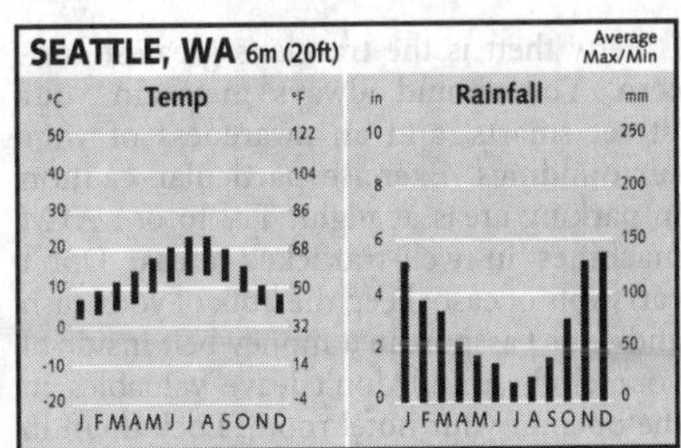

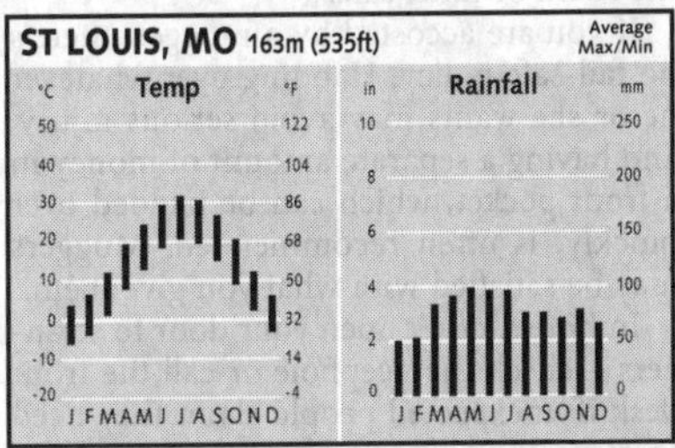

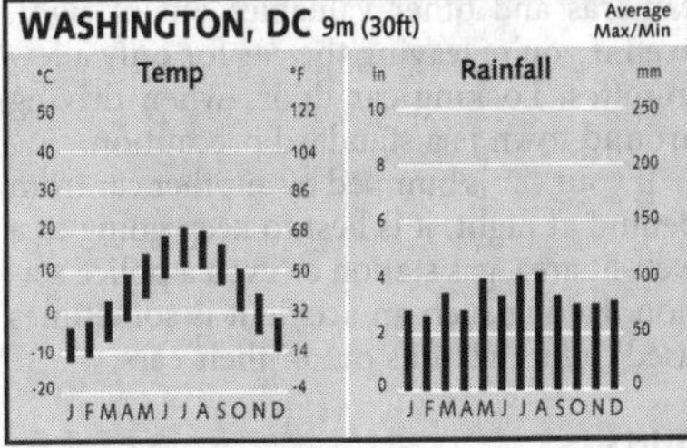

International Trade in Endangered Species. As such, it prohibits the import and export of products made from species that may be endangered in any part of the world, including ivory, tortoise shell, coral, and many fur, skin and feather products. If you bring or buy a fur coat, snakeskin belt, alligator-skin boots or bone carving, you may have to show a certificate when you enter and/or leave the USA that states your goods were not made from an endangered species.

For complete a complete list of US customs regulations, visit www.customs.gov/travel/travel.htm.

DANGERS & ANNOYANCES

Despite its seemingly Babylon-like dangers – guns, violent crime, earthquakes, tornadoes – the USA is actually a very safe country to visit. Perhaps the single greatest danger for travelers is posed by car accidents on America's highways, and the two greatest annoyances will be auto traffic in the cities and crowds at popular sites.

Outdoor activities have their own sets of dangers and annoyances, but these vary with the terrain and the sport. The best advice is to talk to rangers about any risks posed by wildlife or the elements, and whether bugs and mosquitoes will be a particular problem when you'll be visiting.

Crime

Despite the USA's high crime statistics, travelers need not be overly worried. In cities, popular tourist areas tend to be well-trafficked, well-lit and well-protected. Most cities have some areas that are known as 'bad neighborhoods,' and these should be avoided, particularly after dark; ask locals, hotel managers or police officers for advice on what these are. At night, taking a taxi is one way to maximize safety. Outside of the cities, crime of all kinds drops dramatically.

Petty theft is the traveler's greatest concern. You should always maintain your 'street smarts' and an awareness of your surroundings. Exercise particular caution in parking areas at night. Try to use ATM machines in well-trafficked areas. Don't carry lots of cash; keep the bulk of your cash and your passport in a money belt inside of your clothes; and don't leave valuables in the open in your hotel room. Lock them in the room or hotel safe.

If you are accosted by a mugger, there's no fail-safe policy. Handing over whatever he or she wants may avoid serious injury, and having a separate amount of money in a front pocket, which can be handed over quickly, is often recommended. Muggers may be satisfied with what you give them.

In hotels, don't open your door to strangers – check the peephole or call the front desk if unexpected people claim they need to come in. Always lock your car and put cameras and other valuables out of sight, even if you're leaving the car for only a few minutes. Locking car doors when driving around town is a standard precaution.

If your car is bumped by another car from behind at night, it is best to keep going to a well-lit area, gas station or even a police station. Faking such an accident is sometimes used to lure victims out of their cars.

GUNS

Gun violence rarely affects the traveler, though the widespread availability of firearms does present real problems for US society. In cities, muggers and thieves are more likely to be armed with a knife than a gun.

However, be cautious during hunting season. Wear bright clothes if you hike in the woods, or stick to areas where hunting is not allowed. Every year seems to see a handful of tragedies because of incautious hunters.

Cons & Scams

There are no scams unique to the USA. All prey on the gullibility of people or their eagerness to get rich quick. Three-card monte card games, which draw crowds on a city street, are always rigged. Any item for sale that looks too good to be true probably is. A healthy skepticism is your best defense. For a list of current scams and types of fraud, visit the government's website, http://firstgov.gov.

Panhandlers & Homeless People

You're likely to bump into beggars on the streets of many American cities. They are often called panhandlers or transients and are generally harmless. Aggressive or threatening requests for money occur occasionally, but this 'panhassling' is more of an annoyance than a danger.

There's an argument that giving to panhandlers only encourages them to target tourist areas. It is really a matter of conscience. If you want to contribute toward a solution, consider a donation to a charity that cares for the urban poor.

Natural Disasters

With its varied geography and climate, the USA gets its share of fires, floods, tornadoes, hurricanes, snowstorms, dust storms, volcanoes, avalanches and earthquakes. Needless to say, it's very unlikely that you'll experience any of these on a short visit.

However, authorities usually give plenty of warning of an impending disaster, and evacuation may be obligatory, if not merely sensible. Emergency services are very efficient. If an area is prone to certain disasters, detailed precautions will be listed in the front of phone books.

DISABLED TRAVELERS

The USA is a world leader in providing facilities for the disabled. The Americans with Disabilities Act (ADA) requires that all public buildings – including hotels, restaurants, theaters and museums – and public transit be wheelchair accessible. The more populous areas have the best and most widespread facilities, but always call ahead to confirm what is available.

Telephone companies are required to provide relay operators – available via teletypewriter (TTY) numbers – for the hearing impaired. Many banks now provide ATM instructions in Braille. All major airlines, Greyhound buses and Amtrak trains assist disabled travelers; just describe your needs when making reservations, and they will help make whatever arrangements are necessary.

Some car rental agencies – such as Budget and Hertz – offer hand-controlled vehicles and vans with wheelchair lifts at no extra charge, but you must reserve them well in advance.

A number of organizations specialize in serving disabled travelers:

Access-Able Travel Source (☎ 303-232-2979; www.access-able.com; PO Box 1796, Wheat Ridge, CO 80034) An excellent website with many links.

Disabled Sports USA (☎ 301-217-0960; www.dsusa.org; 451 Hungerford Drive, Suite 100, Rockville, MD 20850) Nationwide organization that offers sports and recreation programs for the disabled, selects US athletes for Paralympic Games and publishes *Challenge* magazine.

Mobility International USA (☎ 541-343-1284, fax 541-343-6812; www.miusa.org; PO Box 10767, Eugene, OR 97440) Advises disabled travelers on mobility issues and runs an educational exchange program.

Moss Rehabilitation Hospital's Travel Information Service (☎ 215-456-5995, TTY 456-9602; www.mossresourcenet.org/travel.htm; 1200 W Tabor Rd, Philadelphia, PA 19141) A concise list of useful contacts.

Society for Accessible Travel & Hospitality (SATH; ☎ 212-447-7284; www.sath.org; 347 Fifth Ave, Suite 610, New York, NY 10016) Lobbies for better facilities and publishes *Open World* magazine.

Travelin' Talk Network (☎ 303-232-2979; www.travelintalk.net; PO Box 1796, Wheat Ridge, CO 80034) Offers a global network of people providing service to disabled people.

DISCOUNTS

Travelers will find a plethora of ways to shave costs on hotel rooms, meals, rental cars, museum and attraction admissions, and just about anything else that can be had for a price. Persistence and ingenuity will take you a long way when it comes to finding deals in the USA.

Students and seniors (who are generally considered age 62 and up) are not issued separate discount cards, but they benefit from savings of all kinds. Simply carry proof of age or student status, and ask every time you book a room, reserve a car, order a meal or pay an entrance fee. Most of the time this saves 10% or so, but sometimes the saving is significant, like 50%. American seniors should seriously consider getting a National Park Golden Age Passport, which allows free access to national lands and 50% off use fees like camping.

American Automobile Association (AAA) membership comes with a raft of discounts, and it has reciprocal agreements with several international auto associations. Other people whose status might lead to discounts are war veterans, the disabled, business travelers and foreign visitors. These discounts are not always advertised, so it pays, literally, to ask.

Discount coupons can be found almost anywhere. Most tourist agencies carry publications, brochures, books and flyers with discount coupons. Highway welcome centers and even gas stations will often stock cheap-looking newsprint booklets offering discounts. Also check the advertising circulars in Sunday newspapers. Discounts may have restrictions and conditions, and may be unavailable at peak times, so read the fine print.

Online, you can get hotel discount coupons through Roomsaver.com (www.roomsaver.com) and the Traveler Coupon Guide (www.exitinfo.com).

In addition, children's prices are often discounted, and public museums usually have free or discounted hours once a week or month.

EMBASSIES & CONSULATES

US Embassies & Consulates

The US Department of State Bureau of Consular Affairs website (http://travel.state.gov/index.html) has links for all US embassies abroad.

Australia Yarralumla (☎ 2-6214-5600; Moonah Pl, Yarralumla ACT 2600); Sydney (☎ 2-9373-9200; Level 59 MLC Center, 19-29 Martin Place, Sydney NSW 2000); Melbourne (☎ 3-9526-5900; 553 St Kilda Rd, Melbourne, Victoria 3004)

Austria Vienna (☎ 1-313-390; Boltzmanngasse 16, A-1091, Vienna)

Belgium Brussels (☎ 2-508-21-11; Blvd du Regent 27, B-1000, Brussels)

Canada Ottawa (☎ 613-238-5335; 490 Sussex Dr, Ottawa, Ontario, K1N 1G8); Vancouver (☎ 900-451-2778; 1095 W Pender St, Vancouver, BC, V6E 2M6); Montreal (☎ 514-398-9695; 1155 Rue St-Alexandre, Montreal, Quebec, H3B 1Z1); Ontario (☎ 416-595-1700; 360 University Ave, Toronto, Ontario M5G 1S4)

Denmark Copenhagen (☎ 45-3555-3144; Dag Hammarskjölds Allé 24, 2100 Copenhagen)

Finland Helsinki (☎ 9-171-931; Itäinen Puistotie 14B, Helsinki)

France Paris (☎ 1-4312-2222; 2 Av Gabriel, 75008 Paris)

Germany Berlin (☎ 30-8305-0; Neustädtische Kirchstrasse 4-5, 10117 Berlin)

Greece Athens (☎ 1-721-2951; 91 Vasilissis Sophias Blvd, 10160 Athens)

India New Delhi (☎ 11-2419-8000; Shantipath, Chanakyapuri 110021, New Delhi)

Ireland Dublin (☎ 1-668-8777; 42 Elgin Rd, Dublin 4)

Israel Tel Aviv (☎ 972-3-5103822; 1 Ben Yehuda St, Tel Aviv, POB 26180)
Italy Rome (☎ 6-46-741; Via Vittorio Veneto 119A, 00187 Rome)
Japan Tokyo (☎ 3-3224-5000; 1-10-5 Akasaka, Minato-ku, Tokyo)
Kenya Nairobi (☎ 2-537-800; Mombasa Rd, PO Box 30137, Nairobi)
Korea Seoul (☎ 2-397-4114; 32 Sejongno, Jongno-gu, Seoul 110-710)
Malaysia Kuala Lumpur (☎ 3-2168-5000; 376 Jalan Tun Razak, 50400 Kuala Lumpur)
Mexico Mexico City (☎ 5080-2000; Paseo de la Reforma 305, Cuauhtémoc, 06500 Mexico City)
Netherlands The Hague (☎ 70-310-9209; Lange Voorhout 102, 2514 EJ The Hague); Amsterdam (☎ 20-575-5309; Museumplein 19, 1071 DJ Amsterdam)
New Zealand Wellington (☎ 4-462-6000; 29 Fitzherbert Terrace, Thorndon, Wellington)
Norway Oslo (☎ 22-44-85-50; Drammensveien 18, 0244 Oslo)
Russia Moscow (☎ 95-728-5000; Bolshoy Devyatinsky Pereulok 8, 121099 Moscow)
Singapore Singapore (☎ 6476-9100; 27 Napier Rd, Singapore 258508)
South Africa Pretoria (☎ 12-342-1048; 877 Pretorius St, Box 9536, Pretoria 0001)
Spain Madrid (☎ 91587-2200; Calle Serrano 75, 28006 Madrid)
Sweden Stockholm (☎ 8-783-5300; Dag Hammarskjölds Vag 31, SE-115 89 Stockholm)
Switzerland Berne (☎ 31-357-70-11; Jubilaumsstrasse 93, 3005 Berne)
Thailand Bangkok (☎ 2-205-4000; 120/22 Wireless Rd, Bangkok)
UK London (☎ 20-7499-9000; 24 Grosvenor Sq, London W1A 1AE); Edinburgh (☎ 131-556-8315; 3 Regent Terrace, Edinburgh, Scotland EH7 5BW); Belfast (☎ 28-9032-8239; Queen's House, 14 Queen St, Belfast, Northern Ireland BT1 6EQ)

Embassies & Consulates in the USA

Just about every country in the world has an embassy in Washington, DC. Call ☎ 202-555-1212 for embassy phone numbers, or visit www.embassy.org for links to all international embassies. Many countries also have consulates in other large cities. Look under 'Consulates' in the yellow pages. Most countries have an embassy for the United Nations in New York City.

FESTIVALS & EVENTS

The national festivals and events listed here are celebrated almost everywhere, though with much more fanfare in some places than others. In addition, hundreds of state and county fairs, multicultural events, pioneer days and harvest celebrations fill state and local calendars. Contact a state tourist office to find out what's happening. See also p14 for more festival highlights.

JANUARY

Chinese New Year Two weeks at the end of January. The first day is celebrated with parades, firecrackers, fireworks and lots of food. San Francisco's parade is notable.

FEBRUARY

Black History Month African-American history and famous persons are celebrated across the country.
Valentine's Day The 14th. For some reason, St Valentine is associated with romance.
Mardi Gras In late February or early March, the day before Ash Wednesday. Parades, revelry and abandonment accompany the culmination of Carnival. New Orleans is the most legendary.

MARCH

St Patrick's Day The 17th. The patron saint of Ireland is honored. Huge parades and celebrations occur in New York, Boston and Chicago. Beer will be green, and you should wear green – if you don't, you could get pinched.
Easter In late March or April, the Sunday following Good Friday (which is not a public holiday). Churches are full in the morning, followed by the secular Easter egg hunt, whereby kids search for painted eggs hidden by the Easter bunny.

APRIL

Spring Break (www.springbreakworld.com) Usually near Easter. Colleges take a one-week vacation, and students let loose, descending on various beach towns like ravenous migratory birds to drink, dance and engage in mating rituals.

MAY

Cinco de Mayo The fifth. The day the Mexicans wiped out the French Army in 1862. In the south and the west, parades celebrate Mexico, Mexican heritage and margaritas.
Mother's Day The second Sunday. Children send cards and flowers and call Mom. Restaurants will be busy.

JUNE

Father's Day The third Sunday. Same idea, different parent.
Gay Pride Month (www.interpride.org) In some cities, this is just a week, but in San Francisco, festivities last a month. The last weekend in June culminates with parades.

JULY

Independence Day The fourth. Just about every city and town has a parade commemorating American independence, with fireworks at night. Strangely enough, Chicago pulls out all the stops on the 3rd.

OCTOBER

Halloween The 31st. Kids dress in costumes and go door-to-door trick-or-treating for candy. Adults dress in costumes and act out their alter egos at wild parties. New York and San Francisco are the wildest.

NOVEMBER

Day of the Dead The second. Observed in areas with Mexican communities, this is a day to honor deceased relatives; candy skulls and skeletons are popular.
Election Day The second Tuesday. Annual ritual where Americans engage in participatory democracy.
Thanksgiving The fourth Thursday. A latter-day harvest festival where family and friends gather for daylong meals, traditionally involving roasted turkey. New York City hosts a huge parade.

DECEMBER

Christmas The 25th. The weeks leading up to Christ's birth include a range of religious and secular rituals: tree-lighting ceremonies, church choir concerts, church services, caroling in the streets, parties and, of course, shopping.
Chanukah Date determined by the Hebrew calendar. An eight-day Jewish holiday (also called Hanukkah or the Feast of Lights) commemorating the victory of the Maccabees over the armies of Syria.
Kwanzaa (www.officialkwanzaawebsite.org) From the 26th to the 31st. This African American celebration is a time to give thanks for the harvest.
New Year's Eve The 31st. People celebrate by dressing up, drinking champagne, and/or watching the festivities on TV. The following day people nurse hangovers and watch college football.

FOOD

In this book, prices for restaurants usually refer to an average main dish at dinner; unless otherwise indicated, they do not include drinks, appetizers, desserts, taxes or tips, and the same dish at lunch will usually be cheaper. Budget is usually under $10, midrange from $10 to about $20, and top end is $20 and above. However, most restaurants will have dishes that are cheaper and more expensive than indicated in the review.

See p90 for a full description of cuisine, custom and table manners in the USA.

GAY & LESBIAN TRAVELERS

Most major cities, particularly those on the coasts, have a visible and open gay community that will be easy to connect with. In particular, San Francisco, New York, Los Angeles and New Orleans are centers of vibrant gay life.

The level of acceptance across the country varies greatly, and gay and lesbian travelers should avoid hand-holding and outward displays of affection until they know the lay of the land. In some places, there is absolutely no tolerance whatsoever, and in others tolerance and acceptance is predicated on gays and lesbians not 'flaunting' their sexual preference.

Damron (☎ 415-255-0404, 800-462-6654; www.damron.com) publishes three excellent travel guides: *Men's Travel Guide*, *Women's Traveller*, and *Damron Accommodations*. This website also has lots of information, links and advice. Two travel-oriented gay magazines are *Our World* (www.ourworldmagazine.com) and *Out & About* (www.outandabout.com). *The Queerest Places: A Guide to Gay and Lesbian Historic Sites* (1997) by Paula Martinac is full of juicy details and history, and covers the country.

Other useful national resources include the following:

Gay & Lesbian National Hotline (☎ 888-843-4564; www.glnh.org) A national hotline for help, counseling, information and referrals; see website for hours.
Gay & Lesbian Yellow Pages (☎ 212-674-0120, 800-697-2812; www.glyp.com) Has listings for 25 US cities.
Gay Travel News (www.gaytravelnews.com) Updated quarterly, lists gay-friendly destinations, travel agencies and hotels.
National Gay/Lesbian Task Force (☎ 202-393-5177; www.ngltf.org) A national advocacy group; website has current news and lists of referrals.

HOLIDAYS

On the following national public holidays, banks, schools and government offices (including post offices) are closed, and transportation, museums and other services operate on a Sunday schedule. Many stores, however, do maintain regular business hours. Holidays falling on a weekend are usually observed the following Monday.

January 1 New Year's Day.
Third Monday in January Martin Luther King Jr Day.
Third Monday in February Presidents' Day.
Last Monday in May Memorial Day.
July 4 Independence Day (or the Fourth of July).
First Monday in September Labor Day.
Second Monday in October Columbus Day.

November 11 Veterans' Day.
Fourth Thursday in November Thanksgiving.
December 25 Christmas Day.

INSURANCE

No matter how long or short your trip, make sure you have adequate travel insurance. At a minimum, you need coverage for medical emergencies and treatment, including hospital stays and an emergency flight home if necessary. Medical treatment in the USA is of the highest caliber, but the expense could kill you. See p1126 for complete information.

You should also consider coverage for luggage theft or loss and trip cancellation insurance. If you already have a homeowner's policy, see what it will cover and consider getting supplemental insurance to cover the rest. If you have prepaid a large portion of your trip, cancellation insurance is a worthwhile expense.

A comprehensive travel insurance policy that covers all these things should cost about 5% to 7% of the total cost of your trip.

Finally, if you will be driving, it's also essential that you have liability insurance. Car rental agencies offer insurance that covers damage to the rental vehicle and separate liability insurance (which covers damage to people and other vehicles). See p1120 for details.

Here are some agencies offering comprehensive travel policies:

Insure.com (☎ 800-556-9393; www.insure.com) An independent site that compares quotes among 300 insurance companies and gives advice about the different types of coverage. In the UK, they run Quoteline Direct, www.quotelinedireck.co.uk; in Canada, kanetix.com, www.kanetix.com.

Travelex (☎ 800-228-9792; www.travelex.com) A major insurer with offices worldwide.

Travel Guard (☎ 877-370-4742; www.travelguard.com)

Access America (☎ 800-284-8300; www.accessamerica.com)

INTERNET ACCESS

The USA is as tech-savvy as they come. Travelers will have few problems staying connected.

For quick Internet surfing and email, the best bet is a public library. Nearly every branch has free public terminals, though they do have time limits, and occasionally out-of-state residents are charged a small fee. Even small towns have at least one Internet café or copy center (rates run $10 to $20 per hour). Also, some hotels offer free Internet access to guests; these hotels are identified in the text with an Internet icon, 💻.

If you're traveling with your own computer, setting it up for Internet access while traveling is relatively simple, and it's easy to find a connection. Many hotels have rooms with dedicated modem lines (also called 'data ports'), but check when making reservations. You can also go to an Internet café.

If you're not from the US, remember that you will need an AC adapter and a plug adapter for US sockets. See p15 for Internet resources.

LEGAL MATTERS

The most important and controversial legal development in the USA is the passage of the USA Patriot Act, which has expanded the federal government's powers in order to combat terrorism. There is no way to put a happy face on these laws, which have suspended certain rights of due process in the name of national security. These developments should be taken seriously by all foreign visitors.

However, the majority of US law remains unchanged. A person is still presumed innocent until proven guilty and has a legal right to an attorney.

In everyday matters, if you are stopped by the police, bear in mind that there is no system of paying fines on the spot. Attempting to pay the fine to the officer is frowned upon at best and may result in a charge of bribery. For traffic offenses, the police officer or highway patroller will explain the options to you. There is usually a 30-day period to pay a fine, but the officer has the authority to take you directly to a magistrate to pay immediately.

If you are arrested for a more serious offense, you are allowed to remain silent. There is no legal reason to speak to a police officer if you don't wish, but never walk away from an officer until given permission. All persons who are arrested are legally allowed the right to make one phone call. If you don't have a lawyer, friend or family member to help you, call your embassy. The police will give you the number upon request.

Each state has its own civil and criminal laws, and what is legal in one state may be illegal in others. Federal laws are applicable to the postal service, US government property and many interstate activities.

The USA Patriot Act

Under the Patriot Act, the federal government now has the right to detain foreign visitors and immigrants for an extended period of time without submitting charges or bringing them to trial. Ostensibly, they can only do this by showing a judge that the person is connected to terrorism or an identified terrorist organization, but the standards of proof and oversight are not clear. Since 9/11, several thousand men have been detained – mainly Arabs, South Asians and Muslims – and most have eventually been deported or allowed to leave. Only a handful have been arrested in connection with terrorism.

For more information on the government's powers under the Patriot Act, visit the website of the American Civil Liberties Union (ACLU), www.aclu.org/safeandfree. For information on visas, registration of foreign visitors, and a list of organizations that offer referrals for legal help, see p1103.

Driving

In all states, driving under the influence of alcohol or drugs is a serious offense, subject to stiff fines and even imprisonment. For more information on driving and road rules, see p1118.

Drinking

Bars and stores often ask for photo identification to prove you are of legal drinking age (21). Being 'carded' is standard practice and shouldn't be taken personally. The sale of liquor is subject to local government regulations, and some counties ban liquor sales on Sunday, after midnight or before breakfast. In 'dry' counties, liquor sales are banned altogether.

Drugs

Recreational drugs are prohibited by federal and state laws. Some states, such as California and Alaska, treat possession of small quantities of marijuana as a misdemeanor, though it is still punishable with fines and/or imprisonment.

Possession of any drug, including cocaine, ecstasy, LSD, heroin, hashish or more than an ounce of pot, is a felony punishable by lengthy jail sentences, depending on the circumstances. For foreigners, conviction of any drug offense is grounds for deportation.

THE LEGAL AGE FOR...

- Drinking: 21
- Driving: 16
- Sex: 18
- Voting: 18

MAPS

If you will be driving, a good road atlas is essential. Rand McNally's maps are excellent, as are the Thomas Brothers city guides, which Rand McNally also publishes; both can be found in most bookstores and many gas stations. You can also order them online (www.randmcnally.com). If you are a member of **AAA** (www.aaa.com) or one of its international affiliates, you can get AAA's high-quality free maps from any regional office. Both of the above websites also provide driving directions and free downloadable maps, as does **MapQuest** (www.mapquest.com).

If you will be backpacking, a good topographical (topo) map could be essential. The **US Geological Survey** (USGS; ☎ 888-275-8747; www.usgs.gov; PO Box 25286, Denver, CO 80225) publishes a series of 1:24,000 scale maps (or 7.5-minute maps) that cover the entire country and are ideal for hiking. USGS also publishes a separate series of topo maps of all the national parks. Order maps at the above address; or they can be found at many national park information centers, ranger stations and outdoor stores. The USFS publishes 1:126,720 scale (2 inches = 1 mile) topo maps of the national forests, but they aren't quite as useful as the USGS maps.

The University of Texas maintains an extensive online map library that covers the US and the world; go to www.lib.utexas.edu/maps/index.html.

MONEY

The US dollar is a very stable currency, and it is the only currency generally accepted in the country, except for a few places near the Canadian border that also accept Canadian dollars. For a list of exchange rates, see the inside front cover of this book. For a sample of costs in the US, see p15.

The US dollar is divided into 100 cents (¢). Coins come in denominations of 1¢ (penny), 5¢ (nickel), 10¢ (dime), 25¢ (quarter), the seldom-seen 50¢ (half-dollar) and the $1 coin. Quarters are most commonly used in vending machines and parking meters. Notes, usually called bills, come in $1, $2, $5, $10, $20, $50 and $100 denominations; $2 bills are rare but perfectly legal. Two bill designs are in circulation. The newer one has a larger portrait and several innovations designed to make forgery more difficult.

You can exchange foreign currencies at almost any large bank, and they are usually the best places to do it. Currency exchange counters at the airport and in tourist centers will not have the best rates. In rural areas, however, exchanging money can be a problem, so make sure to exchange plenty of cash, or have US dollar traveler's checks, before heading into the hinterlands.

ATMs

ATMs (automated teller machines) are available 24 hours a day at almost every bank, as well as at shopping centers, airports, grocery stores and casinos. You can withdraw cash from an ATM using a credit card (Visa, MasterCard etc), which will usually incur a fee. Alternatively, most ATMs are linked with one or more of the main ATM networks (Plus, Cirrus, Exchange, Accel), and you can use them to withdraw funds from an overseas bank account if you have a card affiliated with the appropriate network. This is usually cheaper than a credit card transaction. The exchange rate on ATM transactions is usually as good as you'll get.

Check with your bank or credit card company for exact information about using its cards at ATMs in the USA. If you will be relying on ATMs (which isn't a bad strategy), bring more than one card and keep them separate.

Credit Cards

Major credit cards are accepted nearly everywhere throughout the USA. In fact, it's almost impossible to rent a car or make phone reservations without one. (Though, strangely, some US companies, such as airlines, require your credit card billing address to be in the USA – a hassle if you want to book a domestic flight once you're in the country. If you encounter this while buying online or over the phone, visit a travel agent in person.) Even if you prefer to rely on traveler's checks and ATMs, it's highly recommended that you carry a credit card for emergencies, rentals and reservations. If you're planning to rely primarily upon credit cards, bring more than one and include a Visa or MasterCard in your deck, since other cards aren't as widely accepted.

Places that accept Visa and MasterCard are also likely to accept debit cards. A debit card deducts payment directly from the user's bank account, and the user is charged a small fee for the transaction. Check with your bank to confirm that your debit card will be accepted in the USA.

Carry copies of your credit card numbers separately from the cards. If you lose your credit cards or they are stolen, contact the company immediately. Following are toll-free numbers for the main credit card companies:

American Express (☎ 800-528-4800; www.americanexpress.com)
Diners Club (☎ 800-234-6377; www.dinersclub.com)
Discover (☎ 800-347-2683; www.discovercard.com)
MasterCard (☎ 800-826-2181; www.mastercard.com)
Visa (☎ 800-336-8472; www.visa.com)

Traveler's Checks

Traveler's checks offer the possibility of a refund in the event of theft or loss, and traveler's checks in US dollars are almost as convenient as cash. American Express and Thomas Cook are widely accepted and have efficient replacement policies.

Keep a record of the check numbers you purchase and those you have used, and keep the record separate from the checks themselves. The numbers are necessary for obtaining a refund of lost checks.

Buy traveler's checks in US dollars rather than a foreign currency. If you're worried about not using them all, or that your currency might appreciate against the dollar, simply rely on credit cards and/or ATMs instead.

PHOTOGRAPHY & VIDEO

Print film is available everywhere – at supermarkets, drugstores and (most expensively) in the souvenir shops near tourist attractions. Slide film is not as widely available, and black-and-white film is rarely sold outside major cities. Specialized camera batteries may only be available in camera stores. Video cartridges are also widely sold, and don't worry about compatibility: if it fits your camera, it will record just fine. For more details see Lonely Planet's *Travel Photography* by Richard I'Anson (2000).

Drugstores and supermarkets are good places to get your print film processed cheaply – around $6 for a roll of 24 exposures. One-hour processing services are more expensive, usually from around $11.

Restrictions

In the current climate, it's unwise to photograph military hardware or bases. There may be no actual restrictions – in general, if you're allowed to see it, you're allowed to photograph it – but heightened security means that you might attract unwanted attention. It's more likely, however, that you will encounter restrictions for commercial or PR reasons. Many galleries won't let you photograph artwork, and some attractions, such as Disneyland, make it a condition of entry that you won't take photos for commercial purposes.

Photographing People

This can be a very sensitive issue in the USA. There's usually no problem taking medium or long shots, but if you want a close-up, you should always ask. Pointing at the camera and smiling will usually get an affirmative nod. Street people and the destitute may refuse or ask for money.

Photography is commonly prohibited at Native American pueblos, ceremonies and reservations, but sometimes permitted upon payment of a fee. Native Americans usually expect to be tipped if you take their photo.

Airport Security

All airline passengers have to pass their luggage through X-ray machines. Technology as it is today doesn't jeopardize lower-speed film. If you have high-speed film (1600 ASA and above), then you may want to carry your film and cameras with you and ask the X-ray inspector to visually check the film.

POST

The US Postal Service (USPS) is the busiest postal service in the world; it's also inexpensive and reliable. Still, for urgent and important documents, some people prefer the more expensive door-to-door services of **Federal Express** (FedEx; ☎ 800-463-3339; www.fedex.com) or **United Parcel Service** (UPS; ☎ 800-782-7892; www.ups.com).

Postal Rates

As of July 2003, the postal rates for 1st-class mail within the USA were 37¢ for letters weighing up to one ounce (23¢ for each additional ounce) and 23¢ for postcards. First-class mail goes up to 13oz, and then priority-mail rates apply.

International airmail rates (except to Canada and Mexico) are 80¢ for a 1oz letter and 70¢ for a postcard. To Canada and Mexico it's 60¢ for a 1oz letter and 50¢ for a postcard. Aerograms are 70¢ to all countries.

For 24-hour postal information, call ☎ 800-275-8777 or check www.usps.com. You can get zip (postal) codes for a given address, the rules about parcel sizes, and the location and phone number of any post office.

Sending & Receiving Mail

If you have the correct postage, you can drop mail weighing less than 16oz into any blue mailbox. To send a package 16oz or heavier, go to a post office. There are branch post offices and post office centers in many supermarkets and drugstores.

General delivery mail (ie poste restante) can be sent to you c/o General Delivery at any post office that has its own zip code. Mail is usually held for 10 days before it's returned to the sender; you might request your correspondents to write 'Hold for Arrival' on their letters. You'll need photo identification to collect general delivery mail. In some big cities, general delivery mail is not held at the main post office, but at a postal facility away from downtown.

Alternatively, American Express and Thomas Cook provide mail services for their customers, and you can receive letters (not parcels) at their local offices.

SHOPPING

France has its food. England its pubs. The USA has shopping.

It's just not a US vacation if you don't spend some time toting logo-bedecked bags.

Foreign visitors should make a point of visiting at least one shopping mall or Wal-Mart, simply for the cultural experience of epic American consumerism. Plus, US consumer goods are generally cheaper than anywhere else in the world – so you might find some real bargains.

Of course, what most visitors are looking for is a little brand-name American kitsch, which is merely abundant when it isn't bizarre. Truly, some tacky roadside souvenirs achieve the status of folk art, and if nothing else, they prove that Americans really do have a sense of humor about themselves.

Handicrafts

Many regions are known for excellent local handicrafts or native artwork and goods. Traditional quilts, Pueblo jewelry, Navajo blankets, traditional or modern pottery, Gullah sweetgrass baskets and tooled leather cowboy boots are just a few of the things to look for. Good pieces will be expensive; if they are cheap, they are probably not authentic.

Antiques

America is awash in antiques, some bona fide and some merely old junk. Browsing antique shops makes a lovely and interesting afternoon, but as with handicrafts, real antiques are expensive. Bargains are rare and sometimes suspect. The most popular types – anything colonial, Victorian, Amish, Shaker, art deco or '50s moderne – are guaranteed to have a hefty price tag.

Museum Stores

Some of the coolest and most unusual souvenirs can be found in museum stores, which specialize in items that play off the museum's collection. However, they also often sell high-quality original designs by local artists. Sure, they're pricey, but even a paper bag from the Met has its own cachet.

Factory Outlets

Bargain hunters should track down the local factory outlets. These are usually near a freeway exit on the outskirts of a city. They are typically malls where brand-name stores sell their damaged, left over or out-of-season stock at discounts ranging from modest to practically giveaway. Service will be minimal, and choices limited, but for some it's worth the effort to try to find half-price Levi's, Nike shoes or Polo shirts.

CLASSIC SOUVENIRS

- A mini-Statue of Liberty
- An 'I ♥ NY' T-shirt
- A Wall Drug bumper sticker
- A 'jackalope' postcard
- A pair of Disneyland mouse ears
- A 'Vermont is for lovers' coffee mug
- Any sport team logo on a baseball cap
- A Texas-shaped brass belt buckle
- New Orleans Mardi Gras beads
- A velvet Elvis

Thrift Shops & Flea Markets

True bargain hunters will head for thrift shops and flea markets. Ask around or check the local newspaper for information on flea market times. Good ones can provide a delightful slice of local life. Arrive early if you're in the hunt for retro fashions, and expect sellers to ask top dollar.

In many places, weekends are known for sidewalk 'garage sales,' where people put their unwanted belongings up for sale. Look for posted flyers on telephone poles and in grocery stores. They make a great way to strike up casual conversations with locals, and perhaps even find a $1 treasure.

SOLO TRAVELERS

There are no particular problems or difficulties traveling alone in the USA.

Many hotels offer lower rates for a single person, but not all do. These rooms tend to be small and badly located, so if you want more comfort, make a reservation for a double. Similarly, restaurants often shunt single diners to cramped corners. To avoid this, make a reservation for two, and after being seated for a while, look disappointed that your friend isn't coming and order your meal; more than likely, the waitstaff will become extra helpful because of your plight. Or, if you want to meet people, eat at the bar if that is available.

Issues of safety are slightly different for women than they are for men; women should see p1106 for more specific advice.

For anyone, hitchhiking is always risky and not recommended, *especially* hitchhiking alone. And don't pick up hitchhikers when driving.

In general, don't advertise where you are staying, or even that you are traveling alone, if someone strikes you as suspicious. Americans tend to be friendly and very eager to help and even take in solo travelers, and this is one of the pluses of traveling this way. However, don't take all offers of help at face value. If someone who seems trustworthy invites you to his or her home, let someone know where you're going (even your hotel manager). This advice also applies if you go for a long hike by yourself. If something happens and you don't return as expected, you want to know that someone will notice and know where to begin looking for you.

TELEPHONE

The US phone system comprises numerous regional phone companies (many are actually Bell subsidiaries) plus competing long-distance carriers and lots of smaller mobile-phone and pay-phone companies. Overall, the system is very efficient, but it's geared to the needs of local users, and for foreign visitors it can be inconvenient and expensive. Try to bring a telephone card from your home phone company. It may not be the cheapest option, but it will probably offer better information and service than a US pay-phone company or a phone debit card.

Note that most telephone books have complete calling information, as well as local and international area codes, and even list community services, public transportation and things to see and do.

Pay Phones

Local calls cost 35¢ to 50¢ at pay phones. Only put in the exact amount, since phones don't give change. Local-call charges only apply to a small area. If the number you're trying to call is beyond this area, a synthetic voice will tell you to insert more money. Local calls from pay phones can get expensive quickly, and long-distance calls are prohibitive. Instead, use a prepaid phone card, a phone credit card, or the access line of a major carrier, such as **AT&T** (☎ 800-321-0288) or **MCI** (☎ 800-888-8000).

Phone Cards

Phone cards are now almost essential for travelers using the US phone system. There are two basic types.

A phone credit card bills calls to your home phone number. Some cards issued by foreign phone companies will work in the USA – inquire before you leave home. When using a phone credit card in a public place, make sure no one can see you punch in the numbers.

A prepaid phone card is a good alternative for travelers and widely available from vending machines in airports, bus stations, hotel lobbies and other locations. Each card's monetary value is translated into 'units'; one unit equals one minute within the USA, half a minute or less to overseas. Rates vary among different brands, but the cheapest are competitive with domestic phone rates.

Mobile Phones

In the USA cell phones use GSM 1900 or CDMA 800, operating on different frequencies from systems in other countries. The only foreign phones that will work in the USA are tri-band models, operating on GSM 1900 as well as other frequencies. If you have a GSM tri-band phone, check with your service provider about using it in the USA, but be aware that calls will be more expensive than using your home network (because of the US service provider's charges). Your mobile phone number stays the same, and callers at home will be connected to your phone automatically.

You may be able to take the SIM card from your home phone, install it in a rented mobile phone that's compatible with the US systems, and use the rental phone as if it were your own phone – same number, same billing basis. Ask your mobile phone company about using your SIM card for global (or international) roaming. You can rent a phone for about $45 per week, but rates vary.

Phone shops in the USA will allow you to rent a GSM 1900 compatible phone with a set amount of prepaid call time. Pricing plans are complex, but generally this is an expensive option. **T-Mobile** (www.t-mobile.com) is one US company that provides this service.

Telephone Numbers

If you're calling from abroad, the international country code for the USA is 1. To make an international call from the USA, dial ☎ 011, then the country code, followed by the area code and the phone number.

All phone numbers within the USA consist of a three-digit area code followed by a seven-digit local number. If you are calling a number within the same area code, just dial the seven-digit number. If you are calling long distance, dial ☎ 1 plus the area code plus the phone number. New area codes are added and changed all the time, so if a number doesn't work, that may be the reason.

For local directory assistance, dial ☎ 411. For directory assistance outside your area code, dial ☎ 1 plus the three-digit area code of the place you want to call plus 555-1212; this is charged as a long-distance call. For international assistance, dial ☎ 00.

The 800, 888, 877 and 866 prefixes are for toll-free numbers. Most can only be used within the USA, some only within the state, and some only outside the state. To find an organization's 800 number, call ☎ 800-555-1212.

The 550, 554, 900, 920, 940, 976 codes and some other prefixes are for calls charged at a premium rate – phone sex, horoscopes, jokes etc.

TIME

See pp1130–1 for a map of time zones.

TOILETS

The standard of plumbing and sanitation is very high, but public toilets can be scarce on city streets. Public bathrooms (or rest rooms) are generally available at fast-food restaurants and shopping centers, but many bars and restaurants reserve bathrooms 'for customers only.' The desperate can always ask. In addition, most highway rest stops have public toilets.

TOURIST INFORMATION

There is no national tourist office promoting US tourism. However, the federal government does provide some information and resources for travelers (see p15).

Tourist promotion and information is instead provided by states, cities and local areas; see the Information section at the beginning of each regional chapter for the main state agencies. City and county tourist bureaus are listed throughout the book.

Just about every tourist office has a website and will, on request, send out a swag of promotional materials. They also field phone calls; sometimes enthusiastic amateurs in small offices will be much more helpful than their professional colleagues in state bureaus. Some tourist offices maintain lists of local hotel room availability, updated daily, but very few offer reservations services. All tourist offices have self-service racks of brochures, tourist newsletters and discount coupons to local attractions. Some also sell good maps, area histories and other books.

Many cities have an official convention and visitors bureau (CVB), which usually has all the standard tourist literature to hand out. However, some CVBs focus mainly on the convention trade and are not very useful for independent travelers.

In smaller towns, the local chamber of commerce (an organization of local businesses) often runs a tourist information service. They usually provide lists of hotels, motels, restaurants and services, but the lists will mention only chamber members and may not include the cheapest options.

In prime tourist destinations, you'll find additional private tourist bureaus, though some will really be private agents who book hotel rooms and tours on commission. They can offer excellent service and deals, but you won't get unbiased advice or much information on museums or national parks.

Some state governments maintain comprehensive welcome centers along main highways. They are usually open much longer hours, including weekends and holiday times, than other tourist offices. They also stock cheap-looking booklets filled with discount coupons.

TOURS

Companies offer all kinds of tours in the USA; most focus on regions or cities. See the Organized Tours section at the beginning of each regional chapter for recommendations. The following are some of the main activity-based tour companies.

Trek America (☎ 800-221-0596; www.trekamerica.com) specializes in outdoor trips that emphasize activities and hiking; this group has an excellent reputation. On the main Trek America trips, groups are kept to 13 people (age 18 to 38), who travel in a single van and spend most nights camping. Itineraries are kept loose, so that each group to some degree creates its own trip, and stops are often for several nights. However, 'Footloose' trips are gentler; they have less or no camping and participants range from 18 to 55 years old.

Green Tortoise (☎ 800-867-8647; www.greentortoise.com) offers unique adventures for independent budget travelers. What mainly distinguishes Green Tortoise is its buses, which have seats that convert into sleeping bunks, but Green Tortoise is also a state of mind. Buses hold 32 to 40 people, and everyone helps prepare meals, cleans up, enjoys the outdoors and generally gets to know each other. Most people are 18 to 35, but trips include all ages and nationalities. Nearly all trips leave from San Francisco, and they include western national parks, cross-country excursions and jaunts to Central America.

For a more typical cities and sites trip, **Contiki** (☎ 888-266-8454; www.contiki.com) caters to 18- to 35-year-olds and has a wide range of US destinations. Over half of Contiki's travelers are singles, and trips emphasize urban nightlife as much as outdoor activities; most nights are in hotels.

VISAS

The USA is in the middle of overhauling its entry requirements as it establishes new national security guidelines post-9/11. It is imperative that travelers double- and triple-check current regulations before coming to the USA, as changes will continue for several years.

One of the biggest changes so far has been bureaucratic. The Immigration and Naturalization Service (INS) no longer exists. All of its functions have been absorbed into the new Department of Homeland Security; visa and immigrant processing is now handled by the Bureau of Citizenship & Immigration Services (BCIS). There is also a new website with comprehensive visa information: www.unitedstatesvisas.gov.

All foreign visitors (other than Canadians) must bring their passports. Canadians must have proof of citizenship, such as a citizenship card with photo identification, or a passport.

Visa Application

Apart from Canadians and those entering under the Visa Waiver Program (see p1104), foreign visitors need to obtain a visa from a US consulate or embassy. In most countries the process can be started by mail or through a travel agent, but a personal appearance interview is becoming standard; this can add another month or more to the process. The US consular office in your country should also advise you if you must register upon arrival (see p1105).

Another source for visa and immigration information is the website of the US State Department: www.travel.state.gov/visa_services.html. The BCIS website has up-to-date application forms you can download and print out; go to www.bcis.gov.

Your passport must be valid for at least six months longer than your intended stay in the USA, and you'll need to submit a recent photo (2in by 2in) with the application; there is a $100 processing fee, and in a few cases an additional visa issuance reciprocity fee (check the BCIS website for details). In addition to the main nonimmigrant visa application form (DS-156), all men aged 16 to 45 must now complete an additional form (DS-157) that details their travel plans.

In almost all cases, visa applicants are required to show documents of financial stability (or evidence that a US resident will provide financial support), a round-trip or onward ticket and 'binding obligations' that will ensure their return home, such as family ties, a home or a job.

Because of these requirements, those planning to travel through other countries before arriving in the USA are generally better off applying for a US visa while they are still in their home country, rather than while on the road.

The most common visa is a nonimmigrant visitors visa, type B1 for business purposes, B2 for tourism or visiting friends and relatives. A visitor's visa is good for multiple entries over one or five years, and specifically prohibits the visitor from taking paid employment in the USA. The validity period depends on what country you are from. The length of time you'll be allowed to stay in the USA is determined by US immigration at the port of entry (see p1104).

If you're coming to the USA to work or study, you will need a different type of visa, and the company or institution to which you are going should make the arrangements. Other categories of nonimmigrant visas include an F1 visa for students undertaking a recognized course; an H1, H2 or H3 visa for temporary employment; a J1 visa for exchange visitors in approved programs; a K1 visa for the fiancé or fiancée of an American citizen; and an L1 visa for intracompany transfers. Allow at least six months for processing an application.

VISA WAIVER PROGRAM

Under the Visa Waiver Program, citizens of certain countries may enter the USA without a US visa for stays of 90 days or less; no extensions are allowed. Currently, 27 countries are included: Andorra, Australia, Austria, Belgium, Brunei, Denmark, Finland, France, Germany, Iceland, Ireland, Italy, Japan, Liechtenstein, Luxembourg, Monaco, the Netherlands, New Zealand, Norway, Portugal, San Marino, Singapore, Slovenia, Spain, Sweden, Switzerland and the United Kingdom.

Under this program, visitors must produce all the same evidence as for a nonimmigrant visa application: they must be able to prove that the trip is for a limited time, and that they have a round-trip or onward ticket, adequate funds to cover the trip and binding obligations abroad. Your passport must be 'machine readable'; check with your passport issuing agency if you're not sure. You'll be turned back if it isn't.

In addition, the same 'grounds for exclusion' apply (see below), except that you will have no opportunity to appeal the grounds or apply for an exemption. If you are denied under the Visa Waiver Program at a US point of entry, you will have to use your onward or return ticket on the next available flight.

GROUNDS FOR EXCLUSION & DEPORTATION

The visa application form asks, among other things, if you are a drug trafficker, whether you seek to enter the USA to engage in terrorist activities or if you have ever participated in a genocide. If you admit to being a subversive, smuggler, prostitute, junkie or an ex-Nazi, you may be excluded. You can also be refused a visa or entry to the USA if you have a 'communicable disease of public health significance,' a criminal record or if you've ever made a false statement in connection with a US visa application. However, if these last three apply, you can request an exemption; many people are granted them and then given visas.

US immigration has a very broad definition of a criminal record. If you've ever been arrested or charged with an offense, that's a criminal record, even if you were acquitted or discharged without conviction. Don't attempt to enter through the Visa Waiver Program if you have a criminal record of any kind; more than ever, US authorities are linking computer databases, and you should assume they will find every detail.

Communicable diseases include tuberculosis, the Ebola virus, SARS and most particularly HIV. US immigration doesn't test people for disease, but officials at the point of entry may question anyone about his or her health. They can exclude anyone whom they believe has a communicable disease, perhaps because they are carrying medical documents, prescriptions or AIDS/HIV medicine. Being gay is not a ground for exclusion; being an IV drug user is. Visitors may be deported if US immigration finds that they have HIV but did not declare it. Being HIV-positive is not a ground for deportation, but failing to provide accurate information on the visa application is.

Often BCIS will grant an exemption (a 'waiver of ineligibility') to a person who would normally be subject to exclusion, but this requires referral to a regional immigration office and can take some time (allow at least two months). If you're tempted to conceal something, remember that US immigration is strictest of all about false statements. It will often view favorably an applicant who admits to an old criminal charge or a communicable disease, but it is extremely harsh on anyone who has ever attempted to mislead it, even on minor points. After you're admitted to the USA, any evidence of a false statement to US immigration is grounds for deportation.

Prospective visitors to whom grounds of exclusion may apply should consider their options *before* applying for a visa. See p1105 for information and legal advice.

Entering the USA

If you have a non-US passport, you must complete an arrival/departure record (form I-94) before you reach the immigration desk. It's usually handed out on the plane along with the customs declaration. For the question, 'Address While in the United States,' give the address where you will spend the first night (a hotel address is fine). Complete the departure record (the lower part of the form) giving exactly the same answers for questions 14 to 17 as for questions 1 to 4.

No matter what your visa says, US immigration officers have an absolute authority to refuse admission to the USA or to impose conditions on admission. They will ask about your plans and whether you have sufficient funds; it's a good idea to list an itinerary, produce an onward or round-trip ticket and have at least one major credit card. Showing that you have over $400 per week of your stay should be enough. Don't make too much of having friends, relatives or business contacts in the USA; the immigration official may decide that this will make you more likely to overstay. It also helps to be neatly dressed and polite. If they think you're OK, a six-month entry is usually approved.

REGISTRATION

In addition to making sure visitors don't plan to work illegally or overstay, US immigration is now highly concerned with making sure terrorists or others seeking to harm the country aren't admitted. A registration system is being phased in that, by 2005, will include every single one of the 35 million visitors who come to the USA every year.

A 'special registration' called NSEERS (the National Security Entry Exit Registration System) currently applies to citizens of certain countries that have been deemed particular risks. These countries are mainly in the Middle East and Africa; visit www.unitedstatesvisas.gov for a complete list. However, any visitor from any country can be asked to register at a US point of entry, and once the infrastructure is in place, everyone will be. At that time, NSEERS will be called US Visit (Visitor and Immigration Status Indicator Technology).

Registration consists of a short interview in a separate room, having a photo and electronic (inkless) fingerprints taken, and computer verification of all personal information supplied on travel documents; it may also one day include iris scanning and facial recognition technology. US officials claim this process currently takes less than 20 minutes, but if you must register, expect waits and delays. Those who are required to register under NSEERS will be issued a 30-day appointment to return to a regional office, though US immigration can require this of anyone. Missing this appointment is grounds for deportation.

Visa Extensions

If you want, need or hope to stay in the USA longer than the date stamped on your passport, go to the local BCIS office (call ☎ 800-375-5283 or look in the local white pages telephone directory under 'US Government') to apply for an extension well *before* the stamped date. If the date has passed, your best chance will be to bring a US citizen with you to vouch for your character, and to produce lots of other verification that you are not trying to

IMMIGRANT RIGHTS & LEGAL HELP

For independent, up-to-date information about visa issues and immigrant rights, or for attorney referrals, contact the following organizations:

American-Arab Anti-Discrimination Committee (ADC; ☎ 202-244-2990; www.adc.org; 4201 Connecticut Ave NW, Washington DC, 20008) Advocacy group that gives advice on special registrations and immigrant civil rights.

American Civil Liberties Union (ACLU; ☎ 212-549-2500; www.aclu.org; 125 Broad St, New York, NY 10004) Current legal news and civil rights information; *Know Your Rights* pamphlet.

American Immigrant Lawyers Association (☎ 800-954-0254, 202-216-2400; www.aila.org; 918 F St NW, Washington DC, 20004) Attorney referrals.

Immigrant HIV Assistance Project (IHAP), Bar Association of San Francisco (☎ 415-782-8995; www.sfbar.org/vlsp/immigrant.html; 465 California St, Suite 1100, San Francisco, CA 94104) Information on HIV status and immigration.

National Immigration Project, National Lawyers Guild (☎ 617-227-9727; www.nationalimmigrationproject.org; 14 Beacon St, Suite 602, Boston, MA 02108) Information on immigration law, referrals, and lots of website links.

work illegally and have enough money to support yourself. However, if you've overstayed, the most likely scenario is that you will be deported.

Short-Term Departures & Reentry

It's quite easy to make trips across the border to Canada or Mexico, but upon return to the USA, non-Americans will be subject to the full immigration procedure. Always take your passport when you cross the border. If your immigration card still has plenty of time on it, you will probably be able to reenter using the same one, but if it has nearly expired, you will have to apply for a new card, and border control may want to see your onward air ticket, sufficient funds and so on.

Traditionally, a quick trip across the border has been a way to extend your stay in the USA without applying for an extension at a BCIS office. This can still be done, but don't assume it will work. First, make sure you hand in your old immigration card to the immigration authorities when you leave the USA, and when you return make sure you have all the necessary application documentation described above. US immigration will be very suspicious of anyone who leaves for a few days and returns immediately hoping for a new six-month stay; expect to be questioned closely.

Citizens of most Western countries will not need a visa for Canada, so it's really not a problem at all to cross to the Canadian side of Niagara Falls, detour up to Quebec or pass through on the way to Alaska. Travelers entering the USA by bus from Canada can be closely scrutinized. A round-trip ticket that takes you back to Canada will most likely make US immigration feel less suspicious. Mexico has a visa-free zone along most of its border with the USA, including the Baja Peninsula and most of the border towns, such as Tijuana and Ciudad Juárez. You'll only need a Mexican visa or tourist card if you want to go beyond the border zone.

WOMEN TRAVELERS

Women traveling by themselves or in a group should encounter no particular problems in the USA. In these modern times, a woman alone hardly raises an eyebrow, though it does raise a couple of special safety concerns (see p1106).

A Journey of One's Own (1992) by Thalia Zepatos aims to inspire independent female travelers, and it contains loads of advice, anecdotes and resources. Pocketbook-size, *The Bad Girl's Guide to the Open Road* (1999) by Cameron Tuttle is full of more irreverent but equally useful tips and encouragement.

The community website www.journeywoman.com facilitates women talking to each other, and it has links to other sites. Other useful organizations are the **National Organization for Women** (NOW; ☎ 202-628-8669; www.now.org; 733 15th St NW, 2nd fl, Washington, DC 20005), which is a political advocacy group, and **Planned Parenthood** (☎ 212-541-7800; www.plannedparenthood.org; 810 7th Ave, New York, NY 10019), which can offer advice on medical issues and referrals to clinics throughout the country.

Safety Precautions

A single woman is more likely to be the target of harassment or assault, so she should use a taxi, avoid empty streets and be extra cautious about accepting 'help' and invitations from men that lead away from bars and crowded places. For more traveler cautions, see p1100.

Some men may interpret a woman drinking alone in a bar as a bid for male company, whether it is intended that way or not. If you don't want the company, a very firm but polite 'no, thank you' will usually end the conversation.

When driving, it's a good idea to have a sign requesting help, which you can display if you get stuck on the road. At night avoid getting out of your car to flag down help; turn on your hazard lights and wait for the police to arrive. Bringing a mobile phone is good insurance.

If you are assaulted, call the **police** (☎ 911). Cities and larger towns have rape crisis centers and women's shelters that provide help and support; they are listed in the telephone directory.

In addition to being trained in self-defense, some women like to carry a whistle, mace or cayenne-pepper spray in case of assault. If you purchase a spray, contact a police station to find out about local regulations. Laws regarding sprays vary from state to state, but federal law prohibits them being carried on planes.

WORK

If you are a foreigner in the USA with a standard nonimmigrant visitors visa, you are expressly forbidden to take paid work in the USA and will be deported if you're caught working illegally. In addition, employers are required to establish the bona fides of their employees or face fines, making it much tougher for a foreigner to get work than it once was.

To work legally, foreigners need to apply for a work visa before leaving home. A J1 visa, for exchange visitors, is issued to young people (age limits vary) for study, student vacation employment, work in summer camps, and short-term traineeships with a specific employer. The following organizations will help arrange student exchanges, placements and J1 visas:

American Institute for Foreign Study (AIFS; ☎ 800-727-2437; www.aifs.com; River Plaza, 9 West Broad St, Stamford, CT 06902-3788)
BUNAC (☎ 020-7251-3472; www.bunac.org; 16 Bowling Green Lane, London EC1R 0QH)
Camp America (☎ 020-7581-7377; www.campamerica.co.uk; 37A Queens Gate, London SW7 5HR)
Council on International Educational Exchange (CIEE; ☎ 800-407-8839; www.ciee.org; 633 Third Ave, NY, NY 10017)
International Exchange Programs (IEP) Australia (☎ 1300-300-912; www.iep-australia.com; 196 Albert Road, South Melbourne, Vic 3205; Level 2, 333 George St, Sydney, NSW 2000); New Zealand (☎ 09-366-6255; www.iepnz.co.nz; PO Box 1786, Shortland Street, Auckland)

For nonstudent jobs, temporary or permanent, you need to be sponsored by a US employer who will have to arrange one of the various H-category visas. These are not easy to obtain, since the employer has to prove that no US citizen or permanent resident is available to do the job. Seasonal work is possible in national parks, tourist sites and especially ski areas. Contact park concessionaires, local chambers of commerce and ski-resort management. Many menial jobs, such as cleaning, fruit picking and dishwashing, are done by immigrant workers (legal and otherwise) from Latin America, and offer extremely poor pay and conditions.

Transport

CONTENTS

THINGS CHANGE...

The information in this chapter is particularly vulnerable to change. Check directly with the airline or a travel agent to make sure you understand how a fare (and ticket you may buy) works and be aware of the security requirements for international travel. Shop carefully. The details given in this chapter should be regarded as pointers and are not a substitute for your own careful, up-to-date research.

GETTING THERE & AWAY

ENTERING THE USA

Most people arrive in the USA by air. The only land borders are with Canada and Mexico, and arriving by sea is mainly done through cruises.

The first airport that you land in is where you must go through immigration and customs procedures, even if you are continuing on the flight to another destination.

Passengers aboard the airplane are given standard immigration and customs forms to fill out. After the plane lands, you'll first go through immigration. There are two lines: One is for US citizens and residents, and the other is for nonresidents. For details about what documents to have ready for US immigration and about registration of foreign visitors, see Visas (p1103). In the post-9/11 world, immigration officials can be very strict, so expect delays and lots of questions.

After immigration, you collect your baggage and then pass through customs. If you have nothing to declare, you'll probably clear customs quickly and without a baggage search, but don't count on it. For details on customs, see p1089.

If you are continuing on the same plane or connecting to another one, it is your responsibility to get your bags to the right place. Normally, airline representatives are just outside the customs area to help you. Most airports have pay phones and car rentals, but other facilities may be minimal. Outside of the major international airports, don't count on a foreign exchange office, tourist information desk or luggage-storage service – some US airports are not very user-friendly.

AIR

Airports

The USA has 429 domestic airports, and a baker's dozen are the main international gateways. Many other airports are called 'international' but most have only a few flights from other countries – typically links to Mexico or Canada. Even travel to an international gateway sometimes requires a connection in another gateway city. For example, many of the London–Los Angeles flights involve a transfer connection in Chicago.

INTERNATIONAL GATEWAYS

Atlanta Hartsfield International (code ATL; ☎ 404-209-1700; www.atlanta-airport.com)

Boston Logan International (code BOS; ☎ 800-235-6426; www.massport.com/logan)

Chicago O'Hare International (code ORD; ☎ 800-832-6352; www.ohare.com/ohare/home.asp)

Dallas-Fort Worth (code DFW; ☎ 972-574-8888; www.dfwairport.com)

Honolulu (code HNL; ☎ 808-836-6413; www.honolulu airport.com)

Houston George Bush Intercontinental (code IAH; ☎ 281-230-3000; www.houston-iah.com)

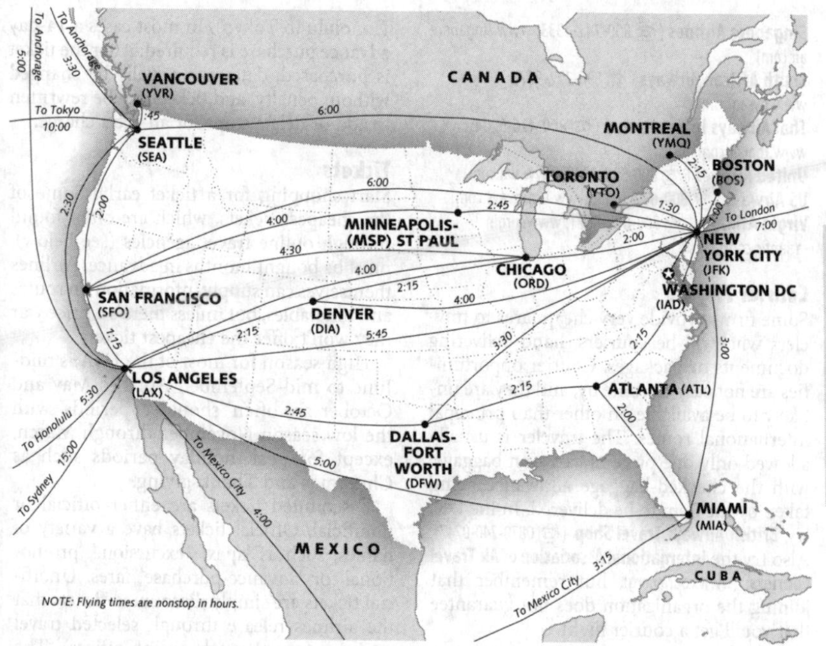

Los Angeles (code LAX; ☎ 310-646-5252; www.lawa.org/lax/laxframe.html)
Miami (code MIA; ☎ 305-876-7000; www.miami-airport.com)
New York John F Kennedy (code JFK; ☎ 718-244-4444; www.panynj.gov/aviation/jfkframe.htm)
Newark (code EWR; ☎ 973-961-6000; www.panynj.gov/aviation/ewrframe.htm)
San Francisco (code SFO; ☎ 650-821-8211; www.flysfo.com)
Seattle Seattle-Tacoma International (code SEA; ☎ 206-433-5388; www.portseattle.org/seatac/default.htm)
Washington, DC Dulles International (code IAD; ☎ 703-572-2700; www.metwashairports.com/dulles/)

Airlines

The national airlines of most countries have flights to the USA, and the USA has several airlines serving the world. Here is a list of the main international carriers.

Aer Lingus (☎ 800-474-7424; www.aerlingus.com)
Aerolíneas Argentinas (☎ 800-333-0276; www.aeroargentinas.com)
Air Canada (☎ 888-247-2262; www.aircanada.ca)
Air France (☎ 800-237-2747; www.airfrance.com)
Air New Zealand (☎ 800-262-1234; www.airnewzealand.com)
Alitalia (☎ 800-223-5730; www.alitalia.com)
American Airlines (☎ 800-433-7300; www.aa.com)
British Airways (☎ 800-247-9297; www.britishairways.com)
Cathay Pacific (☎ 800-233-2742; www.cathaypacific.com)
Continental Airlines (☎ 800-231-0856; www.continental.com)
Delta Air Lines (☎ 800-241-4141; www.delta.com)
El Al (☎ 800-223-6700; www.elal.co.il)
Garuda Indonesia (☎ 800-342-7832; www.garuda-indonesia.com)
Iberia (☎ 800-772-4642; www.iberia.com)
Icelandair (☎ 800-223-5500; www.icelandair.com)
Japan Airlines (JAL; ☎ 800-525-3663; www.jal.com)
KLM (☎ 800-374-7747; www.klm.com)
Korean Air (☎ 800-438-5000; www.koreanair.com)
Kuwait Airways (☎ 800-458-9248; www.kuwait-airways.com)
Lufthansa (☎ 800-645-3880; http://cms.lufthansa.com)
Northwest Airlines (☎ 800-447-4747; www.nwa.com)
Polynesian Airlines (☎ 685-22172; www.polynesianairlines.co.nz)
Qantas (☎ 800-227-4500; www.qantas.com)
Scandinavian Airlines (SAS; ☎ 800-221-2350; www.scandinavian.net)

Singapore Airlines (☎ 800-742-3333; www.singaporeair.com)
South African Airways (☎ 800-722-9675; www.flysaa.com)
Thai Airways International (☎ 800-426-5204; www.thaiair.com)
United Airlines (☎ 800-538-2929; www.ual.com)
US Airways (☎ 800-622-1015; www.usairways.com)
Virgin Atlantic (☎ 800-862-8621; www.virgin-atlantic.com)

Courier Flights

Some firms provide very cheap fares to travelers who will be couriers, hand-delivering documents or packages. Courier opportunities are not easy to come by, and they are unlikely to be available on other than principal international routes. The traveler is usually allowed only one piece of carry-on baggage, with the checked-baggage allowance being taken by the item to be delivered. In the UK, try **British Airways Travel Shop** (☎ 0870-240-0747). Also try the **International Association of Air Travel Couriers** (www.courier.org), but remember that joining the organization does not guarantee that you'll get a courier flight.

Intercontinental Tickets

Round-the-world (RTW) tickets are great if you want to visit other regions as well as the USA. They're usually a bit more expensive than a simple round-trip ticket to the USA, but the extra stops are pretty cheap. They're of most value for trips that combine the USA with another two continents – Europe, Asia or Australasia. RTW itineraries that include South America or Africa as well as North America are substantially more expensive.

Official airline RTW tickets are usually put together by a combination of airlines, or a whole alliance, and they permit you to fly to a specified number of stops and/or a maximum mileage on their routes, so long as you don't backtrack. Other restrictions are that you must usually book the first sector in advance and cancellation penalties apply. The tickets are valid for a fixed period, usually one year. An alternative type of RTW ticket is one put together by a travel agent using a combination of discounted tickets.

Most RTW fares restrict the number of stops within the USA and Canada. The cheapest fares permit only the one stop; others allow two or more. Some airlines 'black out' a few heavily traveled routes (like Honolulu to Tokyo). In most cases a 14-day advance purchase is required. After the ticket is purchased, dates can usually be changed without penalty, and tickets can be rewritten to add or delete stops for an extra charge.

Tickets

Start shopping for a ticket early. Some of the cheapest tickets, which are often found through online travel agencies (see below), must be bought months in advance. Airlines themselves can supply information on routes and timetables, but unless there's a price war they won't offer the cheapest tickets.

High season for most of the USA is mid-June to mid-September. April to May and October are often 'shoulder' periods, with the low season November through March, except for peak holiday periods such as Christmas and Thanksgiving.

Discounted tickets are either official or unofficial. Official tickets have a variety of names, such as 'apex,' 'excursion,' 'promotional' or 'advance-purchase' fares. Unofficial tickets are simply discounted tickets that the airlines release through selected travel agencies (not through airline offices). The cheapest tickets are often nonrefundable and charge a fee for flight changes. Many insurance policies will cover this loss if you have to change your flight for emergency reasons.

When shopping for your air ticket, keep in mind your entire US itinerary. Some deals for travel within the USA can only be purchased overseas in conjunction with an international air ticket. These include various air passes, Greyhound bus line's International Ameripass, and some Amtrak rail passes. Also, you can often get domestic flights within the USA as an inexpensive add-on to your international airfare (see p1115).

ONLINE TRAVEL AGENCIES

Most airlines have their own websites with online ticket sales, often discounted for online customers. To buy a ticket via the Web, you'll need to use a credit card. Commercial reservation networks offer airline ticketing as well as information and bookings for hotels, car rental and other services. Networks include the following:

Atevo Travel (www.atevo.com)
Cheap Tickets (www.cheaptickets.com)
Info-Hub Specialty Travel Guide (www.biztravel.com)
Expedia.com (www.expedia.com)

Hotwire (www.hotwire.com)
LowestFare.com (www.lowestfare.com)
Orbitz (www.orbitz.com)
Priceline (www.priceline.com)
STA Travel (www.sta.com)
Travelocity.com (www.travelocity.com)
Yahoo Travel (www.travel.yahoo.com)

From Africa

A few cities in West and North Africa have direct flights to the USA – Abidjan (Côte d'Ivoire), Accra (Ghana), Cairo (Egypt), Casablanca (Morocco) and Dakar (Senegal). Apart from South African Airways flights from Johannesburg to New York, most flights from Africa to the USA go via a European hub, most commonly London.

SOUTH AFRICA

Flight Centre (☎ 0860-400-747; www.flightcentre.co.za)
Rennies Travel (☎ 011-833-1441; www.rennies travel.com)
STA Travel (☎ 021-418-6570; www.statravel.co.za)

KENYA

Let's Go Travel (☎ 4447-151; www.letsgosafari.com)

From Asia

Bangkok, Singapore, Kuala Lumpur, Hong Kong, Seoul and Tokyo all have good connections to the US West Coast on high-quality national airlines. Many flights to the USA go via Honolulu and allow a stopover. Bangkok is the discounted fare capital of the region, though its cheapest agents can be unreliable.

Four Seas Tours Hong Kong(☎ 2200-7760; www.four seastravel.com/english)
No 1 Travel Japan (☎ 03-3200-8871; www.no1 -travel.com)
STA Travel Bangkok (☎ 662-236-0262; www.sta travel.co.th); Singapore (☎ 65-6737-7188; www.sta travel.com.sg); Hong Kong (☎ 852-2736-1618; www.statravel.com.hk); Japan (☎ 03-5391-2922; www.statravel.co.jp)

From Australia

Some flights go from Sydney and Melbourne direct to Los Angeles and San Francisco. Flights to other US cities will usually involve a stop in Los Angeles, or possibly San Francisco or Honolulu. Qantas, Air New Zealand and United are the main airlines on the route. Fares from Melbourne, Sydney, Brisbane and sometimes Adelaide and Canberra are 'common rated' (the same for all cities). From Hobart and Perth, there'll be an add-on fare.

Low season is roughly February, March, October and November. High season is mid-June to mid-July and mid-December to mid-January. The rest of the year is considered shoulder season. Discounted tickets have minimum- and maximum-stay provisions.

Flight Centre (☎ 1300-133-133; www.flightcentre .com.au)
STA Travel (☎ 1300-733-035; www.statravel.com.au)
Trailfinders (☎ 03-9600-3022; www.trailfinders.com.au)
Travel.com (☎ 1300-130-482; www.travel.com.au)

From Canada

Daily flights go from Vancouver, Toronto and many smaller cities to all the big US centers. Commuter flights to cities such as New York and Chicago can be very expensive. Some of the best deals are charter and package fares to sunny destinations such as Florida, California and Hawaii, with higher prices in the winter peak season.

It may be much cheaper to travel by land to the nearest US city, then take a discounted domestic flight. For example, round-trip fares to New York are much cheaper from Seattle, Washington, than from Vancouver, BC, only 130 miles away.

Expedia (www.expedia.ca)
Travel Cuts (☎ 866-246-9762; www.travelcuts.com)
Travelocity (www.travelocity.ca)

From Central & South America

The main gateway from Central and South America is Miami, but there are also many direct flights to Los Angeles and Houston. Check the international flag-carrier airlines of the countries you want to connect to as well as US airlines such as United and American.

Regular flights link the major cities of Mexico and the USA. At times, depending on prices and exchange rates, it can be much cheaper to fly to a Mexican border town than to the adjacent town on the US side. A flight from Mexico City to Tijuana can cost quite a bit less than a flight to San Diego, just a few miles north on the US side.

Asatej Argentina (☎ 54-011-4114-7595; www .asatej.com)
IVI Tours Venezuela (☎ 0212-993-6082; www.ividio mas.com)
Student Travel Bureau Brazil (☎ 3038-1555; www .stb.com.br)

From Continental Europe

There are nonstop flights to many US cities, but the discounted fares often involve indirect routes and changing planes. The main airlines between Europe and the USA are Air France, Alitalia, British Airways, KLM, Continental, TWA, United, American, Delta, Scandinavian Airlines and Lufthansa. Sometimes an Asian or Middle Eastern carrier will have cheap deals on flights in transit to the USA, if you can get a seat. Also try Icelandair connections via London.

The newsletter *Farang* covers exotic destinations, as does Globe-Trotters **Aventure du Bout du Monde** (☎ 01-45-45-29-29; www.abm.fr).

BELGIUM

Airstop (☎ 07-023-31 88; www.airstop.be)
Connections (☎ 02-550-01 00; www.connections.be)
Nouvelles Frontieres (☎ 02-547-44 22; www.nouvelles-frontieres.be)

FRANCE

Anyway.com (☎ 0892-89-38-92; www.anyway.fr) Auction website for air tickets.
Charters Plus (☎ 01-44-09-06-24)
Havas Voyages (☎ 01-53-29-40-00)
Lastminute (☎ 0892-70-50-00; www.lastminute.fr)
Nouvelles Frontieres (☎ 0825-00-07-47; www.nouvelles-frontieres.fr)
OTU Voyages (☎ 08-25-00-40-27; www.otu.fr) Specializes in student travel.
Usit Connections (☎ 08-92-88-88-88) Specializes in student travel.
Voyageurs du Monde (☎ 01-42-86-16-00; www.vdm.com)

GERMANY

Expedia (www.expedia.de)
Just Travel (☎ 089-747-3330; www.justtravel.de)
Last Minute (☎ 01805-284-639; www.lastminute.de)
Reiseboerse.com (☎ 030 2800 2800; www.reiseboerse.com)
STA Travel (☎ 01805-456-422; www.statravel.de)

ITALY

CTS Viaggi (☎ 06-462-0431; www.cts.it) Student and youth travel.

NETHERLANDS

Air Fair (☎ 020-620-5121; www.airfair.nl)
Holland International (☎ 070-307-6307; www.hollandinternational.nl)
NBBS Reizen (☎ 0900-10-20-300; www.nbbs.nl)

SCANDINAVIA

Kilroy Travels (www.kilroytravels.com); Sweden (☎ 0771-54 57 69); Denmark (☎ 33-11-00-44); Norway (☎ 23-10-23-10)
STA Travel Sweden (☎ 0771-61-10-10; www.statravel.se); Denmark (☎ 33-14-15-01; www.statravel.dk); Norway (☎ 815-59-905; www.statravel.no)

SPAIN

Barcelo Viajes (☎ 90-211-62-26; www.barceloviajes.com)
Nouvelles Frontières (☎ 90-217-09- 79)

SWITZERLAND

Jerrycan Voyages (☎ 022-346-92-82; www.jerrycan-travel.ch)
Nouvelles Frontières (☎ 022-906-80-80; www.nouvelles-frontieres.ch)
STA Travel (☎ 01-297-11-11; www.statravel.ch)

From New Zealand

Air New Zealand has regular flights from Auckland direct to Los Angeles. Flights from Christchurch and Wellington require a plane change in Auckland or the Pacific Islands. You'll find that low, shoulder and peak seasons are roughly the same as for Australia.

Flight Centre (☎ 0800-24-35-44; www.flightcentre.co.nz)
STA Travel (☎ 0508-782-872; www.statravel.co.nz)
Travel.com (www.travel.co.nz)

From Pacific Islands

Hawaii and the US territories of American Samoa and Guam (Micronesia) are the main gateways to the USA from the islands of the vast Pacific Ocean. From some islands, you may have to go via New Zealand, Australia, Papua New Guinea or Japan. There's not much competition on Pacific Islands routes, so don't expect bargain prices.

In addition to domestic carriers Aloha, Continental and Hawaiian Airlines, other airlines in the region include Air New Zealand, Japan Airlines and Polynesian Airlines.

From the UK & Ireland

One of the busiest and most competitive air sectors in the world is from the UK to the USA, with hundreds of scheduled flights by British Airways, American Airlines, United, Delta, Northwest, Continental, Kuwait, Air India, TWA and discount specialist Virgin Atlantic.

Discount air travel is big business in London. Advertisements for many travel agencies appear in the travel pages of the weekend broadsheet newspapers, in *Time Out*, the *Evening Standard* and in the free magazine *TNT*. Discounted fares are highly variable, volatile and subject to various conditions and restrictions. From UK regional airports, discounted flights may be routed via London, Paris or Amsterdam, and will probably not fly direct to smaller US cities such as Las Vegas or Denver.

Most British travel agents are registered with ABTA (the Association of British Travel Agents), which will guarantee a refund or an alternative if you've paid money to an agent who goes out of business. Using an unregistered agent is not recommended.

Bridge the World (☎ 0870-444-7474; www.b-t-w.co.uk)
Ebookers.com (☎ 0870-010-7000; www.ebookers.com)
Flight Centre (☎ 0870-890-8099; www.flightcentre.co.uk)
Lastminute.com (www.lastminute.com) Discounts on everything, including travel.
North-South Travel (☎ 01245-608-291; www.northsouthtravel.co.uk) North-South Travel donates part of its profit to projects in the developing world.
Quest Travel (☎ 0870-442-3542; www.questtravel.com)
STA Travel (☎ 0870-160-0599; www.statravel.co.uk) Discount and student travel specialist.
Trailfinders London (☎ 020-7937-5400; www.trailfinders.co.uk); Glasgow (☎ 0141-353-2224); Dublin (☎ 01-677-7888)
Travel Bag (☎ 0870-890-1456; www.travelbag.co.uk)
Travelocity (www.travelocity.co.uk)

LAND

Border Crossings

Both Canada and Mexico have multiple, and sometimes very busy, entry points. It is relatively easy crossing from the USA into either country; it's getting back into the USA that can pose problems if you haven't brought all your documents. See p1103 for more information.

Car & Motorcycle

If you're driving into the USA from Canada or Mexico, don't forget the vehicle's registration papers, liability insurance and your home driver's license. Canadian and Mexican driver's licenses are valid and an international driver's permit is a good supplement. A vehicle rented in the US can usually be driven into Canada and back, but very few car rental companies will let you take a car into Mexico.

From Canada

BUS

Greyhound has direct connections between main cities in Canada and the northern USA, but you may have to transfer to a different bus at the border. Note that Greyhound US and **Greyhound Canada** (☎ 800-661-8747; www.greyhound.ca) are two different companies. Greyhound's Ameripass is not valid for travel within Canada, but you can use it to get into Canada via certain routes (from Boston or New York to Montreal, from Detroit to Toronto or from Seattle to Vancouver) and back to the USA by the same routes. See p1117 for more on Greyhound bus passes.

CAR & MOTORCYCLE

If your papers are in order, taking your own car across the US-Canadian border is usually quick and easy, but occasionally the authorities of either country decide to search a car *thoroughly*. Canadian auto insurance is valid in the USA. Make sure your policy is current before you cross the border. On weekends and holidays, especially in summer, traffic at the main border crossings can be very heavy, and waits can be long.

TRAIN

Amtrak and Canada's VIA run daily services from Montreal to New York, Toronto to New York via Niagara Falls, Toronto to Chicago, and Vancouver to Seattle. Amtrak rail passes get you to/from Vancouver and Montreal only.

From Mexico

BUS

Greyhound US and **Greyhound Mexico** (☎ 800-710-8819; www.greyhound.com.mx) have cooperative service, with direct buses between main towns in Mexico and the USA. But northbound buses can take some time to cross the US border, as sometimes US immigration insists on checking every person on board.

CAR & MOTORCYCLE

US auto insurance is not valid in Mexico, so even a short trip into Mexico's border region requires you to buy Mexican car insurance, available for about $15 per day at most border crossings. At some border towns, including Tijuana or Ciudad Juárez, there can be very long lines of vehicles waiting to re-enter the USA. For a short visit, it's usually more convenient to leave your car in a lot on the US side and walk or bus across the border. For a longer trip into Mexico, beyond the border zone or Baja California, you'll need a Mexican *permiso de importación temporal de vehículos.* See Lonely Planet's *Mexico* guide for the tedious details.

TRAIN

Amtrak gets close to the Mexican border at San Diego, California, and El Paso, Texas, but there are currently no cross-border services. All of the Mexican train services to towns on the US border have been closed.

SEA

Freighter

It is possible to travel to and from the USA on a freighter, though it will be much slower than a passenger liner. Most cargo ships have a 12-passenger limit, and in recent years comforts and facilities have improved; some are nearly equivalent to cruise ship standards. Prices vary hugely; while they may be as much as half the daily rate of a traditional cruise, you take many more days to get where you're going, so savings may be minimal. Trips range from a one-way, 14-day crossing from Europe to the USA to a 55-day trip round the Pacific from Australia to Los Angeles with many stops. An excellent source of information is the **Cruise & Freighter Travel Association** (☎ 800-872-8584; www.travltips.com; PO Box 580188, Flushing, NY 11358).

Passenger Liner

From about May to October, Cunard's *QE2* sails between Southampton (UK) and New York in about six days. The cheapest fare will be for a bunk bed in an inside cabin; in peak season (June–August) this is about US$2400. For better accommodations, the prices are higher. There are occasional special deals. For details, contact **Cunard's Florida office** (☎ 800-728-6273; www.cunard line.com).

Most other passenger liners in US ports are cruise ships doing all sorts of interesting circuits around the Caribbean, Canada's Maritime provinces, the Pacific Northwest, the Mediterranean and the Pacific. To find out more, contact a specialized agency such as **Cruise Web** (☎ 800-377-9383; www.cruiseweb.com).

GETTING AROUND

AIR

Flying is the only practical way to get around the USA if your time is limited. The domestic air system is extensive, with dozens of competing airlines, hundreds of airports and thousands of scheduled flights every day. Flying is usually more expensive than traveling by bus, train or car, but a special airfare deal can make the cost very competitive.

Main 'hub' airports include all of the international gateways (p1108) plus a number of other large cities. Most cities and towns have a local or county airport, but you usually have to travel via a hub airport to reach them.

The availability of discount deals varies, depending on when you're traveling, how far in advance you buy your ticket (at least two weeks ahead is advised), the route, and a few other factors. In addition to shopping around online (p1110), contact a good travel agent for up-to-the-minute details on fares and discounts. Foreign visitors should also consider buying domestic tickets in conjunction with their international flights; domestic stopovers and 'add-on' fares, when arranged with international tickets, are generally a bargain.

Airlines in the USA

Since 9/11, the US airline industry has been experiencing tremendous financial difficulty; in 2002 alone, the ten biggest US airlines lost $11.3 billion, and United, the world's number two airline, filed for bankruptcy (it continues to operate). Routes, services and even the companies themselves may come and go with little warning, so double-check all your arrangements.

Interestingly, discount airlines are doing well. Southwest and JetBlue have been profitable, and Delta has introduced its low-cost Song fleet. One of the biggest service changes is food; soon, all airlines may do away with free, foil-covered meals and replace them with fancy sandwiches, smoothies and real salads for an extra fee.

Here are the main domestic carriers:

AirTran (☎ 800-247-8726; www.airtran.com)
Alaska Airlines (☎ 800-252-7522; www.alaskaair.com)
America West (☎ 800-235-9292; www.americawest.com)
American Airlines (☎ 800-433-7300; www.aa.com)
American Trans Air (☎ 800-435-9282; www.ata.com)

Continental Airlines (☎ 800-523-3273; www.continental.com)
Delta Air Lines (☎ 800-221-1212; www.delta.com)
Hawaiian Airlines (☎ 800-367-5320; www.hawaiianair.com)
JetBlue (☎ 800-538-2583; www.jetblue.com)
Midwest Express (☎ 800-452-2022; www2.midwestexpress.com)
Northwest Airlines (☎ 800-225-2525; www.nwa.com)
Southwest Airlines (☎ 800-435-9792; www.iflyswa.com)
Spirit Airlines (☎ 800-772-7117; www.spiritair.com)
United Airlines (☎ 800-864-8331; www.ual.com)
US Airways (☎ 800-428-4322; www.usairways.com)

Air Passes

Most US airlines offer some sort of air pass to overseas visitors. They are only sold to

YOU MAY NOW BOARD YOUR FLIGHT

Since 9/11, security measures at US airports have increased. All air travelers now encounter the following general procedures, though some airports differ slightly. For up-to-date information, contact the **Transport Security Administration** (TSA; ☎ 866-289-9673; www.tsa.gov/public). **Airsafe.com** (www.airsafe.com) also has tons of advice on current regulations and information on airline safety.

Note that if you refuse any part of the screening process, you will be barred from flying.

Baggage Screening

All checked luggage is now screened for explosives. In most airports this happens after luggage has been checked at the ticket counter (either behind the scenes or in a separate area), but in a few it happens *before* luggage is checked at the counter. Any bags that are opened for visual inspection will be closed and taped to announce that they have been searched.

It's recommended that you not lock luggage, since locks will be broken if necessary to open a bag. Don't put undeveloped film in checked luggage, since some screening machines will damage it. Don't stack books or papers, avoid packing food and drinks, and put personal items in clear plastic bags if you don't want them handled.

Passenger Screening

To get through the security gate, you need a photo ID and a boarding pass; an airline ticket is no longer accepted. The reason is that a computer system (called CAPPS II) now checks each passenger's name and information against No Fly lists and other data, then encodes a threat assessment on each boarding card. Using this code, security personnel determine what level of search is required or if the traveler should be barred from flying. One early estimate was that the CAPPS II system was prone to a 10% mistake rate, so expect occasional problems. Contact TSA if you feel you have been a victim of discrimination or harassment.

At the security gate, all carry-on bags (limit two small ones per person) are passed through an x-ray machine and all passengers must walk through a metal detector. A secondary screening may be required, and this involves hand wand and pat down checks and opening bags to verify contents. If you wish, you can request a private room to conduct the pat down search or to remove hidden items of clothing that may have set off the alarm.

If you can, avoid wearing hidden body piercings or underwire bras, since they do set off some metal detectors. Shoes may need to be removed and belt buckles opened or removed. Don't wrap gifts, since they may need to be opened. Laptop computers may need to be turned on. Baby strollers and wheelchairs will be thoroughly inspected, so contact the airport or TSA if you have concerns or special needs.

Here is a partial list of everyday items that are prohibited on airplanes. See the TSA website for a full list. These items will be taken from you if you have no other way of disposing of them.

- Pocketknives, even keychain-size
- Scissors (blunt-tipped are okay)
- Corkscrews or pointed-end bottle openers
- Carpentry tools (screwdrivers, wrenches, pliers etc)
- Straight razors (safety razors are okay)
- Heavy-duty tweezers
- All sports equipment

TRANSPORT

foreigners (non-US or Canadian residents) in conjunction with an international airfare, and to get the best deal you have to buy the pass and the international flight from the same airline, or from 'partner' airlines. The passes are actually a book of coupons. Each coupon equals a flight, good for 60 days from the use of the first coupon. One catch is that if a connection is not a direct flight (ie, if it involves a change of flight number), that counts as two coupons.

The conditions and cost structures are quite complicated, so you really have to work out your itinerary and schedule and get a travel agent to provide cost estimates for the options. Alaska and Hawaii are usually excluded, but if these places are on your itinerary, ask if there is a special deal for air-pass holders. Some deals let you leave the flight times open. You reserve your seat at least one day in advance (if seats are available!). Even if you book specific flights when you buy the pass, you can change the dates later without penalty, as long as the last flight is scheduled within the 60-day period. If you decide to change destinations once in the USA, you will generally be charged a fee.

Getting Bumped

Airlines often overbook to guarantee full planes. However, if everyone shows up, some passengers can get 'bumped' off, which usually entails some compensation. This can range from a $200 voucher toward your next flight, to a fully paid round-trip ticket. If you get bumped, airlines will put you on the next available flight. If you want to be first in line for this deal, ask at the gate if the airline will need volunteers on your flight and what the compensation will be. If you will have to spend the night, make sure the airline is going to foot the hotel bill.

BICYCLE

Cycling across the country would be an enormous, though possible, undertaking, but touring regions is easier to do and popular. Long-distance trips can be done entirely on quiet backroads (which is necessary and advisable since bicycles are not permitted on freeways), and most cities have some system of bike lanes, however minimal. Note that cyclists are required to follow the same rules of the road as automobiles, but don't expect drivers to always respect the right of way of cyclists.

Adventure Cycling Association (☎ 406-721-1776, 800-755-2453; www.adventurecycling.org; 150 E Pine St, PO Box 8308, Missoula, MT 59807) is a nationwide bicyclists' club that organizes tours and dispenses tons of advice on routes; it publishes *Adventure Cyclist* magazine. Alternatively, arrange a cycle tour with a bike tour specialist such as **Backroads** (☎ 510-527-1555, 800-462-2848; www.backroads.com; 801 Cedar St, Berkeley, CA 94710). The national advocacy group **League of American Bicyclists** (LAB; ☎ 202-822-1333; www.bikeleague.org; 1612 K St NW, Suite 800, Washington, DC 20006) publishes *Bicycling* magazine, maintains an excellent website with links and touring advice, and offers members a range of discounts, state-by-state resources for touring (in its annual *Almanac*) and other benefits.

If you are transporting your own bike, most international and domestic airlines will carry bikes as checked baggage without charge if they're in a box. Many carriers impose an oversize-baggage charge (for domestic carriers, up to $50) for bikes that aren't disassembled first – check before you buy the ticket. Amtrak trains and Greyhound buses will transport bikes within the USA, sometimes with a small extra handling charge. Call first for details.

Purchase

Buying a bike is easy, as is reselling it before you leave. The best selection and advice is found at specialist bike shops; every city will have several. General sporting goods stores have limited options, and warehouse stores have bargains, but you should know what you want. Used bicycles are sold at flea markets and garage sales and advertised in newspapers and on notice boards at hostels and colleges. These will also be the best places to sell your bike, though stores selling used bikes may also buy from you.

Rental

Long-term rentals are easy to find in any city and most tourist spots. Rates run from $100 per week and up, and a credit card authorization for several hundred dollars is usually necessary as a security deposit.

BOAT

Coastal ferry services, often state-run, provide economical, efficient and scenic links to the many islands off the US coasts. Most larger ferries will transport private cars, motorcycles and bicycles. Windjammer cruises off the coast of Maine are another option. The most spectacular coastal ferry runs are on the south coast of Alaska and along the Inside Passage.

The Great Lakes have a number of attractive islands that can only be visited by boat. Popular trips go to Mackinac Island, Michigan (p417); the Apostle Islands, off Wisconsin (p429); Kelleys Island (p396) and the Bass Islands, Ohio (p396); and the remote Isle Royale National Park (p420).

There is no canal or river public transportation system in the USA, though there are luxury steamboat cruises that ply the waters. Perhaps one of the biggest is the **Delta Queen Steamboat Co** (☎ 800-543-1949; www.deltaqueen.com). It offers three luxurious old-style steamboats making three- to 11-day excursions on the Mississippi, Missouri, Tennessee and Ohio Rivers.

BUS

Greyhound (☎ 800-229-9424 for automated fares & schedules, 214-849-8966 for customer service; www.greyhound.com) is the major long-distance bus company, with routes throughout the USA and to the Canadian cities of Montreal, Toronto and Vancouver.

Greyhound runs buses several times a day along major highways between large towns, stopping at smaller towns along the way. Towns not on major routes are often served by local carriers, and Greyhound will usually have their contact and sometimes their fare information. Local Greyhound office numbers (see individual cities) can be useful for regional specifics such as disabled access. Greyhound doesn't operate in Alaska or Hawaii, but there are local alternatives (see those chapters).

Competing with Greyhound are the 50-plus franchises of **Trailways** (☎ 703-691-3052; www.trailways.com). Trailways may not be as useful as Greyhound for very long trips, but fares are generally a little lower. Here are a few of the regional Trailways bus companies:

Atlantic Coast Trailways (☎ 800-548-8584; www.atlanticcoastcharters.com) On the Atlantic Coast.

Pacific Trailways of Southern California (☎ 714-892-5000; www.pacificcoachways.com) On the Pacific Coast.

Peter Pan Trailways (☎ 800-237-8747; www.peterpanbus.com) In the Northeast.

Most baggage has to be checked in and should be properly labeled. Larger items, including skis and bicycles, can be transported, but there may be an extra charge. Call first to be sure. Don't leave hand baggage on the bus during rest stops.

The frequency of bus service varies, but even the least popular routes will have one bus per day. Main routes will have buses every hour or so, sometimes around the clock. Buses travel mostly on the interstate highways, but bus trips can still be very long because of the great distances. Nonexpress buses will stop every 50 to 100 miles to pick up passengers, and long-distance buses stop for meal breaks and driver changes.

By the standards of most countries, US bus services are really very good. Generally, buses are clean, comfortable and reliable. Buses have air-conditioning, onboard lavatories and reclining seats. Smoking is not permitted. Buses are often the cheapest way to cover long distances, and so are favored by low-budget travelers and the poorer strata of US society. Middle-class Americans tend to prefer the more expensive convenience of flying. Consequently, bus travel provides the traveler with an unvarnished view of American life.

Bus Passes

Greyhound's 'North American Discovery Pass' can be economical if you want to travel a lot in a short period – but be careful of spending all your time on the bus. The pass ranges from four to 60 consecutive days and covers unlimited travel during the time period – Greyhound stamps your pass the first time you use it, and the clock starts from then. Two short-term passes cost more per day, but may better suit your itinerary.

The pass is valid on dozens of regional bus lines as well as on Greyhound and allows short side trips to Montreal, Toronto and Vancouver. For longer journeys inside Canada, a combined pass is available. Passholders can call ☎ 888-454-7277 in the USA for information, but seat reservations do need to be made in person at a bus station.

An International Discovery Pass, or Ameripass, is slightly cheaper and available only to international visitors, not to US or Canadian citizens/residents. International visitors can buy the pass through their home travel agent, on the Internet, or by calling **Greyhound** (☎ 402-330-8552 outside the US, 212-971-0492 Greyhound International Office).

Bus Stations

Some larger towns and cities have a bus station shared by Greyhound and other bus lines, while in others Greyhound and the other companies have separate stations. The better bus stations have clean bathrooms, luggage lockers, information boards, pay phones and snack bars. Some bus stations are depressing and in unattractive, even dangerous, parts of town, so it's better to avoid arriving at night and to budget for a taxi to and from the station.

In small towns with no bus station, Greyhound and other buses stop at a given location, such as a McDonald's, a post office or the Amtrak train station. To board at these stops, know exactly where and when the bus arrives, be emphatic when you flag it down and be prepared to pay the driver with exact change.

Costs

You can usually get a substantial discount on tickets purchased seven days in advance. A round-trip ticket is generally cheaper than two one-ways, but not always. Special promotional fares are regularly offered. If you're traveling with a friend, ask about Greyhound's companion fares, where two can travel for the price of one on a round-trip journey.

There are many discounts available: Tickets for children ages two to 11 are half the standard fare. People over 62 can get a 5% discount, or join the Greyhound Seniors Club and get 10% off. A disabled passenger and a companion can travel together for the price of one. Student discounts are available occasionally on specific routes during certain times of the year – call Greyhound.

Here are some examples of Greyhound's long-distance services:

Reservations

Tickets for some Trailways and other buses can only be purchased immediately prior to departure. Greyhound bus tickets can be bought over the phone (☎ 800-229-9424) or on the Internet with a major US credit card (they often refuse international credit cards); tickets will be mailed to you if purchased 10 days in advance, or you can pick them up at the terminal with proper identification. Greyhound terminals also accept American Express, traveler's checks and cash. Note that only by purchasing a ticket can you reserve a seat. You can buy a ticket as late as 15 minutes before departure, but they will only fill the number of seats on the bus – no standing allowed. Buy your ticket in advance, if possible, to ensure that you get a seat.

CAR & MOTORCYCLE

Among the many cultural, political and economic reasons that the USA is a car-mad society, there is a very practical one: driving a car is the fastest, easiest, most convenient way to cover the continent's long distances and to get to all of its small towns and wide-open spaces. In addition to independence and flexibility, another compelling reason to choose car travel for some or all of your trip is that America's highways and backroads are fun experiences in themselves.

Cars can also be one of the least expensive ways to travel if several people are sharing the costs. Plus, a car can carry all your gear, a cooler and a cookstove, thus making it easier to save on meals and to camp.

There are really only two circumstances when travelers should expressly avoid driving a car. One is in a major city. Traffic will be terrible, parking expensive and usually very difficult, and frequently public transportation in the main downtown areas is excellent (or at least adequate). The best cities for public transportation are New York, Boston, Chicago, New Orleans and San Francisco.

The other circumstance to avoid a car is when you have limited time but want to

Route	Standard fare	Seven-day advance purchase fare	Distance in miles	Duration of quickest service
New York to Chicago	$87	$69	878	16½ hours
New York to Los Angeles	$159	$99	3083	63 hours
Los Angeles to New Orleans	$105	$75	2131	41 hours

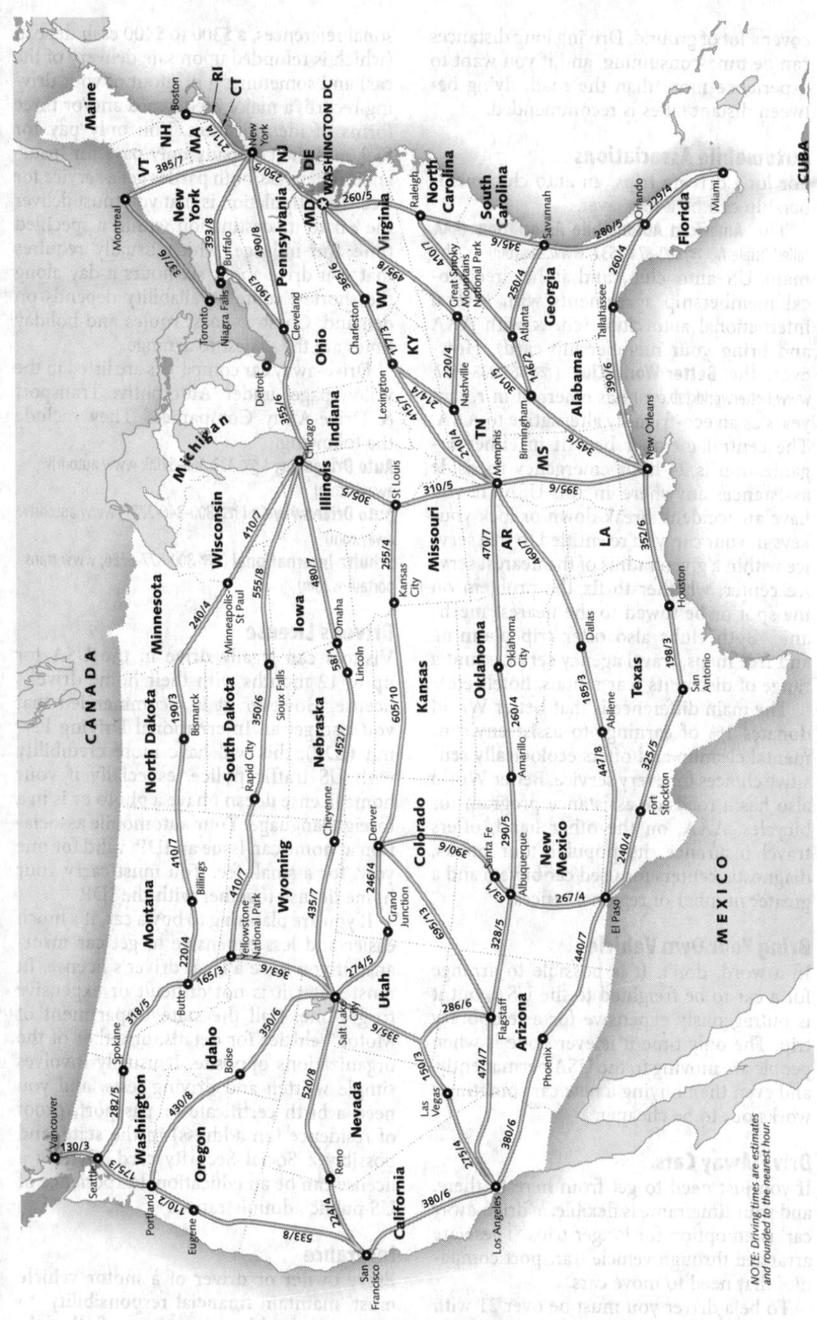
CANADA
MEXICO
CUBA
Vancouver
130/3
Seattle
175/3
282/5
Spokane
318/5
Portland
110/2
Eugene
430/8
Washington
Oregon
Idaho
Boise
Montana
Butte
220/4
Billings
410/7
North Dakota
Bismarck
190/3
Minnesota
240/4
Minneapolis-St Paul
Wisconsin
410/7
Michigan
165/3
Yellowstone National Park
410/7
Rapid City
South Dakota
350/6
Sioux Falls
555/8
350/6
363/6
Wyoming
533/8
224/4
Reno
520/8
Salt Lake City
435/7
Cheyenne
Nebraska
452/7
Lincoln
58/1
Omaha
480/7
Iowa
Chicago
San Francisco
Nevada
274/5
Utah
335/6
Grand Junction
246/4
Denver
605/10
Kansas City
255/4
St Louis
305/5
Illinois
Indiana
California
380/6
Las Vegas
150/3
286/6
695/13
Colorado
Kansas
Missouri
310/5
390/6
275/4
474/7
Los Angeles
Flagstaff
328/5
63/1
Santa Fe
290/5
Albuquerque
Amarillo
260/4
Oklahoma
Oklahoma City
470/7
Memphis
AR
380/6
Arizona
Phoenix
New Mexico
460/7
Dallas
185/3
447/8
Abilene
440/7
267/4
El Paso
240/4
Fort Stockton
325/5
Texas
San Antonio
198/3
Houston
352/6
New Orleans
LA
395/6
MS
Detroit
355/6
Cleveland
Ohio
Toronto
Niagra Falls
Buffalo
393/8
190/3
490/8
Pennsylvania
337/6
Montreal
VT
385/7
NH
New York
MA
Boston
211/4
RI
CT
New York
250/5
NJ
DE
MD
WASHINGTON DC
365/6
Charleston
WV
Virginia
Lexington
177/3
415/7
KY
214/4
210/4
Nashville
220/4
TN
495/8
260/5
Raleigh
North Carolina
410/7
Great Smoky Mountains National Park
South Carolina
301/5
Birmingham
146/2
Atlanta
250/4
Savannah
345/6
Georgia
Alabama
345/6
390/6
Tallahassee
260/4
280/5
Orlando
229/4
Florida
Miami
Maine
NOTE: Driving times are estimates and rounded to the nearest hour.

cover a lot of ground. Driving long distances can be time-consuming, and if you want to experience more than the road, flying between distant cities is recommended.

Automobile Associations

For long driving trips, an auto club membership can be a life-saver.

The **American Automobile Association** (AAA, called 'triple A'; ☎ 800-874-7532; www.aaa.com) is the main US auto club, and it has reciprocal membership agreements with several international auto clubs (check with AAA and bring your membership card). However, the **Better World Club** (☎ 866-238-1137; www.betterworldclub.com) has emerged in recent years as an eco-friendly alternative to AAA. The central member benefit in either organization is 24-hour emergency roadside assistance: anywhere in the USA, if you have an accident, break down or lock your keys in your car, you're entitled to free service within a given radius of the nearest service center, whether to fix the problem on the spot or be towed to the nearest mechanic. Both clubs also offer trip planning and free maps, travel agency services and a range of discounts (car rentals, hotels etc).

The main difference is that Better World donates 1% of earnings to assist environmental cleanup and offers ecologically sensitive choices for every service. Better World also has a roadside assistance program for bicycles. AAA, on the other hand, offers travel insurance, its popular tour books, diagnostic centers for used car buyers and a greater number of regional offices.

Bring Your Own Vehicle

In a word, don't. It is possible to arrange for a car to be freighted to the USA, but it is outrageously expensive for a temporary trip. The only time it is ever done is when people are moving to the USA permanently, and even then buying a new car sometimes works out to be cheaper.

Drive-Away Cars

If you just need to get from here to there, and your timeframe is flexible, a 'drive-away car' is an option for longer trips. These are arranged through vehicle transport companies that need to move cars.

To be a driver you must be over 21 with a valid driver's license; you'll also need personal references, a $300 to $400 cash deposit (which is refunded upon safe delivery of the car) and sometimes a printout of your driving record, a major credit card and/or three forms of identification. You only pay for fuel, and the company only pays for insurance; otherwise, both parties get a service for free. The stipulation is that you must deliver the car to its destination within a specified time and mileage, which usually requires that you drive about six hours a day along the shortest route. Availability depends on demand. Coast-to-coast routes and holiday times are the easiest to arrange.

Drive-away car companies are listed in the yellow pages under 'Automotive Transport & Drive-Away Companies.' They include the following:

Auto Driveaway (☎ 323-666-6100; www.autodriveawayla.com)

Auto Driveaway Co (☎ 800-346-2277; www.autodriveaway.com)

Schultz-International (☎ 800-677-6686; www.transportautos.com)

Driver's License

Visitors can legally drive in the USA for up to 12 months with their home driver's license. However, it is recommended that you also get an International Driving Permit (IDP); this will have more credibility with US traffic police, especially if your home license doesn't have a photo or is in a foreign language. Your automobile association at home can issue an IDP, valid for one year, for a small fee. You must carry your home license together with the IDP.

If you are planning to buy a car, it's much easier and less expensive to get car insurance if you have a local driver's license. In most states it is not difficult or expensive to get one. Call the state Department of Motor Vehicles for details, or either of the organizations opposite. It usually involves simple written and driving tests, and you need a birth certificate or passport, proof of residence (an address) in the state, and possibly a Social Security card. Getting a license can be an educational experience of US public administration.

Insurance

Every owner or driver of a motor vehicle must 'maintain financial responsibility' to protect the health and property of others in case of an accident. The easiest way to do this is to have auto liability insurance, and most states specify a minimum level of coverage. If you already have auto insurance, or if you buy travel insurance, make sure that the policy has adequate liability coverage for a rental car where you will be driving.

Rental car companies will provide liability insurance, but most charge extra. Always ask, though, if liability insurance is included in the rental, and don't be hustled into paying extra if the coverage that's included is adequate. Rental companies almost never include insurance that covers damage to the vehicle itself. Instead, they offer an optional Collision Damage Waiver (CDW) or Loss Damage Waiver (LDW) that has an initial 'deductable' – meaning that you will still have to pay the first $100 or $500 of any repairs. For an extra premium, you can usually get this deductable covered as well. Some credit card companies will cover your CDW if you rent for 15 days or less and charge the total rental to your card. However, if there's an accident, sometimes you must pay the rental car company first and then seek reimbursement from the credit card company. Check your credit card company policy very carefully. Paying extra for all of this insurance increases the cost of a rental car by as much as $10 to $30 a day, but you risk financial ruin to do without it.

If you buy a car, you must take out an independent liability insurance policy, and this can be difficult if you don't have a local license (see opposite). A car dealer or the AAA may be able to suggest an insurer. Even with a local license, insurance can be expensive and difficult to obtain if you don't have evidence of a good driving record. Bring copies of your home auto insurance policies if they can help establish that you are a good risk. Drivers under 25, and especially those under 21, will have problems getting insurance.

Purchase

Foreign visitors should only consider buying a car if they plan on driving for three months or more. Time spent purchasing and then selling the car will negate any monetary savings on shorter visits. Buying a car will be much easier if you have friends or relatives to stay with initially; you'll have an address for the registration and license papers and a private phone to use for calling sellers.

You can buy used cars from dealers or directly from individuals. Dealers cost more but usually offer warranties and/or financing options. To evaluate used car prices, check the model/year in the **Kelley Blue Book** (www.kbb.com) available in libraries and online; also have the car checked by an independent auto mechanic before you buy. Bargaining when buying a used car is standard practice.

Once you buy the car, the transfer of ownership papers must be registered with the state's Department of Motor Vehicles (DMV) within 10 days; you'll need the bill of sale, the title (or 'pink slip') and proof of insurance. Some states also require a 'smog certificate.' It is the seller's responsibility to get a smog emission check; don't buy a car without a certificate (or you may be on the hook for expensive repairs). A dealer will usually submit the paperwork to the DMV for you, but otherwise you need to do this yourself.

Selling a car before you go home can be a desperate business. Selling to dealers will get you the absolute worst price, but it involves a minimum of paperwork. Otherwise, selling for a good price takes luck and persistence. Advertise as widely as possible, especially in hostels, colleges and local papers. Finally, be sure that the DMV is properly notified about the sale, or you may have to pay someone else's parking tickets.

For assistance buying a used car, AAA (see Auto Clubs) offers assistance to members, and **Auto Tour** (☎ 206-999-4686; www.autotourusa.com) specializes in helping foreign US visitors. Based in Seattle, Washington, Auto Tour has referrals for other regions.

Rental

Car rental is a huge business in the USA, and rates are very competitive. Most rental companies require that you have a major credit card, that you be at least 25 years old and that you have a valid driver's license (your home license will do). Alamo, Thrifty, Enterprise and Rent-A-Wreck may rent to drivers between the ages of 21 and 24 for an additional charge. Those under 21 are usually not permitted to rent at all.

Here is a list of the major nationwide car rental companies:

Alamo (☎ 800-462-5266; www.alamo.com)
Avis (☎ 800-230-4898; www.avis.com)
Budget (☎ 800-527-0700; www.drivebudget.com)
Dollar (☎ 800-800-4000; www.dollar.com)
Enterprise (☎ 800-736-8222; www.enterprise.com)
Hertz (☎ 800-654-3131; www.hertz.com)
National (☎ 800-227-7368; www.nationalcar.com)
Rent-a-Wreck (☎ 800-944-7501; www.rent-a-wreck.com)
Thrifty (☎ 800-847-4389; www.thrifty.com)

Companies specializing in RV or camper rentals include the following:

Adventures on Wheels (☎ 800-943-3579; www.wheels9.com)
Cruise America (☎ 800-784-7368; www.cruiseamerica.com)
Happy Travel Camper Rental & Sales (☎ 800-370-1262; www.camperusa.com)

To check the smaller local car rental companies, look in the yellow pages under 'Automobile.'

Car rental prices vary widely from city to city, company to company, car to car and day to day. To get the best rates, shop around. The more flexibility you have with the days of your rental, the better your chances of landing a good deal.

And before you travel, check with your travel agent or with an online reservation network about fly-drive packages. This may offer savings over paying for a plane ticket and car rental separately.

Here are some things to keep in mind when renting a car. Lower prices may apply for renting on weekends, and usually longer rentals are discounted. Unless you aren't driving far, 'unlimited mileage' plans will work out cheaper in the long run than rentals with limited mileage; on the latter, once you go over the mileage limit, per mile fees add up fast. Some rental companies let you pay for your last tank of gas upfront; this is almost never a good deal, since it's always easier to top up before turning the car in than to make sure the tank is empty. Tax on car rentals varies by state, so make sure to ask for the total cost with tax. One-way rentals, where you pick the car up in one place and drop it off in another, are usually more expensive (they add a 'drop off charge) and are only offered by bigger companies; however, occasionally one-way rentals may be cheaper. Be careful about adding extra days or turning in a car early; extra days may be charged at a premium rate, and an early return may jeopardize the low weekly or monthly deal you originally arranged.

Motorcycle

To drive a motorcycle, you need a US state motorcycle license or an International Driving Permit endorsed for motorcycles. A state DMV can give you the rules relating to motorcycle use. Helmets are required in almost every state.

Motorcycle rental and insurance is expensive, especially if you want to ride a Harley-Davidson. **EagleRider motorcycle rentals** (☎ 888-900-9901; www.eaglerider.com) has offices in major cities nationwide.

Bike Tours Amerika (☎ 61-3-5473-4469 in Australia, 49-27-647-824 in Germany; www.biketours.com.au) offers a selection of escorted group tours on motorcycles. They also do rentals and buy-backs for Yamaha XT 600s.

Road Conditions

Many cars are fitted with steel-studded snow tires for winter driving, but you may still be required to use snow chains in mountainous areas. Driving off road, or on dirt roads, is often forbidden by rental car companies, and can be very dangerous in wet weather.

Road Hazards

In deserts and range country, drivers should watch for livestock on highways. High-risk areas are signed as Open Range or with the silhouette of a steer. Deer and other wild animals can be a hazard in some suburban and most rural areas; high-risk areas are signed with the silhouette of a leaping deer.

Road Rules

In the USA, cars drive on the right side of the road. The use of seat belts and child safety seats is required in every state.

The speed limit is generally 55mph or 65mph on highways, 25mph in cities and towns and as low as 15mph in school zones (strictly enforced during school hours). On interstate highways in designated rural areas, the speed limit is 65mph, 70mph or 75mph – always watch for posted speed limits. It's forbidden to pass a school bus when its lights are flashing.

Most states have laws against littering. If you are seen throwing anything from a vehicle, you can be fined $1000 and be forced to pick up what you discarded.

Penalties are very severe for 'DUI' – driving under the influence of alcohol and/or drugs. Police can give roadside sobriety checks to assess if you've been drinking or using drugs. If you fail, they'll require you take a breath test, urine test or blood test to determine the level of alcohol or drugs in your body. Refusing to be tested is treated as if you'd taken the test and failed. The maximum legal blood alcohol concentration is 0.08%.

In some states it is illegal to carry 'open containers' of alcohol in a vehicle, even if they are empty. Containers that are full and sealed may be carried, but if they have ever been opened, they must be carried in the trunk.

HITCHING

Hitchhiking in the USA is potentially dangerous and definitely not recommended. Drivers have heard of so many nasty incidents and lurid reports that they tend to be very reluctant to pick up hitchhikers. Drivers may be more open in rural parts, but traffic can be sparse, and you may well get stranded. Hitchhiking on freeways is prohibited; there's usually a white sign at the on-ramp stating 'no pedestrians beyond this point,' and anyone caught hitching past there can be arrested.

Even hitching to and from a hiking trailhead should be avoided. Try to arrange something at a ranger station or with other hikers. If you're flat broke, there are still alternatives to standing by a roadside with your thumb out. Look for ride shares at hostels, or ask at campgrounds.

LOCAL TRANSPORT

Except in large US cities, public transit is rarely the most convenient option for travelers, and coverage can be sparse to outlying towns and suburbs. However, it is usually cheap, safe and relatively reliable. For regional details, see the Transport sections in the main cities.

Airport Shuttle

Shuttle buses provide inexpensive and convenient transport to/from airports in most cities. Most are 12-seat vans; some have regular routes and stops (which include the main hotels) and some pick up and deliver passengers 'door to door' in their service area; costs are $10 to $15 per person.

Bus

Most cities and larger towns have dependable local bus systems. Most are designed for commuters and provide limited service in the evening and on weekends. Costs range from free to around $1 per ride.

Metro

Some cities have underground subways or elevated metropolitan rail systems, which provide the best local transport. The largest systems are in New York, Washington, DC, Chicago and the San Francisco Bay Area. Other cities have small, one- or two-line rail systems that mainly serve downtown.

Taxi

Taxis are metered, with charges from $1 or $2 to start, plus at least $1.20 per mile. They charge extra for handling baggage, and drivers expect a 10% to 15% tip. Taxis cruise the busiest areas in large cities, but if you're anywhere else, it's easiest to call and order one.

TRAIN

Amtrak (☎ 800-872-7245; www.amtrak.com) has an extensive rail system throughout the USA, with Amtrak Thruway buses providing convenient connections to and from the rail network to some smaller centers and national parks. Compared to other modes of travel, trains are rarely the quickest, cheapest or most convenient option, but they can be close on all counts, and people enjoy them for the experience: trains are comfortable, social and provide a chance to admire the scenery.

Note that Amtrak (a for-profit federal corporation) depends on federal subsidies to operate. Recent budget cuts may lead to the elimination of unprofitable routes, and perhaps even the demise of the entire system, according to Amtrak officials. While it's doubtful the federal government would allow Amtrak to fail, travelers should confirm railroad routes when making plans.

Routes

Long-distance services are on named trains that run most routes daily, though some routes are covered only three to five days

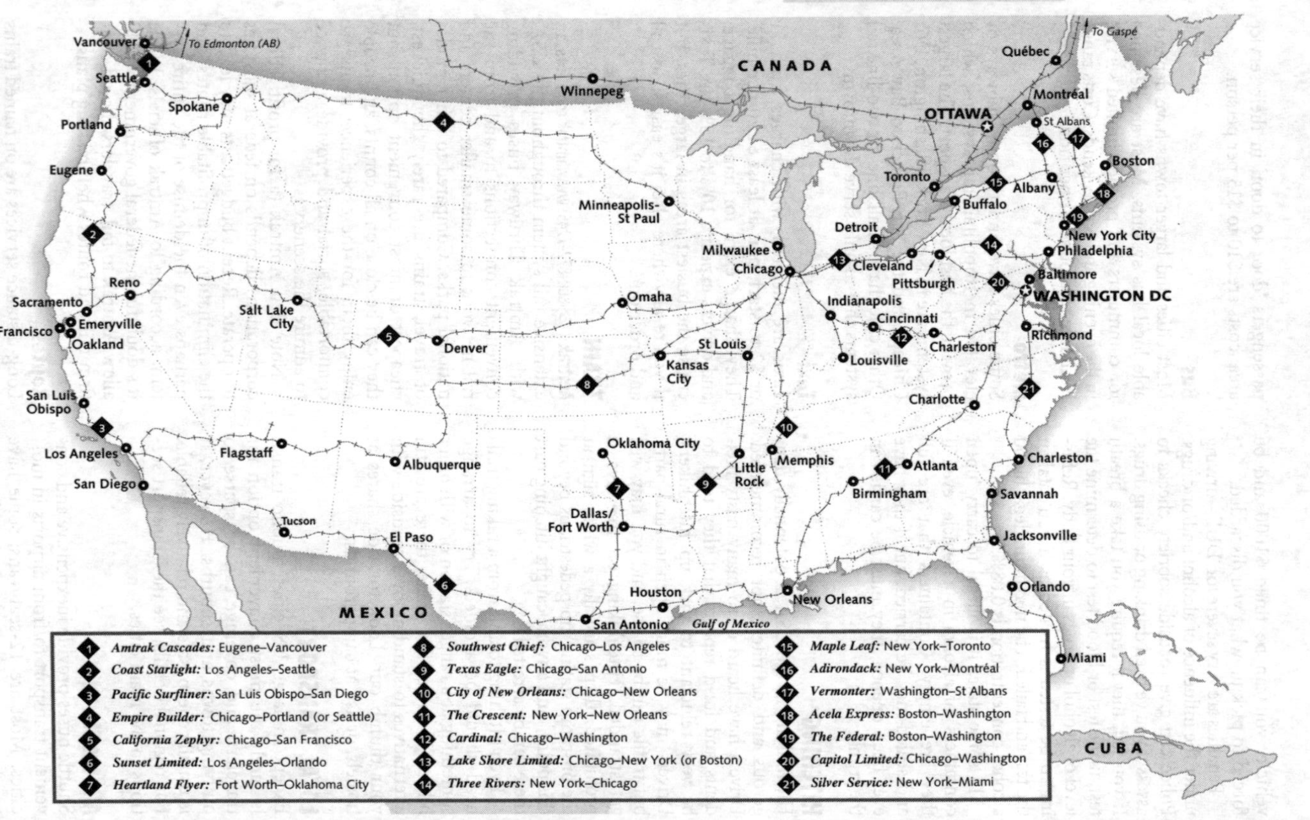
CANADA
MEXICO
CUBA
Gulf of Mexico
OTTAWA
WASHINGTON DC
To Edmonton (AB)
To Gaspé
Vancouver
Seattle
Spokane
Portland
Eugene
Sacramento
Emeryville
Oakland
San Francisco
Reno
San Luis Obispo
Los Angeles
San Diego
Flagstaff
Tucson
Salt Lake City
Albuquerque
El Paso
Denver
Winnipeg
Omaha
Minneapolis-St Paul
Kansas City
Oklahoma City
Dallas/Fort Worth
San Antonio
Houston
Milwaukee
Chicago
St Louis
Little Rock
Memphis
New Orleans
Indianapolis
Cincinnati
Louisville
Birmingham
Atlanta
Detroit
Cleveland
Toronto
Buffalo
Pittsburgh
Charleston
Charlotte
Richmond
Baltimore
Philadelphia
New York City
Albany
Boston
St Albans
Montréal
Québec
Savannah
Jacksonville
Orlando
Miami
1 Amtrak Cascades: Eugene–Vancouver
2 Coast Starlight: Los Angeles–Seattle
3 Pacific Surfliner: San Luis Obispo–San Diego
4 Empire Builder: Chicago–Portland (or Seattle)
5 California Zephyr: Chicago–San Francisco
6 Sunset Limited: Los Angeles–Orlando
7 Heartland Flyer: Fort Worth–Oklahoma City
8 Southwest Chief: Chicago–Los Angeles
9 Texas Eagle: Chicago–San Antonio
10 City of New Orleans: Chicago–New Orleans
11 The Crescent: New York–New Orleans
12 Cardinal: Chicago–Washington
13 Lake Shore Limited: Chicago–New York (or Boston)
14 Three Rivers: New York–Chicago
15 Maple Leaf: New York–Toronto
16 Adirondack: New York–Montréal
17 Vermonter: Washington–St Albans
18 Acela Express: Boston–Washington
19 The Federal: Boston–Washington
20 Capitol Limited: Chicago–Washington
21 Silver Service: New York–Miami

per week. See the Principal Railroad Routes map (opposite). Details are in the Getting There & Around section of each regional chapter; also check the Amtrak website.

Commuter trains provide very fast and frequent services on shorter routes, especially along the Northeast corridor from Boston to Washington, DC. High-speed Acela trains on these routes are especially fast and comfortable, and more expensive. Acela trains also run from New York City north to Albany then west to Buffalo.

Other commuter rail lines serve the Lake Michigan shore near Chicago, the main cities on the California coast and the Miami area. Many of them are included in an Amtrak rail pass (see below).

The only non-Amtrak long-distance passenger railroad in the US is the wonderful Alaska Railroad from Seward to Fairbanks via Denali and Anchorage. See p1032 for more details.

Classes & Costs

Fares vary according to type of seating; you can travel in coach seats, 1st class or in various types of sleeping compartments. Long-distance trains have dining cars, which have decent food at high prices. Train snack bars are also pricey, making it a good idea to bring some of your own comestibles.

Various one-way, round-trip and touring fares are available, with discounts of 15% for seniors age 62 and over and for students (with a 'Student Advantage' card, $20), and 50% discounts for children ages two to 15. Fares are generally lower on all tickets from early January to mid-June and from late August to mid-December.

Generally, the earlier you book, the lower the price, but for short-term offers check the Amtrak website's 'Rail Sale,' which lists dozens of bargain fares for specific routes, available only for limited periods.

Amtrak offers a variety of vacation packages, with options for rental cars, hotels, tours and attractions. Air-Rail packages offer train travel in one direction and a plane trip going the other way. These are good deals if they match your travel plans.

Here are some examples of Amtrak's long-distance services, fares (standard price, one way, coach class) and the shortest travel times on each route:

New York to Chicago $122, 19 hours.
New York to Los Angeles $239, 66 hours.
Los Angeles to New Orleans $112, 46 hours.

Reservations

Reservations can be made any time from 11 months in advance to the day of departure; since space on most trains is limited, it's a good idea to reserve as far in advance as you can. This also gives you the best chance of getting fare discounts.

Train Passes

A USA Rail Pass is available only to international travelers (not to US or Canadian residents). The pass offers unlimited coach-class travel within a specific region for either 15 or 30 days, with the price depending on region, number of days and season traveled (fares in US dollars).

Present your pass at an Amtrak office to buy a ticket for each trip. Reservations should be made as well, as far in advance as possible. You can get on and off the train as often as you like, but each sector of the journey must be booked. At some rural stations, trains will only stop if there's a reservation. Tickets are not for specific seats, but a conductor on board may allocate you a seat. First-class or sleeper accommodations cost extra and must be reserved separately.

A North America Rail Pass is offered by Amtrak in conjunction with Canada's VIA Rail. It allows unlimited travel on US and Canadian railways for 30 consecutive days, and it's available to American and Canadian residents as well as foreign visitors. Other regional rail passes are also offered.

Scenic Railroads

Dozens of historic, scenic and narrow-gauge railroads operate more as attractions than viable transport options. Most only run in the warmer months, and the popular ones book up. Here are some of the most interesting:

Cass Scenic Railroad Appalachian Mountains in West Virginia (p346).
Grand Canyon Railway Williams, AZ, to south rim of Grand Canyon (p826).
Cumbres & Toltec Scenic Railroad Chama, NM, into Colorado's Rocky Mountains (p808).
Durango & Silverton Narrow Gauge Railroad Ends at Silverton mining town in Colorado's Rocky Mountains (p758).
White Pass & Yukon Railroad Skagway, Alaska, to Fraser, British Columbia (p1041).

Health
by Dr David Goldberg

CONTENTS

The North American continent encompasses an extraordinary range of climates and terrains, from the freezing heights of the Rockies to tropical areas in southern Florida. Because of the high level of hygiene here, infectious diseases will not be a significant concern for most travelers, who will experience nothing worse than a little diarrhea or a mild respiratory infection.

BEFORE YOU GO

INSURANCE

The United States offers possibly the finest health care in the world. The problem is that, unless you have good insurance, it can be prohibitively expensive. It's essential to purchase travel health insurance if your regular policy doesn't cover you when you're abroad.

Bring any medications you may need in their original containers, clearly labeled. A signed, dated letter from your physician that describes all medical conditions and medications, including generic names, is also a good idea.

If your health insurance does not cover you for medical expenses abroad, consider supplemental insurance. Check the Subway section of the **Lonely Planet website** (www.lonelyplanet.com/subwwway) for more information. Find out in advance if your insurance plan will make payments directly to providers or reimburse you later for overseas health expenditures.

RECOMMENDED VACCINATIONS

No special vaccines are required or recommended for travel to the United States. All travelers should be up-to-date on routine immunizations, listed below.

ONLINE RESOURCES

There is a wealth of travel health advice on the Internet. The World Health Organization publishes a superb book, called *International Travel and Health*, which is revised annually and is available online at no cost at www.who.int/ith/. Another website of general interest is MD Travel Health at www.mdtravelhealth.com, which provides complete travel health recommendations for every country, updated daily, also at no cost.

It's usually a good idea to consult your government's travel health website before departure, if one is available:

Australia (www.dfat.gov.au/travel/)
Canada (www.hc-sc.gc.ca/pphb-dgspsp/tmp-pmv/pub_e.html)
United Kingdom (www.doh.gov.uk/traveladvice/index.htm)
United States (www.cdc.gov/travel/)

Vaccine	Recommended for	Dosage	Side effects
tetanus-diphtheria	all travelers who haven't had booster within 10 years	one dose lasts 10 years	soreness at injection site
measles	travelers born after 1956 who've had only one measles vaccination	one dose	fever; rash; joint pains; allergic reactions
chicken pox	travelers who've never had chicken pox	two doses a month apart	fever; mild case of chicken pox
influenza	all travelers during flu season (Nov through Mar)	one dose	soreness at the injection site; fever

MEDICAL CHECKLIST

- acetaminophen (Tylenol) or aspirin
- anti-inflammatory drugs (eg ibuprofen)
- antihistamines (for hay fever and allergic reactions)
- antibacterial ointment (eg Bactroban) for cuts and abrasions
- steroid cream or cortisone (for poison ivy and other allergic rashes)
- bandages, gauze, gauze rolls
- adhesive or paper tape
- scissors, safety pins, tweezers
- thermometer
- pocket knife
- DEET-containing insect repellent for the skin
- permethrin-containing insect spray for clothing, tents, and bed nets
- sun block

IN THE USA

AVAILABILITY & COST OF HEALTH CARE

In general, if you have a medical emergency, the best bet is to find the nearest hospital and go to its emergency room. If the problem isn't urgent, you can call a nearby hospital and ask for a referral to a local physician, which is usually cheaper than a trip to the emergency room. You should avoid stand-alone, for-profit urgent care centers, which tend to perform large numbers of expensive tests, even for minor illnesses.

Pharmacies are abundantly supplied, but you may find that some medications which are available over-the-counter in your home country require a prescription in the United States, and, as always, if you don't have insurance to cover the cost of prescriptions, they can be shockingly expensive.

INFECTIOUS DISEASES

In addition to more common ailments, there are several infectious diseases that are unknown or uncommon outside North America. Most are acquired by mosquito or tick bites.

West Nile Virus

These infections were unknown in the United States until a few years ago, but have now been reported in almost all 50 states. The virus is transmitted by culex mosquitoes, which are active in late summer and early fall and generally bite after dusk. Most infections are mild or asymptomatic, but the virus may infect the central nervous system, leading to fever, headache, confusion, lethargy, coma and sometimes death. There is no treatment for West Nile virus. For the latest update on the areas affected by West Nile, go to the **US Geological Survey website** (http://westnilemaps.usgs.gov/).

Lyme Disease

This disease has been reported from many states, but most documented cases occur in the northeastern part of the country, especially New York, New Jersey, Connecticut and Massachusetts. A smaller number of cases occur in the northern Midwest and in the northern Pacific coastal regions, including northern California. Lyme disease is transmitted by deer ticks, which are only 1–2mm long. Most cases occur in the late spring and summer. The CDC has an informative, if slightly scary, web page on **Lyme disease** (www.cdc.gov/ncidod/dvbid/lyme/).

The first symptom is usually an expanding red rash that is often pale in the center, known as a bull's eye rash. However, in many cases, no rash is observed. Flu-like symptoms are common, including fever, headache, joint pains, body aches, and malaise. When the infection is treated promptly with an appropriate antibiotic, usually doxycycline or amoxicillin, the cure rate is high. Luckily, since the tick must be attached for 36 hours or more to transmit Lyme disease, most cases can be prevented by performing a thorough tick check after you've been outdoors, as described below.

Rabies

Rabies is a viral infection of the brain and spinal cord that is almost always fatal. The rabies virus is carried in the saliva of infected animals and is typically transmitted through an animal bite, though contamination of any break in the skin with infected saliva may result in rabies. In the US, most cases of human rabies are related to exposure to bats. Rabies may also be contracted from raccoons, skunks, foxes and unvaccinated cats and dogs.

If there is any possibility, however small, that you have been exposed to rabies, you should seek preventative treatment, which consists of rabies immune globulin and rabies vaccine and is quite safe. In particular, any contact with a bat should be discussed with health authorities, because bats have small teeth and may not leave obvious bite marks. If you wake up to find a bat in your room, or discover a bat in a room with small children, rabies prophylaxis may be necessary.

Giardiasis

This parasitic infection of the small intestine occurs throughout North America and the world. Symptoms may include nausea, bloating, cramps, and diarrhea, and may last for weeks. To protect yourself from Giardia, you should avoid drinking directly from lakes, ponds, streams and rivers, which may be contaminated by animal or human feces. The infection can also be transmitted from person-to-person if proper hand washing is not performed. Giardiasis is easily diagnosed by a stool test and readily treated with antibiotics.

HIV/AIDS

As with most parts of the world, HIV infection occurs throughout the United States. You should never assume, on the basis of someone's background or appearance, that they're free of this or any other sexually transmitted disease. Be sure to use a condom for all sexual encounters.

ENVIRONMENTAL HAZARDS

Bites & Stings

Common sense approaches to these concerns are the most effective: wear boots when hiking to protect from snakes, wear long sleeves and pants to protect from ticks and mosquitoes. If you're bitten, don't overreact. Stay calm and follow the recommended treatment.

MOSQUITO BITES

When traveling in areas where West Nile or other mosquito-borne illnesses have been reported, keep yourself covered (wear long sleeves, long pants, hats and shoes rather than sandals) and apply a good insect repellent, preferably one containing DEET, to exposed skin and clothing. In general, adults and children over 12 should use preparations containing 25% to 35% DEET, which usually lasts about six hours.

TRADITIONAL MEDICINE

American health food stores and many regular groceries abound with so-called 'natural' remedies. These are a few of the more successful ones, in our opinion. They're not guaranteed, of course, but may work great. You never know...

Problem	Treatment
jet lag	melatonin
motion sickness	ginger
mosquito bite	oil of eucalyptus

Children between two and 12 years of age should use preparations containing no more than 10% DEET, applied sparingly, which will usually last about three hours. Neurologic toxicity has been reported from DEET, especially in children, but appears to be extremely uncommon and generally related to overuse. DEET-containing compounds should not be used on children under age two.

Insect repellents containing certain botanical products, including oil of eucalyptus and soybean oil, are effective but last only 1½ to 2 hours. Products based on citronella are not effective.

Visit the **Center for Disease Control's website** (CDC; www.cdc.gov/ncidod/dvbid/westnile/prevention_info.htm) for prevention information.

TICK BITES

Ticks are parasitic arachnids that may be present in brush, forest and grasslands, where hikers often get them on their legs or in their boots. Adult ticks suck blood from hosts by burrowing into the skin and can carry infections such as Lyme disease.

Always check your body for ticks after walking through high grass or thickly forested area. If ticks are found unattached, they can simply be brushed off. If a tick is found attached, press down around the tick's head with tweezers, grab the head and gently pull upwards – do not twist it. (If no tweezers are available, use your fingers, but protect them from contamination with a piece of tissue or paper.) Do not rub oil, alcohol or petroleum jelly on it. If you get sick in the next couple of weeks, consult a doctor.

ANIMAL BITES

Do not attempt to pet, handle, or feed any animal, with the exception of domestic animals known to be free of any infectious disease. Most animal injuries are directly related to a person's attempt to touch or feed the animal.

Any bite or scratch by a mammal, including bats, should be promptly and thoroughly cleansed with large amounts of soap and water, followed by application of an antiseptic such as iodine or alcohol. The local health authorities should be contacted immediately for possible post-exposure rabies treatment, whether or not you've been immunized against rabies. It may also be advisable to start an antibiotic, since wounds caused by animal bites and scratches frequently become infected.

SNAKE BITES

There are several varieties of venomous snakes in the USA, but unlike those in other countries they do not cause instantaneous death, and antivenins are available. First aid is to place a light constricting bandage over the bite, keep the wounded part below the level of the heart and move it as little as possible. Stay calm and get to a medical facility as soon as possible. Bring the dead snake for identification if you can, but don't risk being bitten again. Do not use the mythic 'cut an X and suck out the venom' trick; this causes more damage to snakebite victims than the bites themselves.

SPIDER & SCORPION BITES

Although there are many species of spiders in the United States, the only ones that cause significant human illness are the black widow, brown recluse and hobo spiders. The black widow is black or brown in color, measuring about 15mm in body length, with a shiny top, fat body, and distinctive red or orange hourglass figure on its underside. It's found throughout the United States, usually in barns, woodpiles, sheds, harvested crops and bowls of outdoor toilets. The brown recluse spider is brown in color, usually 10 mm in body length, with a dark violin-shaped mark on the top of the upper section of the body. It's usually found in the south and southern Midwest, but has spread to other parts of the country in recent years. The brown recluse is active mostly at night, lives in dark sheltered areas such as under porches and in woodpiles, and typically bites when trapped. Hobo spiders are found chiefly in the northwestern United States and western Canada. The symptoms of a hobo spider bite are similar to those of a brown recluse, but milder.

If bitten by a black widow, you should apply ice or cold packs and go immediately to the nearest emergency room. Complications of a black widow bite may include muscle spasms, breathing difficulties and high blood pressure. The bite of a brown recluse or hobo spider typically causes a large, inflamed wound, sometimes associated with fever and chills. If bitten, apply ice and see a physician.

The only dangerous species of scorpion in the United States is the bark scorpion, which is found in the southwestern part of the country, chiefly Arizona. If stung, you should immediately apply ice or cold packs, immobilize the affected body part, and go to the nearest emergency room. To prevent scorpion stings, be sure to inspect and shake out clothing, shoes, and sleeping bags before use, and wear gloves and protective clothing when working around piles of wood or leaves.

LOCAL TIME

There are four one-hour time zones across the continental USA, and Alaska and Hawaii cover two more time zones. From east to west, they are as follows:

- **Eastern time zone** Greenwich Mean Time (GMT) minus five hours.
- **Central time zone** GMT minus six hours.
- **Mountain time zone** GMT minus seven hours.
- **Pacific time zone** GMT minus eight hours.

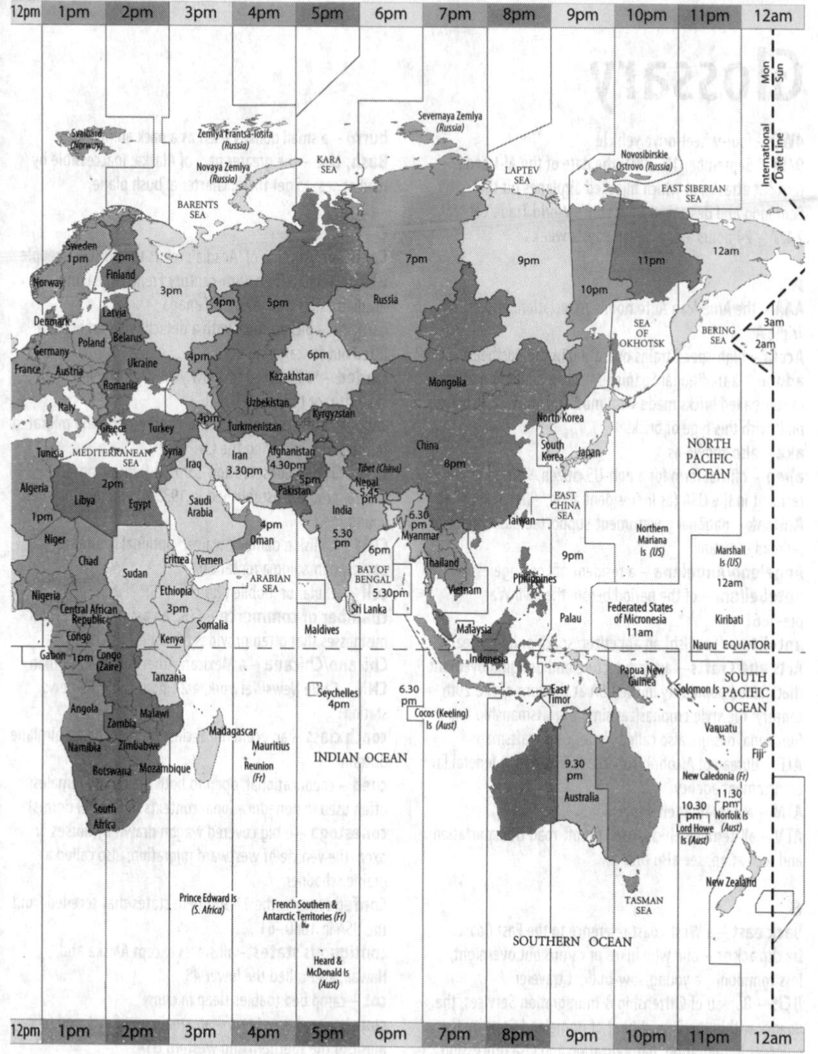

- **Alaska time zone** GMT minus nine hours.
- **Hawaii-Aleutian time zone** GMT minus 10 hours.

When it's 1pm in New York, Detroit, Atlanta and Miami, it's noon in Chicago, Kansas City and Dallas; 11am in Salt Lake City, Denver and Albuquerque; 10am in Seattle, San Francisco and Los Angeles; 9am in Anchorage; and 8am in Honolulu.

Daylight saving time, when clocks are moved forward one hour, runs from the first Sunday in April to the last Sunday in October in most states. Two exceptions are Arizona and Hawaii.

Glossary

4WD – four-wheel-drive vehicle
9/11 – September 11, 2001; the date of the Al-Qaeda terrorist attacks, in which hijacked airplanes hit the Pentagon and destroyed New York's World Trade Center
24/7 – 24 hours a day, seven days a week

A

AAA – the American Automobile Association, also called Triple A
Acela – high-speed trains operating in the northeast
adobe – a traditional Spanish-Mexican building material of sun-baked bricks made with mud and straw; a structure built with this type of brick
aka – also known as
alien – official term for a non-US citizen, visiting or resident in the USA (as in 'resident alien,' 'illegal alien' etc)
Amtrak – national government-supported passenger railroad company
Angeleno/Angelena – a resident of Los Angeles
antebellum – of the period before the Civil War; pre-1861
antojito – (Spanish) an appetizer, snack or light meal
Arts and Crafts – an architecture and design movement that gained popularity in the USA at the turn of the 20th century; the style emphasizes simple craftsmanship and functional design; also called (American) craftsman
ATF – Bureau of Alcohol, Tobacco & Firearms, a federal law enforcement agency
ATM – automated teller machine
ATV – all-terrain vehicle, used for off-road transportation and recreation; see also *OHV*

B

back east – a West Coast reference to the East Coast
backpacker – one who hikes or camps out overnight; less commonly, a young, low-budget traveler
BCIS – Bureau of Citizenship & Immigration Services, the agency within the Department of Homeland Security that oversees immigration, naturalization and visa processing
BLM – Bureau of Land Management, an agency of the federal Department of the Interior that manages certain public land for resources and recreation
blue book – the *Kelley Blue Book*, a used-car pricing guide
bluegrass – a form of Appalachian folk music that evolved in the bluegrass country of Kentucky and Tennessee
bodega – especially in New York City, a small local store selling liquor, food and other basics
boomtown – as during the gold rush, a town that experiences rapid economic and population growth
booster – an avid promoter of a town or university; sometimes has parochial connotations
burro – a small donkey used as a pack animal
Bush, the – the greater part of Alaska, inaccessible by road or sea; to get there, charter a 'bush plane'

C

Cajun – corruption of 'Acadia'; refers to Louisiana people who descended from 18th-century French-speaking Acadian exiles from eastern Canada
camper – pickup truck with a detachable roof or shell fitted out for camping
carded – to be asked to show your ID to buy liquor or cigarettes or to enter a bar
carpetbaggers – exploitative Northerners who migrated to the South following the Civil War
CCC – Civilian Conservation Corps, a Depression-era federal program established in 1933 to employ unskilled young men
CDW – collision damage waiver; optional insurance against damaging a rental car
cell – cellular or mobile phone
chamber of commerce – COC; an association of local businesses that often provides tourist information
Chicano/Chicana – a Mexican-American man/woman
CNN – Cable News Network, a 24-hour cable TV news station
coach class – an economical class of travel on an airplane or train
coed – coeducational, open to both males and females; often used in noneducational contexts (eg hostel dorms)
conestoga – a big covered wagon drawn by horses or oxen, the vehicle of westward migration; also called a prairie schooner
Confederacy – the 11 Southern states that seceded from the USA in 1860–61
contiguous states – all states except Alaska and Hawaii; also called the lower 48
cot – camp bed (babies sleep in cribs)
country and western – an amalgam of rock and folk music of the southern and western USA
coyote – a small wild dog, native to the central and western North American lowlands; also a person who assists illegal immigrants to cross the Mexican border into the USA
cracker – in the South, a derogatory term for a poor white person
CVB – convention and visitors bureau, a city-run organization promoting tourism and assisting visitors

D

DEA – Drug Enforcement Agency, the federal body responsible for enforcing US drug laws

Deep South – in this book, the states of Louisiana, Mississippi and Alabama
Dixie – the South; the states south of the *Mason-Dixon Line*
DMV – Department of Motor Vehicles, the state agency that administers the registration of vehicles and the licensing of drivers
docent – a guide or attendant at a museum
dog, to ride the – to travel by Greyhound bus
downtown – the center of a city, central business district; in the direction of downtown (eg a downtown bus)
DUI – driving under the influence of alcohol or drugs or both; sometimes called DWI (driving while intoxicated)

E

East – generally, the states east of the Mississippi River
efficiency – a small furnished apartment with a kitchen, often for short-term rental
Emancipation – refers to Abraham Lincoln's 1863 Emancipation Proclamation, which nominally freed all slaves in the Confederate-controlled states; in 1865, the US Constitution's 13th Amendment officially abolished slavery
entrée – the main course of a meal
express bus/train – bus/train that stops only at selected stations, and not at 'local' stations
express stop/station – stop/station served by express buses/trains as well as local ones

F

flag stop – a place where a bus stops only if you flag it down
foldaway – portable folding bed in a hotel
forty-niners – immigrants to California during the 1849 gold rush; also, San Francisco's pro-football team (49ers)

G

gallery – a commercial establishment selling artwork; institutions that exhibit art collections are usually called museums
gated community – walled upscale residential area accessible only through security gates
general delivery – poste restante
GOP – Grand Old Party, nickname of the Republican party
graduate study – advanced-degree study, after completion of a bachelor's degree
green card – technically, a Registration Receipt Card, issued to holders of immigrant visas; it's actually pink, and it allows the holder to live and work legally in the USA

H

HI-AYH – Hostelling International-American Youth Hostels; refers to US hostels affiliated with Hostelling International, a member group of IYHF (International Youth Hostel Federation)
Hispanic – of Latin American descent or culture (often used interchangeably with *Latino/Latina*)
hookup – at campgrounds, refers to RV connections for electricity, water and sewerage

I

Imax – specialized, giant-screen theaters and movies
interstate – an interstate highway, part of the national, federally funded highway system
INS – Immigration & Naturalization Service; as of 2002, replaced by the *BCIS* and no longer operating
IRS – Internal Revenue Service, the branch of the US Treasury Department that oversees tax collection

J

Jim Crow laws – in the post–Civil War South, laws intended to limit the civil or voting rights of blacks; Jim Crow is an old pejorative term for a black person
Joshua tree – a tall, treelike type of yucca plant, common in the arid Southwest

K

kiva – a round underground chamber built by Southwestern Native American cultures for ceremonial and everyday purposes
KOA – Kampgrounds of America, a private chain of campgrounds throughout the USA

L

Labor Day – public holiday on the first Monday in September; end of the summer holiday season
Latino/Latina – a man/woman of Latin American descent (often used interchangeably with *Hispanic*)
LDS – from the Church of Jesus Christ of Latter-Day Saints, the formal name of the Mormon church
live oak – a hardwood, evergreen oak, native to the South; dead live oaks make excellent boat-building timber
local – a bus or train that stops at every bus stop or station; see also *express bus/train*
lower 48 – the 48 contiguous states of the continental USA; all states except Alaska and Hawaii

M

Mason-Dixon Line – the 1767 delineation between Pennsylvania and Maryland that was later regarded as the boundary between free and slave states in the period before the Civil War
Memorial Day – public holiday on the last Monday in May commemorating soldiers who died in battle; start of the summer holiday season
MLB – Major League Baseball
MLS – Major League Soccer
moonshine – illegal liquor, usually corn whiskey, associated with backwoods stills in the Appalachian Mountains

morteros – hollows in rocks used by Native Americans for grinding seeds; also called mortar holes

N

NAACP – National Association for the Advancement of Colored People
National Guard – each state's federally supported military reserves, used most often in civil emergencies
National Recreation Area – National Park Service areas of scenic or ecological importance that are also reserved for recreation; they often incorporate public works such as dams
National Register of Historic Places – the National Park Service list of historic sites; designation restricts modifications to help preserve the integrity of original buildings
NBA – National Basketball Association
NCAA – National Collegiate Athletic Association, the body that regulates intercollegiate sports
New Deal – wide-ranging domestic program of public works and regulations introduced by President Franklin D Roosevelt to counteract the effects of the Depression
NFL – National Football League
NHL – National Hockey League
NHS – National Historic Site
NM – National Monument
NOW – National Organization for Women, a political organization dedicated to promoting women's rights and issues
NPR – National Public Radio, a noncommercial, listener-supported national network of radio stations; notable for news and cultural programming
NPS – National Park Service, the division of the Department of the Interior that administers US national parks and monuments
NRA – National Recreation Area; also National Rifle Association, an influential pro-gun lobbyist
NWR – National Wildlife Refuge

O

OHV/ORV – off-highway vehicle or off-road vehicle
out west – the opposite of *back east;* any place west of the Mississippi River
outfitter – business providing supplies, equipment, transport, guides etc, for fishing, canoeing, rafting and hiking trips

P

panhandle – a narrow piece of land projecting from the main body of a state (eg the Florida panhandle); also, to beg from passersby
parking lot/garage – paved area/building for parking cars (the word 'car park' is not used)
PBS – Public Broadcasting System, a noncommercial TV network; the TV equivalent of *NPR*
PC – politically correct; also personal computer
petroglyph – a work of rock art in which the design is pecked, chipped or abraded into the surface of the rock
PGA – Professional Golfers' Association
pickup – small truck with an open bed
pictograph – work of rock art in which the design is painted on a rock surface
po'boy – a fat sandwich on a bread roll
pound symbol – in the USA, the symbol #, not £
powwow – gathering of Native American people
Presidents' Day – public holiday on the third Monday in February, commemorating both Washington and Lincoln
pueblo – Native American village of the Southwest, with adjoining dwellings of *adobe* or stone

R

ranchero – a Mexican rancher; a Mexican-American musical style blending German and Spanish influences
rancho – a small ranch (Mexican Spanish)
raw bar – a restaurant counter that serves raw shellfish
Reconstruction – a period after the Civil War, when secessionist states were placed under federal control before they were readmitted to the Union
redneck – derogatory term for an extremely conservative, working-class or rural person
RV – recreational vehicle, also known as a motor home

S

scalawags – Southern whites with Northern sympathies who profited under *Reconstruction* after the Civil War
schlep – carry awkwardly or with difficulty (Yiddish)
schlock – cheap, trashy products (Yiddish)
shotgun shack – a small timber house with rooms arranged in a line, so you could fire a shotgun straight through from front to back; once-common dwellings for poor whites and blacks in the South
sierra – mountain range (Spanish)
SoCal – Southern California
soul food – traditionally cuisine of Southern black Americans (such as chitterlings, ham hocks and collard greens)
SSN – social security number, a nine-digit ID code required for employment
stick, stick shift – manually operated gearshift; a car with manual transmission ('Can you drive a stick?')
strip mall – any collection of businesses and stores arranged around a parking lot
SUV – sports utility vehicle

T

trailer – transportable dwelling; a trailer park is a collection that doesn't move and provides low-cost housing

TTY, TDD – telecommunications devices for the deaf
two-by-four – standard-size timber, 2in thick and 4in wide

U

Union, the – the United States; in a Civil War context, the Union refers to the northern states at war with the southern Confederate states
USAF – United States Air Force
USFS – United States Forest Service, the division of the Department of Agriculture that manages federal forests for resources and recreation
USGS – United States Geological Survey, an agency of the Department of the Interior responsible for, among other things, creating detailed topographic maps of the country
USMC – United States Marine Corps
USN – United States Navy

W

wash – a watercourse in the desert, usually dry but subject to flash flooding
well drinks – bar drinks with less-expensive, generic brand hard liquor, as opposed to name-brand 'top-shelf' drinks
WNBA – Women's National Basketball Association
WPA – Works Progress (later, Works Projects) Administration; a Depression-era, New Deal program to increase employment by funding public works projects

Z

zip code – a five- or nine-digit postal code; refers to the Zone Improvement Program, which expedited delivery of US mail

Behind the Scenes

THIS BOOK

This 3rd edition of *USA* was written by a team of authors led by Jeff Campbell. He wrote all the front and back chapters and the Northern California section. Authors Loretta Chilcoat (Washington DC & the Capital Region), Susan Derby (Rocky Mountains), Beth Greenfield (New York & the Mid-Atlantic States), Carolyn B Heller (New England), Sam Martin (Texas), Debra Miller (The South), Bob Morris (Florida), Becky Ohlsen (Pacific Northwest), Andrea Schulte-Peevers (California), Kurt Wolff (Southwest) and Karla Zimmerman (Great Lakes) contributed tirelessly to this edition. Tara Duggan wrote Food & Drink, Dr David Goldberg wrote Health, and Ryan Ver Berkmoes wrote History. Scott Freeman wrote the boxed text 'Southern Music: Legends of the South,' Alex Hershey wrote 'On the Ragbrai,' Robert D Hershey Jr wrote 'Spring Training' and Paige R Penland wrote 'Spruce Bark Beetles: Scourge of the Kenai Peninsula.' James Lyon coordinated the 1st and 2nd editions of this book. Erin Corrigan, Alex Hershey and Vivek Wagle assisted in updating information for *USA* 3, drawing from Paige R Penland's, Robert Reid's, Don Root's and Wendy Taylor's text.

THANKS FROM THE AUTHORS

Jeff Campbell A book like this doesn't get made without the help of many hands. Erin Corrigan was our ship's captain, and she was a steady, encouraging presence through sometimes rough waters. I also thank all of *USA* 3's authors, who took on the monumental task of redesigning this book, and did so with excellence and good humor. I relied on the experiences and expertise of a number of people, and my sincerest gratitude goes out to Anne Hayes and Pete Holloran, Bill Metke and Brechin Flournoy, Otis Flournoy, Karen Levine and Mark Nigara, Anna Bushell, David Holmes, Beth Weber, Matt Warshaw, Barbara Archer, Georgia Hughes, Lisa Bach, Jo Beaton, Dick Robinson, Roy Cairo, Kate Hoffman, Nancy Gibbons, Gina Orlando, Alicia Keshishian, Lea Gamble, Don Richards and Caroline Herter. I wouldn't have survived without the love, encouragement and editorial eye of my wife Deanna, or without the daily afternoon walks with my son, Jackson, who proudly proclaimed everything 'my city.'

Loretta Chilcoat Many thanks to Julia Scott for her incredible itinerary planning, Rebecca Pawlowski, Christine Wilson, Mindy Bianca, Caryn Gresham, Jennifer Boes, the very patient commissioning editor Erin Corrigan for enduring my endless Felix questions, and my husband Brad for accepting his absent newlywed wife's hectic travel schedule.

Susan Derby Thank you to the countless amazing people who helped me out with advice (and directions!) on my journeys. To all of the rangers and visitors center staff whom I had the pleasure of meeting, thank you for your patience and guidance. In Denver, Daphne Rice-Allen at the Black American West Museum and James Watson gave invaluable assistance, and Nan Crawford prepped me for the city before the trip. For sharing their homes and vast regional knowledge, thanks to Jacob Uhland in Jackson Hole and Tim Hodsdon in Winter Park. In Crested Butte, Jason Valcourt was a

THE LONELY PLANET STORY

The story begins with a classic travel adventure: Tony and Maureen Wheeler's 1972 journey across Europe and Asia to Australia. There was no useful information about the overland trail then, so Tony and Maureen published the first Lonely Planet guidebook to meet a growing need.

From a kitchen table, Lonely Planet has grown to become the largest independent travel publisher in the world, with offices in Melbourne (Australia), Oakland (USA), London (UK) and Paris (France).

Today Lonely Planet guidebooks cover the globe. There is an ever-growing list of books and information in a variety of media. Some things haven't changed. The main aim is still to make it possible for adventurous travelers to get out there – to explore and better understand the world.

At Lonely Planet we believe travelers can make a positive contribution to the countries they visit – if they respect their host communities and spend their money wisely.

limitless source of information – and a great prom date! I thank Erin Corrigan at LP for trusting me with this assignment and *USA* 2 author Andrew Dean Nystrom for a great chapter to build upon. A million thanks go to Johnny, for his love and support, for his car and for coaching me through my first experience driving a stick shift through an Idaho snowstorm. Finally, thank you to my family, and for making home so irresistible I am indebted to the special people of SF (with a shout-out to Shitzu Bitz).

Beth Greenfield Thanks to Kiki Herold, Mom and Dad, Eileen and Steve Santalarsci, Aimee Szparaga and Richard Nocera, Michael DiFonzo, Patti Greger, Anthony Rodriguez, Bill Miller, Dee Sias and Keith Mulvihill for invaluable tips and support!

Carolyn B Heller Thank you to Anne and Clyde Hanyen for Cape Cod hospitality, to Paula and Howard Luxenberg for company in Connecticut, and to Lou Soltys, Chris Morse and Anna Soltys Morse for always being there to lend a hand. Extra special thanks to my road-trip buddies, Michaela and Talia Albert, and, as always, to Alan.

Sam Martin Thanks to Marty and Nevena at Rocket Buster, Robert at the desert crossing, Scott and Kristin Ryan in Big D, and Brent Hull in cowtown for all their hospitality and tips, and everyone else who pointed me in all the right directions. A big thanks to Anna Martin for the wheels. Biggest thanks to Denise and mighty Ford for tagging along and lending all their loving support.

Debra Miller Thanks to all the chefs who fattened me up with so much good eatin'. I must extend a huge thanks to Tom Downs, who makes New Orleans sizzle. To Randy Peffer for his awesome take on Savannah, to Kate Hoffman, Virginie Boone, Dani Valent and Gary Bridgman for their *Louisiana* research, to Jeremy Gray, Jeff Davis and China Williams for *Georgia & the Carolinas*. Thanks to Erin Corrigan and Jeff Campbell for managing this big book.

On the road, I'm always amazed at the helpful knowledge of visitors center staff – thank you all for sharing your secrets. Thanks to all the booksellers, tour guides, bartenders and passersby, whose friendly conversations make the real South bloom like a magnolia.

Huge thanks to the Atlanta gang for the support, friendship and many cocktail hours. To Scott Freeman, whose casual talk about the Braves, music and literature has taught me much about the South's quirks and charms. To Debra Frank for her killer forehand and to Megan McLaughlin for the glorious morning walks. Finally, thanks to Rob Landau, my husband and best friend, who helps me explore the South with dignity, grace, and a whole lot of wind in my hair.

Becky Ohlsen I would like to thank Erin Corrigan, Jeff Campbell and fellow USA authors for all their hard work; Tom Downs, David Else and Ryan Ver Berkmoes for wisdom imparted over beer; John Graham for expert navigation skills; and Maureen O'Hagan, Bob Young and Audrey Van Buskirk for their help and hospitality.

Andrea Schulte-Peevers I would like to thank all those who provided hot tips, insider information and hospitality during the research of this book. Big hugs to my husband David for his unstinting support and for being such a wonderful travel companion. Thanks also to LP's Erin Corrigan for shepherding this complex project along with aplomb and to Maria Donohoe for allowing me to contribute my share to this book.

Kurt Wolff I would like to thank all who went out of their way to assist, provide information and otherwise encourage my writing and research, including Amy Ventura, Elgy Gillespie, Amy Marr, Carolyn Wolff, Jeanne Kearsley, Tom Downs, Michele Posner, Andreas Schueller, Stephanie Pearson, Katie Arnold, Kim Westhoff, Christine Condino, Lisa Hendrix, Jake Cudek, Tom Mesereau and other tipsters and friendly faces encountered along the way.

Karla Zimmerman I wish to thank the following people for sharing their considerable knowledge of all things local: Paula and Chris Andruss, Jean Belfiore, Lisa Beran, Ted Bonar, Bill Brockschmidt, Carmine Cervi, Lisa Farris, Roger Fatica, Alexis Haspis, Dave Jacobson, Rick Karr, Jeff and Lisa Laske, David Lynch, Rob Levally, Valerie Liberty, Margaret Littman, Helaine and Barry Markowitz, Nancy Moore, Greg Neergard, Erin O'Brien, Jim O'Leary, Keith Pandolfi, Karen Purves, Chris Rowney, Rosemarie Rowney, Laura Samson, Mary Visconti, Sarah Walker, Ray Zielinski, Mitch Zimmerman, the folks at Detroit's Shorecrest Motor Inn and the helpful workers in the Midwest's visitors centers. A special thanks to those above who provided transportation assistance, hand-holding, cookies, humor, beer, and software and tear-drying tissues when my computer crashed. My gratitude to commissioning editor Erin Corrigan and the other LP writers who nudged me along with encouraging words. A big thanks to my parents, Karen and Don Zimmerman, for their love and support. Thanks most of all to Eric, a partner of unfailing generosity and patience.

CREDITS

USA 3 was commissioned and developed in Lonely Planet's Oakland office. Michele Posner contracted all the authors; Erin Corrigan took over from there and developed this title. Graham Neale commissioned and developed the maps, with invaluable assistance from Alison Lyall. Alex Hershey stepped in whenever needed.

Coordinating the production of this title were Rebecca Chau (editorial), Laurie Mikkelsen (cartography), Cris Gibcus (color) and Jacqui Saunders (color and layout). Overseeing production were Rachel Imeson (project manager) and Alison Lyall (managing cartographer).

Editorial assistance was provided by Andrew Bain, Imogen Bannister, Kerryn Burgess, Emily Coles, Peter Cruttenden, Tony Davidson, Susannah Farfor, Thalia Kalkipsakis, Craig Kilburn, Martine Lleonart, Anne Mulvaney, Alan Murphy, Danielle North, Nina Rousseau, Ann Seward, Sally Steward, Linda Suttie, Nick Tapp, Katrina Webb and Gabbi Wilson. The index was prepared by Justin Flynn, and the cover was designed by Pepi Bluck.

Cartographic assistance was provided by Barbara Benson, Piotr Czajkowski, Karen Fry, Joelene Kowalski, Andrew Smith, Herman So, Simon Tillema and Jody Whiteoak. Technical support was provided by Chris LeeAck, Tim Lohnes and Lachlan Ross.

Series Publishing Manager Virginia Maxwell oversaw the redevelopment of the country guides series with help from Maria Donohoe. Regional Publishing Manager Maria Donohoe steered the development of this title. The series was designed by James Hardy, with mapping development by Paul Piaia. The series development team included Shahara Ahmed, Susie Ashworth, Gerilyn Attebery, Jenny Blake, Anna Bolger, Verity Campbell, Erin Corrigan, Nadine Fogale, Dave McClymont, Leonie Mugavin, Lynne Preston, Rachel Peart and Howard Ralley.

THANKS FROM LONELY PLANET

Many thanks to the hundreds of travelers who used the last edition and wrote to us with helpful hints, useful advice and interesting anecdotes:

A Richard Abrams, Shona Addison, Bas Aldewereld, Di Aldrich, Darlinda Alexander, Mark Allison, Thomas Althammer, Maria Amuchastegui, Jon J Anderson, Scott Anderson, Larry Andrews, Alexander Andruska, Elizabeth Arbiter, Allen Armer, Geoffrey Arnold, Hilmir Asgeirsson, Michelle Aslett, Kellie Avery, Victoria Ayres **B** Curtis Bach, Tamara Baldwin, Carl Banner, Sandra Banpenny, OP Bansted, Phillippe and Marie Bardet, Matt Barnette, Mark Bartlett, Geoff Barton, Kirsten Bayly, Darren Beckett, Ray Beebe, Rutger Beekelaar, Eva Behrens, Avi Beigelman, Lesli Bell, Kristina Bellach, Maria and Tony Benfield, Daniel Berenson, Bruce Berger, Brian Bergeron, Caryl Bergeron, Rick Blane, Leah Bloomfield, Rick Blyth, Samantha Blyth, Austin Blythe, Matthias Bode, Malynda Boyle, Clare Braithwaite, Peter Braithwaite, Lui Brandt, Christine Breen, A Bregman, Jack Breisacher, Edwin Breukelman, David Bridgman, Darryl Brock, Liza Brown, Pam Browns, Sheila Bryans, John Bryant, Pam Bryant, Alex Buchanan, Neil and Sandra Burditt, Harry Burgess, Mike Busby, Ben Butchko **C** Peter Camp-Smith, Donna Campbell, Florence Caplow, Claudia Caramanti, Teresa Carpenter, Angela Carper, Hannah Carrick, Pascalle Cartigny, Michael Cartwright, Ben Cassie, Trevor Cassie, Anna Cayley, Errin Cecil-Smith, Carolyn Chapel, Xavier Chavez, Steven Chmielnicki, Brian Choo-Kang, Chungwah Chow, Ton Christiaanse, Caitlin Chun-Kennedy, Rob Ciampa, Bruce Clark, Gee Gee Clemency, Cletus Coble, John Cojeen, Roger Cole, Bram Colen, Mandy Comish, Connie Constan, RS Coon, Jenny Cooper, Ruth Corcoran, John Cornwell, Arthur Corte, Annabel Cowley, Dennis Cox, Adam Crain, Chris Cramer, Jerry Cramer, Scott Crawford, Monique Cremers, Russ Crockett, Gareth Cross, Paul Crowe, Jen Crumpler, Mike Cullom, Meredith Curran, Jean Czerlinski **D** Ake Dahllof, Lucy Dallas, Vicki Daniels, Carl Danzig, B Dark, Helen Daunt, Ian Davidson, Roger Davis, Steven Davis, Richard Davison, Vicki Dawkins, Alan Day, Barbara de Bruine, Anke Dekkers de Wit,

SEND US YOUR FEEDBACK

We love to hear from travelers – your comments keep us on our toes and help make our books better. Our well-traveled team reads every word on what you loved or loathed about this book. Although we cannot reply individually to postal submissions, we always guarantee that your feedback goes straight to the appropriate authors, in time for the next edition. Each person who sends us information is thanked in the next edition – and the most useful submissions are rewarded with a free book.

To send us your updates – and find out about LP events, newsletters and travel news – visit our award-winning website: **www.lonelyplanet.com**.

Note: We may edit, reproduce and incorporate your comments in Lonely Planet products such as guidebooks, websites and digital products, so let us know if you don't want your comments reproduced or your name acknowledged. For a copy of our privacy policy visit www.lonelyplanet.com/privacy.

John Deacon, Matteo Del Grosso, Sara Delaney, Justin Delemus, Christina Demetriou, Richard Desomme, Tony DeYoung, AB DiLucente, Dennis DiLucente, Charlotte Dinolt, Chris DiPalma, Virginia DiPiazza, Joanne Dixon, John Doerr, Nam Van Dong, Mike Dowling, Clara Downey, Sharyn Drabsch, Steve Draper, Sara Drew, Bruce Dribbon, Millie Duke, Charlotte Dyhr **E** Lynne Earle, Richard Earle, Christopher Edwards, John Edwards, C Elkins, Cammy Elquist, Tom Elvin, Nivine Emeran, Chris Enting, Caroline Evans, Gerard Evans **F** Terry Fabiano, Alan Farleigh, Jean Feilmoser, Peter Feldchen, Annette Ferguson, Don Fernandez, Ronela Ferrer, Russell Ferrier, Mark Firmstone, Iris Fischer, Kimberley Flanagan, Grant Fletcher, Danny Flies, Sarah Florenz, Andy Foltz, Cathy Foster, Julia Simeon Foster, Jill Franke, Jerry Franks, Thommy Frantzen, Sandra Friede, Nikolaus Frinke, Alexander Frix, Bob Froehlig, KL Fuchs, Joy Furze **G** Heiko Gabriel, Lantin Gaelle, Nicolas Gaere, Jonathan Gaines, Joe Ganesh, Tom Ganz, Rhona Gardiner, Gideon Gardner, Joanne Garrah, Martina Geig, Nicole Geiger, Lars Gentzen, Natasha George, Indraneel Ghose, Robert Gibson, Emma Giesen, Rafael Gilliam, Paul Gioffi, Brad Gledhill, Peter Glennon, Ben Godfrey, Helena Golden, Z Goldman, Joe Goodfellow, Dayna Gorman, Katie Graves, Deborah Gravrock, Ronalie Green, Jessica Gregory, Chantal Grisanti, Alison Groombridge, Deb Grupenhoff, Joseph Grynbaum, Alexander Guenther, Andac Gursoy **H** Joanne Hackett, Mieneke Hage, Stuart Hale, Ellenise Hall, C Hancock, Kay Hand, Prine Hansen, Tara Hansen, C Harris, Ian Harris, Janine Harris, Lawrence Hauser, Oyvind Henriksen, Marco Heusdens, Lizz Higgins, Ric Higgins, Frank Hill, Mary Hill, Annette Hilton, Whitney Himmel, Eva Himmelberg, Krisztian Hincz, Mike Hoff, John Hoffman, Grainne Hogan, Norma Jean Hogan, Alyson Hogarth, Kai Holderbaum, James Holgate, Henrick Hollesen, Emma Holmbro, Christopher Hook, Jerry Scott Horn, Alain Hottat, Clarissa Howe, Trisha Howell, Jeff Howlett, Simon Huang, David Huff, Arjen Huijs, Graham Hunt, Jamie Hunter, Pennie Hutchins, Garrit Huysman **I** Helle Ingemann, Dave Ingold, Keith Isherwood **J** Kimi Jackson, Toni Jackson, Mary Jacob, Bailey T James, Jane James, Michela Janni, Philippe Jeanty, Geoffrey Joachim, Amelia Johnson, Robert L Johnson, Jamie Johnston, Cheryl Jones, Cliff Jones, Darryl Jones, Geraint Jones, Lindsay Jones, Nick Jones, Paula Jones, James Jordan, Gretchen Joseph, Gerald Joyce, Tim Julou, Christiane Jung, Holger Jung **K** Felicia Kahn, Shawn Kairschner, Dirk Kasulke, Larry Katkin, Michael Keary, Rachel Keary, Joanne Keefe, Shane Kehoe, Rita Keil, John Kelleher, Randy Keller, Madeline Kemna, Bas Kempen, Darren Kendall, Teresia Kevin, Yu Fay Khan, Zia Asad Khan, Derek Kiger, Boz Killebrew, Jim Killebrew, Vanina Killebrew, Eileen King, John King, John Kirk, Karen Kissileff, Michaela Klink, Eberhard Kloeber, Mirjam Knapp, Catherine Koch, Richard Koehler, Arvid E Koetitz, Eric Koh, Mimi Koral, Mark Kral, Jim Krieger, Jeroen Kruis, Jerzy Krupinski, Matthias Kuster **L** Maxime Lachance, Laura LaLonde, Tim Langan Jr, Peter Langridge, Alison Lausten, Susan Lavender, Yuli Law, Adrian le Hanne, Carolyn Lee, Sophie Lefebvre-Blachet, Debra Lehrberger, Franz J Leinweber, Brian Leonard, Ross Leopold, Christine Lepschy, Beverly Leu, Milton Lever, Tim Lewis, Fil Lewitt, Staci Lichterman, Sarah Lieberman, Felicia Lim, Shin Lim, Robson Lin, Gunilla Lindblad, Antje Lindinger, Anne Lindley, Stuart Lipnick, Pieter Lips, Harrison Lipscomb, Paul Littlefair, Andreas Lober, Susan Logan, Heather Lombard, Thomas Lowenburg, Bob Lu, Dermot Luddy, Astrid Lundmark, Marc Lutz, Tracy Lynch **M** Gillian MacKenzie, Joseph MacNeal, Lars Bjoern Madsen, LaTrina Maez, Saleem Mahmood, Scott Malik, Naomi Malone, Gabriel Mandel, Carine Manileve, Garry Mareels, Janna Marks, Youval Marks, Natalya Marquand, James Marshall, Ryan Martin, Jean Martino, Siobhan Marzluft, Julia Mason, Elona Masson, Jonathan Masters, Akiko Masuda, Kate Matthams, Michael Matthes, Jade Mawbey, Sally Maynard, Norma McCarty, Daniel McChesney-Young, Iain McCormick, Lisa McFarlin, Gareth McFeely, Kim McGregor, Jock McJock, Ken McKenzie, Don McManman, Rob McMeekin, Lachlan McMurtrie, Karen McWhirter, Maeve Meighan, Gerrard Meneaud, Rich Mick, Edgar Millard, Mark Miller, Mimi Miller, John Mitchell, Fiona Mocatta, Carrie Mogged, Stephanie Monaghan, Heather Monell, Charlie Monroe, Karina Montgomery, TRW Moore, Elke Moritz, Frances Morrier, Keith Morris, Renate Moser, Emily Mott, Gary Muhrer, Christina Muller, Wendy Mulligan, Jack Munsee, Jean Munsee, Ruth Murphy, Dan Murray, Brian Murrell, Erin Myers, Ron Myers **N** Christina Nagel, Robin Nahum, Jed Nancarrow, Laura Napier, Stend Narti, Mickey Nee, Joe Nekrasz, Lucy Newman, Roy Nicholls, Patrick Nicolai, Dion Nissenbaum, Bob Nitz, Lindsay Noah, Shilene Noe, Jacques Noel, David and Rhonda Norbury, Robert Normandin, Kate Norris, Magnus Norstrom, Eric Nowitzky, Mark Nunez, David Nutt **O** Lars Obel, Pia Obel, Robin O'Donoghue, Cynthia O'Keefe, Shannon O'Loughlin, Clarke Olsen, Mark and Nicole O'Neill, Jan Onno Reiners, April Orcutt, Javier Arias Ortigosa, Sonia Ortiz, Phyllis Oster **P** Markku Paalanen, Donna Page, Leigh Anne Page, Linda Paisley, Shelley Patient, Michelle Pauling, Pamela Paull, Stephen Pearce, Roger Pearson, Gregoire Pellerin, Kara Penny, Eliza Penrose, Sarah Perkins, Matthieu Permentier, Catherine Perrot, Chad Perry, Duke Peters, Dr S Philipp, Jim Pitkethly, PL Plotts, Kylie Polanske, Elizabeth Porter, Stuart Potte, Dierdre Price, Kenton Price, Sue Pritchett, Eulalia Marti Puig, Beth Pullman **R** Maggie Racklyeft, Ofer Rahat, Dr Viven Rajah, Glen Rajaram, Roxana Ramos, Anna Rankin, Thomas Rau, Felix Rayner, Luisa Rayner, John Reeves, Donna Regan, M Rehorst, DE Reibscheid, Lynette Reid, Gerry Renshaw, Maxine Ressler, Brett Rhodes, PJ Rhodes, Michael Richardson, Ronald Jan Rieger, Stephanie Rieke, Sten Rieper, Geoff Rimmer, Walter Rivera, Evan Roberts, Matt Roberts, Andrew Robertson, Judy Robinson, David Rogers, Andrea Rogge, Ben Roman, Aaron Romero, Karen Rowland, Claudia Royston, Roland Rücker, Rob Ruschak, Ken Ryan **S** Norman Sadler, Kenji Saito, Vicki Sales, Hannah Salvidge, V Sameer, John-Paul Sassone, Darren Sault, Lee Savage, Sean Savage, Caryn Schenewerk, Randy Schisler, Mark Schlagboehmer, Martina Schoefberger, Guus Schoonman, Jana Schumann, W Schuurman, Linda Scira, Gabriele Auinger Scnell, Susan Scott, James Sears, Charlotte Seiglow, Gloria Ser, Elizabeth Sercombe, Michel Shames, Alan Sharp, Mary Sheesley, Kristina Shih, Kerri Shimshock, Andrea Shimwell, Andrea and Bob and Ellen Shimwell, Graham Showell, Shyam Shyoid, Jordan Sidaway, Kamer Sidhy, Margaret Sieczkowska, Sandy Sillman, Iain Sim, Chris Simmons, Evy Simon, Gary Sinclair, Sharon Sinclair, Wayne Smatts, Dusty Smith, Grant Smith, Inga Smith, Karen Smith, Maggie Smith,

Marti Benson Smith, Claire Snel, Karia Solano, Paul Soldermann, Tim Somers, Christopher Sonne, Maibritt Sorensen, Jabran Soubeih, Christian Peter Holme Specht, Nadine Spitz, Christopher Staake, Michael Start, J Stefan, Kristine Stevens, Mark Stevenson, Frederick Stewart, Frederick Steyn, Bill and Ann Stoughton, Kerry Strayer, Zach Suckle, Richard Sugiyama, Scott Sutton, Qadri Syed, Joe Szper **T** Ramon Tak, Ignatius Tan, Gabriela Tanaka, K Terlaan, Christobel Thomas, Daniel Thompson, Dennis Thompson, Eric Thomsen, Zoe Thorne, Sheri Thrasher, Brian Tiernan, Gemma Tinsdale, Dawn Toles, Diego Tonelli, Michele Toubhans, Scott Toulson, Masha Traber, Jessica Troy, Wendy Tucker, Brian Turbyfill **U** Christina Urban, Andrea Ursillo **V** Carlijn van Dehn, Rob van den Brand, Cas van der Avoort, Frank van der Heijden, Huub van der Linden, Kris van der Meij, Didier van Hellemont, Ruud van Leeuwen, Stijn van Rest, Harry van Rietschoten, Margo and Fred van Roosmalen, Erica Van Zon, Beth Mary Varhaug, Rok Veber, Jeroen Verhoeckx, Karine Verquin, Marcella Vinciguerra, Alison von Bibra, Monika Vtipil **W** Sally Wade, Helen Wahby, Barbara Wall, Joan Walsh, Michael Ward, Richard A Warriner, Rosemary Watt, Joanne Webb, N Webb, Don Webley, Debbie Weijers, Darian Weir, Gregor Wenig, Kurt Werle, TR Werle, Erik Wettersten, Anna Wexler, Jason White, Jerry White, Carl Whiteley, Jodi Whitlock, Vicki Wilhite, Annabelle Williams, Krissy Williams, Maridowa Williams, Scott Williams, Trevor Williams, Stone Willow, Fiona Wilson, Trevor Wilson, Ben Wimmer, Skip Winitsky, Steve Winwood, Sally Wood, Rachael Woodcock, Gordon Woods, Christopher Wortley, Cathy Wright, Jim Wright **X** Alisha X **Y** Todd Yamaoka, Rochelle Yeo, Terence Yorks, Andrew Young, Janey Young, Robin M Young, Vincent Young **Z** Christine Zardecki

ACKNOWLEDGMENTS

Many thanks to the following for the use of their content:

Mountain High Maps® © 1993 Digital Wisdom, Inc.

Index

ABBREVIATIONS

AK	Alaska	KS	Kansas	NY	New York
AL	Alabama	KY	Kentucky	OH	Ohio
AR	Arkansas	LA	Louisiana	OK	Oklahoma
AZ	Arizona	MA	Massachusetts	OR	Oregon
CA	California	MD	Maryland	PA	Pennsylvania
CO	Colorado	ME	Maine	RI	Rhode Island
CT	Connecticut	MI	Michigan	SC	South Carolina
DC	District of Columbia	MN	Minnesota	SD	South Dakota
DE	Delaware	MO	Missouri	TN	Tennessee
FL	Florida	MS	Mississippi	TX	Texas
GA	Georgia	MT	Montana	UT	Utah
HI	Hawaii	NC	North Carolina	VA	Virginia
IA	Iowa	ND	North Dakota	VT	Vermont
ID	Idaho	NE	Nebraska	WA	Washington
IL	Illinois	NH	New Hampshire	WI	Wisconsin
IN	Indiana	NJ	New Jersey	WV	West Virginia
		NM	New Mexico	WY	Wyoming
		NV	Nevada		

000 Map pages
000 Location of color photographs

D

E

F

000 Map pages
000 Location of color photographs

000 Map pages
000 Location of color photographs

L

M

INDEX

T

000 Map pages
000 Location of color photographs

INDEX

Y

Z

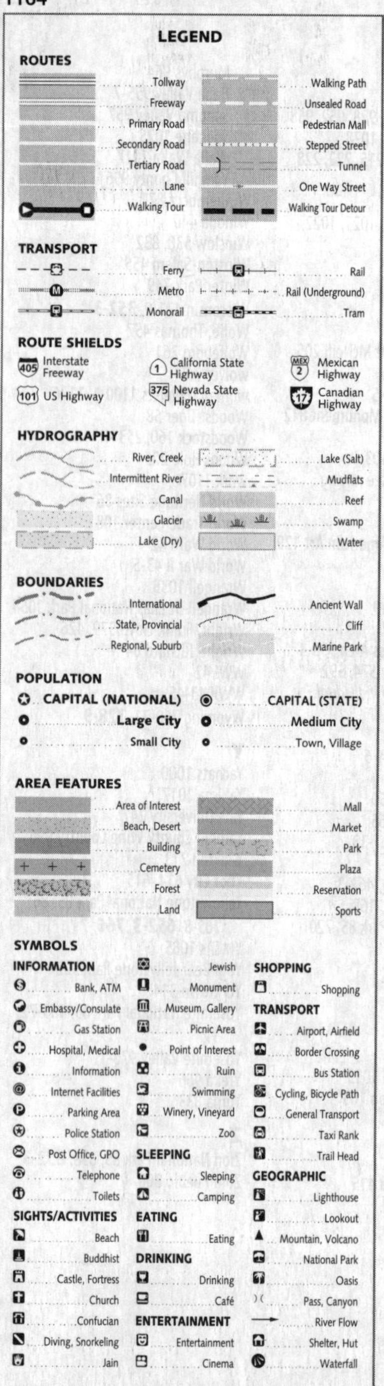

LONELY PLANET OFFICES

Australia
Head Office
Locked Bag 1, Footscray, Victoria 3011
☎ 03 8379 8000, fax 03 8379 8111
talk2us@lonelyplanet.com.au

USA
150 Linden St, Oakland, CA 94607
☎ 510 893 8555, toll free 800 275 8555
fax 510 893 8572, info@lonelyplanet.com

UK
72–82 Rosebery Ave,
Clerkenwell, London EC1R 4RW
☎ 020 7841 9000, fax 020 7841 9001
go@lonelyplanet.co.uk

France
1 rue du Dahomey, 75011 Paris
☎ 01 55 25 33 00, fax 01 55 25 33 01
bip@lonelyplanet.fr, www.lonelyplanet.fr

Published by Lonely Planet Publications Pty Ltd
ABN 36 005 607 983

Cover photographs by Lonely Planet Images: the Statue of Liberty in New York City, Kim Grant (front); the huge red monoliths of Monument Valley in Arizona, Adina Tovy Amsel (back). Many of the images in this guide are available for licensing from Lonely Planet Images: www.lonelyplanetimages.com.

Printed by SNP SPrint (M) Sdn Bhd, Malaysia